THE COLLECTOR'S ENCYCLOPEDIA OF DOLLS

Volume Two

THE COLLECTOR'S ENCYCLOPEDIA OF DOLLS

Volume Two

by Dorothy S.,
Elizabeth A.,
and
Evelyn J.
Coleman

CROWN PUBLISHERS, INC.   NEW YORK

Published by Crown Publishers, Inc., 225 Park Avenue South, New York, New York 10003, and represented in Canada by the Canadian MANDA Group

CROWN is a trademark of Crown Publishers, Inc.

Manufactured in the United States of America

Library of Congress Cataloging-in-Publication Data
(Revised for volume 2)

Coleman, Dorothy S.
  The collector's encyclopedia of dolls

  Includes bibliographies and index.
  1. Dolls—Collectors and collecting.   2. Dolls—
Dictionaries,   I. Coleman, Elizabeth A., joint author.
II. Coleman, Evelyn J., joint author.   III. Title.
NK4893.C6   688.7'221'0321   68-9101
ISBN 0-517-55796-7 (v. 2)

Design by Rhea Braunstein

10 9 8 7 6 5 4 3 2 1

First Edition

CONTENTS

ACKNOWLEDGMENTS

Once again a great many people came to our assistance when we decided to expand and to extend for five more years the information in *The Collector's Encyclopedia of Dolls,* Volume One. Museums, private collectors, and dealers all have been most kind and helpful in providing us with the privilege of examining their dolls and using pictures of their dolls. We gratefully thank the following: Eunice Althouse; Jacqueline Andrews; Dorothy Annunziato; Maria Argyriadis; Suzanne Ash; John Axe; Germaine Bachand; Yvonne Baird; Francis and Paul del Barco-Sacket; Heather and Clifford Bond; Mona and Ken Borger; Cherry Bou; Bourne Gallery in Reigate; Carol Boyd; Sylvia Brockmon; Mary Brouse; Shirley Buchholz; Elizabeth Burke; Robert and Katrin Burlin; Magda Byfield; Astry Campbell; late E. J. Carter; Chester County Historical Society; Jürgen & Marianne Cieslik; Alberta Darby; Betty Davis; Mary de Jong; Deutsche Spielzeug Museum in Sonneberg; Diane Domroe; June Douglass; E.M.I. Collection; Stephanie & Fred Farago; Jim Fernandez; Fogg Museum; Iverna & Irving Foote; Jan & Howard Foulke; late Josephine Garrison; Herb & Kathleen Genelly; Bess Goldfinger; Caroline Goodfellow; Judy Grant; late Edna Greehy; late Alice Grinnings; Gundi Groh-Pracher; Victoria Harper, Ruth Hartwell; Bobby & Reid Hayes; Mrs. Frank T. Heintz; Claire Hennig; Hessische Puppenmuseum; late Irene Blair Hickman; Paula Hill; Mary Hillier; Gladyse Hilsdorf; Melba Hiter; Clara Hobey; Bill Holland; Marion Holt; Helen Huling; Hungarian National Museum; International Doll Library Foundation; A. Jackson; Flora Gill Jacobs; June Jeffcott; Barbara Jendrick; Iris Jenney; Estelle Johnston; Kathleen Joost; Joan Kindler; Violet King; late Sarge Kitterman; Sara Kocher; Vera Kramer; Betty Kudlo; Alice F. La Force; Margie Landolt; Gay Lawson; Ollie Leavister; Annemarie Lohr; Becky & Jay Lowe; Margaret Mandel; Barbara Mansfield; Ruth & R. C. Mathes; May Mauer; Sybill McFadden; Dorothy & Jerome McGonegal; Elizabeth McIntyre; Nancy Menoni; Dorothy Mishler; Gloria Modderno; Becky Moncrief; Winifred Moor; Dr. Eva Horvath Moskovszky; Musée des Arts Decoratifs; Musée National Suisse; Museum of American Architecture and Decorative Arts, Houston, Texas; Museum of the City of Neustadt near Coburg; Museum of the City of New York; Museum of London; Nebraska State Historical Society; Nederlands Kostuummuseum, The Hague; John Noble; Nordiska Museet in Stockholm; Jessica Norman; Kay Orth; Nancy Palazzolo; Jessie Parsons; Jan Payson; Anne-Marie Pelgrims; Marion Poe; Elsie & Al Potter; Helen Ralph; Vivian Rasberry; Mary Lou Ratcliffe; Helen Read; Kathryn Reilly; Judy Reis; late Mary Roberson; Ardelle Ross; Phyllis Salak; Mrs. Schellenberg; Pat & John Schoonmaker; Ben & Martha Sewell; Pamela Brown Sherer; Nancy Slattery; Kitty Smith; Mrs. Moreland Smith; Smithsonian Institution; Margaret Woodbury Strong Museum; Marjorie Tatnall; Mary Alice Thacker; April Thompson; Paige Thornton; Hazel Toon; Bella Traags; Bettyanne Twigg; Hazel Ulseth; late Henrietta Van Size; Jane Walker; Z. Frances Walker; Mathias Wanke; Washington Dolls' House & Toy Museum; Marg Weber-Beck; Jean Nelke West; Ruth Whittier; Margaret Whitton; Betty Lou Wiecksel; late Estelle Winthrop; Richard Withington; Alma Wolfe; Ashley Wright; Richard Wright.

Special thanks go to the following people or companies who graciously provided us with original source material for our research: Maria Argyriadis; Bernard Barenholtz; Bartshe Family; Bethnal Green Museum; Brooklyn Museum; Robert and Katrin Burlin; Poma Casó; Jürgen & Marianne Cieslik; Centre d'Étude et de Recherche Sur les Poupées; Chicago Historical Society; Deutsche Spielzeug Museum in Sonneberg; Katherine Donaldson; Beppe Garella; Margaret Glover; Gordon Gray; Richard Merrill; John Noble; Elizabeth Pierce; Mme. Florence Poisson, curator of the Roybet Fould Museum; Maurine Popp; Anne Marie & Jacques Porot; Phyllis Salak; Salzburger Museum Carolina Augusteum; Pat Schoonmaker; descendant of Mrs. Seyfried; Sotheby Parke Bernet; Margarete Steiff & Co.; Margaret Woodbury Strong Museum; François Theimer; Victoria & Albert Museum; Wenham Museum; Widener Library, Harvard University; Winterthur Rare Book Library.

One of the greatest pleasures in writing a research book is the sharing of information with other dedicated researchers. It has been our particular good fortune to have Jürgen and Marianne Cieslik generously share many of their findings in German records with us. The United States Patent Office has copies of the German D.R.P. patents but not the German D.R.G.M. patents. Practically all of the many references to D.R.G.M. patents in this encyclopedia were based on the findings of the Ciesliks. Mme. Florence Poisson has kindly provided us with the information researched by CERP (Centre d'Étude et de Recherche sur les Poupées) pertaining to French dolls. Dr. Eva Horvath Moskovszky has searched Hungarian records and provided us with the data that she found.

Irving and Iverna Foote have given us valuable assistance, especially in clarifying the directions for the use of this book.

Many people have shared their knowledge of dolls with us and now it is our pleasure and privilege to provide others with the benefits and joys of sharing information.

INTRODUCTION

The identification of a doll is the most frequently sought information: who made the doll, where it was made, when it was made, and how it was made. The first COLLECTOR'S ENCYCLOPEDIA OF DOLLS supplies this information for a large number of dolls made through 1925. For this second volume the cut-off date has been moved forward from 1925 to 1930. These added years were a time of prosperity when markets expanded and many new dolls made their appearance. The terminating year, 1930, brings us almost to the end of the great German bisque doll era, when the rise of militarism in Germany caused toys and especially bisque-head dolls to decline in importance. In a few instances, the history of an important doll or doll maker has been carried past the 1930 date to complete the subject. The variation in dolls is endless. No book on dolls is ever complete or ever will be—the subject is too vast and too complex.

Since the first COLLECTOR'S ENCYCLOPEDIA OF DOLLS was published in 1968, we have done a tremendous amount of primary research both for the period prior to 1925 as well as from 1925 through 1930. It is now our privilege to share this additional information with you. Our ongoing research has brought to light a considerable amount of new and valuable information which we are offering in this second volume. Not wishing to repeat data, a large star (★) has been placed at the end of any entry for which additional information appeared in the first volume.

This volume tries to answer the who, where, when, and how questions as fully and as accurately as possible. Primary sources have been studied and analyzed. Seldom is an entry based on a single source; and where sources give conflicting information, either this fact is noted or the most probable information is given along with an indication of questionability.

Long experience in analyzing data has shown us many pitfalls that must be avoided. Family tradition in dating an antique doll nearly always places the date as one generation too early. In other words, the doll is allocated to the mother who bought it rather than to the child who actually played with it. Information supplied by elderly people who were once involved in the production of dolls must be checked carefully against source material contemporary with the manufacturing of those dolls. Sometimes also, the children or other relatives of people who worked with dolls supply information and this needs to be examined even more critically. Advertising hyperbole, as well, must be discounted to arrive at the truth. Allegations that a doll is the first of its type are often erroneous. Designating a doll as "popular priced" meant that it was a cheap doll. The original prices included for many of the dolls provide an indication of the relative values of various dolls when new. Dolls that look alike were usually made during the same period but not necessarily by the same company or companies. Bisque heads with the same mold number were not always made in the same factory. Two or more factories could have been hired to produce heads from identical molds, or two or more factories could have registered the same number for different molds. If porcelain heads were of different sizes but bear the same mold number, they are not necessarily identical. Different sizes of the same mold number do not necessarily remain identical in appearance as proportions differ with the changing of sizes. See Ill. 1121 in the first COLLECTOR'S ENCYCLOPEDIA OF DOLLS, which shows seven Hertel, Schwab heads all mold number 151, but differing in appearance. Nearly all dolls were hand-painted and therefore differ slightly in appearance. Another cause for differences in the appearance of dolls made in identical molds could arise from the trimming and finishing done by hand, especially when eyes and/or mouths were cut out. Photographs of dolls are preferable to artists' drawings but even the photographer's angle and lighting can sometimes give a distorted impression of a doll.

Many people have difficulty reading marks accurately, so the identification of a doll by its mark has to be done with some caution. It should be noted that stickers, stamps, tags, or even decals with identification can have been added recently. These pitfalls and more have been recognized and every effort has been made to avoid the inclusion of misunderstood or erroneous marks.

Who "made" a particular doll and where was it "made" are very complex questions. It is necessary to understand how dolls were made in order to answer these questions adequately. Rarely were dolls made by a single person, and seldom were they entirely made in a single factory. In fact, the various parts often came from different countries. Parts of dolls were frequently produced as a home industry and brought to a central distributor who, in many cases, assembled the pieces before distribution. This was especially true in Europe, but even in America such dolls as the Kamkins were fabricated in this way. In the German-speaking parts of Europe, where most dolls were made, the person or company that collected the parts, assembled the dolls, and distributed them all over the world was referred to as a *Verleger,* a term for which there seems to be no adequate English translation. (Literally, *Verleger* means publisher.)

The term "French Doll" frequently referred to a particular type of doll and not to the country of origin. Not only the various parts of a doll often came from different countries but the men who manufactured the dolls often worked in several different countries during their careers. For example, Adolph Cohen was educated in Moscow, worked in French and German doll factories for twenty years, then in 1902 came to the United States where he made dolls for many years. The clothes on his dolls after he came to America were based on French models.

When we come to bisque head dolls the who and where becomes even more complicated. Collectors are accustomed to referring to a doll in accordance with the identification on the head. But often heads from the same mold were used by different manufacturers, each of whom would have given their individual doll a different name. This is especially true for the Armand Marseille bisque heads mold #s 370, 390, 341, and 351. One can only distinguish between a Lullabye Baby, My Dream Baby, and Rock-a-Bye Baby by the type of body and original clothes. The bisque heads are all of the same mold. Not only the heads but the entire doll often presents problems in identification.

Also receiving recognition are the designer, the sculptor who made the model, the porcelain factory (or sometimes several factories) that made the head, the factory that made the eyes, the factory that made the wig, and the factory or people who made the body. Last, but not least, there was the *Verleger* who financed the production, owned the designs for the doll and its clothes, engaged the work of the many home workers and/or factories, and arranged the assembling of all the parts as well as the distribution. The names or initials often found on dolls and the ones that collectors usually refer to as those of the manufacturer actually may be those of the *Verleger* or artist. Large toy shops and stores often assembled dolls and dressed them, and in a few cases even painted the faces. Thus many dolls bear the name of a toy shop or store. Collectors do not always realize that Gesland, Simonne, and certain other names were actually those of shops. Sometimes it is the name of the person who designed and/or made the clothes that is associated with dolls as, for example, Madame Alexander and Molly-'es.

Molly-'es is a good example of the variations one finds in names. Records and advertisements often gave different spellings or ways in which names were written. Molly-'es also appeared as Molly 'es, Molly 'Es, Moll-Es and Molly-Es. Molly-'es was chosen for the entry name because that is the way the official trademark registration appeared. Frequently when two different spellings were found both were listed as entries, but one was only cross-indexed. Names for the same model doll often varied according to the language of the country of final distribution. French names were the most frequently bastardized when applied in non-French-speaking countries. Unfortunately, many companies were not always consistent in the manner in which they presented the names of their dolls. For example, Baby Grumpy later became just Grumpy.

Since the various parts of a doll were often made in factories scattered all over the world, it is very difficult to assign a particular country of origin to many of our dolls. There is a considerable amount of evidence that nearly all bisque heads were made in German areas at least a decade prior to World War I. Very little proof has yet been found that in this period bisque heads were made in France, except at the Jumeau factory in Montreuil-sous-Bois, the Gaultier factory in Charenton, and a few other factories. Prior to World War I, there were innumerable statements by various Frenchmen that all other bisque heads came from Germany. The Germans poured their dolls' heads at an earlier date than most of the French doll makers, who continued until at least about 1890 to press theirs. Thus an examination of a porcelain doll's head to see whether it was poured or pressed can sometimes provide clues as to where and when it was made. Dolls in a wide range of quality were produced in most major doll-making countries. The best quality was not necessarily made in France.

The many descriptions of the various processes used in making dolls often provide clues as to possible dates of manufacture. This is especially true of the pressed versus poured porcelain heads and the cold press versus hot press composition heads. Descriptions of manufacturing often reveal the hazardous materials formerly used in the production of dolls.

Dolls have often been given names that depended on their costumes. Thus the same doll can have a different name when it is dressed in a different outfit. This was as true in the past as it is for modern dolls. When the dolls are identical but dressed in different outfits, each of which was given a separate name, these names usually do not have separate entries but are listed in the Index. Identical dolls in identical costumes occasionally had their names changed. For example "Mimi" later was called "Patsy." Often the same name was used for different dolls; that is, companies might change their dolls but keep a popular name such as Effanbee's "Baby Dainty." Popular names were often used by more than one company; a good example is the innumerable "Red Riding Hood" dolls. Dolls from the same mold were sometimes painted differently, and then they became entirely different dolls, Amberg's "Charlie Chaplin" and "Oo-Gug-Luk" is an example.

Primary sources of information about antique dolls are often in languages other than English and must therefore be translated if possible. A dictionary translation often fails to give the true meaning as it relates to dolls. For example, the German word *Täufling*, according to the dictionary, means a baby of christening age. In the 1850s the name "Täufling" was applied to a crying baby doll of the type that bore the 1857 patent stamp of Motschmann. But by 1900 the name "Täufling" was applied to any doll provided it was dressed only in a chemise. These included the dolly-faced bisque head, ball-jointed composition dolls that the purchaser could dress as a child of any age or even as an adult. When it has been found necessary to use words from a foreign language, there usually is an entry for the word, and an attempt to explain its meaning or meanings as applied to dolls.

Historical terms and viewpoints have been quoted, some of which may be offensive to modern readers. These, however, in no way reflect the viewpoints of the authors or the publishers. Wartime propaganda must be understood for what it was. Practically all history is written from a biased viewpoint. However, dolls themselves are tangible artifacts revealing the truth about our past.

The dates given for the dolls usually represent the period for which information was found; that is, when they appeared on the market or were recorded in a copyright or patent. This is not always the entire period during which the dolls were made. When an additional period was indicated, it is noted by "before" or "and later." The beginning dates for makers, producers, and distributors were generally the earliest ones found that indicate an actual involvement with dolls. Precise dates are very difficult to determine. Sometimes three or four different dates were given for the founding or establishing of a company. The date that appeared most frequently was the one generally selected. The formation of a company or partnership could usually be determined but the first creation of dolls by those forming the company or partnership was difficult to date. Seldom did porcelain factories make only dolls' heads; for example, Simon & Halbig was listed in an 1890s directory as a factory that made dishes—no mention of dolls. No one knows when most porcelain factories made their first or last doll's head. Sometimes dolls were produced by entrepreneurs before they actually founded a company. Sculptures and paintings were often the inspiration for many dolls' faces as well as clothing. One can easily recognize Della Robbia cherubs in many of the faces of dolls. Just prior to World War I Käthe Kruse created cloth dolls based on the child's head sculptured by Duquesnois in the early 1600s. This artistic success caused others to create similar dolls in other materials. For example, in bisque the Ciesliks have identified the Kämmer & Reinhardt mold number 115, and similar dolls made by Armand Marseille (Fany) and Bruno Schmidt as well as the cloth dolls made by Erich Klötzer; we have been able to add Schoenhut's Baby in wood as another example. A copy of the Duquenois head was found in the Lenci factory. Information on many of the famous artists who created dolls covers their lifetime because it is uncertain when and for how long they were involved with the creation of dolls. Most successful dolls were copied inexhaustibly. Even cloth dolls with molded faces were often derived from some earlier popular porcelain doll's head.

The pictures, marks, names, tables, and indexes should all assist the reader to identify a particular doll. The additional information found in the first COLLECTOR'S ENCY-CLOPEDIA OF DOLLS, indicated by a star at the end of an entry should always be consulted in order to obtain a full account of a company or a doll. There are numerous references to illustrations in THE COLLECTOR'S BOOK OF DOLLS' CLOTHES that will also be helpful in the identification of a doll.

The reader must be aware of the fact that the prices quoted in this book are the original prices (though they may have been translated from another currency into dollars at the rate of exchange in effect at that time). These prices bear no relationship to prices on today's market. Many of the heights listed were from original catalogs and do not correspond precisely to the heights of dolls as measured at present. Variables enter into the measuring of heights, which account for as much as an inch difference for a large doll. The smaller the doll, the less the variation should be. These variations must be kept in mind when using the many Size-Height Relationship tables. However, these tables can provide a key to those puzzling coded size numbers found on a great many dolls and will help verify the total originality of a doll as intended originally by the manufacturer. The size number is related to the height of a doll and if you can measure the height of your doll and read its size number, you can then compare these numbers with known makers using similar size-height relationships, thus possibly identifying a probable maker.

Nearly all of the items discussed in the Introduction to the first COLLECTOR'S ENCYCLOPEDIA OF DOLLS are pertinent for Volume Two. The reader is urged to study both Introductions, as well as the section How to Use This Book, in order to obtain the greatest benefit from both books.

The authors have endeavored to provide a tremendous amount of information in a readily accessible, clear but condensed form which includes some abbreviations and symbols that are used throughout this book.

ABBREVIATIONS AND SYMBOLS

Ca.	=	about
Cie.	=	Company
cir.	=	circumference
cm.	=	centimeter (centimeters)
Co.	=	Company
Gebr.	=	Gebrüder (Brothers)
in.	=	inch (inches)
h.	=	height (used only in captions)
ht.	=	height (used only in text)
hts.	=	heights (used only in text)
Ill.	=	Illustration
Inc.	=	Incorporated
Mfg.	=	Manufacturing
née	=	maiden name

no.	=	number (used with "style" as style no.)
nos.	=	numbers (used with "style" as style nos.)
Vve.	=	Widow
#	=	number (used with "mold" as mold #)
★		Placed at the end of an entry signifies that additional information on that entry can be found in the first COLLECTOR'S ENCYCLOPEDIA OF DOLLS.
†		Placed at the end of a name indicates that additional information about this name can be found in the first COLLECTOR'S ENCYCLOPEDIA OF DOLLS, but not in Volume Two.
*		Used for a footnote reference.

HOW TO USE THIS BOOK

The reader will find this book useful not only in identifying a specific doll but also in providing a background and understanding of dolls in general and their manufacture in America and Europe, as well as elsewhere.

In order to identify a doll, examine it carefully. Locate any identification on the doll. There may be incised or embossed marks on the head, chest, back of the body or soles of the feet. Sometimes it is difficult to read a mark accurately or part of the mark may be missing. It is wise to check the indexes in this book relating to marks such as those having numbers and/or initials, symbols, etc. This should help to verify your mark, but it must be remembered that slight variations often occur in marks, especially those done by hand. Stamped or decal marks are usually found on the body of the doll. All parts of the body as well as the clothes should be examined for possible marks. Tags, stickers, ribbon cloth labels attached to clothes or cloth bodies, and initials or names on jewelry worn by the doll all aid in the identification. Remember that dolls often had parts made by various people and/or factories and sometimes even stores. Therefore it is wise to examine all parts of the doll as well as its clothes, if original, in order to fully identify it. Many of the marks are only initials or are in code, the various indexes in this book will help to identify these cryptic symbols. Once you have found an entry for your doll or its maker, be sure to read all cross-references denoted by the italicized names. The name is italicized only the first time that it appears in an entry. When the word *Mama* is italicized it refers to a special type of doll that says "Ma Ma" and can "walk" when led.

Unfortunately sometimes recent reproductions of bisque dolls carry the marks of an old doll, a fact that must be kept in mind when examining a doll.

If you are unable to find any marks or other identification on the doll, examine it carefully to see if it is poured or pressed when bisque or china to help determine its origin both geographic and chronological. Look at the pictures in this book and in the first COLLECTOR'S ENCYCLOPEDIA OF DOLLS, (see also the pictures in THE COLLECTOR'S BOOK OF DOLLS' CLOTHES, which is a chronological survey of dolls). Read the captions and accompanying entries for any pictured doll that resembles your doll. General entries for materials such as China, Cloth, Wood, and so forth as well as Chronology, Clothes, entries for Countries, and the various entries on Manufacture should provide information about dolls that are similar to yours. Most popular dolls had numerous imitations which sometimes preclude a definite attribution.

Distributors at various levels have been included in this volume to a greater extent than in the first ENCYCLOPEDIA. The entries for American, British, French, and German stores provide information concerning the types of dolls for sale in these countries at different periods.

The volume of information about dolls is so tremendous that every effort has been made not to repeat facts, either those that have been covered in Volume One or those covered elsewhere in Volume Two. This makes it necessary for the reader to seek in several places the full information about a given doll, doll producing company or doll distributor. Attention is directed to the additional information in three ways: first, all names in italics are shown as separate entries in Volume Two; second, all names followed by a † mark in Volume Two are separate entries in Volume One but not in Volume Two; third, all entries in Volume Two having a ★ at the end have a corresponding entry in Volume One with additional information. When the starred entry in Volume One is consulted, probably it too will have italicized names which should be examined. In order to obtain the complete story, usually it will be necessary to work with both volumes and with a sizable number of entries. If the name does not have an entry, search the indexes for it. Remember that spellings often varied.

Let us take a hypothetical example of a doll for which information is desired. The doll has a bisque head, wig, sleeping eyes, open mouth, teeth, and a fully jointed composition body. It measures 19½ inches (49.5 cm.) tall and has initials and a small number incised on its neck. First the initials are looked up in the index; this leads to the identification of the company that made the doll, or part of it, and the place where it was made. There are long lists of dolls produced by this company over a period of years. The ★ at the end of the entry means that additional names of dolls made by this company may be found in Volume One. Each one of these names in italics or with a † after it should be consulted to see if it corresponds with your doll. You find that in a certain year this company produced a 20 inch (51 cm.) doll that corresponds otherwise with your doll. The difference between 19½ inches and 20 inches is probably due to the fact that originally the wig was fluffier and also producers tended to report slightly exaggerated heights for their dolls. If there is a Size-Height Relationship table in this book for your particular doll, the small number on your doll's head should approximately correspond in size with the 20 inch height as given in the table.

Pertinent general entries will provide further information. For example, if your doll was made in Germany, you should read not only the German Dolls entry but also the entry for Thüringia and for Sonneberg, or wherever the doll was made. Entries for eyes, wigs, and so forth also can be of interest.

If your doll is without clothes, you may be fortunate enough to find a description of its original clothes and perhaps its accessories, if any, under the entry for the name of your doll. If there is no description of the clothes, the entry will give you the dates for your doll so that you can study the Clothes entry and other similar dolls of the same period for which descriptions of the clothes are given. Numerous references are made to the catalog pages in THE COLLECTOR'S BOOK OF DOLLS' CLOTHES. These catalog pages in many instances will show your doll and what it originally wore. Volume Two contains a large number of tables which will enable you to identify readily a doll and its period. Often a doll of the same design was made for many years but its costume was frequently changed. This information usually has been put in tabular form to facilitate identification.

If your doll has a mold number, the many tables and index of mold numbers will be especially useful. Many dolls, especially bisque or celluloid ones, are marked with numbers. These numbers usually represent the mold number and/or the size number. The mold numbers generally have three or more digits; each mold number can be identified with one company or, sometimes, with two or more companies. The number indexes and the mold number tables and examples can help to identify your particular doll.

The size numbers usually have only one or two digits. Sometimes the size is given in centimeters, which can be at least as high as 100 for a large doll. At other times the size is given in inches. Only a few companies were known to have used these standard units of measurement on their dolls and/or dolls' heads. More frequently the size numbers are in code, and the use of given numbers varied not only for different producers, but occasionally the same producer appears to have changed his size code slightly from time to time, possibly due to changes in body styles (see Bébé Jumeau table). By cross-indexing the height and size number of your doll, often you will be able to locate one or two of the Size-Height Relationship tables that approximately match the size number and height of your doll, thus giving you a probable producer (or producers). The Size-Height tables were based on catalog information on a large sample of the designated dolls. Your measurement of height, especially on large dolls, may not tally exactly with that shown in the various tables. The type of body, its condition, and its originality can affect the doll's height. This is especially true in the case of a stuffed kid or cloth body that has settled down with age. Differences in hairstyle or a wig that has changed its shape with the passage of time also can account for variations in height. The coded size numbers represent clues but cannot be relied on as exact identification for some dolls. Porcelain heads that were sold separately would have been attached to bodies of different sizes. In a few cases the location of the size numbers on the doll can suggest possible producers.

Sometimes numbers are difficult to read. Confusion can often arise between certain numbers and similarly shaped letters. Occasionally a good rubbing of a mark can be easier to read than the actual mark on the doll.

The many indexes in both Volume One and Volume Two should be fully consulted since they provide important key information that may lead to the identification of your particular doll.

Names of dolls were sometimes translated into several languages by the manufacturer depending on the country of distribution. There is usually a cross-reference or index entry for these various versions of the name, but when a name does not appear as an entry, sometimes it can be located by translating it into another language. For example, if a German name appears on a doll the English equivalent may be found as an entry instead of the German name. Names of people are listed under the surname unless it is a doll's name, in which case the entry corresponds with the actual name of the doll.

Entries are usually under the name of the Company instead of the name of the Factory or Works. One exception in this volume is the use of the Chad Valley entry instead of Johnson Bros., which was used in the first "Encyclopedia." The exception is made because Chad Valley is a name more readily recognized by doll collectors.

Names for dolls and/or doll producing companies were often derived by onomatopeia, that is, according to the sound of their initials: for example, Effanbee for Fleischaker & Baum. Another frequently used abbreviation was the use of an acronym, that is, taking the first several letters in a long name, such as Mawaphil for Mary Waterman Phillips. Spelling variations often occur but names usually keep the same phonetic pronunciation.

The entry names of Steiff dolls are given in abbreviated form as they originally appeared in the Steiff catalogs. In fact, all doll names correspond to those given in catalogs or advertisements when the doll first appeared on the market.

Black Dolls and Cloth Dolls entries in Volume Two correspond to the Negro Dolls and Rag Dolls entries in Volume One respectively.

States, Shires, Provinces, and so forth are abbreviated according to customary usage, as for example, Thür. for Thüringia, the German province where most dolls were made prior to World War I.

Some of the quotations in this volume contain varying viewpoints concerning certain dolls, thus reflecting social and regional differences. This is especially true for the patriotic bias in wartime. These statements are valuable because they show the thinking about dolls at a particular period or place but do not necessarily conform to modern ideas.

The heights of dolls are listed first in the measurement unit as given in the original source, then in parentheses they are translated into the alternative measurement. For example, centimeters are listed first when found in the original data and are followed by the inch translation in parentheses, or the reverse if indicated.

Prior to 1920, when the American currency remained relatively stable in relation to other currencies, conversion from foreign currencies to American dollars was made on the basis of:

A British shilling = 25¢
A French franc = 20¢
A German mark = 25¢

It is especially important to remember that the prices given for dolls are those for which the dolls were originally offered for sale. *They are NOT today's prices.*

A

A. A. Mascot. See **Road Scout Mascots.**

A. B. C. Doll Shop. 1927. Denver, Colo. Firm members were A. B. Cole, John and Lucinda McCourt. Customers selected the various parts of a doll that they liked best, and these were put together to produce a custom-made doll that was nearly always different from the others.

A. D. T. Société Nouvelle des Etablissements. 1925–30 and later. Paris. Factories at Pont-à-Mousson and Forback, Moselle. The heads and bodies of the dolls were composition.

A Dillar–A Dollar. See **Hug-Me-Tight.**

A. J. Prior to 1927. Mark found on a doll that might have been made or distributed by *Mme. A. Jomin* of Paris. The mark was on a bisque head with a closed mouth.

A. L. Doll Parts Supply. 1929 and other years. U.S.A. Manufactured composition parts such as heads, hands, or arms for dolls.

A la Galerie Vivienne. See **Guillard, François.**

A la Maison Bleue. 1925–30. Paris. Made or distributed dolls ★

A la Récompense. Ca. 1905 and probably other years. Paris. Toy store whose oval paper sticker was found on the sole of a leather shoe worn by a bisque socket head doll wearing a chemise stamped *Eden Bébé.* The lettering was dark green on a white ground and the address appears to have been near the *Nadaud* firm.

1. Paper sticker used by the Paris store A la Récompense and found on a doll wearing a chemise stamped Eden Bébé. See Ill. 851.

A la Tentation. 1889–1900. Trademark of Maison Guyot[†] for dolls and bébés. Paper labels reading "A la Tentation//Guyot//Bébés & Jouets" have been found on several dolls. The bisque head on one of these dolls was marked "C//P 13 G Déposé." P.G. were the initials used by *Pintel & Godchaux.*★

A l'Ancre. 1925–29. Mark used by *A. Hugonnard,* an establishment that produced dolls.

A 1 (A I) Dolls. 1922–27. Brand of high-quality cloth dolls made by *Dean.* These dolls had a black-and-silver-colored pendant attached to them.

1922: Included three *Tru-to-Life* models that came with or without wigs, dressed in 14 styles; six Tru-to-Life models without wigs; 32 designs of flat-face models. Among the models were a baby doll in ankle-length dress with a pacifier in its mouth; a doll representing a little girl wore a dress above its knees and a hat; a boy dressed in a Little Lord Fauntleroy costume; and a character doll dressed as a sailor.

1924: Included *Maisie, Dora, Wendy, Trixie,* and lines called *Popular Dolls* and *Posy Dolls.*

1926: Posy Doll line was still being made; a new doll was *Buster Brown.*

A. 1. Line. 1927. Trade name for a line of toys imported by *Amberg.* This may possibly be the *A 1* line made by *Dean.*

A. P. B. Co. 1920s. Boston, Mass. Made American stoneware dolls' heads. Mark: See Ill. 4. Their heads resembled the *Armand Marseille* dolly-faced socket heads.

A. P. D. Manufacturing Co. World War I period. U.S.A. Made American stoneware dolls' heads; often with a molded Liberty cap, molded hair, and painted eyes. These were usually shoulder heads.

One of these was marked "Made in U.S.A." on the front and "A.P.D. M[f]. Co.//122" on the back. Ht. of shoulder head 5¾ in. (14.5 cm.).

A. & M. See **Moehling, M. J. (Anger and Moehling).**

Abel, Samuel. 1903–30 and later. New York City. Manufactured dolls' eyes.

Abeles & Schnabel. 1912–25. Eger, Bohemia (Czech.). Made dolls.

Aborigines. 1920. Made by *Harwin & Co.* Cloth doll with three-dimensional face. Can stand or sit.

2 & 3. A la Tentation paper label marks found on dolls, including a doll whose head was incised P.G. for Pintel & Godchaux. See Ill. 2109.

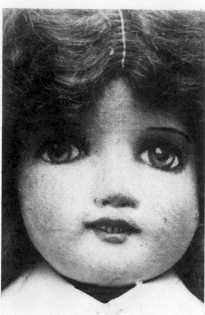

4A & B. A 1 cloth doll made by *Dean,* in their Tru-to-Life line. It has a pressed cloth shoulder head, mohair wig, molded blue eyes. The body was stockinet over a wire armature and the hands were composition. It is dressed in a black Little Lord Fauntleroy-style suit. Mark: Ill. –5. H. 14 in. (35.5 cm.). *Courtesy of Mike White.*

5. Mark on tag of an A 1 doll made by Dean.

Abraham & Straus. 1903–30 and later. Brooklyn, N.Y. In 1915 the store featured dolls dressed to represent various nations.★

Abrahams, Hyman A. 1915–21. London. Distributor established in the 1850s. During World War I, featured dolls of various types, including French dressed dolls, composition dolls, cloth dolls, celluloid dolls, and rubber dolls.

1915: Canadian composition dolls, fully jointed, sold for

6. Mark used by A. P. B. Co., a Boston stoneware doll factory.

7. Mark used on ceramic dolls' heads by the A. P. D. Manufacturing Co.

25¢ to $2.65. Cloth dolls representing soldiers were first named *Territorial* and later called Fall In. *Golliwoggs* were available for 12¢ and 25¢.

1916: The featured doll was a "porcelain" *(British Ceramic) Charlie Chaplin* with movable head. Dressed dolls with bent legs or with straight legs were available.

Abramson, H., & Co. 1918–19. Brooklyn, N.Y. Manufactured composition character dolls with painted hair and painted eyes. The baby dolls wore either long or short baby dresses. Dolls were priced from 14¢ to $1.00.

Abt and Franke. 1865–1930 and later. Hannover, Prussia. Their doll factory named Hannoversche Puppenfabrik made all kinds of dressed dolls, including celluloid dolls and ball-jointed dolls.

1910: Specialized in small dressed dolls 5 to 9½ in. (12.5 to 24 cm.) and character dolls 7½ to 21½ in. (19 to 55 cm.). These included babies in swaddling clothes and dolls dressed in regional costumes.★

Ackermann's Repository of Arts. Ca. 1820s and later. London. A hexagonal box labeled "Ackermann's Repository of Arts, 101 Strand" contained a pair of painted kid piano dolls dressed as a Swiss bridal couple. Ht. 3½ in. (9 cm.).

Acme Toy Manufacturing Co. 1908–30 and later. New York City. Made a variety of popular priced and quality composition head dolls. One of their composition head dolls marked "ACME TOY CO." on its head, had molded and painted hair, metal sleeping eyes, an open mouth, a flange neck, and a cloth body with composition hands and feet. Ht. 24 in. (61 cm.); circumference of the head 18 in. (45.5 cm.).

1919: Stuffed character dolls. Baby dolls with wigs dressed in short baby dresses, caps, and bootees.

1921: Cork-stuffed body with inside joints. Bent-limb baby dolls wore long or short baby dresses and came in five sizes.

8A. Acme composition baby doll with glass eyes, open mouth, two upper teeth, dimples, as advertised by PLAYTHINGS, May, 1929. Note the Acme trademark on the tag.

The straight-leg dolls had sleeping eyes or painted eyes, wigs or painted hair. The wigs were mohair or human hair. Some of these dolls wore knitted sweaters.

1922: Specialized in character dolls.

1923: Cotton- and cork-stuffed bodies. Over 100 numbers in various styles and sizes. Some of these numbers had the new mama-papa voice. Mr. Richlin created new designs for the dolls, but buyers could supply their own designs. Acme manufactured the *Mama* dolls for the *Kiddiejoy* line of *Hitz, Jacobs & Kassler.*

1924: High-grade dolls in various styles, six sizes; all dolls came with mama voices. Dolls had a human-hair wig and

ACME TOY ©

8B. Mark used by Acme on composition heads of dolls.

moving eyes or a mohair wig and stationary eyes. The cheapest dolls had painted hair and eyes. The dolls were dressed in voiles, organdies, silks, or worsted sets with bonnets. There were 40 different costumes, including a long dress on a baby doll.

1926: Mama dolls with composition head, arms, and legs; cotton-stuffed cloth bodies. Dolls with sleeping eyes had eyelashes. Wigs of human hair or sewn mohair were in the latest styles of hair dressing. Also made infant and baby dolls. Acme was sued by *Horsman* for copying *Tynie Baby*, but Horsman lost because they had only "E.I.H." on their dolls and not the full name.

Clothes were advertised as being in the same material and style as those of real children and babies. One baby doll wore a short dress, knitted jacket, and close-fitting cap with rosettes over each ear. The booties were also knitted.

Kaufman, Levenson & Co. distributed Acme dolls.

Acme exhibited a doll at the Philadelphia Sesquicentennial. It had a wig, earrings, teeth, swivel neck, and a ball-jointed composition body with wrist joints. The doll was dressed in a 1920s version of what Dolley Madison might have worn on a formal occasion.

1927: Baby dolls were most important, Mama dolls next in importance. Acme was licensed by *Voices, Inc.* to use their patented voices and criers. A new doll represented a slender-limbed Miss. Dolls were dressed in crepe de chine, taffeta, or rayon costumes. On their heads were either large hair bows or caps.

1928: A new line of baby dolls called *Honey* was introduced. Also new character dolls. The Mama dolls and slim-body types continued to be made. Clothes were colorful. Distributors were Kaufman, Levenson & Co., Salt Lake Hardware Co., and *Vier Bros.*

1929: Quality dolls in original designs; specialized in large Mama dolls with full-length composition legs and human hair wigs. New line of Mama dolls wore sports costumes or fancy dresses, among them brushed wool suits, tam-o'-shanters, coats, and leggings in bright colors or silk coats and bonnets. Many new sizes and styles of Honey baby dolls were made. Small novelty dolls, both black and white, wore felt hats and coats in bright blue, green, red, or yellow.

1930: Factory expanded; continued to make baby, Mama, and slim-body dolls. Honey line was still most important. Cloth-body dolls were stuffed with kapok. Human-hair wigs and silk wigs came in four shades, with long or short curls; some had bandeaux around the hair. Mama dolls with composition head, arms and legs and cloth bodies wore drawers that showed below their very short dresses. One 27 in. (68.5 cm.) doll was dressed in a silk taffeta dress with bonnet to match. This doll came in blue, pink or maize color. ★

Acorn Doll Co. 1919–21. Brooklyn, N.Y. Made dolls with composition heads and cork-stuffed cloth bodies or all-composition fully jointed character dolls. The dolls had either painted or sleeping eyes. The sleeping-eyed dolls had mohair wigs. The dolls came in various sizes from 10 to 26 in. (25.5 to 66 cm.). The trademark was an acorn with "A.D.C.//American Made." in it. ★

9. Mark used by the Acorn Doll Co.

Acrobats. Ca. 1905–24 and probably later. *Schoenhut* wooden dolls dressed as a *Lady Acrobat* and a *Gent Acrobat* in felt one-piece suits.

Acs. Professor. 1920. Central Europe. Distributed museum-quality dolls.

Ad. Rena Co. 1927–28. Brooklyn, N.Y. Manufactured composition heads, hands, etc., for dolls. Licensed by *Voices, Inc.* to use patented mama voices and criers in their dolls. Member of the *American Doll Manufacturers' Association.*

Adalene. 1927–28. Trade name for dolls made by *Ernst Liebermann.*

Adam, George Max. 1922. Chicago, Ill. Listed dolls.

Adelphie. 1918. Paris. Workshop where dolls' clothes were made.

Adler Favor and Novelty Co. 1925–30 and later. St. Louis, Mo. Made cloth dolls with floppy arms and legs. Successor of Stella Adler.[†]

1928: Designed and manufactured *Doodle Dear*, Foppi Doll, *Bobby Doll*, and carriage dolls.

1929: Added *Boo, Sal, Rube, Bathtub* dolls, and infant dolls. Distributed by *Fred W. Voetsch* in New York.

Adler, J., & Co. Mid-1800s–late 1800s. U.S.-made dolls with composition heads, cloth bodies, leather arms, molded black hair, and painted blue eyes. Ht. 24½ in. (62 cm.); head 6½ in. (16.5 cm.); rectangular paper label on back shoulders reads: "J. Adler & Co. // Superior // American Head // No." This descriptive term "Superior" was used on dolls made by various companies.

Admiral George Dewey. 1898–1900 and possibly later. Various portrait dolls represented Admiral Dewey. These dolls had bisque heads with molded mustache and either painted or glass eyes. The hair was partly molded and the

10A & B. Molded and painted composition shoulder head carrying a paper sticker on the back shoulder plate with the mark for J. Adler & Co. (see Ill. 11). The head has black short wavy hair with a center part, the ears are exposed, and the eyes are blue. It is on a cloth body with leather arms and it is wearing its original clothes, including a red-and-white print dress and a white cotton apron. H. 24½ in. (62 cm.). Shoulder head only 6½ in. (16.5 cm.). *Courtesy of Z. Frances Walker.*

J. ADLER & CO.
Superior
AMERICAN HEAD
N⁰ 7

11. Paper sticker attached to the back of a composition shoulder head of J. Adler & Co. seen in Ill. 10.

12. All-bisque doll representing Admiral Dewey. It has molded and painted hair, mustache, and eyes. Original naval costume. H. 3¾ in. (9.5 cm.). *Courtesy of Clara Hobey.*

pates were open or closed; closed mouth, composition five-piece body or cloth body. The dolls wore appropriate uniforms for a U.S. admiral in the Spanish-American War. The Wenham Museum attributes the largest-size dolls to *Cuno & Otto Dressel.* Ht. 15½ in. (39.5 cm.). Smaller sizes were 8, 12, and 14 in. (20.5, 30.5, and 35.5 cm.).

Other similar portrait dolls represented *Admiral William Thomas Sampson, Admiral Winfield Scott Schley, President William McKinley,* and *Richmond Pearson Hobson.*

The 1899 Dewey Doll[†] of *Gebrüder Süssenguth* was probably a portrait doll.

An all-bisque doll also appears to have been a portrait of Admiral Dewey. This doll had molded hair. (See also **Sonneberg.**)

1899: *Butler Bros.* imported and distributed a portrait doll representing Admiral Dewey. It had a bisque head with molded and painted features, including a mustache, and was dressed as Admiral Dewey. Ht. 12 in. (30.5 cm.).★

Admiral Jellicoe. 1915–17. Composition portrait doll distributed by *Hamley Bros.,* was probably made in the *Women's Emergency Corps Workshop.* It had a composition head with molded hair and features, composition hands, and molded boots on a cloth body, and wore a British naval uniform. The soles of the boots are marked "L" and "R" probably indicating left and right. Ht. 19 in. (48.5 cm.).

Admiral William Thomas Sampson. 1898–1903. Portrait doll of Admiral Sampson had a bisque head with molded hair, mustache, and beard, painted or glass eyes, closed mouth, composition five-piece body. Dolls wore appropriate uniforms for U.S. admirals. The Wenham Museum attributed the largest-size dolls to *Cuno & Otto Dressel.* Ht. 15½ in. (39.5 cm.). Other dolls in this series represented *Admiral Dewey* and *President McKinley.* (See also **Sonneberg.**)

Admiral Winfield Scott Schley. 1898–99. Portrait doll of Admiral Schley had a bisque head with molded hair, mustache, and goatee, painted or glass eyes, closed mouth, composition five-piece body. Dolls wore appropriate uniform for a U.S. admiral. Hts. 8, 12, and 15½ in. (20.5, 30.5, and 39.5 cm.). An 8-in. Admiral Schley has been found marked "17 SC." Other dolls in this series represented *Admiral Dewey* and *President McKinley.* (See also **Sonneberg.**)

13A & B. Composition head molded to represent Admiral Jellicoe. It is part of a series made by the Women's Emergency Corps Workshop during World War I, which included representations of important personages on the Allied side. H. 19 in. (48.5 cm.). *Coleman Collection.*

Admiration. 1917–24. Line of dolls made by *Progressive Toy Co.,* handled by *Charles William.*

1923: Walking dolls with cotton floss-stuffed bodies, all-composition walking and talking dolls and dressed dolls. These dolls had sleeping eyes; some of them could roll their eyes.

1924: Same as 1923, but mama voices and wigs were also mentioned. Some of the dolls sold for $1.00.

1927–28: Doll had rubber arms and hands. Ht. 16 in. (40.5 cm.); priced $3.69.★

Adora-Belle. 1927–29. Line of dolls made by *Reisman, Barron & Co.,* both popular priced and quality dolls, included dressed *Mama* dolls with wigs. The trademark for these was "Brighten the HEART of every child// ADORA-BELLE//DOLLS// REISMAN, BARRON & Co." within a circle.

Adrena Doll Co. 1930 and later. New York City. Made dolls.

Adrian, Elizabeth G. 1925–26, New York City. Obtained a design patent for a doll in 1926.★

Adrienne, Mlle. 1927–30 and later. France. Made portrait dolls of *Marshal Foch, Poincaré, Briand,* and others.

Adt. See **A. D. T.**

Advertising. Sometimes advertising is not entirely factual. When an entry reads "Advertised" consideration should be given to this possibility. Dolls were often described as "French" when perhaps they had only been dressed in France.

Names of dolls as advertised were not always the same. This was especially true for dolls having pronouns in their names such as "My," "Our," and so forth, or having adjectives such as "Little," "Sunny," and so forth. Names were sometimes advertised with hyphens and sometimes without hyphens. (See also *Erroneous Claims.*[†])

Advertising Dolls. 1890s–1930 and later. Many manufacturers used dolls to advertise their products, often in the shape of their trademark. Some of these dolls were given away by the manufacturer for publicity purposes; others were made by doll manufacturers because they were widely known products with a household name. These dolls were priced according to the general market. Probably it also happened that an eye-catching doll was taken over by a perceptive company and used for advertising purposes. The dolls were usually labeled or carried an object that made its representation of the advertising company obvious.

Among the companies that manufactured or used dolls for advertising purposes were the following: *Amberg (Vanta Baby);* American Cereal Co. *(Cereta);* American Character Doll Co. *(Campbell Kids);* American Rice Foods and Cook's Flaked Rice Co. *(Miss Flaked Rice; Miss Malto-Rice);* B. T. Babbitt Co. *(Babbitt Boy);* Babcock's Corylopsis *(Baby But-*

When You
Visit
New York

 MEET "ADORA-BELLE"

Address 893 Broadway

Quality Street For Fine Dolls

14. Advertisement for Adora-Belle dolls in PLAYTHINGS, July, 1927. It shows four different costume styles and the Adora-Belle trademark.

15. Mark used by Reisman, Barron & Co. for their Adora-Belle dolls.

terfly); *Baker & Bennett (Spearmint Kid);* Buster Brown Shoes *(Buster Brown);* Cameo *(R.C.A. Radiotrons);* Collingbourne Mills *(Flossie; Baby);* Corn Products Co. *(Cairo Princess);* Curtiss Candy Co. *(Baby Ruth);* Davis Milling Co. *(Aunt Jemima); (Buster Brown);* Force cereal *(Sunny Jim);* Hamilton Brown Shoe Co. *(Twinkie);* Horsman *(Buster Brown; Campbell Kids; Fairy);* Ideal *(Cracker Jack Boy; Uneeda Kid; Zu-Zu Kid);* Imperial Granum (baby food); *Jack Spratt* flour; *Jantzen Knitting Mills (Jantzen Bathing Tots);* Kellogg Co. *(Goldilocks* plus four other characters from children's tales); *Nelke Corp. (Gold Dust Twins);* Quaker Oats Co. *(Puffy);* Sea Island Sugar Co. *(Gretchen; Grocer; Toy Soldier).*

Aerolite. 1923–26. Trademark used by *Chad Valley.*

1923: Used for down-stuffed cloth dolls, especially those with their clothes printed on and with flat faces. These dolls, 11 in. (28 cm.) high, were numbered RD 40 through RD 46. They were named *Beaver, Jean, Peggy, Peter Pan, Pixie, Red Cloud,* and *Sorna.*

Aerolite was also used for the molded-face stockinet La Petite *Caresse* dolls with curls of real hair and hand-colored faces. These came in four heights from 11 to 18 in. (28 to 45.5 cm.) and cost from $1.15 to $2.10 each. They wore either velveteen or plush clothes trimmed with imitation fur.

1924: The following dolls were kapok-stuffed Aerolite dolls: *Baby Doll, Betty,* Caresse, Ching-a-Ling, *Dan, Dolly, Jack, Jack-o-Jingles, Jill,* La Petite Caresse, *Mephistopheles, Olga, Pretty Jane,* and *Tinkle Belle.* Some were stockinet dolls and some were not.

1926: La Petite Caresse kapok-stuffed Aerolite dolls were similar to those shown in the 1924 catalog; there were also new Aerolite La Petite Caresse dolls with felt faces, dresses, and bonnets.

The name Aerolite seems to disappear from catalogs after 1926.

Aetna Doll & Toy Co. 1908–19. Brooklyn, N.Y. In 1907 the Aetna Toy Animal Co. was organized by *Benjamin Goldenberg;* in 1908 this company changed its name to the Aetna Doll & Toy Co. when it purchased the rights for the Can't Break 'Em[+] dolls from the *American Doll & Toy Co.,* also known as the *American Composition Doll Co.*

1912: *Bernard Lipfert* was employed as a painter.

1918: "Art" dolls made for Horsman included the *Campbell Kids, Peterkin, Peek-a-Boo, Middie, Rookie, Army Nurse,* baby dolls, and girl dolls. ★

1919: The company merged with *Horsman.*

Aetna Novelty Co. 1897–1930 and later. New York City. Made dolls' outfits and dressed dolls.

1908: Advertised dolls' fur sets, outer garments, raincoats, dresses, both trimmed and untrimmed hats, bathrobes, corsets, and side garters.

1913: Advertised dolls' dresses, hats, caps, hose supporters, corsets, sets of clothing, furs, and so forth.

1915: *Emil C. and Louis Loewe* were in charge of this company.

1927: Advertised dolls' dresses, coats (including sportcoats), and sets of clothing.

1928–30: *Katherine Rauser* was the factory representative.

African Dolls. Native dolls varied in size, shape, and material according to the region whence they came. Many of them had a religious significance, especially the fertility dolls.

A traveler in Africa reported in 1879 that he had not seen any play dolls for African children. The Kaffirs made leather dolls for museums but not for the African child. (See also **Senegalaise.**)

Age of Dolls. The two most important factors in dating a doll are the type of the doll and the period of its clothes if they can be definitely identified as original.

16. Group of papier-mâché shoulder head dolls with painted eyes, kid bodies, wooden arms. The age of these dolls is indicated by their hair styles and the shapes of the faces. The doll on the left has short hair and a round face suggesting the 1860s. The tall doll with a carton head, wig, and eyelashes indicated by dots is probably about 1810–20. The small doll in the middle with corkscrew curls and a round face dates from the 1850s. The doll on the right has curls on the side and a bun in back, also a longer face than the other small dolls, which puts it around the 1840s. Hs. left to right 10¾, 14, 6½, and 6¼ in. (27.5, 35.5, 16.5, and 16 cm.). *Courtesy of Sotheby Parke Bernet Inc., N.Y.*

Similar dolls were usually of the same period; however, popular dolls were often made over long periods of time. In identifying the type of doll the artistic design, the material, and the construction should all be studied from a chronological viewpoint (see **Chronology**) in order to obtain clues as to the age of the doll. In some cases this will provide an accurate date, such as for the Joel Ellis dolls made by the *Co-operative Manufacturing Co.* But dolly-faced bisque heads on jointed composition bodies, for example, were made well over a half-century. These dolls had similar designs, material, and construction. Therefore the only real clue to their age lies in their original clothes when these have been preserved.

THE COLLECTOR'S BOOK OF DOLLS' CLOTHES is an invaluable tool in helping the collector determine whether

18. Shiny composition shoulder head, lower arms and legs, on a cloth body. The only hair is a fringe across the upper forehead. The hat covers the rest of the head. The head has painted features, a short neck, and arm creases. Original clothes indicate this German doll was made in the 1880s. H. 12 in. (30.5 cm.). *Coleman Collection.*

clothes are original or not. It is not always easy to identify original clothes, and unfortunately the majority of dolls have been re-dressed. Dolls with their original clothes are more valuable both esthetically and monetarily. Commercially dressed dolls often had new outfits every year in order to remain in style, and so it is possible for these clothes to provide a method for precisely dating a doll. The clothes of dolls dressed at home, especially in the 1800s, usually provide a date within a decade for such dolls. However, it takes considerable expertise to identify original clothes and to know their periods.

Almost no collector is clever enough to produce dresses that can be mistaken for original garments if they are carefully studied. Nearly always there is some clue that will disclose that the clothes were made long after the doll had served its role as a child's plaything.

It has often been said of dolls that they are "later than you think." This truism is borne out by the fact that collectors often fail to realize how recently certain types of dolls were still being made. Bisque-head *Bébé Brus* and *Bébé Jumeaus* were produced as late as the 1950s, and in that decade

17. Papier-mâché doll of a type made around the mid-1800s. The original dress with its large sleeves that have been gathered in and its low waistline pointed in front dates this doll as from the 1840s. H. 17 in. (43 cm.). *Courtesy of Sotheby Parke Bernet Inc., N.Y.*

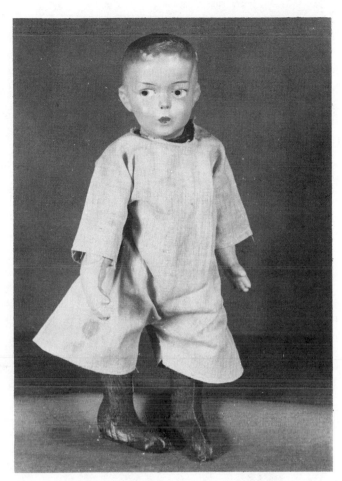

19. Composition flange-neck doll with molded and painted features including short brown hair and roguish blue eyes. The cloth body is pink, green, blue, and brown with composition arms. Original clothes in romper style. This doll was probably made in the early 1910s. H. 12½ in. (31.5 cm.). H. of head only 3 in. (7.5 cm.). *Courtesy of Robert and Katrin Burlin.*

bisque *Bye-Lo Babies* were also made. These were not reproductions, but produced by a continuing use of old molds or new designs made by old firms.

One of the contributions of this volume is the extension of the dates for particular entries given in the first COLLECTOR'S ENCYCLOPEDIA OF DOLLS. Not only has the information been carried forward five years, but many entries have had their dating period otherwise increased. Because the cutoff date in the first COLLECTOR'S ENCYCLOPEDIA OF DOLLS was 1925, many people have mistakenly interpreted that as the terminal date for a doll or company, despite the plus signs following the date.★

Ah Sid. 1908. Cutout cloth doll made by *Saalfield.* The costume of a Chinese boy is printed on the doll. Ht. 7¾ in. (19.5 cm.).

Aicha. 1925. Cloth cutout black doll published by *Fernand Nathan.* It wore a turban, earrings, necklace, and bracelets on its arms and legs. Eyes looked to the side. Ht. 17½ in. (44.5 cm.).

Airman. 1917. Cloth doll made by *Dean.* Made with either a *Tru-to-Life* face or a flat face. A trench coat was supplied as a separate item for this doll.

Akro (Acrobat). 1911–13. Made by *Steiff.* Jointed felt doll representing a circus acrobat dressed in assorted colors, distributed in the U.S. by *Borgfeldt.* Ht. 43 cm. (17 in.); priced $1.60 in Germany in 1911 and $2.10 in New York in 1913.

Al (Alphons, Alfons). 1905–24. Jointed felt doll made by *Steiff;* distributed by *Borgfeldt* in the U.S. and by *Gamage* in England. It had long feet, wore a high collar and a high hat. It was the mate to Gaston *(Ga).* Ht. 35 cm. (14 in.).

1911: Priced 48¢ in Germany. Ht. 35 cm. (14 in.).

1913: Priced 56¢ at Gamage for ht. 11½ in. (29 cm.). Priced $1.00 in New York for ht. 14 in. (35 cm.).

1915: Shown in a painting by *Carl Larsson.*

Alabama Indestructible Doll. See **Smith, Ella.**

Aladin-Lam. 1925–30 and later. Paris. Created *Art Dolls.*

Alart, Eugene. 1913–30 and later. Paris. Factory at Vigneux-sur-Seine and Oise. By 1929 successor was Ernst Alart. Registered a trademark in France in 1913 showing a standing girl doll wearing a chemise. This trademark was pressed into the sole of leather shoes for bébés and dolls. Usually the word "DEPOSÉ" was under the figure.

1916: Supplied leather shoes for dolls made by the *Société Française de Fabrication de Bébés & Jouets* (S.F.B.J.) as well as those modeled by *Albert Marque* and clothed by *Margaine-Lacroix.* Most of these shoes were tied single-strap slippers.

1920s: A long-limbed cloth doll had the Alart trademark on its shoes.

1929–30: Made footwear and other articles of apparel for dolls and character babies.

Alaska Tots. See **Snow Babies.**

Alb (Alb Bauer, Farmer). Before 1911–24. Jointed felt doll made by *Steiff.* Doll represented a peasant with a pillbox-shaped hat. Distributed in the U.S. by *Borgfeldt.* Ht. 35 cm. (14 in.); priced 66¢ in Germany and $1.25 in New York in 1913.

Albert. 1913–16. Jointed felt doll made by *Steiff.* Character doll, dressed as a boy in a pinafore, carried a hoop (see also **Erich**). Distributed in the U.S. by *Borgfeldt.* Ht. in 1913 was 35 cm. (14 in.); priced $2.65. In 1916 hts. were 28 and 50 cm. (11 and 19½ in.).

Albrecht, Frau Spela. 1912. Germany. Designed and made dressed dolls with wax character faces. Some of her dolls were in a Berlin art exhibition according to DEKORATIVE KUNST.

Albrita Dolls. 1915. Cloth dolls made entirely by the *Metropolitan Toy & Doll Co.* The fabric face had painted and pressed features and a curly wig. The cloth body had composition forearms and the dolls came dressed or undressed.

Albritton, Nina Bonner. 1920s and/or 1930s. Clarksville, Tenn. Designed and made "The Albritton Doll." This cloth doll with painted features slightly resembled the *Martha Chase* doll. The unique part of this doll was the way the top of its legs were joined together, above which the legs were jointed at the hips, allowing the legs to swing so that the doll could sit with ease. The dolls were also jointed at the shoulders.

Alcock, Henry. World War I period. Stoke-on-Trent, Staffs. Porcelain manufacturer. Probably made *British Ceramic* dolls' heads.

Alderson, Matthew W. 1890–91. Bozeman, Mont., and Braintree, Mass. U.S., Obtained a German patent (D.R.P.) for dolls' fingers.★

Aldis, Frederic. 1878–1901. London. Handled dolls. (See Ills. 22 and 23.)★

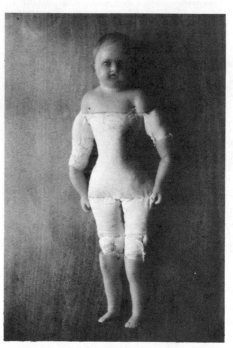

22. Poured wax shoulder head made by Aldis with inserted hair and glass eyes. The cloth body has poured wax limbs which are attached to it with grommets. Mark: Ill. 23. *Courtesy of Marion Poe.*

20. Cloth doll in original 1920s costume including shoes made by Ernst Alart. The doll has a three-dimensional face, painted eyes, and wig. Mark: Ill. 21. H. 21½ in. (57 cm.). *Courtesy of Stephanie and Fred Farago. Photo by Stephanie Farago.*

21. Mark found on the sole of the shoes made by Ernst Alart, successor of Eugene Alart.

23. Mark used by Frederic Aldis.

Alexander Doll Co. 1912–30 and later. New York City. About 1912 the Alexander sisters began designing clothes for dolls. Their father, grandfather, and ancestors for generations had been connected with doll making.

1926: According to an article in PLAYTHINGS, in early 1926 the Alexander Doll Co. was established. "After spending the greater part of their lives working in several of the large doll concerns," the young sisters "Bertha Alexander and Rose Alexander" decided to "devote their talent and creative ability to dolls bearing their own name." Accordingly they went into business for themselves, and "Alexander Dolls" were the result. Their specialty was "dainty costumes for fine dolls."

1927: The Misses Alexander were referred to in PLAYTHINGS as "famous for fifteen years as leading doll designers." They dressed dolls as they had "never [been] dressed before, in gorgeous silks, fine cottons and French voile prints."

The Alexander Doll Co. used the mark "ALEXANDER// WALKING// ADCo.// TALKING// DOLLS// NEW YORK." They were licensed by *Voices, Inc.* to use mama voices and criers in their dolls. The walking-talking dolls must have been the usual *Mama* dolls, a popular type in 1927.

The factory agent and sole distributor was *Kaufman, Levenson & Co.*

1928: The name "Madame Alexander"[†] first appeared in PLAYTHINGS, with the Alexander Doll Co., in reference to a quality line of dolls.

1929: PLAYTHINGS reported that the Alexander Doll Co. had made "splendid progress in the comparatively short time it has been in existence." The Alexander sisters were the designers and makers of an enlarged line of new doll creations known as "Madame Alexander Dolls."

1930: The sister Rose Alexander was no longer mentioned. Florence Alexander appeared at all the large toy fairs and seems to have been in charge of publicity for the Alexander Doll Co. The factory doubled in size and "Madame Alexander" was credited with creating and designing an "original line of strikingly dressed dolls." No two dolls were dressed alike; they wore the newest fashions, and had "attractive blending of colors," according to TOYS AND NOVELTIES. The lines of dolls' clothes were made to fit dolls of all sizes.

The Alexander Doll Co.'s picture in PLAYTHINGS shows Mama dolls and baby dolls. In TOY WORLD, the Alexander dolls are referred to as "personality dolls." There were dolls named *Cherub Baby, Florence,* and *Chubby Baby* as well as novelty dolls.

In 1931 Madame Alexander created and designed a line of clothes for real little girls as well as clothes for dolls. Through the years innumerable dolls' costumes have been designed by Madame Alexander. Among her most famous dolls are the Little Women series, which appeared before 1933, when the name was registered as a trademark by Bertha Behrman doing business as the Alexander Doll Co. Dolls named for the four literary characters have continued to be made until the present day, but both the dolls themselves and the costumes have changed many times through

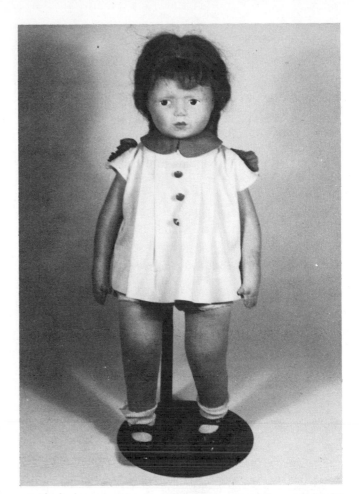

24. Flocked composition head on a pink cloth body, made by the Alexander Doll Co. It has a wig, painted eyes, closed mouth. Original clothes. Marked "Mme//Alexander." H. 19 in. (48 cm.). *Courtesy of Richard Withington. Photo by Barbara Jendrick.*

25. Mark used by the Alexander Doll Co. in 1927.

the years. The same doll was often dressed in various outfits and given different names. For example, the Snow White and the earlier Princess Elizabeth were the same doll but dressed differently.

During the 1930s many names were registered as trademarks by Bertha Behrman doing business as the Alexander Doll Co. Among the most famous ones were Alice-in-Wonderland,[†] 1933; Little Colonel, 1935; Quintuplets, 1936; McGuffy Ana, Scarlett O'Hara, and Snow White,

1937. The registering of a trademark required prior usage. Madame Alexander is Mrs. Behrman.

1939: PLAYTHINGS listed the Alexander Doll Co. under composition dolls, cloth dolls, and wood dolls.

A dressed bisque head doll has been found in a box with the description corresponding to that of the doll. The box was marked "Alexander Doll Co." and "Fashion Academy Award."★

Alexandra. 1876–78. *Silber & Fleming* advertised "New Alexandra Model." Price $1.68. (See also **Queen Alexandra.**)

Alexandre, Henri. 1888–92. Paris. Made dolls, including *Bébé Phénix.*★

26. Bisque head doll made by Henri Alexandre. It has a wig, stationary blue glass eyes, pierced ears, and a closed mouth. Mark on head: Ill. 27. H. 23 in. (58.5 cm.). *Courtesy of Hazel Ulseth.*

27. Impressed mark on the head of the Henri Alexandre Bébé shown in Ill. 26.

Alexandrowicz (-Homolacs), Mme. (Mlle.) Nina. 1916–18. Paris. Born in Poland. Made cloth or wood art dolls. Before World War I she made dolls for children whom she knew. Exhibited sculpture in 1911–12 and paintings in 1919–38.

1916: Made black dolls used for mascots, dolls representing little girls with two plaits, and Mimi, an all-wood doll.

Alfons. See **Al.**

Alfred (Norwegian). 1910–13. Felt character doll made by *Steiff,* dressed as Norwegian boy in removable clothes. He had stitched hair.

1910: Ht. 28 cm. (11 in.).

1911: Hts. 35 and 43 cm. (14 and 17 in.).

Alice. Name of a doll with a bisque shoulder head and hands, glass eyes, open mouth, teeth, on a kid body with cloth legs. The body came stuffed with hair or partly with

cork. The Alice head is mold #191 and the size is in code (see Ill. 28). On the chest of the doll is an oval red sticker with a white border. In the oval is a red ribbon outlined in white with loops and curled ends. On the lower part is the word "Germany" and a 15-petal flower.

Alice dolls have been reported with hts. 10½, 13, and 14 in. (26.5, 33, and 35.5 cm.).

28. Impressed mark on a bisque head reading "Alice."

Alice. 1909–14. Cloth doll dressed as a Quaker lady, made by F. Kaempff.[†]

1912: Had a lithographed linen face and was distributed by *Butler Bros.* Wore a lawn Quaker costume with kerchief and bonnet. The black stockings were attached. Ht. 13½ in. (34 cm.); priced $2.15 doz. wholesale.

1914: Doll came with a celluloid face and its name embroidered on its girdle. Ht. 12½ in. (32 cm.).★

Alice-in-Wonderland. 1905–23. Cloth doll made by *Martha J. Chase.*

1923: Ht. 12 in. (30.5 cm.); price $7.50.★

Alice Marie. 1929. Name of a doll that could count, sing, and say its prayers.

Alice May. 1910. Doll that represented a one-year-old baby wearing a white lawn dress and cap.

Alida (Dutch). 1909–16. Jointed felt character doll made by *Steiff;* dressed in a girl's Marken-type Dutch costume. The felt shoes were shaped like wooden ones. Distributed in U.S. by *Borgfeldt.* Hts. 28, 35, 43, and 50 cm. (11, 14, 17 and 19½ in.). In 1911 hts. 43 and 50 cm. came with and without long combable hair. By 1913 the 35 cm. doll also sometimes had this feature and the 43 cm. doll came with a mama voice. For the 43 cm. (17 in.) doll the prices ranged from $1.80 in Germany in 1911 to $4.30 in New York City in 1913.

1916: A 60 cm. (23½ in.) ht. was added.★

Aliman & Zara. 1919. London. Advertised Mignonettes (*Mignonnettes*).

Alisto Manufacturing Co. 1919–20. Cincinnati, Ohio. Made dolls, including ones with the trade names *American Doll, Cupid, Esther,* and *Love Me.*★

Alkali Ike. 1913–14. Composition head portrait doll of Augustus Carney, a moving picture celebrity, was made by *Amberg.* It had painted features and was dressed as a cowboy riding a horse, from which it was removable. Rights held by the *Essanay Film Co.* Price $1.50.

Alkay Doll & Toy Co. 1919–22. New York City. Made dolls' heads in various sizes with sleeping eyes or with painted eyes.

Alkid Doll Co. 1920–21. Portland, Ore. Made 24 in. (61 cm.) "all kid covered" doll. The dolls were dressed by *Katherine Rauser* and distributed by *Sophia E. Delavan.*

30. Alkid mark stamped in black on a doll with head and body made of kid leather.

29A & B. Alkid doll made entirely of leather. Molded socket head with wig, stationary brown glass eyes, and a closed mouth. The head and shoulder plate are flesh-colored. The rest of the body is a tan color. Mark: Ill. 30. H. 25 in. (63.5 cm.). *Courtesy of the Margaret Woodbury Strong Museum. Photo by Harry Bickelhaupt.*

All British Toy Co. 1918. Bushey, Hertfordshire. Unbreakable dolls were dressed as *Pierrots* and *Crinoline.*

All Nations. See **Le National.**

All Wood. See **Bébé Tout en Bois.**

All-Bisque Dolls. 1860s–1930 and later. In the 1870s *Silber & Fleming* advertised all-bisque bathing dolls with wigs in nine sizes; some had molded and painted costumes.

1883: *Linington* advertised all-bisque dolls jointed at the shoulders and hips; some came with molded, painted hats representing clowns, others came with hair representing girls. Two sizes, priced 40¢ and 70¢ doz. wholesale.

Stern Bros. Advertised all-bisque dolls with wigs, jointed shoulders and hips, molded footwear and wearing a chemise.

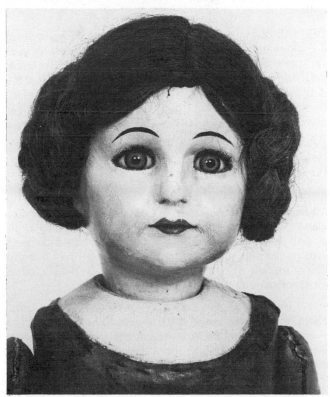

STERN BROS. ALL-BISQUE SIZE–HEIGHT RELATIONSHIP			
Size Number	Height In.	Cm.	Price
0	6	15	$ .50
1	7	18	
2½	8	20.5	
3	9	23	
4	9½	24	$1.10

1884: *Lauer* advertised "Bisque Jointed Babies" which appear to have been all-bisque dolls as follows:

			Price per doz. wholesale		
Size Number	Height In.	Cm.	Long Hair	Curly Hair	Hair not described, probably molded
3/0	2¼	5.5	$ .45		$.25
2/0	2¾	7	$ .45		
2/0	3	7.5		$.36	
0	3¼	8.5	$ .52		
1	3¼	8.5			$.36
5	5½	14	$1.12		
8	7½	19	$1.75		

Table title: LAUER ALL-BISQUE SIZE–HEIGHT RELATIONSHIP

1887: *Wanamaker* advertised all-bisque dolls. Hts. 5½ to 11 in. (14 to 28 cm.).

Lauer advertised that their all-bisque dolls came 1⅞ in. (4.5 cm.) to 4¼ in. (11 cm.) tall; priced 6¢ to 58¢ a doz. They came either without joints or jointed at shoulders and hips. Some of the jointed ones had bent limbs. A few had molded bonnets and a few more had wigs.

1892: *Marshall Field* advertised a variety of all-bisque dolls. They had molded hair or wigs, painted eyes or glass eyes, a few had sleeping eyes and teeth. There were *Frozen Charlottes* without joints or dolls with wired or rubber-strung joints at the shoulders and hips. Most of the dolls had straight limbs but some had bent arms and some had both arms and legs bent. The latter group were called "Boys." For a similar doll see Ill. 75 in the first COLLECTOR'S ENCYCLOPEDIA OF DOLLS. Most of the dolls had molded and painted footwear but were otherwise naked. Fifteen hts. 2¾ to 9 in. (7 to 23 cm.); priced 75¢ to $8.50 a doz. wholesale.

1893: Horsman advertised all-bisque dolls with wigs except for those with bent limbs. A few had sleeping eyes, fully jointed, jointed arms and legs, or jointed arms only.

1904: Fat boy doll, jointed at shoulders and hips with molded footwear, was advertised.

1909: *Siegel Cooper* advertised two all-bisque dolls both with wigs, sleeping eyes, jointed shoulders, and hips. One doll had molded footwear. Ht. 5¼ in. (13.5 cm.); the other doll had bare feet and is reported to have an open mouth. Ht. 5¾ in. (14.5 cm.). Each doll cost 25¢.

1911: *Woodward & Lothrop* advertised all-bisque dolls with movable arms. Hts. 3 and 4 in. (7.5 and 10 cm.); priced 5¢ and 10¢. The all-bisque dolls with wigs and glass eyes were jointed at the shoulders and hips. Ht. 5½ in. (14 cm.); priced 25¢.

1912–13: *Selchow & Righter* advertised "fully jointed" all-bisque dolls with molded hair. Hts. 3½, 4, and 4¼ in. (9, 10, and 11 cm.); priced 40¢ a doz. wholesale. With wigs, hts. 4¼, 5½, and 5¾ in. (11, 14, and 14.5 cm.); priced 40¢ to 85¢ a doz. wholesale. With wigs and sleeping eyes, hts. 5¼ and 7 in. (13.5 and 18 cm.); priced $2.00 a doz. wholesale.

1920: Dolls 3 to 4 in. (7.5 to 10 cm.) tall; priced 45¢ to 90¢ a doz. were advertised. The wire-strung dolls were nearly half the price of the elastic-strung dolls. Dolls were jointed at shoulders only, or at shoulders and hips; had molded hair, some with hair ribbon or hat. Some character-type dolls.

1924–25: *Shackman* and others advertised dolls 1½ to 7½ in. (4 to 19 cm.) tall; jointed at shoulders only, or jointed at shoulders and hips; the latter came with straight or bent limbs. Dolls with molded clothes and jointed at the neck were in this period. Most of the all-bisque dolls had painted eyes and molded hair, but some had wigs and a few had glass sleeping eyes. The *Kewpies*® and *Bye-Lo* Babies were among the most popular all-bisque dolls.

1927: Similar to 1925, except that the molded hair was usually in marcel waves or bobbed, and the eyes were more often glancing to the side.

1927–28: *Charles William* advertised an all-bisque pair of dolls with painted and molded hair, features and clothes. The boy carried a molded slate and the bobbed hair girl carried a molded doll. Ht. 5¼ in. (13.5 cm.); priced 25¢ pair.

1928: The introduction by *Marshall Field* of all-bisque comic character dolls jointed at the neck only, such as *Skeezix, Moon Mullins, Andy Gump,* and so forth.

1931: *Montgomery Ward* advertised a set of three all-bisque dolls representing a boy, a girl, and a baby. The boy and girl had molded bobbed hair and molded footwear, the baby had molded short hair and bare feet. The boy and girl had slim bodies and limbs while the baby had a chubby bent-limb body. All three dolls were jointed at the shoulders and hips. The dolls were naked, but the baby had a pacifier. The boy was 6¼ in. (16 cm.), the girl was 6½ in. (16.5 cm.), and the baby was 5 in. (12.5 cm.); priced 39¢ for the set of three dolls.

1951: All-bisque dolls made in East Germany were jointed at the shoulders and hips, had synthetic wigs, sleeping eyes except for small-size dolls, and molded footwear. The larger dolls had numbers marked on their heads. On the back of the dolls was stamped "Germany" in an ink that allegedly faded. Five hts.: 5¼, 5½, 5¾, 7, and 7½ in. (13.5, 14, 14.5, 18, and 19 cm.).

1950s: All-bisque *Bye-Lo* Babies were made. (See also **Dolls' House Dolls** and entries for major distributors such as **Wanamaker** and **Horsman**.)

All-British Doll Manufacturing Co. 1915–19. Sheffield, England. Made jointed composition child dolls and baby dolls as well as kid-bodied dolls. The jointed dolls had sleeping eyes or sleeping and winking eyes. The dolls had human-hair or mohair wigs. The company also made dolls' clothes for other manufacturers.

1917: The specialty was an exercise doll invented by *Eugene Sandow.* The purpose of this doll was to help the child to exercise by pulling the extensible arms. The exercise dolls were dressed as a Boy Scout or as *Dolly Dimple.* Each of them came with a booklet showing the exercise positions.

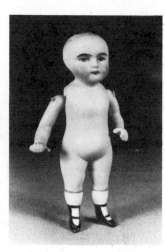

33. All-bisque doll with wig, painted eyes, jointed neck, and molded footwear, having high yellow boots with heels. Marked on back "105//1." H. 4 in. (10 cm.). *Coleman Collection.*

34. All-bisque doll with wig, painted eyes, closed mouth, molded two-strap boots with heels. The doll is jointed only at the shoulders. H. 4½ in. (11 cm.). *Coleman Collection.*

31. All-bisque doll with socket head, wig, glass eyes, closed mouth, and molded footwear. Jointed at the shoulders and with diagonal joints at the hips. H. 7 in. (18 cm.). *Courtesy of Richard Withington. Photo by Barbara Jendrick.*

32. All-bisque doll with socket head, having a wig, glass eyes, and closed mouth. The arms are bent and the footwear is molded. Original blue silk dress. Doll was purchased in Paris. H. 6 in. (15 cm.). *Coleman Collection.*

35. All-bisque dolls left to right: All-bisque doll with brown wig, glass eyes, open mouth with teeth, jointed at neck, shoulders, and hips. Molded single-strap slippers. Ht. 10 cm. (4 in.).

All-bisque doll with wig, blue glass eyes, jointed at neck, shoulders, and hips, molded single-strap slippers. Ht. 10.5 cm. (4 in.).

All-bisque doll with wig, sleeping blue glass eyes, molded two-strap slippers. Ht. 10 cm. (4 in.).

All-bisque doll with wig, blue glass eyes. Clothes are crocheted in red and beige cotton; molded single-strap slippers. Ht. 13 cm. (5½ in.).

All-bisque doll with wig, brown glass eyes, molded single-strap slippers. Dress on the doll is beige with blue trimming. Extra dress is light blue and the hat is straw. H. 14.5 cm. (5¾ in.). *Courtesy of the Collection Nederlands Kostuummuseum, The Hague. Photo by B. Frequin.*

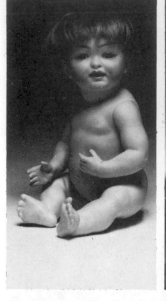

36. All-bisque dolls in original costumes with wigs and molded footwear. The doll dressed as an Italian boy on the left has glass eyes. The doll on the right is wearing a period military costume and it has painted eyes and a swivel neck. H. 3¾ in. (9.5 cm.). *Courtesy of Sotheby Parke Bernet Inc., N.Y.*

37. All-bisque doll with molded and painted hair, features, and footwear. Wire-jointed shoulders and hips. Original clothes; a jacket was probably lost. H. 3¾ in. (9.5 cm.). *Coleman Collection.*

38. All-bisque bent-limb baby with wig, blue glass eyes, and open-closed mouth. Mark on head is "150 1½." H. 10 in. (25.5 cm.). *Courtesy of Sotheby Parke Bernet Inc., N.Y.*

39. All-bisque bent-limb baby doll with wig, sleeping glass eyes, open mouth with teeth, and original Oriental-style costume. H. 7 in. (18 cm.). *Courtesy of Sotheby Parke Bernet Inc., N.Y.*

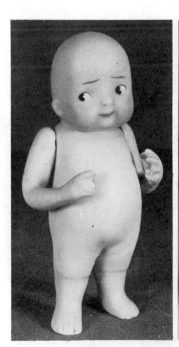

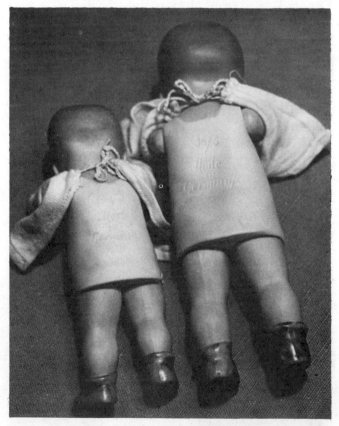

40. Small all-bisque doll with a bald head, painted eyes looking to the side, closed mouth, almost no neck, and jointed at the shoulders. The arms are bent and the legs are apart. *Courtesy of Robert and Katrin Burlin.*

41. All-bisque doll with socket head, wig, blue glass roguish eyes, closed smiling mouth, molded footwear. H. 4½ in. (11.5 cm.). *Courtesy of Sotheby Parke Bernet Inc., N.Y.*

42. Pair of all-bisque dolls with molded and painted hair, glass eyes, closed mouths, swivel necks, molded white chemise and molded blue shoes. See Ill. 1154A for a similar doll. Marks: Ills. 51A & B. Hs. 15 and 18 cm. (6 and 7 in.). *Courtesy of Claire Hennig. Photo by Margie Landolt of Zurich.*

A

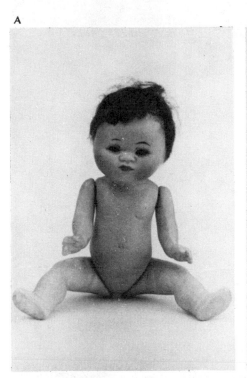

B

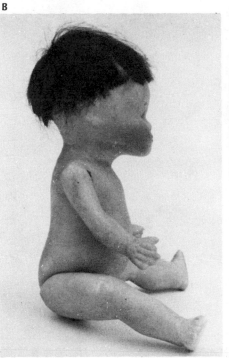

C

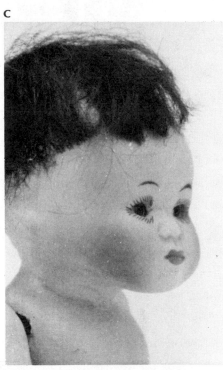

43A, B, & C. All-bisque baby doll with wig, glass eyes, closed mouth, jointed at shoulders and hips. Mark: Ill. 52. H. 6 in. (15 cm.). *Courtesy of Roberta Fiene.*

44. All-bisque doll with molded hair and eyes, looking to the side, closed mouth, molded footwear. H. 6¾ in. (17 cm.). *Courtesy of John Axe. Photo by John Axe.*

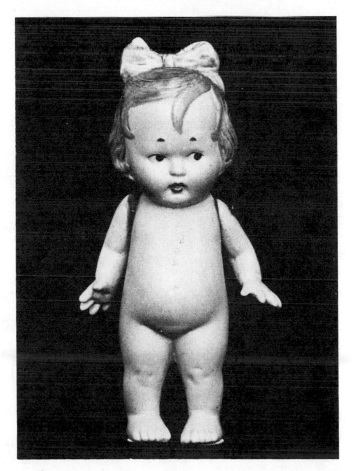

45. All-bisque doll with molded and painted hair and blue bow, black intaglio eyes, closed mouth, wire joints at the shoulders. Mark on the back: "344-10 Made//in Germany." H. 4½ in. (11.5 cm.). *Courtesy of Victoria Harper.*

46. All-bisque doll with molded and painted hair, roguish eyes, jointed only at the shoulders. Made in Japan in the 1920s. H. 5½ in. (14 cm.). *Coleman Collection.*

47. All-bisque doll with a metal leash and bisque dog made in the 1920s. The doll has molded and painted hair, features and footwear; jointed at the shoulders and hips with wire. Original clothes. The leg is impressed "Germany." H. 2¾ in. (7 cm.). *Coleman Collection.*

48. All-bisque doll with molded and painted features. It is only jointed at the neck. The molded red clothes include a hat, coat, leggings, and shoes. A small hole in one hand suggests that the doll originally held an object. Marked "Germany" on the back. H. 3¼ in. (8 cm.). *Coleman Collection.*

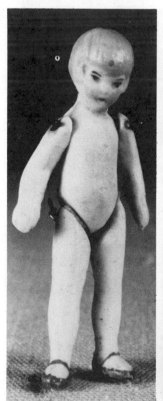

49. All-bisque doll with molded and painted hair, features, and footwear made in the 1920s. H. 2¼ in. (5.5 cm.). *Coleman Collection.*

50. Painted all-bisque doll with molded bobbed hair, closed mouth, molded footwear, original clothes. H. 4¾ in. (12 cm.). *Coleman Collection.*

36/3
Made
in
Germany

36/5
Made
in
Germany

51A & B. Marks incised on the backs of German all-bisque dolls shown in Ill. 42.

Made
in
Germany
1200

M.S.

4
0.

52. Mark incised on back of an all-bisque doll in Ill. 43.

Allen, C. W., & Co. 1921. Aurora, Ill. Made *Polly Wobble* and *Willie Walk*.★

Allen, Frederick H. 1930 and later. England. Advertised dolls in a British toy trade journal.

Allen, Lucking & Co. 1922. England. Advertised dolls in a British toy trade journal.

Alliance Toy Co. 1917. England. Manufactured cloth dolls, character dolls, dressed dolls, and *Golliwoggs*. Cloth doll lines named *Dolletta* and *Conductress*.

Allied-Grand Doll Manufacturing Co. 1915–30 and later. Brooklyn, N.Y. Two factories made inexpensive composition dolls and specialized in black dolls. They made character dolls, including bent-limb babies, with molded and painted features and hair. These dolls wore simple clothes, and in 1930 sold for 25¢ to 50¢.

53. Twin Alma bisque shoulder-headed dolls with wigs and sleeping eyes. They are dressed in original clothes, including blue-and-white plaid dresses and hats. Marks on the heads: left, blue-eyed doll, "Alma 0," right, doll has brown eyes and is marked "Alma 1." The body is marked "Washable Dolls Germany." H. 51 cm. (20 in.) for both dolls. *Courtesy of the Collection Nederlands Kostuummuseum, The Hague. Photo by B. Frequin.*

Allison Novelty Co. 1919–20. U.S. Estelle Allison designed a doll known as *Fan-ie*. During World War I she designed colored postcards with Fan-ies dressed to represent soldiers and sailors, to raise money for war camp entertainment and for injured soldiers. The doll Fan-ie was distributed by *Borgfeldt*. An Estelle Allison copyright was used by *Elizabeth Lesser* for a design-patented doll.

Alma. 1900–01. Bisque head doll produced by *Borgfeldt*.★

Alma
6/0

54. Alma mark incised on bisque shoulder-head dolls.

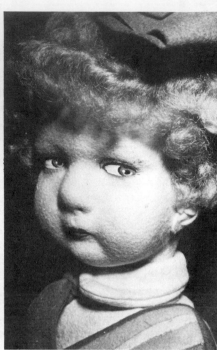

55A & B. Felt Alma dolls were made similarly to the Lenci® dolls with mohair sewed onto the head in strips, painted eyes glancing to the side, closed mouth, hollow felt-covered torso. Original clothes with varicolored felt strips sewn together. Made in the 1920s. Mark: Ill. 56. H. 16 in. (40.5 cm.). *Coleman Collection.*

Alma. 1929–30 and later. Turin, Italy. Felt dolls similar to *Lencis*® had molded head, hollow torso and legs, stuffed arms; fingers were either together or separate. Painted features; hair sewn on the head. The ear of folded felt is one of the identifying attributes. Some dolls have a cloth label reading "Creation Alma//Made in Italy"; others were marked "Alma" on the foot. Various hts. up to 30 in. (76 cm.). The felt clothes were artistically designed.

Alpha. 1915–30 and later. Line of cloth dolls and toys made by *Farnell,* named for their factory, the Alpha Works; Alpha was used as a trade name.

Alphabet Doll. 1917 and other years. Name of a doll with a china head and limbs on a cloth body, having printed alphabet letters and/or pictures on its body, distributed by *Columbus Merchandise Co.* Ht. 15 ½ in. (39.5 cm.); priced $4.50 doz. wholesale. Similar dolls were handled by *Butler Bros.*

Alphabet Man. 1928. Made by *Twinzy Toy Co.* Soft-bodied doll completely covered with letters of the alphabet. On its back was a story or verse that included every letter of the alphabet. Doll had a voice.

Alphons (Alfons). See **Al.**

Alsatian Costume Dolls. See **French Regional Costume Dolls.**

Alt, Beck & Gottschalck. 1854–1930 and later. Nauendorf, near Ohrdruf, Thür. In 1920 there was a consolidation of Alt, Beck and Gottschalck with Alfred Schulze, Alt and Koch and Carl Beck, forming the firm, Carl Beck and Alfred Schulze. *Carl Stahl* was their Berlin agent in 1927. They supplied bisque heads to *C. M. Bergmann* and others. They made bisque *Bye-Lo* heads to be put on composition bodies. Some of their bisque heads were marked with the height of the doll in centimeters.

Création Alma
Made in Italy

56. Alma mark on felt dolls. This mark is printed on a cloth tape and sewed to the clothes.

There is a bisque shoulder head with molded jewelry in the Sonneberg Museum collection that was made by this firm. It is 6½ in. (16.5 cm.) high.

From about 1870 to 1900 a large group of related bisque and china shoulder heads have been found with mold numbers between 639 and 1288. About 85 percent of these mold numbers were even numbers. Of course heads having the same mold number in this series had identical modeling regardless of whether they were china or bisque.

The mold number was followed by ✕ or # or No. in that order of frequency and these were followed by a size number that ranged at least from 7/0 to 13. These marks were usually on the lower back of the shoulder head. When there was a socket head and matching shoulder plate the mark was on the rim of the crown of the socket head and the mold number was found on the upper side of the accompanying

57. One of the Alpha line of cloth dolls made by Farnell. It has a felt face, hair sewed on its head in strips, painted features. Velvet body, jointed at the shoulders and hips. Original Scottish costume. Mark is printed on tape that is sewed on the sole of the foot. H. 14 in. (35.5 cm.). *Courtesy of Richard Withington. Photo by Barbara Jendrick.*

shoulder. Mold numbers 911 and 916 with wigs, glass eyes, and separate shoulder plates had pates cut out with a deep slant, though there was a rim indicating that the head was poured. These heads had two holes in the upper forehead. (See Ills. 64 and 65.)

The various molds having molded hair and/or headwear have been found in both china and bisque. The heads with wigs have been found only in bisque. All of the heads found so far represent Caucasian children or ladies.

The deep shoulders extend over the tops of the arms and there were creases in the front indicating the armpits. Slight modeling suggested busts. Generally two sew holes were found in front and two in back, except on the very large heads that had three holes on both sides.

There was tremendous variation. Some heads had wigs but most of them had molded hair; some of the eyes were glass but the majority were painted blue. A few had open

mouths, usually accompanied by the mold number having ½ after it. Molded bonnets and other headwear such as scarves have been found. Some of the heads had brush marks and some had pierced ears which were generally pierced into the head. There is scarcely any feature found among the porcelain dolls of the late 1800s that was lacking in this series. The same mold number was made with molded black or blond hair, glazed or unglazed. Some of the unglazed heads were tinted and some were untinted. All of these heads were poured rather than pressed.

Unfortunately the manufacturer of these fine quality heads has not been definitely identified as yet. A few of them were marked "Germany" and many of them have been found on *Wagner & Zetzsche* kid bodies. Thus it seems almost certain that they were made by a large porcelain factory in Thüringia. There were almost a hundred porcelain factories in Thüringia but only a third of them were in existence early enough to have made these heads and only a few were large enough to have done so. *Gebrüder Voight* used marks not unlike the X or # but according to the records found by the Ciesliks, Voight produced only a few dolls' heads in the period 1885 to the 1890s. The leading manufacturers, such as *Simon & Halbig* and *Kestner,* seem to be eliminated because their registered mold numbers and general characteristics were different from the ones found in this series. *Kling*'s mold numbers appeared to be less than 500 and their mold and size numbers were separated by a hyphen.

The strongest evidence points to Alt, Beck and Gottschalck as being the makers of this series. This was a porcelain factory in Thüringia known to have made a large number of porcelain dolls' heads. The Ciesliks found an 1888 record that Alt, Beck & Gottschalck was producing boy and girl heads with molded hair, hats, and caps in bisque and in china. Many of the shoulder heads in this group have the features of children and have molded hair, hats, or caps. Examples of this series are in the local Ohrdruf Museum, but Simon & Halbig, Kestner, and Kling were all in this Ohrdruf area.

Probably the strongest evidence in favor of Alt, Beck & Gottschalck is in the mold numbers. According to the Ciesliks at least one of the mold numbers, namely #870, found on a doll in the series (see Ill. 59) was registered by Alt, Beck & Gottschalck in 1895. However, it was possible for more than one company to register the same number. To further prove the Alt, Beck & Gottschalck origin, the Ciesliks found that #1235 was registered by them in the 1890s. #1235 was accompanied on the dolls' heads by "Germany No. [size number] DEP" which means that it was registered in Germany. A few of the molds in the 1200s such as 1234, 1235, 1260, and 1288 had "Germany No." as part of the mark instead of X or #. Known Alt, Beck & Gottschalck mold numbers after 1910 were in the 1300s which would logically follow the earlier numbers found on the series of heads. The corresponding time, place, type, and mold numbers seem to leave little doubt but that Alt, Beck & Gottschalck made the heads which have been found by the authors and are described in the following table, as well as being shown in illustrations 58 to 80 inclusive:

DESCRIPTION OF THE SHOULDER HEADS OF ALT, BECK & GOTTSCHALCK
(X indicates types found)

Mold #	Material		Hair		Eyes		Description	Illustration Number
	China	Bisque	Wig	Molded	Glass	Painted		
639		X	X		X		Bald, turned head	
698		X	X		X		Head with pate cut out	58
772		X		X			Flat top style	
784	X			X		X	Ears exposed, short curls, center part	
812								
830								
870		X	X		X		Pierced ears	59
880	X			X		X	Short curly hair	
882	X	X		X	X	X	Short hair, windblown, locks on forehead	60
890		X		X		X	Short curly hair, molded curl in middle of forehead	61
894		X		X	X	X	Blue scarf, curls on forehead and shoulders	62
898		X		X		X	Lady, braids, pierced ears	63
911		X	X		X		Swivel neck, pierced ears, # on rim of crown. Separate shoulder plate with same mold #	64
916		X	X		X		Similar to 911 except longer face	65
974		X		X		X	Bangs, hair on shoulder	
978		X		X		X	Bangs, curls in back	
980		X						
990		X		X		X	Pink mob cap, bangs	
996		X		X	X	X	Lavender or blue crown, white scarf, bangs	66
998		X		X		X	Molded hat and braids	67
1000	X	X		X	X	X	Bangs and curls [sometimes called Highland Mary]	68, 69, 70
1002		X		X		X	Short wavy hair, pierced ears	71
1008	X			X	X	X	Curls all over, 2 curls on forehead	
1024		X		X	X		Red cap, bangs	72
1028	X	X		X		X	Flat-top type, fat cheeks	
1030	X			X		X	Braids, beads in hair	73
1044		X	X		X	X	Bald head with one hole	74
1046	X			X		X	Curls, part slightly to one side	75, 76
1054		X		X		X	Cap, short hair, baby	77
1056	X	X		X		X	Short curly hair	
1062		X		X			Similar to 1000 but more bangs	
1064		X		X		X	Molded curls	
1086			X	X			Short curls, baby	78
1112	X					X		
1123		X	X		X		Baby with sleeping eyes	79
1127		X	X		X		Turned head	74*
1142	X	X		X	X	X	Center part all the way to nape of neck	80
1154		X					Hair in 1880s style	
1210	X			X		X	Side part	
1214	X	X		X		X	Resembles a boy	
1218		X		X		X	Curls	
1222		X		X		X	Boy or baby style, loose curls	
1226		X		X		X	Child style, short wavy hair. Sometimes found on *Goldsmith* bodies	
1234		X	X		X		Dolly face, open mouth	
1235		X	X		X		Dolly face, closed mouth	
1254		X		X			Short wavy hair	
1260							Reported by Shea	
1288		X		X	X		Bangs and curls	

*Ill. 74 found in the first COLLECTOR'S ENCYCLOPEDIA OF DOLLS.

Mold #1000 was found most frequently, at least in the United States. Many of the heads with wigs, such as 639 and 1127, have turned heads and were often originally dressed in baby-type clothes. Some of the mold numbers were found more frequently in Europe than in America or the reverse was true. The wigged heads usually came with graceful bisque hands. (One type was shown in Ill. 752 in the first COLLECTOR'S ENCYCLOPEDIA OF DOLLS.) The molded heads on original commercial bodies generally had porcelain lower arms and legs of a particular design as seen in Ills. 76 and 80.

What appears to be an identification of the maker of this significant early series of porcelain shoulder heads has been made thanks largely to the persistent work of the Ciesliks and of many other people, including Patricia Hartwell, who shared their information with the authors. (See THE DOLL READER, April/May, 1981, "Ilmenau Dolls???" for an earlier analysis of this group of dolls. Ilmenau is about 12 miles from Ohrdruf.)

According to the Ciesliks, Alt, Beck & Gottschalck registered the following mold numbers: in 1894, 1290 and 1291; in 1895, 866, 867, 868, 869, 870, and 872.

After 1910 they used the following mold numbers: 1322, 1326, 1352, 1353, 1357, 1360, 1361, 1362, 1366, and 1367.

One of the mold #1322 bisque heads represented a character boy with molded hair, intaglio eyes, open-closed smiling mouth having two upper teeth and a tongue, as well as dimples. It was marked "ABG//1322/1//Deponiert." Ht. 12 in. (30.5 cm.). One of the mold #1360 bisque heads had a wig, sleeping eyes, hair eyelashes, pierced nostrils, and an open mouth. It was on a toddler's body with a diagonal hip joint. One of the mold #1362 bisque heads reportedly had incised on the back: "A.B.G// 1362// Made in Germany// 0 ¾." This socket head with sleeping eyes, open mouth, and four upper teeth was 9½ in. (24 cm.) in circumference.

1894: Made bisque heads and all-bisque dolls.

1911: Obtained a German patent (D.R.G.M.) for character heads with sleeping eyes.

1912: Obtained a German patent (D.R.G.M.) for dolls' heads with mechanism for sleeping eyes attached to the voice box.

1913: Obtained a German patent (D.R.G.M.) for dolls' heads with movable tongue.

1915: Obtained a German patent (D.R.G.M.) for dolls' heads with moving eyes and tongue.

1925: Obtained a German patent (D.R.G.M.) for dolls' heads with moving eyes. They advertised a bent-limb baby doll called *Mother's Darling.*

1930: Advertised baby dolls and other dolls dressed and undressed.*

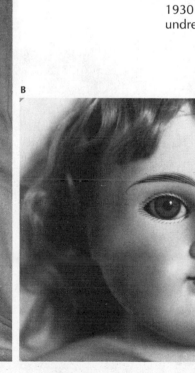
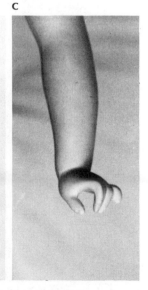

58A, B, & C. Bisque shoulder head probably made by Alt, Beck & Gottschalck, mold #698, has a wig, stationary blue glass eyes, flat eyebrows, closed mouth with a dark lip line, a short neck and arms, creases in the deep shoulders. The open crown is sliced off at an angle and far toward the back. The cloth body made by Wagner & Zetzsche is size 10. The bisque arms are typical for this series of dolls. Mark: Ill. 82. *Courtesy of Mary Alice Thacker.*

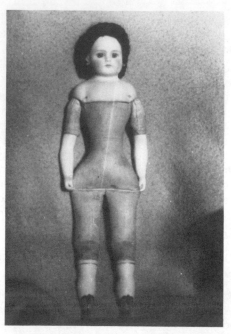

59. Bisque shoulder head mold X 870, made by Alt, Beck & Gottschalck, has glass eyes, nearly flat eyebrows, closed mouth with dark lip line, and a cloth body with bisque arms and legs. The molded footwear includes high-button boots with tassels and heels. Mark: Ill. 85. *Courtesy of Dr. Eva Moskovsky.*

60A & B. Bisque shoulder head mold #882 with molded blond short curls, stationary blue glass eyes. The eyebrows are nearly flat and there is a dark red lip line, characteristic of these heads made in Thüringia, probably by Alt, Beck & Gottschalck. The doll has a homemade cloth body. Mark: Ill. 86. H. of doll 23½ in. (59.5 cm.). H. of shoulder head 5 in. (12.5 cm.). *Courtesy of Cherry Bou.*

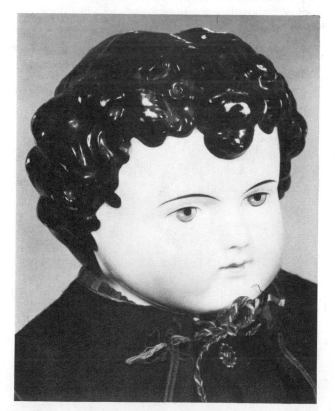

61. China shoulder head made in Thüringia in the late 1800s, probably by Alt, Beck & Gottschalck. Molded short curls in the middle of its forehead. Very short neck, china shoulder extends over top of the arms. Three sew holes are on each side, cloth body. Contemporary clothes for a boy doll. Mark: 890 X 11. H. 24 in. (61 cm.). H. of shoulder head 6 in. (15 cm.). *Coleman Collection.*

62. Molded bisque shoulder head (mold #894) having a blue scarf framing the face, probably made by Alt, Beck & Gottschalck. Mark: Ill. 87. H. 11½ in. (29 cm.). H. of shoulder head 3 in. (7.5 cm.). *Coleman Collection.*

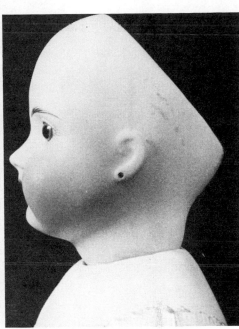

63. Untinted bisque shoulder head with blond molded hair having braids up each side and across the top of the head; molded and painted blue eyes. The dark lip line is typical of the painting in this series, probably made by Alt, Beck & Gottschalck. The ears are pierced into the head. The body is cloth. Mark: 898 X 8. H. of doll 22½ in. (57 cm.). H. of shoulder head 5¾ in. (14.5 cm.). *Courtesy of Margaret Woodbury Strong Museum. Photo by Harry Bickelhaupt.*

64A & B. Bisque socket head on a bisque shoulder plate has a wig, glass eyes, pierced ears, closed mouth, kid lining the neck joint, and a gusset kid body with bisque lower arms. This doll was made in Thüringia, probably by Alt, Beck & Gottschalck. Mark on rim of crown is 911 #7 and there is a matching mark on the shoulder plate. H. 17 in. (43 cm.). *Private collection. Photos by Rick Bromley.*

65. Bisque socket head on a deep bisque shoulder plate having the same characteristics as found on shoulder heads in this series, probably made by Alt, Beck & Gottschalck. The head is cut at a sharp angle like some of the French dolls' heads. Two stringing holes are at the top of the high forehead. It has a wig, glass eyes, and an open-closed mouth. The ears are pierced into the head. It is on a gusseted kid body. Mark: Ill. 88 on shoulder. Mark on rim of crown 916.6. H. 18 in. (45.5 cm.). H. of head and shoulders 5¾ in. (14.5 cm.). *Coleman Collection.*

66. Bisque shoulder head with a molded and painted lavender crown and a white scarf, molded and painted bangs, molded and painted blue eyes, a dark red lip line. This head was made in Thüringia, probably by Alt, Beck & Gottschalck. Mark: 996 X 8. H. of shoulder head 5½ in. (14 cm.). *Courtesy of Margaret Woodbury Strong Museum. Photo by Harry Bickelhaupt.*

68A & B. China shoulder head made in Thüringia, probably by Alt, Beck & Gottschalck. It has molded black short curls and bangs with brush marks, molded and painted blue eyes, nearly flat eyebrows, a dark red lip line, and a cloth body with replaced limbs. The clothes are contemporary with the doll. Mark: 1000 ✗ 3. H. 15½ in. (38 cm.). H. of shoulder head 3¾ in. (9.5 cm.). *Coleman Collection.*

67. Bisque shoulder head probably made by Alt, Beck & Gottschalck has a molded and painted white mob cap and blond hair having a braid on one side. The molded hair falls down the back of the shoulders. There are molded and painted blue eyes and a dark red lip line on the closed mouth. Mark: 998 ✗ 6. H. of shoulder head 4½ in. (11.5 cm.). *Courtesy of the Margaret Woodbury Strong Museum. Photo by Harry Bickelhaupt.*

69. Bisque shoulder head made in Thüringia, probably by Alt, Beck & Gottschalck. It has molded and painted hair and eyes. The bangs end with brush marks. There is a dark red line between the closed lips. The cloth body is a replacement. Mark: 1000 ✗ 8. H. 19 in. (48 cm.). H. of shoulder head 5¼ in. (13.5 cm.). *Courtesy of the Margaret Woodbury Strong Museum. Photo by Harry Bickelhaupt.*

70. Bisque shoulder head made in Thüringia, probably by Alt, Beck & Gottschalck. It has molded and painted hair with bangs, brush marks and short curls. There are stationary blue glass eyes and nearly flat decal-type eyebrows. The closed mouth has a dark lip line. The cloth body has leather arms. Mark: 1000 ✗ 11. H. of doll 25 in. (63.5 cm.). H. of shoulder head 6½ in. (16.5 cm.). *Courtesy of the Margaret Woodbury Strong Museum. Photo by Harry Bickelhaupt.*

71. Untinted bisque shoulder head with molded and painted blond wavy hair and bangs; molded and painted blue eyes; ears are pierced into the head, and there is a dark red line between the closed lips. This head was made in Thüringia, probably by Alt, Beck & Gottschalck. The cloth body has gauntlet-type bisque hands. Mark: 1002 X 8. H. of doll 20 in. (51 cm.). H. of shoulder head 5¾ in. (14.5 cm.). *Courtesy of the Margaret Woodbury Strong Museum. Photo by Harry Bickelhaupt.*

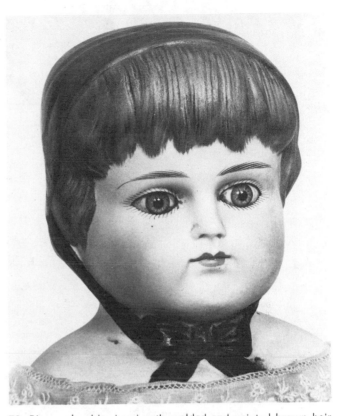

72. Bisque shoulder head with molded and painted brown hair having bangs and brush marks. The molded cap is orange color and has a black bow in back and black ties under the chin. The stationary blue eyes are glass and the nearly flat eyebrows appear to be decals. The lip line of the closed mouth is dark red. This type of head was made in Thüringia, probably by Alt, Beck & Gottschalck. Mark: 1024 X 10. H. of shoulder head 5½ in. (14 cm.). *Courtesy of the Margaret Woodbury Strong Museum. Photo by Harry Bickelhaupt.*

73. China shoulder head only with molded black curls, braids and beads in hair, molded and painted blue eyes, and a closed mouth. The mark 1030 X 5 suggests that it may have been made by Alt, Beck & Gottschalck in Thüringia. H. of shoulder head 5 in. (12.5 cm.). *Coleman Collection.*

74A & B. Bisque shoulder head marked 1044 X 0 made in Thüringia, probably by Alt, Beck & Gottschalck, and dressed as a Scotsman. There is a single hole in the head into which is inserted the blond hair. It has painted blue eyes and a closed mouth. The cloth body has bisque limbs, including the molded heeled boots. Original clothes. H. 12 in. (30.5 cm.). *Coleman Collection.*

A

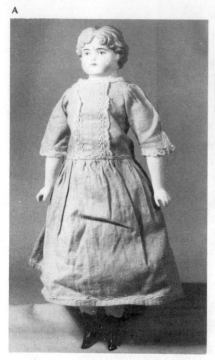

B

C

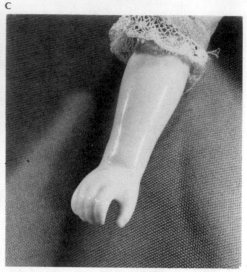

75A, B, & C. China shoulder head and limbs made in Thüringia, probably by Alt, Beck & Gottschalck in the late 1800s. It has molded blond hair, painted eyes, a short neck on deep shoulders. The arms and legs are typical of similar dolls marked in the same manner. This doll is marked 1046 X 4. H. 14 in. (35.5 cm.). H. shoulder head only 3¾ in. (9.5 cm.). *Coleman Collection.*

76. China shoulder head with black molded short curly hair having the part slightly to one side, painted blue eyes, and closed mouth, made in Thüringia, probably by Alt, Beck and Gottschalck. The cloth body has kid arms. Mark: 1046 X 0. H. 10 in. (25.5 cm.). *Courtesy of Richard Withington. Photo by Barbara Jendrick.*

77. Bisque shoulder head with a molded and painted blue cap having dark blue bows and ribbons. The molded short curly hair is blond. The stationary eyes are blue glass and the eyebrows are nearly flat. A dark red line separates the closed lips. This type of head was made in Thüringia, probably by Alt, Beck & Gottschalck. Mark: 1054.8. H. of shoulder head 5¾ in. (14.5 cm.). *Courtesy of the Margaret Woodbury Strong Museum. Photo by Harry Bickelhaupt.*

78. Bisque shoulder head made in Thüringia, probably by Alt, Beck & Gottschalck. It has molded short curly blond hair, stationary blue glass eyes, nearly flat eyebrows, dark red line between closed lips, and a kid body with Universal-type joints. Mark: 1086 #9. H. of doll: 21 in. (53.5 cm.). H. of shoulder head 5½ in. (14 cm.). *Courtesy of the Margaret Woodbury Strong Museum. Photo by Harry Bickelhaupt.*

79. Bisque shoulder head with wig, blue glass eyes near flat eyebrows, open mouth with two upper and one lower square teeth, a type found on early bisque child heads. There is a dimple in the chin, and a kid body with bisque lower arms. Open-mouth dolls in this series usually have ½ after the mold number. It is possible that the ½ was too indistinct to see. Mark: 1123 X 11. H. of doll 24 in. (61 cm.). H. of shoulder head 6¾ in. (17 cm.). *Courtesy of Margaret Woodbury Strong Museum. Photo by Harry Bickelhaupt.*

A

B

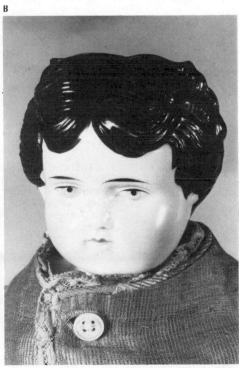

C

80A, B, & C. Thüringian china shoulder head and limbs made in the late 1800s, probably by Alt, Beck & Gottschalck. The molded black hair has a part all the way back to the nape of the neck. China shoulders entirely cover the top of the cloth body. These are typical arms and legs for the group of dolls that are similarly marked. This doll is marked 1142 X 7. H. 21 in. (53.5 cm.). H. shoulder head 4½ in. (11.5 cm.). *Coleman Collection.*

81–92. Marks probably used by Alt, Beck & Gottschalck for their china and bisque shoulder heads.

639 Germany № 6.
81

698   ⅄   12
82

698½   Germany   # 11
83

698½   Germany   #.12
84

870 № 5
85

882 ⅄ 9
86

894 ⅄ 0
87

916 № 6.
88

1064 # 4
89

1123½   Germany.   № 10.
90A

Made in
1123½ Germany № 6
90B

1210 # 9.
91

1235   Germany № 7 DEP.
92

93. Bisque head made by Alt, Beck & Gottschalck. It has molded and painted hair, sleeping brown eyes, open mouth with teeth and tongue. The socket head is on a bent-limb composition baby body. Mold #1322. H. shown on head 28 cm. (11 in.). *Courtesy of Sotheby Parke Bernet Inc., N.Y.*

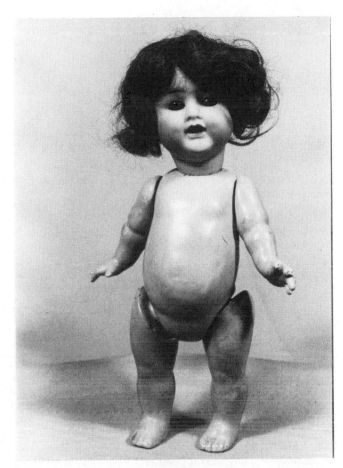

94. Bisque socket head made by Alt, Beck & Gottschalck. It has a wig, sleeping blue eyes, an open mouth with two upper teeth. It is on a five-piece composition toddler body. Mark: Ill. 97. H. 9 in. (23 cm.). *Courtesy of Helen Read. Photo by Steven Read.*

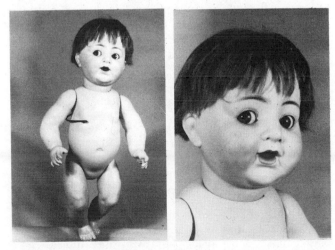

95A & B. Character bisque head made by Alt, Beck & Gottschalck, mold #1352. The flirting glass eyes have metal eyelids that close. The open mouth has two upper teeth and a tongue that flutters. The bent-limb composition baby body is strung with wire. The 45 cm. (17½ in.) h. is incised on the head. *Courtesy of Helen Read.*

96–100B. Alt, Beck & Gottschalck marks on bisque heads of dolls. No. 97 has its mold #1352, the h. of the doll 23 cm. and the size number 4.

A B & G
1322/1
Deponiert

96A

D R G M
(A. B. & G.)
1322
96B   28

AB
1352
23
Made in Germany

97   4

AB
1361
30

98

AB
1367
45
Made in Germany

99   14

2 ½
AB & G
Made in Germany

100A

„ALBEGO"
10
Made in Germany

100B

Altbuch, Mr. H. 1929 and earlier. New York City. Claimed he invented the "French Head" (*Boudoir Doll* type) for dolls. He had formerly been with *Anita Novelty Co.*, but went to the *European Doll Manufacturing Co.* when the two companies merged in 1929.

Althof, Bergmann & Co. 1843–83. New York City. Distributed dolls.★

101. Possible mark for Althof, Bergmann & Co.

Aluminum Doll Head Works. 1919–20. New York City. Obtained a U.S. patent in 1919 for sleeping eyes and for painted eyes.★

Alva Marina. 1917. Dried sea grass packed by *Harley & Miller* was used for stuffing these Alva Marina dolls. The grass was claimed to be vermin proof and nonflammable.

Am Munchen. 1920–22. Bratislava, Czechoslovakia. Shop that sold art dolls made by *Gisella Weyde* and *Elizabeth Neumayer-Somossy.*

Am Torg Trading Corp. 1928. Salesroom in New York City. Sold *Matryoshkas* and other art and handwork made by Russian peasants.

Amaury, Léo. 1911–30 and later. Paris. A sculptor, born in Paris. Modeled dolls' heads during World War I, made busts for which he received several awards.

Amazon. 1884. Name of a composition-head doll distributed by *Lauer,* had glass eyes, molded hair and bangs, composition arms and legs with molded footwear, and wore an embroidered chemise. Seven hts.: 13, 15, 17½, 19, 21½, 26, and 26½ in. (33, 38, 44.5, 48, 54.5, 66, and 67.5 cm.); priced $1.95 to $6.00 doz. wholesale.

Amberg, Louis, & Son. 1878–1930. Cincinnati, Ohio, and, from 1898 on, New York City. Louis Amberg did business under various names prior to 1907. From 1915 through 1921 at least, there was a London office.

Their bisque-head *Baby Nod* was marked Igodi which indicates that it was probably made by *Ernst Heubach* for *Johannes Gotthilf Dietrich.*

1903–04: Amberg and Brill advertised a 10 in. (25.5 cm.) doll with what appeared to be a bisque head. The doll was in a mechanical automobile. (See THE COLLECTOR'S BOOK OF DOLLS' CLOTHES, Ill. 536.)

1907: Joe (Joshua) Amberg joined the firm and the "& Son" was added.

1909: Imported bisque heads and put them on plush bodies with jointed arms and legs.

1910: Amberg was among the first to manufacture completely American-made dolls on a large scale. The dolls were made by the pouring plaster mold, glue composition, method.

1911: Began the use of the *Denivelle*-type cold-press composition method for the heads and arms of their dolls. This was a period of experimentation in the effort to produce an unbreakable composition that would not chip or peel. *Sis Hopkins* doll was introduced.

1912: Among the new dolls were *Miss Broadway,* Hail Columbia,[+] Yankee Doodle,[+] Spearmint Kiddo,[+] *Curly Locks,* and *Daffydils.*

1913: All the 100 new models had a "bisc finish," which was described as "mat, smooth, washable, undipped therefore non-peelable." Amberg claimed that this was the only finish made without the "glue dip," and these dolls were lickable so that children could perform "customary gnawing" without harm to themselves.

The new dolls were *Little Sweetheart, Wonder Baby,* and *Tiny Tots.* There was an all-composition doll with bent limbs, jointed at the shoulders and hips. Composition heads were on either cloth or kid bodies. Special attention was paid to the shaping of the feet and sewing of the toes. Eighteen of the style nos. were baby dolls dressed in long or short white baby dresses and caps. Among the accessories with these were rattles, teething rings, and nipples. The Amberg dolls retailed for 50¢ to $15.00.

1914: New dolls included the *Tango Tots, Pouty Pets,* and *John Bunny Doll.* Another portrait doll of a moving picture actor, previously made, was *Alkali Ike. New Born Babe* was copyrighted in this year.

1915: Many new dolls appeared, among them: Baby Glee,[+] *Beach Boy,* and *Beach Girl, Fishing Boy,* Go-Cart Dolly, Goody Goody,[+] Little Cherub,[+] Pudgie,[+] *Suitcase Dolly, Sweetheart,* Twilite Baby,[+] *Charlie Chaplin,* and *Oo-Gug-Luk.* The last two were made from the same mold but painted entirely differently. In order to keep up with the demand for the Charlie Chaplin doll, they had to discard the usual plaster molds and replace them with brass molds. There were dolls dressed as soldiers of all the Allied nations. They wore approximations of the regulation uniforms and carried national flags and guns. These soldier dolls, made of "bisc" finish composition, were fully jointed, 15 in. high (38 cm.), and retailed for $1.00 or more.

There were many new character dolls, some with mama voices, that sold for only 50¢. *Thomas & Heinrichs* was a factory representative. The "*Little Darling Babies*" were sold through *British Metal & Toy Manufacturers* in London.

1916: An animated version of Charlie Chaplin was made and a multiface doll was patented. Other dolls included First Steps,[†] Pollyanna,[†] *Educational Doll,* and Amberg's Flower. The Ambisc, all-composition and fully jointed, dolls cost between $5.00 and $18.00 a dozen. The boy and girl dolls cost 25¢ to $5.00 each; baby dolls cost 35¢ to $10.00 each. One of the boy dolls wore a double-breasted coat, short trousers, a shirt, four-in-hand tie, and a brimmed hat. One of the girl dolls wore a dress with a low waistline, a wide belt, a full ruffled skirt, and a ribbon-trimmed hat. There were 40 styles of dolls with wigs, costing $5.40 a dozen. Dolls with painted hair came in four sizes. Amberg claimed that he had agents all over the world.

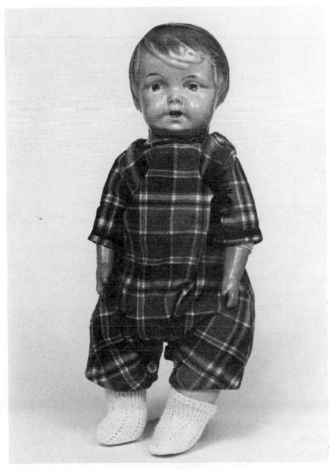

102. Cold-press composition head and hands on a cloth body filled with straw, made by Amberg and copyrighted in 1916. It has molded and painted hair and eyes, an open-closed mouth, and a flange neck. Original clothes except for socks. The cotton rompers are a brown-and-blue plaid. Pearl buttons fasten the crotch. Mark: Ill. 105. H. 14 in. (35.5 cm.). *Courtesy of the Margaret Woodbury Strong Museum. Photo by Harry Bickelhaupt.*

1917: *Otto Denivelle* joined the firm as factory superintendent. Among the dolls in 1917 were Skookum,[†] The Bully Kiddo[†], *Victory Doll,* birthday dolls, and sweater and knit-suit dolls. Amberg also made a *Red Cross Nurse.*

1918: Otto Denivelle introduced the new hot press baking process, which produced composition socket and shoulder heads in nine sizes as well as other dolls' parts. Among the new dolls were the *Happinus* line, *Little Fellow, Regal Sleepers, Amkid* dolls, crybaby dolls, and *Mama* dolls. The Mama dolls had composition heads and limbs on cloth bodies.

1919: Amberg's walking doll with composition shoulder head, arms, and legs was made in 10 styles, and two sizes, 22 and 28 inches (56 and 71 cm.). The price was $42.00 a dozen and up. There was also a fully jointed walking doll. The mama doll that, after being laid down for a short time, opened its eyes and called "Mama" was the company's best seller. Cloth Happifats[†] were introduced.

1920: Joe Amberg was head of the *Doll & Stuffed Toy Manufacturers' Association.*

The American Bisque Dolls *(Fulper)* came in four sizes with foolproof eyes and eyelashes; the imitation "bisc" dolls were made in 10 sizes, fully jointed dolls came in four sizes and character babies were in three sizes. The walking doll was made in three sizes instead of two. The dressed baby dolls had bisque heads, sleeping eyes, and eyelashes. Victory dolls also came dressed.

A short strike occurred in the stuffing department, but since Amberg employed workers of many nationalities with varied ethnic backgrounds it was difficult for them to organize a union. One of the Amberg factory agents was the *Bush Terminal Sales Co.*

1921: Dolls included *Mibs* in composition, *Nature Children,* Freshie[1] (a Happifat youngster), and display dolls. Hts. 30, 36, and 42 in. (76, 91.5, and 106.5 cm.). These large dolls had bisque heads, eyelashes, teeth, tongues, and composition bodies.

1923: Amberg made and imported a wide variety of dolls, including Mama dolls and *Baby Peggy* dolls. Amberg used the slogan "The World Standard."

1924: Amberg advertised 600 style numbers, including some dolls from Germany that were dressed in America, and a reissue of the 1914 New Born Babe. They also made a doll named Ma Chunk. The sleeping-eye Mama dolls retailed for $2.98 to $15.00. Baby Peggy was made with a bisque shoulder head on a kid body. Amberg had an office in Sonneberg.

1926: The New Born Babe doll was exploited as *New Born Basket Babe* and *New Born Bottle Babe.* The novelty in 1926 was the all-felt dressed dolls that sold for 50¢ and $1.00. Mama dolls of all types were leading items. Amberg sold bisque and composition heads for baby dolls.

1927: Otto Denivelle became a firm member. Dolls included *Fairie Princess, Vanta Baby,* and Mama dolls. The voices and criers in the dolls were licensed by *Voices, Inc.*

Amberg registered the trademark "Vanta." They handled an *A 1* line possibly made by *Dean.*

1928: Vanta Baby was made in new styles and new sizes. The *Amfelt Art* dolls were imported from Paris and were designed by Europeans. Amberg registered the trademark "So Big" with a picture of a doll stretching its arms over its head. The *It* dolls, which are jointed at the waist, have been found marked "L.A.&S. © 1928." The 1928 *waist joint* patent was used for several years on dolls having various style heads.

1929: The dolls included "It," *Tiny Tots, Little Amby,* Amfelt Art dolls, Peter Pan, *Sparkle Twins, Twinkle Twins,* and *Teenie Weenies,* as well as the new baby dolls and an extensive line of Mama dolls. "It" and Tiny Tots were jointed at the waistline. The Amberg factory produced 72 dozen Tiny Tot dolls every working day. The prices of the Vanta Baby line were lowered.

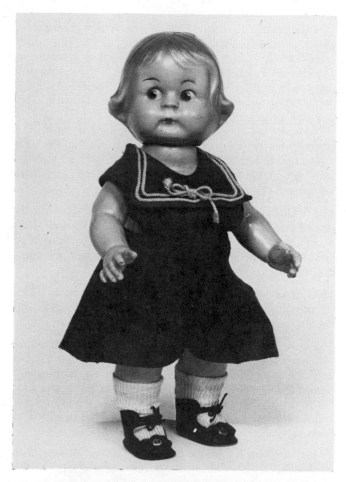

103. All-composition doll made by Amberg in 1928 or later. It has molded and painted hair and eyes, closed mouth. The dome-shaped neck fits into a socket in the head which resembles that found on the Patsy dolls. The sleeveless suit is made of dark blue wool trimmed with white braid. Mark: Ill. 107. H. 13 in. (33 cm.). *Courtesy of the Margaret Woodbury Strong Museum. Photo by Harry Bickelhaupt.*

1930: The Amberg business was sold to *E. I. Horsman,* except for the imported *Amfelt* dolls, which were sold to *Paul Cohen Co.* The "It" doll and others continued to be made in the Horsman factory. (See also **Manufacture of Dolls, Commercial: Made in United States.**)★

© 1916 L.A.&S.
105

L.A.& S.
106   1918

AMBERG
L.A.&S. ©1928
107

AMBERG
DOLLS
THE WORLD
STANDARD
MADE IN
USA
108

AMBERG DOLLS
The World Standard
109

LA&S
RA 241 ⅗
GERMANY
110

105–110. Marks on dolls made by Amberg. No. 105 is on the doll in Ill. 102. No. 107 is on the doll in Ill. 103.

Amberg & Hergershausen. 1925. Berlin. Paul Amberg. Brand name of their dolls was *Elfenhaut* (elf's skin). Their eight-sided trademark has the initials AHABE at top and bottom. This company obtained four German patents (D.R.G.M.) for mama-papa voices in rubber and/or composition dolls.

Ambrose. 1920s. Made by *Farnell.* This was a cloth, long-limbed doll based on a character in James Riddell's book, according to Mary Hillier.

Amerault, Mary. 1889–before 1929. Employed by *Thomas Edison.* She spoke many of the verses recorded for the Edison Talking Dolls.

American Art Dolls. 1915–17. Controlled exclusively by *Strobel & Wilken Co.* These cloth character dolls were made as children or as babies. They had painted features and hair. In 1915 the faces were stockinet, but later treated canvas was used. Joints of their lightweight bodies were at the shoulders and hips. These dolls, made in America, were popular-priced ($2.00 and $2.50) imitations of the *Käthe*

OUTSTANDING **NEW LINES**

NINE (9) NEW

Different

COMPOSITION DOLLS

From:—TEENIE WEENIES—Retailing 75¢

To:—LITTLE AMBY—*So Cunnin'*—*The Baby*

And:—TWINKLE TWINS—UNIQUE BABY GIRLS

And:—Peter Pan Drest Doll

CULMINATING IN

"IT"

*The Crashing
Smashing Hit!*

The DOLL with a
BODY TWIST
all, all its own!

**THE FINEST IMPORTED
SPECIALTIES EVER
SHOWN—FOURTEEN
DIFFERENT
EXCLUSIVE
RANGES**

**Washable—Durable
Colorful—Decorative
Featherweight
Undressable**

Fully Jointed
Handsomely Boxed
From 25c to $5.00

Vanta Baby

"No Pins—No Buttons!"

Lovelier than ever

THE STAPLE LINE

Featuring

New Popular Price Line
RETAILING $1.00
and up

REMEMBER 1929 IS AN AMBERG YEAR

Orders in Hand Prove It, *Absolutely!*

LOUIS AMBERG & SON　*"Toys Since 1879"
Every Known Kind of
Doll and Toy Animal*　**869 Broadway, New York City**

One good turn deserves another—please mention PLAYTHINGS.

104. Amberg's advertisement in PLAYTHINGS, May, 1929, showing some of the dolls made by Amberg.

Kruse dolls. They had black tied single-strap slippers with buckles.

1915: *Susie's Sister* line, ht. 17 in. (43 cm.), and *Tootsie* line.

1916: New dolls included Ulrich, a Dutch boy in long full trousers; Buddy, dressed as a farmer in overalls, and Faith, dressed in Quaker garb.

1917: There were 35 different styles of dolls, but the chief difference was in their costumes. Dolls were dressed to represent various nationalities: Kathrina wore a Dutch girl outfit; Pepe was dressed as an Italian boy, and Pepina as an Italian girl; Hans was dressed as a German boy, and Gretel as a German girl; Robbie and Marion were the American pair, wearing playsuits.★

American Beauty. 1895–1930. A line of *Strobel & Wilken* dolls. One of these with the kid body marked "American Beauty" had a bisque shoulder head with an *Edmund Ulrich Steiner* mark on the back. The shoulders were marked 7 but the rim of the crown was numbered 12. The head had sleeping blue glass eyes and four porcelain teeth. Ht. 26 in. (66 cm.).

American Beauty. 1919–28. Dolls made by Seamless Toy Co.,[+] distributed by Charles William, had composition heads and limbs, mohair wigs and eyelashes, sleeping eyes, open mouths, teeth, tongues, crying voices, cloth bodies. They came dressed. Ht. 24 in. (61 cm.); priced $3.25.★

American Beauty Babies. 1920. Advertised by *Sears.* They had composition heads and forearms, mohair wigs, sleeping eyes, cloth bodies, and were dressed. Hts. 14, 15, 16, and 19 in. (35.5, 38, 40.5, and 48 cm.); priced $3.35 to $5.98.

American Beauty Doll. 1913. Empire Art Doll, a cloth cut-out doll made in hts. 10 and 25½ in. (25.5 and 65 cm.) according to Margaret Whitton.★

American Bisque Co. 1919–20. Williamstown, W.Va. This ceramic factory had gas-fired beehive kilns. They made pink tint all-bisque dolls; most of them had molded hair and footwear; wire joints at the shoulders and hips. There were at least three styles of dolls, a Kewpie type, a girl and a baby, all copied from German examples. The left and right arms generally differed in position. The head and body were made of one type of clay while the arms were made from a different clay. The dolls were usually only 4 or 4½ in. (10 or 11.5 cm.) tall.

American Bisque Doll Co. 1919–21. Newark and Hoboken, N.J. Advertised wood-fiber composition dolls and bisque heads. A picture of a doll with a bisque head looked as if the head had been made by *Fulper.* The dolls came with or without voices, with or without sleeping eyes. (The eyes appear to have been the metal type.) Composition dolls included baby dolls, *Mama* dolls, *Frozen Charlottes,* all-composition ball-jointed dolls, and long-limbed lady dolls. Some of the names used by this company were *Polly Anna, Toddler, Toodles,* and Baby Toddler. The company sold about $200,000 worth of dolls a year.★

American Character Doll Co. 1919–30 and later. New York

City. Made bent-limb and straight-leg wood-fiber composition dolls.

1920: Bent-limb baby dolls with jointed shoulders and hips; ht. 14 and 16 in. (35.5 and 40.5 cm.); dressed in chemise or knitted outfit. The 16-inch doll came in five styles. All-composition novelty dolls jointed at the shoulder, 13 in. (33 cm.) high, came naked with hair and veil or dressed in a knitted suit and cap. Ten styles of this doll were made. Some had painted hair.

1923: Began to use trade name "Petite" for a line of *Mama* and character dolls. Mama dolls came 13 to 26 in. (33 to 66 cm.) tall. Fully jointed character baby dolls were made in a wide variety of sizes. The dolls were dressed in organdy or linen frocks.

1924: New heights 13 to 28 in. (33 to 71 cm.) were added to Petite baby doll line. All the Petite dolls had sleeping eyes.

1925: Claimed an increase of 42 percent in sales of their

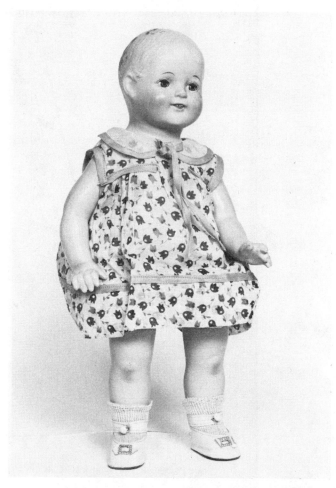

111. Mama doll made by the American Character Doll Co. It has molded and painted hair as well as remnants of a wig; metal covered with celluloid, eyes; hair eyelashes, and painted upper and lower eyelashes; open-closed mouth with two teeth; and dimples. The shoulder head, arms, and legs are composition and the torso is cloth with a round voice box. Original clothes. Mark: Ill. 113. H. 16 in. (40.5 cm.). *Courtesy of the Margaret Woodbury Strong Museum. Photo by Harry Bickelhaupt.*

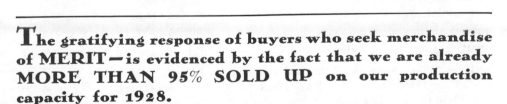

The gratifying response of buyers who seek merchandise of MERIT — is evidenced by the fact that we are already **MORE THAN 95% SOLD UP** on our production capacity for 1928.

AMERICAN CHARACTER DOLL CO., 20 E. 17th St., N. Y.

Start your letter right: "I saw your ad in PLAYTHINGS."

112. Advertisement in PLAYTHINGS, September, 1928, for dolls made by the American Character Doll Co.

dolls. Twin newborn-infant-type dolls were wrapped in a blanket.

1926: Moved to new factory in Brooklyn, where 18,000 square feet was devoted to making dolls. Continued to make walking, talking, crying, and sleeping dolls. Their new dolls included *Bottletot,* created by *J. Brock,* who was in charge of the company, and *Miss Fashion,* a slim doll. "Bottletot, A Petite Baby" was registered as a trademark.

1927: The Bottletot line was changed from those made in 1926. A new line of smiling bent-limb babies called *Happy Tots* was added, as well as *Lucky Aviation Kid.* The Mama dolls were slimmer than formerly and, together with the bent-limb baby dolls in short dresses, were outselling the infant dolls in long dresses. The American Character Doll Co. was licensed by *Voices, Inc.* to use their patent mama voices and criers. Their Mama dolls with wigs and sleeping eyes were sold by *Montgomery Ward.* Ht. 17 in. (43 cm.); priced $3.48. *H. A. Moore* was the London agent.

1928: 100 new numbers of dolls included *Campbell Kids, Puggy,* and *Toddle Tot.* The Petite line of Mama dolls and baby dolls wore lace-trimmed dresses and were made in various sizes. The company claimed that the demand exceeded the supply, as it had done for prior years. *Oakland Stationery and Toy Co.* was one of their jobbers.

1929: Continued to make the same dolls, but some of them wore clothes of new designs. Novelty dolls were mentioned for the first time.

1930: *Sally,* a *Patsy*-type doll, was new. New clothes and new faces appeared in their old lines. There were five new numbers in the Toddle Tot line and a new line of Mama dolls. The baby dolls were now filled with kapok. They registered a doll in a horseshoe surrounded by "A Lovable Petite Doll"; under the doll was the name "Sally." The initials "A C D" have been found on Sally dolls.

1931: Registered "Sally Joy" as a trademark for dolls. Manufactured cloth dolls.★

American Composition Doll Co. 1908 and earlier. New York City. Made dolls with composition heads and sewn arms and legs. In 1908 the company was bought by *Benjamin Goldenberg.* This company was known earlier as the *First American Doll Factory.*

American Countess. 1895. Distributed by *Butler Bros.* It had a bisque head, wig, and came dressed. Ht. 22 in. (56 cm.); priced $3.90 doz. wholesale.

American Doll. 1919–20. Made by *Alisto Manufacturing Co.* Had fingers apart, legs together, molded clothes.★

American Doll Co. 1893–1904. Philadelphia, Pa. Doll factory owned by Francis P. and Harry Knell.† Frank Knell was the half-brother of *Ludwig Greiner*'s daughter-in-law, and had been trained by working for Greiner before Greiner died in 1874.★

American Doll Co. 1907. Attleboro, Mass. Offered a premium doll with bisque head, hands, and feet, wig; dressed in silks and laces.

113–115. American Character Doll Co. Petite marks on baby and Mama dolls.

American Doll Co. 1925–26. Louisville, Ky. Listed in PLAYTHINGS under "Dolls."

American Doll Co. 1920s. Chicago, Ill. Manufactured plaster composition *Kewpie*-type dolls with or without wigs, jointed at the shoulders. Hts. 15 and 30 in. (38 and 76 cm.). "Gloss finished" dolls had movable arms. Ht. 14 in. (35.5 cm.). They also made plaster casts.

AM. DOLL. CO.

116. American Doll Co. mark used on dolls.

American Doll Manufacturers' Association. 1921–28 and probably other years. New York City.

1921: Adopted the slogan "Avoid childhood tragedy—a broken doll. Buy American made dolls."

1925: According to this association, 22 member firms manufactured 85 percent of the dolls sold in the U.S. Only 15 percent were manufactured in foreign countries or by nonmembers, such as the *Alexander Doll Co., Jacobs & Kassler, Regal Doll Manufacturing Co.,* Roth, Baitz & Lipsitz,† Schoenhut, and so forth.

1926: 23 member firms were listed. The association's

trademark was "Durable, Beautiful// 100% American // Made."

1927: 47 member firms. All were in New York City.

American Doll Manufacturing Co. 1912–25 and later. New York City. Made composition dolls' heads and parts. In 1914 they increased their force by a fifth and put on a nightshift in order to handle all their orders.★

American Doll Mold Co. 1928–29. New York City. Claimed that they made the molds for America's biggest manufacturers of dolls. They had an experienced sculptor who improved and finished the rough models supplied by the manufacturers.

American Doll & Toy Co.† See **First American Doll Factory.**

American Dolls (U.S. Dolls). Cloth dolls have been especially important in America, both the homemade and commercial ones. Some of the dolls with cloth heads had a paper face on which the features were drawn. This was stuck onto

the cloth and probably often became detached. Gradual improvements created dolls with treated cloth faces and, finally, molded cloth. Cloth cutout dolls probably were an American innovation. In 1924 the U.S. Department of Commerce described some of the American dolls as having composition heads "with the face covered with fine gauze which makes the tinting or other coloring more effective for 'character' expressions."

As early as the 1820s or '30s dolls' heads of pottery were produced in North Carolina by *John Holland*. However, Americans never produced really fine bisque dolls despite valiant efforts during and shortly after World War I. The greatest success came with the development of composition dolls. Americans strived to make composition-head dolls that were more durable than those made in Europe. *Ludwig Greiner* reinforced his dolls with cloth. In the early 20th century *Benjamin Goldenberg, Otto Denivelle,* and others labored endlessly to produce a durable composition doll. The wood-flour and glue dolls with a glue dip resisted breaking, but they cracked and peeled. This was caused by changes in the weather and excess humidity. Unfortunately this was a serious problem in the East, where most of the dolls were made. As early as 1913 *Amberg* advertised that their dolls were made by the cold-press method and without the glue dip, so they would not crack or peel. Around 1918 the wood-pulp hot-press method of production was inaugurated, with excellent results, and the American baby and

117. Dolls manufactured in the United States in the 1850s and 1860s. The shoulder heads of the rubber dolls at each end were made in accordance with the Goodyear Rubber patent. They have molded black hair and eyes and closed mouths. The Darrow leather doll in the middle has molded and painted black hair and blue eyes. Doll on right is marked "New York Rubber Co.//Goodyear's Pat. 444." All three dolls have cloth bodies and original or contemporary clothes. Left to right, hs. 13½ in. (34 cm.), 15 in. (38 cm.), and 13½ in. (34 cm.). *Courtesy of Sotheby Parke Bernet Inc., N.Y.*

118. Cloth doll made by Martha Chase in America. The head, including the hair and features, is oil-painted. It has blue eyes and a flesh-colored sateen body with oil-painted lower arms and legs. H. 16 in. (40.5 cm.). *Courtesy of Sotheby Parke Bernet Inc., N.Y.*

Mama dolls became real competitors of the postwar European dolls. In 1920 *J. C. Ruben* of *Effanbee* stated: "When you buy a doll you may think it is French or German, and the dealer may even tell you so, but the chances are three out of four that it is American."

In 1927 *Stewart Culin,* curator at the Brooklyn Museum, commented: "The chubby-faced doll with real hair and closing eyes is an adult's idea of what a child should like and not a child's idea at all."

This statement probably influenced the introduction of a new type of slimmer doll in 1927. Mr. Culin went on to say that the "finely finished ornamental dolls could not be played with and were kept in Grandmother's bureau drawer or at the top of a great-aunt's wardrobe." This may partly explain why many more European dolls than American-made dolls of this period have survived.

1928: Charles Hawkes, secretary of the *American Doll Manufacturers' Association,* gave a somewhat chauvinistic description of the American doll industry:

". . . 90 percent of all the dolls sold in the United States in 1927, as for several years past, are of American make, notwithstanding the 'tradition' that most of our dolls come from Germany.

"It is true that dolls today are made to represent little girls and boys and infants. But with a difference strikingly apparent in comparison [with German dolls].

"No longer the expressionless face, the bulging cheeks, the widely staring eyes, the hard, ungainly bodies, but creatures of grace and beauty, approaching closely the appearance and contour of a beautiful, graceful child, with most lifelike and expressive features.

". . . The traditional German doll had a head of bisque, with hard body of composition. Jointed arms and legs were held together with rubber bands. These things are now so rare as to be a curiosity. . . .

"The bisque head, in spite of its beautiful appearance, was ill-fitted for the strenuous life of the up-to-date doll. The jointed arms and legs early succumbed to the infirmities of age and unfavorable climate. The hard body did not respond to the cuddling of the fond owner.

"The composition head of the American doll is at least the equal of the bisque head in texture and far superior on the average in feature and expression.

"American dolls, speaking generally, are "soft-body" dolls, stuffed with pure, clean cotton; limbs securely stitched to the body, but so as to allow free and natural movement. The body is warm and cuddly.

"The Ma-Ma voice, an American invention, has not been imitated by the foreign manufacturer. . . . The American doll "speaks" and says "Ma-Ma" in two syllables and with perfect enunciation.

"Surely we are a far cry in advance of the doll of tradition, and although dolls are still made in imitation of their owners, the approach to perfection is so much closer as to certainly justify a claim to radical change in style.

"The statement that 90 percent of dolls sold in the United States are of domestic production is supported by the results of an extensive survey made in 1927 by the American Doll Manufacturers' Association and reports from several hundred retail dealers, including practically all the large department stores.

"From this it appeared that while American dolls were rarely called for as such, the dolls with the characteristics the buyers wanted were American dolls, and the German dolls, when sold at all, were only in the grades where low price rather than quality was the determining factor." (See also **Benoliel and Braitling.**)★

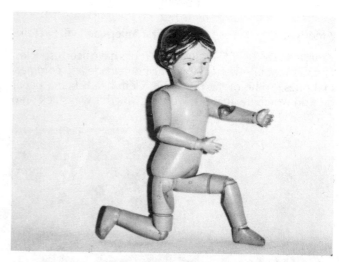

119. All-wood American doll made by Schoenhut with carved and molded hair, hair ribbon, and features. The body is strung with metal springs. Schoenhut mark is on the back shoulders. H. 14 in. (35 cm.). *Private collection.*

120. American composition head doll representing an Indian, created by Mary McAboy. It has a wig, painted eyes, looking to the side, a cardboard body, and wooden legs. Original clothes. H. 14 in. (35.5 cm.). *Coleman Collection.*

American Friendship Dolls. See **Friendship Dolls.**

American Girl. 1908. Cutout cloth doll made by *Saalfield*. Dress was printed on the doll. Ht. 7¾ in. (19.5 cm.).

American Girls. 1914. Distributed by *Butler Bros.* It had a bisque head, wig, sleeping eyes, hair eyelashes, and was on a composition body jointed at the shoulders, elbows, hips, and knees, and had removable clothing. Ht. 17 in. (43 cm.); priced $11.00 doz. wholesale.

American Made Toy Co. 1929. New York City. Louis I. Bloom, doing business as the American Made Toy Company, registered a U.S. trademark with an eagle and the words "American Made// Toy Company." The trademark was for stuffed dolls.

American Maid Dolls. 1900–14. Line of cloth dolls made by *Bruckner,* distributed by *Horsman* and others. Dolls had mitten-type hands and removable clothes. The American Maid Baby and *Topsy* (see *Babyland Dolls*) wore long baby dresses. Topsy and Topsy Baby were black versions. *Red Riding Hood* and *Little Boy Blue* were the same doll as the American Maid dolls; only the clothes were different.

1904: Advertised by *Gimbel Bros.* as having painted faces. Ht. 13 in. (33 cm.); priced 50¢.

1905: Same doll and price advertised by *Siegel Cooper.*★

American Merchandise Co. 1891. New York City. Wholesale distributor of dolls with china heads and limbs on cloth bodies, dolls with bisque heads on kid or on jointed composition bodies, dolls with composition heads and limbs or knock-about dolls with composition heads, as well as all-china and all-bisque dolls.

American Muslin-Lined (Muslin) Head. Ca. 1870s–1880s. Composition heads completely lined with coarse muslin had molded blond or dark Greiner-style hair-dos, painted features. Rectangular paper stickers on the back of the shoulder plates read variously. One was "AMERICAN//MUSLIN-LINED HEAD//No." on a 20 in. (51 cm.) doll with a 5¼ in. (13.5 cm.) shoulder head. Another head had a sticker that read "AMERICAN//MUSLIN-LINED HEAD//No. 9// Warranted Fast Oil Colors." This head was 8 in. (20.5 cm.) tall on a 26½ in. (67.5 cm.) doll. On a third head with a bang hair style the sticker read "AMERICAN//MUSLIN HEAD//Number 4//Warranted Fast Oil Colors" on an 18 in. (45.5 cm.) doll. On the 20 in. (51 cm.) doll the eyes had large black pupils surrounded on the lower three-quarters by a white outline, then a blue outline. There were no highlights. Red dots were in the corner of the eyes and red lines in the nostrils. There was a long lip line and the complexion was light flesh-colored. It was on a commercially made pink-colored cloth body stuffed with hair and had leather arms and leather high-heeled boots with two metal buttons. The stockings had maroon-colored dots and matching maroon ribbon garters. The 18 in. (45.5 cm.) doll was on a home-made cloth body. Another American muslin-lined head was found on a *Goldsmith* body.

American Ocarina & Toy Co. 1919–21. Newark, N.J. Manufactured 75 styles of composition dolls. These came

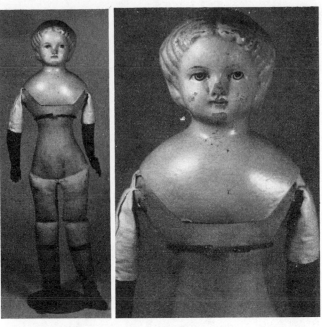

121A & B. Muslin-lined composition shoulder head made in America. It has molded hair painted blond, eyes painted blue, and a closed mouth. It is on a cloth body with lower leather arms. Mark: Ill. 122. *Courtesy Z. Frances Walker. Photo by Barbara Jendrick.*

AMERICAN MUSLIN-LINED HEAD

122. American Muslin-Lined Head mark; printed on a paper sticker attached to the back of the shoulders, found on doll in Ill. 121.

with or without wigs, with painted or sleeping eyes, with straight legs or bent limbs in sizes 10 to 19 in. (25.5 to 48 cm.). The baby dolls wore only a chemise.★

American Pet. 1880s. Name of a doll with a composition shoulder head, wig, glass eyes, cloth body with composition and wood ball-jointed arms and composition lower legs. One of these dolls with the mark shown in Ill. 123 stamped on its stomach was 17 in. (43 cm.) tall. It was made by *Schilling.*

123. American Pet name stamped on a composition doll. Also in the stamp is the name Schillings.

American Produced (Stuffed) Toy Co. 1917–20. New York City. Composition dolls included soldiers, sailors, nurses, and babies. In 1920 dolls were 25 and 32 in. (63.5 and 81 cm.) high.★

American Rice Foods Manufacturing Co. 1899–early 1900s. Used cutout cloth dolls for advertising their products. Dolls included *Miss Flaked Rice* and *Miss Malto-Rice.* (See also **Cook's Flaked Rice Co.**)

American Rose Bud. 1921. Cloth doll made by *Sophia E. Delavan.* Doll had slim legs and neck, worsted hair, wore a percale dress with organdy trim and a pocket containing a printed story. Hat matched the dress.★

American Specialty Doll Co. 1920–30. Brooklyn, N.Y. Exhibited dolls at the New York Toy Fair.

American Stuffed Novelty Co. 1923–30 and later. New York City. Made art and *Boudoir* dolls. These dolls had hand-painted pressed cloth faces, mohair or silk wigs, in a variety of colors. The heads and long-limbed sateen covered bodies were stuffed with white cotton. The original styled clothes were designed by *Morris Politzer,* and were removable. The company used the trade name Life-Like line.

1924: Dolls made as large as 31 in. (78.5 cm.).

1926: The 22 numbers included *Co-Ed Flapper, Collegiate Flapper, Follies Girl, Parisienne Belle, Silk Flapper,* and *Yama Doll.*

1929: Continued to specialize in art and Boudoir dolls but also made *Mama* dolls and baby dolls.

1930: Advertised French-type art dolls with movable heads, cloth faces, and human hair. *Aunt Jemima* dolls were added to their line.

1931: Added all-composition dolls to their cloth dolls, Mama dolls, and baby dolls.★

American Style Doll Manufacturing Co. 1924–28. New York City. Manufactured dolls.

American Tissue Mills. See **Utley Co.**

American Toy & Doll Manufacturing Co. 1917–18. Chicago, Ill. Made $300,000 worth of dolls in their first year. The composition dolls included 15 in. (38 cm.) straight-leg dolls and 15½ in. (39.5 cm.) bent-limb baby dolls. They advertised that their bisque-finish composition would "not crack, peel or chip."★

American Toy & Manufacturing Co. 1917–19. Kansas City, Mo. Made a portrait doll of Marguerite Clark as she appeared in SNOW WHITE, dressed in pink with rose ornamentation, silver crown studded with rosebuds, and a tulle bridelike veil.★

American Toy & Novelty Co. 1917–30 and later. New York City and Philadelphia. In 1930 the company was taken over by the *Frank Plotnick Co.* of Philadelphia. Manufactured all-composition jointed dolls, including bent-limb babies and straight-leg children, with and without wigs. Also made dolls with composition heads and cork-stuffed cloth bodies.

1918: Various character cloth-body dolls, 10¢ up. All-composition dolls, $1.00 up.

1919: Dolls with sleeping eyes. Ht. 14 to 18 in. (35.5 to 45.5 cm.). Dolls dressed in light pink, dark red, and vivid blue.

1919–20: *Tessie,* an all-composition doll.

1921: Doll 10½ in. (26.5 cm.). Cloth body dolls, 25¢ up.

1927: Advertised infant and character composition dolls.

1928: All-composition baby dolls in two sizes. Composition dolls of various types, priced 25¢ to $10. Dolls available in black and white versions. Specialized in dolls for syndicate business.

1929: *Priscilla.*

1930: Cloth dolls stuffed with kapok, dressed as cowboys, soldiers, and in other costumes.★

American Unbreakable Doll Corp. 1923–27. New York City. Made composition dolls, including the *Princess* line.★

American Wholesale Corp. See **Baltimore Bargain House.**

American Wonder Baby. See **Bottletot.**

Amfelt Art Dolls. 1928–30. Line of imported felt dolls in 14 styles produced by *Amberg* as competition with the *Lenci* dolls. Rights to these dolls were sold to *Paul Cohen Co.* in 1930. European designers modeled and costumed these dolls, which had joints at the neck, shoulders, and hips. The faces were washable. Colorful clothes included hats or bonnets; footwear consisted of socks and light-colored single-strap tie slippers.

1928: Price $1.00 to $7.00.

1929: Price 25¢ to $5.00. (See also **Art Felt Dolls.**)

Amico Dolls. 1930. Line of dolls manufactured by *Ammidon & Co.*

Amkid. 1918–early 1920s. Line of real kid- or imitation kid-bodied dolls made by *Amberg.* The heads were usually of composition made by the process discovered by *Otto Denivelle.* One of these dolls has been reported as having a *Revalo* bisque head, but it is not certain this was the original head. Some of the cork-stuffed bodies have kid or imitation kid torsos and upper legs with jointed composition arms, including the wrist joint, and a universal joint at the hips. These dolls were distributed by *Butler Bros.*

124. Amkid mark used by Amberg.

Ammidon & Co. 1930. Baltimore, Md. Manufactured *Amico* line of dolls.

Amor. 1927–28. Trade name of a *Lenci* felt doll, number 566. A black cupid with wings dressed in a girdle of roses and a high hat. Ht. 19½ in. (49.5 cm.).

Amos 'N Andy. 1930 and later. Three companies, Amos 'N Andy Doll Co., *Averill Manufacturing Co.*, and *S. & H. Novelty Co.*, tried to register "Amos 'N Andy" as a U.S. trademark but all were turned down. The Amos 'N Andy Doll Co. then tried unsuccessfully to register "Amos 'N Andy, Check 'N Double Check." The S. & H. Novelty Co. named a pair of their dolls Amos 'N Andy. The pair could be held together with snaps or unsnapped to separate them. They had lightweight composition heads and were dressed in a variety of character costumes.

A black version of the *R.C.A. Radiotrons* doll was supposed to represent Amos and Andy, the radio comedians.

Amusement Novelty Co. 1926– and other years. Elmira, N.Y. Handled baby dolls, *Mama* dolls, *Boudoir* dolls, including those made by *Haskell and Rushton*.

Amuso. 1925. Doll with composition head and limbs on a cloth body made by *August Möller & Sohn*. Some have flirting and sleeping eyes with hair eyelashes, open mouth with teeth and tongue. Ht. of an Oriental version was 14 in. (35.5 cm.).★

AMUSO
100
Made in Germany
30

125. Amuso is a mark found on a German doll. The 100 is the mold number and the 30 is the size of the doll in centimeters.

Anamay Doll Co. 1930 and later. Woburn, Mass. Manufactured cloth dolls.

Anciaux, Mlle. 1918. Paris. Created cloth dolls.

Ancre. See **A l'Ancre.**

Anderegg, Th. Early 1900s. Montreux, Switz. Made and exported carved all-wooden dolls. These dolls with carved hair and painted eyes were jointed. The cream-colored letters on the brown ground of a round paper sticker read "Th. Anderegg//wood//carving// Export// Montreux, Switzerland." Size of one of these dolls, 11 in. (28 cm.).

Anderson, John. 1913. Scotland. Royal Polytechnic. Exhibited Army, Navy, and Red *Indian* dolls at the Ideal Home Exhibit in Glasgow.

Andrew. 1915. One of the dolls promoted by *Mme. Paderewski* to aid Polish refugees. This doll was made in the workshop of *Mme. Lazarski* by Polish refugee artists and represented a boy from Lowiez.

Andri, Ferdinand. 1906. Austria. Designed and made turned wooden dolls entirely by himself. These painted dolls of various sizes could stand either on their feet or on round

disks. They represented villagers in Moravia, Bohemia, and Croatia.

Andrina. 1867. Exhibited dolls in the Paris Exposition.

Andy Gump. 1929. Doll made in Germany for *Marshall Field & Co.*, which gave permission to *Shackman* to also distribute the doll wholesale. It represents a comic-strip character created by Sidney Smith, and was made as an all-bisque doll with molded clothes; only its head was movable. Ht. 4 in. (10 cm.); retail price 25¢.

ANDY
GUMP

Germany

126. All-bisque doll representing Andy Gump as drawn by Sidney Smith. It has molded and painted features and clothes, including a hat. Only jointed at the neck. This doll was produced by Marshall Field, who held the rights. Mark: Ill. 127. Ht. 4 in. (10 cm.). *Coleman Collection.*

127. Mark on the back of the Andy Gump doll.

Anel & Fraisse. 1913–ca. 1920. Anel & Fils. 1921–30 and later. Paris. Factory at Muzy, France. Made celluloid dolls in a wide variety of models and sizes. (See also **Tissier.**)★

Anfray. 1925–30 and later. Paris. Made cloth dolls, *marottes, cymbaliers,* and so on. ★

Angel. 1921. Composition doll made by *Jeanette Doll Co.*

Angela. Ca. 1909. Name of a doll made by *Handwerck* and distributed by *Macy.*

Angermüller, F. 1927–28. Coburg, Germany. Manufactured a doll named *Fancora-Wunder-Baby.*

Anglo-American Novelty Co. 1916. England. Distributed British, French, and American dolls, including celluloid dolls, a doll that said "Mama," and dolls' trousseau sets.

Anielka. 1915. One of the dolls promoted by *Mme. Paderewski* to aid Polish refugees. It was made in the workshop of *Mme. Lazarski* by Polish refugee artists and represented a woman of Lowiez.

Anili. 1927. Trade name of a *Lenci* felt doll. This was a portrait of Madame Scavini's[†] daughter, Anili, at age six. For the straight dark hair a fine fluffy flax product was used.

In the 1980s Anili is still making felt dolls with pressed felt faces. She uses Anili as her trade name.

Anita Novelty Co. Before 1929–30 and later. New York City. In 1929 became affiliated with the *European Doll Manufacturing Co.* Made cloth dolls, especially Flapper dolls and *Boudoir* dolls, which they called "French Head" dolls. *H. Altbuch,* who claimed that he invented the "French Head," was a member of this company.

Ann Boleyn. 1924. "French" cloth doll dressed to resemble the Holbein portrait of Ann Boleyn, featured in the LADIES' HOME JOURNAL. (See Ill. 401.)

Anna. 1891. Trade name of a patented jointed doll made by *Schwarzkopf & Fröber.*

Anna. 1927–28. Trade name of a felt *Lenci* doll of the long-limbed lady type. Number 165/13, ht. 27½ in. (70 cm.). It may represent Anna in ANNA AND THE KING OF SIAM.

Annabelle. 1920s. Trade name of a cloth doll made by *Farnell;* doll represented a character in a book by James Riddell.

Annabelle. 1927. Made by *Royal Toy Manufacturing Co.,* distributed by *Montgomery Ward Co.* This *Mama* doll had composition head, arms and legs, human hair wig, sleeping eyes, hair eyelashes, open mouth with teeth and tongue, and was dressed. Ht. 23 in. (58.5 cm.); price $4.48.

Anneliese. 1926. Trade name used by *Rheinische Gummi und Celluloid Fabrik.* No. 9 and No. 17 had moving arms and legs with footwear. No. 24 also moved its head.

Annette. 1911–14. One of the American Kids,[†] a line of composition head dolls produced by *Horsman.* The head, with molded bobbed hair and a curl on the forehead, was designed by *Helen Trowbridge.* This same head with painted eyes was used for *Fairy, Nancy Lee,* and *Polly Prue,* but the clothes of those dolls differed. Annette wore a striped gingham dress, a lawn pinafore, socks, and felt slippers.★

Annette-Nicolas. 1930. Paris. Made and/or distributed dolls.

Annie Laurie. 1892–95. Distributed by *Butler Bros.* It had a bisque head with "human eyes" and a ball-jointed composi-

tion body, came dressed. Ht. 29 in. (73.5 cm.); priced $7.75 a doz. wholesale.

Annie Rooney. 1925–28. Trade name used by *Borgfeldt.*★

Annin & Co. 1925–26. New York City. Obtained a U.S. trademark for *Liberty Belle.* Lithographed cloth doll made of two pieces.

Annonsbyra, S. Gumaelii. 1899. Stockholm, Sweden. Manufactured dolls.

Anschütz, Hugo. 1895–98. Sonneberg, Thür. In 1898 applied for a German patent (D.R.G.M.) for impregnating fabric in the making of "half dressed dolls."★

Anthony (Anton) [Tyrolean]. 1909–24. Trade name for a felt character doll made by *Steiff* and distributed by *Borgfeldt* in the U.S. It wore the Tyrolean costume of an upper-Bavarian boy. Five hts.: 28, 35, 43, 50, and 60 cm. (11, 14, 17, 19½, and 23½ in.). The 43 cm. doll cost $1.72 in Germany in 1911 and $4.15 in New York in 1913 with a mama voice. By 1924 the 60 cm. (23½ in.) ht. was deleted.★

128. "Anthony," name of a felt doll made by Steiff. It has brown plush hair, painted blue eyes and is wearing a Tyrolean felt costume with a tan coat, black trousers, green suspenders, and a green hat. The buttons and shoes are leather. Voice box is in the torso. H. 13 in. (33 cm.). *Courtesy of Judy Reis. Photo by Mike White.*

Anthony Shield Co. 1903. Chicago. Advertised as a premium a "French" bisque-head jointed doll with sleeping eyes, fully dressed. Ht. 15 in. (38 cm.).

Anzolotta. 1893. Name given to the original *Ida Anzolotta Gutsell* doll, which was painted in oils.

Apache. 1926–28. Name of a French felt doll imported into the U.S. by *Louis Eisen.* Doll was dressed as an Apache—a Paris ruffian—in a large cap, a scarf around its neck, a short coat, and checked trousers.

Apache. 1928. French cloth doll with a flat, silk painted face, sideburns, and hair painted black. A cigarette dangled from the open mouth. The doll wore black-and-white-checked long trousers and large matching cap, a black jacket, a long red silk scarf around its neck, with the ends hanging down the back and front of the doll. Its long pointed shoes were molded and painted black. Ht. 7¼ in. (18.5 cm.).

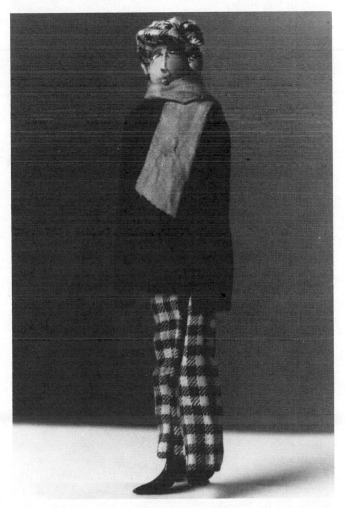

129. Cloth doll representing a French Apache of about 1928, painted features. Note the cap, scarf, long pointed shoes, and cigarette dangling from its mouth, all typical features of an Apache. *Courtesy of Muriel Utteridge.*

Apache. See also **Boudoir Dolls.**

Apfelbaum & Batzner. 1925–27. Fürth, Bavaria. Manufactured doll's house dolls of porcelain and of celluloid; also made dolls' clothes.★

Apollo Knitting Co. 1925–30 and later. Philadelphia, Pa. Manufactured stockings for dolls.

Appel, A. H. & Co. 1920. London. Produced dressed and undressed dolls.

Arab Sheik. 1920. Trade name of cloth doll made by *Harwin.* Doll had a three-dimensional face, could sit or stand, and wore a flowing burnoose.

Arabesque. 1914–27. Line of dolls whose sole distributor was *Strobel & Wilken.*

1926: Line of dolls consisting of baby and *Mama* dolls.★

Arcadia Hosiery Co. 1925–30 and later. Philadelphia. Manufactured stockings and tubing and knit goods for dolls.

Arcadian Babs. 1918. Line of dolls made by *Sutherland Doll Co.* with *British Ceramic* heads.

Archie Pagliacci. 1929–30. Trade name of a doll, made by *Twistum Toy Factory,* of segmented wood and wood composition. It was assembled with wire and painted as a clown with brightly colored enamel. Style No. 611, price $1.50.

Arctic Baby. 1915. Cloth doll with velvet face, body covered with white plush fur, handled by *Whyte, Ridsdale,* came in four sizes.

Arcy Toy Manufacturing Co. 1912–30 and later. New York City. Made dolls with heads of various materials. Had representatives as far away as Sydney, Australia.

1915: Used a new type of composition which they advertised as being unbreakable and unpeelable. Introduced 10 new large size character dolls.

1926: Made 72 numbers of Mama dolls and infant dolls, priced 25¢ to $5.00. Infants were made in bisque or composition head styles.

1927: Made 65 numbers of Mama dolls and baby dolls, which came with either mohair wigs or painted hair and either sleeping eyes or painted eyes. Arcy was licensed by *Voices, Inc.* to use their patented voices and criers in dolls. They also had a line of small celluloid dolls dressed in novelty costumes.

1930: One model had a human-hair wig, teeth, and a silk outfit including underwear and dress with handstitched ruffles. Arcy dolls retailed for $1.00 to $8.00 each, including Mama dolls.★

Arden Studios. See **Heizer, Dorothy.**

Arenz & Büttner. See **Cresco Spielwaren.**

Argentine. 1928. Trade name of a *Boudoir*-type doll distributed by *Louis Eisen.* The doll wore an Argentinian costume in vivid colors.

Argentinian Dolls. Three factories in Argentina specialized in making papier-mâché dolls in 1922. (See also **Gaucho** and Ills. 2200–2201.)

Arhelger, Liddy (née Reidel), and Gummersbach, Franz. 1912–13. Olpe, Westphalia. Obtained several German patents, an Austrian patent, and a British patent for dolls' wigs that can be fastened to and unfastened from the heads by means of metal springs.

Arkadelphia Milling Co. 1914–15. Arkadelphia, Ark. Printed Dolly Dimple cutout dolls on their flour sacks, according to information from Margaret Whitton.★

Arlequin. See **Harlequin.**

Arlette. 1926. French trademark for a doll costumed as a French peasant. Application was made by *Mme. Elisa Rassant.*

Arlette. 1929. Name of a doll with a composition head, wig, jointed body, dressed in a silk costume, and sold by *Bon Marché.* Hts. 25 and 32 cm. (10 and 12½ in.).

Arlington Toy Co. 1920–24 and possibly later. Sonneberg, Thür., and New York City. Produced dolls. Some of the dolls were handled by *Bush Terminal.*

Arlt, Otto. 1895. Görlitz, Germany. Applied for a German patent (D.R.G.M.) for a doll with cloth or leather gloves.

Arm, Ernst. 1913–23. Sonneberg, Thür. Made dolls' heads of porcelain and of celluloid.

1923: Applied for a German patent (D.R.G.M.) for glass eyes and hair eyelashes for dolls, especially character heads.

Armand Marseille. See **Marseille, Armand.**

Armin Spielberger. Hungary. Wholesale distributor of dolls.

Armin Trading Co. 1922. Dealt with dolls in Britain.

Armring. 1922–24 and later. Trademark used by *Steiff* for their celluloid head *Schlopsnies* dolls.

Army Nurse. 1917–18. Trade name of a *Horsman* composition head "Art" doll that wore a dress of blue and white lawn, a nurse's apron, cap, and an armband. (See also **Nurse.**)

Arnaud (Jean), Louis Hubert. 1852–79. Paris. Possibly the maker of a pink kid-over-wood body with an elliptical blue stamp on its stomach having the words "Brevet d'Invention" over script L.A., which was over some indecipherable words. The body had very unusual spherical wooden mortise and tenon joints at the shoulders, elbows, hips, and knees. The body had a low waistline which suggested the 1850s. Ht. of doll including the china head was 16 in. (40.5 cm.).

1856: Louis Arnaud was listed as a maker of dolls in a Paris directory.★

Arno, S., & Son. 1917–18. London. Produced cloth dolls.

Arnola. See **Arnoldia.**

Arnold, J. M. 1918–30 and later. Frankfurt-am-Main, Germany. Produced dressed and undressed celluloid dolls and rubber dolls.

Arnold, Max Oscar. 1877–1930 and later. Neustadt, near Coburg, Thür., and later Bavaria. His son Ernst Arnold joined the company in 1910. The company became affiliated with *Bing* in 1924. Before 1927 it acquired the *Gebrüder Knoch* firm. In 1931 the Max Oscar Arnold porcelain factory was sold to the Rosenthal Porcelain firm. The Arnold factory manufactured dolls of various types, especially walking and talking dolls. Exhibited dolls and took honors in London 1891, Kimberley 1892, and Erfurt 1893.

1899: Advertised ball-jointed dolls of various qualities, wax dolls, leather dolls, and *Mattlack* dolls, including a new type of unbreakable doll and doll's head. They also made dressed dolls and dolls' trousseaux.

1902: Applied for a German patent (D.R.G.M.) for a doll jointed with spiral springs.

1903: Applied for three German patents (D.R.G.M.); one for a doll with a walking and head-turning mechanism; one for a walking doll that said "Mama" and "Papa," raised its arms and moved its eyes, and the third for a walking doll with its voice in the thigh.

1904: Three applications for German patents (D.R.G.M.) for walking dolls with music. Produced dolls with cloth covering over cardboard joints in accordance with a patent of *Gebrüder Süssenguth.*

1905: Another application for a German patent (D.R.G.M.) for jointed dolls of composition.

1906: Applied for two more German patents (D.R.P.) for the talking parts used for dolls. One of these was granted in 1907 and the other in 1909.

1908: Obtained an Austrian patent for a doll containing a speaking device.

1913: Rudolf Dudy was their agent in Hamburg.

1924: Made bisque dolls' heads.

1926: Manufactured dolls for export as well as for domestic use. Advertised for apprentices. (For some of this information we are indebted to the Ciesliks.)★

Arnold Print Works. 1876–20th century. North Adams, Mass. They started to produce cloth cutout dolls in 1892. Some of those shown in their advertisements came with the mark of the *Cocheco Manufacturing Co.* The dolls (printed in colors on cloth) were to be cut out, sewn together, and stuffed with hair, wool, sawdust, or other lightweight material. The printed cloth dolls cost 15¢ each, or 10 dolls for $1.00.

Within a few years after 1892, the Arnold Print Works were producing the following cloth cutout dolls:

Palmer Cox[†] Brownies,[†] Our Soldier Boys,[†] Little Red Riding Hood,[†] Pitti-Sing,[†] another Oriental doll dressed in a kimono, *Pickaninny, Topsy,* Columbian Sailor Boy,[†] an 18 in. (45.5 cm.) doll dressed in its underwear with legs and arms spread out, a white boy and a black boy with removable clothes patented by *Ida Gutsell,* and a jointed cloth doll that could sit on a chair, stand up, or kneel down. This doll was patented by *Charity Smith.*★

Arnoldia. 1906–10. Trade name for a talking and singing doll patented in Germany (D.R.P.) and France by *Max Oscar Arnold*. An advertisement claimed it was entirely unbreakable, but the picture of the head looks more like bisque than composition. It had a wig, sleeping eyes, a fully jointed composition body, and it came dressed in six different costumes, each of which included an elaborate dress, shoes, and stockings, hair ribbon, and/or hat. The doll was 75 cm. (29½ in.) tall. It could count, do arithmetic, and pray, as well as talk and sing in three languages—English, German, and French. The advertisement boasted that children could learn languages and their lessons without a teacher other than the doll! There were 51 records in English, 28 in German, and 20 in French. The English titles were a little strange, such as "The Dead Doll," "Dolly's Funeral," "Mr. Nobody," "Bald-headed Billy, my one-legged doll," "The Groo Groo man," "The Gobles 'uns and the little girl," "Seein' things at night," "A terrible Tale," "There's another picture in my Mama's frame," and "My Morning Prayer, My Evening Prayer."

Arnoldt Doll Co. 1879–1930 and later. Cincinnati, Ohio. Importer; made dolls' clothes and dressed dolls; distributed dolls and repaired dolls.

1886: *Artus Van Briggle* painted the blank faces on the china and bisque heads imported from France by Arnoldt, according to information supplied by the Van Briggle Art Pottery Co.

1912: Advertised dolls of bisque, china, celluloid, kid, and papier-mâché; character dolls, including baby dolls, boy, girl, and lady dolls; *Munich Art Dolls* dressed in regional costumes; *Schoenhut's* wooden dolls; *Campbell Kids*; Munich Art Dolls dressed in native costumes; and "Doll outfits including dresses with buttons and button holes, hats, raincoats, shoes, stockings, gloves, toilet articles, and stationery."

1915: Their Blue Bird line of dolls' clothes was "Fashioned after Children's Apparel."★

Arnould. See Corion.

Arnoult. 1881–82. Paris. Made dolls. Purchased bisque heads from *François Gaultier* according to information from Mme. Florence Poisson, curator of the Roybet Fould Museum.★

Aronsen, The Mohawk. See Hyde, Mathilda.

Aronson, Louis V. 1914–30. Newark, N.J. President of *Voices, Inc.* Obtained U.S. patents for *Mama* doll voices.

1920: Obtained a U.S. patent for a walking doll.★

Arranbee Doll Co. 1922–30 and later. New York. Virgil Kirby, brother-in-law of *Georgene Averill*, was plant manager for Arranbee until it was sold to *Vogue. Miss Ruby Hopf,* sister of Georgene Averill, was the chief designer for this company for many years. Arranbee imported and made dolls and dolls' parts. They used an eight-sided tag. An all-composition doll has been reported marked *Simon & Halbig,* Arranbee.

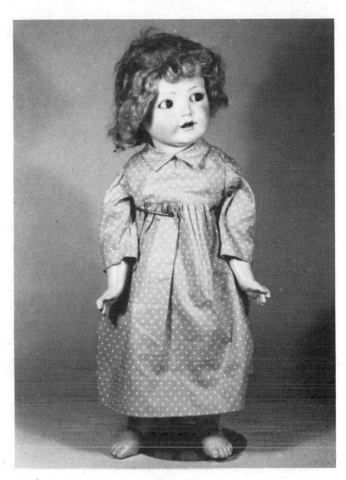

130. Doll made by Arranbee with a Simon & Halbig bisque shoulder head, having a mohair wig, flirting blue sleeping eyes, an open mouth with two upper teeth, and a jointed neck. Cloth Mama-style body with composition lower limbs. Mark: Ill. 134. H. 24 in. (61 cm.). *Courtesy of Richard Withington. Photo by Barbara Jendrick.*

1925: Early in the year *My Dream Baby* was brought out; the factory had to work overtime to fill the orders. My Dream Baby sold for $2.25 to $5.00. A cheaper but similar line sold for $1.00 less.

1926: Produced *Nursing Bottle Baby* in the My Dream Baby line. My Dream Baby was made with *Armand Marseille* bisque head, glass eyes, and rubber hands. Arranbee handled both domestic and imported dolls, including flirting eye dolls. Bisque heads (both shoulder and socket heads), eyes, hands, shoes, and stockings were all sold separately. Agents were Messrs. Rothstein and Artbaum.

1927: New models of My Dream Baby had either bisque or composition heads; some had open mouths with teeth, moving tongue, and rubber hands. The trade name was sometimes shortened to Dream Baby. Other trade-name lines were *Dearest* and *Nursing Bottle Baby.* Arranbee was licensed by *Voices, Inc.* to use their patented voices and criers in the Arranbee dolls.

1928: The lines of *Mama* dolls and infant dolls were given new types of heads and newly designed clothes. *Smiling Face* was a new doll, as well as a talking doll that sold for $4.00 to $12.00. Nursing Bottle Baby still appeared in the advertisements.

1929: Obtained a U.S. patent for joining the head and the arms of dolls to the body, so that they could move in any direction. Dolls made under this patent were put on the market.

1930: Made baby dolls, Mama dolls, and two new dolls—*Nancy* and *Kurly Head*—for which they registered trademarks. The Dream Baby line continued. Some Mama dolls wore coats, dresses, and cloche-type hats. ★

131. Bisque head, bent-limb baby doll produced by Arranbee. It has painted and molded short hair, sleeping brown glass eyes, open mouth with two upper teeth, and a quivering tongue. The cloth body has a crier and celluloid hands, one of which holds a celluloid baby bottle with a rubber nipple. Original clothes. Mark on head: Ill. 135. Mark on the bottle: "Arranbee//Pat. Aug. 10. 26." H. 13 in. (33 cm.). Circumference of head 10¾ in. (27.5 cm.). *Private collection.*

133. All-composition doll made by Arranbee. It has molded and painted hair with a loop for the hair ribbon, blue painted eyes, and closed mouth. The dome-shaped neck fits into the head socket. The body as well as the neck resembles Patsy. Mark: Ill. 136. H. 11½ in. (29 cm.). *Courtesy of Dorothy Annunziato.*

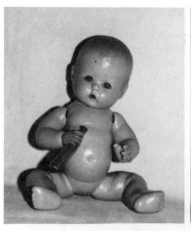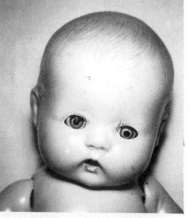

132A & B. Composition bent-limb baby made by Arranbee. It has molded and painted hair; celluloid over metal blue sleeping eyes; open mouth into which the bottle nipple can be inserted; a dome-shaped neck that fits into a head socket. The celluloid bottle with the mark shown in Ill. 137 is held in a celluloid hand. H. 12½ in. (31.5 cm.). *Courtesy of Dorothy Annunziato.*

SIMON & HALBIG

ARRANBEE
PATENT (?)
Germany
134

ARRANBEE
PAT.AUG.10.26.
136

Germany
ARRANBEE
620.13
135

ARRANBEE
DOLL C°.
137

134–137. Arranbee marks. No. 137 is embossed on the body of a composition doll. No. 136 is an embossed mark on a doll with a celluloid bottle. No. 134 is an incised mark on bisque head made by Simon & Halbig.

Arrenberg, Else (née Liedtke). 1920–30 and later. Berlin. Manufactured and exported dolls.★

Arrow Doll Wig Co. 1924–27. New York City. Produced lines of baby dolls, *Mama* dolls, *Boudoir* dolls, and so on, as well as parts for doll hospitals. Company was licensed by *Voices, Inc.,* to use patented voices and criers in their dolls.★

Arrow Novelty Co. 1920–30 and later. New York City. Manufactured composition and cloth dolls. Made some of the *Skookum* Indian dolls designed by *Mary McAboy.*★

Arrowmark Co. 1930 and later. New York City. Manufactured dolls and outfits for dolls.

Art Character Dolls. 1919. Line made by *Ideal,* distributed by *McDonald Bros.* Baby dolls and girl dolls had composition shoulder heads and composition arms, wigs or molded hair, moving eyes that work separately so that the doll could sleep and wink. Hts. 14, 16, 20 in. (35.5, 40.5, and 51 cm.); priced $14.40 a doz. to $4.50 a piece wholesale. Also included were dolls' shoulder heads made to fit stuffed bodies. These came with wigs or molded hair.

"Art" Doll. 1911–20s. Trade name used by *Horsman.*

Art Doll & Novelty Co. 1916–20. Brooklyn, N.Y. Supplied cork and excelsior for stuffing dolls and dolls' bodies with joints on the inside or outside, as well as a variety of dolls' clothes.★

Art Dolls. Dolls designed by well-known artists or inspired by famous works of art and created by the hands of skilled craftsmen. Art dolls have been created through the ages, but during the first three decades of this century there was a special emphasis on this type. Around 1900 many recognizable portrait dolls were created. There was a series of German bisque-head dolls representing the American heroes of the Spanish-American War; wax portrait dolls representing the British royal family and British heroes of the Boer War, as well as French bisque-head dolls representing other celebrities. As early as 1904 a German periodical DEKORATIVE KUNST (Decorative Art) listed the following designers of art dolls: *Otto Gussmann, Karl Gross, Wilhelm Kreis, William Lossow, Oskar Seyfert, Hugo Spieler, Wilhelm Thiele.* (See Ills. 1594 and 2495.) Ten years later *Kate Jordan,* a commercial artist and doll designer in America, referred to doll designing "as in any other form of art—yes, art, for that is what it has come to be." Meanwhile, the *Munich Art Dolls* and the French art dolls had appeared on the market and prospered. During World War I many artists from Eastern Europe fled to Paris and found work designing and making dolls—with *Mme. Lazarski* and others. In the reconstruction period after the war and into the 1920s, many art dolls were created in Paris and elsewhere. Cloth was the favorite material, but wax, wood, leather, and other materials were also used. Some of the most famous dolls were the *Paderewski* dolls. Many dolls were dressed in regional costumes or were part of a historical series; often they were in adult form. One series of cloth dolls represented medieval men and women from various places. These had painted faces, hair of embroidery silk, clothes of silk, velvet, and the like, with appropriate accessories. Ht. was about 8 inches (20.5 cm.). (See Ill. 618.) In 1921 the Bazar de *L'Hotel de Ville* advertised cloth dolls dressed in velvet or knitted costumes. Size 14 in. (35.5 cm.); price $3.40.

138. Composition Marion Kaulitz dolls as shown in STUDIO, January, 1911. *Courtesy of the Brooklyn Museum.*

1929: Among the manufacturers of art dolls were: *American Stuffed Novelty Co.; Richard Haueisen; L. Henze & Steinhauser; Paul Hunaeus; Kley & Hahn; Käthe Kruse; Lenci; Maienthau & Wolff, Marga; Kärl Müller & Co.; Hermann Pensky; Karl Standfuss; Heinrich Zwanger.*

During the 1910s and later many others created and sold dolls that they called "Art Dolls," such as *Horsman* and *Schoenhut.* Sometimes German bisque heads were marked "Künstlerkopf" (artist's head). (See Ill. 2343.)★

Art Fabric Mills. 1899–1910 and later. New Haven, Conn., New York City, and London. Made cloth cutout dolls.

1900: Dolls included *Life Size Doll,* 30 in. (76 cm.), plus two small dolls, price 50¢; Life Size doll, 20 in. (51 cm.), price 25¢; *Cry Baby* doll, price 15¢; *Topsy; Punch & Judy.*

1901: The *Colonial Family* of dolls was added.

1909: *Dolly Dimple* was introduced. The advertising emphasized that these cutout dolls were ideal for shipment all over the world.

After 1910: The dolls also included *Merrie Marie, Belly Good Cook,* and *Da Da Da* (also known as the Newly Wed Kid), as well as most of the previous dolls. (See also **Kirkham.**)★

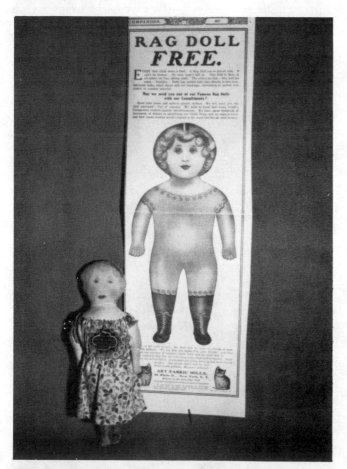

139. Art Fabric Mills' cutout cloth dolls as shown in advertisement and made up into a doll. It has colored lithographed hair, features, underclothes, and footwear. H. of doll 8 in. (20.5 cm.). *Coleman Collection.*

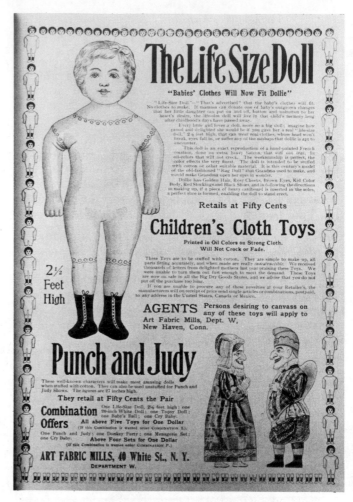

140. Art Fabric Mills advertisement for their cloth cutout dolls as shown in THE DELINEATOR, December, 1901. Besides the Life Size Doll and the Punch and Judy shown in the advertisement, a smaller 20 in. (51 cm.) White Doll, a Topsy Doll, and a Cry Baby are also named. The Life Size Doll is on "heavy Sateen" and has blond hair, brown eyes, "Kid Color" body, red stockings, and black shoes. Punch and Judy are 27 in. (68.5 cm.) high.

ART FABRIC MILLS.
NEW YORK.
Pat. Feb. 13th 1900

141. Printed mark on cloth dolls made by the Art Fabric Mills.

Art Felt Dolls. 1927–30. Trade name of felt dolls imported from Paris by *Amberg.* (See also **Amfelt Art Dolls.**)

Art Metal Works, The. 1914–30. Newark, N.J. They used metal heads on all their dolls and became one of the companies in *Voices, Inc.* They were a member of *Doll Parts Manufacturing Assoc.*

1915: A metal head doll with squeeze wooden bellows had the following label attached to its dress. "Fully patented//Mama Doll//I talk!!//Squeeze me Easy//Made in America/

/Cop. 1915 by Louis V. Aronson." *Aronson* was head of this company. They advertised a new baby doll dressed in white or colors. Ht. 9 in. (23 cm.).

1920: Made *Mama* dolls entirely of enameled brass, also cloth-body dolls. Dolls came with or without sleeping eyes, in several sizes and models, dressed and undressed. Line of dolls called "*Treat 'Em Rough Kiddie.*"

1923: Trade name of their voices was *Ronson* mama voices. They came in large, medium, and small sizes. They also made a crier. Their cleated pinion staff was claimed to be a triumph of mechanical construction.

1929: Made wigs, shoes, and other accessories for dolls as well as voices.★

Art Novelty Dolls Shoe Co. 1925–30 and later. New York City. Manufactured shoes for dolls.

Art Quality//Cameo Toys. 1930. Trademark registered in U.S. by *Joseph Kallus* doing business as the *Cameo Doll Co.*

Art Statue Co. 1917–18. London. Manufactured *Tuftex* composition heads, masks, bodies, arms, legs, and eyes for dolls. Some of their dolls represented celebrities. They also supplied dolls' parts to the trade. Allegedly the eyes can be made round or oval by gently pressing them with a finger, thus making them fit any eyesocket.

1918: Advertised chiefly bent-limb baby dolls with molded and/or painted hair, and "glass eyes." One wonders if these "glass eyes" were the ones that could be pressed into any eyesocket. The picture in their advertisement showed both socket and shoulder heads.

Art Toy Manufacturing Co. 1919–23. London. Represented in New York by the *Bush Terminal.* Made stuffed dolls.

1920: The DAILY SKETCH described them as "Manufacturers of the prettiest dolls in England." Their *Misska* dolls were patented by Serge Kazarin[†] & Mary de Porohovchikova.★

Artcraft Toy Products Co. 1918–20. New York City. 1920–21. Successor, Artcraft Plaything Corp. Brooklyn, N.Y. Products distributed by *Riemann, Seabrey Co.*

1919: Bisquette (wood-pulp composition) heads "designed by portrait artist," but they resembled dolly-face dolls; fully jointed, including wrists; dressed in chemise. Four of the numbers included had sleeping eyes and human-hair wigs.

1920: All-composition bent-limb character baby dolls. Four hts.: 13, 15, 20, and 22 in. (33, 38, 51, and 56 cm.). Fully jointed dolls, four hts.: 19, 21, 24, and 26 in. (48, 53.5, 61, and 66 cm.). Advertised "New glass eyes that automatically keep a snug hold in the socket." The baby dolls had sewn mohair wigs and the fully jointed dolls had either short mohair wigs or long human-hair wigs with curls.

1921: Made 75 numbers of dressed and undressed composition dolls. Also sold separate dolls' heads in various sizes and separate wigs. Baby dolls have chubby arms and dimpled knees.★

Arte e Menage. 1922. Portugal. Shop sold Portuguese regional costumes for dolls.

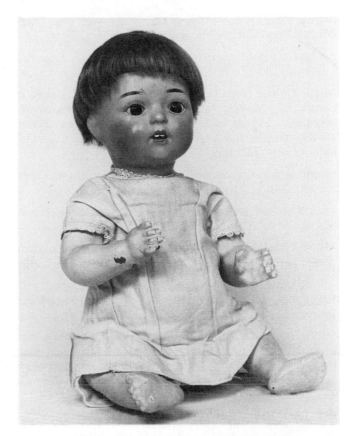

142. Artcraft bent-limb composition baby doll with auburn wig, metal covered with celluloid blue sleeping eyes, open mouth with the upper teeth. The body is made of a hot pressed wood-pulp composition. Original clothes. Mark: Ill. 143. H. 14 in. (35.5 cm.). *Courtesy of the Margaret Woodbury Strong Museum. Photo by Harry Bickelhaupt.*

143–144. Artcraft marks found on composition dolls.

Artel. Early 1900s. Prague, Bohemia. Made wooden dolls with painted clothes. Most of the clothes represented regional costumes of men and women. The arms moved and some of the heads also moved. One group represented acrobats. The dolls stood on a base and were marked "ARTEL PRAHA" in a square.

Artil. Before 1911–16. Felt doll with long feet made by *Steiff.* It was dressed as a German soldier and wore a circular cap. Ht. 28 and 35 cm. (11 and 14 in.). In 1916 ht. 50 cm. (19½ in.) was added.

Artistic Doll Corp. 1930 and later. New York City. Made composition dolls' heads, arms, and legs.

Aschenbach, Eduard. 1917–25. Sonneberg, Thür. Obtained a German patent (D.R.G.M.) for dolls and accessories.★

Asiatic Dolls. ST. NICHOLAS in 1879 described the dolls of Central Asia as being "rag dolls which travelers say are not very pretty." These were found even in the Mohammedan areas where supposedly the religion forbade them. See also **Indian Dolls (East Indian)**.

Asiatic Import Co. 1924–28. New York City. Showed dolls at various U.S. toy fairs.

1926: Oil-cloth dolls represented various fairy-tale characters.

Assael, Gabriel Mentech. 1916–30 and later. London. Distributor who specialized in French dolls and others manufactured on the Continent.

1916: Sleeping and character French dolls, dressed and undressed, sold for 4¢ to $5.00.

1917: French dolls, half and fully jointed, stationary and sleeping eyes, many with eyelashes, dressed and undressed. Hts. 4 in. (10 cm.) to 10 ft. (305 cm.). Baby doll series included a miniature bent-limb jointed baby doll and a fully jointed, partly grown baby doll.

1919: Sold British patent composition dolls.

1926: Sold German dolls made in Waltershausen.★

Assemblers. The English language does not have a precise term for the company that hires someone to model a head; contracts for the making of the parts of the doll, including the clothes; may or may not do the actual assembling; hires sales representatives—and yet this company's name is the one associated with the doll (as, for example, *Borgfeldt, Horsman,* and so on). The Germans use the word *"Verleger,"* which seems to most nearly fit this type of company. Verleger actually means publisher, but it has a special meaning in the commercial toy world.

Associated Toy and Doll Factories. 1930. Represented *P. & M. Doll Co.*

Association d'Aide aux Veuves de la Guerre (Association to Aid War Widows). 1918. Paris. Used porcelain heads and all-porcelain dolls made by *Lanternier,* as well as bodies made by *Ortyz.*

Atascadero Doll and Toy Factory. See **Dooly Dolls.**

Atelier Bordelais des Veuves de Guerre (Bordeaux Workshop of the War Widows). 1918. Bordeaux, France. Made dolls.

Atelier Chrétien de Vaugirard (Christian Workshop of the Rue Vaugirard). 1918. Paris. Made porcelain dolls' heads that had been modeled by the sculptor *Lejeune.*

Atelier des Petites Mains Parisiennes. See **Bricon.**

Ateliers Artistiques.★ See **Lazarski, Mme. Thabée.**

Ateliers Paris-Fantaisies. 1927–30 and later. Paris. Advertised dolls, *mignonnettes,* bébés incassables (bisque-head dolls with jointed composition bodies), and Parisettes.

Athlete. Ca. 1914. Trade name of a doll distributed by *Sears;* doll had a composition head, hair-stuffed cotton-flannel body jointed at shoulders and hips, voice operated by pressing body, wore a sweater. Hts. 9½ and 13½ in. (24 and 34 cm.).

Atlanta Playthings Co. 1930 and later. Atlanta, Ga. Manufactured a line of cloth (possibly felt) dolls, called *Plaything Toys,* which included *Monkey Man.*

Atlantic Excelsior Co. 1930. New York City. Made wood wool for stuffing dolls.

Atlantic Toy and Manufacturing Co. 1917–30 and later. New York City. Made "Atlantic" dolls, which included *Mama* dolls. *Voices, Inc.* licensed them to use mama voices and criers in their dolls. Agent was Joseph Krauss.

1925: Made walking, talking, sleeping, and dressed Mama dolls.

1926: Models had new costumes and sold for 25¢ to $5.00; white or black infant dolls in pink-and-white or blue-and-white blankets, 50¢ up.

1927: Mama dolls, baby dolls, new dolls with slender legs and bodies.

1928: About 100 numbers. Some dolls had painted hair and painted eyes, some had moving eyes and real or mohair wigs. Walking, talking, sleeping dolls included *Da-Da* babies.

1929: Mama dolls, baby dolls, and slim-bodied dolls.

1930: About 80 numbers priced from 25¢ to $10.00—infant, character, and Mama dolls.★

Atlas Doll & Toy Co. 1917–30. New York City. Factory in Baltimore, Md. *Riemann, Seabrey Co.* was factory representative. *Hoest & Henderson* also were agents. Made all-metal dolls, metal head dolls with stuffed bodies, *Mama* doll voices, and criers. They were licensed by *Voices, Inc.*

1919: All-metal dolls with and without sleeping eyes.

1920: All-metal bent-limb dolls, jointed at neck, shoulders, and hips; sleeping eyes. Metal heads, arms, and legs on stuffed cloth bodies with or without wigs; sleeping eyes; dressed in cotton or silk frocks, a knitted costume, or only a chemise. Hts. 14 to 18 in. (35.5 to 45.5 cm.).

1921: 65 style nos. of dolls including all-metal dolls, fully jointed, two sizes; metal shoulder-head dolls, three sizes; metal heads and arms on cloth bodies in hts. 14, 16, and 19 in. (35.5, 40.5, and 48 cm.); baby dolls ht. 12 in. (30.5 cm.). These dolls came with human hair or mohair wigs, some with sleeping eyes; dressed.

1922: All-metal dolls; dolls with metal heads and cork-stuffed bodies, no springs or elastic in the joints. The majority of these were Mama dolls. Some dolls had painted eyes

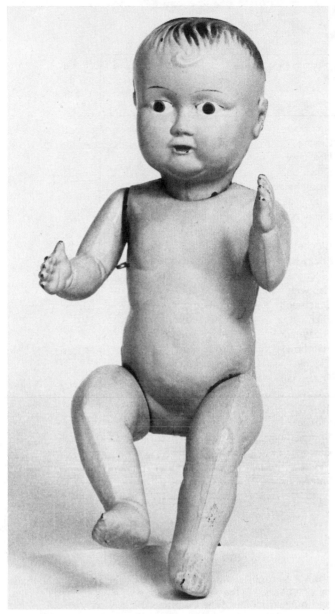

145. All-metal bent-limb baby doll probably of the type made by the Atlas Doll & Toy Co. It has molded and painted hair and features. The neck, shoulders, and hips are jointed with wire springs. The only mark is an O on the head. H. 11½ in. (29 cm.). *Courtesy of the Margaret Woodbury Strong Museum. Photo by Harry Bickelhaupt.*

and painted hair or mohair wigs. The more expensive dolls had real hair wigs and sleeping eyes.

1923: Metal heads on cotton- or cork-stuffed bodies. Featherweight all-metal Mama dolls. Many new numbers of dressed dolls.

1924: All-metal and metal-head, cloth-body, Mama dolls.

1925: Mama dolls with sleeping eyes, priced $1.00 to $5.00, guaranteed not to crack or peel; advertisements said the eyes would not fall out.

1926: Increased line to include dolls up to 26 in. (66 cm.).

1928: Metal-head dolls representing a year-old baby came with metal or cloth body. New line of composition-head Mama dolls. One number of the metal-head dolls jumped through a colored turning hoop; another was "Dolly Jump Rope," with arms and rope moving to give the illusion the doll was jumping rope.

1929: Metal or composition heads on cork-stuffed bodies. Mama dolls and real walking dolls, all-metal dolls. Composition shoulder heads with painted hair, composition arms, and stuffed bodies with straight legs, dressed. Hts. 10, 12, and 13 in. (25.5, 30.5, and 33 cm.).★

Atlas Manufacturing Co. 1914–18. Woodford, Essex, and Walthamstow, England. Agent was F. W. Cox & Co. Made cloth dolls.

1914: *Golliwogs* were their first dolls.

1916: Expanded lines to include *Eskimo* dolls, character dolls, *Summer Girl, Jean,* and *Susie,* as well as a *Tipperary Tom* line and a *Sports Girl* line. Other lines were dressed in Scottish plaids, fancy muslins, and colored sateen. Among the sateen-dressed dolls was a line of baby dolls with *British Ceramic* heads and arms. These dolls squeaked when pressed down.

Attleboro Premium House. 1925. Attleboro, Mass. American and imported dolls were given as premiums, including *Belle of Washington, Dollie Darling,* black dolls, kid-body dolls, undressed dolls, dolls in rompers or in dresses.

Attwell, Mabel Lucie. 1914–30 and later. London and Fowey, England. Artist and illustrator designed exclusive models for dolls made by *Chad Valley* and other doll manufacturers. The doll named *Pooksie* was based on her design and during the war they were made of *British Ceramic* by *Wiltshaw & Robinson* and distributed by *Hamley.*

Some of the Chad Valley dolls carried a tag that read "The Mabel Lucie Attwell Doll (Reg. & Patented). Sole makers Chad Valley Co. Ltd." on one side and "The Chad Valley Hygienic Textile Toys Made In England" on the other side.

The heads and faces were molded, hand-painted felt with veined glass eyes generally glancing to the side. The round faces tended to slope forward, giving a shy look. Their broad mouth suggested a smile. The faces appeared to represent younger children than portrayed by the *Bambina* child dolls, yet one of the dolls resembling a Lucie-Attwell doll has been found with "Chad Valley//BAMBINA//(Regr. & Pat.)" on the bottom of its foot. The Lucie-Attwell dolls had woven combable real hair wigs (mohair), often in short bobbed style and frequently with a large hair bow. The Velvette or velvet bodies were jointed at the neck, shoulders and hips. The chubby hands with sewed fingers resemble those of a small child. More Lucie-Attwell dolls than Bambinas were dressed as boys. The clothes described in the following table were nearly all above the knees in length. The footwear consisted of single-strap slippers and low socks.

1924: Only size 2 was listed. It was 19 in. (48 cm.) tall and cost $4.00.

CLOTHES ON LUCIE-ATTWELL DOLLS				
Style No.	Year	Outerwear	Headwear	Comments and/or Trim
700	1924, 26, 27, 29	Dress, no waist	Hair bow	Cross-stitch
701?	1924	Dress high waist	Cloche	Checked fabric
702?	1924	Dress high waist	Hair bow	Checked fabric
703	1926, 27	Romper & blouse	Dutch bob	Patch pocket
704	1926, 27, 29	Romper & blouse	Frizzy hair	Patch pockets
705	1924, 26, 27	Oliver Twist Suit	Frizzy hair	Buttons
706	1926, 27, 29	Dress, no waistline	Frizzy hair	Printed fabric
711	1926, 27	Dress, high waist	Cap	Ribbons
713	1926, 27	Dress, low waistline	Cloche	Pleated skirt
714	1926, 27	Blouse, short pants	Frizzy hair	Shoulder straps
715	1926, 27	Dress, no waistline	Cloche	Bands
718	1926, 27, 29	Coat, short pants	Cap with visor	Patch pockets
719	1926	Dress, no waistline	Dutch bob	Knitted or crocheted
720	1926, 27, 29	Suit with tails	High hat	Checked long pants
721	1927, 29	Shirt, long overalls	Frizzy hair	Black doll
722	1927, 29	Dress, no waistline	Hair bow	Circle applique
723	1927	Knitted suit	Cloche	Leggings
724	1927, 29	Suit, short pants	Frizzy hair	Button waist
725	1927	Soldier suit	Cloche	Military regalia
729	1929	Dress, low waistline	Tam	Scallops
730	1929	Dress, high waistline	Cloche	Bands
731	1929	Dress, high waistline	Brimmed hat	Print fabric
732	1929	Dress, no waistline	Cloche	Appliqué
733	1929	Coat and cape	Cloche	Print dress
734	1930	Suit long pants	Snookums'curl	Toddler

146A & B. Cloth doll designed by Mabel Lucie Attwell and made by *Chad Valley* in the 1920s. It has a wig, hand-painted flat face, and original clothes. The Bambina mark is on the soles of the feet. *Courtesy of Carol Boyd.*

1927: The Lucie-Attwell dolls were packed in gilt Bye-Bye bedstead boxes. A pair of *Caresse* dolls was also designed by Mabel Lucie Attwell. These were cheaper quality dolls made of felt and velveteen. Style No. 694 wore a short-sleeved dress without a waistline; style No. 695 was similarly dressed except for the high waistline. Both dolls had frizzy hair with large hair bows. Size number 2, ht. 15 in. (38 cm.). Style No. 720 was called *Paddy*, ht. 14½ in. (37 cm.), price $2.90. Style No. 721 was called *Sambo*, ht. 16 in. (40.5 cm.), price $3.20. *Harrods* distributed the dolls designed by Mabel Lucie Attwell.

1930: *Snookums*, the only Lucie-Attwell doll shown in the Chad Valley catalog, was size 1.

	SIZE–HEIGHT RELATIONSHIP OF THE MABEL LUCIE-ATTWELL DOLLS		
		Height	Price wholesale
Size	Inches	Centimeters	1928
0	14½	37	$2.65
1	16	40.5	$3.40
2/A	18½	47	$3.90 simply dressed
2/B	18½	47	$4.40 elaborately dressed

Au Bébé Incassable. 1914–28. Paris. Manufactured and/or handled all-composition bébés as well as making trousseaux and layettes for bébés.

Au Bonheur des Enfants. See **Chaufour.**

Au Chat Botte. 1930. Paris. Made and/or distributed dolls.

Au Defi. Marseille, France. Distributor who handled *Jumeau* dolls.

Au Grand Opera. 1892. Paris. Charles Flyshacker at 37 Boulevard. Haussmann, commissioner and exporter of undressed dolls, dressed bébés, and talking bébés incassables.

Au Nain Bleu. 1836–1930 and later. Paris. Distributed dolls and bébés. Sold walking dolls made by *Roullet & Decamps*. Often the clothes for these walking dolls were made by Au Nain Bleu, according to Anne-Marie and Jacques Porot.

It has been recorded that this shop was still at 27 Boulevard des Capucines in 1907. But by 1924 they had moved to 408 Rue St. Honoré. Dolls having bisque heads marked *Simon & Halbig*, mold #1079, have been found with a paper sticker on the body and a cloth label on the clothes identifying them as having come from Au Nain Bleu at the Capucines address. (See Ills. 299 A & B, 300, and 301 in the first COLLECTOR'S ENCYCLOPEDIA OF DOLLS.)

1889 or later: A marked *Jules Steiner* bisque-head doll was sold at Au Nain Bleu.

1926: Catalog included a doll dressed in swaddling clothes named *Bébé Teteur* and a felt Lenci doll. (See THE COLLECTOR'S BOOK OF DOLLS' CLOTHES, Ill. 760.)

1928: Jointed bébés both dressed and undressed. (See also **Fauvet.**)★

147. Bisque head doll with wig, glass eyes on a five-piece composition body, sold by the Paris store Au Nain Bleu in the 1940s. Original French regional clothes, molded and painted footwear. H. 5 in. (12.5 cm.). *Coleman Collection.*

Au Nain Jaune (At the Yellow Dwarf). Ca. 1900. Paris. A bisque head doll with sleeping eyes, open mouth, teeth and a five piece composition body with molded footwear of black stockings and tan two strap slippers has "293 // 8/0 // S. C. incised on its head and an oval mark on its body reading "Au Nain Jaune// Jouets & Jeux// 64 Avenue de Neuilly 64."

Au Paradis des Enfants. 1864–1925 and possibly other years. Paris. Distributed and probably assembled dolls.

A wax-over-composition head marked *Schmitt* had an Au Paradis des Enfants stamp indicating they handled Schmitt dolls.

1880: Lavasseur and Ouachée succeeded Perreau Fils.[†] A china head doll with short black molded hair has been found on a pink kid body with an elliptical stamp: "Au Paradis des Enfants// Lavasseur & Ouachée." (See Ills. 150 and 151.)

1880s: Several dolls that Queen Wilhelmina of The Netherlands played with as a child wore shoes marked "PARADIS DES ENFANTS PARIS RUE DE RIVOLI 7."

1886: Ouachée alone was listed in the Paris directory.

1897: Catalog advertised only one doll in a chemise, the other dolls were dressed, and several had trousseaux of

148. Paper label found on dolls sold at Au Nain Jaune.

149B. Advertising page and one of the pictures in an ALBUM DE LA POUPÉE distributed by the Au Paradis des Enfants store in the early 1870s. See Ill. 149A for a similar album. Dimensions of the album page 4 x 5.5 cm. (1½ x 2 in.). *Coleman Collection.*

149A. Bisque head, kid body lady doll with original clothes and its original ALBUM DE LA POUPÉE. The album closely resembles the one distributed by Au Paradis des Enfants, part of which is shown in Ill. 149B. The doll has a blond wig, stationary blue glass eyes, pierced ears, and closed mouth. H. 13 in. (33 cm.). *Courtesy of Sotheby Parke Bernet Inc., N.Y.*

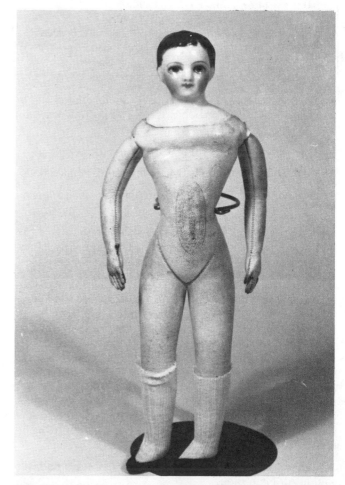

150. China shoulder head on a pink kid body sold at Au Paradis des Enfants when the store belonged to Lavasseur & Ouachée. The china head has dark brown molded short hair with brush marks, molded blue eyes, and both upper and lower painted eyelashes and a darker lip line through the closed mouth. Mark: Ill. 151. Ht. 13 in. (33 cm.). *Courtesy of Clara Hobey. Photo by Barbara Jendrick.*

151. Au Paradis des Enfants mark stamped in blue on the torso of a kid body doll. See Ill. 150.

clothes. A cloth baby doll wore a long dress. (See THE COLLECTOR'S BOOK OF DOLLS' CLOTHES, Ills. 440–441.)★

Au Tapis Rouge. See **Tapis Rouge.**

Audrey. See **Hodge.**

Augstein, S., Co. 1915–29. New York City. Made knitwear for dolls, including sweaters, sacques, caps, leggings, bootees, and so on. They claimed that, before World War I, all dolls' knitwear came from Europe. Their clothes fit dolls 10 to 26 in. (25.5 to 66 cm.).

1915: Clothes cost 10¢ to $1.50.

August. 1916–24. Name of a felt doll made by *Steiff.* Ht. 43 cm. (17 in.). In 1916 there was also a 50 cm. (19½ in.) doll.

Auguste et Vve Caron. 1857 and possibly other years. Paris. Made dolls.

Augustus. 1920s. Name of a cloth doll made by *Farnell;* it represented a character in a book by James Riddell.

Augustus Carney. See **Alkali Ike.**

Aumon & Cie. 1859. Paris. Advertised talking dolls.

Aunt Blossom. See **Auntie Blossom.**

Aunt Caroline. 1921. Trade name of a black cloth doll in the *Rag Shoppe Dolls* series, distributed by *Severn & Long Co.*

Aunt Dinah. 1907–09. Trade name of a cloth cutout doll made by *Saalfield.* This was a black doll 5 in. (12.5 cm.) in height, and was one of the *Tiny Travelers* series of dolls.

Aunt Dinah. 1915–30. Trade name of a black *Effanbee* doll dressed with a bandanna on its head and wearing a kerchief and an apron. Same doll mold with molded hair, painted eyes, open-closed mouth used for a black boy and for a white boy named Brick Bodkins.

1930: Doll had a voice. Ht. 15 in. (38 cm.); priced $1.95.

152. Mark used on the back of the heads of Aunt Dinah dolls made by Effanbee.

Aunt Jemima. 1910–30 and later. Trade name for a black cloth cutout doll used to advertise products of *Davis Milling Co.*, also known as *Aunt Jemima Mills.*

1910: Bandanna on doll had two points. Ht. 15 in. (38 cm.). Later the bandanna had no points. ★

Aunt Jemima. 1923. Trade name of a doll produced by *Louis Wolf.* The doll carried a red polka-dot umbrella and a basket.

Aunt Jemima. 1923–27. A black *Mama* doll with composition head and hands. It carried a diamond-shaped tag that read "AUNT//JEMIMA//MANUFACTURED//ONLY BY//THE//TOY SHOP//NEW YORK." and the usual *Toy Shop* round tag. ★

Aunt Jemima

is more than ever an all year seller. Always keep it on Display.

153. Aunt Jemima doll as advertised in PLAYTHINGS, March, 1927, by the Toy Shop. The doll has two tags, one with the Aunt Jemima mark, Ill. 154, and the other the Toy Shop mark: Ill. 2020.

154. Mark on a paper tag attached to an Aunt Jemima doll.

Aunt Jemima. 1925–30 and later. Trade name of an all-composition dark brown doll distributed by *Butler Bros.* It has painted features and is 12 in. (3 cm.); priced $9.50 a doz. wholesale.

Aunt Jemima. 1930. Trade name of one of the Life-Like line[†] of dolls made by the *American Stuffed Novelty Co.* Black doll wearing a calf-length print dress, large white apron, low socks, and Mary Jane-type shoes. Hts. 15, 18, and 27 in. (38, 45.5, and 68.5 cm.); priced $1.00 to $5.00.

Aunt Jemima Mills Co. 1908–30 and later. St. Joseph, Mo. Registered a U.S. trademark "Diana Jemima" for a black cloth doll in 1924. This trademark had been used since 1908.★

Aunt Jenny "Nigger" Dolls. 1923. Trade name of a black doll made by *Jeanette Doll Co.*

Aunt Mary. 1920s. Des Moines, Iowa. Distributed *"Mary Jane,"* a 15 in. (38 cm.) *Mama* doll.

Aunt Sally. 1899. Distributed by *Butler Bros.* Black bisque-head doll with gray hair, glass eyes. It wore a bandanna and an apron, and held a white jointed bisque baby with painted features. Ht. 15 in. (38 cm.).

Auntie Blossom. 1929. Name incised on back of all-bisque dolls representing a character in the *Gasoline Alley* cartoon drawn by *Frank King.* Doll had a swivel neck and was made in Germany; exclusive distribution rights were held by *Marshall Field,* but they also licensed *Shackman.* The doll had

155. Boy doll in regional costume wears a shoulder sash with the words "Grüss aus Karlsbad" ("Greetings from Carlsbad") on it. Carlsbad was part of Austria prior to World War I. This doll was in the Laura Starr collection around 1900. It has a bisque head made by Armand Marseille, mold #1894, size 10/0. The sleeping eyes are brown and the open mouth has teeth. The five-piece composition body has molded boots. H. 8½ in. (21.5 cm.). *Photo courtesy of Sotheby Parke Bernet Inc., New York.*

painted hair and features; molded and painted clothes. Ht. 3⅜ in. (8.5 cm.). (See Ill. 1231 in THE COLLECTOR'S ENCYCLOPEDIA OF DOLLS. See also **Mrs. Blossom.**)

Aürich, K. W. 1912. Shönau, Chemnitz. Obtained two German patents (D.R.G.M.) for a baby doll with a voice.

Austen & Haben. 1916. Peckham, England. Made dolls with *British Ceramic* heads. New lines had British Ceramic limbs, hair-stuffed bodies, and were dressed; they came in four hts. among them 18 in. (45.5 cm.), and included caricature dolls. The firm also made "Dr. Dolls" and *Eskimo* dolls; the latter came in velvet, plush, or felt and in various sizes.

Austins. 1834. London. Handled dolls.

Australian Dolls. It was reported that Australian natives made dolls of wax and cane between 1912 and 1915.

Companies known to have produced dolls in Australia included *Burkitt, H. Chris, E. F. Co.;* a company that produced *Hush-A-Bye* dolls and used the initials L.C.; and *P. Thomle,* who showed dolls at the Melbourne Exhibition of 1880.

Austrian Dolls (Österreich). From early times, dolls were made in the Tyrol, *Grödner Tal, Bohemia,* and Croatia, but by 1900 the industry had faltered; around 1902 attempts were made to revitalize it. It was not economical for the designers to make the dolls themselves, so instead they became teachers at the Kunstgewerbeschule (School of Applied Arts), the Fachschulen (Craftschool), and the Malschule für Frauen und Mädchen (Painting School for Females).

Dolls have been found with what is believed to be the mark of the *Schlaggenwald* factory of Bohemia. The *Roma P.R.* dolls were made in Carlsbad. Bisque-head dolls have been found marked "Made in Austria" with A & M, *A & M,* or with *Eduardo Juan.* Both these types bear the number 1904 as well.

1922: La Salle & Koch in Toledo, Ohio, with the assistance of the Brooklyn Museum, showed dolls from Vienna, which were described as "the last word in the art of doll making." (See also **Manufacture of Dolls, Commercial: Made in Austria.**)★

Austrian Werkbund. 1924. An organization of artists and manufacturers. They had a commercial staff and a jury of expert artists and artisans who judged every article produced by the Werkbund. Some of their products were sold on the ships of the Hamburg-American Steamship line. One type of doll was a quaint carved wooden one with hair and clothes.

Auto Dolls (Auto Puppen). 1925–30 and later. Term used to describe dolls made to decorate automobiles. The following were among those who manufactured and/or handled this type of doll: *Otto Gans, Heho Art Dolls* made by *Leo Weigert, Bernhard Hermann, Lazarski, Lenci, Carl Möckel, Radiana,* and *Karl Völker.*

Instructions for girls to make these dolls at home were given in LA SEMAINE DE SUZETTE, in 1928.

Autoliebchen (Auto Sweetheart). 1912. Trade name used by Arthur Schoenau of *Schoenau & Hoffmeister* for dolls.

1904

Eduardo Juan

Made in Austria

9

156

157 P&H ³⁄₀ 1904

Made in Austria

P. & R.
1907
15

158

156–158. Marks on Austrian bisque dolls' heads probably made before World War I by the following firms: Moehling (Ill. 156); Pollak & Hoffmann (Ill. 157); Plass & Roesner (Ill. 158).

Automobile Dolls. 1903–26 and later. Many dolls were sold dressed in automobile costumes, usually consisting of a dust cloak and veil and sometimes goggles. Among these were dolls produced by *Amberg* (see THE COLLECTOR'S BOOK OF DOLLS' CLOTHES, Ill. 536); *Horsman* in their Life Like *Babyland* series; *Moritz Pappe*; *W. Payne*; and *Shackman*. *Braitling* made auto goggles for dolls.

Many magazines offered patterns for making automobile costumes for dolls. These included WOMAN'S HOME COMPANION in 1908 (see THE COLLECTOR'S

159. Doll dressed as an automobilist has a bisque shoulder head, arms and legs on a cloth body. The hair with a bun in back, the tan visored cap and the goggles are all molded. Original clothes, tan cotton jacket and skirt; collar and leggings of oil cloth. H. 4½ in. (11.5 cm.). *Courtesy of the Washington Doll's House and Toy Museum.*

BOOK OF DOLLS' CLOTHES, Ill. 580), and LA SEMAINE DE SUZETTE, September, 1911.

1908: Shackman offered one of these dolls, ht. 3½ in. (9 cm.); priced 20¢. (See **Auto Dolls.**[†])

Autoperipatetikos. 1860s–70s. Made in France as well as America and England. A bisque head made by *E. Barrois* was used on a French version. Some of the autoperipatetikos dolls have on the disk at the bottom: "This doll is only intended to walk on a smooth surface. Patent July 15, 1862, also in Europe 20, Dec., 1862." The autoperipatetikos heads represented children, ladies, and men with mustaches and goatees. Such a doll has been found in a box labeled "The Patent//Autoperipatetikos//or//Walking Zouave//*Martin & Runyon.*" In 1863, William Henri Heydecker made a walking doll that resembled an autoperipatetikos.★

Autumno (l'Automne). 1930 and later. *Lenci* felt girl doll (mold #1055) in the *Poupées Salon* series representing Autumn. It wore a dress of leaves, berries, and nuts. Ht. 48 in. (122 cm.).

160. Autoperipatetikos, walking doll with a molded cloth head, painted hair and features, key-wind mechanism, and metal feet. Original clothes. Mark on bottom of mechanism chamber: "Patented July 15th, 1862: also in England." H. 10 in. (25.5 cm.). *Courtesy of Sotheby Parke Bernet Inc., N.Y.*

Aux Enfants Sages. 1870–90s and later. Paris. Distributed and probably assembled dolls. This establishment was found at the same address where the *Maison Munnier* had previously been.

In 1870s handled dolls of E. Barrois.

A doll with a black bisque head marked "Dep//ST." had glass eyes, open mouth, and four teeth. It bore a label of "Aux Enfants Sages// 13, 15, 17 Passage Jouffroy, Paris" on its black composition body. Ht. 19 in. (48 cm.).★

Aux Rêves de l'Enfance. 1870s. Paris. Mark: see Ill. 161.★

Aux Trois Quartiers. 1905–24 and possibly other years. Paris. A store that sold dolls and published catalogs showing dolls.

1905–11: Advertised a walking *Bébé Culotte* with a key-wind mechanism.

1906: Advertised *Bébé Baptême, Bébé Madeleine, Bébé Maillot, Bébé Mignon, Bébé Neva, Bébé Promenette, Bébé Trois Quartiers, Clowns, Le Gracieux, Marottes, Paris Bébé, Polichinelle,* and *Splendide Bébé.*

1910–11. Advertised dolls of felt and wool with removable clothes and a crier. These were dressed as boy and girl peasants and mountaineers. They resembled *Steiff* dolls. Hts. 28, 35, and 43 cm. (11, 14, and 17 in.); priced $1.38 to $2.35. Also sold Bébé Baptême, *Royal Bébé,* cutout cloth dolls of various types, including ones made by *Dean* and regional costume dolls, *Matryoshkas* and *Mignonnettes.* They claimed Bébé Trois Quartiers was made by *Jumeau.*

1919: Advertised *Bébé Chiffon, Bébé Merveilleux,* and *Bébé Parisette.*

1922: This store sold dolls designed by *Beatrice Mallet.* Their doll called "La Petite Bretonne" resembled *Bécassine.* It came in hts. 25, 31, and 43 cm. (10, 13, and 16½ in.).

161. Mark on some of the Aux Rêves de l'Enfance dolls.

Aux Tuileries. Paris. Name of a shop that used an oval stamp on the back of dolls.

Averill, Georgene (née Hopf). Born 1876, died 1963. President of *Georgene Novelties* for many years, up to World War II, when she went to California. Georgene Averill designed many dolls. By 1923, she had created over 2000 costumes for dolls as well as originating the *Mama* doll that could walk without mechanism, thanks to its limber hip joints and low center of gravity. A voice box inside the Mama dolls permitted them to make a two-syllable sound. In 1924 she was superintendent of *Borgfeldt's* toy department and was promoting her own dolls. When the *Bye-Lo* came on the market, it created some rivalry between Averill and *Grace Storey Putnam.*

1926: Created *Bonnie Babe* for Borgfeldt. After World War II Georgene Averill created a Bye-Bye Baby, which she claimed was the first soft plastic doll. These dolls were manufactured by Walter Fleischaker. (See also **Madame Georgene.**)★

Averill Manufacturing Co. 1915–30 and later. New York City. In 1929, the company became associated with the *Bing-Wolf* conglomerate. In 1930, the name became Averill Co. They manufactured composition and cloth dolls, including *Madame Hendren* lines.

1915–16: TOYS AND NOVELTIES, February, 1916, published an article on Averill Manufacturing Co. that said:

"This firm has introduced, within the last year, an absolutely unique method of producing original designs in character dolls. Their youthful model (Mildred Robertson) is carefully dressed in costumes representing nearly every race of people, and it is thus possible to obtain a much greater exactness in the development of their toy models than would be possible by any other means. The house has specialized in producing character dolls which are dressed in thoroly [sic] original costumes, and they use for this purpose dolls selected from the best lines of domestic and imported products. . . . They developed a unique Dutch character for the Easter trade."

162. Bonnie Babe designed by Georgene Averill for Borgfeldt. It has a bisque flange neck, head with molded light brown hair, sleeping brown glass eyes, two lower teeth in an open mouth, and dimples. The cotton-stuffed muslin torso contains a cry box and has composition arms and lower legs. Original clothes. Mark: Ill. 163. H. 17 in. (43 cm.). *Courtesy of Becky Moncrief.*

Copr by
Georgene Averill
1005 / 3652
Germany
1402 / 45

163. Mark incised on some of the bisque heads of Bonnie Babe dolls, designed by Georgene Averill.

The photograph accompanying the article showed four dolls that appear to have bisque heads. Below the picture is "19© 15//Georgene Averill." This may indicate that Averill first used some imported bisque-head dolls but turned to American products when the European supplies were limited because of the war. At this time it seems certain that Averill merely made clothes for dolls and not the dolls themselves.

1916: *Wanamaker* advertised Madame Hendren dolls dressed as an Indian Squaw, a Dutch Boy, and a Dutch Girl. These dolls were 12 in. (30.5 cm.) tall; the Dutch Boy also came in other sizes. Dolls were priced $1.00 to $2.50.

1917: *Yankee Doodle Kids*—Miss U.S.A.[†] and Uncle Sam Jr.[†] Both dolls were dressed in red, white, and blue. Also dolls representing sailor boys and girls, Boy Scouts, and so on.

1918: *Wanamaker* in New York sold about 900 Averill *Mama* dolls priced from $5.00 to $15.00. *Butler Bros.* also distributed them.

1920: Ethnic and regional dressed dolls included Indian Maids, Bucks, Chiefs, Squaws, and Papooses, with jointed shoulders and hips; with or without sleeping eyes; dressed in colored felt. Other dolls with wigs and many with composition arms were designed by Georgene Averill. These included Hilda,[†] *Hans, Lucky Rastus, Toto* the Clown, *Romper Boy,* French Girl, and *Gypsy Queen;* also a doll that could wink and sleep.

1921: Made Indian dolls, *Softanlite dolls, Rock-A-Bye Baby* dolls, *Life Like Doll (Baby), Buddy Boy.* Mama dolls have *Lloyd Voices* and are dressed in many different costumes with square necklines and elbow-length sleeves. There were 400 other numbers of dolls in addition to Mama dolls.

1922: Some dolls wore Irish costumes. There were over 200 different Mama dolls. A special factory was taken over to manufacture the *Dolly Record* dolls.

1923: *Dolly Dingle* dolls, which were designed by *Grace Drayton,* came in both cloth and composition versions. The Madame Hendren line included dolls with wigs, sleeping eyes, either straight legs or infant bent legs; dressed and in various sizes.

1924: All heads were claimed to be made from newly designed dies; 200 Mama dolls had composition heads and forearms. Those with painted hair and eyes and cloth legs came in 4 hts: 15, 16, 19, and 21 in. (38, 40.5, 48, and 53.5 cm.). The Mama dolls also came with mohair wigs, sleeping eyes, and cloth legs or composition legs. The latter type was also made in a 24-in. (61-cm.) size. Of bent-limb baby dolls with voices, those with cloth legs were 16 in. (40.5 cm.); those with composition legs were 18 and 20 in. (46 and 51 cm.). Other dolls included Gold Medal Baby,[†] *Prize Baby, Mah-Jongg Doll* representing a mandarin, *Lullabye Baby,* Mi-Baby,[†] Baby Dingle;[†] *Birthday Dolls* that blow on a horn or play a harmonica; a baby doll with real eyelashes and jointed at the neck and wrists as well as at the usual joints.

1925: Assignees of two U.S. patents obtained by *George Harry Parsons.*

1926: Factory employed 200 people. Among the new dolls were *Cri Dol* and *Pattie Pattie.* Their bisque head Lullabye Baby dolls had *Armand Marseille* heads (mold # 341 or 351) and some if not all of these dolls were made by *Martin Eichhorn,* and were distributed in Britain or her colonies by *L. Rees.*

The company claimed that their Mama dolls were their best sellers. They introduced a new Mama doll with a more slender body and used new models for the heads. The following describes the dolls shown in the company's catalog: The finest Mama dolls had composition heads, arms, and legs, cloth bodies, wigs, sleeping eyes with hair eyelashes, teeth, and were dressed in silk and carried gold tags saying they were walking-talking dolls. These came in 7 hts.: 15½, 16, 17, 18, 22, 24, and 26 in. (39.5, 40.5, 43, 45.5, 56, 61, and 66 cm.). Dolls of 17, 18, and 22 in. came in the greatest number of styles, but all sizes except the 15½ and 16 inch ones came in a variety of wig styles and various costumes. Smaller Mama dolls, 15 and 17 in. (38 and 43 cm.), had painted hair and eyes and cloth legs. These wore either rompers if a boy or a dress if a girl. Some of the 15 in. dolls had criers instead of a mama voice. A group of 14 in. (35.5 cm.) dolls with a wig or short bobbed hair and bangs, sleeping eyes, and eyelashes, as well as composition legs, had a crier instead of a mama voice. Each of these dolls was given a code number. The first digit indicated the type of doll; the next two digits, the size in inches; then came a slash and a number indicating the style and material of the clothes (clothes designated with a 1 in the hundreds column seem to be silk dresses, the other two digits identify the style of the clothes); then after another slash line, a one- or two-digit number denoted the hair style. For example, 2 indicated a wig with short bobbed hair and bangs; 4 indicated a wig with bangs and short curls; 8 indicated a side part and short curls; 11 indicated a side part and frizzy hair; 14 indicated a side part and long curls; 49, 50, 75, 76, and 77 all indicated painted hair. A boy's painted hair was designated by the letter *c* instead of a numeral. A doll marked 226/127/8 would be a Mama doll, 26 inches tall, wearing a silk dress, style 27, and having a wig with a side part and short curls.

Other dolls listed in this Averill catalog included Lullabye Baby, *Lyf-Lyk* baby, and dolls dressed in felt, representing *Indians* and *Dutch* children.

Averill showed a dressed doll in a colonial costume of 1776 at the Sesquicentennial World's Fair in Philadelphia.

1927: Among the new dolls were *Little Brother* and *Little Sister,* designed by *Grace Corry; Dimmie* and *Jimmie; Sunny Girl and Sunny Boy* with celluloid heads; *Snookums,* the moving picture baby; *Baby Marcia; Baby Brite; Bri-tee,* and *Baby 'Aire. Montgomery Ward* distributed *Betty Ann.* Averill applied for the name "Bubbles" to be used as a trademark, claiming that they had used it since 1926, but the application was denied because *Effanbee* already had registered the name as their trademark.

1928: Grace Drayton designed Dolly Dingle dolls to represent her cartoon characters, Dolly and *Bobby.* Sunny Babe was added to the celluloid-headed dolls. Dolly Record recited the prayer "Now I lay me down to sleep." Among the 600 numbers of dolls, other new ones were *Marvel Doll, Val-encia,* and *Mariana.* Sunny Girl was being closed out.

Before 1929: Made a *Father Knickerbocker* with a celluloid head on a cloth body.

1929: New Hendrenite finish. Little Brother and Little Sister dolls were now dressed as *Kiddie Karakters,* namely *Mother Goose, Little Bo-Peep, Little Boy Blue, Mary Had a Little Lamb,* and *Captain Kidd.* Among the new dolls were *Baby Hendren; Babs; Bunchy; Dan;* Dolly Dingle, a black doll; *Rufus,* a black doll; a sailor doll; a cowboy doll; a two-tone whistling doll. The Mama dolls continued to be made with composition heads and arms, cotton-stuffed cloth bodies, Lloyd voices, wigs, sleeping eyes; dressed; ht. 17 in. (43 cm.).

1930: Advertised that the Madame Hendren line of dolls was 100 percent new: Their Mama and baby dolls bore no resemblance to the 1929 dolls, but had newly modeled heads, reconstructed bodies, new-style clothes. Dimmie, Jimmie, Little Brother, and Little Sister were dressed in re-

gional costumes. *Chickie* was a name appearing for the first time in the Averill advertisements. They applied for an *Amos 'N Andy* trademark, but were denied because several other companies had also applied for it. (See also **Manufacture of Dolls, Commercial: Made in United States.**)★

164A & B. Composition head and hands on a cloth body made by Averill Manufacturing Co. It has a braided mohair wig, painted features, felt clothes, and a Madame Hendren cloth label. Mark: Ill. 168. H. 10 in. (25.5 cm.). *Coleman Collection.*

165. Mama doll made by the Averill Manufacturing Co. It has a composition shoulder head and lower arms, a wig, open mouth with two upper teeth and a felt tongue, pink cloth body, including legs. Mark: Ill. 170. H. 18 in. (45.5 cm.). *Courtesy of John Axe. Photo by John Axe.*

166. Averill Manufacturing Co. advertisement in PLAYTHINGS, May, 1927.

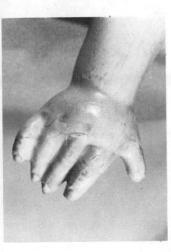

167A & B. Mama doll made by Averill Manufacturing Co. with a composition head, arms, and legs. It has molded hair, sleeping metal eyes, hair eyelashes, open-closed mouth with molded teeth. Original pink clothes. No. 1717. Mark: Ill. 171. H. 17 in. (43 cm.). *Coleman Collection.*

MADAME HENDREN
CHARACTER DOLLS
COSTUME PAT. MAY 9TH 1916

168

GENUINE MADAME HENDREN
DOLL

169

GENUINE
"MADAME HENDREN"
DOLL
617
MADE in U.S.A.

170

GENUINE
"MADAME HENDREN"
DOLL
1717
MADE in U.S.A.

171

MADAME HENDREN DOLLS
PATENT PENDING

172

168–172. Marks used by the Averill Manufacturing Co. Ill. 168 is a cloth label, Ill. 171 is a blue stamp on the back of a Mama doll.

Averill, Maxine. 1927–29. Daughter of Georgene Averill. She worked with her mother and designed dolls, among them Mignonne, which was distributed by *Borgfeldt.*

1929: Obtained a U.S. design patent for a long-limbed cloth doll with a molded face, representing a child. The doll wore a short dress hanging loose from the neckline and a brimmed hat.

Averill, Paul, Inc. 1920–24. New York City. Paul (James Paul) Averill was the husband of Georgene Averill, and the uncle of W. Averill Harriman (former Undersecretary of State). The company manufactured and distributed the walking-talking baby dolls called Wonder[+] Dolls. These *Mama* dolls were designed by Madame Georgene and had names like Peggy, *Polly, Billy Boy, Betty,* and *Jane.* They had composition heads and limbs and were dressed in handmade and hand-embroidered clothes.

1922: Dolls had painted eyes or sleeping eyes; a new number had flirting eyes that rolled from side to side as it walked. Eight or 10 of these Averill dolls were used in a dance in the play TANGERINE.★

Aviator. 1928. Trade name for a doll made by *Twinzy Toy Co.* of artificial leather stuffed with cotton. The doll had a voice; the aviator's suit and parachute were painted on the fabric.

173. All-bisque dolls in original aviator costumes. Molded bobbed hair, aviator's helmet and goggles, painted black dots for eyes, closed mouth, wire joints at shoulders and hips, molded high-heeled slippers. Probably 1920s. H. for both dolls 3½ in. (9 cm.). *Courtesy of Gloria Modderno.*

Aviators (Aviatrixes). 1911–30 and later. A generic term for dolls dressed as aviators. Records have been found indicating the following companies distributed and/or produced these dolls. There were probably other producers of dolls in aviator costumes.

1911: *Karl Stadinger.*

1916: *Dean.*

1917: *Roberts Bros.*

1924–25: *Julius Petri* (Parachute Doll).

1926: *J. Block, W. Payne & Son.*

1927: *American Character Doll Co.; Bleuette* had an aviatrix's costume; *Kämmer & Reinhardt; S. & H. Novelty Co.*

1928: *Louis Eisen; Regal; Squier Twins Toy Co.*

1929: *Butler Bros.; Regal; Woodward & Lothrop;* there were instructions in MODERN PRISCILLA for *Dulcie Daring.*

1930: *Ungarische Gummi Warer-Fabrik.* (See also THE COLLECTOR'S BOOK OF DOLLS' CLOTHES, Ill. 798.)

Aviatrix. 1928. *Boudoir*-type doll distributed by *Louis Eisen.* The aviatrix costume was made in either felt or khaki.

Awender, Josef. 1907. Vienna. Listed in directory under Dolls and Dolls' Heads.

Aylesworth, Jonas. 1909–14. East Orange, N.J. Obtained a French patent for making a composition that could be used for molding various articles, probably including dolls, since the material was a substitute for celluloid, hard rubber, and other such substances.

Ay-Won Toy & Novelty Co. 1919–30. Made and/or distributed dolls, according to PLAYTHINGS.

174A & B. Lady doll with bisque head marked "B. 6 S." It has a wig, dark cobalt blue glass eyes, pierced ears, closed mouth, a short neck and a gusset jointed kid body. H. 21 in. (53.5 cm.). *Courtesy of Eunice Althouse.*

B 1 S

175. Mark on a bisque-head lady doll.

B

B. J. & Cie. Ca. 1860s. Paris. A box top advertised that this company manufactured and exported dressed and undressed dolls. Some of these dolls were patented (S.G.D.G.). Three types were pictured: the undressed doll had a gusseted kid body; one doll wore a plain chemise, and the third wore a costume of the 1860s. It was not possible to determine the material of the head from the picture on the box top.

B. K. B. Dolls. See **Beers-Keeler-Bowman Co.**

B. P. See **S. & Co.**

B. S. 1860s–70s. Initials found on bisque-head lady dolls with kid bodies. *Alphonse Giroux* handled some of these dolls. The size number was between the B and the S. Sizes 0 to 6 have been reported (See Ill. 174).

B. & S. Novelty Co. 1924–30 and later. New York City. Made dolls' shoes in a variety of styles and sizes.

1927–28: Shoes for infant dolls, moccasins for baby dolls,

shoes for *Mama* dolls, high-heeled shoes in all colors for *Boudoir* (Flapper) dolls.

1929–30: Shoes with snaps for Mama dolls, high-heeled cloth or satin shoes in all colors for Boudoir (Flapper) dolls.

Babbit (Babbitt) Boy. 1916–17. Distributed by *Butler Bros.* Composition head, hands, and black shoes; painted hair and features. Doll wore white linen suit and carried a miniature package of Babbitt's cleanser.★

Babie Bouquet. Ca. 1933. Bisque head with a flange neck was imported into the U.S. This was advertised by *Quaker Doll Co.,* which supplied dolls' hospitals. *K & K* used these heads on their cloth bodies. The head sizes, measured according to the circumference, were No. 30, 9¾ in. (25 cm.); No. 34, 11 in. (28 cm.); No. 38, 11¾ in. (30 cm.); No. 45, 13 in. (33 cm.); No. 50, 14½ in. (37 cm.). Price $13.50 to $30.00 a doz. wholesale.

This name is phonetically the same as the earlier *Baby Bo Kaye.*

Babies in the Wood. 1917. Line of dolls made by the *East London Toy Factory.*

Babies of All Nations. See **Saalfield.**

Babis. 1930. Turin, Italy. Made dolls.

Babs. 1917–21. Trade name of a doll with a metal mesh torso and wooden limbs, made by the *Babs Manufacturing Corp.* and distributed by the *International Walking Doll Co.* The five models in the line were jointed, had flexible steel springs and the color was sprayed on them. Babs said "Mama," wore a human hair wig and hand-made clothes. Ht. 28 in. (71 cm.).

Babs. 1920–21. Trade name of a stockinet doll, No. 28, made by *Chad Valley.* Ht. 9 in. (23 cm.).

Babs. 1929–30. Trade name of dimpled baby doll with Hendrenite finish, made by *Averill Manufacturing Co.*

BABS

176. Babs sticker mark on an all-bisque doll.

Babs Baby. 1918. Trade name of dolls manufactured by *Trion.*

Babs Manufacturing Corp. 1917–21. Philadelphia, Pa. Made walking dolls named *Babs.* These were patented in 1917, but there were infringement problems in 1919.★

Baby. 1909 and later. Trade name of a bent-limb baby doll made by *Kämmer & Reinhardt.* Mold #100 was a bisque socket head and mold #200 was a bisque shoulder head. Mold #700 was a celluloid head, made by *Rheinische Gummi und Celluloid Fabrik Co.*

1910: Bisque heads, molded hair, painted eyes; hts. 11 in. and 14 ½ in. (28 and 37 cm.).

Distributed by *John Little & Co.* in Singapore, wearing a chemise it sold for $1.50, $3.25 and $5.75. (Approximately the same as the American dollar.)

1911: Bisque heads with molded hair, painted eyes; hts. 10, 13 and 18 in. (25.5, 33 and 45.5 cm.). With wig and glass sleeping eyes; hts. 9, 11 and 14 in. (23, 28 and 35.5 cm.). Prices were from $1.00 to $3.50 for these sizes. Larger sizes cost up to $5.00 each.

Celluloid heads with painted hair and eyes or with wigs: Hts. 10 and 13 in. (25.5 and 33 cm.). The celluloid-head dolls were a little more expensive than those with bisque heads, but there was also a celluloid-head doll, 17 in. (43 cm.), that cost $5.00. Probably Rheinische Gummi und Celluloid Fabrik Co. always manufactured the celluloid heads of Baby.★

Baby. 1911–16. Name on felt doll made by *Steiff* and called *Do.* The ht. in 1916 was 30 cm. (12 in.).

Baby. 1920s. Cutout cloth advertising doll made by *Collingbourne Mills.* Ht. 6 in. (15 cm.).

Baby. 1926–30. Series of all-celluloid bent-limb baby dolls made by *Rheinische Gummi und Celluloid Fabrik.* These dolls had molded short hair and were jointed at the neck, shoulders, and hips.

Baby Adele. 1930 and later. Trade name of composition dolls designed by *Joseph Kallus* and made by *Cameo.* These dolls representing a two-year-old child had molded hair and straight legs; they wore toddler-type clothes with bonnets and full knee-length skirts. They came in three sizes.

Baby 'Aire. 1927–30. Trade name for an inflatable *Madame Hendren* baby doll made by *Averill Manufacturing Co.* The doll had a composition head, cloth-stuffed legs, and a rubber sack body that could be inflated by pumping the arm or deflated by opening a small valve. It was advertised as taking only a short time to deflate the doll, which could then be rolled up for easy carrying when traveling. It came in two sizes and weighed only about 15 ounces. Comparable stuffed dolls weighed as much as 5 pounds.

1928: Doll made with sleeping eyes. New costumes included a short baby dress, jacket, and cap with ruffles around the face.

1930: Distributed by *Borgfeldt.*

Baby Ann. 1919. Trade name for a stockinet doll designed by *Elizabeth E. Houghton,* made by *Shanklin,* and was dressed in white.

Baby Beautiful. 1910–12. Line of composition character baby dolls made by Hahn and Amberg in 1910 and by *Louis Amberg* in 1911–12.

Baby Beauty. 1914. Trade name for a composition head doll designed by a "noted artist" and produced by *Horsman.* The doll had painted eyes looking either to the side or straight ahead. It came with a mohair wig; some wigs were red, blue, green, or yellow to match the costume of the doll. The composition arms and hands were of a new design, with the fingers separated. Some of the handmade dresses of a French design were made of lawn trimmed with lace and silk ribbons. The chip straw bonnet was trimmed with lace, rosebuds and ribbon rosettes. These dolls came in two sizes, standard and large, only the standard size came with the unusual colored wigs.

Baby Betty. 1912–14. Doll with *Armand Marseille* bisque head on a kid body, came in a box marked *"Columbia."* (See also **Sunshine.**)★

Baby Betty. 1926–28. Trade name for a composition *Mama* doll made by *Joseph Goldstein.* and distributed by the *Chicago Mail Order House.* Ht. 26 in. (66 cm.): priced $3.49 in 1926.

Baby Bibs. 1928. Trade name of a cloth doll designed by *Eileen Benoliel* and made by *Live Long Toys.*

Baby Blanche. 1903–15. Trade name for a bisque-head, ball-jointed composition doll distributed by *John Wanamaker.* Some, if not all, of the bisque heads were made by *Simon & Halbig.* They had sleeping eyes and a wig. The dolls came dressed in a chemise or in a removable outfit.

1903: Came in five hts. 21½, 22½, 24½, 28½ and 30 in. (54.5, 57, 62, 72.5 and 76 cm.); priced $1.00 to $4.00. (See also **Bébé Blanche.**)

Nos. 145 and 245 "Baby Beauty"

177. Composition head doll named Baby Beauty, produced by Horsman as No. 145 and No. 245, the latter being a larger size of the same doll. This doll was listed in the 1914 Horsman catalog under "Unbreakable Art Dolls." Priced $10.50 and $16.50 doz. wholesale. *Catalog courtesy of Bernard Barenholtz.*

1905: Came in hts. 23¼ and 25¼ in. (59 and 65 cm.). Priced $1.00 and $2.00.

1911 or later: Came in hts. 15, 18, and 23 in. (38, 45.5 and 58.5 cm.). Undressed, these dolls cost 75¢ and $1.00. Dressed, the 18-inch doll cost $2.25, or $3.50 if it had a hat. The dressed 23-inch doll cost $5.00.★

Baby Blanche. 1915–18. Name given to several variations of *Effanbee's* composition head dolls.

Baby Blossom. 1913–15. Trade name used by *Horsman* for a composition-head doll. The model of the head was copyrighted in 1911, probably designed by *Helen Trowbridge;* the doll was one of the *Gold Medal Baby* line. Baby Blossom had painted hair and eyes, composition hands, a cork-stuffed cloth body, and was jointed at shoulders and hips. A bone and rubber pacifier fitted into the doll's open mouth. The doll came with either the *Campbell Kids*-type hands or the Gold Medal Baby-type hands, and wore a long baby dress. Various hts. were reported, including 10½, 13, 14, 16, 18 in., and 24½ in. (26.5, 33, 35.5, 40.5, 45.5 and 62 cm.). The junior size sold for $4.50 per dozen; the 16-inch size, $13.50 per doz. wholesale.

1915: Distributed by *Best & Co.,* priced $1.00.★

Baby Blossom. 1927–40 and later. Trade name of a bent limb character baby doll designed by *Joseph Kallus,* made by *Cameo* and distributed by *Borgfeldt.* It had eyes glancing

178. Composition-head doll named Baby Blossom produced by Horsman and shown in their 1914 catalog as No. 140. The head was probably designed by Helen Trowbridge in 1911. The doll has an open mouth and a bone and rubber pacifier. Priced $9.50 doz. wholesale. *Catalog courtesy of Bernard Barenholtz.*

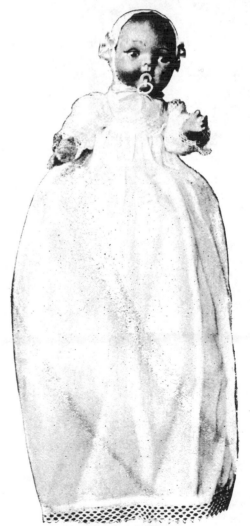

No. 140 "Baby Blossom"

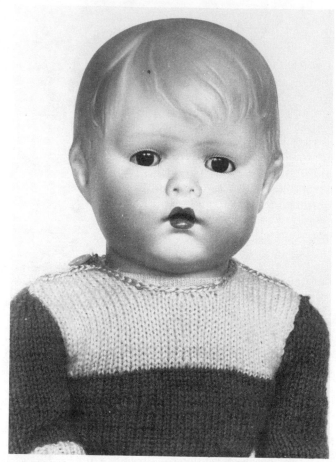

179A & B. Baby Bo Kaye, a bisque head doll designed by Joseph Kallus. It has molded blond hair, sleeping brown glass eyes, open mouth with two lower teeth and a cloth torso with composition arms and legs. Original clothes. Mark: Ill. 180. H. 16½ in. (42 cm.). *Courtesy of the Margaret Woodbury Strong Museum.* Photo by Harry Bickelhaupt.

Copr by
J.L. Kallus
Germany
1394/3

180

BABY BO KAYE
COPR.
BY
J.L.KALLUS
REG. U.S. PAT. OFF.
GERMANY

181

BABY BO-KAYE
REG.U.S.PAT.OFF.
COPYRIGHT BY
JOS. L. KALLUS
GERMANY 84

182

180–182. Marks on bisque or celluloid head Baby Bo Kaye dolls.

to the side, a tiny pug nose and dimples in each fat cheek. The short molded hair had a lock on the forehead. The short baby dress had a full skirt and cape sleeves. Attached to the doll was a tag reading "Baby Blossom" in script. There were composition versions and cloth versions with embossed buckram backed faces. After World War II a 16 in. (40.5 cm.) composition Baby Blossom was made in a version with a flock-spray finish.

Baby Blue Eyes. 1909–28. Cutout cloth doll 12 by 18 in. (30.5 by 45.5 cm.); No. 17 made by *Saalfield.*

Baby Blue Eyes. Ca. 1913. Trade name for a doll with composition head and forearms, which wears a checked gingham dress, bloomers, and a baby cap. Ht. 17 in. (43 cm.).

Baby Blue Eyes. 1925. A *Mama* doll with composition head and arms that was used as a premium. It had painted eyes, a blonde bobbed wig with bangs, and a removable dress. Ht. 12 in. (30.5 cm.). This doll may be the Baby Blue Eyes made by *Averill Manufacturing Co.* in 1928.

Baby Bo Kaye (Baby Bo-Kaye). 1926–28. Trade name for a doll with a *Mama*-type body, but more slender composition legs. Designed by *Joseph L. Kallus* and distributed by *Borgfeldt*, it had molded hair and glass eyes. The head was of composition, bisque, or celluloid, the latter being made by *Rheinische Gummi und Celluloid Fabrik.*

1926: Doll wore a floral print dress with a wide collar and triangular patch pockets. On its head was a wreath of flowers and ribbons.

The name was registered as a trademark in Germany by Borgfeldt. (See also **Babie Bouquet.**)★

Baby Bobby (Bobbie). 1912–15. Trade name of a composition-head doll produced by *Horsman* that represented a younger brother of *Baby Peterkin.* The short molded hair came to a point on the forehead. The painted eyes looked straight ahead. The doll wore a long baby dress and a flannel petticoat, and had a pacifier. Price $8.50 doz. wholesale.★

Baby Bobby. 1928. Trade name of a smiling cloth-body doll made with cloth or composition legs by the *European Doll Manufacturing Co.* Price $3.50.

Baby Bo-Kaye. See **Baby Bo Kaye.**

Baby Boy. 1907–21. Cloth cutout doll made by *Saalfield,* 13 in. by 16 in. (33 cm. by 40.5 cm.).

Baby Bright. 1918. Dressed baby doll with a bisque head on a jointed composition body; distributed by *Eaton.* Hts. 12, 14½ and 18 in. (30.5, 37 and 45.5 cm.); priced $1.75 to $4.95.

Baby Bright Eyes. 1915. Trade name of an *Effanbee* doll with composition head and hands on a cloth body; doll wore short baby clothes. Ht. 15 in. (38 cm.); priced $1.25. (See THE COLLECTOR'S BOOK OF DOLLS' CLOTHES, Ill. 648.)

Baby Brite. 1924–29. Trade name of a composition-head baby doll made by *Averill Manufacturing Co.* The doll had composition arms on a cloth body that contained a *Lloyd* voice. It carried a rectangular tag with a circle design over "Baby//Brite//The Happy Baby// with its first tooth." The

laughing face had sleeping glass eyes, open mouth with one lower tooth, and tongue. This doll wore various styles of clothes, especially short white baby dresses and halo-type baby caps.

1927: Came in four hts. including 18 in. (45.5 cm.).

1929: Came in three hts. 18, 20, and 22 in. (45.5, 51 and 56 cm.).★

183. Mark in PLAYTHINGS for Baby Brite dolls.

Baby Bud. 1915–18. Trade name of an all-bisque doll distributed by *Butler Bros.* It had a wig or painted hair, sleeping glass eyes or painted eyes and was jointed only at the shoulders. Four hts. 3½, 4½, 5½ and 7 in. (9, 11.5, 14 and 18 cm.).★

BABY BUD

184. Mark on a doll named Baby Bud.

Baby Bud. 1918–19. All-composition doll made by *Effanbee.* It had painted hair and eyes, an open-closed mouth and was jointed only at the shoulders. Ht. 6 in. (15 cm.).

Baby Bumps. 1910–17. Trade name for a composition-head doll produced by *Horsman.* Head modeled by an American sculptress. The name Baby Bumps was registered as a trademark in Great Britain.

1910: The doll was manufactured by *Benjamin Goldenberg* for Horsman. The 14 in. (35.5 cm.) version wore a gingham romper suit and cost $1.25.

1911: Three versions were advertised by *R.H. Macy.* These dolls had composition heads and hands. Their cloth body was jointed at the shoulders and hips. The white version wore a long baby dress and was 12 in. (30.5 cm.) tall but with the dress it was 17 in. (43 cm.) tall; price 98¢. The black version, called "Colored Baby Bumps," wore checked rompers. Hts. 9 and 11 in. (23 and 28 cm.); priced 49¢ and 98¢.

Baby Bumps Jr. wore chambray rompers and came in the same heights and prices as the black Baby Bumps.

1912: Dolls had *Campbell Kid* type composition hands and were dressed in either romper suits or in velvet suits. Priced $8.50 doz. wholesale and $15.00 doz. wholesale for the larger size.

1914: New edition with a different model head and a grin on

No. 124 "Baby Bumps"

185. Baby Bumps composition head doll produced by Horsman and shown in their 1914 catalog as No. 124, a "New Edition for 1914 of BABY BUMPS . . . in this new edition he is shown a little older than he used to be with a more grown-up grin. His head, as the name implies takes all kinds of bumps." Priced $8.50 doz. wholesale. *Catalog courtesy of Bernard Barenholtz.*

the face. It was supposed to represent an older baby; the eyes glanced to the side. The cloth body, stuffed with cork, was "fully jointed," according to the Horsman catalog. The 1914 doll wore pink crepe rompers with a matching cap and a bell rattle on a pink ribbon around its neck.

1917: Two sizes with voices and dresses were advertised by the *Columbus Merchandise Co.* Hts. 10¼ and 12½ in. (26 and 31.5 cm.); priced $8.50 to $9.00 doz. wholesale. ★

Baby Bundie. See **Bundie.**

Baby Bunting. 1898 and later. Generic term applied to fur-clad dolls. The fur, usually white, covered the entire doll like a parka and pants. These dolls were generally small in size and relatively inexpensive. For example, the ones sold by *Wanamaker* prior to World War I were 8, 9, 11, and 14 in. (20.5, 23, 28, and 35.5 cm.) tall. Priced 25¢ to $1.00 each. (See also **Eskimo Dolls.**)★

Baby Bunting. 1917. Stockinet doll made by *Shanklin.*

Baby Bunting. 1918. Composition-head, bent-limb baby-body doll distributed by *Butler Bros.* It had a bobbed mohair wig, painted eyes, composition forearms, cork-stuffed body with concealed hip and shoulder joints. This 22-inch (56 cm.) doll wore a "Teddy bear"-type suit and had a pacifier on a ribbon. Price $68.00 doz. wholesale. (See THE COLLECTOR'S BOOK OF DOLLS' CLOTHES, Ill. 719.)

Baby Bunting. 1919. Line made by *Century.* This doll had composition head and forearms, mohair wig, painted eyes in the smaller sizes and sleeping tin or celluloid-over-tin eyes in the larger sizes; open mouth with teeth; cloth body.

The dolls were dressed in short baby dresses and caps, and came in five hts. 12, 14, 16, 17, and 20 in. (30.5, 35.5, 40.5, 43 and 51 cm.). The wholesale prices were from $16.80 per dozen to $3.75 a piece.

Baby Bunting. 1921. English stockinet doll imported by *Meakin & Ridgeway.*

Baby Bunting. 1921–22. Cloth doll made by *Rees Davis.*

Baby Bunting. 1922. Life-size *Mama* doll offered as a premium by NEEDLECRAFT magazine was dressed in rompers with a matching bonnet. Ht. 19 in. (48.5 cm.).

Baby Buster. 1914. Baby doll, made by *Horsman,* had composition head and hands. The hair and eyes were painted and the hands were the baby type. It came dressed in either a short lawn baby dress with a white coat and hood or a long baby dress with a jacket and frilled cap. This doll was the same size as the majority of other Horsman dolls of the period, but it cost a little more than most because of its elaborate clothes.

Baby Butter Ball. 1918. Composition-head baby doll made by *Horsman.* It had chubby arms and wore a short-sleeved baby dress.

Baby Buttercup. 1929. All-bisque cartoon-character doll distributed by *Butler Bros.* It had a movable head, painted features, and molded clothes. Ht. 2¼ in. (5.5 cm.); priced 84¢ doz. wholesale.

Baby Butterfly. 1913–17. This doll with composition head and hands on a cloth body was produced by *Horsman* to represent a Japanese baby. Its fingers were made so that the doll could hold a Japanese parasol. Doll wore a crepe kimono with a wide sash. It came in two sizes—the same size as most other Horsman dolls at that time, and a larger size comparable to that of a real baby. The latter, made chiefly for display purposes, cost $48.00 doz. wholesale; the smaller dolls cost only $8.50 per dozen.

1917: Advertised by the *Columbus Merchandise Co.* Ht. 14 in. (35.5 cm.); priced $18.00 doz. wholesale. ★

Baby Catherine. 1918–20. Trade name of a composition-head doll with metal sleeping eyes made by *Effanbee* distributed by *Butler Bros.* and *Sears.* It was dressed in a short white organdy baby dress and cap, and came in five hts. 13 to 24 in. (33 to 61 cm.). (See THE COLLECTOR'S BOOK OF DOLLS' CLOTHES, Ills. 718 and 719.)★

Baby Charming. 1928. Trade name of a doll distributed by *Hitz, Jacobs & Kassler.*

Baby Dahne. 1926–29. Line of baby dolls made by *Hoest & Henderson,* distributed by *Baker & Bennett* and by *A. S. Ferguson.* The dolls were "featherlight" because of their kapok-stuffed bodies. Their long organdy or batiste baby dresses were made by *Blanche Rowe Cromien.*

1927: Dolls made in four styles.

1928: Priced $4.00.

1929: Two new styles were introduced.

No. 141 "Baby Butterfly"

186. Baby Butterfly composition head doll produced by Horsman. It represents a Japanese baby and was designed by a Japanese artist. It is dressed in a Japanese-type costume, carries a Japanese parasol and is perfumed with "Babcock's Corylopsis of Japan." It was listed in the Horsman 1914 catalog under "Unbreakable Art Dolls" as Nos. 141 and 441. *Catalog courtesy of Bernard Barenholtz.*

"BABY DAHNE"

The Baby's
Real Baby Doll

Soft, cuddly, and light as a feather, Baby DAHNE is making an enviable sales record in Toy, Infant and Gift Departments.

Send for a sample and she'll speak for herself.

Dressed by
BLANCHE
ROWE
CROMIEN

Sole Distributors
HOEST & HENDERSON   45 EAST 17TH ST.
NEW YORK CITY

187. Baby Dahne doll produced by Hoest & Henderson as shown in PLAYTHINGS, February, 1927. This doll was dressed by Blanche Cromien in a long baby dress.

Baby Dainty. 1912 and later. Trade name used by *Effanbee* for various types of dolls with composition heads and limbs. These dolls were distributed by *Butler Bros.* Heights differed from year to year.

1917: Four hts. of baby dolls were 14, 17, 19, and 21 in. (35.5, 43, 48 and 53.5 cm.).

Early 1920s: Name was used for the *Mama*-type dolls.

Late 1920s: Dolls had slender all-composition legs as shown in Ill. 80 of the first COLLECTOR'S ENCYCLOPEDIA OF DOLLS. (See THE COLLECTOR'S BOOK OF DOLLS' CLOTHES, Ill. 716.)★

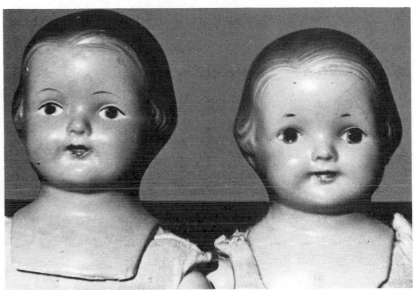

188. Pair of Baby Dainty composition head dolls. They have molded hair, painted eyes, closed mouths and cloth bodies. The variations in appearance are due to the painting. Mark: Ill. 189. *Courtesy of Pat Schoonmaker.*

**EFFANBEE
BABY DAINTY**

189. Mark on composition head Baby Dainty dolls.

Baby Darling. 1914–16. Baby doll came in 5 hts. 14½ to 26 in. (37 to 66 cm.); priced $1.25 to $6.50.★

Baby Dimples. 1927–30 and later. Trade name of a baby doll with a composition head and arms on a cloth body or on a bent limb baby body. The head had molded dimples, an open mouth and sleeping eyes. Doll was made by *Horsman* and marked "E. I. H."
Baby Dimples was distributed by *J.C. Penney.*

1928: The bent-limb doll came in six sizes and seven different styles of clothes. New models with dimples and smiling face, straight dimpled legs and stand-up kapok-filled body, came in four styles of clothes. There were four sizes each of

190. Baby Dimples as advertised by Horsman in PLAYTHINGS, September, 1928.

the Baby Dimples with painted eyes or moving eyes and cloth legs. Some of the dresses were made of a printed fabric depicting Tony Sarg's marionettes.

1929: *Mama*-doll type with *Lloyd* voice was 16 in. (40.5 cm.) tall for the painted-eye version. The sleeping-eye version came in four hts.: 16, 18, 20, and 22 in. (40.5, 45.5, 51 and 56 cm.).

1930: New expression on the faces of the dolls and radical changes were made in the construction of the body. The designs of the clothes were new and one style wore a bib marked "Baby Dimples." (See also **Dimples.**) (See THE COLLECTOR'S BOOK OF DOLLS' CLOTHES, Ill. 773.)

Baby Doll. 1914. Composition character-faced doll produced by *Horsman* was dressed in pink and blue short infant-type dress with lace trimming and rosebuds on the cap. Probable ht. 21½ in. (54.5 cm.); price $27.00 doz. wholesale.

Baby Doll. 1924. Stockinet art doll representing a child, made by *Chad Valley*; body was stuffed with kapok. Doll wore a white knee-length dress and cap, both trimmed with lace. Hts. 8, 10, and 12 in. (20.5, 25.5, and 30.5 cm.).

Baby Doll Manufacturing Co. 1921. U.S.A. Made dolls.

Baby Doll Tinker. 1929. Segmented wood doll made by *Tinker Toys.* Ht. 5½ in. (14 cm.).

Baby Dolls. In 1852 HARPER'S NEW MONTHLY MAGAZINE referred to baby dolls as follows:

"We see advertised some 'Crying Dolls.' We must protest against this new kind of amusement . . . We wish the inventor of this new toy (which might be called the 'disturber of the Peace of Private Families') to be woke up regularly in the middle of the night for the next twelve months to come, by one of his own Crying Dolls! . . . let one of the dolls also be Teething . . . with other infantine varieties."

Most of the *Motschmann*-type dolls of the 1850s–60s were dressed as babies.

1876–80: Baby dolls were distributed by *Silber & Fleming.* They came dressed and undressed, in various sizes. Some had wool-stuffed bodies, some had criers, some were called "Scotch Cap" babies. These last sold for $2.65 doz. wholesale undressed.

1880s–90s: Many of the turned bisque head dolls with bald heads were dressed as babies especially those probably made by *Alt, Beck & Gottschalck.* (See the first COLLECTOR'S ENCYCLOPEDIA OF DOLLS, Ill. 74A.) In 1897 Hall and Ellis of Clark University, Worcester, Mass., wrote A STUDY OF DOLLS and found that children sometimes pulled the wigs off their dolls so that they would be bald like babies.

1920s: Doll designers gave the dolls a very large head because in that period large heads were considered to be cute; the eyes were placed far apart. (See also **Crying Babies, Infant Dolls, Lindner,** and **Swaddling Clothed Dolls.**)★

Baby Dorothy. 1903–14. Trade name of a doll with bisque head made by *C. M. Bergmann* and distributed by *Wanamaker.* The doll had a long curly wig, sleeping eyes, a fully jointed composition body, and wore a chemise.

1903: It came in ten hts. 13, 15½, 17, 18, 21, 23, 25½, 27½, 29½, and 35 in. (33, 39.5, 43, 45.5, 53.5, 58.5, 65, 70, 75 and 89 cm.); priced $1.50 to $9.50 retail.

1905: The four hts. were 22½, 27, 32, and 35 in. (57, 68.5, 81 and 89 cm.); priced $2.75 to $7.50 retail.

Ca. 1912: The 13 hts. were 16, 18, 19, 21½, 24½, 26, 28½, 31, 33, 36, 38, 41, and 43 in. (40.5, 45.5, 48, 54.5, 62, 66, 72.5, 78.5, 84, 91.5, 96.5, 104, and 109 cm.); price $1.00 to $20.00.

Baby Edith. 1913. Name of a doll distributed by *Strawbridge & Clothier.*

Baby Ella. 1918–21. Bisque heads made in Japan and imported into the U.S. by *Morimura Bros.* The dolls had either straight-limb or bent-limb composition baby bodies. The latter came in four hts.: 12, 13, 15, and 17 in. (30.5, 33, 38 and 43 cm.).

1918: Dressed Baby Ella dolls advertised by *Eaton.* Hts. 12, 14½ and 18 in. (30.5, 37 and 45.5 cm.); priced $1.75 to $4.95.★

Baby Fleur. 1920. Distributed by *Montgomery Ward.* It had a composition head with bobbed mohair wig, and was jointed at the shoulders and hips and wore a felt dress. Ht. 12 in. (30.5 cm.); priced $1.00.

Baby Florence. 1910s. Bisque head was made by *Armand Marseille,* mold #370. The imitation leather body had a sticker marked "Baby Florence."

Baby Giggles. See **Giggles.**

Baby Girl. 1907–21. Cutout cloth doll made by *Saalfield.* Cloth size 13 by 16 in. (33 by 40.5 cm.).

Baby Girl. 1919. Trade name of a doll made by *Ideal* with a composition head and hands, molded hair, sleeping eyes, cloth body; hts. 14 and 16 in. (35.5 and 40.5 cm.).

Baby Gloria. 1926–30 and later. Line of baby dolls with bisque, rubber, or composition heads made and/or distributed by Roth, Baitz & Lipsitz[+] and *Maxine.* This line generally had *Armand Marseille* bisque heads and represented a year-old baby with dimples and a smiling face, molded hair. The glass eyes were movable. The dolls wore long or short infant dresses.

1926: The doll carried a round button marked "R. B. L. // New York // Baby Gloria // A head of Safety // beyond harm." Came in 4 sizes.

1927: Line included composition-head baby dolls and a few character dolls. Dolls wore hand embroidered imported dresses or dresses made in U.S.

1928: Armand Marseille bisque heads on straight-limb cloth bodies containing voices; seven hts. 8, 9½, 10, 12, 14, 14½, and 17½ in. (20.5, 24, 25.5, 30.5, 35.5, 37 and 44.5 cm.); priced $4.25 to $27.00 per doz. wholesale.

Bisque heads on bent-limb baby bodies with rivet joints; voices. Seven hts. 10½, 11½, 13, 13½, 15½, 16, and 18 in. (26.5, 29, 33, 34, 39.5, 40.5, and 45.5 cm.). Priced $11.40 per dozen to $3.50 each wholesale.

The composition-head dolls with teeth, tongue, and voice. Four hts. 13½, 15½, 16, and 19 in. (34, 39.5, 40.5 and 48 cm.); priced $27.00 per dozen to $6.25 each wholesale.

1929: Maxine registered "Baby Gloria" as a trademark in the U.S. Dolls had head that turned; made in four sizes.

1930: Five styles of dolls with cloth bodies stuffed with kapok.

Ca. 1933: Distributed by *Quaker Doll Co.* Dolls had imported composition shoulder heads and arms, painted hair, sleeping eyes. Head circumference measured 6, 6¾ and 7½ in. (15, 17 and 19 cm.); priced $12.00 to $18.00 doz. wholesale.★

Baby Glory. 1918. Doll with patriotic-type theme, composition head and hands. It was produced by *Made in America Manufacturing Co.* and advertised as a "Made-in America" doll. Its dress was red, white and blue in horizontal stripes. The doll was a mate of *Teddy.* Ht. 14 in. (35.5 cm.).

Baby Greenaway. 1894. Distributed by *Petit St. Thomas.*

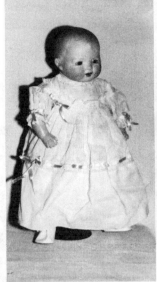

191A & B. Baby Gloria with a bisque head probably made by Armand Marseille. It has molded and painted short hair, brown sleeping eyes, open mouth with two upper teeth, and dimples. The cloth body is the Mama doll type with composition arms and legs. Mark: Ill. 192. H. 18 in. (45.5 cm.). *Courtesy of Dorothy Annunziato.*

192–193. Baby Gloria marks used by the Maxine Doll Co.

Doll was dressed in wool and carried a pail and shovel. Ht. 23 cm. (9 in.); priced 20¢. (See THE COLLECTOR'S BOOK OF DOLLS' CLOTHES, Ill. 429A.)

Baby Grumpy. 1914–30 and later. Trade name for a doll with a frown, made by *Effanbee,* distributed by *Butler Bros., Carson, Pirie, Scott,* and *Marshall Field.*

The name was often shortened to Grumpy during and after World War I. A smaller version of Baby Grumpy was introduced in 1927 with the name "Grumpykins." According to Pat Schoonmaker, Baby Grumpy came in black and white versions and was sometimes marked "DECO//172," for *Otto Denivelle,* 174 and 176 have also been reported on Baby Grumpy dolls. The variation seems to have been in the eyes. A cloth label on the sleeve of a 174 read, "EFFANBEE// Baby Grumpy//Copyrighted."

A doll that looked like Baby Grumpy had a composition

194. Baby Grumpy later known as Grumpykins, as shown and described in PLAYTHINGS, March, 1927. The doll has its original heart-shaped tag.

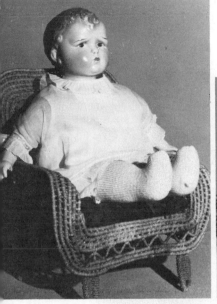

195A & B. Baby Grumpy composition head doll with molded and painted hair and eyes, closed mouth, scowling expression; cloth body having composition lower arms and a cotton twill Effanbee label. Mark on shoulder head: Ill. 196. Ht. 17 in. (43 cm.). *Courtesy of Pat Schoonmaker.*

196–198. Marks for Baby Grumpy and the later version called Grumpykins.

head and forearms, molded hair, intaglio eyes looking to the side, a flange neck with 174 incised on the back, and a cloth body. Ht. 15 in. (38 cm.).

Gebrüder Heubach made a figurine with a face very similar to Baby Grumpy but it is not known whether Effanbee copied Heubach or the reverse.

1915: Round tag on Baby Grumpy dolls with "Guarantee" at top and "Fleischaker & Baum//New York//Effanbee" at the bottom. The black version was called *Baby Snowball*. (See THE COLLECTOR'S BOOK OF DOLLS' CLOTHES, Ill. 648.)

1916–17: Sold by *Gimbel Bros.*; 13 in. (33 cm.) ht. was dressed in various costumes, as girl or boy; priced $1.25. A

10½ in. (26.5 cm.) boy wore a blue jacket with stars, red and white striped trousers and a brimmed hat of matching fabric; priced 65¢.

1924: Made as a *Mama* doll with straight legs, composition forearms and wearing a short dress; ht. 17 in. (43 cm.). Also made with composition bent legs, a voice, and wearing baby clothes. Hts. 18 and 24 in. (45.5 and 61 cm.).

An Effanbee heart-shaped locket was worn by these dolls. A doll of about this period has been found with a label on its sleeve reading: "EFFanBEE//Baby Grumpy//Copyrighted."

1927–28: Grumpykins was described as having a composition head and limbs, "new patented character face," and a cloth body that would stand by itself. The dress was organdy, and made in various colors. Ht. 12 in. (30.5 cm.). These dolls carried a heart-shaped tag reading: "This is// GRUMPYKINS//Trade Mark// A doll so cute, you// just want to hug her//an//EFFanBEE//DOLL." (See THE COLLECTOR'S BOOK OF DOLLS' CLOTHES, Ill. 770 I.)

1930: Grumpy was made so that it could wear roller skates.

1940s: According to Jan Foulke, Baby Grumpy was still being produced.★

Baby Helen. 1905–13. Name of a doll distributed by *Strawbridge & Clothier*. See Ill. 199 for mark.

1912: It had a bisque head, wig, sleeping eyes, fully jointed composition body, chemise and footwear. Ht. 22 in. (56 cm.); priced $1.00.

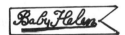

199. Baby Helen mark used by Strawbridge & Clothier.

Baby Hendren. 1929–30. Trade name of a doll made by *Averill Manufacturing Co.* with a composition head, bent arms and legs on a cloth torso. Wore a short lace-trimmed baby dress and halo-type bonnet; a rattle hung on a ribbon around the doll's neck.

Baby Horsman. 1923–24. Trade name of a *Horsman* doll that was advertised as having a body of entirely new design, with the head, hands and body all of the proper proportions. This composition doll had molded hair, large eyes looking straight ahead, dimpled hands, and a cloth body. It was advertised as having a button nose, puckered-up baby mouth and when laid down it assumed a natural attitude without adjustment of arms or legs. It wore baby clothes.

1924: New sizes were introduced.★

Baby Huggins. 1915. Trade name of a line of dolls representing a little baby girl or boy made by *Effanbee*. The dolls had a composition head and hands, cloth body; 15 in. (38 cm.) tall; priced $1.75. According to Pat Schoonmaker these dolls had the number 24 on the back of their heads. (See THE COLLECTOR'S BOOK OF DOLLS' CLOTHES, Ill. 648.)

Baby in Swaddling Clothes. See **Swaddling Clothed Dolls.**

Baby Joan. 1927–28. Trade name for a character baby doll made by *Ernst Liebermann.*

Baby Joy. 1927–29. Trade name of a bent limb doll made by *Royal Toy Manufacturing Co.* This composition doll had molded hair, painted eyes, and dimples; fingers were separated.

Baby June. 1930. Trade name of a doll made by *Carl Kalbitz.*

Baby Land Rag Dolls. See **Babyland Dolls.**

Baby Lindner. Bisque shoulder-head doll with a cloth body composition arms and legs, was made by *Louis Lindner.*

Baby Mae. 1926–27. Trade name for a *Mama* doll made by *Ideal.* This 18 in. (45.5 cm.) doll with composition head and arms was offered as a premium for selling subscriptions to NEEDLECRAFT MAGAZINE. The doll carried a round tag reading: "I can talk//I can walk//I can sleep." It had curly hair and wore a voile bloomer dress and bonnet, knit socks and simulated patent leather shoes.

Baby Marcia. 1927. Made by *Averill Manufacturing Co.;* represented a baby beauty prize winner of this name.

Baby Marguerite. 1912–13. Doll distributed by *Strawbridge & Clothier.*

1912: Bisque head, wig, sleeping eyes, fully jointed composition body. Wore a chemise and footwear. Ht. 32 in. (82 cm.); priced $1.00.

Baby Marlborough. 1904. Doll distributed by *R. H. Macy.* It came with bisque head, sleeping eyes, sewed wig, fully jointed composition body; wore a chemise. Ht. 22½ in. (57 cm.); cost 98¢.

Baby Mine. 1884. Name of a wax head doll distributed by *C. F. Lauer;* it had hair with bangs, sleeping eyes, and wore an embroidered chemise and footwear.

SIZE-HEIGHT RELATIONSHIP OF BABY MINE			
Size Number	Height Inches	Centimeters	Price doz. wholesale
2/0	13½	34	$2.75
0	15½	39.5	$3.00
1	17½	44.5	$3.80
2	19½	49.5	$4.80
3	21½	54.5	$6.00
4	23	58.5	$7.50

Baby Mine. 1910–25. Trade name used by *Ideal* for various dolls.

1910: Combination plush muff and doll made in various colors combined with white.

1917: Doll with sleeping eyes, wore short lace-trimmed baby dress and cap, knitted booties.

1919: All-composition, fully jointed child doll with diagonal

hip joints was advertised as capable of standing alone; it had long curly wig with hair ribbon. Round tag attached to wrist read: "?//Ideal//Baby Mine//moving eyes//?"

1920: Listed as style no. 1920, all-composition, undressed.

1924: *Mama*-doll type distributed by *Montgomery Ward.* Composition head, arms, and legs; cloth body; painted hair and eyes. It wore a dress with matching bloomers and bonnet. Ht. 14½ in. (37 cm.); priced $1.29 each.★

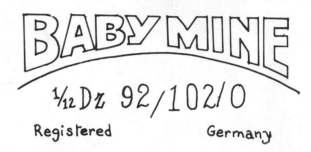

200. Mark on Baby Mine dolls' box.

Baby Nod. 1929 or before. A new born infant type doll produced by *Amberg.* The bisque head was marked "Baby Nod// L. A. & S. N.Y. //Germany//Igodi 12309/4 D.R.G.M." The "Igodi" stood for *Johannes Gotthilf Dietrich* who bought some if not all of his bisque heads from *Ernst Heubach.* Baby Nod had painted hair, glass eyes, a small mouth and a *Patsy*-type neck joint with the socket in the head and a dome shaped neck. The composition hands had a closed fist and the body was cloth.

Baby Olie Ke Wob. See **Little Shavers.**

Baby Patsy. 1926. Trade name for *Mama* doll produced by *Bing.* It had sleeping eyes and hair eyelashes, was 15 in. (38 cm.) tall; priced $12.00 a doz. wholesale.

Baby Patty Cake. 1918. Trade name of a doll made of fleece that simulates clapping its hands. This doll was produced by *Horsman.* (See also **Pat-A-Cake.**)

Baby Peggy. 1923–25. Portrait doll representing Peggy Jean Montgomery, a child actress, who was born in 1919 and appeared in moving pictures in the 1921–25 period; doll was made by *Amberg.* These dolls came in many different versions. Probably the earliest was the composition *Mama* doll with molded Dutch bobbed hair, open-closed mouth, painted teeth; ht. 20 in. (51 cm.).

The bisque-head, kid-body Baby Peggy doll came in a serious-face or a smiling-face version. These dolls are marked "19 © 24//N.Y.//Germany-50-//982/2" or "1924//L.A. & S. N.Y.//Germany//-50-//983/2" for the smiling version, which is 22 in. (56 cm.) tall. It had sleeping eyes and closed mouth; shoulder-length wig with bangs. The 18-inch (45.5-cm.) bisque-head version on a ball-jointed body with jointed wrists had sleeping eyes, hair eyelashes, and the familiar dimples. It was distributed by *Montgomery Ward;* priced $1.98 in chemise and $2.98 dressed.

There were also all-bisque versions of Baby Peggy that

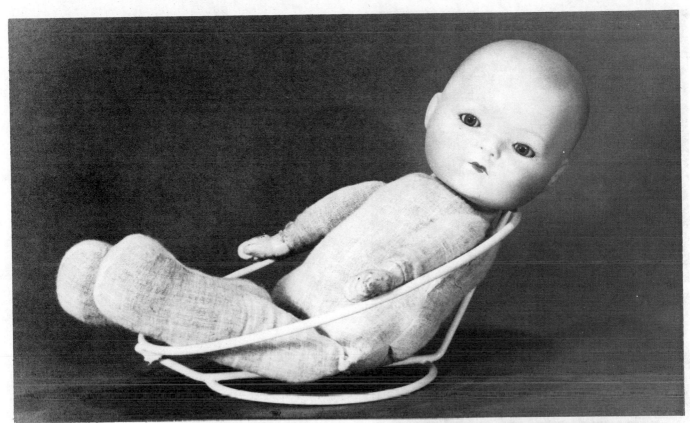

201. Baby Nod, name of a newborn infant bisque head doll produced by Amberg and made by Heubach for J. G. Dietrich (Igodi). This doll has glass eyes, a closed mouth, neck joint with a ball neck going into the socket of the head, and a flange shoulder, over which the cloth body was sewn, composition hands. *Photo by Shirley Buchholz.*

Baby Nod
LA&S. NY
Sermany
Jgodi12309/4 DRGM

202. Baby Nod mark on a bisque head.

came in three sizes 2¾, 4½, and 5¾ in. (7, 11.5 and 14.5 cm.). These were in the pink colored bisque that was used in the 1920s, especially for Amberg dolls. They had a paper sticker on the chest reading "Baby Peggy." Most of these dolls had molded bobbed brown hair; a few had wigs. The shoulders and hips were jointed except on some of the tiniest ones, which had only the shoulders jointed. The footwear, molded and painted, included single-strap Mary Jane-style slippers. ★

Baby Peggy. 1924. Portrait cloth doll representing the moving picture child actress Peggy Jean Montgomery was made by *Dean.* It had a three-dimensional smiling face and wore a wig; it came dressed, and was available in three sizes.

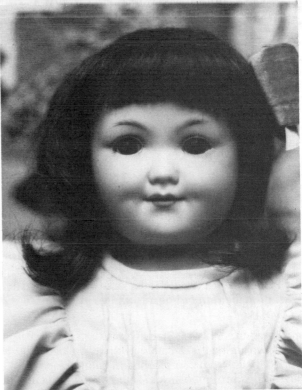

203. Portrait doll of the movie actress Peggy Montgomery, known as Baby Peggy. It has a bisque head and shoulder plate, wig, brown sleeping eyes, a closed mouth, dimples and a kid body with bisque lower arms. H. 22 in. (56 cm.). *Courtesy of Elizabeth Burke.*

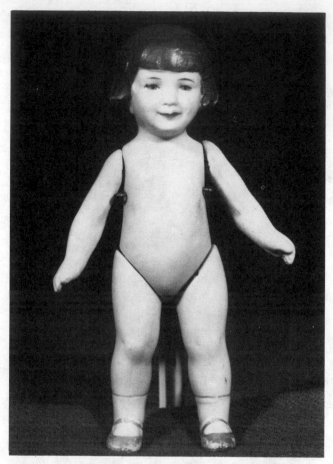

204. Baby Peggy all-bisque portrait doll made for Amberg. It is a pink bisque with molded hair, painted brown eyes, closed mouth, and jointed at the shoulders and hips. H. 5½ in. (14 cm.). *Coleman Collection.*

Germany

19 © 24
L.A.&S. N.Y.
Germany -50-
983/2

205–206. Amberg marks on the back of a Baby Peggy.

Baby Peke-Wu. 1928–29. Trade name of a cloth doll made by *Farnell* in their *Alpha* line, distributed in the United States by *Louis Wolf.*

Baby Peterkin. 1911–15. Trade name used by *Horsman* for a doll shown in the 1912 catalog. It had molded short hair combed back from the forehead, painted eyes looking straight ahead, *Campbell Kids*–type hands. It wore a long baby dress and a flannel petticoat; price was $8.50 a doz. for the larger size. The 1915 Horsman advertisement for Baby Peterkin reads: "New bisque doll, baby smile, big blue eyes, dressed in white pajamas decorated with pink ribbons." (See also **Peterkin** and **Baby Bobby.**)★

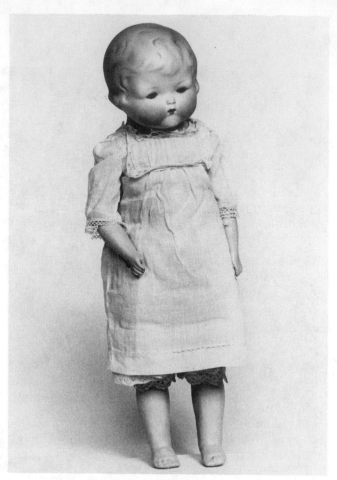

207A & B. Bisque shoulder head doll marked "Phyllis" and probably made for the Baby Phyllis Doll Co. It has molded blond hair, sleeping blue glass eyes, a tiny open mouth with two upper teeth, and a kid body with composition lower arms and legs. The hips have a sewn joint, while the elbows and knees have rivet joints. Mark on head: Ill. 208. H. 20½ in. (52 cm.). *Courtesy of the Margaret Woodbury Strong Museum. Photos by Harry Bickelhaupt.*

Phyllis
Made in Germany

208. Mark on a bisque shoulder head probably made for the Baby Phyllis Doll Co.

Baby Petite. 1916–19. Trade name for an all-composition doll modeled from a real baby by *Jesse M. Raleigh.* It had a bent-limb baby body with metal spring joints.

1919: Wore a short baby dress and bonnet. Came only in hts. 10½ and 12½ in. (26.5 and 31.5 cm.).★

Baby Phyllis Doll Co. 1919–29. Brooklyn, N.Y. until 1928, when it moved to Manhattan. Manufactured "Baby Phyllis" dolls. They were licensed by *Voices, Inc.* to use the patented mama voices and criers in the Baby Phyllis dolls.

1926: Over 200 numbers, including composition dolls made in Brooklyn and imported dolls.

The new bisque heads were made by *Armand Marseille.* The dolls were primarily *Mama* dolls or infant dolls. The *Mama* dolls wore "fashionable costumes." The infants came in many different attires. One infant doll wore a plain dress, two sizes came in fancy clothes, one style number was in a wrapped blanket and one in a blanket coverall. Baby Phyllis dolls came packed in chromolithographed cradle-shaped boxes.

1928: Dressed character dolls were added to their Mama doll, and infant doll lines.

Late 1920s: A bisque head made in Germany and marked "Phyllis" was probably used by this company. The head was on a kid body with composition lower arms and legs. (See Ills. 207A&B.)★

Baby Pierrot. 1913. Name of a doll with a cloth body having a rattle inside the body, dressed as a clown with pompons, and sold by *Gamage.* Price 46¢.

Baby Puck. 1920–28. Trade name of a cloth doll with a *Tru-to-Life* face made by *Dean.*

1920: Style No. D. 256 wore a green, brown or red Puck suit. Ht. 14 in. (35.5 cm.); priced 68¢.

1928: Doll was distributed by *Gamage* and wore a green Puck suit; it came in 14 and 18 in. (35.5 and 45.5 cm.) hts.

Baby Rose. 1919–21. All-bisque doll with wig, sleeping eyes, open-closed mouth, jointed shoulders and hips, arms bent, molded ribbed knee-high stockings and Mary Jane slippers with heels. The round paper sticker has "Baby Rose" on a red ground. Ht. 6 in. (15 cm.).★

497
15
Germany

209A & B. Baby Rose marks, No. 209A is on a paper sticker.

Baby Royal. 1923–24. Life size cloth doll made by *Mabel Bland-Hawkes.*

Baby Ruth. 1893–1907. Trade name of a bisque head doll produced by *Crämer & Héron.*★

Baby Ruth. 1912–19. Trade name of a bisque head baby doll. The smallest size had stationary eyes, six larger sizes, had sleeping eyes. They came dressed or in a chemise.★

BABY RUTH

210. Mark for a bisque head Baby Ruth doll.

Baby Ruth. 1918. Trade name of a doll made by *Effanbee.* It had a composition head and arms, wore a voile dress and nainsook underwear; 27 in. (68.5 cm.) tall.

Baby Ruth. 1927. Trademark registered in U.S. by *Curtiss Candy Co.* for dolls of wax, china, celluloid or stuffed fabric.

Baby Sister. 1918–19. Trade name of an all-composition doll produced by *Jessie M. Raleigh.* The doll had straight legs and was strung with metal springs. In 1918 it had molded short hair.★

Baby Sister. 1924. Doll with composition head and arms, mohair wig, sleeping eyes, open mouth with teeth, cloth body including legs was made by *K. & K.* When the doll was lifted up the eyes opened and it cried "Mama." Ht. 17 in. (43 cm.); price $4.25.

Baby Smiles. 1926–30 and later. Composition head doll made by *Ideal,* was distributed by *Borgfeldt* who registered the name as a trademark in Germany in 1926. This character baby doll had flirting, sleeping metal eyes, dimples in each cheek and rubber arms and hands that permitted it to simulate sucking its thumb, clapping its hands, or praying. The cloth body generally contained a crier. The legs were made of composition or cloth, but later (1928) rubber legs that squeaked when the foot was squeezed were also used. It wore a short baby dress and baby moccasins. A pacifier hung on a ribbon around its neck.

Baby Snowball. 1915. Black version of *Baby Grumpy* made by *Effanbee.* It had a composition head and lower arms, molded hair, painted eyes, cork stuffed cloth body, jointed at the shoulders and hips. The head was marked 172. Striped legs simulated stockings and shoes were made of black felt.

Baby Stuart. 1918–19. Trade name of an all-composition doll produced by *Jessie M. Raleigh.* It had short molded hair, a five-piece metal spring strung body with straight legs, and wore a short dress and baby bonnet.★

Baby Suck-a-Thumb. See **Suck-a-Thumb.**

Baby Sunshine. 1926–29. Trade name for one of the *Happiness* line of composition dolls sold by *Sears.* It had molded hair and painted eyes. Among its costumes were an organdy dress, cap, and sweater.★

Baby Surprise (Baby Surprize). Ca. 1923–25. Trade name of a doll with a composition two-faced head and composition arms and legs. The head turned to show a laughing face or a crying face. A cap hid the face in the rear, and the doll was dressed in rompers.★

Baby Toodles. 1914. Trade name for a doll distributed by *Marshall Field*. It appeared to have the same head as *Suck-a-Thumb* shown in the 1914 *Horsman* catalog, but it does not have the same patented right arm of the Horsman doll although its mouth is open to hold a pacifier. The dolls wore long lace-trimmed dresses and were 22 and 25 in. (56 and 63.5 cm.) tall; prices were $17.00 and $27.00 a doz. wholesale.

Baby Tufums. 1920s. Name of an all-bisque doll produced for *Amberg*. When jointed only at the shoulders and hips it was marked "Baby Tufums//L.A. & S.//107 Germany." When jointed at the neck, shoulders and hips it was marked "Baby Tufums//L.A. & S.//618//Germany."

Baby Tufums
LA&S
107
Germany

211. Mark on a bisque doll named Baby Tufums made for Amberg.

Baby Tunes. 1926–27. Trademark registered in U.S. by *Louis Wolf* for a doll in his *Happiness* line. This doll had a music box inside its body. When squeezed, it played either "Rock-a-bye-Baby" or "Go to Sleep My Baby."

Baby Violet. 1903–25. Trade name of an *Abraham & Straus* doll.★

Baby Violet

212. Mark for a bisque head Baby Violet doll.

Baby Wise. 1921. Trade name of a black cloth doll produced by *Horsman*. This dressed doll represented the baby of *Mammie Wise*.

Baby Wobbles. 1930. Produced by *Paramount*.

Baby Wonder Doll. 1913. Trade name of a composition-head doll with a bisque-like finish, made by *Amberg*. The doll wore a dress trimmed with "drop lace," and held a rattle. It retailed for $3.50 to $15.00.

Babykins. 1931. Trademark applied for by *Borgfeldt*. A bisque head baby doll with molded hair, glass eyes, an open-closed mouth, cloth body having composition limbs

has been reported. This doll was marked "Babykins//Cop. by Grace S. Putnam//Made in Germany//1435//50." The mold # was 1435 and the ht. was 50 cm. (20 in.).

NEEDLECRAFT MAGAZINE reportedly offered a Babykins with sleeping eyes, a crier and wearing a long dress. Ht. of doll 11 in. (28 cm.).

Babyland Dolls (Baby Land Dolls). 1893–1928. Trade name of various types of dolls produced and/or distributed by *Horsman*. Dolls in 1920 or earlier were usually of cloth and were called "Babyland Rag"[+]; some had painted faces, others had lithographed faces.

In 1926 and later the dolls were *Mama* dolls with composition head and limbs.

1893: Cloth doll distributed by Horsman; its removable clothes included a floor length dress, apron and sunbonnet. Priced $8.00 doz. wholesale.

1904: Distributed by *R. H. Macy*, dressed in pink or blue lawn; four hts. 12, 15, 18, and 30 in. (30.5, 38, 45.5 and 76 cm.); priced 24¢ to $4.51.

1908: 34 numbers with *Life Like* faces. The removable dolls' clothes represented those of children. One number was dressed as *Red Riding Hood*. (See THE COLLECTOR'S BOOK OF DOLLS' CLOTHES, Ill. 558.)

1909–10: Macy's advertised four hts. 12, 14, 15, and 18 in. (30.5, 35.5, 38 and 45.5 cm.); priced 24¢ to $1.78. They came dressed in pink or blue lawn.

1910: Horsman catalog shows 14 different dolls, including several babies in long white dresses with ruffles at the shoulder and bonnets. *Buster Brown* and others had lithographed faces; still others were Topsy and Dinah, black dolls; two boy dolls Jack Robinson and an unnamed doll wearing a long blue jacket with white trimming over blue pants and a tam-like hat. The girl dolls were Fancy, Dorothy, Beauty (wearing a lavender blue dress), and Lady in a pink checked dress with white sleeves and ruffles at the shoulders, and a bonnet that tied with a big bow under the chin.

1911: Dolls had removable clothes and wore leather slippers. Hts. 14, and 16½ in. (35.5 and 42 cm.); priced $1.00 and $2.00 at *Woodward & Lothrop*.

Macy's advertised Babyland Rag dolls dressed in lace trimmed colored lawn with a sunbonnet, underwear, and footwear. Four hts. 12, 14, 15 and 18 in. (30.5, 35.5, 38 and 45.5 cm.); priced 24¢ to $1.79.

1911–12: *Gimbel Bros.'* catalog advertised five Babyland dolls: *Topsy Turvy* with a white and a black face, priced $1.00; Red Riding Hood with a painted face, hts. 14, 16, and 17 in. (35.5, 40.5 and 43 cm.); priced 50¢ to $2.00; a girl in a short cape, dress and underclothes, ht. 15 in. (38 cm.), priced $1.00; a boy in a Buster Brown style suit, same ht. and price as the girl; infant with a printed face dressed in long clothes and a cap, priced 50¢ and $1.00.

1912–14: Horsman catalogs show Big Baby doll in a long dress, Red Riding Hood, Tommy Tucker, Dinah, Dorothy, Jack Robinson, and a Topsy Turvy doll.

There were three types of cloth Babyland dolls, the ones with molded faces, 13 in. (33 cm.) tall; the ones with flat

213. Baby Land Rag Doll advertised in the 1893 Horsman catalog. It had removable clothes and cost $9.00 a doz. wholesale. Note that the name later became Babyland Rag, a more familiar spelling.

214. Babyland Rag cloth doll with a flat face, painted features, original clothes. The skirt may have been shortened. (See Ill. 1741.) H. 17 in. (43 cm.). *Courtesy of and Photo by Phyllis Salak.*

215. Babyland Doll marks used by Horsman.

painted faces in small sizes, and 16½, 20 and 30 in. (42, 51 and 76 cm.) tall and the ones with lithographed faces in small sizes, and 14½, 16½ and 24 in. (37, 42 and 61 cm.) tall.

Seven sets of five-piece doll outfits were sold separately for these dolls; each consisted of a union suit, petticoat, dress, hat, and nightgown. The dresses, of lawn or gingham, fit dolls in 11, 13, 15, 17, and 20 in. (28, 33, 38, 43 and 51 cm.). The outfits were priced from $4.00 to $12.00 a doz. wholesale.

1915: Distributed by *Mandel Bros.* Red Riding Hood cost $1.00; black Dinah sold for 60¢.

1926: Mama dolls with composition head and limbs, cloth bodies. The legs had diagonal hip joints and a joint above the knees. Allegedly they could stand alone. The eyes looked straight ahead and teeth were visible. The dresses had ruffles, silk sashes, elbow-length sleeves, and full knee-length skirts. The bonnets tied under the chin. Footwear consisted of socks and tie slippers.★

Bach Bros. 1908–09. New York City. Made black cloth dolls and white cloth dolls named *Bye Bye Kids.* (See Ills. 454 and 455.)★

Back (Bock). 1908–10. Vienna. Listed in a directory under Dolls and Dolls' Heads.

Baer & Strasburger. 1922–28. New York City. Imported various kinds of dolls.★

Baffert, A. 1925–27. Paris. Listed in a directory as making and/or distributing cloth dolls, wax dolls and others.

Bagley, E. W. 1924–25. England. Produced dolls' heads and parts.

Bagnaro, G. 1928–29. Saint Ouen, Seine, France. Made stuffed cloth dolls with mask faces; also made shoulder heads of various kinds. Used the trade name *La Pompadour.* Dolls distributed through jobbers and to bazaars.

Bahner, Doscher Co. 1920–29. New York City. Importer and manufacturer's agent.

1921: Imported bent-limb baby dolls and other dolls. These had mohair or real hair wigs either curly or straight. Nearly all the dolls had sleeping eyes, some with hair eyelashes; some were also flirting eyes. The hand-sewed clothes closed with hooks and eyes.

1922: Advertised an assortment of dressed jointed dolls with kid or kidlyn bodies in four sizes. The girl child-dolls all wore hats except one with a hood and cape and one with a hair bow. The hats generally had brims. The dolls in silk, lace, and velvet dresses retailed for $5.00 to $25.00 each. Various novelty dolls retailed for 25¢ to $5.00 each.

1923: Advertised that all their dolls had real hair, sleeping eyes, and jointed bodies; the imported *Mama* dolls, real hair eyelashes. Grotesque or character dolls made on wire frames with painted stockinet faces and hands included the "fat tummied" Baker, the Butcher, the haughty Butler, the Bell-hop Porter, the supercilious English Tourist, and the self-conceited Beau Brummell.

These dolls have a strong resemblance to the character

cloth faced dolls advertised by *Kämmer & Reinhardt* in their 1927 catalog which showed similar dolls dressed in felt. Ht. 33 cm. (13 in.).★

Bähr & Pröschild. 1871–1930 and later. Ohrdruf, Thür. Made china, bisque and celluloid dolls and dolls' parts. Their bisque dolls' heads, especially mold #s in the 500s were used by *Kley & Hahn, Bruno Schmidt,* and *Wiesenthal, Schindel & Kallenberg* around 1910. Most of the information prior to 1920 is based on the research of the Ciesliks.

1888: Made a bald-type bisque head mold #224 for a nodding head doll patented by *Josef Bergmann* and produced by *Müller & Strassburger.*

1894: There were 200 employees in the factory; owners were Georg and Hans Bähr.

1895: Mold numbers 342, 343, 348 and 350 were used on dolls' necks.

1897: Additional mold numbers were 389, 390 and 393.

1904: Obtained a German patent (D.R.G.M.) for *roguish eyes.*

1905: Advertised wigged bisque heads with and without

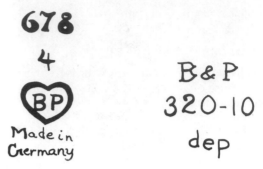

217–218. Marks used on bisque dolls made by Bähr & Pröschild.

219. Mark possibly used by Bähr & Pröschild.

sleeping eyes, hair eyelashes; baby dolls; *Nankeen* dolls, and all-bisque dolls.

1909: Advertised celluloid dolls and dolls' parts. Used the trademark *Buporit* for their celluloid products.

1910: Made all-bisque *Snow Babies.* Introduced mold number 585 for baby dolls.

Other mold numbers used after 1910 were 604, 619, 624 and 678. Mold numbers 585 and 604 have been found on 10, 15, and 25 in. (25.5, 38, and 63.5 cm.) bisque head, bent-limb composition body babies with open-closed mouths. The 15 in. doll was size 7; the 25 in. doll, was size 16.

1912: Obtained a German patent (D.R.G.M.) for fastenings of dolls' heads.

1918: Factory was sold to *Bruno Schmidt* of Waltershausen, and both the Bruno Schmidt factory and the Bähr & Pröschild factory used the heart trademark. However, the Bähr & Pröschild factory put the initials B P in their heart.

1924: Described by U.S. Department of Commerce as making bisque heads and china heads for dolls.

1929: Listed in a directory as making "Bisque dolls, pincushion dolls, modern and antique trinkets." Apparently they were reproducing earlier objects.★

Bail, P. 1928. Paris. Specialized in making bébés.

Bail & Launay. 1920s. France. Made clothes for dolls and was a member of the *Chambre Syndicale.*

Bailey, Doris Sylvia, and Baxter, Sarah Jane. 1916. Longton, Staffs. Their patented process of coating wax over *British Ceramic* was used by the *Dolls' Accessory Co.* and probably *Keats & Co. Nunn & Smeed* and others.★

Bailey & Bailey. 1921–29. U.S.A. Distributed *Gertrude Rollinson's* cloth dolls.

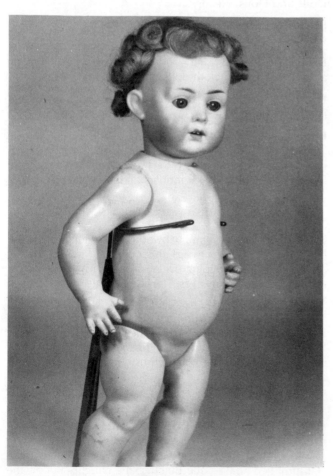

216. Bisque head made by Bähr & Pröschild has wig, sleeping blue eyes, open mouth with teeth, and a toddler type composition body. Mark: Ill. 217. H. 14½ in. (37 cm.). Circumference of head 9 in. (23 cm.). *Courtesy of Richard Withington. Photo by Barbara Jendrick.*

Bainbridge & White. 1922. Britain. Advertised dolls in an English trade journal.

Baird-North. 1921. Distributed *Pudgie*.

Baitz, Lilli & R. 1920s. Berlin. Made art-type character dolls. Elizabeth Folse of Texas reports having a doll with a composition head and limbs on a body made of wire wrapped with thin strips of crepe paper. The hair was mohair; the doll had a label reading "Lilli"//WERKSTATTEN//L. & R. Baitz// Berlin SW68." The dolls representing ladies were dressed in cotton; men dolls were dressed in felt.

Baker, Charles W. 1916–26. London. Wholesale distributor and exporter; specialized in printed cloth, stuffed dolls. Factory agent for *Sunlight, Sieve & Co.*, and *Heinrich Schelhorn*.

1921: Advertised *Kley & Hahn* dolls.

Baker & Bennett. 1900–30. New York City. Factory agents, importers and manufacturers of dolls and dolls' clothes.

1913: Called "Manufacturers" by TOYS AND NOVELTIES. The factory representative was *McClurg & Keen*.

1915: Moved into larger quarters and were agents for the National Toy Manufacturing Co. (See **Q. B. Toy & Novelty Co.**)

1917: Advertised the *Deedle Dum Dolls*.

1918: Advertised dolls costing 10¢ to $1.00 apiece and *Century* dressed dolls 50¢ to $5.00 each. Factory agent for *Wigwam Co.* dolls.

1919: Factory agent for *Giebeler-Falk*.

1921: Distributed dolls made by *Oweenee Novelty Co.*

1922: Made dolls' dresses, both the finished product and those ready to be sewed together. Agent for *Nelke* dolls.

1924: Advertised that many of America's leading toy and doll lines had their headquarters in the Baker & Bennett salesrooms.

1925: Advertised dolls made under their own supervision.

1926: Distributed *Kiddie Specialty Corp.* dolls.

1927: Factory agent for *Baby Dahne, Baby Gloria* and *Tee Wee* Babe.

1929: Advertised several new dolls, some retailed for $5.00.

1930: Agents for *Bimblick*.

Ball, Margaret. 1885–91. Brooklyn, N.Y. Made dolls.

Balleroy, Jullien, & Cie. Limoges, France. A porcelain factory that used the initials J. B. as a mark. These initials have been found on bisque head bébés. (See also **Jacques Berner**.)

Ballet Skirt Girl. 1927. Trade name of a cloth doll made by *Woolnough* and distributed by their factory agent, *Davis & Voetsch*. The dolls were made of powder-puff plush and had hand embroidered facial features.

Balsa Dolls. Dolls made of balsa, linden or similar lightweight wood. (See Ill. 201 in THE COLLECTOR'S BOOK OF

220. Bisque socket head made by Jullien Balleroy on an S.F.B.J. composition body marked. "Fabrication Française S.F.B.J. Paris." It has a wig, blue stationary glass eyes, pierced ears, open-closed mouth with molded teeth. Mark on head: Ill. 221. H. 18½ in. (47 cm.). *Courtesy of Richard Withington. Photo by Barbara Jendrick.*

221–222. Marks found on bisque heads made by Jullien Balleroy in Limoges. No. 221 is on the doll shown in Ill. 220.

DOLLS' CLOTHES. Further examination revealed this doll to be gesso over wood and not composition.)

Balsam Baby. 1930 and probably later. U.S. trademark name for a cloth doll made by *Gre-Poir.* It had a molded cloth mask face with painted features, a partial wig, and the body was jointed at the neck, shoulders, and hips. The fingers were indicated by sewing and the thumb was separate. The dressed dolls had attached to the clothes a square white paper tag with green letters as follows: "Pat. Pending Trade Mark Reg. //Balsam Baby// Healthful Cuddling Doll// Easily cleaned with //Art Gum// Gre-Poir, Inc." One of these dolls dressed in rompers and matching bonnet was 16½ in. (42 cm.) tall.

Baltimore Bargain House. 1881-ca. 1920, succeeded by American Wholesale Corporation, ca. 1920–27 and probably later. Baltimore, Md. Imported and distributed dolls.

1902–03: Advertised dressed so-called "French Dolls" with bisque heads, wigs, sleeping eyes, open mouth with teeth. These dolls with jointed composition bodies were sometimes called "French" because this type of body is believed to have originated in France.

1916: See THE COLLECTOR'S BOOK OF DOLLS' CLOTHES, Ill. 714.

1917: Advertised dolls made of composition, cloth, celluloid, rubber or wood. The dolls included dressed and undressed dolls; some of the baby dolls wore swaddling clothes. Among the dolls were *Buster Brown,* Charlie Chaplin, *Clowns,* Knock-About character dolls, *Queue San Baby,* Red Cross Nurse, *Rough Rider,* Santa Claus, *Uncle Sam* and *Yama Yama Kid.*

1922: Stated "our buyer spent months in Europe visiting all the important centers of production and searching out the newest and most attractive offerings of the foreign makers . . . they have assembled the greatest line of Imported Toys, Dolls. . . . Our tremendous quantity-buying gets us lower prices and our Selling cost by Catalog is only 2.77% as against the 10% to 12% it costs Toy Houses to sell by drummers."

Imported dolls included a bisque-head doll with mohair wig, sleeping eyes, hair eyelashes, open mouth with teeth, fully jointed composition body, tinted and lacquered, wearing a chemise, hair bow and footwear. Ht. 24 in. (61 cm.); priced $24.00 doz. wholesale. All prices of this House were given as wholesale.

Similar dolls without the hair eyelashes or the chemise but on kidlyn bodies with bisque hands came in 6 hts. 11¾ to 22 in. (30 to 56 cm.): priced $6.75 to $24.00 doz.

Dolls with molded low-brow china heads and china limbs on cloth bodies came in 7 hts. 6¼ to 12 in. (16 to 30.5 cm.); priced 40¢ to $1.65 doz.

The imported dressed dolls had bisque heads, wigs, sleeping eyes, open mouth with teeth, jointed limbs; the more expensive dolls were fully jointed. 14 hts. 8 to 19¼ in. (20.5 to 49.5 cm.); priced $2.25 to $42.00 doz.

17 styles of rubber dolls with embossed clothes were advertised, two of the baby dolls closely resembled ones of many decades earlier. There were also clowns, a nurse with

a baby, Buster Brown, girls, boys, and women. 10 hts. 3½ to 8¾ in. (9 to 22 cm.); priced 42¢ to $4.15 doz.

Dolls with celluloid faces, painted features, bellow voices were dressed in flannel or felt. Hts. 5¼ and 5½ in. (13.5 and 14 cm.); priced 82¢ doz.

1924: American Wholesale Corp. had an office in Sonneberg, Thür.

1925: Catalog showed a wide variety of dolls. All-bisque dolls with molded hair, fully jointed, 3½ in. (9 cm.) high, 85¢ doz. dressed; bent-limb baby, rivet-jointed shoulders, 3¾ in. (9.5 cm.) high, 88¢ doz., dressed in knitted sweater; boy and girl dolls 5 in. (12.5 cm.), $1.65 doz., knitted clothes; character dolls, rivet-jointed at shoulders and hips, molded footwear, 4, 5¼ and 6½ in. (10, 13 and 16.5 cm.) high, 77¢ to $1.85 doz.; baby dolls with rivet-jointed shoulders and hips, hts. 3¾, 5¼, and 6¾ in. (9.5, 13 and 17 cm.), 70¢ to $1.75 doz.; boy and girl dolls wearing molded bathing suits, rivet-jointed shoulders and hips, 3¾, 5, and 6½ in. (9.5, 12.5 and 16.5 cm.), 65¢ to $1.95 doz.

Bent-limb character babies with bisque heads, wigs (some bobbed hair, some English mohair), sleeping eyes; dressed in a chemise: 21 hts. from 8 to 25 in. (20.5 to 63.5 cm.). Price $3.85 doz. to $3.50 each.

Bisque heads, ball-jointed composition bodies with jointed wrists and fingers apart, sleeping eyes with eyelashes, wigs; dressed in a chemise: 23 hts. from 11¾ to 32 in. (30 to 81 cm.). Price $7.25 doz. to $12.00 each, wholesale. Similar dolls without jointed wrists and with cheaper chemises came in 6 hts., 11¾ to 17¼ in. (30 to 44 cm.). Price $4.25 to $12.00 doz.

Bisque heads on white kidlyn bodies with universal joints, wigs, sleeping eyes, teeth, pink or blue shoes and socks: 16 hts. from 11½ to 23½ in. (29 to 59.5 cm.). Pink kidlyn bodies with bisque heads and hands: 4 hts. 13 to 22 in. (33 to 56 cm.). Price $10.50 per doz. to $2.25 each. Pink kidlyn bodies with bisque head, composition limbs: ht. 12¾, 15¾ and 21½ in. (32, 40 and 54.5 cm.); price $10.50 per doz. to $2.25 each. Bisque head and lower arms on genuine kid bodies with universal joints: 7 hts., 14¼ to 20 in. (36 to 51 cm.); price $12.00 per doz. to $2.50 each wholesale. Bisque head, composition lower limbs, genuine kid body, universal joints: 4 hts. 14¼ to 20½ in. (36 to 52 cm.); price $1.65 to $3.00 each. Bisque head on a stick, bellows in body, 14 in.; $4.25 doz. Bisque heads on cloth bodies stuffed with hair, German-type sewed knee-joints, mohair wigs, sleeping eyes: ht. 16 in. (40.5 cm.) at $7.50 doz. and 18 in. (46 cm.) at $10.50 doz. Bisque shoulder heads sold separately came in 6 sizes. Price $2.25 to $13.50 doz. Metal-head dolls with molded hair, painted features, hair-stuffed cloth bodies having sewn knee and hip joints and composition arms: hts. 11, 12½ and 15 in. (28, 31.5 and 38 cm.); price $3.65 to $6.75 doz.

All-china dolls (*Frozen Charlottes*) with molded wavy

223. Baltimore Bargain House catalog for July 1917, shows these wartime dolls, which include all-bisque Queue San Babies; composition head, cloth-body dolls; and character dolls representing Charlie Chaplin, Uncle Sam, Red Cross Nurse, Rough Rider, Sailor Boy and Clowns.

IMPORTED BISQUE CHARACTER BABY

T602—Ht. 4½ in., bisque body, painted features, tinted jointed arms, painted cap and shoes. 1 doz. in box..........Doz., **85c**

10-CENT CHARACTER DOLL.

T2041—Height 12 in., unbreakable stuffed body, movable limbs, printed features, calico dress of assorted colors, calico cap to match dress. 1 doz. in box, (gross, $10.20); doz., **87c**

INDESTRUCTIBLE KNOCK-ABOUT CHARACTER DOLLS.

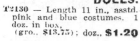

T2130 — Length 11 in., asstd. pink and blue costumes. 1 doz. in box, (gro., $13.75); doz., **$1.20**

"RED RIDING HOOD" DOLLS.

T2126—Length 9¾ in., celuloid face, full jointed, figured calico dress, red cape and hood. 1 doz in box, (gross, $13.75); doz., **$1.20**

SPECIAL ASSORTMENT OF DRESSED CHARACTER DOLLS.

T4111—Boys and girls, height 12¼ inches, movable character heads, embossed hair, painted features, jointed limbs, assorted costumes—romper, dress and blouse effect; assorted colors; 1 doz. in box....................doz., **$2.25**

Staple Toys

INDESTRUCTIBLE WOODEN HEAD DOLLS.

Painted hair and features.

T2026 — Length 9 in., stuffed with sawdust. 1 doz. in box, (gross, $11.25); doz., **98c**

T4100 — Boys and Girls, height 10 inches, character head, gingham rompers and dresses; assorted color trimmings and belts; 1 doz. in box .... doz., **$1.85**

CHARACTER DOLLS

For premium and carnival use. Stout stuffed bodies, jointed limbs, composition head and hands, flesh colored tint, dressed in regulation uniforms. Average ht. 3 in.

T2145   T2149

T2144—Clown .... Each, **$1.35**
T2145—Uncle Sam ...... Each, **$1.45**
T2146—Red Cross Nurse.. Each, **$1.35**
T2147—Rough Rider. Each, **$1.35**
T2148—Yama Yama Kid. Each, **$1.35**
T2149—Charlie Chaplin. Each, **$1.45**
T2150—Baby. Each, **$1.35**
T2151—Sailor Boy. Each, **$1.35**
T2152 — Dotted Clown. Each, **$1.35**
In lots of 1 doz. or more asstd., Doz., **$15.00**

T2150

T4016

T4016—Height .12 in., flesh tint composition hands, romper costume and figured dress, trimmed with lace; ½ doz. in box, doz., **$4.05**

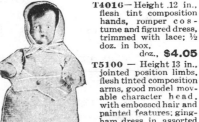

T5100

T5100 — Height 13 in., jointed position limbs, flesh tinted composition arms, good model movable character head, with embossed hair and painted features; gingham dress in assorted colors, white belt with gilt button attached, cap to match dress; ½ doz. in box, doz., **$4.25**

hair, arms and legs apart, ht. 3⅝, 4 and 4¾ in. (9, 10 and 12 cm.). Price 37¢ to 72¢ doz. With gold-painted shoes, these came in hts. 3¼ and 4½ in. (8 and 11.5 cm.); price 37¢ and 70¢ doz.

Low-brow china shoulder-heads on cloth bodies (Nankeen dolls) came in 6 hts., 7 to 12½ in. (18 to 31.5 cm.); price 75¢ to $2.05 doz. These dolls also came with black hair and a floral-design body in the 7¼-inch (18.5 cm.), ht.; 87¢ doz. The shoulder-heads were sold separately, and came in blond and black versions and in 5 hts., 2½, 2¾, 3, 3¼, and 3¾ in. (6.5, 7, 7.5, 8 and 9.5 cm.); price 27¢ to $1.15 doz.

All-celluloid dolls with straight legs, jointed at shoulders and hips, molded hair, painted footwear: hts., 3½, 5½, and 7½ in. (9, 14 and 19 cm.); price 85¢ to $4.15 doz. The same but with bent legs came in 4 hts.: 4 to 7 in. (10 to 18 cm.); price 42¢ to $2.25 doz. Celluloid heads and lower limbs on kidlyn bodies, 6 hts.: 14¼ to 21½ in. (36 to 54.5 cm.); price $1.75 to $4.50 doz. Dressed celluloid dolls with molded hair: ht. 3½, 3⅞ and 5 in. (9, 10 and 13 cm.); price 40¢ to 87¢ doz. The eyes of the 5-inch dolls glance to the side.

Clowns with clapping cymbals, celluloid faces, bellows-type voices, 9 in. (23 cm.); price $1.65 doz. The same, without cymbals but on a stick, 11½ in. (29 cm.), $1.95 doz. Celluloid head on stick, 13½ in. (34 cm.); $1.75 doz. Same as above but with rattle chime, 11 in. (28 cm.); $3.75 doz.

Composition-head dolls in various costumes, 4 hts., 9 to 14 in. (23 to 35.5 cm.); price $1.65 to $4.10 doz. Composition head on a stick with a whistle in the body, 12 in. (30.5 cm.); $1.85 doz. Marottes with music, 12½ in. (31.5 cm.); $4.25 doz.

1927: Catalog advertised over 150 styles of dressed dolls, including infants, child dolls, flappers, and china-head dolls. These were American as well as imported dolls. The dolls made in America cost twice as much as those of European manufacture and similar size. Their dolls included Buster Brown, Traffic Cop, Jackie Coogan, Baby Gloria, Miss Muffet, Boudoir dolls, Topsy, Lucky Lindy, Cymbalier, clowns, Whistling Boy, and imported French novelty dolls. The all-bisque dolls came with molded hair or wigs, jointed at shoulders only or at both shoulders and hips. Heights ranged from 3½ to 5½ in. (9 to 14 cm.). The dolls with low-brow china heads and china limbs on cloth bodies came only in the 8½ inch (21.5 cm.) ht. Those with molded china heads representing boys and girls came in hts. 4½, 7½, and 8 in. (11.5, 19 and 20.5 cm.). Both the china-head and the all-bisque dolls ranged in price from 35¢ to 85¢ per doz. The bisque-head dolls on composition bodies had wigs, sleeping eyes, and open mouths with teeth. The fully jointed ones came in four hts., 15½, 22¾, 23¾, and 31 in. (39.5, 58, 60.5 and 78.5 cm.); priced $9.00 doz. to $9.75 each. The character bisque head dolls on five-piece bent-limb bodies came in four hts. 8½, 12, 14¼ and 16 in. (21.5, 30.5, 36 and 40.5 cm.); priced $4.50 to $19.50 doz.

Bamberger, L., & Co. 1892–1930 and later. Newark, N.J. Distributed dolls and registered trademarks for dolls.

1927: Registered U.S. trademark IKWA for dolls.

1930: Began to use the trademark, "Under the China-berry Tree" for rag dolls. U.S. trademark was registered in 1931. ★

Bambetta Dolls. 1927–29. Made by Chad Valley. These were introduced in 1927 as intermediate in quality and price between the Caresse and Bambina dolls. They had hand-painted velour faces, hair wigs, and jointed arms and legs. The dresses, of various styles, were made of colored organdy or art silk (rayon); the dolls wore felt hats, usually with the brim turned up in front. The style nos. of these dolls were 1202, 1203, 1204, 1205, and 1206. They came in size 1, 14 in. (35.5 cm.) high costing $1.65; size 2, 17 in. (43 cm.) high costing $1.95 and size 3, 19 in. (48 cm.) high costing $2.65. The dolls wore dresses with elbow length sleeves or longer and full short skirts. The footwear consisted of single-strap buttoned slippers and low socks.

1929: The earlier dolls were retained and model 1207 added. It wore a tam and a suit with jacket.

1930: No Bambetta dolls were shown in the Chad Valley catalog.

Bambina. 1918. A black doll made of cotton, a companion to Bleuette.

Bambina. 1924–30 and later. Cloth dolls made by Chad Valley and described as being "models of Italian dolls." This may have referred to Lenci dolls. These were quality dolls, among the most popular series made by the company. Their heads and faces were of hand-painted felt. The faces represented children older than the Mabel Lucie Attwell dolls. The eyes of "veined" glass generally, but not always, looked straight ahead. The wigs were of genuine short hair that could be combed. The necks, shoulders, and hips were jointed. Very few Bambina dolls were dressed as boys. The clothes were removable. The dolls were priced according to their height which varied from 13½ to 19 in. (34.5 to 48 cm.) and to the elaborateness of their clothes. All the dolls wore single-strap slippers and low socks. Cloth labels have been found on the soles of both feet. One label read "Chad Valley 'Bambina' (Regs. & Pat.)": the other label read "Hygienic Toys Made in England by Chad Valley Co. Ltd."

1924: Bambina dolls were advertised as made of "felt and velvette." Style numbers 750–755 came in size 2, were 18½ in. (47 cm.) high.

1926: Size 0 was 14½ in. (40.5 cm.) and came in style numbers 750, 751, 754, 756 and 802; 802 came only in this size. It was chosen by Queen Mary as her purchase at the British Industries Fair. (See Ill. 507.)

Size 1 was 16 in. (40.5 cm.) and came in style numbers: 750, 754, 755, 756 and 778.

Size 2 was 18½ in. (47 cm.). Most of the style numbers from 750–804 came in this size.

Dolls representing babies, some of them in long dresses, were also included in the Bambina series. They had wide baby-type faces and carried the hexagonal Chad Valley tags reading "Bambina//Doll// Chad Valley." Style number 779 came in size 0, ht. 13½ in. (34.5 cm.). Style number 780

224A & B. Cloth doll in the Chad Valley Bambina line. It has a felt head with hair sewed on in strips, blue stationary glass eyes, eyelashes painted at top and side of each eye. The velvet body is jointed at the neck, shoulders, and hips. Original clothes. A white tape with red embroidered letters reads: "Chad Valley-//'BAMBINA'//(REGᴰ & PAT.)." Ht. 15 in. (38 cm.). *Courtesy of Richard Withington. Photo by Barbara Jendrick.*

came in three sizes namely, 0, 1 and 2; hts., 15½, 18½ and 22 in. (39.5, 47 and 56 cm.) (The measurements included the long baby dresses.) Style number 788 was size 0, ht. 13½ in. (34.5 cm.). (See table for style numbers being offered in this year.) A cheaper range of Bambinas was made in 1926.

1927: Dolls were advertised as made of "felt and velvet" and packed in Bye-Bye boxes that simulated a gilt bed with a drawer beneath it. The dolls were made in three sizes: 0, 1 and 2; hts. 14½, 16 and 18 in. (37, 40.5 and 45.5 cm.). (See table for style numbers being offered in this year.)

1928: Some of the earlier models were revised. The baby dolls were made only in size 0, 13½ in. (34.5 cm.) and the price was $2.65 each, the same as for the Bambina child dolls size 0, 14½ in. (37 cm.). Size 1, 16 in. (40.5 cm.) Bambina cost $3.90 dressed in simple clothes, $4.40 in medium-quality outfits and $5.00 each for the deluxe models. All these dolls were still packed in the Bye-Bye boxes. *Gamage,* one of the distributors, advertised that the cloth used for these dolls had a velvety texture but was washable.

1929: The 1929 Chad Valley catalog showed a variety of child models beginning with number 760 but there were no baby dolls. The new numbers included 835 through 892(?). (See table for style numbers being offered in this year.)

1930: The Bambina dolls shown in the 1930 Chad Valley catalog appear to be entirely new models. Instead of size 1 there was now size 1½, ht. 17½ in. (44.5 cm.). Some of the eyes still looked straight ahead, but most now glanced to the side.

Although not so stated, style number 913, the *Princess Elizabeth* doll, appears to belong to the Bambina series. It was size 1½, ht. 17½ in. (44.5 cm.). (See table for style numbers being offered in this year).

Bambino. 1917. Trade name of a stockinet doll designed by *E. E. Houghton* and made by the *Shanklin.*

Bambino. 1928–60. Trade name of an infant doll probably made by *Société Française de Fabrication de Bébés & Jouets* (S.F.B.J.). Distributed by LA SEMAINE DE SUZETTE, a weekly publication that often contained patterns for Bambino's clothes. Bambino had a bisque head similar to a *Bye-Lo Baby's* head, on a composition baby body, until the 1950s, when the head was made of Rholoid and marked "Jumeau 278.3." The *Jumeau* head had painted hair, sleeping eyes, and an open mouth. Prior to this, the head appears to have been unmarked. Bambino represented the baby brother of *Bleuette.*

1928: Wore a handmade white jersey outfit. The doll was 25 cm. (10 in.) high. One of the first patterns was for a christening dress.

1933: Came with either a bisque or composition head. Ht. 26 cm. (10½ in.).

Bamboula. 1931. Trade name of a black baby associated with *Bleuette* and distributed by LA SEMAINE DE SUZETTE. This doll was first shown at a French Colonial exhibition according to M. Theimer.

Bandler, Max. 1925–30 and later. New York City. Made stockings for dolls including novelty stockings.

Bandorf & Co. 1856–1909. Beutelsdorf, Orlamünd, Germany. Successor in 1894 was Carl Robert Saenger. Porcelain factory.

1894: Made porcelain dolls' heads and all-porcelain dolls.

1909: Fifty workers produced dolls' heads.

Banister, John. 1800s. An early trade card with his name read, "All sorts of English & Dutch Toys, with all sorts of Naked and Drest Babies."

Bannawitz, Albert. 1925–29. Schalkau, Thür. Manufactured five-piece and fully jointed dolls with and without voices.★

Bapts & Hamet. 1898. Paris. Made dolls.

Baraja Bébé. 1892. Name of a French doll costing 1¢.

Barbele. Name of a doll made by *Wagner & Zetzsche.* It had a *Haralit* head with molded blond hair having a braided bun and top knot, painted eyes, cloth body with ball jointed composition arms and a flange neck. Some of these dolls were dressed in German regional costumes.

Barbier, George. 1923. Designed a Fragonard group of dolls. The clothes on these dolls were made by *Mme. Pul-*

CLOTHES ON BAMBINAS BY STYLE NUMBERS
Usually short sleeves on dresses, long sleeves on coats and suits.

Style No.	Years	Outer Garment	Headwear	Trim and/or Comments
750	1924–27	Dress, high waist	Cloche	Collar
751	1924–26	Dress, low waist	Brimmed hat	Belt
752	1924–27	Dress, low waist	Military hat	Edging
753	1924–27	Dress, no waistline	Cloche	Scallops
754	1924–26	Dress, low waist	Bonnet	Ribbons
755	1924–27	Coat & dress	Hat	Fur
756	1926–27	Dress, low waist	Cloche	Bow
758	1926–27	Dress, low waist	Cloche	Appliqué
760	1926–29	Dress, no waistline	Cap	Circles
763	1926	Dress, low waist	Cloche	Binding
764	1926	Dress, high waist	Brimmed hat	Panels, uneven skirt
765	1926	Dress, striped	Brimmed hat	Belt
768	1926–27	Dress, skirt trimmed	Cloche	Ruffles
769	1926	Dress, skirt trimmed	Brimmed hat	Panniers
771	1926–29	Dress, pleated skirt	Brimmed hat	Appliqué
774	1926–27	Dress, high waist	Bonnet	Vertical stripe
776	1926	Dress, layered skirt	Bonnet	Bretelles
778	1926–27	Suit with scarf	Cloche	Pompoms
779	1926–29	Short baby dress	Cap	Lace
780	1926–27	Long baby dress	Cap	Lace
781	1926–29	Dress with yoke	Bonnet	Appliqué
783	1926–29	Dress, no waistline	Hat	Appliqué
785	1927	Dress, princess line	Hair bow	Appliqué
787	1926–27	Dress, scalloped skirt	Bonnet	Appliqué
788	1926–27	Suit, knit	Cap	None. Baby.
790	1926–29	Coat & dress	Cloche	Appliqué
791	1926–27	Dress, princess style	Tam	Appliqué
792	1926	Dress, overskirt	Cloche	Appliqué, uneven skirt
793	1926–27	Dress with yoke	Cloche	Uneven skirt
794	1926–29	Dress, no waistline	Frizzy hair	Disks
795	1926–27	Dress, low waist	Cloche	Appliqué
796	1926–29	Dress, high waist	Cloche	Ribbon beading
797	1926–27	Dress, low waist	Cloche	Striped panel
799	1926–29	Dress, high waist	Cloche	Appliqué
800	1926–27	Dress, princess style	Cloche	Appliqué
802	1926–29	Dress, no waistline	Tam	Appliqué. Queen Mary's Choice
803	1926–29	Dress, no waistline	Cloche	Appliqué
804	1926–27	Long-sleeved outfit	Cloche	Vertical stripe
805	1927	Dress, yoke	Brimmed hat	Panels
806	1927	Dress, no waistline	Cloche	Embroidery
807	1927	Dress, Russian style	Tam	Embroidery
811	1927	Coat & dress	Cloche	Bow
813	1927	Coat	Cloche	Vandyked
814	1927	Dress, yoke, toddler	Frizzy hair	Lace
815	1927	Dress, no waistline	Cloche	Checkerboard
816	1927	Dress, low waist	Brimmed hat	Appliqué
817	1927	Knit suit, trousers	Stocking cap	Pompons
818	1927	Coat with cape	Cloche	Darker edges
819	1929	Coat & dress	Cloche	Disks
820	1927–29	Dress, Russian style	Tam	Appliqué
821	1927–29	Dress, no waistline	Hair bow	Appliqué
822	1927	Dress, pleated skirt	Hair bow	
823	1927	Dress, no waistline	Hair bow	Lines and squares
824	1927	Coat, no waistline	Cloche	Triangles
835	1929	Dress, high waistline	Cloche	Bands

Style No.	Years	Outer Garment	Headwear	Trim and/or Comments
844	1929	Dress, high waistline	Hair bows	Box pleats
845	1929	Coat with collar	Cloche	Pockets
846	1929	Dress, low waistline	Hair bow	Appliqué
848	1929	Dress, high waistline	Brimmed hat	Full skirt
851	1929	Suit, short pants	Brimmed hat	Boy
854	1929	Coat with collar	Cloche	Appliqué
858	1929	Suit, long pants	None	Boy
866	1929	Dress, high waistline	Cloche	Scalloped
867	1929	Pajamas	None	Bedroom slippers
872	1929	Dress, no waistline	Bonnet	Squares
873	1929	Suit, short pants	Hat	Boy
874	1929	Dress, no waistline	Brimmed hat	Appliqué
875	1929	Coat	Cloche	Buttons
881	1929	Dress & jacket	Cloche	Appliqué
882	1929	Dress, full skirt	Cloche	Scalloped
883	1929	Dress & underskirt	Brimmed hat	Patch pockets
884	1929	Dress, high waistline	Cloche	Appliqué
885	1929	Dress, high waistline	Bonnet	Full skirt
886	1929	Dress & bloomers	Cloche	Color bands
887	1929	Coat & dress	Cloche	Appliqué
888	1929	Dress, full skirt	Brimmed hat	Appliqué
890(?)	1929	Coat & muffler	Cloche	Buttons
891(?)	1929	Dress, full skirt	Brimmed hat	Printed fabric
892(2)	1929	Coat with collar	Fedora-type	Frog closure
893	1930	Dress with bretelles	Bonnet	Appliqué
894	1930	Dress & drawers	Hair bow	Full skirt
895	1930	Dress, no waistline	Cloche	Appliqué
896	1930	Dress, box pleats	Brimmed cloche	Butterflies
897	1930	Dress, high waistline	Hair over ears	Tiered skirt
898	1930	Dress, low waistline	Bonnet	Appliqué
899	1930	Dress, high waistline	Bonnet	Dragon-fly
901	1930	Coat & dress	Brimmed hat	Flower at neck
902	1930	Russian blouse	Tam	Short pants
903	1930	Suit, short pants	Boy's style hair	Boutonniere
904	1930	Dress, high waistline	Cloche	Scallops
905	1930	Dress, high waistline	Brimmed hat	Full skirt
906	1930	Dress, high waistline	Brimmed hat	Scallops
907	1930	Dress, high waistline	Dutch hat	Appliqué
908	1930	Dress with bretelles	Brimmed hat	Appliqué
910	1930	Dress & scarf	Tam	Checked fabric
911	1930	Suit, short pants	Boy's style hair	Tailored suit

liche; they represented the costumes worn at the Ball du Grand Prix in Paris. The dolls were displayed at the second Silk Exposition held in the Grand Central Palace, New York City.

Barclay Baby Belle. 1908–10. *Bawo & Dotter* trademark. ★

Barefoot Boy. 1919. Trade name of a doll made by *Ideal.* This all-composition doll had molded hair and sleeping eyes. Ht. 15 in. (38 cm.).

Barfuss, Widow Carl. 1909–28. Gotha, Thür. Manufactured dolls.

Bark Dolls. 1918. Dolls made in Florida from the bark of trees. Dolls were dressed with bark, even having hats of bark.

Barker, A. 1926. Britain. Listed in an English trade journal as producing dolls.

Barm, Anna. 1888. Berlin. Made knitted and crocheted dolls.

225. Barclay Baby Belle mark found on dolls.

Barnett, Henry. 1921–26. London. Sole agent in Britain for many continental doll manufacturers, including *A. Bucherer, Buschow & Beck, Dr. Paul Hunaeus,* and *H. Josef Leven.*

Barnett, Isaacs, & Co. 1922–26. Britain. Listed in an English trade journal as producing dolls. Handled Sonneberg dolls.

Barney Google. 1918–28. Trade name of a jointed wooden doll made by *Schoenhut,* designed by Billy de Beck, representing the cartoon character Barney Google. The top hat and other clothes were made of wood and nailed onto the doll, which was 6½ in. (16.5 cm.) tall. With the horse, Spark Plug, it cost $2.75 in 1923.

Barnicol, Carl. 1921–26. Sonneberg, Thür. Manufactured dolls.

Barnicol, Georg. 1913. Sonneberg, Thür. Applied for a German patent (D.R.G.M.) for movable eyelashes for dolls.

Barnikol, Max A. 1927–30. Sonneberg, Thür. Made "unbreakable" dressed art dolls that were distributed by *Hertzog* and called Maba.

Baroness de Laumont. See **Laumont.**

Barr. 1889 and probably other years. St. Louis. Advertised dolls costing 5¢ to $75.00.

Barrett, Mrs. Sara M. 1930. Hollywood, Calif. Owner of *The Doll Shoppe;* made dolls dressed to order.

Barrois, E., and **Barrois, Madame Aimable Ange Lucienne** (née **Desportes**). 1844–77. Paris. Made dolls of all kinds and was one of the earliest manufacturers to use porcelain heads in France. Evidence points to the porcelain dolls' heads marked "E.B." as probably having the Barrois initials, although they did not make the porcelain heads and it is not known whether these heads are from France or Germany. Both dolls' heads of bisque and of china have been found marked "E.B." The bisque heads have had either glass or painted eyes; the china head had painted eyes and painted molded hair. The E.B. bisque heads were also used on autoperipatetikos mechanical bodies and some of the dolls dressed as Boulogne fisherfolk. The E.B. porcelain dolls' heads have been found made by the pressed method. (See Pressed Vers Poured.) E.B. fashion-type dolls with bisque heads were made in at least sizes 3/0 to 7—that is, 23 cm. to 58 cm. (9 to 23 in.) tall.

1848: The inventory of the contents of Madame Barrois' apartment lists: 219 dolls, including numbers 1, 2 and 3; 6,144 dolls' heads; 1,224 varnished dolls' heads; 48 coiffed dolls' heads number 3; 864 dolls' legs; 40 leather legs; a large number of dolls' arms; 144 molds; 36 *carton* dolls' bodies, 144 mechanical dolls' bodies; 1,000 poupards or *Swaddling-clothed Dolls;* a number of *Polichinelles.* Materials for dolls' clothes consisted of 1,000 yards of muslin, 28 yards of jaconas, 22 yards of velvet for dolls' bodices, 90 yards of calico, 110 yards of batiste in various colors, 430 yards of black cotton tulle, 220 yards of white cotton tulle, a quantity of white leather and a quantity of gray paper (the carton dolls and the French papier-mâché dolls were made of gray paper), boxes of flowers and feathers, about 2¼ pounds of pins. Many pins were used in making the carton

and French papier-mâché dolls. Their wigs were pinned on; the shoulder heads were pinned onto the leather bodies, and pins were often used to secure the clothes. These pins were usually the 2-part variety with a separate head and shaft, a type generally found on dolls made prior to 1850.

This inventory was found by Mme. Florence Poisson, conservateur du Musée Roybet Fould, Courbevoie, France. At the Roybet Fould Museum a bisque head doll with bisque arms and a cloth body dressed in an Alsatian costume of about 1871 is marked "Barrois, Paris."

1858: Advertised dolls' heads of composition and of porcelain from French and German factories.

1865: Produced bébés and dolls' heads of composition and of porcelain, as well as other kinds of dolls.

1870s: Supplied dolls or dolls' heads to Benon & Cie., successors of *Munnier* at *Aux Enfants Sages.*★

226. Autoperipatetikos walking doll with a bisque shoulder head having the initials "E B" on its front for "E. Barrois." It has a skin wig, blue glass eyes, closed mouth, pink kid arms.
The body, a cage for the mechanism, has some French printing on it. Original costume. H. 12 in. (30.5 cm.). H. of shoulder head. 3 in. (7.5 cm.). *Coleman Collection.*

227. Bisque shoulder head marked E. B. on the front shoulder for E. Barrois. It has a blond wig, blue glass eyes; closed mouth and a gusset-jointed kid body. Mark: Ill. 230. H. 17 in. (43 cm.). *Courtesy of Iverna and Irving Foote. Photo by Irving Foote.*

228. Bisque head, kid body doll made by E. Barrois. It has a wig, blue glass eyes, pierced ears, closed mouth. The neck swivels on a bisque shoulder plate. Marked E 3/0 B on the front. H. 9½ in. (24 cm.). H. of head and shoulders 2½ in. (6.5 cm.). *Courtesy of Richard Withington and Jim Fernandez. Photo by Barbara Jendrick.*

229. Bisque shoulder head made by E. Barrois. The head is marked "E 3/0 B" along the front shoulder edge. Painted black scallops are at the hairline and probably at one time fancy headwear was replaced by the wig seen in this picture. The large painted eyes have long eyelashes. The mouth is closed. H. of shoulder head 2½ in. (6.5 cm.). *Coleman Collection.*

230   **E 3 B**

231   **E.⁵ DÉPOSÉ B.**

232   **E. 8 DEPOSÉ B.**

230–232. Marks on the shoulders of bisque head E. Barrois dolls. Mark No. 230 is on the doll shown in Ill. 227.

233A, B, & C. Two-faced Bartenstein doll, one face serene and the other face howling. It has a bisque socket head with stationary glass eyes, closed and open-closed mouth, cloth body with composition arms and legs, two strings to activate the voice box. Original chemise. *Courtesy of May Mauer.*

A   B   C

Barry, Bert B., & Associates. 1929–30 and later. Chicago, Ill. Obtained a U.S. trademark, *Pinocchio*, for dolls.

Bartenstein, Fritz. 1879–98. Hüttensteinach, Thür.

1879: Applied for a German patent (D.R.P.) for a dolls' voice. Later he made two-faced dolls.

1887: *Ehrich Bros.* advertised a two-faced doll that cried "Mama-Papa" when its strings were pulled. Ht. 16 in. (40.5 cm.); priced $1.55.★

Barthel Bros. & Warren. 1922. Britain. Listed in English trade journal under Dolls.

Barthélemy. 1929–30 and later. Paris. Made art dolls, including those known as *Marquisette*.

Bartsch, Franz. 1929–30 and later. Jaegerndorf, Czechoslovakia. Manufactured dolls.

Barwig, Franz. 1909. Bohemia. Well-known sculptor in wood; made wooden dolls with painted clothes.

Baseb (Baseball-Player). 1913. Trade name of a jointed felt comic doll made by *Steiff*. It was dressed as a baseball player and had a baseball-type glove. Hts., 50 and 60 cm. (19½ and 23½ in.); priced $6.25 and $7.00 each.

Baseball Catcher. 1914. Trade name of a doll with composition head, hands, and feet on a cork-stuffed cloth body. It wore a baseball suit and had a wire baseball mask over its face. Ht. 15 in. (38 cm.).

DEUTSCHER BARTENSTEIN

U.S.P. N⁰. 243.752

Patented in Deutschland.

234—235. Marks on the bodies of Bartenstein dolls. Mark No. 234 is on the doll in Ill. 233.

Baseball Kid. See **Campbell Kids.**

Baseball-Player. See **Baseb.**

Basia. 1915. Doll promoted by *Mme. Paderewski* for the aid of Polish refugees. It was made in *Mme. Lazarski's* workshop by Polish refugee artists and represented a peasant woman of Posen with long yellow braids.

Basket Baby. 1927. Trade name of a baby doll produced by *Langfelder, Homma & Hayward.* It came in four sizes.

Bass Wood Doll. 1913. A *Bébé Tout en Bois* type doll advertised by *Gamage* as being made of Bass Wood, a "close-grained wood." The doll had a wig and jointed limbs.

It should be noted that *Schoenhut* advertised that their dolls were made of Bass Wood.

236. Bisque head doll in a black challis bathing suit trimmed with red of the 1860s. It has a flange type neck joint on a bisque shoulder plate, a blond wig, molded and painted blue eyes, closed mouth, kid body with bisque lower arms. The bathing cap and shoes are made of oilskin, the latter having a Jumeau mark. H. 18 in. (45.5 cm.). H. of shoulder head 4½ in. (11.5 cm.). *Courtesy of the Margaret Woodbury Strong Museum. Photo by Harry Bickelhaupt.*

Batco Toy & Novelty Co. 1924. Britain. Listed in an English trade journal under Dolls.

Bates, Dewsbury & Co. Ltd. 1918. Hanley, England. Made dolls' heads and limbs including black dolls' heads.

Batger & Co. 1915–22. London. Manufactured dolls with heads, arms, and legs of wax, as well as composition dolls. The wax faces were molded and colored; these dolls had wigs. Dolls' arms and legs were sold separately also.

Bathetzki, A. 1926–30 and later. Köpplesdorf, Thür. Manufactured dolls.

Bathilde. 1926. French trademark for a doll dressed as a French peasant and holding a tray. Trademark applied for by *Mme. Elisa Rassant.*

Bathing Buds. 1917–18. Trade name used by *Effanbee* for dolls with eyes glancing to the side, jointed shoulders, bent arms, with fingers of the left hand in V position, and a rotund body dressed in a one-piece bathing suit. Headgear was a kerchief, in one of several colors. Price was $8.00 a doz. wholesale.

Bathing Doll. 1922. Line of waterproof dolls manufactured by *Wonderland Toymaking Co.*

Bathing Dolls. Several groups of dolls were referred to as "Bathing Dolls." There were dolls dressed in bathing costumes of various types. Naked dolls that could be immersed in water were also called "Bathing Dolls." The German "Badkinder" (Bathing children) usually referred to porcelain *Frozen Charlottes.* Other Bathing dolls were ones that could float such as those made of loofah, sponges and so forth. A few mechanical dolls could actually swim in water.

Among those making, producing and/or distributing Commercial Bathing dolls are those listed below:

1872–89: *Silber & Fleming,* all-bisque or all-china dolls.

1884: *Fiegenbaum.*

1908–10: *Moritz Pappe.*

1910–13 and possibly other years: *Steiff (Daisy, Dora, Ida, Karl, Mabel, Martha,* and *Walter).*

1917 and later: *Dean (Dolly Dips); Morimura (Dolly); Shanklin (Paddlers).*

1917–18: *Butler Bros.*

1918: *Effanbee (Bathing Buds).*

1919: *Colonial (Peachy Pets); Gem* (Bathing Kid).

1920–21: *Beach Knut.*

1922: *Wonderland Toymaking Co.*

1924: *J. Bouton; Eccles.*

1926: *Albert Murphy.*

1927: *Alfred Pensky.*

1928: *Century (Jantzen Bathing Tots).*

1929: *Dr. Paul Hunaeus; Adler Favor and Novelty Co.*

Beginning in the 1870s patterns were given in magazines designed to aid girls in making dolls' clothes at home. Among these magazines were LA POUPÉE MODÈLE (1863–1924). and LA SEMAINE DE SUZETTE (1905–60), both of which included bathing costumes for dolls. (See also **All-Bisque Dolls** and **Gaultier,** Ill. 1009.)

Bathing Girl. 1917–18. Trade name of doll with composition head and hands, molded hair, painted features, and cloth body jointed at the shoulders and hips. Doll wears a black and white checked bathing suit with bloomers under a full skirt, a cap with a colored ribbon, and shoes. This 30-in. (76-cm.) doll was distributed by *Butler Bros.*

Bathing Girls. 1927. Trade name of dolls made by *Alfred Pensky;* they cost $2.75 and up per doz. wholesale.

Bathtub Dolls. 1929. Trade name of dolls advertised by *Adler Favor and Novelty Co.*

Batt, John, & Co. 1883. London. Handled dolls.

237. Mark used by John Batt & Co.

Bätz, August. 1878. Sonneberg, Thür. Made dolls.

Bätz, Berthold. 1928. Sonneberg, Thür. Made dolls. E. Lehman was the firm's British agent.

Bätz, Konstantin. 1913. Sonneberg, Thür. Obtained a German patent (D.R.G.M.) for jointed dolls with movable arms.★

Baudry, Charles Louis. 1917–21. Paris. Obtained French and German patents (D.R.P.) for jointed dolls.

Bauer, Carl. 1911–12. Schwäbisch-Gmünd, Germany. Obtained two German patents (D.R.G.M.) for dolls' clothes.

Bauer & Richter (Rodaer Puppenfabrik). 1922–27. Roda, Thür. Made character babies with bent limbs and toddlers, as well as ball-jointed dolls. These babies and dolls came dressed in a chemise or fully clad. They also made *Mama* dolls, all-porcelain dolls, babies with celluloid heads, and cloth dolls, as well as wardrobes for dolls and supplies for doll hospitals.

1927: They were still advertising Herzkäferchen (Lady Bug)[†], Mein Kleiner Schlingel (My Little Rascal)[†], and Asador[†].★

238. Bauer & Richter's advertisement in DEUTSCHE SPIEL-WAREN ZEITUNG, February, 1927. They advertised ball jointed dolls, character dolls that could sit and also could stand. Their marks were "Herzkäferchen" (Little heart bug or beetle), "Mein Kleiner Schlingel" (My Little Rascal), and "Asador." They had new cloth dolls and babies, Mama dolls, porcelain children, dolls' clothes, celluloid dolls and so forth.

Bauernkinder (Peasant Children). 1914. *Horsman* catalog showed a boy, a girl, and a baby dressed in peasant costumes. These dolls with tanned composition heads allegedly were portraits of real German peasant children; however, the heads for the boy, the girl, and the baby dolls were all identical. The boy and girl dolls came in two sizes. They had molded hair, eyes painted to look straight ahead; the fully jointed body was cloth, stuffed with cork. On the standard-size doll (which appeared to be 14 in. [35.5 cm.]), the composition hands were similar to the early *Campbell Kids* type; the larger dolls had later type hands. The boy wore a short green jacket with brass buttons and cap to match, a loose white shirt, and baggy khaki breeches. The girl doll wore a colored gingham dress with a fancy yoke and hat to match. The baby doll wore a peasant-style knee-length dress and a white lawn cap. Identical dolls were also dressed as a Tyrolean boy and girl. The small-size dolls were $8.50 a doz. wholesale, or retail $1.00 each. The large size dolls were $12.50 doz. wholesale, or retail $2.00 each.

Bauersachs, Emil. 1882–1930 and later. Sonneberg, Thür. In 1910 Victor Roth was the successor. Made and exported dressed dolls, including bisque-head, fully jointed dolls and character dolls.

1890: Advertised ball-jointed dolls.

1910: Member of the Sonneberg group who won a Grand Prize at the Exhibition in Brussels.

World War I: Took over *Butler Bros.* in Sonneberg.

1926: Dolls with clothes distributed by *L. Bremer.*

1927: Manufactured and exported jointed dolls.

1930: Made cloth dolls of various types, including *Boudoir dolls* dressed in pajama-clown suits.★

Bauersachs, Louis. 1850. Philadelphia, Pa. Advertised that he "imported and distributed wax, kid and jointed dolls." The "kid" referred to the doll's body which might have either the early molded-hair papier-mâché head or a china head. The jointed dolls were probably peg wooden dolls.

Bauersachs, Nicol. 1904. Sonneberg, Thür. Obtained a German patent (D.R.G.M.) for a waterproof swimming doll of papier-mâché.

Bauersachs & Henninger. 1878–84. Sonneberg, Thür. 1884–1930 and later. Successor Arthur Schönau. Made dolls.★

Baukastenfabrik. See **Richter, Friedrich, Adolf & Co.**

Baum, Alvin & Co. 1930 and later. New York City. Manufactured outfits for dolls.

Baum, Frank. 1924. Los Angeles, Calif. Registered in U.S. a rectangular trademark with Ⓩ in the center, "OZ//TOYS" on the left "AND//DOLLS" on the right. This trademark was for character dolls, fancy dolls and clown dolls. Frank Baum was the author of the "OZ" books.

Baum, Hugo. See **Effanbee.**

Baumann, Franz, & Brauenschweiger, Alfred. 1915. Würzburg, Germany. Applied for a German patent (D.R.G.M.) for inside joining of dolls' body parts.

Baumann, Victor. 1897–1929. London and Nürnberg. Made dolls.★

Baunton, Elsie R. 1929–30. Seattle, Wash. Designed and made clothes for dolls, especially the *Effanbee* dolls such as *Patsy, Patsy Ann,* and *Skippy.* Her first garment in both time and popularity was a felt cloak. To this 24 numbers were added, including bunny slippers. Mrs. Baunton explained: "You have to copy the children's own clothes. That is why the cretonne overalls, sunsuits, wide-brimmed beach hats, and Kiddie slippers appeal so much to the children. Of course there are romper dresses, coats, etc."

Bautier & Sheller. 1926–27. Sonneberg, Thür. Manufactured dolls.

Bauz. 1911. Name of *Kämmer & Reinhardt's Baby* doll, mold #100.

Bawo & Dotter. 1838–1915. Bavaria and New York City. 1915–30 and later. *Borgfeldt* successor. Made and imported dolls. Company stock and assets were sold for $100,000 in 1915.★

Bayerische Celluloidwarenfabrik. See **Wacker, Albert.**

Bayle, Mlle. Paule. 1918. Paris. Created art dolls.

Bayless Bros. & Co. 1925–30 and later. Louisville, Ky. Made dolls and dolls' heads.

1926: Registered *Honey Child* as a U.S. trademark for dolls.

Bazar de L'Hotel-de-Ville. See **L'Hotel de Ville.**

Bazzoni, Anthony. 1828–78. London. Made wax and composition dolls. Advertised elegantly dressed dolls. According to Henry Mayhew, Bazzoni claimed that he was "the

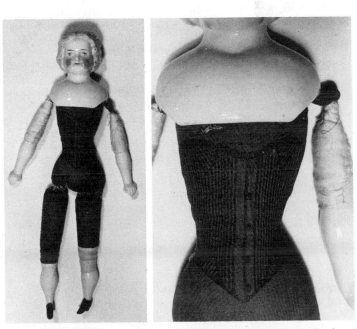

239A & B. China shoulder head bearing the mark of Charles Dotter as shown in Ill. 113 in the first COLLECTOR'S ENCYCLOPEDIA OF DOLLS, except the size no. is 4 instead of 0. This head is on its original body having the printed black stamped corset on the front of the torso. The body is stuffed with sawdust. This example has its original china limbs. H. 16 in. (40.5 cm.). H. of shoulder head 4 in. (10 cm.). *Coleman Collection.*

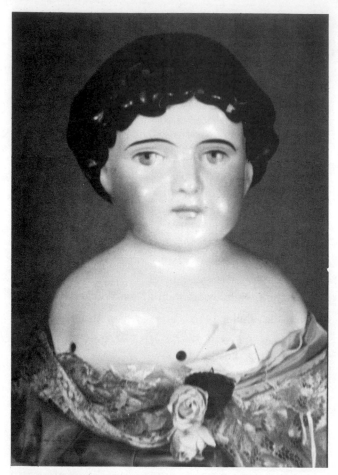

240. China shoulder head doll produced by Bawo & Dotter has molded black hair with curly bangs, molded and painted eyes, and a cloth body. Mark: B & D 10. H. 24 in. (61 cm.). *Courtesy of Richard Withington. Photo by Barbara Jendrick.*

only person who ever made the speaking doll. I make her say 'papa' and 'mama'. . . . I sold one to be sent to St. Petersburg." (Maelzel[†] exhibited a mama-papa doll in 1823.)★

Beach Baby. 1923. Trade name for a *Mama* doll made by *Effanbee.* Hood, apron, and shoes were made of imitation black patent leather; an apron was decorated with the words "Beach Baby" over a picture of a child looking at a sailboat on the water.★

Beach Boy and Beach Girl. 1915. Trade name for barefoot dolls made by *Amberg.* The dolls had sewed lines for toe demarcation; they wore bathing suits and carried a pail and shovel.★

Beach Dolls. 1919. Trade name for dolls made of fibre or wood composition. The dolls represented "alluring girlies," many with veils, and were described as "chic."

Beach Knut. 1920–21. Trade name for a stockinet boy doll made by *Chad Valley.* The doll wore a bathing suit and a beach hat. Ht. 9½ in. (24 cm.).

Beam, Mrs. L. Ca. 1880s and later. Philadelphia. Operated a shop named the French Doll Bazaar.★

Beanie the Clown. 1926. Trade name for a character doll, made by *William P. Beers,* dressed as a clown with a pointed hat. Priced $10.80 a doz. wholesale.

Bear, L., & Son. 1870. New York City. Imported and sold French and German dolls' heads.

Beatrice. 1892. Distributed by *Butler Bros.* It had a bisque head with wig and was dressed. Ht. 22 in. (56 cm.); priced $3.75 doz. wholesale.

Beaudelot (Beaudeloi) 1870s–80s. Paris. Name found on boots belonging to a kid body fashion doll marked "Aux Réves de l'Enfance."[†] Name also found on shoes worn by *Bru* dolls.

Beaufrere, P. 1929–30 and later. Paris. Made dolls.

Beautiful. 1920. Trade name for a composition child doll produced by *Jessie M. Raleigh.* It had a real hair wig with long curls, sleeping eyes, and wore a dress with a high waistline and a skirt made up of three ruffles; also a brimmed hat.

Beauty. 1914. Trade name of a bisque-head doll on a fully jointed composition body. It had a curly wig sleeping eyes and wore a chemise. Four hts. 12, 15, 17, and 22 in. (30.5, 38, 43, and 56 cm.).★

A M Beauty 6/0
Germany

241. Mark found on a Beauty doll.

Beauty. 1928–29. Trade name of a cloth doll in the *Alpha* line of *Farnell,* distributed by *Louis Wolf.*

Beauty. See **Babyland Rag Dolls.**

Beauty Baby. 1926–27. Trade name of an infant *Bye-Lo* type doll produced by *Bing.* The doll wore a long baby dress and carried a tag with the words BING BEAUTY BABY. See Ill. 317.

Beauty Doll Manufacturing Co. (Beauty Doll Co.). 1926–30. New York City. Made *Mama* dolls. Licensed by *Voices, Inc.* to use their mama voices and criers.

Beauty's Daughter. 1884–87. Line of wax dolls distributed by *Lauer.*

1884: Dolls had hair headdresses with bangs, earrings, composition limbs and wore embroidered shirts, cloth stockings and leather boots. Six hts. 13, 16, 20, 23½, 27½ and 32 in. (33, 40.5, 51, 59.5, 70 and 81 cm.); priced $2.25 to $9.75 doz. wholesale.

1887: Dolls had bangs and long hair, wore a chemise and painted footwear. Hts. 16 and 28 in. (40.5 and 71 cm.); priced $1.80 and $5.50 doz. wholesale.

Beaux Art Shade Co. 1924. New York City. Handled *Boudoir* dolls among them one with painted features, dressed in rose colored taffeta, a black satin hat and ruche. Ht. 30 in. (76 cm.).

Beaver. 1923–29. Trade name for one of the down-stuffed cloth *Aerolite* dolls made by *Chad Valley*. Made of printed cloth, it had a flat smiling face, large eyes, a long beard, arms against the body, legs apart; printed clothes. Ht. 11 in. (28 cm.).

Bébé à la Mode. 1923. Trade name for a jointed cloth character doll distributed by *La Place Clichy*. Ht. 17 ½ in. (44.5 cm.).

Bébé Arc-en-Ciel. 1918. Trade name of a bisque-head doll sold by the Paris store *L'Hotel de Ville*. It had sleeping eyes, hair eyelashes, was fully jointed, and wore a silk dress that came in various colors: violet, blue, green, yellow, orange, or red. Doll was 38 cm. (15 in.) tall and sold for $4.20.

Bébé Articulé. Jointed doll. This was also a trademark registered by Friedrich Winkler[†] in 1899.★

Bébé B. H. V. 1921. Trade name of a doll distributed by the Bazar de *L'Hotel de Ville*. The doll had a bisque head, natural hair, sleeping eyes, eyelashes, composition body and wore a chemise trimmed with lace and ribbons. 15 hts. from 29 to 86 cm. (11½ to 34 in.).

Bébé Baiser. See **Kiss-Throwing Bébé**.

Bébé Baptême. 1885–1913 and probably other years. Infant doll either in a long dress or on a pillow. These dolls were sold in Paris stores.

1885: *Louvre* sold a sleeping-eyed Bébé Baptême in a basket with four little boxes containing candy.

1906: *Aux Trois Quartiers* sold a jointed Bébé Baptême wearing long baby clothes trimmed with lace. Five hts. 35, 42, 60, 68 and 78 cm. (14, 16½, 23½, 27 and 30½ in.); priced $1.18 to $5.00.

1910: *Printemps* sold Bébé Baptême with a bisque head, character face, dressed, and held in the pocket of a pillow. Three hts. 33, 42 and 51 cm. (13, 16½ and 20 in.); priced $1.50 to $2.70 each.

1910–11: Advertised by both *Samaritaine* and Aux Trois Quartiers. The doll at the latter store was cloth, ht. 40 cm. (15½ in.). Dressed in a long wool dress, it cost 98¢; in silk, it was $1.58. The Bébé Baptême at Samaritaine had a bisque head portraying an infant with open mouth and teeth; it was fully jointed. The doll came on a pillow in three hts. 35, 42, and 51 cm. (14, 16.5 and 20 in.). These were priced $1.38 to $2.55 but there was also a cheap version for only 88¢. (See also **Bébé Réservé**.)

Bébé Bijou.[†] See **Bébé Tout en Bois**.

Bébé Blanche. Trade name found marked on a box containing a doll with a *Simon & Halbig* mold #1079 bisque socket head on a ball jointed composition body. (See also **Baby Blanche**.)

Bébé Bois. See **Bébé Tout en Bois**.

Bébé Bon Marché. 1894–1925. Trade name for a bisque head, fully jointed, composition body doll made especially for the *Bon Marché* store in Paris. It wore a chemise and footwear. The heights and size numbers were the same as those for the *Bébé Jumeau* in 1894 and there was only a slight variation during the period when it was advertised. Variations in heights can be as much as an inch, especially in the larger versions, without being significant. Bébé Bon Marché was a cheaper doll than the Bébé Jumeau for corresponding types and sizes. (See THE COLLECTOR'S BOOK OF DOLLS' CLOTHES, Ill. 428, which shows the Bébé Bon Marché of 1894.)

BÉBÉ BON MARCHÉ SIZE–HEIGHT RELATIONSHIP (based on the store advertisements)						
Size No.	Height 1894		Height 1903–12 (closed-mouth)		Height 1925	
	cm.	in.	cm.	in.	cm.	in.
1	25	10	26	10½	25	10
2	28	11	28	11	28	11
3	31	12	31	12	31	12
4	35	14	35	14	35	14
5	38	15	37	14½	40	15½
6	41	16	41	16	43	17
7	45	17½	45	17½	46	18
8	49	19½	49	19½	52	20½
9	53	21	53	21	57	22½
10	58	23	58	23	60	23½
11	63	25	63	25	64	25
12	68	27	68	27	69	27

The price of a closed mouth, size number 1, Bébé Bon Marché in the 1894–1912 period was 50¢. A closed mouth Bébé Bon Marché, size number 7, cost $1.65 in the 1894–1903 period and $1.75 in the 1908–12 period; the style with open mouth and teeth, size number 7, cost $2.30 in the 1903–12 period. This was the smallest size open-mouth version in this period. The largest bébé, size number 12, 27 in. (68 cm.), with a closed mouth cost $4.20 in the years between 1894 and 1912. The open-mouth size number 12 cost $5.20 between 1903 and 1906, and $5.00 in the years 1908 to 1912. Thus the open mouth doll always cost more than the closed mouth doll of the same size.

In 1903 the Bébé Bon Marché and Bébé Jumeau were the same height for the same size—numbers 5 through 12. Both dolls were sold by the Bon Marché store.

By 1918 the Bébé Bon Marché seems to have been slightly larger than the Bébé Jumeau for corresponding size numbers, and the Bébé Jumeau prices were considerably higher than the Bébé Bon Marché prices. But they were still advertised as being made by Jumeau in 1921.

Bébé Bon Marché wore chemises that varied in style. The 1894 chemise had bretelles extending from the medium-high waistline over the shoulders; two panels went from the neckline down the front to the lace around the bottom of the skirt. There was lace with ribbon beading around the waistline. By 1904, there was a V-shaped yoke bordered with a lace frill that came down to the high-waisted sash, on which was the name Bébé Bon Marché. The sash tied at the side with long streamers. The sleeves were full; the skirt had box pleats down the front and lace around the bottom. This chemise remained more or less the same, except for variations in the height of the waistline, at least until World War I. In 1925, the chemise had only a small V yoke and a wide collar. The pleat extended down the front. There was no sash, the sleeves were tight, and the skirt was short.

A bébé with the head marked 1907 has been found in a box marked "Bébé de Bon Marché." The size number–height relationships for the dolls marked 1907 were very similar to those shown in the above table, except that a size 15, 78 cm. (30½ in.), has also been reported. Some of these 1907 dolls have been found on Jumeau marked bodies.

243. Bébé Breveté has bisque socket head, shoulder plate, and arms, on a kid body. The head has a skin wig, glass eyes, pierced ears, and a closed mouth. Size 2 marked on shoulder plate. H. 18 in. (45.5 cm.). *Private collection.*

POUPEE

BREVETE

S.G.D.G.

BÉBÉ BREVÉTÉ S.G.D.G.
Tout Contrefacteur sera saisi et poursuivi conformement à la Loi

244A & B. Marks found on Bébé Breveté dolls.

Bébé Breveté. 1870s and later. Name of dolls with bisque head and lower arms on kid bodies. Some of these dolls have a paper label glued on their chest that is identical to the Bru label shown in Ills. 241B and 250 in The first COLLECTOR'S ENCYCLOPEDIA OF DOLLS except for the word Breveté instead of the customary words Bru B^{te}. These Bébés Breveté like the Bébés Bru had molded breasts, a leather band scalloped at the top edge that was placed around the torso just below the breasts. See Ill. 244B. The Breveté's kid body had a seam down the center front of the torso.

An insufficient number of examples has been found as yet to make a valid size-height comparison. ★

242. Bébé Breveté bisque head on a kid body with bisque arms. The socket head has a wig, brown glass eyes, pierced ears, and a closed mouth. The deep bisque shoulder plate is on a gusseted kid body. Original clothes. Head marked 1. H. 16 in. (40.5 cm.). *Courtesy of Sotheby Parke Bernet Inc., N.Y.*

Bébé Bru. After 1872–1954. Line of dolls made by the firm *Bru Jne* until 1899. After 1899 they were made by the *Société Française de Fabrication de Bébés & Jouets* (S.F.B.J.). (See THE COLLECTOR'S BOOK OF DOLLS' CLOTHES, Ills. 319 and 412.)

Bébé Bru dolls were made in sizes at least from number 0 through 16. The table shows the approximate size-height relationship.

The kid-body size-heights are based chiefly on actual dolls, whereas the composition size-heights are those given in the various Paris store catalogs of 1907 to 1912, except for size number 4.

1889–90: Advertised that some of the Bébés Bru had eyelashes.

1894: The *Petit Saint Thomas* catalog advertised a Bru with a composition head, 40 cm. (15½ in.) wearing a chemise and costing $1.50. Bisque-head Brus in this catalog were described as "richly dressed" and came in 46, 54, and 63 cm. (18, 21½, and 25 in.). Prices were $2.00, $2.75, and $4.00. These were less expensive than the *Bébés Jumeau* and some other dolls in the same year. (See **Bébé Caprice.**) (See Ill. 429B in THE COLLECTOR'S BOOK OF DOLLS' CLOTHES.)

1899–1914: Fleischmann, a German, was head of the S.F.B.J. During this period the records present some problems concerning the manufacture of Bru dolls.

1900: The hairdo and chemise on *Bébé Moncey* sold at *La Place Clichy* closely resemble those shown on the Bébés Bru sold in other stores during the 1907–12 period.

1907: The store *Paris Cette* showed their Bébé Bru with hair piled high on the head and falling over the shoulders. The composition-bodied doll came in five sizes (8 to 12) and was priced $1.25 to $3.10 with stationary eyes and $1.35 to $3.30 with sleeping eyes. The distinctive feature about the chemise of the Bébé Bru was that its sash had wide ends that were crossed over and fell down over the front of the skirt. On one of these ends was the label "*Paris Bébé.*" The name "Paris Bébé" was originally the trademark of *Danel & Cie.*

The S.F.B.J. continued the registration of this trademark in the 1900s.

1910: *Modernes,* a store in Paris, advertised the same sizes and type of Bébés Bru as Paris Cette had three years earlier. However, the prices had risen about 20¢ on each doll.

1912: The store *Paris Montpelier* advertised similar Bébés Bru to those offered by other stores since 1907. But, in addition, they had Bébés Bru 76 and 80 cm. (30 and 31½ in.) probably these were sizes 13 and 14. The small Bébés Bru were the same price as in 1910, but the large sizes were considerably more expensive. The 27-in. Bébé Bru cost $4.40 with stationary eyes and $5.00 with sleeping eyes; the 31½-in. Bébé Bru cost $6.40 with stationary eyes and $6.60 with sleeping eyes. But they still cost less than Bébés Jumeau for the corresponding heights.

1952: Bébé Bru dolls were still being produced and marked "Bru Jne." These had bisque heads allegedly made from original molds, glass eyes, open mouth, and jointed composition bodies, some with mama-papa voices. They came

	Kid Bodies		Composition Bodies			
			Heights from available catalogs			
Size No.	Height		1907–12		1952	
	cm.	in.	cm.	in.	cm.	in.
0	28	11				
1						
2	33	13				
3	36	14				
4	39	15½	33	13		
5	43	17				
6	46	18				
7	51	20				
8	54	21½	52	20½		
9	56	22	58	23	46	18
10	63	25	60	23½	51	20
11			65	25½		
12			69	27		
13			76	30		
14	89	35	80	31½		
15			85	33½		

Table title: APPROXIMATE BÉBÉ BRU SIZE–HEIGHT RELATIONSHIPS

dressed and wore single-strap slippers. An advertisement listed $75.00 as the price of the 18-in. Bru, and said that "all dolls are marked." The 1952 Bébés Bru were several inches shorter than their earlier counterparts marked with the same size numbers. This suggests that either they were put on shorter bodies as the years progressed, and there is some evidence of this, or the 1952 Bébés Bru were reproductions. ★

245. Bébé Bru with bisque socket head and a shoulder plate. It has a blond wig, brown glass eyes, pierced ears, closed mouth and a kid body with bisque arms and lower wooden legs. The dress is contemporary with the doll. Marked "Bru Jne 5." H. 16 in. (40.5 cm.). The body appears to have settled and probably it was a little taller originally. *Courtesy of Sotheby Parke Bernet Inc., N.Y.*

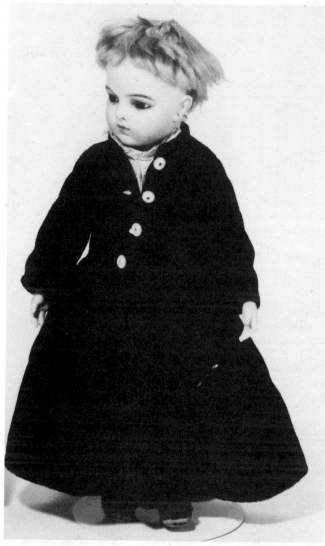

246. Bébé Bru with bisque socket head on a bisque shoulder plate. It has a blond wig, brown glass eyes, pierced ears, closed mouth and a kid body with bisque arms and composition legs. Mark: Bru Jne. 2. H. 13 in. (33 cm.). *Courtesy of Sotheby Parke Bernet Inc., N.Y.*

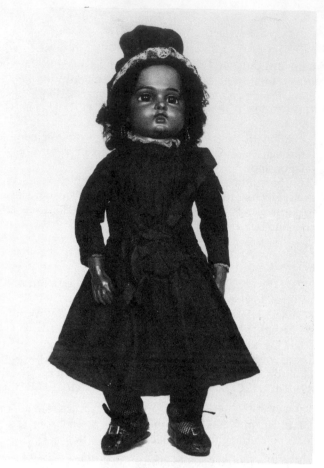

247A & B. Brown bisque circle dot Bébé Bru has a curly black wig, brown glass eyes, pierced ears, open-closed mouth. The white kid body has a brown bisque shoulder plate and lower arms. Original red silk costume including stockings. One of the brown slippers has "N. P." on its sole. H. 17 in. (43 cm.). *Courtesy of the Margaret Woodbury Strong Museum. Photo by Harry Bickelhaupt.*

Bébé Camerose. 1931. Trade name for a bisque-head, composition-body doll made by *Kämmer & Reinhardt*. This doll was sold exclusively in Paris.

Bébé Caprice. 1894. Trade name for a fully jointed doll dressed in satin and sold by *Petit Saint Thomas*. Ht. 46 cm. (18 in.); priced $2.75. (See Ill. 429B in THE COLLECTOR'S BOOK OF DOLLS' CLOTHES.)

Bébé Charmant. 1892–1913. Trade name used by *Pintel & Godchaux* until 1899, and thereafter by the *Société Française de Fabrication de Bébés & Jouets* (S.F.B.J.). A doll wearing a lace-trimmed chemise had, at its low waistline, a cloth label that bore the name "Bébé Charmant" in blue on a white ground. The style of the chemise suggested that the

248. Bisque socket head Bébé Bru with a blond wig, blue glass eyes, pierced ears, closed mouth, on a ball jointed composition and wood body having jointed wrists. Mark: "Bru Jne R 11." H. 24 in. (61 cm.). *Courtesy of Sotheby Parke Bernet Inc., N.Y.*

BÉBÉ BRU BTE.

S.G.D.G.

249. Mark found on some Bébé Bru dolls.

doll was made after 1900 by the S.F.B.J. The doll had a bisque head marked "E. 6 D.," stationary glass eyes, wig, and closed mouth. The poor-quality composition body was jointed at the neck, shoulders, and diagonally at the hips. The neck joint consisted of a metal ring with elastic through it. This 16-in. (40.5-cm.) E. 6 D. doll fits the size–height pattern for *Bébé Jumeau* 1894–1913. Another doll with a bisque head, closed mouth, on a five-piece composition body wore a coarse, starched cotton chemise with a blue flower print and the words "BEBE CHARMANT/Déposé Française" stamped in purple on the chemise. The head of this doll was marked "A//P. 2 G." The P. G. of course were the initials for Pintel and Godchaux and the 2 was the size number which went with a 27 cm. (10½ in.) height. The question arises whether the E. D. head was original to the other Bébé Charmant, whether the chemise was original to this doll; or whether it was a later doll made after Pintel & Godchaux joined the S.F.B.J.

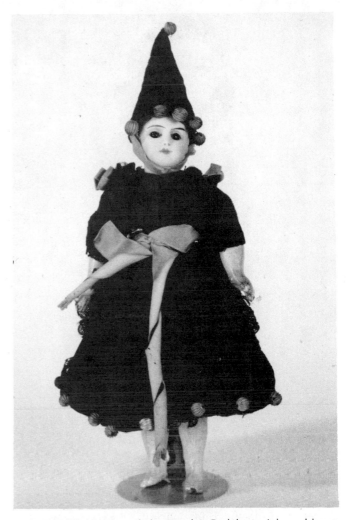

250. Bébé Charmant made by Pintel & Godchaux. It has a bisque head and a five-piece composition body. Original maroon colored dress decorated with gold colored balls over a printed white cotton chemise with a floral print. Mark on head: Ill. 2110. Mark on chemise: Ill. 252. *Courtesy of Annemarie Löhr. Photo by Jürgen Cieslik.*

1904: The *Louvre* store advertised jointed dressed Bébé Charmant in hts. 34 and 40 cm. (13.5 and 15.5 in.) for 58¢ and $1.10.

1912: The Louvre store advertised a pair of walking Bébés Charmant dressed as schoolgirl and schoolboy. They were 39 cm. (15½ in.) high; priced $1.58. These were also referred to as *Bébé Réservé*.

Bébé Charmant. 1928. Trade name of a doll made by *Presles Frères.*

Bébé Chiffon. 1919. Advertised by *Aux Trois Quartiers* as an unbreakable doll, ht. 35 cm. (14 in.); priced $5.40.

Bébé Colosse. 1898–99. Trade name of a doll made by *A. Benoit Gobert.* 1899 and later, this doll was made by the *Société Française de Fabrication de Bébés & Jouets* (S.F.B.J.).

Bébé Cosmopolite. 1895–1910. Trademark used by *Heinrich Handwerck* for dolls. Sometimes used for the LADIES' HOME JOURNAL's doll named *Daisy.* ★

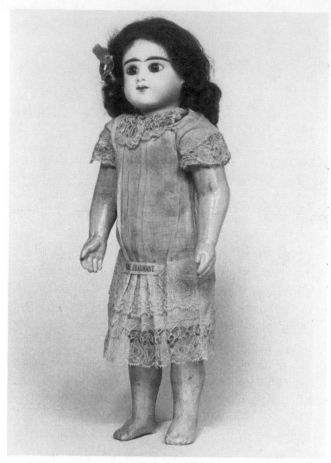

251A & B. Bisque head Bébé Charmant with a brown wig, stationary blue glass eyes, pierced ears and a five-piece composition body. Commercial chemise with the mark shown in Ill. 253 on its belt. The head is marked E 6 D. possibly for E. Denamur or Danel. H. 16 in. (40.5 cm.). *Courtesy of the Margaret Woodbury Strong Museum. Photo by Harry Bickelhaupt.*

BÉBÉ CHARMANT

252–253. Bébé Charmant marks. The mark in Ill. No. 2110 is on the bisque head of a Bébé Charmant. The P. G. stands for Pintel & Godchaux. Mark No. 252 is stamped on the chemise under the dress of the doll in Ill. 250. No. 253 is on the belt of the chemise of the doll shown in Ill. 251.

Bébé Criant. 1911. *Printemps* advertised a bisque-head character baby with this name. It had jointed arms and wore a chemise. Ht. 19 and 23 cm. (7½ and 9 in.). The prices were 29¢ and 39¢.

Bébé Culotte. 1896–1923. Trade name for a bébé wearing a buttoned diaper, leading strings and usually a baby cap. These dolls were sold in most of the leading Paris stores; they had either composition or bisque heads.

1896: *Printemps'* Bébé Culotte was 40 cm. (15½ in.) high and sold for $1.20 with a walker.

1900: *La Place Clichy*'s Bébés Culotte made of carton were priced at 98¢ and $1.40.

Ca. 1900–14: Walking doll named *L'Intrépide Bébé* made by *Roullet & Decamps* was dressed as a Bébé Culotte. It generally had a bisque head made by *Simon & Halbig*, was a small size, and the doll was unable to sit down according to Anne-Marie and Jacques Porot.

1903: *Bon Marché*'s Bébé Culotte had a composition head with open mouth and teeth, a jointed body, and wore a flannel and embroidered piqué outfit. The 35 cm. (14 in.) size cost 78¢ and the 44 cm. (17½ in.) size cost $1.40. At the Magasin (store) de La Ville de Paris these dolls were 37 cm. (14½ in.); priced 59¢.

1904: The *Louvre* store advertised walking composition Bébés Culotte with open mouths, ht. 48 cm. (19 in.); price $1.35.

1905: *Aux Trois Quartiers* had a key-wind walking Bébé Culotte, ht. 35 cm. (14 in.); price $1.58.

1906: The Bébé Culotte at the Louvre store was composition, had an open mouth, and wore a straw baby's helmet. It was 49 cm. (19½ in.) and cost $1.55.

1908–10: *L'Hotel de Ville*'s Bébé Culotte had a composition head. The 32-cm. (12½ in.) size sold for 60¢; the 41-cm. (16-in.) size sold for $1.00.

1909: By this year, the Louvre carried a large stock of these dolls. They advertised them with composition heads. Ht. 33 and 43 cm. (13 and 17 in.); priced 59¢ and 99¢. The bisque-head versions came in hts. 35 and 44 cm. (14 and 17½ in.); priced 78¢ and $1.18. If the bisque heads had sleeping eyes and eyelashes, the prices were 98¢ and $1.55.

Samaritaine advertised unbreakable Bébés Culotte dressed in flannel. Hts. 38 and 45 cm. (15 and 17.5 in.); priced 75¢ and 95¢.

1910: Some stores began to call this type of doll *Bébé Promenette*. The Louvre advertised composition-head dolls with removable clothes. Hts. 33 and 42 cm. (13 and 16½ in.) priced 59¢ and 99¢.

Printemps' Bébés Culotte had bisque character heads. They were 36 and 41 cm. (14 and 16 in.); priced 98¢ and $1.38.

1911: Aux Trois Quartiers' Bébé Culotte with key wind mechanism was 35 cm. (14 in.), and cost $1.70.

1913: The Louvre's Bébé Culotte had a composition head, short hair and no cap. The body was jointed. The doll wore a bib, and there was a single leading string whereas before the doll had been shown with a leading string attached to each shoulder. They came in hts. 33 and 42 cm. (13 and 16½ in.); priced 78¢ and $1.18. The dolls at La Place Clichy were the same price but a little taller: 34 and 45 cm. (13½ and 17½ in.).

1914: Same doll at La Place Clichy as in 1913. Samaritaine's Bébé Culotte was 34 and 43 cm. (13½ and 17 in.); priced 78¢ and $1.18. The *Ville de St. Denis* advertised as a "Poupard promenette" a carton doll dressed like Bébé Culotte.

1923: The dolls at La Place Clichy were smaller, 27 cm. (10½ in.) and 35 cm. (14 in.), but the prices were much higher. (See also **Bébé Promenette** and **Bébé Maillot**.)

Bébé de Paris. 1890–99. Trade name of a doll with a bisque head and fully jointed composition body made by *Rabery & Delphieu*. The chief distributor seems to have been *Petit Saint Thomas.* Beginning in 1899 and possibly later this doll was made by the *Société Francaise de Fabrication de Bébés & Jouets* (S.F.B.J.).

1890–91: Bébé de Paris came in the following hts:

BÉBÉ DE PARIS SIZE–HEIGHT RELATIONSHIP, 1890–91		
Size No.	Height cm.	in.
5/0	28	11
4/0	31	12
3/0	34	13½
2/0	36	14
1/0	40	15½
0	45	17½
1	50	19½
2	57	22½
3	65	25½
4	73	29
5	80	31½

The smallest doll cost 75¢ in a chemise and $1.70 in a silk dress; the largest size cost $9.80 in a chemise. The chemise had a decorated square yoke and a sash with a large bow in front. Lace decorated the bottom of the skirt. The silk dresses came in a variety of styles and had matching hats.

1894: Petit Saint Thomas advertised Bébés de Paris dressed in silk chemises. Five hts.: 43, 47, 53, 58, and 64 cm. (17, 18½, 21, 23, and 25 in.). Prices ranged from $1.75 to $4.00. (See Ill. 429B in THE COLLECTOR'S BOOK OF DOLLS' CLOTHES.)★

Bébé de Réclame. 1898–1902 and possibly later. Trademark registered in Germany by *Heinrich Handwerck* in 1898.

The period of use of this trademark name is not known. Handwerck died in 1902 and his business was taken over by *Kämmer & Reinhardt.* Logically Kämmer & Reinhardt would have received the rights to this trademark.

A bisque head doll with a mohair wig, sleeping eyes, open mouth and on a composition and wood ball-jointed body with jointed wrists, wearing a chemise and footwear, has been found in a box marked "HANDWERCK'S//BÉBÉ DE RÉCLAME." Ht. 61 cm. (24 in.). (See also **Bébé Réclame**.)

Bébé Diamant (Bébé Diamond). 1931. Trademark registered in Germany by *Karl Dehler* for dolls and baby dolls.

Bébé Directoire. 1894. Trade name for a composition-head doll with sleeping eyes and teeth, wearing a satin dress. It was sold at *Petit Saint Thomas.* Ht. 30 cm. (12 in.); priced $1.00. (See Ill. 429A in THE COLLECTOR'S BOOK OF DOLLS' CLOTHES.)

Bébé Disant. Talking doll. See also **Bébé Parlant**.

Bébé Dormeur. 1896–1912. Trade name for a doll with sleeping eyes made by *Bouchet.*

1901–02: *Samaritaine* advertised Bébé Dormeur as having a bisque head with open mouth, composition body, and wearing a silk dress and picture hat. It came in three hts. 56, 60 and 66 cm. (22, 23½ and 26 in.); priced at $1.58 to $2.70.

1903: The store, *La Ville de Paris,* had semi-articulated Bébés Dormeur with wigs, dressed in a chemise, in 7 hts., one for each inch: 7 to 12 in. (18 to 30.5 cm.), plus a 14-inch (35.5-cm.) doll. These were priced 29¢ to 78¢.

1905: *La Place Clichy* advertised dressed Bébés Dormeur. Five hts., 35, 40, 45, 49, and 52 cm. (14, 15½, 17½, 19½ and 20½ in.), priced 90¢ to $1.78.

1911: The dolls at La Place Clichy had teeth and wore silk and lace dresses. Five hts. 27, 29, 33, 35, and 41 cm. (10½, 11½, 13, 14, and 16 in.); priced 39¢ to $1.18.

Samaritaine's Bébés Dormeur with bisque heads were fully articulated and wore silk dresses. They came in four hts.: 38, 41, 44 and 49 cm. (15, 16, 17½ and 19½ in.); priced 95¢ to $1.55.

1912: La Place Clichy sold 3 kinds of Bébés Dormeur. One was undressed, one was in an elaborate dress, and the third style had teeth. The undressed version came in five hts. 30, 33, 35, 39 and 44 cm. (12, 13, 14, 15½, and 17½ in.); priced 29¢ to $1.18.

Bébé Drapeau. 1918. Trade name of fully jointed dolls with sleeping eyes, sold by *L'Hotel de Ville*. These dolls wore silk dresses representing the flags of one of the following countries: France, England, America, Italy, Belgium, Romania, Russia, and Serbia (all allies in the First World War). They were 32 cm. (12½ in.) high and cost $1.95.

Bébé du Bon Marché. See **Bébé Bon Marché.**

Bébé du Louvre. See **Louvre Bébé.**

Bébé Elite. 1900–22. Trademark of *Max Handwerck* for a doll with a bisque head and fully jointed composition body. Advertised this doll as an original model; the trademark was "Marque de Fabrique//Handwerck//Bébé Elite."

Max Handwerck owned the molds but the *Goebel* Porzellanfabrik actually made the socket and shoulder heads. Socket heads had painted hair and eyes; or wig, sleeping eyes, and open mouth with teeth.★

254. Bébé Elite mark on bisque head dolls made by Max Handwerck.

Bébé Esquimaux. See **Eskimo Dolls.**

Bébé Français. 1891–1941. Trademark used by *Danel & Cie., Jumeau,* and *Société Française de Fabrication de Bébés & Jouets,* for dolls that were sold dressed or undressed. The initials B.F. were found on a doll in a box marked Bébé Français.★

Bébé Fruits. 1918. Trade name of dolls with bisque heads, sleeping eyes, and hair eyelashes; fully jointed composition bodies. Their print dresses depicted various fruits, such as oranges, pears, cherries, strawberries, and gooseberries. They were 38 cm. (15 in.) tall. Price $4.00 each. These dolls were sold at the *L'Hotel de Ville*.

Bébé Géant. 1889–99. Trade name for a doll made by *Bouchet*. 1899 and later doll made by *Société Française de Fabrication de Bébés & Jouets*.★

Bébé Gesland. 1860–1924. Trade name for dolls produced by the *Gesland* family and their successors. The bisque heads were made elsewhere and generally had wigs with flowing hair. After 1878, the joints were made of metal instead of rubber so that the doll could sit, kneel, or be dressed easily. The bisque head dolls came in 13 hts. 25, 29, 32, 35, 38, 42, 47, 52, 57, 62, 67, 73 and 78 cm. (10, 11½, 12½, 14, 15, 16½, 18½, 20½, 22½, 24½, 26½, 29 and 30½ in.). Prices for undressed dolls were 90¢ to $5.10; dressed $1.80 to $10.00.★

255. Bébé Français bisque head doll made by E. Danel or Jumeau and later by the S.F.B.J. This doll has a wig, stationary glass eyes, pierced ears, closed mouth and a ball jointed composition body, the wrists are not jointed. Mark III. 257. H. 16 in. (40.5 cm.). *Courtesy of Cherry Bou. Photo by Cherry Bou.*

Bébé Gigoteur. 1862. Name of a mama-papa talking doll patented by *Jules Steiner* according to M. Theimer.

Bébé Gourmand. 1912–13. Trade name for a celluloid doll with a bent-limb baby body, which came with a bottle. It won a gold medal at the Concours Lépine. The *Lafayette* store catalog listed 8 hts. 18, 20, 22, 24, 27, 30, 36 and 60 cm. (7, 8, 8½, 9½, 10½, 12, 14, and 23½ in.); priced 45¢ to $4.40. The 14 inch size was $1.40.★

Bébé Habillé. 1903. Dressed doll. It also seems to have been the trade name of a cloth doll advertised by the store *La Ville de Paris* in 1903. This doll was 30 cm. (12 in.) tall; priced 39¢.

Bébé Incassable. See **Au Bébé Incassable.**

Bébé Jumeau. Ca. 1840–99, line of dolls made by the *Jumeau* family; 1899–1956, line of dolls made by the *Société Française de Fabrication de Bébés & Jouets* (S.F.B.J.). The finest and most popular Bébés Jumeau were made from about 1876 to World War I. These dolls had bisque heads, many of them designed by *Carrier-Belleuse,* on ball-jointed composition bodies. The bisque heads were made at the Jumeau factory in Montreuil-sous-Bois near Paris until 1899, when Fleischmann of *Fleischmann & Bloedel* became head of the firm. 1899–1914. Some of the heads could have also been made in Germany, but using the original Jumeau molds. During World War I and afterward, the Bébés Jumeau were probably all made in France. The Bébé Jumeau heads carry various marks, among them "E. J.," "Tête Jumeau//Bte S.G.D.G.," "Bébé Jumeau," "Jumeau," and others. The "Tête Jumeau" mark is found most often. The heads marked "E. J." are generally pressed; the Tête Jumeau heads are generally poured. According to contemporary reports, probably by Emile Jumeau, the Bébé Jumeau heads were still being pressed as late as 1888, but by 1892 they had

256. Bisque head Bébé Français with a blond mohair wig, stationary blue glass eyes, pierced ears, closed mouth, and a fully jointed composition body. Original clothes and original box. The top part of the paper label has a banner and the 1878 date is still visible which suggests that this doll probably dates from the Jumeau or S.F.B.J. period after Danel lost his court case. Below BÉBÉ FRANÇAIS is FABRICATION//PARISIENNE EXTRA 2. The 2 is in a circle. H. 11½ in. (29 cm.). *Courtesy of Richard Wright. Photo by A. Jackson.*

B G.F

257. Bébé Français mark used on bisque socket heads.

begun to pour the heads. (See discussion of *Pressed versus Poured.*) Bébés Jumeau were made in 16 sizes, and the heads were usually marked with the appropriate size number. The relationship between the size number and the actual height varied slightly. This could have been caused by variations in the body from period to period or simply variations in measurement by the reporting stores. A measuring variation of as much as an inch is frequently found, attributable to wigs, composition body, stringing, and so on. Variations of more than an inch could be indicative of the date of the doll.

If a doll is 15 percent or more shorter than the table indicates, either it probably is a reproduction or the head is on the wrong body.

(See THE COLLECTOR'S BOOK OF DOLLS' CLOTHES for illustrations of Bébé Jumeau that appeared in French store catalogs for the following years: 1887, Ill. 327; 1894, Ills. 428A and 429B; 1902, Ills. 529 and 531; 1911, Ill. 628; 1912, Ills. 629 and 630; 1913, Ills. 639 and 640; 1924, Ill. 656A.)

An unmarked, except for the size number, bisque head with a definitely haunting face, sometimes called a "Long Face" in America and England and called "Bébé Triste" (Sad Baby) in France, always is on a body marked "Jumeau," provided the body is original. In a few instances a shop label on top of the Jumeau mark obliterates it. These dolls are much sought after by present-day collectors, and an examination of over a dozen examples shows the following approximate size–height relationship:

SO-CALLED LONG-FACE JUMEAU SIZE–HEIGHT RELATIONSHIP (based on a small sample)		
Size No.	Height Centimeters	Inches
9	51	20
10	56	22
11	61	24
12	66	26
13	71	28
14	76	30
15	81	32

In 1887 *Wanamaker* of New York and Philadelphia handled Bébés Jumeau dressed in chemises, 11 to 27 in. (28 to 68.5 cm.), and fully dressed dolls 12½ to 29½ in. (31.5 to 75 cm.) tall. The height differences may have been caused by the inclusion of headwear. An 11 in. (28 cm.) doll in chemise cost $2.00; a 12½ in. (31.5 cm.) dressed doll cost $6.00. The 22 in. (56 cm.) doll in chemise cost $6.00 and the 22½ in. (57 cm.) dressed doll cost $16.00. The largest size in chemise 27 in. (68.5 cm.) cost $14.00 while the largest dressed doll 29½ in. (75 cm.) cost $22.00. Wanamaker sold Bébés Jumeau as late as 1896 but did not advertise them in 1902 according to records found so far.

What appeared to be early Jumeau bébés, with only the size number on the head and marked Jumeau bodies, had pressed heads, almond shaped paperweight eyes and eight separate balls for body joints. Their size-height relationship is shown in the 1884–85 column of the accompanying table. One of these early Jumeaus wore a chemise similar in style to that shown on a Bébé Jumeau in the 1884–85 *Bon Marché* catalog.

Another Bébé Jumeau with a pressed head marked "DE-POSÉ//E 3 J." had the ball joints attached to the limbs. This doll wore a chemise similar to that shown in an illustration in LA NATURE, 1888. This doll also wore a maroon colored glass bead necklace that included a brass circle stamped with a "J." The silk ribbon trim on the chemise was also maroon while the ribbon on the chemise of this doll's twin was a light pink. The size-height relationship corresponded with the 1887–89 column in the table.

A Bébé Jumeau with an all-wood ball-jointed body had "DEPOSÉ//E 7 J." incised on its head and "JUMEAU//MEDAILLE d'OR//PARIS" incised on the back of the wooden body. The height 44 cm. (17½ in.) fitted the size-height relationship in the 1887–1924 period.

Practically all of the major Paris stores carried Bébés Jumeau, and the following table is based on the advertisements of these stores as found in their Christmas catalogs. The heights in the 1890–91 period were 1 cm. less than in 1894 for numbers 4 through 12. From 1890 to 1913, the heights were the same for numbers 1 through 3.

The pressed-poured test is the most accurate method of estimating the approximate date of a Bébé Jumeau, but it is not always feasible to remove the wig and investigate the inside of the head in which case the size number-height relationship provides a clue as to whether the doll is early or late. Obviously, most of the Bébés Jumeau have poured heads and their size numbers will correspond with the 1894 to 1924 columns.

The Bébés Jumeau were usually sold dressed in a chemise and the other clothes sold separately. Most of the Paris stores sold dolls' clothes to fit the various-sized Bébés Jumeau, and many other doll manufacturers produced dolls in similar sizes to fit these clothes, which thus became standard sizes.

Many different types of chemises have been found

BÉBÉ JUMEAU SIZE–HEIGHT RELATIONSHIP (based on store catalogs)															
Size No.	1884–85 Bon Marché		1885–86 Bon Marché		1887–89 Louvre		Bon Marché		1890–91 Petite St. Thomas		1894–1913 Various Paris Stores		1916–24 Various Paris Stores			
	cm.	in.	cm.	in.	cm.	.in.	cm.	in.	cm.	in.	cm.	in.	cm.	in.		
1	25	10	23	9	22	8½	23	9	25	10	25	10				
2	26	10¼	25	10	25	10	26	10¼	28	11	28	11				
3	27	10½	29	11½	28	11	31	12	31	13	31	12				
4	31	12	32	12½	32	12½	34	13½	34	13½	35	14				
5	34	13½	35	14	35	14	37	14½	37	14½	38	15	36	14		
6	36	14	37	14½	38	15	40	15½	40	15½	41	16	41	16		
7	40	15½	42	16½	42	16½	44	17½	44	17½	45	17½	44	17½		
8	45	17½	47	18½	47	18½	48	19	48	19	49	19½	49	19½		
9	50	19½	50	19½	50	19½	52	20½	52	20½	53	21	53	21		
10	55	21½	56	22	55	21½	57	22½	57	22½	58	23	57	22½		
11	58	23	69	23½	60	23½	62	24½	62	24½	63	25	62	24½		
12	62	24½	65	25½	65	25½	67	26½	67	26½	68	27	67	26½		
13											72	28½				
14											76	30				
15											81	32				
16											85	33½				

Most of the variations in heights can be attributed to differences in measuring techniques but there was a tendency for dolls of the same size number to be taller in the later years before World War I.

shown on Bébés Jumeau until about 1894. There appear to have been new style chemises almost every year and there was some variation in the styles in the same year as advertised by different stores. The earliest one very plain, was found as late as 1885. By 1887 there was another, more elaborate type with a low waistline. (See Ill. 327 in THE COLLECTOR'S BOOK OF DOLLS' CLOTHES.) The 1888 chemise had a square neckline that appeared to be edged with braid. There were two panels of braid down the front to the low waistline which was shown by a circular band of braid. Another band of braid encircled the hemline and lace trimmed the skirt around the bottom. The short sleeves ended in a band of braid. Some of the chemises had the two panels of braid extending to the hemline and some of the skirts did not have the lace edging. The 1890 chemise had a pointed yoke, two box pleats down the front, and elbow-length sleeves. There were two rows of lace around the bottom. By 1894, the store advertisements showed the familiar chemise with a blue or pink rosebud print that is now often mistakenly called a dress. This same type of printed fabric was used for many decades with only slight variations in style such as the length of the skirt and the amount of pleating. In 1890, the Bébés Jumeau dressed in satin wore Jumeau armbands. Seldom in other years were Bébés Jumeau in advertisements shown dressed.

The mama-papa talking Jumeaus were made at least as late as 1924. At first some came with closed mouths and later only with open mouths; but open-mouth Jumeaus are not necessarily later than the closed-mouth ones. The closed-mouth Bébés Jumeau are recorded as late with and without jointed wrists. Around 1912, when the German influence was strong, Bébés Jumeau began to have their fingernails outlined with paint.

1884: Bon Marché sold Bébés Jumeau with unjointed wrists, ht. 25 cm. (10 in.) in a plain chemise for 58¢ and dressed in a woolen costume for $1.78. The 62 cm. (24½ in.) size sold for $5.00 in a chemise and $11.80 dressed in a wool costume.

1885: Armbands appear to have first been shown on Bébés Jumeau in some of the Paris store catalogs.

1886: A Jumeau advertising card described a Bébé Jumeau as "il est paraphé, marqué; il a son nom sur le corps et quand il est habillé, sur le bras gauche." ("It is initialed, marked; it has its name on the body and when it is dressed, on the left arm.")

1890: Advertisement for Bébés Jumeau listed a 34 cm. (13½ in.) doll as costing $1.30 in a chemise, $2.30 in a wool costume, and $3.90 in a silk dress. A documented source states that Little Alice Smith of Malmesbury, England, received a Tête Jumeau doll in November, 1890. This doll was marked "DEPOSÉ//TETE JUMEAU//B^te S.G.D.G."

1892: *Marshall Field* distributed Bébé Jumeau dolls in rose or blue chemises which had a square yoke, low neckline, sash tied in front, a band around the bottom of the full skirt, and short sleeves. Came in eight size numbers, namely 1 to 8. Priced $18.00 to $54.00 a doz. wholesale.

1893: "French Jumeau Dressed Dolls" were advertised by *Horsman;* priced $5.00 to $25.00 each.

1894: *Petit Saint Thomas* offered Bébés Jumeau both in chemise and dressed in "rich costumes"; the dressed dolls cost about three times as much as the dolls in chemise.

1896: The *Louvre* store advertised closed-mouth Bébés Jumeau 45 cm. (17½ in.) tall for $2.10, but a 45 cm. (17½ in.) open-mouth Bébé Jumeau cost $2.70. The 68 cm. (27-in.) closed-mouth Bébés Jumeau sold for $5.40, and the 68 cm. (27-in.) open-mouth Bébé Jumeau sold for $6.40.

1903: The Bon Marché sold 45 cm. (17½-in.) Bébés Jumeau with closed mouths for $2.30 and for $2.70 with open mouths and sleeping eyes. The 68 cm. (27-in.) Bébés Jumeau were $5.40 for the closed-mouth ones and $6.40 for those with open mouth and sleeping eyes.

1904: *R. H. Macy* sold Bébés Jumeau with real hair eyelashes, and dressed in silk, size 27 in. (68 cm.), for $36.63.

1908–10: *L'Hotel de Ville* sold Bébés Jumeau dressed in chemises, with closed mouth, 45 cm. (17½-in.) size, for $2.20; size 45 cm. (17½ in.), with open mouth and sleeping eyes, $2.90. The largest size, 68 cm. (27 in.), cost $5.80 with a closed mouth and $6.80 with an open mouth and sleeping eyes.

1910: Bébé Jumeau advertised by *Ville de St. Denis* store had natural hair, open mouth with teeth and was fully jointed. It came in eight size numbers, namely 5 to 12; priced $1.58 to $5.80. The "parlant" (talking) bébés with sleeping eyes came in all of the same sizes except for 5 and 6. These dolls cost $2.90 to $6.80.

1912–13: Bébé Jumeau as advertised in the *Lafayette* catalog wore a chemise or came dressed. It had sleeping eyes, eyelashes; the nails were outlined with paint. Hts. 58 cm. (23 in.) and less were "Muet" (silent); those 63 cm. (25 in.) and over were "Parlant."

1913: *Gamage* advertised Bébé Jumeau with bisque head, wig, sleeping eyes, hair eyelashes, ball jointed body, "entirely of wood," a talking Mama-Papa doll, with a flowered chemise and footwear. Six hts. 18, 19½, 21, 23, 27 and 28½ in. (45.5, 49.5, 53.5, 68.5, and 72.5 cm.); priced $4.94 to $10.50. It seems doubtful that the body was "entirely of wood," probably the arms and legs were wood but the torso, hands and feet would have been of a composition, possibly made of wood flour.

1913–14: *Samaritaine* advertised Bébé Jumeau with natural hair, sleeping eyes, hair eyelashes and fully jointed in nine size numbers 5 to 13; priced $1.98 to $8.00. The parlant Bébé Jumeau came in the same sizes but omitted 5 and 6 and cost $3.30 to $9.00.

1915–16: The Louvre catalog showed fully jointed Bébés Jumeau with sleeping eyes and hair eyelashes and wearing a chemise; 44 cm. (17½ in.) high; $3.20 without and $3.80 with "Parlant." The corresponding (67 cm.) 26½ in. size was $8.00 and $9.00.

1923–24: Louvre catalog listed fully jointed Bébés Jumeau with sleeping eyes, hair eyelashes; dressed. ★

BÉBÉS NUS (Jumeau).
tête biscuit, entièrement articulés,
perruque flottante.

Nos		Hauteur	
1.	—	0m25 cent.	2.90
2.	—	0m26	3.75
3.	—	0m27	4.75
4.	—	0m31	5.75
5.	—	0m34	7.50
6.	—	0m36	8.50
7.	—	0m40	10.50
8.	—	0m45	11.50
9.	—	0m50	14.50
10.	—	0m55	17.50
11.	—	0m58	22.50
12.	—	0m62	25 »

BÉBÉS (Jumeau), costumes laine, garnis satin.
très élégants.

No	Haut.		No	Haut.	
1.	0m25,	8.90	6.	0m36,	23 »
2.	0m26,	11.50	8.	0m45,	29 »
4.	0m31,	16.50	10.	0m55,	43 »
5.	0m34,	19.50	12.	0m62,	59 »

258. Advertisement for a Bébé Jumeau and other dolls in the 1884/85 Bon Marché catalog. The Bébé Jumeau in chemise did not have footwear; it was advertised as being fully jointed but the drawing suggests that there were no wrist joints. The dressed Bébé Jumeau wore a wool costume trimmed with satin, and it was more than double the price of the same size bébé in a chemise. In fact in the smaller size the dressed Bébé Jumeau was over three times the price of the bébé in a chemise.

259. Cover of a leaflet published by E. Jumeau and probably given away with the purchase of a Bébé Jumeau. The cover reads: "BÉBÉ JUMEAU//DIPLOME D'HONNEUR//LE PROCÉS [The legal process or trial] // D'UN//BÉBÉ JUMEAU//PARIS." *Coleman Collection.*

260. Box end for a dressed Bébé Jumeau of the 1880s (after the Melbourne Exhibition of 1880). It had blue eyes, a blue satin dress and appears to have been handled by Verchaly of Angers. It was size 11 (58 cm. or 23 in.). Advertising poem for Bébé Jumeau. The first four stanzas are summarized in the last line of the fourth stanza which translated says: "We will put the universe at your feet if you wish!" Then it continues,
"No! said the candid child, with a sweet smile.
A divine smile which we could desire
All this is too much for my little brain
All I want is a Bébé Jumeau." *Courtesy of Magda Byfield.*

261A & B. Bébé Jumeau with a wig, stationary brown glass eyes, pierced ears, closed mouth and a fully jointed composition body. The original chemise has a maroon ribbon with gold letters on its belt proclaiming that it is a Bébé Jumeau. The white chemise has a blue yoke and blue cloth under the lace trimming. The socks are blue and the bronze leather shoes are marked on the sole "7//Bébé// Jumeau//Deposé." The head is stamped in red "DÉPOSÉ//TETE JUMEAU// 8th S.G.D.G.//7." An oval sticker on the back of the body has the printed words. "BÉBÉ JUMEAU// Diplome d'Honneur." H. 44 cm. (17½ in.).

261C. End of the original box in which this Bébé Jumeau came.

261D & E. There are two labels on the box lid. One shows the armband on a dressed Bébé Jumeau and the Bébé Jumeau ribbon on a bébé in chemise. This chemise does not look like the chemise on the bébé which allegedly came in this box. The pictured chemise appears to be earlier than the chemise on the doll. The label advertised that all of the Bébé Jumeau dolls carried the Bébé Jumeau mark on their clothes, the back, and the body. Dressed dolls in the regular (réclame) series came only in the first 8 sizes, and had maroon armbands. The new dressed bébés had red armbands.

The second label on the box lid advertised the new type of Bébé Jumeau shoes for 1890. All of the Bébé Jumeaus then, came with footwear. The shoes were made of a single piece of fine leather; even the sole was leather. At the 1889 Exposition 6 million people visited the Bébé Jumeau showcases. *Courtesy of the Margaret Woodbury Strong Museum. Photos by Harry Bickelhaupt.*

262. Bébé Jumeau with a pressed bisque socket head marked "E 8 J." having stationary brown eyes, pierced ears, closed mouth, ball-jointed composition body with straight wrists. Original clothes including Jumeau shoes. H. 18½ in. (47 cm.). *Courtesy of Cherry Bou.*

263. Bébé Jumeau with wig, stationary blue glass eyes, pierced ears, closed mouth and a ball-jointed composition body. Original clothes including original chemise. Head mark: "Depose 2." Shoes marked "Jumeau." H. 10 in. (25.5 cm.). *Courtesy of Cherry Bou.*

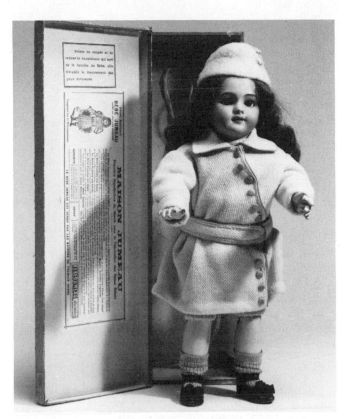

264. Bébé Jumeau with a bisque head marked "Tête Jumeau//5," has a black wig, stationary brown glass eyes, pierced ears, closed mouth, fully-jointed composition body. Original clothes. H. 14 in. (36 cm.). *Courtesy of Sotheby Parke Bernet Inc., N.Y.*

265. Bébé Jumeau with wig, stationary brown glass eyes, pierced ears, open mouth with six upper teeth, fully-jointed composition body. This doll was probably made by the S.F.B.J. Mark on head "Tête//Jumeau//8." Mark on body "Bébé Jumeau// Diplome d'Honneur." H. 50.5 cm. (20 in.). *Courtesy of Sotheby Parke Bernet Inc., N.Y.*

267. Bébé Jumeau with its original box and original clothes. It has a wig, sleeping blue eyes, pierced ears, an open mouth with teeth and a fully-jointed composition and wood body. The words on the box lid are chiefly advertising. At the left are the instructions to cut the rubber elastic which holds the sleeping eyes so they will not move and break in transit. The end of this rubber comes out of the doll's mouth. The figure shows Bébé Jumeau in its chemise. The doll's head is marked "Dep 8//Tête Jumeau" and the body is marked "Bébé Jumeau// Diplome D'Honneur." H. 53 cm. (21 in.). *Courtesy of Sotheby Parke Bernet Inc., N.Y.*

266. "Bébé Jumeau" in its chemise as shown in the 1923 Louvre store catalog. The doll had "natural hair," sleeping eyes with hair eyelashes and a fully jointed composition body. It came in sizes 5 through 12. H. 36, 41, 44, 49, 53, 57, 62, and 67 cm. (14, 16, 17½, 19½, 21, 22½, 24½, and 26½ in.). All sizes except the two smallest were also available as talking dolls.

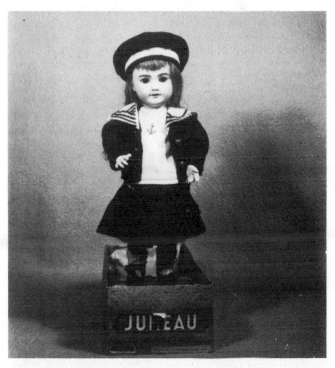

268. Bébé Jumeau made by S.F.B.J. mold #301 has a bisque head with wig, sleeping eyes, hair eyelashes, open mouth and a fully jointed composition body. Original sailor dress. The body has the "Diplome d'Honneur" mark and the shoes are marked "5//Bébé//Jumeau//Deposé//." The head is a corresponding size 5. H. 15 in. (38 cm.). *Courtesy of Cherry Bou.*

Bébé Jumont. Name found on the belt of a doll's chemise. This could have been an attempt to infringe on the popularity of the *Bébé Jumeau.*

Bébé la Georgienne. Bisque-head doll with stationary eyes and closed mouth made by *Lanternier.* Incised on the head was "Fabrication//Française// AL & Cie // Limoges." A sticker on the body read "Deposé Bébé la Georgienne." This doll was 26 cm. (10½ in.) tall.

Bébé la Parisienne. 1900. Trade name of a dressed doll sold by *La Place Clichy* store. It came in three sizes and cost 78¢ to $1.58.

Bébé Lafayette. 1912–27 and possibly later. Trade name of a doll sold exclusively at the *Lafayette* store in Paris. The size number and heights were nearly the same as those for the Bébé Jumeau of the same period. The Bébé Lafayette had a wig, sleeping eyes and eyelashes; it wore a chemise, and some of the popular sizes also came dressed.

BÉBÉ LAFAYETTE SIZE–HEIGHT RELATIONSHIP, 1912		
Size No.	Height Centimeters	Inches
3	31	12
4	35	14
5	40	15½
6	43	17
7	46	18
8	52	20½
9	57	22½
10	60	23½
11	64	25
12	69	27
13	74	29
14	79	31

The 12 in. doll in chemise was priced at $1.15 and the 31 in. doll at $7.40 in 1912. Sizes 3 to 13 came silent while sizes 6 to 14 came parlant. The dressed Bébés Lafayette came parlant. Sizes 6 to 9, hts. 42, 46, 51 and 56 cm. (16½, 18, 20 and 22 in.) priced $4.60 to $7.60. (See THE COLLECTOR'S BOOK OF DOLLS' CLOTHES, Ills. 629, 630, and 639.)

Ca. 1925: Hts. included 28, 36, 43, and 50 cm. (11, 14, 17 and 19½ in.). See Ill. 1599.

1927: Undressed Bébé Lafayette was advertised the same as in 1912 except that the chemise was updated in design and only sizes 6 to 12 were listed.

Bébé l'Avenir (Doll of the Future). 1903–21. This trademark and the German version *Puppe der zukuft* were used by *Gebrüder Süssenguth* and *Guttmann & Schiffnie.* The trademark means "Doll of the Future." Gebrüder Süssenguth was the producer.

1903: This doll was sold at *Tapis Rouge;* it had a "Washable" composition head, was light in weight; ht. 40 cm. (15½ in.); priced 79¢. *Butler Bros.* reported butterfly-shaped tags.

1909: *Siegel Cooper* advertised the "Doll of the Future," with "Hard to Break" head, side-part wig, glass eyes, and fully jointed arms and legs. It wore a chemise and footwear. Ht. 13 in. (33 cm.); priced 50¢.

1911: *Modernes* advertised this doll with a washable "unbreakable" head; it came in 4 sizes, priced 29¢ to 59¢.

1912: Butler Bros. advertised a doll with the tag "DOLL OF THE//FUTURE//UNBREAKABLE." It had teeth and a hollow linen covered body including the limbs. Metal rivet joints were at the hips and knees. Four hts. 14, 16¾, 18, and 21¾ in. (35.5, 42.5, 45.5 and 55 cm.); priced $4.20 to $13.80 doz. wholesale.★

269. Mark on a Bébé l'Avenir made by Gans & Seyfarth and Guttmann & Schiffnie.

Bébé le Parisien. See **Le Parisien.**

Bébé le Radieux. 1904. Trade name of a French articulated doll. The size on a box labeled "Bébé Le Radieux" was No. 9 which corresponded in height roughly with the *Bébé Jumeau* size number 9.★

Bébé le Vrai Modèle. 1910. Trade name of a bébé made by *F. Ch. Rivaillon.* No connection with Bébé Vrai Modèle has been found as yet.

Bébé Lefebvre. Before 1890-ca. 1920s. Made by *Alexandre Lefebvre.* By about 1922 it was made by the *Société Française de Fabrication de Bébés & Jouets* (S.F.B.J.). This doll had either a composition or bisque head with hair eyelashes, wig, mouth with teeth and was on a fully jointed composition body that could kneel on one or both knees. Seven hts. 25 to 72 cm. (10 to 28½ in.).

1919: The son of Alexander Lefebvre claimed that Bébé Lefebvre was the first Bébé Incassable and had been invented in 1869. It is possible that the dolls marked "B. L." are Bébés Lefebvre.

Bébé Leger. 1893–96. Trade name for a doll made by the *Widow Chalory.*

Bébé Loulou. 1891. Mark used by *Wannez et Rayer* for dolls.

Bébé Louvre. See **Louvre Bébé.**

Bébé Madeleine. 1906. *Aux Trois Quartiers* on the Boulevard de la Madeleine, advertised Bébé Madeleine made by *Jumeau.* It had sleeping eyes, hair eyelashes and was fully jointed. The picture showed a sash marked "PARIS BÉBÉ." It came in five hts. 28, 40, 45, 57 and 65 cm. (11, 15½, 17½, 22½ and 25½ in.); priced 78¢ to $4.20. The "Parlant" Bébé Madeleine came only in hts. 45 and 57 cm. (17½ and 22½ in.); priced $2.35 to $3.00.

270. Bisque socket head marked B. L. which probably stands for Bébé Lefebvre. The doll has a wig, stationary brown glass eyes, open-closed mouth and a jointed composition body with a Schmitt mark. The body and head may not have always been together. Mark on head: Ill. 271. H. 14 in. (35.5 cm.). *Courtesy of Richard Withington. Photo by Barbara Jendrick.*

PRICES OF BÉBÉ MAGENTA, 1896					
		Series A	Series B	Series C Completely Articulated—	Series D Completely Articulated—
Height cm.	in.	Shoulder Articulation	Simple Articulation	Cotton Chemise	Satin Chemise
36	14	$ .50			
39	15½			$ .80	$1.05
41	16		$ .60		
42	16½	$ .60		$1.00	$1.50
45	17½	$ .75	$ .80	$1.20	
50	19½	$1.00	$1.00	$1.60	$2.10
54	21		$1.35		
55	21½			$1.90	$2.60
60	23½		$1.60	$2.30	$2.80
65	25½			$2.80	
66	26		$2.20		
69	27		$2.80	$3.70	
70	27½				
76	30			$4.50	
82	32½			$5.80	

There was also a Series E for numbers 1, 2, 3, 4, 5. The dolls in this series may have been fully clad.

**B. L
PARIS
9**

B.12.L

271–272. Marks found on French bisque-head dolls. They may be a Bébé Lefebvre mark, rather than the previously identified Bébé Louvre (Louvre Bébé).

BÉBÉ LEGER

273. Mark used by the Widow Chalory for Bébé Léger celluloid dolls or head in 1893 and probably other years.

274. Mark for Bébé Loulou dolls.

(Warning: The mark "Made in Germany" has sometimes been read "Madeline Germany" when the mark is difficult to decipher.)

Bébé Magenta. 1896–98 and possibly other years. Trade name for a bébé sold only by the *Magenta* store. This doll came with a wig, various degrees of articulation and several types of chemises.

It is possible that Bébé Magenta could have been made by the *Jules Steiner* firm, since it is known that they used similar series identification for varying types of dolls. See **Bébé Premier Pas.** (See THE COLLECTOR'S BOOK OF DOLLS' CLOTHES, Ills. 438 and 444 B.)

Bébé Magnifique. See Magnifique Bébé.

Bébé Maillot. 1880s–1910s. At first this name in France was usually applied to a *Swaddling-Clothed Doll* but later it was often applied to a doll with leading strings.

1885–86: Bébé Maillot, made in Paris, was advertised by *Petit Saint Thomas* as being unbreakable, articulated, and with removable swaddling clothes. It came in four prices from 5¢ to 98¢.

1906: *Aux Trois Quartiers* advertised Bébé Maillot with leading strings and a key-wind mechanism for walking. Hts. 35 and 44 cm. (14 and 17½ in.); priced $1.75 and $3.50. A similar doll has been found with a bisque head made by *Simon & Halbig.* (See THE COLLECTOR'S BOOK OF DOLLS' CLOTHES for illustrations that show Bébés Maillot offered for sale by various French stores, for various years: 1894, Ills. 428B and 429A; 1901, Ill. 526; 1902, Ill. 529; and 1910–11, Ill. 614; and Ill. 562 is of an actual doll.)

Bébé Maison Dorée. 1900–1901 and possibly other years. Trade name of a bébé sold exclusively by the store *Maison Dorée.* This bisque-head doll came in two styles. One did not have jointed wrists and wore a flowered chemise. The other was fully jointed and wore a chemise that somewhat resembled those worn by the *Bébés Jumeau.* The first one, in 1900, came in 9 hts., ranging from 30 cm. (12 in.) to 62 cm. (24½ in.) and was priced from 9¢ to 90¢. In 1901 there were only 8 hts., from 33 cm. (13 in.) to 68 cm. (27 in.), priced

59¢ to $3.10. Because of the size variations, the best price comparison is for a 41-cm. (16-in.) doll. In 1900, the first style cost 29¢ and the second cost 78¢; in 1901 the second style cost 98¢. (See THE COLLECTOR'S BOOK OF DOLLS' CLOTHES, Ill. 447.)

Bébé Marcheur. Many walking dolls were called "Bébé Marcheur" in store catalogs. This name does not necessarily seem to imply a *Jules Steiner* or a *Jumeau*. In 1902 the *Samaritaine* advertised a Bébé Marcheur with the same head and wig as their *Bébé Samaritaine,* which was made by Jumeau. This was a *Kiss-Throwing Bébé* that bore the name "*Eden Bébé*" on the chemise. In fact, various firms made walking dolls.★

Bébé Marcheur. See **Bébés Marcheurs.**

Bébé Mascotte. 1882–1901. Bisque head on a jointed composition body that is sometimes marked "*Jumeau* Medaille d'Or." Although the name Bébé Mascotte was a trademark of May Frères Cie.,[+] the sizes seem to be similar to the early Bébés Jumeau. Sometimes there is an M with the size number but not all dolls marked M are Bébés Mascotte. La Mascotte was advertised by the *Louvre* store in 1882 as being 40 cm. (15½ in.) tall and costing $5.00 dressed in a regional costume. Dolls have been reported as having heads incised "Mascotte" and body stamped "Bébé Mascotte// Paris." Hts. 10 to 27 in. (25.5 to 68.5 cm.).

A poured bisque head with wig and glass eyes was reportedly marked "Mascotte//J." Ht. 23 in. (58.5 cm.). (See THE COLLECTOR'S BOOK OF DOLLS' CLOTHES, Ill. 312 for the Louvre's La Mascotte.)★

276. Bébé Mascotte with a bisque head, blond wig, stationary blue glass eyes, pierced ears, closed mouth, and a fully-jointed composition body. Mark on head: "Mascotte." Mark on body: "Bébé Mascotte//Paris." H. 12½ in. (31.5 cm.). *Courtesy of Sotheby Parke Bernet Inc., N.Y.*

MASCOTTE
I

277. Mark on the head of the Bébé Mascotte shown in Ill. 275.

Bébé Mecanique. See **L'Intrepide Bébé.**

Bébé Ménagère. 1903–13. Trade name of a doll sold exclusively by Nouvelle Galeries à la *Ménagère.* The doll had a bisque head and came in a variety of styles and sizes. Possibly it was not always made by the same firm.

1903: It had an open mouth with teeth and wore a lace-trimmed chemise labeled Bébé Ménagère. Ht. 60 cm. (23½ in.). Price 82¢.

1906: The composition body, fully jointed, wore a silk chemise with Bébé Ménagère on it. The doll was described as *Joli Bébé* and *Bébé Réclame.* Ht. 57 cm. (22½ in.); Price $1.30.

275A & B. Bébé Mascotte with brown wig, stationary blue eyes, pierced and applied ears, and closed mouth, on a jointed composition body. Original chemise. Mark on head: Ill. 277. Mark on body: "Mascotte//Paris." H. 21 in. (53.5 cm.). *Courtesy of Hazel Ulseth.*

1907: The doll had sleeping eyes, a fully jointed composition body; on its lace-trimmed chemise was the name "Bébé Ménagère." It came in five hts. 27, 35, 42, 46, and 52 cm. (10½, 14, 16½, 18 and 20½ in.). The prices ranged from 59¢ to $1.39.

1911–13: The doll was again described as Bébé Réclame, although the lace-trimmed chemise still bore the name Bébé Ménagère. This was a cheaper doll with stationary eyes, and only partially articulated. Hts. 43, 54, and 62 cm. (17, 21½ and 24½ in.); priced 29¢ to 99¢. (See THE COLLECTOR'S BOOK OF DOLLS' CLOTHES, Ills. 628 and 640.) (See also **Bébé Réclame**.)

Bébé Merveille. 1920s. Trade name of a bisque-head doll with a wig, glass eyes and a five-piece composition body made by the *Société Française de Fabrication de Bébés & Jouets* (S.F.B.J.) in their Unis France series. One of these dolls with its head marked "S.F.B.J. 60" was in a box stamped "3 Mai, 1926." This box also had a paper label reading, "FABRICATION PARISIENNE//BÉBÉ MERVEILLE// COMPLETEMENT//ARTICULE."

Another box labeled "Bébé Merveilleux, size 9" has been reported. It contained an S.F.B.J. doll of mold number 238, size 8. However it is not certain that the doll originally came in this box. The fact that two S.F.B.J. marked dolls were found in Bébé Merveille or *Bébé Merveilleux* boxes seems to suggest that *Ulhenhuth* joined the S.F.B.J.

Bébé Merveilleux. 1890–1919. Trade name of a bébé made by *Ulhenhuth*. The bisque head had sleeping eyes, a wig, and open mouth with teeth—at least from 1903 on.

1901: *Pauvre Jacques* advertised Bébé Merveilleux, with jointed shoulders and hips and wearing a printed cloth chemise trimmed with lace. It came in hts. 35 cm. (14 in.) and 45 cm. (17½ in.); price 19¢ and 29¢.

1903: *Tapis Rouge* sold articulated Bébé Merveilleux in four hts. 40, 44, 50 and 63 cm. (15½, 17½, 19½ and 25 in.); price 29¢ to 90¢.

1911–12: This doll dressed in silk was sold at La Place Clichy. The six hts. were 31, 40, 46, 52, 57, and 64 cm. (12, 15½, 18, 20½, 22½, and 25 in.), priced $1.38 to $7.10.

1919: Bébé Merveilleux, fully jointed, was advertised by *Aux Trois Quartiers,* 39 cm. (15½ in.) tall; price $2.90.

Bébé Mignon. 1906. Advertised by *Aux Trois Quartiers* store. It was all-composition, jointed and dressed in silk and wool. The picture hat was trimmed with a plume. Ht. 62 cm. (24½ in.); price $3.70.

Bébé Mignon. See **Leopold Lambert.**

Bébé Miracle. 1886–87. Advertised by the *Louvre* store. Four hts. 28, 35, 41, and 49 cm. (11, 14, 16, and 19½ in.); priced $1.35 to $3.15.

Bébé Modèle. 1900. French trademark registered by *Mme. Caroline Rivaillon.* The trademark had two cherubs and the initials F. C. R. Just the name Bébé Modèle† was registered in 1901 as a trademark by Jules Mettais of the *Steiner* firm. ★

Bébé Moncey. 1900–23. Trade name for a bébé sold at La

Place Clichy. The doll was fully jointed, including the wrists. It wore the same type of chemise with a square yoke throughout this period. (See THE COLLECTOR'S BOOK OF DOLLS' CLOTHES, Ill. 754.)

BÉBÉ MONCEY							
Heights						Prices 1900	
1900				1923			
in chemise		satin & lace dress				in chemise	satin & lace dress
cm.	in.	cm.	in.	cm.	in.		
29	11½					$ .70	
32	12½						
35	14	35	14			$ .98	$1.38
40	15½			40	15½		
43	17	43	17	43	17		
47	18½						
52	20½	52	20½	52	20½		
56	22			60	23½		
61	24	61	24			$2.55	$4.75
				62	24½		
				72	28½		

Bébé Mothereau. 1880–95. Line of bébés made by Alexandre Célestin Triburee Mothereau.† The upper arms and legs are wood. The lower arms and legs have a rounded joint with a metal bracket for attaching it to the elastic stringing.

BÉBÉ MOTHEREAU SIZE HEIGHT RELATIONSHIP		
Size No.	Height cm.	in.
4	38	15
6	45	17½
10	74	29*

*See the first COLLECTOR'S ENCYCLOPEDIA OF DOLLS.

Bébé Nadaud. See **Nadaud, Mlle. A.**

Bébé Neva. 1906. Advertised by *Aux Trois Quartiers* store. It had a bisque head and the clothes consisted of a velvet outfit trimmed with marabou and ribbons. The sleeping eyed version with hair eyelashes was 58 cm. (23 in.) tall and cost $1.75. The stationary eyed version was 38 cm. (15 in.) tall and cost 78¢.

Bébé Nid. See **Leopold Lambert.**

Bébé Ninon. 1927–28. Made by *Bonin & Lefort.*

Bébé Nu. 1884–1923 and probably other years. This appears to have referred to a nude doll, but often it was described as wearing a chemise. Before World War I. Bébé Nu was used in reference to the *Eden Bébé* or in 1884 in reference to *Bébé Jumeau.*

1923: The Paris store *Dufayel* advertised styles of unbreakable washable Bébés Nu; presumably these were composition dolls. One style dressed in a chemise came in four hts. 25, 34, 38, and 45 cm. (10, 13½, 15 and 17½ in.); price $1.05 to $2.95. The second style had a character head with

278. Bébé Mothereau with wig, brown glass eyes, pierced ears, closed mouth, on a jointed composition body. Mark on head is "9//B. M." H. 22 in. (56 cm.). *Courtesy of Sotheby Parke Bernet Inc., N.Y.*

6.
B. M.

279. Mark on a French bébé believed to be a Bébé Mothereau.

sleeping eyes and a toddler's body. Five hts. 33, 46, 52, 60 and 68 cm. (13, 18, 20½, 23½ and 27 in.); prices $6.00 to $24.00. The third style, apparently a child doll with moving eyes, came in five hts. 38, 40, 47, 58 and 66 cm. (15, 15½, 18½, 23 and 26 in.); priced $3.50 to $13.40. The fourth style had an open mouth; three hts. were 36, 43, and 49 cm. (14, 17 and 19½ in.); priced $2.70 to $5.10.

Bébé Nurse. 1890. Advertisement by the *Louvre* store showed a nurse dressed in a satin costume, holding a baby; it was available in four hts. 14, 24, 26 and 31 cm. (5½, 9½, 10½, and 12 in.); priced 38¢ to $1.70. (See also **Nourrice**.)

Bébé Olga. 1896–1930 and later. Trade name of a bébé made by *Gerbaulet Frères*.★

Bébé Palais Nouveauté (Bébé du Palais de la Nouveauté). 1923. Advertised by the store *Dufayel*. These dolls came in six hts. 29, 39, 48, 54, 60 and 68 cm. (11½, 15½, 19, 21½, 23½ and 27 in.). The price ranged from $1.98 to $19.00.

Bébé Parfait. 1904–35. Trademark used by the *Société Française de Fabrication de Bébés & Jouets* (S.F.B.J.).

Bébé Paris. See **Paris Bébé** and **Bébé de Paris.**

Bébé Parisette. 1919. Advertised by *Aux Trois Quartiers* as entirely unbreakable. It was 30 cm. (12 in.), tall and cost $2.70.

Bébé Parisien. 1886–90 and possibly other years. Trade name for a bébé made by *Decoster.* with head and arms of bisque on a jointed composition body.

1886: It was distributed by the store *Petit Saint Thomas,* and wore a dress and hat. Came in three hts. 48, 58, and 68 cm. (19, 23, and 27 in.). The smallest size sold for only 48¢. (See THE COLLECTOR'S BOOK OF DOLLS' CLOTHES, Ill. 320.)

Bébé Parlant. 1884–1912. The many Paris store catalogs seem to indicate that a "Bébé Parlant" probably had an open mouth, but did not always make any sound. The "Muets" (silents) probably had closed mouths. The advertisements sometimes described a bébé as "disant Mama et Papa." if the doll could make sounds.

Samaritaine claimed that they were the exclusive distributor of a doll called Bébé Parlant. The prices were 59¢ for the smallest doll in all years for which records were found, and $1.78 for the largest doll in all years except 1901, when it was $1.50 and 1906 when it was $1.95.

1901: Unbreakable doll that said "Mama, Papa" wore a flowered chemise with Bébé Parlant on the sash. This doll came in four hts. 39, 45, 50, and 54 cm. (15½, 17½, 19½ and 21½ in.).

1902: Described as a completely unbreakable doll that could talk and sleep. It had a wig. Six hts.: 38 to 61 cm. (15 to 24 in.).

1906: Same as 1902, except doll had a Peter Pan-type collar and came in seven hts.: 38 to 65 cm. (15 to 25½ in.).

1908: Same as 1906, except the seven hts. were from 36 cm. (14 in.) to 60 cm. (23½ in.).

1909–11: Same as 1908, except the name was no longer on the sash.

1912: *Bébés Jumeau* 25 cm. (10 in.) to 58 cm. (23 in.) were described as "Muets"; those 63 cm. (25 in.) to 85 cm. (33½ in.) were described as "Parlant." All these had sleeping eyes. See also **Bébé Printemps,** 1896; and **Talking Doll.**★

Bébé Pauvre Jacques. 1901. Trade name for a bébé sold exclusively by *Pauvre Jacques* store. Their catalog listed the following six hts. 33, 36, 42, 47, 57, and 67 cm. (13, 14, 16½, 18½, 22½, and 26½ in.); priced at 45¢ to $1.30. (See THE COLLECTOR'S BOOK OF DOLLS' CLOTHES, Ill. 525.)

Bébé Phénix. 1889–1901. Doll with bisque head, sleeping eyes, fully jointed body including the wrists was sold by *Pauvre Jacques;* it wore a flowered chemise. Five hts. 32, 37, 43, 48 and 53 cm. (12½, 14½, 17, 19, and 21 in.); priced 55¢ to $1.45. (See THE COLLECTOR'S BOOK OF DOLLS' CLOTHES, Ill. 525.)★

280. Bébé Phénix with a bisque head, wig, stationary glass eyes, pierced ears, closed mouth, and a fully jointed composition body. Marks on head; "Phénix" In red and "22" incised H 18 in. (45.5 cm.). *Courtesy of Sotheby Parke Bernet Inc., N.Y.*

281. Bébé Phénix mark on a bisque head.

Bébé Pole Sud. 1910. Doll with celluloid head, plush clothes, and a voice; sold by *Printemps.* Hts. 22, 25, and 27 cm. (8½, 10, and 10½ in.); priced 38¢ to 58¢.

1909–11: This was a period of South Pole exploration.

Bébé Premier. 1911–13. Trade name for a cloth doll produced by *Horsman.* It had an oil-painted head, sateen body and composition arms to above the elbows, and closely resembled the *Martha Chase* dolls. The price was $10.50 doz. wholesale; $12.50 a doz. if it had a jointed body and was dressed in white lawn.

Bébé Premier Age. 1914. Advertised by *Samaritaine* store. It had a character head with hair and sleeping eyes. Five hts. 31, 37, 42, 48, and 65 cm. (12, 14½, 16½, 19, and 25½ in.); price in chemise $1.15 to $3.75; price wearing a silk dress and wool jacket trimmed with ribbon $2.30 to $7.80.

Bébé Ier Age. Ca. 1925. Advertised by *Lafayette* store. It was a dressed cloth doll. Ht. 45 cm. (17½ in.). (See Ill. 1599.)

Bébé Premier Elan. 1892. Name of a walking, talking doll patented by Paul Girard of the *Bru* firm. This doll turned its head and was jointed at the knees according to Anne-Marie and Jacques Porot.

Bébé Premier Pas (Bébé First Step). 1890–92. Trade name used by *Jules Steiner* for a walking, talking bébé that cried when it was laid down. The articulation varied; series A had jointed shoulders and hips; series B had jointed neck, shoulders and hips; series C had jointed neck, shoulders, elbows, hips and knees; series D had jointed wrists also. White kid was usually glued to the bottom of the composition body and top of the thighs in order to hide the mechanism.★

Bébé Premiers Pas (Bébé First Steps). 1912–13. A mechanical, walking dressed doll that was sold by *Bon Marché, Lafayette, L'Hotel de Ville,* and the *Louvre* stores. It was 28 cm. (11 in.) high and cost $2.10. The Louvre also had a 32 cm. (12½ in.) size costing $2.90. Lafayette also had a 33 cm. (13 in.) size. (See Ill. 1598.)

Roullet & Decamps made the mechanical part for this doll. (See also **L'Intrepide Bébé.**)

Bébé Prime. 1930 and before. Name of a simplified walking doll according to Anne-Marie and Jacques Porot.

Bébé Princesse. 1919. Trade name of a doll advertised by *Gebrüder Ohlhaver.*

Bébé Printemps. 1887–1924. Trade name of a bébé sold exclusively by *Printemps,* a Paris store. Bébé Printemps has a bisque head on a jointed composition body.

1887: It came dressed in two types of chemise, one of them a pleated chemise, and sold for 70¢ to $6.90. When the dolls were fully dressed, they cost nearly three times as much.

1896: Bébé Printemps was jointed at the neck, shoulders, and hips; had a closed mouth, stationary eyes, and the smaller sizes were dressed in silk. Size 1 cost only 58¢. Size 4 and over came both with and without "Parlant." Size 4 in chemise and footwear without "Parlant" cost $1.25; with "Parlant" it cost $1.70; but when it came dressed in a rich costume, the price was $3.50. Size 12 in chemise and footwear without "Parlant" cost $7.40; with "Parlant," $7.80. Dressed in a rich costume, this size 12 doll cost $17.00. The small increase for the parlant Bébé Printemps makes one wonder whether the difference was only between an open- and a closed-mouth doll rather than a doll with and without a voice.

1900–1901: Bébé Printemps had a bisque head, sleeping eyes, hair eyelashes, teeth, and natural hair wig. Wearing a chemise and footwear, the 31-cm. (12-in.) doll cost 85¢, and when dressed it cost $2.10. The 86-cm. (34-in.) doll in chemise cost $7.80; when it was "Parlant," it cost $9.00.

1904–5: Same type of doll as in 1900. The chemise had a pleated ruffle around a round yoke and a full skirt. There were 2 box pleats down the front; its name "Bébé Printemps" was on the belt. This doll also came dressed in various costumes.

Bébés-Printemps

BÉBÉ-PRINTEMPS complètement articulé, tête biscuit, avec *dents*, *yeux mobiles*, à cils, chaussé, perruque **cheveux naturels**, chemise fine.

Nos.	Hauteurs.	Prix.	Nos.	Hauteurs.	Prix.
1	0m,31	4.25	7	0m,53	11.75
2	0m,34	5.25	8	0m,58	15.50
3	0m,37	6.25	9	0m,62	17.75
4	0m,40	7.25	10	0m,70	23.50
5	0m,45	8.25	11	0m,76	31. »
6	0m,48	9.75	12	0m,86	39. »

BÉBÉ-PRINTEMPS complètement articulé, tête biscuit, avec *dents*, *yeux mobiles*, à cils, perruque **cheveux naturels**, habillage riche, costumes variés. (Série fine).

Nos.	Hauteurs.	Prix.	Nos.	Hauteurs.	Prix.
1	0m,31	10.50	6	0m,48	25. »
2	0m,34	12.75	7	0m,53	30. »
3	0m,37	14.50	8	0m,58	37. »
4	0m,40	18.50	9	0m,62	45. »
5	0m,45	21. »	10	0m,70	59. »

BÉBÉ-PRINTEMPS PARLANT, articulé, tête biscuit, avec *dents*, *yeux mobiles*, à cils, chemise fine, chaussé, cheveux naturels.

Numéros	4	5	6	7	8	9	10	11	12
Hauteurs	0m,40	0m,45	0m,48	0m,53	0m,58	0m,62	0m,70	0m,76	0m,86
Prix	8.75	10.75	12.75	14.75	18.50	22. »	27. »	34. »	45. »

282. Three versions of Bébé Printemps as shown in the 1901 Printemps catalog. All three have bisque heads, "natural" hair wigs, sleeping eyes with hair eyelashes, and footwear. The two dolls on the left wear a chemise while the doll on the right is fully dressed. The dressed dolls came in a variety of costumes. The doll in the center "talks" and "walks." The size numbers, heights in centimeters and prices in francs (five francs to the dollar) are given in the table. Once again the clothes are the most expensive part of the doll.

1910: The doll and its chemise were the same as in 1904. Sizes 8 to 12 came with and without "Parlant." The 31 cm. (12-in.) size cost 98¢; the 86-cm. (34-in.) size cost $8.60.

1916: The chemise was short and the belt had been lowered so that the skirt was minuscule. There were ruffles over the shoulders, and the chemise was gathered at the neckline and belt.

1918: Dolls similar to those of 1910 cost $2.75 for the 25-cm. (10 in.) size, $3.98 for the 35-cm. (14 in.) size, and $15.00 for the 63-cm. (25 in.) size.

1924: The Bébé Printemps said "Mama, Papa" and cost about $9.00 to $20.00 each.
(See THE COLLECTOR'S BOOK OF DOLLS' CLOTHES for illustrations showing the Bébé Printemps offered in Paris stores for various years: 1887, Ill. 327; 1910–11, Ill. 614; 1924, Ill. 756B.)

BÉBÉ PRINTEMPS SIZE–HEIGHT RELATIONSHIP								
	Heights							
Size	1887		1896–1910		1918		1924	
No.	cm.	in.	cm.	in.	cm.	in.	cm.	in.
1	26	10½	31	12	25	10		
2	29	11½	34	13½	28	11		
3	32	12½	37	14½	32	12½		
4	35	14	40	15½	35	14		
5	38	15	45	17½	40	15½		
6	42	16½	48	19	44	17½	43	17
7	48	19	53	21	47	18½		
8	54	21½	58	23	53	21	49	19½
9	60	23½	62	24½	57	22½	57	22½
10	70	27½	70	27½	60	23½		
11			76	30	63	25	64	25
12			86	34				

Bébé Prodige. 1893–1926. Trademark used by *Jumeau* and the *Société Française de Fabrication de Bébés & Jouets* (S.F.B.J.). These dolls had bisque heads, and composition bodies jointed only at the shoulder and hips. They were made in similar but less numerous sizes than the *Bébés Jumeau,* and were cheaper.

1893: Tour St.-Jacques[†] advertised these dolls dressed in a chemise in the following seven hts.: 25, 30, 35, 40, 45, 50, and 55 cm. (10, 12, 14, 15, 17½, 19½, and 21½ in.); priced 35¢ to $1.18.

1896: The dolls were sold at the *Louvre* store, and came dressed in satin in eight hts. 25, 31, 35, 41, 45, 49, 58, and 63 cm. (10, 12, 14, 16, 17½, 19½, 23 and 25 in.); priced from $1.05 to $4.90.

1913: Bébé Prodige dressed in a chemise and described as "semi-articulated" was sold at the *Ménagère* store. Hts. 37, 46, and 56 cm. (14½, 18 and 22 in.); priced 29¢, 59¢ and 99¢.★

Bébé Promenette. 1906–23 and possibly other years. Similar bébés were also called *Bébé Culotte* in an earlier period.

They were all-composition, dressed in baby drawers and leading strings, and were distributed by *Aux Trois Quartiers, Louvre* store, *Printemps, L'Hotel de Ville* and *Ville de St. Denis.*

Ca. 1910: Ville de St. Denis doll was 35 cm. (14 in.) tall and cost 59¢. Printemps dolls wore a straw helmet and dress. Hts. 35 and 44 cm. (14 and 17½ in.); priced 98¢ and $1.38.

1915: Wore baby drawers, but was otherwise the same as found in 1910 except that there was also a larger size that was a "Parlant" walking doll, ht. 57 cm. (22½ in.); priced $2.55.

1921: There were five hts.

1923: *La Place Clichy* advertised Bébé Promenette. (See THE COLLECTOR'S BOOK OF DOLLS' CLOTHES, Ills. 639 and 754.)

283. Bébé Promenette as advertised by L'Hotel de Ville in its 1921 catalog. This painted cardboard (carton) doll is articulated and has leading strings. Usually a "poupard" is in swaddling clothes. This doll came in five versions.

0 — 41154.
BÉBÉ PROMENETTE
ou POUPARD, *articulé* incassable, carton décoré.
Prix
3.50 4.75 5.95
8.50 et 10.95

Bébé Pygmalion. 1900–1901 and probably other years. Bisque head bébé with wig and a fully-jointed body. Six hts. 32, 37, 43, 48, 58 and 63 cm. (12½, 14½, 17, 19, 23, and 25 in.); priced 59¢ to $2.50. It came in a parlant (talking) version, hts. 43, 53, and 63 cm. (17, 21, and 25 in.). The parlant 43 cm. (17 in.) bébé cost 47¢ more than the same size without the parlant.

Bébé Radieux (Radiant). 1930. Advertised by *Bon Marché* as a doll with an "unbreakable" head, wig, sleeping eyes, hair eyelashes, fully jointed composition body. Ht. 50 cm. (19½ in.).

Bébé Ravissant. 1901. Sold by *Pauvre Jacques;* dressed in silk trimmed with ribbons and lace. Ht. 32 cm. (12½ in.); priced 25¢.

Bébé Réclame (Réclame Bébé or Réclame). 1906–28 and probably other years. Many of the Paris stores advertised Bébé Réclame; literally this name means "Reclaimed Bébé."

1906: A doll with *Bébé Ménagère* on the sash of its silk chemise was sold by the Ménagère store. It was described as

"Bébé Réclame" and had a bisque head, fully jointed composition body, 57 cm. (22½ in.) tall; priced $1.30.

1907: *Paris Cette* advertised a Bébé Réclame for 59¢ but *Pygmalion* charged $1.75 for their 61 cm. (24 in.) Bébé Réclame dressed in satin with a hat and coat. It came with either a blonde or brunette wig.

1910: *Printemps* sold a 49 cm. (19½ in.) Bébé Réclame for $1.98. *Ville de St. Denis'* Bébé Réclame had an open mouth, wore a silk and lace dress and a picture hat. Ht. 55 cm. (21½ in.); priced $1.19.

1911–13: *Ménagère* sold a Bébé Réclame dressed in a blue, rose or red costume; hts. 36, 44, and 48 cm. (14, 17½, and 19 in.). These dolls also came in a chemise and footwear. Hts. 43, 54, and 62 cm. (17, 21½, and 24 ½ in.). The prices were the same 29¢, 59¢, and 99¢ but the dressed dolls were smaller.

The dolls at the Ménagère were jointed only at the neck, shoulder, and hips. The largest dressed version, 48 cm. (19 in.), was not available in 1913.

1912: *Galeries Lafayette* sold Bébé Réclame with sleeping eyes and removable clothes. Ht. 32 cm. (12½ in.); priced 29¢.

1913: Galeries Lafayette advertised only a 32 cm. (12½ in.) Bébé Réclame in a chemise for 29¢.

1921: *L'Hotel de Ville* advertised a bisque head jointed Bébé Réclame with sleeping eyes, hair eyelashes, wig, and chemise trimmed with ribbons, hts. 41 and 47 cm. (16 and 18½ in.). An all-composition Bébé Réclame with a mohair wig, fully jointed and dressed was 42 cm. (16½ in.) tall.

1927: Lafayette advertised a Réclame Bébé as having an "Unbreakable" head with a mohair wig, jointed shoulders and wearing a plaid dress. Ht. 65 cm. (25½ in.).

1928: Bébé Réclame was a trade name used by *Société Industrielle de Jouets Français* for bébés. (See also **Bébé de Réclame.**)

Bébé Regence. 1898. Trade name used in the *Magenta* store. The faces in the catalog are actual photographic representations. 11 hts. 31, 35, 38, 41, 45, 47, 49, 53, 58, 63, and 68 cm. (12, 14, 15, 16, 17½, 18½, 19½, 21, 23, 25, and 27 in.) The dolls in chemise cost 79¢ to $3.90, the dressed dolls cost $2.79 to $7.00. (See THE COLLECTOR'S BOOK OF DOLLS' CLOTHES, Ill. 444B.)

Bébé Réservé (Réservé Bébé). 1909–19. Trade name for various types of dolls distributed by *L'Hotel de Ville* and the *Louvre* store. They usually had bisque heads with sleeping eyes on a jointed composition body, and came in a chemise or dressed.

1909: Hts. of various types, with removable clothes, at the Louvre store:

HEIGHTS OF BÉBÉ RÉSERVÉ (Réservé Bébé)							
Non Parlant (not talking)						Parlant (talking)	
Without Eyelashes		With Eyelashes				With Eyelashes	
		Bébé Baptême		Others			
cm.	in.	cm.	in.	cm.	in.	cm.	in.
26	10½	25	10				
28	11	29	11½				
33	13	31	12	31	12		
37	14½	35	14	39	15½	37*	14½
41	16	40	15½			41	16
42	16½	43	17	43	17		
45	17½	46	18			46	18
47	18½			47	18½		
50	19½	52	20½	51	20		
54	21½			56	22		
				63	25		
				65	25½		
*Kiss-throwing Bébé.				70	27½		

1921: *L'Hotel de Ville* sold composition-head Bébés Réservé in a chemise, ht. 44 cm. (17½ in.), or dressed, 31 cm. (12 in.). The bisque-head version, dressed, came in ht. 42 cm. (16½ in.). There was also a cloth version with wig and hair eyelashes that wore a knitted or wool dress, ht. 40 cm. (15½ in.).

1929: L'Hotel de Ville's Bébé Réservé had a bisque head, sleeping eyes, hair eyelashes, wig, fully jointed composition body. It wore a chemise trimmed with ribbons, and had footwear. Hts. 44 cm. (17½ in.) and 47 cm. (18½ in.) were priced $5.00 and $6.40.

Bébé Rieur (Laughing Bébé). 1912. Trade name for a bent-limb baby wearing a short baby dress and sold by *Bon Marché;* ht. 30 cm. (12 in.) was priced $1.58.

Bébé Rivoli. 1921–29. Trade name used by *L'Hotel de Ville* for a bisque-head doll with sleeping eyes, a mohair wig, fully jointed composition body, and a chemise trimmed with ribbons. In 1929 the doll had eyelashes. It came in the following hts.:

BÉBÉ RIVOLI HEIGHTS							
1921		1929		1921		1929	
cm.	in.	cm.	in.	cm.	in.	cm.	in.
26	10½			57	22½	57	22½
29	11½			60	23½		
33	13	33	13	65	25½	65	25½
36	14			68	27		
40	15½	40	15½	75	29½	75	29½
44	17½			78	30½		
47	18½	47	18½	83	32½		
52	20½			88	34½		

These dolls were about half the price of the *Bébés Jumeau* of similar heights.

Bébé Roulant. 1905. Trade name for a mechanical walking doll on a cone having three wheels—on two in back, and one in front—on the bottom of the cone. The arms moved as the wheels turned. The doll was dressed in a pinafore and a bonnet. Ht. 27 cm. (10½ in.); priced 98¢.

Bébé Sætabis. Label found on a doll in Spain. The circular mark named *Jativa* as its manufacturer.

284. Bébé Sætabis mark found on dolls.

Bébé Samaritaine. 1897–1911 and possibly other years. Bébés made by *Jumeau* and possibly others, to be sold exclusively at the *Samaritaine* store for a slightly cheaper price than for the *Bébé Jumeau*. Until 1901 the doll had a bisque head with stationary eyes and closed mouth for the smaller sizes and sleeping eyes and open mouth for sizes 45 cm. (17½ in.) and larger. After 1901 the doll had sleeping eyes and an open mouth. Some of the open-mouth dolls said "Mama, Papa." These dolls had fully jointed composition bodies. Margaret Whitton found a kiss-throwing and walking Bébé Samaritaine.

Labels on the original top for the box in which the Bébé Samaritaine shown in Ill. 285 came out of. At the left were the instructions to cut the rubber elastic which held the sleeping eyes so that they would not be harmed when the doll was shipped. Similar instructions were on the box top of the Tête Jumeau in Ill. 261C. The larger label read: "To make the Bébé walk, place the hands against the mouth in the position to throw a kiss. Then take the Bébé by the back at the waist and strongly push it forward so that it advances with one foot and then the other and carries itself forward on its heels." Thus this appears to have been a kiss-throwing doll as well as a walking doll. (See THE COLLECTOR'S BOOK OF DOLLS' CLOTHES, Ills. 526 and 531.)

1897: The eight hts. were 26, 31, 38, 45, 58, 63, 68, and 72 cm. (10½, 12, 15, 17½, 23, 25, 27, and 28½ in.). The prices for these dolls wearing a chemise trimmed with ribbons and lace were 45¢ to $6.20. The "Mama, Papa" talking dolls came in hts. 45 to 68 cm. (17½ to 27 in.); priced $2.70 to $5.80.

1901: The hts. were the same as in 1897 except 25 cm. (10 in.) replaced 26 cm. (10½ in.) and 28, 49, and 53 cm. (11, 19½, and 21 in.) were added making 11 hts.

1902: The hts. were the same as in 1901 except the 25 cm. (10 in.) ht. returned to 26 cm. (10½ in.), hts. 34 and 41 cm. (13½ and 16 in.) hts. were added and 72 cm. (28½ in.) ht.

was deleted. These 12 hts. corresponded closely to Bébé Jumeau size numbers 1 through 12.

The Samaritaine catalog claimed that their Bébé Samaritaine had the same head and wig as an *Eden Bébé*.

1906: The Samaritaine catalog stated that Bébé Samaritaine was a Jumeau Medaille d'Or Bébé with open mouth and teeth. It had sleeping eyes and said "Mama, Papa." The first four sizes were the same as the Bébés Jumeau of this period, but the larger sizes differed slightly, they went up only through size 12, which was 69 cm. (27 in.); priced 45¢ to $3.10.

1908–11: Same as 1906, except that nothing was said about Jumeau, and the price of the largest size rose to $3.15.

1913: Bébé Samaritaine in a chemise had sleeping eyes and an open mouth; nothing was said about its being made by Jumeau. It came in 13 hts., 26, 28, 31, 35, 40, 43, 46, 52, 58, 60, 65, 69, and 76 cm. (10½, 11, 12, 14, 15½, 17, 18, 20½, 23, 23½, 25½, 27 and 30 in.); priced 55¢ to $4.80. The largest sizes also came with a speaking apparatus and cost 28¢ to 80¢ more.

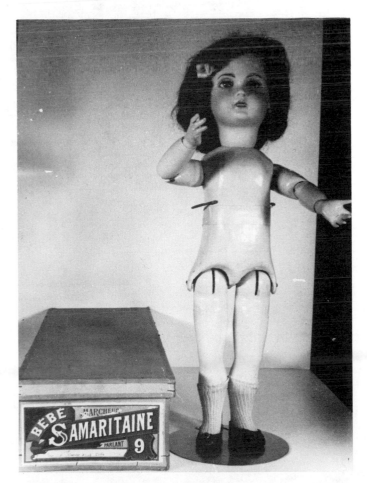

285. Bébé Samaritaine made by Jumeau for the Samaritaine store. It has a wig, sleeping eyes, pierced ears, open mouth with teeth. The original box end proclaims that it "Walks" and "Talks" and is size 9. *Courtesy of Margaret Whitton. Photo by Douglas Dewing.*

1914: Same as 1913 except ht. 60 cm. (23½ in.) became 61 cm. (24 in.). There was also a dressed version with hair eyelashes. It wore a removable silk costume and came in five hts. 54, 60, 63, 67 and 71 cm. (21½, 23½, 25, 26½ and 28 in.); price $4.00 to $7.60.

Bébé Select. 1927–28. Trade name for a doll made by *Bonin & Lefort.*

Bébé Soleil. 1891–1918. In the 1900s made by *Société Française de Fabrication de Bébés & Jouets. By 1918, Henry S. Benjamin* was the distributor in London.★

Bébé Steiner. 1855-ca. 1908. Line of bébés made by *Jules Steiner* and his successors.

1892: Distributed by *Marshall Field* who advertised that their dolls had "human eyes," jointed wrists, wore a promenade costume, shoes and stockings. Hts. 14 and 18 in. (35.5 and 45.5 cm.); priced $60.00 and $90.00 doz. wholesale. (See also **Le Petit Parisien.**)★

Bébé Success. 1894. Trade name for a doll made exclusively for *Petit Saint Thomas.* It wore a silk dress and came in three hts. 30, 40 and 50 cm. (12, 15½ and 19½ in.); prices were $1.50, $2.50 and $3.50. (See THE COLLECTOR'S BOOK OF DOLLS' CLOTHES, Ill. 429 C.)

Bébé Système. 1893–1922. A mechanical walking doll made by *Roullet & Decamps,* similar to *L'Intrepide Bébé,* but without a key wind mechanism and less expensive. Sometimes it was called "L'Intrepide Bébé Marchant Système." It had a fully jointed composition body with wooden limbs and composition hands. The bisque heads on these dolls were first made by *Jumeau* and sometimes they had a Jumeau mark; sometimes they were marked "L'INTREPIDE R.D. breveté S.G.D.G." Among the Bébés Système were black smokers and a character doll, mold #202.

SIZE–HEIGHT RELATIONSHIP OF BÉBÉ SYSTÈME		
Size No.	Height cm.	in.
6	42	16½
7	44	17½
8	52	20½
9	57	22½
10	61	24

After 1899 the heads were generally *Simon & Halbig,* mold #1039 or *Kestner,* marked J.D.K. The dolls were often dressed by the stores in which they were sold for example *Au Nain Bleu.*

The information on Bébé Système was based on the research of Anne-Marie and Jacques Porot.

1893 and later: Sizes 7 and 9 were sometimes known as *Kiss-Throwing Bébés.*

Before 1914: All these walking dolls had flirting eyes and all except size 6 were fully jointed. Size number 6 had straight

286. Bébé Steiner with bisque head, wig, stationary blue glass eyes, pierced ears, closed mouth, and jointed composition body having walking-type legs. Mark on head: "Le Parisien A 9." Mark on body: "Le Petit Parisien// Bébé Steiner//Medaille d'Or, Paris." H. 17 in. (43 cm.). *Courtesy of Sotheby Parke Bernet Inc., N.Y.*

limbs. Size 7 came either in a satin chemise or dressed. Size 9 had hair eyelashes and came in either a satin chemise or dressed.

1920s: Advertised in L'ANNUAIRE de la *Chambre Syndicale.* The dolls wore a cotton or silk chemise or were fully dressed.

Bébé Tanagra. See **Tanagra.**

Bébé Téteur. 1876–1926. Trade name of a doll made by the *Bru* firm until 1899 and later by the *Société Française de Fabrication de Bébés & Jouets* (S.F.B.J.). The agent in Berlin and Dresden was Thode & Knoop. The doll had an open mouth and was able to suck liquid out of a bottle in accordance with a Bru patent. Several Paris stores advertised dolls that could drink from a bottle. These were called "Bébé Téteur," and it seems likely that they were based on the Bru patent that was applied for in 1879 and granted in 1880 in Germany.

1896: *Printemps* sold a Bébé Téteur dressed in swaddling clothes and resting on a pillow similar to Ill. 170 in the first COLLECTOR'S ENCYCLOPEDIA OF DOLLS. The doll was 37 cm. (14½ in.), cost 95¢.

1900: *La Place Clichy* advertised a Bébé Téteur dressed in silk and wearing a bonnet. This doll was only 30 cm. (12 in.) tall and cost 98¢.

1901: Printemps' Bébé Téteur was dressed in silk, had its bottle and was 32 cm. (12½ in.) tall. It cost 95¢, the same as the larger version five years earlier.

1926: *Au Nain Bleu* advertised a Bébé Téteur dressed in swaddling clothes.★

Bébé Tout en Bois (Bébé Tout Bois). 1901–14. Trade name for an all-wood doll sold in most Paris stores. These dolls were made in various types, with or without wigs, with painted eyes or glass eyes that were either stationary or sleeping, five-piece bodies with straight legs or bent-limb baby bodies or fully jointed bodies. They came in many heights from about 27 cm. (10½ in.) to 69 cm. (27 in.) and usually wore only a chemise. Some of these chemises have "Bébé Tout Bois" stamped on them. One of these dolls has been reported wearing a chemise marked "Bébé Bijou† Ex-

clusively Française//Breveté S.G.D.G.//Paris." But it is not certain whether the chemise is original to this doll. Some claims have been made that these dolls were made by *Jumeau*. But by 1901 Jumeau dolls were being made by the *Société Française de Fabrication de Bébés & Jouets* (S.F.B.J.) under the leadership of a German named *Fleischmann*. At the Neustadt near Coburg Museum there are several of these dolls, one of which is a very large all-wooden doll supposed to be the prototype of some dolls made in that region.

Two of the Bébé Tout en Bois dolls have been reported with "Made in Germany" labels. The complete mark on one of the reported dolls was "Holz Baby//Bébé tout bois, fabrication Allemande." (Wooden Baby//All-wood Bébé, made in Germany.) This all-wood doll had a bent-limb baby body, glass eyes and was 40 cm. (15½ in.) tall. Due to the bent-limbs the height cannot be applied to the Heights by Years table.

One of these all-wood dolls had a purple stamp with the *Schilling*-type angel wings over the words "Deponirt//Germany//ALL WOOD." A sticker on another all-wooden doll was marked as shown in Ill. 293A. The angel head with wings appears to have been the trademark of Schilling. The trademark application mentioned wood dolls. But Schilling may have purchased the carved wooden pieces and made them into a doll. Thus it was possible that other companies such as *Löffler & Dill, Rudolf Schneider,* and so forth may have also produced these all-wooden dolls. (See Ills. 288–296.) The similarity of the features and bodies suggests that the carving and turning was possibly done by the same people for all of the Bébé Tout en Bois dolls but the finish, clothes etc. could have been the work of several different companies.

A sticker on another one of these all-wood dolls reads:

287. Bébé Teteur made by Bru. It has a bisque head, a lamb skin wig, stationary blue glass eyes, pierced ears, an open nursing mouth (any intake is controlled by a lever at the back), and a kid body with bisque arms. Original clothes. Mark: "Bru Jne 4." H. 13 in. (33 cm.). *Courtesy of Sotheby Parke Bernet Inc., N.Y.*

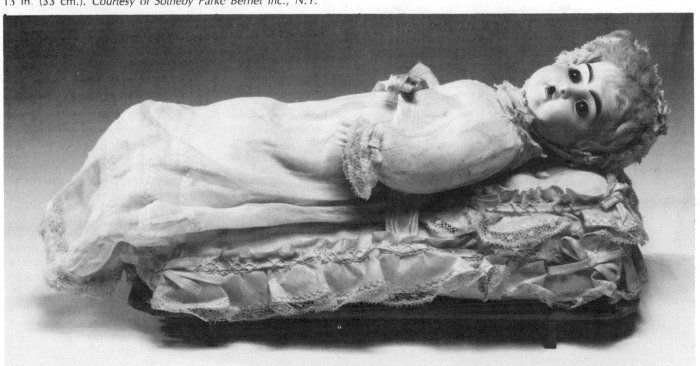

"TOUT BOIS•HOLZ•ALL WOOD//Fabrikmarke//(drawing of angel head with wings)//deponirt//GERMANY."

HEIGHTS BY YEARS, 1902–1914		
Bébé Tout en Bois (All-Wood Dolls)		
Height		Years
cm.	in.	Reported
24	9½	1914
27	10½	1905–14
28	11	1902–11
29	11½	1905
30	12	1911–14
31	12	1902–08
32	12½	1910–14
33	13	1905
34	13½	1902
35	13½	1905–14
37	14½	1908
38	15	1905–14
39	15½	1911–14
41	16	1905–13
42	16½	1908–14
44	17	1911–14
46	18	1905–14
49	19½	1905–14
51	20	1908–09
60	23½	1908
65	25½	1908
69	27	1908

The table is based on 14 catalogs from the stores *Samaritaine, La Place Clichy, Petit St. Thomas, Ménagère, Modernes,* and *Ville de St. Denis.* The prices for the dolls dressed in a chemise ranged from 25¢ for the smallest ones to $4.00 for the largest ones. In 1908 the Samaritaine doll carried a streamer reading "Tête, Corps Bois" (Head, Body Wood).

Motschmann-type wooden dolls had their heads and hands turned and carved in the same manner as found on Bébé Tout en Bois dolls. The elbow and shoulder joints were almost identical to those found on Bébé Tout en Bois dolls. They had painted wisps of hair, glass-threaded stationary eyes, and a flat joint at the neck; the middle torso contained a "voice" and was covered with twill, as were the upper legs. There was a bit of gesso under the paint, whereas the gesso was missing on the later Bébé Tout en Bois dolls.

The Motschmann-type dolls seem to be earlier than the 1901 date when the Bébé Tout en Bois dolls appeared in the Paris stores. The dates 1900–14 given above for Bébé Tout en Bois correspond with the period when the German Fleischmann was the director of the S.F.B.J. Since most Motschmann-type dolls have been found to be much earlier,

it is possible that these wooden dolls had been made in Germany long before they were introduced into Paris. The evidence proclaims that either Motschmann-type dolls were made much later than has hitherto been believed or that the Bébé Tout en Bois dolls were made long before their appearance in the Paris stores.

1900–1901: *Pygmalion* advertised Bébé Tout Bois in chemise, three heights, priced 29¢ to 49¢.

1902: Advertised by *Gamage* and called "Wooden Dolls." Came in four size numbers: 1, 2, 3, and 4; priced $1.23 to $2.48. These were about the same prices as the Bébés Jumeau but the wooden dolls wore simpler chemises and no footwear.

1906: Gamage advertised only the all-wood dolls which they described as "Better quality" in 1913. The sizes, heights and prices remained the same.

1913: Gamage sold all-wood dolls with wigs, jointed limbs and dressed in a chemise. The dolls had a diamond shaped tag on which were the words "The Bass Wood Doll." This doll described as being made of a close grained wood came in two quality grades as follows:

BASS WOOD DOLLS						
	Better quality			Lesser quality		
Size	Height			Height		
No.	in.	cm.	Price	in.	cm.	Price
1	11	28	$ .98	10	25.5	25¢
2	12½	31.5	$1.38	11	28	48¢
3	14	35.5	$1.63	14	35.5	73¢
4	16	40.5	$1.98			

Ca. 1914: Rudolf Schneider of Sonneberg made wooden dolls that carried the label "Bébé Tout en Bois."★

Bébé Trois Quartiers. 1906–11 and probably other years. Bébé named for the *Aux Trois Quartiers* store where it was sold.

1906: It was advertised as having a wig, sleeping eyes and being fully jointed. It wore a chemise with BÉBÉ//TROIS QUARTIERS on the front of the belt. Five hts. 27, 38, 40, 46 and 65 cm. (10½, 15, 15½, 18, and 25½ in.); priced 55¢ to $3.00.

1910–11: Bébé Trois Quartiers was advertised as being made by *Jumeau*. It had a bisque head with wig, sleeping eyes, hair eyelashes and was on a fully jointed composition body. The chemise had "BÉBÉ TROIS QUARTIERS" on its belt. It wore shoes and stockings. Four hts. 20, 40, 46, and

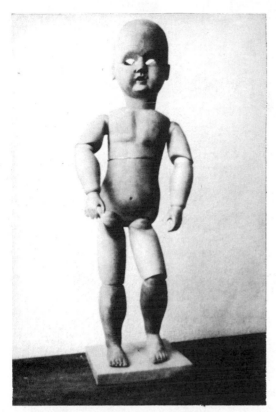

288. An unpainted wooden doll which resembles the Bébé Tout en Bois except that it was never completed. This doll belongs to the Neustadt City Museum which is now in Bavaria but formerly was part of Thüringia. *Courtesy of the City Museum of Neustadt near Coburg.*

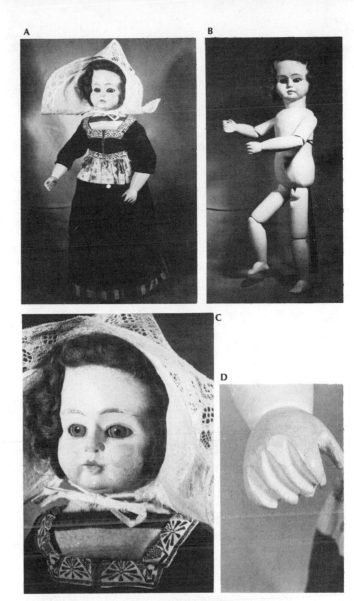

290A, B, C, & D. Bébé Tout en Bois, all-wood doll with brown wig, sleeping blue glass eyes, closed mouth, ball jointed body. Original Volendam Dutch costume. H. 21½ in. (54.5 cm.). *Coleman Collection.*

289. Bébé Tout en Bois (all wood) with mohair wig, stationary blue glass eyes, closed mouth, and original regional costume. Mark: Ill. 293A. This doll was made by Schilling in Germany as shown by the mark. H. 13 in. (33 cm.). *Courtesy of Shirley Buchholz. Photo by John Axe.*

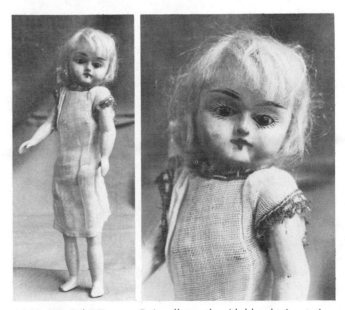

291A & B. Bébé Tout en Bois, all wood, with blond wig, stationary black glass eyes, closed mouth. Original chemise marked as shown in Ill. 294. H. 9 in. (23 cm.). *Coleman Collection.*

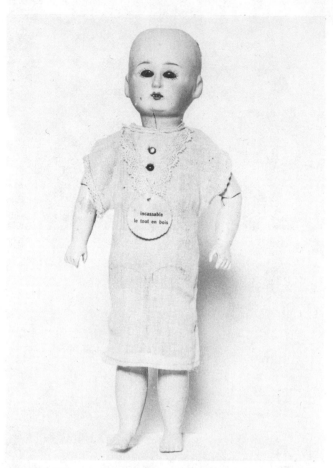

292. Bébé Tout en Bois head and ball jointed body made of carved and turned wood. The wig is missing. The bébé has sleeping glass eyes, an open mouth with upper teeth, and its original chemise. The tag in French reads: "Incassable//Le tout en bois." (Unbreakable//All wood.) H. 15 in. (38 cm.). *Courtesy of the Margaret Woodbury Strong Museum. Photo by Harry Bickelhaupt.*

293A   293B

294A Bébé tout bois   295 B

293–295. Marks found on Bébés Tout en Bois. These all-wood dolls were probably made by several German firms. Ill. 294 is a purple stamp on the chemise. Ill. 293A is a sticker on the body. The winged angel head is the trademark for dolls made by Schilling. Nearly all the large French stores advertised Bébé Tout en Bois from 1900 to 1914. But the marks Ill. 293A, Ill. 294 have the incorrect French "Tout Bois" on them which helps to substantiate their German origin. Ill. 295 is mark shown in Gamage catalog on an all-wood doll.

BÉBÉ BIJOU
Exclusivement Français
Breveté S.G.D.G. Paris

296. Bébé Bijou mark on a chemise worn by an all-wood Bébé Tout en Bois.

57 cm. (8, 15½, 18, and 22½ in.); priced 98¢ to $3.35. The two largest sizes also came "parl" (parlant).

Bébé Unique. 1923. Dressed doll with a washable composition head, a mohair wig, and a fully jointed body was advertised by *Ménagère*. Ht. 54 cm. (21 cm.) sold for $5.00.

Bébé Universel. 1920. Name of a bébé sold by the publishers of the girls' magazine known as FILLETTE. It had an "unbreakable and washable head," a wig, a fully jointed composition body and a chemise. Ht. 28 cm. (11 in.).

Bébé Ville de St. Denis. 1903–14. Bébé advertised as being made by *Jumeau* and sold at the store named *Ville de St. Denis.* It had a wig, an open mouth, was fully jointed and wore a chemise.

1903: The bébé had "BÉBÉ// A LA VILLE DE ST. DENIS" on the low waist band on its chemise. Eight hts. corresponding to *Bébé Jumeau* sizes 1, 3, 5, 8–12.

BÉBÉ VILLE DE ST. DENIS				
1910–1914		Size-height relationship		
Size	Height		Prices in 1914	
No.	cm.	in.	Plain	Sleeping eyes and voices
5	40	15½	$1.10	
6	43	17	$1.30	
7	46	18	$1.50	$2.15
8	52	20½	$1.78	$2.58
9	58	23	$2.38	$3.10
10	60	23½	$2.78	$3.90
11	65	25½	$3.38	$4.70
12	69	27	$3.95	$5.00

It should be noted that the above size-height relations do not correspond with those found for Bébé Jumeau.

297. There is a possibility that this is the type of doll which was sold by the publishers of the magazine FILLETTE, under the name Bébé Universel. It is an all-composition doll except for wooden upper arms and legs. It has a socket head, light brown wig, stationary blue glass eyes, open mouth without teeth, original chemise, cap and footwear. The tag reads, "TETE ABSOLUMENT INCASSABLE//ET// POUVANT SE LAVER." (Head absolutely unbreakable and able to be washed.) Incassable and Laver are in red; the rest is in black letters. Head marked "O." H. 11 in. (28 cm.). *Courtesy of the Margaret Woodbury Strong Museum. Photo by Harry Bickelhaupt.*

Bébé Vrai Modèle. About 1930 and later. Name used on jointed composition bodies of dolls made by the *Société Française de Fabrication de Bébés & Jouets* (S.F.B.J.). The oval sticker on the body usually read "Bébé// VRAI MOD-ÈLE// FABRICATION JUMEAU." Some of these dolls were distributed by *Au Nain Bleu.*

These dolls have been found with S.F.B.J. mold numbers 60 and 301 on bisque heads. One of the dolls was given to Princess Elizabeth of England when she was a small girl in 1930. This doll had a closed mouth, stationary glass eyes, and pierced ears. It was 13 in. (33 cm.). Other sizes have been found. A mold # 301, size number 12, was 68 cm. (27 in.). See Ill. 1360. No connection has been found as yet with *Bébé Le Vrai Modèle.*

Bébé Zephir. 1903–05. Trade name used on a label on the chemise of a fully jointed doll with a composition head

having an open mouth and teeth. Four hts. were 34, 39, 42, and 47 cm. (13½, 15½, 16½ and 18½ in.). These dolls cost 40¢ to 80¢ and were sold at the *Bon Marché* store.

Bébé Zephr (Zephyr). 1925. Trade name of an all-composition doll. With jointed arms it came in four hts. 35, 38, 45, and 48 cm. (14, 15, 17½ and 19 in.); price $2.30 to $4.40. It also came fully jointed in four hts. 34, 42, 47, and 54 cm. (13½, 16½, 18½ and 21 in.).

Bébés Marcheurs. 1929. Trade name used by *Mme. Lazarski.*

Bébés Réclames. 1929–30 and later. Trade name of bébés with composition heads made by the Société Nouvelle des Bébés Réclames. Also see **Bébé Réclame.**

Bécassine. 1905–30 and later. Popular French legendary character. The name is derived from Bécasses near Quimper in Brittany, France. She first appeared and ran for many years in a pictorial story published in the periodical LA SEMAINE DE SUZETTE. Maurice Languereau, the nephew of *Henri Gautier,* was the author of this series as well as of the many

298A & B. Doll dressed as Bécassine has a composition head with molded bonnet, painted eyes, closed mouth and the metal ball multi-joints typical of the dolls made by Bucherer. Original felt costume. H. 7¾ in. (19.5 cm.). *Coleman Collection.*

299. Cloth label on a doll's clothes identifying it as Bécassine.

Bécassine books which began to be published in 1923 by the Henri Gautier firm.

Maurice Languereau used an anagram of his first name, Caumery (with a y instead of the i). Bécassine was drawn by *Emile Pinchon.* Dolls representing Bécassine have been popular for most of the 20th century, and have been made in almost every material: bisque, cloth, composition, rubber, wood, metal and so on. At the Judge's Lodging Museum in England a cloth Bécassine had a white tag reading "Bécassine//Déposé." Another doll dressed as Bécassine had a round face bisque head made by *William Goebel.*

Bleuette, an S.F.B.J. *(Société Française de Fabrication de Bébés & Jouets)* bisque head bébé, had a Bécassine costume comprised of a green dress trimmed with black velvet, a silk apron, a white bonnet and dicky, and cloth shoes. This outfit cost 60¢ for a 27 cm. (10½ in.) bisque head S.F.B.J. doll costing 50¢. Madeline Merrill reported a composition Bécassine 16 in. (40.5 cm.) tall with a French label stitched to the clothes.

1918: Composition head doll with wool hair, cloth body, dressed as Bécassine. Ht. 33.5 cm. (13 in.); priced $1.10. Sold by *L'Hotel de Ville.*

1920s and 1930s: All-metal ball-jointed Bécassine dolls were made by *Bucherer.* Ht. 8 in. (20.5 cm.).

1980: Bécassine dolls were still being sold in Brittany.

Bechmann & Ullmann. 1892–1930. Fürth and Nürnberg, Bavaria. By 1897 they were successors of *Leopold Illfelder & Co.* They were factory agents for *Carl Kalbitz's Kalutu* line of dolls and *Adolf Heller's My Gold Pearl* dolls. These were nearly all dressed dolls. *Ernst Turner* was the London agent.

Beck, Adelbert.† See **Beck & Glaser.**

Beck, Carl, & Schulze, Alfred.† See **Alt, Beck & Gottschalck.**

Beck, Gustav. 1907–10. Vienna. Listed in an Austrian directory under Dolls and Dolls' Heads.

Beck, Louis, & Sohn. 1926–29. Waltershausen, Thür. Manufactured bent-limb baby dolls and dolls with straight limbs, probably fully jointed dolls.

Beck Manufacturing Co. 1888–1921. Brooklyn, New York, and New York City.

1918: Manufactured all-composition dolls with glass eyes, human or mohair wigs. Dolls with bent-limb baby bodies came 13 in. (33 cm.) tall; fully jointed (including wrists) dolls were 18 and 20 in. (45.5 and 51 cm.) tall.

1919: Dolls came in 9 size numbers. The bent-limb baby dolls were 13, 14, and 16 in. (33, 35.5 and 40.5 cm.). The 13-inch size came with either painted eyes or glass eyes. The fully jointed dolls came in five hts. 13, 16, 18, 20, and 24 in. (33, 40.5, 45.5, 51 and 61 cm.). These dolls came with or without eyelashes.

1920: The 14-inch (35.5-cm.) baby doll was no longer made, but a 14-inch fully jointed doll was added; otherwise, the numbers were the same as in 1919 except for the addition of a 27-inch (68.5-cm.) and a 9-inch (23-cm.) fully jointed doll. The latter was described as a dolls' house doll

despite its size. The dolls were said to have bisque as well as composition heads. The dresses were designed especially for the Beck dolls; the larger sizes had hand-embroidered trimming. Beck also advertised a line of silk stockings and buttoned kid shoes with heels, as well as slippers. A new line of cloth dolls by *Van Walkenburgh* was announced. These were made of terry and crepe cloth and included the *Rag Shoppe Dolls;* some of them were dressed in rompers.

1921: The Beck dolls had bisque heads and came in 3 sizes. The clothes included knit outfits, predominately in darker colors so they would not show soil.★

Beck, Richard, & Co. 1903–11. Waltershausen, Thür. Produced dolls with heads of porcelain, wood, or papiermâché. The bodies were of leather or composition, either fully jointed or semi-jointed. They also advertised all-bisque dolls, dolls' parts, dolls' footwear, and wigs. Their mark was a R B W intertwined.

Beck & Glaser. 1892–1926. Königsee, Thür. A porcelain factory was founded in Königsee in 1892. Soon after, it was listed as Beck & Glaser. As early as 1897 they were making all-porcelain dolls' heads. In 1911 Adelbert Beck† took over the factory. This factory used the initials T P K under a tree, or a K in a ragged edge circle, or a B. They specialized in dolls' house dolls.

1926: *Seelig* was the London agent for their porcelain dolls and dolls' heads.

Becker, Georg. 1906. Hagen, Germany. Applied for a German patent (D.R.G.M.) for a "Reform Doll" about 50 cm. (19½ in.) tall.

Beden, Eberhard von. See **Ring, H., & Co.**

Bedington, Liddiat (Liddiatt) & Co. 1875–1930 and later. London. Prior to 1911 Percy Bedington joined Liddiatt to form this import-export firm.

1914: Sole British agent for *Horsman.*

1915: Imported Horsman dolls.

1917: Handled dolls made of *Plastolite.*

1920: Besides importing American dolls including Horsman and *Tinker Toys,* they were the sole agents for some of the Japanese manufacturers.

1926: Advertised the *Huntsmann* series of dolls.

1930: Handled black or white bent limb baby dolls including *Paddy.* These came in various sizes, with or without wigs and wearing a chemise.

Bedtime Baby. 1916–17. Trade name of an all-composition bent-limb baby doll produced by *Jessie M. Raleigh.* Modeled from a real baby, it had painted hair, steel spring joints, wore a sleeping coverall and a pointed cap. Ht. 12½ in. (32 cm.).★

Bedtime Buddies. 1929. A line of cloth dolls designed by *Gertrude Rollinson.* They were made of waterproof, treated fabric and had "real" fingers and toes. *Bobby Lou* was the name given to one of these dolls.

Bedtime Dollies. 1917. Advertised by *Richard Krueger;* cloth dolls representing girls and boys. (See also **Beers-Keeler-Bowman.**)★

FOR THE LITTLE FOLKS

BEAN BAGS; SAND TOYS; BED-TIME DOLLS; CHARACTER CUDDLE DOLLS.

300. Bedtime dolls as shown in a Richard G. Krueger catalog; these dolls came stamped and colored ready for the embroidery to be done. The faces resemble Grace Drayton's drawings.

Bee. 1927. Trade name for a doll representing a child; the doll wore a dress and hat.

Bee Mark. 1891–1921. Trademark registered in France by *Jumeau* and the *Société Française de Fabrication de Bébés & Jouets*. This mark, frequently found on the soles of Jumeau shoes, could have been used prior to 1891 and after 1921 when the registration was renewed.

Beecher, Mrs. Thomas K. (née Jones, Julia). 1893–1910. Elmira, N.Y. Granddaughter of Noah Webster, sister-in-law of Henry Ward Beecher and Harriet Beecher Stowe. Her first doll was made for her niece, Daisy Day. Dolls were made of pink or black cotton or silk, with needle-sculptured, painted features.

Beedle, Claude de Witt. 1912–13. Leominster, Mass. Obtained U.S. and German patents for stringing a doll by joining head and legs. ★

Beers-Keeler-Bowman Co. 1922–30 and later. Norwalk, Conn. In 1924 became William P. Beers & Co. Made char-acter cloth dolls that were "Famous for their originality." These "B. K. B." dolls included *Johnny Rube, Beanie the Clown,* and *Jazette.* Their New York City agent was *Richard Krueger.* ★

Beguin. 1850s. Paris. Made dolls.

Belgian Doll Co. 1918–22. New York City. Produced dressed dolls with composition head and arms called *Dandy Dolls.* This line consisted of 100 different style numbers.

1918: These dolls were new on the American market. *Runnells & Co.* was the factory agent.

Belgian (Belge, Belgium) Dolls. Many dolls were distributed and exhibited as well as made in Belgium. In the 1850s *Van Hollebeké* was a distributor of dolls in Belgium according to his trade card.

During the 1880s and 1890s there were at least four exhibitions of dolls where leading manufacturers of dolls obtained prizes. Then in 1910 there was the international exhibition in Brussels.

Reportedly *De Fuisseaux* of Baudour made bisque heads for dolls before World War I. A group of these dolls came into the Dublin Museum in 1920. Also before the war *Hermann Tietz* had an exhibit of dolls in his store for which a series of postcards were made. In 1916 there was an "Exposition de Poupées, Jouets, Vêtements, & Literies Destinés à la St. Nicholas des Enfants de nos Soldats" (Exhibit of Dolls, Toys, Clothes, and Bedding destined for the Christmas of the Children of our Soldiers). Donations even came from the U.S. Among the exhibitors were *Bon Marché, Bourse, Delhaize Frères,* Fischer Frères, *Hirsch & Cie., La Tentation, Le Jouet Belge, Le Jouet Liégeois S.A.,* and *L'Innovation.*

Also during World War I a Belgian sculptor named *J. Van Rozen* went to Paris, where he created dolls.

Some of the Belgian soldiers after their release from German prison camps of World War I were interned for a period in Switzerland. There they occupied their time by making dolls. These dolls were exhibited by the Art Alliance in New York City in 1918.

1923: An Antwerp firm made seaside souvenir-type dolls, dressed in costumes representing "all the nations that sailed the seas." Several companies in Brussels made dolls dressed to represent opera characters, but these were not successful, as people preferred German dolls. According to an article in TOYS AND NOVELTIES, in 1923 Belgium exported dolls to the Belgian Congo as presents to the native chiefs, who especially liked dolls with sleeping eyes and mama-papa voices. However, the native priests disapproved of all European dolls.

1928–30: *E. Chantrain* of Brussels made dolls named *Marvell.*

Bell, A. 1917–26. London. Agent for dolls of *Dublin Toy Co., Worthitt & Co.,* and *König & Wernicke.*

Bell & Francis. 1906–23. London. Made and/or handled character dolls from miniature to life size.

Before 1917: Made cloth dolls exclusively.

1917: Character dolls included *Colleen, Sunshine, Hockey,*

Tamma Shanta, Red Riding Hood, Pierrot, Pierrette, and *Allies,* representing the Allies. There were also dressed and undressed baby dolls and jointed dolls. The dolls were made of *British Ceramic,* cloth, or composition and were sold for 12 and 25 cents. (See also **British Products Manufacturing Co.**)

1918: The leading line was named *Darling Baby;* it included over a dozen baby-doll numbers. There was also a *Munition Doll* line.

Bellas Hess & Co. 1914–20 and probably other years. New York City. Handled chiefly dressed bisque-head dolls with jointed composition bodies.

1914: The dolls had wigs, sleeping eyes, and hair eyelashes if they were 16 in. (40.5 cm.) or larger.
     The following dolls were on child-type bodies:
Annabel, open mouth with teeth, Ht. 22 in. (56 cm.); priced $2.98.
Dorothy, Ht. 15 in. (38 cm.); priced 50¢.
Edna, Ht. 16 in. (40.5 cm.); priced $1.00.
Elizabeth, Ht. 20 in. (51 cm.); priced $1.98.
Ethel, Ht. 19 in. (48 cm.); priced $2.98.
Gaby de Lys open mouth with teeth, Ht. 23 in. (58.5 cm.); priced $3.98.
Gladys, Five-piece body. Ht. 17 in. (43 cm.); priced $1.50.
Marie, Ht. 18 in. (45.5 cm.); priced $1.98.
Marion, Ht. 16 in. (40.5 cm.); priced $1.00.
Nancy Lee, Ht. 14 in. (35.5 cm.); priced 75¢.
Polly Peeper, Ht. 13 in. (33 cm.); priced 50¢.
Violet, Ht. 16 in. (40.5 cm.); priced $1.00.
     Bellas Hess also sold other bisque head or composition head dolls including Adele, Alice, Aunt Dinah, Beatrice, Bess, Christine, Little Lilly, Little Margaret, Perina, Rose, Sadie Virginia, Whistling Willie and a Horsman *Wilhelmina* as well as celluloid or composition *Kewpies.*® Some of the dolls represented babies.

Belle. 1909. Dressed doll with a bisque head, wig, sleeping eyes. Ht. 20 in. (51 cm.); priced $1.25.

Belle. 1920–21. Stockinet doll made by *Chad Valley.* It had a hand-woven wig and the hair could be combed and brushed. The dress of silk or other material was removable. The doll wore a patented wrist watch. Height 12½ in. (32 cm.).

Belle of Washington. 1925. A premium doll of the *Attleboro Premium House.* It had blue sleeping eyes, teeth, colonial-style white hair, jointed neck, shoulders, and hips. The sleeveless party dress came to the knees.

Belle Tinker. 1927–30. Trade name for a segmented wooden doll made by *Tinker Toys.* Ht. 7 in. (18 cm.).

Bellet, Henri. 1919–20s. Paris. Made *Bébés Culotte, Poupards* including cardboard ones with molded clothes, dolls representing *Swaddling-clothed* babies and girls as well as *Polichinelles.* Henri Bellet was a member of the *Chambre Syndicale.*★

Belly Good Cook. After 1910. Cut-out printed cloth doll representing an Oriental cook made by *Art Fabric Mills.* Ht. 5½ in. (14 cm.).

Belouschek, Franz. 1911. Oeslau, Thür. Applied for a German patent (D.R.G.M.) for a doll's head with stationary eyes.

Belton, Louis-Desirée. 1842–57. Paris. 1842–46, Belton and Jumeau; 1855, Widow Belton; 1856–57, F. Poittier successor. In 1843 Belton was a witness of the birth record of Emile *Jumeau.* Belton lived and worked with Pierre François Jumeau until Jumeau moved away in 1846. The two men made and/or dressed dolls. This information was researched by Mme. Poisson, curator of the Roybet Fould Museum.★

Belton-Type (So-called) Heads. 1870s on. No proof of any head marked "Belton" has ever been reported. Some collectors refer to bisque heads with one, two or three small holes in the pate section but otherwise uncut, as being "Belton Heads." The top of the head can be concave, flat or convex. Heads with these characteristics visible on the exterior when examined on the interior have been found to have been manufactured by the pouring method, a technique used by the Germans before it was used by the French. (See **Pressed vers Poured.**)
     A few of the heads constructed in this manner had identifiable *Limbach* or *Simon & Halbig* marks on them. Unconfirmed reports of *Heinrich Stier* marks have been reported. A large percentage of the "Belton-type" heads had closed mouths and were found on jointed-composition bodies with unjointed wrists, small hands and long wooden stick-type upper legs. There were variations in the faces and quality. Among the mold numbers reported were 100, 116, 117, 120, 127, 137, 154, 183, 185, and 190. The reported hts. range from 9 in. (23 cm.) to 24 in. (61 cm.). The size number-height series is roughly as follows:

Size No.	Height in.	cm.
1	9	23
3	12	30.5
6	14	35.5
8	16	40.5
10	17½	44.5

Occasionally the holes in the pate are indicated but not cut through. (See also *Holes in Head.*)

Benco Dura. 1915–17. Mark found on *British Ceramic* shoulder heads made by *Dura Porcelain Co.*

Benda & Hipauf. 1903–13. London. Displayed jointed dolls of various types, dressed and undressed, as well as dolls' heads, wigs, and so forth.

1913: Applied for a German patent (D.R.G.M.) for dolls' heads.★

Benekendorff, Berger & Co. 1922–24. Made dolls.

Benischek, Karl. 1907–10. Vienna. Listed in an Austrian directory under Dolls and Dolls' Heads.

Benjamin. 1929. *Georges Lang* applied for the name Benjamin as a French trademark. See also **Benjamine (1929).**

Benjamin, Henry Solomon. 1887–1926. London. Agent for American, French, and other continental dolls (dressed and undressed), dolls' heads, limbs, and accessories.

1916: Advertised baby and other celluloid dolls, including the nonflammable *Sicoine* dolls' heads. Distributed various types of dolls.

1919: Advertised *Victory Dolls.*

1924: Handled *Ideal's Soozie Smiles.*

1926: Advertised Goggle Eye dolls.★

Benjamine. Ca. 1915–24. One of the bébés listed in LA POUPÉE MODÈLE for which clothes patterns were published.

Ca. 1915: LA POUPÉE MODÈLE published patterns in the form of two flannel pieces marked "Manteau pour Benjamine" (Cloak for Benjamine); also a bonnet for Benjamine.

1923: Benjamine had sleeping eyes; hair came in several colors; body was fully jointed. Hts. 30, 40, and 46 cm. (12, 15½ and 18 in.).

Benjamine. 1926. Character bébé with sleeping eyes and a smiling face dressed in piqué dress and bib. This doll represented the little sister of *Bleuette* but was only produced for a short time.

Benjamine. 1929. *Georges Lang* applied for the name Benjamine, as a French trademark. (See also **Benjamin.**)

Benledi Works. See **Nunn & Smeed.**

Bennais, Monsieur. See **Biennais.**

Bennati, Mme. Gisela. 1923. Chicago, Ill. Created costumes for 29 dolls, each 24 in. (61 cm.) tall, for the "Story of Silk" exhibit at the Second International Silk Exposition in New York City. Each doll had the characteristics of the person or God whom it represented. Among these were Buddha, Marco Polo, Queen Elizabeth I, and Martha Washington. These dolls appear to have been made of carved wood with articulated arms, and were similar to a group of 36 dolls designed by *Stewart Culin* and *Ruth Reeves,* which were possibly also costumed by Mme. Bennati. These dolls were sent to various colleges and universities to aid in the teaching of the history of costume.

Benoist, Jean-Louis. Ca. 1850–70. Paris. Made dolls; but failed in 1870.★

Benoliel, William A., and Eileen. 1922–30 and later. Chicago, Ill. Co-partners in the firm *Live Long Toys.* Mrs. Benoliel was the designer of the many dolls representing comic cartoon characters.

1926: They had 26 royalty contracts with 7 famous comic cartoon artists.

1928: The following article appeared in the January issue of TOYS AND NOVELTIES:

"How the Idea of a Doll Based on the Newspaper Cartoon of Skeezix Came to two Chicagoans at Same Moment, and How It Was Developed, by Eileen Benoliel.

"It was an interesting coincidence to receive a letter from TOYS AND NOVELTIES on the 9th day of November, 1927, asking for a little article regarding the history of the Skeezix Doll. This date happened to be the fifth anniversary of the day that Live Long Toys shipped the first famous Skeezix baby dolls to ten of the largest toy dealers in the city of Chicago, and on the 11th of November there were twelve prominent windows in the loop displaying Skeezix dolls.

"Both Mr. Benoliel and myself had for two or three years been dabbling around trying to invent some sort of toy that would be a big seller. Then one Sunday afternoon while we were reading the comic page to our two babies of one and three years old we suddenly said simultaneously, 'Why not make a Skeezix doll?' . . .

"Within five minutes after we had uttered the words 'Why not make a Skeezix doll?' I had found a piece of canvas that I happened to have in the house and immediately designed and cut out the first rough-working model of the now famous Skeezix doll. On this particular Sunday afternoon we could find nothing else to stuff this with except some packing excelsior, but within the next half hour Mr. Benoliel went to the nearest drug store to purchase some absorbent cotton with which to stuff the next model.

"This next model was finished that very evening out of a piece of cream colored sanitas cloth and hand painted with my regular artist's oil paints.

"The piece of sanitas cloth used in the first model proved unsatisfactory for the type of toy we wanted to make, as our idea was to make a doll that would be durable, washable, with the colors brilliant and fast. In the later development of the Skeezix doll we tried various materials in order to obtain these features, and at last we found, a high-grade white artificial leather, which proved just the material we were looking for, and this material is what we have been using in our whole line of toys ever since. . . .

"We were so sure that we had something really good that on the following morning, which was Monday, we telephoned the Chicago Tribune office and received information as to the whereabouts of Mr. Frank King, who is the artist and originator of the Gasoline Alley cartoon (which was then and still is to the date of this writing one of the most popular cartoons in the country).

"After receiving this information we immediately telephoned Mr. King and made an appointment to see him the same afternoon and talk to him about his permission to use the character and procedure for contracts of the royalty to be paid to him for the use of his character, Skeezix. His permission was obtained and rough contracts drawn up to turn over to the respective attorneys.

"Now came the problem of how to manufacture and sell this Skeezix doll. But we need have had no fear as to the selling, for, as it proved, our only problem was to be able to manufacture them fast enough to fill the orders which kept coming in. . . .

"I had intended to make these dolls in my spare time at home while still taking care of my babies, but after showing the first hand-made sample to Mr. Grund, Mr. Adams, Mr. Schoenberg, Mr. Paton and other buyers, and receiving their unanimous acceptance of this toy, we were convinced that we had something really big and later events in the history of Skeezix proved the wisdom of their judgments.

"On the strength of this conviction we rented space in a loft near the downtown district of the city. Now, the question of how to *make* the doll kept us both busy going from place to place, getting prices on various materials, cloth and cotton, etc. Then a visit to the Singer sewing machine plant and interviews with machinists and engineers, and we found a machine that would exactly do the work we needed.

"While I was perfecting the various problems in the manufacturing Mr. Benoliel was putting to work his varied experiences gained while working for Sears, Roebuck & Company, Butler Brothers, Marshall Field & Co. and Wright & Ditson. But the time Mr. Benoliel could give to this was very limited, as he was holding a position with an insurance company, where he had been employed for several years. Our capital being very limited, we were obliged to purchase one thing at a time and go very carefully. Within two weeks from the birth of the idea we were established on a floor and were in operation.

"Now things kept going faster and faster, and within another three weeks this business had assumed such large proportions that Mr. Benoliel was obliged to resign from his position and take hold of this rapidly growing business, which had grown too large for me to handle alone, so we formed a partnership.

"From the first day that we started manufacturing, which was exactly forty days before Christmas, we made and delivered over 50,000 dolls, and if it had been possible to have made more we could have delivered them, for we were obliged to cancel many big orders a few days before Christmas. There were messenger boys and porters from various houses lined up waiting to take a package of the dolls as fast as they were finished. It was a case of 'first come, first served.'

"Up to the present time there have been well over 1,750,000 of this model of Skeezix doll sold, and it is still the leader in the line.

"Of course from our success with this first cartoon doll we were approached by many artists with other characters from their pens, but we have tried only to take on those that have the greatest popularity and at the present time we are getting the bulk and volume of our business from about six or seven numbers. The Skeezix doll, Jean, Pal, Puff, Little Orphan Annie, Sandy, Smitty are the leading numbers.

"We are glad to say that our numbers that have proved failures are very few. One thing experience has taught us is that it is not commercially successful to manufacture dolls of any real person—that is, that it is only fictitious characters from cartoons or short books and such that really are the big sellers."★

Benon & Cie. See **Munnier, Maison.**

Benton. 1813. According to TOYS AND NOVELTIES, Benton was an inventor who applied a small engine to dolls' legs so that they could move alternately like a human being's.

Bepi. See **Bergische Puppenindustrie.**

Beppe. 1927–28. Trade name of a *Lenci* doll, series 950, dressed as a little girl, height 28 in. (71 cm.).

Bereinigte Chemische und Metalwaren Fabriken Bernard & Co. 1904–5. Berlin. Obtained a German patent (D.R.P.) for a jumping doll.

Berg, Conrad. 1898. Vienna. Obtained a German patent (D.R.G.M.) for a doll whose body contained a bladder filled with air.

Berg (von Berg), Hermann. 1904–30 and later. Hüttensteinach near Köppelsdorf, Thür. Manufactured dolls and dolls' heads. Used *Schoenau & Hoffmeister* porcelain heads.

Germany
H v B.
500/2 K

301A. Mark found on dolls produced by Hermann (von) Berg.

1922: Advertised celluloid and porcelain heads, jointed bodies, leather bodies, and bodies of treated cloth. Made *Marigold Babies*. Sole British agent was *Gross & Schild*.

1925: Advertised baby dolls with sleeping eyes.

1926: Advertised New Born Baby dolls. London agent was *The London Company for General Trade.*

A socket *Bye-Lo* type baby doll was marked "Germany// H.u.B//500//2/0 X K" on its bisque head. It had glass sleeping eyes and an open mouth.

1926–29: Obtained five German patents (D.R.G.M.) for baby dolls, especially those with voices.

1929: Advertised dressed and undressed dolls.

An Erich von Berg of Steinach near Sonneberg and Köppeldorf was reported as having a doll factory in the 1930s according to the research of the Ciesliks.

E v B
Germany
1

301B. Mark found on dolls produced by Erich von Berg.

Bergfeld, Sol, & Son. 1923–27. New York City. 1927–30, successor was the National French Fancy Novelty Co. with its factory in Brooklyn. Sol Bergfeld remained as sales manager in the new company.

1926: There were 127 style numbers in their *Charlotte* line of dolls.

1927: Made *Mama* dolls with voices licensed by *Voices, Inc.* Used trade name *Carolina Mammy* dolls.

1928: The name of the Charlotte line of dolls was changed to Sunshine Dolls. Labeled a new line, it included a Mama doll named *Miss Sunshine,* baby dolls, and character dolls. *Sears,* carried a Sunshine line of dolls, but it is not known whether these were made by this company or by *Reisman, Barron* which also made a Sunshine line of dolls about this same time. *A. S. Ferguson* distributed the dolls of the National French Fancy Novelty Co.

1929: Sol Bergfeld died.★

Berghold, Albin. 1903–24. Hüttensteinach, near Köpplesdorf, Thür. He applied for 12 German patents (D.R.G.M.) for dolls' heads or voices in 1903, 1905, 1908, 1909, 1911, 1912, 1919, 1921, 1923, and 1924.

1908: Advertised bisque dolls' heads with sleeping eyes.

Berghold, Willy. See **Engelhardt, Hermann.**

Bergische Puppenindustrie. 1926. Remschied, Germany. Made dressed dolls named Bepi. Agent in Hamburg was *Gustav Burmester.*

Bergmann. 1926–30 and later. Berlin. Exported dolls.

Bergmann, Charles M. 1877–88. Waltershausen, Thür. Employee in doll factories. 1889–1930 and later. Waltershausen, Thür. Manufactured dolls.

A C. M. Bergmann bisque socket head doll on a stockinet body with rubber hands has been reported. This doll was marked "B 4/1 //C. M. Bergmann//0//Germany." Ht. 13 in. (33 cm.).

1900–1901: Obtained 2 German patents (D.R.G.M.) for dolls.

1918: Advertised ball-jointed dolls with bisque heads made by *Alt, Beck & Gottschalck, Armand Marseille,* or *Simon & Halbig.* Bergmann made both bent-limb babies and child dolls.

1920: Used mainly Simon & Halbig bisque heads.

1924: Recently made flirty-eye dolls.

1926: Used *My Gold Star* as a trade name.

1927: Advertised baby dolls, child dolls, and older girl dolls. The dolls wore either a chemise or modern attire (1920s-style clothing), and carried a tag with the Bergmann 8-pointed star trademark on it. Registered Schütteläuglein as a trademark in Germany for dolls.

According to auction catalog reports, the size–height relationship for the C. M. Bergmann bisque-head, composition–body, child doll is very roughly as follows.

	Height	
Size	in.	cm.
4/0	13	33
6	23	58.5
6½a	24	61
7a	25	63.5
8	26	66
10a	29	73.5
12	30	76
15	34	86.5★

Bergmann, Josef. 1883–91. Sonneberg, Thür. Made dolls. Patented dolls in Germany, France, and Austria.

1883: He was on the committee to found the *Sonneberg Industrial School.*

1888: Obtained a German patent (D.R.P.) for a doll with a mechanism for the double movement of its head, which simulated nodding when strings were pulled. This doll was distributed by *Müller & Strassburger.*

According to the Ciesliks one of these dolls had a bisque ball-type head mold #224 which was registered by *Bähr & Pröschild* in 1888. The patent number 46547 was stamped on the body of the doll.

1891: Advertised bisque-head dolls with leather bodies or jointed composition bodies. These came dressed or undressed. Bisque heads and composition heads were also sold separately.

Bergner, Carl. 1883–1910. Sonneberg, Thür. Successor to Carl Bergner was Fritz Maaser. 1911–30 and later; manufactured dolls with *multi-faces.* Some of the bisque heads were made by *Simon & Halbig,* according to the records of the Sonneberg Museum. He appears to have used the initials C. B. (for Carl Bergner), and is best known for his three-face dolls. The faces are smiling, crying, or laughing. Sometimes black or mulatto faces were used. Among the heights of the dolls were 11, 13, and 16½ in. (28, 33 and 42 cm.). Often the body was cloth over papier-mâché.

1883: He was on the committee to found the *Sonneberg Industrial School.*

Ca. 1900: Date given for a three-face bisque-head doll by the Sonneberg Museum. It was originally described as the newest novelty made by Carl Bergner. The dolls' three faces each have a different expression. Doll has a ball-jointed body, says "Papa, Mama," wears a blue silk dress, and is 14 in. (35 cm.) tall.

1908: A doll of this date, called a *"Metamorphose,"* made by Carl Bergner is in the Sonneberg Museum.★

Bergner & Brandweiner. 1923–30. Vienna. Made dolls.

Berkeley Crocheters. 1928. Line of dolls' clothes distributed by *Katherine Rauser.*

Berlich, Rolf. 1924. Made cloth (?) dolls that resembled the *Gre-Poir* dolls. They had eyes glancing to the side, wigs and were jointed at the neck, shoulders and hips. Dressed as boys or girls in removable clothes. Hts. 16 and 20 in. (40.5 and 51 cm.); priced $1.30 and $1.70. *Karl Goerlich & Co.* was the London agent.

Berlin, Joseph. See **Fleischmann & Blödel (Bloedel).**

Berliner, Emile. 1890–94. Waltershausen, Thür. Patented a doll that recited prayers or sang children's songs in English, French or German. Ht. 60 cm. (23½ in.) or less. This phonograph type doll was produced by *Kämmer & Reinhardt.*

Berliner Celluloidfabrik. See **Kuntz & Co.**

Berndt, Walter. 1929. U.S.A. Created the cartoon character "Smitty." His designs were used for the all-bisque dolls *Smitty* and *Herby* with jointed necks.

134

C. M. Bergmann. Waltershausen
DOLL FACTORY, THURINGIA, GERMANY
Established 1888
SEND FOR SAMPLES AND PRICE LIST

302. C. M. Bergmann advertisement in PLAYTHINGS, May 1927. Often the factory pictures show an area of buildings larger than the factory actually was. Note the slender legs and bodies.

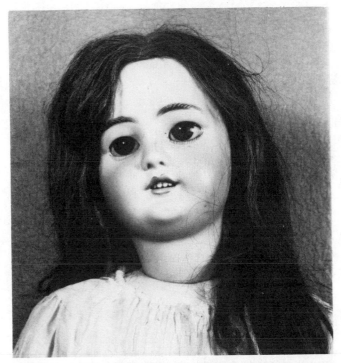

303. Bisque head doll made by C. M. Bergmann has a wig, sleeping blue eyes, open mouth with four upper teeth, and a fully jointed composition body. Simon & Halbig made the head. Mark: III. 304A. H. 25½ in. (63.5 cm.). *Courtesy of Cherry Bou.*

C.M.BERGMANN
SIMON & HALBIG
12

A

S&H
C.M.B

B

B +/
C.M.Bergmann
o
Germany

C

M.BERGMANN
1916
WALTERSHAUSEN

D

304A, B, C, & D. Marks of C. M. Bergmann. No. 304A is on the bisque head made by Simon & Halbig.

Berner, Jacques. 1888. Paris. Registered the initials J. B. as a trademark in France. (See also **Balleroy, Jullien.**)★

Bernhard, Adam. 1926–27. New York City. Factory agent, importer, and jobber.

1927: Sole agent in the U.S.A. for *Rheinische Gummi und Celluloid Fabrik Co.*

Bernhardt, B. 1896–1926. Budapest. Made dolls. He was succeeded by his sons.

Bernhardt, Bauer. 1898. Piesau near Wallendorf, Thür. Made and exported all-bisque dolls and china *Frozen Charlottes.*

Berrick Bros. 1926. London. Imported *Nankeen* dolls, celluloid *Kewpies* and dolls jointed at the shoulders and hips.

Berry & Ross. 1919. New York City. Factory owned by black people and employed black workers who made brown colored composition dolls. Some of the dolls had flowing hair, some had hair with marcel waves and some of the hair was in the Buster Brown style. These dolls were 16 in. (40.5 cm.) tall. Other dolls were dressed as soldier boys. Prices ranged from $1.50 to $3.50.

Bersi (Italian Soldier). 1916. Name of a felt doll made by *Steiff.* Ht. 43 cm. (17 in.).

Bert Williams. 1927. Portrait doll of the comedian of this name. Doll pulling a cart was produced by *Davis & Voetsch.*

Berta. 1913–24. Trade name of a jointed felt character doll made by *Steiff* and distributed by *Borgfeldt.* It wore a calf length print dress trimmed with ribbons. Ht. 28, 35, and 43 cm. (11, 14, and 17 in.). Priced $2.05 to $4.05. The largest doll had a mama voice. In 1916 two heights were added, 50 and 60 cm. (19½ and 23½ in.). In 1924, four hts. 28 to 50 cm. (11 to 19½ in.).

Bertin, M. 1926–28. Le Rainey, Seine & Oise and Paris. Manufactured cloth dolls.

Bertrand, René. 1921–30 and later. Paris. Made dolls.★

Berwick Doll Co. 1918–27. New York City. Made *Famlee* dolls.★

Besnard, Mme. Amant. 1869–1910. Paris. Made dolls and won a silver medal at the Brussels Exhibition in 1910.★

Bessels, Moritz. Ca. 1900–11. Germany. Manufactured dolls. His London agent was H. E. Eckart of *Eckart & Co.*

Besser, Edwin E., Co. 1919–26. New York City. Mr. Besser and his partner Charles Kramer worked for *Borgfeldt* for many years before establishing their own company. They were importers and jobbers but specialized in American lines of dolls. They represented Western Doll Manufacturing Co.† and *Kiddie Specialty Corp.*★

Bessy Brooks. 1921–23. Trade name for a dressed stockinet cloth doll made by *Martha Chase.* Ht. 12 in. (30.5 cm.).

Best & Co. 1902–30 and probably other years. New York City. Sold dolls.

1915: Advertised *Horsman* dolls such as *Campbell Kids, Baby Blossom, School Girl,* cloth dolls including *Red Riding Hood* and *Topsy Turvy.*★

Bestelmeier, Georg Hieronymus. 1793–1812 and probably other years. Nürnberg, Bavaria. Advertised dolls in his catalogs.★

Bester Doll Manufacturing Co. 1919–21. Bloomfield and

Newark, N.J. Made composition dolls which they claimed resembled bisque. The dolls had eyes mounted on springs and long eyelashes. The bodies were fully jointed composition or cork-stuffed cloth with inside joints. The dolls wore American style clothes and were distributed by *Davis & Voetsch.* The Bester factory went into receivership in 1921.★

Bethel Doll Co. 1930. Jamaica, Long Island. Produced dolls.

Betsy Ross. 1917–18. Trade name of a composition doll made by *K & K* and distributed by *Borgfeldt.* The clothes of this doll were claimed to have been made of the same type of material as those worn by children.

1917: TOYS AND NOVELTIES reported: "The story of Betsy Ross and our flag appears in an attractive little red-white-and-blue booklet for little ones, and is packed with every doll. . . .

"The doll is of composition head and hands, painted features and painted hair; full cork-stuffed body, arms and legs with concealed joints. It is dressed in good quality white lawn, with broad national-colored sash over shoulder, with baby pin, and national-colored trimming on hem of skirt; underwear, removable shoes and stockings; straw hat trimmed with national color ribbon. Each doll packed in national-colored trimmed box."

Betsy Ross. 1924. Trade name of a *Mama* doll made by the *National Doll Co.* and distributed by *Borgfeldt.* These dressed dolls had sleeping eyes and came with either composition or cloth legs.★

Betsy Ross. 1926. See **Uncle Sam and Betsy Ross.**

Bette. 1893 and later. Name of a *Kestner* doll stamped on its ball jointed composition body which also had a patent number and the word "Excelsior" stamped on it. The date of the patent was 1893 and the bisque socket head's mold number was 129.

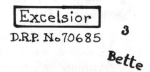

305. Mark found on Bette dolls, made by Kestner.

Betty. 1909–14. Doll with celluloid face and cloth body produced by *Horsman.*

1914: It wore a bloused waistline dress and a frilly bonnet. Priced 50¢.★

Betty. 1916. Cutout cloth doll designed by *Margaret Evans* and made by *Stecher Lithographic Co.* One large doll and two small ones wearing a dress and hair ribbon were on a sheet of cloth 25½ in. by 36½ in. (65 cm. by 93 cm.). Lithographed in five colors. Betty was the mate to *Bobby.*

Betty. 1917. Doll with rumpled hair made by *Shanklin.* It was one of the naughty *Three Little Sisters.*

Betty. 1919–21. Cutout cloth doll made by *Saalfield.* The cloth was 18 in. by 21 in. (45.5 by 53.5 cm.).

Betty (Betty Bobs). 1920–21. A floating doll with a spherical rubber or cork head and hand painted face, made by *Rees Davis.*

Betty. 1920–24. *Mama* doll designed by *Georgene Averill* and manufactured by *Paul Averill.* It was claimed that the doll could dance as well as walk and talk. The head, arms and legs were composition and the body was cloth. It wore a white organdy dress and bonnet to match. The footwear consisted of socks and single strap slippers.★

Betty. 1924. One of the La Petite *Caresse* dolls made by *Chad Valley.* This cloth doll stuffed with kapok had real hair, a hand painted face and wore a dress and hat of velveteen trimmed with imitation white fur, and fancy wool socks. The doll had a 6 sided tag reading: "Chad Valley// Hygienic// Fabric Toys."

It came in the following versions:

Style No.	Height.	
	in.	cm.
256	11	28
257	12½	31.5
258	14	35.5

(See also **Lady Betty**.)

Betty (Betty Bubbles). 1925–27. Trade name for a child doll made by *Effanbee.* It had a wig with long curls but the composition head appears to have been the same mold as that used for *Bubbles,* the baby, with its dimples in each cheek. Also Betty came with six photographs, just as Bubbles did.

Betty. 1927. A doll dressed in a coat and tam representing a child.

Betty Ann. 1927. Made by *Averill Manufacturing Co.,* distributed by *Montgomery Ward,* "Modeled by a European Genius" according to the advertisement. It had a celluloid head, molded hair, glass eyes, composition arms and legs on a cloth body and was dressed. Hts. 14 and 19 in. (35.5 and 48 cm.); priced $3.59 and $5.39.

Betty Bingham. 1926. Trademark for dolls registered in U.S. by *Hills, McLean & Haskins.*

Betty Blue. 1913–20. Cloth doll made by *Dean.*

1913: One of the *Tru-to-Life* series. Ht. 20 in. (51 cm.).

1920: One of the Tru-to-Life series; style No. D192 had printed hair; style No. D201 had a wig. Ht. 18½ in. (47 cm.).

Betty Blue also came as a flat-faced *Knockabout* doll, style No. D3. Ht. 19 in. (48 cm.).

The Knockabout cutout sheet for Betty Blue was style No. S72 and had directions in both English and French. It was suggested that the doll be filled with wood, wool or granulated cork. Ht. of doll 20 in. (51 cm.).

Betty Bonnet. 1918. An all-composition doll with a 5 piece body and steel spring joints made by *Jessie M. Raleigh.* It wore a flowered lawn dress and a brimmed hat with tying strings.★

Betty Bonser. 1930. Cloth doll made by *Bonser.*

Betty Bounce. 1913–19. Line of dolls made by *Effanbee,* distributed by *Montgomery Ward.* Pat Schoonmaker reports one of these dolls marked *Deco* for *Otto Denivelle* on the head and with the Effanbee label on its chest. Some of them were called Tango Kiddies when they had red, blue or green hair.

Betty Bronson Cinderella Doll. 1926. *Topsy Turvy* doll with two composition heads, having wigs and sleeping eyes. This is not a portrait doll but one end was dressed to resemble Betty Bronson as she appeared in the first part of the movie, A KISS FOR CINDERELLA, wearing a laced bodice, calico skirt and mob cap. The other end was dressed as a Princess wearing a silk dress, with bodice covered with lace, and a knitted crown on its head. The skirt was double-faced to effect the change. Ht. 14 in. (35.5 cm.); priced $4.00.

Betty Bubbles. See **Betty (Betty Bubbles).**

Betty Jean. See **Pretty Peggy.**

Betty Lee. 1924–25. *Mama* doll made by *Effanbee,* wore removable clothes including a tam.★

Betty O'Baby (Betty O'Portrait). 1929. Baby doll featherweight and washable created by *Betty Martin.*

Betty SHEbee. See **HEbee SHEbee.**

Betty and Bobby. 1915. Pair of cutout cloth dolls with character faces designed by *Margaret Evans Price.* Ht. 24 in. (61 cm.); plus four smaller versions 6½ in. (16.5 cm.).

Beyler, Albert. 1929. Germany. Obtained a U.S. patent for a pendulum to close each eye of a doll when it is in a horizontal position. The patent was assigned to the *Rheinische Gummi und Celluloid Fabrik.*

Biberian, Gregoire. 1929–30 and later. Nice, France. Registered in France a trademark for dolls consisting of the initials B G intertwined over *La Mascotte* both in a framed square. He made cloth art dolls. *M. Manuel* was the Paris representative.

 306. Mark used by Gregoire Biberian for dolls.

Bico. 1928. Trademark used for their *Rosebud* and *Little Sweetheart* lines by *B. Illfelder & Co.*

Bicot. 1926. Trademark registered in France by *Mme. Julienne Lubecka.*

Biennais (Bennais, Monsieur). Early 1800s. Paris. Made dolls and had a shop called "At the sign of the Violet Monkey" (Au Singe Violette). The shop *Au Nain Bleu* (At the sign of the Blue Dwarf) and *Au Paradis des Enfants* were later located in this same area.

Bierer, L. 1845–1930 and later. Sonneberg, Thür., and Fürth, Bavaria. Handled dolls including ones with porcelain heads made by *Recknagle.*★

101SK
made in germany

307. Mark probably used by L. Bierer on bisque heads made by Recknagle.

Bierschenk, Fritz. 1906–30 and later. Sonneberg, Thür. Manufactured and exported dolls, both dressed and undressed.

1908: Obtained a German patent (D.R.G.M.) for a doll with a mask face.

1926: Obtained a German patent (D.R.G.M.) for cloth dolls in the shape of babies.

1927: Obtained a German patent (D.R.G.M.) for a craft type of doll.

The Sonneberg Museum has a doll with a linen head imprinted with the Bierschenk name. The body was stuffed linen and the dress was of white muslin. This doll was 35 cm. (14 in.) high and dated 1090 by the Museum.★

F3B
Germany

FB
3¾

308A & B. Marks possibly used by Fritz Bierschenk.

Bieseke, Emil. 1900. Berlin. Obtained a German patent (D.R.G.M.) for cutting out a doll.

Big Baby. See **Babyland Rag Dolls.**

Big Baby Doll. 1920. Cloth *Knockabout* doll made by *Dean.* This doll representing a child could be dressed in a baby's cast-off clothes. It came in three versions: No. S73 was a cutout cloth doll with three small dolls also on the sheet; No. D191 had a *Tru-to-Life* face and printed hair; No. D200 had a Tru-to-Life face and a wig. All three versions were 24 in. (61 cm.) tall.

Big Five. 1921. Line of large dolls made by *Effanbee.* They were dressed in French gingham and cambric rompers with matching sunbonnets or caps.

Big Game Hunter. 1928–29. Wooden doll made by *Schoenhut.* This may be *Teddy Roosevelt.* The Roosevelt safari group of dolls was being advertised as late as this.

Big Eyed Gretchen. 1914. Advertised by *John M. Smyth* as having a composition head, arms and legs, painted round eyes looking to the side, cloth body; clothes included a sunbonnet and removable footwear. Ht. 15½ in. (39.5 cm.); priced 69¢.

Bijou Doll Co., The. 1915–17. New York City. Made dolls with composition heads and hands. An 11 in. (28 cm.) doll had a mohair wig and cost 50¢. The following dolls had painted hair and eyes, sewed on shoes and were 13½ to 14 in. (34 to 35.5 cm.) tall. Numbers 50 and 51 were dolls dressed as a boy and as a girl. Numbers 52 and 53 were a sailor girl and a sailor boy doll. Number 56 was a girl doll wearing a plaid Eton jacket. Number 58 was a girl doll wearing a plaid jumper over a striped blouse. Number 61 was a bent limb baby in a short baby dress and bonnet. Number 140 was a larger doll, 15 in. (38 cm.) with removable shoes and stockings. It was dressed as a girl in a lawn dress with lace trimming.★

Bikighaus, Vimie. Late 1800s. Philadelphia. Made clothes for *Jumeau* dolls. See Ill. 309.

309A & B. Bébé Jumeau dressed by Vimie Bikighaus, possibly in Philadelphia. It has a bisque head, blond wig, stationary glass eyes, pierced ears, ball jointed composition body. Original clothes have a cloth tag reading: "Vimie Bikighaus//1634 N. 12th St." Bisque head incised: "E. 6 J." Ht. 15 in. (38 cm.). *Courtesy of Sylvia Brockman.*

Billie. 1921. Trade name of a stockinet doll made by *Chad Valley.* It was number 38 and the wig was not woven. Ht. 11½ in. (29 cm.).

Billiken. 1909–12. "The God of things as they ought to be"

was created by *Florence Pretz. Horsman* secured the rights to produce Billiken dolls and secured the services of *Benjamin Goldenberg* to make this doll. It had a composition head with painted features and a plush body jointed at the shoulders and hips with rivets like the Teddy Bear joints. The smallest size appears to have been 11 in. (28 cm.). Marks were a stamp on the sole of the foot and/or a paper label.

310. Billiken with a composition head, molded and painted features and a plush Teddy Bear type body. Mark: Ill. 311. H. 11½ in. (29 cm.). *Courtesy of Richard Withington, Photo by Barbara Jendrick.*

311. Mark on the sole of the foot of a Billiken doll.

1909: *Macy* advertised a Billiken with composition head and a white "bearskin" body. Ht. 12 in. (13.5 cm.); priced 98¢.

Siegel Cooper advertised The Billiken as a Teddy Doll with a Can't Break 'Em† head and a bear plush body; priced $1.00.

Before 1911–13: *Steiff* made a Billiken-type felt doll which they called *Krack.*

1912: According to a Horsman catalog there were three versions of Billiken, all with a round button having "Billiken //Doll" on it. Number 1 had a white plush body and cost $8.00 doz. wholesale. Number 3 also had a white plush body but was a larger size 16 in. (40.5 cm.) costing $18.00 doz. wholesale. Number 100 was Buster Billiken dressed in pajamas and costing $8.00 doz. wholesale. (**Billiken Tumble It.** See **Tumble It.**)★

Billy. 1922. One of the *Happy Jane* line of cloth dolls made by *Harvard Garment Co.* Its face had hand embroidered features.

Billy. 1930. One of the *Kiddie Pal* line made by *Regal.* It was the mate to *Judy.*

312. Mark used by Regal for their Billy doll, in TOYS AND NOVELTIES, January, 1930.

Billy Bobs. 1920–22. Floating doll with spherical rubber head, hand painted face, made by *Rees Davis.* Mate to *Betty* (Betty Bobs.)

Billy Bounce. 1928–29. Elastic strung doll made for infants by *Petrie-Lewis,* distributed by *Corcoran & Laycock.*

Billy Boy. 1911–14. Two heads copyrighted by *Horsman.* They had short hair and painted eyes which looked straight ahead. The face resembled *School Boy* number 151. Billy Boy came in two hts. Number 168 wore a Russian type cotton suit with striped trim in contrasting colors, while the larger size number 271 wore a white washable suit with knickers. The suit was trimmed with striped "Galatea" facings and the doll cost $13.50 per doz. wholesale.

Billy Boy. 1913–15. Composition head doll made by *Effanbee* resembled *Baby Grumpy.* It was number 115, and had embossed mark "F+B N Y" according to Pat Schoonmaker. Ht. 15 in. (38 cm.).

Billy Boy. 1917. Jointed composition doll made by *Quaddy Playthings Manufacturing Co.* as style no. 906. It was dressed in gingham rompers. Ht. 15 in. (38 cm.).

Billy Boy. 1918–23. Rubber doll made by the *Faultless*

No. 168
"BILLY BOY"
Trade Mark

(Head copyrighted, 1912, by E. I. Horsman Co.)

A smartly dressed likable little fellow. Wears up-to-date, well cut suit of "wash" material, trimmed in contrasting colors, and white socks and buckled shoes. One of our most popular numbers.

Per Dozen........$8.50

No. 168 "Billy Boy"

No. 271 Large "Billy Boy"

No. 271
LARGE SIZE

"BILLY BOY"
Trade Mark

(Head copyrighted, 1911, by E. I. Horsman Co.)

A larger edition of our No. 168 "Billy Boy." This doll is one of the most aristocratic newcomers into our large doll family. "Billy's" suit of wash material is of the newest cut, white, with striped "Galatea" facings. White knickers, and socks and shoes to match complete his effective costume.

Per Dozen...............$13.50

313A & B. Billy Boy advertised in the Horsman catalog of ca. 1914. The composition head for the smaller size had been copyrighted in 1912, for the larger size it had been copyrighted in 1911. It had molded and painted hair and eyes, closed mouth, cloth body with composition Campbell Kid type hands. *Catalog courtesy of Bernard Barenholtz.*

116 **314.** Mark used for Billy Boy by Effanbee.

Rubber Co. It was patented in the U.S. in 1918, according to Faultless. The doll had molded hair, features and clothes, and came in two versions; one was yellow and black, ht. 5½ in. (14 cm.) and the other was red rubber. Ht. 5 in. (12.5 cm.).

Billy (Billie) Boy. 1920–24. *Mama* doll designed by *Georgene Averill* and made by *Paul Averill*. It was claimed that the doll could dance as well as walk and talk.★

Billy Boy. 1924. A cloth body doll made by *Pollyanna Co.* It wore overalls and a colored shirt. Ht. 16 in. (40.5 cm.).

Billy Champion Swimmer. 1912–13. A French celluloid doll with arms that revolve by means of a rubber band. When the rubber band wore out, the head could be removed and the rubber band replaced.

Billy Doll. 1916. Composition doll made by *J. P. Miller*, with molded hair and a bent-limb baby body, came dressed in a chemise in two versions. Number 1 had movable arms and legs, ht. 11 in. (28 cm.). Number 2 had a neck joint as well as arms and legs and was 16 in. (40.5 cm.) tall.

Billy Sitter. 1922. Line of dolls made by *Wonderland Toymaking Co.*

Bimba. 1927–28. Shown in *Lenci* catalog as number 950, a little girl in a ruffled dress. 28 in. (71 cm.) tall.

Bimblick, W., & Co. 1926–30. New York City. Made wooden bead type dolls. The beads had various shapes and were enameled with waterproof colors. The faces were hand painted. The 7 inch (18 cm.) doll cost 25¢. There were also 10¢ and 50¢ dolls. These dolls were distributed by *Borgfeldt, Illfelder, Strobel & Wilken, Louis Wolf, Mossman* and *Baker & Bennett*.

1928: Line called *Joy Doll Family* included a *Soldier Joy.*

1930: Bimblick was the defendant in a case of alleged infringement of the *Cameo* doll named *Margie*. Cameo won this suit.

Bing, Gebrüder (Brothers). 1882–1920. Bing Werke (Corp.), 1920–28; Bing-Wolf Corp., 1928–30 and later.

A large corporation with headquarters in Nürnberg, Bavaria, and branches all over the world. *L. Rees* was the London agent. John Bing was the American representative until the late 1920s when Max Bing represented the Bing-Wolf Corp. In the 1920s Bing Werke was a large conglomerate consisting of 31 subsidiary companies including such doll manufacturers as Gebrüder Bing, *Kämmer & Reinhardt, Max Oscar Arnold, Welsch & Co., Louis Wolf, Waltershauser Puppenfabrik*. They made Bing Künstlerpuppen (art dolls) and dolls designed by the artist *Albert Schlopsnies*. Bing was the only toy factory in Nürnberg that was not closed during World War I.

The word BING has been found on the shoe soles of dolls with composition heads which somewhat resemble the *Käthe Kruse* doll.

1910: Won a grand prize at the Brussels Exposition.

1913: Gebrüder Bing made plush and felt toys.

1924: Applied for a German patent (D.R.G.M.) for jointed dolls. Acquired a license to manufacture and use with certain restrictions the new American "Mama" voices in their dolls.

1925: Bing applied for three German patents (D.R.G.M.)

relating to dolls' heads. One patent was for the eyes in a mask type doll's face, another patent was related to cloth dolls' heads and the third patent pertained to sleeping eyes.

The heads on their dolls were designed by *Prof. Vogt* and *Emil Wagner*. They made newborn baby dolls, baby dolls, unbreakable character dolls, washable dolls, felt dolls and jointed composition dolls representing children. 201 and 301 were used as mold numbers on their S & Q *(Schuetzmeister & Quendt)* bisque heads. Their dolls were 15 to at least 56 cm. (6 to 22 in.) high.

1926: John Bing advertised *Baby Patsy*, a *Mama* doll with sleeping eyes and eyelashes. Ht. 15 in. (38 cm.); price $12.00 per doz. wholesale. Bing also advertised a cloth art doll, hand painted and with sleeping-flirting eyes.

1927: Bing Corp. advertised *Beauty Baby* and "a life-like baby doll having a rubber head covered with imitation skin which makes it feel and look like a real baby." They reported a large reduction in the price of their handmade washable "Künstlerpuppen" (art dolls), some of which had mohair wigs and sleeping eyes. Bing denied rumors of financial difficulties.

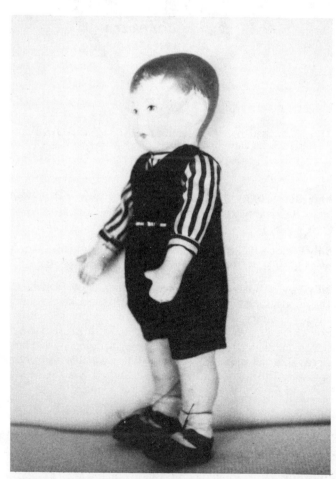

315. Molded and painted cloth doll produced by Bing. It has molded and painted hair and eyes and a closed mouth. The name "BING" is impressed into the shoes. H. 12 in. (30.5 cm.). *Courtesy of Shirley Buchholz. Photo by John Axe.*

316. Small cloth doll marked Bing on the soles of the shoes. It has painted hair and features. Original clothes. *Courtesy of Robert and Katrin Burlin.*

317–318. Marks used by Bing for their Beauty Baby and Beauty Art dolls.

1928: Bing Werke merged with Louis Wolf to form Bing-Wolf Corp. They still handled Kämmer and Reinhardt dolls and dolls of other affiliated factories. Among their dolls were the Beauty Art dolls with composition heads having mohair wigs, cloth bodies and felt clothes. There were 6 different costumes each with a hat. The hts. ranged from 11 in. (28 cm.) to 20 in. (51 cm.). Priced from $1.25 to $5.00. There were also brightly colored rubber dolls representing a sailor, a Dutch boy and girl, an Indian, a fisherman and a cowboy. Priced 25¢, 50¢ and $1.00. A much larger size cost $3.50.

1929: Bing-Wolf advertised "new and striking" dolls including the Kämmer and Reinhardt German dolls. Louis Wolf was in charge of importing dolls into America. *Averill Manufacturing Co.* became associated with Bing-Wolf.★

Bingo Junior. 1914. Shown in the *Marshall Field* catalog as a black baby doll with composition head, painted hair and eyes, cloth body including the hands. It resembled *Baby Bumps.* Ht. 10½ in. (26.5 cm.); priced $8.00 doz. wholesale. (See **Bingo†**)

Bings, Ltd. 1912–15. London. Represented German doll manufacturers, possibly *Bing.*

1912: Registered Sunshine Girl† and Sunshine Kid† as trademarks in England.

1915: Produced dolls representing nursery rhyme characters, such as Mother Hubbard, Mary Had a Little Lamb, Jack Horner, and Little Miss Muffet.

Bing-Wolf Corp. See **Bing, Gebrüder.**

Birkenhead Toy Factory. 1915. Birkenhead, England. Made cloth dolls with celluloid masks as well as *Golliwoggs.*

Birnbaum, Paul. 1914. Cologne, Germany. Applied for a German patent (D.R.P.) for a device for moving dolls' eyes.

Birthday Dolls. Before World War I–1930 and later. According to Agnes Daisey one of her relatives named *Stella Webster* designed by painting in water colors 12 dolls, dressed to represent flowers. The jointed all-bisque dolls themselves were made in Germany at first but during World War I they were made in Japan. The dolls had sleeping eyes and mohair wigs. The colorful costumes made primarily of silk fabrics represented: January, snowberry; February, daffodil; March, violet; April, daisy; May, tulip; June, rose; July, water lily; August, poppy; September, morning glory; October, hops; November, chrysanthemum; December, holly. Ht. 6 in. (15 cm.).★

Birthday Dolls. 1917. Name of dolls advertised by *Amberg.*

Birthday Dolls. 1919. Line of dolls made in England by *Deptford Toy-Making Industry.* Flower dolls were also included in their lines.

Birthday Dolls. 1920. Trade name of a group of dolls that were dressed suitably for each month and were created by *Jessie M. Raleigh.* These appear to have been the all-composition dressed dolls advertised by *Sears.* They had wigs and sleeping eyes. Each doll carried a coin and information on the flower of their birthday month. Ht. 17 in. (43 cm.).

Birthday Dolls. 1924. A new doll made by *Averill Manufacturing Co.* The doll had a horn that when placed in the doll's mouth and the body was pressed the horn would blow. The doll came with the verse, "Little Boy Blue//Come blow your Horn//For this is the day//Billy was born."

The appropriate name of the birthday child would be at the beginning of the last line.

Birthday Dolls. 1927. *Borgfeldt* produced dolls that represented the flower of each month.

Bisc Finish. 1913. This was the finish that *Amberg* used on his composition dolls. He claimed that it would not chip or peel and was washable as well as lickable. The Amberg composition dolls have survived in better condition than many of their contemporary composition dolls. It is believed that *Otto Denivelle* was responsible for the creation of this bisc finish.

Bisc Novelty Manufacturing Co. 1917–19. East Liverpool, Ohio. Genuine bisque dolls' heads were made by *Ernst*

A

B

C

D

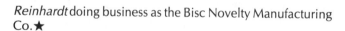

319A, B, C, & D. Birthday dolls dressed by Stella Webster to represent each month. The dolls in this picture are January as a snowberry in white, February as a daffodil in yellow and green, and March as a violet in purple. These small bisque dolls have wigs and molded footwear. *Courtesy of Agnes A. Daisy.*

320. Trademark used by Stella Webster for her Birthday dolls.

Reinhardt doing business as the Bisc Novelty Manufacturing Co.★

Biscaloid (Bisculoid). 1928 or earlier–1930 and later. Trade name for a durable composition used for such dolls' heads imported into the U.S. as those created by *Jeanne Orsini,* the *Gladdie* heads and the *Rock-a-Bye Baby* heads that appeared after 1930. These Rock-a-Bye Baby heads resembled the *My Dream Baby* heads. Similar names were also used, such as Bisculoid *(Hertwig),* Biskeloid, Bisquette[†] *(Artcraft), Bisqueloid (Hitz, Jacobs & Kassler)* and so forth.

Bischoff, Hermann, Jr. 1920–30 and later. Hamburg, Germany. Exported dolls made by *Schreyer, Gebrüder Fleischmann* and others.

Bischoff, Peter. 1909–27. Sonneberg, Thür. Made and exported dolls.

Bishops, W. H., & Co. 1909–24. London. Manufacturer of dressed dolls.

Bismuth Painters. Bismuth is a gray color but the "Bismuth Painters" of Sonneberg painted wooden dolls in bright colors.

Ca. 1750: Wooden dolls carved and/or turned in the Sonne-

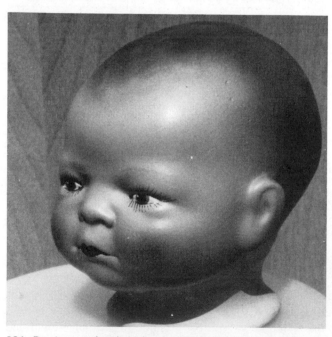

321. Bye-Lo type head made of a Biscaloid-type composition. It has painted hair and blue eyes, closed mouth. The Biscaloid appears to be a hard, smooth white substance, probably having a considerable amount of plaster in it. Mark: Ill. 322. *Courtesy of Mary Alice Thacker.*

BISKELOID

322. Mark incised on the back of the neck of the Biscaloid-type doll in Ill. 321.

BISQUETTE

323. Mark on a doll made of Bisquette.

berg area were painted by the Bismuth Painters and sold elsewhere.

1770: There were 19 master Bismuth Painters in Sonneberg. The Bismuth Painters Guild had trouble with the embossers who painted their own dolls.

Bisque Heads. 1850s–1930 and later. Bisque heads have been one of the most popular types due to their long term durability, their beauty and their relative cheapness. They were produced in Europe and a few in America and Japan. During the 1860s and 1870s most of the bisque heads were put on lady dolls. The all-bisque dolls generally represented children. At the Paris Exhibition of 1878, Emile *Jumeau* showed his French "Bébés Incassable," child dolls with bisque heads on fully jointed composition bodies. A few of this type of doll were recorded as early as 1876. These dolls were a tremendous success and the German manufacturers began to make their versions. During the 1880s and 1890s competition increased, prices dropped and new methods were developed such as pouring the slip instead of pressing it. (See *Pressed vers. Poured*). Earlier refinements were put to use in the making of bisque heads such as; gravity operated sleeping eyes, the affixing of eyelashes, the making of open mouths with teeth and the cutting necessary for the insertion of a voice box. Gradually the supremacy of the French bisque heads was threatened to such an extent that in 1899 the French manufacturers joined together to form the *Société Française de Fabrication de Bébés & Jouets* (S. F. B. J.). The S. F. B. J. almost immediately came under the direction of Salomon Fleischmann, a German who was the largest stockholder. The creation of German character dolls in 1909 added interest to bisque heads. Then the war in 1914 slowed down the production of bisque heads in Germany where most of them had been made prior to the war. France, Britain, the United States, Japan and so forth all tried to produce bisque heads to fill the void but the quality except perhaps for some of the French bisque heads was inferior. After the war recovery was slow in Germany, due to prolonged anti-German feeling and to the wild inflation of Germany's money. The effects of World War I enable us to date many of the German bisque heads as being prior to 1915 or after 1923. During the 1920s, catalogs indicate that German bisque heads were somewhat similar to those made prior to the war. This was probably also true of the French bisque heads of the 1920s when the peak of production was reached by the S. F. B. J. A few examples of catalog advertisements for bisque heads and bisque head dolls give further evidence of the history of bisque heads.

1872: *Bru* had bisque heads on kid bodies and on jointed wooden bodies.

1878: EHRICH'S FASHION QUARTERLY advertised "French dolls, 15 in. (38 cm.) long, bisque turned heads, glass eyes, natural hair, arranged in the most stylish of coiffures, and elegantly attired in either of three styles—ball, wedding or street costume."

1879–80: *Silber & Fleming* in London advertised bisque heads with fancy headdress and necklace, glass eyes, 7 sizes. Possibly these were the so called Parian-type bisque heads.

1884: *Lauer* advertised "French Jointed Dolls Parian Marble bisque Heads to turn. Fine glass eyes, hair head-dresses, and loose hair with bangs, ball jointed limbs with fancy silk and lace trimmed shirts [chemise]."

LAUER FRENCH DOLLS With "Parian Marble Heads" SIZE–HEIGHT RELATIONSHIP			
Size No.	Height in.	cm.	Price per doz. wholesale
2/0	11	28	$ 8.50
0	12	30.5	$ 9.50
1	13½	34	$12.50
2	14½	37	$15.50
3	16½	42	$20.00
4	18½	47	$24.00
5	21	53.5	$30.00

The same dolls at the same prices were also available with skin wigs that could be washed and combed. Separate heads only were obtainable in size numbers 2/0, 1 and 3 with sleeping eyes, priced $7.50 to $10.50 a doz. wholesale. "French Bisque Model Dolls' Heads. Turning heads and beautiful natural hair head-dresses." Size number 3 cost $9.00 doz. wholesale. It was not specified what the eyes were for this head.

1887: Lauer advertised dolls with "French bisque" turning heads and wigs.

LAUER DOLLS With "French Bisque" Heads SIZE–HEIGHT RELATIONSHIP						
	Jointed composition body		Kid body		Cloth body	
Size No.	in.	cm.	in.	cm.	in.	cm.
3/0					8	20.5
0	12	30.5				
1	14	35.5	13	33		
2	15	38	14	35.5	13	33
2½					14	35.5
3	17	43				
4	20	51				
5	23	58.5	16½	42	18	45.5
6			18	45.5		

The prices for these dolls ranged from $1.25 a dozen for the smallest cloth-body dolls to $28.00 a dozen for the largest doll with a jointed composition body. All these dolls were dressed in a chemise. The prices for the dolls in the above table indicate that the bisque head had little effect on the value of the dolls.

1923: *Wanamaker* in Philadelphia advertised dressed bisque head dolls with sleeping eyes, bobbed hair, height 12 in. (30.5 cm.) for only 10¢. These were German dolls.

1927–29: *Butler Bros.* advertised dolls with bisque heads, forearms and lower legs on cloth bodies. They had a molded pair of bows on shoulder-length hair. (This type of hair style has been seen on dolls made in Japan.) Four hts. 5½, 7, 8½ and 13 in. (14, 18, 21.5 and 33 cm.). The largest size was omitted in 1929.

1930s: *Armand Marseille, Kestner* and others made bisque heads in Germany.

Early 1950s: The S.F.B.J. was still making bisque heads. (See also **All-Bisque Dolls** and **Manufacture of Dolls, Commercial: Made in France and Made in Germany.**)★

325. Four untinted bisque-head dolls. They have molded and painted hair and eyes; all except one have ribbons in their hair. The two end dolls have pierced ears and all have closed mouths. The doll on the left has a molded cross. *Courtesy of Sotheby Parke Bernet Inc., N.Y.*

324. Untinted bisque shoulder head and arms on a cloth body. It has molded and painted hair and eyes, closed mouth. Original clothes. H. 9 in. (23 cm.). *Coleman Collection.*

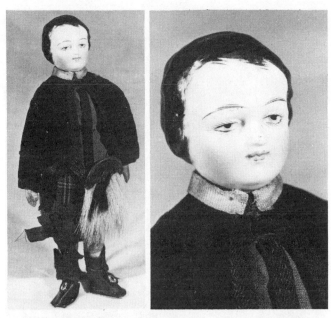

326A & B. Pressed bisque shoulder head with molded hair and features. The painted features include dark reddish brown hair and eyebrows, blue eyes, black eyelashes and the lips are outlined. Head is attached to a stiff kid body; doll has mitten hands. Dressed as a Scotsman in the Royal Stewart tartan. H. 8½ in. (21.5 cm.). *Coleman Collection.*

327. Pressed bisque swivel neck shoulder head on a gusset kid body with bisque arms. It has a wig, cork pate, stationary glass eyes, ears pierced into the head, closed mouth, probably a second generation dress. H. 21 in. (53.5 cm.). *Coleman Collection.*

328. Bisque head doll with a bald pate having a single small hole, wig, stationary glass eyes, open-closed mouth, pierced ears, swivel neck on a shoulder plate and a kid body without joints. Original clothes. Mark: "183//6." H. 17 in. (43 cm.). *Courtesy of Richard Withington. Photo by Barbara Jendrick.*

329. Bisque turned shoulder head with realistic modeling, brown wig, stationary blue glass eyes, pierced ears, closed mouth. The cloth body has leather arms. H. 24 in. (61 cm.). *Private collection.*

330. Bisque socket head with three small holes in the crown; wig, glass eyes, closed mouth. The five-piece composition body has molded footwear including four-strap boots with heels. Contemporary period dress. Mark "2/0 // B." H. 9½ in. (24 cm.). *Coleman Collection.*

331. Bisque swivel neck shoulder head marked XI which may indicate only the size. The eyes are blue and the mouth is closed. The gusseted kid body has bisque hands. H. 16½ in. (42 cm.). Head only: H. 4½ in. (11.5 cm.). *Courtesy of Z. Frances Walker.*

332. Bisque shoulder head with blond wig, sleeping blue eyes, closed mouth, gusset jointed kid body has bisque arms. Original Kate Greenaway style costume. Mark: "7½." H. 21 in. (53.5 cm.). *Courtesy of June Jeffcott.*

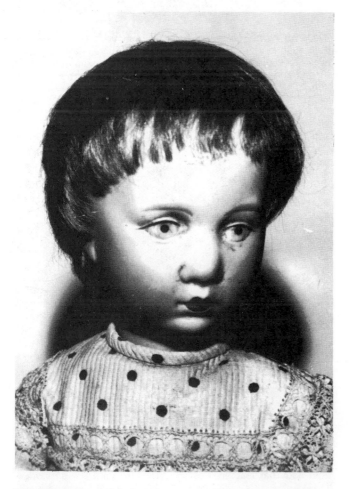

333. Bisque head character face, with mohair wig, molded and painted blue eyes, closed mouth, on a ball jointed composition body. H. 14 in. (35.5 cm.). *Courtesy of Magda Byfield.*

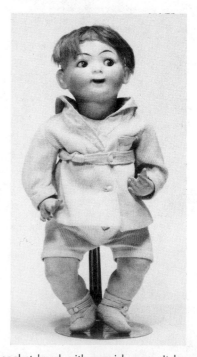

334. Bisque socket head with roguish eyes. It has a blond wig, sleeping blue glass eyes glancing to the side, a closed mouth shaped like a watermelon slice, and a bent-limb composition baby body. It wears contemporary clothes. Mark: "165." H. 14½ in. (37 cm.). Made by Hertel, Schwab & Co. *Courtesy of Sotheby Parke Bernet Inc., N.Y.*

335. Bisque head with wig, stationary glass eyes, smiling closed mouth, jointed composition body, original clothes. H. 14 in. (35.5 cm.). *Courtesy of Sylvia Brockmon.*

X I   **336.** Mark on a bisque-head doll.

Bisqueloid. 1926. U.S. Trademark for dolls applied for by *Hitz, Jacobs & Kassler.*

Bittle, Margaretha. 1894. Fürth, Bavaria. Obtained a German patent (D.R.G.M.) for dolls' clothes made of crêpe paper.

Black Bird. 1927. Trade name of a black baby doll sold by *Whyte, Ridsdale.* These dolls dressed in England came in sizes 13½ and 17½ in. (34 and 44.5 cm.). They cost $1.50 and $2.65.

Black Bottom Doll. 1927. Portrait doll of the stage star, Ann Pennington, created by *Jane Gray* and manufactured by *Gerling.* Arthur A. Gerling, doing business as the Gerling Toy Co., registered Black Bottom Doll as a U.S. trademark.

Black Bottom Vamp. 1927–28. *Charles Stein* obtained a design patent for this floppy doll with a loop at the back of the shoulders so that the doll can be jiggled or hung up. This doll produced by *S & H Novelty Co.* came in 8 different costumes and wore a button marked, "Black// Bottom// Vamp." A picture of one of these dolls shows it wearing an Eton jacket, a cumberbund, long trousers and a tam.

Black Dolls. 1830 or earlier–1930 and later. There were innumerable references to black dolls and a few of them are listed below. Black dolls were often named Topsy.
Kestner, Kämmer & Reinhardt and other German doll producing factories as well as many French doll factories for many years made bisque-head black dolls, all-bisque dolls and black dolls of other materials.
An ethnic black doll with a bisque head made by *Simon & Halbig* had a kinky hair wig, sleeping brown glass eyes, hair eyelashes, closed thick lips, pierced ears. The head was marked, "7//1302//DEP//S & H." The brown composition

body was lady shaped and had long separated fingers. Between its shoulders was a star while a "B" was on its hips. Ht. 19½ in. (49.5 cm.).

1831: THE AMERICAN GIRL'S BOOK described how to make a black cloth doll of rolled linen or muslin covered with black silk or Canton crepe. The dress was of gingham or calico and the bib apron was of a checked fabric. On the doll's head was a white muslin cap. See Ills. 337–339.

Ca. 1860: A German catalog in the Winterthur Museum showed jointed body dolls (probably wooden) dressed as girls and adults. One fifth of these dolls were black. *Pierotti* made black wax dolls representing Topsy and *Uncle Tom.*

1860: *John Robbins* inventoried black china babies and black china dolls, sizes 0 to 3 priced 37¢ to $1.00 doz. wholesale. Black dolls' heads cost 15¢ a doz. wholesale, according to a Day Book in the possession of Elizabeth Pierce.

1861: In May 1861, GODEY'S LADY'S BOOK, one month after the start of the American Civil War, gave the following instructions for dressing a black doll named "Miss Dinah": "Take a black china baby about three inches high, dress it with three black cloth skirts, the third one the longest, and cut with the scissors into scallops, and with a thread drawn into flutes. Over these skirts is a bright scarlet velvet skirt ornamented with braid and beads, over that a short white skirt tied at the waist with a cord and tassel. A ribbon sash passes from the left shoulder to the right side of the waist. On the head is a turban gayly ornamented with feathers and flowers." This doll could be used as a pen wiper.

1876–77: *Silber & Fleming* advertised black dolls undressed, with or without hats, 2 sizes.

1884: All-composition black dolls, ht. 7½ in. (19 cm.) and jointed black rubber dolls, ht. 9 in. (23 cm.) were reported.
Lauer advertised black china *Frozen Charlotte* dolls and black composition head dolls with colored chemises. The 5½ in. (13.5 cm.) doll had woolly hair and jointed limbs; priced 5¢. Larger sizes had glass eyes, composition arms and legs, shoes and stockings. Hts. 10 and 14½ in. (25.5 and 37 cm.); priced 15¢ and 25¢.

1885: *Horsman* advertised all-china black dolls in six sizes.

1887: Lauer in their catalog listed black china babies 3½ in. (9 cm.) for 33¢ a doz. wholesale. These were probably Frozen Charlottes. The black dolls with china head and limbs on cloth bodies were as follows:

SIZE-HEIGHT RELATIONSHIP		
Size	Height	
No.	in.	cm.
10/0	5	12.5
6/0	8	20.5
3/0	10	25.5
0	12	30.5

Prices for these dolls were 36¢ to $1.80 doz. wholesale.

Ehrich Bros. catalog had black bisque head dolls with wigs, jointed at the neck, shoulders, and hips. They wore a striped chemise; priced 49¢.

1889: *Butler Bros.* Sold black wax dolls.

1891–92: *E. Ridley & Son's* catalog listed black jointed dolls with turning heads. Ht. 10 in. (25.5 cm.) for 25¢.

1892: Directions were given for knitting or crocheting black dolls that could be made at home.

1893: *Horsman* advertised multi-head dolls, one head white, one black; black rubber dolls; black all-china dolls in four sizes; priced 5¢ to 33¢ doz. wholesale; and black dolls with composition head in four sizes, priced 38¢ to $2.00 doz. wholesale.

1896: YOUTH'S COMPANION offered a black doll with a bisque head, jointed arms and legs about 10 in. (25.5 cm.) tall as a subscription premium.

1897: A STUDY OF DOLLS by Mr. Hall showed that boys liked black dolls.

Ca. 1900: Mrs. *Beecher* made black dolls of old silk-jersey underwear.

1902: *Gamage* advertised *Golliwoggs* and black dolls with black curly hair, and brown kid jointed bodies. Dressed they were 10 in. (25.5 cm.) for 21¢ and undressed 13 in. (33 cm.) for 73¢.

1904: Mulatto as well as black dolls were described in catalogs.

1906: Gamage advertised Golliwoggs and black felt dolls that were probably made by *Steiff.*

1907: *Kaufhaus* advertised mulatto dolls with kinky hair, sleeping eyes, and wearing a red and white chemise. Four hts. 12, 19, 34 and 43 cm. (4½, 7½, 13½, and 17 in.); priced 19¢ to $1.06.

1908: According to PLAYTHINGS magazine, "The colored National Baptist Association entered a plea endorsing Negro dolls for Negro Children."

1910: Black wax-over-composition head dolls with glass eyes and molded hair, 9½ in. (24 cm.), were reported.

1911: *Catterfelder Puppenfabrik* made black dolls.

1912: TOYS AND NOVELTIES reported, "Negro mothers recommend strongly that only black dolls be given colored children to play with. . . . The result is that the factories turning out negro dolls seem assured of an exceptionally strong demand for that item. . . . And today many negro children were seen fondling black dolls. . . . Doll manufacturers already have prepared to assist this effort 'to instill in the minds of the children race love, race loyalty and race contentment.' "

Horsman catalog listed *Cotton Joe,* a composition head doll, and Topsy, *Topsy Baby,* and Dinah cloth dolls as being black dolls.

Parsons-Jackson Co. made black dolls.

Black dolls were exhibited at the Bavarian Industrial show by *Rat L. Wenz.*

1913: *Aux Trois Quartiers* in Paris advertised a black poupon (baby doll) with an unbreakable head and cloth body. Ht. 30 cm. (12 in.). Price 95¢.

Steiff made several different black dolls including *Sing* which represented a Senegalese African.

1913–14: TOYS AND NOVELTIES in May 1914 reported that "the doll makers of every race of people pattern their dolls after their own. There is just one known exception—the African race. Several efforts have been made in the United States to find a sale for negro dolls, and they have sold as character dolls to the members of the white race, but the blacks refuse to buy them.

"A St. Louis toy dealer who has a store in one of the negro belts of the city last holiday season conceived the idea of offering the little girls of the community some dolls of their own color. He was unable to buy anything from the jobbers that seemed to fill the bill, so he took half a dozen ordinary dolls to a doll hospital to be made black—not black exactly, but brown. They were done up in fine style with a tinge of red in their cheeks and lips, and a wig of kinky hair. The dealer prepared for a great rush, and arranged with the doll hospital man to take care of the orders he was to sell from the samples. But the negroes didn't take to the colored dolls. When the dolls were placed in the window many colored people stopped to look at them. Some went their way without saying anything, while others entered protests. Not one encouraging word was to be had for the dolls, and not one of them was sold."

Probably this failure was because these dolls did not have the proper ethnic features and therefore did not truly represent the black people.

Some all-bisque black and mulatto dolls with ethnic features were shown in the *Marshall Field* catalog. The dolls had curly mohair wigs, glass eyes and were jointed at the neck, shoulders and hips. Ht. 3¾ in. (9.5 cm.); priced $1.80 doz. wholesale.

1915: Information on dolls in Africa was reported in TOYS AND NOVELTIES May, 1915.

"The history of Africa does not extend very far back in the ages, but dolls are common there among the natives and seem to have always been known to them. Among the various tribes, dolls, and this might be said of practically all countries as well, seemed to have a special religious significance, and they are called by many queer names. The most common term in Africa is Mwanna y Kiti, meaning stool-child, for it is there a rigidly forced custom to keep the doll on a stool in the house."

Snowball, one of the *Gene Carr Kids,* was black.

Kley & Hahn made portrait dolls representing the black Senegalese in the Ohrdruf prisoner of war camp.

1916: Cloth black dolls were made by the *De Toy Manufacturing Co.* Ht. 15 in. (38 cm.).

1917–18: Black dolls were made in England by *Doll Pottery Co., East London Toy Factory,* and *Bates, Dewsbury & Co.*

In France a black Bambina appeared in LA SEMAINE DE SUZETTE, with *Bleuette.*

1919: Abundance of black dolls were produced including *Peachy Pets* that were swimmers.

The *Berry & Ross* factory, which was owned by blacks, made black dolls.

1920: Black dolls made in Italy had black faces with white eyes and black bodies. They wore chemises or were dressed as ladies and gentlemen.

1921 or before: *Mlle. Marcelle Giblet* made black dolls.

1921: Black cloth dolls were made by *Grace Corry* for *Century Doll Co.; Buds* and *Buddies* were made by *S. E. Delavan;* and the *Wise Dolls* was made by Horsman. Directions for a homemade black cloth doll were published in THE PRACTICAL TOY MAKER. The doll was to be stuffed with "sawdust, flock, clipped paper or any material to hand." Features were put in with black stitches; a piece of white material served for the mouth, beads for the eyes, and a piece of fur for the hair.

Trego made black dolls.

1922: *Effanbee* made dark brown babies. Kaffirs of South Africa made baked clay dolls.

1923: *Katarina Paar* made black dolls in imitation of Congo art. These dolls were exhibited at the Brooklyn Museum. The *Hitz, Jacobs & Kassler* catalog showed black wooden dolls hts. 6 in. (15 cm.) and 9 in. (23 cm.)

1925: *Shackman* advertised all-celluloid black *Kewpies.* Ht. 2¼ in. (5.5 cm.); price 85¢ doz. wholesale. And an all celluloid black doll dressed as a bride, ht. 2¾ in. (7 cm.); price $2.00 doz. wholesale.

1925–30: *Lenci* catalogs included several black dolls.

1926: Black infant dolls of the *Bye-Lo* and *My Dream Baby* type were being produced.

1927: *Brückner* produced black versions of the cloth *Dolly-pop* and *Pancake Baby* dolls. Several companies made black composition baby dolls.

1928: A dressed life-size black doll was presented to Mrs. Coolidge by the black children of Philadelphia, Pa. as an expression of good will.

TOY WORLD reported, "Where would you think black dolls would be sold? . . . The South or in those sections where a considerable colored population lives. But not so . . . Black babies are sold in Seattle, Portland, and San Francisco, through the high quality stores and in some of the highest priced numbers."

1930: *Chad Valley* listed 4 black dolls in their catalog including *Nabob, Rajah* and *Carolina.*

Allied-Grand specialized in black dolls. *Gerzon* sold black and mulatto bent-limb babies with sleeping eyes. The black baby sucked its thumb and wore a short baby dress and cap. Ht. 40 cm. (15½ in.). Ht. of mulatto baby was 30 cm. (12 in.).

1931: *Montgomery Ward* sold black girl dolls with composi-

tion heads, arms and legs, without elbow or knee joints. These dolls had black wavy mohair wigs, voice boxes, and wore yellow organdy dresses and bonnets. Ht. 18 in. (45.5 cm.); priced $1.00.

In the 1960s PLAYTHINGS reported that black dolls were successful in areas with a large black population.

(See Negro Dolls[†] in the first COLLECTOR'S ENCY-CLOPEDIA OF DOLLS.)

337A & B. Mother in a family of black dolls, made in Newbury-port, Mass., around 1840. The cloth doll is needle sculptured with a crepe head, black wool wig, embroidered eyes, eyebrows and open-closed mouth having teeth. The body is "creative." Original clothes including white kid gloves and a white cotton handkerchief. H. 9 in. (23 cm.). *Coleman Collection.*

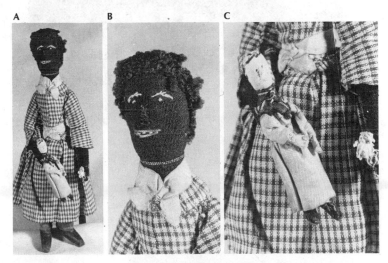

338A, B, & C. The black girl in a family of dolls made in Newburyport, Mass., around 1840. It is needle sculptured with a head of crepe, black wool wig, embroidered eyes, eyebrows and open-closed mouth with teeth. The body is "creative." Original clothes; the black girl carries a white cloth doll in one hand and cloth flowers in the other hand. H. 7¼ in. (18.5 cm.). The doll is 2½ in. (6.5 cm.) tall. *Coleman Collection.*

339. The black boy in a family of dolls made in Newburyport, Mass., ca. 1840. It is needle sculptured with a head of crepe, black wool wig, embroidered eyes, eyebrows and open-closed mouth with teeth. The body is "creative." Original clothes; it carries two buckets made of birch bark. H. 4½ in. (11.5 cm.). *Coleman Collection.*

340. Black cloth dolls ca. 1860s. They are hand-sewn with wig and embroidered features, original clothes. *Courtesy of the Museum of London.*

341. Black cloth needle sculptured doll with embroidered features. Fingers made of wire wound with thread. Original clothes. H. 5¼ in. (13 cm.). *Coleman Collection.*

342. Black china Frozen Charlotte with molded clothes. It has ethnic features, arms at right angles and clenched fists. The white clothes have feather designs and multicolor decorations. The legs with bare feet are apart. H. 4¾ in. (12 cm.). *Coleman Collection.*

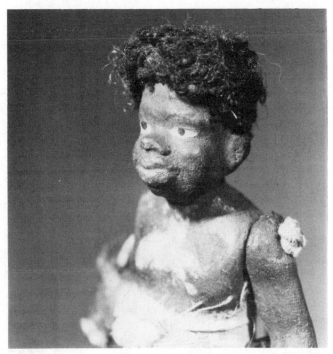

343. Black all-composition doll with kinky wig, painted ethnic features, jointed shoulders and hips, bare feet. H. 4¾ in. (12 cm.). *Coleman Collection.*

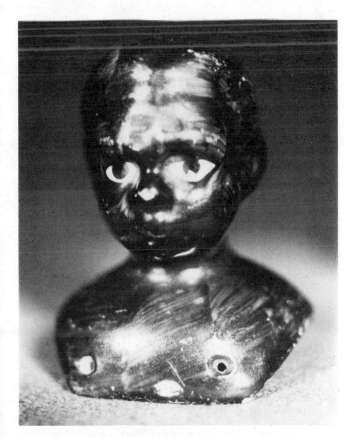

344. Black china shoulder head with ethnic features. The poured head is completely black except for the white eyeballs. It has two sew holes on each side. Mark on back is 4. H. of head only, 2¼ in. (5.5 cm.). *Coleman Collection.*

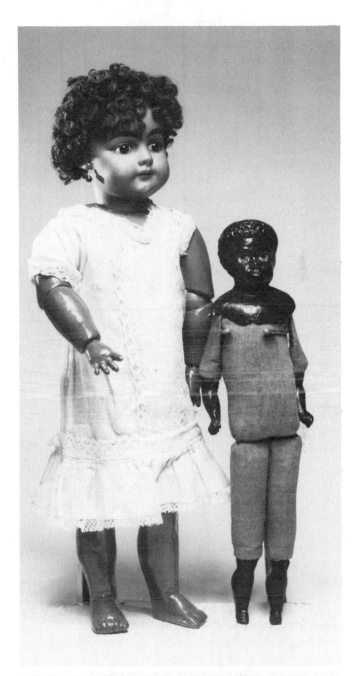

345. Pair of black dolls. Doll on left has a bisque head, black wig, stationary brown eyes, pierced ears, closed mouth, fully jointed brown composition body. Original chemise. Mark on head: "S 10 H// 739// DEP." Mark on body: "Handwerck." H. 17½ in. (44.5 cm.).

Doll on right has a composition shoulder head, lower arms and legs on a brown cloth body. It has ethnic features with short black hair, painted black eyes, and a closed mouth. H. 12½ in. (31.5 cm.). *Courtesy of Sotheby Parke Bernet Inc., N.Y.*

346. Black bisque head doll on a black ball-jointed composition body. The hair is glued to the head, pupilless black eyes, open mouth with teeth. H. 11 in. (28 cm.). *Coleman Collection.*

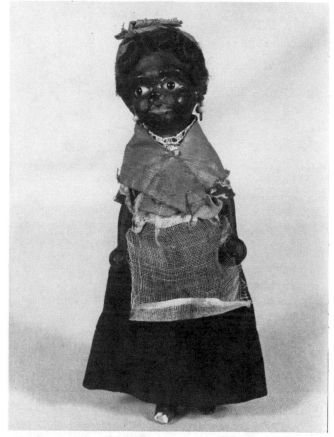

348. Black all-composition doll with a black wig, stationary black glass eyes, pierced ears, closed mouth, and joints at the neck, shoulders and hips. Original clothes include molded and painted red stockings and blue boots. H. 6 in. (15 cm.). *Coleman Collection.*

A JOLLY OLD "MAMMY."

347. Black doll in the collection of Mrs. Hesing of Chicago as shown in THE STRAND MAGAZINE, Sept, 1902. The dress and apron are calico.

349. Three black dolls with ball-jointed composition bodies as shown in DEKORATIVE KUNST, 1912.

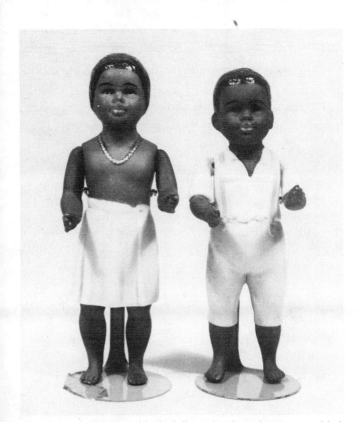

350. Pair of all-bisque black dolls with ethnic features, molded and painted hair, eyes, necklace, and clothes. H. of girl 5¼ in. (13.5 cm.). H. of boy 5 in. (12.5 cm.). *Courtesy of Richard Withington. Photo by Barbara Jendrick.*

Black Eye Susie. 1921. Terry cloth and flannel doll made by *Oweenee,* distributed by *Borgfeldt, Strobel & Wilken* and *Baker & Bennett.*

Black Prince. 1929–30. Advertised by *W. Cohen & Sons.* as having a head made by *Armand Marseille,* mold #351. It also came in a white version called *My Prince.* Hts. 32, 36, 40, 45, 50, 55, and 60 cm. (12½, 14, 15½, 17½, 19½, 21½ and 23½ in.).

Black Sambo. 1920. Stockinet doll made by *Chad Valley.* Number SD 14.

Black Topsie. 1918. Black doll made by *Tyneside Toys.*

Black & White. 1928. Trade name of a *Boudoir*-type doll dressed as a dancer, distributed by *Louis Eisen.*

Blackman, P. J., & Co. 1922. Britain. Produced dolls.

Blair, Camille C. See **Ruffles Co.**

Blampoix, Aîné (Senior). 1847–70. Paris. 1871–85, successor was *Dalloz.*

1861: Supplied dolls' heads to *Mme. Prieur.*

1880: C. Prieur was one of the creditors of Mme. Vve. (Widow) Blampoix.★

Blanca (Winter Sports). 1916. Name of a felt doll made by *Steiff.* Hts. 28 and 35 cm. (11 and 14 in.).

Blanche, Madame. 1913–30. U.S.A. (Could this be *Blanche Rowe Cromien?*)

1930: Designed heads and costumes for dolls made by the *Goodyear Toy Co.*

Bland-Hawkes, Mabel. 1918–30 and possibly later. London and Surrey. Creator and manufacturer of dolls including small cloth dolls, mascot dolls and costumes for dolls. She used the name, "*Cuddley*" for her dressed and undressed dolls.

1921: Advertised *Fluff,* a knockabout doll of colored stockinet.

1923: Made dolls named *Baby Royal,* a life size baby doll in long clothes, Bobbette; Light-weight Fairies; Little Lady Anne, Little Miss Vogue; Princette, a baby doll; and "Tutenkamen" (Tutankhamen).

1927: Her popular lines included: Toots dressed in silk trimmed with marabou; Hazel wearing a silk dress with rosebud trimming; Babs dressed in velvet; My Dollie's Nana; and *Little Miss Vogue* in velvet with white plush trim. Queen Mary purchased a Little Miss Vogue.

1928: Made Caprice, a three-face doll.

1929: The William series of dolls represented naughty boys.★

Blanket Babies. 1926. Single or twin *Kewpie*-like dolls in a blanket were made by *Wolson Novelty Co.* and distributed by *William A. Rich.*

Blasche, Rudolf. 1907–10. Vienna. Listed under Dolls and Dolls' Heads in an Austrian directory.

Blau Bela. 1911–19. Vienna. Listed under Dolls in an Austrian directory. Blau's Puppenfabrik (doll factory) was formerly Rakovsky & Co.

Blay, Louis. 1888–1910. Paris. Won a bronze medal for dolls at the Brussels Exposition in 1910.★

Blazer Dolls. A trade name for dolls advertised by *Reisman, Barron.*

Blechman, S., & Sons. 1922–27. New York City. Registered *Charm* as a U.S. trademark for dolls in 1927. It had been in use since 1922.

Bleuette. 1905–60. Name of a doll made by the *Société Française de Fabrication de Bébé & Jouets* (S. F. B. J.). This doll was distributed by the publishers, first Charles Bleriot and then *Henri Gautier,* of a French weekly periodical for girls 8 to 13 years old. Often in this periodical called *LA SEMAINE DE SUZETTE* (The Week of Suzette), there was a pattern for an outfit for Bleuette.

The publisher of the periodical in the beginning gave away a Bleuette with the first issue of each full year's subscription which cost $1.50. From 1905 to 1918 Bleuette was a bébé with a bisque head and various markings including *Jumeau* and Bleuette. Occasionally it had no mark at all. It had blue or brown stationary eyes, an open mouth, four teeth, a wig, pierced ears and a jointed composition body. Ht. 27 cm. (10½ in.). This height of the earlier Bleuette is based on several actual dolls and is a centimeter less than the reported heights of *Bébés Jumeau,* size 2, by Paris stores. Bleuette was made exclusively for subscribers to LA SEMAINE DE SUZETTE. There were many variations of Bleuette through the years. S.F.B.J. mold number 60 and mold number 301 for bisque heads were used. Bleuette

generally had blue eyes except during wartime when eyes with black pupils only were used. In 1919 sleeping eyes were first used. From 1919–21 both sleeping and stationary eyes were used. After 1921 Bleuette had only sleeping eyes. During World War II the quality deteriorated and according to M. Theimer in 1958 Bleuette was a plastic doll made by Gege without articulation and otherwise resembling a Barbie-type doll. A Bleuette in the Musée du Jouet, Poissy, France was marked "S.F.B.J.//60//Paris// 3/0." This doll was 35 cm. (14 in.) tall. Another Bleuette at the Margaret Woodbury Strong Museum had its bisque head marked "71 Unis/ France 149// 301//1½" and is 30.5 cm. (12 in.) tall. It carried a hexagonal tag with white letters on a blue ground. The tag read, "Marque//Déposée//Bleuette//18 rue Jacob//Paris vie." The blue eyes glanced to the side. This doll was probably made after 1937.

The booklet shown with the doll was dated Winter 1916–17 and is believed to be one of the earliest if not the earliest list of Bleuette's clothes. Bleuette always had up to the minute style clothes. With the early automobiles in 1906 and later she had motoring costumes. In 1910 and for almost every year afterward, she had a *Bécassine* costume. During the wars she had clothes typical of the period. After Lindbergh flew across the Atlantic she had a flying costume. She was elegantly dressed especially in the earlier years. Her clothes had pockets, buttons, and hooks and eyes so the garments were removable. The patterns in LA SEMAINE DE SUZETTE enabled the reader to make the clothes at home or they could be purchased ready-made. The latter were made by home workers who used the patterns in the periodical and were paid by the publishing company for each garment.

1905: 20,000 Bleuettes were made by S.F.B.J. Ht. 27 cm. (10½ in.).

1913: Hair was blonde, brown or tosca (reddish brown).

1914: Some of the dolls were marked "Petite Française// 6/0."

1915: Some of the costumes were inspired by *Jeanne Lanvin* designs.

1922–33: Marks included "S.F.B.J.//60//PARIS//8/0" and "24//FRANCE//S.F.B.J.//60//PARIS//8/0." The 24 stood for the 24th year (1928), 60 was the mold # and the size was 8/0.

1925: Won a silver medal at the Exposition des Arts Decoratifs.

1928: Bleuette with a bisque head cost more than with a composition head.

1933: Size of doll enlarged to 29 cm. (11½ in.) tall. It won a medal at the Lyon Exposition.

1933–60: Mold #301 was used for some of the heads and they were marked "71 UNIS 149//FRANCE//301// 1¼" or a similar type mark.

1937: Bleuette won a gold medal at the Paris Exposition.

1950: Bleuette as a French trademark for dolls was renewed by Gautier-Languereau.

Other dolls for whom clothes patterns were published in

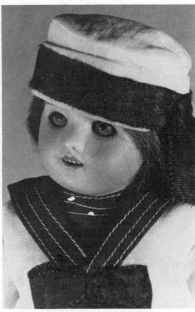

351A & B. Bleuette, a doll with a bisque head and a fully jointed composition body made by the S.F.B.J., as advertised in LA SEMAINE DE SUZETTE, 1919–28, as "Marin." It has a brown bobbed human hair wig, sleeping blue glass eyes (from which the name Bleuette derives), hair upper eyelashes, open mouth with four upper teeth. Original white duck sailor dress with hook fastening, cloche hat with gold letters on the hatband. H. 27.5 cm. (11 in.). *Coleman Collection.*

352. Bisque head Bleuette as made by the S.F.B.J. in the 1930s or later. It has a blond wig, stationary blue glass eyes looking to the side, open mouth with four upper teeth, fully jointed composition body. Original clothes consist of a white organdy dress with blue embroidery, a blue organdy pinafore and blue leatherette shoes. Marks: Ills. 353 and 354. The body is marked "1½." H. 30 cm. (12 in.). The Bleuette booklet dated Winter 1916–17 was the beginning of a series that came out semiannually until 1960. This booklet advertised the commercially made costumes available for Bleuette. *Courtesy of the Margaret Woodbury Strong Museum. Photo by Harry Bickelhaupt.*

LA SEMAINE DE SUZETTE were named *Bambino, Bamboula* and Rosette.

Bloch (Block), J. 1923–26. London. Advertised composition head dolls named Airman and Eton Boy and musical dolls including those representing *Clowns,* page boys, and sailors. He was an importer of dolls.

Bloch, S. 1872. Wheeling, W. Va. A wholesale dealer who handled three different types of wax dolls, crawling babies, and two different styles of rubber dolls priced 87¢ and $1.13.

Bloom, Charles, Inc. 1919–30 and later. New York City. Obtained a U.S. patent for a *Boudoir* flapper-type doll in 1925.★

Bloomin' Kid. 1917. A line of 9 in. (23 cm.) tall dolls distributed wholesale by *Wyman, Partridge.* They were made of leather and felt and had hand-painted features. Included were Indian Chief, Indian Squaw, Cowgirl, and Cowboy.

Bloomingdale's. 1891 and probably earlier–1930 and later. New York City. Distributed dolls.

1891: Advertised bisque head-dolls with wigs, stationary or sleeping glass eyes, open mouth with teeth or closed mouth, ball jointed composition body or cloth body, wearing a chemise or dressed including a hat or bonnet. Hts. 11½ to 25½ in. (29 to 65 cm.); priced undressed 26¢ to $2.98, dressed 56¢ to $4.98.

353–354. Marks on the bisque head and on the paper tag of the Bleuette doll in Ill. 352.

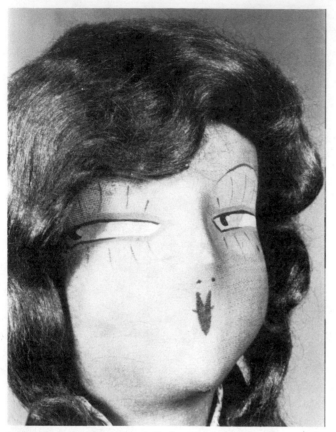

355. Cloth Boudoir doll made by Charles Bloom has mohair glued on head, beauty dot under painted eyes, original clothes including high-heeled shoes. Made about 1925. Mark: Ill. 356. H. 28½ in. (72.5 cm.). *Coleman Collection.*

```
PATENTED  JUNE 2, 1925
     NO. 1540384
CHAS. BLOOM, INC., NEW YORK
```

356. Mark on body of cloth Boudoir doll made by Charles Bloom. See Ill. 355.

Blue Bird. 1915. A line of doll clothes designed from children's apparel by *Arnoldt.*

Blue Bird Co., The. 1929. Baltimore, Md. Registered in 1929 "The Blue Bird Co. Better Bilt Joycraft Toys" as a U.S. trademark for dolls.

Blue Bird Doll. 1920–21. *Horsman* introduced dolls wearing clothing having a blue bird motif in 1920. This costume included a dress with wide pleats and a hooded cape which reached the fingers.

1920: All types of Horsman dolls were dressed in this garb including the *Peek-a-Boos.* ★

Blue Bonnet. 1924. A *Mama* doll handled by *Montgomery Ward.* It had a composition head, arms, cloth body, mohair wig and a voice. The dress and bonnet were made of voile. Ht. 19½ in. (49.5 cm.); price $2.59.

Blue Eyes. 1921. Trade name of a cloth doll designed by *Grace Corry* for *Century Doll Co.* It was advertised that the doll had an artistic face and could jump up and down. The body was stuffed with white cotton. The little girl type costumes came in various colors. ★

Blue Eyes. See **English Rag Dolls.**

Blue Stocking Kid. 1917–18. Made by *Harwin & Co.* as an Educational Doll; distributed by *Hamley.* ★

Blum, Charles B. 1888–1925 and later. New York City. Manufacturer and manufacturer's agent for various companies.

1919: Produced *Liberty Belle* dolls. ★

Blumberg, Erich. 1928–30 and later. Berlin. Manufactured articles required by dolls, including dresses and footwear.

Blumenflirt (Flower Flirtation). 1912. German name used for a doll.

Blum-Lustig Toy Co. 1924–29. New York City. Made and distributed dolls. Specialized in long limbed *Boudoir* type dolls created by *Mme. Emila Milobendzka,* recently of Paris. These dolls were called "French Dolls."

1926: Made black infant dolls and other types of black dolls as well as Boudoir dolls. ★

Bo Peep. 1917–19. Trade name used by H. J. Brown for composition, celluloid and stuffed dolls as well as clothes for dolls. The dolls came in 12 sizes. ★

Bo Peep. See **English Rag Dolls, Bo-Peep,** and **Little Bo-Peep.**

Bob (Scout Boy). Before 1911–16. Trade name for a felt doll made by *Steiff* and distributed by *Borgfeldt* in the U.S. It was dressed as a Boy Scout, had a hat with a low crown and a cord under the chin, knee socks, long shoes and carried a staff. Ht. 30 cm. (12 in.); priced 60¢ in Germany in 1911 and $1.25 in New York City in 1913.

1913: Advertised by *Lafayette* as Boy-Scout. Ht. 35 cm. (14 in.); priced $1.58.

Bob Sleigh. 1920–21. Stockinet doll made by *Chad Valley.* It was dressed in a winter sports costume, came in 3 different colors and 3 size numbers 25/1, small; 25/2, medium; and 25/3 for the large size.

Bobbette. 1927–28. Trade name of a doll produced by *Fibre Toy Mfg. Co.*

Bob-Betty Belongings. 1919–21. Carlsbad, Calif. Company registered in the U.S. Bob-Betty Belongings as a trademark for dolls made of rubber cloth which was hand decorated or colored and stuffed with cotton. Santa Clauses were included in their line.

Bobbie & Coon (Bobby & Coon). 1926–28. Trade name of dolls produced by *Cuno & Otto Dressel.*

Bobby. 1916. Cutout cloth doll designed by *Margaret Evans* and made by *Stecher Lithographic Co.* One large doll and two small ones were shown wearing rompers and having bobbed hair with bangs. They were on a sheet of cloth 25½ in. by 36½ in. (65 cm. by 93 cm.). Lithographed in five colors. Bobby was the mate to *Betty*.

Bobby. 1920–21. *Chad Valley* made a stockinet doll with a hand-woven wig and removable clothes, No. 7SD.

1921: It came with C. V. patent wristwatch and dressed in silk and other materials. Ht. 12 or 13 in. (30.5 or 33 cm.).

Bobby. 1928. All-composition doll distributed by *Paturel*. It wore a shirt and short trousers.

Bobby. 1928–29. Trade name of a character boy doll made to resemble the hero in a comic strip drawn by *Grace Drayton*. These comics appeared in over 50 newspapers and magazines. The doll, designed by Grace Drayton, was made by *Averill Manufacturing Co.* in their *Madame Hendren* line. The doll had a composition head and limbs on a cloth torso. Bobby was the mate to *Dolly* and the two dolls came in a box together.

358. Cloth doll, named Bobby Bobbykins, with its original box. The distributor was the Children's Novelty Co. The doll has a wig only in front and the Drayton type features are chromolithographed on a flat face with blue eyes. Original clothes differ slightly from those shown on the box top. The footwear is lithographed. H. 7 in. (18 cm.). *Courtesy of the Margaret Woodbury Strong Museum. Photo by Harry Bickelhaupt.*

357. Mark on a Bobby doll based on a Grace Drayton design.

1928: It wore an Oliver Twist style suit with a white shirt and short dark trousers that buttoned on the shirt at the waistline.

1929: The doll had new style clothes and came in new sizes.

Bobby. For other listings of Bobby dolls based on the drawings of Grace Drayton, see the first COLLECTOR'S ENCYCLOPEDIA OF DOLLS. See also **Susan & Bobby.**

Bobby Bobbykins. 1909–11 and possibly later. Cloth dolls distributed by the *Children's Novelty Co.* See Ill. 358.★

Bobby Bobs. 1920–21. A floating doll with a spherical rubber or cork head, and hand painted face, made by *Rees Davis*.

Bobby Bonser. 1929–30. Cloth doll made by *Bonser*.

Bobby Bounce. 1923–29. Segmented wooden doll made by *Petrie-Lewis Manufacturing Co.* It was strung on an elastic. Style no. 50, *Billy Bounce* Senior, had bells on its toes.

Bobby Bounce. 1930 and later. Produced by *Borgfeldt*. The doll had a composition head and was probably in competition with the *Averill Manufacturing Co.'s Bobby*.

Bobby Doll. 1928. A bathtub doll that does not sink or shrink, manufactured by the *Adler Favor and Novelty Co.*

Bobby Lou. 1929. One of *Gertrude Rollinson's* cloth *Bedtime Buddies* dolls.

Bobby Sleigh. See **Bob Sleigh.**

Bobby & Coon. See **Bobbie & Coon.**

Bobs Twins. 1920–21. Floating dolls with handpainted faces made by *Rees Davis*.

Boccheciampe. 1925–28. Paris. Made cloth art dolls.★

Bocchin, Ernest. 1925. Passaic, N.J. Obtained a U.S. patent for the insertion of bellows in a tube between the ears of a conventional doll. The doll would then emit sound when the ears were pressed.

Böck. 1916. Name of felt doll made by *Steiff*. Ht. 43 cm. (17 in.).

Bodies of Dolls. Through the years efforts have been directed toward making the doll's body move as much like a human as possible and at the same time keeping the production cost down. Animal skin is the nearest thing to human skin, therefore kid bodies were popular for at least a century. But they were not cheap to produce. In the 1840s and 1850s both pink and white kid bodies were used extensively with china and papier-mâché heads. Dolls with pink kid bodies and unusual wooden or rubber joints were made, possibly by *Arnaud*. When bisque heads became popular in the 1860s they were primarily used on kid bodies. Probably some of the finest bodies were made in the 1860s.

For example the sophisticated wooden bodies with ball

joints made by *Bru,* Benoit Martin[†], and others. Also in this period there were the *Motschmann*-type bodies with floating joints. But in the late 1870s the introduction of the ball-jointed composition body, which was presumably cheaper than the ball-jointed wooden body, revolutionized the production of the dolls' bodies.

The cheapest body of all is usually a cloth body and periodically cloth bodies are promoted because of their cuddly quality as well as the fact that they are inexpensive to produce. Of course some of the least expensive bodies are the ones that are made in one piece, including the head, such as the peg woodens, the *Frozen Charlottes* and so forth.

Many ingenious methods have been devised for joining the head and limbs to the body. Some of the simpler methods are a seam, a gusset, pegs, wire, elastic, rivets or springs. Some of these methods have been elaborated with more sophisticated results. For example the *Lenci* dolls that had their arms sewed on in such a manner that the arm would rotate as well as move up and down.

1884: The *Lauer* catalog listed separate muslin dolls' sitting bodies with leather arms and high leather boots. These came in 14 sizes numbered 2/0 to 12 and cost $1.00 to $9.00 doz. wholesale.

Among the bodies on dolls were ball-jointed bodies with bisque heads, kid bodies with composition heads, bodies with wax heads speaking Mama-Papa, cloth bodies with wooden limbs and wax heads.

1887: The Lauer catalog listed the following types of bodies: double jointed composition bodies; composition jointed bodies; all-wood jointed bodies; muslin bodies with wooden arms and legs; hair stuffed cloth bodies with leather arms; French white kid bodies.

1890: Some *Bébés Jumeau* were advertised as having jointed wrists. But many dolls after this date continued to have non-jointed wrists because they were cheaper.

1891: A store catalog advertised hair stuffed muslin bodies and white kid bodies with and without bisque heads.

1893: Cloth bodies sold at stores cost 25¢ to $1.00.

1912: Cloth bodies were stuffed with cow hair, deer hair, cork chips, cork dust, fine wood shavings, wood-wool, but not with sawdust as formerly, according to a report in TOYS AND NOVELTIES. It might be a little difficult for a modern collector to distinquish between fine wood shavings and sawdust.

1913: PLAYTHINGS reports new types of bodies as being pink silk instead of kid. They also state, "A new line of kid body dolls with turning heads, with bisque breasts as well as heads in order that low neck dresses may be used." This follows an era of high collars.

1918: The introduction of the cloth *Mama* doll body with swinging legs and a low center of gravity that enabled it to simulate walking. This type of body continued to be popular for at least a decade.

1927: Bodies were stuffed with excelsior, kapok, cotton, and wool or wood.

TOYS AND NOVELTIES commented on bodies: "The old skinny body found in practically all dolls made up until a score of years ago has given way to the chubby body characteristic of the dolls made today.

"Some manufacturers have made their doll plump almost to corpulency with the result that within the past two years the public demand is reacting for somewhat thinner dolls."

1928: Mr. Trumpore of Fleischaker & Baum *(Effanbee)* stated in PLAYTHINGS: "The cloth bodies for dolls that were made in America were first stuffed with sawdust, then with excelsior, then with cork which reduced the weight and finally cotton stuffing. Mama voices were inserted in the cotton stuffing."

Ca. 1932: Hair-stuffed cloth bodies were still being produced. China, bisque and composition limbs were used on cloth bodies. Kestner was still making kid bodies. All-composition dolls, jointed without balls, were the principal type. (See also **Manufacture of Dolls, Commercial.**)★

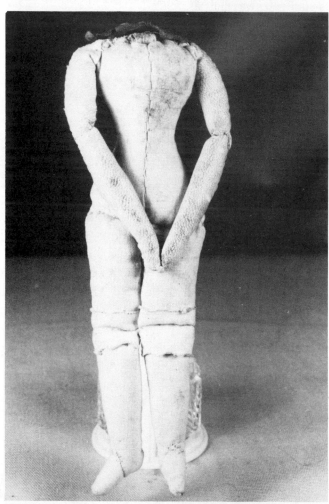

359. German commercial cloth body with kid arms. A wooden dowel sticks out at the top under the blue paper on which 5/0 (the size probably) is written in ink. The fingers and knees are still sewn together just as it came from the factory. The extra piece of cloth at the knee joint is typical of German bodies for dolls. H. of body only: 6 in. (15 cm.). *Coleman Collection.*

360A & B. Wooden body with a china head; the head has black molded hair in the style of the 1860s–70s, blue molded eyes, and closed mouth. The head has a wire mechanism so that it rises up but does not become detached. Footwear is carved and painted, the stockings are orange color and the shoes are blue. H. 9½ in. (24 cm.). *Coleman Collection.*

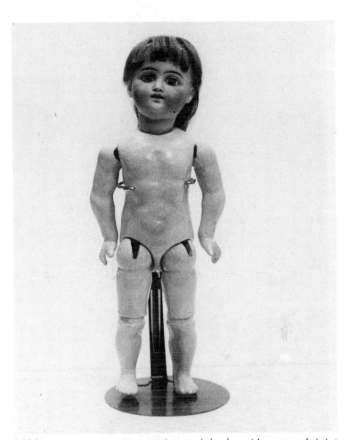

362A & B. Composition and wood body with unusual joint combination. The bisque head is dome shaped with a hole less than an inch in diameter; over this hole is a tin covering with three small holes. Part of the wig was inserted into the center hole and stringing cord was run through the other two holes. There are stationary blue glass eyes, a closed mouth and ears pierced into the head. H. 13 in. (33 cm.). *Courtesy of Violet King.*

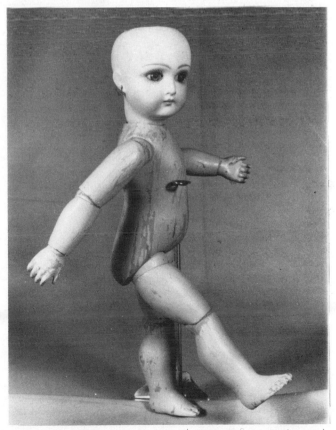

361. All-wood ball-jointed shapely body jointed at the neck, shoulders, elbows, wrists, hips, and knees. The fingers are curved and separated at the ends. Both the fingernails and toenails are painted pink. The bisque head marked 5 is not original to this body. H. of doll 12½ in. (31.5 cm.). *Coleman Collection.*

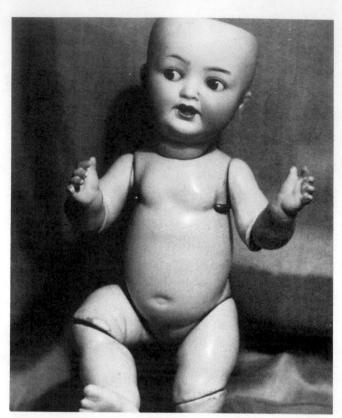

364. Bisque-head toddler with unusual body having slanting joints at the elbows and knees. It has blue glass sleeping and flirting eyes, open mouth with two upper teeth and a quivering tongue. Mark: "Heubach Koppelsdorf//342 2/0//Germany." H. 14½ in. (37 cm.). Circumference of head 9¾ in. (25 cm.). *Private collection.*

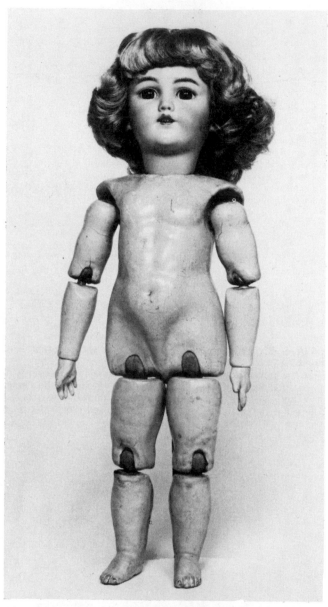

363. Unusual body construction. The composition body has rubber joints. The bisque head has a wig, sleeping brown glass eyes, pierced ears, and an open mouth with four upper teeth. The head is marked "SIMON & HALBIG//1249//DEP//Germany//7." Doll's body based on patents of Heinrich Eckert, and produced by Carl Debes with the trade name "Noris." Doll was advertised in 1905. Upper legs appear to be shown backward in photo. H. 16½ in. (42 cm.). *Courtesy of the Margaret Woodbury Strong Museum. Photo by Harry Bickelhaupt.*

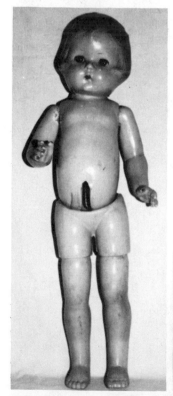

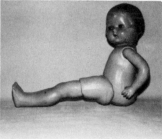

PAT APP'LD FOR

366. Embossed mark on the back of the shoulders of the all composition doll in Ill. 365.

365A & B. Unusual composition body construction. The composition head resembles Patsy and has the Patsy type neck joint; the molded hair is a strawberry blond color; the sleeping blue eyes are celluloid over metal and have hair upper eyelashes; the mouth is closed. The unusual feature of this doll is its hip joints which enable it to sit as well as to stand. Mark: Ill. 366. H. 24 in. (61 cm.). *Courtesy of the late Edna Greehy.*

Body Twist. See **Waist Joints.**

Boggs & Buhl. 1894–95 and probably other years. U.S. Distributed dolls with shoulder heads or socket heads, kid bodies or composition bodies, undressed or in a chemise. Priced 10¢ to $1.00. (See Ill. 432 in THE COLLECTOR'S BOOK OF DOLLS' CLOTHES.)

Bognier-Burnet, Établissement. 1920s. France. Member of the *Chambre Syndicale.* Made undressed dolls.

Bohemian Dolls. Porcelain heads for dolls were made in the environs of Carlsbad, Schlaggenwald and elsewhere in Bohemia. Many types of Bohemian folk art doll were discussed in FOLK TOYS, LES JOUETS POPULAIRES, by Emanuel Hercík, published by Orbis in Prague, Czechoslovakia, in 1952. Among those involved with the production of dolls in Bohemia were the following: *Abeles & Schnabel, Artel, Franz Barwig, Adolf Bornmüller, J. H. Brandeis, K. Budesinsky, Burger & Bentum, Cejka, Prof. H. Folkmann, Fritzche & Thein, Mlle. Marcel Giblet,* Anna Grimm,[+] *J. Grünbaum,* Guth & Eckstein[+], *Rudolf Heinz, V. Heront, Hořické Hrag, A. Kalla, F. Klemperer, Klub der Künstler* Gustave Kmel,[+] *Carl Knoll, Gebrüder Lokesch, Luhacovice, Johann Marschner, Emil Mautner, M. J. Moehling,* C. A. Müller,[+] *A. Mönzberg, Filip Pick, Plass & Roesner, Reinhold Pohl, Theodor Pohl,* Pollack & Samuel,[+] *Pollack & Hoffmann,* Marie Procbázkova,[+] W. M. Propper,[+] *Mme. Raabe, Moritz Resek, Rudolf Richter, Samuel & Söhne, Schlaggenwald, Franz Schubert, H. Stein,* Stoupuv,[+] *Topics, Tunkler Von Treulnfeld, Alois Ullmann, B. Urbanek, V. Vesely,[+] Kopfovi Weiss.*

1920: *Stewart Culin* wrote that no complete dolls were made in Bohemia, only bodies, and German heads were put on them; but these dolls were inferior to the dolls made entirely in Germany.

However there is ample evidence that porcelain factories in Bohemia made dolls' heads. Before World War I Bohemia was part of the Austrian Empire. (See also **Austrian Dolls.**)

Bohm, Professor. 1903–6. Vienna. He taught females how to make dolls in the Kunstschule für Frauen und Madchen (Art School for women and girls).

Bohmer, August. 1907–28. Gotha, Thür. Manufactured knit clothes for dolls including suits, skirts, caps, drawers, and socks.

Bohne, Ernst. 1854–1930. Rudolstadt, Thür. Porcelain factory that manufactured dolls. The marks included a crown with five points over an N which is sometimes mistaken for a similar Capo di Monte[+] mark. Bohne also used marks with anchors, one had a B over the shaft of the anchor and the other had an E on one side and a B on the other side of the shaft. The plain E B found on some porcelain heads is now believed to probably stand for *E. Barrois.*★

Böhnke, Clara, & Zimmermann, Helene. 1909–22. Königsberg, Prussia. Obtained a German patent (D.R.P.) in 1909 for flexible stuffing for jointed dolls. In 1912 they obtained another German doll patent (D.R.G.M.).★

367. Dolls shown in the Bon Marché catalog of 1885. They are dolls in boxes or in a suitcase with their trousseaux, ranging in price from 35¢ to $3.50. There is also a baby doll in swaddling clothes with its baby bottle and a long hair wig, a boy doll in a sailor suit, and a girl doll in a silk costume with high boots having four straps. All three of these dolls have sleeping eyes. The baby cost 70¢, the boy cost 90¢, and the girl cost $1.18.

BOITE contenant un bébé articulé et un trousseau brodé.
8.50, 11.50 et **17.50**

BOITE contenant une poupée miniature et son trousseau **7.50**

BÉBÉS DORMEURS FERMANT LES YEUX
maillot, marin et costume satin.
1re taille, **3.50**   2me taille, **4.50**   3me taille, **5.90**

VALISE CRETONNE
renfermant une poupée et son trousseau . . . . . **8.75** et **4.90**
Petite taille **1.75**

COMPTOIR DES JOUETS

Nº 199.
BÉBÉ ARTICULÉ yeux mobiles, costume soie.

0ᵐ27	0ᵐ32	0ᵐ40
2.45	3.75	5.90

Nº 198.
BEBE MARCHEUR envoyant des baisers, **yeux vivants à cils**, bouche à dents, costume soie orné ruban et dentelle. *Hauteur* sans le chapeau 0ᵐ53 . . . **12.75**

Nº 1906.
BÉBÉ parlant et pleurant, yeux mobiles, bouche à dents, perruque flottante, chemise satin. *Haut.* 0ᵐ57 **8.75**

Nº 19174
BÉBÉ promenette, tête incassable, bouche à dents, costume flanelle et piqué brodé.
Haut. 0ᵐ35. **3.90**
— 0ᵐ44. **5.90**

Nº 1902.
BÉBÉ complètement articulé, tête fine, **yeux vivants**, jolie perruque, costume soie, ruban et dentelle. *Haut.* sans le chapeau 0ᵐ32.
18.75

Nº 1901.
BÉBÉ MAR'N costume lainage, col broderie.

Haut.	0ᵐ28. .	1.45
—	0ᵐ32. .	1.95
—	0ᵐ35. .	2.45
—	0ᵐ38. .	3.75
—	0ᵐ47. .	4.90

BÉBÉ du Bon Marché	1 0ᵐ26	2 0ᵐ28	3 0ᵐ31	4 0ᵐ35	5 0ᵐ37	6 0ᵐ41	7 0ᵐ45	8 0ᵐ49	9 0ᵐ53	10 0ᵐ58	11 0ᵐ63	12 0ᵐ68
complètement articulé et chaussé, de fabrication supérieure.	2.45	3.25	4.25	5.25	6.25	7.25	8.25	9.75	11.50	14.50	17.50	21 »
Le même, parlant, bouche à dents, yeux mouvants.		11.50	13.50	16 »	19 »	22.50	26 »					
BÉBÉ JUMEAU, cheveux naturels.		7.50	8.50	10.50	12.50	15.50	18.50	22 »	27 »			
Le même, parlant, bouche à dents, yeux mouvants.		13.50	16.50	19.50	22 »	27 »	32 »					

BÉBÉ articulé, bouche à dents, perruque flottante, chemise satin et dentelle. *Haut.* 0ᵐ57 **5.90**

BÉBÉ DU BON MARCHÉ

Nº 194. BÉBÉ articulé, tête lavable et incassable, yeux mobiles, bouche à dents.

0ᵐ35	0ᵐ41	0ᵐ50
3.90	5.75	7.75

TÊTE INCASSABLE

Nº 197. BÉBÉ articulé très léger, **tête incassable**, bouche à dents.

0ᵐ34	. . . . .	1.95
0ᵐ39	. . . . .	2.45
0ᵐ42	. . . . .	2.90
0ᵐ47	. . . . .	3.90

BÉBÉ JUMEAU

JE MARCHE SEUL
YEUX VIVANTS

DERNIÈRE NOUVEAUTÉ
Nº 19172.
BÉBÉ mécanique marchant pas à pas, tête fine, **yeux vivants à cils**, bouche à dents, perruque flottante, joli costume soie fantaisie orné ruban et dentelle.
Haut. sans le chapeau 0ᵐ42.
29.50
Le même, avec chemise lingerie.
21.

Nº 19173
BÉBÉ marcheur parlant et envoyant des baisers, **yeux vivants à cils**, joli costume soie Pompadour.
Hauteur sans le chapeau 0ᵐ58. **21.50**

Nº 1907. BÉBÉ articulé yeux mobiles à cils, bouche à dents, costume soie.

0ᵐ28	6.50	0ᵐ40	10.75
0ᵐ31	8.50	0ᵐ43	12.50
0ᵐ35	9.75	0ᵐ47	14.50

Les Petits Marins.
Nº19171. BÉBÉ marcheur articulé, tête fine, joli costume flanelle garçonnet ou fillette. *Haut.* 0ᵐ35.
Exceptionnel 3.90

Nº 1905. BÉBÉ parlant tout articulé série fine, yeux mobiles à cils, bouche à dents, costume riche.

0ᵐ47 .	26.	0ᵐ61 .	43.
0ᵐ52 .	31.	0ᵐ65 .	52.
0ᵐ56 .	36.	0ᵐ70 .	63.

Les Jouets du Bon Marché sont tous, dans chaque genre, de qualité supérieure.

368A & B. Pages from a 1903 Bon Marché catalog showing a Bébé du Bon Marché, Bébé Jumeau, Kiss Throwing bébés, and other bébés and dolls as well as clothes for dolls. The size number for the clothes indicates that they would fit either Bébé Jumeau or Bébé du Bon Marché of a corresponding size number.

TROUSSEAUX ET VETEMENTS POUR POUPEES
Du Comptoir des Layettes.

N° 11. COL lingerie, nansouk garni broderie.
N°s 5-7-9-11-12
» 85

N° 9. BAVOIR piqué garni broderie.
N° 5 au n° 12
» 45

N° 22. VESTE beau drap bleu ou rouge, biais satin et galon.

N°s 5	6-7
1·75	2·10
8-9	10-11	12
2·50	3·10	3·90

N° 39. PARURE palatine et manchon en vraie Mongolie, nœud et ruban satin.
N°s 6-8-10 et 12.
5·75

N° 15. ROBE nubienne crème, ciel, rose ou rouge orné points chainette.

N°s 4-5	6-7	8-9
1·25	1·55	1·85
10-11	2·25	12	2·75

N° 35. CAPOTE lainage nuances assorties.
Du n° 4 au n° 12. 1·60

N° 7. TABLIER basin blanc, décolleté carré orné entredeux et point riche ceinture.

N°s 4-5	6-7
1·10	1·30
8-9	10-11	12
1·50	1·70	1·95

N° 17. ROBE lainage damiers ou rayures, bleu et blanc ou rouge et blanc, col orné galon et guipure.

N°s 5	6-7	8-9
1·95	2·45	2·95
10-11	3·50	4·25

N° 43. BÉRET en feutre garni torsade et pompon soie.
Du n° 4 au n° 12 1·35

N° 21. MANTEAU bengaline crème, ciel, rose ou rouge, broderie soie.

N°s 5	6-7	8-9
6·50	7·50	8·75
10-11	10·	12	11·75

N° 44. DIRECTOIRE soie nuances assorties, broderie soie.
N°5 au n° 12 4·50

N° 19 BURNOUS tissu des Pyrénées bleu, blanc ou rose et blanc, capuchon doublé soie orné cordelière.

N°s 5	7-9	11-13
1·85	2·45	3·10

N° 23. PELISSE tissu des Pyrénées bleu et blanc ou rose et blanc, capuchon doublé soie, orné cordelière, franges boules.

N°s 5	7	9	11
2·75	3·50	4·25	5·25
N° 13	6·25

N° 16. ROBE pongée crème, ciel ou rose garnie jour et dentelle.

N°s 4-5	6-7	8-9	10-11	12
2·25	2·90	3·70	4·50	5·25

N° 43. BÉGUIN velours côtelé crème ciel rose ou rouge.
N° 5 au 9. 1·95
N° 10 au 12. 2·50

N° 12. JUPON taffetas glacé, bleu, rose et cerise, volant 5 ganses.

N°s 6	8
2·25	2·75
10	12
3·25	3·75

N° 20. PALETOT droit, beau drap vieux bleu ou rouge, col orné biais satin et guipure.

N°s 5	6-7	8-9	10-11	12
2·90	3·50	4·15	4·90	5·75

N° 38. DIRECTOIRE velours crème, vieux bleu ou rouge, orné taffetaline et ruban. 5 au 12. 2·25

N° 18. ROBE à taille, lainage damiers ou rayures ciel et blanc ou rose et blanc, berthe ornée guipure.

N°s 5	6-7	8-9	10-11	12
1·75	2·15	2·45	2·90	3·50

N° 37. BONNET nouveauté genre américain en feutre rouge ou vieux bleu.
Du n° 5 au n° 12. 3·75

N° 10. ROBE nansouk blanc côtelé, dessous blanc ciel ou rose, col orné jour et broderie, jupe 3 plis et volant broderie, ceinture.

N°s 4-5	6-7	8-9	10-11
3·15	3·50	3·95	4·40
N° 12	4·90

N° 8. TABLIER nansouk fileté fond blanc, impression ciel ou rose décolleté carré, orné broderie, ceinture, poches garnies broderie.

N°s 4-5	6-7	8-9	10-11	12
1·15	1·35	1·60	1·85	2·10

Pour Enfant

N° 42289. TABLIER brillanté blanc, empiècement petits plis fins, entredeux formant pattes, berthe et épaulettes garnies broderie.

0m50	55	60	65	70	75	80	85
4·75	4·90	5·20	5·40	5·90	6·20	6·50	6·75

TROUSSEAUX ET TOILETTE *pour poupée*, 10 articles *très soignés* livrés dans un carton formant boîte.

1 chemise de jour percale.
1 pantalon garni dentelle.
1 robe de dessous garnie.
1 chemise de nuit genre russe.
1 corset satin blanc.
1 béret feutre.
1 paire soulier mordorés.
1 paire bas fil.
1 robe brillanté garni broderie
1 tablier cretonne fleurettes

N°s 4-5	6-7	8-9	10-11	12
8·75	9·90	11·25	12·50	13·75

TROUSSEAUX LINGERIE *pour poupées*, livrés dans un joli carton moiré contenant une chemise de jour, un pantalon, une robe de dessous et une chemise de nuit.

N°s 4-5	6-7	8-9	10-11	12
2·75	3·35	3·90	4·50	5·25

Pour Enfant

N° 57. ROBE courte, beau pongée crème ciel ou rose, empiècement garni entredeux imitation Valenciennes, double berthe et double volant garnis imitation, Valenciennes à la jupe. Écharpe en pongée.
De 6 mois à 2 ans. 19·50

Les numéros que nous indiquons correspondent pour les tailles aux proportions des Bébés Jumeau ou des Bébés du Bon Marché.

Boli. 1930 and later. Strasbourg, France. Made dolls.

Bolivia. In 1927 dolls were made by the Aymara Indian children, descendants of the Incas in La Paz. The dolls wore native costumes woven by the children for the Y.W.C.A. which in turn distributed the dolls to the Indian children on reservations.

Bologna, Paola. 1920s. Turin, Italy. Artist and illustrator, born 1898. He designed dolls and/or ceramics for *Lenci*.

Bolton, James A. 1926–27. Sayville, N.Y. Obtained a U.S. patent for a kissing doll. The kiss was simulated by pressing the doll's lips against a soft surface such as a child's cheek. When the lips were removed air rushed from a chamber with resilient walls inside the doll's body up through a duct thus producing a sibilant sound simulating the sound of a kiss.

Bon Marché. 1852–1930 and later. Paris. Department store that sold a variety of dolls including: *Arlette, Bébé Bon Marché, Bébé Culotte, Bébé Jumeau, Bébé Maillot, Bébé Premiers Pas, Bébé Radieux, Bébé Rieur, Bébé Zephir (Bébé Zephr), Boudoir* dolls, *Charleston Couple,* cloth dolls, *Francette, Ginette, Gisèle, Gladys, Helyette, Jacqueline, Kiss-throwing* dolls, *La Petite Georgette, Le Bambino, Lily, Linette, Lucette, Lulu (Poulbot), Mado, Monette, Monique,* multi-head dolls, *New Born* baby, *Nono, Odette, Paulette, Petite Écoliers, Riri (Poulbot),* rubber dolls, *Suzette, Swaddling Clothed Dolls, Toto, Venus, walking dolls,* soldier and sailor dolls as well as dolls with wardrobes of clothes in boxes or in suitcases. *Poulbot* designed the cover of their catalog dated 1918.

1880: Advertised that they had an English interpreter. (See THE COLLECTOR'S BOOK OF DOLLS' CLOTHES, Ills. 428, 638, and 642.)

Bon Marché. 1916 and other years. Brussels. Was designated Hors Concours at an exhibition held in Brussels in 1916 to aid the children of Belgian soldiers. The director, M. Blairon, was a member of the jury.

Bonanza. 1887. Trade name of a doll advertised by *Lauer.* This was a "large" composition doll with wig, and molded, painted footwear. It wore a lace trimmed chemise and cost 10¢ to 15¢ a doz. wholesale.

Bonchi (Ponchi) Shokai Ayanmokoji. 1930 and later. Japan. Made dolls.

Bon-Dufour, B. See **Renault & Bon-Dufour.**

Bonin & Lefort (Société). 1923–28. Paris. Registered several French trademarks for dolls and dolls' heads. The one used most often was a circle with a silhouette of a boy and a girl having a tug-of-war with a doll.

1926: Registered *Mon Baby* and *Joli Bébé* as French trademarks.

1927–28: Used the trade names *Bébé Ninon* and *Bébé Select* as trademarks for dolls. ★

Bonini. 1930. Turin, Italy. Made dolls.

Bonnafé. 1876–95. Paris. In 1881 purchased bisque dolls' heads from *François Gaultier* and made dolls, according to

Mme. Florence Poisson, curator of the Roybet Fould Museum. ★

Bonnand Frères. 1927–28. Oyonnax, Ain, France. Made celluloid dolls.

Bonnedol. 1917–18. Line of dolls made by *Cooper & Sons.* Some of these dolls had *British Ceramic* heads and cork stuffed bodies. Mary Hillier reported finding composition dolls in this line also.

1918: Advertised dressed baby dolls with jointed necks and limbs. Some of these dolls had crying voices.

Bonnet Dolls. 1860 or before–1930 and later. Dolls' heads of various materials with molded, painted bonnets or headwear.

1887: *Lauer* advertised bisque bonnet dolls. Hts. 2½, 3½, and 4½ in. (6.5, 9, and 11.5 cm.).

1889: *Butler Bros.* advertised bisque bonnet dolls. These were on cloth bodies with bisque limbs and came 8 in. (20.5 cm.) tall with blonde molded hair and hats decorated with colors and gold for 5¢. The 11½ in. (29 cm.) size cost 10¢.

1898–99: Butler Bros. advertised bisque head dolls with molded and painted decorations on the shoulders and heads which included hats. These represented various nations and were called *International Dolls.* See Ills. 1279 and 1280.

1902: Butler Bros. advertised a bisque shoulder-head doll with molded broad-brimmed, off the face Gainsborough style hat and molded flowing hair. There was a molded gilt necklace with a cross. Four hts. 7¾, 8¾, 10⅝, and 11⅝ in. (19.5, 22, 27, and 29.5 cm.); priced 37¢ to 87¢ doz. wholesale.

1904: Bisque heads with molded picture hats having colored bows. Hts. 9, 11½ and 15½ in. (23, 29, and 39.5 cm.). ★

369. China bonnet shoulder head with molded and painted bonnet and long black curls. *Courtesy of Mary Hillier.*

370. Pair of wax-over composition dolls with molded and painted hats, stationary blue glass eyes, closed mouths and cloth bodies containing voice boxes. The arms are the floating joint type found on the Motschmann-type dolls and the legs are carved and painted wood. Original clothes. H. of girl 14 in. (35.5 cm.). H. of boy 17 in. (43 cm.). *Courtesy of Sotheby Parke Bernet Inc., N.Y.*

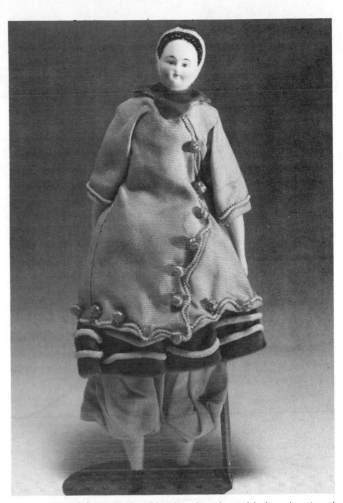

372. Untinted bisque shoulder head with molded and painted headwear, black hair with brushmarks, and blue eyes. The cloth body has bisque arms and legs. Russian style costume. The blue scarf is outlined in yellow and has pink tassels in back. This doll was in the Laura Starr collection around 1900. H. 8¼ in. (21 cm.). *Courtesy of the International Doll Library. Photo by Sotheby Parke Bernet Inc., N.Y.*

371. Untinted bisque shoulder head with a molded and painted brown pill box shaped hat, painted blue eyes, closed mouth and painted footwear. The cloth body has bisque arms and legs. H. 10 in. (25.5 cm.). *Coleman Collection.*

373. China bonnet head with molded and painted hair and features. The white bonnet has a pink rim and pink bows at the top of the head and under the chin. The shoulder head does not have sew holes. H. 6¾ in. (17 cm.). H. of shoulder head including the bonnet 2¼ in. (5.5 cm.). *Courtesy of Paula Hill.*

374. Untinted bisque head with molded and painted bonnet, hair, eyes, and chemisette. The white bonnet has a blue lining and a pink bow. The cloth body has bisque lower arms. Mark: "2." H. 16 in. (40.5 cm.). *Courtesy of Richard Withington. Photo by Barbara Jendrick.*

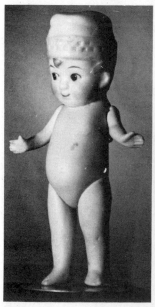

375. All-bisque doll with molded and painted turban, blond hair, black eyes looking to the side, and a smiling mouth. Mark: Ill. 377. H. 4½ in. (11.5 cm.). *Coleman Collection.*

376. All-bisque doll with molded blue cloche on its head, painted and molded hair and features, jointed at the shoulders, marked "NIPPON" on its back. Made in Japan probably in the 1920s. H. 4½ in. (11.5 cm.). *Coleman Collection.*

3/0
1954   *116-4*

377–378. Marks on all-bisque bonnet dolls. For the doll in Ill. 375, the "3/0" is the size number and the "1954" probably is the mold number.

Bonnet Dolls. 1928. Trade name of a *Viscoloid* doll made by the *Pacific Novelty Co.,* a division of the *Du Pont* Viscoloid Co. The doll has molded hair, painted eyes that glance to the side, jointed shoulders and hips; legs are together. It came dressed in crepe paper. Ht. 7 in. (18 cm.).

Bonnet, V., & Cie. See **Martin, Fernand.**

Bonnie Babe. 1926–30 and later. Bisque head baby doll designed by *Georgene Averill* produced and distributed by *Borgfeldt.* The U.S. trademark for this doll was registered by Georgene Averill and transferred to Borgfeldt. The doll represented a grinning year old baby with open mouth and two lower teeth, sleeping eyes, molded hair, composition arms and legs on a cloth body. The label on the doll read, "Madame Georgene Creation." The bisque heads were made in Germany, usually by *Alt, Beck & Gottschalck; K & K* appears to have made the bodies. At first there were only two sizes but the popularity grew so that it was made in six sizes as well as all-bisque versions. The small all-bisque Bonnie Babes were 4½ and 5½ in. (11.5 and 14 cm.) tall. *Butler Bros.* was one of the distributors of Bonnie Babe. A Bonnie Babe having a composition body has been reported but not verified. *Rheinische Gummi und Celluloid Fabrik* made celluloid versions of Bonnie Babe.

1927: *Century* advertised Bonnie Babe in TOYS AND NOVELTIES. Since Century used *Kestner* heads on their baby dolls it is probable that Kestner also made Bonnie Babe heads. Bonnie Babe came with celluloid hands, cloth legs and a voice, ht. 12 in. (30.5 cm.); with celluloid hands and composition legs, ht. 14 in. (35.5 cm.); with composition arms and legs, hts. 15, 17½, and 20 in. (38, 44.5, and 51 cm.).

1946: The U.S. trademark was renewed indicating that Bonnie Babe dolls were still being made.

Bonnie Babs. 1920. Cloth doll produced by the *Three Arts Women's Employment Fund.*

Bonnie Bess. 1930. Premium doll offered by the HOME CIRCLE magazine. It had a composition head and arms, cloth body and legs, jointed at the shoulders and hips, painted hair and eyes, removable clothes except for black cloth ankle boots on the feet. Ht. 16 in. (40.5 cm.).

Bonnie Laddie. 1920. Trade name of dolls made by *Electra.*

Bonny Babs. 1930. Line of dolls made by *Carl Kalbitz;* distributed in London by *E. Turner.*

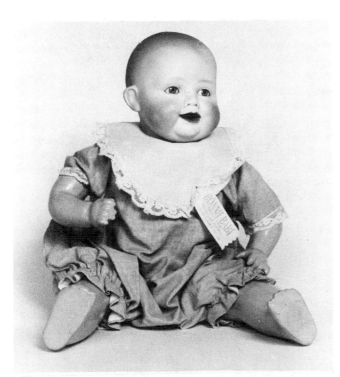

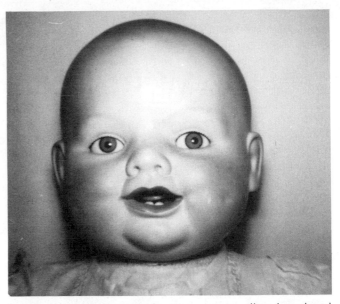

380. Bonnie Babe designed by Georgene Averill and produced by Borgfeldt. Painted hair, sleeping blue glass eyes, open mouth with two lower teeth, dimples in cheeks, cloth body with composition arms. Mark: "Copr. by//Georgene Averill//1005/3652/4//Germany//1386/4 7." H. 22½ in. (57 cm.). *Courtesy of the late Mary Roberson.*

379A & B. Bisque head Bonnie Babe with painted brown hair, sleeping blue glass eyes, open mouth, cloth Mama body having composition arms and legs. Original clothes including the cloth tag that reads: "BONNIE BABE//COPYRIGHTED BY//GEORGENE AVERILL//MADE BY K AND K TOY CO." The mark on the head is "Copr.//Georgene Averill//1005/3652//Germany." H. 16 in. (40.5 cm.) *Courtesy of the Margaret Woodbury Strong Museum. Photos by Harry Bickelhaupt.*

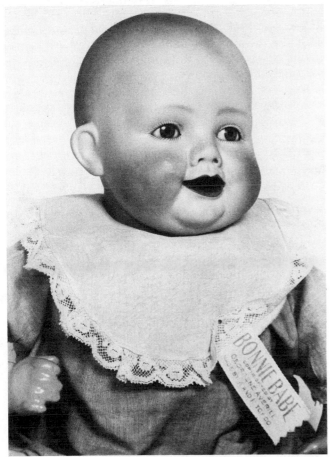

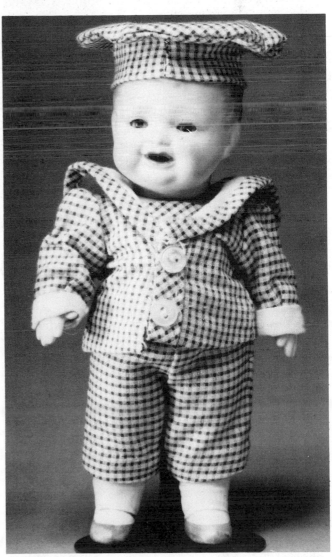

381. All-bisque Bonnie Babe with molded and painted hair and footwear, sleeping brown glass eyes and an open mouth. Toddler-style body has a sticker on its stomach. H. 5 in. (12.5 cm.). *Courtesy of Sotheby Parke Bernet Inc., N.Y.*

BONNIE BABE
COPYRIGHTED BY
GEORGENE AVERILL
382 MADE BY K AND K TOY CO.

383 *Copr by GeorgeneAverill 1005/3652 Germany 1386/36*

384 BONNIE BABE
COPR BY
GEORGENE Ⓜ
AVERILL
REG. U.S. PATENT OFF.
Germany

382–384. Marks found on the bisque head Bonnie Babes.

Bonser Doll Co. 1925–30 and later. Mineola, New York. Founded by Helen Haldane *Wyse*. By 1930 the name appeared both as the Bonser Doll Co. and Bonser Products, Inc. They made washable stockinet cloth dolls with hand decorated faces and colorful clothes. The dolls were generally stuffed with white cotton.

1926: Helen Wyse obtained a U.S. patent for dolls as well as the U.S. trademark, "I am a Bonser Doll." in a checked circle. One of the Bonser advertisements in PLAYTHINGS states, "My Tummy is a rubber ball—that's what makes me lively."

1928: The following directions were given for washing Bonser dolls. "Wash in warm water do not boil; press out water, do not twist or wring doll, dry in shade, not in bright sunshine. Cloth dresses and hats should be washed separately." The doll would float in water. Besides dresses and hats some of the dolls had knitted sweaters and caps. Each doll came wrapped in cellophane. The dolls came in a variety of hts. from 7 to 18 in. (18 to 45.5 cm.). A new large ht. was 30 in. (76 cm.); prices 10¢ and up.

1929: 20 numbers included boy and girl dolls with stockinet and balbriggan material. The boy dolls may have been *Bobby Bonser* and *Buddy Bonser* and the girl doll, *Betty Bonser*.

1930: The stockinet dolls were still being produced but there were also several new types of dolls such as the rattle doll with a composition head on a cloth body and dolls with new faces. The dolls had floppy arms and were dressed in various types of fabric, namely cretonne, rayon, felt, and so forth. Many of the dolls wore felt shoes. One of the dolls called "Kerchief" doll wore a sateen or rayon dress with a child's kerchief in its pocket. Ht. of doll 9½ in. (24.5 cm.). 18 in. (45.5 cm.) dolls sold for $1.00 while larger ones cost $2.00 to $5.00. The small 7 in. (18 cm.) and the large 30 in. (75 cm.) hts. were still being produced.

Bonton. 1927–28. Line of dolls made by *K & K* for *Borgfeldt* who registered the name as a U.S. trademark. The dolls wore felt dresses and picture hats.

Boo. 1929. Trade name of a floppy type doll made by the *Adler Favor and Novelty Co.* It had a round painted face,

385. Bonser cloth doll found having its original cellophane wrapper. Around the neck is a blue silk ribbon with a paper tag reading as shown in Ill. 386. A blue stocking top forms a hat. The features are painted including blue eyes looking to the side. Arms are made from pink stockinet. The lower legs are a printed fabric. The outside seam around the edge is ¹⁄₁₆ of an inch wide. H. 10½ in. (26.5 cm.). *Coleman Collection.*

I AM A
BONSER
DOLL

386. Mark on paper tag of a Bonser cloth doll.

round eyes, tiny mouth and the body contained a voice. The thin floppy arms had mitten type hands. The organdy dress hung from the neckline to the knees without a belt. On its head was a halo-type bonnet. The shoes were removable.

Boob McNutt. 1927. Trade name of dolls produced by *Borgfeldt*.

Boots. 1930. Distributed by *Montgomery Ward*. It was a *Patsy*-type, all-composition doll in a sunbrown color, jointed at the shoulders and came dressed. Ht. 13½ in. (34 cm.); price $1.47.

Bo-Peep. 1921. Trade name of a cloth body doll dressed in felt and made by *Chessler*.

Bo-Peep. 1927–29. Trade name of a stockinet doll with hand-painted face and hair, one-piece body, made by *Nelke* and distributed by *Butler Bros.* and *Charles William.* Ht. 10 in. (25.5 cm.); price $3.90 a doz. wholesale.

Bo-Peep. See **Bo Peep.**

Bord, H. 1926–30 and later. Le Puy, Haute Loire, France. Made dolls.

Borgfeldt, Geo., & Co. 1881–1930 and later. New York; Sonneberg, Thür., and many other places all over the world. They were importers from Japan and Europe, exporters and probably the largest producers of dolls in the United States. They did not actually make dolls in the physical sense, but were what the Germans called *Verlegers*.

Grace Putnam refers to them as "assemblers." They employed designers such as *Rose O'Neill, Grace Corry, Grace Storey Putnam, Joseph L. Kallus, Georgene Averill, Helen Webster Jensen*, and so on.

Various companies made the heads and/or the dolls for them. *König & Wernicke* made dolls, mold #1570M. representing a young girl, for Borgfeldt. Moreover the G. B. on bisque heads probably signified Geo. Borgfeldt. The cloth bodies on many of their dolls were made by the *K & K Toy Co.*, a Borgfeldt subsidiary. In 1930 the Borgfeldt company moved into smaller quarters but they were still active in the doll business in the 1950s.

1889: Ordered over 1000 five-piece composition body dolls from *Martin Eichhorn* according to the Ciesliks.

1897–1904: Borgfeldt obtained two German patents (D.R.G.M.) for dolls with separate clothes.

1901: Registered in Germany a doll with a necklace of imitation jewels according to the Ciesliks' research. This may have been the china head dolls named *Jeweled*.

1909: *Siegel Cooper* advertised *Celebrate* and *Playmate* dolls both of which are believed to have been handled by Borgfeldt.

1915: Bought stock and the assets of *Bawo & Dotter* for $100,000. Imported 30,000 cases of dolls from Rotterdam, a neutral port during World War I.

1917: TOYS AND NOVELTIES gave the following report: "Among the interesting patriotic specialties which have made their appearance since the outbreak of the war are a number of items recently placed on the market by Geo. Borgfeldt & Company.

"Foremost among these is the Betsy Ross Doll."

1918: *Schilling* took over the Borgfeldt business in Sonneberg.

1921: Distributed terry cloth dolls made by *Oweenee* and *Com–A–Long Dolls*.

1923: Tried to restore pre-war conditions in Sonneberg. Sole distributor and licensee for an all-wood doll representing *Happy Hooligan*, made by *Schoenhut*.

1924: Distributor of another doll named *Betsy Ross*, made by the *National Doll Co.*, and *Prize Baby*, made by K & K, as well as the *Bye-Lo Baby*. Georgene Averill was superintendent of the Borgfeldt Toy Department according to Grace Putnam. Had an import office in Sonneberg.

1926: Produced *Bonnie Babe, Buttercup*, Featherweight, and *Rolly-I-Tot;* continued to produce *Baby Bo Kaye*, Bye-Lo Baby, *Kewpies, Little Annie Rooney* and *Pretty Peggy*.

Bonnie Babe and the Bye-Lo Baby enjoyed about equal popularity. Borgfeldt was the agent for *W. Bimblick & Co.'s* wooden bead dolls.

1927: Among Borgfeldt's dolls were *Baby Blossom, Birthday Dolls, Bonton, Captain & Kids, Daisy Dolls, Jackie Coogan, Jiggs & Maggie, Jolly Jester, Käthe Kruse* dolls, *Nobbi Kid, Rag and Tag* dolls, *Rosy-Posy, Rudy, Steiff* dolls and *Virginia*.

1928: *Fly-Lo, Gladdie, Margie, Mignonne, My Playmate, Nifty, Periwinkle, Rose Marie, Sugar Plum*, and *Twinkie Dolls*, as well as many earlier dolls, were distributed by Borgfeldt.

1929: They distributed the *Gertrude Rollinson* dolls, the *Peterson* dolls and *Just Me*.

1930: Borgfeldt was advertising Bye-Lo Baby, *Cuddle Baby*, Daisy, Gladdie, Margie, *Mickey McGuire, Our Gang, Pinkie*, and Rose Marie.

1951: Obtained bisque Bye-Lo heads and all-bisque Kewpies from Germany. It was advertised that the quality was about the same as prior to World War I. An article in SPINNING WHEEL stated that these dolls which also included all-bisque wigged dolls were made in an East German factory. They were stamped "Germany" but the stamp tended to wear off. The Bye-Los and all-bisques came in 5 sizes while the Kewpies came in 3 sizes including size 6.

Trademarks Registered by Borgfeldt[*]			
DATE[*]	U.S.	FRANCE	GERMANY
1923	Mimi		
1925	Jackie Coogan	Bye-Lo Baby	
1926	Bonnie Babe Buttercup Featherweight Rolly-I-Tot		Baby Smiles Baby Bo Kaye
1927	Bonton Jolly Jester Rag & Tag		The Jolly Jester Virginia, Ginny for short
1928	Fly-Lo Gladdie Mignonne Nifty Rosy Posy Sugar Plum		
1929	Just Me		Just Me Gladdie Sugar Plum
1931	Babykins Mary Ann Mary Jane		

[*]See also the first COLLECTOR'S ENCYCLOPEDIA OF DOLLS, p.89.

387. Borgfeldt's advertisement as shown in PLAYTHINGS, January, 1927. Top row, left to right: Bonnie Baby, Bye-Lo, Tiss-me. Bottom row: Dotty Darling, Prize Baby, and Nobbi Kid.

388. Bisque head made by Armand Marseille for Borgfeldt. It has a wig, roguish brown glass eyes, smiling mouth and a composition bent-limb baby body. Reportedly its mark is "253 G.B.//A 0 M//DRGM." H. 11 in. (28 cm.). *Courtesy of Sotheby Parke Bernet Inc., N.Y.*

389. Bisque head doll produced for Borgfeldt. It has a wig, sleeping blue glass eyes, open mouth with two lower teeth, and a five-piece composition body. Mark: "G. 327 B.//D.R.G.M.//A 3/0 M." H. 11 in. (28 cm.). *Courtesy of Sotheby Parke Bernet Inc., N.Y.*

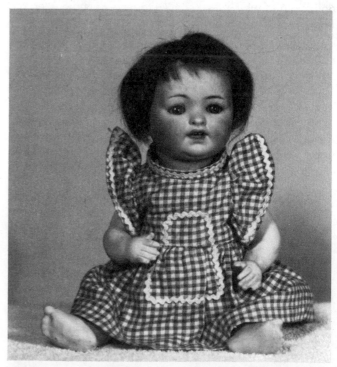

390. Bisque head character baby produced for Borgfeldt. It has a brown wig, sleeping blue glass eyes, an open mouth with two upper teeth, dimples in the cheeks, and a composition bent-limb baby body. Original dress. Mark: Ill. 391. H. 10 in. (25.5 cm.). *Courtesy of Iverna and Irving Foote. Photos by Irving Foote.*

G. B.
0

391

Germany
G. B.

392

G. B
Germany.
A 2/0 M
D. R. G. M.

393

251
G. B.
Germany
A 7/0 M
D. R. G. M.
278/1.

394

G B
A. 5/o. M.
D. R. M. R.

395

396

391–396. Marks on dolls produced and/or handled by Borgfeldt. No. 391 is on the doll shown in Ill. 390.

Bornkessel, F. G. 1891–95. Mellenbach, Thür. Made dolls and *Marottes.*

1895: Won a silver medal at the Lübeck International Exhibition.

Bornmüller, Adolf. 1898. Prague, Bohemia. Produced dolls.

Borough British Dolls. 1915–20. London. Produced handmade dolls, including *British Ceramic* dolls. They made everything from the wig to the clothes and in cheap, medium and high quality. The leading line was of crying dolls, a series with removable clothes and called Borough Baby Dolls.

1915: Dolls had ceramic heads and arms, hair stuffed bodies and came undressed or dressed, as peasants or in the uniforms of the allies. Price $2.10 to $7.35 a doz. wholesale.

1917: Character dolls dressed as Irish girls, Red Cross girls, Russian peasant girls, sailor girls, Serbian peasant girls, Serbian soldiers, and dolls in Spanish or Scottish costumes.

1920: Estimates given for dressing dolls according to customers' own designs.

Borreau. 1878–1930 and probably later. Paris. Ca. 1890, Widow Borreau was the successor; ca. 1895, Bijard was the

successor; ca. 1900–ca. 1920, Paillard was the successor and the firm was called Borreau-Paillard; 1921–27, G. Velter was the successor; 1927–30, H. Lours was the successor.

1881: Bought bisque dolls' heads from *François Gaultier* according to Mme. Florence Poisson, curator of the Roybet Fould Museum.

1927–30: H. Lours advertised dolls, *mignonnettes,* and trousseaux for dolls.★

Borsenius (Borksenin), Valborg. 1926–30 and later. Grudziadz, Poland. Made dolls.

Bosco. 1931. Trademark registered in Germany by *Jos. Susskind* for dolls.

Bossuat, Etienne. 1883–1924. Paris. Factory at Avon, S. et M. France. Made parts for dolls including heads, limbs, wigs and clothes; exported and sold on commission. He belonged to the *Chambre Syndicale.*

1924: Obtained a French trademark with an eight pointed star for dolls and dolls' articles.

Boston Excelsior Co. 1869–1930. New York City. Made stuffing material for dolls.

1926: Material included excelsior, wood-wool, kapok, and all grades of cotton.

Boston Store. 1886–1915 and probably other years. Chicago, Ill. Distributed dolls of various kinds.

1886: Advertised dolls with bisque heads, wigs, jointed composition bodies, wearing a chemise. 8 hts. 10¾ to 18½ in. (27 to 47 cm.); priced 25¢ to 98¢. Similar dolls with sleeping eyes: 9 hts. 16, 17, 18, 20, 22, 24, 25, 27, and 36 in. (40.5, 43, 45.5, 51, 56, 61, 63.5, 68.5, and 91.5 cm.); priced $1.25 to $4.98. Dolls with bisque heads on kid bodies came in three grades: the cheapest in 5 hts. 11 to 19 in. (28 to 48 cm.); priced 17¢ to 69¢; the medium grade in 9 hts. 12 to 20 in. (30.5 to 51 cm.); priced 19¢ to $1.19; the best quality in 6 hts. 20 to 27 in. (51 to 68.5 cm.); priced $1.48 to $2.98. They also sold bisque shoulder heads with glass sleeping eyes, size numbers 4, 5, 6, 7, 8, 9, and 10; hts. of head only 3¼ to 6 in. (8 to 15 cm.); priced 48¢ to $1.10. The rubber dolls were dressed including a hat. Hts. 8, 10, and 12 in. (20.5, 25.5 and 30.5 cm.); priced 25¢ to 75¢.

1909: Advertised all-bisque jointed dolls with wigs and sleeping eyes except for the smallest size which had stationary eyes. 4 hts. 4¾, 5½, 6¾ and 8 in. (12, 14, 17, and 20.5 cm.); priced 10¢ to 49¢. They also had better ones for $1.00. Dolls with bisque heads, wigs, sleeping eyes, hair eyelashes, fully jointed composition bodies dressed in a chemise, shoes and stockings. 7 hts. 16½, 23½, 24½, 25¾, 27½, 30 and 32¾ in. (42, 59.5, 62, 65.5, 70, 76, and 83 cm.); priced 69¢ to $4.48. The smallest size did not have hair eyelashes. The rubber dolls wore worsted dresses and hats. Hts. 6½ and 8½ in. (16.5 and 21.5 cm.); priced 25¢ to 49¢. Knitted clown dolls cost 25¢. All-celluloid dolls with moving arms. 4 hts., 5½, 6⅜, 8 and 10 in. (14, 16, 20.5 and 25.5 cm.); priced 10¢ to 39¢. Other all-celluloid dolls cost up to $5.00. Dolls with celluloid faces and plush bodies called Teddy Bear Dolls. 4 hts. 6½, 12, 14 and 16 in. (16.5, 30.5, 35.5 and 40.5 cm.); priced 24¢ to 98¢. Other dolls with celluloid faces were dressed. Ht. 12 in.; priced 24¢. Separate heads and bodies were also sold. When the body had celluloid arms or hands instead of bisque arms or hands it cost 5¢ more. Bisque heads and *Minerva* metal heads were sold separately. Various styles of kid bodies and pink muslin bodies came in a wide assortment of sizes.

Botta, Aristodème. 1913–21. Paris. Sculptor born in Lyon. Modeled dolls during World War I.

1916: Made doll models often of plaster for *La Francia*. One of the dolls represented a five year old girl with small shoulders, a flat bust, and a prominent stomach.

Botteltot. See **Bottletot.**

Bottle Babe. 1927–29. Bent limb baby made by *Royal Toy Manufacturing Co.* The doll held a bottle with a nipple that fitted into its open mouth; priced $1.00.

Bottle (Bottie) Baby. 1926. Trade name of a drinking doll made by *Century.* The drinking device was patented by John H. Van Winkle of San Francisco, in both the U.S. and Germany. The U.S. commissioner of patents granted an interference on this patent by *Leon Wallach* for a drinking arm doll. A few months later *Paul Seidel* sought a patent for a drinking arm doll to be used for Bottie Baby. The doll had either a composition head or a *Kestner* bisque head, sleeping glass eyes, open mouth with a moving tongue, and a bent limb composition body; four sizes. The doll wore a short baby dress and socks and came with an unbreakable bottle having a rubber nipple.

Bottletot (Botteltot). 1926–28. Trade name of the doll created by *J. Brock,* and made by *American Character Doll Co.* as one of their Petite Babies. Dozens of models were made and discarded before the final one was chosen. The doll had molded hair, sleeping eyes, open mouth, and a crier and could clutch a bottle in its fist. The unbreakable bottle was filled with a white liquid resembling milk and was capped with a rubber nipple. The doll came in a short organdy baby dress or rompers or a dress with a jacket and it wore rubber pants and knitted stockings. Price $4.48 as sold by *Sears.* It seems likely that some of the Bottletots had an embossed mark reading "PETITE//AMERICA'S WONDER BABY DOLL" on the back of the shoulder.

1927: *Montgomery Ward* advertised Bottletot with a composition head on a bent limb cotton body. Hts. 15, 18, and 20½ in. (38, 45.5, and 52 cm.); priced $3.48 to $6.89. The largest size had composition legs. The others had cloth legs.

Bouchet, Adolphe-Henri. 1889–99. Paris. Made and distributed dolls. He obtained several French patents for making dolls.

1899: Joined the *Société Française de Fabrication de Bébés & Jouets* (S.F.B.J.). He contributed commercial property, material for manufacturing bébés, good will and the rights to *Bébé Géant* according to Mme. Poisson, curator of the Roybet Fould Museum.★

Boudoir (Flapper, French Cloth) Dolls. 1915–1930 and

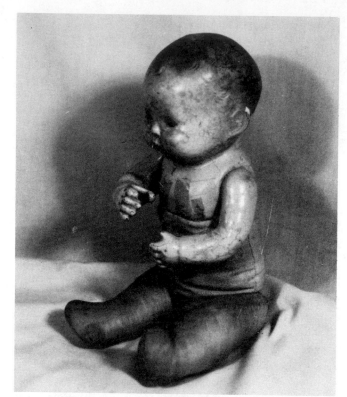

397. Composition baby doll named Bottletot made by the American Character Doll Co. It has molded and painted hair, sleeping metal eyes, an open mouth and a hand made to grasp a bottle. The lower torso is cloth and contains a crier. Mark: Ill. 398. H. 14 in. (35.5 cm.). *Courtesy of Helen Read. Photo by Steven Read.*

398. Mark embossed on a Bottletot made by the American Character Doll Co.

later. Art-type dolls with exaggeratedly long limbs, and heads of various materials such as cloth, composition, ceramics, wax, suede, etc. The hair was often made of silk floss as well as the usual mohair wigs. Features were usually painted. The bodies were generally cloth except for the all-composition Boudoir dolls. Costumes reflected the extreme fashions of the period. There were pants suits, pseudo-Colonial garb, clown outfits, patriotic attire and theatrical clothes. A few of the dolls had a cigarette dangling from their mouth. The shoes usually had very high heels. The long limbed dolls based on *Hilda Cowham* designs may have been the precursors of the Boudoir dolls but the artists in Paris developed these dolls into a real art form.

Marlene Dietrich in satin pants was the inspiration for

some of the Boudoir dolls. Joan Crawford had a portrait in the form of a Boudoir doll. Many artists all over Europe either designed or collected Boudoir dolls. *Lenci* designed some favorite ones including *Fad-ette* with a cigarette. The name "Boudoir" was derived from the use of these dolls as decorations on beds, divans and so forth. Other names include Flapper Dolls, French Dolls and Bed Dolls. During the first half of the 1920s they were chiefly an art doll but as their popularity grew in the second half of the 1920s they came in many types and qualities.

A rather unusual pair of Boudoir dolls made by *Calvare* had large molded cloth faces, spherical glass eyes with narrow blue irises looking to the side, eyelashes only on the side. Blonde "hair" appeared to be artificial raffia. The cloth body was probably built on a wire frame and had hands with separate fingers. These dolls represented a man and a woman in pseudo-eighteenth century attire trimmed with 1920s rosebud type decorations. The heads were 4 in. (10 cm.) in height while the long thin legs were only 2 in. (5 cm.) in circumference. See Ill. 464.

Hermann Steiner made Boudoir-type dolls with composition heads having glass eyes and wigs, on cloth bodies.

1921: The Russian soprano, Lillian Lipkowska, had a collection of Boudoir art dolls.

Lotte Pritzel created Boudoir art dolls with wax heads, dressed in yards of chiffon and lace plus beads and flowers. Her work along with that of *Erna Pinner* was shown in DAS PUPPEN, Berlin, 1921.

Erna Pinner created large cloth Boudoir-type dolls which had flat faces. They wore elaborate costumes generally of silk with pants and ruffs or lace jabots at the neck. The costumes ranged from a Buddha to a clown to her interpretation of period costumes. The clothes were lavishly trimmed with beads, feathers, embroidery, and so forth.

1923: *Marshall Field* provided their Boudoir dolls with verses in defense of Flappers.

1924: The Christmas issue of LADIES' HOME JOURNAL provided instructions for making Boudoir dolls which they called "French Cloth Dolls." The cloth heads were purchased and the bodies and clothes were made at home. The dimensions of the cotton stuffed pink muslin bodies were as follows: 5½ in. (14 cm.) across the shoulders; 11½ in. (29 cm.) length of torso; 2½ in. (6 cm.) thickness of torso; 8 in. (20 cm.) distance around waistline; 13½ in. (34 cm.) length of arms; 18 in. (46 cm.) length of legs.

The dolls were dressed in period costumes based on famous portraits. Each doll wore two white crinoline underskirts gathered at the waistline. The underskirt next to the body was 24 in. (61 cm.) long doubled over to 12 in. (30.5 cm.) instead of being hemmed. The width varied according to the costume. The outer or top crinoline was 25 in. (63.5 cm.) long with a 6 in. (15 cm.) hem and could be as wide as 75 in. (191 cm.). The skirts of the dresses were 1 in. (2.5 cm.) longer than the crinolines and about 3 in. (7.5 cm.) wider. The dresses and headwear were made of taffeta, velvet, silver brocade, fur, lace, gold braid, pearls, and so forth. The legs of the dolls were covered with silk stockings to the knees. They wore taffeta slippers with white kid soles.

1925: *Charles Bloom* obtained a U.S. patent for a cloth Boudoir doll.

1926: Boudoir dolls were made by the *American Stuffed Novelty Co., Blum-Lustig, Kitty Fleischmann, Gerling, Paramount,* and *Unique.* The dolls were about 32 in. (81.5 cm.) high and were sold dressed and undressed.

1927: Among those making Boudoir dolls were *Etta, Mutual Novelty Corp., Mrs. Ethel Westwood, Claire Morris* and *Lady Godwyn* who even made life-size Boudoir dolls. The dolls made in Paris usually wore fur-trimmed clothes. A black version was dressed to represent *Josephine Baker. American Wholesale Corp.* advertised three types of Boudoir dolls, the all-composition dolls with cigarettes, dolls with sateen faces and with painted French mask faces some made of linen. All three types came with either mohair wigs or silk floss wigs with three braided buns. The high heel shoes had ankle ties.

Butler Bros. advertised a variety of Boudoir dolls, most of them with pressed and covered buckram mask faces. These dolls came in hts. 24, 30, and 32 in. (61, 76, and 81.5 cm.).

Montgomery Ward advertised Boudoir dolls with molded sateen faces, mohair wigs, painted eyes looking to the side. Hts. 24 and 30½ in. (61 and 77.5 cm.); priced $1.00 to $1.89.

1928: Boudoir dolls continued to be popular and were made chiefly in America and France. The French ones were described as being "more rangy looking" than the American dolls. The French dolls were more apt to wear bouffant-type skirts. Among the new advertisers were *Katherine Rauser, Kat-A-Korner Kompany, Well Made Doll Co., Dora Petzold, Paturel,* and *Louis Eisen,* an importer. More of the dolls were described as having composition heads than formerly. Some now had white or red hair and some of the sizes had increased to 34 in. (86.5 cm.). These were not cheap dolls, costing as much as $3.50 each.

Bon Marché advertised four styles of Boudoir dolls. The Poupée de Salon had a handpainted head, white hair with curls in the romantic style, a body jointed at the shoulders, hips, and knees, and flat feet. This undressed doll was 75 cm. (29½ in.) tall. The three dressed dolls all had low heels. One wore an organdy dress trimmed with imitation lemons, ht. 73 cm. (29 in.). Another was dressed as a marquise in a colored taffeta dress and a black velvet hat. Ruffs trimmed the neckline, sleeves, panniers and tops of the shoes. Ht. 68 cm. (27 in.). The third doll wore a satin and lamé dress trimmed with flowers. Ht. 73 cm. (29 in.).

1929: Saks Fifth Avenue, New York City, showed Boudoir dolls elaborately dressed as ladies. A new company to join the makers of these dolls was the *European Doll Manufacturing Co.* Imported small sized versions came with porcelain heads. The composition heads came on muslin, sateen or velvet bodies as well as composition bodies. Gerling named one of their Boudoir dolls, "*Whoopee.*"

1930: New manufacturers kept coming into the Boudoir doll market, among them *Mizpah, Sterling Doll Co.* and *Karl Ohlbaum* who made celluloid arms and legs for these dolls. British manufacturers were also making Boudoir dolls by this time. *Morris Politzer* designed and manufactured the Boudoir dolls for the American Stuffed Novelty Co. The sizes grew to 36 inches (91.5 cm.) and rayon was widely used, especially for the clothes. *Victor Keney* used the trademark *Keeneye* for his dolls. He also obtained several U.S. patents for making Boudoir-type dolls. One of these patents was for a head made of composition covered with glue over which was stretched a tubular knit piece of a smaller diameter than the form. Color was then applied to the fabric to form features.

Boudoir dolls were made in the Sonneberg area.

The Boudoir doll sold by *Gerzon* was named "Apache." It had a cigarette in its mouth and its clothes included high-heeled slippers. Ht. 80 cm. (31½ in.).

Bon Marché advertised Boudoir dolls named *Étudiante, Gladys,* and *Mado.*

1970s: A revival of this type of doll took place in France. Many of the heads were made of porcelain and the prices were several hundred dollars. (See also **Gerb's.**)

Boulaye, de la. See **De La Boulaye.**

Boulogne (Boulonnaise). See **French Regional Costume Dolls.**

Boulogne-sur-Mer. 1915–24. France. The porcelain factories of this area, including *J. Verlinque,* made porcelain dolls' heads.

Bourgoin. 1865–ca. 1887. Paris. In 1865 B. Bourgoin sold porcelains. Later a toy man named Bourgoin made mechanical dolls and jointed bébés. The firm was associated with *Jules Steiner* in the 1880s and the name Bourgoin appeared on Steiner bisque heads.

1878: Received a silver medal at the Paris exposition.★

Bournon. 1927. Paris. Made dolls.

Bourse. 1916 and other years. Brussels. Name of a store which was cited with a Hors Concours for its exhibit at an exhibition for the children of Belgian soldiers. A. Sohier who was director of the store was a member of the jury.

Bouton, Dewitt C. 1899. Ithaca, N.Y. Obtained a U.S. design patent for a *topsy turvy* cloth doll. An example of a Bouton doll had sateen faces with painted features. The hair on the white head was painted on the front part of the head. There were two sets of arms with stub hands. The body was two-piece, joined in the middle. The skirt was split up nearly to the waist so that the doll could be turned over easily. A purple stamp stated that the doll was patented and this doll closely resembled the patent drawings of Bouton. See Ill. 403.★

Bouton, J., & Co. 1901–30 and later. New York City. Company founded by Jack Bouton; Harold Bouton was in charge by 1923. In 1929 they became known as the Bouton-Woolf Co. Their dolls were known as the JayBee[+] line, which included imported dolls as well as dolls made by the *Baby Phyllis Doll Co.* They also sold separate bisque heads.

1923: The 350 style nos. included baby dolls with real hair, sleeping eyes, and dressed; *Mama* dolls; dressed character dolls with real hair.

399. Pair of Boudoir dolls with china heads, arms and legs; Pierrot-type painted caps on top of which silver-colored hair is glued. The eyes have heavy shading and the mouths are closed. Original clothes. Hs. 14 in. (35.5 cm.) and 12 in. (30.5 cm.). *Private collection.*

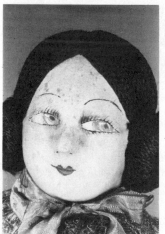 

400A & B. Painted suede face Boudoir doll with black silk yarn hair in buns over the ears. Cloth body in original clothes representing the 1920s version of the romantic period. H. 35 in. (89 cm.). *Coleman Collection.*

401. "French" Boudoir dolls which could be bought ready to dress or could be made of pink muslin stuffed with cotton and having an attached doll's head. The directions for making the clothes were published in the LADIES' HOME JOURNAL, December, 1924. The dolls, in clockwise order, represent: A marquise of the Court of Louis 16th; British lady of the Middle Ages; Empress Eugénie; Venetian lady of the 1700s in Carnival attire; Anne Boleyn; Spanish lady from a Velasquez painting in the Prado.

→

Period Dolls are Exquisite Gifts

When Holbein came to England and found Anne Boleyn's star in the ascendant, he portrayed this tempestuous queen in truly regal splendor. Directly below she is seen wearing a gown of old-blue velvet with a panel of silver brocade faced with silver tissue and lined with old-blue taffeta. The undersleeves, neck binding and coif beneath the velvet headdress are of silver tissue, and rows of brilliants further emphasize her majesty. A Venetian lady of the eighteenth century, ready for the carnival, smiles enticingly beneath her black silk mask and wears a black taffeta frock, ruche and tricorne, bound with gold braid. The front panel is of gold lace over white satin, and on her tight sleeves generous wings of taffeta are gold-edged.

In the Prado, at Madrid, hangs Velasquez' painting of this Spanish lady. Her rose taffeta gown has circular-cut panniers, divided at center front and each side and lined with crinoline and blue taffeta. Changeable blue and red silk braid trims skirt and black velvet bodice, and a bertha of cream lace, matching the full cuffs, falls below an organdie band and row of pearl beads. On her hair a blue, a rose and a tan feather are arranged, with two crystal drops at each side

AND now, besides looking so entrancing that the drawing-room which they adorn becomes the shrine of all hearts, the new dolls furnish inspiration for a bal masque, and assure us that if we follow their silken perfection our gowns will be truly authentic.

They all have two white crinoline underskirts gathered about the waist, the one next to body made from a piece 24 inches long, doubled to 12 inches in length, and varying in width from Anne Boleyn's 42-inch crinoline to Velasquez' 72-inch one. The second crinoline is 25 inches long, with a 6-inch hem, and about 75 inches wide. The Velasquez one has plaits laid in at lower edge to make the skirt stand out in hoop effect. Skirts of all the costumes fall about one inch below the crinoline and are cut about three inches wider.

The left-hand one of the three dolls below represents the Empress Eugénie, who was so charming a figure during the Second Empire. She wears a changeable peach and beige taffeta, ruffled as to skirt and sleeves, each ruffle being edged with apple green ribbon to match the five bows on bodice and the belt. A tiny collar and bell sleeves of organdie and a bonnet of taffeta, with mauve flowers, add to her winsomeness.

She needs no wizard's cap of silver cloth to prove her an enchantress—the lovely lady of the moyen-âge period, whose original is in the Hampton Court museum. Her blue and rose changeable taffeta robe has silver braid edging the bottom of skirt and the silver cloth front panel, which tapers from neck to hem. The basque jacket, flaring from the waist in back, is of bright blue velvet, lined with rose and gold changeable taffeta, and edged with white fur. A mauve chiffon veil is attached to end of cap and one wrist, and the silver lace ruffle on cap is studded with sapphires and rubies.

A marquise of the court of Louis Seize wears an apple green taffeta skirt trimmed with small ribbon rosebuds. Each pannier is made of a piece of rose taffeta one yard long and twenty-three inches wide, gathered on three sides and drawn up to a four-inch width and fastened from center back to center front of the black velvet bodice. Lace bertha and cuffs and lace mittens; powdered hair, in which a rose is placed, and the inevitable pearls are other charming details.

These dolls from Paris may be bought ready to dress or made of cotton-stuffed pink muslin, with attached doll heads. They measure from shoulder to shoulder 5½ inches; from shoulder to end of body, 11½ inches; thickness of body, 2½ inches; across front of waistline, 3 inches; around waistline, 8 inches; legs, 18 inches long; arms, 13½ inches. The legs are covered to knees with silk stockings; feet have taffeta slippers with white kid soles.

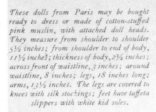

403. Multi-head cloth doll patented by Dewitt Bouton in 1899. This topsy turvy cloth doll has one head white and one head black. Features are painted. H. 18½ in. (47 cm.), measured to bottom of skirt. *Coleman Collection.*

1924: Among their dolls were Folly Girls, Bathing Girls, Indians, and Cowboys.

1925: Advertised bisque head babies with sleeping eyes, priced 50¢ to $5.00. Sole distributor of Baby Phyllis dolls, these came with a picture of the real Baby Phyllis.

1926: Over 200 style nos. The Baby Phyllis dolls were packed in a box shaped like a cradle.

1927: Introduced a musical version of Baby Phyllis labeled "Press me and I will play sweet lullabies." Advertised popular priced dolls called Hot Shots, hts. 11½ in. (29 cm.) and 17 in. (43 cm.).

1929: Used heart-shaped tag with "Phyllis" on it. Some of their dolls had composition heads, hands, and legs, dressed in a wide range of costumes, including coats and hats. Ht. 15 in. (38 cm.); price $1.00.

1930: Imported dolls which sold for $1.00.★

Boutteville. 1920s. France. Made jewelry for dolls. This firm was a member of the *Chambre Syndicale.*

Bow Belles. 1920. Cloth dolls with *Tru-to-Life* faces made by *Dean* as style No. D1080. These dolls had separate skirts and hair bows. Ht. 14 in. (35.5 cm.).

Bowen, J. M., & Co. Ca. 1869. New York City. Bowen and C. M. Nichols imported and distributed dolls including rubber dolls.

402A & B. Boudoir doll with a paper based composition head having a mohair wig, molded and painted brown eyes, closed mouth, on a cloth body with composition arms. Original clothes. Paper tag reads "MADE IN ENGLAND." H. 13 in. (33 cm.). *Courtesy of John Axe.*

BOUTON'S
NEW AND EXCLUSIVE
HOT SHOTS

17 inches high

Retails at a very popular price

11¼" high with wig

Retails at 25c

"PHYLLIS"
The Musical Doll
"Press me and I will play sweet lullabies"

See these latest hits and other controlled specialties at our showrooms — and ask about our two special dolls for Children's Day, June 18th.

Our Complete 1927 Lines Are Ready For Your Inspection

J. BOUTON & COMPANY, Inc.
149 FIFTH AVE. (Through to) 921 Broadway, Cor. 21st St., NEW YORK CITY

404. Advertisement of J. Bouton & Co. as published in PLAYTHINGS, January, 1927. The dolls include "Hot Shots." Hs. 11½ and 17 in. (29 and 43 cm.), and Phyllis.

Bowman, Geo. H., Co. 1910–19. Cleveland, Ohio. Exclusive distributors of *Kant Krack,* Biskoline† dolls.★

Boy (Messenger Boy). 1913. Felt doll dressed as a messenger boy made by *Steiff* and distributed by *Borgfeldt* in the U.S. Hts. 14 and 17 in. (35 and 43 cm.); priced $2.05 and $2.75.

Boy Blue. 1920. Trade name of a stockinet dressed doll made by *Chad Valley*. The doll did not have a hand-woven wig.

Boy Blue. 1924. Doll with composition head and hands, resembling a *Mama* doll. It was advertised by *Mayfair Playthings* as being capable of blowing a horn or blowing bubbles.

Boy Blue. 1926. One of a line of Nursery Rhyme dolls made by *Jeanette Doll Co.* and distributed by *Louis Wolf.* It wore a short jacket, short pants, and a brimless hat.

Boy Blue. See also **Little Boy Blue.**

Boy Dolls. Dolls dressed to represent little boys. It must be remembered that at certain periods especially in the 1800s and early 1900s, little boys wore dresses and had long curls. Many dolls in original clothes probably represent little boys. See the four pictures of boys in 1882 on page 256 of THE COLLECTOR'S BOOK OF DOLLS' CLOTHES. *Silber & Fleming* advertised undressed Boy Dolls with curly hair in 1876.

Boy Scout. 1912. Cloth doll advertised by the *Lafayette* store. The picture resembles a *Steiff* doll. Ht. 35 cm. (14 in.); priced $1.58. (See also **Bob**).

Boy Scout. 1912–13. Trade name of a doll made by *Currie Co.* of white wooden blocks without paint or glue. The blocks were screwed together and the doll was jointed at the neck, shoulder, hips, and knees.

Boy Scout. 1912–14. Trade name of a composition head, cloth body doll produced by *Horsman*. The head was copyrighted in 1912. The composition hands were the same type as those used on *Campbell Kids* at that time. The Khaki colored costume resembled clothes worn by Cowboys. The long trousers were fringed to resemble chaps. The leather belt supported a holster in which there was a metal toy pistol. At the neckline was a plaid bandana and the headwear was a broad brimmed cowboy hat. Ht. 14½ in. (37 cm.). price $8.50 per doz. wholesale. See Ills. 405,406.★

Boy Scout. 1914. A trademark for dolls of *Guttmann & Schiffnie,* according to the Ciesliks.

Boy Scout. 1923. Rubber doll made by *Faultless Rubber Co.* It had molded hair, features and clothes. Came in two versions, one yellow and black, ht. 5½ in. (14 cm.); the other was red rubber, ht. 5 in. (12½ cm.).

Boy Scout. 1926. One of a line of Nursery Rhyme dolls made by the *Jeanette Doll Co.* and distributed by *Louis Wolf.*

Boy Scout. See **Bob.**

Boy Scout. See **Sandow, Eugene.**

Boy Sprout. 1914. Trade name of a doll made by *Dean.*

No. 172
"BOY SCOUT"
Trade Mark

(Head copyrighted, 1912, by E. I. Horsman Co.)

A real "Wild West" youngster in full cow boy rig including f r i n g e d trousers of khaki, shirt to match broad sombrero, bandanna at the neck and leather belt with a real metal p i s t o l in the holster.

Per Dozen........$8.50

No. 172 "Boy Scout"

405. Boy Scout doll as advertised by Horsman in their ca. 1914 catalog. The composition head was copyrighted in 1912. See Ills. 406A & B for the actual Boy Scout doll. *Catalog courtesy of Bernard Barenholz.*

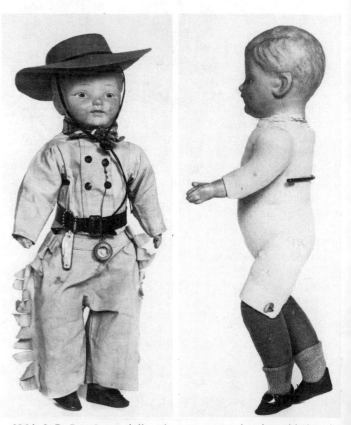

406A & B. Boy Scout doll with composition head, molded and painted blond hair, blue eyes, closed mouth, cloth body with Campbell Kid type composition hands. Note the unusual knee joint for a cloth body. Original clothes except the compass and pen knife are spurious. It should have a gun and holster as shown in Ill. 405. The hat appears to be a replacement. Mark: Ill. 407. H. 14 in. (35.5 cm.). *Courtesy of the Margaret Woodbury Strong Museum. Photo by Harry Bickelhaupt.*

E. I. H. ©

407. Mark on Boy Scout doll produced by Horsman.

Boyard. 1898. Portrait dolls of gentlemen farmers in Rumania. One of these Boyard dolls was in the collection of the *Queen of Rumania.* This doll had a long beard and wore a white cloak trimmed with dark fur. It had a tall fur cap, typical of winter headwear.

Boyer, Mlle Rachel. 1914–18. Neuilly, Seine, France. Designed art dolls for L'Union des Arts.

Boys' Dolls. See **Male Owners of Dolls.**

Bradford & Co. 1925–27. St. Joseph, Mich. Made cloth body dolls and dolls' dresses with fabrics made by the Pacific Mills.

Braesa & Behrend. 1926. Dresden, Germany. Made dolls.

Braitling, Charles F. 1864–1900. Bridgeport, Conn., and New York City. 1900–30 and later Frederick K. Braitling. Made dolls' shoes, wigs, belts, goggles, skates, hosiery and elastic for stringing dolls. In September 1922, TOYS AND NOVELTIES published the following account of the Braitling business:

"In 1864, Charles F. Braitling established himself in the toy business as a retailer, opening a small shop in New Haven. . . . Practically all the stock of dolls which made birthday and Christmas gifts for the shy maids of those antebellum days were imported from England and very different articles from those that now delight the hearts of our modern sub flappers. They were crude, made entirely of china, with china feet painted black to represent shoes with white dots for buttons. This latter objectionable feature impressed Mr. Braitling and he conceived the idea of making real shoes to put on the feet of the dolls he sold and thereby add greatly to their attractiveness and value. He put this idea into effect and in his spare moments designed and made doll shoes from real leather.

"At this period toy stores were opening all over the country and the products which Mr. Braitling had made for his own store exclusively began to have a demand which was national. After quite a bit of serious thought and reflection on the possibilities of this new field he came to the conclusion that the best thing for himself, personally, and for the toy business as a whole would be the development of this refinement in doll outfitting. Accordingly in 1868 he sold his store.

"From that time until the day of his retirement Charles F. Braitling worked constantly and with an unflagging faith in his product to widen the scope of his business and improve his methods of production. At many times it was decidedly uphill work to market his goods in any quantity, but before his death he was gratified by seeing as result of his labor, his business well established as the largest of its kind in the world. At his retirement in 1900 he was succeeded by one of his sons whose name the firm now bears.

"Fred K. Braitling inherited his father's love for the minute and artistic product which was marketed under the family name and early started to learn the trade. At the age of twelve he entered the factory as a sweeper. He passed through the office boy stage and as he grew older he found he had a thorough knowledge of the inside management of the business. He took charge of the sales end of the entire business and the New York office while his father was yet the head of the firm and consequently was well fitted to take complete charge in 1900.

"Since 1900 and the reorganization of the firm, it has constantly expanded. The old lines have been augmented and new ones added. In 1912 the business required new quarters and a new factory was built. This factory was at the time and still remains the only factory in the world built and equipped for the manufacture of doll shoes. Charles F. Braitling died just one month before this plant was to have been occupied.

"The business as it stands in 1922, after its sixty-nine years of leadership in its field, bears little resemblance to the small origin from which it sprang. In 1868 there were two people employed in the business. Today the employees in the plant number 150. . . . The original Braitling doll shoe was put out in one style and six sizes. Today the stock consists of 27 styles in from ten to twenty-two sizes in each style. In addition to these, the Braitling line boasts six lines of doll stockings, house balls, doll goggles, doll belts, and a complete line of wigs. The early production of a few pairs of shoes per week, only enough in fact to meet the demand of Mr. Braitling's own New Haven customers, strikes one as insignificant compared to the present average of seven to eight hundred dozen pairs per week shipped from the Bridgeport factory to customers in all parts of the country.

. . . "A stroll through the factory during working hours is well worth while.

"In a light and airy corner on the top floor the vamps are cut from the raw materials. The shoes are made from both genuine and imitation leather. Up to the time of the war when real leather was impossible to obtain for that purpose, no imitation leather had ever entered the shop, and, at the close of hostilities, when the genuine leather could once more be had, the demand for it was far greater than for its substitute even at the higher price. . . .

"In all but the heaviest selling lines, the vamps are stamped out by hand. These range in length from seven-eights to four and three-quarters inches in the stock sizes. The vamps are one piece, this feature being an innovation made by Mr. Braitling in the doll shoe trade which was carried over into the manufacture of regular shoes and practically revolutionized their production.

"A great part of the stitching and attaching of buckles and buttons is done outside the plant. This is a method used to a great extent in continental toy making which heretofore has not been practiced extensively in America. There are many advantages to this outside work, not the least among which is the gain from an artistic point of view which is realized. The work is, of course, under these conditions done by the piece and generally at the leisure of the workman. In the environment of his own home. . . .

"From the stage in which the uppers are stitched and the buckles and buttons attached the finishing is done entirely in the factory. A score of nimble-fingered girls take the soles which have been previously stamped out and fit them to the uppers. In several deft movements the whole process is completed and the shoe has joined the rapidly rising pile of mates on the bench of each of the operatives. The shoes are packed in boxes made in the Braitling plant, each box containing shoes of each color, generally in the ratio of three black, one red, two pink, two blue, two white and two tan.

"But shoes do not occupy the attention of the entire factory force. The well dressed doll must certainly outfit herself with hosiery coming from this plant, for Mr. Braitling has built up the largest of domestic businesses in doll stockings. These are cut from attractive open work material and are made in several weaves and colors. The sizes correspond to those of the shoes and have as wide a range.

"For the doll motorist Mr. Braitling originated goggles. These are made in several colors of leather, the glass being held in place by small metal rims, and have been protecting the china eyes of their fair wearers for more than fifteen years." (See also **British Dolls**, 1879.)

1918: Shoes made with and without heels, wigs made of real hair or mohair. Auto goggles made for dolls.

1923: Made footwear for *Mama* dolls out of genuine or artificial leather in black, pink, white or blue. Most of these were buttoned slippers. They also made four-button heeled boots and tan leather sandals; goggles came in a variety of colors.

1925: Advertised that their Mama doll footwear would fit either composition or cloth feet. Patent leather and tan leather footwear were mentioned. Artificial leather shoes cost 15¢ to 40¢ a pair while genuine leather shoes cost 25¢ to 75¢ a pair. Moccasins for baby dolls appear to have been a new item.

1926: A new line of brocaded shoes in gold, silver or bronze made to fit Mama dolls and other dolls.

1927: Introduced a line of leather shoes made of alligator, lizard and snake skins. Also a line of gold, silver and Spanish effect artificial leather shoes. Crocheted and knitted bootees for baby dolls.

1928: Introduced high self-locking overshoes for dolls in six sizes. Made high heeled shoes for *Boudoir* dolls. Stockings included mercerized and silk stockings in a variety of styles and colors. Flesh colored stockings and striped socks were advertised. The Dolly Dimples Doll Elastic came in lengths to string dolls, hts. 10 in. (25.5 cm.) to 48 in. (122 cm.). For baby dolls there were pink and blue brushed wool and mercerized wool sets consisting of a jacket, a bonnet and bootees.

1929: Shoes for dolls were ⅞ in. (2.2 cm.) to 4¾ in. (12 cm.) long. They continued to make high heeled satin shoes for Boudoir dolls and overshoes. There were new sizes of overshoes. Shoes were made of artificial leather and real leather including alligator, lizard and snake skins. Advertised that they made shoes to fit any style doll; silk stockings and socks; mercerized stockings with plain or fancy tops. Wigs in various styles were made of real hair or mohair. The knitted wool baby sets came in 4 sizes. Priced $1.00 - $4.50. A new

item was a dolls' bath set consisting of a turkish towel, wash cloth, sponge, and tiny bar of ivory soap that sold for 25¢.

1930: Braitling made the shoes for *Patsy, Patsykins* and *Patsy Ann*. They continued to make shoes of real and artificial leather as well as cloth. A new type was canvas sports shoes. They made roller skates for dolls, especially for *Effanbee*.

1942: Advertised dolls' house dolls.★

Brandeis, J. H. 1915–25. Prague. Produced dolls.

Brandner, Hermann & Co. 1922–30. Sonneberg. Thür. Manufactured dolls of various types such as child dolls, bent limb baby dolls and toddler dolls.

1928: Dolls came in chemises or fully dressed. Advertised *Boudoir* dolls, manikins for shop windows, art dolls and Revue dolls as well as regular types of dolls.★

Branner, Martin A. 1928. Cartoonist whose character Perry Winkle in "Winnie Winkle" was the basis for an all-bisque doll named *Periwinkle*.

Brasseur & Videlier. 1865–82. Paris. In 1881 purchased bisque dolls' heads from *François Gaultier* and used them in making dolls, according to Mme. Poisson, curator of the Roybet Fould Museum.★

Brauenschweiger, Alfred. See **Baumann, Franz.**

Braum, David. 1907–10. Vienna. Listed under Dolls and Dolls' Heads in an Austrian directory.

Braun. See **Brown (Musician).**

Braun, Hugo. 1908–12. Georgenthal, Thür. In 1908 Hugo Braun, a merchant, joined *Franz Schmidt* to form Cellulobrinwerke[†] according to the Ciesliks.★

Braun, Joh. F., & Sohn. 1912. Nürnberg, Bavaria. Obtained several German patents (D.R.G.M.) for jointed dolls.

Brauner, Gustav. 1899–1921. Vienna. Produced dolls.

1907–10: Some of his dolls had metal heads on kid bodies.★

Brauner, Therese. 1899–1920. Vienna. Made dolls.★

Braxted Doll Village Industry. 1918–28. Braxted Park, Witham, Essex. Produced dressed dolls, especially baby dolls with composition heads, arms and legs, cloth bodies, glass eyes, and wigs. They also made cloth dolls, all-leather dolls and carved wooden dolls. Dolls' accessories were also produced. This appears to have been a post wartime domestic industry.

1923: Produced all-leather dolls and carved wood dolls.

Brazilian Dolls. It was reported that in 1914, parts of dolls made in other countries were assembled in Brazil and sold as Brazilian dolls.

Bre (Bretagne Bauer). 1911–16. Fat felt doll made by *Steiff*, dressed as a peasant of Brittany wearing a pork pie style hat. Ht. 35 cm. (14 in.).

Bredow & Dubreuil. 1915–16. London. Distributed American-made dolls of various kinds including *Oteecee* dolls.

Breiner Doll & Toy Co. 1923–27. New York City. Made dolls' heads.★

Brelaz, F. 1865–85. Paris. In 1881 purchased bisque dolls' heads from *François Gaultier* and used them in making dolls, according to Mme. Poisson, curator of the Roybet Fould Museum.★

Bremer, L. 1926. Berlin. Distributed character dolls, art dolls, dolls with clothes, and other dolls made by *Emil Bauersachs, Buschow & Beck, Escher,* and *Elise Israel.*

Brentsend Dolls. World War I–1920s. Grahamstown, South Africa and later Salisbury, Rhodesia. Cloth dolls made by Miss Brent and Mrs. Townsend.

Breton (Brettonne, Brittany). See **French Regional Costume Dolls.** Also see **Bécassine** and **Bre.**

Bretschneider, Gustav. 1896–1930 and later. Neustadt, near Coburg, Thür., and later Bavaria. Made dolls including baby dolls.★

Brettl (Brettlein). 1906 and before. Name for a technique of making dolls by cutting out several layers of small boards and cementing them together to form three dimensional figures. These were then painted. Brettl means "Little board."

Breuer, Ernestin. 1907–10. Vienna. Listed under Dolls and Dolls' Heads in an Austrian directory.

Breul, Clemens. 1919–21. Cologne, Germany. Obtained two German patents (D.R.P.) for dolls' finger movements.

Briand. 1927. Portrait doll created by *Mlle. Adrienne.*

Brick Bodkins. 1915. Doll with composition head and lower arms made by *Effanbee.* It had molded hair, painted eyes, open-closed mouth and dimples. An embossed mark on the back of the neck was "201." The cork-stuffed body had striped legs to simulate stockings and molded composition boots. A similar doll was made in a black version and a similar head was used for *Aunt Dinah.* Ht. 15 in. (38 cm.).

Bricon, M., and Mme. Et. 1916–18. Paris. Made art dolls of cloth, composition or porcelain at the Atelier des *Petites Mains Parisiennes* (The workshop of the Little Hands of Paris, founded by M. Bricon). The dolls were designed by well-known artists, including *M. Gardet.*

Bride and Groom Dolls. See **Wedding Party.**

Brieger & Co. 1895–1901. Breslau, Silesia. Made dolls' bodies.

1901: Obtained a German patent (D.R.G.M.) for a doll's body made of rubberized fabric.★

Briegleb, Adolf. 1909–30 and later. Nürnberg, Bavaria. Produced dolls.★

Brierly, P. L., & Co. 1922–26. London. Distributed dolls.

1926: Sole agent for *Hermann Rogner*'s successors.

Brietsche, D. M. F. 1922–24. England. Produced toys.

Bright Eyes. 1916. Doll made by *Effanbee* with composition head and hands, molded and painted hair and eyes that looked to the side, closed mouth, and a cloth body. The embossed mark was "DECO//144" according to Pat Schoonmaker. Ht. 15½ in. (39.5 cm.). Baby Bright Eyes Jr. was 11 in. (28 cm.) tall.

Bright Eyes. 1927. Name of a cloth doll to be made at home for which instructions were given by the LADIES' HOME JOURNAL. This velveteen boy doll had silk floss curls, a plush cap and jacket and four-in-hand ribbon necktie. Ht. 10 in. (25.5 cm.); width across arms 6 in. (15 cm.); head 3¾ by 4½ in. (9.5 by 11.5 cm.); long legs 4 in. (10 cm.), and long jacket 3 in. (7.5 cm.).

Bringlee. 1919–21. Composition dolls with wigs and glass eyes. Four hts. 18 to 35 in. (45.5 to 89 cm.)   Distributed in London by Yabsley in 1921.★

Brinton-Bruner Co. 1927. America. Made *Mama* dolls.

Bristol, Emma L. 1886–1900. Providence, R. I. Made dolls. (See Ills. 408 and 409).★

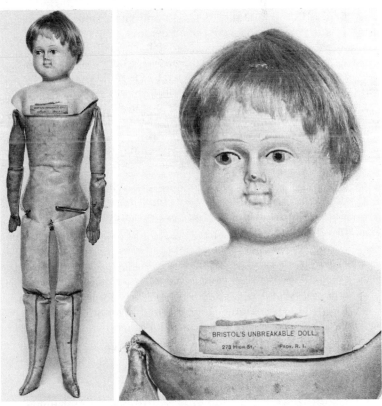

408A & B. Composition shoulder head made by Bristol of Providence, R. I. The thick composition is brown in color with a stark white finish. The doll has a blond wig, molded blue eyes, closed mouth, and a leather body. Mark: Ill. 409. H. 20 in. (51 cm.). H. of shoulder head 5 in. (12.5 cm.). *Courtesy of the Margaret Woodbury Strong Museum. Photo by Harry Bickelhaupt.*

BRISTOL'S UNBREAKABLE DOLL,

273 High St.'   **Prov. R. I.**

409. Mark on paper sticker on front shoulder of a Bristol doll. See Ill. 408.

Britannia Toy Co. 1919–26. London. Manufactured cloth dolls. Some of their dolls were handled by *Bush Terminal* and by *Cowan, de Groot*.

Brite Eyes. 1926. Trade name of a doll made by *Averill Manufacturing Co.* It had one lower tooth and came in five hts. including 16, 18, and 22 in. (40.5, 45.5 and 56 cm.).

Bri-Tee. 1927–28. Trade name of *Mama* doll made by *Averill Manufacturing Co.* It had a composition head with painted hair, blue or brown eyes, slender limbs. The doll representing a 7 year old girl came dressed in several sizes.

British & Foreign Agency Co. 1916. England. Handled *Effanbee* dolls.

British Babes. 1917–18. Line of dressed cloth dolls designed by *E. E. Houghton* and made by *Shanklin*. Some of the dolls were stockinet. The hair was wool. The dolls included George of England with blond hair, Andrew of Scotland with orange colored hair, David of Wales with dark red hair and Patrick of Ireland with brown hair.

British Ceramic Dolls. 1914–30 and later. Dolls made in Britain with ceramic heads or all-ceramic. The ceramic used for this purpose was neither porcelain nor pottery but was of a quality below porcelain and above pottery. It was closely related to stoneware as described by Geoffrey Godden. The heads, limbs and dolls of British Ceramic were fired at a lower temperature than those of porcelain.

Numerous potteries in the Stoke-on-Trent area made British Ceramic dolls and dolls' parts. British advertisements usually described these dolls as "China dolls." "Pot" was also a term used in Britain for these dolls.

1920: Heads of British Ceramic were used in the U.S. on the dolls made by the *New Toy Manufacturing Co.* (See also **British Dolls** and **Manufacture of Dolls, Commercial: Made in Britain.**)

British Doll Manufacturing Co. 1917. Stoke-on-Trent. Made character dolls with *British Ceramic* heads and stuffed bodies. Among their dolls were Gypsy Girl, Italian Girl, Little Bo Peep, Little Boy Blue, Little Jack Horner, Little Red Riding Hood, Marjorie Daw, Pierrette, Pierrot, Policeman, Red Cross Nurse, Robin Hood, Sailors, Scouts and Soldiers.

British Doll & Novelty Co. 1916. Merton, Surrey. Produced dolls with *British Ceramic* socket heads. The bodies were jointed and the dolls came dressed or undressed.

British Dolls. Britain was well known for its wooden and wax dolls during the 1700s. But by the end of the 1800s very few dolls were being made in Britain. They could not compete with the bisque head dolls made in Germany and France. When World War I cut off the supply of German bisque dolls, the potteries in Staffordshire began to make what the British sometimes call "Pot" dolls because they were made in potteries. The British do not usually differentiate between bisque and china. Dolls are most frequently called "china" or sometimes "parian" regardless of whether they are porcelain or pottery. The ingredients of the British dolls appear to have been inferior to the ingredients in porcelain and they were fired at a lower temperature. In the following contemporary accounts about *British Ceramic*

dolls it must be kept in mind that "china" does not mean what American collectors think of as a china doll. The same is true of "porcelain" and "parian." The name British Ceramic seems suitable because these dolls were uniquely British and they were ceramic. It was generally only the head and perhaps the limbs that were made of British Ceramic. Often the molds used for these heads were made from German dolls that were at hand.

In the mid 1920s the supply of German bisque dolls returned to the British markets and competition practically ended the production of the inferior British Ceramic dolls.

Now in the 1980s the interest in bisque dolls by collectors is causing the Staffordshire potteries to return to the manufacture of dolls' heads, and this time they are made of bone china.

Ca. 1850: Henry Mayhew reported an interview with a London maker of dolls, "I made the composition heads for the dolls—nothing else. They are made of papier-mâché. . . . After they go out of my hands to the dollmakers, they are waxed. First, they are done over in 'flake' light [flesh color paint] and then dipped in wax. I make a mould from a wax model, and in it work the paper—a peculiar kind of sugar paper.

"My little girl, fifteen years old, and myself can only make twelve or thirteen dozen a day of the smallest heads. For them I get 4s [$1.00] the gross, and the material . . . costs me 1s 10d [46¢]. . . .

"My wife makes a few dolls' arms of stuffed sheepskin: sawdust is used. She only gets seven farthings [3½¢] a dozen for them. . . . Bodies stuffed with sawdust at 2s 6d [62¢] a gross."

1855: A French article on dolls published in 1924 stated that Britain supplied wax heads for dolls to French manufacturers in 1855.

1876: DEMOREST stated that the British dolls were "dressed without any regard to condition, in hybrid mixtures of lace, muslin and ribbon and flowers."

1878: THE QUEEN, a British periodical, reported, "Ordinary English dolls with wax heads and curling tresses, calico bodies stuffed with sawdust and wax—or, in inferior kinds leather arms—and wax legs are up to 29 inches [73.5 cm.]." The larger dolls were used for advertising purposes. The eyes could open and shut and the hair was arranged so the doll resembled a woman of fashion, a child, or a man.

1879: Olive Thorne in ST. NICHOLAS wrote, "England makes the most beautiful wax dolls in the world. . . . They have real hair, set in the scalp and not a paltry wig; they have glass eyes, each of which is made separately, and is a work of art. There are sixteen manufactories of dolls in London alone.

"The London doll *special* is the rag baby, and a very pretty thing it is, just beginning to come [to America]. The head is of wax covered with very thin muslin, which gives it a peculiarly soft and babyish look, and makes it strong enough for a live baby to play with. Dolls' boots and shoes are also an English trade." (See **Braitling, Charles.**)

1884: LITTLE FOLKS magazine described a visit to one of the largest British doll factories that occupied six floors. It stated:

"The street floor is devoted to the sale of dolls. Its extensive range of window displays [show the] dolls made on the premises.

"Counters and stands are crowded with dolls, some fully dressed, some waiting for the purchaser to choose the outfit. There are young lady dolls of large size, baby dolls in muslin and lace, character dolls like mother hubbard, red riding hood, highlanders and fishwives. In a special compartment are models in wax, single figures and groups, copies of well known paintings or engravings, and mechanical dolls which move their heads and imitate breathing by means of clockwork.

"On the second floor is more work of this kind. There are also curious illustrations of the wax modelers art; casts of faces taken from life, some taken after death, of persons of fame or notoriety, fancy models for displaying the style of the hair dresser or the milliner. . . .

"In the storeroom of the factory thousands of dolls were done up in paper, classified and numbered and packed away in racks ready to meet any order for shipment."

The dolls were actually made on the other four floors of the building. The types of dolls made here included poured wax dolls, wax over composition dolls, composition dolls which were called "papier mache, as well as London rag dolls with wax mask faces covered with muslin."

1895: Dolls came with real hair and real eyelashes; the hair could be combed and brushed. Dolls were made specially to fit baby clothes. A variety of costumes, from peasant costumes to bridal clothes, was worn by the dolls. Black dolls were popular. If a doll was broken, materials could be obtained for its repair.

1899: Advertisement in the Louvre library lists British dolls as follows: wax dolls, demi-wax dolls, multi-faced dolls, cloth dressed dolls. These dolls were sold in France and cost 79¢ to $2.19.

Ca. 1902: Poured wax-head portrait dolls of the Royal Family and other famous British personages were distributed by *Hamley*. (See Ills. 1720, 2142 and 2146.)

1904: THE PRIZE, a periodical, stated, "The dolls made in England[,] which are known all over the world, are mostly of the better class[,] those with pretty wax faces and fluffy hair, nicely dressed in the brightest of muslin."

1913: Imported dolls were required to be stamped "Not British" according to TOYS & NOVELTIES. Actually they were probably required to have the country of origin on them as was the case here in the United States.

1914: Prior to the outbreak of war the old style wax dolls were sold either in a chemise or dressed.

In October, after war broke out, the doll-making industry was started in the Staffordshire area. By this means it was hoped to restart an old English industry, to give employment to Pottery girls, dressmakers and so forth. The art had so entirely died out that inquiries failed to discover anyone who had been trained in the making of any part of the doll.

1914–16: TOYS AND NOVELTIES also reported that at the beginning of World War I Belgian refugees had fled to England and become engaged in making all-felt dolls; even the faces were felt. These wartime dolls were dressed as the soldiers of the Allies, as well as Uncle Sam, John Bull, and so forth. *Horsman* distributed some of these dolls in the U.S.

During this same period Hamley distributed similar felt-faced dolls made by Harwin. There is a possibility that some of the Belgian refugees were employed by Horsman.

1915: The first all-British doll ever produced in the Staffordshire potteries was made with stationary eyes and a cloth body. Other dolls of this period included portrait dolls of *Lord Kitchener, General French* and Scottish soldiers called "Scottish Kilts." An English professional artist modeled these dolls although prior to the war he had never done any of this type of work. *St. Issell's Toy Industry* and the *East London Toy Factory* made dolls of various kinds. A small factory in North Kensington, London, made clowns, and baby dolls dressed in blue frocks and white bonnets.

There was an exhibit of 1000 dolls in costumes of various Nationalities and character at the Southend of London to raise money for wounded soldiers. School children dressed dolls and many of the dolls were donated by titled ladies.

A doll dressed as Edith Cavell was sold to raise money for the Red Cross.

A factory making stuffed dolls in Swansea, Wales, employed 30 girls.

1916: A British toy trade magazine complained that some of the dolls' heads made in Britain were porous and easily soiled.

The British Ceramic heads were put on bodies of cheap cotton, imitation kid, or a shiny material akin to thin oil-cloth. About the only composition and wood bodies available were those of Julius Kohnstam.

1917: About one hundred factories were producing dolls in Britain. British Ceramic heads were made in Staffordshire. (See Ills. 489, 886, 1198.) Celluloid heads were made in Lancashire. The bodies were made of white kid, cloth or composition. It was discovered that the head and whole torso could be cast in one piece of composition. The separate composition arms and legs became jointed at the shoulders and hips.

TOYS AND NOVELTIES reported: "Manufacturers at Stoke are now producing a number of china [British Ceramic] heads and although . . . they have [not] reached the perfection to which they were brought in Germany by years of thought and study yet there is a reason to congratulate ourselves [the British] that [we were able] to do as much as we have done."

Reports in THE TOYSHOP AND FANCY GOODS JOURNAL varied. A February report stated that no wax dolls were made in Britain at that time and that the glass eyes used for dolls were old stock from Austria or from France. This contradicts information in an article in the same journal in July which is as follows: "Jointed dolls have improved most wonderfully. To-day we can purchase the jointed dolls with balanced glass eyes, made at our very doors in Birmingham. I [Sidney Thomas Westwood] am seriously considering at the moment manufacturing dolls myself, as I can improve on the German idea of stringing dolls, so much so that a few weeks ago I was offered a berth as manager of one of the largest English firms of doll makers. . . .

"British-made dolls are rapidly approximating to the German pre-war product. The improvement is especially noticeable this year. Whereas, in the seasons of '15 and '16, we had to be content with papier-mâché faces, and badly shaped figures with clumsy legs and unshod feet, we are to have this year wax heads and wigs, and the rosy cheeks and sparkling eyes to which we have been accustomed. This, together with a much improved figure and shoes to the feet, will be the chief improvement this year. . . .

"My candid opinion as a buyer of British-made dolls is that the improvement shown since the beginning of their manufacture in England, is chiefly in the expression of the faces of the dolls, more especially in the composition ones. In this, as in everything else, it is only a question of time before we get this perfected, and equal to the German article.

"During the past twelve months [1916–1917] the improvement shown in the low and medium priced goods being particularly noticeable, while in rag dolls, Britain undoubtedly holds her own.

"Baby dolls have gone forward by leaps and bounds, and there are many British made dolls of this class which compare favourably with any made either in America or on the Continent.

"In jointed dolls there has been a very big advance, and some beautiful dolls in this class are now being manufactured in the Liverpool district which stand the test of comparison with some of the best German and French goods. . . .

"One of the weak points of the foreign made article which is still taking a far too prominent part in doll design [is the disproportionate sizes of the limbs].

"The arms and legs of the great majority of our dolls are from two to six sizes too small for the heads. . . .

(It is hoped) "that some enterprising manufacturer of arms and legs would awake to the need of the times, and set out to supply this class of article. . . .

"In regard to the dressing of British dolls, here again we are far behind [the Germans]. We lack the details given to the actual finish, and I think the reason of this is that our workers do not give the necessary time to do the work thoroughly, and labour under the idea that because it is only a garment for a doll, any sort of finish will do. . . .

"In dressing dolls, there is still much to be desired. The dresses of the German pre-war models were marvels of ingenuity, tastefulness, and attention to detail, especially in the matter of hats on large-size dolls."

Contrary opinions were also expressed.

"With regard to British dressing, it is infinitely superior to any foreign country, one London firm in particular turning out charming dressed dolls. . . .

"Previous to the war the London dressed doll was always a favourite, and far more saleable than a German dressed one. Not only were the colouring and taste more dainty, but every detail was carried out perfectly. . . .

"Our methods of packing leave much to be desired . . . I [H. H.] helped an assistant to unpack a case of toys the other day. Seven out of twelve dolls had their china faces smashed in, although boxed, and all had to have their bit of very inferior hair disentangled from loose hay, . . .

"There are too many manufacturers who pay little or no attention to packing—indeed, some of the finest British dolls are among the worst packed goods . . . This 'penny-wise' policy is doing more than any one thing to bring British products into bad repute."

Another article in the same issue of the same journal had some interesting comments on the repairing of dolls. The requirements included "Several types and sizes of pliers, several files, a pair of scissors, a light hammer and bar of iron for straightening wire, and a pot of glue. Several spools of wire of various gauges, some spools of round cord elastic and an assorted stock of eyes. . . . There should be an elaborate stock of parts'—heads with or without hair, with real hair, and with painted hair; wigs of all sizes and descriptions; extra arms and legs, classified according to size and character. . . . Four pointers to bear in mind when buying mohair for dolls' wigs are to get the proper shades, the right length of staple, the exact curl and perfect lustre. . . .

"If a doll which has lost its head is discovered to have had brown eyes and brown hair, if possible provide the same kind of hair and eyes for that doll. . . .

"The doll hospital rush will come naturally shortly after Christmas, for that is the time when there are more dolls in children's hands and when breakage becomes acute."

1918: TOYS AND NOVELTIES described the British doll industry as follows: "Throughout the trade everyone is cognizant of the strenuous efforts which are being made by those firms engaged in the manufacture of dolls to secure this industry permanently for this country. Unfortunately the doll manufacturers are being severely handicapped by the difficulty of obtaining sufficient supplies in the way of dolls' heads and limbs. The china [ceramic] heads, which are most required are of course all made in the Staffordshire potteries, but the difficulty is that with the exception of one or two firms which have been started since the war practically all those manufacturing doll heads regard it purely as a side line. The making of pots and crocks is their staple industry, and nothing is allowed to interfere with that. At the present time there is a great shortage of china [ceramic] heads, and the position is rendered more acute by the coal shortage; this factor is reducing the output even of those firms who have gone into the trade whole-heartedly. We hear of a recent case where a whole consignment of heads which were going through was held up for four or five days because the firm required all their coal for their staple business, and could not spare enough to fire the oven. The seriousness of this will be apparent to everyone in the doll trade. The doll head maker is busy enough on his regular lines, and if anything suffers it is the output of the side line; . . . Apart from the shortage there is room for three or four new pot-banks solely making dolls' heads."

1919: TOYS AND NOVELTIES published two articles on British dolls; the first is written from the British viewpoint.

"The British Doll, . . . has a great future before it, if the best that can be done is freely put on the market and the authorities help. How good such dolls can be is to be seen at the doll show at Sunderland House, for which Spencer Thorn, of Hamleys, had some of the most beautiful wax-faced models made, and these can be seen in the theatrical and historical sections. . . .

"The really lovely British doll is not yet cheap, though many models are on the market. There is, however, a great improvement on last year's British dolls. Yesterday one of the big buyers quite frankly said that the future of the British doll lay in protection against German trade. Until that is promised, factories will not be financed for the high-grade doll."

The second article, "Toy manufacturing Today in Great Britain," was written by Joe L. *Amberg,* an American manufacturer, giving his view of British dolls.

"In the doll field, which of course the writer believes he was qualified to judge, as one of the best English authorities put it, Great Britain has not yet shown the 'esprit' and it is hardly possible that the doll industry in higher grade merchandise could grow. . . . The British industry must compete with the Japanese of lengthier duration, the French industry of more than a generation, and last but not least we think the American product.

"The doll that sells in England of course is the one they have been used to, namely the hard-body jointed and character babies. These cannot be made 'over night' even though over night be stretched to a year or more. The English field has not yet developed anything but papier mache or glue composition in the body end, and even in the stuffed bodies of which a few of the lower priced lines are sold, there is ample room in an American's eyes, for improvement. On the other hand they have gotten to what they call a 'Pot' (pottery) head, and this may with proper application work into something. It is not a bisc in that the texture as well as raw material are different, but in many ways it is excellent as a new product. Of course various foreign biscs are still superior. . . . The French product has been sold very freely, and unless Americans or other manufacturers can show a product improved over this at the competing price, the market is hardly open to them."

1920: British companies who made dolls were prospering, among them were *Chad Valley* and others making cloth dolls. Many companies were still using the British Ceramic heads on jointed composition, imitation kid or cloth bodies. All-ceramic dolls as well as ceramic heads were being made. *Meakin & Ridgeway* represented a number of the British companies in Canada and the U.S.

1920s: The social changes in Britain after the war eliminated most of the demand for fragile, expensive dolls. Cloth dolls seemed to be the most popular in this period. Dean, Farnell and other British doll firms prospered. Some British Ceramic dolls continued to be made after World War I but German competition had ruined this industry by the middle of the 1920s.

1927: TOYS AND NOVELTIES reported that the dolls sold by *Harrods* in London were designed by artists. One of the chief designers was the brother of a world-famous sculptor. "Many dolls were sold for one of the many New Year [1928] doll balls, where the dancers either carry dolls or are dressed

to look like them. These doll balls have lately become widely popular, the craze having started with the recent Princess Elizabeth Ball which Queen Mary attended carrying a Princess Elizabeth doll."

1929: *Princess Elizabeth* dolls were dressed in baby clothes. There was a great variety in the dolls sold in Britain; they represented people of all ages, both sexes and many nationalities. The dolls representing young ladies had hair either bobbed or in fashionable long coils around their heads. Prices ranged from a few cents to many dollars.

1930s: Only a few Staffordshire potteries continued to make British Ceramic dolls. Charles *Pierotti* made his last wax doll in 1935. Only producers of cloth dolls seemed to prosper.

1942: The British Board of Trade banned British potteries from making dolls. (See English Dolls[†] in the first COLLECTOR'S ENCYCLOPEDIA OF DOLLS.) (See also **London Doll Market** and **Manufacture of Dolls, Commercial: Made in Britain** and **Manufacture of Wax Dolls.**)

410A & B. Chad Valley doll with a felt head, stitched on wig, painted eyes, closed mouth; cloth body is jointed at the shoulders and hips. Original costume of a guard or conductor on the Great Western Railway. The clothes are of cotton, oil cloth and brown and yellow felt. The chain hanging from the collar had an attached whistle. Marked with cloth label on foot. H. 16 in. (40.5 cm.). *Courtesy of Magda Byfield.*

British Dolls Ltd. World War I period-1921. London. *Miss Muriel Moller* organized this company to distribute the dolls made by *Nottingham,* including the dolls designed by *Helen Fraser Rock,* and the dolls made by *Shanklin* including the dolls designed by *E. E. Houghton.* Among the names of their dolls were: Bather, Baby Bunting, Diver, Joan, Peter and Suzanne.

British Metal & Toy Manufacturers. 1915. London. Sold *Amberg's Little Darling Babies.* No record has been found of these dolls in America and perhaps they were made especially for the British trade.

British National Dolls. Ca. 1930s. London. Made dolls with *British Ceramic* heads marked B.N.D. See Ill. 1765.

British Novelty Co. 1919–20. London. Advertised *Nankeen* dolls, doll's heads, wigs, shoes, and hats.

British Novelty Works, Ltd. 1915–20s. London. This was a subsidiary of *Dean*. They manufactured dolls, especially cloth dolls.

1915: Made a plush doll named *Kuddlemee*.

1916: They produced dolls based on *Hilda Cowham* designs. Their dolls were cloth or had *British Ceramic* heads and came dressed or undressed. Among their character dolls were dolls representing Russian peasant girls.

1917: Line of cloth dolls sold for 12¢ to 25¢.

1920s: Made patented *Evripoze* dolls with flexible limbs. One of their dolls called *Coogan Kid* represented Jackie Coogan.★

British Products Manufacturing Co. 1917–21. London. Specialized in character dolls, both dressed and undressed; exported some of their dolls.★

1917: 250 models of fully dressed dolls with *British Ceramic* heads. These dolls included ones in the costumes of the Allies, Colleen, Hockey, Pierrette, Pierrot, Red Riding Hood, Sunshine, Tamma Shanta Girl, and Wounded Tommy. The dolls were priced 12¢ to $2.50. (See also **Bell & Francis**.)

British Rag Doll Co. Before World War I. One of the *George Kirkham* cloth doll companies. After his bankruptcy in 1913 this company may have combined with the Textile Novelty Co. to become the *British Textile Novelty*. It may have been connected with *Art Fabric Mills* and *Selchow & Righter*.

British Textile Novelty. 1916–25. London. Produced cutout cloth dolls printed on linen. Hts. 20, 28, and 30 in. (51, 71, and 76 cm.); priced 50¢ to 75¢.

British Toy Co. See **Potteries Toy Co.**

British Toys. 1918 and probably other years. London. Handled dolls wholesale and exported dolls made by *Nottingham* and *Shanklin*. These included *British Ceramic* heads known as "Rock China Heads" on jointed *Compolite* bodies with British Ceramic limbs. They also handled *E. E. Houghton* stockinet dolls. Most of their dolls were dressed.

British United (Toy) Manufacturing Co. 1894–1929. Stoke Newington, England. They manufactured *Omega Brand* character dolls that were jointed or had stiff limbs, dressed or undressed, at their Union Works.

Broadway Store. 1911–28. Los Angeles. Held an annual contest to select the prettiest, the smallest, the largest, and the best dressed doll. Society women acted as judges and a tea party was held.

1928: Claimed that 2,500 children attended the party.

Broadway Toy Shop. 1861–1913. New York City. Later proprietor was *George F. Langenbacker*. Handled dolls.

Broches, A. 1927–29. Paris. Made articulated artistic dolls. Used the trade name *Camélia* for their dolls.

Brock, J. 1926. Created *Bottletot* for the *American Character Doll Co.*

Brodeur Doll Shop. 1922–27. Indianapolis, Indiana. Before 1922 Mr. Brodeur was a wax-figure artist, then as demand slackened for wax figures he and his wife turned to repairing dolls. They even did mail order repairs. They sold dolls as well as dolls' parts. Their dolls included bisque, metal, cloth, wax, and wooden dolls.

Brogi, M. Amilcare. 1927–29. Coeuilly-Champigny, Seine, France. Made *Clélia* and other cloth dolls.

1928: Registered Clélia in a diamond as a French trademark for dolls of fabric. See Ill. 599.

Bromilow, John Henry. 1915. Applied for a British patent for dolls' voices.

Brosau, David. 1907–10. Vienna. Listed under Dolls and Dolls' Heads in an Austrian directory.

Brothers, J. A. 1919–23. London. Handled dolls, among them the *Cecily* dolls. They also handled some cheap dolls made by *Tyneside Toys*.

Brouillet, Simon August. 1825–54. Paris. In 1825 he married *Marie-Appoline Cacheleux,* daughter of a well-known toy merchant whom they succeeded but the young couple were inexperienced and extravagant. They made dolls as well as sold them, employing several other workers. Finally in 1854 they went bankrupt and there were many dolls' molds in the inventory. Among the creditors were *Seutter* and *Henry Olhmé*. This information on Brouillet is from Mme. Poisson curator of the Roybet-Fould Museum.★

Brown (Braun) (Musician). 1911. Felt art doll made by *Steiff*. Its felt costume represented a musician but the various instruments were sold separately. Ht. 43 cm. (17 in.); priced $1.74.

Brown, H. J. See **Bo Peep.**

Brown, Hardy. 1928. An artist whose painting of a child's head was used as the basis for the design of *Denny Doll* made by *Jeanette Doll Co.*

Brown Boy. 1917. Cloth doll made by *East London Toy Factory*. The doll was dressed as a native (African?) chieftain.

Brownee. 1929. One of *Twistum's Funny Fuzzee* line of dolls. The doll was made of flexible wire covered with colored knotted yarn. The faces were handpainted with the eyes glancing to the side. Price 75¢.

Brownface Indian. 1927–28. Trade name used by the *Henderson Glove Co.* for dolls.

Brownie. 1917. Character doll made by *Thorne Bros.* A simple movement made the eyes roll.

Brownie Ben. 1927. Wooden doll made by the *Harrison Manufacturing Co.* It was fully jointed and 15 in. (38 cm.) high.

Brownie Doll. 1890s. Cutout cloth dolls made by *Cocheco*. Ht. 16 in. (40.5 cm.).

Brownies. 1892–1927 and later. Dolls representing the figures drawn by Palmer Cox.[+] Besides the cutout cloth Brownies there were all-composition Brownies, jointed at the shoulders and hips and with molded clothes. Brownie dolls came in various materials and sizes.

1904: Six different all-composition Brownie dolls came with thin legs and large feet, allegedly so they could stand. Priced 87¢ a doz. wholesale.★

Palmer Cox Celebrated

BROWNIES

Twelve different figures of the popular little fellows, seven inches long. Printed in colors on one yard of cloth, marked where to cut out and sew together—**20 cts.**

Pat. Jan. 15, '92.
UNCLE SAM.

411. All-composition Brownie designed by Palmer Cox; molded clothes represent a policeman or officer of the law, since "Truant Officer" is inscribed on its cap. Large round bulging painted eyes and thin legs typical of the Brownies. H. 4¾ in. *Coleman Collection.*

412. One of the cloth Brownies as designed by Palmer Cox. This represents Uncle Sam and is one of 12 different figures that were printed in colors on one yard of cloth. These cloth dolls were made to be cut out and sewed together according to a January 15, 1892, U.S. patent. This advertisement was in YOUTH'S COMPANION, in 1894.

Bru (Bru Jne. & Cie.). 1866–99. Paris and the factory at Montreuil-sous-Bois, France. 1866–83, Casimir Bru Jeune; 1883–89, H. Chevrot; 1890–99, Paul Eugene Girard; 1899–1953 *Société Française de Fabrication de Bébés & Jouets* (S.F.B.J.) were the successors. Made dolls and bébés. The *Bébé Brus* with kid bodies are one of the dolls most sought after by collectors today. They are not rare but the demand makes them seem to be so. Bru is a French word meaning daughter-in-law but it does not appear to be a

common French surname. The only Bru listed in the 1865 Paris Directory was a locksmith. However, in Catalonia, the part of Spain adjacent to southern France, Bru is a common surname. In 1952 the then President of the S.F.B.J.. M. Moynot, is quoted as having said that there never was a person named "Bru," that Bru was only a trade name. Of course this was not true but it emphasized the fact that even people in authority often do not know the history of their own company, when they are queried about events of a much earlier period.

An 1872 Bru catalog has provided us with considerable information about Bru dolls. All of the dolls listed in this catalog appear to be of the lady-fashion type and not the Bébé Bru which must have been made later. The bisque heads were of two grades, demi-fine and fine.

According to the catalog: Bru dolls were made in 12 sizes (2/0, 0–10) The bisque head dolls' with white kid bodies wearing a chemise came with painted eyes and fur wig in 5 sizes, 2/0–3. When glass eyes were added size 4 was also added. The dolls with glass eyes and mohair wigs came in all 12 sizes. If the doll had jointed wooden arms on the kid body or a completely jointed wooden body it came in all sizes except the small 2/0 and 0 sizes. A partially articulated wooden body doll came in 5 sizes, 0–4. The two-faced doll on a kid body also came in sizes 0–4.

Dolls were dressed in either removable or non-removable clothes; in wool clothes there were 6 sizes 2/0–4 and in silk clothes, 5 sizes 0–4. If the doll had glass eyes and wore a non-removable double skirt it was only made in 3 sizes, 2/0–1. A doll wearing a nurse maid's costume only came in size 1. All of the articulated dolls wore necklaces and earrings whether they were dressed or not. Some of the undressed dolls were sold naked while others had a mid calf length chemise with a low square neckline.

Bru also made all-rubber dolls in 4 sizes, 0–3. These came in chemises or dressed in bathing suits. Rubber heads of the same sizes could be bought separately. This was also true for the various sizes and kinds of bisque heads even including the 2 faced head.

Prices for undressed dolls ranged from 30¢ for a size 2/0 doll with bisque head, painted eyes, a fur wig and a kid body to a large (size 10) jointed wooden body completely articulated doll with a bisque head having glass eyes which cost $9.60. Undressed wooden body dolls cost about 40¢ more than the kid body dolls.

Without clothes a number 4 doll cost $1.20 to $2.10. If this doll was dressed in wool and had a kid body it cost $4.40 and with a wooden body it was $4.60. But if a number 4 doll was dressed in silk it cost $6.00 to $100 depending on the outfit.

This 1872 catalog contained the same pictures as those found on numerous boxes always containing the smiling type bisque head dolls on kid bodies, kid bodies with wooden arms or all wooden bodies. It seems to be a logical assumption that Bru used these smiling heads on their dolls. But there is no proof that others could not also have used this type of bisque head and we know that Bru sold bisque heads separately. Since the articulated wooden bodies and arms are based on a Bru patent, it seems to be evident that the smiling dolls were definitely Bru dolls if they have wooden bodies or wooden arms. (See THE COLLECTOR'S BOOK OF DOLLS' CLOTHES, Ill. 221 A & B.)

One might expect the smiling Bru dolls to have size numbers corresponding to those shown in the catalog, but this is not the case. Instead the sizes are shown by letters of the alphabet that are usually on both the back of the head and on the shoulder plate. These letters are nearly always the same on both the head and shoulders of the smaller size dolls but for the larger heads the shoulder letter is sometimes the next letter in the alphabet after the letter on the head. One of the smilers with a "b" on one shoulder and 3/0 on the other shoulder was only 9½ in. (24 cm.) tall. This fits the size number in the following table but not the size letter.

Based on a limited sample the size-height relationships for the bisque head so-called smilers appear to be roughly as follows:

Size Letter	Height in.	cm.	Possible 1872 Catalog No.
A	11	28	2/0
B	12	30.5	0
C	13	33	1
D	14	35.5	2
E	16	40.5	3
F	18	45.5	4
G	19	48	5
H	20½	52	6
I	22	56	7
K	25	63.5	8
M	28	71	10

A few of these dolls also have "Déposé" on the forehead. A limited number of opportunities have been afforded to examine the inside of the shoulder plates of these smiling bisque heads. As would be expected they appear to be pressed rather than poured. But what was not expected was the finding of another single letter on the upper part of the inside of the shoulder. (Heads marked F. G. [François Gaultier] on the outside have been found with similar letters on the inside except theirs appear to be larger than those found on the smiling bisque heads.) These impressed letters bear no relationship to the size letters on the outside of the shoulders. The inside letters are somewhat rectangular in shape with the height exceeding the width and with fairly heavy vertical lines. So far the letters B, D, I, H, M, O, and R have been observed. Could these represent dates of manufacture? the symbol of the company for which the doll was being produced or what? The meaning of these letters remains elusive. It has been noted that the bisque hands on some of the dolls with a smiling head, are very similar to the bisque hands on the Breveté Bru dolls.

Some fashion lady type dolls have been found with Bru Jne. incised on them. These dolls are usually on kid bodies and do not appear to be as good quality as the smilers.

Human size heads representing men, women and children were made by the Bru firm. These heads were used as store models. No mention has been found of Bru exhibits prior to the 1878 Paris Exposition at which Bru won a silver medal for dolls and bébés, dressed and undressed. Bru was still making dolls of hard rubber and dolls with wooden bodies. At the Melbourne Exhibit in 1880 Bru won a silver medal for dolls and bébés and a certificate for mechanical figures. It was not until 1885 when Chevrot was head of the Bru firm that they won a gold medal. During the period 1885–88 they won no less than nine gold medals. This suggests that most of the famous Bébés Bru were probably made after 1884. Only a few Bébés Bru were advertised in the Paris store catalogs of the 1890s and early 1900s. The Brus were considerably less expensive than the Jumeaus at that time.

In 1892 Paul Girard patented *Bébé Premier Elan.*

When the S.F.B.J. was formed in 1899 Paul Girard contributed materials, good will and the rights to Bébé Bru estimated at a value of $11,000, according to the research of Mme. Poisson, Curator of the Roybet-Fould Museum. No mention was made of any factory or porcelain products as was the case for *Jumeau* and *Gaultier,* who made bisque heads. Girard was a member of the *Chambre Syndicale.*

According to M. Moynot, President of the S.F.B.J., the Bru molds were used until 1930 but were not used from 1930 to 1950. However the S.F.B.J. renewed the Bébé Bru trademark in 1938 which seems to indicate that they were using it at that time. It was again renewed in 1953 and DOLL NEWS in 1952 carried advertisements for Bébés Bru that were then currently being made.

Sometimes dolls marked with the letters P. G. have been identified as Paul Girard dolls. Evidence seems to point to P. G. as standing for *Pintel & Godchaux.* A doll wearing under its dress a commercial chemise was stamped *"Bébé Charmant,"* the trade name of a Pintel & Godchaux doll. It was marked on its bisque head A//P 2 G. Thus indicating that the initials P. G. probably stood for Pintel & Godchaux.★

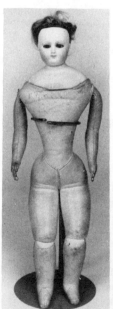

413A & B. Bru lady doll with a bisque shoulder head marked "DEPOSE" on the front and marked as in Ill. 424 on the back of the shoulders. It has a wig, glass eyes, closed mouth, and gusseted kid body. *Courtesy of Vera Kramer, Dolls in Wonderland.*

414A, B, & C. Bru lady doll and its box top showing other Bru lady dolls. The picture on the box lid appeared also in the 1872 Bru catalog and on another Bru box lid. (See Ill. 221 in THE COLLECTOR'S BOOK OF DOLLS' CLOTHES.) The doll shown above has a bisque socket head marked "DEPOSE" on its forehead and "C" (size letter) on the back of its head. It has a wig, stationary blue eyes, pierced ears and a closed smiling mouth. The shoulder plate is bisque and the rest of the body is kid. The dress appears to be original. H. 12¾ in. (32.5 cm.). H. of the head and shoulders 3 in. (7.5 cm.). *Courtesy of the Margaret Woodbury Strong Museum. Photos by Harry Bickelhaupt.*

415. Pressed bisque swivel neck shoulder head on a jointed wooden body which follows the patent obtained by Bru in 1869. The head and shoulder have the size letter "E." It has blue stationary eyes, pierced ears, and closed mouth. The fingernails are a salmon color. The white cotton clothes indicate that the doll was dressed to represent a girl. The shoes have the keystone mark. H. 16 in. (40.5 cm.). *Coleman Collection.*

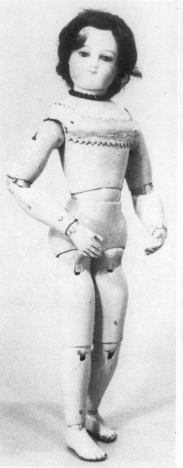

417

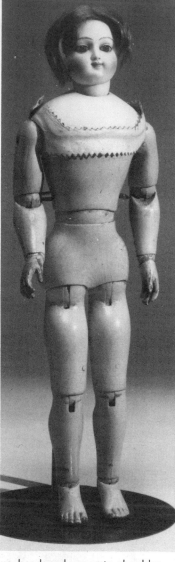

418

417. Bru lady doll with a bisque head and separate shoulder plate on a jointed wooden body, with waist and ankle joints, follows the patent obtained by Bru in 1869. The head has a wig, stationary blue glass eyes, ears pierced into the head, and a closed mouth. Mark: Ill. 425. H. 13½ in. (34 cm.). *Courtesy of Shirley Buchholz. Photo by John Axe.*

418. Bisque head and shoulder plate on a typical Bru patented wooden body. The head has a wig, stationary blue eyes, pierced ears, closed mouth. The wooden body is jointed at the waist and ankles as well as the usual places. H. 17 in. (43 cm.). *Courtesy of Sotheby Parke Bernet Inc., N.Y.*

416. Lady doll with bisque head, blond wig, stationary blue glass eyes, pierced ears, and closed mouth has a kid body. The bisque head and hands of this doll have the same characteristics as known Bru dolls. The light blue dress dating from the late 1870s is original. Marked "B." H. 12 in. (30.5 cm.). *Courtesy of and photo by Dorothy McGonegal.*

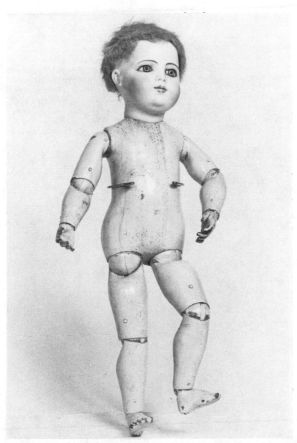

419A & B. Doll believed to be a Bébé Bru with fully jointed wooden body having ankle joints. The bisque socket head fits directly onto the wooden body. The head has a skin wig, stationary blue glass eyes, pierced ears, closed mouth. The head is marked "3." H. 18½ in. (47 cm.). *Courtesy of the Margaret Woodbury Strong Museum. Photos by Harry Bickelhaupt.*

420. Pair of Bru dolls with bisque heads, shoulder plates, and lower arms on kid bodies with wooden lower legs. They have wigs, stationary glass eyes, and pierced ears. The baby is a Bébé Téteur with an open mouth for nursing and the head is marked "Bru Jne// N 3 T." H. 15 in. (38 cm.). The larger doll has a closed mouth and is marked "Bru Jne//10." H. 25 in. (63.5 cm.). *Courtesy of the Washington Dolls' House and Toy Museum.*

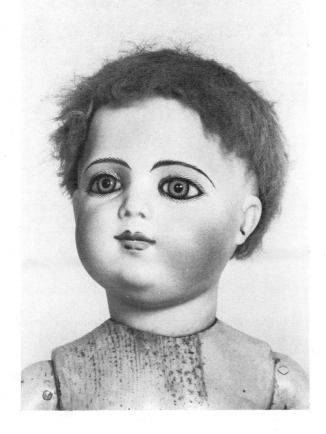

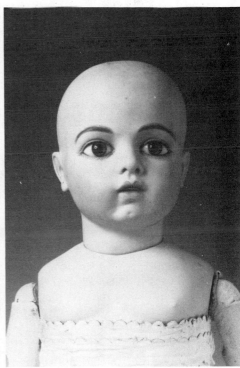

421A & B. Bébé Bru with bisque head, shoulder plate, and lower arms on a kid body. The head was made for a wig. It has stationary blue glass eyes, pierced ears, and an open-closed mouth. The head is marked "Bru Jne. 14." H. 35 in. (89 cm.). *Courtesy of Sotheby Parke Bernet Inc., N.Y.*

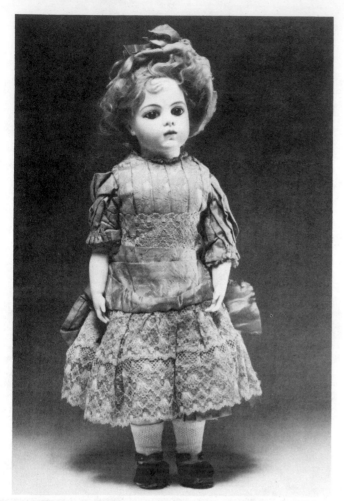

422. Bébé Bru with bisque head, shoulder plate, and lower arms on a kid body with composition legs. It has a brown wig, stationary brown glass eyes, pierced ears, and an open-closed mouth. The head is marked "Bru Jne 8." H. 21 in. (53.5 cm.). *Courtesy of Sotheby Parke Bernet Inc., N.Y.*

423. Bébé Bru with a bisque head on a ball-jointed composition and wood body. It has a blond wig, brown glass eyes, pierced ears, and a closed mouth. The head is marked "Bru Jne R 10." *Courtesy of Sotheby Parke Bernet Inc., N.Y.*

Bruchlos, Georg. 1883–1930 and later. Eisfeld, Thür. Made dressed dolls, exported dolls to America. John Hess was his Berlin agent in the 1920s.

1889: Obtained two German patents (D. R. G. M.) for dolls. One patent was for a jointed doll and the other was for a doll with a parachute.

1905: Obtained another German patent (D.R.G.M.) for a cloth dolls' head.

1914: Advertised dressed dolls, baby dolls and their layettes.

1927: Dressed dolls included ones with 5-piece composition bodies having molded black stockings and tan single strap slippers. Ht. 5½ in. (14 cm.); price 10¢. Other and larger dolls such as a boy and girl in sailor suits and girl dolls in regional costumes cost considerably more.

1930: Advertised jointed cloth body dolls, baby dolls, talking dolls, dancing dolls, inflatable rubber dolls, laughing dolls, dolls with movable features, and dolls' clothes. ★

BRU Jⁿᵉ et Cⁱᵉ Nᵒ 1

424

DEPOSE

E

425

BÉBÉ BRU Nᵒ 1

426

BRU 6

427

424–427. Marks on various Bru dolls. Ill. 424 is on the doll shown in Ill. 413; Ill. 425 is on the doll shown in Ill. 417.

Bruchlos, Valentine M. 1907–27. Eisfeld, Thür. Made dolls and belonged to the *German Manufacturer's Association* in New York City. Sole British agent was *W. Franklin*.

1922: Advertised clowns, a boy doll dressed in overalls and walking dolls.

1927: Advertised walking and tumbling dolls. ★

428. Georg Bruchlos' advertisement for dressed small dolls with wigs, and molded and painted footwear as it appeared in PLAYTHINGS, September, 1927. H. of 6 dolls shown: 5½ in. (14 cm.) each.

Bruckmann, Hattie Bartholomay, (Née Ross). 1917 and later. Portland, Ore. Made dolls of various materials including all-kid dolls, and with various techniques. Dolls were dressed in period, regional and fashionable costumes. Many of the dolls were character dolls. Some of the dolls represented American Indians.★

Brückner, Albert. 1901–30 and later. Jersey City, N.J. and New York City. Albert Brückner died in 1926 but three of his four sons took over the business before his death and the firm was known as Albert Brückner's Sons. These sons were Albert H., Elliott W., and Henry B. Brückner. Albert Brückner's obituary provided the following information:

"In 1901 while watching one of his friends working through the tedious process of stuffing and shaping the faces then used on rag dolls, he conceived the idea of giving form and expression to the faces by stamping out or embossing the features into a mask. His knowledge of lithographing and printing trades enabled him to perfect his idea and he obtained a patent for it in July 1901. His earlier days had been spent with the Gray Lithographing Co. In 1901 he proceeded with the manufacture of the dolls' faces and within a few months had a small factory established for the manufacture of a full line of rag dolls. He held several patents pertaining to the manufacture of dolls and at the time of his death he was treasurer of the *Up-to-Date Manufacturing Co.,* manufacturers of Cry Voices.

429A & B. Molded-face cloth doll with printed features, made by Albert Brückner according to his 1901 patent. Original clothes. H. 12½ in. (31.5 cm.). *Coleman Collection.*

"He had a 'Museum' which contained samples of the various dolls produced from 1901–26, showing their changing dress styles."

As early as 1912 *Horsman* was advertising cloth dolls

with "compressed fabric faces" and their patent date was 1901 which suggests that Brückner made some of these dolls for Horsman. These as well as the flat face dolls were part of Horsman's *Babyland Rag* line of dolls.

1905: *Siegel Cooper* advertised a Brückner boy doll, *American Maid*, *Topsy* and *Topsy Turvy*.

1908: *Macy* advertised a Brückner doll Hts. 12 and 14 in. (30.5 and 35.5 cm.); priced 24¢ and 49¢.

1909: Siegel Cooper advertised a black and white Topsy Turvy doll that resembled the Brückner Topsy Turvy doll. Priced $1.00.

1923: *F. A. O. Schwarz* advertised Brückner's cloth Topsy Turvy dolls with one head white and the other black. Ht. 14 in. (35.5 cm.); priced $2.00.

1925: TOYS AND NOVELTIES stated "Heretofore Brückner dolls have been made for and sold exclusively by one of America's largest doll concerns." Obviously this was Horsman. The article continued by saying that Brückner had been catering to the general trade for only a few months. Brückner's Sons advertised baby dolls and *Mama* dolls, dressed in a variety of costumes. Ht. 14 in. (35.5 cm.) to 31 in. (78.5 cm.). A new doll called *Dollypop* was a cloth doll with its face handpainted in oil colors. The cotton stuffed body contained a squeeze voice patented in the U.S. by Elliott Brückner. This doll came dressed in 12 different outfits. Ht. 13 in. (33 cm.); price $1.00 each.

1926: Registered three U.S. trademarks for cloth dolls, namely *Tubby-Tot*, Tubby and Dollypop written in script. They called their topsy turvy doll *Tu-N-One*. Sought jobbers for their dolls which included infant dolls and Mama dolls.

1927: Added black dolls to their Dollypop line and to their *Pancake Baby* line of dolls. Some of their other dolls were composition dolls which came in several designs.

1928: Advertised terry cloth dolls and continued to make other types. They listed what they deemed necessary in a successful cloth doll made for children aged 1 to 5, as follows:
1. Attractiveness of design of face, body and clothes
2. Durability and ease of removing clothes.
3. Lightweight
4. Suitable for traveling
5. Absence of anything to injure a child.

1930: Continued to make dolls with composition parts and all-cloth dolls, Dollypop, Tu-N-One, and Tubby-Tot were featured. Tubby-Tot was made of flesh colored rubberized cloth stuffed with kapok. It wore a removable rubberized suit and cap. Ht. 13 in. (33 cm.).★

Brückner, Arno. 1925–26. Oeslau near Coburg, Bavaria. Made dolls.

Brückner, Kurt. 1924. Sonneberg, Thür. Used *Schoenau & Hoffmeister* porcelain dolls' heads.

Brückner, Joh. 1905. Oberlind. Thür. Obtained a German patent (D.R.G.M.) for jointed dolls.

Brückner, & Och. 1918–30. Stockheim, Bavaria. Made dolls.

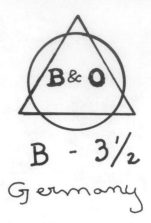

430. Mark possibly used by Brückner & Och.

Brueninghausen, Edward W. 1875–1924. New York City. He was known as "The Major" because of his Civil War service as a major. In 1875 he entered the toy trade and was the first to adopt and the last to use the toy salesman's uniform of a high silk hat and frock coat.

In 1912 he was one of the original members of *Riemann, Seabrey*. He retired in 1922.

1923: Joined *Baker & Bennett* as a director.

1924: Died.

Bruent, Anne Marguerite. 1926. Paris. Registered as a French trademark, *Les Poupées de Mitou*.

Brumback, Jeanne de M. 1927. White Plains, N.Y. Registered The *Cheerio Doll* as a U.S. trademark for dolls.

Brummer & Co. 1922–28. Manchester, England. Distributed wholesale dolls, dolls' parts, and dolls' accessories.

Brümmleef, Phillipp. 1911. Frankfurt, Germany. Obtained a German patent (D.R.G.M.) for dolls.

Brundage, Frances. 1916. Designed the *Dolly Dear* cloth cutout dolls for *Saalfield*. She was a famous illustrator and no doubt her drawings were the inspiration for other doll designs.

Brunet, G., Fils. 1920s. Paris and Herblay, Seine-et-Oise, France. Made sleeping and stationary eyes for dolls. They were members of the *Chambre Syndicale*.

Brunnel, Count and Countess (née de Clermont Tonnerre). 1918. Paris. Created dolls for the Organization des Vents et Concours des Poupées des Allies au Bazar de la Charité.

Brunswick, Hyman. 1853. New York City. Awarded an Honorable Mention for wax dolls at the New York Exhibition.

Brydone-Jack, Katherine S. 1921–23. Glacier, British Columbia, Canada. Obtained a U.S. patent for a doll made of two layers of oilcloth flat seamed around the edges. The limbs were connected to the body or to one another. The doll was stuffed and the surface coated with waterproofing material. The patent drawing showed a sailor type doll.

Brz (Brenzbauer, Farmer of Brenz). 1911–18. Trade name for a jointed felt comic doll made by *Steiff* and distributed in the U.S. by *Borgfeldt*. It wore a blue blouse over its trousers, leather boots, and a fur cap with a tassel. Ht. 50 cm. (19½ in.); priced $3.55 in Germany in 1911 and $4.95 in New York in 1913.

1916: Also had Brenz Bäuerin, farm wife of Brenz.

Bu (Bube, Boy). Before 1911–24. Felt dolls dressed as boys made by *Steiff* and distributed by *Borgfeldt*. In 1911 Bu had long velvet leg coverings. Ht. 28 cm. (11 in.) priced 40¢ in Germany in 1911 and 85¢ in New York in 1913.

Bubbles. 1914–15. Baby doll produced by *Horsman*.

Bubbles. 1924–30 and later. Trade name of a composition head cloth-body doll made by *Effanbee* and designed by *Bernard Lipfert*. Although the copyright date on the doll is 1924, mention of this doll does not appear in PLAYTHINGS until the beginning of 1926. It is first described as having molded hair, real eyelashes, sleeping eyes, two tiny teeth, dimples in its cheeks, says "Mama," puts the forefinger of its left hand into its mouth and wears muslin baby clothes with a piqué cape and lacy embroidered cap. Ht. 21 in. (53.5 cm.). Later in 1926 there were five numbers of Bubbles. But before the year ended Effanbee advertised nine styles and sizes of Bubbles; some were *Mama* dolls with straight legs and some had bent limbs of either cloth or composition. Often their entire arms were of composition. They were dressed in organdy, lawn or silk. Black versions of Bubbles with brown tin eyes came in size 25½ in. (65 cm.).

A variety of marks have been reported on Bubbles: the 13 in. (33 cm.) and 17½ in. (44.5 cm.) size had "EFFANBEE// Bubbles// Copr. 1924// Made in U.S.A." The 16 in. (40.5 cm.) size had "EFFANBEE// Dolls// Walk, Talk, Sleep// Made in U.S.A." The 18 in. (45.5 cm.) size had "19 © 24//EFFAN-BEE//DOLLS//WALK, TALK, SLEEP//MADE IN U.S.A." (See Ill. 585 in the first COLLECTOR'S ENCYCLOPEDIA OF DOLLS.)

1926: Effanbee applied for Bubbles as a U.S. trademark. Doll had a round tag reading "This is// Bubbles//Trademark// Bubbling over with//life and laughter//an//EFFanBee//Doll." Hts. 15½, 18, and 25½ in. (39.5, 45.5 and 65 cm.); priced $4.29 to $9.25. A 19 in. (48 cm.) size costing $5.00 was also advertised. The straight leg Mama doll type was 20 in. (51 cm.) and cost $8.98.

1927: Although a few earlier dolls had dimples, Bubbles seems to have started the popularity of putting dimples in dolls' cheeks. Other companies imitated and copied Bubbles. *Averill Manufacturing Co.* even applied for "Bubbles" as a U.S. trademark for dolls. The Supreme Court of New York County granted Effanbee two injunctions restraining manufacturing or selling dolls which simulated or copied Bubbles. Apparently this was the first time that a doll without a grotesque appearance had been protected by injunction.

There were 50 style nos. of Effanbee Bubbles. They came dressed in short dresses and long dresses some with pink silk coats and bonnets, others wore dimity clothes trimmed with tiny bows and some wore wool jackets. The cloth leg versions came in hts. 13½, 16, and 19 in. (34, 40.5 and 48 cm.). The composition leg version came in hts. 20, 22, and 25 in. (51, 56, and 63.5 cm.). A composition toddler body Bubbles came in ht. 12 in. (30.5 cm.).

Montgomery Ward advertised bent limb cloth body Bubbles in an organdy dress. It came with an Effanbee locket and chain and 6 photographs. 5 hts. 14, 16, 18, 22 and 24 in. (35.5, 40.5, 45.5, 56 and 61 cm.); priced $2.59 to

$9.98. The others had glass eyes. The 2 largest sizes had mama voices and composition legs.

1928: Bubbles had new outfits or could be purchased semi-dressed in baby type silk underwear. The straight leg version could stand alone. The tag read the same as in 1926. 9 hts. 12, 13½, 16, 17½, 20, 22, 24, 25, and 27 in. (30.5, 34, 40.5, 44.5, 51, 56, 61, 63.5 and 68.5 cm.).

Bubbles was distributed by *Butler Bros.* and Montgomery Ward and came with 6 photographs of Bubbles which the little girl owner could give to her friends. The smallest size had a crying voice and painted eyes, while the larger sizes had mama voices and sleeping eyes. The doll wore rubber diapers. Bubbles' big sister was *Mary Lou.*

1929: Full new line of costumes.

1930: The straight leg version could wear roller skates.

Advertised by Montgomery Ward as having blue sleep eyes, open mouth with two teeth, composition head and arms, cotton stuffed cloth body, jointed shoulders and hips, curved arms and legs. Every doll had an Effanbee locket and chain and six photos. Five hts. 16, 17½, 20, 22 and 24 in. (40.5, 44.5, 51, 56, and 61 cm.); priced $4.19 to $9.98. The three smallest sizes had crying voices and imitation leather bootees. The two largest sizes had mama voices and real leather bootees.

Ca. 1933: Domestic composition shoulder head doll came in five sizes. Imported composition shoulder heads with arms, painted hair and sleeping eyes, came in three sizes. All of these dolls were advertised by the *Quaker Doll Co.* (See THE COLLECTOR'S BOOK OF DOLLS' CLOTHES, Ills. 769B and 770 C.) (See also **Betty**.)

431A. Advertisement for Bubbles as shown in PLAYTHINGS, August, 1927. Bubbles as made by Effanbee wore a long or a short baby dress. It had the heart-shaped necklace and carried a paper tag on its wrist.

431B. Six of these photograph postcards of Bubbles were enclosed in the envelope shown in the background and were used for promotional purposes.

"BUBBLES"
NATIONALLY ADVERTISED

The dolls with the Golden Heart

THE GREATEST BABY DOLL OF ALL TIME
Every Mother sees her own baby in Beautiful BUBBLES

FLEISCHAKER & BAUM
NEW YORK

Sales Department:
45 EAST 17TH ST.

General Office:
43 GREENE ST.

Start your letter right: "I saw your ad in PLAYTHINGS."

432. Effanbee's advertisement for Bubbles in PLAYTHINGS, September 1928. Note that the pose is practically the same as in August, 1927 (See Ill. 431A), but the clothes are different. The tag is attached to the dress and reads, "This is//Bubbles// bubbling over with// life and laughter// an Effanbee//Doll."

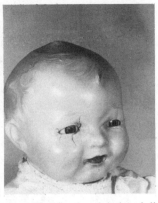

433A & B. Bubbles, a composition shoulder head baby doll made by Effanbee around 1926. It has cloth body with composition arms, molded hair, sleeping metal eyes, dimples, and an open mouth with two teeth; the forefinger of the left hand can go into its mouth. H. 18 in. (45.5 cm.) *Coleman Collection.*

434–435. One of the embossed marks found on the Bubbles made by Effanbee, Ill. 434. Bubbles mark in PLAYTHINGS 1926, Ill. 435.

Bubbly Kid. 1917–18. Trade name of a line of stockinet dolls made by *Fretwell.* The handmade wigs could be combed.

Bube (Schülerpuppen deutsch and französisch [German and French boy]). 1905–16. Felt dolls dressed as schoolboys, made by *Steiff.* The German boy had a knapsack on his back and carried a slate. The French boy had a tasche (schoolbag) and wore simulated wooden shoes. Ht. 28 cm. (11 in.); priced 90¢.

Bubi. 1927–28. Trade name of a *Lenci* doll wearing a hat and coat. Series 950, ht. 28 in. (71 cm.).

Bubi Kopf. 1926. Art doll with bobbed hair made by *Plaut.* (Bubi means bobbed and Kopf means head.). Hts. 32 and 37 cm. (12½ and 14½ in.).

Bubnjek, Stephan. 1907–10. Vienna. Listed under Dolls and Dolls' Heads in Austrian directories.

Buchnauer Porzellanfabrik. See **Plass & Roesner.**

Bucherer, A., & Cie. 1921–30 and later. Amriswil, Switzerland. Made numerous styles of metal body dolls with ball jointed and composition heads, hands and feet. In 1927 it was claimed they had changeable heads. Dolls included *Bécassine, Charlie Chaplin,* a chauffeur in gray or blue clothes, policeman, fireman, *Mutt & Jeff,* Pickwick, many dolls in regional costumes, and dolls known by the name *Saba. Henry Barnett* was the sole London agent. Some of the dolls were only 6½ in. (16.5 cm.) tall some were 7½ in. (19 cm.) tall. The Mutt and Jeff sold for $3.00. (See Ill. 298.)★

Buchreiss, Wilhelm. 1930. Monchröden, Bavaria. Manufactured accessories for dolls.

Bucilla. 1920s. Made cloth dolls to be embroidered; among them was *Dottie Dimple,* a "Stuff-Toy." See Ill. 818.

Buck. 1927. Trade name for stuffed cloth dolls representing Indians with brown faces made by the *Henderson Glove Co.* Price 50¢.

Buck, George H. 1923. Started to manufacture *Doll Debs* in his attic, later expanded to regular factory production.

Buckler, Mary M. 1921–23. Springfield, Mass. Applied for a U.S. patent for dolls' eyes, but died before the patent was granted. Her executrix was Alice G. Buckler.★

Bucquet, Mlle. 1916. France. Founded *L'Adelphie* for making dolls. The clothes on the dolls were of simple design.

Budd, Charles J. 1926–27. New York City. Manufactured handpainted dolls.

Buddeur. Early 1900s. Name found on the sailor hats of boy dolls dressed in sailor suits. These dolls are mold 252 made by the *Société Française de Fabrication de Bébés & Jouets.* When the doll represented a girl the name Buddeuse was used.

Buddie. See **Buds and Buddies.**

Budding Beauty. 1914. Trade name for a doll with "Bisque finish, Washable" composition head and hands, painted hair and eyes, cork stuffed cloth body and wearing a white lawn dress and cap, trimmed with embroidery and ribbons. Ht. 14 in. (35.5 cm.); price $17.00 a doz. wholesale.

Buddy. 1929. Name of a doll advertised by *Reisman Barron.*

Buddy Bonser. 1930. Trade name of a cloth doll made by *Bonser.* Its dress was made of polka dot rayon cloth. Ht. over 18 in. (over 45.5 cm.); price $1.00.

Buddy Boy. 1921. Trade name for one of the *Madame Hendren Mama* dolls made by *Averill Manufacturing Co.* The doll wore rompers.

Buder, Gebrüder. 1913. Sonneberg, Thür. Obtained a German patent (D.R.G.M.) for a two-faced doll.

Budesinsky, K. 1913–22. Prague. Listed under Dolls in an Austrian directory.

Buds and Buddies. 1920–21. Trade names for cloth dolls made by *Sophia Delavan* and dressed by *Katherine A. Rauser,* and *Queen G. Thomas.* The dolls had worsted hair, triangular shaped mouth and dimples. The necks and limbs were slender. Many of the dolls were dressed in regional costumes or as ethnic dolls. Some of the dolls were dressed as clowns wearing a pointed cap and a polka dot clown suit. Other dolls wore rompers or short dresses over wide bloomers. The dresses were self decorated. In the pocket of each doll there was a short printed poem giving the story of its life in order to teach American children to love the needy children of the world.

1921: Dolls included No. 12 American Rose Bud[†], No. 120 Greenwich Village Student[†], No. 122 Holland Bud[†], No. 123A Rag-Bud, No. 132 Buddie Clown[†], No. 804 Scotch Bud[†], No. 914D Greenwich Village Bud[†], No. 915B Buddie.[†]★

436A & B. Bisque head doll resembling Buffalo Bill (Bill Cody). It has molded brown hair, mustache and goatee; molded brown eyes and the eyebrows showing a slight scowl; pierced ears, and closed mouth. One of the composition hands was made so that it could hold an object. Original clothes consist of a brown flannel suit, black felt hat and molded high black boots. H. 8¼ in. (21 cm.). *Courtesy of the Margaret Woodbury Strong Museum. Photo by Harry Bickelhaupt.*

Buffalo Bill. Portrait doll with a bisque head. See Ills. 436A & B.

Bühl (Bühle) H. & Söhne. 1869–98 and later. Grossbreitenbach, Thür. Made porcelain dolls' heads. The factory was founded in 1780 and in the early days there was a connection with *Limbach* which probably explains the use of a trefoil mark.★

437. Mark possibly used by Bühl & Söhne on their porcelain dolls.

Bühner, Caspar. 1914. Empfertshausen, Rhön. Obtained a German patent (D.R.G.M.) for a jointed doll.

Bull, René. 1917. London. A designer for *Tah Toys.*

Bunchy (Bunchie). 1929. Trade name of a doll made by *Averill Manufacturing Co.*

Bundie (Baby Bundie). 1918–25 and later. Designed by *Joseph L. Kallus* made by companies headed by Mr. Kallus. All-composition doll, molded hair or wig, painted eyes or sleeping eyes, jointed shoulders only or shoulders and hips. Clothes were designed by *Blanche Cromien.* No. 102 wore a knitted chemise and cap. Another model was dressed in a Scots outfit. Hts. 8, 12, and 16 in. (20.5, 30.5 and 40.5 cm.).★

Bunney's Ltd. First decade of the 1900s. England. Distributed dolls with bisque heads, ball-jointed composition

438A. Bundie, an all-composition doll designed by Joseph Kallus with molded hair and features, painted in a Kewpie-like manner and dressed in pseudo-Scottish attire. Mark: Ill. 438B. H. 7¾ in. (19.5 cm.). *Coleman Collection.*

438B. Bundie paper sticker mark with blue lettering found on the sole of the feet.

bodies wearing a chemise. Many of these dolls were made in Sonneberg.

Buporit (Bwporit†). 1909 and later. Trademark used by *Bähr & Pröschild* for their celluloid dolls. (See the first COLLECTOR'S ENCYCLOPEDIA OF DOLLS. Ill. 97.).

Bureau, Mme. Louise. Geneva, Switzerland. Made dolls. An orange and white box label read as follows: "AU CHAPERON ROUGE//MADAME LOUISE BUREAU//GENEVA, Rue du Rhone 58//FABRIQUE DE POUPÉES."

Burdines Inc. 1929. Miami, Florida. Advertised that they sold every conceivable type of doll. The dolls were dressed in frilly clothes.

Burgarella. 1929 and later. Rome. Advertised that they made high-priced dolls, each with a distinct personality. New on the American market in 1929, distributed by *Hoest & Henderson*. These all-composition dolls had natural hair and semi-spherical joints. They could be posed in a variety of graceful positions. Their clothes had identifying cloth labels marked "BURGARELLA//MADE IN ITALY." Some of these dolls were dressed in pseudo 1700s costumes.

440A. All-composition doll with mohair wig, painted eyes, body jointed so that it can be put into graceful positions. A similar doll has its clothes labeled "Burgarella." H. 15 in. (38 cm.). *Courtesy of Magda Byfield.*

BURGARELLA
MADE IN ITALY

440B. Cloth label on clothes of composition dolls produced by Burgarella.

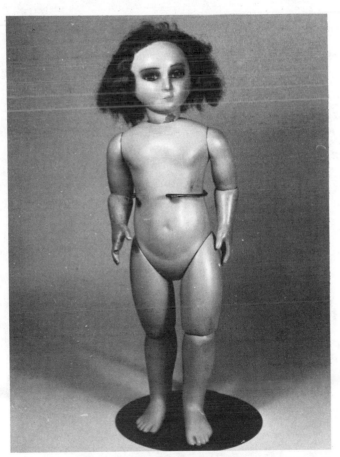

439. All composition doll with wig, molded and painted eyes, heavy eye shadow, and closed mouth. Construction of joints enables the doll to take and hold a variety of unusual poses. A similar doll at the Chester County Historical Society wore what appears to be original clothes of about 1929 that were labeled "Burgarella." H. 17½ in. (44.5 cm.). *Courtesy of Richard Withington. Photo by Barbara Jendrick.*

Burger & Bentum. 1897–1930 and later. Prague (Zizkov), Bohemia, name before World I. Made dolls, dolls' heads and other parts of papier-mâché and wax. ★

Burger, Carl. 1907–10. Vienna. Listed under Dolls and Dolls' Heads in an Austrian directory.

Burgess & Co. 1920. England. Imported French dolls. Handled goods of Pierre Hassid of Paris.

Burghardt, Max. 1920s. Ilmenau, Thür. Registered dolls' eyes as porcelain objects.

Burkitt, H. Chris. 1926. Narrogin, Australia. Made dolls.

Burman, J. and A. J. 1920–28. London. Produced all-British dressed dolls. Did business as The *Zoo Soft Toy Co.* Advertised *Glad Eyed* dolls and dolls' house dolls.

Burmester, Gustav. 1912–27. Hamburg, Germany. Distributed dolls. Represented *Bergische Puppenindustrie, Dorst, P. Hunaeus, H. Josef Leven, Sehm,* and *Hugo Wiegand.*

Burrowes, E. T., Co. 1920. Portland, Maine. Produced dolls with hair nets over their wigs.

Buschbaum, Theodor. 1902–30. Wallendorf, Thür. Manufactured and exported dolls. Specialized in dressed dolls.

Buschmann, Hedwig. 1908. Berlin. Dressed German bisque-head dolls in Renaissance costumes.

Buschow & Beck. 1888–96 Reichenbach, Silesia; 1896–1930 and later Nossen, Saxony. In 1890 they bought the firm of *Dittrich & Schön.* Made metal dolls' heads, celluloid heads and metal heads covered with celluloid as well as all-celluloid jointed dolls. Supplied *Harras & Co., Carl Hoffmeister* and others with metal heads.

1891: Advertised metal dolls' heads.

Buschow & Beck
Puppenfabrik · Nossen i. Sa. 4
Zur Messe in Leipzig: Hansahaus, Grimmaische Str. 13/III, Zimmer 36

„*Minerva*" =

Metallpuppenköpfe, Celluloidpuppenköpfe

Celluloidpuppen ⎰
Celluloidbebi ⎱ *nackt und gekleidet*

*Gekleidete Puppen mit Metall= und Celluloid=
köpfen, Filzpuppen, Werfpuppen, Puppen=
stubenpuppen*

*Puppen=Rümpfe, =Arme, =Beine, =Hände,
=Perücken, =Schuhe, =Strümpfe*

*Christbaumlichthalter, Spez. Kugelgelenklicht=
halter mit Reformklemme.*

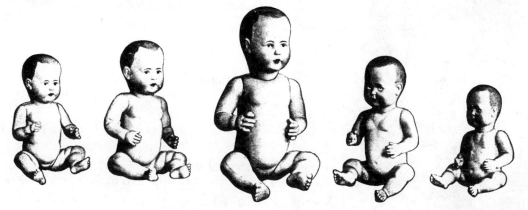

441. Buschow & Beck's advertisement in DEUTSCHE SPIEL-
WAREN ZEITUNG, February, 1927. They list the following products: metal dolls' heads; celluloid babies, undressed and dressed;
dressed dolls with metal or celluloid heads; felt dolls, cloth dolls,
dolls' house dolls, doll bodies, arms, legs, hands, wigs, shoes,
and stockings.

442. Minerva mark on metal-head dolls.

1893: Advertised socket type metal dolls' heads with wigs.

1895: Obtained celluloid for making dolls from *Rheinische Gummi und Celluloid Fabrik Co.*

1902: Obtained a German patent (D.R.G.M.) for celluloid dolls' heads.

1903: Obtained a German patent (D.R.G.M.) for covering metal dolls' heads with celluloid. Began to produce their own celluloid which resulted in an economic boycott policy by Rheinische Gummi und Celluloid Fabrik Co.

1904: Obtained two German patents (D.R.G.M.) for woolen dolls with face masks.

1905: Advertised dolls with celluloid face masks and celluloid dolls called *My Pet.* Obtained a German patent (D.R.G.M.) for a doll's head.

1906: Advertised *Minerva* metal heads covered with celluloid. Minerva ball jointed dolls with metal joints, celluloid heads, patent ball jointed celluloid dolls, dolls' house dolls, dressed dolls, doll bodies of cloth and of leather, wigs and footwear for dolls.

1907: Obtained two German patents (D.R.G.M.) for dolls' heads of metal and celluloid.

1911: Advertised celluloid soldiers with moving joints, all-celluloid dolls and dolls dressed in regional costumes.

(All of the above material, 1891–1911, is based on the research of the Ciesliks.)

1924: Manufactured celluloid dolls, miniature dolls, Minerva metal and celluloid dolls' heads, dressed dolls, dolls' parts and accessories. Sole London agent was *Henry Barnett.*

1925: Obtained a German patent (D.R.G.M.) for ball joints used for celluloid dolls.

1926: Sole British agent was *Lewis Wild.* Advertised *Hansa* dolls. *Bremer* distributed their character dolls.

1927: Made jointed dolls with metal and celluloid heads, separate metal heads and celluloid heads, celluloid dolls with and without clothes, felt dolls. The bent limb baby dolls had swivel necks and painted eyes. Advertised dolls' house dolls, dolls' shoes and parts for dolls. They obtained a German patent (D.R.P.) for a doll drinking from a bottle.

1929: Obtained a German patent (D.R.G.M.) for sleeping eyes.

1930: Made baby dolls, dolls' heads including metal and celluloid heads celluloid dolls, dolls' wigs, and other parts, dolls' house dolls and dolls' footwear. Their dolls came dressed or undressed.★

Bush Terminal Sales Co. 1920–22. Brooklyn, New York. Represented *Amberg, Arlington Toy Co., Deluxe Doll Gerling* Haber Toy Co.,[†] *Highgrade Toy Mfg. Co., Konstructo Co., Marks Bros., Co., Oweenee Trego Doll Co.,* and *U-needa Doll Co.* All of these companies were American doll manufacturers. Bush Terminal Sales Co. also represented the following British doll manufacturers: *Art Toy Manufacturing Co., Britannia Toy Co., Chad Valley* and *Holladay & Co.*

Busgen, Willi. 1919. Milbertshofen near Munich. Obtained an Austrian patent for dolls' bodies that were built on spiral wires.

Bussi. 1928. Trade name used by *Willi Steiner.* The mark was the word "Bussi" in a diamond.

Buster. 1917. Line of *British Ceramic* head dolls with wigs and jointed bodies, manufactured by *Dolphitch.*

Buster. 1928–29. Trade name of a cloth doll made by *Farnell,* distributed by *Louis Wolf.*

Buster Boy. 1914. Trade name of a doll with composition head and hands, molded hair, painted eyes, and cloth body, distributed by *Marshall Field.* It was dressed in a striped cotton suit with belt and short trousers. Ht. 15 in. (40.5 cm.); price $17.00 a doz. wholesale.

Buster Brown. 1903. Cloth doll with painted face and flannel clothes distributed by F. A. O. *Schwarz.* The doll came either with a tam and a suit or a tam and coat. Ht. 10 in. (25.5 cm.); price 50¢.

Buster Brown. Ca 1904. Cloth doll with face lithographed on flesh colored sateen, wore a red suit and tam. One of the *Horsman Babyland Rag* series.

Buster Brown. 1904. Dressed doll fully jointed represented the cartoon character drawn by Richard Outcault for the NEW YORK HERALD. Ht. 18 in. (45.5 cm.).

Buster Brown. 1904. Was given as a souvenir by the Majestic Theatre, Boston, when BUSTER BROWN played there. The small bisque head doll had a five-piece jointed composition body, brown glass eyes, a black sash and molded two strap shoes. The words BUSTER BROWN were stamped on the doll's hat.

Buster Brown. Ca. 1904–10. Cutout cloth doll with pink (red) tunic and short trousers, black tie, white collar and cuffs, socks and single strap slippers, produced by Knickerbocker Specialty Co.[†]

1907: Advertised by *Sears.* Ht. 15 in. (38 cm.). Priced 25¢.

1909–10: Advertised by *Siegel Cooper.* Ht. 16 in. (40.5 cm.) priced 25¢.★

443. Sheet of a cutout cloth doll representing Buster Brown and his dog Tige. Published by the Knickerbocker Specialty Co. from a design by R. F. Outcault. The doll is dressed in a red knicker suit. H. 16 in. (40.5 cm.). *Courtesy of Z. Frances Walker.*

Buster Brown. 1917. Rubber doll distributed by *Baltimore Bargain House,* Ht. 4 in. (10 cm.); priced 75¢.

Buster Brown. 1926. Trade name of a cloth doll with a three dimensional face made by *Dean.* The doll had a bobbed flaxen wig, eyes glancing to the side, the smiling mouth was open-closed and showed teeth. The doll wore a typical suit and tam. The tam had the words, "Buster Brown" on the front of the headband. The shoes had single straps. This doll was made to coincide with the release of a series of six films on Buster Brown by the European Motion Picture Co.

Buster Brown. 1927. An all-celluloid doll with molded hair and molded clothes in various colors. The doll was jointed at the shoulders and hips. Ht. 5 in. (12.5 cm.); price 77¢ a doz. wholesale.

Buster Brown. 1929. Boy doll made by *Ideal.* Price $2.00 each.

Buster Brown dolls. 1902 and later. Various dolls not de-

445. All-bisque doll representing Buster Brown. It has a blond wig, molded and painted eyes and footwear, closed mouth. Original clothes and Tige made of painted cotton batting. H. 5 in. (12.5 cm.). *Coleman Collection.*

BUSTER
BROWN
SHOES

MADE IN JAPAN

446. Buster Brown Shoes, a mark found on all-bisque doll used to advertise the Buster Brown Shoe Co.

scribed above. See Ills. 443, 444, 445, 446, and Ill. 595 in the COLLECTOR'S BOOK OF DOLLS' CLOTHES.★

Buster Brown Hosiery Mills. See United Hosiery Mills Corp.

Butler, Charles. 1826–48. London. Made dolls.

Butler Bros. 1877–1930 and later. Sonneberg, Thür. and New York City, also established in Boston 1877, in Chicago 1879, in St. Louis 1898, in Minneapolis 1907, in Dallas 1911 and in San Francisco 1928. This wholesale establishment was begun as a mail-order house by three brothers, Edward B., Charles H., and George Butler. They were factory agents, importers and jobbers. During World War I Emil Bauersachs took over their Sonneberg office. They reopened their office at least by 1924. (See illustrations in THE COLLECTOR'S BOOK OF DOLLS' CLOTHES for the following years: 1893, Ill. 427; 1906, Ill. 543; 1910, Ills. 617, 618, 619, 620, 621, 622, 623, 624; 1912, Ill. 634; 1918, Ills. 716, 717, 718, 719, 720, 721, 722, 723, 726; 1928, Ill. 770; 1929, Ills. 775 and 776.

From 1899 to 1930 they advertised *Pet Name* china-head dolls.

1890: Advertised "French bisque" dolls with jointed bodies. Hts. 8, 10, 12 and 15 in. (20.5, 25.5, 30.5 and 38 cm.). The largest came with glass eyes. ("French" was probably a type of doll rather than the country of origin.)

444. Doll labeled "Buster Brown Shoes," an advertisement in the form of a flat-faced printed cloth doll. The two pieces are sewn together with gold colored machine stitching. Buster Brown has blond hair, blue eyes, one of which is winking, open-closed mouth, red suit and hat, blue socks and tie. H. 13½ in. (34 cm.). *Courtesy of Margaret F. Mandel.*

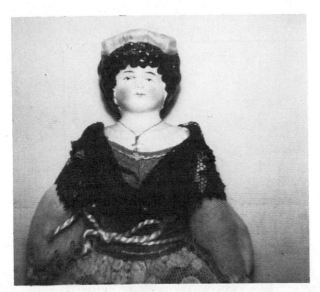

447. Untinted bisque shoulder head distributed by Butler Bros. as the Italian representative in their International Dolls series. It has molded black curly hair, molded headwear, a molded blouse top, and a molded gold color necklace with a cross. The eyes are painted blue and the mouth is closed. Cloth body with bisque limbs, molded footwear. H. of doll 8 in. (20.5 cm.). H. of shoulder head 1¾ in. (4.5 cm.). *Courtesy of the late Josephine Garrison.*

448. Mark used by Butler Bros. Similar marks were used by Butler Bros. on other dolls. (See Ills. 798 and 1498.)

1895: Advertised *American Countess, Annie Laurie, Beatrice, Bonnet Dolls, Carnival, Empress, Exhibition Baby, Fritz Brownies, Lily Langtry,* Parisian, *Prima Donna, Society Belle, Sweet Alice, Tam O'Shanter* and *Trilby.* They also advertised types of dolls including black, all-china, china heads on plain or figured bodies, turning china heads with low brow molded hairdos, and china limbs on cloth bodies. They continued to use the term "French bisque." The accessories included a doll's cutlery set of pewter knife, fork, spoon, knife rest, napkin ring and napkin for 10¢.

1898–99: Advertised the following dolls with painted faces and cloth bodies, imported from a manufacturer; *Admiral Dewey; Dutchman; Englishman; Policeman; Sailor, U.S. Navy;* and *Uncle Sam.* They also advertised *Hottentot* and *International Dolls.*

1912: Advertised *Celebrate* dolls with kid bodies made by *Kestner.*

1914: Advertised the following dolls: *American Girls, Baby Betty*[†] heads, *Debutantes, Dolly Varden, Dottie Dimple, Eskimo, Happy Hooligan, Little Fairy, Little Playmate, Marottes, Matlock* dolls, *Normandy Girls, Red Riding Hood, Rosebud, Society Buds, Summer Girl, Sunny Jim, Sunshine Girl,* and the *Travelers.*

They also advertised various types of dolls including celluloid dolls, rubber dolls and composition head dolls that wore a chemise with one of the following names embroidered on it: Mary, Emma, Edith, Ruth, Mabel or Pauline. The cutout cloth dolls included Dottie Dimple, Red Riding Hood, Japanese, *Greenaway,* Mammy, Topsy Turvey and *Golden Locks.* Felt soldiers with celluloid heads, ht. 6½ in. (16.5 cm.) were advertised. Worsted dolls had stockinet faces, bead eyes, worsted features and hair, worsted clothes in red, blue and yellow. Colored material formed the shoe-feet. Sometimes they wore a knit or muslin peaked cap. Five hts. 7½, 8½, 9½, 12½ and 14 in. (19, 21.5, 24, 31.5, and 35.5 cm.); price 42¢ to $2.10 a doz. wholesale. The four larger heights had bells.

1918: Advertised dolls made by *Amberg, Averill (Mme. Hendren), Effanbee, Ideal* and *Jessie M. Raleigh.* Butler Bros., claimed they were the exclusive distributor of the Jessie M. Raleigh dolls. Butler Bros. refused to accept dolls made in Germany that had been bought and paid for in 1914 and arrived in New York from Holland in October 1918.

1924: Advertised all-bisque, all-celluloid, all-china and all composition dolls as well as china heads and limbs on cloth bodies and composition heads on cloth bodies. Their *Mama* dolls were made by Effanbee and *Gem Toy Co.*

1928: Their catalog advertised cloth dolls up to 30 in. (76 cm.); new born babies with bisque heads; china head and china-limb dolls on cloth bodies. Four hts. 5½, 7, 8, and 13 in. (14, 18, 20.5 and 33 cm.). Pet name china head dolls came in hts. 7½ in. (19 cm.) and 12½ in. (31.5 cm.). Among the dolls were *Boudoir* dolls, *Bubbles, Dainty Miss, Flossie Flirt, Grumpykins, Kiddie Pal, Lenci* type, *Mary Anne,* Mama dolls, *Miss 1928, Nap-Time, Nelke* dolls, *Patsy, Ruth, Smiles, Snow Babies, Sunny Girl, Tootse* and *Topsy.*

1929: Advertised felt dolls with mohair wigs and painted features. Four hts. 12, 14, 17, and 19 in. (30.5, 35.5, 43 and 48 cm.). They had black dolls, china dolls, celluloid dolls, bisque-head dolls on composition bodies, dolls dressed as aviators and as Santa Claus. Their most expensive doll was a dressed Mama doll with an open mouth and teeth, costing $6.75. Among their dolls were *Aunt Jemima, Baby Buttercup, Bo-Peep, Cuddles, Dorothy Darling,* Dutch Boy and Girl, *Kinky Kurls, Kiss-Me, Margie, Mickey McGuire, Miss Sunshine, My Precious, Peggy, Playmate, Rayon Princess, Red Riding Hood, Snow Flake, Sissy, Sister Suzy, Tickletoes* and *Trixie.*★

Butsum Manufacturing Co. 1926. Patented walking mechanism for the *Toddling Toodles* line of dolls distributed by *Louis Wolf.*

Buttercup. 1924–28. Cloth doll with one curly strand of hair, wore rompers in the Oliver Twist suit style.

1926: Trademark registered in U.S. by *Borgfeldt.* Distributed by the *Chicago Mail Order House.* The body was stuffed with cotton and had a squeaker. Ht. 15 in. (38 cm.); priced 89¢. (See also **Baby Buttercup**).★

BUTTERCUP

Copyright, 1924, by King Features Syndicate, Inc.

"THE DOLL OF THE HOUR"

SO COMICAL, SOFT and CUDDLY YOU CAN'T RESIST IT

MANUFACTURED BY PERMISSION OF JIMMY MURPHY, CREATOR OF THE FAMOUS
TOOTS and CASPER COMICS
Which are being read daily by twenty million people all over the country

YOUR TOY DEPARTMENT WILL BE INCOMPLETE WITHOUT "BUTTERCUP

MODERN TOY CO., INC.

Sole Licensees and Manufacturers

Factory and Main Offices:
181 BELMONT AVENUE, BROOKLYN, N. Y.

New York Salesroom:
1133 Broadway

Chicago Representative:
C. A. RIDD
Room 20—Smith Bldg., Wheaton, Ill.

Kindly mention PLAYTHINGS when writing to advertisers.

449. Advertisement for Buttercup in PLAYTHINGS, August, 1924. Modern Toy Co. manufactured this cloth doll. The doll on the left has a "Buttercup" tag attached to its belt.

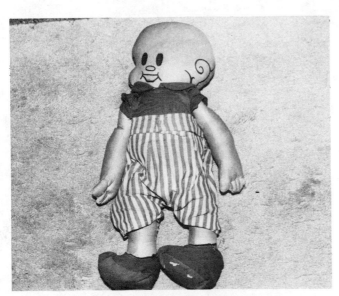

450. Cloth doll representing Buttercup has printed features, black eyes, joints at shoulders and hips. Original clothes. Mark: Ill. 451. H. 18 in. (45.5 cm.). *Courtesy of Phyllis Salak. Photo by Phyllis Salak.*

BUTTERCUP

BY PERMISSION OF

Jimmy Murphy

COPYRIGHT 1924 BY
KING FEATURES SYNDICATE INC.

451. Mark on Buttercup cloth dolls.

Butterfly. 1925–26. Trade name for *Lenci* felt doll No. 189. dressed as an Oriental in a costume inspired by "Madame Butterfly." Ht. 23 in. (58.5 cm.).

Butterick, E., & Co. (The Butterick Publishing Co. [Ltd.]). 1875–1930 and later. New York and London. Published patterns for making dolls' clothes as well as making dolls' bodies and complete dolls. These patterns, sold separately, were described and advertised in the various Butterick publications including BICYCLE, THE DELINEATOR, THE GLASS OF FASHION, and THE METROPOLITAN, as well as the catalogs for their patterns.

All the patterns published in the 1800s for both dolls and dolls' clothes appear to have been available in seven sizes for dolls between the heights of 12 and 24 in. (30.5 to 61 cm.).

1875: Published the No. 1 pattern for dolls' clothes. (See THE COLLECTOR'S BOOK OF DOLLS' CLOTHES, Ill. 272.)

1875 or later: Published pattern No. 5 for making a doll's body.

1882: Published pattern No. 81 for a Cloth Doll. See Ill. 452A. The suggested fabrics to be used for this doll were flannel, stockinet (including that from old stockings or

underclothes); or silesia. Hair for the doll could be made of real hair, jute, mohair, or ravelings from stockings. Eyes were made of black, brown or blue beads; traced with ink or embroidered with silk. The nose and mouth were traced with red ink or red paint, or they were made of silk embroidery or flannel appliqués.

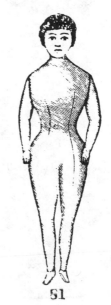

51

No. 81.—PATTERN FOR A RAG DOLL

452A. Butterick pattern No. 81, for a cloth doll, first issued in 1882.

1886: THE DELINEATOR gave instructions on how to draw faces on the cloth dolls that they called Betsy Bobbit. They told the reader to use pattern No. 81. made of twilled cotton, made especially for dolls' bodies, or unbleached muslin. (These same instructions were given in 1898 except then they said to use pattern No. 170.) See Ill. 452B for the designs of the faces that could be traced then painted with watercolors, oil paints, and ink or colored with crayons.

1887: THE DELINEATOR gave instructions for drawing a black face on cloth dolls made of either silesia or sateen from pattern No. 81. The doll was named Mammy Chloe. See Ill. 452C.

Ca. 1891: Published two patterns for dolls including No. 139 for a jointed Lady Doll's body. Pattern No. 140 was a jointed body for a Baby, Girl, Miss, Boy or Man doll. They recommended for each doll also the use of a piece of white leather 5¾ by 9 in. (14.5 by 23 cm.) probably to make the lower arms.

Ca. 1893: Published pattern No. 158 as a Doll's Body; designed for *Santa Claus* or other Corpulent Dolls.

Ca. 1894: Published two patterns for cloth dolls including No. 169 for a Jointed Rag Doll with hair. (Some illustrations of this pattern show it with a seam down the center of the face.) Pattern No. 170 is for a Jointless Rag Doll without hair (Baby, Girl, Miss, Boy or Man). They recommended for each

FIGURE NO. 2.—FACE FOR RAG DOLL.

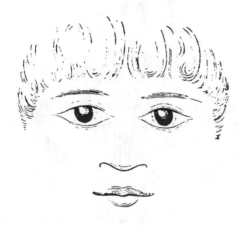

FIGURE NO. 3.

FIGURE NO. 1.

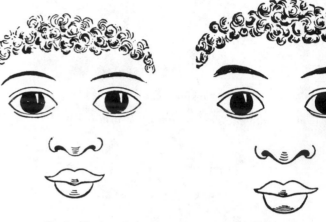

FIGURE NO. 2.   FIGURE NO. 3.
FIGURES NOS. 1, 2 AND 3.—FACES FOR RAG DOLLS.

452C. Three sizes of cloth dolls' black faces published by Butterick's DELINEATOR in December 1887 for use with pattern No. 81.

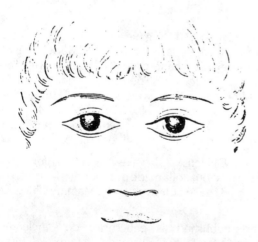

FIGURE NO. 4.
FIGURES NOS. 3 AND 4.—FACES FOR RAG DOLLS.

452B. Three sizes of cloth dolls' white faces published by Butterick's DELINEATOR in December 1886 for use with pattern No. 81.

doll a piece of white leather 5¾ by 9 in. (14.5 by 23 cm.) probably for the lower arms.

1895: Published a pattern for a Corpulent Jointless Rag Doll as No. 186.

1907–8: Butterick offered a cutout cloth doll with patterns for its clothes. It was named the Butterick Rag Doll. Ht. 18 in. (45.5 cm.).★

Butts Works. See Dixon, T. A.

Buzza Co., The. 1927. Minneapolis, Minn. Produced cloth dolls with painted faces, felt hair, removable cotton clothes. Feet were made of black cotton cloth. The dolls were in boxes with a framed picture of the doll and a related poem. A poem in the picture and on the box lid was by Lawrence Hawthorne.

Bye Bye Babies. 1918. Dressed cloth dolls with round faces, made by *Shanklin*. Girl doll wore a lace bonnet and nightgown, the boy doll wore pajamas.

Bye Bye Baby. 1922. Doll designed by *Helen Trowbridge* for *Horsman*. By pulling a cord attached to both arms the doll moved its hands and arms in a lifelike manner imitating a baby's gesture.

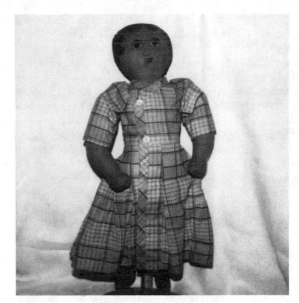

454. Bye Bye Kids, a flat faced brown cloth doll with printed hair and features; jointed at the shoulders and hips. Mark on the lower back torso: "BYE BYE KIDS//STRICTLY SANITARY//OLD MAMMY." H. 14 in. (35.5 cm.). *Courtesy of Joan Kindler. Photo by Phyllis Salak.*

455. Stamped black mark on a Bye Bye Kid.

453. Cloth doll made by Buzza Co. based on a design by Lawrence Hawthorne, copyrighted in 1927. The doll has black felt hair, painted features, and is dressed as "Jolly Jack." It came with a framed picture of Jolly Jack writing on a slate. There is a moralistic poem on the slate extolling the virtues of Jolly Jack. H. of doll 9¼ in. (23.5 cm.). Framed picture is 11 x 18 in. (28 x 45.5 cm.). *Coleman Collection.*

Bye Bye Kids. 1908–09. Cloth dolls made by *Bach Bros.* These flat face dolls with painted hair and features were described as "Strictly Sanitary." One of the black dolls was named *Old Mammy.*★

Bye-Bye Babies. 1918. Dressed dolls that appeared to be cloth; made by *Restall.* Clothes included dresses, suits, rompers, headwear, flannel capes, woolen petticoats, diapers, and footwear. Dolls represented Red Riding Hood, Sammy the Patriotic Kid, Rompy the Romper Boy, and others.

Bye-Bye Twins. See **Susan and Bobby.**

Bye-Lo Baby. 1922–52. Doll representing a three day old baby designed by *Grace Storey Putnam.* Head made by various factories, body made by *K & K,* a subsidiary of *Borgfeldt,* who produced the Bye-Lo Baby and was the sole licensee. There were numerous lawsuits over infringements.

Borgfeldt lost one of these suits in Germany. There were several suits in the United States. The one between Borgfeldt and *Amberg* whose similar *New Born Babe* had come out in 1914, nine years prior to the Bye-Lo Baby was probably the most important. *Alt, Beck & Gottschalck* made some socket bisque Bye-Lo heads that were used on bent limb composition bodies made by *König & Wernicke.*

Some of the competing Bye-Lo-type dolls were very fine quality such as *Siegfried.* The *Armand Marseille My Dream Baby* was the most prolific of the competition dolls. Heads marked only with Roman numerals (II, III, and IV.) have also been found. Allegedly rubber Bye-Los were made after 1925 but they should not be confused with the vinyl Bye-Lo types which were made much later. The wooden Bye-Lo type head made by *Schoenhut* may have been licensed by Borgfeldt since they were the distributors for Schoenhut.

The Museum of the City of New York has a letter written by Grace S. Putnam in 1942, in which she reminisces about the beginnings of the Bye-Lo. "I had copyrighted Bye-Lo plaster head model (under sculpture) in 1922 before, but Borgfeldt copyrighted their manufactured head in 1924–25 just before it went into production. . . . The Bye-Lo was meant to have the original, soft cloth body, which I had designed and patented; I did not model the bisque bodies. They were what they called 'stock bodies.'

"I am just remembering that before I had completed my design for the soft cloth body. . . . I had told them (the Borgfeldt Co.) that they could use one of their 'stock bodies.' It was quite a job for me to get my design of a cloth body that would be easy enough to make at the factory. . . . I finally got it, after making up some twenty different kinds of bodies. . . . When I heard the dolls were being put on with Madame Georgine's [Georgene Averill] bodies (cloth ones) I rushed home to put a stop to it. The cunning celluloid hands on cloth bodies I did not model. They happened to come on the market as separate items just at the right moment. I had modeled some hands but did not need them.

"In Germany there is no doubt but what they sold Bye-Lo dolls without my knowledge (and perhaps some of them had bisque bodies).

". . . They were selling them [bisque-bodied Bye-Los] in great quantities—some time after the Bye-Lo first came onto the market. These little bisque Bye-Los were only about four inches long, had moving arms and legs—fat tummies and the head was a solid part of the body and did not move. The top of head was open to admit the tiny moving eyes; and there was a little wig. It didn't look like a Bye-Lo with hair and especially when it could sit upright. It said on back of body '© G. S. Putnam, 1922 (No) 19.' . . .

"The Quintuplets were the composition head Bye-Los . . . And five of the life sized Bye-Los were sent in a basket . . . as a gift to the five quintuplets. . . . the New York newspaper [Nov. 13, 1934] printed a picture of ten babies in a row—first a live quintuplet, then a Bye-Lo—then another quintuplet, and so on until there were ten, and you were asked to guess which was which.

". . . Of course today [1942] they sell only the composition head Bye-Los, with soft bodies; they come in three sizes; the bisque (from Germany) used to come in seven sizes. (You can imagine what a job I had making patterns for the bodies in seven sizes.)"

Wax head Bye-Lo Babies were first made with pink sateen bodies and mitten type hands. Later they were made with white cloth bodies and celluloid hands.

The all-bisque Bye-Lo Babies with molded hair and painted eyes have been observed as having the mark 20–10 or 20–12 on their back. The last two digits refer to the doll's height in centimeters and corresponding numbers are found on the inside top of the limbs. The tiny arms have 20 over 10 instead of 20–10.

An all-bisque Bye-Lo Baby with wig, blue sleeping eyes, and closed mouth had "G. S. Putnam" incised on its back and the sticker on the chest read "Bye-Lo Baby." This doll had a K & K button on its long baby dress and came with a cap, pillow and blanket in a box, the end of which read "Genuine//Miniature" (drawing of a doll in a short baby dress) "Bye-Lo Baby." Ht. of doll 4½ in. (11.5 cm.).

According to Mr. Joseph L. Kallus, Wanamaker was the first store to sell Bye-Lo Babies.

1925: An advertisement for a Bye-Lo Baby in LADIES' HOME JOURNAL, September 1925, stated: "Grace Storey Putnam, the sculptor, studied hundreds of babies over many years before she finally achieved this triumph."

Bye-Lo Babies came in seven hts. 9 in. (23 cm.) to 20 in.

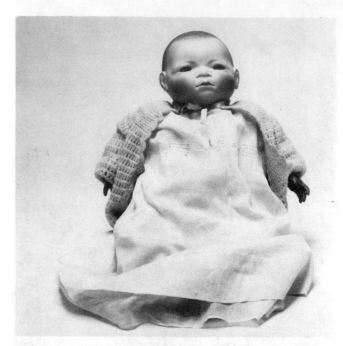

456. Bye-Lo Baby with a bisque head, molded and painted hair, sleeping blue eyes, closed mouth, flange neck, cloth baby-shaped body, celluloid hands, and contemporary clothes. H. 19 in. (48 cm.). Circumference of head 18 in. (45.5 cm.). *Courtesy of Sotheby Parke Bernet Inc., N.Y.*

(51 cm.). *Shackman* advertised all-bisque Bye-Los jointed at the shoulders and hips, hts. 4 and 6 in. (10 and 15 cm.); priced $2.20 and $5.90 a doz. wholesale.

1926: Bye-Lo Babies had sleeping eyes and cried. Nine hts. 9, 11, 14, 16, 18, and 20 in. (23, 28, 35.5, 40.5, 45.5, and 51 cm.) plus three other hts. The 11 in. Bye-Lo cost $2.98, but at *F.A.O. Schwarz* it was $4.50 and the 20 in. size was $16.00. Twin Bye-Los in a pink or blue blanket; hts. 11 and 14 in. (28 and 35.5 cm.) were sold by F.A.O. Schwarz. Schwarz also sold extra dresses, caps, capes, long cashmere coats, jackets, underwear and stork pants for Bye-Los.

The Bye-Lo clothes were made by *M. L. Kahn* and special costumes were made by *Blanche Rowe Cromien*.

Dressed bisque head Bye-Los were sold by the *Chicago Mail Order House;* hts. 16, 19, and 23 in. (40.5, 48 and 58.5 cm.); priced $2.79 to $4.98.

1927: *Butler Bros.* advertised 4 sizes of Bye-Los with composition heads, sleeping eyes and cry voices. Hts. 10 to 17 in. (37 to 43 cm.). Bisque head Bye-Los with sleeping glass eyes, voices, cloth bodies, celluloid hands, and long dresses came in 7 hts. 8½, 9½, 10, 11½, 13, 14½, and 17 in. (21.5, 24, 25.5, 29, 33, 37 and 43 cm.).

Montgomery Ward advertised composition head Bye-Los in long lawn dresses, slips and rubber diapers. 4 hts. 10, 12, 14, and 16½ in. (25.5, 30.5, 35.5, and 42 cm.); priced $3.39 to $8.98.

The all-bisque Bye-Los with painted hair and eyes, bodies jointed at shoulders and hips. Ht. 6 in. (15 cm.); priced 67¢.

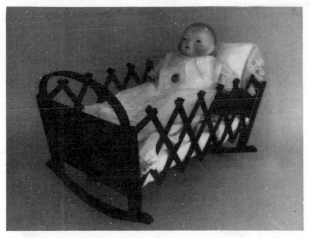

457. Bisque-head Bye-Lo Baby with molded and painted hair, sleeping brown glass eyes, closed mouth, flange neck, cloth body, celluloid hands, and original clothes. Mark on head: "Copr. by Grace S. Putnam//Made in Germany//1373145." Mark stamped on body. See Ill. 460. Metal advertising button on clothes reads "BYE-LO BABY//GRACE//PUTNAM//1922." The expandable wooden cradle is labeled: "C. A. FENNER'S PATENT// NOV. 11, 1873." H. of doll 14 in. (35.5 cm.). *Courtesy of Becky Moncrief.*

458. All-bisque Bye-Lo with painted and molded hair, glass eyes, and its original layette of clothes. It does not have painted bootees. The round paper Bye-Lo sticker is on the doll's chest. *Courtesy of Ben and Martha Sewell.*

© 1923 *by*
Grace S. Putnam
MADE IN GERMANY
7372/45
459

BYE - LO - BABY
PAT. APPL'D FOR
COPY
BY GRACE
STOREY
PUTNAM
460

BYE-LO
BABY
NOT GENUINE
WITHOUT SIGNATURE
461

459–461. Marks found on various types of Bye-Lo Babies.

1933: Bisque Bye-Lo Babies with socket heads were advertised but there is evidence that the socket heads were also among the first Bye-Los produced. Imported *Biscaloid* composition flange neck Bye-Lo heads were advertised. Some of the Bye-Los described as a new model had painted eyes and closed mouths.

1951: DOLL NEWS in 1952 reported that in October, 1951, Borgfeldt had received their first shipment of post World War II German bisque Bye-Lo heads. Borgfeldt claimed that "the quality was about as good as when imported before the War." These heads were made in a German factory near Bonn. They had sleeping eyes and were made from original molds. Came in 5 hts. A few of them were not fired after painting and hence the paint flaked off. (See THE COLLECTOR'S BOOK OF DOLLS' CLOTHES, Ills. 761, 769 B, 777, 778, and 779.)★

Byrd, Lee M. 1928. Oakland, Calif. Obtained a U.S. trademark *Friendly Bugs,* for dolls.

C

C. I. V. Ca. 1900. Stands for "Civil Imperial Volunteer." These initials were used on the upturned brim of a Boer War style military hat of a bisque-head doll with a molded hat and hair, glass eyes, and a closed mouth.

C. Q. Dolls. 1917. Mentioned in GAMES AND TOYS as coming from Southampton, England.

Ça Ne Fait Rien. 1927. French trademark registered by *William Webb Sanders* to designate dolls. Ça Ne Fait Rien (That makes nothing) is in a circle under the figure of a girl.

Cábaña, Charles. 1917–23. Buffalo, N.Y. Obtained two U.S. patents for ball-and-socket joints for dolls.★

Cabaret Girls. 1926. *Boudoir* type dolls representing cabaret girls in France, made by *Katherine Fleischmann.* One of them was named *Noona.*

Cacheleux. 1807–26. Paris. Made dolls and was a wholesale toy merchant. He was succeeded by his son-in-law, *August Brouillet.*

Cadet-Roussel. 1916. Cloth doll created by *Mme. Manson.*

Cadie, Peter. 1898. Manchester, England. Obtained a German patent (D.R.G.M.) for turning a doll's head with a rod on cog wheels. He assigned his patent rights to *Wiele.*

Cahen, Maurice. 1927–30 and later. Paris. Representative for *La Poupée Nicette* dolls of *Perrimond.*

Cahn, Widow Leon. 1930. Strasbourg, France. Made dolls' clothes.

Caho.† See **Canzler & Hoffmann.**

Cairo Princess. 1920. Trade name of a doll representing the trademark of Corn Products Co. and manufactured with their permission by *American Ocarina & Toy Co.*

California Bisque Doll Co. 1925 and probably other years. Berkeley, Calif. Made dolls' heads marked "C.B.D. Co.," under the direction of Mrs. H.T. Epperson.

462. Bisque head doll with wig, glass eyes, closed mouth. The mark on this doll is shown in Ill. 463. *Courtesy of Marion Holt.*

463. Mark used by the California Bisque Doll Co. on their bisque head dolls.

California Toy Shop. 1928. Los Angeles, Calif. *Florence Nichols* was in charge of this dolls' hospital which had 22 kinds of dolls' heads in 95 sizes. Heads were made of bisque, celluloid, composition and metal. The bodies were jointed composition, cloth, kid or *Mama* type. There were 15 different sizes of wigs in blond, tosca, dark brown and red colors. Dolls' clothes were also available. Occasionally a doll over a hundred years old was brought in to be repaired.

Callier, Mlle. Isabelle. 1867. At the Paris Exposition won Honorable Mention for dressing *Huret* dolls.

Calumet Manufacturing Co. 1919–26. New York City. In 1926 they were known as Calumet Importing Co. Manufactured and imported dolls.

Calvare. Early 1920s. France. Made cloth art dolls. These dolls had large molded heads, raffia-like hair, bulging glass eyes looking to the side and surrounded by eye shadow. The hands had wired fingers and both hands and feet seemed to be disproportionately small compared to the large head. The dolls were dressed in period or theatrical costumes. Both dolls and costumes bore labels with a woman's head over the words "CALVARE, MADE IN FRANCE." Ht. 14½ in. (37 cm.).

Calvert Tot. 1916–17. Trade name of a character doll with 12 different styles of dresses made by *Katherine Rauser* who had the selling agency for the dolls. ★

Camberwell (Dolls). 1903–10. An area of doll manufacturers in South London. These dolls were mentioned in the writings of Beatrix Potter.

1903: The dolls were copied from pictures.

1910: Beatrix Potter drew a poster showing a limp doll and saying "Here lies the Camberwell wax doll killed by Free Trade with Germany. Poor Camberwell Dolly is dead."

Camélia. 1926–29. Paris. Trademark registered in France for an artistic, articulated doll by *Silas Guillon*. The word Camélia is enclosed in a diamond. *A. Broches* made these dolls.

Cameo Doll Co. 1922–30 and later. New York City; moved to Port Allegany. Pa., in 1930. This was *Joseph L. Kallus*'s company and they manufactured composition dolls, com-

464. Calvare cloth doll, probably a French art doll of the 1920s. The blond hair is made of a fine raffia-like substance. The stationary brown eyes are round and bulging. The large head has a pressed face made of chiffon. The pink cotton body is formed over a wire frame and has flesh colored silk arms and stockinet legs which are out of proportion to the large head. Original clothes including glass bead necklace. H. 14½ in. (37 cm.). *Courtesy of the Margaret Woodbury Strong Museum. Photo by Harry Bickelhaupt.*

position and segmented wood dolls as well as dolls with composition heads and cloth bodies.

1926: Made "The Selling Fool," a segmented wooden doll with its hat representing a radio tube. This was an *R. C. A. Radiotrons* advertising doll.

1927: Made *Mama* dolls.

1929: Made *Margie.*

1930: Besides Margie made *Lucky Babies.*

1931: Made *Baby Adele* dolls.

According to Mr. Kallus, for many years Cameo was one of the three large doll-making companies that made its own dolls. The other two were *Effanbee* and *Ideal.*

At one period when Cameo received a great many orders for their dolls, their facilities were inadequate and they hired a Canadian manufacturer to meet their production requirements. But only a few Cameo dolls were produced in Canada, because the Canadian dolls did not meet Cameo's quality standards.★

Caminade, Mme. Baptiste. 1918. Paris. Created cloth dolls. She was a sculptress who had exhibited in the Paris salons in 1904–5.

Camp Fire Girl. 1913–14. Composition head doll produced by *Horsman* using a head copyrighted in 1911 and *Campbell Kid* type hands, cloth body and was style No. 173. The doll wore a fringed brown khaki dress, plaid tie, belt with metal pistol in a holster, broad brimmed sombrero. Price $8.50 a doz. wholesale.★

No. 173

"CAMP FIRE GIRL"
Trade Mark

(Head copyrighted, 1911, by E. I. Horsman Co.)

A pretty companion for the Boy Scout. This natty girl wears a jaunty costume, all of brown khaki, fringed; a gaudy bandanna, broad sombrero hat and pistol belt with real pistol in the holster.

Per Dozen.......**$8.50**

No. 173 "Camp Fire Girl"

465. Camp Fire Girl as advertised in a Horsman catalog of ca. 1914. It has a composition head with molded and painted hair and eyes, closed mouth, Campbell Kid type composition hands on a cloth body. The head was copyrighted in 1911. *Catalog courtesy of Bernard Barenholtz.*

Campbell Kid Baby. See **Campbell Kids.**

Campbell Kid Mascot. See **Campbell Kids.**

Campbell Kids. 1910–30 and later. Manufactured by *Horsman* and by *Benjamin Goldenberg* of *Aetna Doll & Toy Co.*, using Can't Break 'Em† composition. These dolls were in the Horsman Art Doll line. The heads were from a model copyrighted in 1910 by Horsman. About 1928 the rights were taken over by the *American Character Doll Co.*

1911: Joseph Campbell Co. licensed Horsman to make these dolls. The boy doll wore plaid or striped gingham rompers with a belt and dark yoke. The girl doll wore a plaid or striped pinafore or jumper over a white blouse.

R.H. Macy advertised that the dolls had "roguish eyes and dimpled chin." The girl's white blouse had a high collar. It wore shoes and the covering of the legs imitated stockings. The boy wore white socks and felt slippers. Ht. 11 in. (28 cm.); price 98¢.

An advertising postcard of the Campbell Kids showed the pink pinafore and blue rompers of plain material. The boy's socks had vertical stripes. One wonders how much of this was artistic license. (See Ill. 466.)

1912: There were 16 styles based on clothes and sizes. Among these were standard size number 125 Boy, 126 Girl, 127 Dutch Boy, 128 Dutch Girl, 129 Baseball Kid, 130 Campbell Kid Baby, 131 Campbell Kid Mascot Boy, 133 Campbell Kid Mascot Girl; large size numbers were 203 Boy, 204 Girl, 205 Cowboy, 206 Cowgirl; extra large size 500 Boy, 501 Girl. The Boy and Girl wore a patented yoke with their striped rompers and dress and the Campbell Kid Baby wore a white lawn short baby dress, two blue hair bows and white felt slippers; price $8.50 a doz. wholesale. The Campbell Kid Mascot Boy wore a striped pull-over type blazer in assorted college colors and khaki breeches. The Mascot Girl was dressed the same as the Boy except for a white duck skirt instead of the breeches.

1913: The boy wore a double-breasted jacket and knickers. The Girl, the Baby, and Mascot were dressed the same as in 1912. *Gamage* advertised their Campbell Kid Girl dressed in a pinafore and the Boy in rompers; price $1.25 each.

1914: Changes were made in the Campbell Kid dolls, instead of a flange neck there was a shoulder head so the dolls could wear clothes with lower necklines. A few of the dolls had wigs. The hands on some of the dolls had some of the fingers separated and composition part way up the arm so that the dolls could wear short sleeves. The cork stuffed cloth bodies were jointed at the knees as well as the shoulders and hips except for the smallest size. The standard size was enlarged to 12½ in. (31.5 cm.) and a Junior size, 10 in. (25.5 cm.), Boy (style no. 75) and Girl (style no. 76) were introduced; priced $4.25 a doz. wholesale. A new size, 14 in. (35.5 cm.) Campbell Kid Baby style no. 129, had bent limbs. Its white lawn short baby dress was trimmed with lace and had a matching cap; price $8.50 a doz. wholesale.

The Campbell Kid Boy, style no. 125, wore a low necked striped or printed rompers with a belt; the Girl, style no. 126, wore either a dress similar to the Boy's rompers or a dress of dotted lawn with pink or blue trim. In the standard size the Boy and Girl had circular striped stockings. The Boy, number 165, was the same as 125 except it had a mohair wig with bangs and bobbed hair and wore a white beach cap. The Girl number 166 was the same as 126 except for the same type mohair wig as the boy's (165) plus a silk hair bow. These wigged dolls cost $10.50 a doz. Number 127 was the same as 126 except the hair was colored red, blue, green or yellow to match the costume and had a silk hair-ribbon. Number 169 was a boy wearing a red double-breasted jacket with belt and white duck knickers. Number 170, the corresponding Girl, had a red jacket, white skirt and plaid bandanna tie. These dolls had early type hands. (See Ill. 266 in the first COLLECTOR'S ENCYCLOPEDIA OF DOLLS.) The standard size of these red jacket dolls cost $8.50 doz. wholesale.

Larger-sized dolls but similar to 125 and 126 were numbers 203 (Boy) and 204 (Girl). Their clothes had longer sleeves and they cost $13.50 a dozen. The larger sized dolls with wigs were numbers 265 (Boy) and 266 (Girl), costing $16.50 a doz. wholesale.

A new doll was named Miss Campbell; it came in painted hair and wigged versions. The eyes looked straight ahead and not to the side as found on nearly all other Campbell Kids.

1915–16: The dolls in Dutch costumes wore striped stockings and felt "wooden shoes." The girl's costume consisted of a red blouse, blue skirt and white apron; the boy wore a striped shirt and khaki pants. Ht. 12½ in. (31.5 cm.).

The dressed Campbell Kids were distributed by *Best & Co.* priced $1.00.

1917–19: Campbell Kid boy wore checked rompers and the girl wore a figured lawn Mother Hubbard style dress. A 7 in. (18 cm.) Campbell Kid cost 25¢. A 12 in. (30.5 cm.) Campbell Kid, distributed by *Eaton* cost 75¢. They were also distributed by the *Columbus Merchandise Co.* Ht. 12½ in. (33 cm.): priced $17.00 doz. wholesale.

1928: American Character Doll Co. in their Petite doll line had Campbell Kid dolls, with exclusive permission from the Campbell Soup Co. These dolls bore only a slight resemblance to the earlier Horsman Campbell Kids.

1929–30: The American Character Doll Co.'s Campbell Kids were all-composition, with molded hair, round eyes looking to the side, jointed shoulders and hips. The doll was slightly pigeon-toed when it stood alone. Raised letters on its back read "A//PETITE//DOLL." It came in various costumes, most of them copied from Campbell Soup advertisements. One of the dresses had a band or a diamond design around the bottom and the doll wore a matching bonnet. Ht. 12½ in. (31.5 cm.). Price $2.95 each. *Puggy* was called the man of the Campbell Kid family. ★

Campfire Girl. 1925–26. Line of Nursery Rhyme dolls made by *Jeanette Doll Co.,* distributed by *Louis Wolf.*

Canadian Dolls. Over half of the dolls in Canada were imported from Germany except during the First World War years. *Dominion Toys* made dolls in Canada in 1915. In 1917 some of the handmade dolls that were made as a home industry in Quebec Province were shipped to Europe. ★

466. Advertising postcard of Campbell Kid dolls, dated May, 1911. The card reads, "The Campbell Kids [left] Manufactured by License from Joseph Campbell Company. Copyright by Joseph Campbell Co. [right]. Heads Reproduced from Plastic Model. Copyright 1910 by E. I. Horsman Co. Protected International Copyright Law. [Bottom] The Jolliest Dolls of All." *Coleman Collection.*

No. 587—"Campbell Kid"

No. 587—"Campbell Kid." This is another of the famous character dolls, and on account of its continued popularity, we decided to again offer it to our club raisers. Any little girl will appreciate a couple character dolls more than any other kind. This doll is ten inches tall, strongly made, with unbreakable head. Sent, carefully packed, for four yearly subscriptions at 35c each, or one subscription at 35c and 60c extra.

467. Small Campbell Kid offered as a magazine subscription premium in 1913. This doll appears to have cloth stub hands. H. 10 in. (25.5 cm.).

Horsman Unbreakable
Trade "Art Dolls" Mark

No. 169 Miss Campbell

THE "CAMPBELL KIDS" Trade Mark

New Super Grade with INDIVIDUAL MOHAIR WIGS
(Heads Copyrighted 1910 by E. I. Horsman Co.)

No. 165. **CAMPBELL KID BOY WITH WIG.** Same size as No. 125, dressed in new design Romper Suit, figured material and broad binding. White beach cap, short socks and felt shoes. Wig is of fine mohair made on the doll's head..........Per Dozen, $10.50

No. 166. **CAMPBELL KID GIRL WITH WIG.** Companion Doll to No. 165, dressed in new design figured lawn frock. The glossy, well-arranged wig is surmounted by a broad silk ribbon of color to match the dainty costume......................Per Dozen, 10.50

No. 167. **MISS CAMPBELL WITH WIG.** Similar style of costume to No. 130; white lawn, lace trimmed, over pink under-dress. In this doll we have painted the eyes looking **straight forward** instead of in the usual Campbell Kid manner. The wig is trimmed with a silk ribbon bow.................Per Dozen, 10.50

Nos. 165 and 166 Campbell Kids

No. 204   No. 203   2   No. 210

The "Campbell Kids" have Caught the Colored Hair Craze

No. 127. **CAMPBELL KID GIRL.** Hair colored in red, blue, green or yellow to match costume and with silk hair-ribbon.
Per Dozen, **$8.50**

"Campbell Kids" in Larger Sizes
To Retail for $2.00 or over
(Heads Copyrighted 1910 by E. I. Horsman Co.)

No. 203. **CAMPBELL KID BOY.** Large size. New design, with exposed neck and jointed knees. Romper suit, belted, of striped percale, short socks and felt shoes..Per Dozen, **$13.50**

No. 204. **CAMPBELL KID GIRL.** Large size. Companion doll to No. 203, dressed in pretty lawn frock with broad binding and open neck. Short socks and felt shoes...Dozen, 13.50

No. 210. **MISS CAMPBELL.** Large size. Similar to No. 130 in dress design, the lace trimmed white lawn pinafore having a pink under-dress ....Per Dozen, 13.50

Large Super-Grade with Mohair Wigs

No. 265. **CAMPBELL KID BOY.** Large size. Same as No. 203, but with mohair wig and with a white beach hat..............Per Dozen, **$16.50**

No. 266. **CAMPBELL KID GIRL.** Large size. Same as No. 204, but with wig and broad silk hair ribbon ....Per Dozen, 16.50

No. 267. **MISS CAMPBELL.** Large size. Same as No. 210—pink and white party dress—with wig and hair ribbon...........Per Dozen, 16.50

---

468. Campbell Kids in various costumes and with or without wigs as advertised by Horsman ca. 1914. The hands on these Campbell Kids have the forefingers and little fingers partly separated from the other fingers that have a greater curvature. These hands are not the same as the early Campbell Kid hands that were used on many other dolls; shown in this same ca. 1914 catalog. *Courtesy of Bernard Barenholtz.*

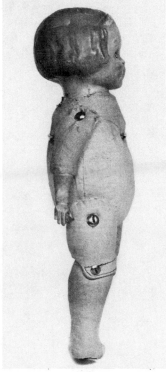

469A & B. Campbell Kid with composition head and hands on a cloth body with a flange neck and jointed at the knees as well as the shoulders and hips. The head is similar to those shown in the catalog of ca. 1914 but the hands and neck indicate that this is an earlier doll or a doll made by a competitor. Original clothes. Mark on head "2/0." H. 13½ in. (34 cm.). *Courtesy of the Margaret Woodbury Strong Museum. Photos by Harry Bickelhaupt.*

THEY HAVE COME TO LIFE!
THE *Campbell Kids*

I'm all ready to play with you on Children's Day [Saturday, June 15th]

I've been looking at little girls from all the Campbell soup ads so long, and longing to play with them, that now my fairy godmother has made me into a real live doll, so I can play with you all day long. Now, you can be my little mother and hug and squeeze me. We will be *so* happy together. I will be the best dollie you ever had. I have a funny little face, and lovely clothes, and I can turn my head any-way at all, and move my arms and legs, and stand up all by myself in all kinds of cunning positions, just like a real little girl! If you will ask DAD or MUMMY to let me be your little Campbell Kid, I'll promise to love you as much as you love me. Be sure to tell them to look for my name, "Campbell Kid" on the tag, because that means I'm a genuine PETITE unbreakable doll and will live for a long, long time.

$2⁹⁵

LOOK for this TAG. It is your guarantee.

and up in all department stores and better toy shops.

To MOTHERS and FATHERS and brothers, sisters, uncles and aunts, too.

The Campbell Kids are the most charming and lifelike dolls you ever saw. They are completely moveable, heads, arms, and legs—too cute for words. Your little girl has had all the other types of dolls. NOW, she deserves a NEW one—a doll that is different and more interesting—that she is sure to love devotedly. Give her one for Children's Day and she will have wholesome company for a long time.

Be sure to look for the Petite Campbell Kid tag which identifies the genuine Campbell Kid—an UNBREAKABLE Petite Doll.

Send for a free copy of the picture book of Campbell Kids and Petite Dolls

Just fill in and mail the coupon below

A PETITE DOLL Campbell Kid

whether its a "mamma" doll - a baby doll or a novelty doll - its the best made if its a
PETITE DOLL
The best is none too good for your child - and it costs no more

We introduce the *Campbell Kids* and other PETITE Dolls

AMERICAN CHARACTER DOLL CO., Inc.
20 East 17th Street, New York
Gentlemen: Please send me a FREE copy of the colored picture booklet of Campbell Kids and Petite Dolls.

Name_____

Address_____

City and State_____

470. Campbell Kids advertisement in PLAYTHINGS, May, 1929. The two costumes on these dolls as shown in this picture are also seen on actual dolls in Ills. 471 and 472. Note the Campbell Kid tag in the lower left corner.

472. Campbell Kid as made by the American Character Doll Co. and advertised in PLAYTHINGS in 1929. (See Ill. 470.) It is all-composition with molded and painted hair and eyes, closed smiling mouth. The neck joint has the socket in the head. Original clothes. H. 12½ in. (31.5 cm.). *Courtesy of Pat Schoonmaker.*

←**471.** Campbell Kid all-composition doll as made by American Character Doll Co. and advertised in PLAYTHINGS, May, 1929. See Ill. 470. It has molded and painted brown hair and blue eyes, pink pug nose, smiling Drayton type mouth, neck with socket in the head. Original dress. Mark: Ill. 473. H. 12½ in. (31.5 cm.). *Courtesy of the Margaret Woodbury Strong Museum. Photo by Harry Bickelhaupt.*

473A & B. Marks of Campbell Kid dolls made by American Character Doll Co.

Canastota Sherwood Stamping Co. 1930 and later. Canastota, N.Y. Made adjustable roller skates of rolled steel for dolls. They could be taken off or put on without removing the dolls' shoes; they fit shoes 2⅜ in. (6 cm.) to 3½ in. (9 cm.). An advertisement showed a *Patsy* doll wearing these skates.

Candy Kid. 1910–14. Composition head designed by *Helen Trowbridge,* copyrighted 1910 and described as a smiling two-year-old. Appears to be the same head as that used for *Carnival Baby.* Doll produced by *Horsman* as number 147

No. 147 "Candy Kid"

No. 147. "CANDY KID"
Trade Mark
(Head copyrighted, 1912, by
E. I. Horsman Co.)
A jolly little chap with a two-year-
old smile that's catching. Wears ging-
ham rompers, socks and felt slippers.
Per Dozen........**$8.50**

474. Candy Kid doll advertised in a Horsman catalog of ca. 1914. It has a composition head with molded and painted hair and eyes, closed mouth, Campbell Kid type composition hands, and a cloth body. The head was copyrighted in 1912. *Catalog courtesy of Bernard Barenholtz.*

of Can't Break 'Em† composition head and hands, cloth body. This doll had painted hair and eyes, *Campbell Kid* type hands.

1911: Listed as a premium for YOUTH'S COMPANION. It came dressed in striped rompers with red yoke, belt and cuffs. Ht. 12 in. (30.5 cm.); price $1.25.

1912: It wore rompers identical to those worn by the Campbell Kid Boy, socks and flannel slippers.

1914: The striped rompers were belt-less for the standard size. There was a Junior size, number 81. that had the same head as the Junior *Football Kid* and Junior *Farmer Boy.* This Junior size had a belt. Price $4.24 a doz. wholesale. Head shown in Ill. 474 was copyrighted in 1912.★

Candy Kid. Ca. 1929. Trade name of a doll made by *Ideal* with composition head and lower legs, metal flirting eyes, rubber lower arms, cloth body. Ht. 15 in. (38 cm.), according to Patricia Schoonmaker.

Candy Stick Man. 1928. Oilcloth or soft-bodied doll made by *Kat-A-Korner Kompany.*

Canyon Kiddies. See **Kallus, Joseph L.**

Canzler & Hoffmann. 1906–30 and later. Berlin and Sonneberg, Thür. Made their own dressed dolls. Used the trademark Caho.† Obtained porcelain dolls' heads from *Schoenau & Hoffmeister.*

1906: Advertised "The Crying Baby on a pillow" with automatic voice, style no. 684, price $6.60 per doz. wholesale; dressed dolls of all kinds; dolls' clothes, hats, shoes, stockings and fur trimmed garments; *Täuflinge;* dolls' bodies; heads, wigs, and other articles for dolls' hospitals.

1911: Advertised dressed dolls of all kinds, bodies, heads, mohair and real hair wigs; character baby 28 cm. (11 in.) dressed in baby clothes. Style no. 1801, price $3.60 per doz. wholesale. Latest novelty was a baby that drank.

1923: Applied for a German patent (D.R.G.M.) for a doll's body.

1925: Applied for a German patent (D.R.G.M.) for a *Mama* doll.

1927: Applied for a German patent (D.R.G.M.) for a stuffed doll with a "leather cloth body," celluloid head and celluloid arms. Advertised miniature dolls.

1928–29: Advertised dressed and undressed dolls, dolls' house dolls and trousseaux for dolls.

1930: The "new celluloid heads" had molded short bobbed hair with bangs or straight hair. Also advertised cloth dolls, dolls' house dolls, baby dolls and dolls' trousseaux.★

Cape Cod Sailor. Ca. 1926. Bisque-head dolls' house Grandfather type with molded grey hair and side burns, black molded boots, dressed in yellow paper reinforced with a network of threads. Came in a box marked "Made in Germany//Nr. 1720//CAPE COD SAILOR." Ht. 6¼ in. (16 cm.).

Capital Toy Co. 1923–30. New York City. Manufactured

Ceetee line of *Mama* dolls, baby dolls, character dolls. Dolls had either composition or cloth legs.

1929–30: Style no. 100 Sp. wore a dress of percale trimmed with white piqué. Price of dolls 25¢ to $10.00. ★

Capitol Hat Frame Works. 1925–26. Des Moines, Iowa. Made outfits for dolls.

Capo Di Monte.† See **Ernst Bohne** for a similar mark.

Caprice. World War I. Name found on a bisque socket head made by *Lanternier*. It had a wig, glass sleeping eyes, and an open-closed mouth with molded teeth. The head was incised "DÉPOSÉ//FABRICATION//FRANÇAISE//CAPRICE//NO. 12//A. L. & Cie//LIMOGES." Ht. 24 in. (61 cm.). ★

Captain. See **Ka (Captain).**

Captain Kidd. Ca. 1910. Trade name of a cloth doll with painted features and long black hair representing a pirate. The doll wore a big straw hat, carried a papier-mâché sword and was described as having a "fierce appearance."

Captain Kidd. 1929. One of the *Kiddie Karakters* made by *Averill Manufacturing Co.* The doll's composition head was designed by *Grace Corry* and first appeared under the name *Little Brother.* This doll wore a pirate costume consisting of a white shirt, a wide roman-stripe cumberbund, dark trousers that covered the knees and a high hat with the brim turned up off the face. It had a rectangular tag on which was printed "Captain Kid //The//Pirate//Bold."

Captain Kiddo. 1912. A printed cloth doll with a *Grace Drayton* style face. It carried a sword at its belt.

Captain & Kids. 1927–28. Trade name for dolls produced by *Borgfeldt.*

Capuano. See **Non-Breakable Toy Co.†**

Carael, J. 1929–30. Paris. Made dolls' clothes including hats, footwear and lingerie as well as mohair wigs.

Card, E. B. See **Carevelle Doll Co.**

Cardon-Laghez. 1920s. France. Made jewelry for dolls and was a member of the *Chambre Syndicale.*

Carevelle Doll Co. 1922. Made *Daddy Dolls* originated by E. B. Card.†

Care of Composition Dolls. 1926–27. PLAYTHINGS gave the following advice: "Composition heads and arms of dolls should be cleaned with Vaseline or cold cream. The doll's hair can be cleaned and rearranged by brushing with a hair brush of medium bristles.

"If some enamel chips off, such spots can be retouched with enamel selected to closely match the complexion of the doll. A torn body can be patched. Dresses, underwear and stockings should be washed and ironed when they become dirty."

To this advice it should be added that bleaches and starches should never be used in washing dolls' clothes. Mild soap and sun bleaching are best. Also the repainting is not advised.

Carene. 1929. Name of a series of dolls made by *Chad Valley.*

Caresse. 1923–1930 and later. Inexpensive cloth dolls made by *Chad Valley.*

They were also known as "La Petite Caresse" dolls. Usually they had stockinet heads but later their movable heads were also made with felt or velour faces. The faces were hand-painted and the wigs were of real hair. The *Aerolite* bodies were generally stuffed with kapok. Most of these dolls came in size 1, 11 in.; size 2, 13 in.; size 3, 16 in.; or size 4, 18 in. The largest size came with or without a mama voice. These dolls usually carried a hexagonal tag reading "Chad Valley //HYGIENIC //Fabric Toys." (See also *Lucie-Attwell Caresse* dolls.)

1923: The knee-length plain garment of the Caresse dolls had imitation white fur around the neckline. This fur was also around the rim of the cloche. For about 15 cents extra a matching muff could be obtained.

1923 CARESSE DOLLS			
Style	Height		
No.	in.	cm.	Clothes
169	11	28	
170	13	33	Velveteen
171	16	40.5	gown
172	18	45.5	
173	11	28	
174	13	33	Plush
175	16	40.5	gown
176	18	45.5	

1924: The 1923 dolls continued to be made, but with buttons down the front of numbers 169–180.

The following numbers were new in 1924.

Style	Height		
No.	in.	cm.	Clothes
177	11	28	
178	13	33	
179	16	40.5	Woolly fur gown
180	18	45.5	
260	11	28	
261	13	33	Velveteen garments trimmed with
262	16	40.5	white woolly fur around hat rim,
263	18	45.5	neck, cuffs, bottom of flared skirt,
264	21	53.5	and down front above the waist-
265	25	63.5	line.

Some of the Caresse dolls were given special names such as *Olga, Pretty Jane* and *Betty.*

1926: There were several innovations in 1926. Felt faces and dresses were mentioned for the style nos. 430–433 girl models and for the 426–429 models which were baby dolls. Nos. 169–172 and 260–265 were the same as in 1924. 172 was available in three hts. 18, 21 and 25 in.

New style nos. were:

Style Nos.	Height in.	Height cm.	Clothes
272	11	28	Velveteen dresses trimmed with scalloped felt around the neckline, bottom of skirt and on hat. Very short flared skirt.
273	13	33	
274	16	40.5	
275	18	45.5	
276	21	53.5	
277	25	63.5	
420	11	28	A bonnet and short-sleeved organdy dress trimmed with felt flowers in contrasting colors.
421	13	33	
422	16	40.5	
423	18	45.5	
426	11½	29	Height includes long baby dress trimmed with lace and having a high waistline. Doll wore baby caps.
427	14½	37	
428	17½	44.5	
429	19	48	
430	12½	30.5	Bonnet and short-sleeved felt dresses trimmed with appliqués. Slippers are strapless.
431	14	35.5	
432	16½	42	
433	18½	47	

1927: The Caresse dolls were made in accordance with three patents. Number 169–172 were dressed in colored velveteen and trimmed with fur plush around the hat rim, the collar and bottom of the skirt. The two larger sizes of number 172 had been reduced to 20 and 24 inches and the same was true for numbers 276 and 277. Numbers 272–277 wore a colored velvet cloche, scarf and low waisted, full skirted dress, all trimmed with scalloped felt edging. Numbers 480 and 481 were each made in the same sizes as the other dolls but had size designations from 1 to 6. Number 480, which was new, wore a close fitting velvet hat and a high waisted velvet dress with colored embroidery trimming around the hat rim and skirt bottom. Style No. 481, also new, was attired in a velvet hat and coat trimmed with imitation leopard skin. The Caresse dolls were packed in Bye-Bye bed boxes.

1928: Some of the Caresse dolls had movable felt heads and hand-painted velour faces, while others still had stockinet heads, bodies and arms which made a slightly cheaper doll. None of the Caresse dolls were packed in Bye-Bye bed boxes. Several of the Caresse series were withdrawn; these included the two largest sizes of style number 172 and all of 272, 480 and 481.

Style No.	Height in.	Height cm.
169	11	28
170	13	33
171	16	40.5
172	18	45.5

When a mama voice was included in No. 172 the cost was raised by about $2.25 per dozen.

1929: There was no change in attire on number 169–172. New numbers were: 469, 13 inches wore cloche and coat trimmed with imitation fur around the hat rim, the collar and cuffs. 487 came in 4 sizes 11 to 18 inches and wore a hat with the brim turned up in front and coat with imitation fur cuffs and around the bottom of the coat. 488 size 16 had a tam with an imitation fur band and imitation fur muffler with pompon ends. The coat had a patch pocket. 489 size 18 inches, wore a cloche and a coat with a narrow band of imitation fur around the neckline, down the front, and around the bottom as well as on the cuffs.

1930: None of the earlier Caresse dolls were listed in the 1930 Chad Valley catalog. Even the sizes were different in the 465 and 609 series. 465 came in four hts. 15, 18, 20 and 22 in. while 609 came in 11, 13 and 14½ inch hts.

Numbers 424, 464, 465, 613 and 655 were made in colored velvet, 453 and 609 were made in silk plush and 656 was made in velvet and plush. Number 424 represented a boy and wore a brimmed hat, Eton jacket and very short pants. Number 464 had a cloche, a coat above the knees in length, imitation fur cuffs and strip around the neckline and down each side of the closure. 465 wore a brimmed bonnet and full coat over a print dress. The bonnet and coat were trimmed with imitation fur around the edges. 609 represented a child in a silk plush garment, the tunic covered the thighs and the tight fitting cap had a pompom on top.

Caresse Imps. 1928–30 and later. Made by *Chad Valley*. These 14 in (35.5 cm.) dolls had hand-painted faces, bobbed or shingled hair, slim bodies and long legs showing beneath the extremely short clothes. They were dressed in variously colored art felt and sometimes in velvet.

1928: Style No. 643, a brunette, wore a cloche and a garment with an uneven bottom. No. 645 represented a boy with bobbed dark hair with bangs. It wore short trousers. No. 646 represented a girl with a hairbow on its dark hair. It wore a short-sleeved coat.

1929: The dolls of 1928 continued to be produced, plus the following: No. 649 with dark bobbed hair, a brimmed hat and a two-piece romper suit; No. 652 wore a bonnet on its dark hair and a sleeveless dress with no waist line. The bloomers showed below the dress. No. 654 had bobbed blond hair with bangs and wore a short-sleeved, high-waisted dress with a full paneled skirt.

1930: No. 655 represented a boy in velvet clothes. It had a tam on its blond, bobbed hair and wore a belted jacket and short trousers. No. 656 represented a girl dressed in velvet and felt. It wore a cloche; both hat and dress were trimmed with six-pointed stars.

Carette. See **Huret, Maison.**

Carina Dolls. 1928–29. Made by *Chad Valley*. They were velveteen dolls jointed at the neck, shoulders and hips and made so that they could either sit or stand. They had hair wigs and removable velveteen clothes in various colors. Style No. 1200 wore a hat with the brim turned up in front and a coat with a yoke, a button closing and imitation fur collar and cuffs.

CARINA DOLLS		
Size No.	Height in.	cm.
1	14	35.5
2	17	43
3	19	48
4	22	56
5	24	61
6	30	76

Carl, Hermann. 1912. Oeslau, Thür. Obtained a German patent (D.R.G.M.) for a doll's head with sleeping eyes.

Carl, Max, & Co. 1891–1905. Neustadt near Coburg and Sonneberg. Thür. Produced dolls with wax heads, wax-over-composition heads, bisque heads and china heads on bodies of composition, kid or colored cloth. The bodies were stuffed with hair. The dolls came dressed or undressed. *H. E. Eckart* was the factory agent in London.

1902: Obtained a German patent (D.R.G.M.) for a nursing doll.

1904: Exhibited dolls at the St. Louis World's Fair.

1905: Advertised that they had over 1,000 style numbers selling for 2¢ to $6.25 in London. Their dolls included the *Carl Hartmann Globe Baby;* "Full Model" wax dolls, hts. 6½ to 20½ in. (16.5 to 52 cm.); priced 2¢ to 25¢. Other dolls in the same price range were "Full Model" dressed dolls, hts. 12½ in. (31.5 cm.) and 14½ in. (37 cm.); "Half Model" wax dolls, some with sleeping eyes and some with mama-papa voices, hts. 15½ to 25 in. (39.5 to 63.5 cm.). "Half Model" dressed dolls, ht. 23 in. (58.5 cm.); wax dolls in colored chemises hts. 9 and 12 in. (23 and 30.5 cm.); dressed wax dolls seven hts. 6, 7½, 10, 11, 12, 15, and 16 in. (15, 19, 25.5, 28, 30.5, 38 and 40.5 cm.) undressed, and hts. 9 in. (23 cm.) and 15 in. (38 cm.) dressed; composition dolls, ht. 9 in. (23 cm.); washable dolls, ht. 12 in. (30.5 cm.) and clapping dolls.★

Carl, Robert. 1895–1910. Köppelsdorf, Thür. 1910–25, Frickmann & Robert A. Lindner; 1925–30 and later. Karl Frickmann, successors of Robert Carl. Their dolls should not be confused with the earlier lady dolls marked R. C. DÉPOSÉ or DÉPOSÉ R. C., which appear to have a French origin. (See **Radiguet & Cordonnier.**)

1883: Attended the *Sonneberg Industrial School.*

1900: Applied for two German patents (D.R.G.M.), one for a doll's head with moving eyelashes of goat hair.

1905: Applied for two German patents (D.R.G.M.), one for sleeping eyes and one for a doll's head with pacifier.

1907: Novelty was a doll's head with sleeping eyes and a voice.

1908: Applied for a German patent (D.R.G.M.) for dolls' eyes with lashes.

1910: Advertised character dolls with artistic heads of bisque or celluloid; doll bodies of leather; ball-jointed *Täuflinge* with Mama voice in the head; porcelain heads from their own models (possibly the heads were made by *Armand Marseille* which was a nearby porcelain factory). Robert Carl had 50 factory workers and numerous cottage workers.

1911: Advertised character dolls; dolls' heads with natural eyebrows.

Applied for a German patent (D.R.G.M.) for a baby doll's head with a voice.

1912: Advertised that the latest novelty was a cloth doll that cried when touched.

1915: Applied for a German patent (D.R.G.M.) for voices in dolls' heads.

1925: Karl Frickmann advertised leather dolls, babies, jointed dolls, and babies and dolls with Mama voices in their heads; leather bodies; wax-cloth, cloth, bisque and celluloid heads with or without wigs.

A considerable part of the above information was based on the research of the Ciesliks.★

475. Mark on dolls produced by Robert Carl.

Carlègle, Charles-Emile, and Hellé, André. 1918. France. Made wooden toy figures representing cowboys, Indians, sailors, poultry keepers, children, ladies, officers, and merchants. These were sold in *Printemps* store. Carlègle was born in 1877 in Aigle, Canton Vaud, and died in 1940. He was a humorist, illustrator, painter, and engraver. (See also **Hellé, André.**)

Carles, Jean. 1926. Nice, France. Registered *Mousmé* as a French trademark for dolls.

Carlier, Fournelle & Gibon. 1925–30 and later. Paris. Made dolls.★

Carlton Works. See **Wiltshaw & Robinson.**

Carluccio. 1927. Trade name of felt doll made by *Lenci*. It had golden curls made of a fine fluffy flax product and the expression and chubby body of a three-year-old boy. The doll carried a wooden stick horse and portrayed the little brother of *Anili.*

Carmen. 1927–28. Trade name of a felt doll made by *Lenci*, representing the opera character with this name. It was style No. 561 and wore a yellow dress with red poppies on it, a high red comb, high heeled red slippers and carried a basket of red apples. Ht. 32½ inches (82.5 cm.).

Carmen Sylva. See **Queen Elizabeth of Romania.**

Carmencita (Bébé Carmencita). 1912–30. Trade name used by *Arthur Schönau.*★

Carnival. 1895. Trade name of a dressed doll distributed by *Butler Bros.* It had a bisque head with wig. Ht. 22½ in. (57 cm.); priced $3.35 doz. wholesale.

Carnival Baby. 1910–16. Trade name for two different composition-head dolls produced by *Horsman* as number 132. The first doll had a head designed by *Helen Trowbridge* and copyrighted in 1910. This appeared to be the same mold as *Candy Kid,* and had painted hair, eyes looking straight ahead, face painted white with at least one face patch. Its black and white sateen costume was similar in design to the girl *Campbell Kid*'s dress, but shorter with bloomers showing, and white shoes.

A new style of head was copyrighted in 1912 and was used on the Carnival Baby number 132 shown in the Horsman 1914 catalog. The eyes were painted looking to the side. There were two colored face patches on the white face. Campbell Kid type hands were still used. Broad ruffs were around the neck, cuffs and trousers of the black and white Pierrot costume. It had a white felt pointed clown's hat. Price $8.50 a doz. wholesale. A smaller doll, Junior size number 79 was similarly dressed and cost $4.25 a doz. wholesale. Ca. 1916. This doll was identified with the *Gene Carr Kids.*★

No. 132 "Carnival Baby"

476. Carnival Baby dolls produced by Horsman and advertised in their catalog of ca. 1914. The composition clown head was copyrighted in 1912 and the doll has the early Campbell Kid type composition hands. *Courtesy of Bernard Barenholtz.*

Carnot, François. World War I. France. The founder of *Jouets de France;* his toys seem to have influenced the development of wooden dolls.

Caro (Silly Guss). 1911–13. Name of a jointed felt doll made by *Steiff* and distributed by *Borgfeldt.* It was a comic doll representing Silly Guss, a clown and wore a coat with long tails. Came in assorted colors. Ht. 17 in. (43 cm.); priced $2.32 in Germany in 1911, $2.50 in New York in 1913.

Carolina. 1930. Black girl doll made by *Chad Valley,* number 698/2 with fuzzy hair. It wore a grass skirt, head band, bracelets and anklets. Ht. 15 in. (38 cm.).

Carolina Mammy. 1927. Trade name of dolls made by *Sol Bergfeld.*

Caron,[†] **Vve. (Widow).** See **Auguste et Vve. Caron.**

Carrie Cuddler. 1914. Trade name of a cloth character doll made by *Dean.*

Carrie Joy. 1924–28. Trademark used by *Ideal* for dolls.★

Carrier-Belleuse, Albert Ernest. Before 1887. Sèvres, France. A sculptor who designed a doll's head (or heads) for Emile *Jumeau.* Carrier-Belleuse was born in 1824 in Anizy-le-Chateau, Aisne; he died in 1887 in Sèvres.

Various dates have been given the designing of the Jumeau head of Carrier-Belleuse. If his granddaughter was the model, it would have had to have been after 1880 for she was born about 1877. M. François Theimer believes that the ca. 1558 picture of Henry of Navarre as a boy of four was the inspiration for the Jumeau head. Henry of Navarre became King Henry IV of France and in 1608 he settled the dispute between the Bimbellotiers (Makers of playthings) and Poupetiers (Makers and dressers of dolls) as to the rights to produce dolls, by passing a statute which gave the monopoly of the doll making to the Poupetiers.

Carrier-Belleuse had nearly 20 people in his workshop and one of them could have modeled the head under his supervision. It is possible that it was his son, Louis Robert Carrier-Belleuse, born in 1848 in Paris died in 1913 in Paris who designed the Jumeau head. The son was also a sculptor and after his father's death he was Art Director of the Faïencerie de Choisy-le-Roi, for which he designed models. He was a Chevalier de la Légion d'Honneur.

1851: Albert Carrier-Belleuse had his first exhibit in the Salon.

1864–69: Rodin studied under Carrier-Belleuse.

1867: Won a Medal of Honor at the Salon and was decorated with the Legion of Honor by Napoleon III.★

477. Bébé Jumeau with a bisque head designed probably by Carrier-Belleuse. It has a wig, stationary blue glass eyes, pierced ears, closed mouth. The head is incised "E. 4 J." and the composition body is marked "Jumeau //Medaille d'Or." Original shoes. H. 12 in. (30.5 cm.). *Courtesy of Sotheby Parke Bernet Inc., N.Y.*

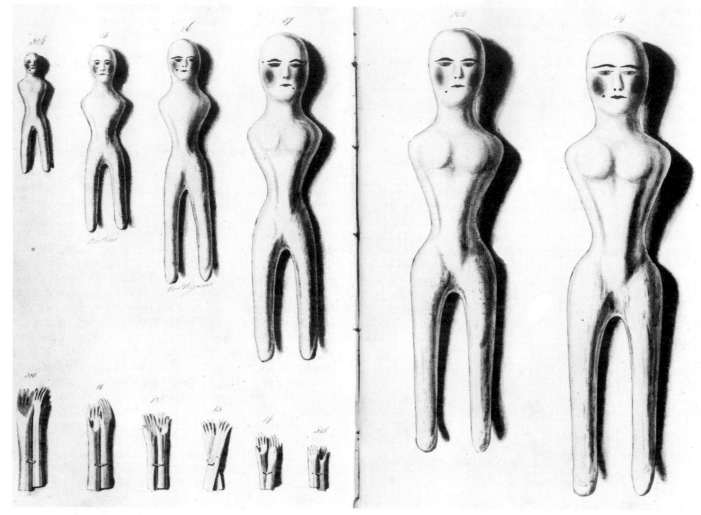

478. Undressed Carton Moulé dolls of various sizes with appropriate wooden lower arms. This picture is in a French catalog of the late 1700s or ca. 1800. Note that these dolls all have beauty marks on their cheeks as found on the dolls in Ills. 480 and 482. *Courtesy of Henry Francis du Pont Winterthur Museum, Joseph Downs Manuscript Collection.*

Carroll, The Thomas, Co. 1927. Chicago, Ill. Factory agent for doll manufacturers.

Carson, Pirie, Scott & Co. 1911–30 and later. Chicago, Ill. Store that sold dolls, including dolls produced by *Cuno and Otto Dressel.*

1914: Advertised *Fairy Dolls;* dolls dressed in European regional costumes; *Baby Grumpy,* priced 95¢; dolls with sleeping eyes and mama voices, priced $1.25; jointed composition dolls with wigs and sleeping eyes, priced $1.25; large jointed baby dolls with wigs and eyelashes, priced $3.50.★

Cartier, M. Roger. 1928. Bourg-la-Reine, Seine. Registered *Nez d' Hareng* as a French trademark for dolls.

Carton (Carton Moulé). French term for a kind of *papier-mâché.* The word "carton" is used by some collectors to designate the material used in France for dolls in the 1700s

and early 1800s. At first these dolls had their head and torso of carton; later it was the head and upper torso which finally developed into the French papier-mâché heads on kid bodies. The head of the doll shown in illustration 836 of the first COLLECTOR'S ENCYCLOPEDIA OF DOLLS is made of carton and not gesso-over-wood.★

Cartwright, A. S. 1880–1917. Birmingham, England. Manufactured rubber dolls, bottles and comforters for dolls.

Carvaillo, Adrien. 1923–30 and later. Paris. Used the trademark *Venus* for his cloth dolls. See Ills. 2647 and 2648.★

Cascelloid Co. 1919–30 and later. London. Made celluloid dolls based on the drawings of *Mabel Lucie Attwell.* These included *Diddums* and Little Happy.

Casey the Cop. 1926. Doll made by *Wolf Doll Co.* It shuffled along and gave the appearance of toppling over but kept its footing. Ht. 9 in. (23 cm.).

480   481

479

479. Carton shoulder head with a dark brown wig, molded brown eyes and a closed mouth. The body has kid-over-carton down to the waist and wooden hands, the rest of the body is kid. H. 14½ in. (37 cm.). *Courtesy of Estelle Johnston.*

480. Doll with carton head and torso, wooden arms, strands of hair around edge of cap, molded and painted eyes, beauty marks on cheeks, closed mouth, and original clothes. H. 19 in. (48 cm.). *Courtesy of Estelle Johnston.*

481. Doll with carton head and stuffed body. Wears original silk and gauze dress with cotton underdress. Costume ca. 1820. H. 31.5 cm. (12½ in.). *Courtesy of the Nordiska Museet in Stockholm, Sweden.*

482A & B. Pair of Carton Moulé dolls in original costumes. The large doll has a few strands of hair under its headwear, molded and painted brown eyes, three black beauty marks on its cheeks, a dimple in the chin, earrings attached to its head, and wooden hands. There is a wooden base and a string that when pulled raises the arms. The small doll is seated on a cushion and has painted blue eyes. It has two black beauty marks and one white beauty mark on its cheeks. Its hands are leather. Hs. 24½ in. and 7 in. (62 and 18 cm.). *Courtesy of the Margaret Woodbury Strong Museum. Photos by Harry Bickelhaupt.*

Cass, N. D., Co. 1918–27. Athol, Mass. Made the *Funny Face Family*, which were peg-jointed dolls of white wood. The parts for these dolls—Reddy, Whitie (Whitey), and Bluey their son—were interchangeable. A labeled Cass dolls' trunk contained a molded felt face doll and its wardrobe of clothes, some of which were made of felt. Another labeled trunk contained the wardrobe of a *Kamkins* doll. *Strobel and Wilkin* and *Louis Wolf* were their agents.

483. Doll with a flocked cardboard socket head, a blond wig, painted eyes, closed mouth, cloth body. The doll and its extra clothes are in a trunk marked "Cass" (Ill. 484). Head of doll marked "76//S." H. of doll 10 in. (25.5 cm.). *Courtesy of the Margaret Woodbury Strong Museum. Photo by Harry Bickelhaupt.*

TRADE MARK

TOYS   QUALITY

MADE IN U.S.A.

484. Mark on trunk shown in Ill. 483. This mark has also been found in a trunk containing the wardrobe of a *Kamkins* doll shown in Ill. 1376.

Cassanet, A., & Cie. 1881–90s. Paris. Purchased bisque dolls' heads from *François Gaultier* for some of the dolls that he made, according to Mme. Poisson, curator of the Roybet-Fould Museum. ★

Catholic Sister. 1914. Doll made by *Effanbee*.

Catterfelder Puppenfabrik. 1894–1930 and later. Catterfeld near Waltershausen, Thür. Carl Christian Trautmann, 1904–5, Hugo and Richard Gross 1910, Walter Gross 1917, Franz Kundy, 1920–22, were in charge of the factory.

Made dolls generally using *Kestner* bisque heads on composition bodies. The size number on these heads usually indicated the height of the doll in centimeters except for mold #264.

The size-height correlation for mold #264, a doll representing a child, has been found as follows: 1—46 cm. (18 in.), 2—48 cm. (19 in.), 4½—68.5 cm. (27 in.). Among the molds that have their hts. given in centimeters were 201 (a baby), 208, 220 and 263.

1894: Won a medal in Erfurt at the Thüringian Industry Fair.

1902: Reported by some sources as the founding date.

1904: Applied for two German patents (D.R.G.M.), one for a jointed doll and one for a talking doll.

1906: Advertised ball-jointed dolls and 5—piece standing dolls, bisque shoulder heads and socket heads, solid wooden limbs, shoes, stockings, and leather bodies.

1908: Advertised the finest and medium grade ball-jointed dolls, the finest mohair and angora wigs, dolls' heads of the finest bisque.

1911: Advertised a ball-jointed child doll called *Mein Herz'l* (My Sweetheart) and a child doll with the mold # 219 also character baby dolls with the mold # 200. These babies with painted hair and eyes closely resemble the *Kämmer & Reinhardt* mold # 100 babies. Mold #200 was made in a

black and a white version. Mold # 201 babies with painted eyes and hair had dimples in their cheeks. They also advertised novelty babies in celluloid with painted hair and lashes and sleeping eyes. Applied for a German patent (D.R.G.M.) for a doll's head with a pacifier.

1912: Advertised "Mein Sonnenschein"[†] (My Sunshine); new babies with painted hair and sleeping eyes; babies with moving tongue, marked 208; mohair wigs and wigs made of animal skins.

1920: Used the trademark "Mein Sonnenschein." Specialized in the finest ball-jointed dolls, bent limb and standing babies with and without wigs; doll and baby heads with and without wigs; dolls' wigs, character dolls marked 219.

1922: Trademark, "Kleiner Sonnenschein"[†] (*Little Sunshine*) was registered. Some of the above information was supplied by the research of the Ciesliks. In the early 1920s this factory was a supplier for *Dennis Malley & Co.*★

Cave & Easterling. 1924–30. London. Factory agent for *Eccles* in Britain and the colonies. Sole agent for *August Schelhorn.*

Caversham Doll. Name found on a doll produced by *Henry Jeffrey Hughes* or *Henry John Hazel,* both having the initials H. J. H. found on the doll's head. Mr. Hazel's address was on Caversham Road. The *British Ceramic* shoulder head, lower arms and legs were made by *Crown Staffordshire Porcelain Co.* See Ill. 489.

489. British Ceramic head with molded and painted hair, features and footwear. The eyes are enameled, the head named Caversham was made by Crown Staffordshire during World War I. The cloth body and the Scottish costume were made by Henry Jeffrey Hughes or Henry John Hazel. Mark: Ill. 490. H. 12 in. (30.5 cm.). H. of shoulder head 3¼ in. (8.5 cm.). *Coleman Collection.*

CP
208
‾‾
45
N

485

S

CP
208/38
Deponiert

486

Catterfelder
Puppen
fabrik
91
3/0

487A

Catterfelder
Puppenfabrik
No
5

487B

S & H

C. T.

7

488

485—488. Marks used by the Catterfelder Puppenfabrik for dolls.

490. Brown stamp mark on a British Ceramic head named Caversham made by Crown Staffordshire Porcelain Co. (See Ill. 489.)

Cayetano. Name attached to the clothes of an all-bisque doll dressed as a *swaddling-clothed* baby. See Ill. 491.

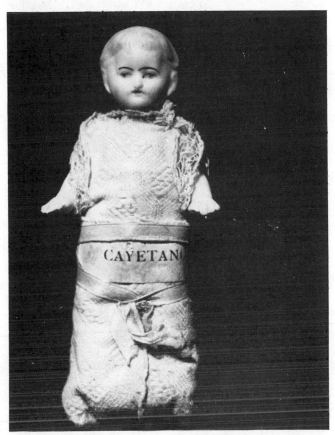

491. All-bisque doll in swaddling clothes that has "Cayetano" on a label attached to the clothes. The blond hair is molded and has brushmarks. The eyes painted blue; mouth closed. Original clothes. H. 4 in. (10 cm.). *Coleman Collection.*

Cecille. 1926. Trade name of a child doll with cloth body and limbs made by *L. Rees.* These dolls were dressed and had a round tag.

According to the Ciesliks these *Lenci*-type dolls were made by *Martin Eichhorn.*

Cecily Doll, The. 1918–20. Made by *Speights Ltd.* and distributed by *Edwards & Pamflett* as one of the *Classic* line. The *British Ceramic* character baby head had a wig and glass eyes.★

Cee Bee Doll Manufacturing Co. 1919–27. New York City. Made and/or distributed dolls. Cee Bee stood for *Charles Blum.*★

Ceetee. See **Captital Toy Co.**

Ceine Steward Co. 1929. Los Angeles, Calif. Imported dolls.

Cejka. 1920. Prague. A painter who designed wooden dolls which were seen in many shops according to *Stewart Culin.*

Celebrate (Celebrated). 1895–1925 and later. Trademark sometimes used for some of the *My Playmate* line of dolls made by *Kestner* and *König & Wernicke* for *Borgfeldt.* Celebrated was also used with the *My Dearie* line of dolly-face

492. Celebrate, a mark used by Borgfeldt for dolls.

dolls that had *Simon & Halbig* bisque heads on bodies made by *Wiesenthal, Schindel & Kallenberg.*

1904: *Butler Bros.* advertised these dolls as having long flowing hair, sleeping eyes and cork-stuffed kid bodies. Some of the dolls wore Scottish plaid stockings and single strap slippers and rosettes. Four hts. 14, 17, 20, and 22½ in. (35.5, 43, 51, and 57 cm.).

1909: *Siegel Cooper* advertised Kestner Celebrated dolls with bisque heads, side part wigs, sleeping eyes, fully jointed composition bodies, chemise, and footwear. Ht. 22¼ in. (56.5 cm.); priced $1.50.★

Celestia. 1887. Trade name of a wax doll with model features, glass eyes, wig with bangs, chemise and painted footwear. Distributed by *Lauer.* Four hts. 14½, 22, 26, and 30 in. (37, 56, 66, and 76 cm.), priced $1.75 to $7.50 doz. wholesale.

Cellba. 1927–30 and later. Brand name of celluloid dolls made by *Schöberl & Becker.* Cellba is an acronym for Celluloidwarenfabrik Babenhausen. (See Ills. 2334 and 2335.)

Cellowachs. Before 1927–30 and probably later. Name of material used for dolls by *Kämmer & Reinhardt* and *König & Wernicke.*

Cellulobrinwerke Georgenthal. See **Braun, Hugo.**

Celluloid. 1869–1930 and later. PLAYTHINGS in 1908 reported that prior to 1905 celluloid dolls were clumsy looking and could not withstand the knocking about that children gave them. Between 1905 and 1908 celluloid dolls improved in appearance and durability. Most of the celluloid dolls were made in Germany but many of them were painted by girls from Italy. All types of boys and girls were represented in celluloid dolls. (See *Manufacture of Celluloid Dolls[+]* for a description of their manufacture in 1908.)

A 1924 U.S. DEPARTMENT OF COMMERCE REPORT stated that it was not until 1905 the *Rheinische Gummi und Celluloid Fabrik* furnished doll makers in Sonneberg and surrounding areas with celluloid dolls' heads. However, Rheinische Gummi und Celluloid Fabrik had registered the Turtle trademark for celluloid dolls as early as 1899.

TOYS AND NOVELTIES, in 1920 reported that before 1910 D. Harmonica perfected the making of pyroxylin plastic toys by the blowing method. About the same time this was also done by the Rheinische Gummi und Celluloid Fabrik. The patent rights were in dispute for years. Finally the issue was decided giving both litigants the right to produce celluloid toys. By 1920 five or six American factories were also making types of celluloid. The largest ones were: *Exeloid Co.* of East Stroudsburg, Pa., which moved to Newark, N.J., in 1918; Du Pont, which supplied Pyralin sheeting for making celluloid dolls. These sheets made in pink, blue or white were 5/1000 to 20/1000 of an inch thick (.0125 to .05 cm.).

Celluloid was produced in Germany, France, the U.S., Japan and probably elsewhere. Among the companies that produced celluloid dolls, including both those who actually made celluloid dolls and those that used celluloid for the various parts of their dolls were:

Bähr & Pröschild	*Dr. Paul Hunaeus*
Buschow & Beck	*Kohl & Wengenroth*
Catterfelder Puppenfabrik Co.	Rheinische Gummi und Celluloid Fabrik Co.
Cuno & Otto Dressel	*Max Rudolph*
Kämmer & Reinhardt	*Bruno Schmidt*
Kestner	*Franz Schmidt & Co.*
König & Wernicke	*Schöberl & Becker* (Cellba)
Hagendorfer Celluloid Warenfabrik	*Karl Standfuss*
	Albert Wacker

In America there were:

Averill	*Irwin*
Bo Peep *(H. J. Brown)*	*Marks Bros.*
Du Pont Viscoloid Co.	*Parsons-Jackson Co.*
Horsman	*Celluloid Novelty Co.*

Probably the best known French celluloid dolls were made by *Petitcollin* (Profile head of an Eagle). Other French celluloid factories were *Widow Chalory; Convert;* Cie. Parisienne de *Cellulosine; Société Industrielle de Celluloid* (S.I.C.)—their celluloid was called "Sicoid," *Société Nobel Française* (S N F).

The center of the French celluloid industry was at Oyonnax and the celluloid from this area was called "Naxöid." Celluloid from Rhone-Poulenc was called "Rhodöid" and acetate celluloid was called "Acelöid."

The *Wilson Doll Co.* made celluloid dolls in England.

Dolls associated with the *Zast* company, bearing the initials "A. S. K.," were made of celluloid in Poland.

Celluloid dolls have been found with a wide variety of marks indicating that they had been made in Japan.

These companies were among those who made and/or used all-celluloid dolls, or celluloid heads on composition bodies, kid bodies or cloth bodies.

The short hair which became fashionable in the 1920s eliminated the demand for celluloid hair ornaments and the celluloid factories turned to making dolls.

The earlier all-celluloid dolls came in heights from about 5 to 13 in. (13 to 33 cm.) or even larger. From W.W. I. on the size variation seems to have been even greater, that is from about 1½ to 18½ in. (4 to 47 cm.).

The all-celluloid dolls had either straight legs or bent limbs. They were jointed at the shoulders only, or at the hips and shoulders, and sometimes they had no joints at all. Generally the hair was molded but occasionally on the

larger dolls there was a wig. The molds often resembled the then currently popular bisque heads. For example in 1917 some of the all-celluloid dolls 6½ and 9 in. (16.5 and 23 cm.) tall, closely resembled the bent limb Kämmer & Reinhardt, mold #100 *Baby*. By 1927 Kämmer & Reinhardt produced many all-celluloid dolls in three hts. 12, 15½ and 18 in. (30.5, 39 and 46 cm.), and in a variety of types. Some had molded hair and some had wigs with short or long hair. The usual joints were at the neck, shoulders, and hips, but a novelty in 1927 was a knee joint. The heads usually were marked with three digits. The hundred digit was "7," which indicated that the doll was made of celluloid. The unit and tens digit denoted the mold # of the head and generally corresponded with a similar mold # on the Kämmer & Reinhardt bisque head dolls in their one hundred series. The celluloid version was more expensive than the bisque version. The most common all-celluloid doll made by Kämmer & Reinhardt in 1927 was number 717.

In the early 1900s a celluloid spray paint was used on dolls, especially metal dolls' heads and metal dolls' eyes. When it became difficult to obtain glass eyes from Europe during World War I, many of the doll makers used these celluloid covered metal eyes. (See **Buschow & Beck**.) Later some of the felt dolls were coated with a celluloid paint.

1904: *Macy* advertised a celluloid head on a jointed wooden body. The doll had a wig and was 17½ in. (44.5 cm.) tall.

1908–10: Celluloid dolls began to appear in Paris stores. At first the head or mask was made of celluloid and the body was plush. Often these were called Esquimaux *(Eskimo)* dolls or "Bébés Pole North" (North Pole Babies). Celluloid shoulder heads came on bodies of composition, wood, kid, or cloth.

1909: *Siegel Cooper* advertised various celluloid or celluloid head dolls or masks of celluloid for dolls. An all-celluloid doll with painted features and jointed shoulders came in seven hts. 4, 5¾, 6½, 7¾, 9¾, 12½ and 14¼ in. (10, 14.5, 16.5, 19.5, 25, 31.5 and 36 cm.); priced 10¢ to $1.65. A doll with a celluloid shoulder head, cloth body, kid forearms, and footwear. Ht. 18 in. (45.5 cm.), was priced 50¢. A doll with a celluloid head on a jointed plush body, called a "Teddy Bear" doll, had a voice. It came in three hts. priced 25¢ to $1.00. A doll with a crochet head having a celluloid mask face had a cloth body, a voice, and wore a crocheted dress and hat. Ht. 9½ in. (24 cm.); priced 50¢.

The *Boston Store*'s catalog stated that celluloid arms cost 5¢ more than bisque arms.

1912: The Horsman catalog advertised boy and girl dolls in the 10½ inch (26.5 cm.) ht. Style Nos. 30c and 40c; the 13½ inch (34 cm.) ht., numbers 62 c and 63 c; 15 inch (38 cm.) ht., number 105c; 16 inch (40.5 cm.) ht. number 110c; and 17½ inch (44.5 cm.) ht. number 160c. The smaller girl dolls wore dresses with berthas and the larger girl dolls wore pinafores over their dresses. The boys wore long trousers or knickers. Some of the dolls wore sailor outfits. There were also dolls with celluloid mask faces: one designated H. C., one named *Stella,* and another, number 52c. Prices ranged from $2.00 to $12.00 a dozen.

1913: According to TOYS AND NOVELTIES German celluloid was known as "Parisian Ivory."

1914: Horsman advertised the same 13½ inch (34 cm.) numbers 62c and 63c; 16 inch (40.5 cm.) number 110c, and 17½ inch (44.5 cm.) number 160c. as in 1912. Their new 12 inch (30.5 cm.) dolls were numbers 35c and 36c; the 15 inch (38 cm.) ones were numbers 105B, 105 SB, 105 G, and 105 SG. The B stood for Boy, the G for Girl and the S for Sailor. There was a new 111c number for a 16 inch (40.5 cm.) doll. The same pictures were used for the mask-face dolls as in 1912 but they were given new names H.C. was called Nancy and 21c was called Betty.

National Cloak & Suit Co. advertised an all-celluloid bent limb baby with painted hair and eyes, jointed at the neck and hips. Hts. 7, 9, and 14 in. (18, 23 and 35.5 cm.); priced 25¢ to $1.00.

1920: Many of the all-celluloid dolls wore molded clothes, especially bathing suits. Prices varied from 45¢ a dozen for a 3 inch (7.5 cm.) doll with jointed limbs to $4.50 for an 18½ in. (47 cm.) bent limb baby.

1925: The all-celluloid *Kewpies* came in small sizes and in black or white versions. Many of them were dressed in crêpe-paper clothes.

494. All-celluloid doll with molded hair, painted features, jointed shoulders. Original regional costume. H. 6½ in. (16.5 cm.). *Coleman Collection.*

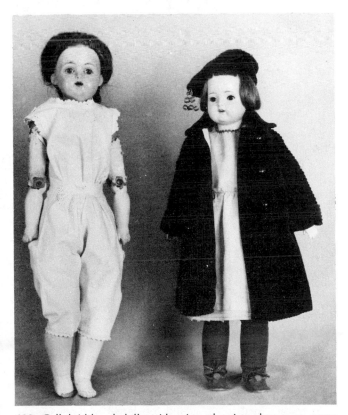

493. Celluloid-head dolls with wigs, sleeping glass eyes, open mouths. Left, head marked "K ☆ R//255" and the Turtle mark. H. 53 cm. (21 in.). Right, head marked "K ☆ R//255 Germany// No. 6." and the turtle mark of Rheinische Gummi und Celluloid Fabrik Co. H. 49 cm. (19½ in.). *Courtesy of the Collection Nederlands Kostuummuseum, The Hague. Photo by B. Frequin.*

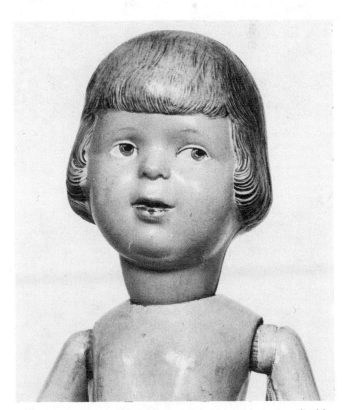

495. Celluloid socket head with molded blond hair, intaglio blue eyes, closed mouth, on a composition and wood ball-jointed body. Mark: Ill. 499. H. 16 in. (40.5 cm.). *Courtesy of the Margaret Woodbury Strong Museum. Photos by Harry Bickelhaupt.*

Small bent limb babies also came in black or white versions. Some of the novelty all-celluloid dolls included a *Mutt & Jeff* pair. The variety of clothes on all-celluloid dolls included regional costumes.

1927: *Butler Bros.* advertised celluloid dolls 2½ to 9 in. (6.5 to 23 cm.). The black dolls were 3½ and 6 in. (9 and 15 cm.). All-celluloid dolls also came with jointed shoulders and mohair wigs in 4, 6, and 9 inch (10, 15 and 23 cm.) hts.

1928: Kämmer & Reinhardt introduced their all-celluloid *My Rosy Darling* doll.

1929: Some of the all-celluloid dolls had rolling beads as pupils for their eyes.

After World War II. All-celluloid dolls were made in France and dressed by Minor in lavish Brittany costumes. ★

496. All-celluloid doll with molded hair, painted eyes, closed mouth, bent limbs. Original layette. Mark is the turtle of Rheinische Gummi und Celluloid Fabrik. H. 9 in. (23 cm.). *Courtesy of Jacqueline Andrews.*

498. All-celluloid type doll made of Loveloid has molded and painted features and clothes. The mouth is closed. Jointed at the shoulders so that the doll can simulate playing with the ball and tennis racquet which are in its hands. Mark on the back: "LOVELOID//REG. U.S. PAT. OFF.//PATENT 41045." Mark on bottom of skirt in the back: "133//   //JAPAN." *Courtesy of Pat Schoonmaker.*

497. Three celluloid shoulder heads made from the same mold. They have short blond hair, blue eyes and closed mouth. There are some differences in the handpainting which causes each head to appear slightly different. H. 2½ in. (6.5 cm.). *Courtesy of Mathias Wanke.*

499–500. Marks on celluloid dolls. No. 499 is on the doll in Ill. 495.

Celluloid Novelty Co. 1869–81. Newark, N.J. Made celluloid dolls.★

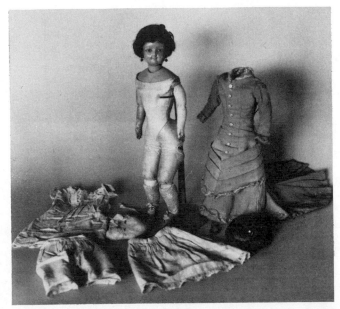

501A & B. Celluloid head and shoulder plate on a gusseted kid body. It has an auburn hair wig, stationary blue glass eyes, earrings pegged into the head with wood, closed mouth. Original clothes with a blue faille dress, a straw hat and a separate bustle that buttons around the waist. There is a possibility that this doll may have been made by the Celluloid Novelty Co. *Courtesy of the Museum of American Architecture and Decorative Arts, Houston, Texas. Photos by Becky Moncrief.*

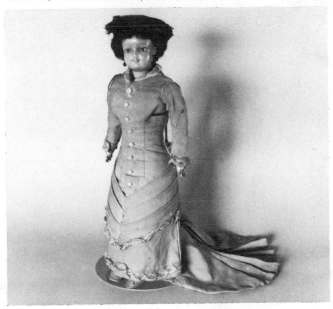

Celluloidwarenfabrik. See **Hunaeus, Dr. Paul.**

Celluloidwarenfabrik Babenhausen. See **Schöberl & Becker.**

Cellulosine (Cie. Parisienne de Cellulosine). 1925–28. Factory at Oyonnax, offices in Paris. Made celluloid dolls. Paris agent was *Jacques Helft.*★

Celtid. 1914. Trade name used by Rheinische Gummi und Celluloid Fabrik for a type of celluloid doll. (See Ill. 2215.)

Central Committee of Toy Industries. 1916. Britain. Committee of manufacturers who made wax, composition and cloth dolls.

Central Doll Manufacturing Co. 1917–21. New York City. Manufactured character dolls, child dolls, bent-limb baby dolls, and carnival dolls that were as large as 30 inches (76 cm.). Some of these dolls were dressed as soldiers, sailors, Red Cross nurses and clowns.★

Central Fibre Co. 1930 and later. South Gardiner, Me. Made dolls.

Century Doll Co. 1909–30. New York City. The company was founded by Max Scheuer, a pioneer in the toy business, and his sons Bert and Harold. Max Scheuer retired in 1926 and died in 1933. Century used *Kestner* bisque heads on many of their later dolls. In 1928/29 they merged with *Domec* to become the *Doll Corporation of America*, located in Lancaster, Pa.

1917: Advertised that their composition-head dolls had a few grooves through which the body was sewed to the head. The hands were wired to the cloth arm, making it almost impossible for the hands and head to come off. Their character dolls had a "velvet finish" and the heads were painted or wigged. They made the shoes worn on their dolls. Dolls came in hts. 10½ to 16½ in. (26.5–42 cm.).

1918: Introduced a new line of large dolls with sleeping eyes and wigs that cost up to $60 a dozen. These dolls were sold in Canada as well as the U.S.

1919: Advertised 250 new style Nos. with or without sleeping eyes and 8 new models which included the *Baby Bunting* line.

1920: They were among the first companies to advertise bisque-head dolls after World War I. These were jointed composition baby dolls with glass sleeping eyes and wigs. They came in a variety of hts. dressed and undressed; also 250 new style Nos. of cloth-body dolls with wigs and glass sleeping eyes.

1921: Introduced the *Fiji-Wigi* line of dolls designed by *Grace Corry*. Other dolls had bisque heads or composition heads on composition bodies. The bent limb babies and the straight limb child dolls with glass sleeping eyes and wigs came in 4 hts. and were dressed and undressed. There were 200 style Nos. and eight models of composition heads, hands and feet on cloth bodies that were dressed and had glass sleeping eyes and wigs. They called their composition "Wood Bisc."

1922–24: Listed *Mama* dolls, jointed dolls, and stuffed dolls.

1926: Kestner's bisque heads were used on baby doll, Mama doll and child doll bodies made in America. The Mama dolls began to have more slender legs. Century claimed they were the exclusive American agent for Kestner bisque heads. Some of these heads had eyelashes. The dolls wore lace trimmed dresses, silk socks and leather single strap slippers. Some of them had a ribbon bandeau in their hair. The child dolls came in 18 to 30 inch (45.5 to 76 cm.) hts. One of their new dolls was *Bottle Baby,* a doll that appeared to drink from its bottle but the liquid flowed from the bottle into its arm and back into the bottle.

1927: Many new character dolls with composition heads

were added, among them *Chuckles,* a smiling baby doll that could stand alone. Century Doll Co. was licensed by *Voices* to use their mama voices and criers.

1928: New dolls included *Pudgy Peggy* and the *Jantzen Bathing Tots* which were made under special arrangement with the Jantzen Knitting Mills. Century also featured a special Spring and Summer doll assortment. ★

502. Advertisement for Century dolls in PLAYTHINGS, August 1924.

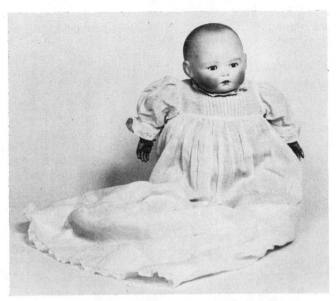

CENTURY DOLL C°.
Kestner Germany
505

CENTURY
DOLL CO.
506 N. Y.

504–506. Marks of Century dolls. No. 505 is on the doll in Ill. 503.

503A & B. Century baby doll made by Kestner. The bisque head has slightly molded and painted hair, sleeping blue glass eyes, and closed mouth on a "frog"-shaped cloth body with dimpled celluloid hands. Original clothes consisting of a long white cotton dress, flannel slip, underskirt, flannel diaper, and long stockings. Mark: Ill. 505. H. 14 in. (35.5 cm.). *Courtesy of the Margaret Woodbury Strong Museum. Photos by Harry Bickelhaupt.*

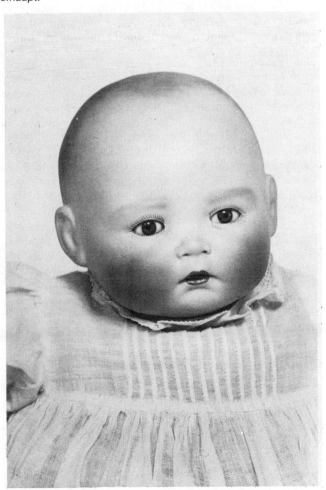

Cerbelaud, Edouard. 1860–75. Paris. Made dolls. Purchased the toy business from his brother-in-law but went into bankruptcy in 1875. One of his creditors was *Roth & Rau.*

Cereta. 1904. Trade name for a premium doll of the American Cereal Co. of Chicago, manufacturers of cereals including Quaker Oats. The doll had a bisque head, sleeping eyes, fully jointed body, gauze dress, picture-type hat, stockings, and kid slippers with buckles. Ht. 17 in. (43 cm.); price 75¢ plus 2 Cereta checks.

Cerveau, Joseph. 1829. Philadelphia, Pa. Advertised "Improved dolls."

Chable, Jean. 1830s, Bonnétable. 1842–67. Paris. Made dolls. He failed in 1863 and again in 1867 according to Mme. Poisson, curator of the Roybet-Fould Museum.

Chad Valley. 1917–30 and later. Harbonne near Birmingham, England. (Also known as Johnson Bros.[†]) Around 1849 two brothers, Joseph and Alfred Johnson, established a printing firm in Birmingham. The Chad Valley plant was built in 1897 and toys were made there. Dolls do not appear to have been made until about 1917. The director of the firm in 1919 was A. J. Johnson, son of Alfred Johnson. At that time they exported to Canada, South Africa and Australia. In the early 1920s they were represented in New York by *Bush Terminal.* In the late 1920s, *Louis Wolf* was their sole agent in the U.S. and Canada. After World War I they took over the firm of *Roberts Bros.* of Gloucester. They were part of the National Scheme for the employment of disabled men and were contractors to His Majesty's Government. They made various types of cloth dolls, and their earliest dolls predominately had stockinet faces; around 1924 they began to produce hand-painted felt faces on dolls made of velvet or velveteen. They made dolls of various qualities; the cheapest ones were cloth dolls with their clothes printed on them and without modeling. These were listed in Chad Valley catalogs, 1923–1929, and were named *Beaver, Jean,*

Peggy, Peter Pan, Pixie, Red Cloud and *Sorna*. Their best dolls had hand woven combable wigs, "veined glass" eyes, molded hand-painted faces, removable fashionable clothes which nearly always included a hat. They used imitation fur trimming from 1923 on, but felt appliqué trimming was even more extensive, beginning in 1926. The dresses and suits were extremely short, exposing long legs on many of the dolls. Cloches were favorites. Some dolls wore coats as well as dresses and hats. Only a few dolls were dressed as boys. Five out of the many hundreds of doll types shown in Chad Valley catalogs, 1920–1930, were dressed as babies and one of these had a bisque head, which was probably purchased elsewhere and the doll assembled by Chad Valley. Most of their dolls represented children; there do not appear to have been any long-limbed lady dolls. A considerable number of their dolls were novelty dolls such as *Jack-O-Jingles,* the *Road Scout Mascot*, Rattle dolls, *Mephistopheles,* the *Tango Tar Baby,* the *Rajah, Golliwoggs,* Pierrot, Pierette, Nurse, Footballer and so forth.

Probably the most famous Chad Valley dolls in the 1920s were those based on the designs of *Mabel Lucie Attwell*. Another famous doll designer was *Norah Wellings,* who worked for Chad Valley from 1919 to 1926. Later *Hilda Cowham* also designed some of their dolls. In 1930 Chad Valley made a *Princess Elizabeth* doll to represent the little four year old princess. This doll is not to be confused with the Chad Valley dolls representing an older Princess Elizabeth and Princess Margaret. These were made in the late 1930s.

1917: Chad Valley made character dolls, dressed dolls and mechanical voices for dolls.

1919: 12 designs of stockinet dolls with stationary or sleeping glass eyes and combable wigs; jointed or unjointed; dressed as girls or boys.

1920: The following stockinet dolls were listed in the Chad Valley catalog and numbered in the order given: *Susanne, Joan, Lady Betty, Belle, Jack, Peggy, Bobby, Red Riding Hood, Irish Molly, Pretty Prue, Zoe, Peter,* Jack-O-Jingles, *Black Sambo,* Nurse, Chef, *Pierrot, Pierette,* Welsh Girl, *Dorothy, Poppy,* Footballer, *Boy Blue, Nora, Bob Sleigh, Little Cresta, Miss Muffet, Babs, Marjorie, Seaside Sue* and *Beach Knut.* Also there was a cloth doll named *Pat M'Gee.*

The first 12 dolls in the above mentioned stockinet group were the most expensive ones. These dolls had hand woven wigs that could be combed. Their cheapest dolls were smaller, and lacked these refinements.

1921: Almost the same group of dolls was listed in this year as in 1920 except Black Sambo and Pat M'Gee were replaced by *Dickie, Billie,* a *Jester* and *Dancing Doll,* girl and boy. The most expensive dolls, hts. 12 or 13 in. (30.5 or 33 cm.) came with "C. V." (Chad Valley) patent wrist watches. The smaller dolls were 9 to 11½ in. (23 to 29 cm.) tall. All the dolls were stockinet.

1923: The stockinet dolls were named *La Petite Caresse* and given the trademark *Aerolite*. They had real hair wigs, handcolored faces and wore velveteen or plush costumes of a single style trimmed with imitation fur around the neck and rim of their turbans. Muffs could be purchased separately. The dolls came in four hts. 11, 13, 16 and 18 in. (28, 33, 40.5 and 45.5 cm.).

1924: There were several innovations in this year. The hexagonal tag with the words "Chad Valley //HYGIENIC// Fabric Toys" becomes evident on the dolls. Except for *Baby Doll* (dressed as a child), Jack, *Jill* and Jack-O-Jingles, the dolls were no longer described as stockinet but they were "kapok-stuffed," had handpainted felt or fabric faces. Some of the Caresse dolls were described as late as 1928 as having stockinet faces, so presumably both types of faces were made. Velvette was used for the bodies.

They still had woven combable wigs of real hair and removable clothes. The least expensive of the La Caresse dolls was *Pretty Jane* dressed in a check print cloth. Other La Petite Caresse dolls included *Caresse* dressed in mohair plush or woolly fur; *Olga, Betty* and others dressed in velveteen came in five hts. 11, 16, 18, 21 and 25 in. (28, 40.5, 45.5, 53.5 and 63.5 cm.).

Some of the large sizes also came with a mama voice for 40¢ extra. The quality dolls were the new *Bambina* and Lucie-Attwell dolls. These were both 19 inches (48 cm.) tall, and had handpainted felt faces and velvette bodies. The Lucie-Attwell dolls represented a child younger than the Bambinas; the faces of the Lucie-Attwell dolls were broader. Both types of dolls had the eyes glancing to the side. Two novelty dolls only appeared for this one year. They were *Dan* and *Dolly* based on the designs of *Mr. Williamson* whose drawings were featured in several newspapers.

1924–25: Obtained a British patent for putting glass eyes into a doll's head made of textiles or felt that had been stiffened with shellac or starch.

1926: Innovations this year were the Tango Tar Baby that could walk and dance and the Caresse dolls riding tricycles. There were new costumes for many of the La Petite Caresse dolls including a group of organdy frocks. The Lucie-Attwell dolls came in style Nos. 700–720 and the Bambinas from 750–804, according to their costumes. About half of the Lucie-Attwell dolls were dressed as boys while all of the Bambinas were young girls or babies. Bent-limb baby Bambinas and La Petite Caresse dolls were introduced this year; they had chubby faces and were dressed in baby attire including some in long dresses. The babies each came in four hts. 11½ to 22 in. (29 to 56 cm.) including long dresses. Both Lucie-Attwell and Bambina child dolls were in size 0, 14½ in. (37 cm.); size 1, 16 in. (40.5 cm.) and size 2, 18½ in. (47 cm.). The veined glass eyes of the Lucie-Attwell dolls glanced to the side, while many of the Bambinas looked straight ahead. The Bambina and Lucie-Attwell dolls were used in a school setting along with a doll dressed to represent the School Mistress. Another doll was dressed in a Peter Pan outfit. Cheaper versions of Bambina were produced.

1927: The Tango Tar Baby, the dolls on tricycles and the Peter Pan doll were no longer shown. The largest sized Caresse doll was now 24 in. (61 cm.) instead of 25 in. (63.5 cm.). Some new costumes were found on Caresse dolls. Over half of the Bambina dolls were in new style costumes while less than half of the Lucie-Attwell dolls had new type outfits. A black doll, *Sambo,* was new among the Lucie-Attwell dolls as were a pair of less expensive Caresse type girl dolls, ht. 15 in. (38 cm.). Jack-O-Jingles was back, dressed in velveteen and still 15 in. (38 cm.) high. As an innovation the dolls were packed in Bye-Bye boxes shaped like a bed and with a drawer beneath the bed to hold bedclothes. The Bambina and Lucie-Attwell dolls were packed in gilt bedsteads while the cheaper Caresse dolls had wood-grain bed boxes.

1928: Some of the Caresse dolls had movable felt heads and hand-painted faces, while other Caresse dolls had stockinet heads, bodies and arms. The largest size Caresse dolls had mama voices. The Bambina baby dolls were made only in the smallest size. The Lucie-Attwell Caresse dolls were deleted. Jack-O-Jingles remained. New in 1928 were the *Caresse Imps,* 14 in. (35.5 cm.) high; the *Carina* dolls that would sit and stand and came in 6 hts. up to 30 inches (76 cm.); and Bambetta dolls of a quality between the Caresse and Bambina dolls that came in 14 inch (35.5 cm.), 17 inch (43 cm.) and 19 inch (48 cm.) hts. The Bambetta dolls had the highest model numbers—over 1200.

1929: All the groups of dolls, Caresse, Caresse Imps, Carene, Carina, Bambetta, Bambina, and Lucie-Attwell, had some old models and some new models. Jack-O-Jingles and the School Mistress were still listed. A new doll was the black Golliwogg, made in four hts. *Woolly-Wag* was used as a trademark.

1930: Numerous innovations were made in 1930. A 17½ inch (44.5 cm.) doll was made to represent Princess Elizabeth. A group of black dolls called *"Niggers"* including *Nabob, Rajah, Carolina* and three others, numbered 616, 618 and 623 were new as were also the *Road Scout Mascots* A A. and R. A. C. of felt. A baby doll with a bisque head came in four hts. 16, 17, 23 and 25½ in. (40.5, 43, 58.5 and 65 cm.). This appears to include the long baby dress. A 14 inch (35.5 cm.) doll style No. 613 was dressed as a pixie and No. 453 in hts. 13½ and 14½ in. (34 and 37 cm.) was dressed as a rabbit with a human face. All of the Caresse, Caresse Imp, Bambina, and Lucie-Attwell dolls wore new costumes. Only one Lucie-Attwell doll was shown in the catalog, this was *Snookums.* An entirely new doll was made of washable imitation flesh cloth and dressed in felt. It was made in three hts. 14, 17, and 19 in. (35.5, 43 and 48 cm.) and given the number 1211, the highest number shown in the Chad Valley catalogs up through 1930. This does not mean that there had been 1211 different models as the various series were assigned groups of numbers with some spare ones. For example the Lucie-Attwell dolls began with number 700 and went up to 734 but the Bambina dolls started at 750, skipping 735–749, and rose to 911. Usually a single model in various sizes was designated as 1211/1, 1211/2 and 1211/3 or 700/0, 700/1, and 700/3 for example. (See Ills. 146, 224, and 410.)

1938: Chad Valley was granted the Royal Warrant of Appointment "Toymakers to Her Majesty the Queen." Cloth labels on the soles of the feet of the Chad Valley dolls have been found to read "THE CHAD VALLEY CO. LTD.//[British royal coat of arms]// TOYMAKERS TO//H. M., THE QUEEN." Another cloth label on the other foot was "HYGIENIC TOYS//MADE IN ENGLAND BY//CHAD VALLEY CO. LTD." The cloth label used on the clothes read "MADE IN ENGLAND//—BY THE—//CHAD VALLEY Co. Ltd."★

507A & B. Bambina series felt face doll made by Chad Valley. A doll just like this was chosen by Queen Mary (wife of George V), as her favorite Chad Valley doll. Its blonde mohair is sewn on in strips. The glass eyes are blue. The mouth is closed and the lips are of different shades as seen on Lenci dolls. The body is velvet. Original clothes. Pink rayon dress has blue felt circles and edging. Marks: See Ills. 510 & 511. H. 14 in. (35.5 cm.). *Courtesy of Margaret Woodbury Strong Museum. Photos by Harry Bickelhaupt.*

508. Chad Valley doll designed by Mabel Lucie Attwell. It has a felt head that turns; a mohair wig; brown glass eyes looking to the side, smiling single line mouth; velvet body jointed at the shoulders and hips. Original footwear. Cloth label stitched onto the sole of the foot. H. 14 in. (35.5 cm.). *Courtesy of Magda Byfield.*

509. Chad Valley doll with a felt head having a zigzag seam similar to the Lenci seams. It has a brunette wig glued on, painted brown eyes, closed mouth, velvet body and original regional costume; white cloth label with red letters on foot reads, "HYGIENIC TOYS//MADE IN ENGLAND BY//CHAD VALLEY CO., LTD." H. 18½ in. (47 cm.). *Courtesy of the Margaret Woodbury Strong Museum. Photo by Harry Bickelhaupt.*

510

–Chad Valley–
"BAMBINA"
511 (REGᵈ.& PAT.)   **512**

510–512. Marks on Chad Valley cloth dolls. Usually the mark is on the bottom of a foot. No. 510 shows a Chad Valley tag. No. 511 shows mark on the bottom of the foot of Queen Mary's doll.

Challenge Patent Washable Dolls. 1890s–1902. Trade name of a doll with composition head, glass eyes, wig, composition arms and legs with painted footwear, on a cloth torso. Distributed by *Butler Bros.*

1890s: Seven Hts. 18, 20, 24, 28½, 30, 32 and 35½ in. (45.5, 51, 61, 72.5, 76, 81, and 89.5 cm.).

1902: Same as 1890s except instead of an 18 in. (45.5 cm.) doll, there was one 26 in. (66 cm.).

Chalory, Vve (Widow). 1893–96. Paris. Produced all-celluloid and part celluloid dolls, including dolls named *Bébé Leger.*★

Chalté, François (Chalté & Leborgne). 1852–68. Paris. Made dolls. In 1860 he had nine employees but he later fell ill and failed in 1868, according to Mme. Poisson, curator of the Roybet-Fould Museum.★

Chambre Syndicale des Fabricants de Jouets et Jeux et Engins Sportif. 1886–1928 and later. Paris. Trade organization composed of French toy manufacturers. In 1927–28 *M. Pintel* was the president and *Decamps* was the treasurer of this organization.

1886: Registered in France "ARTICLE//FRANÇAIS." in a triangle as a trademark.

1897: Registered in France the same trademark but with MARQUE above one side and DÉPOSÉE above the other side. Under the bottom of the triangle was No. where the appropriate number was to be inserted.

1920s: The following numbers have been recorded but the same number was not always listed with the same company and a company was often found having different numbers listed. As yet the significance of the numbers has not been determined.

MEMBERS OF THE CHAMBRE SYNDICALE	
1. *G. Vichy*	149. *Société Française de Fabrication de Bébés & Jouets*
5. *Henri Alexandre*	
13. *Falck-Roussel*	
71. *Unis France*	161. *Alexandre Lefebvre*
85. *L. Lambert*	226. *G. Geoffroy*
106. *Dehais*	264. *G. Renault & Bon-Dufour*
131. *M. Pintel Fils*	
134. *G. Decamps* (*Roullet & Decamps*)	316. *E. Bossuat*

Other members included: *Henri Bellet, Boutteville, G. Brunet Fils, Cardon-Laghez, N. Clerc* (Les Fils de N. Clerc), *Delasson, Delattre, H. Delcourt, B. Derolland & B. Delacoste, Établissement Bognier-Burnet, Giraud-Sauveur, Grout, Guénucho, Mme. J. Hecquet, Hubert, Jeux & Jouets Français, Lang-Guillemaut, Les Poupées Artistiques Française, André Martel, Masson, Migault Fils, Charles Rouaud, Société du Caoutchouc Manufacturé, Société Industrielle de Celluloid, Tanagra, Tissier & Cie., Armand Weill.*★

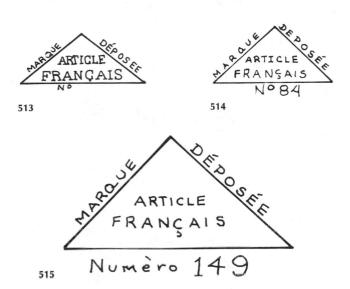

513   514

515

513–515. Marks used by members of the Chambre Syndicale des Fabricants de Jouets Français.

Chantilly, Cie. 1924–28. Paris. Factories at Montreuil and Lilas. Specialized in unbreakable dolls' heads of silica. These appear to be a ceramic head.★

Chantrain(e), E. 1928–30. Brussels, Belgium. Manufactured and exported dolls called *Marvell. W. Seelig* was the factory agent in London.

Chaperon Rouge (Red Riding Hood). 1910. Cloth doll dressed as a girl in removable Red Riding Hood style cape and sold at *Printemps.* Hts. 35 and 43 cm. (14 and 17 in.); priced $1.78 and $2.50. (See also **Little Red Riding Hood** and **Red Riding Hood.**)

Chapsal, E. 1928–29. Paris. Made dolls that sucked.

Character Art Dolls. 1919. Line of dolls with composition heads, arms, and feet made by *Ideal.* These dolls had molded hair, sleeping eyes, and some of them had molded boots. The line included *Barefoot Boy, Knickerbocker Boy, Middy Girl, Sunbonnet Girl* and *Uneeda Boy.* Five hts. 12, 13, 14, 15 and 16 inches, (30.5, 33, 35.5, 38 and 40.5 cm.). Not all of the dolls came in all of these sizes.

Character Dolls. The primary definition of a character doll is the representation of real people especially babies and children. However the toy trade often refers to unusual looking dolls especially those representing the comic cartoon characters such as *Happy Hooligan, Max and Moritz* and so forth

as character dolls. Most of the character dolls were products of the twentieth century and the *Munich Art dolls* in the first decade of this century aroused the interest in character dolls. Soon *Kämmer & Reinhardt,* the *Société Française de Bébés & Jouets* (S.F.B.J.) and many others were making dolls that resembled real children and babies. In 1913 TOYS AND NOVELTIES defined character dolls as "Ones modeled and painted from living models of the nations they represent." In the 1920s *Boudoir* dolls were called character dolls.

1910: *Gebrüder Heubach* dolls represented children and ladies.

1911: Nouvelles Galeries *(Ménagère?)* advertised a character bébé that was demiarticulated, had stationary eyes, what appeared to be flocked hair, and wore a chemise. Four hts. 33, 37, 42 and 49 cm. (13, 14½, 16½ and 19½ in.); priced 59¢ to $1.45 each.

Character dolls with sleeping eyes began to be advertised.

1913: TOYS AND NOVELTIES reported, "Word comes from Germany that the popularity of the character doll is waning. But the orders for some of these dolls continues to be strong." Then a few months later the same magazine reported that character dolls were very popular: "These dolls represent infants with short hair, wondering eyes [flirting eyes], tongues protruding from the mouth and a general air of babyhood. Other character dolls look like school girls and boys, their expression being more stern than the babies' expressions."

Lafayette advertised Character Babies with sleeping eyes and wig. The two smallest sizes were dressed in a chemise, the others in a silk tricot costume. Seven hts. 20, 25, 31, 37, 42, 48 and 65 cm. (8, 10, 12, 14½, 16½, 19 and 25½ in.); priced $2.15 to $7.00 each for the babies in the silk tricot outfits.

1914: TOYS AND NOVELTIES in May 1914 told of the part that H. G. Wells had in the development of character dolls.

"Rag baby dolls and character dolls are a prominent feature of the doll trade and the latter especially has provided some sensational features for the coming season. The old style wax doll, either put out in a little shift or dressed, is still of course a tremendous seller, but since the ice was first broken some years ago with the Golliwog a thousand other varieties of dolls have been marketed. Since H. G. Wells, the famous English novelist, wrote his big-selling book on floor games the trade in character dolls has been still further stimulated. It will be remembered that in this book Wells described how he provided extensive indoor games for his children. . . .

" . . . The children were encouraged to draw islands, countries, peninsulas, lakes and what not on a large scale. Then toys were bought to enable them to build cities, harbors, lighthouses, churches, town halls and the rest. . . . It was then that he hit his big difficulty. How was population to be supplied? Soldiers could be secured and sailors, too, but he found the market short of policemen and other well known types of this world's inhabitants. Since then, as I have indicated, the trade in these character figures has been wakened up and an up-to-date father following Wells' lines would find himself capable of making a country almost down to its most minute details."

This appears to be a broader interpretation of the meaning of the term "character doll" than is used by many collectors. Here the costumes appear to be the important factor.

1915: The *New Era Novelty Co.* advertised their "Original character dolls such as soldiers, sailors, jockeys, baby dolls, etc."

1919: *Character Art Dolls* made by *Ideal.*

1923: *La Place Clichy* advertised two types of character bébés; both had sleeping eyes. The smaller ones were dressed in chemise and had a hair bow and pacifier. They came in four hts. 17, 20, 24 and 39 cm. (6½, 8, 9½ and 15½ in.). The larger ones were dressed in a tricot suit and came in four hts. 38, 46, 52, and 60 cm. (15, 18, 20½ and 23½ in.).

The *Louvre* store also advertised character bébés. These dolls representing children had bisque heads, sleeping eyes, hair eyelashes. Five hts. 34, 36, 46, 52 and 68 cm. (13½, 14, 18, 20½ and 27 in.). (See also **Chronology** and **Horsman.**)★

„Fräul'n, noch a Halbe!"

516. Puppen Reform character dolls shown by Hermann Tietz as illustrated by DIE WELT DER FRAU, November, 1908. The caption reads "Fraulein still another half."

518. Bisque head character doll on composition body. S.F.B.J. mold #236 with wig, sleeping eyes, and an open-closed mouth. *Courtesy of Sotheby Parke Bernet Inc., N.Y.*

517. Group of character baby dolls with bisque heads and bent-limb composition baby bodies. The dolls are Simon & Halbig mold #1428, size 9; and unmarked baby with an open/closed mouth. Hs. 15 and 12 in. (38 and 30.5 cm.). *Courtesy of Sotheby Parke Bernet Inc., N.Y.*

519. Bisque head character boy made by Gebrüder Heubach with molded hair, blue intaglio eyes, open-closed mouth, and a ball-jointed composition body. Mark: 7604 and the Heubach sunburst (See sunburst in Ill. 1190). H. 14½ in. (37 cm.). *Courtesy of Sotheby Parke Bernet Inc., N.Y.*

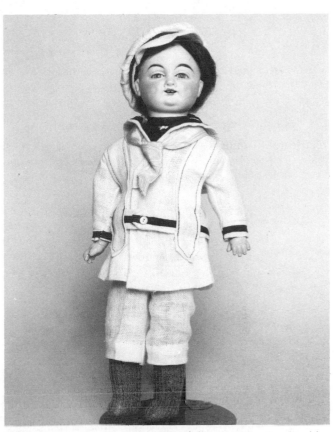

520. Bisque head character dolls dressed in commercial regional costumes, with composition bodies. The small pair in Tyrolean costumes have wigs, blue sleeping eyes, open mouths with teeth. The heads are marked "1309//L.//1." There is a possibility that these heads were made by Simon & Halbig for Louis Lindner. H. 10 in. (25.5 cm.). The large doll, marked "6969//5//Germany," in Dutch costume has a wig, brown sleeping eyes and a closed mouth. H. 17 in. (43 cm.). *Courtesy of Becky and Jay Lowe. Photo by Bill Holland.*

522A & B. Bisque head character doll with wig, sleeping blue glass eyes, open mouth, 2 upper teeth, dimples; has a jointed composition body. The mark on the head is embossed; see Ill. 523. H. 12 in. (30.5 cm.). *Courtesy of Paige Thornton.*

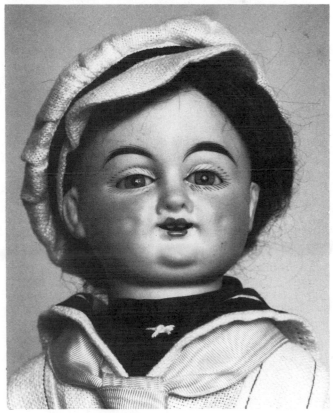

521. Bisque head character doll with skin wig, sleeping eyes, an open mouth, and a fully jointed composition body. Mark: "141." H. 14 in. (35.5 cm.). *Courtesy of Sotheby Parke Bernet Inc., N.Y.*

523. Mark embossed on character faced bisque head shown in Ill. 522.

Charles Lindbergh. See **Lindbergh** and **Our Lindy.**

Charleston Toddlers. 1926. Black all-composition dolls made for *Amberg* in Germany. They have wigs, painted eyes, molded and painted footwear.

524. Mark used for the Charleston Toddlers.

Charlie Chaplin. 1915–16. Made by *Amberg* using the same mold for the composition head as was used for *Oo-Gug-Luk.* This mold was designed by *Jeno Juszko.* The Charlie Chaplin hats were sold separately.

1915: TOYS AND NOVELTIES reported that in order to keep up with the demand, "they have been forced to discard the usual plaster moulds replacing them with metal ones." The metal ones were of brass. The dolls came in hts. 13 and 14½ in. (33 and 37 cm.).

1916: An animated version was made by Amberg. ★

Charlie Chaplin. 1916. *Hyman A. Abrahams* was the London agent for a "porcelain" (*British Ceramic*) doll version of Charlie Chaplin with a moving head.

Charlie Chaplin. 1916–20 and possibly later. Cloth doll made by *Dean.* It was a flat-faced printed *Knockabout* doll with a derby hat, cane and large feet. Ht. 11½ in. (29 cm.).

1920: Designated style no. 208.

1981: Dean reissued this doll.

Charlie Chaplin. 1917. Walking doll made by *Horsman.* Ht. 12 in. (30.5 cm.). Price $1.80.

Charlie Chaplin. 1917. Cloth doll made by *Hammond.*

Charlie Chaplin. 1917–18. Doll with composition head and hands, molded and painted hair and mustache, painted features, cloth body jointed at the shoulders and hips. It wore a black coat, black and white checked trousers, black felt derby and carried a cane. Distributed by *Butler Bros.* Ht. 30 in. (76 cm.).

Charlie Chaplin. 1920. Trade name of a doll manufactured by *Elektra.*

Charlie Chaplin. 1927. Trade name of a doll made of metal by *A. Bucherer.*

Charlier. 1925–30 and later. Paris. Made and exported dolls dressed in felt, silk and so forth.

1930–31: Advertised that they "executed all models after patterns."★

Charlot. 1916–22. Cloth doll created by *Mme. Vera Ouvré.* in 1916; one of many French dolls representing Charlie Chaplin.★

Charlotte Bubbles. Ca. 1926. Doll made by *Effanbee* as one of the *Bubbles* line. (See also **Betty.**)

Charlotte Dolls. 1923–28. Line of *Mama* dolls made by *Bergfeld* and his successor, the National French Fancy Novelty Co. The label on these dolls read: "I AM//CHARLOTTE//The New//Unbreakable Doll//I've come to make//You Happy and Jolly//I Talk while you Walk//And Walk while you Talk//I'm dressed in the very//best and Sleep while//you Rest."

1927: The line had slim bodies, wigs, moving eyes and came dressed.

1928: Name of the line was changed to Sunshine dolls which included *Miss Sunshine.*★

"CHARLOTTE"
DOLLS
AND
National French Animals
"CHARLOTTE" DOLLS offer one of the market's finest lines featuring slim body dolls with wigs, moving eyes and dainty costumes.
National French Fancy Novelty Co.
Factory: 2055 Pitkin Ave., Brooklyn, N. Y.
Salesrooms: 215 4th Ave., New York

525. Charlotte dolls as advertised in PLAYTHINGS, May, 1927. These dolls were made in Brooklyn, N.Y. by the National French Fancy Novelty Co.

Charm. 1927. U.S. trademark for dolls registered by *S. Blechman & Sons.*

Charmant Bébé. 1918. Advertised by *Printemps* as a newborn character baby with sleeping eyes, hair eyelashes, wig, and wearing a chemise. It came in a bent limb version. Six hts. 20, 25, 31, 37, 42 and 48 cm. (8, 10, 12, 14½, 16½ and 19 in.); priced $1.65 to $7.40. The straight-limb fully jointed version came in six hts. 33, 38, 45, 52, 60 and 69 cm. (13, 15, 17½, 23½ and 27 in.); priced $4.40 to $13.80. (See also **Bébé Charmant.**)

Charms. 1920–21. Trade name of dolls made by the *Mutual Doll Co.*

Charpentier, Thomi. 1923. Los Angeles, Calif. Former Follies dancer who made *Boudoir* type dolls.

Charterhouse Brand. 1917–18. Line of baby dolls with *British Ceramic* heads and cloth bodies dressed in long or short baby clothes. Dolls were advertised by *Turnbull.*

Chase, Martha Jenks (née Wheaton). Ca. 1889–1930 and later. Pawtucket, R.I. In 1919 her son, R. D. Chase, joined the firm. Martha Chase died in 1925 and her husband and/or her son carried on the business. The stockinet dolls were made for at least ten years after her death. In 1952 her grandson, Robert Chase, made vinyl-head dolls. These were still being made in the 1970s.

Martha Chase made dolls with heads of stockinet stretched over a mask. The masks were made in molds reproduced from bisque-head dolls. The stockinet was sized and then painted with oils. Pink sateen and later other materials were used for the bodies. It is possible that some of the dolls that resemble Chase dolls may have been made by other doll makers.

Mrs. Florence Smith Mitchell worked for Mrs. Chase for a number of years and experimented with making dolls. Allegedly one of these had hair made of string.

1903: *F. A. O. Schwarz* advertised Chase dolls, hts. 16 and 20 in. (40.5 and 51 cm.); priced $3.75 and $4.50.

1904: *R. H. Macy* sold four hts. 16, 17, 21 and 24 in. (40.5, 43, 53.5 and 61 cm.).

1907: R. H. Macy advertised a 19 in. (48 cm.) ht.

1908: R. H. Macy advertised five hts. 14, 16, 20, 23 and 26 in. (35.5, 40.5, 51, 58.5 and 66 cm.); priced $2.79 to $6.89. This was their most expensive undressed doll.

1909: The Chase advertisement for their dolls in the LADIES' HOME JOURNAL read: "Made of clean cotton cloth by skilled art workers. Beautifully handpainted. May be easily washed and cleansed with warm water. . . . Sold undressed, but suits to fit can be procured if ordered. When old and worn they may be repaired and repainted by sending to the makers. Made in five hts. 16, 20, 24, 27, and 30 in. [40.5, 51, 61, 68.5, and 76 cm.]. All first-class dealers in the United States sell these dolls."

1911–12: Advertised by *Gimbel Bros.* Had handpainted faces and limbs. Six hts. 9, 15, 20, 23, 25½ and 29½ in. (23, 38, 51, 58.5, 65 and 75 cm.); priced $3.00 to $10.00. These dolls were almost twice as expensive as Gimbel's finest bisque-head dolls.

1916: *Wanamaker* advertised dressed Chase dolls; four hts. 12, 16, 20 and 24 in. (30.5, 40.5, 51, and 61 cm.); priced $2.50 to $5.25.

1917: TOYS AND NOVELTIES commented on Martha Chase and her dolls. "The big toy stores of Boston, New York and other cities learned of these dolls, and begged her to let them sell some. It was then that the fame of this woman and her beautiful creation began to spread. Orders reach her now from every part of the country, from China, Sweden, India, Australia, and all of the countries of the globe—from royalty itself."

Also TOYS AND NOVELTIES quoted the following letter from Martha Chase: " 'I first made the dolls about 28

years ago [1889] as an amusement and to see what I could do. For several years I did this and gave the dolls away to the neighborhood children. Then, by chance, a store buyer saw one and insisted upon my taking an order. That was about 20 years ago, and since then there has been a gradual increase in the business. The dolls have gained recognition by their merits, as I have advertised them but very little. Then some one who knew about them asked me to make one adult size, to use in the hospital training schools and from that has developed another new industry. Now [1917] we are making dolls that can be immersed in water and used in child welfare work."

1920: Dolls included character dolls, educational dolls and bathtub dolls. Hts. 12 to 30 in. (30.5 to 76 cm.). Priced $4.00 to $10.00.

1923: Dolls were made with Princess Sateen covered bodies or with stockinet bodies that were waterproofed and thickly covered with paint. Some of the sateen body dolls had molded bobbed hair. All of them came in six hts. 12, 16, 20, 24, 27 and 30 in. (30.5, 40.5, 51, 61, 68.5 and 76 cm.); priced $3.50 to $9.00 retail. The following separate clothes were available for all of the sizes; girls' and babies' suits, boys' suits, bloomer suits, rompers, dresses, girls' underwear of Berkeley, boys' underwear of stockinet, caps, shoes and stockings.

The following special Chase stockinet dolls were made: *Alice-in-Wonderland, Duchess,* Frog Footman, *George Washington, Mad Hatter, Mammy Nurse, Pickanninies,* and *Tweedle-dum and Tweedle-dee.* Soft cloth dolls named *Bessy Brooks, Silly Sally* and *Tommy Snooks* were also made.

F. A. O. SCHWARZ ADVERTISED CHASE DOLLS			
Size No.	Height in.	cm.	Price
0	13	33	$3.50
1	17	43	$4.50
2	20	51	$5.50
3	24	61	$6.75
5	30	76	$8.75

1927: The baby doll used by the nursing service at Knoxville, Tenn. was named Knoxanna.

1930: Advertisement showed dolls with short hair and dolls with the later Dutch bobbed hair. Dolls came dressed and undressed.★

Chatel et Louapt. Before 1867. France. Distributed dolls and failed in 1867. One of their creditors was *Wislizenus,* a German doll maker.

Chatterbox. 1923. Trade name of a doll made by *Progressive Toy Co.* The doll had a painted face, sleeping eyes, a wig and wore rompers. It called "Mama" at regular intervals for 60 times in 15 minutes even when it walked, slept or sat. Ht. 24½ in. (62 cm.).

Chaufour. 1871–75. Paris. Dressed and distributed fashion-

526. Chase stockinet doll with painted brown hair, gray-blue eyes, applied ears, and a closed mouth. The head and limbs are heavily covered with oil paint. H. 21½ in. (54.5 cm.). *Courtesy of Sotheby Parke Bernet Inc., N.Y.*

527. Chase stockinet doll with a heavy oil paint covering on the head, arms, and legs; painted blue eyes; ears attached; closed mouth; jointed at the shoulders, elbows, hips, and knees. H. 23 in. (58.5 cm.). *Courtesy of Sotheby Parke Bernet Inc., N.Y.*

528. Chase stockinet doll with painted blond hair and blue eyes, closed mouth. Contemporary clothes. H. 12 in. (30.5 cm.). *Courtesy of Sotheby Parke Bernet Inc., N.Y.*

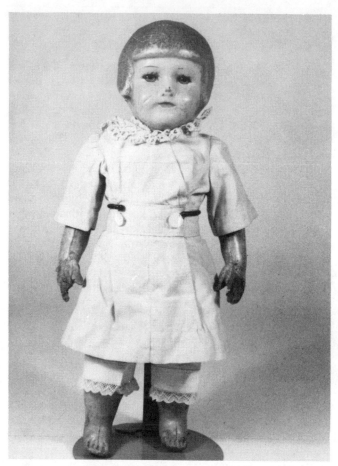

529. Chase cloth doll with molded and painted hair and eyes, closed mouth, probably made in the 1920s. H. 12½ in. (31.5 cm.). *Courtesy of Richard Withington. Photo by Barbara Jendrick.*

type dolls with bisque heads, lower arms and legs; especially those with kid over wood bodies, jointed at the shoulders, elbows, hips and knees. A white paper label on the chest of some of these dolls read, "AU BONHEUR DES ENFANTS// MAISON//CHAUFOUR//PASSAGE DU SAUMON 29, 31, & 33//PARIS." Apparently the name of Chaufour's shop was Au Bonheur des Enfants.

One of these dolls was 18 in. (45.5 cm.) tall.★

Check Marks. Marks often found on *Jumeau* dolls' heads. These marks usually in red, and varying in shape and size are also found on marked E. D. heads and on heads that have no other mark. It should not be assumed that all heads with check marks were made by Jumeau or their successor *Société Française de Fabrication de Bébés & Jouets.*

Checkeni, Dominico. 1866–85. Marion and New Haven, Conn.; Brooklyn, N.Y. Patented a waxed multi-face doll. See Ill. 530.★

Checker Betty and Checker Bobby. 1922. Trade name of dolls with checkered cloth faces made by *Sherwin.* These dolls were also referred to as "Greenwich Village Creation."

Chedebois. 1927–30 and later. Paris. Made art dolls and fetishes.

A

B

530A, B, C, & D. Wax-over-composition dolls' head made according to the Checkeni patent of 1866. The head rolls around to show all four faces as seen in the group of pictures above. The composition is a dark substance similar to the pseudo gutta-percha used for daguerreotype cases. Three of the faces have blue glass eyes. Two of the mouths are closed and two have round holes. H. of head only, 6 in. (15 cm.). *Courtesy of the Margaret Woodbury Strong Museum. Photos by Harry Bickelhaupt.*

C

D

Cheerio Doll. 1927. U.S. trademark for dolls registered by *Jeanne de M. Brumback.*

Cheery Boy. 1916. Trade name of doll style no. 201. made by *Trion.* The doll wore a striped shirt with a pocket and short pants.

Chelsea Art Doll Makers. See Puslowski.

Cheney Bros. 1923. Exhibited dolls at the second International Silk Exposition at the Grand Central Palace. Their dolls included the Fragonard group designed by *George Barbier* representing the costumes worn at the Bal du Grand Prix in Paris and executed by *Mme. Pulliche.*

Chéret & Moreau. 1900. France. Moreau won a bronze medal at the Paris Exposition.★

531. Chérie bisque shoulder head has a blond wig, stationary blue glass eyes, pierced ears, open mouth with teeth. Mark: "Limoges//Chérie." H. 17½ in. (44.5 cm.). *Courtesy of Sotheby Parke Bernet Inc., N.Y.*

532. Chérie doll made by Lanternier in France. The bisque socket head is yellow in color and the painting of the usual dolly face gives it an Oriental appearance. It has a black wig, brown glass eyes, pierced ears, open mouth with seven upper teeth and a fully jointed composition and wooden body. Mark: Ill. 533. H. 22 in. (56 cm.). *Courtesy of Iverna and Irving Foote. Photo by Irving Foote.*

FABRICATION
FRANCAISE

AL ε Cᴵᴱ
LIMOGES
Cherie 8

FABRICATION
FRANÇAISE

AL ε Cⁱᵉ
LIMOGES
cherie 7

533–534. Marks on the Chérie bisque heads. No. 533 is on the doll in Ill. 532.

Chérie. Name on bisque heads made by *Lanternier* in Limoges. See Ills. 531, 532, 533 and 534.★

Cherub Baby. 1930. Cloth doll designed and created by *Madame Alexander.* The doll was stuffed with kapok and dressed in a variety of costumes. It represented a baby younger than *Chubby Baby.*

Cherub Jenny and Cherub Johnny. 1923. *Tru-to-Life* cloth baby dolls made by *Dean.* Hts. 10½, 13 and 16 in. (26.5, 33 and 40.5 cm.).

Cherubs. 1920s. Cloth dolls made by *Dean* and dressed as boys in art silk suits or as girls in embroidered dresses and bonnets. Ht. 3 in. (7.5 cm.).

Cherubs. 1926. A new born baby doll with unbreakable head, bent limb jointed composition body. Distributed by *Whyte, Ridsdale* in England. Ht. 8½ in. (21.5 cm.).

Chervy, M. See Mail.

Chesham Brand. 1916. Dolls with shoulder heads of composition or of *British Ceramic;* came with or without wigs. The arms on the cloth bodies were usually of the same material as the head. These dolls were distributed by *Ellison, Rees* under the trademark Ellarco.

Chessa, Gigi. 1922 and later. Turin, Italy. A painter who worked for *Lenci* and probably designed some of their dolls' clothes. Born 1898 in Turin, died in 1935. One of his paintings was in the Gallery of Modern Art, in Florence, Italy.

Chessler Co., The. 1920–30 and later. Baltimore, Md. Manufactured cloth dolls and dolls with composition heads.

1920: Made two types of cloth dolls with embroidered features and ribbon trimming. One type was made of Ratine stuffed with kapok so that it could float. These dolls were made in 12 style Nos. and were 10 in. (25.5 cm.) tall. The other dolls were made of colored flannel or felt stuffed with cotton. These dolls came in 16 style Nos. and were 16 in. (40.5 cm.) tall.

1921: Advertised that their new dolls were stuffed with either kapok or silk floss. The eyes were hemstitched and the dolls were dressed in felt garments. They included a clown, *Dutch Boy, Red Riding Hood, Bo-Peep,* and *Society Miss* wearing a cape and able to be undressed.

Nursery emblems were appliquéd with different colored silks on some of the dresses. A few of the dolls were dressed in black and burnt orange for Halloween.

1924: Some of the cloth dolls were made of terry cloth. A new type of doll had composition face, hands, and feet, a mohair or human hair wig or painted hair. Some of these dolls had sleeping eyes and were dressed in organdy.

1926: Advertised infant and *Mama* dolls with composition heads in many styles and sizes.

1927: Licensed by *Voices, Inc.* to use patented mama voices and criers in their dolls. Used the trade name "Chessler Durable" for their line of dolls.

1928: Specialized in infant dolls and character dolls. Some of their dolls wore dresses of crepe de chine and other rich fabrics. They made twice as many style Nos. as in 1927.

1929: Their new featured dolls had long curls, smiling faces, straight legs, mama voices and wore handmade dresses.★

Chester Gump. 1923–24. Stuffed artificial leather (oilcloth) doll, made by *Fleming.* The hair was red and the nose was long. The body of red, blue and black showed a polka dot shirt, wide collar and large tie, short trousers and low boots with "Chester Gump//by Sidney// Smith" written diagonally on them. Ht. 13 in. (33 cm.).★

Chester Gump. 1926–29. Oilcloth doll made by *Live Long Toys.* It bears the names "Chester Gump" and "Sidney Smith," who designed the cartoon figure which the doll represents. The doll was a profile likeness of a small boy wearing a red and blue suit. The washable "Art leather," as the oilcloth was described, was soft stuffed. The doll itself, designed by *Eileen Benoliel,* was 13 in. (33 cm.) tall and sold for $8.00 a doz. wholesale.

535. Stamped mark on Chester Gump oilcloth doll made by Live Long Toys.

Chester Gump. 1929. All-bisque doll with jointed neck and molded clothes represented the cartoon character drawn by Sidney Smith. These dolls were made in Germany and distributed wholesale exclusively by *Marshall Field* and *Shackman.* Retail price 15¢.

Chev (German Soldier). 1911 and before. Name of a felt doll made by *Steiff,* dressed as a German soldier with two rows of buttons down the upper front, a white belt and sword. It had long feet. Hts. 28 and 35 cm. (11 and 14 in.).

Chevalier, D. 1930. Paris. Made or distributed dolls.

Chi (Chinaman). 1911–13. Name of a jointed felt doll representing a Chinaman. It was made by *Steiff* and distributed by *Borgfeldt.* Silk clothes came in assorted colors. Ht. 17 in. (43 cm.) priced $2.55 in 1911 in Germany and $3.50 in 1913 in New York.

Chic. 1908–11. Name of dressed dolls made by *Franz Frankl.*

Chicago Mail Order House. 1926–27 and probably other years. Chicago, Ill. Distributed dolls, among them bisque head *Bye-Los;* bisque head dolls with mohair wigs, sleeping eyes, jointed composition bodies, ht. 20½ in. (52 cm.), priced $1.99; bisque shoulder head dolls with sleeping eyes, hair eyelashes, kidlyn bodies; composition head *Mama* dolls, ht. 21 in. (53.5 cm.); priced $2.98; metal head dolls, ht. 15½ in. (39.5 cm.); priced 39¢. They also advertised *Baby Betty, Buttercup, Margie* and *Effanbee's Pat-a-Pat Baby.*

Chicago Toy House. 1927–28. Chicago, Ill. Factory representative that was associated with *Live Long Toys.*

Chickie. 1930. Trade name of a baby doll made by *Averill Manufacturing Co.*

Chicos. 1929. Trademark registered in U.S. by the *Curtiss Candy Co.* for dolls of china, wax or celluloid.

Chief. 1919–20 and probably other years. Handmade doll representing an American Indian. This was No. 2 among the dolls created by *Mary Frances Woods.* It had an individualistic face and blanket pattern and wore a single feather on the back of its head. Ht. 14 in. (35.5 cm.).★

Children of Today. 1930. A line of cloth dolls made by *Live Long Toys.* They represented boys and girls. Their hands had snaps so they could simulate clasping hands and were thus enabled to stand by themselves. Some of these dolls had voices.

Children's Novelty Co. 1909–11. Philadelphia, Pa. Distributed cloth flat faced dolls with lithographed features. Their dolls included *Bobby Bobbykins* and *Dolly Dollykins* with *Drayton* type faces. On the box lid of Dolly Dollykins is "DOLLY//DOLLYKINS// [then in smaller letters] THE CHILDREN'S NOVELTY COMPANY//SELLING AGENTS//813 FILBERT STREET//PHILADELPHIA//[and in the corner] REGISTERED U.S. PATENT OFFICE 1909."

Children's Press, The. 1928–29. Chicago, Ill. Registered U.S. trademark *Joey* for dolls.

Childs & Sons. Mid 1800s. Brighton. Doll with a papier-mâché head, pushing a carriage, is marked with a label reading: "CHILDS & SONS//51 KINGS ROAD//BRIGHTON //DESK & DRESSING CASE MAKER//TOYS, BASKETS, LEATHER WORKS, GLASS, PAPIER MACHE//CUTLERY, BRUSHES, COMBS & C."

Chillingworth, Thomas. See **Mechthold, Georg, & Co.**

Chiltern Toy Works. 1915. England. Manufactured stuffed dolls.

Chime Dolls. 1911–12 and probably other years. Chimes inside the doll's body played music when the doll was shaken. It was distributed by *Sears* and had a composition head and arms, painted hair and eyes, cloth body. The 16 in. (40.5 cm.) size had a wig.★

Chin Chin. Ca. 1918. Celluloid doll representing a Japanese baby. Ht. 4 in. (10 cm.); price 5¢.

Chin Chin. See **Pollyanna Co.**

Chin Chin Baby. 1920s. All bisque dolls made by *Gebrüder Heubach.* The square Heubach mark was on the bottom of the feet but was frequently difficult to see. These dolls were similar to *Queue San Baby.* Chin Chin Baby had a red and gold triangular sticker on its chest. The words "Chin Chin Baby" in black formed a triangle and in the center there was a red dragon over the word "Germany." These dolls had various types of molded headwear and a molded queue. Its brown eyes had a black pupil whereas Queue San Baby had only black pupilless eyes. The index finger and little finger were separated on Chin Chin but not on Queue San. The arms were jointed at the shoulder but the hips were rarely jointed. Ht. 4¼ in. (11 cm.).★

536. Three all-bisque Chin Chin dolls made by Gebrüder Heubach in the 1920s out of a pink bisque. They have Oriental features including brown painted slanting eyes and a molded and painted queue. The cap and slippers are also molded and painted but vary slightly from one doll to another. The doll in the center was once made into a pin cushion. The Chin Chin sticker is on the chest of each doll. The Heubach square mark is on the bottom of the feet. H. 4¼ in. (11 cm.). *Coleman Collection.*

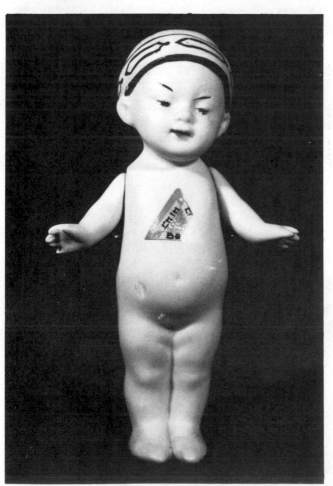

537. All-bisque Chin Chin doll made by Gebrüder Heubach of pink bisque. H. 4¼ in. (11 cm.). *Coleman Collection.*

538. Mark on sticker found on the chest of Chin Chin dolls. This is printed in red, yellow and black.

China Head Dolls. Most china heads, that is, glazed porcelain heads, were made in Germany from about 1840 on. During the period 1840–80 there was a great variety of hairdos on the china heads. Those with short hair and/or short necks generally represented children while those with longer necks usually represented adults. Many of the heads came in a wide variety of sizes. 7/0 to 14 have been noted. Usually the number on the back or front of the shoulder plate referred to the size code which often differed from factory to factory. However some factories used numbers for their mold identification.

Unfortunately most china heads had no decipherable marks at all. Several flat top style china heads have been found with crossed hammers and the word "Germany."

(Possibly *Metzler & Ortloff.*) A rare hairdo china head has the initials D E on the front. The kid body of this doll was marked with the name of *Carl Stephan*'s dolls' hospital in Vienna.

Prior to about 1880 most of the china heads were pressed. Pressed heads can be identified by the rough surface inside the head and the unevenness of the thickness of the porcelain. (See **Pressed vers Poured.**) Usually the later poured china heads had a smooth interior surface and there was often evidence of bubbles. The thickness of the porcelain tended to be uniform in the poured heads.

Certain variations in techniques have been noted such as the eyebrows having a gray outline around the black arch. The shapes of the shoulders and the size and position of the sew holes may all be indicative of the factory where the dolls' heads were made. But we cannot be sure that the variations signify a difference in factories or a difference in the period in which the heads were made. Studies have been under way to analyze the chemical ingredients, which it was thought might help to identify the factories or at least indicate the areas of origin. But these studies were terminated when it was learned that many of the factories purchased their slip from the same place, which might have been a considerable distance from where the heads were eventually made. Unfortunately the hard paste/soft paste analysis did not seem to provide an answer because most of the heads were neither distinctly hard paste or soft paste but a combination of the two.

Certain recognizable faces are often found with a variety of hairdos and it is tempting to assign these heads to the same factory. On the other hand there are numerous examples of similar hairdos with different faces. Often the hairdos appear to be identical until they are carefully examined and then slight variations are found which suggest that the heads were made in the same period but by competing factories.

Prior to 1880 most of the china heads appear to have been sold separately and the purchaser either bought a commercially made body or in most cases made the body at home. The result was that some rather strange-looking bodies were often found with china heads. These original bodies should be preserved. Some of the very early china heads were on commercially made wooden bodies with china limbs. One of the hands on these dolls usually had a hole formed by joining the fingers and thumb. A few of these dolls have been found holding a staff which was used as a pointer on a fortune telling disc.

Rarely does one find a china-head doll dressed in its original commercial costume. Most of the original clothes on china head dolls are rather plain cottons that were homemade.

During the 1870s and 1880s a few china heads had pierced ears and blond china heads began to appear. Earlier unusual features were glass eyes or eyes painted brown. The glass eyes were more common among the china heads that we suppose to have been made in France by *Huret, Rohmer* and so forth. The brown eyes are extremely rare on certain types such as bun chinas and those with upswept hair in back with puffs at the side, a style sometimes referred to as "Dress Makers" types. Brown eyes were more common on the simple hairdo types such as the one resembling the usual 1858 *Ludwig Greiner* hairdo. This type was made in a three

part mold with mold lines on either shoulder and down the center back.

After about 1880 lady dolls went out of fashion and most of the china heads represented children with short hair and short necks. A few corkscrew curl hairdos that were popular earlier were still on the market, but the flat tops and stereotype low-brows were made in vast quantities. Many very fine china child-doll heads were made during the period 1880–1910 in a Thüringian factory (*Alt, Beck & Gottschalck*). This group of heads usually had the mold number, a #, X or No. and the size number along the back edge of the shoulder plate. The shoulder plate was extensive and had an upper arm crease. There was a wide variety of hair-dos with both black and blond hair. Mold number 1000 with bangs was most often seen but there were many curly types of hairdos and a few had headwear. See Ills. 61, 68, 73, 75, 76, and 80.

In 1887 flat-top china head dolls with cloth bodies having china arms and legs, the latter with high boots with tassels, were advertised by *Ehrich Bros.* Hts. 13 and 15½ in. (33 and 39.5 cm.); priced 35¢ and 40¢.

The common wavy low-brow hairdo of the late 1800s continued to be produced in Germany at least through the first half of the 1900s and thereafter appeared frequently in reproductions. Unfortunately because the early fancy hairdo china heads are now somewhat rare, it is easy for collectors to think only of these late low-brow chinas as representing china heads.

Among the factories known to have produced china shoulder heads and/or all-china dolls were:

Alt, Beck & Gottschalck
Bähr & Pröschild
Bawo & Dotter
Bohne Ernst
Conta and Boehme
Royal Copenhagen
Dressel, Kister & Co.[+]
William Goebel
Hertwig & Co.
Kestner
C. F. Kling & Co.
Kloster Veilsdorf
Königliche Porzellan Manufaktur (K. P. M.)
Orben, Knabe & Co.
Jacob Petit
F. Pfeffer (Gotha)
Theodor Pohl
Pollack & Hoffmann
A. H. Pröschold
Reideler
Rörstrand
Schlaggenwald
Sèvres
Wallendorf

1840–55: *Orin Woodford* sold dolls with china heads on cloth bodies. He used some K. P. M. heads on his dolls in the 1850s.

1860–61: Elizabeth Pierce has an American Day Book of *John D. Robbins,* who appears to have imported many china heads. The heads were size 1 to 14 and cost 56¢ to $4.00 a dozen. Black china heads came in the smaller sizes and a china head with a cap, size 3, cost $1.12 a dozen. The china heads on bodies came as small as size 4/0 and the entire doll cost $1.25 a dozen.

1884: *C. F. Lauer* advertised dolls with china heads and limbs on muslin bodies. These came in 17 size numbers from 10/0 to 9 with hts. from 4 to 25½ in. (10 to 65 cm.); priced 30¢ to $8.50 doz. wholesale. Most of them had painted boots but for slightly more money and up to a ht. of 21½ in. (54.5 cm.) some of the dolls had gold boots. These appear to have been glazed china but the differentiation between china and bisque is rather vague in the Lauer catalog.

1885: *Horsman* advertised 15 sizes or styles of dolls with china heads and limbs on cloth bodies. These ranged in price from 31¢ to $8.00 a doz. wholesale. In addition there were six sizes or styles of black and of white china "Babies." These both ranged in price from 6¢ to 75¢ a doz. wholesale and were probably all-china dolls. Separate china heads came in seven sizes or styles costing 31¢ to $2.00 a doz. wholesale.

1887: C. F. Lauer advertised dolls with china heads and limbs on muslin bodies in the following sizes and prices:

LAUER CHINA HEAD DOLLS			
Size No.	Height in.	cm.	Price per doz. wholesale
0	10½	26.5	$1.00
1	11	28	$1.10
1½	12	30.5	$1.25
2	12½	31.5	$1.35
2½	14	35.5	$1.75
4	17	43	$2.50
8	22	56	$6.75
9	25	63.5	$8.00

1904: A curly haired child's head with side part came in either black hair or blond hair and five Hts. of shoulder heads, 3¼, 4, 4½, 5 and 5¾ in. (8.5, 10, 11.5, 12.5, and 14.5 cm.), according to Western News Co.

1927: Reideler advertised that he manufactured china dolls of all kinds, dressed and undressed. The picture in the advertisement shows what looks like a china head and china limbs on a cloth body. The hairdo is a simple style but not the regular low brow.

1928: Kestner was still making china dolls, according to PLAYTHINGS.

1938: Kimport advertised china dolls with "blonde or jet hair." Four hts. 6, 9, 12, and 18 in. (15, 23, 30.5 and 45.5 cm.). The larger sizes had blue garters.

1940s: Ruth Gibbs in New Jersey made original china-head dolls inspired by the early flat top and plain hairdo types. (See also **Clear, Emma C.**)

1950s: Both Kimport and Elsie Krug advertised china head dolls as old stock, made prior to World War II.★

539A & B. Turned, flesh-tinted china shoulder head. Black hair is in ringlets conforming to the shape of the head. The eyes are brown. Cloth body has china arms and feet with boots lacing up the front. H. 16½ in. (42 cm.). H. shoulder head 4 in. (10 cm.). *Courtesy of Frances Walker.*

540A. Two china shoulder head dolls, both on wooden bodies with china limbs. Both have molded hair painted black, and blue painted eyes. The smaller doll has a braided bun with loops over the ears in the so-called Gothic hair style. One of the hands is clenched while the other is not. The original clothes are made of a cream colored silk ribbon.

540B. The larger doll has molded long ringlets which reach the shoulder, as can be seen in this close-up.

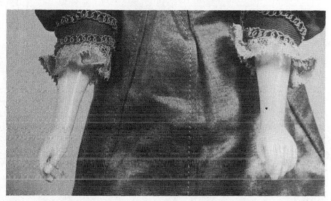

540C. The close-up of the hands of the larger doll. H. of the larger doll 13 in. (33 cm.). H. of shoulder head 2½ in. (6.5 cm.). H. of the smaller shoulder head 1½ in. (4 cm.). *Courtesy of Frances Walker.*

541A, B, & C. China shoulder head with curls in front and bun in back, painted blue eyes, a small closed space between the lips, a cloth body and kid arms. Original clothes. H. 16 in. (40.5 cm.). *Coleman Collection.*

542. Pink-tinted china head with molded dark brown hair that encircles the ears and has a bun in back. This style was popular in the 1840s. The kid body has wooden arms and legs. H. 17 in. (43 cm.). *Courtesy of Richard Withington. Photo by Barbara Jendrick.*

A

B

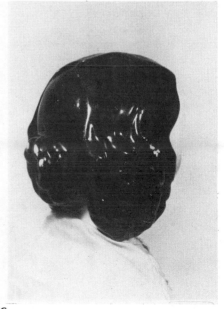

C

543. China head, arms, and legs. The molded black hair has a coiled bun in back; blue painted eyes; cloth body. The molded shoes have no heels. H. 13 in. (33 cm.). *Courtesy of June Jeffcott.*

544A, B, & C. China shoulder head with molded hair, full at the sides and bun in back; painted features; 3 sew holes on each side; homemade cloth body. H. 24 in. (61 cm.). *Coleman Collection.*

545A & B. China shoulder head doll with braids on the side and a braided bun in back, molded blue eyes, closed mouth and a cloth body with china lower arms and legs. Contemporary clothes. The molded boots have flat heels. H. 13½ in. (34 cm.). H. of shoulder head 3½ in. (9 cm.). *Coleman Collection.*

546A & B. China shoulder head doll with molded bows and snood, molded blue eyes, closed mouth, and cloth body having kid hands. Original clothes. H. 16½ in. (42 cm.). H. of shoulder head 4 in. (10 cm.). *Coleman Collection.*

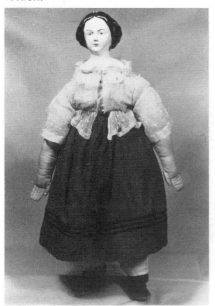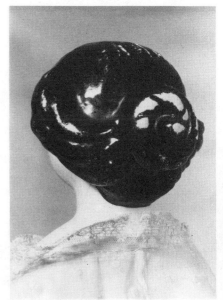

A   B   C

1 Wooden doll of around 1760 with glass eyes and gesso-covered face. H. 4¾ in. (12 cm.). *Courtesy of the Strong Museum.*

Seven wooden dolls dating from about 1820 to 1850. The doll on the left, H. 5½ in. (14 cm.); the pair in the box, H. 7½ in. (19 cm.); and the one in the right front, H. 4½ in. (11.5 cm.), are all peg wooden dolls from the Grödner Tal. In the center is a baby in carved and painted swaddling clothes, H. 3¾ in. (9.5 cm.). The two larger dolls on the right have faces covered with gesso (see Ill. 2752) Hs. 8 in. (20.5 cm.) and 7 in. (18 cm.). *Coleman Collection.*

Wax-head doll of about 1815 with glass eyes, cloth body, and kid arms. H. 15 in. (38 cm.). *Coleman Collection*.

Carton doll of about 1815 holding a small doll (see Ill. 482). Hs. 24½ and 7 in. (62 and 18 cm.). *Courtesy of the Strong Museum*.

Three all-wood dolls. *Left:* A peg wooden doll made in the Grödner Tal, dressed as an Arab (see Ill. 2189). H. 13 in. (33 cm.). *Center:* A doll probably made in the first quarter of the 1800s (see Ill. 2755). H. 11 in. (28 cm.). *Right:* Bébé Tout en Bois made in Germany after 1900, dressed in a commercial chemise (see Ill. 291). H. 9 in. (23 cm.). *Coleman Collection.*

Five dolls with composition or papier-mâché heads. *Left to right:* Doll in Greek costume (see Ill. 2190); doll in bathing outfit ca. 1860 (see Ill. 2496); doll with French papier-mâché head, kid and cloth body, original commercial clothes of the 1820s–1850s (see Ill. 965); papier-mâché head doll on a kid with wooden limb body wears an Amelia Bloomer–type costume; papier-mâché head doll dressed as a Zouave with gun (see Ill. 1898). Hs. 16, 11½, 15½, 9, and 7½ in. (40.5, 29, 39.5, 23, and 19 cm.). *Coleman Collection.*

An 1860s wax-over composition head on a doll bearing the label of Charles Dummig (see Ills. 841 and 842). H. 24½ in. (62 cm.). *Courtesy of Frances Walker.*

Composition shoulder-head doll marked "J. ADLER & Co.// Superior AMERICAN HEAD//No. 7" (see Ills. 10 and 11). H. 24½ in. (62 cm.). *Courtesy of Frances Walker.*

Dolls with china heads, arms, and legs on jointed wooden bodies. The man doll has a molded cap, mustache, and goatee. H. 6¾ in. (17 cm.). The girl doll has long curls onto its shoulders. H. 4½ in. (11.5 cm.). *Courtesy of Jay and Becky Lowe. Photo by Bill Holland.*

Pair of china-head dolls. The boy doll has wooden hands and a Woodford, Boston sticker on its chest (see Ills. 2765 and 2766). H. 13 in. (33 cm.). The lady doll has a V-shaped part and bun in the back. H. 17 in. (43 cm.). *Coleman Collection.*

China head and arms on a pink kid body; original commercial clothes of about 1860. H. 21 in. (53.5 cm.). *Courtesy of the International Doll Library Foundation.*

11

Three china-head dolls with unusual molded hairdos. *Left:* Hair has a comb, snood, and a spit curl on each side (see Ill. 552). H. 17 in. (43 cm.). *Center:* Hair has a molded rose in front and a gilt ornament in back (see Ill. 551). H. 19 in. (48 cm.). *Right:* Hair has a molded braid that coils around the head (see Ill. 1113). H. 19½ in. (49.5 cm.). *Coleman Collection.*

12

13

Five china-head dolls all dressed in flimsy original commercial clothes. All have unusual hairdos except the smallest doll which has corkscrew curls (see Ills. 632, 633, and 638). Hs. *left to right*, 11¾ in. (30 cm.), 10 in. (25.5 cm.), 12 in. (30.5 cm.), 7½ in. (19 cm.), and 14½ in. (37 cm.). *Coleman Collection.*

Untinted bisque dolls with molded hair. *Left to right:* Puffs in back, glass eyes, pierced ears, mark "5Y6," Goldsmith body; blue molded ribbon, curls in back, glass eyes, pierced ears, mark "114 5," probably a Kling cloth body; short curls, glass eyes, kid body; snood and blue bows on side, painted eyes, cloth body; coronet braid, painted eyes, pierced ears, cloth body. Hs. 17, 18, 13, 17, 15, and 23 in. (43, 45.5, 33, 43, 38, and 58.5 cm.). *Courtesy of Frances Walker.*

15

Bisque-head lady or girl dolls in original clothes. *Left to right:* Doll has a bald head and bisque lower arms (see Ill. 1591), H. 18 in. (45.5 cm.); German girl doll (see Ill. 636), H. 17 in. (43 cm.); regional costume doll with cloth body, H. 15 in. (38 cm.); Bru lady doll with kid body and wooden arms, head marked with the size letter D. H. 15 in. (38 cm.). *Coleman Collection.*

16

Group of lady and girl dolls. *Left to right:* Painted eye bisque-head doll, kid body, possibly French; china-head doll with wig; bisque-head doll possibly made by Terrene (see Ill. 2595); celluloid-head doll; composition-head doll, glass eyes, pierced ears, swivel neck, cloth body, mark on front shoulder "Waschecht"; wax-over composition-head doll, glass eyes, swivel neck; bisque-head doll with a blown kid–type body, pierced ears; Hs. 16, 10½, 17½, 13, 18, 16, and 17 in. (40.5, 26.5, 44.5, 33, 44.5, 40.5, and 43 cm.). *Courtesy of Frances Walker.*

Bisque head with swivel neck, kid body, and bisque arms. These long face heads are usually found on lady bodies, some of which are marked Jumeau or were made by Philip Goldsmith, Lacmann, or others. H. 20 in. (51 cm.). *Coleman Collection.*

Bisque-head doll with molded hair made by Simon & Halbig, marked "S 3 H" (see Ill. 2391). H. 11½ in. (29 cm.). *Coleman Collection.*

Four dolls dressed in Scottish outfits. *Left to right:* British ceramic head with molded hair made by Crown Staffordshire (see Ill. 489); composition head with wig, glass eyes, molded and painted mustache; bisque head probably made by Alt, Beck & Gottschalck (see Ill. 74); molded blond hair bisque head, kid body that is possibly French (see Ill. 2193). Hs. 12, 11¾, 12, and 12½ in. (30.5, 30, 30.5, and 31.5 cm.). *Coleman Collection.*

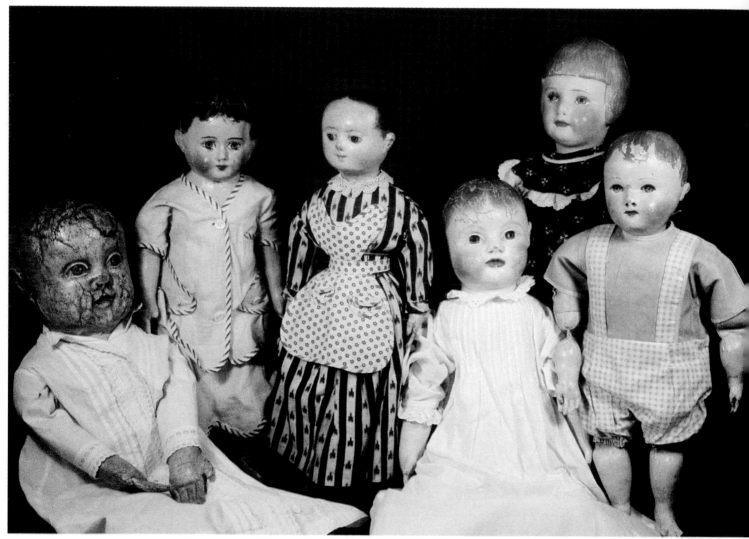

Group of cloth dolls. *Left to right:* Reinforced, oil painted and molded stockinet head doll made by Wellington; molded and painted Alabama baby with applied ears, blue shoes; Izannah Walker doll with molded and painted head, curls in back and brush marks in front, black boots; Sheppard baby with molded and painted stockinet head; girl doll with bobbed hair and baby doll with short hair and cavities in nostrils and ears, both of these dolls have molded and painted heads and were made by Martha Chase. Hs. 21½, 18, 18, 21½, 20½, and 16½ in. (54.5, 45.5, 45.5, 54.5, 52, and 42 cm.). *Courtesy of Frances Walker.*

Cloth doll of the type shown in the Horsman catalog for the 1893 Chicago World's Fair and identified as a "Worsted Doll." Doll has a needle sculptured stockinet head with black bead eyes, embroidered features, worsted hair, hat, collar, and dress trimming of worsted French knots. H. 8 in. (20.5 cm.). *Coleman Collection*.

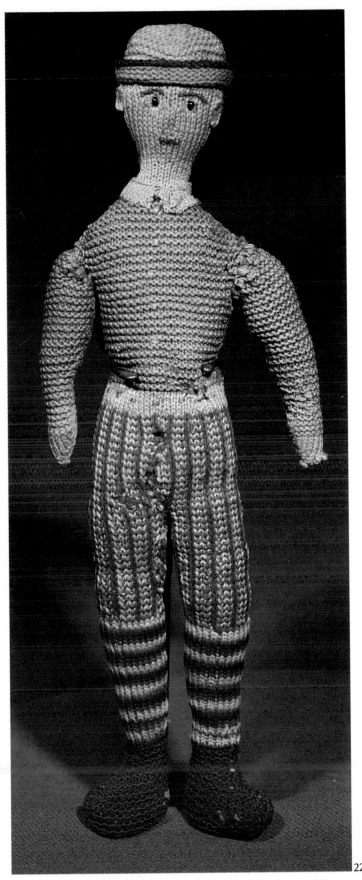

22

Knitted boy doll, probably homemade in the 1890s, has black bead eyes and other features embroidered. All the clothes, except the separate hat, form part of the doll. H. 13 in. (33 cm.). *Coleman Collection*.

21

All-bisque dolls with swivel necks and glass eyes. The doll on the left has sleeping eyes and joints at the knees, molded boots. H. 5¾ in. (14.5 cm.). The other two dolls have elbow joints, center doll has joints of bisque balls, doll on right has wooden balls in its joints. Both dolls have bare feet and are 5½ in. (14 cm.) tall. *Courtesy of Jay and Becky Lowe. Photo by Bill Holland.*

547A & B. Molded and painted china shoulder head is on a kid body. The café au lait-colored hair has braids in back of the brush marks. The hair is caught up into a black snood in back; across the crown is a black ruffled band which forms a kind of widow's peak. The single-stroke eyebrows are the same color as the hair. The blue eyes are semi-outlined and have highlights. The three-piece wool dress of the 1870s period has a purple ground with white dots. H. 19 in. (48.5 cm.). H. shoulder head 6 in. (15 cm.). *Coleman Collection.*

548A & B. Flesh tinted china shoulder head made in Germany in the 1860s. Molded hair has wings and brushmarks in front, a large loop in back, 3 sew holes in front and back. H. 12 in. (30.5 cm.). H. of shoulder head 3 in. (7.5 cm.). *Coleman Collection.*

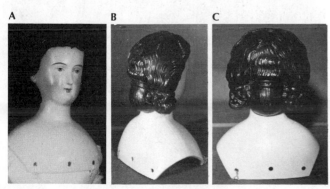

549A, B, & C. China head with braided loops on each side and a comb holding an unbraided loop in the center back. It has molded blue eyes and a closed mouth. H. of shoulder head 7½ in. (19 cm.). *Coleman Collection.*

550. China head with molded black hair, shoulder length in back, braids on sides; blue eyes; molded blouse top; replaced cloth body. H. 24 in. (61 cm.). *Coleman Collection.*

551A & B. Decorated china shoulder head. It has a molded rose in front and a gilt ornament in the back of the hair. There are brushmarks, molded and painted blue eyes, the exposed ears are pierced; closed mouth; molded and painted blouse top; cloth body. H. 19 in. (48 cm.). H. of shoulder head 5 in. (12.5 cm.). *Coleman Collection.*

552A & B. China head with black hair arranged with a comb and snood in back and a spit curl on each side. It has brushmarks, molded and painted blue eyes, closed mouth, cloth body with china arms and legs. H. 17 in. (43 cm.). H. of shoulder head 4¾ in. (12 cm.). *Coleman Collection.*

554A, B, & C. China head with black hair having a side part and with the ears showing. It is on a homemade cloth body. Original clothes. H. 8¼ in. (21 cm.). H. shoulder head 2½ in. (6.5 cm.). *Courtesy of Dorothy Annunziato.*

553. China shoulder head with molded short black hair, brush marks following the hairline, molded and painted blue eyes, closed mouth and a double chin. The face is flesh color. *Courtesy of Z. Frances Walker.*

555. Pinkish china head, lower arms and legs. The chubby limbs denote a young child. The head has molded and painted curly hair and features, with a slight space between the color of the lips. A flange neck enables the head to turn on the cloth body. H. 6¼ in. (16 cm.). *Coleman Collection.*

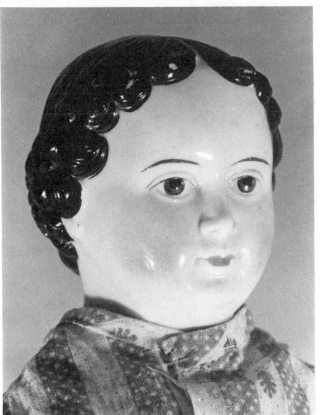

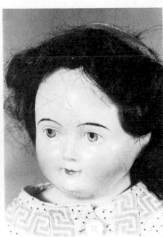

558A & B. Bald pink china head with a slit on top in which the wig was to be inserted; painted features including lower lashes; two sew holes on front and back of the shoulders; cloth body with leather hands. Clothes are contemporary with the doll. H. 21 in. (53.5 cm.). H. of shoulder head 5½ in. (14 cm.). *Coleman Collection.*

556. China head with molded tight black curls, brown eyes, partly exposed ears, closed mouth on a cloth body with red leather hands. Redressed in a contemporary dress. H. 18 in. (45.5 cm.). *Coleman Collection.*

557. Doll has china head, arms, and legs; wig and glass eyes; dressed in original clothes. H. 67 cm. (26½ in.). *Courtesy of the Nordiska Museet in Stockholm, Sweden.*

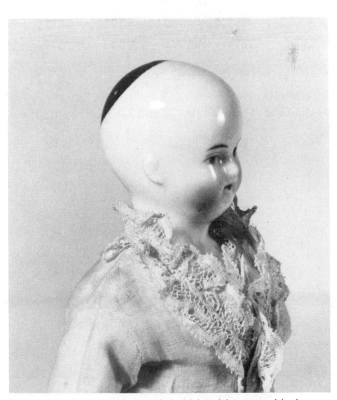

559. China shoulder plate with bald head having a black pate. Probably made ca. 1860 in Germany. It has painted features. *Courtesy of the Museum of the City of New York.*

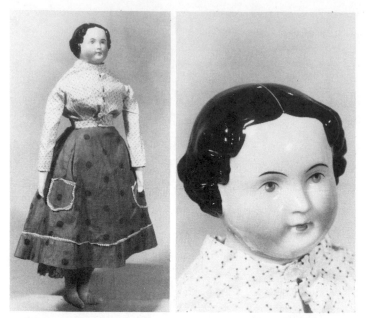

560A & B. Pinkish china shoulder head with molded hair, having a flat top and corkscrew curls; painted eyes; circular nostril lines; mouth has a slight space between the lips; three sew holes on each side. H. 19 in. (48 cm.). H. of shoulder head 4¼ in. (11 cm.). *Coleman Collection.*

561. China shoulder head with a molded flat-top curly hairdo, two sew holes front and back, painted features. Cloth body, kid arms. Original clothes. H. 13½ in. (34 cm.). H. shoulder head 3¾ in. (9.5 cm.). *Coleman Collection.*

562A & B. China shoulder head doll with flat-top type hair-do, painted eyes, closed mouth, with lip line, and cloth body jointed at shoulders and hips. Clothes contemporary with the doll. H. 21½ in. (54.5 cm.). *Coleman Collection.*

563A & B. China shoulder head with hair having wings, curls on forehead; and a cluster in back held by a comb, brushmarks, pierced ears; two sewholes on each side; cloth body with leather hands and boots. H. 18 in. (45.5 cm.). H. of shoulder head 4¼ in. (11 cm.). *Coleman Collection.*

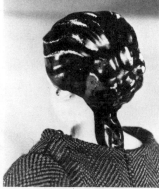

564A & B. China shoulder head with molded hair, brushmarks, bangs, bun, and loop on neck, molded and painted features, pierced ears, cloth body. It wears a dress of a period contemporary with the doll. H. 10½ in. (26.5 cm.). H. of shoulder head 3 in. (7.5 cm.). *Coleman Collection.*

567. Pair of china head dolls with almost the same hairdos. Both have what is sometimes called "spill curls." Both have black hair, blue eyes, closed mouth, cloth body. But there is a slight difference. The doll on the left has wisps of hair at the end of its curls, its face is plumper, the mouth is flatter, and a tiny piece of the ears show. It wears a contemporary dress, while the other doll has been redressed. H. of doll on left 11 in. (28 cm.). H. of doll on right 13 in. (33 cm.). *Courtesy of Richard Withington. Photo by Barbara Jendrick.*

565. China shoulder head on a kid body. The head has brush-marks, pierced ears, original clothes. H. 19½ in. (49.5 cm.). *Courtesy of the Hungarian National Museum, Budapest.*

566A & B. China shoulder head with molded hair, ears pierced into the head, painted eyes, closed mouth. Cloth body with china limbs. Contemporary period wrapper. H. 17½ in. (44.5 cm.). H. of shoulder head 4½ in. (11.5 cm.). *Coleman Collection.*

568A & B. China shoulder head with molded and painted hair and features, two sew holes front and back; cloth body contemporary with the head. Back of shoulder marked "4." H. 18 in. (45.5 cm.). *Coleman Collection.*

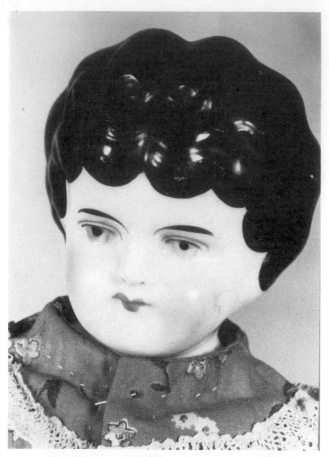

569. China shoulder head with so-called, low-brow hairdo, painted features, no sew holes, cloth body, china arms and legs with molded footwear. Original dress. H. 16 in. (40.5 cm.). H. shoulder head 4 in. (10 cm.). *Coleman Collection.*

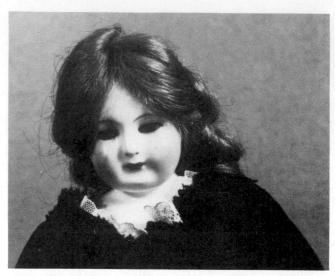

571. China shoulder head with wig, stationary blue glass eyes, closed mouth, kid body gusset jointed at the shoulders, hips and knees. H. 15 in. (38 cm.). *Courtesy of Cherry Bou.*

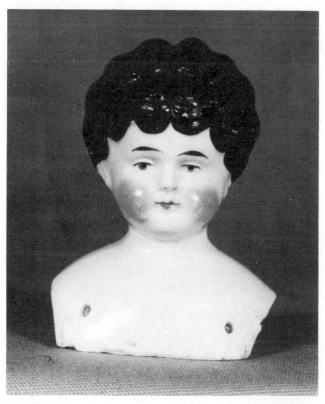

570. China shoulder head with molded wavy hair that comes down low on the forehead, painted and molded features, sew holes. This style of hairdo was popular from the 1880s to 1930s. H. of shoulder head 3¼ in. (8 cm.). *Coleman Collection.*

572. China-head doll with wig, stationary blue glass eyes, closed mouth, and a pink kid body with china arms. Original clothes of the 1850s have never been removed to find a mark. H. 20 in. (51 cm.). *Courtesy of Sotheby Parke Bernet Inc., N.Y.*

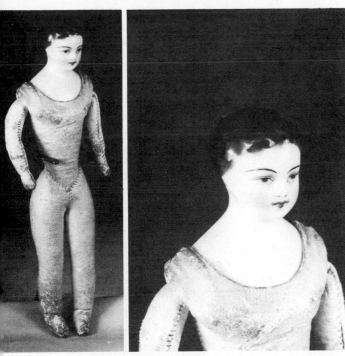

573A & B. Pressed china flesh colored head with molded and painted features. Dark brown eyebrows and mottled hair, blue eyes. The dots in the corners of the eyes and lower lashes are a reddish purple as are the lines above the eyes, the nostril lines, and the outline of the mouth. A lighter shade forms shadows for the eyes, nose, mouth and ears. The body is kid. H. 8½ in. (21.5 cm.). H. shoulder head only, 2¼ in. (5.5 cm.). *Coleman Collection.*

575. Pressed china shoulder head has painted and molded features and hair. The brown painted hair is molded into a coiled bun at the nape of the neck. It has blue eyes which are highlighted with eye shadow above and below the eye and in the eyelashes. The eyebrows are feathered. This type of head is usually found on kid bodies. The cloth body with china limbs is a replacement. H. 14½ in. (37 cm.). H. of shoulder head 3¼ in. (8 cm.). *Coleman Collection.*

574. China head with molded blond hair, blue eyes, highly colored cheeks, closed mouth, cloth body and original clothes. H. 10½ in. (26.5 cm.). H. of shoulder head 2 in. (5 cm.). *Coleman Collection.*

576–577. Unidentified marks found on china shoulder head dolls.

Chinaman. 1929. Trade name of a doll made of California redwood by the *Poppy Doll Co.* These wooden dolls were hand painted with a harmless washable enamel. Their movable parts were controlled by a lever in the back.

Chinaman Acrobat. Ca. 1906–24. *Schoenhut* wooden doll; hair was in a queue. This acrobat doll wore a Chinese-style tunic and trousers. Came in one size. See Ill. 2357.★

Chinese Crying Babies. 1853–61 and probably later. These dolls were mentioned in GODEY'S LADY'S BOOK in 1853 and listed in the Day Book of *John D. Robbins.* The price was $10.00 doz. wholesale in 1860. The question arises as to whether these Oriental dolls were the Japanese *Motschmann*-type with crying voice or actually Chinese dolls.

Chinese Dolls. The oldest known doll in China was a roly-poly doll. Many of the dolls were made of baked clay. Some of the Chinese dolls most frequently found in the Occident were the *Door of Hope* Mission dolls made in 1900–40. Those made in Shanghai had wooden heads; those made in Canton had composition heads. Evidence has been found that indicates that most of the Chinese dolls with white lacquered composition faces, hands with long fingers (or fingernails), easily movable joints, and wearing elaborate clothing and headwear were made during the 1910s and 1920s. Many of these dolls appear to have been produced and Estelle Johnston has found a note attached to one of them indicating that it was made in a missionary school. The handwritten note is as follows:

"Doll made by Chinese women in the mission school at Hwaiking, Province of Honan, China. This school has an enrollment of 350 and is conducted by Mrs. Joseph A. Mowatt, Canadian Missionary. Quebec, Aug. 1924." The note was written on a doctor's form dated 191–.

1913: According to TOYS AND NOVELTIES: "Chinese dolls were produced in abundance in Kiauchau, the Sonneberg of China. The work was done by families in humble homes for the most part. Each member of the family became a specialist at some small task and then the family assembled and completed the doll. The heads, bodies, limbs and features were made with remarkable rapidity.

"Generally the head is made of waxed paper, the inside of which is filled with any kind of cheap stuffing. The painting of the face is a task frequently allotted to adult women.

"The hair and eyebrows of these Chinese dolls generally consists of fine silk threads, and these are sometimes decorated with a bit of gold or silver paper. The body and limbs consist of wire cores around which colored silk string is wound. The feet are made in a most ingenious way, the principal portion being cuttlefish shell. The shell is first boiled, after which the outer part is pared off. The remaining material is durable and yet it can be easily cut to the desired shape. These shell feet are only fitted to the larger dolls, however, or those which sell at the highest prices. The cheaper playthings are content with feet of paper. The process of making and selling these Chinese dolls is simple in the extreme. The manufacturers keep no samples. They merely execute orders given them verbally by dealers, according to the requirement of the trade. These dolls are not manufactured for export, although a few of them find their

way to Europe and America, generally in the hands of travelers returning home. They suffice for the Chinese child, however, and they are to be found in every corner of the great Chinese Republic."

There were also some other Chinese dolls probably made in a Canton mission found by Americans. They had what appear to be composition heads. Jo Gerken has investigated one of these dolls that contained a piece of Cantonese newspaper. She described the head as being stockinet that had been gessoed and then painted. These dolls had painted features and either painted hair or a wig. The cloth bodies were painted with an oil paint up to the elbows and knees. The bodies closely resembled those made by *Martha Chase* and were jointed at the shoulders, elbows, hips and knees. The legs were attached to the bottom front of the torso. The body and the clothes were all hand-made. Frogs served as fastenings and the bride doll wore a beaded headdress with red embroidery. The doll representing a man wore a blue and black costume; size 9½ inches (24 cm.).

These dolls are superior in quality to the glazed composition dolls of the Canton *Door of Hope Mission.* See Ill. 814.

In 1923 *Stewart Culin* purchased a "Chinese Mandarin Tea Doll" in a Munich shop for $2.00.★

Ching Chow. 1929. All-bisque doll with jointed neck and molded clothes represented the cartoon character drawn by *Sidney Smith* in the "Gumps." These dolls were made in Germany and distributed wholesale exclusively by *Marshall Field* and *Shackman.* Retail price 25¢.

Chinkie (Chinkee). 1911–12. Composition head doll with painted hair and eyes made by *Horsman,* Number 160 in the 1912 catalog.★

Chinn, Howard Thomas. 1923–30. Inglewood, and Atascadero, Calif. He patented in Germany a doll that could simultaneously move its arms and hair. It was called *Scarey Ann* and was made by the *Poppy Doll Co.* Mrs. Chinn made cloth dolls for Bullock's Department Store.★

Chins, Movable. 1904. Novelty dolls had movable chins and voices to simulate talking. They came dressed. Ht. 12 in. (30.5 cm.).

Chiquet, F., & Le Montréer. 1865–85. Paris. Made talking bébés. *Le Montréer* appears to have left the firm around 1870.

1878: Chiquet received an Honorable Mention at the Paris Exposition.

1881: Purchased bisque dolls' heads from *François Gaultier* and used them on some of the dolls that he made according to Mme. Poisson, curator of the Roybet-Fould Museum.★

Chirkoff. Ca. 1800. Russia. Made wooden dolls in the style of *Tatyha.*

Cho-Cho San. Ca. 1920. All-bisque doll made by *Morimura Bros.;* jointed at the shoulders, with painted features and clothes. Ht. 4¾ in. (12 cm.).

Chocolate Drop. 1923–24. Brown cloth doll, painted features, 3 yarn pigtails. Ht. 11 in. (28 cm.). See Ill. 801.★

578. Cho-Cho San mark on all-bisque doll with molded cap and slippers.

Chotz (Cschotz), Josef. 1816–36. Vienna. Made toys of pressed paper. This probably included papier-mâché dolls.

Choumara. 1928–30 and later. Paris. Made cloth dolls.

Christening Baby. 1918–19. Trade name of a doll made by *Effanbee* according to Pat Schoonmaker.

Christensen, E. GK. 1928–29. Aalborg, Denmark. Obtained a British patent for a doll with its mouth formed by an opening in a sheet of rubber which was connected to movable eyes and a control device which was manually operated so that the mouth and eyes moved simultaneously. The pressure also collapsed the bellows from which the sound was emitted.

Christensen, Peder Jensen, 1925–26. Ellidshøj, Denmark. Obtained a Danish and a German patent for a doll with changeable facial expression.

Christiansen, Bertha Christine. 1925–26. Copenhagen. Obtained a British and a German patent for a doll with mechanically movable limbs.★

Christie, Walter Edward. 1907–26. London. Produced dolls and was the agent for *Löttler & Dill.*★

Christine. 1915. One of the dolls promoted by *Mme. Paderewski* for the aid of Polish refugees. It was made in *Mme. Thabée Lazarski's* workshop and represented a little peasant girl from Cracow.

Christmas Dolls. 1860–61. Name given to a group of dolls listed in the account book of *John D. Robbins.* Price $3.00 a doz. wholesale.

Christobel. 1927–28. A *Mama* doll distributed by *Montgomery Ward.* This doll had a composition head and limbs, painted eyes and a mohair wig. It wore a pink striped crepe de chine dress with organdy trimming and a matching bonnet. Size 24 in. (61 cm.); price $2.59.

Christopher. 1917–18. Line of cloth dolls made by *Shanklin.* Its head was covered with wool hair using a new treatment. The legs were jointed. It was a mate to *Shirley.*

Christopher Robin. 1930. Made by *Teddy Toy Co.* It wore an oilskin coat and sou'wester.

Chronology. Two articles on the chronology of dolls were published in TOYS AND NOVELTIES in 1913 and in 1915. The history of dolls as reported by Dr. Fritz Hoeber in October 1913 is interesting for two important reasons, namely the 1913 view of the history of dolls and the origin of many of the statements that have appeared in later versions of the history of dolls. However, the accuracy of some of the statements is open to suspicion, but the majority of the account is probably accurate.

Les Poupées à travers les âges.

I : Préhistoire. — II : Rome. — III : Grèce. — IV : Égypte. — V : Moyen-Age. — VI : Renaissance. — VII : XVIIᵉ siècle. — VIII-VIII : Premier Empire. — IX : 1830. — X : 1892. — XI : 1922. — XII : 1923. — XIII : 1916.

579. Chronology of dolls as shown in LES JOUJOUX written by Calmettes and published in 1924: I Prehistoric, II Rome, III Greek, IV Egypt, V Middle Ages, VI Renaissance, VII 17th century, VIII (Dressed and undressed) First Empire, IX 1830, X 1892, XI 1922, XII 1923, XIII 1916. *Courtesy of the Widener Library, Harvard University.*

"The savages of Africa, America and Australia, the inhabitants of Eastern Asia and the Malay Archipelago, all have known dolls from the beginning. . . . The Chinese doll consists of a sack-like piece of gay colored cotton or silk material, to the upper end of which is fastened a papier-mache head, whose delicate traits are rendered in painting, and whose hair consists of black silk threads. . . .

"When we pass over into the realm of our European culture development, we find . . . all kinds of dolls, costly ones of elegantly modeled wax, of carved, painted and gilt wood, and even of Ivory. There are also cheap ones for the great masses of the people, of the universal material, terra cotta. It is probable that many of the well known figures, which in the fourth century, were produced in large quantities at Athens and the Boestian [sic] border town of Tanagra, of which we admire such charming types in our large museums, those fine little fashion dames and veiled matrons, the graceful dancing girls, and the wonderfully jolly character figures of the new (classical) comedy, were intended for the amusement of the children. Besides these motionless figures of the plastic art, there also were, in Greece and Rome, clay dolls with flexible limbs, in principle not different from our own, of rather crude formation of the body and limbs, which latter are fastened with little wood pins to the shoulder and hip limbs. A better specimen belonging to the fourth century was found on the Kimmeric Bosphorus, in the peninsular Krim, settled by inhabitants of Athens.

"The Greek word for doll is 'Kora' meaning girl. As is the case with us, with them also, the feminine dolls were in the majority. Plutarch's little daughter possessed such a doll. The demand for dolls seems to have been considerable. It was supplied by a special trade called the 'Koroplastixi,' which supported its workers. . . .

"Of the dolls of the middle ages unfortunately much less is known than of the antique. From the second half of the Fifteenth Century there exist two little carved wood pictures of workmen, finished as rather primitive dolls, evidently wooden limbed dolls. . . . For the epoch of the Renaissance a better record is made.

"The Nuremberg toy industry reaches back to those days. Paris showed then, progressive development in the production of very expensive fashion dolls, of which we mention two by way of example, one from the time of Francis I, belonging to the Darville Collection [This Derville or Darville doll was later proven to be a fake], and one somewhat younger from the time of Henry III belonging to the well-known Vienna collection [of Figdor, also suspect]. Both are dressed in elegantly fashioned gay colored brocade gowns, which are trimmed with rich embroidery and lace. They are strictly in the style of that period [sixteenth century], with neatly folded linen collars surrounding the carefully carved heads. The faces in their gay colored paint, smile rather stiffly. The French Renaissance is also the inventor of the dolls of a pressed paper mass, papier mache or papier moule, so much in demand until far into the Nineteenth Century.

"The central position which France occupied in the succeeding centuries is surely also illustrated by the immense Paris doll industry. Under Louis XII, dolls were even admitted at court. They were permitted to ride in the state carriage of the king, and were the acknowledged favorites of the king as well as of the princes and princesses. The most illustrious minds at the court of the Sun King [Louis XIV], such as Bossuet and La Fontaine, did not disdain them. Altogether, that period of the grotesque which distinguishes itself through conditions exaggerated into the colossal, prides itself of quite fabulously luxurious and costly dolls and doll outfits.

"Louis Epernon, Bishop of Toulouse, presented the daughter of Louis XIV, Mademoiselle de Bourbon, with a magnificent doll and doll room, with little bed, complete

furnishings, night gowns and many costumes for change.

"This refinement, it is true, extended only to dresses and outfits. The dolls themselves at that time were still quite primitive, with their heads, hands and feet carved out of wood and painted in a manner that does not individualize. The bodies, the arms and legs were made of stuffed pads held together with ribbons.

"In the early Nineteenth Century doll heads of wax with glass or enamel eyes made their appearance. During this century the work of perfecting progressed more rapidly. The body was formed of a covering of sheep skin filled with sawdust or bran. About the year 1850 there were dolls of gutta percha. A little later came the first porcelain heads with genuine hair wigs, which were produced either of untwisted silk or of the hair of the Astrachan or the Tibet goat.

"In the greater enlivening of its figures the doll industry then made forward strides. Talking dolls, which by means of a spring mechanism, say 'Mamma' and 'Papa,' were constructed in 1823. In the same year we find for the first time the so-called 'sleeping eyes,' which in a horizontal position of the doll, close by means of a counterweight fastened to the eye-ball.

"For doll fashions, the same as for their human prototypes, Paris, of course, ruled. The figure parts were produced in Germany and England and were then imported into France. Very pretty wax and porcelain heads came from London; porcelain busts were made principally in Bavaria, Prussia, and also in Austria. Above all, however, these were made in the famous house industry towns of Southern Thuringia, such as Coburg, Sonneberg and Holdburghausen [Hildburghausen]. These Thuringian workshops, noted for the manufacture of everything in the way of toys, also enjoyed a good reputation for busts of papier mache. Those of wax, on the other hand, were largely drawn from England. Thus the dolls were produced until far into the Nineteenth Century, in all parts of the world.

"The sale of dolls offers much that is historically noteworthy. The most luxurious business houses were found in Paris towards the end of the Eighteenth Century. Then they were eight in number. One of the most favored stores was located in the Rue Honore, going by the name of 'At the Violet Monkey.' The proprietor of this store [was] Mr. Bennais. . . .

"The French doll was always an elegant lady of fashion. This seems to have been the case going back to the most ancient times. It did not only serve as an innocent plaything for children, but it also filled an important role as arbiter of Paris elegance.

"As far back as 1391, Queen Isabeau of Bavaria, the spouse of King Charles VI, of France, ordered a number of beautifully attired dolls to be sent to the Queen of England for the purpose of showing her the beautiful French gowns worn at her wedding.

"The two magnificently dressed French Renaissance dolls have already been mentioned. But later the Paris dolls reflect all fashion variations of the Seventeenth, Eighteenth and Nineteenth Centuries down to the smallest details. A whole branch of the industry, which had its seat in the Saint Martin Quartier, was able to support itself on the dressing of this mondain society in miniature. The custom followed to this day, to produce model dolls dressed in the newest fashion which reproduce, in a small way, with perfect exactness, the cut and finish of the costumes for the tailor shops and the ladies in foreign countries eager after the Paris fashions, was gaining more general extension in the course of the Eighteenth Century. Charming, indeed, are the little 'Incredibles' of the time of the Revolution. There is also a series of empire dolls which a toy manufacturer of that period illustrates in his sample book, in their low cut, light colored ball dresses, with short waist girdled with a large bow, and with a turban-like head-dress crowned with large ostrich feathers. [This sounds as if it came from the so-called Maury Catalog.]

"And not less charming in style and distinguished taste in all that refers to costume are the periods of the Restoration of the Citizen King and of the Second Empire.

"The city fashion dolls are not the only costume dolls. Noted also are the costume dolls as they are found since the close of the Eighteenth Century, in all parts of Germany, but also in the different sections of the Alpine countries of France and particularly Italy. These have been added to by the modern artistic reform movement in the doll industry, at first in Munich, and thereupon also in Berlin, Dresden and Karlsruhe. These are supplemented by different vocation types, chimney sweeps, huntsmen and soldiers of all classes and grades of service."

Another article published in TOYS AND NOVELTIES in May 1915 was entitled "A BIT OF DOLL HISTORY."

"Just exactly where and when dolls had their origin has never been determined, for so far back through the ages have they been traced, that it is quite more than likely that like Topsy, they 'just grew.' They have been known in every land and clime, and there is scarcely a corner in this old world of ours that has not possessed a doll of some sort of character. In Egypt, remarkable modern looking dolls have been known to exist in the eighteenth dynasty and they were common both in Greece and Rome. The Vatican and Museum Carpegna have quite a few well preserved dolls which were found in the catacombs.

" . . .It is most noticeable, too, that throughout all the ages, and in all the queer places that they have been found at one time or another, the baby form has been adhered to almost exclusively in a manner that might be termed universal. . . .

"Doll making as an industry was first developed by the Germans, and there are records existing today which go to show that their manufacture had been made a means of livelihood as far back as the 17th century. The real developments in doll making, however, have all taken place in comparatively recent years, while the American industry dates back less than a decade. [Actually dolls had been made commercially in America for over five decades.]

"Dolls, as we know them today, [1915] really did not come into very much prominence until about 1860, when the long, slender kid and cloth bodied dolls with heads of papier mache or china became very popular. In fact they have maintained their popularity even to the present day, and are to be found in considerable quantities among the imported lines each year.

"Following these came the beautiful but perishable wax dolls with natural hair and sleeping eyes. These dolls, too, met with great favor, but they were too expensive and perishable to last, and are no longer manufactured. A few years later came the wooden-bodied, jointed dolls which were invented by a Frenchman named Jumeau [Bru was the inventor]. These dolls had a considerable run and were the immediate forerunners of the present day jointed dolls with china and bisque heads, and stuffed or composition bodies, which are made almost entirely in Germany.

"The American unbreakable character doll, now so well known throughout practically the entire world, was originated some eight or nine years ago [1915–1895 = 20 years] in Russia by a man named Hoffman. His composition for making unbreakable heads was rough and rather unsatisfactory, but he had hit upon the fundamental principles which were later developed, and it was through him entirely that the American doll has taken its own place in history. Mr. Hoffman succeeded in securing patents which covered his process of manufacture to a certain extent, whereupon he organized a company in America and started to make unbreakable dolls. The value of his idea was early appreciated by one of our few large toy companies who bought up the patents and proceeded to make dolls in earnest. Their success soon attracted many men to this field, and at the present time [1915] there must be several hundred manufacturers of dolls and doll parts in the United States."

GREEK PERIOD: The Fogg Art Museum has a marble bas-relief which they date as 4th. century B. C. The translation of the grave's inscription reads: "Melisto, Daughter of Kteskartes, House of Potamos." The sculpture shows a small girl playing with her dog and clutching a doll in her hand. The doll appears to be simply a plaything and not a religious object. See Ill. 580.

MIDDLE AGES: Two part molds were filled with a soft wet dough which hardened to form dolls when it dried.

1500s: The better informed members of the German toy industry in the early 1900s believed that French Huguenot refugees originated the doll industry in Thüringen. This theory is substantiated by the fact that the majority of the inhabitants of Sonneberg were Protestants.

The 1550 British Customs records reported babies and babies' heads of earth from Germany. These were dolls and dolls' heads possibly ceramic.

1600s: Allegedly Louis XIII was given dolls when he was two years old and he played with dolls until he was seven.

A French publication mentions dolls of wood and of plaster given to a little girl.

A letter of 1604 written by a member of the Swedish court requested a fashion doll to be sent from the English court.

Three dolls in Swedish museums were made of metal wire covered with "unspun silk thread." The stuffed cloth heads had slight modeling and embroidered features. The coiffured hair appeared to be made of animal hair and had elaborate trimming including pearls. The dresses of a 1600s style were made of silk trimmed with braid. The largest and probably oldest doll allegedly belonged to a daughter of Charles IX of Sweden; it had a bodice, skirt, two petticoats, a

580. Marble grave relief on an Attica Greek Sculpture of the 4th century B.C. The little child is obviously playing with the dog while clutching a doll. Size 37½ by ca. 19½ by ca. 3¼ in. (95x ca. 49.5 by ca. 8 cm.). *Courtesy of the Fogg Art Museum, Harvard University.*

581A & B. Ca. 1660. Front and back of a pair of cloth dolls that allegedly were made in Sweden. The heads with embroidered features were made of iron wire covered with silk and stuffed. The bodies consisted of wire armatures. The original clothes were silk dresses with leading strings, metal lace underskirts, and linen chemises. H. of doll on left 7.5 cm. (3 in.). H. of doll on right 8.5 cm. (3½ in.). *Courtesy of the Nordiska Museet in Stockholm, Sweden.*

chemise and a beaded muff. The two smaller dolls had leading strings suggesting that they represented children. Hts. 7.5, 8.5 and 15 cm. (3, 3½ and 6 in.). See Ill. 581.

1700s: British Customs records show that painted babies could not be imported. The duty on babies that were imported then exported was considerably less than on babies that remained in England. British ships carried dolls to New England, West Indies, Italy, Spain and Holland.

Artists such as François Boucher molded wax-headed dolls. Other artists included dolls in their pictures.

TOYS AND NOVELTIES in August 1913 reported that in the late 1700s bread dough dolls were made by pressing a mass of paper into a mold and letting it harden, then it was covered with dough and modeled. In 1764 *Anne Hume* of

New Jersey advertised "common pressed dolls." These may have been what collectors called *carton* dolls. Wood and cloth dolls were also popular.

In 1759 George Washington ordered from *Unwin & Wigglesworth* in London, "a neat dress'd Wax Baby" for his three year old stepdaughter and in 1762 he purchased from London two fashion-dressed dolls, one costing a guinea ($5.25).

The most common description of dolls in orders and advertisements was "Fash. Drest." The VIRGINIA GAZETTE in 1769–75 contained advertisements for dressed and undressed imported dolls. Some of these had glass eyes and wigs. Among those handling these dolls and possibly dressing them fashionably were: 1769–71, Sarah Pitt; 1771,

Mary Dickinson; 1772–73, Margaret Hunter; 1774, John Carter; 1774–75, Cathrine Rathell.

In 1774 Samuel and Henry Dixon of Virginia ordered a dozen dressed dolls and another dozen dressed dolls with glass eyes.

About 1784 Thomas Davis, also of Virginia, paid 15 shillings ($3.75) for an "English Doll with red silk dress for Betty." Betty his daughter was less than two years old at the time.

In 1785 a new fashion periodical named CABINET DES MODES OU LES MODES NOUVELLES claimed to have a circulation in England, France, Germany, Italy and Spain as well as for the inhabitants of the North. An early issue of this magazine stated:

"They will no longer have to make dolls which are always imperfect mannequins and very expensive and which do not give all the nuances of our new modes." Obviously this referred to fashion dolls which the magazine was attempting to replace.

Some cloth dolls made around the end of the 1700s can be dated approximately by their clothes. These dolls usually had rolled cloth limbs and sometimes rolled fingers. Often the faces were featureless; possibly the features have been worn away but it also seems likely that these dolls originally had paper faces on which the features were drawn and that the paper had become lost. The Ohio Historical Society has a family of dolls reportedly from the Boston area made in this fashion. The lady doll of the family was a wooden so-called Queen Anne type doll with a flattish face having painted eyes, cloth arms, rolled fingers and carved legs and shoes with heels. The gentleman, the two sons and black female all had arms and legs like the lady doll but their heads were elongated cloth spheres with paper faces glued onto the cloth. The features were drawn in ink on the paper. The black doll's face had reverse drawing with the paper blackened except for the features which were left white. The white dolls had flax hair and the black doll had wool hair. The clothes were fastened with numerous pins on all of these dolls. The pins were of the early type with a shaft encircled at the top with wire, thus proving an early date for these dolls which apparently belonged together as a group.

1822: Thomas Anners[+] distributed dolls in Philadelphia.

1830s: Peg wooden dolls, some with combs and some with round heads as well as homemade cloth dolls were used for dolls' house dolls. "Smartly dressed dolls" were attached to the May garlands in Northhampton, England.

THE GIRL'S OWN BOOK by Mrs. Child, 1833, tells us: "The dressing of dolls is a useful as well as pleasant employment for little girls. . . . I once knew a little girl who had twelve dolls, some of them were given her; but the greater part she herself made from rags, and her elder sister painted their lips and eyes. She . . . would dress the dolls in the costumes of different nations. . . . The sewing was done with the most perfect neatness."

1840s–50s: Henry Mayhew in his book LONDON LABOUR AND THE LONDON POOR, 1861, based on information gathered in 1849–50, described the British doll industry. Armless penny dolls (priced 2¢) were sold by street peddlers

582. Gesso-over-wood doll of the second quarter of the 1700s with wig and painted eyes; dressed as a man in a red suit with coat, vest, and knee breeches. The costume was named "habit à la française" and also included a three cornered hat. H. 42 cm. (16½ in.). *Courtesy of the Collection Nederlands Kostuummuseum, The Hague. Photo by B. Frequin.*

583. Cloth doll made of rolled white fabric; no legs; black cloth forms the hair. The features were drawn on the cloth but have nearly all worn off. Original clothes of the late 1700s. H. 6 in. (15 cm.). *Coleman Collection.*

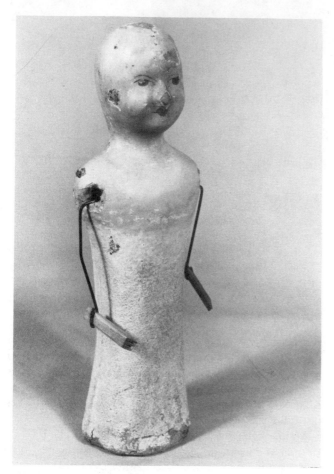

584. Carton head and torso with wire arms and wooden hands; a type made in France around 1800. The wig was nailed on the head; the features were molded and painted. A hole in the bottom had a wooden dowel in which a stick was inserted. H. 11½ in. (29 cm.). *Coleman Collection.*

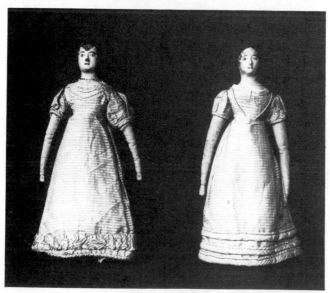

585. Pair of dolls in original linen clothes of the early 1800s. H. 24 cm. (9½ in.). *Courtesy of the Nordiska Museet, Stockholm, Sweden.*

who either carried the dolls in a basket or on a "Swag-barrow."

The German jointed dolls were too expensive for the peddlers. The German heads were sent to London where they were sold by Alfred Davis, White's, or Joseph's. Sellers in London made up the dolls and the dolls were sold either by the makers or by swag shops. These dolls cost about 6¢ to 8¢ and came in size numbers 1, 2, and 3. One dozen of the small-size bodies required 1½ yards of calico.

Plaster dolls with match legs were considered old-fashioned but one never saw a chandler's window without one. Wax and wax-over-composition dolls were sold in the Barbican. Nearly half a million dolls were sold each year in London.

GODEY'S LADY'S BOOK, 1853, reported "Young lady[ies] of seven . . . with their dolls, gutta percha, wax or chinese crying babies which ever they maybe."

LES JOUJOUX, a French publication, reported in 1924 that in 1855 German doll manufacturers furnished papier-mâché and porcelain heads to the French doll makers. Often the dolls played with in France had only clothes that were French. The dolls' heads were made in Saxony, Bavaria, Prussia, Austria, or England. England kept a monopoly of the wax heads.

1860s: THE ENGLISHWOMAN'S DOMESTIC MAGAZINE for December, 1865, described dolls. At first they spoke of an earlier period when the dolls sold by the peddlers from their baskets had "very red cheeks, and very little mouths, and very large eyes and very curly wigs, and very gouty

586. Poured wax head and arms, inserted hair, blue glass eyes; doll wears a crinoline type dress with five tucks and long pan-talettes suggesting the 1850s. H. 47 cm. (18½ in.). *Courtesy of the Collection Nederlands Kostuummuseum, The Hague. Photo by B. Frequin.*

calico limbs." The earlier doll "might be a mere lump of uningeniously [sic] carved wood; it might be a jointed figure with a rudely painted face and shining locks also painted; it might be a calico carcass, stuffed with sawdust, with a composition head and neck sewn on the top; it might be a plaster contrivance with match legs." The article continued, "We saw the other day two neat specimens of handicraft in the doll line made by Hottentots[,] wonderfully clever figures of a lady and gentleman—made of rough leather—in the costume (not by any means elaborate) of their race.

"... Encouragement is given to foreign manufactures. ... Artists, ... hairdressers, ... dressmakers, ... milliners, ... shoemakers, glovers, staymakers, ribbon weavers, jewellers, hosiers ... are employed in the manufacture of dolls and the fitting-up of dolls with dolls' appurtenances. Here are journeymen positively earning a very respectable income out of ... the manufacture of dolls' eyes. Blue eyes and black eyes, eyes that move and can't move. ... Wax, which, after a laborious process of classification shall be employed in the formation of dolls' heads, necks, arms, and lower extremeties [sic]." (See also **Cremer & Son**.)

1870s: There was a bewildering array of dolls and numerous store advertisements of dolls began to appear. *Bru* published a catalog of their dolls in 1872.

1880s: In ST. NICHOLAS, 1888, Olive Thorne Miller wrote about dolls: "For a long time they have enjoyed complete outfits of clothes, jewelry and 'belongings' ... they have been able to sit down and to stand up; to move their eyes and turn their heads, to walk and to say 'Papa' and 'Mamma'."

1890s: A STUDY OF DOLLS by Hall in 1897 showed that for children under 6, 98% of the girls and 82% of the boys played with dolls. For children 6 to 12, 99% of the girls and 76% of the boys played with dolls. There were 12 female dolls to 1 male doll and baby dolls were relatively few

587. Nürnberg catalog page of ca. 1860 showing various Täuflinge and dolls. The drawings indicate the relative size of the dolls. The four-digit numbers in the 4500s appear to designate the type of doll; when there is further variation a capital letter follows the number. The number or fraction after the slash denotes the size. Note that all of these dolls wear a chemise. Hs. 3 to 14½ in. (7.5 to 37 cm.). *Courtesy of Henry Francis du Pont Winterthur Museum, Rare Book Room.*

588. Left: Bisque-headed doll with molded hair, blue glass eyes, dressed in a two-piece costume. H. 35 cm. (13½ in.). Right: Bisque-headed lady doll with wig, blue glass eyes, blue costume of ca. 1870–75 with a blue parasol. H. 36 cm. (14 in.). *Courtesy of the Collection Nederlands Kostuummuseum, The Hague. Photo by B. Frequin.*

despite the fact that they were preferred by little girls. Boys did not like baby dolls. They preferred ethnic dolls especially black dolls. Dolls representing adults were the least popular.

The CHICAGO SUNDAY TRIBUNE, December, 1898, described the popular dolls for Christmas as follows:

"The eyes of this year's dolls are a clear open-and-shut proposition. Jointed bodies, also, that once were costly beyond price, are now cheaper than sawdust. . . . Baby Bunting in snowy white rabbit skin is shown shoulder to shoulder with the grotesque red and blue French clown. . . . The favorite doll of the year is by all odds the French jointed clown that may have any kind of a face. . . . The body is indestructible, and will remain in whatever ludicrous position it may be placed. The woolly hair is in patches of four distinct colors. . . .

"Dolls' wardrobes often making the price of a doll, and few expensive dolls are sold with but a single dress. Clothes include a variety of corset waists, bonnets and shoes.

"A fad that was introduced a year or more ago, and that has continued to grow in favor, is to have the doll named after some actress and dressed in the costume she uses in her favorite role. . . .

"One doll used to be all that was necessary; now a whole trunkfull are none too many. . . .

"Dolls are cheaper this year. . . . Dolls that cannot sleep however costly have been dug out of last year's stock."

Ca. 1900: Mr. Trumpore of *Effanbee* wrote in 1928 that around 1900 American dolls sold for 10¢ and up. The factories consisted of scattered units specializing in various

589A & B. Bisque-head lady doll with its original picture taken when it was new in 1877. It has a wig, stationary eyes, a closed mouth, a bisque shoulder plate, and a kid body. Original clothes as seen in the 1877 picture. H. 18 in. (45.5 cm.). *Courtesy of Cherry Bou.*

parts. One factory was devoted to heads, another to arms, another to bodies and a fourth to assembling. Composition heads were made by the cold-press process.

During the Spanish-American war the windows of stores were filled with khaki clad dolls.

1903: Baby dolls were becoming more popular partly because of the new self feeding doll with a bottle filled with liquid. By pressing a bulb located in the doll's head it appeared to drink the contents of the bottle.

1909: *Siegel Cooper* advertised a bent limb baby with painted hair and eyes. Ht. 14 in. (35.5 cm.). It cost $1.50 with a stationary head and $2.00 with a movable head.

Ca. 1910: Manufacturers began to make chubby dolls.

1912: TOYS AND NOVELTIES reported the following notes about dolls: "Bodies are stuffed with cow's hair or deer's hair, corkchips, cork dust, fine wood shavings, wood or [wood-] wool, not with sawdust."

"Dolls . . . lie on their back and kick, throw up their hands, move their heads and occasionally call for their parents."

"Nowadays well-known artists, painters and sculptors design dolls. . . .

"Formerly a doll consisted of a leather body and a porcelain head. . . . Now hardly any doll can be found which does not sing with the aid of a clockwork or which does not say 'Papa' and 'Mama' and wear gowns of the latest style."

In Germany, "In the line of doll-making each manufacturer produces a certain part. This has even sub-divided itself among the parts of the doll eyes, a given factory producing a given part."

The French at the first of the year put a duty of 60% on toys and stamped all their articles "French Manufacture."

"Taste has been diverted somewhat from the so-called character dolls and interest revived again in the idealized doll-head of old."

1913: TOYS AND NOVELTIES made various comments about dolls.

In London a group of dolls was dressed for a charity Toy Fair under the direction of the queen. These dolls were dressed in the latest French fashions for ladies.

Germany supplied 60 percent of the dolls sold in America. Most of them came from Sonneberg but the finer ones came from Waltershausen. German doll factories were running full time and increasing their output.

"The new custom in America of buying undressed dolls and dressing them in American-made clothes has caused a considerable decrease in the demand for dressed dolls." (See **Clothes.** 1909.)

Character dolls were popular, both babies and school-age girls and boys as represented by dolls.

"The dolls that go to sleep hold their own, too, although the tiny tots poke the eyes out just to see what will happen. There is the celluloid doll that baby can take along when he has his bath; there is the unbreakable doll of wood and of canvas; in fact, there is such a wide range of dolls from the very cheapest 10-cent one to the most expensive and elabo-

590. Postcard picture of a little girl pretending to have a sale of some of her dolls. The Spanish postcard has a French picture of the early 1900s.

591. Three bisque head dolls' house dolls of the early 1900s. Two dolls with wigs have glass eyes and the doll in the center has molded and painted hair and eyes and is made by Simon & Halbig. The dolls have on cloth bodies with bisque lower arms and legs. Original clothes. H. 5¼ in. (13 cm.). *Courtesy of Claire Hennig. Photo by Margie Landolt of Basel, Switzerland.*

rate. . . . it seems awful to think even one little one should be deprived—even if it should only be a rag doll."

1914: The declaration of World War I (1914–1918) had a profound effect on the production of dolls, for it cut off the supply of dolls to the enemies of Germany. In England a pottery in Staffordshire began to produce dolls. By the end of the war, England had a large doll industry. In France there were reports of the revival of the doll industry which the German competition had destroyed before the war. Even in the colonies during World War I, such as South Africa and Canada, doll manufacturers began to produce dolls to fill the void left by the lack of the German doll.

In America the industry was encouraged as the war progressed from 1914 to 1918, and this was especially true after the U.S. entry into the war in 1917. In 1914 German dolls came to the U.S. via Holland. TOYS AND NOVELTIES reported that no word had been received from France and apparently no dolls were coming from there to America. During World War I Japan appears to have begun making bisque heads with Occidental features.

Googly-eyed dolls with Drayton-type mouths were popular. *Kate Jordan,* a designer of dolls, wrote in TOYS AND NOVELTIES, April 1914: "There is nothing so far to compare with the European bisque, which we cannot imitate. Yet bisque is both heavy and brittle. Our American unbreakables are heavy, too heavy for babies' dolls and also very uncertain as to reproduction of the model. One American firm is doing creditable work in wood [probably *Schoenhut*], but how unsympathetic it is to the touch! How lacking in the precious quality of cuddlesomeness! A doll of any hard substance is such a long, long way from the ideal. A more or less yielding body is an essential to the perfect doll all designers are striving toward.

"I would almost say that we need strive no further, that perfection has been attained in Frau Kate Kruse's adorable 'toy babies,' but that their necessarily high price puts them out of general reach. And I am for the democratic spirit in dolldom as elsewhere.

"Here occurs to me a question that I have often asked myself in view of the fact that certain extremely homely character babies have had a surprising success. Is the homeliness an aid to the child's illusion of reality, or is it only the far swing of the pendulum away from Florabella of the infinitesimal mouth and preposterous eyes?

"For a while I doubted the child's preference; I thought the choice was probably of the buyers themselves pleased with novelty and that the doll mothers accepted the ugly babies and loved them just as real mothers do, but now it does not seem so certain to me that this is the case. Yet there surely is no reason why moderate comeliness should lessen the human quality. It is risky in doll designing, as in any other art—yes, art, for that is what it has come to be—to make prettiness the first consideration. Insipidity is apt to result, or cold, classic regularity. But in my work I shall try to avoid either extreme, in the belief that character may exist with some degree of attractiveness."

1915: Prices increased for materials used in making dolls and some materials were in short supply such as skins and mohair used for soldiers' clothes. Metals were used for

canning. Textiles from Europe were difficult to obtain. New American factories began to make composition heads. Dolls of rubber and celluloid also helped to replace the porcelain dolls formerly obtained from Germany.

1916: TOYS AND NOVELTIES had several articles that told about dolls in 1916.

"Some few months after war broke out in Europe, when there were large quantities of imported dolls in the warehouses of many merchants and when shipments were still coming to this country more or less frequently, the writer was engaged in conversation with one of New York's large buyers of toys on this very subject. The opinion was expressed that domestic doll makers had produced many very good values during the season just passed, and that they should be complimented for the rapid development shown and the high standard attained. 'Bah,' said the buyer, 'the domestic doll manufacturers turn out the poorest lot of junk I have ever seen. I wouldn't have one in the place if it wasn't necessary. Why on earth don't they take lessons from the Germans and produce something worth looking at?' He stepped over to a counter and picked up a beautiful bisque creation which would retail around $4 or $5. 'Look at this doll,' he continued. 'Isn't it beautiful? They don't produce anything like it in the whole United States.' . . .

"Sometime later the writer again had occasion to broach the same subject in an interview with the head of one of the country's largest and best doll manufacturing firms. Viewed from the other side of the fence, the situation took quite a different aspect, and in substance this is how the manufacturer put it:

"Domestic or American dolls constitute a totally different class of merchandise from imported dolls, and belong in a distinct and separate field of their own. It is no fairer to draw a comparison between them than it would be to compare oil painting with photographs or the renditions of a pianist with the mechanical strains from a pianola. They perform a definite function, they are designed for certain purposes, . . . but they do not compete with the bisque dolls from other countries, and are not even intended to look like them. Certain it is that Yankee ingenuity could produce better imitations of foreign dolls if that were the goal.

"As far as quality is concerned, however, the average character doll made in this country is not of a particularly high standard, from an artistic point of view, at least. It is true that with a few exceptions, practically all domestic doll lines represent a rather poor standard of quality in workmanship, and material too, and that they do not show the evidence of much effort on the part of their maker to do extremely high-class work. But there is a perfectly good and sufficient reason for this apparent failing, and it points directly back at the merchants who yearly sell them by the thousands. They are almost wholly responsible for the standards which have been set in doll production, yet they blame it all on the manufacturer.

"In the first place, the buyers who purchase the dolls to be sold at Christmas, really handle dolls but once a year, and are by no means thoroughly familiar with the various materials and processes of manufacture. They can tell, perhaps, when a doll is attractive and apparently well made, they can pick out the ones which will probably sell well and quickly, or they can criticize the poorer products, but they know nothing about material and labor, . . .

"[T]he great bulk of toy buyers know little and care less about how dolls are made; their principal concern is that of price, and the lower they can squeeze the manufacturer, the more satisfied they become that a clever deal has been made. If a factory produces an attractive number which looks like a good seller the buyer will say, 'That is quite good, I like that number, turn it out for me at a certain price and I will give you an order for so many.'"

Katherine Rauser expressed her views in TOYS AND NOVELTIES, January 1916.

"Because of the war the toy trade, and most particularly the doll market, is left high and dry. Germany has been the source of the bulk of the supply. Submarine activities, international embargoes and limited factory output have affected the German exportation so drastically that to be colloquial the annual business of Santa Claus . . . has been all shot to pieces.

"There was rejoicing in the hearts of dealers in dolls when the embargo was lifted about ten days ago from a shipment of $600,000 in toys from Germany. The greater portion of this is invoiced as dolls, either complete, or in the embellishing sections, such as heads, eyes, wigs or legs and arms. The best bisque heads and the finest bodies are fashioned in Germany, where the trade passes down thru generations in families. Only one house in this country puts out a standard doll that parallels the German product. It has been discovered, according to commercial reports, that the majority of French dolls get their heads from Germany, altho the best real hair wigs come from the United States, and the best novelty dolls from here.

" 'But it isn't novelty dolls the trade wants,' Mrs. Rauser said . . . 'Little girls don't want that kind to mother, or to dress, either. They want beautiful, up-to-date babies. That knowledge has been my success.'"

Red paint prices soared and caused dolls to have less ruddy complexions than formerly.

Foulds & Freure of New York received a small shipment of bisque socket dolls' heads from Germany.

Susan Tucker Mori of Atascadero, California, applied for a German patent.

1917: Spring joints began to be used because of the scarcity of rubber. Imitation leather replaced real leather.

A five reel motion picture was made using dolls and changing their position frame by frame. The dolls appear to have been Schoenhut dolls.

1918: A Dutch ship arrived in New York with German dolls which had been bought and paid for in 1914. These dolls were refused by nearly all of the doll companies in America. Dolls donated by stores and manufacturers were auctioned to raise funds for the American Red Cross. One group of 9 dolls brought $920.00.

1919: German dolls were not acceptable in the United States.

1920: TOYS AND NOVELTIES tells of the strike problems: "The doll strike in New York is over. . . . It was a case of radicalism of the worst type pitted against an iron clad determination on the part of manufacturers to fight for the basic American rights of an employer to regulate his own private enterprise . . . .

"That the domination of the doll-making industry either by manufacturers or by labor unions, depended on the outcome of the strike waged against Fleischaker & Baum, was declared in no uncertain terms by J. L. Amberg, of Louis Amberg & Sons, . . .

" 'Only two shops worthy of mention have been unionized,' said Mr. Amberg' 'All the rest are working as open shops. Experience in this industry has conclusively taught the impossibility of operating under a dictatorship which specifies the sort of labor, amount of pay, hours and the scores of other limitations imposed by unions. The general unrest throughout the trade has brought about several strikes, most of which, however, have amounted to little or nothing.'

"He cited the strike at the factory of the Modern Toy Company which lasted for over six weeks and then completely collapsed. The Liberty Doll Company, manufacturers of heads, was somewhat inconvenienced by a strike, but the management replaced all the strikers and the factory is now going ahead successfully, just as well in fact as was previously true with the old force of workers.

" 'The real fight, which was to settle whether or not the industry is completely unionized,' said Mr. Amberg, 'centered on the Fleischaker and Baum strike. Had the preposterous demands of the strikers been met, including the unquestioned dictatorship of a 'shop chairman' and a 35 per cent increase of wages it would have meant that the control of individual plants had passed from the hands of their owners, and the control of the industry at large gone to the hands of the union. Now that German dolls are coming into this country in large numbers, and often sold at a figure less than those of American products, you can readily see what the result would be with the curtailment of production and the increased cost of operation. The domination by unions in the doll-making industry would pave the way for increased importations and cripple the future of American trade.'

"Mr. Amberg said that the usual intimidations incident to strikes had been active in the Fleischaker & Baum situation, which was waged entirely by Italians. The immediate neighborhood of the factory was so well policed that all assaults had taken place at some distant point, workers in some cases having been attacked in their homes. But through a persistent show of strength the shop was kept running. Twelve arrests have been made and conviction secured in each case. Others are expected. Not only were the police active in preventing any outbreak of violence but other doll factories in New York gave their aid freely.

"The Amberg plant, according to Mr. Amberg, has been well fortified against the possibilities of a strike. An interesting situation prevails here which points to the foresightedness of the management. Many different nationalities are represented among the workers, and because of their varied ideas, temperament, racial influences and traditions it is very difficult for them to get together on an organized basis.

"This was recently tried, trouble having started in the stuffing department, but the strike lasted less than a day. While Mr. Amberg is more than willing to listen to the grievances of all the individual demands of workers, he positively refuses to entertain any demands presented to him from the workers as a body. The person who comes to him on such a mission and insists on trying to carry it through is discharged on the spot.

"One hour after the strike was declared fifty men, known as the Amberg Police, were organized into squads of ten each, having a lieutenant in charge of each squad and a captain over the platoon. The leaders were selected by the men themselves and they all quickly received comprehensive instructions which they acted upon with alacrity. One of the main duties of the Amberg Police was to protect the women workers of the factory. The effectiveness of the plan is told in the brief statement that the strike lasted less than a day."

Dolls dressed in regional costumes were used by libraries to teach history and geography.

Around 1920 composition dolls' heads made by the hot press method changed from having "ring" (flange) necks that were sewn into the body to regular shoulder heads, according to PLAYTHINGS.

1921: French women started the vogue of carrying dolls.

1922: Portrait dolls of famous actors and actresses and grotesque character dolls were popular.

1923: Popular dolls called "grotesque" were made out of odds and ends by impoverished women in Europe who had been wealthy at one time. These dolls were priced for the well-to-do only.

Small celluloid dolls served as mascots. The finding of King Tut's tomb led to the introduction of dolls with an Egyptian motif.

TOYS AND NOVELTIES reported that *Strobel & Wilken* had been established permanently in Sonneberg trying to restore old market conditions. The few lines offered there were mostly prewar ones.

1924: *Mama* dolls wore short dresses with their bloomers showing. LES JOUJOUX described French dolls as made of porcelain, cloth, molded carton, celluloid or rubber. The cloth dolls were plush, gauze or linen. Dolls came in hts. 6 cm. to 1 meter (2½ to 39½ in.). The bébés could talk, had moving eyes and eyelashes, threw kisses; the mouth was open with teeth. They could walk alone without help. Their nails were outlined with paint.

1925: United States imported a million dollars' worth of dolls from Germany.

Plump baby dolls were the most popular type. But slim bodied dolls began to appear. A doll society of superior artists was formed in Tokyo.

1926: Many of the dolls in the United States were dressed in Colonial costumes to celebrate the sesquicentennial, but for the most part these were cheap souvenir dolls.

Boys under 5 prefer girl dolls but older boys preferred boy dolls, clowns, *Brownies* and ethnic dolls.

Inflation in Europe and Japan hindered their competition with American dolls. In America the dollar doll created competition problems. American dolls tended to have soft cuddly bodies and big heads, with the space between the eyes exaggerated allegedly to improve their appearance. About one-fourth of the dolls sold were the *Bye-Lo Baby* types. *Bubbles* started the trend toward the smiling dolls with dimples.

A group of women protested against the "sophisticated" French dolls (probably the *Boudoir* type dolls). They claimed the appearance of these dolls was enough to corrupt the morals of the young. As a result the toy merchants did not stock these dolls heavily.

The copies of DEUTSCHE SPIELWAREN ZEITUNG in most of the American libraries, starting in 1926, indicated a renewed interest in German bisque head dolls.

The sending of *Friendship Dolls* to Japan began in 1926 and continued into 1927.

1927: TOYS AND NOVELTIES claimed that 90 percent of the dolls sold in the United States were made here and that a large number of dolls were exported all over the globe. There were problems in importing German bisque dolls nevertheless they were still highly favored.

Dolls represented every age. The infant dolls in long dresses were losing favor to the year old baby dolls in short dresses. These two groups accounted for nearly half the dolls. Mama dolls still predominated but they could not stand alone and newer dolls that could do so were supplanting them. Mama dolls were slimmer than formerly and were dressed in a variety of clothes. Other dolls represented school girls and nurses in uniforms. Large hair bows were popular. *Wanamaker* sold baby dolls in short dresses for $5.00 to $15.00.

1927 saw labor troubles in doll factories. There were strikes which hindered production and pressure to unionize. The strikes were not for money or hours. In New York, workmen received $30.00 to $80.00 a week; sprayers got $40.00 to $50.00 a week while sandpaperers and painters received $70.00 to $80.00. This contrasts with the minimum wages of women working in Massachusetts toy factories where they received only $10.00 to $13.50 depending on age and experience.

Dolls were used in schools in many cities to teach the care of babies. For this purpose cloth dolls, wax dolls, china dolls, bisque dolls and other types of dolls were used.

1928: Nearly 25 million dolls were produced in the United States and a few of these were even sent to Germany. TOYS AND NOVELTIES reported that the "largest and most expensive ones come from Germany, some of the prettiest ones from France." But the American dolls were most popular especially the baby dolls, one of these went to sleep when you rocked it but stayed awake if you did not rock it. Smiling baby dolls were the chief favorites.

PLAYTHINGS stated that 55 percent of the dolls were baby dolls, 35 percent were Mama or child dolls and 10 percent were novelty dolls. Dolls with rubber arms were preferred over those with composition arms. A strong Art Deco influence was shown in dolls from Paris. Boy dolls enjoyed greater popularity than formerly.

Patsy started a trend toward all-composition dolls that were strung so that they could be put into a variety of positions and could stand alone.

An article on "Santa Claus and Company" in the December, 1928, LADIES' HOME JOURNAL told us: "As for dolls, they are a crowning achievement. Whether they are baby dolls, modeled from a week-old baby, or little-girl or school-girl dolls, they have poise, individuality and charm. Some laugh, some cry and some speak; some stand, some pose and some walk; some have real hair, some have dimples, some drink milk; but all alike have beautifully formed, life-like figures. The babies are chubby and precious with an infant's fat little body and legs and an infant's crumpled hands and feet, and the young ladies are exquisitely slender.

"Their wardrobes follow the French, as is natural with folk who maintain a resident Paris correspondent, and they display a variety that shames many a trousseau. There are rain sets with galoshes, umbrella, hat and weatherproof coat matched in smart plaids; there are lounging robes and dressing gowns and smocks; there are slippers in snake's skin, leather, velvet and satin; there are gloves and fans and jewelry and sweaters; and there are dresses and hats and wraps for every time and occasion, neatly packed in traveling trunks."

In 1928 Mussolini issued an edict that all dolls made in his country have long hair. But many *Lenci* dolls known to be of this period had short hair.

Moscow's teachers' union decided that little girls should not be allowed to play with dolls. The doll represented the bourgeois idea of family life. (See also **Russian Dolls.**)

592. Felt doll of the 1920s, possibly a Lenci, has hair sewn on in strips, eyes painted looking to the side, closed mouth, and a felt body. Original clothes. This doll resembles model 111/4 in the 1925-26 Lenci catalog, but is 12 in. (30.5 cm.) and not 13 in. (33 cm.), as indicated in the catalog. *Courtesy of Sotheby Parke Bernet Inc., N.Y.*

1929: Dolls had slim bodies and legs; fully jointed dolls were scarcely seen at the Leipzig Fair. Bobbed hair was still popular but blond hair was in the minority. Some of the dolls had darker complexions to simulate sunburn. Dresses were a little longer than previously. Many of the new dolls were creations of artists and sculptors.

1930: The catalog for the Leipzig Fair boasted that 900 toy manufacturers from many countries were represented. The catalog stated "Little girls of Today . . . want dolls that are different—peasant dolls, character dolls and dolls of royal lineage besides the ever popular baby doll and the doll that can 'do' things." At the fair girl dolls, baby dolls, lady dolls and doll accessories were shown in a wide selection.

Kapok filling was used for most cloth-bodied dolls. Some baby dolls had very short sleeves for economic reasons. *Woodard* claimed that their dolls were made almost entirely by machinery without being touched by human hands.

TOYS AND NOVELTIES reported that "scruffy" dolls were bought for very little boys. Dolls made by convicts in prisons were causing concern because of the cheap competition they offered doll manufacturers.

1930s: Bisque-head dolls were still being produced in Germany and France and they were still using skin wigs. But the Depression followed by the rise of Hitler discouraged many of the German doll makers and they were enticed to emigrate, especially the Jews. Thus ended an era. (See also **Manufacture of Dolls.**)★

Chu Chin Chow. 1922. All-bisque Oriental type doll with shoulder joints, fingers together and hands at right angles to the wrist. It had earrings, a pigtail and wore a silk outfit including the hat. Came in 2 sizes. Distributed by *Hamley Bros.*

Chubby. 1915–16. All bisque character doll with jointed shoulders, legs together and a molded knit shirt and ruffled drawers. *Louis Wolf* distributed this doll.★

593. Mark on an all-bisque doll named Chubby.

Chubby. 1916–20. Trade name of a doll manufactured by *Elektra.*★

Chubby. 1929. A plump baby doll wearing a knit sacque and bonnet. Price $16.75.

Chubby Baby. 1930. Art doll with face painted on sateen, designed and created by Madame *Alexander.* It was dressed in a variety of costumes representing an older baby than *Cherub Baby.*

Chubby Boy. 1911. Distributed by *R. H. Macy;* it had composition head and hands on a cloth body that was jointed at the shoulders and hips. It wore a blue and white checked shirt with pearl buttons, a silk tie, slippers and socks. Ht. 12½ in. (31.5 cm.); price 98¢.

THIS IS A CENTURY YEAR

"CHUCKLES"

The "STANDING" SMILING "Dimpled" Face Baby, America's Most Beautiful Baby Doll, and

"PUDGY PEGGY" The Chubby Little Charmer With a Bow in Her Hair

Head the Century Line of Outstanding Doll Hits

CENTURY DOLL CO. 62 WEST 14th STREET, NEW YORK

594. Chuckles made by Century Doll Co. and advertised in PLAYTHINGS, September, 1928.

Chubby Buds. 1924. All-composition doll with painted hair and footwear, distributed by *Butler Bros.* Hts. 4½ and 5¾ in. (11.5 and 14.5 cm.).

Chubby Chancy. Late 1920s. All-bisque doll with jointed neck; wore molded clothes, consisting of light green shirt, short green trousers, red cap, and brown shoes. Ht. 3½ in. (9 cm.).

Chubby Kid. 1920–22. All-composition *Kewpie*-type doll made by *Columbia Doll & Toy Co.* The legs were apart and had high molded boots. The various knitted costumes were trimmed with marabou. One costume had a wide skirt and a hat.

1922: *Sears* advertised Chubby Kid with joints at the shoulders.★

Chubee. 1917. Line of composition dolls made by *J. P. Miller.* The line included spring strung bent-limb baby dolls jointed at the neck, shoulders and hips. It was claimed that the doll was washable. Some of these dolls wore long clothes and some wore only a chemise. Hts. 11, 15 and 25 in. (28, 38, and 63.5 cm.).

Chuckles. 1927–29. Doll with hot-press composition shoulder head, arms and legs, made by *Century.* The mark embossed on the back of the shoulder plate was "CHUCKLES//A CENTURY DOLL." The round tag read "The new standing //CHUCKLES//Baby Doll." It had molded short hair, painted eyes or sleeping metal eyes or glass eyes, open mouth with two upper teeth, and dimples in each cheek. The arms and legs were slightly bent and there was a diagonal hip joint so the doll could stand or sit. It also came with bent baby legs. The cloth body contained a mama voice. It was created by *Bert & Harold Scheuer.*

1927: Wore a short baby dress, real kid shoes and a halo type baby bonnet. Came in 8 hts. including 14, 16, 18, 21 and 23 in. (35.5, 40.5, 45.5, 53.5, and 58.5 cm.).

1928: Priced $3.50 to $12.00.

1929: 7 hts.

CHUCKLES

A CENTURY DOLL

595. Mark for dolls named Chuckles.

Chums. 1927–28. Twin doll sets with two boy dolls and two girl dolls dressed in various costumes and made by the *Primrose Doll Co.* They had "never-stick" patented moving eyes. Priced $1.00 and up.

Chunky Toys. World War I period. Small articulated wooden dolls made by disabled soldiers in the *Lord Roberts' Memorial Workshops.*

Cie. Parisienne de Cellulosine. See Cellulosine.

Ciechanowoka, Hélène (née Varsovie). World War I period.

Paris. A Polish artist and refugee who dressed dolls in cast-off clothes.

Cigarette Buck. 1920. A doll representing an American Indian with a cigarette in its mouth, made by *Mary Frances Woods* as No. 4. Each doll was handmade and had an individual face and blanket pattern. It wore a single feather at the back of its head. Ht. 12 in. (30.5 cm.). (See **Cigarette Friend.**[†])

Cigarette Girl. 1923–28. Also known as *Fad-ette, Parisienne* or Smoking Cigarette Girl. These *Boudoir* dolls with a cigarette in its mouth were made by *Lenci* with felt heads and by *Mutual Novelty Corp.* with composition head. Design patents for similar dolls with cigarettes in their mouths were obtained by *Max Goodman* in 1925 and by *Eugene Goldberger* in 1926. The Goldberger doll had a felt head but the material of the Goodman dolls is not known. (See also **Haskell, Samuel.**)

Cigarette Girl. 1926. A *Boudoir* type doll created by *Kitty Fleischmann* and manufactured by *Gerling.* It had fuzzy hair and wore a cretonne pants suit.

Cincinnati Doll Factory. 1896–1930 and later. Cincinnati, Ohio. Manufactured dolls.★

Cinderella. 1925–26. Nursery Rhyme Dolls made by *Jeanette Doll Co.* and distributed by *Louis Wolf.*

Cinderella. 1927. One side of this *Twinjoy* doll was dressed as Cinderella in rags and the other side represented Cinderella dressed in silk. This doll was created by *Berry Kollin.*

Cinderella. See Betty Bronson Cinderella Doll.

Cinderella Baby. 1906. Advertised by *Hutzler.* It had a bisque head with wig, ball-jointed composition body, and wore a chemise and footwear. Its name was on a ribbon attached vertically. Ht. 26 in. (66 cm.); priced $4.00.

Cinderella Dainty Dolly Dresses. 1922. Made by *Eade* in four styles.

Cinderella Wash Dresses. 1924. Line of dresses that can be easily put on or taken off dolls and can be easily washed and ironed. The 37 numbers included a middy suit; dresses with pockets, aprons and so forth. The clothes were made to fit dolls in hts. 16, 18, and 20 in. (40.5, 45.5, and 51 cm.).

596. Mark for Chums made by the Primrose Doll Co.

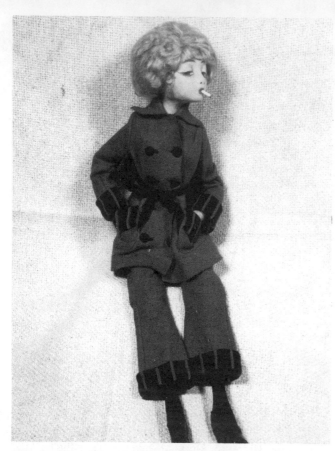

597. Smoking Cigarette Girl made by Lenci with a felt head, shoulders, arms, and legs; blond mohair stitched on the head in strips; molded and painted brown eyes; applied ears; open-closed mouth made to hold a white wood cigarette. Original green felt pants suit trimmed with black which appears to have been copied by Haskell. This is Lenci doll style no. 162; the label on the coat has the standard Lenci patent data used on dolls 1922–28. This doll was purchased in Venice in 1928. H. 25 in. (63.5 cm.). *Courtesy of Alice F. La Force. Photo by Ron Marquette.*

598. Cigarette Girls, all-composition Boudoir dolls with imitation cigarettes in their mouths. These dolls were probably made by the Mutual Novelty Corp. in the second half of the 1920s. They have hair of silk embroidery twist, painted eyes, and are jointed at the neck, shoulders, elbows, hips, and knees. Original clothes. H. 25½ in. (65 cm.). *Courtesy and photo by Stephanie Farago.*

Cissna, W. A., & Co. 1897–98 and probably other years. Chicago, Ill. Importers and jobbers who distributed dolls through their catalog called THE HUSTLER. Most of their dolls had bisque shoulder heads, wigs, teeth, and kid bodies.

	DOLLS AS ADVERTISED BY CISSNA			
	Height		*Price*	
Name	*in.*	*cm.*	*Wholesale*	*Description*
Bright Eyes	12½	31.5	$2.00 doz.	(25¢ retail)
Cinderella	18½	47	$6.26 doz.	Sleeping eyes, open mouth
Columbia	18½	47	$5.75 doz.	Body trimmed with colored thread
Mary Maiden	15½	39.5		(75¢ retail,) "French bisque head," sleeping eyes
Our Adele	22¼	56.5	$9.50 doz.	Sleeping eyes, open mouth
Our Beauty	16	40.5	$5.90 doz.	Sleeping eyes
Our Bell	20½	52	$7.25 doz.	
Our Cadet	16	40.5	$4.50 doz.	Open mouth
Our Crescent	21	53.5	$8.90 doz.	Open mouth
Our Favorite	15	38	$2.20 doz.	(25¢ retail)
Our Halma	23	58.5	$9.90 doz.	*Show Doll*, sleeping eyes, open mouth
Our Solitaire			$8.75 doz.	Sleeping eyes
Our Steinway	16½	42	$3.00 doz.	
Our Sunshine	14½	36		(50¢ retail) Sleeping eyes
Priscilla	16½	42	$4.50 doz.	Blue eyes, open mouth
Ruth	18½	47	$6.50 doz.	
Royal	24½	62	$1.25 each	"French bisque head," blue eyes, open mouth

Cissna also advertised dolls representing *Indians* and *Orientals,* as well as *Worsted Dolls.* The Orientals were also named Woo Chang and Hip Lung. ★

Cita. 1916. Cloth doll made by *Mme. d'Eichthal.* It was dressed in Kate Greenaway style clothes including a cabriolet hat.

Civil Imperial Volunteer. See **C.I.V.**

Cl. (Clown). Before 1911–24. Trade name of a jointed felt comic doll representing a circus clown. It was made by *Steiff* and distributed by *Borgfeldt.* It came in seven hts. 28, 35, 43, 50, 60, 80 and 100 cm. (11, 14, 17, 19½, 23, 31½, and 39½ in.); priced $1.00 to $9.00.

Claflin, H. B., & Co. 1912–14. New York City. Paris and Manchester, England. Factory representative and importer.

1913: Advertised *Cupid-Eye, Snow Bird* and *Spree-wald* dolls. ★

Clair, Madame Corine. 1923. U.S.A. Designed and created dolls for *Regal*.

Claire. 1926. French trademark for a doll dressed as a serving maid. It was registered by *Mme. Elisa Rassant*.

Clairette. 1921. Trade name of cloth dolls made by *Les Poupées Artistiques Française*. This doll represented a little sister.

Clarabel. 1916. Cloth doll with a smiling expression; had sequins sewed on its eyes to represent the pupils. This dressed doll was made by *Mlle. Duvall*.

Clarendon Works. See **Smith & Hoyle.**

Claretie, Mlle. Germaine. 1918. Paris. Created wax dolls.

Clarisse. 1923–24. Trade name of a cloth articulated doll with a mohair wig and felt clothes sold at the *Louvre* store. Ht. 40 cm. (15½ in.).

Clark, Albert J. 1925–28. Los Angeles, Calif. Doing business as Clark's Dollar Store, he registered as a United States trademark *Dollar Store* for dolls.

Clark, Ellen M. 1926. El Cajon, Calif. Obtained a United States patent for making dolls.

Clark, E. O. 1917. Scotland. Designed *Pixie* dolls.

Classic. 1900–24. Name of the works where *Speights Ltd.* made dolls. The name "Classic" was also used as a brand name. These dolls came dressed and undressed. During World War I. Classic dolls had *British Ceramic* heads, some of which were made by *Mayer & Sherratt*—such as the *Melba* dolls which usually came on jointed composition bodies. A bisque shoulder head doll with a cloth body and bisque limbs has been reported with "6 Classic England" incised on it. This doll was 20 in. (51 cm.) high. Another doll has been reported marked "Classic—Cecily." See Ills. 1855 and 1857.

Clauderies. World War I–1930 and later. Clauderies, a French word meaning waddlers or toddlers was used as a name for mechanical dolls that swayed from side to side as they advanced. The bisque heads were made by *Limoges* at first and later by *Unis France*. The earliest of these dolls had dolly type faces and wore short baby clothes. Later the dolls had character faces and came with composition heads as well as bisque heads. One type of Clauderies was described by Anne-Marie and Jacques Porot as having a crude carton and wood body with gauntlet hands on iron wire arms. The composition legs were connected to the body by iron arcs. The composition feet had lead soles to enable the doll to stand upright on one foot.

Claudette. 1918. Trade name of a doll created by *Jean Ray* and distributed by *L'Hotel de Ville* store in Paris. It had a painted head, cloth body and removable clothes. Hts. 36 and 42 cm. (14 and 16½ in.); price $5.60 and $8.20.

Claudine. 1927. *Lafayette* store advertised it as a cloth doll with wig, wearing a felt dress. Ht. 55 cm. (21½ in.).

Clausen & Co. 1922. Baltimore, Md., and Hamburg, Germany. Imported dolls made by Thüringian cottage industries.

Clay Pipe Doll. 1908. LADIES' HOME JOURNAL described how to make a doll out of a clay pipe. The face was outlined with ink and the dress was made of "holly paper." (See also **Unusual Materials for Making Dolls.**)

Clear, Emma C. 1888–1930 and later. Buffalo, N.Y., Cleveland, Ohio and Los Angeles, Calif. Successor in 1950s was Lillian Smith. Repaired, reproduced and made porcelain-head dolls.

1888: Began repairing and dressing dolls.

1890s: Made clothespin dolls for children in hospitals. She was a high school student at that time.

1917: Emma Clear moved to California and stated "I have lived to see the day when the most intelligent people in the country are coming to agree with me that the finest art of the last few generations went into dolls."

1939: Advertised "The First American China Doll makes her bow to the World of dolls." This was a reproduction of a china shoulder head with her hair in a bun. The cloth body had a corset on it. Price $10.00. Mrs. Clear also sold carved wood hands and feet for early composition and wax dolls. These were more expensive than her porcelain limbs. Wigs were made of Caucasian hair, Oriental hair or mohair.

1940: Designed Martha and George Washington which were sculptured by Martha Oathout Ayers. Other original dolls sculptured by Martha Ayers for Emma Clear were 2 versions of Danny Boy which were portraits of Martha Ayers' son, and the Modern Madonna, for which her daughter was the model. The exact date of the creation of these dolls is not known.

The pink china reproductions with a bun in back came in hts. 16, 18 and 32 in. (40.5, 45.5 and 81.5 cm.).

1946: Prior to this date Mrs. Clear made the following reproductions:
Jenny Lind
Mona Lisa
Nancy Lee (bonnet doll)
Kaiserin
Blue Scarf Doll
Gibson Girl (reproduction from a parian statue). There were two versions of this doll, had differences in the neck.
Dolly Madison
Toinette.

At first the reproductions were not marked but later they had a C around the year, thus C41 lear. Sometimes the dolls were marked H.D.D.H. (Humpty Dumpty Doll Hospital) or Clear but these were usually made later. ★

Clefs. 1908. Name of a French town in Maine-et-Loire that appears on a French trademark registered by Mme. Demarest[+] for a doll.

Clélia. 1927–31. French trademark in a diamond-shaped frame, registered by *Amilcare Brogi* for felt or muslin dolls.

599. "Clélia" trademark for cloth dolls.

Cleo. 1926. Trademark registered in Germany by *Albert Wacker* for dolls.

Cleo Corporation. Ca. 1883–1924. New York City, Toronto, Paris, Nürnberg, and Sonneberg, Thür. Imported dolls, especially dolls from *Lehmann. Miss Frances Schalleck* designed the costumes for their dolls.

Clerc, Les Fils de N. 1908–27. Paris and Plaine - St.-Denis, Seine. Member of the *Chambre Syndical.* Manufactured dolls in *swaddling clothes* or with leading strings and diapers, made of wood and/or cardboard. They had articulated heads and arms. They also made jointed bébés and undressed bébés.

1924–26: Obtained a French patent and a German patent (D.R.P.) for making composition dolls and dolls' parts.

1925: Won a Diplome d'Honneur at an Exhibition.★

Clichy. See **La Place Clichy.**

Clifton Works. See **Mayer & Sherratt.**

Climax Rubber Co. 1926–30 and later. New York City. Made outfits for dolls.

Cliquot (Club) Kid. 1924. *Mama* doll dressed to represent the Cliquot Club trademark. This doll with a composition head and cloth body was made by the *Gem Toy Co.* and distributed by *Supplee-Biddle.* The doll had baby ostrich feathers around its face. Ht. 18 in. (45.5 cm.).

Closter Veilsdorf.† See **Kloster Veilsdorf.**

Cloth Bodies. Hollow cloth bodies were advertised in 1910. These bodies were covered with linen including the legs. The arms were jointed at the shoulders, elbows and wrists. The rivet jointed legs were articulated at the hips and knees. The dolls came in four hts. 14, 16¾, 18, and 21¾ in. (35.5, 42.5, 45.5 and 55 cm.). In the late 1920s *Lenci* and *Alma* made felt dolls with hollow torsos.

As late as 1928 there were no state or federal laws, only local laws, regarding the sanitary treatment of stuffing used for cloth-body dolls. (See also **Nankeen Dolls.**)★

Cloth Dolls. Also known as Rag Dolls.† Cloth dolls have been popular throughout historical times and were made in many forms from the front and back variety with two pieces of cloth sewn together to sophisticated types with three dimensional molded features. Often they were made at home out of used fabrics, but many important doll manufacturers included a line of cloth dolls. The artistic felt dolls of the 1920s were among the most expensive dolls of that period. *Dorothy Heizer* cloth dolls of the 1920s–30s often originally cost several hundred dollars. Cloth dolls are most appropriate for babies and young children because they are soft and present few possibilities for harm. It has been found that some advertisements for "Rag Dolls" or "Cloth Dolls" may have referred to dolls with cloth bodies rather than all-cloth dolls.

Cloth dolls' heads have been found dating from as early as the 1860s that were obviously molded from pre-existing bisque heads; for example the heads made by Hawkins (See Ills. 785 and 786 in the first COLLECTOR'S ENCYCLOPEDIA OF DOLLS). A more recent example of the cloth

doll called *Flora's Famous Dolls,* made in South Africa, had heads molded from an A. M. #390 10½ for the 17 in. (43 cm.) ht. and S ⓅⒷ H 1906 for the 21 in. (53.5 cm.) ht.

1700s: Cloth dolls were made of rolled fabric as shown in Ill. 583. A similar dressed doll had an embroidered face and feet. The arms were made of quills and a mob cap was on its tiny head. Ht. 4¼ in. (11 cm.).

1831: THE AMERICAN GIRL'S BOOK described how to make a jointed and a plain linen or muslin doll stuffed with bran. The doll had a stick inside to provide support. This doll could be made in a black or white version. It was suggested that by renewing the outside covering the doll should last for years. Its face and hair were painted with water colors.

1860–61: *John D. Robbins* imported "Linen Dolls," size 2, price $1.25 a doz. according to his account book owned by Elizabeth Pierce.

1872: *Silber & Fleming* sold four sizes of dressed cloth dolls.

1873: Directions for making a cloth doll were given in a book titled HOME GAMES FOR YOUNG AND OLD. The doll was made of white cotton stuffed with rags or cotton wool. The hair and features were embroidered with cotton or silk thread or were painted. The hands were made of old white kid gloves. The body was made so that the doll could sit down.

1876–77: Silber & Fleming sold seven sizes of cloth dolls in two grades.

1878: Molded cloth dolls made in Houndsditch, England, by young children were sold for a pittance at such places as Ascot race course. These dolls were generally dressed as infants in muslin trimmed with lace. The *London Rag* dolls of this period cost considerably more.

1882: *Butterick* issued its first pattern for making a cloth doll.

1885: *Horsman* advertised "Model Rag Dolls" in six sizes.

1893: Horsman advertised cloth *Baby Land Rag* dolls, *Clowns,* and baby dolls made of jersey. (See Ill. 2449.)

1898: THE LADIES' HOME JOURNAL gave directions for making two girl dolls, a baby doll and a sailor-boy doll. "The rag dolls . . . have heads and bodies cut to-gether of white muslin. The fronts and backs are the same shape, and are then sewed together and stuffed with bran. The arms and legs are made, and sewed to the bodies. The faces are painted on lawn in water colors and sewed over pink muslin. The girl doll has a frock and flaring bonnet of pink gingham. Oil colors are used on the faces of the baby, the sailor boy and the little girl in the plaid bonnet. Bronze shoes and black stockings are used on these dolls. The sailor-boy doll's suit is made of blue linen, and the other of figured lawn and cambric. The baby doll has a dress and sunbonnet of white cambric."

> The prices given for dolls are those for which the dolls were originally offered for sale. They are *not* today's prices.

1899: *Cuno & Otto Dressel* advertised jointed cloth dolls according to the Ciesliks.

1902: *Wanamaker* sold cloth dolls dressed in an apron and bonnet for 50¢ to $5.00.

Early 1900s: Cloth dolls, usually a pair representing a man and a woman, were made in the Madeira Islands and dressed in native costumes. The man doll wore white clothes, including white leather boots. The features were usually embroidered and the woman doll wore a cone-shaped hat. These dolls have been erroneously ascribed to a much earlier period and to other areas, such as southern Russia.

1906: LADY HOLLYHOCK AND HER FRIENDS gave instructions for making cloth dolls. "First make a paper pattern then cut out and sew the cloth together and stuff it with cotton." Dolls could also be made from handkerchiefs or towels. Hair was made with black thread and for "topsies" (black dolls) the thread was sewed on with french knots. The features could be embroidered, drawn with water colors or with ink thinned a little. "Put the stockings and kid shoes on first." Mittens were also made of kid.

1912: Winters & Reinecke *(Anton Winters)* advertised cloth dolls.
    Strawbridge & Clothier advertised an "Imported Stockinette Doll, washable, fully jointed, light colored painted hair." Price $6.00. It closely resembled a *Martha Chase* doll.

1912–13: *Selchow & Righter* advertised flat surface cloth dolls stuffed with cork and sawdust. The names of their dolls were, *Gretchen, Hans, Miss Muffet,* and *Tom Thumb.* Similar dolls were also available as *Cutout Cloth* dolls. *Daisy Velvet* was printed in colors on velvet.

1913: TOYS AND NOVELTIES reported, "The indestructible rag baby is wholly American and is manufactured in several large cities. A few of these have been exported but they have not proved very popular with the European child."
    LADIES' WORLD advertised *May Manton* patterns for making cloth dolls and their clothes; three-quarters yard of pale sateen was required for a 22 in. (56 cm.) doll which would have been stuffed with bran, sawdust or cotton batting. "The portion of the pattern representing the face is perforated so that the features may be stamped and afterwards gone over with watercolor. A doll wig may be bought, or one made of yarn or even hemp rope unraveled." Patterns for a child doll's coat, cape, hat, nightgown, chemise, drawers, petticoat; baby doll's dress, long coat, petticoat and cap were all available for dolls 18, 22, and 26 in. (45.5, 56 and 66 cm.) tall.
    F. Kaempff[†] advertised cloth dolls.
    Gamage advertised cloth dolls with *Life Like* faces; priced 60¢.

World War I period [1914–18]: Art dolls of cloth were made in France. These were usually richly costumed.

1917: In England *Tah-Toys, Fretwell* and *Shanklin* produced cloth dolls of stockinet. A couple of years later *Chad Valley* made similar dolls. (See also **Chase Martha.**)

1920: A wholesale catalog advertised a cork stuffed, printed cloth doll made of Turkish toweling with pinked edges. Ht. 8½ in. (21.5 cm.); price 85¢.

1925: Cloth dolls, made by European artists, were dressed to represent a tourist, tradesman, music leader, monk, tennis player, footman, cowboy, cobbler, chef, and so forth. Ht. 12½ in. (31.5 cm.).

1925–26: *Heinrich Müller* obtained a U.S. patent for a doll made of pressed sheet metal covered with cloth.

1927: *Bing Corp.* made a baby doll with a rubber head covered with imitation skin.
    Felt finish composition dolls were advertised.

1928: *Albert Brückner*'s Sons, makers of cloth dolls, list the following qualifications for a satisfactory cloth doll:
    1. Attractiveness and novelty of design of face, body and clothes.
    2. Durability and ease of removing clothes for laundering.
    3. Absence of anything to injure a small child.
    4. Light weight and cuddliness, so they can be taken to bed by the child.
    5. Suitable for traveling and camping.
    6. Educational value for prekindergarten children.
    The *Bonser* doll advertisements stated: "Good cloth dolls are stuffed with soft, white cotton and when washed will dry out as soft and fluffy as new dolls." See directions for washing Bonser dolls at the Bonser entry. (See also **Manufacture of Dolls, Commercial: Made in France, Cloth Dolls; Made in United States, Cloth Dolls;** and **Worsted Dolls.**)★

600. Cloth doll in original linen clothes of the early 1800s. H. 24 cm. (9½ in.). *Courtesy of the Nordiska Museet, Stockholm, Sweden.*

601. Cloth over wood doll made from a twig. It has a wig, embroidered eyes, nose, and mouth. Original clothes. *Courtesy of R. C. and Ruth Mathes.*

602. Cloth over wood doll. The wooden doll underneath appears to be one of the so-called Queen Anne type. The features of the cloth face are embroidered. Original clothes including extra garments of the mid 1800s. H. 13 in. (33 cm.). *Courtesy of Joan Kindler.*

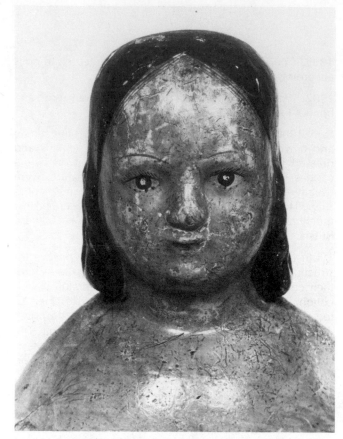

603. Cloth doll's head that has been heavily covered with paint and perhaps other substances. It has shoulder length black cork-screw curls, painted brown eyes, dots for lower lashes, brown cloth body. The fabric may have darkened with age. Jointed at shoulders and hips. H. 19 in. (48 cm.). H. of shoulder head 5¼ in. (13.5 cm.). *Courtesy of the Margaret Woodbury Strong Museum. Photo by Harry Bickelhaupt.*

604. Sized and molded cloth head with wire around edge of shoulders. Black hair molded into corkscrew curls, painted eyes, closed mouth, commercially made cloth body with wooden arms. Original clothes. H. 20½ in. (52 cm.). *Courtesy of Sylvia Brockmon.*

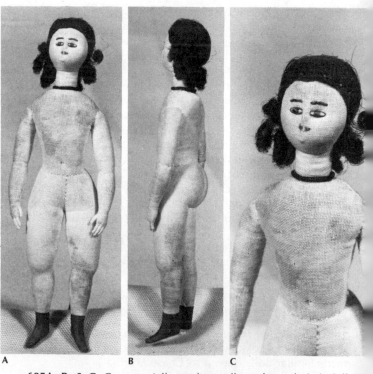

A   B   C

605A, B, & C. Commercially made needle-sculptured cloth doll with embroidered features, rolled fingers. Necklace of coiled wire suggests a mid 1800s date. H. 4½ in. (11.5 cm.). *Coleman Collection.*

606. Needle-sculptured cloth doll with embroidered features. Silk yarn braided hair, rolled fingers, original clothes and bead earrings. H. 5¾ in. (14.5 cm.). *Coleman Collection.*

607A & B. Cloth-covered peg wooden doll; hair made of yarn and paint; painted face. Clothes were probably made in the 1870s when the earlier wooden doll was covered with cloth for a second generation's use. H. 7 in. (18 cm.). *Coleman Collection.*

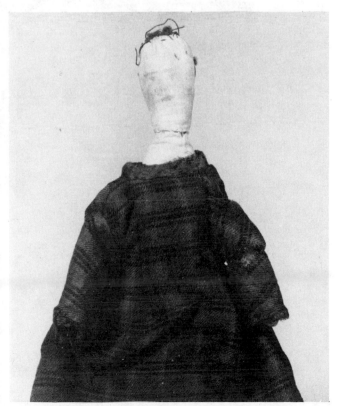

608. Homemade cloth doll with wool yarn hair, features drawn on the face, stub hands and feet. Original clothes of the 1870s. H. 7 in. (18 cm.). *Coleman Collection.*

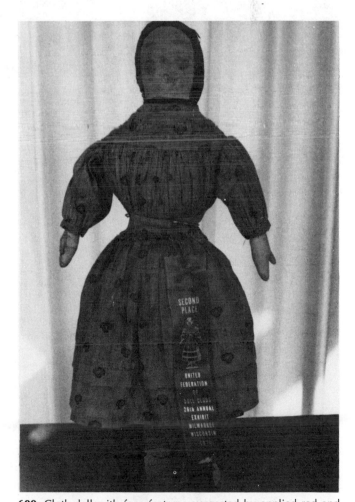

609. Cloth doll with face features suggested by applied red and black fabric; black silk head covering for hair; black velvet choker. Original clothes include a quilted petticoat. A card with the doll reads "Rag Doll 'Bettydear' made by 'Loving Hands' about 1850." H. 19 in. (48 cm.). *Courtesy of Margaret Mandel.*

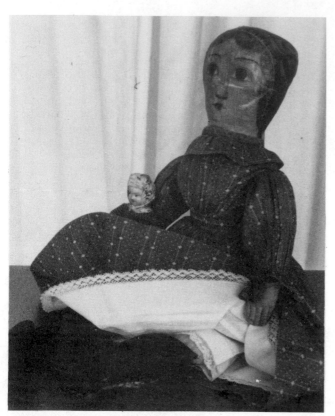

610. Cloth doll has hair and features painted with oils. The face has no contours. It has brown eyes, and there is a cotton-stuffed body. Original clothes. H. 17 in. (43 cm.). Holds a composition head doll with stick legs, dressed in a Russian ethnic outfit. H. 4 in. (10 cm.). *Courtesy of Margaret Mandel.*

611A & B. Canvas head cloth doll has a flat face and the back of the stuffed head is rounded. Face and hair are delineated with oil paint and lead pencil marks. Blond hair, blue eyes, closed mouth, kid arms to shoulders, jointed shoulders and hips. Contemporary dress and shoes. H. 26 in. (66 cm.). *Private collection.*

612. Cloth body doll with embroidered silk yarn hair and features, bead eyes. Original clothes of the 1890s. H. 5¼ in. (13 cm.). *Coleman Collection.*

613. Two-piece lithographed cotton sateen doll with brown hair and eyes, dressed in blue lithographed sailor suit with red bows, red stockings and black shoes with gold buckles. Dated by original owner as being about 1910. H. 18 in. (45.5 cm.). *Courtesy of Margaret Mandel.*

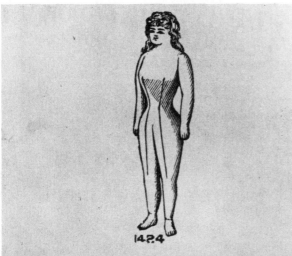

Rag Doll Pattern. 4 sizes, for dolls from 1.
to 24 inches from crown to sole. The 16-inch
size requires ⅝ yard of material 27 to 36 inche
wide. Price, 5d. or 10 cents.

614. Cloth doll pattern as shown in THE DESIGNER, a Standard publication, December, 1901. This pattern came in four sizes for dolls. Hs. 12, 16, ?, and 24 in. (30.5, 40.5, and 61 cm.).

Transfer pattern
for doll's face

No. 2928—Rag Doll,
including Transfer
Pattern for Face.
Cut in one size only,
18 inches high. Price
of this pattern, ten
cents

615. Advertisement for patterns for a cloth doll as shown in the WOMAN'S HOME COMPANION, ca. 1915.

616. Pair of needle-sculptured cloth dolls with embroidered features, including mustaches. Original clothes representing men wearing large visored caps. H. 10 in. (25.5 cm.). *Coleman Collection.*

617. Cloth doll with wig and wire armature. The features of the face are painted but without contours; it has brown eyes, closed mouth. Original Russian costume with painted boots. The feet rest on two cardboard rectangles which enable the doll to stand. H. 5¾ in. (14.5 cm.). *Courtesy of Cherry Bou.*

618A & B. Cloth dolls with molded and painted faces, hair of embroidery silk probably made in France in the 1920s. Original clothes and accessories representing the period of the 1300s. The clothes are made of silks and velvet; some of the velvet is marked to imitate ermine. The long shoes have the medieval turned-up toes and have "Carcassonne" written on the soles. The man has gold thread chains for a necklace and for a belt from which hangs a wooden dagger painted gold. The lady holds a prayer book and has a leather purse hanging on a gold thread chain. H. 7¾ in. (20 cm.). *Coleman Collection.*

619A & B. Sateen cloth doll with brown mohair wig, molded features, brown painted eyes, dots for eyebrows, closed pursed mouth with highlight on lower lip, flange neck. Original clothes except for the hat. H. 18 in. (45.5 cm.). *Courtesy of Margaret Mandel.*

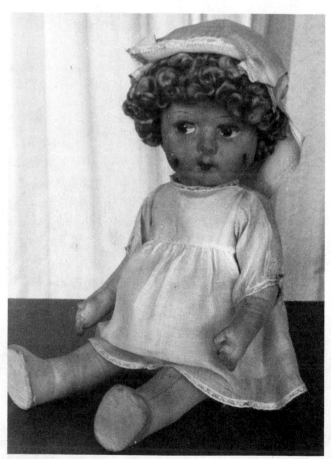

620. All-cloth 1920s doll with wig, molded features, brown painted eyes glancing to the side, upper and lower eyelashes, straw stuffed head and torso, cotton stuffed limbs. Contoured legs have seams in back and front. Original clothes. H. 16 in. (40.5 cm.). *Courtesy of Margaret Mandel.*

621A & B. Stockinet doll with painted face, not molded; wool yarn hair. Original pseudo-peasant clothes. H. 12 in. (30.5 cm.). *Coleman Collection.*

622. Molded cloth head with seam down the center, painted hair and features. Pink cloth body with painted high black boots. Original Hungarian clothes for a boy doll. H. 14 in. (35 cm.). *Coleman Collection.*

623. Ragline mark on a cloth doll having molded features.

Cloth Papier-mâché. 1920. Name of material used by the *New England Doll Co.* for their dolls with ball-jointed bodies.

Clothes. The original clothes on a doll are an extremely important part of the doll. They help to date the doll. They tell what age and sex the doll is supposed to represent. They can evoke some understanding of the original environment of the doll. They add immeasurably to the artistic appearance of a doll. In 1922 a museum curator stated: "Costumes are the most formal demonstration of people's art." Collectors appreciate original clothes more and more as their knowledge of them grows. Original clothes are defined as the clothes that belonged to the doll while it was played with during the childhood of the original owner.

If a collector is unable to obtain the original clothes, then contemporary clothing, that is, clothing made in the same era as the doll, should be sought. If a doll is dressed in contemporary clothes this information should be passed along as part of the history of the doll.

One important piece of evidence that collectors should be able to recognize is the presence of the two-part pins on early dolls. About 1839 a new type of pin was invented but some of the old pins were still used for as much as several decades later. The early pins have a shaft to which is affixed at the top a doughnut shaped head. If the doll's clothes have machine stitching the earliest possible date is about 1860.

Bébés Jumeau were usually sold dressed in a chemise and footwear. The purchaser bought other garments to suit his or her taste. Most of the garments were stamped or had a cloth label with a number to correspond with the size number on the doll's head, thus assuring their fit. There was a corresponding number on the sole of the Jumeau shoes.

The following French establishments were among those who made clothes for dolls:

> *Bail & Launay;*
> *Barrois;*
> *Delattre;*
> *Desrues;*
> *Doucet;*
> *Jeux et Jouets Français*
> *Jumeau;*
> *Lanvin;*
> *Margaine-Lacroix;*
> *Nicholas & Keller;*
> *Paul Poiret;*
> *Prieur;*
> *Rouaud;*
> *Simonne;*
> *Société Française de Fabrication de Bébés & Jouets*
> *(S.F.B.J.) and possibly*
> *The House of Worth.*

For further details on dating and recognizing original clothes, see THE COLLECTOR'S BOOK OF DOLLS' CLOTHES. (For dolls in period or regional costumes, see *French Regional Costumes, Historical Costumes,* etc.)

Ca. 1860: A German catalog at Winterthur Museum showed jointed-body dolls (probably wooden) dressed as girls and adults. One of the lady dolls wore a reform-type costume like that advocated by Amelia Bloomer. Hts. 3 to 9 in. (7.5 to 23 cm.). Cloth body dolls were dressed as children. Hts. 8½ to 20 in. (21.5 to 51 cm.). (See Ill. 140 in THE COLLECTOR'S BOOK OF DOLLS' CLOTHES.)

1860–61: *John D. Robbins* in his Day Book listed dolls dressed as boys, girls, crying babies, as well as *Polichinelle* and *Santa Claus*.

1863: In 1928 Queen Mary of England gave a doll representing Queen Alexandra as a young girl to the London Museum. This doll was described by PLAYTHINGS in March 1928 as follows: "The doll, which is 15 inches in height, was made in 1863 and is perfectly dressed according to the fashion of the day, including a crinoline. The dress is made of silk in the Queen's favorite mauve shade. A little panne velvet jacket is worn over the dress.

"The correct hairdressing fashion of the time is illustrated in this unique doll. Pads were then worn at the nape of the neck and the hair tucked under. A net was worn over the head. The doll's jewels consist of a large brooch at the neck of the dress and a small pearl necklace. There is also a long gold chain. A bouquet of pink roses is carried. All the garments are beautifully made by hand."

This doll was shown on postcards published by the London Museum.

1867: DEMOREST'S YOUNG AMERICA provided directions for making a pattern for dolls' house dolls' clothes. "Take a piece of paper a finger long and a little over, half the width, double it over double it again the other way and cut it. Shorten or lengthen as you require and for sacks cut the opening to the bottom."

1873: The book HOME GAMES FOR OLD AND YOUNG advised people to dress their dolls at home using cotton cloth, calico, muslin-delaine, ribbons and so forth. "Do not buy elegantly dressed dolls which can be used only on great occasions. . . . Small dolls made entirely of china are rather troublesome to dress, because the arms are generally fastened to the sides as far as the elbow. . . . Make a skirt of ribbons wider than the whole length of the doll, and gather it close under the arms; the skirt being longer than the doll, and the ribbon stiff, the doll will stand upon it, and the naked feet will be concealed. . . . For rather large dolls a piece of lace should be put across the body first and ribbon over it. The china dolls with pretty painted boots and hair dressed in nets, etc., must of course have short petticoats, and drawers of cotton or fine cambric, and skirts of ribbon with or without lace over them. . . . Tiny shoes can be made of a scrap of kid or morocco, or stout silk or ribbon."

A boy doll was dressed in trousers and a short sleeved bodice of scarlet merino or flannel, over which was worn a brown linen pinafore tied around the waist with "scarlet braid, and edged around the armholes with narrow broderie Anglaise or crochet."

1875: THE ELITE DRESSMAKER sold dolls accompanied by patterns with cloth models for the doll's wardrobe of 12 pieces. The doll had a wig and sleeping eyes. The cloth models showed how to put the garments together and how they looked when finished. Hts. of doll: 12, 18 and 22 in.

(30.5, 45.5 and 56 cm.); priced with cloth models $1.75 to $2.75.

1876: *Silber & Fleming* advertised boy and girl dolls in sailor costumes.

A dolls' dressing contest for girls up to age 15 was held in Boston. The child had to cut and sew all of the garments herself.

1878: At the Paris Exhibition French dolls were dressed as fashionable ladies; Alsatian nurse; Breton girl; Normandy peasant; a barefoot fisherwoman; an Incroyable with short waistcoat, double watch chain, cocked hat and huge necktie; a soldier in full red trousers, wasp-waisted coat and conspicuous epaulettes; a sailor in striped jersey, open jacket with brass buttons and Tarpaulin hat. The accessories for dolls included skipping ropes, feeding bottles, picnic items, brushes, combs, hairpins, nail scissors, tweezers, trunks, hand boxes, portmanteaus carpet bags, medicine chests, pouches, dressing cases, reticules, pocketbooks, skates furlined boots, satin shoes with Louis XV heels, collars, cuffs ivory tablets, opera glasses, powder boxes, babies' basket and playthings for dolls.

THE QUEEN, THE LADY'S NEWSPAPER in June 1878 advised: "If doll dressing is intended as an amusement for children, we would suggest that the toilette should be as much like that of the youthful sempstress [seamstress] as possible, as this gives the work an air of reality. . . . [And when dressing a doll in historic costume or foreign costume] The costume should be minutely copied not only from a print or picture often incorrect and lacking details, but perfected by information gained by research."

1880: THE GIRLS' OWN PAPER stated, "It is a great mistake to dress dolls too grandly; they do not give half so much pleasure as plainer ones." Knit clothes were suggested even for boy dolls.

1882: Silber & Fleming advertised dolls' outfits ranging in price from 43¢ to $15.00 depending on the size of the doll and the type of material. Besides selling separate clothing, dolls were sold in boxes or trunks with additional clothes.

1895–96: The *Louvre* store offered separate clothes for bébé type dolls in varying sizes that corresponded with the size number of the doll. These included bicycle costumes for male and female dolls.

1899: A doll's bicycle costume consisted of a shirtwaist, jacket with belt, bloomers, cap with feather, over-gaiters, shoes, and stockings.

1903: Children's costumes for dolls tended to replace grown-up costumes. The Paris stores sold separate clothes for *Bébé Jumeau, Bébé Bon Marché* and similar dolls that were generally sold dressed in a chemise and footwear. The dolls' corsets came in various colors. Felt slippers for dolls had fancy cords running through them and were decorated with tiny jewels.

1904: Fur automobile coats for dolls.

1908: At the Paris Exhibition a number of French ladies won prizes especially for dressed wax dolls. These ladies included Mmes. *Lafitte & Désirat, Jungbluth, Soulié, Mlle. Riera,* and others. (See THE COLLECTOR'S BOOK OF DOLLS' CLOTHES, p. 415.)

1909: *Siegel Cooper* had its own workshop where clothes were made for their exclusive bisque-head dolls. These clothes were designed by Americans. A bisque-head doll with wig, sleeping eyes and ball jointed body when fully dressed cost $1.75 but when wearing only a chemise and footwear cost 35¢. Ht. 9 in. (23 cm.).

Separate clothes came in many sizes and styles. The prices for dresses ranged from 50¢ to $1.75 depending partly on the material and partly on size. Hats priced 25¢ to $1.50 were sold separately and included an Italian straw hat, white lingerie hat, lawn hat or poke bonnet. There were five styles of dolls' parasols priced 25¢ to $2.00.

1911: HARPER'S gave the following account on the methods used in Germany for making dolls with special reference to the manufacture of dolls' clothes.

"When one speaks of a doll factory in Bavaria one does not mean the sort of factory that is known in America. The owner of a doll-factory where dressed dolls were handled, for instance, assembles the dolls in his place of business, and has the clothing cut out there. Then women call and take away ever so many little garments to be stitched at home according to the model which they have seen. This pleasant and profitable employment is not confined to the women of the poorer classes, although it is mostly executed by them. Quite a number of women of refinement make pin-money by dressing dolls for some such factory.

"Doll-making abroad is a real home industry, because nearly all the work is done in the homes of the poor. Some families make limbs, others bodies, still others manufacture heads of dolls, and anyone who will may dress them. So individual have dolls become that many are known in the trade by the Christen [*sic*] names of the children who posed for them. Hans, Peter, Marie, Gretchen, Annie and the Royal dolls, are known to all the shops which handle them." (These names were used by *Kämmer & Reinhardt* in 1911.)

Before 1913: Society people in Philadelphia imported clothes for their dolls in order to dress them as various members of the royal houses.

1912: TOYS AND NOVELTIES in January and February, 1913, described the making of dolls' clothes in the previous year:

"Dressmaking for dolls furnishes work for scores of women all over the world as dolls are shipped in many instances minus clothing and are dressed by the women of the different countries to which they are sent. . . .

"Delicate lingerie, tiny silk stockings, slippers and even gloves go with the modern doll's outfit. Hats, too[,] must be made and of the very latest style. The Parisian fashions are copied to the letter, and in many instances the miniature copies compare favorably with the original. Changes of clothing are required, for one of the chief delights of a child is the dressing and undressing of her doll, [writing] of her Christmas wants she invariably asks for a 'doll with a trunk full of clothes.'

"The dolls made in France, especially at Vincennes, have an exquisite finish. This is accounted for from the fact that each year there is a prize offered for the best design for dolls and new ideas in their manufacture. Doll dressmaking in Paris is a genuine science, for the Parisian article, like her human counterpart of that city, takes the fashions with her everywhere. All her dainty clothing are perfect copies of the apparel of the women who are seen on the boulevards of the French capital.

"The dressmakers have found it no easy matter to clothe the character dolls, for in many lands the national costumes are a thing of the past, having been superceded by the styles from Paris, and the museums of costumes of different countries had to be examined before the exact style of dress could be made. This year [1912] on Christmas morning [the little girl] found a little Swiss peasant or a German nurse or a French lady of fashion in her stocking. . . . They impress upon the mind of the child the salient characteristics both in feature and dress of the children of foreign lands."

"The gown makers of Paris and New York have their counterpart in the toy industry. . . . It is a fact that the makers of doll gowns and outfits sometimes step beyond the dictates of the adult fashion centers in the creation of modish doll styles.

"The rivalry in dress among women is no keener than that among the gown designers and makers. And so well does the toy world portray the world of affairs that makers of quality doll clothing and outfits vie with each other keenly to keep in the van of advancing Dame Fashion. There are makers of doll clothing in every land. Australia, with practically no toy industry boasts a score of doll outfit houses. Japan, Germany, France, Italy, England—each has its leaders in the design and manufacture of gowns, dresses, hats, shoes, under-clothing and miscellaneous outfits for the doll. It might be expected that America, with its militant toy industry, would jump quickly into a leading place in doll outfitting, and that result has surely been achieved. There are a score of houses which are today in America making as fine doll outfits as any Old World designers.

". . . Mrs. Rauser is probably the leading manufacturer of fine doll outfits, dresses, underwear, aprons, hats and novelties in America."

1913: It was the vogue to dress dolls as French Bohemian girls. The *May Manton* patterns were available for girl, boy and baby dolls.

1915: TOYS AND NOVELTIES in August reported: "Dolls Show Fashions of Past and Help Set Fashions of Present.

"Thirty dolls, each fourteen inches high, were placed on view in the Museum of Art, New York, Aug. 4, to illustrate fashions for women from the middle ages to the twentieth century. This was in response to the increasing demand for costume material by American designers cut off from European sources of inspiration. The models have been chosen from paintings of the old masters, tapestries and standard authors on costume. Every detail has been carefully worked out and fabrics have been selected in texture and design as nearly as possible like those of the period reproduced. The display follows along the Foucault collection of dolls in the Musee des Arts Decoratifs, Paris. The costuming offers fresh proof that fashions move in circles, thus enabling modern designers to draw on the centuries for the next evolution in woman's dress."

The same model was used for each doll. It had a bisque head, slightly turned, glass eyes and a wig. The difference in the dressing of the hair and the various headwear types provided the dolls with an individuality. The doll had composition arms and the proportions of a lady. The clothes represented the French style for the most part and covered the period from the early fourteenth century to the late nineteenth century.

Dolls, hts. 14 to 19 in. (35.5 to 48 cm.), were the most desirable because they were the easiest to dress.

Novelties for dolls were fur-trimmed shoes and ankle watches.

1917: *Doucet* dressed a series of historic costume dolls which were purchased by the Toledo Museum of Art.

1920–21: Kits were available containing clothes stamped on cloth ready to embroider, cutout and sew together. Included were embroidery cotton, dress snaps, and needle. The wardrobe consisted of a dress, apron, teddy type chemise, petticoat, cap, and booties. Price $1.50.

1922: TOYS AND NOVELTIES in March 1922 reported on an address by M. D. C. Crawford before the Fashion Art League in Chicago. In his talk on "The Relationship Between the Dressmaker and the Doll [he] expressed the belief. . . . that the history of costumes be studied by all dressmakers and in all art schools via the delightful medium of the doll, and that costume dolls be made expressing not only the charming history of the past, but local characteristics, that the masculine dolls receive consideration equal with the feminine dolls. . . .

"There are types of men and women determined by their occupation and race that could be immortalized in dolls and delightfully expressed through the medium of miniature mannikins. Imagine what a sensation it would create in this metropolis, or in any other, if every year there were 100 or 500 dolls made by dressmakers, typifying some local character or reaching backward expressing some incident in local history, with charm and gaiety. I believe if the great dressmakers in the centers of population where are gathered the great art collections, would address themselves to the task of reducing fashion history to 10 or 15 principal types, created in beauty and accurate detail and spirit, that this collection could move about the country and perform educational services of the highest order. It could be made at trifling expense in duplicate and multiply its potentialities for good. But each year to this convention should come from all over, your own members not alone, but from art schools and private craftsmen, dolls expressive of this age, interpretive of its functions and showing its relationship to costume."

1925: Handkerchiefs were used to dress dolls.

1926: American dolls were usually commercially dressed while the undressed dolls were nearly all imported.

1927: According to TOYS AND NOVELTIES the dolls at *Harrods* in London were so beautifully dressed that some ladies brought their dressmakers to see whether they could copy the dresses for the ladies.

1928: At the 1928 New Year balls some of the women were dressed to look like dolls.

WOMEN'S WORLD MAGAZINE distributed as premiums commercially dressed dolls with composition heads and hands on cloth bodies.

Sadie P. Le Sueur designed embroidered dresses for these dolls based on designs that had won first prize at a Tennessee State Fair. Each stamped pattern and floss for a doll's dress with matching bonnet and bloomers was sold together with an identical stamped pattern for a little girl's dress. All of the patterns had white collars and cuffs, five had patch pockets.

The dolls' dresses were as follows:

Name of Doll	Height in.	cm.	Material of Dress	Color of Dress	Embroidered Trimming
Beatrix	14	35.5	Gingham	Yellow	Roses
Bertha	14	35.5	Gingham	Peach	French knot flowers
Blanche	16	40.5	Gingham	Yellow	Appliqué flowers
Betsy	16	40.5	Gingham	Blue	Multicolored flowers
Barbara	21	53.5	Voile	Blue	Roses
Belle	21	53.5	Voile	Green	Cherries
Beth	26	66	Voile	Blue	Roses and French knots
Bess	26	66	Voile	Pink	Roses and Forget-me-nots

Colors for dolls' clothes in the order of their preference:
1. White
2. Off-white such as cream, mauve-white, pink white and so forth
3. Yellow and green
4. Gray. Black and white tweed trimmed with gray or white fur. (Furs were especially important this year.)
5. Rose, mauve and blue-mauve
6. All blue shades from navy to aquamarine

1929: Exhibits of smartly dressed dolls often served as style shows from which clothes for the juvenile population often developed.

Effanbee encouraged clerks to sell extra dolls' clothes when selling a doll.

1930: Madame *Alexander* designed a complete line of dolls' clothes made to fit "dolls of all sizes," according to PLAY-THINGS. (See also **William Henry Cremer, Jr., and Manufacture of Dolls, Commercial.**)

625A & B. Queen Anne type wooden doll with gesso covered head. It has a real hair wig, pupil-less black glass eyes and a closed mouth. Original clothes of ca. 1760. The watch bears the name "Eliz Bootle," and the doll was given to the museum in 1980 by the Wilbram Bootle family. *Courtesy of the Victoria and Albert Museum, London.*

624. Wooden doll of the mid 1700s has a wig, stationary pupil-less black glass eyes, dots indicating eyebrows and eyelashes, closed mouth. The head is covered with gesso. Original clothes. H. 4¾ in. (9.5 cm.). *Courtesy of the Margaret Woodbury Strong Museum. Photo by Harry Bickelhaupt.*

626A & B. Wooden doll with a gesso covered face, wig, stationary black pupil-less glass eyes, dots around the eyes and eyebrows, and a closed mouth. The torso, lower arms and legs are wood. The upper arms are cloth thus providing movement. The feet resemble hooves. Original clothes of ca. 1810–25. H. 17 in. (43 cm.). *Courtesy of the Margaret Woodbury Strong Museum. Photos by Harry Bickelhaupt.*

627. Original clothes on a papier-mâché head doll of the 1840s or 1850s. It has black hair molded in long curls, painted eyes, closed mouth, kid body with wooden lower arms and legs. *Courtesy of the late Estelle Winthrop.*

628. Original clothes on a wax-over papier-mâché head doll. It has a black wig, stationary black pupil-less glass eyes, pierced nostrils, closed mouth, kid body. H. 25 in. (63.5 cm.). *Courtesy of Sotheby Parke Bernet Inc., N.Y.*

629. Pair of papier-mâché head dolls with molded hair, brown glass eyes. Doll on left has china arms. Both have original cotton dresses. Left, H. 67 cm. (26½ in.); right, H. 34 cm. (13½ in.). *Courtesy of the Collection Nederlands Kostuummuseum, The Hague. Photo by B. Frequin.*

630. Clothes of the 1850s on a papier-mâché head doll, with black hair having brushmarks; there is evidence of a former wig. It has stationary black pupilless glass eyes, pierced nostrils, open mouth with upper and lower teeth, pink kid body jointed only at the shoulders. The clothes are all handsewn; it wears a pink-and-white-checked silk dress trimmed with silk fringe. The initials "C. F." are embroidered at the top of the white stockings. The gray suede boots lace up the inside and are without heels. H. 23½ in. (59.5 cm.). H. of shoulder head 7 in. (18 cm.). *Courtesy of H. B. Christianson.*

631A & B. Pair of china shoulder head dolls on stiff kid bodies; one is pink and the other white. The heads have molded hair, with side parts painted black with brush marks, and blue painted eyes. They are wearing dresses made from the same pattern. Both have low square necklines, full sleeves of white net, imitation stomachers, low waistlines with four tabs below. However, the doll with the pink kid body is wearing a dress of blue satin with a pink satin underskirt, while the other doll is wearing a white cotton dress. Both dresses are trimmed with suitable braid. The one in white has black cloth square-toed slippers while the other doll has blue leather slippers marked "4." H. 10½ in. (27 cm.) and 11½ in. (28.5 cm.). *Coleman Collection.*

632. China-head lady doll with original commercial clothes. The molded black hair is held in a white snood with purple luster and gold trimming. The doll has painted blue eyes, closed mouth and a cloth body with kid arms. The dress is white gauze trimmed with ribbons. H. 10 in. (25.5 cm.). *Coleman Collection.*

634. Clothes of a gentleman of the mid 1800s on a doll with an untinted bisque head; black hair, molded with a side part and brush marks; molded and painted blue eyes; white line between the lips; cloth body with kid arms. The three-piece gray wool suit has a matching high hat. The shirt is white linen. H. 20 in. (51 cm.). H. of shoulder head 5 in. (12.5 cm.). *Courtesy of Jesse Parsons.*

633. China shoulder head with molded snood and blouse top, painted blue eyes, narrow white area between lips, cloth body and china lower limbs. Original commercial clothes; the molded ankle boots have flat heels. H. 12 in. (30.5 cm.). H. of shoulder head 3 in. (7.5 cm.). *Coleman Collection.*

635. A very long baby dress on a tiny peg wooden doll. The doll has a ball head with painted hair. H. of doll ¾ in. (2 cm.). H. of doll and dress 5½ in. (14 cm.). *Coleman Collection.*

636. Bisque head doll dressed as a fashionable girl of the late 1860s in an original blue outfit. It has a bisque socket head and bisque shoulder plate, blonde wig, stationary blue glass eyes, pierced ears, closed mouth, kid body with German type joints at shoulders, elbows, hips, and knees. H. 17 in. (43 cm.). *Coleman Collection.*

637. Lady doll of the 1870s in original clothes and with an extra dress. The bisque shoulder head has a swivel neck, a blond wig, stationary blue glass eyes, pierced ears, closed mouth, and a kid body. H. 19 in. (48 cm.). *Courtesy of Sotheby Parke Bernet Inc., N.Y.*

638. China shoulder head with molded hair has a braided loop on the shoulders in back, a gold comb in front, ears pierced into the head, cloth body, bisque arms. (See also Ill. 1790.) Original commercial clothes of the 1880s. Mark: "2." H. 14½ in. (37 cm.). H. of shoulder head 4½ in. (10 cm.). *Coleman Collection.*

639. Group of lady or girl dolls in original clothes. They each have a wig, stationary blue glass eyes, pierced ears, a closed mouth, and a kid body. Reading from left to right: The lady doll in the 1860s dress has a stationary neck and is marked "E. B." H. 13½ in. (34 cm.). The girl doll in the 1870s dress has a swivel neck. H. 10 in. (25.5 cm.). The girl doll in the 1880s dress has a swivel neck. H. 15½ in. (39.5 cm.). The lady doll in the 1870s dress also has a swivel neck. H. 12 in. (30.5 cm.). *Courtesy of Sotheby Parke Bernet Inc., N.Y.*

641. Lady doll in fashionable clothes of the 1880s. It has a bisque head on a shoulder plate, wig, stationary blue glass eyes, pierced ears, closed mouth, kid body. Mark: "0." H. 12½ in. (31.5 cm.). *Courtesy of Richard Withington. Photo by Barbara Jendrick.*

640. Bisque head lady doll dressed as a bride. It has a wig, glass eyes, closed mouth, porcelain hands and feet with molded boots. Original clothes. H. 22 in. (56 cm.). *Courtesy of Elsie and Al Potter.*

642. Bisque-head doll wearing a coat and hat of the 1890s. It has a brown wig, sleeping blue glass eyes, closed mouth, jointed composition body. Mark on head: "15." H. 17 in. (43 cm.). *Courtesy of Sotheby Parke Bernet Inc., N.Y.*

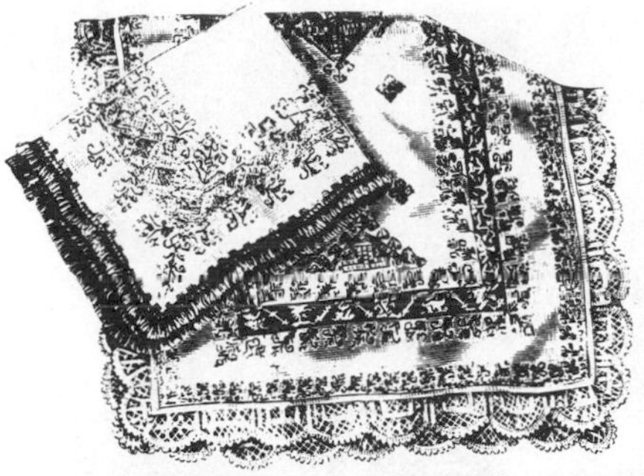

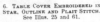

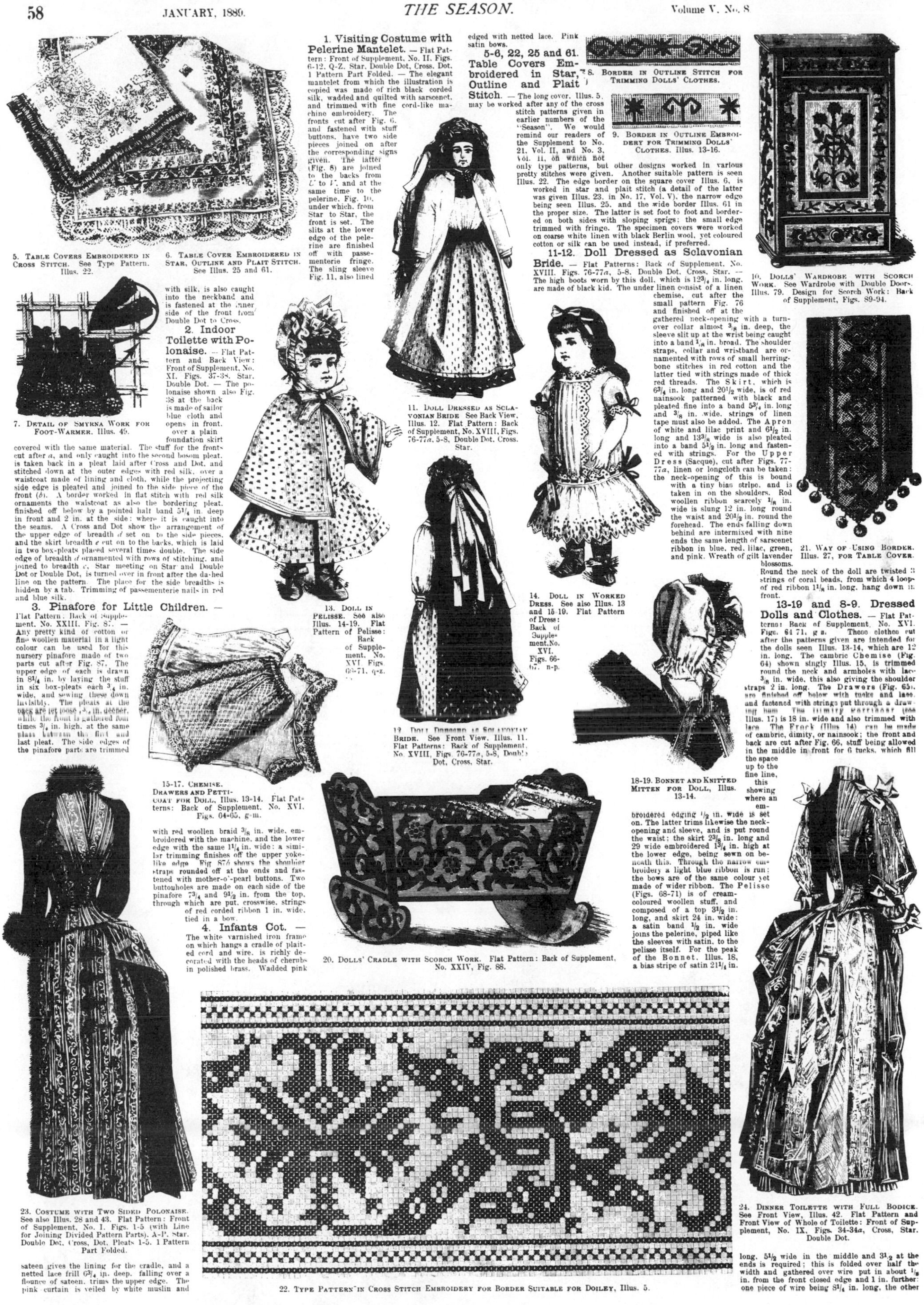

5. Table Covers Embroidered in Cross Stitch. See Type Pattern. Illus. 22.

6. Table Cover Embroidered in Star, Outline and Plait Stitch. See Illus. 25 and 61.

1. Visiting Costume with Pelerine Mantelet. — Flat Pattern: Front of Supplement, No. II. Figs. 6-12. Q-Z. Star, Double Dot, Cross, Dot. 1 Pattern Part Folded. — The elegant mantelet from which the illustration is copied was made of rich black corded silk, wadded and quilted with sarscenet, and trimmed with fine cord-like machine embroidery. The fronts cut after Fig. 6. and fastened with stuff buttons, have two side pieces joined on after the corresponding signs given. The latter (Fig. 8) are joined to the backs from U to V, and at the same time to the pelerine, Fig. 10, under which, from Star to Star, the front is set. The slits at the lower edge of the pelerine are finished off with passementerie fringe. The sling sleeve Fig. 11, also lined with silk, is also caught into the neckband and is fastened at the inner side of the front from Double Dot to Cross.

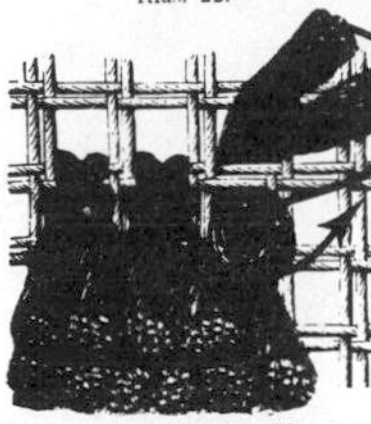

7. Detail of Smyrna Work for Foot-Warmer. Illus. 49.

2. Indoor Toilette with Polonaise. — Flat Pattern and Back View: Front of Supplement, No. XI. Figs. 37-38. Star, Double Dot. — The polonaise shown also Fig. 38 at the back is made of sailor blue cloth and opens in front, over a plain foundation skirt covered with the same material. The stuff for the fronts cut after *a*, and only caught into the second bosom pleat, is taken back in a pleat laid after Cross and Dot, and stitched down at the outer edges with red silk, over a waistcoat made of lining and cloth, while the projecting side edge is pleated and joined to the side piece of the front (*b*). A border worked in flat stitch with red silk ornaments the waistcoat as also the bordering pleat, finished off below by a pointed half band $5\frac{1}{4}$ in. deep in front and 2 in. at the side: where it is caught into the seams. A Cross and Dot show the arrangement of the upper edge of breadth *d* set on to the side pieces, and the skirt breadth *e* cut on to the backs, which is laid in two box-pleats placed several times double. The side edge of breadth *d* ornamented with rows of stitching, and joined to breadth *c*, Star meeting on Star and Double Dot or Double Dot, is turned over in front after the dashed line on the pattern. The place for the side breadths is hidden by a tab. Trimming of passementerie nails in red and blue silk.

3. Pinafore for Little Children. — Flat Pattern: Back of Supplement. No. XXIII. Fig. 87. — Any pretty kind of cotton or fine woollen material in a light colour can be used for this nursery pinafore made of two parts cut after Fig. 87. The upper edge of each is drawn in $8\frac{1}{4}$ in. by laying the stuff in six box-pleats each $\frac{3}{4}$ in. wide, and sewing these down invisibly. The pleats at the back are let loose $\frac{3}{4}$ in. deeper, while the front is gathered four times $\frac{3}{4}$ in. high, at the same place between the first and last pleat. The side edges of the pinafore parts are trimmed with red woollen braid $\frac{3}{8}$ in. wide, embroidered with the machine, and the lower edge with the same $1\frac{1}{4}$ in. wide: a similar trimming finishes off the upper yoke-like edge. Fig. 87*b* shows the shoulder straps rounded off at the ends and fastened with mother-o'-pearl buttons. Two buttonholes are made on each side of the pinafore $7\frac{3}{4}$ and $9\frac{1}{2}$ in. from the top, through which are put, crosswise, strings of red corded ribbon 1 in. wide, tied in a bow.

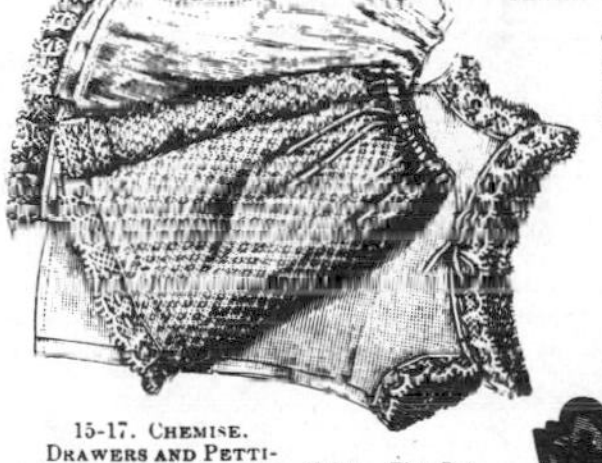

15-17. Chemise. Drawers and Petticoat for Doll, Illus. 13-14. Flat Patterns: Back of Supplement. No. XVI. Figs. 64-65, g-m.

4. Infants Cot. — The white varnished iron frame on which hangs a cradle of plaited cord and wire, is richly decorated with the heads of cherubs in polished brass. Wadded pink sateen gives the lining for the cradle, and a netted lace frill $6\frac{3}{4}$ in. deep, falling over a flounce of sateen, trims the upper edge. The pink curtain is veiled by white muslin and edged with netted lace. Pink satin bows.

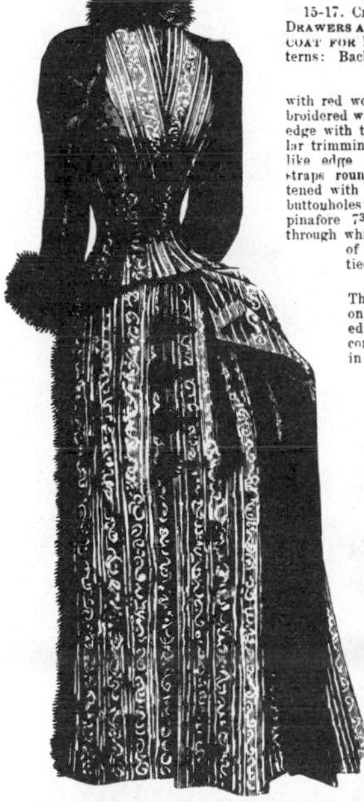

23. Costume with Two Sided Polonaise. See also Illus. 28 and 43. Flat Pattern: Front of Supplement, No. I. Figs. 1-5 (with Line for Joining Divided Pattern Parts). A-P. Star. Double Dot. Cross, Dot. Pleats 1-5. 1 Pattern Part Folded.

5-6, 22, 25 and 61. Table Covers Embroidered in Star, Outline and Plait Stitch. — The long cover, Illus. 5, may be worked after any of the cross stitch patterns given in earlier numbers of the "Season". We would remind our readers of the Supplement to No. 21, Vol. II, and No. 3, Vol. II, on which not only type patterns, but other designs worked in various pretty stitches were given. Another suitable pattern is seen Illus. 22. The edge border on the square cover Illus. 6, is worked in star and plait stitch (a detail of the latter was given Illus. 23, in No. 17, Vol. V), the narrow edge being seen Illus. 25, and the wide border Illus. 61 in the proper size. The latter is set foot to foot and bordered on both sides with sloping sprigs; the small edge trimmed with fringe. The specimen covers were worked on coarse white linen with black Berlin wool, yet coloured cotton or silk can be used instead, if preferred.

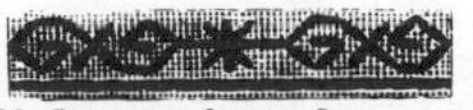

8. Border in Outline Stitch for Trimming Dolls' Clothes.

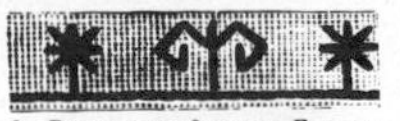

9. Border in Outline Embroidery for Trimming Dolls' Clothes. Illus. 13-16.

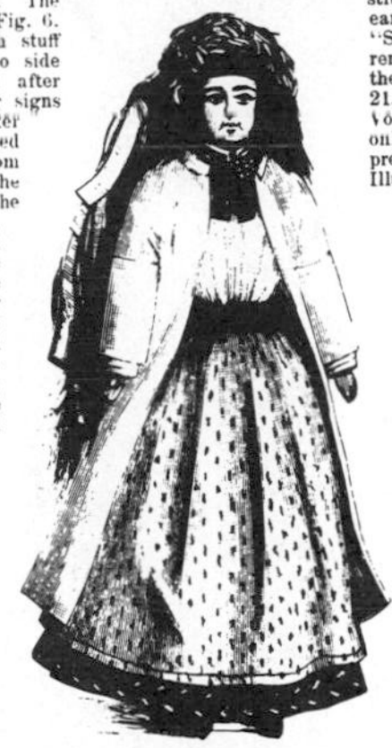

11. Doll Dressed as Sclavonian Bride See Back View, Illus. 12. Flat Pattern: Back of Supplement, No. XVIII, Figs. 76-77*a*, 5-8, Double Dot, Cross. Star.

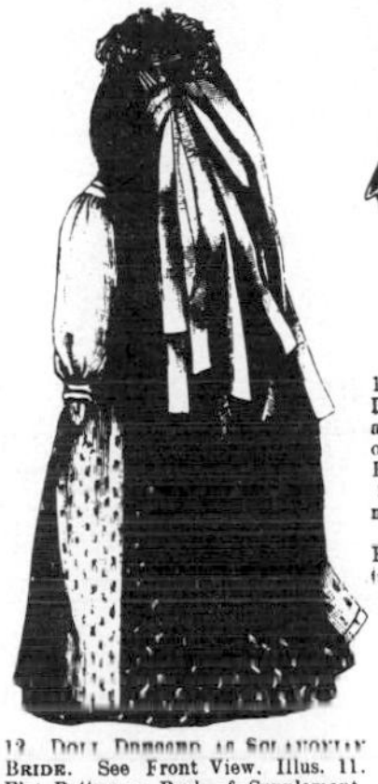

12. Doll Dressed as Sclavonian Bride. See Front View, Illus. 11. Flat Patterns: Back of Supplement, No. XVIII, Figs. 76-77*a*, 5-8, Double Dot, Cross, Star.

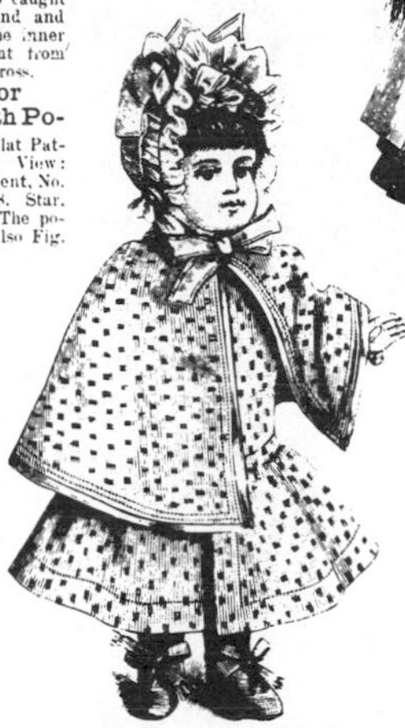

13. Doll in Pelisse. See also Illus. 14-19. Flat Pattern of Pelisse: Back of Supplement, No. XVI. Figs. 66-71, q-z.

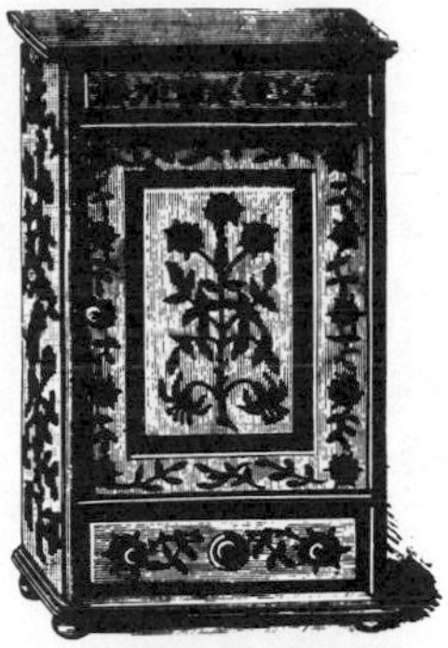

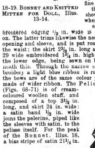

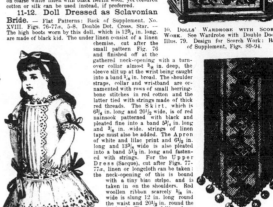

10. Dolls' Wardrobe with Scorch Work. See Wardrobe with Double Doors, Illus. 79. Design for Scorch Work: Back of Supplement, Figs. 89-94.

11-12. Doll Dressed as Sclavonian Bride. — Flat Patterns: Back of Supplement. No. XVIII. Figs. 76-77*a*, 5-8. Double Dot. Cross, Star. — The high boots worn by this doll, which is $12\frac{3}{4}$ in. long, are made of black kid. The under linen consist of a linen chemise, cut after the small pattern Fig. 76 and finished off at the gathered neck-opening with a turn-over collar almost $\frac{3}{8}$ in. deep, the sleeve slit up at the wrist being caught into a band $\frac{1}{8}$ in. broad. The shoulder straps, collar and wristband are ornamented with rows of small herring-bone stitches in red cotton and the latter tied with strings made of thick red threads. The Skirt, which is $6\frac{3}{4}$ in. long and $20\frac{1}{2}$ wide, is of red nainsook patterned with black and pleated fine into a band $5\frac{3}{4}$ in. long and $\frac{3}{8}$ in. wide, strings of linen tape must also be added. The Apron of white and lilac print and $6\frac{1}{2}$ in. long and $13\frac{3}{8}$ wide is also pleated into a band $5\frac{1}{2}$ in. long and fastened with strings. For the Upper Dress (Sacque), cut after Figs. 77-77*a*, linen or longcloth can be taken: the neck-opening of this is bound with a tiny bias stripe, and is taken in on the shoulders. Red woollen ribbon scarcely $\frac{1}{8}$ in. wide is slung 12 in. long round the waist and $20\frac{1}{2}$ in. round the forehead. The ends falling down behind are intermixed with nine ends the same length of sarscenet ribbon in blue, red, lilac, green, and pink. Wreath of gilt lavender blossoms. Round the neck of the doll are twisted 3 strings of coral beads, from which 4 loops of red ribbon $1\frac{1}{8}$ in. long, hang down in front.

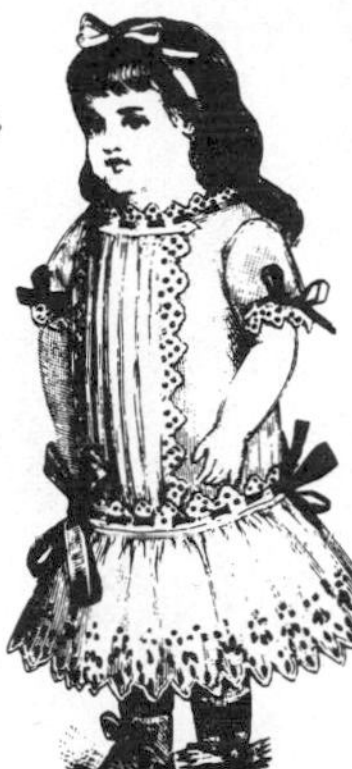

14. Doll in Worked Dress. See also Illus. 13 and 15-19. Flat Pattern of Dress: Back of Supplement. No. XVI. Figs. 66-67. n-p.

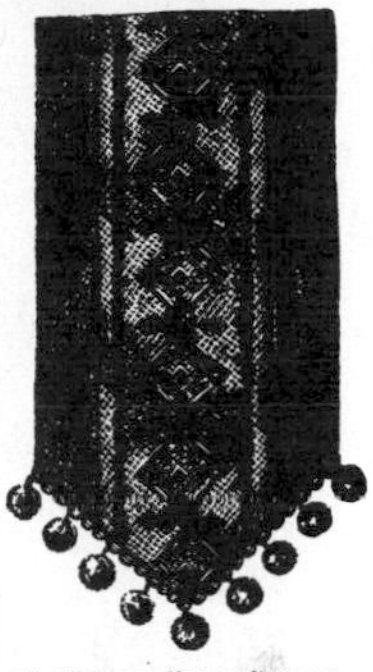

21. Way of Using Border. Illus. 27, for Table Cover.

13-19 and 8-9. Dressed Dolls and Clothes. — Flat Patterns: Back of Supplement. No. XVI. Figs. 64-71, g-z. These clothes cut after the patterns given are intended for the dolls seen Illus. 13-14, which are 12 in. long. The cambric Chemise (Fig. 64) shown singly Illus. 15, is trimmed round the neck and armholes with lace $\frac{3}{8}$ in. wide, this also giving the shoulder straps 2 in. long. The Drawers (Fig. 65), are finished off below with tucks and lace, and fastened with strings put through a drawing hem. The dimity Petticoat (see Illus. 17) is 18 in. wide and also trimmed with lace. The Frock (Illus. 14) can be made of cambric, dimity, or nainsook; the front and back are cut after Fig. 66, stuff being allowed in the middle in front for 6 tucks, which fill the space up to the fine line, this showing where an embroidered edging $\frac{1}{2}$ in. wide is set on. The latter trims likewise the neck-opening and sleeve, and is put round the waist: the skirt $2\frac{3}{8}$ in. long and 29 wide embroidered $1\frac{3}{4}$ in. high at the lower edge, being sewn on beneath this. Through the narrow embroidery a light blue ribbon is run; the bows are of the same colour yet made of wider ribbon. The Pelisse (Figs. 68-71) is of cream-coloured woollen stuff, and composed of a top $3\frac{1}{2}$ in. long, and skirt 24 in. wide: a satin band $\frac{1}{2}$ in. wide joins the pelerine, piped like the sleeves with satin, to the pelisse itself. For the peak of the Bonnet, Illus. 18, a bias stripe of satin $21\frac{1}{4}$ in. long, $5\frac{1}{2}$ wide in the middle and $3\frac{1}{2}$ at the ends is required; this is folded over half the width and gathered over wire put in about $\frac{1}{8}$ in. from the front closed edge and 1 in. further: one piece of wire being $8\frac{1}{4}$ in. long, the other

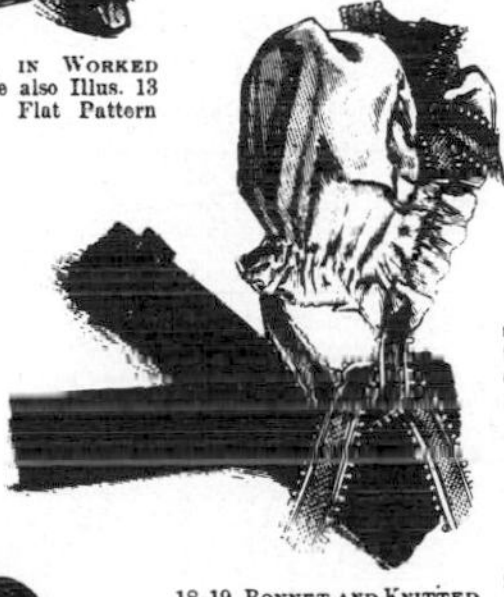

18-19. Bonnet and Knitted Mitten for Doll, Illus. 13-14.

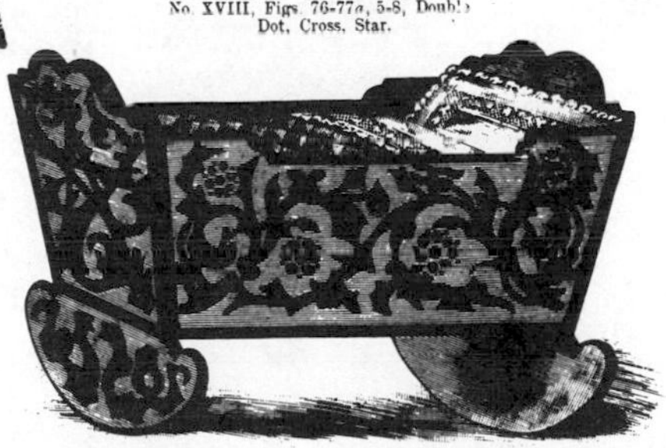

20. Dolls' Cradle with Scorch Work. Flat Pattern: Back of Supplement, No. XXIV, Fig. 88.

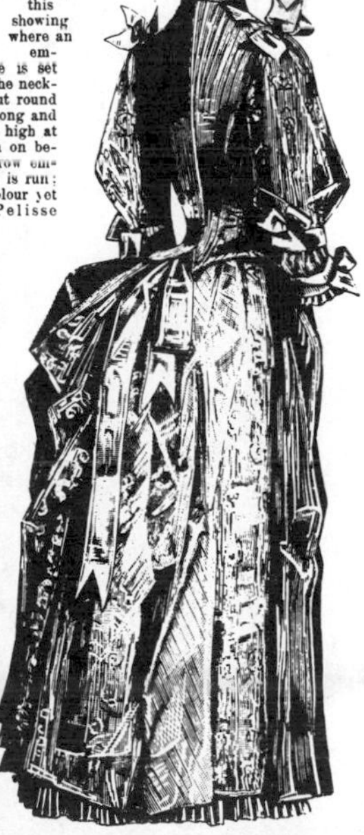

24. Dinner Toilette with Full Bodice. See Front View, Illus. 42. Flat Pattern and Front View of Whole of Toilette: Front of Supplement, No. IX, Figs. 34-34*a*, Cross, Star. Double Dot.

22. Type Pattern in Cross Stitch Embroidery for Border Suitable for Doiley, Illus. 5.

643. Page from THE SEASON, January 1889, showing dolls' clothes, including a doll dressed as a Slavonian Bride. H. $12\frac{3}{4}$ in. (32.5 cm.). The other clothes are a dress embroidered in white work, pelisse, bonnet, and knit mittens for a 12 in. (30.5 cm.) doll.

644. Bisque head with a wig, pupilless glass eyes, closed mouth, flange neck on a five-piece composition body. Molded footwear and original commercial clothes. H. 9 in. (23 cm.). *Coleman Collection.*

645. Pair of bisque head dolls with showy commercial clothes of the 1890s. The dolls have wigs, stationary glass eyes, pierced ears, closed mouth, fully jointed composition bodies. *Courtesy of the late Irene Blair Hickman.*

646. Bébé Jumeau with its trunk of clothes and accessories. The bébé has a bisque socket head with brown glass eyes, pierced ears, closed mouth, composition body with separated wood balls at the joints, no wrist joints. Doll wears original chemise and an ivory silk hat labeled "AU BON MARCHE//LAYETTES//Taille 7// 4 E44// 2^f. 75" (Size 7, price 55¢). The trunk, marked on its handles "H <> A DÉPOSÉ," contains three dresses, underwear, a heart-shaped necklace marked "J," and two pairs of leather shoes, one with the Jumeau bee mark (Ill. 1362) and the other with the Alart girl over DÉPOSÉ. Marks on the doll: Incised on the head "DÉPOSÉ//10" and a blue stamp on the back of the body "JUMEAU//MEDAILLE D'OR//PARIS." H. 22½ in. (57 cm.). *Courtesy of Becky Moncrief.*

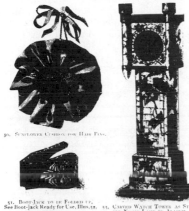

647. Pages from the THE SEASON, January, 1892, showing dressed dolls in and outside of a display window. The doll on the extreme right in the window is dressed as a gardener maiden in south Germany. H. 15 in. (38 cm.). Next to it is a doll dressed as a milkman in South Germany. H. 14½ in. (37 cm.). Behind the milkman is a doll dressed in a black-and-white-checked woolen frock with a "waistband bodice." H. 14 in. (35.5 cm.). Note "Alice" with its trunk and trousseau in the foreground.

648. Page from THE SEASON, January, 1895, showing dolls' clothes including dolls in knitted Norwegian costumes for "Sky Runners," H. 3¼ in. (8 cm.); a dressed doll with its wardrobe including a knitted petticoat, H. 10¾ in. (27.5 cm.); and a baby doll in a long dress with its layette in a basket. THE SEASON was the English edition of the MODENWELT and the German influence is seen here in the "German Tap Room for Doll's House."

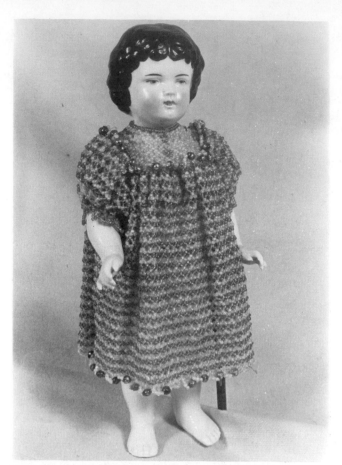

649. Frozen Charlotte has molded curly black hair and blue painted eyes. The knee length beaded dress made of blue and white beads is trimmed with silver beads. H. 9¼ in. (23.5 cm.). *Courtesy of Z. Frances Walker.*

650. Bisque-head doll with original clothes of the 1890s. It has a light blond mohair wig, sleeping blue glass eyes, closed mouth, and jointed composition body. The silk dress has tucks, lace inserts, and ribbon bows. The bonnet is straw in back. Mark on head: "14." H. 22 in. (56 cm.). *Private collection.*

Clothes for Christmas Dolls
By Anna Lent

THESE clothes for dolls have been designed with a twofold purpose: first, to please the little people, and then to assist the grownups who undertake the pleasant task of dressing dolls that will delight the hearts of the children at Christmastime.

The patterns contain few pieces, and this greatly simplifies the work. The wee garments are all cut like real babies' and children's clothes; for children find the greatest delight in the fact that Dolly's clothes are just like their own, and quite as easily put on and off.

A COMPLETE set of clothes for the baby-doll. Flannelette is suggested for the "flannel" petticoat and for the little wrapper that is cut the same way as the nightgown; and, by-the-way, lap and pin the petticoat band—also the shirt—with tiny safety-pins just like a real, live baby's clothes. Make the cloak of cashmere or challis, and the little cap of lawn or silk. The patterns for these doll's clothes are cut in four sizes to fit dolls 12, 16, 20 and 24 inches high, and cost 15 cents a set.

2892   DRAWN BY GRACE G. WIEDERSEIM

Frequently the piece-box will supply the necessary materials for Dolly's outfit; but sometimes it may be necessary to buy new. Lawn, at ten cents a yard, is suitable for the undergarments; it will also be pretty for the baby's dress, and, in combination with lace, at eight cents a yard or less, for the little girl's befrilled frock. Narrow lace, at three or five cents a yard, will trim the

2895

ALL the underclothes for the little girl-doll; a kimona and a nightgown, too. There are patterns in four sizes to fit dolls measuring 14, 18, 22 and 26 inches, which cost 10 cents a set.

underclothes. The dress of dotted material for the little girl-doll is made by the same pattern as the frilled frock; lawn, dimity or challis with a tiny yoke of lace or embroidery is suggested for this.

For the same Dolly, cashmere or broadcloth will make a cute little coat, but I am sure Dolly's small mother would think a coat of taffeta or velveteen "perfectly dear."

651. Clothes for a baby doll and for a little girl doll drawn by Grace G. Weiderseim (Drayton) for THE LADIES' HOME JOURNAL, December, 1906.

652. Molded and painted clothes on a cardboard doll with molded and painted hair and features. The doll is jointed at the shoulders. H. 17½ in. (44.5 cm.). *Courtesy of Ruth and R. C. Mathes.*

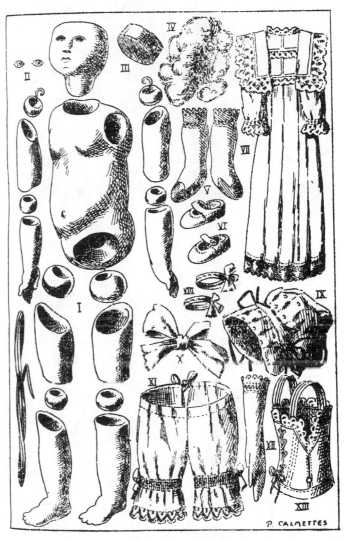

Anatomie et trousseau d'une poupée.

I : Corps et tête. — II : Yeux. — III : Crâne en liège. — IV : Perruque. — V : Bas. — VI : Souliers. — VII : Chemise. — VIII : Jarretières. — IX : Capote. — X : Nœud de tête. - - XI : Pantalon. — XII : Gants. — XIII : Corset.

653. "Anatomy and clothes of a doll" by Calmettes in LES JOUJOUX, 1924. I. Body and Head, II. Eyes, III. Cork pate, IV. Wig, V. Stockings, VI. Shoes, VII. Chemise, VIII. Garters, IX. Bonnet, X. Hair bow, XI. Drawers, XII. Gloves, XIII. Corset. *Courtesy of the Widener Library, Harvard University.*

654. All-bisque doll with molded and painted hair, features and footwear; jointed at the shoulders and hips. It wears a crepe paper outfit including a hat with a crepe paper tassel. H. 4 in. (10 cm.). *Coleman Collection.*

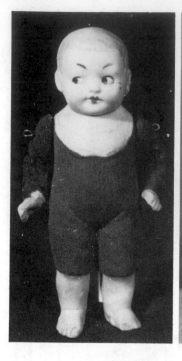

655. The clothes on this all-bisque doll are flocked. The bisque is light pink and the suit is a dark green. The doll has molded blond hair, painted eyes, wire joints at the shoulders. H. 4½ in. (11.5 cm.). *Coleman Collection.*

656. Flange neck composition-head doll on a cloth body, jointed with the so-called teddy bear type joints. Molded and painted features include the short blonde hair, mauve intaglio eyes, and a closed mouth. Original clothes include a two-piece blue suit trimmed with a band of black and white over the edges including the side opening. The black shoes are a part of the body. H. 13½ in. (34 cm.). *Courtesy of Robert and Katrin Burlin.*

657. Clothes, accessories, trousseau trunks and boxes as advertised by L'Hotel de Ville in their 1921 catalog. The items include dresses, outerwear, underwear, headwear, footwear, kimonos and aprons. Many of the garments are wool. The bonnets are silk. The sizes correspond to the size numbers of the Bébé Jumeau.

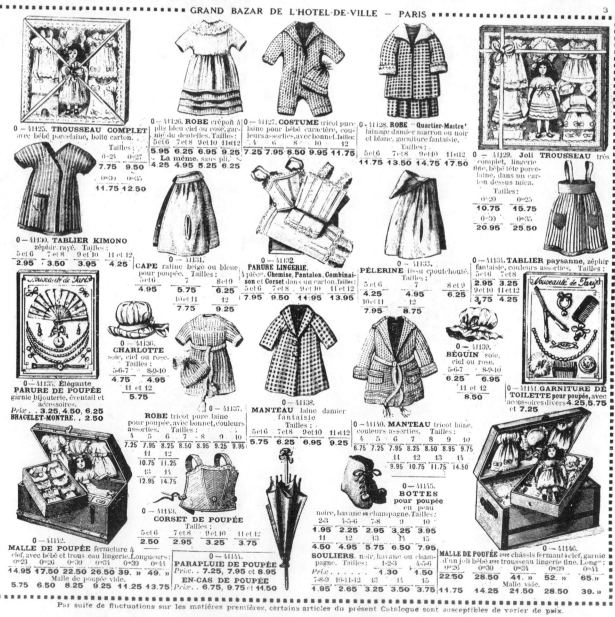

Par suite de fluctuations sur les matières premières, certains articles du présent Catalogue sont susceptibles de varier de prix.

37260. TROUSSEAU
avec Bébé articulé dormeur, modèle riche.

1	2	3
25.50	28.50	35. »

Modèle plus simple.

8.75	10.25	12.50

658. Clothes for a sleeping jointed bébé as advertised by the Louvre store in 1923. The dolls came in sizes 1, 2, and 3, in a fine quality or in an inexpensive quality, the latter costing about a third as much as the former.

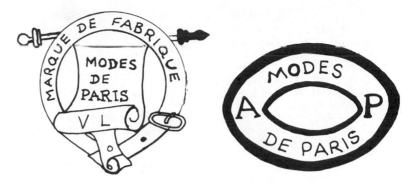

660–661. Modes de Paris labels found on dolls' clothes.

659. Bisque socket head baby doll with its layette in a hamper. It has a blond wig, sleeping light gray glass eyes, hair eyelashes, open mouth with two upper teeth, and a composition toddler body. There are an organdy and two cotton dresses, two pairs of shoes, and two pairs of bootees plus underwear and accessories. Mark: K ✡ R//SIMON AND HALBIG//126//GERMANY//14. H. 10 in. (25.5 cm.). *Private collection.*

Clothespin Dolls. 1906. A book named LADY HOLLY-HOCK AND HER FRIENDS gave directions for making clothespin dolls, including those dressed as Indians, John and Priscilla Alden.

Clowns. Dolls dressed as clowns have been popular ever since clowns and jesters originated. Various kinds of dolls made in almost all types of materials were made into clowns. Sometimes clown dolls have had special names such as *Coloro, Cracker Jack, Krack, Pierrot, Yama, Zu-Zu Kid* and so forth. Clown dolls often had designs painted or decaled on their faces. In the 1890s and before World War I nearly all the large French stores carried dolls dressed as clowns. Clowns came in many sizes and prices. The following are a selected sample:

1891: The Swedish catalog of *Printemps* showed a papier-mâché doll dressed as a clown and wearing a conical hat. Ht. 70 cm. (27½ in.).

1893: The *Horsman* catalog showed knitted worsted clown dolls some with "voices;" priced 90¢ to $8.00 doz. wholesale.

1898: See **Chronology.**

1901: Clowns believed to have been made by the *Société Française de Fabrication de Bébés & Jouets* (S.F.B.J.) were exhibited at the Crystal Palace in London. (See Ill. 1334.)

Ca. 1904: Wooden clowns similar to *Schoenhut's* clowns were made by *Dorst.*

Before 1911–1913: Several types of felt dolls made by *Steiff* were dressed as clowns. One of these wore a suit that was vertically half light and half dark, with three pompons down the front and a tiny cylindrical hat. These dolls came in seven hts. from 28 to 100 cm. (11 to 30½ in.). In 1911 they cost 48¢ to $4.28 in Germany. (See also **Caro, Coloro, Gusto, Noso,** and **Oro.**)

1912: The *Lafayette* store advertised clown dolls with pointed hats. Four hts. 28, 35, 43, and 50 cm. (11, 14, 17, 19½ in.); priced 49¢ to $1.30.

1912–14: *Horsman* produced a cloth doll dressed as a clown with each vertical half of its costume a different color. These dolls retailed for 25¢.

1917: *Baltimore Bargain House* advertised clown dolls with composition head and hands, cloth bodies. Ht. 36 in. (91.5 cm.); priced $1.35.

World War I period: Some of the Staffordshire potteries in England produced clown heads for dolls.

1920: *Averill* produced a clown called *Toto*.

1920s: S.F.B.J. was still making clown dolls.

1921: *Grace Corry* designed a jumping cloth clown for *Century*.

The Schoenhut clowns were named Cracker Jack, *Humpty*, and *Dumpty*. They came in two sizes when dressed in cotton and one size when dressed in silk.

Terry cloth and flannel dolls representing clowns were made by *Oweenee*.

1922: *Bruchlos* made walking clowns.

A cloth clown named Billy Clown was distributed by *Montgomery Ward*. It had shoe-button eyes, squealed when squeezed and wore a red and blue felt suit and a colored, pointed cap with a bell on the tip top. Ht. 6½ in. (16.5 cm.); priced 98¢.

1923: *Faultless Rubber Co.* made three types of clown dolls: one had a laughing face on both sides, one had frowning faces on both sides and the third had a laughing face on one side and a frowning face on the other side. These dolls had molded hair, features and clown suits. They came in yellow with black trimming, red or white. The white clown had a whistle. Ht. for all the clowns was 5 in. (12.5 cm.).

1924: *Frank Baum* designed a clown.

1926: William P. *Beers* & Co. and *Gustav Förster* made clown dolls.

1927: Cloth clowns were made of powder puff plush by *Woolnough. Etta* also made clown dolls.

1928: Small wooden clown made by *Poppy Doll Co.; Live Long Toys* and Steiff made cloth clowns.

1929: *Twistum Toy Factory* made *Archie Pagliacci* and *Clownee*. (See also **Cymbalier, Pierrot, Pierrette, Polichinelle** and **Worsted Dolls**.)★

Clownee. 1929. One of the *Twistum Funny Fuzzee* line made of twisted fexible wire covered with colored knitted yarn. The clown face is handpainted. Price 75¢.

Cocheco Manufacturing Co. 1827–1893 and later. Boston, Mass. Successor was Lawrence & Co. They did not make dolls until 1889 when they made a 16 in. (40.5 cm.) cutout cloth doll designed by *Celia and Charity Smith*. By 1893 they had also made *Darkey Doll*, a *Japanese* doll and *Brownie Doll*.★

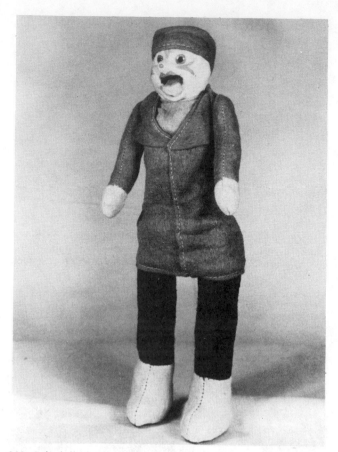

662. Felt doll, face marked as a clown, shoe button type glass eyes; mouth opens and shuts when squeaker in torso is pressed. Original clothes. H. 11½ in. (29 cm.). *Coleman Collection.*

663. Clown advertised in Bon Marché catalog in 1903. The jointed doll had a "washable, unbreakable" head and a silk costume. Six hts. 37, 40, 44, 48, 53, and 59 cm. (14½, 15½, 17½, 19, 21, and 23 in.).

No. 2672—Clown Doll and Costume. Cut in one size only. The costume in white with red trimmings is effective. Pattern, ten cents

664. Clown doll made by Steiff. It has a felt head, blond plush wig, shoe button eyes, closed mouth, cloth and felt body. Original felt clown suit in red and yellow with vandyked edges. H. 19. in. (48 cm.). *Courtesy of Richard Withington. Photo by Barbara Jendrick.*

666. Clown costume pattern for a cloth doll advertised in the WOMAN'S HOME COMPANION, December, 1916.

665. Pair of felt clowns made with seams down the center of their faces in the manner of the Steiff dolls. The hats are sewn on the heads. The eyes are black buttons; the mouths are closed. The clown costume forms the bodies which are stuffed with straw. Hts. are 12 in. (30.5 cm.) and 11 in. (28 cm.). *Courtesy of Richard Wright. Photo by A. Jackson.*

17585. **Clown articulé,** tête incassable, habillage soigné.

19.50, 12.50 et **7.50**

667. Jointed clown doll with an unbreakable head and well-made costume advertised by Printemps in 1918. Priced $1.50, $2.50 and $3.90.

0 -- 41150. **CLOWN** tête incassable inaltérable au lavage, habillage satin garni de dentelles.

Hauteurs :

0ᵐ42	0ᵐ46	0ᵐ52
16.50	**19.95**	**24.95**

0 -- 41156.

CLOWN *complètement articulé,* tête feutre caractéristique, perruque peluche habillage soigné. Hauteurs :

0ᵐ35	0ᵐ45	0ᵐ55	0ᵐ65
11.75	**18.75**	**24.95**	**30.** »

668. Clown dolls sold by L'Hotel de Ville in 1921. The clown on the left has an unbreakable, washable head and is dressed in satin trimmed with lace. H. 42, 46, and 52 cm. (16½, 18, and 20½ in.). The clown on the right has a felt character face, plush wig; it is fully jointed and carefully dressed. Four hs.: 35, 45, 55, and 65 cm. (14, 17½, 21½ and 25½ in.).

Cochet. 1807–74. Paris. According to the research of Mme. Poisson, curator of the Roybet Fould Museum, Cochet, Jeune, was making dolls around 1824 at his shop in Sannois (Seine-et-Oise). Meanwhile in Paris the doll shop Cochet-Dehenne also made dolls. The dolls were of several kinds but most of them appear to have had carton or composition heads on kid bodies. They were still making this type of doll in 1854.★

Codeg. See **Cowan, de Groot & Co.**

Co-Ed Flapper. 1925–27. *Boudoir* type doll made by the *American Stuffed Novelty Co.* It had a pressed cloth face, mohair wig, wore a silk double-breasted coat, trousers, and a bowtie. The clothes were designed by *Morris Politzer.*★

Co-Ed Kids. 1929. One of the *Folly Dollies* advertised by *Reisman, Barron & Co.*

Cohen, Adolph.[+] See **Trion Toy Co.**

Cohen, Alec, & Randall. 1930. London. Agents for *Carl Kochniss* and *Arthur Schoenau.*

Cohen, Edward. 1922–23. London. Made and imported dolls.

Cohen, Jack. 1929–30. New York City. President of *King Innovations;* directed the production of *Cuddle-Kewpies.*

Cohen, L., & Sons. 1923–29. New York City. Made Elco line of *Mama* dolls with composition head, arms and legs on cloth bodies. These came with or without sleeping eyes. The trademark was shaped like a seal with white letters "FOR QUALITY//Elco//Dolls//GUARANTEED THE BEST."

1923: They had 28 style nos. in hts. 19 and 23 in. (48 and 58.5 cm.).

1926: Elco Baby Dolls were added.

1927: Advertised singing and talking dolls.

669. Mark for L. Cohen on composition-head dolls.

Cohen, Paul, Co. 1930. New York City. Bought *Amberg*'s import business including the *Amfelt Art Dolls.*

Cohen, W., & Sons. 1924–30 and later. London. Produced art *Mama* dolls in various sizes as well as *Snowdrop* babies and Snowdrop jointed dolls. Used heads made by *Armand Marseille* and *Ernst Heubach.* The doll factory was in Schalkau, Thür. Cohen's trademark found on tags on dolls was "MILLENDO" in a diamond.

1930: Made the following exclusive lines Angela (newborn baby doll), Baby Bette, Barbara, *Black Prince,* Billie Boy, *Curly,* Dolores an art doll, Irene, Jeanie, Muriel, My Favorite, *My Prince* and *My Queen.*

Cohn, Aaron. 1907–26. New York City. After 1912 Toronto, Canada. Made dolls.

1925–26: Obtained a United States patent for a doll whose arm movements simulated clapping its hands while it emitted a sound of merriment. This was produced by alternately squeezing and relaxing a yielding part of the body.

Cohn, Grete. 1918–20. Berlin. Applied for a German patent (D.R.G.M.) for dolls' heads.★

Cohn, Irwin E. 1926. New York City. Obtained a U.S. patent for a doll with a voice and movable features.

Coiffe, A. 1872–1930 and possibly later. Limoges, France. Successor was Henri Coiffe; and by 1909 Couty, who had been a porcelain decorator joined the firm which began to make dolls' heads. Mme. Couty claimed that her husband had broken the head of one of his daughter's dolls to see how it was made. This porcelain factory supplied dolls' heads to *Prieur* and is believed to have made some of the heads marked *Masson.*★

Cold-Press Composition. 1890s–1929. *Solomon D. Hoffmann* was credited with originating cold-press composition but *Benjamin Goldenberg* and *Otto Denivelle* improved its making, although the problem of peeling was never completely solved.

Mr. Trumpore of Effanbee described this type of composition calling it "soup" in its original state. He said it contained glycerin, flour and so forth and that it was poured into plaster molds. He complained that this product was too heavy and tended to soften in hot weather. The heads usually had a flange type neck although shoulder heads were also made. Composition limbs were made by the same method as the heads. The cold press method was still being used by a few manufacturers as late as 1929. (See Manufacture of Composition Heads in the first COLLECTOR'S ENCYCLOPEDIA OF DOLLS, and **Manufacture of Dolls, Commercial; Made in United States**).

Cole, Roxanna Elizabeth McGee (Mrs. A. R.). 1868–1930 and later. She was assisted by her daughter-in-law, Molly Hunt Cole, who carried on the business of making cloth dolls after Roxanna's death in 1907. Roxanna's dolls were made of a fine muslin and had delicate needle sculpture such as the shape of the chin and the dimples in the hands of the baby dolls. The clothes also showed fine needlework. The faces were artistically painted. These dolls were sold in Memphis, New Orleans, New York, Massachusetts, and other places including Europe. Molly Cole apparently used the same patterns as Roxanna but Molly's dolls were less delicate, had rounder faces and reflected twentieth century styles.

1898: THE BOSTON ADVERTISER published an article about Roxanna Cole entitled "A Famous Dollmaker."

1899: A Boston collector, Mrs. Elizabeth Richards Horton, bought five dolls from Roxanna Cole. These dolls were named Grandma Cole, Cinderella, Josie June, Mae—a matinee doll, and Baby. It has been recorded that Grandma Cole was the thousandth doll made by Roxanna Cole and that it appeared as one of the dolls that was copied as a painting in the INDEX OF DESIGN, published by the National Gallery of Art.★

670A & B. Roxanna Cole cloth dolls made in the last quarter of the 1800s. These dolls were handsewn. They have painted hair and eyes, original clothes. H. of girl doll 20 in. (51 cm.). *Courtesy of Mrs. Jon (Estelle) Johnston. (Jon Johnston is a descendant of Roxanna Cole.)*

Coleman, S. Before 1867. London. Made and/or handled wax dolls. Estelle Johnston reported a wax doll with inserted hair and glass eyes that had a paper label reading "FROM//S. COLEMAN, Nos. 6, 7, 11, 12 and 26//Ground Floor, Pantheon//Oxford Street Entrance." The Pantheon burned down in 1867.

Colette. 1923–24. Name of a doll with a velvet head, wig, dressed in taffeta, and sold by the *Louvre* store. Four hts. 30, 40, 50 and 60 cm. (12, 15½, 19½ and 23½ in.).

Colette. 1927. Cloth doll with wig, dressed in felt and sold by the *Lafayette* store. Ht. 60 cm. (23½ in.).

Colette. 1928. All-composition dressed doll sold by *Paturel.*

Colette. 1928–30 and later. French trademark name for a mascot doll made by *Mme. Germaine Douche.*

Collecting Dolls. TOYS AND NOVELTIES in 1917 stated:

"Dolls are by no means exclusively to be classed as toys for children, says the Milwaukee Free Press. They belong to the field of art, to the economic world to say nothing of their interest as a spontaneous expression of the human spirit. Not the children who played with them, quaint pantaletted shades, are revived by a look at the rare authentic survivals, so much as the grown people who provided these puppets for the sport of their little folks.

"Dolls minister to one of the child's deepest instincts, that of make-believe. The baby doll is tended fondly; more advanced dolls figure in whole dramas of thrilling interest, from a general attack of measles to the last wedding or journey in the family.

"What makes doll collecting worth while is that dolls repeat in miniature the looks and clothes of the country and age they belong to.

"Eugene Field helped to popularize doll collecting, now

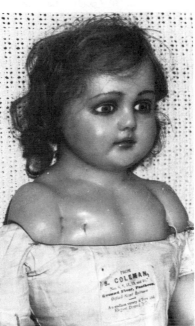

671A & B. Poured wax head doll made and/or produced for S. Coleman. It has inserted human hair, stationary blue glass eyes, inserted hair eyebrows, and eyelashes, closed mouth, cloth handsewn body. The original Scottish costume has a velvet jacket with Sheffield silver buttons. Accessories have identical Celtic design. Paper label on body (See Ill. 672). H. 32 in. (81 cm.). *Courtesy of Estelle Johnston.*

FROM

S. COLEMAN,
Nos. 6, 7, 11, 12, and 26

Ground Floor, Pantheon
Oxford Street Entrance

An endless variety of Toys and
Elegant Dressed Dolls

672. A label identifying a doll as being handled by S. Coleman.

dignified into a rewarding pursuit. Nothing could be queerer than the slim ladies with china heads and dangling limbs that our grandmothers dressed in brocades and taffetas, except the dolls with papier-mâché countenances and painted features cherished by the generation before that."

"Museums count a collection of dolls a priceless treasure."

Collecting dolls is determined by many motives. The most important are the artistic appeal of the doll, the quality of the doll, the current fad for the various types of dolls, the extent of one's pocket book, nostalgia, the ability to find dolls, and the space to house them.

Beauty is in the eye of the beholder and each of us prefers a different type of doll. Most collectors buy a doll with their heart rather than their head. Often, however, one's taste changes and a doll that is thought to be beautiful today may not appeal as much tomorrow when one has learned more about dolls and has become more sophisticated in collecting them.

The demand for certain types of dolls rises and falls with the passage of time. There are finite fads for various dolls, and the origin of these fads is often difficult to pinpoint. Sometimes a book written about a certain type of doll will increase interest in that particular type of doll. Once a doll starts to rise in popularity, demand accelerates and of course supply is limited.

In general the greatest interest recently is in collecting antique dolls; and antique dolls are defined as dolls over 75 years old. However, a new book on a specific kind of doll can spurt a tremendous interest in the more recent dolls. This is evidenced by the books on Madame *Alexander*'s dolls.

Before World War I. relatively few antique dolls were found in collections. In the 1700s and early 1800s not many dolls existed and few of these survived. Some of the so-called Queen Anne type dolls and the early molded hair papier-mâché dolls that were among the earliest ones found in most collections, were less than 75 years old in 1900. Porcelain dolls were not available until about 1840. After World War I. when some of the china dolls would have been 75 or more years old they became the popular dolls to collect. After World War II when some of the bisque-head dolls were over 75 years old, they became the most popular type for collectors. At first it was the parian-type dolls, then the bisque-head lady types sometimes called "French Fashion." These were followed by the child dolls, especially the early French bébés.

Around 1970 interest began to develop in bisque-head character dolls even though they were not yet 75 years old. A little later this included the Googly-eyed type of character doll. Throughout the 1970s most collections comprised largely dolls with bisque heads that were made less than a century before. Relatively little interest was shown in the earlier types of dolls and dolls of other materials with the possible exception of cloth dolls and composition dolls.

Great age and rarity often seem to be negative factors as far as interest in dolls is concerned. Most of the very old dolls are rare but not all rare dolls are old. It is not true that the only reason for a doll being rare is that it was unsuccessful and therefore few were made. Many other reasons caused dolls to be rare. One is that they were perishable. Few rubber dolls survived although many were made in the 1800s and 1900s. Wax dolls also have had a high casualty rate. Elaborate hairdo chinas are extremely rare because they required more skilled talent and were more difficult to produce because of the necessary multipart molds and the undercutting. Thus they cost more to produce than the plainer heads and manufacturers probably found them less profitable. Dolls made in times of economic depressions were frequently rare. Wars can also affect the quantity and types of dolls produced. Obviously during wartimes fewer dolls were made. *Amberg's New Born Babe* came out in 1914 and the early examples were extremely rare whereas the *Bye-Lo Baby*,

which was very similar, came out in 1924 and millions were produced.

Strange as it may seem rarity can be a deterrent to demand. Collectors are seldom interested in really rare dolls that they know nothing about. When erroneous statements have been published that only a small number of a certain type of doll was made collectors vie for the privilege of owning one of these dolls. The *A. Marque* doll is a good example of this phenomenon. One of the most sought after dolls at present is the *Bru*. Although they are plentiful, few come up for visible sale because of the large demand. Originally they were cheaper than the *Jumeaus* which always held top place among the bisque-head dolls when new. Owning a Bru is somewhat of a status symbol among collectors. Other dolls of similar artistry and quality can go unnoticed until information about them has been widely publicized.

Finally and probably most important of all for collecting dolls is the size of one's pocket book. When you buy a doll, you are going to live with it and you want something that has genuine appeal for you regardless of whether it is the current fad. Many collectors say they cannot afford old dolls and buy reproductions instead. This may be short sighted because reproductions probably will not rise in price nearly as much as the playdoll of past eras. If a collector can forget the high-priced old dolls that are in top demand and seek other quality types that are often less expensive even than reproductions the pocket book will benefit and there will probably be a far better investment for the future. Chinas and so-called parian-type dolls have actually fallen in price during the 1960s and 1970s when an adjustment is made for inflation.

Another alternative is to collect modern dolls. Since most of these are vinyl and there is evidence that these are not durable and possibly toxic, they should not be considered for long-lasting collections. There are, however dolls made by various modern artists and manufacturers especially for collectors.

Most of these dolls are produced in small quantities and limited editions. However these limited editions probably all go into collections and are preserved whereas dolls that are given to children as toys have an extremely high rate of destruction and often few survive for collectors.

Attributes that increase the desirability of a doll for collecting are as follows (The order of preference depends on the individual doll and the individual collector):

1. Dolls in excellent condition without repairs. (No repair should be made that cannot easily be undone if one so desires.)

2. Dolls made of durable material including the finish on the doll. Wooden and metal dolls frequently have the paint chipped off.

3. Dolls with identifiable marks.

4. At the present time bisque head dolls with closed mouths. (These were not necessarily earlier dolls but were cheaper and less desirable originally and therefore fewer were made, which increases their popularity with current collectors.)

5. Dolls with extra clothes that are contemporary with the doll.

6. Dolls in original clothes.

7. Dolls dressed as males.

8. Dolls with ethnic features as well as ordinary dolls painted black or any shade of brown.

9. Dolls with documented histories or early pictures of the doll.

10. Dolls that really walk, talk, or perform some other human-like function.

11. Dolls in original boxes. (Make sure the doll actually came in the box.)

12. Dolls with original tags, buttons, etc. (Unfortunately tags and buttons are easily reproduced and can readily be changed from one doll to another.)

The head is considered by collectors today to be the most important part of a doll but it should be on its original body. Sometimes the parts of the body are old but did not come together originally.

Original clothes, especially on old dolls, are often difficult to find. The next best thing is to find clothes contemporary with the doll and if these are the right size and period they will usually fit the doll perfectly. Making new garments that are suitable requires a great deal of study and knowledge. The textile and trims as well as the style and sewing techniques must be of the appropriate period.

Dolls with movable eyes should always be stored face down. Wax, rubber, and dolls with paint that peels should be kept in as constant temperature and humidity as possible. Expensive dolls should be insured with fine arts insurance and frequent revisions in their values are necessary.

Periodic upgrading of a collection is advisable. Quality is always preferred to quantity. If someday a collector wishes to dispose of all of his or her dolls variety will be found to be an advantage. Lovely as they are a dealer or an auction house might find it difficult to dispose of a hundred Brus in a short time at top value. Flooding the market always drives the price down. Many of our finest collections have been put on the market a few dolls at a time and the prices have remained high while many other collectors have had the opportunity of obtaining these treasures.

In studying the information in this book relative to dating and evaluating a collection it should be recognized that the dates are not necessarily the entire period covered by a company or doll. They only represent the period for which information has been documented. Little if any research has been done after 1930 for this book. (See also **Chronology, Clothes, Manufacture of Dolls, Measurement of Dolls, Pressed versus Poured, Prices of Dolls,** as well as Custodianship[+], Display,[+] and Storage[+].)

Collections of Dolls. Among the notables who collected dolls in the 1800s and early 1900s were George Sand, author, and grandmother of *Mme. Lauth-Sand:* Eugene Field, poet; Frances Hodgson Burnett, author; Josephine Daskam Bacon, author of children's stories; *Sarah Bernhardt,* actress—who dressed many of her own dolls; Ellen Terry, actress; May Robson, actress; Clyde Fitch, playright; Tony Sarg, puppeteer; William Trier, painter who illustrated books on dolls—possibly the dolls were from his own collection; *Jeanne Lanvin,* a couturière; Edward Lovett, who in 1914 exhibited his dolls at the National Museum of Wales—

the catalog for this exhibit explained that the "Collection illustrates a scientific standpoint of ethnography and folk lore, rather than a quaint curious" display; Baroness Dora Groedel of Hungary; Ernst of Budapest, who collected dressed, carved wooden dolls and dolls with wax heads on kid bodies.

1897: LADIES' HOME JOURNAL reported that a 14 year old girl had a collection of 20 dolls. It included a "Bride, a large wax doll which she had won at a fair. . . . Boy dolls, baby doll in long clothes. French lady dolls in gorgeous dinner dresses and carriage toilettes, with head turned haughtily to one side; dolls with bold shiny black eyes and dolls with languishing blue ones, dolls that went to sleep and dolls that stayed awake, and tiny wax and china dolls with their clothes." The largest doll was "Big Sue" dressed in long baby clothes. "Tiny Totsie" was a tiny bisque doll.

1902: Mrs. Washington Hesing of Chicago, Ill. had a collection of over 100 dolls from all parts of the world. Many of the dolls were given to her by friends who had traveled. Often they were dressed in regional peasant costumes.

1905–7: The Société des Amateurs de Jouets et Jeux Anciens (Society of Lovers of Old Toys and Games) published a series

A CHICAGO WOMAN'S DOLLS.

A PRETTY SWISS PEASANT.

A NORWEGIAN GIRL. A SWEDISH GIRL.

673. Three dolls in the collection of Mrs. Hesing of Chicago as shown in THE STRAND MAGAZINE, September 1902. The Swiss doll has flaxen hair and a large black lace hat. The two Scandinavian dolls have costumes trimmed with beads. The dolls were probably made in Germany and dressed in Switzerland and Scandinavia in clothes accurately representing the costumes worn by the peasants in their respective areas.

of bulletins titled LE JOUETS ET JEUX ANCIENS which showed the dolls in various collections. Among the collectors were Fernand Laurent, who collected dolls in regional costumes, and Mme. Laumonier, who had ivory, leather, wax, and wood dolls of the 1700s and 1800s. The president of this Society was Léo Claretie and the vice presidents were Henri d'Allemagne and Arthur Maury.

1913: TOYS AND NOVELTIES reported that Mme. Martin-Guelliott had 600 dolls showing all the popular costumes of France, of the rest of Europe and even countries such as Mexico, Barbary, and Greenland. "Mme. Menard-Dorian's collection contained both ancient and modern dolls." The reports continued:

"The Queen of Holland reveled in her dolls, which varied from statesmen, court dignitaries, soldiers, maids of honor and sailors to those representing other countries in national costumes, and she took great pride in the varied array, but it is said that whenever any of her dolls offended or displeased her, she would threaten to make them a Queen. This she considered the worst punishment that could befall them. She also hated the formality of bowing, so that when she inflicted such a penalty upon her dolls, she thought it would have a chastening effect. The different costumes representing the different parts of Holland are most picturesque when seen gathered together in so gay an assemblage, and one notes especially, the charming specimen, dressed as a fishwife of Schevenigen, with her scoop bonnet and bright cloak."

It has been reported that Queen Wilhelmina as a child was obliged to speak French to her French dolls, German to her German dolls, and so forth, thus enabling her to be proficient in languages.

1914: TOYS AND NOVELTIES reported: "There are many [Japanese dolls] in private collections. The Schwerdtmann Toy Company, of St. Louis, has quite a collection that was once used in an exhibit. The Japanese doll is considered one of the valuable items of a doll exhibit and is especially desired for private collections. One of the finest private collections in America, probably, is owned by Mrs. Howard W. Lang, of Springfield, Mass., who has a collection of more than 400 dolls from all parts of the world, including Japan. Her collection of Japanese dolls is a most interesting one, since each is intended to represent some of the important personages of Japan.

". . . In Mrs. Lang's collection is a doll an exact replica of an Italian wine merchant."

1915: The Musée des Arts Decoratifs had the Foucault collection of dolls in historical costumes and the Metropolitan Museum had a similar collection bequeathed to it by Mrs. Maria P. James.

1916: Collecting old dolls was becoming a popular hobby. Mrs. Wilbur Macey Stone started her collection by obtaining dolls from New England attics and far off lands.

World War I period: Helen Nyce, the illustrator, collected dolls, including *Hilda*.

1921: Lillian Lipkowska, Russian opera star, collected *Boudoir* type dolls.

674. Pair of bisque shoulder head dolls dressed in Tyrolean regional costumes; molded hair, painted eyes, they have cloth bodies and mitten-type hands. These dolls were in the collection of Undi, an illustrator who won a prize for his watercolors in 1925. H. of man doll 9 in. (23 cm.). H. of woman doll 8¾ in. (22.5 cm.). *Courtesy of the Hungarian National Museum, Budapest.*

1922: TOYS AND NOVELTIES told of the collection of the late Mr. Seifu Shimizu of Tokyo. "He kept his dolls hidden under the mat-covered floors of his rooms." He wrote a set of books about them. These books were illustrated with hand-colored pictures.

1923: Eva Laza Griffen, wife of the former American consul to Colombia, collected dolls from all over the world.

1925: The former Kaiser Wilhelm of Germany gave his doll collection to a Berlin museum. Most of his dolls were in regional costume and included what appears to have been character dolls manufactured by *Kämmer & Reinhardt.*

1926: TOYS AND NOVELTIES reported: "Parisian women have always been keen on dolls, and many of them possess huge collections."

1927: The Moscow Museum in Russia had a varied collection of dolls. It included German dolls and a full representation of the different racial types which inhabited Russia. There were dolls in the costumes of the then modern Western European and the American business woman as well as American blacks.

Mrs. E. Westwood of New York City collected Boudoir type dolls. She preferred to dress them in mid-1800s styles.

1930: Mrs. Charles Walcott, wife of a former curator at the Smithsonian, collected early American dolls.

1935: There were enough collectors of dolls in New England

to form an organization known as "The Doll Collectors of America."★

Colleen. 1917. Trade name of a character doll made by *Bell & Francis.*

College Kids. 1914. Composition head dolls made by *Horsman* and distributed by *Marshall Field.* It is believed that these dolls were also known as *Campbell Kid* Mascot dolls. They represented a boy, and a girl in a dress. The duck fabric outfits came with appropriate college letters and colors. Ht. 13 in. (33 cm.); price $17.00 doz. wholesale.

Collegiate Dolls. 1925–26. All-celluloid dolls distributed by *Shackman.* They represented college boy and girl graduates, with a mortar board hat and diploma. The boy was in a black gown and the girl in a white dress. Football players wore a sweater with a letter for Princeton, Harvard or Yale. Ht. 2¾ in. (7 cm.); price $1.50 doz. wholesale. See Ill. 2499.

Collegiate Flapper. 1926–27. *Boudoir*-type doll made by the *American Stuffed Novelty Co.* It had a handpainted pressed cloth face, silk or mohair wig, long limbed body stuffed with cotton. The removable clothes were designed by *Morris Politzer.*

Collegiate HEbee. See **HEbee-SHEbee.**

Collingbourne Mills. 1920s. Manufactured sewing sets for making dolls' dresses. They also made cloth cutout dolls such as the Happy Family including *Flossie* and *Baby.*

675. Mark on a cloth doll produced by Collingbourne Mills.

Colombina. 1925–26. Felt doll made by *Lenci* as No. 165/4, dressed in pseudo 1700s attire with a tricorn hat and carrying a walking stick. Ht. 26½ in. (67.5 cm.).

Colonial Belle. 1928. *Boudoir* doll distributed by *Eisen.* The doll wore a white wig and pseudo-Colonial type clothes.

Colonial Doll. 1917. Cloth doll made by *Dean's.* It came in two versions: one had a flat face and the other had a *Tru-to-Life* three dimensional face. A sleeveless, jacket length trench coat trimmed with simulated fur was supplied for the doll as a separate item.

Colonial Doll. 1918. One of the *Next to Nature* all-composition dolls made by *Colonial Toy Manufacturing Co.* and distributed by *Butler Bros.* The doll had a mohair wig, sleeping eyes, hair eyelashes, a movable tongue, jointed neck and metal spring joints. It wore a chemise. Hts. 24 and 26 in. (61 and 66 cm.). Without the eyelashes and movable tongue it came in hts. 14, 16½ and 18 in. (35.5, 42 and 45.5 cm.). When it had painted eyes it was made only in the 18 inch (45.5 cm.) ht.

Colonial Family. 1901–9. Cutout printed cloth dolls made by *Art Fabric Mills.* They consisted of a Mother, Father, Brother and Sister dressed in costumes that simulated those of the 1700s. They were used as premiums for Malted Cereal Co. and National Medicine Co. Mother and Father were nearly 24 in. (61 cm.) and Brother and Sister were about 15 in. (38 cm.). Sometimes these dolls were erroneously called George and Martha Washington. Later *Elms & Sellon* advertised these dolls. Hts. 18 in. (45.5 cm.) and 12 in. (30.5 cm.).

Colonial Girls. 1926. *Boudoir* type dolls made by *Kitty Fleischmann.*

Colonial Novelty & Doll Manufacturing Co. 1930 and later. New York City. Manufactured dolls.

Colonial Toy Manufacturing Co. 1915–20. New York City. Made "Bisque finish" composition dolls until 1920 when they also used *Fulper* real bisque heads. *David Zaiden,* the president of the company (1915–18), had spent many years perfecting the composition used for these dolls. Some of the dolls were all-composition with fully jointed bodies or bent limb bodies that tried to imitate the pre-war German dolls. Other dolls had a composition head on a cork stuffed cloth body.

1915: Advertised wig, sleeping glass eyes, teeth, and moving tongue on the bisque finish dolls which came in various sizes.

1917: Advertised straight leg dolls and bent limb babies as well as the fact that they were exclusive agents for the *Drayton Hug-Me-Tight* cloth dolls.

They had 12 numbers of all-composition dolls which they claimed were washable; six of these were dressed and six were undressed. Seven of the 12 numbers had painted hair and eyes, two had painted eyes and a wig and 3 had sleeping eyes and wig. Their clothes had pearl buttons and button holes.

1918: The jointed all-composition dolls came in 50 types with sleeping eyes. Price $14.00 to 96.00 a dozen. Hts. mentioned were 14, 18, 24 and 30 in. (35.5, 45.5, 61, and 76 cm.) An 18 in. (45.5 cm.) all-composition doll with painted hair and eyes cost $20.40 a dozen in a chemise and $36.40 a dozen when dressed in a three-piece outfit of white lawn trimmed with lace.

1919: Advertised over 100 numbers including black dolls, swimmers and cloth body dolls with sleeping eyes. There were baby dolls, child dolls and "little ladies" who wore bathing suits. *Peachy Pets* were swimmers or waders. *Miss Colonial* had a white wig, gloves, a fan and two strands of pearls around its neck.

1920: They continued to make all-composition dolls but they also obtained bisque heads made by Fulper which they claimed were exclusive models. The bisque heads came in six sizes and had wigs, sleeping eyes, and teeth. They came on bent limb baby bodies or on fully jointed child bodies. Prices ranged from $14.00 to $175.00 doz. wholesale. An all-composition doll had bent baby limbs, wig, metal eyes, open mouth with tongue. On the back of the socket head neck were raised letters in an arc, that read "COLONIAL TOY MANUFACTURING CO."★

Colonial Works. See **Ibbetston, Leonard.**

Coloro (Clown). 1911–13. Jointed felt art doll designed by *Albert Schlopsnies,* made by *Steiff,* and distributed by *Borgfeldt* in the U.S. It represented a circus clown and wore velvet clothes with hand coloring in assorted colors. Ht. 17 in. (43 cm.). Priced $2.20 in Germany in 1911 and $3.30 in New York in 1913. See Ills. 2309 A & B.

Columbia. 1904–15. Line of *C. M. Bergmann* dolls with bisque shoulder heads made by *Armand Marseille* and found on kid bodies with rivet joints. The bisque socket heads found on composition bodies were also made by *Simon & Halbig.*

An elliptical paper sticker on the front of a kid body was marked "COLUMBIA//W CORK-STUFFED" in a ribbon design. Pat Schoonmaker found a *Baby Betty* doll in a box marked "Columbia."

1914: Dolls had bisque heads with mohair wigs, sleeping eyes, hair eyelashes, kid bodies with composition forearms and lower legs. Four hts. 19, 20½, 23, and 26 in. (48, 52, 58.5 and 66 cm.).★

676A & B. Marks on kid-body dolls with "Columbia" label.

Columbia. 1912. Line of dressed, jointed dolls produced by *Carl Hartmann.* This might be the dolls with *Armand Marseille* heads.

Columbia Doll Co. 1926. New York City. Made *Mama* and infant dressed dolls in a variety of sizes. Their $2.00 doll had a wig and sleeping eyes.

Columbia Doll & Toy Co. 1917–22. New York City. Made all-composition dolls jointed at neck, painted side-glancing eyes, with or without wigs; the wigs were covered with a

veil. High button boots were molded on. The costumes were assorted knit outfits that were trimmed on the hat and wide, flaring skirt with marabou or its imitation. Ht. 12 in. (30.5 cm.). The Columbia twins were named Miss Columbia and Columbia Jr.★

Columbian Sailor. 1893–94 and possibly later. Cutout cloth doll representing a sailor of the period of Christopher Columbus. This doll was patented in January, 1893. Ht. 17 in. (43 cm.). See Ill. 677.

Pat. Jan. 31, '93.

SAILOR BOY, 10c.

677. Cutout cloth doll representing a Columbian Sailor of 1492. This advertisement was in YOUTH'S COMPANION; in 1894. The lithographed cutout doll wore a blue, red, and gold costume and the patent date of January 31, 1893 was on the back of the cap. H. 17 in. (43 cm.).

Columbine. Name of a figure that represented the Lady's Maid in the COMMEDIA DELL'ARTE, which dates back to at least the 1600s.

1911–15: Doll with composition head and hands, cloth body made by *Steinhardt.* A label in printed letters on the front hemline read: "Columbine's//???" Its dress of white moire had a lace ruff collar and cuffs. The peaked hat had two bells and a red plush pompom. In 1915 NEEDLE-CRAFT MAGAZINE offered this doll as a premium.

1918: Name of a doll created by *Adolphe Willette* according to "Les Jouets," an article in ARTS FRANÇAIS. This doll was made of a substance like *Prialytine* and was signed on the foot by the publishing house, *Gallais.* Ht. 24 cm. (9½ in.).

1929: Name of a cloth doll made in Florence, Italy.★

Columbus Doll. 1893–94. Trade name of a doll distributed by *Montgomery Ward.* The doll had a bisque head, wig, glass eyes and teeth and was dressed in a pseudo late 1400s costume. The broad cap was trimmed with an ostrich plume and marked on the front "1493 C. Columbus 1893." Hts. 15, 18, and 21 in. (38, 45.5, and 53.5 cm.); priced $1.80 to $3.25.

Columbus Doll Co. 1926. U.S. Advertised a jobbing line of dolls.

Columbus Merchandise Co. 1917 and probably other years. Columbus, Ohio. Wholesale distributor who handled dolls.

1917: Among the dolls offered for sale according to their catalog were the *Gebrüder Heubach* infant dolls with a molded cap decorated with painted flowers, all-bisque dolls with either molded hair or wigs. These dolls were jointed at the shoulders and hips. They were all-china dolls in either black or white with molded hair. They also were jointed at the shoulders and hips. Their *Nankeen* dolls had china heads and limbs.

Among the composition-head dolls were *Amberg's* Koaster Kids; *Horsman's Baby Bumps, Baby Butterfly,* and the *Campbell Kids; Ideal's* baby dolls and dolls with molded boots such as *Goldie* and *Zu-Zu Kid.* Other composition dolls included *Charlie Chaplin* and a Japanese boy and girl.

The wooden dolls were made by *Schoenhut.*

Other types of dolls included celluloid dolls, cloth dolls with lithographed faces, and rubber dolls. They also advertised dolls dressed as *Eskimos,* and babies in either short or long dresses.

Colwell, W. E. 1927–28. Zion, Ill. Obtained a British patent for a key wind walking doll.

Com-A-Long. 1920–21. Doll with composition head and cloth body produced by *Borgfeldt.* It had movable arms and legs and wore a colored lawn or gingham dress or rompers.★

Comfort. Early 1900s. Name found stamped on a cloth doll possibly made by *Jessie M. Raleigh.* See Ill. 678.★

COMFORT   **678.** Mark found on Comfort cloth dolls.

Comic Kid. 1919–30 and later. Cloth cutout doll made by *Saalfield.* The doll was 18 in. (45.5 cm.) tall.

Commercial Manufacturing & Pattern Works. 1921. Chicago, Ill. Advertised *Johnny Joints.*

Compo Doll & Novelty Co. 1925–27. New York City. Made dolls and dolls' heads.

Compolene. 1918. Trademark for an "unbreakable" material registered in Britain by *J. P. Miller.*

Compolite. 1918–19. Name registered as a British trademark by *J. P. Miller* for an "unbreakable" light material used for entire dolls produced by *Nottingham* and for dolls' bodies with *British Ceramic* heads.

1918: Advertised by *British Toys* as used for dressed dolls having British Ceramic heads, glass eyes, and jointed bodies.

Composition ("Indestructible") Dolls. Throughout history dolls have been made of various types of composition. (See also **Cold-Press Composition, Hot-Press Composition** and **Manufacture of Dolls, Commercial.**)

1927: TOYS AND NOVELTIES, stated that, "Composition heads and parts are impossible to make under certain condi-

tions of temperature and humidity which are not uncommon in the Summer in New York City. Every year there are days and even weeks when work can be carried on only at extreme risk, if at all."★

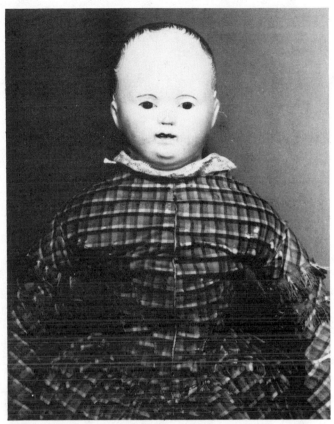

679. Composition shoulder head of the 1840s has black painted hair with brushmarks, no molding, stationary black pupilless glass eyes, open mouth with 2 upper and 2 lower teeth, kid body. Original clothes. *Courtesy of Nancy Palazzolo.*

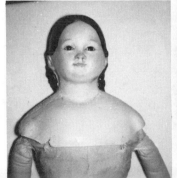 

680. Composition shoulder head with long black molded corkscrew curls, stationary black pupilless glass eyes, and closed mouth. The cloth body is hand woven and hand sewn. It has white leather arms. H. 28½ in. (72.5 cm.). H. of the shoulder head 9 in. (23 cm.). *Courtesy of Betty Lou Weicksel.*

681. Composition shoulder head with molded and painted features. The blond hair has a flat top with curls in the back. The pupils of the eyes are heavily outlined. The head was probably made in Thüringia sometime in the last three decades of the 1800s. H. of the head only, 3½ in. (9 cm.). *Coleman Collection.*

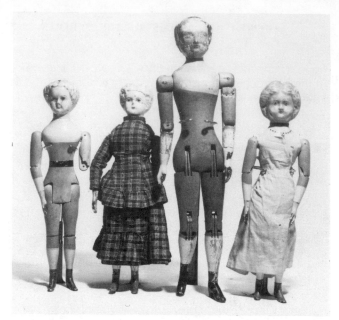

682. Three dolls with composition heads on wooden bodies, made by the Jointed Doll Co. ca. 1880s. The tall doll, made by the Cooperative Doll Co. (Joel Ellis) ca. 1873, had a wooden head as well as a wooden body. All of these dolls have metal hands and feet. Each doll has a different molded hair style. Some of the eyes are painted blue and some are brown. All have closed mouths and are jointed at the neck, shoulders, elbows, hips, and knees. Note the molded necklace on the doll at the right. Hs. left to right: 11½, 11½, 15¼, and 12 in. (29, 38.5, and 30.5 cm.). *Courtesy of Sotheby Parke Bernet Inc., N.Y.*

683. Shiny composition shoulder head, lower arms and legs, on a cloth body. Molded hair with brushmarks, blue threaded glass eyes. Original clothes of the 1890s. Mark: Ill. 694. H. 18½ in. (47 cm.). *Coleman Collection.*

684. Composition shoulder head doll of the 1880s has a wig, glass eyes, closed mouth, cloth body with leather lower arms, red circular striped legs and high heeled red leather boots. Original red dress. H. 14 in. (35.5 cm.). *Courtesy of Richard Withington. Photo by Barbara Jendrick.*

685. Dark brown all-composition doll with kinky hair wig, glass eyes, closed mouth, swivel neck on a five-piece body. The ethnic features and color suggest that this doll represents an African but the costume is almost identical to the clothes on several different dolls representing North American Indians. The varicolored fringed braid, black shiny belt and shoulder sash are typical of American Indian garb as conceived by German doll makers. H. 4¾ in. (12 cm.). *Coleman Collection.*

686A & B. Composition shoulder head, lower arms and legs on a cloth body, wig, sleeping glass eyes, open mouth with teeth, dimples in cheeks. Plaster type composition with glossy finish. Original clothes of ca. 1900. H. 17 in. (43 cm.). *Coleman Collection.*

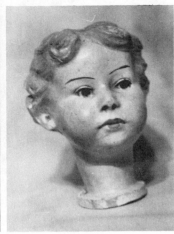

688A & B. Pair of composition cold pressed heads made from a mold similar to that of Gebrüder Heubach boy and girl dolls. They have molded hair, intaglio eyes, closed mouth, and neck ending in flanges. *Courtesy of May Maurer.*

687. Composition-head lady doll of ca. 1910 has a blond wig, glass eyes, closed mouth, cloth body with composition hands. Original clothes. H. 16¾ in. (42.5 cm.). *Courtesy of May Maurer.*

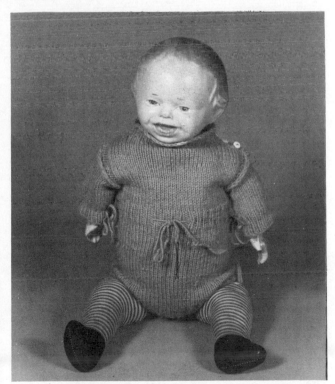

689. Composition-head doll with light brown molded hair, molded eyes and an open-closed laughing mouth. The cloth body has composition hands; the legs are covered with circular red-and-white-striped fabric to simulate stockings, with black sateen for shoes. This doll is probably pre-World War I since it resembles the early Campbell Kids in construction. The knitted suit may be original. H. 14 in. (35.5 cm.). *Courtesy of Shirley Buchholz.*

690A & B. Composition swivel neck doll with mohair wig, painted eyes, closed mouth, cloth body jointed at the shoulders and hips. Original clothes of the late teens. *Courtesy of Magda Byfield.*

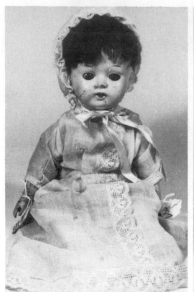

692A & B. Composition shoulder head doll of the 1920s with a wig, sleeping metal-type eyes, closed mouth, on a cloth body with composition lower arms. Original clothes. H. 13 in. (33 cm.). *Courtesy of Richard Withington. Photo by Barbara Jendrick.*

691. Composition face mask over a felt head; the mohair wig is stitched onto the felt scalp. The face has painted eyes, closed mouth. The felt body is jointed at the neck, shoulders and hips. Original clothes of the 1920s consisting of a velvet coat and hat, muslin chemise, woolen socks, and oilcloth boots. H. 14 in. (35.5 cm.). *Courtesy of Magda Byfield.*

693. Flocked composition head with a black wig, painted blue eyes, closed mouth; cloth body. The original costume suggests a 1920s date. The dress is blue and the shoes are made of oil-cloth. H. 15 in. (38 cm.). *Courtesy of Richard Withington. Photo by Barbara Jendrick.*

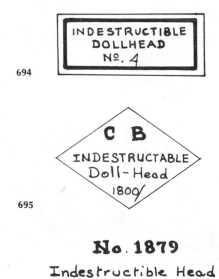

694

695

696

694–696. Marks on composition doll heads, describing the composition as "Indestructible."

Conductress. 1917. Character doll representing a war worker, made by the *Alliance Toy Co.*

Conkling, Mme. Henri. 1916. France. She founded *L'Ouvrier du Gros-Caillou* (The worker of the large pebble), an organization to produce dolls.

Conrad, P. 1926. Dresden, Germany. Manufactured dolls.

Conselman, Bill. 1925. Created with *Charlie Plumb* the cartoon character *Ella Cinders* which was made into a doll by *Horsman* in 1928.

Conta & Boehme. 1878–1914 and probably other years. Pössneck, Thür. A porcelain factory that made dolls' heads and all-porcelain dolls, especially china *Frozen Charlottes* (so-called).

Their mark was found on the feet of the Frozen Charlottes which came with short blond or black hair, short necks, chubby bodies with fingers curved, bent arms away from the body and feet apart. Hts. 33, 35, and 40.5 cm. (13, 14 and 16 in.). The largest one reported also had 4/0 on the right foot.

Several examples of an 1870s style hairdo china head have been seen. These were pressed china shoulder heads glazed inside and out. The molded black hair was arranged in a braided coronet with five small curls at the nape of the neck. The heads had painted eyes and brush strokes. One of the heads had pierced ears. Inside the heads were incised with the shield having a bent arm holding a dagger, the Conta & Boehme mark. Below this mark were incised roman numerals such as V, VIII and IX, over 37, 35, and 36 respectively. The Roman numerals appear to have indicated the size since V was the smallest and IX the largest head.

1878: They registered several numbers in Germany.

697. China shoulder head made by Conta & Böhme. The pressed head has black molded hair, brushmarks, molded and painted blue eyes, and closed mouth. The body is cloth with china arms. Mark: See Ill. 698. H. 17 in. (43 cm.). *Courtesy of Sybill McFadden.*

698. Conta & Böhme mark on the inside of a china shoulder head.

Contessa Maffei. 1925–26. Felt doll made by *Lenci,* number 165/0, dressed in a Romantic period costume, carrying a green carriage parasol. Ht. 29½ in. (75 cm.).

Continental Toy & Novelty Co. 1929. New York City. Made *Boudoir* type dolls and stuffed toys. Merged with *Blum-Lustig,* Pompeian Art Works, and Sil-Kov Art Pillow Co.

Contortionist Doll. 1908. A line of dolls whose supple bodies could be twisted and bent into various positions. The line included *Polly of the Circus, Peter Pan, Sandy MacGregory,* and representations of other celebrities.

Converse, Morton E., & Son. 1925–26. Winchendon, Mass. Made a jointed wooden doll called *Flexy* which was created by *Mrs. Ripley Hitchcock.* This firm was the successor of Converse Toy Woodware Co., the successor of Mason & Converse founded in 1878.

Convert. 1911–30 and later. Oyonnax and Péncran, France. Made celluloid dolls.

1930: Introduced dolls named *Nani* and *Nano.*

Coogan Kid. 1920s. A patented *Evripoze* cloth doll with flexible limbs representing Jackie Coogan and made by the *British Novelty Works,* a subsidiary of *Dean.* It had a mohair wig and came in two sizes.

Cook (Ko). See **Mi (Missis).**

Cook, Henry. See **Fluffy Ruffles.**

Cook's Flaked Rice Co. Ca. 1900. New York City. Offered a cutout cloth doll as a premium. Boasted that thousands of these dolls were made. The dolls wore printed combination underwear which was printed in color on muslin. Ht. 25 in. (63.5 cm.). (See also **American Rice Foods Manufacturing Co.**)

Coon. 1926. Name of some dolls produced by *C. and O. Dressel.*

Cooper, Frederick, & Sons. 1915–20. London. Manufactured *Bonnedol* line of baby dolls and *Mama* dolls with composition or *British Ceramic* heads. Some of their dolls had plush bodies. The jointed cloth bodies were stuffed with cork and most of them had composition limbs. The dolls came dressed or undressed.

Co-operative Manufacturing Co. 1873–74. Springfield, Vt. Manufactured wooden dolls patented by Joel Ellis. (See Ellis, Britton & Eaton.[+]) About 60 people, mostly women, were

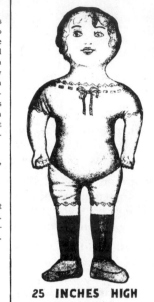
699. Cook's Flaked Rice Co. cloth premium doll as advertised in HARPER'S MAGAZINE. H. 25 in. (63.5 cm.).

employed in making these dolls. The head was cut into roughly a cube shape, then steamed until softened and compressed in a hydraulic press with steel dies to form the features. The body and limbs were turned on a lathe and the head fastened to the body with a dowel. The metal hands and feet were usually painted black but sometimes they were a bright blue. The hair was generally black but some blondes have been found and even some with painted necklaces.

Elsie Krug tells us that the business was terminated after such a short time, "because the man who made the machine for pressing the dolls' heads charged excessive royalties."★

Coppélia. 1928–29. Paris. Trade name for makers of cloth dolls, art dolls and toy dolls. These dolls were offered for the wholesale trade and for export. The name Coppélia was derived from a ballet character representing a doll.

Copyrights. In the 1920s it was required that the full name and not just the initials be on the product.

In 1926 a new copyright law was proposed (H R 6249). According to this new law industrial designs formerly classified as design patents would come under copyrights. "It is not essential that the design shall be new, but only that it shall be original in its actual application to, or embodiment in some manufactured article." Design was defined as "Any conception in relation to a manufactured product, either as to pattern, shape, or form which is original in its application to or embodiment in such manufactured product and is for the purpose of ornamentation of surface or other decoration."

The design could be registered for a short period at a small expense with the privilege of an extension.★

Coquelin, Monsieur. Ca. 1902. French actor who reportedly had a porcelain head portrait doll made at Montreuil. Both *Damerval Frères & Laffranchy* and the *Société Française de Fabrication de Bébés & Jouets* (S.F.B.J.) had porcelain factories at Montreuil-sous-Bois.

Coquette. 1916. Trade name of a doll distributed by *Tootle Campbell Dry Goods Co.*

Coquette. 1927. All-composition doll imported by *Butler Bros.* It had painted features, a wig, jointed arms, and wore only a silk ribbon sash. Ht. 4¼ in. (11 cm.).

Cora. 1927. Trade name of a line of portrait cloth dolls made by *Norah Wellings.* They had felt faces, glass eyes, real hair wigs, and were articulated. Bodies were made of velvet with sewn labels. One of these dolls was given to Queen Mary when she visited the Victoria Toy Works in 1927 according to Mary Hillier.

Corazon Heart. 1930. Doll made by *Bruno Schmidt.*

Corcoran & Laycock. 1928–30. New York City. Factory agents for *Petrie-Lewis, Poppy Doll Co., S. & H. Novelty Co.,* and *Veelo Mfg. Co.*

Corinthian Bazaar. After 1867. London. Sold wax dolls.

Corion. Before 1927–30. Paris. Produced art dolls. Successors were Menvielle & Arnould, then Arnould in 1930.

Corky. 1928. Oilcloth doll representing the then new Gasoline Alley baby, brother of *Skeezix.* It was made by *Live Long Toys* and wore a long baby dress.

Cornelius, W. H. 1924. England. Produced dolls.

Corona. 1917. Brand name for dolls, used by *Hancock.*

Corona Pottery. See **Hancock, S., & Sons.**

Corry, Grace (Grace Corry Rockwell). 1920–29. New York City. Designed and made dolls for various companies. Bisque heads and composition heads were made from her designs.

1926: She designed and copyrighted *Pretty Peggy* which was produced and distributed by *Borgfeldt.* Originally this bisque-head doll was called Betty Jean.

1927: Designed *Little Brother* and *Little Sister,* composition head dolls, for *Averill Manufacturing Co.*

Later these dolls were dressed in various costumes such

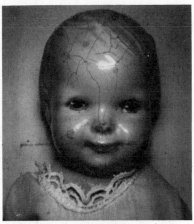

700A & B. Composition shoulder heads designed by Grace Corry in the mid-1920s. Dressed as a girl it was called Little Sister, dressed as a boy it was called Little Brother. The same head with molded and painted blond hair, blue eyes and closed mouth was used for a girl or boy doll. The cloth body has composition arms and legs. Mark: See Ill. 701. H. 14 in. (35.5 cm.). H. of shoulder head 5 in. (12.5 cm.). *Courtesy of the late Edna Greehy.*

© BY

GRACE CORRY

701. Embossed mark on composition head designed by Grace Corry.

as nursery rhyme characters, regional costumes and so forth and given names appropriate to their costumes.

1928: Created a doll named *Merriwinkle* for *Schoen & Yondorf.*★

Cosgrove Bros. 1922–26. Milton, Mass. Made *Elizabeth.*★

Cossack. 1922. Line of dolls made by *Wonderland.*

Costers. 1917. Cloth dolls made by *Hammond.*

Cosy Kids. 1920s. Cloth (felt and/or plush) dolls made by *Dean* with *Tru-Shu* feet. They wore a double breasted coat, cloche or bonnet, leggings or single strap slippers and socks.

1920: One of the flat-faced *Knockabout* series, made of muslin, style No. D 252. There were six printed costumes. Ht. 9½ in. (24 cm.); price 35¢.

Cotton Joe. 1910–16. One of the American Kids in Toyland† line of composition head dolls made by *Horsman.* It had molded hair, painted eyes looking straight ahead.

1911: *R. H. Macy* advertised a black Cotton Joe wearing a red shirt with pearl buttons, brown denim knee-length overalls, simulated stockings and black shoes. Ht. 13 in. (33 cm.); price 98¢.

1912: Listed in the catalog as No. 149; priced $8.50 doz. wholesale.

No. 149 "Cotton Joe"

702. Cotton Joe is a black version of Farmer Boy produced by Horsman and advertised in their catalog of ca. 1914. The composition head was copyrighted in 1912. It has composition hands like those used on the early Campbell Kids. *Courtesy of Bernard Barenholtz.*

1914: Cotton Joe's head was the black version of No. 159, Farmer Boy. It also came in a larger size 14 in. (35.5 cm.); priced $17.00 doz. wholesale and a smaller, "Junior" size, No. 80 $4.25 doz. wholesale.★

Country of Origin. Due to the use of paper stickers and other perishable methods of marking, the country of origin often cannot be determined. In America and Britain laws, especially after 1890, required some sort of labeling as to the country of origin, but as late as 1913 France did not have a similar requirement.

Often parts of the doll came in various shipments and the assembling and dressing were completed in the country of distribution, thus complicating and confusing the origins of the doll. Porcelain heads were sometimes painted in countries other than those in which they had been manufactured. (See **Van Briggle, Artus.**)

Court Dolls. Name given by modern doll collectors to sexed wooden dolls with gesso finish. Several of these dolls had old round paper tags with scalloped edges and red letters on a white ground. The letters read "Douanes?//Paris//Exposition." (Duties//Paris//Exposition.)

Couterier (Couturier), Alice. Before 1865–94. Paris. Factory was at Grenelle. Successor appears to have been Gustav Couterier. Made fashion-type dolls with bisque heads (purchased elsewhere). One of the Couterier dolls had painted short hair, painted eyes, and an unjointed kid body on which was an elliptical blue stamp that read "Maison// Alice Couterier//Paris." (See Ill. 704.) Another doll with

703. Wooden court dolls with carved, gessoed, and painted hair and features have jointed anatomically correct (sexed) bodies. The doll on the right is a Hermaphrodite. Original costumes represent the 1700s but appear to be later. These two dolls have paper tags that read "Douanes?//Paris//Exposition." Apparently they were shown at a Paris Exposition but the date of that exposition is unknown. Hs. 10½ in. (26.5 cm.). *Courtesy of Elsie and Al Potter.*

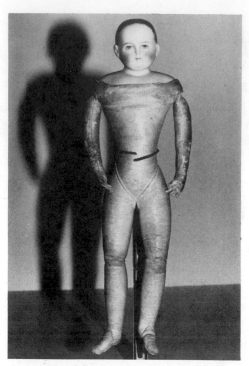

704. Untinted bisque shoulder head on a fashion type kid body made and/or handled by Alice Couterier (Couturier). It has black painted hair with brushmarks, blue molded and painted eyes, closed mouth. It has the short neck of a child but the proportions of the body suggest an adult. Oval mark with blue letters: "Maison//Alice Couterier//Paris." H. 13 in. (33 cm.). *Courtesy of Estelle Johnston.*

bisque head and hands had a wig, blue glass eyes, and a paper label (See Ill. 705) on the front of its wooden body which could turn at the waist. The original clothes were of the 1860s and included a pair of Congress style boots with a mark on their soles. Ht. of doll 17½ in. (44.5 cm.).

Besides dolls this house dressed marottes.

1891: Called one of their bisque-head dolls *La Poupée Volante.* This doll probably wore a flounced dress.★

Couty. See **Coiffe, A.**

Cowan, de Groot & Co. 1919–30 and later. London. Founded by S. D. Cowan and A. de Groot, who used the trade name "Codeg." They were doll importers and distributors.

1919: Handled *Britannia* dolls.

1923: Produced *Sonny Boy.*

Cowan, de Groot & Ross. 1922–30. London. Produced dolls. It is probable that this may not have been a separate firm from Cowan, de Groot & Co.

1924: Agent for *S. D. Zimmer*

1926: Agent for dressed dolls made by *Chr. Reisenweber.*

Cowboy (Cow Boy, Cow Girl). Many dolls have been dressed to represent people both male and female who looked after the cattle on ranch lands in various parts of the world including the American West, Mexico and Argentina. Among those manufacturing or distributing these dolls and the names of some of these dolls were:

705. Couterier paper label mark found on Alice Couterier dolls.

1889: *Montgomery Ward.*

1895: *Butler Bros, Wild West.*

1912: *Horsman, Campbell Kids.*

1913–16: *Steiff,* Mexican *Cowboy.*

1916: *Averill Manufacturing Co.,* Cowboy.† (See THE COLLECTOR'S BOOK OF DOLLS' CLOTHES, Ill. 711.)

1917: *Langrock Bros.,* Cowboys and Cowgirls, *Wyman, Partridge, Bloomin' Kids; Western Art Leather, Cow Boys and Cow Girls.*

1918: *Charles-Emile Carlègle and André Hellé; T. Eaton,* Cowboy.

1923: *Hitz, Jacobs & Kassler,* wooden dolls.

1924: *J. Bouton & Co.*

1926: *Horsman, HEbee SHEbee.*

1927–28: *I. & M. Helvetic Corp.*

1929: *Effanbee, Skippy; Averill Manufacturing Co. Cowboy.*

1930: *Etta; Lenci* an Argentine Gaucho; *Gebrüder Schmidt.* (See also the separate listings for specific **Cowboys,** and **Cowboys and Cowgirls.**) (See also the **Horsman Boy Scout.** Ills. 405 and 406.)

Cowboy (Mexican Cow Boy). 1913–16. Jointed felt comic doll representing a Mexican cowboy made by *Steiff.* It wore fur-type trousers or chaps, and a large sombrero style hat.

1913: Distributed in the U.S. by *Borgfeldt.* Four hts. 40, 45, 55, and 100 cm. (15½, 17½, 21½, and 39½ in.).

1916: In Germany the hts. were 40, 55, and 100 cm. (15½, 21½, and 39½ in.).

Cowboy. 1914. Doll with composition head, hands and feet, painted hair, cloth body, jointed at the shoulders and hips. It wore a shirt and leather cuffs, imitation sheepskin chaps, patent leather belt with buckle, leather holster, metal pistol, lariat and tan sombrero hat. Ht. 13 in. (33 cm.).

Cowboy. 1918. Doll with a celluloid head sold by *Eaton.* Ht. 6 in. (15 cm.); priced 25¢.

Cowboy. 1929 and possibly earlier. Doll with composition head and arms, painted hair and eyes, with a cotton-stuffed cloth body made by *Averill Manufacturing Co.* This whistling doll, which whistled in two tones, wore a cowboy suit with chaps and a hat. Ht. 14 in. (35.5 cm.).★

Cowboy and Cowgirl (Cow Boy, Cow Girl). 1917. Stuffed, colored leather dolls made by *Western Art Leather Co.* The boy had "Cow Boy" on his belt and the girl had "Cow Girl" on her belt. Both had a gun in a holster.

Cowham, Hilda (Hilda Gertrude Lander). 1915–30 and later. Illustrator who designed dolls for *Dean* and its subsidiary *British Novelty Works* as well as *Laurie Hansen.* In the 1930s Hilda Cowham also designed dolls for *Chad Valley* according to Mary Hillier. The Cowham dolls represented children with long stilty legs that resembled her drawings. There were cloth dolls and dolls with *British Ceramic* heads. An example of the latter is a shoulder head of deep flesh color with a wig, painted eyes, open-closed mouth and teeth. It was made by *Hancock* for Laurie Hansen and is incised "Hilda Cowham//Hancock's 2." The ht. of the shoulder head was 5 in. (12.5 cm.). The Laurie Hansen dolls came with eyes wide open or eyes nearly closed. The Cowham dolls were advertised as play dolls and as display dolls. *Hilda Cowham Rag Dolls* were made by Dean.

1916: Hilda Gertrude Lander registered *Hilda Cowham Doll* as a trademark in Britain. She designed *Hilda Cowham Kiddies* for British Novelty Works.

The Laurie Hansen dolls had laughing flesh-tone faces probably like the British Ceramic example described above. These dolls had long limbs.

1917: Designed *Gaiety Girl, Skating Girl* and *Golf Girl* for Laurie Hansen.

"HILDA COWHAM HANCOCK'S 2"

706. Pink British Ceramic head designed by Hilda Cowham and made by Hancock. It has a black wig, painted blue eyes, open-closed mouth with white between the lips. Mark: See Ill. 707. H. of shoulder head 5 in. (12.5 cm.). *Courtesy of the Margaret Woodbury Strong Museum. Photo by Barbara Jendrick.*

707. Hilda Cowham's mark on a British Ceramic head that she designed for Hancock.

Cox, Galatine. 1910. Edinburgh and New York City. Produced a cloth cutout advertising doll dressed as a Scottish boy. Ht. 15 in. (38 cm.).

Coxeter, Mrs. Clara. 1865–70. London. Made dolls.

Crabet Shape Co. 1916–10. London. Manufactured cloth dolls with mask faces and wigs. The dolls came dressed in a variety of costumes, usually a dress, bonnet, and underclothes. Price 13¢ to 25¢.

Cracker Jack. 1921. Name of a *Schoenhut* clown; it wore various clown costumes.

Cracker Jack Boy. 1917–18. Made with movable limbs by *Ideal.* Ht. 15 in. (38. cm.); price $1.00.★

Cradle Babe. 1927. One of the *Kiddiejoy* line made by *Hitz, Jacobs & Kassler. My Dream Baby* type doll with a bisque head and glass eyes. It wore a long dress of lawn, and came in a decorated cradle with blanket and pillow. Price for the entire item was $1.00.

Cradle-Time. 1928. Cloth doll made by Twinzy Toy Co. *(Squier Twins Toy Co.).*

Craigcraft. See **Tillicum Toys.**

Crämer, Eduard. 1896–1927. Schalkau, Thür. Made dolls.

1927: Made felt dolls.

Crämer & Co. Early 1900s–1930 and later. Nürnberg, Bavaria. They exported *Snow Babies* until World War II.

Crämer & Héron. 1892–1920s. Sonneberg and Mengersgereuth near Sonneberg, Thür. Made dolls. In 1909 Crämer and Héron founded the Porzellanfabrik Mengersgereuth which had the initials P. M. and might be the factory that made the many German bisque heads marked "P. M." Other factories known to have used P. M. in their mark included: Porzellanfabrik Martinroda of Eger & Co., founded in Thüringia in 1901; Porzellanfabrik Hof-Moschendorf, founded by Otto Reinecke in Bavaria in 1878; a Porzellanfabrik founded in 1890 in Selb, Bavaria, by Paul Müller and taken over in 1917 by Hutschenreuther, whose own factory was also located in Selb.

The unidentified bisque heads were marked with the initials P. M., the outline of a heart and sometimes the name Herzi.[+] The P. M. initials have been found on bisque heads marked *Trebor* or *Grete*. Most of these P. M. heads were on bent limb composition baby bodies. The Ciesliks found that *Carl Harmus, Jr.*, obtained dolls' heads from this factory. P. M. mold numbers included 23 and 914. Lois Kirkpatrick reported that her 914 head was on a doll that had a label "*Little Sister*" on it. Hts. reported from 9 to 22 in. (23 to 56 cm.).

1892–93: Crämer & Héron exhibited dolls at the Chicago Exposition.

1910: Member of the Sonneberg group that won a grand prize at the Brussels Exposition.★

708. Bisque head baby doll; possibly the head was made by Crämer & Héron. It has a dark brown wig, blue glass eyes, an open mouth and a bent limb baby body. Mark: "P.M.//914//1." H. 11½ in. (29 cm.). *Courtesy of Sotheby Parke Bernet Inc., N.Y.*

P. M.
914
Germany.
2/0

709. P. M. marks on bisque head dolls possibly made by Crämer & Héron.

Crandall, Charles M. 1874–81 and later. U.S.A. Made acrobatic jointed wooden dolls that were handled by *Selchow & Righter*, Strasburger, Pfeiffer,[+] *Millikin & Lawley* and H. Jewitt.

1875: Applied for a U.S. patent for his dolls' joints. Later Jewitt obtained the British patent for Crandall.

Craven Novelty Co. 1922. England. Produced dolls.

Crawford, Mr. M. D. C. 1925. New York City. Designed dolls together with *Stewart Culin* for an exhibit used to display the History of Costume, which was used with lectures on the subject at numerous colleges and universities.

Crawling Baby. 1914. A celluloid *(celtid)* character baby with its head having painted hair and eyes. The doll "crawls" by moving its feet, activated by a spring. This doll was distributed by *Marshall Field*. Ht. 6 in. (15 cm.); price $17.00 a doz. wholesale.

Créations de Grande Luxe. 1927–28. Paris. Name used by Tony Deluy for the workshop where modern art dolls were made.

Creeping Baby. 1884–85. Distributed by *Selchow & Righter* who gave the instructions "To make the baby creep draw it along the floor holding the cord in an upright position." 5¼ in. long by 4 in. high. (13½ cm. by 10 cm.).

Creeping Baby. 1926. Doll made by *Schoen & Yondorf* in their Sayco line.

Cremer, Eversfield & Co. 1923–24, New York City. Advertised all-composition character dolls, jointed at the shoulders and hips. 12 numbers. Ht. 14 in. (35.5 cm.).★

Cremer & Son. 1862–ca. 1900. London. Sucessor was Henry Cremer in 1873. William Henry Cremer Jr. was in charge of this famous toy shop at least from 1862 to 1873. In 1862 he claimed that he made dolls. See Ill. 710 for his mark. A dolls' Carte de Visite Album 2 in. (5 cm.) high having 8 photographic prints of dolls was attributed to "W. H. Cremer European Toy Warehouse, 27 Bond Street."

In 1865 THE ENGLISH WOMAN'S DOMESTIC MAGAZINE had an article, "Lilliput of Regent Street," which described the dolls and their accessories in the Cremer store. In the article Cremer Jr. was referred to as "Merlin" because of his wizardry. The article was as follows:

"The doll made for, and dressed by, a famous magician in Dollyland, is an astounding marvel of what may be done with taste and ingenuity in the make and fitting-up of little ones for the little ones. . . . We found the mighty Merlin. . . .

"He reigned in the kingdom of Lilliput; sole master, not of a toyshop, but of a world in miniature, a state wherein the rights of dolls were admitted, and they were treated in every respect as fellow-creatures.

"They received us very kindly. A charming girl, about twelve inches high, with flaxen curls and lips as ruddy, if not ruddier than the cherry, performed on a pianoforte.

"A gay party of picnicking friends were the next to greet us. . . . It quite prepared you for the bride in her robes of virgin purity, her veil of modesty, and coronal of orange blossoms. . . . It led you on . . . to see her in her well-fitting

710. Mark used by W. H. Cremer, Jr.

riding-habit. . . . [Next] a grandmamma, spectacles on nose, teaching a very tiny one. . . . We saw her in her morning dress, her walking dress, her evening dress, ready for dinner or the opera. . . .

"We grew inquisitive . . . and drawers and doors flew open at the magician's bidding, and we were freely admitted into all the marvels and mysteries of our little lady's toilet.

"Here were her jewel-boxes, full of brooches, and buckles, and earrings, and bandeaux, and bracelets, and chains, and necklaces, and watches, gold and silver, and diamonds and pearls, rubies, emeralds, sapphires, amethysts, carbuncles, and all the rest that are known to the lapidary . . . earrings a quarter of an inch long, watches half-an-inch in circumference. Here were her shoes—exquisitely made shoes—of all shapes, and intended for all sorts of wear; white satin slippers that Cinderella could not have got on; patent-leather boots, comfortable fur-edged, double-soled winter boots, warranted to stand all weathers—surely a fairy cobbler must have made them, stockings to match—silk, cotton, worsted, light, dark, and all the colours of the rainbow; gloves also, so delicate and beautiful that they seem to be flung down as a challenge to fall in love with the wearer; collars, cuffs, furs, tippets, muffs, boas, comforters—everything stays, not quite so heavy as the iron stays . . . stays and crinolines (for her dollyship must be in the fashion), the pinching in and filling out must be exercised upon her as well as on her maturer sisters. The corsets of the most fashionable cut are triumphs of art. They are the sole work of one young lady, who does not do anything else. Then as to the crinolines; they are made to suit the purse of dolly, or that of her guardians—some of the very best, some mere fly-cages—for there are poor dolls as well as rich ones.

"Merlin kindly showed us the trousseaux of many miniature ladies, all containing everything that a lady can require, and many of them everything a lady might desire. She has her carte-de-visite book [photograph album] and her portemonnaie [purse].

"There is a singular advantage enjoyed by dolly in one of the toilet operations—namely, her hair. Many a lady grows weary under the hands of the coiffeur. . . . Now dolly simply shifts her head of hair. Cunning she is, and may sometimes be seen in curlpapers, knowing well that her ringlets are all ready for her in a drawer up-stairs. Whatever be the prevailing fashion of the hair, dolly's wigs are made accordingly; for morning calls, for the park, for dinner, for the opera, she takes one off and puts another on.

"As to dolly herself, her face and head and neck are made of wax, so are her limbs; her body is made of kid, stuffed with fine wool. Some of her poorer sisters are compelled to be content with a linen epidermis, but kid is aristocratic. Most of the miniature ladies can be made to move their heads and to exercise their joints; some of them open and shut their eyes, and we were introduced to a baby that shrieked and kicked its arms and legs about after the manner of a child waking up in not the best of humours. But one of the most ingenious things . . .—is the shifting of heads. Thus dolly, to-day a girl in the middle of her teens, is to-morrow a coquette looking out of them, and the next day a bride, and the next a matron, and the next a very mature and stately lady, and the next wrinkled and white-headed, to be the next, by merely twisting her head off and substituting another, a blooming girl again.

"Everything exhibited by Merlin in his miniature world was remarkable for its extreme accuracy of detail and the excellency of the taste displayed in its manufacture. There were coats, trousers, and vests for gentlemen-dolls; boots, gloves, hats, cravats, and cigars and cigar-cases to match. The pockets were all practicable, the copy faithful to the original in every particular.

"As to the amount of material consumed, and the number of hands employed, and the arrangements of the trade with regard to their employment, Miss Wren [OUR MUTUAL FRIEND by Charles Dickens] and Mr. Riah's 'pieces' seem out of count altogether. Merlin plainly said he had never seen anything like Miss Wren's way of doing business in all his experiences in Lilliput.

". . . dressing tables, dressing-cases, brushes, hairpins, pin-cushions, swing glasses, cheval glasses, chimney-glasses. . . . there is nothing in the world of civilization you can think of, or that a well-brought-up doll, accustomed to the elegancies of life, might not obtain at Merlin's. And who is Merlin but Cremer, Junior."

An 1873 Cremer report was given in THE COLLECTOR'S BOOK OF DOLLS' CLOTHES, pp. 157–158.★

Crepe Cloth Dolls. Dolls have been found made of this material. In THE AMERICAN GIRL'S BOOK, first published in 1831, a description of how to make a black crepe doll was given.

1927: *Butler Bros.* advertised such dolls with flat faces. They represented a Dutch boy, a Dutch girl and a *Tiny Tot*. (See also **Cloth Dolls**.) (See Ills. 337, 338, and 339.)

Crescent Toy Manufacturing Co. 1907–21. Brooklyn, New York. Manufactured stuffed character dolls.

1920: Advertised "Sweater dolls."★

Crescent Works. See **Sunlight, Sieve & Co.**

Cresco Spielwaren. 1921–24. Schweinfurt a Main, Germany. Successor was Arenz & Büttner. Obtained several German patents (D.R.P.) for a doll with a movable head.

Cressall, A. A. 1922. London. Produced dolls.

Cresta. 1926. Line of velvet face dolls made by *Dean*. They came in two styles and three sizes.

Cri-Dol. 1926. Bent-limb baby doll with a composition head, painted hair and sleeping eyes, made by *Averill Manufacturing Co.* in their *Mme. Hendren* line. Rectangular tag reads "Cri-Doll// Patented// © cries like a real baby// to operate wind crank at// side of doll's body."

Criest, Frank. 1918. Sharpsville, Pa. Obtained a United States patent for a walking doll with a plurality of legs adapted to frictionally engage a base.

Crinoline. 1918. Trade name of an "unbreakable" doll made by the *All British Toys Co.*

Croisat, Dame Vve. (Widow, née Josephine Hely). Before 1874. Paris. Made dolls. She failed in 1874 according to the research of Mme. Poisson, Curator of the Roybet-Fould Museum.

Cromien, Blanche Rowe. 1925 or earlier—1930 and later. Rockaway, New Jersey. Designed and made clothes for dolls. Many of the clothes were handmade. She dressed dolls for *Borgfeldt,* such as special costumes for *Bye-Lo Babies.* She designed and made most of the clothes for the *Cameo* dolls as well as the clothes for the dolls of *Hoest & Henderson* such as *Baby Dahne.* Blanche Cromien made doll outfits that were sold separately often in hat boxes or suitcases.

TOYS AND NOVELTIES in 1931 reported that she manufactured dolls, but as far as is known she only made the clothes. However it is sometimes stated of people that they made certain dolls when actually they only dressed the dolls.

Crosby, Percy. 1929. Creator of *Skippy,* his design was used for a doll made by *Effanbee.*

Crosthwait, Ota. 1926. Kansas City, Mo. Obtained a United States design patent for a doll.

Crouilbois, Mme. 1918. Paris. The Art Institute of Chicago has some dolls with wax heads and hands dressed in period costumes of the 1700s and mid 1800s. The dolls were purchased new in 1918 and bear the label "Mme. Crouilbois// Maison Crouilbois// Paris, France."

LES JOUETS published in 1918 a statement that Mme. Crouilbois created stylish costumes for dolls.

Crown. 1909. Brand name of dressed and undressed rubber dolls advertised in London.

Crown Doll (Kronenpuppe). 1895–1930 and later. Trademark registered and used by *Kestner.*★

Crown Doll Manufacturing Co. 1927–29. New York City. Manufactured dolls and was licensed by *Voices, Inc.* to use their patented mama voices and criers in the Crown dolls.

Crown Staffordshire Porcelain Co. 1889–1930 and later. Minerva Works, Fenton, Staffordshire. During World War I they made *British Ceramic* dolls' heads. They supplied heads to the *Doll Pottery Co.,* to *Henry Jeffrey Hughes* or *Henry John Hazel* for the *Caversham* dolls and probably to other British doll-making companies.

Cruchet, Marie. Ca. 1850–57. France. Obtained several patents for making dolls. One related to the doll that said "Mama" and "Papa." Another related to the making of a shoulder head in one piece rather than the customary two pieces. Yet another related to the articulation whereby the sockets in the ball joints were covered with kid.

CRY BABY DOLL

(CRY BABY AS SOLD)

These Dolls are for very Little Folks and are in high favor with the Tots—when made up the Cry Baby is as Broad as is long and presents a very comical appearance.

Retails at 15c.

711. Cutout cloth doll named Cry Baby. These dolls were designed for "very Little Folks." This advertisement was in THE DELINEATOR, December, 1901.

Cry Baby. 1900–2. Cloth cut-out doll made by *Art Fabric Mills.* The printed clothes on the baby consisted of a shirt and diaper. The legs are foreshortened to give the doll the appearance of being seated. Price 15¢.

Crying Babies. 1851–1930 and later. Baby dolls that emitted crying sounds. In February 1852 HARPER'S NEW MONTHLY MAGAZINE reported on the new "Crying Dolls." (See **Baby Dolls.**) The *Motschmann*-type doll introduced about 1855 in Europe usually had a squeaker that might cause it to be called a crying baby. The Day Book of *John D. Robbins* in 1860–61 listed numerous styles and sizes of crying babies, dressed and undressed, among them were wax dolls and "chinese style babies." Sizes ranged from 3/0 to 4; prices 50¢ to $30.00 a doz. wholesale. This information was provided by Elizabeth Pierce. (See also **Chinese Crying Babies.**)★

Crying Voice. A mechanism, usually a bellows, that caused the doll to emit a single tone. This should be distinguished from the two-tone mama voice. (See **Crying Dolls.**[†])

Cuddle Baby. 1930. Dressed dolls with cloth bodies produced by *Borgfeldt.*

Cuddle Baby. See **Gem Toy Co.**

Cuddle Body. See **Baby Dimples.**

Cuddle Dolls. 1926. Soft dolls with handpainted faces made by *Kitty Fleischmann.*

Cuddle (Cuddly) Kewpies. 1929–30 and later. A *Kewpie* doll in cloth form designed, copyrighted and trademarked by *Rose O'Neill.* They were made exclusively by *King Innovations, Inc.* under the direction of Jack Cohen, the concern's president. He worked with Rose O'Neill to turn a Kewpie into a cloth doll. The jersey and satin dolls had mask faces, molded top knots and wings. Their hands were mitten shaped.

According to PLAYTHINGS, King Innovations was capable of making Cuddly Kewpies by the millions and they were the chief wholesale distributors. *Vier Bros.* jobbers were also distributors. *Wanamaker'*s sold 600 of these dolls

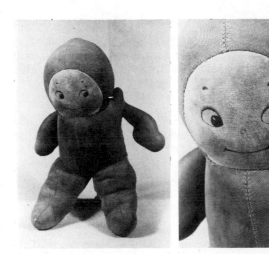

712A & B. Cloth doll, shaped like a Kewpie with topknot and wings, named Cuddle Kewpie. Painted flat face in the Kewpie style. Doll made of red fabric, except for the white face; no clothes. H. 11 in. (28 cm.). *Coleman Collection.*

in one day thanks to Rose O'Neill being at the store to autograph them.

Richard Krueger was also one of the producers of the Cuddle Kewpies.

CUDDLE KEWPIES			
Size	Height		
No.	in.	cm.	Price
0	11	28	$1.29
1	14½	37	
2	17	43	
3	22	56	$3.75

Cuddlekins. 1917–27. Line of soft body dolls designed for infants. Some of these dolls were made of stockinet or terrycloth. They were distributed by *Strobel & Wilken.*★

Cuddlekins. 1930. Line of soft dolls made by *Oakhurst Studios.* These dolls represented a boy, a girl, a clown, a Dutch girl, an American Indian, a Chinaman, and an Eskimo.

Cuddles. 1927. Doll created by *Jane Gray* and manufactured by *Gerling.* (See also **Kuddles.**)

Cuddles. 1929. Trade name of a jersey cloth doll with hand-painted features and hair, one piece body. It was manufactured by *Nelke* and distributed by *Butler Bros.* Ht. 10 in. (25.5 cm.); price $2.00 a doz. wholesale.

Cuddles. 1930 and later. Name of a doll with composition head, rubber arms, and sometimes rubber legs, made by *Ideal.* (See Ill. 713.)

Cuddley Dolls. 1923–28. Doll advertised as "indestructible." It had real hair, hand-colored molded face and cloth body stuffed with kapok. The dress was velveteen trimmed

713A & B. Cuddles made by Ideal. It has a composition head with molded hair, sleeping metal eyes, open mouth with two upper teeth, dimples, cloth body containing a crier, rubber arms to above the elbows and composition or rubber legs. Original pink and white clothes and tag with red and black letters on a white ground. Mark on body: "U.S. Patent//1621434//1793395." (These patents were dated 1927 and 1931). The 1927 patent was used on earlier dolls. H. 14 in. (35.5 cm.). *Private collection.*

with plush, to resemble fur. *Gamage* distributed this doll. Four hts. 11, 13, 16, and 18 in. (28, 33, 40.5 and 45.5 cm.). This was one of a line of dolls made by *Mabel Bland-Hawkes,* others came dressed or undressed and some wore bathing suits because these dolls could float in water.

Cuddley Ones. 1916–18. Dressed cloth dolls made by *Three Art Women's Employment Fund.* Price $8.25 to $25.50 a doz. wholesale.

Cuddly Dimples. 1930. Trade name of a doll made by *Horsman.*

Culin, Alice (Mrs. Stewart). 1920s. New York City. A painter who designed dolls including portrait dolls and "fantasy dolls."

Culin, Stewart. 1902–28. Brooklyn, N.Y. Curator at the Brooklyn Museum. In the 1920s he had several doll exhibitions and purchased many dolls on his trips to Europe and Africa. He invented a flat type doll with jointed arms that could be used to display miniature costumes.

1908: Assisted Laura Starr in writing THE DOLL BOOK.

1921: He supplied dolls to be dressed by the *Syndicate de la Couture Parisienne.*

1923: THE BROOKLYN CITIZEN reported. "Brooklyn going ahead of Paris in setting fashions for U.S. . . . Culin is the ultimate fashion dictator of America; he is the Czar of the designers."

Cuming, M. A., & Co. 1920–30. New York City. Made doll presses.★

Cupid. 1916 and probably other years. Trade name of an all-bisque doll jointed at the shoulders and hips made in Germany and distributed by *Butler Bros.* Eyes glanced to the side. The numbers 10414, 10950 and 10954 have been found on these dolls. Hts. 5, 5⅛ and 5¼ in. (12.5, 13 and 13.5 cm.).

Cupid Doll. 1919–20. Doll made by *Alisto*. It was jointed at the shoulders, stood on a base with legs together, and was dressed and had a hair ribbon.★

Cupid. 1919–20. Doll advertised by W. C. Eck & Co.✝ The dressed doll had eyes glancing to the side, had its legs together and stood on a base.

Cupid Knitwear Co. 1926–30 and later. New York City. Manufactured handmade knit outerwear for dolls, especially for *Mama* dolls and infant dolls.

1926: Advertised knit doll outfits including a matching cape and hat that would accurately fit dolls of each size.

1929: Advertised knit jackets, robes, and other accessories for dolls.

Cupid Love. 1923. Trade name of a doll shown at the British Industries Fair. It was claimed that there was an annual production of a million a year.

Cupid-Eye. 1913. Trade name of a coy looking doll produced by the *Claflin Co.*

Cupido. 1913. Name of a small baby doll advertised by *Standfuss*.

Cupids. 1920–22. London. All-composition *Kewpie*-type dolls made by the *Lawton* Doll Co. 12,000 of these dolls were made in the London factory per week. Many of them were used as mascots.

Cupids. 1924. Dolls of all sizes and styles made by *Kletzin* for export only.

Cupids. 1924. Dolls distributed by *L. Meyer*.

Cupids. 1926. Dolls manufactured and exported by *August Schelhorn's* successors.

Curly. 1930. Advertised by *W. Cohen & Sons* as having a head made by *Ernst Heubach*, mold #342. It had a bisque head on a five piece composition body with straight lower legs. Seven hts. 30, 36, 42, 46, 50, 55, and 60 cm. (12, 14, 16½, 18, 19½, 21½ and 23½ in.). Dolls with a cheaper finish and a bent limb body came in six hts. 38, 43, 45, 51, 55, and 60 cm. (15, 17, 17½, 20, 21½, and 23½ in.).

Curly Locks. 1912–13. Composition head doll with molded curls, painted eyes, cloth body with gauntlet-type composition hands, made by *Amberg*. Marked "574 ©// L. A. 1912."★

Curly Locks. 1916–18. All-composition doll made by *Jessie M. Raleigh* had a wig and a five-piece body with steel spring joints. One of the 13½ inch. (34 cm.) dolls wore a lawn skirt, blouse and a ribbon headband.★

Curly Locks. 1917. Cloth cutout, *Hug-Me-Tight*, doll.

Curly Locks. 1918. Doll with composition shoulder head and forearms on a cork stuffed cloth body, distributed by *Butler Bros.* It had a wig, sleeping eyes, open mouth, and wore a one-piece knit union suit and ribbon headband. Hts. 13, 16 and 20 in. (33, 40.5 and 51 cm.); price $19.50 to $34.50 a doz. wholesale.

Curly Locks. 1920. Cloth doll made by *Dean* in three versions. Style No. S 71 was a cutout *Knockabout* doll with the directions given in English and French. It was suggested that the doll be stuffed with wood wool; price 41¢. The other two versions had three-dimensional *Tru-to-Life* faces. Style No. D. 193 had printed hair and cost 83¢; style no. D 202 had a wig and cost $1.10. All three versions were 14 in. (35.5 cm.) tall.

Curly Locks. 1922. One of a Mother Goose series. This handpainted cloth doll with a voice was made by *Rees Davis.*

Currie & Co. 1912–13. London. Made dolls of white wood blocks screwed together, but they were jointed at the neck, shoulders, hips and knees. They advertised that these dolls were made without paint or glue and that they had harmless coloring. One of the dolls was given the trade name *Boy Scout.*

Curtis Product Co. 1925–26. Hibbing, Minn. Made dolls' heads and hands of a "non-breakable material."

Curtiss Candy Co. 1927–29. Chicago, Ill. Registered *Baby Ruth* as a U.S. trademark for dolls in 1927, and in 1929 they registered *Chicos* as a trademark.

Custodianship of Dolls.★

Cutie Dolls. 1921. All-composition *Kewpie*-type doll made by *Phoenix Doll Co.* The doll had a wig with a veil, legs apart and wore various dresses trimmed with marabou.

Cutie Dolls. 1927. All-celluloid dolls with molded hair; jointed at shoulders and hips. Five hts. 3, 4¾, 5¾, 7, and 8½ in. (7.5, 12, 14.5, 18, and 21.5 cm.); priced 25¢ to $3.50 a doz. wholesale. Those jointed at the shoulders only, and flesh colored, came in five hts. 3½, 4, 5, 5½, and 8 in. (9, 10, 12.5, 14, and 20.5 cm.); priced 30¢ to $1.75 per doz. wholesale. Same doll in a black version, hts. 4, 5, and 7¾ in. (10, 12.5, and 19.5 cm.); priced 35¢ to $1.75 doz. wholesale.

Cutout Cloth Dolls. Dolls printed on muslin were to be cutout, sewed together and stuffed. Many companies produced these dolls, among them were *Arnold Print Works, Art Fabric Mills, Dean, Elms & Sellon, Fernand Nathan, Saalfield* and many others. These dolls were especially popular as advertising dolls.

1906: *Gamage* advertised several cutout cloth dolls including a jointed doll, a 20 in. (51 cm.) doll, a *Life Size Doll* and *Foxy Grandpa;* priced 22¢ to 47¢.

1912–13: *Selchow & Righter* advertised the following cutout cloth dolls: *Daisy, Dolly Dimple, Gretchen, Hans, Juanita, Laddie,* Life Size Doll, *Little Bo Peep, Little Boy*

Blue, Little Red Riding Hood, Marie, Miss Muffet, Tiny Tim, Tom Thumb, and *Topsy.*

Cymbalier. 1882 or earlier–1927 and possibly later. Doll holding cymbals that were attached to each hand. When the body was pressed the cymbals were brought together thus making a noise or some other simple action causing the cymbals to strike one another. These dolls were especially popular in the Paris stores and were often dressed as clowns.

1882: *Ehrich Bros.* advertised a Cymbalier clown with a small doll on its shoulders.

1887: *Lauer* advertised dressed Cymbaliers, priced 5¢ to $1.00.

Ehrich Bros. advertised a Cymbalier with a wax head and glass eyes; priced 65¢.

1891: The Swedish catalog of *Printemps* advertised a bisque-head Cymbalier.

1892: The *Louvre* store advertised a doll with cymbals, dressed as a Russian in silk and velvet. Ht. 30.5 cm. (12 in.); priced 58¢.

1893: *Horsman* advertised Cymbaliers, described as "clapping figures"; priced 38¢ to $9.00 doz. wholesale.

1900–1: Printemps advertised bisque head Cymbaliers dressed in silk for 45¢ and 78¢.

1902: *Wanamaker* advertised a doll dressed as a clown, which clapped cymbals, for 25¢.

1903: *Ville de St. Denis* advertised Cymbaliers with moving eyes. Ht. 35 cm. (14 in.); the one in wool clothes cost 29¢ and in satin clothes it cost 58¢.

1904: *Simpson-Crawford Co.* advertised Cymbaliers.

1905: *Petit Saint Thomas* advertised a doll with cymbals, dressed in a pseudo-Arabian costume. Hts. 33, 37 and 42 cm. (13, 14½ and 16½ in.); price 29¢ to 58¢.

1907: *Paris Cette* advertised Cymbaliers dressed in wool for 13¢.

1909: La *Samaritaine* advertised Cymbaliers. Hts. 35 and 38 cm. (14 and 15 in.); priced 29¢ and 39¢.

1910: Ville de St. Denis advertised a Cymbalier with sleeping eyes, clothes trimmed with lace and gold braid. Ht. 42 cm. (16½ in.); price 29¢.

Ca. 1910: *Shackman* advertised a Cymbalier dressed in silk. Ht. 4½ in. (11.5 cm.); price 25¢.

1912: *Modernes* advertised a Cymbalier with a movable mouth and eyes. Ht. 38 cm. (15 in.); price 59¢.

Paris Montpelier advertised a bisque head Cymbalier for 29¢.

Sears, advertised Cymbaliers with painted composition heads representing *Foxy Grandpa, Happy Hooligan* and a Policeman. Ht. 10½ in. (26.5 cm.); price 90¢ doz. wholesale. The cymbals were activated by pressing the chest of the doll.

1913–14: Samaritaine advertised a Cymbalier with moving eyes and mouth. Hts. 35 and 38 cm. (14 and 15 in.): priced 29¢ and 39¢.

1914: The Ville de St. Denis Cymbalier had a fantasy costume and cost 13¢ to 29¢.

1927: The *American Wholesale Corporation* advertised Cymbaliers with composition heads and painted features, and wooden limbs dressed in felt clown costumes. Ht. 12 in. (30.5 cm.); price $1.75 doz. wholesale. (See also **Clowns.**)

714. Cymbalier dressed as a clown. It has a bisque head, wig, stationary blue glass eyes and an open mouth with two upper teeth. The body is made of wood and wire so that pressure enables the wooden arms to bring the cymbals together. Original clothes. Head marked "70.195." H. 13½ in. (34 cm.). *Courtesy of Cherry Bou.*

17581.
Clown cymbalier.
4.90 et 4.25

715. Cymbalier dressed as a clown and sold by Printemps in 1918 for 85¢ and 98¢.

Czar Nicholas. See **Tzar (Nicholas).**

Czecho-Slovak Commercial Corp. 1921. Produced dolls.

Czechoslovakian Dolls. Moravia was the Toy Center of Czechoslovakia according to PLAYTHINGS. In 1928 the Czechoslovakian government granted interest free loans to small manufacturers in Moravia.

Stewart Culin bought many dolls in Prague on his various visits to Czechoslovakia; among these were the dolls made by *Mlle. Marcel Giblet.* He also listed a considerable number of "leather dolls."

1920: Stewart Culin reported on a large Moravian doll with knit clothes and described it as "not having distinction of similar dolls seen elsewhere but was practical and interesting." (See also **Bohemian Dolls.**)

D

D. A. Script mark found on bisque socket head. Size 6 is a 24 in. (61 cm.) doll. Maker is not known as yet.

D. R. G. M. 1891–1930 and later. Deutsches Reichs Gebrauchs Muster, a German-registered design or *patent* that is a lesser patent than the *D.R.P.*

D. R. M. R. Deutsches Reichs Muster Rolle (German Model Register). (See also **Patents.**)

D. R. P. 1877–1930 and later. Deutsches Reichs *Patent* (German registered patent).

Da Costa, Arthur V. 1921–25. Providence, R.I. Obtained a U.S. patent for hollow bulbous body parts for dolls.

Da Da Da. After 1910. A cutout printed cloth doll made by the *Art Fabric Mills.* It represents the baby in the cartoon NEWLY WED KID[+] published by the Press Publishing Co. Ht. 5½ in. (14 cm.).

Da-Da. 1928–29. Baby doll with composition head and arms, painted hair; made by the *Atlantic Toy and Manufacturing Co.* The doll had two lower teeth and wore a short baby dress and a halo style bonnet.

Dach (Dachauer). Before 1911–24. Jointed felt comic doll made by *Steiff* and distributed by *Borgfeldt* in the U.S. It wore the costume of a peasant from Dachau with two rows of buttons down the front of the vest and pork pie hat. Ht. 14 in. (35.5 cm.); Price 83¢ in Germany in 1911 and $1.25 in New York in 1913.

Daddy Doll. 1922. Doll's head of a painted rubber ball with a hair mustache, made by *Carevelle Doll Co.* based on the design of E. B. Card.[+] It wore a black felt evening costume. Ht. 36 in. (91.5 cm.).

Daddy Longlegs. 1915. Made by *Effanbee,* advertised by Marks & Knoring.[+]

Daddy Scott. 1925. U.S.A. Trademark for wooden dolls registered by *Walter B. Scott.*

Daddy Warbucks. 1929. All-bisque doll with jointed neck, represented the *Little Orphan Annie* cartoon character called Daddy Warbucks drawn by Harold Gray. The doll

716. Bisque head doll with wig, brown glass eyes, open mouth and teeth. The composition body is ball jointed. Mark: "D A 6." H. 24 in. (61 cm.). *Courtesy of Richard Withington. Photo by Barbara Jendrick.*

717. Mark found on bisque heads of dolls.

was made in Germany and distributed wholesale exclusively by *Marshall Field.*

Daffydils. 1912–13. Composition doll made by *Amberg.* It represented the cartoon character named "Daffydils" drawn by Tad.★

Daheim. 1919. Line of fully jointed dolls dressed by *Carl Hartmann.*

Dahne Dolls. See **Baby Dahne.**

718A & B. Steiff felt doll named Dach. It also represents one of the musicians in "The Village Band." (See Ill. 2506.) It has painted gray hair, black button eyes, closed mouth and a body jointed at the neck, shoulders and hips. There is a Steiff button in each ear and all of the buttons on the vest have the Steiff marks. The seam is not down the center of the face but around the nose, with diagonal seams extending outward down from the nose. Original clothes. H. ca. 30 cm. (12 in.). *Courtesy of the Washington Dolls' House and Toy Museum.*

719. Dach (Dachauer Bauer) representing a peasant of Dachau, is a felt Steiff doll. It has painted gray hair, black button eyes, closed mouth, Steiff buttons in each ear and in two rows down the vest. Original clothes similar but slightly different from those shown in Ill. 718. H. ca. 30 cm. (12 in.). *Courtesy of Richard Wright. Photo by A. Jackson.*

Dainti-style Edinburgh Dressed Dolls. 1917. Leading line of the *Edinburgh Toy Factory.* Jointed dolls had removable clothes.

Dainty Doll. 1929. *Segmented Wooden Doll* with enamel finish made by the *Essenel Co.* It consisted of a ball for the head and a ball for the body, three balls for the arms and four segments for the legs.

Dainty Dolls. 1929. Cloth dolls made by *Dean* with hand-painted faces.

Dainty Dorothy. 1910–30. Trade name of a line of dolly-faced dolls distributed by *Sears* and *Eaton.* The bisque heads were made by *Kestner,* or *Simon & Halbig* mold 1080 with the kid bodies, and *Gebrüder Heubach.* Heubach used their square mark and the number 10,633. One of the Dainty Dorothy dolls had marked on its head, "Germany// S H 1080 DEP 7" and on its body, "Dainty Dorothy//Sears Roebuck & Co."

1912: Sears advertised this doll as having a bisque head, mohair wig, sleeping eyes, hair eyelashes, kid body with rivet joints at the elbows, hips and knees, and patented shoulder joints. There were composition forearms and lower legs. Dressed only in footwear. Five hts. 18½, 20½, 23, 25½ and 28 in. (47, 52, 58.5, 63.5, and 71 cm.); price $1.75 to $4.98.

1918: Eaton advertised all-composition Dainty Dorothy fully jointed doll.

1922: Sears' Dainty Dorothy had a bisque head with mohair wig, sleeping eyes, hair eyelashes, rivet jointed kid body with composition lower arms and legs. Hts. were the same as in 1912 without the largest size.

1930: Sears registered Dainty Dorothy Doll in the U.S. as a trademark for dolls. ★

Dainty May. 1923. Name of a doll produced by *Demacol.*

Dainty Miss. 1928. A composition head *Mama* doll distributed by *Butler Bros.* It had a sewed wig, sleeping eyes, hair eyelashes and wore a voile or organdy dress with matching bonnet and a locket and chain. Hts. 20, 24, and 28 in. (51, 61, and 71 cm.); priced $4.00 to $7.25.

Daisey. 1884. Line of wax-head dolls distributed by *Lauer,* came in two versions with flowing hair and with "crimped hair bangs over the forehead." It had earrings, composition arms and legs with painted stockings and boots, and wore an embroidered chemise. The second version had sleeping eyes.

DAISEY DOLLS SIZE–HEIGHT RELATIONSHIP				
Size No.	Height in.	cm.	Price doz. wholesale	
2/0	13½	34	$2.00	
0	15½	39.5	$3.00	Sleeping eyes
1	17½	44.5	$3.00	
2	19½	49.5	$5.00	Sleeping eyes
3	21½	54.5	$4.85	
4	23	58.5	$7.25	Sleeping eyes
5	25½	65	$8.20	

Daisy. 1903–4. Trade name of a doll distributed by *Montgomery Ward*. It was a cloth doll, cotton stuffed with a lithographed face. The clothes were removable. Ht. 13 in. (33 cm.); priced 50¢.

Daisy. 1904 and possibly other years. Trade name of a line of china-head dolls with molded black or blond hair, painted eyes, and molded necklaces having a jewel in them, cloth bodies with china lower arms and lower legs. Four hts. 8¼, 10, 14, and 16 in. (21, 25.5, 35.5 and 40.5 cm.); priced 40¢ to $2.00 doz. wholesale. Retail price of the largest size was 25¢. See also **Jeweled** and **Vanity Fair Dolls.**

Daisy (Bather). 1910–11. Felt character doll with stitched hair, made by *Steiff*, dressed as a girl in a bathing suit. Hts. 28 and 35 cm. (11 and 14 in.); priced $1.57 in 1911 for the larger size.

Daisy. 1911. Name of a bisque head composition-body doll offered as a premium by the LADIES' HOME JOURNAL. The dolly-faced bisque heads were made by either *Kestner* or *Simon & Halbig*. The latter were usually on *Heinrich Handwerck* bodies. Several different mold numbers appear to have been used as a result of the great demand. These included Kestner mold #171, and the Simon & Halbig *Bébé Cosmopolite*. Ht. 18 in. (45.5 cm.).★

Daisy. 1912–13. Cutout cloth doll with its own cutout cloth outfit of clothes, produced by *Selchow & Righter*. Ht. 7½ in. (19 cm.); priced 83¢ doz. wholesale.

Daisy. 1914. Trade name of a cloth doll with lithographed face, produced by *Horsman*. Most of the Horsman cloth dolls were made by *Brückner*. This doll was shown in the 1912 Horsman catalog but without a name; priced 25¢.

Daisy. 1918. Name of a dressed doll with a brimmed hat, made by *Harwin & Co.* Ht. 24 in. (61 cm.).

Daisy. 1927. One of the *Twinjoy* line of *Flower Dolls* created by *Berry Kollin*. These dolls with a face on each of two sides wore petal dresses.

Daisy. 1928. Cloth doll made by *Dean.*

Daisy. 1928. Trade name of a doll produced by *Kindel & Graham.*

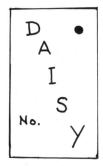

720. Tag mark on a Daisy doll produced by Kindel & Graham.

Daisy. See **Daisy Dolls.**

Daisy Bell. 1906. Advertised by *Hutzler,* had a bisque head, blonde or brunette wig, sleeping eyes, ball-jointed composition body, wore a chemise and footwear. Ht. 23 in. (58.5 cm.); priced $1.00.

Daisy Bell. 1908. Trade name of a bisque head dressed doll with a wig. One of the distributors was the *Boston Store,* where it came dressed in four style nos. Ht. 13 in. (33 cm.); priced 25¢.

Daisy Bella. 1908. Trade name of an imported doll advertised by *Samstag & Hilder.*

Daisy Darling. Early 1900s. Cutout lithographed cloth doll produced by *Horsman*. The little girl doll wore an ankle-length red dress with a bertha-style collar and yellow and white trimming. See Ill. 721.

721. Sheet of a cutout cloth doll representing Daisy Darling which is produced by E. I. Horsman. The doll wears a red dress with blue sash and blue stockings. H. 13 in. (33 cm.). *Courtesy of Margaret Whitton.*

Daisy Dimple. 1911–12. Composition head designed by *Helen Trowbridge* for *Horsman* and copyrighted in 1911. The doll's head had molded bobbed hair and bangs, painted eyes, dimples and smiling open-closed mouth with teeth. The cloth body had composition hands. This doll, No. 137, was one of the American Kids in Toyland,[†] and the same head appears to have been used for *Hans* and *Gretchen, Happy Hiram, Jack Tar, Prince Charlie* and *Robbie Reefer.* The head on this Daisy Dimple differed from the 1914 Horsman Daisy Dimple.

Daisy Dimple. 1912. Trade name of a bisque-head doll distributed by *Sears*. It had a mohair wig, sleeping eyes, hair eyelashes, bisque hands on a kid body with rivet jointed hips and removable footwear. Tilting activated the mama-papa voice. Four hts., 16½, 19¼, 22½, and 25¼ in. (42, 49, 57, and 64 cm.); price 98¢ to $2.65.

Nos. 137 and 138

"DAISY DIMPLE"

Special EXTRA SIZE Unbreakable Doll at same price as dolls of
Standard Size

Heads copyrighted, 1913, by E. I. Horsman Co.)

No. 138. UNDRESSED DOLL—full jointed. This is a particularly desirable unbreakable doll, the largest ever
made at the price here offered. The finely made full
jointed cloth stuffed body is clothed in a tight fitting
union suit of stockinette..............Per Dozen, **$8.50**

No. 137. DRESSED DOLL. This is the same doll as the fore-
going (No. 138) but in a pretty lawn costume, lace
trimmed, and with a ribbon sash; half length socks
and buckled slippers. The dress cut to show the neck
and bare arms......................Per Dozen, **8.50**

No. 138 and No. 137 Extra Size "Daisy Dimple"

722. Daisy Dimple dolls were advertised in the Horsman catalog of ca. 1914 as being "EXTRA SIZE." These dolls have a composition shoulder heads, molded and painted hair, painted eyes, closed mouth, cloth body with composition arms. They came wearing a stockinet union suit or a lawn dress. *Catalog courtesy of Bernard Barenholtz.*

Daisy Dimple. 1914. Composition shoulder head copyrighted by *Horsman* in 1913. The eyes look straight ahead and
there were dimples and teeth. The jointed cloth body had
all-composition arms. The undressed version, No. 137,
wore a jersey union suit and the dressed version, No. 138,
wore a lace trimmed lawn sleeveless dress with a ribbon
sash. Both dressed and undressed dolls cost $8.50 a doz.
wholesale and were advertised as being "Extra Size." The
head on this doll resembled No. 150 School Girl and was
different from the 1911–12 Horsman Daisy Dimple Doll.

Daisy Dolls. 1919. Line of dolls made by *Nottingham* included *Joyce Joslyn, Peter and Pauline.* This line was cheaper than *Helen's Babies.*

Daisy Dolls. 1924–28. Trade name of one of the *Posy* line of
cloth dolls made by *Dean.* The dolls wore a low waisted
dress with flaps around the neckline and around the knee
length skirt. It had a hat with a brim and carried a flower in its
right hand.

Daisy Dolls. 1927–30. Trade name of a *Mama* doll produced by *Borgfeldt.*

Daisy Velvet. 1912–13. Stuffed doll printed in colors on
velvet and advertised by *Selchow & Righter.* Ht. 7½ in. (19
cm.); priced 83¢ doz. wholesale.

Dalaba. See **Das Lachende Baby (The Laughing Baby).**

Dalloz. 1871–85. Paris. Successor of *Blampoix,* made dolls.

1881: Purchased some of his dolls' heads from *François
Gaultier,* according to Mme. Poisson, curator of the Roybet
Fould Museum. ★

Dallwig Manufacturing Co. 1918–22. Chicago, Ill. Their
dolls designed by a noted sculptor had sleeping eyes and
fully jointed composition bodies. Both real hair and mohair
were used for their interchangeable wigs. The dolls had extra
head tops which were adjusted to the face of the doll with a
patented attachment. ★

**Damerval Frères & Laffranchy (Jules and Charles Damer-
val).** 1910 and probably earlier–1916. Montreuil-sous-Bois,
France. This company appears to have made the dolls
marked D. L. found with "Montreuil//s/Bois//France" or
"Montreuil//France" on bisque dolls' heads that generally
represented men. The men sometimes had a molded mustache and occasionally wore period or military costumes. It
has been recorded that a doll representing *M. Coquelin* had
a bisque head made in Montreuil. The Damerval Frères &
Laffranchy dolls had composition bodies and came in hts.
12½ and 13 in. (31.5 and 33 cm.).

A small doll-face doll has been found with the mark
shown in Ill. 726.

1915: They showed an assortment of bisque dolls' heads. ★

Damio Doll. 1800s. Japan. Type of dolls made in Japan.

723. Bisque head doll probably made by Damerval & Laffranchy of Montreuil-sous-Bois. It has a wig, stationary brown glass eyes, closed mouth, and gusseted kid body. Mark: "D L." H. 13 in. (33 cm.). *Courtesy of Sotheby Parke Bernet Inc., N.Y.*

724A & B. Damerval & Laffranchy probably made this bisque head doll. It has an open crown and molded dark gray hair below the hat. The molded mustache and eyebrows are also dark gray. The molded eyes are blue, the mouth is closed, and the composition body is fully jointed. The fat, dimpled hands resemble those of a baby. Original black wool suit and high hat. Mark: "Montreuil //France//D. L." H. 13 in. (33 cm.). *Courtesy of the Margaret Woodbury Strong Museum. Photo by Harry Bickelhaupt.*

Dan. 1924. One of the *Aerolite* velveteen dolls made by *Chad Valley* based on *Mr. Williamson*'s design and given the number 270. It wore a one-piece suit with long trousers and carried a six-sided tag labeled "Chad Valley// HYGIENIC//Fabric Toys." Ht. 11 in. (28 cm.).

Dan. 1929. Doll with composition head and arms on a cotton stuffed cloth body, made by *Averill Manufacturing Co.* It had painted hair and eyes with a two tone whistle. It wore overalls and a hat. Ht. 14 in. (35.5 cm.).

Dancing Doll. 1921. Stockinet dolls made by *Chad Valley*. Style no. 50 was dressed as a girl and No. 51 was in boys' clothing.

Dancing Katharina. 1925. Made by *Schoen & Yondorf*, it had two braids and wore Dutch silhouette long trousers and a tall hat.

Dancing Marionettes. See **Radio Dancing Couple.**

Dan-Dee Strap & Specialty Co. 1930 and later. Manufactured cloth dolls.

Dandy. 1927. Trade name of a felt *Lenci* doll. It had hair of a fine fluffy flax, a monocle, straw hat, button hole bouquet and white spats with shiny shoes.

Dandy Doll Co. 1918–21. New York City and Brooklyn, N.Y. Made dolls.

1924: A company named Dandy Toy and Novelty Co., in Brooklyn, N.Y., made Dandy Dolls.

725A & B. Bisque-head doll probably made by Damerval & Laffranchy. It has painted brown hair, except on top of the head which is partly open, and blue eyes, closed mouth, and a crude five-piece composition body. Original flannel clothes: blue tunic, red hat, and trousers. Mark: "Montreull//s Bois//France//D. L." H. 12½ in. (31.5 cm.). *Courtesy of the Margaret Woodbury Strong Museum. Photo by Harry Bickelhaupt.*

Montreuil
France
D₂L

726. Mark found on a dolly-faced doll probably made by Damerval & Laffranchy.

Danel & Cie. 1889–95. Paris. Factory at Montreuil-sous-Bois. Before 1889, Danel had been director of the *Jumeau* factory. Danel & Cie. was formed in 1889 by Messieurs Danel and *Guépratte.* M. Theimer has records of a doll marked E. 6 D.; on its head the Eiffel Tower *Paris Bébé* mark on its body, and the star Paris Bébé mark on the soles of its shoes. Both of these Paris Bébé marks were registered by Danel & Cie. in 1889. (See also Ill. 733.) This suggests that the E. D. mark may have been used by Danel.

A 24 in. (61 cm.) Paris Bébé has been reported to have had the following marks: on the head "Paris Bébé Tête Dep. 11."; on the jointed composition body was a paper label that read, "Poupées Nues 7 Habilles Gros et Demi-Gros Mme. Vve. Vivet Rue de la Palud 51 Marseille. On se charge des Réparations." (The *Widow Vivet* of Marseille advertised undressed dolls, and her dressed dolls were large or medium size. She also made repairs.)

Later the term Paris Bébé was printed on the sash in a picture of a doll which was advertised by various Paris stores as a *Dru.*

1890–91: Jumeau et Douillet sued Danel & Cie. for copying *Bébés Jumeau.* After Danel and Guépratte left Jumeau they established a factory for making dolls almost opposite the Jumeau factory. Danel's factory produced about 50,000 bébés a year. It was claimed in the lawsuit that Danel had borrowed molds and tools from the Jumeau factory and had enticed Jumeau workers to come and work for him. Furthermore it was claimed that Danel had taken Jumeau heads and bodies which he had copied. It was pointed out that Danel used metallic articulation (probably springs), while Jumeau used rubber (elastic). Danel denied that he had taken dolls and molds from the Jumeau factory but the court ruled in favor of Jumeau. Mme. Anne-Marie Porot and M. François Theimer found this information about the court case. (See POLICHINELLE, No. 7, pp. 4–6 for further details.)★

Daniel Novelty Co. 1927. New York City. Advertised raincoats and hats for dolls, in three sizes. Priced $1.00 to $2.00.

Daniels, Miss E. See **Jungle Toys.**

D'Annunzio. 1917. An Italian poet who was the subject of wooden portrait dolls carved in the wartime trenches by soldiers from the Austrian Tyrol.

Danny Dangle. 1926. Dolls made of enameled wooden beads by *Louis Hoffman.* Price $2.25 a doz. wholesale.

Daphne. 1924. Small art doll of wax or plaster created by *J. S. Sant.*

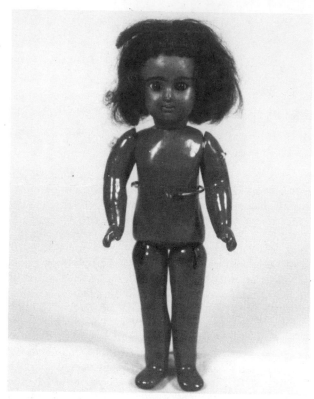

727. Brown bisque-head doll probably made by Danel with a wig, brown glass eyes, open mouth with teeth, and a brown straight limb composition body. Mark: Ill. 730. H. 10 in. (25.5 cm.). *Courtesy of Richard Withington. Photo by Barbara Jendrick.*

729. Bisque head bébé probably made by Danel and/or Jumeau. It has a wig, stationary blue glass eyes, pierced ears, closed mouth, fully jointed composition body. Mark: Ill. 731. H. 20 in. (51 cm.). *Courtesy of Cherry Bou. Photo by Cherry Bou.*

728. Bisque-head bébé marked E 9 D probably made by Danel. It has a wig, stationary blue glass eyes, pierced ears, open mouth with teeth, fully jointed composition and wood body. The footwear is original. H. 21 in. (53.5 cm.). *Courtesy of Sotheby Parke Bernet Inc., N.Y.*

$$E1D$$
730   DEPOSÉ

$$E.8.D$$
731

E 5 D
DEP
732   FRANCE

730–732. E. D. marks on Danel bisque-head dolls.

PARIS, DÉPOSÉ

733. Danel mark found on soles of shoes; registered in 1889 in France.

Dapper Dan. 1930. A segmented doll made of birchwood by *Pickering*. It had a ball shaped head with a derby hat, three balls constituted the arms. Heavily coated colored lacquer represented the clothes which included long bell-bottom trousers. Ht. 7¾ in. (19.5 cm.).

Darbo. Early 19th century. Paris. Toy shop at the sign of the three monkeys on the Rue de Richelieu. Here they made and sold dolls.

Darcy, M. Robert. 1928. Registered a French trademark *Mon Fétiche* (My Fetish) for dolls made of turtle leather.

Darkey Doll. 1893 and later. Cutout cloth doll made by *Cocheco Manufacturing Co.* Ht. 16 in. (40.5 cm.).

Darkie. 1922. Line of dolls made by *Wonderland Toymaking Co.*

Darkie Baby. See **Dickie & Darkie Baby.**

Darling. 1905–15. One of these kid-body bisque-head dolls marked "Darling" on its head and body had a wig, molded eyebrows, sleeping eyes, hair eyelashes, universal joints, bisque lower arms and cloth lower legs.★

735–736. Marks on Darling dolls. No. 735 is on the back of the bisque shoulder plate. No. 736 is a blue sticker on the front of the kid body.

Darling (Darling Toddler). 1926 and probably later. A trademark for dolls registered in the U.S. by *Irwin*. A walking composition-head doll produced by Irwin was named Darling Toddler. It had painted features and a closed mouth and was dressed. Its tag read, "DARLING//TODDLER//PAT. PEND.//WIND ME UP//AND I//WILL WALK//AN IRWIN//PRODUCT." See Ill. 737.

734. Bisque shoulder-head doll named Darling. It has a black wig, sleeping eyes, hair eyelashes, open mouth with upper teeth and a kid body with bisque arms, cloth feet and universal-type joints. Mark on head: Ill. 735. Sticker on body: Ill. 736. H. 24 in. (61 cm.). *Courtesy of Richard Withington. Photo by Barbara Jendrick.*

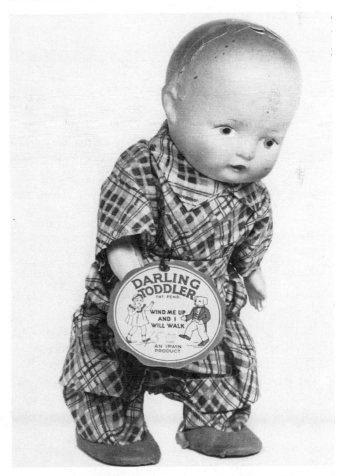

737. Composition head and hands on a walking doll named Darling Toddler. It has painted blond hair and blue eyes, closed mouth and original clothes. The round tag reads: "DARLING//TODDLER//PAT. PEND.//WIND ME UP//AND I//WILL WALK//AN IRWIN//PRODUCT." H. 9 in. (23 cm.). *Courtesy of the Margaret Woodbury Strong Museum. Photo by Harry Bickelhaupt.*

Darling. 1928. Trade name of a doll with a bisque head, wig, sleeping eyes, ball-jointed composition body, fully dressed, sold at *Gamage*.

Darling Baby. 1918. Line of dolls produced by *Bell & Francis*.

Darneval et Lafranchi. See **Damerval Frères & Laffranchy.**

Das De Ha. 1930. Name used by *Dr. Paul Hunaeus* for a standing baby with *Igodi* moving celluloid head.

Das Lachende Baby (The Laughing Baby). Late 1920s–30s. Made by *Schoenau & Hoffmeister*. It had a socket bisque head with a wig and open mouth. Slightly resembles the *Princess Elizabeth* doll. Sometimes the name appeared in the shortened form, Dalaba.

Porzellanfabrik
Burggrub
Das lachende Baby
1930-2
Made in Germany
D.R.G.M.

738. Mark for the German Das Lachende Baby (The Laughing Baby).

Das Lebende Steiner Auge (The Living Steiner Eye). 1927. Trademark registered in Germany in 1927 by *Hermann Steiner*.

Das Wunderkind (The Wonder Child). Multihead doll made by *Kestner*. There were three extra bisque heads to go on the jointed composition body; the doll had jointed wrists. Two heads had blonde wigs and two heads had brunette wigs. The heads had either glass or painted eyes.

Dattelzweig & Meir. 1920–25. Haid, Bohemia. Made dolls.

Daum. 1913. Jointed felt comic doll representing a pigmy and wearing a large hat. Made by *Steiff* and distributed by *Borgfeldt*. Ht. 11 in. (28 cm.); priced $2.10.

Daum, Carl (Karl). 1921–25. Sonneberg, Thür. His dolls were handled by *Salzedo Bros.* in London.

Davey (Dawny), Cecilia E. 1928. Culver City, Calif. Obtained a U.S. design patent for a doll wearing a cloche and a low waisted dress with a tight short skirt. The patent picture suggests a cloth doll.

David Copperfield. Ca. 1916. Produced by *Horsman*, in "Greenaway" style. Later version was *Master Sam*.

Davies, J., & Co. 1919–20. London. Advertised dolls in a British trade journal.

Davis, Geo. M. 1856. Boston, Mass. His catalog at Winterthur advertised painted and unpainted India rubber dolls and dolls' heads including Boy with Bouquet, Flower Girl, *Fireman*, Fille du Régiment (Daughter of the Regiment), Old Woman and Children in a Shoe, Red Riding Hood, Roly Poly, Sailor Boy, *Santa Claus* and Soldier. There were full length baby dolls and black dolls' heads. All of the painted dolls' heads could be obtained in laughing versions by special order. The painted heads cost $1.50 to $9.00 a doz. wholesale, unpainted heads were $1.00 to $4.00 a doz. wholesale. The painted baby dolls cost $1.25 to $21.00 a doz. wholesale.

Davis, M. S., Co. 1902–9. Chicago, Ill. Manufactured all-leather stuffed dolls that lace up the front. The natural leather color was retained except for the features and hair. Ht. 12 in. (30.5 cm.). This appears to be the doll patented by Gussie Decker[+] in 1902–3 and distributed by *Butler Bros.*

1904: Several of the toy catalogs listed an all-leather doll that had been patented the preceding year by Gussie Decker. This doll was described as "impossible for baby to hurt itself. . . . one doll will do for several generations of children. . . . Leather is very fine for a baby to chew on when teething." The dolls were stuffed with cotton and priced $4.00 to $8.50 doz. wholesale.

1907: *Sears* advertised them. Ht. 12½ in. (31.5 cm.); priced 40¢.

1908: Priced 50¢.

1909: The leather doll was advertised by *Siegel Cooper* as being "Baby's First Doll"; priced 50¢. See Ill. 2379, number 45.

Davis Milling Co. 1910–30 and later. St. Joseph, Mo. By 1924 it was called *Aunt Jemima Mills Co.* They made the cutout cloth *Aunt Jemima, Uncle Mose, Wade Davis, Jemima* and *Diana* dolls.

Davis, Rees. 1920–27 and later. Chicago, Ill. She was a retired actress who went into the business of making dolls. Her business at first was named Rees Davis Toy and Novelty Shop, then Rees Davis Toy Co. In 1922 the business was taken over by *Pollyanna Co.* In 1939 Rees Davis Studios made cloth dolls. Miss Rees Davis' dolls were distributed by *Marshall Field.*

1920: Made rubber or cork floating dolls called *Billy Bobs, Betty, Bobby Bobs, Bobs Twins* as well as cloth dolls representing *Mother Goose* characters. These handpainted cloth dolls included, *Little Boy Blue, Little Miss Muffet, Red Riding Hood* and *Tommy Tucker.*

1921: New dolls were called *Baby Bunting, Handsome Hans,* and *Humpty Dumpty,* all advertised as being washable. "Fi-Fi, Milady of Fashion" was a lady doll with a wig. There were other character dolls.

1922: New style nos. were *Pierre, Pierrot,* and *Jasbo* the clown. In the Mother Goose cloth series *Curly Locks, Little Bo-Peep* and *Sally Jane* were added making a total of 35 styles. *Tommy Toodles* and other slumber dolls were made for children to take to sleep with them.

1927: Listed in the Chicago directory. ★

Davis & Voetsch (The Dee Vee Doll Co.). 1917–30 and later. New York City. From 1929 to 1937 Fred Voetsch was the successor. Prior to 1917 Isaac H. Davis and Fred Voetsch

739. All-leather doll made by M. S. Davis Co. and patented by Gussie Decker. It has a seam down the middle of the face to give it shape. The hair and eyes are painted black; closed mouth. The cotton stuffed body laces up the front. H. 12 in. (30.5 cm.). *Courtesy of Margaret Woodbury Strong Museum. Photo by Harry Bickelhaupt.*

had worked together for Joseph Hahnesend & Co.[†] They were manufacturers' agents, jobbers and importers of dolls and used Dee Vee as a trade name.

1919: Represented the *Bester* dolls, which had sleeping eyes and real eyelashes. They also advertised cork-stuffed dolls dressed in American styles.

1924: Advertised 150 style nos. in their *Mama* doll line with composition head, arms, and legs, with or without sleeping eyes, with mohair or real hair wigs, cotton-stuffed cloth body, dressed. Five hts. 16, 18, 20, 22 and 25 in. (40.5,

45.5, 51, 56, and 63.5 cm.). There were eight style nos. of baby dolls with Mama voices.

1927: Exclusive agent for *Woolnough* cloth dolls made of powder-puff plush with long legs. These dolls represented clowns, sunbonnet girls, Ballet Skirt Girls, snow girls, snow boys and French Gamins. One of their pull toys was a black doll that walked like the actor *Bert Williams.*

1928: Advertised a large assortment of Mama dolls and infant dolls.

1929: Factory representative for *Live Long Toys, Twistum* and *Adler.*★

Day Novelty Co. 1923–24. Seymour, Iowa. Made dolls.

Dazzle Dazzle. 1919–20. One of the dolls in the *Classic* line made by *Speight.* It had composition arms and legs and a hair stuffed body. Ht. 16 in. (40.5 cm.).

De Beck, Billy. See **Barney Google.**

De Brzeska, Mlle. Aline. 1924. Fontenay-sous-Bois, Seine Val-de-Marne, France. Registered as a French trademark the name Lutetia[†] with the initials N. B. and a coat-of-arms.

De Carlègle. 1918. France. Created dolls.

De Carlo. 1920. Italy. Designed dolls.

De Felice, Mlle. Marguerite. 1916–18. Paris. Created dolls.

1916: Molded dolls in kid.

1918: Created dolls dressed in historical costumes.

MARGUERITE DE FÉLICE   *Poupée.*

740. This doll was attributed to Marguerite De Felice by Léo Claretie in 1918.

De Fontenay, Mme. Adam. 1878. Awarded an honorable mention for her dolls at the Paris Exposition.

De Fuisseaux (Finsseau). Probably before World War I. Baudour, Belgium. Manufactured bisque shoulder heads and socket heads. These came in several sizes and usually had character faces. They used the initials "D.F.//B." over a letter and a number. The letter probably represented the mold and the number the size. One of the socket heads had a wig, open mouth, sleeping eyes. Ht. 48 cm. (19 in.). See Ills. 741A & B for another socket-head doll.

The shoulder heads extended over the top of the shoulders and the edge ended in the same plane all around. Most of these had bald heads, painted eyes and closed mouths. Some examples were as follows:

Mark on head	Height		Type
	cm.	in.	
F1	52	20½	Doll
F1	15	6	Head only
F2	13	5	Head only
F3	11.5	4½	Head only
B3	6	2½	Head only, man
B4	5	2	Head only, child

Dolls slightly similar in concept to the De Fuisseaux heads were designed in Paris by the Belgian refugee artist *J. Van Rozen* during World War I.

741C. Mark of De Fuisseaux found on the socket head in Ill. 741.

742. Belgian bisque character shoulder head made by De Fuisseaux of Baudour. It has a bald head for a wig, painted blue eyes with orange eye shadowing, closed mouth. H. of shoulder head 6 in. (18 cm.). *Courtesy of Marianne Cieslik.*

De Jaham, G. Ca. 1900–1920. New Orleans, La. Made cloth dolls especially black ones. The dolls' head, hands and feet were oil painted.

De Kasparek, Mme. Jeanne. 1922–30 and later. Paris. Made art dolls.

1925: Awarded Diplome d'Honneur at the Paris Arts Exhibit. ★

De la Boulaye. 1916. France. Sculptor who made models in clay or wax; one of his heads was made for the dolls of *Baroness de Laumont.*

MADE BY

G. DE JAHAM

NEW ORLEANS

743. Mark found on an oilcloth doll made by G. De Jaham.

741A & B. Belgian bisque character socket head doll made by De Fuisseaux of Baudour. It has a wig, painted eyes, and a closed smiling mouth. There is a ruddy color to the bisque head, which is filled with wood shavings. The cloth body has molded composition shoes. Original clothes are those of a flower vendor, with a furled umbrella and a basket of flowers. Mark: Ill. 741C. H. 12 in. (30.5 cm.). *Coleman Collection.*

De la Thuilerie, A. 1873–82. Paris. A label on a fashion-type kid body doll read as follows: "A. DE LA THUILERIE// Grand Magasin de Jouet// Rue St. Honoré, 366//PARIS// ENGLISH SPOKEN." (See also **Thuillier, A.**)★

De Laumont. See **Laumont, Baroness de.**

De Liauty. 1927. Trademark for mascot dolls registered in France by *M. Louis Dedieu.*

De Luxe Babies. 1918. Dolls with composition shoulder heads, sleeping eyes, and cloth bodies made by *Effanbee.* The dolls wore accordion pleated organdy dresses, lace caps and lace trimmed petticoats. Hts. 12 to 30 in. (30.5 to 76 cm.).

De Luxe Manufacturing Co. 1925–29. New York City. Made dolls' shoes.

De Rochefort. 1914–15. France. Created dolls.

De Sannier. 1920–21. Paris. Obtained a German patent (D.R.P.) for a jointed doll.

De Toy (Detoy) Manufacturing Co. 1916. Detroit, Mich. Formerly the Colonial Detroit Garment Co. In 1916 they manufactured exclusively a large line of character cloth dolls. The heads, arms and legs were stuffed with cotton; the bodies were stuffed with excelsior. The hair and features were painted. These dressed dolls comprised Mother, Brother, Sister, Baby, Black Mammy, and Nurse. Brother wears a short jacket and long Dutch-type trousers. Ht. 15 in. (38 cm.). Price 25¢.★

De Veriane, Mlle. Renée. 1907–18. Paris. Created dolls.★

De Villers, Yves, & Co. 1924–26. New York City. Registered in the U.S., "Poupées//Raynal//Modèle Déposé" in an oval within a rectangle as a trademark for dolls.★

De Vovonne. 1927 and later. Trademark registered in France by *Mme. Yvonne Spaggiari* for peasant dolls.

De Zerbi, A. 1929. Paris. Made dolls.

Dean & Sons. 1917. Advertised dressed dolls. The other Dean Co. *(Dean's Rag Book Co.)* made nearly all of the dolls attributed to Dean.

Dean's Rag Book Co. 1903–30 and later. London. *British Novelty Co.* was one of their subsidiaries. They made cloth dolls of various types, including cutout cloth dolls.

1908: The cutout cloth dolls called *Knockabout* had separate clothes provided for them. A large cloth baby doll could wear the cast-off clothes of a real baby. A printed *Pearly* wore clothes covered with pearl buttons.

1910–11: *Aux Trois Quartiers* advertised Dean's cutout cloth dolls named Le Petit *Sambo* and Mademoiselle *Nini.*

1912: Cloth cutout dolls called *Teddie* and *Peggie* resembled the *Drayton* drawings. These dolls were reprinted by Dean in 1980.

1913: *Tru-to-Life* molded-face dolls were patented. Buckram, calico or paper was stiffened and pressed into shape between dies or molds. These dolls came in three sizes.

Betty Blue was 20 in. (51 cm.). Baby doll was over 24 in. (61 cm.). Price 37¢ to 87¢. *Goo Goo Petlings, Pauline Guilbert* dolls and *Puck* dolls were also shown.

1914: Dolls included *Boy Sprout, Carrie Cuddler, Diana, Joyful Joey, Miss Moppietopp, Nautical Nancy, Piccadilly Knut, Pierette, Ragtime Kids, Sarah Starer, Shrieking Susan.* Each was produced in three sizes. Size 1 cost 88¢, size three cost $1.13 and size five cost $1.50.

1915: 30 numbers of Tru-to-Life cloth dolls with removable clothes including babies in long dresses and girls, some with coats and bonnets. Some of these dolls had wigs. Price 62¢ to $6.26.

Dean obtained a U.S. patent for Tru-to-Life dolls. Cloth dolls with long legs based on the designs of *Hilda Cowham* and called *Hilda Cowham Kiddies,* were introduced as well as *Gilbert the Filbert,* a cloth doll with a monocle. The doll could stand on its feet. Price $1.00. Character dolls such as Punch and Judy, soldiers and so forth were produced. One of the two-piece soldier dolls wore a khaki uniform with three chevrons under a crown on its arm, a kepi-type cap, and puttees. It carried a gun and had a knapsack on its back. The white cloth label in the foot seam read "RAG DOLL N°3//SOLDIER PAINTED BY SAMUEL FINBURGH 5 JUNE 1915."

1916: The cloth Knockabout dolls included *Charlie Chaplin.* Various types of dolls seem to have been called "Knockabout." These cloth dolls were advertised as being suitable for export. There were many numbers of Tru-to-Life dolls, both dressed and undressed. Possibly one of these dressed dolls had a molded painted face and long blonde wig. It belonged to Bettyanne Twigg and had footwear stamped in color. There were marks on the sole of each foot. One appeared to be "The Numbered (?)//Certificate// on the heel// Hygienic stuffing registered." The label on the other foot appeared to read "Dean's Rag Knockabout Doll// Registered in all countries//British Manufacture."

1917: Tru-to-Life dolls included baby dolls, Hilda Cowham Rag Dolls, *Airman, Colonial Dolls* and *Dolly Dips.* The last three were also made in a flat face version, as were other dolls. Miniature Hilda Cowham dolls were an innovation. Hilda Cowham designed cutout figures representing boys and girls. *Chloe Preston* designed dolls for Dean during World War I, according to Mary Hillier.

There were five different designs in the *Ta-Ta* series. *Kuddlemee* soft dolls were new, as were the *Tru-Shu* feet. New names that appeared were *Ham* and Charlie, both movie stars; "Charlie" was Charlie Chaplin.

1918: Dolly Dips came with jointed or unjointed legs.

1920: Dean's catalog lists: Hilda Cowham Kiddies, Hilda Cowham Rag Doll, Gilbert the Filbert, Goo Goo series, Knockabout series, *Lucy Locket, Mother Goose* series, and Pauline Guilbert dolls.

After February 2, 1920, all the prices for the dolls were raised 10 percent.

1921: Advertised *Wooly Wally,* a *Golliwogg.*

1922: The inauguaration of the *A 1* dolls and the patented

Evripoze dolls. Tru-to-Life dolls were described as "Doll with the Disc." They were dressed in 13 styles and came in three heights.

A cloth doll with Tru-to-Life face and Tru-Shu feet had on the sole of its right foot the Dean trademark and "HY-GIENICALLY STUFFED//DEAN'S A 1 DOLL//MADE IN ENGLAND." On the sole of the left foot was "DEAN'S A 1 DOLL//MADE IN ENGLAND//TRU-TO-LIFE PATENTED// BRITISH N° 25151, USA APL 13/15// TRU-SHU FEET, PATENTED//USA APL 9/18. DÉPOSÉ, FRANCE." The doll had a pressed face, painted features, open-closed mouth showing four teeth, stump type hands and shaped feet but no toes. Ht. 23½ in. (59.5 cm.).

1923: *Cherub* dolls were made including *Cherub Jenny and Cherub Johnny.* The A 1 series included Sunbonnet Babies dressed in checked rompers and matching bonnets. The down stuffed baby dolls included Betty Blue, *Big Baby Doll,* Curly Locks, and Kuddlemee. Hts. 10½, 13 and 15 in. (26.5, 33 and 38 cm.).

1924: Dean had an agent for dolls in Australia, Belgium, Canada, France, Holland, New Zealand, South Africa, Straits Settlement and East Indies. Their A 1 brand included *Popular Dolls, Dora, Maisie, Wendy* and *Trixie.* Trixie and Wendy were in the Tru-to-Life series. Other dolls included *Baby Peggy* and the *Posy* dolls named *Poppy, Rose, Daisy* and *Marigold.*

1926: The A 1 dolls included *Buster Brown.* Other dolls were Dickie Blob and The Inkwell Fairy, a character on a then current record. *Dinkie Dolls,* which came in four models, ht. 12 in. (30.5 cm.), price 25¢; *Playtime Dolls;* Posy Dolls; *Princess Dolls* dressed in velvet outfits with white fur trim and a muff, eight sizes, priced 95¢ and up; *Cresta* dolls; and *Elegant* dolls. Dinkie Dolls and Elegant dolls, highly fashionable lady dolls, were described as being hygienically stuffed. Floral dolls were also advertised.

1927: New lines include Frilly Dolls & *Smart Set* dolls.

1928: Baby dolls; Daisy Dolls; Erbie Brown; *Grumpy;* Pierrette made of art silk with a flat face; *Luvly* dolls; *Sunshine* dolls; *Thirsty; Travel Tots;* patented *Wabbly Wally, Willow Pattern* dolls, and dolls à coudre (dolls to sew) which were advertised in France.

1929: *Borgfeldt* distributed their dancing dolls for which there was a design patent; nevertheless there were legal battles because of the similarity of these dolls to those made by some other manufacturers. These dolls came in eight styles and three heights.

1930: *Husheen* dolls with mask faces, Princess Dolls, *Modern Dolls,* Sunshine dolls, *Sylvie Dolls* and Ta-Ta dolls.★

Dearest. 1927. Trade name of a baby doll made by *Arranbee.*

Dearie. 1916–18. All-composition, five-piece, straight-leg, steel spring jointed doll made by *Jessie M. Raleigh.*★

Debes, Carl, & Sohn. 1905. Hof, Bavaria. Advertised *Noris Puppen,* a patented jointed doll. (See Ill. 363.)★

744. Dean's cloth doll representing a chimney sweep. It has a plush wig, lithographed features, cloth body, and is jointed only at the neck. Original clothes and accessories including a chimney brush, sack and sticks. It is alleged to have been purchased in 1924. Mark: Ill. 746. H. 15 in. (38 cm.). *Courtesy of Magda Byfield.*

745A & B. Dean's cloth doll representing Charlie Chaplin. The cloth face is impregnated, molded, and lithographed. It has wool yarn hair, blue eyes and a closed mouth. The floppy feet appeared in 1929. Original black felt tail coat, black and white checked trousers and red felt vest. H. 13 in. (33 cm.). *Coleman Collection.*

746. Mark stamped on the center of the back of a cloth doll made by Dean. (See Ill. 744.)

Debutante. 1918. All-composition, five-piece, straight-leg, steel spring jointed doll made by *Jessie M. Raleigh*. It had a wig and wore a lawn dress with a ribbon headband.★

Debutantes. 1914. Trade name of bisque-head dolls distributed by *Butler Bros*. They had a wig, sleeping eyes, and hair eyelashes, on a composition body jointed at the shoulders elbows, hips and knees. The clothing was removable. Ht. 17 in. (43 cm.); price $11.25 doz. wholesale.

Decalco Litho Co. 1925–27. New York City. Made cloth-body dolls.

Decalcomania Decorations. Some of the features on dolls especially the eyebrows were often applied with decals after the first firing of the bisque heads. The majority of these decal transfers were made in Nürnberg.

Decamps. See **Roullet & Decamps.**

Decker, Gussie.† See **Davis, M. S., & Co.**

Deco. 1912 and later. Mark used by *Otto Denivelle* on some of the dolls made by *Effanbee*, among them *Baby Grumpy* and *Betty Bounce* according to Pat Schoonmaker. (See Ill. 762.)

Decoster, J. 1890. Paris. Made *Bébé Parisien*, bébé heads, dressed and undressed bébés, dolls and *Mignonnettes*.

FᵠᵁᵉFʳᵃⁿˢᵍ ᴅᵁBÉBÉ PARISIEN
ARTICULÉ
221 Boulᵈ Voitaire à PARIS
FABRIQUE
de Ietes de Bébés
J. DECOSTER
Bébés Nᵘˢ
et habillés
POUPÉES MIGNONNETTES

747. Mark of J. Decoster who produced many kinds of dolls.

Dedieu, Louis. 1927. Paris. Registered *De Liauty* as a trademark for mascot dolls in France.

Dee Vee. See **Davis & Voetsche.**

Deedle Dum Dolls. 1917. Wooden dolls composed of blocks patented by *Richard Humbert* and distributed by *Baker & Bennett*. These included Addie, Bonnie, Cookie, Daddy, Dewdrop, Dolly, Duncie, Lanky Dink, Ma, Mandy, Middie, Reggie, Squee, and Tumbley.

Deerfield Dolls. See **Hyde, Mrs. Mathilda.**

Deffonds, Mme. 1916. Paris. Created dolls.

Definitions of a Doll. The 1851 edition of WEBSTER'S DICTIONARY gives two definitions of the word Doll. First, it is an "image" or "idol." Second, it is "A puppet or baby for a child; a small image in the human form, for the amusement of little girls." Puppet, from the same derivative as the French word Poupée and the German Puppe is defined as "A Doll." The second definition of Baby is "A small image in the form of an infant, for girls to play with; a doll."

The name "Baby" was still generally used with dolls in 1878 as shown by an excerpt from THE QUEEN, "The baby dolls in this class particularly excel, and they can be had with the hair arranged in a variety of ways, suitable either for dressing as men, women of fashion or children."

1981: Collectors define a doll as a child's plaything in human form. No distinction is made as to the sex of the child playing with the doll, nor to the age represented by the doll. In France, bébé is used for dolls representing babies and small children, while Poupée represents older children and adults, a distinction no longer made in the English language. It is not certain whether the same distinction was made between the German words *Täuflinge* and Puppen. Translations are sometimes difficult because English used only one word where other languages used two different words.

Dehais. 1836–1930. Paris. In 1873 Verger became the successor. 1890–1928, Louis Marie Renou was the successor; he was a member of the *Chambre Syndicale*. They made *poupards* and mechanical dolls.

1865: Known as Dehais & Verger; advertised poupards, dolls with movement, and dresses.

1881: Purchased bisque dolls' heads from *François Gaultier* according to the research of Mme. Poisson, curator of the Roybet-Fould Museum.

1928: Advertised *Polichinelles, Marottes* with music, and mechanical toys with music.★

Dehler, E. 1908–28. Coburg, Thür. and later Bavaria. In 1911, I. Herzog was the successor. Manufactured and exported dolls.

1911: Advertised jointed *Täuflinge* in chemises, character babies and wooden dolls dressed and undressed. It is possible that some of these were *Bébés Tout en Bois*.

1928: Made dressed dolls; listed in a French directory.★

Dehler, Karl. 1931. Waltershausen, Thür. Registered in Germany *Bébé Diamant* as a trademark for dolls and baby dolls.

Dehler, Wilhelm. 1878–92. Neustadt near Coburg, Thür. Produced dolls. The initials W. D. have been found on a bisque head doll with three small holes in the pate. See Ill. 2664 for another bisque head marked W. D. It is a poured head with an open crown.★

Dehmer, A., & Zeicher, H. 1930. Strasbourg, France. Manufactured dolls.

Dehors, A., & Mme. 1860–90. Paris. Made dolls. It has been reported that they used the initials A. D. (See **Delhaye**.)

1865: Mme. Dehors made bébés, dolls, and clothes for dolls.

1878: Received a silver medal at the Paris Exposition.★

Dehut, M. 1929–30 and later. France. Made dolls called *Poupées Georgia.*

d'Eichthal, Mme. 1916. France. She founded *La Francia* and made cloth dolls called *Cita* and *Bébé Yves.*

Dekline, Mr. World War I period. Pompton Lakes, N. J. PLAYTHINGS credited Dekline with being the first manufacturer to produce a wood pulp composition dolls' head by pressing it in hot dies known as the *Hot Press* method.

Dell & Co. 1917–30. London. Produced dolls. Sole agent for *Gustav Förster.*

1926: Advertised New Born baby dolls, walking and talking dolls.

Delacoste, B. See **Derolland, Basile.**

Delarue, Mme. See **Mabire, Mlle.**

Delasson. 1920s. France. Made rubber bébés and belonged to the *Chambre Syndicale.*

Delattre. 1920s. Paris. Made dressed bébés, *mignonnettes* (little dolls), dolls with trousseaux including some with trunks and jewelry sets for dolls. Member of the *Chambre Syndicale.*

Delavan, Sophia E. 1916–21 and possibly other years. Chicago, Ill. Advertised that she made dolls and wigs for dolls. A wig carrying her paper label has been found marked "AMERICAN//[a picture of a young girl with a curly wig]//TRADE MARK//WIG." within a circle, and beneath it "Made in Germany//Size 2," thus indicating that she imported some of her wigs.

1921: Represented the *Alkid Doll Co.*★

748. Mohair wig with a Sophia Delavan paper label in it. The label shows that the wig was made in Germany but was called an "American Wig."

Delbek (Delbeck), Luise. 1907–10. Vienna. Listed under Dolls and Dolls' Heads in an Austrian directory.

Delcourt, H. See **Gesland.**

Delcroix (Delacroix), Henri. 1865–87. Paris and Montreuil-sous-Bois, Seine, France. Made porcelain dolls' heads. The size of the mark varied with the size of the head. See Ill. 751. Grandjean probably used some of these heads which were marked "G.D." Delcroix also made dolls marked "*Pan.*" See Ills. 2047 and 2048.★

749   750   751

749–751. Marks on porcelain heads made by Henri Delcroix.

Delft Girl. 1907–9. Cutout cloth doll made by *Saalfield* as one of their *Tiny Travelers* series. The doll represented a Dutch Girl. Ht. 5 in. (12.5 cm.).

Delhaize Frères et Cie. (Le Lion). 1916 and probably other years. Brussels. Handled dolls and won the grand prize at an Exhibition of dolls for the benefit of the children of Belgian soldiers. M. Jules Delhaize was the Honorary President of the Exhibition.

Delhaye Frères (Bros.). 1900–12. Villemomble, France. Produced dolls and in 1912 used the initials "A. D." for Alexandre Delhaye.

Deller, Alfred. 1907. Vienna. Produced jointed dolls and *Täuflinge,* dressed and undressed as well as dolls' parts. He also repaired dolls.

Delphieu. See **Rabery & Delphieu.**

Delphine, Flosse. 1850–55. Paris. It is reported that she worked for *Jumeau* and was helped by members of her family.

Deluxe Doll & Toy Co. 1918–21. New York City. Made dressed dolls with composition shoulder heads and cork stuffed cloth bodies. Dolls were distributed by the *Bush Terminal.*★

Deluy, Tony. See **Créations de Grand Luxe.**

Dely, Anna. 1921. Hungary. She taught doll-making to classes in the *MOVE.* Among the dolls made by Anna Dely were *Iluska* representing a character in a Hungarian fairy tale and a doll representing the god *Janos.*

Demalcol (Demacol). 1921–24. Catterfeld Thür., Neustadt, Bavaria and London. Originators of *Dainty May, Little Sunshine* and *May Blossom.* The trademark for May Blossom was registered in Germany by Alfred Lange.[†] Demalcol also advertised baby dolls, jointed dolls, dressed dolls and undressed dolls. Demalcol was an acronym for *Dennis Malley & Co.* of London.

752. Demalcol bisque socket head with wig, glass eyes, closed mouth. Mark: See Ill. 753. H. of socket head only, 2½ in. (6.5 cm.). *Coleman Collection.*

753. Demalcol mark on a bisque socket head.

754. Bébé with a bisque head that has a mark believed to be that of Denamur. The socket head has a wig, stationary blue glass eyes, pierced ears, and closed mouth. Mark on head: Ill. 757. H. 21½ in. (54.5 cm.). *Courtesy of Hazel Ulseth.*

Demische, Anneliese. 1930 and later. Hannover, Germany. Made clothes and trousseaux for dolls; also made little dolls.

Denamur, Etienne. 1857–99. Paris. Made porcelain-head dolls with either open or closed mouths. Probably some of the bisque heads marked "E. D." were made by Denamur.

1890: Won a gold medal at the London *Exhibition.*

1893: The dolls described as made by the gold medal winner at London in 1890 and distributed by Tour St. Jacques[†] were possibly E. Denamur dolls. (See **French Dolls, 1893.**)★

Denise. 1923–25. Trade name of a doll that was to be stuffed; it came in a box along with the material and equipment needed for making a wardrobe of clothes for the doll.

Denise. 1925. Cutout printed cloth doll published by *Fernand Nathan.* It was a small version of *Suzy.* Ht. 27 cm. (10½ in.).

Denivelle, Otto Ernst. 1910–30 and later. Mount Vernon and Pleasantville, N.Y. During 1910–12 in Mount Vernon, N.Y., he worked with his brother on perfecting *cold-press* glue-type composition to be used for making dolls' heads. The heads made of this type of composition were produced by using collapsible molds. The Denivelle heads and the similar Can't Break 'Em[†] heads competed with each other for superiority. *Joseph L. Kallus,* then attending school, worked with the Denivelle brothers on week-ends. By 1912 the

755. Bisque head bébé marked "E 8 D" (Ill. 758) probably for Denamur. It has a wig marked 8, stationary glass eyes, pierced ears, closed mouth, fully jointed composition body. The head is pressed and has a cork pate. H. 20 in. (51 cm.). *Courtesy of Richard Withington. Photo by Barbara Jendrick.*

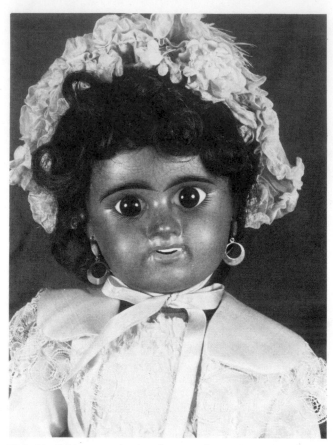

756. Black bisque socket head is on a brown ball jointed composition body. The head is marked (Ill. 759), possibly for Denamur. The wig is black, as are the glass eyes. The mouth is open with four upper teeth. The clothes are replacements. H. 24¾ in. (63 cm.). H. of head only, 5¾ in. (14.5 cm.). *Courtesy of Sara Kocher.*

E. ⚆ D.
DEPOSE

757

E ⚆ D

758

E 10 D.
DEPOSE

759

757–759. Marks on bisque heads of bébés probably made by Denamur. No. 757 is on doll shown in Ill. 754. No. 758 is on doll shown in Ill. 755 and No. 759 is on doll shown in Ill. 756.

problem of the distortion in this glue-type composition when it dried was pretty well overcome and the Denivelles began to sell their dolls' heads and arms to various doll makers who put them on cloth bodies. Unfortunately the brother died young leaving Otto Denivelle in charge of the business. *Amberg* was one of the first companies to buy Denivelle heads and arms. By 1915 Fleischaker & Baum, *Effanbee*, also used Denivelle products. The 1915 Effanbee catalog states: "Ours [dolls] are made under the Denivelle method, which is the most expensive method known on account of the tremendous manufacturing plant required."

Denivelle's mark *DECO* in an ellipse was put on some of the molds of dolls' heads designed by Kallus, according to Mr. Kallus. This mark was found on several of the Effanbee dolls such as *Baby Grumpy* and *Betty Bounce*. It is known that Mr. Kallus worked with both Denivelle and Hugo Baum. As World War I ended, the cold press method for making dolls' heads was superseded by the *hot press* method.

Later Denivelle worked for *Gund* and for *Regal* when it was affiliated with *Horsman*. After that Otto Denivelle worked for *Cameo* in Port Allegany, Pa. under Joseph Kallus.

1915: Denivelle was granted a U.S. patent for sleeping eyes for dolls. The eyeballs were mounted on a pivot rod so they could swing in the socket. The rod was embedded in the walls of the head and passed through the sockets and the eyeballs so that the eyes maintained their proper alignment and position.

1917: TOYS AND NOVELTIES reported that Denivelle joined the Amberg firm as factory superintendent having been President of the Denivelle Co. He was called, "A leader in the American doll industry." He had been supplying Effanbee for sometime. "As a pioneer in the industry, he is a remarkably clever plaster and mould man."

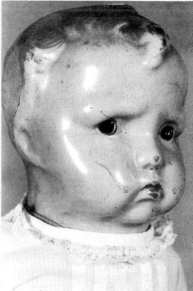

760A & B. Composition head doll marked DECO probably made for Otto Denivelle. It has the cold press type composition head and hands. This doll has molded hair, painted eyes, and a bent-leg cloth body and closely resembles Baby Grumpy. Mark: Ill. 761. H. 14 in. (35.5 cm.). *Coleman Collection.*

DECO

761–762. Embossed marks on the necks of dolls created by Otto Denivelle. (See Ill. 760.)

1918: Denivelle's new baking process for composition dolls was used by Amberg for *Little Fellow* and *Happinus.* This appears to be the introduction of the hot press method.

1926: Denivelle obtained a U.S. design patent for a doll. (See **Manufacture of Dolls, Commercial: Made in the United States.**)★

Denne, Mme. 1817. Paris. Sold dressed dolls with "enamel" (a form of glass) eyes. One price was $5.40 according to Mme. Poisson, Curator of the Roybet-Fould Museum.

Dennis, Malley & Co. 1921–24. London. Specialized in dolls made in Catterfeld, Neustadt, and Waltershausen, Germany. They had a London Warehouse and showrooms in Friedrichroda, Hof and Leipzig, Germany.

The acronym *Demalcol* which was their telegraphic designation was used on some of their bisque heads for dolls made in Germany.

1922: An exhibit of Dennis, Malley & Co. dolls at a British trade fair contained "fully jointed and character dolls dressed in a variety of beautiful dresses and costumes." Among the dolls shown at the Leipzig Fair were *Little Sunshine,* fully jointed dolls, and character dolls. *May Blossom* was also a fully jointed doll.★

Dennis, Thomas R. 1927. Joplin, Mo. Sold and repaired dolls.

Dennison Manufacturing Co. 1896–1927 and later. Framingham, Mass. Manufactured crepe paper and made dolls' clothes.

1896: Dressed small bisque-head or all-bisque dolls in crepe paper. The dolls represented Little Lord Fauntleroy, a Princess, Brides, Widows and so forth. Hts. 4 to 6½ in. (10 to 16.5 cm.).

1911: Used crepe paper to make dolls' dresses.

1927: Registered *Nancy* as a trademark in the U.S. for crepe paper dolls' outfits.

Denny Doll. 1928. Trade name of a doll representing a child with arms bent; made by *Jeanette Doll Co.* The head of the doll was designed to resemble the child's head in a painting by the artist *Hardy Brown.* Various hts. 11 to 27 in. (28 to 68.5 cm.); price $1.00 and up.

Dent & Co. 1897. Windsor, England. Name of a company on a box containing a doll with a bisque head, sleeping eyes, and jointed composition body. The head is marked "261 Dep Germany." Allegedly this 8 in. (20.5 cm.) doll was a present from Queen Victoria to a God-daughter.

Dep. These letters are frequently found incised on bisque dolls' heads. They stand for either the French "Déposé" or the German "Deponirt" (Deponiert). Both indicate a registration claim. The German DEP. signifies a design registered in a German City Court. It is generally impossible to identify a doll if it has no other identification. Many German manufacturers marked their doll "DEP." plus identifying names or initials. *Simon & Halbig* often placed their DEP. under the name or initials so that it is often seen below the wig while the Simon & Halbig or S & H remains hidden by the wig. Similarity of some dolls marked DEP. to *Bébés Jumeau* have been noted by collectors but a study of the size-height relationship of the two types reveals a noticeable difference. The DEP. dolls are usually larger in size than the Bébés Jumeau for corresponding size numbers.

Department. 1884. Name of a line of wax-head dolls distributed by *Lauer;* they had "hair head-dresses," glass eyes, composition legs with painted shoes. Hts. 7, 8¼, and 11 in. (18, 21, and 28 cm.); priced 5¢ to 10¢.

763. Bisque head doll with wig, sleeping blue glass eyes, pierced ears, open mouth with teeth, and a ball-jointed composition body. Mark on head: 275 DEP. Mark stamped on body: JUMEAU MEDAILLE D'OR. H. 19 in. (48 cm.). *Courtesy of Richard Withington. Photo by Barbara Jendrick.*

764. Bisque head marked DEP 306 has a wig, sleeping brown glass eyes, pierced ears, open mouth, and a ball-jointed composition body. H. 19½ in. (49.5 cm.). *Courtesy of Sotheby Parke Bernet Inc., N.Y.*

765. Bisque head marked DEP has a blond wig, stationary brown glass eyes, pierced ears, closed mouth, and a fully jointed composition body. Original clothes. H. 15½ in. (39.5 cm.). *Courtesy of Sotheby Parke Bernet Inc., N.Y.*

Deptford Toy-Making Industry (Deptford Fund Toy-Making Industry). 1917–19. London. Made dolls of various materials.

1917: Baby doll and cloth character dolls representing Cinderella, Jester, *Pierrot, Red Riding Hood* and others.

1918: Made dressed dolls of plush and felt, baby dolls, and wood Punch and Judy dolls.

1919: Made *Birthday Dolls,* Flower dolls, jointed dolls representing *Eskimos,* Jesters, Pierrot, and Red Riding Hood.

Der neue Mensch (The New Man). 1926. Trademark registered in Germany by *Mittelland Gummiwerke* for dolls.

Der Unart.[+] See **Naughty.**

Derdzakian, Eugenie. Ca. 1908. Made the body and dress of a doll representing a Munich Street-car Girl. The head was created by *Marie Marc-Schnür.* The doll wore an apron and a brimmed low-crown hat with a big bow under the chin.

Derolland, Basile. 1860–1928 and later. Paris. Factory at Asnières-sur-Oise; successors by 1914 were B. Derolland & B. Delacoste; successor by 1921 was B. Delacoste. Made rubber bébés.

1910: Won a grand prize at the Brussels Exposition, where they showed rubber dolls undressed and dressed with molded clothes or with knit or crocheted outfits.

1927: Company had a million dollars capital, and was a member of the *Chambre Syndicale.*★

Derombies, A. 1925–28. Paris. Advertised porcelain doll busts for candy boxes, tea cosies, pincushions and so forth. He was the agent for Dressel, Kister & Co.[+]

D'Erophine, Alexandrine. 1886. Paris. Distributed dolls. Registered in France the initials A d' E in her trademark.

Des Loges, M. Hubert. 1916. Paris. Registered as a French trademark for dolls the initials H. C. L. in the outer part of two concentric circles. A baby was shown in the inner circle.

Desaubliaux, Mlle. 1915–18. Boulogne-sur-Seine. Made "French type" cloth dolls and supervised the making of dolls in the homes. The group was named "L'Assistance par le Travail." The project was called "Oeuvre du Travail à domicile." Some if not all of these dolls were dressed as children.★

Desfosses. 1824. France. Made molds for dolls according to Mme. Poisson, Curator of the Roybet-Fould Museum.

Designers. The designers of dolls were probably the most important persons in the creation of dolls. Their talent or lack of it often determined the success or failure of a doll. There were specially trained artists who made a business of designing dolls. These people were hired by the *Verlegers* and producers of dolls but only a few of their names are now known. They often based their designs on some fine art portraits. Sometimes important artists such as *Albert Marque; Carrier-Belleuse,* the chief designer of Sèvres; and *Joseph Wackerle,* the Nymphenburg designer, turned their talents toward the designing of a doll or two. Probably the greatest source of designing skills used for dolls were popular illustrators. The design for a doll usually began as a two dimensional illustration from which the three dimensional model was made, frequently by an art student. Often the illustrator had a hand in the creation of the doll, or at least it had to meet his (or her) approval. Finally there were the artists who designed a doll or two from an illustration, a portrait or an actual person and created dolls based on these designs; some of these designers protected their work with U.S. design patents or copyrights of the design.

The following people were among those known to have designed dolls or whose designs were used for making dolls: Estelle Allison (Alison Novelty Co.), *Mabel Lucie Attwell, Florence Attwood* (Merry thought), *George Barbier, Frank Baum,* Hugo Baum, *Benoliel, Walter Berndt, Botta, Martin Branner, Frances Brundage,* Bucherer, *Rene Bull,* Wilhelm Busch, Carrier-Belleuse, Ad Carter, *Bill Conselman, Grace Corry, Hilda Cowham,* Palmer Cox,[+] *Percy Crosby, De la Boulaye, Rudolph Dirks, Katherine Dodge, William Donahey, Grace Drayton,* **Hazel Drukker,**[+] *Dudovich, Mr.*

Eckardt, Carl Ed, *Margaret Evans, Maude Tousey Fangel, Samuel Finburgh,* Helen *Rock Fraser,* Fernel French, *Gardet, Harold Gray,* Adolph Graziana, *J. Green,* Milt Gross, *Pauline Guilbert, Gumery, Hansi, Dorothy Harwin,* John Hassall, *Dorothy Heizer, André Hellé,* Elizabeth Houghton, *Kate Jordan, Jeanne Jozon, Jeno Juszko, Joseph L. Kallus,* Ernst Kämmer (Kämmer & Reinhardt), Brin Kerhof, *Frank King, Käthe Kruse,* Louis-Aimé Lejeune, Mr. Leslie, *Bernard Lipfert, Beatrice Mallet, Julius Mangiapani, Mme. Manson,* Albert Marque, *Mary McAboy, Winsor McCay, Valerie McMahan, George McManus, Antonin Mercié,* Berthe Noufflard, Gottlieb Nussle, Richard Oberender, *Rose O'Neill,* F. Opper, *Jeanne Orsini,* Richard Outcault, *Mary L. Parker, Ernesto Peruggi,* Mary Waterman Phillips,[+] *Erna Pinner,* Poulbot, *Chloe Preston, Florence Pretz,* Probik, *Grace Storey Putnam, Jessie M. Raleigh, Jean Ray, Franz Reismann,* Mr. Richlin, *Heath Robinson,* Karl Krausser *Rohlinge, Penny Ross, Elena Scavini, Albert Schlopsnies, Caesar Schneider,* Harry *Schoenhut, Sidney Smith, Hugo Spieler, Karl Stadinger, Marga Szerelemhcgyi, Sophie Taeuber,* Helen *Trowbridge, Sandro Vacchetti, Paul Vogelsanger,* Prof. *Vogt, Joseph Wackerle, Emil Wagner, Frank Willard, Adolphe Willette,* Mr. *Williamson, Mary Frances Woods,* Richard Zetzsche *(Wagner & Zetzsche)* and *Mlle. Zitzmann.* (See also **Advertising Dolls; German Dolls, 1920; Manufacture of Dolls.**)

Designs for Dolls. Probably one of the most important parts in the creation of a doll is designing it. Usually the designing begins with a drawing; this could be an original sketch, or a copy of the work of an illustrator, a cartoon artist or a painter. Even when a sculptor makes a model, a sketch would usually be drawn first so the producers of the doll could approve or disapprove. The next step would be the making of the model. This was usually in clay or wax and was often done by a student in art school under the supervision of the originator of the design. This was the known procedure in creating *Rose O'Neill's Kewpies* and *Jessie M. Raleigh's* dolls. From the model the molds or dies were made and the doll itself was made from these molds or dies if it had a three dimensional face, which is usual for almost all materials.

A prototype of the new doll was generally shown at an exhibit or Toy Fair and its design value tested. If it did not receive approval, it was scrapped and the artist returned to the drawing board. If it did receive approval often others tried to copy its design.

In 1884 HARPER'S BAZAR described the work of the modellers of dolls as follows: "The most surprising fact about dolls is that their facial features are made to vary equally with those of the human. . . . the modellers have faithfully reproduced in clay the features of the successive generations of children. If there were in existence a museum containing one of each type of feature manufactured every year, it would comprise a faithful panorama of humanity as it appeared in infancy year after year. It is the duty of the modeller of dolls to examine consecutive generations of the human family in different countries in order that the styles in faces may keep pace with the changes of countenances of children."

In 1914 according to TOYS AND NOVELTIES, *Henry Fabricius,* one of the large importers of dolls in St. Louis,

stated, "The German factories, like American factories, come so nearly to duplicating each other's products of dolls that often it is difficult to tell which line of dolls belongs without looking at the tag."

PLAYTHINGS in 1928 explained the process: "A doll manufacturer produces a rough model which is sent to a company that makes molds. There an experienced sculptor improves and finishes the rough model and from the work of the sculptor a mold is made."

TOYS AND NOVELTIES in 1927 commented on designing dolls: "Detail is much harder to produce in sculpture than in painting. Dolls are a form of sculpture. . . . Most of the dolls which prove to be big sellers are designed by expert women designers who have spent years in the study of children and their toy habits. . . . Shape of mouth, curve of lip, slant of eyebrow are all studied."

Further comments in 1926 were: "High prices are paid to women artists and sculptors to design new faces that combine the baby appearance with the toy spirit. As much as $25,000 a year has been made by some women doll designers. A new doll design is hazardous. After spending thousands for moulds and machinery the public may turn 'thumbs down' on the new doll."★

Désirat. See **Lafitte & Désirat, Mmes.**

Desrues. 1920s. France. Made clothes for dolls and was a member of the *Chambre Syndicale.*

Dessain. 1867. Exhibited dolls at the Paris Exposition.

Dessin. 1930. Paris. Made and/or distributed dolls.

Detourbet, Mme. Claude (née Eulalie Fabre). 1817–44. Paris. Sold dolls. In the 1820s her shop was called Au Polichinelle Vampire.

Detoy. See **De Toy Manufacturing Co.**

Deubener Shopping Bag. 1925–26. St. Paul, Minn. Made outfits for dolls.

Dew Drop. See **English Rag Dolls.**

Dewey Doll Co. 1930 and later. Summit, N.J. Manufactured dolls.

Dhomont, Mme. 1916. France. Made artistic cloth clown dolls.

Di (Dienstmann Porter). Before 1911–16. Felt doll with long feet, made by *Steiff.* It wore a porter's uniform with a kepi. Ht. 35 cm. (14 in.); priced 83¢.

Diamant, L. 1924. Listed under Dolls in a British trade journal.

Diamond Hat Frame Co. 1927–28. New York City. Exhibited dolls' faces at the Toy Fair.

Diana. 1902–8. Metal dolls' heads made by *Alfred Heller;* distributed in the U.S. by *Strobel & Wilken* and others. The shoulder heads came in nine sizes with molded hair and seven sizes with wigs.

1904: *Western News Co.* advertised Diana metal heads with painted hair and glass eyes. There were five hts. ranging from 3¼ to 6½ in. (8.5 to 16.5 cm.). Priced $6.00 to $12.00 doz. wholesale.

DRGM 160638

766. Mark on Diana metal dolls' heads.

1908: *R. H. Macy* advertised Diana shoulder heads with wig and glass eyes. Size numbers 1, 2, 3, 4, 5, 6, and 7. Measurement around the shoulders 7 to 13 in. (18 to 33 cm.); priced 44¢ to $1.14.★

Diana. 1914. Cloth doll made by *Dean*.

Diana Jemima. 1908–30 and later. A printed cloth doll used as a premium by the *Davis Milling Co.* and their successors, the Aunt Jemima Mills Co. This black doll varied in form through the years.

1910: Diana Jemima was shown holding a small black doll. Ht. 11½ in. (29 cm.).

1924: Diana Jemima was shown holding a kitten. The name was registered as a U.S. trademark for dolls by the Aunt Jemima Mills Co.

Diane. 1928. *Boudoir* doll distributed by *Eisen*. It was dressed as a sportswoman.

Dick (British Soldier). 1911 and before. Felt doll with long feet, made by *Steiff* and dressed as a British soldier with kepi and rifle. Ht. 35 cm. (14 in.).

Dickie. 1921. Stockinet doll made by *Chad Valley*. This style no. 37 did not have a hand-woven wig. Ht. 11½ in. (29 cm.).

Dickie & Darkie Baby. 1928. Names of dolls manufactured by *Cuno & Otto Dressel*.

Diddums. 1920. All-ceramic doll with molded hair, jointed shoulders, feet apart. The thumb on the right hand was in a sucking position, the left hand fingers were wide apart. It was a mascot doll and appeared to be made in Britain of *British Ceramic*. Price 56¢.

1921: *Hamley* advertised four versions of Diddums, namely: Bath Boy with soap, towel, and sponge; Miss Dainty dressed in silk; Little Adam dressed in ivy leaves and a silk ribbon; Pierrot dressed in silk.★

Diddums. 1920s–30s. Trade name of a series of character dolls made of velvet and felt by *Chad Valley* and based on the drawings of this name by *Mabel Lucie Attwell*. The doll wore rompers. Similar dolls were also later produced, both in rubber and in celluloid by the *Cascelloid Co.,* according to Mary Hillier.

Didi. 1920. All-bisque doll designed by *Jeanne I. Orsini*.★

Dienstmann. See **Di**.

Dies for Manufacturing Dolls. See **Molds for Dolls.**

767. Mark on an all-bisque doll named Didi.

Dietrich, Johannes Gotthilf. 1915–30. Berlin. Obtained many patents for dolls in Germany, the U.S., Britain, and France throughout this period. Used the acronym Igodi for his dolls (I and J are interchangeable in German.). Used porcelain heads made by *Ernst Heubach*. Some of the *Amberg* bisque-head dolls including *Baby Nod* bore the Igodi mark.

1926: Obtained Kowenko celluloid heads from *Kohl & Wengenroth*.

1930: *Dr. Paul Hunaeus* stated that he used Igodi heads on some of his baby dolls.★

768

8192

Igodi
·9·

769

Heubach-Köppelsdorf
Igodi
Revalo - 22-7
Germany

770

768–770. Marks on dolls made by Johannes Gotthilf Dietrich who used the acronym Igodi. Various companies made the bisque heads for these dolls.

Diétrich. 1929–30 and later. Paris. Made dolls.

Diez (Dietz). 1874–1927. Sonneberg, Thür. Exported dolls.★

Diffloth, Albert (Diffloth & Fils.). 1870–81. Charenton, France. One of several people involved with porcelain products who were selected in 1881 to evaluate the inventory of

François Gaultier, according to Danckert and Mme. Poisson, Curator of the Roybet-Fould Museum.

Dilly Dick. 1917. Cloth character doll made by *Tah Toys.*

Dimmie. 1929–30. All-composition doll with a Hendrenite-finish head made by *Averill Manufacturing Co.* This doll, representing a girl, mate to *Jimmie,* had molded hair, eyes glancing to the side, a tiny pursed mouth, and joints at the neck, shoulders, and hips. One arm was bent. It was advertised as being "pleasingly plump" and "able to stand and pose a thousand ways." Clothes included a short dress with short sleeves, no waistline, and a bonnet. It had a rectangular tag with "Dimmie" on it. This doll was one of the competitors of *Patsy.*

1930: Dimmie was also dressed in regional costumes.

Dimple Dolls. 1929. Distributed by *Hale Bros.*

Dimpled Baby. 1928. Trade name of a doll with composition head, arms and legs, sleeping eyes, dimples, a voice, and an above the knees dress. It was advertised as being able to stand alone and to sit. Ht. 15 in. (38 cm.); price $2.69.

Dimples. 1927–29. All-composition doll representing a baby of the age that would be learning to walk, made by *Horsman.* It had creases around its moving eyes to give the impression of laughter. There were dimples in each cheek. The body was jointed at the neck, shoulders and hips and contained a mama voice. It wore white, pink or blue and sometimes had a silk coat and cap. The clothes were made by *M. L. Kahn.*

1928: Price $4.00 to $12.50. (See also **Baby Dimples.**)

Dimples. 1930. Line of dolls made by *Karl Kalbitz* and distributed in London by *Turner.*

Dina. 1927–28. Felt doll representing a school-age girl. It wore a dress with a high waistline and a full skirt that covered the knees. This was *Lenci* doll no. 700/4. Ht. 37½ in. (95 cm.).

Dinah. 1914. Trade name of one of the cloth dolls made by *Dean.*

Dinah. See **Aunt Dinah.**

Dinah. See **Babyland Dolls.**

Dinkie Dolls. 1920. Dolls made by *Speights* with *British Ceramic* heads, composition arms and legs, removable garments that fastened with hooks and eyes, hat and footwear; five sizes.

Dinkie Dolls. 1926. Cloth dolls made by *Dean* in four style nos. Ht. 12 in. (30.5 cm.).

Dirks, Rudolph. 1904 and later. He designed the Katzenjammer family which included Fritz, one of the Katzenjammer Kids that was made into a cloth cutout doll by *Saalfield.*

Steiff made felt dolls representing the various members of the Katzenjammer family.

Distribution of Dolls. Prior to about 1800 most dolls were sold in stalls at fairs, or by pedlars. Then Toy and Fancy Shops began to appear. The Manufacturers displayed their dolls at the great toy fairs such as the annual Leipzig Fair in Germany. Wholesalers and jobbers purchased the dolls from the manufacturers then sold the dolls to the retail toy stores.

Often distributors were unable to travel the long distances to toy fairs and factory agents went around the world showing samples of their dolls. Since carrying a large number of dolls long distances was impractical around the beginning of the 1800s hand colored catalogs appeared. Some of these catalogs were named for the town from whence they came, such as the Nürnberg or Biberach catalogs; and some were named for producers, such as the Bestelmeier[†] or *Lindner* catalogs. Catalogs grew in importance and eventually were used by retail distributors as well as producers and wholesalers.

In the 1870s–80s there were several innovations in distribution; there was the rise of the mail-order businesses such as *Ehrich Bros.* and *Montgomery Ward,* who sold dolls directly to the consumer by means of catalogs. Magazines offered premiums to those who sold subscriptions. For example, YOUTH'S COMPANION published long premium lists which included dolls. In 1881 *Borgfeldt,* who was a producer *(Verleger)* rather than a manufacturer, opened a large display area from which retailers could choose the dolls they wanted. Borgfeldt hired designers of dolls; contracted the production of dolls with various factories; owned at least one subsidiary, namely *K & K,* where dolls' bodies were made. Borgfeldt had exclusive distribution rights for several makers of dolls such as *Steiff.* In other words "Big Business" began to operate in the doll trade.

During the last quarter of the 1800s the department stores and chain stores began to sell dolls especially prior to Christmas. But chain stores did not become important until the 1900s. In order to compete with them mail order houses in the 1920s began to establish retail branches. Meanwhile the individual small toy store was being forced to join with others in order to buy competitively. For the consumer and for the collector there were certain advantages in these trends. Competition held prices down and yet Dr. Paul Nystrom, Professor of Marketing at Columbia University, in 1926 stated that the "Rate of growth of the United States toy industry since 1914 was one of the greatest of all industries in America." For the collector the records of dolls in the mail order catalogs and in the large department store catalogs are of tremendous importance.

1927: PLAYTHINGS described the process of distribution as follows: Factory Representatives or Factory Agents were firms handling the sales of a given manufacturer. They or the manufacturer himself sold to the Jobber, Wholesaler, Chain Store or Buying Syndicate. Many manufacturers did not like to carry a large stock. The Jobber bought a quantity of dolls from the manufacturer and kept them in a warehouse from which he could supply the needs of other distributors. The wholesaler was the oldest type in the chain of distribution to the retailer. Chain stores sold to retailers or consumers. Syndicate buying occurred when a group of stores, large or small, combined so that their orders were of a sufficient size to enable them as a group to eliminate the wholesaler and thus reduce costs. ★

Dittrich & Schön. 1886–90. Reichenbach, Silesia. Joseph Schön obtained a German patent (D.R.P.) for a metal doll's head which he produced. In 1887 Max Dittrich joined Schön and they formed a firm which was taken over in 1890 by *Buschow & Beck*. This information was researched by the Ciesliks.

Dixie Doll. 1921. Name registered as a U.S. trademark for dolls by the *United Hosiery Mills Corp.* The doll was made by taking a long sock, stuffing it with knitted ravelings and tying the sock in a knot at the top of the head which was covered with a tight-fitting cap. The faces including the cheeks and the edge of the hair were painted. The dolls were dressed in colorful clothes.

Dixon, T. A. 1918–20. Worcester, England. Made "unbreakable" (Noxid composition) dolls with glass eyes at the Butts Works.

Djénane Co. 1929. Paris. Registered its name as a trademark in France for dolls.

Djibre, H. See **Israël & Prieur.**

Dlouhy & Seidl. See **Hertzog, G. F., & Co.**

Do (Baby). Before 1911–13. Name of a felt, jointed character doll made by *Steiff* and distributed by *Borgfeldt* in the U.S. "Do" had a mama voice and wore a red and white felt costume with the word "Baby" or a baby's name on the chest. Ht. 30 cm. (12 in.); priced 90¢ in Germany in 1911 and $1.40 in New York in 1913.

Doane, Foster P. 1927. Boston, Mass. Factory agent for manufacturers of dolls.

Dockstader. 1902. Black cloth doll with woolly hair and bead eyes; represented a male minstrel; distributed by *Butler Bros.* Priced $2.15 doz. wholesale.

Dodd, Thomas. See **Roxy Factory.**

Dodge, Katherine. 1918. U.S.A. Illustrator whose drawings were used to design a doll named *Peeps* which was made by *Jessie M. Raleigh.*

Dodo. 1927. Trade name of a doll representing a child. It wore a frilly dress and a broad brimmed hat.

Doebrich, George. 1893–1915. Sonneberg, Thür., and Philadelphia, Pa. In 1896 he applied for a German patent (D.R.G.M.) for a hinged joint on a leather or cloth body of a doll.★

Doebrich, Julius. 1897. Sonneberg, Thür. Applied for a German patent (D.R.G.M.) for the moving joints on a stuffed doll.

Doebrich, N. B. 1899. Sonneberg, Thür. Applied for a German patent (D.R.G.M.) for a washable coating on poured wax and cast wax dolls' heads. This patented procedure was used by *Cuno & Otto Dressel* in 1899.

Doléac, L., & Cie. 1881–1908. Paris. In 1881 purchased bisque dolls' heads from *François Gaultier* for the dolls they made, according to an inventory found by Mme. Poisson curator of the Roybet—Fould Museum.★

Doll.† See **Definitions of a Doll.**

Doll, George. 1831–85. Baltimore, Md. Until 1837 when he went to Philadelphia. He joined his brother, *John Doll, Sr.,* in business in Philadelphia. They imported dolls, made dolls, and were doll jobbers. Their place of business was called "Temple of Fancy."

Doll, John, Sr. 1837–79. John Doll, Jr., 1879–1915. Philadelphia, Pa. They were doll jobbers and John Doll, Sr., was in business with his brother *George Doll*. John Doll, Jr., took over the business from his father in 1879.

1862–63: Imported dolls including "plain babies" and "dressed babies." He sold the former for 75¢ to 95¢ doz. wholesale, and the latter for $1.00 to $1.50 doz. wholesale.

771. Bisque head doll possibly produced by L. Doléac. It has a wig, stationary blue glass eyes, pierced ears, open mouth with six upper teeth, and a ball jointed composition body. Mark: Ill. 772. H. 22 in. (56 cm.). *Courtesy of Paige Thornton.*

LD.
DEP.
9

772. Mark on bisque-head dolls possibly made by L. Doléac.

1866: John Doll, Sr., arranged for 17 year old Albert Schoenhut to come to America. Both of these men were natives of Germany.

1880: John Doll, Jr., started *Wanamaker*'s Toy Department.

1915: John Doll, Jr., was on the LUSITANIA, a British ship sunk by the Germans.

Doll Accessory Co. 1921. Longton, Staffs. Advertised Flesho dolls.

Doll & Stuffed Toy Manufacturers' Assoc. 1920. An association of over 50 leading doll makers under the leadership of J. L. *Amberg*. The companies organized to further the advancement of the industry and for protection in case of a strike. (See **Chronology, 1920.**)

Doll Corporation of America. 1928–30. New York City. Had a doll factory at Lancaster, Pa. This Corporation was formed by the merging of *Century* and *Domec*.

One of their trademarks was a girl holding a globe across which was written "Doll Corporation// of America// makers of // Century & Domec// Dolls." The other trademark showed a girl holding streamers in front of a globe with "Doll Corporation of America// Century Dolls, Domec Dolls" on the streamers. The Century dolls were high quality while the Domec dolls were popularly priced.

1929: 150 numbers included *Chuckles* a baby of the Century line, *Moody* a two-faced baby, and *Giggles* in the Domec line. New glass eyes were used and snap fasteners replaced pins.

Doll Debs. 1923. Trade name of dolls made by *George H. Buck*.

Doll Dorothy. 1913. Trade name of a doll with a bisque head, wig, jointed composition body and a wardrobe of clothes.

Doll Exerciser. 1917. Designed by *Eugene Sandow* and made by the *All-British Doll Manufacturing Co.* These dolls, distributed by the *National Doll League,* had stretchable arms and were dressed as Boy Scouts, *Dolly Dimple* and Red Cross nurses. Exercise charts came with the dolls, which had a composition head, real hair wig, with shoulder-length curls, a jointed body, and removable clothes.

"Doll" Manufacturers. 1917–20. Tunbridge Wells, England. Made dolls with *British Ceramic* head and limbs on cloth bodies. Also made dolls with mask faces. They specialized in black and *Hindu* dolls.

Doll of Character. 1925–28. Trade name used for dolls by *Domec*.

Doll of the Future. See **Bébé l'Avenir.**

Doll Parts Co. 1926. New York City. Arms, forearms and hands for dolls made of wood composition.

Doll Parts Manufacturing Assoc. 1929. U.S.A. An association to help manufacturers of parts with their problems and to bring about a better understanding between the doll manufacturer and the parts manufacturers. Membership was open to companies making composition heads, hands,

arms, and kindred products. The members included *Eagle Doll & Toy Co., Fiberoid Doll Products, Co., Frisch Doll Supply Co., Metropolitan Doll Co., Nibur Novelty Co., Novelty Doll Manufacturing Co., P. & M. Doll Co., Roma Doll Co., Roxy Doll & Toy Co., Saxon Novelty Co.* and the *Toy Products Manufacturing Co.* Associate membership was available for manufacturers of voices, wigs, shoes, and other doll accessories. The associate members included *Art Metal Works* and *Markon Manufacturing Co.*

Doll Pottery Co. 1916–22. Fenton, Staffs. Made and distributed dolls through their London showroom using *British Ceramic* heads and parts manufactured by the *Crown Staffordshire Porcelain Co.* In 1916 the Doll Pottery Co. registered that they had a capital of $10,000, "to carry on the business of manufacturer of dolls' heads in parian and other pottery ware, manufacturer and dealers in dolls' heads, bodies and clothing." They claimed they were one of the first in this field when war broke out. Often they used molds taken from German dolls' heads. They made a wide variety of styles: shoulder heads and socket heads; molded hair and wigged heads; glass eyes, intaglio eyes, and plain painted eyes; dolls representing boys and girls; white dolls and black dolls; multi-head dolls with three heads, one of them black. The black color was applied to the outside of the white ceramic. There were also Pierrots, clowns and many other types in varying degrees of quality. The words "English Make" are often, but not always, found with the D. P. Co. mark.

Various numbers have been reported with the D.P. Co. mark. One number 654,305 is a 1916 design registry number. The dolls reported have all been between 11 and 15 in. (28 and 38 cm.). A 14 in. (35.5 cm.) doll came with three heads and two sets of limbs. Part of the above information was supplied by Caroline Goodfellow, Curator at the Bethnal Green Museum. A sunburn-colored shoulder head representing a young woman was pointed at the bottom of the front, had painted hair with a lock extending down on the shoulders and a hole in back for a ribbon bow. The open-closed mouth had teeth and the painted eyes were intaglio. Ht. of head from point to top of head was 5¼ in. (13.5 cm.).

The mark on the pointed part of this doll was "ENGLISH//D.P.//C°. //MAKE." The first and last words were vertical and the rest horizontal.

1917: Advertised 120 different models. Their expensive dolls had splayed fingers.

1918: Advertised all-"porcelain" bent-limb baby dolls, hts. 11 and 13½ in. (28 and 34 cm.); shoulder heads with molded hair in four models that come in four to six sizes each; shoulder heads with wigs and either painted or glass eyes, in 10 sizes. All of these heads appeared to have had teeth. Heads could also have been obtained with the eye sockets cut out but without the glass eyes inserted.

Doll Shoppe, The. 1930. Hollywood, Calif. Doll dresses were made to order by *Mrs. Sarah M. Barrett* and her staff.

Dollar Leader. 1898–99. Line of dolls dressed in the regional peasant costumes of Holland, Germany, Sweden and Austria; distributed by *Butler Bros.* Ht. 13¾ in. (35 cm.).

773. British Ceramic head made by the Doll Pottery Co. It has molded and painted hair and eyes and an open-closed mouth with teeth. Mark: Ill. 774 on the pointed neck. *Courtesy of Richard Withington. Photo by Barbara Jendrick.*

Dollar Princess. 1909 and later. The mark "Dollar Princess //62//Special" has been found on dolls with bisque head, sleeping eyes, wigs, open mouth with four teeth, a ball jointed composition body with nails on the hands and toes outlined. These dolls were produced by *Kley & Hahn*. Hts. 24½ to 26 in. (62 to 66 cm.). They may have come in other sizes.★

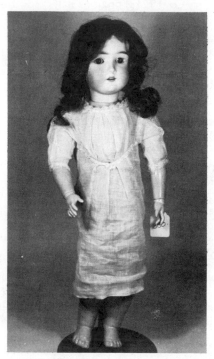

778. Bisque socket head doll named Dollar Princess. It has a wig, sleeping glass eyes, open mouth and a fully jointed composition body. Original chemise. Mark: Ill. 779. H. 24½ in. (62 cm.). *Courtesy of Richard Withington. Photo by Barbara Jendrick.*

774.

D·P·C° 46-6
775

D·P·C°

ENGLISH MAKE
49-10
776

67-9
BRITISH MAKE
D·P·C°
777

774–777. Marks found on heads made by the Doll Pottery Co. of British Ceramic.

779. Mark on the bisque head of the Dollar Princess dolls.

Dollar Prinzessin. See **Petzold, Dora.**

Dollar Store. 1925–28. A U.S. trademark for dolls registered by *Albert J. Clark* doing business as Clark's Dollar Store.

Dollcraft Company of America. 1918–19. Newark, N.J. Jobbers and manufacturers of dolls. Made dolls with clay heads, sleeping eyes, real hair wigs, rubber jointed wooden bodies. They used the trade name Gie-Wa for their dolls.

Dolleries. 1915–23 and later. Trade name for dressed dolls and dolls' accessories distributed by *Ellison, Rees & Co.* and their successor L. Rees. These dolls had wigs, teeth and composition bodies with straight or bent limbs.

Dolletta. 1917. Line of cloth dolls made by *Alliance.* Priced 13¢ to 25¢.

Dollie. 1893. Name of a waterproof apparel for dolls advertised by *Horsman;* priced $1.75. doz. wholesale. (See also **Rosie.**)

Dollie Darling (Dollie Doolittle). 1925. A premium doll advertised by the *Attleboro Premium House.* This *Mama* doll had eyes that slept and winked. It was jointed at the neck, hips, and shoulders. It wore a print dress, a red raincoat, bonnet, footwear and carried a beaded wrist bag. Ht. over 16 in. (50.5 cm.).

Dollie Doll. 1921. Trade name for a dressed composition doll with wig, made by the Metro Doll Co.[†]

Dollie Doolittle. See **Dollie Darling.**

Dolliettes. 1917. Dolls with "life like" faces made by *Huvan.*

Dollit. 1906. Trade name used for dolls by *Annie Alice Ivimey.*

DOLLIT

780. Dollit mark used for dolls by Annie Alice Ivimey.

Doll-O'-My Heart. 1918. Composition doll made by *Jessie M. Raleigh.* It had long dark curls and was handpainted as well as air-brushed. Ht. 22½ in. (57 cm.).

Dolls' Accessory Co., The (Parkhall Works). 1917–21. Longton, Staffs. According to THE TOY AND FANCY GOODS TRADER: "This firm originally produced what was known as a wax finish china head. This was a china head made and fixed in the ordinary way then dipped in wax, which gave it a coating of wax and an appearance similar to the old wax doll. The idea was only a partial success, however, and the makers . . . scrapped the idea, and set out to make something which could be produced cheaply and which would not be open to the objections which were levelled against the china-wax doll. After some experiments, they succeeded in producing a head which could be sold to the trade considerably cheaper than the ordinary china head. . . . Let there be no mistake; the head which the Dolls' Accessory Co. is producing is a real china head, but as a result of the special process of finishing and decorating, these heads only require one firing where the ordinary head has to be fired twice. Again, the makers of these heads are also makers of another article which, when it is being fired, allows of two or three doll heads being placed inside. In effect, this means that the firing of these heads costs practically nothing, so it will be seen that in producing a cheap doll's head the makers have reduced the cost of manufacture. They therefore give their customers the advantages of

this method without sacrificing the quality of the head itself. These heads can be obtained in several sizes, from something like 10 shillings [$2.50] per gross upwards. For doll makers requiring something cheaper still, the Dolls' Accessory Co. produces a porcelain mask at 8 shillings and 6 pence [$2.15] per gross. These have a superior appearance and look infinitely better than the celluloid or silk mask."

The "china heads" mentioned in this article are *British Ceramic* heads.

The method of coating the heads was a process patented by *Doris Sylvia Bailey and Sarah Jane Baxter.*

It was advertised that dolls' limbs as well as all-ceramic dolls could be waxed in this manner and that they were washable in hot and cold water.

Dolls' House Dolls. These small dolls generally under 8 in. (20.5 cm.) were usually dressed as members of a family or in the costumes of household related occupations. Often they were sold as a group. The dolls could be made of any material but by the 1880s bisque-headed dolls predominated. In one series of dolls' house dolls the 6½ in. (16.5 cm.) men dolls were size 8/0 and the 5½ in. (14 cm.) lady dolls were size 10/0.

Late 17th century: A dolls' house known as the "Chambre du Sublimé" was given to the Duke du Maine along with a group of wax portrait dolls. These portrait dolls of Racine, Boileau, La Fontaine and Bossuet were each given by the individual whom the doll portrayed.

Ca. 1860s: *Rock & Graner* showed dolls' house dolls in their catalog.

1889: *Nöckler & Tittle* advertised dolls' house dolls.

1900: *La Place Clichy* store advertised dolls' house dolls.

1901: *T. Eaton,* store advertised dolls' house dolls.

1902: *Butler Bros.* Advertised a black doll dressed as a chef. It had woolly hair, wore a white flannel costume with a muslin apron and had a spoon in its belt. Ht. 7 in. (18 cm.); priced 96¢ doz. wholesale.

Emil Paufler advertised a variety of dolls' house dolls.

1903: PLAYTHINGS ADVERTISED that dolls dressed representing a waiter to serve dinner in a dolls' house were new.

1908: *Moritz Pappe* advertised dolls' house dolls.
Shackman advertised a 5½ in. (14 cm.) chambermaid.

Ca. 1910: Shackman advertised the following dolls' house dolls; Chambermaid, Cook, and Bride dressed in silk. Ht. 6 in. (15 cm.); priced 15¢ to 40¢. A housemaid Ht. 5½ in. (14 cm.) cost 15¢.

1911: *Simon & Co.* advertised dolls' house dolls. Adelbert Beck made bisque heads for dolls' house dolls.

1920: *Beck Manufacturing Co.* advertised a fully jointed dolls' house doll. Ht. 9 in. (23 cm.).
R. F. Novelty Co. advertised the Happy Doll Family.

1920s: A group of Dolls' House Dolls made in Germany had bisque shoulder heads, arms, and legs on cloth bodies, molded hair or wig, painted eyes and sometimes molded mustache or sideburns. They came dressed and their costumes included for the lady dolls, a wrapper or morning frock (Morgenrock); a housemaid's (Zofe) black uniform with a white apron and cap over a wig; a cook's (Köchinen) outfit with a white coat over a print dress and a white cap over a molded bun; a Red Cross nurse's (Kranbenfleger) outfit in a blue and white striped uniform, white apron and cap with a red cross at the neckline and on the armband, its hair style appeared to be the same as that on the cook; the dress for Grandmother (Grosmutter) was a print with the low waistline of the period for her molded grey hair had a black bow in back and she carried a lorgnette. The lady in the wrapper was mold #699 and the housemaid was mold #701. These lady dolls were 6 and 6¼ in. (15 and 16 cm.) tall, but probably came in other heights as found with the men dolls.

A man doll mold #702 wore pajamas (Pyjama) and a multi-colored lounging robe; the butcher (Fleischer) wore the occupational costume of a European butcher consisting of a blue and white striped cotton jacket, white shirt, black bow tie, gray flannel trousers, black cap, and had a meat cleaver. The black waiter (Kellner) is shown in Ill. 788. The Grandfather (Grossvater) had a bald head with a grey fringe and mutton-chop sideburns. The men came in hts. 6¼ and 7¼ in. (16 and 18.5 cm.). All of these dolls may have come in smaller and in larger sizes than those listed here.

The above group of dolls have been found in their own individual boxes each with a label identifying the type of doll to be found in the box. These names were either printed on the label or hand written. The size and style of the boxes differed, and the numbers on the boxes ranged from 28/3 to 4732/3.

Before 1924: *Kennedy North* made dolls' house dolls.

1925–26: Cloth dolls' house dolls were made by *Dorothy Heizer* to go with Tiny Toy Furniture. Ht. 1 in. (2.5 cm.) to the foot (30.5 cm.).

1927: *Carl Horn* made dolls' house dolls dressed in various costumes including boys, girls, maid, chimney sweep, Santa, a doll in a bathing suit and dolls in various regional costumes. Hts. 1¼ to 3½ in. (3 to 9 cm.). (See Ill. 1212.)

DEUTSCHE SPIELWAREN ZEITUNG listed the following concerns under Dolls' House Dolls: *Apfelbaum & Batzner, Buschow & Beck, Hedwig Eitner, Friedmann & Ohnstein, Kling, G. Kreiss, Alfred Pensky,* and *M. Sehm.*

1928: *Montgomery Ward* advertised dolls with bisque heads and limbs on cloth bodies dressed as a bride in net trimmed with wool and the groom in a black felt suit. Both dolls had black molded shoes with heels. Ht. 4 in. (10 cm.).

1930: DEUTSCHE SPIELWAREN ZEITUNG listed the following manufacturers of dolls' house dolls: Buschow & Beck, *Canzler & Hoffmann, Dr. P. Hunaeus,* Hedwig Eitner, Friedmann & Ohnstein, Carl Horn Nacht, *Kestner,* Kling, *H. Josef Leven,* Alfred Pensky, M. Sehm, *Sorneck, Sperrhake, Standfuss,* and *Albert Wacker.*

1931: All-bisque dolls with molded hair and/or headwear and molded footwear, no other clothes. Eight of these dolls came in a set representing Grandma, Grandpa, Mother,

Dad, Maid, Big Brother, little twin Sisters. Dad wore a high hat. Hts. 2½ to 2⅞ in. (6.5 to 7.5 cm.); priced 69¢ for the set.

Ca. 1932: Kestner and other German firms were still making bisque-head dolls' house dolls. About twice as many of these represented females as the ones representing males, and they included maids, chambermaids, waitresses, cooks, chauffeurs, chefs and so forth. (See also **Mignonnettes; Kämmer & Reinhardt.**)★

781. Dolls' house doll with bisque shoulder head, arms, and legs on a cloth body. It has a blond wig, painted eyes, and a closed mouth. Original pink and cream colored clothes and molded footwear. H. 5¼ in. (13.5 cm.). *Courtesy of Eva Moskovsky.*

782A & B. Dolls' house doll with a bisque head having a wig, blue glass eyes, and a molded white beard suggesting an elderly man. The five-piece composition body has molded black boots with heels. Original smoking robe and cap. H. 4¾ in. (12 cm.). *Courtesy of the Washington Dolls' House and Toy Museum.*

783. Dolls' house doll with a bisque head having the features of an elderly woman, a white wig and blue glass eyes. The five-piece composition body has molded black slippers. Original costume consists of a felt dress and a white mob cap. H. 4¾ in. (12 cm.). *Courtesy of the Washington Dolls' House and Toy Museum.*

784. Dolls' house doll with a bisque shoulder head, molded hair, eyes, and mustache. The cloth body has bisque limbs including molded high black boots. Original costume consists of a felt suit trimmed with paper buttons, a silk bow tie and cumberbund. H. 6¼ in. (16 cm.). *Courtesy of the Washington Dolls' House and Toy Museum.*

785. Bisque head dolls' house lady doll with blond wig in a pompadour style, molded blue eyes, and closed mouth on a cloth body with bisque limbs. Original pink clothes with molded two-strap black slippers and white stockings. H. 6¼ in. (16 cm.). *Courtesy of the Washington Dolls' House and Toy Museum.*

786. Dolls' house doll with a bisque shoulder head, molded hair pompadour style and bun in back, molded blue eyes. The cloth body had bisque limbs; the white stockings and single-strap slippers with heels were molded. Original striped dress with black ribbon trim. H. 6¼ in. (17 cm.). *Courtesy of the Washington Dolls' House and Toy Museum.*

787. Bisque-head dolls' house doll with molded hair and mustache, painted eyes, closed mouth; the cloth body has bisque lower arms and legs. Original clothes and box marked "No. 15/3. 1.20//Herr in Smoking." H. 6¼ in. (16 cm.). *Courtesy of the Washington Dolls' House and Toy Museum.*

788. Black dolls' house doll with bisque head and limbs on a cloth body; molded kinky hair and molded and painted features. Original clothes; doll is dressed as a waiter in a black felt suit with tails, and metal buttons on the vest. H. 7½ in. (19 cm.). *Courtesy of the Washington Dolls' House and Toy Museum.*

789. Black dolls' house doll with bisque head and limbs on a cloth body; it has molded kinky hair, molded and painted features. Original clothes consist of a bandanna, a black-and-white-print dress, and a white lace-trimmed apron. H. 7¼ in. (18.5 cm.). *Courtesy of the Washington Dolls' House and Toy Museum.*

790. All bisque dolls' house doll with molded and painted hair, maid's cap, features, and footwear. The doll is jointed at the shoulders and hips with wire stringing. Original black and white maid's uniform. H. 2 in. (5 cm.). *Courtesy of Magda Byfield.*

791. Pair of all-bisque dolls' house dolls with molded and painted hair and features, with a hat for the girl and footwear for both dolls. Original felt and cotton clothes. H. 3½ in. (9 cm.). *Courtesy of Magda Byfield.*

Dolls' Supplies. 1915–21. Liverpool and London. Made composition dolls, dolls' heads and parts which they supplied to small doll makers. The parts included socket heads, arms, and legs. Most of the legs had molded footwear in color. They also supplied *British Ceramic* heads.

1917–18: Their special doll had a jointed neck and was called *My Girlie Girl.*

1918: Added two more sizes in their line of jointed character dolls.

Dolly Doll. World War I period. All-bisque doll, with eyes glancing to the side, made by *Morimura Bros.* It wore a molded bathing suit with horizontally striped short trousers. Its diamond shaped paper label was gold, red and white with the word "Dolly" on it. ★

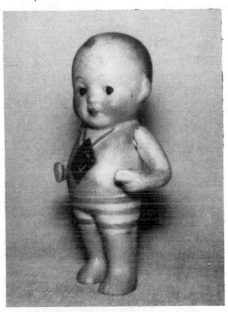

792. All-bisque doll named Dolly made in Japan. It has molded and painted hair, features, and a bathing suit; doll is jointed only at the shoulders. Marks: Ills. 793 & 794. H. 3½ in. (9 cm.). *Coleman Collection.*

NIPPON

793–794. Marks on a Dolly doll: one mark is on a sticker and the word Nippon is impressed on back. (See Ill. 792.)

Dolly. 1924. *Aerolite* velveteen cloth doll based on a design of *Mr. Williamson* and made by *Chad Valley.* This doll with wings and feelers, wore a full scalloped skirt; was No. 271. It carried a six-sided tag that read "Chad Valley// HYGIENIC// Fabric Toys." Ht. 11 in. (28 cm.); price $1.00.

Dolly. 1928–29. Doll with a composition head and limbs made by *Averill Manufacturing Co.* It was designed by *Grace Drayton* to represent the character of this name in her comic strip DOLLY AND BOBBY, which was published in over 50 newspapers and in the PICTORIAL REVIEW.

1928: It wore an unbelted short floral print dress with lace-trimmed bloomers showing. There were very short sleeves on the dress; the doll wore a large hair bow.

1929: Came in new sizes and new styles of clothes. (See also **Dolly Dingle.**)

Dolly Betty. 1914. One of the *Dolly Varden* series of cutout cloth dolls distributed by *Marshall Field.* The printed fabric showed combination underclothes with red ribbons, a red hair ribbon, red stockings and black laced boots. Ht. 21½ in. (54.5 cm.); price $2.25 doz. wholesale.

Dolly Bubbles. Ca. 1926. One of the *Bubbles* family of dolls made by *Effanbee.* (See also **Betty.**)

Dolly Bunting. 1906. Advertised by *Gamage.* It was dressed as a white bunny and came in size numbers 1, 2, and 3; priced 22¢ to 47¢.

Dolly Dainty. 1914. One of the *Dolly Varden* series of cutout cloth dolls distributed by *Marshall Field.* The printed fabric showed combination underclothes with blue ribbons, a blue hair ribbon, white socks and black Mary Jane style slippers. Ht. 14 in. (35.5 cm.); price 90¢ doz. wholesale.

Dolly Dear. 1916–30 and later. Cutout cloth doll made by *Saalfield* and designed by *Frances Brundage.* Dolls were 24 and 7 in. (61 and 18 cm.) tall on one sheet. It also came in a 15 in. (38 cm.) size.

1919: Advertised by *Sears,* as having lithographed colors. Priced 25¢.

1922: Advertised by Sears for 21¢.

Dolly Delight. 1926. Name of a cloth doll to be made at home for which instructions were given in MODERN PRIS-CILLA. The doll was made of pink sateen stuffed with cotton. Its flat face had embroidered features. Brown yarn constituted the hair. The arms and legs were joined to the body with elastic cord to form joints. The removable clothes consisted of a dress, rompers, jacket, coat, bonnet, petticoat, drawers, nightgown, socks, and kid slippers.

Dolly Dimple. 1907–14. Trademark name of bisque socket head dolls with wigs, glass eyes, open mouth with upper teeth dimples in each cheek and in the chin. These heads bear a *Gebrüder Heubach* sunburst mark. See Ill. 798 for a socket head Dolly Dimple mark. The marks include an H which might stand for *Hamburger,* who appears to have produced these dolls. Jan Foulke reported that the mold number was 5777.

795. Sheet of a cloth cutout doll called Dolly Dear, made by Saalfield Publishing Co. from a design by Frances Brundage and copyrighted in 1916. The larger model number indicates that this is a later version of the sheet having a larger doll, and two smaller dolls on the side. *Courtesy of Hazel Toon.*

ROUGH SIZE-HEIGHT RELATIONSHIPS OF SOCKET HEAD VERSIONS OF DOLLY DIMPLE				
Size No.	Height		Circumference of head	
	in.	cm.	in.	cm.
5	14	35.5		
6½	15½	39.5	9½	24
7½	19	48		
8	20	51	10¾	27.5

Dolly Dimple bisque shoulder head dolls produced by Hamburger and distributed probably by *Butler Bros.* and *Marshall Field* also appear to have had heads made by Gebrüder Heubach; sometimes the square Heubach mark was found on these dolls. The dolls had wigs, sleeping eyes, open mouth, dimples in each cheek and in the chin. The heads were on kid bodies with joints at the shoulders, hips and knees. Six hts. 14½, 17, 17¾, 19, 21, and 22½ (37, 43, 54, 48, 53.5, and 57 cm.).★

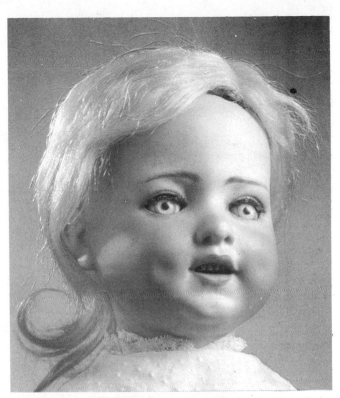

797A. Dolly Dimple, name of a bisque socket head made by Gebrüder Heubach. It has a wig, blue sleeping eyes, decal-type eyebrows, hair eyelashes, open mouth with four upper teeth, dimples in the cheeks and chin. The ball-jointed body is composition and wood. Mark: "DEP.//DOLLY DIMPLE//H//GERMANY//8." H. 20 in. (51 cm.). Circumference of head 10¾ in. (27.5 cm.). *Courtesy of Jay and Becky Lowe. Photo by Bill Holland.*

796. Dolly Dimple, name of a bisque head made by Gebrüder Heubach. It has a wig, sleeping brown glass eyes, an open mouth with two upper teeth, dimples and is on a ball jointed composition and wood body. Mark: Ill. 797B. H. 19 in. (48 cm.). *Courtesy of Sotheby Parke Bernet Inc., N.Y.*

797B. Dolly Dimple mark incised on a bisque socket head made by Gebrüder Heubach. (See Ill. 797A.)

798. Paper label found on a kid body marked Dolly Dimple with a crown and branches below it. Other paper labels with names associated with Butler Bros. have had these same symbols.

Dolly Dimple. 1909–16 and probably other years. Cutout cloth doll produced by *Art Fabric Mills* and *Selchow & Righter* depicting a girl wearing an ankle length dress with a high neckline. This was the same dress design as that worn by *Gretchen*. This doll was the mate to *Tiny Tim*. It was distributed by various companies including the National Cloak and Suit Co. and *Thompson's Mail Order Premium House*. Ht. 13¼ in. (33.5 cm.); priced 10¢ or 75¢ doz. wholesale.

Dolly Dimple. 1917. A rattle doll made by the *East London Toy Factory*.

Dolly Dimple. 1917. All-composition doll made by *Nunn & Smeed*. It had a wig with long ringlets and sleeping or stationary glass eyes.

NUNN & SNEED
Dolly
Dimple
No. 4
LIVERPOOL

799. Dolly Dimple mark used by Nunn & Smeed.

Dolly Dimple. 1917. A *Doll Exerciser* made by the *All-British Doll Manufacturing Co.* using *Sandow*'s patent. The doll came in a box with a chart of exercises.

Dolly Dimple. 1922. Doll with a head of pink *British Ceramic* coated with wax; it had a wig and a ball-jointed composition body.

Dolly Dimple. See **Arkadelphia Milling Co.**

Dolly Dimples. 1927. Trade name of a doll representing a child. It wore a dress and cap.

Dolly Dimples. 1929. A crying baby doll; wore a pink dress; price $5.75.

Dolly Dimples Doll Elastic. 1906–18 and later. Made by *H. W. Meier Co.* It came in seven sizes to fit dolls from 10 to 36 in. (25.5 to 91.5 cm.).

1906: Priced 25¢ to $1.00.★

800. Dolly Dimples one-piece Doll Elastic as advertised in the LADIES' HOME JOURNAL, December, 1906, by H. W. Meier & Co. of Baltimore. An instruction book for stringing dolls came with each of these elastics. The elastics came in 7 sizes for dolls, 10 to 36 in. (25.5 to 91.5 cm.) tall and larger.

Dolly Dingle. 1923–29. Name used for a variety of dolls made by *Averill Manufacturing Co.* The dolls were based on the designs of *Grace Drayton*.

1923: Came as a cloth doll with painted flat face or with a composition head that had a pug nose. Ht. of cloth doll, 11 in. (28 cm.).

1928: Advertised as a cutout cloth doll.

1929: Came as a two-tone whistling black doll with a composition head and arms on a cloth body. It wore a shirt, knee-length overalls and the three pigtails were tied with ribbon. Ht. 14 in. (35.5 cm.). (See also **Dolly,** 1928–29.)★

801. Dolly Dingle, Chocolate Drop, Happy Cry, and Sis made by Averill Manufacturing Co. and advertised in PLAYTHINGS, August, 1924.

802. Dolly Dollykins cloth doll with its original box. The distributor was the Children's Novelty Co. The doll has a wig only in front and the Drayton type features are lithographed on a flat face with blue eyes. Original clothes as seen on the box top except for the bonnet. The footwear is lithographed. H. 7 in. (18 cm.). *Courtesy of the Margaret Woodbury Strong Museum. Photo by Harry Bickelhaupt.*

Dolly Dips. 1917–20 and possibly later. Made by *Dean* with a flat face or with a three dimensional *Tru-to-Life* face. It came with *Tru-Shu* feet and with or without jointed legs. It wore a bathing suit with a separate skirt and a bathing hat. Ht. 14 in. (35.5 cm.).

1920: Number D 232 had a flat face; number D 236 had a Tru-to-Life face.

Dolly Dollykins. 1909–11. Trade name of a cloth flat faced *Drayton*-type doll. It was distributed in Philadelphia by the *Children's Novelty Co.* See Ill. 802.★

Dolly Double and Topsy Turvy. Cutout cloth dolls with two heads, one white and one black. Made by *Elms & Sellon.* The black head was named *Dinah.*★

Dolly Duds. 1922–29. Line of dolls' clothes and accessories made by the *Lodge Textile Works.*

Dolly Dumpling. 1918–22. Composition doll made by *Effanbee* and distributed by *Butler Bros.* It came with a composition shoulder head having molded hair and composition hands on a cloth body. There were six versions, namely a little girl with three styles of dresses, the Romper Baby with two styles of rompers and a "new born" baby in a short white lawn baby dress. The latter came with a 24 page booklet © in 1918 containing the story of the baby's birth and pictures of its house; on the cover, the doll was being carried by *Aunt Dinah.* Ht. of Dolly Dumpling 14½ in. (37 cm.); priced $1.00.

1922: It was a *Mama* doll according to Pat Schoonmaker.

Dolly Fairy. 1914. One of the *Dolly Varden* series of cutout cloth dolls distributed by *Marshall Field.* The printed fabric showed a dress with pink ribbons, a pink hairbow in the doll's curls, white socks, and black slippers with pink bows. Ht. 14 in. (35.5 cm.); priced 90¢ doz. wholesale.

Dolly Jane. 1914. A large version of *Dolly Fairy.* Ht. 29½ in. (75 cm.); priced $3.70 a doz. wholesale.

Dolly Kit. 1928. Name of a line of tiny bags for carrying a doll's nursing bottle and clothes made by Ideal Products Co. The bags contained clips which held the bottles always in an upright position.

Dolly Marion. 1923. Composition-head doll made by *Effanbee.* It wore horn-rimmed glasses. (See also **Dolly Rose Mary.**)

Dolly May. 1926. Doll with composition head and hands on a cloth body, made by *Ideal.* It had flirting tin eyes and a paper tag reading "I can talk, I can walk, I can sleep," as well as streamers reading "Dolly May." "Watch my rolling eyes when I walk." It wore a white organdy dress trimmed with pink embroidery and a Dutch style cap, patent leather slippers with buckles. Ht. 18 in. (45.5 cm.).

Dolly Mine. 1926–28. Cutout cloth doll distributed by *Charles William.* Ht. 19 in. (48 cm.); price 20¢. Shown wearing a petticoat and footwear. (See THE COLLECTOR'S BOOK OF DOLLS' CLOTHES, Ill. 761.)

Dolly Modiste. 1916–17. Line of clothes made by *Katherine Rauser;* it included a traveling outfit in a traveler's case and dolls' millinery.★

Dolly Penn. 1913. Name of a doll distributed by *Strawbridge & Clothier.*

Dolly Pop. See **Dollypop.**

Dolly Rainbell. 1928. Rubberized raincoat and hat made of Fairfield fabric by *Du Pont* and distributed by *Butler Bros.* It came in various colors. Price $12.00 a doz. wholesale.

Dolly Raindear. 1927–28. A raincoat, hat and umbrella outfit made by *Harris Raincoat Co.* and distributed by *Regal* and *Butler Bros.* It was made of waterproof Scottish plaids in red, green or blue combinations. Price $18.50 a doz. wholesale.

Dolly Record (Dolly-Reckord[†], Marvel Doll). 1922–28. A doll that "sings, recites, prays and dances." Made by the *Averill Manufacturing Co.*

1928: TOYS AND NOVELTIES reported "Marvel Doll [Dolly Record] previously not available for over the counter sales. It has a phonograph record device which enables it to pray, sing and recite in a human voice." The doll had composition head, arms and legs; human hair wig; sleeping eyes; open mouth and teeth. It wore a white organdy dress trimmed with lace, ribbons, and rosebuds. The undergarment was a colored panty combination. Footwear consisted of knit socks and white shoes. Ht. 26 in. (66 cm.).★

Dolly Rose Mary. 1923. Composition-head doll made by *Effanbee.* It wore horn-rimmed glasses. (See also **Dolly Marion.**)

Dolly Rosebud. 1926–30. *Mama* doll with a composition head and limbs made by *Horsman.* It had dimples in its cheeks.

1926: Dressed in printed and white piqué with matching hat; priced $4.95.

1928: It had sleeping eyes and wore an organdy dress and bonnet or came dressed in the Wexbar silk marionette prints designed by Tony Sarg. The dress and matching hat illustrated the marionette plays and children's books by Tony Sarg, such as THE WOODEN SOLDIER and THE CIRCUS. Dolly Rosebud came in six sizes; price $1.98 to $9.90.

1930: New expression given to the face; new body construction and new costumes. Six sizes. See Ill. 2077. (See also THE COLLECTOR'S BOOK OF DOLLS' CLOTHES, Ill. 774.)

Dolly Strong. 1910 and later. Doll with composition head

DOLLY ROSEBUD

803. Dolly Rosebud as advertised by Horsman in PLAYTHINGS, September, 1928.

made by *Amberg* using the poured plaster mold glue process. The hair was molded at first but later some of these dolls had wigs. It had a sateen body jointed at the shoulders and hips. Three sizes, priced 50¢ to $2.00.★

Dolly Sunshine. 1914. One of the *Dolly Varden* series of cutout cloth dolls distributed by *Marshall Field.* The printed fabric showed a blue print dress, a blue hair ribbon, white socks and black Mary Jane type slippers. Ht. 17½ in. (44.5 cm.); priced $1.50 doz. wholesale.

Dolly Togs. 1930 and later. Melrose, Mass. Manufactured dolls' outfits.

Dolly Varden. 1881 and probably earlier. Rubber doll made by *Goodyear.*

Dolly Varden. 1898. Cloth doll with lithographed face. Doll made of muslin or stockinet.

Dolly Varden. 1899. Doll with a multicolored face printed on cardboard. The hair-stuffed cloth body was jointed at the hips. It wore a dress, a bonnet that encircled the cardboard face, underwear, and footwear. This doll, distributed by *Butler Bros.,* was advertised as being "A revival of an old favorite." Ht. 16 in. (40.5 cm.). (See **Chronology,** 1700s.)

804A & B. Dolly Varden cloth doll with a chromolithographed paper face. No arms under the cape. Original clothes chiefly of colorful flannel. H. 8½ in. (21.5 cm.). *Coleman Collection.*

Dolly Varden. 1902. Cloth doll with painted linen face and hair, stubby arms, distributed by *Butler Bros.* It wore a long dress or a short baby dress and hood. Ht. 11½ in. (29 cm.); priced $2.25 doz. wholesale.

Dolly Varden. 1906–14. Distributed by *Butler Bros.* It had an embossed lithographed linen face, cotton stuffed cloth body, and came dressed.

1914: Hts. 8¾ and 13 in. (22 and 33 cm.); priced 35¢ and 45¢ doz. wholesale. (See THE COLLECTOR'S BOOK OF DOLLS' CLOTHES, Ills. 617 and 634.)★

Dolly Varden. 1914. Cutout cloth doll series printed on cloth that was treated to make it germ proof. It was distributed by *Marshall Field.* The series included *Dolly Betty, Dolly Dainty, Dolly Fairy, Dolly Sunshine, Jacky Tar,* and *Sunny Boy.*

Dolly Walker. 1917–23. Walking doll with human hair or mohair wig or without a wig; made by the Wood Toy Co.[†]

1919: It had springs and spring hinges.

1920: It did not have springs and spring hinges. Style no. 100 wore a gingham dress; nos. 101 and 107 wore organdy dresses; no. 109 wore a net dress. ★

Dollypop. 1925–28. Line of cloth dolls made by *Brückner* had handpainted faces and either a squeeze or balancing cry voice. They wore a dress, hat and footwear.

1926: There were 12 different styles. Nos. 102 and 106 were dressed as girls with bows in their hair; priced $1.00 to $1.50.

1927: There were black and white versions.

1928: New style no. was a "sitting baby doll." This No. probably had bent limbs. Some of the dolls wore bonnets. ★

Dolly-Reckord.[†] See **Dolly Record.**

Dolphitch Manufacturing Co. 1915–18. Acton, Middlesex and Oxford, England. Previously *D. A. Fitch* and Mrs. W. Fitch had manufactured dolls and dolls' clothing. In 1915 they formed this company and were in charge of it. They produced various types of dolls with composition heads or masks, *British Ceramic* heads, cloth heads, or wax heads, as well as short and long clothes, baby dolls' clothes sets, jersey suits, straw hats, shoes, socks, and wool boots.

1917: There were two lines of cloth dolls. The *Buster* line had a British Ceramic head and a jointed composition body. The dressed jointed baby dolls came in both wax and in composition.

1918: The leading line was dressed dolls. Character baby dolls and wax baby dolls were articulated; the latter were on composition bodies.

Domec Toy Co. 1918–30 and later. New York City. In 1928 Domec merged with *Century* to form the *Doll Corporation of America;* the factory was located in Lancaster, Pa. The name Domec was kept after the merger as a trade name. They manufactured popular priced dolls for Carnivals; premiums and syndicated stores.

1924: Line of 150 different dolls, costumed in 111 styles of dresses, including Ma Jong, baby dolls, Carnival dolls, Fair dolls and *Mama* dolls with sleeping eyes that sold for $1.00 to $10.00.

1925: Used the trade name Doll of Character.

1926: Made *Kaddy Kid.*

1927: Made Mama dolls with sleeping eyes. Domec was licensed by *Voices, Inc.* to use mama voices and criers. Their new-born baby doll *Giggles* was made in several sizes.

1928: Giggles was dressed in pink, blue or white and was made in three sizes. The new doll was a singing doll that played a 7 in. (18 cm.) disc record regardless of the position of the doll. Ht. 28 in. (71 cm.); price $15.00.

1930: *Kewty* was one of their line of dolls; prices in the line ranged from $1.00 to $15.00.★

Dominik. 1915. Trade name of one of the dolls promoted by *Mme. Paderewski* for the aid of Polish refugees. It was made in the workshop of *Mme. Thabée Lazarski* by Polish refugee artists and represented a bridegroom from Cracow. The festival attire included the characteristic peacock feather cockade.

Dominion Toy Manufacturing Co. 1911–19. Toronto, Canada. Made Dominion Brand composition character dolls jointed with rivets at the shoulders and hips. The neck was also jointed. Their label read, "Dominion Brand, Made in Canada." They wore various styles of dresses and came in several sizes. London agent was *Lewis Wild.*

Donahey, William. 1920–26. Chicago, Ill. His design for the *Teenie Weenies* was used by *Live Long Toys.* ★

Donald. 1919–21. Cutout cloth doll made by *Saalfield;* mate to *Dorothy.*

Doodle Dear. 1928–29. Long-limbed cloth doll made by *Adler Favor and Novelty Co.* It had a molded, washable, handpainted smiling face with a spit curl on its forehead. The clown suit was removable.

1928: Wore a checked clown suit.

1929: Wore a polka dot clown suit.

Dooly Dolls. 1916–19. Atascadero, Calif. Kewpie-type all-composition dolls made by the Atascadero Doll and Toy Factory.

1916: *Susan Tucker Mori* of Atascadero obtained a German patent for a doll's head.

1918: Dolls made of wood pulp fiber, came jointed at the shoulders only or jointed at the shoulders and hips. The clothes were cut out in high stacks of cloth. Many thousands of dolls were produced.

1919: Advertised that the dolls were made of light weight diatomaceous earth (fossilized shellfish). Many women were employed in the production of these dolls and one company ordered 250,000 dolls.

Door of Hope Mission Dolls. 1901–50. Shanghai and Canton, China.

A Protestant mission called The Door of Hope was founded in Shanghai in 1901 to rescue destitute children, slave girls, and unhappy child widows. It was not attached to any religious denomination nor did it receive much if any church support. It was funded largely by the Shanghai Municipal Council, the Shanghai Health Department, the Rotary Club and the American Women's Club. The Shanghai Police Court frequently turned over children who needed protection.

The girls were taught needlework, embroidery, knitting and other skills. These skills were put to work in the dressing of the Door of Hope dolls. The fine sewing on the dolls shows how careful were the instructions. The textile industries were pressured into giving their scraps of fabric to the Door of Hope Mission and the girls who made and dressed the dolls received wages for doing so. The dolls were distributed through representatives in China, England, Australia, the United States and South Africa. The missionary workers came from these same countries.

Some of the dolls had tags reading "N.E. Branch Woman's Foreign Missionary Society."

The 1902 Annual Report of the Door of Hope Mission stated:

"During the year, seven Chinese girls and one foreign girl have been received into the Home. . . . The year closed with eight in the Home. . . . Regular study hours are kept during five mornings of the week. . . . The girls are taught to read Chinese characters and . . . simple arithmetic and hygiene. . . .

"Five afternoons each week are given to sewing. Plain sewing and knitting have been done, and in addition over 150 Chinese dolls have been dressed and sold. A sewing machine has been purchased. The net proceeds of the industrial work, . . . have more than covered the expense of the girls' food and clothing. . . . We shall be very glad if friends will help the work by sending us plain sewing, knitting, or orders for dolls. The charge for sewing is three to five cents an hour. Knitting is done by the piece. The price of dolls varies, according to the work and materials from 75¢ to $5.00."

The relatively high price of the dolls reveals the many hours of work that must have gone into their making at only three to five cents an hour. The girls averaged only about one doll a month. The cost of material accounted for about half of the sale value. This ratio was fairly consistent as is shown in the following table:

Year	Receipts from Sale of Dolls		Expenditures for materials in doll making
1908	$ 960	Mexican dollars	$ 563
1909	2,467	Mexican dollars	1,218
1912	2,644		1,445
1913	1,976		1,105
1920	3,773		1,946
1921	4,376		2,467
1924	3,529		1,595
1925	1,711		810
1926	1,458		740
1927	960		426
1928	846		383
1929	947		492
1930	1,540		868
1938	3,674	Chinese dollars	

The yearly fluctuations may have been partly influenced by currency valuations.

At the beginning of 1913 there were 98 girls in the First Year Home and the count remained under 100 although there were large numbers coming and going. For example at the beginning of 1924 there were 84 girls; during the year 90 girls were rescued from brothels and slavery, 22 married, 8 died, 17 returned to relatives and 30 were sent to the Industrial Home, an adjacent part of the Door of Hope Mission, thus leaving 97 girls in the First Year Home at the end of 1924. According to a later Annual Report, "All stay one or two years, at least, in the First Year Home, so that they can have the advantages of studying in the classes held each morning in the Primary School."

The average productivity of each girl must have been only about a dozen dolls a year—no wonder they were relatively expensive. The 1940–41 Door of Hope Report comments:

"The usual activities of the homes have been continued as before. Both girls and teachers in the doll industry . . . have praised God for keeping them supplied with work and orders. . . .

"It really is a wonderful thing that girls who cannot even hold a needle when they come to us, can learn in a few months to do such fine work."

The total production for the entire 48 years (1902–1949) when these dolls were being produced probably did not exceed 50,000 dolls, a tiny amount when compared with the millions of dolls produced each year by single companies in other countries. However, a large proportion of the Door of Hope dolls have survived because they were used for educational purposes or purchased for collections.

The 1940–41 Door of Hope Report went on to say, "Miss P--- has proved invaluable in her efficient and patient training of girls to make the miniature garments—exact copies of the clothes worn by all classes of Chinese people, both men, women and children. These 22 model dolls are made by the First Year Home girls, and sold to friends, who desire to use them in educational or missionary talks in the homelands."

The head, hands and arms to the elbow were of pearwood carved by a man and his assistants possibly from Ningpo where the Chinese pearwood carving art flourished. Mr. Ashley White has supplied much of the information about the Door of Hope dolls and a letter from him provided the information that Mr. Fong had a woodcraft shop in Kui Kiang Road, Shanghai. He carved the heads, hands and some of the feet. Mr. Wright met the woman who "picked up the doll parts from Mr. Fong's shop often over a 16 year period between 1916 and 1932." The wood was as smooth as satin and needed no paint or varnish to resemble the ivory yellow Chinese skin. The hair, eyes and lips were painted. Some of the dolls wore their hair in a carved bun; others wore fancy head-dresses. The palm of the hand was rounded and the thumb was separate. The bodies were stuffed with raw cotton.

A sample of the wood from one of the Door of Hope dolls was tested by the U.S. Government and found to be similar to pearwood but of the genus *Euonymus* according to Eveline Sicard.

In 1916 Mary Ninde Gamewell wrote in THE GATEWAY TO CHINA: "The Door of Hope dolls are famed far and wide. The little wooden heads, beautifully carved, are the only parts of the dolls not made by the girls. Shanghai firms gladly donate in abundance bright-coloured scraps of silk, satin, and cotton cloth. The dolls are dressed to represent all grades and classes of society and a set consisting of sixteen, is of real value educationally.

"The first-year girls spend the morning in study and the afternoon in work. They begin by learning to make their own clothes, cloth shoes and all, then when the tailor's trade has been thoroughly mastered, they are set to dressing dolls. For this work a slight compensation is given which acts as a spur and encouragement."

The costumes on the dolls were all made by hand. The outer garments were Chinese silks, satins, or cottons. The under-garments showed in miniature exactly what was worn by the Chinese people. Every garment can be taken on and off. The gentlemen's trousers were tied at the ankle just as in real life. The old style bride and groom are in formal dress as it was worn at Court in the days of the Empire. Their costumes were hand-embroidered. The bride was dressed in red, the color of happiness. The embroidered squares on the front and back of the groom's robe stand for the so-called "Mandarin Squares" or badges of office which the old-style officials were entitled to wear. The bridegroom's cap had the official button as well as a feather. High satin boots were obligatory for formal occasions.

Prior to 1911: The dolls had cloth hands and feet and the dolls representing men and boys had long black braided hair queues. Among the dolls were the bride and groom, the mourner, the boy and girl in silk, the Elder Gentleman of high rank, Policeman, Amah and baby in two sizes. The Manchu Lady, Ht. 16 in. (40.5 cm.) was a larger size than those made later.

The boy in silk wore a velvet sleeveless jacket and a brocaded silk outfit with tunic and trousers. The long full sleeves ended considerably below the hands, probably indicating that he represented a class that did no work with its hands. Ht. 8½ in. (21.5 cm.).

1916: Sixteen different types of dolls were made by the Door of Hope girls.

1922: The dolls included Table Boy, same clothes as Student. Grandmother, the hat worn only in winter. Grandfather, well-to-do elderly man. School Boy dressed in cotton. Young Lady and her Husband of the upper classes; their children, a School Girl in cotton dress and Small Boy in holiday dress of silk. Young Man dressed for funeral of his father—three balls of his hat are for catching his tears, and the paper wand is for driving off evil spirits. Widow in sack cloth. Bridegroom on his wedding day in "official" dress, rank denoted by design on the embroidered square and color of button on hat. Bride in traditional old style costume. Farmer with grass raincoat for working in wet weather. The Buddhist priest with long yellow gown, shaved head; gown has no buttons. Municipal policeman in Shanghai police dress.

1920s–30s. 24 different types of dolls were produced: Bride and Groom, the favorites; Old Lady and Old Gentleman with queue; Young Lady and Young Gentleman; Young Lady in long garments; Boy in silk and Girl in silk; small boy in cotton and girl in cotton; Kindergarten Child; Baby; Cantonese Amah, a nurse with baby on her back; Amah; Table Boy; Priest, Buddhist of the Tibetan Lama Temple in Peking; Mourner in sackcloth with girdle of straw; Widow with bonnet that acts as a veil covering her face; Policeman; Farmer with carved feet; Manchu woman, with carved headdress and feet.

Other dolls were sometimes made for special orders.

1939: Plans for a new building were disrupted by war and orders for dolls could not be completed.

1940: Kimport advertised the following 20 Door of Hope Dolls: Chinese Bride, old style with face covered; Chinese Groom; Modern Bride with face showing; Young Gentleman; Young Lady; Amah and baby; Amah without baby; Girl in silk; Boy in silk; Little Girl; Little Boy; Chang the barefoot Farmer, dressed in a straw coat and woven coolie hat; Mourner in sackcloth; Widow in sackcloth; Buddhist Priest; Table Boy; Old Grandfather; Old Grandmother; Shanghai Policeman; Manchu Lady in Satin with carved headdress and feet. The dolls representing adults were 11 in. (28 cm.) tall except for the Farmer who was 12 in. (30.5 cm.) and the Young Lady who was 10 in. (25.5 cm.). The Boy in silk was 8 in. (20.5 cm.) and the Girl in silk was 7 in. (18 cm.); the Boy and Girl were 6 in. (15 cm.).

By 1940 the war had caused prices to increase and silk materials were almost unobtainable. Kimport had to charge as much as $9.95 for the bride and groom which were the favorites.

1950: The Door of Hope Mission had been a War Casualty but some of the girls escaped to Taiwan with an American, Miss Clara Nelson, and the mission work was carried on there but few if any dolls appear to have been made after World War II.

There was a similar Door of Hope Mission in Canton. After the First World War this mission was not prospering and a missionary named Florence Drew came to its rescue. In order to teach skills dolls had previously been made in this mission also. They continued to make dolls but most of them were sold only locally. These dolls had head, hands and feet made of a clay-like composition material with a glazed surface. The business man and wife of the professional man had white faces; the rest are pink in color. The Canton dolls were cruder and generally slightly smaller than the Shanghai Door of Hope dolls, being 7½ to 10 in. tall. The fingers were longer and the handmade clothes less well made on the Canton dolls. These Canton dolls usually wore pants with ties on them. Each coat or jacket had three frog loops for fastenings.

The Canton Door of Hope dolls in the 1930s included a barefoot female farmer with gray hair in a top-knot, a bald-headed farmer with painted mustache and beard; both of these farm people were dressed in cotton clothes. The professional man and his wife wore silk clothes. His paper hat was six-sided. She wore a coat which had been removed to show her embroidered shirt in the illustration (See Ill. 814). Another woman, all in black, wore a heavy coat over cotton pants. The business man had a molded hat, a black mustache and a heavy blue coat.

World War II also caused the closing of the Canton Door of Hope Mission. The production of the dolls at this Canton Mission is unknown but the surviving ones seem to be extremely rare.

Another slightly different type of doll attributed to Canton, had a body similar to those found on the *Martha Chase* dolls. Possibly these dolls were designed by a Missionary from the New England area who was familiar with the Chase dolls.★

806. Door of Hope carved wooden-head doll portraying a Chinaman of the upper class. It has a hair queue and cloth stub hands. This doll was part of the Laura Starr collection soon after 1900, thus making it one of the earliest Door of Hope dolls. Original silk clothes. *Courtesy of the International Doll Library Foundation. Photo by Sotheby Parke Bernet Inc., N.Y.*

807. Door of Hope doll known as the Manchu Lady, with a carved headdress and cloth stub hands. This exquisite doll was part of the Laura Starr collection soon after 1900. It differs in many ways from the Manchu Lady of the 1930s in Ill. 808. Original blue silk dress and pink pants. H. 16 in. (40.5 cm.). *Courtesy of the International Doll Library Foundation. Photo by Sotheby Parke Bernet Inc., N.Y.*

805. The First Year girls at the Door of Hope Mission in Shanghai busy making dolls. *Courtesy of Ashley Wright.*

808A & B. Carved wooden-head, hands and feet on a cloth body made by the Door of Hope Mission in China in the 1930s. It has elaborate carved and painted wooden headwear which with its original handmade clothes represents a Manchu Lady. H. 11½ in. (29 cm.) including the headwear and shoe platforms. *Coleman Collection.*

809A & B. Carved wooden-head doll made by the Door of Hope Mission in China. It has a real-hair queue, carved and painted features, a cloth body including hands and elaborate handmade clothes representing a boy in an affluent family. Made between 1901 and 1914. H. 8¼ in. (21 cm.). *Coleman Collection.*

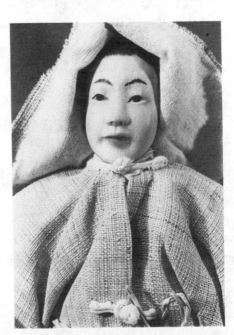

810. Dolls with carved wooden heads and hands, painted features, and cloth bodies, made by the Door of Hope Mission in China. Original handmade clothes. The Amah (nurse) does not wear the type of shoes made for bound feet which were worn by the upper classes. H. 11 in. (28 cm.). *Coleman Collection.*

811. Carved wooden head and hands on a cloth body made by the Door of Hope Mission in China in the 1930s. The original sackcloth clothes represent a mourning widow. Pink roses encircle the bun which is carved on the back of the head. H. 11 in. (28 cm.). *Coleman Collection.*

812. Door of Hope dolls with carved wooden heads and hands and painted features. The variations in countenance is extremely evident. This group was probably made in the 1920s or 1930s. Original clothes. *Courtesy of Ashley Wright.*

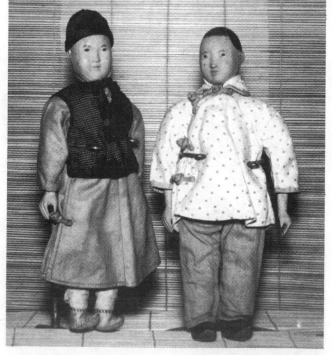

813. Pair of Door of Hope dolls with carved wooden heads and hands, painted hair and features. The similarity in carving suggests that it could have been done by the same person or at least at the same time. Original clothes. *Courtesy of Ashley Wright.*

814. Dolls made at the Door of Hope Mission in Canton, China. These dolls have composition heads and hands. *Courtesy of Ashley Wright. Photo by Mary Lou Estabrook of the LAKEVILLE JOURNAL.*

Dora (Bather). 1910–11. Felt character doll with stitched hair made by *Steiff* and dressed as a girl in a bathing suit. Hts. 28 and 35 cm. (11 and 14 in.).

Dora. 1924. Flat faced cloth doll made by *Dean* in the *A-1* line. It came in three designs with printed clothes. Ht. 12 in. (30.5 cm.).

Dora. Name of a "Washable" doll made in Germany.

Dora-Petzold-Puppen. See **Petzold, Dora.**

Doremus & Benzer. 1921. New York City. Distributor of the *Muncie Doll.*

Doremus, I. W., & Co. 1922. New York City. Selling agent for *Lincoln.*

Doris. 1916. Doll with wig, jointed body, and dressed in a chemise; handled by *Whyte Ridsdale.*

Dorn, Max. 1922–23. Chicago, Ill. Factory agent for imported and domestic dolls.

Dorn, Max. 1926–27. New York City. Made outfits for dolls.

Dornheim, Koch & Fischer. See **Dernheim, Koch & Fischer.**† The correct spelling is Dornheim.

Dorogi & Co. (Dr. Dorogot). 1924–29. Budapest. Manufactured rubber. Obtained several Hungarian, German and British patents for various uses of rubber in the manufacture of dolls. One of the British patents was for a process by which celluloid heads could be affixed to rubber bodies.

1926: Employed 33 skilled and 212 unskilled workers.

Dorothea. 1926. Doll with a *British Ceramic* head made by *Wolstan Doll Co.* It had sleeping eyes and a fully jointed body. (See also **Dorothy.** 1918–20.)

Dorothy. See **Babyland Rag.**

Dorothy. 1913. Name of a doll with a wig, sleeping eyes, and ball jointed body advertised by Gamage. Ht. 10½ in. (26.5 cm.); priced 25¢.

Dorothy. 1918–20 and possibly later. Doll made by *Wolstan Doll Co.* It came in a variety of styles, with or without wigs, with or without sleeping eyes, undressed or dressed, as children or girls with fancy hats.

1918: Priced $7.50 to $45.00 doz. wholesale.

Dorothy. 1918–19. All-composition doll with straight legs made by *Jessie M. Raleigh.* It had a wig, a steel spring jointed five-piece body and wore a figured lawn dress and a ribbon head band. ★

Dorothy. 1919–21. Cutout cloth doll made by *Saalfield.* Mate to *Donald.*

Dorothy. 1921–22. Stockinet doll with removable clothes, made by *Chad Valley* as No. 205D. Ht. 11½ in. (29 cm.).

DOROTHY
9082
made in England

815. Mark on a British doll named Dorothy.

Dorothy. 1927–28. Doll with composition head and limbs distributed by *Montgomery Ward*. It had sleeping eyes, mohair wig, mama voice, and wore a rayon dress over organdy underwear that was not removable. Ht. 22 in. (56 cm.); priced $4.89.

Dorothy Dainty. 1911–12. Trade name of a composition-head doll made by *Amberg*.★

L.A.S. ©
414
1910

816. Dorothy Dainty mark impressed on an Amberg composition head.

Dorothy Dainty. 1915–18. Composition head doll made by *Effanbee*.

1915: It was a baby doll with a curly wig, a pacifier in its mouth, composition hands and dressed in a long baby dress and cap. (See THE COLLECTOR'S BOOK OF DOLLS' CLOTHES, Ill. 646.) Price $1.25.

1918: A line of Effanbee dolls with natural hair wigs. They wore party frocks and straw bonnets. Ht. 14 to 30 in. (35.5 to 81 cm.).

Dorothy Darling. 1929. Composition shoulder head, bent-limb baby doll distributed by *Butler Bros.* It had painted hair, sleeping eyes, painted teeth, crying voice, jointed shoulders and hips and was dressed in various styles of short baby clothes. Hts. 17, 23 and 25 in. (43, 58.5 and 63.5 cm.).

Dorothy Jane. 1930. One of the *Kiddie Pal* line of *Regal*, Dorothy Jane was advertised as "My Sweetheart."

817. Mark for a Dorothy Jane doll, one of the Kiddie Pal line.

Dorothy Perkins. 1910. Doll with molded hair and footwear; had removable crocheted clothes. Ht. 4 in. (10 cm.).

Dorris & Co. 1923–26. London. Made dressed dolls including the "Little Pet" series.

Dorst. Sonneberg, Thür. Made machinery for doll factories.

Dorst, G. 1928. Sonneberg, Thür. Exported dolls.

Dorst, Julius. 1839–1930 and later. Sonneberg, Thür. Produced wooden and wood-pulp composition dolls, and exported dolls.

1865: Made wooden toys.

1873: Won a medal at the Vienna Exhibition.

1878: Made wooden dolls' heads and five-piece jointed wooden dolls.

1880: Won first prize at the Melbourne Exhibition.

1883: Was one of the founders of the *Sonneberg Industrial School*.

1887: Won a bronze medal at the Antwerp Exhibition.

1897: Applied for a German patent (D.R.G.M.) for changing dolls' heads.

1898: Georg Friedrich Dorst followed in his father's footsteps.

Ca. 1904: Their catalog showed patented (D.R.G.M.) circus dolls that resembled those of *Schoenhut*.

1905: Applied for a German patent (D.R.G.M.) pertaining to a doll that said "Mama" and "Papa," moved its arms and turned its head.

1909: The Crown Prince of Prussia gave his children a large group of Dorst toys for Christmas.

1910: Employed up to 175 workers. A catalog of dolls and dolls' heads listed dressed composition dolls. Wooden dolls with felt clothes. Wooden dolls with knit clothes. Jointed wooden dolls in felt. Jointed dolls entirely of wood.

Dorst was a member of the Sonneberg group who won a grand prize at the Brussels Exposition.

1926: Manufactured and exported dolls. His dolls were distributed by *Gustav Burmester*.

1927: Advertised wooden toys and used the clown trademark.★

Dory, Mme. Myrtha. World War I period. France. Made dolls dressed to represent wartime women in the following occupations: Bus drivers and conductors, chauffeurs, coachmen, mail carriers, mechanics, parcel carriers, subway employees, and workers on shells for guns.

Dots Dolls. See **Harwin & Co.**

Dottie (Dotty Dimple). 1907–19. Cutout cloth doll made by *Saalfield*.

1914: Distributed by *Butler Bros.* They made a 15 in. (38 cm.) doll; priced 79¢ doz. wholesale.★

Dottie Dimple. 1920s. Cloth doll to be embroidered and stuffed, made by *Bucilla* as one of their "Stuff Toys." It had a flat face with outlines of the hair and features to be embroidered. This set, number 5390, also contained material and embroidery floss for making a blue sateen dress and hat for this doll. Ht. 11 in. (28 cm.); priced 75¢.

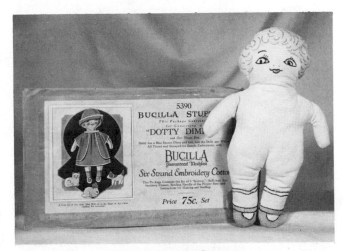

818. Cloth doll named Dottie Dimple, made from a Bucilla pattern, and the envelope from which it came. The two-piece cloth doll had stamped features which could then be embroidered with the outline stitch. In addition this package contained a dress for the doll. H. 11 in. (28 cm.). *Coleman Collection.*

Dotty (Dolly Dimple). 1927. Doll with composition head, arms and legs, mohair wig, sleeping eyes, new slender cotton filled cloth body. This dressed *Mama* doll was distributed by *Montgomery Ward.* Hts. 18, 21, and 23 in. (45.5, 53.5, and 58.5 cm.); priced $3.48 to $4.59.

Dotty Darling. 1927. Doll with a composition head having a felt finish, produced by *Borgfeldt* and distributed by *Butler Bros.* It had a mohair wig, painted eyes looking to the side and a cotton stuffed torso and limbs. The doll wore a felt dress trimmed with flowers and buttons, a hat, slippers with straps that were tied. It had a round tag with "Dotty//Darling" on it. Hts. 14, 17, and 18½ in. (35.5, 43, and 47 cm.). This doll was made in competition with the *Lenci* dolls. See Ill. 387.★

Dotty Dimple. 1912–13. Nodding-head doll advertised by *Selchow & Righter.* It had molded clothes and represented a lady with a large hat. This doll came in two sizes; priced $2.00 doz. wholesale.

Dotty Dimple. See **Dottie Dimple.**

Doucet, Maison. 1917 or before. Paris. Dressed in historic costumes some wax dolls which were exhibited in Boston and later sold to the Toledo Museum of Art for, reportedly, $30,000. The dolls represented French fashions in dress from the sixth century to the then modern times and included dolls dressed as Louise de La Vallière, François I, Empress Eugénie, and Ninon de l'Enclos among others. (See also **Historical Costume Series, 1917.)**

Douche, Mme. Germaine. 1928–30 and later. Paris. Made dolls.

1928: Applied for two French trademarks, *Colette* and *Puppet's Mary,* for dolls and mascots.

Douglas Fairbanks.[+] See **Robin Hood.**

Douillet, Emile. 1890s. Montreuil-sous-Bois, France. Member of the *Jumeau* firm and partner of Emile Jumeau in their lawsuit against *Danel & Cie.*

Douwes, Gebrüder. Amsterdam. Dressed a doll with a ball-type bisque head, painted features, and bisque arms on a cloth body. It wore a Dutch style costume labeled with a cloth tag reading: "Gebr. Douwes// National Costuum// Damrak 69 Amsterdam."

GEBR. DOUWES
NATIONALE COSTUUMS
DAMRAK 69 AMSTERDAM

819. Cloth tag used by Gebrüder Douwes.

Dow, Stanley Thomas, and Trautman, Frederick Otto. 1921–24. Leicester, England. Applied for a British patent and a German patent (D.R.P.) relating to a doll with a spring.

Dr. Pill. 1914. Bisque doll that represented a character in the *Little Nemo* comic strip created by Winsor McCay. This doll was distributed by *Strobel & Wilken.* It wore a long coat with three large buttons on its vest and carried a doctor's satchel with "Doctor//Pill" on the side. Two sizes; priced 25¢ to $1.00.

Drag. Before 1911–16. Felt doll with long feet made by *Steiff* and dressed as a German Dragoon with a sword. Ht. 28 and 35 cm. (11 and 14 in.).

Drake, H. G., & Co. 1920–26. London. They processed kapok down for filling dolls' bodies.

Drayton, Grace Gebbie (Wiederseim). 1909–29. Philadelphia, Pa. She was an illustrator from whose designs many dolls were made, especially in composition and cloth. Grace Drayton drew Bobby Blake[+] and Dolly Drake[+] as early as 1905 and these figures with their googly eyes inspired the creation of many dolls. One of these had a composition shoulder head and arms, molded hair, painted eyes looking straight ahead, and a curved line mouth. Ht. 16 in. (40.5 cm.). (See Ill. 651.)

1926: Grace Drayton obtained a U.S. design patent for a doll.

1928: The *Dolly* and *Bobby* dolls based on her drawings were manufactured by *Averill Manufacturing Co.*★

Dream Baby. All-composition doll marked "Dream Baby." Had painted hair and eyes, (fat face unlike the *My Dream Baby,*) toddler body with bent arms. Ht. 11 in. (28 cm.).

Dream Baby. See **My Dream Baby.**

THE dress, which may be made very simple or trimmed with frills of lace and ribbon bows; the cloak and the hat are for the little girl-doll. Patterns for these little garments are made in four sizes to fit dolls 14, 18, 22 and 26 inches tall, and cost 10 cents a set. The hat may be made of material to match the coat, or of white or colored felt.

DRAWN BY GRACE G. WIEDERSEIM   2894

Patterns for the set of doll clothes illustrated on this page can be supplied. Order by number, stating size, and inclosing price which includes a Guide-Chart, from the Pattern Bureau, The Ladies' Home Journal, Philadelphia.

820. Clothes for dolls drawn by Grace Drayton in the LADIES' HOME JOURNAL, December, 1906. (See also Ill. 651.)

Dreamland Doll Co. 1905–8. Detroit, Mich. Importers and manufacturers of Dreamland dolls. The jointed dolls cost $4.25 to $8.25 doz. wholesale.★

Dreifuss, Isidore. 1921. Strasbourg, France. Registered *La Poupée Ideale* as a trademark in France.★

Dresden, Augustin. Lindenauplatz, Germany. His tradecard states that he "can furnish articles from the simplest to the most elegant" obtainable from the manufacturers of Germany and Austria. The articles for sale included dolls, dolls' heads, porcelain dolls, and parts for dolls.

Dresdener Werkstätten für Handwerkskunst. 1904. Dresden, Germany. It was a workshop for handmade art products including the making of wooden dolls designed by *Eugen Kirchner.*

Dressel (Known as Cuno & Otto Dressel from 1873 on). Ca. 1700–1945. Sonneberg, Thür. Opened branches in 1894 in London; 1917 in Leipzig; 1919 in Nürnberg; 1920 in Berlin; 1920s Grunhainichen in the Erzgebirge area. Produced, distributed and exported dolls. In the early 1900s they designated buyers of their dolls' by numbers; for example *Eaton* was number 16/10 according to the Ciesliks.

Johann Georg Dressel (b. 1686, d. 1740) was in the toy business and probably handled dolls. His grandson Johann Philipp Dressel (b. 1735, d. 1804) expanded the business and took over a former ducal estate in 1764 which he named Dresselhof. This large estate became the premises for the Dressel business as long as it existed. In 1789 the Duke of Saxe-Meiningen, the dukedom where Dresselhof was lo-

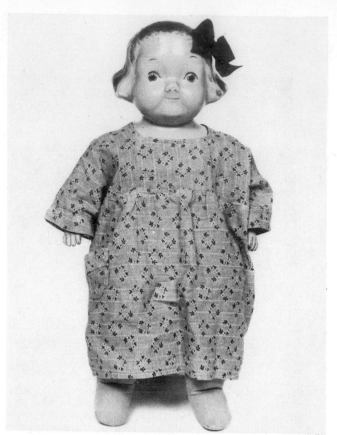

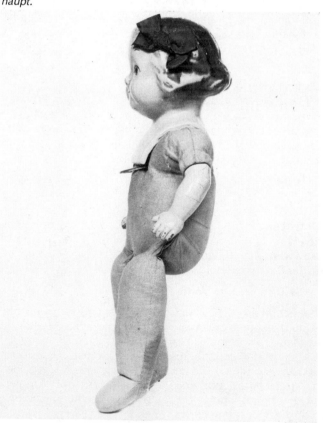

821A & B. Doll designed by Grace Drayton. It has a wood-pulp type composition shoulder-head and arms, molded and painted hair with fabric hair ribbon, molded and painted eyes. The pug nose and single line smiling mouth are typically Drayton. The pink cloth body has a voice box. Original black and gray print dress. Mark: Ill. 823. H. 16½ in. (42 cm.). *Courtesy of the Margaret Woodbury Strong Museum. Photo by Harry Bickelhaupt.*

822A & B. Printed cloth baby doll designed by Grace Drayton. The face is flat and the clothes are printed on the doll. Mark: Ill. 824. *Courtesy of the late Henrietta Van Sise.*

G. G. DRAYTON

G.G. Drayton

823–824. Marks found on dolls designed by Grace Drayton. No. 824 is printed on the back of the doll in Ill. 822. No. 823 is on the composition head of the doll in Ill. 821.

cated, inaugurated a statute for Industry and Trade. This Duke, George I (1782–1803), gave 26 Sonneberg citizens— among them Johann Philipp Dressel—the privilege of trading with toys which was largely a home industry. When Johann Philipp Dressel died in 1804 the firm became known as Johann Philipp Dressel's Sons. These sons were Johann Balthasar Dressel (b. 1775, d. 1819), Martin Dressel (b. 1780, d. 1860), Gabriel Dressel (b. 1782, d. 1838) and Ernst Friedrich Dressel (b. 1797, d. 1870). In 1830 the firm be-

came known as Ernst and Carl Dressel. The three older brothers had died or retired, leaving Ernst Friedrich Dressel and Carl, the son of Johann Balthasar Dressel, as heads of the business. Otto Dressel (b. 1831, d. 1907) became a member of the firm in 1856. In 1862 the statute for Freedom and Trade was enacted in Saxe-Meiningen thus permitting the Dressels to have a factory for making dolls, as well as to produce dolls made as a home industry, in the area. In 1873 the firm was known as Cuno & Otto Dressel. After Cuno Dressel died in 1893, the business was run by Otto Dressel, who died in 1907, and his sons, Otto Dressel, Jr. (b. 1857, d. 1926), and Ernst Friedrich Dressel (b. 1858, d. 1939). Dr. Hans Dressel (b. 1883, d. 1942) joined the firm in 1911. He traveled extensively in North and South America. In 1914 Otto Dressel retired and Herman Ortelli, Ernst Friedrich Dressel's son-in-law, joined the firm. Just before or during World War II all of these men died and in 1945 the business was nationalized.

The Dressel family information was graciously supplied by Marianne Eichhorn, a descendant of Ernst Friedrich Dressel, Jr.

The Dressels used wood, wax, wax-over-composition, papier-mâché, "solid paste" (a hard composition), china, or bisque heads on their dolls. The bisque heads were made by *Simon & Halbig, Armand Marseille, Ernst Heubach, Gebrüder Heubach, Schoenau & Hoffmeister* and possibly others.

Dressel supplied heads for other doll manufacturers. A Dressel composition head has been found on an original cloth body made by *Philip Goldsmith.*

In the 1920s G. Greiner was their sole London agent.

1875: Holz-Masse trademark was registered in Germany for dolls, dolls' heads and *Täuflinge.* This mark had the initials of E D with the E reversed for Ernst Dressel, father of Cuno and Otto Dressel.

The word Holz-Masse was sometimes impressed on the inside of the composition or wax-over-composition shoulder heads as seen in Ill. 831.

Before 1882: A child who died in 1882 owned a doll with a composition head having a skin wig, painted eyes with painted lower eyelashes and a cloth body with composition limbs. On the upper right leg the Dressel caduceus mark (See Ill. 488 in the first COLLECTOR'S ENCYCLOPEDIA OF DOLLS) was stamped. This mark on a corresponding leg was also found on a somewhat similar composition head doll that also had a Dressel mark on its shoulder head and on its chemise. This second doll had the German type reinforced knee joints and molded footwear on the lower composition legs.

1883: Otto Dressel Senior was one of the founders of the *Sonneberg Industrial School.*

1890: Date given by the Sonneberg Museum to a papier-mâché shoulder head with molded hair and glass eyes. This head is attributed to Cuno & Otto Dressel. Ht. of head 14 cm. (5½ in.).

1894: Applied for a German patent (D.R.G.M.) for cloth dolls' bodies that were painted or printed.

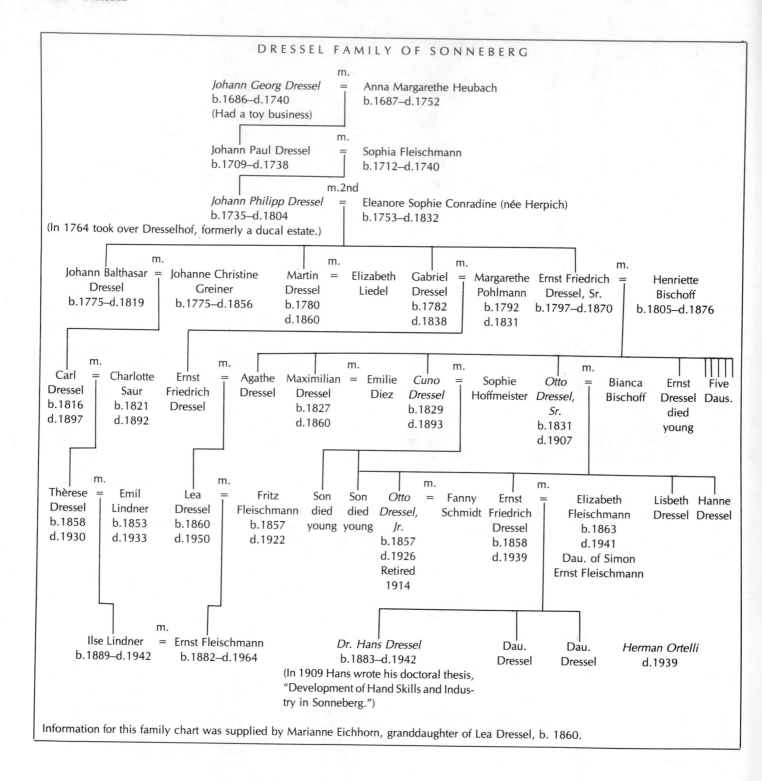

DRESSEL FAMILY OF SONNEBERG

Johann Georg Dressel b.1686–d.1740 (Had a toy business) **m.** = Anna Margarethe Heubach b.1687–d.1752

Johann Paul Dressel b.1709–d.1738 **m.** = Sophia Fleischmann b.1712–d.1740

Johann Philipp Dressel b.1735–d.1804 **m.2nd** = Eleanore Sophie Conradine (née Herpich) b.1753–d.1832
(In 1764 took over Dresselhof, formerly a ducal estate.)

Johann Balthasar Dressel b.1775–d.1819 **m.** = Johanne Christine Greiner b.1775–d.1856

Martin Dressel b.1780 d.1860 **m.** = Elizabeth Liedel

Gabriel Dressel b.1782 d.1838 **m.** = Margarethe Pohlmann b.1792 d.1831

Ernst Friedrich Dressel, Sr. b.1797–d.1870 **m.** = Henriette Bischoff b.1805–d.1876

Carl Dressel b.1816 d.1897 **m.** = Charlotte Saur b.1821 d.1892

Ernst Friedrich Dressel **m.** = Agathe Dressel

Maximilian Dressel b.1827 d.1860 **m.** = Emilie Diez

Cuno Dressel b.1829 d.1893 **m.** = Sophie Hoffmeister

Otto Dressel, Sr. b.1831 d.1907 **m.** = Bianca Bischoff

Ernst Dressel died young

Five Daus.

Thèrese Dressel b.1858 d.1930 **m.** = Emil Lindner b.1853 d.1933

Lea Dressel b.1860 d.1950 **m.** = Fritz Fleischmann b.1857 d.1922

Son died young

Son died young

Otto Dressel, Jr. b.1857 d.1926 Retired 1914 **m.** = Fanny Schmidt

Ernst Friedrich Dressel b.1858 d.1939 **m.** = Elizabeth Fleischmann b.1863 d.1941 Dau. of Simon Ernst Fleischmann

Lisbeth Dressel

Hanne Dressel

Ilse Lindner b.1889–d.1942 **m.** = Ernst Fleischmann b.1882–d.1964

Dr. Hans Dressel b.1883–d.1942
(In 1909 Hans wrote his doctoral thesis, "Development of Hand Skills and Industry in Sonneberg.")

Dau. Dressel

Dau. Dressel

Herman Ortelli d.1939

Information for this family chart was supplied by Marianne Eichhorn, granddaughter of Lea Dressel, b. 1860.

1897: E. F. Dressel was the assignee of a German patent (D.R.G.M.) obtained by *Frederick B. Schultz* for stringing dolls.

1899: *Gebrüder Süssenguth* assigned a patent for jointed dolls to Dressel. Applied for a German patent (D.R.G.M.) for dolls' chemises with flags or coats of arms on them.

Advertised latest novelty dolls' heads, the molded cloth dolls' heads, patented in all countries, unbreakable, washable, and ideal for export. Another new novelty was jointed composition dolls with cloth covering, unbreakable and light. These dolls came dressed in all possible designs. Their wax dolls and wax heads were made washable in accordance with the German Patent of *N. B. Doebrich.* They had factory representatives in Berlin, Hamburg and London.

1901: Applied for German Patent (D.R.G.M.) for dancing dolls and walking dolls.

1903: Advertised their own make of dressed dolls, leather body dolls, and bodies, washable *Täuflinge* and heads.

Sometimes used the name *Mercurius* with their Mercury logo.

1907: *Jutta* was registered in Germany as a trademark by Otto Dressel.

1908: In the Sonneberg Museum there is a collection of *Munich Art Dolls* designed by *Wackerle* and attributed to the production of Cuno & Otto Dressel in this year.

1909: Applied for a German patent (D.R.G.M.). Dr. Hans Dressel wrote THE DISTRIBUTORS AND INDUSTRY OF SONNEBERG, published in Gotha.

1910: Applied for a German patent (D.R.G.M.) for dolls' heads with eyelashes. The Dressels were members of the group who won the grand prize at the Brussels Exposition.

In the Sonneberg Museum, dated by the Museum, there was a Cuno & Otto Dressel doll with a Simon & Halbig bisque head. It had sleeping eyes, a real hair wig, a ball jointed body shaped like a lady and it wore a silk dress and hat. Ht. 56 cm. (22 in.).

1911–14: A *John Wanamaker's* catalog advertised a "Dressel Baby with Human-looking eyes." Hts. 9½, 11½ and 13½ in. (24, 29 and 34 cm.).; price $1.25 to $2.25.

1916: Advertised jointed dolls and babies marked Jutta; dressed dolls marked "C O D"; leather bodies and cloth bodies with and without heads.

1920: Applied for a German patent (D.R.G.M.) for a doll's head with sleeping eyes. Used mainly Simon & Halbig bisque heads.

1920s: Produced a doll named *Kissie* (Kissmequick) in Britain.

1923: Applied for a German patent (D.R.G.M.) for dolls' bodies with voice.

Mid 1920s: Advertised their Jutta line, *Lotte* dolls; and all-wood babies with bent limbs and painted hair, ht. 28 cm. (11 in.). Dolls with composition heads came on either cloth bodies or cardboard bodies. Eight hts.: 28, 31, 36, 38, 42, 46, 51, and 52 cm. (11, 12, 14, 15, 16½, 18, 20, and 20½ in.). The 38 cm. (15 in.) doll also came in a mulatto version. Dolls with composition heads having wigs or painted hair were on bodies with composition arms and sometimes composition legs. These dolls had universal joints and were 40, 41, and 48 cm. (15½, 16, and 19 in.) tall. Dolls with metal or celluloid heads were on pink cloth bodies stuffed with animal hair and having composition or wooden arms. Five hts.: 42, 45, 46, 48, and 50 cm. (16½, 17½, 18, 19, and 19½ in.). They also advertised dolls with leather or cloth bodies, dolls in chemise, dressed dolls and dolls in boxes with a wardrobe of clothes.

1924: They claimed their jointed dolls were as good as the ones made in Waltershausen. Advertised wooden dolls made in the Erzgebirge.

1925: Manufactured *Rock-A-Bye* babies, *Susie,* Jutta jointed dolls, *Mama* dolls and leather body dolls.

1926: Applied for a German patent (D.R.G.M.) for a bent limb baby with movement. Advertised Jutta, fully jointed dolls, bent limb dolls, five-piece standing dolls and a baby doll named *Sonny* as well as a black doll named Sammy.

1927: Advertised babies' and dolls' bodies.

1928: Their dolls included *Bobby & Coon, Dickie & Darkie Baby,* and Jutta dolls.

1929: *Heinerle* was one of their new baby dolls designed by *Helene Haeusler.* Advertised Our Baby and Rockabye.★

825. Composition shoulder-head produced by Cuno & Otto Dressel. It has molded black hair with brushmarks, painted eyes, closed mouth, and a single sew-hole in the front and in the back. Mark: Holz-Masse. *Courtesy of Margaret Whitton.*

826. Wax-over-composition shoulder head possibly produced by Cuno & Otto Dressel ca. 1870s out of a wood-pulp composition. The wax cover extends only to the line of the painted yoke. The head originally had a wig. The eyes are painted blue. On the inside of the back shoulder is impressed a mark (see III. 831). A doll with a similar impression had on its body an oval stamp with the interior of the stamp very similar to the mark shown in the first COLLECTOR'S ENCYCLOPEDIA OF DOLLS, III. 488. On the front shoulder is painted XV. H. of shoulder head 5½ in. (14 cm.). *Collection of Robert and Katrin Burlin.*

828A & B. Composition shoulder head produced by Cuno & Otto Dressel on a cloth body with leather arms and boots made by Philip Goldsmith. See Ill. 1079A & B. It has molded hair and painted features. Holz-Masse mark is the same as that shown in Ill. 481B in the first COLLECTOR'S ENCYCLOPEDIA OF DOLLS. H. 16 in. (40.5 cm.). H. of head only, 4½ in. (11.5 cm.). *Coleman Collection.*

827. Wax-over composition doll's shoulder head produced by Cuno & Otto Dressel. It has a wig, painted eyes, closed mouth and a molded blouse top. Impressed mark inside the back shoulder is shown in Ill. 831. On the lower front shoulder in gold is XXXVIII. *Courtesy of the Wenham Museum.*

829. Doll produced by Cuno & Otto Dressel. It has a bisque head made by Simon & Halbig, a wig, sleeping brown glass eyes, pierced ears, open mouth with four teeth and a fully jointed composition body. Original dress. Mark shows that the head is mold #1349. H. 17 in. (43 cm.). *Courtesy of Sotheby Parke Bernet Inc., N.Y.*

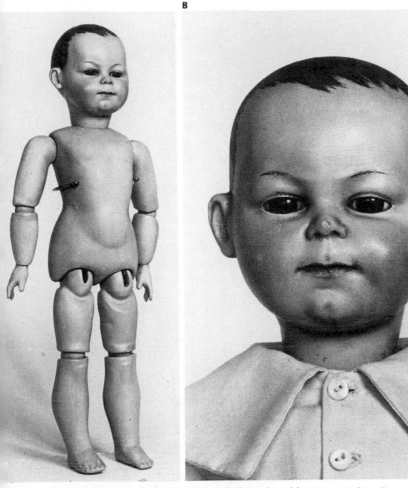

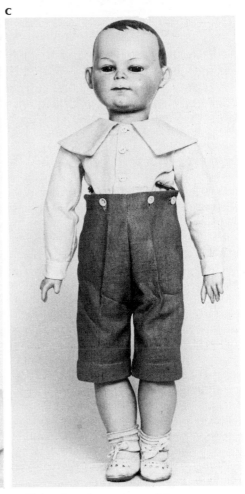

830A, B, & C. All-composition doll produced by Cuno & Otto Dressel. It has painted hair with brushmarks, stationary blue glass eyes, ears stick out, closed mouth, dimple in the chin, and outlined nails on the hands. Mark on body is a red stamped "Holz-Masse" figure. Original Oliver Twist style suit with blue trousers. H 19½ in. (49.5 cm.). *Courtesy of the Margaret Woodbury Strong Museum. Photo by Harry Bickelhaupt.*

O PATENTED O
HOLZMASSE

831

(1896 COD 1 DEP MADE IN GERMANY)

832

A. 1776. M
C.O.D 3/0 D E P.
made in Germany

835A

833

2/0

S & H
1349
Dressel
3

834

6/0X

A M
COD93-A-DEP
made in Germany

835B

Heubach · Köppelsdorf
Jutta-Baby
Dressel
Germany
1922

836

831–835A & B–836. Marks on dolls produced by Cuno & Otto Dressel. No. 831 is found on early composition shoulder heads seen in Ills. 826 & 827. Nos. 835A and 835B are on bisque heads made by Armand Marseille. No. 834 is on one of the bisque heads made by Simon & Halbig. No. 836 is on one of the bisque head Jutta dolls. No. 833 is the "Holz-Masse" mark on a composition shoulder head.

Dressel, Wilhelm. 1881–1920. Sonneberg, Thür. He was probably the Wilhelm Dressel (b. 1849, d. 1928), a descendant of Martin Dressel (b. 1780, d. 1860) and cousin of Cuno & Otto Dressel. Wilhelm was a doll manufacturer and exporter.

1910: Member of the Sonneberg Group who won the Grand Prize at the Brussels Exposition.

1913: The son, Fritz Dressel, was the President when this business was sold to *F. W. Woolworth.* (See also **Sonneberg Industrial School.**)

Dressel & Koch. 1893–1905. Köppelsdorf, Thür. Porcelain factory where dolls' heads were made. In 1897 it became Koch & Weithase[+] and, in 1902, Hering & Weithase. The Hering was *Julius Hering.*★

%

D&K dep

837. Mark used by Dressel & Koch on their porcelain dolls' heads.

Drinking Doll. 1904. The bisque head on the doll contained a rubber bulb that with applied pressure sucked up the liquid in a glass nursing bottle that was attached to the mouth by a long rubber tube. Ht. 13 in. (33 cm.). (See also **Bébé Teteur.**)

Drobik. Early 1900s. Sonneberg area, Thür. He designed some of the *Armand Marseille* dolls' heads.

Drowsy Dick. 1914. Composition head *Horsman* baby doll; wore a long lawn dress and cap; style no. 142; priced $8.50 doz. wholesale.★

Drusilla Dolls. 1920s. Six original Drusilla dolls were shown at a New York exhibition of dolls.

Druzba, Th. 1894. Altona, Germany. Applied for a German patent (D.R.G.M.) for aluminum dolls and dolls' heads.

Dschang-Go. 1925–26. Trade name of a *Lenci* doll, no. 188, representing an Oriental playing a musical instrument. Ht. 23 in. (58.5 cm.).

Du Pont de Nemours, E. I., & Co. 1919–30 and later. Wilmington, Del., and elsewhere. They made materials that were used in the production of dolls. This was especially true of the Du Pont *Viscoloid Co.,* a subsidiary.

1927: Fairfield, Conn., factory, made coated rubber materials and gum rubber products used for dolls, dolls' voices and dolls' clothes. Arlington, N.J., and Leominster, Mass., factories made Pyralin, also known as Pyroxylin plastic, which was used for dolls' faces.

1928: *Pacific Novelty Division,* New York City, advertised a

No. 142
"DROWSY DICK"
Trade Mark

838. Drowsy Dick produced by Horsman and advertised in their catalog of ca. 1914 has molded hair and half closed eyes. The composition head is affixed to the body so that it appears to move forward as if nodding.

large line of Viscoloid dolls including *Vamp* and Bonnet Dolls dressed in crepe paper. Some of the dolls dressed in crepe paper were 7 in. (18 cm.) tall.★

Du Pre Studios. 1930 and later. St. Paul, Minn. Made cloth dolls.

Du Serre, J. 1904–10. Paris. Was awarded a Diplome d' Honneur for his display of dolls at the Brussels Exposition.★

Duabeck, Paul. 1921. Berlin. Applied for a German patent (D.R.P.) for dolls.

Dublin Toy Co. 1915–17. Dublin, Ireland. A philanthropic company that put girls to work making cloth dolls and wax heads, arms and legs for dolls to go on cloth bodies. The dolls were dressed or undressed. *A. Bell* was the sole agent.

Duborjal, J. & A. 1930. Paris. Made and/or distributed dolls.

Duchess. 1903–8. Trade name of a doll imported by *Samstag & Hilder.*★

Duchess. 1914. Name of a doll with a bisque *Armand Marseille* head. Size number 10 was 26 in. (66 cm.) tall. See Ill. 839.★

839. Duchess, name of a doll with a bisque head made by Armand Marseille. The doll has a wig, sleeping blue glass eyes, open mouth and a fully jointed composition body. Mark: "Duchess//A 3 M." H. 17 in. (43 cm.). *Courtesy of Sotheby Parke Bernet Inc., N.Y.*

Duchess. 1921–23. Dressed stockinet doll made by *Martha Chase.* Ht. 12 in. (30.5 cm.); price $7.50.★

Duckme Doll Co. 1920. New York City. Produced *Vamps,* dolls made of wood-fiber composition.★

Ducrot, Aîné (Sr.). 1823. Paris. Distributed dolls and dolls' clothes.

Dudovich, Marcello. 1920s. Italy. Name of the artist whose designs were used for some of the *Lenci* dolls. He was a painter and designer, born in 1878 in Trieste. He exhibited in Milan in 1905.

Dudu. 1930. Cloth doll made by *Norah Wellings.*

Dufayel. Before 1924. Paris. By 1924 it had become the Palais de la Nouveauté. Distributed dolls.

Duha, Melanie. See **Our Shop.**

840. Postcard showing a lady doll in the exact pose shown in the Lenci catalog of 1925/26. The card picture which also dates from the 1920s is signed by Dudovich, who was one of the principal designers for the Lenci firm in the 1920s.

Dulcie Daring, The Flying Doll. 1929. A homemade gingham cloth doll representing an aviatrix for which instructions were given in MODERN PRISCILLA. The doll had short curly auburn hair made of crewel wool, a flat face and a stuffed body with long slender arms and legs. It wore a tan Palm Beach cloth suit with brown leather buttons, belt and sleeve straps. Brown leather was also used for the helmet, goggles, gloves and high boots. It had removable beige colored sports shirt, brown tie, and athletic underwear (shirt and shorts).

Dumas, Mme. 1836–52. Paris. Made dolls with wax shoulder heads.

Dummig, Charles. 1848–65. Philadelphia, Pa. Handled wax-over-composition head dolls. See Ills. 841 and 842 for a doll distributed from his 1865 address.

Dumont, Ray W. 1926. New York City. Registered in U.S. the trademark *Widget* for dolls.

Dumpty. 1903–30 and later. Name of a clown in the *Schoenhut* Circus. Partner of *Humpty.*

1921: It came in two sizes when dressed in cotton.

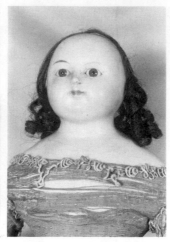

841A & B. Close-up and overall of a wax-over-composition shoulder head doll handled by Charles Dummig of Philadelphia. The black hair is inserted into a slit in the crown. It has stationary blue glass eyes and a closed mouth. The body is cloth with stamped leather arms. The original clothes represent a girl. Mark: Ill. 842. H. 24½ in. (62 cm.). Head only 6¾ in. (17 cm.). *Courtesy of Frances Walker.*

842. Charles Dummig's paper label attached to the back of a wax-over-composition shoulder head.

Dun Lany (Dunlany), William P. 1917–18. Chicago, Ill. Obtained a U.S. patent for a rotatable doll joint with a disc on the torso. This patent was assigned to *Sears.*

Duncan, Mrs. Josephine Angèlique. Before 1923. Daughter of a founder of St. Joseph, Mo. Made cloth dolls.

Duncan, William. 1926. Los Angeles, Calif. Applied for a U.S. patent for a multi-face doll.

Dupont. See **Du Pont.**

Dura. 1925. Trademark used by *H. Josef Leven.*

843. Dura mark used by H. Josef Leven for dolls.

Dura Porcelain Co. (Empress Pottery). 1915–18. Stoke-on-Trent, Staffs. This firm had two potters and one color expert. Their only products were *British Ceramic* dolls' heads and dolls' limbs. They made shoulder heads and socket heads,

heads with painted hair, and bald heads for wigs. The heads had hand-painted eyes that were enameled in blue, brown, or grey or had eyesockets for glass eyes. The heads came in various sizes. One head was reported to have been marked "Benco Dura." A shoulder head with black glass eyes and an open-closed mouth was marked "DU 12 RA."

844. British Ceramic shoulder head made by the Dura Porcelain Co. at their Empress Pottery during World War I. It has a wig, sleeping eyes, and an open mouth. The body is cloth. Mark: "DU 12 RA." H. 17½ in. (44 cm.). *Courtesy of Marianne Cieslik. Photo by Jürgen Cieslik.*

DU(28)RA

845. Incised mark found on British Ceramic heads made by the Dura Porcelain Co.

Durabel. 1909. Name used as a mark by *Kley & Hahn.*

Durand. 1824. France. Made dolls and shoulder heads for dolls.

Durand, E. 1927–28. Paris. Agent in France for *Dean's.*

Durrel Co. 1930. Boston, Mass. Produced *Trixy Toys.*

Düsel, Heinrich. 1911. Neustadt near Coburg, Thür. Applied for a German patent (D.R.G.M.) relating to dolls.

Dutch, B. 1922–26. Listed under dolls in British directory.

Dutch Boy. 1921. Cloth doll made by *Chessler Co.,* dressed in felt garments.

Dutch Boy & Dutch Girl. 1917. Stuffed leather dolls made by *Western Art Leather Co.* The leather was colored and the dolls were dressed and had their hands in their pockets. "Hans" was on the boy's belt and the girl had two long braids.

Dutch Boy & Girl. 1929. Cloth dolls with hand-painted features and hair made by *Nelke.* They had one-piece jersey bodies. Ht. 10 in. (25.5 cm.); price $3.90 doz. wholesale.

Dutch Cleanser Dolls. See **Old Dutch Cleanser Dolls.**

Dutch Costume Dolls. 1911–14. Dolls made by *Horsman,* sometimes with a *Campbell Kid* head, named Hans (Dutch Hans[+]), Gretchen, Willem and Wilhelmina.

1914: Girl wore a red waist, blue skirt, white apron, striped stockings, and felt "wooden shoes." Ht. 12¾ in. (32.5 cm.); price $17.00 doz. wholesale.

Dutch Costume Dolls. 1917–26. Composition head dolls dressed by *Georgene Averill* in felt Dutch style costumes. The dolls had painted features and molded hair; later some of them came with wigs. Their cloth bodies were jointed at the shoulders and hips. They were produced by *Averill Manufacturing Co.* and distributed by *Butler Bros.*

1917: Hts. 11, 14½ and 17½ in. (28, 37, and 44.5 cm.).

1926: Hts. 10, 13, and 14 in. (25.5, 33, and 35.5 cm.). The shoes were part of the feet on the 10 in. (25.5 cm.) dolls and the larger sizes wore wooden shoes.

Dutch Dolls. In 1923 according to TOYS AND NOVELTIES Dutch dolls were dressed as a Volendam fisherman wearing a knit jersey, baggy gray trousers held up by a wide belt furnished with two silver bosses, and a strangely shaped cap. The Volendam woman doll wore a voluminous skirt and a white coif covering its plainly arranged hair.

Scheveningen fisher maidens wore countless petticoats standing out stiffly. Their Sunday attire included a lace headgear and heavy coral necklace.

Brabant peasants wore flower laden bonnets.

Spakenburg women wore gaily colored aprons and tiny straw hats. Milk maids had heavy wooden clogs, long white aprons, gay shawls and linen caps.

There were also dolls representing judges, lawyers and policemen.

In 1924 Dutch dolls were described as being long limbed and dressed as *Pierrot.* (See also **Regional Costume Dolls and Douwes.**)

Dutch Dolls.[+] See **Peg Wooden Dolls** and **Grödner tal.**

Dutchman. 1899. Imported doll distributed by *Butler Bros.* I had a painted face with a mustache, cloth body and was dressed as a Dutchman. Hts. 9 and 11½ in. (23 and 29 cm.)

Duty on Dolls. In 1912 the U.S. duty on imported dolls (see **Imports, Dolls**[+]) was 35 percent of the value and the duty plus the shipping and insurance cost amounted to nearly 80 percent of the value of a typical German doll according to a study made by TOYS AND NOVELTIES. Thus a doll costing $1.00 in Germany would cost about $1.80 when it reached New York. The 1922 act raised the duty from 35 percent to 70 percent. By 1926 the duty on dressed dolls was 90 percent when the dress was made of artificial silk or trimmed with lace or embroidery. PLAYTHINGS in 1908 stated that the U.S. was the only country where the duty was based on value; other countries based their duty on weight. As a result the cheaper and heavier dolls were imported into the U.S., while the lighter and more expensive dolls went to other countries. The U.S. was the largest buyer of German dolls, with Great Britain ranking next. Sometimes dolls bore a tag marked "Douane," which referred to the duty in France. (See also **Show Dolls, German Dolls, 1921,** and **Tariff.**)

Duval & Dizengromel. 1930 and later. Paris. Made dolls.

Duvall, Mlle. Fannie E. 1916–18. Paris. Created cloth dolls with smiling three dimensional faces and simple clothes. The dolls had a sequin sewn on to represent the pupil of the eye. Also made clothes for dolls.

CRÉE par FANNIE E. DUVALL
OUVROIR
180, Rue de G

846. Duvall mark stamped on dolls.

Duvinage & Harinkouch (Harinkouck). See **Giroux, Alphonse, & Co.**

Duyts, Abraham. 1924–26. London. Imported and distributed dolls.

Dwarf. See **Snik.**

Dykman, Howard. 1921–23. East Orange, N.J. Obtained a U.S. patent for a doll having a reversible garment affixed to it.

1922: Applied for a German patent (D.R.P.) for usable dolls.

Dymaob, A. C. Komcko Go. Name found on a bisque head that may have been made in Russia. (See Ill. 2266.)

E

E. D. E. D. heads were often found on marked *Jumeau* bodies especially the Diplôme d' Honneur ones. Some E. D. heads had the check marks that were associated with heads having Jumeau markings. The size-height relationship between some of the marked E. D. dolls and the marked Jumeau dolls was very similar. The E. D. Bébés had a small size 1/0 that is 8½ in. (21.5 cm.) tall which has not been found for Jumeau Bébés. Sizes 15 and 16 have not been found on E. D. Bébés. One of the E. D. heads on a marked Jumeau body has been found in a box marked *Bébé le Radieux,* but it is not known whether the doll was originally in this box. (See also **Danel & Cie.** and **Denamur, Etienne.**)

E. F. Co. Ca. 1930. Sydney, Australia. Doll with an aluminum head; molded hair; wooden sleeping eyes; dimples in cheeks; cloth body wired to the flange neck; composition lower arms; long slim straight legs. Rectangular mark on the lower back of the body is undecipherable. Body seams of the cloth body were up the middle front and middle back of the body.

Eade, G. W., & Co. 1922–26. Aurora, Ill. Made *Cinderella Dainty Dolly Dresses,* a line of washable percale, gingham, and sateen clothes for dolls. The dolls' dresses were reproductions of the dresses made for people by this same concern.

1922: Advertised four styles.

1923: Line included 37 numbers including no. 230 a two piece middy suit with a red tie and white collar; no. 130 with four aprons and a bonnet.

1924: A variety of aprons including a rubberized apron were in the line. One outfit called a "Chink" suit had a black sateen tunic and trousers trimmed with bright colored binding. A dress of sateen also trimmed with contrasting colors had matching medallion "cat head" pockets.

Eagle Doll & Toy Co. 1927–29. New York City. Made composition dolls' heads, hands and similar products which enabled them to be members of the *Doll Parts Manufacturing Assoc.*

Eagle Works. See **Harwin & Co.**

Ears. *Ernest Bocchin* in 1929 obtained a U.S. patent for placing compressible protruding ears in a conventional doll's head and activating a bellows in these ears to produce a sound.★

East London (Federation of Suffragettes) Toy Factory. 1915–28. London. Made cloth dolls; dolls with *British Ceramic* or wax heads and limbs in original designs as well as dolls' clothes. Sizes varied up to life size. Sometimes used the initials E.L.S.F.

1915: Cloth dolls had molded faces, movable heads and arms. The British Ceramic and wax-headed dolls represented British Babies, Japanese babies, brown babies, Belgian peasants, *Pierrots,* soldiers, Boy Scouts and Girl Guides. They also made wooden dolls.

1917: Dolls included *Puck, Babies in the Wood, Dolly Dimple,* and a rattle doll.

1924–28: Made long-limbed mascot dolls.

Eastern Doll Manufacturing Co. 1923–24. New York City. Made character and *Mama* dolls with or without wigs, and with sleeping eyes. The character dolls came in hts. 12 to 24 in. (30.5 to 61 cm.) and cost 25¢ and up.★

Eaton, T., Co. Possibly before 1901–30 and later. Toronto. Distributed various kinds of dolls. Designated as buyer No. 16/10 by Cuno & Otto *Dressel* according to the Ciesliks.

1901: Advertised bisque-head dolls with stationary or moving eyes, composition body; priced 25¢ to $8.50. Undressed kid-body dolls with stationary or moving eyes cost 15¢ to $7.00. Other dolls included ones with china heads and limbs on cloth bodies; *Eaton's Beauty;* Ma and Pa talking dolls; black dolls; rubber dolls; dressed dolls' house dolls; and dolls' heads of bisque, china, or metal.

1914: Advertised 2 styles of dolls with bisque heads on bent limb composition bodies. Ht. 11 in. (28 cm.); priced 49¢. Dolls with bisque heads on composition bodies came undressed 8 and 10 in. (20.5 and 25.5 cm.) tall; priced 10¢ and 49¢. Similar dolls came dressed in 4 styles. Hts. 14 to 20 in. (35.5 to 51 cm.); priced 25¢ to $2.00. Bisque heads on cloth bodies. Hts. 13½ and 17 in. (34 and 43 cm.); priced 25¢ and 49¢. Bisque heads on kid bodies. Ht. 16 in. (40.5 cm.); priced 49¢. Bisque heads on imitation kid bodies. Ht. 12½ in. (31.5 cm.); priced 25¢. Other dolls included Ma and Pa voice dolls with composition head and limbs, *Rex Kid, Golden Locks,* and an all-celluloid baby. Ht. 8½ in. (21.5 cm.); priced 25¢. There was also a doll with a celluloid face on a cork stuffed body. Ht. 11½ in. (29 cm.); priced 24¢.

1918: Advertised all-bisque dolls, jointed at shoulders and hips. Ht. 5½ in. (14 cm.); priced 19¢. A bisque-head baby, ht. 9 in. (23 cm.); priced 95¢. Other bisque-head dolls were named *Baby Bright, Baby Ella,* and *Baby Ruth.* Composition-head dolls came with wigs, ht. 15 in. (38 cm.); priced $1.25 to $2.25; or with painted hair, hts. 10½, 13½, and 18 in. (26.5, 34, and 45.5 cm.); priced 25¢ to $1.00. Other composition-head dolls included *Campbell Kids* and Red Cross Nurses, all-composition *Dainty Dorothy,* and a Japanese doll dressed in a kimono. Ht. 9 in. (23 cm.); priced 25¢. The all-wood dolly-faced *Schoenhut* with wig wearing a union suit was 15 in. (38 cm.) tall; priced $5.25. All-celluloid dolls jointed at the shoulders and hips. Hts. 4 and 6 in. (10 and 15 cm.); priced 15¢ and 29¢. A celluloid head with molded hair and a cloth body. Ht. 10 in. (25.5 cm.); priced 29¢. A *Cowboy* doll had a celluloid head and an *Eskimo* doll had a celluloid face.★

Eaton's Beauty. 1901–15 and probably later. Name of a special doll sold by *Eaton.* It had a wig and a ball-jointed composition body; the heads were also sold separately.

1901: Doll priced $1.00 to $6.00.

1914: Hts. 21, 25 and 27 in. (53.5, 63.5 and 68.5 cm.); priced $1.00 to $4.50. A separate head and a wig each cost 35¢.

Ebaso. Ca. 1930. Trade name used by *Emil Bauersachs.* See **Bauersachs, Emil.**

Eccles (New Eccles Rubber Works). 1921–26. Eccles, Lancashire. Manufactured rubber dolls with molded clothes of various designs including those representing men, boys, girls, a Scotsman, and a bather. Their agent for Britain and the Colonies was *Cave & Easterling.*

Ecco. See **Eckstein & Co.**

Echold, Rudolf. 1912. Waltershausen, Thür. Applied for a German patent (D.R.G.M.) for dolls.

Echovarria, Eduardo. 1926. Granite City, Ill. Applied for a U.S. patent for a talking doll.

Eckardt, Ges. Geb. 1926–30. Sonneberg, Thür. Obtained a British patent for dolls made of wood or porcelain with the upper part of the doll made of the same material as the body and the lower limbs made of flexible soft fabric. (See also **Adolph Strauss.**)

Eckardt, Mr. It has been reported that before World War I he made the doll models for *Wislizenus;* after World War I he made the doll models for *König & Wernicke.*

Eckardt, Hermann V. 1927–28. Brooklyn, N.Y. Obtained a U.S. patent for a doll that was jointed at the neck, shoulders, and hips. It had a baby bottle of opaque glass with a red rubber nipple that fitted into the doll's mouth. The doll came with a play pen. This patent was assigned to *Strauss-Eckhardt.*

Eckardt, Reinhold. 1913. Neustadt near Coburg, Thür. Applied for a German patent (D.R.G.M.) for a doll's head with eyes that moved vertically.

Eckart & Co. (H. E. Eckart). 1820–1930 and later. Nürnberg, Bavaria; Sonneberg, Thür., and London. Founded in 1820 by Georg Phillip Eckart who was succeeded by his son C. R. Eckart, and then Georg's grandson, Hans Englebert Eckart, who started a business in London in 1895. Hans was succeeded in 1928 by his sons, Walter Eckart and Ronald Eckart[+] in London, but Walter and Ronald had already been in charge of the Sonneberg branch and were known as W. & R. Eckart. Hans Eckart prior to World War I was the factory agent for several German manufacturers of dolls including *Bessels, Max Carl* and *Wittzack.*

In 1928 THE TOY TRADER, a British periodical, gave the following account of the business of Mr. H. E. Eckart:

"With the retirement of Mr. H. E. Eckart there passes from the trade a well-known personality who has been prominent as a toy importer in London for many years past. The name of Eckart's is almost as old as the toy trade itself, at least the trade as we know it today. The original business of Eckart & Co. was founded at Nurenberg, as long ago as the year 1820, by Mr. George Philipp Eckart, grandfather of the subject of these notes. . . .

"The original founder of the firm used to travel with his samples on horseback, and it is interesting to learn that even at that time, nearly a hundred years ago, his complaint was about the keen competition and price-cutting which was then prevalent. At the outset the business of Eckart & Co. was carried on mostly with Belgium, Holland and France, but later on business connections were opened up with England. At a later date, Mr. C. R. Eckart, a son of the founder of the business, began visiting this country twice a year, opening temporary showrooms; this was about 1865, and when his son, Mr. H. E. Eckart . . ., was seventeen years of age, he made his first trip to London.

"In 1895 Mr. H. E. Eckart started a business in London under the style of H. E. Eckart & Co. This was carried on at Bradford Avenue, Redcross Street, and later in Barbican. From the commencement of the firm, Mr. Eckart continued to develop an ever-increasing business, and when the war broke out in August, 1914, he had over £30,000 worth of orders on his books which he was unable to execute. Such a set back might have staggered a weaker man, but Mr. Eckart

faced the situation and without wasting much time he started a doll factory in London, where he ultimately employed about one hundred and twenty workers, producing London-made dolls, taking for his designs the best models of certain German manufacturers. This venture was a great success and helped to fill the shortage of dolls which was experienced in this country during the early years of the war.

"When the war was over, Mr. Eckart, in common with other manufacturers who had started making toys in this country, found that it was no longer possible to compete with the German-made dolls, and accordingly he went over to Sonneberg, where he bought a large combined warehouse and factory, which he established under an experienced local manager, with a view to producing dolls and toys for the English market.

"In the meantime, his two sons, Mr. Walter and Mr. Ronald Eckart, who both served in the British Army during the war, were now of an age to assist him in the business, and after being discharged from the army they joined him, assisting in the managing and travelling, and as a result have built up a successful business in the Sonneberg trade.

"It will thus be seen that although Mr. H. E. Eckart is retiring from the business the name of Eckart still continues to be a big factor in the toy trade in London, and, we understand, it is the intention of the present proprietors who are now trading as W. & R. Eckart, Ltd. to open up a house in Nurenberg very shortly. Mr. W. Eckart has a fourteen months old son, Derrick, and in due course this young man will no doubt take his place in the business, making the fifth generation since the founding of the business in 1820."

1922: W. & R. Eckart announced "That they have cleared their Sonneberg Warehouse from top to bottom and have shipped the whole stock of dolls, dressed and undressed to their London warehouse. The shipment represents the value of about ten million marks. . . .

"In view of the fact that Messrs. W. & R. Eckart have their own factory in Sonneberg and ship direct to London, they are able to offer these dolls on the most advantageous terms." The shipment of dolls from Sonneberg to London was due to the "collapse of the German Exchange."

Sometimes they used bisque heads made by *Ernst Heubach.*

1925: W. & E. Eckart advertised "The Mother's Darling," a new born infant type doll which had a wobbly head, tiny moving eyes, and a self-activated voice.

1926: Advertised New born baby dolls, Pierrots and a doll with sleeping eyes that fed itself and said "Mama."

Ecker, . . . Co. 1926. New York City. Made molds for dolls.

540 – 4
GEO
5

847. Mark used by Eckart & Co.

Eckert, Heinrich. 1901–5. Munich, Bavaria. Obtained several patents in Austria for ball and socket joints for dolls in addition to his French, British and German patents. (See Ill. 363.)★

Eckert, Rudolf. 1903. Waltershausen, Thür. Applied for a German patent (D.R.G.M.) for dolls.

Eckhardt, Gebr. Used *Schoenau & Hoffmeister* bisque heads according to the research of the Ciesliks.

Eckhart, C. F., Co. 1925–26. Port Washington, Wis. Made dolls.

Eckner, Heinrich. 1898. Grossenhain, Germany. Applied for a German patent (D.R.G.M.).

Eckstein, Hermann. 1899–1929. Neustadt near Coburg, Thür., and, later, Bavaria. Manufactured dolls.

1914: Applied for a German patent (D.R.G.M.) for dolls.

1927: Used in some of his dolls the *H. Steiner*'s "life like moving eyes"—sleeping eyes that also moved sideways. Eckstein made bent-limb baby dolls, new born baby dolls, dolls with bisque heads having bangs and bobbed hair wigs; open mouth and teeth. The jointed composition bodies had heads which hid the neck joints. There were also stuffed felt dolls.★

Eckstein & Co. 1926–30 and later. Sonneberg, Thür., and Nürnberg, Bavaria. Manufactured dolls including baby dolls, dolls with mask faces, long limbed dolls, and cloth body dolls.

1926: Belonged to the *German Manufacturer's Assoc.* in New York City.

1927: Line of flexible dolls called Ecco. A new doll was named *Revue Girl.*★

Eclipse Doll Manufacturing Co. 1919–21. Springfield, Mass. Successor was Worthy Doll Manufacturing Co. Made dolls.

1919: Made fully jointed all-composition dolls. Hts. 15, 19, and 22 in. (38, 48, and 56 cm.).

1920: 50 new styles of stuffed dolls; 18 new styles of baby dolls; three new styles of fully jointed dolls. Six styles of the jointed dolls came in four hts.: 15, 17, 19, and 22 in. (38, 43, 48, and 56 cm.). A ball-jointed composition doll was shown wearing a dress with a high waistline and a hat with a soft crown.

1921: Made eight lines of dolls with 24 style nos. The dolls had composition heads, molded hair or mohair wigs, painted features, cloth bodies stuffed with excelsior. Ht. 12 to 18 in. (30.5 to 45.5 cm.).★

Écolière (Écolier). 1913. Name of a doll representing a school girl (school boy) with wig, fully jointed, dressed, and carrying a schoolbag, but the doll can be undressed. It was distributed by *Samaritaine.* Ht. 34 cm. (13½ in.) priced $1.38.

Eddy, W. Osgood. 1925–26. Middleboro, Mass. Made dolls' shoes.

Edel, Anton, Jr. Early to mid 1800s. Munich, Bavaria. Distributed dolls. Among the dolls that he advertised were: wooden dolls with movable limbs; dolls with wood or papier-mâché heads on leather bodies; some of these had molded hair and some had real hair; these dolls also came dressed in various costumes; carved wooden soldiers; *Polichinelle* figures with wooden or papier-mâché heads. This information was provided by a German toy list in the possession of R. C. and Ruth Mathes.

Edelkind. 1918–28. Trademark registered in Germany by *Hugo Wiegand* for dolls.

1925: Advertised "Lieb Edelkind" (Beloved Noble Child) as a new wonder doll.

1928: Edelkind dolls came with wigs, glass eyes and composition baby, toddler or child bodies.★

Edelman, H. M. 1926. New York City. Created stockinet handpainted dolls.

Edelmann, Edmund. 1921–30 and later. Sonneberg, Thür. Manufactured and exported dolls of various types under the brand name *Melitta, Mine* and *Mona.* He made bent limb baby dolls, fully jointed composition dolls, stuffed dolls, dressed and undressed dolls, dolls' heads, wigs and other supplies for doll hospitals. He used *Schoenau & Hoffmeister* or *Armand Marseille* bisque heads. The London agent was Martin Raphael & Co.

1921: He had sample rooms at Düsseldorf, Hamburg and Leipzig.

1924: Sole London agent was *L. & A. L. Goodman.*★

Eden Bébé (Eden Puppe). 1890–99, made by *Fleischmann & Blodel;* 1899–1953, made by *Société Française de Fabrication de Bébés & Jouets* (S.F.B.J.). This was a popular doll in the Paris stores prior to World War I. It was less expensive than many of the other French Bébés and came in many versions—black, white, walking, talking, *Kiss-Throwing,* dressed, undressed, with bisque heads or composition heads. A bisque-head Eden Bébé marked "Eden Bébé//Paris //11// Déposé" had a teen-age type body.

A doll with a bisque head marked "C//10/0" and red check marks over the ear had a wig on the typical brownish composition pate that matched the brownish composition body of the type made by the S.F.B.J. after 1899. On the upper forehead were three holes—one in front and the other two on either side beside the large hole for the pate. This doll had stationary blue glass eyes, an open mouth and teeth. Under its regional costume it wore its original flimsy flowered chemise on which was stamped in red a rectangle with the words "EDEN BÉBÉ//Breveté S.G.D.G." On the sole of one of its shoes was the paper sticker of *A la Recompense* for the shop from which it was originally purchased. Ht. 10½ in. (26.5 cm.).

Eden Bébé heads have been reported marked *Simon & Halbig.*

Because of all the variations a size-height table for Eden Bébés can only be considered a rough approximation and no chronological trends are discernible. Only because of the

APPROXIMATE SIZE–HEIGHT RELATIONSHIPS FOR EDEN BÉBÉS		
Size No.	Height cm.	in.
1	28	11
2	31	12
3	35	14
4	39	15½
5	42	16½
6	44	17½
7	47	18½
8	50	19½
9	54/55	21½
10	59/60	23½
11	64	25
12	67	26½
13	70	27½
14	75	29½
15	78	31

abundance of available height data in Paris store catalogs does a table seem to be of some value.

1896: *Magenta* store offered a 28 cm. (11 in.) Eden Bébé caucasian for 10¢ and Mulatto for 13¢.

1898: Magenta advertised a talking, sleeping Eden Bébé. Ht. 39 cm. (15½ in.) for 55¢.

1900–1901: *Pont Neuf*, a Paris store, advertised three style nos. of Eden Bébés in chemises. No. 15 had a wig, sleeping eyes, open mouth with teeth and a fully jointed composition body. The chemise was made of satinette. Five hts.: 29, 36, 46, 53, and 58 cm. (11½, 14, 18, 21, and 23 in.); priced 50¢ to $2.25. No. 17 was similar to No. 15 but it was not fully jointed. Ht. 47 cm. (18½ in.); priced 35¢. No. 20 was similar to No. 17 but with a composition head instead of a bisque head. Ht. 49 cm. (19½ in.); priced 98¢.

1901: *Samaritaine* advertised Kiss-throwing Eden Bébés, ht. 57 cm. (22½ in.) for $2.05.

1902: Samaritaine described their Kiss-throwing Eden Bébé as having the "head and wig of a Bébé Samaritaine": *Bébé Samaritaine* was made by *Jumeau* (S.F.B.J.) in this period. A walking Eden Bébé "Walks on wheels."

1910: *Ville de St. Denis* advertised a bisque-head jointed Eden Bébé in a chemise. Hts. 35 and 37 cm. (14 and 14½ in.); priced 13¢ and 19¢.

The composition head, jointed Eden Bébé in chemise came in eight hts.: 33, 36, 40, 41, 43, 47, 49, and 53 cm. (13, 14, 15½, 16, 17, 18½, 19½, and 21 in.); priced 58¢ to $1.45.

1911: *La Place Clichy* advertised Eden Bébé with mama-papa pull strings. Ht. 36 cm. (14 in.) for 58¢.

Modernes described their Eden Bébé character heads as being "absolutely infantine."

1912: *Paris Montpelier* advertised Eden Bébé character dolls with bisque heads. Ht. 34 cm. (13½ in.); costing 29¢, and with composition head 35 cm. (14 in.) costing 58¢.

1913: *L'Hotel de Ville* advertised Eden Bebé with a bisque head, sleeping eyes, hair eyelashes, sewn wig, fully jointed composition body, wearing a chemise. Hts. 28 to 78 cm. (11 to 31 in.); price 59¢ to $5.40.

1914: Ville de St. Denis advertised composition head, jointed Eden Bébé in a chemise. Eight hts.: 32, 37, 41, 45, 47, 48, 51 and 57 cm. (12½, 14½, 16, 17½, 18½, 19, 20 and 22½ in.); priced 32¢ to $1.58.

1919: *Aux Trois Quartiers* advertised Eden Bébé with sleeping eyes. Ht. 40 cm. (15½ in.).

1920s: A bisque-head doll in its original box marked "EDEN BÉBÉ//FABRICATION FRANÇAISE" also had the *Unis France* mark on the box and "JE FAIS DODO" on the doll's skirt.

1950: According to a letter from M. Moynot, the then current President of the S.F.B.J., they were still using the Eden Bébé molds.

1953: S.F.B.J. renewed their Eden Bébé Trademark. (See THE COLLECTOR'S BOOK OF DOLLS' CLOTHES for illustrations which show various store offerings: for 1894, Ill. 428 A; 1896, Ill. 438; 1898, Ill. 444A; 1901, Ill. 526; and 1902, Ill. 531.)★

848A & B. Bisque socket head produced for Fleischmann & Blödel and known as an Eden Bébé. It has a blond wig, stationary blue glass eyes and a closed mouth. It is on a five-piece composition body. The clothes are replacements. Mark: Ill. 853. H. 13½ in. (34 cm.). *Courtesy of Sara Kocker.*

848C. Eden Bébé with a bisque head having a wig, stationary blue eyes, pierced ears, closed mouth and a ball jointed composition body. Mark: Ill. 854. H. 22½ in. (57 cm.). *Courtesy of Hazel Ulseth.*

849. Pair of Eden Bébé dolls with wigs, blue glass eyes, pierced ears, open mouths with teeth, and jointed composition bodies. Doll on left, mark: Ill. 856. Doll on right has the same mark except the size is 1 instead of 7. Hs. 17 and 11 in. (43 and 28 cm.). *Courtesy of Richard Withington. Photo by Barbara Jendrick.*

850. Bisque head doll with wig, stationary blue glass eyes, pierced ears, open mouth with four teeth, and a ball-jointed composition body. Mark: EDEN BÉBÉ//PARIS//11//Deposé. H. 25 in. (63.5 cm.). *Courtesy of the Washington Dolls' House and Toy Museum.*

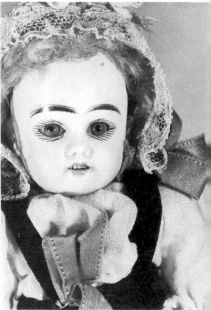

851A & B. Bisque head doll produced for Fleischmann & Blödel under the name Eden Bébé. See Ill. 857 for the mark. The head has a blond wig, blue glass eyes, and an open mouth. The pate is a wood flour composition which is similar to the material used in the five-piece body. It is dressed in a regional costume including a white wool blouse, black velvet belt and shoulder straps, cream satin apron, red wool skirt, black shoes marked "A LA RECOMPENSE" (see Ill. 1), and stockings. Under this costume is the commercial chemise made of a blue floral print cotton material. H. 10¼ in. (26 cm.). *Coleman Collection.*

B **C**

852A–C. Eden Bébé in its original box marked "UNIS FRANCE." The label on the skirt reads "Couchez Moi//Je Fais Dodo//Fabrication Française," which means: "Lay me down// I go sleepy bye// Made in France." The doll has a bisque head marked "Unis France," a wig, brown sleeping eyes, open mouth with teeth, and a composition body jointed only at the neck, shoulders, and hips. The original clothes indicate that this doll was made in the 1920s. H. 13½ in. (34 cm.). *Courtesy of the late Henrietta Van Sise.*

A

855
EDEN BEBE
PARIS
5

853
EDEN
PARIS
G

856
EDEN BEBE
PARIS
7
DEPOSÉ

854
EDEN·BEBE
PARIS
N

857

EDEN - BÉBÉ
Breveté S.G.D.G.

858
C
10/0

853–858. Marks on Eden Bébé dolls. Ill. 857 is on the chemise. Ill. 858 is on the bisque head. Ill. 1 is on the sole of the shoe. All three marks are on the doll shown in Ill. 851.

Edgar, E. C. 1924–25. Chatham, Kent, England. Obtained a British patent for moving the head and/or the eyes of a doll by means of levers.

Edgar & Co. 1920–21. New York City and Philadelphia, Pa. Imported dolls.

Edinburgh Toy Factory. 1917. Edinburgh, Scotland. The leading line was "Dainti-style Edinburgh Dressed Dolls." The removable clothes were designed by "experts" and worn by jointed dolls. Among the character dolls were: Scottish Fishwife, Red Cross Nurse, Her Ladyship, Little Jack Tar, and Boy Scout.

Edinburgh Women's Emergency Corps. 1915. Edinburgh, Scotland. A philanthropic group who made dolls.

Edison, Thomas Alva. 1878–94 and later. Orange, N.J. According to TOYS AND NOVELTIES in 1929, the Edison talking doll was made by the thousands in the U.S. and abroad. *Mary Amerault* in 1889 recited "Mary had a little lamb" for the doll's record. In 1929 Edison gave one of the original talking dolls to Mr. and Mrs. Henry Ford.

Between 1891 and 1894 the Edison Phonograph Toy Mfg. Co. was located in Boston.★

Edith Cavell. 1915–16. Doll dressed as Edith Cavell was sold to raise money for the Red Cross.

1916: Portrait doll produced by *Manchester Doll Makers*.

Edlin's. 1811–50. London. Toy shop that sold dolls.

Edma. See **European Doll Manufacturing Co.**

Eduard. 1916. Trade name of a felt doll made by *Steiff*. It was dressed to represent a Tennis Player. Ht. 50 cm. (19½ in.).

Eduardo Juan. See **Moehling, M. J.**

Educational Doll. 1916–17. Made by *Amberg*. Attached to the bodice of the doll's dress was a tiny booklet telling a nursery tale.★

Educational Doll. 1916–17. Made by *Harwin*. It wore a round button on which was printed, "The//Educational//Doll//[??]." It had the days of the week on the front of its blouse, numerals around the cuffs and the bottom of the blouse, the alphabet on its skirt and there were words written on its babushka.

Edvige. 1927–28. Lenci doll No. 700/2, represented a school-age girl with braids over its ears. It wore a dress with a high waistline and a full skirt covering the knees.

Edwards, Emily. 1924. San Antonio, Texas. Obtained a U.S. patent for a cloth doll.

Edwards, John Paul. Ca. World War I. U.S.A. Designed clothes for dolls including *Mary Jane.* (See also **German Dolls.**)

Edwards & Pamflett, Mesdames. 1918–23. London. Made cloth dolls with composition heads and limbs on cloth bodies as well as character baby dolls and fully jointed dolls with composition bodies. Produced *Cecily Dolls,* which were distributed by Bairn Toys.★

Edwina. 1928. Trade name of a composition doll made by *Amberg*. Ht. 13 in. (33 cm.).

Eegee Dolls.[†] See **Goldberger, Eugene.**

Effanbee (EFFanBEE). 1910–30 and later. New York City. An onomatopoetic acronym for Fleischaker & Baum,[†] manufacturers of composition dolls. Hugo Baum had worked as a salesman for *Samstag & Hilder* before the formation of Effanbee.

Joseph Kallus stated that he worked closely with Hugo Baum and designed some of the Effanbee dolls. Mr. Kallus also stated that his Company *(Cameo),* Effanbee, and *Ideal* were the only large American doll-producing companies that actually made their own dolls at one time. *Butler Bros.,* one of the companies distributing Effanbee dolls, referred to certain dolls as being of "Effanbee quality." One of these dolls was listed as a "French Baby"; this seems to indicate that an Effanbee doll was considered by Butler Bros. to be high quality but that popularly priced dolls were also made.

Effanbee used a pin with a blue bird in flight on it, at least through 1925; and a golden heart, often in metal, was their symbol from 1923 on. (See THE COLLECTOR'S BOOK OF DOLLS' CLOTHES, Ills. 645, 646, 647, 648, 649, 716, 769B and 770 C.)

1910: Claimed that their composition dolls had the strength of concrete.

1915: Used the *Otto Denivelle* cold press composition. Some of the dolls were marked "Deco" for Denivelle.

Their dolls included *Aunt Dinah, Baby Bright Eyes, Baby Grumpy, Baby Huggins, Baby Snowball, Billy Boy, Brick Bodkins, Daddy Long legs, Dorothy Dainty, Fifi, Jumbo Boy and Girl, Our Baby, Tiny Tads, Whistling Jim,* and other character dolls; most of the dolls had molded short hair; some had wigs and sleeping eyes. Nearly all of these dolls were dressed.

1916: *British Foreign Agency Co.* was one of their distributors.

Effanbee used a round tag with "GUARANTEED//THIS TOY//IS MADE UNDER//SANITARY CONDITIONS OF //THE MOST DURABLE AND // EXPENSIVE MATERIALS AND//BY THE MOST MODERN MA-//CHINERY.//IT IS GUARANTEED TO //GIVE SATISFACTORY//WEAR// EFFANBEE." on one side and on the reverse side, "IF IT IS EFFANBEE (in a 3-sided banner)//WHEN //BUYING A// DOLL OR ANY//STUFFED TOY//LOOK FOR THE// *EFFANBEE*//LABEL."

1917: Sleeping eyes were used on some of the cloth-body dolls. Besides *Mary Jane* there were War Nurse dolls in three sizes; price $1.00 and up. The factory was partially destroyed by fire.

1918: The company adopted a new plan of co-operative benefits for employees.

There were 200 models including Aunt Dinah, *Baby Catherine, Baby Dainty, Baby Ruth, Bathing Buds, Betty Bounce, Christening Baby, De Luxe Baby, Dolly Dumpling, Johnny Jones,* Little Girl, *Our Baby* and *Sweater Baby.* Many of the dolls had composition shoulder heads with molded hair or wigs, painted or sleeping eyes, and cork stuffed cloth bodies but allegedly the favorites had eyelashes and fully jointed composition bodies. Some of the cloth-body dolls were sold undressed but most of the dolls were sold dressed. The War Nurse in clothes that simulated official uniforms came in hts. 12 to 24 in. (30.5 to 61 cm.). A line of character babies with composition shoulder heads and painted eyes wore white percale rompers with pink or blue trimming and came in four sizes. Another line of dolls, dressed in silk clothes came in three sizes. There were also dolls in Japanese costumes that had realistic Japanese faces, according to TOYS AND NOVELTIES.

1919: The dolls were increased by 200 new models making a total of 300 styles or models. Effanbee used the label, "They Walk, They Talk, They Sleep." especially on *Mama* dolls. Miss *Katherine Fleischmann* was in charge of the designing of dresses. The doll named Mary Jane wore a silk gown and hat. J. Hopkins was the London distributor.

1920: The Union staged a four-week strike against Effanbee.

The new cloth dolls were dressed in rompers or dresses with or without belts. A baby wore a long dress. The black doll wore an apron, a kerchief on its head and striped stockings.

1921: New dolls included, *Little Miss Muffet, Margie, Mildred,* a *Boudoir* doll, and a crying baby in real baby clothes.

1922: 50 styles of dolls with voices, many of them said both "Papa" and "Mama." One baby doll played 15 tunes—a waltz, a foxtrot, a one step, and some classics when a spring-type mechanism was wound. Dressed Mama dolls came in hts. 10½ to 27 in. (26.5 to 68.5 cm.). A 26 in. (66 cm.) Mama doll had a fabric face. The *Sambo Family* included dark brown babies. There was also a *Hawaiian* Reed dancer doll.

1923: Line of 150 numbers with composition heads and arms, painted hair, mohair or real hair, cloth bodies with composition legs except for the cheaper numbers that had cloth legs.

New dolls included *Dolly Marion* and *Dolly Rose Mary,* both wearing horn rimmed glasses and *Honeybunch. Mary Ann* was a smaller sized version of *Nancy Ann.* No. 232 was a Mama doll shown in TOYS AND NOVELTIES in January dressed in colored rompers with a pocket in the shape of a chicken or rabbit and a sunbonnet. It had a tag or button with a flying blue bird over the words "Effanbee//Dolls."

1924: Effanbee dolls, especially Mama dolls, were popular in Britain. Mama dolls came in five hts.: 17, 18, 21, 24 and 28 in. (43, 45.5, 53, 61 and 71 cm.). Some of the new dolls were *Betty Lee,* Alice Lee† and Barbara Lee.† A Pierrot ht. 26 in. (66 cm.), cost $5.00. Dressed cloth infant dolls with rubber panties came in three sizes.

1925: Made *Rosemary* and a New Born Baby doll. London agent was *H. A. Moore.*

1926: *F. A. O. Schwarz* advertised an 18 in. (45.5 cm.) Effanbee Mama doll. The new dolls were *Bubbles* in 5 styles, *Rose-Marie* and *Lovey Mary;* the latter had the new slender composition legs. *Chicago Mail Order House* distributed Pat-a-Pat Baby.

1927: Bubbles was made in 50 styles including the ones with the composition shoulder plate extending below the arms. Some of the Mama dolls had slender legs and were dressed in silks, organdies and novelty materials. New dolls were Grumpkins, a small version of *Baby Grumpy; Mary Lou,* the big sister of Bubbles; and *Mimi* or *Patsy*—the latter was designed by *Bernard Lipfert.* The advertisements first showed the doll with the name "Mimi," but later the doll was called "Patsy" after the registering in the U.S. of Mimi as a trademark was refused. TOY WORLD reported that Patsy was named for Patricia Fitzmaurice the little daughter of a trans-Atlantic aviator. Walter E. Fleischaker stated that the bent-limb baby dolls were the best sellers and the ones in short baby dresses were preferred ten to one over those in long baby dresses. Effanbee obtained two injunctions in order to protect Bubbles from infringements. They were licensed by *Voices, Inc.* to use patented mama voices and criers.

Montgomery Ward claimed that a doll with a composition shoulder head, mohair wig, sleeping eyes, and hair eyelashes was "made exclusively for us by Effanbee with their name on back of each head." 5 hts.: 5¼, 5½, 6, 8 and 8¾ in. (13.5, 14, 15, 20.5 and 22 cm.); priced $1.43 to $3.79. If the 5¼ in. (13.5 cm.) doll had a bisque head it only cost 95¢. Besides Bubbles, Montgomery Ward sold *Mary Sue, Naughty Eyes* and Rose Mary.

1928: Fan Tuerst was known as "The Effanbee Lady."

The registration of "Patsy" as a trademark was accepted by the U.S. patent office. Effanbee claimed that they had used Patsy since September 15, 1927, however, the advertisements at the end of 1927 named the doll "Mimi." Effanbee issued warnings to possible imitators of Patsy and they won an infringement case when they sued *Maxine* for producing *Mitzi,* an imitation of Patsy. Other Effanbee dolls were *Marylee* (Marilee), Mary Sue, *Lovums,* and Laughing Eyes. Patsy wore a dress and drawers trimmed with lace. Bubbles was dressed in crepe-de-chine with a wool cap and hand crocheted jacket as well as other costumes. They advertised mechanical dolls such as dancing girls who twirled their parasols and a clown that swung on a trapeze bar; as the figure went up it turned its head, paused and then turned and flipped over.

1929: Advertised that all their dolls had Patsy-type necks wherein the socket was in the head and the neck had a rounded upper portion to fit into the socket. All the dolls still came with a golden heart identification. New dolls included *Lilibet; Patsy Ann; Skippy,* mate to Patsy; and Marilee. There were new costumes for Patsy and Bubbles. Effanbee stated that their dolls were "durable" and that "there is no such thing as an unbreakable doll unless it is the rag doll and that is not indestructible because it can be torn."

1930: New dolls were *Patsykins, Tousel Head* and *Sugar Baby,* a baby doll. Roller skates were made to fit all of the Patsy family. ★

1161-2
65c.
1161-4
$1.25
1161-6
$1.75

Semi-dressed baby dolls. Some with knitted booties and some with stockings.

1114-2
$1.00
1114-4
$1.50
1114-6
$2.50

Semi-dressed dolls with mohair wigs; Stockings - Booties.

19

═══ *Made in Sanitary Workrooms* ═══

859. Effanbee composition-head baby dolls as advertised in their 1915 catalog. The dolls pictured appear to be the ones with mohair wigs, painted eyes, "semi-dressed," and with stockings and booties.

860. Doll made by Effanbee with composition head and arms. It has a wig, sleeping metal and celluloid eyes. Original clothes. Mark: Ill. 864. H. 21 in. (53.5 cm.). *Courtesy of Patricia Schoonmaker.*

861. Mama doll made by Effanbee in the mid 1920s and named Rosemary. It has a composition shoulder head, composition arms and legs, brown human hair wig, sleeping metal and celluloid eyes with hair upper eyelashes, open mouth with four celluloid teeth and a felt tongue, cloth body. Original clothes and the Effanbee heart-shaped locket. Shoulder plate is marked: "EFFANBEE//ROSEMARY//WALK TALK SLEEP." H. 27 in. (68.5 cm.). *Courtesy of John Axe. Photo by John Axe.*

The doll YOUR child would choose

BETTY LEE is 20 inches tall and costs $7.50. She has two bigger sisters, just like her, Alice Lee who is 23 inches tall and costs $10, and Barbara Lee who is 29 inches tall and costs $15. They wear the sweetest organdie frocks, trimmed with baby Irish lace. There are many, many dolls in the Effanbee Family—all sizes and from very moderate prices up to $25. If your dealer does not carry them write to us and we will see that you get what you want through him.

THE most perfect thing about Betty Lee is her precious adorable face—pink, dimpled cheeks, wee red mouth, big blue really eye-lash eyes that go fast asleep. And dimpled arms and legs—just like a baby's—curly hair and a soft round body to hug.

She won't wear out

BUT the next-to-the-best thing is that like a real baby Betty Lee *won't wear out.* You can wash her face, dress and undress her, drop her on the floor. Of course she doesn't *like* being dropped, but it isn't likely to hurt her much. She is made that way—to last until daughter grows up.

For character-building play

BETTY LEE is so life-like she teaches gentle care and kindness. She wears clothes that can be taken off and put on again, washed and ironed. Her floppy legs dance with you like a real person. She really loves you and says "Mamma" in the prettiest way. Everything to a little girl that a real baby is to her mamma—just as absorbing and just as much loved.

Betty Lee is an Effanbee Doll—of course. If you want to know all about her, and all of her flocks and flocks of pretty sisters—a few of whom are sketched on this page—just drop into any good department or toy store and ask for Effanbee Dolls—the *"dolls with the golden heart."* You will know them by their darling little golden heart necklaces.

Every mother wants this booklet

SEND THE COUPON for our free booklet, "THE PROPER DOLL FOR MY CHILD'S AGE." It will tell you a lot about the best dolls for various ages, with a few hints on lessons children learn through doll play.

FLEISCHAKER & BAUM
Dept. 16, 45 Greene Street, New York City

EFFANBEE DOLLS

Fleischaker & Baum. Dept. 16. 45 Greene Street, New York City

Please send me your free booklet, "THE PROPER DOLL FOR MY CHILD'S AGE."

Name ....

Address ....

862. Effanbee advertisement in PLAYTHINGS, August, 1924, for Betty Lee, h. 20 in. (51 cm.); Alice Lee, h. 23 in. (58.5 cm.); and Barbara Lee, h. 29 in. (73.5 cm.). These three dolls had composition heads, arms and legs, wigs and were typical Mama dolls. They wore organdy dresses and the Effanbee heart locket as seen on the doll in the upper right. They cost $7.50 to $15.00 and other Effanbee dolls cost up to $25.00.

863 −4 G
F +B [CO] NY

864 *Effanbee*

865A *Effanbee*

865B *Effanbee*

866

867

863–867. Marks on Effanbee composition-head dolls. No. 864 is on the doll shown in Ill. 860.

The word Effanbee when it first appeared as a mark on dolls usually had the letters after the first E in lower case. For those dolls whose molds were first made in 1923 the word EFFANBEE was in all capital letters. After 1923 the "AN" in the middle continued to be capitalized but as time progressed it often tended to be smaller in size, compared with the first three and last three letters.

Efird's. 1927. Charlotte, N.C. Distributed dolls. Advertised dolls dressed as brides and grooms with the bride's veil carried by a *Kewpie.*

Egelhaaf, Oskar. See **Rock & Graner.**

Egler & Gondrand. 1925–29. Paris. Made dolls.

Ehrendfeld, William. 1906–28. New York City. Worked for *Horsman* for 22 years and was in charge of the manufacturing processes part at that time. He worked with *Benjamin Goldenberg* and was involved in the designing of dolls.

Ehrich Bros. 1872–1907 and possibly other years. New York City. Distributed dolls.

1887: Advertised bisque head dolls on composition, kid or cloth bodies. Some of the composition body dolls had sleeping eyes, some had choker necklaces to hide the neck joint and one of these dolls had mama-papa pull strings. These dolls came in a chemise or dressed. There were also china-head dolls, composition-head dolls, rubber dolls in chemise or worsted outfits, and wax dolls. The dressed French dolls were 13½ to 17 in. (34 to 43 cm.) tall; priced $1.75 to $3.85. Other dolls included *Bartenstein*'s two-faced doll, *Cymbalier, Gypsy Countess,* Jack the Sailor, *London Rag Baby,* and *Nancy Lee.* (See THE COLLECTOR'S BOOK OF DOLLS' CLOTHES, Ills. 226, 227, 302, 304, and 305.).★

Ehrlicher, Arthur. 1911. Sonneberg, Thür. Applied for a German patent (D.R.G.M.) for dolls.

Eichhorn, Albin. 1926 and other years. Steinach, Thür. Porzellanfabrik Göritzmühle had been founded in 1868 and by 1920 was owned by Günther and Otto Eichhorn. In 1926 Albin Eichhorn was reported making dolls' heads according to the Ciesliks.

Eichhorn, Christian, & Söhne (Sons). 1909–30. Steinach, Thür. This porcelain factory had been founded by Max and Albert Eichhorn in 1860 according to the Ciesliks. At the Leipzig Fair in 1910 this firm showed porcelain dolls and dolls' heads. Other members of the Eichhorn family succeeded Christian Eichhorn.

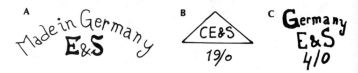

868A, B, & C. Marks used by Christian Eichhorn & Söhne on their porcelain dolls' heads.

Eichhorn, Leonhard, Jr. 1910–26. Sonneberg, Thür. Made dolls including baby dolls. He obtained five German patents (D.R.G.M.) relating to dolls. One of the patents was with *Jakob Grünbeck* and another one was with another firm member according to the Ciesliks.

Eichhorn, Martin. 1889–1930 and probably later. Sonneberg, Thür. Made and exported dolls including dressed dolls. He was born in 1864. His wife Ida joined him in making dolls. One of their first large orders was from Fred

869. Advertisement of Louis Eisen, an importer of felt dolls made in France. This advertisement was in PLAYTHINGS, July, 1927. The three dolls shown represent a peasant of Gascony with its sabots, a Parisian Apache, and a French child doll similar to the Lenci-type dolls.

Kolb, the agent for *George Borgfeldt,* for over 1,000 five-piece composition-body dolls. By 1921 he was making fully jointed composition-body dolls and cloth-body dolls. Besides supplying dolls to Borgfeldt, he also supplied dolls including *Lenci* types to *L. Rees & Co.* Some of the Eichhorn dolls had heads made by *Armand Marseille* such as the *My Dream Baby* head (mold #s 341 and 351) on the *Lullabye Baby,* a name trademarked by *Averill Manufacturing Co.*

1949: Martin Eichhorn died.
Most of this information is based on the research of the Ciesliks.

Einco. See **Eisenmann & Co.**

Einenkel, Brunhilde. 1922–47. Greizi, Thür. Made Art dolls in picturesque and fanciful clothes. These cloth body dolls were made in *Else Hecht's* workshop.★

Eisen, Louis. 1927–29. New York City. Manufacturer and importer of dolls, especially from Paris. Most of the dolls had felt heads and represented French peasants, clowns, French *Apaches* and so forth.

1927: Advertised dolls with felt heads named *Gascon* and *Jeanette.*

1928: Innovation was putting a suedine head on their *Boudoir* dolls and dressing them as "romantic characters."

Dolls included the Apache, the *Argentine,* the *Aviatrix,* Black Dancer, *Colonial Belle, Diane, Jockey, Russian Boy,* Sailor Girl, *Suzanne,* White Dancer, and so forth.

Eisenmann & Co. (Einco). 1881–1930 and later. Fürth, Bavaria; London. Company founded by Joe and Gabriel Eisenmann produced and distributed dolls. Among the dolls' heads which they used were Gebrüder Heubach bisque heads. Joe Eisenmann was called "King of the Toy Trade."

1908: *Leon Rees* married Maud Eisenmann and soon thereafter became a partner in the company.

1912: Applied for a German patent (D.R.G.M.) for dolls.

1920s: London agent for *Amberg* and *Mittelland.*

Eisenstädt, Isidor, & Co. 1895–1903. Waltershausen, Thür.; Berlin. Manufactured ball-jointed dolls. Specialized in walking dolls including cloth walking dolls.

1899–1902: Applied for four German patents (2 D.R.G.M. and 2 D.R.P.) for walking dolls.

1900: Obtained an Austrian patent for a Walking doll.★

Eisenstädt, Paul. 1901. Waltershausen, Thür. Applied for a German patent (D.R.P.).

Eisner, Hermann. 1896. Berlin. Applied for a German patent (D.R.P.) for dolls.

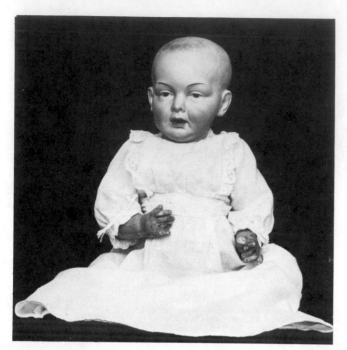

870. Bisque head character baby doll made by Eisenmann & Co. It has molded hair with brushmarks, enameled intaglio eyes, open-closed mouth, five-piece composition body. Original clothes. Marked: "Einco//2//Germany." H. 15 in. (38 cm.). *Courtesy of Victoria Harper.*

**Germany
Einco
2**

**Einco
0
Germany**

871–872. Einco marks used by Eisenmann & Co..

Eitner, Hedwig. 1901–30 and later. Leipzig, Saxony. Made dolls' dresses, underwear, headwear, trousseaux, and shoes.

1926–27: Listed in a German toy trade journal under "Dolls' House Dolls."

1930: Listed in a German toy trade journal under Dressed Baby Dolls, Child Dolls and Dolls' House Dolls.

Elaine. Ca. 1904–12. Trade name of a *Heinrich Handwerck* doll made for *Gimbels.* It had a *Simon & Halbig* bisque head,

mohair wig, sleeping eyes with hair eyelashes, chemise, silk stockings and satin slippers.

1904: 11 hts.: 15, 16½, 20½, 22, 24, 25, 27, 28, 30, 31 and 33 in. (38, 42, 52, 56, 61, 63.5, 68.5, 71, 76, 78.5 and 84 cm.); priced $2.00 to $8.75.

1911: Eight hts.; the 20½ in. (52 cm.) was replaced by 19¼ in. (49 cm.) and the 25, 28 and 31 in. (63.5, 71 and 78.5 cm.) dolls were eliminated. Prices were $2.25 to $10.00.

El-Be-Co. See **Langrock Bros. Co.**

Elco. See **Cohen, L., & Sons.**

Eldon, Albert J. 1926. Mount Vernon, N.Y. Obtained a U.S. design patent for a rubber doll.

Elegant Dolls. 1926. Trade name used by *Dean* for dolls representing young ladies. These cloth dolls had three-dimensional faces and wore 12 different costumes; one of them had a "fur" trimmed coat and high-heeled ankle boots. Ht. 22 in. (56 cm.).

Elektra Toy & Novelty Co. 1912–20. New York City. Made dolls.

1920: Dolls included *Honey Babies, Charlie Chaplin, Yama-Yama, Bonnie Laddie* and Boy Scout.★

873. Composition head cloth-body doll made by Elektra Toy & Novelty Co. It has molded and painted hair and eyes. Original baseball uniform on this large doll. *Courtesy of Robert and Katrin Burlin.*

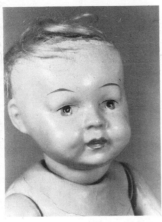

874A & B. All-composition bent-limb baby doll made by Elektra with early-type American composition. Hair is inserted in a hole in the pate. It has painted features and is wire strung. Mark: Ill. 875. H. 11¼ in. (28.5 cm.). *Coleman Collection.*

875 ELEKTRA TOY & NOVELTY Co

NEW YORK

876 ELEKTRA
TOY & N.Co.

877 E.T & NCo.
N.Y.
COPYRIGHT

875–877. Embossed marks on composition-head dolls made by Elektra Toy & Novelty Co.

Elfenhaut. 1925. Brand name of dolls made by *Amberg & Hergershausen.* Elfenhaut means elf's skin.

Elie. 1925–29. Name of cloth body art dolls and toy dolls advertised by *Karl Müller & Co.*★

Elise. 1919. Doll made by *Jessie M. Raleigh,* described as a sedate, demure Miss with long dark curls.

Elite. Name found on a group of bisque socket head dolls that appeared on the market in some quantity in the early 1980s. They probably have some age and may have come from a stored stock. This group had molded headwear that represented various nations including Austria, Turkey and the United States. The incised mark (see Ill. 878) has the name "Elite" and a single letter or pair of letters that are the initials of the country represented by the molded headwear. For Austria there is an O (Österreich) indicating a Germanic origin, as does the D for Deutschland; for Turkey a T, and for the United States a U.S. Other nations were also represented in this series. All of these heads have round glass eyes looking to the side and watermelon slice shaped mouths. Some of these Elite dolls had two faces, each side with a different hat. These dolls might have been made for *Bawo & Dotter* in Germany or Austria or they might have been made by *William Goebel,* for Max Handwerck, all of whom used the name Elite, or *Bébé Elite.* Possibly they were made by someone else.

Elite Doll Co. 1915–18. Tunstall, Staffs. Made *British Ceramic* shoulder heads and socket heads for dolls. They made three lines of wigged heads, with painted eyes, or fixed glass eyes, or the third line called *Silver Series* line with sleeping eyes. The first two lines came in six hts. Seven hts. in the silver line were: 10, 12, 14, 16, 18, 22 and 26 in. (25.5, 30.5, 35.5, 40.5, 45.5, 56 and 66 cm.).

Dep.
Elite
U.S. 1

878. Elite mark on a German bisque character doll's head that resembles Uncle Sam. The initials "U.S." in the mark may stand for United States.

Elizabeth. Name stamped in green on the neck of a doll's head bearing the *Gebrüder Heubach* square mark according to Jan Foulke. The doll had a bisque socket head with sleeping eyes glancing to the side, a closed mouth and a composition body. Ht. 7 in. (18 cm.).

Elizabeth. 1922–26. Name of a cloth body doll made by *Cosgrove.*★

Elizabeth, Princess. See **Princess Elizabeth Doll.**

Elizabeth Series. See **Princess Elizabeth Doll.**

Elk Knitting Mills Co. 1918 and later. Made *Nelke* Dolls. Later it appears to have been part of the Nelke Corp.

Ella Cinders. 1928–29. Doll representing the character of this name created by *Charlie Plumb* and *Bill Conselman* in their comic strip which was published by the Metropolitan News Service. The composition head version was produced by *Horsman* and marked with raised letters on the back of its neck "© //1925// M.N.S." Stamped across the thigh was "Patent Applied For" and the rose and white tape tag on the dress read, "ELLA CINDERS // TRADEMARK REG. U.S. PAT. OFF.//COPYRIGHT 1925// METROPOLITAN NEWSPAPER SERVICE." Another similar tape tag on the dress read "HORSMAN//DOLL//M'F'D IN U.S.A." In 1926 Colleen Moore had starred in a moving picture about Ella Cinders written by Bill Conselman. The doll resembled Colleen Moore in this moving picture. The composition head version had painted black hair or a wig, round painted eyes with freckles under the eyes, an open-closed mouth, a cloth body and four different styles and colors of clothing, all with a

Peter Pan collar on the dress, white combination under-clothes, black and white socks and black single-strap slippers. PLAYTHINGS described the doll as "Wide of eyes, freckled of face, human in expression." Ht. 18 in. (54.5 cm.). The cloth version of Ella Cinders had painted hair and eyes.

1929: Wore a checked dress and an apron. Cost $2.75.

879. Composition head doll produced by Horsman and representing the comic character, Ella Cinders. It has molded black hair, round blue eyes looking to the side, freckles under the eyes, open-closed mouth, cloth torso and composition arms and legs. The original clothes include a pink and white checked cotton dress with a black sash and white apron. Marks: Ill. 880 is on the head; Ill. 881 is on the sleeve; and there is a square blue stamp on the body with a letter or Roman numeral in the center of it. H. 17¾ in. (45 cm.). *Courtesy of the Margaret Woodbury Strong Museum. Photo by Harry Bickelhaupt.*

1925
M.N.S.

"ELLA CINDERS"
TRADE MARK   REG. U.S. PAT. OFF.
COPYRIGHT 1925
METROPOLITAN NEWSPAPER SERVICE

880–881. Mark: Ill. 880 is on the composition head of an Ella Cinders doll produced by Horsman. The M.N.S. stands for Metropolitan Newspaper Service. Mark: Ill. 881 is on a cloth label attached to the sleeve. It has red letters on a white ground.

Ellar. Ca. 1925. Name of an Oriental looking bisque head made by *Armand Marseille.* Size number 2/OK was a doll 9¾ in. (25 cm.) tall.★

Ellarco. See **Ellison, Rees & Co.**

Ellice, John, Co. 1929–30. New York City. Prepared cotton used for stuffing dolls.

Ellinger, Johann. 1910. Vienna. Listed under Dolls and Dolls' Heads in an Austrian directory.

Ellis, Joel. See **Co-operative Manufacturing Co.**

Ellison, Rees & Co. 1915– Ca. 1920. London and Chesham, England. Leon Rees helped to form this Company which later became *L. Rees & Co.* Ellison, Rees & Co. used the trademark Ellarco and the trade names *Chesham Brand* and *Dolleries.* The dolls that they produced were dressed as girls or boys.

1916: Their lines included a cloth-body character doll called *Impy* and *Union Jack Baby.*

Elm, H. 1878. Gera, Thür. Distributed small inexpensive porcelain-head dolls, dressed and undressed.

Elms & Sellon. 1910–18 and possibly other years. New York City. Probably also known as Elms & Co. at one time. Produced cutout cloth dolls including *Dolly Double and Topsy Turvy; the Standish No Brake Life Size Doll; Colonial Family; Punch & Judy.* These dolls had been made by *Art Fabric Mills* and/or *Arnold Print Works.*

Eloise Novelties. 1928–29. Los Angeles, Calif. Made outfits for dolls.

Else (Winter Sports). Before 1911–13. Felt character doll made by *Steiff,* dressed in winter sports attire, and mate to *Kurt.* Four hts.: 28, 35, 43, and 50 cm. (11, 14, 17, and 19½ in.); price $1.18 to $2.85.

Elsey, Francine. 1925–30. Paris. Made and/or distributed dolls.

Elsó Magyar Játékbabagyár (First Hungarian Doll Factory). 1926 and other years. Hungary. This factory of Gusztáv Ormos made composition dolls.

882   ELMS & CO.
TOY DEPARTMENT
NEW YORK

883   ELMS & SELLON
40 & 42 E. 19th St.
NEW YORK

THE STANDISH
—"NoBrake"—
LIFE SIZE DOLL

884   ELMS & SELLON
NEW YORK

882–884. Elms & Sellon marks on cloth dolls.

885. Else, felt doll made by Steiff and dressed for winter sports. Most of the costume is original. *Courtesy of Vivian Rasberry.*

Eltona Toy Co. 1919–21. New York City. Imported dolls including quality dolls with bisque heads, sleeping eyes, hair eyelashes, and real hair wigs as well as popular priced dolls.

1919: Some of the eyes on the dolls were large black painted dots. One doll number cried "Mama" when pressed in the center of its stomach.

Embossers. 1700s—early 1800s. Thüringen and Bavaria. The name embosser had an entirely different meaning than it has in the 20th century. At first embossers covered carved or wooden figures with gesso. Before 1780 they began to mold dolls out of lime-water and black flour, so called "bread dough." Dolls' faces or masks were modeled and put on conical wooden figures. It was chronicled that "In Neuenbau [a village near Sonneberg] they turn the bodies for the dolls that are modelled of dough at Sonneberg." The work of the embosser soon included modelling, at first small, later large figures out of dough, modelling them free hand. Since the embossers painted their own dolls, they began to have trouble with the *Bismuth Painters'* Guild. So they formed an Embossers' Guild. Eventually the dough used by the Embossers became moldy and began to be eaten by mice and mites which brought an end to the embossers' making dolls. ★

Emde, Heinrich. 1925–26. Elberfeld, Germany. Obtained a German patent relating to the hair on celluloid dolls' heads.

Emdee. See **Marcuse, Day & Co.**

Emell Toy Manufacturing Co. 1917–20. London. Manufactured dolls and used the initials "M.L." in a circle or rectangle.

Emily Marie. 1926. Oil-cloth doll based on a design by Harold Gray, made by *Live Long Toys.* It represented one of the characters in the comic cartoon, LITTLE ORPHAN ANNIE.

Emmeluth, Ludwig. 1928. Düsseldorf, Germany. Applied for a German patent (D.R.P.) relating to dolls' wigs.

Emmy Schmaltz. 1929. All-bisque doll with a turning head, made in Germany and distributed exclusively by *Marshall Field.* It represented one of the characters in the comic cartoon MOON MULLINS, drawn by *Willard.*

Empire. 1926 and later. Mark used on dolls in accordance with British law.

Empire Art Doll. See **American Beauty Doll.**

Empire Porcelain Co. 1916–25 and later. Empire Works, Stoke-on-Trent, Staffs. Founded in 1896, still in business in the 1960s. During World War I they made *British Ceramic* heads for dolls. One of their shoulder heads had molded blonde hair with a blue molded ribbon through it, enameled eye pupils and lips, open-closed mouth with teeth. On the back of the shoulder was incised "70. EMPIRE//Stoke-on-Trent." Ht. of shoulder head 4½ in. (11.5 cm.).

70. EMPIRE.
Stoke-on-Trent

886A. British Ceramic head made by the Empire Porcelain Co. during World War I. It has molded and painted hair and features. The eyes are enameled. The cloth body has ceramic hands and feet. Mark: Ill. 886B. H. 18 in. (45.5 cm.). H. of shoulder head only, 4¾ in. (12 cm.). *Coleman Collection.*

886B. Mark on back shoulder of dolls made by the Empire Porcelain Co.

Empress. 1895. Name of a bisque-head doll distributed by *Butler Bros.* It had a wig and was dressed. Ht. 21 in. (53.5 cm.); price $2.75.

Empress Eugenie. 1924. The LADIES' HOME JOURNAL gave directions for making period clothes for a French Cloth Doll that resembled the Journal's idea of what might have been worn by the Empress. The dress was of changeable peach and beige taffeta. The bodice had five bows of apple green ribbon down the front, a tiny collar, ruffled sleeves edged with green ribbon, bell shaped undersleeves of organdy and a belt matching the ribbon bows. The ruffled skirt also had each ruffle edged with the apple green ribbon. The matching taffeta bonnet was trimmed with mauve flowers.

Empress Pottery. See **Dura Porcelain Co.**

Enders & Wagner. See **Harrass (Harras), Adolph.**

Engel, George, & Associates. 1925–26. New York City. Advertised imported and domestic dolls. James E. Engel of New York City who applied for a U.S. patent in 1926 for a "figure Toy," may have been one of the Associates.

Engelhardt, Hermann. 1873–1928. Sonneberg, Thür. Successor in 1928 was Willy Berghold. Made and exported dolls.

1910: One of the Sonneberg group of Grand Prize winners at the Brussels Exhibition.

1928: Advertised bent-limb baby dolls with molded hair, long-limbed dolls and various other dolls. Specialized in dressed dolls.★

English Doll Manufacturing Co. 1916–17. Derby, England. Made dolls with *British Ceramic* heads and "Sham" (presumably cloth) bodies, with or without wigs, good quality dolls with sleeping eyes and cheap dolls with stationary glass eyes. The dolls came dressed and undressed. Hts. 11 to 16 in. (28 cm. to 40.5 cm.). Price $2.13 to $3.94 a doz. wholesale. Cloth dolls were also available for 94¢ a doz. wholesale.

English Dolls.† See **British Dolls.**

English Rag Dolls. 1892. Line of dolls distributed by *Marshall Field.* These cloth dolls had linen faces with glass eyes, soft arms and legs. They were dressed in costumes representing *Little Red Riding Hood,* Bo Peep, Blue Eyes and Dew Drop.

ENGLISH RAG DOLLS SIZE–HEIGHT RELATIONSHIP		
Size No.	Height in.	cm.
00	13½	34
0	15	38
1	17	43
2	19	48
Price per doz. wholesale was $4.00 to $12.00.		

English Toy Manufacturing Co. 1914–15. Stoke-on-Trent, Staffs. Established by two ladies to provide work for unemployed women and girls at the beginning of World War I. By the end of their first year they were producing 1,000 dolls' heads and 300 "ready made dolls" every week. All of the parts of the dolls were made in this factory. The eyes were described as follows: "Even the eyes, the manufacturing process of which offers the greatest difficulties, but has been developed to such a perfection that they closely resemble natural eyes and are wonderfully approaching the German make."

Englishman. 1899. Doll imported and distributed by *Butler Bros.* It had a painted face, sideburns, cloth body and wore a checked suit and high boots. Hts. 9 and 11½ in. (23 and 29 cm.).

Enslins. World War I and later. Graaff Reinet, South Africa. Made cloth dolls with painted hair.

Ens-Puppen. 1922 and possibly other years. Trade name for dolls made by *Katarina Paar* and Elizabeth Neumayer-Somossy, who derived the name from her initials E. N. S. Their workshop was called, "Werkstätte fur Künstlerische Dekorationspuppen und Kunstgewerbe." The dolls were dressed in national costumes of various countries, including Egypt, East India and so forth. They cost around $4.00.

Epperson, Mrs. H. T. See **California Bisque Doll Co.**

Epstein, Hugo. 1921–24. Chicago, Ill. Imported dolls.

Erhard, Stephen. 1887–1930. London. By 1926 it was S. Erhard & Son. Made and imported dolls especially from France and Japan. They used a diamond with the initials S. E. & S. in it as a trademark. They advertised celluloid dolls, jointed dolls, Kewpies, dressed dolls and dolls' trousseaux.

1916: Advertised dressed and undressed dolls.

1921: Advertised India rubber dolls.

1926: Imported Japanese dolls. Specialized in celluloid dolls. These included black dolls and white dolls, standing dolls and bent-limb baby dolls. The latter came in four hts.: 3, 4½, 7 and 9 in. (7.5, 11.5, 18 and 23 cm.).★

Erich. 1913–24. Jointed felt character doll made by *Steiff* and distributed by *Borgfeldt.* This boy doll wore a pinafore. Hts. 11, 14, and 17 in. (28, 35.5, and 43 cm.). The largest size had a mama voice. (See also **Albert.**)

Erika. 1916–24. Name of a felt doll made by *Steiff.* In 1916 there were five hts.: 28, 35, 43, 50 and 60 cm. (11, 14, 17, 19½, and 23½ in.). In 1924 they advertised only the first four hts.

Erika. 1922–30. Line of dolls produced by *Carl Hartmann;* included baby dolls, fully jointed composition body dolls,

Erika

1489
SIMON & HALBIG

887. Mark on a Simon & Halbig doll identifying it as being named Erika.

and cloth-body dolls. Name found on *Simon & Halbig* bisque head mold # 1489; this doll was distributed by *Sears*.★

Erisman Doll Hospital. 1925–26. Lancaster, Pa. Made cloth-body dolls.

Erlich, M. & D. 1924. Advertised dolls in a British trade journal.

Ernenmein. 1930 and later. Paris. Made dolls.

Ernst, Charles & Hermann. 1920–23. New York City. Sole distributor of *Lenci* dolls in the U.S.★

Erskine, Albert H. 1923–27. Calif. He worked in the *Borgfeldt* firm from 1910–17. Went west in 1923 and represented several toy and doll producers.

Erste Steinbacher Porzellanfabrik. See **Wiefel & Co.**

Erzgebirge. 1800s–1900s. An area in Germany noted for its wooden dolls and toys (See also **German Dolls** and **Nöckler & Tittel.**)

Esanbe. See **Schranz & Bieber Co.**

Escher, E. Jün. (Jr.). 1880–1927. Sonneberg, Thür. Made and exported dolls and dolls' heads.

1899: Applied for a German patent (D.R.G.M.) for dolls.

1902: Applied for another German patent (D.R.G.M.) for dolls.

1903: Advertised dressed and undressed dolls.★

Escher, J. G. (J. G. Escher & Sohn). 1790–1928 and later. Sonneberg, Thür. Manufactured dolls of various materials. Used the initials I. G. E. S. (I and J are interchangeable in German.).

1790: Founding date.

1897: Advertised wooden dolls' heads and wooden jointed dolls.

1910: One of the Sonneberg group of Grand Prize winners at the Brussels Exposition.

1913: According to the firm's catalog, *Armand Marseille* bisque heads, mold # 390, were used on their fully jointed dolls and five-piece dolls. Clothes were made of silk, wool or cotton.

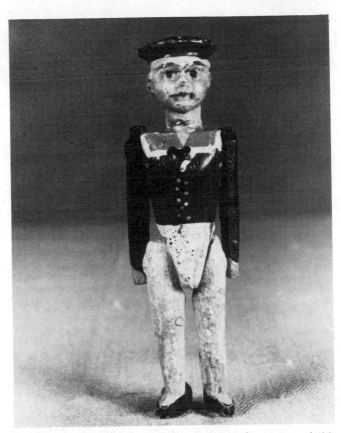

888. Carved, turned, and painted all-wooden doll probably made in the Erzgebirge area of Germany prior to World War I. The painted clothes represent those of a sailor. This doll was a gift to the authors from Mary Hillier. H. 2½ in. (6.5 cm.). *Coleman Collection.*

1914: Advertised dressed dolls; celluloid dolls; baby dolls, dressed and undressed; jointed dolls and jointed babies; celluloid heads, and articles for doll hospitals.

1916: Eduard Förster was head of the firm.

1920: Their catalog showed dressed and undressed dolls; double-jointed dolls with hair eyelashes; bent-limb character babies with sleeping eyes made of bisque or celluloid; bent-limb babies with jointed cloth bodies and papier-mâché hands; celluloid five-piece bodied dolls with sleeping eyes; fully jointed wooden dolls; wooden five-piece jointed dolls; Nankeen dolls with porcelain heads; washable dolls with papier-mâché heads; jointed bodies of art leather (oil cloth) with porcelain heads and sleeping eyes; all-bisque and china dolls. Dolls wore black stockings as well as white stockings.

1926: Dolls distributed by *Bremer*.

1927: Listed under Art dolls in a German toy trade journal.

1928: Catalog showed unbreakable jointed dolls made of wood with celluloid heads, based on a German patent (D.R.G.M.).

A considerable part of the above information was based on the research of the Ciesliks.★

889. Mark used by J. G. Escher for their dolls in 1928.

Esk. (Eskimo). See **Esq.**

Eskimo Baby. 1919. Doll with composition head and hands, mohair wig, sleeping eyes, cork stuffed cloth body, jointed at shoulders and hips; it wore an all-wool suit. Distributed by *Montgomery Ward.* Ht. 22 in. (56 cm.).

Eskimo (Esquimo, Esquimaux) Dolls. Dolls made by Eskimos representing their own people. The dolls were often made of bones, teeth, wood or Walrus tusks and sometimes of animal skins. These dolls were usually dressed in fur or skins.

1879: According to ST. NICHOLAS magazine the Eskimo doll "is made of ivory or wood, carefully carved as nearly like the human figure as possible, with eyes of bits of pearly shell, inlaid. Some of them are twelve or eighteen inches tall, but most of them are six or eight inches only. . . . the girls keep house with their ivory dollies, get the meals and make the clothes, all in Eskimo fashion."

1902: Dolls of Iglulik tribe were made of crudely tanned reindeer skin with native dressed fur trimming. They used clumsy iron or stone needles to sew the strong animal sinews used in making the dolls, according to TOYS AND NOVELTIES.

1907–13: *Elizabeth Scantlebury* showed school children three dolls all in furs representing Eskimos.

Eskimo Dolls. 1893–1930 and probably other years. Commercially made dolls dressed in fur or plush which usually covered all of the doll except for the face and limb extremities. Occasionally these dolls were called *Baby Bunting.*

Sometimes these same dolls had large ears attached to the top of their heads in order to represent bunnies.

Interest in Eskimo dolls was increased by the notoriety about Peary's[†] daughter who was known as the Snow Baby (see **Snow Babies**).

1893: Bisque-head doll with a white fur-covered jointed body was advertised by *Horsman.* Two styles came with voices and two styles came without voices; priced $2.00 to $8.50 doz. wholesale.

1896: One of the premium dolls offered by the YOUTH'S COMPANION had a bisque head, joints at shoulders and hips and was dressed as an Eskimo. Ht. 7 in. (18 cm.).

890. Eskimo doll of chewed leather made by an Eskimo. Tiny pieces of leather were sewn together with black thread to form designs; this same thread was also used to embroider the facial features. A few of the small pieces at the bottom of the skirt and on the boots were sewn with light colored thread. The hood is trimmed with strips of red leather. Tiny reverse triangles decorate the hemline of the skirt. The reason for the triangle above the left eye is not known by the authors. H. 9 in. (23 cm.). *Coleman Collection.*

ESKIMO DOLLS OF FLEXIBLE MATERIALS

891. Dolls representing Eskimos, as shown in INTERNATIONAL STUDIO, April, 1923. The dolls were probably made by Eskimos.

892. Peg jointed wooden doll with carved features not painted; hair arranged in typical style of Greenland Eskimos. Original regional costume. H. 9½ in. (24 cm.). *Coleman Collection.*

1899: Dolls with white or other colored fur covering distributed by *Butler Bros.* These dolls had bisque heads that turned, glass eyes and open mouth with teeth. Hts. 5½, 9¾ and 11 in. (14, 24.5 and 28 cm.). The smallest ones came with painted eyes and only with white fur.

1902: Butler Bros. advertised dolls similar to those of 1899. Priced from 87¢ to $2.10 a doz. wholesale.

1907: *Sears* advertised a bisque-head doll with a white fur covered composition body called an "Esquimo" doll. Hts. 10½ and 11½ in. (26.5 and 29 cm.); priced 25¢ and 50¢.

1909: *Louvre* Store advertised a composition-head doll with a white or beige plush covering the body. Four Hts. 24 to 35 cm. (9.5 to 14 in.); Price 29¢ to 70¢.

Samaritaine advertised similar dolls but the hts. were 25, 29, and 31 cm. (10, 11½ and 12 in.); price 35¢ to 59¢.

1910: Two-thirds of the fur clad bisque-head dolls wore white fur and one third wore colored fur. The 6 in. (15 cm.) doll had painted features and the 9¾ in. (24.5 cm.) one had glass eyes and an open mouth. *Moritz Pappe* advertised Eskimo dolls.

Ville de St. Denis advertised Eskimo dolls with celluloid heads and jointed plush bodies. Hts. 25, 31 and 37 cm. (10, 12 and 14½ in.); priced 25¢ to 59¢.

1912: The *Lafayette* store named one of these girl dolls, "Eskima." The doll wore a parka and carried a muff. Four hts.: 25, 27, 30 and 36 cm. (10, 10½, 12 and 14 in.); priced 27¢ to 55¢.

The Louvre store continued to advertise "Les Esquimaux," but they had added a crier and the six hts. were 26 to 45 cm. (10½ to 17½ in.); priced 29¢ to $1.05. The dolls at *L'Hotel de Ville* and *Paris Montpelier* had celluloid heads. *Bon Marché* advertised celluloid heads, wool plush and leading strings. Hts. 32, 39 and 44 cm. (12½, 15½ and 17½ in.); priced 58¢ to $1.10.

1913: The Louvre again changed the hts. of their dolls. This year they had 26 to 50 cm. (10½ to 19½ in.); priced 29¢ to 98¢.

The L'Hotel de Ville dolls with celluloid heads were 35, 38 and 54 cm. (14, 15 and 21½ in.) tall; priced 40¢ to 80¢. (See also **Esq.**)

1913–14: Samaritaine advertised Eskimo dolls with composition heads and plush bodies. Hts. 28, 34, and 39 cm. (11, 13½ and 15½ in.); priced 29¢ to 78¢.

1914: Butler Bros. advertised fur clad Eskimo dolls with bisque heads, painted features, composition bodies having jointed limbs and painted shoes. The fur was white or in various colors. Ht. 6 in. (15 cm.); price 92¢ doz. wholesale.

Ville de St. Denis advertised Eskimo dolls that were 32 and 40 cm. (12½ and 15½ in.) tall; priced 29¢ and 45¢.

Marshall Field advertised Eskimo dolls with bisque heads, glass eyes, and fur covering in white or four other colors. Ht. 9 In. (23 cm.); priced $4.00 doz. wholesale.

This year the Louvre dolls were in six hts. 28 to 54 cm. (11 to 21½ in.); priced 29¢ to $1.15; otherwise they were the same as in previous years.

1915: The Louvre store again changed heights. This year there were five hts. 29 to 44 cm. (11½ to 17½ in.); priced 38¢ to 98¢.

1915–17: *Hawksley & Co.* made plush and felt Eskimo dolls with celluloid or xylonite faces.

J. Fred Scott made masks for Eskimo dolls.

1916: Cloth dolls entirely covered with white plush except for the face were made by *Atlas Manufacturing Co.* in 7 sizes.

1917: *Wyman, Partridge & Co.* distributed Eskimo dolls with celluloid mask faces, felt hands and feet and brown plush bodies. Ht. 13 in. (33 cm.).

1918: *Eaton* distributed celluloid-head Eskimo dolls. Ht. 9½ in. (24 cm.); priced 35¢.

1919: *Aux Trois Quartiers* advertised their composition-head Esquimau doll in four hts. 25 to 40 cm. (10 to 15½ in.).

1920: *Société Française de Fabrication de Bébés & Jouets* (S.F.B.J.) advertised Eskimo dolls.

1921: L'Hotel de Ville's plush Eskimo dolls had composition heads and came in four hts. 32 to 49 cm. (12½ to 19½ in.).

1922: Dolls dressed in sheepskin were made by the *Novelty Manufacturing Co.*

893. Fur covered Eskimo type commercial doll with bisque head, glass eyes, open mouth, five piece composition body dressed in white fur. Head marked 14/0. H. 7¾ in. plus ½ in. fur cap (19.5 cm. plus 1 cm.). *Courtesy of Richard Withington. Photo by Barbara Jendrick.*

1923: Louvre store advertised Eskimo dolls in only two hts., 32 and 36 cm. (12½ and 14 in.).

1928: The many trips to the North Pole caused continuing interest in Eskimo dolls in Paris. *Paturel* advertised ones that were jointed at the shoulders and hips with elastic. (See also **Klondike Dolls.**)★

Eskimo Tots. 1928. Cloth dolls made by *Kat-A-Korner Kompany* in two sizes.

Esquimaux Dolls. See **Eskimo Dolls.**

Esq. (Esk. [Eskimo]). 1909–16. Jointed character doll representing an Eskimo with felt face and hands on a mohair-plush body made by *Steiff,* distributed in U.S. by *Borgfeldt.* It had a pointed plush cap and came in white, light brown or other colors. The doll wore skis and carried ski poles but these accessories were sold separately. Five hts.: 28, 35, 43, 50 and 60 cm. (11, 14, 17, 19½ and 23½ in.). The 28 cm. ht. cost 75¢ in Germany in 1911 and $1.00 in New York in 1913.

1913: *Gamage* advertised Steiff felt dolls in brown plush clothes. Ht. 11 in. (28 cm.); priced 62¢. (See also **Samojede.**)

894. Esquimaux (Eskimo) doll sold at the Louvre store in 1916. It has an "unbreakable" head, jointed body and a crier. It is advertised as a toy for a young child. Five hs. 29 to 44 cm. (11½ to 17½ in.); priced 38¢ to 98¢.

895. Esquimaux (Eskimo) doll sold by the L'Hotel de Ville, Paris, in 1921. It has an "unbreakable" head and is clothed in plush. Four hs. 32 to 49 cm. (12½ to 19½ in.).

Essany Film Co. 1913–15. U.S.A. Held the rights for making portrait dolls representing *Alkali Ike* and *Charlie Chaplin.*

Essenel Co. 1929–30. Providence, R.I. Made all-wood dolls including *Dainty Doll.*

Estate (L'été). 1930 and later. Felt doll made by *Lenci* in the *Poupées Salon* series representing Summer. It wore a green skirt and apron and held a yellow bird as style no. 1054. Ht. 48 in. (122 cm.).

Esther. 1919–20. Trade name of a dressed doll made by *Alisto*. It had joints at the shoulders; its legs were together; and it wore a hair ribbon.★

Esther. 1926. Cloth doll made by *Käthe Kruse* representing a girl. It wore a hat with a flat crown and small brim. Distributed by *F. A. O. Schwarz*. Ht. 16 in. (40.5 cm.); price $16.50.

Esther. See **Pet Names.**

Esther Starring. 1924–26. Designed by *Penny Ross;* made by *Live Long Toys.* This oilcloth doll representing Esther Starring in "MAMMA'S ANGEL CHILD" had its legs together and wore a dress, bonnet and high socks.★

896. Oilcloth doll designed by Penny Ross and made by Live Long Toys to represent the actress Esther Starring. This nearly flat doll had printed hair, face, and clothes. Mark: Ill. 897. H. 10 in. (25.5 cm.). *Coleman Collection.*

ESTHER STARRING

Penny Ross

897. Mark in black on Esther Starring oilcloth doll.

Établissement Bognier-Burnet. See **Bognier-Burnet, Établissement.**

Établissements Gerbaulet Frères. See **Gerbaulet Frères.**

Établissements di Giotti. See **Giotti, Établissements di.**

Établissements Niceray. See **Niceray, Établissements.**

Etienne, Eugene. 1876 and earlier. Paris. Made dolls.

Etna. See **Société Etna.**

Eton Boy. See **Bloch, J.,** and **Schwarz.**

Etta Inc. 1927–30. New York City. Miss *Etta Kidd,* a designer of dolls and President of the firm with all-women workers, made cloth art dolls of various types.

1927: They made *Boudoir* dolls dressed as male or female clowns, ladies, and dolls representing boys and girls. *Voices, Inc.* licensed Etta to use patented mama voices and criers in their dolls.

1928: Every doll had a handpainted face and wore a different style dress. There were baby dolls, big dolls, little dolls, dolls with long curls, and dolls with bobbed hair.

1929: The handmade cloth bodies had jointed necks. Some of the dolls had human hair wigs and hair eyelashes.

1930: Scores of new numbers were designed by Etta Kidd. They included babies, girls, boys, adults, pairs, pirates, cowboys, and long limbed dolls in romantic period costumes. Dolls' outfits, hats and shoes were also sold separately. Price of the doll was around $5.00, slightly lower than formerly. (See Ills. 898 and 899.)

Etudiante. 1930. Trade name of a *Boudoir* type doll dressed in taffeta and wearing a hat, as advertised by *Bon Marché*. Ht. 65 cm. (25½ in.).

Eugenic Babies. 1914. Trade name of a group of dolls advertised in a British trade journal. These lightweight composition dolls had sleeping eyes and were fully jointed.

Eureka Doll Co. (Eureka Doll Manufacturing Co.). 1923–30 and later. New York City. Made *Mama* dolls and baby dolls including crying dolls. *S. O. Ludwig* was their factory agent.

1924: Dressed Mama dolls cost 50¢ to $1.00.

1926: Increased number of doll models and variety of costumes.

1927: Made dolls with wigs and with sleeping eyes. A new doll was dressed as a clown in a flowered satin suit. Eureka was licensed by *Voices, Inc.* to use patented mama voices and criers in their dolls.

1928: Made large variety of baby dolls including their new doll-in-cradle. Mama dolls came with painted hair or wigs, painted eyes or sleeping eyes. Some of the sleeping-eyed dolls wore silk dresses. Some of the dolls had composition arms and legs on the cloth bodies. Hts. were 12 to 30 in. (30.5 to 76 cm.). Most of the larger dolls were Mama dolls. Popular prices for the dolls ranged from 25¢ to $5.00.

FOR *the first time in the history of America the attempt to* rival European Creations of Boudoir Dolls, Art Novelties, Pillows has been successful.

Etta, Inc., claims this distinction by offering a varied and increasing line of extraordinarily attractive Boudoir Dolls, Novelties D'Art, Pillows and Bags of the Vogue, Animals and Toys of Topical Interest.

Every Buyer is cordially invited to visit our New Display Room at 23 West 45th Street, New York—where what is whispered about in this message is shouted aloud by the models themselves.

Etta Incorporated

23 West 45th Street New York

PHONE: BRYANT 2061

898. Etta's advertisement for their Boudoir and novelty dolls as shown in PLAYTHINGS, January, 1927.

899. Etta's mark used for Boudoir and novelty dolls.

European Doll Manufacturing Co. 1911–30 and later. New York City. Despite their name they claimed that all their dolls in the 1920s were made in their own factory in America, "the line complete from head to heel." They specialized in *Mama* dolls, baby dolls, and infant dolls, and used the acronym EDMA. Most of their dolls were sold to jobbers. *Anita Novelty Co.* merged with this company but they kept the name European Doll Manufacturing Co.

1924: Advertised 70 numbers, which came with wigs or painted hair. The higher priced dolls had composition heads, arms and legs. Also there were lines of cloth dolls and crying dolls costing as little as 10¢ or 25¢. Mama dolls came in hts. 11 to 30 in. (28 to 76 cm.); priced 25¢ and up.

1925: A black doll 26 in. (66 cm.) tall cost $1.50.

1926: Over 200 numbers of Mama dolls and infant dolls,

cost 10¢ to $6.00. A sleeping eyed baby doll in a blanket cost $1.00. A sleeping eyed Mama doll in a lace trimmed outfit was 24 in. (61 cm.) tall.

1927: Licensed by *Voices, Inc.* to use patented mama voices and criers in their dolls.

1928: Over 300 numbers including a new doll, *Baby Bobby* and slim legged Mama dolls with marcelled hair and rayon silk dresses. Dolls were priced 25¢ to $10.00. Bags and pillows with composition dolls' heads on them were a novelty.

1929: Advertised over 300 numbers with an assortment of dolls retailing for 25¢ to $8.00. The baby dolls were able to stand. There were smaller dolls than previously and the emphasis was on dressed and undressed "Flapper" dolls (*Boudoir* dolls). "French," Flapper and felt dolls were brought in by the Anita Novelty Co. merger. According to TOY WORLD, February 1929: "The European Doll Manufacturing Co., . . . has affiliated . . . with the Anita Novelty Co.

"The latter concern has been a pioneer in the manufacture of pillows, flappers, bags and other French head novelties. . . .

"*M. Altbuch*, inventor of the French head, is also a member of the novelty concern."

1930: Made the *Famlee Dolls*. A trademark for the EDMA line was "Edma Dolls// Walks and Talks." Besides the various Mama dolls in this line there were baby dolls in short dresses, infant dolls and novelty dolls; price 25¢ to $10.00. A new featherweight line of dolls cost $1.00 to $5.00. A composition doll with a voice based on a pending patent was 11½ in. (29 cm.) tall; priced 50¢.★

900. Mark of the European Doll Manufacturing Co. (EDMA).

Euston, H. R., & Co. 1922–24. London. Agents for *Friedrichroda Doll Factory* and doll factories in Sonneberg and Neustadt. Sold dolls to wholesalers.

Eva. 1926–27. See **Topsy**, 1926–27.

Evangelina. 1930. Cloth doll with flat face and wig made by *Kat-A-Korner Kompany*; price $1.50 to $3.00.

Evans, Ewart. 1924–26. Advertised dolls in a British trade journal.

Evans, Margaret. 1916. An American children's artist who designed cutout cloth dolls named *Betty* and *Bobby* for *Stecher Lithographic Co.*

Evans & Co. 1928. Philadelphia, Pa. Produced dolls.

Eveline. 1927–28. *Boudoir* dolls wearing a period costume, made by *Lenci* as number 800. Size 45 in. (114.5 cm.).

Evelyn. 1918–19. All-composition doll made by *Jessie M. Raleigh* with wig, five-piece body, straight legs, steel spring joints; it wore a flowered dress and ribbon head-band.★

Everlasting Doll. 1876. Distributed by *Silber & Fleming*. It came dressed as a sailor, as a soldier or in a woolen dress. There were three sizes for each of these costumes.

Everlasting Doll Co. 1929–30 and later. New York City. Produced dolls.

Evripoze. 1920s. Name of a cloth doll patented in 1922 with a pressed head and a shoulder plate of stiffened fabric, a mohair wig, painted eyes, and a neck jointed so that the head turned. The stockinet body had cotton stuffing around a wire armature, and composition lower arms; the lower legs appeared to be wood, and were fully jointed, but reportedly

without ball and socket or spring joints. It was capable of standing on its own feet. This was one of the *A-1, Tru-to-Life* dolls made by *Dean* through its subsidiary the *British Novelty Works*. It carried an A-1 triangular tag and the bottom of one foot was stamped with "MADE IN//ENGLAND" in a rectangle; the other sole carried the patent number. These dolls wore dresses or suits representing regional or character costumes. Ht. 14 in. (35.5 cm.) and probably other heights.

Excelsior. 1890–1914. Trade name of dolls made by *Kestner* and distributed by *Butler Bros.* These dolls came with various types of bisque heads and various types of bodies.

1890: Doll's bisque head had sleeping eyes, wig and open mouth. Kid body had bisque hands. Hts. 17¾, 20½ and 25¾ in. (45, 52 and 65.5 cm.); price $17.50 to $39.00 doz. wholesale. The largest doll sold for $5.00 retail.

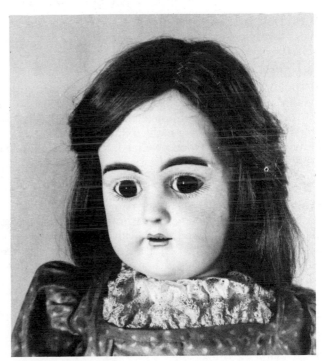

901. Bisque head doll with a wig, brown glass eyes, pierced ears, open mouth with four teeth and is on a ball-jointed composition body. Mark on head: Ill. 902. Mark on body: Ill. 903. H. 25 in. (63.5 cm.). *Courtesy of Hazel Ulseth.*

289 Dep

Excelsior Germany 5

902–903. Excelsior mark found on the body of a doll, Ill. 903, and the mark found on the head, Ill. 902.

1899: One type of doll had a molded bisque shoulder head, bisque arms and legs on a cloth body. The head and arms were tinted flesh color and white stockings and high black laced boots were represented on the legs. Hts. 6, 9½ and 13 in. (15, 24 and 33 cm.). Another type was a bisque socket head with a curly hair wig, glass sleeping eyes, and open mouth with teeth. The ball-jointed composition body was jointed at the wrists and the fingers were separated. The footwear consisted of black or plaid stockings and real patent leather shoes. Hts. 27 and 28¾ in. (68.5 and 73 cm.). A third type had a bisque head that turned, with glass eyes and open mouth with teeth. The composition body was jointed at the shoulders and hips and the shoes and stockings were painted on the legs. Hts. 8 and 9½ in. (20.5 and 24 cm.).

1902: Doll had a bisque head with glass eyes, wig, open mouth and teeth; on a ball-jointed composition body. Six hts.: 13¼, 16, 19, 23, 27 and 30 in. (33.5, 40.5, 48, 58.5, 68.5 and 76 cm.); priced 69¢ to $3.69 each wholesale.

1914: Doll had a bisque head with mohair wig and sleeping eyes. It was on a kid body with rivet joints. Four hts.: 15¾, 18, 20½, and 22½ in. (40, 45.5, 52, and 57 cm.).★

Exeloid Co. Before 1918–20. Prior to 1918, Newark, N.J.; 1918–20, East Stroudsburg, Pa. Made celluloid dolls using Pyralin† (Pyroxylin Plastic) sheets 20 in. by 50 in., 5/1000 to 20/1000 of an inch thick supplied by *Du Pont*. These pink, white or blue sheets were molded into celluloid dolls by a blowing process developed earlier in Germany. Wooden dolls were made in another factory in South Sterling, Pa.

Exercise Doll. See **Sandow, Eugene.**

Exhibition Baby. 1895–99. Trade name of a doll with composition head, arms and legs on a cloth body. It had a wig, glass eyes, an open-closed mouth with teeth and was distributed by *Butler Bros.* The doll had the proportions of a real baby and it was claimed that it could be used in show windows.

1895: It came in five hts.: 20, 22½, 25½, 27 and 31 in. (51, 57, 65, 68.5, and 78.5 cm.); priced 69¢ to $3.45.

1899: There were four hts.: 15, 21¼, 22½, and 25½ in. (38, 54, 57, and 65 cm.).

Exhibitions (Expositions). Dolls were a major attraction at the large industrial exhibitions which showed the newest and finest dolls produced at that time. The Jury Reports provided valuable information about these dolls and the awards show the names and relative importance of the various doll manufacturers. Most of this information has been reported in the first COLLECTOR'S ENCYCLOPEDIA OF DOLLS (see the entries for the various manufacturers, the chronology and the entry for each individual country) or in the appropriate entry in this volume. But these multitudinous entries do not provide overall information or a means for studying comparisons which the following exhibition data gives graphically.

The exhibition lists are not complete because details have not been found for all the awards. It should also be noted that many of the porcelain manufacturers who made

A BRIDE AND GROOM FROM
PONDICHERRY.

904. A bride and groom from Pondichéry, a French city in India. These dolls were part of a group of French costume dolls sent to the Rouen Exhibit of 1896. Later they were exhibited in Mlle. Koenig's museum in Paris and in the 1900 Paris Exposition. This picture was shown in ST. NICHOLAS, January, 1910.

905. The largest Nelke doll ever made. This doll was exhibited at the 1926 sesquicentennial celebration in Philadelphia. The two children are Harry and Jean Nelke, grandchildren of the founder Harry Nelke. Mrs. Moreland G. Smith, another grandchild, kindly made this old picture available.

dolls and dolls' heads had displays in the exhibition but are not included in the following lists because their products were primarily types of porcelain other than dolls.

Dolls were also shown at many other exhibitions for special purposes: philanthropic, artistic, mercenary, and to encourage sewing. The following are examples:

INTERNATIONAL AND NATIONAL EXHIBITIONS

1823 PARIS
Award unknown. France: Maelzel.[†]

1839 PARIS
Silver Medal. France: *Giroux.*
Award unknown. France: *Guillard.*

1844 BERLIN
Silver Medal. German States: Kummer[†]; Sonneberg Group; Voit & Fleischmann.[†]
Bronze Medal. German States: *A. Fleischmann*; Rau[†]; Voit.[†]
Award unknown. German States: Grossman[†]; Kraatz[†], Löwenthal[†]; Möwes[†]; Poppe[†]; Selzen[†]; Trognitz.[†]

1844 PARIS
Honorable Mention. France: *Belton & Jumeau; Brouillet & Cacheleux;* Dumont.[†]
Award unknown. France: François[†]; Greffier.[†]

1849 PARIS
Bronze Medal. France: Jumeau; *Théroude.*
Honorable Mention. France: Testard.[†]

1850 LEIPZIG
Bronze Medal. German States: *Hülse.*

1851 LONDON
(This was the first International Exhibition.)
Prize Medal. Austria: *Haller; Kietaibl.*
England: *Montanari.*
France: Jumeau.
German States: A. Fleischmann; Rock & Graner[†]; Sonneberg Group showed "Gulliver among the Lilliputians" made of bread dough and "Fair at Rosenau near Coburg." Rosenau was the birthplace of Prince Albert, Queen Victoria's consort.
Honorable Mention. Austria: C. A. Müller & Co.[†]
England: A. Bouchet.[†]
No Award. Austria: Purger.[†]
England: Trebeck.[†]
German States: Albert[†]; Bahn[†]; Lang[†]; Löwenthal; Neubronner.[†]

1853 NEW YORK
Bronze Medal. France: Leblond.[†]
German States: *Lange.*
Honorable Mention. German States: Fleischmann; S. Krauss[†]; Rock & Graner.
United States: *Brunswick;* H. Rogers[†]; Tuttle[†]—his exhibit is shown in Ill. 139 in THE COLLECTOR'S BOOK OF DOLLS' CLOTHES.

1854 MUNICH
Prize Medal. German States: Helm & Wellhausen[†]; Poppe.
Honorable Mention. German States: Hawsky[†]; Rock & Graner.

1855 PARIS
Silver Medal. France: Jumeau; Théroude.
German States: Rock & Graner.
Bronze Medal. France: *Huret.*
Award unknown. England: Montanari.
France: *Arnaud;* Dartheny[†]; Greffier; *Guillard;* Testard.[†]
German States: G. Liedel[†]; Poppe; Voit.

1862 LONDON
Prize Medal. France: Jumeau; Théroude.
German States: G. Benda[†]; Fromann[†]; L. Köhler[†]; Nöthlich & Falk[†]; Rock & Graner; Chr. Witthauer.[†]
Honorable Mention. German States: Hawsky; Helm & Wellhausen.
Award unknown. England: Burley[†]; *Cremer;* Montanari; *Peacock; Pierotti;* Rich.[†]
German States: Hutschenreuther.[†]
Russia: Han.[†]

1867 PARIS
Silver Medal. France: Jumeau; Potiers.[†]
Bronze Medal. France: *Caron; Roullet.*
Medal. France: Théroude.
Honorable Mention. France: Simonne.
Award unknown. Brazil: Hospice de Pedro II.[†]
England: Cremer.
France: *Andrina;* Bereux[†]; *Dehors; Dessain;* Fialont[†]; *Giroux, Guillard;* Huret & Lonchambron; *Loisseau;* Rémond[†], *Ruhmer;* Schanne[†]; *Schudze; Verdavainne.*
German States: Duffner[†]; Frank[†]; Kirschkamp[†]; G. Simon.[†]
Malta: Polito[†]; Zammit.[†]

1868 PARIS
Silver Medal. France: Caron.

1873 VIENNA
Gold Medal. France: Jumeau (medals of cooperation were given to four members of Maison Jumeau including Mme. Pannier.[†])
Medal of Merit. France: Giroux; Marchal & Bouffard[†]; Pannier.
Diploma of Merit. France: Guillard.
Awards unknown. Austria: *Insam & Prinoth; Moroder; Scholz;* Thilen.[†]
England: Cremer.
Germany: F. Bischoff[†]; Chr. Bischoff & Co.[†]; *J. Dorst; C. & O. Dressel;* Dressel, Kister & Co.[†]; *Engelhardt;* T. Escher[†]; A. Fleischmann & Co.; J. & P. Fleischmann[†]; *Hachmeister;* Jacob[†]; Krauss; *Lambert & Samhammer[†];* J. C. Lindner[†]; *Louis Lindner & Son;* J. N. Lützelberger; C. G. Müller[†]; J. F. Müller[†]; Rock & Graner.
United States: Vermont Novelty Works *(Co-operative Manufacturing Co.).*

1875 CINCINNATI
Award unknown. United States: *P. Goldsmith; Strobel & Wilken.*

1875 CHILE
Prize. Germany: *Fischer, Naumann & Co.*

1876 PARIS
Honorable Mention. France: *Ulhenhuth.*

1876 PHILADELPHIA
Gold Medal. France: Jumeau.
Award unknown. Germany: C. & O. Dressel; Schünemann[+]; Sichling.[+]
  Norway: Gram.[+]
  United States: *Althof, Bergmann & Co.;* Ives[+]; Lacmann[+]; *New York Rubber Co.*
  A picture of the French and German doll exhibit is shown in Ill. 225 in THE COLLECTOR'S BOOK OF DOLLS' CLOTHES.
  Newport, R. I. contributed a special "Centennial Doll" to the exhibition. This 10 in. (25.5 cm.) wax doll was allegedly imported from Paris and bought in Philadelphia by the Hon. Benjamin Bourne of Bristol, R. I. He was a member of Congress from 1790 to 1796 and gave the doll to his niece, Lilly Turner, born 1792. The doll wore original clothes and it was claimed that it had moving eyes.

1878 PARIS
Gold Medal. France: Jumeau; Potiers.
Silver Medal. France: *Bourgoin; Bru;* Caron; Choumer & Collet[+]; *Derolland; Gaultier; Rossignol;* Roullet; *Schmitt; J. Steiner; Vichy.*
Bronze Medal. France: *A. Blampoix.*
Honorable Mention. France: Borreau[+]; Pannier.
Award unknown. Austria: Insam & Prinoth; Moroder; Thilen.
  Bolivia: Artola.[+]
  China: Knight.[+]
  Denmark: Brix[+]; E. Hansen.[+]
  England: Montanari.
  France: Bereux; *Chiquet;* Dehors; Devanaux[+]; Estivalet & Martin[+]; Guillory[+]; *Jullien;* Keller[+]; *Lefebvre; Lejeune;* Elie Martin; Merle[+]; Montanari[+]; *Nadaud; Petit & Dumontier;* Quivy[+]; *Rabery & Delphieu;* P. Rauch[+]; Schudze; Simonne; Ulhenhuth; *Villard & Weill.*
  Guatemala: Mayorga.[+]
  Japan: Yamagawa.[+]
  Spain: Macazaga.[+]
  LITTLE FOLKS, a periodical, reported in 1879 that French girls, ages 5 to 15 years, had made for wax dolls in this exhibition "elaborate doll's clothes all muslin and lace."

1879 CHERBOURG
Silver Medal. France: Vichy.

1879 PARIS
Bronze Medal. France: Guimmoneau.[+]
Medal. France: Ulhenhuth.

1879 SYDNEY
First Degree Merit. France: Jumeau.
Highly Commended. France: Villard & Weill.
  Germany: Fischer, Naumann & Co.
Commended. Germany: Lambert & Samhammer; Motschmann & Hüffner[+]; Rock & Graner; *D. H. Wagner.*

1880 BRUSSELS
Bronze Medal. France: Gaultier.

1880 MELBOURNE
Gold Medal. France: Jumeau (dolls, bébés).
Silver Medal. France: Bru (dolls, bébés); *Falck.*
Bronze Medal. France: Jumeau (mechanical); Lejeune; Vichy.
  Germany: Fischer, Naumann & Co.; Unger[+], Schneider & Co. (mechanical).
Certificate. France: Bru (mechanical): Martin; Potiers.
  Germany: Wagner.
No Award. Germany: Dorst; C. & O. Dressel; Fleischmann Bros.[+]; R. Heinze[+]; J. C. Lindner; L. Lindner & Son; *Müller & Strassburger.*
  Japan: T. Hayashi[+]; Kiriu Koshokuwaisha & T. Akiyama.[+]
  Queensland (Australia): *P. Thomle* (mechanical).

1881 PORTE ALEGRE, BRAZIL
Award unknown. Germany: D. H. Wagner.

1883 AMSTERDAM
Gold Medal. France: Martin.
Silver Medal. France: Gaultier; Rabery & Delphieu.
Award unknown. France: Pannier.

1884 NEW ORLEANS
Gold Medal. France: Jumeau; Vichy.
Award unknown. United States: Darrach[+]; Wishard.[+]

1884 NICE
Silver Medal. France: Gaultier.

1885 ANTWERP
Hors Concours (Member of Jury). France: Péan Frères.[+]
Diploma of Honor. France: Jumeau.
Gold Medal. France: Derolland.
Silver Medal. France: Gaultier; Rabery & Delphieu.

1885 PARIS
Gold Medal. France: Bru; Jumeau.
Bronze Medal. France: Joanny.[+]

1886 LIVERPOOL
Gold Medal. France: Bru.
Medal. France: Ulhenhuth.

1886 PARIS
Gold Medal. France: Bru.

1887 LE HAVRE
Gold Medal. France: Bru.

1887 TOULOUSE
Gold Medal. France: Bru.

1888 BARCELONA
Gold Medal. France: Bru.
Silver Medal. France: L. Lambert[+]; Rabery & Delphieu.

1888 BRUSSELS
Prize. Germany: *Buschow & Beck.*

1888 CINCINNATI
First Prize. United States: *Arnoldt.*

1888 MELBOURNE
Gold Medal. France: Bru; Vichy.
Silver Medal. Austria: *Frankl.*
            France: Falck & Roussel.
Award unknown. France: Bru (Chevrot).
    Germany: *M. O. Arnold;* C. & O. Dressel; Heubach; Kämpfe &
    Sontag[†]; *P. Recknagel.*

1888 PARIS
Gold Medal. France: Bru.
Silver Medal. France: *Guyot.*

1889 BARCELONA
Prize. Germany: Buschow & Beck.

1889 LINZ
Gold Medal. Austria: Frankl.

1889 PARIS
Hors Concours. France: Jumeau; L. Lambert; Péan.
Foreman of Jury. France: Jullien.
Member of Jury. France: Derolland.
Gold Medal. France: Steiner; Villard & Weill.
Silver Medal. France: Bru (Chevrot); Gaultier; Niquet & Bouchet.[†]
Award unknown. France: Duhotoy[†]; Dumont[†]; Duthiel[†]; Petit &
    Dumontier; *J. A. Runggaldier;* Vichy.

1890 LONDON
Gold Medal. France: *E. Denamur,* Tour St. Jacques.[†]

1890 PARIS
Diploma of Honor. France: Steiner.

1892–93 CHICAGO
(World's Columbian Exposition)
Diploma of Merit. United States: Adams.[†]
Award unknown. France: *Bawo & Dotter;* L. Delachal[†]; *Couturier;*
    Desiré & Lamane[†]; P. E. Girard (Bru); A. Hesse (Vitu[†]); Jumeau
    (exhibited large lady dolls dressed in historical costumes);
    Lambert (mechanical); Maltête[†]; *Fernand Martin; Pintel &
    Godchaux;* Al. Rabery; Roullet & Decamps (mechanical); G.
    & H. Vichy (mechanical & music).
    Germany: M. O. Arnold; *Alt, Beck & Gottschalck; Crämer &
    Héron;* C. & O. Dressel; Dressel, Kister & Co.; *Wilh. Dressel;*
    A. Fleischmann & Crämer; Edm. Fleischmann & Sohn[†]; Fleis-
    chmann Bros.; *C. Geyer & Co.;* H. Hachmeister; *H. Hand-
    werck;* Heinrich Bros.[†]; *H. Horn;* Kämmer & Reinhardt; *J. D.
    Kestner, Jr.;* Joh. Chr. Lindner; L. Lindner & Son; *A. Luge &
    Co.*[†]; *F. Luge;* Limbach Porzellanfabrik; Rueckert & Co.; *Phi.
    Samhammer;* F. M. Schilling; O. Schmidt[†]; *Schuetzmeister &
    Quendt;* O. Treuter[†]; *Wiesenthal, Schindel & Kallenberg; E.
    Wittzack.*
        Many of the above exhibitors contributed to the Sonneberg
    group, which had a carriage with dolls in it dressed as children
    and surrounding it. This was designed by the Sonneberg In-
    dustrial School under the supervision of *Prof. Möller* and many
of the "cottage manufacturers" participated in its preparation;
according to an 1895 periodical, ATHLETIC SPORTS, GAMES
& TOYS.
Jamaica: W. H. Nash[†] (cashew dolls).
Japan: Iwasa Buemon[†]; Shimizu Hatsuzo[†]; Wada Heibei[†]; Kan-
    sai Trading Co.[†]; Hattori Manji[†]; Sato Torakiyo.[†]
Mexico: Galindo[†]; Hernandez[†]; Herrera y Hoyo.[†]
Norway: Husflidsforening Norsk[†]; Kristian Olson.[†]
Spain: Jaime Pujol e Hijo[†] (cardboard).
Sweden: Emma Kraepelin.[†]
United States: Horsman; Ives (mechanical).

1893 ERFURT
Silver Medal. Germany: *E. Bauersachs.*

1894 VIENNA
Silver Medal. Austria: Frankl.

1895 DRESDEN
Bronze Medal. Germany: E. Bauersachs.

1895 PARIS
Gold Medal. France: Bouchet.

1896 ROUEN
Gold Medal. France: Bouchet.
    Mlle. Koenig exhibited 200 dolls in the costumes of Brittany
and other French provinces and colonies.

1897 BRUSSELS
Gold Medal. France: Bouchet.

1897 VIENNA
Gold Medal. Austria: Frankl.

1900 PARIS
Hors Concours & Member of Jury. France: Fernand Martin; *Société
    Française de Fabrication de Bébés & Jouets.*
Grand Prix. France: *Roussel & Dufrien;* Vichy.
    Germany: Bauersachs; *Geo. Borgfeldt & Co.;* Crämer & Héron;
    Dorst; C. & O. Dressel; Wilm. Dressel; Engelhardt; *J. G.
    Escher & Sohn;* Fleischmann Bros.; Fleischmann & Crämer; C.
    Geyer; *Haag Bros.;* H. Hachmeister; *C. Harmus, Jr.; R. Hart-
    wig;* Hugo Heubach[†]; C. Hoffmeister[†]; *M. Hofmann & Co.;
    H. Horn;* A. König[†]; *Rich. Leutheuser;* J. C. Lindner; L. Lind-
    ner & Son; *Löffler & Dill;* H. Lützelberger[†]; *J. N. Lützelberger;*
    F. Luge; A. Luge & Co.; Carl Meyer[†]; R. Möller[†]; Müller &
    Fröbel[†]; P. Samhammer; *C. Schaitberger;* F. M. Schilling;
    Schmey (successors); A. Schönau[†]; G. Spindler[†]; G. Stier[†]; F. E.
    Winkler[†]; Zeuch & Lausmann.[†]
        (This was a Sonneberg Collective exhibit.)
Gold Medal. France: Villard & Weill.
    Germany: *Bing Bros.*
Silver Medal. France: L. Delachal; Delhaye Bros.[†]; J. Mettais
    (Steiner); Roullet & Decamps.
    Japan: Seijiro Misaki[†]; Yazo Yaseihara.[†]
Bronze Medal. France: Ch. & H. Collett (Maison Derolland); A.
    Duclos[†]; J. Fournier[†]; Gaultier; Jullien, Jr.; T. Lamagnère[†]; H.
    LeConte & Co.[†]; Maison F. Martin; Moreau *(Chéret & Mor-
    eau);* Muller & Delattre[†]; *L. M. Renou.*

Germany: Heinrich Bros.; Maison Hugo Heubach.

Japan: Z. Kishikawa[†]; K. Okada[†]; M. Sakuda[†]; K. Shimizu[†]; H. Wada[†]; S. Wakano.[†]

Honorable Mention. France: Maison A. Duclos[†]; A. Lefebvre.

Japan: Y. Bamba[†]; Furukawa[†]; M. Matsubashi[†]; Nishikawa.[†]
   The doll collections of the queen of Romania and of Mlle. de Bourbon were on display at this Exhibition.

1904 ST. LOUIS

Grand Prize. France: Villard & Weill.

   Germany: A. König; *Armand Marseille; M. Steiff.*

Award unknown. France: L. Lambert (mechanical with music); Mme. Marcat[†]; F. Martin (mechanical); *J. du Serre.*

   Germany: Collective exhibit of Sonneberg, designed by Director Professor Möller, used dolls to portray a fair.
   E. Bauersachs; Geo. Borgfeldt & Co.; *M. Carl;* Cramer & Héron; J. Dorst; C. & O. Dressel; W. Dressel; E. Escher, Jr.; A. Fleischmann & Cramer; Fleischmann Bros.; Hamburger & Co.[†]; C. Harmus, Jr.; R. Hartwig; Hugo Heubach; C. Hoffmeister; H. Horn; R. Leutheuser; L. Lindner & Son; H. Lützelberger; J. N. Lützelberger; A. Luge & Co.; Müller & Fröbel; W. Pfarr[†]; P. Samhammer & Co.; F. M. Schilling; G. Schmey (successors); A. Schönau; *L. Wolf & Co;* Zeuch & Lausmann. (For the official report from the catalog of the exhibition of the German Empire, see the first COLLECTOR'S ENCYCLOPEDIA OF DOLLS, under German Dolls.)

1905 LIÈGE

Grand Prize. France: Villard & Weill.

   Primitive Russian and Brazilian dolls in exhibit, also contemporary French and German bisque head dolls as well as dolls from Belgium and Japan. Old dolls included early wooden ones.

1906 PARIS

Grand Prize. France: Roullet & Decamps.

1907 PARIS

Grand Prize. France: Roullet & Decamps.

1908 LONDON

Award unknown: *Clerc.*

1908 PARIS

Hors Concours. France: *Mmes. Lafitte & Désirat.*

Grand Prize. France: Roullet & Decamps.

First Prize. France: *Mlle. Riera.*

Second Prize. France: *Mme. Jungbluth, Mme. Soulié.*

Honorable Mention. Mmes. Bausmann, Derauvo, Dulong, Leroy, Létang, Natanelli, Pillois, and Saratoff.

1909 BERLIN

Award unknown. Germany: Kaulitz.

1909 PARIS

Grand Prize. France: Roullet & Decamps.

1910 BRUSSELS

Hors Concours & Members of Jury. France: Fernand Martin.

Grand Prix. France: Derolland & Delacoste; Widow Decamps, *Kratz-Boussac.*

   Germany: Gebrüder Bing; Steiff; The Sonneberg collective group depicting a fair in Sonneberg, designed by Director

Professor Möller and still exhibited in 1980 in the Sonneberg museum. The contributors included Emil Bauersachs; Cramer & Héron; C. & O. Dressel; Wilm. Dressel; Engelhardt; J. G. Escher; Fleischmann & Cramer; Gebrüder Fleischmann; C. Geyer; H. Hachmeister; C. Harmus, Jr.; R. Hartwig; Hugo Heubach; M. Hofmann & Co.; H. Horn; R. Leutheuser; Louis Lindner & Son; Löffler & Dill; F. Luge; H. Lützelberger; J. N. Lützelberger; A. Mansert[†]; Müller & Fröbel; W. G. Müller[†]; Pulvermacher & Westram[†]; P. Samhammer; C. Schaitberger; *M. F. Schelhorn*[†]; F. M. Schilling; Schmey successors; G. Spindler; F. E. Winkler; W. Zurkuhl.[†]

Gold Medal. Germany: Gebrüder Fleischmann[†] of Nürnberg; Marion Kaulitz.

   England: *Dean.*

Silver Medal. Denmark: Magasin des Poupées Parisiennes in Copenhagen.

Bronze Medal. France: *Le Montréer.*

1911 LONDON (Crystal Palace)

Gold Medal. England: Dean.

1918 NEW YORK CITY

American, Belgian, French, and Polish dolls.

1924 ? Jubilee

Silver Medal. Germany: Löffler & Dill (Sico).

1926 PHILADELPHIA

United States: *Acme; Annin; Averill Manufacturing Co.; Dorothy Heizer; Nelke*

Dolls dressed by Women's Clubs in various states.

1861–65: During the American Civil War, Dolls were exhibited at the Sanitary Fairs that were held in various cities to raise money for the Sanitary Commission (Later known as the Red Cross). (See Ills. 155, 162, and Color Plate 7 in THE COLLECTOR'S BOOK OF DOLLS' CLOTHES.)

1875–77: Yearly exhibits of dolls were held in London. Children competed for prizes in dressing the dolls which then were either sold to obtain money for orphanages or were given to children in hospitals. There were four classes of dolls in 1877: dolls dressed as brides, baby dolls, single dolls in regional or period costumes, and a group of dolls in regional or period costumes. The prizes were books.

1876: A doll exhibit in Boston was described in WIDE AWAKE: Dolls of all kinds and sizes, dressed entirely by readers of the child's periodical WIDE AWAKE. The dolls wore any type of costume so long as they had a chemise, drawers, underskirt and dress. Headwear and footwear were optional. The patterns for the clothes could be made by others but the garments must have been made by the child herself. Suggested costumes were Quaker ladies, Martha Washingtons, Swiss peasants, Roman Girls, plain waiting-maids, cooks, etc. The prizes will be given *not* for handsome dress, but for the *best-made* clothing." The ten prizes were books grouped according to the ages of the contestants, that is, under 10 years, 10 to 12 years, and 12 to 15 years of age. The dolls shown in the exhibition were later sent to children in hospitals in various cities as Christmas presents.

1. DRESSING DOLLS. 2. UNPACKING THE DOLL CASES.

NEW YORK CITY.—THE CHARITY-DOLL SHOW, OPENED DECEMBER 15TH, AT FIFTH AVENUE AND SIXTEENTH STREET.
DRAWN BY MISS G. A. DAVIS.—[SEE PAGE 371.]

906. Drawing from FRANK LESLIE'S ILLUSTRATED NEWSPAPER, December 20, 1890, showing the preparation for a charity doll show in New York City.

A

B

C

907A, B, & C. Three bisque head dolls exhibited at a Dolls' Fair in Denver, Colorado, 1891. One of these dolls is black and dressed in a regional costume. They all appear to have wigs, glass eyes, and jointed composition bodies; probably made in Germany. These three Carte de Visite photographs are part of a series of similar pictures in the Coleman Collection.

1890: FRANK LESLIE'S ILLUSTRATED NEWSPAPER reported an exhibition of dolls dressed by famous people such as First Ladies Mrs. Cleveland and Mrs. Harrison, and many stage stars. As usual the dolls later were either sold for charity or given to children's hospitals and missions. (See THE COLLECTOR'S BOOK OF DOLLS' CLOTHES, Ill. 415, for the dolls shown at this exhibition.)

1892: Dolls dressed in a historical costume series were exhibited in Paris. These later became part of the Musée des Arts Décoratifs' collection in the Louvre Museum.

1894: THE GIRLS' OWN PAPER, a British periodical, described a competition which was somewhat similar to those held in the 1870s. Again there were four categories, namely: "Historical, National, Rag Dolls and Dolls in Present-Day Fashions.

". . . In the class of 'rag dolls' three classes will be admitted, i.e., the old-fashion rag doll, as made up altogether at home; the new-fashion one, made of the flat models [Cutout Cloth Dolls] as now sold in most shops, and those with the head and shoulders of wax or Composition, the bodies only being of home manufacture. Rag dolls to be dressed as children of all ages; only not as grown people. The clothes should invariably be made to take on and off. . . . After the [exhibit] the dolls will be presented to the children of hospitals, poor children's societies and workhouses.

". . . We had only one bride come to our competition, four nurses, a charming gentleman of the reign of George III., and a beautiful Incroyable damsel of the year 1793, hailing from Paris, and dressed in blended hues of yellow and pink even to her stockings; the patches and powder period is also represented and the millinery of our competition leaves nothing to be desired." The dolls were sent to hospitals, orphanages, and industrial schools.

1896: Some of the 10,000 dolls at a show in Buffalo, N.Y. were described in HARPER'S ROUND TABLE. The charity show had most of the dolls arranged in scenes such as a "Hunt Breakfast" which depicted the annual fox hunting meet of "The Duke of Beaufort and his huntsmen wearing blue broadcloth coats with buff facings, while the Earl of Bathurst's . . . men wore pink broadcloth, the clothing being imported from England expressly for these tiny huntsmen. . . .

"The doll which attracted the most attention was one which had come all the way from Paris—where she had just taken a prize at a doll show there. . . . Her gown was of pink brocaded satin, her coat and high poke bonnet were of moss-green velvet. In one hand she held a lace fan and in the other a ruffled chiffon parasol and a point-lace handkerchief peeped from a jeweled shopping-bag which she carried on her arm." According to this same account another doll wore a Worth gown which contrasted with a Salvation Army group.

1897: 3,000 dolls were exhibited in Philadelphia, Pa. to raise money for Howard Hospital. Entrance fee was 10¢ a doll. A large variety of dolls was exhibited: old dolls, dolls in historical costumes, and dolls in regional costumes; some of these were loaned by the Archaeological Department of the

FIRST PRIZE. *(Five Guineas.)*

908. The Exhibit of 1894 sponsored by THE GIRLS' OWN PAPER awarded the first prize of $26.25 to the doll shown in this picture. This doll representing a four year old girl, wore a lined white cashmere pelisse, a trimmed beaver bonnet, and a "Dutch hood." The white dress had a pink silk yoke and sleeves. The underclothes were knitted.

University of Pennsylvania. A doll sent by *Au Nain Bleu* was costumed by a celebrated modiste of Philadelphia, Pa.

1899–1901: 1,300 dolls collected by *Queen Elizabeth of Romania* were exhibited in various cities in Europe and America. The exhibits raised money for charity.

1902: The "Art in Child Life" exhibit in Vienna featured dolls made by *Wilhelm Pohl.*

1908: Dolls created by *Poulbot* were exhibited in the Salon des Humaristes, Paris. See Ill. 912.

1908–11: The Munich Art Dolls were shown at several Art Exhibits, by *Marion Kaulitz.*

Ca. 1910: *Léonhard Tietz* had a doll exhibit and competition in his store to raise money to buy milk for children and for the Society to Protect Infants. The exhibit had various dolls in scenes. A Flemish Fair included an Italian shooting gallery; Buffalo Bill's Wild West show; Mme Blanche, a fortune teller; a photography studio with special pictures of automobiles, airplanes and electric lights. One room-setting had 17 stylishly dressed lady dolls similar to the art dolls made by *Mlle. E. V. Riera.*

SECOND AND THIRD PRIZES. (*Three Guineas and One Guinea.*)

909. Dolls winning second and third prizes, as shown in THE GIRLS' OWN PAPER, 1894. The exhibit prizes were $15.75 and $5.25. The gray-green velvet coat and hat were trimmed with gray-green fluffy "galon." The stockings were knitted and the shoes were homemade. The third prize went to a doll dressed in a Japanese style frock of pink and green satin and gold embroidery.

910. The 1894 Exhibit sponsored by THE GIRL'S OWN PAPER, awarded a prize of $5.25 to each of the two girls who made the clothes for this baby doll and this cloth doll.

1912–13: At the Bavarian Industrial show, *Rat L. Wenz* exhibited regional costume dolls.

1914: Mr. Edward Lovett exhibited dolls in Cardiff, Wales. (See **Collections of Dolls.**)

1915: The Metropolitan Museum exhibited a series of dolls dressed in historical costumes. These dolls were still at the Metropolitan Museum until World War II.

1916: An exposition of Decorative Arts organized by M. Metman in Paris featured the art dolls of *Mme. Thabée Lazarski* and *Mlle. Fiszerowna.*

In Brussels there was an exhibit entitled "Exposition de Poupées, Jouets, Vêtements & Literies Destinés à la St. Nicholas des Enfants de nos Soldats. (Exhibition of Dolls, Toys, Clothes, and Bedding for the Christmas of the Children of our Soldiers). Donations for this exhibit even came from the U.S. Prizes were as follows: Hors Concours: *Bourse, Hirsch & Cie., Bon Marché, L'Innovation Fischer Frères.*

Grand Prize: *Delhaize Frères, Le Jouet Belge, Le Jouet Liégeois.* 1ˢᵗ Prize: *La Tentation.*

1918: THE TOYSHOP AND FANCY GOODS JOURNAL,

911. Doll in period costume created by Wilhelm Pohl and shown in the "Art in Child Life" exhibit in Vienna in 1902.

912. Dolls representing urchins of Paris created by Poulbot and exhibited in the Salon des Humaristes as shown in THE STUDIO, November, 1908.

„In Reih' und Glied" — so gut es gehen will.

913. Puppen Reform dolls exhibited by Hermann Tietz in Munich, as reported in DIE WELT DER FRAU (The Ladies' World), November, 1908. The German caption is "In rank and file as good as possible."

February, 1919, reported an exhibit of dolls held in London the previous December.

"It was amusing to find the Premier's drawing-room inhabited by wondrous dolls recently. Mrs. Lloyd George was giving a tea, where the plans of the doll show for the Children's Jewel Fund were being discussed, and some of the more famous dolls, including the Welsh one which Queen Alexandra has sent now that her children and grandchildren are grown up, had been brought for the occasion. . . . Lady Drogheda, who is doing the air-dolls, was in a black frock, with brushed wool embroidery, an adornment also adopted by Mlle. de Bittencourt, who is in charge of the Ninette and Rentintin [sic] dolls. Lady Henry, Lady Tree, Mrs. Archibald Weigall, and Lady Newnes, who is organizing the historical section of the show were all enthusiastically discussing plans, and the Duchess of Marlborough, in whose Curzon Street house the show is to be held on December 10 to 20 hurried in rather late."

The Art Alliance had an exhibit of dolls which included a French *Pandora* doll.

1922: An exhibit of dolls dressed in costumes of the Coimbra area of Portugal was held in Coimbra. These dolls were manufactured in nearby Feguera de Foz. After the exhibit *Stewart Culin* purchased about half of these dolls. (21 of them for the Brooklyn Museum).

1923: The Brooklyn Museum exhibited cloth dolls created by *Katarina Paar.*

29 carved wooden dolls dressed in silk to represent famous historical celebrities were made by *Gisela Bennati* and exhibited at the Second International Silk Exposition.

Ca. 1925: Texas College of Industrial Arts exhibited 100 dolls dressed to represent periods and places in American History. Work began on the creation of this series in 1923.

1925 and earlier: 36 carved wooden dolls with articulated arms were dressed in historical costumes and exhibited in numerous Colleges and Universities to illustrate courses in the History of Costume.

1926: The Art Alliance of America exhibited dolls, among them the cloth dolls of *Dorothy Heizer,* the wooden dolls of *Helen Hitchcock,* and the paper dolls of Helen Dry. On the committee for this exhibition were John Martin, *Rose O'Neill,* Tony Sarg and Mrs. *Stewart Culin.* Tony Sarg loaned some of his antique wooden and wax dolls for this exhibit.

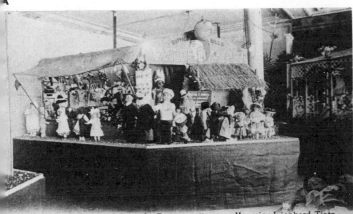

Kermesse Flamande de la «POUPÉE CHARITABLE,» aux Magasins Léonhard Tietz,
au profit des œuvres «Le Lait pour les Petits» et Soc. prot. des «Enfants Martyrs»
Phot. G. Hauck Anvers

Kermesse Flamande de la «POUPÉE CHARITABLE,» aux Magasins Léonhard Tietz,
au profit des œuvres «Le Lait pour les Petits» et Soc. prot. des «Enfants Martyrs»
Phot. G. Hauck Anvers

Kermesse Flamande de la «POUPÉE CHARITABLE,» aux Magasins Léonhard Tietz,
au profit des œuvres «Le Lait pour les Petits» et Soc. prot. des «Enfants Martyrs»
Phot. G. Hauck Anvers

914A–C. Dolls exhibited by Léonhard Tietz in Antwerp, Belgium, ca. 1910, as shown on a series of postcards. The first group of dolls is at Buffalo Bill's Wild West Show. The second scene is at a photographer's studio on a street corner. The shop window shows formal photographs of dolls. The third scene is along an amusement area. On the left is a music grinder and on the right a queue waiting at an entrance. The dolls in all three scenes appear to be German bisque or celluloid head dolls. (See Ills. 2606 and 2607.)

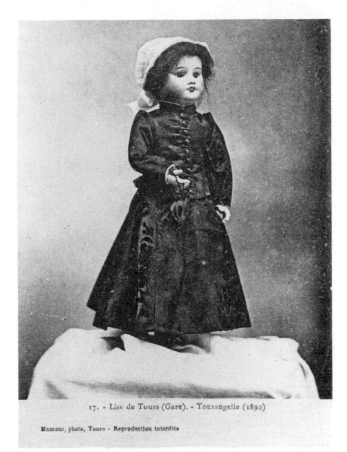

17. - Lise de Tours (Gare). - Tourangelle (1890)

Mamour, photo, Tours - Reproduction interdite

915. Postcard picture of a doll representing a lady of Tours, France, in 1890. This doll appears to have been part of an exhibit in Tours during or after World War I.

Expert Doll & Toy Co. 1926–30. New York City. Made popular priced stuffed dolls of velvet or plush. Used "Expert Dolls" as a trademark.

Exposition Doll & Toy Manufacturing Co. 1921–30 and later. New York City. Manufactured *Mama* dolls, baby dolls and character dolls. Used the trade name "Exposition Dolls."

1927: They were licensed by *Voices, Inc.* to use their patent mama voices and criers.

1928: Advertised a new group of baby dolls, a new line of 27 in. (68.5 cm.) popular priced dolls with "French wigs." Their best dolls had hair eyelashes, mohair wigs, composition arms and legs. Other dolls came with cloth legs. The height range of their various types of dolls was 12 to 28 in. (30.5 to 71 cm.).

Expositions. See Exhibitions.

Eyebrows. The painting of eyebrows with a darker center line surrounded by a lighter area appeared to be typical of a porcelain factory that made china heads dating from the 1850s–60s. This similarity of eyebrows on dolls from a given factory often suggests that decals were used for these eyebrows rather than hand-painting. (See also **Decalcomania.**)★

Eyeglasses. Many dolls have been found wearing eyeglasses. These could be representations of the types of glasses that are used for improving vision or they could be goggles to protect the eyes when in a fast-moving vehicle. Prior to World War I dolls that wore glasses often represented comic characters such as *Foxy Grandpa* and *Gilbert the Filbert.* The following is a list of some of the dolls that wore eyeglasses or goggles and some of the manufacturers.

1902 and later: Foxy Grandpa.

Before 1906–11 and later: *Gr.* (Grandpa), *Steiff.* (See Ill. 1082.)

1915–21: Gilbert the Filbert, the Nursery Knut, *Dean.*

1918: *Braitling,* auto goggles.

1923: *Dolly Rose Mary* and *Dolly Marion,* horn rim glasses, *Effanbee.*

1926: *School Girl, Chad Valley; Harold the College Boy, Whyte Ridsdale.*

1927: Kurt, *Käthe Kruse; Dandy* (monocle), *Lenci;* and "Funny," *Dora Petzold; Grandma and Red Riding Hood, Twinjoy Dolls.*

1929: *Dulcie Daring,* pattern in MODERN PRISCILLA; *Lindbergh, Shuco.* (See THE COLLECTOR'S BOOK OF DOLLS' CLOTHES, Ill. 798.)

Eyes. Apparently glass eyes were made in many European countries. In Germany most of the glass eyes were made in Lauscha but a 1924 U.S. Department of Commerce report stated that making dolls' eyes was an old established craft in Germany and many homes and factories supplied eyes to the local trade. This report credited *Otto Gans* with the invention of flirting eyes. However dolls have been found with a flirting eye mechanism which dated from probably the time Otto Gans was born. Setting eyes was the best paid job in the manufacturing of dolls in the Sonneberg area.

As late as the early 1900s *Lucy Peck* and probably others still used a wire pull method for making sleeping eyes in wax dolls' heads. See Ill. 2074.

The natural looking French glass eyes used for French bébés are called "émaillé" (enameled) in France but in America they are usually described as "paperweight." Henry Mayhew in London (see 1840s–50s below) referred to eyes that were "glass spheres made of white enamel." (See **French Dolls** before World War I.)

"Enameled" eyes in the U.S. refers to eyes that are painted with a shiny enamel paint.

During World War I and in the 1920s metal eyes were used for American dolls; sometimes wax or a thin layer of a celluloid substance was placed over the metal. Many of these eyes were made by *Margon* in Newark, N.J.

1840s–50s: Types of eyes were described by Henry Mayhew in his book LONDON LABOUR AND THE LONDON POOR, 1861, based on information gathered in 1849–51.

There were only two makers of dolls' eyes in London but many of the eyes were made in Birmingham. The common eyes were small hollow glass spheres made of white enamel and colored either black or blue. "Natural Eyes" were super-

ior but similarly made and used only on the best dolls. Nine tenths of the eyes are exported. "The eyes that we make for Spanish America are all black. Here however nothing but blue eyes goes down; that's because it's the colour of the Queen's eyes, and she set the fashion in our eyes as in other things. We make the same kind of eyes for the gutta-percha dolls as for the wax. It is true the gutta-percha complexion isn't particularly clear; nevertheless the eyes I make for the washable faces are all of natural tint, and if the gutta-percha dolls look rather bilious, why I ain't a going to make my eyes look bilious to match."

1851: Mayhew wrote in the MORNING CHRONICLE:
"A Man may make about twelve dozen pairs of the commoner [eyes], and about two or three dozen pairs of the better ones in the course of a day. . . . I make eyes for a French house at L'Havre that exports a vast quantity."

1861: *John D. Robbins* imported dolls' heads with sleeping waxed glass eyes.

1882–83: *Printemps* advertised a 15 cm. (6 in.) *Mignonnette* with sleeping eyes.

1893: *Horsman* advertised eyes with hair eyelashes.

1913: Dolls that roll or wink their eyes were reported to be "new from Paris."

916. Wax-over-composition head doll with dark brown hair inserted in a slit, black glass wire-pull sleeping eyes, closed mouth and a cloth one-piece body with kid arms. Original clothes. H. 27 in. (68.5 cm.). *Courtesy of Cherry Bou.*

917. Wax-over-composition shoulder head with black weighted sleeping eyes. A black band is in the molded blond painted hair and the cloth body has wooden limbs. Original clothes. H. 12 in. (30.5 cm.). *Coleman Collection.*

918A & B. Pressed bisque head doll with wig; the flirting brown glass eyes are operated by a lever at the back of the neck. Similar to the Tête Jumeau shown on page 28 of Margaret Whitton's THE JUMEAU DOLL. It has pierced ears and a closed mouth. Mark on outside of neck: Ill. 921. Written in ink inside the head just below the rim: "Breveté France et Etranger//A??." Ht. 26 in. (66 cm.). *Courtesy of Heather and Clifford Bond.*

1915: It was claimed that the dolls' eyes made by the *English Toy Manufacturing Co.* approached the quality of the ones made in Germany.

E. Greiner made eyes with moving lids.

1917: A British trade journal in 1917 reported that glass eyes were still being made in Birmingham but most of them were imported from France during the war. It was also reported that dolls' eyes were a monopoly of the Austrian glass blowers. Could Thüringen have been erroneously located in Austria?

Another British toy trade journal reported that prior to World War I eyes all came from Germany, "but now they are made and even exported by Italian firms."

Ca. 1920: A paper tag attached to a *Fulper* bisque head read, "NOTICE//The eyes action is tied//to secure safe transit// please untie//the cord."

1926: TOYS AND NOVELTIES reported: "In dolls of foreign manufacture eyes are cast in plaster of Paris on a rod which is immovable when the plaster has set. The eyes often do not fit the holes in the head. . . . In the United States patents permit the adjustment." Otto Gans of Waltershausen advertised dolls with "patented Flirting and Solid Eyes having Reflex Action."

Paul Krannich patented dolls' eyes consisting of electric lights.

1927: *Hermann Steiner* patented eyes with moving pupils. (See Ill. 2520.)

1928: American trade journals commented as follows on the eyes in American dolls: "More blue eyes than brown eyes are painted on composition dolls." Thanks to the ideas of *Isaac A. Rommer* of *Ideal* many of the American dolls have moving eyes. Mr. Trumpore of *Effanbee* stated about the developments in moving eyes: "The slightest details and objections have had to be foreseen and overcome. The objection to the staring . . . was overcome largely through the adoption of the eyelashes."

1929: PLAYTHINGS reported that "Dolls' eyes are made by painting the design on metal disks attached to a weighted bar inside the head, the weight moving the eyes as the position of the doll is changed." These were used chiefly on popular priced dolls. Celluloid eyes had been used for many years but they were not always successful. PLAYTHINGS continued: "In seeking to reduce the cost the manufacturer

experimented with eyes of celluloid. He contracted for 300,000 dolls' eyes but the shells lacked uniformity in size, color and expression, and the balancing apparatus entailed a larger expense than the metal eyes did."

The case went to court where it was demonstrated "that after exposure to heat or cold, dolls with celluloid eyes turned out to be a cross-eyed brood." Rolling beads were used as pupils in the eyes of some celluloid dolls. "Unbreakable glass," probably a plastic, appears to have been new for use as dolls' eyes. All types of eyes came with or without eyelashes. Margon made celluloid and metal or "unbreakable glass" eyes.

As late as 1933 metal sleeping eyes covered with a celluloid paint were advertised. These eyes were used for *Smiles, Tickletoes,* and *Suck-a-Thumb.* (See also **French Dolls** and **Manufacture of Dolls, Commercial.**)★

920. Bisque head with roguish (googly) eyes, a wig, stationary blue glass eyes, and closed mouth shaped like a watermelon slice. It is on a five-piece bent-limb composition baby body. Mark on head: 165/10. H. 18 in. (45.5 cm.). *Courtesy of Sotheby Parke Bernet Inc., N.Y.*

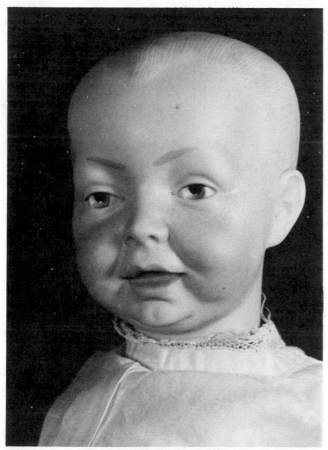

919. Bisque head with intaglio eyes, molded and painted hair, an open-closed mouth and a composition body. *Courtesy of Robert and Katrin Burlin.*

921. Mark on bisque head with unusual eye movement. See Ill. 918.

F

F. & M. Novelty Co. 1918–27. New York City. Made eyes for dolls of various sizes. Assignee of two U.S. patents obtained by Samuel Marcus[+] relating to the partial rotary movement of the eyes and the movement toward and from the front of the doll's head.

1918: Advertised that their movable eyes were adjustable to fit any head and were not affected by the shrinkage of the head.★

F. C. R. 1900. Trade name of *Mme. Caroline Ricaillon*.

F + G. See **Reproductions.**

F. R. 1908. Line of dressed dolls with composition heads and arms on cloth bodies, made by the *American Doll & Toy Co.*

Fabbrica Giocattoli. 1927–29. Turin, Italy. Made dolls.

Fabbrica Italiana Bambole. 1911–30 and later. Milan, Italy. Made dolls.

1911: Exhibited dolls in Turin Exhibition.

1916: Giovanni Galimberti worked for this factory.

1917: Listed in a British toy trade journal.

1929–30: Line of dolls called "La Rosa."

Fabco Doll. 1918. Trade name of a washable cloth doll with wig; jointed at the shoulder and hips; made by *Utley*. This doll came in many sizes.

Fabric Products Corp. 1930 and later. Indianapolis, Ind. Made dolls.

Fabrication Feminine Française. 1918. Paris. Workshop where dolls were made.

Fabricius, Henry. 1858–1914. St. Louis, Mo. In 1884 business burned and shortly afterward Henry Fabricius died. His three sons carried on the business which became known as Fabricius Toy & Novelty Co. This company was a jobber and importer of dolls and dolls' heads from Germany and France. These were distributed in the middle west and far-west areas of the U.S.

1911: Claimed that they carried thousands of dolls and dolls' heads including over 200 styles of large dolls with bisque heads and ball-jointed composition bodies. There were composition dolls, celluloid dolls, all-bisque dolls, and kid-body dolls.

Fad-ette. 1923. *Boudoir* type doll made by *Lenci*. It wore a suit, vest, and brimmed hat, and carried a hatbox. A cigarette was in its mouth.★

Faerie Princess. 1930. Trade name of a doll created by *Charles Thierer*.

Fair Trading Co. 1921–27. New York City. Manufactured and distributed dolls.

1927: Lost an infringement suit to the *American Doll Manufacturers' Assoc.*

Fairee. 1929. One of the *Funny Fuzzee* line of *Twistum* made of twisted flexible wire covered with colored knotted yarn. The faces were handpainted. Price 75¢.

Fairie (Fairy, Faerie) Princess. 1927–28. Fully jointed *Mama* doll made by *Amberg* in six sizes.

Fairy. 1911–15. Trade name of a doll designed by *Helen Trowbridge*, made by *Horsman*. The composition head was copyrighted in 1911 and appeared to be the same mold as that used for *Annette, Nancy Lee* and *Polly Prue*. Fairy came as no. 134 with molded bobbed hair, a curl on its forehead and light colored clothes. Ht. 12 in. (30.5 cm.); priced $8.50 doz. wholesale. No. 180 was the same doll except that it had a wig and dark colored clothes; priced $12.00 doz. wholesale.

1913: *Gamage* advertised a dressed Fairy with *Campbell Kid* type hands; priced $1.12.★

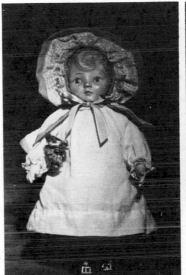 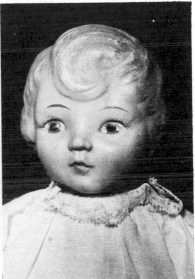

922A & B. Fairy doll designed by Helen Trowbridge and produced by Horsman, starting in 1911. It has a composition head and hands on a cloth body, molded hair and painted features. The hands are the early Campbell Kid type. Mark: Ill. 923. H. 13 in. (33 cm.). *Coleman Collection.*

EIH © 1911

923. Embossed mark on Fairy doll produced by Horsman.

Fairy. 1914. Trade name of a doll with bisque head, mohair wig, sleeping eyes, hair eyelashes, and ball-jointed composition body; dressed only in a chemise. Four hts.: 16½, 22, 26½ and 29 in. (42, 56, 67.5 and 73.5 cm.).

Fairy. 1919. Doll dressed in fanciful costume with tinsel trimming; distributed by *Harrods*. Ht. 8½ in. (21.5 cm.).

Fairy Belle. 1930. Doll made by *Arthur Schönau*.

Fairy Dolls. 1914. Dolls dressed in regional costumes, distributed by *Carson, Pirie, Scott & Co.*

924. All-bisque doll in a sewing box created by the Fairy Gift Co. The doll has a wig, painted blue eyes, closed mouth, body jointed at shoulders and hips, molded and painted footwear. The Fairy Play Box contains five pieces of fabric, ribbons, crude lace, artificial flowers, two spools of cotton thread, six pearl buttons, blunt scissors, needle, and thimble. H. of doll 5 in. (12.5 cm.). *Courtesy of the Margaret Woodbury Strong Museum. Photo by Harry Bickelhaupt.*

Fairy Gift Co. 1925–26. Cincinnati, Ohio. Produced dolls.

Fairy Lilyan. 1884. Line of wax-head dolls distributed by *Lauer* had "hair head-dresses with bangs; earrings," painted stockings and boots and wore embroidered chemises. Ten hts.: 12, 13, 14½, 15½, 17½, 20, 21½, 23½, 27½, and 32 in. (30.5, 33, 37, 39.5, 44.5, 51, 54.5, 59.5, 70, and 81 cm.); priced $1.30 to $8.75 doz. wholesale.

Fairy Moonbeam. 1884–87. Line of wax-head dolls distributed by *Lauer*, had various hair head-dresses with hair bangs, sleeping eyes, earrings, and composition arms and legs with painted stockings and boots. It wore a lace trimmed morning wrapper.

SIZE–HEIGHT RELATIONSHIP OF FAIRY MOONBEAM DOLLS				
Size No.	Height in.	cm.	Price per doz. wholesale 1884	1887
0	15½	39.5	$3.75	
2	19½	49.5	$5.00	$3.75
4	23	58.5	$8.00	$5.50

Fairy Princess. Early 1900s. Trade name of a doll made in Switzerland with carved wooden shoulder head and on a twill cloth body. The facial features were painted. See Ills. 925.

Fairy Tale Dolls. 1915. Group of four or five dolls representing the principal characters in a given fairy tale. Made by *Indestructo Specialties Co.* These groups came in 16 differ-

925A & B. Fairy Princess, name of a doll with carved wooden head and hands, made in Switzerland in the early 1900s. Carved hair and features. Original clothes, tag on skirt reads, "Catalogue//No. 11.//Fairy Princess" in longhand; on the reverse side is a shield with a cross under which is "S.G.F. Bern." H. 15 in. (38 cm.). *Coleman Collection.*

ent boxes; for example, a box with Red Riding Hood characters, another box for Babes in Woods, another box for Robinson Crusoe, a box for the Three Bears, and so on. Price $1.00 per box set.

Fairy Tale Dolls. Many companies made dolls which they named after Fairy Tale characters. These dolls were made in various materials for many years.

Fairyland Doll Co. 1903–9. Plainfield, N.J. Made dressed cloth dolls with handpainted faces, and bodies stuffed with raw cotton.

1907: Style no. 50 was 15 in. (38 cm.); cost $1.00. Style no. 42 was 20 in. (51 cm.); cost $2.00.★

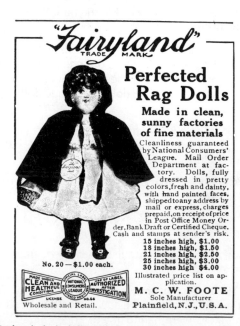

926. Fairyland cloth doll made by M. C. W. Foote and advertised in the LADIES' HOME JOURNAL, December, 1906. The dolls came in hs. 15 to 30 in. (38 to 76 cm.).

Falck & Roussel (Falck, Adolphe). 1880–1902. Paris. Made dolls and composition-bodied bébés that bore a rectangular tag reading "TÉTÉ ABSOLUMENT INCASSABLE//EN POUVANT SE LAVER." (Unbreakable head//Washable.)

1856: Adolphe Falck, born in Paris, was the younger brother of Joseph Falck who later owned a sawmill and sold wood.

1888: Purchased a considerable number of bisque dolls' heads from *François Gaultier.* There were various types of heads including ball heads with painted hair and black or blue eyes, according to Mme. Poisson, curator of the Roybet Fould Museum. ★

Fall In. See **Territorial.**

Fam Doll Co. World War I period. Made all-composition dolls with metal eyes, open-closed mouth with upper teeth, and ball-jointed composition bodies. One of these dolls was 14 in. (35.5 cm.) tall.

927. Mark of the Fam Doll Co.

Family of Dolls. See **Colonial Family.**

Famlee Dolls. 1918–30 and later. Multi-head dolls, with composition heads that screwed onto a cloth body, made by *Berwick.*

   The boxed sets each contained from two to twelve heads and one body, with clothes that were appropriate to the various heads. Some of the heads were unmarked and some had "PAT. APR. 12–21" as an embossed mark.

1931: The manufacture and distribution of the Famlee Dolls was taken over by the *European Doll Co.;* price $1.00 and up. ★

C   D

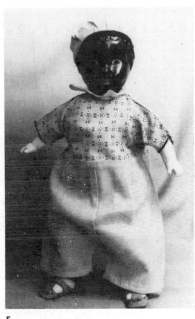

E   F

B

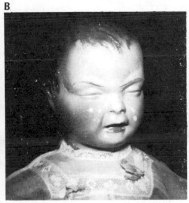

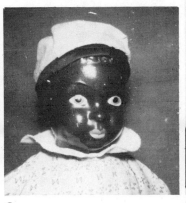

G

H

928A–H. Famlee doll with a single body having a neck into which various composition heads can be screwed. The heads have wigs or molded and painted hair, painted eyes or metal eyes covered with celluloid or closed eyes, and a closed mouth. There is a special costume to go with each head whether it is black, yellow, or white, boy, girl, or baby. Mark: Ill. 929. H. 16 in. (40.5 cm.). *Coleman Collection.*

"PAT. APR. 12. 21"

929. Embossed mark on the neck of a Famlee Doll head and the mark on the metal screw part of the body's neck.

Famous Doll Studio. 1906–22. New York City. Made dolls with bisquette (bisque finish) composition head and arms on cloth bodies. These character dolls, called "Sani-Dolls,"† had mohair or real hair wigs, painted eyes or sleeping glass eyes, and were advertised as washable in hot or cold water.

1919: Dolls wore long or short dresses, or knitted outfits.

1921: Hts. 12, 14, and 20 in. (30.5, 35.5, and 51 cm.).★

Fan and Fannie. 1928. Dolls representing the characters in a book by *Valerie McMahan* titled FAN AND FANNIE, THE BASEBALL TWINS, published by Barse & Co. Fan was a boy doll with vertical stitching on its spherical body and Fannie was a girl doll with horizontal stitching on its body. Fannie had a big red ribbon bow in back. A similar black doll was called Ginger.

Fan Bush Co. 1929–30 and later. New York City. Manufactured cloth dolls.

Fan Kid. Before 1923. Composition head doll made by *Adolph Strauss.* It was dressed in a baseball catcher's uniform. See Ill. 930.

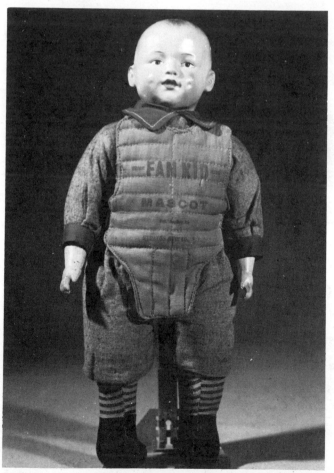

930. Composition-head doll named Fan Kid. It has brown molded hair, blue intaglio eyes, open-closed mouth, dimples, flange neck, cloth body, composition lower arms. The gray flannel suit has a red collar and cuffs. The catcher's apron is made of a coarse cotton to simulate canvas. The cloth lower legs and feet simulate footwear. Mark in red ink: "TRADE FAN KID MARK// MASCOT//Pat. Applied for//STRAUSS MFG. CO. N.Y." H. 14 in. (35.5 cm.). *Courtesy of Patricia Schoonmaker.*

Fancora-Wunder-Baby. 1927. Doll manufactured by *F. Angermüller* who claimed that the doll cried and drank; according to information supplied by the Ciesliks.

Fancy. See **Babyland Dolls.**

Fangel, Maude Tousey. 1920–30 and later. Designed cloth dolls with flat printed faces. One of the baby dolls had mitten-type hands. Ht. 14 in. (35.5 cm.). Another doll was a Georgene doll named *Sweets.* Some of these dolls had three-piece heads and three-piece feet.

931. Cloth doll with flat face designed by Maude Tousey Fangel. *Photo courtesy of Kathryn De Fillipo.*

Fan-ie. 1919. Baseball doll designed by Estelle Allison *(Allison Novelty Co.)* and distributed by *Borgfeldt.* The head and body each simulated a baseball; the arms and legs were appendages, with the legs made together; and there were joints at the shoulders. The eyes were painted looking to the side and a single line represented the mouth. The doll was undressed and had a square paper label on its chest.

Fannie. See **Fan and Fannie.**

Fanny. 1916. Name of a felt lady doll made by *Steiff.* It was dressed in a fashionable felt attire. Ht. 50 cm. (19½ in.).

Fantaisies Parisiennes. 1930 and later. Decorative dolls made by the Société Anct. Sustrac.

Fany. Name on bisque dolls' heads made by *Armand Marseille.* When Fany had molded hair, it was mold # 230, and when it had a wig it was mold #231.★

Fany
2 3 0
A. 3 M.
D.R.M.R.248

231.

DRMR248

Fany.

932–933. Marks on the bisque heads of dolls marked Fany and made by Armand Marseille.

Fapowlea Co. 1926. London. Imported Japanese celluloid dolls including *Kewpie* types, which were sold wholesale.

Farcy. See **Maison Farcy.**

Farina. 1926. Black dancing doll representing one of the Hal Roach, *Our Gang,* moving picture stars. It was made by *Schoen & Yondorf* and wore a jacket with a single button, a collar, bow tie, checked cap, long trousers and had a scroll shaped paper tag. Ht. 11½ in. (29 cm.); priced $1.25. This doll also came in a box with the other Our Gang dolls.

Farina. Late 1920s. Black all-bisque *Our Gang* doll with molded clothes and articulated neck.

Farmer. Ca. 1908–24. Wooden doll made by *Schoenhut.* It came in one size and wore a striped shirt, short trousers, a straw hat and carried a rake.★

Farmer Boy. 1907. Celluloid face doll distributed by *Sears.* It had a cloth body and removable overalls. Ht. 13½ in. (34 cm.); priced 50¢.

Farmer Boy. 1912–14. Had a composition head resembling those of *Toodles* and *Carnival Baby* on a cloth body. The composition hands were similar to those of the Campbell Kids. It had painted eyes looking to the side. The doll produced by *Horsman* as No. 159, wore a plaid cotton shirt, khaki overalls and a wide brimmed straw hat. Priced $8.50, doz. wholesale.

1914: A smaller size doll called Jr. Farmer Boy, No. 77, had the same head as Jr. *Candy Kid* and Jr. *Football Kid.* Jr. Farmer Boy had no hat. Price $4.25 doz. wholesale.

Farmer Boy Cy. See **Lifelike Babyland Dolls.**

Farmerette. 1919. Doll with composition head made by *Ideal* using the former *Zu-Zu Kid* model. It had molded hair, painted eyes, composition hands, cloth body and wore overalls and a hat with stars on it. Ht. 13 in. (33 cm.).

Farnell, J. K., & Co. Before 1915–30 and later. Alpha Works, Acton, London. The firm was founded before 1867 according to a British toy trade journal. Another journal stated that it was founded in 1871 by Miss Farnell and that for many years they made plush and cloth mascots especially animals. During the 1920s *Chloe Preston* designed dolls for this Company. Many dolls had felt faces and plush or cloth bodies. *Louis Wolf* distributed the dolls in America.

Ca. 1915: Made a cloth doll named *Ole Bill.*

1921: Among their dolls were ones representing the cartoon characters Mutt and Jeff that were called "Butt" and "Biff." Other dolls were named Little Britain, Little Miss Cracker, which had a detachable nightie, and Pal Peter.

1924: Advertised cloth dolls dressed in rompers and bonnets.

1925: They made dolls named *Annabelle, Augustus* and *Ambrose* representing characters in James Riddell's book, which was published by Hutchinson according to Mary Hillier. Farnell applied for the use of *Alpha* as a U.S. trademark for cloth dolls.

1926: Advertised a cloth doll that wore a short jacket, long checked trousers, and a tam; another cloth doll represented a short, fat boy. Farnell obtained a British patent for a doll

No. 159 "Farmer Boy"

934. Farmer Boy doll produced by Horsman and advertised in their catalog of ca. 1914. The composition head was copyrighted in 1912 and appears to be the same as that used for Carnival Baby and Cotton Joe. *Courtesy of Bernard Barenholtz*

whose body and limbs consisted of four pairs of lazy tongs, one pair for each arm and one pair for the body and one leg. The fourth pair served as the other leg. The extensible tongs were roughly covered by the clothes. The joints were stiff so that the doll would stay in any position in which it was placed. "Nizza" was a new line of dolls.

1928–29: Advertised *Baby Peke-Wu, Buster, Scotty,* and *Beauty.* It is not certain whether these were dolls or mascots.

1937: Made a series of dolls representing participants in the coronation of George VI. Several different uniforms were used on the portrait dolls of the king. One of these dolls in a Scottish outfit bore an acorn-shaped tag reading "H.M.// King//Made in England//by J.K. Farnell & Co. L^td.//Acton, London//W3."

Another doll, with a felt face, velvet body, painted features, hair sewn in strips on the head, and jointed at the neck, shoulders, and hips, had a tape on the sole of its foot with the words "Farnell Alpha Toys."

935A & B. Brown velvet cloth doll made by Farnell. It has wool hair and painted features. Original boy's costume. The sole of the foot is marked with a cloth label as seen in Ill. 936. H. 14 in. (35.5 cm.). *Coleman Collection.*

936. Cloth label on the sole of the foot of the brown Farnell boy doll.

Fashion Dolls. There were many fashionably dressed dolls advertised in the 1860s and 1870s that were designed as children's playthings. (See **Bru, Chronology, Cremer & Sons; Exhibitions; French Dolls 1869 and 1913–16; Lady Dolls; Poupée Pompadour; F. A. O. Schwarz;** see also THE COLLECTOR'S BOOK OF DOLLS' CLOTHES for further details.)

1913: TOYS AND NOVELTIES described "A new type French doll attired in gowns of the latest model used in . . . stores to show the latest styles in miniature. The clothes are not removable."

1916: A French author (Doin) commented that prior to World War I fashion dolls had existed but were disdained. By 1916 sculptors had modernized fashion dolls and these dolls carried French dresses and knickknacks overseas. ★

Fata, SA. 1929–30 and later. Milan, Italy. Manufactured dolls.

Father Christmas. 1917. Cloth doll made by *Hammond.*

Father Knickerbocker. Before 1929. Doll made by *Averill Manufacturing Co.* with a celluloid head that had a Dutch-bob style hair. It had the number 200/14 and the tortoise mark of the *Rheinische Gummi und Celluloid Fabrik Co.* on it. The cloth body had stamped in blue on the back: "Genuine//Mme Hendren//Doll//1917// Made in U.S.A."

Fat Baby. 1892. Trade name of a composition doll which said "Mama, Papa," distributed by *Marshall Field.* Ht. 13 in. (33 cm.). Price $2.00 doz. wholesale.

Fatty. 1926. One of the Hal Roach *Our Gang* dancing dolls made by *Schoen & Yondorf.* It was pudgy and wore a pull-over sweater, long trousers, a stocking cap and had a scroll shaped tag. Ht. 11½ in. (29 cm.); price $1.25.

Fatty Hoarder. 1918. A soft (cloth?) character doll made by *Harwin.*

Faudel's Ltd. 1909–20. London. Importer, exporter and distributor of dolls. Agent for *Ilford, Ludlow Guild,* and *Steiff.* Handled British, French and Japanese dolls made of celluloid, ceramic, cloth, composition, rubber, and wax.

1915: Advertised French-made celluloid dolls representing infantry and cavalry soldiers.

1917: Advertised character dolls, baby dolls, French sleeping dolls, dressed and undressed dolls; price 8¢ and up.

Faultless Rubber Co. 1916–23 and probably later. Ashland, Ohio. Made molded all-rubber dolls generally without joints.

1917: Four models of red-colored dolls: two were molded naked; one had a molded smocked dress; and one represented a boy with molded bloomers.

1923: Their dolls included *Billy Boy, Boy Scout, Clowns, Nurse,* Pat-Biddy,† Sailor Boy,† and *Sweetie.* They also made inflatable rubber dolls. Hts. 8½, 14½ and 17½ in. (21.5, 37 and 44.5 cm.). ★

Faunalia. 1884. Line of composition-head dolls distributed by *Lauer* that had "hair head dresses" and kid bodies.

FAUNALIA DOLLS SIZE–HEIGHT RELATIONSHIP				
Size No.	in.	cm.	Price doz. wholesale	
1	11	28	$3.00	
2	12	30.5	$4.50	"French eyes"
3	13	33	$4.50	
4	15	38	$6.00	"French eyes"
5	16	40.5	$6.50	
6	18	45.5	$8.00	"French eyes"
7	20	51	$9.00	

Fauré, Ph. 1881–96. Paris. Made dolls.

1881: Purchased bisque dolls' heads from *François Gaultier,* according to Mme. Poisson, Curator of the Roybet Fould Museum.★

Faustine. Ca. 1920. Elaborately dressed wax doll made by *Lotte Pritzel.*

Fautereau-Gradowska, Mme de. 1929–30. Paris. Made dolls.

Fauvet. 1924–28. Paris. Made jointed bébés, dressed and undressed, which were sold by *Au Nain Bleu.*★

Favor Toy & Novelty Importing Corp. 1922. Advertised walking and talking dolls with hair eyelashes, up to 34 in. (86.5 cm.).

Favorite. 1896–99. Trade name of dressed dolls with bisque heads, wigs, glass eyes, open mouth with teeth, jointed bodies with "soft limbs," distributed by *Butler Bros.* Hts. 15 and 20 in. (38 and 51 cm.); priced $3.00 to $8.35 doz. wholesale.

Favorite. 1900–27 and later. Line of dolls produced primarily by *Kämmer & Reinhardt,* distributed by *F. A. O. Schwarz.* The doll usually had a bisque head, wig, sleeping eyes, hair eyelashes, open mouth with teeth and a fully jointed composition body. Some of these dolls were dressed but generally they wore a chemise and footwear. The Favorite dolls nearly always had a number at the base of the neck in back which indicated the approximate height of the doll in centimeters.

1903: The doll had a ball-jointed composition body. 10 Hts. 12 to 35 in. (31 to 89 cm.); priced $1.50 to $12.00. Five Hts. 13 to 22 in. (33 to 56 cm.) had Mama-Papa voices and cost $2.00 to $4.50. Four hts. 13 to 20 in. (33 to 51 cm.) had celluloid heads and cost $2.00 to $4.00.

1923: Favorite doll was a dolly-faced doll, K ☆ R mold # 155, and similar to the 1903 dolls except the knee joints were above the knees. There were still 10 hts. but went from 12 to 31 in. (30 to 80 cm.) and cost $1.50 to $16.50. Only

937. Favorite line of dolls handled by as shown dressed in F. A. O. Schwarz's 1923/24 catalog. The prices are considerably higher when the doll is dressed in silk. Hs. from 13 to 29 in. (33 to 73.5 cm.).

three hts. came with a mama voice, namely 16, 18, and 19 in. (39, 46 and 50 cm.); priced $5.00 to $6.75. This line also included dressed dolls in seven hts. 12 to 29 in. (34 to 76 cm.). The prices for the dressed dolls ranged from $5.50 to $30.00 for the 29 in. (76 cm.) doll in a lawn dress, coat and hat. When the large size doll wore silk clothes the price rose to $38.00.

The Favorite line also included a bent-limb baby doll, K ✡ R mold #126; this came with a bisque head, bobbed mohair wig, and glass eyes with hair eyelashes. There were 10 hts. 10 to 28 in. (26 to 72 cm.) dressed in a chemise; priced $2.00 to $15.00. Four hts. 13 to 20 in. (32 to 50 cm.) were available with mama voices; priced $4.25 to $8.50. Five hts. 11 to 20 in. (28 to 50 cm.) were available dressed; priced $6.00 to $30.00. (The centimeter heights indicate the size numbers actually on the doll's head and were not estimated from the inches which were reported in the F. A. O. Schwarz catalog.)

1926: Schwarz gave the same heights as in 1923 except for the bent-limb baby dolls with mama voices and plush wigs in hts. 13 to 22 in. (32 to 56 cm.).

A doll with a rubber head, wig and painted eyes was new in this series. It came in three hts.: 16, 18 and 22 in. (39, 46 and 58 cm.). A rubber head baby doll wearing a long dress came in hts. 13 and 15 in. (32 and 36 cm.).

1927: The Kämmer & Reinhardt "My Darling" line molds #155 and 126 were called "Favorite" by Schwarz in their earlier catalogs. 155 was a standard dolly-faced doll and 126 was a character baby which was made for many years. The heights of the Schwarz and K & R dolls corresponded except there were additional heights especially smaller and larger ones reported in the K & R catalog. There were 24 hts. 19 to 100 cm. (7½ to 39½ in.) of the mold #155 dolls and 13 hts. 17 to 72 cm. (6½ to 28 ½ in.) of the mold # 126 dolls. Kämmer & Reinhardt reported the same three hts. for their rubber head dolls as Schwarz had in 1926.

Favorite. Late 1910s–early 1920s. Bisque-head dolls made by *A. Lanternier & Co.* Sizes from Number 2/0 to 13 were 17 to 28 in. (43 to 71 cm.).★

Favorite. 1930. Line of *Mama* and baby dolls made by the *Novelty Doll Manufacturing Co.* A dressed doll with moving eyes, ht. 16 in. (40.5 cm.); cost $1.00.

Favorite Saxonia. 1910. Name used for dolls by *Nöckler & Tittel.*

Feather Doll. See **Federdocken.**

Feather Light Brand. Ca. 1914. Doll with celluloid head and lower limbs; mohair wig; sleeping eyes; hair eyelashes; cork-stuffed white kid body with footwear. Distributed by *Sears.* Five hts.: 14½, 16½, 18¼, 21, and 26 in. (37, 42, 46.5, 53.5, and 66 cm.); prices $1.35 to $3.75.

Federal Doll Manufacturing Co. 1917–26. New York City. They had two factories: one made composition heads and limbs and the other factory assembled the dolls. In 1918 they consolidated the two factories, with Michael Schoen as the general manager. They also sold dolls' heads separately.

938. Favorite bisque shoulder head on a kid body with small bisque lower arms. This doll has a wig, brown glass eyes, ears pierced into the head, open mouth with teeth. Mark on head: "FABRICATION//FRANÇAISE//FAVORITE//No. 2/0 Ed Tasson//A. L. & Cie.//LIMOGES." H. 14 in. (35.5 cm.). *Courtesy of Richard Withington. Photo by Barbara Jendrick.*

1918: Advertised 150 styles of composition shoulder head dolls, with or without wigs, on undressed cloth bodies. Four hts.: 14, 18, 22, and 26 in. (35.5, 45.5, 56, and 66 cm.).

1919: Advertised 350 styles of dolls including *Liberty Belle* and *Roze.* Most of the dolls had composition heads and full arms, torsos stuffed with excelsior and legs stuffed with cork.

1920: The Roze doll had its composition arms joined to the shoulder head with elastic; the body and legs were stuffed with cork.

One of their factories suffered a fire.

1921: Dolls with composition shoulder heads and full composition arms on cork stuffed bodies came with or without wigs, dressed or undressed, in three heights.

1922: Advertised dressed walking and talking dolls; probably these were *Mama* dolls.

1924: Advertised over 200 styles of walking and talking dolls that could be used as premiums. One of these was a Mama doll dressed in rompers and a bonnet. Ht. 26 in. (66 cm.).★

Fédération du Jouet Français (Federation of French Toys). 1914–18. Paris. Workshop founded by *Mme. Sautter* for making "new types of dolls."

Federation of the Doll. 1912. England. An English organization of girls 10 to 15 years old. Each girl was given a porcelain doll to name and care for as if it were a sister. The group then met periodically to discuss the problems of caring for this "sister."

Federdocken (Feather Doll). Late 1700s–1930 and later. Wooden dolls with real feathers on their hats were made for generations as a home industry in *Viechtau near Gmunden* in the Balkans; similar dolls were probably made elsewhere. It was claimed that *Pesendorfer* made the first Federdocken around 1800.

1881: These dolls with movable arms cost 3¢ a doz. wholesale.

Fehn, Gustav, & Co. 1921–30. Köppelsdorf, Thür. Advertised dolls and dolls' heads.★

Fehrle. Carved wooden-head boy doll had a button reading "FEHRLE". Ht. 12 in. (30.5 cm.).

Feiler, Carl, & Co. 1898–1903. Jena, Thür. Manufactured jointed dolls, kid bodies, and dolls' accessories.

939. Turned wooden doll of the type called Federdocken, made probably in the Viechtau during the 1800s. The face and features are painted. The feather in the brim of the hat gives the doll its name and is typical. The torso contains pebbles which rattle when the doll is moved. H. 7½ in. (19 cm.). *Courtesy of the International Doll Library.*

1898: Used a German patent (D.R.G.M.) obtained by *Gustav Zeiner* for dolls' joints.

Feisenberger, Gebrüder. 1928–30 and later. Berlin. Listed in a German toy trade journal under dolls and babies including celluloid dolls and babies.

Fekete, J. H. 1908. Vienna. Advertised a kiss-throwing walking doll that could sing two melodies; 50 cm. (19½ in.) tall as well as a doll that could say "Mama Papa" that was 100 cm. (39½ in.) tall.

Feldstein, Zadek, Co. 1926–27. New York City. Registered "*San-I-Toy*" in U.S. as a trademark for dolls.

Felertag & Beyer. 1926. Buchholz, Saxony. Advertised baby dolls, *Mama* dolls, talking dolls double jointed and stiff jointed dolls.

Felice. See **De Felice, Mlle. Marguerite.**

Felix. Before 1911–16. Felt character doll made by *Steiff*. It wore a knit coverall in white, blue or red. Hts. 28 and 35 cm. (11 and 14 in.).

Felix, Max. 1925. Vienna. Distributed dolls including those of *Wagner & Zetzsche.*

Felt Dolls. 1893 or before–1930 and later. Felt was used for bodies and/or heads of dolls. Among the manufacturers and/or producers who used felt for dolls were:

Alma, Amberg, Brogi, Carvaillo, Chad Valley, Charlier, Eduard Crämer, Dean, Deptford Toy-Making Industry, Dittrich & Schön, Eisen, Farnell, Fleischmann & Bloedel, Gustav Förster, French Fashion Importing Co., Furga, Giotti, August Grams, Gre-Poir, Carl Harmus, Jr., Harwin, Richard Haueisen, Hawksley, Bernhard Hermann, Horsman, Koedever, Krauhs, Mme. Thabée Lazarski, Magit, Marcuse Day & Co., Marga, Messina-Vat, Meyer & Lorang, Nowytsky, Ourine, Pappe, Perrimond, Emil Pfeiffer, Raynal, Franz Reuther, August Schelhorn, Gustavus Schmey, Sloan, Twinjoy Doll Co., Anna Vogt, Norah Wellings, and so on. Additional companies such as *Lenci* and *Steiff* were enumerated in the first COLLECTOR'S ENCYCLOPEDIA OF DOLLS, I.

1927: TOYS AND NOVELTIES reported that dolls shown in London were works of art, made entirely of felt and designed by a real artist.

1929: TOY WORLD published an article by John Paul Edwards on the Leipzig Fair that stated:

"The trend is noticed on the part of a number of European manufacturers to make felt dolls of the Italian type. A vast improvement in quality and in design is to be seen in the product of these factories.

"The result will be that the Italian volume may be cut down by the competition of the better lines of the manufacturers of other countries. But the better Italian factories still dominate the European market for the finer felt dressed dolls."★

Fémés, Játékárugyár. 1925–29. Oroshaza, Hungary. Made dolls.

Ferguson, A. S., & Co. 1886–1929. New York City. Factory agent, importer and jobber. PLAYTHINGS claimed that this was the first factory agency in the U.S. toy trade. William M. Ferguson succeeded his father before 1890 and in 1929 he liquidated the company.

1926: They represented *The French Doll Makers* as well as *Ideal, Katherine Rauser, Ross & Ross,* and *Schoenhut.*

1927: They also represented *Hoest & Henderson, Live Long Toys, Nelke,* and *Schoen & Yondorf.*

1928: *Knickerbocker* and *National French Fancy Novelty Co.* were added.★

Ferguson Novelty Co. 1915. New York City. Applied for a U.S. patent for their *Zig Zag Chap* which wiggled as it walked. They made five different characters including Charlie Chaplin and a black man wearing a tailcoat.

Fernel. Before World War I. France. Artist whose models were used to create expensive dolls.

Ferny, Alex. 1925–28. Paris. Made art dolls with kid heads.★

Ferrant (Ferrand), Mme. J. See **Laumont, Baroness de.**

Fétiche Porte Bonheur//Pretty (Mascot Brings Happiness). 1929. French trademark for mascot dolls, applied for by *Pablo Valdivielso.*

Fiberoid. 1923–30 and later. Term used by *K & K* for composition dolls.

Fiberoid Doll Products Co. 1927–30. New York City. Made dolls, composition heads, hands, arms and similar products. They were members of the *Doll Parts Manufacturing Assoc.*

Fibre Toy Manufacturing Co. 1923–28. South Gardiner, Me. Made *Bobbette* dolls which they claimed were light and durable.

Ficter, R. 1930. Strasbourg, France. Manufactured dolls.

Fiegenbaum & Co. 1884. San Francisco, Calif. Importers and distributors of dolls with bisque, china; or wax heads, some of these came with trousseaux. Fiegenbaum also advertised creeping babies and swimming dolls. The French bébés had kid bodies.

Field. See **Marshall Field & Co.**

Fifi. 1915. Baby doll with composition head and hands, cloth body, made by *Effanbee.* It was style No. 100 dressed in short baby clothes. Ht. 15 in. (38 cm.); priced $1.25. (See THE COLLECTOR'S BOOK OF DOLLS' CLOTHES, Ill. 648.)

Fi-Fi, Milady of Fashion. 1921. Lady doll with wig but no joints, made and dressed by *Rees Davis.*

Fifth Avenue Dolls. 1903–4. Dolls with bisque heads, wigs, glass eyes, ball-jointed composition bodies, produced by *Cuno & Otto Dressel.* The two smaller dolls had stationary eyes while the three larger dolls had sleeping eyes. Five hts.: 12, 15¼, 17, 21, and 24 in. (30.5, 39, 43, 53.5 and 61 cm.). Distributed in the U.S. by *Western News Co.*

Fiji-Wigi. 1921. Black cloth dolls with bobbing heads, designed by *Grace Corry* for *Century.* Dolls were stuffed with cotton and wore colored costumes.★

940. Doll with felt head, arms and legs on a cloth body. It has a blond mohair wig, painted eyes, closed mouth with a highlight on the lower lip. Joints are at the neck, shoulders and hips. The arms and legs are felt. Mitten type hands have stitching to designate fingers. Original felt costume. H. 15½ in. (39.5 cm.). *Courtesy of Richard Withington. Photo by Barbara Jendrick.*

941. All-felt doll with wig, painted blue eyes, closed mouth with lower lip highlighted, fingers apart except for the two middle fingers. The clothes are organdy and felt except for the babushka which is rayon and has felt fringe and trimming. H. 20 in. (51 cm.). *Courtesy of Margaret Mandel.*

942. Felt doll with painted eyes, highlights on the lower lip, fingers apart except for the two middle fingers. Original clothes, quilted soles on the shoes. H. 18 in. (45.5 cm.). *Courtesy of Herb and Kathleen Genelly.*

Finburgh, Samuel. World War I period. Manchester, England. Made cutout cloth dolls including dolls representing soldiers and a girl holding a toy bear. The soldier design was from a painting by Finburgh for *Dean* in 1915. It was reprinted by H. M. Stationary Office ca. 1970.

Fingerhut, Jacob. 1902–10. Kalisz, Poland. Successors of Jacob Fingerhut, 1910–30 and later. Manufactured dolls.

Finzi & Bianchelli. 1910s. Rome and Florence, Italy. A doll with a bisque head incised "M. R.// 48–3/0." on a stick-type composition body, wore a dress to which was attached a paper sticker saying "Finzi e Bianchelli//Roma, Firenze." At least two porcelain factories in *Limoges,* France, used the initials "M. R." Finzi & Bianchelli may have only dressed the doll or they may have actually produced it using a Limoges head. Ht. 12 in. (30.5 cm.).

Fiorella (Little Flower). 1927–28. *Lenci* doll style No. 165/20, dressed as a red rose. Ht. 27½ in. (70 cm.).

Filipino. 1899. Doll with china shoulder head and limbs on a cloth body; it had the brown color and ethnic features of the Philippine aborigines. *Butler Bros.,* the exclusive distributor, included these dolls in their *War Doll* line. Three hts.: 7¼, 10 and 13¼ in. (18.5, 25.5 and 33.5 cm.).

Filipino Belle. 1899. Doll with bisque head, short woolly hair, glass eyes, open mouth with teeth, body jointed at the neck, shoulders, elbows, and hips. *Butler Bros.* distributed this doll dressed as a native Philippine girl in their *War Doll* line. Ht. 15 in. (38 cm.).

Fillaux, E. 1902–3 and probably other years. Paris. Specialized in *swaddling clothed* dolls and called their establishment Au Poupard. Their papier-mâché dolls had molded and painted features and clothes. See Ills. 944 and 945.

Fillette. 1909–14 and probably later. Name of a doll for which the clothes patterns published in the periodical FILLETTE were designed.

1912: The doll was advertised as "absolutely unbreakable," presumably composition but the head may have been bisque. Ht. 38 cm. (15 in.); priced 59¢.

Fillette. 1911. Name of a doll with bisque head and sleeping eyes advertised by *Aux Trois Quartiers.* Ht. 30 cm. (12 in.).

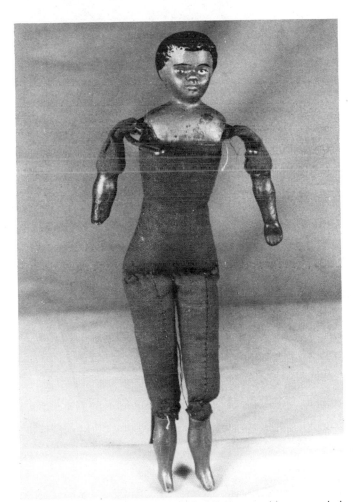

943. Dark brown bisque shoulder head, arms, and legs on a dark brown cloth body. This doll was advertised as a Filipino doll by Butler Bros in 1899, just following the Spanish-American War, which had aroused interest in the Philippines. It has molded kinky black hair and painted features, closed mouth. The legs appear to represent boots with heels. H. 7¼ in. (18.5 cm.). H. of shoulder head 1½ in. (4 cm.). *Coleman Collection.*

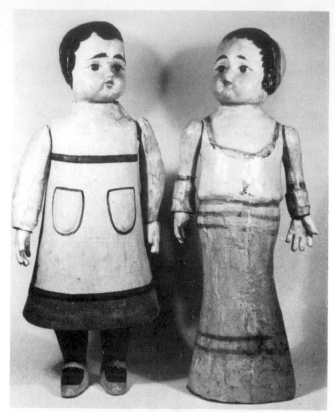

944. All papier-mâché dolls made by E. Fillaux. These dolls have molded and painted features and clothes. They are jointed at the neck and shoulders. They are light in weight for their size. The girl has a grey pinafore over a red dress and the baby in swaddling clothes has a bib. Both dolls have caps. Mark on each doll: Ill. 945. H. 29 in. (73.5 cm.). *Courtesy of Richard Withington. Photo by Barbara Jendrick.*

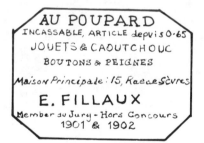

AU POUPARD
INCASSABLE, ARTICLE depuis 0.65
JOUETS & CAOUTCHOUC
BOUTONS & PEIGNES
Maison Principale: 15, Rue de Sèvres
E. FILLAUX
Membre du Jury - Hors Concours
1901 & 1902

945. Mark used by E. Fillaux. This was a paper sticker on the bottom of the dolls. See Ill. 944.

Fircks, Franz. 1920–22. Schwerin, Germany. Obtained a German patent (D.R.P.) for dolls.

Fireman. 1856. India rubber doll representing a fireman was distributed by *Geo. N. Davis.*

First American Doll Factory. 1892–1908. Brooklyn, N.Y. In 1896, became the American Doll & Toy Co.[†]; in 1908, sold to *Benjamin Goldenberg.* Made dolls with composition heads. The later dolls had Can't Break 'Em[†] heads and hands on cloth bodies.

1905: *Siegel Cooper* advertised dolls with composition head and hands, wig, glass eyes, and a dressed cloth body. These dolls were made entirely in America and since the America Doll & Toy Co. was the only American company known to have been making composition heads at that time it seems likely that these dolls were made by this company. Ht. 13 in. (33 cm.); priced 50¢.

1908: Dolls wore black stockings and slippers with buckles. The *F. R.* line wore a jacket, blouse, skirt, and hat. Other lines were dressed in a chemise. One line had Rembrandt style wigs; another had sewed curly wigs, and the third line had painted hair and glass eyes. (See also **Hoffmann** and **Manufacture of Dolls, Commercial: Made in United States.**)

First Prize Baby. 1919–21. Doll with bisque head and pink colored body, dressed in a shirt and having a nipple pacifier. It was imported from Japan by *Morimura Bros.*★

Fischer, Albert. 1907–30 and later. Schalkau, Thür. His widow ran the business in 1929–30 and later. Made dolls. (See **August Albert Fischer**[†].)

Fischer, Anna V. 1910. Vienna. Listed under dolls and dolls' heads in an Austrian directory.

Fischer, Arno. 1907–30 and later. Ilmenau, Thür. Made porcelain dolls.

Fischer, Bernhard. 1907–8. Vienna. Listed under dolls and dolls' heads in an Austrian directory.★

Fischer, Johannes. 1904–30. Hildburghausen, Germany. Manufactured dolls especially mechanical dolls.

1904: Applied for two German patents (D.R.G.M.) for a talking doll.

Fischer, Leonhard. 1923–24. Fürth, Bavaria. Obtained a German patent (D.R.P.) for a doll with a voice box.

Fischer, Louis. 1866–1918. Schalkau, Thür. Applied for four German patents relating primarily to the joints on the dolls. Some of his dolls had detachable masks, and some had porcelain heads. Dolls with *Gebrüder Heubach* heads have been found with detachable masks. These dolls were dressed in exotic costumes.

1912: Doll had a voice in its body.

1918: Doll dressed in winter costumes.★

Fischer Frères. 1916 and probably other years. Brussels. One of the Grand Prize winners at the Brussels exhibit of dolls that was to aid the children of Belgian soldiers.

Ed Loriaux of Fischer Frères was a member of the Jury at this exhibit.

Fischer, Naumann & Co. 1852–1930 and later. Ilmenau, Thür. By 1898 Wilhelm Doellstaedt was the successor. Rudolf Wernicke worked for this firm before he founded *König & Wernicke.*

1860: The British patent for a cloth body that enabled the doll to sit was applied for by Fr. Haas & Co. on behalf of Fischer, Naumann. Haas' name was stamped on some of these cloth bodies (See Ill. 950) which suggests that Haas probably handled these Fischer, Naumann bodies.

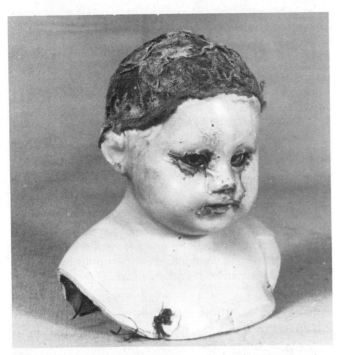

946. Composition shoulder head made by the First American Doll Factory in 1892–95. This head had a wig, glass eyes, a closed mouth and two sew holes on each side. Mark: Ills. 948 and 949. H. of head only, 4 in. (10 cm.). *Coleman Collection.*

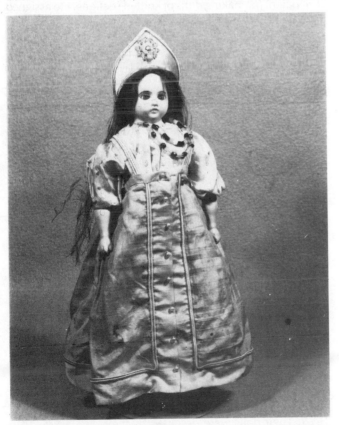

947. Composition head; probably made by the First American Doll Factory. It has a wig, glass eyes, cloth body with composition arms. The original costume suggested a Russian type but the paper backing for the headwear has printing in English on it. H. 14 in. (35.5 cm.). *Courtesy of Cherry Bou.*

F. A. D. F.

Solomon Hoffmann
Patented Aug 2nd 1892

948–949. Marks on the shoulder of a "Can't Break 'Em" type composition shoulder head. Ill. 948 is incised. Ill. 949 has a faint blue stamp.

1890s: Made articles for dolls. Employed 174 men and 176 women; one of these was Moritz Rieth who later became co-owner.

1927: Advertised dolls' bodies, dresses, shoes, and stocking. Also listed celluloid and porcelain toys.

1930: Advertised dolls, baby dolls, dolls' bodies and parts, wigs, trousseaux, shoes, and stockings. ★

Fisher's Famous Kiddies. See **Western Art Leather Co.**

Fishing Boy. 1915. Character doll made by *Amberg.*

Fishman, S. Z. 1924–28. Advertised dolls in a British toy trade journal.

Fiszerowna, Mlle. 1915–16. France. Worked in *Mme. Thabée Lazarki's* doll making workshop. Mlle. Fiszerowna created cloth dolls with blue cloth circles for the eyes and pink cloth circles for its cheeks. Her dolls were shown in VIE FEMININE, May, 1916.

Fitch, Darrel Austen. 1909–20. Hounslow, Middlesex. Also known as Fitch & Co. Manufacturer and distributor of dolls.

1910: Obtained an Austrian patent for dolls' moving eyes.

1913: Obtained a second British patent for moving eyes. Claimed their dolls were designed by "a well-known sculptor." The dolls had ball-jointed composition bodies and sold for 62¢ and up. (See also **Dolphitch Manufacturing Co.**)★

Fitzpatrick, James. 1905–13. Philadelphia, Pa. Made and imported dolls.

Flag Printed Dolls' Bodies. 1898–1901. Dolls having printed flags on their cloth bodies were included in the *War Doll* line of *Butler Bros.*★

Flanders Boy. 1924. *Mama* doll with composition head and arms, mohair wig, and felt clothes was made to resemble *Jackie Coogan* in his role as the Boy of Flanders. It was distributed by *Montgomery Ward.* Ht. 22 in. (56 cm.); priced $4.09.

Flapper Doll. 1929. Advertised as all-composition *Miss 1929* by *Butler Bros.;* it had a bobbed mohair wig, painted features, facsimile cigarette in its mouth, jointed body, and was dressed in pajamas. Ht. 25 in. (63.5 cm.); price $2.85.

Flapper Doll. See **Boudoir Dolls.**

Flapper Kid. 1923. Long-limbed doll with bobbed silk hair, made by *Pollyanna Co.* The satin doll wore a beach-cloth dress, hat set on its head at a rakish angle, silk stockings, and patent leather slippers.

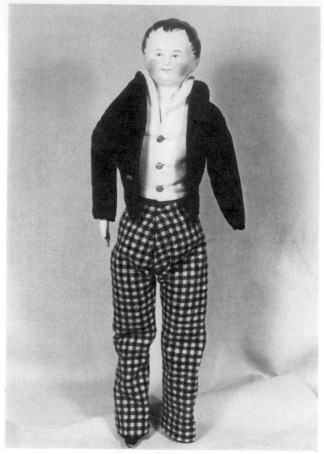

950. China shoulder head doll with a cloth body marked Fr. Haas & Co., who was apparently the British agent for Fischer, Naumann & Co. Haas was probably the distributor of the Fischer, Naumann dolls. The china head has black molded hair with a side part, molded and painted blue eyes, closed mouth and a cloth body with china arms and legs. Allegedly the doll belonged to Caroline Gore of England, born 1856. A wardrobe of men's clothes was made for the doll by Caroline's nurse and was found stored in a doll-size chest with the label of Izzard, a London toy shop. Mark on body: See Ill. 951. H. 18 in. (45.5 cm.). *Coleman Collection.*

951. Mark of Fr. Haas stamped in blue on the cloth body of a china-head doll. The cloth body was made according to an 1860 Fischer, Naumann patent. See Ill. 950.

952. Fischer, Naumann mark found on shoes for dolls.

Flapper Novelty Doll Co. 1922–24. New York City. Made long-limbed dolls including Flapper College dolls dressed in satin or cotton clothes of various college colors, *Floppy Flo*, *Mah Jong* and *Kiki*.★

Flappy Flap (Flopy Flapper). 1923. Cloth doll with colored woolen yarn wig, face painted with red cheeks simulating those of a clown, long, dangling arms and legs, distributed by *Marshall Field*. Hts. 24 and 30 in. (61 and 76 cm.); priced $1.50 and $2.50.

Flavia. 1927. Trade name of a doll.

Flechter, Samuel. Before 1894. Cincinnati, Ohio. Worked in the doll-making factory of his relative *Wolf Flechter*.★

Flechter, Wolf. Before 1875–1890s. Repaired and sold dolls until 1875, when he joined *Philip Goldsmith* in the manufacturing of dolls. In 1878 he sold his interest in the Goldsmith company and went into producing dolls by himself. Later he was joined by his relative *Samuel Flechter*.★

Fleet Novelty Co. 1914. London. Advertised dolls with "goo-goo eyes," probably painted. Price 16¢ doz. wholesale.

Fleischaker, Walter. See **Averill, Georgene.**

Fleischaker & Baum. See **Effanbee.**

Fleischer, Horace T. 1919–20. Elkins Park, Pa. Obtained a U.S. patent for making dolls of knitted sections. He assigned the patent to the *Notaseme Hosiery Co.*

Fleischer Toy Manufacturing Co. 1917–24. New York City. In 1924 they advertised "High Grade Mama Dolls." Earlier it was popular-priced *Mama* dolls.★

Fleischmann, Adolf. 1844–81. Sonneberg, Thür.; 1881–1930 and later, Fleischmann & Crämer, successor, also of Neustadt near Coburg. Manufactured and distributed dolls of various kinds.

1844: Produced 360,000 papier-mâché heads.

1851: Represented in London by *Spurin*.

1858: He organized an extensive trade campaign sponsored by Crown Prince George II of Saxe-Meiningen.

1881: Registered a trademark in Germany that included a winged angel head that closely resembled the trademark registered by *Schilling*.

1883: Fleischmann & Crämer were among the founders of the *Sonneberg Industrial School*.

1904: Advertised dressed dolls, *Täuflinge*, wax dolls' heads, kid and cloth bodies.

1910: One of the Sonneberg group of Grand Prize winners at the Brussels Exhibition.

1925–26: London agent was Henry Jackson & Co.

1926: Their dolls were designed by their own artists.

1927: Berlin agent was *Carl Stahl*.

Part of the above information was researched by the Ciesliks.★

953A. Trademark registered by Fleischmann & Crämer in 1881. The head with the wings at the bottom of this trademark resembles the trademark of Schilling.

953B. Paper label used by Adolf Fleischmann on their "Superior" dolls.

Fleischmann, G. 1930. Sonneberg, Thür. Made cloth dolls. *Seelig* was the London agent.

Fleischmann Gebrüder (Bros.). 1880–1930 and later. Sonneberg, Thür. Manufactured and exported dolls. The Fleischmann Bros. were probably the sons of Johann Paul Fleischmann. In the 1930s they became amalgamated with the firm of Louis *Lindner* & Sons.

1910: One of the Sonneberg group of grand prize winners at the Brussels Exhibition.

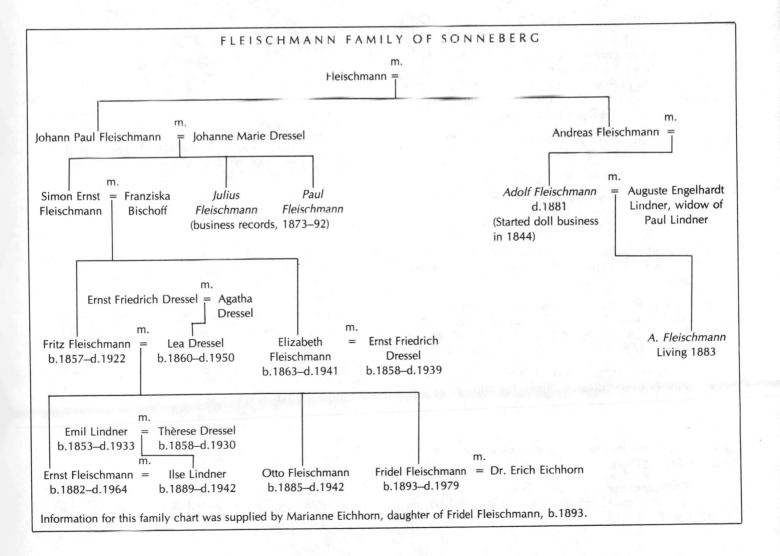

FLEISCHMANN FAMILY OF SONNEBERG

Information for this family chart was supplied by Marianne Eichhorn, daughter of Fridel Fleischmann, b.1893.

Fleischmann, Miss Katherine (Kitty). 1910–27. New York City. Designed and made dolls.

1910–18: Toy buyer for *Gimbels*.

1919: In charge of designing dresses for *Effanbee* dolls.

1926: Advertised that she would design special dolls for lines of dolls on order. Her baby dolls were *Cuddle Dolls* with handpainted faces. She also made dolls named *Jane, Susie,* or *Sally* in hts. 14 to 16 in. (35.5 to 40.5 cm.). The long-limbed dolls included *Cigarette Girl, Spiffy, Greenwich Village Artist,* Artist from the Latin Quarter, and Dancing Girls from France such as *Noona.* Kitty Fleischmann also made outfits for dolls.★

Fleischmann (Salomon) & Bloedel (Blödel). 1873–1926. Fürth, Bavaria; Sonneberg, Thür.; and Paris. Soon after 1871 Fleischmann had contacts in Paris. In 1908 Joseph Berlin was the successor in Fürth and Sonneberg. Firm was liquidated in 1926 but their successors were still manufacturing toys in 1928, according to a Paris directory. Fleischmann and Blödel manufactured, distributed, and exported dolls. Salomon Fleischmann was in charge of the *Société Française de Fabrication de Bébés & Jouets* (S.F.B.J.) until 1914 when he fled to Spain, where he later died.

1898: Registered "Bébé Triomphe"[†] as a trademark in Germany.

1899: Fleischmann contributed land, factories, machinery, materials, good will, and rights to *Eden Bébé* to the S.F.B.J. This contribution, valued at $200,000, was the largest one made when the S.F.B.J. was formed, according to Mme. Poisson, curator of the Roybet Fould Museum.

1900–1914: Exported dolls to France, according to a Frenchman writing before 1916.

1908: Advertised regional costume doll series.

1910: Registered *Perlico-Perlaco* as a trademark in Germany for dolls with moving heads and legs. There was a new regional costume doll series.

1913: Advertised caricature dolls and their German patented (D.R.G.M.) Perlico-Perlaco dolls. *Henry Benjamin* was their sole British agent.

1914: They manufactured felt and plush dressed and undressed dolls. Special lines were for export. A group of their dolls in a Cologne Carnival procession consisted of dolls representing nobles, athletes, family members and so on.

1915: There were 100 style Nos. of various baby dolls with wigs, in long or short dresses. Prices 25¢ and up.

1920s and earlier: Used mainly *Simon & Halbig* bisque heads.

1922: Advertised they were the sole producers of a doll representing *Fridolin.*

1925: Advertised a wide choice of dolls.

Part of the above information was supplied by the Ciesliks.★

954. Bisque head doll made by Fleischmann & Bloedel. It has a black wig, stationary glass eyes, pierced ears, closed mouth and is on a ball-jointed composition body with straight wrists. Original clothes. Mark on head: "EDEN BÉBÉ//PARIS//0." H. 11 in. (28 cm.). *Courtesy of the Margaret Woodbury Strong Museum. Photo by Harry Bickelhaupt.*

Fleming Doll Co. 1922–24. Kansas City, Mo. Made *Tum Tum* rubber dolls and floating oil-cloth dolls.

1923: *Chester Gump* was a new oil-cloth doll.★

Flesho. World War I period. Name used by *The Dolls' Accessory Co.* for their *British Ceramic* heads which were coated with wax.

Flexy. 1926–29. Two-dimensional wooden dolls designed by *Mrs. Ripley Hitchcock* and made by *Converse* who claimed the name was a registered trademark. The hair, facial features, underwear and footwear were printed on the wood. The dolls jointed at the shoulders, hips, and knees were sold dressed in a variety of costumes and came in various hts.; price 10¢ and up.

Flip. 1914. Bisque doll representing the character of this name created by Winsor McCay in his *Little Nemo* comic series, distributed by *Strobel & Wilken.* The doll wore a long coat, big bow tie, vest with three large buttons, vertically striped trousers and a high hat. A "cigar" was in its mouth. It came in two sizes, priced 25¢ and $1.00.

Flips and Flops. See **Miami Wood Specialty Co.**

Flirt, The. 1907–30 and later. Flirting-eye dolls made by *Kämmer & Reinhardt*. The eyes were called by different names in different periods such as "Roguish" ("Schelm"), "Knavish," "Roli," and so on. They were used on bisque heads or on celluloid heads and often had hair eyelashes. ★

Flirt, The. 1924–27. All-composition doll with wig, painted eyes looking to the side, jointed arms, silk dress, distributed by *Butler Bros.* Ht. 4 in. (10 cm.); price $1.25 doz. wholesale.

Flopper Flo. See **Floppy Flo.**

Floppidolls. 1928–29. "Natural position," long-limbed cloth dolls designed and manufactured by *Adler*. They had pressed, handpainted faces which were claimed to be washable. The removable clothes were in the styles worn by children.

Floppy (Flopper) Flo. 1922–24. Long-limbed *Boudoir* doll with carrot colored worsted hair, made by *Flapper Novelty Doll Co.*

1923: Advertised by *Lola Carrier Worrell* as being a "flirtatious flapper doll" made for children. ★

Flopy Flapper. See **Flappy Flap.**

Flora. 1927–28. *Lenci* felt doll style No. 700/3 dressed as a school-age girl with a high waist and a full skirt covering the knees. Ht. 37½ in. (95 cm.).

Flora McFlimsey. 1861–65. A generic name for dolls with wardrobes of clothes especially those sold at the Sanitary Commission Fairs. The Sanitary Commission was the forerunner of the American Red Cross during the American Civil War. Known surviving examples of these Flora McFlimsey dolls were from Fairs in Boston, Brooklyn, Poughkeepsie, New York, and Philadelphia. (See **Exhibitions,** 1861–65.) ★

Flora's Famous Dolls. 1915–28. Made by *Mrs. Grace Wheeler* and her daughter Florence who supplied the information about these dolls. Two helpers made the bodies and the dresses and an agent traveled with samples. These cloth dolls were inspired by the *Laubscher* dolls, and were based on German bisque-head dolls. The 17 in. (43 cm.) size was cast from an A.M. 390 10½ head (*Armand Marseille* mold #390, size number 10½) and the 21 in. (53.5 cm.) size was cast from a head marked "S ☆ PB—H//1906//11//Germany" (*Schoenau & Hoffmeister*, mold #1906, size number 11). The face which was made of plaster of Paris was covered with mercerized lawn after being built onto the body and then handpainted. The wig of angora skins were washed, dyed and shaped to the dolls' heads. The golden curls could be combed.

The bodies made of unbleached calico stuffed with sawdust had sewn joints at the shoulders and hips. The arms and legs were enameled in flesh color and shoes were painted on the feet.

At peak periods production was 100 dolls a month and each doll dressed in cotton cost about 70¢ to make. In the beginning the hts. were 17, 18, and 21 in. (43, 45.5, and 53.5 cm.) but later only the 17 in. (43 cm.) ht. was produced.

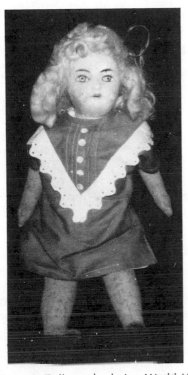

955. Flora's Famous Doll, made during World War I by Flora Wheeler. This was a molded cloth doll covering a plaster cast taken of an Armand Marseille #390 bisque socket head. It has an angora skin wig, blue painted eyes, and closed mouth. Original clothes including painted shoes. H. 17 in. (43 cm.). *Courtesy of Victoria Harper.*

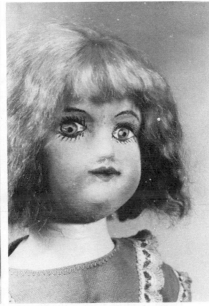

956. Molded and painted cloth doll made by Flora Wheeler in 1981 in South Africa. This doll is a duplicate of the dolls she and her mother made during World War I which they named "Flora's Famous Dolls." It has a wig and painted shoes. H. 16 in. (40.5 cm.). *Coleman Collection. Gift of Flora Wheeler.*

Flor-El-Lyn. 1930 and later. Line of dolls manufactured by *Franklin Studio.*

Florence. 1930. Doll with human hair wig advertised by *Alexander Doll Co.* It wore a velvet coat and hat.

Florence. See **Pet Name.**

Florensa, Ramon. See **Hosta Porcelain Factory.**

Floresta. 1925–26. Line of dolls made by *Scheyer* The name was used as their trademark.

Florida Dolls. It was reported in 1918 that dolls were made and dressed entirely of the bark of trees from the interior of Florida. These were possibly Seminole Indian dolls.

Florodora. 1901–21. Bisque heads with wigs, sleeping eyes, open mouth, and teeth, made by *Armand Marseille.* The dolls usually came on kid bodies but since the heads were also sold separately they can be found on composition or imitation kid or even cloth bodies.

The Florodora heads were used by *Borgfeldt* in their *My Playmate* and *Celebrate* lines.

The following size numbers have been reported: 7/0, 6/0, 5/0, 4/0, 3/0, 2/0x, 0, 0½, 1, 2, 2½, 3, 4, 5, 5½ 6, 7, 8, and 9. The most frequently found were the size 3/0 which has been reported to make dolls ranging in ht. from 13 to 18½ in. (33 to 47 cm.). The total reported range for all sizes was 10 to 30 in. (25.5 to 75.5 cm.). Generally the dolls with shoulder heads were taller for their size number than those with socket heads.

1909: *Siegel Cooper* advertised Florodoro *(sic)* as having a bisque shoulder head and hands, wig, sleeping eyes, kid body with gusseted knee joints and universal type hip joints. It had an oval sticker on its chest and had footwear. Ht. 14½ in. (37 cm.); priced 50¢.

1911: WOMAN'S HOME JOURNAL, August, 1912, gave directions for crocheting a Florodora cap and sacque.

1914: *John Smyth* advertised kid body Florodora dolls with bisque head and arms, wig, sleeping eyes, hair eyelashes, open mouth. Seven hts.: 17, 18½, 21½, 23¾, 26¼, 28, and 29½ in. (43, 47, 52, 60.5, 66.5, 71, and 75 cm.); priced 98¢ to $3.98. There was also a Florodora doll with a voice mechanism. Hts. 18 and 22 in. (45.5 and 56 cm.); priced $1.38 and $1.89.

1921: A kid body Florodora doll 21 in. (53.5 cm.) tall cost $1.49.★

Florrie the Flapper. 1920. Cloth doll with *Tru-to-Life* face and wig, made by *Dean.* It wore flapper style clothes and carried a flapper handbag. Style No. D 212 was 14 in. (35.5 cm.). Style No. D 213 had *Tru-Shu* feet and was 17 in. (43 cm.) tall. Dean also used the name Florrie the Flapper for one of the *Hilda Cowham Kiddies.*

Flossie. Ca. 1912. Composition head doll made by *A. Steinhardt & Bros.* The hair was molded with pigtails that stuck out at each side. Eyes were painted.

Flossie. 1920s. Cutout cloth advertising doll made by *Collingbourne Mills.* Hts. 6 and 15½ in. (15 and 39.5 cm.).

957A & B. A pair of Florodora dolls with bisque heads on five-piece composition bodies. One has a blond wig and the other has black hair. Both have brown sleeping eyes and original commercial clothes. H. 14 in. (35.5 cm.). *Courtesy of Sotheby Parke Bernet Inc., N.Y.*

958. Florodora bisque head doll with wig, sleeping blue eyes, open mouth with teeth, and a five-piece composition body; original clothes. H. 16 in. (40.5 cm.). *Courtesy of Sotheby Parke Bernet Inc., N.Y.*

959. Mark found on Florodora dolls.

Flossie. See **Heizer, Dorothy.**

Flossie Flirt. 1921–30 and later. Line of dolls with patented sleeping eyes that rolled from side to side as well as winked, made by *Ideal* and distributed by *Butler Bros.* and *Sears.* It generally had a composition head with a mohair wig and a *Mama* type cloth body.

1924: Ht. 20 in. (51 cm.).

1925: Seven hts.; 100 costumes.

1926: Advertised that the heads were modeled by artists and that some of the heads had eyelashes. The hands were either composition or rubber and the legs were composition. Four hts.: 14, 17, 19, and 23 in. (35.5, 43, 48, and 58.5 cm.); priced $1.65 to $4.95.

1927: Some of the dolls wore rayon dresses. Attached to each doll was a label with the Ideal trademark above "Flossie//Flirt//WATCH MY//EYES ROLL // AS I WALK." 4 hts.: 18, 19, 22, and 23 in. (45.5, 48, 56, and 58.5 cm.). The 23 in. size was the only height that came with either composition or rubber hands.

Sears advertised Flossie Flirt with composition head, arms and legs, in four hts.: 14, 15½, 17, and 20 in. (35.5, 39.5, 43, and 51 cm.); priced $1.98 to $4.98.

Flossie Flirt's "half sister" was *Vanity Flossie.*

1928: The dolls were dressed as children in either lawn or dimity dresses; the smallest height had a crying voice instead of a mama voice. The heights were the same as in 1927 except for the 20 in. (51 cm.) which replaced the 19 in. (48 cm.); priced $24.00 doz. to $3.75 each wholesale.

1929: Doll was no longer a Mama doll. It represented an older child and had a crying voice and sometimes teeth. The rubber arms were not painted and it was claimed that they could hold any object. Flossie Flirt wore an organdy dress, above the knees in length. The smaller hts. had bonnets while the larger dolls had "satine" bandeaus or felt hats. There were six hts.

1945: Ideal renewed its Flossie Flirt trademark. (See THE COLLECTOR'S BOOK OF DOLLS' CLOTHES, Ills. 770 D and 775 F.)★

Flo'T Me Novelty Co. 1924–26. Philadelphia, Pa. Advertised in a toy trade journal cloth body dolls with or without voices. One of their dolls was 8 in. (20.5 cm.) tall.

Flower and Fruit Dolls. Dolls have been molded so that they appear to carry flowers. Some of these were handled by *Geo. N. Davis* in 1856 or made by *Rheinische Gummi und Celluloid Fabrik* in the 1920s. Other dolls have had flowers

Another "Ideal" Achievement

Flossie Flirt
Reg. U. S. Pat. Off. Pat. Pend.

Flossie Flirt—is her name. She walks, says "Mama," is dressed adorably, and is practically indestructible. But best of all—she not only sleeps or winks mischievously at you—but rolls her eyes from side to side and flirts gaily as she toddles along.

960. Flossie Flirt made by Ideal and advertised in PLAYTHINGS, August, 1924. This is a Mama doll with eyes that sleep, wink, and roll from side to side.

or fruit molded into their headwear such as the bisque head line named *Marguerite.* Amberg's *Sunny Orange Blossom* had an orange as its headwear.

There were instructions in books for making dolls out of flowers or fruits. (See **Unusual Materials for Making Dolls.**)

Sometimes dolls' clothes represented flowers or fruits as shown in the following list:

Before World War I: *Stella Webster* created a series of dolls called *Birthday Dolls* which were dressed to represent various flowers associated with each month.

1919: *Deptford Toy-Making Industry* advertised Flower dolls.

1920: *Jessie M. Raleigh* advertised *Birthday Dolls* dressed as flowers.

1924: *Dean* advertised the *Posy* doll line.

1926: Part of *Mama's Angel Child* line of cloth dolls designed by *Penny Ross* and made by *Live Long Toys* included tulips, morning glories, and so on. The dolls were marked on their hips.

1927: *Borgfeldt* produced dolls that represented the flower of each month.

1927–28: *Lenci* made a doll named *Fiorella* (little flower) dressed as a red rose.

Two dolls in one type created by *Mrs. Berry Kollin* and made by the *Twinjoy Doll Co.* The doll had composition heads, cloth bodies and wore flower shaped dresses with petals representing a rose, a sweet pea, a daisy, a pansy, a lily or other flowers. Most of these dolls had names that corresponded with girls' names. Priced $2.00.

Fluegelman, M. F. 1917–30. New York City. Manufactured dolls' pressed faces. Claimed "any special design and expression made to your individual order."

1927–28: Made *Kewpie* masks for faces of cloth Kewpies. ★

Fluff. 1921–24. Lightweight knockabout cloth doll made by *Mabel Bland-Hawkes.*

Fluffidown. 1916. Cloth doll made in Britain.

Fluffy Ruffles. 1907–9. Doll representing Hattie Williams in the stage play FLUFFY RUFFLES.

Fluffy Ruffles. 1908. According to Mary Hillier, Henry Cook and John Solomon made cloth dolls named Fluffy Ruffles in Britain.

Fly-Lo. 1926–30 and later. Trade name of a baby doll with a ceramic (including bisque) or composition head with glass or metal sleeping eyes, molded and painted hair, flange type neck, and a cloth body.

Since the heads were sometimes sold separately, the bodies could vary; however, they were usually similar in shape to the *Bye-Lo* bodies with celluloid hands. The doll was designed by *Grace Storey Putnam* for *Borgfeldt.* The head was incised or had embossed words, "Copr. by//Grace S. Putnam." One of the features of this doll was its wings which had a wire running through the edges. The wings had their tips attached to the doll's wrists but they could be put into various positions. Color of the wings varied.

1927: Came with sleeping eyes or painted eyes. It usually wore a suit of shiny satin. Ht. 16 in. (40.5 cm.).

1928: Name registered in U.S. as a trademark for dolls by Borgfeldt. Came with green and gold wings.

Ca. 1933: According to the *Quaker Doll Co.* catalog bisque Fly-Lo heads came in sizes 7¼, 8, 9½, and 11 in. (18.5, 20.5, 24, and 28 cm.) head circumference; price $4.50 to $9.00 doz. wholesale.

Flyshacker, Charles. See **Au Grand Opera.**

Folie. See **Marottes.**

Folkmann, Professor H. 1920. Prague, Czeckoslovakia. Sculptor who designed and carved wooden dolls inspired by paintings of old masters. The articulated dolls were made of lime wood, painted and elaborately costumed. They represented Faust (young and old), Mephistopheles, *Salome,* Fatima and so on.

Follender, Otto, Wig Corp. See **Manufacture of Wigs.**

Follies Girl. 1926. Trade name of a doll with hand-painted pressed cloth face, mohair or silk wig, long-limbed cloth body stuffed with cotton, made by the *American Stuffed Novelty Co.* The removable clothes were designed by *Morris Politzer.* One of these dolls wore a silk dress with a big bow under the chin and a full skirt. Ht. 26 in. (66 cm.).

Folly Dollies. 1929. Novelty dolls made by *Reisman Barron.* Dolls represented clowns, chorus girls, dancers and so on.

Folly Dolly. 1924. Trade name of dolls dressed as boys or girls, made by *Henry J. Hughes.* Price 25¢ and up.

961. Fly-Lo bisque head designed by Grace Putnam. It has molded and painted hair, sleeping blue glass eyes, closed mouth. The body is a replacement. Mark: Ill. 962. H. of flange head 3¼ in. (8.5 cm.). Circumference of head 8½ in. (21.5 cm.). *Courtesy of the Margaret Woodbury Strong Museum. Photo by Harry Bickelhaupt.*

*Copr. by
Grace S. Putnam
Germany
1118/25*

962. Mark on Fly-Lo bisque heads copyrighted by Grace Putnam.

Football Kid. 1914. Jr. style no 78. Composition head same as those used for Jr. *Candy Kid* and Jr. *Farmer Boy,* made by *Horsman.* Doll wore a striped pull-over in various college colors and khaki knickers; priced $4.25 doz. wholesale.

Football Player. See **Fu.**

Foote, Luther R. 1925–26. Rochester, N.Y. Made shoes for dolls.

Foote, Mary. See **Fairyland Doll Co.**

Forbes & Wallace. 1886–87 and possibly other years. Springfield, Mass. Advertised German dolls with bisque, composition, china or wax heads, dressed or undressed. They also had cloth dolls and all-bisque dolls; priced 5¢ to $1.00.

Ford, Gladys. 1928. Brooklyn, N.Y. Obtained a U.S. patent for a washable stuffed doll that appeared to represent a girl and a cat.

Foreign. 1926 and later. Mark used on dolls in accordance with British law. (See Ill. 1313.)

Forest. 1930. Paris. Made and/or distributed dolls.

Forest Fur Co. 1917. New York City. Made fur clothes for dolls including coney, ermine, eider down or imitation leopard skin coats, fur turbans, cloth tam-o'-shanters, two animal sets of neck pieces and muff, and fur sets of turban, stole and muff. Coats fit dolls 18, 20, 22, and 24 in. (45.5, 51, 56, and 61 cm.) tall: priced up to $7.00 per coat.

Forster. Ca. 1900. New York City. Made cutout printed dresses for dolls. One of these dresses had full sleeves, a high waistline and a red print skirt. It would have fit a 16 to 18 in. (40.5 to 45.5 cm.) doll.

Förster, Albert. 1928–29. Neustadt near Coburg, Bavaria. Manufactured *Mama* dolls.

Förster, Christian. 1913, Neustadt near Coburg, Thür. Obtained a German patent (D.R.G.M.) for a cloth-body doll with a self activating whistle.

Förster, Elfriede. 1910. Bonn, Germany. Obtained a German patent (D.R.G.M.) for the movement of dolls' eyes.

Förster, Gustav. 1922–30 and later. Neustadt near Coburg, Bavaria. Made and exported various kinds of dolls including *Mama* dolls, character baby dolls, mascots, black dolls, Indian dolls, bisque dolls, papier-mâché dolls, felt dolls, ball-jointed dolls, and so on. The cloth bodies were generally stuffed with hair. His sole British agent was *Del & Co.*

1925: Introduced *Wee Baby*, a line of baby dolls.

1926: Patented fully articulated, papier-mâché *Jackie Coogan* doll.

1927: Advertised walking clowns.

1928: Advertised jointed dolls and dressed dolls.

Fortune-telling Dolls (Fate Lady). These dolls were generally small with their skirts made of folded papers, which were usually colored. Concealed on each paper was a motto which was often handwritten. The papers were threaded by a string which held them up around the waist. Or the doll was attached with a wire to a round board covered with white paper on which various mottos were written. Each motto was on a pie-shaped section with a point at the outside edge. Examples of mottos were given with the instructions for making these fortune telling dolls.

1830s: THE GIRL'S OWN BOOK gave the following instructions: "This is a toy made of about a quarter of a yard of pasteboard, cut round and covered with white paper. The outside edge should be neatly bound with gilt paper. The flat surface is ruled for mottos, and all the lines meet in the centre. The writer should be careful to draw a line of red or black ink between each, to make them distinct. Exactly in the centre of the circle, a wire is inserted; and on that is fastened a neatly-dressed jointed doll, of the smallest size. In one hand she holds a small straw wand, with which she points to the poetry beneath her. The wire is made steady by fastening it in the centre of a common wafer-box, covered

and bound to correspond to the rest of the toy. The doll is just high enough above the pasteboard to turn round freely. When you wish your fortune told, twirl her round rapidly, and when she stops, read what her wand points to.

1860: THE GIRL'S OWN TOY-MAKER gave the following instructions:

"Take a piece of pasteboard about twelve inches square; draw a circle upon it, and cut it out. The outside edge should be coloured or bound round with gilt-edge paper. The flat surface must then be ruled, all the lines meeting in the centre; in these the mottoes are written, taking care to draw a distinct line in red or black ink between each. Insert a wire exactly in the centre of the circle, and on it fasten a neatly jointed dressed doll, altogether not more than five or six inches (12.5 or 15 cm.) high. In one hand fix a small wand, pointing towards the motto beneath her. The wire can be made steady by fastening it in the centre of any common round box, covered and bound to correspond with the other portions. The doll must be just high enough above the pasteboard to turn about freely. When you wish to tell a fortune, turn the doll round rapidly, and when she stops read what her wand is pointing to.

1860s: A German publication (HERZBLÄTTCHENS ZEIT-VERTREIB) provided a pattern for making pieces of paper used to form the skirt of a fortune-telling doll. (See also Ill. 1276 and **Sibyl Fortune Telling Doll Co.★**

Fould, Mme. Consuélo.[†] See **Poupées Consuélo Fould.**

Foulds & Freure. 1911–30 and later. New York City. Robert Foulds came from Scotland to New York in 1842 and founded a jobbing and dry goods business. In 1857 the business, then owned by his nephew Robert Foulds, changed to specializing in toys. In 1911, Richard Freure, who had been engaged in the toy and fancy goods business, joined the descendants of Robert Fould to form Foulds & Freure. This firm imported dolls and dolls' parts as well as being a doll jobber.

1915: Advertised dolls' heads, hands, wigs, eyes, and so on. They imported from Germany via Holland bisque heads molds #390 and #370 made by *Armand Marseille* and a mold #03468 character baby socket head with wig. They also sold dressed dolls.

1916: They were receiving small shipments of bisque socket heads from Germany.

1917: Germany was still supplying a few dolls with bisque heads and celluloid dolls. Foulds & Freure advertised metal and celluloid dolls' heads, cloth bodies, kid arms for dolls, and limbs for character dolls. They obtained exclusive rights for the bisque dolls' heads made by two Japanese firms. These heads had sleeping glass eyes, came with or without wigs, and had open mouths with teeth. They also advertised entire dolls, separate wigs, bodies, limbs, clothes and accessories.

1918: They claimed a large shipment of Japanese dolls' heads was on its way. This included socket heads, shoulder heads, dolly-faced heads, character heads, and baby heads.

1919: Advertised 81 different shoulder heads made of bisque, metal or composition. 14 of these appear to have had molded hair and the rest had wigs. Their supply of socket heads had even greater variation. They had imported kid-body dolls as well as composition body dolls. The celluloid heads had sleeping or painted eyes and came with or without wigs.

1920: Low-brow type china heads and limbs on cloth bodies and all-bisque dolls of various styles, *Kewpies*, Kewpie-types, *Santa Claus*, a policeman, and over 40 different styles of celluloid dolls, most of them with molded clothes, were advertised. They claimed that they had reduced their prices on bisque heads and on glass eyes.

1921: Composition heads were listed as well as socket and shoulder bisque heads with wigs or painted hair.

1924: *My Dream Baby* mold #341 and #342 with closed mouth were sold by Foulds & Freure. Later the open mouth My Dream Baby mold # 351 became available. *My Honey* dolls were also offered for sale as well as dolls' dresses.

1926: Stated that they were factory agents as well as being importers and jobbers. They specialized in doll hospital supplies including heads and outfits for dolls.

1930: Advertised imported and domestic dolls, supplies for doll hospitals, novelty dolls and dolls' outfits.

963. Mark used by Foulds & Freure who handled dolls.

Fouillot, Mme. 1927–30 and later. Paris. Made dolls.

Fouquet, Mme. 1925–30 and later. Paris. Made dolls.

Foxy Grandpa. 1902–12 and later. Made in several versions all based on the Carl E. Schultze[†] drawings and distributed by *Butler Bros. Gamage, Sears, F. A. O. Schwarz* and others. The small cloth doll 11 or 12 in. (28 or 30.5 cm.) tall showed Grandpa with his hands in his coat pockets and wearing a derby hat, while the large 20 in. (51 cm.) cloth version made by *Art Fabric Mills* showed grandpa with his hands in his trouser pockets and without a hat. There was a rabbit under one arm and a watch fob having a masonic insignia. The latter was also sold by *Elms & Sellon. Steiff* made a felt doll named *Gr* that closely resembled Foxy Grandpa. Also there were at least two composition versions of Foxy Grandpa; one all-composition doll jointed at the shoulders and hips had molded clothes. The other composition doll was fully jointed including the wrists; it was dressed and wore a straw hat. Ht. 18 in. (45.5 cm.).

1902: Advertised by Butler Bros. as having a "stout face"

(composition?), cotton body, and wearing a flannel suit and straw hat. Ht. 11¾ in. (30 cm.).

1903: Advertised in a F. A. O. Schwarz catalog.

1912: Sears sold a Foxy Grandpa *Cymbalier.*★

964A & B. Printed, stuffed, cloth two-sided (front and back) doll representing Foxy Grandpa with his eyeglasses, bow tie, and spats. (Also see Gr.) H. 11¼ in. (28.5 cm.). *Coleman Collection.*

Francette. 1930. Dressed cloth doll with "washable" head, wig, and felt clothes sold by *Bon Marché.* Ht. 47 cm. (18½ in.).

Francia. See **La Francia.**

Franck, Carl, & Co. 1867–1930. Ohrdruf, Thür. Manufactured heads of dolls.

Francke, F. 1926–28. Dresden, Germany. Manufactured dolls.

Franek. 1915. One of the dolls promoted by *Mme. Paderewski* to aid Polish refugees. It was made in the workshop of *Mme. Thabée Lazarski* by Polish refugee artists. This doll was dressed in the holiday attire of a Polish peasant from Cracow. These were clothes that would have been worn at weddings and special celebrations including a white coat made of "Sukmana," a coarse woolen fabric supposed to wear forever.

Frank, M. J., & Co. 1926. New York City. Registered *"On My Lap"* as a U.S. trademark for dolls.

Franke, Carl Friedrich. 1912. Berlin. Obtained a German patent (D.R.P.) for stringing a doll's body.

Franke, Friedrick Carl. 1914–30 and later. Berlin. Distributed and exported dolls, among them *Kestner* dolls.

Frankel, G., & Sons. 1884–1926. New York City. Importer of dolls and a jobber.

1926: Specialized in celluloid dolls.

Franken, T. 1893. Paris. Name in the registration of French trademark, *Bébé Moderne.* †

Franken & Co. 1915. London. Sole agent for porcelain headed French dolls which came in 12 models dressed in the uniforms of the various Allied soldiers. Priced 25¢ to 62¢.

Frankenberg. L. 1922–26. Listed under dolls in a British toy trade journal. Imported German dolls.

Frankfurter Gummiwaren-Fabriken. 1927. Berlin. Made rubber bathing dolls and nursing dolls.

Frankl, Franz. 1888–1930. Vienna. 1908–30. Successors were Otto Ernst Frankl and Robert Frankl. Produced dolls.

1887: Advertised composition dolls, *Täuflinge,* and trousseaux for dolls.

1908–10: Advertised *Chic* Dolls. Maintained a display shop in London and Leipzig.

1914: Advertised tango dancer dolls.

Franklin, J. G. 1925. Produced cuddley dolls.

Franklin Studio. 1930 and later. Covington, Georgia. Manufactured *Flor-El-Lyn* line of dolls, a line of dressed nursery rhyme character dolls, other dressed dolls, and dolls' outfits.

Franklin, W., & Son. 1922. London. Sole agent in Britain for *V. M. Bruchlos,* also agent for *Übler & Beck* and *Victor Steiner.*

Frankowska, Mlle. 1916–18. Paris. Created deluxe cloth dolls.

Franz (Fisherman). 1911–16. Felt art doll made by *Steiff,* dressed in a Dutch regional costume of a fisherman. It had a black fisherman's hat or a sou'wester and the clothes were in assorted colors. Ht. 50 cm. (19½ in.).

Franz, Johannes. 1871–1913. Sonneberg, Thür. In 1895 he obtained a German patent (D.R.G.M.) for a jointed doll with rubber arms. ★

Franz, Otto. 1899–1908. Vienna. Made dolls and dolls' heads. ★

Fraser Rock. See **Rock, Helen Fraser.**

Frear, William H. 1880s. Troy, N.Y. A trade card advertised dolls at Frear's Troy Cash Bazaar.

Freckles. 1926. Dancing doll that represented one of the Hal Roach *Our Gang* moving picture stars. It was made by *Schoen & Yondorf* and carried a scroll-shaped tag. Ht. 11½ in. (29 cm.); priced $1.25.

Freckles. 1929. A stuffed oil-cloth doll representing the cartoon character in FRECKLES AND HIS FRIENDS, created by Merrill Blosser. The doll made by *Live Long Toys* had freckles and wore a print shirt, short trousers, circular striped stockings and large shoes. Ht. 11 in. (28 cm.); priced $6.00 doz. wholesale.

Freitag. See **Frey Tag, F. W., & Co.**

Fremont, L. E. Before 1865. Paris. According to Mme. Poisson, Curator of the Roybet-Fould Museum, he sold dolls and dolls' trousseaux.

1864: He failed and *Jumeau* was one of his creditors. 18 percent of his inventory was dolls.

French, James W. 1903–16. Los Angeles, Calif. Claimed that he had patented a secret hardening process to enable him to make dolls' heads out of egg shells which a child could not smash. He used various kinds of eggs from Humming bird to Ostrich eggs. The eggs were broken open at the place that corresponded with the doll's hair line and the contents of the eggs were sold to restaurants and bakeries. A doll representing the Merry Widow was made from a bantam hen's egg. A doll representing President Wilson was made from a duck's egg. These dolls were not too successful until the war came and German dolls were no longer available.

French Baby. 1918–19. Name of a dressed composition-head doll made by *Effanbee.* It had a bobbed mohair wig and sleeping eyes. Ht. 15½ in. (39.5 cm.).

French Doll Bazaar. See **Beam, Mrs. Louisa.**

French Doll Makers, The. 1925–30 and later. New York City. Made cloth-body dolls and was represented by *A. S. Ferguson.* In 1929–30 *Gre-Poir* became part of this company.

French Dolls. According to the United Federation of Doll Clubs' GLOSSARY: "the term 'French Doll' is to be applied only to dolls made entirely in France . . . According to this definition any doll with an unmarked or unrecognizably marked head cannot be called 'French' . . . French-type dolls are those made partially in France." During the period 1900–1914 when the *Société Française de Fabrication de Bébés & Jouets* (S.F.B.J.) was controlled by *Salomon Fleischmann* of Germany, one cannot be certain that even dolls with recognizable French marks were made entirely in France. Often it is not certain whether French refers to a country or to a quality.

1608: King Henri IV granted by statute the monopoly of making dolls to the "poupetiers" (makers and dressers of dolls) and denied rights to the "bimbelotiers" (makers of playthings). However, the guild of poupetiers seems to have disappeared by the time of Louis XIV (middle 1600s).

Ca. 1800: A French catalog at Winterthur shows dolls with head and torso of cardboard and painted features. Lower arms and hands of wood were shown separately.

1844: French dolls had pink kid bodies and according to a French critic the heads were not as beautiful as those on English or German dolls.

1860s: M. Rondot, a Frenchman, wrote: "making porcelain heads in France. . . . neglected by us, has been introduced in Bavaria, Prussia and Austria."

1869: HARPER'S BAZAR stated, "The chief French toy is a doll, not a representation of an infant. . . . but a model of a lady attired in the height of fashion, a leading manufacturer changing the costume every month to insure accuracy."

1870: LA POUPÉE MODÈLE, published by *Mme. Lavalée-Peronne,* gave the heights that corresponded with the size numbers for French lady-type dolls.

Size No.	Height in.	cm.
0	12	30
2	14–15½	36–40
4	17½	45
5	19½	50
6	21½	54

1872: See *Bru.*

1875–76: Bébé Incassable (unbreakable baby) was introduced. These dolls had bisque heads and jointed composition bodies. They represented a child of about four years old. In 1876 the *Louvre* store advertised Bébés Incassable, the model for which they claimed was owned by them and which they described as new.

1876: DEMOREST commented: "French doll indicates at once her position in society. Lady dolls are dressed in complete walking costumes, dinner or evening dresses, bonnes [nursemaids] in caps, neat plain dresses and aprons, waiting maids in pretty print dresses, fancy muslin aprons and smart caps with ribbons." The bodies were of jointed kid; priced $3.00 to $10.00 undressed, $5.00 to $25.00 dressed; trousseaux cost extra.

1878: THE QUEEN mentioned French bébés with jointed composition bodies dressed as children; Wooden body lady dolls articulated even at the wrists and ankles. Hts. 10 to 16 in. (25.5 to 40.5 cm.); and a walking bébé that said "papa" and "mama."

1879: EHRICH'S FASHION QUARTERLY listed the following sizes for French-type lady dolls with bisque heads and kid bodies. Eight hts.: 12½, 14½, 16, 17½, 19, 20½, 22, and 23½ in. (31.5, 37, 40.5, 44.5, 48, 52, 56, and 59.5 cm.). Other sources of this period gave approximately the same heights.

1880: The Oscar Strasburger & Co. catalog (Strasburger & Pfeiffer[+]) listed "French Kid body Dolls with fine Bisque Turning Heads, Natural Hair, Glass Eyes, jointed Bodies."

STRASBURGER "FRENCH" DOLLS		
Size No.	Height in.	cm.
2/0	11½	29
0	12¼	31
1	13½	34
2	14½	37
3	16	40.5
4	17	43
5	18½	47
6	21	53.5

1885: *Horsman* advertised "French Bisque Dolls" and separate "French Bisque Heads" with natural hair in 10 sizes or styles. The heads were $10.50 to $48.00 a doz. wholesale.

1887: *Lauer* advertised "French Bisque" dolls' heads, turning and non-turning; size numbers 0 thru 6 as shown for *Stern.* The turning heads cost $4.50 to $13.50 doz. wholesale and the non-turning heads cost $4.00 to $12.75 doz. wholesale. These heads came with wigs.

1893: Tour St.-Jacques[+] advertised dolls of "French manufacture (gold medal at London 1890)." These dolls had bisque heads, wigs, and fully jointed composition bodies including wrists. 11 hts. 38 to 90 cm. (15 to 35½ in.). Prices with chemise and footwear were 78¢ to $5.80.

1894: *Linington's* "French Bisque Dolls" had teeth.

1897: A STUDY OF DOLLS by Hall reported that the Russian Toy Congress protested against the large, elegant French dolls that taught love of dress and suggested luxury.

1904 and later: *Henry S. Benjamin* handled the dolls of the S.F.B.J. in London.

1912: TOYS AND NOVELTIES stated that all French-made dolls were stamped "French Manufacture."
LESLIE'S ILLUSTRATED WEEKLY NEWSPAPER reported: "At Vincennes, France, there is a large factory where the very best type of French doll is made. Parts of all dolls are imported from Germany, for that country has a monopoly on the heads, and the factories all over the world depend on the German factories for their supply of this part of the dolls." (Montreuil-sous-Bois adjoins the better known Vincennes area.)

1913: TOYS AND NOVELTIES reported: "The dolls made in France, especially at Vincennes, have an exquisite finish. This is accounted for from the fact that each year there is a prize offered for the best design for dolls. . . .
"New French fashion dolls [are] attired in gowns of the latest model used in show windows and women's stores to show the latest styles."
French dolls could say several words, roll or wink their eyes and walk. The clockwork mechanism was activated by winding a key inserted at the waistline. Price $15.00 and up.

Before World War I period: TOYS AND NOVELTIES reported later: "Years ago France was once noted for the toys and dolls which she manufactured for all the world. Never was the industry as large or as extensive as it is in Germany . . . but there are many among us who can remember the popularity of the beautiful but fragile wax dolls which came from France.
"Before the war nearly all the dolls' heads and enameled [glass] eyes were purchased by the French manufacturers from Germany."
Claretie in ARTS FRANÇAIS (1918) wrote: "Dolls were dressed in France but the bodies were almost entirely German. Even in Paris the grand Société du Bébé [S.F.B.J.] was composed in part of the capital of German stock holders."

1914–16: Jeanne Doin wrote a report in 1916 entitled "La

Renaissance de la Poupée Française" (The rebirth of the French Doll") which was published in the GAZETTE DES BEAUX ARTS. This report as translated follows:

"The Germans had ruined the French doll industry in a few years by methodically copying and underselling. . . . Before 1900 many companies, Rabery, Bru, Pintel, Eden Bébé, gave up the struggle and were absorbed by Bébé Jumeau. This Société had a virtual monopoly but it should be noted that among its largest stock holders was a German. Its facilities were the only ones in France that permitted it to make entire bébés. Other firms had to get their porcelain heads and glass eyes from Germany. Germany could deliver in Paris their heads for only 2¢ all charges paid while the same head made in France cost 8¢. The reason of this difference was that the German ovens fired the porcelain dolls' heads simultaneously with expensive luxury items whereas in France the heads were fired without other objects.

"After 1900 Fleishmann & Bloedel, Gutmann & Schiffnie and Margarete Steiff pursued their peaceful conquest with energy.

"At Sonneberg, the great doll manufacturing center, a number of firms concerned themselves especially with exporting to France under the protection of the Imperial Government and the Chamber of Commerce. Nürnberg, Eisfeld, Georgenthal, Ilmenau, Neustadt and Waltershausen also sent thousands of dolls across our frontiers. The Germans did not send trash, the factories beyond the Rhine produced high class objects. Thanks to their perfection and regularity others could not produce equivalent merchandise. This explains why at the beginning of the war the situation in France was critical.

". . . In August, 1914, Mme. la Baronne de Laumont created her first dolls. [Some of her dolls had porcelain heads made in Limoges.] The following month L'Association de Petites Fabricants engaged certain master porcelain-makers to undertake as quickly as possible the manufacture of bisque heads. Six months later Damerval & Laffranchy formed its collection. Limoges and Boulogne-sur-Mer followed the example. Soon in a Polish refugee workshop the cloth doll appeared.

"Thus, from private and collective efforts that were very different as to cause and effect, came the movement about which we are writing. Today [1916] the cloth doll or those of composition with porcelain heads form the fairest kinds. The first is a toy for the clumsy hands of a small child while the second pleases young girls who enjoy combing, dressing and copying the appearance of the doll. . . .

"The cloth doll is not a modern invention as is generally believed. . . . For my part I know 5 cloth dolls, all little and indeed French, that were made at the beginning of the 19th century. . . . It is reasonable to think that the dolls from Germany were formerly derived from our dolls of bran. We know that Mme. Margarete Steiff's grotesque cloth dolls have hideous squinting typical of German humor. Unbelievably, French Mothers liked these horrors, and the disastrous result was that their children imitated their dolls.

"In England, German dolls were copied without being excessively grotesque. In France lighter weight cloth was used to form amusing fantasies. . . . The cloth doll is ever changing according to the material used and the hands that fashion it.

"The first was created by Mme. Lazarski in 1914. These dolls wore Polish costumes like the ones that she had made the year before in her native Poland. Mme. Lazarski's dolls were simplified in features and form. . . . In the same workshop Mlle. Fiszerowna applied pink or blue circles to give color to the cheeks and clarity to the eyes. The dolls of these two ladies were shown at the 1916 Exposition. . . .

"The cloth dolls propagated and in some Polish workshops the character of the foreigner persisted while in others it tapered off. Soon dolls of true French character began to appear. The doll of Mme. Ambroise Thomas is an example. . . . Each workshop has its own particular type of doll and details vary greatly. The metal skeleton, the stuffing, the way the parts are assembled lead to notable differences. Imitations are rare but borrowing of ideas is constant. The form of the hands and feet are similar but some are elongated while others are stubby. As for hair, one sees all kinds, tow, cotton, wool, fur, silk; sometimes they are sewed, sometimes quilted or embroidered.

"Certain types are especially popular. The yellow and black races which are easily and unmistakably represented, enjoy great favor. At the 14th Concours Lépine one is able to buy a Japanese doll for $3.20 and a black doll for $2.00 which is not expensive. Perhaps rather than the dolls of Mme. Deffonds one would prefer the little black doll of Mme. Alexandrowicz, which is more comical and is a mascot. Are the dolls from Japan a future menace? M. D'Allemagne in his 1907 report on the St. Louis Exposition mentions that the only serious competition with Sonneberg were the Japanese entries. The doll factories of Osaka and Kyoto make good dolls at low prices. These are European not oriental models. After the rebirth of the French doll will it be necessary to speak of the influx of dolls from our yellow ally? . . .

"Cloth dolls can be classified into 2 groups, those with the face sewed down the middle and those without this sewing. The latter sometimes have a nose and sometimes do not. All of these features depend on the wishes of the artist creating the doll. The type of material used is a factor. Some dolls have no necks, others have 2 pink dots for a nose. Often this is because the creator wishes to simplify the doll. The well-stuffed body and legs tend to remind one of the rigidity of the antique wooden dolls with which our grandmother played. The bright pink color of the satin and of the cottons also evoke memories of antique dolls. But the modern costumes remind us that these are the dolls of to-day.

"Besides the costume, the variations in the shape of the head indicates the workshop where the doll was made. Some of the deformities may be caused by the attempt to produce a comic effect, while others represent natural irregularities that might be found in a child. The dolls are made especially to imitate and appeal to children in regard to the shape of the head, the suppleness of the body and the charm of the costume. Dolls are made for children's enjoyment." The following is a list of producers of cloth dolls and some of the names of their dolls:

"*Mlle. Swiecka* made Zobéida and Haroun-al-Raschid. *Mme. Alexandrowicz.*

Mlle. Desaubliaux.

Mme. Roig made Bébé Gallia.

Mme. d'Eichthal made Yves and Cita.

Mme. Manson made Sophie and Cadet-Roussel and Marlborough.

Mme. Vera Ouvré made Gavroche and Charlot [Charlie Chaplin].

Mlle. Verita.

Mlle. Duvall made Clarabel.

Mme. Dhomont made clowns.

La Francia made dolls dressed as Bretonnes.

Mlle. Lloyd.

Mlle. Rozmann made *Parmentier* [names not italicized in original].

"Among the producers of wooden dolls and some of their dolls are: M. Georges Lepape made Gilles and Marion with wooden heads on cloth bodies. Mme. Alexandrowicz who made an all wooden doll called Mimi.

"The toys of M. F. Caront seem to have influenced the development of wooden dolls.

"It is feared that after the war Germany will again take over the doll market despite the efforts to make dolls in France. The porcelain head dolls with composition bodies are still commercially most desired. . . . The regional dolls of Mme. de Laumont represent the areas of France. . . . Made in large quantity the dolls of Mme. de Laumont show our national costumes everywhere and this is at a time when they tend more and more to disappear.

"Mme. Pierre Goujon designs new costumes for dolls that differ from the old pink and blue satin with their falballas, plumes, bows, and laces. . . . It was so stupid to have the old clothes that all looked alike. The new clothes are plainer and more diversified. Fancy clothes are replaced by chemises, drawers, skirts and especially buttons. . . . Mme. Bertha Noufflar, Mlles. Lloyd and Duvall, l'Adelphie have participated in this transformation. In the same way the dolls of La Francia charm with their elegance and high quality. . . . But on the subject of La Francia I wish to speak of the doll of M. Botta [He made dolls for La Francia].

"For a long time composition dolls have been badly proportioned. Too bad to influence the taste of children who undress their dolls ten times a day by giving them such ugliness. . . . M. Botta makes his dolls with bodies typical of a true 5 year old, small shoulders, prominent stomach, flat bust, strong back, a mixture of robustness and grace.

"Other sculptors who have made clay or wax models are MM. Masson and de la Boulaye who have each made a head for Mme. de Laumont. M. Gardet has made the model for a doll for M. Bricon. M. Lejeune has made a head for Mlle. Thomson and M. [Albert] Marque has sculptured a doll for a large store. The head of the Infanta is by M. Gumery. . . . The model of M. Antonin Mercie was made to carry the Parisian modes through the ages. It has a woman's body and is a doll figurine. On the contrary the little girl and the baby of Mme. Bertha Noufflar are toys. . . . The Sèvres factory adopted one of her models. . . .

"The artist carries the idea. The manufacturer applies it. The dependence on Germany is at an end. . . . Other artists have devoted themselves to the delicate and minute creation of the deluxe doll. Mlle. de Felice has modeled dolls in kid. Mme. Martet has made dolls representing the characters of Balzac. Mlle. Frankowska made dolls representing the Romantic eras of the past.

"Mme. Lauth-Sand created cloth dolls representing gypsies. . . .

"Of the fashion doll, I shall say only a few words in passing. Before the War she existed but she was a little disdained. Sculptors have modernized her. And because voyages are risky and salesmen are rare [due to the war] the fashion dolls to-day carry across the seas our dresses and knick-knacks. Therefore by the forces of circumstances we return to the customs of an earlier time. Nevertheless the fortunes of the fashion doll and the deluxe doll are full of vicissitudes. Women are capricious and hard to please but the constancy of children is admirable. To enter into life without a doll is inconceivable. That is why the doll will always be demanded and beloved. . . ."

Claretie in ARTS FRANÇAIS's Les Jouets, written in 1918, added the following names to Doin's names of French doll makers who started to work at the beginning of the war or earlier: *Rachel Boyer, De Rochefort, Renée de Vériane, Mmes. Lafitte & Désirat, Margaine-Lacroix, Mégard,* Prévost-Huret, *Mme. Sautter, Eugéne Simon,* Mlle. *Valentine Thomson,* and *Maria Verone.* A model made by *M. Antonin Mercié* was based on a child's head by Donatello.

TOYS AND NOVELTIES in 1919 reported that at the beginning of the war "It was noticed that the dolls were nearly all German, so artists had to create a French type of doll.

"Antoine *[sic]* Mercié made a model. [Other] great artists furnished models for dolls though, of course, these were too expensive for general use. But several societies worked on dolls and china [porcelain] heads were made at *Sèvres* and Limoges."

TOYS AND NOVELTIES quoted an article written by Henri Clouze:

"It is a question whether the term industry can be applied to the production of French toys. . . . [which] remained in France a craftsman occupation, in most instances a craftsman on a small scale, too. One or two houses before the war had a capital over a million francs [$200,000]. . . .

"With the best intention imaginable, talented women produced dolls of such elegance and distinction as had never been on the other side of the Rhine. The Artists, deprived at a time of orders, took the wrong direction, and the renaissance of the French toy industry turned toward making show pieces for the showcases, made entirely by artists as unique specimens. A young girl who made a Breton doll demanded 100 francs [$20.00] for it, and refused to sell it to a manufacturer for the purpose of reproducing it in quantities. The result was a few articles in the press, a few purchases by collectors but the trade suffered a rebutal.

" 'It was impossible to let things remain there. Since it was seen that the small artisans were not capable, single handed, to intensify and modernize their production, much less, owing to their lack of solidarity, to combine their efforts, the capitalist stepped in to help.'

"New companies were founded. A few among the old

ones, purged of their former German association, resumed manufacture."

The workshop of *Mlle. Valentene Momson* was discussed by TOYS AND NOVELTIES in 1915:

"At the present time, under Mlle. Momson's direction, and suggestion . . . dolls of many kinds are being made. . . .

"Toy making seems especially adaptable for disabled soldiers. It involves the sort of work that can be done even in bed, and many wounded soldiers are already beginning to learn their new trade. It will not only give work to the men, but to widows of soldiers who can paint and dress dolls."

Mlle. Momson's organization in Paris, known as *La Vie Femmes,* distributed all over France material and directions for making dolls. A former doll factory was reorganized and began full operation turning out dolls' heads which were supplied to soldiers and homes where the bodies were sewed and the dolls dressed. Many of these dolls were brought to sell in America in 1915 by Mme. Charles Le Verrier, the wife of a Paris College President.

1917: TOYS AND NOVELTIES continued to tell about the French dolls: "Beautiful hand cut, hand painted . . . dolls of every age and facial expression into which each individual soldier seems to have put some twist of whimsical humor. . . .

"In this work Paris is having the co-operation of some of her greatest artists. Another interesting feature of the work, which could not exist except for war, is the utilization of a very high class of labor among the convalescent soldiers, who under ordinary circumstances, would be engaged in other pursuits. It is a gathering of painters, sculptors and skilled artizans who are now making toys for pastime as much as for pay.

"Among the new things are wonderful dolls sculptured from life by great men in their line of work, and stuffed fabric dolls with perfectly articulated bodies and faces painted from designs made by well-known portrait artists.

"Many of the new toys are being sold for the benefit of the war sufferers and thus both their manufacture and their sale is philanthropic. In the distribution of these lines there is often a co-operation with the United States. This is true in connection with the dolls manufactured under the patronage of the Baroness Laumont and those which are dressed by French war orphans, who, thereby, gain their livelihood. The former are high priced dolls, while the latter are very simple ones, such as a child could make the clothes for."

1918: TOYS AND NOVELTIES printed two articles on French soldiers released from German camps and interned in Switzerland, whose dolls were exhibited by the Art Alliance in New York City. Among the exhibits from the house of Callot were dolls representing French soldiers, ladies of the demi-monde, French children, Cinderella and her sisters.

1919: TOYS AND NOVELTIES printed two articles on French dolls. The one by Joe L. *Amberg* gave an American's viewpoint:

"The French have a certain 'esprit' which prompts them to make. . . . the most beautiful creations in Toys.

"Dolls. Once upon a time the storekeeper used to tell the buyer that 'this is a French doll' and this was the acme of recommendation. The old Joumet [*Jumeau*] doll which has been made for more than a generation we might even today say is a splendid item. This with the *Paris Bébé* are the two fine lines shown there. The bisc heads are good but when it comes to the bodies they 'fall down' badly in comparison with Americans. The finer grades are fully jointed similar to the old German ones, and excel in finish, but they are frightfully high at present. Our finest American wood pulp bodies are just as light, much more durable, and at least in our estimation, much better in shape.

"The fact that we may sell our dolls there particularly when it came to the bodies rather proves that this idea prevails with their buyers as it does with the writer. Their heads as stated are excellent finish, but not pleasing in expression from our viewpoint. Most French dolls are controlled by one association [S.F.B.J.] and they show cheaply finished papier-mâché affairs as well, and of course although all priced items are offered they are not really 'cheap' in price by any means. The French, however, are making very small dolls with papier-mâché bodies with bisc heads from a few inches up. These unfortunately, although fair in quality are too high, I believe, to stand importing.

"Here, as in England, the jointed baby doll or fully jointed girl doll is the one that sells. Without doubt in dolldom 'hard body dolls', as they are called, are the only ones desired in France."

The other article stated: "It is feared that when more normal conditions prevail, foreign, and especially German, competition will seriously handicap the French doll trade. In Germany the largest factories are in remote districts, where the work is done by the peasants, whereas in France the factories are situated in or near the large cities, where the cost of living is much higher. Before the war nearly all the dolls' heads and enameled [glass] eyes used were purchased by the French manufacturers from Germany. Since 1914 these essential parts of dolls have been made in France at Limoges, [*Lanternier* and *Coiffe*, Couty & Co.], Boulogne-sur-Mer [*Verlingue*], and in the suburbs of Paris [S.F.B.J.].

"A business was organized in Paris last year with a capital of [$800,000] which is attempting to make dolls' heads, besides dressing the dolls. This firm is receiving large orders, and its dolls are meeting with considerable success.

"It appears from a report by the United States Consul-General at Paris, that until its recent revival, the French toy industry had been on the decline for some years."

Wounded French soldiers in Paris continued to make cloth dolls with three dimensional faces. These represented Normandy peasants wearing sabots, old women, men, girls and children.

A novelty was "Poupée Chiffon," a long limbed cloth doll.

1920–21: The Baroness de Laumont sent dolls to French villages where they were dressed by local peasants and shepherdesses. These were called *Rural Dolls.*

According to TOY AND FANCY GOODS TRADER a new series of dolls was made by a "well known French manufacturer. The animals and dolls' faces are made of papier mache, and are quite original in their grotesqueness. The dolls are dressed in the very latest Parisian style, but many models are being brought out dressed in true English fashion."

In 1921 and probably other years, German toy manufacturers had branches in France which were not stated to be German and parts of dolls were sent to France where they were assembled into dolls.

1922: Dolls wore copies of creations of famous Parisian Modistes.

1923: High quality dolls of porcelain or composition wore silk, velvet and lace clothes. Inexpensive dolls were made of wood or molded cardboard and wore poorly made chemises. Artistically painted cloth dolls represented American Indians, cowboys, black Africans, Pierrots, Gnomes and Salomé. These dolls were more expensive than the pre-war porcelain dolls. Good luck dolls were popular to use in parlors, automobiles, on bicycles and so on.

1926: The Paris dressmaking salons sold doll models and from *Poiret* came laughing dolls with supple legs.

Dolls were made with chamois-skin faces and limbs or with painted georgette fabric. Other dolls were made by Russian and Romanian refugees.

TOYS AND NOVELTIES in 1926 reported that before World War I ". . . the reputed French-made dolls sometimes came from Nürnberg, the finishing touches having been added in Paris. . . . French products are notoriously bad and appallingly dear."

The same magazine described the French dolls of 1926 as follows: "The dolls, for example, exploit the last thing in short skirts, rakish little hats, skeleton shoes and gossamer-like stockings, the miniature sticks which they carry when in walking costume, being provided with an elaborate handle."

1927: Long limbed expensive dolls with wardrobes of fine clothes were popular in Paris. These had pressed, hand-painted cloth faces and were similar to *Boudoir* dolls except with more elaborate clothes. Fur trimming was popular even on pajamas. Thibet fur was used for a "great mop of hair." One of these dolls was black and represented *Josephine Baker*. Other dolls were created by *Mme. Emilia Milobendzka* and *Consuélo Fould*.

1928: PLAYTHINGS contained an article on French dolls: "Today France is producing many of her own toys and is giving them the distinctive French touch. . . . The real novelty toys last year were . . . talking dolls. . . . Likewise there were most childlike dolls which rolled the eyes, walked, talked and one which actually drank. Down its throat can be poured the contents of a nursing bottle, but at the end of the day, the hinged back must be opened and a sponge taken out and pressed dry. . . . There are many Eskimo dolls."

A German toy trade journal reported that the great fashion houses and couturiers of Paris occupied themselves as much with a doll's dress as with a lady's clothes.

The following marks have been found on French-type dolls but so far have not been definitely identified. All of these dolls have a size number but the samples are too small to draw any conclusions except that they roughly seem to follow the French size-height patterns. However it should be noted that some of the *Simon & Halbig* dolls had somewhat similar size-height relationships.

The marks are: A. T.; G. V. (lady doll); H. (Both bébé and lady types); M. (the size-height relationships are different from those found with Mascotte dolls). (See also **E. Barrois, Bébé Bru, Bébé Jumeau, Danel & Cie., Etienne Denamur, French Regional Costume Dolls, Manufacture of Dolls Made Commercially in France, Pintel and Godchaux, Société Française de Fabrication de Bébés & Jouets (S.F.B.J.), Société Industrielle de Celluloid.)**★

965A & B. French doll wearing original commercial clothes. The papier-mâché shoulder head has a thin coating of wax. The doll has blue painted eyes. Placed over the black painted hair are the remains of the original wig which was pinned in place. The dress is likewise pinned in place with the early wrapped head pins. (The 1848 inventory for Madame E. Barrois of Paris listed over two pounds of pins.) The upper torso is molded carton while the legs and arms are leather. The original dress is of white gauze trimmed with red silk ribbon and gilt thread. The apron is pink brocade. Inside the hat is paper with French printing. H. 15½ in. (39.5 cm.). *Coleman Collection.*

French Fashion Importing Co. 1930. New York City. Imported *Poupées Ninon.*

French Gamin (Urchin). 1927. Cloth doll made by *Woolnough* of plush with embroidered facial features. *Davis & Voetsch* were the factory agents for this doll.

French Heads. See **Anita Novelty Co.**

966. French bisque head doll with blond wig, stationary blue glass eyes, pierced ears, and a closed mouth. It has a socket head on a bisque shoulder plate and a kid body without joints. The original clothes represent saint Genevieve, patron saint of Paris. The metal coat of arms on the doll's breast are those of the city of Paris. H. 8½ in. (21.5 cm.). *Courtesy of the Margaret Woodbury Strong Museum. Photo by Harry Bickelhaupt.*

967. Bisque pressed shoulder head with molded and painted hair and eyes, closed mouth, and kid body jointed only at the shoulders. The fact that this doll has a pressed head and a kid body suggests that it may have been made in France. Original regional costume. The mark, Ill. 970, is found on the inside of the shoulder in a manner similar to marks found on François Gaultier's shoulder plates. Shoulders on bodies that follow the Bru patent of 1869 also often have similar marks. H. 12 in. (39.5 cm.). *Coleman Collection.*

968. Unmarked French-type doll resembles dolls marked Breveté. It has a wig, stationary blue glass eyes, pierced ears, closed mouth, kid body with bisque arms. Original dress. H. 14½ in. (37 cm.). *Courtesy of Cherry Bou.*

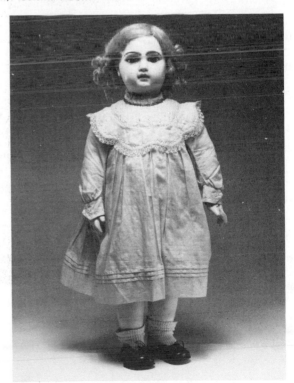

969. Bisque head doll marked Tête Jumeau has a wig, stationary brown glass eyes, pierced ears, closed mouth and a fully jointed composition body. Probably original clothes except shoes. H. 24 in. (61 cm.). *Courtesy of Sotheby Parke Bernet Inc., N.Y.*

H

970. Mark on the inside of a bisque shoulder head, possibly French.

French Novelty Dolls. 1927. All-composition art dolls in elaborate costumes made for decoration and distributed by the *American Wholesale Corp.* Six hts. 14¾ to 16¾ in. (37.5 to 42.5 cm.); priced $3.75 to $5.00.

French Regional Costume Dolls. Probably most of these dolls were made and dressed in France but some of the dolls were made in Germany or elsewhere. *Lenci* dressed a few dolls in French regional costumes. During the late 1800s and early 1900s many people made the "grand tour" of Europe and brought home regional costume dolls. Most of the Paris stores carried French regional costume dolls and they could also have been purchased in local shops in the various regions. Among the manufacturers of dolls in French regional costumes were *Fleischmann & Bloedel, François Gaultier* (heads), *La Francia, Limoges (Lanternier), Ravca* and *Société Française de Fabrication de Bébés & Jouets.*

Occasionally one finds a *Bébé Jumeau, Bru* or other French doll dressed in regional costume. The most popular costumes were those representing Alsace, Boulogne-sur-Mer, Brittany, Normandy and Provence. For each area there was a tremendous variation in the costumes depending on the occupation, the social station, the occasion—such as a wedding—Sunday outfits, festival and of course the period in time represented. Usually the Alsatian women wore a large black bow decorated with a tri-colored rosette on their heads. Many of the Boulogne-sur-Mer dolls were dressed to represent fishermen and fisherwomen. Many of the peasants of France wore wooden shoes (sabots) which should not be confused with the Dutch wooden shoes.

1890: The Musée Pédagogique was established in Paris by Mlle. Marie Koenig. The feature of this Museum was a series of dolls dressed in French regional costumes. Mlle. Koenig wrote two books on this collection namely POUPÉES ET LÉGENDES DE FRANCE. published in 1900 and MUSÉE DE POUPÉES, in 1909.

1896–1900: Paris stores were advertising dolls dressed as Brittany couples in silk and wool. The dolls were about 29 cm. (11 in.) tall.

1908: Fleischmann & Blödel made a series of dolls dressed in French regional costumes.

1910: *Marion Kaulitz* dressed dolls in French Regional costumes.

World War I period: *Baroness de Laumont* dressed Lanternier dolls in French regional costumes. La Francia and probably other organizations also made these costumes.

LA POUPÉE MODÈLE published patterns for making French regional costumes and dolls in regional costumes were shown in LA SEMAINE DE SUZETTE. Mascot dolls such as *Nénette* and *Rintintin* as well as *Yerri, Gretel* and *Suzel* wore regional costumes.

1921–22: Bisque-head dolls dressed in Alsatian or Brittany costumes were available in Paris stores in at least eight sizes. TOYS AND NOVELTIES reported that dolls in French Provincial costumes were appealing to doll collectors.

1927–28: Dolls dressed as French peasants were exported from France to America. (See also **Regional Costume Dolls.**)

971. French regionally dressed composition head dolls with bisque legs and bare feet, bisque fish and a bisque basket. Hair painted black appears only in front on the man and is a ball pate in front on the woman. The man has painted brown eyes and the woman has painted blue eyes. Each has a closed mouth, except that the man has a cigar in the corner of his mouth. The cloth bodies have kid arms with stub hands. The woman has a large padded bosom. On the life preserver that the man carries over his shoulder is written the words "Société Humane." H. 9¼ in. (23.5 cm.). *Coleman Collection.*

972. French regional costume dolls wearing the clothes of Boulogne fisherfolk. They have pressed bisque heads, painted black hair (the man also has sideburns), painted blue eyes, and closed mouth. The cloth bodies have pottery limbs. The hands are made to hold objects and the girl has bare feet while the man has sea-boots. He has a pottery fish and casket. She has a pottery basket. Her bosom is padded to make it larger. She is marked "F. G." for F. Gaultier. H. 9¼ in. (23.5 cm.). *Coleman Collection.*

FISH-GIRLS OF BOULOGNE AS THEY DRESS FOR FÊTE-DAYS
AND WORKING-DAYS.

973. French dolls in the costumes of Boulogne fisherwomen. The doll on the left is dressed in holiday attire while the girl on the right is wearing work clothes. The bisque heads were probably made by François Gaultier. Note that the underskirts with vertical stripes and the large bead earrings are similar on the two dolls. These dolls, exhibited in Mlle. Koenig's Musée Pédagogique, were shown in a U.S. magazine, ST. NICHOLAS, January, 1910.

974. Group of bisque head dolls dressed in French regional costumes as Boulogne fisherfolk. They have glass eyes, closed mouth, pierced ears (except for the Lanternier), cloth bodies, and pottery hands made to hold the various pottery accessories. Left to right: Man with pottery boots. Head marked F. G. 2/0" for Gaultier. H. 13 in. (33 cm.). Woman marked "F. G." in a scroll for Gaultier. H. 13½ in. (34 cm.). Woman wears sabots and is marked "A. L." with an anchor for Lanternier. H. 13 in. (33 cm.). Woman wears sabots and is marked "F. G." in a scroll for Gaultier. H. 14½ in. (37 cm.). *Courtesy of Sotheby Parke Bernet Inc., N.Y.*

975. Dolls with German-type bisque heads dressed in original French regional costumes as Boulogne fisherfolk. They have molded black hair (the man has sideburns), painted brown eyes, closed mouths, cloth bodies with pottery hands. The man's boots and fish are also pottery. They are jointed only at the shoulders and the woman has a large padded bosom. H. 9¾ in. (25 cm.). *Coleman Collection.*

READY FOR THE WEDDING-TRIP, LA MARTYRE,
FINISTÈRE.

976. Bisque head dolls in French regional costumes represent a bride and groom of La Martyre, Finistère, Brittany. These dolls in Mlle. Koenig's Musée Pédagogique were shown in ST. NICHO-LAS, January, 1910.

A BRIDE OF OLÉRON. HERE ARE WORN THE BIGGEST PEASANT HATS IN FRANCE.

977. French doll dressed as a bride on the island of Oléron, and displayed in the Musée Pédagogique by Mlle. Koenig, shows the enormous headdress of that region. Illustration is from ST. NICHOLAS, January 1910.

978. Molded and heavily painted cloth doll with wool yarn hair. Tag reads: "France, Pyrenees//Woman from Basque section." Original clothes. H. 36 cm. (14 in.). *Coleman Collection.*

A DOLL FROM LORRAINE.

979. French doll with a bisque head probably made by François Gaultier. The doll wears a native costume of Lorraine and was exhibited by Mlle. Koenig in the Musée Pédagogique. This picture is from ST. NICHOLAS, January, 1910.

AN ALSATIAN MAIDEN.

980. French regional costume of Alsace exhibited by Mlle. Koenig in the Musée Pédagogique and shown in ST. NICHOLAS, January, 1910.

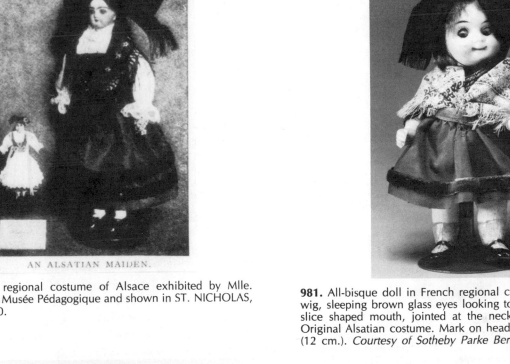

981. All-bisque doll in French regional costume. It has a black wig, sleeping brown glass eyes looking to the side, watermelon slice shaped mouth, jointed at the neck, shoulders and hips. Original Alsatian costume. Mark on head: "202.10." H. 4¾ in. (12 cm.). *Courtesy of Sotheby Parke Bernet Inc., N.Y.*

982. Cloth doll dressed in Alsatian costume. It has painted brown hair and eyes, closed mouth. The head is heavily painted and the body made of coarse cotton is jointed at the shoulders and hips. The mitten hands have stitched fingers. Original costume with black ribbon headwear, black satin bodice and apron, ribbed skirt. Shoes may be replacements. H. 13 in. (33 cm.). *Courtesy of the Margaret Woodbury Strong Museum. Photo by Harry Bickelhaupt.*

983. French cloth doll in regional costume. It has a flocked fabric face, blond silk braided hair, painted blue eyes, closed mouth, body jointed at the shoulders and hips. Original Alsatian style costume with a black blouse and head bow, flowered silk apron and shawl and a corduroy skirt. H. 10 in. (25.5 cm.). *Coleman Collection.*

984. Bisque head doll in French regional costume. It has a dark brown wig, sleeping glass eyes, hair upper eyelashes, open mouth with four upper teeth and a fully jointed composition body. Original Alsatian costume. Mark: "UNIS//71 FRANCE 149 //60//2/0." H. 13¾ in. (35 cm.). *Courtesy of Richard Withington. Photo by Barbara Jendrick.*

French Rubber Dolls. See **Rubber Dolls.**

Fretwell Manufacturing Co. 1917–18. London. Made wigged stockinet dolls including *My Kiddie, Bubbly Kid* and *Snowbell.*

Freuding, Karl. 1928–29. Wemding, Bavaria. Obtained a German patent (D.R.G.M.) for a jointed doll.

Freundlich, Ralph A. 1923–30 and later. New York City. He was with the *Jeanette Doll Co.* until 1929 when Ralph Freundlich, Inc. was formed. Made various types of dolls especially dolls with composition heads and limbs on cloth bodies.

1930: Most of the composition-head dolls were large, 27 or 28 in. (68.5 or 71 cm.) tall, but on light weight cloth bodies. They appear to have been *Mama* dolls, and weighed only one and one-half pounds. Price $1.00. Leatherette dolls representing fairy-tale characters were also made. (See also **Silver Doll Co.**)★

Frey Tag (Freitag), F. W., & Co. Before 1924–30. Ohrdruf, Thür. Successor in 1924 was the *Thüringer Spielwarenfabrik.* They made jointed dolls.

Frey Tag, R. P. 1926–27. New York City. Produced dolls.

Frickmann, Karl. See **Carl, Robert.**

Fridolin. 1922. According to the Ciesliks this was a doll representing a character in HEITER FRIDOLIN (Cheerful

Fridolin), published by Ullstein for young people. The sole producer of the doll was *Fleishmann & Bloedel.*

Friedel, Alban. 1911. Nürnberg, Bavaria. Applied for a German patent (D.R.G.M.) for a doll with musical works.★

Friedman, Jean L. 1918–19. New York City. Registered *"Nosy// Rosy"* as a U.S. trademark for dolls.

Friedmann, Hermann. 1912. Berlin. Applied for two German patents (D.R.G.M.) relating to dolls' bodies and head coverings.

Friedmann, Miss. 1920 and later. Tetschen, Silesia. Made leather dolls, some of which were in regional costumes. The dolls were distributed by *Kopfovi Weiss.*

Friedmann & Ohnstein. 1925–30 and later. Breslau, Silesia. Made and exported dolls including dolls' house dolls. Hts. 4 to 22 cm. (1½ to 8½ in.). Also advertised cloth dolls.

1930: Advertised dolls, baby dolls, dolls' house dolls, cloth dolls, "sofa dolls" and dolls' clothes. These products were distributed by *Hertzog.*★

Friedrichrodaer Puppenfabrik. 1902–30. Friedrichroda near Waltershausen, Thür. Manufactured dolls.

1911–13: Fritz Jäger[+] obtained several German patents (D.R.G.M. and D.R.P.) for dolls' wigs which were assigned to the Friedrichrodaer Puppenfabrik.

1924: London agent was H. R. Euston & Co.

Friendly Bugs. 1928. Trademark registered in U.S. by *Lee M. Byrd.* for dolls.

Friendship Dolls. 1926–27. Nearly 200,000 dolls were sent by the children of America to the children of Japan including the Princess Shigeko, daughter of the Emperor. The project was sponsored and organized by the Federal Council of the Church of Christ in America. It was supported by Protestant, Jewish and Catholic groups as well as the National Congress of Parents and Teachers, the Y.W.C.A., Camp Fire Girls, Junior Red Cross and so on. Each doll had a transportation ticket costing 99¢ and a passport visaed by the Japanese Council General costing one cent. The dolls sailed from the West Coast of America in January 1927 and were distributed in Japan on the following Doll Festival Day, March 3.

Most of the dolls sent from America had composition heads and were of the *Mama* doll type. They were dressed in the current fashions for American children. The specifications for the dolls were that they "were priced as moderate as quality would permit; face, arms and legs of unbreakable material [composition or cloth]; joints and wigs hand-sewn; eyes that opened and closed and a voice that should say unmistakably 'Mama'." A few of the dolls did not meet these standards but they were sent anyway. Carl E. Milliken recorded this venture on motion picture film.

In return 58 (another account said 49) very fine Japanese dolls were sent to America as a show of appreciation. Each doll cost $200.00 and was paid for by collecting one yen from each Japanese school child. The dolls were 32 in. (81 cm.) tall and their clothes were specially woven, designed and dyed. With each doll there was a trunk, chest of six drawers, a chair, a desk, and a mirror stand, all in black laquer trimmed with gold. Receptions and teas were given in their honor. Most of these dolls eventually became part of museum collections.

Unfortunately many of the American dolls were destroyed by the Japanese during World War II. But during the 1970s there was an exhibition in Japan of the few surviving American Dolls. One of these was an *Averill Manufacturing Co.* doll.

Frigeri, Achille. 1900. Canneto, Province of Mantua, Italy. Employed 20 workers including children to produce handmade dolls. (See also **Furga, Luigi, & Co.**)

Frilly Dolls. 1928. Advertised by *Gamage*. These were cloth-body dolls dressed in rayon of various colors. Clothes were trimmed with frills. Five hts.

Frisch Doll Supply Co. 1927–30 and later. New York City. Manufactured dolls' heads, arms and other composition parts, as well as outfits for dolls. They were members of the *Doll Parts Manufacturing Assoc.*

Fritsch, Heinrich. 1928–30. Ilmenau, Thür. Made shoes and stockings for dolls.

Fritz. Before 1911–24. Felt character doll made by *Steiff*. It was dressed as a boy in a red sweater, tam and striped stockings. Four hts.: 28, 35, 43 and 50 cm. (11, 14, 17 and 19½ in.). In 1924 there was only ht. 28 cm. (11 in.).

Fritz. 1914–22. Cutout cloth doll made by *Saalfield* representing one of the *Katzenjammer Kids* drawn as a cartoon by *Rudolph Dirks*. This doll was style no. 143. Ht. 16 in. (40.5 cm.).

Fritz, Anton. 1834–47. Vienna. Made and/or handled wooden dolls.

Fritz Brownie. 1895. *Butler Bros.* advertised three styles of character dolls under this heading including Uncle Sam Dutchman and Policeman. They had stockinet faces, painted very stout cloth bodies and all wore hats. Ht. 11½ in. (29 cm.); price $4.20 a doz. wholesale.

Fritzche & Thein. 1906–25. Prague, Czechoslovakia. Produced porcelain dolls.

Frizzi. 1927. Trademark registered in Germany by *John Hess* for dolls.

Frobenius, Lilian (Lilli). 1908–18. Germany. Created art dolls in the *Puppen Reform* movement. She worked with *Marion Kaulitz* and dressed dolls that had heads designed by *Joseph Wackerle* and *Marie Marc-Schnür*. These dolls with hard composition heads and painted eyes were exhibited by *Hermann Tietz* in 1908.★

Fröber, Franz. 1930. Hüttensteinach, Thür. Manufactured dolls.

Fröber, Richard. 1895–1918. Hüttensteinach, Thür. He obtained two German patents (D.R.G.M.) related to joining the head and body of a doll.★

Froebel. Early 1800s. Thür. Made dolls. One of his descendants, Auguste Engelhardt, married Paul Lindner (son of

Johann Simon Lindner), who died in 1847, and in 1848 Auguste married *Adolf Fleischmann.*

Froebel-Kan. World War I period–1920s. Tokyo. Made bisque-head babies and used a triangular-shaped mark.

Frozen Charlottes. 1850s–1920s. These dolls were called "Nacktfrosch" (Naked Baby) in Thüringia, Germany. They were also called "Badekinder" in Germany. Most of these dolls are non-sexed but occasionally one is found sexed as a boy. An example of the sexed dolls has molded short black hair, a dot for the eyes, arms against the body, legs apart and on its back 4433 was incised. Ht. 5¾ in. (14.5 cm.).

Among the German companies who made these dolls were *Conta & Boehme* (mark found on the bottom of the right foot.), *Ritter & Schmidt*[†], and *Schuetzmeister & Quendt*. The records of these three companies relate to the late 1800s. Conta & Böhme appears to have made large china Frozen Charlottes of up to 14 in. (35.5 cm.) or more.

CHINA FROZEN CHARLOTTES SIZE–HEIGHT RELATIONSHIP				
Size No.	1880 Oscar Strasburger & Co.		1887 C. F. Lauer	
	in.	cm.	in.	cm.
5/0	1	2.5		
4/0	1¼	3		
3/0	1½	4		
2/0	2	5	2⅜	6
0	2¼	5.5	2¾	7
01/0	2½	6.5	3	7.5
1	3	7.5	3⅓	8.5
1½	3½	9		
2	3⅝	9.5	3½	9
2½			3½	9.5
3	4	10	4⅓	11
4	4½	11.5		
5	5	12.5		
6	5⅜	13.5		
7	6	15		
8	6¼	16		

The 1880 dolls ranged in price from 6¢ to $2.35. doz. wholesale. Numbers 2/0 to 3 cost 14¢ to 30¢ doz. wholesale, while comparable dolls in 1887 cost 13¢ to 42¢ doz. wholesale.

1884: The *Lauer* catalog listed "Glazed China Babies" which were probably *Frozen Charlotte*-type dolls Nos. 1, 2, 3, 4, 5, 7, 8, 9, 11, 12, 13, and 15. These retailed for 1¢ to 10¢. No. 1 with gold boots cost 3¢ while No. 4 with gold boots cost 2¢ The prices were approximately the same for both the black and white versions.

1880s: Two of the large Frozen Charlottes, ht. 14 to 15 in. (35.5 to 38 cm.), have been found dressed as babies. One in a German Museum wore a long infant style dress. The other was one of Queen Wilhelmina's dolls which lay on a pillow with a ruffled edge. The doll was completely covered with white work embroidered material except for its face and forearms with clenched fists.

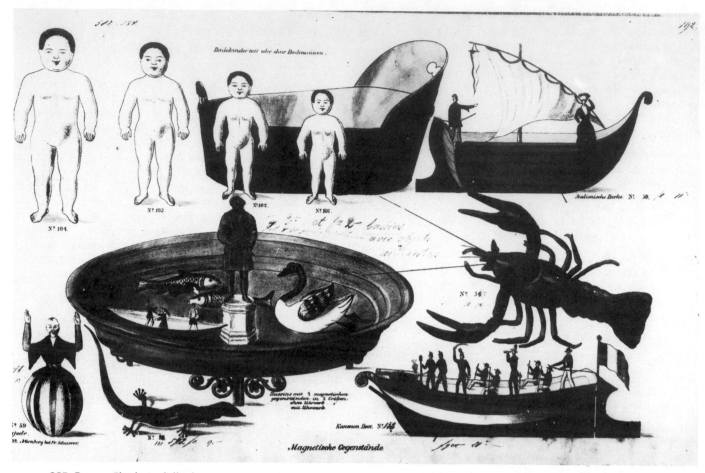

985. Frozen Charlotte dolls shown on a page in a Nürnberg toy catalog ca. 1850s. These dolls came in four sizes and were sold with or without a bathtub. They were called "Badekinder" (bathing children). *Courtesy of Marg. Weber Beck from Franz Carl Weber, Zurich.*

By 1913 *Marshall Field* was selling for 16¢ a doz. wholesale the same size china doll Lauer had sold for 13¢ a doz. in 1887.

1912: *Lyra-Fahrrad-Werke,* advertised porcelain "Badepuppe" (Bathing dolls). Hts. 18 and 26 cm. (7 and 10½ in.).

1924: Butler Bros. was still advertising the small 1¾ and 2½ in. (4.5 and 6.5 cm.) Frozen Charlottes.★

Fry, Roger. 1913–19. London. Born 1866, died 1934. He was a painter and art critic who championed Paul Cézanne. He ran the Omega Workshop which produced futuristically decorated dolls "full of subtle meaning," according to PLAYTHINGS.★

Fu (Fussballer). 1903–25. Felt doll with a long nose and long feet made by *Steiff* and dressed as a European football player. Ht. 35 cm. (14 in.).

Fuerst, Fan. 1928. Worked for *Effanbee* and was known as "The Effanbee Lady." She was an internationally known entertainer and accompanied by actresses dressed as dolls, she told children's stories.

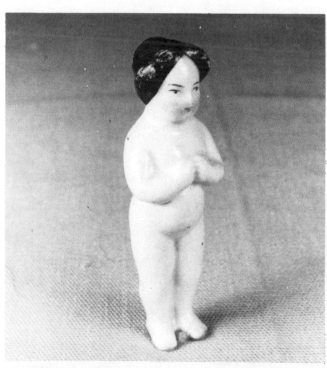

986. Pink china Frozen Charlotte with fancy hairdo of wings in front and bun in the back. Arms folded across chest and the legs are together. H. 2½ in. (6.5 cm.). *Coleman Collection.*

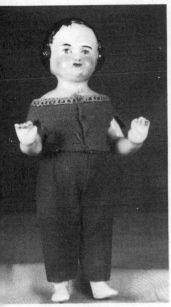 

987A & B. China Frozen Charlotte with a molded boy's hairdo and original boy's clothes. The weight suggests that this is a solid china doll. H. 7 in. (18 cm.). *Coleman Collection.*

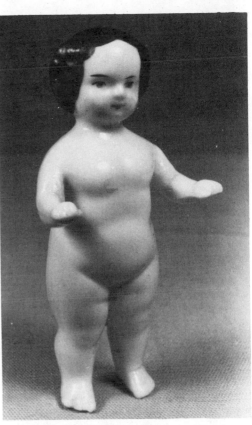

988. Frozen Charlotte of china with flat top type hairdo, arms away from the body, legs apart. H. 3¼ in. (9½ cm.). *Coleman Collection.*

989. Black china Frozen Charlotte type, arms at right angles, feet apart, dress contemporary with the doll. H. 2¼ in. (5.5 cm.). *Coleman Collection.*

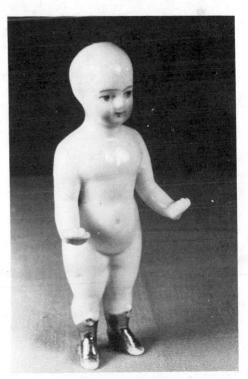

990. China Frozen Charlotte type with a wig, molded gold boots. H. 4 in. (10 cm.). *Coleman Collection.*

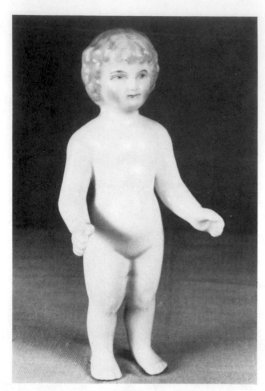

991. Frozen Charlotte type with blond molded curly hair, bangs on forehead, arms away from the body and at right angles with palms of hands facing each other, legs apart from the knees down. H. 5¼ in. (13.5 cm.). *Coleman Collection.*

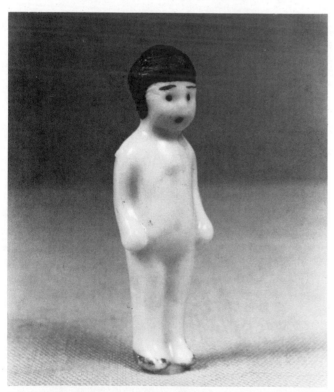

992. Frozen Charlotte type china doll with painted bobbed hair and gold slippers. Made in the 1920s. H. 2 in. (5 cm.). *Coleman Collection.*

Fukuruko. 1925–26. *Lenci* felt doll No. 190 dressed as Japanese God of Wisdom. The doll had an exaggeratedly high forehead and carried a staff. Ht. 12 in. (30.5 cm.).

Ful. 1916–24. Name of a felt doll made by *Steiff.*

1916: Hts. 28, 35, and 43 cm. (11, 14, and 17 in.).

1924: Ht. 35 cm. (14 in.).

Fulper Pottery Co. 1918–22. Flemington, N.J. Made bisque dolls' heads and all-bisque dolls. TOYS AND NOVELTIES reported that "Fulper Pottery received the medal of Honor, the highest award for foreign and domestic pottery and nine other awards at the Panama Pacific International Exposition in 1915." (This took place before they started to make dolls.)

Among the Companies that used Fulper bisque heads were *Amberg, Colonial Toy Manufacturing Co.* and *Horsman.* Each company appears to have had its own models. There were socket heads and shoulder heads. Horsman often used their adtocolite[+] bodies with the Fulper heads.

The initials "M. S." usually found in Fulper marks stood for Martin Stangl who was in charge of the production of bisque dolls' heads. His wife's sister painted eyelashes on the heads according to an interview with Martin Stangl published in SPINNING WHEEL in 1973.

1920: There were at least 100 numbers and many of the dolls had human hair wigs and exclusively designed dresses. Amberg had child and baby dolls in four sizes.

An advertisement for Fulper bisque-head child dolls listed hts.: 14, 21 and 26 in. (35.5, 53.5 and 66 cm.). Price $42.00 to $93.00 doz. wholesale. Bent-limb baby dolls came in four hts.: 14, 16, 20 and 24 in. (35.5, 40.5, 51, and 61 cm.); price $43.00 to $87.75 doz. wholesale.

Sears advertised that their Fulper bisque shoulder and socket heads with or without wigs, with sleeping eyes, arrived too late to list in their catalog.

1922: The manufacture of bisque dolls' heads was terminated, but Fulper continued to produce pincushion type heads and novelties, some of which were designed by Tony Sarg.

1927: Fulper still had a sizable number of heads and both shoulder heads and socket heads, without eyes or wigs, were offered in seven hts.: 10 to 12, 13 to 14, 15 to 16, 17 to 20, 21 to 23, 24 to 30 and 31 to 36 in. (25.5 to 30.5, 33 to 35.5, 38 to 40.5, 43 to 51, 53.5 to 58.5, 61 to 76 and 78.5 to 91.5 cm.). An assortment of 100 heads was offered for $22.75.★

Fumsup. 1914–22. *Hamley Bros.* registered this name as a trademark and used it for bisque, celluloid, or rubber dolls which they distributed. *S. Hancock & Sons* was the sole manufacturer of the bisque line. This was an all-bisque mascot doll with a four-leaf clover above its forehead, thumbs pointed upward, and wings on its heels. A heart shaped label read "British//Fumsup//Reg //-." The "bisque" was probably *British Ceramic.*

1917: Fumsup came dressed as Pierrot or Pierrette. Fumsup Fairy cost $3.12 doz. wholesale.

1920: The rubber version of Fumsup with a squeaker came

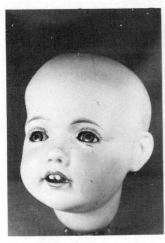

993. Bisque socket head made by Fulper, probably Kestner's Hilda head was used for the model. The head has a wig, blue glass sleeping eyes, an open mouth with two upper teeth. H. of head only, 6 in. (15 cm.). *Coleman Collection. Gift of Joseph Kallus.*

994. Fulper bisque head on a Horsman adtocolite body. It has a wig, celluloid-over-metal eyes, open mouth with teeth and tongue. Marks: See Ills. 612 and 844 in the first COLLECTOR'S ENCYCLOPEDIA OF DOLLS. H. 16 in. (40.5 cm.). *Coleman Collection.*

995. Mark on bisque heads made by Fulper. The M S monogram at the top stands for Martin Stangl.

in three sizes, costing 25¢ to 98¢. The celluloid version came in two sizes; priced 48¢ and $1.69.

1922: Fumsup had a woolen wig with the "hair in assorted colors and standing straight up." It was dressed in a silk ribbon with a big bow in back and came in three sizes. (See also **Thumbs Up.!**)★

Funny. See **Petzold, Dora.**

Funny Face Family. 1918–27. Wooden dolls named Reddy, Whitey, and Bluey made by *N. D. Cass Co.* Reddy represented the husband, Whitey the wife, and Bluey the son. They were made of jointed wooden pegs and their eyes, ears and noses could be twisted into various positions.

1918: Price $1.00.

Funny Fritzie. 1912. Trade name of a composition head doll advertised by *Sears.* It had molded hair and painted eyes on a cloth body with composition hands. The crying voice was activated by squeezing. It wore striped rompers. Hts. 9¾ and 12¾ in. (25 and 32.5 cm.); price 25¢ and 48¢.

Funny Fuzzee. 1929. Line of dolls made by *Twistum,* including *Brownee, Clownee, Fairee* and *Jerree.*

Fur-clad Dolls. See **Eskimo Dolls.**

Furga, Luigi, & Co. 1872–1930 and later. Canneto Sull' Oglio, Mantua Province, Italy. Both PLAYTHINGS and DANCKERT reported that the Furga porcelain factory was founded in 1872 at Canneto. The following paragraph written by A. R. Brovarone and Barbara Rorchetti was published in PUPEIDE and translated into English:

"In the 1870s Luigi Furga, an Italian nobleman, who owned property in Canneto, decided to begin making dolls with the help of Ceresa, who had acquired the art of making papier-mâché masks in Germany before returning to his native home, Other natives especially females were recalled from Germany to work in the factory."

In 1881 a Chamber of Commerce report stated that the firm employed 33 people of whom 22 were adults and 11 were children. The first Furga dolls had wax heads with papier-mâché bodies and limbs. A little later dolls were also made with cloth bodies and wax or papier-mâché heads. Many of these dolls were exported to other European countries.

By 1895 the business had grown so that there were 178 workers employed. In 1900 a report on the industrial conditions in the Province of Mantua stated that there were 158 workers in the Luigi Furga & Co. factory. Men, women and children of both sexes performed most of the work by hand. About half a million dolls were produced each year. The papier-mâché was modelled by hand into plaster molds by women workers.

As the demand for bisque-head dolls grew, Furga imported bisque heads from Germany and put them on bodies made by Furga in Canneto. Meanwhile Furga was making its own heads of "pastello," a kind of composition made of plaster, paste and paper pulp. Their quality dolls had real hair wigs while the cheaper dolls had mohair wigs.

In 1910 Furga was exporting dolls to England, Brazil and other South American countries. Strong competition with German dolls forced Furga to make smaller, more popular priced dolls. With the outbreak of World War I, difficulties increased because they could no longer obtain bisque heads, glass eyes and coloring matter for finishing their dolls. All of these products were imported from Germany before the war.

After the war Furga began to make its own bisque heads and all-bisque dolls. Their bisque was made by pouring slip into molds. The all-bisque dolls were called "*mignon-nettes.*" These had their heads and torsos in one piece and had the arms jointed at the shoulders and legs jointed at the hips. The shoes and socks were molded and painted. The wigs were mohair and the eyes made of glass.

Between 1925 and 1930 some of the Furga dolls were made of pressed felt.

1929: PLAYTHINGS reported that the Furga bisque dolls' heads rivaled the German bisque ones. In a workshop adjoining the porcelain factory dolls' bodies were made. Some of the finished dolls had glass eyes, real hair, and were fully dressed.

1950s: Furga produced composition dolls.

1980s: Furga dolls were vinyl. (See also **Mantuan Dolls.**)★

996. Mark used by the Furga porcelain factory. This mark may or may not have been used on Furga dolls.

Fürstenberg. Ca. 1750–1930 and later. Fürstenberg, Brunswick. One of the early and important porcelain factories. It is not certain that dolls were made at Fürstenberg. China shoulder heads have been found with marks similar to those used by Fürstenberg. See Ills. 997 and 998. However it is known that there was a considerable amount of copying of the marks of famous porcelain factories by lesser porcelain factories such as Wallendorf, Rudolstadt and so on.

Fussballer. See **Fu.**

Fuzzee. See **Funny Fuzzee.**

G

G. & S. Novelty Co. 1927. New York City. Made shoes for dolls.

Ga. (Gaston). 1905–24. Trade name for a jointed felt doll made by *Steiff* and distributed in the U.S. by *Borgfeldt.* This long-nosed, long-limbed doll with a small high hat and spats represented Gaston, mate to Alphons. Ht. 50 cm. (19½ in.)

1913: Sold by *Gamage,* priced 62¢.

Gabriel, Samuel, Sons & Co. 1916–28. New York City. Made dolls.

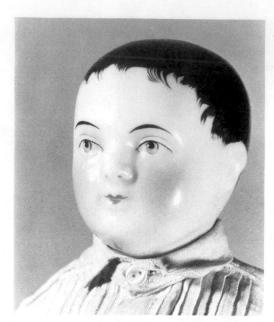

997. Pink tinted china head doll with an F mark (see Ill. 998) inside the back shoulder, similar to the mark used by the Fürstenberg porcelain factory. This doll has black painted hair with no molding. It has white molded eyeballs and painted blue eyes, and a slight white area between the lips. The cloth body is a replacement but the shirt is contemporary. H. 13 in. (33 cm.). *Coleman Collection.*

998. Mark on china head dolls which resembles the mark used by the Fürstenberg porcelain factory.

1918: 56 dolls listed in their Mother Goose series.

1928: "Sew Dress Dolls" were printed back and front on heavy cardboard. They had movable arms and wore cloth clothes.★

Gaby. 1927. Dressed cloth doll with wig, sold by *Lafayette* store. Ht. 40 cm. (15½ in.).

Gaby. 1929–30. A ventriloquist named "Mr. Gaby" was supposed to have designed these dolls made by *Alfred Munzer.* The composition doll with long limbs had a wide moving mouth and eyes looking to the side; it came with or without a mama voice. There were various versions. Gaby was a boy dressed in an evening type jacket, vest, collar, and short pants. Gaby Buttons (style no. 1016) wore a short jacket with two rows of buttons, a wide collar and long trousers. Also there were Gaby Frank, Gaby Joe (no. 1014) in a shirt and overalls and several Gaby Kids (nos. 1005 and 1012) dressed as clowns. These dolls cost $2.00 to $5.00.

Gaess & Hollander. 1930 and later. Long Island City, N.Y. In 1931 they registered *Phenox Products* in the U.S. as a trademark for composition figures.

Gaessler, Antoine. Before 1862. Strasbourg, France. Distributed toys. When he failed in 1862 dolls were six percent of his stock according to Mme. Poisson, curator of the Roybet Fould Museum.

Gaillard, Arnoul. Paris. Name in gold letters found on a kid band attached to the clothes on a doll with a Tête *Jumeau* head.

999. Bisque head doll made by Jumeau and dressed by Arnoul Gaillard. It has a wig, stationary light brown glass eyes, pierced ears, closed mouth, and a ball-jointed composition body. Original clothes except for the bonnet; part of the skirt is missing. Mark on head: "8" incised, Tête Jumeau in red ink. Mark on body stamped in blue: "JUMEAU//MEDAILLE D'OR//PARIS." Mark on clothes: Ill. 1000. H. 21 in. (53.5 cm.). *Private collection.*

ARNOUL GAILLARD
17 RUE DE ROME 17
PARIS

1000. Mark in gold on kid found on the clothes made by Arnoul Gaillard for a Jumeau doll. See Ill. 999.

Gaiety Girl, The. 1917–18. Character doll designed by *Hilda Cowham* and made by *Laurie Hansen.*

Galabert, Mme. 1925–30. Paris. Made and/or dressed art dolls and bisque *mignonnettes.*★

Galalita, Messrs. 1915. London. Manufactured dolls' eyes especially for cloth dolls.

Galatoize. 1924–26. London. Distributed dolls. Agent for C. Hopf.

Galeries Lafayette. See **Lafayette.**

Galimberti, Giovannni. See **Fabbrica Italiana Bambole.**

Gallais, P. J., & Cie. 1917–25. Paris. Distributed books with the works of *Poulbot* and *L'Oncle Hansi* in them as well as the *Yerri* and *Gretel* dolls based on the Hansi drawings. Also produced Columbine, Pierrot and Pierrette designed by *A. Willette.*

1001. Trademark of P. J. Gallais & Cie.

Gallia. 1916. A cloth bébé made by *Mme. Roig.*★

Galluba & Hofmann. 1888–1926. Ilmenau, Thür. Porcelain factory that made dolls. It is not known what the connection was with the *Ilmenauer Porzellanfabrik.*

1891: Hugo Galluba and Alfred Teufel took over B. Küchler & Co. with its 70 workers.

1897: Galluba & Hofmann employed 500 workers and won a gold medal in Leipzig.

1914: A catalog in the Sonneberg Museum listed many examples of Galluba & Hoffmann's elegantly dressed dolls. (See also **German Dolls,** 1914.)★

G & H
J

1002. Mark of the Galluba & Hofmann porcelain factory.

Gamage, A. W. 1878–1930 and later. London. Imported and distributed dolls.

1902: Advertised *Jumeau* dolls; all-wooden dolls *(Bébé Tout en Bois); Polichinelles; Golliwoggs* and other black dolls; walking dolls both mechanical and nonmechanical; dolls made of celluloid, cloth or rubber; dolls with pink or white leather bodies; dressed dolls with bisque heads on fully jointed composition bodies or with wax over composition heads; trunks containing dressed dolls and their wardrobes of clothes.

1906: Advertised all-wooden dolls (Bébé Tout en Bois); wood "Dutch" dolls *(Peg Wooden); Schoenhut* wooden

Circus dolls; Golliwoggs; Dolly Bunting; Japanese dolls; fairy dolls suitable for Christmas trees; dolls made of celluloid; dolls made of cloth including *Steiff* felt dolls; dolls made of rubber; dolls with metal heads; dolls with leather bodies. Some of the dolls were dressed as Red Riding Hood or sailor boys and sailor girls. The dressed dolls were up to 26 in. (66 cm.) tall; priced $1.25.

1913: Advertised *Baby Pierrot,* Bébé Tout Bois made of bass wood, *Campbell Kids, Dorothy, Fairy,* Japanese dolls, Jumeau, *Kiddieland,* Laughing Black *Sambo (Société Française de Fabrication de Bébés & Jouets* [S.F.B.J.]), London Dressed doll, *Marvel, Phyllis, Red Riding Hood,* Sailor Boy (S.F.B.J.), *Salome, Sambo's* Baby Brother, *Sambo's* Little Sister, Steiff dolls, and bent-limb character baby dolls with wig and chemise; sitting hts. 14 to 25 in. (35.5 to 63.5 cm.).

1928: The following dolls were sold by Gamage: *Baby Puck, Bambina, Cuddley Doll, Darling, Frilly Dolls, Greta, Lifelike Dolls, Marvell Doll, My Daisy, My Daisy Baby, Princess, Sico, Tee Wee,* and *Tru-to-Life.*

Gans, Otto. 1901–30 and later. Waltershausen, Thür. He obtained innumerable patents for dolls, especially for dolls' eyes. The earliest was in 1901, but PLAYTHINGS in 1927 reported that the Otto Gans firm was established in 1908. The Ciesliks tell us that Otto Gans was in the Gans & Seyfarth firm from 1908 when it was established until 1922 when he had his own porcelain factory. Information from various toy trade journals in the 1920s indicates that Otto Gans made entire dolls. This is probably one of many cases where it is impossible to obtain a clear record of the functions of related doll designers, makers and producers.

1901: Applied for two German patents, one (D.R.G.M.) for moving eyelids and one (D.R.P.) for flirting eyes.

1902: The flirting eye patent was used by *Kämmer & Reinhardt.*

1908–13: Obtained two German patents (D.R.G.M.) and six German patents (D.R.P.) for dolls. Two of these patents were taken out with *Kraemer & Von Elsberg* of Cologne.

1916–18: Obtained two German patents (D.R.G.M.) and (D.R.P.) and an Austrian patent for sleeping eyes.

1922: According to the Ciesliks, Otto Gans made porcelain heads and all-porcelain dolls and he used the trademark *My Dearie.*

1923–25: Applied for and/or obtained 13 German (D.R.G.M.) patents, six German (D.R.P.) patents and one Austrian patent. Most of these pertained to walking dolls and/or talking dolls. A U.S. Department of Commerce report credited Otto Gans with the invention of flirting eyes and stated that he had exploited them. Perhaps there was a connection between Otto Gans and Kämmer & Reinhardt both of Waltershausen. In 1925 Otto Gans advertised *Oga* dolls.

1926: Obtained two U.S. patents pertaining to dolls' voices as well as another German patent. He belonged to the *German Manufacturers Assoc.* in New York City.

1927: Produced bent-limb baby dolls and ball-jointed composition body child dolls. These dolls had bisque heads with flirting eyes and "solid eyes having reflex action" which he called "Lifelike Eyes." They were dressed or wore only a chemise.

Otto Gans obtained a British patent relating to dolls' eyes and two more German patents (D.R.P. and D.R.G.M.).

1929: Made felt dolls and applied for two German patents (D.R.G.M.), one was for dolls' eyes and the other pertained to the dolls' head.

1930: Advertised dressed and undressed dolls and character baby dolls including *auto dolls,* walking dolls and painted dolls' heads. Registered Kindertraum as a trademark in Germany.★

1003A. Mark on dolls produced by Otto Gans.

Gans & Seyfarth. 1908–30 and later. Waltershausen, Thür. According to the Ciesliks *Otto Gans* was a member of this company until 1922 when the company split into two new firms, Otto Gans and *Seyfarth & Reinhardt.* The exact relationship and functions are difficult to determine. Through the years Otto Gans, Gans & Seyfarth and Seyfarth & Reinhardt all obtained innumerable German patents, both D.R.G.M. and D.R.P., for dolls and doll-related items.

Ca. 1910: Gans & Seyfarth obtained an Austrian patent for fastening and unfastening the parts of a doll.

1913: They were licensed by *Kämmer & Reinhardt,* the patentee, to use their patent relating to flirting eyes. Gans & Seyfarth advertised and distributed character dolls, baby dolls and dolls that could be transformed. The latter probably used the fastening and unfastening patent.

1926–30: Gans & Seyfarth were still listed in the DIDOT Paris directory as being doll manufacturers.★

Garconne Dolls. 1926. Parisian dolls dressed in smoking jackets that reflected the current fashion.

Gardet, M. 1916. France. Sculptor who made a model used by *M. Bricon* in making dolls.

Gardner, A. J. 1868–1930 and later. London. Distributed art dolls in the 1920s.

Garfield, James, & Co. 1920–29. London. Made dolls. (See **Kohnstam.**)

HERE ARE SOME OF MY NOVELTIES

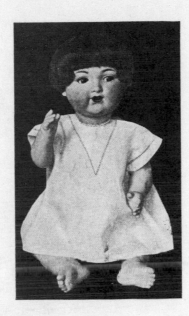

Send For Samples

Send For Samples

FINEST QUALITY DOLLS

With patented Flirting and Solid Eyes having Reflex Action. None but these Lifelike Eyes will satisfy you!

As an introduction, I offer a sample collection of various principal numbers for $20.

Convince yourself of my advantageous offer.

OTTO GANS

WALTHERSHAUSEN (THUR)   **GERMANY**

Established 1908

1003B. Bisque-head dolls advertised by Otto Gans in PLAYTHINGS, November, 1927. These dolls have wigs; flirting or "reflex action" eyes, both of which were referred to as "Lifelike Eyes." The bodies are jointed composition and the dolls wear chemises.

G.&S.

1004   8

G. & S.6
Germany

1005

G. & S 6

Germany

1006

G & S
It.
Germany

1007

Gans & Seyfarth
126.
Germany

1008   6

1004–1008. Marks used by Gans & Seyfarth on their dolls.

Garis, Howard R. 1924. East Orange, N.J. Registered *Nurse Jane Fuzzy Wuzzy* as a U.S. trademark for dolls.

Gascon. 1927. French felt doll imported into America by *Louis Eisen*. It wore a smock, striped trousers, and matching stocking cap as well as wooden sabots (shoes). (See Ill. 869.)

Gasoline Alley. 1923–30. Comic strip drawn by *Frank O. King* inspired the creation of many dolls representing the characters in this cartoon. Among the characters were *Auntie Blossom, Mrs. Blossom, Corky, Rachel, Skeezix* and *Uncle Walt.*★

Gaspar, Engert. 1926–29. Fürth, Bavaria. Obtained a German patent (D.R.G.M.) for dolls with a writing movement.

Gasparez. 1925–30 and later. Paris. Made dolls.

Gaston. See **Ga.**

Gaston & Alphonse. 1914. Pair of dolls representing characters in comics.

Gatty, Nicholas. 1916. England. His calendar dolls were dressed in costumes of the Romantic period by a group of ladies and these dolls were distributed by *Liberty & Co.*

Gaucho (Argentinian). 1916. Name of a felt doll made by *Steiff.* Hts. 35 and 43 cm. (14 and 17 in.). Other companies, such as *Lenci,* made Argentine Gauchos. (See Ills. 2200 and 2201.)

Gaujard, Alexandre. 1852–70. La Capelle and Paris, France. Made toys including dolls. His business failed in 1870 according to Mme. Poisson, curator of the Roybet Fould Museum.

Gault, J. Roger. Before 1916–18. Paris, London, Zurich, and Milan. He appears to have been a producer *(Verleger)* and manufacturer. He used porcelain dolls' heads made in *Limoges.* These shoulder heads and socket heads were advertised as being in ten sizes. There were also dolls' eyes, arms and legs. 52 girls were employed in making glass eyes for dolls. *Bedington, Liddiat & Co.* as well as *C. Melin & Co.* were the British agents.

1917: Fully jointed dolls, dolls' heads and parts were made of lightweight, patented "washable, unbreakable" *Plastolite.* Many of these French Plastolite dolls were shipped to Britain and there were plans for building a Plastolite factory in England. Gault also advertised other French dolls, dolls' clothes, and accessories.★

Gaultier (Gauthier prior to 1875**), François.** 1860–99. After 1899 it was part of the *Société Française de Fabrication de Bébés & Jouets* (S.F.B.J.). It was located in St. Maurice and Charenton, adjacent towns in the province of Seine. Both of these towns were on the outskirts of Paris and only a few miles from Montreuil-sous-Bois. Made porcelain dolls' heads and dolls' parts for lady dolls and for bébés. These were sold to many of the principal French makers of dolls. All-bisque dolls have been found marked "F. G." See Ill. 1009.

Mme. Poisson, curator of the Roybet Fould Museum, has researched the Gauthier (Gaultier) history and published her findings in No. 7 of the CERP reports. In brief the history is as follows:

In 1837 François Gauthier, son of Silvain Gauthier, was born in Berry near Vierzon and Foécy. This area had many porcelain factories and Silvain worked in one of them. In 1857 François Gauthier married Louise Elizabeth Pilorgé in Paris and they had seven children.

Eugène-Louis born 1857
Emile-Jules born 1860
Louise born 1862
Elisa-Louise born 1865
A child
Ernestine-Eugènie born 1870
Blanche-Emile born 1873
When François Gauthier was married he was listed as a

maker of porcelain products and his new wife was a burnisher of porcelain. At first the couple lived with Louise's parents, the Pilorgés, in Charenton. In 1865 Alexandre-Silvain Pilorgé, Louise's brother, was described as a "maker of porcelain heads."

François Gauthier prospered and in 1867 he bought 600 meters in the vicinity of Saint Maurice, where he built a porcelain factory and went to live. In 1872 he obtained a French patent for cutting out and inserting glass eyes in bisque dolls' heads. There was a court action against François Gauthier in 1875 but it was a case of mistaken identity. Since the town records had been burned in 1871 proof was difficult and François Gauthier changed his name to François Gaultier to prevent further problems.

APPROXIMATE SIZE–HEIGHT RELATIONSHIP FOR F.G. LADY DOLLS WITH BISQUE HEADS AND KID BODIES		
Size No.	Height in.	cm.
0/3	10	25.5
0/2	11	28
0	12	30.5
1	13½	34
2	15	38
3	17	43
4	18½	47
5	20½	52

In 1881 Mme. Gaultier died and an inventory was made of the Gaultier property. Some of the valuations were made by *Albert Diffloth*, a porcelain manufacturer in Charenton, and by Claude Bastide *Prieur*, a distributor of dolls and articles for dolls in Paris. The inventory included two furnaces and two stones to beat the paste. At that time porcelain was in the form of paste rather than slip. It is not known whether these important stones were used in the mixing process or the rolling out process, or perhaps both.

The dolls' parts included in the inventory were:

Swivel heads	1,835 F
Shoulder heads with glass eyes	1,767 F
Shoulder heads with painted eyes	1,103 F
Heads for bébés	4,165 F
Various heads	1,392 F
Arms and legs	910 F
All-bisque dolls	634 F

Glass eyes which were probably bought elsewhere. (No mention was made of any material for dolls' bodies.)

Among the 54 customers who still owed money for their most recent deliveries were: *Arnoult, Bonnafé, Borreau, Brasseur, Brelaz, Cassanet, Chiquet, Dalloz, Doléac, Fauré, Gesland, Jacquin, Jullien, Lessieux, Petit & Dumontier, Prieur, Rabery & Delphieu, Rungaldier, Schneider, Simonne, Thuillier, Verger,* and *Vichy.*

In 1882 François Gaultier made his eldest son, Eugène-Louis Gaultier, director of the firm which was then called Gaultier & Fils Aîné (Fils Aîné—eldest son). Three years later

in 1885 Emile-Jules Gaultier took his father's place in the business and the name was changed to Gaultier Frères. The following year François Gaultier became mayor of Saint Maurice, an office that he held until 1892.

In 1888 another inventory was made which listed the following products:

FINISHED PRODUCTS FOR SALE		
Type	Number of heads	Medium price per head
Swivel head	414	30¢ (including shoulders)
Complete heads for bébés	864	15¢
Shoulder heads with glass eyes	1,044	12¢
Shoulder heads with painted eyes	1,896	7¢
Ball-type heads with painted hair	5,196	3¢
Heads decorated but not finished:		
Swivel heads without eyes	5,298	
Swivel heads without eyes for bébés	965	
Turning shoulders	1,040	
Some arms and heads were for *Falck*		
Some bébés were for R. D. (probably Rabery & Delphieu)		
Undecorated heads in the white:		
Swivel heads without shoulders	2,105	
Swivel heads for bébés	1,025	
Heads for Falck	22,950	
Head and so forth in paste form before firing:		
Swivel heads without shoulders	1,920	
Heads for bébés	2,421	
Ball-type heads	1,355	
Turning shoulders	412	
Heads for Falck	18,510	

It appears that Gaultier was filling a large order for *Falck & Roussel* in 1888 but they do not appear to have been listed in the 1881 inventory. No doubt there were other companies who used Gaultier heads but did not happen to have an unpaid bill in 1881 or 1888 when these inventories were made.

In 1899 Gaultier Frères of Saint Maurice joined the Société Française de Fabrication de Bébés & Jouets (S.F.B.J.). They contributed porcelain dolls, dolls' parts, and other material as well as molds, patents, trademarks, and good will, estimated to be valued at $10,000. The factory appears to have been rented to the S.F.B.J. (See also **Gautier et Lehujeur.**)★

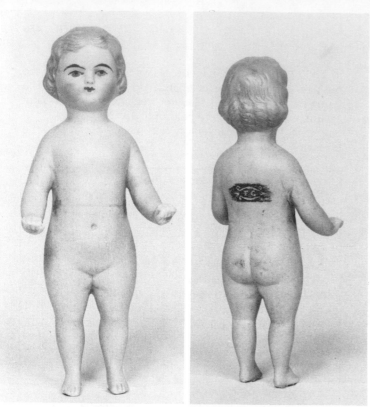

1009A & B. All-bisque doll made by François Gaultier. It has molded blond hair, painted blue eyes, closed mouth, no joints in the body, and the hands are clenched. Marks on the back: "F.G." in a scroll and "1" lower down. H. 6½ in. (16.5 cm.). *Courtesy of the Margaret Woodbury Strong Museum. Photos by Harry Bickelhaupt.*

1010A & B. Bisque socket and shoulder head made by François Gaultier. It has a wig, stationary blue glass eyes, pierced ears, closed mouth and a lady type gusseted kid body. Original commercial chemise. Mark: "F.G." on the side shoulder. H. 14 in. (35.5 cm.). *Courtesy of Helen Read. Photo by Steven Read.*

1011A & B. Bisque head made by François Gaultier's successor S.F.B.J. The head has a pinkish color, a mohair wig, stationary glass eyes, pierced ears, and a closed mouth. The bisque shoulder plate is almost white in color and the kid body has no joints. The original commercial dress of the 1920s style is on the doll. Mark: "F. G." in a scroll. H. 16 in. (40.5 cm.). *Coleman Collection.*

1012. Bisque head made by François Gaultier with wig, blue glass eyes, pierced ears, closed mouth. It has a gusset jointed kid body with bisque lower arms that were probably also made by Gaultier. See also hands on doll in Ill. 1013. Original dress. Mark: "F. 1. G." H. 17 in. (43 cm.). *Courtesy of Sotheby Parke Bernet Inc., N.Y.*

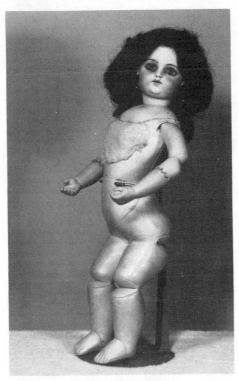

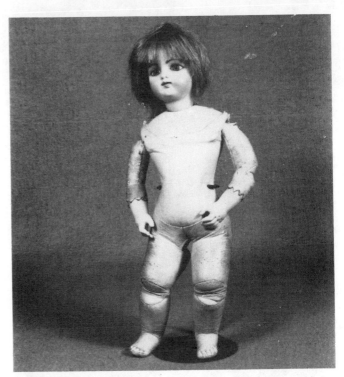

1014. Bisque shoulder head made by François Gaultier. It has a wig, stationary blue glass eyes, pierced ears, and an open-closed mouth. The kid body has bisque arms and gusset joints. Mark: "F.2 G." H. 11½ in. (29 cm.). *Courtesy of Cherry Bou.*

1013. Bisque socket head, shoulder plate, and lower arms made by François Gaultier. See also arms on doll in Ill. 1012. It has a wig, stationary blue eyes, pierced ears, open-closed mouth, and gusseted kid body with padding for the bosom. Mark: Ill. 1021. H. 15¾ in. (40 cm.). *Courtesy of Iverna and Irving Foote. Photo by Irving Foote.*

1015. Bisque head made by François Gaultier. The doll has a wig, stationary brown glass eyes, pierced ears, closed mouth and a ball jointed composition body. Mark: Ill. 1022. H. 18 in. (45.5 cm.). *Courtesy of Iverna and Irving Foote. Photo by Irving Foote.*

1016. Bisque head made by François Gaultier. It has a wig, stationary blue glass eyes, pierced ears, and a closed mouth. The fully jointed composition body has metal hands. Mark: "F 5 G." H. 15 in. (38 cm.). *Courtesy of Sotheby Parke Bernet Inc., N.Y.*

1017. Bisque head made by François Gaultier. It has a wig, stationary blue glass eyes, applied pierced ears, and a closed mouth. The body is a jointed bébé type made of composition and wood. Mark: Ill. 1023. H. 22½ in. (57 cm.). *Courtesy of Hazel Ulseth.*

1018. Bisque head made by François Gaultier. It has a wig, stationary blue glass eyes, pierced ears, closed mouth. It is not known who made the composition body. Mark: "F. G." H. 14 in. (35.5 cm.). *Courtesy of Sotheby Parke Bernet Inc., N.Y.*

1019. Bisque head made by François Gaultier. The doll has a mohair wig, stationary brown eyes, closed mouth, five-piece composition body with painted and molded footwear. Original clothes. Marked "F. G." between wavy lines on the back of the head and "C" on the front of the neck socket. H. 5 in. (12.5 cm.). *Private collection.*

1020. Bisque head made by François Gaultier. It has a wig, stationary blue glass eyes, pierced ears, open mouth with teeth and is on a ball-jointed composition body. Mark: "F. G.//6." H. 18 in. (45.5 cm.). *Courtesy of Sotheby Parke Bernet Inc., N.Y.*

1021

F.2/oG.

1022

F.1.G

1023

9

·F.G·

1024

F.I.G

5/o

1025

F G

1021–1025. Marks on bisque heads made by François Gaultier.

T. D.

1026. Mark on a body having a head made by François Gaultier.

Gaume, Mme. 1815–19. Paris. Distributed dolls.

Gaume, Henriette. 1929–30 and later. Paris. Made art dolls of wax and of cloth.

Gauthier. See **Gaultier, François.**

Gautier. Paris. Name on an all-celluloid doll labeled *Les Poupées Blanche.*

Gautier, Henri. 1905–60. Paris. Published LA SEMAINE DE SUZETTE, which included information about the clothes for *Bleuette, Bambina, Bambino, Bamboula* and Rosette. Clothes could be made from patterns or purchased ready-made.

Gautier et Lehujeur. 1865. Paris. Listed in the Paris directory as maker and painter of porcelain. (See also **Gaultier, François.**)

Gavinet, Mme. (née Jeanne Désirée Lespagnier). 1862–66. Paris. Made dolls and failed according to Mme. Poisson, curator of the Roybet Fould Museum.

Gavroche. 1916. Name of a cloth doll created by *Mme. Vera Ouvré.*

Gay, Benjamin. 1826–43. London. Made dolls.

Gay Stuffed Toy & Novelty Co. 1926. Brooklyn, N.Y. Made stuffed dolls.

Gee, E. M. 1927–28. Philadelphia, Pa. Made outfits for dolls.

Gee Gee Dolly. 1912–13. Mask model based on a *G. G. Drayton* design copyrighted in 1912 had hair only painted on the composition mask, the rest of this doll was cloth. No. A wore a white, pink, or blue dress and bonnet. Ht. 20 in. (51 cm.); priced $12.00 doz. wholesale. No. B wore same type clothes as No. A. No. BB (boy) wore a blouse, coat, knickers, and cap. Hts. of these two dolls 16½ in. (42 cm.); priced $8.50 doz. wholesale.

1913: Late in the year the name was changed to *Peek-A-Boo.*★

Gef. (Gendarme). 1911–13. Felt art doll made by *Steiff.* It had a mustache and goatee and was dressed as a French gendarme with a sword. Ht. 50 cm. (19½ in.).

Geffers, Carl, & Co. 1911–26. Erfurt, Thür. Made dies for stamping out dolls' parts including heads. Produced machines for making ball-jointed bodies for dolls.★

Geh, Chr. M. 1883. Berlin. Advertised dolls' heads, cloth bodies and wigs.

Gehren, Haneiseri. 1920. Swingen, Germany. Made cloth dolls competing with *Steiff.* Dolls were handled by *Kopfovi Weiss.*

Gem Toy Co. 1913–30 and later. New York City. Appears to have changed its name to Gem Doll Corp. in 1929. Made dolls with composition heads on cloth bodies and all-composition dolls. Specialized in baby dolls and *Mama* dolls. They were sued by *Horsman* for copying *Tynie Baby,* but Horsman lost the suit because they only had their initials, E.I.H. on the doll. *Butler Bros.* distributed Gem dolls.

1915: Advertised that all their character dolls were stuffed with cork and had inside joints. Jumbo doll was 24 in. (61 cm.) tall. Price $1.00.

1919: Advertised dolls with painted hair or wigs, stationary or sleeping eyes. The *O. U. Kids* which included Grass Widow, Dough Boy and Bathing Kid were 11 in. (28 cm.) high.

1921: Made Ballet Girl dolls dressed in stiffened silk and marabou.

1924: Advertised *Cliquot Kid.* Mama dolls with composition forearms and legs and painted hair came in hts. 18 and 21 in.

GEM DOLLS

In the Quality Group at a Popular Price

Holiday
Deliveries
Guaranteed

GEM

Offers the Trade Exceptional Values in Dolls of Real Beauty

Every Size and Style Available — Daintily Dressed for
Your Most Critical Clientele

Act Now ——

GEM TOY CO., INC.

42 Greene Street   New York

1027. Dressed Gem doll made by the Gem Toy Co. and advertised in PLAYTHINGS, August, 1927. Note the round tags on the Gem dolls.

(45.5 and 53.5 cm.). Mama dolls with wigs were 16½ in. (42 cm.) and with sleeping eyes and movable tongue, 26 in. (66 cm.) tall.

1926: New Gem baby doll in short dress cost $1.00 and up. Some of the dolls had silk jackets and rubber panties.

1927: Advertised 150 to 200 numbers, all dressed. Mama dolls came with new slim legs as well as regular styles. There were also infant dolls and bent-limb baby dolls. Some had wigs and some had molded hair. A bent-limb baby with painted hair and features called Cuddle Baby wore dresses or rompers. There were six styles including a figured percale romper outfit. Hts. 9½ or 10 in. (24 or 25.5 cm.); priced $4.15 doz. wholesale. Larger bent-limb babies with cloth bodies, sleeping eyes and some with wigs, wore short baby dresses. Five hts. 13½, 14, 14½, 17 and 21 in. (34, 35.5, 37, 43, and 53.5 cm.). The largest size had eyelashes. Gem was licensed by *Voices, Inc.* to use their patented mama voices and criers in the Gem dolls.

Montgomery Ward advertised Gem dolls with composition head, arms, and legs, mohair wig, sleeping eyes, hair eyelashes, and mama voice in a cotton-stuffed cloth body. Ht. 18 in. (45.5 cm.); priced $3.98.

1928: Smiling baby dolls with dimples were the new feature. Priced up to $1.00.

1929: Doll representing children wore knee length dresses and hairbows. Baby dolls had composition head and limbs, painted hair, sleeping eyes, a voice, and cotton-stuffed cloth body. It wore a short baby dress, jacket, and halo-type baby bonnet. Hts. 14 and 15 in. (35.5 and 38 cm.)

1930: Introduced *Hug-Me* baby doll.

1931: Advertised *Patsy* type dolls.★

1028. Mark on dolls made by the Gem Toy Co.

Gemilla. 1907–13. One of the dolls created by *Elizabeth Scantlebury,* dressed as a Turkish girl to show schoolchildren a foreign costume.

Gend. 1911. Felt doll made by *Steiff* and dressed in a German gendarme's uniform. Hts. 28 and 35 cm. (11 and 14 in.); priced 75¢ and $1.00.

Gene Carr Kids. 1915–16. Dolls with composition heads and hands, molded hair, painted eyes either open round or in a squint that appeared closed. For some of the dolls the wide smiling mouth had only one or two teeth, the ears were large, and the nose bulbous. The dolls were named Snowball or Smoke No. 184 (a brown boy), Mike No. 183 and Jane No. 182 with eyes open, Blink No. 181 and Lizzie or Skinney No. 182 with eyes closed. A white cloth tag with aqua-colored letters read "MADE GENE CARR KIDS U.S.A. //FROM NEW YORK WORLD'S//'LADY BOUNTIFUL'

The Baden-Powell doll. General Buller as a doll.

1029. Portrait wax doll representing General Baden-Powell, the founder of the Boy Scouts, as shown in THE LONDON MAGAZINE, 1902. The doll was one of a series of Hamley dolls.

1030. Portrait wax doll of General Buller, produced by Hamley, the wax parts were possibly sculptured by Pierotti. This illustration was in THE LONDON MAGAZINE, 1902.

COMIC SERIES// [?] By E. I. HORSMAN CO. N.Y." Ht. 13½ in. (34 cm.); priced $1.25. Blink and Mike also came as *Carnival Kids* dressed in Pierrot-style costumes, Nos. 131 and 132.★

General Baden-Powell. Ca. 1902. Wax head portrait doll of the founder of the Boy Scouts. It had a mustache and wore a field uniform including a broad brimmed hat, revolver and sword.

General Buller. Ca. 1902. Wax head portrait doll with mustache. It wore a military uniform with kepi, service ribbons and sword.

General French (Sir John French). 1915–17. A composition portrait doll modeled by a professional English artist, produced by the *Women's Emergency Corps Workshop* and distributed by *Hamley.*

General Joffre. 1915–17. A composition portrait doll distributed by *Hamleys* and produced by the *Women's Emergency Corps Workshop.*

General Trade Ltd. 1926. London agent for *Hermann von Berg*.

General White. Ca. 1902. Wax head portrait doll.

Geneviève. 1927. All-felt doll with wig, felt dress, sold by the *Lafayette* store. Ht. 52 cm. (20½ in.).

Gent Acrobat. Ca. 1905–24. Wooden Humpty Dumpty circus doll made by *Schoenhut*.★

Gentille Poupée (Pretty Doll). 1918. Name of a dressed doll with bisque head, stationary eyes and jointed composition body sold at *Printemps*. Hts. 21 and 22.5 cm. (8½ and 9 in.); priced 45¢ and 65¢.

Genty. See **Rabery & Delphieu.**

Géo. 1930. French trademark registered by *M. Georges Stergard* for dolls.

George Washington. 1905–23. Dressed stockinet doll made by *Martha Chase*.

1923: Ht. 25 in. (63.5 cm.); price $25.00.★

George Washington. 1930. *Shackman* advertised a candy box figure of George Washington on a horse. The portrait head was bisque.

Georgene Novelties. 1920s–30 and later. Georgene Averill used her first name for a doll shop and for certain dolls. Early *Raggedy Ann* and *Raggedy Andy* dolls had Georgene Novelty Co. tags. A cloth doll named *Sweets* designed by *Maude Tousey Fangel* was called a Georgene doll. (See also **Madame Georgene.**)

Georgette. 1919–20. One of the *Classic* dolls made by *Speights*. It had a *British Ceramic* head, mohair wig with curls, sleeping eyes, and wore a blue, rose or pink georgette dress trimmed with white net. Ht. 23 in. (58.5 cm.).

Georgia. See **Poupées Georgia.**

Gerbaulet Frères (Bros.) Établissements. 1850–1930 and later. Paris. Produced and exported dolls especially *Bébé Olga*.

1926: *L. & A. L. Goodman* was their sole London agent.★

Gerb's (Poupées Gerb's). 1927–30 and later. Paris. Created, made, and exported cloth dolls. One of these dolls with a flocked fabric head, white silk hair, composition hands and feet was labeled "Poupées Gerb's//29 Rue Gauthey, Paris//Made in France."

1929: Advertised a girl doll with hair to its shoulders, dressed in a coat and scarf. The boy doll wore a short jacket and long trousers.

Gerhardt, Herbert. 1930 and later. Gera, Thür. Obtained an Austrian patent for a sucking doll.

Gerl, Auguste. 1910. Vienna. Listed under Dolls and Dolls' Heads in an Austrian directory.

Gerling Toy Co. 1912–30 and later. New York City, London, Paris and Neustadt near Coburg, Thür. or Bavaria. This company appears to have been a *Verleger* which also made voices for dolls. They produced character dolls, infant dolls, *Mama* dolls and *Boudoir* dolls. Arthur A. Gerling was head of the company.

1918–19: Advertised a line of character dolls, Mama dolls and patented stuffed dolls.

1920: Dolls had painted eyes or sleeping eyes, the cloth bodies were stuffed with cork or with excelsior.

1926: Introduced the *Hotsy Totsy* line of Boudoir dolls and the *Winsome Babies*. A brown newborn baby doll of about this period had a bisque head, painted hair and eyes, pierced nostrils, composition hands, cloth body and a voice. It was marked "3// Arthur A. Gerling//Made in Germany//D.R.G.M." Ht. 16½ in. (42 cm.). A similar white infant doll with sleeping eyes and pierced nostrils was 15 in. (38 cm.) high.

1927: *Jane Gray* created for Gerling the *Black Bottom Doll*, which was registered in the U.S. as a trademark for dolls by Arthur Gerling.

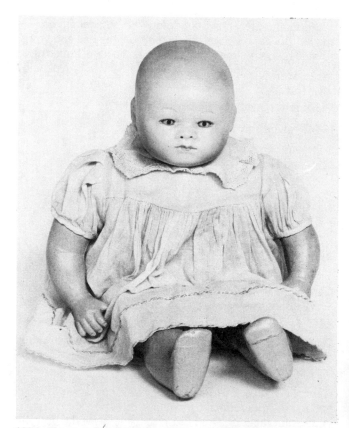

1031. Bisque infant head on a Mama body produced by Arthur Gerling. The head has painted short blond hair, sleeping brown glass eyes, pierced nostrils, closed mouth, projecting chin (a Gerling characteristic). There is a flange neck joint, a white cotton torso, and composition arms and legs. Mark: Ill. 1032. H. 18½ in. (47 cm.). *Courtesy of the Margaret Woodbury Strong Museum. Photo by Harry Bickelhaupt.*

1928: Advertised "Genuine French Art and Novelty Dolls." Continued making Mama dolls and the baby dolls had smiling faces.

1929: Advertised Boudoir dolls, Whoopee and The Dancing Dollies.★

3

ARTHUR A GERLING

1032. Gerling mark on bisque head baby dolls.

Germain (Mer). 1899–1930. Paris. Made dolls.★

Germaine. 1878. Name of a lady doll dressed in a silk costume to represent an operetta character. Ht. 37 cm. (14½ in.).

German Dolls. Sonneberg and other parts of Thüringia were ruled by the dukes of Saxe-Meiningen (Sachsen-Meiningen) until the consolidation of the German states in 1870. George I, duke of Saxe-Meiningen, in 1789 enacted the Statute of Industry and Trade. This gave to 26 citizens of Sonneberg all the rights to trade with dolls and toys. (It should be pointed out that Waltershausen, Ohrdruf, Ilmenau and many other places in Thüringia were not in the dukedom of Saxe-Meiningen but in other dukedoms which made up Thüringia.) Among these 26 was Johann Philipp *Dressel.* These 26 citizens were not permitted to engage in the actual making of dolls. But in 1862 the Statute of Freedom and Trade was enacted in Saxe-Meiningen by Duke Bernhard Erich Freund which permitted the companies to engage in manufacturing dolls as well as to trade in them.

It was claimed that by far the largest percentage of the dolls made between 1870 and World War I came from Germany and most of these originated in Thüringia. In 1855 the French admitted that most of the papier-mâché and porcelain heads used by French doll makers had been made in Saxony, Bavaria, Prussia or Austria, all Germanic areas.

THE QUEEN, a British periodical, in 1878 published the following, "Germany supplies the pretty doll with stuffed bodies and china heads, arms and legs from 2 in. [5 cm.] to 12 in. [30.5 cm.] or 14 in. [35.5 cm.] in height. They are molded to represent boys or girls, the latter with light or dark hair, dressed à la Impératrice in nets or plaits, and having holes for earrings in the ears. They are well adapted for dressing in costume and moreover are very inexpensive." The term "china" probably included bisque.

Dr. Axel Munthe, a Swedish physician and author who lived in Paris, in 1898 commented that "German manufacturers of dolls were incapable of producing pretty and expressive dolls' faces. Therefore they bought their dolls' heads from the factories at Montreuil-sous-Bois and at St Maurice [the François Gaultier factory], where fine models were made by artists such as Carrier-Belleuse and others." This was written just before the formation of the *Société Française de Fabrication de Bébés & Jouets* (S.F.B.J.), which was headed by *S. Fleischmann,* a German.

FRANK LESLIE'S, in 1912, stated: "Parts of all dolls are imported from Germany, for that country has a monopoly on the heads, and the factories all over the world depend on the German factories for their supply of this part of the dolls. . . .

"Germany . . . has made rapid strides in the perfection of the doll, and as far back as 1851 there was a school for the purpose of teaching the art of coloring the faces, and the beautiful, lifelike baby dolls, with faces painted from living models, are the work of some of its pupils."

The reasons were many for German predominance: wages were low, raw materials were at hand, the industry was subsidized to some extent. Industrial art schools were established and there was an art protection law which enabled artists and artisans to flourish. In 1900 German workers in Sonneberg made about $4.00 to $5.00 a week while women made about $1.50 to $3.00 a week. A late 1800s stereoptican picture of papier-mâché doll making in Sonneberg described the process:

"The work is systematically divided. Certain workers mould the heads, bodies, arms and legs; others paint them; others put the parts together. Certain employees do nothing all day but fasten bright eyes into empty sockets; others make wigs; the adjusting of the wigs is a separate job.

"If one is inclined to criticize the quality of the workmanship put into these flimsy undergarments and gay frocks and hats, it should be remembered that the girls who make the wardrobes work twelve hours a day for [usually] less than three cents an hour.

"Living expenses are not small in proportion; these women and girls have difficult problems to meet. But they have never known any easier life, so they take it as it comes, make the best of it, and get a good deal of pleasure out of small opportunities.

"These finished dolls are largely for export. Some are sold direct to foreign buyers, some through commission agents in the large Prussian cities."

A report a few years later, ca. 1908, by Laura S. Farlow, stated: "Fifty thousand souls, old and young are employed in making toys in the Thüringian forest region alone,—all of them in their own home. . . . Grandfathers and fathers; mothers and brothers and sisters; and even tiny children."

TOYS AND NOVELTIES in 1913 described the Thüringian doll industry as reported by the American consul as follows:

"A typical and long-established Thüringian industry, of which the work in many branches is still performed in the homes of the workers is the manufacture of dolls. . . . The development of the doll industry began about 1850 and its principal center in this district is Waltershausen. The chief raw material in the manufacture of toys was originally wood, which was cheaply supplied from the extensive forests of this region; but papier mache has now largely taken the place of wood. A remarkable feature of the Thüringian toy industry, and one which so largely operates to keep it in the same localities and in the same hands of home workers, is the almost unlimited diversity of its output, as a well-equipped sample room of toys would contain 15,000 to 20,000 different articles.

"Such variety of production is impossible with machinery. The great diversification of manufacture and the demand each season for many novelties call for the exercise of so much originality, art, individual taste, and skill of hand that there is at present no prospect that machinery and large scale factory production will supplant entirely the work still so extensively done in the home."

ST. NICHOLAS in 1879 described German dolls as being "Wooden dolls." Yet collectors chiefly associate bisque and china head dolls with Germany. TOYS AND NOVELTIES discussed German wooden dolls in a 1913 article:

"Formerly German toy production was almost exclusively limited to the four well known districts, Berchtesgaden, Nuremberg, Meininger Overland and the Saxon Erzgebirge. Whether these places of production were created exactly in the order mentioned, and whether one district saw and learned the production of toys from the other, rests only on supposition . . .

"One of these universal toys is the wooden doll. Its oblong or round head, the arched bosom, the lower body which appears roller like, owing to the downward hanging woman's skirt, all these parts can be produced with the turning chisel. As for the head covering of a round hat, as found on the Tyrolese and Erzgebirge dolls, or of a crown, as seen on the Sonneberg dolls, this has been carved out of one piece. The Tyrolese product shows small, corpulent forms, the Sonneberg types distinguish themselves through slender forms, and the Erzgebirge wood doll excels all of the others in size and opulence of the bust.

"The hollow, rattle dolls, provided with tiny stones or peas in the Sonneberg or Saxon make-up[,] are found in the Viechtau, a small, but ancient, Austrian toy district, situated on the Salzkammergut Lakes. The 'pull' dolls, which by pulling a cord, raises and lowers its arms, has apparently remained limited to the Sonneberg district, while, to the contrary, the dancing doll, supported on hog bristles and moving around in a circle, passes as having home rights both in Sonneberg and also in the Erzgebirge districts."

Around 1908: *Marion Kaulitz* instigated the *Puppen Reform* movement which brought character dolls into being and gave added impetus to the German doll industry.

TOYS AND NOVELTIES provides some interesting comments on the German toy industry from the time of the Puppen Reform to World War I:

"After the radical reform of 1908 nothing remained to reform, and the doll children really could not be made more child-like." A little later it was reported: "Before the war nearly all the dolls' heads and enameled [glass] eyes used were purchased by the French manufacturers from Germany."

In 1913 it was reported that German doll factories were running full time and increasing their output. Most of the dolls came from Sonneberg but the finer ones came from Waltershausen. Large factories were located in both places.

"Dolls for the entire world are now made in Germany, although each country generally dressed its own consignments in its own national garb."

In 1914 TOYS AND NOVELTIES discussed Art Dolls:
"It has become popular with art loving society ladies,

women artists, kindergarten leaders, etc., to devote themselves with zeal to toys and in that line to create after their own whims and fancy articles which only too readily are described by the daily press as artistic specialties, this notoriety greatly pleasing the ladies. At Christmas last year [1913] special attention was given to the dolls, . . . The latest dolls are probably most correctly described with the mark 'Phantastic,' for there is about them a breath of peculiar oddity, daring absence of expression, peculiar way of clothing, and, besides this, over-slender bodies in exalted positions. If these figures were not described as dolls, one would take them for ornaments; and they really are more suitable for an elegant drawing room than for a nursery. But this is by no means the result those ladies wish. They wanted to carry art into the life of the child. Our little doll mothers shall early be educated to an 'artistic' taste. They are to be able to recognize the difference between factory ware and art products. There were, therefore, around the Christmas time in Dresden, Munich, Berlin, Vienna, etc., quite a number of separate exhibitions of these new artists dolls, which are reported to have aroused intense interest.

"The question of what is to be done regarding the German exhibit at San Francisco is still a topic of discussion. . . .

"Firms of the Sonneberg toy industry have expressed themselves firmly in favor of representation at the Universal Exposition in San Francisco. . . . It would have been all right to decline participation at Paris, Brussels, etc., whose only well known and sufficiently worked markets came in question, but it is absolutely wrong to neglect the western portion of America."

Also in 1914 a St. Louis importer named *Henry Fabricius* was reported as saying, "Not all of the dolls sent by German factories are good enough to market in America. Most of the German dolls have bisque heads but about one third have composition heads with molded hair and usually voices. The bisque-head dolls have sleeping eyes for the most part. Some have googlie eyes and watermelon type mouth. About half of the dolls have wigs and the rest have molded hair. Baby dolls have straight hair wigs, either short or bobbed. . . . The German factories like American factories, come so nearly duplicating each other's products of dolls that often it is difficult to tell to which line a doll belongs without looking at the tag."

1916: According to *Katherine Rauser* shipments of dolls from Germany to the U.S. included complete dolls as well as heads, eyes, wigs, or legs and arms:

"The best bisque heads and the finest bodies are fashioned in Germany where the trade passed down through generations in families. Only one house in this country [America] puts out a standard doll that parallels the German product. It has been discovered, according to commercial reports, that the majority of French dolls get their heads from Germany."

1917: A British doll expert stated in a British trade journal: "Before the war Germany unquestionably held a master key to the doll industry. If other countries were successful in the manufacturing of bodies, they had often to go to Germany for the heads. Even those who made dolls' heads were frequently compelled to call upon the Germans for the eyes."

1918: TOYS AND NOVELTIES discussed the shortages in Germany due to the war. Poor quality felt and paper took the place of leather. Paper dresses for dolls were unsatisfactory. Before the war, Sonneberg alone worked up several million marks worth of mohair annually. But artificial mohair was expensive and it was placed under embargo for army requirements. Doll makers had to use human hair but the supply of this was limited and the price high.

1919: Skilled labor before the war received $3.00 and in 1919 they got $7.80. All raw materials were scarce.

1920: Dr. *Culin,* Curator at the Brooklyn Museum, wrote about the German dolls that it was a "well recognized custom for artists of distinction to make models for the . . . dolls which are manufactured for commerce. The superior excellence, the perfection of the German doll . . . was in no sense an accident, but the result of the most painstaking endeavor. There can be no possible competition in Europe with the products of the great German factories, and indeed it would be difficult to find among all the dolls manufactured for children more engaging objects than those delightful infants made by *Käthe Kruse.*"

According to an article on German dolls in TOYS AND FANCY GOODS TRADER: "China factories [are] closing or they only fire their oven once per fortnight instead of daily as in pre-war days. This affects the doll industry which is dependent on these factories for heads and limbs. The only toys in this part of the country which are being made in anything approaching large quantities are articles made by small homeworkers in the mountain district, and composed principally of wood, papier-mâché and composition."

1921: A British toy wholesaler wrote that German dolls had been aging in damp warehouses and crumbled when taken out. He also complained that the British Merchandise Marks Act was being bypassed by stamping packing cases with country of origin instead of stamping the dolls themselves or by attaching to dolls made in Germany large labels describing them as "English Dressed."

1922: A British trade journal claimed that German celluloid dolls were cheaper and better quality than Japanese celluloid dolls.

1923: The year of incredible inflation. In October two billion marks were worth 50¢. Before 1914 one mark was worth 25¢. Fewer lines of German dolls were offered than before the war and most of these lines were prewar ones. Several American doll firms had established themselves in Sonneberg in an effort to restore prewar conditions. Some dolls 14 to 16 in. (35.5 to 40.5 cm.) were available but priced very high and there were almost no small dolls. Sleeping-eye dolls were scarce and the Leipzig Fair was a disaster, according to TOYS AND NOVELTIES. *Hitz, Jacobs*

& Kassler, who had offices in Fürth, Bavaria, and New York City, in their wholesale catalog advertised an extensive selection of bisque head dolls including those with sleeping eyes. These dolls were of the regular baby face or dolly face variety.

1924: The United States Department of Commerce published a report (No. 267.) on the German doll industry. It stated "It is believed that French protestant immigrants who came to Germany to escape persecution took to toy-making as the simplest occupation accessible to them. Majority of the Sonneberg inhabitants are protestants." The old craftsmen of the 18th century by their teaching caused the evolution of more expressive dolls in the 19th century. The two great doll centers were Waltershausen including Ohrdruf, where dolls of the highest grade were made in factories, and Sonneberg. Whereas in Sonneberg and Neustadt dolls of medium and better grades were made by home workers. U.S. import duty on dolls before the war was 35 percent but by 1924 it had been raised to 70 percent.

1927: TOYS AND NOVELTIES reported that a new all-celluloid doll was able to move a few steps and roll its eyes.

In 1953 John Paul Edwards, foreign sales manager for Hale's Department Store in California, gave a lecture on his early experiences and observations:

For 41 years he had designed and bought dolls, usually from overseas. Mr. Edwards said that the Bavarians were very clever at their doll making. The collector who owns a *Mary Jane* doll made in a factory in Steinach, Thüringia, has one of Mr. Edward's dolls. The doll had a bisque head and wore a pea jacket and sailor cap designed by Mr. Edwards. It was the doll dress designer that he dealt with when he went to Bavaria or Thüringia. If he had an idea he wished made for a doll, he gave a sketch or description to the artist. Later the same day the model was ready and it was a well-made replica. His suggestions for new ideas were warmly welcomed by the artists.

The finest German dolls were made in Gotha and Waltershausen in Thüringia. The cheaper dolls were made around Coburg and Sonneberg. The *Kestner* doll factory of Waltershausen made the highest quality dolls in Germany.

The high grade *Miblu* dolls of 1925 were the finest celluloid dolls and had transparent skin like that of a real baby. These were made by the *Rheinische Gummi und Celluloid Fabrik.*

The Germans made dolls representing people of every country of the world, except possibly of Tibet. It was not just to have a dark skinned doll to represent Africa, the doll had to have African features and dress. No matter what the country, Liberia, Africa, Arabia, or Argentina, the doll had to look like it came from those lands. Germany was noted for its ability to accommodate every country. The cheap labor of Germany resulted in cheap but good dolls and most of the children of the world played with German dolls until 1914. The American doll industry began to be really active around 1910 and that year marks the beginning of the end of the German doll monopoly. (See also **Manufacture of Dolls Made Commercially in Germany**). ★

1034A & B. Bisque shoulder head probably representing the empress of Germany with its molded coronet braid and pierced ears as described in THE QUEEN in 1878, except for its size. The necklace and blouse top with shoulder bows are molded. There are two sew holes on either side through which the head is attached to the cloth body with leather arms. H. 24 in. (61 cm.). H. of shoulder head 6 in. (15 cm.). *Coleman Collection.*

1033. Papier-mâché shoulder head with molded curls over the ears and a bun high up in back, painted features, kid body and wooden lower arms and legs. Original dress. *Courtesy of the late Estelle Winthrop.*

1035. Group of four china shoulder heads with black molded hair and blue eyes made in Germany. From left to right they have: curly hair and pierced ears, h. 15 in. (38 cm.); side part, h. 12 in. (30.5 cm.) and h. 11½ in. (29.5 cm.); and a molded bow in the hair, h. 16½ in. (42 cm.). *Courtesy of Sotheby Parke Bernet Inc., N.Y.*

1036. Composition shoulder head doll made in Germany has a molded black flat-top hair style, painted eyes and a closed mouth. *Courtesy of Sotheby Parke Bernet Inc., N.Y.*

1038. German bisque head made by Simon & Halbig on a ball jointed composition body made by Kämmer & Reinhardt. It has a wig, sleeping blue glass eyes and a closed mouth. Mark: "K ✡ R//S & H.//117 A." H. 20 in. (51 cm.). *Courtesy of Sotheby Parke Bernet Inc., N.Y.*

1037. Pair of bisque-head dolls on composition bodies made in Germany. They have wigs, glass eyes, closed mouths. Original clothes. Hs. 13½ in. (34.5 cm.) and 12 in. (30.5 cm.). *Courtesy of Sotheby Parke Bernet Inc., N.Y.*

1039. German bisque-head dolls with composition bodies. Doll on the left has a wig, sleeping glass eyes, open mouth with teeth, and a fully jointed body. Original commercial chemise. Kestner mark mold #167. H. 16 in. (40.5 cm.). Doll on the right has molded and painted blond hair, blue intaglio eyes, open-closed mouth and a bent-limb baby body. Probably original clothes. Kämmer & Reinhardt mold #100. H. 14½ in. (37 cm.). *Courtesy of Sotheby Parke Bernet Inc., N.Y.*

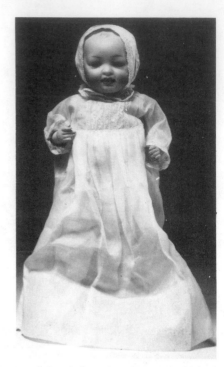

1040. Bisque head baby doll made in Germany, probably by Hertel, Schwab & Co. The painted hair shows brush marks. It has stationary brown glass eyes, closed mouth, five piece bent limb composition body. Mark: "142." H. 10½ in. (26.5 cm.). *Courtesy of Sotheby Parke Bernet Inc., N.Y.*

1041. German baby doll with a bisque head on a bent-limb composition body, probably by Hertel, Schwab & Co. It has painted blond brush marks for the hair, sleeping blue glass eyes, and an open-closed mouth. Mark: "151//2." H. 11½ in. (29 cm.). *Courtesy of Sotheby Parke Bernet Inc., N.Y.*

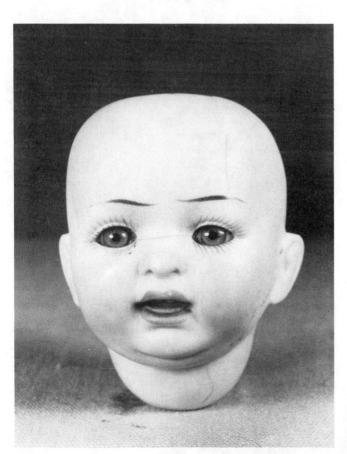

1042. German bisque head with wig, stationary blue glass eyes, open mouth with teeth, probably by Hertel, Schwab & Co. Mark: Ill. 1046. H. of head only, 2½ in. (6.5 cm.). *Coleman Collection.*

1043. China shoulder head doll made in a Germanic area in the early 1900s. It has a wig, painted features, and china arms. Original clothes represent the mid 1700s. *Courtesy of the Smithsonian Institution.*

1045. Bisque head doll made in Germany. It has a mohair wig, with braids over the ears, sleeping eyes, open mouth with teeth, ball-jointed composition and wood body. Original German regional costume. H. 7½ in. (19 cm.). *Coleman Collection.*

A GERMAN NURSE-GIRL AND BABY.

A FRUIT-SELLER OF HAMBURG.

1044. German dolls in the collection of Mrs. Hesing as shown in THE STRAND MAGAZINE, September, 1902. The Nurse-Girl and Baby came from Mechlenburg. Its short stiff full skirt is under an apron that ties around the waist. The customary nursemaid's cap has a big starched bow in front. The Fruit Seller of Hamburg has long hair and a gaily ornamented costume. It was that "costumes like this may even now [1902] be seen in Hamburg, but not with the frequency of days gone by."

Made in Germany
152
3/0

1046. Mark on a bisque head doll made in Germany probably by Hertel, Schwab & Co. See Ill. 1042.

German Export Service Bureau. 1930. Solicited orders from American toy buyers.

German Manufacturers Association. 1926. New York City. This association represented about 50 German toy manufacturers, including *V. M. Bruchlos, Eckstein & Co., Otto Gans,* Arthur *Gotthelf, Alexandre Greiner,* and *Käthe Kruse.*

German Novelty Co. 1914–15. New York City. Advertised unbreakable character dolls and dolls with voices.★

POPPEN

37-30-73/0 — Gelukspopje, solide celluloid. Beweegbare armen. Geschikt als badpopje en als theewarmer-pop. 8½ centimeter hoog **25** c

11½ centimeter hoog .... **35** c

17½ centimeter hoog .... **60** c

37-30-381 — „Duimzuigstertje"
Ideal-Baby. Steenen kop, beweegbare tong en slaapoogen. Gekleed met mutsje, luierbroekje, hemdje, jurkje, manteltje, kousjes en babysokjes. 44 centimeter hoog **5**⁷⁵

37-30-8468 — Onbreekbare Baby.
Beweegbare kop, armen en beenen, met slaapoogen, wimpers en page-haar, in nachthemd met zijden strikjes.

Hoogte 25 centimeter	1.75
Hoogte 30 centimeter	2.40
Hoogte 36 centimeter	3.60
Hoogte 45 centimeter	4.50
Hoogte 50 centimeter	5.90
Hoogte 60 centimeter	8.25

37-30-858 — „Lievelingsbaby" met zeer fijnen biscuitkop, schelm-slaapoogen en beweegbaren tong, met hemdje.

34 cm. hoog	6.75	52 cm. hoog	10.75
43 cm. hoog	8.75	62 cm. hoog	15.75

37-30-390 — Stofpopje, geheel onbreekbaar, in aardige viltkleeding met appliques, geheel uitkleedb. 33 cm. hoog **2**⁴⁰

37-30-328 — Eenvoudig Stofpopje in aardige viltkleeding, met modern hoedje. 32 cm. hoog **1**⁴⁵

37-30-391 — Geheel onbreekbaar Stofpopje in pyama met lederen riempje, uitkleedbaar. 31 cm. hoog **2**⁴⁰

37-30-7635 — Onbreekbare Celluloid-Pop, beweegbare kop met glazen oogen, 40 cM. hoog ongekleed **5**⁷⁵
Beweegbare armen en beenen, 50 cM. hoog, ongekleed **7.50**

Complete onder- en bovenkleeding .... EXTRA **3.90** en **2**⁹⁰

Een klein overzicht uit een zeer groote sorteering!

37-30-862 — Fijnste kwaliteit geheel onbreekbare Baby met celluloid kop, schelmslaapoogen en wimpers, in batisten luierbroekje, met „mama"-stem.

36 cm. hoog	9.75	50 cm. hoog	16.75
41 cm. hoog	12.75	60 cm. hoog	24.75

37-30-1567 — Mignonnette-popje, 17 cm. hoog, met trousseau, die op borduren na klaar is. Compleet met borduurgaren, in doos 30 × 23 cm. **2**¹⁰

37-30-1566 — Mignonnette-popje, 18 cm. hoog, met complete trousseau, 2 garnituren, in doos 32 × 23 cm. **3**⁶⁰

Breekbare Speelgoederen worden verzonden in extra stevige doozen, welke à 40 cents berekend worden.

37-30-550 — Popje in kleederdracht van het eiland Marken, Volendam of Goes, zeer origineel. 24 centimeter hoog **1**⁹⁰

37-30-550

37-30-380 — Geheel onbreekbare Stofpop met babygezichtje. Kruse-genre, met geschilderd haar. Complete onderkleeding, bovenkleeding (jongen of meisje) van gehaakte wol. 46 centimeter hoog **8**⁷⁵

42 cm. hoog	6.75	35 cm. hoog	4.75

37-30-862

37-30-380

Eigen inkoopbureaux te Paris, Lyon, London en Chemnitz

111

1047. Dolls advertised by the Gerzon store in Holland in 1928. Left to right: All celluloid dolls. Hs. 8.5, 11.5 and 17.5 cm. (3½, 4½, and 7 in.). Ideal Baby with sleeping eyes. H. 44 cm. (17½ in.). Unbreakable (?composition) baby with sleeping eyes and hair eyelashes. Six hs. 25, 30, 36, 45, 50 and 60 cm. (10, 12, 14, 17½, 19½, and 23½ in.). K★R bisque head baby with "naughty" sleeping eyes. Four hs. 34, 43, 52, and 62 cm. (13½, 17, 20½ and 24½ in.). Celluloid doll with molded hair, glass eyes, hs. 40 and 50 cm. (15½ and 19½ in.). Three cloth dolls, hs. 31, 32, and 33 cm. (12, 12½, and 13 in.). Toddler with celluloid head, naughty sleeping eyes and hair eyelashes. Four hs. 36, 41, 50 and 60 cm. (14, 16, 19½, and 23½ in.). Doll dressed in the regional costume of the Island of Marken, Volendam or Goes. H. 24 cm. (9½ in.). Two boxes of "mignonnettes" (small dolls with their trousseaus). Hs. of dolls 17 and 18 cm. (6½ and 7 in.). Käthe Kruse type cloth doll (does not appear to be a Käthe Kruse doll, only similar in style). Hs. 35, 42, and 46 cm. (14, 16½, and 18 in.). *Courtesy of the Collection Nederlands Kostuummuseum, The Hague.*

A   B   C

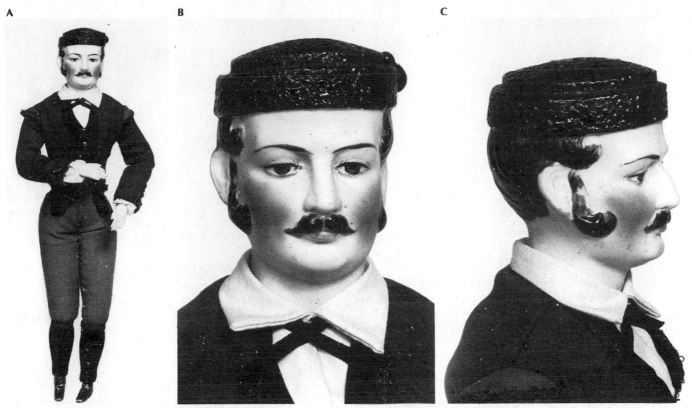

1048A–C. Bisque head man doll with a Gesland-type body that has a cloth covering, metal inner structure including the joints, bisque arms, and molded boots. It has a molded and painted hat, hair with sideburns, and mustache. The eyes are also molded, and painted brown; it has a closed mouth. The matador costume was re-created by Margaret Whitton. H. 19 in. (48 cm.). *Courtesy of the Margaret Woodbury Strong Museum. Photos by Harry Bickelhaupt.*

Germanus, August. 1899. Erfurt, Thür. Applied for a German patent (D.R.G.M.) for a jointed doll.

Gerwig, Moritz. 1920s. Pforzheim, Germany. Name appeared on the leather shoe of a *Käthe Kruse* type doll.

Gerzon. 1925–30. Holland. Imported and distributed dolls, especially celluloid and composition-head dolls.

1925: Advertised dolls with composition heads and cloth bodies that resembled *Käthe Kruse* dolls. The ones dressed as boys or girls were 40 cm. (15½ in.) tall while the dolls in chemise with footwear, came in hts. 35, 37.5 and 40 cm. (14, 14½ and 15½ in.).

1926: Advertised celluloid dolls dressed as boys or girls, ht. 22 cm. (8½ in.); and cloth-body dolls, hts. 33 and 38 cm. (13 and 15 in.).

1928: Advertised an *Ideal* baby; *Kämmer & Reinhardt's* Liebling *(Mein Liebling)* baby; *mignonnettes;* the Käthe Kruse type dolls; all-celluloid *Kewpie*-type dolls; dressed cloth dolls; and dolls dressed in regional costumes.

1930: Advertised most of the dolls listed in the 1928 catalog plus *Boudoir* dolls, black dolls, mulatto dolls, Chinese dolls and a doll sucking its thumb that came in black or white versions. The dressed Chinese dolls had sleeping eyes. Four hts. 30, 35, 39, and 44 cm. (12, 14, 15½, and 17½ in.).

Geschwister, L. 1920s. Germany. Created dolls; may have been related to *Heinrich's Geschwister.*

Gesland. 1860–1928. Paris. By 1926 the successors, H. Delcourt and J. Ortyz, were succeeded by the Société Industrielle de Jouets Français for whom a factory at Antony, Seine, was listed. They also had factories at Lyon, Cancale, Paramé and Boulogne-sur-Mer. They made, repaired, exported and distributed dolls. In 1928 they had a capital of a million francs. Several patents including a German D.R.G.M. patent of unknown date, appear to relate to a doll's body that closely resembled the body of the *Bébé Gesland* as shown in the first COLLECTOR'S ENCYCLOPEDIA OF DOLLS, Ills. 634 and 635. An advertising leaflet for this "new jointed doll with noiseless movements" is in the Margaret Woodbury Strong Museum. The Gesland firm was a member of the *Chambre Syndicale.*

1881: Purchased bisque heads from *François Gaultier* according to Mme. Poisson, curator of the Roybet Fould Museum.

World War I and later: Used the *Petite Française* bisque heads made by *J. Verlingue.* In 1921 they were at the same address in Paris as *J. Verlingue.*

1927: Manufactured cardboard *poupards.*

1928: They specialized in Bébé *Tanagra* and *Bébé Réclame.* Their dolls had a porcelain or composition head, stationary or sleeping eyes, and came dressed or undressed. ★

1049. Bisque-head lady doll with typical Gesland body having a stockinet covering, metal joints, and bisque arms. It has a wig, stationary blue glass eyes, pierced ears. The bisque parts may have been made by François Gaultier. H. 16 in. (40.5 cm.). *Courtesy of Sotheby Parke Bernet Inc., N.Y.*

1050. A Gesland doll with a head marked "R. 3 D." for Rabery & Delphieu. Both of these firms are known to have purchased bisque heads from François Gaultier. This bisque head has a wig, brown glass eyes, pierced ears, a closed mouth, and is on a ball-jointed composition body. Mark: Ill. 1053. H. 23½ in. (59.5 cm.). *Courtesy of Hazel Ulseth.*

1051. Advertisement for E. Gesland in 1893. It gives the address which had been the same since 1875 and gives the admonition that the House of Gesland is not a shop. It is a factory and store. They can repair Bébés and Dolls of all makes in ten minutes. They replace damaged heads and are open 8 A.M. to 7 P.M. but on Christmas Eve and New Year's Day they stay open until 10 P.M.

1055. Mark used by Carl Geyer for dolls in 1911.

1053–1054. Marks on bodies of Gesland dolls. Ill. 1053 is on a sticker on the composition body of the doll in Ill. 1050. Ill. 1054 is a stamp on a doll's body.

Gessert, Schmidt & Co. 1923–30. Engelsbach near Waltershausen, Thür. Made dolls.★

Geuther, Theodor. 1892–1930 and later. Sonneberg, Thür. Produced bent-limb baby dolls, ball jointed dolls, stiff legged jointed dolls, *Mama* dolls, and dancing dolls. These came in a chemise or dressed.

Gévrinette. 1927. *Lafayette* store sold two cloth dolls with this name. One had a wig and a silk or felt dress. Ht. 52 cm. (20½ in.). The other was all felt, had a wig, wore a silk dress and a coat and hat. Ht. 65 cm. (25½ in.).

Geyer, Carl, & Co. 1885–1913. Sonneberg, Thür.; 1913–29, Carl Geyer & Sohn; 1929–30 and later, Carl Geyer Sohn. Made and exported dolls and doll related items. A partner *Carl Meyer* in 1899 left this company and formed his own firm.

1902: Applied for a German patent (D.R.G.M.) for a doll.

1910: Applied for a German patent (D.R.G.M.) for a box containing materials for dolls' clothes and a sewing machine.

One of the Sonneberg group of Grand Prize Winners at the Brussels Exposition.★

1052. Gesland's 1893 advertisement for their "greatest Novelty Bébé Gesland, patented. Not sold in any other store or Bazar in Paris, Parian manufacture. House founded in 1860. Bronze medal at Paris Exposition. The bébé metal articulation replaces rubber, the only bébé with feet, arms and bust of hard wood. Bisque head, flowing hair, wig, the Bébé can sit or kneel and can be easily dressed." Then follows the prices for various sizes of undressed bébés, bébés dressed in silk of various colors, and bisque heads for bébés. This is followed by a list of other items sold by Gesland such as wigs, dolls' clothes, talking bébés, black dolls and so forth. (Margaret Whitton has found a German patent for a doll that appears to be exactly like the Gesland doll.)

Gibbon & Son Ltd. See **Welsh Toy Industries.**

Gibbs, Messrs. 1870. London. Made leather shoes.

Giblet, Mlle. Marcel (Marcelle). Before 1920–22. Prague, Czechoslovakia. She fled to Prague with her sister and they supported themselves by making art dolls of a type that originated in Paris during World War I. The dolls had an ethnic style. The curator of the Brooklyn Museum, *Stewart Culin,* purchased some of her dolls for an exhibit. One of these dolls Mr. Culin described as a "fine lady with a very small head with tow hair and wonderful clothes." Other dolls were black or brown with "fuzzled" hair and legs that curved limply. Mr. Culin worried that her dolls would be copied in America, but she replied, "No one could copy them. Each one is different, they have a character quite their own."★

Gibson, Edward Tinkham. 1909–12. Brooklyn, N.Y. Patented a cloth doll with a skirt that hung free. Several of these dolls have been seen dressed in red sailor-style dresses. There was an identification stamp on the upper leg.★

Gibson Girl. Ca. 1910. Trade name of a doll made by *Kestner,* often mold #172. Hts. included 10 and 21 in. (25.5 and 53.5 cm.).★

Gibson & Sons. 1919–20. London. Handled *Houghton* cloth dolls.

Giebeler-Falk Doll Corp. 1918–21. Made dolls with aluminum heads and wooden or composition bodies. Their agents were *Baker & Bennett; Borgfeldt; B. Illfelder; Owens-Kreiser Co.; Samstag & Hilder; Steinhardt; Strobel & Wilken;* and *Louis Wolf.* These dolls were distributed all over the world. The tallest doll, 25 in. (63.5 cm.), weighed only 2¼ pounds.

1919: Advertised that they produced 1000 dolls per week. ★

Giely, C., & Co. 1929–30 and later. Paris. Produced porcelain shoulder heads and wax shoulder heads.

Giesecke & Schulte. 1885–1930 and later. Lippstadt, Westphalia. Produced dolls.

Giestes, Gusta. 1922–23. Erfurt, Thür. Obtained a German patent (D.R.P.) for movable dolls.

Gie-Wa. 1918–19. Trade name used by *Dollcraft.* There were three hts. 18 to 26 in. (45.5 to 66 cm.).

Giggles. 1927–30. Trade name of a baby doll made by *Domec.* It could "suck" its thumb and turn its head. The cloth body was filled with kapok and it wore a pink, blue, or white dress.

1928: Three hts., priced $1.00, $2.00, and $3.00.

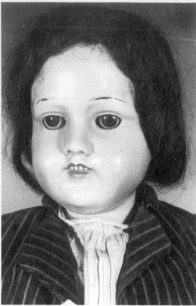

1056A & B. Doll with metal head, hands and legs on a ball-jointed wooden body made in America ca. 1919 by Giebeler-Falk. It has a wig, metal sleeping eyes, open-closed mouth with four teeth. The body is jointed even at the wrists and ankles. Mark III. 1057. H. 22 in. (56 cm.). *Coleman Collection.*

1057. Mark used by Giebeler-Falk on their metal and wood dolls.

1930: Called "Baby Giggles." Came in four hts.

1947–69: *Cameo* made a doll designed by *Rose O'Neill* and *Joseph Kallus,* made in composition until 1954 when it began to be made in vinyl. This doll was also called Giggles and represented a giggling girl.

Gilbert, A. C., Co. 1924. Listed in a British toy trade journal under Dolls.

Gilbert the Filbert, the Nursery Knut. 1915–21. This British Music Hall hit was represented by a cloth doll that could

stand on its feet. It was made by *Dean* and wore a variety of costumes but usually had a monocle, spats, hat, and flower.

1915: Price $1.00.

1920: Number D 188 was 14 in. (35.5 cm.) tall. Number D 189 was 10½ in. (26.5 cm.) tall.

Gilles. 1916. Doll with a wooden head on a cloth body stuffed with fabric, made by *M. Georges Lepape.*

Gilt Dolls. 1860–61. Name listed by *John D. Robbins* as among his imported dolls, priced 63¢ a doz. wholesale. According to information supplied by Elizabeth Pierce.

Gimbel Bros. Ca. 1900–30 and later. New York City and Philadelphia, Pa. Prior to World War I it was customary for six or seven large German manufacturers to compete for the annual Gimbel "order of 2,000 dolls of a special kind." The war stopped these German orders and after the war Gimbels looked elsewhere for dolls. Gimbels operated a dolls' hospital.

1904–5: Catalogs showed *American Maid;* Dollar dolls, 22 in. (56 cm.) tall; *Elaine* dolls; *Heinrich Handwerck* lady dolls; infant dolls and kid body dolls. (See Ill. 540 in THE COLLECTOR'S BOOK OF DOLLS' CLOTHES.)

1911: Catalog showed Dollar dolls, 22 in. (56 cm.) tall; Elaine dolls; Handwerck dolls; *Martha Chase* dolls; *Babyland Rag* including *Topsy Turvy,* Red Riding Hood, Girl, Boy, and Infant; Mr. *Twee Deedle;* celluloid dolls; kid-body dolls; dolls' clothes and accessories.

1912: Advertised composition character dolls; jointed kid-body dolls; life-size dolls; all-bisque dolls; all-celluloid dolls; and the many *Horsman* dolls, such as Baby Bumps[†] and *Campbell Kids;* Dutch Dolls and so on.

1916–17: Catalog showed *Baby Grumpy;* baby doll with voice; celluloid dolls and other dolls.

1918: Displayed 45 dolls dressed to represent the Allied nations in costumes based on designs furnished by the University of Pennsylvania.

1926: Created a window display in Milwaukee, Wis. The display, called "Dance of the Nations," was composed of cloth dolls with various colored yarn hair. The group represented a doll orchestra surrounded by dolls in regional costumes.

1930: Advertised a special doll called "Gimbel Baby." This was an infant doll with composition arms and legs on a cloth body. Ht. 26 in. (66 cm.); priced $3.95. They handled French, German, Italian dolls including *Lenci* dolls. Their American dolls came from *Effanbee,* Horsman, and *Averill Manufacturing Co.* and included *Mama* dolls. They also had dolls' clothes and dolls' accessories. ★

Ginette. 1928. Name of a bisque-head doll with wig, sleeping eyes and hair eyelashes sold by *Bon Marché.* It wore a silk costume. Ht. 35 cm. (14 in.).

Ginger. See **Fan and Fannie.**

Ginsburg & Wolfe. 1925–27. Brooklyn, N.Y. Made wigs, shoes, and accessories for dolls.

Beautifully Dressed Dolls at Moderate Prices

Gimbels for Dolls. At both the New York and Philadelphia stores a vast collection covering almost everything made in the way of dolls, dolls' clothing, etc. No true father or mother but is deeply interested in the display, while of course the little girls extract great joy and excitement from it.

No. K 10200. Dressed Doll. Thirteen inches in height and very appropriately dressed; closing eyes. 50c.

No. K 10201. Dressed Doll. A prime favorite with little girls. Closing eyes; picture hat—the real goods; 18 inches. $1.00.

No. K 10202. Jointed Doll. Sleeping eyes; sewed wig; shoes and stockings; 15 inches. A splendid doll for the price. 50c.

No. K 10203. Gimbel Dollar Doll. Fine, full, sewed, mohair wig parted on side; sleeping eyes, either blue or brown; shoes and stockings; 22 inches high. This is the best doll ever sold for so low a price and is our "leader." $1.00.

No. K 10204. Dressed Doll. Closing eyes; 11 inches; a very attractive little doll. 25c.

No. K 10205. Gimbels' "Elaine" Doll. The finest product of the famous "Handwerck" factory. Hand-sewed mohair wig side parting; sleeping eyes with eyelashes; satin slippers; silk stockings. It's a greatly pleased little **girl** that gets one of these elegant dolls. 15 inches, $2.25. 16 inches, $2.50. 19¼ inches, $3.00. 22

inches, $4.50. 24 inches, $5.00. 27 inches, $6.00. 30 inches, $7.50. 33 inches, $10.00.

No. K 10206. Jointed Doll. Sleeping eyes; sewed wig; shoes and stockings; 12 inches. Fine for its price, which is but 25c.

No. K 10207. "Handwerck" Jointed Doll. A doll that is a standard and very fine value. Full sewed wig; closing eyes; shoes and stockings. 22 inches, $2.50; 24 inches, $2.75. 27 inches, $4.25. 30 inches, $5.50. Same doll with eyelashes, 25c additional.

NOT ILLUSTRATED.

Doll's Rain Coats. 50c, $1.00, $1.50.
Doll's Rubbers. 25c and 40c pair.
Doll's Buttonhooks and Glove Buttoners. 5c and 15c.
Doll's Hair Brushes. 15c, 25c, 50c.
Doll's Clothes Brushes. 25c and 50c.
Doll's Fancy Hair Pins. 5c each.
Doll's Gloves. 25c and 50c.
Doll's Curling Irons. 5c.
Doll's Parasols. 35c, 50c, $1.00, $1.50, $2.00.
Doll's Umbrellas. 75c, 85c, $1.00.
Doll's Ice Skates. 15c.

Doll's Roller Skates. 15c.
Doll's Corsets. 25c, 50c, 75c.
Doll's Leggings. 35c and 50c.
Doll's Red Coats with Brass Buttons. $1.50, $2.00, $3.00.
Doll's Watches for Boys or Girls with Fobs, Chains or Pins. 25c, 50c, $1.00.
Doll's Gold Chain Hand Bags. 25c, 50c, 65c.
Doll's Ornaments for Hair. 10c and 25c.
Doll's Hat Pins. All sizes and lengths. 25c and 50c.
Rubber Toys for Little Babies. Assorted animals, rattles and dolls. 15c, 25c, 50c, $1.00.
Doll's Brass Beds. $4.00, $5.00, $8.00, $10.00, $12.00.
Doll's Slippers. Assorted colors. 15c, 20c, 30c, 35c.
Doll's Leather Slippers. 25c.
Doll's Patent Leather Slippers. 25c.
Doll's Gold Slippers with High Heels. 85c and $1.50.
Doll's Sandals, Russet. 25c.
Doll's Suede Slippers. Assorted colors. 25c.
Doll's Wooden Dutch Shoes. 10c.
Doll's Stockings. Silk. Assorted colors. 20c, 35c, 50c.
Doll's Socks. Assorted colors. 10c, 15c, 25c.

Philadelphia   **GIMBEL BROTHERS**   **New York**

102

1058. Gimbel's 1912 catalog page showing dressed and undressed dolls; the third and fifth doll in front row were made by Heinrich Handwerck. Dolls' clothes and accessories are also listed.

All Babyland Loves the Gimbel Store

All kinds and manner of dolls—dainty ones, beautiful ones, ugly ones—unbreakable ones, but each to bring happiness and content to some child. Write us about any doll dress or doll furniture you may want.

Postage:—Celluloid, 25c; Rag, 18c; Bisque, about 60c.

No. K 10300. Jointed Stockinette Doll. Hand painted face and limbs; unbreakable. 9-inch doll, $3.00. 15-inch doll, $4.00. 20-inch doll, $5.00. 23-inch doll, $6.50. 25½-inch doll, $8.00. 29½-inch doll, $10.00.

No. K 10301. "Babyland" Topsyturvy Rag Doll. Reversible, showing white and colored face. $1.00.

No. K 10302. Celluloid Doll. Jointed arms and legs; painted shoes, stockings, eyes and hair; 6 inches, 25c. 7½ inches, 50c. 9½ inches, 75c. 11 inches, $1.00. 13¼ inches, $1.50.

No. K 10303. Sailor Boy Doll. Painted face; 12 inches high, 25c.

No. K 10304. Kid Body. Bisque head and hands; closing eyes; shoes and stockings; 12 inches, 25c. 14 inches, 50c.

No. K 10305. Rag Doll. Dressed as a boy; 13½ inches, 50c.

No. K 10306. Teddy Bear Baby Bunting Doll. Celluloid face; unbreakable body; has fur body like Teddy Bears; stands 12 inches high; movable joints, 25c and 50c.

No. K 10307. "Babyland" Red Riding Hood Rag Doll. Painted face; 14 inches, 50c. 16 inches, $1.00. 17 inches, $2.00.

No. K 10308. Sailor Girl Doll. Painted face; 12 inches high, 25c.

No. K 10309. Mr. Twee Deedle Doll. One of the most humorous dolls created for the children; has a "can't break 'em" head, and is dressed in red and yellow jacket, green stockings and red and yellow cap; stands 18 inches to the top of his cap. $1.00.

No. K 10310. Babyland Girl Doll. Dressed in cape, dress and underclothing; 15 inches high. $1.00.

No. K 10311. Babyland Boy Doll. Neatly dressed; 15 inches high. $1.00.

No. K 10312. Babyland Infant Doll. Printed face; long clothes and cap. 50c and $1.00.

NOT ILLUSTRATED.

Doll Dresses. Latest style and fashion. Made of fine lawn assorted colors, all white or dotted, pink and blue. For doll, 22 inches high. $1.00.

Gingham Dresses. Well made and nicely finished. To fit dolls 16 inches high, 50c; 22 inches, $1.00 and $1.25.

Fine White Lawn Dresses. With low neck. Sizes for 16-, 18-, 22- and 24-inch dolls. $1.75.

We carry a full line of dresses for dolls. 14 inch, $1.00; 16 inch, $1.50; 18 inch, $2.00; 20 inch, $2.50; 22 inch, $3.00; 24 inch, $3.00 and up, to silk dresses for large dolls at $10.50.

Doll's Knit Booties. Assorted colors, pink and blue trimmings. 19c, 20c and 35c pair.

Doll's Knit Sacques. Assorted colors 25c, 50c $1.00.

Infant Doll's Long Dresses. Nicely trimmed with lace. 14 inch, 85c; 16 inch $1.00; 18 inch, $1.50 and up to $4.00 each.

Doll's Rompers. Pink and blue. 50c.

Doll's Untrimmed Felt Hats. 25c, 50 $1.00.

Doll's Wire Frame. For making hat 10c and 15c.

Doll's Fine Trimmed Hats. Latest d sign. $1.00, $2.00, $3.50.

New York   **GIMBEL BROTHERS**   **Philadelphia**

103

1059. Another page from the 1912 Gimbel's catalog showing various dolls such as a Martha Chase cloth doll, several Babyland cloth dolls, Mr. Twee Deedle, and other cloth dolls as well as an all-celluloid doll and a doll with a celluloid face. Various dolls' clothes and accessories are also listed.

Dolls and Toys for the Younger Children

Most of these dolls are known as character unbreakable dolls, and are really almost indestructible, while faces are really true to infant life. The other toys are also of excellent quality and will please the small boy or girl. Gimbel's Restricted Delivery Offer applies.

R-19800. Infant Doll. Large size. Dressed with cap and bootees. Stands 25 inches high; special....... **$1.25**

R-19801. Infant Doll. 19½ inches high. Short dresses, cap and bootees. This pretty doll will delight any child... **$1.50**

R-19802. Large Plush Bear. Brown. Collar around neck with bells. 18 inches high. **$1.00**

R-19803. Rattle Doll. 15 inches high. Doll and rattle combined. Will afford great amusement to the little tot.... **15c**

R-19804. A Large Boy Doll. Dressed with rompers and cap. 20 inches high. Very unusual. Will be sure to please .. **$1.50**

R-19805. Dressed Carnival Doll. 19 inches high. With cap and shoes....... **$1.00**

R-19806. Grumpy Girl Doll. Including dress and cap. 13 inches high. Its grumpy expression makes it most unusual....... **$1.25**

R-19807. The Woody Tiger Plush Toy. 6 inches high, 8 inches long, 50c, 8½ x 11, $1.00. 11 x 13, $1.50. 12 x 15, $2.00. 13⅓ x 17...... **$2.50**

Charlie Chaplin

R-19808. Charlie Chaplin Mechanical Toy. When wound it just walks like Charlie Chaplin. Very funny.................... **75c**

R-19809. Baby Doll. With Voice. Completely dressed, and with pacifier. 19 inches high...... **$3.00**

R-19810. The Victor Dog. Fine velveteen. 9 inches high, $1.00. 11 in. $1.50. 14 in. $2.00.

R-19811. Rattle Doll. Celluloid head. 9½ inches tall. Nice gift for the tiny tot....... **35c**

R-19812. Grumpy Boy. Blue jacket; red and white trousers. 10½ ins. **65c**

R-19813. Dressed Infant Doll. 11 inches high, 16½ high from the hem of dress. Cap included. **75c**

R-19814. Jumbo Boy. Doll dressed in rompers. Stands 17 inches high. Very attractive....... **75c**

R-19815. Grumpy Doll. Dressed 13 inches high. a dozen different ways... **$1.25**

R-19816. Featherweight Crying Doll. 10 inches. Celluloid head; knit clothing **$1.00**

New York — Gimbel Brothers — Philadelphia

198

1060. Gimbel's 1916–17 catalog page showing wartime dolls. Most of these dolls have composition heads; one doll has a celluloid head. Three of the dolls appear to be Effanbee's Baby Grumpy.

Giotti, Établissements di. 1925–30 and later. Nice, France. Factory in Nice, agent in Paris. Made felt art dolls. Used *Magati* (Magali) as a trademark.

Girard, Alexandre. 1925–29. Montreuil-sous-Bois, and Paris, France. Made dolls. (Also see **Société Française de Fabrication de Bébés & Jouets.**)★

Girard, Paul Eugène. See **Bru.**

Girardet, Mme. P. 1918. Neuilly, Seine, France. Created heads for dolls.

Giraud-Sauveur. 1926. Léon, Champagnole, Jura, France. Manufactured composition dolls. This may refer only to composition bodies; the material of the head is uncertain. They also advertised *Bébés Maillot,* walking bébés, dressed and undressed dolls. They belonged to the *Chambre Syndicale.*

Giraudet (A.), Vve. (Widow), Fils & Cie. 1926–29. Lorette, Loire. 1929–30 and later, J. Giraudet. Made dolls.

Girlie. 1919. Trade name of a stuffed muslin doll made by *Saalfield.* Ht. 10½ in. (26.5 cm.).

Giroux, Alphonse, & Cie. 1839–before 1865; before 1865–1880s and probably later, successors were Duvinage & Harinkouch (Harinkouck). A box with a blue stamp inside the box top which read "Exposition Publique//ALPHONSE GIROUX & Cie.//43 Boulv. des Capucines, Paris//Peinture Papeterie Encadremts//Objects d'Art, de goût et de fantaisie //Vente et Location de Tablux" contained a French-type doll with a papier-mâché shoulder head having five corkscrew curls of hair glued to the nape of the neck below the painted black hair. The body of the doll was pink kid and the box contained numerous clothes of the 1850s period. There were three dresses besides the one on the doll. Two of the dresses were silk lined with stiffened gauze. In addition there were three straw hats and one brimmed hat, three pairs of slippers, a silk dressy apron, a chemise, and a handkerchief. Ht. of doll 25 cm. (10 in.).

1860s: Advertised baby dolls that cried and called "Mama."

1880s: Advertised children's toys: "original articles of the firm's own invention, can be obtained nowhere else."★

1061. Mark on dolls handled by Alphonse Giroux & Cie.

Gisèle. 1930. "Unbreakable" head doll with sleeping eyes, a cloth body, felt clothes sold by *Bon Marché.* It said "Mama." Ht. 42 cm. (16½ in.).

Givjoy. 1920–29 and other years. Triangular trademark, " 'GIVJOY'//[TRADEMARK]//TOYS" registered for dolls in Britain by *Holladay.*

Glad Baby (Glad Eyes). 1927–28. Bisque head with mohair wig, sleeping googly-style eyes, and closed, wide, smiling mouth, on a composition body, jointed at the neck, shoulders, and hips. One of the Glad babies had a mark reading "Armand Marseille//Germany//323// A 6/0 M." It was dressed in beige colored felt rompers with red buttons and red trimming, white shoes and socks. This doll was in a box marked with a wreath around "M//W," with numbers 48/2647 and "Made in Germany." This doll was 9 in. (23 cm.) tall. These dolls were sold by *Montgomery Ward.* Another Glad Baby wore rompers with a red bow at the neckline and in its hair.

1927: Hts. 7⅜ and 9½ in. (18.5 and 24 cm.); priced 62¢ and $1.00.

Glad Eyed Doll. 1928. Boy or girl dolls sold by *Harrods.* They had glossy composition mask faces, felt heads with plush fabric hair, glass (or imitation glass) eyes stuck firmly into the felt head. Over the eyes were placed large socket holes in the mask so the eyes protruded but could not fall out. The bodies of stuffed pink felt were straw filled and had composition movable limbs attached with outside metal washers. There was a squeaker inside the body. Hts. 10 and 14 in. (25.5 and 35.5 cm.).

Gladdie. 1928–30 and later. Trade name of a doll designed by *Helen Webster Jensen.* The head was made in Germany, probably in the Ohrdruf area since an original mold is in the Ohrdruf Museum. The body was made by *K & K.* Both head and body were made for the *Verleger, Borgfeldt.* The heads were made of "biscaloid," an imitation bisque composition. The hair was molded and the doll had glass eyes, open-closed mouth with teeth, composition arms and lower legs on a cloth torso with cloth upper legs. The mark on the head in script had the word "copyright" misspelled: "Gladdie// Copyriht By// Helen W. Jensen//Germany." This doll was first copyrighted as "Happy Ann" according to one report. The name Gladdie was registered in the U.S. for dolls by Borgfeldt. Some of the Gladdies had a mama voice. Four hts. 16, 18, 20, and 23 in. (40.5, 45.5, 51, and 58.5 cm.).

Gladeye. 1915–21. Name of a cloth doll made by *Imperial Toy Co.* in velveteen or sateen in bright colors. Ht. nearly 20 in. (51 cm.). (See also **Burman.**)

Gladys. 1914. Name of a cloth doll with a celluloid face. The name "Gladys" was on its belt. Priced 19¢.

Gladys. 1930. *Boudoir* doll wearing a silk dress and velvet hat, sold by *Bon Marché.* Ht. 70 cm. (27½ in.).

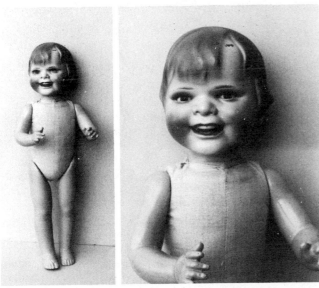

1062A & B. Gladdie has a biscaloid head designed by Helen Jensen. The hair and eyes are molded and painted. The open-closed mouth shows two upper teeth in a laughing expression. There is a flange joint at the neck. Concealed joints at the shoulders and hips connect the composition arms and legs to the cloth torso, which contains a voice box. Mark: Ill. 1063. H. 18 in. (45.5 cm.). *Courtesy of Sybill McFadden.*

1063. Mark on Gladdie dolls designed by Helen Jensen.

1064A & B. Pair of Globe Babies with bisque heads, sleeping eyes, open mouths with teeth. They are on five-piece composition bodies made by Carl Hartmann. Original regional costumes, molded footwear. Mark: Ill. 1065. H. 8½ in. (21.5 cm.). *Coleman Collection.*

Glaser, F. C. & L. 1896–1902. Berlin. Obtained patents pertaining to dolls. (See also **Granz, Leonhard.**)

Glevum Works. See **Roberts Bros.**

Globe Baby. 1898–1927 and later. Line of dolls with bisque or celluloid heads, that were produced and dressed by *Carl Hartmann* who registered the name as a trademark in 1898. In 1914 he advertised Globe *Kämmer & Reinhardt* babies and Globe *Paladin Babies.* The catalog (ca. 1905) of *H. E. Eckart,* a factory agent, described Globe Baby as a specialty

Globe Baby
C. HARTMANN
Germany
3/0
DEP

1059..

Globe Boby
D. R. G.M.
C. Hartmann
Germany
Dep
6/0

1065A & B. Marks on Globe Baby bisque dolls' heads produced by Carl Hartmann.

of *Max Carl.* But Globe Baby definitely belonged to Carl Hartmann as is seen by the marks (see Ills. 1065A & B): "Baby// DEP//Germany// C.3 H.//0."; "Globe Baby// C. Hartmann//Germany//3/0//DEP."; and "10598// Globe Baby //D.R.G.M.//C. Hartmann// Germany//Dep// %." The doll with the incised mark listed last also had a green number with many digits stamped on it which suggested that it might have been made by Gebrüder Heubach. It was wearing its original commercial clothes which included a very short red skirt. The style of the clothes that it was wearing indicated that the doll was made either in the 1920s or later.

The bisque-head Globe Babies had mohair curls, sleeping eyes, open mouth with teeth and jointed five-piece composition bodies with footwear, generally two strap slippers, and socks molded and painted on them. They wore various costumes, often regional clothes representing boys and girls. One pair of these dolls was 8½ in. (21.5 cm.) tall.

1914: *Marshall Field* distributed Globe Babies wholesale. These dolls were dressed as girls or boys and some of them came in baskets with two complete outfits of clothes. Hts. 7, 8½ and 9 in. (18, 21.5 and 23 cm.).★

Globe Doll Works. 1926–29. New York City. Made *Mama* dolls and was licensed by *Voices, Inc.* to use their patented mama voices and criers.

Globe Trotter. See **Spo. (Sportsman).**

Gloria. 1913. Unbreakable dolls representing soldiers, made by *E. & H. Landgrof.*

Gloria. 1927. Name of a doll with composition head, hands and legs, mohair wig, sleeping eyes, crying voice, distributed by *Montgomery Ward.* Ht. 17 in. (43 cm.); priced $1.89.

Gloria. See **Kitts, J. DeLancy.**

Gloria Family. 1930 and later. Gloria, Gloria Lou, and Gloriette were made by *Maxine.*

Gluck, Schmideck & Rosenberg. 1922. Budapest. Produced dolls according to the Ciesliks.

Glukin, William, & Co. Probably 1920s. New York City. Made cloth mask faces with lithographed features for dolls. The necks were stamped with the mark seen in Ill. 1066.

7001 Patent Pending WM. GLUKIN & CO., INC., N.Y.C.

1066. Glukin mark on dolls.

Gmunderdocken. 1800s until the early 1900s. Wooden dolls (docken) representing the people of the Gmunden area, made as a home industry in the *Viechtau* near the Gmunden area of the Balkans. These dolls had movable arms. Hts. 4¾ to 5½ in. (12 to 14 cm.).

1881: Priced 12½¢ doz. wholesale.

Gnome. See **Snak** and **Snik.**

Gobert, Adolphe-Benoit. 1898–99. Paris. Contributed materials, good will, and the rights to *Bébé Colosse,* valued at $8,000, to the *Société Française de Fabrication de Bébés & Jouets* in 1899; according to the research of Mme. Poisson, curator of the Roybet Fould Museum.★

Gobert's Toy Bazar. 1880s. Philadelphia, Pa. Advertised dolls.

Goblin Toy Co. Ltd. Reading, England. Produced wooden dolls similar to the Grödner Tal peg wooden dolls. Their trademark was a circle with a goblin in the middle and the words "Goblin Toy Co. Ltd."

Godchaux. See **Pintel, Henri, and Godchaux, Ernest.**

Godchot. 1927. Paris. Made dolls.

Goebel, William. 1871–1930 and later. Oeslau, Bavaria. Factory was founded in 1871 by Franz Detlev Goebel to make porcelain and earthenware ornamental objects. In 1879 it was inherited by his son William Goebel, whose son Max Louis Goebel took over the factory in 1911. The Ciesliks supplied the following information concerning the various numbers for dolls registered by the William Goebel firm. These numbers indicate the widespread use of porcelain heads made by this factory.

1888: Registered #46 through #54 with and without open mouth and teeth.

1889: Registered a trademark of a doll's head, #Z1.

1892: Registered a trademark of an embossed doll's head.

1893: Registered porcelain dolls' head mold #s 330, 340, and 350.

1894: Advertised 120 models of heads, including shoulder

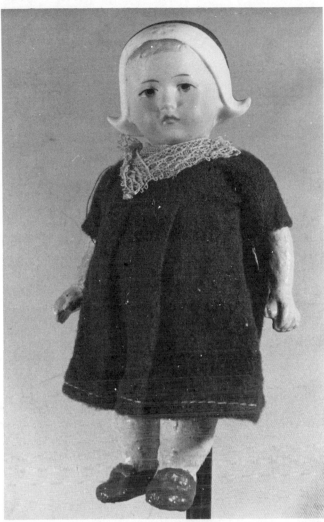

1067. Bisque bonnet head made by William Goebel. The Dutch-style hat has brown flocking with a white band in front decorated with an impressed floral pattern. The socket head is on a five-piece composition body with molded and painted footwear including reddish brown slippers with gold buckles. The original commercial brown flannel dress is high-waisted. Mark: Ill. 1068. H. 6½ in. (16.5 cm.). *Coleman Collection.*

1068

1069

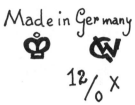

1070

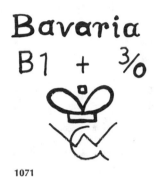

1071

1072

plates. Heads came in 21 sizes. Applied for a German patent (D.R.G.M.) for a porcelain doll's head with eyes and teeth set in.

1908: Advertised all-bisque dolls and baby dolls.

1913: Registered porcelain dolls' head #s 317/3/0, 319, 320/12/0, 321, 322/13/0.

1914: Registered porcelain babies and porcelain dolls' heads.

1921–32: Registered porcelain dolls' head mold #s 106, 107, 110, 111, 114, 122, 123, 124, 125, 126.

1073

K.L. 839 A

1074

1068–1074. Marks on bisque head dolls made by William Goebel.

The number 126 is usually associated with *Kämmer & Reinhardt-Simon & Halbig,* but here it is William Goebel. More than one company often registered the same number.

Among the numbers found on William Goebel bisque heads were K 7 3/0; B 5 – 3¾; B 1 + 0½. The latter was on a doll dressed as *Bécassine.* Some of their marks included a "K" for Knabe (boy) or an "M" for Madchen (girl).★

Goerlich, Karl, & Co. 1923–24. Berlin and London. Agent for *Rolf Berlich* dolls and *Maha* dolls made in Waltershausen.★

Goetz, C., & Co. 1896–98. Hildburghausen, Thür. Manufactured dolls; the factory employed 16 people.

Goggles. See **Eyeglasses.**

Göhring, Max. 1918–30 and later. Oberlind near Sonneberg, Thür. Manufactured dolls. Used *Mago Puppen* as a trade name.

1927: Advertised character dolls and *Mama* dolls, dressed and undressed.★

Gold Dust Twins. 1920s. Brown stockinet twin dolls made by *Nelke* and used as premiums by the Fairbanks Soap Co., maker of Gold Dust Soap Powder. Ht. 4½ in. (11.5 cm.).

Gold Herz. See **Schmidt, Bruno.**

Gold Medal Baby (Gold Medal Prize Baby). 1911–15. The head was modeled by *Helen Trowbridge* from a real baby and was copyrighted by *Horsman* in 1911. The doll had a composition head and hands, painted hair, and eyes that looked straight ahead. The cloth body with bent legs was cork stuffed. Later the name was applied to a line of baby dolls.

1912: Came dressed in short or long baby dresses; when it was in a long dress a ½ was added to the size number but the prices remained the same.

GOLD MEDAL BABY, 1912			
Size No.	Height in.	cm.	Price doz. wholesale
0	Junior size		$ 4.25
1	12	30.5	$ 8.50
2	14	35.5	$13.50
3	16	40.5	$21.00
5	23	58.5 (life size)	$39.00

Numbers 0 and 1 also came in boxes with two complete costumes, one a romper suit and knitted undergarments. These were called "Trousseau Baby."

1913: Came in 20 styles. Priced 50¢ to $10.00.

1914: Became a line of baby dolls, undressed or wearing short dresses or long dresses, which included *Baby Blossom* and *Suck-a-Thumb* baby.★

GOLD MEDAL BABY, 1914		
Style No.	Height in.	cm.
85; G/0	10½	26.5
171; G c/1	13	33
2; 239; 240	16	40.5
3; 4	18	45.5
720; 725	21½	54.5
5; 7	23½	59.5

Goldberg, I. A., & Sons. 1917–20. Birmingham, England. Made dressed and undressed dolls with *British Ceramic* heads on cloth bodies.

Goldberg, Louis. 1924–30 and later. Britain. Advertised dolls in British toy trade journals.

Goldberger, Eugene. 1917–30 and later. Brooklyn, N.Y. Founded by Mr. and Mrs. E. Goldberger. H. B. Eckardt was head of the manufacturing of dolls. From 1923 on they used the trademark "EEGEE." Their mark was a circle with the words "TRADEMARK//EEGEE//DOLLS//MADE IN U.S.A." in it. *Monroe Hitz & Co.* was Goldberger's distributing agent in the late 1920s.

1917: Made dolls in 100 styles priced from 25¢ to $5.00. They included baby dolls in long or in short dresses; romper dolls; eight different Fair dolls. Hts. 25 to 30 in. (63.5 to 76 cm.).

1919: The cloth-body dolls ranged in ht. from 8 to 30 in. (20.5 to 76 cm.). A featured doll was dressed as a boy wearing an overseas cap. The listing of *Globe [Baby]* moving-eye dolls suggests that they may have imported German dolls or simply used this name for their own dolls.

.5. GOLDBERGER

1075A & B. Mark used by E. Goldberger.

The following numbers were advertised for 16 in. (40.5 cm.) dolls: #s 202; 202W; 204; 205; 206 girl dolls; #212 baby doll in floor-length dress. #401W came with or without wig, assorted dresses, and headwear. #502 W had sleeping eyes, mohair wig, dress and hat.

1920: There were 100 numbers in their doll line, with or without sleeping eyes. Featured character ladies included *Mrs. Tom Thumb*. A picture in TOYS AND NOVELTIES showed a Goldberger doll with a net over its wig.

1921: Advertised character dolls with real or mohair wigs and cloth bodies, stuffed with excelsior or cork, with or without composition arms and legs.

1922: Added an import department. The imported dressed dolls had jointed kid bodies. Their own dolls had wood pulp composition heads, hands and feet, painted hair or mohair wigs and cloth bodies. These were character dolls, carnival dolls or *Mama* dolls which came in five sizes.

1923: Produced three million dolls a year. Mama dolls had composition or cloth legs and their cloth bodies were stuffed with cotton. Dressed dolls were 15, 18, and 20 in. (38, 45.5, and 51 cm.) tall. Priced $1.00 to $5.00. Carnival dolls were made of wood-fibre composition in a variety of styles. Produced 75 cases of carnival dolls per day.

1924: Increased their capacity. Advertised dolls with composition heads, arms and legs, sleeping eyes, cloth body. Hts. 11 to 30 in. (28 to 76 cm.); priced 25¢ to $15.00.

1925: New Long Island factory was supposed to triple output. A new line of quality dolls was made for department stores. A *Cigarette Girl* with a felt head and long limbs was featured.

1926: At least three U.S. design patents for Cigarette Girl dolls were obtained by Eugene Goldberger. They brought out *Steppin' Baby*. Also advertised composition baby dolls.

1927: Obtained bisque heads from *Armand Marseille*. These were used to make baby dolls dressed in white with colored wool jackets, caps and bootees. Also advertised slim legged dolls with natural hair wigs and Dutch girl and boy. Goldberger was licensed by *Voices, Inc.* to use their patent mama voices and criers.

1928: Advertised 150 numbers of dolls, including those with painted hair, mohair or real hair wigs, painted or sleeping eyes with hair eyelashes, chubby faces, slender or fat legs, and clothes in either pastel or brilliant colors. Dolls were dressed in silk, wool or cotton in new styles. Baby dolls wore long or short dresses.

1929: Over 75 numbers of dolls, including a bent-limb baby doll with sleeping eyes and full composition legs. Ht. 14 in. (35.5 cm.); price $1.00.

1930: Advertised that they were increasing their lines of dolls which included Mama dolls and Carnival dolls.★

Golden Jane. See **Heizer, Dorothy.**

Goldenberg, Benjamin. 1907–27. New York City. He bought the *American Doll & Toy Co.* and renamed it the *Aetna Doll & Toy Co.* Improving the type of composition used for dolls, he could compete with *Otto Denivelle* and worked with *Horsman* in producing their Can't Break 'Em[†] dolls. In 1919 the Aetna and Horsman companies merged. When E. I. Horsman died, Goldenberg became president of the company but he also died a short time later, in 1927. His obituary stated: "His genius in designing and manufacturing artistic dolls found prompt recognition throughout the country and in foreign lands."★

Goldenberg, L. 1918. England. Made cloth dolls.

Goldenlocks (Golden Locks). 1909–19. Cutout cloth doll made by *Saalfield*. There was a large doll and two similar small ones. Sometimes the doll had a ribbon bandeau in its hair. These dolls were used as premiums by magazines such as COMFORT and WOMAN'S WORLD.

1914: Advertised by *Butler Bros.* and *T. Eaton*. Priced 19¢. (See Ill. 1076.)★

Goldfoot & Sayer, Ltd. 1922–24. London. Producer and importer of dolls, especially from Sonneberg.

Goldherz. See **Schmidt, Bruno.**

Goldhill & Co. 1837–1929. London. Wholesale distributors. Their dolls in 1929 included New Born Babies, Cuddly, dressed and undressed dolls.

Goldie. 1917. Trade name of a doll advertised by the *Columbus Merchandise Co.* It had a composition head with an open mouth with teeth, and molded hair. The arms and tan shoes were composition. Ht. 16 in. (40.5 cm.); priced $17.50 doz. wholesale.

Goldie Girl. 1916. Girl doll with two ribbons across its chest; it wore a hat. This was No. 334 made by *Trion*.

Goldie Locks. 1926. Nursery rhyme doll made by *Jeanette Doll Co.*, in their Jedco line. It was distributed by *Louis Wolf*.

Goldilocks. 1919–20. Trade name of an all-composition doll made by *Jessie M. Raleigh*. It had a wig, a five-piece body with straight legs and it was strung with steel springs. It wore a dress, a pinafore with three bears stenciled on the skirt, and a sunbonnet. Ht. 11½ in. (29 cm.).★

Goldilocks. 1920. Trade name of an all-composition doll with a wig and a pinafore with three bears on it, advertised by *Sears*. Four hts. 13½, 17, 20 and 22 in. (34, 43, 51, and 56 cm.); priced $4.95 to $9.95.

Goldilocks. 1924. *Mama* doll with composition head, arms, and legs, mohair wig, and sleeping eyes, on a cloth body with a silk-like dress and hair bow. Ht. 26 in. (66 cm.); priced $7.39. Distributed by *Montgomery Ward*.

Goldilocks. 1926. Cloth cutout advertising doll of *Kellogg Co.* Ht. 14 in. (35.5 cm.).

Golding, W. E., & Co. 1920. London. Advertised dressed dolls in "china and celluloid" including *Kewpies*. It is not known whether "china" means porcelain or *British Ceramic*.

Goldman, Molly. See **Molly-'es.**

Golden Locks and Her Twin Babies Given To You

Here Is a Splendid Christmas Present for that Little Girl of Yours

Be Sure and Read About the Chocolate and Tea Set Given for Promptness. It Would Look Well on Your Christmas Tree

Just As Big As a Real Baby

You Will Fall In Love With Golden Locks

ONE OF THE TWINS

In every home where there are little girls or boys there should be plenty of dolls. There is no little girl or boy who will not fall in love with GOLDEN LOCKS AND HER TWIN BABIES. The illustrations on this page of Golden Locks and her Twins do not begin to show to you what these dolls really are.

Golden Locks herself is as big as a real live baby. She and her twins are different from any dolls which you have now, and no matter how many dolls you have you should have Golden Locks and Her Twins.

Golden Locks is over two feet high. Baby clothes will fit her and you can bend her legs and arms without fear of breaking them. Just think, she can sit up in a chair or sleep in baby's own bed. You will be proud to have her as a playmate and you will fall in love with the twins. Just think what fun it would be to have a doll family; all of them are practically unbreakable and will stand hard usage for years. These dolls are lots better for little folks than bisque or china dolls, because they will not break. You cannot soil their pretty hair or lose their eyes, and my offer to you makes them within the reach of every girl or boy in every home.

THE OTHER TWIN

Every little girl must have dolls, and many little boys want dolls too, and here is your opportunity to get all three—Golden Locks and her Twins instead of just one doll. You surely will be delighted with these beautiful dolls and many a happy hour can be spent with them.

MY PLAN

I Have a Plan That I Know Will Please You!

Anyone who wants Golden Locks and her Twins may have them by sending one yearly subscription, either new or renewal, to Woman's World for 50c and 15c additional, or 65c in all

SAVE 15 CENTS

If you will put the names and addresses of the heads of five families who have children in their homes on the five lines in the bottom of coupon in right hand corner below, I will credit you with 15 cents, or in other words for this coupon filled in with the names of five persons who are the heads of families where there is a little girl, I will allow you 15 cents credit and I will send you Golden Locks and her Twin Babies and Woman's World for one year for only 50 cents. Remember, this coupon saves you 15 cents. If you don't fill it out it will cost you 65 cents for a year's subscription to Woman's World and Golden Locks and her Twins.

Just fill out the coupon below right away and send it to me, with 50 cents, and it will entitle you to Golden Locks and Her Twin Babies and a year's subscription to Woman's World, and if you write me at once I'll send you one of Golden Locks' own Chocolate and Tea Sets as an extra reward for promptness.

1076. Cutout cloth doll named Goldenlocks (Golden Locks) consists of a large doll over two feet high, and two smaller dolls. This advertisement appeared in WOMAN'S WORLD, December, 1913.

Goldman, Meyer. 1931. Philadelphia, Pa. Registered in March 1931 Molly-'es as a trademark for dolls' clothes.

Goldmann, Franziska. 1907–10. Vienna. Listed in an Austrian directory under Dolls and Dolls' Heads.

Goldsmith, Alfred. 1924–29. London. Imported dolls, especially celluloid dolls. He was the sole agent for *Seligmann & Mayer*. He sold only to wholesalers. By 1924 he claimed he had 2,000 *Waltershausen* dolls; 2,000 *Mama* dolls: 127,500 dressed dolls; *kewpies;* etc.

Goldsmith, Philip. 1870–94. Cincinnati, Ohio, and Covington, Ky. Made cloth bodies and composition heads. Both Philip Goldsmith and his wife Miss Heller were born in Germany and came to this country where they were married. They lived first in Milwaukee, then Chicago where they had a fancy goods store, then moved to Covington where he made dolls and his wife made clothes for the dolls. Goldsmith dolls can usually be traced back to the area west of the Allegheny Mountains and east of the Mississippi River.

The Goldsmith patented corset was often part of the body and had braid or rickrack trimming in contrasting colors. The color of the corset usually corresponded with the color in the footwear but corsets of the same color as the rest of the body have been found. A few of the corsets had stamped closures but the 1885 patent provided string for lacing up the corset. A unique feature of the patented Goldsmith corset was that one of the top ends of the laces was not fastened down so that theoretically the lacing could be pulled tighter. Not all Goldsmith dolls have the patented corsets on the body but they can be identified usually by the leather hands with sewed fingers, stiffened with small wooden sticks. Another indication was the high curved top boots with beige colored string lacings and a pair of string tassels at the top. These boots were made of leather, imitation leather or a cotton fabric, generally red, blue, or black.

There was great variation in the stockings. Some were plain, some had circular stripes, some had vertical stripes, some had plaids or checks. Goldsmith must have used whatever fabric was available. A few of the Goldsmith legs had painted or stamped floral designs on a plain fabric. The boots on these dolls with floral designs generally were leather, had more crossings of the laces and were possibly earlier than the dolls with other types of legs. (See Ill. 374 in THE COLLECTOR'S BOOK OF DOLLS' CLOTHES.)

Sometimes the entire lower leg was covered with the material of the stocking; at other times the knee-high stocking was separate above the boot and worn over the leg itself. Usually a narrow band of cloth in a contrasting color encircled the stocking near the top to represent a garter.

The bodies were often stamped with the size number and the ones with the patented corset usually had the patent date stamped under the shoulder head. Some of the Goldsmith dolls have been found with a purple stamp of the name "My Dolly" in Gothic style letters on the front of the body just under the shoulder plate.

Various types of heads have been found on Goldsmith bodies, including china heads and bisque heads, but the majority were composition. Among the latter were *Cuno & Otto Dressel* heads and *American Muslin* heads. Several bisque swivel neck shoulder heads similar to the head shown in Ill. 1053 in the first COLLECTOR'S ENCYCLOPEDIA OF DOLLS have been found on Goldsmith bodies. Heads of this type were also found on marked *Jumeau* bodies which suggests a possible French origin. It is known that French porcelain heads were imported to the Cincinnati area at the time that Goldsmith was making his bodies but before the patent corsets. (See **Arnoldt.**)

1889: Goldsmith bodies were distributed by *Montgomery Ward.* The bodies came in five hts.: 10, 12½, 15, 17, and 20 in. (25.5, 31.5, 38, 43, and 51 cm.); priced 20¢ to 60¢.

1893: *Horsman* advertised Goldsmith muslin bodies with corsets kid arms, imitation shoes, and stockings. They came in 12 sizes, numbers 0–11; priced $1.35 to $8.00 doz. wholesale. (See Ills. 1077–1080.)★

Goldstein, Joseph. 1922–28. New York City. Factory representative and manufacturer of dolls.

1926: Advertised 50 sizes and styles of bisque infant dolls as well as bisque-head baby dolls.

1927: Made *Baby Betty* dolls.★

Golf Boy. 1904. Bisque head doll; wore golf suit with knickers, vest, golf stockings, and golf hat, and carried a golf stick. Ht. 14 in. (35.5 cm.).

Golf Boy. 1926. Doll with composition head, arms, and legs, cloth body; dressed in a black and white plaid suit with knickers and matching cap. Over his shoulder was slung a golf bag holding one golf club. Ht. 14½ in. (37 cm.); priced $1.25. This doll was distributed by Charles William.

Golf Boy. 1927–28. Was shown in the *Lenci* Catalog. He wore a pull over, visored cap, knickers formed by square patches, and carried a golf stick. Style No. 300 F. Ht. 17½ in. (44.5 cm.).

Golf Girl. 1917–18. Character doll designed by *Hilda Cowham*, manufactured by *Laurie Hansen*.

Golliwog. See **Gow.**

Golliwogg (Golliwog, Gollywog). 1890s–1930 and later. According to Margaret Hutchings, in the late 1800s when the British occupied Alexandria, Egypt, native workers were called "GHULS" and they wore armbands bearing the letters W.O.G.S. (Working On Government Service). British troops began calling these workers "Golliwogs," and when dolls representing them appeared and were taken back to Britain as souvenirs, the name remained with them. Then Florence Upton wrote her popular children's stories about Golliwoggs (she used two "gs") and Robinson adopted them as the advertising symbol for their marmalade.

1902: Advertised by *Gamage* in a small and large size; priced 12¢ and 25¢.

1905: *Wanamaker* advertised Golliwogs. Hts. 7½, 10½, and 11 in. (19, 26.5, and 28 cm.); priced 10¢ to 50¢.

1906: Gamage advertised six sizes; priced 12¢ to 88¢.

1911–16: Golliwoggs made by *Steiff* were called *Gow*.

1914: *Atlas Manufacturing Co.* made Golliwogs.

  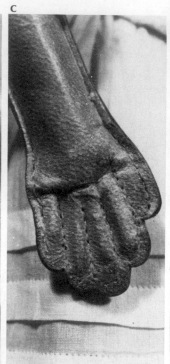 

1077A, B, C, & D. Composition shoulder head, probably German, on a cloth body made by Philip Goldsmith. It has a blond wig, stationary brown glass eyes and a closed mouth. A leather lower arm of this doll is shown in Ill. 1077C and a leather boot and circular striped cotton stocking are shown in Ill. 1077D. For a description of the other clothes see THE COLLECTOR'S BOOK OF DOLLS' CLOTHES, Ill. 362. H. 26 in. (66 cm.). *Coleman Collection.*

1915: *Birkenhead Toy Factory* made cloth Golliwogs.

1916: *Gray & Nicholls* made Golliwoggs, as did *Sunlight, Sieve & Co.,* who called their dolls Gollywogs.

1917: *Alliance Toy Co., Hammond Manufacturing Co.* and *Star Manufacturing Co.* all made and/or advertised Golliwoggs.

1921: *Dean* made a Golliwogg named *Wooly Wally.*

THE PRACTICAL TOYMAKER published directions for a homemade Golliwogg. The head was of painted and varnished plaster, hair was inserted, the limbs and body were on a wire frame and the feet were made of cardboard.

1923: *Mabel Bland-Hawkes* made an Egyptian Golliwog.

1929: *Chad Valley* made a Golliwogg with round eyes and a broad mouth. This black doll had a fur plush wig and wore a red, blue, and yellow satinette suit.

CHAD VALLEY GOLLIWOGGS, 1929		
Size No.	Height in.	cm.
629/1	10½	26.5
629/2	12	30.5
629/3	15	38
629/4	17	43

1930: *Ouida Pearse* gave instructions for making Golliwoggs in her book SOFT TOY MAKING.★

Goo Goo.† See **Kämmer & Reinhardt** and **Roguish Eyes.**

Goo Goo Petling. 1913–20. Trade name for cloth dolls made by *Dean.* In 1920 *Teddie* and *Peggie,* cutout cloth dolls, were part of the Goo Goo series.

Good Sisters. See **Three Little Sisters.**

Goodman H., & Sons. 1929. New York City. Registered *Goody* as a U.S. trademark for dolls.

Goodman, L. & A. L. (Goodman, Louis). 1922–26. London. Made *Goody Goody* line of dolls. Sole London agent for *Gerbaulet Frères* and *Edmund Edelmann.*★

Goodman, Leon. 1926. Philadelphia, Pa. Obtained two U.S. Design patents for dolls.

Goodman, Max. 1925–26. New York City. Obtained a U.S. design patent for a *Cigarette Girl* doll. The doll had fuzzy hair and wore a pants suit without a belt. The cuffs and pockets had horizontal striped trimming.

Goodwyn, Lady. 1926–27. Los Angeles, Calif. Made dolls including life-sized ones with long limbs. Oil paint was used for the features. Wigs were of real hair. The dolls and their clothes were of silk. TOYS AND NOVELTIES reported that these dolls cost up to $3,000.

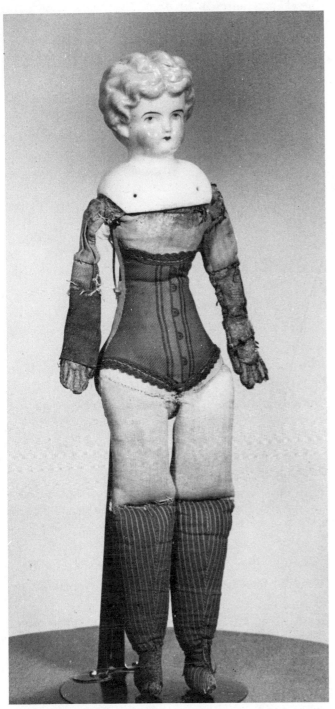

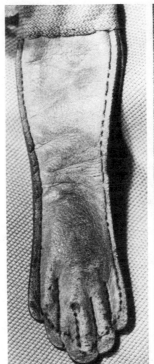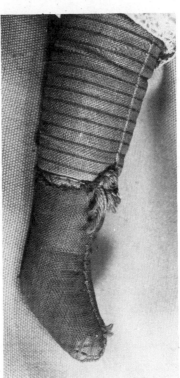

1079A. Hand on a cloth body made by Philip Goldsmith. The doll, including its composition head produced by Cuno and Otto Dressel, is shown in Ill. 828. The fingers and thumb of the leather hand are indicated by stitching and stiffened with the insertion of pieces of wood. The fingers on this hand are longer and thinner than those shown in Ill. 1077C. The lower legs are similar to those in Ill. 1077D. except that these are blue where the others are red and these legs have blue garter bands around the top of the stockings which were not found on the other legs. *Coleman Collection.*

1079B. Leg on a cloth body made by Philip Goldsmith. The entire doll is shown in Ill. 351 in THE COLLECTOR'S BOOK OF DOLLS' CLOTHES. This entire lower leg is made of the circular-striped red and white fabric and has a seam up both the front and back. The boots are red cotton cloth and have the pair of string tassels at the top but the lacings have disappeared. Other boots have been found made of leather or oilcloth, and the stockings of the doll with corset bodies are generally plain red or blue cotton cloth. *Coleman Collection.*

1078. China shoulder head on a cloth body made by Philip Goldsmith. The corset is only in the front and has stamped fastenings but it is edged with real braid. The leather fingers are stiffened with the usual insertions of tiny sticks. The entire lower leg and foot are made of striped fabric over which the boot is placed. This is not the corset body patented in 1885, but its similarities and Cincinnati Provenance indicate that it probably was made by Goldsmith. A similar stamped body has been found with the purple stamp "My Doll." *Private collection.*

My Dolly.

1080. Mark found stamped on the upper shoulder of a cloth body made in the same manner as Philip Goldsmith's dolls' bodies.

Goody. 1929. Trademark registered in U.S. by *H. Goodman & Sons* for dolls.

Goody Goody Dolls. 1923–26. Line of dolls made by *L. & A. L. Goodman.* They came with and without voices and bore the trademark "Goody//Goody//Series" in an oval.★

Goodyear Rubber Co. 1839–90. New Haven, Conn., and New York City. Made dolls and dolls' heads of rubber. In the 1881 catalog they showed nine styles of naked dolls, including two with joints and three male sexed; 25 styles of shoulder heads; six dressed babies (see Ill. 2258); six dressed as girls, including *Dolly Varden;* and three dressed as "Boy Soldiers."

Goodyear Toy Co. 1923–30 and later. New York City. Manufactured *Mama* dolls and infant dolls. Heads and costumes were designed by *Madame Blanche.* Factory agent was *S.O. Ludwig.*

1924: Mama dolls were with and without sleeping eyes. Ht. 13 in. (33 cm.) and up.

1930: *My Darling* was one of the new dolls in their baby line.★

Google (Googly) Eyes. See **Roguish Eyes.**

Goo-Goo. 1923. Rubber doll made by *Pneumatic Toy Co.* When the body was squeezed, air was forced through a sound box in the neck. It was claimed that one store sold nearly 10,000 of these dolls in two months.

Gordon, Lady Duff. 1918 and other years. A famous British couturière.

1918: One of her assistants designed dresses for *Trion* based on imported models, according to Trion. (See also **Rauser, Mrs. Katherine A.**)

Gordon, M. 1904 and probably other years. Boston, Mass. Advertised all-bisque dolls. Ht. 4 in. (10 cm.); priced 39¢ to 42¢ doz. wholesale. Bisque-head dolls, wig, glass eyes, jointed composition body, wearing a chemise. Hts. 7, 9½, and 21½ in. (18, 24, and 54.5 cm.); priced 42¢ to $1.98 doz. wholesale. Dressed bisque-head dolls, with wig, sleeping eyes and fully jointed body. Ht. 14 in. (35.5 cm.), priced $4.10 doz. wholesale. A similar doll not fully jointed. Ht. 13½ in. (34 cm.); priced $3.90 doz. wholesale.

When the dolls had stationary glass eyes, hts. 6 and 10½ in. (15 and 26.5 cm.), price was 42¢ and $1.95 doz. wholesale. Kid-body dolls with bisque heads, wigs, sleeping eyes, "real shoes and stockings." Ht. 17¼ in. (44 cm.); priced $4.29 doz. wholesale. These dolls bore *Kestner* marks. A similar doll but poorer quality, with stationary eyes, imitation stockings and paper shoes. Ht. 13½ in. (34 cm.); priced $1.98 doz. wholesale.

A bisque shoulder head with molded hair and painted eyes on a cloth body. Ht. 10 in. (25.5 cm.); priced 85¢ doz. wholesale. A dressed cloth doll. Ht. 13 in. (33 cm.); priced 83¢ doz. wholesale. A *worsted doll* with a bell on its pointed hat. Ht. 13 in. (33 cm.); priced 85¢ doz. wholesale.

Gordon Highlander. 1899. Doll dressed in Scottish costume with fur cap and claymore, distributed wholesale by *Butler Bros.* Ht. 8¼ in. (21 cm.).

Gordon Works. See **Hancock, S., & Sons.**

Gorgellino, Francesco. 1918–24. Turin, Italy. Applied for Italian and German patents (D.R.P.) for mechanical dolls.

Goria, Lamberto. 1920s. Italy. Designed dolls and/or ceramics for *Lenci.* He was a painter and sculptor, born in 1863 in Tortona.

Gorleston (Toy) Industry. 1920–22. London and Gorleston on the Sea, England. Listed in the British buyer's directory under Dolls. They made cloth dolls including those with celluloid faces. Their sole selling agent was J. B. Newman in 1920.

Göschel, Johana. 1853 and possibly other years. Vienna. Distributed dolls.

Goss, Gladys. 1920–21. Nevada, Mo. Obtained a U.S. patent for a jointed cloth doll.★

Gotha Porzellanfabrik. See **Pfeffer, Fritz.**

Gotham Toy Co. 1923–24. Listed under Dolls in TOYS AND NOVELTIES.

Gothania. See **Puppenfabrik Gothania.**

Gotthelf Firm. 1873–1929. Remscheid, Germany. Made dolls including baby dolls and *Ulla Puppe.*

1926: Belonged to the *German Manufacturers Assoc.* in New York City.★

Gottschaldt, Hermann. 1899. Ilmenau, Thür. Applied for a German patent (D.R.G.M.) pertaining to the joints of a doll.

Gottschalk & Davis. 1888–1926. London and Manchester, England. Imported and distributed dolls.

1915: Advertised dolls with composition or celluloid faces, molded hair, plush bodies; and stuffed calico dolls without any molding. There were nine models of the latter. One sold for 2¢, five sold for 12¢ and three models ht. 22 in. (56 cm.), sold for 25¢.

1926: Advertised Japanese celluloid toys.

Gottwald, Johannes. 1925–30 and later. Vienna. Made dolls.

Gotze, Berta. 1897. Berlin. Applied for a German patent (D.R.G.M.) pertaining to a cloth doll that could stand erect.

Gotzke, Gustav. See **Nöckler & Tittel.**

Goubeaux, M. 1921–30 and later. Paris. Made and repaired dolls of all makes. Distributed wigs and dolls' clothes.★

Goujon, Mme. Pierre. 1916. France. She founded Les Veuves de la Guerre (Widows of the War), an organization whose function was to make dolls. Mme. Goujon claimed that she dressed the dolls in simpler and more attractive clothes than had been done in the past.

Gould & Baum. 1920. U.S.A. Claimed that they made sleeping eyes that equaled the appearance of the German eyes but were more durable and less expensive.

Gourdel Vales & Co. 1921. London. Herbert Nalty doing

POUPÉES, PAR Mᵐᵉ PIERRE GOUJON
(Œuvre des « Veuves de la Guerre ».)

1081. Dolls created by Mme. Pierre Goujon in her workshop which employed widows of World War I. Their work was chiefly dressing the dolls. *Photo from LA RENAISSANCE DE LA POUPÉE FRANÇAISE by Jeanne Doin, in 1916.*

business as Gourdel Vales & Co. registered a French trademark of a *Kewpie*-type figure, with arms raised. Over the figure were the words *"Thumbs up!// Haut les Mains!"* and under the figure *"Touche du Bois// Touch Wood."*★

Gove Manufacturing Co. 1928–29. Williamsport, Pa. Helen N. Gove doing business as Gove Manufacturing Co. registered *UNEKE* in an ellipse as a U.S. trademark for dolls.

Gow. (Golliwogg). Before 1911–16. Name of a jointed felt black *Golliwogg* made by *Steiff* and distributed in the U.S. by *Borgfeldt.* It had a single line curved mouth, separate fingers and large feet. Seven hts.: 28, 35, 43, 50, 60, 80, and 100 cm. (11, 14, 17, 19½, 23½, 31½, and 39½ in.). The smallest size cost 60¢ in Germany in 1911 and $1.40 in New York in 1913. Gamage sold the four smallest sizes of these dolls in 1913; priced 62¢ to $1.88.

Gowdy, John. 1916–17. Philadelphia, Pa. Obtained a U.S. patent for a tumbling doll with a two part tubular body.

Gr. (Grosspapa, Grandpa). Before 1906–11 and later. Felt doll made by *Steiff,* representing a grandfather that bore a strong resemblance to *Foxy Grandpa.* It had long feet, a bulbous nose with spectacles perched on top and a broad smile. It wore a high collar shirt, a red bow tie, a beige vest with three buttons, a blue suit—the coat having notched lapels and two pockets—a small white brimmed hat, beige spats and black shoes. This doll was portrayed as a character called "the Professor" in a 1929 English translation of the French book PIERRE PONS, illustrated by Paul Guignebault.

1906: Distributed by *Gamage,* priced 62¢.

1911: Listed in Steiff catalog. Ht. 35 cm. (14 in.); priced 85¢.

Graaff-Reinet. See **Laubascher's Puppen Fabrik.**

Grab, Berta. 1907–10. Vienna. Listed in an Austrian directory under Dolls and Dolls' heads.

Grabo, Max. 1909–30 and later. Berlin. Made and exported dolls.

1930: Advertised dressed and undressed dolls, celluloid dolls, baby dolls and dolls' outfits including knit wear.

Graefe, Otto. 1912–13. New York City. Imported *Minerva* metal dolls' heads and *Knockabout* dolls.

Gräfenthal Porzellanfabrik. 1861–1885 and later. Grafenthal, Thür. A porcelain factory founded with the Duke's concession. It was operated by Unger, a modeler; Schneider, who had previously been at Wallendorf employed as the shopkeeper; and Hutschenreuther. Before 1885 the name was Schneider & Hutschenreuther but in 1885 the factory came into the possession of the heirs of Schneider. The Sonneberg Museum had a china shoulder head with molded hair and glass eyes which they attributed to this factory. The height of the shoulder head was 15 cm. (6 in.).

Grams, August. 1927–29. Judenbach, Thür. Manufactured and exported felt dolls and *Mama* dolls. The dolls came dressed or undressed.

Grand Bazar de L'Hotel-de-Ville. See **L'Hotel de Ville.**

Grand Doll Manufacturing Co. 1923. Brooklyn, N.Y. Manufactured dolls.

1082A & B. All-felt doll named Gr. for Grandpa, made by Steiff around 1910. Doll has wool hair sewed onto its head, shoe button type eyes, felt eyeglasses, a bulbous nose, and is dressed as Foxy Grandpa. H. 14½ in. (37 cm.). *Coleman Collection.*

Grande, Giovanni. 1920s. Italy. He worked for *Lenci,* was involved with the Lenci Ceramics and perhaps contributed to Lenci doll designs. He was a painter and sculptor, born in 1887, died 1937. One of his works was in an Art Gallery in Florence, Italy.

Grander Doll Co. 1923–24. New York City. Made dressed *Mama* dolls with composition heads, arms, and legs, with or without wigs, and with sleeping eyes. Hts. 16 in. (40.5 cm.). Priced $1.00 and up.★

Grandjean. 1887–90. Paris. Made jointed bébés with bisque heads, probably made by *Delcroix.* Examples found have had pressed bisque heads and were small dolls.★

Grandma and Red Riding Hood. 1927. One of the *Twinjoy* line of cloth dolls created by *Mrs. Berry Kollin.* One side of the doll was dressed as Grandma with horn-rimmed spectacles, the other side represented Red Riding Hood. A round tag identified this doll.

Grandpa. See **Gr.**

Granic (Gra-Nic). 1917. Line of dolls made by *Gray & Nicholls.*

Gräning, Eduard. 1924–27. Leipzig, Saxony. Obtained a German patent (D.R.P.) for a moving doll.

Granitol. 1909. Name used by *Carl Hoffmeister* for imitation leather bodies for dolls.

Grant, McEwan & Co. 1924. Listed in British toy trade journal under Dolls.

Granz, Leonhard. 1902. Paris. He assigned to *Glaser* his German patent (D.R.G.M.) for a doll whose arm movement operated its voice.

Gratieux, M. Fernand. 1919. Billancourt near Paris. Registered several trademarks in France for dolls and toys. These were all in an ellipse; one was "F.G."; another was "Gratieux//Paris"; and the third was *Tout Va Bien* (All goes well). This F.G. must not be confused with the *François Gaultier* (Gauthier) F.G.

Graves, Charles Watson. 1892–98. Newark, N.J. Obtained two German patents (D.R.P.) for dolls' joints. Emil Verpillier[†] was a partner in these patents.★

Graves, Jennie H. See **Vogue Doll Shoppe.**

Gray, Harold. 1926–29. U.S.A. The designs for dolls were based on cartoon characters drawn by Harold Gray. The *Live Long Toy Co.* made oilcloth dolls representing *Little Orphan Annie* and *Emily Marie.* Little Orphan Annie was also made in all-bisque.

Gray (Grey), Jane, Co. 1915–29. New York City. Designed and made cloth-body dolls, including *Kuddles* (Cuddles) cloth dolls.

1927: Designed Easter dolls, The *Poster Girl,* and *Black Bottom Doll;* the latter was made by *Gerling.*★

Gray & Dudley Co. 1918 and probably other years. Nashville, Tenn. Distributed dolls.

1918: Advertised 33 style nos. with composition heads, 11 had wigs, 22 had molded hair. Hts. 9½ to 17 in. (24 to 43 cm.); priced 40¢ to $1.50. Two similar dolls were dressed in silk rompers, one had molded hair. Ht. 13½ in. (34 cm.); priced 87½¢. The other doll had a wig. Ht. 14 in. (35.5 cm.); priced $1.50.

Gray & Nicholls. 1902–20. Liverpool, London. Made *Granic* (Gra-Nic) line of dolls including *Eskimo* dolls and *Golliwoggs.* Their dolls were cloth or "china" which probably meant *British Ceramic.* Proprietors were Foster, Blackett and Wilson.

Greek Dolls. There was a doll producing industry in Athens around 1914. After World War I, the *Near East Industries,* with headquarters in Athens, made dolls.

Green (Lakey, Lackai; Footman). 1911. Felt art character doll made by *Steiff.* It wore a felt livery outfit and came in assorted colors. Ht. 43 cm. (17 in.); priced $2.18.

Green, Mr. J. 1930. Designed *Lialla* dolls and *Valencia* dolls for *Penn Stuffed Toy Co.*

Green Parrot. 1700s. London. Advertised "fine babies" (dolls).

Greenaway. 1907–19. Cutout cloth doll made by *Saalfield.*

1914: Distributed by *Butler Bros.* They made a 15 in. (38 cm.) doll; priced 79¢ doz. wholesale.★

Greenwich Village Artist. 1926. Name of a long-limbed *Boudoir* doll made by *Kitty Fleischmann,* dressed in a cretonne smock, black trousers, and artist's-type hat.

Greenwich Village Bud and Buddie (Student).[†] See **Buds and Buddies.**

Gregg, Marjorie T. 1914–15. Brookline, Mass. Obtained a U.S. patent for making dolls' bodies by winding a strip of material over a wire frame.

Gregori-Olivier. 1879. France. Handled dolls named *Poupée Nana.*

Greif Puppenkunst. 1927–28. Dresden, Germany. Made felt and plush art dolls, some of which had celluloid heads or bisque heads made by *Ernst Heubach.*

"Greif."
Puppenkunst
Germany
7/0

1083. Mark used by the Greif Puppenkunst factory.

Greiner, Alexandre. 1925–30. Steinach, Thür. Produced dolls and belonged to the *German Manufacturers Assoc.* in New York City.

Greiner, Anton. 1910. Sonneberg, Thür. Applied for a German patent (D.R.G.M.) for a baby doll with a voice.

Greiner, E. 1915. Heidersbach, Suhl, Thür. Applied for a German patent (D.R.G.M.) for dolls' moving eyelids.

Greiner, G., & Co. 1924–29. London. Sole British agent for *Steiff, Cuno & Otto Dressel,* and Bayerische Celluloidwarenfabrik *(Albert Wacker).*

1926: Advertised *Jutta* dolls and baby dolls, *Rock-a-Bye* and *Sonny* baby dolls, *Susie* dolls, dressed and undressed dolls.

Greiner, Ludwig. 1840–74. Philadelphia, Pa. 1874–83, Ludwig's sons, Greiner Bros., were the successors; 1890–1900, Francis B. Knell (Knell Bros.) was the successor. Made composition reinforced with cloth shoulder heads for dolls, usually with molded hair and painted eyes. A few marked Greiner dolls had glass eyes. The heads when made into dolls usually formed large dolls. A 13 in. (33 cm.) doll is about the smallest size. ★

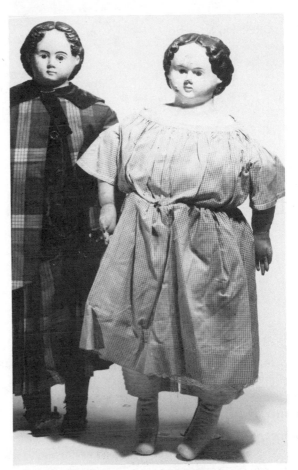

1085. Two Greiner papier-mâché shoulder head dolls. They have molded and painted hair and eyes, homemade cloth bodies and clothes. H. of each doll 31 in. (78.5 cm.). *Courtesy of Sotheby Parke Bernet Inc., N.Y.*

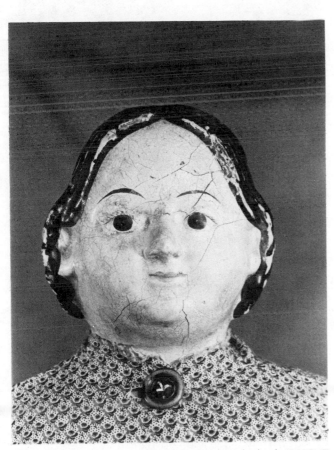

1084. Composition shoulder head stamped on the back "PATENT HEAD" which is believed to have been an early Ludwig Greiner mark. It has molded corkscrew curls, painted brown eyes, a cloth body with leather arms. H. 25 in. (63.5 cm.). H. of shoulder head 6 in. (15 cm.). *Coleman Collection.*

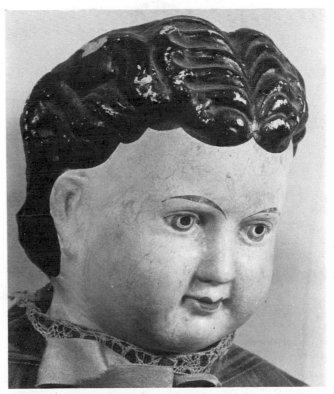

1086. Greiner shoulder head with an 1858 mark has molded and painted black hair, painted blue eyes, closed mouth and a cloth body. Clothes are contemporary with the doll. H. 20½ in. (52 cm.). H. of shoulder head 5 in. (12.5 cm.). *Courtesy of Z. Frances Walker.*

1087A PATENT HEAD 1087B

GREINER'S
PATENT DOLL HEADS.
No. 8
Pat. Mar. 30, '58. Ext.'72
Factory 414 N. 4th St. Phila.

GREINER'S PATENT HEADS.
No. O.
1088 Pat. March 30th, '58.

GREINER
Everlasting
1089 Doll Heads

1087–1089. Marks found on the back shoulder of Greiner papier-mâché dolls.

Greiner, N. 1898. Steinach, Thür. Made dolls.

Greiner, Richard. 1903. Sonneberg, Thür. Applied for a German patent (D.R.G.M.) relating to a doll's body.

Greiner & Co. 1860–1929. Steinach, Thür. Manufactured kid-body dolls and dolls' bodies.★

1090. Mark used by Greiner & Co.

Gre-Poir, Inc. 1927–30 and later. New York City. Produced the line of Gre-Poir dolls under the directions of I. Alvin Grey. According to Sybill McFadden, Eugenie Poir of Paris designed these dolls which came with molded heads made of felt or a textile mask face. The name Eugenie Poir did not appear in Paris directories of this period. These dolls had mohair wigs, painted features, eyes glancing to the side, and hair upper eyelashes set into the fabric. The bodies were of pink cloth, jointed at the neck, shoulders and hips; thumbs were separate, the other fingers were indicated by sewing. The dolls carried a square tag. Hts. 16, 19, and 23½ in. (40.5, 48, and 59.5 cm.) have been reported.

1929: Gre-Poir dolls were included in a catalog issued by *William E. Peck & Co.* of American toy lines exported to the British Empire.

1091. Cloth Gre-Poir doll. It has a light brown wig, painted brown eyes looking to the side, eye shadow, closed mouth, and joints at the neck, shoulders, and hips. The mitten hands have fingers indicated by sewing. Original clothes. H. 17 in. (43 cm.). *Courtesy of Estelle Johnston.*

1930: Registered in the U.S. the trademark *Balsam Baby* for cloth body dolls.

Gre-Poir became part of *The French Doll Makers.* Jan Foulke reported a tag reading "French Doll Makers//an ORIGINAL//Eugenie Poir// Model// Bimba//'I can be cleaned with Art Gum'//New York//Paris."

Greta. 1928. Name of a doll with bisque head, sleeping eyes, wig, ball-jointed composition body. The doll wore a lace trimmed chemise and was distributed by *Gamage.* Seven hts.: 11, 14, 16½, 19, 23, 24½, and 31 in. (28, 35.5, 42, 48, 58.5, 62 and 79 cm.) tall.

Gretchen. 1908–11. Cutout cloth doll made by *Saalfield.* It had a printed Dutch girl costume. Ht. 7½ in. (19 cm.).

Gretchen. 1911. Trade name of a ball jointed doll made by *A. Wislizenus.*

Gretchen. 1911–12. Doll with composition head designed by *Helen Trowbridge* and copyrighted by *Horsman.*

It had molded bobbed hair and bangs, painted eyes, smiling open-closed mouth with teeth, and appeared to have come from the same mold as *Daisy Dimple, Hans, Happy Hiram, Jack Tar, Prince Charlie,* and *Robbie Reefer.*

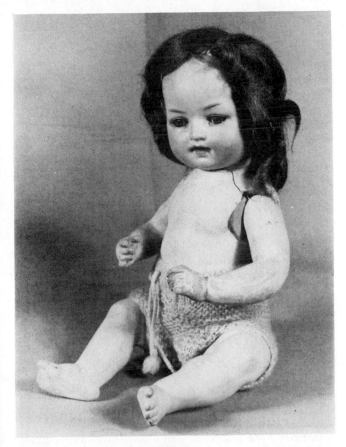

1092A & B. Bisque character head incised Grete has a wig, sleeping blue eyes, an open mouth with two upper teeth and a bent-limb composition baby body. Mark: Ill. 1093. H. 14 in. (35.5 cm.). *Coleman Collection.*

It was number 141 and wore a Dutch-type costume with a waistline apron, striped stockings, and felt shoes in the shape of wooden shoes. Its mate was Hans.

Gretchen. 1912–13. Name used by *Selchow & Righter* for a flat faced cloth doll stuffed with cork and sawdust. Its ankle length dress with a high neckline was similar to the dress worn by *Dolly Dimple.* Ht. 12½ in. (31.5 cm.); priced 10¢ retail, 80¢ doz. wholesale.

Gretchen. 1912–13. Cutout cloth doll produced by *Selchow & Righter* as a "Dutch Doll." Ht. 8 in. (20.5 cm.); priced 40¢ a doz. wholesale.

Gretchen. 1915. Name given by MODERN PRISCILLA to a baby doll with composition head and hands that resembled *Horsman's Gold Medal Babies.* Directions were given in MODERN PRISCILLA for making a wardrobe of clothes for this doll.

Gretchen. 1925–26. *Lenci* felt doll #165/2 dressed in Tyrolean regional costume with a wide brimmed hat trimmed with flowers. The doll carried a handkerchief. Ht. 29½ in. (75 cm.).

Gretchen. Cutout advertising doll on sugar sacks of *Sea Island Sugar.* Printed clothes of a Dutch girl. Ht. 8 in. (20.5 cm.).

Grete. 1916–24. Name of felt doll made by *Steiff.* In 1916 it came in five hts.: 28, 35, 43, 50, and 60 cm. (11, 14, 17, 19½, and 23½ in.). In 1924 it came only in the first three heights.

Grete. Name incised on bisque character heads. See Ills. 1092 and 1093. The identification of the "P M" initials has not been confirmed as yet.

P.M.

Grete

O.

1093. Mark on baby doll named Grete.

Grete. See Life Like Babyland Dolls.

Gretel. 1917–18. Doll representing a little Alsatian girl as drawn by *Hansi* has painted eyes and hair, body jointed at neck, shoulders, and hips. It was dressed as a school girl in velvet and taffeta with large Alsatian bow on its head. In one hand is a school slate with the signature of Hansi on it and in the other hand is an umbrella. It was made of a substance called *Prialytine* and was distributed by *P. J. Gallais & Cie.* who published Hansi's books. It was also distributed by Marshall Field. Gretel was a mate to *Yerri.* Ht. 8½ in. (21.5 cm.).

1094A & B. All-Prialytine doll named Gretel based on the design of the artist Hansi and representing an Alsatian school girl during World War I. It has molded and painted hair, eyes, and footwear. The mouth extends in curved lines on each side to show a broad smile. The original Alsatian costume is made of silk and velveteen.

Accessories include a folded umbrella, a school slate and sponge. On the front of the slate is written in script, "Vive la//France!//Gretel" and on the back is "Hansi" and the Gallais trademark. See Ill. 1001. The original box lid has the name Gretel and a picture of Gretel drawn by Hansi. H. 8½ in. (21.5 cm.). *Coleman Collection.*

1094C. Mark on Gretel dolls indicating the name of the material of which they are made.

Gretel. 1924. Name of a felt doll made by *Steiff.* Hts. 28, 35, and 43 cm. (11, 14, and 17 in.).

Greuling, Adolf. 1894. Sonneberg, Thür. Applied for a German patent (D.R.G.M.) for the joints of a doll.

Greuling, Carl. 1904. Sonneberg, Thür. Applied for a German patent (D.R.G.M.) for a jointed doll with a nodding head.

Grey, I. Alvin. See Gre-Poir, Inc.

Grillet, Albert. 1926–30 and later. Annecy, Haute-Savoie, France. Made celluloid dolls including dolls' rattles and Poupées Grillet.

Grinnell Lithographic Co. 1917–24. New York City. Made cloth dolls not molded. One of these had Mary on one side and her lamb on the other side. Ht. 9 in. (23 cm.).★

Grocer. Cutout advertising doll on sugar sacks of *Sea Island Sugar.* Printed clothes. Ht. 8 in. (20.5 cm.).

Grödner Tal Wooden Dolls. 1700s–1930 and later. Centered around St. Ulrich, Austria, until World War I, then this area became part of Italy. It is in the South Tyrol. The wooden dolls and dolls' heads were carved from Zirbel pine according to one source; another source said Arollas or Pinus Cembra, a fine grained firm but soft white wood. The early dolls were grounded with a local clay, then painted with water colors or glue colors and finally varnished. Women and children over 6 years old as well as men carved the dolls. Among the famous carvers and *Verlegers* were *Franz Runggaldier, Johann Anton Runggaldier,* Peter Wellponer[+], *Josef Purger, Johann Baptist Purger,* Johann Baptist *Moroder,* Johann Peter Moroder and his sons Josef and Dominik Moroder, *Josef Meingutscher, Johann Perathoner,* the *Obletters, Insam & Prinoth,* the *Sanoners* and *Vogler.* Dolls were made from ½ to 24 in. (1.3 to 61 cm.) tall and taller.

1700s: The dolls and dolls' heads were sent to Oberammergau and elsewhere to be painted. In the late 1700s the people of the Grödner Tal began to paint their dolls in addition to carving them. There were about 40 wood carvers.

1800–20: There were 300 workers carving dolls by hand. Salesmen from the Grödner Tal went all over the world selling these dolls.

1820s: Foot driven wheels began to be used to turn the wood; later, water driven wheels were used.

Mid 1800s: Austrian laws forbade men of military age to leave the country thus hindering the sale of these dolls.

1873: Population of the Grödner Tal was 3,500 and there were 2,000 carvers plus the painters and gilders. A good carver turned out 240 jointed dolls a day. Ht. 1½ in. (4 cm.). *Insam & Prinoth* bought 30,000 a week all year round of this size, making a total of 1,560,000 a year. Insam and Prinoth and Purger had the two largest warehouses in St. Ulrich. Insam & Prinoth had 30 large storerooms containing millions of dolls, large and small, painted and unpainted. One room contained dolls' heads to be exported after painting. The verlegers or wholesale dealers usually bought the dolls directly from the carvers, stored them until wanted and only gave them out to be painted as the orders came in from London or elsewhere. Women did most of the painting.

1914: Carved wooden dolls were crude-looking according to TOYS AND NOVELTIES. The entire doll was never made by one person and often as many as 25 people worked on it, especially before machinery began to be used.

1929: PLAYTHINGS reported that carved dolls in natural or painted wood, dressed or undressed, were made in the Grödner Tal. Some of the dolls were rigid and some skillfully jointed. Each workman displayed his own individuality but the dolls preserved their distinctive character. Some of the workmanship was better than that found on earlier dolls.

Groll, Carl. 1909–30 and later. Ilmenau, Thür. Made dolls.★

Groom, Gertrude E. 1921–23. Waltham, Mass. Obtained a U.S. patent for a doll made of unshorn sheepskin with the woolly side out.

Gross (Hugo, Richard, and Walter). See **Catterfelder Puppenfabrik.**

Gross, Karl. 1904. Dresden, Germany. Designed art dolls dressed in regional or historical costumes. See Ill. 2495.

Gross & Schild. 1922–30 and later. London. Distributed and imported dolls. Agent for Britain and the colonies of the following companies: *Carl Harmus, Hermsdorfer Celluloidwaren Fabrik, Carl Heumann, Kestner, Rudolf Langguth & Co., Heinrich Schmuckler,* and *Hermann von Berg. Gross & Schild* sold only to wholesalers.

1926: Obtained a British patent for a doll that opened and closed its jaw. A sound was emitted by the opening of the jaw.★

Grossbreitenbach. 1861–1930. Thür. There were at least three porcelain factories located here for which there was evidence that they made dolls' heads and all-porcelain dolls. These factories were:

1861: Grossbreitenbach Porzellanfabrik, founded by *Adolph Harrass*; his successors were Enders & Wagner.

1886: *Jul. Eginh. Harrass* founded a porcelain factory.

1899: *Marienfeld Porzellanfabrik* was mentioned.

Grossmann, August. 1912. Brombach, Germany. Applied for a German patent (D.R.G.M.) for a dolls' head with moving eyes.

Grossmann, Ernst. 1880. Sonneberg, Thür. Made ball-jointed bodies of wood and/or composition similar to those made in France for the early *Jumeau* bébés. He obtained two G.M. patents and some of his bodies had waist joints. He used two round stamps one—with his initials "E. G." and the other with "Gesetzlich//Geschützt." Some of his dolls had bisque bald heads with small holes.

Grossmann, S., & Co. 1907–10. Vienna. Listed in an Austrian directory under Dolls and Dolls' Heads.

Grosspapa. See **Gr.**

Grotesque Dolls. World War I period–1923. Formerly well-to-do women who were impoverished by the war and had artistic talents turned to making dolls out of odds and ends. Some of these dolls were made of wire wrapped with wool and the faces were stuffed patches of linen. Flower and perfume shops as well as department stores sold these dolls at prices only within the reach of the well-to-do.

INTERNATIONAL STUDIO commented on these dolls as follows: "They are intended to be caricatures and their make-up often betrays no little artistic taste. The larger ones are flexible even the heads being made of soft material, and they may be bent and posed in any way desired." The article was accompanied by a picture of one of *Lotte Pritzel*'s wax dolls. (Other dolls have been advertised as having Grotesque features in the 1890s through the 1930s.)

Grout. 1920s. France. Member of the *Chambre Syndicale*; he made undressed dolls and bébés in swaddling clothes and in underclothes as well as cardboard *poupards* with molded clothes.

Grout, William Edward. See **Trotman, Walter Knowles.**

Grove, Rene D. 1926. Middletown, Pa. Obtained U.S. patent for a jointed doll.

Gruber, Clemsen. 1907–10 and probably other years. Vienna. Listed in an Austrian directory as "King of the dolls." He was a large distributor of Austrian and foreign dolls.

Grubman Engineering and Manufacturing Co. 1923–29. Long Island City, New York. Leo J. Grubman was in charge of this company which made voices and sleeping eyes for dolls. He was also one of the officers of *Voices, Inc.,* to which he assigned some of his many patents.

1923: Leo Grubman applied for a U.S. and a German patent (D.R.P.) for mama voices. The sound device was placed in the lower torso of the doll and mounted so that it would not be damaged if the doll were dropped or abusively handled.

1924: Applied for a German patent (D.R.P.) for eye movement in dolls' heads. A new type of voice said "Mama" or "Papa" depending on how the doll was manipulated.

1925: Applied for two British patents relating to the movement of the dolls' eyes.

1095A & B. Two stamped marks found on dolls' bodies made by Ernst Grossmann.

1926: Produced 35,000 voices for dolls per day; used 1,200,000 pounds of steel per year. Obtained two U.S. patents for mounting eyes in dolls' heads.

1927: Used the trade name "Grubman" for dolls' voices.

Grumery. 1918. Paris. Created dolls.

Grump. 1915. Character boy and girl dolls made by *Joseph Roth.*

Grumpy. 1928. Cloth doll made by *Dean.*

Grumpy (Grumpykins). See **Baby Grumpy.**

Grünbaum, J. 1929–30. Prague, Czechoslovakia. Made dolls.

Grünbeck, Jakob, and Eichhorn, Leonhard, Jr. 1910. Coburg, Thür. Applied for a German patent (D.R.G.M.) for a sleeping-eyed doll with hair eyelashes.

Grundig, R., & Co. 1913–27. Mengersgereuth near Sonneberg, Thür. Advertised dolls' heads of wood and of composition, claiming they were cheaper than porcelain heads. By 1925 *Henry Barnett* was their distributor.

Grünebaum, J., & Son. 1919–30 and later. Brooklyn, N.Y., and Woodhaven, L.I. Made clothes for dolls.

1919: Advertised knit goods made of wool or imitation silk and including sweaters, sweater suits, jackets, caps, and bootees.

Grunhaus (Greenhouse). Ca. 1880–1921. London. Successor in 1921 was P. Silverman. Wholesale distributor of cheap dressed dolls.

Grüning, Armin. See **Nöckler & Tittel.**

Gruss aus. German words attached to some dolls, followed by the name of a Germanic town. "Gruss aus" means "Greeting from."

Guatemalan Dolls. In 1926 PLAYTHINGS advertised dolls dressed in "picturesque rags" to show the doll fashions of Quezaltenango, Guatemala.

Gucggenheimer, Theodor. See **Huck, Adolf & Co.**

Gudauner. Before 1838. Grödner Tal. A *Verleger* who sold dolls.

Guenucho. 1920s. France. Member of the *Chambre Syndicale.* Made jewelry for dolls.

Guépratte, Jean Marie. Before 1881–98. Paris and Montreuil-sous-Bois. Before 1889 one of the Guéprattes made glass eyes for *Jumeau.* In 1889 Jean left Jumeau and went with *Danel* to form Danel & Cie. Danel and Guépratte were sued by Jumeau in 1890–91 for copying *Bébé Jumeau* and they lost the suit. Some of the heads marked E. D. look very much like Bébé Jumeau heads and may have been made by Danel and Guépratte.

1891: In September both Jean Marie Guépratte of Paris and Danel & Cie. of Montreuil-sous-Bois registered trademarks for dolls. Danel registered *Bébé Français* and Guépratte registered *BÉBÉ SOLEIL* (see Ill. 1098) with the words Bébé Soleil in a sun with a face and rays within a five pointed star.

1096. Bisque head souvenir dolls with a shoulder sash reading "GRUSS AUS KARLSBAD." (Greeting from Carlsbad.) It has a wig, sleeping blue glass eyes, open mouth with teeth, a five-piece composition body. Original regional costume of the Carlsbad, Austria, now Czeckoslovakia, area. Molded and painted footwear. H. 7 in. (18 cm.). From the collection of Laura Starr, 1845–1917. *Courtesy of the International Doll Library. Photo by Sotheby Parke Bernet Inc., N.Y.*

Previously, in 1889, Danel & Cie. had registered a somewhat similar mark. (See Ill. 733.) The initials in the points of the star were D L G R C which could stand for Danel, Guépratte Cie. The mark has been found on the soles of shoes and it is known that Guépratte Fils specialized in footwear.★

Guerchoux, Rémy. 1843–52. Paris. He was made the adjudicator when Mme. Jugelé[+] failed. They started to live together and made dolls. But in 1850 Mme. Jugelé ran off and married M. Popineau (Poupinot) who was the best doll maker. M. Guerchoux failed while the Popineaus continued to make dolls. This information is based on the research of Mme. Poisson, curator of the Roybet-Fould Museum.

Guggenheimer, Theodor. See **Huck, Adolf, & Co.**

Gugusse. 1920s. Name of some dolls made by the *Société Française de Fabrication de Bébé & Jouets* (S.F.B.J.).

Gugusse de l' Hippodrome. 1903–5. A doll representing an actor with its hair going up to a point wore a dress suit with tails and a large bow tie. This doll was distributed by the stores *Pygmalion* and *Petit Saint Thomas.* Ht. 45 cm. (17½ in.); priced $1.38.

1097. Wax-over-composition shoulder head doll possibly made for Guépratte. It has a wig, stationary blue glass eyes, closed mouth and a cloth body with kid arms. The jointed body is similar to those made by Sarah Robinson. Clothes are contemporary with the doll. Stamped mark: Ill. 1098. This mark is similar but not the same as the mark registered by Guépratte in 1891. H. 15 in. (38 cm.). *Courtesy of Richard Withington. Photo by Barbara Jendrick.*

1098. Mark resembles the one registered by Jean Marie Guépratte.

1099. Bébé Soleil mark registered by Jean Marie Guépratte in 1891.

Guilbert, Pauline. 1913–20. England. Designed cutout cloth dolls for *Dean.* These dolls were No. 98 Antoinette, No. 100 Eugenie, No. 102 Josephine; Marguerite; and Mignonne. Ht. 12 in. (30.5 cm.).

1100. Mark of Pauline Guilbert for dolls she designed for Dean.

Guillard, François. 1835–50. Nantes, France. Successor, Widow Guillard (née Agathe Francheteux). 1850–59. Paris. Handled dolls at a shop named A la Galerie Vivienne, according to the research of Mme. Poisson, curator of the Roybet Fould Museum.

1865: Maison Guillard was a wholesale distributor of dolls.★

1101. Guillard mark found on a kid body lady doll from the Galerie Vivienne. *Courtesy of The Museum of the City of New York.*

Guillaume, Albert. 1917. Paris. Designed the molded faces for *Émile Lang's* cloth dolls. Born in 1873 in Paris and died in 1943 in Faux, Dordogne. He was a painter, humorist, and illustrator, and took many prizes for his works.

Guilleré. 1918. Paris. Director of the Primavera workshop for toys and dolls, located in the *Printemps* store.

Guillon, Silas. 1925–29. Paris. Made art dolls.

1926: Registered *Camélia* in France as a trademark for dolls' bodies and heads.

Guillow, Paul K. 1930 and later. Wakefield, Mass. Made clothes for dolls.

Guinzburg, E. A. 1925–27. New York City. Made dolls.

Guiterman, S., & Co. After 1871–1924. Handled dolls, especially American dolls after World War I.

Guiton.† See **Munnier, Maison.**

Guitry, Mme. Amie. 1918. France. Dolls made by *Mme. J. Ferrant* were dressed in the workshop of Mme. Guitry.

Gumery, M. 1916. France. A sculptor who modeled a doll's head representing the Infanta.

Gund Manufacturing Co. 1898–1930 and later. New York City; 1927–29, successor J. Swedlin. During the 1920s *Otto*

Denivelle did some work for Gund. Made dolls with composition heads and cloth bodies.

1915: Advertised a creeping doll that lifted its hands and legs. It was dressed in pink rompers.★

Günther, Emma. 1918–30 and later. Berlin. Manufactured and exported dolls, dolls' clothes and accessories. *Seelig* was her London agent and Van der *Kolk* was her agent in Amsterdam. *Hertzog* also handled her dolls' clothes.

Gussmann, Otto. 1904. Dresden, Germany. Designed art dolls dressed in regional or historical costumes. See Ill. 2495.

Gusto. (Circus Usher). 1911. Felt doll made by *Steiff*. It had long feet, spats, and was dressed as a circus clown in a black felt coat with tails. Ht. 35 cm. (14 in.); priced $1.75.

Gutberlet, H. W. 1897. Buchholz, Germany. Applied for a German patent (D.R.G.M.) for dolls' heads.

Gutmann, Ludwig. 1896. Osterburken, Germany. Applied for a German patent (D.R.G.M.) for a clockwork operated revolving doll.

Gutschke, Wilhelm. 1894. Berlin. Applied for a German patent (D.R.G.M.) for a celluloid-head doll.

Gutsell, Ida Anzolotta. 1893 and later. Ithaca, N.Y. The original Gutsell doll was painted in oils and called *"Anzolotta."* Ida Gutsell's boy dolls were made in a white version with a brown or blue suit. The black version, "Darkey Doll," had a white shirt and red, blue or black short pants. Its clothes were not removable like the white version's clothes. Ht. 16 in. (40.5 cm.).★

Gutta-percha. Name applied to various materials used to make dolls; most of them were not real gutta-percha but it is often difficult to distinguish real gutta-percha, which is reddish white in color in its original state, brittle and will not float. It is entirely different from rubber in appearance and in chemical, and physical properties. It is a fibrous substance. At 120 degrees Fahrenheit it could be molded by pressure and when cold it would retain its shape. Oil and saline solutions have no effect on gutta-percha but strong acids would decompose it.

The words "gutta-percha" mean gum tree in the Malaysian language.

The early descriptions of gutta-percha dolls lead one to believe that these dolls were made of substances that were not actually gutta-percha. An 1878 quotation from THE QUEEN suggested that rubber which could be pressed to squeak was mistakenly called "Gutta Percha" which could not be pressed. (See 1878, following.)

Ca. 1840: TOYS AND NOVELTIES in 1913 stated that gutta-percha was used around 1840 to make dolls in Sonneberg.

Ca. 1850: Henry Mayhew wrote about gutta-percha heads. They "have no gutta-percha in their composition but are solely made of glue and treacle [molasses]. The heads are small coloured models of the human face, usually with projecting nose and chin, and wide distorted mouth, which admit of being squeezed into a different form of features, their elasticity causing them to return to the original caste." Mayhew also reported an interview with a maker of eyes for gutta-percha dolls. "We make the same kind of eyes for the gutta-percha dolls as for the wax. It is true, the gutta-percha complexion isn't particularly clear, nevertheless the eyes I make for the washable faces are all of the natural tint; and if the gutta-percha dolls look rather bilious, why I ain't agoing to make my eyes look bilious to match."

1853: Gutta-percha dolls were mentioned in GODEY'S LADY'S BOOK.

1872–82: *Silber & Fleming* advertised unbreakable gutta-percha dolls, some of which were described as having glass eyes. They came in as many as eight sizes.

1878: THE QUEEN reported: "There is the gutta percha doll, which will stand a great deal of nursery ill-treatment, and is much in favour, on account of its power of squeaking in anything but euphonious tones. These are mostly dressed in bright-colour wools, crocheted either to simulate a Zouave,

1102A & B. A doll made entirely of a reddish tan hard substance that resembles identified samples of gutta-percha. It has molded hair and features, painted eyes and is heavier than rubber. Original clothes. H. 8½ in. (21.5 cm.). *Coleman Collection.*

a drummer or nigger boy or sometimes a baby in long clothes, with cloak and hood, which are all worked in . . . red, blue, and yellow blending most happily with the gutta percha."★

Guttmann, Julius. 1895. Berlin. Applied for a German patent (D.R.G.M.) for a doll's head.

Guttmann & Schiffnie (Société Guttman & Schiffnie). 1897–1930 and later. Sonneberg, Thür., and Nürnberg, Bavaria. This company used the same trade name as Gebrüder Sussenguth and both names appeared on a catalog. The relationship and function of each firm is not known. *Bébé l'Avenir* (Doll of the Future) was their most popular doll. Jeanne Doin reported in 1916 that since 1900 Guttmann & Schiffnie were one of the largest German exporters of dolls to France.★

1103–1104. Marks found on Guttmann & Schiffnie dolls.

Guyot.† See **A la Tentation.**

Gwendolyn. 1927. Name of a dressed doll with composition head, arms and legs made by *Royal Toy Manufacturing Co.* and distributed by *Montgomery Ward.* It had a human hair wig, sleeping eyes, hair eyelashes and a cotton stuffed cloth body. Ht. 27 in. (68.5 cm.); priced $5.79.

Gym Tinker. 1929. Jointed doll with tension spring construction so that it can keep various positions. Made by *Tinker Toy Co.* Ht. 8¾ in. (22 cm.).

Gymnastik Doll. 1930. Trademark registered in Germany by *Albin Hess.*

Gypsy Countess. 1887. Bisque-head doll advertised by *Ehrich Bros.* It was jointed at the neck, shoulders, elbows, hips, and knees. It was dressed in a regional-style costume and carried a bouquet of flowers.

Gypsy Doll. World War I. Mme. *Lauth-Sand* dressed a doll to represent a Gypsy. (See Ill. 1615.)

Gypsy Queen. 1920. Doll with composition shoulder head and arms, wigged, was designed by *Madame Georgene* for *Averill Manufacturing Co.*

H

H. Unidentified mark found on some fine quality bisque heads. These heads have a size number that suggests a French origin; also, they are often found on ball-jointed composition bodies marked Jumeau. See Ill. 1105.

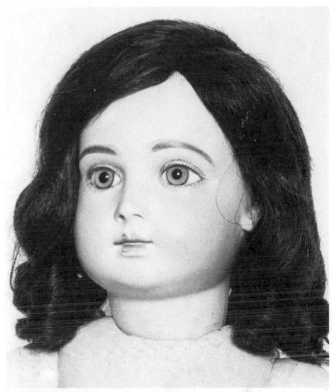

1105. Bisque head doll with brown wig, stationary blue glass eyes, pierced ears, closed mouth with a small space between the lips. It is on a fully jointed composition body. Mark on head: 3 H. Blue stamp mark on the body: "JUMEAU//MEDAILLE D'OR //PARIS." H. 21 in. (53.5 cm.). *Courtesy of the Margaret Woodbury Strong Museum. Photo by Harry Bickelhaupt.*

H. C. Unidentified mark found on some closed-mouth bisque heads. See Ills. 1106 and 1107.

H. & Z. Doll Co. 1919. New York City. Manufactured 50 styles of fully jointed, including wrist, composition body and cloth body dolls, representing babies, children and ladies. All-composition dolls had wigs and sleeping eyes. Baby dolls: Hts. 21 to 26 in. (53.5 cm. to 66 cm.). Children and lady dolls: Hts. 25 to 30 in. (63.5 to 76 cm.).★

Haag, Gebrüder (Bros.). 1886–1928. Sonneberg, Thür. Manufactured and exported dolls.

1925: Advertised ball-jointed dolls and bent limb baby dolls, dressed and undressed.★

Haas, Fr. See **Fischer, Naumann & Co.**

Haas & Cžižek. See **Schlaggenwald.**

Haase, Konstantin. 1922–25. Grossbreitenbach, Thür. Obtained a German patent (D.R.P.) for stuffing dolls.

1106. Bisque head doll with blond wig, stationary blue glass eyes, closed mouth, a fully jointed composition body. Mark: Ill. 1107. *Courtesy of Richard Withington. Photo by Barbara Jendrick.*

ℋ 10 C

1107. H. C. mark found on bisque head dolls.

1108. Mark of the H. & Z. Doll Co.

Habermann, Gebrüder (Bros.). 1926–30. Steinach, Thür. Manufactured dolls. These Habermanns were probably related to Wilhelm Habermann.[†]

Habor, Nikolaus. 1907–10. Vienna. Listed in an Austrian directory under Dolls and Dolls' Heads.

Hachmeister, Hermann. 1872–1930 and later. Sonneberg, Thür. Made and exported dolls and dolls' clothes. The dolls came dressed and undressed. By 1926 he represented *Gustavus Schmey.*

1910: One of the Sonneberg group of Grand Prize winners at the Brussels Exhibition.

1912: Advertised jointed dolls, Art dolls, dolls' clothes and dolls' linens.

1926: Advertised *Mama* dolls; underwear was included with the dolls' clothes. Had a London office.

1927: Advertised a doll wearing a pre-World War I. style dress. Trade name *Hapusa-Puppe* was used for dolls.

1930: Advertised Mama dolls, Art dolls, baby dolls and dolls' clothes.★

Haeusler, Helene. 1927–30 and later. Sonneberg, Thür. Created a cloth baby doll called *Heinerle.* Until 1932 she worked for *Cuno & Otto Dressel* in a managerial capacity. Later she set up an independent workshop where dolls were made of wood, composition and cloth.

Hagemann, Alice. See Kaulitz, Marion Bertha, and Munich Art Dolls.

Hagendorn & Co. 1913–14. Osnabrück and London. Manufactured and exported celluloid dolls.

Hahn, Curt. 1926. Blumenau. Saxony. Made *Erzgebirge* wooden dolls.

Hahnesend, Joseph, & Co. 1915–17. New York City. Joseph Hahnesend and I. H. Davis formed Joseph Hahnesend & Co. Later Davis left and formed *Davis & Voetsch* with Fred W. Voetsch. Hahnesend & Co. handled dolls.★

Haidinger, Benedict. 1853 and possibly other years. Distributed dolls. (The Haidingers had a porcelain factory in Elbogen, Bohemia, but the connection if any is not known.)

Hair. A STUDY OF DOLLS by G. Stanley Hall and A. Caswell Ellis of Clark University, Worcester, Mass. was published in 1897 and listed the following materials used for dolls' hair: mohair, human hair, hemp ravelings, wool, split grass, corn silk, bits of fur, shavings, feathers and hair painted on the head. If a wig came off, the doll was treated as a baby and sometimes children pulled the wig off so the doll would be bald like a baby. Children preferred curly hair to straight hair and blonde hair to dark hair, according to the Hall-Ellis study.

1909: *J. Stellmacher* applied for a German patent for dolls' heads with spun glass hair.

1917: *Max Handwerck* applied for a German patent for dolls' wigs made of "Glass." (See also **Wigs.**)★

1109. Hermann Hachmeister's advertisement in DEUTSCHE SPIELWAREN ZEITUNG, February 11, 1927. The advertisement tells us that Hachmeister of Sonneberg, founded in 1872, made dressed dolls, dressed and undressed baby dolls, dolls with mama voices and art dolls in "all" sizes and prices as well as dolls' dresses and underwear.

1110. 1830s papier-mâché head with Apollo Knot hair style, curls at each side, brown painted eyes, and a kid body with wooden lower arms and legs, painted slippers. H. 25 in. *Courtesy of Sotheby Parke Bernet Inc., N.Y.*

1111. 1840s papier-mâché head with black molded hair that has long curls at the side and a bun in the back, painted blue eyes. It is on a kid body with wooden lower arms and legs. Original blue cotton and net dress. H. 21 in. (53.5 cm.). *Courtesy of Sotheby Parke Bernet Inc., N.Y.*

1112A & B. Hair wig on a china shoulder head doll with braids around the ears, and a bun in back, molded and painted blue eyes (eyeballs are white on the flesh-colored head), closed mouth. The body is cloth with kid arms. Original dress on this large doll. *Courtesy of the Chester County Historical Society.*

1113. Black molded hair china shoulder head with a braid that starts from the center back and coils around to form a band across the top of the head. The wavy hair in front is drawn down over the ears. There are six waves on one side and only five on the other. The blue eyes have highlights and are semi-outlined. The nose has a red oval while the mouth is painted open. The cloth body has leather arms and wears an 1840–50s cotton dress. H. of doll 19½ in. (49.5 cm.). H. of shoulder head 5¾ in. (14.5 cm.). *Coleman Collection.*

1114A & B. China head with an elaborate hair style and great detail including brushmarks. The head has molded and painted blue eyes and a closed mouth. H. of shoulder head 3½ in. (9 cm.). *Coleman Collection.*

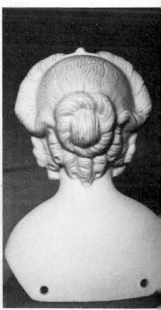

1115A & B. Untinted bisque shoulder head with fancy molded hairdo that has wings in front, curls and a bun in back. The exposed ears are encircled by the hair. The painted features include a closed mouth. There are two sew holes on each side. H. 16 in. (40.5 cm.). H. of shoulder head 4¼ in. (11 cm.). *Coleman Collection.*

1116A & B. Pair of porcelain shoulder heads with identical 1860s hair styles having loops and puffs with bead ornaments and painted features. **A.** is a bisque head with blonde hair and glazed gold beads. H. 11 in. (28 cm.). H. of shoulder head 3 in. (7.5 cm.). **B.** is a pinkish china head with black hair and black beads. There are no sew holes on this poured head marked "5" on the back shoulder. H. of shoulder head 2⅛ in. (5.5 cm.). Both heads in *Coleman Collection*.

1118A & B. Unusual hair treatment with a cork pate for a wig and molded blond hair encircling the head which has stationary blue glass eyes and a closed mouth. The bisque head has a flange type joint where it fits onto the bisque shoulder plate. The kid body has wired fingers of kid, a gusset joint at the hips. H. 18½ in. (47 cm.). H. shoulder head 6 in. (15 cm.). *Courtesy of the Margaret Woodbury Strong Museum. Photo by Harry Bickelhaupt.*

1117A & B. Untinted bisque shoulder head with molded and painted hair with a gold bead hair ornament, blue and gold necklace and decorated blouse top, brush marks, stationary blue glass eyes, pierced ears, closed mouth. It is on a cloth body with leather arms. H. 18 in. (45.5 cm.). H. of shoulder head 3½ in. (9 cm.). *Courtesy of and photo by Becky Moncrief.*

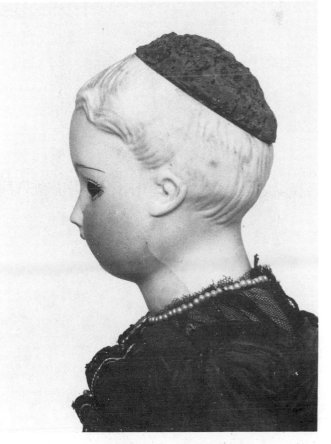

1119. Untinted bisque shoulder head doll has blond molded hair and blue stationary threaded glass eyes, and feathered eyebrows. The body is cloth with bisque arms. H. 13½ in. (34 cm.). H. of shoulder head 4½ in. (11.5 cm.). *Courtesy of Z. Frances Walker.*

1120. Untinted bisque turned shoulder head with blond molded hair with ringlets that reach the shoulders. The eyes are stationary threaded blue glass with painted eyelashes and feathered eyebrows. It is on a cloth body with leather arms. H. 12¾ in. (35 cm.). H. of shoulder head 3½ in. (9 cm.). *Courtesy of Z. Frances Walker.*

1121. Bisque shoulder head with blond molded hair parted on the side, stationary blue glass eyes, open-closed mouth, and a kid body with bisque hands. H. 14 in. (35.5 cm.). *Courtesy of Richard Withington. Photo by Barbara Jendrick.*

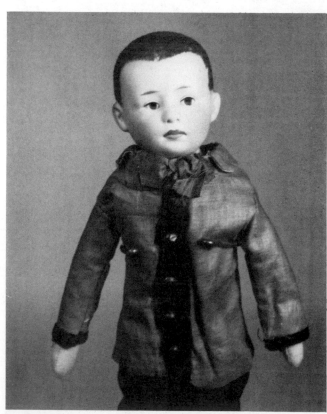

1122. Flocked brown hair on a bisque shoulder head doll, with intaglio blue eyes, closed mouth and a cloth body. Mark on head: "O Germany." H. 14 in. (35.5 cm.). *Courtesy of Richard Withington. Photo by Barbara Jendrick.*

1123. Bisque head with flocked hair, stationary brown glass eyes, open-closed mouth, on a jointed composition body. H. 16 in. (40.5 cm.). *Courtesy of Sotheby Parke Bernet Inc., N.Y.*

The Paris Craze for Colored Hair

ought to Toyland by Horsman Dolls

No. 145X
FINE DRESSED BABY GIRL

th mohair wig of red, blue, green or
v. Costume to match of lace-trimmed
and beautiful lace bonnet trimmed with
rosettes and colored ribbons,

Per Dozen.............$10.50

No. 145 X

1124. Baby Doll produced by Horsman and advertised in their catalog of 1914. It had a mohair wig that came in red, blue, green, or yellow. *Courtesy of Bernard Barenholtz.*

BSGDG

1125. Mark inside a mohair wig, found on a lady type doll.

Hakata Dolls. See **Japanese Dolls.**

Halbig. See **Simon & Halbig.**

Hale Bros. 1926–30 and later. San Francisco, Calif. Doll distributor.

1926: Registered in U.S. the trademark *Over the Bridge to Fairyland* for dolls. Later this trademark was renewed by the company known as Nancy Ann Story Book Dolls, Inc.

1929: Sold *Dimple Dolls.*

Halka. 1915. Cloth doll stuffed with cork or straw, hand painted or embroidered face, bobbed hair style with bangs, made by refugee Polish artists in the work shop of *Mme. Lazarski.* This doll representing a little peasant girl was one of the most popular dolls promoted by *Mme. Paderewski.* Ht. ca. 15 in. (38 cm.).

Hall, Carrie. 1920s–30 and later. North Platte, Nebr. Created "Handicraft Dolls." These were dressed dolls; most of them had composition heads and arms but a few had china heads or *Minerva* metal heads. The dolls were dressed to represent historical characters, fictional characters or Biblical characters. Four hts.: 8, 12, 14, and 16 in. (20.5, 30.5, 35.5, and 40.5 cm.). Carrie Hall also designed dresses for people.

Haller, Johann. 1770–1840. Vienna. 1840–ca. 1858. Anna Haller, wife of Johann, and her son-in-law *Franz Lutzenleithner* were successors. Probably there were two generations of Johann Hallers. The records indicate that the Hallers were *Verlegers* in the early 1800s if not earlier.

1770: Founded and produced wooden dolls and mechanical dolls.

1825: Berchtesgaden and *Grödner Tal* wooden dolls as well as dressed mechanical dolls were distributed from their shop at 707 Fleischmarkt, an address which appeared on labels found on Haller dolls.

1838: About 2,000 items were produced by the Hallers including papier-mâché dolls' heads, leather dolls' heads and walking dolls.

1853: Anna Haller was listed as a doll distributor.★

Hallett, Wm. 1826–37. London. Made composition and leather dolls.

Halloween. Dolls have been dressed to represent Halloween, like those done by *Chessler Co.* in 1920.

Halpern, D. 1930 and later. Paris. Distributed *Kestner* dolls.

Halpern, J., Co. 1923–30 and later. New York City, Pittsburgh, Pa., and Sonneberg, Thür. *Verleger* who had a seven story building in Sonneberg where dolls were collected from home workers in Sonneberg and 20 surrounding villages. These dolls of many styles and sizes were then exported to America.★

Haltrich, Friedrich. 1853 and possibly other years. Vienna. Distributed dolls.

Ham. 1917–18. Cloth doll made by *Dean.* It represented the moving picture star of this name.

Hamburger & Co. 1889–1909. Berlin, Nürnberg, and New York City. Produced dolls.

Dolly Dimple bisque heads have an incised H. probably for Hamburger, as well as the *Gebrüder Heubach* sunburst mark. See Ills. 796 and 797.

1907: Sent postcards from Nürnberg, picturing and announcing the shipment of *Viola* and other dolls to the Goldzcher store in New Jersey. (See Ill. 2656.)★

Hameau, J. Name on a stamp on a lady doll. (See Ill. 1126.)

1126. Hameau stamp on a fashion lady type doll.

Hameler, Franz. 1910. Vienna. Listed in an Austrian directory under Dolls and Dolls' Heads.

Hamley Bros. 1760–1980 and later. London. William Henry Hamley was born in 1843 and died in 1916. He was succeeded by his son, John Hamley. The firm made dolls and also imported, exported and distributed dolls both wholesale and retail. According to Vivien Greene the original Hamley family was still involved with the manufacture of dolls in 1980 at Croydon near London. During World War I and shortly afterward they obtained *British Ceramic* heads and dolls from *Hancock* and *Hewitt & Leadbetter*.

1760: Ancestors of the Hamleys started a toy-shop named Noah's Ark.

Ca. 1880s: A dressed wax lady doll in a box marked "Hamley's// European Toy Warehouse// 202 Regent Street//London" has been reported.

1902: THE LONDON MAGAZINE reported, "Mr. Hamley, an expert in doll portraiture, gives . . . details of the dolls he has made." These dolls with wax or with porcelain heads included portraits of the royal family, and famous military and theatrical persons. Mr. Hamley probably designed and financed these dolls but it is doubtful if he actually made the porcelain heads. The *Pierottis* made most of the wax dolls for Hamley's.

1905: A Hamley catalog listed five addresses one of which was "Imperial Toy Warehouse," 59 Knightsbridge.

1908–14: Hamley's received a steady flow of German and Austrian dolls.

1912: TOYS AND NOVELTIES reported that Hamley's could supply wax, china, celluloid, and composition dolls in 14 sizes with "clothes to match" as well as all kinds of dolls' parts. "Dolls supplied with regular trousseaus, each garment

most beautifully finished with lace and insertion. . . . the wardrobes of a doll would often run to a considerable figure." Regular stock dolls cost up to $55.00; special dolls cost more.

1914: John Green Hamley registered in Britain the trademark *Kolly Kid* for dolls.

1915: "Unbreakable" (composition) portrait dolls of *Lord Kitchener, General French, Tzar Nicholas, King Albert, General Joffre, King George V,* and *Admiral Jellicoe* all in detailed costumes, were produced by the *Women's Emergency Corps Workshop* and sold by Hamley.

1917: Sold *Fumsup, Pooksie,* LuLu,[†] *Wu Wu,* and *Kewpies* that were jointed at the neck and shoulders. These Kewpies sold for $1.12 and $2.12 a doz. wholesale.

1919: Elfie was a Kewpie type made of *British Ceramic.*

1920: Fumsup came in celluloid and in rubber versions.

Na Poo was No. 1 of the Sister Suner series.

1922: Advertised *Ping Pong,* Fumsup and *Chu Chin Chow* as well as other British dolls and dolls imported from the Continent.

1920s: Advertised New Born Baby dolls, fully jointed art dolls, cloth body dolls, and undressed and dressed dolls with clothes made by Hamley. These dolls were in Hamley's wholesale department. Wax fairy dolls were available retail. These dolls had a wig and wore very full knee-length skirts and a crown. They were barefoot and carried a long wand with a big bow tied to the middle.

1930: Wax portrait dolls of *King Edward VII* and *Queen Alexandra* were still available.★

1127. Mark used by Hamleys for dolls.

Hammond Manufacturing Co. 1916–19. Burton-on-Trent, England. The manager *Mr. Simmonds* was a doll maker in London prior to joining this company, which made dolls of "porcelain", composition and cloth. They bought heads and made the bodies, wigs, and clothes. The dolls were stuffed with wood-wool and pine chips that were available in the factory. The dolls were jointed or unjointed and came with fixed or sleeping eyes.

1917: Advertised cloth dolls representing *Father Christmas, Charlie Chaplin, Costers, Golliwoggs,* and three different designs representing girls. Hts. 15 and 29 in. (38 and 71 cm.). Other dolls came as small as 11½ in. (29 cm.).

Hampshire Pottery. See **Taft, James Scholly.**

Hancock, S., & Sons (Gordon Works, Corona Pottery).
1857–1937. Stoke-on-Trent, Staffs. Made *British Ceramic* dolls, dolls' heads and limbs in 1914 through 1918 using a variety of designs; also made exclusive designs. Some of their dolls' heads were designed by *Hilda Cowham.* Hancock was the sole manufacturer of *Fumsup.* They made their own stationary and sleeping eyes for dolls.

One of the Hancock heads was marked "NTI//GIRL// ENGLISH MAKE," and on the right in smaller letters off by itself was what appears to be "C/R."

1917: GAMES AND TOYS described a visit to the Hancock factory. First plaster of Paris molds were created by modellers working from dozens of designs. Then "slip" was made of china clay, water and other materials. The article told us: "The two parts of the mould are put together and the slip is poured in until the mould is quite full. . . . We see the slip very slowly receding down the aperture or orifice; . . . [while] the mould is drawing away by capillary attraction the water from the slip, . . . a film is forming on the mould. This process goes on so rapidly that in about five minutes the film is sufficiently thick to enable the mould to be turned upside down and the remaining slip poured away. In a very short time the mould can be opened and in it will be found the china [British Ceramic] head, which is placed after one day in an adjacent drying stove.

"Next the eyes are cut out. . . . the apertures must be carefully bevelled inside the head to allow the eyes to be inserted later. Inequalities in the surface of the head are now removed by means of a heavy camel hair brush dipped in water; and after drying, the head is now ready for the ovens. . . .

"One of these great ovens . . . is built in circular form, of brick, and is some fifteen feet across, gradually sloping up to a pointed dome over twenty two feet (7 meters) high. It is heated by means of external fires built in its walls; these kept going day and night, [and] soon produce in it heat of about 1,200 c.

"We are next taken to see the heads being packed ready to go in the oven. They are placed in large earthenware pans made of marl and having a practically flat bottom. These pans or 'Saggars' are taken one by one to the oven, where the first are placed on the ground next to the wall until a ring of them is formed round it. Others are brought in and stood on top of the first ring. . . . then others are built on these until they form a complete lining. Next, the door is closed and the fires are made up and kept going night and day until they are drawn, the oven opened and the saggars removed.

"Damaged heads are now discarded, and the remainder pass to the decorators. The lips are painted in by hand, also the eyelashes, and little touches are given to the nostrils. Sometimes the complexion too is hand-painted; sometimes it is entrusted to aerograph operators. Then the decorating work has to be baked in; so the head must go again to what is known as the enamelling kiln, which makes the colouring permanent."★

Handicraft Dolls. See **Hall, Carrie.**

Handsome Hans. 1921–22. Cloth doll made by *Rees Davis.*

1128. Mark of Hancock on their British Ceramic heads.

Handwerck, Heinrich. 1876–1930. Gotha near Waltershausen, Thür. Worked for *Wislizenus* in 1878. After 1902, when Heinrich Handwerck died, the factory and business was sold to *Waltershauser Puppenfabrik.* The W found on the forehead of many of the Handwerck or Kämmer & Reinhardt dolls probably related to the Waltershauser Puppenfabrik.

In the early 1920s Heinrich Handwerck, Jr., started a new doll-making business using his own name.

In the late 1880s Heinrich Handwerck, Sr., had originated large scale machine production of composition dolls' bodies made possible through die-forming and stamping processes. Steam was used for the manufacturing. A U.S. Department of Commerce report in 1924 supplied the above information. (See **Manufacture of Waltershausen Dolls, Commercial: Made in Germany in Waltershausen Region.**)

Simon & Halbig bisque heads made from Handwerck molds were used on Handwerck composition bodies. The trademarks included an eight pointed star with French or with German wording, a shield and the words *Bébé Cosmopolite,* Bébé de Réclame[+] and Bébé Superior[+]. The better quality dolls had real hair and fancy chemises. The second quality dolls had mohair wigs and plain chemises.

1885: Made leather bodies stuffed with cork and pink cloth bodies stuffed with sawdust.

1888: Advertised ball jointed dolls. The composition bodies were made of lime soaked paper pulp placed while still damp in sulphur molds. After hardening they were removed and sanded, then painted with a white lime wash followed by a pink colored paint, and finally varnished. This work was done chiefly by workers in their own homes.

1897 on: A lady doll with a shapely ball jointed composition body has been reported stamped "D. R. Patent No. 100279." This patent was applied for in 1897 and was granted in 1898. The body had straight wrists. The socket head, made by Simon & Halbig, was mold # 1159. It also had the red "Wimpern"[+] stamp.

1898: Advertised ball jointed dolls and *Täuflinge.* Some of the body parts were wood and generally steel molds were used instead of the sulphur ones.

1904: *Gimbels'* catalog showed the following Handwerck dolls: *Elaine* dolls; Lady dolls with lady style wigs, sleeping eyes, eyelashes, chemise; five hts.: 20, 22, 24, 25 and 27 in.

(51, 56, 61, 63.5 and 68.5 cm.); priced $2.50 to $5.85; infant dolls with short curly wigs, sleeping eyes, eyelashes, long chemise; six hts.: 15, 18, 19½, 21, 24, and 28 in. (38, 45.5, 49.5, 53.5, 61, and 71 cm.); priced $1.25 to $4.50. Other Handwerck dolls of lesser quality than the Elaine dolls had mohair wigs, sleeping eyes, chemise and footwear; four hts.: 24, 27, 29, and 31 in. (61, 68.5, 73.5, and 78.5 cm.); priced $2.50 to $3.75. See Ill. 540 in THE COLLECTOR'S BOOK OF DOLLS' CLOTHES.

1904–10: *R. H. Macy* catalogs listed Handwerck dolls with bisque heads, wigs, sleeping eyes, some with eyelashes, ball jointed composition bodies, except for the 18 in. (45.5 cm.) doll which came with and without ball joints.

In 1904 the 26 in. (66 cm.) doll dressed in a chemise cost $3.49; the 25 in. (63.5 cm.) doll dressed as a lady in a tailored costume cost $21.62; and the 30 in. (76 cm.) doll dressed as a lady in silk cost $38.99.

HANDWERCK DOLLS SIZE–HEIGHT RELATIONSHIP		
Size	*Height*	
No.	in.	cm.
2¼	18	45.5
2½	20	51
3	22	56
4	25	63.5
5	26	66
6	30	76

1129. Bisque head doll of ca. 1900 with wig, sleeping blue glass eyes, hair eyelashes, fully jointed composition and wood body. Head marked "Germany//Handwerck//Halbig//0." A red stamp mark on the body reads "Heinrich Handwerck//Germany//0." One of the garments is marked "Modes de Paris 4." H. 39 cm. (15½ in.). *Courtesy of the Collection Nederlands Kostuummuseum, The Hague. Photo by B. Frequin.*

1911–12: *Gimbel's* catalog showed a Handwerck doll with bisque head, wig, sleeping eyes, composition body, chemise, and footwear. Four hts.: 22, 24, 27, and 30 in. (56, 61, 68.5, and 76 cm.); priced $2.50 to $5.50.

1912: Handwerck dolls were distributed by *Winters & Reinecke* in Philadelphia, Pa.

1913: Advertised dolls with stationary or sleeping eyes and crying babies with moving tongue.

1914: *Montgomery Ward* catalog advertised Handwerck character bisque heads with wigs, sleeping eyes, moving tongues, and on bent limb composition bodies; hts. 10 and 13½ in. (25.5 and 34 cm.); priced $17.50 and $33.00 a doz. wholesale. Without the moving tongue but with eyelashes and jointed wrists on ball jointed composition bodies, the hts. were 22, 25, and 28 in. (56, 63.5, and 71 cm.); priced $60.00 to $90.00 a doz. wholesale.

1915: Celluloid dolls were listed. Handwerck dolls were handled by *Borgfeldt.*

1923: A large group of pre-World War I Handwerck dolls were sold in various Latin-American countries.

1925–27: Applied for German patents (D.R.G.M.) for sleeping eyes in dolls' heads.★

1130A & B. Brown bisque head doll made by Heinrich Handwerck. It has a black wig, stationary brown glass eyes, pierced ears, open mouth with four upper teeth and a fully jointed composition body. Mark: Ill. 1133A. H. 19 in. (48 cm.). *Courtesy of Iverna and Irving Foote. Photo by Irving Foote.*

1131. Heinrich Handwerck bisque head doll with a blond wig, sleeping blue glass eyes, pierced ears, open mouth with teeth, and a fully jointed composition body. H. 21 in. (53.5 cm.). *Courtesy of Sotheby Parke Bernet Inc., N.Y.*

1132. Bisque head doll made by Heinrich Handwerck with a blond wig, sleeping brown glass eyes, pierced ears, open mouth with two upper teeth, and a fully jointed composition body. Original clothes. Mark: "HANDWERCK//6." H. 29½ in. (75 cm.). *Courtesy of June Jeffcott.*

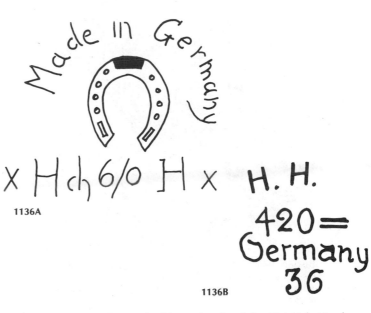

Germany

HEINRICH HANDWERCK
SIMON & HALBIG

1133A

Germany

HEINRICH
HANDWERCK
SIMON & HALBIG
6½

1133B

79-3 X
HW
GERMANY

1134

119 -10½ X
HANDWERCK
Germany
2¼.

1135

Made in Germany

X H ch 6/0 H X

1136A

H. H.
420 =
Germany
36

1136B

1133–1136. Marks on the bisque heads of the Heinrich Handwerck dolls.

Handwerck, Max. 1900–30 and later. Waltershausen, Thür. Made dolls and dolls' bodies. Created his own models, many of which were produced as bisque heads by *William Goebel.* These heads were either socket or shoulder-head type with wigs and sleeping eyes or painted hair and eyes, on composition bodies. There were also all-porcelain dolls. One of the most successful dolls was *Bébé Elite.*

1902: *Triumph Bébé* was a new doll.

1917: Applied for a German patent for dolls' wigs made of "Glass."

1922: Advertised the "Handwerck Celebrated Doll."

1924: Made flirting-eye dolls. Applied for a German patent (D.R.G.M.) relating to spring joints for dolls.★

1137. Bisque head doll made by Max Handwerck. It has a wig, blue glass eyes, an open mouth with teeth, and a fully jointed composition body. Size mark: 3. H. 24 in. (61 cm.). *Courtesy of Sotheby Parke Bernet Inc., N.Y.*

1283/285

MAX
HANDWERGK
GERMANY

1138

283/285

MAX
HANDWERGK
GERMANY
2/4

1139

Made in Germany

Max Handwerck

1140

421
6
M.Handwerck
Germany

1141

1138–1141. Marks on the bisque heads of dolls made by Max Handwerck.

Hänel, C. Paul. 1926. Grünhainichen, Erzgebirge. Made artistic dolls.

Hanington, A. W., & Co. 1915–16. New York City. Made *Kutie-Kins* dolls.★

Hanisch, Luise. 1907–8. Vienna. Listed in an Austrian directory under Dolls and Dolls' Heads.

Hank. 1917. One of the El-Be-Co line of dolls made by *Langrock Bros. Co.* This chubby composition character doll sold for $1.00.

Hanka. 1924–26. Name of a *Mama* doll with bobbed hair made by *Gebrüder Pfeiffer*. In England Hanka was advertised by *L. Meyer*.

Hankyland Dolls. 1926. Trademark registered in U.S. by *Brush Heiss* for dolls.

Hanna. 1920 and probably other years. A *Schoenau & Hoffmeister* bisque head usually found on a bent limb composition body. Size 12/0 was 6¾ in. (17 cm.) tall. Other hts. reported were 7 and 9 in. (18 and 23 cm.).★

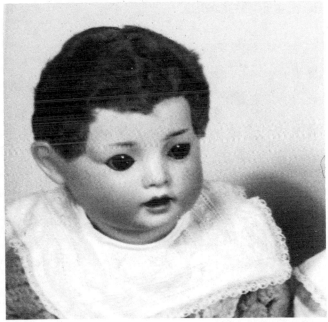

1142. German bisque head baby marked Hanna, made by Schoenau & Hoffmeister. It has a wig, blue glass eyes, open mouth with teeth. It is on a bent limb composition baby body. Head marked: Germany S✡H Hanna 3. H. 15 in. (38 cm.). *Courtesy of Richard Withington. Photo by Barbara Jendrick.*

Hannoversche Gummi-Kamm Co. 1883–1926. Hannover, Prussia. Made rubber dolls.

1926: Applied for a German patent (D.R.G.M.) for rubber dolls.

1143. Mark possibly used by Hannoversche Gummi-Kamm Co. on celluloid or rubber dolls.

Hannoversche Puppenfabrik. See **Abt & Franke.**

Hans. 1908–11. Cutout cloth doll made by *Saalfield*. It had a printed costume of a German boy. Ht. 7¾ in. (19.5 cm.).

Hans. 1911–12. Doll with composition head designed by *Helen Trowbridge* and copyrighted by *Horsman*. It had molded bobbed hair and bangs, painted eyes, smiling open-closed mouth with teeth, and appeared to come from the same mold as *Daisy Dimple, Gretchen, Happy Hiram, Jack Tar, Prince Charlie* and *Robbie Reefer*. It was number 140 and wore a Dutch costume without a hat but with circular striped stockings and felt shoes in the shape of wooden shoes. Hans was a mate to Gretchen.

Hans (Farmer Boy). Before 1911–24. Jointed felt character doll made by *Steiff* and distributed in the U.S. by *Borgfeldt*. It was dressed as a peasant boy with a red vest, short trousers and a hat. Five hts.: 28, 35, 43, 50, and 60 cm. (11, 14, 17, 19½, and 23½ in.); price for the 35 cm. doll in Germany in 1911 was $1.50 and in New York in 1913 it was $2.25.

Hans. 1912–13. Cloth doll stuffed with cork and sawdust produced by *Selchow & Righter*. It had a printed Lord Fauntleroy style boy's suit. The jacket of which had rounded corners. Ht. 12½ in. (31.5 cm.); priced 10¢ each or 80¢ a doz. wholesale. Hans also came as a cutout cloth doll. Ht. 13¼ in. (33.5 cm.); priced 10¢ each or 75¢ doz. wholesale.

Hans. 1920. Dressed doll designed by *Georgene Averill* and made by *Averill Manufacturing Co.* It had composition arms and a shoulder head with a wig.

Hans. See **Dutch Boy.**

Hansa. 1902–12. Trade name used by *Carl Hartmann* for a line of dolls jointed at the shoulders and hips.

Hansa. 1926. Dolls with celluloid or rubber heads made by *Buschow & Beck* and distributed by *W. Reinicke*.

Hänsel. 1924. Name of a felt doll made by *Steiff*, representing a boy. Hts. 28, 35 and 43 cm. (11, 14, and 17 in.).

Hansel & Gretel. 1906. Advertised by *Moritz Pappe*.

Hansen, Karen Marie (née Petersen). 1918–20. Silkeborg, Denmark. Obtained Danish and German patents for dolls.★

Hansen, Laurie, & Co. 1915–21. London. Manufactured and/or dressed composition, wax, and cloth dolls. Exported dolls. Specialized in the *Hilda Cowham*, long legged black-stocking dolls with *British Ceramic* or composition heads. Distributed *Vera* dolls made at the *Lord Roberts' Memorial Workshops*. Advertised English dressed French dolls; the heads on these dolls are not specified as to the material. Called their dolls "Laurie" dolls.

1917: Advertised over 100 numbers; some of these had jointed cloth bodies, others had fully or partially jointed composition bodies. Among the dressed dolls were: The *Skating Girl, The Gaiety Girl, The Golf Girl,* Pierrot and Pierrette. These cost as much as $12.37 each, wholesale. Wax dolls wore six different costumes copied from Continental designs. "Rag pattern" dolls, possibly cutout cloth dolls, sold for 80¢ a doz. wholesale.

1918: Advertised Hilda Cowham dolls "Reg. No. 371990," child dolls, bent limb baby dolls with British Ceramic heads, and Pierrettes dressed in silks of various shades.

Hansi (L'Oncle Hansi) (J. Jacques Waltz). 1918–19. Landscape painter and illustrator. He drew the Alsatian characters *Yerri* and *Gretel*, which were made into dolls. Born in 1873, he died in 1951; he was an officer of the Legion d'Honneur and designed toys in the style of d'Epinal.★

1144. Gretel, a doll designed by Hansi and made entirely of Prialytine. It has molded and painted light brown hair and blue eyes, closed smiling mouth. Original clothes and accessories. Mark on doll: Ill. 1094C. Mark on slate: Ill. 1001 H. 8½ in. (21.5 cm.). *Courtesy of the Margaret Woodbury Strong Museum. Photo by Harry Bickelhaupt.*

Hansi. World War I period–1930 and later. Name of a portrait doll designed by the sculptor Herr *Kaiser* and representing the little daughter of *Max Zetzsche*. The *Haralit* head had molded hair, painted or decal eyes, open-mouth with two teeth and dimples. It came on various types of bodies, usually cloth or imitation kid. Often the arms were made of Haralit. (See also **Harald** and **Inge.**)

Hanska. 1914–15. Cloth doll representing one of the "Waifs of Cracow" made by Polish refugees in Paris under the direction of *Mme. Paderewski.*

Happifat. 1913–21. Doll designed by *Kate Jordan,* and produced by *Borgfeldt.*

1920: The composition-head version girl wore a pinafore over its dress and a bonnet.

1921: All-bisque Happifats came in three sizes. Freshie[+] was the name of the Happifat baby.★

Happi-Kiddie Dolls. 1930. Line of dolls distributed by *Monroe Hitz.*

Happiness Dolls. 1925–29. Advertised dressed dolls with composition head and arms, molded hair or wig and sleeping eyes. Dolls were produced in America and included infant dolls of various sizes, *Baby Tunes,* and mechanical walking dolls that it was claimed could walk by themselves for 25 feet. Walking dolls came in four hts.: 14, 18, 20, and 24 in. (35.5, 45.5, 51, and 61 cm.).★

Happinus. 1918. Line of all-composition dolls made by *Amberg* using *Otto Denivelle* type composition. The baby doll came with or without a wig, with or without flirting eyes. There was also a Coquette[+]-type doll with a molded ribbon in its hair. This doll had a diagonal hip joint. Price 75¢.

Happy. 1915–16. Boy doll made by *Trion,* style no. 240, wore a sailor suit; no. 241 wore a Russian-style blouse with a pocket, and pants.★

Happy Ann. See **Gladdie.**

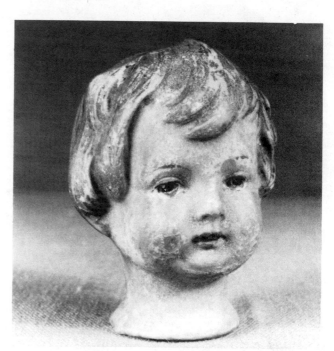

1145. Hansi portrait head made of a special composition called Haralit. This head made by Wagner & Zetzsche in the 1920s has molded and painted brown hair, intaglio blue eyes, an open-closed mouth with teeth, and a flange neck. Mark: Ill. 1146. H. of flange neck head 2 in. (5 cm.). *Coleman Collection.*

1146. Mark found on the Haralit head made by Wagner & Zetzsche and named Hansi.

Happy, Cry. 1924. Trade name of a cloth doll. See Ill. 801.★

Happy Doll Family. 1920. Small dolls, jointed at neck, shoulders and hips, were advertised by *R.F. Novelty Co.* as representing a father, mother, little sister, little brother, infant, French maid, and black nurse. Price $3.75.

Happy Family. See **Collingbourne Mills.**

1147. Felt doll representing Happy Hooligan, a comic character. The only hair on the head is the eyebrows which are embroidered with black yarn in vertical satin stitches. The round almost spherical eyes are the type often found on stuffed animals. The mouth, nose, and ears are appliquéd felt. The five-piece straw filled body has a wooden box with a hinged door that opens in the doll's back. Original clothes of wool except for the cotton waistcoat. The red felt hat represents a tin can with the white felt serving for the label. The green bottle is made of wood. Mark on foot: "Made in Germany." H. 19 in. (48 cm). *Courtesy of the Margaret Woodbury Strong Museum. Photo by Harry Bickelhaupt.*

Happy Flossie. 1927. Baby doll made by *Ideal,* distributed by *Sears.* It had flirting eyes, rubber hands, pacifier and wore an organdy dress and bonnet.

Happy Gallagher. 1914. Composition-head doll advertised by *John Smyth.* It had painted eyes looking to the side, cloth body jointed at the shoulders and hips, straw hat and removable shoes and socks. Ht. 14 in. (35.5 cm.); priced 69¢.

Happy Go Lucky. 1920. Jointed cloth doll with wool hair, dressed in gingham and made by the *Beck Manufacturing Co.*

Happy Helen. 1927–28. Handled by *Charles William.* It had a composition head and arms, cloth body, crying voice, and came dressed. Ht. 15 in. (38 cm.); priced 48¢.

Happy Hiram. 1911–12. One of the American Kid Dolls with a composition head designed by *Helen Trowbridge,* and produced by *Horsman.* The head with molded bobbed hair and bangs, painted eyes, and a smiling open-closed mouth with teeth, appeared to be the same mold as *Daisy Dimple, Hans, Gretchen, Jack Tar, Prince Charlie,* and *Robbie Reefer.* Happy Hiram wore Khaki or blue overalls and a cotton shirt. *Wanamaker* sold it for $1.00.

Happy Hooligan. 1910–14. Trade name of a composition-head doll sold by *Butler Bros.* It had a cloth body and was dressed, representing the comic character drawn by F. Opper.★

Happy Hooligan. 1912. Trade name of a composition head doll sold by *Sears.* It came dressed and by pressing the chest cymbals were activated. Ht. 10½ in (26.5 cm.); priced 90¢ doz. wholesale.

Happy Hooligan. Felt doll made in Germany. See Ill. 1147.

Happy Hooligan. 1923–27. Comic character drawn by F. Opper and made into an all-wood doll by *Schoenhut. Borgfeldt* was the sole licensee and distributor. Ht. 9½ in. (61 cm.).★

Happy Hooligan. 1929. Doll made of California redwood by *Poppy Doll Co.* It was hand painted with washable enamel; the movable parts were controlled by a lever in the back.

Happy Hooligan. See **Ho.**

Happy Jane Line. 1920–23. Washable cloth doll and doll's dress line made by *Harvard Garment Co.* There were 50 style numbers of dolls with hand-embroidered faces. One of the dolls was named *Billy.* Price $2.00 and up a doz. wholesale.★

Happy Tot. 1927–30 and later. Part of the Petite[†] line made by *American Character Doll Co.* This doll had composition head and limbs on a cloth body.

1927: A dimpled, smiling bent-limb baby doll usually with an unbreakable bottle containing a white fluid and with a rubber nipple that could be put into the doll's mouth. The doll wore an organdy baby dress and a halo-style bonnet. It came in four sizes; priced $2.00 and up.

1928: Advertised as having sleeping eyes and a voice. Baby moccasins were part of the costume. Hts. 15, 18, and 21 in.

1148. Happy Tot made by the American Character Doll Co. and advertised in PLAYTHINGS, June 1927. It came with or without its "unbreakable bottle with milk fluid and a real rubber nipple."

(38, 45.5, and 53.5 cm.); priced $2.98 to $4.49.

1929: A new baby doll with a bottle was introduced. It wore new style clothes.

1931: Besides the baby doll there was a Happy Tot *Mama* Doll with composition head and limbs, wig, sleeping eyes, and cloth body. Hts. 18 and 21 in. (45.5 and 53.5 cm.).

Hapusa-Puppe. 1927. Name of a jointed art doll made by *Hermann Hachmeister.*

Harald. 1915–30 and later. Name of a portrait doll designed by the sculptor *Franz Reismann* that represented the little son of Max Zetzsche. This doll was made by *Wagner & Zetzsche.* The Haralit head had painted hair and features; sometimes the eyes were made by using decals. The bodies

varied. They were made of real or imitation leather, or cloth, including stockinet. Sometimes they had ball jointed composition arms and universal leg joints. Celluloid and composition were also used for the arms and legs. (See also **Hansi** and **Inge.**)★

Haralit. See **Wagner & Zetzsche.**

Harania, Joachim. 1912–22. Frankfurt am Main, Hesse.

Harald

W. Z.

1149. Mark on Harald, head of doll made by Wagner & Zetzsche of Haralit.

Obtained several German patents for dolls' heads.★

Harder & Schöler. 1928. Hamburg, Germany. Manufactured and exported dolls.

Hardy, M. 1925–30 and later. Hartford, Conn. Made cloth-body dolls.

Hare, Henry. 1863–1926. Hull, England. Distributor and warehouseman of dolls. A doll with a wax-over-composition shoulder head and limbs, wig, stationary glass eyes, a mouth with four teeth, and a cloth body has "H. Hare, Hull" stamped on its upper leg.

Harlequin (Arlequin). Name for a figure in the COMMEDIA DELL'ARTE, which dates back to the 1600s. Harlequin represented the Valet. Other figures from the COMMEDIA DELL' ARTE which have been made into dolls included *Columbine, Pierrot, Polichinelle,* and *Scaramouche.* Among the makers and/or the distributors of Harlequin were the following:

1830s: *Kestner* in his day book listed Harlequins.

1840s: *Louis Lindner & Söhne* advertised in his catalogs dolls that resembled Harlequins.

1893: *Horsman* advertised Harlequins in his catalog.

1916–18: *Butler Bros.* distributed a doll which they called Harlequin. It had a composition head and hands. It had molded hair, painted features, cloth body jointed at shoulders and hips, and was dressed in a yellow sateen clown suit with brown stars printed on it. The cap was pointed. (This was not a true Harlequin.)

1920: Felt doll made by *Lenci* as number 118 was dressed in a felt Harlequin costume. Ht. 17½ in. (44.5 cm.).

1925: *Fernand Nathan* had a cutout cloth doll named Arlequin in his catalog. The doll had slant eyes and a chromolithographed Harlequin costume. Ht. 17½ in. (44.5 cm.).

1929: Name of a cloth doll made in Florence, Italy.★

Harley & Miller. 1917. Listed in a British toy trade journal as supplying *Alva Maria* (Marina), a dried sea grass used for stuffing dolls.

Harmus, Carl, Jr. 1873–1930 and later. Sonneberg, Thür. By 1919, he was succeeded by Viktor Sachsenweger. Harmus appears to have been a *Verleger* who produced and exported dolls. Some of the bisque heads on his dolls were marked P. M. and/or *Trebor,* which possibly indicated that they were made at the Porzellanfabrik Mengersgereuth in Sonneberg by *Cramer & Héron.* Some Harmus dolls had the Revalo mark of *Gebrüder Ohlhaver.* Other marks were also used; see Ill. 1150.

1896: Applied for a German patent (D.R.G.M.) for a felt-faced doll.

HARMUS
Germany

1150. Mark on a bisque head produced by Carl Harmus.

1900: Applied for a German patent (D.R.G.M.) for a jointed boy doll dressed in pajamas.

1907: Applied for a German patent (D.R.G.M.) for a doll with a voice.

1910: Applied for two German patents (D.R.G.M.): one for a doll with a drinking device; one for a voice in a doll's body. Harmus was one of the Sonneberg group of Grand Prize winners at the Brussels Exhibition.

1911: Advertised felt dolls, character dolls, dolls dressed in regional costumes and a drinking baby.

1913: Applied for a German patent (D.R.G.M.) for a doll's face mask.

1914: Advertised dressed baby dolls.

1919: Advertised jointed composition body and cloth body dolls.

Ca. 1920: Stockinet cloth doll made by Harmus over a pliable iron armature is in the Sonneberg Museum collection. Ht. 27 cm. (10½ in.).

1922: Advertised art dolls.

1924: *Gross & Schild* was their London agent.

1926: Advertised dressed dolls. Made *Our Bobby. Heller & Co.* was the sole British agent.★

Harmuth, Anna. 1908–10. Vienna. Listed in an Austrian directory under Dolls and Dolls' Heads.

Harold Lloyd. Cutout cloth doll representing the moving picture actor of this name. Ht. 12 in. (30.5 cm.). (See also **Harold, The College Boy.**)

Harold Teen. 1929. All-bisque doll with turning head, representing the cartoon character drawn by Carl Ed. It was made in Germany and distributed wholesale, exclusively by *Marshall Field* who also licensed *Shackman.*

Harold Teen. 1929. Oil cloth doll representing the cartoon character of this name drawn by Carl Ed. The doll made by *Live Long Toys* had a spring in its legs and wore a yellow sweater and blue trousers. Ht. 15 in. (38 cm.). Price $10.00 doz. wholesale.

Harold, The College Boy. 1926. Composition doll resembling the motion picture star *Harold Lloyd.* The design for this doll with horn-rimmed glasses was registered by *Whyte, Ridsdale.* It came in two sizes: one was dressed in a sport-shirt, soft collar, belt and flannel trousers; the other wore a sports-jacket.

Harper, G. W. 1918–22. London. Advertised *Eskimo* dolls in various colors in a British toy trade journal.

Harras & Co. 1890–1910. Sonneberg, Thür. Advertised metal dolls' heads and limbs which they obtained from *Buschow & Beck,* according to the Ciesliks' research.

1910: Advertised imitation porcelain dolls on jointed bodies.

Harrass (Harras), Adolph. 1861–1911. Grossbreitenbach,

Thür. Successors were Enders & Wagner. This porcelain factory made dolls.

1911: Advertised character dolls with and without wigs, dressed and undressed, according to the Ciesliks' research. (See also **Grossbreitenbach.**)★

Harrass (Harras), Jul. Eginh. 1886–1898. Grossbreitenbach, Thür. Operated a porcelain factory that made dolls' heads and all-porcelain dolls. (See also **Grossbreitenbach.**)

Harris, Marcus & Lewis. 1925–30 and later. London. Advertised Japanese celluloid baby dolls and *Kewpies*.

Harris Raincoat Co. 1926–30 and later. New York City. Manufactured dolls' clothes including the *Dolly Raindear* outfits. Products were distributed by *Regal.*

Harris, Seymour. 1922. Listed in a British toy trade journal under Dolls.

Harrison, Martha R. 1914–19. Jersey City, N.J., and New York City. Obtained a U.S. patent for a doll's hand with a rubber band threaded through it so that when the fingers were moved they automatically resumed their original position.★

Harrison Manufacturing Co. 1927. Shelby, Mich. Made a wooden doll named *Brownie Ben.*

Harrods. 1859–1980 and later. London. Distributed dolls. It is not certain when they began to distribute dolls.

1912: Catalog advertised jointed child type dolls and baby dolls. These had sleeping eyes, except for a doll with a character face; several of the larger dolls had hair eyelashes. The baby doll was dressed in England and wore removable long clothes. Some of the other larger dolls also wore removable clothes made in England. The other dolls were probably dressed elsewhere in clothes that were sewed on the dolls. Hts. ranged from 10 to 19 in. (25.5 to 48 cm.).

1918: Catalog advertised jointed dressed dolls including *Mimi.*

1919: Catalog advertised jointed dressed dolls including *Fairy* Dolls.

1927: Catalog showed *Mabel Lucie Attwell* dolls, Knockabout Dolls, and other dolls representing girls.

1927–28: Harrod specialized in *Princess Elizabeth* Dolls and dolls for doll balls. (See THE COLLECTOR'S BOOK OF DOLLS' CLOTHES for references to dolls in other Harrods' catalogs.)

Harry (Dutch Fisherman). Before 1911–24. Jointed felt doll made by *Steiff* and distributed in the U.S. by *Borgfeldt.* It was dressed as a fisherman in a So'wester type hat, short trousers and felt shoes shaped like wooden ones. Five hts.: 28, 35, 43, 50, and 60 cm. (11, 14, 17, 19½, and 23½ in.). The 35 cm. size cost $1.00 in Germany in 1911 and $1.90 in New York in 1913. The 43 cm. size cost $1.89 in Germany in 1911 and $3.65 in New York in 1913 but it included a mama voice.

Gamage sold the four smallest sizes in 1913 and described the removable costume as Dutch; priced $1.12 to

$3.62. By 1924 ht. 60 cm. (23½ in.) was discontinued.

Hart Doll, The. 1930. Trademark registered in U.S. by *Violet D. Steinmann* for dolls.

Hartleys Sports Stores. 1928. Melbourne, Australia. Advertised dressed and undressed bisque-head dolls, composition-head dolls, cloth dolls and rubber dolls, including *Jutta* dolls, *New Born Baby, Lucille* dolls, *Lenci* and imitation Lenci dolls; *Mascot* dolls; *Tennis* dolls, and *Mama* dolls.

Hartmann, Carl. 1889–1930. Neustadt near Coburg, Thür., and later Bavaria. Produced and exported dressed dolls especially small dolls in regional costumes which were usually *Globe Babies.* Hartmann obtained his bisque and celluloid heads from *Kämmer & Reinhardt* and/or their sources.

1893: Advertised dressed dolls and their trousseaux.

1899: Applied for a German patent (D.R.G.M.) for a bisque-head doll dressed in wool or silk.

1902: Advertised *Hansa* dolls.

1903: Advertised *Paladin Baby.* Applied for three German patents (one D.R.G.M. and two D.R.P.); one of the latter patents, with Kämmer & Reinhardt, pertained to sleeping eyes in celluloid dolls.

1905: Globe Baby dolls were distributed in London by *Max Carl.*

1908: Advertised *Marta* and *Viktoria Luise* dolls.

1910: Mentioned *Pionier [sic]* dressed dolls.

1912: Advertised *Columbia* line of dolls.

1914: Applied for a German patent (D.R.G.M.) for a jointed doll.
　　Advertised dressed Waltershausen, Kämmer & Reinhardt ball-jointed babies.

1919: Advertised *Daheim* dolls.

1921: Produced dressed and undressed jointed dolls. Sole British agent was *Joseph Layfield.*

1922: Advertised *Erika* dolls.

1926: Applied for two German patents (D.R.G.M.) for dolls' arms.

1927: Advertised Erika and Globe Baby as well as dressed felt dolls and dolls with "unbreakable washable heads."★

Hartmann, Karl. 1914–26. Stockheim. Bavaria. Manufactured and exported bent-limb and ball-jointed composition body dolls.

1914: Applied for a German patent (D.R.G.M.) for jointed dolls.

1926: Became bankrupt according to the research of the Ciesliks.

Hartung, Kuno. 1908. Sonneberg, Thür. Applied for several German patents (D.R.G.M.) relating to dolls' eyes.

Hartwieger, L. 1908–10. Vienna. Listed in an Austrian

1151. Bisque head doll produced by Carl Hartmann. It has a wig, glass eyes, and a ball-jointed composition body. The crocheted outfit is probably contemporary with the doll and the footwear appears to be original. H. 8 in. (20.5 cm.). *Courtesy of Victoria Harper.*

directory under Dolls and Dolls' heads.

Hartwig, Robert. 1879–1929. Sonneberg, Thür. Manufactured and exported dolls.

1879: Obtained a German patent for dolls.

1910: One of the Sonneberg group of Grand Prize winners at the Brussels Exposition.★

Harva. 1928–30. Line of rubber dolls in red and other colors, imported and distributed by *Julius Schmid.* The dolls had molded clothes and hair, no articulation, and legs apart. There were at least 12 models representing boys and girls.

Harvard Boy. 1904. Bisque-head doll with white shirt having a frilly collar, a big bow tie, short red trousers and a square red hat. Ht. 14 in. (35.5 cm.).

Harvard Garment Co. 1920–23. Harvard, Ill. Advertised *Happy Jane* line of cloth dolls and dolls' dresses.★

Harvard Toy Works. 1930 and later. Malden, Mass. Manufactured cloth dolls.

Harvey Manufacturing Co. 1928. Columbus, Ohio. Listed in an American toy trade journal under Dolls.

Harwin & Co. 1915–21. London. Made *Steiff*-type felt dolls. The dolls were designed by Miss Dorothy Harwin and were named "Dots Dolls." They copied Steiff dolls during World War I, because nations at war are not required to recognize their foe's patents, etc.

The dolls came dressed or undressed. The costumes included various uniforms of the Allies as well as boys and girls.

1915: No. 1, Tommy, a British soldier doll; no. 2, Kiltie, a Scottish soldier doll; no. 3, sailor doll; no. 4, French soldier doll; Boy Scout; British officer; and clown dolls.

1916: Brownie doll, Eyes Right doll, Family dolls including Pa, Ma, Nurse, Baby, Boy, Girl, and Cook.

1917: *Blue Stocking Kid* and *The Educational Doll; Reggie Rations* and *Daisy dolls* were 24 in. (61 cm.) tall.

1918: *Fatty Hoarder* dolls.

1919: John Bull, Elsie Janis, Enchanted Princess, Sweet Lavendar, and Uncle Sam dolls.

1920: Advertised that they had a new line of dolls with three-dimensional faces and the ability to sit or stand. The dolls were as follows: *Aborigines, Arab Sheik,* Boy Blue, Boy Scout, Italian Boy, *Kathleen Mavoureen,* Minni Ha-Ha, Pierrot, Red Cross Nurse, Scottish Soldier, South Sea Islander, and Topsy.

1921: Advertised Bo-Peep, Dutch Girl, The Educational Doll, Eyes Right, Father Christmas, Fumsup, Jazz Clown, Pan, Red Indian, Rosebud, Snow Boy, Squaw, Tinkles, Wobbles, and Zulu Chief.

Harwood, William A. 1862–80s. Brooklyn, N.Y. Produced composition shoulder heads resembling *Lerch* dolls' heads. They had a rectangular sticker on their backs reading: "Manufactured for//Wm. A. Harwood."★

Manufactured for
WM. A. HARWOOD.

1152. Paper label on a papier-mâché shoulder head made for William A. Harwood.

Haskell, Samuel. 1914–26. Brooklyn, N.Y. Obtained several U.S. patents for dolls including one used by the *Mutual Novelty Corp.* This was a *Cigarette Girl* that had bobbed hair and wore a pants suit with a belt and vertical striped fabric for the cuffs and trimming on the pockets. The clothing closely resembled that found on marked *Lenci* lady dolls with cigarettes.★

1153. All-composition Boudoir dolls based on a 1925 design patented by Samuel Haskell and made by the Mutual Novelty Corp. These dolls have wigs, molded and painted eyes; the mouth is made to hold the cigarette. Original clothes as shown in the design patent. H. 24 in. (61 cm.). These dolls also resemble Butler Bros., Miss 1928. *Courtesy of Stephanie and Fred Farago. Photo by Stephanie Farago.*

Hassall, John. 1914–18. England. Artist who designed *Papooski* for *Three Arts Women's Employment Fund.* The dolls that he designed were generally caricatures, for he drew some of the comics found in PUNCH.★

Hattori, Mamil (Mamji). 1904. Tokyo. Exhibited dolls at the St. Louis Exhibition.

Haueisen, Richard. 1908–29. Gehren, Thür. Made cloth dolls especially felt ones which resembled those made by *Steiff,* and Art dolls dressed and undressed. *Kopfovi Weiss's* Store in Prague distributed his dolls.

Created Tyrolean costume dolls that were lent by the Brooklyn Museum for an exhibit in New York City in the 1920s. His dolls were purchased by *Stewart Culin.*

Hausman & Zatulove. 1919. New York City. Made Hau-Zat line of dolls including *Ku-tee* cloth dolls.★

Hausser, Otto. See **Pfeiffer, Emil.**

Haven & Barouck. 1930. Paris. Made and/or distributed dolls.

1917–18: Made *Blue Stocking Kid.*

Hawaiian Dolls. 1921–29. *Lucinani* was one of the few Hawaiian dolls reported. Probably there were native dolls. *Effanbee* and *Langrock Bros.* created dolls representing Hawaiian dancers. Shackman distributed *Yaaka Hula.*

Hawksley & Co. 1895–1920. Liverpool, England. Made dressed and undressed cloth dolls; some had celluloid or Xylonite faces and were stuffed with hair.

1915: Advertised printed dolls and *Eskimo* dolls.

1916: Advertised character baby dolls, calico dolls, and jointed dolls.

1917: Hawksley's nursery rhyme dolls included Dick Turpin, Dick Whittington, Red Riding Hood, Mother Hubbard, Bo-Peep, Cinderella, and Mary Had a Little Lamb. They also advertised "Fur" Pierrot and Pierrette with celluloid faces and dolls' hats.

1920: Produced the Hawcoll series of stuffed dolls.

Hazel, Henry John. 1882–1929. London. Factory at Wolsey Mews. Dressed dolls and made cloth dolls. Hazel called himself a "Doll Costumier" and claimed that he supplied the European continent with better dressed dolls, using the finest jointed dolls made on the Continent. His initials H. J. H. and his address on Caversham Road suggest that he may have produced the dolls with British Ceramic heads marked *Caversham.*

THE TOY AND FANCY GOODS TRADER included the following article on H. J. Hazel in 1922:

"We had the pleasure recently of visiting the works of Messrs. H. J. Hazel, Wolsey Mews, Caversham Road, Kentish Town, London N.W. 5.

"Messrs. Hazel is one of the oldest established firms in London, the business having been established forty years ago. The founder of the business is still alive and taking an active interest in it, but has relinquished the management to his son, who carries on the business according to the old traditions of the firm. It is to Messrs. H. J. Hazel that the toy trade in this country owes the evolution of the English dressed doll. For many years Hazel's have specialized in this department of the business, and to-day they supply the trade all over the world. All the dresses are made in their own workrooms and a tour around the workrooms is more reminiscent of the West-end costumiers than a toy factory.

"We have pleasure in illustrating two or three of the most popular lines run by this firm. We recommend particular attention to a Scotch [sic] doll which is a popular favourite not only in this country but with overseas buyers." See Ills. 489 & 490.

1915: Dressed dolls priced up to $10.50 wholesale.★

Headworth, F., & Co. 1920. London. Listed in a British Toy trade journal under Dolls.

Heap & Co., Messrs. 1916–17. Anerley, London. Made cloth dolls and dolls with *British Ceramic* heads for export and the wholesale trade, including *Pierrette* dolls.

HEbee-SHEbee. 1925–27. All-bisque or all-composition dolls based on the drawings of *Charles Twelvetrees* in the PICTORIAL REVIEW. They had painted features, and molded undershirt and booties—blue booties for the HEbees and pink booties for the SHEbees. These dolls were produced by *Horsman* and came in various costumes. The all-bisque version was marked "Germany" between the shoulders and "60" on the torso's edge; often it wore a paper bib; it was 5 or 9 in (12.5 or 23 cm.) tall; the all-composition version was 10½ in. (26.5 cm.) tall.

1926: Costumes included Collegiate HEbee (No. 204) dressed in a knitted outfit with a big "Y" on its chest and wearing a stocking cap. Sunbonnet Sal SHEbee (No. 207) wore a printed dress and sunbonnet. Betty SHEbee (No. 209) was in a short dress trimmed with lace and had a big bow on the top of its head. Pancho HEbee (No. 216) was dressed in a colorfully decorated sombrero and a long fringed scarf. Also, Brides, Grooms, Ballet Dancers, Charleston Dancers, Cowboys, Sailors, Toreadors, and others.

1927: New styles of clothes were available.★

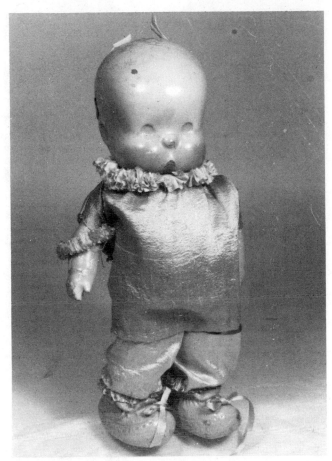

1155. All-composition HEbee-SHEbee; molded and painted features and shoes. Jointed at the shoulders and hips. Original clothes. H. 11 in. (28 cm.). *Courtesy of Richard Withington. Photo by Barbara Jendrick.*

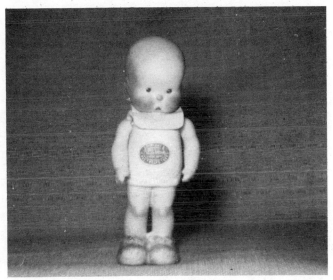

1154A. All-bisque HEbee-SHEbee doll based on the illustrations of Charles Twelvetrees. All the features and clothes are molded and painted. It is jointed only at the shoulders. The doll wears a molded shirt and shoes and a paper bib. Mark: Ill. 1154B. See Ill. 42 for other dolls similarly constructed. H. 4 in. (10 cm.). *Courtesy of the late Henrietta Van Sise.*

1154B. Mark on a paper sticker found on the stomach of an all-bisque HEbee-SHEbee doll.

Heber, P. 1926. Strasbourg, France. Made dolls.

Hecht, Else. 1920–30. Munich, Bar. The following artists made dolls in Else Hecht's workshops: *Brunhilde Einenkel, Elise Israel, Betty Krieger, Dora Petzold, Lotte Pritzel* and *Strasser.*★

Hecht, Pfeiffer. 1926. London. Listed in a British toy trade journal under Dolls.

Heckerau. 1890s. Waltershausen, Thür. According to a U.S. Department of Commerce report this was one of the first companies in Germany to make celluloid dolls' heads.

Hecquet, Mme. J. 1920s. Paris. Member of the *Chambre Syndicale.* Made clothes and accessories including jewelry and watches for bébés.

Hegemann, Alice. 1908–9. Germany. Artist who worked with *Marion Kaulitz.* She dressed dolls that had heads designed by *Josef Wackerle* and *Marie Marc-Schnür.*★

Hegone Studio. 1930 and later. New York City. Made cloth dolls.

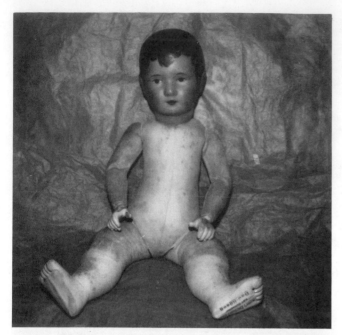

1156. Cloth doll made by Heine & Schneider with molded face that has painted features, and composition hands. Mark: Ill. 1158A. H. 17½ in. (44.5 cm.). (Note that this doll was made in the same town as the Käthe Kruse Dolls.) *Courtesy of Joan Kindler.*

1157. Doll made by the Heine & Schneider art doll factory entirely of pressed cardboard covered with muslin. It has molded and painted hair, brown eyes, and spring joints at the neck, shoulders, and hips. Original clothes. Mark: Ill. 1158B. H. 17 in. (43 cm.). *Courtesy of Betty Kudlo.*

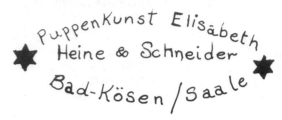

Schneider's Kunstpuppen-Atelier
Karl Schneider
Bad-Kösen

PuppenKunst Elisäbeth
★ Heine & Schneider ★
Bad-Kösen/Saale

1158A & B. Marks stamped on the foot of cloth dolls made by Heine & Schneider. See Ills. 1156 and 1157.

Heho Art Dolls. 1928. New models from Paris were sold by *Leo Weigert* of Nürnberg. These were sofa dolls, *auto* dolls, other decorative dolls and dolls representing characters in theatrical revues.

Heideröschen (Wild Rose). 1928. Trademark registered in Germany by *E. W. Mathes* for dolls.

Heidler, Heinrich. 1898. Neustadt near Coburg, Thür. Made cloth bodies for dolls.

Heimann, Oskar. 1909. Erfurt, Thür. Applied for a German patent (D.R.G.M.) relating to a doll's leather body.

Heimbrodt, Adolf. 1928. Sonneberg, Thür. Made character dolls and *Boudoir* dolls. One of the latter had a wig and wore a pants suit.

Heimlich, Isaak. 1910. Vienna. Listed in an Austrian directory under Dolls and Dolls' Heads.

Heincke (Heinecke), Hans. 1903–11 and later. Waltershausen, Thür. Obtained a German patent (D.R.P.) for making pressed forms to be used as dolls' parts. By 1911 he was the owner of the *Adolf Wislizenus* firm.

Heine. 1917. Trade name of one of the El-Be-Co line of dolls made by *Langrock Bros. Co.* This chubby composition character doll sold for $1.00.

Heine & Schneider. Before 1920–22. Bad-Kösen, Saale. Art doll factory started by Elizabeth Heine and Schneider. Successors in 1920 were Karl Schneider and Günther Heine. By 1922 Günther Heine was the sole successor. Made dolls of pressed cardboard covered with flesh-colored muslin. A doll has been reported with a purple stamp on the bottom of its foot reading "Puppen Kunst Elizabeth//Heine & Schneider //Bad-Kösen/Saale" (Art Doll Elizabeth). The features and hair were hand painted with oil paint. The cheeks were almost as red as the lips and the ears were pink in color. This chubby doll had spring joints at the neck, shoulders and a diagonal hip joint. It wore a vestee with black velvet ribbon forming pseudo lacings. The one piece undergarment formed a guimpe and a petticoat. The dress was completely lined with organdy. Footwear consisted of white socks and black oil cloth slippers with ankle ties. Ht. 17 in. (43 cm.).

1922: Advertised hts. 30, 45 and 47 cm. (12, 17½ and 18½ in.).

Heineck, Otto. 1919–20. Kiel-Gaarden, Germany. Obtained a German patent (D.R.P.) for the articulation of dolls.

Heinecke. See Heincke.

Heinerle. 1929–30. Trade name of a stockinet baby doll created by *Helene Haeusler* and made by *Cuno & Otto Dressel*. It had a pressed face, painted eyes and hair. The thumb was separate from the rest of the fingers, which were indicated by sewing. It carried a red and white cloth tag with the Dressel winged helmet mark on it. Ht. 31 cm. (12 in.).

Heinrich's, Geschwister (Brother and Sister). 1925–30 and later. Nürnberg, Bavaria. Made art dolls, including cloth dolls. (See also Geschwister Heinrich's Kunstlerpuppen[†].)

Heinz. 1924. Name of a doll made by *Steiff*. Ht. 20 cm. (8 in.).

Heinz. 1925. Name of a doll made by *Rheinische Gummi und Celluloid Fabrik*.

Heinz, Alfred. 1906–25 and later. Sonneberg, Thür. Made dolls. From 1906 to 1912 he applied for several German patents (D.R.G.M.) for dolls.★

Heinz, M. See Tietz, Hermann.

Heinz, Rudolf. 1911–28. Prague, Bohemia. His successors took over in 1925. Manufactured composition body dolls.

1912–13: Advertised dolls' heads.★

Heinz, Rudolph, & Co. 1858–1922 and probably later. Neuhaus am Rennweg, Thür. Ernst Heinz was the owner of this porcelain factory in 1913. By 1922 it was called the Aelteste Volkstedter Porzellanfabrik where dolls' heads were made.

1160. Mark on porcelain dolls' heads made by Rudolph Heinz.

1159. Advertisement in DEUTSCHE SPIELWAREN ZEITUNG, February, 1927, for Geschwister (Brother and Sister) Heinrich's Art Dolls.

Heinze, Arthur. 1910–11. Unna, Germany. Obtained a German patent (D.R.P.) for a mechanical doll.

Heinze, Carl. 1861 and probably other years. Hildburghausen, Thür. He was named as one of the creditors when Louise Amadine *Prieur*, a Paris dollmaker, went bankrupt, according to Mme. Poisson, curator of the Roybet-Fould Museum.★

Heio-Beio. 1927. Name advertised by *Scherzer & Fischer* for new born twin dolls.

Heise, Richard. 1929–30. Germany. Made shoes, overshoes and clogs for dolls. *M. Michaelis & Co.* was his Berlin agent.

Heiss, Brush. 1926. Registered *Hankyland Dolls* as a U.S. trademark for dolls.

Heizer, Dorothy Wendell. 1920–30 and later. Essex Fells, N.J. Made cloth dolls with wire armatures. The three dimensional faces were usually of hand painted crepe individually molded. Many of these were portrait and/or period costumed dolls.

1920: Made clothes for dolls.

1161A & B. Cloth doll molded over a form designed and made by Dorothy Heizer to represent the portrait of Mme. Récamier. Gold beads form a comb in the silk yarn hair and trim the dress. Probably made in the 1940s. H. 9½ in. (24 cm.). *Coleman Collection.*

1921: Made flat-faced cloth dolls with painted features. Began to made three-dimensional face dolls with a portrait of Galli-Curci. Made a doll representing a flapper and an 1845 period dressed doll. Hickson's of New York distributed her dolls.

1922: Made dolls by wrapping wire with woolen yarn. The yarn was wrapped around a pencil to make a coil which was sewed in place for the hair and clothes. Also made cloth dolls representing a Bedouin, an Egyptian and a portrait of 10 year old Kate Warriner.

1923: Made dolls representing Cinderella, the Prince, Footman and two Sisters as well as several dolls dressed in period costumes of 1750 and 1820.

MODERN PRISCILLA published an article by Dorothy Heizer concerning a cloth doll named *Penelope* for which there were descriptions of the 13 in. (33 cm.) doll and its wardrobe. For $2.50 the uncut cloth Penelope with its hand-painted face and directions for making it into a three dimensional doll could be purchased together with the patterns for the wardrobe of clothes.

1924: Made inch (2.5 cm.) to the foot (30.5 cm.) cloth dolls for General Electric displays. Also made larger dolls dressed as a man and lady (called Golden Jane) of 1845 and a lady of 1860.

1925: Made large dolls in a proportion of 3 in. (7.5 cm.) to the foot (30.5 cm.), as well as small dolls only 4½ in. (11.5 cm.) tall.

1926: Made dolls in costumes of 1776, 1826, 1876 and 1926 for the Sesquicentennial Exhibition in Philadelphia. Also made portrait dolls of John Alden, Priscilla and a modern girl with an Airedale which went into the Newark Museum collection. Continued to make inch to the foot dolls which were distributed through the Arden Studios to be used with Tiny Toy Furniture in dolls' houses.

1928: Made dolls dressed in period and modern costumes; priced $10.00 to $45.00. In later years prices for new Heizer dolls were quoted as high as $1,000. It is claimed that she used real gold beads to trim some of the clothes.

MODERN PRISCILLA had an article and pictures of a pattern for a long-legged doll named Flossie which was designed by Heizer. In the editor's note she remarks that "little girls like dollies that are 'real.' College girls get the thrill of a lifetime out of such swagger mascots."

1929: Made dolls representing contemporary brides and Alice-in-Wonderland as well as the Duchess.

1930: Made George and Martha Washington, Lafayette and Benjamin Franklin for the Newark Museum. Began to make period costume dolls for Mrs. Frank Noyes whose collection later went to the Smithsonian. Made a group of nursery rhyme characters 5 in. (12.5 cm.) tall.★

Held, Adolf. 1928–29. Munich, Bavaria. Obtained a German patent (D.R.P.) for a walking doll.

Held, Rosa. 1923–28. Nürnberg, Bavaria. Obtained a German patent (D.R.P.) for jointed dolls.

Held, Willy. 1926–30. Listed in a British toy trade journal under Dolls.

Helen. Mid 1800s. Porcelain shoulder head with molded hair and hat, marked "Helen." Ht. of shoulder head 18 cm. (7 in.) according to the Sonneberg Museum. (Not to be confused with the *Pet Name* "Helen.")

Helen. Name of a bisque head made in Germany.

1162. "Helen" mark on a German porcelain head.

Helen. 1919. Trade name of a composition doll with a full-bodied wig, representing a little girl; made by *Jessie M. Raleigh.*

Helen. See **Hellen.**

Helen. See **Pet Name.**

1163. Felt doll named Hellen (Helen), made by Steiff, has a button in the ear. The doll has light brown mohair sewn to the scalp, beadlike glass eyes with black pupils, closed mouth, and joints at the shoulders and hips. Original clothes, including felt "wooden" shoes. H. 48 cm. (19 in.). *Courtesy of Richard Wright. Photo by A. Jackson.*

Helena. See **Pritzel, Lotte.**

Helen's Babies. 1884. Trade name of a dressed bisque-head, composition-body doll, jointed at the neck, shoulders and hips. Four hts.: 5½, 6½, 7½, and 9 in. (14, 16.5, 19, and 23 cm.); priced 25¢ to 40¢.

Helen's Babies. 1915–18. Dolls modeled by sculptress *Helen Fraser Rock* from real children. Made by *Nottingham*. Dolls had "Rock China" (a form of *British Ceramic*) heads, wigs, cloth bodies and were dressed as babies, little boys in suits or little girls in short dresses. They had removable clothes and some of them were 18 in. (45.5 cm.) tall.

Helft, Jacques. 1925–28. Paris. Handled celluloid dolls including swimmers. Agent was Joyard, Sr. ★

Helk, Berthold. 1913–18. Neustadt near Coburg, Thür. Applied for a German patent (D.R.G.M.) for dolls' bodies. ★

Hellé, André. Ca. 1912–18. Paris. Before World War I this French artist made models that were used to create expensive dolls. During the War he carved wooden dolls with *M. Carlègle*. These dolls were sold by *Printemps*.

Hellen (Helen) (Dutch Fisherwoman). Before 1911–24. Felt character doll made by *Steiff* and distributed in the U.S. by *Borgfeldt*. It was dressed as a fisherwoman in a plaid blouse, an apron and felt "wooden" shoes. Five hts.: 28, 35, 43, 50, and 60 cm. (11, 14, 17, 19½, and 23½ in.). The smallest size cost $1.25 in Germany in 1911 and $2.20 in New York in 1913. The 43 cm. size cost $2.50 in Germany in 1911 and $4.30 in New York in 1913 with a mama voice.

Gamage sold all five sizes of Helen in 1913 and described the removable costume as Dutch; priced $1.23 to $3.75.

1924: Four hts. were 28, 35, 43, and 50 cm. (11, 14, 17 and 19½ in.).

Heller, Adolf. 1914–30. Waltershausen, Thür. Made ball-jointed dolls, character babies, new born infants, *Mama* dolls, dolls with flirting eyes, dolls with moving tongues, small dolls, child dolls and lady dolls. The specialty was *Meine Goldperle (My Gold Pearl)*.

1930: London agent was *E. Turner*.

Heller, Alfred. 1901–10. Meiningen near Coburg, Thür. Made metal dolls' heads named *Diana*.

1901: Applied for a German patent (D.R.G.M.) for metal dolls' heads. ★

Heller, William M. See **Stein, Charles.**

Heller & Co. 1926. London; Nürnberg, Sonneberg and Olbernhau, Germany. Importers and factory agents. Sole British agent for *Carl Harmus, Jr.* Advertised *Our Bobby*.

Helma (Dutchwoman). 1911–16. Felt art doll made by *Steiff*. It wore a Dutch costume in various colors and wooden (?) shoes. In 1911 the ht. was 50 cm. (19½ in.). In 1916 the five hts. were 28, 35, 43, 50, and 60 cm. (11, 14, 17, 19½, and 23½ in.).

Helmut. 1924. Name of doll made by *Steiff*. Ht. 20 cm. (8 in.).

Helvetic, I. & M. (H. M.), Corp. 1927–28. New York City. Made musical mechanical dolls with squeeze bellow musical movements in the cloth bodies. Many of their dolls were mounted on horses including cowboys, cowgirls, Indians, Arab Sheiks and George Washington.

Helyette. 1928. Name of a cloth doll sold by *Bon Marché*. It had a felt head, wig, and wore a lace-trimmed organdy dress. Ht. 52 cm. (20½ in.).

Hempel, John. 1817 and other years. Sold in England dolls of papier-mâché and wood representing a cobbler and wife.

Hendeles, S. 1926–29. London. Made dolls.

Henderson Glove Co. 1927–30 and later. Creston, Iowa. Manufactured cloth dolls representing American Indians. These came already stuffed or as cutout cloth dolls representing an Indian chief named *Buck* and a *Squaw*. Dolls short and fat had printed clothes. The trademark was a shield with the word "Master built" above an Indian head with a swastika on each side of the head. Under the head were the words *"Brownface Indian."* Dolls sold for 50¢ and $1.00. Similar dolls had been made by *Tambon Co.*

1164. Mark used by the Henderson Glove Co. for their cloth Indian dolls.

Hendrenite. 1928–29. Trade name for composition used by *Averill Manufacturing Co.* for their Madame Hendren dolls. They claimed it would not crack or peel, could be cleaned with a damp cloth, was durable and registered greater molding detail than was formerly possible.

Hendrix. Roberta W. 1919–23. Chicago, Ill. Obtained a U.S. patent for a walking doll.

Hengerer, Wm., Co. 1929. Buffalo, N.Y. Imported dolls including a *Lenci* boy and girl, price $18.50 each; and Alice Marie, a doll that could sing and say her prayers, priced at $22.50. They had to pay the required 90 percent duty on their dolls if the clothes were trimmed with lace.

Henio. 1915. One of the dolls promoted by *Mme. Paderewski* to aid Polish refugees. It was made in the workshop of *Mme. Lazarski* by Polish refugee artists. The clothes of this boy doll represented the holiday attire of country people and were similar to those worn by *Romano* but of different material.

Henn, Martin. 1899–1910. Vienna. Manufactured dolls and dolls' heads.

Henry, Beulah I. 1926. New York City. Obtained a U.S. patent for a doll.

Henze, L., & Steinhauser. 1869–1930 and later. Erfurt and Gehren, Thür. Founded by Laura Wacker (Mrs. Henze) and Anna Wacker (Mrs. Steinhauser) in Erfurt. Later moved to Gehren and Kurt Steinhauser, son of Anna, was the succes-

sor in 1907. Made cloth dolls, art dolls and dressed many of their dolls in regional costumes.

1886: Factory employed 400 workers. Made "wool dolls."

1895: Advertised dolls with wool heads, celluloid heads, celluloid face masks or composition heads.

1910: Advertised plush dolls with mama-papa voices, *Eskimo* dolls, dolls dressed in military uniforms of various countries and Chantecleer dolls. Dolls exported to America had special marks.

1912: Advertised character babies.

1920: Advertised plush dolls, jointed dolls and babies.

1925–27: Produced Art dolls.
   (Part of the above information was based on research by the Ciesliks.)★

Herber, P. 1926–30. Strasbourg, France. Made dolls.

Herberg, Paul. 1930. Advertised dolls dressed in chenille in a German toy trade journal.

Herbert. 1911 and earlier. Felt doll made by *Steiff.* It had long feet and was dressed as a boy wearing a sweater. Ht. 35 cm. (14 in.).

Herbillon. 1858–63. Paris. He was one of several important makers of dolls on the rue de Choiseul.

1858: Obtained a French patent for reinforcing a doll's porcelain head with a cloth lining.★

Herbst, Richard. 1910–23. Steinach and Neustadt near Coburg, Thür. Applied for a German patent (D.R.G.M.) for a doll with its head and torso in one piece.★

Herby. 1926–29. One of the oil cloth comic cartoon characters made by *Live Long Toys* based on the drawings of *Walter Berndt* published in the CHICAGO TRIBUNE and NEW YORK NEWS. Herby, *Smitty*'s little brother, was No. 21, dressed as a small boy in a red coat and cap. The names "Herby" and "Walter Berndt" were on the doll. Ht. 11 in. (28 cm.); priced $4.00 a doz. wholesale.

Herby. 1929. All-bisque doll with jointed neck and molded clothes, made in Germany and distributed wholesale exclusively by *Marshall Field* and *Shackman.* It represented the comic character drawn by *Walter Berndt* in the *Smitty* cartoons. Price $1.10 doz. wholesale or 15¢ retail.

Herby. Cutout cloth comic character doll, licensed by Famous Artists Syndicate. Ht. ca. 8 in. (20.5 cm.).

Herculean. 1884. Line of composition-head dolls distributed by *Lauer,* had various "Hair head-dresses," glass eyes, embroidered chemise, painted shoes and stockings. Seven hts.: 13, 14½ 16, 18, 19½, 21½ and 23½ in. (33, 37, 40.5, 45.5, 49.5, 54.5 and 59.5 cm.); priced $1.75 to $5.75 doz. wholesale.

Hercules. Another name for *Schoenhut*'s *Gent Acrobat.*

Hergershauser (née Baehr). 1925–26. Berlin. Obtained a British patent for a rubberlike coating for dolls that were cast around wire cores or joints. The coating was made of colloidal-glue gelatine or vegetable mucilage with glycerine added.

Hering, F., & Co. 1926. Köppelsdorf, Thür. Made porcelain dolls' heads

Hering, Julius. 1893–30 and later. Köpplesdorf, Thur. 1908–30 and later, J. Hering & Sohn. Made porcelain dolls' heads among them bisque heads marked *VICTORIA*. (The Vililaria in the first COLLECTOR'S ENCYCLOPEDIA OF DOLLS is a misreading of this mark.) (See also **Dressel & Koch.**)★

1165A & B. Marks used by Julius Hering on bisque dolls' heads.

1166A. Hermsdorfer Celluloidwarenfabrik advertisement in DEUTSCHE SPIELWAREN ZEITUNG, February, 1927, showing one of their patented Drinking Babies. This has a detachable drinking mechanism hand to facilitate dressing, a flask with refill liquid, and a funnel to replace the milk liquid.

Herirel, W. 1919–21. London. Imported and exported dolls and dolls' heads.

Herman, L. 1927. U.S.A. Made *Mama* dolls. He was licensed by *Voices, Inc.* to use their patented mama voices and criers in his dolls.

Hermann, Bernhard. 1925–28. Sonneberg, Thür. Produced ball-jointed dolls, felt dolls, *Mama* dolls, sofa dolls, and *auto* dolls. Many of the dressed dolls represented adults. (See also **Herrmann, Bernhard.**)

Hermann & Co. 1920–30 and later. Coburg, Bavaria. Made plush dolls.

Hermsdorf, Georg. 1917. Chemnitz, Saxony. Applied for a German patent (D.R.G.M.) for military dolls.

Hermsdorfer Celluloidwarenfabrik. 1925–27. Berlin-Hermsdorfer. Made celluloid dolls, baby dolls and dolls' heads. London agent was *Gross & Schild.*

1925: Applied for a German patent (D.R.G.M.) for a drinking celluloid baby doll.

1926: Applied for a German patent (D.R.P.) for a jointed doll with a drinking mechanism.★

1166B. Trademark of Hermsdorfer Celluloidwarenfabrik representing a ladybug.

Herold, Christoph. 1909–26. Schalkau, Thür. Made dolls.

Heront, V. 1921–27. Prague, Czechoslovakia. Made dolls.

Herrmann, Bernhard. 1914. Sonneberg, Thür. Applied for a German patent (D.R.G.M.) for a jointed art doll with a head of pressed and soft stuffed leather. (See also **Hermann, Bernhard**).

Herrmann, Carl. 1914. Osnabrück, Germany. Applied for a German patent (D.R.G.M.) relating to the shoulders of a doll.

Herrmann, Carl. 1924–26. Potsdam, Germany. Made dolls and dolls' parts.

1926: Obtained a German patent (D.R.P.) for the compositions and processes used in making dolls and dolls' parts.★

Herrmann, Carl Albert Georg. 1905–6. Dresden, Germany. Obtained an Austrian patent for dolls' heads.★

Hertel, Schwab & Co. (Stutzhauser Porzellanfabrik). 1910–30 and probably later. Stutzhaus near Ohrdruf, Thür. Founded by August Hertel and Heinrich Schwab, both of whom designed dolls' heads. Their dolls' heads were used by *George Borgfeldt (Bye-Lo Baby); Kley & Hahn* (mold #s 133, 135, 138, 158, 160, 161, 162, 166, 167, 169, and 180); *König & Wernicke* (mold #s 98, 99, 157 and 170); Albert Schachne (mold #148); *Strobel & Wilken* (mold #s 163, 165, 172, and 173); Rudolf Walch (mold #142); *Wiesenthal, Schindel & Kallenberg* (mold #150); *Louis Wolf* (mold #s 152, 200 and 222). Other mold numbers made by Hertel, Schwab & Co. according to the research of the Ciesliks were 130, 132, 134, 141, 143, 147, 151, 159, 170, 176, 208, 217, and 220. Dolls bearing the marks of either 142 or 154 also seem to belong to this group.

They made china and bisque dolls' heads as well as all-porcelain dolls. Most of their heads had character faces. They came with wigs or molded hair; painted or glass eyes; open mouths usually with tongue or closed mouth; socket or shoulder heads. The heads usually had a mold number and either "Made// in//Germany," or the mark of the company that owned the mold such as Kley & Hahn, Louis Wolf and so forth.

1913: Applied for a German patent (D.R.G.M.) for a doll's moving tongue.★

See Ills. 521, 1041, 1042, 1046, 2232, and 2233.

Hertwig & Co. 1864–1930 and later. Katzhütte, Thür. A porcelain factory was founded here in 1762 by J. W. Hamann, and was still in existence in 1945. The successors, Ernst and Hans Hertwig, began to make dolls' heads and dolls in 1864. In 1894 C. & F. Hertwig were the successors. This Company made *Snow Babies* and *Pet Name* china heads. Old products from the factory are appearing on the market in the 1980s.

1884: Registered mold #s 150A, 150B, 150C for porcelain dolls' heads representing children according to the research of the Ciesliks.

1894–1925: Applied for nine German patents (D.R.G.M.) pertaining to dolls' heads and bodies.

1167A. Bisque head with a wig, blue glass eyes that both sleep and look to the side—a type called "roguish." It has a bent-limb composition baby body. Clothes are contemporary with the doll. The bisque head appears to have been made by Hertel, Schwab & Co. for Strobel & Wilken. Mark: "173.5." H. 12½ in. (31.5 cm.). *Courtesy of Sotheby Parke Bernet Inc., N.Y.*

150
13

1167B. Mark found on a bisque baby doll's head that has an open-closed mouth, made by Hertel, Schwab & Co. for Wiesenthal, Schindel & Kallenberg.

1901: Began to make Snow Babies. The earliest ones were commissioned by *Johann Moll*. Made other types of all bisque dolls.

1911: The bisque upper half of the dolls with molded clothes above the waist line were 2, 2½, and 3 in. (5, 6.5, and 7.5 cm.).

1929: Registered *Bisculoid* as a trademark in Germany for dolls.★

Hertzog (Herzog), G. F., & Co. 1878–1930 and later. Berlin. Successor was Wilh. Dlouhy & Leop. Seidl. Distributed and exported dolls.

1930: Was the agent for *Max Barnikol, Friedmann & Ohn-*

stein, Emma Günther, Karl Kalbitz, König & Wernicke, Hermann Meyer, Müller & Kaltwasser, H. Scharf, Gebr. Schmidt, Karl Standfuss, Margarete Steiff, Gustav Wolf and *Georg Zöllner.*★

Herzi. After 1909. Name found on a bisque-head doll possibly made by *Crämer & Héron.* Ht. 10 in. (25.5 cm.).★

1168. Bisque head doll made by Hertwig has molded and painted hair, features, clothes on torso above the waist, and footwear. The brown trousers and white upper arms are cloth to simulate clothes. H. 4¾ in. (12 cm.). *Coleman Collection.*

Herzlieb (Sweetheart). 1913–25. Trademark registered by *Hugo Wiegand.* This line was advertised by *Scherzer & Fischer.*★

Hess, Albin. 1913–30 and later. Schalkau, Thür. Made dolls.

1913: Applied for a German patent (D.R.G.M.) for dolls' shoes.

1930: Registered *Gymnastik Doll* as a trademark in Germany.

1169. Mark on dolls produced by Albin Hess.

Hess, John. 1909–27. Hamburg, Germany. In 1927 registered *Frizzi* in Germany as a trademark for dolls.★

Hess, Theodore, & Co. 1918–20. New York City. Produced all-composition dolls, dolls with composition heads and hands on cloth bodies stuffed with cork, and all-celluloid dolls. The dolls came with wig or painted hair, with or without sleeping eyes, with shoulder heads or socket heads, dressed or undressed. A band with the word "Hessco" printed on it was attached to the dolls.

1919: Some baby dolls had a milk bottle. Seven Reported heights of dolls were: 14, 15, 16, 16½, 18, 18½, and 21 in. (35.5, 38, 40.5, 42, 45.5, 47, and 53.5 cm.); priced $10.50 to $37.50 a doz. wholesale.

1920: The number of heights was increased so that they ranged from 10 to 24 in. (25.5 to 61 cm.).★

Hessische Spielwaren-Manufaktur. See **Sutter, Prof. Conrad.**

Hett, Oscar. Several googly-eyed dolls have been reported with "Copr// by//Oscar Hett// Germany" marked in script. The dolls had a flange neck and a cloth body. Another reading of this mark is Oscar Hitt.

1170. Mark found on Oscar Hett (Hitt) dolls.

Hett, Wilhelm. 1912. Berlin. Applied for a German patent (D.R.G.M.) for a doll's head with indestructible eyes.

Hetty. 1929. Cloth doll made by *Dean.* In a circle on the chest is "I AM//HETTY//THE//HELP YOURSELF//GIRL."

Hetzel, Louis. 1894–1915. Sonneberg, Thür. Applied for a German patent (D.R.G.M.) pertaining to a doll.★

Hetzel, Peter. 1870s. Sonneberg, Thür. A *London Rag Doll* type bearing this name is in the Sonneberg Museum collection. The doll has a wax head covered with gauze, glass eyes, and a cloth body, and is dressed in a christening robe. Ht. 30 cm. (12 in.).

Heubach, A. Friedr. 1912. Sonneberg, Thür. Applied for a German patent (D.R.G.M.) for a doll's head with sleeping eyes.

Heubach, Ernst (Köppelsdorfer Porzellanfabrik). 1886–1930 and later. Köppelsdorf, Thür. The son of *Armand Marseille* (Herman) married Beatrix, the daughter of Ernst Heubach, and a few years later in 1919 the porcelain factories of Ernst Heubach and Armand Marseille merged to become the Köppelsdorfer Porzellanfabrik. They made bisque dolls' heads with molded hair or wigs, with painted eyes or sleeping eyes. Based on a sample survey mold # 250 was by far the most popular. This was followed by mold #s 300,

1171A. Bisque head doll made by Heubach of Köppelsdorf, dressed in a Hungarian costume of the early 1900s. *Courtesy of the Hungarian National Museum.*

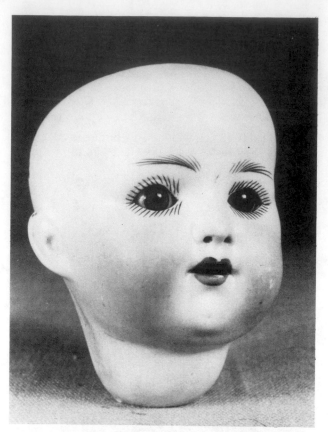

1171C. Bisque socket head made by Ernst Heubach of Köppelsdorf. It has a wig, sleeping blue glass eyes, and an open mouth with two upper teeth. Mark: Ill. 1178. H. of head 2½ in. (6.5 cm.). *Coleman Collection.*

1171B. Bisque head doll made by Ernst Heubach of Köpplesdorf. It has a wig, sleeping dark gray glass eyes, open mouth with 4 upper teeth, and a five-piece composition body. Mark: Ill. 1175. H. 11 in. (28 cm.). *Courtesy of Helen Read. Photo by Steven Read.*

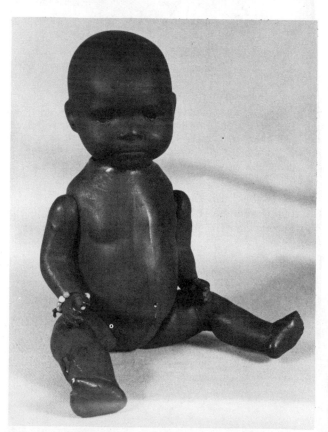

1173. Black bisque head baby marked as shown in Ill. 1180, on a bent-limb composition baby-style body. The socket head has glass eyes, closed mouth, and pierced ears. Dressed in a long white infant's dress. H. 10 in. (25.5 cm.). Circumference of head 7¼ in. (18.5 cm.). *Coleman Collection.*

1172A & B. Bisque head doll made by Ernst Heubach of Köppelsdorf with a wig, sleeping brown glass eyes, pierced nostrils, open mouth with teeth, and a five-piece composition toddler body. Original clothes. Mark: Ill. 1179. H. 8½ in. (21.5 cm.). *Courtesy of Iverna and Irving Foote. Photo by Irving Foote.*

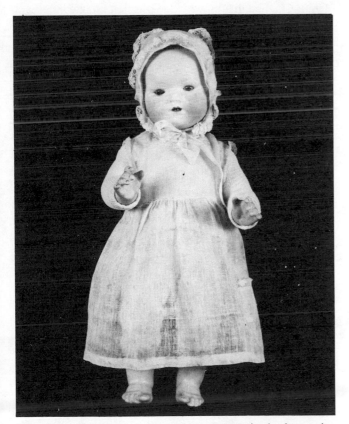

1174. Bisque head baby doll made by Ernst Heubach of Köppelsdorf. It has molded and painted hair, blue glass eyes, open mouth with two lower teeth. The bent-limb composition body is of the late 1920s type that could sit or stand. Original clothes. Note the pocket near the hem of the skirt. Mark: "Heubach Köppelsdorf//400 2/0//Germany." H. 37 cm. (14½ in.). *Courtesy of the Collection Nederlands Kostuummuseum, the Hague. Photo by B. Frequin.*

1175
Heubach.
250·12/0
Koppelsdorf
Thuringia

1176
Heubach
267·7/0
Köppelsdorf
D·R·G·M·
Thuringia

1177
275·14/0
E H·Germany·
D·R·G·M·

1178
Heubach-Koppelsdorf
320·14/0
Germany

1179
Heubach-Koppelsdorf
321·14/0
Germany

1180
Heubach·Köppelsdorf
399 13/0·D·R·G·M·
Germany

1181
1900 7/0

1175–1181. Marks of Ernst Heubach of Köppelsdorf, found on bisque dolls' heads.

320, and 399. Mold numbers ranged from 250 to 452. Size numbers ranged from 18/0 to 9. There was considerable variation in the size-height relationships probably due to different types of bodies. Size 9/0 tended to be 11 in. (28 cm.); size 4/0, 14 in. (35.5 cm.) tall and size 2/0, 19 in. (48 cm.) tall. Sometimes the body was marked with a number denoting the doll's height in centimeters.

This factory made porcelain dolls' heads for *Cuno & Otto Dressel (Jutta), Johannes Gotthilf Dietrich (Igodi)*—sometimes used in *Amberg* dolls, *Gebrüder Ohlhaver (Revalo), Seyfarth & Reinhardt* (S U R), *Adolf Wislizenus* and others. Many of these dolls were dressed in regional costumes.

1915: Factory employed about 140 workers according to the Ciesliks.

1923: Supplied bisque heads to W. & R. *Eckart* including molds #250 and #300 with sleeping eyes and hair eyelashes. They came in various sizes.

1930: Supplied mold #342 to W. *Cohen & Sons* for a doll named *Curly*.

Heubach, Gebrüder (Bros.). 1820–63. Lichte near Wallendorf, Thür. 1863–1930 and later. Successors of Gebrüder Heubach. According to the Ciesliks, Christoph and Philipp Heubach bought the factory of Wilhelm Liebmann in 1840. Later they made bisque heads for dolls and all-bisque dolls. By 1894 Philipp Ottakar and Richard Heubach were the successors. The factory was still operating in 1945. The heads were either socket or shoulder heads and came with molded hair or wigs, with intaglio eyes or sleeping glass eyes. The size numbers range from 14/0 to 8 and perhaps beyond. The heights are at least from 4 to 26 in. (10 to 66 cm.) tall. The mold numbers appear to go from 5636, one of the most popular molds with an open-closed mouth and two lower teeth, to mold #10,633. Most of the mold numbers in the 5,000s, 6,000s, and 7,000s have the sunburst mark, while the mold numbers of the 8,000s and 9,000s are more likely to have the square mark.

A sample showed over twice as many dolls with the square mark as were reported with the sunburst mark. Several of the square mark dolls were known to have been on the market between 1910 and 1914. Among the Heubach dolls given names were *Chin Chin Baby, Dainty Dorothy, Dolly Dimple, Elizabeth,* and *Whistling Jim.* Heubach supplied dolls to *Cuno & Otto Dressel, Eisenmann,* Carl Hoffmeister[+], *Wagner & Zetzsche* and others. *Au Nain Bleu* sold dolls with Gebrüder Heubach heads. Heubach may have made heads for *Globe Baby* dolls.

Heads bearing the incised mark 1907 which is often associated with *Jumeau,* have also been found with the green stamp having several numbers which were associated with Gebrüder Heubach. One of these heads was made of the pink bisque, a type that was known to have been used by Gebrüder Heubach for some of their dolls.

1882: Sunburst mark was registered.

1894: Factory had about 400 employees.

1911: Advertised artistically modeled heads. Applied for a German patent (D.R.G.M.) for dolls' heads.

1912–13: *Selchow & Righter* advertised imported dolls that closely resembled Coquette[+] and the molded bonnet baby heads made by Heubach. The dolls were described as "A most unique and handsome line which cannot be duplicated elsewhere." Some of the dolls had bent limbs and some had straight limbs. 10 hts. 6 to 16 in. (15 to 40.5 cm.); priced $1.50 to $9.00 doz. wholesale.

1914: *Marshall Field* advertised tinted bisque character heads that appear to have been made by Gebrüder Heubach. These were shoulder heads with molded hair.

1915: Mlle. Zitzmann modeled some of the Gebrüder Heubach heads according to the Sonneberg Museum.

1917: The Columbus Merchandise Co. advertised bisquehead dolls that appear to resemble those made by Gebrüder Heubach. One style of socket head had a laughing baby face. The body had bent arms and legs. It was jointed at the shoulders and hips. The short lawn baby dress had a matching bonnet. It also wore flannel underwear and shoes. Hts. 10½ and 12 in. (26.5 and 30.5 cm.). Priced $24.00 and $36.00 wholesale. Another version had a molded Dutch style cap with painted flowers. It was on a bent limb composition body. Hts. 8 and 12¾ in. (20.5 and 32 cm.); priced $4.50 to $8.50 doz. wholesale.

1928: Claimed that they made dolls that imitated the Capo Di Monte[+] products.★

Heubach, Gustav. See **Wiefel & Co.**

Heubach, Hugo. 1894–1930 and later. Sonneberg, Thür. and London. Made and exported dolls.

1910: One of the Sonneberg group of Grand Prize winners at the Brussels Exposition.★

Heubach, Oscar. 1883. Thür. Distributed dolls. One of the members of the committee formed to found the Sonneberg Industrial School, according to the Ciesliks.

Heublein, Georg. 1915–30 and later. Sonneberg and Oberlind, Thür. Made dolls, including cloth body dolls and babies.

1927: Advertised Art Dolls.

1931: Advertised dressed baby dolls and dolls in chemise, with cloth bodies.★

Heumann, Bernhard, & Batz, Ernst. 1922–23. Sonneberg, Thür. Obtained a German patent (D.R.P.) for a doll with a voice.

Heumann, Carl. 1918–30 and later. Sonneberg, Thür. Made dressed and undressed dolls, baby dolls and dolls representing children and ladies. Most of the dolls had bisque heads, wigs and jointed composition bodies.

1926: The sole London agent was *Gross & Schild* who handled orders from the colonies as well as Britain. Many of the dressed dolls wore skirts above the knees and large bows or hats. Some of the dolls wore high-heel, single-strap slippers.

1927: Produced a celluloid drinking baby doll.

1928–29: Among their dolls was *Suck-Thumb-Baby.*

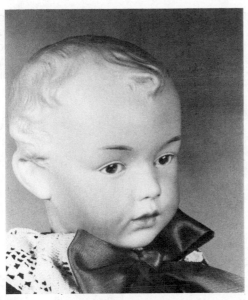

1182. Molded hair bisque character head made by Gebrüder Heubach. It has intaglio eyes and an open-closed mouth. This socket head is on a replaced composition body. Mark: Ill. 1190. H. 17½ in. (44.5 cm.). *Coleman Collection.*

1183. Bisque socket head made by Gebrüder Heubach. It has molded hair and hair ribbon, intaglio eyes, closed mouth, and is on a jointed composition and wood body. Mark: Ill. 1192. H. of head only, 5 in. (12.5 cm.). *Courtesy of the late Magda Byfield.*

1184. Two bisque heads made by Gebrüder Heubach are on five-piece composition bodies. Doll on left: molded and painted hair, intaglio eyes glancing to the side, and a tiny closed mouth. Original clothes. Mark: Ill. 1197. H. 7 in. (18 cm.). Doll on right has flocked hair, intaglio eyes, closed mouth, and original chemise. H. 6 in. (15 cm.). *Courtesy of Richard Withington. Photo by Barbara Jendrick.*

1185. Bisque shoulder head made by Gebrüder Heubach has molded Dutch bob style hair, intaglio eyes glancing to the side, a closed smiling mouth and is on a kid body with bisque forearms. Clothes contemporary with the doll. Mark: "[the square Heubach mark] // 2/0 D //Germany." H. 11¼ in. (28.5 cm.). *Courtesy of June Jeffcott.*

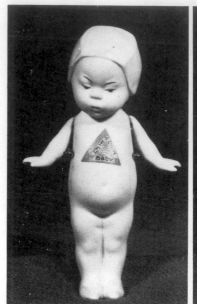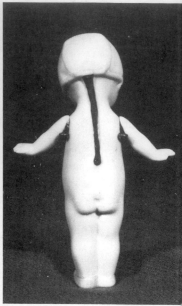

1187A & B. All-bisque doll bearing the label of Chin Chin Baby. See Ill. 538. The square Heubach mark is incised on the bottom of the feet of this doll. It has molded and painted Oriental features, including a queue, yellow shoes, and a purple cap trimmed with black. H. 4¼ in. (11 cm.). *Coleman Collection.*

1186. Bisque head made by Gebrüder Heubach has a pink color throughout the porcelain. It has a reddish brown Rembrandt style wig, sleeping blue glass eyes, open-closed mouth, and is on a fully jointed composition body. The nails on the hands are outlined. Mark: "6" over the square Heubach mark. H. 18 in. (45.5 cm.). *Coleman Collection.*

8 4 2³

8428

Germany
Gebrüder Heubach

G. 1 H.

1188

6⅘   0   86

70   12

DEP
Germany

1189

G

HEU
BACH

1193

6

HEU
BACH
Germany

1194

16   22
DEP

'7
Germany

1190

HEU
BACH
4

1191

10586
11

W. u. J.
J.
Germany

germany
7

1196

90 Heu. 95 Germc

1197

83   81
HEU
BACH

1192

HEU
BACH

1195

1188–1197. Marks found on dolls with bisque heads, made by Gebrüder Heubach.

Heumann, P. 1929. Sonneberg, Thür. Made dolls. His exclusive agent in Belgium and Holland was Jack Van de Kamp.

Heusel, G. I., & Co. 1926. Nürtingen, Germany. Advertised dressed dolls.

Hewitt & Leadbeater (Willow Pottery). 1914–20. Longton, Stoke-on-Trent, Staffordshire. After World War I began, they were the first British firm to manufacture *British Ceramic* dolls' heads, according to THE TOY AND FANCY GOODS TRADER. Later they took over another factory solely for the manufacture of dolls' heads and parts. They made both shoulder and socket heads but appear to have made more shoulder heads than socket heads. Their heads had molded hair or bald heads or heads with pate cut out for wigs, painted eyes or holes for glass eyes. They also made all-bisque dolls including a *Kewpie* type, Some of the shoulder heads were marked on the back of the shoulder "WILLOW ENGLAND" under a number in a square.

1919: 30 ovens were used and over 1,000 people were employed in the making of dolls' heads, arms and legs.

1920: Also known as Hewitt Bros.[†] Made dolls under the name "Willow Crest China."

1198. Doll's shoulder head made of British Ceramic at the Willow Pottery by Hewitt & Leadbeater. Molded hair and pair of bows, painted features, cloth body. Original dress. Mark: Ill. 1199. H. 8 in. (20.5 cm.). *Coleman Collection.*

1199. Mark used by Hewitt & Leadbeater at their Willow Pottery for their British Ceramic heads and limbs.

Heyde, Hermann. 1909–26. Dresden, Germany. Manufactured dolls and dolls' wardrobes.

1910: Registered in Germany the trademark for dolls shown in Ill. 1200.

1200. Marks found on bisque-head dolls probably produced by Hermann Heyde.

Heydecker, William Henri. 1863. Made a walking doll that resembled an *Autoperipatetikos,* according to Mme. Poisson, curator of the Roybet-Fould Museum.

Heyer Brothers. 1855 or before–90s. Boston, Mass. Imported, dressed, and distributed dolls. In the 1855 Boston City Directory, Heyer Brothers, importers and wholesale dealers, were located on Congress Street. By 1860 they had moved to Federal Street and later they moved to Summer Street, where in November, 1872, they suffered tremendous losses in the Boston fire. At least two of their dolls' heads that went through this fire have survived: one is a china shoulder head with a luster snood and brushmarks, ht. 7 in. (18 cm.), now in the Wenham Museum collection, and the other is an untinted bisque shoulder head with a flat-top hairdo now in the possession of a Heyer's descendant. Ht. 6 in. (15 cm.).

The HISTORY OF THE GREAT FIRE IN BOSTON, written in 1873 by Colonel R. H. Conwell, states: "Of the 30,000 women and girls thrown out of employment by the great fire were 200 girls who were employed 16 weeks each year in doll-dressing. Others worked in toymaking." No doubt some of these women and girls were employed by the Heyer Brothers. Apparently they imported the dolls' heads from Germany and probably made the bodies and clothes in their shop, especially during the four months prior to Christmas. After the fire Heyer moved in with Samuel Greech, another toy handler, on Washington Street.

In 1875 Heyer Brothers, importers of toys, appear to have had a factory and/or warehouse on Franklin Street and a retail store on Washington Street. A trade card of Heyer Brothers that appeared to date from the 1880s read: "Importers of Paris Dolls. Large assortment of Dolls' Jewelry." By 1893 they were again located on Federal Street.

Heymann, Armand. 1919–27. Paris. Imported porcelain dolls and celluloid bébés from Japan.★

Heyne, Franz, & Co. 1911–12. Leipzig, Germany. Applied for a German patent (D.R.G.M.) for dolls' heads with a voice mechanism.★

Heywood, Abel. 1918–20. Manchester, England. Advertised dressed and undressed dolls.

Hiasl (Tirolese Boy). 1911–16. Felt character doll made by *Steiff.* It was dressed as a Tyrolean boy. Ht. 35 cm. (14 in.); priced $1.58.

Hiawatha. 1908. Cutout printed cloth doll made by *Saalfield.* This was an American Indian papoose. Ht. 7½ in. (19 cm.).

Hiawatha. 1926. One of the Jedco line of nursery rhyme dolls made by *Jeanette Doll Co.,* and distributed by *Louis Wolf.*

Hiawatha. Name of an all-bisque doll representing an American Indian.

1201. Paper label mark for Hiawatha found on an all-bisque doll.

Hibernian Novelty Co. 1916–17. Dublin. Listed in a British toy trade journal. Manufactured cloth dolls with silk faces and dolls' composition heads and limbs. Specialized in dolls' clothing. Cloth dolls cost 13¢ and up.

Hibsch, Fraulein Hilda. 1891. Schreiberhau, Silesia. Made dressed and undressed dolls, specializing in ball-jointed dolls.

Hicks, H. C. S., & Co. 1930. London. Wholesale agent for rubber dolls made in Germany.

Hickson. See **Heizer, Dorothy.**

Hidoux. 1930 and later. Paris. Made dolls.

Higgs, William. 1733. London. Made wooden dolls. The doll shown in Ill. 836 in the first COLLECTOR'S ENCYCLOPEDIA OF DOLLS and "possibly" attributed to William Higgs is not wood but carton, a type of doll found in French catalogs at the end of the 1700s and therefore unrelated to William Higgs' dolls.★

Highgrade Toy Manufacturing Co. 1916–21. New York City, and Astoria, L.I. Manufactured dolls with painted eyes that sold for $1.00 and up, or with sleeping eyes that sold for $1.50 and up. The cloth bodies were stuffed with cork or excelsior. The factory agent was *Bush Terminal.*★

Highlander. 1913. Felt doll dressed in a Scottish costume with a busby, was made by *Steiff* and sold by *Gamage.* Hts. 17, 20 and 24 in. (43, 51 and 61 cm.); priced $1.37 to $1.88. It was one of the characters portrayed in the 1929 English version of the French book PIERRE PONS, illustrated by Paul Guignebault.

Hi-Jinx. See **Kitts, J. DeLancy.**

Hilcker (Hilker). 1829–48. Paris. Made kid-body dressed dolls.

Hilda. 1914 and later. Name of a bisque-head baby doll made by *Kestner* with sleeping eyes, open mouth and two upper teeth. The name "Hilda" was often, but not always found on these dolls. The painted hair version generally had the copyright symbol and Ges. Gesch. 1070 included in the mark. Dolls with molded and painted hair sometimes had no mold number or 190. These were probably made by Kestner and possibly were versions of Hilda because of their close resemblance. Hilda mold numbers 237 and 245 had wigs. A

black Hilda has been reported marked "Made in Germany// 245//J.D.K. Jr.//1914//©//Hilda." There were also mulatto Hildas. Usually the bodies were bent-limb composition baby bodies. These dolls were probably made in the 1920s as well as prior to World War I. See Ill. 993 for a *Fulper* head that resembles Hilda.★

1202. Bisque Hilda head made by Kestner, with wig, sleeping glass eyes, open mouth with two upper teeth, is on a bent-limb composition body. Mark: "245//J.D.K. Jr. //1914 © Hilda." H. 25 in. (63.5 cm.). Circumference of head 19¼ in. (49 cm.). *Courtesy of Sotheby Parke Bernet Inc., N.Y.*

1203. Bisque Hilda head made by Kestner with wig, sleeping glass eyes, and open mouth with two upper teeth is on a bent-limb composition body. Marked "L. Made in Germany 245 15// J.D.K. Jr.//1914 © Hilda//Ges. Gesch n. 1070." H. 21½ in. (54.5 cm.). Circumference of head 14½ in. (37 cm.). *Courtesy of Richard Withington. Photo by Barbara Jendrick.*

1204. Bisque socket head marked Hilda, made by Kestner. It has molded blond hair, sleeping blue glass eyes, open mouth with two upper teeth, and is on a bent-limb composition body. Clothes are probably contemporary with the doll. H. 11 in. (28 cm.). *Courtesy of Sotheby Parke Bernet Inc., N.Y.*

Hilda Cowham Kiddies. 1916–20. Designed by *Hilda Cowham,* produced by *British Novelty Works,* a subsidiary of *Dean.* These dolls had long legs and were made in a life size and a small size.

Queen Mary purchased one of these dolls.

1920: Number D 258 came dressed and named as follows: Motherly Molly, Spiffkin's the sport (a boy), Mademoiselle, Cheeky Charlie (a boy), Dainty Daphne, *Florrie the Flapper,* Miss Folly, Saucy Sally, Scuttie the Scout (a boy), Nurse Norah, Demure Dora, Jolly Jack (a boy). Height 12 in. (30.5 cm.).

Hilda Cowham Rag Dolls. 1920. Designed by *Hilda Cowham,* produced by *Dean.* These cloth dolls had *Tru-to-Life* faces, hair wigs with either a ribbon band or bow except for Thora with a tam. Their legs were jointed and they wore dresses, long, dark mercerized stockings, and patent shoes. These patent shoes were of polished wood and Dean advertised that "When placed on a slanting wooden board the stilty dolls hobbled from top to bottom." The style numbers were:

D 1029 Flaxen Flora, embroidery on the dress.
D 1030 Darling Dora, white dress with red dots;
D 1031 Tantalizing Thora, felt costume and tam;
D 1032 Captivating Cora, rosebud print dress;
D 1033 Laughing Laura, floral spray print dress;
D 1034 Natty Nora, dotted blouse and black and white checked skirt.

Hilde (Toddler). 1911–16. Felt character doll made by *Steiff* and distributed by *Borgfeldt* in the U.S. It represented a toddler and wore a white dress and baby cap. Hts. 28 and 35 cm. (11 and 14 in.). The 28 cm. doll was priced $1.31 in Germany in 1911 and $2.20 in New York in 1913. In 1916

the five hts. were 28, 35, 43, 50, and 60 cm. (11, 14, 17, 19½, and 23½ in.).

Hilde. 1925. Trade name used by *Rheinische Gummi und Celluloid Fabrik* for dolls.

Hildebrand, Fritz. 1920–22. Berlin. Obtained a German patent (D.R.P.) for a doll.

Hildebrand, Robert. 1909. Leipzig, Germany. Applied for a German patent (D.R.G.M.) for dolls.

Hilgendorf, M. See **Petsch, C. L.**

Hill, Ernest Walter, & Cushing, Edwin Charles. 1914. England. Manufacturers of dolls who applied for a British patent for dolls.

Hiller, Robert. 1887–95. Breslau, Silesia. Made dolls' bodies and dressed dolls. Used R. H. in a circle with a drawing of a swan as a mark.

1205. Mark used by Robert Hiller on dolls.

Hillmann, Friedrich. 1902–9. Sebnitz, Saxony. Applied for a German patent (D.R.G.M.) for a cloth body doll. ★

Hills, McLean & Haskins. 1926. Binghamton, N.Y. Registered in U.S. *Betty Bingham* as a trademark for dolls.

Hilmar. 1924. Name of a doll made by *Steiff.* Ht. 20 cm. (8 in.).

Hindu Dancer. 1922. A limp sock stockinet doll made by the *Sardeau* sisters. The face was molded over a plaster cast and had a greenish tinge. The doll wore cerise colored Turkish style silk trousers trimmed with blue, a blue turban, blue sandals and long strings of beads.

Hipauf, Bruno. 1913. Applied for a British patent for dolls.

Hirsch, Louis. 1902. Braunschweig, Germany. Applied for a German patent (D.R.G.M.) for rubber used for stringing dolls.

Hirsch & Cie. 1916 and other years. Brussels. They were awarded an Hors Concours for their dolls shown at the Exhibit for the Benefit of the Children of the Belgian Soldiers. M. Pintal, who was one of the directors of Maison Hirsch, was a member of the Jury for this exhibit.

Historical Costume Series. Exhibits of dolls dressed in historical costumes sometimes provide more information about the dolls themselves of a given period than the costumes worn by them. The dolls in these series are important because they reflect the interest and skill of their own times, rather than the supposed period of the costumes.

1206. Dolls with poured wax heads and hands; hair is inserted and also forms mustaches and beards. Renaissance style clothing suggests that these dolls probably belonged to a historical group. H. 13 in. (33 cm.). *Courtesy of Sotheby Parke Bernet Inc., N.Y.*

1892: Mme. Charles Cosson dressed and exhibited in Paris sixteen fashion-type lady dolls with bisque heads and kid bodies. These dolls were dressed in costumes representing ladies of Roman Gaul, and the years 1000, 1450, 1520, 1550, 1575, 1600, 1640, 1700, 1750, 1780, 1792, 1810, 1830, 1860, and 1892. After being exhibited many times this series of dolls became a part of the doll collection at the Musée des Arts Décoratifs in Paris.

1893: Another historical series of costume dolls was sent to the Chicago Exhibition. The surviving dolls from this group of 25 dolls have been *Jumeau* lady dolls with bisque heads and composition bodies. This series represented French costumes through the Middle Ages and modern times. These dolls were dressed by workers and patrons of the French doll industry.

1908: *Strawbridge & Clothier* showed "The Court of Historic Dolls." These dolls were made and dressed by *Mlle. Riera.*

1915–17: A group of 30 lady dolls with turned bisque shoulder heads was dressed to illustrate historical fashions. These 14 in. (35.5 cm.) dolls were exhibited at the Metropolitan Museum of Art in 1915.

The dolls represented ladies dressed in period costumes: Flemish, 1300s; two Burgundian, late 1400s; French, 1430, end of the 1500s, 1605, 1646, 1675, 1690, 1725, 1740, 1755, 1775, 1780, 1795, 1819, 1828; two German, early 1500s; Italian, end of the 1300s; Venetian, 1560; English, early 1300s, two for 1563, one for 1560,

1649, 1858; and American, 1842, 1860, 1874. TOYS AND NOVELTIES in 1917 commented on this Historical Series of dolls:

"The Metropolitan possesses a series illustrating the historical development of costume from the Middle Ages to the twentieth century with meticulous accuracy. The designer, Miss Lightfoot, was an expert who had spent years in the libraries and art galleries of Europe.

"The collection comprises the wired head-dress of Holbein's portraits, framing the face in the form of a heart; the slashed sleeves, wide collars and flowing lines of the Medici; the seventeenth century gown of grayish green which Pepys would have noted as 'a very fine and handsome garment.' The Frans Hals era shows the formal cut, stiff collars and cuffs, and gilt stripings familiar to his canvases. Only the very costliest of colored prints, designed by artists, give so lively a representation of the taste in costume of the past as these elaborately dressed dolls."

1915–18: Mesdames *Lafitte and Désirat* created wax dolls showing costumes worn by French women during World War I.

1916 and later: *Ligue du Jouet Français* produced a series of dolls with either bisque heads made by *Lanternier* or with composition heads; these dolls were dressed in costumes representing ladies in history.

1917: TOYS AND NOVELTIES reported on the acquisition of the Doucet Dolls by the Toledo Museum of Art as follows:

"A few weeks ago the historical collection of Doucet dolls was purchased for $30,000 for the Toledo Museum of Art. They had been on exhibition at the allied bazaar in Boston and were sold for the benefit of the Permanent Blind Relief Fund. These dolls afford probably the most complete and detailed reproduction extant of French fashions in dress from the sixth century to the present time. Each represents an historic French personage, and stands about two feet high." (See also **Doucet, Maison.**)

World War I: Dolls were dressed to represent George Washington, Betsy Ross and other American patriots.

1922: *Mme. Pulliche* dressed six dolls representing Venetian women of the 1700s. The dolls were modeled by *Salemme*, a New York sculptor, and their clothes were designed by *George Barbier* of Paris.

1923–26: The finding of King Tutankhamen's tomb caused a group of dolls to be dressed as ancient Egyptians.

1923–30 and later: *Dorothy Heizer* dressed dolls in historical costumes. Some of these are in the Newark Museum, the Smithsonian Institution and elsewhere.

1923 and later: *Minna Schmidt* dressed dolls to represent famous Women in history.

Hitchcock, Helen (Mrs. Ripley). 1924–26. New York City. Designed a jointed wooden doll called *Flexy* that was manufactured by *Converse*. Mrs. Hitchcock was President of the Art Center and Charles Dana Gibson was First Vice President.

1924: Obtained a U.S. design patent for a doll.

1926: Exhibited dolls at an Art Alliance of America Exhibition.

Hitchy Koo. 1913–14. Trademark registered in Britain by Horsman for dolls.

Hitt, Oscar. See **Hett, Oscar.**

Hitz, Jacobs & Kassler. 1918–30 and later. New York City, and Fürth, Bavaria. By 1925 they were known as Jacobs & Kassler and used the initials "J and K." Factory agents, they imported dolls to America and handled American-made dolls. *Kiddiejoy* was their principal line.

Some of the dolls sold in the Hitz, Jacobs & Kassler line of Kiddiejoy dolls were *Mama* dolls made by *Acme*.

1923: The wholesale catalog of this Company listed four types of undressed, bisque-head, ball-jointed, composition-body dolls. All of these had sleeping eyes and hair eyelashes. They wore chemises, shoes and stockings except in the smaller sizes. The dolls with ringlet wigs came in 17 hts. ranging from 14½ to 33¾ in. (37 to 86 cm.) tall. The 18 and 27¼ in. (45.5 and 69 cm.) dolls came only with flirting eyes and mama voices. The 27½ and 28 in. (70 and 71 cm.) dolls came only with flirting eyes. The 20 and 23¼ in. (51 and 59 cm.) dolls came with flirting eyes and with or without mama voices. The 24 and 25¼ in. (61 and 64 cm.) dolls came with or without flirting eyes and with or without mama voices. These dolls were priced from $12.50 a doz. for the 14½ (37 cm.) doll to $48.00 a doz. for the 27¼ in. (69 cm.) doll with flirting eyes and mama voice.

The dolls with bobbed hair wigs came in seven hts.: 13¾, 15¼, 17¼, 18½, 20, 20¾, and 21 in. (35, 40, 44, 47, 51, 52.5, and 53.5 cm.) and were priced from $27.50 to $50.00 a doz.

Character baby dolls with bisque heads, bent limb composition baby bodies, sleeping eyes, and wigs; came in nine hts.: 9¾, 11¼, 12¾, 14¼, 17¾, 20, 22¼, 25¼, and 28 in. (25, 28.5, 32.5, 36, 45, 51, 56.5, 64, and 71 cm.) and were priced from $10.00 to $116.00 a doz. These dolls wore a chemise.

Dolls with bisque heads, hands, and feet; sleeping eyes and wigs on both jointed kidolyne and real kid bodies came in five hts.: 14¾, 15½, 17¾, 20, and 24 in. (37.5, 39.5, 45, 51, and 61 cm.). They also came only on the kidolyne bodies in five hts.: 14, 16½, 18¾, 21¾, and 23¼ in. (35.5, 42, 47.5, 55, and 59 cm.). These dolls wore nothing except pink slippers and socks. The kidolyne body dolls were priced at $17.00 to $43.00 a doz., while the real kid-bodied dolls cost from $22.00 to $52.00 a doz. The 24 in. (61 cm.) composition-bodied dolls cost $25.00 a doz., while the kidolyne and real kid bodied dolls of the same heights were $43.50 and $52.00 a doz. respectively.

Hitz, Jacobs & Kassler handled 189 numbers of dressed dolls with bisque heads, sleeping eyes, wigs and composition bodies.

These dolls came in nine hts. from 10 to 18 in. (25.5 to 45.5 cm.) with straight legs and wore 47 different costumes. They cost $4.25 to $15.00 a doz. The variation depended solely on height. The dressed dolls with jointed knees came in eight heights from 11 to 18½ in. (28 to 47 cm.) and they wore 60 different costumes. These dolls cost $8.00 to

Miss 1928

Miss 1928

Painted Eye
$9.00 dozen

Moving Eye
$12.00 dozen

13 in. high   A REAL STANDING DOLL   13 in. high

JOINTED ARMS   ASSORTED DRESSES   JOINTED LEGS

AND FOR IMMEDIATE DELIVERY

REED ROCKERS   BRITAINS SOLDIERS   CEREAL SETS
"BABY CHARMING"   CHINA DISHES   DOLL BASSINETS
                  JUVENILE ROLL AND FLAT TOP DESKS
IMPORTED TOYS   DOMESTIC TOYS

BOOKLETS ON REQUEST

Jacobs & Kassler

Ⓚ

9-11 East 16th Street   **New York**

1207. Hitz, Jacobs & Kassler's advertisement in PLAYTHINGS, September, 1928. Miss 1928 came dressed with painted eyes or sleeping eyes, and jointed at the shoulders and hips. H. 13 in. (33 cm.).

$25.00 a doz. Ball-jointed dolls with eyelashes came in six hts. 19¼ to 25¾ in. (49 to 65.5 cm.). Thus dolls under 19 in. had jointed or straight knees but ball joints were used only on the larger dolls. The ball-jointed dolls wore 23 different costumes and cost between $27.00 and $63.00 a doz. Dolls dressed in white coats came in 13 hts. from 11½ to 25¾ in. (29 to 65.5 cm.) costing $8.70 to $63.00 a doz. Over a third of these heights were not listed in any of the above mentioned groups. The dolls in silk dresses came in the same heights and prices as the dolls in white coats except that the three that were 23¼, 24½, and 25¾ in. (59, 62, and 65.5 cm.) tall were omitted.

Hitz, Jacobs & Kassler also handled a "Cheaper line" of dressed dolls. Those with straight legs came in nine hts. 10 to 16 in. (25.5 to 40.5 cm.) costing only $3.35 to $9.20 a doz. The fully jointed doll, in seven hts. from 12 to 19½ in. (30.5 to 49.5 cm.), cost from $8.00 to $21.60 a doz., not much cheaper than their better grade of dressed dolls described above.

Jointed novelty dolls with wigs and clothes, usually a bathing suit, came in three hts. 4, 4½ and 5 in. (10, 11.5, and 12.5 cm.). These cost $3.40 and $3.80 a doz., unless they had sleeping eyes, then the price almost doubled to $6.00 and $6.30 a doz. *Frozen Charlotte* type novelty dolls with wigs and clothes cost only 80 cents a doz. for the 5 in. (12.5 cm.) ones and $1.20 a doz. for the 6 in. ones.

Dolls with bisque heads, wigs, sleeping eyes and jointed composition bodies were sold in boxes, wardrobe trunks, and steamer trunks with their trousseaux. The dolls came in various heights from 6 in. to 10½ in. (15 to 26.5 cm.). The prices rose with the height of the doll and the container. A 10½ in. (26.5 cm.) doll in a trunk with its clothes cost $7.00 each. A layette for a 7½ in. (19 cm.) baby doll in a box cost $3.00 each.

Hitz, Jacobs & Kassler imported turned and carved wooden dolls that were handpainted. These dolls were $2.00 a doz. for the 6 in. (15 cm.) ones and $4.00 a doz. for the 9 in. (23 cm.) ones. The smaller dolls were dressed as "Small baker," Coachman, Dutch boy, German boy, or girl, Black boy, Bull fighter or Turk. The larger dolls were costumed as a Master baker, Coachman, German man or woman, Dutchman with cap, Dutchwoman, Swedish man or woman, Italian Gondolier, Spaniard, Bull Fighter, Spanish Peasant, Japanese woman, Cowboy, Turk with fez, Negro, Clown, Nurse, Chinese, Hindoo, and Moroccan. (See Ill. 2762.)

1926: Registered *Bisqueloid* and Kiddiejoy as U.S. trademarks for dolls. They ran into problems with Kiddiejoy but in 1927 their opponents' claim was dismissed.

Kiddiejoy Baby doll resembled *My Dream Baby.*

1927: Advertised baby and Mama dolls including *Cradle Babe.*

1928: Dolls included *Me Too,* an infant doll; *Miss 1928;* and *Baby Charming.*★

Hitz, Monroe, & Co. 1926–30 and later. New York City. Distributed *E. Goldberger* dolls and was factory agent for the *Happi-Kiddie* dolls.

1208. Mark used by Monroe Hitz in 1931 for Happi-Kiddie Dolls.

Hitzegrad, Clemens. 1907. Oldenburg, Germany. Applied for a German patent (D.R.G.M.) for filling dolls' bodies with sponges.

Ho. (Hoolygan, Happy Hooligan). 1905–24. Felt doll with long feet made by *Steiff* and dressed to represent the comic character, Happy Hooligan, drawn by F. Opper. Ht. 35 cm. (14 in.).

1906: Distributed by Gamage with the name Hooligan; priced 62¢.

Hobo. 1904–24. Wooden doll made by *Schoenhut.* It wore a suit and striped shirt.

1921: Made in two sizes.★

Hochmayer, Rudolf. 1910–11. Vienna. Produced dolls.

Hockey. 1917. Character doll advertised by *Bell & Francis.*

Hodge, Alfred R. 1914–15. Chicago, Ill. Obtained a U.S. patent for a doll.

Hodge and Audrey. 1921. Pair of British stockinet dolls distributed in America by *Meakin & Ridgeway.* The dolls were dressed as an English farm boy and girl.

Hoefler, George John. 1916–18. Stapleton, N.Y. Obtained a U.S. patent for a weeping doll. There was a closure in the neck connected by a tube with a reservoir in the head of the doll. This provided the water for the "tears."

Hoest & Henderson. 1926–29. New York City. 1929–30 and later, successor was Hoest & Co. The firm members were Arthur V. Hoest and George Henderson. They were manufacturers and distributors of baby dolls and *Mama* dolls.

1926: Distributed dolls made by *Atlas Doll & Toy Co.* Produced dolls' dresses and *Baby Dahne* line, dressed by *Blanche Rowe Cromien.*

1927: Baby Dahne came in four styles. The cloth bodies of their dolls were filled with kapok. Their factory representatives were *Baker & Bennett, A. S. Ferguson, Strobel & Wilken* and *Louis Wolf.*

1929: Advertised two new numbers in the Baby Dahne line and bathing girls, priced $1.00. Distributed the *Burgarella* Italian dolls.

1930: Distributed *Scarey Ann* line of dolls.

Hofbauer, Franz. 1907–10. Vienna. Listed in Austrian directory under Dolls and Dolls' Heads.

Hoffman, Louis, & Co. 1926. New York City. Made wooden dolls called *Danny Dangle,* which was a *Segmented Wooden Doll.*

Hoffmann, Solomon D. 1880s–97. Moscow, Russia, and Brooklyn, N.Y. 1897–1909, successor was his widow and son. Solomon Hoffmann called his factory the *First American Doll Factory* and he put the initials F.A.D.F. on the composition heads that he made. Despite the fact that these heads were advertised as so durable that "you can pound one against the counter, drop on the floor or throw across the room without breaking it," the head peeled badly and few have survived. They were made of a very early cold-press type composition which was later improved by *Benjamin Goldenberg*.

1899: Dolls distributed by *Butler Bros.* had composition heads and limbs, wigs, glass eyes and cloth bodies. The dolls wore a ribbon marked "Patented Absolutely Unbreakable."

1902: Butler Bros. listed eight dolls' hts.: 13½, 14, 14½ 16, 18, 18½, 19½ and 23 in. (34, 35.5, 37, 40.5, 45.5, 47, 49.5, and 58.5 cm.); price 38¢ to $1.75 each wholesale. ★

Hoffmeister, Carl. 1890–1925. Sonneberg, Thür. In 1892 he bought the *Albert Pulvermacher* factory. Carl Hoffmeister was one of the founders of *Schoenau & Hoffmeister*. In 1920 the son, Wilhelm Hoffmeister, joined his father but in 1925 they went bankrupt. They made bodies of kid, imitation leather which they called *granitol*, silk, felt, and other cloth as well as composition. They used heads of bisque made by *Gebrüder Heubach* and Schoenau & Hoffmeister; composition heads; *Buschow & Beck*'s metal heads; *Rheinische Gummi und Celluloid Fabrik Co.*'s celluloid heads; and wooden heads. ★

Hofmann, Ernst. 1902–29. Chemnitz, Saxony. Made outfits for dolls including sweaters, sacques, diapers, socks, stockings and combination sets.

Hofmann, Johannes. 1923–26. Neustadt near Coburg, Bavaria. Manufactured dolls. ★

Hofmann, M., & Co. 1900–10. Sonneberg, Thür. One of the Sonneberg group of Grand Prize winners at the Brussels Exposition. ★

Hogue-Bigot. 1929. Paris. Made footwear for dolls.

Hohenstein & Lange. 1894. Berlin. Applied for a German patent (D.R.G.M.) for making patterns for dolls' clothes.

Holden & Cutter. 1845 and probably other years. East Cambridge, Mass. Imported and distributed dolls. Advertised that they arrived via monthly steamer from France and Germany. Also distributed American toys.

Holes in Head. The holes in bisque heads can be clues as to the origin and/or dates of the head. When the wig is removed and the inside of the bisque head is examined it becomes evident whether the head was pressed or poured. The pressed head is rougher than the poured head and has no lip which is characteristic of the poured head. The roughness of the pressed head is often in thin, fine ridges, probably related to the instrument used to roll it out or to the sponge that was used in pressing it into the mold. (See **Pressed versus Poured**.) The Germans usually poured their slip for bisque heads while the French up until the late 1800s usually pressed their heads. Thus a pressed head is probably French and earlier than about 1890, when *Jumeau* changed from the pressed method to the poured method.

Some dolls have very high foreheads and one or two small holes in front of the large wig pate hole. These holes appear to have been used for the stringing of the head with a hook when it had one hole or a cord if there were two holes. But often there is no evidence of the functional use of the holes. It is presumed that the porcelain factory made the heads with these holes and the company who purchased the heads may or may not have used this feature. Since the wig has to be partially removed to find these holes, they are probably found on many more heads than currently realized. Thus far the heads with these small forehead holes all appear to have been made in Germany. Some marked *Simon & Halbig* socket heads on bisque shoulder plates have the two forehead holes. Similarly the bisque socket heads on the bisque shoulder plates, both parts having a three digit mold number, the symbol # and a size number, have the two forehead holes (see Ill. 65). Most of the dolls with one forehead hole are marked "Germany." A Simon & Halbig-*Handwerck* head has been found with one forehead hole. However, a doll marked "*Eden Bébé*" on its original chemise and having red check marks on its head has one hole on its forehead as well as holes over the ears. This doll was probably made in the 1899–1914 period when the *Société Française de Fabrication de Bébé & Jouets* was controlled by *Fleischmann*, a German, and many of its bisque dolls' heads were probably made in Germany. Sometimes holes facilitated mechanisms such as those for eyes. (See also **Belton-Type** and **French Dolls**.) ★

Holladay, A. J., & Co. 1916–30 and later. London and Paris. Imported, manufactured and exported dolls.

1916: Advertised French and English, dressed and undressed dolls as well as plush jointed *Eskimo* dolls.

1918: Advertised *Cecily* dolls made by *Edwards & Pamflett* and Rosebud.

1920: Represented in New York by *Bush Terminal*.

1923: Distributed dolls produced by *Le Jouet Liégeois S.A.* ★

Holland, John. 1796–1843. Salem, North Carolina. He worked at the Moravian Pottery and his inventory listed four types of dolls selling for 5¢, 8¢, 10¢ and 15¢. The mold for a doll's head has been found among the artifacts of this Pottery. This was a round mold with a pouring hole at the neckline which would produce a cylindrical neck. Another mold was in the form of a figurine or a *Frozen Charlotte* type doll with molded clothes.

Holland Bud. 1921. Cloth doll made by *Delavan*. It had worsted hair in two braids, a triangular mouth, slim limbs and neck. It wore a blue, white and yellow Dutch Costume with bloomers showing below the short skirt, and there was a printed story in the pocket of the dress. ★

Hollmann, Rudolf. 1926–27. Leignitz, Silesia. Manufactured dolls.

Hollywood Babes. 1930. Washable cloth dolls with painted faces made by *O. J. Lafayette & Co.* Limbs were long but not as long as the *Boudoir* dolls. Clothes were all removable. These dolls were called "Movie dolls."

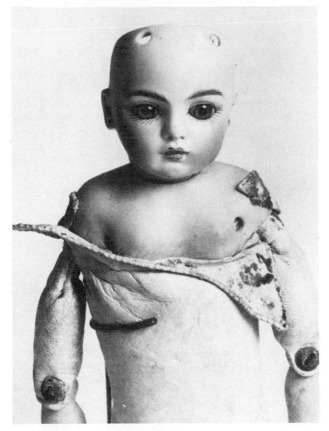

1209. Bisque shoulder head with a swivel neck, a wig, stationary glass eyes, a closed mouth, two holes on the upper forehead, and a finely modeled breastplate. The rivet- and gusset-jointed kid body has bisque lower arms and composition lower legs. This bisque head is poured, a technique used by the Germans earlier than by the French manufacturers. Mark on the back of the pate rim is "132." H. 13 in. (33 cm.). *Courtesy of Vera Kramer, Dolls in Wonderland.*

1210A & B. Bisque head with three small holes in the top of the head. These holes served a dual purpose: they are used for the stringing of the doll and also for attaching the wig. This doll has stationary blue glass eyes, an open-closed mouth, ears pierced into the head, and a ball-jointed composition body with long wooden upper limbs and small hands that has the fingers together, no wrist joints. The body is typical of most dolls with small holes in the crown. This doll is mold # 100, size 9, and there is also an X under the 9. H. 20 in. (51 cm.). *Coleman Collection.*

Hollywood Imps. 1929–30. Cloth dolls with handpainted faces of an impish or flapper type. They were made by *Woodard* The hair was either yarn or felt; bodies were stuffed with kapok.

1930: Some of the dolls were as follows:

Style No.	Height in.	cm.	Name and/or Clothes
1	23	58.5	Eva, a pajama girl in pink
4	23	58.5	Farm boy
11	21	53.5	Dutch Girl
13	21	53.5	Dutch Boy
18	18	45.5	Girl wearing short pants
22	18	45.5	Girl in a swim suit
23	22	56	Boy in a college sweater
24	19	48	Aviator
25	20	51	Football player
?	?	?	Aviatrix

Dolls priced 50¢, $1.00 and $1.50.

1211. Illustration used to advertise Hollywood Imps in PLAY-THINGS in 1929.

Holmgreen, Ch. Martin Voldemar. 1913. Copenhagen, Denmark. Applied for a German patent (D.R.G.M.) for dolls.

Holmquist, Dorothy B. 1930. Berkeley, Calif. Made clothes for dolls including dolls' linens, fur and fur-lined garments.

Holtschmidt, Walter. 1900. Coburg, Thür. Applied for a German patent for jointed dolls.

Homer, M., & Son. 1836–86. United States. Their trade card suggests that this firm was a doll distributor.

Honey. 1927. Composition head doll distributed by *Montgomery Ward.* It had painted hair, sleeping eyes, open mouth, and composition arms on a dressed cloth baby body that contained a crier. Ht. 18 in. (45.5 cm.); price $2.98.

Honey. 1928–30. Composition-head dolls made by *Acme* and carrying a round tag with the word "Acme" over the picture of a girl with a doll.

1928: Dolls came in six sizes with bent limbs, five sizes with sitting bodies and three sizes with standing bodies. The baby dolls had composition arms and wore short, sheer baby dresses, halo-type bonnets, and baby moccasins.

1929: New sizes and styles.

1930: Wigs were made of human hair or silk hair in four shades of color and with long or short curls.

Honey Babies. 1920. Manufactured by *Elektra.*

Honey Bunch. 1918. All-composition doll with five piece, straight leg body having spring joints, made by *Jessie M. Raleigh.*

Honey Bunch. 1931. U.S. trademark registered for dolls by *Ideal.*

Honey Child. 1926. U.S. trademark for dolls registered by *Bayless Bros. & Co.*

Honeybunch. 1923. Composition head and hands on a cloth body, made by *Effanbee.* According to Pat Schoonmaker this doll was marked "EFFANBEE//HONEYBUNCH //MADE IN U.S.A." and the head resembled *Bubbles.* It had sleeping eyes and an open mouth with teeth. Ht. 12½ in. (31.5 cm.).★

Höning, Hans. 1926–28. Sonneberg, Thür. Obtained a German patent (D.R.P.) for a doll's articulation. He was a successor of *Emil Pfeiffer.*

Hooligan (Hoolygan). See **Ho.** and **Happy Hooligan.**

Hooper, M. S., & Co. 1919–20. London. Advertised dolls in a British toy trade journal.

Hopf, A. C. 1928. United States. Representative of *Averill Manufacturing Co., Nelke,* and *Knickerbocker Toy Co.*

Hopf, A. Paul. 1925–26. Nürnberg, Bavaria. Obtained a German patent (D.R.P.) for a ball-jointed doll similar to the *Bucherer* doll. (See also **A. Huck.**)

Hopf, C. 1924. Neustadt near Coburg, Bavaria. Manufactured Mama dolls, which were distributed by *Galatoize* Ltd. in London.

Hopf, H. E. Neustadt near Coburg, Germany. Made composition dolls marked *Libra.*

Hopf, Miss Ruby. United States. Sister of *Georgene Hopf Averill.* Ruby Hopf was *Arranbee*'s chief designer for many years.

Hopf, Verne. 1920s. United States. Sales manager of *Georgene Novelties.*

Hopkins, Joseph. 1917–24. England. Advertised character dolls in several British toy trade journals. He was the agent for *Telma* and *Wholesale Toy Co.*

Hopkins & Co. 1916–17. London. Factory agent and distributor of *British Ceramic* dolls, cloth dolls and French dolls including undressed and dressed dolls such as the series named *My Clothes Take Off.*

Höppner, Max. 1919. Plauen, Germany. Applied for a German patent (D.R.G.M.) for dolls' clothes.

Hořické Hrag. Early 1900s. Czechoslovakia. Name on two-dimensional wooden dolls with attached and articulated arms. The features and decorations of the clothing were painted or burned into the wood. The dolls carried the mark ᴴH and "HOŘICKÉ HRAG//DRUZSTVE."

Horinek, Franz. 1910. Vienna. Listed in an Austrian directory under Dolls and Dolls' Heads.

Hörler, Karl. 1910. Vienna. Listed in an Austrian directory under Dolls and Dolls' Heads.

Horn, Carl. 1906–30 and later. Dresden, Saxony. His successors made small dolls especially those dressed in regional costumes and *dolls' house dolls.*

1906: Advertised soldiers.

1927: Made dolls dressed as boys, girls, chimney sweeps, maids, Santa Claus and so on. Some of the dolls wore bathing suits. Hts. 1¼ to 3½ in. (3 to 9 cm.).★

Horn, Heinrich. 1895–1927. Sonneberg, Thür. Made dolls' bodies of kid or cloth.

1927: He specialized in dolls with bisque or celluloid heads on kid bodies. The Berlin agent was Carl Stahl.★

1212. Miniature dressed dolls and dolls' house dolls as advertised by Carl Horn in PLAYTHINGS, 1927. H. of dolls 1¼ to 3½ in. (3 to 9 cm.).

1213A. Small dressed all-bisque dolls of the type made by Carl Horn. They have molded and painted hair, black dots for eyes, closed mouth, and are jointed at the shoulders and hips. Original clothes with molded and painted footwear. H. 1¼ to 1½ in. (3 to 4 cm.). *Courtesy of Clara Hobey. Photo by Neil Hobey.*

1213B. Pair of small all-bisque dolls in crocheted clothes similar to the dressed dolls advertised by Carl Horn. The dolls have molded and painted hair, black dots for the eyes, closed mouths, wired joints at the shoulders and hips. Original clothes with molded and painted footwear. H. 1¼ to 1⅜ in. (3 to 3.5 cm.). *Courtesy of Clara Hobey. Photo by Neil Hobey.*

Horne, Elizabeth. 1890. South Hampstead, Middlesex. Made dolls but not dolls' houses despite the fact that she called her business The Real Dolls House Female Toy Making Depot.

1214. Mark used by Elizabeth Horne, according to Gwen White.

Horne, Joseph. Before 1927–30 and later. Pittsburgh, Pa. Distributed dolls.

1927: Gave an annual Christmas dolls' tea party for children ages four through 12 on the roof of their store to receive Santa's airplane. Over 2,000 children attended.

Hornier (Harnier), Henri. 1861. Paris. A doll has been reported with a holograph tag reading, "This is a collector's doll made by the artist Henri Hornier [Harnier] in Paris in the year 1861."

Hornlein, Theodor. 1909–25 and later. Sonneberg, Thür. Made dolls.

1909: Applied for a German patent (D.R.G.M.) for jointed dolls.

Horsman, Edward Imeson. 1865–1980 and later. New York City. Known as E.I. Horsman Co. *Aetna Doll & Toy Co.* merged with Horsman to form the E.I. Horsman & Aetna Co. but they soon resumed the name E.I. Horsman Co. again.

Edward Imeson Horsman, born 1843, in 1859 started to

work as an office boy with Paton & Co. of New York City for $2.00 a week.

An 1881 Horsman catalog does not mention dolls. However, according to several Horsman obituaries, by 1878 he had a large showroom of dolls and soon began to handle many aspects of the doll industry and function as an American *Verleger*. With the help of *Benjamin Goldenberg* they produced the Can't Break 'Em[†] composition dolls. These dolls were described as "always with heads modeled from life by an American Sculptress and such original models duly protected by copyright." The name *Helen Trowbridge* appeared as the artist who designed these copyrighted dolls. Cloth dolls were made by *Albert Brückner* exclusively for Horsman from 1901–25. Cutout cloth dolls such as *Daisy Darling, Little Fairy, Tommy Trim* and *Willie Winkle* were made for Horsman. When Edward Imeson Horsman died in 1927 and Benjamin Goldenberg died a few weeks later, the business was taken over by William Ehrenfeld and Harold B. Bowie, both of whom had been employed by Horsman for 22 years. They promised to carry on the designs and manufacture of dolls as formulated by E. I. Horsman and Benjamin Goldenberg.

At least from 1913–20 *Bedington, Liddiat & Co.* had a showroom of Horsman dolls in London.

The early years of Horsman's business were described rather chauvinistically in an article, "The Toy Man of Toy Town," published in McCLURES MAGAZINE in 1913.

"Five years ago [1908] the doll world was made up chiefly of vacuous-faced figures from over the sea—all cut pretty much from the same pattern, empty of character, unbending in demeanor, and having the same wearisome mother's-angel look about their mouths. Of course, the real flesh-and-blood children loved these doll babies, for that was human nature. The children's mothers bought the dolls, for that was human nature too. But, for all that, there wasn't a single doll, among the whole vacant featured lot on the market, that had ever made a name for itself in doll society. All dolls were just dolls. . . .

"In the doll society of those days there were no such doll persons as the Campbell Kids, Kewpies, Hug-me Kiddies, Sis Hopkins, Baby Dainty, Klippity Klop Kids, Country Cousins, Boy Scout, or Middy Girl. . . .

"Mr. Horsman belonged to the minority, and he had his ear to the ground. He got to thinking, one day, about the strange fascination the image Billiken seemed to possess for the public at large, and about the manner in which the Teddy Bear had got into the hearts of the children. He made up his mind to combine the two and make a doll.

"About eighteen years before this, a Russian inventor [*Solomon D. Hoffmann*] had got up an 'unbreakable' composition for doll heads. Finding himself unable to do anything with it in Europe, he brought it to America. In this country his success was scarcely any better. The few doll manufacturers here took no interest in it—they already had papier-mâché and various substances that passed as unbreakable, so why should they bother their heads over this other material? A few dolls were made of it, so far as the heads were concerned, but for eighteen years one of the biggest opportunities in the doll industry went begging.

"Mr. Horsman was beginning to see a glimmer through the fog of conventional dolls. Not only did he combine the Teddy Bear and Billiken and make a doll of the two, but he got control of this doll-head composition, gave it a catchy trade-name Can't Break 'Em, and began to use it in the manufacture of the so-called Billiken doll. A million Billiken dolls were sold!

"But this was only the beginning. Mr. Horsman . . . was still thinking. Why was it, he asked himself, that the children and their parents liked the Billiken doll and so often gave it preference over the old-fashioned angel-faced doll? The answer seemed clear enough. Because it had character! It wasn't a mere dummy!

"The logic of the situation, pointed to a character study of real children as models for dolls. An artist was secured to make the study, and 'Baby Bumps' was the first real character doll produced. This doll baby made a great sensation in the doll trade. 'Baby Bumps' is now passé, but the memory of him lingers in considerably over a million homes in America.

"Then came the 'Campbell Kids.' These dolls sprang into instant popularity. No best seller among books ever took hold with such sudden vigor as did these dolls. They passed the million mark in a hurry, and still the people wanted more. Ever since then, the history of the doll business in the United States has kept step with the history of fiction. Other manufacturers jumped into the game, and there has been an intense rivalry among them to produce the best sellers.

"There have been many of these—like the Candy Kid, Toodles, Miss Mischief, Suck-a-thumb Baby, Serious Baby Bobbie, Little Sunshine, and Laughing Baby Peterkin. Each manufacturer has his own group of characters, like a company of actors and actresses on the stage. Every season these groups are changed by the addition or retirement of dolls. There is always a chance that a new character will sweep the country, make big money for its promoters, and attain for itself a temporary place in this new and strange doll society. There is another and bigger chance that it will fall flat, or, at most, amount to nothing but a 'filler.' Usually the first two months of its career tell its fate. But one thing is certain: every doll, like every character on the greater stage of life, must sooner or later step down to make way for some new star. No one product can long hold a market single-handed, for the world is full of ideas—once somebody 'starts something.'

"But the odd thing about this character-doll business is the fact that in all the doll trade nobody started anything of the sort until five years ago. . . . American manufacturers had so long been accustomed to the waxen corpses of Germany that the idea of anything else hadn't occurred to them. . . .

"To-day Germany finds itself wholly unable to compete in this branch of the trade—for two reasons. In the first place, the few character dolls Germany has tried to place in the American market haven't been successful because the types were not the sort American children loved. Little girls in this country, take more kindly to 'Willie and Lillie,' 'Dottie Dimple,' 'Johnny Tu Face,' and familiar patterns of that sort, rather than types from the Tyrol. In the second place, Germany can't make the character dolls as cheaply as America can. This may sound heterodox, but it is a fact. Once American manufacturers get started on a thing, they invent machinery and methods that leave everything else in the shade. The impossible things quickly become commercially possible.

"Then, if you get back of the scenes, you will find that the toy-makers have publicity ways all their own. If you go to a vaudeville show and hear a catchy song about Miss Jumpity Jump, just for instance, it may be that up in the studio of some character-doll manufacturer you could find the original sculptor's model of that ambitious doll, awaiting the psychological hour for her début."

Actually the evidence points to the fact that *Kämmer & Reinhardt's* "Baby" (mold # 100) came out before its American imitation "Baby Bumps." Moreover, Germany could produce dolls more cheaply than American manufacturers, but there was a sizable tariff which raised the price of the imported dolls so that competition was advantageous to the American producers.

1885: Advertised a large variety of dolls as follows (the prices were all wholesale):

Bisque head dolls, composition bodies, ten sizes, priced $4.00 to $36.00 a doz. French bisque dolls, ten sizes undressed, priced $12.00 to $96.00 a doz.; nine sizes dressed, priced $36.00 to $250.00 a doz.

Separate bisque heads were available in nine sizes with white fur wigs and in ten sizes with natural hair wigs; the former cost up to $15.00 a doz. and the latter up to $48.00 a doz. and were described as "French bisque." All-china dolls came in white or black, six sizes, price 6¢ to 75¢ a doz. Dolls with china shoulder heads and limbs on cloth bodies came in 15 sizes; priced 31¢ to $8.00 a doz. Separate china heads came in seven sizes, 31¢ to $2.00 a doz.

Composition dolls came in ten sizes, 75¢ to $12.00 a doz. With white fur hair there were six sizes, $4.00 to $15.00 a doz. Separate composition heads came without hair in eight sizes at 75¢ to $3.00 a doz.; with hair in nine sizes, at $1.75 to $6.00 a doz. When the composition heads were washable and had hair there were six sizes, priced $4.00 to $9.00 a doz.

Model Rag (Cloth) dolls came in six sizes priced $6.00 to $18.00 a doz.

"Model wax dolls" with footwear, 11 sizes, priced $4.00 to $36.00 a doz.; extra large wax dolls in 12 sizes 75¢ to $18.00 a doz. Speaking dolls came in five sizes, $12.00 to $48.00 a doz. Separate kid bodies came in eight sizes, some had bisque arms and some had footwear; priced $2.75 to $18.00 doz. (See Ill. 1215.)

1893: The Horsman catalog for the Chicago World's Fair listed a wide variety of dolls at wholesale prices.

They had all-bisque dolls and all-china dolls; the latter came in black or white and with or without gilt feet. The bisque-head dolls had wigs and generally sleeping eyes except in the smaller sizes. One of the smaller sleeping eye dolls could say "Papa" and "Mama." The dolls with fully jointed composition bodies had jointed wrists in the larger sizes, wore a chemise and no footwear. These dolls came in hts. 6 to 35 in. (15 to 89 cm.) and cost 38¢ to $120.00 doz. depending on size and quality. One group of these dolls with open mouth and teeth wore a silk chemise, bonnet and footwear. Hts. 16 to 27 in. (40.5 to 68.5 cm.); priced $9.00 to $39.00 doz. The open mouth appears to have been a new feature.

Most of the bisque-head dolls with kid bodies were made by *Kestner.* They had wigs and sleeping eyes, or a few had "turning eyes" instead of sleeping eyes; as a novelty a few also had hair eyelashes; the hands were bisque and the bodies had gusset joints. Hts. 10 to 28 in. (25.5 to 71 cm.); priced $1.00 to $42.00 doz.

The low-brow china head dolls with china limbs and cloth bodies came in ten sizes 7 to 20 in. (18 to 51 cm.); priced 31¢ to $3.50 a doz. The bonnet china heads with china limbs on cloth bodies came in four sizes; priced 38¢ to $2.00 doz.

Composition-head dolls with wigs, glass eyes, composition arms and legs on cloth bodies came in eleven hts. 14 to 31 in. (35.5 to 78.5 cm.); priced $9.00 to $72.00 doz. Similar dolls with cloth imitation footwear came in ten hts. 18 to 36 in. (45.5 to 91.5 cm.); priced $1.75 to $10.00 doz.

Composition-head dolls with painted hair, glass eyes, and cloth sitting bodies having imitation footwear came in four hts. 12 to 18 in. (30.5 to 45.5 cm.); priced 75¢ to $2.00 doz.

Baby dolls had bisque or composition heads on short fat bodies. Multi-face composition-head dolls said, "Mama-Papa." There were black dolls and multihead (topsy turvy?) dolls with one head that was of a white baby and the other head black.

The finest dressed dolls were "French *Jumeaus*" costing $5.00 to $25.00 each. Other dressed dolls had bisque heads and either fully jointed composition bodies or cloth bodies. Hts. 8 to 21 in. (20.5 to 53.5 cm.); priced $1.50 to $240 doz. Dolls with composition heads on jointed bodies or cloth bodies were 9 to 21 in. (23 to 53.5 cm.) tall; priced 75¢ to $3.75 doz. The clothes represented boys, girls, and babies in long dresses. Some of the girl dolls wore floor-length dresses. "Mourning Dolls" were dressed all in black. Other types of dolls included rubber dolls; knitted *Worsted Dolls,* including harlequins, clowns, and Santa Claus as well as jersey baby dolls with voices; *London Rag Dolls; Babyland Rag Dolls; Marottes; Cymbaliers; Eskimo* dolls; American *Indian* dolls and *Zulu* dolls.

Dolls' parts and accessories included: Bisque, china and composition heads; kid and cloth bodies, including *Goldsmith* corset bodies; shoes, gloves, headwear and so forth. (See Ill. 1216.)

1903: Babyland Rag Dolls were advertised.

1905: *Siegel Cooper* distributed the following Horsman dolls: *American Maid,* Bruckner cloth dolls, boy dolls, *Topsy,* and *Topsy Turvy.*

1906: *Life Like (Lifelike) Babyland Dolls* were introduced.

1911: Horsman Art Dolls appeared on the market in three sizes: standard, 10½ in. (26.5 cm.); large, 13 in. (33 cm.); extra large, 15½ in. (39.5 cm.).

1912: Advertised that for the past three years they had produced an average of 3,000 dolls a day (about a million a year) in over 100 style numbers. The composition mixture and first casting of these dolls was a carefully guarded secret.

The 1912 Horsman catalog provided the following information: Horsman was still producing *Billiken* and *Baby Bumps* but they had several dozen new model composition dolls' heads, most of these were the work of Helen Trowbridge. It is probable that she actually sculptured the model for the *Campbell Kids* based on *Grace Drayton*'s drawings. This was a procedure often followed in that era. Most of the composition heads had painted hair but at least five numbers came with wigs. The eyes were painted with most of them looking to the side but some of the eyes were painted looking straight ahead. Quite a few of the dolls had open-closed mouths with teeth. The flange neck fitted into the cloth body and the join was covered by a high neckline.

There appears to have been three types of composition hands. The child dolls, Baby Bumps and a few other babies had the same type of hands as the Campbell Kids. Entire composition arms and legs were developed for the *Gold Medal Babies*. These limbs copied the more graceful positions of the German composition bodied babies. A special type of right hand was made for Baby *Suck-a-Thumb* to enable it to put its thumb into its open mouth. The rest of the bodies were cloth with joints at the shoulders and hips.

The same head was often used for several different numbers, the only difference being in the clothes. For example, *Daisy Dimple, Hans, Gretchen, Happy Hiram, Jack Tar, Prince Charlie* and *Robbie Reefer* all appeared to be the same doll, simply dressed differently. *Pocahontas* was a Campbell Kid, darkened in color and dressed as an Indian. The Indians and black dolls did not have ethnic features.

There was a similarity in many of the designs of the clothes. For example *Candy Kid*'s rompers were identical in design to those worn by the Campbell Kid Boy. Both *Carnival Baby* and *Toodles* wore the same style "Carter's" smock and knickers. Most of the dolls wore socks and either single strap slippers or pumps with buckles on them. The four dolls in Dutch costume wore striped stockings and simulated wooden shoes made of fabric.

Style numbers and names of composition head dolls offered for sale in 1912, in standard size:

1	Billiken	146	Suck-a-Thumb
2, and 2½	Gold Medal Baby	147	Candy Kid
100	Buster Billiken	148	Toodles
125	Campbell Kid Boy	149	*Cotton Joe*
126	Campbell Kid Girl	151	*School Boy*
130	Campbell Kid Baby	152	*Kickapoo*
131	Campbell Kid Mascot Boy	153	Pocahontas
132	Carnival Baby	154	*Baby Bobby*
133	Campbell Kid Mascot Girl	155	*Baby Peterkin*
134	*Fairy*	156	*Little Nemo*
135	*Jap Rose* Boy	157	Jack Tar
136	Jap Rose Girl	159	*Farmer Boy*
137	Daisy Dimple	160	*Chinkie*
138	*Nancy Lee*	161	Baby Bumps
139	Robbie Reefer	164	Polly Prue
140	Hans	180	Fairy (wigged)
141	Gretchen	188	*Miss Mischief* (wigged)
142	Happy Hiram	192	School Girl (wigged)
143	*Sunbonnet Sal*	193	*Willem* (wigged)
143	*Annette*	194	*Wilhelmina* (wigged)
144	Trousseau Baby		

Horsman showed in their catalogs three types of cloth Babyland dolls. The celluloid head dolls came on cloth bodies with cloth limbs, the smallest size with only a celluloid mask. The celluloid head dolls came in five hts.: 10½, 13½, 15, 16 and 17½ in. (26.5, 34, 38, 40.5 and 44.5 cm.).

1913: Advertised 100 new styles.

1914: In their catalog Horsman stated, "We speak invariably as either the Producers or First-hand Distributors of the goods enumerated." Actually Horsman was an American version of a *Verleger*.

Innovations on their composition dolls for 1914 were the enlarging of the standard size and the introduction of a junior or smaller size. The junior size was around nine inches tall while the standard size seems to have varied between 11 and 13 inches. The large size was around 16 inches. There seems to have been considerable variation in sizes; for example, the Campbell Kids' height has been reported as 8½, 9, 9½, 10, 10½, 11, 11½, 12, 12½, 13, 15½ and 16 in. (21.5, 23, 24, 25.5, 26.5, 28, 29, 30.5, 31.5, 33, 39.5 and 40.5 cm.). There must always be some allowance for height variations due to the way a doll is measured but this variation seems greater than would occur solely due to this fact.

Other innovations were the use of a shoulder head which permitted some of the costumes to have low necks. A composition arm with some of the fingers separated began to be used on child dolls. This enabled the dolls to wear short sleeves. The cork stuffed cloth bodies were jointed at the shoulders, hips and knees. These new types of structures were used for Campbell Kids and some other dolls but not for all of the dolls. Many of the dolls were still made with the old-style heads, hands and bodies.

Many new models were made and there were more numbers in 1914 than previously. They still used some of the same heads and gave the doll a new name or they used different heads for dolls with the same name. Baby Bumps was totally different from the earlier version of Baby Bumps. The difference was explained by saying Baby Bumps had grown older. Sometimes dolls with the same number had the same name in 1914 as previously and sometimes they did not. Sometimes more than one doll model had the same number. Consistency was not one of the Horsman virtues.

Among the innovations in 1914 were dolls with variously colored hair, both painted and wigged. Two of the wigged doll numbers now came with glass eyes. One group of dolls was dressed in Bavarian regional costumes. Other groups were sold dressed only in underclothes. A few of the dolls were sold with outerwear such as coat, cape and so forth. None of the babies appear to have had composition legs as was seen in 1912. The legs on the babies were bent cloth legs and many of them wore booties. Other footwear remained the same as that worn in 1912. Most of the other clothes had been updated except for some of the junior size dolls that wore the same designs as were found in 1912.

Numbers and names of composition head dolls offered for sale, 1914, in standard size:

GC/1 Gold Medal Baby (short dress)	150 School Girl
124 Baby Bumps (older baby)	151 School Boy
125 Campbell Kid Boy	152 Kickapoo
126 Campbell Kid Girl	153 Pocahontas
127 Campbell Kid Girl (colored hair)	157 Jack Tar
129 Campbell Kid Baby	159 Farmer Boy
130 *Miss Campbell*	163 *Miss Janet*
132 Carnival Baby	165 Campbell Kid Boy (wigged)
134 Baby *Bauernkind*	166 Campbell Kid Girl (wigged)
135 Girl *Bauernkind*	167 Miss Campbell (wigged)
135½ *Tyroler* Girl	168 *Billy Boy* (wigged)
136 Boy *Bauernkind*	169 Campbell Kid Red Jacket Boy
136½ *Tyroler* Boy	170 Campbell Kid Red Jacket Girl
137 Daisy Dimple (dressed)	171 Gold Medal Baby (long dress)
138 Daisy Dimple (undressed)	172 *Boy Scout*
139 Robbie Reefer	173 *Camp Fire Girl*
140 *Baby Blossom*	174 *Sunshine*
141 *Baby Butterfly*	180 *Baby Buster* (short dress)
142 *Drowsy Dick*	181 Baby Buster (long dress)
143 Sunbonnet Sal	183 Our Baby (wigged)
144 *Our Baby*	187 *Oliver Twist* (wigged, glass eyes)
145 *Baby Beauty* (wigged)	188 *Little Emily* (wigged, glass eyes)
145X Baby Beauty (wigged, various colors)	
146 Suck-a-Thumb	
147 Candy Kid	
148 Toodles	
149 Cotton Joe	

(See Ill. 1218.)

1915: The trade names included *Nature Babies;* Irish Mail Kids; Rosebud Babies; Baby Peterkin, a new bisque doll and its younger brother called Baby Bobby; Cycle Kids in style No. 104, Boy Cycle Kid; No. 105, Sambo Cycle Kid; No. 106, Cycle Kid Monk; No. 107, Clown Cycle Kid. The Campbell Kids had new style clothes including two Dutch costumes.

An important innovation this year was a composition head doll with glass eyes and a wig designed by a "celebrated New York Artist" on a fully jointed body. The doll was described as having a "bisque finish . . . bare neck and arms." Horsman was advertising in British toy trade journals.

1916: The numbers and names of the Horsman dolls in 1916 were as follows: 124–126, 134–136, 138–141, 143, 146, 150–151 were the same as in 1914. 160–161, 200–208, 213–217, 225–227 were wigged versions. 75–99 Junior sizes including 90–95 *Peek-A-Boos. Peterkin* dolls included: 111 Willy, 113 Tommy, 114 Betsy, 115 Fancy, 117 Canton Kid, 119 Baby. Others included 127 Campbell Dutch Boy; 128 Campbell Dutch Girl; 131 Carnival Kid, eyes shut; 132 Carnival Kid, eyes open; 133 Our baby, long dress; 137 Mandy Bumps; 138 Sandy Bumps; 142 *Phoebe Snow;* 145 Our Baby, short dress; 147 *Bubbles;* 148 Topsy; 148½ Sambo; 152 *Polly Prue;* Baby *Darling;* 154 Baby Rosebud; 157 Paul Pry; 163 Miss Molly; 164 Peasant Boy; 165 Peasant Girl; 177 *David Copperfield;* 178 Little Em'ly; 179 Miss Nancy; 181–185 are *Gene Carr Kids* including 181 Blink, 182 Jane, 184 Smoke, 185 Lizzie; 195 Peek-A-Boo wigged; 196 Jubilee Girl; 197 Peasant Boy; 198 Peasant

Girl; 221–227 Girls in large sizes; 225½ Boy in large size.

Other new dolls were The *Raggedy Man* and *Thomas Edison Jr.*

Cloth dolls included the Babyland Rag dolls with Brückner type faces. Binks a boy; and Binney a girl.

1917: Dolls included Campbell Kids, Peasant Children, Peterkin, Miss Sam,[+] *Master Sam,* Rookie, a baby ht. 13½ in. (33 cm.), *Lady Fuller,* Phoebe Snow, *Our Darling,* and Farmer Boy; the last four dolls were 16 in. (40.5 cm.) tall.

1918: Advertised over 200 new numbers with new models of the heads and/or new costumes. All the Horsman dolls had a purple and gold shoulder sash with the words "GENUINE HORSMAN 'ART' DOLL."

According to TOYS AND NOVELTIES the line of all-felt dolls made by Belgian refugees who had fled to England at the beginning of the war represented soldiers of all Allied nations plus sailors, clowns, nurses, Uncle Sam, John Bull, peasants and so forth. The dolls were described as "most life-like characters in felt ever produced"; even the faces were felt.

Other dolls included: *Miss Liberty, Baby Butter Ball, Baby Patty Cake* and dolls representing school girls. The ball-jointed dolls had unjointed wrists, real hair wigs and glass eyes; on some, the eyes could go to sleep. Baby dolls wore long or short clothes or no clothes at all; a few of them said "Mama." Peterkin came in an all-adtocolite[1] version.

1919: TOYS AND NOVELTIES reported, "The E. I. Horsman & Aetna Doll Co . . . occupies over 60,000 square feet of space . . . exclusive of its auxiliary plants devoted to the manufacture of doll dresses.

"Three hundred and fifty employes [sic] carry on in this factory not only all the process of doll manufacture proper, but also related operations.

"Every Horsman doll is not only the complete product of their own factory as regards head, body and costume, but also the wig, the paint with which the doll is finished, and the box in which it is contained.

". . . This company was the first in America to produce a pasted wig, . . .

"Their box factory not only produces five thousand paper boxes a day, but also all washers used in their dolls.

"The policy of the E. I. Horsman & Aetna Doll Co., . . . is to manufacture every part that goes into their dolls so as to control not only quality but also supply, . . ."

Composition-head infant dolls with molded hair and painted eyes were 11 and 14 in. (28 and 35.5 cm.) tall; dressed in short or long baby dresses. An 18 in. (45.5 cm) tall doll had sleeping eyes or roguish eyes with a wig. The largest sizes, 21 and 22 in. (53.5 and 56 cm.), had both wigs and sleeping eyes and wore short baby dresses and caps.

Composition-head girl dolls with molded hair and painted eyes came 14 and 16 in. (35.5 and 40.5 cm.) tall; price dressed $9.00 and $12.00 a doz. wholesale. These dolls also came with mohair or human hair wigs and painted, stationary glass or sleeping eyes. Various heights have been reported from 16 to 20 in. (40.5 to 51 cm.); prices depended on clothes, but they were at least as high as $4.25 each wholesale.

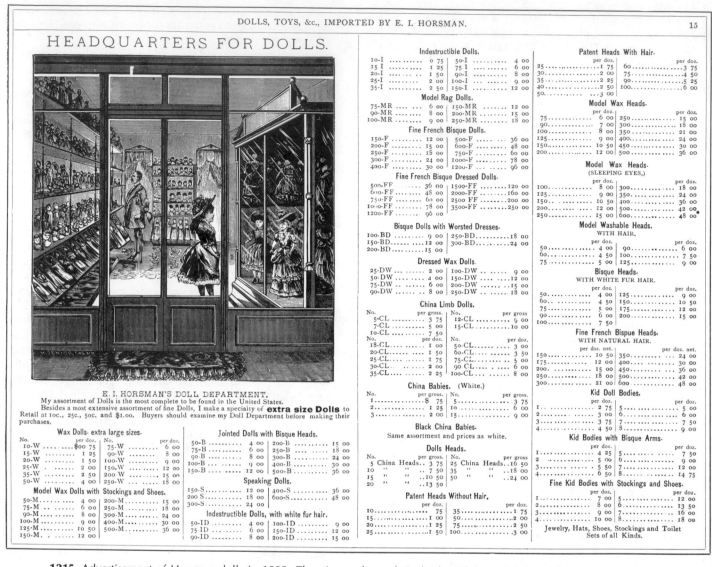

1215. Advertisement of Horsman dolls in 1885. The picture shows their display of dressed dolls, dolls in chemises, and dolls' heads. The scope of their Doll Department is emphasized by the comprehensive list of items that they sold wholesale.

1920: Advertised bisque-head *(Fulper)* dolls with wigs or with molded hair on bent limb or fully jointed adtocolite composition bodies. These came dressed or undressed in a variety of heights including 16 and 18 in. (40.5 and 45.5 cm.) for the fully jointed dolls.

1921: Various types of dolls were dressed in pinafores with felt bunnies appliquéd on their clothes, and named "Pinafore" dolls. The family of *Wise* dolls were dressed, cloth, black dolls and included *Baby Wise, Lizzie Wise, Mammie Wise,* and *Miss Polly Wise.*

Another new doll was an all-composition walking doll with the walking mechanism in its body. It had molded hair, was jointed at the neck, shoulders and hips and wore rompers, hat, socks, and single strap slippers.

1922: Advertised Chubby dolls and over 100 other new style numbers in various sizes. These came with painted hair or wigs. *Bye Bye Baby* and *Red Riding Hood* were new lines of dolls.

Sears advertised Horsman dressed *Mama* dolls with *Lloyd* voices, mohair wigs, and painted eyes. Hts. 14, 17, and 19 in. (35.5, 43, and 48 cm.); priced $2.98–$4.25. The two smaller sizes came with sleeping eyes and cost $3.68 and $4.59.

1923: *Baby Horsman* was one of the new dolls. (See also **Manufacture of Dolls, Commercial: Made in United States.**)

1924: The emphasis seemed to be on Mama dolls; one of these with a wig and dressed cost $6.98.

A new face finish was claimed to be washable. Other new features included hair eyelashes on moving eyes and human hair wigs.

1925: Horsman registered *Pat-A-Cake* in the U.S. as a trademark.

1926: *HEbee-SHEbee* dolls were dressed in various costumes. Babyland dolls were Mama dolls with composition head and limbs. Horsman advertised all-new costumes on their dolls; 1925 clothes were discontinued. The new costumes copied the latest styles of children's clothes.

1927: *Baby Dimples* was a new doll. Baby dolls wore short dresses at a three to one ratio to long dresses. Over three times as many dolls were dressed as little girls as those in baby clothes. Most of the little girl dolls wore bonnets but a few wore wide bandeaus in their hair or cloches (hats). Mama dolls were dressed as a little girl of beginning school age.

Sears advertised dressed Mama dolls with composition head, forearms, and legs, mohair wigs, sleeping eyes with hair eyelashes. Ht. 18 in. (45.5 cm.); priced $2.98.

Late 1920s: Horsman sued *Acme* for copying *Tynie Baby.* Horsman lost the case because they had put only E. I. H. on their dolls' heads.

1928: *Dolly Rosebud* was a new Mama doll. A new model head for Mama dolls was made and the dolls came in eight heights, some larger than formerly. Dolly Rosebud and Baby Dimples were dressed in prints depicting Tony Sarg's marionettes, as well as in other fabrics. Clothes of wexbar silk and coats and hats of chinchilla or velvet were introduced.

Made Ella Cinders doll based on cartoon character.

1929: Felt used for dolls' clothes; boy wore wide Dutch-type trousers and short jacket; girl wore full skirt and tight bodice. Mama dolls with composition heads and limbs, wigs, sleeping eyes, hair eyelashes, and cotton-stuffed cloth body wore organdy dresses and came in four hts.: 16, 18, 20, and 23 in. (40.5, 45.5, 51, and 58.5 cm.).

Baby Dimples had a kapok stuffed soft body with dimpled composition legs. Peterkins were dressed as boys or girls.

1930: Acquired *Amberg* business including *Vanta Baby, It* and so on. Horsman produced these dolls but used the Amberg name.

Peggy was a new name for a Horsman doll. They advertised that their entire line of dolls had new clothes made in the latest fashion. (See THE COLLECTOR'S BOOK OF DOLLS' CLOTHES, Ills. 715, 730 and 773.)★

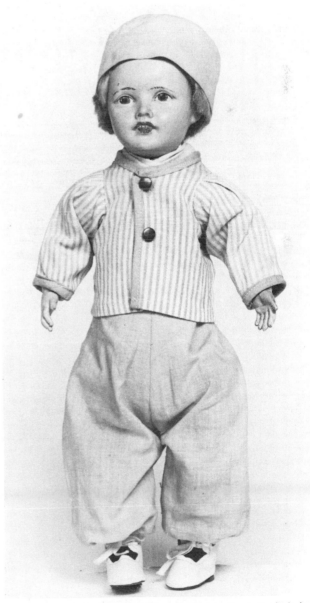

1216. Front page of the E. I. Horsman FANCY GOODS AND TOYS catalog for their display at the 1893 Chicago World's Fair. This shows some of their dolls.

1217. Composition head with a flange neck on a cloth body, produced by Horsman. It has a wig, painted blue eyes, open-closed mouth with four upper teeth, and Campbell Kid type composition hands. H. 13½ in. (34 cm.). *Courtesy of the Margaret Woodbury Strong Museum. Photo by Harry Bickelhaupt.*

Horsman Unbreakable TRADE "Art Dolls" MARK

Trade Mark "Bauernkinder" A New Doll Departure

PEASANT CHILDREN

Artistic, Lovable

A new doll departure, these are real life studies of German peasant child types, —the pretty lovable kind, which you will see in the little villages where German toys are made. They are artistic as well as lovable creations and are offered at a price never before placed on dolls of this class.

No pains have been spared to make them perfect in every detail of design, dress and finish.

No. 135½ and 136½ Tyrolers

No. 134 Baby Bauernkind

No. 136 Boy Bauernkind

No. 135 Girl Bauernkind

No. 134. **BAUERNKIND BABY.** A cute little tot dressed in a peasant style costume with a quaint white lawn cap, lace trimmed, and tied with ribbon. Has the best quality cork stuffed cloth body, fully jointed.........................Per Dozen, **$8.50**

No. 135. **BAUERNKIND GIRL.** A little older child of the same type dressed in colored gingham costume, hat to match. This little lady is well tanned by the sun and is altogether a unique and winsome plaything ....Per Dozen, **8.50**

No. 136. **BAUERNKIND BOY.** Just such a sturdy sun-tanned little tot, such as one may see all through the black forest country. His costume consists of a short green jacket with brass buttons and cap to match, loose white shirt and baggy khaki breeches, short socks and felt shoes...........................Per Dozen, **8.50**

No. 135½. This is a merry little maiden, dressed prettily in a bright red petticoat and green blouse with a green Tirolean hat feather, short socks and felt booties. A doll which will delight every little girl.................................Per Dozen, **8.50**

No. 136½. A companion doll to No. 135½. The green and red costume consists of blouse, overdress and Tirolean hat. Short stockings and booties............Per Dozen, **8.50**

LARGE SIZE "BAUERNKINDER." (To Retail for $2.00.)

No. 211 **BAUERNKIND BOY.** Similar to No. 136, but larger and finer. Costume of green and khaki..Per Dozen, **$13.50**

No. 212. **BAUERNKIND GIRL.** Companion doll to No. 211. Costume of green and red.
Per Dozen, **13.50**

3

No. 211 Large Bauernkind

No. 212 Large Bauernkind

1218. Horsman "Bauernkinder" (peasant children Art dolls.) These composition head dolls have molded and painted hair and eyes and are on cloth bodies. The smaller size dolls have Campbell Kid type composition hands, while the larger girl and boy dolls have a different shaped composition hand. The statement that "these are real life studies of German peasant child types, . . . which you will see in the little villages where German toys are made" suggests some authenticity to these costumes. This is a page from a Horsman catalog of ca. 1914. *Courtesy of Bernard Barenholtz.*

1219. Composition shoulder head doll produced by Horsman. It has molded hair, painted features, cloth body with bent legs, and adtocolite composition hands. Clothes are contemporary with the doll. Mark: Ill. 1227. H. 14 in. (35.5 cm.). Probably named "Baby Darling" in Ca, 1916 Horsman Catalog. *Coleman Collection.*

1220. Bisque socket head made in Japan for Horsman probably during or shortly after World War I. It has a dark brown wig, sleeping blue glass eyes, and an open mouth with four upper teeth. Mark: Ill. 1228. H. of head 5 in. (12.5 cm.). *Courtesy of the Margaret Woodbury Strong Museum. Photo by Harry Bickelhaupt.*

1221. Horsman composition head Mama doll with human hair wig, sleeping blue eyes, hair eyelashes, open mouth with two upper teeth, and a cloth body with composition arms. Original clothes. Marked "E.I.H. © A.D.C." H. 25 in. (63.5 cm.). *Courtesy of Viola Endersbee.*

1222. Rosebud, a composition shoulder head Mama doll produced by Horsman. It has a reddish wig, sleeping metal eyes with hair eyelashes, open mouth with teeth and tongue, dimples, and a cloth body with composition arms and lower legs. Original dress is labeled "HORSMAN//DOLL." Mark on head: "© E.I.H. CO. INC." Stamped on back of body is 4; stamped on cloth part of leg is "PATENT APPLIED FOR." H. 19½ in. (49.5 cm.). *Courtesy of John Axe.*

1223. A display of Horsman dolls as shown in PLAYTHINGS, January, 1927.

"CAN'T BREAK 'EM"

1224

"Can't Break 'Em"

1225

EIHCO

1226

E.I.H. ©A.D.C°

1227

No - 11
HORSMAN
NIPPON

1228

EI©HC°.
E.I.HORSMAN
INC.

1229

© 1924
E.I. HORSMAN
CO. INC.

1230

©1924by
EI Horsman Co.ING
MadeinGermany

1231

1224–1231. Marks on dolls produced by Horsman. These marks are usually embossed on the back of the composition head or shoulder.

Horsnell Bros. Ltd. 1926. London. Imported dolls and advertised "Dolls of all kinds" and dolls' accessories in a British toy trade journal, also exported dolls.

Horstmeyer, Mme. (née Burkhardt, Hedwig). 1899. Berlin. Applied for a German patent (D.R.G.M.) for a walking doll that turned its head.★

Horvath, Josef. 1853. Vienna. Manufactured toys.

Hospitals for Dolls. See **Repairing Dolls.**

Hosta Porcelain Factory. 1867–97 and later. Barcelona, Spain. In 1897 *Ramon Florensa* sought the correct type of slip for making dolls' heads which he was starting to produce.

Hot-Press Composition. Ca. 1918–30 and later. According to Mr. Trumpore of *Effanbee, Mr. Dekline* was the originator of hot press, wood pulp composition dolls' heads. This method required a "gang mold" or a group of molds joined together rather than the single molds used earlier. These gang molds or doll dies were originated and made by *J. E. Steinmeier Bronze Works.* At first the heads had "ring" (flange) necks that were sewn into the body, but around 1920 composition shoulder heads began to be made using the hot press method.

(See **Manufacture of Composition Heads** in the first COLLECTOR'S ENCYCLOPEDIA OF DOLLS, and **Manufacture of Dolls, Commercial: Made in United States.**)

Hot Shots. 1927. Name of dolls made by *J. Bouton & Co.* These dolls with wigs were 11½ and 17 in. (29 and 43 cm.) tall.

Hotel de Ville. See **L'Hotel de Ville.**

Hotsy Totsy. 1926. Line of *Boudoir* dolls made by *Gerling* and including dolls dressed as Flappers and *Cigarette Girls.*

Hottentot. 1899. All-composition black doll distributed by *Butler Bros.* It had kinky hair, painted features, earrings, and was jointed at shoulders and hips; dressed in African type costume. Hts. 5¾ and 8½ in. (14.5 and 21.5 cm.).

Hough, S. Wolfe. 1919. Dronfield, England. Manufacturer and importer of dolls and dolls' parts including dolls with porcelain or celluloid heads.

Houghton, Elizabeth Ellen. 1915–21. London Designed the cloth dolls made by *Shanklin.* She was a well-known artist according to a British toy trade Journal. When World War I broke out Mrs. Houghton organized the local ladies in Shanklin on the Isle of Wight into a doll-making and doll dressing cottage industry group. This endeavor grew and they moved to London where they had a factory in Greenwich and were funded by *The Three Arts Women's Employment Fund.* Later the business was known as *The British Toys,* which handled Houghton dolls made by both Shanklin and *Nottingham* The dressed dolls were made of cloth, usually stockinette, and had sculptured faces designed by Mrs. Houghton. The modeling was so detailed that even the temple marks were indicated. The dolls had yarn hair and came in black or white versions. Mrs. Houghton's signature was used as a trademark on these dolls.

1916: Made dolls representing three sisters and named *Patty, Prudence,* and *Suzanne.* These dolls were exported to America by *Meakin & Ridgeway.*

1917: Dolls included the Three *Good Sisters* named above, the Naughty (Bad) Sisters, *British Babes, Kate Greenaway* children, *Paddlers, Picaninnies* and so on.

1921: *Roberts Bros.* of Gloucester made Houghton dolls.★

1232A & B. Dark brown all-composition doll with black wig, painted and molded ethnic features, jointed at the shoulders and hips, and it wears a fur, skirt, earrings, and necklace. This doll closely resembles the Hottentot doll advertised by Butler Bros. in 1899. H. 5¾ in. (14.5 cm.). *Coleman Collection.*

Houghton & Dutton. 1880. Boston, Mass. Catalog listed French dolls, priced $1.25 to $4.50; china or wax dolls, priced 7¢ to $1.00; composition dolls, 15¢ to 54¢; dolls' heads, 8¢ to $2.00; dolls' bodies, 22¢ to $1.08; dolls' boots, 13¢ to 37¢; dolls' hose, 6¢ to 12¢; dolls' toilet sets, 75¢ to 98¢.

Houla-Houla Hawaiian. 1917. One of the El-Be-Co dolls of *Langrock Bros.* It came in three sizes; price $1.00 and up.

Hourdeaux-Bing Inc. 1923–26. Lichtenfels, Bavaria. Made dolls.

Hourtret, Suz & Giely, Cam. 1927–28. Paris. Made shoulder heads and *mignonnettes.*

House of the Seven Gables. Salem, Mass. Distributed peg wooden type dolls with curls on the side of the head. See Ill. 1233.

Hovenden, R. C., Sons Ltd. Before 1820–1929. London. Handled dolls, used the monogram mark of R H//& Sons. The 5-sided mark has the RH in the center of the word London.

1233. Carved and turned peg wooden dolls sold at the House of the Seven Gables in Salem, Mass. These dolls with carved wooden curls on each side of their head are shown on a period postcard in the Coleman Collection.

Howard Pottery. 1925–30 and later. Shelton, Staffordshire. Made *British Ceramic* dolls.

Hu Sun. 1925–26. *Lenci* felt doll style no. 251 represented a kneeling Oriental smoking an opium pipe. Ht. 23 in. (58.5 cm.).

Huard, Mon. (R.G.F.). 1880–1929. Paris. Made heads, bodies and wigs for dolls.

Hubbard (Mother Hubbard). 1911 and earlier. Felt doll made by *Steiff* to represent Mother Hubbard. Doll resembled a witch with a conical brimmed hat and a cane. Ht. 43 cm. (17 in.).

Hubenthal, L. 1890s. Budapest. Store that advertised "French Dolls."

Hubert. 1920s. France. Member of the *Chambre Syndicale.* Made jewelry for dolls.

Hubertus (Hunter). 1909–25. Felt character doll made by *Steiff* and distributed in the U.S. by *Borgfeldt.* It was dressed as a hunter with a brimmed hat turned up on one side, and spats. Five hts.: 28, 35, 43, 50, and 60 cm. (11, 14, 17, 19½, and 23½ in.). In 1913 the 43 cm. doll came with or without a mama voice; the two tallest dolls came only with a mama voice. The price in 1911 in Germany for the 60 cm. doll was $4.81 and in 1913 in New York it was $6.55.

1913: *Gamage* described this doll as wearing a red jersey shirt, grey trousers, a hat, and gaiters.

1924: There were three hts.: 28, 35, and 43 cm. (11, 14, and 17 in.).

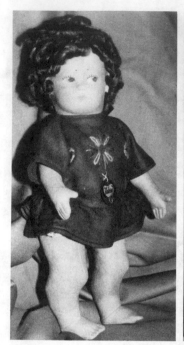

1234A & B. Hubsy, a felt doll produced by E. Pfeiffer, with a reddish wig, molded and painted blue eyes, closed mouth, jointed at the neck, shoulders, and hips. The mitten hands have sewn fingers. Original clothes, including a brown felt dress. Mark on tag: Ill. 1235. *Courtesy of Astry Campbell.*

1235. Hubsy mark on a tag attached to the doll's dress.

Hubsy. 1923. Felt doll produced by *Emil Pfeiffer.*★

Huchez, Maurice. 1925–27. Paris. Produced bisque and porcelain dolls' shoulder heads.

Huck, Adolf, & Co. 1923–27. Nürnberg, Bavaria. Successor by 1927 was Theodor Guggenheimer. Both A. Huck and H. Huck obtained German patents (D.R.P.) in 1924 for jointed dolls.

1927: Advertised that they were a celluloid factory making dolls' accessories, especially toilet sets.

Hudson, P. G., & Hepworth, F. N. 1927. Carlisle, England. Obtained a British patent for a doll whose torso consisted of a box.

Hug Me Dollies. 1926. Line of *Mama* and baby dolls with cloth bodies, made by the *Modern Toy Co.* Ht. 11½ in. (29 cm.).

Hug Me Kiddies (Hug-Me-Kiddy). 1912–1914. Dolls with round googly eyes made by Monroe M. Schwarzschild.[†] (See Ill. 1236.) (See also **Hug-Me-Tight Kiddies.**)

1912: It was claimed that one New York firm had sold 200,000 of these dolls. McCALL'S MAGAZINE offered these dolls in the 11½ in. (29 cm.) ht. as a premium.★

Hug-A-Bye. 1916. Trade name of a line of cloth dolls produced by *Horsman* for infants. The line included Binks and Binney.

Hughes, Francis L. (Hughes & Jacobs, Jacobs and Hughes). 1864–1909. Rochester, N.Y. Imported, assembled and distributed dolls wholesale.

1876: Invoice listed "China Babies" (probably all-china), china dolls and wax dolls.

1882: Advertised in their catalog "China limb dolls;" wax dolls; jointed dolls (probably from the *Jointed Doll Co.*); and doll heads including "*Parian* Marble Doll Heads."

1890: Catalog listed 100 styles of china doll heads; 500 styles of wax dolls; "Bisk jointed dolls, flowing hair."

Hughes, Henry Jeffrey. 1887–1929. London. By 1911 "& Son" was added. Made, distributed, and exported dolls including Folly Dolly dolls, Eskimo dolls and possibly *Caversham* dolls. See Ills. 489 and 490. Dolls had cloth bodies, *British Ceramic* or celluloid heads. The dolls were dressed as a Boy Scout, Dutch girl, a nurse, Pierrots, and as a sailor. The better dolls were dressed in velvet.

1924: Advertised that they made "all-English dolls," including Knockabout dolls, Rag dolls, Picture dolls, New Folly dolls, New velvet Jester dolls, Scotch, Irish and Welsh dolls.

1925: Advertised male and female *Golliwogs* and a doll named Miss Cross-Word.★

Hug-Me. 1930. Baby doll with kapok stuffed cloth body made by *Gem.* It had a wig, sleeping eyes, voice, and came dressed. Various sizes and prices were available.

Hugme. 1930. One of the *Kiddie Pal* line of dolls made by *Regal.* It had a composition head and arms, painted eyes, open-closed mouth, flange neck, cloth body and legs.

Hug-Me-Tight. 1915–17. Cloth dolls with flat faces and printed clothes, designed by *Grace Drayton,* advertised by *Colonial Toy Manufacturing Co., Montgomery Ward,* and *Wyman, Partridge & Co.* The Mother Goose[†] line included A Dillar–A Dollar, Bow Wow, Ding Dong Bell, I Like Little Pussy, *Little Boy Blue,* Little Mousie Bride, Goosey Gander, Ride a Cock Horse, *This Little Girl, Wee Willie Winkie* and so on.

1916: Ht. 11 in. (28 cm.).

1917: These were made as cutout cloth dolls.★

Hug-Me-Tight Kiddies. 1914. TOYS AND NOVELTIES reported that a "Clock work mechanism caused their eyes to move in a natural fashion." It seems more likely that these were *Hug Me Kiddies* and that manipulation of a rod caused the eyes to move.

1236A & B. Hug Me Kiddy doll with a composition mask face, brown plush hair, round roguish brown glass eyes, closed mouth, and flesh-colored felt torso with stub hands. Original clothes. See Ill. 2279. H. 10 in. (25.5 cm.). *Courtesy of the Margaret Woodbury Strong Museum. Photo by Harry Bickelhaupt.*

Hugo, Hugh. 1930 and later. London. Antiques dealer who specialized in producing dressed all-wooden dolls with elaborate wigs and glass eyes, slightly resembling all-wooden dolls of the 1700s but with longer necks. The period clothes were made of old fabrics. These dolls were usually large and some of them represented characters in the play *"School for Scandal."* (See also **M. & Mme. Georges Lepape.**)

Hugonnard, A. 1925–29. Paris. Advertised "Poupées universelles" marked *A l'ancre* (Universal dolls marked with an anchor.).

Huguette. 1929. Name of a cloth doll (or cloth body doll) sold by *Bon Marché.* This dressed doll had a wig. Ht. 33 cm. (13 in.).

Huldschinsky, Hedwig Maria. See Strasserpuppen Werkstatten.

Hülse. 1850. Germany. Won a bronze medal at Leipzig for dolls.

1237. Hugh Hugo's wooden doll made ca. 1930 to somewhat resemble the wooden dolls of 150 years earlier. The white hair wig is over a black painted area similar to that found on early peg wooden dolls. The stationary blue glass eyes are threaded and there is a composition area around the eyes to hold them in place. Similar composition forms the nose. The mouth is almost a straight line. The turned wood body has cloth joints at the shoulders and elbows and mortise and tenon joints at the knees and hips. The original dress is in pseudo-1700s style made of old fabrics and laces. The footwear is painted black. H. 28 in. (71 cm.). *Courtesy of the Margaret Woodbury Strong Museum. Photo by Harry Bickelhaupt.*

1238. Wooden doll produced by Hugh Hugo. The wooden doll itself was made in England ca. 1930. It has a wig, stationary black pupilless glass eyes, and a closed mouth. The original clothes were made by Hugh Hugo of old materials. H. 19 in. (48 cm.). *Courtesy of Sotheby Parke Bernet Inc., N.Y.*

Hülss, Adolf. 1915–30 and later. Waltershausen, Thür. Made dolls with bisque heads and jointed composition bodies, representing bent-limb babies, toddler and child dolls with ball joints. These dolls came dressed or undressed.

1927: Registered *Nesthäkchen* in Germany as a trademark. It should be noted that the H in the Hülss mark found on dolls resembles a B. See Ill. 853 in the first COLLECTOR'S ENCYCLOPEDIA OF DOLLS. ★

Hülss, Georg. 1930. Waltershausen, Thür. Made baby dolls and other dolls including dolls' heads.

Humbert, Richard Edward. 1916–17. Montclair, N.J. Made *Deedle Dum* dolls using toy blocks. Claimed this was patented in the U.S.

Hume, Anne. 1764. Burlington, N.J. Advertised "common pressed dolls." The material that was pressed is not known.

Humpty. 1903–30 and later. Name of a clown in the *Schoenhut* Circus, partner of *Dumpty*.

1924: When dressed in cotton they came in two sizes.

Humpty Boy. 1928. Cloth doll designed by *Eileen Benoliel* and made by *Live Long Toys*.

Humpty Dumpty. 1921–22. One of the *Mother Goose* cloth doll series with real hair and a handpainted face made by *Rees Davis*.

Humpty Dumpty. 1928. Cloth body dolls made by *Ross & Ross;* represented boys and girls.

Humpty Dumpty. 1929. One of the *Playpet Doll* line of Mother Goose characters made of segmented wood by the *Sun Enamel Works.* It had a handpainted egg-shaped head with eyes glancing to the side and wore a narrow brimmed bowler hat. Price $7.50 doz. wholesale.

Humpty Dumpty Doll Hospital. See **Clear, Emma.**

Humpty Dumpty Toy Co. See **Schoenhut, A., & Co.**

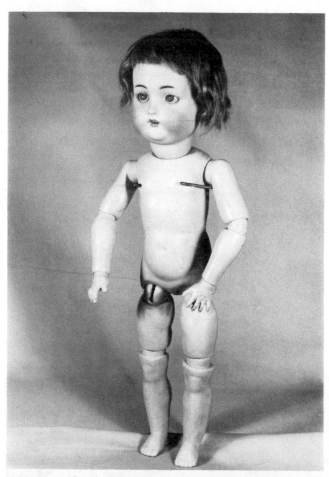

1239. Bisque head made by Simon and Halbig for a doll made by Adolf Hülss. It has a wig, sleeping eyes, open mouth with four teeth, and is on a ball-jointed composition and wood body with wooden arms and composition hands. H. 20 in. (51 cm.). Mark: Ill. 1240. *Coleman Collection.*

1240–1241. Marks found on bisque heads made for Adolf Hülss. See III. 1239.

Hunaeus, Dr. Paul. 1895–1930. Linden near Hannover, Germany. 1925, successor was Carl Scheu. Manufactured celluloid dolls and dolls' heads. His British agent in the 1920s was *Henry Barnett.*

1900–1901: Applied for seven German patents (5 D.R.G.M. and 2 D.R.P.) for dolls.

1911: Registered his intertwined PH initials in Germany. Obtained a German patent (D.R.P.) for dolls.

1912: Obtained a German patent (D.R.P.) for dolls.

1926: Dolls were distributed by *Gustav Burmester.*

1927: Registered *Natura* in Germany as a trademark for dolls and dolls' heads.

1928: Obtained a German patent (D.R.P.) for sleeping eyes in a doll's head. Advertised baby dolls, dolls' house dolls, and art dolls.

1929: Advertised swimming dolls.

1930: Distributed celluloid dolls for *Rheinische Gummi und Celluloid Fabrik Co.* according to the Ciesliks. Advertised a baby doll that could sit or stand. It had a moving head made by *Igodi.*★

1242. Mark used by Dr. Paul Hunaeus on celluloid dolls.

Hundorf, Walter. 1926–27. Munich, Bavaria. Obtained a German patent (D.R.P.) for a machine to stuff dolls.

Hungaria. 1930 and later. Hungary. Made composition dolls and dolls' heads.

Hungarian Dolldom. See **Magyar Babavilag.**

Hungarian Dolls. Many of the dolls in characteristic Hungarian costumes were made in Germany. Sometimes only the doll's head was imported and the rest of the doll was made in Hungary. The costumes represented the nobles, the soldiers—especially the Hussars, and the holiday costumes of the peasants. Shepherds were a favorite subject.

Among those in the doll business in Hungary were the following people or concerns: *B. Bernhardt* (1896–1926); *Anna Dely* (1921); *Dorogi & Co.* (1924–29); *Elsó Magyar Játékbabagyár* (1925)[+]; *Fémés Játékárugyár* (1925–29); *Gluck, Schmideck & Rosenberg* (1922); *Hunnia (Humnia)* (1913–25); *Berta Kunõdi* (1907–10); *Zsigmond Liebner* (1920–30); *Magyar Asszonyok Nemzeti Szövet Sége* (1909–26); *Magyar Babavilag* (1920); *Magyar Müvészeti Mühely* (1920s); *Magyar Ruggyantaárugyár Rt.* (1925–26); *Országos Magyar Háziipari Szövetség* (ca. 1925); Ignác Redö[+] (1925–26); *Ignác Rosenberg* (1925–30); *Armin Spielberger* (1920–30); *Marga Szerelemhegyi* (1920s–30s); *Frau Károly Tóbiás* (1920); *Tódor Kertèsz* (1861–1926); *Ungarische Gummi-waren-Fabrik* (1894–1930); *G. Weszely* (1906); *Zboray* (1920).

After World War I many artistic dolls were made in Hungary.

1914: TOYS AND NOVELTIES in an article on Hungarian dolls stated: "Dolls often are made in the image of some well-known army officer."

1921: PLAYTHINGS referred to earlier dolls dressed as shepherds wearing long sheep skin skirts, milk maids and popcorn men. All of these dolls as well as Hungarian dolls, representing boys and girls were exhibited at the Brooklyn Museum in New York. Some of these dolls were made by *MOVE* and by Hungarian Dolldom *(Magyar Babavilag).* The Brooklyn Museum's curator, *Stewart Culin,* described the Hungarian dolls as "Triumphs of taste and ingenuity."

1920s–30s: Mrs. Marga Szerelemhegyi made and exported the *Marga* dolls. Some of her dolls were shown at the New York World's Fair in 1939 and are now in the collection of the Strong Museum. (Many of the Hungarian companies began their names with a Hungarian term for Hungary, that is, either Magyar or Ungarische.)

Hunnia (Humnia). 1913–25 and later. Budapest. A doll factory that was listed under Wax Dolls' Heads in an Austrian directory.★

Hunt, Arthur. 1926. Shrewsbury, England. Made art dolls.

Hunter, William Crosby, and Sims, Frederick Walter. 1922–26. Obtained a U.S. patent for dolls' eyes.★

Huntsmann. 1926. Series of dolls advertised by *Bedington, Liddiat.*

Huret, Maison. 1812–1930 and later. France. A. Lemoine was the successor in 1885, Carette in the 1890s and Prévost in 1902. Huret dolls have been seen and/or reported as having bisque, china, gutta-percha, metal or wooden heads. These had either painted or glass eyes. The bodies were composition, gutta-percha, kid or wood with bisque, china, composition, gutta-percha, or metal hands. It is not known whether real gutta-percha was used or a substance called gutta-percha. Observations suggested the latter. Barbara Spadaccini found a reference that Huret porcelain heads were made in a French town where a porcelain factory was known to have existed.

1868: M. Henri Nicolle wrote that Huret made 1,200 to

1244A & B. Bisque socket head on a marked Huret body. The head has a blond wig, blue paperweight stationary eyes, and a closed mouth. The body is ball-jointed including the waist. The hands are metal, possibly pewter. H. 17¾ in. (45 cm.). H. of head only, 3¼ in. (8 cm.). *Courtesy of Sara Kocker.*

1243. Bisque head Huret doll has a wig, blue glass eyes, closed mouth, and metal hands and feet with shoes marked "Huret," according to the owner, Elsie Potter. H. 18 in. (45.5 cm.). *Courtesy of Elsie and Al Potter.*

1,500 dolls a year. At first they used astrakhan fur for wigs but later found mohair to be more satisfactory. The dolls were dressed as ladies or children in a workshop on the rue de Choiseul. The dolls dressed as Pierrettes wore simple skirts, wooden sabots, and blue stockings. Another popular doll represented Normandy milkmaids. Nita Loving was the owner of this rare book by M. Nicolle.

1914–18: Prévost Huret at 58 (68) rue de la Boétié, Paris, made dolls and heads of dolls according to an article written by Claretie.

1927–30 and later: Made bébés, art dolls and dolls to be used as favors.

1929: Advertised porcelain and composition heads, mask faces, cloth bodies, eyes, and voices for dolls. (See THE COLLECTOR'S BOOK OF DOLLS' CLOTHES, Ill. 145.)★

1248A. Hush-A-Bye baby doll with bisque head made by Armand Marseille. It has molded blond hair, sleeping brown glass eyes, open mouth with two upper teeth, and a flesh-colored cloth body with celluloid arms and legs. Original clothes. Mark on head: "A. M.// Germany." Mark on stomach: "PAT. 6944-13-4-32//L. C. //Hush-A-Bye Doll." The body construction was patented by L. Cohen of Australia in 1932. See Ill 1248B for the box in which this doll came. H. 12 in. (30.5 cm.). Courtesy of the Margaret Woodbury Strong Museum. Photo by Harry Bickelhaupt.

1245. A bisque head lady doll with a wig, blue glass eyes, closed mouth, pierced ears, a swivel neck on a bisque shoulder plate, and a cloth body with leather arms. The hat on the doll is stamped "HURET." (The doll itself may have no relationship with the Huret concern.) H. 15½ in. (39.5 cm.). Courtesy of Richard Withington. Photo by Barbara Jendrick.

BREVET D'INV: S.G.D.G.
MAISON HURET
Boulevard Montmartre, 22
PARIS.

EXPOSITION UNIVERSALS DE 1855.

1246–1247. Marks found on Huret dolls or their clothes.

HURET
34 Bould Haussmann
PARIS

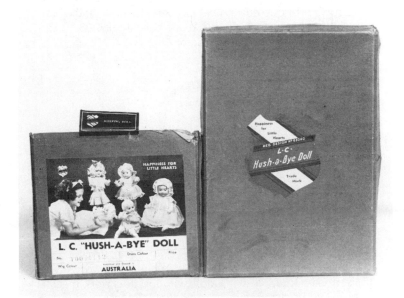

1248B. Hush-A-Bye doll's box end and box top. The dolls pictured were assembled and dressed in Australia as was the doll in Ill. 1248A that came in this box.

Hush-a-Bye Baby. 1922–23. Name of a doll made by *Farnell*. In 1923 it came in several sizes.

Hush-a-Bye Baby. 1925–28. Name of a baby doll with composition head and cloth body made by *Ideal*. It had painted hair, sleeping eyes, a mouth open so that it could simulate sucking its thumb and a crying voice. There were two models, one pouting and one in repose. Some of the dolls had composition hands and others, in 1926–27, had flexible rubber hands modeled from a real baby's hands. A few dolls had rubber legs. The dolls wore long or short baby clothes. A few of the dolls in 1926 were sold with a complete wardrobe. The 11 in. (28 cm.) ht. cost $1.35 dressed. The 19 in. (48 cm.) ht. cost $1.85 dressed and included a pillow and blanket. *Spiegel* advertised a Hush-a-Bye doll. Ht. 14½ in. (37 cm.); priced $1.35.★

Hush-A-Bye Doll. Name of a baby doll with a bisque head made by *Armand Marseille.* It had molded hair, sleeping eyes, open mouth with teeth, a pink cotton covered body, and celluloid arms and legs. The short baby dress and bonnet were blue organdy. This doll was assembled and dressed in Australia and had a label on its stomach with "Pat. 6944-13-4-32" over a shield on which was "L.C.//Hush-A-Bye Doll." Ht. 11½ in. (29 cm.).

Husheen Dolls. 1930. Cloth dolls made of silkeen plush except for the mask face, hands, and soles of the feet. These dolls were made by *Dean* in three hts. 7½, 9, and 10½ in. (19, 23, and 26.5 cm.).

Hustler Toy Corp. 1925. Sterling, Ill. Made turned *Segmented Wooden Dolls.*

Hutkinow, Theodore. 1924–25. Brooklyn, N.Y. Obtained a U.S. patent for a "double voice" for dolls.

Hutschenreuther, Lorenz. 1856–1930 and later. Selb, Bavaria. According to KERAMOS, a ceramic industry magazine, "china" heads for dolls were made by this porcelain factory. A bisque doll's head has been found with the Hutschenreuther factory's mark. At one time about 3,000 workers were employed by this factory.

1249. Mark found on Hutschenreuther dolls.

Hüttinger & Buschor. 1920–26. Nürnberg, Bavaria. The owners were Lucius Hüttinger and Traugott Buschor. Advertised Casadora,† a living doll without clockwork mechanism, and moving dolls in swaddling clothes.

1920–23: Applied for six German patents (5 D.R.G.M. and 1 D.R.P.) pertaining to dolls with movement and voice.★

Hutzler Brothers. 1906 and other years. Baltimore, Md. Their 1906 catalog listed *Cinderella Baby; Daisy Bell;* bisque heads with wigs on ball-jointed composition bodies, wearing chemise and footwear; stockinet dolls; kid-body dolls; rubber dolls; dolls' clothes, including automobile coats in plain colors and in checks; doll accessories, including opera bags and chatelaines. Dressed dolls cost up to $20.00 each.

Huvan Manufacturing Co. 1917. Ilford, Essex. Advertised crying baby dolls with lifelike faces and *Dolliettes*.

Hyde, Mrs. Mathilda. Ca. 1915–17. Mrs. Hyde created a set of costume dolls. In 1912 she went to Deerfield, Mass. where she studied for two years about the six little captives taken in 1704 when Deerfield suffered an Indian Massacre. Besides the captives, the dolls also represented Aronsen, the Mohawk who married one of the captives. These "Deerfield Dolls" were tagged with the name of the person represented; among them was William, Stephen.

Hyde & Co. 1882–94. Boston, Mass. Imported and distributed dolls wholesale.

Hygrade Cut Fabric Co. 1930 and later. New York City. Made outfits for dolls.

I

I Am A Bonser Doll. See **Bonser Doll.**

I. R. Comb Co. See **India Rubber Comb Co.**

Ibbetston, Leonard. 1917–20. Ilford, Essex. Factory known as Colonial Works; made cloth dolls, dolls' parts and accessories. The jointed cloth dolls were stuffed with hair and came dressed or undressed. The parts and accessories included wigs, bodies, arms, legs, dresses and shoes, but the specialties were dressed dolls and dolls' dresses.

1918: Also advertised dolls with unbreakable (composition?) heads on washable kid (imitation kid?) bodies.

Ickel, Edmund. 1890 and later. Kloster Vessra, Saxony. Porcelain factory made bisque dolls' heads and all-porcelain dolls. The heads were made with molded hair or for wigs, with painted eyes or with eye sockets for glass eyes, with closed mouths or open mouths and teeth. The shoulder heads had jointed necks. This information was supplied by the research of the Ciesliks. Danckert shows their marks as having the initials "F & L" or "P.V."

I-C-U Baby. 1927. Name of a doll made by the *Wolf Doll Co.* When the head was pressed down and then released it sprang back to its normal position while emitting a cry.

Ida (Bather). 1911 and earlier. Felt character doll made by *Steiff.* It was dressed as a girl in a bathing suit. Ht. 35 cm. (14 in.); priced $1.20.

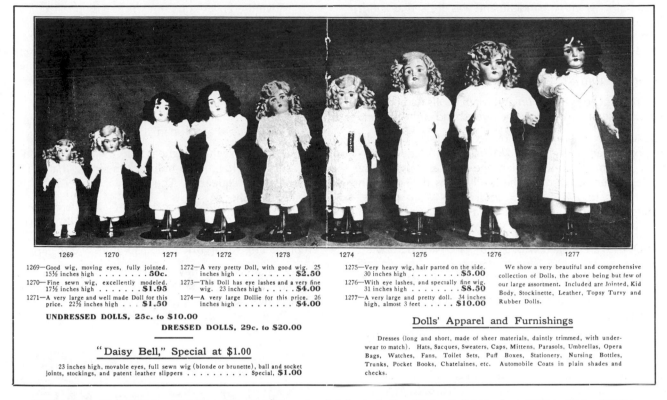

1269—Good wig, moving eyes, fully jointed. 15½ inches high . . . . **50c.**

1270—Fine sewn wig, excellently modeled. 17½ inches high **$1.95**

1271—A very large and well made Doll for this price. 22½ inches high . . . **$1.50**

1272—A very pretty Doll, with good wig. 25 inches high **$2.50**

1273—This Doll has eye lashes and a very fine wig. 23 inches high **$4.00**

1274—A very large Dollie for this price. 26 inches high **$4.00**

1275—Very heavy wig, hair parted on the side. 30 inches high **$5.00**

1276—With eye lashes, and specially fine wig. 31 inches high **$8.50**

1277—A very large and pretty doll. 34 inches high, almost 3 feet **$10.00**

We show a very beautiful and comprehensive collection of Dolls, the above being but few of our large assortment. Included are Jointed, Kid Body, Stockinette, Leather, Topsy Turvy and Rubber Dolls.

UNDRESSED DOLLS, 25c. to $10.00

DRESSED DOLLS, 29c. to $20.00

"Daisy Bell," Special at $1.00

23 inches high, movable eyes, full sewn wig (blonde or brunette), ball and socket joints, stockings, and patent leather slippers . . . . Special, **$1.00**

Dolls' Apparel and Furnishings

Dresses (long and short, made of sheer materials, daintily trimmed, with underwear to match). Hats, Sacques, Sweaters, Caps, Mittens, Parasols, Umbrellas, Opera Bags, Watches, Fans, Toilet Sets, Puff Boxes, Stationery, Nursing Bottles, Trunks, Pocket Books, Chatelaines, etc. Automobile Coats in plain shades and checks.

1250. Hutzler Bros. 1906 catalog page showing bisque-head dolls, including "Daisy Bell." Hs. from 15½ to 34 in. (39.5 to 86.5 cm.). Hutzler also advertised other types of dolls, dolls' clothes and accessories.

Ideal Novelty & Toy Co. 1906–80 and later. Brooklyn, N.Y. One of the few large companies that actually made their own composition dolls. They were pioneers in making "unbreakable" dolls in America. Morris Michtom and A. Cohn, the founders of the Company, began to make dolls in 1906 but Cohn left in 1911.

1913: Made a baby doll 38 in. (96.5 cm.) tall. Price $2.00 and up.

1915: TOYS AND NOVELTIES reported: "Mr. Michtom displayed a large variety of unbreakable dolls in many attractive characters. Throughout this entire line every number, from the 50¢ items up, has a new feature of composition feet which enables the doll to stand up without support. This line also includes some washable kid dolls, which is an entirely new feature in that kind of body, but the most prominent character we have seen this year is the 'Uneeda Kid'."

The *Uneeda Kid* doll had the molded high black boots to enable it to stand.

1917: Dolls included *Baby Mine, Cracker Jack Boy, Kimono Baby, Pajama Baby,* four Patriotic Dolls dressed in army or navy uniforms, and a Sweater Girl. There were also 24 styles and sizes of infant dolls in long or short baby dresses as well as dolls representing boys and girls. Some of the dolls not only had sleeping eyes but the eyes also moved from side to side. The dolls came with molded hair or wigs. The cork stuffed cloth bodies had steel joints; the all-composition dolls had spring joints and some of them represented babies.

One of the distributors of their dolls was the *Columbus Merchandise Co.*

1918: All-composition dolls included bent-limb babies, straight leg child dolls and *Liberty Boy.* The all-composition babies with painted hair and sleeping eyes came in six hts. 12 to 24 in. (30.5 to 61 cm.). Babies with composition heads and hands, painted hair, sleeping eyes and cloth bodies came in three hts.: 13½, 14½, and 16 in. (34, 37, and 40.5 cm.). The smallest size wore either long or short baby dresses; the 14½ in. size had an open mouth and pacifier and wore a long lawn dress; the largest size also wore a long lawn dress and had a nursing bottle with a crocheted cover.

Ideal advertised composition baby dolls with wigs, dressed in silk jersey outfits consisting of sweaters, leggings and caps; a line of bathing suit dolls with wigs and sleeping eyes. Hts. 13 to 18 in. (33 to 45.5 cm.).

1919: Advertised over 200 numbers including the Art character dolls, Red Cross Nurse, Baby Mine, *Pinafore Girl, Farmerette* (formerly *Zu-Zu Kid*), *Summer Girl, Pantalette Girl.* Dolls came in 12 sizes and 78 characters. Some of these had molded composition boots with either plain or circular striped cloth legs representing stockings. Eyelashes, human hair wigs and mama voices began to be advertised. One of the dolls cried when it was raised from lying down.

1920: Advertised over 200 numbers, all with moving eyes and some that could wink and blink. The dressed dolls wore fancy fabrics designed by artists. Style no. 1471 had a bobbed hair wig with a bandeau and was dressed as a girl. Style no. 1659 had a curly wig and hat and was dressed as a girl. Style no. 1667 was a baby doll in a short dress and cap and had a bottle. Style no. 1677 had a wig and veil and was dressed as a girl. Style no. 1920 was Baby Mine. Prices of dolls ranged from $1.00 to $30.00 each.

1921: Introduced *Flossie Flirt* and *Mama* dolls named *Rosy Cheeks*. Some of the dolls' clothes were hand embroidered.

1923: Advertised 83 numbers of sleeping dolls. Boy dolls were popular and some cried, "Mama-Papa." A new walking doll was made so that when one leg was touched the other leg came forward mechanically. This doll came in three hts. up to 27 in. (68.5 cm.). Dolls wore dresses, playsuits, or rompers. *Nancy Jane* was listed as a premium doll.

1924: Dolls were tagged with a baby pin. New dolls were *Carrie Joy* and Sucker Thumb[†] (Suck-a-Thumb). *Soozie Smiles* was distributed in England by *H. S. Benjamin*.

1920s: *Kandy Kid,* a doll with metal flirting eyes, was marked Ideal.

1925: Advertised that all their dolls were washable and had sleeping eyes.

1926: Introduced flexible rubber hands with fingers that could be opened and closed to hold objects. *Baby Mae* was a new Mama doll. *Hush-a-Bye Baby* came out in a new design with rubber hands and Flossie Flirt as well as *Vanity Fair* also had rubber hands. *Smiles* may have been a shortened form of the name Soozie Smiles. *A. S. Ferguson* was one of the distributing agents for Ideal.

1927: Smiles was described as a new baby doll with rubber arms and flirting eyes. Other new dolls were *Kindergarten Baby, Happy Flossie, Nightingale Baby,* and *Twinkle Toes.*

Ideal filed several suits against infringers on their flirting-eye patents. They claimed they had made improvements in their flirting eyes. The Mama dolls had rubber hands and Mr. Michtom asserted that the Mama dolls "sold way ahead of the baby dolls." Ideal was licensed by Voices, Inc. to use their patented mama voices and criers in Ideal's dolls.

Butler Bros. advertised Mama dolls with composition head and limbs made by Ideal with wigs, in three hts. 21, 27, and 30 in. (53.5, 68.5, and 76 cm.). The two largest sizes also had sleeping eyes and hair eyelashes.

1928: New doll was named *Peter Pan.* The baby dolls had rubber arms and legs that emitted a crying sound when pinched; standing dolls had only rubber arms. The patent for the rubber limbs was assigned to Ideal by *Maurice Sanders.* Most of the dolls had sleeping and flirting eyes. A novelty was the Dolly Kit made of red, blue, green, and black *Du Pont* Fabrikoid and containing two miniature nursing bottles with nipples and aluminum bottle holders which would hold the bottle in an upright position.

Gerzon sold a dressed bent limb composition baby doll made by Ideal. Ht. 44 cm. (17½ in.).

1929: New dolls were *Buster Brown, Tickletoes, Wendy* and *Winsome Winnie.*

Advertised over 200 numbers and emphasized the fact that since the rubber arms were not painted they were washable, would not crack or peel and were guaranteed for three years. A two-part mold was used, preferably with unvulcanized rubber for each arm and each leg. The hands and feet were hollow but the fingers and toes were solid. The upper leg was made of cloth and had a swing hip joint on a cloth torso.

1930: Advertised a doll named *Cuddles.*

1932: Ideal was the assignee of a U.S. patent obtained by Abraham M. Katz for a hollow rubber leg that emitted a sound when squeezed. The patent also pertained to the stringing of the leg.

1930s: Made Composition Shirley Temple, Snow White and the seven Dwarfs as well as dolls with "Flexi-Wire" bodies representing Fanny Brice and Mortimer Snerd.

1952: Claimed that they employed 3,000 people and produced 24,000 to 25,000 dolls a day. (See THE COLLECTOR'S BOOK OF DOLLS' CLOTHES, Ills. 717, 770 and 775.) (See also **Rommer, Isaac.**)★

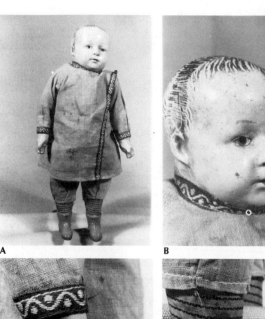
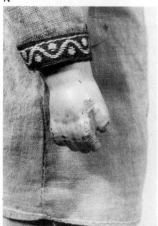

1251A–D. Boy doll with composition head, hands, and molded boots, made by Ideal around 1915. Molded hair, painted features; heavy, shiny composition. Original clothes. H. 12 in. (30.5 cm.). *Coleman Collection.*

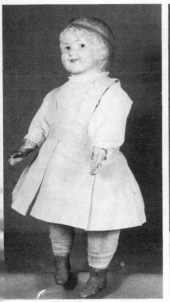

1252A & B. Composition head doll that resembles a coquette and may be Ideal's version which is called Naughty Marietta.† The features and hair with band are molded and painted. The eyes are glancing to the side. The cloth body has composition hands and low boots. This style of boot was a feature of Ideal. H. 14½ in. (37 cm.). H. of head only, 3½ in. (9 cm.). *Collection of Robert and Katrin Burlin.*

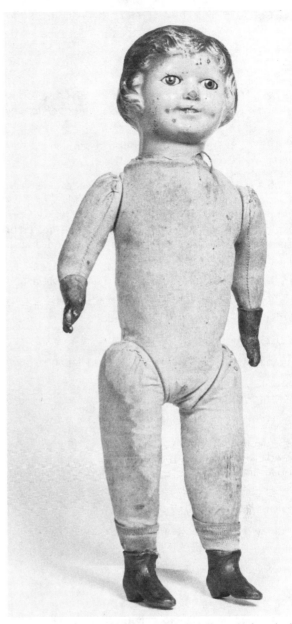

1253. Cold press composition-head doll made by Ideal. It has molded brown hair, sleeping and winking blue metal eyes covered with celluloid, open-closed mouth with teeth, dimples, flange neck on a cloth body with composition hands and boots. The cotton socks are attached to the boots. H. 16 in. (40.5 cm.). *Courtesy of the Margaret Woodbury Strong Museum. Photo by Harry Bickelhaupt.*

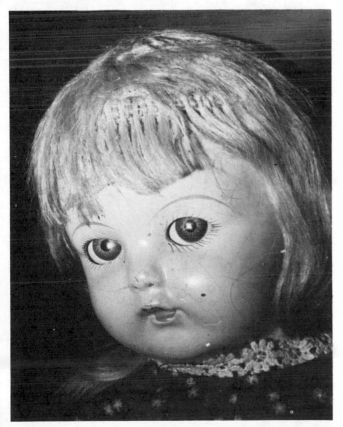

1254. Composition-head doll made by Ideal. It has a blond Rembrandt style wig, sleeping and flirting blue metal eyes covered with celluloid, open-closed mouth with white dots suggesting two upper teeth, and a flange neck on a cloth Mama doll body with composition lower arms and legs. Dress appears to be contemporary with the doll. Mark: Ill. 1255. H. 19½ in. (49.5 cm.). *Coleman Collection.*

1255–1256. Marks on Ideal composition head dolls.

Ideal Toy Co. 1915. Hackney, London. Made cloth *Eskimo* dolls.

Idéale. See **L'Idéale.**

Igodi.† See **Dietrich, Johannes Gotthilf.**

Ihle, Herbert. 1924. Birmingham, England. Advertised dolls in a British toy trade journal. Agent for *Catterfelder Puppenfabrik.*

I K W A. 1927–28. Trademark for dolls registered in U.S. by *L. Bamberger & Co.*

Ilford Doll Co. 1917–21. Ilford, Essex. Made dolls with *British Ceramic* heads and hair stuffed cloth bodies, or composition bodies. The leading line was the *Kissy Kissy Doll.* Some of the dolls were baby dolls and dolls came dressed or undressed. *Faudels* was the agent for these dolls. Advertised "French Dolls."

Illfelder, B., & Co. 1862–1930 and later. Fürth, Bavaria, and New York City. Imported and distributed dolls.

1915: Advertised American character dolls.

1917: Advertised Japanese dressed dolls.

1918: Franz B. Illfelder visited China and Japan seeking dolls.

1919: Agent for *Giebeler-Falk.*

1920: Advertised rubber dolls.

1926–28. Agent for *Bimblick, Domec, Kämmer & Reinhardt,* and other European companies. *Sweetheart* (My Sweetheart, Little Sweetheart) and *Rosebud* (Our Rosebud) continued to be the principal lines.

1929: Distributed *Peterson* dolls.

1930: Handled American and imported dolls.★

1257. Mark found on dolls, probably produced by Illfelder. (I. and J. are interchangeable in German.)

Illfelder, Leopold, & Co. 1882–1930. Sonneberg, Thür.; Fürth, Bavaria, and London. Successors by 1897 were *Bechmann & Ullman.* Produced and distributed dolls.

1897: Applied for a German patent (D.R.G.M.) for a metal doll.★

Ilmenauer Porcelain Factories. 1777–1930 and later. Ilmenau, Thür. There were several references to the manufacture of porcelain dolls' heads in Ilmenau in the late 1800s. At that time three porcelain factories existed according to DANCKERT and DIDOT. These were Ilmenauer Porzellanfabrik, *Galluba & Hofmann* founded in 1888, and *Gebrüder Metzler & Ortloff* founded in 1875.

Mr. Rolf Wernicke of *König and Wernicke* was born in

1910, the son of Rudolf Wernicke, who was born and grew up in Ilmenau and whose family had lived in Ilmenau and worked in the doll industry for generations. Unfortunately the statements of those who have been involved in the doll business sometimes prove to be incorrect unless they can be verified by other documentation and so far no documentary proof has been found for this 1977 statement regarding the manufacture of porcelain dolls in the first three quarters of the 1800s in Ilmenau, which Mr. Rolf Wernicke wrote. "At the same time [1840] there were in Ilmenau porcelain factories as well as production units for making kid gloves. What would have been more natural than to start manufacturing kid bodies with shoulder heads. Moreover the knowledge of kid-leather manufacture could be applied to the production of dolls' shoes." *Fischer, Naumann & Co.* and *Wagner & Zetzsche,* both located in Ilmenau, made shoes as well as kid bodies for dolls. Earlier the Wernickes had worked for Fischer, Naumann. Numerous marked Wagner & Zetzsche kid bodies have been found with bisque or china shoulder heads having the mold and size number along the back edge. This was the type of head probably made by *Alt, Beck & Gottschalck* in Nauendorf only a few miles away.

J

1258. Mark associated with the Ilmenauer Porzellanfabrik. (In German I & J are interchangeable.)

Iluska. 1921. Name of a doll representing a Hungarian fairy tale character. This doll was made by *MOVE* under the direction of *Anna Dely.*

Imhof, Ferdinand. 1898–1909. Berlin. In 1908 he moved to Westfalen, Germany. He applied for four German patents (1 D.R.G.M. and 3 D.R.P.) and an Austrian patent for a doll that "walked" on wheels. These patents were used by *Franz Schmidt.* The 1900 D.R.P. patent number and the name A. Länder were on the soles of the shoes of some of these walking dolls. (See Ill. 1259.)★

Imp, Caresse. See **Caresse Imps.**

Imperial. 1898–1910. Line of dolls with bisque heads and kid bodies handled by *Hamburger.* A doll has been reported by Donald Mitchel marked "S & H 1260 DEP Germany 4½ IMPERIAL." This doll had a bisque head made by *Simon & Halbig* on a gusseted kid body with bisque lower arms and cloth lower legs.

Imperial. 1930 and later. Hungary. Made composition dolls and dolls' heads.

Imperial Granum. 1914 and later. Name on cutout cloth dolls advertising an unsweetened food for babies. The doll was made in several versions and came 8 in. (20.5 cm.) tall.

Imperial Toy Co. (Toyland Works). 1915–19. Hull and London. Made long-limbed cloth dolls and *Eskimo* dolls of white plush with blue markings in various styles and sizes.

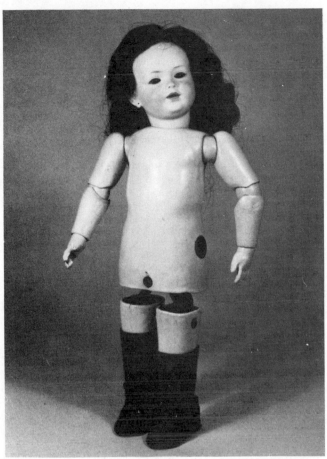

1259. Bisque head on a mechanical walking doll made by Imhof. It has a wig, sleeping brown glass eyes that squint, pierced ears, an open-closed mouth, and a composition body containing the walking mechanism. The hole on the hip is for the key to wind the mechanism. The wheels extend through the soles of the shoes. On the soles is the mark: "D.R.P.//No. 119, 857//Patent A. Länder." Mark on the bisque head: "536//4." H. 16 in. (40.5 cm.). *Courtesy of Richard Withington. Photo by Barbara Jendrick.*

Eskimo dolls also came in felt. The proprietor was S. Barkoff.

1915: Made *Gladeye* dolls.

1919: Cloth dolls were made in nine sizes.

Impersonating Doll Co. 1925–26. St. Louis, Mo. Made dolls.

Imports, of Dolls. The total value of imports of dolls and dolls' parts into the U.S., in thousands of dollars, was:

	1912	1922	1923	1924	1925	1926	1927	1928
Germany	1,538	1,493	1,794	642	583	545	755	752
Japan	2			73	108	146	112	
France	9	145	162	30	33	47	45	252
Other	15			54	37	48	87	
Total	1,564	1,638	1,956	799	761	786	999	1,004

1922, 1923, and 1928 appear to be incomplete reports.

1926: Only five percent of the value of dolls and dolls' parts sold in U.S. were imported: $786,000 imported value and about $15,720,000 American dolls and dolls' parts value. (See also **Duty on Dolls.**)★

Impy (Impie, Im). 1914. Name of a black bisque doll with large eyes and mouth representing the comic strip character of this name drawn by Winsor McCay in the *Little Nemo* series. The doll was imported and distributed by *Strobel and Wilken*. It was a scantily clad African child adorned with necklace, earrings, arm and wrist bracelets and anklets; came in two sizes and cost 25¢ to $1.00.

Ind. (Indian). 1911–16. Jointed felt art doll representing an American Indian, made by *Steiff* and distributed in the U.S. by *Borgfeldt*. Ht. 35 and 43 cm. (14 and 17 in.). The 43 cm. size cost $2.38 in Germany in 1911 and $3.65 in New York in 1913. In 1916 there was also a 100 cm. (39½ in.) height.

Indestructible. See **Composition Dolls.**

Indestructo Specialties Co. 1915–16. New York City. This company handled dolls with composition bodies, flirting and sleeping eyes. Ht. 15 in. (38 cm.). Dolls weighing less than an ounce were dressed as soldiers in the military costumes of various nations. Ht. 4 in. (10 cm.).

16 different boxes held dolls representing the four or five principal characters in *Fairy Tale Dolls.*★

India Rubber Comb Co. 1851 and later. New York City. Made dolls and dolls' heads of hard rubber.

1860–61: *John D. Robbins,* a distributor, purchased I.R. Comb Co. dolls in 2 sizes, priced 42¢ to 74¢ a doz. wholesale, according to a Day Book owned by Elizabeth Pierce.

Indian Dolls (American). Dolls made by Indians representing their own people. Most of the American Indians used wood, bark of trees, clay, animal skins, rags, corn husks or corn cobs for dolls. The Alaskan Indians used walrus tusks or carved stones for their dolls.

The importance of the collection of North American Indian dolls at the Smithsonian Institution was discussed by TOYS AND NOVELTIES in this 1914 article:

Indian Dolls of North America. "These dolls represent the expenditure of a vast sum of money. The dolls are not as a rule of such great value, but much time and money were spent in collecting them. Even now it is said the list is not complete, and occasionally a new doll is added to the already large collection. . . . It was discovered that the dolls possessed real value to the scientist, and from a display to satisfy the curious, the doll collection became one of the units in Uncle Sam's research work.

". . . They study the characteristics of the various tribes by studying the dolls. . . . The ethnologists are able to gain information of the characteristics of the remote ancestors of the people who made and played with the dolls. The discovery has been made that the particular characteristics of a people or tribe, especially those which they had inherited, were shown more strongly in the playthings of their children and especially in their dolls. This was found to be especially true among the savage tribes, for the doll is the recognized

1260. Leather and cloth doll made by American Indians, probably of the Sioux tribe. The leather head has eyes and mouth made of glass beads, and cheeks painted red. The hair which once framed the face has nearly all disappeared. Cowrie shells hang from the sides of the head as if they were earrings. The cloth body was made from a flour or sugar sack. The arms are much shorter than the sleeves; the dress and boots are white buckskin trimmed with blue, white and pink glass beads, and red paint. There are numerous bead necklaces. H. 15 in. (38 cm.). *Coleman Collection.*

1261. Pair of Indian dolls of cloth and leather with wig, embroidered features, earrings, rolled cloth fingers. Original clothes claimed to have been made by Jean Scott Failing. Hs. 7½ in. (19 cm.). *Courtesy of Richard Withington. Photo by Barbara Jendrick.*

universal plaything of children both savage and civilized. Through the present large collection of dolls at the National Museum at Washington experts have been able to trace kinship between two native tribes of North America living thousands of miles apart. . . .

"Through the study of these dolls the government is gaining possession of an immense amount of information regarding the people who inhabited America thousands of years before the arrival of Columbus. For instance, from a report lately made by these experts it is shown almost certainly that the Indians who first settled the country along the Pacific Coast even as far down as Central America, came across from Asia by way of Bering Strait or the islands of the Bering sea. Much of the information leading to this belief came from a study of these dolls. There are not many pretty dolls in the collection; indeed, most of them are uglier than the homeliest rag doll any white child ever had. Many of the dolls of the savage children have faces that have been made as hideous as possible. The experts say that this ugliness was intended to denote great physical strength, so that a very ugly man-doll would mean to the savage child a very strong man. Some of the dolls are very richly dressed. This is especially true of the dolls obtained from the Indians of the western section of America. There is a Sioux doll with a robe designed after the robe of a chief, which is covered with elks teeth. It is worth several thousand dollars."

ST. NICHOLAS magazine had several articles on American Indian dolls. In 1879, Western Indian dolls were described, "The dolls are of rags with hideous faces painted on them, and daubed with streaks of red in the style admired by the race."

The 1881 article told how Indians made dolls. "Their favorite method is to use corn-husks, from which they will fashion dolls that are almost as pretty as those made of costlier material, and sometimes more shapely. . . . Thorns are used to form features, as well as to fasten the clothes." A corncob formed the body and head, corn silk the hair and a bonnet was made from a leaf.

In 1888 ST. NICHOLAS published descriptions of American Indian dolls from various regions by Olive Thorne Miller and L. A. Higgins:

Dolls of the Gros Ventre tribe in the Dakota Territory.

"They are a queer-looking pair, dressed in the most elegant Gros Ventre style. They are eighteen inches tall, made of cloth, with their noses sewed on, and their faces well colored; not only made red, like the skin, but with painted features. The Indian doll has a gentle expression, with mild eyes, but the squaw has a wild look, as though she were very much scared. . . . Both have long hair in a braid over each ear, but the brave has also a quantity hanging down his back, and a crest standing up on top—perhaps as 'scalp-lock.'

"The dress of the lady resembles, in style and material, a bathing-suit. It is of blue flannel, trimmed with red braid, a long blouse and leggings of the same. She has also moccasins, and a string of blue beads around her neck, besides little dots of beads all over her waist. The suit of the warrior is similar in style, but the blouse is of unbleached muslin, daubed with streaks of red paint, and trimmed with braid, also red. Across his breast he wears an elaborate ornament of white beads, gorgeous to behold."

A Sioux doll named Bonita was about a foot tall and had "real skin, and real hair,—real buckskin, and real horse-hair. Charming pink cheeks on her very yellow face; expressive bead eyes, and a very unique little group of beads that does service for both nose and mouth surprisingly well. Two black beads, placed in line between two white ones, form each of the cleverly made eyes. Her raven hair is plaited in eighth-of-an-inch braids, and tied behind with a tiny buckskin ribbon. Not to be sparing of her charms, she has also two graceful braids falling in front of her shoulders.

"If Bonita had stayed in her wigwam home, she probably might have had two or three dresses, put on outside of this one—to refresh her soiled toilet, after the manner of her tribe. But we think her quite fresh enough in this gorgeous red-flannel dress, bound with yellow calico! She has square sleeves that quite envelop her spare arms, and marvelous square side-breadths that dip lower than the rest. She wears six strands of milk-white beads about her throat, and others dotted over her dress yoke. An indescribable pendant of tin bangles is suspended from her buckskin belt, which is also trimmed in tin ornaments. Excelling all else in deft workmanship are her wonderful little moccasins. . . . They are exquisitely embroidered in blue and red floss, and have tiny silk binding, sewed with invisible stitches." This dress apparently is the every-day dress, for a more elegant costume is described as being of "doe-skin" and having a "mouse-tooth necklace."

Southwest dolls. The Moquis dolls of the Hopi tribe of the Southwest "have wooden dolls of different sizes and degrees. The best have arms and legs, are dressed in one garment of coarse cotton, and instead of hair have feathers sticking out of their heads, like the ends of a feather duster.

"A Lower grade of Moquis doll has no limbs, but is gayly painted in stripes, and wears beads as big as its fist would be, if it had one. This looks as you would with a string of oranges around your neck. The poorest of all, which has evidently been loved by some poor little Indian girl, has in place of a head a sprig of evergreen." (See *Italian Dolls* for another use of a sprig for a doll's face.)

Oregon Territory dolls. A Nez Percé doll. "A Nez Percé girl has contributed to us [a] doll in its cradle of basket work. It is a rag-baby about eight inches [20.5 cm.] long, and as tightly tied into the cradle as the poor little Nez Percé girl herself was tied into hers. . . . Many a swing has it enjoyed hanging from a bush; and many a greasy dinner has it shared with its little owner,—at least, so one must judge from its looks."

Alaskan Indian dolls (See also **Eskimos.**). "The dusky damsel of Alaska has an ivory doll. It is carved from Walrus tusk, any length from one to six inches [2.5 to 15 cm.] with nose carved, and eyes, eye-brows, and mouth of black enamel. Even the inch-long baby has features carefully made. She has also a doll of wood, six or eight inches [15 or 20.5 cm.] long, with its face carved and a curious ornament just below the corners of the mouth. This is a blue bead, and is in imitation of the fashion of her tribe, of making in the lower lip an opening like a buttonhole, through which a desired ornament may be thrust. None of the Alaska dolls have joints, but this unnatural stiffness has apparently not been altogether satisfactory to the small damsels, for some are carved in a sitting posture.

"The most humble doll is simply a stick with a head carved on the end. But the most elaborate of all the Indian dolls I have seen belongs also to Alaska. It is carved from dark-colored wood, with mouth open, showing three white teeth, and it has real hair, in locks six inches [15 cm.] long, stuck into holes in the wooden head, with the drollest 'patch' effect."

Dolls of the Sitka tribe of Alaska are of "leather; black, greasy-looking creatures, with beads for eyes and mouth, and dressed of fur. They have also a poorer doll, of clay, with the nose formed, when the clay was soft, by summary process of a good pinch in the face; and a lavish display of beads made by small punches in the same soft material. The dress of these Sitka babies is simple,—a piece of coarse Indian cloth wound around the body and tied on with a rag."

Canadian Indian dolls. "The squaw dragging a six inch-long toboggan loaded with tent and poles, while the warrior carries his snow-shoes. She is dressed in red and black flannel, with calico blouse and cloth hood; tin bracelets are on her arms, and her breast bears an ornament like a dinner-plate, also of tin. Her lord and master wears a dandyish suit of white canton-flannel, fuzzy side out, a calico shirt, red necktie, and likewise a hood and tin dinner-plate. They are made of wood, with joints at hip and shoulder, and the faces are carved and painted.

"Micmac dolls of the Algonquian tribe in Eastern Canada are of leather but these are finer than the dolls of Sitka. . . . The leather is light colored; and it has a nose not pinched up in front, but pinched out from behind, and held in shape by something hard. It has black beads for eyes, and mouth and eyebrows of black paint. In dress it is quite grand; moccasins, leggings and calico gown, with a liberal amount of bead trimming and necklaces."

The *H. H. Tammen Co.* of Denver, Colorado, published a catalog in 1886 which listed crude pottery dolls of the Santa Clara, Apache and Zuni Indians for sale.

The STRAND magazine in 1902 described a Sioux baby doll in the collection of Mrs. Washington Hesing. This was a flat dressed doll made of chamois and came from the Standing Rock Reservation in North Dakota, U.S.A.

TOYS AND NOVELTIES, in 1913, described the North

1262A & B. Commercial needle-sculptured cloth doll representing an American Indian. Rolled fingers and toes, trimming of coiled wire suggests a mid 1800s date. H. 8¼ in. (21 cm.). *Coleman Collection.*

1263. Bisque head doll dressed as an Indian has stationary glass eyes, a five-piece composition body. Original clothes include velvet "buckskin" trousers and vest. Several beaded necklaces and wire bracelets on both arms adorn the doll. H. 8½ in. (21.5 cm.). *Collection of Robert & Katrin Burlin.*

American Indian dolls as "made of the bark of trees, clay, rags and wood. They are used not only as playthings, but they often symbolize their various gods . . . through them the children are instructed in the symbolism with which they are connected. The dolls of the Indian tribes of today [1913] are truer likenesses of the squaws and braves, and the bodies are made of some substantial material, as rags, wood, or even corn cobs, and are very beautifully attired in embroidered or beaded clothes with tiny moccasins. The features of the faces are indicated on a cloth, either with charcoal, color or occasionally with beads. Sometimes the children, themselves, make small dolls of clay which are rather crude but which give them the pleasure of a beloved plaything. The native Sioux dolls are dressed entirely in leather, with fringes made of the same material and the hair is long and thick, hanging down in long plaits. Sometimes beads are used to represent hair."

Also in 1913 *Elizabeth Scantlebury* exhibited dolls dressed as a Chippewa Indian Mother and her baby.

TOYS AND NOVELTIES, 1916–20, had several articles on American Indian dolls. It was stated again that the Sioux dolls in Dakota were made of buckskin decorated with bright colored beads. The wood of the sacred cotton wood trees was sometimes used to make dolls with religious significance. Other dolls were made of clay, rags, knots and the bark of trees. The Passamquoddy tribe called dolls "Ampskudahekanek."

In 1925 *Stewart Culin* wrote that "Indian dolls of buckskin and beads are of recent foreign introduction according to Mr. Rumpf, but Indian children make and play with dolls made of a thin slab of board with shell beads for eyes that date from the beginning of time." It should be noted that before the white man brought beads to the Indians, dyed porcupine quills were often used to decorate clothes.

PLAYTHINGS in 1925–26 contained articles on various Indian dolls especially those in the Wisconsin State Historical Museum. There were the usual buckskin dolls, fringed and beaded, made by Cheyenne Indians in South Dakota. A corn-husk doll with a wasp-like waist was made by the Ottawa Indians in Michigan. Native dolls of the lake country of California were made of slats of redwood with shell beads for eyes. Three unusual dolls had heads of dyed orange skins and hair of braided darning cotton.

Indian (American) Commercial Dolls. Bisque-head dolls, probably made in Germany in the late 1800s, were sometimes given to little Indian girls. They were dressed as Indians generally in buckskin clothes. These dolls have been found with Belton-type bisque heads on five piece composition bodies as well as with the more normal style with the head cut open.

Many ethnic dolls representing Indians had bisque heads made by *Armand Marseille* and other porcelain factories. Cloth or composition dolls were often simply darkened in color and dressed as Indians.

The U.S. Customs Court in 1929 ruled that souvenir Indian dolls were children's playthings.

Some of the commercial Indian Dolls were made and/or distributed by: *John Anderson* of Scotland, *Averill Manufacturing Co., J. Bouton, Butler Bros., Chad Valley, Cissna,*

1264A & B. Bisque-head doll representing an Indian Brave made in the 1890s. It is tan color and has glass eyes, open mouth, teeth and a scowl. The five-piece composition body is also tan and has molded shoes. Original Indian costume. The head is marked "8/0." H. 8½ in. (21.5 cm.). *Coleman Collection.*

Gustav Förster, Helvetic, Henderson Glove Co., Horsman, Jeanette Doll Co., O. J. Lafayette Lenci of Italy, *Live Long Toys*, Marshall Field, Mary McAboy, Nelke, Oakhurst Studios, Mme Paderewski, Saalfield, Sears, Shackman, Gebrüder Schmidt, Steiff, Strauss-Eckhardt Co., Tambon, Trego, Louis Wolf, Mary Frances Woods, Wyman, Partridge & Co. and YOUTH'S COMPANION.

Both Mary McAboy and Mary Frances Woods made real Indian portrait dolls while Horsman simply took dolls like the *Campbell Kids* and dressed them in pseudo-Indian attire. Generally squaws, papooses and Indian Chiefs were represented in various sizes.

1893: Horsman advertised two sizes of Indian dolls; priced 38¢ and 75¢ a doz. wholesale.

1907: Sears advertised bisque head dolls with composition bodies dressed as Bucks and Squaws in imitation buck skin. Ht. 10½, 12, and 14 in. (26.5, 30.5, and 35.5 cm.); priced 19¢ to 69¢.★

1265. All-composition pair of dolls representing an Indian Brave and an Indian Squaw probably made in the 1890s. They have wigs, molded and painted features, including war paint on the Brave. The composition body has a swivel neck, is jointed at shoulders and hips. Original clothes trimmed with string fringe; molded shoes. H. 5½ in. (14 cm.). *Coleman Collection.*

1266. Kämmer & Reinhardt bisque-head mold #101 doll dressed as a German version of an American Indian girl. It has a wig with braids, molded and painted blue eyes, closed mouth, and a ball-jointed composition body. Original clothes. H. 19 in. (48 cm.). *Courtesy of Richard Withington. Photo by Barbara Jendrick.*

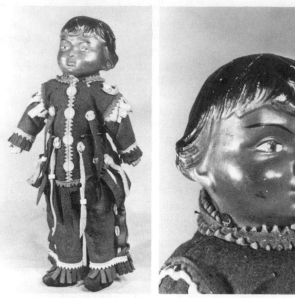

1267A & B. A reddish brown composition-head doll with molded and painted features and a flange neck. It is on a cloth body with composition hands, and is dressed in felt to represent an American Indian. This doll shows an American Indian as visualized by a commercial doll manufacturer, possibly the Averill Manufacturing Co. H. 15 in. (38 cm.). *Coleman Collection.*

1268. Composition-head doll dressed in felt as an American Indian. It has molded and painted hair and features. The eyes look to the side, closed mouth. Original clothes. *Courtesy of Dorothy Annunziato.*

1269. Pueblo Indian Brave smoking a pipe as portrayed by Mary Frances Woods' dolls. It has a face of crepe paper over a form, black pin heads for eyes; the body is blue cloth over a cardboard cylinder and the lower legs and feet are wood. Mark on sole of foot: Ill. 2770. H. 12½ in. (31.5 cm.). It is accompanied by a Squaw. *Coleman Collection.*

Indian Dolls (East Indian). Most of the dolls that represented East Indians with which children played were made in Germany prior to World War I. Dolls were cast into the Ganges by little girls to replace former human sacrifices according to an article in PLAYTHINGS. TOYS AND NOVELTIES reported that white dolls were "dressed to represent British military officers in khaki uniforms, complete with sun hat, cartridge bag and rifle. . . . The doll makers of India pattern many of their dolls after church dignitaries." Native dolls were difficult to find but crudely baked clay dolls were made in remote villages of the plains.

"Dolls in the Himalayan jungle are more skillfully made. These dolls wear gaudy clothes furnished with fringes of gold and silver tinsel. There are nose rings, jingling anklets in which fragments of polished turquoise glisten, rock crystal necklaces and bangles, tiny rings, shawls into which shreds of a looking glass have been inserted. These dolls are dressed by the local women."

1879: ST. NICHOLAS reported that the girls of India have dolls made of wood, cut out, all dressed and painted in gay colors, as though they wore real clothes. They have them of all sizes and indeed the doll is a very important member of the family. "In many houses dolls have a room to themselves, . . . A Bengal paper gives an account of the wedding of two dolls belonging to very wealthy Hindu families. There was a grand procession through the streets as though they were two people. . . .

"[The dolls are] curiously dressed in paint and gilt, with ears of some bright color, spots on nose and chin, and a head that 'comes off'—though the clothes do not."

1896: Bride and Bridegroom of Pondichéry. See Ill. 904.

1911–13: Steiff made a felt doll representing a Singhalese (Sing).

1917–30: The following people or companies made dolls representing East Indians: Chad Valley; Hitz, Jacobs and Kassler; Kelvedon Village Industry; Katarina Paar; and Sardeau.

Indra Kunstwerkstätten (Art Workshop) Inc. 1922–23. Munich, Bavaria. Produced showy type dolls, according to Stewart Culin.★

Industria Bambole Artistiche. 1928–29. Turin, Italy. Made dolls.

Industrial Art Schools. According to TOYS AND NOVELTIES in 1923 the major sources of designers and craftsmen for making dolls were the Industrial Art Schools in the various countries. There were 350 schools in England, 59 in Germany, 200 in Italy and France, and only two in the U.S. The best designers and craftsmen in American factories were trained in European schools. (See also **Sonneberg Industrial School.**)

Inf. (German Infantry Man). Before 1911–16. Generic term for felt dolls representing German infantry soldiers made by Steiff. They came in uniforms with or without gun and equipment. The dolls carried swords if appropriate to their rank. The uniforms included those for fatigue duties, sentry duties; Private, Sergeant, Lieutenant and Major. Most of these came 43 and 50 cm. (17 and 19½ in.) tall. The Lieutenant was 45 cm. (17½ in.) tall.

Infant Dolls. During the second half of the 1920s infant dolls in long dresses were popular but gradually baby dolls in short dresses superseded them. About 1927 some infant dolls began to have rubber arms. Most infant dolls had cloth bodies containing crying devices.

Inge. (Dutch Vollendam). 1911 and earlier. Felt character doll made by Steiff. It was dressed in the every day costume of a woman of Volendam, Holland, and wore wooden (?) shoes. Four hts.: 28, 35, 43, and 50 cm. (11, 14, 17, and 19½ in.). This doll in the largest sizes came with or without long hair. Without the long hair the 50 cm. doll cost $2.55 and with the long hair it was $3.50.

Inge. 1916–20s and probably later. Trade name of a doll made by Wagner & Zetzsche. This portrait doll of the little daughter of Max Zetzsche was sculptured by Franz Reismann and came in two versions, one with short hair and one with braids and a red bow in front. The composition-type (Haralit) head with molded hair, painted or decal or sten-

1270A–C. Felt doll called Inf, representing a German infantry soldier, has painted hair, dark blue bead-like eyes, open-closed mouth, and a flange neck. The body is jointed at the shoulders and hips. Original clothes and equipment except the rifle is missing. The uniform is dark blue with red trimming and gold buttons. The black boots, belt with two cartridge boxes and spiked helmet are made of leather. The cleats on the soles of the boots are Steiff buttons. H. 35 cm. (14 in.). Courtesy of the Washington Dolls' House and Toy Museum.

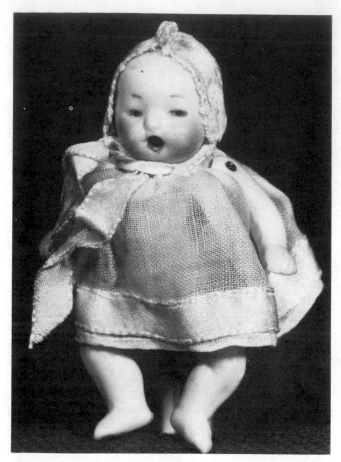

1271. Pink all-bisque infant doll with painted blond hair and blue eyes, round open mouth to receive a bottle, wire-jointed shoulders and hips, The bent arms and legs have dimples at the elbows and knees. Original clothes. Marked "Germany" on one arm and "7" on the upper back. H. 2½ in. (6.5 cm.). *Coleman Collection.*

ciled eyes and open-closed mouth has been found on an imitation kid body with universal joints at the hips and knees. The arms had ball joints at the shoulder, elbows and wrists and were constructed like a regular arm of a ball-jointed composition body. Marks found incised on the head were "2//Jnge// W. Z." and "Jnge//3// 1924." The 2 and 3 were size numbers. Number 3 was 14½ in. (37 cm.) tall. (See also **Hansi** and **Harald.**)

Insam & Prinoth. 1820–1930 and later. St. Ulrich, Gröden Tirol; Nürnberg, Bavaria. One of the largest *Verlegers* in St. Ulrich, they handled peg wooden dolls and wooden dolls' heads.

Before 1838. Insam Bros. were Verlegers who sold dolls in Barcelona, Cadiz, Messina and Venice.

1873: They had 30 large storerooms containing millions of dolls, large and small dolls, painted and unpainted dolls. One room contained only unpainted dolls' heads. Insam & Prinoth bought the dolls and dolls' heads from carvers who worked at home. These were stored until the orders came from London or elsewhere, when they were given out to the

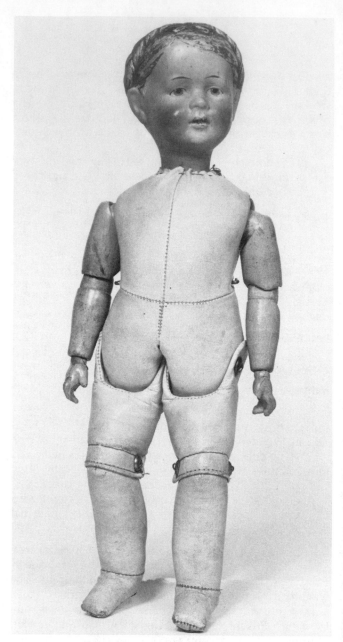

1272. Inge doll made by Wagner & Zetzsche. The head, a portrait of Max Zetzsche's daughter, is made of Haralit, a celluloid-type composition. It has molded blond hair, with a braid around the top of the head, blue intaglio eyes and an open-closed mouth with two teeth. The Kidaline body has Ne Plus Ultra joints at the hips and knees. The ball-jointed arms are wood and the hands are made of Haralit. Mark: Ill. 1273. H. 13 in. (33 cm.). *Courtesy of the Margaret Woodbury Strong Museum. Photo by Harry Bickelhaupt.*

$$\overset{2}{J\tilde{n}ge}$$
W. Z.

1273

Jnge.
3
1924

1274

INGE
1
1924
W Z

1275

1273–1275. Marks found on Inge Haralit head dolls made by Wagner & Zetzsche.

people who painted them in their homes. Insam & Prinoth bought 30,000 peg wooden dolls, 1½ in. (4 cm.) high each week all year round making a total of about 1,500,000 a year of just this one size and type of doll and there were many sizes of dolls as well as styles of dolls.

1890: Insam & Prinoth catalog listed the following dolls with their heights in zolls which are nearly the same as inches.

Painted wooden dolls, price per doz. wholesale:

Without noses, five hts.: ½, ¾, 1, 1½, and 2 zolls (1.5, 2, 2.5, 4, and 5 cm.); price for ½ zoll was 20¢ and for the 2 zoll only 1.7¢. More skill was needed for small dolls.

With noses, 8 hts.: 3, 14, 15, 16, 18, 20, 22, and 24 zolls (7.5, 35.5, 38, 40.5, 45.5, 51, 56, and 61 cm.); 3 zolls was 2.8¢, 14 zolls was 34¢, and 24 zolls was $2.70.

With curls, hts. 3 and 4 zolls (7.5 and 10 cm.): priced 2.3¢ and 2.5¢.

With nose and curls, four hts.: 3, 4, 5, and 6 zolls (7.5, 10, 12.5, and 15 cm.); priced 27¢ to 4.3¢.

With nose, curls, arms and knee joints, eight hts.: 4, 5, 6, 7, 8, 9, 10, and 12 zolls (10, 12.5, 15, 18, 20.5, 23, 25.5, and 30.5 cm.) priced 3¢ to 17¢.

Wooden *Täuflinge* with hair, seven hts.: 6, 8, 9, 10, 12, 14, and 16 zolls (15, 20.5, 23, 25.5, 30.5, 35.5, and 40.5 cm.); priced 86¢ to $5.40.

Wooden doll bodies, six hts.: 3, 3½, 4, 4½, 5, and 5½ zolls (7.5, 9, 10, 11.5, 12.5, and 14 cm.); priced 6¢ to 15¢.

All leather dolls with wooden heads, eight hts.: 6, 8, 10, 12, 14, 16, 18, and 20 zolls (15, 20.5, 25.5, 30.5, 35.5, 40.5, 45.5, and 51 cm.); priced 38¢ to $3.60.

Half leather dolls with wooden heads, 12 hts.: 5, 6, 7, 8, 9, 10, 12, 14, 15, 16, 18, and 20 zolls (12.5, 15, 18, 20.5, 23, 25.5, 30.5, 35.5, 38, 40.5, 45.5 and 51 cm.); priced 14¢ to $2.80.

Wooden shoulder heads representing boys, eight size numbers: 3/0, 2/0, 0, 1, 2, 3, 4, and 5; priced 3¢ to 58¢.

Wooden shoulder heads representing ladies, same as for boys plus a size 6; price 3¢ to 54¢ for size 5 and 66¢ for size 6.

Better Grade wooden shoulder heads representing ladies. 15 sizes: 3/0, 2/0, 0, 1, 2, 3, 4, 5, 6, 7, 8, 9, 10, 11, and 12; priced 44¢ to $2.40.

Poupards (Swaddling Clothed Babies) came in 11 hts., 4, 5, 6, 7, 8, 9, 10, 11, 12, 13, and 14 zolls (10, 12.5, 15, 18, 20.5, 23, 25.5, 28, 30.5, 33, and 35.5 cm.); priced 2.6¢ to 76¢.

Wooden lady with a child that it raises and lowers. Same heights as poupards; priced 3¢ to 76¢.

Wooden Polichinelle heads, assorted styles, nine hts.: 2, 2½, 3, 3½, 4, 4½, 5, 5½ and 6 zolls (5, 6.5, 7.5, 9, 10, 11.5, 12.5, 14 and 15 cm.); priced 17¢ to $1.68.★

International Commission Agency. 1922. Cleveland, Ohio. Advertised that they were direct factory representatives for 86 factories making dolls and toys in Germany, Czechoslovakia and Austria.

International Doll Co. 1920s–30 and later. Philadelphia, Pa. This was Molly Goldman's company. She designed and created clothes for dolls using the trade name *Molly-'es.* The dolls were usually composition or cloth.

1276. Peg jointed wooden doll of the type made by Insam and Prinoth with painted black hair and brushmarks, pierced ears, closed mouth. This doll has been adapted in a domestic craft as a fortune teller. Original clothes. H. 5½ in. (14 cm.). *Courtesy of Sotheby Parke Bernet Inc., N.Y.*

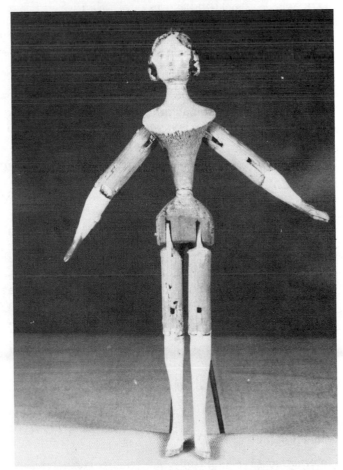

1277. Peg-wooden doll with carved wooden curls on the side of the head and bun in back in a style first made popular in the 1840s. This type of doll was advertised by Insam and Prinoth as late as the 1880s. H. 6½ in. (16.5 cm.). *Coleman Collection.*

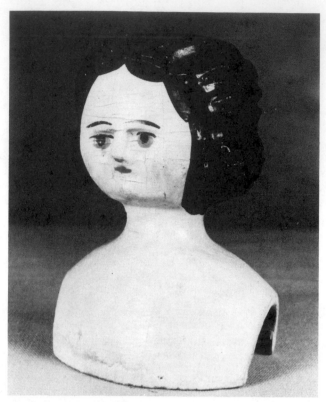

1278. Wooden shoulder head with carved hair having a bun in back, painted features, probably made in one of the Germanic wooded areas, possibly by Insam & Prinoth. H. head only, 4¼ in. (11 cm.). *Coleman Collection.*

International Doll Manufacturing Co. 1920–21. New York City. Handled dolls with composition heads and hands on cloth bodies.

1921: Advertised "Life-Like dolls with wigs, painted or sleeping eyes, cork-stuffed bodies." Hts. 12, 16, 21, and 22 in. (30.5, 40.5, 53.5, and 56 cm.). The 21 inch doll was dressed as a boy in a knitted outfit.

International Dolls. 1898–99 and probably later. Name of a group of dolls with molded headwear and molded blouse tops representing various regions such as Cuba, Italy, Russia, U.S.A., and elsewhere. The shoulder heads were a stone bisque with painted features and usually there was some gold trimming. The cloth bodies had a colored panel down the front of the torso and bisque or china arms and legs. These dolls were made by the same company as the 12 in. (30.5 cm.) *Admiral Dewey* and as stated by their distributor *Butler Bros.* Four hts.: 7½, 10⅝, 14, and 15½ in. (19, 27, 35.5, and 39.5 cm.); priced 37¢ to $1.80 doz. wholesale. Separate shoulder heads were also sold by Butler Bros.★

International Toy Co. 1926–30. London and U.S.A. Made wooden dolls. The *Ted Toy-lers* that made Ted Toys was a branch of this company.

International Walking Doll Co. 1917–21. New York City. Advertised *Babs,* a Japanese walking doll.★

1279. Untinted bisque shoulder head with molded hat and blouse top sold by Butler Bros. in 1899 as part of their International doll series. This doll is supposed to represent Cuba. It has molded and painted hair and features and is on a cloth body with porcelain limbs. *Courtesy of Richard Withington. Photo by Barbara Jendrick.*

1280. In 1899 Butler Bros. advertised a series of dolls under the heading International dolls. These dolls wore the headdresses of various costumes of the world. This one represents Italy. Molded on top of the black curly hair is a blue and gold headpiece. The eyes are painted blue. On the shoulder section is molded a gold beaded necklace ending in a crucifix on the upper portion of the chemise. The cloth body has porcelain limbs. *Courtesy of Sara Kocker.*

Inverno (L'Hiver). 1930 and later. Felt doll made by *Lenci*, style no. 1056 representing Winter in the *Poupées Salon* series. It wore a white fur hood and cape and carried a sprig of mistletoe. Ht. 48 in. (122 cm.).

Iris. 1913. Name of a doll style no. L. 3104 handled by *Whyte, Ridsdale*. Ht. 14 in. (35.5 cm.); priced $3.37 doz. wholesale.

Iris. 1927. Bisque head fully jointed doll with wig, handled by *Bedington, Liddiatt & Co.*

Iris Drollery. 1921. Stockinet doll made by *Chad Valley* as style no. 9. It had a woven wig that they claimed could be brushed and combed. It was dressed in silk and other materials and wore a Chad Valley patent wrist watch. Ht. ca. 12½ in. (31.5 cm.).

Irish Dolls. Some of the people and/or factories who were involved in the doll business are as follows: *Dublin Toy Co.* (1915–17), *Kingram Industries* (1915–21), Orwell Art Industries[+] (before 1908), and *Peskin* (1918–19).★

Irish Molly. 1920. Stockinet doll made by *Chad Valley* as style no. 9 SD. It had a woven wig and removable clothes.

Irle, Johann. 1809–16 (?) Vienna. Made wooden toys probably including dolls.

Irwin & Co. 1926–30 and later. New York City. Made dolls with cloth bodies; advertised celluloid dolls. The trademark "MADE IN//IRWIN//U.S.A." in a circle below "NON-FLAM" appears to belong to Irwin & Co. The Irwin is within a ribbon having notched ends. This mark has been found on all-celluloid bent limb babies and straight leg dolls without joints.

1926: Registered *Darling* as a U.S. trademark for dolls.

1929: Advertised rattle dolls with moving celluloid eyes.

1930: Advertised *Tawka Toys,* a line of stuffed dolls.

Irwin-Smith Co. 1920. Chicago, Ill. Advertised Oriental dolls.

Isco. See **Indestructo Specialties Co.**

Israel, Elise. 1921–26. Zittau, Saxony. Made dolls and dolls' heads and applied for six German patents (D.R.G.M.). Elise Israel made art dolls in *Else Hecht*'s workshop. Some of these dolls were distributed by *Bremer*.

1925: One of the dolls was a rattle doll.

1926: Used the name *Muk* for some dolls and *Lisa* for art dolls.

Israël (& Prieur). 1859–1930 and later. Paris. Successor was L. Salomon. In 1930 and later, H. Djibre was the Paris manager. They assembled, repaired and distributed dolls. Advertised wigs of real hair or mohair, parts of dolls, clothes of all kinds, accessories such as parasols and jewelry.★

It. 1928–30 and later. All-composition doll with a ball joint at its waist called a "body twist" *(waist-joints).* The doll was made by *Amberg* until the business was sold in 1930 to *Horsman* who continued to make the It doll. This doll had molded bobbed hair, painted eyes looking to the side, a small mouth, and neck joint similar to *Patsy*. The doll wore a variety of clothes. There was usually a label on the hem of the skirt and a tag hanging from the wrist. An accessory was a puppy on a leash. The 14 in. (35.5 cm.) high doll sold for $3.00. Similar dolls in the It line were *Peter Pan Drest Dolls, Sue* and *Tiny Tots*.

1930: It was dressed in a Horsman costume, but the doll was marked "Amberg Pat. Pend.// L. A. & S. © 1928."

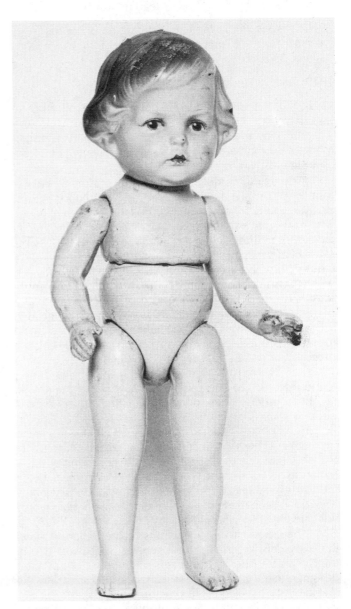

1281. All-composition doll made by Amberg and called "It". This doll has blond bobbed molded hair, painted brown eyes and a closed mouth. This 1928 doll has a neck joint similar to Patsy, with the socket in the head. Similarly the waist joint has the socket in the breast part of the body. This joint allows the doll to twist its body in various ways. Mark: "AMBERG//PAT. PENDING //L.A. & S. © 1928." H. 13½ in. (34 cm.). *Courtesy of the Margaret Woodbury Strong Museum. Photo by Harry Bickelhaupt.*

Italian Dolls. Prior to 1870, for centuries in Italy small craftsmen and artisans had made dolls. In 1872 the *Furga* porcelain factory opened in Canneto sull 'Oglio, Mantua.

However, prior to World War I few dolls were made in Italy. TOYS AND NOVELTIES in 1914 reported that most of the Italian dolls were portrait dolls and were made of composition, rubber, metal, or celluloid. Furga used some bisque heads imported from Germany. After World War I, Italy received the Val Gardena (Grödner Tal) area and the wooden doll industry that had existed there for several centuries. In the 1920s there were doll factories in Florence, Milan, Rome, Turin and other leading towns.

1916: Among the companies making dolls besides Furga were *Mr. O. Pogliani, Mr. Ernesto Landriani* and *Fabbria Italiana Bambole.*

1919: The *Lenci* dolls began to be made.

1920: TOYS AND NOVELTIES published the following report on Italian dolls:

"Italy now making toys to take the place of those formerly imported. Some of the dolls being produced are of unusual interest and are decidedly artistic. . . .

"The ugly little dolls that under their clothing hid deformed limbs have been replaced by well-shaped figures; and for a long time now Italian dolls have been exported wholesale, and have been popular on account of their pretty faces. But marionettes and dolls have other ambitions besides being merely 'pretty' in Italy. If the Italian industry wished to survive the inevitable dumping of foreign articles, when these could once more be freely obtained from countries that could turn out a greater variety and a greater number cheaper than the Italians were able to do, it had to set out on new lines 'typically' Italian and create a demand for really beautiful toys which would be an ornament to a nursery and an inspiration to the children, . . .

". . . The most artistic types of Italian dolls have [not] found their way to England yet; perhaps they have not, so far, been produced in sufficient quantities to make them popular 'lines' for the wholesale toy trade. The buying public not knowing of their existence has not created a demand for them over here, but in Italy they are great favourites with the children; the most beautiful dolls not being given to babies to play with, who would readily destroy them, but to little girls, who take pride in their 'Bambok' [dolls]. Collections have been made of the different character dolls which will survive even when lesser toys flood the market.

"There are so many newcomers into the Italian doll-land that they defy description; but generally speaking, one of their characteristics is the special attention given by their designers to the expression of their faces; they are so life-like that they take the place dolls were originally meant to hold— that of 'a child's child.' Some of them have most winning smiles, not at all like the ordinary vacant grin so common on a doll's face.

"Just as in olden times, fine arts found ready patrons in Italy, so to-day many ladies of the nobility are interested and foster new schemes and developments for the Italian toy industry, and they have periodical local exhibitions which vie with each other to produce the finest toys and especially dolls. Amongst these patrons of doll-land are: the Princess di Poggio Surasa, the Marchioness Farace di Villaforesta, the Marchioness Dusmet, the Countess of Roascio, Mme Bona Luzzatto, Mme. Elia, etc., who co-operated with such artists as De Carlo, Toddi, and others in fostering all that is most beautiful in the doll industry. Toddi's masterpiece is, I think, his 'Salome,' which is turned out by a large Turin factory. Salome is a wonderful little dancer, beautiful of face and figure, most artistically got up, with bracelets at her wrists and ankles, and a suitable headdress and a skirt in original design. The little Salome's corset is a poem in itself; she is a most fascinating new doll.

"There is a great variety of what might be termed 'The exotic doll family.' These are real 'darkies'—not frightfully ugly dolls, but dear little Pickaninnies—too cute for words, with dark faces and bodies and wonderful white eyes, with dark pin-like pupils in the centre. These are dressed in all sorts of styles. Some have merely a little white chemise on, nicely finished off at the neck and arms; others have proper little gentlemen's and ladies' costumes on, and suitable playmates on which to ride, such as crocodiles, that give the right local 'atmosphere' to these little swarthy dolls. Another character of doll-land is a fat little Redskin lady, made of plush. She has a little bolero coat, beads round her neck, a skirt in strips of material, her hair done up in many saucy pigtails in real Red Indian style. Italians turn out a great variety of Dutch dolls (these can be bought in small sizes, . . .). Other attractive Italian dolls are Esquimaux with costumes which are a copy of the real ones, and dolls of every nationality from the tiny, naked baby doll to the beautiful lady in bridal array, with veil and orange blossom and happiness written on their faces.

". . . true-to-life dolls with human expressions and real hair on their heads, will never go out of fashion.

"Italy is aiming a capturing of the 'true-to-life' doll trade, reproducing the types of all countries East and West with a characteristic 'Italian' finish. Recently doll exhibitions have had great success in Turin and Rome. A very fine show of them took place in the garden of the English Embassy, under the patronage of the Ambassadress Lady Rodd, who is an enthusiast of the new industry. Italian children will play this Christmas with Italian dolls marvelously beautiful, unbreakable, soft, supple, with sentimental faces of exquisite sweetness in their expressions. Italian dolls have been a labour of love harnessed to vivid imagination and industry."

1922: A group of dolls were dressed to represent opera characters such as Faust, Mephistopheles, Don Giovanni, Zerlina, Rodolfo, Mimi, Manrico, Leonora, and a portrait doll of Caruso as Canio. The dolls were somewhat crude but expensive.

1928: Mussolini issued an edict that all dolls made in Italy must have long hair. Some of the dolls shown in the Lenci catalogs had short hair.

Boys and girls made dolls wrapped in swaddling clothes. The faces were made of sprigs of fresh thyme and carnations. These dolls were taken before the image of St. John and christened on St. John's Day after which the children played with them.

1929: Felt dolls were made by several factories in Turin: Lenci, *Alma* and so on. Bisque and possibly China dolls were made in Mantua. 500 workers were employed at the Furga factory.

Composition dolls were made in Rome and Florence. Roman dolls were anatomically correct. Cloth dolls were made in Florence, especially Pierrots, Columbines, Harlequins and so on. Wooden dolls were made in Val Gardena (Grödner Tal). These were mostly peg wooden; and in Florence especially Pinocchio.

1930: DEUTSCHE SPIELWAREN ZEITUNG listed the following Italian dolls: jointed dolls with porcelain or composition heads on papier-mâché bodies, felt art dolls, celluloid dolls, Tyrolean wooden dolls, miniature dolls, dressed dolls, and musical dolls. (See also **Mantuan Dolls.**)★

Itco Works. See **Peskin, J.**

Ivimey, Annie Alice. 1906. East Molesey, Surrey. Used *Dollit* as a mark for dolls. See Ill. 780.

Ivorine Manufacturing Co. 1919. London. Made dolls' masks. Advertised that they would make new patterns to fill requirements.

Izon, Russell, & Co. 1922. Britain. Advertised dolls in a British toy trade journal.

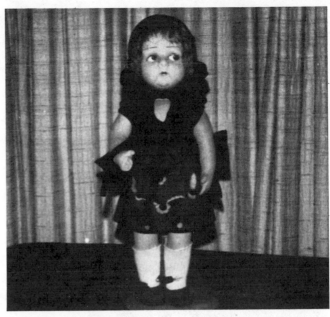

1283. Italian all-felt doll with wig, painted brown eyes looking to the side, pins in back of each ear, closed mouth, and a five-piece body. Original clothes except for the socks. Foot marked: "Made in Italy." H. 17½ in. (44.5 cm.). *Courtesy of Vivian Rasberry.*

1282. Bisque socket head marked Italy with wig, glass eyes, closed mouth, on a five piece composition body. The original costume is that of a Vatican Swiss Guard and includes a metal helmet and a wood and metal pike. The footwear is molded and painted. Mark Ill. 1285. H. 6½ in. (16.5 cm.). *Coleman Collection.*

1284A & B. Felt-head Lenci doll made in Italy. The hair is attached in strips and the painted eyes look to the side, closed mouth. Original felt clothes. *Courtesy of May Maurer.*

Ital̈y
I/o

1285. Mark on a bisque head. The doll is dressed as a Vatican Swiss Guard. See Ill. 1282.

J

J. M. Initials found on a bisque-head doll with a closed mouth. See Ills. 1286 and 1287.

Jaccouz, A. 1865. Paris. Made dolls.

Jack. 1920–21. Stockinet doll with hand woven wig, removable clothes of silk or other material. Style no. 5, made by *Chad Valley*.

1921: Wore a patented wrist watch. Ht. ca. 12½ in. (31.5 cm.).

Jack. 1924. Stockinet art doll stuffed with kapok wore white

knickers and a stocking cap. Style no. SD54, made by *Chad Valley*. Mate to *Jill*. Ht. 10 in. (25.5 cm.).

Jack and Jill. 1921. British stockinet dolls imported to the U.S. by *Meakin & Ridgeway*.

Jack and Jill. 1927. *Twinjoy* doll created by *Mrs. Berry Kollin;* one side was dressed as Jack and the other side as Jill with a little tin bucket.

Jack and Jill Tots. 1921. Terry cloth and flannel dolls made by *Oweenee Novelty Co.* and distributed by *Borgfeldt, Strobel & Wilken* and *Baker & Bennett*.

Jack Robinson. See **Babyland Dolls.**

Jack Spratt. Cutout cloth doll printed on large flour sacks advertised Jack Spratt flour. A separate hat brim and bow tie provided a third dimension.

Jack Tar. 1911–14. Composition head doll designed by *Helen Trowbridge,* made by *Horsman.* The head appears to be the same mold as *Daisy Dimple, Hans, Happy Hiram, Gretchen, Prince Charlie* and *Robbie Reefer.* It had molded bobbed hair and bangs, painted eyes looking straight ahead, smiling open-closed mouth, teeth, dimples, and a cloth body with *Campbell Kid* type hands. It wore a white or blue duck long trouser two-piece sailor suit with a broad collar, and a black tie. Mate to *Nancy Lee.* Style no. 157; price $8.50 a doz. wholesale. Distributed by *Marshall Field* with the name "Jack."★

1286. Bisque head doll with a wig, stationary blue glass eyes, pierced ears, closed mouth and a fully jointed composition body. Mark: Ill. 1287. A similar marked head appears to be pressed, a French characteristic. H. 26½ in. (67.5 cm.). *Courtesy of the Margaret Woodbury Strong Museum. Photo by Harry Bickelhaupt.*

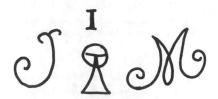

1287. It is not known as yet to whom the "J. M." mark belongs. In fact it is not certain whether it is a J. M., since J and an I were often made similarly. (See Ill. 1286.)

No. 157

"JACK TAR"

Trade Mark

(Head copyrighted, 1912, by E. I. Horsman Co.)

A jolly sailor boy, all spick and span in white duck yachting rig—or in blue if you prefer. Broad collar and cuff bands or reverse collar, and black tie. Wears buckled shoes.

Per Dozen........$8.50

No. 157 "Jack Tar"

1288. Jack Tar as advertised in a Horsman catalog of ca. 1914. It has a composition head with molded and painted hair and eyes, closed mouth, Campbell Kid type composition hands on a cloth body. The head was copyrighted in 1912. *Catalog courtesy of Bernard Barenholtz.*

Jack the Sailor. 1887. Bisque head dressed doll, jointed at the neck, shoulders, and hips, distributed by *Ehrich Bros.* Ht. 8 in. (20.5 cm.); priced 35¢.

Jackie. 1918. Doll with composition head, hands and high boots possibly made by Ideal. It had molded hair, painted eyes, closed mouth, and cloth body jointed at shoulders and hips. It wore a removable sailor suit with a white blouse and colored collar, cuffs and belt. This doll was given as a premium by NEEDLECRAFT MAGAZINE. Ht. 12 in. (30.5 cm.).

Jackie. 1926. One of the Hal Roach *Our Gang* dancing dolls made by *Schoen & Yondorf.* It bore a scroll-shaped tag.

Jackie Coogan. 1924. Doll named *Flanders Boy* resembled Jackie Coogan as he appeared in the moving picture DOG OF FLANDERS.

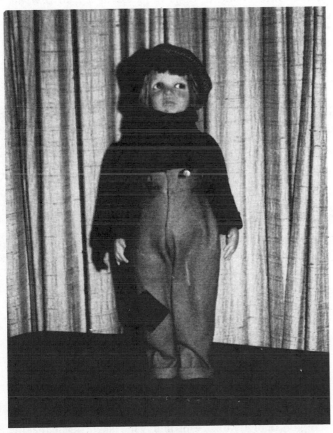

1289. All-felt doll resembling Jackie Coogan in THE KID. It has a Dutch bob wig, painted brown eyes looking to the side and no ears. Original clothes. H. 21 in. (53.5 cm.). *Courtesy of Vivian Rasberry.*

Jackie Coogan. 1925–27. Trademark registered by *Borgfeldt* in the U.S. for dolls.★

Jackie Coogan. 1926–28. Patented line of portrait dolls representing the moving picture star of this name; made by *Gustav Förster.*

Jackie Coogan. 1927. All-celluloid doll with molded bobbed hair and molded clothes consisting of red trousers, blue sweater, suspenders and a jaunty cap; representing the moving picture star of this name and distributed by the *American Wholesale Corp.* Ht. 6½ in. (16.5 cm.); priced $1.75 doz. wholesale.

Jackie Coogan Kid. 1921–22. Doll with composition head and hands, molded hair, painted eyes, cloth body; made by *Horsman.* Wore a turtle-neck sweater, long gray pants and a checked cap with visor at the side. On this portrait doll was a round button reading "HORSMAN DOLL// JACKIE// COOGAN//KID//PATENTED." Hts. 13½ and 15½ in. (34 and 39.5 cm.).★

1290. Mark on a Jackie Coogan doll produced by Horsman.

Jack-O-Jingles. 1920–1929. Made by *Chad Valley* as one of their Novelty Art dolls. It had a pointed cap with pompoms, a collar with points over the shoulders and in the center front with a bell attached to each point. Pompoms hung from the short skirt. The doll appeared to have mitten hands and the clothes were part of the doll itself so that this was a fairly cheap doll. It started out in 1920 as a stockinet-faced doll, style no. 13, ht. 9½ in. (24 cm.).

1924: It was still a stockinet doll, now stuffed with kapok and dressed in red, blue, green, and gold. The height had been increased to 15 in. (38 cm.). It bore a hexagonal tag reading "Chad Valley// HYGIENIC//Fabric Toys."

1927–1929: Changes had been made and the doll no longer had a stockinet face but was a *Caresse*-type velveteen doll and had the style no. 485. The 15 in. height remained the same, as did the general appearance. The pompons were made of silk in various colors.

Jacky Tar. 1914. Cutout cloth doll in the *Dolly Varden* series distributed by *Marshall Field.* The printed doll had a Buster Brown style hairdo and wore a blue sailor suit with a red belt, anchors on the collar and stockings, short trousers and black boots. Ht. of doll 17½ in. (44.5 cm.); priced $1.50 doz. wholesale.

Jacob, Gustave. 1920. Paris. Advertised *mignonnettes,* including "new porcelanite" jointed ones; dressed and undressed dolls, 4 to 10 in. (10 to 25.5 cm.) tall; bisque dolls' heads.

Jacob, Louis. 1865. Sonneberg, Thür. Distributor of dolls; used a hand-drawn sample book.

Jacob, Son & Co. 1920–30. London. Agent for gray and colored Hungarian rubber dolls (probably *Ungarische Gummiwaren-Fabrik*), including dolls representing children and an aviator.

1924: Advertised Nankeen dolls.

Jacob & Petit. See **Petit, Jacob.**

Jacobs & Hughes. See **Hughes & Jacobs.**

Jacobs & Kassler. See **Hitz, Jacobs & Kassler.**

Jacqueline. Ca. 1925–29. Name of various dolls sold in French stores.

Ca. 1925: *Lafayette* advertised Jacqueline as having a cloth body and dressed in wool with gold trimming. Ht. 60 cm. (23½ in.).

1927: Lafayette advertised Jacqueline as being a cloth doll with a wig, wearing a silk dress trimmed with felt. Ht. 50 cm. (19½ in.).

1928: *Bon Marché* advertised Jacqueline with a character head, wig, fully jointed body, dressed in a silk costume with a bonnet. Ht. 55 cm. (21½ in.).

Jacqueline, Tante (Aunt). 1910–19 and probably other years. Designed the patterns for making *Bleuette*'s clothes and for making other items as published in LA SEMAINE DE SUZETTE. Her successor by 1924 was *Suzanne Rivière.*

Jacquin. 1881. Paris. Made dolls and bought bisque dolls' heads from *François Gaultier,* according to Mme. Poisson, curator of the Roybet Fould Museum.

Jafferian, Kinias M. 1918–19. New York City. Obtained a U.S. patent for a doll with a hollow tube body and a turning head.

Jäg (Hunter with Gun). 1913. Jointed felt doll made by *Steiff* and distributed by *Borgfeldt.* The doll represented a hunter with a gun and hunting bag. Ht. 19½ in. (49.5 cm.): priced $4.45. (See also **Hubertus.**)

Jäger, Fritz.[†] See **Friedrichrodaer Puppenfabrik.**

Jäger, Josef, & Co. 1850–53. Vienna. Josef Jäger, Alois Jäger and Josef Koch handled "Nürnberg wares" which would have included dolls.

Jaham, G. De. See **De Jaham, G.**

Jakob (Jacob), H., & Co. 1930 and later. Sonneberg, Thür. Made dolls.

Jan. 1915. One of the "waifs of Cracow" cloth dolls made under the inspiration of *Madame Paderewski.* It was designed and made by Polish refugee artists in the workshop of *Mme. Lazarski* in Paris. Most of these dolls were sent to America. The handpainted head of heavy cloth was stuffed with cork; the body was stuffed with cork or straw. It represented a boy-gardener; wore a brimmed hat, blouse, short trousers with shoulder straps, low socks and buckles on its slippers. Ht. ca. 15. in. (38 cm.).

Jan. See **Life Like Babyland Dolls.**

Jan Carol. 1929. A costume variant of *Rosemary,* made by *Effanbee.*

Jane. 1918. Composition-head dolls made by *Jessie M. Raleigh.*

Jane. 1918. Line of cloth dolls made by *Shanklin.*

Jane. 1919–22. Cutout cloth doll made by *Saalfield.*

Jane. 1920. Name of a *Mama* doll with composition head, arms and legs made by *Paul Averill.* It wore a colored organdy dress and bonnet, socks and single strap slippers.

Jane. 1921. Name of an English stockinet dressed doll with its hair in two braids. *Meakin & Ridgeway* imported this doll into America.

Jane. 1926. Name of dolls made by *Katherine Fleischmann;* with handpainted faces. Hts. 14 to 16 in. (35.5 to 40.5 cm.).

Jane. 1928. Name of dolls designed by *Eileen Benoliel;* made of oilcloth by *Live Long Toys.*

Jane.[†] See **Gene Carr Kids.**

Janos. 1921. Doll representing the God Janos, purchased in Budapest and probably made by *Anna Dely.*

Jánosne Zboray. See **Zboray, Jánosne.**

Jansen (Dutch Boy). Before 1911–13. Felt character doll made by *Steiff.* It wore the every day costume of a man in Holland including wooden shoes. Four hts.: 28, 35, 43 and 50 cm. (11, 14, 17 and 19½ in.); priced $1.10 to $2.60.

Jantzen Bathing Tots. 1928. Dolls made by *Century* under special arangements with Jantzen Knitting Mills. Jantzen made bathing suits, for dolls and people.

Jap Rose Kids. 1911–12. Boy and girl dolls with composition heads and hands, painted hair and eyes, cloth bodies. The girl had hair bows and the boy had a bowl-shaped hairdo. Both wore Kimonos.★

Japanese Dolls. These seemed to be more than just children's playthings. There was a religious association and a decorative purpose but they were meant largely for children. The dolls were made of clay, porcelain, wood, bamboo, sawdust, straw, paper, celluloid, cotton, flannels, and other fabrics, shells, rubber, metals, and so forth. TOYS AND NOVELTIES told us that quality dolls were produced by "master-hands in doll-making receiving the reputation of sculptors of high rank." One family in Hakata began making dolls in 1596 and was still making them in 1955 with 200 home workers. The clay for these dolls came from the Oburayama district where it was refined. The dolls were cast in molds and the clothes painted on them after carefully mixing paints to achieve the right shades of color. In 1927 TOYS AND NOVELTIES stated that "Practically all dolls intended for [Japanese] domestic consumption had sex organs portrayed in detail."

LA POUPÉE MODÈLE reported in 1863 that a true Japanese doll was a real curiosity in the Western World.

In 1879 ST. NICHOLAS reported,

"The girls of Japan have . . . dolls that walk and dance;

dolls that put on a mask when a string is pulled; dolls dressed to represent nobles, ladies, minstrels, mythological and historical personages. Dolls are handed down for generations, and in some families are hundreds of them. They never seem to get broken or worn out. . . . though the little owners play with them, they do not dress and undress them and take them to bed as you do. A good deal of the time they are rolled up in silk paper and packed away in a trunk."

The dolls packed away in a trunk would have been the dolls of the Girls' or Boys' Festival, but there were other dolls played with all through the year. The latter usually represented boys or girls aged two to five, bought undressed in a shop and dressed by a female relative in the current style. A girl would have several of these dolls called "ningyo." When the girl married, these dolls were sent to the husband's house. These dolls were not part of the Festival dolls but attended it as visitors.

The families of Japan celebrated the Doll Festival days and the Emperor and Empress gave a reception on behalf of the dolls of the Imperial family. The Yamanaka collection of 150 of these ceremonial dolls from the palace included dolls dating back to 1420. Some of the Festival dolls represented historical persons; all were gorgeously costumed in non-removable clothes. The materials for the clothes were specially woven in miniature patterns.

TOYS AND NOVELTIES in 1914 discussed Japanese dolls and the Doll Festival:

"The Oriental type is to be seen in every portion of the Japanese doll. It is to be seen in the almond-shaped eyes with the extreme expanse of forehead, between, the short, broad nose and the small mouth. . . .

"Among the poorer classes one often sees a very small child bearing upon her back a doll in exactly the same position as the mother carries her baby. This doll is changed for a larger one as the years go on, until she becomes so accustomed to its weight that she is able to carry and care for the new baby brother or sister when it arrives.

"The tiny rag doll of Nippon is a fine piece of work; the material is soft crepe and there is a drawstring in the hem of the short dress that makes the garment far more sensible than the long dress of civilized countries.

"There are finely modeled dolls showing every occupation of the country, viz., flower sellers, perambulating restaurants, basket peddlers, sponge cake sellers, etc. . . .

"The Japanese dolls are patterned after the Japanese idea of the beautiful to be found in the upper classes. . . .

". . . There are dolls representing the gods from which sprang the first Mikado of the Island Empire. There are bewitching little dolls representing the sacred dancers, who live at the beautiful temple at Nara and who posture and jingle their bells and wave their wisteria branches with infinite grace. The numerous little bells fastened to the handle resemble an ordinary rattle that entertains the American baby, but as a matter of fact it is a model of the sacred Suzu, which the virgin priestess used in her dance before the gods in olden times.

"The dolls . . . show the Mikado and his wife panoplied with all the insignia and regalia of their high office. Every minutia of their costumes, even to the jewels in their crowns and the long tasseled court fan carried by the aristocratic lady are typical of the class to which she belongs. The Japanese dolls portray three distinct classes of people of that country. There is the doll with the chubby cheeks portraying the peasant class; the Samurai family and the royal group. The doll maker of Japan makes a distinction in the face only between the two upper classes and the peasant, the doll representing the lowly being always lacking in beauty. The only distinguishing difference between the two upper classes is to be found in their costumes.

"One of the unique customs of Japan . . . is the purchasing of seven dolls for every female child born. As soon as the sex is announced, it is the duty of the father or some friend to go straight to a toy shop and purchase the group of seven dolls. These dolls represent the Mikado and his family and form a marvelous exhibit of workmanship. Later there may be other dolls, including the court musicians and attendants.

"The festival is looked forward to by the children for months. The ceremonies are much the same in all houses of the same class. The festival lasts a week, and never were children so busy 'toing and froing' as the little Japanese maidens during the time.

"The tiniest cherry blossom has her own mon, or crest, which adorns the beautiful rice paper upon which with a pen which is really a camel's hair brush, she writes the invitation to her doll festival in most ceremonious and stilted language. She sends and receives dozens of these charming epistles. On the soft, white mats of the drawing-room, as we would call it, there is arranged a set of five graduated shelves covered with red, the color of joy and pleasure. Upon these shelves are set in proper order all the dolls of the household, and for an entire week dolls and children are feasted and feted. . . .

". . . When the small girl for whom this congery [sic] of dolls has been bought marries and goes to her new home she takes the collection with her and keeps it carefully intact until her eldest son marries, when it becomes his property and is handed down from generation to generation. Thus it will be seen that in course of time a family becomes the possessor of a fine and valuable collection of dolls. The family of the late Shogun, the Tokogwas, are said to own the most valuable and expensive collection in Japan, among them are several examples of the no-dancers, exquisitely modeled and finished by the best artists in the country."

PLAYTHINGS in 1928 gave the history and further details about the Festival Dolls:

"A Boston woman, Miss Jessie M. Sherwood, first thought of having American and Japanese youngsters learn to know each other better by exchanging playthings. She communicated with friends in Tokyo and Kyoto, suggesting her plan to them. . . .

"In Japan, dolls are held in high esteem. The annual doll festival, held each year on the third of March, is the principal holiday in the lives of Japanese children. It has a religious significance, almost but not quite forgotten by the Japanese themselves.

"Not hundreds but thousands of years ago, March 3 was the day of purification according to the ancient creed of Japan. It was obligatory for every pious citizen, on that day, to bathe in the river, washing away all sins of the past 12 months.

1291. Seven Japanese dolls shown in a painting by the British artist Miss Eliza Turck (b. 1832, fl. 1854–86). In 1881 she exhibited this picture, named "Little Haru at Home—Tea and Dolls" at the Royal Society of British Artists. The Japanese dolls were probably ones that Miss Turck had seen in England. Note that several of the dolls representing babies or small children have floating joints which allegedly were copied by the Germans after being shown at the 1851 London Exhibition. *Courtesy of the Bourne Gallery, Reigate, England.*

"Gradually, as the centuries passed—and as the climate . . . seemed to change open air baths in early March grew unpopular. It became the custom for each family, on the festival day, to attire two dolls in the costumes of master and mistress of the house and then duck these dolls in the river in symbolic observance of the tradition of purification.

"More centuries passed. Few families now bothered to inflict March river-dips even on the dolls. The doll festival, however, held its place on the calendar.

"So it does today. It is nearly as much a red-letter occasion for boys and girls as is our Christmas. Every household in Japan observes it with a doll display only limited by the family resources.

"However much the dolls may differ in excellence of workmanship and richness of attire, they are always arranged with the same formality. They sit on five scarlet upholstered steps.

"On the top step are two dolls clad in royal attire. They represent the emperor and empress, and they symbolize the never-ending protection which the heads of the nation extend over all subjects.

"On the next lower step are three dolls dressed as ladies-in-waiting at the royal court. These symbolize the womanhood of Japan.

"The third step holds two trees in boxes, an orange tree and a cherry tree. They symbolize the two trees which flank the gates of the royal palace at Kyoto. Between the toy trees are five figures; two sentinels, clad in armor, and three coolies, one laughing, one angry, and one weeping. The sentinels remind boys and girls that they live in safety because of the valor of the army which defends them. The coolie dolls represent the common people and their pleasures, griefs and passions. [Another account calls these "drunkards of the three humors."]

"The lower steps contain tiny models of every household utensil and piece of furniture which the family uses. The more elaborate displays include little figures of servants and children, all occupied in mimic tasks. Occasionally more than five steps are needed for the whole collection.

"On the lowest step of all, or on tiny tables in front of the steps, refreshments are set out for all comers. Neighbors exchange calls and gifts. The doll festival is of particular importance, too, to unmarried girls. It is their duty, as they grow from childhood, to arrange and care for all the doll display equipment."

The Girls' Festival of dolls called "Hina Matsuri" was on March 3rd, while the corresponding Boys' Festival was May 5th and was called "The Feast of Flags." The dolls for the boys were bought when they were born and represented famous warriors such as Monotaro, Yoshitsumen and Kato Kiyomasa as well as commanders, generals and wrestlers, all dolls expressing strength, valor and adventure. *Kintarō,* the hero of a popular folk tale, and Shoki, a Chinese hero, were two popular dolls for boys. The dolls representing military personages usually wore suits of armor.

In the early years of the twentieth century many dolls with Oriental-type faces and clothes were made in Europe and America. Among the producers of these dolls were *Averill* and *Horsman.* These dolls should not be confused with Japanese dolls made in Japan.

In 1906 *Gamage* imported boy and girl dolls from Japan. Six hts.: 8½, 9½, 12½, 14, 16, and 18 in. (21.5, 24, 31.5, 35.5, 40.5 and 45.5 cm.); priced 12¢ to 56¢.

In 1907 *Sears* advertised dolls with bisque heads, wigs, sleeping eyes, and fully jointed composition bodies dressed in Japanese style clothes. Hts. 12¾, 14, and 15½ in. (32.5, 35.5, and 39.5 cm.); priced 40¢ to 85¢.

In 1913 Gamage advertised imported Japanese dolls in native dress.

During World War I Japanese dolls began to replace the missing German bisque and celluloid dolls. (See **Imports.**) The Japanese dolls tried to copy Western dolls but the copies were generally inferior in quality. A British toy trade journal stated in 1922 that large quantities of Japanese dolls had to be returned to their manufacturers owing to poor quality.

The distinction in age between Japanese dolls marked Nippon or Japan is difficult to ascertain and the two appear to have been used simultaneously in some cases. Of course dolls marked "Occupied Japan" can be dated as 1945 or later.

The A.A. Importing Co. of St. Louis, Mo., claimed in 1969 that two decades earlier (late 1940s) they had handled the new china and bisque shoulder heads like the one shown in Ill. 889 in the first COLLECTOR'S ENCYCLOPEDIA OF DOLLS, with molded hair, painted eyes, pierced ears and tiny sew holes. The shoulder heads sometimes bore a paper label reading "Made in Japan." One would expect "Made in Occupied Japan" at that time. Ht. of head 3¼ in. (8.5 cm.). (See also **Friendship Dolls.**)★

403884.

Poupée Japonaise,
robe crépon de couleurs
variées.

Hauteur 0ᵐ,15.

0.95

1293. Japanese doll as shown in Printemps catalog, 1918. It wears a crepe kimono. H. 15 cm. (6 in.). *Courtesy of Margaret Whitton.*

1294. Oriental yellow-tint bisque-head made by Simon & Halbig with a black mohair wig, stationary brown glass eyes, pierced ears, open mouth with four upper teeth, and a fully jointed composition body painted with a yellowish cast. Original clothes. Mark on head: "S. H. 1129//DEP.//4." H. 13½ in. (34 cm.). *Courtesy of the Museum of American Architecture and Decorative Arts, Houston, Texas. Photo by Becky Moncrief.*

1292. All-composition Japanese bent-limb baby doll with glass eyes, pierced nostrils, open-closed mouth with tongue. Original kimono. H. 11½ in. (29 cm.). *Coleman Collection.*

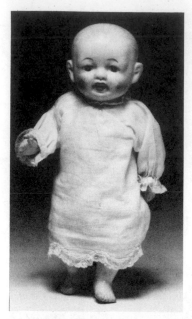

1295. Japanese bisque head with painted blond hair, intaglio blue eyes, open-closed mouth, and a five-piece bent-limb composition body. Mark: "NIPPON//22." H. 22 cm. (8½ in.). *Courtesy of Sotheby Parke Bernet Inc., N.Y.*

1296. Bisque socket head made in Japan on a bent-limb composition body. It has a black wig, sleeping brown glass eyes and an open mouth with teeth. H. 13½ in. (34 cm.). *Courtesy of Sotheby Parke Bernet Inc., N.Y.*

1297. All-bisque doll with molded and painted hair, features and clothes, jointed only at the neck. Marked "JAPAN" on the soles of the shoes. H. 4 in. (10 cm.). *Coleman Collection.*

1298

1299

1300

1301

1298–1301. Marks on dolls made in Japan and/or representing a Japanese person.

Japanese Kimono Doll. 1907–25. Cutout cloth doll made by *Saalfield.*

Jaques. 1902. London. Store that sold dolls.

Jasbo. 1922. Doll dressed as a clown, made by *Rees Davis.*

Jasio. 1915. Doll promoted by *Mme. Paderewski* to aid the Polish refugees. It was made in the workshop of *Mme. Lazarski* by Polish refugee artists and was dressed as a boy (son of a tinsmith) from the Tatra mountain area of Galicia.

Jaszay, Jolán. See **Our Shop.**

Jativa. Early 1900s. Spain. Name found on a doll's label claiming that they made *Bébé Sætabis.*

Jaulmes. See **Jouets de France.**

Jay-Bee. See **Bouton, J., & Co.**

Jazette. 1926. Name of a *Boudoir* doll made by William P. *Beers* & Co. It wore a conical hat. Price $15.00 doz. wholesale.

Jazz Baby. 1921. Name of a carnival-type doll.

Jazz Hound. 1922–27. Doll designed by *Jane Gray Co.*

1927: Made by *Gerling.*★

Jazz Nigger. 1922. Line of dolls made by *Wonderland.*

Jazza. 1923. Name of a cloth doll made by *Mabel Bland-Hawkes.*

Je Dors. French for "I sleep." *Samaritaine* in 1901 sold dolls with these words on the tag.

Je Fais DoDo. Childish French for "I sleep." *Modernes* in 1911 sold dolls with these words on the tag. *Société Française de Fabrication de Bébés & Jouets* (S.F.B.J.) dolls of the 1920s have also been found with these words on a label attached to the doll's skirt. One of these dolls had "UNIS//FRANCE" on its head and on its original box which was also labeled "EDEN BÉBÉ//FABRICATION FRANÇAISE."

Je Marche. French word for "I walk" has been found on dolls able to walk.

Je Parle. French for "I speak." It is not certain that all dolls so labeled could actually speak, that is, say, "Mama-Papa." A large number of dolls were described as "Je Parle" in the French store catalogs, so that it seems possible that the term might sometimes simply have been used to describe a doll with an open mouth.

Je Suis Tout en Bois. French for "I am all wood." (See *Bébé Tout en Bois.*)

Jean. 1916. Cloth doll made by *Atlas Manufacturing Co.* It had stub hands and wore a plaid dress and matching bonnet.

Jean. 1923–29. Down-stuffed cloth body doll made by *Chad Valley* as style no. 41. The legs were apart but the bent arms were next to the body. Its printed clothes were a light shirt, short dark trousers and a close fitting hat. Ht. 11 in. (28 cm.).

Jean. 1925–29. Name of oilcloth doll stuffed with cotton; made by *Live Long Toys* and bearing the names "Jean" and

Frank King. The printed costume on the doll consisted of a red, blue or green coat, hat and high button leggings. Style no. 9. Ht. 13 in. (33 cm.).★

Jean, M. Elie. 1919. Caen, France. Registered his initials "E. J." superimposed to form a monogram as a French trademark for dolls.

Jean, Maison. Brussels, Belgium. Made and repaired dolls with ball jointed composition bodies. A green and white sticker has been found with the mark of this shop.

Jean-Jacques. See **Poum.**

Jeannette. Ca. 1925. Name on a bisque head made by *Schuetzmeister & Quendt.* This name often was used on mold # 301.

Jeanette. 1927. Name of a doll representing a little girl, imported into America by *Eisen.* It wore a coat, cloche (hat) and single strap slippers.

Jeanette. 1927. Cloth doll dressed in taffeta advertised by *Lafayette* store. Ht. 52 cm. (20½ in.).

Jeanette Doll Co. 1919–28. New York City. Made composition and cloth dolls especially *Mama* dolls and baby dolls. Jedco. was their trademark.

1919: Advertised *Pantless Jimmie* and *Miss Jeanette's* trousseau trunk.

1920: Style no. 300 dressed in a lace-trimmed plaid dress and bonnet. Ht. 14½ in. (37 cm.); price $7.00 without wig, $8.90 with wig.

1921: Advertised 150 numbers including *Angel, Our Ann Ella,* and *Our Trixie.* These had arms folded over the chest and legs apart.

1923: Mama dolls had composition heads, hands and legs and were stuffed with cotton. Some of the dolls had a papa voice instead of a mama voice. They came in a variety of heights but the most popular were 23 to 27 in. (58.5 to 68.5 cm.). The best of the Jedco line was a 30 in. (76 cm.) baby doll. The cheaper $1.00 dolls had cloth legs. One of their trade names for a black doll was *Aunt Jenny.*

1924: Advertised 500 numbers of Mama dolls. They came with painted hair, mohair or real hair wigs, painted eyes or sleeping eyes, composition legs or stuffed legs. Among the new dolls there were Laddie, (Little) Miss Muffet, (Little) Boy Blue, (Little) Red Riding Hood,[†] Sailor Boy, *Salvation Nell* and a doll dressed in Shriner regalia, including a black suit with proper emblems and a fez. Ht. 10 in. (25.5 cm.). Red Riding Hood was also made in a leatherette version.

1925: Advertised Fairyland dolls including Campfire Girl in a khaki uniform, *Cinderella* in a brocade gown, Peter Piper, Pocahontas, Simple Simon, Tommy Atkins, and a Bell Hop with roly-poly eyes from flirting with Suzie Ann. Prince Charming dressed in gold and with a sweeping plume in his hat as well as the Boy Scout were dolls made of leatherette.

The composition-head dolls with wigs were 19 in. (48 cm.) tall.

1926: Displayed dolls in London. Miss Muffet came in two

sizes. The Nursery Rhyme line of dolls was distributed by *Louis Wolf.* New numbers in this line included Goldie Locks, Hiawatha, Soldier Boy and Policeman.

1927: Jeanette was licensed by *Voices, Inc.* to use their patented mama voices and criers. The dolls sold for 10¢ to $10.00.

1928: Used the trade name *Denny Doll.*★

Jeanson, Jules Joseph. 1891. Paris. Produced dolls. See Ills. 1302 and 1303.

1302–1303. Marks used by Jules Joseph Jeanson, according to Gwen White. The mark shown in 1302 was found on a bisque-head doll. The 1303 mark was reported by Gwen White.

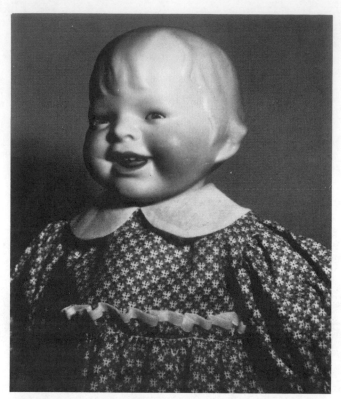

1304. Helen Jensen's Gladdie doll with a biscoloid head, molded blond hair, blue glass eyes and an open-closed mouth with two upper teeth. The cloth torso has composition arms and legs. Mark: Ill. 1063. *Courtesy of the late Sarge Kitterman. Photo by Winnie Langley.*

Jedco. See **Jeanette Doll Co.**

Jedrek. 1915. Paris. A sculptor who made the models for the *Paderewski* dolls, according to a contemporary account in the CRAFTSMAN.

Jedrek. 1915. Name of one of the dolls promoted by *Mme. Paderewski* for the aid of Polish refugees. The dolls were made in the workshop of *Mme. Lazarski* by Polish refugee artists. Jedrek represented a mountain guide from Zakopane in the Tatra mountains of Galicia, a fashionable resort area prior to World War I.

Jellicoe. See **Admiral Jellicoe.**

Jenny Lind Doll Co. 1916. Chicago, Ill. Made phonograph dolls called Jenny Lind that wore a chemise and hairbows. Ht. 22 in. (56 cm.).★

Jensen, Helen Webster. 1928. U.S.A. Designed *Gladdie* which was copyrighted as Happy Ann. *Borgfeldt* produced these dolls.

J'envoi des Baisers. French for "I throw Kisses" a popular feature of dolls of the early 1900s. (Also see **Kiss-Throwing Bébé.**)

Jernoid Works. 1915. Merton Abbey, Surrey. Made mask-type faces for dolls to be used by doll manufacturers. The masks were advertised to be non-inflammable; presumably they were celluloid.

Jerree. 1929. One of the *Funny Fuzzee* line of *Twistum.* It was made of twisted flexible wire covered with colored knotted yarn. The smiling face was handpainted. It sold for 75¢.

Jerry. 1930. Name of a doll with composition head and wooden limbs, advertised by *Pressman* in TOYS AND NOVELTIES.

Jersey Boy and Girl. 1917. Made by *Royal Crown Pottery Co.*

Jester. 1921. Stockinet doll made by *Chad Valley* as style no. 49.

Jeux & Jouets Française. 1920s. France. Member of the *Chambre Syndicale;* made clothes, dolls and dressed dolls.

Jeweled. 1902–7. Name of china shoulder heads that had a molded gold necklace around the front half of the neck with colored glass in a gilt setting. The smallest size head had only one "jewel."★

Jiffy. 1930. Trademark registered in U.S. for dolls by *Kleinert Rubber Co.*

1305. China shoulder head doll named Jeweled and handled by Butler Bros. It has molded and painted hair and eyes. The body is cloth with china arms and legs. Footwear is molded and painted on the legs. A molded gold necklace is halfway around the neck with two colored glass imitation jewels in a gilt setting. H. 12 in. (30.5 cm.). *Courtesy of Richard Withington. Photo by Barbara Jendrick.*

Jiggs & Maggie. 1927. Wooden dolls representing the cartoon characters of this name drawn by *George McManus.* The dolls were made by *Schoenhut,* distributed by *Borgfeldt* and bore a paper label reading, "Pat. appl. for// International// Features Service//© 1924." The cartoon was copyrighted in 1924 by International Features Service.

Jill. 1914. Composition-head doll with painted hair, round glass eyes, cloth body, distributed by *Marshall Field.* It wore a lace-trimmed dress and bonnet. Ht. 14 in. (35.5 cm.); price $17.00 doz. wholesale.

Jill. 1920. Name of a composition doll made by *Jessie M. Raleigh.*

Jill. 1924. Stockinet art doll stuffed with kapok, made by *Chad Valley* as style No. SD 55. Mate to *Jack.* Ht. 10 in. (25.5 cm.).

Jill. See **Jack.**

Jim. 1918. Line of cloth dolls made by *Shanklin.*

Jimmie. 1929–30. All composition doll with "Hendrenite" finish made by *Averill Manufacturing Co.* It had molded hair, eyes glancing to the side, tiny pursed mouth, jointed neck, shoulders and hips, one arm bent, wore various costumes. The tag on the doll read "Jimmie// Dimmie's//Boy Friend."

Jimmy. 1919–30. Cutout cloth doll made by *Saalfield.*

Jimmy Jounce. 1924–29. Wooden doll for infants made by *Petrie-Lewis.* Dolls were strung with rubber bands and came in white with red or blue.

Joachimstal & Wagner. 1893–1909. Berlin. Manufactured dolls.

1893: Applied for a German patent (D.R.G.M.) for a doll with a rubber head.★

Joan. 1920–21. Stockinet doll with hand-woven wig that could be brushed and combed; made by *Chad Valley* as style no. SD2. It had removable clothes.

1921: Had a Chad Valley patented wristwatch. H. 12½ in. (31.5 cm.).

Joan. See **Peter.**

Joanny, Joseph. 1884–1921. Paris. Made dolls and bébés. See Ills. 1306 and 1307.★

J.G.J

J. J.

1306–1307. Marks used by Joseph Joanny for dolls, according to Gwen White. 1306 was found on a bisque head doll. The 1307 mark was reported by Gwen White.

Jobard, A. 1852–64. France. He worked for six years in a doll factory and in 1853 established his own doll-making business.

1855: He failed and his inventory gave manufacturer's prices as follows:

Dressed doll	7¢
Dressed doll with wig	15¢
Dressed doll with wig and hat	20¢
Swaddling-clothed baby	4¢

This information was researched by Mme. Poisson, Curator of the Roybet Fould Museum.★

Jockey. 1928. Name of a *Boudoir* doll dressed as a jockey distributed by *Eisen.*

(There were many other dolls dressed as jockeys including those made by *Kämmer & Reinhardt* and *Steiff.*)

Joey. 1928. Trademark registered in U.S. by *The Children's Press* for dolls.

Joffre. See **General Joffre** and **L'École Joffre.**

Johann. 1916. Name of felt doll made by *Steiff.* Ht. 43 cm. (17 in.).

John. 1921. Name of an English stockinet doll imported into the U.S. by *Meakin & Ridgeway.*

John. 1922. Name of a doll with a highly painted face, a wire frame and a stuffed body, designed by Miss Rees Davis and made by *Rees Davis* Toy Co. It was the mate to *Judy.*

John Bunny Doll. 1914–15. Portrait doll with composition head made by *Amberg*. It had a smiling mouth with teeth, a rotund head and body and came with various costumes; one was a sailor suit and another was a Norfolk jacket and bow tie. Marked on head "34//©//L.A. & S 1914." Cloth label on suit read, "JOHN BUNNY DOLL// COPYRIGHT L.A. & S. 1914 TRADEMARK REGISTERED// MADE EXCLUSIVELY BY LOUIS AMBERG & SON, N.Y.//WITH CONSENT OF JOHN BUNNY [name in script]//THE FAMOUS MOTION PICTURE HERO OF THE VITAGRAPH CO." See Ills. 1308, 1309, 1310, and 1774.

1914–15: *Bellas Hess* & Co advertised a John Bunny doll with a white shirt and colored long trousers. Hts. 11 and 14 in. (28 and 35.5 cm.); priced 69¢ and $1.39.★

Johnny Joints. 1921. Name of a doll that was jointed so it could obtain a variety of positions; made by *Commercial Manufacturing & Pattern Works*.

Johnny Jones. 1915–18. Name of a doll made by *Effanbee* with composition head and hands, molded hair, painted eyes, closed mouth, cloth body.

1915: Wore a Russian-style suit.

Johnny Rube. 1926. Name of a cloth doll with chin whiskers and dressed as a farmer; made by *Beers-Keeler-Bowman Co.* Marked "B.K.B." Price $10.00 doz. wholesale (Maker was also listed as William P. Beers & Co.).

Johnny Tu Face (Johnny-Tu-Face). 1912. Doll with composition head and limbs made by *Effanbee*. Ribbon tag read "To Have Me Cry, Just Turn My Head//I Laugh When You *? ?*//Johnny Tu Face."★

Johnson Bros. Ltd.† See **Chad Valley.**

Johnson, G. F. 1901. Berlin. Applied for a German patent (D.R.G.M.) for a doll with two heads.

Johnston, G. R. 1885–86. U.S.A. Imported dolls, dolls' heads, and dolls' bodies. In 1886 became Johnston, Tallman & Co. Dolls were distributed by *Selchow & Righter*.

Joibelles. 1920. Name of dolls distributed by *Three Arts Toy Industry*.

Jointed Doll. 1893. Cutout cloth doll made by *Arnold Print Works*.

Jointed Doll Co. 1874–85. North Springfield, Vt. Advertised "We also furnish an improved jointed doll with an elastic body so designed as to fit all heads of American manufacture."★

Joints. See **Bodies of Dolls.**

Jok (Jockey). 1913. Jointed felt doll representing a jockey; made by *Steiff,* distributed by *Borgfeldt*. Ht. 17 in. (43 cm.); price $4.50.

Jol Lee Jays. 1929. Trademark registered in U.S. by *Lee Rubber & Tire Co.* for sponge dolls.

Joli Bébé. 1901–26. Trademark registered in France by *Damerval,* then in 1926 registered by *Bonin & Lefort* for dolls and dolls' heads. These were bisque heads.

1308A & B. Amberg's composition-head portrait doll of John Bunny, the moving picture actor. It has molded and painted hair and eyes, open-closed mouth with upper and lower teeth. The composition of the head and hands was made by the cold press method and there is a flange neck. The body is cloth with composition hands. Original clothes. Mark on head: Ill. 1309. Mark on clothes: Ill. 1310. H. 13 in. (33 cm.). *Courtesy of the Margaret Woodbury Strong Museum. Photos by Harry Bickelhaupt.*

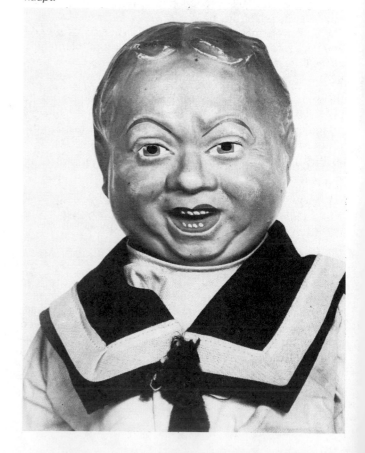

© 34.
L.A.S. 1914

JOHN BUNNY DOLL
Copyright L.A.&S. 1914 Trademark Registered
Made Exclusively by Louis Amberg & Son, N.Y.
With consent of *John Bunny*
The Famous Moving Picture Hero of the Vitagraph

1309–1310. Marks on Amberg's John Bunny Doll. No. 1309 is on the composition head and No. 1310 is sewn on the coat sleeve.

1901: *Louvre* store advertised Joli Bébé with an open mouth, wearing a chemise and bronze slippers. Ht. 59 cm. (23 in.); price $1.58. It was $3.15 if it was dressed in silk and lace.

The fully jointed Joli Bébé dressed in velvet; hts. 38 and 46 cm. (15 and 18 in.); priced 75¢ and $1.10. The same doll dressed in silk came in seven hts. 31, 38, 41, 45, 49, 53, and 58 cm. (12, 15, 16, 17½, 19½, 21, and 23 in.); priced $1.95 to $6.20.

1903: *Pygmalion* advertised Joli Bébé in a blue or rose colored silk dress. Ht. 60 cm. (23½ in.); price $1.38. *Tapis Rouge* advertised Joli Bébé, fully jointed, open mouth, dressed in a chemise. Seven hts. 28, 34, 45, 53, 62, 74, and 84 cm. (11, 13½, 17½, 21, 24½, 29, and 33 in.); priced 59¢ to $5.80.

1904: Louvre store advertised jointed dressed Joli Bébé; eight hts. 28, 34, 36, 40, 45, 48, 50, and 55 cm. (11, 13½, 14, 15½, 17½, 19, 19½, and 21½ in.); priced 30¢ to $2.15.

1905: *La Place Clichy* advertised Joli Bébé with a streamer reading "Je Parle." and dressed in silk; ht. 37 cm. (14½ in.); price 90¢.

1908: Louvre store sold fully jointed Joli Bébé with sleeping eyes, dressed in silk and with a boa, pocket book and umbrella. Ht. 45 cm. (17½ in.); price $3.15.

1911: La Place Clichy advertised that Joli Bébé was an entirely new doll with a character head, dressed as either a boy or girl. It was described as *"Je marche."* Ht. 39 cm. (15½ in.); priced $1.10.

1912: La Place Clichy added another size, namely, 47 cm. (18½ in.) tall.

1920: *L'Hotel de Ville* advertised Joli Bébé with bisque head, mohair wig, sleeping eyes, semi-jointed with straight legs, wearing a chemise and footwear. Eight hts.: 36, 39, 43, 45, 49, 52, 55, and 61 cm. (14, 15½, 17, 17½, 19½, 20½, 21½, and 24 in.). Joli Bébé was offered the same as above except with a "washable" composition head instead of the bisque head.★

Jolly Dutch. See **Marcuse, Day & Co.**

Jolly Injun. 1916. All-bisque doll representing an American Indian; painted and molded hair, loin cloth and shoes; distributed by *Sears*. Hts. 2 and 3½ in. (5 and 9 cm.).

Jolly Jack. 1913. Name of a composition-head doll.

No. 583—"Jolly Jack"

No. 583. "Jolly Jack" Character Doll, composition head, stuffed body. Eight inches tall. This doll will be appreciated by children of any age, and is an ideal "baby boy" doll. Neatly dressed in gingham rompers and sent carefully packed, charges prepaid, for two yearly subscriptions at 35c each, or one subscription at 35c and 20c extra.

1311. Jolly Jack, a composition head doll, was offered as a magazine premium in 1913. It has molded and painted hair and features, a cloth body with stub hands, wears checked gingham rompers. H. 8 in. (20.5 cm.).

Jolly Jack. 1927. Cloth doll with painted face, felt hair, removable clothes, except for black cloth serving as shoes. A pocket contained a handkerchief that matched the doll's shirt. Doll made by *Buzza Co.* It came in a box with a framed picture and poem written by Lawrence Hawthorne. See Ill. 453.

Jolly Jester. 1926. Trademark registered in U.S. by *Borgfeldt* for dolls.

Jolly Jumps. 1912–20. Composition-head doll made by *Elektra*.★

Jomin, Mme. A. Before 1925–30. Paris. Successor by 1925 was J. Launay. Handled dolls' heads and accessories for dolls.★

Jones, Robert. 1826–48. London. Made wooden dolls.★

Jones, William Henry. Before 1915–22. London. Prior to 1915 he had been an agent for dolls for many years. Made printed cloth dolls and dolls with *British Ceramic* heads.

1915–16: Made *Eskimo* dolls with linen faces.

1917–18: Advertised a 25¢ line of dressed dolls with British Ceramic heads, shoes and socks.

1920–22: Made plush dolls.

Jonnie Jingles Co. 1918–20. New York City. Obtained a U.S. design patent for an indestructible sanitary doll. ★

Jordan, Arthur. 1926. Birmingham, England. Distributed dolls wholesale.

Jordan, Kate. 1904–20. New York City. She began in 1904 to draw illustrations of dolls for a large American importer of dolls, probably *Borgfeldt*. Later she designed dolls including the *Happifats*. She had studied art for years and claimed that designing dolls was an art. She strived not to make her dolls insipid or with cold classic regularity. (See also **Chronology, 1914.**) ★

Jordan, Marsh & Co. 1895–1930 and probably other years. Boston, Mass. Distributed dolls.

1895: Advertised French and American style dolls especially bisque-head dolls with curly wigs, sleeping eyes, fully jointed bodies, priced $1.00 to $10.00.

1897: Advertised bisque-head dolls in chemise and dressed dolls as well as *Yankee* cloth dolls.

Jordan & Wilder. 1867 and probably other years. Boston, Mass. Advertised toys and hard rubber goods, probably included dolls.

Jörg. 1916. Felt doll made by *Steiff*. Hts. 30, 40, and 50 cm. (12, 15½, and 19½ in.).

Joseph. 1926. Trademark registered in France by *Mme. Elisa Rassant* (née Blum) for a doll dressed as a bellhop and holding a tray.

Joseph, Isidore. 1917–20. London. Advertised dressed and undressed dolls in a British toy trade journal, including French dolls.

Josephine Baker. 1927–28. Long-limbed black doll made in Paris to resemble the famous dancer of this name. This *Boudoir*-type doll wore an exotic outfit. Various other dolls were also made to represent Josephine Baker.

1928: Art dolls, chiefly of composition, were made in France as caricature portraits of Josephine Baker.

Jou Jou. 1919. Trademark registered in France by *Lepinay* for dolls. The trademark had Jou at the top and at the bottom with a chef's head in the center.

Jouets Artistique Français. World War I–before 1924. Bordeaux, France. One of several workshops in which wounded soldiers made dolls. It was not in existence by 1924 because the dolls were too expensive. (See also **L'École Joffre.**)

Jouets de France. World War I–before 1924. Environs of Paris. Founded by *François Carnot*. Mme. Le Bourgeois, *Rapin* and Jaulmes were the artists who designed the models

that were made in this factory by wounded soldiers who made dressed dolls and painted wooden dolls. It was not in existence by 1924 because the prices were too high. (See also **L'École Joffre.**)

Joy Doll Corp. 1920–22. New York City. Made wood-fibre composition dolls, dolls' heads and limbs.

1922: Made two designs, with or without wigs, dressed in six different costumes. Ht. 16 in. (40.5 cm.). ★

Joy Doll Family, The (Joy Dolls). 1928–29. Name of wooden bead dolls made by *Bimblick*.

Joyce. 1929. Name of a doll representing a little girl with red wig and blue eyes; wore a floral print dress and hat. Price $5.50 according to TOYS AND NOVELTIES.

Joyce & Josylin. World War I period. Twin dolls with *British Ceramic* heads made by *Nottingham* in the *Daisy* line.

Joyful Joey. 1914. Name of a doll made by *Dean*.

Joyland Toy Manufacturing Co. 1923–24. Milwaukee, Wisc. Made dolls.

Jozon, Jeanne. 1918. Paris. Created carved wooden dolls. One of these was dressed in a Bretonne regional costume. Mlle. Jozon was a sculptress born in 1868; she died in 1946. She won Honorable Mention for her sculpture in 1897.

Juanita. 1908. Cutout cloth doll made by *Saalfield*. It had a printed costume of a Spanish girl. Ht. 7¾ in. (19.5 cm.).

Juanita. 1912–13. Cutout cloth doll representing a Spanish girl, advertised by *Selchow & Righter*. Ht. 8 in. (20.5 cm.); priced 40¢ doz. wholesale.

Juanita. 1927. Trade name of a child doll wearing a hat and coat according to TOYS AND NOVELTIES.

Jubilee. 1905–28. Line of various types of dolls handled by *Strobel & Wilken*. Prior to World War I the dolls had jointed composition or kid bodies. After World War I they had cloth bodies. Their heads were bisque, celluloid or, later, composition. Some of the bisque heads resembled those made by *Gebrüder Heubach*; others were made by *Armand Marseille*.

1907: Called "Jubilee Art Dolls" with composition heads and hands, painted features; cotton stuffed bodies, jointed at shoulders and hips; wore simple dresses in pastel shades. One was dressed as a Dutch girl. Hts. 10½, 17, and 20 in. (26.5, 43, and 51 cm.). ★

Judge, Edward S. 1867–78. Baltimore, Md., and Philadelphia, Pa. In 1875 it was Judge & Early. Made papier-mâché dolls' heads. See Ills. 1314, 1315, and 1316 for marks. See Ills. 1314–1316. ★

Judy. 1922. Name of a doll with a highly painted face, a wire frame and a stuffed body, designed by Miss Rees Davis and made by *Rees Davis*. It was the mate to *John*.

Judy. 1930. One of the *Kiddie Pal* line of dolls made by *Regal*. Advertised as "Girl friend of Billy." See Ill. 1317.

Juge (Jugendwehr [Young Defender]). 1913–16. Felt doll made by *Steiff*. Hts. 35 and 43 cm. (14 and 17 in.).

1312. Jubilee dressed dolls with composition head, faces painted by hand and cloth bodies, as advertised by Strobel & Wilken in PLAYTHINGS, February, 1927.

1314–1316. Marks found on Judge or Judge and Early papier-mâché dolls' heads.

1317. Mark on Judy dolls made by Regal.

2034 H.W. 3/0
"Jubilee"
foreign. reg. design

1313. Jubilee mark for dolls. Probably made for the British trade after 1925 because of the use of the word foreign.

Jugelé, Mme. See **Guerchoux, Rémy.**

Jügelt, Walter. 1924–26. Neustadt near Coburg, Bavaria. Manufactured dolls.★

Juhel. 1777 and other years. Paris. Shop on the rue Saint Denis that specialized in dolls, according to LES JOUJOUX.

Jullien. 1827–1904. Paris, Conflans, and Saint-Léonard. 1827–56. A person named Jullien had a porcelain business in Conflans, a part of Charenton where the Gauthiers (Gaultiers) later were located. In 1840 Jullien of Conflans founded a porcelain factory in Saint-Léonard where unpainted porce-

lain was produced. This factory was still in existence in 1889. It is not known when or if Jullien began to produce porcelain dolls' heads but it seems likely that this firm was one of the early French doll makers.

1855: Won a first class medal at the Paris Exposition for his "porcelains and novelties." This probably included dolls' heads.

1865: Jullien fils aîné (eldest son) was listed in the DIDOT directory with the initials N.C., meaning "notable merchant," and a reference to his porcelain factory in Saint-

Léonard. A few doors away on the same street another Jullien was listed as having a porcelain warehouse.

1878: Jullien was one of the award winners at the Paris Exposition.

1881: Purchased bisque dolls' heads from François Gaultier, according to Mme. Poisson, curator of the Roybet Fould Museum.

Size-height relationship for dolls with five-piece child type composition bodies. (The small sample makes the relationships as shown very rough estimates.)

JULLIEN BÉBÉS, SIZE–HEIGHT RELATIONSHIP		
Size	Height	
No.	In.	Cm.
4	15	38
5	17	43
6	19	48
7	21	53.5
8	23	58.5
9	25	63.5

Dolls have been reported with JJ marks but it is not known whether they are Jullien Jeune, *Jules Jeanson*, or Joseph *Joanny* Dolls. See Ills. 1302, 1303, 1306, and 1307.★

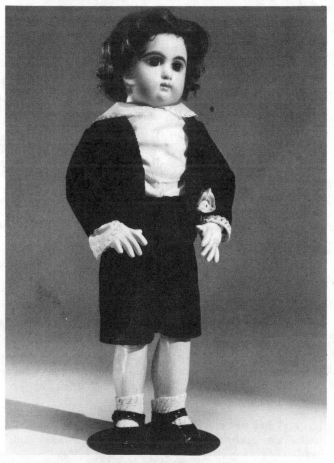

1318. Bisque socket head on a Jullien doll. It has a wig, blue glass eyes, closed mouth and is on a ball-jointed composition body. Mark: "Jullien//7." H. 18 in. (45.5 cm.). *Courtesy of Sotheby Parke Bernet Inc., N.Y.*

1319. Bisque-head doll made by Jullien has a wig, blue glass eyes, pierced ears, an open mouth with teeth, and is on a jointed composition body. Mark: Ill. 1320. H. 18 in. (45.5 cm.). *Courtesy of Richard Withington. Photo by Barbara Jendrick.*

5
JULLIEN

1320. Mark on bisque heads on Jullien dolls.

Jullien, H. J., & Son. 1917. Britain. Made *Eskimo* dolls with celluloid mask faces, white or brown plush bodies.

Jumbo. 1915. Name of a composition-head doll with cork stuffed cloth body made by *Gem*. Ht. 24 in. (61 cm.).

Jumbo Boy and Girl. 1915. Composition-head dolls with molded hair, cloth body, made by *Effanbee*. The boy, style no. 212, wore a one-piece belted suit with the trousers nearly to the ankles. The girl, style no. 214, had bobbed hair and wore a belted ankle-length dress. Price of each doll 75¢.

Jumeau. 1842–99. Paris and Montreuil-sous-Bois; 1899–1958, successor was the *Société Française de Fabrication de Bébés & Jouets* (S.F.B.J.). Pierre François Jumeau married in 1833 and his second son, Emile, was born in 1843. One of the witnesses of the birth record was *Louis-Désirée Belton* who was living and working with Jumeau at that time, according to Mme. Poisson, curator of the Roybet Fould Museum.

Pierre Jumeau made fashion-type dolls with kid or wood bodies. These came in at least sizes 0 to 9 and probably larger. The smallest size was similar to that of the *Bébé Jumeau* but the increments were larger. Most of these dolls had only the size number incised on the head and the bodies were stamped "JUMEAU//MEDAILLE D'OR//PARIS."

The so-called "Long-Face Jumeau" also had only a size number on its head and the jointed composition body was stamped "JUMEAU//MEDAILLE D'OR//PARIS."

Several other closed mouth dolls with only size numbers on their heads and "JUMEAU//MEDAILLE D'OR//PARIS" stamp on their composition bodies have been called "Portrait Jumeaus" by present day collectors. However, it seems likely that nearly all Jumeau dolls were inspired as portraiture. M. François Theimer quoted from an 1892–94 report in LE JOUET PARISIEN that the portrait of Henri IV of France as a four year old child was the inspiration for the Bébé Jumeau dolls. There is a remarkable resemblance between this picture of Henri IV and illustration 914 in the first COLLECTOR'S ENCYCLOPEDIA OF DOLLS. The Jumeau bébés have larger eyes than the child in this portrait.

Prior to 1873 Jumeau appears to have made chiefly kid bodies, wooden bodies and clothes for dolls.

In 1873 Jumeau started to make bisque dolls' heads at Montreuil-sous-Bois and soon thereafter Emile Jumeau took over the business and began to make Bébés Jumeau. These appear to have been advertised by 1878 and shown at the International Exhibition that year. The large porcelain kilns required a separate factory at Montreuil-sous-Bois away from the rest of the Jumeau factory because of the enormous fires required for the kilns.

PRODUCTION OF BÉBÉS JUMEAU	
Year	Approximate Number of Dolls Produced
1879	10,000
1881	85,000
1883	115,000
1884	220,000
1886	130,000
1889	300,000
1897	3,000,000 (black, white & mulatto)
1910	over 5,000,000 (Reported by McCALL'S Magazine)

Thus more than twice as many Bébés Jumeau were produced by the S.F.B.J. in one year than were made in all the years prior to 1890.

A Jumeau advertisement of about 1890 stated that Bébé Jumeau was marked on the back of the head, on its chemise, on the box, and if the doll were dressed it was on its left arm.

The name was on a maroon band across the front of the chemise or around the upper arm, when dressed. By 1890 undressed bébés wore a fancy chemise and footwear while dressed bébés had elaborate clothes including a hat.

The Jumeau dolls' heads until about 1890 were pressed. (See **Pressed versus Poured.**) The so-called fashion-type dolls and the E.J. Jumeaus that have been examined have nearly all had pressed heads. The Tête Jumeaus that have been examined have all had poured heads. Those with the "DÉPOSÉ//TÊTE JUMEAU//Bte. S.G.D.G." red stamp appear to have been placed on bodies with "JUMEAU//MEDAILLE D'OR//PARIS" purple stamp on the body. A few of these heads have been found with the "BÉBÉ JUMEAU//DIPLOME d' HONNEUR" oval paper sticker, attached to the body. The heads with the large "TÊTE JUMEAU" red stamp and the incised DEP appear to always be found on the bodies with the paper sticker reading "BÉBÉ JUMEAU//DIPLOME d'HONNEUR."

According to an article by Gaston Tissandier in an 1888 issue of LA NATURE found by Margaret Whitton, the process for making pressed heads at the Jumeau factory was as follows:

"The paste taken from the tanker is kneaded, spread by rollers, and fashioned to the thickness desired, according to the size of the head to be made. Then this paste is cut into squares and placed in a mask-shaped mold. This molding is executed very quickly by women. When the heads are sufficiently firm within the molds, they take them out and dry them on boards in a special room."

This work was done chiefly by women. It took about 27 hours for the firing of the heads. Then about 350 men and women decorated the heads, each person performing one small job. The second firing was at a lower temperature and took only about seven hours.

The body parts were made of a papier-mâché composition forced into cast iron molds with a small wooden tool. After molding, the body parts were first painted with zinc white, then five coats of flesh tone paint and finally a coat of varnish.

Christine Anderson of Dewsbury, Yorkshire, England, discovered in the May 14, 1892, DEWSBURY REPORTER an article entitled "How French Dolls were Made." This article was first published in PEARSON'S WEEKLY and described a visit to the "most famous doll factory in the world" at Montreuil. This must have been the Jumeau factory which was further verified by the description, "The factory has a courtyard, flanked on either side by hundreds of small paned windows through which I caught glimpses of some 500 men, women and children bending over their work.

"The model of the famous Paris doll is always the human baby, the child from one to four years old. . . .

"The head is made [by] women and girls. . . . filling face moulds and a white liquid that runs from a tankard with taps. This liquid is of the same ingredients as Sèvres and Limoges ware. When the contents of the mould are dry they are emptied on trays, and before they become hard the ears are pierced to receive earrings. The faces are then put in a huge oven to bake 28–30 hours."

The description of these two visits to the Jumeau factory is extremely important because the 1888 visit described the pressing of the dolls' heads while the 1892 visit described the pouring method.

From these two descriptions we know that the change from pressing to pouring must have occurred in or after 1888 and before 1892. Thus giving the change from one method to the other probably within the three year period 1889–91, and it can be said that pressed Jumeau heads were made prior to about 1890 and the poured heads were made after about 1890. This provides a benchmark for dating Jumeau heads.

A bisque head Bébé Jumeau marked "Déposé E 5 J" had a wax pate with inserted hair. Its 38 cm. (15 in.) height suggested that it may have been a late version E. J. It is not known whether the head was pressed or poured.

Bébé Bon Marché, Bébé Trois Quartiers, Louvre Bébé and *Bébé Samaritaine* were all attributed to Jumeau, according to advertisements by these Paris stores. Their size-height relationship corresponded with those for Bébé Jumeau. This was also true for some of the dolls marked 1907. Dolls have been found with the number 1907 and the Jumeau name but it is not certain that all dolls marked 1907 were Jumeau. Some of the dolls' heads marked 1907 also have had the green numbers typical of the *Gebrüder Heubach* heads. These heads were made of a pinkish bisque typical of some late Gebrüder Heubach dolls. It is also questionable whether the dolls marked B.L. were Louvre Bébés and hence made by Jumeau.

Around 1900 a group of character dolls were produced which bore a Tête Jumeau mark. The dating of these dolls was verified by pictures that resemble them very closely in a 1901 issue of BLACK AND WHITE, a British periodical. These dolls with poured heads had approximately the same size-height relationship as had been found on other Tête Jumeaus. However, these dolls had a mold number, which was more of a German characteristic than a French one. *Simon & Halbig* registered in Germany one of these numbers in conjunction with Jumeau in 1889 according to the research of the Ciesliks. On these character dolls the mold number was usually followed by "DÉPOSÉ// TÊTE JUMEAU//B^te S.G.D.G."

Mold numbers have been reported from 201 through 225 for this group of Jumeau dolls. These numbers were either on the back of the neck or sometimes inside the head. Mold numbers 226 and above were also character dolls but they bore the S.F.B.J. mark. At least one of the 201–225 group represented a lady and the size-height relationship of the lady dolls differed from the other dolls.

After World War II the S.F.B.J. made a group of small lady dolls (See Ill. 1340) and the bisque heads were marked 221. These heads closely resembled the earlier mold 221 Tête Jumeau heads except for size. Presumably mold # 221 was a standard head for S.F.B.J. lady dolls for at least 50 years.

Recent research has revealed that statements made by M. Moynot, one of the last presidents of the S.F.B.J. firm, must be checked for accuracy. In many instances it is not wise to accept information about a company from its President or other official without documentary verification for the period involved.

Sheets of decals with Jumeau labels corresponding to the labels found on Jumeau bodies have been reported found for sale in Europe in the 1980s.

Many of the dolls made during the time that *Fleischmann* was in charge (1899–1914) had Simon & Halbig heads on bodies with Jumeau labels, usually the "BÉBÉ JUMEAU//DIPLOME d' HONNEUR" oval paper label. A Jumeau doll supposedly in its original box has been reported as having the F. E. Winkler[†] mark on the box, but it must be remembered that boxes have often been replaced. (See **Manufacture of Dolls, Commercial: Made in France.**)

1863: Jumeau Dolls were shown in THE COLLECTOR'S BOOK OF DOLLS' CLOTHES, Ill. 142B.

1882: Size numbers 1 through 8 had ears molded with the head. Size numbers 9 through 16 had applied ears. The dolls wore a necklace of Paris pearls to hide the neck joint. Bébés with kid bodies were also advertised but not recommended.

(A pressed shoulder plate for a socket head has been found with the incised mark "E. DÉPOSÉ J. 10." There was a pair of sew holes front and back to attach it to a body.)

1884: Jumeau began to make dolls with two pull strings that enabled them to say "Mama-Papa."

1885: Emile Jumeau called kid body dolls "Parisiennes."

1886: On a Jumeau advertising card a composition body Bébé Jumeau was called "la petite Parisienne."

1890–91: Mme. Porot and M. Theimer have found Court records of a lawsuit of this date wherein the firm of Jumeau and *Douillet* sued *Danel & Cie.,* composed of Messieurs Danel and *Guépratte,* for copying Bébé Jumeau. Jumeau appeared to have won this case against M. Danel, a former director of the Jumeau factory, and M. Guépratte, formerly in charge of making the glass eyes for Jumeau.

According to François Theimer the Jumeau factory employed 200 female workers and 30 male workers.

1892–1900 and possibly later: Jumeau made the bisque heads for the mechanical dolls made by *Roullet & Decamps* according to Anne-Marie and Jacques Porot.

1893: At the Chicago Exposition, Jumeau showed 25 bisque head lady dolls dressed in a series of historical costumes dating from 1000 to the time of the Exposition. Ht. 24 in. (63.5 cm.).

1897: Emile Douillet was referred to as a partner of Emile Jumeau.

1899: When the S.F.B.J. was formed Emile Louis Jumeau and his wife contributed the goodwill of the Company and the rights to their marks including "Bébé Jumeau." The Jumeaus rented their two factories in Montreuil-sous-Bois and their shop in Paris at 8 rue Pastourelle to the S.F.B.J. according to Mme. Poisson, curator of the Roybet Fould Museum; two of the Jumeau daughters served on the S.F.B.J. board.

1900–14: *Bébé Tout en Bois* (All-wood Doll) was advertised in Paris stores. It has sometimes been attributed to Jumeau but no proof has been found, whereas several of these dolls are known to carry labels reading "Made in Germany" or "Allemand Fabrication."

Margaret Whitton has found a wooden head with a paper sticker label, "BÉBÉ JUMEAU//DIPLOME d'HON-NEUR" on the back of its neck. Similar paper stickers are usually found on Jumeau composition bodies. This head does not look like the usual Bébé Tout en Bois head and it is on a composition body instead of a wooden one.

1902: *Gamage* advertised Jumeau Dolls with sleeping eyes, and chemise and footwear. Six hts.: 12, 14, 16, 20, 24, and 28 in. (30.5, 35.5, 40.5, 51, 61, and 71 cm.); priced $1.23 to $6.25. Jumeau at that time was part of the S.F.B.J. The dressed Jumeau dolls were size numbers 4, 5, 6, 7, 8, and 10; priced $2.75 to $10.50. Walking dolls that could say "mama" and "papa" had stationary eyes, and came in size numbers, 6, 8, and 10; priced $3.75 to $5.00. When dressed the walking, talking dolls cost up to $12.75.

1903: Open mouth doll marked "BÉBÉ//A LA VILLE DE ST. DENIS" was advertised as being made by Jumeau.

1905–50s: *Bleuette* and *Bambino* had various types of Jumeau (or S.F.B.J.) marks. A late Bambino head made of Rholoid was marked "Jumeau 278.4." *Bébés Vrai Modèle* had the name Jumeau on their paper label.

1906: *Aux Trois Quartiers* advertised *Bébé Madeleine* as made by Jumeau. The picture of this doll showed it wearing a sash marked *"Paris Bébé."*

1910–14: *Ville de St. Denis* advertised that their Bébé Ville de St. Denis was made by Jumeau. The picture of this doll in 1910 showed it wearing a sash marked "Bébé Parlant."

1911: Aux Trois Quartiers advertised a Jumeau doll that wore an *Eden Bébé* type of chemise.

1931: A group of dolls usually in French Provincial costumes had "Unis France" on the back of their bisque heads. They had composition bodies and on their apron or dress a blue and white circular paper label with three concentric circles and the words, "EXPOSITION // BÉBÉ//PARIS 1931// JUMEAU//INTERNATIONALE." Some if not all of these dolls were 8 in. (20.5 cm.) tall.

1938 and later: Large Jumeau dolls were made especially for the two little English princesses. These bisque head, composition body dolls had extensive wardrobes of clothes and accessories. Similar dolls were later made in two hts., 18 and 32 in. (45.5 and 81 cm.), according to Margaret Whitton.

1940s–50s: A group of bisque-head dolls with wigs, glass eyes, closed mouths, composition bodies, dressed in historical costumes carried a Jumeau tag and came in a Jumeau labeled box. These dolls, mold # 221, represented Madame de Sévigné, Mme. de Pompadour, Marie Antoinette, Empress Josephine, Marie Louise, Empress Eugénie, Queen Victoria and Sarah Bernhardt. These dolls carried a silver colored paper tag reading "fabrication//JUMEAU//PARIS// Made in France." Ht. 10 in. (25.5 cm.); price $15.00 (See Ill. 1340).

After World War II: It is not known exactly when the all-composition Jumeau dolls were made but they appear to have been made during or after World War II. They carry various marks; some have "Paris 301" on the head, others have "Unis Paris 301" or "Jumeau 319" on the head. The following paper labels have been found attached to the costumes of these dolls: "FABRICATION//JUMEAU//PARIS //MADE IN FRANCE," "Bébé Française//FABRICATION JUMEAU//PARIS," "POUPÉE//JUMEAU//PARIS//MADE IN FRANCE."

1950: M. Moynot, President of the S.F.B.J., described their dolls, "Bébé Jumeau doll moves, sleeps, talks; head of porcelain made in our factory at Montreuil and has natural hair; clothes made in our studio at 160 rue de Picpus, Paris. We manufacture under the name of 'Jumeau.'

1952: Advertised that the Jumeau dolls of 1952 were entirely different from those produced in 1951. There were a variety of style numbers made in three sizes, small, medium and large. Bisque head Jumeau dolls were still being made.

1953: A portrait doll of Queen Elizabeth II dressed in coronation robes was produced as a Jumeau doll.

1956: The Bébé Jumeau trademark for baby dolls and dolls was renewed by S.F.B.J.

1958: The liquidation of Jumeau and S.F.B.J. occurred. Some very late Jumeau heads were a celluloid type rather than bisque or composition. ★

1321. Girl doll with bisque head and shoulder plate, wig, stationary blue glass eyes, pierced ears, closed mouth and a kid body. Original 1880s clothes. The shoes are marked "E. Jumeau." Head marked "5." H. 19½ in. (49.5 cm.). *Courtesy of Sotheby Parke Bernet Inc., N.Y.*

1322A & B. Bisque head Jumeau doll with a lady-type kid body. It has a wig, stationary blue glass eyes, pierced ears, closed mouth and a kid body without gussets. The swivel neck, head and bisque shoulder plate appear to have been poured which would probably date this doll after 1890. Head marked with red check marks, Jumeau mark on the body. Ill. 1343. H. 19½ in. (49.5 cm.). *Courtesy of Richard Withington. Photo by Barbara Jendrick.*

1323. So-called "Long-Face" Jumeau doll with bisque head having a wig, stationary blue glass eyes, pierced and applied ears, closed mouth, and a fully jointed composition body. Dress contemporary with the doll. H. 27 in. (68.5 cm.). *Courtesy of Cherry Bou.*

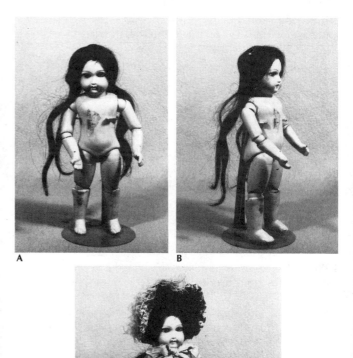

1324A & B. Pressed bisque head doll made by Jumeau. It has a wig, stationary blue glass eyes, pierced ears, a closed mouth and a ball-jointed composition body with wrists that are not jointed. Original clothes. Mark on head: "3"; Jumeau mark on body. H. 13½ in. (34 cm.). *Courtesy of Cherry Bou.*

1325A–C. Bisque head Jumeau doll with black wig, stationary blue glass eyes, pierced ears, closed mouth, and a jointed composition body with wooden balls. The wrists are not jointed. Original clothes. Cartouche Jumeau mark on the head. H. 11½ in. (29 cm.). *Courtesy of Cherry Bou.*

1327. Jumeau chemise for a bébé as advertised by Printemps in 1887. See Ill. 327 in THE COLLECTOR'S BOOK OF DOLLS' CLOTHES. *Courtesy of Mary Brouse.*

1326. Pressed bisque head Jumeau bébé with wig, stationary glass eyes, pierced ears, closed mouth, and a ball-jointed composition body. Original clothes of the 1890s. This doll came with a wardrobe of clothes some of which are stamped "9." Mark on head: "E. 9 J." H. 20 in. (51 cm.). *Coleman Collection.*

1328. Poured Jumeau bisque-head doll with blond wig, stationary blue glass eyes, pierced ears, closed mouth, and a fully jointed composition body. Original clothes. Mark: "DÉPOSÉ //JUMEAU//9." H. 20 in. (51 cm.). *Courtesy of Cherry Bou.*

1329. Bisque head Jumeau bébé with a brown wig, stationary brown glass eyes, pierced ears, open-closed mouth, and a composition and wood ball-jointed body. Mark: "DÉPOSÉ JUMEAU //8." H. 18 in. (45.5 cm.). *Courtesy of Sotheby Parke Bernet Inc., N.Y.*

1331. Bisque head Jumeau Bébé with a blond wig, stationary blue glass eyes, pierced ears, closed mouth, and a fully jointed composition body. Mark on head: "TÊTE JUMEAU//3." Mark on body: "JUMEAU//MEDAILLE D'OR//PARIS." H. 12 in. (30.5 cm.). *Courtesy of Sotheby Parke Bernet Inc., N.Y.*

1330. Bisque head Tête Jumeau bébé with wig, stationary brown glass eyes, pierced ears, closed mouth and a jointed composition body. Mark on head: Ill. 1351. Mark on body: Ill. 1343. H. 14 in. (35.5 cm.). *Courtesy of Richard Withington. Photo by Barbara Jendrick.*

1332. Jumeau doll with a poured bisque head, blond wig, stationary blue glass eyes, pierced ears, closed mouth and a fully jointed composition body. Original clothes. Mark on head: "DÉ-POSÉ//TÊTE JUMEAU// B^te S.G.D.G.//1." It has a maroon colored silk armband with gold lettering. H. 9½ in. (24 cm.). *Courtesy of Cherry Bou.*

1334. Two dolls dressed as Pierrots shown in the British periodical BLACK AND WHITE, 1901. These dolls had been displayed at the Crystal Palace and appear to be in the numbered Jumeau character series. Probably the doll on the left is mold # 208. This picture would have been after Jumeau became part of the S.F.B.J. under the German, Fleischmann, but before the Puppen Reform and the introduction of character face dolls by Kämmer & Reinhardt.

1333A & B. Two-faced Jumeau bisque head with one face smiling and one face crying. It has a wig, stationary blue glass eyes, open-closed mouth with teeth, and a fully jointed composition body. Original bonnet. Size 7. H. 18 in. (45.5 cm.). *Courtesy of Sotheby Parke Bernet Inc., N.Y.*

1335. Bisque head doll marked "1907//14." Probably a Jumeau doll made under the S.F.B.J. It has a poured head, a wig, brown glass eyes, open mouth with four upper teeth and is on a ball-jointed wood and composition body. The wrists are not jointed. H. 31 in. (78.5 cm.). *Courtesy of Sotheby Parke Bernet Inc., N.Y.*

A

1336. Jumeau bisque head doll with wig, brown glass eyes, pierced ears, open mouth with teeth, is on a ball-jointed composition body having straight wrists. Mark on head: "275 DEP." Several dolls with this mold number have been found on bodies marked "JUMEAU //MEDAILLE D'OR//PARIS." as is this one. The head is poured in a German manner. H. 14½ in. (37 cm.). *Courtesy of Richard Withington. Photo by Barbara Jendrick.*

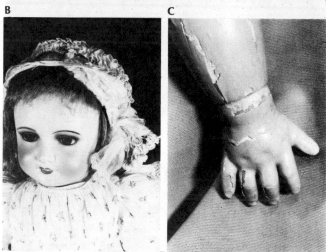

B   C

1337. Bisque head Jumeau Bébé with a reddish brown wig, sleeping blue glass eyes, hair upper eyelashes, open mouth with four upper teeth, and a fully jointed composition body. Original chemise, hat, corset and shoes all marked with the size number of 12, and the doll has the Unis France 301 mark on its head and a sticker on its body reads, "BÉBÉ JUMEAU//Diplôme d' Honneur." H. 26½ in. (67.5 cm.). *Courtesy of Ruth Hartwell.*

1338. Bisque head Jumeau doll with wig, sleeping glass eyes and hair eyelashes, pierced ears, open mouth with four upper teeth, and a ball-jointed composition body. Original clothes except footwear. Mark incised: "S.F.B.J. 25 301 11" over the red stamp "TÊTE JUMEAU." H. 24 in. (61 cm.). *Courtesy of Sotheby Parke Bernet Inc., N.Y.*

1339. Bisque head Jumeau doll with a black wig, blue sleeping glass eyes, an open mouth with four upper teeth, and a jointed composition body having wrists with joints. Original clothes. H. 11½ in. (29 cm.). *Courtesy of Cherry Bou.*

1340. Jumeau lady dolls with bisque heads having wigs, stationary glass eyes, closed mouths, and five-piece composition bodies. Original clothes represent, top row left to right: Empress Josephine, Empress Eugénie, Queen Victoria, Sarah Bernhardt; bottom row: Empress Marie Louise, Queen Marie Antoinette, Mme. de Pompadour, and Mme. de Sévigné.

These dolls were made in the late 1940s–early 1950s. Mark on head: "221." Mark on round tag: "fabrication// JUMEAU//PARIS// Made in France." H. 10 in. (25.5 cm.).

E.DEPOSE J. 10

1341

208
DEPOSE
TETE JUMEAU
BTE
VXI

1350

DÉPOSÉ
TÊTE JUMEAU
Bᵀᵉ SGDG

X A HVI II

1351

E J.
A
10

1342

JUMEAU
MÉDAILLE D'OR
PARIS

1343

8
E J

1344

E. 7 J.

1345

DEPOSE
TÊTE JUMEAU
Bᵗᵉ S.G.D.G.
10

1352

JUMEAU

1346

DEPOSE
JUMEAU
X II T
7

1347

1907
TÊTE JUMEAU
9

1354

1907/
4

1353

∨
TETE JUMEAU
Bᵀᴱ S.G.D.G.

1348

214
DÉPOSÉ
TETE JUMEAU
Bᵀᴱ S.G.D.G.
11

1349

UNIS
FRANCE
21   149
306
JUMEAU
1938
PARIS

1355

1341–1355. Marks on Jumeau heads. Ills. 1353, 1354, and 1355 are marks on the heads from the S.F.B.J. period.

BÉBÉ JUMEAU
Déposé

1356

BÉBÉJUMEAU
Déposé

1357

BÉBE JUMEAU
Diplome d'Honneur

1358

1359

BÉBE
VRAI MODELE
FABRICATION JUMEAU

1360

1356-1360. Marks on Jumeau bodies.

BÉBE
JUMEAU

MED.OR
1878

PARIS
DÉPOSÉ

1361

PARIS

DÉPOSÉ

1362

1361-1362. Marks on Jumeau shoes.

Jumper Dolls. 1920. Cloth flat face doll made by *Dean* as one of the Knock-about series. It was style No. D 253 and wore a pull-over, skirt, and tam. H. 12 in. (30.5 cm.).

June Babies. 1917–19. Line of cloth-body dolls made by *Nottingham.* They had composition masks and represented *Wounded Tommies,* Sailors and Red Riding Hood.

Jungbluth, Mme. 1908. Won a second prize in a Paris Exhibition for wax dolls in Historical Costumes.

Junghans, Simon. 1892–1908. Rittersgrun, Saxony. Made and distributed dolls with composition heads reinforced with metal strips. The heads had painted hair or wigs and sleeping eyes.

1900: Applied for two German patents (D.R.G.M.) for these "unbreakable" heads.

Jungle Toys. 1918. London. Miss E. Daniels, doing business under the name Jungle Toys, advertised that she would make dolls to order.

Junior. 1922. Name of a sponge rubber doll made by *Miller Rubber Co.*

Juno. See **Standfuss, Karl.**

Junon. 1917. Name inscribed on a china socket head with a Sèvres mark. This Sèvres head had a wig and painted eyes. Ht. of head only, 5 cm. (2 in.). See Ill. 2369C.

Jurischitz (Jurisic), Mathias (Anna). 1907–10. Vienna. Listed in an Austrian directory under Dolls and Dolls' heads.

Just Born. 1925. Name of a baby doll made by *Gem.*

Just Me. 1928–30 and later. Trademark registered in U.S. by *Borgfeldt* for dolls. The bisque head was mold # 310 made by *Armand Marseille.* It had a wig, glass eyes glancing to the side, a tiny closed pursed mouth, similar to the *Patsy* mouth and a composition body with one arm bent. The bisque head was sometimes a painted bisque, that is the surface was covered with an overall coat of paint which was not fired into the bisque. The body was jointed at the neck, shoulders and hips. Some of the Just Me dolls were dressed by *Vogue.*

Hts. 8 and 10 in. (20.5 and 25.5 cm.). A composition head Just Me was marked "Registered Germany A 3/0 M." It had a closed mouth, sleeping eyes and a cloth body and was apparently also made by Armand Marseille. See Ills. 1363 A & B and 1364 A & B.

Just-Lyk. 1930 and later. Line of dolls made by the *Natural Doll Co.*

Juszko, Jeno. 1911–20. New York City. Designed the head of *Amberg's Charlie Chaplin* doll in 1915 and this same head was also painted black and called *Oo-Gug-Luk.*★

Jutta. 1906–28. Line of bisque, composition or celluloid head dolls produced by Cuno & Otto *Dressel* and named for the famous 14th century Countess Jutta who was the patroness of Sonneberg. These dolls were either child dolls or baby dolls. They came with molded hair or wigs. Some of them had flirting eyes. The bisque heads were made by *Simon & Halbig, Ernst Heubach* and probably others. Dolly-face Simon & Halbig mold #s 1348 and 1349 were used on Jutta

1363A & B. Bisque socket head Just Me doll produced by Borgfeldt in competition with Patsy. The bisque head was made by Armand Marseille and has a dark brown wig, sleeping blue glass eyes looking to the side. Sometimes the eyebrows are a line and sometimes a dot; closed pursed lips. It is on a five-piece composition body with one arm bent and long legs. Original clothes. Mark on head: Ill. 1365. H. 10 in. (25.5 cm.) *Courtesy of the Margaret Woodbury Strong Museum. Photos by Harry Bickelhaupt.*

1364A & B. Just Me doll with a painted bisque head, that is, the painting was not fired into the bisque, a technique usually found after 1930. It has a blond wig, sleeping blue glass eyes looking to the side, closed pursed lips and a composition body with one arm bent and long slender legs. Original clothes. Mark on head: Ill. 1365. The dress has a Vogue cloth label on it. H. 10 in. (25.5 cm.). *Courtesy of the Margaret Woodbury Strong Museum. Photos by Harry Bickelhaupt.*

Just ME
Registered
Germany
310/7/0

1365. Mark on bisque heads of Just Me dolls.

dolls. The mold #s 1914 and 1922 were also used on some of the Jutta heads. These dolls had wigs, molded eyebrows, sleeping eyes, open mouths with four teeth, and pierced ears. Examples of their marks were "1348//Jutta//S & H //16" and "1349// Dressel//S & H //8." The latter was found on a doll 20 in. (51 cm.) tall. Mold #s 1914 and 1922 were used on Jutta character dolls. The mold # 1914 marks were "SIMON & HALBIG//Jutta//1914//9" and "Jutta//1914//8½." The latter was on a doll 16 in. (40.5 cm.) tall. One of the composition-head versions of Jutta which had a dolly face was marked "M & S //40." on the head; the ball-jointed composition body was marked "Jutta" under the Cuno & Otto Dressel caduceus mark. Two concentric circles surrounded this red stamp mark. Ht. of doll was 23½ in. (59.5 cm.).

1920s: Jutta bent limb baby dolls came in five hts. 48, 54, 58, 63, and 70 cm. (19, 21½, 23, 25, and 27½ in.). Bisque head child dolls came in 15 hts. 33, 42, 44, 46, 48, 51, 55, 57, 64, 70, 74, 78, 87, 96, and 105 cm. (13, 16½, 17½, 18, 19, 20, 21½, 22½, 25, 27½, 29, 30½, 34, 38, and 41½ in.) When bisque-head child dolls had "Parisian eyes," wooden arms and jointed wrists they were only in the six hts. 46 to 64 cm. (18 to 25 in.). Dolls came dressed or undressed.

1928: *Hartleys Sports Stores* in Australia advertised Jutta dolls. Composition head baby dolls with molded hair came 13 and 17 in. (33 and 43 cm.) tall; undressed child dolls were 14½, 18½, 20, and 24½ in. (37, 47, 51, and 62 cm.) tall; dolls dressed as boys and jointed at the knees were 17½ in. (44.5 cm.) tall; dressed girl dolls with real hair were 17 in. (43 cm.) tall.★

K

K. K. See **Kruse, Käthe.**

K. M. Dolls. 1899. Name of dolls with bisque heads, glass eyes, open mouth with teeth, distributed by *Butler Bros.* Four hts. 7¾, 9¾, 11, and 15¾ in. (19.5, 25, 28, and 40 cm.).

K. & K. Toy Co. 1915–30 and later. New York City. Made dolls for *Borgfeldt* with whom they were affiliated. Many of their dolls were distributed by *Butler Bros.* Most of the bisque heads on their dolls were made in Germany. They called their composition heads bisquette. (See also **Kaempfer.**)

1918: Made hundreds of style numbers including *Suffragette; Betsy Ross; Red Riding Hood.* Ht. 15 in. (38 cm.);

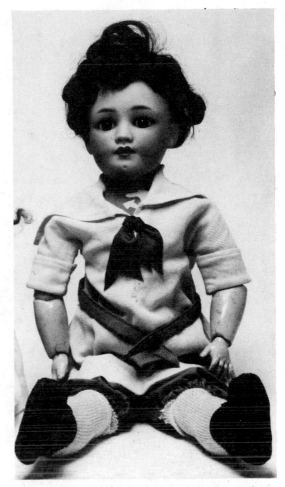

1366. A Jutta doll produced by Cuno & Otto Dressel with a bisque head made by Simon and Halbig. It has a wig, sleeping blue glass eyes, and an open mouth with four upper teeth. The ears are not pierced as is usual on Simon & Halbig heads. The composition body is fully jointed. Mark: "SIMON & HALBIG// 1348//JUTTA//10." H. 24 in. (61 cm.). *Courtesy of Sotheby Parke Bernet Inc., N.Y.*

baby dolls in long dresses; child dolls in nurse's outfit, dolls dressed as little girls in clothes made of the same fabrics as real children wore. Ht. 14½ in. (37 cm.).

1919: Advertised dolls with composition heads and hands, cork stuffed cloth bodies. Dolls with molded hair were 14½ in. (37 cm.) tall. Dolls with wigs were 12½, 14½, 16, and 18½ in. (31.5, 37, 40.5, and 47 cm.) tall. When they had sleeping eyes the 12½ in. ht. was omitted and 21 and 23½ in. (53.5 and 59.5 cm.) hts. were added. The 23½ in. ht. cost $10.50.

1920: Bisquette-head doll with human hair wig, sleeping eyes and dressed in a fancy little girl's outfit was advertised as being a doll for display purposes. Ht. 21 in. (53.5 cm.); priced by *Butler Bros.* $12.00 doz. wholesale.

1921: The new feature was flesh-colored imitation kid legs.

1924: *Mama* dolls were featured. Their cloth bodies were

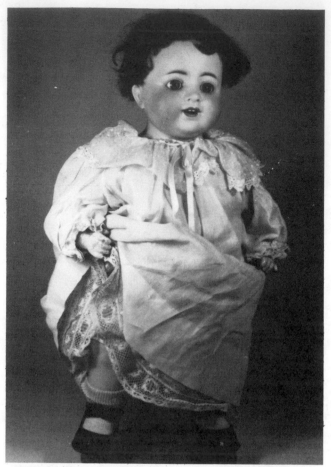

1367. Bisque shoulder head doll made by K & K. It has a mohair wig, blue glass eyes, open mouth with two upper teeth and a tongue. The composition lower arms and legs are on a cloth Mama-type body. Mark: "K & K //56// Made in Germany." H. 18 in. (15.5 cm.). If the head had been on a regular child body it would probably be 56 cm. (22 in.). *Courtesy of Richard Withington. Photo by Barbara Jendrick.*

38

K. & K.
45
Made in Germany

K AND K
TRADE MARK

1368–1369. Marks used on dolls made by K & K. They imported their bisque heads from Germany.

stuffed with cotton. The bisque shoulder heads on Mama dolls were usually marked K & K and "Germany//Thüringia" or "Made in Germany" and a size number that corresponded to the height of the doll in centimeters.

Dressed Mama dolls with composition heads, arms and legs, mohair wigs, sleeping eyes, and cotton stuffed cloth bodies were 18 in. (45.5 cm.) tall and sold for $4.98.

Among their dolls were *Baby Sister, Bye-Lo Baby* and *Prize Baby.*

1927: They were licensed by *Voices Inc.* to use their patented mama voices and criers. They made bodies for *Bonnie Babe.*

1928: *Rose Marie* was one of their dolls. (See THE COLLECTOR'S BOOK OF DOLLS' CLOTHES, Ills. 721 and 757.)★

Ka. (Kaptain, Captain). 1905–16. Name of a jointed felt doll made by *Steiff;* it was distributed in U.S. by *Borgfeldt* and in Great Britain by *Gamage.* It was a rotund doll representing a Captain with whiskers in the cartoon known as the *Katzenjammer Kids.* The fingers were separate on the large hands. Ht. 35 cm. (14 in.).

1906: Gamage sold the doll for 62¢.

1911: It was sold in Germany for $1.12.

1913: The price in England was 81¢ and in New York $1.55.

Kabrle, Heliodor (Anna). 1910. Vienna. Listed in an Austrian directory under Dolls and Dolls' Heads.

Kaddy Kid. 1926. *Mama*-type doll with eyes glancing to the side and teeth showing, made by *Domec Toys* and distributed by *B. Illfelder & Co.* It wore a checked golf suit with knickers and cap and carried a golf bag and clubs. Came in two sizes, priced $1.00 and $3.00.

Kader. Name found on celluloid dolls.

B 3520
KADER

1370. Mark on a Kader celluloid doll.

Kaempfer, Joseph G. Before 1912–25 and later. New York City. He was licensed by *Borgfeldt* to make composition *Kewpies.*

1918: Made bisquette jointed dolls in various sizes. (See also **K. & K.**)★

Kago Doll Co. 1921. Maspeth, N.Y. Made composition Kewpie-type dolls with or without wigs. The wigs were covered with veils. The dolls wore fanciful costumes. ★

Kahn, Albert, & Co. 1920–27. New York City. Advertised "Unbreakable Kanko" dolls, dressed dolls, walking and dancing dolls.★

Kahn, Ed. 1898. Schalkau, Thür. Made *marottes.*

Kahn, Lucien. 1926–29 and possibly later. Paris. Factory at Montreuil-sous-Bois. Made cloth dolls. He registered in France *Moglette* as a trademark for dolls.

Kahn, M. L., & Co. See **Kahn & Mossbacher.**

Kahn & Mossbacher. Before 1900–30 and later. New York City and Philadelphia, Pa. Successor Maurice L. Kahn, 1910–30 and later. Made clothes for dolls excluding shoes and stockings.

1911: Made dresses, hats, caps and worsted goods, specialized in outfits for character dolls.

1919: Advertised plain or flowered lawn, organdy and silk dresses, worsted booties and bonnets.

1921: The baby clothes were white, other clothes were generally solid colors with white trimming.

There were knitted dresses, sports sweaters with pockets, and brimmed hats with worsted designs embroidered on them.

1923: Advertised dolls' outfits for many makes of dolls including dresses, sweaters, capes, sacques, hats, tams, hoods, and booties.

1924: Dresses for *Mama* dolls were made of organdy or voile, in pastel shades, trimmed with tiny flowers and sheer laces.

1926: Designed and made party frocks, afternoon tea-gowns and infant dresses for dolls, including *Bye-Lo Baby,* jointed composition body dolls and Mama dolls.

1929: Made new outfits for *Bubbles, Dimples* and *Patsy* family including a snowsuit for Patsy. The line of doll outfits ranged in price from 10¢ to $10.00.★

Kaiser, Mr. World War I period. Thür. Sculptured *Hansi,* a portrait doll, for *Wagner & Zetzsche.*

Kalbitz, Carl (Karl). 1866–1930 and later. Sonneberg, Thür. Made baby dolls, cloth-body dolls, jointed composition-body dolls and dressed dolls.

1924: *Luckham & Co.* was their London agent.

1929: His London agent, *Ernst Turner,* registered *Kalutu* as a trademark in England.

1371. Mark used for the Kalutu line of dolls made by Carl Kalbitz.

1930: *Bechmann & Ullmann* was the factory agent. The London agent, E. Turner, dressed the dolls. *G.F. Hertzog* distributed some of the Kalbitz dolls. Kalbitz made the Kalutu line of art dolls which bore a round label reading "Genuine//Kalutu//Production."★

Kalco. 1927. Trade name used by *Kaufman, Levenson & Co.* for dolls.

Kalla, A. 1910–18. Shmiedeberg, Bohemia. Listed in an Austrian directory under Dolls and Dolls' Heads; specialized in papier-mâché dolls in various sizes.

Kallenberg. See **Wiesenthal, Schindel & Kallenberg.**

Kallgruber, Emma. 1907–10. Vienna. Listed in an Austrian directory under Dolls and Dolls' Heads.

Kallus, Joseph L. 1912–82. New York City. 1922–30 and later, he was doing business as *Cameo.* While still attending school Joseph Kallus worked week-ends with *Otto Denivelle* and his brother in Mt. Vernon, N.Y. At that time the Denivelle brothers were trying to develop improvements in cold-press composition used for dolls' head and hands.

Borgfeldt tried to have their subsidiary *K & K* make wood-pulp composition dolls but they were not successful and soon after 1925 Cameo took over the manufacture of these dolls. For many years thereafter Cameo made composition *Kewpies, Scootles* and *Bye-Lo Babies.*

1927: *Baby Blossom, Canyon Kiddies* and cloth Kewpies were produced.

1928: *Sissy* was copyrighted.

1929: *Margie* was the feature doll.

1930: *Baby Adele* and *Pinkie* were copyrighted. A segmented wooden doll marked *R.C.A. Radiotrons* was used for advertising by R.C.A. (Radio Corporation of America). A black skin version of the R.C.A. doll representing *Amos 'n' Andy,* a favorite radio team of that era, was also made.

Mr. Kallus applied for a U.S. patent relating to the molded limbs of a doll with a composition and wood body. The Cameo Company registered in the U.S. a trademark for dolls which was an ellipse with a drawing of a child doll's head in profile and the words "Art Quality" above the head and "Cameo Toys" below the head.

1932: Betty Boop and Joy were copyrighted.★

Kalner. See **Well Made Doll Co.**

Kalo (Austrian Hunter). 1911–13. Felt art doll made by *Steiff,* dressed as an Austrian lieutenant and described as "Kaiserjager" (King's Hunter). Ht. 60 cm. (23½ in.).

Kalutu. 1929–30 and possibly other years. Registered trademark by *Ernst Turner* in England for dolls made by *Carl Kalbitz.*

Kamauf, Karl. 1925. Vienna. Obtained an Austrian patent for dolls.

Kamimura. 1927–28. *Lenci,* Oriental doll, style no. 562 wore a kimono and elaborate headdress. Ht. 40 in. (101.5 cm.).

1373. Betty Boop doll with a composition head on a segmented wooden body, made by Joseph Kallus. It has molded black hair, painted eyes, closed mouth and a molded and painted costume. The doll portrayed the cartoon character made famous in the movies by Fleischer Studios. H. 12½ in. (31.5 cm.). *Courtesy of Jessica Norman.*

1374. Decal mark on the chest of a Joy doll made by Joseph Kallus.

1375. Red heart with BETTY BOOP in white letters and the rest in black letters. This mark is on the doll in Ill. 1373.

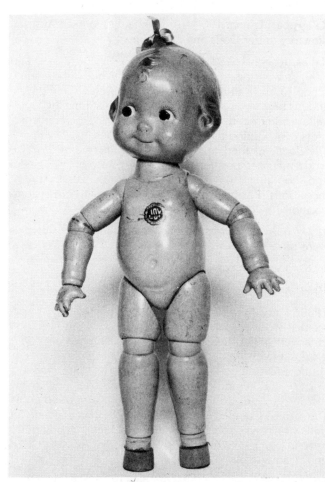

1372. Composition head doll named Joy made by Joseph Kallus. It has molded and painted hair, and eyes looking to the side, a curved linear mouth, neck socket in the head and a ball jointed wooden body with composition hands. Mark Ill. 1374. H. 15 in. (38 cm.). *Courtesy of the Margaret Woodbury Strong Museum. Photo by Harry Bickelhaupt.*

Kamkins. 1919–28. Cloth doll made by *Louise R. Kampes Studio*. Several types of marks are found on these dolls. One of them, a heart-shaped sticker placed over the left side of the chest is as shown in Ill. 1377. The making of the clothes and the sewing on these dolls were done by workers at home using prescribed patterns.

Kamkins with a voice box was marked in ink at the top back of its head, "L. R. KAMPES ATLANTIC CITY//PAT. NOV. 2–20."

1928: Louise Kampes registered "Kamkins—A Dolly to Love." as a U.S. trademark for dolls. (See THE COLLECTOR'S BOOK OF DOLLS' CLOTHES, color Ill. 26.)★

Kamlish & Cass (Kamlish, J., & Co.) 1916. London. Produced dressed and undressed dolls with *British Ceramic* heads and limbs including *Eskimo dolls*.

 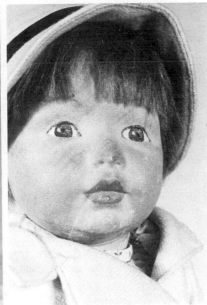

1376A & B. Kamkins cloth doll with molded and painted features bearing a heart-shaped sticker with the words as shown in Ill. 1377. It has a flange neck, reddish blond hair and blue painted eyes. Inside the body is a voice mechanism. This doll has a trunk with the mark "Cass." (See Ill. 484.) H. 19 in. (48 cm.). *Courtesy of Elizabeth Anne Pierce.*

1377. Mark found on Kamkins cloth dolls, which includes the trademark registered in 1928.

Kämmer & Reinhardt. 1886–1930 and later. Waltershausen, Thür. Firm was founded by Ernst Kämmer, a designer and modeler who died in 1901, and Franz Reinhardt, an administrator and salesman born 1858. *Karl Krausser* worked under Ernst Kämmer and when Kämmer died, Krausser took his place. Shortly after the death of *Heinrich Handwerck* in 1902 Kämmer & Reinhardt bought the Handwerck factory, which was managed by Gottlieb Nüssle who became a firm member by 1911. Kämmer and Reinhardt designed dolls' heads but usually did not actually make them. *Simon & Halbig* made most of the bisque heads and was part of the company by 1920. Beginning in 1918 *Schuetzmeister & Quendt* also supplied bisque heads. *Rheinische Gummi und Celluloid Fabrik Co.* made most of the celluloid heads. Kämmer & Reinhardt was a *Verleger* but the dolls were generally distributed by other companies such as *Bing, Borgfeldt, B. Illfelder, L. Rees & Co., Strobel & Wilken,* and *Louis Wolf.* By 1924 the company was part of the Bing group and they advertised that they made their own celluloid heads.

Before 1927 they used the *Miblu,* and the *Cellowachs* heads attributed to *König & Wernicke.* These heads usually carried the tortoise mark of Rheinische Gummi und Celluloid Fabrik Co.

Bing seems to have had some control over all of these companies which were sometimes referred to as the *Waltershauser Puppenfabrik.* The W found on the forehead of some of the Kämmer & Reinhardt dolls probably relates to the Waltershauser Puppenfabrik.

From 1886 to 1909 Kämmer & Reinhardt made only dolly-face dolls according to their 25th anniversary booklet. However, advertisements in the 1890s state that they specialized in jointed *Täuflinge* with bisque heads and dolls' heads of bisque, wood or composition. They claimed they were the first company to put teeth in dolls' heads. Of course teeth had been used for dolls much earlier but they may have been among the first to use them in bisque doll heads. Some of the teeth in Simon & Halbig heads could be early ones and Kämmer & Reinhardt used Simon & Halbig heads. In the 1920s Kämmer & Reinhardt produced or handled cloth dolls and dolls with rubber heads. Earlier they had handled Käthe Kruse cloth dolls. Most of the Kämmer & Reinhardt dolls had their approximate height in centimeters marked on their heads. The character heads also have a mold number. The heights ranged from 12 cm. (4½ in.) to at least 120 cm. (47 in.). The hundreds digit of the mold number usually identified the head as follows:

1. Bisque socket head.
2. Shoulder heads of various materials, as well as the socket heads of black and mulatto babies.
3. Bisque socket heads or celluloid shoulder heads.
4. Heads having eyelashes.
5. Black heads, "Goo-Goo" heads called "Grotesque" heads, busts and arms for pincushions, and so forth.
6. Mulatto heads and others.
7. Celluloid heads, bisque-head walking dolls.
8. Rubber heads.
9. Composition heads and some rubber heads.

ABBREVIATIONS USED BY KÄMMER & REINHARDT
"Sch" (Schelm) means *roguish* (flirting) *eyes.*
"Ma" means mama voice.
"N" means new.

Most of the other letters refer to the style and/or material of the wig or clothing. There is no indication whether a doll has an open or closed mouth as far as the codes have been deciphered.

Mold # 100, usually representing a six-week-old baby, came with molded hair or wig, painted eyes or glass eyes. At first the eyes were painted. This doll's head was on a bent-limb composition body or on a fully jointed composition body. Size number 100, indicating the doll is about 100 cm. or 39½ in. tall, is sometimes found on dolly-faced dolls and must not be confused with the character babies of mold # 100. Mold # 109 was Elise[†], (not Elsie, a typographical error in the Kämmer & Reinhardt entry in the first COLLECTOR'S ENCYCLOPEDIA OF DOLLS.)

MOLD NUMBERS FOUND ON KÄMMER & REINHARDT DOLLS' HEADS

Mold No.	Name of Doll	Years Produced (+ = and later)	Description of examples observed. Other types may exist.
100	Baby	1909+	Molded hair, or wig, painted or glass eyes. Baby or jointed child-type body. Black or white.
101	Peter Marie	1909+	Wig, painted or glass eyes, closed mouth. Child-type jointed body. Black or white.
101x			Same as above except with flocked hair.
102		1909+	Molded, painted hair with bangs, painted eyes, closed mouth. Child-type jointed body.
103		1909	Wig, painted eyes, closed mouth on a child-type body.
104		1909+	Wig, painted eyes, open-closed mouth with teeth, child-type body.
105		1909	Wig, painted eyes, closed mouth, child-type jointed body.
106		1909+	Wig, painted eyes, closed mouth, child-type jointed body.
107	Carl	1909+	Wig, painted eyes, closed mouth, child-type jointed body.
108		1909+	
109	Elise	1909+	Wig, painted eyes, closed mouth. Child-type jointed body.
110			
111		1909+	Wig, glass eyes, open mouth.
112		1909+	Wig, glass eyes, or painted eyes, open-closed mouth with teeth, jointed child body.
112X		1909	Same as above except with flocked hair.
114	Hans or Gretchen	1909	Wig, glass or painted eyes, closed mouth, jointed child body.
114X			Same as above except with flocked hair.
115		1911–27	Molded hair, open mouth, glass eyes. Jointed child body. Käthe Kruse dolls resembled this doll. Her dolls were handled by Kämmer & Reinhardt.
115A		1911–27	Wig, closed mouth, glass eyes, jointed child body or baby body.
116		1911–27	Molded hair, open-closed or open mouth with two teeth. Glass eyes. Dimples. Jointed child body.
116A		1911–27	Wig, open mouth, glass eyes. Baby body. Black or white.
117		1911–27	Wig, closed mouth, glass eyes. Jointed child body.
117A		1911–27	Wig, closed mouth, glass eyes. Jointed child body.
117n		1916–27	Wig, open mouth, glass eyes. Jointed child body, composition or rubber hands.
117X		1911–27	Wig, open mouth, glass eyes. Jointed child body.
118		1912+	Wig, open mouth, glass eyes. Baby body.
118A			Wig, open mouth, glass eyes. Baby body.
120		1912+	Baby or child body.
121		1913+	Wig, open mouth, glass eyes, dimples. Baby or child body.
122		1913+	Wig, open mouth, glass eyes. Baby or child body. Some have D.R.G.M. 2425 granted, 1913.
123	Max	1913+	Wig, closed mouth forming a line. Roguish glass eyes, jointed child body.
124	Moritz	1913+	Wig, closed mouth forming a U. Roguish glass eyes, jointed child body.
125			
126		1914–27	Wig, open mouth, glass eyes which sometimes flirted. Baby or toddler body.
127		1922–27	Molded hair, open mouth, glass eyes. Baby or toddler body.
128		1927	Wig, open mouth, sleeping or flirting eyes. Baby body.
129		1922	Wig.
131		1922–27	Wig, curved line mouth, roguish flirting sleeping eyes. Toddler body.
135		1927	Wig, painted eyes.
138		1927	Painted hair.
144		1927	Painted hair.
150		1927	Glass eyes.
155		1927	Dolly face, wig, sleep glass eyes.
156		1927	Wig, painted footwear.
165		1927	Painted hair.
170		1925	Painted hair. New Born Baby style.

MOLD NUMBERS FOUND ON KÄMMER & REINHARDT DOLLS' HEADS

Mold No.	Name of Doll	Years Produced (+ = and later)	Description of examples observed. Other types may exist.
171			
172		1925	
173		1927	Painted hair. Toddler or baby body.
191		1922	Mulatto.
196			
200–214			Shoulder bisque heads corresponding to 100–114 which are socket heads.
225			Shoulder celluloid head, wig, glass eyes, open mouth, cloth body.
226		1922	Mulatto shoulder head.
246			Mulatto or black shoulder head, wig, glass sleeping eyes.
248		1922	Same as above.
252			Same as above.
255			Celluloid shoulder head, wig, sleeping eyes, hair eyelashes.
256		1922	Sleep eyes. Celluloid or Miblu shoulder head.
265		1922	Painted hair, glass eyes. Celluloid or Miblu shoulder head.
301			Celluloid shoulder head corresponding to 101 bisque socket head.
355		1927	Sleep eyes, wig, slender body.
402		1927	Wig, sleep eyes or painted eyes, slender body.
403		1927	Wig, open mouth, sleep or flirting eyes. Jointed child body. Dolly face.
406			
442			Painted eyes, open mouth, wig. Jointed child body.
509		1927	Googly eyes, curved line mouth. White.
510		1927	Googly eyes, round eyes glancing to the side.
511		1927	Googly eyes.
526			Sleep eyes. Mulatto or black.
531		1927	Googly eyes. Black.
626		1922	Sleep eyes. Mulatto or black.
631		1927	Googly eyes. Mulatto.
651			Sleep eyes. Mulatto.
652			Sleep eyes. Ethnic black.
700	Baby		Painted hair; resembles 100.
701	Marie		Wig, painted eyes, closed mouth; resembles 101.
715			Painted hair and eyes.
716			Painted or wig hair, painted or glass sleeping eyes or flirting eyes.
717		1927	Painted or wig hair, painted or glass sleeping or flirting eyes.
721			Painted eyes and hair.
723			Painted hair and eyes.
727		1922–27	Painted hair and eyes or glass eyes on a baby body.
728		1922–27	Wig, sleeping or flirting eyes, moving tongue.
785			Bisque head with sleep eyes, wig, on a walking body.
787			Same as above.
788			Same as above.
835			Rubber head and hands, painted eyes, closed mouth, wig.
917			Composition head.
926		1922	Composition head, wig.
952			Wig, ethnic black or mulatto.
1126			All-bisque version of mold #126.

The thousands and ten thousands digits generally identified body types as follows:

1. Jointed composition body, no knee joint, except for "Goo-Goos." Straight or bent legs, black or white.
2. Jointed composition baby body that can stand, no knee joints, toddler body.
3. Jointed composition body, no knee joints.
4. Jointed composition bent-limb baby body.
5. Black baby bodies.
7. Celluloid body except for a few composition bodies jointed at shoulders and hips.
8. Cloth baby body.
14. Jointed composition body usually with joints above the knee.
16. Cloth standing body.
17. Celluloid standing body.

1888: Advertised washable patent dolls' heads according to the Ciesliks.

1893–95: Advertised talking and singing dolls based on the phonograph patent of *Emile Berliner*. The phonograph part of this doll was made by Grammophon-Fabrik Kämmer & Co. Kämmer & Reinhardt also advertised all-bisque dolls with jointed shoulders according to the Ciesliks.

1896: Advertised several styles of jointed dolls, bisque heads, composition heads, and wooden heads as well as all-bisque dolls with jointed arms and legs.

1897–98: Applied for four German patents (D.R.G.M.) relating to dolls' arms and legs. Two of these patents pertained to the limbs on cloth or leather dolls.

1899: Advertised bisque dolls' heads with hair eyelashes.

1900–01: Applied for seven German patents (five D.R.G.M. and two D.R.P.) for walking dolls, sleeping eyes and so on.
Registered *"Mein Liebling"* (My Darling) and Majestic Doll[+] as trademarks for dolls in Germany.

1900 and later: Made dolls for *F.A.O. Schwarz* which they called *Favorite*.

1902: Advertised *Rohlinge* (Ruffian) dolls designed by Karl Krausser; walking dolls with heads that turned as the doll walked; sitting and standing dolls. The flirting eyes used in the dolls were based on a patent by *Otto Gans*.

1903: The German patent (D.R.P.) for sleeping eyes in a celluloid doll's head was obtained with *Carl Hartmann*.

1909: Introduced character dolls which owed their inception to models exhibited at a Munich Exhibit.

1910: Grandchildren of Franz Reinhardt were the models for mold # 101, named Peter or Marie, and mold # 114, named Hans or Gretchen.

1911: Advertised *Käthe Kruse* dolls, Baby "Bauz," Annie[+] and Walter[+] *Mattlack* and *Lama-Lack* finish were used for dolls.
According to HARPER'S, "So individual have dolls become that many are known in the trade by the Christen [sic] names of the children who posed for them. Hans, Peter, Marie, Gretchen, Annie and the royal dolls are known to all the shops which handle them." These were the dolls in Kämmer & Reinhardt's Royal[+] line.

This November 1911 HARPER'S article on dolls pictured "An Indestructible Canvas Doll" and "The New Jointed Doll." The heads of these two dolls were strikingly similar. The text discussed the new Käthe Kruse canvas dolls and the Kämmer & Reinhardt Royal Dolls. The head of "The New Jointed Doll" was obviously Kämmer & Reinhardt mold # 115. Both of these dolls were produced by Kämmer & Reinhardt in 1911. This suggests that both the cloth and bisque heads could have been designed from a sculpture of François Duquesnois. (See also **Clothes.**)

1912: Advertised boy dolls with moving tongue and with real hair or skin wigs. Mold # 117 came with open or closed mouth. Frequently there was a letter after the # 117. The 117 and 117 A usually have a closed mouth; the 117n and 117X usually have open mouths with teeth. The *n* stood for neu (new) and these dolls were not made until 1916.
LADIES' HOME JOURNAL published clothes patterns for Kämmer & Reinhardt character dolls.

1913: Applied for four German patents (two D.R.G.M. and two D.R.P.) for dolls' heads.
Advertised a new baby head, *Mein Kleiner Liebling* (My Little Darling), mold #s 121 and 122, and *Max and Moritz* with flirting eyes, mold #s 123 and 124. All the Kämmer & Reinhardt dolls also came with Lama-Lack finish.

1914: The new bisque-head doll was mold # 126. A British toy trade journal reported that a new jointed baby doll named Wunderschoen (*Wunderschön*) was made of composition.

1915: Applied for two German patents (a D.R.P. and a D.R.G.M.). The D.R.P. patent was for a device whereby a pin fell automatically when the head or the doll was turned to the right which prevented the doll from closing its eyes. When turned to the left the pin returned automatically thus enabling the doll to close its eyes when laid down. The dolls with this device were named *Naughty (Der Unart)*.

1916: Obtained an Austrian patent for a doll's head with sleeping eyes.

1917: Became part of the Bing Werke (a conglomerate).

1920: Kämmer & Reinhardt Actien Gesellschaft (Joint Stock Company).
Acquired the Simon & Halbig factory. Wademar Sörgel became a Director of the company.

1921: Made dolls, dolls' heads, dolls' bodies, dolls' limbs, dolls' clothes and dolls' wigs.

1922: Character babies, fully jointed composition body dolls, walking dolls, dancing dolls, dolls with mama voices and dolls with flirting eyes were among those arriving monthly in New York. A Kämmer & Reinhardt catalog showed mold # 18, a lady doll; mold # 60, a "complete" doll; and other mold #s.

1923: A case of 42 assorted baby and a case of 48 assorted jointed standing dolls, hts. 23 to 70 cm. (9 to 27½ in.), were advertised.

1924: Applied for a German patent (D.R.G.M.) for a walking doll with voice. (See also **Manufacture of Dolls, Commercial: Made in Germany in Waltershausen Region.**)

1925: L. Rees & Co., their London distributor, advertised My Darling line of jointed dolls, baby dolls, New Born Babies, dolls' clothes including millinery.

1926: Obtained a German patent (D.R.P.) for sleeping eyes. Applied for two German patents (D.R.G.M.), one for dolls' eyes and one for dolls' joints. Advertised *Me-Lie-Ba.*

1927: Advertised "My Darling" and "My Darling Baby" lines made of Rosewax and dolls with the new waxy Miblu heads. Dolls included Mauseli, Schnucki and Susi, baby dolls with Naughty patent device said "mama" and had flirting eyes from ht. 35 cm. (14 in.) up. Little dolls 12–26 cm. (4½ to 10½ in.) had Simon & Halbig heads; some were all-bisque dolls. Rubber hands were used on some dolls, as well as rubber heads which had painted eyes. (See THE COLLECTOR'S BOOK OF DOLLS' CLOTHES, Ills. 762, 763, 764, 765, and 766.)

Character dolls representing men of various occupations had painted cloth faces, wire frames, felt clothes. Ht. 33 cm. (13 in.). Smaller dolls had painted and molded composition heads, cloth bodies with movable arms and legs attached with wire. These dolls represented many different professions, trades, soldiers and sailors including railway-men, firemen, airmen, porters, chauffeurs, cooks and other servants. All were men dolls except one dressed as a maid. Kämmer & Reinhardt advertised that "For large orders also trades and soldiery of other nations can be delivered if colored illustrations are sent in." The size-height relationship for most of these dolls was as follows:

Size No.	Height cm.	in.	Price per doz. wholesale
4/0	9.5	3½	$1.35
3/0	10	4	$1.55–1.75
2/0	12	4½	$1.75–2.00
0	13	5	$2.00–2.40
1	15	6	$2.40–3.10
1½	20	8	$3.00–3.75
2	23	9	$3.50–4.20

Dolls dressed as jockeys also came in size numbers 2½ and 3 which cost considerably more than the smaller dolls. A cabman with a bisque head came in sizes 1, 1½ and 2; priced $3.30, $3.85 and $4.40 doz. wholesale.

These prices were from a Kämmer & Reinhardt catalog with the prices in U.S.A. dollars.

1928: Advertised My Rosy Darling (Mein Rosiger Liebling) and dolls made of bisque, celluloid or wax.

Applied for two German patents (a D.R.G.M. and a D.R.P.) for a doll with a voice.

Gerzon advertised celluloid Mein Liebling Dolls.

1929: Applied for two German patents (a D.R.G.M. and a D.R.P.) for dolls' eyes.

1930: Advertised My Darling (Mein Liebling); line made of *Porzellanit*, bisque, porcelain, celluloid or Cellowachs. Dolls had sleeping eyes or flirting eyes, open mouth or closed mouth. A large assortment of jointed dolls included *Nollipolli*, a new model. *Panta* heads, advertised as being unbreakable and incombustible, were described as an "export novelty." Dolls without knee joints were made with straight legs or legs slightly bent. Allegedly these dolls could stand without support and simulate walking or running.

1931: Advertised that their *Bébé Camerose*, a bébé incassable, was sold exclusively in Paris.

A pottery head of the Russian type of manufacture, marked "K ☆ R" on a body marked "Made in Russia," has been reported. This doll had a wooden pate and may have been a World War I reproduction of a Kämmer & Reinhardt doll.

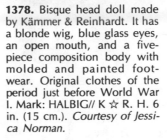

1378. Bisque head doll made by Kämmer & Reinhardt. It has a blonde wig, blue glass eyes, an open mouth, and a five-piece composition body with molded and painted footwear. Original clothes of the period just before World War I. Mark: HALBIG// K ☆ R. H. 6 in. (15 cm.). *Courtesy of Jessica Norman.*

1379. Doll made by Kämmer & Reinhardt with a Simon & Halbig bisque head having a wig, sleeping glass eyes, open mouth and teeth. It has a ball jointed composition body. Original clothes. Head marked: "S & H.// K ☆ R.//66." H. 66 cm. (26 in.). *Courtesy of the Collection Nederlands Kostuummuseum, The Hague. Photo by B. Frequin.*

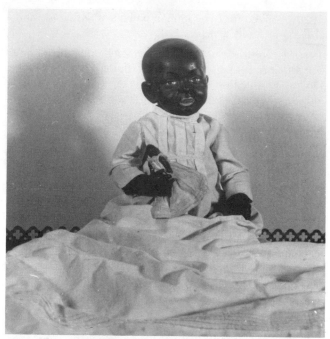

1380. Black Kämmer & Reinhardt mold # 100. The bisque head has molded and painted hair and eyes. The mouth is open-closed and the composition body has bent limbs. Clothes are contemporary with the doll. H. 13 in. (33 cm.). *Courtesy of June Jeffcott.*

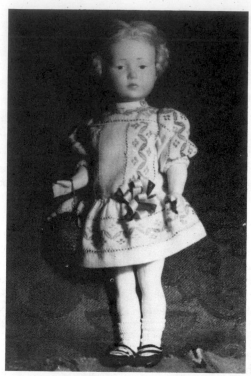

1381. Kämmer & Reinhardt bisque head doll mold #101 has a wig, intaglio eyes, a closed mouth, and a five piece composition body. H. 8¼ in. (21 cm.). *Courtesy of Dr. Eva Moskovszky.*

„Прогулка". Современныя куклы въ Германіи.

1382. Illustration in a Russian book, UTPYWKA, by N. D. Bartram, published in 1912 in Moscow, showing two bisque-head dolls made by Kämmer & Reinhardt. The girl appears to be mold # 101 and boy is either mold #107 or 109.

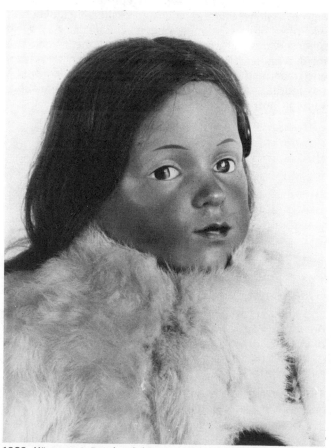

1383. Kämmer & Reinhardt bisque head doll, mold # 103. It has a wig, painted eyes glancing to the side and a closed mouth. H. 23 in. (58.5 cm.). *Courtesy of Vera Kramer, Dolls in Wonderland.*

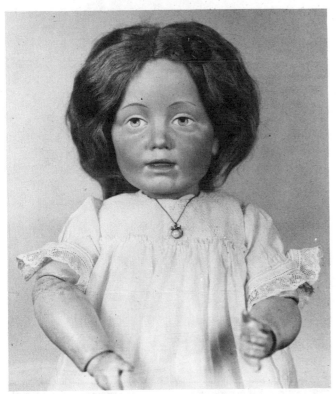

1384. Kämmer & Reinhardt bisque-head doll with wig, painted eyes, closed mouth, and a ball-jointed composition body. The head is mold #105. H. 20 in. (51 cm.). *Courtesy of Vera Kramer, Dolls in Wonderland.*

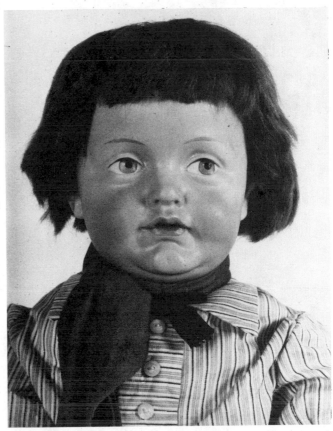

1385. Bisque-head doll with the mold # 106 painted on it in red. This may be a Kämmer & Reinhardt character doll. It has a wig, painted eyes, a closed mouth, and a composition body. H. 20 in. (51 cm.). *Courtesy of Vera Kramer, Dolls in Wonderland.*

1386. Kämmer & Reinhardt bisque head doll with wig, painted eyes, closed mouth, and a five-piece composition body with molded and painted footwear. This doll is mold # 112A. H. 8¼ in. (21 cm.). *Courtesy of Dr. Eva Moskovszky. (This number has been found frequently in Hungary.)*

1387. Bisque-head doll made by Kämmer & Reinhardt using their mold #114. It has a wig, molded and painted eyes, closed mouth, and a jointed composition body. *Courtesy of Dr. Eva Moskovszky.*

1388. Bisque head, bent-limb baby body doll made by Kämmer & Reinhardt. It has a wig, sleeping brown glass eyes, closed mouth, and is on a composition body. This is mold # 115A and on the head it also has "V K ☆ R A// 38." H. 12½ in. (31.5 cm.). It would probably be 38 cm. (15 in.) if it had straight legs. *Courtesy of Sotheby Parke Bernet Inc., N.Y.*

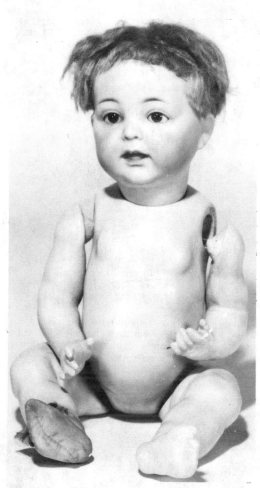

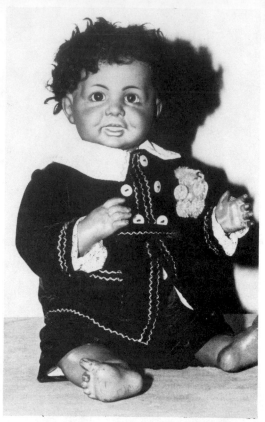

1390. Brown bisque head and brown five-piece bent-limb baby composition body made by Kämmer & Reinhardt from mold # 116 A. It has a wig, brown glass eyes, and an open-closed mouth with two upper teeth and tongue. Note the way the big toe sticks out. H. 15 in. (38 cm.). *Courtesy of Elsie and Al Potter.*

1389. Kämmer & Reinhardt bisque head mold #116 has a wig, sleeping brown glass eyes, an open-closed mouth with two teeth and a bent-limb composition baby body. H. 14 in. (35.5 cm.). *Courtesy of Sotheby Parke Bernet Inc., N.Y.*

1391. Kämmer & Reinhardt mold #116. A bisque head with a wig, sleeping blue glass eyes, open-closed mouth with two upper teeth and tongue. It has a bent-limb composition baby body with a big toe that sticks out. H. 18½ in. (47 cm.). *Courtesy of Sotheby Parke Bernet Inc., N.Y.*

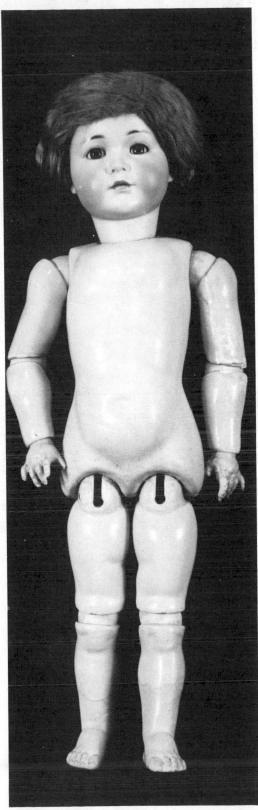

1393. Kämmer & Reinhardt mold # 117A bisque head with a wig, sleeping blue glass eyes, closed mouth, on a fully jointed composition body. The head is marked 70 and the height is 70 cm. (27½ in.). *Courtesy of Sotheby Parke Bernet Inc., N.Y.*

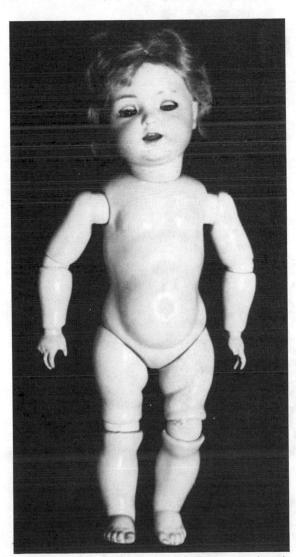

1392. Kämmer & Reinhardt bisque socket head doll mold # 117. The head made by Simon & Halbig has a wig, sleeping blue glass eyes, closed mouth and is on a ball-jointed composition body. Head marked: "K ☆ R//SIMON & HALBIG// 117." H. 68 cm. (27 in.). *Courtesy of the Collection Nederlands Kostuummuseum, The Hague. Photo by B. Frequin.*

1394. Bisque-head doll made by Kämmer & Reinhardt with wig, sleeping brown eyes, open mouth and teeth, composition toddler body. Head marked "Simon & Halbig//122//128." H. 34 cm. (13½ in.). *Courtesy of the Collection Nederlands Kostuummuseum, The Hague. Photo by B. Frequin.*

1395A & B. Profile of bisque head mold # 123 representing Max, a mischievous character in a story for children, written by Wilhelm Busch before 1870. This doll was made by Kämmer & Reinhardt. It has a wig, glass eyes glancing to the side, closed smiling mouth. *Courtesy of Pat Schoonmaker.*

1396. Bisque head doll made by Kämmer & Reinhardt from their mold # 124. It represents Moritz, the mischievous boy partner of Max shown in Ill. 1395. This doll has glass eyes glancing to the side and a closed smiling mouth. The wig and clothes are recent additions. For a more suitably clothed Moritz see Ill. 1854. *Courtesy of Pat Schoonmaker.*

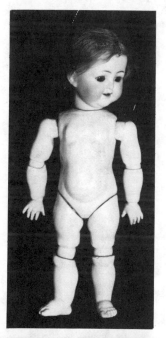

1397. Bisque head doll made by Kämmer & Reinhardt with wig, sleeping brown eyes, open mouth with teeth on a composition toddler style body. Head marked: "K ☆ R //Simon & Halbig//126 //32." H. 37 cm. (14½ in.). If this head had been on the designated bent-limb baby body the ht. would have corresponded with the ht. mark on the head. *Courtesy of the Collection Nederlands Kostuummuseum, The Hague. Photo by B. Frequin.*

1398. All-bisque Kämmer & Reinhardt bent limb baby doll. It has a wig, sleeping glass eyes and an open mouth with two upper teeth. The manufacture of these dolls was discontinued by 1927. Mark on head: Ill. 1407. Mark on torso: Ill. 1408. Mark on arm: Ill. 1409. Mark on leg: Ill. 1410. The 1126 number appears to designate an all-bisque version of head mold #126. H. 21 cm. (8½ in.). The 21 in the mark on the body indicates the height in centimeters. *Courtesy of Ardelle J. Ross.*

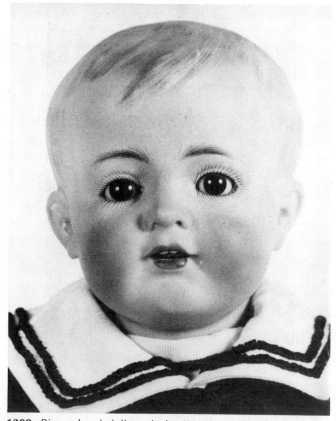

1399. Bisque-head doll made by Kämmer & Reinhardt. It has molded and painted hair, sleeping glass eyes, an open mouth with two upper teeth and a jointed composition body. The mold # is 127. *Courtesy of Vera Kramer, Dolls in Wonderland.*

1402. Celluloid shoulder head doll made for Kämmer & Reinhardt and having mold #225. It has a wig, blue glass eyes, an open mouth with teeth and a pink kid body with composition and wood arms. Clothes are contemporary with the doll. The turtle mark is on the head as well as the Kämmer & Reinhardt mark. H. 16 in. (40.5 cm.). *Courtesy of Sotheby Parke Bernet, Inc., N.Y.*

1400. Kämmer & Reinhardt bisque head doll made from mold # 131. It has a wig, stationary roguish blue glass eyes, and a closed smiling mouth. The composition body has ball joints. H. 14½ in. (37 cm.) A small size version marked "131-16" is shown in Ill. 2714. *Courtesy of Sotheby Parke Bernet Inc., N.Y.*

1401. Bisque head made by Simon & Halbig mold # 403 on a Kämmer and Reinhardt ball-jointed composition body. It has a wig, sleeping brown glass eyes, and an open mouth with teeth. Mark: Ill. 1411. H. 22½ in. (57 cm.). *Courtesy of Richard Withington. Photo by Barbara Jendrick.*

1403A & B. Celluloid doll made by Rheinische Gummi und Celluloid Fabrik for Kämmer & Reinhardt. It has mold # 717 (see mark for head: Ill. 1412). It has a brown wig with two plaits, blue glass sleeping and flirting eyes, and an open mouth with four teeth. Like the head the body is also marked: Ill. 1413. The 39 stands for the centimeter size. Original clothes include a dress having a red felt skirt and black rayon sleeveless bodice. The helmet shaped hat is also of red felt. The shoes are leather with a pompon. H. 39 cm. (15½ in.). *Coleman Collection.*

1404. Celluloid socket-head doll made for Kämmer & Reinhardt and having the mold # 728. It has a wig, sleeping and flirting brown glass eyes, open mouth and teeth, and a toddler type composition body. Original Tyrolean costume with edelweiss embroidery and stag antler buttons. The size is marked 29/31 indicating that it is 29 cm. on a bent limb baby body and 31 cm. on a toddler body as this one is. H. 31 cm. (12 in.). *Courtesy of Richard Withington. Photo by Barbara Jendrick.*

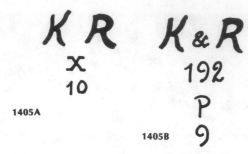

1405A

1405B

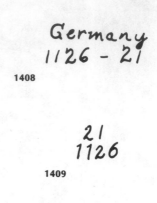

1408

1409

1410

1406A

1411

1406B

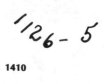

1412

1407

1413

1405–1413. Marks on Kämmer & Reinhardt dolls. No. 1412 is on a celluloid head and No. 1413 is on the celluloid body with the celluloid head. Nos. 1407, 1408, 1409, and 1410 are on an all-bisque doll. Most of the other marks are on bisque heads.

Kampes, Louise R., Studio. 1919–30 and later. Atlantic City, New Jersey. Made *Kamkins.*

1927: Licensed by *Voices, Inc.* to use patented mama voices and criers in her dolls. Made *Mama* dolls.

1928: Registered "A Dolly to Love" as a trademark in U.S. for dolls.★

Kämpfe & Heubach (Wallendorf Porzellanfabrik). 1897–1930. Wallendorf, Thür. Porcelain factory, made dolls. Used marks almost identical to those used by *Meissen, Königliche Porzellan Manufaktur* (K.P.M.) and *Nymphenburg.* This factory probably made the dolls shown at the 1908 Munich exhibit.★

Kandy Kid. 1920s. Composition head, arms and legs, molded painted hair, metal flirting eyes, cloth body jointed at the neck, shoulders and hips, made by *Ideal.* Ht. 15 in. (38 cm.).

Kandy Kids. 1918. Line of dolls with *British Ceramic* heads made by the *Royal Crown Pottery Co.*

Kane, Mathilde. See **Sardeau, Miss Hélène.**

Kanko.[†] See **Kahn, Albert, & Co.**

Kant, Krack. 1912–19. Trade term used for all-celluloid dolls made by *Parsons-Jackson.* The material of these dolls was referred to as "biskoline."

1914: Hts. 10, 12, 14 in. (25.5, 30.5, and 35.5 cm.).

1919: *George H. Bowman* of Cleveland was the exclusive distributor.★

Kapok. 1919–30 and later. A cotton-like fibre that covered the seeds of the ceiba tree. It was light in weight and was used to stuff cloth body dolls.

Kaptain. See **Ka.**

Kaptain Kid Co. 1923. Rochester, N.Y. Made dolls.

Kaptain Kiddo. Cloth doll designed by *Grace Drayton* and representing a cartoon character in the SUNDAY NORTH AMERICAN comics.

Karakter Kiddies. See **Kiddie Karakters.**

Karakters. See **Averill Manufacturing Co.**

Karl, August Friedrich. 1926–27. Sonneberg, Thür. Produced cloth dolls, *Mama* dolls, New Born Baby dolls, fully jointed and sitting baby dolls of Waltershausen quality. Claimed his dolls came "with first-class dresses."

Karl (Bather). Before 1911–16. Felt character doll made by *Steiff,* dressed in a striped bathing suit and cap. Six hts. 28, 35, 43, 50, 60, and 75 cm. (11, 14, 17, 19½, 23½, and 29½ in.); priced 90¢ to $4.05. By 1916 the 75 cm. (29½ in.) size was omitted.

Karmen Corp. 1921–24. New York City. Advertised Tub[†] and *Tubbins.*★

Kase-Quinby Rubber Co. 1925–26. New York City. Made outfits for dolls.

Kashner Co. 1928. New York City. Jobber and distributor of dressed dolls. Ht. 7½ in. (19 cm.); priced 10¢.

Kasia. 1915. Name of a cloth doll sponsored by *Mme. Paderewski* to aid Polish refugees. The doll was dressed as a housewife in Cracow and made by Polish refugee artists in *Mme. Larzarski*'s workshop.

Kasparek, Jeanne de (Mme). 1922–30 and later. Paris. Made dolls in a workshop called *Sans Rival.*

1922: Registered in France a trademark for dolls consisting of a coat-of-arms with a crest having a crown and three feathers.

1925: Won a Diplôme d'Honneur award at the Arts Decoratif exposition in Paris.

Katagini Bros. 1930. New York City. Made celluloid dolls, especially *Mama* dolls. Used the initials "C.K."

Kat-A-Korner Kompany. 1925–30 and later. Nashville, Tenn. Manufactured cloth dolls including ones made of oilcloth.

1927: Advertised Garden Girl made of oilcloth and a cloth clown that would "perform when squeezed."

1928: Made over 100 style nos., including *Candy Stick Man, Eskimo Tots* and *Sunshine Girl.* A new doll was of the *Boudoir* type covered with cretonne and over 36 in. (91.5 cm.) high.

1930: Advertised cloth dolls including *Fvangelina, Rattle Head* dolls and *Kollege Klowns.*

Kate Greenaway, Jack and Jill. 1917. Name of dolls made of stockinet or other fabric, by *Shanklin.* These dolls were designed by *E. E. Houghton.*

Kathi. Before 1911–13. Name of a felt doll made by *Steiff,* dressed in regional costume with a dirndl and broad-brimmed hat. Ht. 35 cm. (14 in.).

Kathleen Mavoureen. 1920. Name of a cloth doll with a pressed face made by *Harwin.* The doll could sit or stand and was dressed as an Irish girl.

Katie Kroose. 1918 and possibly earlier. *Effanbee*'s composition head imitation of *Käthe Kruse* dolls. It came with painted hair or wig, dressed as a girl or boy and was similar to *Baby Blanche.* Head was marked 334 according to Kelly Ellenburg.

Katinka. 1925–26. *Lenci* felt doll style no. 257 wore a Russian-type costume with a very high headdress. Ht. of doll 31½ in. (80 cm.).

Katz, Abraham. 1932. Brooklyn, N.Y. Obtained a U.S. patent which he assigned to *Ideal,* pertaining to a rubber leg that would produce a noise when squeezed.

Katz, Leo. 1924–30 and later. Vienna. Made dolls.★

Katzenjammer Kids. 1904 and later. Name of dolls representing characters in the Sunday comics. (See also **Ka.** and **Mi.**)★

Kauders, Glass & Co. 1907. Vienna. Listed in Austrian directory under Dolls and Dolls' Heads.

Kaufhaus des Westens. 1907 and other years. Berlin. Department store that sold bisque head dolls with painted eyes and cloth bodies; *Cymbaliers; Marottes; Mein Liebling* made by *Kämmer & Reinhardt;* white and mulatto ball-jointed *Täuflinge.* They also sold a variety of dressed dolls. Hts. 20 to 48 cm. (8 to 19 in.); priced 11¢ to $1.81.

Kaufman, I., & Son. 1929–30. Brooklyn, N.Y. Made stockinet for dolls in various colors and widths as well as various grades of stuffing cotton.

Kaufman, Irving. See **Modern Doll Co.**

Kaufman, Levenson & Co. 1925–30. New York City. Distributed dolls, especially those of *Acme.* Used *Kalco* as a trade name for dolls.

1927: Sole distributor of *Alexander* dolls.

1930: Advertised *Paramount* line of dolls.★

Kaufmann & Gordon Co. 1921. New York City. Advertised stuffed dolls in TOYS AND NOVELTIES, priced 25¢ to $10.00.

Kaulitz, Marion Bertha. 1901–20s. Munich, Bavaria. She was English on her mother's side and best known as the instigator of the *Puppen Reform,* a movement in Bavaria towards the creation of realism in dolls. STUDIO TALK reported that about 1901 "When the artistic conscience began to invade this industry [dolls] it fell to some artists of Dresden and Munich to introduce a change."

An article in the November, 1911 issue of HARPER'S discussed the Marion Kaulitz dolls:

"Perhaps the most interesting feature about the jointed child dolls is the fact that each type is made after the portrait or photograph of a real child, and is often a copy of a living child model. One traces the incentive to realism in doll manufacture to a lovely elderly lady in Munich. She is an artist, and one with a deep love for childhood. It seemed to her that when one considered all the passion of love which a doll inspires in the breast of its owner, that little girl ought to have a pet that looked more human than dolls have been wont to look. With this idea she developed, in plaster, dolls that were exact imitation of the various peasant folk who came to Munich from Bavaria and other provinces of a Sunday. The holiday attire of each native village was represented. . . . The Empress of Germany . . . was delighted with the human-looking manikins, and this fact did not take long to spread throughout the Empire and reach the ears of Americans. Now the artist in Munich has several artist assistants to aid her in developing new peasant faces and types, and factories eagerly await models from her studio to dress according to her designs."

The hard composition heads of the Art Dolls were designed by *Marie Marc-Schnür, Paul Vogelsanger* and *Josef Wackerle.* Various types of bodies were used; some were fully jointed composition bodies made by *Cuno & Otto Dressel.* Marion Kaulitz, *Lilian Frobenius* and Alice Hagemann dressed the dolls which were distributed by *Hermann Tietz* in Munich. The faces of the dolls were handpainted usually by Marion Kaulitz and could be washed without damage. Most of the dolls had composition faces but a few had cloth faces. The costumes of the dolls were very colorful and resembled clothes worn by children. The Kaulitz dolls were not mass produced.

1908: At the Munich Exhibit she showed dolls with character faces representing boys and girls. The girls all had wigs but the boys had various kinds of hair. The hard composition heads had painted eyes. These "puppen reform" dolls were exhibited by Hermann Tietz.

Some of her dolls were given by Auguste-Victoria, Empress of Germany, to the children of the Royal household as Christmas presents.

1910: A report written by M. P. Verneuil and published in ART ET DECORATION, July, 1910, in Paris stated:

"Marion Kaulitz's . . . dolls are not like the ordinary dolls of today which are grotesque by comparison with their heads too large, their stupid faces, dull looks and rediculous clothes. The Kaulitz dolls are totally different. Each one seems to have a different head and their very own face. However, the artists modeled only seven different heads but the colors of the eyes and hair varied and at the same time the coiffeur and clothes were never the same on any two dolls. Moreover Mlle. Kaulitz charmingly varied the clothes, dressing some grandly in silk while others wore cotton or knitted wool. Some are dressed for school, some are urchins wearing sabots. These realistic dolls represent children of all classes and colors.

"At the time of the visit of the author, Marion Kaulitz is preparing to show her dolls at the Leipzig Fair where it is certain she will have the same success as she had in Munich. These are true living dolls unlike the unformed poupards or the pretentious deformed dolls that our children have been accustomed to having.

"Many of the dolls wear accurate provincial costumes. For Brittany there is a whole series with the headdresses of Nantes, Pluvinier, Auray, the isle of Moines, Rosporden, Vannes or Quimperlé, and with aprons and fichus of brillant colors that are separate from the somber dresses; and the 'bigoudaines' of Pont-l'Abbé with their strange coiffures and dresses embroidered in bright colors. Also dolls dressed as all the swell young lads with their short round jackets, beautifully embroidered vests and round hats with velvet ribbons. There are similar provincially dressed dolls for Normandy, the Basque country, Provence, Savoy, Vendée. These costumes are simple but accurate and greatly surpass the dolls that one usually sees in France.

"Mlle. Kaulitz does not consider these dolls to be art objects that require high prices. They are priced about the same as other dolls despite their artistry. Their clothes are exquisitely made and the materials well chosen but not costly. The prices must remain within reasonable limits or else they would become collector's items rather than toys for children. They are not like the little 15 centimeters high [6 inches] carved wood dolls that cost 50 francs [$10.00] and are too expensive for the average child to play with. Dolls must be enjoyed by children and probably eventually replaced. It is rediculous for a child to have its doll only on Sunday. The Kaulitz dolls are made sufficiently robust so that they will last a long time and they are priced so that they can easily be replaced when they are finally broken."

The Kaulitz dolls were made in their German workshop for art handwork in/or near Munich.

1911: Dolls were exhibited in Berlin, Paris, and Vienna. All of the dolls passed through the hands of Marion Kaulitz before being sent all over the world.

1912: She won a first prize at the Breslau Fair. Most of the dolls represented School Boys and Girls.

1915: Doll-type heads on beverage warmers were a new Kaulitz product. These heads generally represented women with ethnic type features, often of the black race. A Kaulitz doll's head representing a child had cloth arms, a full skirt forming a beverage warmer for the nursery and a hooded cloak.

1923: Kaulitz dolls represented various races.★

Ein kleines
„Tschapperl".

1414. Picture of a Kaulitz baby doll in the Hermann Tietz exhibit as shown in DIE WELT DER FRAU, November 1908, a month after the first showing. The caption reads, "A little gentle, awkward baby."

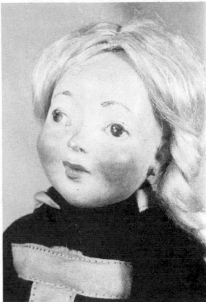

1416A & B. All-composition doll made by Marion Kaulitz in the Puppen Reform period. It is not known which artist designed this head but similar dolls are seen in articles on Kaulitz dolls in DEKORATIVE KUNST and DIE WELT DER FRAU, 1908. The socket head is made of a plaster type composition and has a blond wig, molded and painted bulbous eyes, open-closed mouth, and a fully jointed composition and wood body. Original clothes. H. 12 in. (30.5 cm.). *Coleman Collection.*

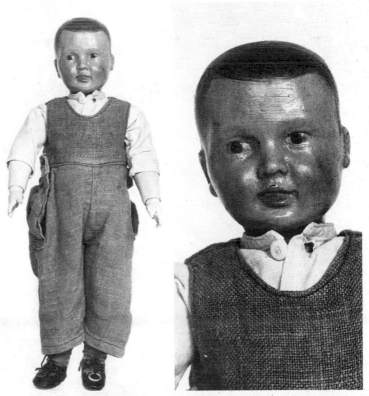

Kinderreigen

1415. Puppen Reform dolls exhibited by Hermann Tietz as shown in DIE WELT DER FRAU, November, 1908. The caption reads "Children dancing in a ring."

1417A & B. Painted hair boy doll created by Marion Kaulitz. This composition doll has painted blue eyes, open-closed mouth with teeth, and a fully jointed composition and wood body. Original clothes. Mark: Ill. 1425. H. 14½ in. (37 cm.). *Courtesy of the Margaret Woodbury Strong Museum. Photos by Harry Bickelhaupt.*

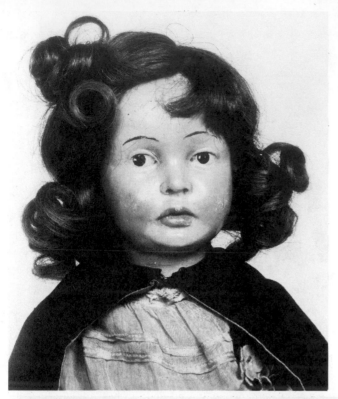

1418. Marion Kaulitz all-composition doll with wig, painted blue eyes, closed mouth, a fully jointed body. Contemporary clothes. Mark: Ill. 1426. H. 17 in. (43 cm.). *Courtesy of the Margaret Woodbury Strong Museum. Photos by Harry Bickelhaupt.*

1419. Munich Art Dolls created by Marion Kaulitz and her associates. This illustration of these composition dolls appeared in THE STUDIO, May, 1909.

BY MARION KAULITZ

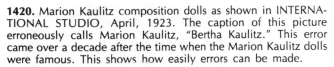

"KAULITZ DOLLS" NAMED FROM THEIR CREATOR, BERTHA KAULITZ, WHO INITIATED A GREAT REFORM IN DOLL MAKING ABOUT 1910

1420. Marion Kaulitz composition dolls as shown in INTERNATIONAL STUDIO, April, 1923. The caption of this picture erroneously calls Marion Kaulitz, "Bertha Kaulitz." This error came over a decade after the time when the Marion Kaulitz dolls were famous. This shows how easily errors can be made.

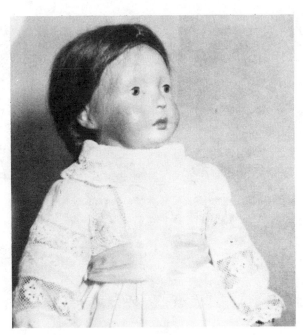

1422. Marion Kaulitz composition doll with wig, painted eyes, closed mouth, and a composition and wood body. H. 14 in. (35.5 cm.). *Courtesy of Jane Walker.*

DOLLS   BY MARION KAULITZ

1421. Marion Kaulitz dolls shown in THE STUDIO, January 1911.

„Время кринолина". Современныя куклы въ Германіи. Изъ колл. Г. Гитцъ.

1423. Marion Kaulitz's, composition dolls as shown in UTPYW-KA by N. D. Bartram, a Russian book published in 1912. *The book is in the Widener Library at Harvard University.*

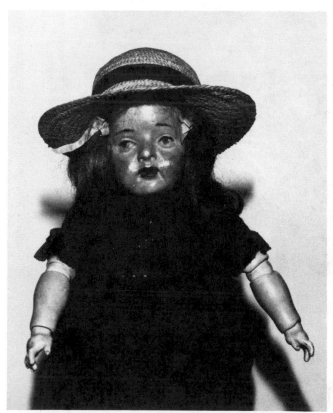

1424. Kaulitz type composition doll with wig, painted eyes, closed mouth, and fully jointed composition and wood body. H. 13 in. (33 cm.). *Courtesy of the late Magda Byfield.*

K 2   K .Ⅎℂ

1425–1426. Marks on plaster composition-headed dolls created by Marion Kaulitz.

Kawashima, Sijiro. 1930 and later. Kyoto, Japan. Manufactured dolls.

Kaybee Doll & Toy Co. 1917–19. Los Angeles, Calif. Made composition heads set into composition shoulder plates. These washable heads had sleeping eyes and human hair wigs. The bodies were cloth. Some of the dolls were carnival dolls.★

Kayborn Novelty Co. 1924–27. Brooklyn, N.Y. Made soft-body terry cloth and leatherette character and floating dolls.

Kaye, Benjamin. 1926. Brooklyn, N.Y. Obtained a U.S. design patent for a doll.

Kaye Toy & Fancy Goods Co. 1916–17. London. Wholesale distributor of dolls including French and British jointed dolls priced $2.00 to $8.12 and up. Dolls with celluloid or ceramic mask faces priced $1.00 to $3.12 and up.

Kayo. Cutout cloth doll representing a comic character and licensed by Famous Artists Syndicate. Ht. 8 in. (20.5 cm.).

Kayo. 1926–30. Doll made of oilcloth by *Live Long Toys* was based on the design by *Frank Willard* representing a cartoon character in the *Moon Mullins* comic series.

1927: Doll wore a dark sweat shirt, a single suspender, long polka dot trousers and a Derby hat.

1928: *Eileen Benoliel* designed a new version.

1929: This washable doll bore the names "Kayo" and "Frank Willard." Its clothes were red and yellow. Ht. 11 in. (28 cm.); priced $8.00 doz. wholesale.

Kayo. 1929. All-bisque doll with jointed neck and molded clothes, made in Germany and distributed exclusively by *Marshall Field* and *Shackman*. The doll represented one of the cartoon characters in the *Moon Mullins* comic drawn by *Frank Willard.*

It wore polkadot long trousers. Priced $1.10 doz. wholesale.

Kean (Keen) & Co. See **Kohnstam, M., & Co.**

Keats & Co. 1916 and later. Burslem, Staffs. Wedgewood Toy Factory, name of the Keats factory, used *British Ceramic* dolls' heads coated with a special preparation that gave a velvet surface similar to wax dolls. This may have been the patented process of coating ceramic heads with wax, a process patented by *Doris Sylvia Bailey and Sarah Baxter* in 1916. These dolls of Keats & Co. came in a variety of styles and sizes; priced $2.50 to $3.00.

Keeler, Fanny. 1929. New York City. Registered in U.S. "Keeler Dolls" as a trademark for dolls.

Keenan, Mrs. Anna M. 1921–28. Seattle, Wash. Manufactured *Sweetie* dolls.★

1427. Keeneye Boudoir doll patented by Victor Keney. It has a composition shoulder head with wig, painted eyes and hair eyelashes, a cloth body with composition arms and feet. It has molded footwear. Original clothes are of a patriotic red, white, and blue design. Marks: Ills. 1428 and 1429. H. 25 in. (63.5 cm.). *Coleman Collection.*

1428. Embossed mark on the back on Keeneye dolls shoulder plate.

1429. The sticker mark on Victor Keney's Keeneye Boudoir doll.

Keeneye. 1931. Trademark registered in U.S. by *Victor Keney* for *Boudoir* dolls. See Ill. 1429.

Kefi. 1927–28. Trademark of *Christian Kern* used for dolls' articles.

Keilich, Bernh. 1926–28. Berlin. Manufactured dolls.

Keity, S., & Sons. 1922. England. Distributed dolls.

Keller Toy Manufacturing Co. 1930 and later. Columbus, Ohio. Manufactured dolls' outfits.

Kellogg Co. 1926–28. Battle Creek, Mich. Used cutout cloth dolls representing nursery rhyme characters such as *Goldilocks, Little Bo-Peep, Mary and Her Little Lamb, Little Red Riding Hood* and *Tom, Tom the Piper's Son* as advertising dolls.

Kelly (Sgt. Kelly[+], American Soldier). 1909–13. Jointed felt doll with a long nose and long feet, made by *Steiff* and distributed by *Borgfeldt* in the U.S. It wore the blue uniform of an American soldier, with a kepi. Ht. 35 cm. (14 in.); priced 90¢ in Germany in 1911 and $1.55 in New York in 1913.

1430. Kelly, a U.S. soldier as represented by a Steiff felt doll. The hat is sewed to the top of the head; sideburns and hair at the back are painted on the felt. Eyes are black buttons; closed mouth, neck turns and there are joints at the shoulders and hips. Original clothes consist of a blue coat, gray trousers with a felt stripe down the outside of each pant's leg. The letters U.S. are on each side of the collar. The Steiff button is in the ear. H. 15 in. (38 cm.). *Courtesy of Richard Wright. Photo by A. Jackson.*

Kelty, E., & Sons. 1921. Southport, England. Advertised fully jointed dolls with composition bodies, sleeping eyes, dressed and undressed. These were in the K-AN-ESS series.

Kelvedon Village Industry. 1918. Kelvedon, Essex. A village industry that made dressed Fairy dolls, character dolls, dolls in East Indian costumes and tumbling dolls.

Keney, Victor. 1930 and later. New York City. Registered in U.S. *Keeneye* as a trademark for dolls and obtained a U.S. patent for dolls. He made primarily *Boudoir* dolls.

Kerduff. 1930 and later. Paris. Made dolls.

Kermit Roosevelt. 1909 and later. Jointed wooden portrait doll made by *Schoenhut* as part of their "Teddy in Africa" set. Kermit often had a camera.

Kern, Christian. 1876–1928. Sonneberg, Thür. Manufactured dolls' articles.

Kern, Wilhelm. 1898. Wallendorf, Thür. Made dolls.

"Kersa" Spielwaren Werkstatte. 1920–30 and later. Mindelheim, Schwaben. Made cloth body dolls.

Kertèsz, Tódor. See **Tódor Kertèsz.**

Kestner, J. D., Jr. 1805–1930 and later. Waltershausen, Thür. 1860–1930 and later, owned a porcelain factory in Ohrdruf known as Kestner & Co. This Ohrdruf porcelain factory had been in existence since the 1840s. Kestner later became affiliated with several other porcelain factories. Kestner supplied most of the bisque heads used by *Catterfelder Puppenfabrik. Rheinische Gummi und Celluloid Fabrik Co.* supplied celluloid heads and parts to Kestner. *Borgfeldt, Butler Bros., Century Doll Co., Horsman, R.H. Macy, Sears, Siegel Cooper, F.A.O. Schwarz,* and others distributed Kestner dolls. Kestner was one of the first firms to make dressed dolls. A considerable number of Kestner heads have the height of the doll in centimeters incised on them but this practice was not as widespread for the Kestner dolls as for the *Kämmer & Reinhardt* dolls. Some dolls have been attributed to Kestner because they have a mold number that is found on marked Kestner dolls from a different mold; also because the way "Made in Germany" is written is similar to that used by Kestner. However, dolls with the same mold number must have the same face in order to have been made by the same company except for slight variations due to size, painting, whether the mouth is open or closed and whether it has glass or painted eyes. Different companies could and did use the same mold numbers for their individually designed heads. However, these designs would vary from one company to another though the mold number was the same.

Some bisque shoulder heads with the customary Kestner size mark on the back edge of the shoulders had in the same location on the inside of the shoulder a stamped incised numeral which may have indicated a code number for a mold, a distributor or a date.

1816: Kestner produced wooden dolls.

1830s: Harlequins with Kestner heads were made in various sizes.

1867: The grandson of J. D. Kestner was Adolf Kestner who made dolls with papier-mâché or wax-over-composition heads on leather or cloth bodies according to the Ciesliks.

1874: A Kestner invoice for dolls sent through the port of Philadelphia listed mostly "Nankin" dolls. These would have had china or bisque heads and limbs on cloth bodies. The duty was 35 percent.

1892–93: Obtained three German Patents (D.R.P.) for dolls' heads and bodies.

1893: Horsman advertised Kestner dolls with bisque heads, wigs, sleeping eyes, gusset jointed kid bodies, bisque hands, with or without footwear. 15 hts. 15 to 28 in. (38 to 71 cm.); priced $9.00 to $42.00 doz. wholesale.

1894: Applied for three German patents (D.R.G.M.) for bathing or swimming porcelain dolls *(Frozen Charlottes).*

1897: Registered the following mold numbers according to the research of the Ciesliks: 11, 12, 120, 121, 122, 123, 124, 125, 126, 127, 128, 129 (Dolly face), 131a, 131b, 132, 133, 134, 135, 136, 137, 138, 140, 141a, 141b, 142b, 143, 144, 145. A 129 head has been found on a body stamped *Bette* (See Ill. 305).

1898: Specialized in dolly-face bisque-head dolls with jointed composition bodies or kid bodies. The Ohrdruf Kestner factory made bisque heads and all-bisque dolls.
  Butler Bros. distributed Kestner's *Marvel* dolls.

1899: Dolls included the *Excelsior* line and all-bisque dolls with and without molded clothes. The dolls with molded clothes including headwear, represented girls and boys. The largest size had jointed shoulders. Hts. 2½, 3¾, and 6 in. (6.5, 9.5, and 15 cm.). All-bisque dolls representing Orientals with pigtails, almond-shaped glass eyes, jointed at the neck, shoulders and hips were 4½ in. (11.5 cm.). tall.
  Butler Bros. also distributed dressed Kestner dolls with bisque heads and composition bodies. Five hts. 20½, 22½, 23, 26 and 27 in. (52, 57, 58.5, 66 and 68.5 cm.).

1899–1914: According to Anne-Marie and Jacques Porot, Kestner made some of the bisque heads for the *Roullet & Decamps* walking dolls, namely *Bébé Système* and *L'Intrépide Bébé* with glass eyes, marked J. D. K. or with painted eyes marked 141 (a reported Kestner mold number).

1902: Butler Bros. advertised Marvel, Excelsior and *Par Excellence* lines as well as baby dolls with bisque heads having a "real baby face," sleeping eyes, open mouth with two teeth, and a fully jointed composition body. Hts. 12¼, 16½, and 19¼ in. (31, 40.5, and 49 cm.); price 72¢ to $1.49 each. Dolls with bisque shoulder heads on cloth bodies had high black boots. Hts. 6, 9½, and 13 in. (15, 24, and 33 cm.); price 42¢ to $1.95 doz. wholesale. All-bisque dolls with mohair wigs, glass eyes, jointed arms, free standing legs and painted footwear came in hts. 3⅛ and 5 in. (8 and 12.5 cm.); price 88¢ and $1.65 doz. wholesale. The 5 in. (12.5 cm.) ht. with sleeping eyes cost $1.82 doz. wholesale. Larger sizes came with jointed hips; hts. 6¾ and 9¼ in. (17 and 23.5 cm.).

1903: Applied for a German patent (D.R.G.M.) for a walking doll.
  Montgomery Ward advertised Kestner dolls with bisque

head, wig, sleeping eyes, teeth, and on a kid body stuffed half with cork, riveted knee and hip joints, composition arms and ball joints at the shoulders, elbows and wrists. Hts. 23, 24½ and 28 in. (58.5, 62 and 71 cm); priced $3.75, $5.00 and $5.75.

They also sold Fat Baby which had a bisque head and kid body. Ht. 8½ in. (21.5 cm.); priced 25¢.

The bisque shoulder heads with wigs, sleep eyes and teeth were sold separately. 10 hts. Price 45¢ to $2.25.

1904: Dolls included china-head dolls with molded hair, china limbs, and a cloth torso. Most of the dolls, including the *Celebrated* dolls, had bisque heads on kid bodies. Some of the kid bodies had Universal (rivet-type) joints. The bisque heads had sleeping eyes and wigs. Kid-body dolls had bisque hands and sold for 19¢ to $5.00 each wholesale. Came in 15 Hts.: 8¼, 11, 13, 15, 17, 19, 20, 22, 23, 23½, 24, 24½, 25½, 26 and 28½ in. (21, 28, 33, 38, 43, 48, 51, 56, 58.5, 59.5, 61, 62, 65, 66, and 72.5 cm.). The 8¼ in. (21 cm.) doll was the chubby dwarf doll which may have been the "Fat baby doll" advertised in 1903.

Kestner also sold dolls with bisque heads on ball-jointed composition bodies with jointed wrists. These dolls with sleeping eyes and wigs were 19½ and 23 in. (49.5 and 58.5 cm.) tall. The 23 in. doll cost $3.50, while the 23 in. kid body doll cost $3.00 each wholesale.

1907: Sears advertised bisque-head, kid-body dolls made by Kestner. They had wigs, sleeping eyes, bisque lower arms, composition lower legs and Universal type joints. Five hts.: 18, 20, 23½, 26, and 28½ in. (45.5, 51, 59.5, 66, and 72.5 cm.); priced $1.75 to $5.00. Sears also sold separate Kestner shoulder heads in five hts.; priced 59¢ to $1.89.

1907–08: R. H. Macy advertised Kestner dolls with bisque heads, wigs and sleeping eyes, on a ball-jointed composition body, dressed in a chemise, shoes and stockings. Came in nine hts. 15, 17, 19, 21, 22, 23, 25, 29, and 33 in. (38, 43, 48, 53.5, 56, 58.5, 63.5, 73.5, and 84 cm.).

1908: Sears had the same hts. as in 1907. They also advertised all-bisque Kestner dolls with wigs, sleeping eyes and hair-eyelashes on all the dolls except the smallest. These dolls were jointed at the shoulders and hips. Hts. 5, 6½, and 10 in. (12.5, 16.5, and 25.5 cm.); priced 25¢, 50¢ and 98¢.

1909–10: Siegel Cooper advertised the Kestner Celebrated dolls as having "Bohemian bisque" heads. This may have meant that the slip (see *Carl Knoll*) or some of the ingredients of the bisque came from Bohemia. Other Kestner kid-body dolls had bisque heads, wigs, sleeping eyes, and rivet joints. Ht. 16½ in. (42 cm.); priced $1.00.

1910: Kidlyne (imitation kid) bodies for small dolls were introduced. Dolls with hair eyebrows and eyelashes were 22½, 25, and 29 in. (57, 63.5, and 73.5 cm.).

Kestner applied for a German patent (D.R.G.M.) for dolls' eyes.

Siegel Cooper advertised bisque head, kid body Kestner dolls with wigs and sleeping eyes in various hts. priced 58¢ to $12.50. Their bisque head, ball-jointed composition body doll with wig, sleeping eyes, dressed in a chemise was 22 in. (56 cm.); priced $1.45.

1911–12: Kestner character heads were used on the Roullet & Decamps dolls that wore a sash reading "DONNEZ MOI LA MAIN, JE MARCHE" (Give me your hand, I walk), according to Anne-Marie and Jacques Porot.

1912: Kestner dolls were imported into Philadelphia by *Winters,* Reinecke. Celebrated dolls with kid bodies were distributed by Butler Bros. Kestner applied for a German patent (D.R.G.M.) for sleeping eyes.

1913: Bisque character baby dolls cost 79¢ each.

1914: Kestner made *Kewpies* and *Hilda* dolls about this time. *John M. Smyth* advertised composition body Kestner dolls. The bisque heads had wigs, sleeping eyes, hair eyelashes, open mouth; dressed in a chemise. Seven hts.: 23, 24½, 27, 29½, 31½, 33, and 34½ in. (58.5, 62, 68.5, 74.5, 80, 84, and 87.5 cm.); priced $2.89 to $11.48.

1915: Borgfeldt handled kid-body Celebrated dolls, jointed composition dolls, and character baby dolls made by Kestner.

1916: Advertised ball-jointed dolls; bent-limb character babies; dolls' heads of bisque, celluloid or papier-mâché; all-bisque and all-china dolls; wigs for dolls.

1918: After the death of Adolf Kestner the firm was managed by Eduard Prechtl, Ernst Florschütz and Ernst Bufe.

1921: Advertised jointed composition body dolls, bent limb character babies, kid body dolls, all-bisque dolls, Kewpies, Googlies, dolls with china heads and limbs and cloth torsos. Dolls' parts included bisque, celluloid and composition heads, arms, legs, torsos, as well as wigs, shoes and stockings.

1923: A large portion of the dolls sold to the various Latin-American countries was pre-World War I stock.

1926: Century advertised Kestner bisque heads exclusive on Century dolls. The bisque heads were on "new type *Mama* dolls with slender bodies and legs and cuddling and sitting babies." Cuddling babies probably had cloth bodies and sitting babies had the bent-limb composition bodies. Kestner bisque heads were used on *Bottle Baby*. There were 10 new head models, some of them with smiling faces. The Kestner heads were put on American-made bodies. Bisque head dressed dolls with wigs and hair eyelashes on slim jointed composition bodies came 18 to 30 in. (45.5 to 76 cm.) tall. Applied for a German patent (D.R.G.M.) for baby dolls.

The sole London agent for Kestner was *Gross & Schild.*

1928: Kestner still was making china dolls. They also made baby dolls with toddler bodies, display dolls, pincushion dolls, tea cosy dolls, and bisque heads for newborn babies and children. Applied for a German patent (D.R.G.M.) for dolls' eyes. Sleeping eyes had hair eyelashes. They used the crown trademark without the streamers.

1930: Advertised Nankeen dolls, dressed and undressed dolls and babies, miniature dolls, leather bodies and other dolls' parts, wigs, shoes, stockings and other dolls' clothes.

ca. 1932: A Kestner catalog reportedly of 1932 showed a wide variety of bisque-head and all-bisque dolls. Many of them resembled dolls that were on the market prior to World

War I. There were bent-limb babies, googlies, all-bisque Kewpie types, all-bisque *Max and Moritz,* all-bisque children with boots having several straps up the front, Frozen Charlotte types, and dolls' house dolls with cloth bodies.

Only two all-bisque black dolls and one fully jointed bisque head black child doll were shown. There was a considerable variation in the types of composition bodies. About 10 percent had bent limbs. The remaining 90 percent was divided nearly equally among regular fully jointed bodies, toddler-type bodies, and the newer slender leg bodies. The diagonal hip joint was found especially on the toddler type bodies. Some kid bodies with entire or lower composition arms and lower composition legs were still being offered.

Most of the dolls had wigs with short hair, either the Dutch bob type with bangs or wavy with a side part. The few dolls without wigs (other than the dolls' house dolls) had molded and painted short hair.

Over two thirds of the dolls were sold dressed and the others wore a chemise in nearly every case. This did not include the many small all-bisque dolls about half of which were sold naked. Only about one in twenty of the dressed dolls represented a boy, the rest were girls or babies.

The Ciesliks reported that the following mold numbers were registered by Kestner in addition to those listed under 1897. The new numbers were 72, 146, 147, 152 (dolly face), 154 (shoulder head dolly face), 155, 168, 171 *(Daisy),* 174, 180, 184 (closed mouth), 186, 187, 195 (shoulder heads, some with holes for hair eyebrows, some brown skin), 201 (some celluloid shoulder heads), 211 (baby), 234, 239, 241 (character face), 237 and 245 (wigged Hilda ca. 1914), 243 (Oriental), 255 (1921 bawling baby also marked O.I.C.), 257 (baby), 260 (toddler baby), 1045 (black), 1070 (painted hair Hilda).

Other mold numbers identified as being Kestner were: 150 (all-bisque), 162 (teenager), 167 (dolly face), 172 *(Gibson Girl),* 173 (Googly), 208, 214 and 215 (hair eyebrows), 220 (baby or toddler with dimples), 221 (Googly); 226 (wig and glass eyes); 249 (dolly face); 263 and 264 (dolly faces) were used by Catterfelder Puppenfabrik.

Kestner made several dolls with additional interchangeable heads. One group with four heads had molds 171, 182, 183 and 190; another group had molds # 171, 180, 186 and 187. The last two heads had painted eyes. A doll reported with three interchangeable heads had mold 174 with an open mouth, 178 with a closed mouth, and 185 with an open mouth; all three of these heads had sleeping glass eyes.

No doubt Kestner made dolls with heads having other mold numbers. However, caution should be used to distinguish the Kestner mold numbers from dolls' heads with the same mold numbers that were used by other factories. It is most unlikely that the baby heads numbered 152, 154 and so on were made by Kestner since these mold numbers on baby heads were used by *Hertel, Schwab.*★

1431. Kestner bisque shoulder head with wig, sleeping eyes, open-closed mouth with teeth. Mark on back of shoulders, "B. Made in Germany 6." H. 19 in. (48 cm.). H. of shoulder head 5 in. (12.5 cm.). *Coleman Collection.*

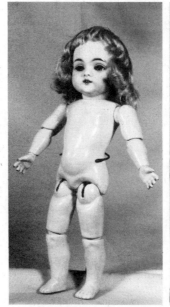

1432A & B. Kestner bisque socket head mold # 143 with wig, sleeping eyes, hair eyelashes, open mouth, two teeth; on a ball-jointed composition body. Mark on neck: III. 1457; a 12 is on the rim of the crown in back and a red stamp "Germany//2/0" on the back of the torso. H. 12½ in. (31.5 cm.). *Coleman Collection.*

1433. Bisque shoulder-head doll made by Kestner using mold # 148. It has a wig, stationary brown glass eyes, open mouth, and a gusseted kid body with bisque lower arms and cloth legs. H. 15 in. (38 cm.). *Courtesy of Sotheby Parke Bernet Inc., N.Y.*

1435. Lady-type bisque socket head doll made by Kestner with mold # 162. It has a wig, sleeping brown glass eyes, open mouth with teeth and a ball jointed composition body. H. 18 in. (45.5 cm.). *Courtesy of Richard Withington. Photo by Barbara Jendrick.*

1434. Bisque shoulder-head doll made by Kestner with their mold # 154. It has a wig, sleeping brown glass eyes, open mouth with four upper teeth, and a tongue. The kid body has lower arms of bisque and lower legs of composition. Mark on head: Ill. 1458. H. 26 in. (66 cm.). H. of shoulder head 6 in. (15 cm.). *Courtesy of Helen Read. Photo by Steven Read.*

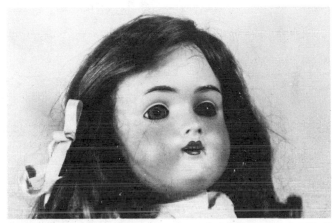

1436. Bisque head made by Kestner using their mold # 168. It has a wig, sleeping blue glass eyes, and an open mouth with teeth molded in the bisque. Mark on head Ill. 1459. H. of head only, 5¾ in. (14.5 cm.). Circumference of head 11 in. (28 cm.). *Courtesy of Helen Read. Photo by Steven Read.*

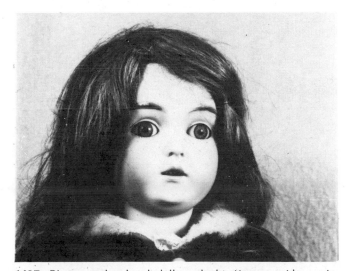

1437. Bisque socket head doll made by Kestner with a wig, sleeping blue glass eyes, hair eyelashes, pierced ears, open mouth, and a ball jointed composition body with wrist not jointed. Mold # 171. This number was often used by THE LADIES' HOME JOURNAL as their premium for a doll called Daisy which was distributed around 1910. H. 24 in. (61 cm.). *Courtesy of and photo by Cherry Bou.*

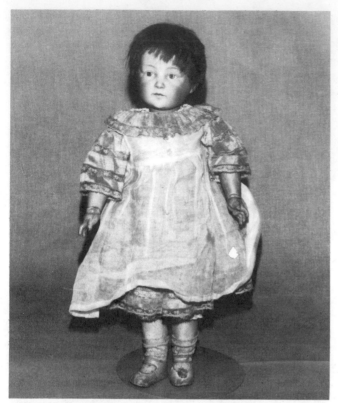

1438. Kestner bisque socket head doll mold # 187. This head was also used for the multi-head Kestner dolls. This doll has a wig, painted eyes, closed mouth and a fully jointed composition body. Original clothes. The doll came in its original Kestner box. H. 17 in. (43 cm.). *Courtesy of the late Magda Byfield.*

1439. Bisque shoulder head doll made by Kestner. It has a wig, fur eyebrows, sleeping blue glass eyes, open mouth with four upper teeth, and a kid body with bisque lower arms. It is mold # 195. Mark on head: Ill. 1462. Oval paper label on the chest for Kestner. H. 17½ in. (44.5 cm.). *Courtesy of Helen Read. Photo by Steven Read.*

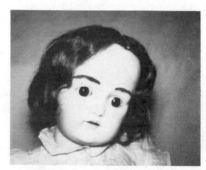

1441. Kestner bisque head mold # 215 with fur eyebrows. It has a wig, sleeping glass eyes, open mouth with teeth and is on a ball jointed composition body. Mark on head: "made in//K. Germany 14 //J. D. K.//215." H. 25½ in. (65 cm.). *Coleman Collection.*

1440. Kestner bisque socket head baby doll mold # 211. The wig is missing. It has sleeping blue glass eyes, open-closed mouth and a five-piece bent limb composition body. H. 15½ in. (39.5 cm.). *Courtesy of Sotheby Parke Bernet Inc., N.Y.*

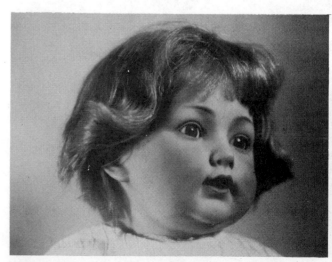

1442. Kestner bisque head doll mold # 220. It has a wig, sleeping blue glass eyes, open mouth with two upper teeth, and a toddler-type jointed composition body. Mark: Ill. 1463. H. 22 in. (56 cm.). Circumference of head 15 in. (38 cm.). *Courtesy of Helen Read. Photo by Steven Read.*

1443. Kestner bisque head doll mold # 221 has a wig, round brown glass eyes looking to the side, closed smiling mouth; a type of doll sometimes called a "googly." The fully jointed composition body has short, plump legs. H. 11 in. (28 cm.). *Courtesy of Sotheby Parke Bernet Inc., N.Y.*

1444. Hilda bisque head doll made by Kestner. It has molded and painted hair, blue glass eyes, and is on a composition bent limb baby body. Original clothes. H. 16 in. (40.5 cm.). *Private collection.*

1445. Kestner bisque socket head doll mold # 243, with Oriental features. It has a black wig, sleeping dark glass eyes, open mouth with two upper teeth, and an olive-colored bent-limb baby composition body. H. 13 in. (34 cm.). *Courtesy of Sotheby Parke Bernet Inc., N.Y.*

1446. All-bisque doll made ca. 1914 with wig, painted eyes, open-closed mouth, molded footwear. The head, arms and legs are all marked "130//2." Dolls with similar marks and similar molded footwear were attributed to Kestner by Genevieve Angione. H. 5 in. (12.5 cm.). *Coleman Collection.*

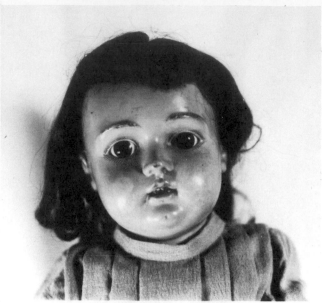

1447A & B. Pair of all-bisque dolls made by Kestner and representing Max & Moritz. They have molded and painted hair, features and shoes; jointed at the neck, shoulders and hips. The faces and hands portray the mischievousness of these two characters. The tops of their legs are marked 187, probably a mold number. All-bisque dolls with molded clothes have been found in a Kestner catalog with the No. 186. These dolls also resemble Max and Moritz. H. 4½ in. (11.5 cm.). Moritz's topknot extends a little above this height. *Coleman Collection.*

1448. Celluloid-head doll made for Kestner from their mold # 201. It has a wig, stationary brown glass eyes, open mouth with four teeth; and a kid body. Mark on head: Ill. 2221. The J. D. K. part is incised and the turtle part is embossed. H. 21 in. (53.5 cm.). *Courtesy of Helen Read. Photo by Steven Read.*

No. 585

No. 585—Kid Body Doll. Extra quality, fourteen inches tall, movable arms and legs. This is also an **imported** doll of great popularity on account of its wearing qualities. Will outlast any of the stuffed dolls, as the kid covering is extra strong and carefully sewed. Has beautiful bisque head with curly hair and movable eyes. Sent complete with slippers and stockings for four yearly subscriptions at 35c each, or one subscription at 35c and 60c extra.

1449. Doll made by Kestner offered as a magazine subscription premium in 1913. This bisque-head doll with wig, sleeping glass eyes and a kid body cost 60¢ plus a 35¢ subscription. H. 14 in. (35.5 cm.).

Girls—This Large, Magnificent Doll
Given for only 6 McCall subscriptions

Premium 741

Premium 741—This is the biggest value in dolls we have ever offered. Think of it! This doll is 22 inches high. Among the special features of this genuine bisque doll are its beautiful eyes, which open and close; and very pretty hair. Being jointed, it can be placed in any position. Price $2.50. This is the best doll we have ever offered because it is made by the famous Kestner factory in Germany. Sent express collect for only 6 yearly subscriptions at 50 cents each. Express prepaid for 3 extra subscriptions.

1450. Kestner bisque head doll on a fully jointed composition body offered as a subscription premium by McCALL'S in 1913. It has a wig, sleeping glass eyes, a fancy chemise and footwear. H. 22 in. (56 cm.); price $2.50 or six 50¢ subscriptions. The express delivery cost three extra subscriptions, making a total of nine subscriptions.

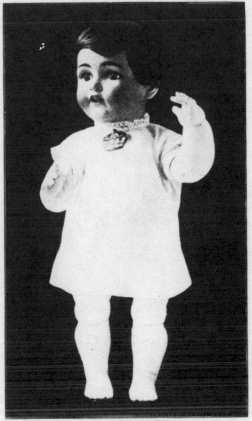

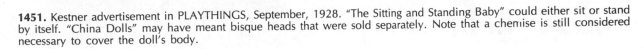

1451. Kestner advertisement in PLAYTHINGS, September, 1928. "The Sitting and Standing Baby" could either sit or stand by itself. "China Dolls" may have meant bisque heads that were sold separately. Note that a chemise is still considered necessary to cover the doll's body.

b Germany 3

1452

19

C$\frac{1}{2}$ made in Germany

1453

made in Germany. G.

1454

made in Germany L

1455

E made in Germany 9
129.

1456

12
made in
A. Germany 5
143.

1457

154.12. dep.

H. made in Germany.

1458

E$\frac{1}{2}$ made in 9$\frac{1}{2}$
Germany.
168
08.

1459

185.

1460

made in Germany.

E.198.9.

1461

Dep. 195.6$\frac{1}{2}$

1462 A   +

B$\frac{1}{2}$ made in Germany

1462 B

M. made in   16.
Germany.
J. D. K.
220.^{15}

1463

made in
A. Germany. 5.
J.D.K.
221.
1464   Ges. gesch.

J.D.K.
221.
Ges. gesch.

1465

F made in
Germany 10
243
J.D.K.

1466

J.D.K.
made in Germany

1471

y made in 13.
Germany.
247.
J.D.K.
13.

1467

J.D.K.
made in 12
Germany

1472

J.D.K.
Made in 13. Germany

1473

J.D.K.
257
made in
Germany
31

1468

Germany
J. D. K.
257
made in
Germany
31.

1469

Kestner
Made in Germany

1474

1475

1476

made in
Germany
JDK
257

1470

1477

1452–1477. Kestner marks usually on bisque heads. These include mold #s 129 through 257. Mark No. 1474 is a red stamp on the back of a composition body. One- and two-digit numbers are sometimes also found in various places on Kestner heads. For example, mold #143 (Ill. 1457) has a "12" not with the rest of the mark but incised on the rim of the crown at the back. Ill. 1463 has the 15 in its proper place.

Ketsy Piper. See **Little Shavers.**

Kewpie®. 1912–80 and later. Designed by Rose O'Neill, who held the design patents. *Borgfeldt* had the manufacturing rights for many years and later passed them on to *Joseph Kallus.* Many companies made Kewpies either under contracts or special licenses. In 1982 Joseph Kallus still controlled the Kewpie trademark and copyright but by 1984 Jesco had taken over the rights for the Kewpies after the death of Mr. Kallus. There were many legal battles over the manufacture of Kewpies without consent of the copyright or patent owners. During World War I and thereafter companies in Japan were often found guilty of infringements. Kewpies were made of all-bisque, celluloid, cloth, composition, rubber, vinyl, zylonite and probably other materials.

Kewpie figurines, sometimes called "action Kewpies," had mold numbers at least from 4843 through 4883; 4868 and 4871 had A and B versions. 4844 and 4861 had A, B, and C versions. These mold #s were registered in Germany according to the research of the Ciesliks.

A round paper sticker on the back of a Kewpie was marked as follows: Clockwise "KEWPIE DES. PAT. III. 4. 1913." "Germany" was counter-clockwise at the base. In the middle ring clockwise was "REG. U.S. PAT. OFF." In the center was the copyright symbol ©. This mark resembled in style but differed in words from the mark in Ill. 1482. On the front of this doll is the heart shaped sticker marked "KEWPIE //REG. U.S.//PAT. OFF."

1909: Mr. Kallus stated that small Kewpie figurines were made.

1913: Rose O'Neill wrote an article on the origin of the Kewpies that was published in the June issue of TOYS AND NOVELTIES, as follows:

"To come to the Kewpies; they were born about four Christmases ago in the LADIES' HOME JOURNAL. For several years before, when I illustrated love stories for the magazines, I used to make headings and tail pieces with a few top-knotted cupids in them, doing some quaint thing connected with the story. The editor of the LADIES' HOME JOURNAL cut out some of these little fellows, sent them to me and asked me to make a series for children with them, kindly offering to have the verses written for me.

"'I'll write my own verses,' said I proudly; and I sent him an illustrated letter full of Kewpies; the name I invented, as being 'little' for cupid. In that letter I put fragmentary verses and drawings and outlined the Kewpish character and possible future deeds to be distinguished by kindliness and funniness and philosophy, besides being cheerfully idiotic.

"The Kewpies moved later to the WOMAN'S HOME COMPANION, where they are in their third year. The numbers of the first year are already out in book form and the later ones will be in their turn. Hundreds of letters about them arrive from children all over the world, also from their kind parents, grandmas, maiden aunts and bachelor uncles. Well, they began to utter such things as, 'I wish we had a Kewpie we could hold,' or 'Could you make us a Kewpie to hang on the Christmas tree?'

"I put my finger to my brow and—produced Kewpie Cut-outs. Kewpie Klubs were formed. New mothers wrote me their babies were Kewpies, and they were training their

hair in top-knots. Then about two years ago doll factories began to write, saying 'Make a real Kewpie doll. Can you model one in clay?' I had never modeled in clay—but I did. I made a Kewpie doll. Then I picked a doll house and they told me to go to Germany, to the Thüringer Forest, where the people do nothing but make toys, never stopping to play with them. I did.

"I left my lovely Capri in the Bay of Naples, where I live a good deal of the time, completely surrounded by roses, and I went to Germany. And, the Thüringer toy makers said, 'Look, here comes a new woman.' But they were not afraid of me long, because they found me so harmless and Kewpish.

"And some months after, when I had returned to New York, Kewpies were coming into the harbor by the ship-load and people were writing to me every day to let them make Kewpie ice cream moulds, Kewpie postcards, Kewpie calendars, Kewpie shirties, Kewpie cradles, Kewpie eartads, Kewpie cups and saucers, Kewpie spoons, knives, forks, shoes, stockings, baby carriages, Valentines, dinner cards, table decorations, cotillion favors, Christmas hangings, nursery friezes, hoods, coats, union suits, caps, baby jumpers, rattles, writing paper, slates, tablets, nursing bottles—must I go on?"

A single store in Indianapolis ordered 1,000 Kewpies. They came in several sizes and in bisque or celluloid.

1914: All-bisque Kewpies came in four hts. 5½, 6¼, 7⅜, and 8¾ in. (14, 16, 18.5 and 22 cm.). All-celluloid Kewpies were jointed at the shoulders. Hts. 4¾, 5½, 7¼ in. (12, 14 and 18.5 cm.); priced 23¢ to 69¢.

1915: All-celluloid Kewpies came in hts. 4½, 5½ and 6½ in. (11.5, 14, and 16.5 cm.); priced 23¢ to 69¢. Rose O'Neill lost a case to William Hecht for the use of the name and trademark "Kewpie" for children's suits. She had recently contracted with a third party for a similar use for children's suits.

1916: TOYS AND NOVELTIES reported "One does not see as many Kewpies now as formerly, but they are buying them by the millions in Australia, New Zealand, Japan and elsewhere."

1917: Dolls called "Kewpies" were made by the *Lord Roberts' Memorial Workshops.* They were composition with shoulder joints. Hts. 6 and 8 in. (15 and 20.5 cm.); price 25¢ and 50¢. *Hamley* distributed Kewpies with moving heads and arms; priced $1.12 and $2.12 doz. wholesale.

Wyman, Partridge advertised all-bisque Kewpies with painted hair and eyes, jointed at the shoulders. Hts. 6 and 10 in. (15 and 25.5 cm.).

1918: Composition Kewpies were made by *K. & K.* A trademark for Kewpies was registered in France.

Shackman advertised 2 in. (5 cm.) celluloid Kewpies for 10¢. The bisque Kewpies were 4 and 6 in. (10 and 15 cm.). These bisque Kewpies came undressed costing 25¢ and 50¢; and dressed ones costing 60¢ to $1.25. The most expensive ones were dressed as a bride and groom.

Kewpies were used for pillow dolls, to adorn candy boxes and for other decorative purposes. Rose O'Neill and Borgfeldt won an infringement suit against Cinquini.†

1919: *Katherine Rauser* dressed Kewpies as flowers with matching headdresses. Among these flowers were roses, pansies and Easter lilies. Other Kewpies wore dresses and sweaters.

Sears distributed all-composition Kewpies with jointed arms. Ht. 8½ in. (21.5 cm.); priced 98¢ naked and $1.15 to $1.98 dressed.

1920: Celluloid Kewpies with jointed shoulders came in five hts.: 3¼, 6, 7, 9 and 11½ in. (8, 15, 18, 23 and 29 cm.).

1921: Innovations for Kewpies distributed by *Butler Bros.* were all-composition Kewpies with wigs. Hts. 9, 10½ and 12½ in. (23, 26.5 and 31.5 cm.) had mohair wigs. The 12½ in. ht. also came with human hair wigs. Some Kewpies with composition heads and hands had cork stuffed cloth bodies jointed at shoulders and hips. These dolls wore lawn dresses and came in hts. 12½ and 21½ in. (31.5 and 54.5 cm.); price $7.80 and $9.00 doz. wholesale. (See THE COLLECTOR'S BOOK OF DOLLS' CLOTHES, Ill. 726.) Kewpies were dressed in various costumes. Rose O'Neill herself dressed Kewpies in a silk cap and a matching ribbon sash with a big bow. One group of Kewpies wore regional costumes such as that of a Hindu girl, a lady from a harem, and a naked Kewpie with a French hat according to TOYS AND NOVELTIES. Large Kewpies wore removable, washable pinafores and dresses. These clothes had buttons and tiny handmade button holes.

1922: Kewpies were manufactured by the *Phoenix Doll Co.*

1924: *Nelke* advertised stockinet Kewpies in two sizes priced 50¢ and $1.00.

1925: Shackman advertised all-bisque and all-celluloid Kewpies dressed in crepe paper. The all-celluloid Kewpies came in black or white versions; hts. 2¼ and 3¼ in. (5.5 and 8 cm.). All-bisque Kewpies came in five hts. 4½, 5¾, 6½, 8 and 10 in. (11.5, 14.5, 16.5, 21.5 and 25.5 cm.).

There was also a 9 in. (23 cm.) dressed all-bisque Kewpie. Many of the Kewpies were dressed as members of bridal parties.

1926: Celluloid Kewpies were imported into Britain from Japan by *Fapowlea Co.*

1927: Featherweight Kewpies were made with handpainted cloth mask faces made by *M. F. Fluegelman.*

1929: *Cuddle* (Cuddly) Kewpie, a cloth doll, was introduced.

PLAYTHINGS in November 1929 published an article signed by Rose O'Neill. The article was as follows:

"Rose O'Neill Tells How She Created Cuddle Kewpies

"The idea of the Kewpies first came to me about twenty years ago in a dream. But their origin dates still farther back to my childhood, when I used to be enraptured with my baby brother and was always making little drawings of his funny little looks and gestures.

"It was all those stored-up memories of babyism that came out in the Kewpies—the things that made me call the baby, 'The Tender Clown.'

"Kewpie top-knot was the little lock that used to stand up from the baby's head on the pillow. The tiny wings came naturally from the baby character, half elf, half angel.

"The name Kewpie was baby-talk for 'Cupid,' spelled with a 'Kew,' because it looked funnier.

"I had been publishing the Kewpie drawings and verses in magazines about a year when I modelled the first Kewpie figure.

"Children had begun writing to me from various places in the world, asking if I would not make a Kewpie they could hold in their hands.

"The toy-factories, too began to ask the same question. So I modelled nine sizes of Kewpie dolls and they went all'round the earth, made in hard materials, bisque, celluloid, rubber, composition.

"But I was not satisfied. I wanted a Kewpie that would be soft to the touch, a Kewpie that would melt in your arms.

"So I planned that huggable Kewpie for years, and at last my youngest sister, Callista O'Neill, helped me work out the jolly little patterns, because scizzors [sic] and needles are not my strong point.

"She would cut and stuff and cut and stuff: each time submitting the little soft thing to me for criticism.

"And at last, we got the perfect cuddle-Kewpie.

"She knows as much now about his little round contours as I do.

"And now Mr. Jack Cohen of the King Innovation, Inc., Novelties, knows all about it too."

And the article goes on to say: "The Kewpie Philosophy is soft. It has no angles. There's nothing implacable, hard or horny about it."

1931: An advertisement of *Eckstein & Co.* showed a Cuddle Kewpie with similar body construction but a slightly different face from the one introduced in 1929.

1951: All-bisque Kewpies made in a factory in East Germany and imported to America by Borgfeldt who claimed "the quality is about as good as when imported before the War" (presumably World War II). These Kewpies came in three heights, one of which was 6 in. (15 cm.) and were stamped "Germany" on the body. This mark rubbed off easily and it became difficult to distinguish these 1950s Kewpies from the early ones.

1983: Taken over by Jesco after the death of Joseph Kallus. ★

1478. All-bisque Kewpie with usual molded and painted hair and features including the wings. Mark on soles of feet: "O'Neill." H. 4½ in. (11.5 cm.). *Coleman Collection.*

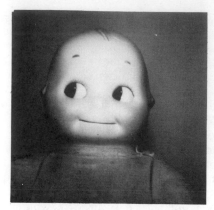

1479. Bisque head Kewpie with molded and painted hair and eyes, flange neck on a cloth body, blue wings, starfish shaped bisque hands. Mark on back of neck: Ill. 1483. H. of doll 12 in. (30.5 cm.). H. of head 4 in. (10 cm.). *Courtesy of the late Mary Roberson.*

1481

1482

1483

Made in Germany
1377

KEWPIE
Germany

1484

KEWPIE
DES. & COPYRIGHT
ROSE O'NEILL

1485

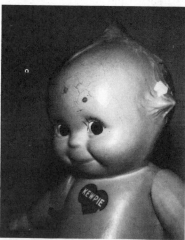

1480A & B. All-composition Kewpie with jointed shoulders and a red heart-shaped decal mark; molded hair and painted features. Mark: Ill. 1485 H. 11 in. (28 cm.). *Coleman Collection.*

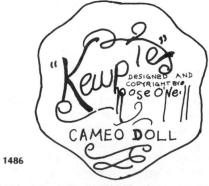

"Kewpie"
DESIGNED AND
COPYRIGHT BY
Rose O'Neill
CAMEO DOLL

1486

1481–1486. Marks found on Kewpie dolls produced by Borgfeldt. No. 1486 is a tag found on a composition Kewpie with a wig.

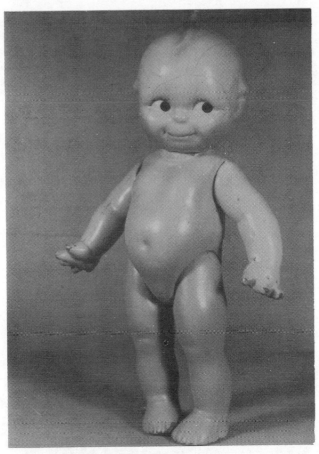

1487. All-composition Kewpie-type jointed at the neck (socket in head), shoulders, and hips. Molded hair and painted features, no wings and no mark. H. 12½ in. (31.5 cm.). *Coleman Collection.*

1488. Kewpie-type all-composition doll, a Japanese imitation without wings or joints. Small doll. *Coleman Collection.*

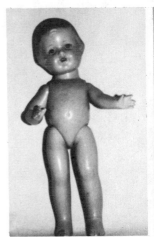

1489A & B. All-composition doll named Kewty with molded and painted hair, sleeping blue metal and celluloid eyes, open mouth with two upper teeth, neck socket in the head and a five-piece body. Mark: Ill. 1490. H. 13½ in. (34 cm.). *Courtesy of Dorothy Annunziato.*

KEWTY

1490. Kewty mark embossed on the back shoulders of an all composition doll.

Kewty (Kewtie). 1930. All-composition jointed character doll made by *Domec.* Ht. 15 in. (38 cm.).

Kickapoo. 1911–14. Doll's head copyrighted in 1910, produced by *Horsman* and probably designed by *Helen Trowbridge.* This composition doll, style no. 152, represented a dark-skinned Indian boy with molded hair and painted eyes. It wore the same style rompers as the *Campbell Kids* of this period. Instead of a belt on these khaki colored rompers there were red tabs across the bottom of the yoke and down the side of the garment. A red head-band held gaudy feathers. *Pocahontas* was the mate to Kickapoo.★

Kicker. 1916. Felt doll made by *Steiff.* Hts. 43 and 50 cm. (17 and 19½ in.).

Kid, The. See **Jackie Coogan Kid.**

Kid Bodies. At least as early as the beginning of the 1800s–1930 and later. Many of the early china heads were on kid bodies which often had no joints except where the arm was attached. Lady bodies of gusseted kid were popular after about 1860. Kid was used extensively for the bodies of dolls representing children, especially in Germany during the 1880s to 1930s. The similarity of kid to human skin and its adaptability to small shapes made it desirable for dolls' bodies. Around 1900 imitation kid began to be used on less expensive dolls.

1860: The Day Book of *John D. Robbins,* made available

No. 152 "Kickapoo"   No. 153 "Pocahontas"

No. 152 "KICKAPOO" and
No. 153 "POCAHONTAS"
Trade Mark
(Head copyrighted, 1910, by
E. I. Horsman Co.)
The picture tells the whole story
about these attractive and comical little
Indians' boy and girl. Their costumes
are of brown khaki trimmed with bright
red. Head bands are red with gaudy
feathers.
Either Doll. Per Dozen, $8.50

1491. Kickapoo and Pocahontas as advertised in a Horsman catalog of 1914. They have dark composition heads with molded and painted hair and eyes, closed mouth, Campbell Kid type composition hands on cloth bodies. The heads were copyrighted in 1910. *Courtesy of Bernard Barenholtz.*

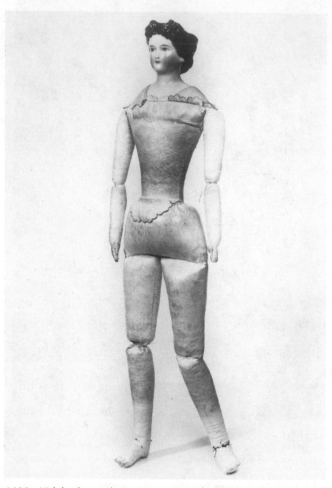

1492. Kid body made in Germany. The edges of the kid are scalloped and the joints are sewn and not gusseted. This body has a low waist and with the hair style of the china head an 1870s date is suggested. *Courtesy of the Worthing Museum.*

through the courtesy of Elizabeth Pierce, listed 12 sizes of kid body dolls, 8/0 to 4 undressed and sizes 7/0 to 2 dressed. The undressed dolls cost 31¢ to $2.01 doz. wholesale and the dressed dolls cost 88¢ to $3.24 doz. wholesale.

1878: *Printemps* store in Paris advertised fully jointed kid body dolls: [probably the French lady dolls] in four hts. 32, 35, 36 and 38 cm. (12½, 13½, 14, and 15 in.); priced 75¢ to $1.35.

1885: *Horsman* advertised eight sizes or styles of kid bodies priced $2.75 to $9.00 doz. wholesale; with bisque arms the prices rose to $4.25 to $14.75 doz. wholesale, and the "Fine Kid" bodies with shoes and stockings cost $7.00 to $18.00 doz. wholesale.

Ca. 1933: Kid bodies had arms of kid, bisque, composition or celluloid.★

Kid Dolls and/or Dolls' Heads. See Leather Dolls.

Kidd, Etta. 1927–30. New York City. President of *Etta Inc.* designed dolls for this company.

Kiddie Karakters. 1929. Line of dolls made by *Averill Manufacturing Co.* distributed by *Bing Wolf.* These dolls had the same heads as *Little Brother* and *Little Sister* designed by *Grace Corry.* They were dressed in costumes representing Mother Goose characters such as *Mother Goose, Little Bo-Peep, Mary Had a Little Lamb* and *Little Boy Blue.* One of this line was dressed as *Captain Kidd,* the pirate. Each of these dolls had a rectangular tag pinned to its clothes.

Kiddie Pal. Ca. 1925–30. Line of composition head dolls made by *Regal* distributed by *Butler Bros.* These dolls had molded hair, painted or sleeping eyes, cloth body with composition limbs and usually a mama or a crying voice.

1927: Advertised Kiddie Pal Dolly and Kiddie Pal Babies.

1928: Registered a heart-shaped trademark in U.S. for dolls. Dolls dressed in lawn with a matching bonnet and colored

1493. Shapely kid body without joints made of 14 pieces of leather, straight edge around the shoulders, stub hands; the original poured bisque head has the so-called Alice-in-Wonderland hairdo popular in the 1860s. This head was probably made in Germany but the origin of the kid body is uncertain. H. 8½ in. (21.5 cm.). *Coleman Collection.*

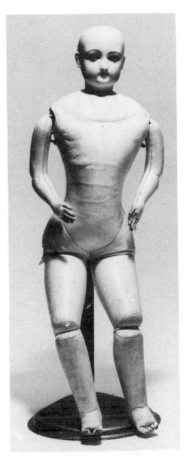

1494. Shapely kid body with bisque head and shoulders made by François Gaultier. It is not known who made the body which has gusset joints at the elbows, hips, and knees. Each finger and toe is separate. Mark on shoulder, "F. G." H. 21½ in. (54.5 cm.). *Courtesy of Sotheby Parke Bernet Inc., N.Y.*

slippers came 20 and 27 in. (51 and 68.5 cm.) tall; priced $21.00 doz. and $3.25 each wholesale. The larger dolls had hair eyelashes.

1929: The 20 in. (51 cm.) ht. came without hair eyelashes and voice. A 26 in. (66 cm.) doll with eyelashes and mama voice cost $3.10 each wholesale. (See THE COLLECTOR'S BOOK OF DOLLS' CLOTHES, Ills. 770E and 775E.)

1930: Line included dolls named *Billy, Dorothy Jane, Hugme, Judy, Kinky, Kiss Me, Love Me, Smiles* and *Sonny Boy.* (See also **Kiddie Pale Baby.**)★

Kiddie Pale Baby. Label on a doll made by *Regal.* The doll has a composition head, painted hair and eyes, an open–closed mouth with two upper teeth. Ht. 16½ in. (42 cm.). The word Pale in the mark may have been a misspelling of Pal. See Ills. 1497 and 1498.

Kiddie Specialty Corp. 1924–27. New York City. Made popular priced dolls with cloth bodies. Their line of dolls were distributed by *Baker & Bennett, Edwin E. Besser, Owens-Kreiser, Strobel & Wilken* and *Louis Wolf* and were priced 25¢, 50¢, and $1.00.

Kiddiejoy (Kiddie Joy). 1922–30 and probably later. Line of domestic and imported dolls handled by *Hitz, Jacobs & Kassler* and their successor Jacobs & Kassler specialized in composition or bisque head baby dolls and Mama dolls. Some if not all of these bisque heads were made by *Armand Marseille.* Among these were mold #s 372 and 375, a Mama doll with a shoulder head on a cloth body size number 6, 24 in. (61 cm.) tall, and other mold #s such as 991 and 993.

1923: Some of the Kiddiejoy Mama dolls advertised in the Hitz, Jacobs and Kassler 1923 catalog were made by *Acme.* The Kiddiejoy dolls had composition heads and hands with cloth bodies and came in the following variations:
Painted hair and eyes, came in nine hts. 14½, 15, 16, 17, 18, 19, 20, 21, and 24 in. (37, 38, 40.5, 43, 45.5, 48, 51, 53.5, and 61 cm.).
Wig and painted eyes came in six hts. 15, 17, 19, 20, 21, and 25 in. (38, 43, 48, 51, 53.5, and 63.5 cm.).

"*Madame Hendren*"
KIDDIE KARAKTERS

HENDRENIZE YOUR DOLL DEPARTMENT

LITTLE BO PEEP

MOTHER GOOSE

MARY HAD A LITTLE LAMB

LITTLE BOY BLUE

From out the pages of rhyme and story come these nursery "Karakters"—Display them—they'll sell on sight.

Space permits showing just a few of the many numbers.

Write or wire for sample dozen via Express Prepaid.

CAPTAIN KIDD
The Pirate Bold

AVERILL CO. INC. - 37 UNION SQUARE, N.Y.

We will appreciate your courtesy in mentioning PLAYTHINGS.

1495. Kiddie Karakters made by Averill Manufacturing Co., shown in a PLAYTHINGS, May 1912 advertisement. All of the dolls except Mother Goose are from the Grace Corry Little Brother mold.

1496. Mark on a Kiddie Pal composition body doll made by Regal Doll Manufacturing Co.

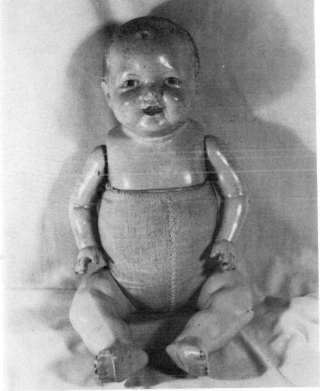

1497. Kiddie Pale, name on a composition head doll made by Regal. This may be one of the line of Kiddie Pal dolls. It has molded blond hair and blue eyes, open-closed mouth with two painted upper teeth. The composition extends down to a waist flange that fits into a lower cloth torso. The arms are rubber and the bent legs are composition. Mark: Ill. 1498. H. 19 in. (48 cm.). *Courtesy of Helen Read. Photo by Steven Read.*

"KIDDIE PALE DOLLY"

REGAL DOLL MFG. CO. INC.

1498. Kiddie Pale mark on a composition head doll made by Regal.

Wig and moving eyes, hts. 16 and 18 in. (40.5 and 45.5 cm.).

Black version, painted hair and eyes, ht. 20 in. (51 cm.).

Dolls with composition heads, arms and legs came in the following variations:

Painted hair and eyes, ht. 20 in. (51 cm.).

Wig and painted eyes came in four hts. 18, 20, 21 and 24 in. (45.5, 51, 53.5, and 61 cm.).

Wig and moving eyes came in four hts. 16, 18, 20 and 24 in. (40.5, 45.5, 51 and 61 cm.).

The cheapest doll was the 17 in. (43 cm.) one with painted hair and eyes at $13.50 a doz. wholesale. This doll was dressed in a "cheap bowered [?flowered] dress and cap. All cotton." The most expensive dolls were the 24 in. (61 cm.) ones with composition heads, arms and legs, wigs and sleeping eyes at $60.00 a doz. wholesale. These dolls were dressed in dotted Swiss or a basket weave dress, both with matching bloomers. A total of 66 numbers of Kiddiejoy Mama dolls were listed in the 1923 catalog, some of these dolls differ only in costume. Of the 38 dolls illustrated all had caps or bonnets except four with ribbon bows in their wigs. The dresses were about knee length and when shorter the matching bloomers showed. Six of the dolls were dressed in rompers and two of these, the ones with belts, are designated as boys. The "Chocolate Drop" wore poplin rompers without a belt. The more expensive dolls wore dotted swiss, organdy, dotted voile or basket weave fabric. The cheaper dolls wore crepe, poplin, checked or flowered voile. The most popular dress, shown on four of the 38 illustrated dolls, is a light colored voile dress, trimmed with black lace around the scalloped skirt bottom, the neckline and the sleeves as well as a piece of lace down the upper center front. Four of the dolls had patch pockets on their dresses. All the dolls wore white socks and dark single strap slippers.

1926: Advertised a newborn baby type with bisque head, painted hair, brown or blue sleeping eyes, celluloid hands, bent-limb cloth body with crier, dressed in a short baby dress of voile and booties. This doll came in four sizes, priced $4.00 a doz. and up wholesale. The picture looks like *My Dream Baby.* There were other Kiddiejoy babies as well as accessories such as bathrobes, rubber pants, blankets, knitted cap and jackets. Jacobs & Kassler registered Kiddiejoy as a trademark in U.S. for dolls.

1927: New Born baby sold in a cradle was called *Cradle Babe.*

1928: Dolls were named *Baby Charming* and *Me Too,* an infant doll.

1930: PLAYTHINGS advertised Kiddiejoy dolls with light weight bodies, dressed in baby clothes with cap and booties.★

Kiddiekins. 1921. Line of dolls designed by *Gertrude Rollinson.*

Kiddieland. 1913. Name of a googly eyed doll sold by *Gamage,* who advertised that the expression could be changed by moving the eyes. It came dressed in a coat and hat; the most expensive version also had a muff. Two hts. priced 46¢ and 98¢.

1499. Kiddiejoy line of dolls advertised in PLAYTHINGS, May, 1927. One of these dolls named "Cradle Babe" had a bisque head, sleeping glass eyes and was dressed. Other dolls in this line included composition head Mama dolls.

1500. Bisque head infant doll in the Kiddiejoy line produced by Jacobs & Kassler. It has a dome-shaped head, sleeping blue glass eyes, closed mouth, and a bent limb composition baby body. H. 9½ in. (24 cm.). *Courtesy of Sotheby Parke Bernet Inc., N.Y.*

1501. Mark on a Kiddiejoy bisque head made by Armand Marseille for Jacobs & Kassler.

Kiddie Doll. 1924. *Mama* doll with composition head and arms, wig, cloth body and a bloomer frock, distributed by *Montgomery Ward.* Ht. 15½ in. (39.5 cm.); priced 83¢.

Kiddlums. 1917–18. Trademark registered by *Tah Toys* in Britain. The flesh colored stockinet dolls in this line had wigs, glass eyes and removable clothes. The dolls representing girls were dressed in silk with lace trimmed combination underclothes. The boy dolls wore silk shirts with large turned down white collars and velveteen knickers.

Kiddykin. See **Perls, Charles.**

Kidette. 1917–20. Name of a line of dolls with *British Ceramic* heads, wigs, sleeping or stationary glass eyes, and jointed imitation kid, hair or wool stuffed bodies, made by *Speights.* Some of these dolls came in five different styles of wigs; price $4.62 and up.★

Kidlet. Ca. 1917–18. Name given to imitation Kewpie dolls of bisque or celluloid by *Shackman.* The all-bisque Kidlets were dressed as Indians, Dutchmen, farmers, fishermen, clowns and so on. Ht. 4¾ in. (12 cm.); price 50¢. All-celluloid Kidlets, ht. 6 in. (15 cm.); price 10¢. A baby doll with a Kidlet face emitted a cry when pressed down. Ht. 5 in. (12.5 cm.); price 15¢.

Kidlyn. A box marked "Kidlyn Doll" contained a dolly-faced doll with a bisque head having a *Heubach* of Köppelsdorf mark, mold # 275 and a size no. 16/0; on an imitation kid body. Ht. 12 in. (30.5 cm.).★

Kidlyne. 1906–24. Imitation kid body used by *Kestner* in their *Marvel* line, distributed by *Butler Bros.*

1910: Dolls had bisque heads with wigs, glass eyes, open mouth with teeth. The Kidlyne bodies were stuffed with cork and sawdust. Hts. 11 and 12½ in. (28 and 31.5 cm.). The larger size had sleeping eyes.

1924: Dolls had bisque heads with wigs and sleeping eyes on Kidlyne bodies. Hts. 12½ and 15 in. (31.5 and 38 cm.) had bisque hands; hts. 13¼ and 17¼ in. (33.5 and 44 cm.) had bisque forearms, and were jointed at the shoulders, hips, elbows, and knees. ★

Kidolene. 1920–30 and later. Imitation kid used for dolls' bodies. Ca 1933. came with bisque forearms or celluloid hands; distributed by *Quaker Doll Co.*★

Kiemayer, Heinrich. 1931. Vienna. Obtained an Austrian patent for a walking doll.

Kienel, Jul. 1907. Sonneberg, Thür. Applied for a German patent (D.R.G.M.) for a jointed wooden doll.

Kiesewetter. See **Petz Spielwarenfabrik** and **Wiefel**.

Kiesewetter, Alwin. 1920–28. Coburg, Thür., and Bavaria. Made dressed dolls. ★

Kieswetter, Anton. 1898–1925. Neustadt near Coburg, Thür., and later Bavaria. Succeeded by his widow before 1918. Made dolls. ★

Kieswetter, Georg B. 1895. Sonneberg, Thür. Applied for a German patent (D.R.G.M.) for a doll's feeding bottle that activated the eyes.

Kieswetter, Reinhardt. 1898. Neustadt, near Coburg, Thür. Made cloth bodies for dolls.

Kietaibl, Franz. 1834–63. Came from an area that sometimes belonged to Austria. He was born in 1803 and died in 1863. He patented dancing dolls and other automata. His shop in Vienna was named "Zum Chineser" and there he handled dolls of various kinds from 1834 to 1863.

1851: Won a prize medal at the International Exhibition in London.

Kigan. 1927–28. *Lenci* felt doll no. 556 represented an Oriental man. It wore a jacket and trousers. The foot was made with the big toe separated from the rest of the toes. The doll carried a spear-like weapon having a curved end.

Kiki. 1924. Long-limbed character doll (*Boudoir* type) represented *Lenore Ulric* in "Ki-Ki." Permission to make this doll was granted by Mr. Belasco to the *Flapper Novelty Doll Co.*

Killy, Sever P. 1917–18. Rhame, No. Dak. Obtained a U.S. patent for eyeball movement in a doll's head.

Kimono Baby. 1917. Trade name of a doll with painted hair or wig, sleeping eyes made by *Ideal*.

1502. Bisque shoulder head doll with a Kidlyn body. The head was made by Heubach of Köppelsdorf from mold # 275 and imported by A. Strauss. It has a wig, sleeping blue glass eyes, and an open mouth with teeth. The Kidlyn body is jointed only at the shoulders and hips and has bisque hands. Original clothes. H. 12 in. (30.5 cm.). *Courtesy of Sotheby Parke Bernet Inc., N.Y.*

Kindel & Graham. 1917–29. San Francisco. Clarence C. Graham and Walter N. Kindel made and exported dolls as well as importing them.

1917: Company was founded.

1928: One of their dolls carried a rectangular tag marked *DAISY*.

1929: They made "French Art Dolls" at one location and at another location, the House of Novelties, they sold dolls.

Kindergarten Baby. 1927. Doll with rubber arms made by *Ideal.* It had a pencil in one hand and a notebook in the other hand.

Kindergarten Emporium. 1902 and probably other years. London. Sold Dolls.

Kindergarten Girlie. 1918. All-composition doll with wig, straight legs and spring joints, made by *Jessie M. Raleigh.* Ht. 11½ in. (29 cm.).★

Kindertraum (Children's Dream). 1930. Trademark registered in Germany by *Otto Gans.*

King, Frank O. 1922–29. Glencoe and Chicago, Ill. Created the cartoon characters that were made into all-bisque dolls with jointed necks. These dolls represented *Uncle Walt, Skeezix, Rachel* and *Auntie Blossom.*★

King, G. W. 1929–30. Sideup, Kent, England. Obtained a British patent for causing movement of dolls' heads or other parts.

King, John Paul. 1891–93. Philadelphia, Pa. Obtained patents in various countries for dolls. Agents in Berlin were C. Fehlert and G. Loubier.

King Albert of the Belgians. 1915–17. Portrait doll with a composition head, hands and molded boots, molded hair and painted eyes, probably made by the *Women's Emergency Corps Workshop* and distributed by *Hamley.* The doll wore a navy blue dress uniform with tails and a white belt. Ht. 19 in. (48 cm.).

King Alfonso of Spain. Before World War I. Portrait doll dressed in the uniform of the English 16th Lancers of which this King was Colonel-in-Chief.

King Alfonso of Spain. 1914–23. Portrait doll dressed in the uniform of a Spanish General.

King Edward VII of England. 1902–30 and later. Wax portrait doll made by *Pierotti* family and distributed by *Hamley.* The hair was inserted into the wax. One early version was dressed in a scarlet military uniform. Another version wore coronation robes. Ht. 26 in. (66 cm.) and possibly other costumes and sizes.

King George V of England. 1915–17. Portrait doll with composition head, hands and molded boots, molded hair, beard and mustache and painted eyes, probably made by the *Women's Emergency Corps Workshop* and distributed by *Hamley.* Ht. 19 in. (48 cm.).

King Innovations. Before 1918–30 and later. New York City. Jack Cohen, President of King Innovations, was responsible for making cloth *Kewpie* dolls called *Cuddle Kewpies.* These Kewpies were designed by *Rose O'Neill,* manufactured and distributed by King Innovations.

King Tut Dolls. 1922 and later. *Boudoir* type dolls with long necks, long limbs, long earrings and Egyptian style clothes, high heel shoes. These dolls came out soon after the discovery of King Tutankhamen's tomb in 1922. (See also **McAuley, Claire P.**)

Kingram Industries. 1915–21. Dublin, Ireland. Produced a line of dolls which were advertised in a British toy trade journal. Their dolls included black cloth dolls named Kurly-Koon and Kaffir Kiddy.

1915: Kingram Toys was a trademark registered by Ryall King and Ethel Margaret Graham for dolls and toys.

Kinky. 1930. One of the *Kiddie Pal* line of dolls made by *Regal.*

1503. Mark on Kinky, one of the Kiddie Pal line of composition head dolls.

Kinky Kurls. 1929. Doll with dark brown composition head and arms, two worsted pigtails, painted eyes, cotton stuffed body, jointed at the shoulders. It was dressed in printed percale rompers and was distributed by *Butler Bros.* The right arm was bent. Ht. 15 in. (38 cm.); priced $8.00 doz. wholesale.

Kintarō. Before 1920 and probably afterwards. All-bisque with molded and painted clothes represented the hero of a Japanese folk tale and often appeared as one of the dolls at the Boys' Day Festival, May 5th. An axe head in a circle was depicted on its chest and its sash was yellow. The arms and legs were bent and the fists were clenched. The porcelain tongue fell in and out as the doll was tipped backwards and forwards.

Kintzback, Martin. 1869. Philadelphia, Pa. Obtained a U.S. patent for a porcelain hand to be attached to a leather arm. See Ill. 1504.

Kirchner, Adolf. 1907–10. Vienna. Listed in an Austrian directory under Dolls and Dolls' Heads.

Kirchner, Eugen. 1904. Dresden, Germany. Designed turned wood dolls that were made by the *Dresdener Werkstätten für Handwerkskunst* (Dresden workshop for art handwork). These dolls had flat wooden arms jointed at the shoulders. Their painted clothes represented occupational and peasant costumes. The dolls came in various sizes and had accessories such as umbrellas, police billies, tools, rakes and so on.

Kirchner, Oscar. 1925–26. Schalkau, Thür. Manufactured composition dolls including bent limb babies; white and mulatto versions.

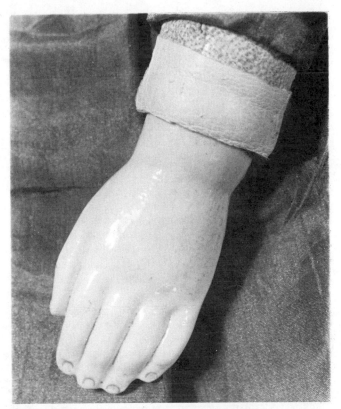

1504. Wrist length china hand made according to the patent obtained by Martin Kintzback in 1869. It is attached to a leather arm and found on a body with a china shoulder head possibly made by Rörstrand. (See Ill. 2245.) *Courtesy of Z. Frances Walker.*

1505. Wooden dolls designed by Eugen Kirchner and made in the Dresden workshops as shown in STUDIO, May 1904. These turned and carved dolls are generally jointed at the shoulders and stand on wooden platforms. The clothes are part of the wooden dolls.

Kirkham, George William Chambers. 1891–1913. London. He did business as G.W.C. Kirkham Jr., The British Rag Doll Co., The Shynall Rag Doll Co., The Textile Novelty Co, and the *Art Fabric Mills*. In 1904 he purchased the business from his employers. In 1913 he went bankrupt and among his creditors was *Selchow & Righter*.

Kirn-Reinick Co. 1925. New York City. Advertised "The Doll of a Thousand Characters" in TOYS AND NOVELTIES.

Kirsch, S., & Co.† See **S. K. Novelty Co.**

Kirsch & Reale. 1927–30. New York City. Distributed dolls. Sole agent for *Lenci* dolls in the U.S.

Kisenstaedt, P. 1901. Waltershausen, Thür. Obtained a German patent (D.R.P.) for a walking doll.

Kiss Me (Kiss-Mee). 1929–30. One of the *Kiddie Pal* line of dolls made by *Regal,* distributed by *Butler Bros.* and *J.C. Penney.* This was an all-composition character doll that raised its hands to throw kisses. It had painted hair and eyes. The body, jointed at the shoulders and hips, could stand on its feet.

1929: The doll came dressed in 50 different costumes and carried a heart-shaped Kiss Me tag. Ht. 12½ in. (31.5 cm.); priced $4.90 doz. wholesale. (See THE COLLECTOR'S BOOK OF DOLLS' CLOTHES, Ill. 775 G.)

1506. Mark on Kiss Me, one of the Kiddie Pal line of composition head dolls.

Kissie. 1920s. Name of a *Cuno & Otto Dressel* bisque head doll. It had a short wig, glass eyes, open mouth and was on a toddler-type body. Hts. 30, 35, and 40 cm. (12, 14, and 15½ in.). May be the doll named Kissmequick in 1929.

Kiss-Throwing Bébé (Bébé Baiser). 1890s–1930. Nearly all of the large French stores sold Kiss-Throwing dolls between 1900-and 1930. These dolls were Bébés with bisque heads on jointed composition bodies that could usually walk, the performance of which activated the kiss throwing mechanism. The directions on a *Bébé Samaritaine* read, "Push the doll forward and it moves one leg, then the other as it throws kisses with one of its hands." They had wigs, glass eyes and generally open mouths. Most of these bébés carried a tag or ribbon with the words, "Je Marche, Je Parle, J'envoi des Baisers." (I walk, I speak, I throw kisses) or similar phrases.

The occasional use of the words "Je dis Papa, Maman" (I say Papa, Mama) no doubt indicates that the Kiss-Throwing doll had Mama-Papa strings.

One of these dolls that cried "Mama-Papa" had a head marked "S. H., 1039//10½ DEP." Ht. 22 in. (56 cm.).

Speaking phonograph dolls were made in this era but so far none of these have been reported with Kiss-Throwing mechanisms.

1893: According to Anne-Marie and Jacques Porot *Bébé Système* could throw kisses as well as walk and talk. It came in size numbers 7 and 9, hts. 44 and 57 cm. (17½ and 22½ in.).

1894: *Bon Marché* advertised a kiss-throwing doll that said "papa-mama." Ht. 47 cm. (18½ in.); priced $2.95. (See THE COLLECTOR'S BOOK OF DOLLS' CLOTHES, Ills. 428A and 429.)

Petit St. Thomas advertised dressed kiss throwing dolls. Hts. 30 and 39 cm. (12 and 15½ in.); priced $1.25 and $2.50.

A 12 inch Kiss-Throwing *Bru* has been found with a closed mouth and strings to operate the kiss throwing arm.

1900: *La Place Clichy* advertised kiss-throwing and "Je Parle" dolls. Hts. 47, 57, and 67 cm. (18½, 22½, and 26½ in.); priced $1.75 to $2.95.

1900–01: *Pont Neuf* advertised a kiss-throwing doll that they claimed was exclusive with them and could sleep, talk, walk and turn its head as well as throw kisses. It had a "washable, unbreakable" head with a wig, sleeping eyes, open mouth and teeth, and a lace trimmed silk chemise. Ht. 57 cm. (22½ in.); priced $2.18.

1901: The *Louvre* store advertised dolls that threw kisses with both hands, 56 cm. (22 in.) tall, cost $2.15 in a chemise and $5.10 in a silk and lace dress.

1901–02: The *Eden Bébé* at *Samaritaine* could throw kisses and say "Papa-Mama." Ht. 57 cm. (22½ in.); price $2.05. (See THE COLLECTOR'S BOOK OF DOLLS' CLOTHES, Ills. 526 and 531.)

1903: Bon Marché advertised kiss-throwing dolls with hair eyelashes, silk costume and picture hat. Hts. 55 and 58 cm. (21½ and 23 in.); prices $2.55 and $4.30 depending on the elaborateness of the costume.

1904: The advertisement for the Louvre store was the same as in 1901 except the doll had hair eyelashes and the cost in a chemise was $2.55.

1906: Samaritaine advertised kiss-throwing and "Je Parle" dolls with heads that turned as they threw kisses. Hts. 58 and 65 cm. (23 and 25½ in.); prices $2.30 and $3.90. The latter was dressed in silk with a picture hat.

1908: Louvre advertised a kiss-throwing "Je Parle" doll with hair eyelashes. Ht. 57 cm. (22½ in.); price in chemise $2.55, in silk and lace costume $5.10.

J. H. Fekete advertised a tall singing kiss-throwing doll.

1908–09: *Hotel de Ville* advertised *Bébé Marcheur* as a kiss-throwing doll with hair eyelashes, dressed in silk chemise. Ht. 57 cm. (22½ in.); price $2.59.

Samaritaine had the same advertisement as in 1906.

1909: Louvre advertised a kiss-throwing *Bébé Réservé*. Ht. 37 cm. (14½ in.); priced $2.55.

1910: Hotel de Ville had the same advertisement as in 1908–09, except a ht. 47 cm. (18½ in.) was added. This doll cost only $1.50.

Printemps advertised a kiss-throwing, "Je Parle" doll. Ht. 60 cm. (23½ in.); priced in chemise $3.18, in removable clothes $4.50.

The *Ville de St. Denis'* kiss-throwing doll was advertised as talking and fully jointed. Dressed in a chemise. Ht. 58 cm. (23 in.); it cost $2.35.

1912: The Louvre advertisement was the same as in 1908 except the prices had risen to $2.75 for the doll in a chemise and $5.30 for a dressed doll.

Bon Marché's kiss-throwing doll had sleeping eyes, hair eyelashes and removable Empire style clothes. Hts. 48 and 58 cm. (19 and 23 in.); priced $2.35 and $2.95.

Lafayette advertised a doll that threw kisses with both hands. It had a wig, sleeping eyes, hair eyelashes, removable cotton or silk dress. Ht. 58 cm. (23 in.); priced $2.85. Other kiss-throwing dolls could speak (parlant); the girls were dressed in silk. Hts. 52, 55 and 58 cm. (20½, 21½, and 23 in.); priced $4.70 to $5.70. A similar doll 55 cm. (21½ in.) was dressed as a boy in a blue and red sailor suit. (See THE COLLECTOR'S BOOK OF DOLLS' CLOTHES, Ills. 629 and 630.)

1913: *Gamage* advertised a "Paris dressed" kiss-throwing doll that could walk and talk. It had a wig, flirting eyes, a fully jointed body and removable clothes. Ht. 22 in. (56 cm.); priced $6.87.

Samaritaine advertised that their dolls had jointed wrists and threw kisses with both hands. They were also "Parlant" and wore a satin costume. Ht. 60 cm. (23½ in.); priced $5.70.

1913–14: La Place Clichy's advertisement was the same as in 1900 except the 67 cm. (26½ in.) doll cost $3.50.

1914: Louvre's kiss-throwing doll was the same as in 1912, except the dressed doll's price had risen to $5.70 and a smaller doll had been added. Ht. 52 cm. (20½ in.); priced $3.15 in a cotton dress and $4.70 in a silk and lace dress.

1915: The Louvre's kiss-throwing doll, still a "Je Parle" doll, came in two hts. 53 and 57 cm. (21 and 22½ in.); price dressed in a silk costume $5.90 and $7.00. The 57 cm. (22½ in.) size in a chemise cost $3.75.

1916: *Printemps'* kiss-throwing and "Je Parle" doll was 57 cm. (22½ in.) tall and cost $5.40 in a blue silk costume.

1918: Printemps' kiss-throwing doll came in three hts. 49, 55, and 70 cm. (19½, 21½, and 27½ in.); the dressed prices were $7.30, $11.00 and $16.00.

1921: Hotel de Ville's kiss-throwing dolls came in four hts. 42, 49, 50, and 53 cm. (16½, 19¼, 19½ and 21 in.).

1923: The Louvre advertised a kiss-throwing, "Je Parle" doll dressed in silk trimmed with cashmere. Ht. 56 cm. (22 in.).

1924: See THE COLLECTOR'S BOOK OF DOLLS' CLOTHES, Ill. 756A for a Printemps' kiss-throwing doll.

1927: Lafayette store advertised two kiss-throwing dolls. The "Je Parle" (I speak) doll wore a silk dress, coat and hat trimmed with plush, and silk stockings. Ht. 57 cm. (22½ in.). The other kiss-throwing doll had an "unbreakable" head, a mohair wig, sleeping eyes, hair eyelashes and wore a chemise.

1928–29: Bon Marché advertised two kiss-throwing dolls, *Monette* and a bisque head walking bébé with sleeping eyes, hair eyelashes and dressed. Ht. 49 cm. (19½ in.).

1930: Bon Marché's kiss-throwing dolls had bisque heads, mohair or human hair wigs, sleeping eyes with eyelashes and wore a chemise. Hts. 52 and 56 cm. (20½ and 22 in.). The larger one was "parlant" (speaking). Bon Marché still advertised Monette.★

Kissy Kissy. 1918. Leading line of the *Ilford Doll Co.* These were fully jointed dolls.

Kister, A. W. Fr., Inc. 1834–1930 and later. Scheibe in Schwarzburg, Rudolstadt, Thür. Porcelain factory, made china and bisque heads and all-bisque dolls. It is not known when they began making dolls. They imitated Meissen products and used "K.P.M.//X" as a mark.

1894: According to the Ciesliks, Fridolin Kister was the successor and they made cloth body dolls and all-bisque or all-china dolls. The factory employed 170 workers but they made other products as well as dolls.

1913–14: Listed in a German directory under Jointed Dolls.★

Kita Shimizu & Co. 1929. Kyoto, Japan. Manufactured dolls.

Kitchener. See **Lord Kitchener.**

Kitson, Arthur. See **Specialty Toy Co.**

Kitts, J. DeLancy. 1918. San Francisco, Calif. Made character dolls with faces handpainted with water colors. The dolls were dressed in silk and their names included Gloria, a patriotic doll; Sum Fun, an Oriental doll and Hi-Jinx, a clown.

Klafer & Co. 1919–21. Munich, Bavaria. Obtained a German patent (D.R.P.) for a doll's body.

Kleiner Spatz (Little Sparrow). 1926. Trademark registered in Germany by *Albert Wacker* for dolls.

Kleinert, I.B., Rubber Co. 1926–30 and later. New York City. Made dolls of rubberized material filled with stuffing. These dolls represented Goldilocks and the three bears. Kleinert's "Bubble Apron" had a *Kewpie* doll in the pocket. They made dolls' clothes including capes with hoods, bathing caps and baby Jiffy pants.

1930: Registered *Jiffy* in U.S. as a trademark for dolls and apparel.

Klem, Anna Mariahilf. 1809–16. Vienna. Manufactured wooden toys which probably included dolls.

Klemperer, F. 1923–30 and later. Prague, Czechoslovakia. Made dolls.

Klenberg, Benjamin Wolf. 1904. Plauen, Germany. Applied for a German patent (D.R.G.M.) for a phonograph doll.

Kletzin, Johann Heinrich, & Sons. 1922–26. Hassenberg near Neustadt, Thür. Kletzin, Ltd. was a British branch. A feudal castle was converted into a factory to make dolls; 300 workers were employed in this factory. The clay used to make the dolls was obtained from the grounds adjoining the estate. A special process was used to mold the material and dry it with hot air. The entire doll was made on the premises except for the glass eyes. The dolls had wigs, hair eyelashes and jointed composition bodies. The clothes were made by home workers. Kletzin specialized in *Mama* dolls and *Cupids.* Their dolls were all exported and sold to wholesalers, England being their largest market. The packing cases were made from the wood of the trees in their own forest. One time they chartered an entire ship to transport 4,000 cases of dolls from Bremen to London. *L. Meyer* was their London distributor.

1924: Mama dolls were 55 and 65 cm. (21½ and 25½ in.) tall.

1926: Dolls were advertised as "Character Art Dolls."

Kley & Hahn. 1902–30 and later. Ohrdruf, Thür. Made dolls with bisque heads and jointed composition bodies or leather bodies. Exported dolls. Appear to have used Kestner bisque heads on some of their dolls. The Ciesliks reported that *Kestner* & Co. of Ohrdruf made the *Walküre* bisque heads. Kley and Hahn also used *Hertel, Schwab* heads.

1902: Albert Kley and Paul Hahn established the doll factory with 15 workers.

1903: Advertised that the heads were their own models. Most of the bodies were five-piece.

1905: Made shoulder heads for their leather bodies.

1906: Advertised double jointed *Täuflinge* with bisque heads, also celluloid heads. Many of these were exported to North America.

1907: Made *Majestic* dolls, patented in the U.S. according to the research of the Ciesliks.

1908: Applied for a German patent (D.R.G.M.) for joints for a doll's body.

1909: Applied for two German patents (D.R.G.M.) for dolls' joints and advertised *Schneewittchen, Prinzess* and *Durabel* as trade names according to the Ciesliks. Besides the Princess Line, there was the *Dollar Princess.*

1910: The company employed 250 workers. They made character babies with painted eyes and hair; dolls representing young girls with painted eyes and closed mouths; all-bisque *Snow Babies;* and other character dolls. They applied for a German patent for sleeping eyes.

1911: Some of the baby dolls with painted hair had sleeping eyes and came with or without voices.

1912: The innovation was a moving tongue. *Reisenbaby* was introduced.

1913: Dolls and dolls' heads were made of composition as well as porcelain. Fully jointed baby dolls, walking baby dolls, and dolls representing *Max and Moritz* were introduced according to the Ciesliks.

1914: Advertised baby dolls with celluloid heads, having wigs, sleeping eyes and moving tongues. Both the celluloid and bisque heads came as shoulder heads or as socket heads. Some of the wigs were made of washable fur. The ball-jointed dolls included *Meine Einzige, Schneewittchen* and Walküre. Rodler babies were introduced as well as Art Dolls.

1915: Advertised dolls representing various prisoners in the Ohrdruf prisoner of war camp. These bisque-head portrait dolls included black Senegalese, French and English.

1918: Advertised baby dolls, fully jointed dolls, Meine Einzige, Schneewittchen and Walküre. The dolls' heads were made of bisque or celluloid and had wigs, moving tongues, sleeping eyes and sometimes baby voices. There were new art model baby dolls.

1921: Distributed in London by *Charles W. Baker.*

1924: The factory employed 300 workers and their primary dolls were ball jointed including Meine Einzige, Schneewittchen and Walküre.

1926: Applied for a German patent (D.R.G.M.) for sleeping and flirting eyes.

1927: Advertised character babies and fully jointed dolls dressed and undressed ranging from the cheapest to the finest quality. They also advertised dolls' parts. Their principal dolls were still Walküre, Schneewittchen and Meine Einzige.

1928: Advertised *Waltershausen* babies, art dolls, painted heads, dresses, shoes and stockings for dolls.

1930: Same as in 1928 plus parts for dolls and wigs.

1931: Celluloid dolls and babies were added to the list.

Kley & Hahn heads were marked K & H or K H and included the following mold numbers: 133, 135, 138, 158 (baby), 159, 160, 161 (Baby), 162, 166, 167 (baby), 169 (toddler), 176, 180, 250 (Walküre), 266, 282, 292, 520, 525 (baby), 526, 531, 546, 548, 549, 554, 567, 568, 571, and 680.

A 158 with molded and painted hair, glass eyes, and an open-closed mouth with two upper teeth was on a ball-jointed composition child body which gave it a ht. of 15 in. (38 cm.) for size 4. The head circumference was 9¼ in. (23.5 cm.).★

APPROXIMATE SIZE–HEIGHT RELATIONSHIPS OF KLEY & HAHN DOLLS (based on a very small sample) BENT LIMB CHARACTER BABY DOLLS		
Size Number	Height in.	cm.
2/0	9	23
1	11½	29
6	15	38

1507. Pair of seated dolls with bisque heads and bent limb composition bodies were made by Kley & Hahn. Doll on the left, mold # 161, has stationary blue glass eyes and an open-closed mouth with two upper teeth and tongue. The body contains a voice box. Doll on the right, mold # 167, has sleeping blue glass eyes and an open mouth with two upper teeth. Both dolls are size 6. H. 15 in. (38 cm.). The maker of the bisque-head doll in the center with the dimples, mold # 151, is not known. Size 13. H. 22 in. (56 cm.). These three heads were made by Hertel, Schwab. *Courtesy of Sotheby Parke Bernet Inc., N.Y.*

1508. Bisque head character baby with molded and painted hair, sleeping brown glass eyes, open-closed mouth and a bent-limb composition baby body. Mark: "1 Germany K & H [in a banner] 525." H. 12 in. (30.5 cm.). Circumference of head 8 in. (20.5 cm.). *Courtesy of Richard Withington. Photo by Barbara Jendrick.*

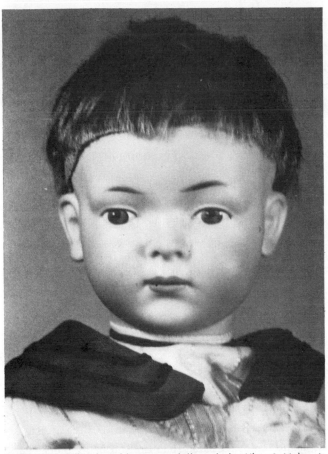

1510A & B. Doll made in Germany possibly by Kley and Hahn. It has a bisque socket head having molded hair, brushmarks, glass eyes, open–closed mouth and dimples. It has a German-type ball-jointed composition body with fingernails outlined in red. Original knitted suit. The bisque head is only marked "531," and was possibly made for Kley & Hahn. H. 14 in. (35.5 cm.). *Coleman Collection.*

1509. Bisque head mold # 526, doll made by Kley & Hahn. It has a mohair wig, molded and painted eyes, closed mouth and a fully jointed composition body. Mark on head: Ill. 1513. Mark on body: "Germany." H. 19½ in. (49.5 cm.). *Courtesy of Richard Withington. Photo by Barbara Jendrick.*

1511. Kley & Hahn advertisement in PLAYTHINGS, January, 1927. Note that the dressed girl doll wears a choker necklace to hide the neck joint, while the bent-limb baby in a chemise does not have a necklace. "Schneewittchen" means Snow White and "Meine Einzige" means My Only One.

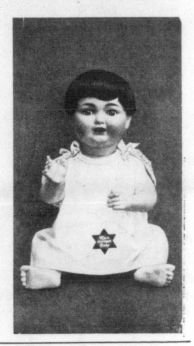

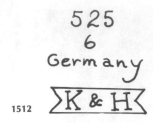

1512–1514. Marks on bisque heads of Kley & Hahn dolls. No. 1514 has a five-pointed star and "S. H.," which suggests a Schoenau & Hoffmeister connection.

Kling, C. F., & Co. 1836–1930 and later. Ohrdruf. Thür. Porcelain factory that made dolls and dolls' heads. From 1901 on they made all-bisque *Snow Babies*. Their china heads usually had a pink tint. The hair and eyes were generally painted on the china heads. Heads with mold #123 have been found with cork pates.

1881: Registered the K in a bell as a trademark for dolls according to the Ciesliks.

1899: Advertised all-bisque dolls and dolls with bisque heads having sleeping eyes and open mouths with teeth. They also sold *Nankeen* dolls with porcelain heads and limbs on cloth bodies as well as separate porcelain arms and legs for dolls.

1926: Kling had rooms to display samples in Amsterdam, Berlin, Hamburg and Vienna. They specialized in all-porcelain dolls including bathing ladies. The Nankeen dolls came with wigs or with molded hair.

1927: Advertised dolls' house dolls, Nankeen dolls, small dolls, porcelain heads and other parts for dolls. *Kolk* was their agent.

1928: William Straube took possession of the Kling factory. Advertised porcelain dolls; Nankeen dolls with wigs or

molded hair; one style had a rococo type wig and bisque limbs which appear to resemble the dolls with the *Simon & Halbig* mold # 1160 heads having rococo style wigs.; dolls' house dolls; dolls with diagonal hip joints; black dolls; all-bisque dolls and all-bisque figures in a crawling position; bathing ladies; porcelain parts for dolls.

1930: Advertised porcelain busts for pincushion dolls, tea cosies and other novelties.

1934: Published a picture of the various types of dolls that they had produced over the years and among them was a china head on a peg wooden body with china limbs.

Among the Kling mold numbers were: 114, 116, 119, 122, 123, 128, 129, 131, 133, 135, 137, 140, 141, 142, 148, 151, 160, 167, 176, 182, 185, 186, 188, 189, 190, 200, 202, 203, 214, 216, 217, 220, 222, 223, 247, 254, 266, 285, 303, 305, 370, 372, 373, and 377.

The 305 had a molded hat and represented a boy. These numbers were found on the back shoulders of china or parian type shoulder heads usually with molded hair and sometimes with pierced ears and/or fancy collars. After each number was a dash and the size number. Later the K in a bell separated the mold and size numbers. ★

Kling, John Paul. 1893. Philadelphia, Pa. Applied for a German patent (D.R.P.) for crying dolls.

Klingenschmid, Barbara. 1853 and probably other years. Vienna. Distributed dolls.

Klinger Manufacturing Co. 1926–27. New York City. Made dolls.

Klippety Klop Kids. 1912–13. Trade name for some composition-head dolls made in America.

1515. Kling bisque shoulder head with molded hair and collar, glass eyes, pierced ears, closed mouth. Mark: "135–6." *Courtesy of Dr. Eva Moskovszky.*

1516A & B. China shoulder head made by Kling. It has molded and painted hair and blue eyes, ears pierced into the head, closed mouth and a marked Webber cloth body (lacking the Webber mechanism). It is jointed at the shoulders, hips, and knees. Head is marked: Ill. 1526. H. 19 in. (48 cm.). H. of shoulder head 4½ in. (11.5 cm.). *Courtesy of Ruth Hartwell.*

1517A & B. Untinted bisque shoulder head probably made by Kling, mold # 170, size 10. It has molded blond hair and a molded collar, stationary blue glass eyes, ears pierced into the head, closed mouth and a cloth body with kid forearms. H. 25½ in. (65 cm.). H. of shoulder head 6¾ in. (17 cm.). *Courtesy of Clara Hobey. Photo by Neil Hobey.*

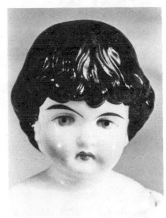

1518. Kling molded hair bisque shoulder head mold # 186. It has blue threaded glass eyes and the mouth is closed. Replaced cloth body. Mark Ill. 1527. H. 14 in. (35.5 cm.). *Coleman Collection.*

1519. Pinkish china shoulder head, mold # 188 made by Kling. It has molded and painted curly hair and facial features. There are two sew holes on each side. The body is a replacement. Mark: Ill. 1528. H. 12 in. (30.5 cm.). H. of shoulder head 3¼ in. (8 cm.). *Coleman Collection.*

1520. Kling bisque shoulder head mold # 200. It has molded hair, painted eyes, closed mouth, and a cloth body. Mark Ill. 1529. H. 11 in. (28 cm.). *Courtesy of Richard Withington. Photo by Barbara Jendrick.*

A

B

C

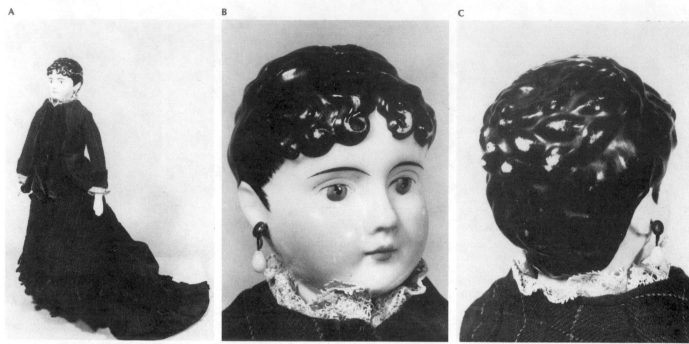

1521A–C. China shoulder head made by Kling around the 1880s, mold # 223, size 6. It has a molded braided coronet hairdo, painted blue eyes, ears pierced into the head and a cloth body with china limbs. Original dress. H. 18½ in. (47 cm.). H. shoulder head only, 4¾ in. (12 cm.). *Coleman Collection.*

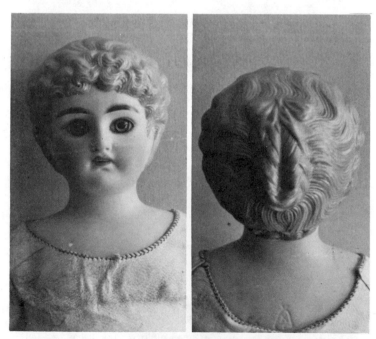

1522A & B. Kling bisque shoulder head mold # 266 with molded hair, blue glass eyes, open-closed mouth on a kid body. Mark: Ill. 1530. H. 14 in. (38.5 cm.). *Courtesy of Suzanne Ash.*

1523. All-bisque doll made by Kling. It has a wig, glass eyes, open mouth and teeth, and molded footwear. Mark on head: Ill. 1532A. Mark on arms: Ill. 1532B. Mark on back: Ill. 1532C. Mark on tops of legs: Ill. 1532D. *Courtesy of Jan Foulke. Photo by Howard Foulke.*

1524. All-bisque doll made by Kling. It has a wig, glass eyes, closed mouth, wire jointed shoulders and hips, and molded footwear. Mark on head: Ill. 1533A. Mark on arms: Ill. 1533B. Mark on back: Ill. 1533C. Mark on top of legs: Ill. 1533D. *Courtesy of Jan Foulke. Photo By Howard Foulke.*

Klondike Dolls. 1899–1901. Distributed by *Butler Bros.* to commemorate the Klondike gold rush. These dolls had bisque turning heads and the bodies with high painted boots were covered with fur or plush to simulate a "parka." The 6 in. (15 cm.) doll had painted eyes and a closed mouth; the 9½ in. (24 cm.) doll had glass eyes and an open mouth with teeth. These dolls came with a metal gun, a pick and two knives. (See also **Eskimo Dolls.**)★

Kloster (Closter†) Veilsdorf Porzellan Fabrik Co. 1765–1930. Kloster Veilsdorf between Hildburghausen and Eisfeld, Thür. Made bisque and china dolls. Some if not all of their low-brow china heads were marked on the back of the shoulder with the size number and "Germany." A Kloster Veilsdorf parian-type shoulder head had a hairdo like the one shown in illustration 310 in THE COLLECTOR'S BOOK OF DOLLS' CLOTHES.

1850: Date of one of the china shoulder heads with molded hair attributed to the Kloster Veilsdorf factory by the Sonneberg Museum. This head is 5 in. (12.5 cm.) tall.

1909: Produced all-porcelain dolls, jointed dolls, dolls' heads and *Nankeen* dolls; 460 workers were employed according to the Ciesliks.

1926: Made porcelain dolls of many types including *Frozen Charlotte* types, all-porcelain dolls jointed at the shoulders, or shoulders and hips; dolls with molded clothes and various molded hairstyles or molded hats; dolls with porcelain heads and lower limbs on cloth bodies.★

Kloster Vessra. See **Ickel, Edmund.**

Klötzer, Erich. 1910–30 and later. Sonneberg, Thür. Made Art dolls resembling the *Kruse* dolls, but marked "E. K."

Klub der Künstler. 1920. Prague, Czechoslovakia. A club of German women artists who made dolls. The President of the club and distributor was *Mme. Raabe.*

Kluge, Anna. 1901. Chemnitz, Germany. Applied for a German patent (D.R.G.M.) for making dolls' clothes of crepe paper.

Kluge, Joh. Ernst. 1826–1909. Berlin. Wholesale distributor of inexpensive dolls and dolls' accessories.

Knäbe (Boy). 1916. Felt doll made by *Steiff.* Ht. 28 cm. (11 in.).

Knauth, Edm., & Knauth, Guido. 1872–1930 and later. Orlamünde, Thür. A doll marked Knauth has been reported with mold # 301, size number 2/0, ht. 13 in. (33 cm.).★

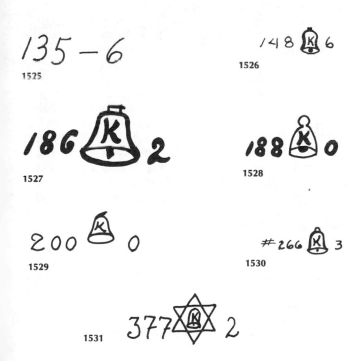

1525–1533. Kling marks on china or bisque heads and on all-bisque dolls. The marks usually have the mold number followed by the size number.

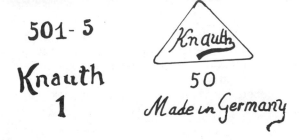

1534A & B. Knauth marks on bisque head dolls.

Knecht Ruprecht. Before 1926. Name of dolls representing attendants of St. Nicholas or the infant Jesus. These dolls were displayed in the Sonneberg Museum.

Knickerbocker Boy. 1919. Doll with composition head, arms and molded boots made by *Ideal*. It had molded hair, sleeping eyes and wore an Oliver Twist style suit. Ht. 16 in. (40.5 cm.); priced $11.40 doz. wholesale. (See also **Shoe, Molded.**)

Knickerbocker Doll Co. 1920–25. New York City. Made wood-fibre composition dolls. No. 106 was 9½ in. (24 cm.) tall and No. 121 was 13½ in. (34 cm.) tall. They specialized in a doll that turned its head as it walked.

Knickerbocker Kid. 1914. Trade name for doll with composition head, hands and feet, cloth body and dressed in a long belted jacket and knickers. Ht. 12 in. (30.5 cm.).

Knickerbocker Toy Co. 1925–30 and later. New York City. Made stuffed dolls. Leo L. Weiss was the President and *A. S. Ferguson* represented the company.

1938: Made Snow White and the Seven Dwarfs.

Knight Bros. & Cooper. 1916–20. Derby, Derbyshire. The leading line was named Reliance Brand after their Reliance Works. This included character dolls with *British Ceramic* heads having wigs, glass eyes and jointed bodies which came in two sizes. Some of these dolls had bald heads. Cheaper dolls had mask faces on stuffed bodies. These came in four sizes. *T. M. Wheeler* was their London agent.

An expert was employed to design the clothes in the latest fashions for the dolls. These included baby dolls wearing long white gowns trimmed with lace and ribbon; character dolls dressed as Dutch, Fairy, Flapper, Gypsy, Irish, Little Red Riding Hood, *Pierrot, Pierrette,* Quaker, Sailor, Scottish, Shepherdess, Soldier, or Welsh girls as well as sports clad boys and girls. There were Summer and Winter costumes.

Most of the clothes were removable and had buttons and/or hooks.

1919: Sold dolls' parts as well as dolls.

Knitted Dolls. Knitted dolls representing soldiers were mass produced by cutting up larger pieces of knitting or crocheting. The features were embroidered and the hands were made especially for the dolls. These dolls usually wore a soldier's uniform of the Franco-Prussian War, that is, a blue coat, white sash at the waist, a yellow shoulder sash, black trousers with a red stripe, a black cap with tassels perched on light colored hair. One of these soldiers belongs to the Swiss National Museum. The above information was obtained from this museum.

Knitted bodies were made for shoulder heads of dolls. One of these bodies' made of fine natural wool had sloping shoulders and broad hips suggesting an 1860s or 1870s date. The fingers were separate and the feet were well shaped. The crotch was open so that the shoulder head could be inserted and only the head could be pushed up through the neckhole. When stuffed this would have made a durable and very satisfactory body.

Many of the periodicals for ladies provided directions for making various styles of knitted dolls.

1881: The NEW YORK TRIBUNE published a booklet, "Knitting and Crochet," which gave instructions for making a girl and a boy doll of zephyr wool. For the girl the head was knitted and included shaping for the nose, ears and chin. It was stuffed with cotton wadding. The eyes, mouth and hair were embroidered and the eyes contained a glass bead. The hands were mitten shape and attached to the crocheted jacket which had a collar. The skirt was crocheted as were also the pantaloons which formed the upper part of the legs. The legs, simulating stockings, could be crocheted with or without stripes and they ended with high black boots. A Scottish cap completed the outfit.

The boy doll's head was made similar to that of the girl doll but his clothes were knitted instead of crocheted. They commenced with his shoes working up through the stockings, trousers, sweater and finally the hands.

1892: Various fashion periodicals such as BUTTERICK, HARPER'S BAZAR and so forth published directions for making knitted dolls of wool yarn. These were generally for boy dolls and described as playthings for either boys or girls. They came in various sizes and various colors. The nose and ears were often knitted appendages but the rest of the facial features were embroidered and beads sometimes were used for eyes. The hair was made by knitting a long narrow strip. This was dampened and pressed with an iron, then cut in two lengthwise and unraveled to a desired length. The clothes formed parts of the doll and decorative elements such as caps, collars, pockets and so forth were knitted or crocheted separately and sewed onto the doll. The boy dolls usually had circular striped stockings and short trousers. Some of the most elaborate knitted dolls were described in a book "The Art of Knitting," published in London by Butterick in 1892. These included a 22¼ inch bearded Harlequin with a pointed hat and bells on his vandyked collar and tunic bottom. A Soldier doll wore a helmet; buttons and bars were embroidered on the jacket, and the trousers had pockets one of which contained a white lawn handkerchief. A knitted boy doll named "Sambo" could be made with a black or white face and hands. (See also **Worsted Dolls.**)★

Knoch, Edmund. 1896–1930 and later. Mönchröden near Coburg, Thür. Later Bavaria. Made dressed and undressed dolls. He used bisque heads made by *Schoenau & Hoffmeister*. *Richard Oberender* modeled Knoch's early porcelain heads.

1916: The ball-jointed *Täuflinge* came with or without a chemise.

1930: *M. Michaelis & Co.* was their Berlin agent for dressed dolls.★

Knoch, Gebrüder. 1887–1918, or later. Neustadt near Coburg, Thür. Founded by Christian Knoch; later joined by Gotthelf Knoch to form the Gebrüder (Brothers) Knoch. After 1918 *Max Oscar Arnold* became their successor. Made porcelain heads of dolls. Molds #s included 192, 193, 199, 201, 205 and 216. Size numbers usually included a number

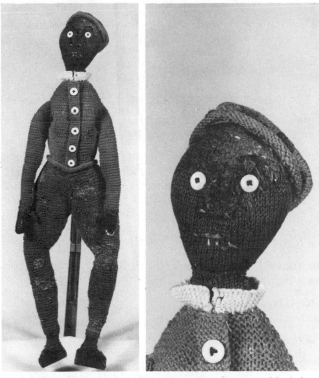

1535A & B. Doll made of knitted wool represents a black boy; eyes are pearl buttons sewed on with black thread, teeth are indicated in the open closed mouth. Knitted clothes form the body. H. 15½ in. (39.5 cm.). *Coleman Collection.*

1536A & B. Doll made of knitted wool represents a white boy; knitted short hair, black glass bead eyes, embroidered features. Knitted clothes form the body. This doll was probably made following a published pattern done at the end of the 1800s. H. 12½ in. (31.5 cm.). *Coleman Collection.*

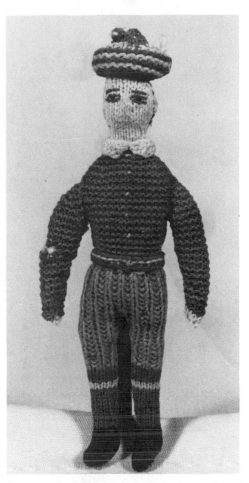

1537. Doll made of knitted wool, following a published pattern, represents a white boy; knitted short black hair, embroidered features. Knitted clothes form the body. H. 6 in. (15 cm.). *Coleman Collection.*

in the teens, a slash and 0. The teens number decreased as the size increased.

1888: Registered numbers 2999 and 3001 for jointed dolls with bisque or with composition heads according to the Ciesliks.★

Knock About (Knockabout, Knock-About) dolls. 1891–1927 and probably other years. These were inexpensive light-weight dolls. They included cloth dolls or dolls with heads of bisque, composition, celluloid, or celluloid mask faces.

1891: Dolls with composition heads were distributed by the *American Merchandise Co.*

1893–1913: Dolls with bisque shoulder heads on felt bodies distributed by *Butler Bros.* In 1899 eight hts. 10, 11, 12½, 13½, 14½, 16½, 18, and 23 in. (25.5, 28, 31.5, 34, 37, 42, 45.5, and 58.5 cm.).

In 1902 with stationary glass eyes Knock About dolls came in four hts. 10, 11, 12½, and 16½ in. (25.5, 28, 31.5, and 42 cm.); priced $1.75 to $4.20 doz. wholesale. With

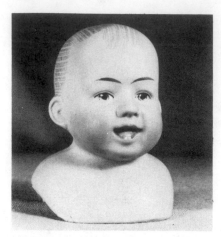

1538. Poured bisque shoulder head made by *Gebrüder Knoch*. It has painted baby hair, intaglio eyes, open-closed mouth with two lower teeth and a tongue showing. The neck is very short. The flesh tint is of a high color. Mark: Ill. 1539. H. shoulder head only 3¼ in. (8 cm.). *Coleman Collection.*

1539. Mark found on Gebrüder Knoch bisque shoulder head.

sleeping glass eyes, hts. 12 and 15¾ in. (30.5 and 40 cm.); priced $2.25 and $4.25 doz. wholesale.

1908–27: Cloth cutout dolls, flat faced or *Tru-to-Life* dolls made by *Dean.*

In 1920 cloth flat-faced dolls included *Pinafore Dolls* and *Charlie Chaplin.* The cutout sheets included *Betty Blue, Big Baby Doll* and *Curly Locks.*

1909: *Siegel Cooper* advertised these Knock About dolls as having a celluloid shoulder head, painted features, cloth body with kid arms. Ht. 18 in. (45.5 cm.); priced 50¢.

1917: Baltimore Bargain House advertised Knock-About dolls.

1922–24: Mabel Bland-Hawkes made knockabout *Worsted Dolls.*

1927: *Harrods* advertised Knock-about Doll that wore a velvet coat and dress. This may or may not be one of *Dean's* Knockabout Dolls which had separate clothes provided for them.★

Knoll, Carl (Karlsbaden Porzellanfabrik). 1844–1930 and later. Fischern near Carlsbad, Bohemia. Made bisque heads for dolls and also sold slip to German companies. In 1886 he

claimed he had the finest porcelain slip and clay. (See **Kestner,** 1909.)

1905: Registered three porcelain dolls' heads.

Knudsen, Krestine. 1928. Oakland, Calif. Registered *The Old Country Dolls* as a trademark in the U.S.

Knut (Dutchman). 1911–16. Felt art doll made by *Steiff* and dressed as a Dutchman with "wooden" shoes and fur cap. The clothes came in assorted colors. Ht. 50 cm. (19½ in.); priced $2.55.

Knut. See **Dean.**

Ko (Cook). See **Mi (Missis).**

Ko Ko. 1927. Trade name for the Inkwell Clown doll advertised by *Borgfeldt.*

Köbel, Jac. 1898. Neustadt near Coburg, Thür. Made cloth bodies for dolls.

Koch, Josef. See **Jäger, Josef.**

Koch, Otto, & Sohn. 1930. Steinach, Thür. Made dolls' bodies and arms. Their Berlin agent was *M. Michaelis & Co.*

Koch, Paul. 1915–28. Neustadt near Coburg, Thür., later Bavaria. Manufactured dolls.

1926–28: Joined with the successors of *August Schelhorn* in exporting dolls.

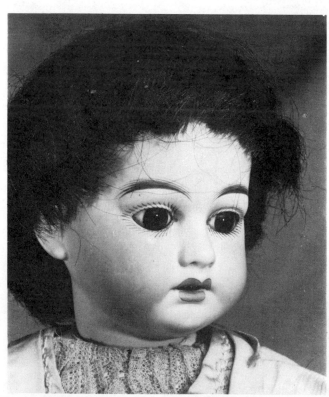

1540. Knoll Porzellanfabrik bisque socket head with wig, stationary brown glass eyes, open mouth with four upper teeth in a poured head. It is on a replaced composition body. Mark: Ill. 1544. H. 16 in. (40.5 cm.). *Coleman Collection.*

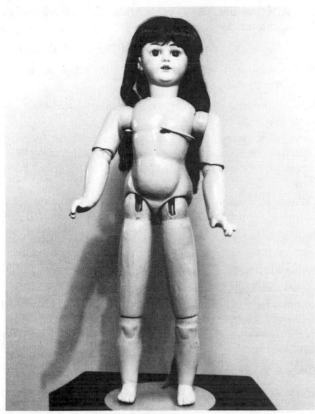

1541. Bisque socket head made in the Carl Knoll porcelain factory. It has a wig, sleeping blue eyes, pierced ears, open mouth, four upper teeth and a felt tongue. The ball jointed composition body has unusually long upper legs, a characteristic sometimes found on other doll bodies with an Austrian provenance. H. 27 in. (68.5 cm.). *Courtesy of Barbara Mansfield.*

Koch, Wilhelm. 1853 and possibly other years. Vienna. Made dolls' heads.

Kochendörfer, Fritz. 1891–1927. Sonneberg, Thür. Made and exported dolls.★

Kochniss, Carl. 1888–1930. Sonneberg, Thür. Made art dolls and novelty dolls. *Alec Cohen & Randall* were his London agents.

Kochniss, Victor. 1914. Oberlin, Germany. Applied for a German patent (D.R.G.M.) for dolls' eyelids.

Kocsis, Louis (of Newark, N.J.), and **Yagoda, S.** (of Brooklyn, N.Y.). 1926. Applied for a U.S. patent for making dolls' parts.

Ko-Ed Kids. 1929. Trade name of dolls advertised by *Reisman, Barron.*

Koedever. 1911. Nürnberg, Bavaria. Advertised felt and plush toys including *Eskimo Dolls.*

Koenig & Wernicke. See **König & Wernicke.**

Kofem (Soldier in a field uniform). 1916. Felt doll made by *Steiff.* Hts. 28 and 35 cm. (11 and 14 in.).

Kohl & Wengenroth. 1902–26. Offenbach am Main, Germany. Made celluloid dolls and dolls' heads.

1912: Advertised bathing dolls, baby dolls and dolls' heads.

1924–25: Applied for three German patent refinements (D.R.G.M.) for dolls, relating to joints, voice, and eyes.

1926: Supplied the special Kowenko heads to *Johannes Gotthilf Dietrich.* These heads were made in accordance with Dietrich's patents. ★

1545–1546. Kohl & Wengenroth's mark, used for their celluloid dolls.

293 ⚷ 0

1542

⚷ 701 5

1543

⚷ 1906 8

1544

1542–1544. Marks on bisque heads made by the Knoll Porzelanfabrik.

Köhler, Eduard. 1895. Treuchtlingen, Bavaria. Applied for a German patent refinement (D.R.G.M.) for dolls made of combined materials.

Köhler & Rosenwald. 1925. Nürnberg, Bavaria. Their factory was called Nürnberger Stoffspielwarenfabrik (Nürnberg Cloth Toy Factory). They applied for a German patent (D.R.P.) for producing dolls.

Kohn, Berta. 1907–10. Vienna. Listed in an Austrian directory under Dolls and Dolls' Heads.

Kohnstam, M., & Co. 1867–1930 and later. Sonneberg, Thür, Fürth, Bavaria, London. The trademark MOKO[+] came from the name of Moses Kohnstam, the founder of the firm, who died in 1912. He was succeeded by Kohnstams not only in Germany but also in England, by Julius Kohnstam who was a naturalized British subject. Julius established a doll factory in London which was named Keen & Co.[+] but maintained his connections in Germany.

A doll with a paper tag that read MOKO and *Princess Charming* had a head marked *Heubach* of Köppelsdorf mold #320.

1913: Julius Kohnstam made dolls including *Vera* and supplied German bisque heads for jointed dolls made in Britain.

1916: By this date Lord Roberts' Memorial Workshop had taken over Kohnstam's Keen & Co because of Kohnstam's German connections.

1920: Julius Kohnstam established another doll company in London which was called *James Garfield & Co.*

1922: Julius Kohnstam reestablished the Kohnstam doll business in London this time using his own name.

1924: Julius Kohnstam advertised fully jointed dolls with sleeping eyes, hair stuffed kid body dolls and all-wood dolls. These dolls had the trade names of *Lola Baby* and *Violet.*

1926: Meanwhile the German branch of the Kohnstam family registered *Nanette* as a trademark in Germany.

1929: The German Kohnstam obtained a German patent (D.R.P.) for stuffed dolls.

1930: The German Kohnstam advertised *Tessie* dolls and dressed dolls.

1933: Julius Kohnstam brought a group of Germans to England in order for the Germans to teach English workmen the art of making composition dolls. These dolls were made by Dollies Ltd., another company established by Julius Kohnstam.

The Kohnstam companies continued to make dolls and in 1935 Dollies Ltd. joined *Dean* to form Dean's Dollies Ltd.★

1547

1548

1549

1547–1549. Marks used by Kohnstam for dolls in 1930 and probably other years.

Kolk, A. A. Van der. 1836–1927. Amsterdam. Was a distributing agent for dolls and toys.

1925: Agent for *Emma Günther* and *Wagner & Zetzsche.*

1927: Distributed dolls for Kämmer & Reinhardt, *Kling* and *Willy Weiersmüller.*

Kollege Klowns. 1930. Cloth dolls made by *Kat-A-Korner Kompany.*

Kollin, Mrs. Berry. 1926–27. Designed dolls for *Twinjoy,* including *Cinderella, Flower Dolls, Grandma and Red Riding Hood, Jack and Jill, Topsy* and *Eva, Uncle Sam and Betsy Ross.*

Köllner, Hermann. 1913. Ilmeneau, Thür. Applied for a German patent (D.R.G.M.) for a method of stringing dolls.

Kolly Kid. 1914. Trademark for certain dolls distributed by *Hamley Bros.*

Komie Klown. 1929. Trademark for dolls registered in U.S. by *Pat Page.*

Kommerzienrat, Frau. 1908. Munich, Bavaria. Dressed dolls in 1700s style costumes. The dolls had porcelain heads made by *Nymphenburg* and probably were designed by *Josef Wackerle.*

König & Rudolph. See **König & Wernicke.**

König & Wernicke. 1911–30 and later. Waltershausen, Thür. In 1911 Max König, August Rudolph and Max Rudolph established a doll factory, but in 1912 Rudolph Wernicke took over from August and Max Rudolph who retired. They made dolls with bisque or celluloid heads on composition bodies.

1912: Advertised baby dolls and child dolls; dolls with sleeping eyes; dolls' accessories. The mark "Königskinder" was registered according to the research of the Ciesliks.

1913: Applied for a German patent (D.R.G.M.) for a doll with a moving tongue.

Made bisque-head dolls with composition bodies. The following mold #s have been found on the necks of König & Wernicke dolls' heads.

1040 Baby doll with molded hair, sleeping eyes and bent limbs.

1070 Baby doll, wig, sleeping eyes, closed mouth and bent limbs.

1090 Same as 1070 but with an open mouth and two teeth.

1080 Baby dolls with mohair wigs, movable googly eyes, bent-limbed bodies. These dolls were in the *Mein Stolz* (My Pride) line. Seven hts. 26, 29, 32, 35, 40, 45, and 50 cm. (10½, 11½, 12½, 14, 15½, 17½, and 19½ in.).

1570 M. was a toddler with baby face, wig, sleeping eyes, one of the Mein Stolz line of dolls made for *Borgfeldt.*

1590 J.S. Same as 1570 M except for hair, mouth and chemise.

1580 "Pfiffikus" (Sly Boy), name of a doll with googly eyes, mohair wig, fully jointed body. Three hts. 30, 40 and 53 cm. (12, 15½ and 21 in.).

1583 Urchin Boy with googly eyes; dressed without footwear; mate to 1584. Hts. 40 and 48 cm. (15½ and 19 in.).

Bru Bébé with bisque head, shoulders, and hands, on a kid body, open-closed mouth with molded teeth, original clothes. Marks on forehead "B^te SGDG" and on back of the head a circle and dot over 2/0. H. 14 in. (35.5 cm.). *Courtesy of Jay and Becky Lowe. Photo by Bill Holland.*

Falk & Roussel Bébé with closed mouth, original clothes, including an armband reading "PETIT CHERUBIN." Bisque head marked "F. R.//8." H. 18 in. (45.5 cm.). *Courtesy of Jay and Becky Lowe. Photo by Bill Holland.*

Bisque-head doll made by the Jules Steiner firm in the 1890s has a closed mouth, pierced ears, a ball-jointed composition body, and original clothes. H. 13 in. (33 cm.). *Courtesy of Sylvia Brockman.*

26

Paris Bébé made by Danel in 1889, or later by Jumeau. Marked on bisque head "PARIS BÉBÉ//TÊTE DEPOSE//10." Eiffel Tower mark on jointed composition body. H. 24 in. (61 cm.). *Courtesy of Jay and Becky Lowe. Photo by Bill Holland.*

Four Bébés Jumeau in original clothes. The one with the red hat has its original armband. *Left to right* marks: Jumeau in a cartouche, size 1 (see Ill. 1325); Jumeau marks on body and shoes, size 2 (see Ill. 263); Tête Jumeau size 2. Hs. 11½, 10, 9½, and 10½ in. (29, 25.5, 24, and 26.5 cm.). *Courtesy of Cherry Bou.*

Bébé Jumeau with an armband and its original box. Ht. 20 in. (51 cm.). *Courtesy of and photo by Cherry Bou.*

Bébé Jumeau dressed in original wizard costume has a closed mouth and is marked on its head "DEPOSE//TÊTE JUMEAU//B^te SGDG//9"; marked on body "BEBE JUMEAU." H. 22 in. (56 cm). Character Jumeau with closed mouth having a small round hole in it, pierced applied ears, and ball-jointed composition body. Incised mark on head "216//10." Between these two numbers is a red stamp, "DEPOSÉ//TÊTE JUMEAU//B^te SGDG." H. 22½ in. (57 cm). The "GRAND JEU DE BÉBÉ JUMEAU" is a game published in 1889 to celebrate the opening of the Eiffel Tower. *Courtesy of Jay and Becky Lowe. Photo by Bill Holland.*

31

Bisque head with smiling closed mouth, composition body, original clothes of about 1910–15. H: 14 in. (35.5 cm.). *Courtesy of Sylvia Brockmon.*

32

Bébé Jumeau in original clothes of the 1880s. *Courtesy of Sylvia Brockmon.*

Bisque head representing a lady, painted eyes, closed mouth, pierced ears, marked 10. H. 24½ in. (61.5 cm.). *Courtesy of Jay and Becky Lowe. Photo by Bill Holland.*

33

Bisque head with closed mouth made by Simon & Halbig. Mark: "SIMON & HALBIG//S & H//IV." H. 17½ in. (44.5 cm.). *Coleman Collection.*

34

Black bisque head made by Simon & Halbig as mold #116 A for Kämmer & Reinhardt (see Ill. 1390). H. 15 in. (38 cm.). *Courtesy of Elsie Potter.*

36

Bisque head with wig and closed mouth made by Armand Marseille, based on the sculpture of François Duquesnois (1594–1646). The doll was named Fany. H. 13 in. (33 cm.). *Coleman Collection.*

35

Bisque-head dolls with composition bodies. *Left to right:* Kestner with closed mouth, marked "made in //b Germany 3//212"; Franz Schmidt & Co. doll with closed mouth, marked "A. P.//MADE IN GERMANY//S & C//4"; black so-called Belton-type, skin wig, no mark. Hs. 12½, 14, and 11½ in. (31.5, 35.5, and 29 cm.). *Courtesy of Jay and Becky Lowe. Photo by Bill Holland.*

German bisque-head dolls on composition bodies. *Left to right:* Dolls have sleeping eyes, closed mouth, marked "111 - 4//Germany"; molded and painted eyes, open-closed mouth with painted teeth, marked "151//S & H//0 ½"; painted eyes, closed mouth, marked "S & H//152//7," lady-shaped body; sleeping eyes, closed mouth, marked "1307//7," lady-shaped body. Hs. 17, 17½, 20½, and 19¾ in. (43, 44.5, 52, and 50 cm.). *Courtesy of Jay and Becky Lowe. Photo by Bill Holland.*

Left: Bisque head De Fuisseaux of Baudour doll with painted features and wig, cloth body, composition molded shoes (see Ills. 741 and 742). H. 12 in. (30.5 cm.). *Coleman Collection.*

Pandora bisque-head fashion doll (so described when it was produced), created by Valentine Thompson, has bisque head and hands sculptured by Louis-Aimé Lejeune. The pink cloth body has composition lower legs. Dolls of this type are known to have been costumed by the Callot Sisters and shown at the Art Alliance in New York City in 1918. The embroidery and braid trimming on this flannel suit are typical of the Callots' work. The cloth label on the skirt reads "No. 21 Frileuse" (Chilly), referring to the fact that this is a winter outfit. H. 13 in. (33 cm.). *Coleman Collection.*

Schoenhut all-wood Oriental baby dolls with queues, painted Oriental-shaped eyes, and five-piece baby bodies. Mark is a blue decal "H. E. SCHOENHUT//©." These dolls copyrighted by Harry Schoenhut closely resemble the sculptured head of a child made by François Duquesnois before 1646. Many German firms used the same sculpture as their inspiration for doll models. (See Ill. 92 in The Collector's Encyclopedia of Dolls, Volume One.) *Courtesy of Jay and Becky Lowe. Photo by Bill Holland.*

Indian portrait dolls of Sacajawea and her papoose made by Mary Frances Woods (see Ill. 2272). H. 10 in. (25.5 cm.). *Coleman Collection.*

Composition-head doll designed by Grace Corry Rockwell and called "Little Brother" (see Ills. 1701 and 1702). H. 14 in. (35.5 cm.). *Coleman Collection*.

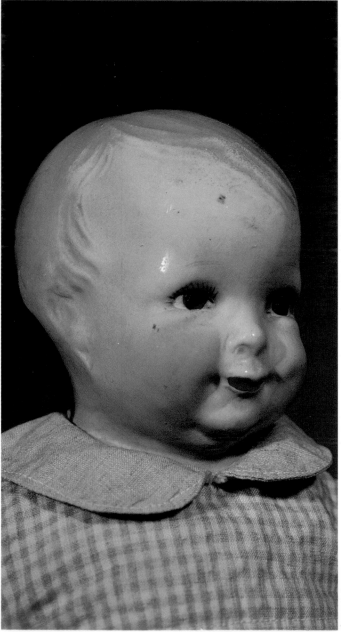

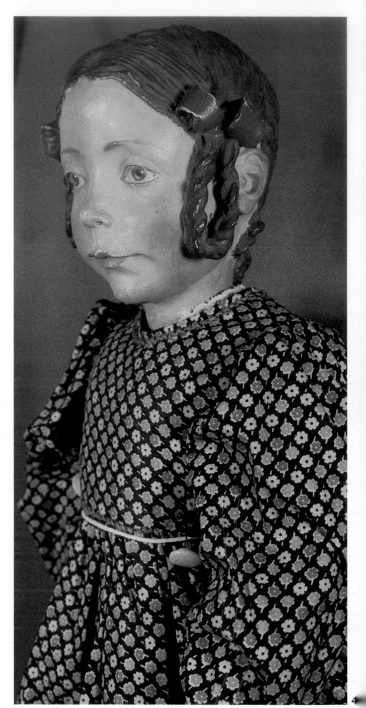

Munich art doll type with a composition head on a ball-jointed composition body. The head closely resembles a watercolor painting of his daughter by Carl Larsson. H. 24 in. (61 cm.). *Courtesy of the Chester County Historical Society*.

Lenci Lady doll. *Courtesy of the Strong Museum.*

"Balsam Baby" cloth doll made by Gre-Poir in 1930. The cloth torso is filled with balsam needles. H. 17 in. (43 cm.). *Coleman Collection.*

Oilcloth doll representing Skeezix (see Ills. 2441 and 2442). H. 13½ in. (34 cm.). *Coleman Collection.*

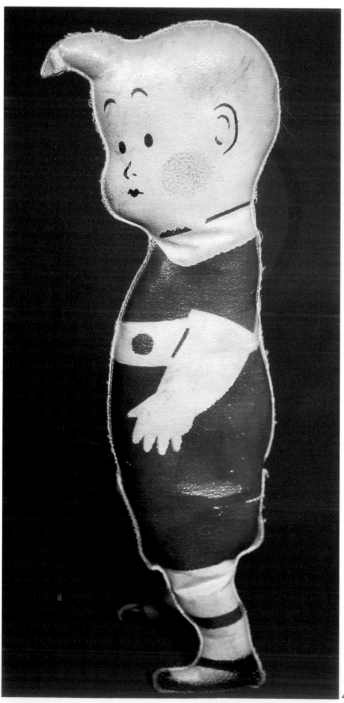

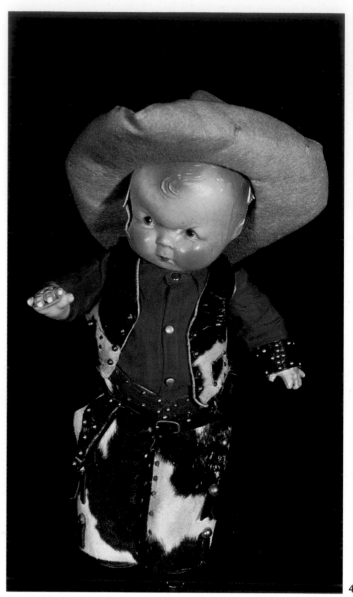

Composition doll made by the American Character Doll Co. and named "Puggy." Original cowboy-style clothes. H. 13 in. (33 cm.). *Courtesy of the Nebraska State Historical Society, Rathburn Collection.*

1584 same as 1583 except dressed as a girl.

It should be noted that some of the socket-type baby heads have the same mold numbers as Simon & Halbig shoulder heads for example 1040 and 1080.

4711 Dolly face, wig, with or without eyelashes, fully jointed child doll with jointed wrists, one of the "Mein Stolz" (My Pride) line made for Borgfeldt.

7000 Dolly face, human hair or mohair wig, with curls, sleeping eyes; fully jointed child body with jointed wrists; 13 hts. 28, 32, 37, 40, 48, 50, 54, 57, 60, 62, 64, 67, and 70 cm. (11, 12½, 14½, 15½, 19, 19½, 21½, 22½, 23½, 24½, 25, 26½, and 27½ in.).

1035 Doll was the same as mold # 1090 except it had a celluloid head.

1916: Applied for a German patent (D.R.G.M.) for sleeping eyes.

1919: Rudolph, Alfred and Paul Wernicke were firm members. Advertised bent-limb babies and fully jointed babies as well as dolls' heads and wigs.

1920: Advertised "Mein Stolz" (My Pride) for export.

1925: Dolls had diagonal hip joints on toddler bodies. The knee joints were made to show under short clothes.

1926: Advertised baby dolls with *Cellowachs* heads and celluloid heads of the Schildkröte variety, made by *Rheinische Gummi und Celluloid Fabrik Co.*

A. *Bell* was the London agent.

1927: Advertised baby and child dolls with celluloid heads of their own design. The reflex action eyes in their dolls were made by *Seyfarth & Reinhardt.* The Mein Stolz dolls were still being made with bisque heads.

1928: Baby head mold # 1600 was used on a toddler body with disc joints.

1929: Applied for three German patents (D.R.G.M.): one was for sleeping eyes, one for a voice in a celluloid head and one was for a doll's hand.

1930: Applied for a German patent (D.R.G.M.) for a hard rubber doll.

Advertised dolls and babies with Zello wax (Cellowachs) heads. One of these was mold # 1610. Some of the dolls had reflex eyes and were marked "Mein Stolz." *Hertzog* was their Berlin Agent.

1932: Head mold # 2600 was used on toddler type bodies or bent limb baby bodies.

Other König & Wernicke mold #s were 88, 90, 98, 106, 111, 112, 222, 298 celluloid, 333, 555, and 777.★

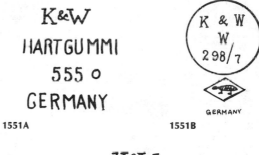

1551A & B–1553. Marks on heads of rubber and celluloid dolls made for König & Wernicke. Some of the heads have the turtle mark of Rheinische Gummi und Celluloid Fabrik as well as the König & Wernicke mark.

1550. Celluloid socket head made by Rheinische Gummi und Celluloid Fabrik Co. for König & Wernicke using mold # 1070. It has sleeping glass eyes and an open mouth. Rolf Wernicke in 1975 dated this style of head as ca. 1929. Mark: Ill. 1551 B. H. of the head 4¼ in. (11 cm.). *Coleman Collection.*

Königliche Porzellan Manufaktur. 1761–1930 and later. Berlin. A doll head having a K.P.M. red orb and blue eagle mark has been found on a doll body marked *Woodford & Merrill*, Boston. Only in 1851 was this establishment listed in any of the Boston City Directories. From 1840 to 1850 and from 1852 to 56 just Woodford was listed at the address on the label.★

Königsee Porzellanwerke. See **Beck & Glaser.**

Konrad, Hurwart. See **Sauerzapf, Georg Andreas.**

Konstructo Co. 1920–21. Portland, Ore., and New York City. Sole distributor of Indian dolls made by *Mary Frances Woods. Bush Terminal* represented this firm in New York City.

Konti, J. 1923–30 and later. Vienna. Made dolls.

Kopfovi, Weiss. See **Weiss, Kopfovi.**

Koppe, Louis, & Son. 1925–30 and later. New York City. Made outfits for dolls.

1555A & B. China shoulder head and arms probably has the mark of the Königliche Porzellan Manufaktur (K.P.M.). It has molded brown hair with a bun, painted eyes, cloth body. Dressed in a regional Dutch costume. The doll has a summer and a winter skirt, a separate pocket and a black wool apron. H. 19½ in. (50 cm.). *Courtesy of the Collection Nederlands Kostuum-museum, The Hague. Photo by B. Frequin.*

1554. Pressed china shoulder head in the white, made in König-liche Porzellan Manufaktur (K.P.M.). Mark: Blue stamp with KOENIGLICHE PORZELLAN MANUFACTUR. in a circle around a spread eagle. This shoulder head is a second due to a tiny flaw on the crown and for this reason it was never painted. H. of shoulder head 4½ in. (11.5 cm.). *Coleman Collection.*

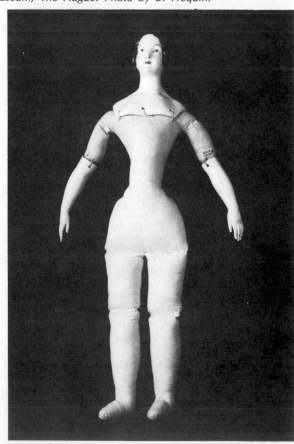

1556. China shoulder head made by the Königliche Porzellan Manufaktur (K.P.M.). It has brown molded hair with three ringlets on each side in front and a bun in back, a style popular in the 1840s; painted eyes, and a sternum molded with detail. The body is cloth with wooden limbs. A K.P.M. mark is found inside the shoulders. H. 7½ in. (19 cm.). *Courtesy of Sylvia Brockmon.*

1557. Mark of Königliche Porzellan Manufaktur, also known by its initials K.P.M. These marks were usually found on the inside of the china shoulder heads.

Köppelsdorfer Porzellanfabrik. See **Heubach, Ernst.**

Korean Dolls. In 1913 TOYS AND NOVELTIES reported Roly Poly dolls were among the early Korean dolls. "Korean girls made their own dolls from a bamboo stem and wisps of grass stuck on top of bamboo to represent hair. A sort of white paste or powder does duty for the face. This is then dressed." (See also **Oriental Dolls.**)

Kösel, Hermann. 1921–23. Nürnburg, Bavaria. Obtained a German patent (D.R.G.M.) for covering a doll's body.

Kospa. (Cossack, parade uniform). 1916. Felt doll made by *Steiff.* Hts. 28 and 35 cm. (11 and 14 in.).

Koustari. 1906. Trade name of Russian dolls handled by *Leon Snéquireff.*

Kovar's Inc. 1926. New York City. Distributed the hand carved and handpainted wooden peasant figures and *swaddling-clothed babies* made in their own workshops in Czechoslovakia.

Kowenko. See **Kohl & Wengenroth.**

Krack (Krackjack). 1910–16. Felt comic doll made by *Steiff,* distributed by *Borgfeldt* in the U.S., resembled a *Billiken.* It had stitched hair, separate fingers and removable clothes. 1910 ht. 35 cm. (14 in.). 1911–16 ht. 30 cm. (12 in.). Price in 1911 in Germany $1.09 and in 1913 in New York $1.50.

Kradle Babe. Before 1926. *Bye-Lo* type doll made by *Domec.* Production was stopped in 1925, when Domec lost an infringement suit to *Borgfeldt* because Kradle Babe resembled the Bye-Lo too closely.

Kraemer & Von (Van) Elsberg. 1913–14. Cologne, Germany. Applied for three German patents (D.R.G.M.) for dolls' eyes. All except one of these patents was with *Otto Gans.*★

Krailsheiner & Sohn. 1899. Stuttgart, Germany. Applied for a German patent (D.R.G.M.) for a cloth doll.

Kramer, Adolf. 1924–26. Hamburg, Germany. Obtained a German patent (D.R.P.) for dolls' movement.

Kramer, Emil. 1906. Taura near Burgstadt, Germany. Applied for a German patent (D.R.G.M.) for cork balls for a jointed doll.

Kramer & Lange. 1925. New York City. Imported dolls.

Krampe, Otto. 1902–03. Schalksmühle, Westfalen, Germany. Applied for an Austrian patent relating to the sleeping eyes for a doll.★

Krannich, Paul. 1926. Neustadt near Coburg, Bavaria. Obtained a patent for a doll with electric lights for eyes.

Kratz-Boussac, Henri Othron. 1892–1910. Paris. Made celluloid dolls.

1906: Registered in France L'Aiglon (The eagle) for dolls. This should not be confused with *Petitcollin's Tête d'Aigle* (eagle's Head) mark.

1910: Won a grand prize for dolls at the Brussels Exposition as the Établissements Kratz-Boussac.

Krauhs. Vienna. Made felt dolls. On the foot of a doll was *Diana Veller* and a metal tag on the leg had the name Krauhs.

Kraus, Frederik. 1930 and later. Köppelsdorf, Thür. Advertised dolls, baby dolls and clothes for dolls.

Krause & Wessely. 1926–28. Gehren and Königsee, Thür. Advertised small dressed porcelain and celluloid dolls, as well as art dolls.

Krauss, Gebrüder. 1863–1930 and later. Eisfeld, Thür. Made dolls. It seems more likely however that the bisque dolls' heads marked G. K. were made by *Gebrüder Kühnlenz* in their porcelain factory than by Gebrüder Krauss.★

Krauss, Hermann. 1925–30. Rodach near Coburg, Thür. In 1930 it was the widow Bertha Krauss & Sons. Made composition dolls.

Krauss, Kaspar. 1878. Sonneberg, Thür. Made dolls.

Krausser, Karl. 1900–30 and later. Waltershausen, Thür. Perfected the process for coloring and giving a durable finish to celluloid heads. He designed celluloid dolls' heads for

Kämmer & Reinhardt. These heads were made by *Rheinische Gummi und Celluloid Fabrik Co.* When Ernst Kämmer died Krausser took his position in Kämmer & Reinhardt.

Krausz (Krats), Samuel. 1875. Rodach near Coburg, Bavaria. Made dolls' heads and registered two trademarks for dolls in Germany.

Krayer, Hilde Lotte. 1929. Berlin-Wilmersdorf. Registered a trademark in Germany for dolls. See Ill. 1558.

1558. Trademark used by Hilde Lotte Krayer for dolls.

Krautwurst, Ernst. 1907–10. Vienna. Listed in an Austrian directory under Dolls and Dolls' Heads.

Krebs, Stengel, & Levy. 1915–24. New York City. Advertised bent-limb baby dolls in TOYS AND NOVELTIES.★

Kreis, Wilhelm. 1904. Dresden, Germany. Designed art dolls dressed in regional or historical costume. See Ill. 2495.

Kreiss, Georg. 1926–28. Fürth, Bavaria. Made dolls' dresses and trousseaux. Advertised dolls' house dolls and pincushion dolls.

Kremer, Carl Josef. 1911. Waltershausen, Thür. Applied for a German patent (D.R.G.M.) relating to sleeping eyes in dolls' heads.

Kresge, S. S., & Co. Before 1914–30 and later. Sonneberg, Thür. and Detroit, Mich. Distributed dolls. During World War I the Sonneberg office was taken over by *Josef Leven.*

Kretschmer. Before 1867–90s. Illustrator of books on regional costumes especially of the German-speaking areas.

1867: SELECT HISTORICAL COSTUMES was "selected from the great works of . . . Kretschmer and others of equal authority."

1890s: DEUTSCHE VOLKSTRACTEN (German Folk Costume), a book illustrated by Kretschmer, was used for the designs of the regional costumes on dolls made by *Ernst Reinhardt* and dressed by his wife and helpers around 1900 and later.

Kreutzer, Georg. 1910–30. Unterlind, Sonneberg, Thür. Made dolls.

1910: Applied for a German patent (D.R.G.M.) for a bent limb baby doll with a voice in its torso.

1926: Manufactured dressed dolls and baby dolls.

1930: Advertised bent-limb babies, jointed child dolls, mulattoes, art dolls and *Mama* dolls. ★

Kreuzer, Johann. 1910. Vienna. Listed in an Austrian directory under Dolls and Dolls' Heads.

Krieger, Betty. 1920s. Germany. Made art dolls in *Else Hecht's* workshop.

Krieger, Frau. 1909. Germany. Created handmade regional and historical Bavarian costumes for small dolls.

Kringle Society Dolls. 1914 and probably other years. Name under which dolls were sold by *Marshall Field* according to their catalog.

Kringle Tots. 1914. All-bisque dolls with eyes glancing to the side, movable arms, distributed by *Marshall Field.* Seven hts. 4¾ to 9 in. (12 to 23 cm.); priced $1.70 to $17.00 a doz. wholesale.

Kris Kringle Kid Co. 1924–25. Jersey City, N.J. Trademark registered in U.S. for dolls by Elsie Dinsmore Landfear doing business as Kris Kringle Kid Co.★

1559. A hat marked Krohn of Paris is on a Bébé Jumeau with a mohair wig, stationary brown glass eyes, pierced ears, closed mouth, and a ball jointed composition body. Original clothes. H. 13 in. (33 cm.). *Courtesy of Elsie and Al Potter.*

Kröhl, Adolph. 1830–98. Berlin. Made and exported dolls and dolls' heads of wax, bisque, papier-mâché, wood, leather, metal and china. Also handled *Täuflinge,* dolls' bodies of leather and cloth, dolls' wigs; dolls' shoes and stockings and other accessories including jewelry. Used A K as a mark. Listed in Paris directory under Dolls.

1883: Advertised a doll with shoulder head, braided wig and "A.K." on its chest.

Krohn, Alexandre. 1882–90. Paris. Made dolls' clothes including hats.★

Kröning, Hermann. 1927. Gotha, Thür. Listed in toy trade journals under Dolls.

Krueger, Richard G. 1917–30 and later. New York City. Made cloth dolls and cloth-body dolls. Probably after 1930 they made the *Cuddle Kewpies.* (See Ill. 300.)

1920: Advertised handpainted dolls, stuffed dolls and bent-limb babies.

1926: Agent for *Beers-Keeler-Bowman.* (See also **Wurzburg.**)★

Kruse, Käthe. 1910–80 and later. Bad Kösen, Silesia and Charlottenburg, Prussia. After World War II moved to Donauwörth, Bavaria. Made dolls of waterproof nettle cloth (a type of muslin), cotton wool and stockinet. The heads and hair were handpainted with oil paints. Most of these dolls were on a skeleton frame with rigid and movable parts. The early ones were stuffed with deer hair. The earliest type was described by Käthe Kruse in an article published in LADIES HOME JOURNAL, November 1912, and also shown in THE COLLECTOR'S BOOK OF DOLLS' CLOTHES, Ill. 631. The construction of the early type thumbs was shown in this article. The thumb was a part of the hand while by 1914 the thumb was sewed on separately and much later the thumb was again part of the hand. An early Käthe Kruse doll (in the Schloss Schleusingen Museum near Sonneberg in 1981) had a seam across the bridge of its nose. The dolls were usually marked on the bottom of the left foot with a number and the name Käthe Kruse. The numbers usually ranged from three to five digits and the marks were in black, red or purple ink. The dolls in Series I generally were 43 cm. (17 in.) high. Series II, V and VI were made in the 1920s. Then in 1927 a smaller Series VII, 35 cm. (14 in.) tall, was also made. By ca. 1946 there were four hts., 35, 45, 47, and 52 cm. (14, 17½, 18½, and 20½ in.), in Series IX, XII, XIV and VIII respectively. Most of these 1946 dolls had wigs but some of the smallest size ones came with painted hair, as well as wigs.

F.A.O. Schwarz and the Sonneberg Museum measured their Käthe Kruse dolls as being 16 in. (40.5 cm.) but this appears to have been a measuring variation of the standard 43 cm. (17 in.) dolls.

There is evidence that supports the theory that Käthe Kruse used as her model a piece of sculpture by François Duquesnois (1594–1643) known as Francesco Fiammingo.

1911: Käthe Kruse dolls were advertised by *Kämmer & Reinhardt,* but this was not a continuing association. The ball jointed and 45 cm. (17½ in.) dolls were probably produced during the Kämmer & Reinhardt era.

1912: An article in TOYS AND NOVELTIES in 1912 tells about the Käthe Kruse dolls that were new on the market at that time:

"She had two jolly little girls who wanted to play and a very decided sculptor husband who wouldn't give them shop toys to play with. So she tied a knot in a towel in such a manner that it acquired two arms and a waist-line and then every time she had to make a new one—which was often enough as Mimmele and Pfiffele dealt none too kindly with their only plaything—she improved upon the last until she evolved the most wonderful baby. . . .

"In this evolution her husband, Max Kruse, who carved the modern 'Runner of Marathon' and 'Youthful Love' rendered indispensable service, for it is after his models that the muslin infants are fashioned. He suggested and criticised while his wife's deft fingers fashioned the little forms with scissors, needle and thread, muslin and cotton batting. Four years they labored before they attained the ideal. . . .

"The rag dolls of former days had heads the flatness of which suggested a steam roller massage; of expression there was none, and of profile not even a suggestion. Not so the new Käthe Kruse doll. She boasts not only a bona-fide profile, arms, legs that are more useful than ornamental, but two perfectly moulded, truly shell-like ears. Some of them even boast the luxury of a dimple.

". . . The craze for dolls grew . . . she consented to teach young girls to make them for a large toy shop, with the condition that she or some other artist of worth should paint the faces by hand. . . .

"The doll stands about a foot and a half high, has movable limbs and a head as hard as that of a bisque or china doll. Every bit of it is made of ordinary muslin, sewed by hand and stuffed with the most ordinary cotton; the head is dipped into some chemicals, also a factory secret. . . . The body is full of little seams, the placing and direction of which presented the most difficult problem to the makers. There is a tiny little seam over the bridge of the nose between the brows . . . and one on either side of the chin. . . . The ear with all its complicated little crevices is moulded with the head."

These early dolls were exhibited in a Berlin show, at *Hermann Tietz's* Department Store.

1913: The dolls were also discussed in TOYS AND NOVELTIES, March, 1913:

"The Käthe Kruse dolls [are] made of fine canvas and painted to look about as much like a real baby as anything heretofore seen. [One of them is dressed] in her dainty red dress and tilted straw hat. . . .

"When Mrs. Kruse first began working out the 'perfect doll' problem she set a high ideal for her product. The doll must be unbreakable, or as nearly so as possible. It must be a character doll, one closely resembling a real child. And it must be a real 'play doll,' one with which the little girl can play to her hearts content without injuring the doll or herself. . . . The Kruse work shop is always under the personal guidance of Mrs. Kruse. The heads are painted by young artists, and each one is inspected and given distinct individuality."

The hair was painted blond or brown and the eyes were blue or dark.

TOYS AND NOVELTIES also reported that the "Käthe Kruse dolls seldom find their way into any homes other than the rich. They are stocked even in large stores by the dozen and not by the gross."

The Käthe Kruse dolls won the grand prize at the Ghent Exhibition. *Strobel and Wilken* was the sole U.S. agent. It has been reported that *Fischer, Naumann* in 1913 produced a few dolls for Käthe Kruse, but she was not satisfied with them and again the association was terminated.

1914: Käthe Kruse won several infringement cases. She obtained a German patent (D.R.P.) for the articulation of a doll. This patent was also obtained in Austria in 1915. In Germany Käthe Kruse dolls sold for $5.00 undressed and $6.60 to $8.00 dressed. Dolls representing soldiers in field gray uniforms were especially popular; some of these were only 11 cm. (4½ in.) tall and sold for about 30¢. (See THE COLLECTOR'S BOOK OF DOLLS' CLOTHES, Ill. 643.)

World War I: In a Käthe Kruse catalog of this period many of the dolls wore costume components that were similar to one another but they were put together in different arrangements. One of the illustrations from this catalog is identical to one shown in STUDIO in 1913. Both the early and later type hands were shown. A few of the dolls had also been shown as early as 1911 and as late as 1923/24 in the F.A.O. Schwarz catalog.

1916: *Borgfeldt* distributed Käthe Kruse dolls.

1922: DEUTSCHE SPIELWAREN ZEITUNG gave the following account in English in 1928. " 'The Toddler', the next most important type came out in 1922. In this model, nature with her characteristics, and the sense of touch are even more perfectly followed up. The little one's body is soft . . . while the limbs are supple and loose. . . . the wohle [sic] is carried by a skeleton-frame, composed of rigid and movable parts. The 'flesh',—cotton-wool and gauze,—is put on and covered with the 'skin', a tricot material. This kind of jointed doll need not be covered. 'The Toddler' when naked has a natural and beautiful child-like body." These dolls called "Schlenkerchen" in German were 33 cm. (13 in.) tall. (Series II.)

1923: F.A.O. Schwarz advertised 35 styles of girl dolls and 20 styles of boy dolls; priced $10.00 undressed and $15.00 to $18.00 dressed.

Ca. 1923: Bambino, a smaller version of the Series I dolls, was made. Ht. 25 cm. (10 in.).

1924: In London *W. Seelig* was the sole British agent.

1925: Little Dreamer[+] was introduced. This was a life-size baby doll made for nursing practice. Its size and weight corresponded to that of a real baby. It was known as Series V and VI and came in sleeping (Träumchen) and awake (Du Mein) versions. Series V was 45 to 50 cm. (17½ to 19½ in.). Series VI was 55 to 60 cm. (21½ to 23½ in.).

1926: The bodies were washable except for one that was made of stockinet fabric. The heads and limbs were movable.

In London the agent, Seelig, advertised: Undressed dolls cost $4.32 and dressed they were $7.32; 25¢ of the purchase price of each doll was contributed to the National Council for Maternity and Child Welfare.

At F.A.O. Schwarz dolls in plain clothes cost $12.00, in better clothes $13.50, in fine quality clothes $15.00 and the best quality cost $16.50.

1927: Introduction of Series VII. Ht. 35 cm. (14 in).

1928: According to an English report in DEUTSCHE SPIEL-WAREN ZEITUNG, July, 1928: " 'Little' Käthe Kruse Doll is a type within the reach of every class of society. It combines the advantages of Doll I., the soft limbs of stuffed Massel; the painted plastic, little head, so easily washed and an exceptional cheap price." This was a smaller doll than those made previously and probably was designated Series VII. *Gerzon* sold dressed Käthe Kruse-type dolls. Hts. 35, 42 and 46 cm. (14, 16½ and 18 in.).

1929: Wigs were put on Series I dolls, and Series VIII, ht. 52 cm. (20½ in.), and Series IX, ht. 35 in. (14 in.), were introduced.

1930: Dolls with wigs were made in four styles including a girl with two braids and a short-haired boy. Dolls have more slender bodies than formerly. A group of novelty dolls such as those representing elves were exhibited.

The early Käthe Kruse catalogs were undated but approximate dates could be arrived at by comparison with dated sources such as the identical pictures shown in the STUDIO for 1913 and DEUTSCHE KUNST UND DEKORATION for 1914, plus dolls in identical costumes shown in other publications during the 1910s. The presence of nine World War I military costumes also substantiated the dating of one of the catalogs. A few of the dolls in this World War I catalog were also shown in the 1923–24 F.A.O. Schwarz catalog. Most of the Series I Käthe Kruse dolls were the same; only the clothes differed and determined the names in the following table.

The presence of a doll known to have been exhibited in 1922 as well as the presence of dolls in costumes identical to those shown elsewhere made possible the approximate dating of a later undated catalog.

Several of the dolls listed below continued to be dressed in the same type of costume for possibly as long as a decade. Generally it was the policy among doll makers (especially American manufacturers) to give their dolls new costumes nearly every year. Either Käthe Kruse did not follow this custom or the pictures used for the catalogs and advertisements were not always up-to-date.

One of the catalogs stated "The right is reserved to make changes in material, style and colour." This accounts for the variation even in the same catalog.

Klaus, Max and Thomas are shown with military tunics and accoutrements over their regular clothes. Also in the World War I catalog is a nameless doll in a nightgown and nightcap and a coffee warmer with a doll's head and arms. *Marion Kaulitz* was also making coffee warmers during World War I.★

KÄTHE KRUSE DOLLS
(All have high necklines)

Name*	Years	Series	Clothes description and height other than the 17 in. (43 cm.).
Agnes	1927–28	I	Print dress, panel down front, hat, toy in hand.
Alix	Ca. 1920s	I	Pink voile dress, full knee-length skirt, pink underwear, Biedermeier period style hat of pink voile with ruches.
Alma	1914–W.W.I	I	Dress without waistline. Four buttons down front, baby bonnet. (See Ill. 1562.)
Almut	1930	?	Wig. High-waisted plaid dress, bonnet. Height not given.
Annchen	W.W.I	I	White pinafore over a dotted print dress or blouse, conical hat.
Anneliese	1927	VII	Dress below calf length; carries flowers; mate to Leopold; 35 cm. (14 in.) ht.
Annemirl	1913–W.W.I	I	Print dress to ankles, large apron, shawl, high conical hat. (Called Gretchen in 1914.)
Bäbchen	1927–28	I	Dark jumper over light blouse, hat, carries a basket of flowers.
Babu	Ca. 1922	I	Jumper buttoned in front to waistline over long-sleeved print dress, matching cap.
Barbel	Ca. 1922–24	I	Knee-length floral print dress, white collar and cuffs matching cloche.
Bauz	1911	I	Baby doll.
Beate	W.W. I	I	Ankle-length print dress, high waistline, ¾ length sleeves, carries a parasol.
Bettina	Ca. 1922	I	Knee-length dress, high-waisted sash tied in front, lace shawl, modified tam with wide band.
Biball	1927	I	Sweater, knitted cap; carries flowers.
Bobo	1930	?	Wig, boy in shirt, tie and short pants. Height not given.
Bridgette	1927	I	Light dress and cloche.
Brigittchen	1930	?	Wig, two braids, girl in print jumper over a light blouse, carries a basket. Height not given.
Charlotte	Ca. 1922	I	Calf-length dark dress without a waistline, trimmed with rickrack. Revers at neckline reveals a blouse or dickie. Matching baby bonnet. Carries a cane.
Christinchen (Christichen)	1914–W.W.I	I	Knee-length, long-sleeved print dress trimmed at hemline with feather stitching, apron. Straw hat with narrow brim. (See Ill. 1562.)
Christkind	1914–W.W.I	I	Chemise, cap and bare feet. (See Ill. 1562.)
Conrad	W.W.I	I	Knee-length suit, buttons and tucks down front of the blouse. Wide collar and cuffs, bow tie, hat with turned-up brim.
Der Maxel	1927	II	Crocheted leotard and cap.
Dora	W.W.I	I	Dark costume with smock.
Dorchen	W.W.I	I	Print dress constructed like an 18th century robe. Dark footwear.
Elfriede	W.W. I	I	Dark ankle-length dress under striped smocked, baby bonnet with large bow under the chin.
Elschen	Ca. 1922	I	Knee-length low-waisted print dress. High cylindrical hat, sandals.
Emmy	Ca. 1922	I	Nearly ankle length full skirt. Panel down front to high waistline. Matching hood. Has a dog on a leash.
Erika	Ca. 1922	I	Knee length print dress, V neckline, no waistline. Bonnet has rosettes over each ear.
Erna	Ca. 1922–24	I	Knee-length print dress, matching hood, trimmed pinafore.
Esther	1926	I	Dressed as a girl with a hat.
Evchen	W.W.I	I	Same as Emmy except skirt and sleeves are longer.
Fanny	Ca. 1922	I	Dress of floral print on light ground, above-knee length, natural waistline. Cap has rosettes over each ear. Carries a parasol.
Felix	1914–24	I	Knitted sweater, leggings, scarf and cap.
Fifi	1927		
Finucke	Ca. 1922	I	Knee-length dark jumper, no waistline, light colored blouse, cloche, boots.
Freddy	W.W.I–1924	I	See Fritz in this Käthe Kruse table. See Ills. 1561 and 1562.
Friedel	Ca. 1922–28	I	Above-knee length vertical striped dress, square yoke, belt at low waistline. Cap with high crown. Holds the reins of a toy horse.
Friedebald	1929	VIII	German child with wig. Ht. 52 cm. (20½ in.).
Friedericke	1913–W.W.I	I	Checked knee-length dress, white Peter Pan collar and cuffs. String sash with fringed ends. Cloche. Carries a cane.
Fritz	1911–28	I	Knee-length trouser suit with wide pointed collar and cuffs. Pinafore trimmed with blanket stitch. Cloche (slight variation in the style of hat in the various pictures. See Ills. 1561 and 1562.) Also called Freddy.

KÄTHE KRUSE DOLLS
(All have high necklines)

Name*	Years	Series	Clothes description and height other than the 17 in. (43 cm.).
Frühsahrsamantel	W.W.I–Ca. 1922	I	Morning or summer coat, W.W.I; coat is plaid. Ca. 1922 has vertical stripes. Matching cloche.
Gänseliessel	Ca. 1922	I	Checked knee-length dress, button in front of upper part; dark full apron over skirt. A bandana on the head. Carries milk pails.
Gertraud	W.W.I	I	Light colored dress trimmed with tucks and eyelet embroidery, high waistline, full skirt to mid calves. Brimmed bonnet with large bow under the chin.
Gretchen	1914	I	See Annemirl in this Käthe Kruse table.
Gretel	1927		
Hannerle	W.W.I	I	Above the knees length print dress, normal waistline. Bonnet with very large bow under chin.
Hans	1913–27	I	Dark print smock, above-knee length, no waistline. Large light collar and cuffs. Matching cloche with high crown. See Ill. 1562.
Hedi	1926–28	I	Wears dress and cloche.
Henriette	1914–W.W.I	I	Light dress, mid-calf length, high waistline, puffed sleeves, mob cap. Carries a parasol.
Hermann	W.W.I	I	Same dress and hat as Friedericke except with a pinafore instead of collar and cuffs.
Hilde	W.W.I	I	Light colored dress trimmed with a dark print, as a pseudo-jacket and at the bottom of the mid-calf-length skirt. Cloche.
Inge	1927		Light dress and cloche.
Itzebumsack	Ca. 1922	I	Knee-length jumper with V neckline over a blouse. Bonnet with very full crown.
Jacky	Ca. 1920	I	Colored shirt, green pants, knitted cap (same as Jockerle). See Ill. 1562.
Jaköble	W.W.I	I	Long overcoat, dark vest, long checked trousers, bowtie, high collar, hat with a brim turned up.
Jockerle	W.W.I–1924	I	Striped shirt, knee-length pants with suspenders, knitted long stockings and cap. Carries books on back. (Same as Jacky.) See Ill. 1562.
Jordi 2	1930	?	Wig, bobbed, side part. High waist print dress above the knees. Height not known.
Karlchen	Ca. 1922	I	Boy's winter outfit, Dutch silhouette pants with fall. Helmet type headwear. See Ill. 1045 in ENCY I.
Kathel	Ca. 1922–24	I	Above the knees full skirt, high waistline, ribbon beading around neck and on turned-up brim of cloche.
Kathrinchen	1913–28	I	Dutch costume, mid calf length dress. White apron and fichu. Dutch cap. Wooden shoe shaped footwear.
Klärchen	W.W.I	I	High-waisted long sleeved pinafore over knee-length dress. Bonnet.
Klaus	W.W.I–1924	I	Apron with pocket, over dark romper suit. Brimmed hat. See Ill. 1562.
Klein-Datti	Ca. 1922	I	Knee-length dress trimmed with blanket stitch, including the armholes and cap. High belted waistline.
Kurt	1927–28	I	Striped short trousers, white shirt, brimless tall hat. Wears glasses, and carries a cane.
Leopold	1927	VII	Boy mate to Anneliese. Long coat and long trousers, waistcoat and high hat. Ht. 35 cm. (14 in.).
Liesel	1914–W.W.I	I	Dotted print above the knees length dress. Short dark jacket tied together in front. Dotted Dutch-shaped cap. See. Ill. 1562.
Lieselotte	W.W.I	I	Ankle-length dress, sash at high waistline, ruffle on skirt. Short printed jacket. High cylindrical hat matches jacket.
Lilli	W.W.I	I	Mid calf-length dress, light color, trimmed with dark rickrack. Shirt slit at sides, high waistline. Brimmed conical hat.
Lisebill	1929	VIII	German child with wig. Ht. 52 cm. (20½ in.).
Lu	Ca. 1920	I	Printed knee-length jumper, short-sleeved blouse. Described in the catalog as a "play-dress." Brimmed white felt hat.
Lutt Matten (Little Martin)	1913–W.W. I	I	Full knee-length pants, long sleeved jacket with three buttons down the front. Long scarf, wooden shoe shaped footwear. Dutch-type cylindrical hat.
Männe	Ca. 1922–24	I	Printed rompers with wide pocket on front. Blanket stitch around all the edges, including the cylindrical hat.

KÄTHE KRUSE DOLLS
(All have high necklines)

Name*	Years	Series	Clothes description and height other than the 17 in. (43 cm.).
Mareile	W.W.I	I	Ankle-length dress, high waistline, wide collar and cuffs. Full-crown bonnet with wide ties. See Ill. 1562.
Margaretchen	1911–W.W.I	I	Floor-length print dress, full skirt, knitted vest, cardigan and cloche.
Matten	1913–28	I	Dutch boy with light colored knitted jacket, dark full short pants, scarf and cylindrical hat. Wooden shoe shaped footwear. See Ill. 1562.
Max	1913–W.W.I	I	Knee-length dotted dress, string sash, dark yoke, brimmed hat. Carries a butterfly net. Also shown as a Prussian soldier.
Michel	1913–27	I	Dark full collarless shirt, light long trousers with seam pockets. Stocking cap. See Ills. 1562 and 1563.
Mimerle	W.W.I–1927	I	Ankle-length dress with long full sleeves, sash at high waistline. Baby-type bonnet. Named for Käthe Kruse's daughter.
Mimi	Before 1910	I	First doll made for daughter Mimerle. This was probably the baby doll filled with sand, having a potato head.
Minka	1926–27	I	Girl with cloche. Sold for $16.50 at F.A.O. Schwarz.
Moritz	W.W.I	I	Jacket with notched collar, knitted short pants and circular striped cap. See Ill. 1561.
Muche	Ca. 1922	I	Knee-length high waisted dress trimmed with embroidery, triangular shaped hat with tassel on side.
Nellie	1927–28	I	Striped dress, bonnet, carried a parasol and bunch of flowers.
Olga	Ca. 1922	I	Knee-length dress of striped fabric, hangs from yoke. Long sleeves have caps at shoulders. Cloche trimmed with fur.
Oskar	Before W.W.I	I	One of the early dolls made for Käthe Kruse's daughter Fifi.
Otto	1926	I	Boy with hat.
Pepi	Ca. 1922	I	Tyrolean type boy's outfit. Simulated lederhosen. Double-breasted jacket. Conical hat with feather. Carries a staff.
Peter	W.W.I	I	Knitted snowsuit with matching stocking cap and mittens.
Pumpernella	Ca. 1922	I	Knee-length printed fabric, narrow collar, two buttons down front. Tam with side extensions.
Ralph	Ca. 1920s	I	Red suit with short pants, light shirt, four-in-hand tie of printed fabric. Tam. Carries a cane.
Red Riding Hood			See Rotkappchen in this table.
Redcap			See Rotkappchen in this table.
Robert	1913–W.W.I	I	Knee-length print dress, sleeveless pinafore. Cloche.
Rotkappchen (Red Riding Hood, Redcap)	1914–26+	I	Red checked knee-length dress. Red knitted jacket and cap. Carries a basket.
Röschen	W.W.I–1914	I	Ankle-length A-line dress, knitted sweater trimmed with flowers. Cloche matches the sweater.
Rudi	Ca. 1922	I	Middy blouse buttons down the front, short pants. Wide brim straw hat. Carries a cane.
Rumpumpel	Ca. 1922	I	Mid-calf length print dress hangs from a square yoke. Plain band around the bottom of the skirt. Cloche extends down on both sides. Carries a rope of flowers.
Ruth	1926	I	Girl with hat.
Semper	W.W.I	I	Long trousers, short jacket, high waistline. Poke-bonnet with large bow under the chin. Carries a cane.
Seppi (Called Hans in 1914)	1913–W.W.I	I	Regional costume, short pants and vest, shirt trimmed with embroidered bands. Suspenders. Hat with frilled brim. Carries a staff. See Ills. 1561 and 1562.
Sofie	1914–W.W.I	I	Knee-length light dress, natural waistline, full skirt. Bonnet with large bow under the chin. Carries a parasol.
Soldiers	W.W.I	I	The dolls represented an infantryman, Hussar officer, Lancer officer, Mounted officer wearing a cuirass. The officers were described as German of Hindenburg. Four other dolls had military tunics over their regular attire and wore military caps or helmets. The helmets had either the pointed projection or a square projection on top. These dolls carried swords, rifles and/or pistols.

KÄTHE KRUSE DOLLS
(All have high necklines)

Name*	Years	Series	Clothes description and height other than the 17 in. (43 cm.).
			Small dolls only 11 cm. (4½ in.) tall were also dressed as soldiers.
Susannchen	W.W.I	I	Printed dress and plain pinafore.
Talla	1914–W.W.I	I	Ankle-length dress with sash at high waistline, printed coat with raglan sleeves. Bonnet with eyelet brim and full crown. See Ill. 1561.
Thomas	W.W.I	I	Shown as a soldier and also as a schoolboy wearing a pinafore.
Trudel	1914–W.W.I	I	Ankle-length dress trimmed with embroidered bands above high waistline. Short jacket with blanket stitch trimming. Knitted cloche.
Trudila	Ca. 1922	I	Knee-length floral print dress, with matching jacket. Bonnet has a high crown, lace around the face.
Ullrich	1913–W.W.I	I	Printed tunic with ruffle at bottom, open down the front, wide collar, matching short pants and tight fitting cap.
Ursel	Ca. 1922	I	High waisted, knee-length dress, striped full skirt, short jacket. Dress and jacket trimmed with blanket stitch. Band on tam matches the skirt, full crown.
Violet	Ca. 1920s	I	Silk dress without a waistline, above the knees in length, very short sleeves, hand embroidered trimming. Baby type cap.
Wera	Ca. 1922	I	Mid-calf length printed dress, high waistline, full skirt. Bonnet with ruffle around the face.
Wihelminchen	Ca. 1922	I	Ankle-length print dress, ruffle at hem, lace collar. Dark hip length jacket.
Willi	W.W.I	I	Striped pinafore and striped short pants. Short knitted sweater. Cloche. Books carried on his back.

*Some of these names were also used for dolls of various series made after 1930. There were other names for Käthe Kruse dolls of this period that the authors have not been able to verify. Sometimes there were slight variations in the clothes, but this did not change the original name. The heads of series I and VII were made of nettle cloth, while the heads of series II, V, and VI were made of stockinet.

UNBREAKABLE DOLLS   DESIGNED AND EXECUTED BY KÄTE KRUSE

1560. Käthe Kruse cloth dolls in a chemise-like garment; two of the dolls have headwear but none of them have footwear. The dolls were shown in STUDIO, March, 1911, a few months after they had first appeared on the market. The thumbs on these dolls were part of the hands and not a separate piece sewed onto the hand. The feet appear to have been longer and thinner than those found on later dolls.

1561. Pictures of Käthe Kruse dolls as shown in DEUTSCHE KUNST UND DEKORATION ("German Art and Decoration"), December, 1914. These dolls are left to right at top: Moritz, Talla, Seppi; at the bottom is Fritz; all Series I dolls.

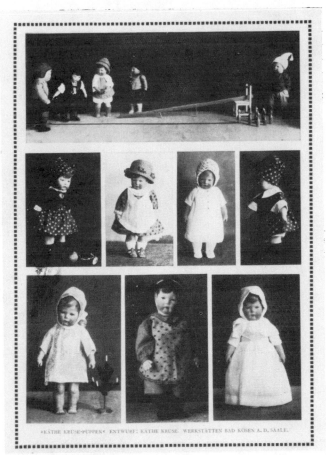

1562. Pictures of Käthe Kruse cloth dolls in DEUTSCHE KUNST UND DEKORATION ("German Art and Decoration"), December, 1914. The dolls, left to right, top row: Jockerle (?), Seppi, Fritz, Matten, Michel; middle row: Liesel, Christichen, Alma, Hans; bottom row: Christ child, Klaus or an early Fritz (?), Mareile (?). The costumes showed some variation but the principal features appeared to remain the same for a doll with a given name. All of these dolls are Series I.

UNBREAKABLE DOLLS DRESSED AS PEASANT CHILDREN MADE BY MISS KAETHE KRUSE, OF BERLIN, WHO ACHIEVES A REMARKABLE REALISM IN HER FIGURES

1563. Pair of Käthe Kruse dolls shown in INTERNATIONAL STUDIO, April, 1923. The doll on the left is named Michel. Both of these dolls are 17 in. (43 cm.) high.

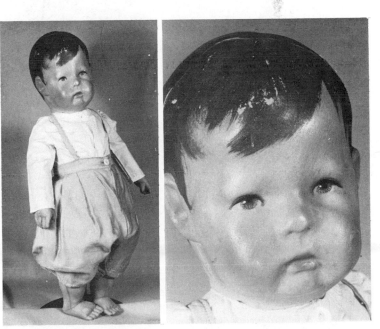

1564A & B. Cloth doll with its left foot bearing the stamp of Käthe Kruse. The molded features are painted with oil including the brown eyes and hair. This doll has a separate thumb, a feature found in Kruse dolls made at least by 1914.

It is wearing orange-yellow sateen trousers with suspenders and a white cotton blouse that are contemporary with the doll. H. 17 in. (43 cm.). *Coleman Collection.*

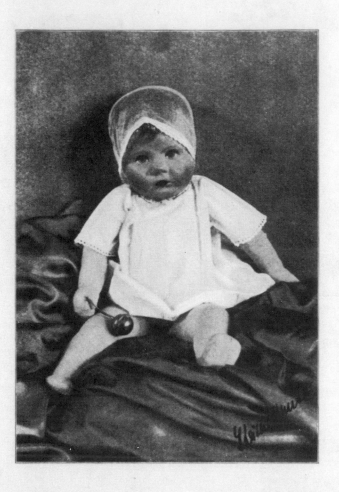

Käthe Kruse=Puppen
waschbar, weich, dauerhaft

Werkstätten der Käthe Kruse=Puppen, Bad Kösen
Zur Messe in Leipzig: Wagnerhaus, Grimmaische Straße.

1565. Advertisement for Käthe Kruse dolls in DEUTSCHE SPIELWAREN ZEITUNG, February 1927. Picture is of the baby dolls of that period. Note the Käthe Kruse signature in the lower right corner of the picture. The dolls are described as being "washable, soft, durable." Compare this baby with the ones shown in 1911, Ill. 1560.

KATHE KRUSE-DOLLS

THE WORLD-FAMED SOFT DOLLS

IB-137—Agnes

LIFELIKE REPRODUCTIONS
SOFT, DURABLE, WASHABLE

Made Entirely by Hand
of Impregnated Nettle-Cloth

TWO SIZES:

SERIES I.......17″ high
SERIES VII.....14″ high

Each series can be delivered in numerous
styles and dresses.

For particulars please write to the manufacturers:

WERKSTÄTTE DER KÄTHE
KRUSE-PUPPEN

BAD KÖSEN XI / Germany

DURING THE LEIPZIG FAIRS:

Messhaus Wagner, Grimmaische Strasse

IA-132—Nellie

IA-131—Bäbchen

VII—Leopold   VII—Anneliese

IB-136—Kurt

Good business and good fellowship suggest mentioning PLAYTHINGS.

1566. Advertisement for Käthe Kruse dolls in PLAYTHINGS, December 1927. These dolls were made in two sizes. Series I, the earlier type, was 43 cm. (17 in.) high. Series VII, which appeared around 1927, was 35 cm. (14 in.) high. All of these dolls are shown with accessories.

1567. Composition head Käthe Kruse doll with the composition only to the top of the neck; the rest of the sand-weighted body is a pink stockinet. The hair is knotted through a muslin cap. It has painted eyes and a closed mouth. The ears are large and protruding. The hands have curved fingers. Original clothes. It is signed Käthe Kruse on the sole of the foot. H. 19 in. (48 cm.). *Courtesy of the late Magda Byfield.*

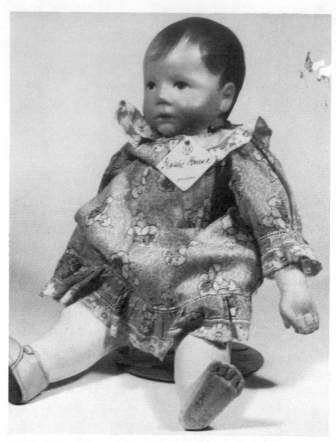

1568. Käthe Kruse cloth doll with painted hair and features. Original clothes. The mark (Ill. 1571), and no. 33947, on the bottom of the foot. Note the original Käthe Kruse tag. This is a Series VII doll made in 1927 or later. H. 14 in. (35 cm.). *Courtesy of the late Mary Roberson. Photo by Barbara Jendrick.*

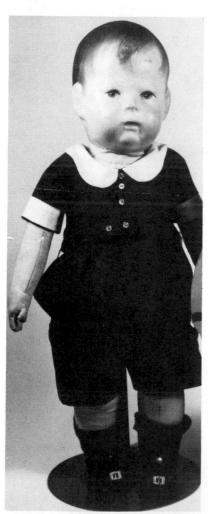

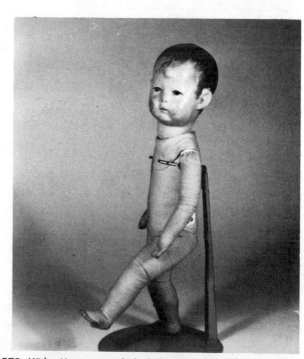

1569. Käthe Kruse cloth doll with painted hair and eyes, closed mouth, body jointed at the shoulders and hips. The fingers are together and the thumb is an extra piece sewed onto the hand. Mark on foot: "Käthe Kruse 89960." H. 17 in. (43 cm.). *Courtesy of Richard Withington. Photo by Barbara Jendrick.*

1570. Käthe Kruse type cloth doll jointed at the neck, shoulders and hips. Painted hair and features on a socket-type head. The thumb is part of the hand and not an added piece sewed onto the hand. Marked "183" in red on the sole of its foot. H. 35 cm. (14 in.). *Courtesy of Richard Withington. Photo by Barbara Jendrick.*

Käthe Kruse
33947

1571–1572. Marks on Käthe Kruse cloth dolls. Ill. 1571 is on the sole of a foot; Ill. 1572 is on a paper tag.

Kruse-type dolls. 1928. Dressed dolls sold by *Gerzon.* Hts. 35, 42 and 46 cm. (14, 16.5, and 18 in.). (See also **Susie's Sister, Heine & Schneider, Klötzer,** and **Bing** dolls, 1927.)

Kubelka, Josef. 1884–1910. Vienna. Patented processes for affixing dolls' hair.

1907–10: Listed in directories under Dolls and Dolls' Heads. The Business was called *Zur Puppendoktorim* (At the Dolls' Lady Doctor). Advertised "A choice of the finest specialty Dolls, Toy Dolls. The biggest and oldest repair house in Vienna." This information was researched by Dr. Eva Moskovszky.

1909: Obtained an Austrian patent for affixing dolls' hair by piercing the scalp in several places, drawing the hair through from the inside with a crochet needle and gluing it in place.★

Küchler & Co. See **Galluba & Hofmann.**

Kuddle Mee (Kuddlemee). 1915–18. Plush dolls made by *British Novelty Works,* a subsidiary of *Dean.*

Kuddles. 1915–17. Cloth dolls made of Turkish toweling by *Jane Gray Co.* These dolls had handpainted flat faces. They were washable, floatable and filled with kapok. The clothes were painted on the dolls. (See also **Cuddles.**)★

Kufi. 1925–26. *Lenci* felt doll, style no. 261, represented a little black girl dressed in checked pattern felt and having a large hairbow.

Kühles (Kühle), Franz. 1904–30 and later. Ohrdruf, Thür. Manufactured dolls, especially ball-jointed dolls.

1904: Advertised bisque heads and wooden heads with wigs; ball-jointed and five-piece bodies, as well as parts for dolls.

1910: Advertised bisque shoulder heads and socket heads; babies and character dolls; leather bodies and composition bodies. Dolls that were 60 cm. (23½ in.) tall cost 60¢.

1913: Named a line of dolls *Spezial.* Specialized in five hts. 56, 60, 63, 65 and 68 cm. (22, 23½, 25, 25½, and 27 in.).

1925: Applied for a German patent (D.R.G.M.) for a seamless aluminum doll's head. (See also **Manufacture of Dolls, Commercial: Made in Germany in Waltershousen Region.**)★

Kühn, Berthold. 1927–30. Georgenthal, Thür. Made socket and shoulder heads for dolls, including baby dolls. The heads had molded hair or wigs and were placed on ball-jointed composition bodies, bent-limb baby bodies or cloth bodies. One style baby shoulder head had bent baby arms attached at the shoulder joints.

Kühn, Ernst. 1925–26. Catterfeld, Thür. Manufactured and exported dolls including ball jointed child dolls and character baby dolls. Most of the dolls wore only a chemise.

Kühnlenz, Gebrüder. 1884–1930. Kronach, Bavaria. Made dolls and/or dolls' heads in their porcelain factory. Registered 44/20 through 44/35 mold #s for dolls according to the research of the Ciesliks. Other mold numbers probably used by Kühnlenz were: 13, 21, 28, 32, 38, 41, 56 and 165. A dash and a size number usually followed these mold numbers with the exception of 165. Other size numbers besides 20 through 35 have been observed on bisque heads bearing the mold # 44.

1907: Bisque head dolls with wigs, stationary glass eyes, open mouth, and five-piece composition bodies, dressed as soldier boys. Some of the heads were marked "G K 44–14" and the costumes included those in red, red and blue, pale blue and dark blue. These dolls were distributed by *Butler Bros.* Ht. 6 in. (15 cm.).

1914: Marshall Field also distributed these dolls. ★

Kummer, Robert. 1910–11. Prössneck, Bohemia. Listed in a Vienna directory under Wooden Dolls.

Kundy, Franz. See **Catterfelder Puppenfabrik.**

Kuni (Swiss, Berne). Before 1911–13. Felt doll made by *Steiff* and dressed in the regional costume of a boy of Berne, Switzerland. Ht. 35 cm. (14 in.).

Kunnin-Kids. 1921–23. Trade name of 11 styles of stockinet dolls stuffed with kapok, made by the *Ontario Textile Co.* The faces were handpainted and the dolls were dressed in scarlet, blue, orange, and white. Hts. 9, 14, and 19 in. (23, 35.5, and 48 cm.); priced $4.00 to $21.00 a doz. wholesale.★

Kunōdi, Berta. 1907–10. Hungary. Listed in a Vienna directory under Dolls and Dolls' Heads.

Kunst, Anton. 1920–26. New York City. Advertised that he was the "Largest doll die maker in America." They did all the modeling, plastering and molding in this bronze and brass foundry, known as the Kunst-Art Bronze Founderies. The picture in the advertisement shows molds with six dolls' heads, six dolls' bodies and six pairs of dolls' arms and legs.

Kunstanstalt, Grimme & Hempel. 1905. Leipzig, Germany. Applied for a German patent (D.R.G.M.) for celluloid dolls' heads.

Kunstler Kopf (Art Head). See **Schoenau & Hoffmeister.**

1573A & B. Bisque swivel-neck shoulder head possibly made by Gebrüder Kühnlenz. It is on a gusseted kid body with bisque hands and cloth feet. The head has a wig, plaster pate, stationary glass eyes, pierced ears and an open-closed mouth. Mark: Ill. 1041 in the first COLLECTOR'S ENCYCLOPEDIA OF DOLLS on the socket head and 27 is incised on the shoulder plate. H. 17½ in. (44.5 cm.). H. of shoulder head 5½ in. (14 cm.). *Coleman Collection.*

1575–1577. "G K" marks used by (or possibly used by) Gebrüder Kühnlenz on their bisque heads.

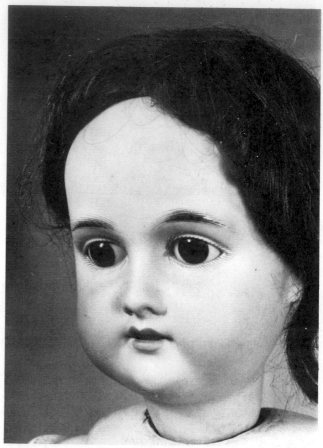

1574. Doll marked "G K" possibly for Gebrüder Kühnlenz has a bisque head, sleeping brown eyes, an open mouth with four upper teeth, and a ball-jointed composition body. Mark Ill. 1575. H. 26 in. (66 cm.). *Courtesy of Cherry Bou.*

Kuntz & Co. (Berliner Celluloidfabrik). 1895. Berlin. Applied for a German patent (D.R.G.M.) for celluloid dolls' limbs. ★

Kurly Head. 1930 and later. Trademark registered in U.S. by *Arranbee.* The trademark was "KURLY HEAD//TRADE MARK//ARRANBEE//DOLL CO." and a circle within which was a full face doll's head.

Kurt (Winter Sports). 1911 and earlier. Felt character doll made by *Steiff.* It was dressed for Winter sports in a white sweater. Mate to *Else.* Four hts. 28, 35, 43 and 50 cm. (11, 14, 17 and 19½ in.); priced $1.05 to $2.35.

Ku-tee. 1919. Cotton stuffed cloth dolls made by *Hausman & Zatulove* (Hau-Zat). The dolls had handpainted faces. They were washable and had no metal on them. The clothes represented boys and girls. Three hts. 15, 18 and 21 in. (38, 45.5 and 53.5 cm.).

Kutie. 1930. Stockinet doll made by *Plotnick.* It had painted features, stub hands and feet and came in assorted colors, wearing a tight fitting knitted cap. Dolls were 12½ to 13 in. (31.5 to 33 cm.) high; price 50¢.

1578. Mark on Hausman & Zatulove's cloth Ku-Tee dolls.

Kutie-Kins. 1915–16. Felt dolls stuffed with cotton, made by *A. W. Hanington.* They wore a variety of costumes including style No. 3, Little Bo-Peep, with a peaked hat and carrying a crook.

No. 6, Soldier Boy, dressed as a boy in short trousers but wearing an army-type kepi and carrying a rifle and pistol. No. 10, Dutch Boy, with suspenders over its shirt, full short trousers and wooden shoes.★

L

La Bambola. 1930. Turin, Italy. Made dolls.

La Bèrgère de Trianon. 1917. Inscription found on a china socket head made by *Sèvres.* It had a wig, painted eyes. Ht. of head only, 6 cm. (2½ in.) (See Ill. 2369B.)

La Boulaye. See **De la Boulaye.**

La Fabrication Féminine. World War I. Group that created dolls designed by well-known artists.

La Fossa. 1893–1894 and later. M. La Fossa made dolls until his death in 1894 and his widow continued the business. One of the La Fossa dolls was a whistler. Ht. 10 in. (25.5 cm.) according to Eleanor Haight.

La Francia. 1915–19. Paris. Group founded by *Mme. d'Eichthal* for the creation of dolls designed by well-known artists. *M. Botta* was among those who made dolls for La Francia. Some of their dolls were called "Bretonnes de la Francia."★

La Georgienne. One of the *Favorite* line made by *Lanternier.* A La Georgienne doll marked size number 1 was 19 in. (48 cm.) tall.★

La Mascotte. 1929–30 and later. Trademark registered in France by *M. Gregoire Biberian* for cloth art dolls made in Nice. (See also **Bébé Mascotte.**)

La Moglette. See **Moglette.**

La Mouche. 1918. Trademark registered in France by *Mme. Poulbot.*

La Nicette. See **La Poupée Nicette.**

La Parisienne. 1913. Name of a *mignonnette* advertised by *Bon Marché.* It came dressed as a lady in various costumes. Ht. 19 cm. (7½ in.); priced 49¢.

La Parisienne. 1921–22. Trade name of an "Unbreakable" doll designed by *Jean Ray* and sold by *Bon Marché.* It was dressed in a velvet coat trimmed with fur. Ht. 35 cm. (14 in.).

La Parisienne. 1925–30 and later. Trade name of dolls made by *Carlier, Fournelle & Gibon.* The name was attributed to *Maurice Millière,* possibly he was the designer (See the first COLLECTOR'S ENCYCLOPEDIA OF DOLLS for other La Parisiennes.).

La Patricienne. 1906–08. Name of a doll made by the successors of *Jules Steiner.*★

LA PATRICIENNE
(DEPOSE)

E.
D. B.
Paris

1579–1580. Marks on La Patricienne doll's head (No. 1579) and on its body (No. 1580).

1581. Cloth doll named La Poupée Nicette with molded features, wig, painted brown eyes and a closed mouth. *Courtesy of Iris Jenney.*

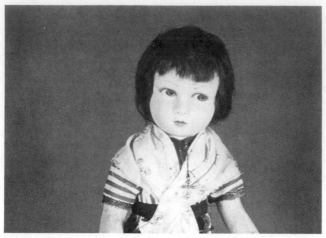

1582. Cloth doll, probably a La Poupée Nicette made in Nice, France. It has a wig, molded and painted features, eyes looking to the side and a closed mouth. Original regional costume. *Courtesy of Robert & Katrin Burlin.*

La Patrouille. 1911. Trade name of a doll patented by *Edmond L'Hotte.*

La Perfezionata Bambola Marciante Universale. Name on a box containing a bisque-head walking doll.

La Petite Americaine. 1918. Name of a fully jointed doll with wig and sleeping eyes, distributed by *Printemps.* The doll wore a red, white and blue satin costume. Ht. 41 cm. (16 in.); price $5.18.

La Petite Bretonne. See **French Regional Costume Dolls.**

La Petite Caresse. See **Caresse.**

La Petite Dolls. 1922. Small bisque-head dolls distributed by *Montgomery Ward.* They had mohair wigs, sleeping eyes and were jointed at the shoulders and hips. Ht. 10 in. (25.5 cm.); with teeth cost 89¢. Six other heights without teeth were 6½, 8½, 9½, 9¾, 11¾ and 13 in. (16.5, 21.5, 24, 25, 30, and 33 cm.); priced 49¢ to 79¢.

La Petite Georgette. 1921. Chromolithographed cutout cloth doll advertised by *Bon Marché.* Ht. 50 cm. (19½ in.).

La Place Clichy. 1896–1923 and probably other years. Paris. A large department store that advertised dolls in their catalogs.

1900: Advertised *Bébé Bru, Bébé Culotte, Bébé La Parisienne, Bébé Marcheur, Bébé Moncey, Bébé Teteur, Eden Bébé, Marotte, Mignonnette,* dolls' house dolls, clowns, soldiers, and dolls dressed in regional costumes.

1905: Advertised *Bébé Dormeur,* Bébé Moncey, *Bébé Tout en Bois,* and Eden Bébé.

1907: Bébé Tout en Bois was advertised.

1911: *Bébé Merveilleux,* Bébé Dormeur, Bébé Moncey and Bébé Tout en Bois were advertised.

1913: Advertised *Bébé Maillot* and *Bébé Promenette.*

1914: Advertised Bébé Moncey, and *Rintintin* and *Nénette* designed by *Poulbot.*

1923: *Bébé à la Mode,* Bébé Culotte, and Bébé Moncey were advertised. See Ill. 754 in THE COLLECTOR'S BOOK OF DOLLS' CLOTHES.

La Pompadour. 1928–29. Cloth dolls made by *G. Bagnaro.*

La Poupée de France. World War I period. Name of a group who created artistic dolls designed by well-known artists.★

La Poupée de Poche. Pocket-size dolls. (See also **Le Poupon.**)

La Poupée Ideale. 1921. Trademark registered in France by *Isidore Dreifuss* for a special type of doll.

La Poupée Nicette (La Nicette). 1924–30 and later. Cloth, usually felt, art dolls made by *Gaston Perrimond.* The Paris agent was *Maurice Cahen.*

1930: Exported by *Leprestre & Guilleray.* Dolls were for children and for decoration.★

La Poupée T. S. F. 1928. Paris. Made patented dolls.

La Poupée Volante. 1891. Trade name of an *Alice Couterier* French bisque-head doll.

La Princess. 1930. Paris. Name of a shop that made and/or distributed dolls.

La Princesse. 1918. Trademark registered in France by Mme. *Poulbot* for dolls.

La Rosa. See **Fabbria Italiana Bambole.**

La Semaine de Suzette. 1905–30 and later. France. Weekly publication that included information about clothes for *Bleuette, Bambino* and other dolls. There were many stories about dolls in this journal, as well as characters that were the inspiration for dolls such as *Bécassine.*

1928: Gave instructions for making Doll Fetishes (Mascots) for the automobile out of wooden beads.

La Superba. 1906–09. Patented phonograph doll made by *Max Oscar Arnold.* The doll was also called *Arnoldia.* It could both sing and talk.

La Tentation. 1916 and probably other years. Belgium. A store that won first prize for its exhibit of dolls at an Exposition in Brussels for the benefit of the children of Belgian soldiers.

La Vénus.† See **Vénus.**

La Vie Femmes. 1915. Company organized by *Mlle. Momson* to put widows and wounded soldiers all over France to work sewing bodies and clothes for dolls. The heads were supplied from a former commercial doll-making factory. *Mrs. Le Verrier* sold the dolls in America.

La Ville de Paris. 1903 and probably other years. Paris. A store that distributed *Bébé Culotte, Bébé Dormeur* and a cloth doll listed as *Bébé Habillé* (dressed doll).

Laar, Pauline Henriette Van (née Petit Maître). 1925–26.

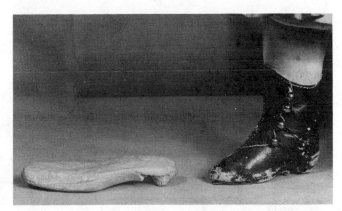

1583. Composition shoe sole and heel made according to the 1874 Lacmann patent to provide a firm base for a doll's shoe. On the right is the finished Lacmann boot having the solid sole. The doll wearing the boot is shown in the first COLLECTOR'S ENCYCLOPEDIA OF DOLLS, Ill. 1053.

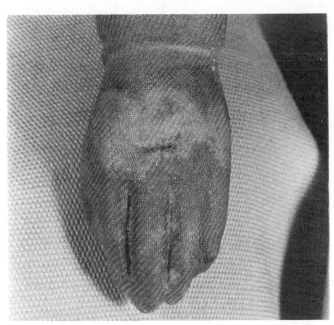

1584. Doll's hand made of cotton fabric over a composition molded form according to Lacmann's 1874 patent. This is the hand of the doll shown in the first COLLECTOR'S ENCYCLOPEDIA OF DOLLS, Ill. 1053.

Gerzenfer, Switzerland. Obtained a German patent (D.R.P.) for a doll.

Labat, Mme. 1925–30. Paris. Made and/or distributed dolls.★

Labrador dolls. Dolls whittled out of bits of wood by *Eskimos*. The dolls were dressed in fur with fur caps on their heads. The fur coats of the dolls representing men had a longer "tail" or base than those representing women. According to TOYS AND NOVELTIES in 1915 a boat came only once a year to pick up these dolls.

Lackey (Lackai). See **Green.**

Lacmann, Jacob. 1860–83. Philadelphia, Pa. Patented dolls' hands and feet in the U.S. in 1874.★

Lacombe, Jean Gaspard (called Camille). 1848–51. France. Made and distributed dolls. He married in 1848 and with the dowry money purchased a business which failed in 1851, according to Mme. Poisson, Curator of the Roybet Fould Museum.

Lacroix, Mme. Margaine. See **Margaine-Lacroix, Mme.**

Laddie. 1912–13. Cutout cloth doll representing a "Scotch" (Scottish) boy, advertised by *Selchow & Righter.* Ht. 8 in. (20.5 cm.); priced 40¢ doz. wholesale.

Laddie. 1922. Line of dolls made by *Wonderland.*

L'Adelphie. 1915–16. France. Founded by *Mlle. Bucquet.* L'Adelphie created dolls that were dressed simply.

Ladies Sewing Society of the Moravian Church. See **Polly Heckewelder.**

Lady Acrobat. Ca. 1905–30 and later. One of the *Schoenhut* wooden circus dolls. It is similar to the *Lady Circus Rider* but it wore tights instead of a skirt.★

Lady Betty. 1920–21. Stockinet doll with long curled wig that could be brushed and combed, made by *Chad Valley.* Removable clothes were made of silk or other material. The

dress was above the knees and the doll, style No. 3, wore a picture hat. Ht. 13 in. (33 cm.).

Lady Charmana. 1922. Line of dolls made by *Wonderland.*

Lady Circus Rider. Ca. 1905–30 and later. *Schoenhut* wooden doll.

1924: Came in two sizes.★

Lady Di. 1922. Dolls made by *Wonderland,* of red and cream colored plushette. These came in four hts.

Lady Dolls. Nearly all of the bisque-head lady dolls on French type bodies that have been examined have had pressed heads. (See **Pressed versus Poured.**) Sometimes these dolls came with painted eyes and swivel neck or glass eyes and stationary necks or with painted eyes and stationary necks, although most of them had both the glass eyes and swivel neck.

The heads had various marks including F. G. for *Gaultier,* E.B. for *Barrois, Bru Jne.* and others but most of the heads had only a size number or letter and many have no mark at all. Ralph Griffith reported a lady doll with "Breveté 1292" on the front and "M.4 T." on the back. The bodies often carried the name *Jumeau, Simonne,* and so forth, or the name of the store from which it was sold. (See also **French Dolls.**) The type of clothes designated a Lady doll.

The bisque heads of lady dolls made in Germany were usually poured. Most of the porcelain factories, especially in the Ohrdruf area, made heads for lady dolls.

The bodies were made of a variety of material: wood, kid, wood and kid, blown kid, or cloth. Lady dolls of cloth including felt were popular in the 1920s. (See **Boudoir Dolls.**) All-composition lady dolls as well as those with celluloid, suede, kid, or composition heads have been found. Many of the post World War I art dolls represented ladies.

1904: DEKORATIVE KUNST showed a group of Lady dolls. See Ills. 1594 and 2495.

1908: Among those who won prizes for their Lady dolls in the Paris *Exhibition of 1908* were *Lafitte & Désirat* for wax Lady dolls and *Mme. Riera* for bisque-head Lady dolls.

1912: DEKORATIVE KUNST showed *Steiff* Lady dolls dressed in the height of the then current fashions.

1913: Mignonnette dressed as a lady was sold by *Bon Marché*.

1916: The Baroness de *Laumont* founded the *Ligue du Jouet Français* where her Lady dolls were made. They had either bisque or composition heads.

1931: Bisque-head Lady dolls with wig, composition body with long thin legs without a knee joint were sold by *Montgomery Ward.* In a chemise they cost $2.98; dressed, they cost $4.98.★

1586. Queen Anne–type wooden doll with a wig, stationary black pupilless glass eyes, dots for eyelashes and along the eyebrows, and a closed mouth. The body is cloth and kid. Original costume of the early 1800s. H. 12½ in. (31.5 cm.). *Courtesy of Sotheby Parke Bernet Inc., N.Y.*

1587. Lady doll with a papier-mâché shoulder head and an open mouth with teeth. It is on a kid body and is wearing a bridal costume of ca. 1850. H. 14½ in. (37 cm.). *Courtesy of Sotheby Parke Bernet Inc., N.Y.*

1585. Carved and painted wooden lady doll with black windswept hair, painted gray eyes, pierced ears, closed mouth, and ball joints at the shoulders, elbows, hips and knees. The bosom and upper part of the chemise as well as the footwear are painted. H. 10 in. (25.5 cm.). *Courtesy of Estelle Johnston.*

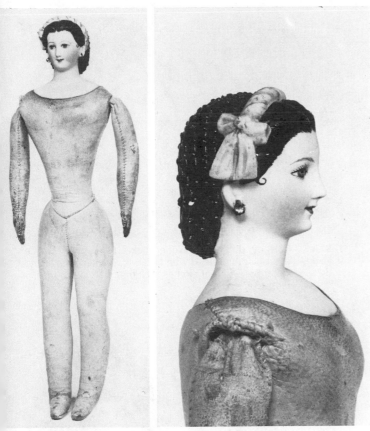

1588A & B. Untinted bisque shoulder-head doll with molded dark brown hair in a green and lavender snood, and a spit curl on the cheek. The molded blue eyes have an enamel finish. The ears are pierced and the mouth is closed. The pink kid body has no joints but the fingers are indicated by sewing. (A head with similar molding can be found under the china section, in Ill. 326 A & B, in the first COLLECTOR'S ENCYCLOPEDIA OF DOLLS.). H. of doll 16¼ in. (41.5 cm.). H. of shoulder head 4¼ in. (11 cm.). *Courtesy of the Margaret Woodbury Strong Museum. Photos by Harry Bickelhaupt.*

1589. Three bisque-head lady dolls. They have wigs, stationary glass eyes, closed mouths and kid bodies. The doll on the right has bisque arms. All have original clothes. *Courtesy of Elsie and Al Potter.*

1590. Pair of wax-over-composition shoulder head dolls with curly blond wigs, stationary blue glass eyes, wire loop earrings, closed mouths, and cloth bodies. The wax-over-composition lower arms have simulated gloves. The smaller doll has an opening indicated between two buttons at the wrists. The legs have cloth stockings and garters fitting into molded composition buttoned boots. Original clothes. Hs. 15 and 19 in. (38 and 48 cm.). *Courtesy of Estelle Johnston.*

1592A & B. Lady doll with bisque socket head on a bisque shoulder plate, neck joint lined with kid, wig, painted eyes, cloth body with kid arms. Original clothes including hat. H. 13 in. (33 cm.). *Coleman Collection.*

1591A & B. Bisque shoulder head on a cloth body with bisque lower arms and wooden upper arms is dressed as a lady of the late 1870s. The bald head has blue threaded glass eyes, closed mouth, and pierced ears. It wears a commercial dress with a train made of deep maroon and cream satin trimmed with metallic embroidery, lace, and maroon and cream satin ribbons. Footwear includes bronze boots and red and white circular striped stockings. H. 18 in. (45.5 cm.). *Coleman Collection.*

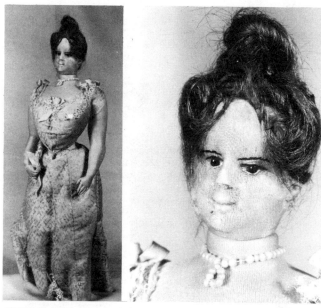

1593A & B. Needle sculptured silk cloth doll representing a lady, with glass bead eyes, embroidered features, rolled fingers. Original clothes suggest an 1890s date. H. 13 in. (33 cm.). *Coleman Collection.*

1594. Group of dolls representing ladies in historical costumes as shown in an exhibition where dolls were designed by Karl Gross, Otto Gussmann, Wilhelm Kreis, William Lossow, Oskar Seyfert, Hugo Spieler, and Wilhelm Thiele. These dolls were exhibited in Dresden, 1904, according to DEKORATIVE KUNST. (See also Ill. 2495.)

1595. Poured wax shoulder-head lady doll with inserted hair, threaded blue glass eyes. The body is cloth with poured wax lower limbs. The underclothes are original. Reportedly this doll was purchased in England in 1912. H. 16¼ in. (41 cm.). *Courtesy of Katrin and Robert Burlin.*

Concours de la « POUPÉE CHARITABLE, » aux Magasins Léonhard Tietz, au profit des œuvres « *Le Lait pour les Petits* » et Soc. prot. des « *Enfants Martyrs* »
Phot G. Bauck, Anvers

1596. Postcard picture of a group of lady dolls as shown by Léonhard Tietz in his store in Antwerp, Belgium, ca. 1910. These dolls appear to be like the ones made and dressed by Lafitte and Désirat. (See Ill. 1609.)

Lady Fuller. 1917. Doll with Can't Break 'Em[†] head and limbs on a cloth body, distributed by *Charles William*. The doll had molded hair, parted lips with teeth showing and wore a hat and coat. Ht. 16 in. (40.5 cm.); priced 98¢.

Lady Sheila. 1922. Line of dolls made by *Wonderland*.

Lady Sylvia. 1928. *Mama* dolls with sleeping eyes and dress of silk. Price $12.00.

Lafayette, Galeries. 1895–1930 and later. Paris. Large department store that sold dolls.

1912: Advertised dressed *Kiss-Throwing* Bébé.

1913: Dolls included *Bébé Gourmand, Bébé Jumeau, Bébé Lafayette, Bébé Réclame, Nénette* and *Rintintin* (designed by *Poulbot*), *Steiff* Boy-Scout *(Bob)*, and a whistling boy doll *(Le Petit Siffleur)*. See Ills. 1598 and 1599.

1926–27: Advertised Kiss-Throwing Bébé as well as a bébé with bisque head, wig, sleeping eyes, hair eyelashes, fully jointed body, a silk dress and stockings, leather slippers. Ht. 50 cm. (19½ in.).

Lafayette also advertised dressed dolls with composition heads on cloth bodies. Hts. 55 and 65 cm. (21½ and 25½ in.).

1927: Dolls included Bébé Lafayette, *Claudine, Colette, Gaby, Geneviève, Genvrinette,* Jacqueline, *Jeanette,* Kiss-Throwing dolls, Mignonnettes, New Born Babies, Pierrette, Pierrot, Réclame Bébé (Bébé Réclame), *Régini* and *Suzon* as well as bisque head bébés, "unbreakable" head bébés and cloth dolls. They sold separate dolls' heads of cloth with or without hair, mask faces with or without hair and dolls' bodies. (See THE COLLECTOR'S BOOK OF DOLLS' CLOTHES, Ills. 630 and 639.)

Lafayette, O. J., & Co. 1930 and later. Los Angeles, Calif. Made washable cloth dolls with painted features; some of the dolls represented moving picture stars and were called *Hollywood Babes*. Other models included Indians, black dolls, and *Little Red Riding Hood*.

1597. Bisque head lady doll made in the 1920s. It has silk embroidery-yarn hair, painted and molded features and the body is of wire covered with silk fabric. Original clothes. The base of the doll is marked "Made in// Japan." H. 5¼ in. *Coleman Collection.*

1598. Lafayette catalog page showing dolls in 1913. Among their dolls were dressed talking Bébés Jumeau with sleeping eyes and hair eyelashes. Similar Bébés Lafayette cost only a little over half as much as the Jumeaus. Most of the dolls were advertised as being able to walk. Some were mechanical walking dolls such as the "Bébé Premiers Pas." Even the Mignonnette only 23 cm. (9 in.) was a walking doll. Two of the dolls could throw kisses and several could talk. Some of the dolls had removable clothes, including the small, 18 cm. (7 in.) celluloid dolls. *Courtesy of the Collection Nederlands Kostuummuseum, The Hague.*

1599. Dolls sold at the Lafayette store in 1925. Most of the dolls are cloth. Only Bébé Lafayette and the mignonnette with its trousseau have bisque heads. Several of the dolls have composition heads. Only one doll is described as walking and none of them as talking. *Courtesy of the Collection Nederlands Kostuummuseum, The Hague.*

Lafitte & Désirat, Mmes. Before 1908–18 and possibly later. They designed and created wax-headed dolls, with the help of the Musée de Grevin (a wax works museum). Mme. Désirat was the sister of Mme. Lafitte who was the sister-in-law of the founder of the fashion periodical FEMINA. The dolls were dressed to show the fashions each season, each year, beginning with about 1900. The date of the costume style was on the base of each doll. By 1908 they had already won so many prizes that they were designated as "Hors

Concours" when they exhibited in Paris a series of wax dolls dressed as contemporary dancers and wearing hats. A group of their dolls had costumes of the type worn by women in wartime factories, women engaged in wartime transportation, and so forth during World War I.

1924: The Lafitte & Désirat dolls were exhibited at the Musée de la Guerre.

Lakenmacker Co. 1921–24. New York City. Imported dolls

1600. Two wax-head lady dolls created by Lafitte, Désirat. They have mohair wigs, painted eyes, closed mouth. The bodies are made of wrapped wire armatures, some of the hands are wax, others kid, presumably to represent gloves. The painted kid boots with heels form the feet. The original velvet, fur, and silk costumes are trimmed with beads, flowers and feathers. Mark on base "LAFITTE DESIRAT." Label on bottom of base: "MADE IN FRANCE." *Courtesy of Estelle Johnston.*

especially small bisque baby dolls, jointed dolls, and novelty dolls.

1922: Advertised dressed jointed dolls.

1923: Advertised bisque baby dolls, 1½ to 8 in. (4 to 20.5 cm.) tall. The smallest dolls had joints only at the shoulders while the others were jointed at the shoulders and hips.★

Lama-Lack. 1911–13. A lacquer-like finish used by *Kämmer & Reinhardt* on some of their dolls.

Lambert, André. 1924–30. Paris. Advertised that *Zina* dolls were produced in his factory. He also had a store.★

Lambert, John. 1918. Paris. Created dolls.

Lambert, Leopold. 1880–1920s. Paris. Mary Hillier reported that Lambert served as an apprentice to *Vichy* and later had his shop near *Roullet & Decamps*. Leopold Lambert was no. 85, a member of the *Chambre Syndicale*. Among his mechanical dolls were Bébé Mignon, Bébé Nid, and clowns. He also provided accessories for dolls.★

Lambert & Samhammer. 1872–84. Sonneberg, Thür.

Mathias Lambert and *Philipp Samhammer* founded a doll and toy factory in 1872. The partnership was terminated in 1881 and Lambert sold the factory to *Armand Marseille* in 1884. Meanwhile Samhammer had started his own business. Their dolls were chiefly composition and wax-over-composition. They used an anchor with the entwined initials L S near the top of the anchor.

Lambin-Cousin. 1926–30 and later. Nogent-sur-Oise, France. Made dolls.

Lamhammer, Philip. See **Samhammer, Philipp.**

Lamkin (Lamkins). Ca. 1930. *Effanbee* doll with composition head, arms, and legs, molded hair, sleeping eyes. Ht. 16 in. (40.5 cm.).

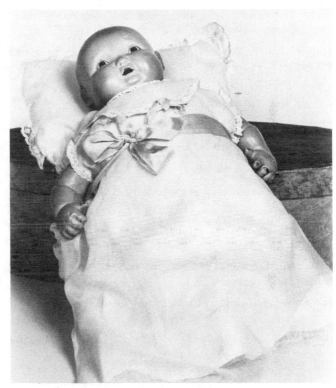

1601. Composition head doll named Lamkin, made by Effanbee. It has painted hair slightly molded, blue celluloid-type eyes, open mouth with tongue, and a pink cloth body with curved composition arms and legs. Original clothes and pillow. Mark: Ill. 1602. H. of doll 16 in. (40.5 cm.). The original box top's fine print is as follows:

"Dolly will surely love her new home and you will have lots of fun caring for her. And you will find her such a wonderful playmate, with her nice pink cheeks, pretty eyes, little tilted nose, and her dainty clothes. Perhaps you want to name her after someone you love. It will be great fun to pick out a name that will be just right.

"Remember Dolly has feelings like yourself, so play with her as you would with your little friends. Treat her gently and be sure to put her to bed on time. Of course, we hope your Dolly never gets sick, but no matter how strong dolls and children are sickness will happen and they get hurt. If anything like this occurs, our Service Department will be glad to repair the doll, charging only for the new parts required. The address is EFFan-BEE Doll Company, 42 Wooster Street, New York City." *Courtesy of the Margaret Woodbury Strong Museum. Photos by Harry Bickelhaupt.*

1602. Trademark of a Lamkin doll made by Effanbee.

Lammel, Paul, & Lipmann, Franz. 1912. Deuben near Dresden, Germany. Applied for a German patent (D.R.G.M.) for a doll's head with moving eyes.

Lamp Studio. 1930 and later. Utica, N.Y. Made cloth dolls and registered *Lynda-Lou* as a U.S. trademark for dolls.

Lämpel (Lehrer, Teacher). 1916. Felt doll made by *Steiff.* Ht. 43 cm. (17½ in.).

Lancelin. 1929. Paris. Used waste pieces of leather for making art dolls' heads, dolls' shoes, gloves and so forth.

Länder, A. See **Imhof, Ferdinand.**

Lander, Hilda Gertrude. See **Cowham, Hilda.**

Landfear, Elsie Dinsmore.[†] See **Kris Kringle Kid Co.**

Landgrof, E. & H. 1913. Nürnberg, Bavaria. Made a line of character dolls named *Perplex* and unbreakable *Gloria* soldiers.

Landolt, Dr. 1918. Paris. Carved wooden dolls.

Landriani, Ernesto. 1916. Exhibited composition dolls in Milan, Italy.

Landsberger, Adolf. 1907–09 and possibly other years. Magdeburg, Saxony. Manufactured dolls. (See Ill. 1603.)★

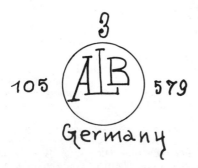

1603. Mark used by Adolf Landsberger.

Landsturm (Landsturmann). 1916. Felt doll made by *Steiff.* Hts. 28 and 35 cm. (11 and 14 in.).

Lang, Émile. 1915–28. Paris. Made a line of cloth dolls with molded faces based on the designs of artists named *Albert Guillaume* and *Jean Ray.* These dolls included ones dressed as soldiers and dolls in "Quaint costumes." The bodies were articulated. Ht. 14 in. (35.5 cm.) and up.

1917: The Lang stand at the Paris Fair was described in TOYS AND NOVELTIES as "one of the most attractive displays of dolls."

1928: Advertised dancing pairs of dolls.★

Lang, M. Georges. 1929. France. Registered *Benjamin* and *Benjamine* as two trademarks for dolls in France.

Langbein, Carl. 1913. Neustadt near Coburg, Thür. Applied for a German patent (D.R.G.M.) for a doll with a mama voice.

Langbein, Johannes. 1898. Neustadt near Coburg, Thür. Made cloth bodies for dolls.

Langbein, Oscar. 1908–30 and later. Sonneberg, Thür. Manufactured dolls.

1911: Applied for a German patent (D.R.G.M.) for a doll with a voice and moving arms and eyes.★

Lange, Erben G. 1853 and probably other years. Germany. Made wooden dolls and won a bronze medal for these dolls at the 1853 New York International Exhibition.

Langenbacker, Geo. F. See **Tibbals, Lewis P.**

Langer-Schlaffke, Marta J. 1911. Silesia, Germany. Dressed dolls designed by *Wackerle* and others in Silesian costumes. She and her husband had a school for embroidery and textile work. The costumes for the dolls were made by her and her pupils. The dolls including a representation of a wedding party and a Christening ceremony were exhibited at the Museum of Applied Arts in Silesia.

Langfelder, Homma & Hayward. 1921–30 and later. New York City. In 1922 they took over the import department of *Morimura Bros.* Imported bisque and celluloid dolls especially from Japan and Germany. The *Chin Chin* dolls made in Germany by *Gebrüder Heubach* were slightly smaller versions of *Queue San Baby* which had been a Morimura product but it is not known whether Langfelder, Homma & Hayward or some other company produced the Chin Chin dolls.

1926: Also handled American-made dolls and rubber dolls. Most of their dolls cost 5¢ to 25¢.

1927: Advertised dressed and undressed dolls. One of their new dolls was a bisque baby in a hooded cradle; priced 50¢ and $1.00 each.

1930: Advertised bisque dolls, celluloid dolls, composition babies and rubber dolls representing boys and girls. ★

Langford Bros. & Co. 1920. London. Agent for French manufacturers of dolls.

Lang-Guillemaut. 1920s. France. Member of the *Chambre Syndicale;* made cloth dolls.

Langguth, August. 1926. Sonneberg, and Oberlind, Thür. Made and exported jointed dolls and baby dolls that wore a chemise and said "mama."

Langguth, Ernst. 1929. Oberlind, Thür. Manufactured dolls.

Langguth, Rudolf, & Co. 1921–25. Hüttensteinach, Thür. Made dressed and undressed dolls. The London agent was *Gross & Schild.*

Langlois. Prior to 1862. France. Distributed dolls; failed in 1861 according to Mme. Poisson, Curator of the Roybet Fould Museum.

Langrock Bros. Co. 1916–23. Brooklyn, N.Y. Their line of composition character dolls was named El-Be-Co.[†]

1917: Some of the dolls, dressed in felt, represented American Indian boys and girls, cowboys and girls, Dutch boys and girls and soldiers of all nations. There were 15 character styles 14 in. (35.5 cm.) tall; priced $1.00. The *Averill Manufacturing Co.* also dressed dolls in similar felt costumes at this time. Another part of the El-Be-Co line were baby dolls and character dolls dressed in various fabrics such as lawns or silks. These retailed for 50¢ and up and included a group of 12 styles of boy and girl dolls that were cork stuffed. Ht. 16 in. (40.5 cm.); priced $1.00. Two of their chubby dolls were named *Heine* and *Hank* and a doll representing a Hawaiian was called *Houla-Houla.* The dolls came with or without wigs.

1923: Obtained a U.S. patent for attaching the legs to a doll's body.★

```
COPYRIGHT 1917
LANGROCK BROS.
BROOKLYN, N.Y.
```

1604. Langrock Bros. mark on composition dolls.

Lanky Tinker. 1926. Wooden doll with elongated leather arms and legs made by *Tinker Toys.* Ht. 12 in. (30.5 cm.).

Lanternier, A., & Cie. 1915–24. Limoges, France. Porcelain factory engaged in making porcelain dolls and dolls' heads. The heads have been found with *Caprice, Chérie, Favorite, La Georgienne, Lorraine* and *Toto* on them. Many of the Lanternier lady dolls were dressed in French provincial costumes, especially those of peasants from Alsace, Arles, and Bourg.

1918: The bodies for the Lanternier heads were made by *Ortyz.* These dolls were produced for the *Association d'Aide aux Veuves de la Guerre* (Association to Aid War Widows).

1924: Lanternier was described as being "renowned for its bébé heads."★

Lanvin, Jeanne. World War I–1927 and possibly other years. Paris. Famous couturière who dressed dolls and collected dolls.

World War I period: Dressed some of the dolls which had heads made by *Sèvres.* These dolls, gifts of *Margaine-*

1605A & B. Bisque socket-head lady doll made by Lanternier using a sculpture by J. E. Masson. This doll was made under the auspices of the Baroness de Laumont. The poured bisque head with a hole above the ears has blue paperweight eyes, and an open-closed mouth. The wig is a dark brown. Inside the head was found a French newspaper dated 1916. The same date as when the Louvre store advertised a lady doll under the name of Masson. (See Ill. 1608.) The long-limbed lady composition body has molded high heeled slippers. Dressed in a regional costume. H. 17½ in. (44 cm.). *Coleman Collection.*

1606. French doll named "Lorraine" with a bisque socket head designed by Masson and made by Lanternier during World War I. The doll has a wig, stationary blue glass eyes, an open-closed mouth and a jointed composition body. The assembling of the doll and the making of its original clothes were probably done in the workshop of Mme. de Laumont. The footwear is molded and painted. Mark: Ill. 1608. H. 17½ in. (44.5 cm.). *Courtesy of the Margaret Woodbury Strong Museum. Photo by Harry Bickelhaupt.*

1607. Bisque head made by Lanternier during World War I and named "Favorite." It has a wig, large sleeping blue glass eyes, pierced ears, open-closed mouth with teeth, and a composition lady-shaped body. Mark: "Fabrication Française, Favorite No. 1. A. L. Cie., Limoges." H. 17 in. (43 cm.). *Courtesy of Sotheby Parke Bernet Inc., N.Y.*

JE masson
S.C.

LORRAINE
Nº0
AL&Cº
LIMOGES

1608. Mark found on bisque doll's head made by Lanternier.

Lacroix in 1918, were in the Louvre collection of dolls in 1970.

1923: Dressed three dolls in modern costumes for an exhibit at the Brooklyn Museum, New York. Two of the dolls wore evening gowns; one of these was pale pink with a long tulle skirt trimmed with narrow shirred ribbon and the other evening gown was made of "peace" taffeta with a full pointed skirt trimmed with silver ribbon. The third dress was a canary colored afternoon dress trimmed with the same kind of material in a French blue color. Later these dolls were also exhibited at Bonwit Teller.

1927: Dressed lady dolls in contemporary costumes.

Larbaud, Charles Amédée. Born 1820–65. Paris. When he failed in 1862 his inventory listed dolls at manufacturers' prices according to Mme. Poisson, Curator of the Roybet Fould Museum. He also failed in 1865.

Largo, Rosa. 1900. Leignitz, Germany. Applied for a German patent (D.R.G.M.) for a wool doll with a face of celluloid or pasteboard.

Larkin Co. 1875–1930 and later. Buffalo, N.Y. Advertised dolls in their catalogs.

1913: Advertised dolls with "Full ball-jointed body made of papier-maché" (composition) and with bisque heads having sleeping eyes and curly wigs. The dolls wore a chemise, shoes, and stockings. Hts. 18 and 23 in. (45.5 and 58.5 cm.); priced $1.51 and $2.84. Another bisque-head doll, this time with molded hair and painted eyes, resembled the *Gebrüder Heubach* Coquette type doll. It had a kid body with bisque arms and came with shoes and socks. Ht. 18½ in. (47 cm.); priced $1.45. A composition head doll similar to the Coquette wore "a blue cotton dress with white collar, cuffs and belt" as well as a petticoat and drawers with lace trim. Ht. 14¾ in. (37.5 cm.); priced $1.29. *Horsman's Campbell Kid* wore a romper suit with a "yoke decorated with Campbell Kid pictures." Ht. 12 in. (30.5 cm.); priced $1.39. A bent-limb baby doll described as "almost unbreakable. Made of a clay composition." Ht. 14 in. (37 cm.); priced $2.29. The *Schoenhut* Circus which included two clowns, Ht. 9 in. (23 cm.) along with two animals and furniture sold for $2.26.

In addition they had four styles of dolls' dresses which would fit dolls of sizes corresponding to the ball-jointed composition body with bisque head dolls described above; priced $1.33 to $2.33.

1920: Advertised all-composition dolls as premiums. These were bent-limb baby dolls with wigs or painted hair as well as child dolls with ball-jointed composition bodies.

L'Arlequin. 1927–30. Paris. Made dolls, especially dolls to be used as favors.

Larsson, Carl. After 1900. A composition head doll that resembles the *Marion Kaulitz (Munich Art Dolls)* type appears to have been inspired by the painting of Larsson's daughter entitled "Lie-abed's Sad Breakfast." Larsson's self-portrait shows him holding a *Steiff* doll.

Lassie. 1921. Jointed composition doll made by the *Mutual Doll Co.* These dolls had wigs and came in a chemise or dressed in various outfits such as play clothes, tailored clothes, or in originally designed clothes.★

1609A & B. Composition plaster head doll with molded and painted hair, hair ribbons, and features. The head is made of a material similar to that used for the Munich Art Dolls. The head looks like Kersti, the daughter of Carl Larsson, shown in his 1900 portrait titled "Lie-abed's Sad Breakfast."

It seems possible that this doll was a portrait doll based on designs and/or pictures made by Carl Larsson. It has a regular German ball-jointed composition body like the ones found on the Munich Art Dolls. *Courtesy of the Chester County Historical Society.*

Lassie. 1922. Line of dolls made by *Wonderland.*

L'Association des Petits Fabricants. 1914. France. This Association engaged master porcelain makers to manufacture bisque heads for dolls.

L'Atelier Bricon. See **Bricon.**

Laubscher's Puppen Fabrik. 1915–27. Graaff-Reinet, South Africa. Founded by Miss Anna Laubscher. Made cloth dolls. The first dolls had round flat faces with painted features and wavy golden blonde painted hair. The body was made of unbleached calico dipped in red ink water and filled with sawdust. There were disc joints at the shoulders and hips. Later improvements were made by pushing a hard round object under the face fabric to form a nose and the body was filled with crushed cork which made it lighter in weight. The shape of the legs varied; some were straight and some were bent. As time progressed changes in the doll were made, some as improvements such as using a plaster cast under a linen covering to provide configuration to the face and some due to necessity. The supply of cork ran out and it became necessary to use crushed corn husks with the sawdust as stuffing. At first Anna Laubscher painted the heads and her sister, Mary, dressed the dolls. As business grew girls were employed to paint the dolls and to sew the bodies; boys came after school to dip the bodies in the ink water and old men stuffed the bodies. At the height of production 250 dolls a week were made. Some of these dolls were exported to Kenya and Rhodesia but most of them were distributed in South Africa. A few of the dolls were marked with a rubber stamp on the back: "MISS A. LAUBSCHER//GRAAFF-REINET." A Laubscher doll was the heroine of one of the first Afrikaner children's books. This story of Riena Reinet had illustrations depicting a real doll. Other people in the area tried to copy these dolls but the faces were less artistic and the colors faded.

1916: Laubscher dolls were advertised as being 38 cm. (15 in.) high. Price 88¢.

The information on the Laubscher dolls was supplied by Victoria Harper of South Africa.

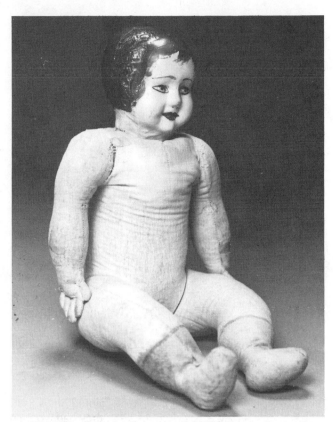

1611. Laubscher cloth doll with molded and painted features. A plaster mask under the cloth gave the face its formation. This doll was made ca. 1918. H. 22 in. (56 cm.). *Courtesy of Victoria Harper.*

1612. Laubscher Doll Factory and personnel during World War I. This cloth doll factory was in Graaff-Reinet, South Africa. *Photo courtesy of Victoria Harper.*

Lauer, C. F. 1842–88 and possibly later. New York City. Imported and distributed wholesale a wide variety of dolls and dolls' parts. Lauer handled dolls from England, France and Germany as well as domestic American lines of dolls. Their 1884 and 1887 catalogs listed bisque dolls, china dolls, composition dolls, parian dolls, rubber dolls, wax

1610. Three Laubscher cloth dolls. These various versions were made at different times. *Courtesy of Bella Traas.*

dolls; black dolls as well as white dolls; dolls with composition bodies, kid bodies in 1884 and cloth bodies in 1887. Among the dolls with special names in both years were *Beauty's Daughter, Fairy Moonbeam, Miss Merryheart, Naiad* dolls, Penny China Babies and *Sleeping Beauty.* The hair on the dolls was described as hair headdresses (probably molded), flowing hair or skin wigs.

From Germany came dolls with bisque heads and patented jointed bodies. Described as "French" were "parian marble" bisque heads on ball jointed bodies. Most of the dolls had composition or wax (probably wax-over-composition heads). Some of the rubber dolls had moving heads and moving arms.

1884: Special name dolls were also *Amazon, Baby Mine, Daisey, Department, Fairy Lilyan, Faunalia, Herculean, Regina, Stella* and *Sunshine.* The dressed wax dolls were claimed to be in the "Latest Paris Dresses" and cost up to $36.00 doz. wholesale.

1887: Special name dolls were also *Bonanza, Celestia, Little Maid from School, My Darling, Pretty Face,* and Trousseau Dolls.

Musical dressed dolls had a music box in the doll's body.

All-china dolls ranged from 1¼ to 5 in. (3 to 12.5 cm.); priced 5¢ to $1.00 a doz. wholesale.

Dressed all-composition dolls with jointed limbs 6 in. (15 cm.); cost 41½¢ a doz. wholesale. If they had wooden jointed limbs they were only 33¢ a doz. wholesale. Ht. 6 in. (15 cm.) imported rubber dolls cost $2.00 a doz. wholesale, while the domestic 6 in. (15 cm.) rubber dolls cost $2.40 a doz. wholesale.

Dolls' stockings came in assorted colors and were described as cloth stockings, open-work stockings, and "Fancy perforated design." Size numbers 1 to 9; priced 60¢ to $1.25 doz. wholesale.

A Lauer firm handled dolls in Pittsburgh, Pa., according to a postcard which also stated that the firm was founded in the 1840s. It is not known whether there was any connection with C. F. Lauer of New York City.

Laughing Cavalier. 1923. Name of a doll made in Holland, representing the man in the portrait painting of this name by Frans Hals.

Laughing Dolls. 1876 and later. Advertised by *Silber & Fleming* as a new model doll.

1876: Undressed, price $1.18.

1879: Dressed as boys or girls; price $1.13. (There may have been earlier laughing dolls and many later ones are known to have existed.)

Laughing Eyes. 1928. Trade name of a composition doll made by *Effanbee.* It wore a pink organdy dress, a pink bandeau trimmed with yarn flowers and the Effanbee locket and chain.

Laughton. 1919. A small size *Leda* doll with composition head and limbs, glass eyes; jointed at the shoulders and hips.

Laumaunier, Charles. 1882–1900. Paris. Produced dolls.★

Laumont, Baroness de (Mme. J. Ferrant). 1914–21. Paris. Produced dolls.

1914: Produced her first doll.

1915: Her dolls were shown in VIE FEMININE.

1916: Founded the *Ligue du Jouet Français* (League of the French Toy) where women made dolls for children. One of the doll's heads was modeled by the sculptor M. *Masson* and another by the sculptor *De la Boulaye.* These dolls were dressed in historical, modern or regional costumes. The French regional costume dolls were sent all over the world to preserve the knowledge of these costumes. *Lanternier* usually made the bisque heads for the Baroness de Laumont's dolls.

1918: Made dolls from the models of *Antonin Merciê.* These

C. L.

1613. Mark used by Charles Laumaunier who produced dolls.

1614. Doll created by Mme. de Laumont, representing a lace-maker of Puy and made by the League of the French Toy. The bisque head was made in Limoges. *Source: LA RENAISSANCE DE LA POUPÉE FRANÇAISE by Doin. 1916.*

dolls, made by Mme. J. Ferrant, were dressed in the workshops of *Mme. Amie Guitry.*

1920: Displayed novelty dolls dressed in the various peasant costumes of the French Provinces. She also created what she called *Rural Dolls.*

Launay, J. See **Jomin, Mme. A.**

Launing, Alex. 1929. Paris. Made dolls.

Laura (German Spreewald). 1911–16 and earlier. Name of a felt character girl doll made by *Steiff,* dressed in a Spreewald regional costume. Ht. 35 cm. (14 in.).

Laurens, Vve. 1856–58. Paris. A doll with a composition head on a pink kid body was marked "Laurens." It had pierced nostrils and wore a regional costume.★

Laurie Dolls. See **Hansen, Laurie, & Co.**

Lauritzen, H. 1922–24. Advertised dolls in a British toy trade journal.

Lauth-Sand, Mme. Aurore. 1914–18. Paris. Made cloth dolls representing Spanish Gypsies. The dolls had prominent cheekbones, strong arches of the nose and pointed chins, all

1615. Doll created during World War I by Mme. Lauth-Sand, the granddaughter of George Sand. The doll represented a Gypsy of Grenada. *Source: LA RENAISSANCE DE LA POUPÉE FRANÇAISE by Doin, 1916.*

Gypsy characteristics. The hair was done in a bun in back and "heart breaker" curls in front. The unusual fabrics of the dresses and shawls showed a close knowledge of the Spanish Gypsies. The dolls wore necklaces and flowers. Mme. Lauth-Sand was the granddaughter of George Sand.

L'Automne. See **Autunno.**

Laval. See **Max-Laval.**

Lavalée-Peronne. See **French Dolls,** and **Peronne.**

Law, Miss Anna N.A. 1927. Pittston, Pa. After considerable research she made and dressed 45 to 55 dolls in historical costumes representing famous American women in the various states. Among the people represented by the dolls were Betsy Ross (dressed by one of her descendants); Dona Dolores, sweetheart of Ponce de Leon; a Hopi Indian squaw; Frances Slocum; and Miss Alice Robertson, Oklahoma's former representative in Congress, modeled from life.

These dolls were loaned to Arnold Constable & Co. in connection with their centennial celebration. Ht. of dolls 10 to 14 in. (25.5 to 35.5 cm.).

Lawrence, Mr. J. W. 1908–18. London. Made dolls that were dressed or undressed especially *Crying Babies.* Some of these were the Japanese type dolls.

1915: Undressed dolls cost 25¢, dressed dolls were 50¢.

1916: Baby doll in a long dress cried when it was laid down.

1917: Made criers, squeakers and growlers and other parts for dolls including whistlers, for rubber dolls.

Lawrence & Co.† See **Cocheco Manufacturing Co.**

Lawton Manufacturing Co. 1920–30 and later. This Company began as the Lawton Doll Co. in Blackpool, England, in 1920 and was founded by Mr. C. A. E. Lawes. By 1922 it was also in Manchester and London.

1922: Claimed that the London factory made 12,000 dolls a week. These were chiefly the *Kewpie*-type *(cupids)* composition dolls used as mascots or souvenirs. (See also **Manufacture of Dolls, Commercial; Made in Britain.**)

Layfield, Joseph. 1916–22. Southport, Lancs. & London Manufacturer, exporter and distributor of dolls.

1916: Advertised dressed and undressed dolls.

1917: Advertised a baby doll line and hair-stuffed knockabout dolls.

1921: Distributed *Carl Hartmann* dolls.

Lazarski, Mme. Thabée. 1913–30 and later. Poland in 1913. Paris from 1914 on. Made dolls in Poland prior to World War I. She simplified the form and features of her dolls so that they would appeal to children. The dolls were dressed in Polish costumes. After the outbreak of World War I, Mme. Lazarski fled to Paris where she gathered together other Polish refugees and established a workshop. Under her guidance in her workshops, cloth dolls, felt dolls, leather headed dolls, and wax dolls were created. These dolls, designed by well-known artists, were exhibited at the great art exhibits of the entire world.

1915: Several hundred Polish refugee families including illustrators who designed dolls, art students and wood carvers who made dolls, worked in Mme. Lazarski's ateliers (workshops). These people were known as La Groupe Polonaise (Polish). Part of this work, under the direction of *Marie Mickiewicz,* was financed and publicized by *Mme. Paderewski.* The people came from various parts of Poland and various strata of society all of which was reflected in the dolls made in the workshops. The Lazarski dolls were shown in the May 15 issue of VIE FEMININE.

1918: The group had grown so that there was a workshop at one address in Paris and the "Ateliers Artistiques" (Artistic Workshops) at another address. The workshops continued to make dolls after the War ended.

1921: Used the description "Le Plus Bel Enfant de France" (The most beautiful baby in France) for some of her dolls.

1926: A French Directory reported that Mme. Lazarski's workshop made dolls of cloth including felt, as well as leather or wax. She had registered the name "Mascotte." The dolls had been exhibited at the Beaux Arts, Salon d'Automne, Musée des Arts Decoratifs, and Salon des Humoristes.

1927: Advertised deluxe dolls; contemporary decorative dolls of cloth, leather, and wax; souvenir dolls; fetish dolls for automobiles, and character bébés of felt.

1928: Bébés Incassables (Composition body child dolls) were also made in the Atelier Artistiques. Some dolls were made for export.

1929: Only cloth, leather, and felt character dolls were mentioned. The registered names continued to be Mascotte and *Bébés Marcheurs,* according to the advertisements, but these names appear to have been used also for dolls other than those produced by Mme. Lazarski.

1930: Artistic luxury dolls were advertised without mention of the materials used in the manufacture of the dolls.★

Le (Lehrer Schoolmaster). Before 1911–16. Name of a felt doll made by *Steiff* with long limbs and dressed as a schoolmaster. Ht. 50 cm. (19½ in.). First of the Steiff character-type dolls according to THE STUDIO, December, 1911. (See Ill. 2505.) (See also **Lämpel.**)

Le Baby. 1920s. Celluloid doll made by the *Société Industrielle de Celluloid.* It came in 21 heights.

Le Bambin. 1890–98. Name of a Bébé Incassable made by *E. Denamur.* The doll could stand, sit or kneel and its wrists were jointed. It came in a chemise and footwear with a label reading "Le Bambin" sewn to the front of the belt or it came fully dressed.

1890: Won a gold medal at the London Exhibition.★

Le Bambino. 1928–30. Cloth doll wearing a dress and bonnet sold by *Bon Marché.* The doll could sit. Ht. 37 or 38 cm. (14½ or 15 in.).

Le Bébé. 1911. Atlantic City, N.J. Distributed dolls including *Schoenhut* dolls.

1616. Pair of cloth dolls created by Mme. Lazarski and shown by Léo Claretie in his article "Le Jouet de Pays de France" (The Native Toys of France), published in LES ARTS FRANÇAIS, 1918.

1617. Cloth dolls created by Mme. Lazarski and shown in an article, "Le Jouet de Pays de France" (The Native Toys of France), by Léo Claretie, which appeared in LES ARTS FRANÇAIS, 1918.

Le Bey, Mme. 1925–30 and later. Paris. Made dolls.

Le Bos D'Espinoy, Charles. 1922. Neuilly-sur-Seine, France. Obtained an Austrian patent for a doll with moving eyes.

Le Chat Botté (Puss in Boots). 1929. Paris. Listed in a Paris Directory as making dolls.

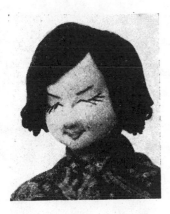

Mme LAZARSKI.   *Têtes de poupées en peau.*

1618. Pair of leather heads on Mme. Lazarski dolls made in her Paris workshop during World War I. *Source: LES ARTS FRANÇAIS, 1918.*

Le Gracieux. 1906. Name of a bisque-head doll with teeth, jointed body, velvet clothes trimmed with lace and a picture-type hat. Ht. 54 cm. (21½ in.); priced $1.38. Advertised by *Aux Trois Quartiers.*

Le Groupe Polonaise de Mme. Lazarski. See **Lazarski, Mme.**

Le Jouet Belge. 1914–16. Belgium. Name of a woodshop founded by Mme. Franchomme, where people wounded or harmed by the War could make dolls.

1916: 50 people were employed in this workshop and a group of dolls dressed in regional costumes by Mme. Meunier received a Grand Prize at an Exposition in Brussels for the benefit of the children of Belgian soldiers.

Le Jouet Liégeois S.A. 1914–23 and possibly other years. Liége (Liège), Belgium. The accent mark changed from time to time. Name of a workshop created by M. Stevaert for making dressed dolls.

1916: Exhibited dolls dressed in regional or occupational costumes at an Exposition in Brussels for the benefit of the children of Belgian soldiers. These dolls won a Grand Prize. (See Liège Dolls.†)

1923: Their unbreakable headed dolls were distributed in London by *A. J. Holladay & Co.*

Le Jouet Natura. 1928–30 and later. Paris. Made cloth dolls.

Le Joujou Français. 1919. Trademark registered in France by *M. V. Lepinay* for dolls.

Le Marvel. 1930 and later. Line of popular priced dolls made by the *Marvin Toy Co.*; came in a variety of costumes. Price $1.00 and up.

Le Montréer. 1867–1921. Paris. Distributed dolls.

1910: Won a bronze medal at the Brussels Exposition.★

Le National. 1906–13. Name of small dolls *(Mignonnettes)* dressed in regional costumes. They usually came in boxes containing five, 10 or 20 dolls. These boxes were sold at the *Louvre* and *Aux Trois Quartiers* stores.

1906: Ht. 6 cm. (2½ in.); price 58¢ for five and $1.15 for 10.

1911: Ht. 9 cm. (3½ in.); price 59¢ for five, $1.18 for 10 and $2.35 for 20.

Le Parisien. 1892–1908. Trademark used by the successors of *Jules Nicholas Steiner.* (See also **Bébé Steiner** and **Le Petit Parisien.**)★

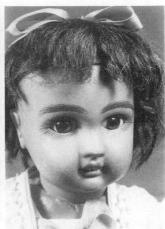

1619A & B. Black bisque socket head made by J. Steiner, on a ball-jointed composition body, stamped "Le Parisien//Bébé Steiner." The head has a black wig, brown paperweight eyes, open mouth with six upper teeth, and pierced ears. The joints of the body include the wrists. Redressed. H. 12¼ in. (31 cm.). H. of socket head 2¾ in. (7 cm.). *Courtesy of Sara Kocher.*

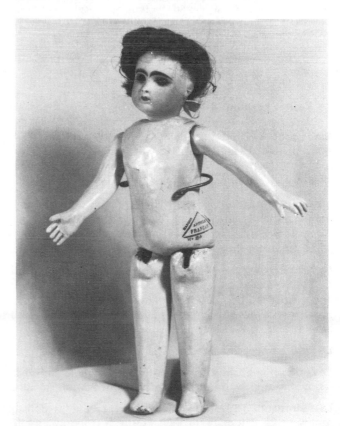

1620. Bisque head Le Parisien Bébé made by the successors of Jules Steiner. It has a wig, stationary blue eyes, pierced ears, closed mouth and a five-piece composition body. Mark on head: Ill. 1624. Mark on body: Ill. 514. H. 10 in. (25.5 cm.). *Courtesy of Helen Read. Photo by Steven Read.*

LE PARISIEN
Bᵀᴱ S.G.D.G.
1621   A 13

A-19
PARIS

"LE PARISIEN"
1622

BEBE "LE PARISIEN"
MEDAILLE D'OR
PARIS
1623

LE PARISIEN
A 23
PARIS
1624

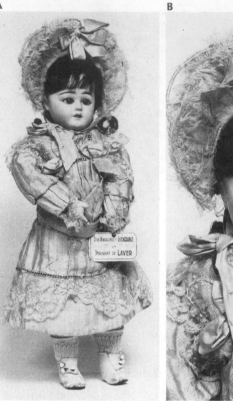

1625   BÉBÉ LE PARISIEN

1621–1625. Marks on Le Parisien bisque head, composition body dolls made by the Jules Steiner firm. No. 1624 is on a head. No. 1623 is on a body. No. 1625 is on a shoe.

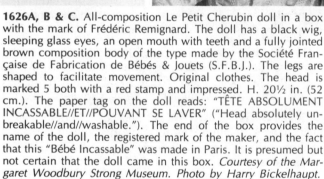

1626A, B & C. All-composition Le Petit Cherubin doll in a box with the mark of Frédéric Remignard. The doll has a black wig, sleeping glass eyes, an open mouth with teeth and a fully jointed brown composition body of the type made by the Société Française de Fabrication de Bébés & Jouets (S.F.B.J.). The legs are shaped to facilitate movement. Original clothes. The head is marked 5 both with a red stamp and impressed. H. 20½ in. (52 cm.). The paper tag on the doll reads: "TÊTE ABSOLUMENT INCASSABLE//ET//POUVANT SE LAVER" ("Head absolutely unbreakable//and//washable."). The end of the box provides the name of the doll, the registered mark of the maker, and the fact that this "Bébé Incassable" was made in Paris. It is presumed but not certain that the doll came in this box. *Courtesy of the Margaret Woodbury Strong Museum. Photo by Harry Bickelhaupt.*

Le Petit Chérubin. 1888–99. Bébé incassable made by *Frédéric Remignard*. Tag read "TÊTE ABSOLUMENT INCASSABLE//ET//POUVANT SE LAVER." The box for this doll had a picture of a kneeling bébé with arms bent at the elbow, long curly hair with a hair ribbon and wearing a knee length dress (or chemise) with a low belt.

1899: Frédéric Remignard transferred his rights to this trademark to the *Société Française de Fabrication de Bébés & Jouets* (S.F.B.J.), according to the research of Mme. Poisson, Curator of the Roybet Fould Museum.★

Le Petit Parisien. 1889–91 and probably later. Bisque-head doll with jointed composition body made by *Jules Steiner* and distributed by *Petit St. Thomas*.
    Some of these dolls had walking bodies. (See also **Bébé Steiner** and **Le Parisien**.)★

Le Petit Sambo. See **Sambo**.

Le Petit Siffleur (The Little Whistler). 1912. Doll dressed as a boy and sold by the *Lafayette* store. Ht. 28 cm. (11 in.).

Le Pétomane. 1892. Edouard Philippe created a doll to represent Le Pétomane (Joseph Pujol), a celebrity in café concerts.

LE PETIT CHÉRUBIN
BÉBÉ INCASSABLE
FABRICATION PARISIENNE
Nº

1627. Bisque head Le Petit Parisien doll made by the Jules Steiner firm. It has a wig, stationary blue glass eyes, pierced ears, a closed mouth and a jointed composition body. Original clothes. Mark on head: "Fi^{re} A 9." Mark on body is a "Le Petit Parisien" sticker. H. 16½ in. (42 cm.). The label on the box has:

Marque de Fabrique	BÉBÉ INCASSABLE
[Picture of a Doll]	habillé Cost. American Rose
	—Serie 1638 No. 7
A. H.	PARIS [?]

Courtesy of Sotheby Parke Bernet Inc., N.Y.

1628A & B. Le Petit Parisien bisque-head doll made by the Jules Steiner firm. It has a wig, sleeping blue glass eyes that are operated by a lever in the side back of the head, closed mouth, and a jointed composition body. Mark on head: Ill. 1629. Mark on body: Ill. 1630. Label on stomach "Au Nain Bleu//E. Chauviere//Boul. des Capucines 27// Paris." H. 22 in. (56 cm.). *Courtesy of Richard Withington. Photo by Barbara Jendrick.*

FIGURE C № 4
J. STEINER B^{te} S.G.D.G.
PARIS

Le Petit Parisien
BÉBÉ STEINER
MEDAILLE d'OR
PARIS 1889

1629–1630. Marks on Le Petit Parisien bisque head, No. 1629, and the label on the composition body, No. 1630.

Le Poupon. 1879. Trade name for a tiny French doll available from Mme. Lavallée *Peronne,* according to POUPÉE MODÈLE. This doll was also known as *La Poupée de Poche.* Price 35¢.

Le Printemps. See **Primavera.**

Le Radieux Bébé. 1925. Advertised by the *Bon Marché* store. This articulated bébé had sleeping eyes and came in three heights.

Le Rêve. 1905–11. Bébé incassable, with wig, sleeping eyes, eyelashes, fully jointed body distributed by *Petit St. Thomas* store. It wore removable clothes made of satin and lace.

1905: The doll's costume included a Bergère (shepherdess') hat and footwear. Ht. without hat was 53 cm. (21 in.); price $2.50.★

Le Saint. 1921–30. Paris. Made and/or distributed dolls.★

Le Sonneur. 1897. Two-faced composition clown with a bell in each hand advertised by the *Samaritaine* store. Ht. 31 cm. (12 in.); priced 28¢.

Le Splendide Bébé. See **Splendide Bébé.**

Le Sueur, Sadie P. 1928. American. Designed dresses for dolls. (See also **Clothes.**)

Le Verrier, Mrs. 1915. American. Distributed the dolls of *La Vie Femmes.*

Leach, M. P. 1917. Britain. Made various styles of stuffed dolls and dressed jointed dolls as well as dolls' clothes, including shoes.

Leading Doll Manufacturing Co. 1919. New York City. A new company founded by Mr. Greenberger. Advertised carnival dolls plus 50 style nos. ranging in price from 25¢ to $2.00.

Leather Dolls. Dolls' heads, bodies and entire dolls were made of leather. American Indians especially liked to use animal skins for making dolls. Eskimos and others also followed this practice. In Europe leather was used extensively for the bodies of dolls. In the early 1800s leather-faced pedlar dolls were made: on the bases of some of these were labels reading "C. & H. White//Milton//Portsmouth." Small all-kid baby and child dolls were made in France in the 1920s. These had painted and molded hair and features. They were jointed at the shoulders and hips. Also in the 1920s a few of the *Boudoir* type dolls had kid or suede heads.

1826–37: *Hallett* produced leather dolls.

1838: *Haller* produced leather dolls.

1860–61: The Day Book of *John D. Robbins* listed "leather dolls," priced $1.50 a doz. wholesale. It is not known whether these "leather dolls" were all-leather or only had leather bodies.

1893: See **Manufacture of Dolls; Homemade: Leather:** for homemade leather head dolls.

1902–09: Kid dolls made under the patent of Gussie Deck-er,[†] primarily by *M. S. Davis Co.,* were advertised as "Baby's First Doll" and in 1904 as being "impossible for baby to hurt itself . . . one doll will do for several generations of children. Leather is very fine for a baby to chew on when teething."

1914: *Bernard Herrmann* made pressed leather heads.

1915: *Mlle. Swiecka* produced leather dolls.

1915–16: *Mlle. de Felice* modeled dolls in kid.

1917: Dolls made of leather and felt were called *Bloomin' Kids.*

Stuffed leather dolls with colors on the leather were made by *Western Art Leather Co.* in nine styles. *H. Bruckmann* produced leather dolls.

1918: *Mme. Lazarski* created dolls with leather heads. *Mme. Morel* produced leather dolls.

1920–21: All-Kid dolls were made by the *Alkid Doll Co.* Ht. 24 in. (61 cm.).

Dolls with composition heads covered with chamois were made by disabled French soldiers. Some of these dolls were sold at *Wanamaker's* store.

Miss Friedmann made leather dolls.

1923: *Gertrude E. Groom* obtained a U.S. patent for a doll made of unshorn sheepskin.

1925: Alex Ferny[†] made kid heads.

1925–27: *E. H. Taillandier* produced dolls with leather heads.

1925–30: *G. Ourine* made leather versions of *Poupée Royal.*

1926: *Marie Vassilief* produced leather dolls.

1926–28: *M. E. Todhunter* obtained a patent for using leather over molded clay for dolls' heads.

1928: *Maison Yvonne* handled leather dolls. These may have been leather-body dolls.

1929: *Lancelin* made leather art dolls' heads.

1930s: Leather-head dolls were still being made in the workshops of Mme. Lazarski.★

Leavens, E. M., Co. 1921. Rochester, N.Y. Made walking dolls.

Lebel, Mme. (née Stapfer, Rachel). 1916–18. Paris. Created dolls.★

Lechleitner, Aloys. 1860–1930. Berlin. Manufactured dolls.

L'École Joffre. World War I-1924. Lyon, France. Also known as *Lyons French Toy Co.* Wounded soldiers made dolls at this workshop. By 1924 the high prices caused its extinction. (See also **Jouets Artistique Français, Jouets de France and General Joffre.**)

Leda. 1917–19 and later. Line of composition-head dolls made by *Spencer & Co.* and their successor, Leda Dolls. These dolls had glass eyes and their paint allegedly would not wash off. Their soft bodies were fully jointed. They came dressed in short baby clothes, long baby dresses or wool dresses. The babies often had pacifiers in their mouths.★

1631A & B. Leather head and hands on a cloth body with a wooden spool base. This folk art doll was recorded as having been made in Newburyport, Mass., by "Grandma Kimball" ca. 1840 for the Piper children whose mother had died in 1835. The face is needle sculptured with black bead eyes, embroidered eyebrows and mouth. Original clothes. H. 10 in. (25.5 cm.). *Coleman Collection.*

1632A & B. Leather-head doll recorded as having been made in Newburyport, Mass. by "Grandma Kimball" ca. 1840. The features are embroidered and there is needle sculpturing. Black beads form the eyes. The body is partly cloth and has a wooden spool base and leather hands. Original clothes. H. 10½ in. (26.5 cm.). *Coleman Collection.*

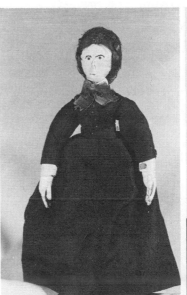

1633A & B. Leather-head doll representing a man of ca. 1840 when it was reportedly made by "Grandma Kimball" for the Piper children. The needle sculptured face has embroidered features including a closed mouth. The cloth body with sewn joints has leather hands. Original clothes, plus a red handkerchief, and watch fob. H. 9 in. (23 cm.). *Coleman Collection.*

1634A & B. Leather-head doll recorded as having been made by "Grandma Kimball" in Newburyport, Mass. for the little Piper children whose mother had died in 1835. The face is formed with needle sculpture and the features are embroidered. Real hair is arranged in a snood. The cloth body has sewn joints and leather hands. Original clothes. H. 8¼ in. (21 cm.). *Coleman Collection.*

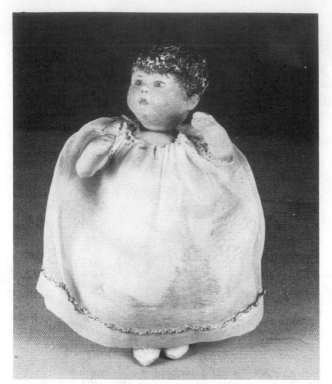

1635A. All-leather bent-limb baby doll made in France in the 1920s. The hair and features are molded and painted. Original clothes. H. 5½ in. (14 cm.). *Coleman Collection.*

1635B. Mark found on leather baby dolls.

1636A & B. All leather doll of a tan color. It has a black wig, painted brown eyes, earrings sewed onto the ears, closed mouth and a five-piece bent-limb baby body. Original clothes that may represent a North African costume. H. 12 in. (30.5 cm.). *Courtesy of Iverna and Irving Foote. Photo by Irving Foote.*

Ledieu, E. 1928–30 and later. Paris. Made dolls.

Lee, Allan, Co. 1930 and later. Philadelphia, Pa. Manufactured cloth dolls.

Lee, Arthur H., & Sons. 1915–20. Birkenhead, England. Made celluloid dolls' faces in several sizes.

Lee Rubber & Tire Co. 1929–30. Conshohocken, Pa. Registered in U.S. *Jol Lee Jays* as a trademark for sponge dolls.

Lefebvre, Alexandre, & Cie. 1860–1926. Paris, Lagny, Seine-et-Marne and Saumur, M. et L. Made dolls and dolls' parts. Member of the *Chambre Syndicale.*

By 1922 Lefebvre belonged to the *Société Française de Fabrication de Bébés & Jouets* according to Anne-Marie and Jacques Porot.

1912: Won a gold medal at an exhibition.

1920s: Advertised that they were the only company who made a Bébé that could kneel on one knee or both knees. These dolls had either bisque or composition heads with eyelashes and came in seven hts. from 25 to 70 cm. (10 to 27½ in.). *Bébé Lefebvre* was dressed in a chemise.

Clown dolls, dressed in silk, were able to assume all the positions of an acrobat and came in five heights 45 to 65 cm. (17½ to 25½ in.).

There were six models of jointed dolls with painted features including a Zouave with mustache. Each model came in six hts. 31 to 75 cm. (12 to 29½ in.). There were also carton *Poupards,* dolls in swaddling clothes with leading strings and diapers. These came in seven hts. 26 to 75 cm. (10½ to 29½ in.). Some of the dolls were undressed.★

1637. Mark probably used by Alexandre Lefebvre for bébés.

Leger, E. 1896. Nürnberg, Bavaria. Applied for a German patent (D.R.G.M.) for a jointed doll with or without music.

Leh, Hans. 1890–1930 and later. Coburg, Thür., and, later, Bavaria. Made dolls.

1927: Made jointed character babies, stuffed cloth character dolls, and dressed dolls.★

Lehmann, Ernst Paul. 1881–1930 and later. Brandenburg, Prussia; later, Nürnberg, Bavaria. Made mechanical walking dolls that had celluloid heads made by *Buschow & Beck.* These were patented in Germany and were made from 1902 until at least World War I.★

1638. Mark used by Ernst Paul Lehmann for mechanical dolls.

Lehmann, Martha (née Kohl). 1928. Dresden. Registered *Muschi* in Germany as a trademark for dolls.

Lehrer. See **Le.**

Leibe & Hofmann. 1772–1888. Gera, Thür. The Porzellanfabrik Untermhaus when it was founded in 1772 was known as Gerarer Porzellanfabrik.

1882: The factory belonged to Leibe & Hofmann. They employed 130 workers and made dolls' heads.

1888: The factory was sold and they no longer made dolls' heads. (This information was according to the research of the Ciesliks.)

dep L & H 9

1639. Mark found on bisque dolls' heads with open mouths possibly made by Leibe & Hofmann.

Leick, Agnes. 1914. Berlin. Applied for a German patent (D.R.G.M.) for dolls' heads.

Leipzig Messe (Fair). Before 1200–1980 and later. Buyers from all over the world came to Leipzig, usually twice a year (Spring and Fall) to buy dolls from the German dealers and *Verlegers.*

Ca. 1900: The fair was rejuvenated.

1914: 800 temporary wooden structures were erected, some of them palatial, to show the wares of the 4,000 dealers for only a week. About 400,000 buyers crowded the area and in one day often gave all their orders for at least ten months.

1925: Business was still limited by postwar prejudice against the German dolls. TOYS AND NOVELTIES described the Autumn Fair as a "fiasco."

1929: TOYS AND NOVELTIES reported that the fair broke all previous records with four times as many exhibits and 10 times the attendance of any prewar fair.

Lejeune, Louis-Aimé. 1915–24 and probably later. Saint Maur-des-Fossés, France. Sculptor who designed and made the models for many dolls. He specialized in the bébé heads for *Société Française de Fabrication de Bébés & Jouets.* He also made models for portrait dolls such as the one of Dorothy Ward, a famous English actress who performed in Paris.

Lejeune (born 1884, died 1969) won several medals including a gold medal in 1920. He was a member of the Legion of Honor and his works are in several museums including the Brooklyn Museum.

1915: The center part of the trademark registered by M. Lejeune appears to be his monogram.

1916: Lejeune made a model for a doll to be made by *Mlle. Thomson.*

1918: He designed dolls' heads that were made in the *Atelier* (workshop) *Chrétien de Vaugirard.*★

L'Elégante. 1905. Name of a doll with sleeping eyes, hair eyelashes, satin clothes, and a picture hat, sold by the *Petit St. Thomas* store. Ht. without the hat was 38 cm. (15 in.); priced $1.18.

Lemaire, Mme. 1821–58. Paris. Made and/or distributed dolls, according to Florence Poisson, curator of the Roybet Fould Museum.

Lemoine, A. See **Huret, Maison.**

Lenci®. 1918–80 and later. Turin, Italy. Trademark and name of a firm where felt dolls with pressed faces were made. The Lenci trademark has been used continuously throughout the long existence of this Company which has made not only felt dolls but also composition head dolls, wooden dolls and porcelain figurines and dolls.

In 1919 the acrostic for Lenci "Ludus Est Nobis Constanter Industria" (Play is work for us) as devised by Ugo Ojetti was registered as a trademark in Italy by Enrico Scavini. Three years later in 1922 Enrico Scavini registered the name Lenci as a trademark in Italy and Britain. When in 1924 he registered Lenci as a trademark in the U.S. he stated that it had been used since 1920. An advertisement in PLAYTHINGS, October 1920, used the name the "Scavini Dolls," while the PLAYTHINGS November 1922 advertisement used the name "Lenci di E. Scavini." In 1923 and thereafter the advertisements were for "Lenci Dolls." No mention has been found as yet in American publications of the acrostic which was registered in Italy in 1919.

Elena König, born in Turin, Italy, in 1886, was the daughter of Francesco König, a German chemistry professor, who in 1885 became Director of the Regia Stazione Agraria in Turin. From 1906 to 1908, Elena studied art in Düsseldorf, Germany, and appears to have remained in Germany until shortly before her marriage to Enrico Scavini, February 1, 1915. He was born in Milan, Italy, in 1888. A letter written by Elena in German and dated August 22, 1914, addressed to "Rico Mio," was signed "Lenci." A bronze plaque dated 1915 and signed by the artist *Giovanni Riva* portrays the head of Elena Scavini and has the name Lenci on it. Riva was one of the many artists who later designed some of the Lenci ceramics.

Enrico went off to war and in 1918 Elena and her brother, Bubine König, made their first felt dolls in the Scavinis' apartment in Turin. Elena's autobiography tells us: ". . . to understand better how my dolls were born the doll of which I had always dreamed and thought in my heart in the profound grief of having lost my little girl." According to this Autobiography, Bubine operated the machine to steam press the faces and Elena did the rest of the work. Their first doll was named Lencina (Little Lenci) and was dressed in a checked red and white felt dress. The head, arms and legs were flesh colored felt. Early in 1919 the firm was officially founded but the dolls were still made in the Scavinis' apartment. In this same year 1919 Enrico Scavini applied for a patent in the U.S. for pressing the heads. The Scavini dolls advertised in 1920 were chiefly character type dolls, ethnic dolls and broad faced little girl dolls. These dolls were designed by Elena but as business grew the firm expanded and well-known artists began to also design the dolls and porcelain figurines. Among these artists were:

Beltramo, Berzoni, *Paola Bologna*, Principessa Bona, *Gigi Chessa*, Damilano, *Marcello Dudovich*—one of the chief designers, Claudia Formica, Goria, *Giovanni Grande*, Jacopi, *Giulio Da Milano, Giuseppi Porcheddu* who helped design dolls' clothes, *Massimo Quaglimo*, Regis, Giovanni Riva, Rosina, Seglie, *Mario Sturani, Felice Tosalli* and *Sandro Vacchetti* who joined the firm in 1920 and later became the Art Director. The names of most of these artists were supplied by Mr. Beppe Garella, the present owner of the Lenci firm.

The earliest marked Lenci dolls that have been found to date have a tiny silver colored round metal button attached to the clothes. A little later possibly as early as 1922 the button was enlarged to a diameter of about ⁵⁄₁₆ in. (0.8 cm.) and bore the name Lenci on it. Various cardboard tags were attached to the clothes of the Lenci dolls. These came in different shapes with a variety of information but always the "Lenci" trademark. In the mid 1930s the cardboard tags simulated the earlier metal button in color but in a slightly larger size. They were marked "Lenci// Torino// Made in Italy." At about the same time parchment type heart-shaped paper tags also began to be put on the dolls identifying the name or area represented by the doll. Other forms of Lenci identification were the cotton ribbon strips sewn onto the clothes. These, marked "Lenci//Made in Italy," began to be used about 1925 and continued in use until about 1950. In the mid 1930s a silk or rayon ribbon was sometimes substituted. A purple or black ink stamp "Lenci" is sometimes found on the sole of the foot of the dolls, but the Lenci heads and bodies were not otherwise marked. Some Lenci dolls can be identified by their dark wooden accessories trimmed with painted flowers. Many other companies copied the Lenci dolls so that it is difficult to discover any entirely unique feature of the Lenci dolls.

Nearly all Lenci dolls in 1930 and earlier had a model number on their tags by which the approximate date of the doll can be determined. For dolls without a model number the height can be a clue when used with the tables on pages 90–92 in the LENCI book by Dorothy S. Coleman. The heights given in Lenci catalogs were sometimes a little more than the heights measured currently for corresponding dolls, probably due to the flattening of the hair. The model numbers began with 100 and rose chronologically until they were over 2000 in 1930. However it must be remembered that popular models were often made for many years. One of the most popular models was series 300 with a hollow felt covered torso. This model first appeared about 1925. Other companies also used this same body technique for their dolls.

1922: The firm moved to larger quarters on the Via Marco Polo. *Gigi Chessa* began to work for the Lenci factory.

1923: TOYS AND NOVELTIES published the following article: "A doll reaching America by the way of Italy, has become the fashion among grown-ups. . . . Known as the Lenci doll, it has had an impressive effect on feminine fashions here. Fifth Avenue designers and milliners admit-

tedly are receiving demands for gowns, sport coats, pajamas and hats, such as grace the more than one hundred models of dolls, according to a writer in the New York Times.

"Over in Turin where the Lenci dolls are made, 300 workmen are turning out these artificial folk—each with an individuality of its own . . .

"Because of the artistry and care in manufacture, the Lenci doll is likely to remain a high priced toy, each saucy doll being a hand-made product.

"J. C. Messina, American representative of Lenci di Scavini, manufacturer of the doll . . . said that the original Lenci doll was born out of necessity of the young wife of an aviator to meet the differences between his army pay and his peace time earnings as an artist.

"Surrounded by several hundred Lenci dolls, Spanish dancers, French manikins, Dutch girls, American flappers, and 'angel faces,' Mr. Messina told the story of the new plaything of grown-ups.

" 'The creator of the doll was Mrs. Enrico Scavini, wife of an Italian artist of Turin . . . Lenci was a pet name Scavini had given to his young wife, whom he married just before the world war. When Scavini, a young man in his twenties, enlisted in the flying corps, Mrs. Scavini, a woman of culture, faced the problem of living on the pay of a soldier, which in Italy is very small.

" 'An artist herself, she sat down one day and made a doll out of a few pieces of felt. She dressed the doll in a style of her own, and painted a face of a little girl she knew. Friends who came to the home were enraptured over the remarkable life-like features. The suggestion naturally followed that she make and sell these dolls, and the enterprise was successful from the start.

" 'Mrs. Scavini engaged leading artists to devote their talents in developing the individual character of the dolls. One of the earliest models which was very popular—and still is—had bobbed hair, fluffy and wavy. Soon human dolls copied the idea and the bobbed hair craze spread over Europe and extended to the United States, . . .

" 'When Enrico Scavini returned home from the war, he found himself partner in a business which had grown to large proportions and in which the demand exceeded the output.'

"The craze for the Lenci dolls was not limited to women. . . . Many men were among the purchasers generally favoring the sophisticated French chorus girls, legs crossed, with a cigarette tilted at an angle."

F.A.O. Schwarz advertised Lenci series 109, ht. 20 in. (51 cm.), for $18.00 with a hat and $15.00–$16.00 without a hat. Lenci series 110, ht. 18 in. (45.5 cm.), cost $15.50 and $16.50 with a hat. The smaller Lenci dolls cost $7.50, $10.00 and $12.00. It was suggested that Lenci dolls could be cleaned with a piece of bread.

Lenci dolls were exhibited in Paris and at the Leipzig Fair.

1925: The Lenci firm moved to a larger factory on the Via Cassini and Mario Sturani joined the firm. A doll dressed in an elaborately embroidered Russian costume was produced.

1926: The Schwarz catalog listed series number 109, 110, 149 and 300. The prices were about the same as in 1923.

Saks Fifth Ave. advertised imported burnt orange and copenhagen blue felt coat and hat sets for little girls two or three years old, priced $39.50. These were exact copies of the costumes on Lenci dolls which were also available for $25.00.

Liberty of London sold Lenci dolls through their agents including Metz & Co. in Holland.

1928: TOYS AND NOVELTIES reported that Mussolini had ordered all dolls to have long hair but the Lenci catalogs of the period show dolls with hair of varying length.

1929: An Italian publication printed an article addressed to children on the life of Signora "Lenci" and the then current work of the Lenci factory.

The article stated: "I have also visited the studio of Signora Lenci, where she herself with her tireless and valuable collaborators Sandro and Emilio Vacchetti, model and create the new doll . . ."

PLAYTHINGS reported that the hollow felt bodies (series 300) were shaped and sewn by machinery. The dolls were painted by "special artists." Felt was the only material used for the clothes which consisted of regional costumes, historical costumes, sports costumes and theatrical costumes.

The prices of Lenci dolls were reduced early in the year because of competition.

Display manikins began to be made.

TOY WORLD had an article on Lenci as follows: "The widespread popularity of Lenci dolls makes their origin and history interesting. 'Lenci' is the pet name of Elena, and Madame Lenci is the owner of that name.

"Madame Lenci created the first dolls for charity aims, and encouraged by the success of her first productions, she started producing them as a commercial undertaking. She began in 1919 and with four work[ing] girls made 50 samples to show the world what she could do. They had [a] good welcome both in Italy and overseas.

"With Madame Lenci in the production of dolls was joined her husband and Sandro Vacchetti, a clever painter.

"They got to work seriously, and at the end of the first year 150 persons were working at the Lenci dolls.

"Afterward they began the creation and study of cushions, quilts, carpets, furniture; as a matter of fact, everything that related to home decoration and especially children's bedrooms and nurseries.

"Meanwhile, at the end of four years, workers were getting so numerous that they had to be housed in a factory. Today 800 people are employed in a factory suited to artistic kinds of production."

Dolls dressed in Fascist costumes were produced as well as a series dressed in various sports outfits.

1930: Competition grew stronger and Lenci inaugurated a washable felt that was covered with a cellulose paint.

1931: Some of the innovations were dolls with what appear to be glass eyes, dolls with wooden heads and the selling of separate outfits for the dolls.

An entirely new code for the identification of the Lenci dolls was inaugurated in the 1931 catalog.

LENCI DOLLS IN 1931 CATALOG CODE COMPARISON				
Height of doll*		**Code**	**Old Code**	
cm.	**in.**	**Letter**	**Number**	**Type of doll**
12	5	X		Wood
18	7	XX		Small mascots
22	8½	S		Mascots
22	8½	V		Lady
26	10½	F		Child
35	14	N		Child
35	14	P		Child
35	14	V		Lady
40	16	V		Lady
40	16	Bambino		Bent limb baby
42	16½	C	149	Child sometimes with teeth
44	17½	E	300	Child with hollow felt torso
44	17½	L	1500	Child with pouty face
44	17½	O		Washable, child
48	19	B	110	Child
48	19	M		Child with glass or plastic eyes
50	20	V		Lady
53	21	OO		Baby
55	21½	G	500	Child
58	23	A	109	Child
58	23	AA		Child
60	24	R	165	Lady or Man
65	26	T		Lady
70	28	T		Lady
72	28½	J	950	Child
73	29	HH		Lady
86	34	D	169	Child
86	34	H	700	Girl
120	48	Z		Lady

*Conversion of centimeters to inches is according to the Lenci 1931 catalog.

1933: Mr. Pilade Garella and his brother Flavio joined the firm. Pilade was in charge of the commercial part and his brother took charge of the production.

1936–37: In December 1936 a formal contract was drawn up between "Signora Elena Lenci Koenig in Scavini" and "Lenci S A" signed by Pilade Garella. The Garellas were then head of the Lenci corporation which owned the rights to the Lenci trademark. They hired Elena Scavini as Art Directress for five years (1937 thru 1941). Under the contract she was "to proceed in the creation . . . of new types whether of dolls or costumes" as part of her work. These were necessary to form the annual catalogs. She and her family retained the rights to live in the premises of the business as they had been doing.

1937: Enrico Scavini left the Lenci factory; he died the following year.

1942: Beppe Garella, son of Pilade, joined the Lenci firm.

1943: Beppe Garella, son of Pilade, fought with the Italian Partisans against the forces of Mussolini and the Garella Family received a citation from the British Army for their aid.

After the Lenci factory recovered from the damage of World War II, Pre-War production was resumed and the dolls continued to be made, often using some of the original early molds. (See also **Felt Dolls**.)★

1641A & B. Lenci all-felt doll with green color hair, painted brown eyes, gray eyeballs, green eyebrows, closed mouth. Body has sewn joints at the shoulders, elbows, knees and hips. The original Pierrot type costume is made of beige, green, and black felt. The musical instrument is wood. Lenci rectangular tag is on the clothes. H. 26 in. (66 cm.). *Courtesy of Iverna and Irving Foote. Photo by Irving Foote.*

1640A & B. Felt Lenci with red hair, painted blue eyes looking to the side, open-closed mouth, and four teeth. The head has a socket into which the neck fits. The body is jointed at the shoulders, elbows, hips and knees as well as the neck. Original Russian type outfit with embroidered rose colored tunic, and embroidered green felt boots with high heels. H. 10 in. (25.5 cm.). H. with hat 11½ in. (29 cm.). *Courtesy of Iverna and Irving Foote. Photo by Irving Foote.*

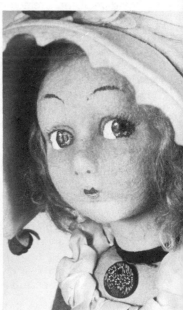

1642A & B. Felt Lenci lady doll similar to the one shown in PLAYTHINGS, May, 1923, and appearing on the cover of an early Lenci catalog. The blond mohair curls are put on in strips, painted brown eyes look to the side, closed mouth. Original felt clothes, a wooden locket with painted flowers and a bouquet of felt flowers. H. 24½ in. (62 cm.). *Coleman Collection.*

1644A & B. All-felt Lenci doll of the 110 series with the larger metal Lenci button attached to the underclothes. Fingers indicated by stitching, thumb separate. Original orange felt jumper with matching coat. H. 18 in. (45.5 cm.). *Coleman Collection.*

1643. Lenci Cigarette Girl with a felt head, shoulders, arms and legs, mohair stitched on the head in strips, painted brown eyes, mouth with opening to hold the white wood cigarette. Original pants suit similar to those that are on dolls designed by Haskell in America for the Mutual Novelty Corp. This model 162 has a Lenci label on the coat but the patent numbers on it refer only to the 1921 head patent and not to the cigarette or costume. Ht. 25 in. (63.5 cm.). *Courtesy of Alice F. La Force. Photo by Ron Marquette.*

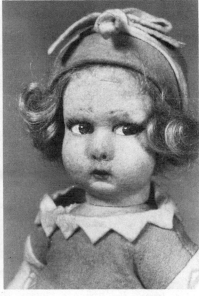

1645A & B. Felt Lenci doll, appears to be in the no. 160 series of 1923. It has mohair curls, painted features, felt body. Original pink with white trimming felt clothes. H. 10 in. (25.5 cm.). *Coleman Collection.*

1646. Lenci felt doll Series 111. It has hair attached in strips, painted brown eyes looking to the side, closed mouth. Note the two highlights on the lower lip which is lighter in color than the upper lip. This is a typical Lenci mouth. There is a dimple in the chin. The cloth torso has felt limbs and there are joints at the neck, shoulders and hips. Original clothes. H. 12½ in. (31.5 cm.). The Lenci catalog lists this doll as 13 in. (33 cm.). *Courtesy of the Margaret Woodbury Strong Museum. Photo by Harry Bickelhaupt.*

1647. Group of Lenci felt-head dolls. All five have hair, painted eyes looking to the side, closed mouth, and original clothes. Left to right: Hs. 12½ in. (31.5 cm.), cloth label; 13 in. (33 cm.), Japanese girl, paper tag; 16 in. (40.5 cm.), cloth label; 12 in. (30.5 cm.), possibly Series 111, paper tag; 16 in. (40.5 cm.), wears Val Gardena costume, ca. 1940, two paper tags. *Courtesy of Sotheby Parke Bernet Inc., N.Y.*

1648. Five Lenci felt dolls; all except the second from the left are Series 300 with hollow felt torsos. The dolls have mohair applied to their heads in strips, painted eyes glancing to the side, and closed mouths. Original clothes. Left to right: Fascist boy with rectangular paper label, H. 17½ in. (44.5 cm.); girl in Italian regional costume with heart-shaped tag, H. 18½ in. (47 cm.); Swiss Guard with pike, H. 17½ in. (44.5 cm.); Scottish boy and girl, boy has brown hair and blue eyes. H. of both dolls 17½ in. (44.5 cm.). *Courtesy of Sotheby Parke Bernet Inc., N.Y.*

1649. Two Lenci felt dolls with hair, painted eyes looking to the side, closed mouths, and original clothes. The doll on the left is probably the 1500 series. Hs. 18 and 19½ in. (45.5, 49.5 cm.). *Courtesy of Sotheby Parke Bernet Inc., N.Y.*

1650. Black felt Lenci girl doll with hair sewed on in strips, round eyes, and ethnic features is jointed at the neck, shoulders, and hips. H. 16 in. (40.5 cm.). *Courtesy of and photo by Phyllis Salak.*

1651A & B. Felt Lenci doll in the Mascotte series. It has a braid down the back, painted features, fabric body, felt arms, and the costume of a French peasant with wooden sabots. H. 8½ in. (22 cm.). *Coleman Collection.*

1652. Pair of felt bent-limb babies made by Lenci ca. 1930. They have blond hair, painted brown eyes looking to the side, closed mouth, body jointed at the neck, shoulders, and hips. Original clothes. H. 20 in. (51 cm.). *Courtesy of Sotheby Parke Bernet Inc., N.Y.*

1653. Lenci felt bent-limb baby doll with blond mohair in strips, painted brown eyes looking to the side, and closed mouth. Original clothes. H. 17 in. (43 cm.). *Courtesy of Helen Huling.*

1654. Lenci felt doll, Series 450, has mohair applied in strips, painted brown eyes looking to the side, closed mouth, and original clothes. H. 13 in. (33 cm.). *Courtesy of Sotheby Parke Bernet Inc., N.Y.*

1655A & B. Lenci felt doll, Miniature size, Series 310, No. 306 in a Lenci box. The heart-shaped paper sticker on the box has green lettering. The doll has painted eyes and an open-closed mouth. Original clothes and five brass-head pins in its hair. The parchment type tag on the wrist reads: "Lucia//Lombardia." On the back of the round silver paper Lenci label is "310/413". A cloth label on the skirt reads "Lenci Torino." H. 9 in. (23 cm.). *Courtesy of Richard Withington. Photo by Barbara Jendrick.*

1656. Lenci Miniature series of felt dolls made ca. 1930 or later. They have mohair, painted eyes looking to the side and an open-closed mouth. Original clothes. Doll on left is dressed as a bride and the lower part forms a pillow. Girl on right wears blue and pink. Both 9 in. (23 cm.). *Courtesy of Sotheby Park Bernet Inc., N.Y.*

1657A & B. Felt Lenci doll in the Miniature series. Mohair curls, painted features, fabric body, felt arms, original clothes of white organdy and red felt. H. 9 in. (23 cm.). *Coleman Collection.*

1659

1660

1661

1662   1663

1659–1663. Marks on Lenci cloth dolls. Some of the marks are on the clothes.

1658. Pair of large Lenci felt dolls with the later type smoother faces and non-felt clothes. They have mohair hair, painted eyes looking to the side. The doll on the left has brown eyes, a closed mouth, and original clothes. H. 22 in. (56 cm.). The doll on the right has round painted blue eyes and an open-closed mouth. H. 19 in. (48 cm.). *Courtesy of Sotheby Parke Bernet Inc., N.Y.*

Lenore Ulric. 1921–22. Portrait doll of Miss Ulric as she appeared in Ki-Ki,[†] made by *Hélène and Mathilde Sardeau.* The face was modeled in plasterine and a canvas was stretched over it and appropriately painted.

Another version of *Kiki* was made by the *Flapper Novelty Doll Co.*

Leonhardt, Paul. 1926. Eppendorf, Germany. Produced dolls. London agent was Gross & Schild.

Leonia Doll Co. 1929–30. New York City. Made and/or distributed dolls.

Lepape, M. & Mme. Georges. Before World War I–1918. France. Artists whose models were used to create expensive dolls. They made wooden dolls. M. Lepape (born in 1887, died 1971) was a painter and illustrator who worked with *Paul Poiret.* He drew many of the covers for VOGUE until 1933. He also collaborated with GAZETTE DU BON TON, VANITY FAIR and FEMINA.

1916: The wooden heads were on cloth bodies, stuffed with fabric. Among their dolls were ones named *Gilles* and *Marion.* They also made marionettes.

1918: Their wooden dolls resembled the *"School for Scandal"* type dolls.

1664. Wooden dolls made by M. and Mme. Georges Lepape, as shown in LES ARTS FRANÇAIS, 1918.

Lepinay, M. V. 1919. Paris. Registered two trademarks in France for "Toys of all kinds." One trademark was *Le Joujou Français*. The other trademark was a square with *Jou* across the top and bottom and a chef's head in the center.

Leprestre & Guilleray. 1930 and later. Paris. Handled exports of *La Poupée Nicette*.

Lerch, Edmund. 1927–28. Eppendorf, Saxony. Made dolls' outfits and trunks, baskets, boxes, and "bath-houses" with a doll and its clothes in them. He also made empty trunks and swings with dolls in them.

September, 1927   **PLAYTHINGS**   183

Sample Assortments Sent Upon Receipt of $15.00, $20.00 or $25.00

DOLL OUTFITS Retail from $1.50 to $3.00

SWINGS Retail from 75c. to $2.00

DOLL OUTFITS IN TRUNK Retail at $3.00

EDMUND LERCH, EPPENDORF, SAXONY, GERMANY
Manufacturer of Furnished Doll Trunks, Bath Houses, Boxes, Baskets. Also Decorated White Lacquered Swings, Folding Chairs, School Benches, Swinging Chairs and Settees.

1665. Edmund Lerch's advertisement in PLAYTHINGS, September 1927. He made boxes, baskets and trunks containing dolls and their outfits.

Lerch, Philip. 1858–ca. 1875. Philadelphia, Pa. Made papier-mâché dolls' heads. ★

Leredde, Vve. (Widow, née Leonie Alphonsie Monnet), & Sonnet, Charles Eugène. 1888. France. Made dolls and used the initials "M. S." according to Gwen White.

Les Nations. See **Le National.**

Les Originaux. 1927 and later. Trademark registered in France by *Mme. Yvonne Spaggiari* for peasant dolls that appear to resemble the *Ravca* dolls.

Lerch & Co.,
MANUFACTURERS
No 6.

1666. Mark used by Philip Lerch on papier-mâché shoulder heads of dolls.

M.S
DEPOSE
PARIS

1667. Mark incised or raised on dolls' heads made by Veuve (Widow) Leredde & Charles Eugène Sonnet.

Les Petites Mains Parisiennes. See **Petites Mains Parisiennes.**

Les Poupées Artistiques Française. 1920s. Paris. Member of the *Chambre Syndicale.* They advertised cloth dolls, undressed and dressed dolls including clowns. Three of their dolls were named *Yves* and *Yvette* (Boy and a Girl) and *Clairette* (Little Sister).

Les Poupées Blanche Gautier, Paris. Label found on an all-celluloid doll having a wig, painted features and dressed. Ht. 14 in. (35.5 cm.).

Les Poupées de Mitou. 1926. Trademark registered in France by *Mme. Anne Marguerite Bruent* for luxury dolls, mascot dolls and fan dolls.

Les Veuves de la Guerre. See **Mme. Pierre Goujon.**

Leschhorn, Rudolf. 1925–27. Sonneberg, Thür. Manufactured dolls including soft stuffed dolls. His trademark was *LESCHI*. According to the Ciesliks he used *Schoenau & Hoffmeister* heads.

Leschi. 1925–27. Trademark used by *Rudolf Leschhorn.*

L'Espérance. World War I period. Name of a group who created dolls designed by well-known artists.

Lesser, Elizabeth. 1911–19. New York City. Designed and created dolls for *Horsman.*

1912: Copyrighted "Figurine" dolls, a new type of character doll with "Slim, well bred forms, refined faces." These dolls with wigs and various costumes represented boys and girls. Ht. 13 in. (33 cm.); price $8.50 a doz. wholesale.

1913: One of her multi-face dolls was patented by Horsman.

1919: She obtained two design patents for dolls. One was based on an Estelle Allison *(Allison Novelty Co.)* copyright and the other was Impie,† a Ben-Arthur Studios† copyright. ★

Lessieux. 1871–82. Paris. A doll maker who purchased bisque dolls' heads from *François Gaultier* in 1881, according to Mme. Poisson, Curator of the Roybet Fould Museum. ★

Spezialitäten:

Gekleidete Puppen

Filz-Puppen

Mama-Puppen

Charakter-Puppen
und Babys

Leder- und
Stoffpuppen

Puppenköpfe

Puppen-Bälge

Plüsch- u. Filztiere
aller Art

Mascottes.

H. Josef Leven,
Puppenfabrik.

Sonneberg i.Th.
Spielwarenfabrik.

Zu den Messen:
In Leipzig
Dresdner Hof, III Etage
Zimmer 199.
In Frankfurt a. M
Haus Offenbach, St. 3061
Musterläger:
Hamburg,
Gustav Burmester,
Südseehaus, Lange Mühren
Berlin,
Walter Richter, SW 68,
Ritterstraße 39
Düsseldorf,
Alfons Riedinger
Kaiser-Wilhelm-Straße 34
München
Adolf Reiß,
Rosenheimer Straße 17

1668. Advertisement of H. Josef Leven in DEUTSCHE SPIELWAREN ZEITUNG, February, 1927. He produced dressed dolls, felt dolls, Mama dolls, character dolls and babies, dolls with leather or cloth bodies, separate dolls' heads, and cloth bodies for dolls.

L'Eté. See **Estate.**

Letitia Penn. The famous wooden doll whose ownership was traced by the LADIES' HOME JOURNAL in 1902. Allegedly it was given in 1692 by Letitia Penn, daughter of William Penn, to Miss Rankin of Philadelphia. This early date is suspect both from the point of view of the doll's clothes and the family genealogy. Miss Rankin gave the doll to Mrs. Prior who gave it to Miss Anne Massey; Miss Massey became Mrs. Brown and gave the doll to Miss Mary B. Kirk of Sandy Springs, Maryland (a Quaker area). In 1882 Miss Kirk died and the doll went to Dr. Mahlon Kirk who still owned it in 1902.

L'Etoile. World War I period. A French group who created artistic dolls designed by well-known artists.

Leube. See **Schoenau & Hoffmeister.**

Leuchars, William. 1867 and before. London. His catalog stated "The Largest assortment in London of dolls, both dressed and undressed, in wax, composition, china and India rubber." These dolls were in a toy warehouse. Prices ranged from 25¢ to $26.25.

Leutheuser, Friedr. 1914. Sonneberg, Thür. Applied for a German patent (D.R.G.M.) for a doll's body.

Leutheuser, Richard. 1894–1928. Sonneberg, Thür. Manufactured and exported dolls.

1910: One of the Sonneberg group of Grand Prize winners at the Brussels Exposition.

World War I: Took over the *Louis Wolf* office during the War period.★

Levallois. 1930 and later. Paris. Made dolls, dolls' heads, dolls' shoulder heads, dolls' face masks and dolls' bodies.

Levavaseur et Ouachée. See **Au Paradis des Enfants.**

Leven, H. Josef. Before 1914–30 and later. Sonneberg, Thür. Manufactured and exported dolls. He had agents in Berlin, Hamburg, Düsseldorf, Munich and London. *Henry Barnett* was his British agent. Before 1918 Josef Leven was associated with several firms, namely *Leven & Sprenger, Johannes Franz,* and *Siemens & Schuckert* according to the Ciesliks. Leven used the mark *DURA.*

World War I: Took over the *S. S. Kresge* office during the war period.

1919: Advertised baby dolls, child dolls, cloth dolls, leather dolls, dolls' heads and dolls' bodies.

1924: Advertised baby dolls, hair stuffed dolls, real and imitation kid dolls' bodies, dressed and undressed dolls.

1925: Applied for a German patent (D.R.G.M.) for a cloth doll. Henry Barnett was the sole London agent. Advertised dressed dolls, including New Born Baby dolls, artistic unbreakable dolls, mantel dolls, and *Eskimo* dolls. Among their mascot dolls were *Kewpie* types and Flippant Flappers, a *Boudoir* type doll. They also had a series of dolls which represented Fairy Tale characters and characters from other tales. These included "Red Riding Hood," "Snow White and the Seven Dwarfs," "Baby Bunting," "Off to the Seaside," "Winter Sports in Switzerland," "Where are you going my pretty maid?" "A-Hunting we will go," "By the side of the Zuyder Zee," "Mother Goose," and "Come into my Garden, Maud."

1926: Advertised a *Boudoir Doll* named "Flippant Flapper." Dolls distributed by *Gustav Burmester.*

1927: Continued to advertise dressed dolls of all kinds, jointed dolls, Eskimo dolls and mantel dolls as well as little dolls and cloth doll molds.

1929: Advertised dressed and undressed dolls, character dolls, baby dolls, dolls' house dolls, *Mama* dolls, leather and cloth dolls, Eskimo dolls, "Over coat" dolls, mascot dolls' heads, dolls' bodies, castings for dolls, dolls' trousseaux, and dolls' shoes.

The sole London agent was David S. Tiebel.★

Leven & Sprenger. 1896–1927 and later. Sonneberg, Thür. Manufactured dolls. *Josef Leven* was a member of this firm at one time.

1896: Advertised dolls with and without joints and the new doll with three heads (or faces).

1909: Advertised leather dolls.

1912: Advertised baby dolls, *poupards,* dolls' heads and other parts.

Leverd & Cie. 1869. Paris. A Leverd marked doll had a bisque head, wig, swivel neck; the joints permitted it to obtain a variety of positions as indicated by the French patent.★

Leverrier, Mme. 1918. Paris. Directress of a shop on the Champs Elysées called *Pandora* for which *Mlle. Valentine Thomson* created dolls.

Levert, François-Eugene. 1849–56. France. He sold dolls until he failed, according to Mme. Florence Poisson, Curator of the Roybet Fould Museum.

Levie, J. 1925–26. Sonneberg, Thür. Advertised *Mama* dolls, ball-jointed dolls, dressed dolls, and *Eskimo* dolls. Hts. of the ball-jointed dolls were 60 to 70 cm. (23½ to 27½ in.).

Levy, I., and Co. 1889–1928. London. Made dolls.

1917: Advertised dressed and undressed dolls that were designed and made by this company. The dolls came in a variety of sizes and styles. Price $1.50 and up a doz. wholesale.

1918: Dolls cost 3¢ to 14¢.

1928: Handled Beautikin, Baby Ruth and Duchess dolls.

Lévy, Pierre, & Cie. 1919. Paris. The trademark "Bébé Bijou"† has been found on the chemise of a *Bébé Tout en Bois* but it is not certain that this chemise was original to this doll.★

Lewis & Owen. 1917–18. London. Handled dolls of *Kaye Toy Co., Kean & Co.,* and Dell & Co.†

Ley, H. 1893–1925. Coburg, Thür., and, later, Bavaria. Advertised dress dolls including *Mama* dolls.

Leydel, Mme. 1828–50s. Paris. Manufactured dolls according to Mme. Florence Poisson, curator of the Roybet Fould Museum.★

L'Hiver. See **Inverno.**

> The prices given for dolls are those for which the dolls were originally offered for sale. They are *not* today's prices.

L'Hotel de Ville. 1900–29, possibly earlier and later. Paris. A large store with catalogs that listed the following dolls.

1908: Advertised *Bébé Culotte, Bébé Jumeau, Eden Bébé, Kiss-Throwing* dolls.

1909–10: The same as 1908 plus *Mignonnette, Polichinelle,* and soldiers.

1912: *Bébé Premier Pas* was featured.

1913: Advertised *Bébé Esquimaux,* Bébé Jumeau, *Bébé Tout en Bois,* Eden Bébé.

1918: Advertised *Bébé Arc-en-Ciel, Bébé Drapeau, Bébé Fruits, Bécassine, Petites Marraines de Guerre.*

1921: Catalog showed *Bébé B.H.V., Bébé Marcheur, Bébé Promenette, Bébé Réclame, Bébé Réservé, Bébé Rivoli, Clown,* Kiss-throwing Doll, *Marotte,* Mignonnette, Polichinelle, Doll in Alsatian costume, new born character baby and rubber dolls.

1929: Advertised Bébé Réservé, Bébé Rivoli, bisque head dolls on composition bodies, all-composition dolls, all-felt dolls with molded cloth faces.

L'Hotte, Edmond Louis. 1911. Bois-Colombes, France. Patented *La Patrouille* and used initials E. L. in script as a trademark.

Li Tia Guai. 1925–30 and later. *Lenci* felt doll representing an Oriental with slanting eyes and wearing a coolie hat, wooden clogs and carrying a lamp.

1925: It was style No. 188 A. Ht. 58 cm. (23 in.).

1930: It was style No. 300/60. Ht. 44 cm. (17½ in.).

1931: It was style No. E 39. Ht. 44 cm. (17½ in.).

Lialla Dolls. 1930 and before. Designed by *Mr. J. Green* and made by the *Penn Stuffed Toy Co.* Some of these were *Mama* dolls with composition arms and legs. They came with various faces and sizes. Style No. 1000 was 13 in. (33 cm.) tall and cost $1.00.

Libby Doll & Novelty Co. 1930 and later. New York City. Manufactured cloth and composition dolls.

Liberty Belle. 1918–19. Composition doll with hat in the shape of the Liberty Bell, made by *Federal,* and distributed by *Charles Blum.* The doll wore a silk cape; one side was blue and the other side was stars and stripes. This life-sized doll cost $5.00 and up. It also came in a smaller size wearing a white silk dress with the blue cape lined in red. Ht. 11 in. (28 cm.).★

Liberty Belle. 1925–26. Trademark registered in U.S. by *Annin & Co.* for dolls. This was the cloth doll in the shape of the Liberty Bell that was sold as a cutout doll on a sheet or made up into a doll. These dolls had the name "Liberty Belle" on their printed cap. Reproduced in 1976.

Liberty Boy. 1917–18. All composition soldier doll made by *Ideal.* The different colored cord on the hat denoted the different branches of the service. The demand was so great that an entire factory floor was needed to supply these dolls. Ht. 12 in. (30.5 cm.); priced $2.00.★

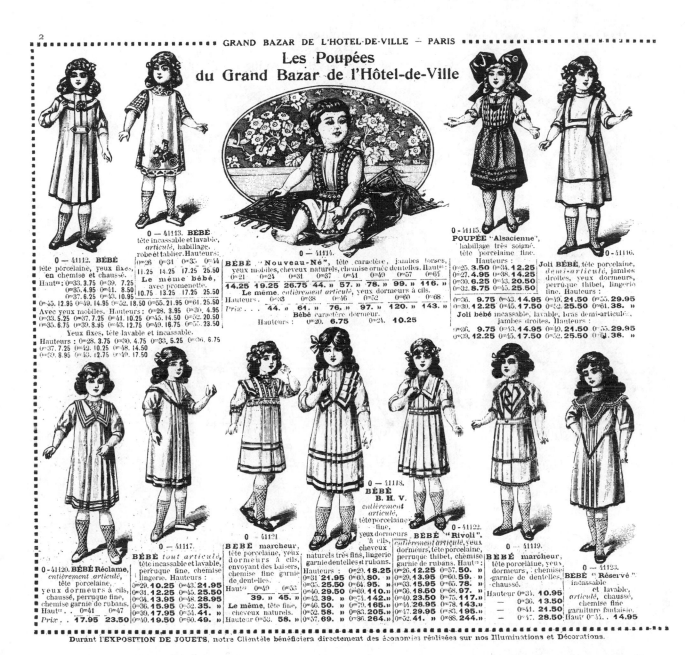

Les Poupées
du Grand Bazar de l'Hôtel-de-Ville

1669. Dolls in chemise (undressed) as shown in the 1921 catalog of L'Hotel de Ville. These dolls include Bébé B.H.V., Bébé Réclame, Bébé Réservé, Bébé Rivoli, walking dolls some of which also threw kisses, and a newborn bent-limb baby doll with a character face. In addition one of the dolls wore a dress and pinafore and another wore an Alsatian costume. Over half of the dolls had bisque heads.

1670. Dressed dolls shown in a 1921 L'Hotel de Ville catalog. The types of dolls and the percentage with bisque heads were about the same as for the "undressed" dolls. The bisque-head dolls were generally a little more expensive than the composition-head dolls. The price differential between dressed dolls and dolls in chemise was not nearly as great as it had been prior to World War I. As usual dressed dolls usually came with headwear.

1671. Back cover of the 1921 catalog of L'Hotel de Ville. The dresses on the bébés and dolls have much shorter skirts than those shown elsewhere in the catalog. This is probably due to different artists' drawings. Several of the dolls are called "Poupée" instead of "Bébé." These seem to be cloth dolls. None of the dolls are described as having bisque heads. In several instances the same doll was shown in two different costumes.

Liberty Doll Co., The. 1918–22. Made "unbreakable" dolls' heads.

1920: Strike caused the management to replace the strikers with new workers.★

Liberty & Co. Probably 1906–30 and later. London and Birmingham, England, Amsterdam and possibly elsewhere. Distributed dolls. Metz & Co. was their Amsterdam agent.

1913: Advertised dolls dressed in ethnic costumes, in Quaker costumes, and in a *Santa Claus* costume.

1920s: Sold *Lenci* child dolls with the Liberty Co. label sewed onto their clothes.

1926: Advertised black dolls made of plush, ht. 32 cm. (12½ in.); white dolls made of suede, ht. 40 cm. (15½ in.); Lenci dolls, hts. 32 and 50 cm. (12½ and 19½ in.).

Libra. Trade name of dolls made by the *H. E. Hopf* family of Neustadt near Coburg. A small composition doll with painted footwear and a blue gauze chemise, ht. 5¾ in. (14.5 cm.), has been reported in a box marked: "Made in Germany //LIBRA//H E [picture of an eye between the two parts of a scale.] Hopf//In North, South, East and West//'Libra ware' are the Best."

Librairie Gallais. 1918. Paris. *Hansi, Maurice Neumont* and *A. Willette* all designers of dolls were associated with the Librairie *Gallais*.

Lichtenfels Puppenfabrik. 1903 and possibly other years. Bavaria. Manufactured five-piece jointed dolls, jointed *Täuflinge*, bathing dolls, and composition arms for dolls.

Lichtenstein. 1889. U.S. Their fashion catalog advertised bisque-head dolls with wigs, sleeping eyes, jointed composition bodies, priced 75¢ to $3.50; rubber dolls, 23¢ to 73¢; *worsted* dressed dolls 19¢ to 48¢; and dolls' clothes.

L'Idéale. 1927–30 and later. Trademark registered in France and used by *Mlle. Marie Georgette Rigot* for cloth art dolls. Mlle. Blanche Fouillot[†] had registered this same trademark for dolls in 1906.★

Lie, Erik. 1896. Berchtesgaden, Bavaria. Applied for a German patent (D.R.G.M.) for a doll's head with changeable features.

Lieb Edelkind. See **Edelkind.**

1672. Liberty & Co. 1913 catalog page from their Dutch distributor, Metz. This shows, left to right, top to bottom: Dolls dressed in costumes of Russia and English Indonesia, an Eskimo, Santa Claus, a Quaker, Tyrolean, Laplander, Matryoska dolls, and a regional peasant. The centimeter heights of the dolls can be converted into inches by dividing by 2.54. *Courtesy of the Collection Nederlands Kostuummuseum, The Hague.*

1673. Liberty & Co. 1926 catalog page from their Dutch distributor. Dolls nos. 1, 4, and 10 appear to be Lenci dolls. Nos. 2, 6 and 8 are called Liberty dolls and probably were made in England. No. 5 is a black doll. These dolls are dressed as children and not in regional costumes as seen in Ill. 1672 before World War I. The centimeter height can be divided by 2.54 to obtain inches. *Courtesy of the Collection Nederlands Kostuummuseum, The Hague. Photo by B. Frequin.*

Liebermann, Christian. 1894–1912. Judenbach and later Coburg, Thür. Made dolls.

1894: Applied for a German patent for a suspended doll (angel type) with a voice in its body.

1906: Applied for a German patent (D.R.G.M.) for a doll with musical works in its body.

Liebermann, Ernst. 1894–1930 and later. Neustadt near Coburg, Thür. and later Bavaria. Made dolls and used *Schoenau & Hoffmeister* heads on some of them. He also advertised Waltershausen jointed dolls with celluloid heads and wigs. By 1925 Franz Albert Liebermann was the owner and he specialized in wholesale distribution and export.

1904: Applied for a German patent (D.R.G.M.) for a doll with a mama-papa voice.

1927–30: Advertised *Baby Joan, Violett* and *Adalene.*★

1674. Mark used by Ernst Liebermann for various types of dolls.

Liebermann, Georg Nicole, & Liebermann, Louis. 1902–13 and probably other years. Neuhaus near Sonneberg, Thür. Besides French and German patents they obtained in 1903 an Austrian patent for a doll with a moving mouth piece. Louis Liebermann applied in 1912 for a German patent (D.R.G.M.) for a doll with moving tongue and teeth. The following year he applied for another German patent (D.R.G.M.) relating to porcelain dolls' heads.★

Liebermann, Oskar. See **Steiner, Albin.**

Liebling lernt laufen (Darling learns to walk). 1927–30 and later. Name given to dolls with toddler bodies that were made by *Kämmer & Reinhardt* in their *Mein Liebling* line. Various head molds were used and the dolls came dressed in short clothes. They usually had bisque or celluloid heads with flirting eyes and mama voices. The dolls were black or white and some of the black dolls had ethnic features. These dolls could sit or stand as well as "walk." There was no walking mechanism in the body. They were a type of *Mama* doll.

Liebner, Zsigmond. 1920–30 and later. Budapest. Known as "Uncle Liebner," he distributed dolls.★

Life Like (Lifelike) Babyland Dolls. 1906–16. Cloth dolls with lifelike lithographed faces produced by Horsman. Some of their costumes differ from the *Babyland Rag* dolls which had handpainted faces.

Life Like Babyland dolls were shown in 1912 and 1914 catalogs. All were standard size selling for $8.00 or $8.50 a doz. wholesale, except Babyland Beauty which was 16 in.

(40.5 cm.); priced $33.00 in 1912 and $27.00 in 1914 a doz. wholesale.★

LIFELIKE BABYLAND DOLLS		
Style No.	Name	Costume or type
200 B	Jan	Dutch boy with wooden shoes
200 C	Cy	Farm boy, overalls and brimmed hat
200 G	Grete	Dutch girl with wooden shoes
200 P	Miss Priscilla	Quaker girl with kerchief and bonnet
202	Girl	Lawn dress
202 RH	Red Riding Hood	Red Riding Hood
203	Baby	Long dress
204	Topsy	Black doll, girl
205	Topsy baby	Black doll, long dress
206	Boy	Boy's outfit
208	Fancy	
209	Babyland Beauty	Girl in print dress and bonnet
215	Marjorie	Finely dressed girl
220 B	Sunbonnet Sue	Girl with sunbonnet
220 BP	Little Bo-Peep	Dolly Varden outfit
225	Automobile Girl	Coat over a dress and a bonnet
230 B	Golf Boy	Handknit sweater, plaid knickers and cap
230 G	Golf Girl	Handknit sweater, skirt, brimmed hat

Life Like Doll (Baby). See **Lyf-Lyk Line.**

Life Like Doll. 1910s–20s. Name of a bisque head doll produced by *Cuno & Otto Dressel* with a *Gebrüder Heubach* head mold #6969. The head had a wig, sleeping eyes and a closed mouth. The composition body was ball jointed. See the first COLLECTOR'S ENCYCLOPEDIA OF DOLLS, Ill. 816 A, for a Gebrüder Heubach doll bearing this same number 6969. The doll shown in THE COLLECTOR'S BOOK OF DOLLS' CLOTHES, Ill. 691, has a Gebrüder Heubach head on a marked Cuno & Otto Dressel body.

Life Size Doll. 1899–1941. Cutout dolls made by the *Art Fabric Mills* and *Selchow & Righter,* the successor, in 1911. It was used as a premium by the National Medicine Co. and others. See Ills. 1675 and 1676.

1909: 30 in. (76 cm.) size was advertised by *Siegel Cooper.*

1912–13: Selchow & Righter advertised Life Size Dolls printed on heavy drill, or on Sateen for the larger size. Hts. 20 and 30 in. (51 and 76 cm.).

1940–41: There were advertisements for a reissue of the *Merrie Marie* Life Size Doll.★

Lifelike Dolls. 1926. Line of *Mama* dolls and infant dolls made by the *Maxine Doll Co.* These dressed dolls came in several sizes. In 1928 *Gamage* advertised "Lifelike" baby dolls with sleeping eyes. Those in long clothes were 12, 13½, and 16 in. (30.5, 34, and 40.5 cm.) tall; priced 88¢ to $2.23. Those in short clothes came in four hts. 9½, 11, 13, and 16 in. (24, 28, 33 and 40.5 cm.); priced $1.13 to $3.13.

LIFE SIZE DOLL

"Babies' Clothes Will Now Fit Dollie"

"Life-Size Doll"—"That's advertised" that the baby's clothes will fit. No clothes to make. If mamma can donate one of baby's outgrown changes, that her little daughter can put on and off, button and unbutton to her heart's desire, the life-size doll will live in that child's memory long after childhood's days have passed away.

Every little girl loves a doll, more so a big doll; imagine how proud and delighted she would be if you gave her a real "life-size doll," 2½ feet high, that can wear real clothes, whose head won't break, eyes fall in, or suffer any of the mishaps that dollie is apt to encounter.

This doll is an exact reproduction of a hand-painted French creation, done on extra heavy Sateen, that will not tear. In oil-colors that will not crock. The workmanship is perfect, the color effects the very finest.

The doll is intended to be stuffed with cotton or other suitable material. It is this Century's model of the old-fashioned "Rag Doll" that Grandma used to make, and would make Grandma open her eyes in wonder.

Dollie has Golden Hair, Rosy Cheeks, Brown Eyes, Kid Color Body, Red Stockings and Black Shoes, and in following the directions in making up, if a piece of heavy cardboard is inserted in the soles, a perfect shoe is formed, enabling the doll to stand erect.

2½ Feet High

Doll Made Up.

Retails at 50c.

20 inch Life Size Doll

Same as the 2½ feet size, only smaller.

(DOLL AS SOLD.)

Retails at 25c.

1675. Life Size cutout cloth dolls as advertised in the DE-LINEATOR, December 1900. Hs. 20 and 30 in. (51 and 76 cm.).

Life-Like line. 1930. Advertised as *Mama* dolls, baby dolls, art dolls in pastel shades, and Aunt Jemima, a black doll. It is not known whether this line had any connection with one of the above Life Like lines.

Lifraud, Suzanne. 1915. Paris. A sculptress who modeled dolls' heads. She was born in 1892 and obtained a medal in 1929.

Ligue du Jouet Français (League of the French Toy). 1914–16 and possibly later. Paris. Founded by *Mme. la Baroness de Laumont* for the purpose of producing dolls for children and to give work to women. Tags on composition-head lady dolls read "Ligue du Jouet Français." These dolls resembled the bisque-head dolls known to have been made under the supervision of Mme. de Laumont.

Life Size Rag Doll

Premium No. 381

20 inches tall, printed in nice bright colors on strong cloth. Sent for 1 new subscription at 35c and 5c extra.

1676. Life Size cutout cloth doll offered as a magazine subscription premium in 1913. H. 20 in. (51 cm.).

1915: An article in REVUE DES DEUX MONDES by Georges d'Avenel, May 15, 1915, reported on the Ligue du Jouets Français:

"The manufacturers of toys have seen with surprise the rebirth last autumn (1914) of the lady doll dressed coquettishly. Some of our fashionable ladies being anxious to procure the work of 'little hands' have suggested that they put their leisure in the service of the country by making dolls. The light and flexible bodies stuffed with cotton were covered with leather or cloth. The metal-wire armatures were surmounted with composition heads having painted eyes. The original models for these heads were created by talented sculptors who in peacetimes were engaged in fine arts. Instead of being stereotyped dolls their expressions were alert or ingenuous, haughty or sly, naive or unruly and the costumes match the expression of the faces. The clothes are made of remnants and leftovers from stores, the end of a piece of silk, a damaged piece of linen, cast-off trinkets but the costumes always reflect true Parisian fashions. The dolls represented personable women, marquises, working girls, peasants or fisherwomen, all looking life-like. The large stores and bazaars have welcomed these creations of the 'League of the French Toy.' They were admired in London in March and have since gone to San Francisco where they represent the grace and taste of our country. The dolls were produced by the inventive fingers of our workers, using material found by chance in our familiar workshops. At present the 'League of the French Toy' has no other shop than a room in the private house of the lady who initiated this work. Here the French and foreign distributors come to make their purchases. The capital for this industry at first was only made available by a good lady who economised on the clothes allowance given to her by her husband. The success of this enterprise proves again that an intelligent effort to produce something new is more important than the availability of capital."

1677. Composition-head doll produced by the Ligue du Jouets Français (League of the French Toy). It has a wig, painted eyes and closed mouth. This doll of about 1916 is in a Series VI and dressed in pseudo 1700s style to represent Queen Anne of Austria. The high-heeled shoes are molded and painted. Mark: Ill. 1678. H. 14 in. (35.5 cm.). *Courtesy of the Margaret Woodbury Strong Museum. Photo by Harry Bickelhaupt.*

1678. Mark on tag on dolls produced by the Ligue du Jouet Français.

Lila. 1914. Mark registered in Germany by *William Goebel* to be used on porcelain babies.

Lili. 1928. Name of a dressed cloth doll sold by *Paturel.*

Lilibet. 1929. Portrait doll of *Princess Elizabeth* of England made by *Effanbee*. The doll wore a golden yellow dress, the same color as was worn by the Princess herself.

Liliput. 1894–1908. Dolls imported by *Samstag & Hilder.*★

Lilith. Ca. 1920. Name of an elaborately dressed wax doll created by *Lottie Pritzel.*

Lilith Dolls. 1930. New York City. Made and/or distributed dolls.

Lillen, S. B. 1893–94. Liverpool, England. Obtained a German patent for a cloth doll with a movable head.

Lilli. See **Baitz, Lilli & R.**

Lilliputians. 1892. Trade name of all-bisque dolls with jointed bodies distributed by *Marshall Field*. The dolls wore brimmed hats and high multi-strap boots. Ht. 3½ in. (9 cm.); price $2.75 doz. wholesale.

Lilliputians.[+] See **Mignonnettes.** (See THE COLLECTOR'S BOOK OF DOLLS' CLOTHES, Ill. 309.) (See also **John Mason,** 1785.)

Lillums. 1929. All-bisque doll with a turning head, based on a character in the *"Harold Teen"* cartoon drawn by Carl Ed. The dolls were made in Germany and distributed wholesale exclusively by *Marshall Field* and their licensees.

Lilly. Before World War I. Name found on a bisque shoulder head with wig, glass eyes and open mouth. The kid body had bisque arms. This doll made in Germany was probably the doll "Lilly" handled by *Borgfeldt*. It came in at least three hts. 10, 16, and 18 in. (25.5, 40.5, and 45.5 cm.).★

1679. Bisque shoulder head marked "Lilly" has a wig, stationary blue glass eyes, open mouth with four upper teeth, and a kid body with bisque lower arms and cloth lower legs. Mark on head: Ill. 1680. H. of doll 21 in. (53.5 cm.). H. of shoulder head 5½ in. (14 in.). *Courtesy of Helen Read. Photo by Steven Read.*

Lilly

3/0.

Made in Germany

1680. Lilly mark on a bisque shoulder head.

Lilly. 1913. Felt character doll made by *Steiff* and distributed by *Borgfeldt*. It was dressed as a girl in a coat and leggings or high spats. Ht. 17 in. (43 cm.); priced $6.00.

Lily. 1913. Name of a doll handled by *Whyte, Ridsdale*. Ht. 10½ in. (26.5 cm.); priced $2.13 doz. wholesale.

Lily. 1917–18. A doll with a painted head and cloth body created by *Jean Ray* and distributed by *Bon Marché and L'Hotel de Ville*. It had removable clothes. Hts. 36 and 42 cm. (14 and 16½ in.); priced $5.50 and $7.50.

Lily. 1927. One of the *Twinjoy* line of *Flower Dolls* with a petal dress. This was two dolls in one created by *Berry Kollin*.

Lily. 1928. Composition-head doll advertised by *Bon Marché*. It had a wig, sleeping eyes, jointed body, and wore a wool dress. Ht. 42 cm. (16½ in.).

Lily Langtry. 1895. Distributed by *Butler Bros*. It had a bisque head, wig and came dressed. Ht. 23 in. (58.5 cm.); priced $5.25 doz. wholesale. The doll was named after the famous English Actress.

Limbach Porzellanfabrik. 1772–1927 and later. Limbach near Alsbach, Thür. The Limbach trefoil marks are frequently found on dolls although one similar trefoil mark was also used by the *Ilmenauer Porzellanfabrik*.

One of the Limbach doll's heads was marked *Wally*. Another Limbach doll's head was a bisque shoulder head with molded black hair and a molded blouse, painted eyes, and a closed mouth. This head with its trefoil or shamrock mark is sometimes referred to by collectors of the 1980s as the "Irish Queen."

1850: A china shoulder head with molded hair at the Sonneberg Museum was identified as having been made by Limbach at this date.

1894: The factory manager was Victor Dressel and there were 166 employees. They produced bisque dolls' heads, dolls' house dolls and all-bisque and all-china "bathing dolls."

1926: Advertised dolls' heads and small jointed dolls.

1927: Advertised glazed china baby dolls and jointed bisque dolls.★

Limber Lou. 1921. Advertised by *Riemann Seabrey* as "a doll having a thousand expressions." It was made of wire and dressed. Ht. 18 in. (45.5 cm.).★

Limoges. 1867 or earlier–1925 and later. Several of the porcelain factories in Limoges made dolls' heads and dolls. Some of these were made without color in the white and were painted and given additional lower temperature firing elsewhere. (See also **Clauderies, J. Roger Gault, A. Lanternier & Cie.** and **Montastiers & Perier.**)

Lincoln Import Sales Co. 1922–23. New York City. Imported dressed and undressed German dolls. Their selling agent was *I. W. Doremus*.

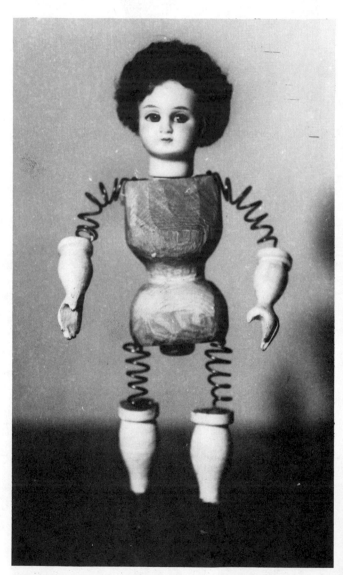

1681. Bisque head made by Limbach is dome-shaped under the wig. It has stationary glass eyes, a closed mouth and the neck appears to fit over a dowel. The torso, lower arms and lower legs are wood while the upper arms and legs are wire springs. H. 7½ in. (19 cm.). *Courtesy of Dr. Eva Moskovszky.*

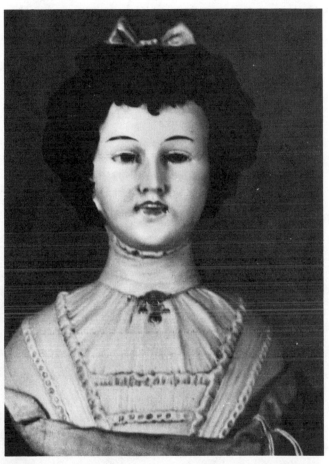

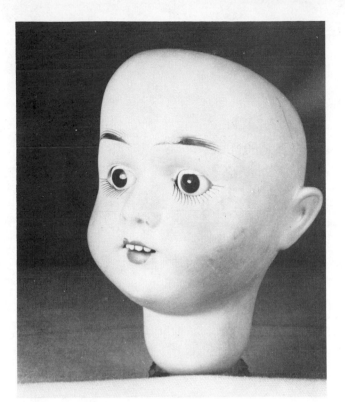

1683. Bisque head with the Limbach trefoil and "Wally" mark: Ill. 1695. It has a wig, sleeping glass eyes, and an open mouth with four upper teeth. H. of head only 4 in. (10 cm.). *Coleman Collection.*

1682. Untinted bisque shoulder head marked with the Limbach trefoil. It has molded and painted black hair, intaglio eyes, open-closed mouth with teeth. The hair style and molded bodice top suggest that the head was made ca. 1900. The cloth body has leather arms. Mark: Ill. 1685. H. 19 in. (48 cm.). *Courtesy of Richard Withington. Photo by Barbara Jendrick.*

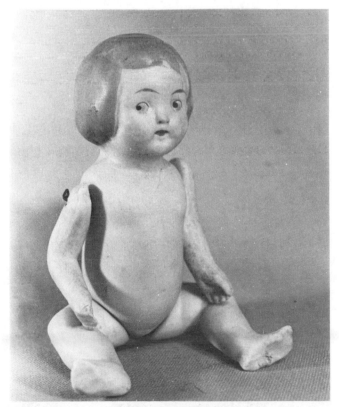

1684. All-bisque doll made by the Limbach Porcelain Factory. It has molded hair, painted features including round roguish eyes, and a bent-limb body. Mark: Ill. 1689. H. 4½ in. (11.5 cm.). *Coleman Collection.*

8552 ☘

1685

GERMANY
8682
☘ 4

1686

GERMANY
8822
☘

1687

9109
GERMANY
☘

1688

9307 2/0
GERMANY
☘

1689

☘

10

1690

Germany
☘

4

1691

P 23
MADE IN GERMANY
☘

1692

👑

1695

⊙ ⊙

Limbach

1693

Wally 4

👑
☘ L
17 72
Limbach

1694

Rita
3/0

👑
☘ L
17 72
Limbach

△ A S
MADE IN GERMANY

1685–1695. Marks used by the Limbach Porcelain Factory.

Lindbergh. 1927. Non-portrait dolls were dressed to represent Lindbergh and were available in the stores by the time he returned to New York City. Later the Lindbergh portrait doll was produced and called *Our Lindy.*

Lindbergh. 1929. Doll made by *Shuco* with a mask face having aviator's goggles. The body was plush.

L'Indestructible. 1894–95. Bébé with rubber head and hands, glass eyes, open mouth with teeth. It was patented and advertised by *A. Bouchet.*

Lindner, Edmund. 1851 and later. Sonneberg, Thür. According to records written by *Adolf Fleischmann* whose wife was a Lindner, Edmund Lindner attended the 1851 London Exhibition and on his way home he saw in a toy shop a Japanese doll of a type that was new to him. When he reached home he made some dolls of wood similar to the Japanese dolls that he had seen and thus probably produced in Germany the first commercial *Täufling* or baby doll which collectors also know as the *Motschmann-type* doll. This Täufling baby doll with its hard hip section was soon copied by many other German and French manufacturers. (See **Munnier.**) The research of the Ciesliks discovered the Fleischmann record. It is interesting to note that the first Täuflinge were made of wood and what appears to have been the latest Täuflinge because of their similarity to *Bébé*

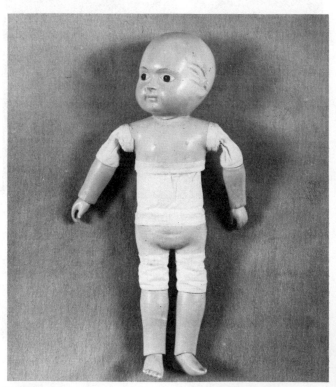

1696. Baby doll or Täufling composition head, breast area, hip area, hands and feet; cloth stomach area, upper arms and upper legs; wooden lower arms and lower legs with floating joints; molded and painted hair; painted eyes. Edmund Lindner probably introduced this type into Germany. Marked in ink "C. E." on sole of left foot. H. 32 cm. (12½ in.). *Courtesy of the Collection Nederlands Kostuummuseum, The Hague. Photo by B. Frequin.*

LINDNER FAMILY OF SONNEBERG

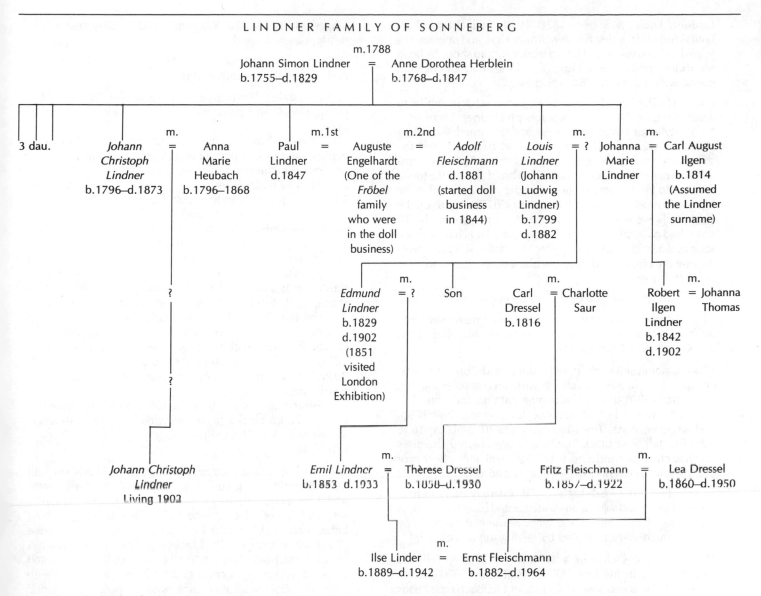

Information for this family chart was supplied by Marianne Eichhorn, a relative of Emil Lindner, b.1853.

Tout en Bois dolls, were also made of wood. See Ill. 1228 in the first COLLECTOR'S ENCYCLOPEDIA OF DOLLS.

(Note: in the Peabody Museum in Salem, Mass., many items of Japanese origin were accessioned into the collection before 1852 when Admiral Perry allegedly set out to open Japan to Western trade.) (See also **Crying Babies.**)

Lindner, Johann Simon. Late 1700s–after 1831. Sonneberg, Thür. Founder of a very important doll *Verleger* family. He was born in 1755, married in 1788. His oldest son was Johann Christoph, born in 1796, died 1873. His other sons involved with dolls were Johann Louis (Ludwig) Lindner, born 1799, and Carl Ilgen Lindner (son-in-law). Carl's son Robert Ilgen Lindner was born in 1842 and died in 1902. (See Family Chart.) Some of the doll and toy catalogs of Johann Simon Lindner and his son Louis Lindner are in the Sonneberg Museum and one of these was reproduced in 1979. *Lewis Page* distributed Lindner dolls around 1830.

Ca. 1830: The catalog showed dolls with molded hair, papier-mâché heads, kid bodies and wooden limbs having red, yellow or blue shoes. Pinked paper covered the joining of the limbs to the bodies. See Ills. 368 and 1290 in the first COLLECTOR'S ENCYCLOPEDIA OF DOLLS. Similar heads on wooden bodies with ball joints at the shoulders, hips, elbows and knees were also shown. The leather-body dolls came in 16 sizes from number 0000 to 12 and the wooden-bodied dolls came in 20 sizes from number 00000000 (eight zeros) to 12; some of the largest sizes had earrings. There were four styles, articulated at the shoulders and with turned or carved clothes. These held a swaddling clothed baby that was raised or lowered by a string extending from the back of the doll representing the Mother. Three of the four other wooden dolls with turned or carved clothes were called "Tiroler docken" and had hats of various shapes. The fourth doll was similar to the Tiroler docken but had pebbles inside to form a rattle.

Lindner, Louis, & Söhne. 1830–1928. Sonneberg, Thür. Louis Lindner founded his own firm in 1830 and later he was joined by his sons. A doll with a bisque turned shoulder head on a cloth body with composition limbs had an elliptical stamp with the words "Baby//Lindner."

Ca. 1841: The Louis Lindner catalog showed dolls similar to those in the ca. 1830 catalog of Johann Lindner. There were seven styles of babies in carved and/or turned swaddling clothes *(poupards.)* One of these had dark hair and the shoulders were outlined with pinked strips. The new items included a papier-mâché head with a braid around the top of the Apollo knot. Some of the kid bodies were jointed at the hips and knees and had entire arms of kid. The heads on the baby dolls were similar to the heads of the poupards. 10 styles had painted short hair, five styles had real hair and one style had a bald head. There were also dolls with glass eyes. Among the character dolls were black dolls, Turks, soldiers and *Harlequins.*

1842: Advertised black or blue glass eyes.

1859: Lindner & Söhne were creditors of *Pierre Ringel* when he failed according to Mme. Florence Poisson, Curator of the Roybet Fould Museum.

1880: Catalog shows dolls with china heads, bisque heads, composition heads including varnished papier-mâché. There were all-bisque and all-china bathing dolls, hts. 2 to 16 cm. (¾ to 6½ in.). Most of the dolls came in both black and white versions. The Täuflinge were 20 to 50 cm. (8 to 19½ in.) tall. The black Täuflinge wore colored chemises and had curly hair and glass eyes. Dolls with either leather or cloth bodies often had wooden arms and legs.

1881: The Lindner catalog showed a variety of Täuflinge. Some of them had wax heads with painted hair, hts. 20 to 58 cm. (8 to 23 in.); others had wigs. Some had mama-papa voices which were activated by raising the arms.

1911: The Louis Lindner advertisement in PLAYTHINGS (See Ill. 1099 in the first COLLECTOR'S ENCYCLOPEDIA OF DOLLS) showed several Gebrüder Heubach type heads on Lindner dolls. It should be noted that Louis Lindner's sister-in-law was a Heubach.

1922: Advertised dolls and dolls' heads.

1930s: The firm Louis Lindner & Söhne and Gebrüder Fleischmann were amalgamated.

Part of the above information was researched by the Ciesliks.★

Lindstrom, Frank. 1926. Bridgeport, Conn. Doing business as the Lindstrom Tool & Toy Co. obtained a U.S. design patent for a doll. Advertised "Dancing Bettys and Clowns."

Lindy Doll. See **Our Lindy.**

Lines Bros. See **Hamley Bros.**

Linette. 1928. Advertised by *Bon Marché.* The doll had a character head, wig, felt body, and was dressed. Ht. 48 cm. (19 in.).

L'Infernal Brise-Tout. 1918. French trademark registered by *Mme. Poulbot* for dolls.

Linger, Esther L. 1926. Washington, D.C. Obtained a U.S. design patent for a doll.

Linington, C. M. 1866–late 1890s. Chicago, Ill. Importer and wholesale distributor of dolls.

1883: Catalog listed wax (i.e., wax-over-composition), composition, and china head dolls as well as all-bisque dolls.

Nearly all of the wax-head dolls had hair, glass eyes, earrings and those up to 22 in. (56 cm.) had "bisque" arms and legs. Sleeping eyes were reported on 14½ and 28 in. (37 and 71 cm.) dolls. Dolls came in 14 hts. 6 to 29 in. (15 to 73.5 cm.); priced 48¢ to $9.60 doz. wholesale.

One style of composition-head doll had hair, glass eyes, and bisque limbs with garters and shoes on the legs. Four hts. 11¾, 12½, 17½, and 21 in. (30, 31.5, 44.5, and 53.5 cm.); priced 80¢ to $4.50 doz. wholesale. The other style had painted hair, leather body with cloth shoes; ht. 10½ in. (26.5 cm.); priced $1.65 doz. wholesale; with leather shoes, ht. 12½ in. (31.5 cm.); cost $2.10 doz. wholesale.

The drawing of the china-head dolls shows a flat top hair-do, china lower arms and legs and a seam down the middle front of the cloth body. Nine hts. 5½, 6½, 7½, 8, 10½, 11, 14, 16, and 20 in. (14, 16.5, 19, 20.5, 26.5, 28, 35.5, 40.5, and 51 cm.); priced 30¢ to $3.80 doz. wholesale.

Jointed all-bisque dolls included representations of clowns, Turks, blacks, babies and girls. They came in several sizes from 3 in. (7.5 cm.) and up, and cost 35¢ to 70¢ doz. wholesale.

Late 1880s: Catalog listed French bisque heads on ball jointed bodies, long curly hair, glass sleeping eyes, teeth, and wore a chemise; four hts.: 19, 19½, 21, and 24 in. (48, 49.5, 53.5, and 61 cm.). The 24 in. size cost $2.00. China babies came as blondes or brunettes; ht. 4 in. (10 cm.); price 35¢ a doz. wholesale. The black china babies were only 2¼ in. (5.5 cm.) tall. The white all-bisque dolls with jointed arms, ht. 2¼ in. (5.5 cm.), cost 6¢ a doz. wholesale with painted hair. These also came with flowing hair. Bisque dolls with Kate Greenaway bonnets were 2¾ in. (7 cm.) tall.

Late 1890s: French bisque heads on ball-jointed bodies, open mouth with teeth, wore a chemise; hts. 10, 12¾, and 14½ in. (25.5, 32.5, and 37 cm.); priced $1.25 to $2.00 a doz. wholesale. There were two kinds of dolls with bisque heads on kid bodies; one kind had gusset joints and the other had metal joints. The former ranged in ht. from 13 to 19½ in. (33 to 49.5 cm.) while the latter were 11 to 18½ in. (28 to 47 cm.). They all had wigs and glass eyes. All of the china heads were of the wavy hair low-brow style. They came on cloth bodies with china limbs; the ones with plain white cloth bodies ranged in ht. from 7 to 20 in. (18 to 51 cm.) and the ones with colored printed bodies were 7 to 16 in. (18 to 40.5 cm.) tall.

The composition ("washable non-destructible") head dolls on cloth bodies came in three styles. The regular ones were 17 to 32 in. (43 to 81 cm.) tall; the talking versions with two strings, one "mama" and one "papa," were 24 and 28 in. (61 and 71 cm.); a fat baby girl with long hair was 13 and 24 in. (33 and 61 cm.) tall while a similar fat baby boy with

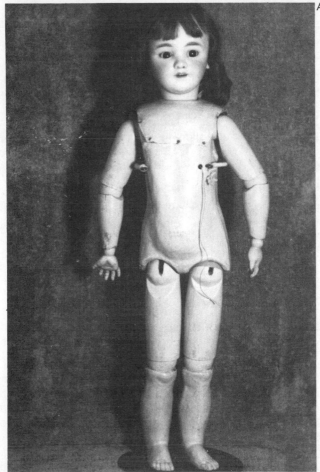

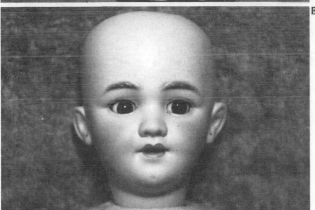

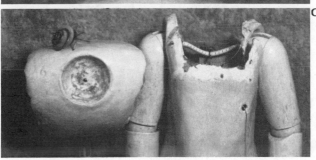

1697A, B & C. Child doll produced by Louis Lindner & Söhne. The bisque head was made by Simon & Halbig, mold #1339. It has a new wig, sleeping brown glass eyes, pierced ears, open mouth with four upper teeth, composition and wood fully jointed body. The shoulder plate was cut out to enable the voice to be placed inside the doll. The voice is activated by a string emerging at the breast area of the doll. The above pictures show the shoulder plate removed and also in place. Note the narrowness of the shoulders when not attached to the shoulder plate. Mark on head: Ill. 1698. Stamped mark on torso: "D.R.G.M.// 357529." This German patent for a doll's voice was obtained by Hermann Wegner, October 12, 1908. H. 28 in. (71 cm.). *Private collection.*

1339

S & H

L L & S

13

1698. Mark on the Simon & Halbig bisque head of a doll produced by Louis Lindner & Söhne.

short hair was 22½ in. (57 cm.) tall. The large sized girl with long hair cost $1.50 each while the slightly smaller boy with short hair cost $7.25 a doz. wholesale.

Knitted *Worsted Dolls* dressed in bright colored knitted worsted suits with matching caps represented girls, boys and clowns. No two suits were alike. Ht. 13 in. (33 cm.); price $3.75 a doz. wholesale. It is interesting to note that these were considerably more expensive than dolls with French bisque heads or with composition heads of similar sizes.

A novelty rattle had a gauze faced baby head with a rattle inside and a knitted cap and cape. Ht. 9¼ in. (23.5 cm.). ★

Link, A., & Co. 1917. Glasgow, Scotland. Made accessories for dolls.

L'Innovation. 1916. Brussels. Name of a store that exhibited dolls at the Brussels Exposition to benefit the children of Belgian soldiers. Herman of L'Innovation was a member of the Jury at the Exposition, therefore they were Hors Concours.

Linster, Mlle. 1916. Belgium. She dressed some of the dolls shown at the Exposition for the benefit of the children of Belgian soldiers.

L'Intrepide Bébé. 1892–1930 and later. Generic name of mechanical walking dolls made by *Roullet & Decamps.* At first they were called "Marchant Mécanique" (Mechanical Walkers), then "*Bébé Premiers Pas"* (Not to be confused with *Steiner's "Bébé Premier Pas"*); later they were called *Marchant Systême; Bébé Systême* or Bébé Mécanique, according to Anne-Marie and Jacques Porot. Bébé Systême walked without a key wind. At first Jumeau made the bisque heads but most of the bisque heads were made in Germany. *Simon & Halbig* supplied the heads marked 1039 or 1079. *Kestner* supplied bisque heads marked J. D. K. with glass eyes. There were also heads marked DEP 289. The bodies were composition except for wooden limbs on the larger sizes. The Porots' research found that the wooden arms were similar to those found on some *Bru* dolls and presumably the same factory supplied both Bru and Roullet & Decamps. This wood factory supplied the unpainted wooden balls which were then painted at the same time as the rest of the body by

Roullet & Decamps. White kid covered the mechanism in the lower part of the torso. The dolls wore a chemise or were dressed as boys or girls in various costumes; they were often dressed by the store where they were sold.

A walking bébé has been found with a *Jumeau*-like head incised "L'intrepide R.D. B^te, S.G.D.G. 8." Ht. 51 cm. (20 in.).

1906 or later: Gaston Decamps, son of Ernst Decamps, designed bodies for these dolls.

SIZE–HEIGHT RELATIONSHIP OF L'INTREPIDE BÉBÉ			
Size	*Height*		
Number	*cm.*	*in.*	*Description*
5	35	14	Composition limbs, doll unable to sit
7	44	17½	Composition limbs, doll unable to sit
8	47	18½	
9	57	22½	Jointed wrists, flirting eyes
10	61	24	Jointed wrists, flirting eyes and talking
12	75	29½	Jointed wrists, flirting eyes and talking

1920s: Doll had a bisque head, wig, glass eyes, open mouth and teeth, jointed wrists, and came dressed. It wore a ribbon on which was "Donnez moi á main// je marche, je parle." (Give me your hand// I walk, I talk.)

1930 and later: *Petitcollin* made celluloid heads for L'Intrépide Bébé. These dolls were usually size 2. Ht. 33 cm. (13 in.).★

Linzerdocken. During the 1800s. Wooden dolls wearing the high cap of the Linz women were made for generations as a home industry in the Viechtau near Gmunden area of the Balkans.

1881: Linzerdocken with movable arms, ht. 4¾ in. (12 cm.), cost 2½¢ a doz. wholesale.

Lion Tamer. Ca. 1905–24. *Schoenhut* wooden doll, wore a coat with three rows of decorations across the chest and a fez type hat, carried a whip.★

Lioret, Henri. 1893–1900 and perhaps later. France. His 1893 patent was used by *Jumeau* to make Bébé Phonographe† that could talk and sing. These dolls were generally about 25 in. (63.5 cm.) tall. See Ill. 2096.

Lipfert, Bernard. Ca. 1910–30 and later. He was born in 1888 and around 1910 worked as a designer of dolls for *Armand Marseille*. In 1912 he came to America and later designed many famous American dolls including *Bubbles*, *Patsy* and the Patsy family dolls. He modeled the heads in clay and then made the plaster-of-paris molds.★

Lipmann, Franz, and Lammel, Paul. 1912. Deuben near Dresden. Applied for a German patent (D.R.G.M.) for dolls' heads with moving eyes.

Lippert & Haas. See Schaggenwald.

Lisa. 1916–24. Felt doll made by *Steiff*. Five hts. 28, 35, 43, 50 and 60 cm. (11, 14, 17, 19½ and 23½ in.). By 1924 the 60 cm. (23½ in.) size was discontinued.

Lisa. 1926. Art doll made by *Elise Israel*.

Liselotte. 1926. Line of celluloid child dolls with molded Dutch bob hairdos; fully jointed (diagonal hip joints); made by *Rheinische Gummi und Celluloid Fabrik Co.*, and advertised in a British toy trade journal.

Lisette. 1925. Printed cutout cloth doll published by *Fernand Nathan*. This was a smaller version of *Suzy*. Ht. 45 cm. (17½ in.).

Lisk, S., & Bro. 1922–30 and later. New York City. Handled American dolls and imported dolls from the Orient and Europe.★

Lisl (Lizzie, Loni, Bavarian Tirolese). Before 1911–24. Various names of a felt character doll made by *Steiff* and dressed as a girl of the Bavarian Tyrol. Five hts. 28, 35, 43, 50, and 60 cm. (11, 14, 17, 19½, and 23½ in.); priced $1.63 to $5.71 in Germany in 1911.

In 1913 this doll with the name Lizzie was in the *Borgfeldt* catalog. Hts. 28 and 35 cm. (11 and 14 in.); priced $2.30 and $2.95 in U.S.

In 1924 Lizzie was listed in the Steiff catalog as being 28, 35, 43 and 50 cm. (11, 14, 17 and 19½ in.) tall.

Lissy. Probably before World War I. Name of a doll with a German bisque head, wig, sleeping eyes, open mouth, and teeth on a pink imitation kid body. Hts. 20 and 22 in. (51 and 56 cm.).

1699. Lissy marks on German bisque heads of dolls.

Lithographed-face Cloth Dolls. Technique used in the manufacture of cloth dolls in the late 1800s and early 1900s, such as *Life Like Babyland Dolls*, *Little Fairy*, and *Little Tots*.

Little, John, & Co. 1910. Singapore. Their catalog listed the *Kämmer & Reinhardt* mold #100 "Baby," celluloid swimming dolls, and "French Dressed Dolls"; priced $1.00 to $11.50. (These were Singapore dollars.)

Little Amby. 1929. Composition doll made by *Amberg*, jointed at the shoulders and hips, with a diagonal hip joint; came dressed as a boy in short trousers. It had various hair styles. Priced $2.50.

Little Annie Roonie. 1925–26. Composition and all-bisque versions of this doll were made.★

Little Athlete. 1912. Trade name of a composition-head doll distributed by *Sears.* It had a hair stuffed cotton flannel body which was jointed at the shoulders and hips; dressed in a knitted sweater with buttons on the shoulders. The voice was activated by squeezing. Hts. 9½ and 13½ in. (24 and 34 cm.); priced 48¢ and 89¢.

Little Bo Peep. 1912–13. Cutout cloth doll wearing a necklace and a skirt extending below the knees, advertised by *Selchow & Righter.* Ht. 18 in. (45.5 cm.); priced 25¢, $2.00 doz. wholesale.

Little Bo-Peep. 1917. Cloth cutout doll in the *Hug-Me-Tight* line.

Little Bo-Peep. 1922. One of the handpainted *Mother Goose* cloth dolls with real hair made by *Rees Davis.*

Little Bo-Peep. 1928. A cloth cutout advertising doll of *Kellogg Co.*

Little Bo-Peep. 1929. One of the *Kiddie Karakter* line of dolls made by *Averill.* The *Little Sister* doll mold designed by *Grace Corry* was used for this doll which wore a floral print, Bo-Peep type costume, carried a crook and had pinned to its clothes a rectangular tag with the Bo-Peep nursery rhyme on it.

Little Bo-Peep. See **Life Like Babyland Dolls.**

Little Bob-Sleigh. See **Bob Sleigh.**

Little Boy Blue. 1912–13. Cutout cloth doll dressed in a Lord Fauntleroy style suit with rounded corners on the jacket, advertised by *Selchow & Righter.* Ht. 18 in. (45.5 cm.); priced 25¢, $2.00 doz. wholesale.

Little Boy Blue. 1912–14. Cloth boy doll wore a Buster Brown type suit and a stocking cap, produced by *Horsman* in the American Maid line of dolls. Priced 50¢ retail.

Little Boy Blue. 1915–17. Cloth cutout doll in the *Hug-Me-Tight* line.

Little Boy Blue. 1920. One of the handpainted *Mother Goose* cloth dolls with real hair, made by *Rees Davis.*

Little Boy Blue. 1929. One of the *Kiddie Karakter* line of dolls made by *Averill.* The *Little Brother* mold designed by *Grace Corry* was used for this doll which wore very short trousers, and a tam, had a horn on a string around its neck and had pinned to its clothes a rectangular tag with the Little Boy Blue nursery rhyme on it.

Little Boy Blue. 1929. Doll made of segmented turned wood with handpainted face and a novelty hat. This doll with eyes looking to the side was made by the *Sun Enamel Works.* Price $7.50 a doz. wholesale.

Little Boy Blue. See **Nursery Rhymes.**

Little Brother. 1927–29. Doll with composition head, molded hair, painted eyes, cloth body with composition arms and with or without composition legs. The head was sculptured by *Grace Corry* and the doll was made by the *Averill Manufacturing Co.* It wore a variety of costumes and when dressed as a girl it was called *Little Sister;* when it wore a nursery rhyme or fairy tale costume it was called a *Kiddie Karakter.* Ht. 14 in. (35.5 cm.).

1927: It wore an Oliver Twist type suit with short trousers buttoned onto a white shirt.

PLAYTHINGS, July 1927, described Little Brother and Little Sister as being the "creation of Grace Corry who has caught in clay that delightful moment in child expression just before a radiant child breaks out in a smile."

1929: Besides the Oliver Twist suit it was dressed in playsuits that were made in plain colors with print tops. These were designed by *Katherine Rauser.* An advertisement also showed it dressed in a double breasted coat, and tam.

Vivian Rasberry reported a Little Brother doll dressed in a felt Dutch boy costume with wooden shoes. This doll had a string wig over its molded hair and contained a voice box.

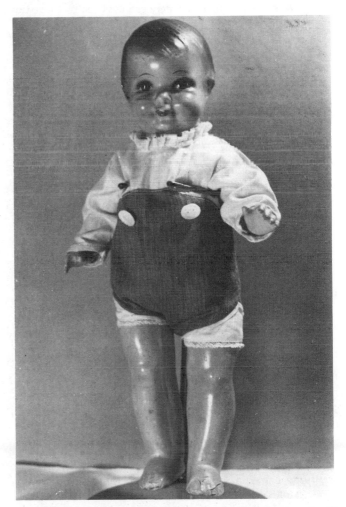

1700. Little Brother doll designed by Grace Corry for Averill Manufacturing Co. It has molded brown hair and eyes, a closed mouth, a cloth body with composition arms and legs and a cry box. Mark on head "© //By//Grace Corry." H. 14 in. (35.5 cm.). *Courtesy of Jan Payson.*

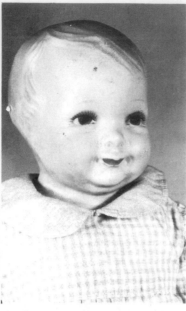

1701A & B. Composition shoulder head designed by Grace Corry. It was called Little Brother when it first appeared on the market in 1927, but the head was later used for dolls with other names. It has molded hair and painted features. Mark: Ill. 1702. H. 14 in. (35.5 cm.). *Coleman Collection.*

©

BY

GRACE CORRY

1702. Mark on Little Brother, an all-composition doll.

Little Buck. 1920. An Indian-type doll made by *Mary Frances Woods*. It had a portrait type face of crepe-paper over a mold, and wore a blanket and a single feather at the back of its head. Ht. 10 in. (25.5 cm.). See Ill. 2768.

Little Carrot. 1915. Represented a waif of Cracow, and was one of the *Paderewski* dolls made in *Mme. Lazarski*'s workshop in Paris. The name came from its carrot-colored hair.

Little Cherub. 1912–15. Name of a doll with bisque head, mohair wig, sleeping eyes, ball-jointed composition body including jointed wrists; came in a chemise and footwear. This doll was distributed by *Sears*. There were four hts. 10, 13½, 15, and 18 in. (25.5, 34, 38, and 45.5 cm.); priced 25¢ to $1.19. The largest size had hair eyelashes. ★

Little Cresta. 1920–21. Stockinet doll dressed in a winter sport costume of fleecy material made by *Chad Valley*. The costume came in various colors and three size numbers, 26/1 (small), 26/2 (medium), 9½ in. (24 cm.) and 26/3 (large).

Little Darling. 1929. Name of a bisque-head doll that came in a basket with a trousseau and was sold by *Butler Bros*. Ht. 11 in. (28 cm.); price $6.00.

Little Darling Babies. 1915. Dolls made by *Amberg* and distributed in Britain by the *British Metal & Toy Manufacturers.*

Little Dressmaker. 1926–28. Name on a box containing a sleeping-eyed doll, a sewing machine, assorted dress patterns stamped for embroidery, silk and embroidery yarn, fasteners, silk ribbon, and a thimble. These boxes were produced by the *Standard Solophone Manufacturing Co.*

Little Emily. 1914. Had a composition head with a mohair wig and glass eyes, on a cloth body. The composition hands had some of the fingers separated. This "new art model" made by *Horsman* was style No. 188. It wore a pink and white costume with a golden straw, brimmed hat with roses and ribbons on it. This doll was slightly larger than the standard Horsman doll and cost $13.50 doz. wholesale.

Little Fairy. Early 1900s. Cutout lithographed cloth doll produced by *Horsman*. The blond hair little girl doll wore an ankle-length red dress with a wide collar and cuffs. Ht. 9½ in. (24 cm.). ★

Little Fairy. 1914. Name of a dressed doll distributed by *Butler Bros*. It had a bisque head, sleeping eyes, and a wig. Ht. 14½ in. (37 cm.); priced $5.10 doz. wholesale.

Little Fellow. 1918. Composition doll made by *Amberg* using the *Denivelle* process for making durable composition.

No. 188 "Little Emily"

1703. Little Emily produced by Horsman and advertised in their catalog of ca. 1914. It has a composition head and hands, a mohair wig, glass eyes, and wears a straw hat. *Courtesy of Bernard Barenholtz.*

Little Imp. Early Kewpie Era. All-bisque doll with tiny horns, hoofed feet, and tiny curling tail. It had starfish type hands like those on a Kewpie and was jointed at the shoulders. *Illfelder* copyrighted this doll. Hts. 4½ to 7 in. (11.5 to 18 cm.).

Little Lucille. 1919–20. Composition doll with long curls and sleeping eyes made by *Jessie M. Raleigh.* It wore a silk mull cape and hat with the brim turned up in front. Ht. 24. in. (61 cm.). (See Ill. 2175.)

Little Lulu. 1929–30. One of the *Sayco* line of character dolls made by *Maurice Long & Meyer Yondorf.* It was dressed as a child.

Little Maid from School. 1887. Name of an American-made rubber doll with a fan, distributed by *Lauer.* Ht. 6 in. (15 cm.); price $2.40 a doz. wholesale.

Little Mary. 1911–30 and later. Cutout cloth doll made by *Saalfield.*

Little Mary Mix-Up. 1919–30. *Horsman* art doll based on the Brinkerhof drawings. It had a composition head and arms, molded hair or wig, painted eyes or glass sleeping eyes, and a cloth body, jointed at the shoulders and hips. One Company made dresses in 12 styles for this doll. Hts. 16 and 18 in. (40.5 and 45.5 cm.). The 16 in. (40.5 cm.) doll cost $16.50 a doz. wholesale but it is not known whether this doll had molded hair and painted eyes or wig and glass eyes.★

Little Mary Mix-up. 1924. Oil cloth doll based on the Brinkerhof drawings and distributed by *Butler Bros.* Ht. 18 in. (45.5 cm.); priced $8.25 doz. wholesale.

1704A & B. Composition-head doll labeled Little Mary Mix-Up, made by Aetna for Horsman. Molded hair and features except for the bow which is glued to the back of the head. It has painted features. Cloth body is jointed at the shoulders and hips and has composition arms. Original commercial clothes. Sewn to the sleeve is the cloth label. See Ill. 1705. H. 16¼ in. (41 cm.). *Courtesy of Robert and Katrin Burlin.*

Little Mary Sunshine. 1927–28. Doll with composition head and limbs, sleeping eyes, crying voice on a toddler-type body. It wore an organdy dress, petticoat and flannel diaper and was distributed by *Montgomery Ward.* Ht. 13¼ in. (33.5 cm.); price $2.79.

Little Merry Sunshine. See **Merry Sunshine.**

Little Miss. 1929. *Mama* doll with composition head and forearms, cloth body, distributed by *Butler Bros.* Ht. 20 in. (51 cm.).

Little Miss Muffet. 1920. One of the handpainted cloth *Mother Goose* dolls with real hair, made by *Rees Davis.*

Little Miss Muffet. 1920–21. Decorative-type doll designed by Hugo Baum,[†] who obtained the design patent for this doll with a spherical body having a circumference of 36 in. (91.5 cm.). The doll was made by *Effanbee* and had a composition head with teeth and a baby-type cap on its head. It came in 12 pastel colors and was lace trimmed. Ht. 18 in. (45.5 cm.); price $5.00.

Little Miss Muffet. Ca. 1927–28. A *Lenci* felt girl doll with a felt spider sewn to its skirt. Style No. 178/M. Ht. 35 in. (89 cm.).

Little Miss Muffet. See **Nursery Rhymes.**

Little Miss Vogue. 1924–27. A cloth doll made by *Mabel Bland-Hawkes.* It was dressed in velvet trimmed with white plush, wore a stocking cap and carried a white muff. The clothes came in six different colors.

Little Nemo. 1911–14. *Horsman* doll based on the comic-strip character of this name drawn by *Winsor McCay* and published in the NEW YORK HERALD under the title "Little Nemo in Slumberland." The doll, made with the permission of the NEW YORK HERALD, had a composition head with short molded hair and painted eyes. One version wore striped pajamas with three buttons on the jacket. In 1909 there was a stage play called "Little Nemo" and one of its characters was called "The doll-faced girl."

1914: A bisque version of Little Nemo came in two sizes and was distributed by *Strobel & Wilken.* Some of the Little Nemo dolls wore short suits with long sleeves and a wide collar, horizontally striped capes and large brimmed hats with feathers. Little Nemo dolls cost 25¢ to $1.00.★

Little Orphan Annie. 1919. Name of a dressed doll distributed by *Sears.* It had a composition head with wig, painted eyes, composition arms on a cloth body that was jointed at the shoulders and hips. Ht. 14½ in. (37 cm.); price $2.45.

LITTLE MARY MIX-UP
TRADEMARK
BY PERMISSION
New York Evening News
MFG'D BY E.I. HORSMAN & AETNA DOLL CO.

1705. Cloth label sewn to the sleeve of a doll called Little Mary Mix-Up produced for Horsman with permission from The New York Evening World.

Little Orphan Annie. Cutout cloth doll licensed by *Famous Artists Syndicate.* Ht. ca. 8 in. (20.5 cm.).

Little Orphan Annie. 1925–30 and later. Oilcloth doll made by *Live Long Toys,* based on a cartoon of this name drawn by *Harold Gray.* The doll was designed by *Eileen Benoliel* with arms and legs attached at an angle to a flat pillow shaped doll. The doll wore various costumes and came in several sizes; the largest reported size was 15½ in. (39.5 cm.). Both names, "Little Orphan Annie" and "Harold Gray," were usually printed on the dolls.

1926: The name was on the belt of the removable percale dress. There were also panties.

1927: The large size wore a polka dot dress with its name on the belt. The small size was dressed in a coat and hat. The dog named "Sandy" was made to accompany "Little Orphan Annie."

1929: Style no. 14 wore a red dress. Ht. 10¾ in. (27.5 cm.); price $4.00 a doz. wholesale. Style No. 15 wore a red coat and hat. Ht. 13 in. (33 cm.); price $8.00 a doz. wholesale. ★

Little Orphan Annie. 1929. All-bisque doll, jointed at the neck, represented the *Harold Gray* cartoon character of this name. It had molded clothes and was made in Germany. *Marshall Field* and *Shackman* were the exclusive wholesale distributors. Ht. 3½ in. (9 cm.); priced $1.80 doz. wholesale.

Little Orphan Annie. 1930. One of the *Trixy Toys* line made by *Durrel Co.*

1706. Segmented wooden doll representing Little Orphan Annie as drawn by Harold Gray. This was probably one of the Trixy Toys made by Durrel Co. in 1930 and later distributed by Butler Bros. The clothes are part of the wooden doll. Mark: Ill. 1707. H. 5 in. (12.5 cm.). *Coleman Collection.*

LITTLE ORPHAN ANNIE
HAROLD
GRAY—

1707. Stamp on skirt of Little Orphan Annie, a segmented wooden doll probably made by Durrel.

Little Peary. 1908. Cutout cloth doll made by *Saalfield.* It had printed *Eskimo* clothes and was named after the famous arctic explorer, Robert Edwin Peary. Ht. 7¾ in. (19.5 cm.).

Little Pet. 1923. Line of dolls made by *Dorris & Co.*

Little Pink Lady. 1919. All-composition doll made by *Jessie M. Raleigh* had a shoulder length wig with a ribbon in the hair and wore a high-waisted dress with a full skirt and tucks around the hemline.

Little Playmate. 1914. Name of a doll distributed by *Butler Bros.* It had a bisque head, wig, sleeping eyes and was jointed at the shoulders and hips. Ht. 11½ in. (29 cm.); price $2.25 doz. wholesale.

Little Polly Flinders. 1929. One of the Mother Goose nursery rhyme characters in the *Playpet* doll line made by the *Sun Enamel Works.* This segmented wooden doll had a hand-painted face with eyes glancing to the side. Its costume included a brimmed hat. Price $7.50 a doz. wholesale.

Little Princess. 1920–28. Cutout cloth doll made by *Saalfield.* Size: 23 by 17 in. (58.5 by 44.5 cm.).

Little Queen. 1909. Bisque-head doll with wig and sleeping eyes distributed by the *Boston Store* in Chicago. Ht. 17 in. (43 cm.); price dressed, 50¢.

Little Rascal. 1915. Made by *Trion.* Dressed in a Sailor blouse with a high dickie and a skirt. Style No. 232. ★

Little Red Riding Hood. This was one of the most popular names in the doll-making trade. Almost any doll could have a red hood and cape put on it and be given the name Little Red Riding Hood or Red Riding Hood (Rotkappchen in German). *English Rag Dolls, Hug-Me-Tight* line, *Käthe Kruse, Mawaphil* and many others as well as those listed separately in both ENCYCLOPEDIA One and Two used this name for some of their dolls. (See also **Red Riding Hood** and **Nursery Rhymes.**)

Patented July 5 & Oct. 4, '92.
**LITTLE RED
RIDING HOOD, 10c.**

1708. Cutout cloth version of Little Red Riding Hood[†] as advertised in YOUTH'S COMPANION, 1894. The printed fabric was made by Arnold Print Works.

Little Red Riding Hood. 1907–19. Cutout cloth doll made by *Saalfield*. Size: 18 by 18 in. (45.5 by 45.5 cm.).

Little Red Riding Hood. 1909. Dressed cloth body doll advertised by *Siegel Cooper*. It wore a white dress, red cape and bonnet. Hts. 12 and 15 in. (30.5 and 38 cm.); priced 50¢ and $1.00.

Little Red Riding Hood. 1912–13. Cutout cloth doll advertised by *Selchow & Righter*, probably made by Art Fabric Mills. Ht. 16 in. (40.5 cm.); priced 85¢ doz. wholesale.★

Little Red Riding Hood. 1918. Doll made by *Mogridge*.

Little Red Riding Hood. 1926. Composition-head doll on a cloth body having stub hands and feet was distributed by *Charles William*. It wore a dress, cloak and hood made of red oilskin. Ht. 13 in. (33 cm.); priced 45¢.

Little Red Riding Hood. 1928. Cutout cloth doll advertising *Kellogg Co.* products.

Little Red Riding Hood. 1929. Segmented, turned wood doll made by the *Sun Enamel Works*. It had a handpainted face with eyes looking straight ahead. Price $7.50 a doz. wholesale.

Little Red Riding Hood. 1930. Cloth dolls line made by *O. J. Lafayette*. It had removable clothes.

Little Rosebud. 1911–12. Doll offered as a premium by YOUTH'S COMPANION. It had a *Minerva* metal head, wig, glass eyes, teeth and came with paper patterns for its clothes.★

Little Rosebud. See Rosebud.

Little Shavers. 1919–30 and later. A group of handmade, handpainted dolls created by Elsie Shaver[+]. These dolls with their strange and artistic clothes warranted an article in ART & DECORATION. The dolls, supposedly residents of the land of Olie-Ke-Wob, were named Baby Olie-Ke-Wob, Ketsy Piper, Patsay Dobla, Princess of Olie-Ke-Wob, and Thomas Squeelik.

1937: Littler Shaver was made by the *Alexander Doll Co.* after having obtained the rights from Elsie Shaver.★

Little Sister. The round label on a chemise read, "LITTLE// SISTER//COPYRIGHTED//GERMANY." The chemise was found on a doll with a bisque head marked "G. 326 B.// A. 1 M.//D.R.G.M. 25 [or 29]" on a bent-limb composition body. The mark indicates an *Armand Marseille* head, mold #326, on a *Borgfeldt* doll but it is not certain that the chemise was original to the doll.

Little Sister. 1920s. Bisque-head doll with wig, sleeping eyes, open mouth and teeth on a bent limb composition baby body. The head, possibly made by *Crämer & Héron*, was marked "P.M.//914// Germany." Size number 4/0 was 10 in. (25.5 cm.) tall.

Little Sister. 1924. Bisque-head doll with bobbed wig, sleeping eyes, open mouth with teeth, on a bent-limb composition baby body wearing a chemise was distributed by *Charles William*. Hts. 11 and 16 in. (38 and 40.5 cm.); priced 98¢ and $1.98. It is possible that this doll could have

been one of the Little Sister dolls described above. (See THE COLLECTOR'S BOOK OF DOLLS' CLOTHES, Ill. 757.)

Little Sister. 1927–29. Doll with composition head, molded hair, painted eyes, cloth body with composition arms and with or without composition legs. The head was sculptured by *Grace Corry* and the doll was made by the *Averill Manufacturing Co.* It wore a variety of costumes and when dressed as a boy it was called *Little Brother;* when it wore a nursery rhyme or fairy tale costume it was called a *Kiddie Karakter*. Ht. 14 in. (35.5 cm.).

1927: It wore a lace trimmed beltless dress.

1929: Several styles of playsuits in plain colors with print tops were designed by *Katherine Rauser* for this doll. Among other new costumes were a print dress with lace around the square neckline, no waistline, short sleeves and a double breasted coat with matching tam. The panties showed below the dress.

Little Sister. 1930 and later. All-composition doll with sleeping eyes, hair eyelashes, jointed at the neck, shoulders and hips, wore a silk crepe dress and an *Effanbee* locket. This doll was made by Effanbee and distributed by *Montgomery Ward*. Ht. 19 in. (48 cm.); priced $6.98.

Little Squaw. 1920. Indian style doll with crepe-paper over a mold form made by *Mary Frances Woods*. These dolls each had an individual face and blanket pattern according to an advertisement. This was style No. 7, ht. 10 in. (25.5 cm.). (See Ill. 2768.)

Little Sunshine. 1923–24. Name of character baby series originated by *Demalcol*, made by *Catterfelder-Puppenfabrik* and distributed by *Ihle*.

Little Sweetheart. 1902–28. Line of dolls made by *Illfelder*.★

1709. Little Sweetheart mark of B. Illfelder & Co. for dolls.

Little Sweetheart. 1913–15. Doll with composition head and hands on a bent-limb baby body made by *Amberg*. It wore a knitted white angora wool jacket, leggings and cap.★

Little Sweetheart. See Sweetheart.

Little Tot Bumps. 1914. Name of a doll with composition *Campbell Kid* type head and hands. It wore a lace trimmed white lawn dress with a high neckline and long sleeves. The clothes were not like any shown in the 1914 *Horsman* catalog. This doll was in the *Marshall Field* 1914 catalog and the clothes could have been made by Marshall Field. Hts. 10½ and 12¾ in. (26.5 and 32.5 cm.); priced $8.00 and $17.00 a doz. wholesale.

Little Tots. 1927. Name of a flat-faced cloth doll; entire doll lithographed in color including the clothes. Ht. 9 in. (23 cm.).

Little Tynie Tots. See **Tiny Tots.**

Live Long Toys. 1923–30 and later. Chicago, Ill. Made oilcloth dolls designed by *Eileen Benoliel.* Most of these dolls represented cartoon characters.

1923: Made *Skeezix* as a baby in rompers and *Uncle Walt.* Claimed that they sold 500,000 dolls.

1924: Added Skeezix as a boy in short trousers, *Mrs. Blossom* and *Rachel* as well as the *Teenie Weenies* and *Esther Starring* as she appeared in *MAMMA'S ANGEL CHILD,* a cartoon by *Penny Ross.*

1925: New dolls were *Little Orphan Annie, Herby* and *Red Grange.*

1926: Added *Chester Gump; Kayo; Emily Marie,* Little Orphan Annie's doll, *Smitty,* three *Flower* dolls, girl dolls dressed as a tulip, a morning glory, and one other flower. Skeezix wore overalls, pajamas or a bathing suit as well as his earlier costumes. Advertised that there were 12 new dolls making a total of 40 dolls representing cartoon characters.

1927: Opened a display house known as the *Chicago Toy House. A. S. Ferguson* was the factory representative. Skeezix came in two toddler sizes and two child sizes. Little Orphan Annie came in two sizes. *Moon Mullins* was represented as a doll.

1928: Several thousand of the *Corky,* Skeezix's baby brother, were ready for sale as soon as Corky appeared in the Cartoon. Other dolls not seen in prior lists included a new Kayo, *Jane, Humpty Boy, Clown, Baby Bibs.*

1929: Factory representative was *Fred W. Voetsch.* New names were *Pat, Jean, Harold Teen, Perry Winkle* in two sizes and *Freckles.* They claimed that over a million Skeezix as a Baby had been sold. A new Skeezix cost $1.00. A new line of eight different cartoon characters sold for 50¢ each.

1930: Advertised *Snappy Dolls* with snaps concealed in their hands. Another new line was called "children of today." Many of the Live Long dolls had imported voices.★

Livesey, Milton, & Co. 1919–21. Accrington, Lancs. Manufactured celluloid dolls' masks as well as jointed dolls and leatherette dolls.

Lizzie. See **Lisl (Lizzie, Loni).**

Lizzie Wise. 1921. Black, dressed cloth doll made by *Horsman;* represents the young daughter of *Mammie Wise.*

Llacer, E. Ca. 1925. Madrid. Distributed dolls. A gold sticker with this name and an address has been found on the clothes of bisque-head oriental infant-type dolls.★

1710. Art leather (oilcloth) dolls made by Live Long Toys. The dolls represented Skeezix as a toddler and as a little boy, Uncle Walt, Orphan Annie, Herby, Smitty, Kayo, Red Grange, Chester Gump, and so forth. This page is from PLAYTHINGS, January, 1927.

Llord, Ricardo. 1928–30 and later. Paris. Made bébés, dolls and dolls' heads of various kinds.

Lloyd George. Wax portrait doll with inserted hair including mustache, stationary glass eyes. (See Ill. 1711.) This doll was probably made in England during or prior to World War I.

Lloyd Manufacturing Co. 1917–29. West New York, N.J. The many patents used by this company were obtained by Burt Edward Lloyd of Woodcliff, N.J., and New York City. These patents pertained to sound producing voices, especially *Mama* doll voices.

1917: A sound producing device was patented in America and Canada. The device had an aperture and movable valves through the aperture to successively close and open it. The device was activated by moving the dolls' arms.

1918: *Averill's Lyf-Lyk Baby* was the first doll made with Lloyd's mama voice.

1919: Obtained a U.S. patent for a tubular member fitted into the open side of a hemispherical resilient diaphragm.

1711. Wax portrait doll of Lloyd George. It has inserted red hair, including a mustache, stationary glass eyes, and a closed mouth. Original clothes. *Courtesy of Elizabeth McIntyre.*

1922: Obtained a German patent and a U.S. patent for mama-papa voices.

1924: Lloyd voices constructed entirely of metal were also made by a Canadian doll manufacturer, named Lloyd-Harlam Toy Co. They were distributed in London by J. R. Stern. Mark was "TRADE//LLOYD'S [over A 1]//MARK" in a diamond.

1925: Applied for a British patent and a German patent for the sleeping eyes of a doll.

1926: Obtained a U.S. patent for a sound producing device placed below the neck and between the arms of a doll. The sound was produced by pressure on the doll's body or on the head or by movement of the arms.

1929: Lloyd Mama voices were used by Averill in their *Sunny Babe, Sunny Boy, Sunny Girl* and *Baby Brite. Horsman* used Lloyd Mama voices in *Baby Dimples, Rosebud Babies* and other Mama dolls.★

Lloyd & Magnus Co. 1886–87 and other years. New York City. Distributed dolls as a wholesale dealer.

Lloyd, Mayer & Co. 1919–20. London. Manufactured composition Poppy dolls. Hts. up to 24 in. (61cm.).

Lodge Textile Works. 1918–30 and later. Albany, N.Y. Made various types of clothes for dolls including outerwear and underwear. Their line was called *Dolly Duds.*

1919: Some of the clothes were knitted.

1923: Made knitted union suits and blankets for dolls, as well as other clothes and accessories.

1925: Advertised that their dolly bunting fitted many sizes of baby dolls.

1926: The doll blankets were made in three sizes and many designs.

1927: Advertised dolly bunting, doll blankets and doll capes.

1929: Advertised doll outfits.

Loewe, Emil, Co. 1897–1927. New York City. Made outfits for dolls. He and Louis Lowe were in charge of *Aetna Novelty Co.* in 1915. Emil Loewe died in 1927.

Loewenheim, I. N. Late 1800s. New York State. Advertised china, cloth, and rubber dolls and dolls' heads.

Löffler, Ignaz. 1899–1910. Vienna. Listed in Austrian directory under Dolls and Dolls' heads.★

Löffler & Dill. 1887–1930 and later. Sonneberg, Thür. and Coburg, Bavaria. Eduard Schmidt was their successor. Manufactured and exported dolls of various kinds. Used Sico and Sicora† as trademarks; also called some of their dolls *Wunderpuppen* (Wonder dolls).

1910: One of the Sonneberg group of Grand Prize winners at the Brussels Exposition.

1924: Won a silver medal at the Jubilee Exhibition. Made a composition head *Mama* doll with painted hair and eyes, open mouth and teeth, pink cloth body with wooden lower arms, which resemble those found on the *Bébé Tout en Bois* dolls, and composition lower legs. There was a stringing arrangement through the upper legs to just under the shoulder plate. A patented clamp went around the waist to which a long round wooden stick could be attached to enable the doll to simulate walking. The heel and toe caps were made of sandpaper which enabled the feet to grasp the floor firmly. The sole of one of the shoes between the caps was marked "I walk, I talk,//and when I fall,//Loudly//Mamma//Mamma,//I call,//"Sico"//the wonder-doll.//Patented Silver Medal,//Jubilee Exhibition 1924." Ht. 20 in. (51 cm.).

1926: *W. E. Christie* and *W. Seelig* were the London agents, who advertised the Sico Mama dolls with composition heads, wigs or molded hair, wooden arms, removable clothes. Ht. 17 and 21 in. (43 and 53.5 cm.).

1928: Had showrooms in Amsterdam, Budapest, Carlsbad, Copenhagen, Hamburg, London, Milan, Paris, Stockholm, Vienna, and Zurich. Hts. of dolls 38, 43, and 53 cm. (15, 17 and 21 in.).

Gamage sold Sico dolls that turned their heads as they

102   DEUTSCHE SPIELWAREN-ZEITUNG   Februar II / 1927

Sico-Sicora-Wunderpuppen

Preisgekrönt mit der silbernen Medaille und patentamtl. geschützt.

„Sico-Sicora"-Puppen sind weich gestopft und unzerbrechlich, haben vorzügliche' selbsttätige Garantie-Stimme. „Sico-Sicora"-Puppen sind die einzigen auf dem Weltmarkte bekannten **weichgestopften** Puppen, welche infolge der patentamtlich geschützten, verstellbaren Laufvorrichtung das Laufen eines Kindes in vollendeter Weise, ohne besonderen Mechanismus, nachahmen und **beim Laufen den Kopf nach links und rechts drehen.** Der „Sico-Sicora"-Verwandlungs-Künstlerkopf ist unerreicht schön, kann mit und ohne Perücke benutzt werden und ist unzerbrechlich. (Patentamtlich geschützt) Sico-Sicora-Wunder-Puppen laufen am **patentamtlich geschützten Laufstock** und haben **patentamtlich geschützte Laufschuhe** für glatten Boden. Sico-Sicora Puppen erregen in allen Weltteilen Aufsehen.

Alleiniger Hersteller:

Eduard Schmidt, Coburg

Neuer Meßstand Leipzig: Zentralmeßpalast, 4. Obergeschoß, Nr. 351—355

1712A & B. "Sico-Sicora-Wunder-Puppen" composition head Mama dolls made by Eduard Schmidt, the successor of Löffler & Dill, as pictured in DEUTSCHE SPIELWAREN ZEITUNG, February, 1927. Sico is the boy doll on the left and Sicora the girl doll on the right. These are walking and talking dolls.

A

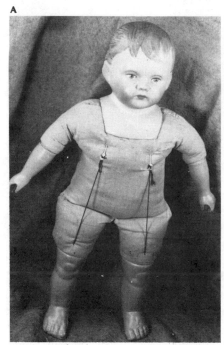

B

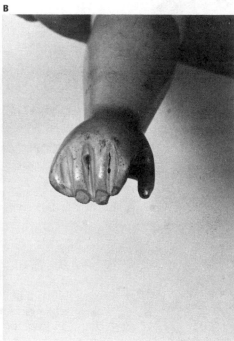

C

I walk, I talk,
And when I fall,
Loudly
Mamma,
Mamma,
I call.

„Sico"
the wonder-doll
Patented. Silver Medal.
Jubilee Exhibition 1924

1713A-C. Mama doll made by Eduard Schmidt, successor of Löffler & Dill, and purchased new in South Africa in 1927. It has a molded and painted composition shoulder head, open mouth with teeth, wooden lower arms, composition lower legs and a pink cloth body. The two elastic cords raise the legs so that it walks. A wooden handle like a broomstick has two wire hooks that fit into a metal clamp that surrounds the waist and has "D.R.G.M." on the front. When this device is on the doll and the stick is pushed forward the doll appears to walk. The wooden hands resemble those found on the German Bébé Tout en Bois dolls. The bottom of the original shoe states that this "Sico" doll can walk and talk and is "Patented. Silver Medal// Jubilee Exhibition 1924." The heel and toe caps are sandpaper to facilitate the walking. H. 20 in. (51 cm.). *Courtesy of Victoria Harper.*

walked. These dolls had wigs, wore rompers and a hat and also talked.

1930: *O. Widmann* was the sole British agent.★

Lofgren, Ulrika. 1913–18. Obtained a U.S. patent for a doll with a cover for the head and body over a wire frame, plus stuffing.

Loisseau. 1863–67. Paris. Made dolls.

1867: Exhibited dolls at the Paris Exposition.

Lokesch, Gebrüder. 1902 and probably other years. Lieben near Prague, Bohemia. Applied for a German patent (D.R.G.M.) for dolls' heads with hair eyelashes and moving eyes. Their metal dolls' heads were marked *Venus* over a heart.

Lola Baby. 1924. Name of a doll advertised by *Kohnstam*.

Lolita. 1927–28. *Lenci* felt doll dressed in a Spanish costume. Style No. 165/15. Ht. 27 in. (68.5 cm.).

1714. Mark found on dolls possibly produced by Löffler & Dill.

1715. Venus mark used by Gebrüder Lokesch on their metal dolls' heads.

Lona Art Dolls. 1927 and probably other years. Celluloid-head doll with molded hair, intaglio eyes, open-closed mouth, cloth body made by *A. Schmidt*. The celluloid head was made by *Rheinische Gummi und Celluloid Fabrik*. There were 11 styles of these dolls. The dolls were dressed as children, both boys and girls, as well as in regional costumes. They carried red and black circular tags tied on to the wrists. Ht. 14 and 15½ in. (35.5 and 39.5 cm.).

L'Oncle Zeppelin. See **Zep.**

London Company for General Trade, The. 1926–30. London. Imported dolls.

1926: They were agents for *Hermann Von Berg.*

London Doll Market. In 1927 the London Doll Market showed popular baby dolls representing three-week-old infants, child and lady dolls dressed in the height of fashion wearing felt dresses and hats.★

London Dressed Doll. 1913. Dressed doll with wig, advertised by *Gamage;* priced $1.73 to $2.25.

London Rag Dolls (Babies). 1865–1905. Dolls with cloth-over-wax mask faces. Black pins were often used for eyes.

1884: Six hts. 14½, 16, 19½, 22, 26, and 28 in. (37, 40.5, 49.5, 56, 66, and 71 cm.). (See also **Manufacture of Dolls, Commercial: Made in Britain.)**

1887: *Ehrich's* advertised London Rag Babies with muslin covered wax faces, painted features, wearing a long baby dress or a Red Riding Hood costume. Hts. 20 and 25 in. (51 and 63.5 cm.); priced 85¢ and 90¢.

1893: *Horsman* advertised London Rag Dolls in long or short baby clothes or dressed as Red Riding Hood. There were eight styles or sizes ranging in price from 75¢ to $10.00 doz. wholesale.

1900: The GIRLS' OWN ANNUAL reported on a doll maker in Shoreditch, England: "Taking up a ready-made wax face, she pressed it into a heated mould, previously lined with white muslin; which adhered to the warm wax and came away with it. Upon this surface her employer would paint the features and complexion. For effecting this little opera-

"LONA"-DOLLS

1716A. Pair of Lona dolls with celluloid heads and cloth bodies made by August Schmidt and advertised in PLAYTHINGS, February, 1927.

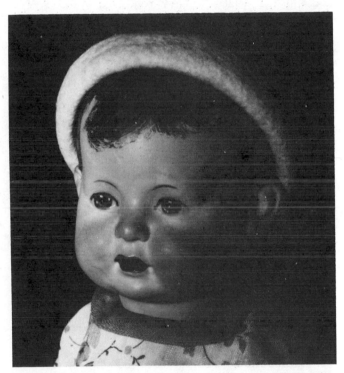

1716B. Lona celluloid head doll made by August Schmidt. It has molded and painted hair, intaglio brown eyes, open-closed mouth with tongue but no teeth, and a cloth body. Original clothes. There is a red and black circular tag tied onto the wrist with a red ribbon. The tag states that it was made in Germany with a D.R.P. patent. H. 14 in. (35.5 cm.). *Courtesy of Germaine Bachand.*

1717. Mark for Lona dolls.

tion, which required some deftness, the doll maker was paid 6d [12¢] per gross. . . . She had neither to supply faces nor muslin." (See also **Peter Hetzel.**)★

Long, J. W. See **OO-Gug-Luk.**

Long, Maurice, & Yondorf, Meyer. 1929–30. New York City. Factory representative and producers of *Sayco* dolls.

Long Jack and Little Jack. 1917. Doll with limbs that could be pulled out for Long Jack and retracted for Little Jack, made by *Thorne Bros.*

Long-limbed Dolls. See **Boudoir Dolls.**

Long & Praeger. 1924–25. New York City. Advertised dolls of various kinds.

Loni. See **Lisl (Lizzie, Loni).**

Loose, Hilda. 1920–21. New York City. In TOYS AND NOVELTIES, Miss Loose was described as "One of the leaders in the field of Novelty dolls [and] is absolutely original in her creations. . . . Both professional and laymen . . . have searched for the causes that give her designs such a wonderfully artistic effect and popularity. The causes are the enigmatic proportioning—noble lines of a tendency toward the slim and the wonderful distribution of the mass, coupled with touches of classic harmony." She designed the *Pepita Dolls.*

Lord, Charles. 1921. London. Manufacturers' agent for Sonneberg, and Nürnberg dolls.

Lord Jellicoe. See **Admiral Jellicoe.**

Lord Kitchener. Ca. 1902. A portrait doll with a wax head.

Lord Kitchener. 1914–17. Portrait doll modeled by an English artist, probably made in the *Women's Emergency Corps Workshop,* and distributed by *Hamley Bros.* The doll had composition head, hands and feet with molded boots. The hair and mustache were molded, the eyes were intaglio. The khaki uniform included a hat with a visor and puttees. Ht. 19 in. (48 cm.). (See COLLECTOR'S BOOK OF DOLLS' CLOTHES, Ill. 744.)★

Lord Plushbottom. 1929. All-bisque doll that represented a character in the *Moon Mullins* comic series drawn by *Frank Willard.* It was made in Germany and distributed wholesale exclusively by *Marshall Field* and their licensees. Ht. 3½ in. (9 cm.).★

Lord Robert Cecil, Marquis of Salisbury. Ca. 1902. Portrait doll with wax head, dressed in robes representing those worn by Lord Cecil at the coronation of *King Edward VII.*

Lord Roberts' Memorial Workshops. 1915–22. Named in honor of Lord Roberts who was a Field Marshall; the Principal workshop was in Fulham, London; branch workshops were in Belfast, Birmingham, Bradford, Brighton, Colchester, Edinburgh, Liverpool, Manchester, Newcastle and Yorkshire with trade connections all over the world. These workshops to help wounded soldiers and sailors were founded by Lord Cheylesmore who had seen service with the Grenadier Guards many years previously. The machinery in the workshops had been installed through the munificence of comrades in arms. Engraved plates were attached to each

1718. All-bisque doll representing Lord Plushbottom as drawn by Willard and produced by Marshall Field. It has molded and painted features and clothes. There is a mustache; the doll holds a high hat and the neck is jointed. Mark: Ill. 1719. H. 3½ in. (9 cm.). *Coleman Collection.*

1719. Incised mark on back of all-bisque Lord Plushbottom.

machine indicating the corps, battery or company making the gift. The workers were employed at work best suited to their physical capacities and received fair wages. Special machines were designed to be operated by one-armed men. The dolls were molded, sprayed, assembled, and finished all on the premises. The dolls were designed so they would sell at competitive prices. They were constructed to withstand wear and tear and to be attractive to children.

1915: Earliest dolls were clumsy and sombre in color.

1916: Made 16 varieties of dolls. They had taken over the British patents and equipment for making *Vera* dolls which were dressed and then distributed by *Laurie Hansen.*

1917: The work had improved and the wooden dolls were artistic and colorful yet had commercially competitive prices. Most of the dolls had moving arms and legs and painted clothes. The dolls represented soldiers in khaki with high boots, kepi, and so forth; sailors with white blouse and cap, blue trousers and black shoes; Red Cross nurse with white apron and cap, blue dress, red cross on the cap and bodice of apron; officer in blue uniform with a sword; boys and girls. The heads were spherical and the arms were two-dimensional. These dolls, called *"Chunky Toys,"* could stand alone.

They also made the dressed Vera dolls and baby dolls that could sit, as well as *Kewpie* dolls and other Mascot dolls. The baby doll hts. were 12, 13, and 14 in. (30.5, 33, and 35.5 cm.). The Kewpie hts. were 6 and 8 in. (15 and 20.5 cm.).

1919: They took over the business of Kean (Keen) & Co., a subsidiary of the German *Kohnstam* firm.

Lord Roberts as a doll.

1720. Wax portrait doll of Lord Roberts as shown in THE LONDON MAGAZINE, 1902.

Lore. 1930. Advertised by *Franz Schmidt* as a mate to *Peter.* It had flirting eyes and a toddler type five-piece body.

Lorenz, E. C., & Bahrmann-Kohn. 1915. Berlin and Leipzig. Applied for a German patent (D.R.G.M.) for jointed dolls.

Lori. Name impressed on character bisque heads; accompanied by the green mark of *S. & Co.* See Ill. 1721.

Loriot, A. 1797 and possibly other years. London. Advertised "Dressed Wax Dolls" 8/- (price $2.00).

1721. Lori mark on a doll's bisque socket baby's head.

1722. Bisque head doll marked Lorraine, designed by Masson for Mme. de Laumont and with a head made by Lanternier. The doll has a brown wig, stationary blue glass eyes, open-closed mouth with teeth, and a composition body. Original clothes. Mark on head: Ill. 1608. One of the tags on this doll indicates that the Red Cross sold these French dolls during World War I. H. 18 in. (45.5 cm.). *Courtesy of the Margaret Woodbury Strong Museum. Photo by Harry Bickelhaupt.*

Lorraine. World War I period. Name of bisque socket head designed by *Masson* and made by *Lanternier;* came with open mouth or open-closed mouth. The dolls were created by *Mme. de Laumont.* Hts. 14½ and 17 in. (37 and 43 cm.).★

Lorraine. See **French Regional Costume Dolls.**

Lossow, William. 1904. Dresden, Germany. Designed art dolls dressed in regional or historical costumes. See Ill. 2495.

Lothar. 1916. Felt doll made by *Steiff.* Hts. 28, 35, 43, 50 and 60 cm. (11, 14, 17, 19½, and 23 in.).

Lotte. 1916. Felt doll made by *Steiff.* Hts. 28, 35, 43, 50 and 60 cm. (11, 14, 17, 19½, and 23½ in.).

Lotte. 1920s. Name of a doll made by *Cuno & Otto Dressel.* It had a wig, glass eyes, a bent-limb baby body or ball-jointed child's body and wore a chemise.

Lotte. 1927–28. *Lenci* felt doll of the *Boudoir* doll type with long limbs. Its skirt was mid-calf length. Style No. 800/A. Ht. 45 in. (114.5 cm.).

Lotte Talking Baby. 1922. Patented talking doll made by *Viktor Steiner.*

Lotus Blossom. 1907–13. One of the *Elizabeth Scantlebury* dolls dressed as a Japanese girl to show school children how the Japanese dress. Sister to *Toyo.*

Lotze, Widow & Daughter. Before World War I. Nürnberg, Bavaria. Made chemises for bisque-head dolls.

Louise, Brongn (Art?). 1917. Inscription in a china socket head made by *Sèvres.* It had a wig and painted eyes. Ht. head only, 7.5 cm. (3 in.). (See Ill. 2369B.)

Louisville Doll & Novelty Manufacturing Co. 1927. Louisville, Ky. Made *Mama* dolls and were licensed to use mama voices made by *Voices, Inc.*

Lours, H. See **Borreau.**

Louvre. 1855–1930 and later. Paris. Large store that sold dolls, especially *Bébé Jumeau* and *Louvre Bébés* made by *Jumeau* and from 1899 on made by *Société Française de Fabrication de Bébés & Jouets* (S.F.B.J.).

1876: LA MODE ILLUSTRE (French version of HARPER'S BAZAR) in the possession of the Ciesliks contained an advertisement for the Louvre store which contained the following information:

Size No.	Height cm.	in.	Prices undressed Kid body	Wood body	Prices dressed Kid body
			DOLLS (POUPÈES) WITH MOVABLE BISQUE HEADS, WIGS, GLASS EYES		
0	30	12	$ .58		$1.75–$2.75
1	35	14	$ .78	$2.30	$2.30–$4.00
2	40	15½	$ .98	$2.70	$3.55–$5.40
4	46	18	$1.32	$3.50	$4.50–$8.00
6	52	20½	$2.10	$4.40	

When the Kid body dolls were sold with three costumes, including hats, footwear and jewelry in a trunk, they cost from $4.60 to $33.00.

A doll in a costume with an elaborate train. Ht. 48 cm. (19 in.); cost $15.00.

The Louvre also advertised undressed "Talking" bisque head bébés, made in Paris. These had wigs, glass eyes, and the arms and legs were also made of bisque.

Height cm.	in.	Prices
40	15½	$2.15
45	17½	$2.55
47	18½	$2.90
52	20½	$3.50

Bisque head bébés with wigs and fully jointed composition bodies came undressed. The model for these was owned by the Louvre and they were described as being new.

Height cm.	in.	Prices
40	15½	$2.10
45	17½	$2.55
50	19½	$3.15
55	21½	$3.70

The crying rubber dolls and bébés were dressed in knitted wool and were made especially for the Louvre store. The Louvre catalogs listed the following dolls:

1882: *Bébé Mascotte.*

1885: *Bébé Jumeau* dressed and undressed, *Polichinelle,* Bébé in *Swaddling Clothes, Marotte, Bébé Baptême,* rubber bébés dressed in wool, four hts. 22, 24, 26, and 32 cm. (8½, 9½, 10½, and 12½ in.).

1892: Clown *Cymbalier,* Bébé Jumeau, Louvre Bébé, *Miss Helgett,* Polichinelle and a Zouave.

1895–96: Bébé Jumeau, *Bébé Prodige;* composition bébé in swaddling clothes, Louvre Bébé; Marotte; Nurse with bébé; rubber bébé dressed in wool, five hts. 24, 26, 28, 33 and 38 cm. (9½, 10½, 11, 13, and 15 in.); rubber doll in swaddling clothes.

1901: Louvre Bébé.

1902: Louvre Bébé.

1904: *Bébé Charmant, Bébé Culotte, Bébé Réservé.*

1909: *Bébé Réservé, Bébé du Louvre.*

1910: Bébé du Louvre.

1912: *Bébé Premiers Pas,* Bébé du Louvre.

1913: Bébé Culotte, Bébé du Louvre.

1914: Bébé du Louvre.

1915–16: Alsacienne costume doll, Bébé du Louvre, Bébé Jumeau, Bébé Parlant, Bébé Promenette, Character Bébé, *Eskimo, Kiss-throwing, New Born Baby, Paris Bébé,* parlant and walking, Polichinelle, Red Cross Nurse, Soldiers of the Allies. See Ills. 1723 and 1724.

1921: Bébé du Louvre.

1923–24: Bébé du Louvre, Bébé Jumeau, *Clarisse, Colette,* cutout cloth doll, *Denise,* Eskimo, Marotte, *Mimi, Nisette, Pierrot,* Polichinelle, *Suzette, Zezette.* See Ills. 1725 and 1726. (See THE COLLECTOR'S BOOK OF DOLLS' CLOTHES, Ills. 312 and 592.)★

> The prices given for dolls are those for which the dolls were originally offered for sale. They are *not* today's prices.

AU LOUVRE – PARIS
VÊTEMENTS DE POUPÉES

375039. TROUSSEAU complet « Lingerie Vêtements », avec mignonnette dormeuse.
0m21 **2.90**
0m27 **4.25**
0m32 **5.75**

375040. NOUVELLE MALLE garnie avec penderie pour les robes, tiroir contenant la lingerie, bébé entièrement articulé, dormeur avec cils.

0m30	0m35	0m39	0m42	0m45
19.50	22. »	28. »	34. »	40. »

375041. TROUSSEAU MIGNONNETTE en celluloid, avec chaise transformation.
0m27 **4.90**
0m31 **5.90**

375044. TROUSSEAU layette, bébé articulé, yeux mobiles à cils. Hauteur des bébés.
0m25 **8.50** 0m28 **9.25** 0m30 **10.75** 0m32 **12.50** 0m35 **16.75**

375042.

BÉBÉ JUMEAU, cheveux naturels, entièrement articulé, dormeur à cils.

5	6	7	8
0m36	0m41	0m45	0m49
11.50	13.»	16.»	18.»
9	10	11	12
0m53	0m57	0m62	0m67
23.»	27.»	33.»	40.»

Le même parlant.
0m45 0m53
19.» 21.50 27.»
0m57 0m62 0m67
01.50 08.» 15.»

375043. BÉBÉ nouveau né dormeur.
0m32 0m37 0m42
6.50 9.90 11.75
0m49 0m58 0m66
15.50 19.50 22.»
Le même articulé.
0m34 0m38 0m46
8.50 11.95 15.50
0m52 0m61 0m70
18.25 22. » 25. »

375045. BÉBÉ entièrement articulé, tête incassable et lavable, bouche avec dents.
0m31 0m38 0m45
3.90 6.25 8.50
11.50 15.75

Le **BÉBÉ du LOUVRE** dormeur, fabrication supérieure, articulations complètes.

1	2	3	4
0m25	0m29	0m32	0m36
3.90	4.90	6.75	8.25
5	6	7	8
0m40	0m43	0m47	0m52
9.50	11.50	12.75	14.75
9	10	11	12
0m57	0m60	0m64	0m69
18.50	21.»	25.»	29.»

Le même parlant.
0m57 0m60
22. » 25. »
0m47 0m52
15.50 19.50
0m64 0m69
29. » 33. »

375046.

375047. QUARTIER-MAITRE en serge marine, garni piqué blanc et broderie.
5-6 7-8-9 10-11-12
4.90 5.50 5.90

375047 bis. ROBE soie ciel ou rose, garnie dentelle et ruban.
5-6 7-8-9 10-11-12
3.75 5.25 5.90
Chapeau assorti.
3.25 3.90 4.50

375048. ROBE lingerie, pour bébé caractère, garnie de petits plis et dentelle.
4-6 8-10 11-12
3.75 5.90 7.25
Bonnet lingerie assorti.
2.45 2.75 2.90
Choix de lingerie et chaussures.

375048 bis. MANTEAU joli lainage, damier bleu et blanc, col velours assorti.
5-6 7-8 9-10 11-12
3.90 4.75 5.50 6.25

375050. CHEMISE de nuit nansouk, garnie imitation valenciennes.
5-6 7-8-9
1.75 2.25
10-11-12
2.50
Chemise de jour.
.75 1.05 1.45

375050 bis. ROBE dessous en nansouk garnie imitation valenciennes.
5-6 7-8-9
1.15 1.45
10-11-12
1.75
Pantalon assorti.
.70 .95 1.15

375051. ÉTOLE ou **MANCHON** fourrure blanche, garnie de têtes et queues.
5 au **8.2.25** 9 au **12.2.45**

375051 bis. ROBE soie ciel ou rose, recouverte tulle brodé soie.
5-6 7-8-9 10-11-12
2.90 3.75 4.50
Chapeau assorti.
2.25 2.90 3.25
Bottines champagne claque verni noir.
5-6 7-8 9-10 11-12
1.25 1.50 1.60 1.90

375049. ROBE avec bretelles lainage rayé marine et blanc, chemisette lingerie.
5-6 7-8 9-10 11-12
3.75 4.25 4.50 4.90
Chapeau soie assorti.
2.40 2.75 2.90 3.25

375049 bis. TABLIER batiste blanche, avec motifs broderie main.
5-6-7-8 9-10-11-12
2.75 3.25

Toutes les commandes sont expédiées FRANCO DE PORT à partir de 25 francs.

1723. Louvre store catalog page for 1915–16 showing Bébé Jumeau, Bébé du Louvre, New Born Bébé, and a composition head bébé, all in chemises, as well as clothes that could be purchased separately for these dolls. The sizes of the clothes probably correspond with the Bébé Jumeau sizes. There are several boxes and a trunk with a small doll and its trousseau.

1724. Dressed dolls shown in a Louvre store catalog for 1915–16. Two of the dolls are babies, two throw kisses, several walk and talk. The doll with a head designed by Masson wears an Alsatian costume. Three or four of the dolls wear removable clothes.

LES POUPÉES DU LOUVRE

37241.
BÉBÉ CARACTÈRE
entièrement articulé,
dormeur à cils, tête
porcelaine, robe
lingerie.
fine.0 34. **64.** »
0ᵐ36   0ᵐ46
88. »   **110.** »
0ᵐ52   0ᵐ68
138. »   **197.** »

37241.

37254.

37254.
BÉBÉ A. articulé,
tête incassable,
cheveux Thibet fins.
0ᵐ20   0ᵐ26
4.90   **6.75**
0ᵐ30   0ᵐ34
8.90   **14.50**
0ᵐ38   0ᵐ42
19.50   **22.50**

37252. " **Zézette** ". Très grande **POUPÉE**
chiffon, tête artistique, articulée, perruque
fine, habillage taffetas, nuances mode,
rubans Pompadour.
Hauteur 0ᵐ76. . . . . . . **230.** »

37242.
BÉBÉ L.
marcheur,
tête
porcelaine
fine,
dormeur,
cheveux fins, costume
guipure avec trans-
parent.
Haut. 0ᵐ35. **25.50**
0ᵐ46   0ᵐ52
49. » **59.** »

37255.
BÉBÉ F., bébé riche,
articulé, dormeur
à cils, cheveux
naturels, habillage
guipure soie, garni
velours couleur.
0ᵐ31 0ᵐ36 0ᵐ40
34. » **48.** » **58.** »
0ᵐ45 0ᵐ52 0ᵐ57
69. » **89.** » **125.** »

37250. DÉDÉ C.
complètement articulé,
tête porcelaine fine,
dormeur à cils, costume
fantaisie.
0ᵐ29   0ᵐ34   0ᵐ39
18.50 25.50 33. »
0ᵐ43 0ᵐ48 0ᵐ54 0ᵐ57
44. » **57.** » **76.** » **89.** »

37247.
BÉBÉ K.
articulé,
tête
incassable,
habillé, tablier
fantaisie,
se déshabillant.
0ᵐ27   0ᵐ32
12.50 15.50
0ᵐ35   0ᵐ45
17.75 26.50

37248. BÉBÉ D.
tête incassable,
dormeur,
perruque fine,
entièrement articulé,
costume toile
de Jouy.
0ᵐ29 . . **16.50**
0ᵐ34   0ᵐ39
21.75 29. »
0ᵐ43 0ᵐ48 0ᵐ54 0ᵐ57
39. » **49.** » **65.** » **78.** »

37249. BÉBÉ M.
marcheur,
envoyant
des baisers, parlant, entièrement
articulé, dormeur à cils, cheveux
naturels, habillage soie, garniture
cachemire
Hauteur 0ᵐ56 . . . . . **110.** »

37243.
" **Clarisse** ".
POUPÉE en
tissu bourré,
articulée,
cheveux
Thibet,
costume feutre. Haut. 0ᵐ40 **30.** »

37245.
Jolie
POUPÉE en étoffe, tête
caractère, costume drap
fantaisie avec motifs
animaux.
Haut. 0ᵐ40 **29.90**

37251.
" **Colette** "
Jolie **POUPÉE**
chiffon, tête
velours artistique,
habillage taffetas,
nuances mode.
Haut. 0ᵐ30. **45.** »
0ᵐ40   0ᵐ50   0ᵐ60
62. » **89.** » **134.** »

37253. " **Mimi** ".
POUPÉE
bourrée, tête
satinette,
articulée, per-
ruque Thibet,
costume drap.
Hauteur 0ᵐ75.
149. »

37246.
" **Nisette** ".
POUPÉE en
étoffe bourrée,
costume drap
couleur. Haut. 0ᵐ50. **69.** »

37244.
" **Suzette** ".
POUPÉE chiffon
articulée,
costume fantaisie.
Hauteur 0ᵐ28.
24.50

Grand Choix de **TROUSSEAUX DE POUPÉES**   1

1725. Dolls shown in a 1923–24 Louvre store catalog. Three of these dolls had bisque heads, three had composition heads. Seven had cloth heads and two do not reveal the type of head. All except one of the dolls had names; the names were Clarisse, Colette, Mimi, Nisette, Suzette and Zezette. Generally the composition dolls were cheaper than the bisque-head dolls and the cloth dolls were most expensive for corresponding heights. All of the dolls were fully dressed.

37226.
BÉBÉ DU LOUVRE
dormeur, à cils,
articulations complètes,
fabrication   supérieure.

1	2	3	4
0ᵐ25	0ᵐ28	0ᵐ31	0ᵐ35
12.50	**14.75**	**16.75**	**21.50**
5	6	7	8
0ᵐ40	0ᵐ43	0ᵐ46	0ᵐ52
25.50	**29.75**	**35.»**	**49.»**
9	10	11	12
0ᵐ57	0ᵐ60	0ᵐ64	0ᵐ69
56.!»	**65.»**	**79.»**	**92.»**

Le même, parlant. 6. **34.»**
7. **46.»** | 8. **54.»** | 9. **62.»**
10. **72.»** | 11. **87.»** | 12. **108.»**

1726. Bébé du Louvre in its chemise as shown in the 1923–24 Louvre store catalog. The doll had a wig, sleeping eyes, hair eyelashes and a fully jointed composition body. It came in 12 sizes. H. 25 cm. to 69 cm. (10 to 27 in.). Sizes 6 through 12 were also available as talking dolls. This doll was about half the price of the Bébé Jumeau at the same store in 1923.

Louvre Bébé. 1892 or earlier–1908. In 1909 the name appears to have been changed to Bébé du Louvre. Both bébés were distributed by the *Louvre* store. *Jumeau* made Louvre Bébé and the sizes were the same for the Louvre Bébé and *Bébé Jumeau*. The size-height relationship for the Louvre Bébé and for the Bébé du Louvre corresponded with that for the Bébé Jumeau but a limited sample of dolls marked "B.L." does not seem to fit this pattern. (See **Bébé Lefebvre.**)

1892: Louvre Bébé wearing a belted chemise with a fancy lace panel down the front and bronze slippers came in 12 hts. 26, 29, 32, 35, 39, 42, 45, 49, 55, 59, 66, and 71 cm. (10½, 11½, 12½, 14, 15½, 16½, 17½, 19½, 21½, 23, 26, and 28 in.); priced 55¢ to $5.40.

All except the five smallest sizes came plain or "parlant" (open mouth?). The 45 cm. (17½ in.) size cost $2.10 plain and $2.50 "parlant." The Louvre Bébé also came dressed in 12 hts. from 31 to 82 cm. (12 to 32½ in.). There nearly always seemed to be variations in sizes between dressed and undressed French dolls.

1895–97: The chemise had a diagonal shoulder sash with the name "Louvre Bébé" on it. The yoke and sleeves were fancy and the skirt was plain except for the lace around the bottom. The 12 hts. were almost the same as in 1892 except

for the four largest dolls which were 53, 58, 63 and 68 cm. (21, 23, 25 and 27 in.). The prices had dropped to 49¢ to $4.20 and the six smallest sizes came only without "parlant." The 45 cm. (17½ in.) doll plain cost $1.65 and "parlant" $2.50. The dressed Louvre Bébés came in 12 hts. 28 to 76 cm. (11 to 30 in.).

1901: The sizes and prices were the same as in 1896 but the "parlant" versions had sleeping eyes.

1902–08: Same as in 1901.

1909: The name was changed to Bébé du Louvre but the sizes and heights were the same as the earlier Louvre Bébé. The chemise was the same except the sash was larger.

1912: Same as earlier dolls except the shoulder sash had only "Louvre" on it. It still wore bronze slippers.

1913: Same as 1912 except prices had risen to 59¢ for the smallest doll and $5.30 for the largest doll. The smallest "parlant" doll was 45 cm. (17½ in.); cost $2.25.

1914: Same as 1913.

1915–16: Sizes were the same or within one cm. of those for the earlier dolls but all of the dolls were listed as sleeping and "parlant" (open mouth?); prices ranged from 78¢ to $6.60.

1921: The chemise had no sash.

1923–24: Hair eyelashes were added to the sleeping eyes. The sizes and hts. were identical to those of 1915 except for four that were one cm. (less than ½ in.) smaller. Some of the dolls were no longer "parlant." (See THE COLLECTOR'S BOOK OF DOLLS' CLOTHES, Ill. 529.)

L'Ouvrier du Gros-Caillou (The Workers of the Large Pebble). 1916. France. Doll-making workshop founded by *Mme. Henri Conkling*.

Love Doll Co. 1928. Los Angeles, Calif. Made clown dolls with composition heads and hands, faces painted by artists, bodies stuffed with felt. The pierrette costumes were made of Baronette satin in black, white, turquoise blue, maize, old rose, red or nile green colors and trimmed with marabou or malines.

Love Me. 1919–20. Doll with legs to-gether and molded clothes made by *Alisto*. Ht. 12 in. (30.5 cm.).

Love Me. 1923. *Mama* doll with a *Ronson* voice made by *Oweenee*.

Love Me. 1930. One of the *Kiddie Pal* line made by *Regal*.

Lovey Mary. 1926–28. Composition head doll with a slim body and slender legs made by *Effanbee*. This was a *Mama* doll with curly hair, sleeping blue eyes and hair eyelashes. It wore matching organdy dress, bonnet, "petties" and bloomers and came in pink, blue or lavender. Around its neck was the golden-heart necklace. The doll was named for the girl portrayed by Bessie Love in the Metro-Goldwyn-Mayer moving picture based on the story "Lovey Mary" by Alice Hegan Rice. Bessie Love had the slender legs needed to portray this part and so the doll was made with slender legs. Various sizes including 19 in. (48 cm.) tall which cost $5.00.

Lovie. 1920. Doll made by the *S.K. Novelty Co.* It had a wig with a net.

Lovums. 1928–30 and later. Trademark registered in U.S. by *Fleischaker & Baum.* This usually had a composition head with a laughing expression and a neck joint like *Patsy.* It had sleeping eyes and a kapok filled cloth bent-limb body. One doll marked "Effanbee//Lovums//©" was reported as a *Mama* doll with a wig and an open mouth; Lovums came with a variety of costumes. Hts. 16 to 29½ in. (40.5 to 75 cm.).

One version of a large size Lovums came with a record device in its body like the *Dolly Record* and the *Mae Starr* dolls. It is possible that all of the phonographs in these dolls were made by the same company.

1930: Three style nos. wore dresses or rompers. Hair was red, tosca or blond.★

1727. Composition head Lovums made by Effanbee. It has a wig, sleeping eyes, hair eyelashes, open mouth with teeth, cloth body, and composition bent arms and legs. Mark on head: Ill. 1728. Metal heart tag on wrist. *Courtesy of Mary Alice Thacher.*

EFFANBEE
LOVUMS.
©
MADE IN U.S.A.

1728. Mark on composition head of Lovums dolls made by Effanbee.

Lowe, Mrs. M. 1913–30 and later. Birmingham, England. Made removable dolls' clothes for manufacturers of dolls as well as dolls' wardrobes of clothes.

1913: Advertised dresses and coat sets for baby dolls; knitted novelty goods.

1915: Made dresses, hats, bonnets, underclothing sets for baby dolls; Red Cross nurse outfits; khaki uniforms.

1917: Made over 40 styles of dresses, each in at least four sizes; woolen coats, baby doll long clothes, jersey suits in 14 sizes and underclothing in 10 sizes. Also made caps, vests, shoes, and gloves for dolls.

1927 or before: Granted a Royal Warrant.

Lowry, Mrs. Adj. 1922. U.S.A. Made clothes for dolls, available either from a special order or from the selection on hand. Dolls dressed in her wedding costumes were used in a Hollywood moving picture. The Queen's outfit, costing $50.00, was worn by a doll.

Loyrion, A. 1929 and earlier. Paris. Made cloth heads and face masks for dolls as well as straw and felt hats for dolls.

Lubecka, Mme. Julienne. 1926. Paris. Registered *Bicot* as a trademark in France for dolls.

Lucette. 1929. Name of a dressed doll with a character head and felt body sold by *Bon Marché.*

Lucie-Attwell. See **Attwell, Mabel Lucie.**

Lucille. 1920. Dressed composition doll made by *Jessie M. Raleigh.* It represented a sub-debutante and wore an orchid and a large hat.

Lucille Doll. 1926–28. Art doll distributed by *L. Rees* in London and *Hartley* in Australia. It was a child doll with sleeping or painted eyes, came with or without a voice, and had cloth body and limbs. It had a round tag and came dressed. Ht. 20 in. (51 cm.).

According to the Ciesliks these *Lenci*-type dolls were made by *Martin Eichhorn.*

Lucinani. 1926. Name of a doll dressed in a Hawaiian costume of orange silk and plaited grass.

Lucinda. 1926. Name of a doll that could stand and had blond hair, made by *Effanbee.* It wore a blue voile dress, matching bonnet and blue underclothes. Price $3.95.

Luckhan, Charles & Co. 1921 and other years. London. Imported dolls. He took the entire output of three doll factories in Sonneberg and dressed these dolls in English style clothes. Agent for *Bechman & Ullman.*

Lucky Aviation Kid. 1927. Regular composition child doll dressed in an aviator suit similar to that worn by *Lindbergh,* including goggles; made by the *American Character Doll Co.* This doll was available on the market, "when Lindy marched up Fifth Avenue" according to the advertisements. See Ill. 1729.

Lucky Babies. 1930. Lightweight doll dressed in a short baby dress, a bonnet, and baby moccasins made by *Cameo.* Several sizes were made.

Lucky Lindy. 1927. Child-type doll with a cloth body wearing a crude khaki aviation suit including helmet, large boots, and small goggles. Made by the *S. & H. Novelty Co.* and distributed by the *American Wholesale Corp.* There was a large square tag hanging from the doll's chest. From this tag saying "Lucky Lindy" a tiny model airplane was suspended. Ht. 15 in. (38 cm.); priced $8.75 doz. wholesale.

Lucky Rastus. 1920. Composition shoulder head with wig;

1729. Lucky Aviation Kid is a doll representing Lindbergh, made by the American Character Doll Co. and advertised in PLAY-THINGS, June, 1927, only one month after Lindbergh's successful flight.

doll usually had composition arms. It was designed by *Madame Georgene* and made by *Averill Manufacturing Co.* Doll came with a chicken on its back.

Lucy Locket. 1920. Cloth doll with flat face made by *Dean* carried a pocket book on a cord handle. Style No. D 172, ht. 8½ in. (21.5 cm.).

Lüders, Richard. 1897. Görlitz, Germany. Assignee of a German patent (D.R.G.M.) by *Karl Ring* for movement of the upper and lower eyelids of dolls' eyes.

Ludlow Guild of Toymakers. 1917. England. Made baby dolls and *Eskimo* dolls. *Faudel's* was their agent.

Ludwig, Samuel O. 1928–30. New York City. Factory representative for *Eureka Doll Co., Goodyear Toy Co., Maxine Doll Co.* and *Baby Gloria* Dolls.

Luge, A., & Co. 1880–1930. Sonneberg, Thür. Made dressed and undressed dolls.

1914: Applied for a German patent (D.R.G.M.) for the non-natural material of dolls' wigs.

1930: Advertised *Südsee* Baby with a tag reading *South Sea Baby.*★

Luge, Ferdinand. 1880–1928. Sonneberg, Thür. Made and exported dolls.

1893: Won a prize at the Chicago Exhibition.

1910: One of the Sonneberg group of Grand Prize winners at the Brussels Exposition.

1912: Advertised *Täuflinge* and jointed dolls dressed in a chemise and having a mama-papa voice.

1919: Specialized in baby dolls and jointed standing dolls.

1926–28: Proprietor was Ernst Strassner.

Luhačovice. Early 1900s. Bohemia. Made two- and three-dimensional wooden dolls with painted clothes, which generally represented regional costumes.

Lukács, Sarolta. See Our Shop.

Lullabye Baby. 1924–28. Trademark of a baby doll made by *Averill Manufacturing Co.* and distributed in England by *L. Rees.* It had a rectangular cloth label or a round tag.

1926: Came in two versions: one had a composition head and the other had a bisque head, both had celluloid hands, painted hair, sleeping eyes. The composition version also came with painted eyes and wore rompers. Ht. 10 in. (25.5 cm.). The doll wore long or short baby dresses and sometimes a knitted jacket. The six hts. of the composition head dolls were 10, 12, 14, 16, 18, and 22 in. (25.5, 30.5, 35.5, 40.5, 45.5, and 56 cm.). The hts. of the bisque head dolls were 12, 14, and 18 in. (30.5, 35.5, and 45.5 cm.). Sometimes the 12 in. (30.5 cm.) size came as twins wrapped in a blanket with a teddy bear or kitten design on it. These twins had sleeping eyes and criers.

Some if not all of the bisque head version were made by *Martin Eichhorn* using *Armand Marseille*'s bisque heads known as *My Dream Baby* (mold #s 341 or 351).

Lulu. 1928. Name of an "unbreakable" doll designed by *Poulbot* and distributed by *Bon Marché.* It wore short pants, suspenders, and slippers with ribbon tied around the ankles. Ht. 40 cm. (15½ in.).

Lund Art Co. 1924. New York City. Made a doll named Sandy with a composition head.

L'Union des Arts. See Boyer, Mlle. Rachel.

Luta. 1929–30. Trade name of all-felt or all-leather dolls made by *Eg. Mich Luthardt.* The dolls had removable baby or child clothes. Some of them were character dolls. They had wigs and straight legs that enabled them to stand or sit.

Lute Player, The. 1923. Doll representing the figure in Frans Hals' painting "The Lute Player" has a well-modeled face closely resembling the one in the picture. The doll was made in Holland and provided with a lute. Ht. 18 in. (45.5 cm.).

Luthardt, Eg. Mich. 1868–1930 and later. Steinach, Thür. Made dolls and dolls' bodies. Used *Schoenau & Hoffmeister* heads according to the Ciesliks.

1908: Advertised dolls' bodies of leather, imitation leather, cloth or felt with arms and legs of celluloid, wood or porcelain and cloth.

1927: Advertised *Mama* dolls; leather dolls; leather dolls' bodies; dolls' heads of porcelain, celluloid or composition; voices for dolls.

1929: Made *Luta* dolls.★

Luthardt, Louis Philipp. 1928 Neustadt near Coburg. Made a line of dolls named "Revue Dolls".

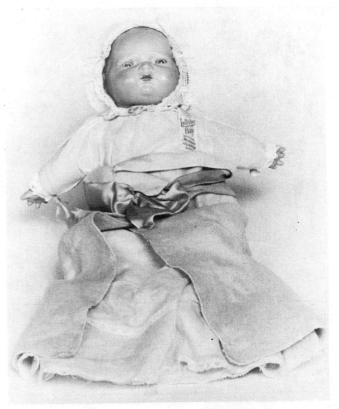

1730A. Composition head infant doll made by Averill Manufacturing Co. and named Lullabye Baby. It has molded blond hair, sleeping blue metal and celluloid eyes, closed mouth, cloth body containing a voice box, composition hands and bent legs. Original clothes. Marked on head: "Madame Hendren//Doll." Mark on body: "Genuine// 'Madame Hendren'//Doll//316//Made in U.S.A." Label on dress: Ill. 1730B. H. 15 in. (38 cm.). *Courtesy of the Margaret Woodbury Strong Museum. Photo by Harry Bickelhaupt.*

1730B. Lullaby Baby mark on a cloth label attached to the dress of a doll (Ill. 1730A).

1731. Mark for Eg. Mich. Luthardt.

Lutin. 1915 and later. Doll with bisque shoulder head made by *J. Verlingue.* It had a bent limb composition baby body. Size number 3/0 was only 5 cm. (2 in.).★

1732. Lutin mark used by J. Verlingue on bisque heads.

Lütz, Georg. 1887–1906. Sonneberg, Thür. Made composition heads for dolls. See Ills. 423 and 424 in the first COLLECTOR'S ENCYCLOPEDIA OF DOLLS.

Lützelberger, Hermann. 1895–1930 and later. Sonneberg, Thür. Made dolls.

1910: Applied for four German patents (D.R.G.M.) pertaining to hair for dolls.

He was one of the Sonneberg group of Grand Prize winners at the Brussels Exposition.★

Lützelberger, J. N. 1828–1930. Sonneberg, Thür. Produced and distributed dolls. In 1883 Eduard Müller was the successor and in 1913 *L. Steiner* was the successor.

1894: Applied for a German patent (D.R.G.M.) for cutting patterns and materials for dolls' clothes.

1910: One of the Sonneberg group of Grand Prize winners at the Brussels Exposition.★

Lutzenleithner, Franz. 1853 and probably other years. Vienna. *Johann Haller*'s son-in-law; he distributed dolls.

Luvly Dolls. 1928. Trade name of cloth dolls made by *Dean.*

Lydia Figures. Ancient times. In Sardes, the capital of ancient Lydia, terra cotta figures with arms and legs that could be moved by pulley strings were manufactured. Among these dolls were black dolls and Harlequin types.

Lyf-Lyk Line (Life Like Doll[+] [Baby]). 1917–28. Dolls made by *Averill Manufacturing Co.* had composition heads with painted hair; one version had a curl in the middle of its forehead. The eyes were either painted or sleeping eyes. These *Mama* dolls were claimed to have been patented in 1918 and to have been the first dolls made with a *Lloyd* mama voice.

1918: *Wanamaker* sold about 900 of these dolls. They came in three sizes.

1924: The dolls could wear real baby clothes.

Ca. 1926: Had a rectangular tag reading "Lyf-Lyk//Baby." Ht. 24 in. (61 cm.).

1928: Line included *Baby Brite, Val-encia,* and *Mariana.*★

Lynda-Lou. 1930. Trademark registered in the U.S. for dolls by the *Lamp Studio.*

Lynn & Co. ca. 1903. New York City. Made silver-plated small dolls that were put in cakes or elsewhere. Ht. 1¼ in. (3 cm.); priced two for 1¢.

Lynwood Toy Co. 1919. Birmingham, England. Advertised national character dolls.

Lyon Doll Co. 1917–22. New York City. Made dressed dolls, priced 50¢ and up.★

Lyons, Messers. B. & Co. 1915. London. Exported and distributed cloth dolls.

Lyons French Toy Co. 1919 and later. Lyons, France. Formerly the *L'École Joffre* (School). Registered in France a trademark for dolls, consisting of two concentric circles with a crowing rooster in the center.

Lyra-Fahrrad-Werke. 1912 Prenzlau, Germany. Hermann Klaasen G.m.b.H. Handled dressed dolls including *dolls' house dolls,* undressed dolls including large *Frozen Charlottes,* and *celtid* dolls.

Lyro-Puppen-Co. 1924. Berlin. Made Lyro dolls. These were stuffed unbreakable dolls with wigs and dressed as children. Their tag had a six pointed star.

M

M. D. C. See **Modern Doll Co.**

M. F. Initials found on bisque head dolls. See Ill. 1733.

M.M. S.I. R.E. Anonima. 1928. Turin, Italy, Manufactured dolls.

M. & S. Superior. See **Müller, Friedrich.**

Ma. (Matrose, Sailor). Before 1911–24. Felt doll dressed as a sailor, made by *Steiff* and distributed by *Borgfeldt* in the U.S. Ht. 35 cm. (14 in.); priced in 1911 in Germany 75¢ and 1913 in New York $1.25. The clothes in 1924 differed from the earlier ones.

1929: Doll portrayed a character called "sailor" in an English translation of a French book, PIERRE PONS, illustrated by Paul Guignebault.

Ma. 1922. Sponge rubber doll made by the *Miller Rubber Co.*

Ma Chunk. 1924–27. Name of a doll made by *Amberg.*

Maar, E., & Sohn. 1917–30 and later. Mönchröden near Coburg, Thür, and later, Bavaria. The senior member of the firm was Ernst Maar. Manufactured dolls using *Schoenau & Hoffmeister, Armand Marseille* and perhaps other bisque heads.

1930: Specialized in standing babies, dressed and undressed. *M. Michaelis & Co.* were their Berlin agents.★

1733A & B. Bisque head doll with a bobbed hair wig, stationary blue glass eyes, open mouth with five upper teeth, and a ball jointed composition body. Original regional clothes. Mark. Ill. 1734. H. 14 in. (35.5 cm.). Circumference of head 7 in. (18 cm.). *Courtesy of Dorothy Annunziato.*

1734–1735. "M. F." marks found on bisque head dolls.

Maar, Oskar. 1925–27. Mönchröden near Coburg, Bavaria. Made baby dolls in baby walkers. These came in two styles and three sizes; priced $1.25 to $3.00 each.★

Maaser, Robert. 1911–30 and later. Sonneberg, Thür. Made and exported dolls.

1913: Applied for two German patents (D.R.G.M.) for baby dolls with moving jaws.

1920: Advertised dolls with bisque or composition heads on jointed or non-jointed bodies. Some of the baby dolls had moving jaws.

Maba Art Doll. See **Barnikol, Max A.**

Mabel (Bather). 1911. Felt character doll made by *Steiff* and dressed as a girl in a bathing suit or middy dress. The doll had stitched hair and removable clothes. Hts. 28 and 35 cm. (11 and 14 in.).

Mabel. Name on bisque shoulder heads made in Germany. The doll had a wig, glass eyes, and an open mouth, and was usually placed on a kid or imitation kid body with bisque arms. Ht. 13 in. (33 cm.) and possibly others.★

1736. Ma (Matrose, sailor), name of a felt doll made by Steiff. The hat is sewed onto the head but the red beard is made of mohair sewed onto the face. It has black button eyes, closed mouth and a seam down the center of the face and neck. The body is jointed at the shoulders and hips. Original clothes. H. 35 cm. (14 in.). *Courtesy of Richard Wright. Photo by A. Jackson.*

Germany

Mabel 7/0

Germany

Mabel 11/0

1737–1738. "Mabel" marks on bisque shoulder heads.

Mabel. See **Pet Name.**

Mabel Lucie-Attwell. See **Attwell, Mabel Lucie.**

Mabire, Mlle., et Delarue, Mme. 1929. Paris. Made dolls.

Macy, R. H. 1858–1930 and later. New York City. A picture of their Christmas 1875 doll display is shown in Ill. 212 of the COLLECTOR'S BOOK OF DOLLS' CLOTHES. Macy distributed the following dolls:

1884: Macy advertised the following *Jumeau* dolls: "Jumeau Doll, with long flowing hair . . . Jumeau Doll, short Lamb's Wool Hair . . . Jumeau Dressed Dolls." All three of these came in 13 hts. 8½ to 31½ in. (21.5 to 80 cm.). The relationship of the code numbers and the heights did not agree with the size-heights of the Jumeau dolls offered by the Paris stores at that time. The code numbers may have referred to Macy's stock numbers. The 8½ inch size is smaller than any of the known Paris Jumeau dolls which suggests that either these were made especially for the American trade or that they were not real Jumeau dolls. The heads with long flowing hair were generally slightly more expensive than the "Lamb's Wool Hair" dolls. The dressed dolls averaged about three times the price of the undressed dolls of corresponding heights. A large Jumeau doll cost $12.98 undressed and $39.98 dressed. The flowing hair dolls cost about 2⅓ times as much as the flowing hair Jumeau heads alone, while the Lamb's Wool Hair dolls cost nearly 3 times as much as the Lamb's Wool Hair head alone.

"German Jointed Dolls" came in only a few small hts. 15½ in. (39.5 cm.) or less and were a little less expensive than similar "Jumeau" dolls. Wax Dolls, with closing eyes, "hair flowing at back, banged in front," came in 8 hts. 14 to 32 in. (35.5 to 81 cm.). These were nearly half the price of the German jointed dolls. The "Composition Wax Dolls" with closing eyes were about half the price of the other wax dolls of corresponding sizes. But when they were dressed in "French aprons, with colored ribbons and hat to match" the price was often three or more times as much. "Composition Boy Dolls" came in four hts. 11½ to 17½ in. (29 to 44.5 cm.). These were a little less expensive than similar size "patent Dolls, with long hair," which came in six hts. 13⅓ to 20 in. (34 to 51 cm.).

Bisque dolls' house sized dolls came jointed with closing eyes, in five hts. 2½ to 7 in. (6.5 to 18 cm.), priced 8¢ to 89¢. All-bisque unjointed dolls came in six hts. 2½ to 5½ in. (6.5 to 14 cm.); priced 3¢ to 14¢.

"Nankeen Dolls [china head on cloth bodies], china limbs, long hair" came in eight hts. 8 to 12 in. (20.5 to 30.5 cm.); priced 16¢ to 49¢, slightly less than the Composition Boy Dolls. But the Nankeen Dolls, china limbs, no hair came in 12 hts. 3 to 16¾ in. (7.5 to 42.5 cm.); priced 4¢ to 39¢.

Undressed cloth dolls came in three hts. 10, 11, and 13½ in. (25.5, 28, and 34 cm.); priced 32¢ to 39¢. Dressed cloth dolls also came in three hts. 13½, 16, and 17 in. (34, 40.5, and 43 cm.); priced $1.49 to $1.98. Small rubber dolls hts. 5 and 8 in. (12.5 and 20.5 cm.) cost 19¢ and 34¢ while jointed rubber dolls hts. 9 and 12 in. (23 and 30.5 cm.) cost 74¢ and 84¢.

In addition to dolls and dolls' heads, Macy sold muslin

bodies and leather arms in numerous sizes as well as a large variety of dolls' clothes and accessories. There were "Dolls' Wardrobes in boxes with Dolls," priced 59¢ to $7.98. About one fourth of the clothes were for Baby Dolls. Baby probably corresponded to bébé not infant. "Baby Sets of Underwear" for dolls cost up to $6.99.

1904: *Baby Marlborough,* Macy's Special doll had a bisque head. *Babyland Rag,* hts. 12 and 30 in. (30.5 and 76 cm.); priced 24¢ and $4.51. *Handwerck* dolls with bisque heads, probably made by *Simon & Halbig,* had ball-jointed composition bodies. Hts. 25, 26, and 30 in. (63.5, 66, and 76 cm.); priced $21.62 dressed, $3.49 in chemise and $38.99 dressed, for the respective heights. The two dressed dolls wore clothes representing a lady. A "Jumeau" doll with a bisque head that looked German was dressed as a child. This was the *Société Française de Fabrication de Bébés & Jouets* (S.F.B.J.) period when Simon & Halbig and other German porcelain factories supplied many of the bisque heads for French dolls. Ht. 27 in. (68.5 cm.); priced $36.63. Thus the dressed Handwerck and "Jumeau" dolls were similarly priced but the dressed dolls were many times the price of similar dolls in a chemise. Dressed bisque head dolls: Ht. 12½ in. (31.5 cm.); priced 24¢. Macy also sold separate clothes for dolls including a variety of hats (see Ill. 1739).

1905: Macy's catalog advertised a "Jumeau French Jointed Doll; dressed handsomely in silk, covered with lace overdress, shoes and stockings; hat to match; wig of beautiful hair, closing eyes with lashes; 23 in. long; priced $28.29." There were also several Handwerck dolls, a "Rag Doll" and bisque or tin dolls' heads and dolls' clothing.

1906: Handwerck dolls; cloth dolls. Ht. 15 in. (38 cm.); priced 99¢. Clothes for dolls were sold as sets.

1908: Bisque heads on composition bodies, wearing chemise, a special Macy doll. Ht. 22 in. (56 cm.); priced 98¢, with hair eyelashes $1.24.

Bisque heads on cork-stuffed bodies, undressed.
Kestner dolls came in eight sizes.
Dressed bisque-head dolls. Hts. 13 to 26 in. (33 to 66 cm.); priced 24¢ to $9.81.
Dressed Handwerck bisque-head dolls, priced $2.76 to $4.76.
Diana metal head dolls. All-celluloid dolls; hts. 6 to 13 in. (15 to 33 cm.); priced 24¢ to 98¢.
Cloth dolls included five sizes of *Martha Chase* babies; *Brückner*-type dolls. Hts. 12 and 14 in. (30.5 and 35.5 cm.); priced 24¢ and 49¢. A 30 in. (76 cm.) cloth doll with removable clothes cost $4.56.

1909: Macy's Special doll was about the same as in 1904. Babyland Rag dolls now came in four hts. 12 to 18 in. (30.5 to 45.5 cm.); priced 24¢ to $1.78. Martha Chase dolls came in four hts: 16, 17, 21, and 24 in. (40.5, 43, 53.5, and 61 cm.); priced $2.49 to $4.96. Celluloid dolls came white or black. Hts. 5 to 13 in. (12.5 to 33 cm.); priced 24¢ to 98¢. The Handwerck bisque head, jointed composition body dolls. Hts. 18 and 22 in. (45.5 and 56 cm.); priced $4.49 dressed for the smaller size and $1.24 in chemise for the larger size. A bisque-head dressed doll. Ht. 13 in (33 cm.);

priced 24¢. Undressed dolls had hts. up to 32 in. (81 cm.); priced $4.76. Dolls with celluloid head, wigs, sleeping eyes on plush Teddy Bear type bodies. Hts. 10 and 13 in. (25.5 and 33 cm.); priced 98¢ and $1.49. Composition head Billiken dolls had "white Bearskin" bodies. Ht. 12 in. (30.5 cm.); priced 98¢. Small dolls in boxes or trunks with their trousseaux were also sold by Macy.

1911: *Horsman* dolls included *Baby Bumps, Babyland Rag, Campbell Kids, Cotton Joe* and *Chubby Boy;* all celluloid dolls and child dolls with bisque heads having wigs, sleeping eyes, and open mouth with teeth, on ball-jointed bodies. They wore a chemise and footwear or were fully dressed.

1926: Baby dolls.

R. H. Macy & Co., New York
DOLLS AND DOLL CLOTHING

For Descriptions and Prices See Opposite Page
54

1739. Macy's 1904 catalog page showing dolls. Nos. 9800 and 9805 are Babyland Rag Dolls. No. 9810 is Baby Marlborough, Nos. 9811, 9813, and 9823 are Handwerck dolls with bisque heads. No. 9815 is a "Jumeau." The relative heights of the dolls are not as shown in this illustration. For example, No. 9815, the "Jumeau," is 4½ in. (11.5 cm.) taller than No. 9810, the Baby Marlborough.

LIFELIKE DOLLS' DAINTY CLOTHES

12E 3830. Genuine Heinrich Handwerck Jointed Doll. Bisque head, closing eyes, curly wig; with shoes and stockings; size 22 inches..............................**$1.24**

12E 3831. Jointed Doll Dressed in Lawn, lace hat, shoes and stockings; good jointed body, bisque head with closing eyes. Colors Pink, Blue or White; size 18 inches **98c**, size 16 inches **49c**, size 13 inches........................**24c**

12E 3832. Fine Quality Jointed Doll. Bisque head, closing eyes, curly wig. Silk dress trimmed with lace; lawn bonnet; shoes, stockings; lawn underwear; size 21 inches. .**$5.94**

12E 3833. Handwerck Jointed Doll, dressed in fine White Lawn Suit, lace hat, white shoes and stockings; size 18 inches **$4.49**

12E 3834. MACY Special Doll; full jointed doll; is positively the best doll bargain obtainable. Stands 22 inches high; full jointed papier mache body; well formed bisque head, moving eyes with eyelashes; with shoes and stockings, full banged or parted wigs........**98c**

12E 3835. Lawn Suit. Dress of good quality lawn trimmed with Lace, White lawn skirt and drawers. Dress in Pink or Blue; size for 18, 20 or 22 inch doll...........................**$1.89**

12E 3836. Doll's Fine Flannel Coat, with narrow braid to match; brass buttons; Pink or Blue; for Doll 18 to 22 inches...........**$1.14**

12E 3837. Doll's Jumper Suit. Linen skirt, Lawn waist, Good Lawn underwear; size for dolls 18 to 22 inches..................**$1.19**

12E 3838. Doll's Set consisting of Necklace, Bracelets, Comb, Looking Glass and 2 fancy Pins, put up in a neat box.......................**49c**

12E 3839. Straw Hat with Ribbon Bow to fit dolls from 18 to 22 inches..............**49c**

12G 3830. Doll's Set consisting of Watch, Earrings, Necklace, Fancy Hair Pins, put up in good box...................................**19c**

12G 3831. Doll's Worsted Set, consisting of Sacque, Muff, Cap, and Bootees. Colors Pink or Blue.....................................**44c**

12G 3832. Doll's Plaid Waterproof Mackintosh. Well made and finished; size for dolls, 18 to 22 inches..........................**98c**

12G 3833. Jointed Doll (not illustrated), of extra fine grade; body made of papier mache, full ball jointed; bisque head; moving eyes; silky hair with long curls; shoes and stockings.

A, 26 inches high,	$2.39
B, 28 inches high,	3.24
C, 30 inches high,	3.74
D, 33 inches high	4.74

1740. Page from a 1909 Macy's catalog shows 12E3830 a bisque head Handwerck doll in chemise; 12E3831, 12E3832, and 12 E3833 dressed bisque head dolls; the 12E3833 is a Handwerck doll; N12E3834 is the Macy Special Doll about the same size and same price as in 1904. The Special Doll and Handwerck in chemise are the same size but do not appear to be the same in the picture. Various dolls' clothes were sold separately. The jewelry sets (Parures) were called "Nouveauté de Paris."

DOLLS MENTIONED BELOW CAN BE HAD WITH LIGHT OR DARK HAIR

12E 3820. Stockinet Dolls, indestructible and washable; fine cloth body, composition head, arms and legs, all hand finished; carefully made; a doll that will give good satisfaction; 16 inches $2.49, 17 inches $2.97, 21 inches $3.89, 24 inches................................$4.96

12E 3821. Unbreakable Dressed Doll, Muslin body stuffed with cotton; Lawn dress, Kid arms, shoes and stockings, celluloid head; size 14 inches $1.29, 16 inches $1.44, 18 inches................$1.79

12E 3822. Jointed Celluloid Doll, with Lawn dress, worsted sweater and cap; size 8½ inches.......................98c

12E 3823. Jointed Dressed Doll, Pink and Blue Gingham dress; Sunbonnet; shoes and stockings; 12 inches.......................98c

12E 3824. Babyland Rag Doll, dressed in Pink or Blue lawn; shoes and stockings; Lawn underwear; 18 inches $1.78, 15 inches 98c, 12 inches 24c, 14 inches.......................49c

12E 3825. Kid Body Doll With Bisque Head, moving eyes and curly wig; shoes and stockings; 19 inches 98c, 14 inches.......................49c

12E 3826. Doll's Satin Parasol, with Lace insertion; size 12 inches; colors Pink or Blue. Other Parasols 39c, 49c, 79c, up to.......................$3.96

12E 3827. Doll's Trousseau; set consists of dressed jointed doll, 8 inches high, Bisque head, closing eyes; extra dress, underskirt, apron and coat; 10x14 inches.......................98c

12E 3828. Doll's Trunk Trousseau, good wood trunk; contains one dressed 6 inch doll, extra set of underwear, dress cape, handkerchief and apron.......................$1.39

12E 3829. Doll's Celluloid Bath Set, consists of Bath Tub, Mirror, Soap, Soap Dish, Powder Box, Wash Cloth, Towel, Fine Comb, Dressing Comb and Celluloid Doll.......................49c

12G 3820. Doll's Real Hair Wig, with long flowing curls: 8 inches 98c, 9 inches $1.24, 10 and 11 inches $1.34, 12 inches $1.39, 13, 14, 15 inches $1.59, 16 and 17 inches.......................$1.89

12G 3821. Dressed Baby Doll, good quality jointed body, Bisque head, moving eyes, long baby clothes neatly made of fine lawn, trimmed with embroidery; full set of fine underwear and lace cap; size 14 inches $2.08, 18 inches $2.69, 22 inches.......................$3.29

12G 3822. Celluloid Doll, jointed arms, painted shoes and stockings, light and washable; 6 inches 24c, 9 inches 39c, 11 inches 59c, 13 inches.......................98c

12G 3823. Small Celluloid Dressed Baby Doll, good quality lawn dress and skirt; Worsted Jacket and Cap; Doll 5 inches long......98c Same in Negro Doll.......................98c

12G 3824. Dressed Unbreakable Doll, Muslin body: composition head, legs and arms; short wooly wig; Pink or Blue gingham Dress with sunbonnet White apron; 12 inches.......................69c

12G 3825. Red Riding Hood Rag Doll, dressed in Lawn, with White apron and Red Cape and Hat; Shoes and Stockings: 15 inches.......................98c

12G 3826. Doll's Fur Set; consists of 11 inch Stole and good size round Muff.......................$1.29 Other Fur Sets from 24c up to.......................3.49

1741. Macy's 1909 catalog page shows No. 12E3820, a Martha Chase Doll; Nos. 12E3821, 12G3822 and 12G3823 celluloid dolls; Nos. 12E3824 Babyland Rag Doll; Nos. 12E3825 and 12G3821 bisque head dolls; Nos. 12G3824 composition head dolls; Nos. 12E3827 and 12E3828 small dolls with their trousseaux; No. 12G3820 a wig; and 12G3826 fur tippet and muff.

And some crocheted clothes for the other dolls

A SLIP-ON sweater, hood, and booties of white Iceland wool for a 13-inch baby doll have pale blue edges and pompons

DOLLS FROM R. H. MACY

FOR a little girl doll of 17-inch size an ensemble costume of dress, cape, and cap is popular. Miss Flapper, 24 inches high (at the right), wears a sports cap and coat sweater with attached scarf. Directions for making all the dolls' crocheted things will be sent for fifteen cents in stamps. Order CK-274 and address Crochet Dept.

Crochet designs by Helen Marvin

1742. WOMAN'S HOME COMPANION, December, 1924, used dolls from R. H. Macy to model the crocheted clothes for dolls designed by Helen Marvin.

Mad Hatter. 1921–23. Dressed stockinet doll made by *Martha Chase;* represented the drawing of John Tenniel. Ht. 12 in. (30.5 cm.); price $6.50.

Mad Hatter. Cloth doll made by *Dean.* See Ills. 1743 and 1744.

Madame Alexander. First appeared in PLAYTHINGS in 1928. See **Alexander Doll Co.**

Madame Blanche. See **Blanche, Madame.**

Madame Bovary. 1927–28. *Lenci* felt doll dressed in a romantic period-type costume, carried a parasol, represented the title character in a novel by Gustave Flaubert. Style No. 165/21. Ht. 27½ in. (70 cm.).

Madame Butterfly. 1902. Bisque-head doll on a ball-jointed composition body dressed in a blue sateen Japanese style costume with a tinsel necklace and locket, metal ornaments and flowers in its hair wig. This doll, representing the title character in Giacomo Puccini's opera, was distributed by *Butler Bros.* Ht. 14½ in. (37 cm.). (See also **Butterfly.**)

Madame de Pompadour. Ca. 1920. Wax portrait doll made by *Lottie Pritzel* and elaborately dressed.

Madame Georgene. 1920–27. Designed and handled dolls. Name used by *Georgene Averill* and her husband, before and after they left *Averill Manufacturing Co.*

1920: Designed a French girl doll, *Gypsy Queen, Lucky Rastus, Romper Boy* and *Toto* the Clown.

1927: Created for *Borgfeldt,* Birthday Dolls with the flowers of each month. (See also **Georgene Novelties.**)★

Madame Hendren. 1915–30 and later. Line of dolls manufactured by *Averill Manufacturing Co.*

1916: Composition head dolls dressed in felt clothes. (See THE COLLECTOR'S BOOK OF DOLLS' CLOTHES, Ills. 711, 712 and 713.)

1918: Dressed baby dolls with composition heads. (See THE COLLECTOR'S BOOK OF DOLLS' CLOTHES, Ill. 720.)

1920: *Mama* dolls and *Indian* dolls.

1924: Advertised *Dolly Record, Gold Medal Baby, Life Like,* Mama dolls with *Lloyd* voices, and *Rock-A-Bye.*

1926: The line included *Betty Bronson Cinderella Doll, Brite Eyes, Lullabye Baby, Whistling* Cowboy, Whistling Dutch Boy, Whistling Indian, Whistling Sailor. The new Mama dolls had composition heads with wigs and child-like faces, slender bodies with flexible rubber arms and long legs. Tags read "Genuine Madame Hendren Doll." The dolls were dressed and wore hairbows. Hts. 17, 20, and 24 in. (43, 51 and 61 cm.).

1927: Advertised *Baby 'Aire, Baby Brite, Little Brother, Little Sister, Sunny Babe, Sunny Boy* and *Sunny Girl.*

1928: Among the dolls offered for sale were *Bobby* and *Dolly* based on the drawings of *Grace Drayton,* and *Father Knickerbocker.*

1929: *Dimmie* and *Jimmie, Kiddie Karakters* including *Cap-*

1743A & B. Mad Hatter cloth doll made by Dean. It has a molded mask face, hair glued under the hat, painted blue eyes, open-closed mouth with four teeth, velvet hands and shoes. Original clothes partly of felt. Mark: Ill. 1744. On the back of the tag is "Made in//England." H. 15 in. (38 cm.). *Courtesy of the Margaret Woodbury Strong Museum. Photo by Harry Bickelhaupt.*

1744. Mad Hatter mark on tag of a cloth doll made by Dean.

tain *Kidd, Little Bo-Peep, Little Boy Blue* and *Mary Had a Little Lamb* were among the dolls advertised.

1930: Mama dolls and baby dolls had newly modeled heads, reconstructed bodies and re-styled clothes; claimed that the line was one hundred percent new.★

Madame Pompadour. 1927–28. *Lenci* felt doll dressed as a lady in a pseudo-1700s costume. Style No. 165/16. Ht. 27½ in (70 cm.).

Madame Royal. 1917. Inscription on a china socket head with wig and painted eyes, made by *Sèvres*. Ht. head only, 5 cm. (2 in.). See Ills. 1745 and 2369C.

Madame the Baroness de Laumont. See **Laumont, Baroness de.**

Mädchen (Schülerpuppen deutsch and französisch [German and French schoolgirls]). Before 1911–16. Felt dolls made by *Steiff,* dressed as French or German schoolgirls with tasche (schoolbags). The French girl dolls wore simulated wooden shoes. Ht. 28 cm. (11 in.); priced $1.12.

Made in America Manufacturing Co. 1915–18. New York City. Made dolls.

1915: Lines included Baseball Boy, Jockey, Sailor, Soldier and so forth.

1918: *Baby Glory* and its mate *Teddy* had composition heads with molded hair and composition hands. Ht. 14 in. (35.5 cm.).★

Made Well Doll Hand Co. 1927. New York City. Made parts for dolls and was a member of the *American Doll Manufacturers' Association.*

Madeira Dolls. Made of white kid and later made of cloth. Flat faces except for the nose, embroidered features. The fingers were rolled separately and the dolls wore regional costumes of the Madeira Islands. The men dolls usually had high white boots.

Madelon. See **Zette.**

Mademoiselle Nini. See **Nini.**

Madingland. 1917. Line of baby dolls in colored long clothes and a line of *Eskimo* dolls made by the *South Wales Manufacturing Co.*

Mado. 1930. *Boudoir* doll wearing a silk dress and velvet hat sold by *Bon Marché.* Ht. 70 cm. (27½ in.).

Madonna. 1920. Doll representing an Indian Squaw with a papoose on its back, style No. 3 made by *Mary Frances*

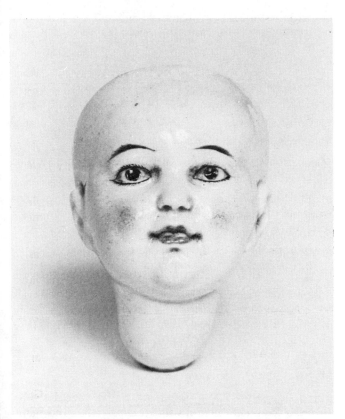

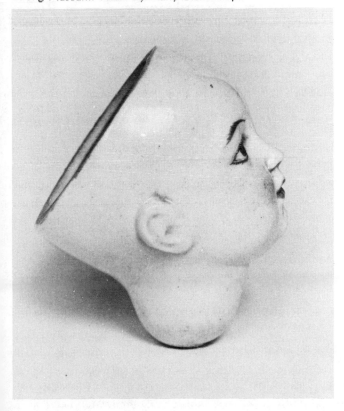

1745A & B. Glazed china head made by Sèvres during World War I and incised "Madame Royal." It was made to have a wig. The painted brown eyes are intaglio. There is a small white space between the pink-orange lips. A dimple is below the lips. H. of head only, 3 in. (7.5 cm.) *Courtesy of the Margaret Woodbury Strong Museum. Photo by Harry Bickelhaupt.*

Woods. Each handmade doll had its individual face and blanket pattern. Ht. 12 in. (30.5 cm.).

Madonna. 1925. *Lenci* felt doll representing a Madonna with an infant doll in swaddling clothes. Style no. 262. Ht. seated 10 in. (25.5 cm.).

Mae Starr. Ca. 1928. Doll with composition shoulder head, molded hair or wig, sleeping eyes, open mouth or open-closed mouth, cloth body with composition arms and legs, possibly made by *Effanbee.* The body contained a talking mechanism for records that appear to have been similar to those found in *Dolly Record.* Doll marked "MAE//STARR //DOLL." Ht. 29 in. (73.5 cm.).

Mag, Andhrée. 1928–29. Paris. Made dolls.

Magali.† See **Magati.**

Magasin de la Ville. See **La Ville de Paris.**

Magasin des Enfants, Passage de l'Opéra. Paris. Late 1800s–1910. Mark on the ball jointed composition body of a so-called "Long Face" *Bébé Jumeau* (Bébé Triste). See Ills. 1748 and 1749.★

Magati (Magali). 1926–30 and later. Trademark registered in France by *Giotti* who made felt art dolls. The name Magati was in a triangle with the apex at the bottom.

1746. Mae Starr talking doll with its talking cylinder in the lower right corner. The doll has a composition head and arms, sleeping eyes, hair eyelashes, open mouth, and a cloth body. *Courtesy of the E.M.I. Collection.*

1747. Mark on Mae Starr composition head dolls.

1748. So-called "Long-Face" or "Bébé Triste" Bébé Jumeau with a Magasin des Enfants (Store of the Children) stamp on its ball-jointed composition body. The bisque head has a wig, stationary blue glass eyes, pierced and applied ears and a closed mouth. Original clothes. Head incised "15" and mark on body "JUMEAU //MEDAILLE D'OR//PARIS." Original clothes. H. 32 in. (81 cm.). *Courtesy of the Washington Dolls' House and Toy Museum. Doll was formerly in the Nancy Menoni Collection.*

1749. Mark for Magasin des Enfants (Store of the Children).

1750. Magati mark used by Giotti for felt dolls.

Magenta (Grand Bazar Magenta). Before 1896–1908 and probably later. Paris. Name of a store that sold dolls. See THE COLLECTOR'S BOOK OF DOLLS' CLOTHES, Ills. 438, 439 and 444 A & B.

1896: Advertised *Bébé Magenta.*

1898: Continued to advertise Bébé Magenta and added *Bébé Regence.*

Maggie & Jiggs†. See **Jiggs & Maggie.**

Magic Dolls. 1925–30 and later. Trade name for various kinds of dolls made by *Le Saint.*

Magit. 1925–27. Trade name for felt art dolls (Poupées Artistiques) made in Argenteuil, Seine & Oise, France. Dolls sometimes were marked with the initials M.A.P.I.

Magnifique Bébé. 1908. Name of a doll sold at the *Louvre* store. This "parlant" doll had natural hair, sleeping eyes, hair eyelashes, a fully jointed body, dressed in a silk removable costume with lace trimming and jewelry. The accessories included a watch, purse of gold metal and a flask of perfume. The 10 hts. were 39, 43, 47, 51, 56, 63, 65, 70, 75, and 79 cm. (15½, 17, 18½, 20, 22, 25, 25½, 27½, 29½, and 31 in.); priced $4.70 to $27.00.

Magny. 1930. Made and/or distributed dolls.

Mago Puppen. 1927. Trademark name used by *Max Göhring* for character dolls and *Mama* dolls. The name Mago Puppen was written in an oval beside the picture of a swing.

Maguy. 1925–28. Name of cloth dolls made by *Boccheci-ampe.*★

Magyar Asszonyok Nemzeti Szövetsége (National League of Hungarian Women). 1909–26. Budapest. Produced dolls in Hungarian costumes.

Magyar Babavilag (Hungarian Dolldom). 1920 and probably later. Budapest, Hungary. Made and exported hand-sewn cloth dolls dressed in Hungarian regional costumes, historical costumes or as character dolls. Five or six girls were employed in this work. The dolls had removable clothes and the group advertised that they would make any desired doll on order and if the material was provided the price would be correspondingly lower.

1920: According to *Stewart Culin* they had in stock the following dolls representing:
A man and a woman of the Mezökövesd area; a man and a girl of the Kalotaszeg area; a Slovak man and young woman; a Sarkoz girl; an old shepherd; a market woman; and a clown. Hts. 8 to 15 in. (20.5 to 38 cm.).
Later a group of these dolls were loaned by the Brooklyn Museum for an exhibition in New York City.

Magyar Müvészeti Mühely (Hungarian Art Workshop). 1920s. Budapest. Created dolls representing Swabian occupations in Hungary. Some of these dolls were lent by the Brooklyn Museum for an exhibit in New York City.

Magyar Ruggyantaárugyár Rt. (Hungarian Rubber Articles Factory). 1922–26. Budapest. Made rubber dolls and celluloid dolls. (See also **Ungarische Gummiwaren-Fabrik.**)

1922: Marked "Made in Hungary."

Mah Jong. 1924. Long-legged doll dressed in silk or cotton, representing a chinaman and made by the *Flapper Novelty Doll Co.*

Maha Dolls. 1924. Line of baby dolls and straight-limbed child dolls made in Waltershausen. The London agent was *Karl Goerlich & Co.*

Mah-Jongg. 1923–24. Cotton stuffed doll with long pigtail and Oriental costume, made by the *Averill Manufacturing Co.* Ht. 10 in. (25.5 cm.).★

Mahlknecht. 1800s. St. Ulrich. *Verleger* family who collected and distributed wooden dolls, made in the Grödner Tal.★

Maiden Toy Co. (Maiden America). 1915–19. New York City. Company known as Maiden America Toy Co. from 1917–19 or thereafter. Maiden America dolls carried the label "Des. Pat. 8-24-15//1915//Kate Silverman// ©."

1917: Dolls were distributed by *Wyman, Partridge.* Ht. 8 in. (20.5 cm.).

1918: The all-composition "Maiden America" doll was jointed at the shoulders and wore a red, white, and blue ribbon with a large bow in back; price 50¢ or more.

1919: Advertised dressed character dolls representing boys, girls, nurses or sailors with painted molded hair or wigs, bent arms, straight legs that enabled the doll to stand alone.★

Maienthau & Wolff. 1927–30 and later. Nürnberg, Bavaria. Made and/or distributed dolls including art dolls and baby dolls, dressed and undressed.

Maier, Imannuel. 1921–24. Plochingen, Würtemberg. Obtained a German patent (D.R.P.) for dolls' bodies.★

Mail. Before 1927–30 and later. Paris. M. Chervy was the successor in 1927. Made decorative dolls with porcelain molded-hair heads (possibly pincushion tops) and cloth bodies as well as fetishes.

Mailaender, Relly. 1920s. Germany. Created dolls.

Maisie. 1924. Flat face cloth doll with printed clothes made by *Dean* as one of their *A 1* brand. Ht. 14 in. (35.5 cm.).

Maison d'Italle. See **Salzedo Bros. & Co.**

Maison Dorée. Around 1900–01. Paris. Store that sold *Bébé Maison Dorée.* See THE COLLECTOR'S BOOK OF DOLLS' CLOTHES, Ill. 447.

Maison du Petit Saint-Thomas.† See **Petit St. Thomas.**

Maison Farcy. 1927–30 and later. Paris. Store that sold bébés and other types of dolls as well as dolls' clothes and trousseaux.

Maison Huret. See **Huret.**

Maison Munnier. See **Munnier.**

Maison Yvonne. 1928–29. Paris. Made and exported dressed dolls with wax heads and in leather.

Majestic. 1894–1914. Trademark for dolls of *Edmund U. Steiner.* (See THE COLLECTOR'S BOOK OF DOLLS' CLOTHES, Ill. 557.)★

Majestic Doll. 1894–1914. Bisque heads for some of these dolls were made by *Kley & Hahn* according to the Ciesliks.★

Majestic Doll Co. 1918–20. New York City. Manufactured dressed dolls.

1919: Over 50 style Nos. of composition dolls that were claimed to be washable in hot or cold water and would not be injured by soap. They had painted hair or human hair wigs or mohair wigs, sleeping eyes and cost $1.00 to $5.00. *Charles Blum* was a selling agent.

1920: 30 style Nos. with stuffed bodies, hts. 15 to 20 in. (38 to 51 cm.). They also made moving eyes for dolls.★

Makers of Dolls. A name or initials on the head or body of a doll is usually assumed to be that of the maker of the doll. Of course occasionally a name simply signifies a particular model. But often even these names can be traced to a given maker. Some makers can be determined by the symbols or way in which the size is denoted as for example the alphabet and number markings used by *Kestner* to denote sizes. Dolls with identifiable marks usually have greater value than similar unmarked dolls. Moreover an unmarked doll that closely resembles a marked doll is not necessarily made by the same company but it is probably made around the same period as the marked doll when this type of doll was popular.

Makers seldom marked their dolls until about the fourth quarter of the 19th century. Since then the labeling of dolls has shown increasing popularity. Probably this is partly due to the ever-growing interest in collecting and identifying dolls. By 1950 some dolls were marked not only with the maker's name but also where the doll was made, when the doll was made, and the name of the model.

Collectors should be careful in assuming that any name or identification on a doll refers to the maker of the doll. Dolls can be complex objects and their production often involved the work of many people and companies. There is the designer, the modeller, the factory or factories that produced the heads, the factory or factories that made the bodies and assembled the dolls. The designers and creators of the clothes for the dolls. The *Verlegers* who held the rights and hired or subcontracted all of these people and processes. Last but not least were the distributors such as the factory agents, the jobbers, the wholesale distributors and finally the retail distributors. Often one of these distributors held the rights for a doll and their name or symbol appears on the doll. Many bisque-head dolls carry the initials "G. B." which stands for *George Borgfeldt*, one of the largest verlegers and distributors of dolls in America. Borgfeldt owned the rights for the *Kewpies* and *Bye-Lo* babies but instead of the G. B. these dolls have the names of the designers *O'Neill* and *Grace S. Putnam* respectively. Some collectors refer to a Bye-Lo as though Grace S. Putnam were the maker. Actually she was the designer who worked under contract for Borgfeldt. The bisque Bye-Lo heads were made by various porcelain factories in Germany. The bodies were made by the *K & K Toy Company*, a subsidiary of Borgfeldt. Often collectors refer to *Armand Marseille* or *Simon & Halbig* dolls. Actually all they produced were the heads and various companies used these heads in creating dolls. This is also true for *Gebrüder Heubach* and many other porcelain manufacturers. However the majority of the Armand Marseille heads were used by *Heubach* of Köppelsdorf. These two Heubach firms are sometimes confused, but Gebrüder Heubach made bisque heads while Heubach of Köppelsdorf made bodies and assembled dolls.

Although a large number of Simon & Halbig heads were used by *Kämmer & Reinhardt,* they were also used by *Heinrich Handwerck, C. M. Bergmann* and even *Jumeau* in France, when it was part of the *Société Française de Fabrication de Bébés & Jouets,* as well as Eekhoff[†] in Holland.

Dolls dressed in regional costumes often have the name of the area represented on their labels rather than the name of the maker. Unless one has a detailed geographic knowledge this can cause confusion.

Research is helping the modern collector to identify many of the makers of their dolls. However it should be clearly understood that even when the marks on a doll are deciphered or the names are given, this does not necessarily tell who actually made the total doll. Since the head is most likely to carry an identification and it is the most important part of a doll, collectors generally attribute their dolls to the maker of the head. This method of attribution also allows for the fact that a great many of the heads are not original to their bodies. Both heads and bodies were replaced with tremendous frequency from the time the doll was first made until the present day. (See also **Manufacture of Dolls, Commercial** for various places, and **Marks.**)

Male Owners of Dolls. Louis XIII of France played with dolls as a boy and kept some of them all of his life. Napoleon I played with dolls until he was seven years old. Kaiser Wilhelm II of Germany had a doll collection.

1897: Hall and Ellis of Clark University, Worcester, Mass., made A STUDY OF DOLLS which, according to a questionnaire, revealed that among boys under six years old 82 percent had played with dolls, among boys 6 to 12 years of age 76 percent of the boys had played with dolls. Possibly some of the older boys did not wish to own up to having played with dolls. Boys preferred "colored dolls, brownies, German, Chinese and other dolls . . . because they are 'funny' or exceptional.

"That boys are naturally fond of and should play with dolls as well as girls there is abundant indication. . . . Boys as well as girls might be encouraged to play with boy dolls more than at present, with greater advantage. . . . Dolls representing heroes of every kind and non-existent beings, dragons and hobgoblins, find their chief admirers among boys. . . . Boys are little prone to doll luxury or elaborate paraphernalia."

1905: McCALL'S reported that little boys in England brought their dolls to Mrs. *Marsh* to be repaired.

1923: A Harvard Professor wrote that boys should be given dolls because of their educational value. Boys generally preferred special types of dolls such as dolls dressed as clowns, brownies, soldiers or ethnic representations.

1928: PLAYTHINGS reported that a psychologist interviewed a large number of boys under six years of age and 82 percent answered that they enjoyed playing with dolls. (See also **Collections of Dolls.**)

Mallet, Beatrice. 1922–27. France. Created dolls for the *Société Française de Fabrication de Bébés & Jouets* (S.F.B.J.).

1922: *Aux Trois Quartiers* store advertised the Beatrice Mallet cloth dolls. They had round faces, colored cheeks, wigs and removable clothes; one costume was an Oliver Twist suit on a boy doll. Ht. 14 in. (35.5 cm.).★

Malloy, William, & Co. 1922. Detroit, Mich. Imported dolls.

Malter, Carl. 1909–12. Sonneberg, Thür. Applied for two German patents (D.R.G.M.) for dolls.

Malter, Gustav. 1905. Sonneberg, Thür. Applied for a German patent (D.R.G.M.) for dolls' joints.

Mama (Mamma) Dolls. 1918–30 and later. A special type of doll with a two syllable voice that said "Ma-ma" and with a cloth body having swinging legs sewed onto the torso slightly toward the front, and a low center of gravity so that when the doll was held by the hands and moved forward the legs simulated walking as a toddler. These dolls were originated by *Georgene Averill* and the early ones had insipid faces, squatty bodies and the voices made a rasping or wailing sound. The public was slow to respond to these dolls at first and Georgene Averill promoted them by touring stores. The straight legs soon yielded to slightly curved legs with dimpled rosy knees and the stiff arms that jutted from the body at right angles were replaced with fully formed arms with chubby hands.

1921: By 1921 demand for Mama dolls had grown and they were patented in Britain as well as the U.S. *Seymour, Russell* as well as many others made Mama dolls.

1922: According to TOYS AND NOVELTIES demand for the Mama dolls exceeded all expectations. In a Western store's Toy department five dozen Mama dolls were sold in 25 minutes. The customers fought for them. They practically ended the reign of the German bisque dolls by their strong competition, aided by the 70 percent tariff.

A 26½ in. (67.5 cm.) tall Mama doll cost $2.69. Nevertheless this was more expensive than some of the contemporary bisque head dolls.

Among the companies making Mama dolls were *Atlas Doll & Toy Co.; Averill Manufacturing Co.; Paul Averill; Century Doll Co.; Effanbee; Fleischer Toy; E. Goldberger; Horsman; Reisman, Barron.*

1923: TOYS AND NOVELTIES reported that 80 percent of the doll requests were for Mama dolls and described how they were made. "Within the past five years special machinery for baking arms, heads and legs of dolls have been evolved [*Hot Press* method]. This type of machinery is improved every year. The use of this machinery required specially trained people. . . . Even in cheap Mama dolls flesh tinted cloth is used for the body and limbs. . . . to [make an] efficiently stuffed doll requires special skill. Yet there are 60 different operations required to make a doll. When Mama dolls were first made they were sometimes sold without hands or shoes. Mama dolls now walk, talk, sleep and even dance. Two innovations of the present time [1923] can dance. . . . Gone are the pink pop-eyed dolls. Real artists paint lovely complexions, eyes painted with roguish or innocent expression, real eyebrows. Eyelashes are not just streaks of black or brown paint—real hair eyelashes are often on sleeping eyed dolls. Magenta lips cupid-bowed are a thing of the past. Contour of the head and features are those of a toddler. Painted hair or wig-bobbed or ringlets. Gone are long gooey curls. New sleeping eyes can no longer fall out with one good poke.

"Several years ago voices were improved further. Antiquated are Mother Hubbard dresses or dresses with a sash around the middle. Now several manufacturers have designers who devote their entire time to originating frocks for dolls. . . . Wardrobes are made by outside workers, i.e. homeworkers."

F. A. O. Schwarz advertised Mama dolls with composition head and hands, mohair wig, cloth body, dressed and with a bonnet as follows:

| Height | | Price | Style | |
in.	cm.	Dollars	No.	Description
13	33	$2.00	113	Stuffed legs, painted eyes
18	45.5	$3.00	212	Stuffed legs, painted eyes
18	45.5	$5.00	400	Stuffed legs, sleeping eyes
19	49	$4.50	1300	Composition legs, painted eyes

1924: Joe *Amberg* stated: "Cost of production is prohibiting the making of bisque doll heads; and in recent years there has been a steadily decreasing demand for bisque or papier-mâché dolls. I prophesied in Germany four years ago that they would have to come to the Mama doll with a durable composition head—and I could not get a single manufacturer to even try to make one. But to-day a hundred factories are producing them—not to mention an indefinite quantity of home-workers." This was shortly after the mark had plummeted in value.

Bing had acquired the license to manufacture, to use, and to sell under certain restrictions one of the new American Mama voices in their dolls. Among the manufacturers of mama dolls were Amberg; Averill; Bing; *Davis & Voetsch;* Effanbee; *Gem;* Horsman; *Ideal; J.H. Kletzin; Pollyanna Co.; Schoenhut; Toy Shop.* Mama dolls were distributed wholesale by *Butler Bros.; Montgomery Ward; Sears; Supplee-Biddle; Charles William,* and many others.

1925: Mama dolls were very plump and tended to be less tall. Infant dolls began to usurp the Mama doll popularity. One store in Missouri reported to PLAYTHINGS that they sold three baby dolls to one Mama doll. K. & K. were among the manufacturers of Mama dolls.

1926: Mama dolls were thinner and had longer legs than earlier. *Kestner* bisque heads were used on these new style Mama dolls. Mama dolls began to appear in German records more frequently than formerly. Knitted outfits were popular for Mama dolls. *M. L. Kahn* specialized in making clothes for Mama dolls.

In addition to previously named companies Mama dolls were made and/or distributed by:

Acme Toy Manufacturing Co.;

American Character Doll Co.;
Arcy Toy Manufacturing Co.;
Atlantic Toy & Manufacturing Co.;
Baby Phyllis Doll Co.;
Albert Brückner's Sons;
Chessler Co.;
L. Cohen & Sons;
Domec;
European Doll Manufacturing Co.;
Goodyear Toy Co.;
L. Herman;
Bernhard Hermann;
Hitz, Jacobs & Kassler;
Hoest & Henderson;
Jeanette Doll Co.;
Kämmer & Reinhardt;
Kampes;
Katagini Bros.;
Löffler & Dill;
Louisville Doll & Novelty Manufacturing Co.;
Metropolitan Doll Co.;
Modern Doll Co.;
Modern Toy Co.;
Mutual Novelty;
National Doll Co.;
Nibur Novelty Co.;
Original Doll Co.;
Paramount Doll Co.;
Penn Stuffed Toy Co.;
Perfect Toy Manufacturing Co.;
M. Pressner & Co.;
Primrose Doll Co.;
R. B. & L. Manufacturing Co.;
Regal Doll Manufacturing Co.;
S. & S. Doll Co.;
Self Sell Doll Co.;
Shaw Doll Co.;
Star Doll & Toy Co.;
Uneeda Doll Co.;
Well Made Doll Co.;
Louis Wolf & Co.

All 23 members of the *American Doll Manufacturers' Association* made Mama dolls in 1926.

1927: TOYS AND NOVELTIES reported, "Nearly all of the American dolls have the so-called unbreakable hot-press composition heads. They are made from special wood pulp composition which upon baking becomes almost as hard as wood. . . .

"The old skinny body found in practically all dolls made up until a score of years ago has given way to the chubby body characteristic of the dolls made to-day. Doll makers found that plump bodied dolls are preferred to those of thin gawky stature. . . . No mother loves a skinny baby. Some manufacturers have made their dolls plump almost to corpulency with the result that within the past two years the public demand is reacting for somewhat thinner dolls. . . .

"Another modification of the doll's anatomy . . . is the enlarging of its head. Babies with big heads are cute, reasoned the designers."

1928: Most of the Mama dolls were sold dressed. They were 20 to 30 in. (51 to 76 cm.) tall and cost $2.00 to $7.00 each.

1930: Most of the companies previously mentioned, as well as a few others, were still making Mama dolls.

Ca. 1933: K. & K. Mama dolls had imported bisque shoulder heads. At one time *Armand Marseille* made bisque shoulder heads for *Kiddiejoy* Mama dolls. Black composition shoulder heads were made in America for Mama dolls.

Rubber crying legs for Mama dolls were sold separately in America. (See also **Manufacture of Dolls, Commercial: Made in United States.**)★

Mama Doll Voices. 1918–30 and later. The *Lloyd* voice was the first real Mama-type voice with two tones. It was remarkably clear and this stimulated interest in *Mama* dolls.

1927: A new type of voice for Mama dolls was made by *Markon.* (See also **Manufacture of Dolls, Commercial; Kinds of Materials Used.**)

1928: PLAYTHINGS warned: "Technically Mama dolls should have a two tone voice and not a one tone crying voice. But many dolls are sold or advertised as Mama dolls that do not have the two tone voice." A campaign was inaugurated to correct this misuse of the name.

1929: "Dolls Will Say 'MA-MA' this Year" according to the following article which appeared in TOY WORLD, February 1929: "A National campaign to create an insistent public demand for dolls that say 'ma-ma' will be carried on through 1929 by Voices, Inc., Newark, New Jersey. This is in protest to the manufacturers who, to save the cost of an extra syllable, have put on the market dolls which only say 'ma'.

"Hundreds of newspapers throughout the country this past Christmas printed articles pointing out the superiority of ma-ma voices, and poking fun at the single syllable ma dolls. . . .

"Such newspaper headings as 'Doll Manufacturers Try to Put It Over on the Children,' 'Bootlegging in Dolls is Developing Rapidly,' and 'The Doll Scandal' are typical of the stories that appeared in newspapers all over the country."(See also **Voices, Inc.**)★

1751. Mama doll produced by Horsman with composition head, arms and legs, a wig, sleeping metal eyes, hair eyelashes, open mouth, cloth body. Original clothes. Mark Ill. 1229. H. 37 in. (94 cm.). *Courtesy of April Thompson.*

1752. Mama dolls advertised by Reisman, Barron & Co. in PLAYTHINGS, August, 1924. These have wigs or painted hair, sleeping or painted eyes. Mama dolls must have a two-tone voice that says, "Mama" or "Papa," as well as a body with legs attached so that when led, the doll simulates walking.

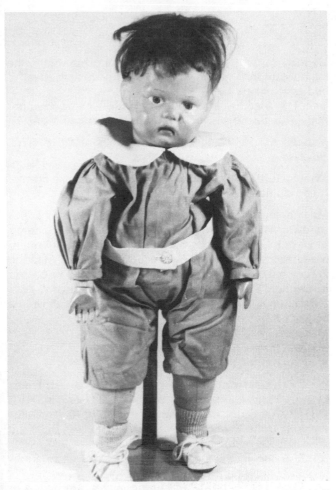

1753. Wooden shoulder head and hands on a cloth Mama doll body, made by Schoenhut. It has a wig and painted features. H. 17 in. (43 cm.). *Courtesy of Richard Withington. Photo by Barbara Jendrick.*

1754A & B. Pair of Mama dolls with bisque heads, wigs, sleeping eyes, open mouths and teeth on cloth bodies with composition arms and legs. The legs are affixed to the torso in the typical swinging manner. The body is chubby with a low center of gravity to enable the doll to simulate walking; the outline of the circular Mama voice box can be seen in the "undressed" picture. Original clothes. Mark: "K & K//45//Made In Germany." The 45 probably indicates the height in centimeters. Actually the doll is nearer to 15 in. than the 17½ indicated by the 45 cm. The 4 in. (10 cm.) shoulder head may have been made for a taller doll or the body may have settled downward due to age. *Courtesy of Mary Lou Ratcliff.*

Mama and Papa Dolls. See **Talking Dolls.**

Mama's Angel Child. 1919–20. Doll made by *Jessie M. Raleigh* based on a *Penny Ross* design, had a wig and wore a print dress with a sash and a ribbon in its hair. (See Ill. 2175.)★

Mama's Angel Child. 1924–26. A group of four dolls, made of oilcloth by *Live Long Toys*. These were based on the designs of *Penny Ross* and included *Esther Starring* and three *Flower Dolls*. They wore a dress and bonnet.

Mamie Lou. 1921. A black *Rag Shoppe* doll distributed by *Severn & Long.*

Mammie Wise. 1921. Black cloth dressed doll made by *Horsman* represented the mother of *Miss Polly Wise, Lizzie Wise* and *Baby Wise.*

Mammy. 1903. Black cloth doll distributed by *Montgomery Ward.* It was dressed as a Southern nursemaid. Ht. 16 in. (40.5 cm.); priced 75¢.

Mammy. 1910–19. Cutout black cloth doll made by *Saalfield.*

Mammy Nurse. 1905–23. Black stockinet doll made by *Martha Chase.* Came dressed or undressed.

1923: Ht. 27 in. (68.5 cm.); priced $8.00 undressed.★

Mancel, Peter. Ca. 1870s. Paris. Name on a pressed bisque shoulder head with wig, glass eyes, ears pierced into the head, open mouth with six teeth.★

1755. Mark of Peter Mancel on a pressed bisque shoulder head.

Manchester Doll Makers. 1916. Manchester, England. Advertised, seeking orders for over 7,000 portrait dolls of *Edith Cavell,* the World War I heroic nurse. The doll had real hair, a woman's face and was dressed in a nurse's uniform.

Mandel Bros. 1915–27 and possibly other years. Chicago, Ill. Distributed dressed dolls including *Babyland* and *Kewpies.*

1927: A doll with a voice 21 in. (53.5 cm.) tall cost $6.95.

Mandel, H., and Sichert, C. 1893. Applied for German and French patents for dolls and dolls' heads of celluloid.

Mangiapani, Julius. 1930 and before. Designed a *Quaker Doll* for *Penn Stuffed Toy Co.* Claimed he had had years of experience with leading manufacturers in America and Europe.

Mangold, Hans. 1924–27. Fürth, Bavaria. Obtained two German patents (D.R.P.) for dolls.

Manhattan Doll Co. 1890–1922. New York City. Importers and jobbers of dolls.

1919: Advertised a composition and wood doll that would walk when led by the hand, no mechanism. Came dressed as a girl, boy soldier or sailor; without a wig it cost $10.00 and with a wig $12.00. In Parisian style dress it was $15.00.

1920: The same doll with a long curly wig still cost $12.00 but when wearing a silk dress it was $20.00. The style, with sleeping eyes, was $15.00 and $25.00 if dressed in silk; or in a handmade gown with a hat it cost $40.00.

Manifatture Aritistiche. 1928. Turin, Italy. Manufactured art dolls.

Mann & Mann. 1923. London. Made *Mimosa* dolls and dressed character baby dolls.

Mannheimer Maschinenfabrik Mohr & Federhaff. 1919–20. Mannheim, Germany. Obtained a German patent (D.R.P.) for a process and a composition for making dolls and dolls' parts.

Mannikins for Display. These were made by *Käthe Kruse, Lenci* and many other doll manufacturers. (See also **Show Dolls.**)

Manning, Joseph Alexander. 1913–14. Pawtucket, R.I. Obtained a U.S., a British and a German patent (D.R.P.) for a doll's head with hollow eyes having a rolling ball within them.★

Manning, Mrs. Will S. Ca. 1900. Saugerties, N.Y. Made and/or distributed dolls.

Manon. 1927–28. *Lenci* felt doll representing the operatic character of this name in MANON LESCAUT by Giacomo Puccini. The doll held a mirror. It was in style no. 165/14. Ht. 27½ in. (70 cm.).

Mansert, August. 1908–25 and later. Sonneberg, Thür. Made and exported dolls.

1910: One of the Sonneberg group of Grand Prize winners at the Brussels Exposition.

Manson, Mme. 1916–18. Paris. Created cloth dolls including Cadet-Roussel, Marlborough, and Sophie.

Manton, May. 1913. America. Made patterns for cloth dolls and their clothes. (See also **Cloth Dolls.**)

Mantuan Dolls. Ca. 1880–1930. PLAYTHINGS in 1929 described doll-making in Mantua, Italy: "Mantua has specialized in china [bisque] dolls for the last 50 years, steadily improving their workmanship and finish. Some 500 workers are regularly engaged in this business. One of the factories [probably *Furga*] has a special department fitted with up-to-date machinery and special oven for firing the pottery and turn out dolls' heads which can compare with the finest

German 'bisquit' [bisque]. Workshops are annexed to the main establishment and in them other parts such as dolls' bodies are made.

"The leading articles are high-class china-[bisque-] dolls with glass eyes, real hair and fully dressed."

Manuel, M. 1930 and later. Paris. Representative of *G. Biberian.*

Manufacture Géneral du Nord. 1926–30. Roubaix, France. Made cloth dolls and dolls' heads.

Manufacture of Dolls. The divisions of the entries are as follows: **Manufacture of Dolls, Commercial; General; Kinds of Materials Used; Made in Austria; Made in Britain; Made in France; Made in France, Cloth Dolls; Made in France and Germany, Compared; Made in Germany; Made in Germany, Sonneberg region; Made in Germany, Waltershausen region; Made in United States; Made in United States, Cloth Dolls.**
Manufacture of Dolls, Homemade: Leather.
Manufacture of Wax Dolls.
Manufacture of Wigs.

(See also **American Dolls; Austrian Dolls; British Dolls; Chinese Dolls; Eskimo Dolls; French Dolls; German Dolls; Grödner Tal Dolls; Indian [American] Dolls; Italian Dolls; Japanese Dolls; Sonneberg Dolls; Waltershausen Dolls** and other nations and regions that made dolls.

Plus the many Manufacturers of Dolls and various named Materials.

Other entries of Manufacturing interest are **Bodies of Dolls, Boudoir Dolls, Chronology, Clothes, Cold Press, Designs for Dolls, Holes in Head, Hot Press, Knitted Dolls, Makers of Dolls, Mama Dolls, Pressed vers. Poured, Production of Dolls, Reproductions, Spring-Jointed Bodies.**)

Manufacture of Dolls. Commercial: General. Collectors usually give a single name for the manufacturer of a doll and think of the doll in its entirety being produced by this one company. In most cases a doll is the product of several companies and many people.

First a doll must be designed. This was usually done by an artist; often the drawings of a famous person were used. These drawings then became the basis for making a three dimensional model or prototype. This work was often done by an art student, generally under the direction of the designer. The molds were made from the models or sometimes they were supplied by a company specializing in making molds.

The various parts of the doll such as the eyes, the wig, the metal stringing pieces and so forth, were purchased from various factories. In many cases the heads themselves were made elsewhere but from the molds owned by the original *Verleger.* If the doll was an extremely popular one like the Bye-Lo Baby, several factories made the heads. The body was usually made where the doll was assembled. But in some cases, especially in the home industries of Europe, each part of the body was made by a different person or family.

One of the most important parts of a doll from a sales and financial point of view was its clothes. Often these were designed by a member of the firm or an employee and then made up by various women in their own homes. Or the dolls' clothes were purchased from one of the many companies that specialized in making dolls' clothes. Since the clothes had to be of up-to-date design and changed practically every year, this was an important part of the production of the dolls. Often the same doll was given several names depending on its costume. (See **Käthe Kruse**.)

Collectors are sometimes more familiar with the names of the distributors of dolls than with the actual manufacturers, for example *Louis Wolf, Strobel & Wilken* and so forth. Usually another company acted as the factory representative for a given doll manufacturer. Then there were jobbers, importers, wholesale distributors, as well as retail distributors.

Generally a doll was the work of a great many people and of a sizable number of companies. These companies in many instances were located in several different countries. This is why it is almost impossible to designate a single country of origin or even a single manufacturer for many of the dolls. As far as is known *Armand Marseille, Simon & Halbig, Gebrüder Heubach* and others were porcelain factories that made only dolls' heads. Other factories bought these heads, added wigs and eyes, put them on bodies and dressed them. Collectors usually name the manufacturer of a doll according to whatever name is identified by marks on the doll, regardless of whether the mark indicates the Verleger, the maker of the head or the body or even the distributor.

McCALL'S MAGAZINE, December, 1910, gave a report on German composition dolls and added: "Russia manufactures dolls also and so does England. The United States has its doll factories. In New York City there are establishments that turn out some very good examples of papier mache dolls, but by far the most elaborate dolls in the world come from France. Preeminent among the French dolls is the famous Bébé Jumeau—the talking doll. At the Jumeau manufactory just outside Paris, over five million of these dolls are made annually."

Many dolls, especially in Germany, were made as a home industry. This was especially true of dolls' clothes, even in America. The clothes for the Kamkins dolls were made by women in their homes. Even the uppers of the Braitling shoes were made by workers in their homes. TOYS AND NOVELTIES in September 1922 explained why home industry produced a better doll than one made entirely in a factory. "In the environment of his own home and without the constant urging for speed which factory supervision entails, he is far more likely to interest himself in the perfection of his product and put his soul into it. This is not pure theory and has been conclusively proven."

1927: PLAYTHINGS in September, 1927, described the function of a Manufacturer's Representative. He "stands as an intermediary between manufacturers on one side and retailers and jobbers on the other. Overhead of showrooms are divided among many firms."

Manufacture of Dolls, Commercial; Kinds of Materials Used.

1848: The *Barrois* inventory listed materials used for the manufacture of dolls.

1902–21: An article of 1902 was reported in ANTIQUE WORLD, December 1971.

"Porcelain and composition dolls' heads are made by similar processes. Little machinery is used. The hot liquid is poured into lead or plaster molds. Holding the mold in one hand the man allows the steaming white mixture to fill all the cavities. Quickly reversing the mold the workman allows the slip that does not adhere to the mold to run back into the tank. Another workman seizes the mold when it is cool enough to handle and with two movements his hands separate the leaden sides and pull out the doll's head . . . Next the ragged seams are trimmed and the head is dipped in flesh colored paint, the doll's complexion resembles a boiled lobster but under the white wash it will be flesh colored.

"A girl or youth next paints the eyebrows, the cheeks, and a man puts in the eyes. If the eyes are to open and shut the balancing of the lead becomes a matter of skill. Nothing remains but to put on the wig which is curled and arranged by an expert.

"The best doll-bodies are stuffed with shavings of cork; hair, excelsior, cotton and sawdust are also used. The arms and legs are molded exactly as the heads and are sewed into their places."

Parts of this article were published in TOYS AND NOVELTIES, June, 1921.

1924: The U.S. Department of Commerce Report No. 267 discussed the materials used in making dolls: "dressed doll is made up of about 20 different types of raw material, most of which come from English speaking countries or countries controlled by them. Use of substitute materials is not always satisfactory but cheaper especially in view of the very high tariffs."

1927: PLAYTHINGS, July 1927 reported on the material used by manufacturers of dolls.

"A few of the products that go into the manufacture of a doll [are] starch, glue, wood flour, rosin, enamel, lacquer, paint, talcum, mohair, human hair, cotton goods, silk, ribbons, marabou, stockings, shoes, cases, boxes, eyes, springs, washers, pins, cord and other materials and parts too numerous to mention in this limited space.

"In mentioning the doll voices that are used, we can make this serve to illustrate the quantities of raw materials that are used. Just think, one company alone, in a year's manufacture of Ma-Ma voices, used 1,200,000 lbs. of steel, 3,500,000 paper tubes, 150,000 lbs. of tin plate, and 60,000 yards of rubberized cloth. It is almost inconceivable to think that this material, together with large quantities of brass, fibre, aluminum, and rubber cement, would be required by one manufacturer of doll voices, but these are authentic figures."

Also in July PLAYTHINGS devoted an entire article to glue. This was written by Wilbur L. Jones and entitled "Use of Glue in Toy-Making."

"There is not one glue but many. Some smell foul; some are 'sweet.' Some are water-resistant; some are not. Some are used hot, others cold. Some are expensive, others cheap. There is a glue for every use, and a use for every glue. . . .

"A word or two concerning some of the better known types. . . . Hide glue [is] made by extracting a low-grade gelatin from the skins of cattle. A cheaper grade of animal glue is made by boiling bones; the process is akin to that by which the housewife makes soup out of beef bones. From the choicest hide glue to the cheapest bone glue there are innumerable gradations in properties and in price. . . .

"Animal glue has been superseded in some . . . factories by vegetable glue—or 'tapioca pudding' as it is sometimes called. Vegetable glue is made by cooking treated tapioca flour with caustic soda. It is a transparent amber-colored glue, which is used cold. I have made numerous tests which prove that vegetable glue will give just as strong . . . joints as animal glue. It is an excellent adhesive in every respect, being especially advantageous for use in large-scale operations. Besides being considerably cheaper than animal glue it is less liable to bacterial decomposition.

". . . Casein glue is prepared by sifting a powdered casein mixture into cold water and stirring it until a smooth liquid has been obtained. Casein glue is a whitish solution, resembling condensed milk. It is always used cold. When casein glue hardens and sets, it undergoes a chemical change whereby it becomes insoluble in water. Hence, it is unlike animal and vegetable glues in that it is water-resistant. It is not absolutely waterproof, as some erroneously assume.

"These three are the glues most commonly found. . . . There is an interesting newcomer, soya bean glue, which is somewhat like casein glue, only cheaper. In addition to soya bean glue there are several other vegetable protein glues, which are made of cotton seed meal, linseed meal, peanut meal, etc. They possess varying degrees of water-resistance and usefulness.

"The cheapest of all possible glues is sodium silicate (water glass). This is not used extensively . . . because of lack of confidence in its strength and durability. . . .

"The most nearly waterproof glue that I know of is blood albumin. This material, which is obtained from the stockyards, is dissolved in water, brushed on the joint, and then 'set' in a hot press. This gives a decidedly water-resistant bond. The advantage which this glue possesses by virtue of its water-resistance is offset, to a degree, by the difficulty of using it. A hot-press is a cumbersome and expensive piece of apparatus. There are times, however, when blood albumin is the logical adhesive to use.

"The above enumeration does not exhaust the list of glues which the toy-maker might find adaptable to his purposes. There are many glues of minor importance which could be used to fill some special need."

1929: The following supplies were advertised in PLAYTHINGS in January 1929.

Colors, dry
Cutting dies
Doll faces, any special design and expression could be made
   to individual orders.
Dolls' hair and wigs
Dolls' heads
Dolls' molds; an experienced sculptor would improve and
   finish your rough models. This sculptor served America's
   biggest doll makers according to the advertisement.
Dolls' stockings
Dolls' voices
Dolls' eyes
Glue pots

Labels
Machinery
Marabou
Mohair
Paints, varnishes and lacquers
Paper boxes
Patent attorneys
Ribbons
Rubber products and parts
Stockinet material
Stuffing materials
Wire and wire parts
Wood turning and wooden parts

PLAYTHINGS in January 1930 advertised "Wood Wool and Cotton for stuffing dolls" as well as "All grades of stuffing cotton."

Manufacture of Dolls, Commercial: Made in Austria.

TOYS AND NOVELTIES in 1912 described the manufacture of dolls in Vienna, an area that has seldom been covered before. Speaking of Viennese dolls:

Formerly they were "all completed by hand work and the little bodies, and all other parts, were put together in laborious manner.

"Despite the machine activity a large number of persons are busied around the making. The little hands and feet are each made by a separate machine. She entrusts her head to other hands and gets a wig put on by others. The eyebrows can only be made by a specialist, the little dresses only by the tailoress, the tiny chemises only by the seamstress, the little shoes only by workers accustomed to tiny feet. Yes, even the cheeks, an artist in this line must make red.

"From the large wood storerooms and cardboard stocks one proceeds to the stencil and press department. There, rattling unceasingly, the machines are directed by men. Heavy steel stencils press, with the utmost precision, the gray, wet cardboard, in order to bring out the form of the little body. After this has been done, the cardboard is dried, and on another machine the two body parts are fastened together. Then they are jointed with wood so the form remains exactly the same. As simple as it is to manufacture the bodies, just as complicated a proposition it is to make the feet and hands.

"These require much machine power and agility of hand. A machine is set in motion which mixes and kneads the mass. Next it, is working still another machine which works the masses into rods, and thus prepares them for stencils. This machine resembles a sausage machine. The rods come in a warm condition into the press and stencil department and there they are worked over into feet and hands. This is accomplished by pressing this mass into forms of heavy steel and driving it together with machine power. When the little legs and hands have the desired form, they go into the drying ovens, where they get solidity and durability. All this pressing was formerly done by hand; now it is accomplished exclusively by machines.

"After the component parts of the dolls have been produced, they go into a division where women's hands are awaiting them. There they also meet, for the first time, all the different parts of which a doll is composed. Workers grind, file and polish without the use of a machine. From there on everything is handwork.

"Close to this department there is a work hall, which has been finished entirely into a rosy red line. Wherever one may look everything appears in a delicate rosy color. Here the body parts are given flesh color and are varnished, stuck on wood sticks and dried in the drying-chamber in an atmosphere of a fixed temperature. When the preparatory work has proceeded to this point the assembling begins.

"The porcelain heads, which are made in another factory, are stored in large store-rooms, and are still preferred to the little heads of composition. These doll heads are, in expression, very different in recent times. The face of a character doll has something about it which interests the child immensely and gives more pleasure than the ever smiling antiquated doll face. There are now, obstinant, stupid, peasant-like and weeping faces that are pretty to look upon.

"These faces now receive their charming complexion in a special compartment. After this last turn the dolls come into the adjusting department. There the little bald heads receive the first attention. The glued or sewed wig of real hair, or of the hair of the angora goat, prepared, dyed and dressed, is now placed on the doll. A very modern fashion is the wheel-dressing, which is fastened with real hairpins.

"Then the doll, beginning with the underclothes, is treated like a little girl. First comes a little lace-trimmed chemise, delicate embroidered drawers, perfumed underskirts, shoes and drawn-work stockings. According to its distinction, the doll gets an evening toilet, a becoming sport costume or a smart street gown. But there are also national costumes and outfits, which are much in demand, such as Tyrolians, Spanish Ladies, Ladies in Hungarian National Costumes, the Karlsbad Spring maid, the Automobilist, etc."

On the whole the making of dolls in Vienna appears to be similar in method to that used elsewhere in Europe. Note that the porcelain heads are made in another factory; no doubt this was generally true everywhere. The statement that the faces receive their complexion in a special compartment is rather puzzling. Does this refer to porcelain heads? If so the heads must have been received in the white and were decorated in the factory where the rest of the doll was made. It appears that the reference was to the porcelain heads but on the other hand there is the possibility that composition heads were meant.

It is interesting to find that dolls and little girls still wore chemises as late as 1912. The perfumed underskirts are a novel idea and perhaps collectors will wish to add a touch of scent to their dolls' underskirts for the sake of authenticity.

Manufacture of Dolls, Commercial: Made in Britain.

An 1884 article in LITTLE FOLKS MAGAZINE, described the methods of doll manufacture used in a large English doll factory as follows:

"In the modeling and casting rooms, at well lighted benches, men and boys work making heads and limbs of various sizes; some of wax, some of papier mache, others of a combination of the two materials. The clay model is first made, then the plaster cast is made which is used as the mould. Into this the wax is poured. This is really a mixture of spermaceti and clarified wax. When melted it has the consistency of cream. It is poured into the mould and immediately solidifies. This begins next to the mould and extends toward the center. When a layer is sufficiently thick, the workman turns the mould upside down to pour off the liquid portion left. Thus a hollow copy of the mould is obtained.

"Heads and limbs cast in wax break easily. As a precaution against accidents, many dolls have a foundation of papier mache beneath the wax. The paper is soaked in starch to soften it and is then pressed into the mould. When dry it is firm and hard and will stand a good deal of knocking about. Dipped into wax it assumes an appearance of being entirely wax. Scraping and trimming remove the marks of the joints of the mould and the surface has an even look.

"The heads then pass to workmen who cut the apertures for eyes, and these, globes of glass with one side coloured to represent the eye ball, are inserted. The eye is warmed slightly and then pressed into the socket, exactly adjusted, so the eye has no squint.

"The doll then receives its hair. On the cheaper ones, an opening is made from front to back in the head. Two tufts of hair are inset and fixed with paste. Hair to imitate natural growth is put in by women. The operator puts a doll head on her knee, resting the palm of her right hand on it. A small bundle of hair to be inserted is taken between finger and thumb of the left hand, and between finger and thumb of the right hand a tool resembling a flattened bodkin is held. A few hairs are caught at a time and forced into the wax. The hair is inserted in rows from the nape of the neck upwards. The wax pressed firmly down on the inserted ends to hold them firmly. The ends are then trimmed, the locks curled with a tiny pair of curling tongs.

"The last steps to complete the doll in the doll factory consists of painting the lips and applying rouge to the cheeks. Then the head, limbs and body are brought together, in a special department, and are assembled. A few stitches with stout thread is sufficient to unite the various parts and the doll is ready to receive clothing.

"The dress making department is an important one. In it young women cut out and make diminutive clothing, sewing machines of toy-like size being used for the work. A large order for India was just completed and included an extensive array of dolls dressed according to the quaint styles of those artists who have distinguished themselves by illustrating children and their ways." In this same factory the making of the *London Rag Dolls* was described in 1884 by LITTLE FOLKS MAGAZINE as follows:

"One variety of doll was being made in large numbers, namely the rag doll. Not remarkable for its beauty, it is nevertheless highly appreciated by children of the working classes, for whom it is designed. The body, limbs and head of the doll are all in one piece, and composed of sawdust enclosed in a casing of calico. The face consisting of a mask of wax, is covered with a layer of fine muslin, which being pressed into the wax is scarcely observable. The object of this covering is to strengthen it against rough usage. The face is glued upon the sawdust head and then the doll is ready for dressing. Her clothes are permanently fixed by the dressers and she is soon quite smartly attired."

This type of doll was first made by Richard Montanari. The stuffing found in dolls of this type does not appear to always be of sawdust.

Irene Pierotti in COUNTRY LIFE, 1974, wrote about the making of wax heads for dolls by her ancestor Harry Pierotti, who made wax models of prominent people and wax dolls by the poured-wax method.

"The best-quality models had eyebrows and eyelashes, and in some of them the hairs were actually inserted singly to give full realism." (A few of the Pierotti molds are in the Bethnal Green Museum.)

THE GIRLS' OWN ANNUAL, in 1900 described how a doll maker in Shoreditch, England made cloth bodies, "with black calico feet, and arms and hands of flesh-coloured leather. . . . Had to take the cloth to a machinist to be stitched up. . . .

"Bodies would be filled with sawdust up to the hips and with shavings above, so that the larger part of the body should be light. The waist part should be stuffed very firmly so as to give a center of gravity to balance the weight of the head, but the bust and shoulders must be loosely filled. . . . German and British bodies made so that the legs will bend at the place where the knees are supposed to be."

According to THE PRIZE in 1904: "The dolls made in England . . . are manufactured in large works, where they go through many processes. The first step is the making of the head. A quantity of East Indian wax is melted, and when it is near boiling point some red colouring matter is stirred in. Hollow moulds are then placed in rows, the part which forms the crown of the head being downwards, after which the maker takes a canful of the melted wax and pours it into the moulds. When he has filled about a dozen, he returns to the first one, and pours back into the can whatever of the wax remains fluid. If he did not do this, the head would, of course, be solid. He serves the second mould in the same way, and so on with the rest.

"In a short time the heads can be removed from the moulds—a very simple matter, as the latter are in three pieces. Then they go to a man who puts in the eyes. He takes a knife and cuts out holes for the sockets, and, for small dolls, warms the glass eyes over a gas jet and sticks them in the holes, securing them by running a little melted wax into the skull. But in the case of large dolls wax is run over the eyes, and the eyebrows and eyelids are afterwards carefully modelled with little tools.

"Next the head is trimmed and cleaned and rubbed over with violet powder. After this the cheeks are tinted with rouge, to make them look rosy, and the lips and nostrils touched up with vermilion, and then the article is taken in hand by a woman, who puts in the hair. Sometimes this is human, being obtained from abroad—many little girls in Switzerland, for example, part with their tresses for a very small sum—but the light flaxen locks generally used are mohair, specially manufactured for dolls' heads. The woman, however, puts the head on a block, and presses hair into it with a knife, finally closing up the small gashes she makes by rubbing a roller over the scalp. Now the head is finished.

"Doll bodies, as everybody knows, are usually made of calico stuffed with sawdust. This also is done by women, who work at home. One of these bodymakers obtains so many yards of calico from a master, and, buying her own sawdust, makes the material into dolls. As she usually is helped by her children, she makes many dozens every week. Arms are made by other women, but those of wax are cast in moulds, just like the heads.

"We have thus the various parts of a doll, and all that remains is the putting of these together. The maker, working in the factory, soon does this with glue and thread, and then the doll is ready for sale. If, however, it is to be dressed, it afterwards goes to women, who put on it fancy clothes." (See also **Manufacture of Wax Dolls.**)

According to a British periodical, THE TOYSHOP AND FANCY GOODS JOURNAL, February 1917, an article entitled "Common Sense" discussed British dolls.

"Of doll factories there are now in the country about one hundred, all struggling through various stages of experiments. Some are coming out very well, especially regarding dolls made of celluloid and papier-mâché. The china heads of Staffordshire and those made of celluloid in Lancashire are excellent. The heads, or masks, as they are technically called, lack little of the fine finish of the German article, and some of the papier-mâché bodies and jointed limbs are being moulded from beautifully executed models. The white kid bodies, too, are well done. As a rule, however, our makers have not yet attained to the symmetrical lines of the German doll. The papier-mâché material appears to lend itself well to doll-making. The whole body and head can be cast in one piece, and the limbs afterwards cast and jointed into place.

"There is a difficulty about the inserted eyes. In prewar days these were the monopoly of Austrian glass-blowers, who are very clever in producing the most natural-looking. There are still, I believe, a few stocks in this country, but any fresh supplies are reaching England from France. Futile attempts have been made to induce British glass-blowers to take up the manufacture of dolls' glass eyes. They either cannot or will not, though one might have thought that some of the glass factories of this country that have developed such enterprise and introduced so many reforms in the past year or so would have found it worth while to add still another department to their activities.

"No wax dolls have made their appearance yet—that is, none of British make—so that in this and some other directions there is room for a considerable amount of development."

Actually glass eyes as well as *wax dolls* were being made by a considerable number of British firms in 1917.

(See also **Hancock** for a description of the making of *British Ceramic* dolls.)

THE TOYSHOP AND FANCY GOODS JOURNAL, July 5, 1917, reported: "Nearly every manufacturer has a 'compo' of his own, differing in porosity and texture, so that the matter of the right kind of paint is not the easy problem it looks. . . .

"There are two methods of finishing dolls where paint is used—dipping and spraying. Dipping being the cheapest method, most dolls are finished this way, but spraying is the best method of finish—of that there is no doubt, as it gives a natural and more finished appearance. . . .

"The manufacturers of dolls will also be well advised to place themselves in the hands of those who are specialists in all that appertains to colouring in oil or spirit bases. Whilst the dolls are being improved and perfected in details, the life-like tinting of the limbs should be studied and improved. Many there are who do not like experimenting because of the cost. This is no excuse since without experimenting one cannot make progress. There is another more important reason, however, viz. that to-day the experimenting in getting the desired tints for the particular material of which the doll is used will be made by any progressive house specialising in colourings. In fact, they are out to benefit the trade just as much as to sell their specialties.

"At the moment practically every doll manufacturer possesses a secret composition which he is using for his dolls' limbs and this being so, I need hardly say how important it is to get a colouring that will suit the material used. Each compo. must to an extent differ in porosity, and surface texture which makes it all the more necessary why doll-makers should leave it to the specialist in paint to suit the material employed. This in my mind is highly essential whether brush, dip or spray is used."

TOY AND FANCY GOODS TRADER, October, 1917, described the manufacture of British Ceramic dolls' heads in the Staffordshire Potteries:

"The history of the British toy industry offers no more interesting development than that which surrounds the doll head industry which has grown up in the Potteries district of North Staffordshire. . . . Before the war . . . pottery manufacture was largely divided into two classes, the useful and the artistic, . . . but the manufacture of doll heads was something quite apart from either, and when one remembers that the pottery manufacturers had to discover everything for themselves it will be seen that the progress which they have made in the manufacture of doll heads is no mean achievement. To-day there are those who compare Staffordshire Pottery heads with those formerly imported from Germany, generally to the disadvantage of the former, forgetting that the German doll head maker has had thirty or forty years' experience, whereas the Staffordshire firms have had three years in which to create what was to them a new industry. . . .

"Buyers had been so long accustomed to look to Germany for supplies that when those supplies were summarily cut off the whole position quickly became a problem of where to obtain supplies. At first few firms ventured into the doll making trade, and it was well on in 1915 before we saw anything really presentable in dolls. The question of the bodies, wigs, and dresses was an easy one, but the porcelain head looked like being the stumbling block. It was then that the Staffordshire Pottery came to the rescue; first one and then another firm took up the doll head problem, and eventually a fair supply of heads was forthcoming. It would be idle to pretend that these heads were or are as good as the German article, but taking into consideration the fact that the making of this article is practically new, the British-made head compares very favourably with the imported goods[;] when the decorators have had as much practice as the Continental producers, it is no idle boast to say that the Staffordshire goods will eventually eclipse and supplant the foreign articles. . . . They have been carefully modelled, the features finely pencilled, but we personally consider that if they were made prettier, it would be a distinct acquisition to the already well-potted head. We are also of the opinion that a greater variety of 'smiles' should be introduced, . . .

"The British head has a truly British appearance inasmuch as the features are typically English. . . .

"There are now a considerable number of firms in the Potteries District producing doll heads. Each of these firms have their own ideas as to designs, etc., and while some are content to produce only the very high-class article, others specialise in cheaper heads. . . .

"The standard of wages in the Potteries, particularly for women and girls, was a very low one; there was an abundance of labour upon which to draw, and other conditions were equally favourable. . . .

"It is, of course, well known that all the china [porcelain] heads used for doll making in this country [Great Britain] are produced in the Staffordshire Potteries."

In February, 1919, THE TOYSHOP AND FANCY GOODS JOURNAL reported: "Four years ago there was not a single firm in the kingdom that made china or composition heads for dolls. At this moment not only is Stoke-on-Trent producing good work, but there is actually a large factory turning out dolls within the area of the City itself—a sufficiently striking proof of the importance of the new industry when the rents within the area of the 'one square mile' [city of London] are considered. And it is characteristic of the times that it is entirely directed by women. The modelling of the faces, the limbs, the hands is entirely done here. You are taken through rooms which seem peopled by hosts of tiny faces, whether of babies, of toddling tots, or those who can wear fashionable costumes. Here are rows of wires on which thousands of tiny hands are drying; there is a room given over to eyes and the simple device which closes the lids. . . . Moreover, there is a useful auxiliary industry growing up in the making of their clothes. Girls who [are] crippled and living in the country have been traced out and taught to make exactly what is wanted. There are special lists for dolly's summer millinery. The young lady wants her fur coat and muff for winter wear. . . .

"Jointed dolls are likely to come on the market in considerable numbers. Up till twelve months ago it was a reproach to the manufacturers that no particular firm had laid themselves out to produce jointed dolls on anything like a big scale. More than one trading concern has since recognised the opportunity to make a name. . . . La Belle France sent a few of these goods."

Later in 1919 the same journal stated: "In England the Toy Trade Association discussed whether elementary schools should be approached with a view to teaching children to make dolls as was done in Germany to procure cheap labor, and thus enable competition with Germany."

An article in the British periodical GAMES AND TOYS, February, 1922, quotes an earlier issue of the DAILY MAIL which discussed the manufacture of composition Cupid Dolls by the *Lawton Manufacturing Co.*

"On the top floor huge presses, with high pressure gas, bake and press out the shape. The material composed chiefly of wood fibre makes them almost indestructible, as they can be banged about without breaking. They are then glued together, cleaned, scraped, filed and polished. On the next floor are dipping tanks and drying racks, while on the next floor are hairdressers who put on the lovely little coiffeur . . . while artists give them that individual hand-painted expression. . . . Then they are dressed, boxed and packed. On the ground floor they are examined as to first and second quality, and are ready for shipment."

A British publication GAMES AND TOYS, February 1922, reported on the making of dolls: "A Doll Maker . . . states that, . . . each doll requires the joint labour of from ten to thirty workers. . . .

"Ordinarily a doll's body is built up of brown paper. Sheet after sheet is well moistened with paste. The paper is then placed in an iron mould and hammered well with a mallet until it takes the required form.

"As soon as the trunk of the body is moulded the same process is repeated in the case of the legs, feet, and hands. The moulds thus filled are hung up to dry, a process which occupies from one to four weeks.

"From the drying-room the moulds pass to the painters, who give each part or member its first layer of 'skin' by means of a coat of flesh-tinted paint.

"Next, the doll's head is made. This is done by filling face-moulds with a milk fluid, which flows from a tankard with faucets somewhat like those of a soda fountain.

"When the contents of the moulds have set they are placed in a huge oven and baked. This takes from 24 to 30 hours.

"After this each face is given a flesh tint by means of paint, the rouge is put on the cheeks, and the eyelashes and eyebrows are formed.

"The heads are then dried in some airy place, and subsequently they are put in the ovens again for a further 30 hours' baking.

"The heads are now ready to receive the eyes. These are of glass and enamel. Each eye is made in a darkened room into which the sunlight rarely peeps.

"The eyes are carefully matched and then glued into the head, while the head is 'rounded out' by means of cork clipping.

"Not until each portion of the body has received at least five coats of paint and varnish are they all ready for 'assembling.' This process calls for the highest art in the doll's creation.

"First, the different members are 'assembled' on pieces of elastic. Wooden sockets are put in the shoulders, elbows, and knees, and little wires or 'articulators' are inserted and the necessary adjustments made until every limb moves in a more or less 'human' fashion.

"The doll now passes to the coiffeur. Great boxes of hair, varying in colour from palest gold to raven black, are tried in turn, until the shade best suited to the complexion is found. When the correct shade has been found the locks are tacked on to the head by small brass nails.

"Next, and finally, the hair is dressed, the dimpled feet are put into dainty Louis XIV slippers, a white chemise is put on the figure. The doll is ready for sale."

Apparently the dolls described above had heads with cork pates and it is not certain whether they were made in France or in Britain.

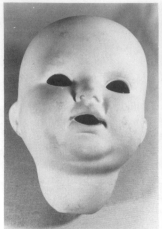
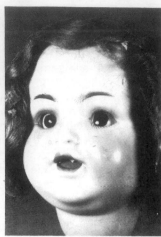

1756A & B. British Ceramic head partially manufactured. It has been fired once but not painted and has not had a final firing to make the paint permanent. This head could be painted later by a middleman. The head lacks a wig and eyes. Marked: "B.N.D.// LONDON." B. Finished version of "B.N.D." head has wig, glass eyes, but has not had the paint fired. H. of both heads 4½ in. (11.5 cm.). *Coleman Collection. Gift of Joseph Kallus.*

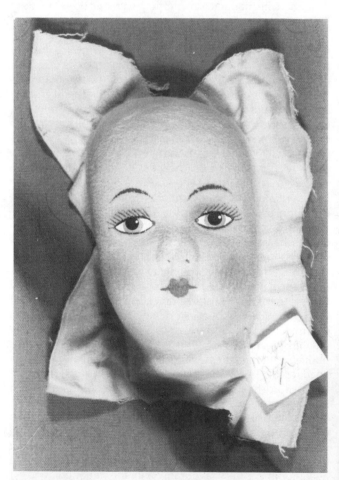

1757. Shaped mask face of painted cotton velvet over buckram, marked "British Made." This face was used by Molly-'es for her Margaret Rose Dolls. H. of head 5 in. (12.5 cm.). *Coleman Collection. Gift of Molly Goldman.*

Manufacture of Dolls, Commercial: Made in France. Descriptions of the manufacture of French bisque head dolls were found in the following publications; contradictions often were evident.

1885: THE JUMEAU DOLL STORY, published anonymously but probably written by *Emile Jumeau,* translated by Nina Davies in 1957.

1888: LA NATURE published an article by Gaston Tissandier which has been translated in THE JUMEAU DOLL, by Margaret Whitton. The heads were still being pressed when this visit to the Jumeau factory was made.

1892: DEWSBURY REPORTER published an account of another visit to the Jumeau factory. The heads were being poured when this visit was made. Thus it appears that the change in method from pressing to pouring of Jumeau heads was made around 1890.

1897: PEARSON'S MAGAZINE printed an article entitled "A Village of Dollmakers," by M. Dinorben Griffith. (Reprinted in part in the first COLLECTOR'S ENCYCLOPEDIA OF DOLLS, pp. 405–7.)

1898: LES JOUETS HISTOIRE FABRICATION, by Léo Claretie. (This has been partially translated in the first COLLECTOR'S ENCYCLOPEDIA OF DOLLS, p. 405.) Léo Claretie himself in 1918 attributed that his own book was published in 1898.

Ca. 1900: Laura S. Farlow wrote the following article entitled "In the World of Toys."

"In one half yearly season Paris will send to New York alone over a quarter of a million dollars' worth of dolls. . . . Only there is little or no home work in the French industry. Instead of the mild-eyed peasants in [German] forest huts you have roaring factories, giant chimneys, steaming engines and whirling presses.

"Each great establishment maintains a special Invention Department whose doors are fast closed against the inquisitive. Inside sit anxious eyed men, upon whose brainwork may depend the bread of five thousand people. In some cases the very workmen are not let into the secret, for each section of a new mechanical toy will be made separately thousands at a time. . . .

"But perhaps the great doll factories are the most interesting. The dainty plaything originates in somewhat unpromising surroundings. Few would think the pink and white darling emerges at first from a great trough, into which men stir shreds of old kid gloves and scraps of cardboard, saturated with tragacanth, an adhesive gum made from the goat's horn!

"All around machinery is groaning and creaking. One workman stripped to the waist is shuffling sawdust into a pan of boiling water. Another throws masses of paste into the mixing trough whose fans are worked by horizontal shafts. The pulp thus formed is carried away to the weighing tables, where it is parceled out molded and compressed, until it assumes with miraculous celerity the forms of busts, arms and legs.

"In one factory a quarter of a million sections will be turned out every day providing material for at least fifty thousand dolls. Later you will see these separate greenish-hued busts and limbs heaped up in baskets, like the relics of some Herodian massacre! They now go into the painting shops, where magical brushes paint them a delicate rose. In the next department are made myriads of copper wire hooks whereby arms and legs are secured to the trunk.

"Dolly is now on her feet but is still without a head—the crowning point of her creation. An original model will be some lovely portrait by a special artist of the house, who has copied types of beauty in the museums and galleries of the world. This copy is reproduced in pure porcelain clay poured into a mold; and then apertures for the eyes are made, the face tinted, eyebrows and lashes traced, and the cheeks touched with carmine. The painted heads are then placed on round trays called 'gazettes,' and put in the oven to be baked in immense batches. [The narrator fails to mention the first (porcelain) firing which was done in immense kilns located at a distance from the main factory. The heads came out in the white from this firing and were then painted.]

"Thereafter, if they emerged safe and sound—there is an element of doubt about this—they only need eyes, cranium and wig. Very weird places are the dark shops where women glass-blowers are making millions of eyes. The only light is from the lurid jets of the blow-pipes. Little drops of molten glass fall like tears, and are swiftly colored blue, black or hazel and then borne away in thousands, heaped up in baskets.

"According to price, dolls' eyes are fixed or movable. This latter process is effected by cleverly arranged levers that give a very natural expression. A practised woman can put in position one thousand five hundred eyes in a day and thereby earn one dollar which is considered a fair day's pay. As to the wig, for a cheap doll this is a simple matter. A chosen tress of wool is tied together with a cord, then opened and divided into four; after which it has only to be stuck onto the head with a little pasteboard cap.

"Locks of soft silky Tibetan wool, combed, curled and waved make much more coquettish coiffures. A clever girl can turn out one hundred and twenty dozen such wigs in a working day! Dolly is entirely created now, yet still without her dresses. And you may be sure dressmaking for smart dolls is a mighty elaborate business, to which Paris devotes much of her marvelous art.

"Dolls' shoe making is a distinct industry; and hats, frocks and lingerie all come from separate sources. There is one great concern in France known as the 'Societe du Bebe Francais' [*Société Française de Fabrication de Bébés & Jouets*] which employs thousands of hands and in certain cases takes as much trouble over frocks and hats as Worth or Paquin do in the case of real live grown-ups! . . .

"The plant involved in this immense industry is worth scores of millions of dollars and includes engines, both steam and electrical, of every conceivable kind; as well as turning-lathes, drilling, filing and drawing machines. Grindstones, ovens, molds and melting pots, too. As to the material employed, I need only mention gold, silver, iron, brass, tin, pewter, zinc, copper, lead, nickel and aluminum as well as mother of pearl, ivory, all kinds of wood, Indian rubber, silk, satin, velvet, lace, cloth, cotton, kid, leather and skins of every kind. Rags and pasteboard, too—but anything like a complete inventory is impossible.

"Practically every trade and handicraft on earth is represented. You will find painters and mechanics, clock-makers, armorers, scabbard-makers, coachbuilders, carpenters, jewellers, gemsetters, molders, smelters, tailors, dressmakers, milliners, shoe-makers, hairdressers, and a hundred others. The men receive about a dollar and seventy-five cents a day, and the women less than a dollar on the average.

"In all the great toy houses of France and Germany, inventive ability is encouraged among the humblest; and in some cases original models are brought forward that have been dug out of Egyptian tombs and were played with, perhaps by infantile Pharoahs five thousand years ago!

"Even the humblest toy-maker is given a share in the profits of his invention; and although it seems strange to see grown men making dolls . . . who shall say that their share in the world's work is without importance."

According to LESLIE'S ILLUSTRATED WEEKLY NEWSPAPER, December, 1912: "At Vincennes, France, there is a large factory where the very best type of French dolls is made. Parts of all dolls are imported from Germany, for that country has a monopoly on the heads, and the factories all over the world depend on the German factories for their supply of this part of the dolls.

"A special branch of the industry is devoted to making dresses and hats. The latest styles are copied. The woman in charge is ever on the alert for novelties, and this year the 'character doll' has given her no little study. These dolls are made to represent different nations. They are clothed in the picturesque costumes worn in Germany and other European countries before the French fashions spread over the world, and the doll dressmakers have been compelled to study various museums of costumes in order to fashion the proper dresses. Dolls of this type have an educational value and will likely prove popular.

"In Paris there is a large doll dressmaking establishment where hundreds of girls (many of them fashion experts) are employed. Prizes are offered each year for the most artistic creations in doll dressing and manufacture. This accounts for the fine finish of the French doll, which is a genuine counterpart of the stylish French woman of the period."

TOYS AND NOVELTIES reported in 1913: "Head is cast from the finer Kaolin. One girl cuts out the eye sockets. [No mention is made of the firing to produce porcelain.] Another touches up the cheeks with rouge, and a third blackens the eyebrows. Down the table journeys the head getting its finishing touches from these specialists, ending at last in a bake oven. It comes from the oven both eyeless and hairless. [This must be the second firing], but these additions are . . . quickly made. A cork is driven into the hole at the top of the head before the wig is attached.

"There is a gloomy air of witchcraft about the room devoted to making the eyes. . . . Girls are 'blowing' eyes by the hundred with a blow pipe. The eyes themselves are blown from cream colored molten glass and the pupils of brown or blue are added in the same manner.

"At last the doll is sent to the robing room, if she is to be sold dressed, and there the complete outfits which many French dolls possess are added."

In 1924 Pierre Calmette wrote a report on his visit to the Société Française de Fabrication de Bébés & Jouets (S.F.B.J.)

factory which was published in LES JOUJOUX: "The creating of a plaster model was the first step. Then this model was reproduced in a hollow form and from this the steel mold was made. Molds were made for the torso, hands, arms, thighs, and legs. . . . The body was molded out of old paper which was liquified by adding a glue paste and then poured into the hollow mold and pressed by a positive matrix or mold. Sometimes the dough put into the hollow molds was composed of plaster of Paris, gum tragacanth and scrapings of the skins of gloves. The hands were stamped by machine.

"All of these parts were taken from the molds and dried. After they had dried the seams from the molds were filed down, the opening in each piece was equalized so that they could fit together. These pieces were then segregated as to type, put into wide baskets and carried to the painting workshop. Up to this time the pieces were a dirty grey color. After several coats of paint they became a rosy color which was applied by young workers either by means of a brush or mechanically by an airbrush. The parts were then placed on sticks which were stuck into holes against the wall. When dried they were carried to the workshop where they were put together. There a cross-bar of wood was inserted in the torso to support the copper wire and stringing parts which would be attached to the various parts of the doll; to provide easy movement at the joints of the legs and shoulders, hollow wooden half ball and socket were placed opposite to each other. They were linked together by hooks attached to rings. When thus the arms were attached to the shoulder, the forearms to the arms and the hands to the forearms, then the legs to the thighs and the thighs to the torso, only the head was lacking. The head must never be ugly.

"Formerly the French manufacturers bought the heads from Germany. But by 1924 they had found it best to make the heads themselves. In our day some excellent artists sculpture the faces, smiling or serious, for the fashionable dolls. A sculptor named M. Lejeune was a specialist in this work. The Maison Lanternier in Limoges is renowned for its bébé heads.

"The dolls' heads are in effect a special article of commerce. They are found in stores especially small shops which contain in their windows only dolls' heads surrounded by clothes and accessories. These shops for repairing dolls are found all over Paris. One of them opposite the store Bon Marché advertises that they replace bad heads. Alas, the porcelain head breaks more often than any other part of a doll. The manufacture of dolls' heads is an important industry as well as the making of wigs for dolls.

"The large factories have their own sculptors who prepare the models, mold makers, painters, and assemblers. The sculptor's model is used to make a hollow mold. This mold serves to cast a number of examples using a slip of extremely fine kaolin porcelain that has been put through a sieve many times. When the greenware is removed from the mold it looks like the original sculpture. It is a head without a pate.

"According to the future price of the doll the head must be more or less perfect the simpler ones have painted eyes. Better eyes are of enamel paste [glasslike paste jewelry]. The best dolls have moving eyes.

"For the heads in the last two groups the workers cut the eyeholes while the head is still soft greenware. They are then sent to the ovens for baking, and are baked at a temperature of 1500 degrees. They are only heads and necks, no pates.

"The pates are made of cork. Before the cork is attached, the eyes have to be inserted. Using a pair of pinchers, a blow pipe and sticks of enamel [glass] of different colors the worker picks up the enamel with the pinchers and brings it near the flame, which comes from the blow pipe. Agilely turning and twisting the pinchers the enamel becomes incandescent and slowly takes the shape of an eye. The worker takes care that it does not cool before he places the colored parts of the eye which make up the iris and pupil thus giving life to the eye. The white mass is softened in the flame and in the center a bit of blue, brown or black is placed. The finished eye is placed in the eye socket. The agile and expert workers each produce 400 to 500 pairs of eyes in a day and from 100 to 120 pairs if they make the more complicated eyes called 'Fibres' [paperweight]. In addition the workers also produce 240,000 or 300,000 black eyes for bébés each year. According to the price of the doll, the eyes are painted on the porcelain head at the same time as the cheeks and lips or they are the enamel eyes as described above. The better eyes are movable by a counterweight and the best eyes called 'Vivants' [living] move in all directions and are operated by a spring at the back of the doll. After the eyes are put into the head, it is closed with a cork pate.

"Next the heads are painted and a different worker paints each part of the face. Each worker always uses the same color for the same feature, never varying it. The method is like a production line. . . . There are no waste movements; the same rapidity of execution is found among the wig makers, some of whom work in a special workshop and others work at home.

"The ones at home work alone or with assistants and they supply the large factories or the small shops, especially the repair shops. Wigs come in all colors, straw blondes, auburn blondes, red or brown, carrot colored or black as ebony. There are even albino wigs that are all white. The luxury wigs are made of human hair. Medium grades are of silk and the cheapest are of mohair. The mohair comes in bales that are divided into locks of hair. These are rolled on spools, washed, then boiled, dried in a stove, curled, sewed on cloth foundation or on nets and finally nailed or glued to the cork pate. Supplied with their wigs the heads are finished as blonde heads, brunette heads with curled hair, plaited hair, waved hair, well combed or disordered. They go to the repair shops or are put on the type of bodies for which their price fits them. Some dolls have moving heads articulated at the neck in the same manner as the limbs are articulated. Those with immovable heads have the heads glued onto a piece of wood which extends from the inside of the body. . . .

"But the dolls that we have described so far are medium priced ones. The rare dolls are those that talk and walk, which necessitates numerous additional operations. They need bellows, springs, valves, air boxes which must be mounted carefully in the stomach of the doll so that it can say 'Papa and Mama' or to put the mechanism inside the doll so that it can walk or throw kisses.

"The popular doll which has articulated arms and legs and is provided with stationary or sleeping eyes is not finished when the wig is placed on the head. It lacks only a chemise before being sent to the distributors. This chemise is cut, assembled and sewn at the factory. The dolls generally also have shoes and stockings. The shoes have uppers of leather, two soles, buttonholes, flaps, ribbons and are all quilted and sewn. The doll will often be more luxuriously shod than its mother.

"Far more elegant than many little girls are the expensive dolls with lace trimmed chemises, drawers and petticoats; embroidered dresses of silk, surah taffeta, satin, voile, percale or wool; hats trimmed with ribbons, flowers and conspicuous plumes. When they leave their couturiers the dolls are so attractive that it is difficult to recall their beginnings. However, these various steps are performed in all the big and little factories, even in the prisons where cheap handwork is available and dolls are made in large quantities. The prison at la Santé and some provincial prisons make dolls.

"At the S.F.B.J. factory 25 to 30 people worked on each doll. They included the sculptor, the mold maker, the one who filled the molds, the one who removed the greenware from the mold, the people who put the heads on trays to go into the ovens, the people who put them into the ovens, the cooks who man the ovens, the painters of the background colors, the painters of the various features of the face, the eye makers, the finishers, the turners who prepared the wooden parts, the molders who made the body, hands and limbs, the joiners who finished the parts, the dippers who colored the parts, the varnishers who varnished the parts, the assemblers who strung the dolls with rubber, the wig makers, the hair dressers who put the wigs on the dolls, the dressmakers, the shoemakers, the dressers who put the chemise and footwear on the bébés and the packers who put the dolls in boxes.

"The wages of molders, painters, weighers, dressers, etc., in the factories were 6 to 10 francs per day before the War. In 1924 wages are 4 or 5 times the 1914 ones. In 1914 people worked 10 hours, in 1924 they worked 8 hours a day. The profit on a doll costing 25 francs is less in 1924 than it was on a doll costing 6 francs before the war. There are almost no labor troubles in the doll factories."

[The above translation is not literal in some instances in order to make it more comprehensible.]

Manufacture of Dolls, Commercial: Made in France, Cloth Dolls.

In 1924 Pierre Calmette in LES JOUJOUX discussed the manufacturing of cloth dolls in France: "The ultra modern dolls are made of tricot cloth. They have amusing and more lively heads than the porcelain ones. These heads are made with a mask of silky fabric made like the cardboard masks, with the aide of hollow molds. After molding they are dried, stiffened, painted, then placed on top of the body. But these are only faces, a large wig must cover the joining of the mask and the body. In order to avoid this joining the manufacturers have devised a method of pulling the tricot in such a way as to look good even without hair.

"Half heads or whole heads, they are carefully painted so that each doll has a slightly different face. The eyes have a very amusing unruly expression and these dolls have superiority to all others, their heads are works of art and unbreakable."

1759. Bisque head doll manufactured in France. It has stationary blue glass eyes, pierced ears, open mouth with teeth, and a fully jointed composition body. Mark on head: "Tête Jumeau." Mark on body: "JUMEAU//DIPLOME d' HONNEUR." H. 20½ in. (52 cm.). *Courtesy of Sotheby Parke Bernet Inc., N.Y.*

1758. Bisque head Bébé Teteur manufactured by Bru in France. It has a wig, stationary brown glass eyes, pierced ears, open mouth into which a bottle nipple will fit, bisque shoulder plate, bisque lower arms, kid body, and wooden lower legs. Marked: "Bru Jne. 6." H. 15 in. (38 cm.). *Courtesy of Sotheby Parke Bernet Inc., N.Y.*

1760. Bisque socket head doll manufactured in France by the Société Française de Fabrication de Bébés & Jouets (S.F.B.J.). It has a poured bisque head with wig, stationary blue glass eyes, open mouth, and a fully jointed composition body. Mark: "S.F.B.J.//238//4." H. 15 in. (38 cm.). *Courtesy of Sotheby Parke Bernet Inc., N.Y.*

Manufacture of Dolls, Commercial: Made in France and Germany, Compared.

In the REVUE DES DEUX MONDES, for May 15, 1915, George d'Avenel wrote an article entitled "Jouets Française Contre Jouets Allemande" ("French Toys Compared with German Toys"): "Those who played with dolls prior to 1873 had to imagine that their doll was a baby since it was shaped and dressed as a young girl or a lady. In 1873 M. Jumeau perfected a true bébé with a child's figure. This bébé had a porcelain head and a molded cardboard body. The body had hollow wooden parts into which ball joints were juxtapositioned. The hands were made of a composition derived from silicate of potash mixed with glue and sawdust. Carrier Belleuse sculptured the model of an artistic head for M. Jumeau. At the 1889 Paris Exposition these dolls were awarded the highest honors for their quality but not for their price. The fact that the Bébé Jumeau was expensive increased competition which was heavily felt especially after 1890. French exports to the United States diminished by half in some years, while the Germans made similar but much cheaper dolls in order to lessen the effect of the raising of the McKinley Tariffs. The Germans also made lighter weight dolls than the French in order to circumvent the French laws of 1892 which imposed a duty of $12 per 220 pounds.

"France still monopolized the luxury bébé trade but few of these expensive bébés were sold and the German bébés were the popular dolls because of their cheaper price. In 1899 the principal manufacturers in Paris joined together and formed the Société Française de Fabrication de Bébés & Jouets [S.F.B.J.]. Prior to this the expenses of all these firms, except one, had absorbed nearly all of their profits. With the joining of the group, rents, patents, travel and various other expenses, that had burdened the individual companies, became less of a problem. Skillfully directed, the S.F.B.J. has doubled its business over the past fifteen years [1899–1914]. Today [late 1914 or early 1915] they have a five million Franc [one million dollar] business with 2,000 workers and a dividend of 8 or 9 percent. In spite of this progress the S.F.B.J. is still dependent on Germany for much of its raw material and parts. In 1913 its imports from Germany amounted to a million Francs [$200,000]. However patriotic the French manufacturers are and even if they decide to import nothing from Germany, they will not be able to sell their products in Paris at the same price as the Germans. The most patriotic distributors will be constrained to withdraw their clientele because they themselves will be unable to sell the merchandise. . . .

"The S.F.B.J. uses more than 300,000 pounds of sized cardboard in the body casting molds. This costs nearly a third less in Germany than in France. Formerly one worker made 24 bodies of bébés per hour. Now one machine makes 400 bodies in the same time. They are turned out with perfect details and are strong enough to bear the weight of a man standing on them. This machine was originally a Bavarian model but it was so well improved by the factory at Montreuil that it could stamp and finish both sides of the doll with one stroke. When the German armies threatened to swoop down on Paris last August, the precaution of dismantling this machine was taken so that the Germans could not discover its secrets.

"The wooden parts with which only bébés of a certain price can expect to be endowed, are composed of eleven pieces and come from l'Ain and la Nievre. Mere composition bébés have their arms and legs made in a mold from a mixture of potatoes, rice, wood flour and other mysterious substances. They are worked up in huge machines which turn the arms and legs out twenty at a time, hollow within and well modelled on the outside. They then pass through the stove for drying. The output of five and a half million of these bébés and soldiers a year at the Montempoivre factory is imposing numerically but of small value.

"However large are the numbers of composition dolls, rubber dolls, non-inflamable celluloid or metal dolls, none of these will be able to replace the bisque heads since most of them have the disadvantage that in time they will warp and peel.

"During the past 15 years the S.F.B.J. have replaced the old Jumeau oven of 2 meters [6½ feet] with two ovens of six meters [19½ feet] which hold thirty thousand ceramic heads at a time on the earthen gazettes. They are presently in the process of constructing a third oven. All porcelain is composed of kaolin, an unctuous element that is unfusible and gives plasticity; of feldspar which is fusible at a high temperature and gives the transparency; and of quartz or black silica which is neither plastic nor fusible but permits the change into a solid substance. If too much feldspar is used the object becomes deformed and with too much kaolin it has a yellowish tint. Each manufacturer adds other ingredients which remain secret. Dolls' heads are cast as slip into molds, and because of the liquid state the amount of silica must be adjusted to avoid shrinkage and to keep the adherence to the mold. The procedure is based on the property possessed by a dry plaster mold to absorb the water in the slip and thus form the walls of the object in the desired shape. The excess slip is then poured off.

"One worker is able to cast 1200 to 1500 heads a day and although this slip is more expensive than that of dinnerware, hopefully we must not fear our rivals. The manufacturers working in Germany have certain advantages. One of the most popular businesses in Sonneberg belongs to a French family which migrated to that area around 1830 [no substantiation for a date this early has yet been found but the reference is possibly to the Marseille family.] The kaolin in the Sonneberg area cooks at 200 degrees less than the French kaolin, a fact that affords considerable economy in the use of fuel in the furnaces. The extra cost of the fuel for the 200 degrees can be likened to the fact that in the boilers of steamships it is necessary to double the force of the machines in order to increase the speed only a few kilometers. The very high temperature above a certain degree requires the consumption of coal entirely disproportionate to the additional heat obtained. The S. F. B. J. cook their heads at 1200 degrees for 20 hours. Not only is coal expensive in France but also are salaries. It seems to be of little consequence to pay a renowned artist $200 for a beautifully modelled head that does not please the child customers as much as a head sculptured by a simple factory worker. The little girls themselves are the judges and their approval is sovereign.

"The bébé's head before as well as after cooking must

pass through the hands of a dozen workers. They perform the cleaning, the removal of seams, the opening of the mouth and eyes and the scooping out behind the eyes where the porcelain must not be more than a millimeter (.04 inches) in thickness. This is difficult work but necessary so that the eyes do not squint.

"The teeth for the fine heads are sculptured and enameled. Those for the common heads are usually placed five at a time. A good woman worker can fill 1,200 jaws a day for which she is paid 5 cents a hundred. In Germany the placing of the teeth is performed twice as quickly because it is done by cutting a band of molded teeth without worrying whether they are placed correctly. When the heads come from the ovens they are painted including the pink cheeks, red lips and interior of the nostrils as well as the dark eyebrows and eyelashes.

"Fifty years ago [1865] the eyes were made of enameled porcelain, twenty-five years ago [1890] they were made of plain glass [This is refuted by the "Jumeau Story" written in 1885]. Today both common eyes and fine ones are made by a special method of fabrication. In deep darkness the workers sit side by side each having a blow-pipe that is activated or subsided by the workers as required. The end of a tube of opal glass is presented to the blue gas flame. The tube lengthens in the flame and turns red. The worker blows immediately the other end of the tube and thus obtains a round ball which becomes the cornea of the eye. Into this ball is fused a stalk of heated colored glass to form the black or blue pupil of the eye. Scissors cut the globe from the tube and the eye falls into a basket. This is a common eye which can be made in any color but will not have the advantage of moving. Fine eyes for the expensive dolls have both mobility and are endowed with tiny threads so that they resemble human eyes more closely. . . . These threads are created by applying 8 rays of opaque white glass on a small stick of transparent crystal. This is turned into a paste by heat, stretched and placed on the pupil.

"In the eye-making workshop at Montreuil fifteen years ago three workers produced some dozens of pairs of eyes per day. At present 14,000 eyes per week are made, most of them the fine type. Both the common types of eyes and the common porcelain heads are sold to Paris manufacturers by German firms because they can be produced in Germany for about half the cost. The attempts to make eyes mechanically in France have not been successful. At Lauscha in Thuringia where eyes are made in homes, the children almost seem to be born with a blow-pipe in their hands. The children earn money thus from their earliest years. The women earn only 1 mark 50 [37¢] a day out of which they must pay for the gas and raw materials. Their net wages for their labor is less than 20 cents. Before sticking these eyes in the interior of a head it is necessary to match a pair and to choose them carefully because almost every head differs slightly. The eyes can vary in the making process and only a hundredth of a millimeter will produce eyes that appear to squint or to look wild, either cross-eyed or wall-eyed. At one time the sleeping bébés were supplied with a complicated mechanism. The Germans invented the use of a counter weight of lead with the eyes held in plaster sockets so they could seesaw automatically. This method has been adopted everywhere, instead of

the eyelid being lowered, the eye turns and seems to shut because the upper part of the orb is painted in skin color.

"In place of a pate [this does not appear to be the cork pate] which has no useful purpose the bébé will be coiffed with a cap of nansook on which the hair is glued. In Germany the wig is bought already made. In France the S.F.B.J. make their own wigs. The most expensive wigs are made in small numbers using Chinese hair bought at Marseille where it is drawn thinner and dyed. The medium quality wigs are of mohair, that is the hair of the Tibetan goat. The cheapest wigs are made of ordinary wool. The S.F.B.J. factory consumes over twenty-two tons of these three kinds each year.

"The hair is first carefully weighed, allowing 15 grams [about ½ ounce] per head, then it is combed and passed on to the 'tress dresser' and finally to the person who arranges the hair. This work is paid for by the piece and it is surprising to see the rapidity with which the combs disentangle, the scissors cut and the hammer nails down the curls of this demoiselle.

"For the boys a machine places the mohair in clumps of one or two millimeters [.04 or .08 inch] on their heads which have first been coated with a glue imported from Germany. Analysis of this glue has thus far not revealed its secret production. Then the hair is brushed or raised so that it stands on end by another machine with compressed air. After this the male bébé is a faithful image of Champignol after his passage through the military shearing machine [this is flocked hair].

"The doll enters the world not only naked but in a score of pieces. After inspection its limbs are gone over by a manicurist and pedicurist who with a brush or scissors remedy any apparent defects. Before being supplied with a wig, the heads in the assembling workshops had been placed on torsos to which arms and legs were affixed by means of interior wire hooks and rubber elastic.

"The costume accounts for almost half of the price for the doll and requires a multitude of workers. Houses of shoemakers working only for dolls, furnish leather boots and gaiters as well as satin slippers in various shades. There is a great amount of difference in the costumes depending on price, from a doll costing $16 or more and dressed with the best and most expensive layette with many accessories to the wooden bébé with painted hair wearing a muslin chemise like a poultice. At the S.F.B.J. there are 200 chemise makers earning about $1.65 to $2.00. The better chemises are made of silk or fine French muslin trimmed with lace. The chemises are cut out in quantity with a saw. The slippers for the dolls in chemises are made of blue or rose paper bordered with nansook sewed by hand and ornamented with nickel metal buckles. . . . Their price is only 3 cents per pair. . . . The great majority of the dolls are unable to afford much for their toilette. They are limited by the declining international economy. During the past sixteen years the average price of a bébé has fallen by half. At retail, prices begin at less than 20 cents but the greatest number are sold at 30 cents and 50 cents. The 30 cent dolls cost the wholesaler 20 cents and for this amount he receives a doll 20 centimeters [8 inches] high with a porcelain head, sleeping eyes, the body jointed at the neck, knees, hands and feet [sic] and wearing a hood and jacket of black velvet, underclothes, shoes and stockings.

These German mignonnettes varied from $1.00 to $4.00 a dozen and sold by the millions. Not a single Frenchman has been able to meet this competition as yet. The clothes on these dolls were extremely cheap but it is because of the cheaper porcelain heads (costing 30¢ a dozen postpaid in Paris) that these mignonnettes avoided competition and the agents in Fürth and Nürnberg triumphed. Despite reproaches for buying these cheap dolls no one is able to abstain from selling them and have thus driven some of the French manufacturers out of business. Moreover, the porcelain makers of Limoges do not show any great haste in coming out of their routine apathy regarding the making of dolls' heads. Let us hope that the S.F.B.J. due to their experience and extensive resources will profit by the war to enable them to put a French mignonnette on the market."

Manufacture of Dolls, Commercial: Made in Germany.

The success of any industry depended on the availability of skilled workmen, fuel and the raw materials that were required. Thüringia and adjacent Northern Bavaria had a plentiful supply of all of these elements needed in the manufacture of porcelain dolls' heads.

Forests abounded in Thüringia and from early times the inhabitants had achieved skills in making wooden dolls. But the wood also served to provide fuel for the large kilns of the porcelain factories. Thus both skilled workmen requiring reasonable wages and a convenient source of fuel were readily available as well as necessary raw materials to produce porcelain dolls.

According to GERMAN AND AUSTRIAN PORCELAIN, a book written by a porcelain collector named George Ware after World War II, Thuringia and the surrounding area were far richer in all of the raw materials required to produce porcelain than any other area in Europe. Here were rich deposits of kaolin, feldspar and quartz.

Kaolin is a white clay-like substance that withstands very high temperatures and does not discolor in the firing but fuses very slowly or is non-fusible. Feldspar is a group of crystal minerals found in nearly all crystalline rocks. It is usually white or pinkish in color. Quartz is a form of silica, the most common of all solid minerals. The feldspar and quartz under high temperatures form a fusible glass and act as a flux. A flux promotes the melting and fusion of metals and minerals. The more kaolin, the harder the porcelain is. Hard paste porcelain is less transparent than soft paste porcelain and more transparent than stone bisque. Hard paste porcelain cannot be scratched with a steel knife while soft-paste porcelain is not only more transparent but also softer. Hard paste porcelain is more resonant than soft paste porcelain. The French were more likely to use the soft-paste porcelain than the Germans who generally used a hard paste. Bisque usually has slightly more feldspar than china. Stone bisque has less feldspar and kaolin, more quartz and other ingredients are added. Flint, a very hard quartz, is often used for stoneware. In addition stoneware is not fired to quite as high a temperature as true porcelain.

Porcelain is generally made from about half kaolin and a quarter each of quartz and feldspar. Pegmatite, also plentiful in Thüringia, was sometimes substituted for the quartz and feldspar in lower grades of porcelain. Often other minor ingredients were added and many companies had secret formulas which they carefully preserved.

The above ingredients after being carefully washed were pulverized and mixed together to form a paste. For bisque the ingredients were ground to a finer texture than for china or stone bisque. Excess water was pressed out of the paste and then it was formed into cakes which were stored in cellars for about a year. The cellars kept these cakes at a low temperature and proper humidity. After the necessary aging the dough-like cakes were ready for molding.

In the nineteenth century the porcelain paste was actually rolled out like dough and then pressed into the molds. The rough insides of a doll's head and the lack of uniform thickness reveal the fact that the paste was rolled out and the head was pressed rather than poured. Towards the end of the nineteenth century it was discovered that by adding water to the paste, slip was formed which could be poured into the molds. Poured dolls' heads have smooth interiors and are of uniform thickness. Sometimes remnants of bubbles are visible. In general poured heads are after about 1870 but for some years thereafter both methods were used. *Jumeau* did not change from pressed to poured until about 1890.

The molds, made of plaster of Paris, absorbed the water contained in the paste in a short time, thus permitting the dough-paste to shrink away from the mold without changing its shape. When slip was used the plaster of Paris molds were filled with slip which hardened next to the walls of the mold and then the remaining slip was poured off. Most of the molds for dolls' heads were two-part, but some of the more elaborate heads required three or even more parts. These parts after being removed from the mold were joined together with a thin slip paste, surplus slip was removed and necessary refinements made in the greenware. The head before it was fired was called "greenware." This must then have been allowed further drying prior to being taken in clay saggers (trays) to the kilns for firing. The decorations on some of the heads were not molded but put on by hand in the greenware stage.

After the first high temperature firing the heads were decorated and/or glazed. In the twentieth century *decalcomanias* and/or stencils were frequently used for some of the features on bisque dolls' heads. On glazed (china) heads only a few colors could be used successfully under the glaze. The decorations were usually fused in or on the glaze during the second firing.

Ordinarily the porcelain heads were fired twice or more but bisque heads can be made with only one firing; when this is done the paint will wash off, a circumstance that happily does not often occur. For very fine quality, highly decorated porcelain heads three or more firings were needed.

The method of making porcelain dolls' heads was about the same wherever they were produced but certainly the greatest number were made in Germany.

In 1893 OUR LITTLE MEN AND WOMEN explained the process of making Porcelain heads as follows: "The clay heads are then put into great ovens. Sometimes five thousands are put into a single oven, and there are great doll factories in Germany that have thirty of these immense ovens all going at the same time.

"When the ovens are full the furnaces are set at work, and for seven days and nights the fires are kept up to turn the clay into china. Every moment they are watched with the greatest care—all day and all night—for the slightest mistake will spoil everyone. And after all this care it often happens that only one in five comes out a perfect china doll's head."

LESLIE'S ILLUSTRATED WEEKLY NEWSPAPER in 1912 stated: "Parts of all dolls are imported from Germany, for that country has a monopoly on the heads and the factories all over the world depend on the German factories for their supply of this part of the dolls." It is difficult to believe that this was entirely true, but it certainly indicates that Germany was the principal source. Moreover, most of the German factories making porcelain dolls were in Thuringia and Northern Bavaria.

TOYS AND NOVELTIES in May 1915 described the making of bisque-head dolls in Germany prior to World War I:

"The beautiful imported dolls with real hair, sleeping eyes, etc., which are so common in every toy store, are made principally in factories scattered throughout Germany. It is a more or less common belief that all German dolls are made in the homes, but though a large portion of the routine labor is accomplished in this manner, all the important steps are done by machinery or skilled labor in the factories, themselves. Uniformity in a product is one of the primary requisites, and it would be impossible to obtain sufficiently symmetrical results, were the work not controlled by an organized factory. Let us take one of the better grades of imported dolls from the shelf and see how its various parts are made and assembled.

"The head of this particular doll is composed of bisque, a porcelain-like clay which is found in large deposits throughout Germany, and it was formed in a steel mould [The use of steel for the porcelain mold seems unlikely] at some factory. The moulds and machinery for turning out doll heads represent a very large investment of money, and since the profits depend in a large part on quantity, moulding is seldom if ever done in the home.

"This head, with many others exactly like it, was then sent out to some family in a nearby district, where the eyes were inserted, eyebrows, lips, nose, etc., painted and the cheeks tinted by skilled workers who have spent their entire lives doing these special operations and nothing more. The eyes and paints are all supplied by the factory and a very remarkable degree of uniformity is attained in this manner. The wigs of long beautiful hair, which are next glued to the head, are often made at the home by other skilled workers, but in many instances of expensive dolls, even these are made in a factory.

"The limbs which are jointed at elbows, wrists and knees, are composed of papier-mâché or a similar composition, and these parts too are all moulded or pressed with steel dies in a factory. Each part is then dipped in a flesh color paint, and when dry they are sent out to the homes to be assembled. The cloth which forms the shell of the body is all machine cut in a factory, though the shell itself is sewed up and stuffed with sawdust, cork or a similar material, in the homes. The various parts, that is head, limbs and body, are then sent to still other homes where they are completely assembled and finishing touches put on. In the meantime, other families have been making dresses, hats, etc., from the machine cut materials sent to them, and in these homes the finished doll is finally dressed and forwarded to the factory for packing and shipping.

"The wages received by these home workers are very low compared to our American standards, an entire family of father, mother and four or five children often receiving but 50 or 60 marks ($12.50 to $15.00) per week, and since through long practice they become very proficient, a very large amount of work is accomplished at an exceedingly low cost. The United States consumes about $1,750,000 worth of imported dolls every year, almost all of which come from Germany."

Some of the statements in this account are suspect. Porcelain-like clay is not found throughout Germany but only in certain areas. The use of steel molds and the painting of the heads in the homes without additional firing sounds as though the description has turned from bisque heads to composition heads. The reference to cloth bodies also suggests this confusion.

The above article was also published in 1917 in the British Periodical THE TOYSHOP AND FANCY GOODS JOURNAL, plus the following additional paragraphs.

"Few people realized the immensity of the capital and organization that go to—and are absolutely necessary to—the production of dolls, and that to produce them in perfection, and the different sizes, at least five factories are required. To the uninitiated this sounds preposterous, but is nevertheless true, viz.:

1. Bodies of stuffed dolls—all sizes.
2. Arms, heads, and legs. Compo.
3. Wigs, all sizes, and light and dark; with eyelashes.
4. Arms, heads, and legs. China [Bisque].
5. Heads. Compo.
6. Elastic of varying strengths; for stringing jointed dolls.
7. The factory for fitting, tinting and finishing off. . . .

"One has to admit that they [Germans] did excel in doll-making over all other countries."★

1761. Manufacture of dolls' heads in Germany. This picture shows various pouring molds and a worker pouring slip into one of these molds. Both rabbits and dolls are shown in the greenware. Two of the Kewpie-type dolls appear to have been fired. Under the shelf it looks as if there are broken pieces. *Courtesy of the Museum of the City of Neustadt near Coburg.*

1762. This picture shows dolls' heads stacked on trays in a German doll factory. The men in the foreground appear to be cutting out the eyes but it is possible that they are painting the eyes. This picture was probably taken before World War I. *Courtesy of the Museum of the City of Neustadt near Coburg.*

1763. Steps in manufacturing bisque head dolls in Germany. The men on the left are assembling the dolls. The men on the right in the back are painting the composition bodies which can be seen drying on sticks. *Courtesy of the Museum of the City of Neustadt near Coburg.*

1764. Dressing bisque head dolls of various types in Germany prior to World War I. In the background can be seen girls making dolls' clothes with sewing machines. *Courtesy of the Museum of the City of Neustadt near Coburg.*

1765. A china shoulder head probably made in Germany has a china glaze but has not been painted as yet. This head will need to be fired once again at a lower temperature than previous firings so that the colors will not come off. H. of shoulder head 5 in. (12.5 cm.). *Coleman Collection.*

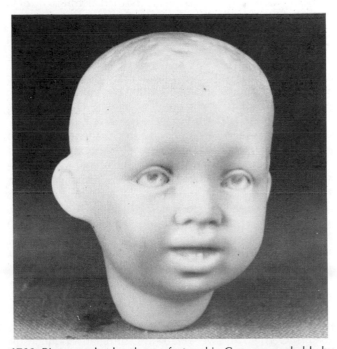

1766. Bisque socket head manufactured in Germany probably by Th. Recknagel. This all-white head has the features of a black boy but is entirely white without any painting. It has been through the first firing to become bisque but it has not been painted or had subsequent firings. Two teeth show in the open-closed mouth. Mark: Ill. 2181. H. of head only, 2 in. (5 cm.). *Coleman Collection. Gift of the Ciesliks.*

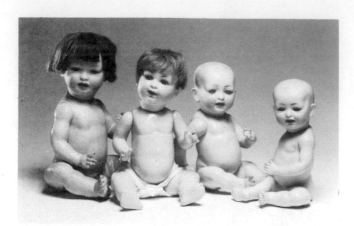

1767. Bisque socket head baby doll manufactured in Germany. These dolls have five-piece bent limb composition bodies popular from 1910 through the 1920s. The heads have wigs or painted hair, sleeping blue glass eyes, an open mouth with teeth except for the doll on the right which has an open-closed mouth. The positioning of the fingers and toes varies among the dolls. Left to right the marks are: "8½,"; "980 A 2 M" (Armand Marseille); "151"; and "2 141." Left to right the hs. are: 16 in. (40.5 cm.); 13½ in. (34 cm.); 12 in. (30.5 cm.); and 11 in. (28 cm.). *Courtesy of Sotheby Parke Bernet Inc., N.Y.*

Manufacture of Dolls, Commercial: Made in Germany in Sonneberg Region.

Ca. 1900 a Stereoptican card by Underwood & Underwood described workers dressing dolls in Sonneberg, Thür, as follows:

"It is not a particularly good farming district, and large numbers of people here abouts have for many generations earned their living by working . . . in small factories . . . or in their homes. As usual in such cases, Sonneberg people have a specialty—it is work in papier-mâché. The doll business is one of its most important applications.

"The work is systematically divided. Certain workers mould the heads, bodies, arms and legs; others paint them; others put the parts together. Certain employes do nothing all day but fasten bright eyes into empty sockets; others made wigs; the adjusting of the wigs is a separate job.

"If one is inclined to criticize the quality of the workmanship put into these flimsy undergarments and gay frocks and hats, it should be remembered that the girls who make the wardrobes work twelve hours a day for (usually) less than three cents an hour.

"Living expenses are not small in proportion; these women and girls have difficult problems to meet. But they have never known any easier life, so they take it as it comes, make the best of it, and get a good deal of pleasure out of small opportunities.

"These finished dolls are largely for export. Some are sold direct to foreign buyers, some through commission agents in the large Prussian cities."

PLAYTHINGS in February, 1908, reported: "Although the first German toys were made in Thüringian Mountains, it was the city of Nuremberg that first became known to the world at large as the home of toyland. However, in the seventeenth century the Thüringian toy industry again became independent and sought its own markets. Since then

its development has been in giant strides. Toward the close of the eighteenth century the discovery of the 'taig,' a dough composed of black flour, glue and water, and used for modeling dolls' bodies and figures, revolutionized the industry. Of still greater importance was the discovery of papier-mâché, in 1820, by a Sonneberg modeler.

"The doll-manufacturing industry did not begin to assume conspicuous proportions until 1850. Before that time only wood and leather were used in this trade. At the time of the first London World's Fair a Sonneberg doll manufacturer [See *Lindner*] brought home and improved a Chinese doll, made of heavy colored paper, and with movable head and limbs [See *Täuflinge*]. Next came hairless wax heads. To begin with, the wax and varnish were put on the prepared head with a brush in a more or less crude or uneven manner, whereby the face was left expressionless. A thimble, so the story goes, one day fell into a dish of fluid wax. When its owner drew it forth it was found to be beautifully covered with a uniform coating of wax. The manufacturer caught the idea and established a factory for wax papier-mâché dolls prepared by the dipping process. By giving the papier-mâché a flesh tint, and through the use of wheat powder, he attained a very good imitation of the human skin. Painting completed the process of facial expression. Next came the setting of artificial eyes, which are principally made in the little town of Lauscha. These eyes soon were made movable, and the result was a sleeping doll. But the hairless head had to be improved. Human hair was originally used, but the discovery of mohair wigs opened up large possibilities in this line, as the fine, glossy hair of the Angora goat was found to be unsurpassable for this purpose. When mohair grew more expensive wool was added. In rapid succession there followed further inventions and discoveries until the modern life-like, jointed speaking doll was the result.

"At the head of this industry are the large exporting houses, both German and foreign, doing business directly with merchants in all quarters of the globe. They correspond in all modern languages, and are organized on the most approved modern style. Some of them do a commission business almost exclusively, gathering up the toys in small lots, packing and shipping them, and doing little or no manufacturing business themselves.

"Next in rank are found smaller exporter and manufacturers doing some foreign business directly, and delivering also to the great exporting houses. These vary from large and wealthy establishments to lesser factories handling but small quantities. There are, of course, houses which confine themselves exclusively to manufacturing. The output of many of the factories is entirely or in large part controled by some of the big exporters."

McCALL'S MAGAZINE, December, 1910, published an article about Sonneberg dolls entitled, "Where Toys Come From" by Brunson Clark. According to this article the composition dolls made in Sonneberg were: "the best dolls in all Germany. One of the largest factories sends to America over one million dolls a year and it possesses a secret formula for making the powder from which the enamel paint used on papier-mâché dolls is manufactured.

"All these dolls are made in practically the same way. First the papier-mâché, in the form of a more or less dirty paste, is kneaded in a trough almost as bread is kneaded, until it reaches the proper consistency. Then it is put to one side to cool, and as soon as it is ready it is put into different machines and dolls' hands and sometimes also arms and legs are stamped out of it.

"It would certainly come near to breaking the heart of any especially tender-hearted little girl to stand in front of one of these machines while it was running at full speed and have her see a continuous stream of tiny hands pouring out of it. I don't know exactly why but they look so pitiful and helpless, these miniature hands, almost as if they had been cut off of something alive.

"The heads are always made in molds; the paste is reduced to a liquid form and then is poured from curious German pitchers with sharp-pointed noses into plaster molds. . . . Legs and arms are molded exactly like the dolls' heads. When the new-made doll's head first emerges from its chrysalis it is not a pleasing object to view. It is all uneven and ragged-looking from the rough surface of the mold and the empty eye sockets stare gruesomely at you. The first thing done is to trim off the ragged edges and paint the whole head a bright flesh color. It is then set on one side to dry until the next day, when the eyebrows are painted on, the cheeks tinted and the bright red lips brought out with a scarlet paint. This work is done by women, who, from long practice, are exceedingly expert, and are able to give Miss Dolly her complexion, lips and eyebrows with scarcely more than 'a twist of the wrist.'

"When this is finished the head is once more set aside to dry, when it is ready for the eyes to be put in. These are the most difficult part of the doll to manufacture. And it is a curious fact that different countries like different colored eyes in their dolls. For instance, the majority of the little girls in Italy, France and Spain have dark-brown or black eyes, so the dollies intended for those countries are made with dark eyes. America on the other hand, likes the bulk of her dolls blue-eyed, though she also imports a few dark-eyed beauties in case any of her fair daughters prefer that kind. England likes blue-eyed dolls with flaxen hair, as the typical English beauty is a blond.

"Miss Dolly's head is now complete with the exception of her wig. This, whether golden or dark brown, is curled and arranged in the very latest fashions for doll children. . . .

"Next the completed head must be sewed to a body, for even the smallest doll mother knows that a head without a body is no use at all, so in another department of the factory the doll's body is cut out and stuffed with hair, excelsior, cotton or sawdust, according to whether she is to be a cheap or expensive doll lady.

"She is now complete, except her costume. If she is to start on her travels properly dressed she is at once taken to the dressmaking department of the factory, where she is fitted out with underclothes, stockings and shoes, a dress, and often a coat and hat besides, all in the very latest fashion. Other dolls are clad only in a coarse cotton chemise and sent out in the world to be clothed by their future purchasers."

LESLIE'S ILLUSTRATED WEEKLY NEWSPAPER, December 5, 1912, described the making of composition dolls in Germany:

"Away up in the forests of Thuringia and Bavaria, men, women and children are working day after day fashioning dolls—dolls of every description, which will be shipped to . . . America. . . . Many of these dolls are the products of the cottage industry, for hundreds of them are made in the homes of the peasants. They are not as fine and beautiful, perhaps, as those which are turned out in the large factories; but they are nevertheless unique in many ways, and their very quaintness is attractive to the restless little American who, like the grown-ups of the present day, is ever longing for something new—something different. . . .

"In Sonneberg the greater part of the population is engaged in this industry, and it is the chief source of revenue for the town and gives employment to whole families during the entire year.

"The making of the composition dolls as seen in the German factories is an interesting process, even though some of the rooms are hot, steamy places where one does not care to stay long at a time. First, there is the kneading-room, where a big mixing trough is set up, and in this all sorts of rag-bag materials are found—old gloves, rags, bits of cardboard, etc., and gum tragacanth. This mixture is kneaded by hand to the consistency of paste, heated and carried into the mold-room. There it is dipped up by women and poured into the patterns, which are set up in rows. The molds are put away until they are cold enough to handle, when a workman, by a dexterous movement of his hands, separates the leaden sides, and the doll's head is revealed. The polisher then trims off the ragged seams and sends the heads to another room, where the holes for the eyes are cut out. This is an extremely delicate task, as all the sockets must be of uniform size. The work is done by hand, a long sharp knife being used.

"The heads are next painted, waxed or glazed, depending upon the character of the material from which they are made. The arms, legs and hands are molded in the same manner as the heads—a special machine being used for stamping out the hands. These parts are painted in flesh color, while the heads must have rosy cheeks, red lips and dark or light eyebrows, as the color of the eyes used may require. Putting in the eyes is a simple operation, unless the eyes are to open and shut, in which case the balancing of the lead becomes a matter of skill. Germany possesses a secret formula for the enamel used on the faces, and the dainty natural flesh tint of the better grade of dolls is the result of this process. The making of the eyes is a dreary task, for it must be done away from the sunlight, and in some parts of Germany the eye makers work in the cellars. It is said that one town [Lauscha] supplies three-fourths of all the dolls' eyes used. Violet is the most difficult color to mix, and few violet-eyed dolls are found.

"The wig is the final touch, and this is usually made of real hair imported from China. The hair used for blonde dolls is the same, except that the color is extracted. The assembling of the parts is often very complicated, as the best jointed dolls have a stout elastic cord on the inside, to which the movable parts are attached. The bodies are stuffed with shavings of cork, sawdust, excelsior or cotton, and the arms and legs must be sewed in place with precision, or a crippled doll would be the result. The entire work demands practice and skill, both of which are acquired early in life by the workers. . . .

"Germany . . . has made rapid strides in the perfection of

the doll, and as far back as 1851 there was a school for the purpose of teaching the art of coloring the faces, and the beautiful, lifelike baby dolls, with faces painted from living models, are the work of some of its pupils."

TOYS AND NOVELTIES, January 1913, reported: "Thuringia, perhaps, furnishes the greatest number [of dolls] for in that province whole families are engaged in the industry. There is a sort of unwritten law that doll making is hereditary in certain families and the greatest secrecy is maintained by these families as to some of the formulas used in coloring, wig making, etc. Sonneberg, a little German city in Thuringia, contains several large factories where a small army of men, women and children are employed—in fact, the doll making industry is the source of revenue for the entire population of the town. The factories there use a certain kind of enamel which gives a beautiful life-like appearance to the faces of the dolls. The formula is the work of a German chemist who discovered it after many experiments and it is known only to a few of the employees who guard the knowledge of its ingredients with the greatest secrecy.

"Some of the very best dolls are made in Sonneberg, too, for there is an academy of design where the children are taught modeling and coloring by artists. The school was established in 1851 and its model room contains many excellent pieces of sculpture and rare old prints. Modelling dolls is no easy task, and it is remarkable what perfect figures the students of this school are able to turn out. Moulds are made from the models, and from these leaden patterns the heads, arms and legs are turned out—a special machine being used for stamping the hands. The factories, especially the kneading room, are hot and filled with steam, and for this reason the big, brawny Germans who knead the mixture wear as few clothes as possible while at work. The makeup of the composition dolls is composed of old rags, and paper with a large amount of gum tragacanth. The mixture is kneaded to a paste and heated. In a nearby room the moulds are set up in rows and here the women workers fill the moulds one after another in rapid succession. After they cool, a man by a peculiar twist of his hands separates the lead patterns and pulls out the doll's head, leg or arm as the case may be. The polisher then trims off the rough edges and carries the heads to the socket cutter, where holes are made for the eyes. This work is done by skilled workmen who use long, sharp knives. The sockets must be absolutely uniform or the eyes will not fit. The eye cutter rarely makes a mistake, and it is astonishing how rapidly he works. The waste material from the socket cutting is gathered up and reheated, and moulded again. Nothing is allowed to go to waste. The next stage is the painting of the heads, and this is usually done by girls who make some pretense to being artists. The cheeks are given the natural rosy tint, the mouth is touched with the lip color and the eyebrows are painted either dark or light to match the color of the eyes to be used. Setting the eyes is an easy task unless they are to open and shut, in which case some skill is necessary in balancing the small weight hung to the bow joining the two eyes at the back.

"When the doll is upright the weight does not move the eyes but when dollie is laid upon her back the weight maintaining its own position moves around and brings down

the upper part which is colored to resemble the eyelid. The wig is the finish of the doll's head and the crowning glory of its beauty. The hair used for the cheap dolls is usually goat hair and for the better grade real hair is imported from China. Hairdressing is a special branch of the industry and the wig makers watch the hair-dressing fashion plates for new ideas with as much eagerness as the most fashionable city coiffeuer does to give her human patrons something new. The same hair is used for blonde dolls except that the color is extracted by a certain process—another secret of these German doll makers. The bodies are stuffed with sawdust, cork, excelsior, cow's hair or wool, depending on the quality of the doll. The arms and legs are sewed in place by girls and the greatest care must be used to have them in exactly the proper angle.

"Making the eyes for 'Miss Dollie' is a dreary work for the coloring used must not be exposed to the sunlight until the eye is completed. The majority of the eye makers do their work in cellars. They are most secretive as to their methods and visitors rarely, if ever, penetrate these underground workshops. Few violet eyed dolls are on sale owing to the fact that the violet eye is the most difficult to make.

"Wax dolls are old fashioned, the composition doll having taken its place from the fact that it is quite as pretty and much more durable. . . . The doll must have her face washed and here the wax face has proved a failure. . . .

"In the forests of Thuringia doll making is a home industry as many of the peasants fashion them in their cottages. These dolls are, of course, not as perfect as the ones turned out by the large factories, but they are unique and please children. . . .

"The entire doll is never made by one person alone, and years ago before the art of machinery had been perfected a doll passed through the hands of at least 25 persons before it had been completed, and even after this handling it was a clumsy, awkward thing as compared with the dolls of today. The bodies in those days were stiff, being without joints and often covered with kid."

Manufacture of Dolls, Commercial: Made in Germany in Walterhausen Region.

The U.S. DEPARTMENT OF COMMERCE REPORT No. 267 reported in 1924 on the Manufacture of Composition Bodies in the Waltershausen Area: "An old composition for bodies and limbs still in favor is made of a mass worked up in mixing mills of light ground selenite (gypsum), flour, and glue, pressed in cast sulphur molds. But in the late eighties large-scale machine production was made possible through the die-forming and stamping process originated by Heinrich Handwerk, whose name was erroneously accepted by American patrons as indicative of handwork. The plant and the entire business was later taken over by the Waltershauser Puppenfabrik G. m. b. H. This firm makes its own wooden parts for dolls' joints and also supplies an affiliated concern Kaemmer & Reinhardt A. G. A son of Heinrich Handwerk, bearing the same name has recently gone into business and has revived the old firm name. The die forming and stamping process calls for the use of long fiber cardboard and involves the use of the new familiar heated steel die and a combination forming and cutting punch.

"The nonstuffed bodies are usually made in either one of two materials: (a) 'Pape,' which is made of a fine grade wood pulp and is machine pressed in molds; (b) 'papier-mâché,' which is strawboard or cardboard stock, mixed with sawdust, flour, glue, or resin (in each case using the proper solvent), all hand-pressed in plaster of Paris molds made from positive sulphur models. The 'pape' type is sometimes called 'papier-mâché' by non-German doll makers. The jointed doll and the doll with closing eyes were first introduced about 50 years ago. The trade gives much credit for the improvements in these lines to Ernst Kaemmer, one of the founders of the firm Kaemmer & Reinhardt A. G. Among these improvements may be mentioned hair eyelashes, articulated teeth, adjustable joints with removable rubber tendons, and the paint dipping method in place of brush painting. . . .

"Limbs and arms are made in three grades. They are made of 'pape' if they are parts of dolls of fine quality; of papier-mâché and hand pressed for cheaper dolls; while in the case of the cheapest grades of dolls they are made of either fir or pine, jointed with rubber tendons, or in the very low grades with wire. The dolls with movable arms and limbs are almost all ball-jointed. Franz Kuehle, of Ohrdruf, makes quite a specialty of this line. Another firm in this town making a complete line of these dolls is Kley & Hahn, normally employing about 300 workers. Some of the brands are 'My Only One' (Meine Einzige), 'Snow Fairy' (Schneewittchen), and 'Walkuere.' Other firms in Ohrdruf are Ohrdrufer Puppenspielwarenfabrik, Franz Kuehles, and the Thueringer Spielwarenfabrik (formerly F. W. Freytag & Co. G. m. b. H.). However the first position in the superiority of their jointed dolls in the Walthershausen-Ohrdruf district is still being accorded by the trade to J. D. Kestner, Jr., and Kaemmer & Reinhardt A. G." (An e was used with the vowel instead of an umlaut.) (See also **Heinrich Handwerck, Embossers,** and **Friedrich Müller,** as well as names listed above.)

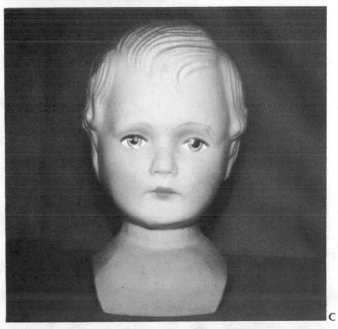

1768. Workers in a German home making parts for composition dolls. The little boy is kneading the composition paste and the man is filling a mold. A lower leg stands upside down on the table. *Courtesy of the Museum of the City of Neustadt near Coburg.*

1769A,B & C. Photographs relating to the manufacturing of composition dolls in the southern Thüringian area.

A. Shows left to right the metal mold, the composition head in the mold, the composition head with the eyes cut out and the edges trimmed.

B. Shows women workers sanding or smoothing the parts of the doll that the machines on the right have stamped out.

C. Shows the finished painted composition (Pappe) head. *Photos Courtesy of the Museum of the City of Neustadt near Coburg.*

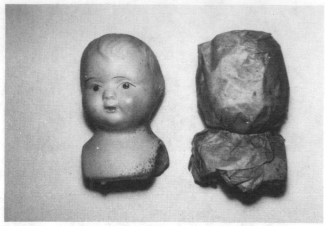

1770. Composition shoulder head and a similar head in its original paper wrappers just as it came from the factory. The heads have molded blond hair, painted blue eyes, and closed mouth. H. of head 4 in. (10 cm.). *Courtesy of the late E. J. Carter.*

1772. Composition shoulder heads probably manufactured in Germany on cloth bodies probably made in the U.S. The dolls have molded and painted hair and eyes, closed mouths. Original or contemporary clothes. Doll on left has brown eyes, homemade body with leather arms. H. 20 in. (51 cm.). Doll second from left has brown eyes and a body made by Philip Goldsmith. "M. & S. Superior" label is on the shoulders (Müller & Strassberger?). H. 22 in. (56 cm.). Doll second from right has blond hair and blue eyes. H. 14 in. (35.5 cm.). Doll on right has blue eyes and a body made by Philip Goldsmith. H. 17 in. (43 cm.). *Courtesy of Sotheby Parke Bernet Inc., N.Y.*

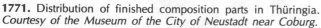

1771. Distribution of finished composition parts in Thüringia. *Courtesy of the Museum of the City of Neustadt near Coburg.*

Manufacture of Dolls, Commercial: Made in the United States.

According to *Mr. Joseph Kallus,* the late president of *Cameo* only three American Companies made their own entire dolls. These were Cameo, *Effanbee* and *Ideal.* The other companies generally bought their dolls from specialized manufacturers of dolls. These other producers hired various modelers often suggesting changes in the model to suit their standards. One or more manufacturers of dolls then made the dolls from the molds based on the model. Occasionally one company permitted another company to use its models for a stipulated fee. This was a more common practice among companies who did not actually make their own dolls. It can readily be seen that this presents problems to the collector who tries to identify a doll by its looks without marks for its identification. Collectors must realize that if two dolls look alike they are probably of the same period but not necessarily made by the same company. In many instances the idea for a doll's design was originated by one person or company, the doll was modeled by an artist who was commissioned for the purpose and the parts were made by various manufacturers who specialized in them. The company designated by the mark often assembled the parts, hired someone to dress the doll and performed the promotional activities necessary to market the doll. (This would correspond to the activities of the German *Verleger.*)

In addition to the process of developing the *designs for dolls,* the producer could hire a separate firm to make the *molds for dolls.* Ready-made molds were also obtainable. TOYS AND NOVELTIES in August, 1915, commented: "[There is] No one industry existent between the North and South Poles in which the custom of infringement is so prevalent as in the manufacturing of toys. No sooner does [a] company place an attractive doll of a new design on the market than a half-dozen doll manufacturers immediately go and do likewise. . . .

"If the present laws of this country [United States] were more rigid, it is probable that fewer infringements would be made, but at the present time the designer of a new toy is afforded very little protection for his invention."

The U.S. Department of Commerce Report No. 267, 1924, commented that doll-making depends on the novelty and number of its models to attract sales. One of the reasons why doll-making has not graduated in its entirety into the factory stage is that new ideas which must be created from year to year can naturally be suggested only by a large number of ingenious workers. It is the home workers who are forever bringing out new models based upon original ideas and it is they who frequently stimulate a vogue for a particular type of doll.

Most of the "manufacturers" should be called "collectors" and they simply collected and assembled the dolls.

Grace Putnam described this process, "Assemblers hire someone for $50.00 to model a head, getting someone to sew up the bodies and someone to make the clothes, etc. The final doll being named by and being put out as the creation of the assembler."

In 1929 *Grace Corry* the artist wrote to Averill: "All workers in clay realize that it is one thing to produce a character of interest—and that it is quite another thing to find a manufacturer who is able to retain the art features when the product must be manufactured and sold in huge quantities, and at a price within the reach of modest pocket books."

TOYS AND NOVELTIES, May, 1915, gave considerable information about the manufacture of composition dolls in America: "There must in general be more than one hundred different kinds of dolls on the market today, each necessitating slightly different methods of manufacture. . . .

". . . We turn to the present day unbreakable character dolls of American manufacture, for no industry in the country has shown a more rapid growth, or made greater strides than have the domestic manufacturers in the past six or eight years.

"The idea of making an unbreakable doll's head was originated in Russia by a man named Hoffman [Hoffmann] who obtained patents on a rather crude process of manufacture and brought it to America for development. The value of such a doll was early appreciated by the toy trade, and although the first doll was made but eight or nine years ago [it was longer than this] there are several hundred firms engaged today in this lucrative business. The most important part of these dolls, the composition of which heads, hands, feet, etc., are made, is made up in many different ways and of many different constituents, though in general they may all be divided into two distinct classes, each employing certain rather regular methods and similar materials. In one class belong the pressed heads, etc., which are made with steel dies under varying pressures while in the other class all parts are formed by pouring a composition in liquid form into plaster moulds.

"Each manufacturer has his own private composition, the components of which are kept carefully secret, but the general materials used are known to all. For pressed heads, a mixture of sawdust or woodpulp, flour, glue, talc and several other materials and chemicals is brought up to the consistency of a thick paste that is nearly dry, and formed under pressures varying from 500 to 8,000 pounds per square inch in the desired shapes, with steel dies operated by electric or hydraulic presses. The dies themselves are generally heated to a high temperature by gas jets or other means, which introduces a sort of baking process at the same time. The heads and other parts are made in halves which are later glued together and dipped in a thick paint, filling the pores and leaving a smooth finish of flesh color.

"With poured heads, the procedure is materially different and an entirely different composition is used throughout. In the better class of heads, glue is used as a base, the other materials used being principally wood pulp, talc and glycerine. This mixture is made up in large vats or tubs, and when it has been brought up to the exact consistency, it is ladled into plaster of paris moulds which are immediately emptied and set aside to dry. A thin layer of the composition adheres to the inside of each mould and as soon as the head is sufficiently firm, it is taken out of the mould and placed upon a rack for further hardening.

"These heads are all of a dull grey color and they are generally dipped in a thick paint to fill up all small holes and give the head a flesh tinted ground color. Some of the best heads, however, come out with such a smooth finish that this step is not necessary and the cheek tinting, etc., is all done directly upon the bare compositions. The moulds themselves have a comparatively short life, for being of plaster they soon become worn, so a casting of the original model is made of a stiff rubber-like glue and from this, fresh moulds are continually being made. So important is this in fact, that in the larger factories, a corps of men are kept continually busy, turning out fresh moulds. Before the heads have become too firm, they are all carefully examined for imperfections, and the edges and other projections are trimmed smooth with a sharp knife, after which they are replaced on the racks to harden.

"When hard, they are removed to the painting department where eyebrows, lips, etc., are painted on by skilled workers. In the process of hardening this composition shrinks slightly, and if a head were to be painted before it had entirely set, the complexions would present a wrinkled and cracked appearance, not altogether desirable in a brand new doll. In painting a doll the eyebrows, eyes, nose and lips are put on with a fine brush, which requires considerable skill in producing uniformity and the right expression. The complexion and hair effects are obtained by means of an air brush, which sprays a very fine cloud of paint under great pressure, and this latter operation is exceedingly rapid as the workers soon become very dexterous in manipulating the brushes. The process of making hands and feet is precisely similar to that for heads excepting the final operations of painting for these parts are simply dipped in a tub of flesh colored paint and allowed to dry.

"To produce bodies and limbs for these dolls which are positively uniform in size, shape and weight is not as easy a task as might be imagined, for all of this work is hand labor. The material for the shells is cut by large hand operated knives which shear through a hundred thicknesses of cloth with as much ease as one, and they are sewed up on electrically driven machines. The stuffing, if it is excelsior, is packed in cone shaped metal containers which are slipped inside the skins and then withdrawn. When cork or a similar filler is used the material is generally poured directly in the skins as it is an easy matter to obtain a uniform density and weight in this manner.

"In most factories a very large dressmaking department is maintained, for in comparison to the other operations, the process of dressing a doll is particularly a tedious one, and a number of women and girls are kept continually busy. Here again the patterns are cut out in great quantities by large cutting knives, and the sewing is done on electrically operated machines which are controlled by the feet of the workers. This latter process is in reality one of the most important in the entire manufacture of dolls, for though clothes may not make a man, they come pretty close to making a doll, the selling qualities of which are governed largely by the attractiveness of its appearance.

"From the above brief outline it may be seen that the manufacture of these particular kinds of dolls is almost entirely hand labor, which is one of the principal reasons why Germany can produce dolls at an exceedingly low cost. Materials, too, are considerably cheaper in that country than in America and in spite of our best attempts at business organization and efficiency it has proved impossible so far to produce dolls in this country which can compete with imported products on a price basis. Originality and design, however, is another matter, and there is undoubtedly a large market here for our domestic products. A certain style and character has been created by our leading doll manufacturers, and the demand for American dolls is increasing rapidly each year."

During 1915 TOYS AND NOVELTIES had other short comments on the manufacture of composition dolls.

In February: An "Innovation is the use of hydraulic pressure of over 3,000 pounds by the *New Era Novelty Co.* to produce a light weight composition doll that they claim is unbreakable, unburnable and washable."

In June: *Amberg* installed a special set of brass molds for their Charlie Chaplin doll. In order to keep up with the demand "They have been forced to discard the usual plaster moulds, replacing them with metal ones."

In December: "Modern machinery can now mix, roll out flat and press into moulds entirely automatically the composition for dolls' heads." This new machine was inspired by similar machines used in large bakeries.

TOYS AND NOVELTIES, February, 1916, reported: "In the manufacture of American dressed character dolls, many chemicals are used in making the unbreakable composition for heads, hands, feet, etc., and the prices of practically all of these have gone up from 15 to 200 per cent. Composition heads, which are made by the pouring process, contain a large proportion of glycerine and the cost of this chemical has increased more than 40 cents per pound. When it is known that the largest doll manufacturers frequently use more than 1,000 pounds of glycerine a week during their busy season, the effect of this rise may be better appreciated. The paints used for these heads have also experienced a sharp increase in price, particularly red paints, and it would not be at all surprising if the domestic dolls appeared less ruddy this year than in the past. As far as the bodies of the dolls are concerned, an added cost is to be found there also. A material known as Percale, which is flesh colored and used for the limbs and bodies, has gone up from two to three cents a yard, while the prices of practically all dress materials, ribbons, laces, etc., have shown a noticeable increase. . . . So it will be small wonder if the dolls of this country are more expensive or of a poorer quality for the money, than they have been for some years past.

"It is true, of course, that some manufacturers have foreseen this climb in the market value of materials, and have bought large stocks of supplies far in advance, but these instances are few and far between, for the average doll maker is not in a position to buy the materials for a season's output a whole year in advance. His overhead expenses during Spring and Summer are enough of a risk as it is."

TOYS AND NOVELTIES, May, 1920, gave the following information on the jobs and wages of factory workers who made dolls in the United States:

"The following statistics of wages is based on a 45 to 48 hour week.

"The following listings are in the composition department:

Pressers—mostly piece work $32 to $60 a week; this work brings as high as $75 a week.

Polishers—$25 to $90 a week; on piece work they average from $50 to $60 a week usually.

Sprayers—$35 to $90 a week, and have been known to go as high as $123 a week.

Painters—$40 a week and up; it is very common for a painter to receive from $60 to $80 a week.

Eye setters—time or piece work, $18 to $30 a week.

Eye fitters—time or piece work, $25 to $60 a week.

Dippers—$30 to $50 a week.

(The remaining workers make cloth bodies and clothes.)

Body operators—piece work, up to $45 a week.

Stuffers—piece work, from $30 to $50 a week.

Joiners—mostly piece work, from $35 to $50 a week.

Dress operators—piece or time work, depending upon efficiency, from $15 to $35 a week.

Doll dressers (young girls)—piece or time work, from $16 to $26 a week.

Head sewers—mostly piece work $30 to $50 a week."

For comparative purposes at that time, 1920, firemen made $30 to $40 a week, mail carriers received $23 to $27 and New York school teachers had just been raised from $19 a week to $30 a week.

The TIP TOP TOY catalog of 1920–21 described: "The Making of a Tip Top Doll. Wood pulp is the foundation of most modern dolls and each manufacturer has his particular method, very often a secret one, of treating the pulp. Once the pulp is ready it is run into flame-heated, brass molds, and allowed to remain there until it has set. On being removed it is given a rough finish and placed on racks to dry. After the drying, the doll part is given a finer polish and is cemented to its mate. The now complete body, head, arm or leg is given a third polish, and is ready for the painters.

"The body coat is given to the doll by means of the air brush, which throws a fine, even spray over the entire surface. It is interesting to note that some of the ingredients of this coat are the same as those used in strengthening and protecting the wing surfaces of airplanes. Powerful fans exhaust the gases that are given off when the paint is applied.

"The flesh tints and rosy cheeks finished, the doll's head goes through a very important operation. Fully fifty percent of a doll's expression depends on the eyes, and a good deal of the remaining expression is created by the wig or hat. In a doll like Pudgie the eyes demand particular attention. In the kid body and baby dolls, which are equipped with sleeping eyes, these eyes are inserted later. The eye painters are among the most highly paid members of the organization. Their hands are steady and sure; they are able to give the illusion of sight to a painted eye.

"Assembly of the dolls follows. Joints are strung together with strong elastic and wigs of many styles are attached."

TOYS AND NOVELTIES in May, 1923, described how *Mama* dolls were made: "Benjamin Goldenberg of E. I. Horsman Co. explains his processes of manufacture. . . .

" 'The right making of dolls is far more of an art, far more of a science, than we had imagined; it is founded on modeling and sculpture; it includes many departments of chemistry; . . .

" 'To begin with, the head of the future doll is first modeled in plaster from a living baby, and an exceptionally well favored baby. The first stage is exactly the same as if a marble portrait bust were in contemplation.

" 'From the plaster model, metal moulds are prepared by casting and then working up and polishing the metal casting. For the doll's face there are a pair of moulds, one concave and the other convex; and the same for the back of the head. There are a pair of moulds, concave and convex for the front of each arm, with another pair for the back of the arm; a pair for the front and a pair for the back of each leg, from the knee down. We are speaking now of dolls with stuffed bodies, only the extremities being made of unbreakable composition.

" 'The material of this composition is wood flour, mixed with starch and moistened with water, till it looks like a bran mash. When this composition has been pressed between the heated concave and convex moulds for four or five minutes, the water evaporates, leaving a substance which is practically reconstituted wood; and this is almost unbreakable. Powdered white wood and hardwood make the best composition.

" 'The concave moulds, in sets of half a dozen, are filled with the wet mixture of wood and starch, which is worked into the hollows of the moulds by the fingers of skilled workmen; the convex moulds are then pressed down on the soft composition, and the set of moulds is put into a complicated gas heater and left there for four or five minutes. The steam and wood fumes are carried off by exhaust pipes working in the hood over each gas heater.

" 'If the faces are being made, the result, when the moulds are opened, is a set of masks lying flat like a tray, and joined together at the ears, and of the color and weight of light brown wood. The masks are broken apart by hand, and the rough edges are broken off in the same way. Sharp knives later trim the edges smooth.

" 'The backs of the heads are made in the same way, and then back and front are struck [*sic*] together with carpenter's glue.'

"The heads we saw were about the size of the head of a baby four or five months old, with real baby features; they had about the color of the dark brown babies of India.

" 'The head is then dipped into a pail of sticky pink enamel, which has the general appearance of melted strawberry ice cream; it dries rapidly, and forms a very firm, smooth surface, the skin of the future doll baby, under which the glued joint between the back and front of the head becomes completely invisible.

" 'Then come the roses on the chubby cheeks. They are done with an air brush, a fine jet of air carrying rose colored paint, as a spray carries perfume. The expert who does this can adorn two thousand heads with rosy cheeks in an average working day.

" 'Then there are the eyes which open and shut. They are artistically made, of celluloid with a glazed surface, and are wired together in pairs. From the center of the wire there is another stiff wire with a small lead weight at the end, and, when the doll baby is laid on its back, this weight hangs down like a pendulum in the center of the head, making the eyes roll forward until they show the pink eyelid instead of the white of the eye with the colored iris and black pupil. To adjust the eyes, the top of the head is removed by an operation like trepa[n]ning; when the eyes are fitted, the top of the head is glued on again, and the line of junction is completely hidden by pink enamel.

" 'The doll baby's head is now ready to receive its crowning glory, which comes in the form of a diminutive wig, generally made of real hair, whether blond or dark. The doll baby's head is smeared with white paste, and the little wig is pulled on. . . . A covering of brown tissue paper is then twisted round the head like a veil, to keep the wig trim and clean until the paste is thoroughly dry. A barber lady gives a final touch of elegance by clipping the hair evenly across the forehead.

" 'The arms and legs are moulded, glued and covered with pink enamel in the same way. The body is made of strong pink muslin, stitched on a machine, turned inside out to hide the seams, and then stuffed with cotton.

" 'Half way through the stuffing process, the voice is inserted. Outwardly, the voice looks like a brown card cylinder, three or four inches high, two or three inches across, and closed at both ends, with the lid perforated like a salt-shaker. The voice is sent out by means of a piston moving in an air chamber; two soft rubber stops on the rod of the piston break the current of air twice as it comes out, and the result is a plaintive call, "Mama!" with a tone peculiarly appealing. The cardboard cylinder holding the voice is inserted in the middle of the body with the perforated end toward the front, and the rest of the stuffing is firmly packed in above it.

" 'To the body thus fortified with a voice, the head, arms and legs of wood composition are firmly attached, and the doll baby is ready to be dressed. . . .

" 'For the most part, no special materials for doll's clothing are made. . . .

" 'Fifty seamstresses with fifty sewing machines are ceaselessly busy with the garments, which are designed, cut out and made by exactly the same processes . . ., as for the garments of animated human beings: the same layers of material, laid out on the same long tables; the patterns marked in the same way, and the same cutting with the Eastman machine. . . .'

"The making of their shoes is a great matter, too; here, we understand, some special qualities of black enameled cloth are used which are made solely for this purpose. Many layers are cut at once by a steel die in a heavy press.

"The sewing is done by machine, and then the soles are fixed on with glue, the whole process taking a few seconds only. The socks for the doll babies come from the knitting mills. . . .

"The baby heads moulded by women who love babies, have a genuine baby look, and the dresses are chosen on exactly the same principle of taste which was applied when it was a question of dressing Mr. Goldenberg's own babies."

Ca. 1926: An Averill catalog described how they made their Madame Hendren dolls. "The parts of the heads, arms and legs were made by the hot press method and the small hands by the cold press method. The parts were reamed out and filed to provide smooth even surfaces before they were glued to-gether. The heads, arms and legs were then dipped and sanded for smoothness. The painting was done with spray guns and the heads were held over large drums to collect the dripping. Some of the dolls had painted hair and eyes while others had sleeping eyes and wigs, a few had eyelashes. The head and limbs were attached to the stuffed cloth bodies and finally the dolls were dressed in clothes that were made on the premises."

TOYS AND NOVELTIES in March 1927 reported that a New York factory employing 60 to 70 men "makes heads and arms for several of the leading high grade doll manufacturers in New York City." The workmen in one of the largest composition factories making dolls' heads went on strike. These workmen had been making $30.00 to $80.00 a week; sprayers got $40.00 to $50.00, sandpaperers and painters got up to $70.00 or $80.00 a week.

PLAYTHINGS, in July 1927, commented. "Wood in the form of sawdust, flour, pulp and the like is sometimes mixed into various shapes."

PLAYTHINGS, in September 1927, reported on the wood flour used to produce dolls.

"The estimated annual production of wood flour in the United States is slightly in excess of 24,000 tons, which has a total value of about $750,000. In addition to the domestic supply, which is practically all consumed within the country, 6,413 tons were imported from Europe in 1926. Norway, the Netherlands, Sweden, and Germany, in the order in which they appear, were the chief nations furnishing this material.

"In spite of a 33⅓ per cent ad valorem import duty the very close utilization abroad of all wood substances and the cheap ocean freight rates into the port of New York allow the foreign product to successfully compete with that manufactured by American concerns.

"Fully 75 percent of the wood flour manufactured in the United States is made from white pine . . . under the present rates of duty foreign manufacturers are successful in laying their products down in New York at prices competitive with those of domestic manufacturers, whose rail freight is often the determining factor of profit or loss.

"Wood flour might properly be considered as a by-product of the lumber industry, because over 60 percent of that produced is made from wood shavings and sawdust, but the sawmill or planing mill owner who is a prospective manufacturer of this material should not labor under the impression that all of his sawdust, chips and mill ends can be led through any type of grinder and be made to yield handsome profits. . . .

"It is not only necessary for the successful producer of wood flour to study the most approved and efficient grinding methods, but he must also study carefully the requirements of the consumers. Each consuming industry has its particular demands.

"The wood flour used for a filler in synthetic resins must be of a fine grade. One manufacturer reports that it must pass through a 60-mesh sieve, but it is thought that most other manufacturers demand even finer grades. The wood flour is thoroughly mixed with the phenolic resin, coloring matter, etc., into a plastic mass. After mixing, this material is ground to a very fine powder and is then ready for molding. It is molded in presses that are capable of exerting a pressure of about 2,000 pounds per square inch and the molds are heated to a temperature of approximately 350 F.

"The use of wood flour as a filler is not limited to the products made with phenol resin. It is made into a variety of products which are as widely different as the binding materials used in them. Among these molded products might be mentioned, . . . dolls, etc.

"In practically all cases where a plant has developed a satisfactory binding material it regards the formula as a trade asset and thus is very reluctant to divulge any information regarding it. Starch, rosin, sodium silicate, and many other materials are used—sometimes alone and sometimes in combination.

"In the above group of products employing wood flour as a filler, the most important is the manufacture of dolls. In this industry the wood flour is thoroughly mixed with rosin, gums, and other binding constituents and is then molded under pressure in bronze molds. Heat is applied along with the pressure by means of jets of gas flame along the upper and lower sides of the molds. In manufacturing larger dolls, the arms and legs, and heads are made in two sections which are later glued together. This hollow construction results in a saving of materials and at the same time facilitates the other work, such as jointing the arms and legs and setting the eyes.

"The time required for the baking in the mold varies with the thickness of the shell being made. It is usually from four to six minutes.

"These dolls are termed 'unbreakable' in distinction from those made of china or bisque. Their high quality, lifelike appearance, and freedom from breaking with the least knock or fall have gained for them a very fine reputation and they have largely supplanted the German-made dolls which were so widely purchased in this country before the war.

"Doll manufacturers seem to prefer the light-colored, semifibrous, imported grades of wood flour. Light color is really not essential, since the parts after molding are dipped in a very heavy flesh-colored glue solution, but it is necessary that they have wood flour of a slightly fibrous nature which adds to the strength of the finished product."

TOYS AND NOVELTIES in October 1928 reported: "The American made doll . . . is fabricated in large and sanitary factories. The heads are moulded from patterns designed by real artists, of wood pulp or wood flour, glue and other materials by either a hot or cold process.

"When thoroughly dried and seasoned it is smoothed by a buffer and then dipped in a flesh-colored sizing which fills in all pores in the material and furnishes a smooth surface for the enamel or finish. This finish is put on, after another drying, with an air brush, which gives the soft, velvety appearance characteristic of the well-made American doll head, and is at the same time moisture proof, adding materially to the wearing qualities and cleanliness.

"After again drying, the rosy cheeks and blue or brown eyes are painted by men and women who are real artists in this work. When moving eyes are required these are inserted and securely fastened by machinery or by hand.

"Dresses must follow and even suggest the vogue for smart children who abide by prevailing styles, and these are designed for the most part by women dress designers who make doll clothing their life's work.

"Best of all, your American doll is a durable doll, for she can be dropped time without number and never break her own pretty head or her little mother's tender heart.

"Her body is stuffed with cotton that is immaculately clean, and the body has the soft human feel of a real baby's. Wigs of real hair on the better class of dolls are carefully woven and secured in place. Curls, braids and bobs are all there and all clean and neat.

"Then there is the Ma-Ma voice, an American invention which clearly cries 'Ma-Ma' when the doll is tilted, and which lasts as long as the doll.

" 'Moving Eyes' are now so well made that they will withstand the hardest usage without being displaced—many of them with real lashes."

In the same month, October 1928 PLAYTHINGS also reported: "When the humidity is high dipping and finishing operations on composition dolls' heads and parts cannot be done. One manufacturer explained that the glue in the dip is ordinarily slow in drying and on humid days it is impossible to do anything. Another manufacturer said 'It isn't in the dip at all. We run into trouble caused by excessive humidity on our spraying operations.'

"The solution seemed to be to make the heads and parts during the winter months when humidity is low, but demand does not always permit this seasonal work. . . . And still the trouble of doll heads cracking, peeling, flaking and blushing made us feel that there must be some way out. . . . As far as the difference of opinion between the two authorities with respect to this trouble . . . both of them are right.

"It is, of course, essential that any material be completely dry, not only on the surface, but through and through, before it is sprayed. If it isn't, the moisture contained in the material will be continually striving to get out. . . . This bears out the contention of the first manufacturer who said 'it was all in the dip.' But no matter what the material, no matter how dry it is, the minute it is sprayed the action of the spraying substance is that of a refrigerant . . . this sudden cold applied to a warmer surface collects moisture on the sprayed surface, that is it collects it if the percentage of moisture in the air (humidity) immediately around the sprayed surface, is higher than that occasioned by this refrigerating action of the spray."

In July 1930 TOYS AND NOVELTIES reported: "Composition dolls cannot be made on hot days. This means June, July, August and part of September."

TOYS AND NOVELTIES in November 1928 reported on a demonstration of the processes used to make dolls in October at the *Jordan, Marsh* store in Boston. The dolls were "made of wood and rosin, of flour and cornstarch, . . . experts daftly painting in her blue or brown eyes. (mostly blue) and her rosy lips."

PLAYTHINGS in December, 1928, had an article on the *Louis Amberg* & Son firm to celebrate their fiftieth year. It explained how the Amberg composition heads were made in their two factories which started operations in 1910 and were among the first to make composition head dolls in America. "Then came the war. . . . During this period the Amberg plant was developed from the old poured mould glue composition method into the more modern heavy dough composition known as cold-press, finally, into the present wood pulp baked composition," which is referred to as the hot-press method.

TOY WORLD in August 1929 reported: "The American

dolls . . . are manufactured in sanitary factories. The heads are molded from patterns designed by artists of ability. Wood pulp, wood flour, glue and other materials are used in both the hot and cold molding processes. These heads are then dried and seasoned and polished with a buffer before being dipped in the flesh-colored sizing which fills all pores, adds to sanitary qualities and completes the smooth surface for the enamel or other finish.

"This finish is applied by an airbrush which gives the soft velvet appearance. This finish is moisture proof which adds to sanitary and cleaning qualities. The rosy cheeks and the blue or brown eyes are added by hand. If moving eyes are required, these too, are put in by hand work.

"The body is made by a very different process. The body, like the head, is carefully designed. Then it is carefully stuffed with cotton that has been carefully cleaned and processed. Much skill is required to get this cotton at exactly the required density to give the body the 'human feel.'

"Wigs of real hair for the better class of dolls are carefully woven and secured in place. Coiffures are in prevailing modes, although curls are more popular in the doll world than for human juveniles.

"Moving eyes and the voices have many variations. The biggest difference in these features in recent years is that they are now installed with sufficient security to last an average doll lifetime."

The same magazine in December 1929 described a demonstration in the California Toy Shops of Los Angeles:

"The different stages and processes of doll making. . . . The glue foundation with half of the face painted with its first coat, then with its coat of enamel on, then with its features painted on, and finally the finished head with eyes and wig.

"The making of doll legs, the leg molded in two parts, showing how it is put together, and the different stages in outer paint coats, was also shown.

"Ingredients used in making dolls were included with explanatory labels, celluloid teeth and tongue, a bottle of glycerine, a pile of flakes of glue, wheat flour used to give the smooth surface, and wood pulp, the principle ingredient. There was also a doll partly stuffed with silk floss." (See also **Hot Press Composition.**)

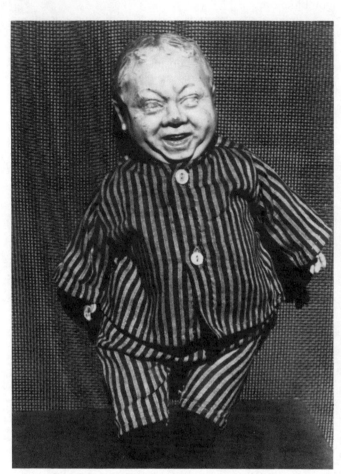

1774. Composition portrait head of John Bunny made by Amberg ca. 1915. John Bunny was a popular moving picture star. The composition was based on a formula created by Otto Denivelle. *Courtesy of Mrs. Frank T. Heintz.*

1773. Composition portrait head of Charlie Chaplin made by Amberg in 1915. Original clothes. Mark is a cloth label on the sleeve: "CHARLIE CHAPLIN DOLL//WORLD'S GREATEST CO-MEDIAN//MADE EXCLUSIVELY BY LOUIS AMBERG & SON, N.Y. //by SPECIAL ARRANGEMENT WITH ESSANAY FILM CO." H. 14½ in. (37 cm.). *Coleman Collection.*

Manufacture of Dolls, Commercial: Made in United States, Cloth.
TOYS AND NOVELTIES in January 1913 reported: "New York doll quarantine possible . . . it is unlikely that a doll quarantine will be established to prevent the spread of tuberculosis—not among the doll population—but among their flesh and blood foster mothers. A child labor investigator tells of hearing a woman who had just bought a doll in one of the fashionable Fifth Avenue toy shops remark to the salesman: 'My little girl will take it to bed with her tonight.' Two days before, the inspector had seen the same doll sewn

together in a crowded tenement room where two members of the family who were working on it were affected with tuberculosis. It has been proposed to seize all dolls made in such places and hold them in quarantine until a law can be passed prohibiting home work in tenements entirely."(See also **Benoliel** and **Kewpie**.)

Manufacture of Dolls, Homemade: Leather.

1893: THE GIRLS' OWN ANNUAL, gave the following directions for making suede leather dolls:

"The body of this doll is made of pink sateen; the length of the doll is fifteen inches, divided into three for the head, six for the body, and six for the legs. Length of arm four and a half inches, two and a half in circumference. Waist measure is six inches, neck three inches, breadth at shoulders three inches, but round the shoulders six inches. The face is two inches in length, with an inch beyond for hair; it is two inches broad where shown, but is five inches in circumference. The head is the most difficult part of the doll to make. It is first formed of a piece of linen stuffed with good cotton wool, and made in the shape of an egg. The stuffing of the shaped piece of linen must be firm and full without being hard. Then a piece of flesh coloured suéde leather is required (this can always be taken from the clean part of a . . . suéde glove), and this is fitted to the head, and hair and features traced out upon it. The nose is made slightly prominent by the leather being pinched together at that place so as to shape it, and these pinches are secured with a few stitches at the nostrils and where the nose and eyes are on a line together. To paint the face, use water-colours mixed with aquarella medium. Make the hair of burnt sienna and vandyke brown, and mark the eyebrows out with vandyke brown. Use cobalt and black for the eyes, with a little ultramarine blue. The cheeks are made bright with a touch of vermilion, but previously to that the face is washed over several times with a wash made of Chinese white and crimson lake. The lips are touched in with crimson lake. A good deal of careful stitching is required to fit the glove leather to the doll's head; but as the doll's cap conceals all of this, it is better to shape the head by so doing correctly, than to leave it to chance. Some people sew a little real hair on to dollie's forehead instead of painting it in. This hair can be bought as a doll's fringe at any dollmakers.

"The baby's dress consists of one long undergarment, a baby's robe and cape. These are all made of fine Indian muslin and take off and on."

If the doll is too difficult to make it was suggested that "a lady who works for charitable purposes will . . . make up the doll."

Manufacture of Wax Dolls.

GODEY'S LADY'S BOOK in 1856 provided detailed instructions for making wax dolls at home: "There are no imitations of natural objects more exact and pleasing than those made of wax: . . . So exact indeed are they, if well made, that the most practised eye cannot sometimes detect the real from the artificial. . . . [I]n truth no art is of more easy attainment; a little patience and a little taste are the whole mental requisites; these, superadded to ordinary care in the manipulation, cannot fail very shortly to render proficient the most inexperienced. . . . The chief thing is to know how to select

1775. Directions for making this baby doll with a suede face are given in THE GIRLS' OWN ANNUAL, December, 1893. The face is needle sculptured and the hair and features are painted with watercolors. A fringe of hair for the forehead could be bought "at any doll makers" and substituted for the painted hair. The body is made of pink sateen. H. 15 in. (38 cm.).

the proper materials, and how to set about the work in a proper manner.

"In large towns, the requisite materials can always readily be procured, and it is not worth while that any of them should be home made; yet as persons who desire to practise this art may live far in the country where it is difficult to obtain even the simpler requisites, and as circumstances often arise in which it is absolutely impossible to procure what may be wanted for a particular purpose, we intend to include in this every available information; that the learner, however remotely situated may be his residence, or unique his model, may have as much as possible his difficulties removed, his mind stimulated and his fingers directed to attain excellence.

"The art of making Waxen Fruit includes every small object made in a mould; thus the same instructions that direct to make an orange, are equally applicable to form . . . a doll, a bust or any similar article, observing that the principal upon which all are formed is that a mould is requisite. This first to be made or procured, then wax is to be cast in it, sometimes solid, sometimes hollow. In many cases the objects will now be completely finished, with the exception of just trimming around where the mould joined; in other cases, the wax castings are to be painted with dry colors for some, and wet colors for others; and in different manners, according to the effect desired to be produced. Thus the imitation of solid objects in wax necessarily resolves itself into three distinct portions, each of which we must consider in detail; and first to . . .

MAKING MOULDS OF TWO PARTS

"The materials and implements requisite for making the proper moulds are plaster of Paris; some slips of stiff paper, or ribbons of tin cut from thin tin plates of their full length, and about three inches wide; some damp sand in a bowl; a pint basin; large spoon; small dinner knife; and jug of water. The plaster of Paris should be quite fresh, and of good quality, superfine if it can be procured, if not, the common plaster of the oil shops; the superfine is very much to be preferred, as it is whiter, finer, harder and more durable.

MOULD WITH TWO PARTS

"Sink nearly one-half the [doll model] into the sand which has been previously damped; and it will be better, for a reason afterwards explained, to sink that part of the [doll model] so that the widest part of the [model] shall be just above the sand. Make the sand smooth around it. Then take one of the longest pieces of tin, bend it around into a hoop a little more than an inch wider than the [doll], and keep it of this form and size, by a bit of string tied round it; stick this hoop in the sand so as to inclose the [doll] and be at an equal distance from it on every side, the upper edge of the tin standing up above the [doll], which is now prepared for casting from. If you have no tin, a piece of stiff and smooth brown paper, folded double, and one end fastened to the other by a wafer or wax, and the slip then made to surround the [doll], will do as well as the tin, though it is more troublesome to insert into the sand.

"Now prepare the plaster of Paris, which is to be poured on to the [doll]. First pour water into the basin (it may be half or three-quarters full), sprinkle the plaster into the water quickly, till it comes up to the top of the water, or till you think you have enough to cover the exposed half of the [doll] in depth, pour off the superfluous water, and stir the whole together quickly, till well mixed, to about the consistence of thick cream or honey; then pour the mixed plaster upon the [doll], so as to cover it all over equally, or as nearly so as possible; the plaster will, of course, be stopped from running away by the tin edging. If it should be too thin, and therefore run too much off the [doll], so as to leave the top bare, or nearly so, you must, after pouring it on the [doll], watch till it begins to harden, and then with a knife plaster it on the deficient parts, or else quickly mix up a little more to pour on; the whole of this must not take up above a minute or two, or the plaster will begin to set, as it is called, that is, it will commence solidifying, for it is the property of calcined plaster of Paris to unite itself with water with so strong a chemical affinity that from an impalpable powder it becomes a hard and solid substance.

"While the half mould, now roughly formed is becoming hard enough to handle, the basin and spoon must be carefully washed, ready for use again presently, for a second quantity of plaster must never be mixed up in any vessel till all former quantities be carefully washed away; and be it remarked, also that if plaster gets hard and dry in a basin, spoon or other vessel, the best way to remove it is to pour in a little water, when it will readily separate in one piece.

"We will now suppose the plaster, which has been poured on the [doll], to have gotten about as hard as the flesh of a soft pear, or just hard enough to handle; when this is the case, take the whole up from the sand, take away with the point of the knife all sand which will drop from it, carefully remove the tin rim, and hold the mould by the [doll]; now cut away any superfluous parts around the outside with a knife, as quickly as convenient, for it is now momentarily getting harder; turn it up, and holding the mould itself in the hand [doll] uppermost, remove the [doll model] if it can be done readily without hurting the mould. Lay the [doll] aside, cut away the lower edge of the mould where it has touched the sand, till the mould is exactly that of half the [doll model], which is easily seen by the shape of it internally. This is somewhat important, in order that the second half of the mould shall fit the [doll]. If the tin has been of proper size, the mould will be half an inch thick around the edge.

"The next operation is to prepare the second half of the mould, and that is easier and quicker to do than the first. First make two, three or four holes with the round point of the knife in different parts of the former half, to such a depth and of such a size that each will hold half a small marble or large pea. Then grease with tallow and salad oil, melted together in equal proportions, and laid on with a small brush, the edge of the finished half, holes and all. Wipe the [doll model] from all sand, and place it in the half mould exactly as it came out so that it shall fit in every part; surround the finished half mould with a long slip of stiff paper or tin, which you must tie on with a string, or fasten with a wafer. Place the whole, thus prepared, on a table or flat surface, [doll] uppermost; prepare some liquid plaster, as in the former instance, pour it upon the [doll], and let it partly harden. Then take off the edging, trim up the outside, and when quite hard, insert the blade of the knife between the two halves and separate them. The whole mould will now be complete and the [doll model] being taken out, it will be ready to cast in.

ELASTIC MOULDS

"The body to be moulded, previously oiled, must be secured one inch above the surface of a board, and then surrounded by a wall of clay, about an inch distant from its sides. The clay must also extend rather higher than the contained body; into this, warm melted glue, as thick as possible, so that it will run, is to be poured, so as to completely cover the body to be moulded; the glue is to remain till cold, when it will have set into an elastic mass, just such as is required.

"Having removed the clay, good glue is to be cut into as many pieces as may be necessary for its removal, either by a sharp-pointed knife, or by having placed threads in the requisite situation of the body to be moulded, which may be drawn away when the glue is set, so as to cut it out in any direction. The portions of the glue mould having been removed from the original are to be placed together and bound round by tape.

"In some instances it is well to run small wooden pegs through the portions of the glue, so as to keep them exactly in their proper positions. If the mould be of considerable size, it is better to let it be bound with moderate tightness upon a board, to prevent its bending whilst in use; having done as above described, the wax is to be poured into the mould, and left to set. The wax must not be poured in whilst too hot, as it cools so rapidly, when applied to the cold glue, that the sharpness of the impression is not injured.

"When the moulds are not used soon after being made, treacle [molasses] should be previously mixed with the glue, to prevent it becoming hard.

"The description thus given is with reference to casting those bodies which cannot be so well done by any other than an elastic mould; but glue moulds will be found greatly to facilitate casting in many departments, as a mould may be frequently taken by this method in two or three pieces, which would, on any other principle, require many.

WAX TO OBTAIN AND PREPARE

"The wax should be put in a moderately fine hair bag, well tied up and be boiled briskly in a clean saucepan or large pipkin [small earthenware jar with a horizontal handle, often used for boiling liquids] with sufficient water to well cover the bag, and half an ounce of aqua-fortis [commercial nitric acid] to each quart of water; a weight should be placed upon the bag to keep it down. As the wax rises to the top of the water, it is to be skimmed off with a spoon, and be put into a pan, and when no more rises, the bag must be pressed by having a flat board and a heavy weight placed on it to squeeze out any wax that may remain. The wax so obtained should be re-boiled in fresh water, and treated the same way as before, and even a third boiling may be necessary in order to have it quite pure; after the last boiling, it is to be poured into moulds to form cakes. The quantity of aqua-fortis at the second boiling may be reduced one-half; and if it is boiled a third time, it may still further be reduced to the same extent. If wanted white, it is bleached.

WAX, TO WHITEN

"The process of bleaching wax in order to give it that beautiful whiteness which it has in commerce is effected generally by chemical means; but it may be bleached in small quantities as follows: Take the best and cleanest beeswax you can obtain; melt it in hot water; skim it off into a cup or basin, previously oiled; when quite cold, cut the wax into thin slices; expose these to the action of the sun and air upon white dishes, sprinkling it—unless there be rain—once or twice a day with clean water; at the end of a week melt the wax again, and proceed as before. In hot weather the wax may be floated on water in the middle of the day, as it is best not to allow it to melt.

GENERAL OBSERVATIONS ON CASTING WAX

"The wax may be, and often is congealed around the hole as well as the sides; in this case it is evident that the hole must be cleared before the liquid within can escape; it is scarcely worth while to pour any out of a . . . small object. In casting a large object through a hole, there should only be a small quantity of wax allowed to congeal first; in a few minutes a second coat may be poured in and afterwards a third; this method will prevent cracking. The object of the water to soak the mould in at first and between each casting is to prevent the wax and mould sticking together; and the reason hot water is preferred is that it may not congeal the wax too rapidly. In a mould which is too cold, the wax will often settle in ridges or streaks. The mould, when filled or partly filled, as the case may be is, after such filling, plunged and turned about in cold water, merely to hasten the congealing of it. Wax should be melted always by a very slow and gentle heat, the heat of boiling water pot is an excellent thing to melt it in. This because, if not hot, it will be apt to adhere to the mould, and also, because when any color has been mixed with it, this color becomes darker, especially when there is chrome yellow in it; this turns by heat dark olive. If great toughness is required in a wax cast or mould, one ounce of yellow rosin, or, still better, of Canada balsam, is to be added to every pound of wax. Wax moulds for plaster casting, or the electrotype, should have the above, and also one fourth its weight of flake white and red lead, mixed together previous to melting. Modeling wax, and that used for wax dolls, hair-dressers' blocks, & c. are colored with flake white and vermilion, the latter in very small quantity.

"Wax is sometimes adulterated with white lead, tallow, suet, potato, starch, or resin. When wax is bought, it is proper to break each cake, for it is not unfrequently the case that some impurities are in the center, the outside being good.

SECOND PROCESS—CASTING THE [DOLL]

"For casting the [doll] in the moulds, the following articles will be required: A wash-hand basin of cold water, another of hot water, two or three pipkins, tin saucepans or other vessels to melt the wax in, a towel, and the following colors in fine powder, or better still, ground in oil, such as artists use and which are usually sold for 4d. [8¢] the tube, viz: light chrome yellow, lake, Prussian blue, and raw umber; also, some red lead in powder, and a sufficiency of wax. The best wax is not necessary; the remaining pieces of half-burnt wax or composition candles will do equally well; . . . A bone knife or a teaspoon is also necessary to stir up the melted wax. Thus furnished, set to work as follows: The method being exactly the same of every [doll] which is to be cast hollow, the color alone differs, and this must be always in accordance with the [doll] that is to be imitated; . . .

"Casting a [doll].—Prepare the mould by soaking it for ten minutes in water, as hot as the hand can conveniently bear. While the mould is soaking, melt a sufficiency of wax; when melted, put in a little red lead in powder, stir it up well; then take out the mould from the water rubbing it, lest you should rub out the fine irregularities on the inside of the mould, which constitute the beauty of the [doll]. The mould will now be penetrated with water, but without having the surface wet, thus preventing the wax sticking to it. Thus ready, hold one-half the mould in the left hand; nearly fill this half side with the melted wax just stirring up, taking care that none of it has run over the edge or joint; put the other half of the mould on it, squeeze the two pieces tight together with the hands, and, still holding them tight, turn them over and over in every manner, so that the melted wax shall, before it congeals, pass equally over the whole internal surface of the mould. The mould being warm with the water, and still further warmed by the wax, it would take perhaps ten minutes before the whole were congealed; save time, you must have recourse to the basin of cold water, and dip your hands and the mould in the water, still turning it about, thus keeping it immersed, and turning it for two or three minutes, the wax will have become hard, which may be known by shaking it, and the same time listening whether there is the sound of a liquid within. If set, leave it to rest for a few minutes in cold water. Then the halves of the mould may be pulled off and the [doll] will be found perfect in form, and of a natural color. The only thing now to be done is to take off with a penknife any mark of the joint of the mould, and if the knife itself leaves a mark, smooth it off with a bit of a rag, damped with turpentine. Solid [dolls].—Small [dolls] cannot be well cast in the above manner. The best process then is to tie the parts of the mould together, and pour the wax through a hole at the top, until the mould is full; then place this in cold water, but not so that the water can run into the hole at the top; let it stop a minute, then pour out again all the wax not congealed, so that the [doll] will be solid or not, according to the management pursued.

FINISHING THE [DOLL]

"After the waxen [dolls] are cast, they require first to have the mark or ridge left by the joints of the mould carefully pared off with a penknife, and then generally the knife-marks smoothed off with a small piece of rag, dipped in turpentine or spirits of wine; . . . The material now required are various colours as carmine in powder, together with the same colours used in casting; also there will be required a small piece of flannel, two or three camel-hair brushes, . . .

PUTTING ON A ROSY TINT

"Take up a little of the powder carmine on a small piece of flannel, and rub it gently and regularly over such part of the [doll] as is to be thus ornamented; it will soon communicate all the effect desired. . . . Mix carmine or other color with turpentine, spirits of wine, or varnish, so as to be very weak of color; take up a little in a hard tinting brush. . . .

"If a person is not furnished with oil or powder colors and dislikes the use of varnish or turpentine, he may use for all purposes of finishing the cast [doll], the ordinary water colors of the paint boxes, rubbed up in the customary way with water, to which a drop or two of oxgall has been added. This last is necessary to make the colors adhere to the wax, which is of a greasy nature. It is to be observed, however, that [dolls] colored with water colors, cannot be washed, as that may which has been finished in turpentine or varnish.

WAX, TO REMOVE FROM A DRESS

"It not unfrequently happens that, when wax is melted, some is spilt on the dress; it may be removed as follows: Toast the crumb of a small piece of bread, and while hot apply it to the droppings of wax, a portion of which it will absorb and take up, and by repeating this process, the whole wax will be gradually removed."

The directions for making wax dolls seem to be far more complicated than the reader of *Godey's* was first led to

believe. However, the detailed description of the process would make the task less difficult. The use of the pronoun "his" and the spelling with "ou" in such words as "mould" as well as the use of the British currency 4d. shows that these directions were probably copied from an earlier British publication. Of course in the 19th century many of the poured wax dolls were made in Britain.

The glue mold was to facilitate molding when undercuts were necessary. The model could be made of any material that was as hard as a piece of fruit. It could be a figurine or clay model as well as an actual doll's head that was to be reproduced in wax. The harmfulness of lead was not realized in the 1850s.

THE QUEEN AND LADY'S NEWSPAPER in 1877 gave the following report on how wax dolls were made.

"The number of people employed in the manufacture of dolls is astonishing, and in large establishments nearly the whole work takes place on the premises, every person having his or her own particular work or specialty. In some of the wholesale establishments in London thousands of dolls are turned out in the course of a week.

"The work of one man is the making of the head. This is done by pouring melted wax into a mould or cast of the head and features. Some of the wax, however is poured off before it has time to become all perfectly solid. In this way the more expensive ones are made. The others are of composition, or paper coated over with wax, and are much more generally used, as they are less expensive, and not so easily cracked or broken. Another man's entire work is to put in the eyes. With a sharp knife he cuts away the wax for the sockets. After properly adjusting the glass eyes, he fastens them in by pouring a little melted wax in the skull, which, coming in contact with the glass, cools, and keeps them in place. With the more expensive dolls he models, the eyelids and eyebrows with his hands. This requires considerable skill and long practice to accomplish successfully.

"These little glass eyes are imported from Germany. Hundreds of gross of them, assorted in sizes and packed in large cases, are sent over to England annually.

"When the eyes are inserted in the head, the next point is the putting on the hair. This is an important consideration with the manufacturer, being the most costly part of the whole toy. In many of the best dolls the hair and its insertion cost as much as the rest of the head put together, for no doll would be considered perfect unless its hair were natural, that is, unless it could be combed and brushed without injury. This work is all done by women. The head to be adorned is placed on a block, the operator holding in her left hand the hair, carefully combed and cut to a uniform length; in her right hand a dull knife, with which she lifts a small piece of wax, and pushes the hair underneath. When she has finished this process, by inserting only two or three hairs at a time, she takes an iron roller and gently but firmly rubs it over the surface, thus fastening the hair securely on the head. This is a very tedious process, and only used in the more expensive dolls. In the less expensive or composition ones, a deep groove is cut completely through the skull, along the top of the head where the parting is to be, and the uncurled ends of the ringlets are pushed in with a blunt knife, and then fastened down with paste.

"Black hair, which is seldom used for dolls, is almost entirely human, and is imported from the Continent, while the flaxen locks so universally preferred are made of mohair. This material is specially manufactured for the purpose, and there is one house in London which supplies nearly all the English as well as the best French and German makers. It is of a remarkably soft and silky texture, and is sold in little bundles of different lengths.

"Having finished with the doll's head, the body is now to be considered. Upon this a number of people are employed, chiefly women, assisted by the younger members of their families, each of whom takes one special part. The manufacturer gives out so many yards of cotton, and he knows to an inch how much material each dozen dolls will require, according to their size. The body-maker takes it home, and accomplishes the work in the following manner: One person cuts out the body of the doll, another sews it; a third rams in the sawdust, a fourth makes the joints and in this way a family will produce many dozen in a week. The payment of this work is by the piece.

"The arms form another branch of this manufacture, upon which certain persons are almost exclusively employed. Except for the very commonest class of dolls, the arms are made of kid below the elbow, and cotton above; and in every case there is an attempt at fingers, although their number may not always be correct. The price paid for these arms completed is incredibly small. The work-woman furnished the kid, cotton and sawdust, and for large arms about six-inches long receives 6½ d. [13¢] for a dozen pair. Small arms for cheaper dolls are supposed to be worth only 1½ d. [3¢] dozen pairs. As these poor people furnish the material, it must be difficult to keep starvation from their doors, unless they have other means of support.

"The putting of the head and arms together is the last process. This is done with glue and thread. The doll is then wrapped up in tissue paper, and ready for the market.

"At least twenty different people are employed in making a doll, not counting those who manufacture the raw material, that is the wax, the eyes, the cotton, and the hair. In London there are sixteen wholesale establishments or manufactories."

(This article also appeared in HARPER'S BAZAR in the same year.)

OUR LITTLE MEN AND WOMEN in 1893 told how "A wax doll's head is made in two hollow parts of plaster of Paris. The eyes and nose and mouth are carved out with a knife the two parts are stuck to-gether, and then the head is dipped in hot wax or a preparation made from petroleum[,] probably paraffin[,] and set away to cool and harden. Then the artist works up on them with his paints and tiny brushes and the hairdresser takes his turn."

THE PRACTICAL TOY MAKER, a Home Industries booklet published in London in 1921, gave directions for making a wax doll: "This is a class of toy for which there is a constant demand, and one that can be made a paying proposition even though produced on a modest scale. The real wax-headed doll is perhaps the most attractive production in the doll line, . . . the beauty of the wax head has never been surpassed. . . . A plain style of doll has the head and

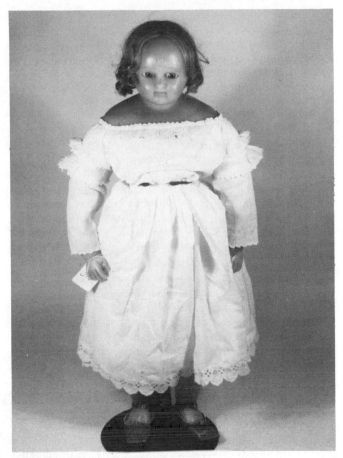

1776. Manufacture of poured wax dolls is shown by this doll with its wax shoulder head, arms and legs. The hair is inserted in the scalp. There are blue glass eyes and a cloth body. H. 25½ in. (65 cm.). *Courtesy of Richard Withington. Photo by Barbara Jendrick.*

shoulders in wax, arms and legs in composition and a cloth body stuffed with sawdust or hair. The head is cast in a thin layer of wax which is backed with composition with inserted glass eyes and hair of mohair or 'tow'. The first step of the work is to make a plaster two-piece mould, from which a succession of casts can be taken. The mould may be made from an existing head, the first stage being to build a strap of plasticine round it to divide it. Cover one side with plaster and allow to set, then remove the plasticine strips and scrape a few circular hollows in the edge of the half mould and oil it. The other half of the model is then covered similarly and allowed to dry, after which the two halves of the mould are moved from the model. They are tied together ready for receiving the wax, a great deal of time being saved if a number of moulds are made and stood in a row crown downward ready to receive the wax.

"Any good white wax that sets hard may be used, the material being melted in a can stood in hot water. It is tinted a pink shade by stirring in a little rouge. The plaster moulds are well saturated with water before pouring, but there must be no actual drops inside. They are filled with wax right up to the top, then after 20 minutes, when the wax in contact with the plaster has had time to set, the liquid [wax] inside can be poured back into the can, leaving a shell of wax about 1/8 in. thick. When hard, this shell is backed with a composition layer composed of glue, whitening and tow, which will greatly strengthen it. When hard and dry, separate the halves of the mould and trim up the cast, when it is ready for applying the hair and eyes, and colouring.

"The next operation is rather peculiar, the scalp being cut away . . . [In the same way as you find with German bisque-head dolls] a cardboard substitute being glued in its place. These may be made of several thicknesses of paper pasted together and compressed into a wooden mould. Before glueing in place, make a hole in it, and brush up and tie together some tow or hair and apply glue to the tied-up part and press into the hole. Before fixing the scalp in place the doll's eyes should be fitted, these being procurable by the gross from dealers in dollmakers' requisites. Sockets are cut to accommodate them, a little melted wax being poured inside to embed them in. They should be worked about until a realistic appearance has been obtained. The cardboard scalp is then glued to the head, and the hair glued down to cover it as naturally as possible. The face is then finished by dusting violet powder over it and rouging the cheeks, then with a fine brush, the eyebrows, lashes and nostrils are painted in, the lips being tinted vermillion.

"The legs and arms are cast in a simple two piece mould that includes perhaps a dozen or more limbs. The surface is well oiled and the casts made in plaster, these being finished by painting and varnishing. The groove serves for tying on the calico shapes, these being afterwards turned back. . . . Make up the calico body and stuff, together with the stuffed portions of the limbs, with hay straw, wood shaving, or other convenient material. Lastly the head is carefully glued to the stuffed body." (See also **Manufacture of Dolls, Commercial: Made in Great Britain.**)

Manufacture of Wigs for Dolls. PLAYTHINGS, January, 1927, contained a Rosen & Jacoby advertisement stating, "Send us your doll heads and we will return them to you dressed in wigs best suited to their character."

Also in PLAYTHINGS, January, 1927, and continued in March, 1927, Otto Follender Wig Corp. described how they made wigs:

"There are three distinct kinds of hair which go to make up wigs, mainly. MOHAIR, or hair from a certain type of goat, ORIENTAL HAIR, or human hair gathered in the Orient, and OCCIDENTAL HAIR, or hair gathered in the European countries. The former is commonly called Chinese Hair and the latter First Quality Hair. These three kinds are again divided into several grades each, which will be taken up in detail.

"There is one outstanding feature of hair, whether real or imitation, it is grown expressly for the market. Mohair . . . is originally the hair of goats of certain species. Some of the best product comes from Angora, Persia, and Turkey. Then there is Australia, and in recent years Texas has grown a considerable quantity of mohair. The hair is shorn from the animals, baled to grades and length, dyed to the proper shades and spun into a sort of rope or braid when it is to be used for WIGS. . . .

"The European countries produce much of the world's supply [of hair]. The most productive regions are Italy, followed by the Balkan States, Germany and Switzerland. Each country produces a distinctive grade or quality hair. Although each is termed First Quality Hair, that coming from Germany or Switzerland is the best. It is soft, and may be had in natural light colors. Rumania and the Balkan Section produces the next best grade. Here the hair is noticeably coarser and runs in darker shades. While Italy produces the greatest quantity of raw hair, this is coarser than the other grades and is almost entirely dark.

"When the writer claims that hair is grown for the Market he does not mean in the same sense as wool or cotton, although there is little difference in the methods employed. The original source of hair in Europe is the peasant woman. When a woman's tresses reach a certain length she travels to the market place of a village or community where there are dealers of hair and sells either part or most of her braid while it is still on the head. After the required amount of bargaining is done, the required amount of the hair is cut off, and the woman receives her pay and returns to her home. This process is repeated as often as there is a demand for the hair. There are also many itinerant dealers or peddlers who travel about the country selling, buying and exchanging wares and household goods, who also buy the hair from the head, and in turn sell it to the town establishments. The product secured in this manner is termed cut-hair. There is still another form of raw hair collecting and this is called the combings method. When combing the hair a certain amount of hair is bound to break off or fall out. All this is collected by the comb and is removed to some receptacle, generally a vase or dish and when several pounds have been accumulated, it is sold to a dealer.

"From the small dealers scattered all over the country the hair finds its way to the large collectors or dealers, usually located near a seaport, where the hair is combed out, the colors matched, sizes sorted, and made into convenient bundles. It is then cleaned, sterilized and shipped all over the world. It is interesting to note that Europe consumes a considerable quantity of the raw hair it produces.

"The greatest factor in the Human Hair market today is China. It is estimated that China with her enormous population produces about 5,000,000 pounds of Human Hair annually. Chinese hair is of greater length comparatively than European hair, and is grown not only by the women but by the men as well. With the exception of the orthodox Chinese the natives grow their hair long. His que [sic] must be at all times properly cut and barbe red. The religions of the country makes the que [sic] imperative so the male quite properly mixes business with custom."

The second installment of the article by Otto Follender continues the story of the origin of the hair for dolls' wigs.

"Let us follow the hair from a source in China to the time that it is used on a doll. . . . The collector or barber . . . has saved or stored a quantity of hair. This is sent to the dealer in a seaport with whom he does business. This dealer then has workers who comb out this hair and sort it out into lengths of from about 6 inches to about 50 inches. During this sorting process the hair is cleansed and bundled, each size separately, in bundles of about a half pound each. These are then disinfected, packed in cases and the case is fumigated after which it is passed by the port doctor, and if the hair goes to the States, by the U.S. Consular office.

"On arrival in this country after clearing customs it is distributed to the different trades . . . the shorter lengths are used mainly for doll wigs. . . .

"For our purpose the hair is first given several chemical baths, which serve two purposes. It is further cleansed and softened, and is changed to any desired light shades. The original hair being of a bluish black color, it is necessary that we do this. Then it is woven, several hairs at a time, into long strings and these strings are sewed on forms of cloth. Each style of wig requires a different method of sewing. Then the hair is either curled into the desired long curls, ringlets, roll curls, marcelles, and any number of other styles or is made into any desired bob.

"Although doll wigs seem a simple product it is really a most complex problem to make out of material that varies in so many characteristics a more or less uniform and stable product. Although we are living in a machine age these same reasons are responsible for the fact that with one or two exceptions doll wigs are made by hand by the same method used twenty years ago." (See also **Wigs.**)★

1777. German girls working on dolls' wigs and curling the hair. The bundle of sticks in the foreground are used to curl the hair. Just behind the sticks are the swatches of hair and in the distance are the dolls with wigs lying flat, while farther back at an angle are the dolls waiting for their wigs. *Courtesy of the Museum of the City of Neustadt near Coburg.*

Mara. 1925–26. *Lenci* felt doll style no. 165/1 dressed as a peasant woman with long lappets on its headdress. Ht. 29½ in. (75 cm.).

Maranette Doll Co. 1929–30. New York City. Distributed and/or made dolls.

Marca Registrada. Spanish for Trademark.

Marceau. 1929–30 and later. Paris. Made dolls.

Marcel. See **Marseille, Armand.**

Marcel. See **Roth, Joseph, Manufacturing Co.**

Marceline. 1910–15. Name of a portrait doll with composition head and hands made by *A. Steinhardt & Bros.* and offered as a premium by NEEDLECRAFT magazine. The label on its coat read: "Marceline//The Hippodrome Clown."★

Marcella. 1915. One of the *Paderewski* dolls made by Polish refugees in *Mme. Lazarski*'s workshop. Marcella represented a mountaineer girl in church clothes.

Marchant Mécanique. See **L'Intrépide Bébé.**

Marchant Système. 1913. According to Anne-Marie and Jacques Porot this doll was a simplified walking doll patented by *Roullet & Decamps.* Later they used the patent on a *Kiss-Throwing* doll called *Bébé Système.*

Marcoux, Charles. 1920–23 and probably other years. Montreuil-sous-Bois, Seine. Made porcelain heads for dolls.★

SERIE O

FRANCE

3

1778. Mark probably used by Charles Marcoux for porcelain dolls' heads.

Marc-Schnür (Maré-Schur[+]), Marie. 1908–18. Munich, Germany. One of the principal artists who designed heads for *Marion Kaulitz* dolls. These art dolls with hard composition heads and painted eyes represent babies, children or adults. At first they were known as Schnür dolls but they were based on Kaulitz's ideas. Marion Kaulitz dressed them in regional or occupational costumes. Marie Marc-Schnür was a portrait painter born in 1869. She also designed wax head dolls. (See Ill. 1779.)

1908: Dolls were exhibited by *Hermann Tietz.*

Marcus, L., & Co. 1922. Advertised dolls in a British toy trade journal.

Marcuse, Day & Co. 1916–22. St. Albans, Herts., and London. Made Emdee line of felt and cloth character dolls, including those with *British Ceramic* heads.

1916: Style nos. included a Jolly Dutch series, *Pierrot* and *Pierrette.*

1917: Advertised dolls with and without sleeping eyes.

1780A & B. Felt face Marga doll with mohair wig, painted features, cloth body, elaborately costumed as a Hungarian girl from one of the provinces. H. 13½ in. (34 cm.). *Coleman Collection.*

1779A & B. Dolls with wax heads designed by Marie Marc-Schnür as shown in DEKORATIVE KUNST, April, 1912.

1781A & B. Felt face Marga doll with mohair wig, painted features, pipe inserted in the mouth, cloth body dressed as a Hungarian boy. The name of the province is on a heart shaped tag. H. 13½ in. (34 cm.). *Coleman Collection.*

Marga. 1920s and later. Trade name of the dolls made by *Mrs. Marga Szerelemhegyi.* These dolls had either felt or composition heads, hair attached to the heads, painted features and cotton bodies. Their clothes were very elaborate and usually represented Hungarian regional attire. They carried a heart-shaped tag with the name "Marga" on it and the clothes sometimes bore a black stamp, "Made in Hungary." 14 in. (35.5 cm.) was a popular size.

1929: *Meier & Frank* sold Marga dolls.

1939: Marga dolls were shown at the New York World's Fair.

Margaine-Lacroix (Margaine Lacroix), House of. 1873–1918. Paris. French couturière and doll maker who dressed dolls for the *Société Française de Fabrication de Bébés & Jouets* (S.F.B.J.). Some of the cloth-body dolls that she dressed had china heads made by *Sèvres.*

Her dolls' clothes often represented those worn by inhabitants of French, Russian and other provincial regions as well as royal historical personages. She sometimes copied costumes shown in famous portraits. The clothes usually

bore a woven silk label with the identification "Margaine-Lacroix, 19 Boulevard Haussmann, Paris."

1914/15: According to an article by Léo Claretie in ARTS FRANÇAISE, Margaine-Lacroix created dolls.

1916: Carnegie Museum in Pittsburgh purchased 40 of her dolls: 35 were marked S.F.B.J. and five were marked *A. Marque.* The A. Marque dolls were dressed as Queens of France while the S.F.B.J. dolls were dressed in various costumes; six as Russians, one as an Italian, one as a Swiss girl, one English, and the rest in French costumes. Among these were dolls dressed to represent the following portraits: D'Artagnan from the THREE MUSKETEERS; Isabel de Beauvaise, Queen of France; M. and Mme. Gavarni; Princesse de Lamballe; Musette from LA BOHÈME; Pamela from NANINE;

1782. Composition head Marga doll has braided mohair wig, decorated with ribbons, black velvet headband edged with rick-rack, painted blue eyes, and a closed mouth. The head and torso are one composition piece while the arms and legs are cloth, jointed at the shoulders and hips. Original Hungarian costume. Stamp on petticoat "Made in Hungary// MARGA." H. 11½ in. (29 cm.). *Courtesy of Estelle Johnston.*

Mme. Marie Jeanne Roland; Mrs. Sarah Siddons as portrayed by Gainsborough; and Elizabeth Louise Vigée-Lebrun. All of the dolls had a hat or headdress, a lace and ribbon trimmed batiste combination undergarment, and silk or leather shoes made by *Eugene Alart.* The A. Marque Queens cost $35 while the S.F.B.J. dolls cost $10 to $23. To facilitate the passage of the dolls through U.S. Customs it was advised that they should be called "Modéles Coutumes," not "Poupées" (Models of Costumes, not Dolls).

1918: Created dolls and dolls' clothes.

Margie. 1921. Name of a doll with composition head and hands made by *Effanbee.* The doll had molded hair with a large bow affixed to the top, painted eyes and a cork stuffed cloth body. Its dress was figured lawn trimmed with white, and had a bluebird pin affixed to it. Ht. 15 in. (38 cm.).

Margie. 1926. Name of a composition head *Mama* doll distributed by the *Chicago Mail Order House.* Ht. 26 in. (66 cm.); priced $1.89.

Margie. 1928–30 and later. Name of a doll with a composition head, and segmented wooden body designed by *Joseph Kallus,* made by *Cameo,* and distributed by *Borgfeldt* and *Butler Bros.* It had molded hair and head band, painted eyes glancing to the side, open-closed mouth with painted teeth, and a separate neck piece that was attached by a spring wire or hook. The 18 pieces of turned wood comprising the body were strung together with elastic. On its chest was a heart-shaped decal with "Margie" in white letters over two lines of black letters reading "DES. & COPYRIGHT BY JOSEPH KALLUS." Several hundred thousands of these dolls were produced.

1929: It came wearing a ribbon bandeau and bow; a rayon knitted shirt or full lawn skirt. The hands were knobs and it could stand alone. Ht. 10 in. (25.5 cm.); price $1.00. Another company made an imitation of Margie and lost a Court battle over their doll. (See THE COLLECTOR'S BOOK OF DOLLS' CLOTHES, Ill. 776A.)

1930: The doll was made with hands having fingers. It could sit or stand and wore various styles of dresses or rompers. The doll was slightly taller than in 1929.

According to Mr. Kallus, Margie was later made as a cloth-body doll with an embossed covered buckram face.

1783A & B. Margie, designed and made by Joseph Kallus with a composition head and segmented jointed wooden body. This doll with the stub hands was made in 1929, later the hands had fingers. It has molded hair and painted features including an open-closed mouth with teeth. Mark, decal: "MARGIE// © by J. L. Kallus." H. 10 in. (25.5 cm.). *Coleman Collection.*

1784. Red decal mark on the chest of Margie, designed by Joseph Kallus.

Margon. 1917–30 and later. Trade name for metal eyes with a celluloid covering, patented by Samuel Marcus[†] and made in Newark, N.J. Margon was an acronym for Marcus, Grubman and Konoff. In the 1920s Marcus and Konoff bought out Grubman. Later the name Margon was used for plastic eyes. (See also **Markon.**)

Margot, Pierre François. 1850–68. Paris. In 1850 he married and acquired a business of making and selling dolls, which failed in 1858. The inventory showed dolls at manufacturer's prices. In 1868, he failed again as a maker of dolls. This information was supplied by Mme. Florence Poisson, Curator of the Roybet Fould Museum.★

Marguerite. 1927. Trade name of a German-doll with a bisque head, wig, glass eyes, open mouth and teeth on a fully jointed composition body.

Marguerite Clark. See **Snow White.**

Marguerite Dolls. 1901. Stone bisque shoulder-head dolls with molded decorations on the heads and front shoulders. They had cloth bodies and came in four styles, including a clover leaf, a morning glory, one other flower, and a butterfly (see Ills. 1785, 1786 and 1787). Four heights; priced 40¢ to $2.00 doz. wholesale.

1786. A series of Marguerite dolls include this shoulder head ornamented with a butterfly. This ornament is painted blue as are the eyes. The cloth body has bisque lower arms and china legs. H. 11¼ in. (28.5 cm.). H. of shoulder head 3¼ in. (8 cm.). *Courtesy of Sara Kocher.*

1785A & B. Untinted stone bisque shoulder head with molded hair and two four leaf clovers as molded headwear and another pair on the front shoulders. All of the clovers have gold trimming. This doll may be in the Marguerite series which was advertised in 1901 and shown as a doll with similar hair arrangement or it may be part of Butler Bros.' International series and representing Ireland. The cloth body has a wide maroon strip of cloth all the way down the center front of the torso, a typical Butler Bros.' feature. The china legs are replacements. H. 10½ in. (26.5 cm.). H. of shoulder head 3 in. (7.5 cm.). *Coleman Collection.*

1787. Untinted bisque shoulder head with molded headwear in the shape of a morning glory which is painted pink with a green stem. The long curls and bangs are molded and painted as are the features. It has a molded yoke with a band of green points around the neck. The body is cloth with bisque lower limbs. This style of head may belong to the Marguerite dolls advertised by Butler Bros. H. 13¼ in. (33.5 cm.). H. of shoulder head 4½ in. (11.4 cm.). *Courtesy of Sara Kocker.*

Maria. 1927–28. Black *Lenci* felt doll, style no. 565. The doll was barefoot and wore a shirt with vertical stripes and a broad brimmed hat. Ht. 19 in. (48 cm.).

Maria-Cheliga, Mme. 1918. Paris. Created cloth dolls.

Mariana. 1927–28. *Lenci* felt doll, style No. 564, dressed as a Dutch girl. Ht. 10½ in. (26.5 cm.).

Mariana. 1928. Name of a *Madame Hendren Lyf-Lyk* doll made by *Averill Manufacturing Co.* It had a mohair wig, sleeping eyes and a mama voice.

Maria-Teresa. 1925–26. *Lenci* felt doll, style No. 252, dressed in a pseudo 18th century dress, held a small cage. Ht. 20 in. (51 cm.).

Marie. 1908–11. Cutout cloth doll made by *Saalfield*. It had a printed French girl's dress with a big red bow in back and in the hair. Ht. 7¾ in. (19.5 cm.).

Marie. 1912–13. Cutout cloth doll representing a French girl, advertised by *Selchow & Righter*. Ht. 8 in. (20.5 cm.); price 40¢ doz. wholesale.

Marie. 1920. One of the *Classic* dolls made by *Speights* with a *British Ceramic* head, mohair wig, sleeping or stationary eyes. When Marie had a hair-stuffed body it cost less than half as much as when it had a jointed composition body. There were six different styles of removable clothes with hooks and eyes.

Marie-Jeanne. 1926. Name of a doll representing a French peasant holding a tray. This doll was used as a trademark registered in France for dolls, by *Mme. Elisa Rassant.*

Marlenfeld Porcelain Factory (Porzellanfabrik). 1892–99 and later. Grossbreitenbach, Thür. This factory, owned by *A. Voigt*, made china and bisque dolls' heads and limbs.

1788. Mark of the Marienfeld Porcelain Factory.

Marigold. 1924. One of the *Posy* line of cloth dolls made by *Dean*. It wore a knee-length skirt trimmed with shamrock designs. Bands of a light colored fabric encircled the neckline, the bottom of the skirt and sleeves. Its hat had a brim.

Marigold Babies. 1922–24. Line of character-face baby dolls made by *Hermann von Berg*. They had wigs and the jointed bodies could stand. They came dressed or undressed.

Marilee (Marylee). 1928–30. *Mama* doll with *Patsy* type neck joint, made by *Effanbee*. It had composition head, arms and legs, mohair wig, sleeping eyes, hair eyelashes, smiling lips, teeth, a cloth cotton-stuffed body jointed at the shoulders and hips. It also had a crying voice and came dressed. If it had a crying voice instead of a mama voice it was not a real Mama doll even though described as such in the advertisements.

1929: It had an extensive new wardrobe of clothes including dresses, coats and hats.

1930: It came in hts. 11 and 21 in. (28 and 53.5 cm.). *Montgomery Ward* charged $5.00 for the larger size doll.

1789. Marilee mark on a composition head of the Patsy type made by Effanbee.

Marilyn. 1927–28. Name of a doll with composition head and limbs on a cotton stuffed cloth body distributed by *Montgomery Ward*. It had a human hair sewed wig. Sleeping eyes with hair eyelashes, open mouth with teeth and tongue and a mama voice. Its dress was of silver cloth in a two-tone rose effect and there was a bandeau on its head. Ht. 25 in. (63.5 cm.); priced $5.48.

Marion. Before 1914–16. Name of a doll with a wooden head on a cloth body stuffed with fabric, created by *Georges Lepape*.

Marion, Mlle. 1918. Paris. Created dolls.

Marjean. 1920s or earlier. U.S.A. Brand name of a large assortment of accessories for dolls. These included bracelets, buckles, tortoise shell combs, fans, hat pins, lockets, necklaces, fancy pins, and purses. A salesman's sample card showed a wide variety of doll size items. Label read: "MARJEAN [with head of a child below and beneath that] BABY DOLL//JEWELRY."

Marjoric. 1912–14. See **Life Like Babyland Dolls.**

Marjorie. 1917. Flat face cloth doll with printed hair and clothes, distributed by *Wyman, Partridge*. Shown holding an animal. Ht. 10½ in. (26.5 cm.).

Marjorie. 1918. All-composition doll with five-piece spring jointed body made by *Jessie M. Raleigh*. It had molded short hair.★

Marjorie. 1920–21. Dressed stockinet doll with a hand-woven wig, made by *Chad Valley* as style no. 29. Ht. 9 in. (23 cm.).

Märklin. See **Rock & Graner.**

Markmann, Sigismund. 1909–30 and later. Berlin. Manufactured and exported dolls. Specialized in outfits and accessories for dolls.

1921: Advertised a doll and its wardrobe contained in a cardboard Easter Egg.

1927: Advertised bodies for baby dolls.★

Markmann, Wilhelm. 1929–30. Berlin. Made dolls' clothes.

Markmann, Wilhelm. 1930 and later. Ohrdruf, Thür. Manufactured porcelain dolls.

Markon Manufacturing Co. Before 1926–30. New York City. Manufactured voices, eyes, teeth, tongues, wigs, shoes and other accessories for dolls as well as the dies for doll-making machinery. The metal part of the sleeping eyes was marked "OMN Co. Inc.//Pats.//Pend."

1927: Made a new crying voice that could be used in smaller dolls than was previously possible. The edges of the metal case for the voice were rounded.

1928: Assignee of a patent by *John N. Whitehouse* for a doll with sleeping eyes.

1929: Manufactured "unbreakable" glass eyes; celluloid eyes that had been "popular for many years"; metal eyes "designed for popular priced dolls." All the eyes were furnished with or without hair eyelashes. The small crying voice was named "Midget." The teeth and tongues were made separately or in combination, of celluloid or of metal. They were members of the *Doll Parts Manufacturing Assoc.* (See also **Margon**.)

Marks. It is usually impossible to identify a doll, especially the bisque and china ones without a mark. A single letter or number does not generally constitute a decipherable mark. Dolls that closely resemble one another may or may not have been made by the same manufacturer. Successful dolls were frequently copied by other manufacturers. Dolls that look alike were probably made in the same period but not necessarily by the same manufacturer.

Often dolls are marked "Patented" and a date is given. When the patent referred to is examined it sometimes has little to do with that particular doll. It may be an earlier patent obtained by the maker and not really applicable to the doll on which it is found. For example, the 1892 design patent of *Celia Smith* specifies its use for "animal statuettes." But later she used this patent date on her dolls.

Names do not serve as identifiable marks unless they are registered as a trademark and are actively in use such as "*Kewpie.*" This accounts for the fact that one finds innumerable "Little Red Riding Hoods" and other popular named dolls made by different manufacturers.

Unfortunately a few modern makers of reproduction dolls leave the original mark on the doll that they are reproducing. Care must be taken to recognize these reproductions. Marks are not always easily read even by experienced collectors. Familiarity with the mark is often necessary in order to read it properly. Many collectors have reported having dolls marked "Madeline Germany." When actually the mark is only "Made in Germany," the "l" and "e" being extraneous scratches. Often parts of a letter are missing.

Marks can be found in many places on the heads and shoulder plates of dolls. They were sometimes made on the rim of the crown, on the top of the forehead, on the curved bottom of the head, near the edge of the shoulder plate or inside the shoulder plate. Stickers were usually placed on the body of the dolls, but *Kestner* sometimes placed their crown sticker on the front of the dolls' neck. Cloth labels often were sewed on dolls' feet or on their clothes. Many of the French Bébés had their names on a ribbon sash or a ribbon sewed onto their belt. Stamped marks have been found on dolls' heads, bodies and/or clothes, especially commercial chemises.

Sometimes the mark described an attribute of the doll such as "Wimpern"[†] (eyelashes). Often the mark was a code number or letter; the ones designating size numbers, mold #, or style no. can sometimes be deciphered and hopefully further study will reveal the meaning of more of these marks and lead to the identification of the makers who used them.

Sometimes it is necessary to be able to recognize and read the old German alphabet. This alphabet is shown in Ill. 1791. Note the similarity between the lower case f, s, and k. Lower case n and u are also very similar. Upper case I and J are identical. Umlauts (two dots) were sometimes placed over a, o or u to indicate diphthongs æ, œ and ue.

In the English alphabet which was also used by the Germans during recent times and some earlier periods, a "B" and an "E", a "B" and an "R", an "F" and a "P", and so forth are sometimes difficult to distinquish. Confusion arises frequently between a "C", a "G", and a "6".

The word "Germany" sometimes had a line over the lower case "y." According to the Ciesliks this practice comes from an early usage.

A paper sticker, tag or a button on a doll can usually identify the doll but the collector should be aware of the fact that these articles can easily be removed from a doll and placed on another doll; also, they can be made readily and even feloniously placed on any doll. This has been known to have occurred with some collectibles but it is hoped that doll dealers and collectors are more ethical than this.

One of the best ways to study incised or embossed marks is to make a rubbing or exact tracing of the mark, and place it on a white index card. The configuration on the card is actually easier to study than on the doll for several reasons: it includes some details not always noticeable on the curved surface of the doll; a group of cards can be compared more easily than the heads or dolls themselves; and comparison with published marks is facilitated. When the mark is partially concealed such as under the wig or under the kid of the body or even under the original clothes it is Not Recommended to attempt to obtain such marks.

Throughout the 1970s and early 1980s nearly all the books published in America and in Europe that contained marks on dolls appear to have simply copied the marks shown in the first COLLECTOR'S ENCYCLOPEDIA OF DOLLS. Apparently it was not understood that marks on dolls although similar can often be different not only in the order in which the information was given but in the manner in which it was written. Actually the variation was tremendous. Ralph Shea made a detailed study of the way various companies wrote just the word "Germany." He showed over 20 different calligraphic examples of "Germany" found on Armand Marseille dolls' heads alone. Most of the incised marks on dolls' heads are holographs, that is hand-written. The marks were generally incised in the master mold or on the original sculpture.

Large doll producers would have hired many artists and the incision of the mark may or may not have been done by the original artist or mold maker. No doubt it was often done by one of the many assistants. Moreover these artists and assistants could have worked for various companies during their lifetime. In view of all the possible variations it is not surprising that one finds so many differences in the incised marks. Nevertheless the marks of each company are generally sufficiently similar in content to provide identification. Marks are often in code, for example mold numbers, size codes, initials and/or symbols. It is these that reveal the origin of the dolls rather than the handwriting variations or similarities.

THE TOY TRADER gave the following account in 1926: "The new Merchandise Marks Bill . . . reads as follows: 'It shall not be lawful to sell, expose for sale or distribute by way of advertisement in the United Kingdom, any goods which bear any name or trade mark being, or purporting to be, the name or trade mark of any manufacturer, dealer or trader in the United Kingdom, not being goods produced or wholly or mainly manufactured therein, unless the name or trade mark is accompanied by an indication of origin.

"'Indication of origin' means, at the option of the person applying the indication, either

(a) in the case of goods manufactured or produced in any foreign country, the words 'foreign manufacture' or 'foreign produce' and in the case of goods manufactured or produced in a part of His Majesty's Dominions outside the United Kingdom the words 'Empire manufacture' or 'Empire produce'; or

(b) a definite indication of the country in which the goods were manufactured or produced; the indication being given, in either case in a conspicuous form. . . .

"It is expressly provided that a wholesale dealer may sell goods . . . wholesale to a purchaser unmarked, provided he secures from the purchaser an undertaking in writing that they will either be marked before they are offered for further sale, or that they will be exported or sold for exportation."

The "Marks" entry in the first COLLECTOR'S ENCYCLOPEDIA OF DOLLS should be read in its entirety in order to fully understand the meaning and importance of marks. (See also **Measurement of Dolls.**)★

1790. Bisque shoulder head with molded and painted hair and features. This 2½ in. (6.5 cm.) head marked 2 on the back of the shoulder is from a mold that is identical to a 4½ in. (11 cm.) china shoulder head (see Ill. 638) that is also marked 2 on the back of the shoulder as Is the tiny China head. Usually single digit numbers on the shoulder indicate the size, but here it appears to be a mold number. *Coleman Collection.*

1791. German Script Alphabet used in Germany until the end of World War II. Familiarity with this Alphabet is often necessary in reading marks on dolls made in areas that used the German language.

A. a.   B. b.   C. c.   D. d.   E. e.   F. f.   G. g.

H. h.   J. t.   J. j.   K. k.   L. l.   M. m.   N. n.

O. o.   P. p.   Q. q.   R. r.   S. f. s.   T. t.   U. u.

V. v.   W. w.   X. x.   Y. y.   Z. z.

Marks Bros. 1918–30 and later. Boston, Mass. Made and imported dolls and dolls' heads. They were affiliated with the *New England Toy Co.* Some of their dolls were handled by *Bush Terminal.* On their celluloid shoulder heads a number was often placed on the back indicating the height of the shoulder head in inches. They sometimes used the mark "Made In Germany//Marks Brothers Co. Boston," or for their American dolls, "Made in U.S.A.//Marks Brothers Co. Boston." These words were usually within a shield.

1918: Advertised *Sweetheart* line of cloth dolls and dolls with composition heads on cork stuffed bodies. Also celluloid shoulder heads with painted eyes and hair.

1919: Claimed they were exclusive manufacturers of the Bellow Crying Doll sometimes called "Squeak Doll." Advertised celluloid socket heads. *W. E. Peck* was their British agent.

1924: Advertised complete equipment for manufacturing *hot-press composition* heads and stuffed dolls including the dies for the heads. They also had celluloid faces, celluloid heads, composition heads and voices, both tipping and squeeze types. The trousseaux for dolls came in boxes or trunks and cost 25¢ to $5.00.★

Marks Doll Co. 1914. Canton, Ohio. Advertised dolls in TOYS AND NOVELTIES.

1792. Celluloid shoulder head made by Marks Bros. It has molded hair and painted features. Mark: III: 1793. H. of shoulder head only, 6 in. (15 cm.). *Coleman Collection.*

MARKS BROS. CO.
BOSTON, MASS.
U.S.A. 6

1793–1794. Mark on celluloid heads made by Marks Bros.

Markus. Before 1911–16. Felt character doll made by *Steiff.* and distributed by *Borgfeldt* in the U.S. and by *Gamage* in London. It wore a vertical-striped boy's suit and tam. Six hts. 28, 35, 43, 50, 60 and 75 cm. (11, 14, 17, 19½, 23½ and 29½ in.). The 43 cm. size was priced $2.12 in Germany in 1911 and in 1913 $3.95 in New York and $1.98 in London. In 1916 the hts. were 28, 35, 43, 50 and 60 cm. (11, 14, 17, 19½ and 23½ in.).

Marlborough. 1916. Belligerent looking cloth doll created by *Mme. Manson.* It represented "Going off to War."

Marlborough Manufacturing Co. 1918. London. Made dolls representing Charlie Chaplin and Red Cross Nurses. Used the initials M.M.C.

Marot, Maison. 1870s–80s. A china head doll with a wig and a kid body had a circular stamp on its chest which read "MAISON MAROT//PALAIS//ROYAL//GALERIE d'OR-LEANS, 46."

Marottes (Folie). Doll's head on a stick, often made music when twirled. Sometimes the stick was in the form of a whistle.★

Marque, Albert. 1910–16 and probably other years. Paris. Sculptor who made the model for a doll that was sold in one of the large department stores in Paris, according to a 1916 contemporary article by Jeanne Doin. These were the dolls marked "A. Marque" with bisque heads, wigs, closed mouth, pierced ears, ball jointed composition body with bisque forearms.

A. Marque was born in Nanterre, Seine, in 1872. He exhibited at many of the Paris Salons beginning in 1899. At first he was known for his Art Nouveau sculptures and he specialized in representations of babies and children, until World War I. Later he made sculptures of famous adults. He worked in bronze, marble, terra cotta and plaster and won many prizes.

A contemporary writer on art described A. Marque's work: "In seeking the true form of his model, he made rough models 10, 20 and even 50 times or more, until he found just what he sought." This same writer stated that A. Marque's infants rivaled those of Della Robbia and Houdon.

1902: He sculptured "Deux enfants à la poupée" (Two doll-like babies) for *Sèvres.*

1905 or 1906: At one of the Paris Salons (probably the Salon d'Automne of 1905), A. Marque exhibited a little girl's head in bronze inspired by Donatello's work. This was put in the same room with paintings by Matisse and other famous early 1900s artists. Allegedly Louis Vaucelles, a well-known critic

1795. Bisque dome shaped head on a Marotte. It has a blond wig, stationary blue eyes, and a closed mouth. The lower part of the doll is a stick. Original costume. H. 13 in. (33 cm.). *Courtesy of Sotheby Parke Bernet Inc., N.Y.*

0 — 41155. **FOLIE** à soufflet.
tête porcelaine, costume soie
et dentelle.
3.50, 4.50, 6. », 7. » et 8. »
A musique.
12. », 14. », 16. » et 20. »

1796. Advertisement in a 1921 catalog of L'Hotel de Ville for a Marotte or Folie. It has a bisque head, wig, and a silk costume trimmed with lace. In the end of the stick is a whistle. It makes music when twirled or is also made without music. Several prices are quoted for each type but the marottes with music cost 2½ or more times the price of the ones without music.

of the day, wrote, "Ah, Donatello au milieu des fauves." (Ah, Donatello in the midst of the wild beasts) and thus the name Fauvism was given to one of the most important artistic movements of Paris painting of that era.

1910: Won a silver medal at the Brussels Exposition in the toy class, presumably for his dolls.

1916: The Carnegie Museum in Pittsburgh purchased from *Margaine-Lacroix* five dolls with heads marked "A. Marque," clothes labeled "Margaine Lacroix," shoes with the *Alart* mark, stands marked "H. Gaudermen." These dolls were dressed as Queen Isabel, wife of Charles VI; Queen Marie, wife of Louis XV; Queen Marie Antoinette, wife of Louis XVI; Empress Josephine, wife of Napoleon I; Empress Eugénie, wife of Napoleon III. These dolls representing French Queens and Empresses came in custom-made boxes covered with French wallpaper. The Museum purchase also included 35 other dolls that were marked "S.F.B.J." *(Société Française de Fabrication de Bébés & Jouets)* but were wearing similarly labeled clothes, and had similar stands and similar boxes, to those of the A. Marque dolls. This suggests that the S.F.B.J. could have made the Albert Marque dolls, using the model designed by A. Marque. François Theimer claims that he has seen Albert Marque dolls in clothes carrying Worth labels. At the time of the A. Marque dolls it was fairly common practice to reproduce French couturier labels and attach them to clothes. Hts. of the five Queens reported was 24 in. (61 cm.); priced $35 each according to the invoice from Margaine-Lacroix. Other A. Marque dolls had measured 22 in. (56 cm.) tall. Their costumes included those of children and regional clothes, usually with the Margaine-Lacroix label.

1797. Doll designed by Albert Marque shown in this illustration from the pamphlet RENAISSANCE DE LA POUPÉE FRANÇAISE by Doin, written in 1916. The book is in the collection of the Widener Library, Harvard University. The doll has a wig, bisque head and lower arms on a composition body.

1798A–D. Bisque head doll designed by the sculptor Albert Marque. It has a wig with a Rembrandt style hairdo, stationary blue glass eyes, pierced ears, closed mouth, and a ball jointed composition body with bisque lower arms. Original regional costume. Mark on the head: "A. Marque." Shoes have the Alart mark on their soles. H. 22 in. (56 cm.). *Courtesy of the Margaret Woodbury Strong Museum. Photos by Harry Bickelhaupt.*

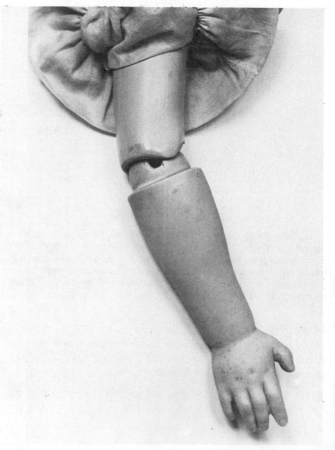

a. Marque

Margaine Lacroix

18. Boulevard Haussmann   PARIS

1799–1800. Marks on dolls designed by A. Marque (No. 1799) and dressed by Margaine Lacroix (No. 1800).

Marque Déposée. French for Trademark.

Marquer & Garnot. 1929. Paris. Manufactured aluminum molds for making dolls.

Marquis of Salisbury. See **Lord Robert Cecil.**

Marquisette. 1917. Mark on a socket head made by *Sèvres* and having a Sèvres mark. The head had a wig and painted eyes. Ht. of head only 7.5 cm. (3 in.). (See Ill. 2369A.)

Marquisette. 1929. Name of dolls made by *Barthélemy.*

Marschner, Johann. 1927. Hainspach, Czechoslovakia. Listed under Dolls in a directory.

Marseille, Armand. 1885–1930 and later. Sonneberg and Köppelsdorf. Thür. According to the Ciesliks, Herman Marseille, an architect, was a Huguenot born in St. Petersburg, Russia, in 1822. His son, Armand Marseille, was born in 1856 also in St. Petersburg. They were still in St. Petersburg in 1859 when Armand's brother, Mischa, was born but they left Russia sometime later.

The family appears to have settled in Coburg which was then Thüringia and now Bavaria. Armand married and had a son, Herman Marseille, in 1885, the year in which Armand took possession of the porcelain factory of Liebermann & Wegescher. This factory made porcelain articles including heads for whistles and pipes. In 1884 Armand Marseille had purchased the *M. Lambert* Toy factory. It is believed that Armand Marseille made his first bisque doll's head ca. 1890. Herman Marseille Senior died in Coburg in 1903. In 1915

Herman Marseille Junior married Beatrix Heubach, daughter of *Ernst Heubach* and in 1919 the Marseille and Heubach factories merged to become the Vereinigte (United) Köppelsdorfer Porzellanfabrik and Herman Marseille became the manager. Armand Marseille died in 1925 in Köppelsdorf.

According to contemporary directories the factory was known as Porzellanfabrik Armand Marseille in 1926 and in 1928 the union was dissolved. Herman continued to make bisque heads and later made composition heads. The factory continued operations until the 1950s. In Sonneberg the name Marseille was pronounced like "Marcel."

Ernst Reinhardt was one of the employees in the Armand Marseille factory before he came to Philadelphia, Pa., around 1909. Louis Marseille, brother of Armand, died in Philadelphia in 1896.

Armand Marseille was one of the largest suppliers of bisque dolls' heads in the world from about 1900 to 1930 and later. Among the many companies who used Armand Marseille heads were: *Amberg; Arranbee; C. M. Bergmann; Borgfeldt; J. Bouton; Butler Bros.; W. Cohen & Sons; Cuno & Otto Dressel; Eckart; Edelmann; Foulds & Freure; Otto Gans; E. Goldberger; Hitz, Jacobs & Kassler; B. Illfelder; E. Maar; Montgomery Ward; Wilhelm Müller; Emil Pfeiffer; Quaker Doll Co.; Joseph Roth; Samhammer; Peter Scherf; Sears; Seyfarth & Reinhardt; Siegel Cooper; E. U. Steiner; Wagner & Zetzsche; Wanamaker; Hugo Wiegand; Wislizenus;* and *Louis Wolf.*

The Armand Marseille bisque heads were usually marked "A. M." and/or "Armand Marseille" as well as "Germany" or "Made in Germany." There was considerable variation in the way in which these words were written, sometimes they were printed and sometimes they were in script. The first letter was capitalized in the names and the rest of the letters were lower case (not capitals). Sometimes the A was written Λ on what appears to be the 1920s dolls; often the early y in Germany had a line over it. The size number usually was found between the A and the M but sometimes it was after the A. M. Occasionally the mark on the bisque heads had an Armand Marseille mold number and the initial or initials of the owner of the mold but did not have any other Armand Marseille designation.

		ARMAND MARSEILLE MOLD NUMBERS			
Mold No.	D.R.M.R. or D.R.G.M. No.	Description of Head	Type of Neck	Name of Doll	Company Who Used the Head
93		Dolly face	Shoulder head		Dressel
95		Dolly face	Shoulder head		
110?		Molded hair	Shoulder head		
121					
189		Dolly face	Socket		
200	243	Wigged, eyes to side, closed mouth	Socket		
205		Baby			
210	243	Molded bobbed hair, eyes to side. Girl	Socket		
210e		Mate to the above. Boy	Socket		
223		Eyes to side			
230	248	Molded hair, closed mouth	Socket	Fany	
231	248	Wigged, closed mouth	Socket	Fany	
233			Socket		
240		Bald head baby	Flange	Baby Phyllis	Baby Phyllis Doll Co., J. Bouton

ARMAND MARSEILLE MOLD NUMBERS

Mold No.	D.R.M.R. or D.R.G.M. No.	Description of Head	Type of Neck	Name of Doll	Company Who Used the Head
241					
242		Painted bisque			
244		Painted bisque			
246		Painted bisque			
250	248	Molded hair and features	Socket		Borgfeldt
251	248	Wig, glass eyes, open mouth	Socket		Borgfeldt
252	248	Painted eyes to side, watermelon mouth, molded hair	Socket		Borgfeldt
253		Wig, glass eyes to side, watermelon style mouth	Socket	Nobbikid	Borgfeldt
254		Molded hair, painted eyes, watermelon style mouth	Socket		
255		Wig, painted eyes to side, watermelon style mouth	Socket		
256		Baby			E. Maar
258		Eyes to side, watermelon style mouth	Socket		
259		Baby			Borgfeldt
266		Molded curly hair	Socket		
270			Shoulder head		
273			Shoulder head		
300		Dolly face	Socket		
309			Shoulder head		
310		Wigged, glass eyes and closed mouth	Socket	Just Me	Borgfeldt, used later by Vogue
318		Black, painted hair, sleeping glass eyes			
320	255	Bald head, eyes painted to side, closed mouth	Socket		
322		Painted hair, eyes painted to side, closed mouth	Socket		
323		Wigged, glass eyes to side, closed mouth	Socket		
324	255	Molded hair, painted eyes to side, closed mouth	Socket		
325		Wigged, glass eyes to side, closed mouth	Socket		
326	259	Baby. Sleeping eyes, molded hair, open mouth	Socket		Borgfeldt
327	259	Baby. Molded hair, sleeping eyes, open mouth	Socket		Borgfeldt
328	267	Baby. Molded hair, sleeping eyes, open mouth	Socket		Borgfeldt
329	267	Baby. Wigged, sleeping eyes, open mouth	Socket		Borgfeldt
333		Black or Oriental. Painted hair			
341		Infant, painted hair, closed mouth	Flange	My Dream Baby Rock-a-Bye Baby	Arranbee, Dressel
341K		Infant, painted hair, closed mouth	Socket		
341Ka		Infant, wigged, closed mouth	Socket		
342		Painted hair, sleeping eyes, open mouth, infant	Flange		
345				Kiddie Joy	Hitz, Jacobs & Kassler
347		Sleeping glass eyes, open-closed mouth	Shoulder head		
350		Sleeping eyes, closed mouth	Socket		
351		Infant, painted hair, open mouth	Flange	My Dream Baby	Arranbee, W. Cohen
351K		Infant, painted hair, open mouth	Socket		
352		Baby, molded hair, open mouth	Shoulder head		
353		Oriental infant. Open mouth	Flange		
353K		Oriental infant. Open mouth	Socket		
354					

ARMAND MARSEILLE MOLD NUMBERS

Mold No.	D.R.M.R. or D.R.G.M. No.	Description of Head	Type of Neck	Name of Doll	Company Who Used the Head
356		Oriental			
360a		Baby. Sleeping eyes, open mouth			
362		Black	Socket		
370	377439	Dolly face	Shoulder head		
370	374830	Dolly face (This D.R.G.M. was issued in 1909)	Shoulder head		
371					Amberg
372		Molded girl's hairdo, glass eyes, open mouth	Shoulder head	Kiddie Joy	Hitz, Jacobs & Kassler
375		Wigged, glass eyes, open mouth	Shoulder head	Kiddie Joy	Hitz, Jacobs & Kassler
376			Shoulder head		
377		Young girl or boy			
378		Glass eyes, open mouth (Biscaloid)	Socket		
382		Painted hair, sleep-eyes, open mouth			
384			Socket		
390		Dolly face	Socket		
390	374830	Dolly face (see #370)	Socket		
390n	246	Dolly face	Socket		
391			Socket		
395		Sleeping eyes, open mouth	Socket		
396		Mulatto	Socket or straight		
398		Oriental			
399		Character			
400	343	Lady face with closed mouth	Socket		
401		Lady face with open or closed mouth	Socket		Louis Wolf
406		Black			
411		Baby			
414					
449		Painted eyes, closed mouth	Socket		
450		Wigged, sleeping eyes, closed mouth	Socket		
451		Indian, sleeping eyes, open mouth	Socket		
452		Wigged, sleeping eyes	Socket	Shirley Temple style	
452H		Molded hair version of 452	Socket	Shirley Temple style	
454					
458		Indian			
500	232	Character. Molded hair, painted eyes, closed mouth	Socket		
504					
505		Painted eyes			
510					
513		Black, sleeping eyes, open mouth			
515					
516					
518		Black, molded hair, sleeping eyes, open mouth	Socket		
519			Flange		
520	232	Molded hair, intaglio or glass eyes, open or open-closed mouth	Socket		Wilhelm Müller
540					Gebr. Eckardt
542		Sleeping eyes, open mouth	Flange		
550		Wigged or painted hair, sleeping eyes, closed mouth	Socket		
550a		Wigged, sleeping eyes, closed mouth	Socket		
551					

Mold No.	D.R.M.R. or D.R.G.M. No.	Description of Head	Type of Neck	Name of Doll	Company Who Used the Head
551K			Socket		
560	232	Molded hair, intaglio eyes, closed mouth	Socket		
560a	232	Wigged, glass eyes, open mouth	Socket		Emil Pfeiffer
570	232	Character face			
590		Character face, wigged, glass eyes, open mouth	Socket		
599		Oriental			
600	234	Molded hair, painted eyes, closed mouth	Shoulder head		
620	234	Character			
621	234	Character			
630	234	Painted hair and eyes, closed mouth	Shoulder head		
640a	234	Painted eyes, closed mouth	Shoulder head		
640b	234	Character head	Shoulder head		
670			Shoulder head		
696		Sleeping eyes, open mouth			
700		Sleeping eyes, closed mouth	Socket		
701		Sleeping eyes, closed mouth	Socket		
710		Indian			
711		Glass eyes, closed mouth	Shoulder head		
750	258	Baby. Wigged, glass eyes, open mouth	Socket		
760	258	Character. Wigged, glass eyes, open mouth	Shoulder head		
790		Baby			
800	234	Character, molded hair, glass eyes, open mouth	Socket		
810		Sleeping eyes, open-closed mouth	Shoulder head		
820		Sleeping eyes, open-closed mouth			
900		Baby			
920		Wigged, glass eyes, open mouth	Shoulder head		
927		Baby			
950		Painted hair and eyes, closed mouth			
951		Character			
957		Wigged, glass eyes, open mouth	Shoulder head		
966	267	Biscaloid, wigged, glass eyes, open mouth	Socket		
970		Baby			Otto Gans
971	267	Baby			
971a	267	Baby. Glass eyes, wigged, open mouth	Socket		
972		Wigged, glass eyes, closed mouth		Baby Peggy	Amberg
973		Wigged, glass eyes, closed mouth		Baby Peggy	Amberg
975		Baby. Wigged, glass eyes, open mouth	Socket		Otto Gans, Louis Wolf
980		Baby, wigged, glass eyes, open mouth	Socket		
984		Baby			
985		Baby, wigged, glass eyes, open mouth	Socket		
990		Baby, wigged, glass eyes, open mouth Black or white	Socket		
991		Wigged, glass eyes, open mouth	Shoulder head	Kiddie Joy	Hitz, Jacobs & Kassler
992		Baby, wigged, glass eyes, open mouth	Socket	Our Pet	Gebr. Eckardt
993				Kiddie Joy	Hitz, Jacobs & Kassler
995		Baby, wigged, glass eyes, open mouth	Socket		Seyfarth & Reinhardt
996		Baby, wigged, glass eyes, open-closed mouth	Socket		
997				Kiddie Joy	Hitz, Jacobs & Kassler
1321					Hugo Wiegand
1330		Baby or Toddler, wigged, glass eyes, open mouth (also marked Köppelsdorf)	Socket		Wilhelm Müller
1333		Baby			
1353				My Dream Baby (Type)	
1361					Quaker Doll Co.

ARMAND MARSEILLE MOLD NUMBERS

Mold No.	D.R.M.R. or D.R.G.M. No.	Description of Head	Type of Neck	Name of Doll	Company Who Used the Head
1369		Painted eyes, open mouth			
1370		Painted eyes, open mouth			
1374		Dolly face, fur eyebrows		Florodora	
1776		Dolly face, wigged, glass eyes, open mouth	Shoulder head		Dressel
1890			Shoulder head		
1892			Shoulder head		Dressel
1893			Shoulder head		
1894		Dolly face, wigged, glass eyes, open mouth	Socket & shoulder head versions		Found on Dressel dolls
1895					
1896			Shoulder head		Dressel
1897		Dolly face, wigged, glass eyes, open mouth	Shoulder or socket head		
1898			Shoulder head		Dressel
1899		Dolly face, wigged, glass eyes, open mouth	Shoulder head		Peter Scherf
1900					
1901		Dolly face, wigged, glass eyes, open mouth	Shoulder head		Peter Scherf
1902					Peter Scherf
1903			Shoulder head		
1905					
1909			Shoulder head		
2000					
2010			Socket		
2015		Wigged, glass eyes, open mouth	Shoulder head		
2966		Wigged, glass eyes, open mouth	Shoulder head		
3091			Shoulder head		
3093			Shoulder head		
3200		Wigged, glass eyes, open mouth	Shoulder head		
3300		Wigged, glass eyes, open mouth	Shoulder head		
3500		Wigged, glass eyes, open mouth	Shoulder head		
3600		Wigged, glass eyes, open mouth	Shoulder or socket head		
3700		Wigged, glass eyes, open mouth	Shoulder head		
4008			Shoulder head		

The above mold numbers have been seen by the authors or have been reported. It is not certain that all of the latter group are correct. There is some confusion between the mold numbers and the numbers which follow D.R.G.M. or D.R.M.R.

Sometimes Armand Marseille dolls' heads had names without mold numbers. These included: *Alma, Baby Betty, Baby Gloria, Baby Florence, Baby Phyllis, Beauty, Columbia, Duchess, Ellar, Florodora, Jubilee, Mabel, Majestic, Melitta, My Playmate, Nobbi Kid, Our Pet, Princess, Queen Louise, Rosebud, Superb, Sunshine,* and *Tiny Tot.* The Armand Marseille heads representing Indians often did not have a mold number. The names of other dolls' heads possibly made by Armand Marseille were *Darling, Lilly,* and *Lissy.*

In the marks on Armand Marseille heads "A" seems to stand for "Ausgeschnitten" (Cutout) which probably meant the pate was to be cutout. "H" stood for "Halsrand" (neck edge) which referred to the neck of the doll. "K" stood for "Kurbelkopf" (socket head). "N" stood for "Neu" (new). The meaning of x is not known but it sometimes appeared on the *My Dream Baby.* K was generally found on the socket heads of My Dream Babies.

1892: Registered (DEP) a doll's head that was made for Cuno & Otto Dressel. This head was marked "C.O.D. 93 DEP" according to the Ciesliks. It came in sizes 0 to 10.

1893: The factory had 550 employees making bisque dolls' heads and all-bisque dolls.

1902: The bisque shoulder heads had wigs and the larger sizes had sleeping eyes. They were often used on Superb kid bodies that also had bisque hands.

A doll marked "1894//A.M. 5 DEP" on its bisque head and with a ribbon marked "John Wanamaker//Philadelphia //New York, Paris" was shown as style no. 4370 in the 1902 Wanamaker catalog. This doll appeared in color plate 19 in THE COLLECTOR'S BOOK OF DOLLS' CLOTHES. Thus it is evident that 1894 cannot be used as a date for dolls with this mark without further proof.

ARMAND MARSEILLE BISQUE SHOULDER HEADS SIZE–HEIGHT RELATIONSHIP

Size No.	Height of just the Shoulder Head in.	cm.
10/0	3	7.5
7/0	3⅝	9
5/0	4¼	11
0½	4⅜	11
2/0	4½	11.5
0½x	5	12.5
2½	5½	14
4	6¼	16
6	6¾	17
8	7¾	18.5

1909: *Siegel Cooper* advertised "Marcel" bisque-head dolls with sleeping eyes, sewed curly wigs, jointed papier-mâché bodies, dressed in a chemise and footwear. Ht. 14½ in. (37 cm.); priced 50¢. Their Florodoro (Florodora) bisque-head dolls had sleeping eyes with eyelashes, kid bodies and wore only shoes and stockings. Ht. 14½ in. (37 cm.); priced 50¢.

Applied for six German patents (D.R.G.M.) for dolls' heads.

1913: Mold # 401 lady doll made for Louis Wolf.

1914: Made the head for *Nobbikid,* mold # 253. It had googly eyes.

1915: Supplied Foulds & Freure with their 390 line and 370½ line.

1918: Supplied C. M. Bergmann with some bisque heads.

1920s: Made bisque socket heads for Tiny Tot dolls.

1922: Montgomery Ward advertised Armand Marseille bisque heads on Princess Dolls with composition bodies. Ht. 18½ in. (47 cm.). Armand Marseille bisque heads and hands were on imitation kid bodies with universal joints. Ht. 18 in. (45.5 cm.). Separate bisque heads made by Armand Marseille had mohair wigs, sleeping glass eyes and hair eyelashes. Four hts. of head only: 3¾, 4⅜, 5, and 5⅜ in. (9.5, 11, 12.5 and 13.5 cm.).

1926: Made bisque heads for the Baby Phyllis line of dolls for *J. Bouton & Co.*

1927: Factory had eight kilns, a very large number of kilns. They supplied *E. Goldberger* with bisque heads.

1930: Supplied mold #s 390, 520 and 1330 to *Wilhelm Müller.*

Ca. 1933: Supplied *Quaker Doll Co.* with bisque heads including mold # 390 and # 1362. # 390 came in 27 sizes, from 8/0 to 18. These made up into dolls 8 to 38 in. (20.5 to 96.5 cm.); priced $3.00 to $60.00 a doz. wholesale.

1936: Armand Marseille bisque mold # 390 heads listed in a Wagner & Zetzsche catalog:

Size No.	Socket Head Circumference cm.	in.	Approximate Ht. of Doll cm.	in.
6/0	17	6½	28	11
4/0	19	7½	31	12
2/0	22	8½	36	14
0	23	9	39	15½
1	24	9½	41	16
2	25	10	44	17½
3	26	10½	47	18½
4	27	10½	48	19
5	28	11	50	19½
6	29	11½	52	20½
7	29	11½	54	21½
8	30	12	57	22½
9	32	12½	60	23½
10	33	13	63	25
11	34	13½	67	26½
12	36	14	70	27½

Earlier the 390 heads were usually on taller dolls for the same size number as given above. The variation could be as much as two inches; especially with the taller dolls. Since Armand Marseille heads were put on a variety of bodies the heights of dolls with the same size heads often differed considerably. The dolls with shoulder heads were usually taller than those with socket heads having the same size number. This difference was especially apparent between the mold #s 370s and 390s. The heads on bent-limb baby bodies and on toddler or *Mama* doll bodies were larger in size number relative to the height of the doll than those on child type bodies.

Examples of the following size numbers have been found and no doubt others also exist.
17/0, 16/0, 13/0, 12/0, 11/0, 10/0, 9/0, 8/0, 7/0, 6/0, 5/0, 5/0x, 4/0, 3/0, 2/0, 2/0x, 1/0, 0, 0½, 1, 1½, 2, 2½, 3, 3½, 4, 4½, 5, 5½, 6, 6½, 7, 7½, 8, 8½, 9, 10, 11, 12, 13, 14, 15, 16, 17, 18.
Size 16/0 was on dolls as small as 5 in. (12.5 cm.) tall.
Size 2/0 was on dolls 15 or 16 in. (38 or 40.5 cm.) tall.
Size 6 was on dolls about 22 in. (56 cm.) tall.
Size 12 was on dolls about 29 in. (73.5 cm.) tall.

These general size-height relations seem to show taller dolls than those given for 1902. This difference might be due to a changing trend over the years, or to the fact that the dolls on which the 1902 relationship was based were abnormally short dolls. *Kestner* made a very short doll with a kid body around 1902.★

Taking a sample of nearly 300 Armand Marseille heads it was found that:

Mold # or Name	Per-centage Found	
390 Socket head	45	The proportions given represent those found in collections of dolls in the U.S.A. and Britain; and may not be a true representation of the real relative numbers of these dolls produced at any given time or for the whole production period of these dolls (ca. 1890–1930 and later).
370 Shoulder head	15	
Florodora	9	
1894 Shoulder head	8	
My Dream Baby	4	
3200 Shoulder head	3	
Googlies (eyes looking to the side)	3	
Others	13	
TOTAL	100	Percent

Marseille, François Emile. 1888. Maisons Alfort, France. Registered in France a trademark "M" in a shield over an anchor for dolls.★

1802. One of Armand Marseille's bisque heads, mold # 258, with roguish (googly) glass eyes. It has the watermelon slice shaped mouth and is on a bent limb composition baby body. H. 14 in. (35.5 cm.). *Courtesy of the late Magda Byfield.*

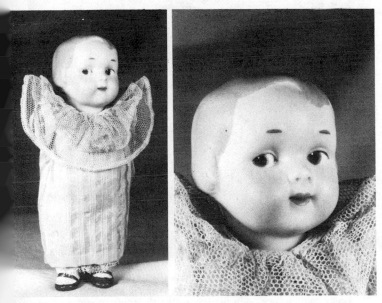

1801A & B. Bisque head made by Armand Marseille, mold # 210, intaglio roguish eyes, closed mouth on a five piece body. Original clothes, molded footwear. Mark: Ill. 1819. H. 6½ in. (16.5 cm.). *Coleman Collection.*

1803. Armand Marseille's bisque head mold # 310 has a blond wig, sleeping and flirting blue glass eyes, closed pursed mouth, and a five piece composition body. Mark on head, "Just ME// Register Germany//A. 310/3/0 M." (See also Ill. 1365.) *Courtesy of Bess Goldfinger.*

1805. Pair of bisque socket heads representing Orientals, made by Armand Marseille. They have painted black hair, sleeping brown glass eyes, closed mouths and bent limb baby composition bodies. Left to right, marks: A M //353// 8K and AM//353// 3½ K. Hs. 20 and 13 in. (51 and 33 cm.). *Courtesy of Sotheby Parke Bernet Inc., N.Y.*

1804. Pair of bisque socket heads mold # 323 made by Armand Marseille. They have wigs, roguish (googly) glass eyes, smiling closed mouths and composition bodies. Doll on the left has straight legs and the doll on right has a bent limb baby body (possibly replaced). Mark on both dolls "Germany 323//A 11/0 M." H. of doll on left 6 in. (15 cm.). H. of doll on right 7 in. (18 cm.). *Courtesy of Richard Withington, Photo by Barbara Jendrick.*

1806. Bisque head made by Armand Marseille; mold # 390 has a wig, glass eyes, and an open mouth with teeth. The arms are composition. Original regional costume. H. 12 in. (30.5 cm.). *Courtesy of Sotheby Parke Bernet Inc., N.Y.*

1807. Bisque socket head mold # 390 made by Armand Marseille. This doll has the final painting of the bisque after the firing. It has a wig, with two long braids, sleeping glass eyes, open mouth, and a fully jointed composition body. Original regional costume. Mark "Armand Marseille//Germany//390//A 5/ 0 M." H. 12½ in. (31.5 cm.). Circumference of head 7 in. (18 cm.). *Courtesy of Richard Withington. Photo by Barbara Jendrick.*

1808. Character bisque head mold # 400 made by Armand Marseille with a wig, sleeping blue glass eyes, hair eyelashes, closed mouth, and a ball jointed composition body. Contemporary clothes. Mark 400//A 3 M. II. 18 in. (45.5 cm.). *Courtesy of Sotheby Parke Bernet Inc., N.Y.*

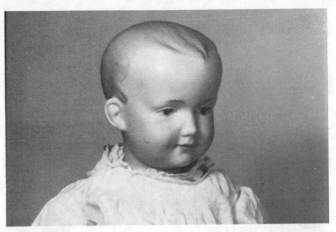

1809. Bisque socket head mold # 500 made by Armand Marseille. It has painted hair, intaglio blue eyes, closed mouth and a composition bent limb baby body. Mark: Ill. 1828. H. 14 in. (35.5 cm.). Circumference of head 10 in. (25.5 cm.). *Courtesy of Richard Withington. Photo by Barbara Jendrick.*

1811. Character bisque socket head mold # 550 made by Armand Marseille, has a wig, sleeping blue glass eyes, closed mouth, and a ball jointed composition body. Mark: "Germany //550//A 4 M //D.R.G.M." H. 19½ in. (49.5 cm.). *Courtesy of Jessica Norman.*

1810. Bisque socket head made by Armand Marseille, mold # 520. It has molded hair, brown intaglio eyes, an open-closed mouth, and is on a ball jointed composition body. H. 15 in. (38 cm.). *Courtesy of Sotheby Parke Bernet Inc., N.Y.*

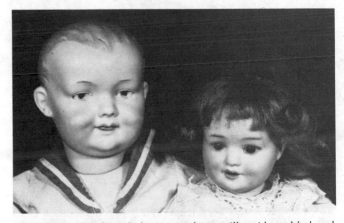

1812. Bisque head made by Armand Marseille with molded and painted hair and features. The eyes are intaglio, the mouth is open-closed with two upper teeth, molded dimples. This mold 560 differs in appearance from the same mold (560a) which has the eyes and mouth cut out, and has a wig. (See Ill. 2094.) Mark: Ill. 1829. H. 15 in. (38 cm.). *Coleman Collection. Purchased in Europe.*

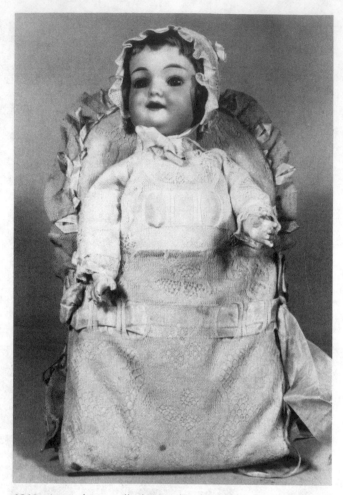

1814. Pair of bisque character heads made by Armand Marseille, mold #971. They have wigs, sleeping glass eyes, open mouth with two upper teeth, and a five piece bent limb composition baby body. Mark: Ill. 1831. H. 13 in. (33 cm.). *Courtesy of Jan Payson.*

1813. Armand Marseille bisque head mold # 560a on a doll probably produced by Emil Pfeiffer in the 1920s. It has a wig, sleeping glass eyes, open mouth with teeth, dimples, and is on a toddler style composition body. Original lace, net and ribbon pillow into which the doll fits. Only the upper half of the doll is dressed. Mark on head: Ill. 1830. The back of the body is marked 30, its cm. height (12 in.). *Coleman Collection.*

1816. Bisque socket head mold # 1894 made by Armand Marseille has a blond mohair wig, stationary black glass eyes, open mouth, and is on a ball jointed composition body. Original clothes. Mark: "Made in Germany//Armand Marseille//1894." H. 21 in. (53.5 cm.). *Private collection.*

1815. Bisque socket head made by Armand Marseille. It has a wig, key wind moving blue glass eyes that go from side to side, an open mouth with two upper teeth and a composition toddler body. Mark: "A 980 M//Germany 16// D.R.G.M." H. 26 in. (66 cm.). *Courtesy of Sotheby Parke Bernet Inc., N.Y.*

1817. Bisque shoulder head mold # 1894 made by Armand Marseille. It has a blond wig, sleeping glass eyes, open mouth with teeth, and a kid body with bisque forearms. Mark: "1894//A M O DEP." H. 17 in. (43 cm.). *Courtesy of June Jeffcott.*

$\mathcal{A}M$ 95-1 DEP

1818

210
A10/0M.
Germany
D.R.G.M.

1819

Germany
M.H.
A 300 M.
12/0X.

1820

Armand Marseille
Germany
323
A.4/0.M.

1821

Germany
G 326 B
A 15 M.
D. R. G. M. 259

1822

AM
Germany
352 /2/2 K

1823

Armand Marseille
Germany
370
A 7/0 M

1824

Armand Marseille
Germany
390
A 9/0 M

1825

390
Made in Germany
A 9/0 M

1826

Armand Marseille
Germany
390
A 7/0 M

1827

500
Germany
A 4 M

D.R.G.M

1828

560
Germany
A. 2 M.
D.R.G.M.

1829

Made in Germany
Armand Marseille.
560 a
A 7/0 M
D.R.M.R. 232

1830

Germany
971.
A. O. M.
D.R.G.M. 2674.

1831

Germany.
A 985 M
1.

1832

1818–1843. Marks used on bisque heads made by Armand Marseille. The ones without the mold numbers may have been earlier than the others or in some cases they were marked with the initials of the doll maker for whom the head was made.

A.M.
Köppelsdorf.
Germany.
1330.
A. 8. M.

1833

1894
AM 2/0 DEP

1834

1894
AMDEP
made in Germany
8

1835

Germany.
1894
3600
A.M.ODEP.

1836

37⁰⁰
AM8 DEP.
made in Germany

1837

D.R.G.M.377439.
Made in Germany
D.R.G.M.374830/374831
◠
A 5 M.
390

1838

A.5 M.
D.R.G.M. 201013

1839

E.U. ST.
AW&Co
A   M3
made in Germany

1840

E.U.St.
made in Germany
A.M.
6

1841

Made in Germany
A 1 M

1842

A 14. M

1843

Marsh. 1865–1914. London. An article published in COUNTRY LIFE, 1974, reported that "Charles Marsh" claimed that he had originated the Royal *Model Doll.* Other wax doll makers also claimed that they originated the portrait dolls representing the children of Queen Victoria.

1905: McCALL'S MAGAZINE in December, 1905, had an article on the Marsh concern and included a listing of the services performed by Mary Ann Marsh.

DOLLY'S HOSPITAL
FULHAM ROAD, S. W.
Operation daily from 9 a.m. till 8 p.m.
M. MARSH
"Cures all Complaints incidental to Dollhood: Broken Heads or Fractured Limbs made whole; Loss of Hair, Eyes, Nose, Teeth, Fingers, Hands, Toes, or Feet replaced: Wasting away of the Body restored to Soundness. All Accidents are successfully treated by M.D. (Mender of Dolls.). Patients leave the Institution looking better than ever.
DECAPITATIONS AND AMPUTATIONS DAILY.
"Heads, Arms, Legs, or Bodies to be had separately. New Heads put on Old Shoulders, or New Shoulders put on Old Heads. Wigs and Heads for the French-jointed Dolls. Not responsible for Patients left after Three Months from Date of Admission to Hospital.

Children's own Hair inserted in their Dolls
Dolls dressed to order.
Dolls cleaned and repaired."

Both boys and girls brought their dolls to Mrs. Marsh to be repaired.

1908: M.A. Marsh was listed in a directory as a Manufacturer of dolls. ★

1844. Mark on dolls made by Charles Marsh.

Marshall Field & Co. 1852–1930 and later. Chicago, Ill. In 1927 Marshall Field celebrated their 75th Anniversary but it is not known when they first began to handle dolls. By the 1880s, Marshall Field was offering imported dolls wholesale. This continued at least until the 1910s period when their toy department was called The Kringle Society, and they offered dolls which were made both in the U.S. and Europe. PLAYTHINGS in 1929 listed Marshall Field as a maker of dolls.

1888: Most of the dolls shown in their catalog had bisque heads, wigs, glass eyes, jointed composition bodies and were dressed. Some of these dolls when in chemise were 15

to 17 in. (38 to 43 cm.) tall. They had sleeping eyes and/or mama-papa voices. The gusseted kid body dolls had bisque or composition shoulder heads with wigs, glass eyes, bisque lower arms even with the composition heads. Only the 25 in. (63.5 cm.) bisque-head dolls came with teeth and only some of the 15½ in. (39.5 cm.) bisque heads had pierced ears.

"Bébé Dolls" had bisque heads, sleeping eyes, jointed arms and legs and wore long baby clothes. Eight hts. 10½ to 20 in. (26.5 to 51 cm.).

There were also undressed composition-head dolls and china limb dolls; dressed rubber dolls and wool *(worsted)* dolls. The latter included dolls dressed as clowns, milkmaids, Russians and sailors.

1889: The catalog showed dolls similar to those in 1888, except more of the bisque heads had sleeping eyes and teeth and more of the bodies were gusseted kid. New dolls had bisque heads, jointed composition bodies and were dressed as Admirals, Jockeys, Little Lord Fauntleroy, sailors, and others. Five hts. 11 to 15 in. (28 to 38 cm.). But most of the dolls were still dressed as little girls. Also new were the "Jointed Mongolian Dolls" dressed as a Chinese Mandarin or a Japanese tea planter. Hts. 10 to 13 in. (25.5 to 33 cm.).

1892: Advertised that they distributed the following: *English Rag* dolls, composition-head dolls, Mama-Papa dolls, *Bébé Jumeau* in chemise, dressed *Bébé Steiner;* black dolls; dolls with nursing bottles that empty; all-bisque bent limb naked baby dolls called "boys"; other all-bisque dolls; infant dolls in long dresses; *Lilliputians;* bisque shoulder heads; dolls' stockings, dolls' slippers, and dressed dolls of china, bisque or composition.

1913: Advertised character dolls, lady dolls, men dolls, boy dolls, girl dolls and baby dolls; dolls with kid bodies and dolls with ball-jointed composition bodies; dolls with heads of bisque, celluloid, felt, cloth, stockinet, rubber or wood. The dolls were undressed, or dressed in a variety of costumes; clothes and accessories were sold separately.

1914: The Marshall Field's Kringle Society catalog shows dolls made by the following companies: *Amberg, Borgfeldt, Heinrich Handwerck, Carl Hartmann, Hertwig, Gebrüder Heubach, Horsman, Kämmer & Reinhardt, New York Rubber Co., Katherine Rauser, Rheinische Gummi, Schoenhut, Simon & Halbig, Trion Toy Co.,* Vischer[+] and many others.

1919: Advertised dolls dressed as soldiers of the Allies, nurses, and so on. There were black dolls, Oriental dolls, Indian dolls and white dolls.

1920: Distributed the *Rees Davis* floating dolls. Imported hand-carved wooden dolls from Switzerland. These dolls came in 15 to 20 different regional costumes.

1923: Among the dolls advertised were the *Flappy Flap* cloth dolls, *Grumpy* and various *Mama* dolls. One of their dolls was dressed in an Egyptian type costume.

1929: Exclusive wholesale distributor of the all-bisque dolls with jointed necks and molded clothes, representing various cartoon characters including *Skeezix, Uncle Walt, Aunty Blossom, Rachel, Orphan Annie, Daddy Warbucks, Smitty,*

Herby, Mr. Bailey (Boss), Andy Gump, Chester Gump, Ching Chow, Min, Uncle Bim, Tilda, Moon Mullins, Kayo, Emmy Schmaltz, Lord Plushbottom, Mushmouth, Harold Teen, Lillums, Winnie Winkle and Perry Winkle. They licensed Shackman to sell these dolls in the New York area. These dolls had their names incised on their back.

The 24 above-named dolls advertised in 1929 were later increased to include other members of these particular comics as well as dolls representing the Just Kids. Our Gang, The Nebbs, Mutt & Jeff and other comics. According to Becky Lowe there were 62 different "nodder" dolls in the group excluding the animals. Hts. 2½ to 3½ in. (6.5 to 9 cm.); priced $1.10 to $1.80 doz. wholesale.

PLAYTHINGS carried a Marshall Field advertisement stating "Dolls range from old fashioned stockinet ones to modern dolls that can sing 'London Bridge is Falling Down.' A large percentage of the Marshall Field dolls are dressed under our own supervision in styles copied from the latest children's models, and finished off with zip fasteners, kid gloves, umbrellas, and other amazing accessories.

"Baby dolls are completely outfitted. . . . Dresses for dolls, sweaters, print play dresses, party frocks, fur trimmed coats, raincoats and lingerie.

"Individually dressed dolls $5.50 up. Other dressed dolls 75¢ up. Baby dolls dressed $1.00 up. Wardrobe trunk for dolls include: play dresses, party dresses, coats, hats, sports outfits, raincoats, kimonos, night gowns, toilet articles and jewelry $26.00 to $110.00."

Marshall Foch Doll. 1927. Portrait doll of Marshall Foch, created by Mlle. Adrienne.

Marta. 1908. A doll with a wardrobe made by Carl Hartmann. The wardrobe included accessories.

Martel, André. 1920s. Paris, factory at Billom (Puy-de-Dôme). Member of the Chambre Syndicale. Made dolls' clothes of wool, cotton, silk and so forth including bonnets and footwear. Gloves and mittens were made of silk or cotton. Boots were made of leather or felt; slippers were leather; bootees were cotton. The dolls' underwear was a combination style.

Martet, Mme. 1916. Paris. Created dolls.

Martha (Bather). 1911 and earlier. Felt character doll made by Steiff. It was dressed as a girl in a bathing suit or middy dress. Hts. 28, 35 and 43 cm. (11, 14, and 17 in.); priced $1.05 to $2.06.

Martha Ann. 1927. Composition head dressed Mama doll distributed by Montgomery Ward. It had a mohair wig, sleeping eyes, open mouth, composition arms and legs on a cloth body. Ht. 20½ in. (52 cm.); priced $2.59.

Marti, Paul, & Co. 1926–29. London. Made dressed and undressed dolls.

Martin, Betty. 1929. Chicago, Ill. Created Betty O'Baby and Betty O'Portrait dolls. The babies were washable and very light in weight.

Martin, Fernand. 1880–1928. Paris. The successor in the 1920s, V. Bonnet & Cie., made walking dolls.★

Martin, Robert. 1899. Chemnitz, Saxony. Applied for a German patent (D.R.G.M.) for a doll's pattern.

Martin & Runyon. 1862–65. London. Name found on the box of a Zouave autoperipatetikos.★

Martine. 1924. Name of a cloth, dressed art doll sold by Printemps.

Martineau, Miss. Name inscribed on a poured wax-head doll with inserted hair, wax arms and linen body. Ht. 25 in. (63.5 cm.).

Maruei-Oki Doll Co. 1925–30. Kyoto, Japan. Made dolls.

Marvel. 1898–1913 and probably other years. Line of bisque-head dolls made by Kestner and sold by Butler Bros. The heads had wigs, some had stationary glass eyes and some had sleeping eyes; some of the mouths were closed and some open with teeth.

1899: Dolls had kid bodies with gusset joints and bisque lower arms. They wore black or plaid socks and shoes. Five hts.: 11, 13, 15¾, 17½ and 21 in. (28, 33, 40, 44.5 and 53.5 cm.).

1902: Kid bodies were stuffed with cork and sawdust. Larger sizes 23¾ and 24¾ in. (60.5 and 63 cm.) were added; prices ranged from $2.25 doz. to $1.80 each wholesale.

1910: A Kidlyne (imitation kid) body was used on the 11 in. (28 cm.) doll. The heads had sleeping eyes, open mouth and teeth. 19 and 28 in. (48 and 71 cm.) hts. were added.★

Marvel. 1913: Doll advertised by Gamage as having a wig, ball-jointed composition body; it wore a chemise. Ht. 11 in. (28 cm.); priced 13¢.

Marvel Doll. See **Dolly Record.**

Marvell Doll. 1928–30. Doll resembled a Lenci made by E. Chantrain; claimed to have been washable with sponge and soap. Hts. 17 and 23 in. (43 and 58.5 cm.); priced $2.87 and $4.69.

1928: Distributed by Gamage.

Marvin Toy Co. 1930 and later. New York City. Manufactured Le Marvel line of dolls.

Mary. 1921. British stockinet doll imported into the U.S. by Meakin & Ridgeway.

Mary. 1926. Doll with clockwork mechanism, represented one of the Hal Roach "Our Gang" members. It was made by Schoen & Yondorf, came dressed and bore a scroll shaped tag. Ht. 11½ in. (29 cm.); priced $1.25.

Mary and Her Little Lamb. 1926–28. Cutout cloth doll used to advertise products of Kellogg Co.

Mary Ann. 1920s. Name of an all-composition black doll with molded hair and painted features; jointed at the neck, shoulders and hips; made by the P. & M. Doll Co. Ht. 16 in. (40.5 cm.).

Mary Ann. 1922. Cloth doll stuffed with silk floss or kapok. It was made by Ross & Ross.

Mary Ann. 1923. *Mama* doll made by *Effanbee* with composition head, shoulders, bent arms and legs with dimpled knees. It wore an organdy dress trimmed with lace and a matching bonnet. The dress was knee length with elbow-length sleeves. The ankle strap slippers had buckles on the toes.★

Mary Ann. 1930. Trademark for dolls registered in U.S. by *Borgfeldt.*

Mary Anne. 1928. Name of a bisque-head doll with a bent-limb baby body distributed by *Butler Bros.* It came dressed in various outfits. This might be the *Borgfeldt* doll with an "e" added to the name. Spelling was often variable.

Mary Had a Lamb. 1919–20. Doll made by *Jessie M. Raleigh;* and came with a white lamb. (See Ill. 2175.)★

Mary Had a Little Lamb. 1908–24. Wooden doll and lamb made by *Schoenhut,* distributed by *Siegel Cooper* in 1909. The doll wore a shepherdress style dress and a large hat. Box was labeled "MARY HAD A LITTLE LAMB//HUMPTY DUMPTY." Came in one size; priced $1.50 including a school bench and desk.

Mary Had a Little Lamb. 1916–17. One of the *Hug-Me-Tight* line of cloth dolls, designed by *Grace Drayton* and made by the *Colonial Toy Manufacturing Co.*

Mary Had a Little Lamb. 1929. One of the *Kiddie Karakters* dolls in the *Madame Hendren* line made by *Averill Manufacturing Co.* The doll was made from the *Little Sister* mold designed by *Grace Corry.* It wore a checked dress and bonnet and carried a stuffed lamb. The rectangular tag pinned to its clothes had the corresponding nursery rhyme on it.

Mary Hoyer Doll Manufacturing Co. 1925–30 and later. Reading, Pa. Made all-composition dolls. Booklets describing how to make knitted and crocheted costumes for these dolls were available as well as accessories. Ht. 15 in. (35.5 cm.).

Mary Jane. Ca. World War I. Doll made in Steinach, Thür., wore a pea jacket and sailor cap, clothes designed by *John Paul Edward* in the United States.

Mary Jane. 1917–20. Line of dolls with composition head, wig, sleeping eyes, open mouth and teeth made by *Effanbee.* The body varied; it was a ball jointed composition or a cloth with composition limbs or kid body with Universal joints. It came semi-clad in combination underwear trimmed with ribbon beading or dressed in a silk gown with matching hat.

1919: Lenox[†] made Mary Jane bisque heads for Effanbee.

1920s: *Aunt Mary* and *Sears* handled dolls called Mary Jane; perhaps these were the Effanbee dolls since the descriptions were similar. The all-composition Mary Jane doll at Sears came in four hts. 16, 18, 20 and 24 in. (40.5, 45.5, 51, and 61 cm.); priced $6.95 to $11.75.★

Mary Jane. 1922. Cloth doll stuffed with silk floss or kapok, made by *Ross & Ross.*

Mary Jane. 1931. Trademark for dolls registered in U.S. by *Borgfeldt.*

Mary Lee. See Marilee.

Mary Lois. 1923. *Mama* doll that could wink and go to sleep probably made by *Ideal.* It had a Dutch bob wig, wore an embroidered blouse, checked gingham skirt and a matching tam. Its round tag read, "I am a // walking // Doll." Ht. 16 in. (40.5 cm.).

Mary Lou. 1927–28. Composition head *Mama* doll with curly hair made by *Effanbee* as *Bubbles'* big sister. Ht. 18 in. (45.5 cm.); price $5.00.

Mary Louise. 1927–28. Composition head and limbs, ringlet bobbed human hair wig, sleeping eyes, mama voice, distributed by *Montgomery Ward.* It wore a crepe-de-chine dress and a silk bandeau in its hair. Hts. 21½ and 24 in. (54.5 and 61 cm.); priced $7.39 and $8.48.

Mary Lu. 1928. Trademark for dolls registered in U.S. by *J. C. Penney Co.*

Mary Mix Up. See Little Mary Mix-up.

Mary Pickford. 1922–23. According to the BROOKLYN EAGLE in 1923, Mary Pickford "commissioned the famous doll creators to make a character doll of herself, offering to pay a large sum for the most successful likeness."

Allegedly 60 models were made by the eight contending artists and sculptors before one was selected.★

Mary Quite Contrary. 1919–20. Composition doll made by *Jessie M. Raleigh.*

Mary Sue. 1925–28. *Mama* doll made by *Effanbee* and distributed by *Montgomery Ward.* It had a human hair wig, sleeping eyes, hair eyelashes, an open mouth, composition arms and legs. One of its costumes was an organdy dress scalloped around the bottom and a ribbon bandeau and bow in its short curly blonde hair. It differed from *Rose-Marie* only by the length of its hair. Mary Sue was described as being able to dance as well as walk when it was led by the hand. It came with six photos and a heart necklace. Four hts. 18, 21, 23, and 26 in. (45.5, 53.5, 58.5, and 66 cm.); priced $6.29 to $10.93.

Mary Sunshine. 1929. *Mama* doll distributed by *Sears.* It wore an organdy dress and matching bonnet.

Marylee. See Marilee.

Mascot (Mascotte). Generic term used chiefly for dolls in the 1910s and later, such as *Nénette and Rintintin.*

Mascot. 1912–14. Composition-head doll made by *Horsman.* It had the same head and hands as the *Campbell Kids.* But it wore a striped blazer with a college letter for various colleges and in corresponding college colors. Worn with the blazer were knickers and a skullcap.★

Mascot Dolls. 1928. Cloth dolls in assorted shades with contrasting hair, distributed by *Hartley Sports Stores.* Ht. 16 in. (40.5 cm.).

Mascots. 1915–17 and later. Name of dolls made by *Farnell,* included *Ole Bill.*

Mascotte. 1925–29. Name used by Mme. *Lazarski* for dolls.

Mascotte. See **Bébé Mascotte** and **La Mascotte.**

Mascottes. 1927–30 and later. Line of felt dolls made by *Lenci.* Ht. 8½ in. (22 cm.) as reported in the 1930 Lenci Catalog.

Masin Wenzel. 1910. Vienna. Listed in a directory under Dolls and Dolls' Heads.

Mask Faces. Only the front half of the head was delineated and the back half was simply rounded and often covered with headwear. These masks were frequently used on *Boudoir Dolls* and the silk-faced art dolls of the 1920s. They were made of almost any material such as woven cloth, stockinet, felt, celluloid or bisque. Some of the stiffened cloth mask faces were marked "Made in England."

The following companies were among those who made and/or distributed mask faces:

1904: *Buschow & Beck*

1914: *Nottingham Toy Industry.*

1915: *Jernoid Works; J. Fred Scott.*

1917: The *Dolls' Accessory Co.* made a once-fired mask for dolls; *H. J. Jullien, Knight Bros. & Cooper;* Nottingham made *Vogue* dolls with mask faces.

1920: *M. Pintel.*

1927: The *Lafayette* store advertised mask faces with or without hair.

1928: *Ch. Ruchot & Fils.*

1930: *Dean* made a *Puck* with a mask face. (See also **Brückner** and **Glukin.**)★

Maskot. 1928. Long-limbed doll made by the *East London Toy Factory.*

Mason, John. 1765–85. Philadelphia, Pa. Imported and distributed dolls.

1771: Imported a large assortment of toys from Bristol, England, on the ship Warwick.

1773: Imported from London on the Ship Catherine and other ships from Bristol "a very large and neat assortment of toys such as drest dolls, . . . naked dolls."

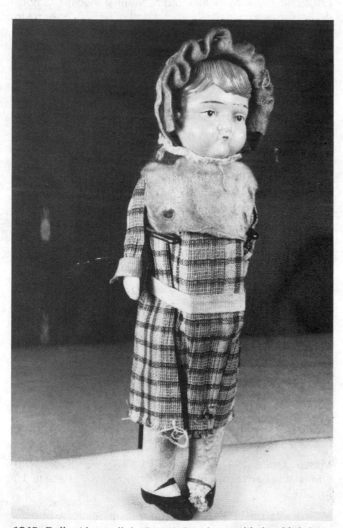

1845. Doll with a celluloid mask face has molded reddish hair, molded blue eyes, closed mouth and a cloth body with composition hands and legs. A squeaker voice is in the torso. Original clothes. H. 7½ in. (19 cm.). *Coleman Collection.*

1846. Cloth mask face doll in a 1900s version of a 1700s man's attire. The hair is white silk with curls on the side and a black ribbon to hold the queue in back. Painted blue eyes and features including a beauty mark on the cheek. The body is flesh colored silk. Original costume. H. 27½ in. (70 cm.). *Courtesy of the Margaret Woodbury Strong Museum. Photo by Harry Bickelhaupt.*

1847. Front and back view of British-made cotton velvet over buckram mask face with painted features used by Molly-'es to make her dolls. Similar mask faces were used by Norah Wellings. H. of head 2¼ in. (5.5 cm.). *Coleman Collection. Gift of Molly Goldman.*

1785: The INDEPENDENT GAZETTEER reported "John Mason-Toys, a curious assortment for sale at John Mason's Upholster's Store between Chestnut and Walnut Street, viz. Drest dolls, Naked ditto, Lilliputian dolls . . . wigs for dolls."

Mason & Taylor. Many dolls are erroneously attributed to Mason & Taylor. They did *not* make the wooden dolls with composition heads that have the black band around their waists. These bands have the patent dates belonging to the members of the Jointed Doll Co.[†] Mason & Taylor made other types of wooden dolls with composition heads.★

Masson, Jules Edmund. 1914–16. France. Sculptor born in 1871 in Paris. He made models of clay or wax for art dolls. Later he won several medals for his sculptures and engraved medals. Mme. de Laumont used one of his models for dolls' heads. The bisque dolls' heads were made in *Limoges* by *Lanternier* and by *Couty*. The Lanternier heads were usually marked "*Lorraine*"[†] (see Ill. 1849). The *Louvre* store sold dolls with heads designed by Masson and dressed in Alsatian regional costumes. These dolls had stationary glass eyes. Ht. 36 cm. (14 in.); priced $1.05. The same doll with an ordinary head and sleeping eyes, cost only 59¢. (See Ill. 1724).

Masson. 1920s. France. Member of the *Chambre Syndicale*, he made jewelry for dolls.

Master Sam. 1917 and possibly later. Name of a doll produced by *Horsman*. It had a composition head and hands, molded and painted features, wore a blue jacket and cap edged with red and white striped fabric, and red and white striped long trousers. At the neckline was a wide white collar with a red, white and blue bow tie having the words "TEDDY //BULL MOOSE" woven into it. This appears to have been a Teddy Roosevelt 1912 campaign ribbon which could have been added to the doll later or it could have been old stock used by Horsman. Except for the words on it, the ribbon looks like the tie shown in the patent papers.

A cloth label sewn on the jacket read, "UNCLE SAM'S KID//Trade mark//Design Applied For//E. I. Horsman Co. New York." *David Copperfield* had the identical clothes, except that doll had no bow tie.★

Mastercraft Doll Co. 1921–24. New York City. Made cloth dolls.★

1848. Bisque head designed by J. E. Masson, made by Lanternier for a doll created by Mme. de Laumont. It has a wig, stationary blue glass eyes, an open closed mouth with six teeth, and a cloth body with composition lower arms and legs. Original regional costume with white painted stockings and black shoes having heels. Mark: Ill. 1849. A round cardboard tag edged with metal and attached to the petticoat reads on one side "No 11" and on the other side "Vendéene." (inhabitant of Vendée). H. 15½ in. (39.5 cm.). A similar doll dressed in a Renaissance costume belongs in a historical series and is 14½ in. (35.5 cm.) tall. *Courtesy of the Margaret Woodbury Strong Museum. Photo by Harry Bickelhaupt.*

JE masson
S.C.

LORRAINE
Nº0
ALEC⁰
LIMOGES

1849. Mark on bisque heads designed by J. E. Masson and made by Lanternier.

Materials of Dolls. In 1897 G. Stanley Hall of Clark University, Mass., made a survey of about a thousand children, aged three to 12, seeking their preferences as to the material of their dolls with the following results:

CHILD PREFERENCES, 1897	
Material	Percentage
China	26 percent
Wax	20 percent
Paper	17 percent
Cloth	15 percent
Bisque	12 percent
Rubber	7 percent
Other	3 percent

Others, including celluloid, clay, glass, knitted wool, papier-mâché, tin, and wood, amounted to 3 percent, making a total of 100 percent. It is likely that some of the children did not understand the distinction between china and bisque, therefore the china may be too high and the bisque too low a percentage. It is possible that some of the children could have called glazed china dolls "glass."

Mathes (Matthes), E. W. 1853–1930 and later. Berlin. Founded in 1853 by Ida Mathes, by 1913 it was owned by Franz Mathes. Made dolls, used the names Ursula[+] and Friedel[+] for their dolls.

1928: Registered the name *Heideröschen* in Germany for dolls.★

Mathewman (Matthewman), Winifred. 1915–18. Ingleton, Yorkshire. Obtained a British patent in 1915 for dolls' eyes that winked and gradually glanced sideways.

Matlock Patent Washable Doll. 1899–1914. Composition head dolls with wig or molded hair, glass eyes, composition limbs and a cloth body, distributed by *Butler Bros.*

1899: Four hts. 11, 16½, 18 and 24 in. (28, 42, 45.5 and 61 cm.).

1902: Six hts. 12¼, 16½, 18½, 23, 24 and 30¼ in. (31, 42, 47, 58.5, 61 and 77 cm.); priced 96¢ to $8.35 doz. wholesale.

1914: Nine hts. from 11 to 31 in. (28 to 78.5 cm.); price $1.10 to $10.00 doz. wholesale. (See also **Mattlack**.)★

Matryoshka. There are varying accounts as to the origin of these Russian multiple nesting dolls. One account says that they were made principally in the villages of Bogorodskoye and Zagorsk. Dolls representing Napoleon and other military heroes were popular. It has been reported that the figures in some of these matryoshkas represented various characters in Russian fairy tales and that each group would tell one such tale.

1910–11: *Aux Trois Quartiers* sold these dolls under the name "Poupées Siberiennes." Ht. 14 cm. (5½ in.); price 49¢.

1928: PLAYTHINGS described these nested dolls which opened to display a smaller and still a smaller object of the same kind. They were made by Russian peasants in their own homes and had been made by the same families for generations. In 1928 they were sold by the Russian Peasant Art & Handicraft Department of *Am Torg Trading Corp.* in their New York salesroom.

"These wooden dolls are brilliantly colored. Red predominates with flashes of green and orange. The dolls have a highly polished surface."

Matthes.[+] See **Mathes, E. W.**

Matthewman. See **Mathewman, Winifred.**

Mattlack. Name used by *Kämmer & Reinhardt* for the mat finish on their celluloid or composition dolls. They used this term at least from 1912–27. *Max Oscar Arnold* and *Wislizenus* also used this term to describe some of their ball jointed dolls. (See also **Matlock**.)

Maurice Chevalier. 1928. A composition portrait art doll made in France.

Mauroner. Before 1838–96. Grödner Tal, Austria. *Verlegers* of dolls.

Before 1838: Joseph Mauroner of the Grödner Tal sold dolls in Madrid.

1853: Anton Mauroner and Christian Mauroner were Toy Verlegers, no doubt including dolls. (See also **Moroder**.)★

Maus, Widow Edith (née Westphal). 1925–28. Brunswick, Germany. Made art dolls and dolls' clothing. Max Lichterfeld was the distributor in Berlin and *Herman Bischoff Jr.* was the distributor in Hamburg.

1926: Advertised dressed dolls with wigs and rubber bodies. These carried a round tag with a mouse shown on it.

1927: Advertised dolls with washable soft rubber bodies, dolls' wigs and clothes.★

Mautner, Emil. 1912–25. Prague, Austria and later Czechoslovakia. Made composition dolls and dolls' heads.

Mavrogordato, Frau Geheimrat. 1930 or before. Germany. Created dolls.

Mawaphil Dolls. 1921–30 and later. Line of stockinet art dolls made by *Rushton Co.* The name Mawaphil, an acronym, came from the name of the artist who designed them, Mary Waterman Phillips. They were handmade and had handpainted, round faces, painted hair and eyes. They represented *Mother Goose* characters and 40 other types.

1922: 20 new style nos. each in various colors; priced 50¢ to $2.50. A Dutch boy and girl were among the styles.

1923: 23 new style nos. came with or without voices. A clown was one of the dolls, as were *Noble Ned* and *Willie Frog*.

1926: 48 style nos., 12 of which represented Mother Goose characters. Each Mother Goose doll had a Mother Goose shaped tag with the appropriate rhyme on it. Dolls included *Dutchy Boy, Hello Bill, Jack, Jill, Little Bo-Peep, Noble Ned*, and *Simple Simon*. Four hts. 8 to 20 in. (20.5 to 51 cm.).

1929: All of the dolls had voices.

1850A & B. Cloth doll with a tag that indicates that this doll was made for the Rushton Co. in their Mawaphil line of dolls and that this is Georgy Porgy with the appropriate nursery rhyme. Also on the tag are numbers 790 and Z12521. The doll has a hand-painted face done in oils on a canvas type material. The hair is blond and the eyes are blue. The stockinet body has lime green pants and matching helmet shaped hat, plus a white shirt and pink vest and the under portion of the crown of the hat. Black shoes and flesh colored hands. H. 12 in. (30.5 cm.). *Coleman Collection.*

1851. Plush cloth doll in the Mawaphil line of Rushton Co. with hand painted features including blue eyes. Wisps of blond hair extend from under the cap. Original clothes, pink plush panties are part of the body. Pink ribbed socks and white flat shoes are sewn onto the legs. A similar doll was advertised in PLAY-THINGS as new in 1928. H. 9 in. (23 cm.). Circumference of hips 10 in. (25.5 cm.). *Courtesy of Alma Wolfe. Photo by David Nelson.*

1930: New style nos. were made of plush, velveteen, terry cloth and stockinet; priced 50¢ to $4.00. A girl doll had a plush head, arms and legs and wore a print costume, felt shoes, and mercerized stockings. ★

Max and Moritz. Two bad boys drawn by Wilhelm Busch for a book first translated into English in 1870. Many dolls portrayed these little rascals. Often the dolls had *Roguish* (googly) eyes. This may have been the origin of the googly eyes. Max usually had the watermelon slice shaped mouth.

There were several all-bisque versions of Max and Moritz, including a pair of nodders.

Among the earliest Max and Moritz dolls were those made by *Sehm.* Other known Max and Moritz dolls were:

1907–24: *Schoenhut* wooden dolls. Max had a flat top hair-do painted black, and wore a blue coat, red vest and shoes, black and white checked trousers. Moritz had a top-knot hairdo and wore a green coat, black and white checked trousers and tan shoes. They came in one size.

1910–23: Celluloid dolls made by *Rheinische Gummi und Celluloid Fabrik* with joints at the shoulders and molded clothes. Ht. 14 cm. (6 in.).

1910–24 and possibly other years: *Steiff* made jointed felt dolls which were distributed by *Borgfeldt* in the U.S. These dolls had stitched hair and removable clothes. Ht. 30 cm. (12 in.); priced 67¢ in Germany in 1911 and $1.15 in New York in 1913. In 1916 there was also a 35 cm. (14 in.) size.

1912: Mold #s 31 and 32 were made by *Th. Rechnagel* according to the research of the Ciesliks.

1913: Both *Kämmer & Reinhardt* and *Kley & Hahn* made Max and Moritz dolls. The K & R head molds were #s 123 and 124 and usually the bodies had molded footwear.

1923: *Rheinische Gummi und Celluloid Fabrik Co.* made celluloid versions of Max and Moritz dolls.

1925: *Phoenix* in their Harburger Gummiwaren Fabrik made molded and painted rubber versions of Max and Moritz.

Ca. 1930: *Kestner* made all-bisque versions of Max and Moritz. These had molded hair, painted features, jointed shoulders and hips, and were mold # 186 for the ones with molded clothes and mold # 187 for the ones without molded clothes. Ht. 4½ in. (11.5 cm.). (See Ill. 1853.)

1980: Max and Moritz dolls were sold in German stores. ★

Max-Laval. 1927–30 and later. Paris. Made heads for dolls.

Max-Schudze. See **Schudze, Max.**

Maxine Doll Co. 1926–30 and later. New York City. Made *Mama* dolls, infant dolls, baby dolls and all-composition child dolls. They called one of their lines *lifelike* Dolls. In 1929, *B. Silverman* took over the Company and they moved into larger quarters. In this same year Sam Ward joined the Company. *Samuel O. Ludwig* was the factory representative.

1926: Dolls came in various sizes and their dresses were of original design.

1927: Licensed by *Voices, Inc.* to use the patented mama voices and criers in their dolls.

1928: The baby dolls had smiling faces, came with composition or cloth legs and some of them could stand without support. *Baby Gloria* came in five hts. Maxine Doll Co. made a doll called *Mitzi* that was similar to *Patsy. Effanbee* sued them for infringement and obtained an injunction. Then Maxine sued Effanbee and won their case in the New York Supreme Court, which gave them the rights to make and sell Mitzi. But the appellate court reversed this decision and Effanbee finally won all rights to a doll having the features, characteristics and general appearance of Patsy as well as the trade name.

1931: Advertised Baby Gloria; *Gloria* Lou and Gloriette; a doll's wardrobe packed in an overnight case with lock and handle and dolls packed in a box that could be converted into a cradle; priced $1.00 to $5.00.

May, Otto. 1913. Chemnitz, Germany. Applied for a German patent (D.R.G.M.) for a voice in a doll dressed in swaddling clothes (poupard).★

1853A & B. Pair of all-bisque dolls representing Max and Moritz and made by Kestner ca. 1914. They have molded and painted hair, intaglio eyes looking to the side, closed impishly smiling mouths. The bodies are jointed at the neck, shoulders and hips. Original clothes except that Moritz has lost his pants. H. 6½ in. (16.5 cm.). *Courtesy of the late Magda Byfield.*

1852. Felt Max has the Steiff button in its ear. The black mohair is sewn onto the head. There are black button eyes, closed smiling mouth, a turning neck and joints at the shoulders and hips. The seam down the center of the face ends at the bottom of the nose where it meets a horizontal seam. Original felt clothes include a gray coat, orange shirt and tan pants. H. 30 cm. (12 in.). *Courtesy of Richard Wright. Photo by A. Jackson.*

1854A & B. Pair of bisque socket heads mold #s 123 and 124 on the dolls made by Kämmer & Reinhardt and Simon & Halbig. They represent the characters named Max and Moritz in the Wilhelm Busch children's story. Moritz is the doll on the left. They have wigs, glass eyes glancing to the side, closed smiling mouths that portray their mischievousness, and five-piece composition bodies with molded footwear. Original clothes. H. 16 in. (40.5 cm.). *Courtesy of Vera Kramer, Dolls in Wonderland Museum.*

May Blossom. 1922–23. Name of a doll originated by *Demalcol.*★

May Manton Patterns. See **Clothes.**

Maya. 1925–27. Name of an art doll made by *Heinrich Geschwister.*★

Maybelle. 1912–22. Name of dolls made by the Bell Toy Co.[†]

1912–14: Dolls had socks and leather slippers. Four hts. 17½, 24½, 26¾ and 28 in. (44.5, 62, 68 and 71 cm.); price $1.75 to $4.95. (See also **Arcy Toy Manufacturing Co.**)★

Mayer, Otto. 1929. U.S. Made and/or distributed American character dolls.

Mayer & Sherratt. 1915–20. Longton, Staffordshire. Made *British Ceramic* dolls' heads and limbs at their Clifton Works. They marked their dolls *Melba* and/or *Classic* and sometimes M.&S. Some of their dolls had wigs and sleeping eyes. Other dolls had molded hair.

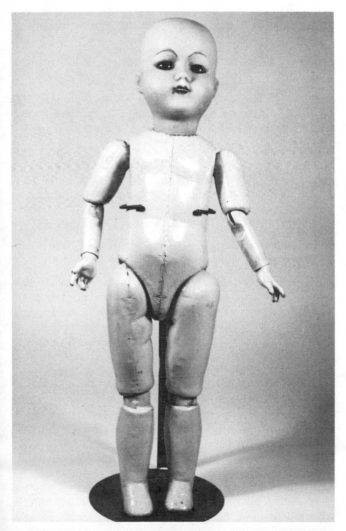

1855. British Ceramic socket head made by Mayer & Sherratt for Speights. It has a wig, stationary brown glass eyes, open mouth with teeth and a composition and wood body. The parts of the torso and upper legs are joined together with staples. Marks on head: Ills. 1856 and 1857. H. 20 in. (51 cm.). *Courtesy of Richard Withington. Photo by Barbara Jendrick.*

1856–1857. Mayer & Sherratt marks on British Ceramic dolls' heads. No. 1856 is incised. No. 1857 is a paper sticker.

Mayers, Francis. 1924. Advertised dolls in a British toy trade journal.

Mayfair Gifts & Playthings. 1921–29. New York City. Produced dolls.

1924: Advertised *Boy Blue.*★

Mayossen, P. 1930. Paris. Made and/or distributed dolls.

McAboy, Mary. 1913–30 and later. Missoula, Montana. By 1916 *H. H. Tammen* made the Indian dolls and Mary McAboy supervised the dressing of the dolls which was done as a home industry chiefly by young married women who were supplied with the material, instructed by Mary McAboy and paid by the piece. (See Ill. 1858.)★

McAuley, Claire P. 1926. Obtained a U.S. patent for a doll which she assigned to Becker K. Morris and Jeremiah H. Boullester. The doll was called a *King Tut* flapper (*Boudoir* doll).

McCall Co. 1872–1930 and later. New York City. Published patterns for dolls' clothes.

1912: Published a transfer pattern for a five-piece cutout cloth doll. The underclothes and boots were to be embroidered in outline stitch.

1923: They sent several hundred identical patterns of doll's dress to Stewart's of Louisville where a doll dressing contest was held for children aged six to 12. Over 300 dresses were made and dolls were given as prizes.

McClellan & Sidebottom. 1928–30. San Francisco, Calif. Represented *American Toy & Novelty, Arranbee Doll Co., Century Doll Co., Blanche Rowe Cromien, King Innovations* and *Love Doll Co.* in the Western U.S.

McClurg, A. C., & Co. 1909–29. Chicago, Ill. Distributors and jobbers of imported and domestic dolls.

1929: They had a retail store that sold dolls in Forest Park, Ill.★

McClurg & Keen. 1913. Chicago, Ill. Factory agents for *Baker & Bennett* and *Mitred Box Co.* It is not known whether this McClurg was connected with *A. C. McClurg.*

1858. Dried apple head doll made by Mary McAboy. The hair is made of cotton yarn, the black eyes are beads (or the round heads of pins), black cloth body, wooden legs. The arms are simulated by folds in the wool blanket. The suede boots are painted with Indian-type designs. Feathers in the headband are nearly all missing. Original clothes. H. 11½ in. (29 cm.). *Coleman Collection.*

McConnell, Mrs. M. S. 1926. North State Street (town and state unknown) where she had a store known as "The Doll Shop." She made individually styled, handmade clothes for dolls.

McCrosby, Aubrey D. 1918. Los Angeles, Calif. Obtained a U.S. patent for a hollow doll's head having eyesockets and eyeballs that were pivotally mounted.

McDonald Bros. Co. 1919 and probably other years. Minneapolis, Minn. Wholesale distributors of dolls with bisque heads, metal heads, and composition dolls. Imported dolls from Japan and sold dolls produced by *Borgfeldt, Horsman, Ideal* and others.

McEwen, Mary. After 1910–30 and later. Seattle, Wash. Made wax-over composition heads for dolls in both black and white versions. They usually had glass eyes and sometimes inserted hair according to Jenny Jones.

McKim Studios. 1931 and later. Independence, Mo. Mail order house that advertised stamped materials to be made up into cloth dolls. The dolls had handtinted faces and everything was supplied except the stuffing. The names of their dolls were Fanchon, a girl with yarn hair and an orange colored oilcloth dress; Soldier Doll, made of colored felt and with black oilcloth busby, belt and shoes; and Tink, a clown doll with a black felt nose and shoes, an oilcloth coat and a bell on top its stocking cap. Later in the 1930s they became one of the leading distributors of Foreign dolls and Antique dolls.

McMahan, Valerie. 1928. Created *Fan and Fannie,* the baseball twins, and a black doll named Ginger.

McManus. Ca. 1910. The *Newlywed's Kid* (Baby doll) was based on a comic character drawn by McManus. In 1924 International Features Service copyrighted McManus' cartoon of JIGGS AND MAGGIE, the designs of which were used by *Schoenhut* for their wooden dolls named *Jiggs and Maggie.*

McPhesters, Clara. 1926. Baldwin City, Kansas. Obtained a U.S. patent for a doll with its arms and legs fastened to the torso by bolts and thumb nuts. The doll was jointed at the shoulders, elbows, hips and knees. The arms and legs formed a series of links which permitted it to assume many different positions.

McSherry & Co. 1880s. Lodi, Calif. Advertised dolls on their trade card.

Me Too. 1928. Name of a doll in the *Kiddiejoy* line of *Hitz, Jacobs & Kassler.* It was made with either straight legs or bent legs and wore either short or long baby dresses.

Meakin & Ridgeway. 1919–21. New York City. Imported English stockinet dolls including *Baby Bunting, Jane, John, Mary, Patty, Prudence, Toddler, Tomboy,* and the pairs *Hodge and Audrey, Jack and Jill, Peter and Joan, Susan and Bobby.* Other dolls came with *British Ceramic* dolls' heads on composition, kid, imitation kid or cloth bodies.★

Mealy Manufacturing Co. 1920. Baltimore, Md. Made jewelry and watches for dolls.

Measurement of Dolls. Most of the measurements in this book are from published records, that is catalogs or other forms of early advertisements. Either inches or centimeters are given as originally published, the measurement shown in the parentheses is a conversion of the original measurement. Many bisque-head dolls have an incised size number. It is usually on the lower back of the neck of the socket head or along the back edge of the shoulder head. The *Kämmer & Reinhardt* dolls generally have the approximate height in centimeters as their size number. A few *Kestner* and other German dolls also follow this pattern, but most Kestners have the common letter and number series that identifies the height. Obviously the height will vary with the body type; bent limb babies will not be the same height as toddler or fully jointed dolls having the same size head. But generally a given model head is found on the same type of body. Dolls with kid or cloth bodies sometimes change their height because the stuffing settles or leaks out. A celluloid shoulder head often has its shoulder head height in its mark. The height is in centimeters for European made dolls and in inches for American or British dolls.

In early advertisements shoulder heads were usually measured according to the height of the head and the length across the shoulder plate. It is not known whether the size numbers on the shoulder heads, especially on the bisque shoulder heads, were sometimes keyed into these dimensions. For example in 1896 *Montgomery Ward* showed the following size-height relationship for bisque shoulder heads with teeth:

MONTGOMERY WARD SIZE–HEIGHT RELATIONSHIP—HEAD ONLY				
Size No.	Height of Shoulder Head in.	cm.	Length of Shoulder Head in.	cm.
4	3¼	8	1¾	4.5
5	3¾	9.5	2	5
6	4¼	11	2¼	5.5
7	4½	11.5	2½	6.5
8	4¾	12	2¾	7
9	5½	14	3	7.5
10	6	15	3	7.5
11	6¼	16	3½	9

French bébés usually have coded size numbers; these often differed over the years for a given manufacturer, which provides a clue in dating a doll. Bébés whose size number-height relationships fit known historical patterns were probably made by the same manufacturer. For example *Bébé Bon Marché* has approximately the same size number-height relationship in any given period as *Bébé Jumeau* and both of these dolls were made by *Jumeau*.

China heads sometimes have a size number and heads from one manufacturer can be differentiated from those made elsewhere based on the size number–height relationships but unfortunately the names of most of the china head manufacturers are still unknown.

What can these size number height relationships tell you about a given doll? First the doll must be measured as accurately as possible. Measuring a doll is not always precise due to the wig, the joints and the position of the doll when measured. But not more than an inch should be generally allowed and less than an inch for a small doll though more than an inch for a doll over 30 inches is acceptable. Knowing the height and size number of a doll with identifiable maker's marks, the appropriate size number-height table should be consulted and this will verify the authenticity of your doll. If the body is not original it may not fit the table. If the doll is a reproduction the height will be at least one seventh less than the height given in the table due to the shrinkage in reproducing the head, unless the body is disproportionately long.

Factories changed the heights of their dolls from time to time so that it is often possible to find an approximate date from the height of a doll. This is true for cloth, composition and dolls of other materials as well as for bisque head dolls. The height can sometimes help to identify the original name and costume of the doll. A company such as *Horsman* made many versions of the *Campbell Kids* but only a few in the small or large sizes in certain years and wearing specific costumes. Knowing the height of a *Lenci* or *Chad Valley* doll can be of tremendous help in identifying the doll and ascertaining its approximate date. Lenci catalog heights tend to be slightly larger than a measured height.

Many heights of specific dolls in various years are given in this book but this information is not always complete. However for dolls made in 1930 and earlier the heights provide a valuable identification tool.

As collectors and persons interested in the older dolls become more interested in the identification of their dolls and in verifying that the dolls are not reproductions, the significance of the height measurement and the importance of size related information becomes evident. The height of a doll can be a valuable indicator of its origin, age and originality. Early German catalogs of the 1800s often gave the heights of dolls in zolls. A zoll was approximately one inch (2.5 cm.).

Mechanical Rubber Co. 1925. London. Advertised rubber dolls.

Mechano. 1925–28. Vienna. Made dolls including metal ones.

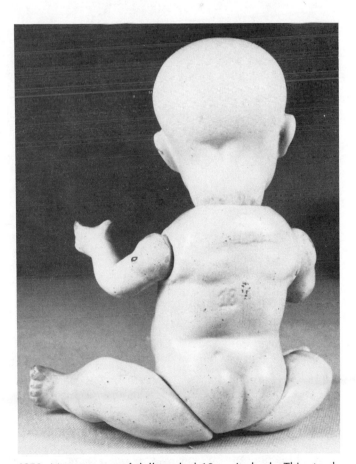

1859. Measurement of doll marked 18 on its back. This stands for 18 cm. (7 in.). This bisque head doll is also shown in Ill. 2095 and is believed to have been handled by Emil Pfieffer. *Coleman Collection.*

1860. Bisque head and shoulder plate marked D, which indicates that this head is size D. It has a wig, stationary glass eyes and a closed mouth which is slightly smiling. It is on a kid gusseted body. Heads similar to this have been found on wooden bodies which follow the Bru patent of 1869. H. 12½ in. (31.5 cm.). *Courtesy of Sotheby Parke Bernet Inc., N.Y.*

Mechthold, Georg, & Co. 1894–1915. Oberlind and Sonneberg, Thür. and Fürth, Bavaria. Manufactured and exported dolls.

1894: Applied with Thomas Chillingworth for a German patent (D.R.P.) pertaining to dolls.

1895: The Mechthold-Chillingworth D.R.P. patent was granted. Georg Mechthold sought another German patent (D.R.G.M.) for an "unbreakable" cloth doll.★

Meech, Herbert John. 1865–1917. London. Made and repaired poured wax dolls and wax-over composition dolls. One of his poured wax dolls was reported stamped "H. J. Meech, Doll Maker, Old Dolls Cleaned & Repaired, 50 Kennington Road S E., Doll Maker to the Royal Family, 6 prize Medals Awarded."★

Meg. 1915. Cloth doll with a velvet face, plush wig, handled by *Whyte, Ridsdale.* It was dressed in a red frock with a white collar and belt. Three hts.; priced $4.50 to $5.50 doz. wholesale.

Mégard. 1914–15. France. Created dolls.

Meier, Harry W., & Co. 1905–18. Baltimore, Md. Made *Dolly Dimples Doll Elastic* for stringing dolls. Their logo was a diamond within which was "LEXINGTON & LIBERTY STS//H. W. MEIER & CO. //BALTIMORE."

1906: Advertised dolls, dolls parts, and "everything for dolls."

1909: Their advertising postcard showed a large group of dolls in a hospital scene and the store sign reading: "THE DOLL SHOP AND DOLL'S HOSPITAL."★

Meier & Frank Co. 1903–29. Portland, Ore. Imported and distributed dolls. Held annual Doll Shows.

1917 and later: According to Janet Johl they distributed dolls made by *Hattie Bartholomay Bruckmann.*

1928: Imported 50 tons of toys by ship.

1929: Sold *Marga* dolls.

Mein Dicker Kleiner Liebling (My Fat Little Darling). Before 1927–30. Dolls made by *Kämmer & Reinhardt* in their *Mein Liebling* line.

1927: Bisque or rubber heads with wigs on various styles of composition bodies usually jointed only at the neck, shoulders, and hips. The rubber-head dolls all seem to have had molded footwear. Mold #s 126 and 131 also came on all-bisque dolls. Mold #s included 126, 131, 156, 526 (black or mulatto), 626 (black or mulatto), 651 (mulatto), 826, 831, 856, and 886 (walking). The mold # 856 rubber-head dolls came in eight sizes 12, 13, 14, 17, 19, 21, 23 and 26 cm. (4½, 5, 5½, 6½, 7½, 8½, 9, and 10½ in.). The size number was the height in centimeters. (See Ill. 2714.)

1861–1862. Marks on Meech wax dolls.

Mein Einzige Baby. See **Meine Einzige.**

Mein Glückskind (My Lucky Child). 1919–21. Registered trademark of *A. Wislizenus*.★

Mein Goldherz (My Golden Heart). 1904–30. Registered trademark of *Bruno Schmidt*. It was used especially for ball-jointed dolls and character babies.

1930: Doll had bisque or celluloid head.★

1863. Mein Goldherz mark used by Bruno Schmidt.

Mein Herz'l (My Sweetheart). 1911. Trade name of ball-jointed dolls with wigs and wearing a chemise, manufactured by *Catterfelder Puppenfabrik*.

Mein Kleiner Liebling (My Little Darling). Before 1913–30 and later. Dolls made by *Kämmer & Reinhardt* in their *Mein Liebling* line.

1913: Bisque-head mold #s 121 and 122 were advertised with this name.

1927: Bisque, celluloid or composition heads with wigs, sleeping or roguish eyes on composition bodies that represented a baby of one or two years of age or the slimmer older child. The latter became available in 1927. Mold numbers:

126	Some of these dolls that were 40 cm. (15½ in.) and more tall had *Naughty* eyes.
509,510 and 511	Had sleeping googly eyes and the mouth was shaped like a watermelon slice.
531 X	Black googly.
631	Mulatto googly.
728 W	Celluloid head had roguish or flirting eyes, movable tongue.
952 B	Black with sleeping eyes.

Mein Liebling (My Darling [English], Mon Chéri [French], or Mi Liebling [Spanish]). 1901–30 and later. Line of bisque, composition, celluloid or rubber head dolls made by *Kämmer & Reinhardt*. The bisque heads were made by *Simon & Halbig*. *Liebling lernt laufen* (Darling learns to walk); *Mein Dicker Kleiner Liebling* (My Fat Little Darling); *Mein Lieblings-Baby* (My Darling Baby); *Mein Neuer Liebling* (My New Darling); *Mein Rosiger Liebling* (My Rosy Darling); *Mein Süsser Liebling* (My Sweet Darling); Me•Lie•Ba (acronym for a Mein Lieblings-Baby); and Roli were all part of this line.

Most of the Mein Liebling dolls had a shield shaped tag and wore a choker of simulated pearls over the neck joint.

1907: *Kaufhaus* advertised dolly-faced Mein Liebling dolls with various style wigs.

1922: Line included bisque heads with mold numbers:

115	Closed mouth.
117	Generally known as Mein Süsser Liebling.
126	23 cm. (9 in.) and up, also came with hair, eyelashes and flirting eyes. 32 cm. (12½ in.) and up also came with the *Naughty* apparatus. It was found on bent-limb baby bodies or toddler bodies.
131	Some heads with sleeping eyes but without hair eyelashes. Bodies were toddler or sometimes older children types.
226	Mulatto shoulder head without hair eyelashes.
228	Shoulder head with sleeping eyes and hair eyelashes.

Mold #727 was all-celluloid with painted hair and eyes or glass eyes and moving tongue.

Mold #728 head was on an all-celluloid doll with sleeping eyes, hair eyelashes and moving tongue.

A bisque head without a mold number had a wig, hair eyelashes and was on a lady-type body. Ht. 40 to 80 cm. (15½ to 31½ in.).

1927: Mein Liebling dolls in Kämmer & Reinhardt's catalog included the following mold numbers:

117	Bisque socket head, wigged with sleeping or flirting eyes. Not all mold #117s were identical. The ones shown in the 1927 catalog were number 317 but were described as having a head mold #117. These differed slightly in appearance from the mold #117 doll shown in Ill. 1241 in the first COLLECTOR'S ENCYCLOPEDIA OF DOLLS.
122	Bisque socket head, wig, sleeping eyes, hair eyelashes, movable tongue, on a bent limb baby body. See Ill. 1394.
126	Bisque socket head baby with wig and eyes that could either sleep, flirt or were naughty. It was found on a bent limb baby body or the toddler style body or the new slender legged body with jointed composition arms. See Ills. 1397 and 1398.
127	Bisque socket head baby with molded hair and glass eyes. See Ill. 1399.
131	Roguish face with wig, round glass eyes and watermelon slice shaped mouth. See Ill. 1400.
150	Mulatto with wig and glass eyes on a ball-jointed composition body.
155	Bisque socket head with wig and sleeping eyes with hair eyelashes.
156	Bisque socket head with wig and glass eyes, on a body jointed at the neck, shoulders, hips and above the knees.
170	Newborn infant style with painted hair or wig and sleeping eyes. It usually had a cloth body.
171	Newborn infant style with painted or wigged hair and sleeping eyes.
173	Newborn infant style with painted or wigged hair and sleeping eyes. It resembled mold #873, a rubber version. It came on a toddler composition body or a cloth body.
248	Bisque shoulder head with wig and sleeping eyes.

252   Bisque socket head with racial features of a mulatto or black, wig and sleeping eyes. It was on a composition bent limb baby body. It resembled mold #952 which was a composition version.

256   Bisque shoulder head with wig and sleeping eyes.

265   Celluloid shoulder head with molded hair and painted eyes.

403   Bisque socket head with wig, sleeping eyes, hair eyelashes, and came on a ball-jointed composition body. See Ill. 1401.

509   Googly faced doll with wig, sleeping eyes, watermelon slice shaped mouth and a ball jointed composition body.

510   Similar to 509.

511   Similar to 509.

526   Black bisque socket head baby with wig and sleeping eyes, on a five-piece bent limb composition body. The head resembled mold #126.

531   Black head with wig, sleeping googly eyes and a watermelon slice shaped mouth.

626   Mulatto bisque socket head baby doll with wig and sleeping eyes. The head resembled mold #126.

631   Mulatto bisque socket head with sleeping googly eyes and a watermelon slice shaped mouth.

651   Mulatto with wig and glass eyes.

715   Celluloid head with molded hair and painted eyes. One all-celluloid version, called a bathing doll, came without a chemise while another version had a cloth body with celluloid arms and a chemise.

717   Celluloid head with wig, sleeping or flirty eyes. It came on a body of all celluloid, a composition body or a cloth body with celluloid arms. See Ill. 1403.

727   All-celluloid doll with molded and painted hair and eyes. It resembled mold #127.

728   Celluloid head with wig and sleeping eyes, sometimes with hair eyelashes and a movable tongue. It came on the new slender legged or bent limb body. The body was composition or all-celluloid or cloth with celluloid arms. See Ill. 1404.

785   Bisque head with wig, sleeping eyes with hair eyelashes. The body had an iron mechanism that enabled it to walk and turn its head.

787   Celluloid head doll with the same iron walking mechanism as 785.

788   Similar to 785.

817   Rubber head with wig and painted eyes on a cloth body with rubber hands.

826   Head had wig and was on a five-piece body.

831   Head with wig and round glass eyes looking to the side. The mouth was shaped like a watermelon slice.

835   Rubber head came with molded hair or with a wig, the eyes were painted. It came on a cloth body with rubber hands or on a composition body.

856   Bisque socket head with wig and glass eyes, came on a five-piece straight legged composition body. Came without a chemise.

873   Rubber head came with molded hair or with a wig, the eyes were painted. When not wearing a wig it resembled mold #173.

886   Head with a wig and glass eyes was on a stiff jointed composition body.

926   Composition head and body with wig and sleeping or flirting eyes, similar to mold #126.

952   Black or mulatto composition head baby with racial features, had a wig and sleeping eyes. Similar to mold #252.

1126   All-bisque baby doll jointed at shoulders, neck, and hips, had a wig and glass eyes. It is similar to mold #126. (1927 was the last year in which these dolls were available.) See Ill. 1398.

2131   All-bisque doll with wig, and roguish glass eyes. The head was mold #131. (1927 was the last year in which these dolls were available.)

At least one version of Mein Liebling that was made from about 1902 to 1927 could walk and turn its head.

In the 1927 Mein Liebling mold # code the hundreds digits appear to have designated the heads as being:

1. Bisque socket head.
2. Shoulder head of various materials except socket head for black and mulatto dolls.
3. Bisque socket heads.
4. Heads having hair eyelashes.
5. Black and/or googly heads.
6. Mulatto heads.
7. Celluloid heads, except for bisque heads on walking dolls.
8. Rubber heads.
9. Composition heads.

A four digit number appeared to designate an all-bisque doll.

There were probably some exceptions as is always the case in analyzing doll data.

1928: Mein Liebling dolls distributed by *Gerzon* had bisque heads with sleeping and flirting eyes, moving tongues. Four hts. 34, 43, 52, and 62 cm. (13½, 17, 20½, and 24½ in.). The bent-limb baby dolls had either bisque or celluloid heads. The celluloid babies came with sleeping and flirting eyes, hair eyelashes, mama voices and a chemise. Four hts. 36, 41, 51, and 60 cm. (14, 16, 20, and 23½ in.).

Ca. 1932: Bisque or celluloid heads usually had wigs except for the new-born infant type dolls. There was a larger percentage of the dolls with celluloid heads than in 1927 and a smaller percentage with rubber heads. There were sleeping or flirting eyes and often a mama voice. Black dolls wore grass type skirts. There were more bent arms and fewer knee joints than in 1927. Cloth body dolls came with a slip or dressed. Families of dolls' house dolls were new; these came with a Mother, a Father, a boy, a girl and two servants. The dolls were advertised as "movable with wire in legs and arms, can sit and stand alone."

Mein Lieblings-Baby (My Darling Baby). Before 1927–30 and later. Baby dolls made by *Kämmer & Reinhardt* in their Mein Liebling line. Some of these dolls had bisque heads made by *Simon & Halbig*.

1927: These dolls included the following mold numbers:

126   Bisque head, wig, sleeping eyes with eyelashes, open mouth with teeth, and was on a bent limb

composition baby body or a toddler body that could stand. Sizes over 35 cm. (14 in.) included "Naughty" mechanism and a movable tongue.

127   Bisque head, painted hair, glass eyes, on a bent limb composition baby body.

170   Newborn infant type, bisque head with painted hair or wig, sleeping eyes, cloth body.

171   Similar to 170.

173   Bisque baby with painted hair or wig, sleeping eyes, came on a composition bent limb baby body.

252   Black or mulatto ethnic bisque head with wig, sizes 28 and 30 cm. (11 or 12 in.) had stationary eyes; sizes 35 to 51 cm. (14 to 20 in.) had sleeping eyes. It was on a composition bent limb baby body.

626   Mulatto baby doll without ethnic features, had a bisque head with wig. Sizes 17 to 30 cm. (6½ to 12 in.) had stationary eyes, 35 to 63 cm. (14 to 25 in.) had sleeping eyes. It was on a bent limb composition baby body.

727   All-celluloid doll, painted hair, bent limb baby body.

728   All-celluloid doll with wig, on a bent limb baby body or with celluloid head, wig, sleeping or roguish eyes, open mouth, teeth, movable tongue, on a composition or cloth bent limb baby body.

835   Rubber head and arms, painted hair and eyes, mama voice, cardboard baby body with bent limbs including papier-mâché legs.

835J   Same as 835 except it had a wig, came with a toddler body and was called Liebling lernt laufen.

926   Composition head with wig, hair eyelashes, sleeping eyes, movable tongue, bent limb composition baby body.

952   Same as mold 252 except the head was composition instead of bisque.

Ca. 1932: Catalog number 33 was a bisque head bent limb baby with wig. Mold # s 126, 127, 626, 727, 728, 926, and 952 (black) that were shown in the 1927 catalog as Mein Lieblings-Baby dolls were shown only as separate heads.

Mein Neuer Liebling (My New Darling). 1916–30 and later. Bisque, celluloid or rubber head dolls made by Kämmer & Reinhardt in their Mein Liebling line; all the heads had wigs except for the celluloid mold #715 which had painted hair. This was a new series in 1916. The dressed dolls all had bisque heads, roguish eyes, rubber hands and slender composition bodies in 1927.

1916: Mold #117 was 117n, the n stood for neuer (new).

1927: These dolls included the following mold numbers:

317   Bisque head, flirting eyes, rubber hands, slender type composition body. The mold number was followed in the catalog by H, N, S T or X probably indicating the hair style.

355X   Bisque head, sleeping eyes, hair eyelashes, slender type composition body including composition hands.

715   Celluloid head and arms, painted hair and features, cloth body.

717X   Celluloid head, sleeping or roguish eyes, hair eyelashes, rubber hands, composition or cloth body.

728   Celluloid head and arms, cloth body. The mold number was followed by an X or W which probably indicated the hair style.

817   Rubber head and arms on a cloth body.

835   Rubber head and hands, painted eyes on either a slender composition or corpulent cloth body.

Most of the dolls had Dutch bob (straight hair and bangs) style wig and their mold # was followed by an X. The mold # 117 for the bisque head and mold # 717 for the celluloid head followed by an N had bushy bobbed hair wigs. Mold #s 117 T and 728 W had short frizzy wigs. Mold # 715 had no letter following the mold number and it had molded hair.

Mein Rosiger Liebling. See **My Rosy Darling.**

Mein Stolz (My Pride). 1913–30 and probably later. Trademark used by König & Wernicke for a line of bisque-head dolls. ★

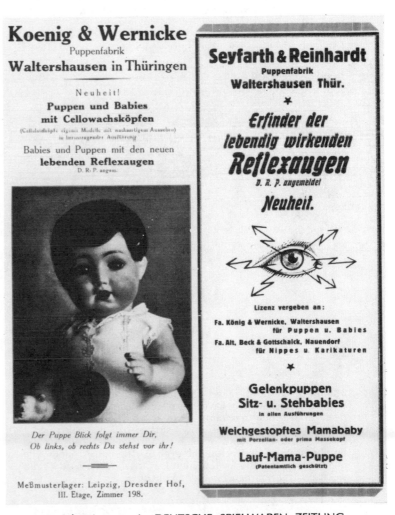

Koenig & Wernicke
Puppenfabrik
Waltershausen in Thüringen

Neuheit!
**Puppen und Babies
mit Cellowachsköpfen**
(Celluloidköpfe eigener Modelle mit wachsartigem Aussehen) in hervorragender Ausführung

Babies und Puppen mit den neuen
lebenden Reflexaugen
D. R. P. angem.

Der Puppe Blick folgt immer Dir,
Ob links, ob rechts Du stehst vor ihr!

Meßmusterlager: Leipzig, Dresdner Hof,
III. Etage, Zimmer 198.

Seyfarth & Reinhardt
Puppenfabrik
Waltershausen Thür.
✳
*Erfinder der
lebendig wirkenden*
Reflexaugen
D. R. P. angemeldet
Neuheit.

Lizenz vergeben an:
Fa. König & Wernicke, Waltershausen
für Puppen u. Babies
Fa. Alt. Beck & Gottschalck, Nauendorf
für Nippes u. Karikaturen
✳
**Gelenkpuppen
Sitz- u. Stehbabies**
in allen Ausführungen
Weichgestopftes Mamababy
mit Porzellan- oder prima Massekopf
Lauf-Mama-Puppe
(Patentamtlich geschützt)

1864. Advertisement in DEUTSCHE SPIELWAREN ZEITUNG, February, 1927, for a Cellowachs (celluloid) head doll made by Koenig (König) & Wernicke in their Mein Stolz line. The doll has the new reflex eyes patented by Seyfarth & Reinhardt. These eyes can look in several directions. Mark: Ill. 1865.

1865. Mark on tag of Mein Stolz line of dolls made by König & Wernicke.

Mein Süsser Liebling (My Sweet Darling). 1912–27. Bisque head doll made by *Kämmer & Reinhardt* in their *Mein Liebling* line. It usually was mold # 117 and came with an open or closed mouth and flirting and/or sleeping eyes. In 1927 the body generally represented an older girl.

Meine Einzige (My Only One). 1907–27. Trademark used by *Kley & Hahn* for a line of dolls.★

Meine Goldperle. See **My Gold Pearl.**

Meingutscher, Josef Anton. Before 1838. Grödner Tal, Austria. A *Verleger* who distributed dolls as far away as Philadelphia.

Meissen. 1710–1930 and later. Meissen, Saxony. TOYS AND NOVELTIES in 1912 claimed that Meissen porcelain heads were used on tea cosies exhibited by *Eugenia Woerlein* at the Bavarian Industrial Exhibit.★

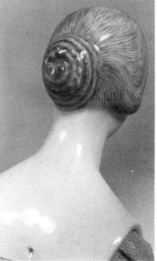

1866A & B. Flesh tinted china shoulder head marked with crossed swords which have been attributed to Meissen. Other heads with similar modeling and marks have also been marked "Made in Germany." The brown striated hair is molded into a bun in back. The pupils of the eyes are grey and there is a red line both above and below the eyeball. The body is cloth with china limbs. H. 10½ in. (26.5 cm.). H. of shoulder head 2¼ in. (6 cm.). *Courtesy of Z. Frances Walker.*

1867. Mark attributed to Meissen.

Melba. 1915–20. *British Ceramic* heads made by *Mayer & Sherratt* and named for the opera singer Dame Nellie Melba. These heads were marked "MELBA//ENGLAND." The heads came with molded hair or wig; painted eyes or sleeping eyes; open mouth usually with four teeth or closed mouth. Some of the smaller heads were bald and covered with a wig. The cloth bodies often had British Ceramic arms and legs. These dolls came in various sizes. ★

Me•Lie•Ba. 1926–30 and later. Bisque head dolls made by *Kämmer & Reinhardt.* They had a mohair wig, sleeping eyes, hair eyelashes, movable tongue, usually a chemise and were in the *Mein Liebling* line, but they carried a round tag instead of the usual shield-shaped Mein Liebling tag. The bisque heads were made by *Simon & Halbig.*

1927: Mold # 122 was on a bent-limb baby body. "Special" was the designation of some of the dolls with ball-jointed composition bodies.

Ca. 1932: Catalog numbers 32 and 34 were on bent-limb baby bodies; numbers 71 and 72 were on slender ball-jointed composition bodies.

1868. Five Melba British Ceramic heads all marked "MELBA//ENGLAND." The three dolls also have British Ceramic hands, wigs, glass eyes, and open mouths with four teeth. Doll on left has sleeping brown eyes. H. 20 in. (51 cm.). Doll in center has sleeping blue eyes. H. 25 in. (63.5 cm.). Doll on right has stationary brown eyes. H. 14 in. (35.5 cm.). The two small shoulder heads in the foreground both have blue painted eyes; one has a closed mouth and one has an open mouth. *Courtesy of Melba Hiter.*

MELBA
ENGLAND

1869. Melba mark on British Ceramic dolls' heads.

Melin, C., & Co. 1916–25. London and Paris. Wholesale distributor of dolls, dolls' heads, *mignonnettes*, wigs, and eyes.

1919: Advertised *Limoges* porcelain dolls' heads.

Melitta. 1924 and probably other years. Line of bisque head dolls made by *Edmund Edelmann*, usually with *Armand Marseille* heads. Among these dolls was a character baby with a wig, glass eyes, hair eyelashes, pierced nostrils, open mouth with teeth and a felt tongue. Size number 11 was 20 in. (50 cm.) tall.

Another Melitta on a toddler body was size 4½. Ht. 15½ in. (40 cm.). Distributed in England by *Martin Raphael & Co. Ltd.*

1870–1871. Melitta marks on bisque heads.

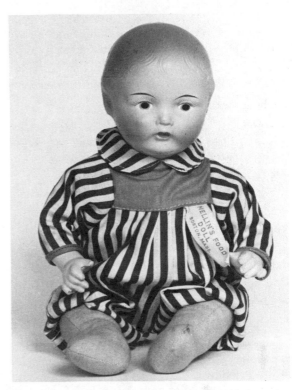

1872. Composition head doll produced by Horsman and representing the Mellin's Food Baby. It has molded and painted hair and blue eyes, closed mouth, and a pink cotton body with composition lower arms. Original clothes. Mark on head: "E.I.H. © Inc." Mark on rompers: Ill. 1873. Mark on box: "Horsman 900 Broadway, New York//E. I. Horsman Co. Inc.//Genuine Horsman ART DOLL." H. 10½ in. (26.5 cm.). *Courtesy of the Margaret Woodbury Strong Museum. Photo by Harry Rickelhaupt.*

```
MELLIN'S  FOOD
    DOLL
BOSTON, MASS.
```

1873. Mark on a cloth tag attached to Mellin's Food Doll's clothes.

Mellinger, Leopold. 1903. Berlin. Applied for a German patent (D.R.G.M.) for the head of a speaking doll.

Mellin's Food Doll. Ca. 1920s. A doll with a composition shoulder head and composition arms had molded hair, painted eyes and a bent-limb cloth body. It wore red and white striped rompers with a blue yoke and blue at the bottom of the sleeves. It had a cloth label reading "MELLIN'S FOOD//DOLL//BOSTON, MASS." and was found in a *Horsman* box.

Melton & Kidder. 1925–26. Portland, Ore. Produced dolls.

Ménagère. 1900–24 and possibly for a longer period of time. Paris. Store that sold dolls, among them:

1902–14: *Bébé Tout en Bois.*

1903–13: *Bébé Ménagère.*

1906–13: *Bébé Réclame.*

1912: Washable composition doll in a chemise came in four hts. 30, 36, 40, and 47 cm. (12, 14, 15½, and 18½ in.); price 60¢ and up.

1913: *Bébé Prodige* and *Paris Bébé.*

1923: *Bébé Unique.*

See THE COLLECTOR'S BOOK OF DOLLS' CLOTHES, Ills. 628, 640.

Menco Importing Co. 1922–23. New York City. Henry M. Marks, formerly with *Bawo & Dotter*, was president of this company. They imported dolls.★

Mendelsohn, Jos. 1901. Leipzig, Germany. Applied for a German patent (D.R.G.M.) for jointed dolls.

Mendelson, Leo. 1898. Hamburg, Germany. Applied for a German patent (D.R.G.M.) for a jointed doll.

Menier-Reihoffer, J. N. Before 1894–1921. Vienna. By 1894 it had become Vereinigte Gummiwaren-Fabriken (United Rubberware Factory). They applied for five German patents (D.R.G.M.) for various types of rubber dolls.

Menthe. 1929. Paris. Made and exported footwear for dolls.

Menvielle & Arnould. See **Corion**.

Mephistopheles. 1924. *Aerolite* or kapok stuffed cloth art doll made by *Chad Valley;* dressed as a devil in turkey red, it was style no. 165. Ht. 10½ in. (26.5 cm.).

Mercié, Antonin (Antoine). Before World War I–1919. Paris. A sculptor who made models for dolls including a historical series of Paris Fashion Dolls.

Before World War I: He created models for expensive dolls.

1914: He used the Donatello child heads as his inspiration and later worked with *Sèvres* in designing dolls.

1916: Sculptured the heads for fashion type dolls with lady shaped bodies.

1918: Created models for dolls made by *Mme. de Laumont*.

Mercurius. 1903 and other years. Name found on a cloth tag worn by a doll with a bisque head made by *Armand Marseille,* produced by *Cuno & Otto Dressel* and distributed by *Wanamaker's.* (See color plate 19 in THE COLLECTOR'S BOOK OF DOLLS' CLOTHES.)

Meresnky, H. 1898. Berlin. Applied for a German patent (D.R.G.M.) for dolls' dresses.

Mermaid Doll & Toy Co. 1921–27. New York City. Made *Mama* dolls.

1927: Licensed by *Voices, Inc.* to use their patented mama voices and criers in the Mermaid dolls.★

Merrie Marie. 1900–41. Cutout cloth *Life Size Doll,* made by *Art Fabric Mills,* after 1910 made by *Selchow & Righter.*

In 1940–41 it was distributed by Velvalee Dickinson who stated that they were reprints.★

Merrill, John William. Before 1910. Sheffield, England. Imported and distributed dolls.

1909: Went bankrupt and among his creditors were *Cuno & Otto Dressel, Insam & Prinoth* and *C. E. Turnbull.*

Merriwinkle. 1928. Doll representing a three year old girl designed by *Grace Corry* and made by *Schoen & Yondorf,* in their Sayco line. It was described as "Half angel, half imp, has a tip tilted nose, snapping blue eyes and a mischievous smile."

Merry Sunshine. 1927. Dressed composition head toddler doll distributed by *Montgomery Ward.* It had sleeping eyes, a crying voice, composition arms and legs. Ht. 13¼ in. (33.5 cm.); priced $2.79.

Merrythought, Ltd. 1930 and later. Telford, Shropshire, and London. Manufactured cloth dolls. Directors were H. C. Janisch, chairman of the Toy Manufacturer's Association, formerly with *Farnell,* and C. J. Rendle. Rendle and Florence Atwood had worked for *Chad Valley* and had designed dolls. Atwood worked under *Norah Wellings.*

Merveilleuse. 1886. Name of a doll in the Sonneberg Museum Collection. It had a porcelain head, mohair wig, sleeping eyes, ball jointed composition body and wore a dress and hat of cotton piqué. Ht. 70 cm. (27½ in.). Possibly this could be a *Bébé Merveilleux.*

Merville, Edouard. 1925–30 and later. Made dolls.★

Merz, Emile. 1918. Beauvais, France. Registered in France "E M //B" in a circle as a trademark for dolls' clothes and accessories.

Messalina. Before 1923. Name of an elaborately dressed wax doll made by *Lottie Pritzel.* This is not to be confused with the bisque head doll dressed as Messalina by *Mlle. Riera* in her historical series.

Messenger Boy. See **Twinjoy Doll Co.**

Messin, Jullien. 1928–30 and later. Paris. Exported *mignonnettes* and dressed bébés. He was an agent for *Max Seifert.*

Messina-Vat. 1924–30 and later. Turin, Italy, and New York City. Mr. J. C. Messina, who had been in charge of some of the *Lenci* dolls in 1923, later imported the Italian Vat felt dolls. These dolls, the work of Italian artists, wore gay colored felt costumes and closely resembled Lenci dolls. Their teddies were hem stitched with red thread and their feet had a thread which ran from one toe to the other.

Besides the dolls, Messina-Vat made bright colored felt coats for children and women as well as felt animals and flowers.

1924: Messina-Vat dolls included black dolls with large turbans and colorful costumes, *Pierrots* and dolls representing girls.

Messing, Albert. 1913–15. Georgenthal, Thür. Applied for a German patent (D.R.G.M.) for a doll's head with moving teeth and palate.★

Metal Cast Products Co. 1923. New York City. Manufactured metal casting forms for metal and rubber dolls.

Metal Devices Corp. 1926. Chicago, Ill. Made a Phonograph Doll that could sing and recite nursery rhymes. The motor was placed inside the body and required only a single turn to wind. The cylinder type records were made of a special composition that did not necessitate changing the needle.

Exquisite Beauties To Brighten Your Doll Dep't
Nothing in all Dolldom can compare with them. Many popular-priced numbers. Shipments from our N. Y. stock. Write for catalog No. 12.
MESSINA-VAT
58 West 45th St., New York
Other N. Y. C. Display Rooms:
Bush Terminal Sales Bldg., 9th floor;
130 W. 42nd St.
ITALIAN DOLLS
MADE IN TORINO, ITALY

1874. Messina-Vat advertisement in PLAYTHINGS, May 1927. These dolls were in competition with Lenci dolls.

1875. Felt doll made by Messina-Vat. It has painted eyes, closed mouth and is jointed at the neck, shoulders and hips. Original clothes. Mark: III. 1877. *Courtesy of Shirley Buchholz.*

1876. Pair of Messina-Vat felt dolls made in Turin, Italy. Note the similarity to Lenci dolls. These dolls have mohair hair, painted eyes looking to the side, closed mouth with a lighter lower lip on which is a highlight. The bodies are jointed at the neck, shoulders, and hips. Mitten-type hands have sewed finger divisions. Original clothes. Mark on underwear: III. 1877. Hts. 11 and 16 in. (28 and 40.5 cm.). *Courtesy of Stephanie and Fred Farago. Photo by Stephanie Farago.*

1877. Messina-Vat cloth label on dolls' underclothes.

Metal Dolls. Ca. 1850–1930 and later. Numerous dolls were made with metal heads or were all-metal. The all-metal mechanical toys are not considered to be dolls. One of the earliest metal-head dolls had a molded hairdo with a braided bun and comb in back. This lead-colored metal head was painted and affixed to a kid body with wooden arms and legs. Thus the doll closely resembled the early molded hair papier-mâché head dolls.

The chief manufacturing center for making metal heads in Germany was Nossen, Saxony *(Buschow & Beck)*. The heads were stamped out of sheet metal and the two halves were welded together. *A. Kröhl* was one of the exporters. Most of the American mail order houses advertised metal heads for dolls, especially *Minerva*. These shoulder heads came with molded hair and painted eyes, with wig and painted eyes or with wig and sleeping eyes. They were available in a variety of sizes. Various metals were used including aluminum, brass and other alloys. The metal shoulder heads were usually put on cloth bodies but the socket heads went on composition or metal bodies. In Germany *Alfred Heller* made *Diana* metal heads and *Karl Standfuss* made *Juno* metal heads.

In Austria *Gebrüder Lokesch* made *Venus* metal heads.

One of the American companies that made metal dolls' heads was the *Art Metal Works*. Their dolls with cloth bodies usually had *Ronson* voices.

1857: *Jules Roy* patented zinc dolls' heads.

1886: *Joseph Schön* used sheet metal for dolls.

1897: *Leopold Illfelder* patented metal dolls.

1897–98: *Karl Sommereisen* produced aluminum heads.

1912: *Erika Morf* patented a metal doll's head.

1917–30: *Atlas Doll & Toy Co.* made all-metal dolls.

1918–21: *Giebeler-Falk* made dolls with aluminum heads.

1919–20: *Aluminum Doll Head Works* made aluminum heads for dolls.

1924: A metal head was used on a kid body with rivet joints at the shoulders and hips. Hts. 13½, 19, and 20 in. (34, 48, and 51 cm.).

1925–28: *Mechano* made metal dolls.

1928: *Atlas Doll & Toy Co.* made an all-metal doll representing a year old baby.

1929: Metal shoulder heads were advertised with painted

hair and painted eyes in two heights but with a wig and painted eyes it came in six heights.

1930: *Montgomery Ward* advertised a baby doll with a metal head having painted hair and sleeping eyes on a cloth body containing a crying voice, and wearing a long dress. Ht. 13 in. (33 cm.); priced $1.00. A doll with a similar head on a bent limb composition baby body wore a short dress. Ht. 16¾ in. (42.5 cm.); priced $2.83.

A doll representing a child had a metal head on a cloth body. Ht. 19 in. (48 cm.). The price with painted hair, composition arms and cloth legs was $1.47. The price with mohair wig, sleeping eyes, composition arms and legs and a crying voice was $2.83.★

Metamorphose. 1908. A multi-face bisque head patented by *Carl Bergner* and made by *Simon & Halbig*. The head had four different expressions and color and an example is in the Sonneberg Museum collection. Ht. of head only was 8 cm. (3 in.).

Metropolitan Doll Co. 1924–29. New York City. Made various kinds of dolls some of which were designed and modeled by *Ernesto Peruggi*.

1924: A composition head with a molded loop in its hair to accommodate a hair-ribbon was marked "Metropolitan Doll © 1924." The doll had painted eyes and composition hands.

1879. Metal head doll made in America has molded blond hair, painted blue eyes, open-closed mouth with two upper teeth, a flange neck, and a cloth body with metal hands. The body contains a bellows type voice. Contemporary clothes. Mark stamped in ink on the body: "PATENTS PENDING//MADE IN U.S.A." H. 11½ in. (29 cm.). *Courtesy of Jan Payson.*

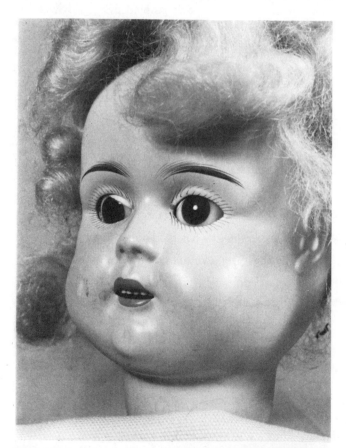

1878. Metal socket head made in Germany with wig, sleeping eyes, open mouth and teeth, Mark: Ill. 1881. H. of head 4 in. (10 cm.). *Coleman Collection.*

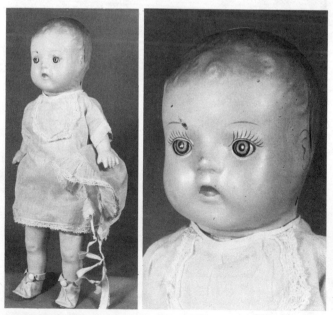

1880A & B. Flange neck metal head doll on a cloth body with composition lower limbs. It has molded hair, blue metal sleeping eyes with painted eyelashes. Original clothes. *Collection of Robert and Katrin Burlin.*

4
GERMANY

PATENT

1881–1882. Marks on metal heads.

1926: Made dolls for jobbers and retailers. The dolls included infant dolls, *Mama* dolls, crying dolls, with painted eyes or sleeping eyes, with human hair or mohair wigs.

1927: Specialized in sleeping-eyed dolls. They were licensed by *Voices, Inc.* to use their patented mama voices and criers in the Metropolitan dolls.

1929: Belonged to the *Doll Parts Manufacturing Assoc.*, which required that its members make dolls' heads, hands, arms, and other composition products.

Metropolitan Toy & Doll Co. 1914–15. London. Made cloth *Albrita* dolls and *Eskimo* dolls, as well as clothes for dolls. Formerly this was named F. Mitchell.

Metz & Co. See **Liberty & Co.**

Metzel (Metzels), Erich. 1898 and later. Pössneck, Thür. Made dolls.★

Metzler, Gebrüder (Bros.), & Ortloff. 1875–1930 and later. Ilmenau, Thür. The brothers Rudolph, Robert, and Hugo Ortloff made heads for dolls in their porcelain factory. The painting and making of the doll articles were done as a home industry. According to the Ciesliks they began to produce dolls' heads around 1894. (See Ills. 1885 and 1886.)★

Metzler, Martin. 1912–13. Sonneberg, Thür. Applied for two German Patents (D.R.G.M.) for dolls' bodies. One was for a cloth body stuffed with hair and having ball joints. This patent was obtained with *Richard Metzler.* The other patent was for stringing a doll.

Metzler, Richard (Sr. & Jr.). 1885–1927. Sonneberg, Thür. Made wooden dolls and wax dolls.

1888: Advertised jointed and unjointed dolls.

1894: Advertised wooden dolls and wooden dolls' heads with real hair.

1912–13: Obtained a patent with *Martin Metzler* for cloth dolls' bodies.

Metzner, Edmund. 1915–27. Sonneberg, Thür. Manufactured dolls.★

Meunier, Mme. 1916. Belgium. Dressed dolls in regional costumes for *Le Jouet Belge.*

Meusel, Walt. 1929. Oberlind, Thür. Manufactured dolls.

Mexican Dolls. Mexico was famous for its wax dolls and for its tiny dolls.

In 1869 THE GIRLS' OWN BOOK described the dolls

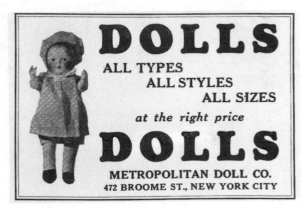

1883. Advertisement for dolls made by the Metropolitan Doll Co. as it appeared in PLAYTHINGS, May, 1927.

C **METROPOLITAN 1929**

1884A, B & C. Marks on composition head dolls probably made by the Metropolitan Doll Co. The attribution of the No. 1884A mark is not certain.

that were made in Mexico by coating cloth figures with wax. These were made in various sizes and represented people of various ages. Some of these waxed dolls were sent to *Mme. Montanari* in London where they were distributed.

Elsie Krug described old Mexican wax dolls as having well modeled faces, hands and feet. No two were exactly alike. They showed occupations and accessories such as market men or women with vegetables, a man with a cock, a water carrier and a woman with flowers. The clothes were made of fabric dipped in wax and they stood on a base. Hts. 5¾, 7, and 12 in. (14.5, 18, and 30.5 cm.).

A group of Mexican wax-head dolls with molded hair and glass eyes had adult portrait type faces.

The men had beards or mustaches. The torsos were wood and the arms and legs had cloth upper parts and wax forearms and lower legs. The shoes were molded and painted and had small heels. The clothes suggested the late 1800s or early 1900s. Hts. ca. 9 in. (23 cm.).

TOYS AND NOVELTIES in 1914 gave the following description of some Mexican dolls:

"The tiniest dolls in the world are said to be made by the Mexican Indians. Many of them are not more than three-quarters of an inch in length, yet they are perfect in every detail. The Indians make these dolls by first making a framework of small wire. Then they wind about this

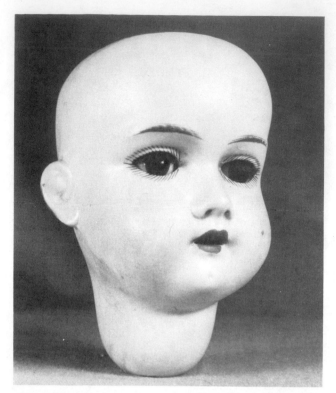

1885. Bisque socket head probably made by Gebrüder Metzler & Ortloff. It has a wig, sleeping eyes, open mouth with four teeth. Mark III. 1886. H. head only 4 in. (10 cm.). *Coleman Collection.*

Made in Germany
890
EM2½

1886. Mark on bisque heads made probably by Gebrüder Metzler & Ortloff.

framework very fine silk thread until the figure has the proper shape. The costumes are then fitted to the doll, cut according to the character it is to represent.

"With needles that can scarcely be held in the fingers, the eyes of which are almost invisible, various designs are embroidered on the dolls' clothes with the finest of silk thread. So cleverly do the Indians execute these designs that even under a powerful glass no imperfect details are to be found.

"Once properly dressed the doll is given its hair. Even to the details of the braids and ribbons this work is carried out.

Then there are formed the eyes, the nose and the mouth, hands and feet. Some dolls are provided with tiny baskets of flowers, fancy sombreros, water jars and other paraphernalia. The baskets are made of hair by the Indians of Guarajuato. The bits of pottery are made of clay in exact imitation of the practical articles. All of these accessories are sewed to the dolls. Miniature roses are embroidered in the costumes of the dancing girls and ornaments are arranged in their hair. Other characters are as carefully made."

Similar dolls were made by Isabel Belaunsaran[+] in the Cuernavaca Valley in 1914. These sold for 25¢ retail and took two hours to make.

Among the companies that dressed dolls in Mexican costumes were *Horsman, Lenci* and *Steiff.*★

Meyer, Armand. 1930 and later. Made dolls.

Meyer, Carl. 1899–21. Sonneberg, Thür. Made character dolls and babies, including cloth dolls with celluloid faces and *Waltershausen* dolls. Before 1899 he was a partner in *Carl Geyer & Co.*

1910: Dressed dolls in regional costumes, as *Red Riding Hood,* as Toboggan dolls, and so on. Exported dolls to England and South America.★

Meyer, Florence. 1926. San Francisco, Calif. Obtained a U.S. design patent for a doll.

Meyer, H. 1930. Dresden, Germany. Manufactured dolls.

Meyer, Hermann. 1926–30. Hannover, Saxony. Made and/or distributed celluloid dolls and babies and rubber dolls.

1926: *Rheinische Gummi und Celluloid Fabrik* supplied the celluloid dolls which had wigs, painted or glass eyes. These dolls were dressed by Hermann Meyer.

1930: Rubber dolls were distributed by *Hertzog.*

Meyer, L. 1922–29. London. Made and/or distributed dolls.

1922: Distributed dolls of *Kletzin.*

1924: Advertised *Hanka* dolls, *Cupids,* dressed and undressed dolls.

1926: Advertised *Mama* dolls and British-made Art dolls. Some of their dolls sold for 13¢ to 88¢.

Meyer & Lorang. 1929–30 and later. New York City. Made felt dolls with "natural hair and washable faces." They also imported dolls and were factory agents. The felt dolls pictured had eyes that looked straight ahead, arms slightly bent and a thumb separate from the fingers which were indicated by stitches.

1929: No. 3170 came in four styles and wore a bonnet; cost $1.50.

No. 3173 came in two styles and wore a brimmed hat; cost $2.00. All of these dolls came with clothes in assorted colors and there were large bows on the shoes at the ankles.

Meyers, Gladys. 1930. America. Made clothes for dolls following the principle that "children like their dollies to have the same kind of clothes they are wearing and if possible made of the same material." First she made reefer jackets, then tailored suits and sunsuits until she had 41 different numbers. She made clothes for *Patsy* and her family. In a wedding party group *Skippy* was the groom dressed in a black tailored suit and the eight bridesmaids were dressed in organdy.

Mezg (Metzger, Butcher). 1913–16. Felt jointed doll representing a butcher, made by *Steiff* and distributed by *Borgfeldt*. Ht. 14 in. (35 cm.); priced $2.35 in 1913.

M'Ginn, Peter. Before 1926–30. London. In 1926 the successor was L.A. Wolff. Made and/or distributed dolls. Advertisement showed a bent-limb baby doll with a Dutch bob hairdo and wearing a chemise.

Mi (Missis). 1905–16. Felt jointed doll made by *Steiff* and distributed by *Borgfeldt*. This fat doll was dressed as a woman with a dotted blouse, long skirt, a wide apron, a conical hat and heavy shoes. Ko (Cook) was similar except it had a plain blouse and was a tea cosy. Mi represented the Mother in the *Katzenjammer Kids*. Ht. 35 cm. (14 in.); priced $1.12 in Germany in 1911 and $1.55 in New York in 1913.

This doll was shown in paintings by *Carl Larsson* in 1906 and 1915.

1906: Distributed by *Gamage* with the name of "Mrs. Fatty"; priced 62¢.

1913: Distributed by Gamage with the name "Mrs. Captain"; priced 81¢.

Mi Corazón de Oro (My Dear Heart). 1930. Name of a doll advertised by *Bruno Schmidt*.

Mi Encanto. 1930. Trademark name registered by *Seligmann & Mayer* in Germany for dolls.

1887. Felt Steiff doll known as Mi (Missis), and when in tea cosy form known as Cook (Ko). It represented Mrs. Katzenjammer, mother of the Katzenjammer Kids. Original felt clothes. H. 18 in. (45.5 cm.). *Courtesy of and photo by Phyllis Salak.*

Mi Liebling. See **Mein Liebling.**

Miami Wood Specialty Co. 1923–24. Dayton, Ohio. Made wooden circus figures similar to the Schoenhut ones and specialized in clowns. Among these were "Flips and Flops the Flying Clowns." (The name Miami is derived from an Ohio River.)

Miblu. 1925–30 and later. A waxy celluloid material made by *Rheinische Gummi und Celluloid Fabrik Co.* for *Kämmer & Reinhardt* dolls. The name Miblu was the acronym for the German words for milk and blood.

1926: Miblu was registered as a trademark in Germany by Rheinische Gummi und Celluloid Fabrik.

1930: *Max Rudolph* advertised Miblu dolls' heads.

Mibs. 1921–24. All-bisque or composition head on cloth body dolls made and/or produced by *Amberg*. It was designed by Hazel Drukker[†] and represented a three-year-old child. The composition version was dressed in either a pink or white pinafore, blue rompers or a white lawn dress.

The all-bisque version was marked "© //L.A. & S. 1921 //Germany." Hts. 3 and 4¾ in. (7.5 and 12 cm.).

1921: Advertised in British Toy Trade Journals.

1922: *Sears* advertised the dressed composition head version.

1924: Was advertised in a "new version"; priced $1.50. (See THE COLLECTOR'S BOOK OF DOLLS' CLOTHES, Ill. 725.) (See Ills. 1888 and 1889.)★

Mich (Bauer [Peasant] Michel). 1911–16. Felt character doll made by *Steiff* and distributed by *Borgfeldt*. It was dressed as a peasant wearing a velvet vest, a white cap and leather boots. Ht. 50 cm. (19½ in.); priced $3.56 in Germany in 1911 and $4.75 in New York in 1913. (See Ill. 1890.)

Michaela. 1915. One of the *Paderewski* dolls made by Polish refugees in *Mme. Lazarski's* workshop. It represented a bride from Sieradz dressed in a wedding costume consisting of a red moiré silk skirt and flowered apron. The bonnet was adorned with yellow and blue ribbons and the veil of cerise brocaded silk was embroidered.

Michaelis, Amandus, & Co. 1870–1930. Rauenstein, Thür., and London. In 1911 the company was owned by Albin Michaelis and *Hermann Pensky*. Made various types of dolls, specialized in dolls with kid bodies.

1890: Advertised *Täuflinge*, wax dolls, and dolls that were jointed as well as not jointed.

1904: Applied for a German patent (D.R.G.M.) for waterproofing papier-mâché for dolls.

1910: Made a mourning doll for the English trade because of the death of King Edward VII.

1911: Advertised jointed character dolls, one of which had a voice.

1926: Advertised baby dolls, *Mama* dolls, a walking clown, black and white boy dolls with a harmonica and a voice. (See Ill. 1891.)★

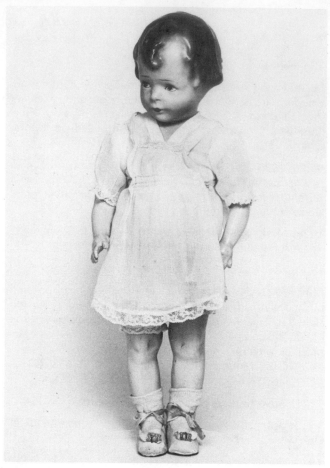

1888. Composition shoulder head doll representing Mibs, designed by Hazel Drukker and made by Amberg. It has molded and painted hair and blue eyes, closed mouth and a cloth torso with composition legs and lower arms. Original clothes. H. 16 in. (40.5 cm.). *Courtesy of the Margaret Woodbury Strong Museum. Photo by Harry Bickelhaupt.*

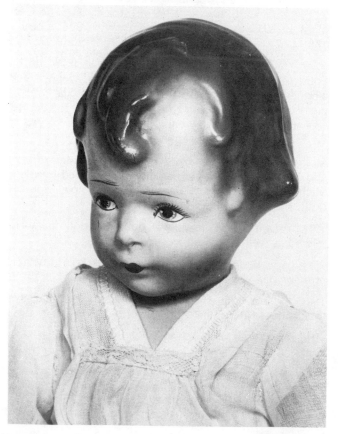

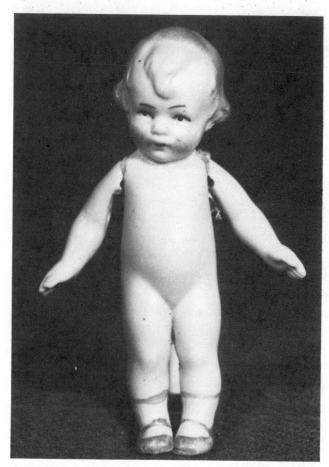

1889. All-bisque Mibs doll designed by Hazel Drukker and produced by Amberg. It has molded blond hair, pink socks and green shoes. The bisque is pink throughout. Mark on back: "©//L. A. & S. 1921//Germany." H. 3 in. (7.5 cm.). *Coleman Collection.*

1890. Mich (Bauer Mich), farmer Michel, is a Steiff felt doll with brown mohair sewn to the head, bead-like blue glass eyes, seam down the center of the face, closed mouth, turning neck and joints at the shoulder and hips. Original clothes except for the hat. H. 54 cm. (21½ in.). *Courtesy of Richard Wright. Photo by A. Jackson.*

1892A & B. Marks probably used by the successors of Hugo Michaelis at the Porzellanfabrik Rauenstein.

Michaelis, Hugo. 1887–1930 and later. Rauenstein, Thür. Owned the Porzellanfabrik Rauenstein that had once belonged to the Greiner[†] family. In 1892 his successors took over the factory. Made bisque dolls' heads including those named *Alice* (mold #191), *Dora*, and those marked with crossed Fs as shown in Ill. 1892. By 1927 there were 500 employees according to the Cieśliks' research.

Michaelis, M., & Co. 1890–1930. Berlin. Exporters who handled dolls, dolls' parts, dolls' clothes. They represented *Richard Helse, Edmund Knoch, Otto Koch & Sohn, F. Maar & Sohn, Max Rudolph, Victor Steiner, Max Vogel, Hugo Wiegand,* and *August Wiener* in 1930.

Michel, Nicholas. 1926. Sulphur Springs, Tex. Obtained a U.S. patent for a resilient neck that connected a doll's head and body making the head slidable and rotable.

Michèle. 1915. A painter and designer of the *Paderewski* dolls according to a contemporary account in the CRAFTSMAN.

Michtom, Morris. See **Ideal Novelty & Toy Co.**

Mickey. 1920. Stockinet dolls manufactured and distributed by the Bandeau Sales Co.[†] The doll was made of a single piece of white jersey cloth filled with floss stuffing and advertised as being washable. The features and blue or pink sweater were painted.★

Mickey. 1926. Trademark registered in U.S. by *Performo Toy Co.* for toy figures.

Mickey McGuire. 1929. Name of an all-bisque doll with painted features and molded clothes representing the cartoon character of this name, distributed by *Borgfeldt* and *Butler Bros.* Ht. 2¼ in. (5.5 cm.); priced 84¢ doz. wholesale.

Mickiewicz, Miss Marie. 1915–16. Directed the making of the *Paderewski* dolls in *Mme. Lazarski*'s workshop. Miss Michiewicz was the granddaughter of the Polish poet Adam Mickiewicz.

1891. Mark possibly used by the successors of Amandus Michaelis.

Middie. 1917–18. One of the *Horsman* "Art" dolls, it wore a white sailor suit with puttees (or high boots) and a white brimmed cap.

Middy Girl. 1913–19. Doll with composition head and arms, molded hair, sleeping eyes, made by *Ideal.* It wore a middy blouse and a checked cotton skirt. Ht. 14 in. (35.5 cm.); price $10.80 doz. wholesale.

Midolly. 1919–20. Line of baby dolls and child dolls made by the *New Toy Manufacturing Co.* The dolls had wigs, sleeping eyes, hair eyelashes, and their composition bodies were steel strung. They came in an organdy chemise or fully dressed.

MIDOLLY LINE IN 1920			
	Height		
Style No.	in.	cm.	Description of body
400	20	51	Bent-limb baby
405			Fully jointed child
410	22½	57	Bent-limb baby
415	26	66	Fully jointed child
425	29	73.5	Fully jointed child
451	22½	57	Bent-limb baby
462	25	63.5	Bent-limb baby
498	29	73.5	Fully jointed child

When dressed these doll wore gingham, crepe-de-chine, muslin, or dotted mull. The child dolls had hair ribbons or hats and kid slippers. The baby dolls wore long or short dresses and had kid bodies.

1893. Midolly mark used by the New Toy Co.

Migault, Établissement. 1878–1930. Briare, Loiret, and Paris, France. Made jewelry and parures for dolls. Member of the *Chambre Syndicale.*

Migault & Papin. 1908. France. Used the initials M. P. as a mark for dolls.

Mignon. 1903. Doll jointed at the shoulders and wearing a molded bathing suit. It was called "Mignon" by *F. A. O. Schwarz.*

Mignon. 1912. The *Louvre* store advertised a baby doll on a cushion as being "Mignon." Ht. 17 cm. (6½ in.); priced 58¢.

Mignon. 1912–13. Name of a celluloid doll, jointed at the shoulders and having a "painted bathing suit." It was adver-

tised by *Selchow & Righter.* Hts. 5¾, 9, and 10 in. (14.5, 23 and 25.5 cm.); priced $2.00 to $6.00 doz. wholesale.

Mignon. 1918–20. Name of a bisque head doll produced by Félix Arena.[†] It had a mohair wig, sleeping eyes, open mouth with teeth, a jointed composition body and the head was marked "Mignon 1" on a 21 in. (53.5 cm.) doll.

Mignon. 1927. A cloth doll made in Paris and dressed as a French peasant wearing sabots. It carried an eight-sided paper tag bearing the name Mignon. Ht. 25 in. (63.5 cm.).

Mignonne. 1928–29. Art doll designed by *Maxine Averill.* The sole distributor was *Borgfeldt* who registered the name as a trademark in the U.S. The doll had a modernistic painted face and hair, a stuffed flesh-colored suede body and wore a figured linen dress with a matching hat. A dog was tucked under the doll's arm.

1929: Price $7.50.

Mignonnettes (Mignonettes). 1875–1930 and later. Name usually applied to small dolls, but dolls as large as 35 cm. (14 in.) have been called "Mignonnettes." The term was used extensively in France and occasionally elsewhere. Some of the advertisements for dolls were as follows.

1882–83: *Printemps* advertised two styles of mignonnettes. The first represented a coquettish peasant. Ht. 15 cm. (6 in.); priced with stationary eyes 58¢ and with sleeping eyes 98¢. The other mignonnette was dressed in wool and silk tricot. Hts. 11, 15, and 17 cm. (4½, 6, and 6½ in.); priced 29¢ to 78¢.

1890: Mignonnettes were made by *J. Decoster.* There were also advertisements for bisque dolls in satin costumes. Ht. 11 and 13 cm. (4½ and 5 in.); priced 19¢ and 29¢.

1891: Printemps in their Swedish edition catalog, advertised bisque head mignonnettes. Hts. 12 and 14 cm. (4½ and 5½ in.).

1897: *Samaritaine* advertised bisque head girl and boy dolls dressed in satin and velvet Russian costumes, costing 29¢ for the pair.

Au Paradis des Enfants advertised mignonnettes dressed in religious garb.

1901: Samaritaine advertised dolls with sleeping eyes, dressed. Ht. 24 cm. (9½ in.); priced 29¢.

1902: Samaritaine's couples in regional costumes including Russian, cost 29¢.

1903: *Tapis Rouge*—Black or white dolls jointed at the neck, shoulders and hips, hts. 15 or 20 cm. (6 or 8 in.) cost 19¢. When they had long hair wigs, sleeping eyes and were dressed, ht. 21 cm. (8½ in.), they cost 29¢. A doll in swaddling clothes with a bottle, ht. 15 cm. (6 in.) cost 15¢.

1905: *Petit Saint Thomas'* Mignonnettes came in a box with a wardrobe of clothes.

La Place Clichy's Mignonnettes came with sleeping eyes. Ht. 21 cm. (8½ in.); priced 29¢.

For Christmas *Bleuette* was offered as a 10 cm. (4 in.) mignonnette.

1906: *Louvre* store's mignonnette dolls called *Le National* were dressed in regional costumes. Ht. 5.5 cm. (2¼ in.).

Samaritaine's dolls were dressed in silk, ht. 22 cm. (8½ in.); priced 29¢.

1908: *L'Hotel de Ville* advertised bisque-head, fully jointed, dressed mignonnette dolls. Ht. 19 cm. (7½ in.); priced 50¢. Also at Hotel de Ville there were dolls with sleeping eyes and able to walk; dressed in silk and lace. Ht. 23 cm. (9 in.); priced 55¢.

1910–11: *Aux Trois Quartiers* advertised dressed mignonnettes in regional and in historical costumes. These came in glass covered boxes containing three to 20 dolls. Ht. of dolls 7 cm. (2¾ in.); priced 39¢ to $2.35 according to the number of dolls.

1911: Printemps called their composition character head dolls mignonnettes. Hts. 30 and 35 cm. (12 and 14 in.); priced $1.35 and $1.90.

Samaritaine's mignonnettes were jointed dolls with wigs and sleeping eyes. Ht. 20 cm. (8 in.); priced 29¢.

1912: *Bon Marché* advertised six mignonnettes in regional costumes. Hts. 7 and 9 cm. (2½ and 3½ in.); priced 55¢ and $1.18 for the six dolls.

Paris Montpelier's mignonnettes were bisque-head dolls with sleeping eyes, 29¢ and 58¢ if fully jointed.

Lafayette advertised a dressed walking mignonnette with sleeping eyes. Ht. 23 cm. (9 in.); priced 58¢. Other mignonnettes were in boxes with their trousseaux.

Aliman & Zara of London advertised mignonnettes.

1921: L'Hotel de Ville offered dressed mignonnettes.

1923: *Dufayel* advertised mignonnettes with sleeping eyes. Ht. 12 cm. (4½ in.).

La Place Clichy advertised mignonnettes.

1925: *Shackman* offered bisque head mignonnettes with a bow in the hair, sleeping eyes, composition body, jointed at shoulders and hips. They came dressed as a girl. Ht. 7 in. (18 cm.); priced $3.75 doz. wholesale.

1927: Bisque head dolls with sleeping eyes, "satinette" dresses, various style hats, sold by Lafayette store as mignonnettes. Ht. 25 cm. (10 in.).

1928: *Gerzon* advertised mignonnettes, hts. 17 or 18 cm. (6½ or 7 in.) in boxes with their trousseaux. See THE COLLECTOR'S BOOK OF DOLLS' CLOTHES, Ills. 428B, 526, 531 and 754 (See also **Dolls' House Dolls, Lilliputians; Manufacture of Dolls, Commercial: Made in France and Germany, Compared.**)★

Mik, Johann, & Kamauf, Karl. 1924. Vienna. Obtained an Austrian patent for a walking doll.

Mikado Shokai (Ima Kumancho). 1926–30 and later. Kyoto, Japan. Made dolls.

Mike.† See **Gene Carr Kids.**

Milano, Guilio Da. 1920s. Italy. Born in 1897 in Nizza Marittima. He was one of the artists who designed dolls and/or ceramic figures for *Lenci*.

1927: Won a silver medal.

0—41158.**MIGNONNETTE**
habillage fantaisie.
3.75, 4.50, 5.50 et **6.75**

1894. Mignonnette, a small dressed doll advertised by L'Hotel de Ville in their 1921 catalog. The doll sold for four different prices.

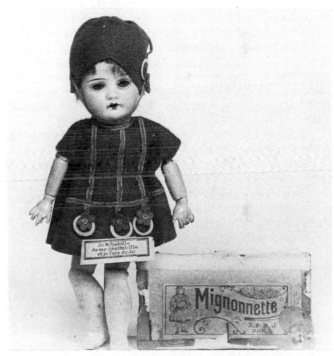

1895. Bisque head Mignonnette doll made by the Société Française de Fabrication de Bébé & Jouets (S.F.B.J.) with its original box. The doll has a wig, sleeping blue glass eyes, open mouth with four upper teeth, and a ball jointed composition body. Original felt dress and cloche probably of the 1920s. The paper tag on the dress reads: "Je m'habille//Je me déshabille//et je fais dodo." (I dress myself//I undress myself//and I go to sleep.) The box end has on it: "Mignonnette//7 unis france 149//No.2 ___ S.F.B.J.//PARIS." H. 8½ in. (21.5 cm.). *Courtesy of the Margaret Woodbury Strong Museum.*

Mildred. 1921. Name of a doll made by *Effanbee*. It wore a blue dimity dress with a canary yellow sash and hat to match. Came in three heights.

Mildred. See **Prize Baby.**

Milendo. See **Cohen, W.**

Military Costume Dolls. Popular throughout the ages these dolls were dressed by commercial concerns as well as persons at home to represent various nations and various military branches and ranks. Portrait dolls of military heroes and a few military costume dolls with special names have been listed according to their names. Some of the famous Generals, Admirals or Marshalls who inspired portrait dolls were *General Baden-Powell, Admiral Dewey, Marshall Foch, Admiral Jellicoe, General Joffre, Lord Kitchener, Lord Roberts, Admiral Sampson, Admiral Schley, Von Hindenburg.*

Also dolls representing Royalty have been found wearing military attire. (See *King Albert, King Edward VII,* and so forth.)

Around 1900 Boer War costume dolls were in evidence, but during World War I an even larger percentage of dolls wore military outfits. Between these wars and after World War I relatively few dolls were dressed in military costumes.

The French *Pioupiou* (foot soldier), the American Doughboy and the British *Tommy* were especially popular. Dolls with round pill-box shaped hats (like bell-hops wore) were likely to represent the British Tommy during and after the Boer War period. During World War I some of the dolls were dressed as Airmen. Various dolls had a molded German helmet with a spike on top. These included *Kewpies,* Doll heads made by *Gebrüder Heubach,* and those marked *Elite.*

Steiff and other manufacturers dressed their dolls in the military uniforms of various nations.

During World War I many of the *Käthe Kruse* dolls were dressed in German military uniforms.

A papier-mâché head doll with an Austrian insignia on its helmet which had lost its spike stood on a green wooden base. (See Ill. 1897.)

A lancer officer came in the same type of German box as the 1920s *Dolls' House Dolls* with bisque heads. This doll with a mustache had hands painted brown to represent gloves. It wore a hussar-type hat, a sword and pistol holster. Ht. 9 in. (23 cm.). (See Ill. 1907.)

In a 1927 *Kämmer & Reinhardt* catalog a series of dolls was advertised, the tallest one being 23 cm. (9 in.). They were designed to be placed in settings such as small military groups, shops, etc. In addition the catalog stated that "soldiery of other nations can be delivered if colored illustrations are sent in." See THE COLLECTOR'S BOOK OF DOLLS' CLOTHES, Ills. 428, 496, 522 and 530.

1831: The *Lindner* catalog showed dolls in military costumes.

1856: *Geo. Davis* advertised rubber dolls in soldier and sailor costumes.

1894: *Montgomery Ward* advertised "Indestructible soldier" dolls dressed in oilcloth. Ht. 10½ in. (26.5 cm.); priced 10¢.

1896: *La Place Clichy* advertised Pioupiou, the familiar French term for a private.

1897: *Samaritaine* advertised jointed composition dolls dressed as a French Corporal, a sailor or orderly, and an African hunter. Ht. 46 cm. (18 in.); priced $1.05.

1899–1901: *Butler Bros.* advertised Rough Rider dolls.

1900: La Place Clichy advertised composition dolls with felt hats and leather boots dressed as English soldiers with mustaches and as Boer soldiers with beards and cartridge belts. The dolls representing Boers were slightly more expensive than those representing the English soldiers.

1901: *Louvre* store advertised a composition doll dressed as a corporal wearing a kepi. Four hts. 48, 60, 72, and 87 cm. (19, 23½, 28½, and 34 in.); priced 95¢ to $2.75.

1902: Butler Bros. advertised a glass-eyed doll dressed in a Hussar's uniform with a red, braided tunic, belt and sword. Ht. 5¼ in. (13.5 cm.); priced 96¢ doz. wholesale.

Louvre advertised a jointed composition doll with mustache dressed as a corporal in a wool outfit with a short jacket, long trousers and a kepi. Four hts. 45, 53, 63, and 80 cm. (17½, 21, 25, and 31½ in.); priced 95¢ to $3.50. Louvre also advertised a jointed composition doll with beard, dressed in a khaki Boer costume with a cartridge shoulder belt, brimmed hat, high boots and carrying a rifle. Hts. 45 and 54 cm. (17½ and 21½ in.); priced $1.58 and $1.95.

1904: Butler Bros. advertised bisque-head dolls in various uniforms representing Cavalry, Infantry, Hussars, Rough Riders and sailors. Ht. 6 in. (15 cm.). The Russian red Hussar uniform with epaulettes and sword came also in a slightly larger size.

1905: *Bon Marché* advertised jointed composition dolls dressed as Japanese soldiers with a rifle and Cossacks with a sword. Hts. 36, 40, and 44 cm. (14, 15½, and 17½ in.); priced 58¢ to $1.10.

Worsted dolls dressed as soldiers were made by *Emil Wittzack.*

1906: *Carl Horn* dressed miniature dolls as soldiers and each doll had a rifle.

1908: Louvre advertised jointed composition dolls dressed as Lieutenants in the French cavalry and in the infantry. Ht. 40 cm. (15½ in.); priced 58¢.

1909: Samaritaine advertised dolls dressed as Infantry Lieutenants. Ht. 45 cm. (17½ in.); priced 59¢.

L'Hotel de Ville advertised jointed dolls with composition heads dressed in various military uniforms. Hts. 37 and 43 cm. (14½ and 17 in.); priced 59¢ and 99¢.

1910: Louvre advertised composition-head dolls dressed in various uniforms. Hts. 31, 37, and 42 cm. (12, 14½, and 16½ in.); priced 35¢ to 99¢.

Moritz Pappe advertised dolls dressed as soldiers.

Printemps advertised jointed composition dolls dressed in uniforms with fringed epaulettes and kepi. Hts. 32, 38 and 44 cm. (12½, 15 and 17½ in.); priced 35¢ to 99¢.

Before 1911–16 and later: *Steiff* dressed their felt dolls as various soldiers and sailors. The German soldiers included various ranks from Private to Major and various branches of the army such as Infantry, Artillery, Dragoons and so forth.

The uniforms of other nations included American, Austrian, Belgian, English, French and Dutch.

1911: *Karl Standfuss* patented a celluloid soldier doll.

1912: *Lafayette* store advertised dolls in various uniforms. Hts. 35, 40 and 45 cm. (14, 15½ and 17½ in.); priced 35¢ to 98¢.

Modernes store advertised a cloth soldier doll. Ht. 35 cm. (14 in.); priced 29¢.

Butler Bros. advertised celluloid head dolls with painted features, cloth bodies and felt military costumes including a Zouave uniform. The costumes included headwear, patent leather belts and cartridge boxes. Ht. 7 in. (18 cm.); priced 89¢ doz. wholesale.

1912–14: *Horsman* advertised Sailor dolls.

Louvre advertised composition-head dolls dressed in various military uniforms. Hts. 31, 37, and 46 cm. (12, 14½, and 18 in.); priced 35¢ to 98¢. In 1914 dolls dressed as Infantry Cavalry, and Artillery Officers and a ht. of 48 cm. (19 in.), priced $1.35, were added.

1913: *Gamage* and *Borgfeldt* advertised Steiff soldiers.

World War I Period: Among the many companies that made dolls dressed in military uniforms were the following: *Hyman Abrahams, Borough British Dolls, British Doll Manufacturing, British Products Manufacturing, Dean, Lelia Fellom[+], Harwin, Horsman, Ideal, Knight Bros. & Cooper, Käthe Kruse, Langrock, Nottingham Toy, Potteries Toy, Albert Schoenhut, Shropshire Toy Industry, W. H. Smith, Société Française de Fabrication de Bébés & Jouets, Standard Doll Co., Steiff, Sunlight, Sieve & Co., Trion Toy Co., Western Art Leather* and *Wigwam.*

1915: The *Henry S. Benjamin* showroom in London showed French dolls dressed to represent whole French infantry regiments, officers and enlisted men; all reproduced exactly to scale even to buttons and rifles.

TOYS AND NOVELTIES on its inside front cover showed composition dolls in the military uniforms of various nations. These dolls each weighed less than an oz. Ht. 4 in. (10 cm.).

Louvre store advertised dolls dressed as soldiers of the Allies. The cloth dolls were 37 cm. (14½ in.) tall, costing $1.30. The composition-head dolls were 40 cm. (15½ in.) tall, costing 85¢.

1916: Printemps advertised composition-head dolls dressed in the uniforms of the Belgians, French, English, Italians and Russians. Ht. 40 cm. (15½ in.); priced 85¢.

1917: Sailor boys and girls made by the *Star Manufacturing Co.* A composition head doll dressed as a Sailor boy was distributed by the *Baltimore Bargain House.* It had a cloth body with composition hands. Ht. 36 in. (91.5 cm.); priced $1.45.

1917–18: Horsman made British Tommy dolls.

1918: Dolls with composition heads and hands, molded hair, painted features, cloth bodies with shoulder and hip joints were dressed as soldiers and distributed by Butler Bros. Ht. 13 in. (33 cm.).

Printemps advertised "Soldiers of the Allies." These jointed dolls had composition heads. Ht. 40 cm. (15½ in.); priced $1.30.

Early 1920s: A few of the *Lenci* dolls were dressed as soldiers.

1924: Cloth doll made by *Nelke* was dressed as a sailor with middy blouse, bell bottom trousers, feet apart and a cap on the side of its head.

1925: *Shackman* sold all-celluloid dolls dressed as soldiers and sailors. Ht. 2¾ in. (7 cm.); priced $1.50 doz. wholesale.

1928: *Poppy Doll Co.* made small all-wooden dolls dressed as sailors.

1929: Composition head doll made by *Averill Manufacturing Co.* had painted hair and eyes, a cotton stuffed cloth body with composition arms and a two-tone whistle. It was dressed as a sailor in a white suit and hat. Ht. 14 in. (35.5 cm.).

Cloth dolls made by Nelke wore a jacket with two rows of buttons down the waist length front and it had tails in back. The long trousers were lighter in color than the jacket and the doll wore a busby.

Cloth dolls representing soldiers and sailors were made by *Twinzy.* (See also **Aviator.**)

A special type of military uniform called Zouave[+] was often found on dolls because of its picturesqueness. These uniforms resembled the Moorish costumes worn in French Algeria and were adopted in 1830 by some units of the French Army. Other armies later also adopted this style of uniform, which existed until after World War I.

The following are examples of some of the dolls dressed in Zouave uniforms:

1860s: Some of the *Autoperipatetikos* dolls, having molded cloth heads with features resembling a man with a mustache and goatee, wore Zouave style clothes.

1878: THE QUEEN described *Gutta Percha* dolls dressed as Zouaves.

1892: The Louvre store advertised a jointed composition doll dressed as a Zouave. Ht. 41 cm. (16 in.); priced $1.18.

1903: Bon Marché sold composition head dolls dressed as Zouaves. Hts. 35, 40, and 45 cm. (14, 15½ and 17½ in.); priced 39¢ to $1.30.

1917: The *Standard Doll Co.* advertised a doll with a composition head and hands, painted hair and eyes, dressed in a Zouave costume. Ht. 16 in. (40.5 cm.).★

Milk Maid. Ca. 1908–24. *Schoenhut* wooden doll wore an apron over a long dress and a bonnet; carried a milk pail. Came in one size.★

Milkmaid Mary. 1911–12. Doll made by *Horsman* with a head designed and copyrighted by *Helen Trowbridge.* The clothes were similar to those worn by *Sunbonnet Sal,* but Milkmaid Mary style No. 187 was larger and cost $10.80 doz. wholesale.

1896. Pair of composition-over-wood head dolls on peg wooden bodies dressed in military uniforms. The molded black hair has a bun in back and a mustache was painted on the face. They have painted blue eyes and closed mouths. Original clothes trimmed with gold paper and gold colored beads. Paper shoulder sashes and belts. H. 3¾ in. (9.5 cm.). *Courtesy of the Margaret Woodbury Strong Museum. Photo by Harry Bickelhaupt.*

1897. Papier-mâché head doll in a military costume. It has molded and painted features including a mustache. There is a hole in the mouth possibly for the insertion of a horn or other musical instrument. The hands are wood. Original felt clothes with red jacket, white pants and high black boots. A black tabard is trimmed with gold paper. The epaulets are also gold paper. The helmet has an Austrian insignia and the spike is missing. H. 8 in. (20.5 cm.). *Courtesy of the Washington Dolls' House and Toy Museum.*

A CANTEEN CARRIER OF THE
IMPERIAL GUARD IN 1862.

1898. Composition head doll dressed in a Zouave military uniform has painted blue eyes, closed mouth, and a carton body with wooden three finger hands. It is jointed only at the shoulders. Original clothes with painted footwear. It carries a metal musket. H. 7½ in. (19 cm.). *Coleman Collection.*

1899. A French doll exhibited ca. 1900 in Mlle. Koenig's Musée Pédagogique. This doll represents a Vivandière of 1862 and was shown in ST. NICHOLAS, January, 1910.

1901. Knitted and crocheted fabric doll in a military uniform. The hair is wool yarn; the features and details are embroidered, creating needle sculpture. Machine sewing in evidence where parts of larger pieces of fabric are joined, suggests that this was a mass produced doll. Original clothes. H. 30 cm. (12 in.). *Courtesy of the Musée National Suisse.*

1900. Pressed china shoulder head with brushmarks and painting but no molding of the hair. Original all-leather clothes encase the body and represent a military man. Hands are flat pieces of kid with incisions to show fingers; large high black boots serve as legs and feet. A similar but later doll dressed all in oilcloth was described as a "Soldier" in an 1894 Montgomery Ward Catalog, H. 9½ in. (24 cm.). H. of shoulder head 2 in. (5 cm.). *Coleman Collection.*

N° 19073. SOLDATS
habillage drap, tête
lavable incassable.

0ᵐ35	0ᵐ40	0ᵐ45
1.95	3.90	6.50

1902. Military dolls advertised by Samaritaine in their 1897 catalog. These composition jointed dolls were dressed as ordinance soldier, a corporal, a sailor or an African soldier. H. 4 cm. (1½ in.); price $1.05. This extremely small height may be a misprint. *Courtesy of Margaret Whitton.*

1903. Soldier with Zouave uniform as advertised by Bon Marché in 1903. It has a "washable unbreakable" head. Hs. 35, 40 and 45 cm. (14, 15½ and 17½ in.). *Courtesy of Margaret Whitton.*

1904A & B. All-composition doll in a Zouave military costume has its black hair glued onto the scalp, painted mustache, stationary glass eyes, an open mouth with teeth, a body jointed at the neck, shoulders, and hips. Original uniform. Mark in red on back of neck "3." H. 18½ in. (47 cm.). *Courtesy of Richard Withington. Photo by Barbara Jendrick.*

1905. Doll dressed in a soldier's khaki uniform with cartridge belt and high molded brown boots, probably of the Boer War period. It has a bisque head mold # 1902, size number 15/0, with a skin wig, glass pupilless eyes, open mouth, and teeth; on a five-piece composition body. H. 9 in. (23 cm.). *Coleman Collection.*

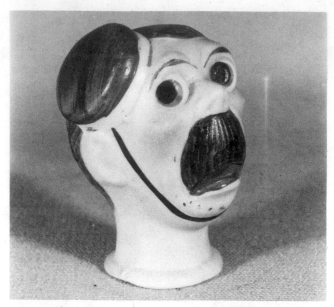

1906. Flange neck bisque head representing a British Tommy has molded and painted features, including a pill box style hat set off to the side, brown hair, round blue eyes looking to the side, a large mustache between the turned-up nose and a mouth which is turned down. H. of head 2¼ in. (5.5 cm.). *Coleman Collection.*

1907. Bisque shoulder head doll in a military costume. It has molded and painted hair, mustache and eyes, closed mouth and a cloth body with bisque arms and legs. The hands are painted brown to represent gloves. Original clothes and accessories include a brown suit with paper buttons and string trimming, a sword and pistol holster. The cylindrical hat has a red silk ribbon on the top and side. The original box is marked: "89/27 M/1.90 Ulanen Offizier feld gr." This indicates that the doll represents a Lancer officer and cost 48¢. H. 9 in. (23 cm.). *Courtesy of the Washington Dolls' House and Toy Museum.*

1908. Military uniform on a bisque-head dolls' house doll with molded and painted hair and features, cloth body. Original clothes consisting of a red jacket, blue pants, brown cylindrical hat, all trimmed with gold embossed paper, molded boots. H. 7½ in. *Courtesy of the Washington Dolls' House and Toy Museum.*

1909A & B. Bisque socket head doll in a French military uniform made by the Société Française de Fabrication de Bébés & Jouets (S.F.B.J.). It has white cotton wool for its hair, stationary black glass eyes, open mouth with three upper teeth and a five-piece composition body with typical S.F.B.J. brownish base to the composition. Original costume. Mark: "S.F.B.J.//60//PARIS." H. 11 in. (28 cm.). *Coleman Collection.*

1910. All-bisque dolls in original military costumes. They have wigs, painted eyes and molded footwear. H. 3½ and 3¾ in. (9 and 9.5 cm.). *Courtesy of Sotheby Parke Bernet Inc., N.Y.*

1911. Felt Scottish soldier made in the manner of a Steiff doll, but also resembles "Kiltie" made by Harwin. It has painted hair, black button eyes, and a seam down the center of the face. A hole back of the ear suggests that a button may have been attached there. Original clothes except for the hat. It has a gold colored coat and spats, green tartan kilt, black leather shoes with felt soles. The coat is the same cut as that worn by Soldat, englisch (English Soldier) except for the color. H. 14½ in. (37 cm.). *Courtesy of Richard Wright. Photo by A. Jackson.*

1912. Bisque head doll dressed as a French soldier of World War I, made by the Société Française de Fabrication de Bébés & Jouets (S.F.B.J.). It has flocked hair, stationary blue glass eyes, open mouth with teeth, and a ball jointed composition body. Original uniform. Mark "S.F.B.J.//237//PARIS 4." H. 16 in. (40.5 cm.). *Courtesy of Sotheby Parke Bernet Inc., N.Y.*

AU LOUVRE -- PARIS
POUR LES TOUT PETITS

375084. **SUJETS** tout en étoffe Alsacienne.
Lorraine, infirmières ou soldats alliés. Haut. 0ᵐ37. **6.50** | 375085. **SOLDATS** carton incassable fin, costumes des alliés, assortis, haut. 0ᵐ40. **4.25**

1913. Dolls dressed in the uniforms of the World War I allies and a Red Cross Nurse as shown in a 1916 Louvre store catalog. The three dolls on the left are cloth dolls. Other cloth dolls were dressed as Alsatians or inhabitants of Lorraine. H. 37 cm. (14½ in.); priced $1.30. The East London Federation of Suffragettes in 1915 made similar cloth dolls dressed as Tommy Atkins (British soldiers).

The three dolls on the right are made of composition and dressed as various allied soldiers. H. 40 cm. (15½ in.); priced 85¢.

1914. All-bisque doll with wig, painted features, dressed as a French soldier of World War I; metal helmet. H. 4½ in. (11.5 cm.). *Coleman Collection.*

Miller, Bradley & Hall. 1857 and probably other years. New York City. Imported and distributed India rubber dolls and dolls' heads.

Miller Bros. 1916. London. Produced *Eskimo* dolls, dressed dolls and limbs for dolls.

Miller Doll Manufacturing Corp. 1930 and later. New York City. Manufactured dolls.

Miller, J. P., & Co. 1916–19. Liverpool, England. Made composition dolls which included the *Chubee* line, *Billy Doll* and other bent limb baby dolls. They modeled and made the dolls in their own factory.

1918: Registered in Britain *Compolene* and *Compolite* as trademarks for "unbreakable" composition material for dolls. *Nottingham* referred to this material.

Miller Rubber Co. 1922–23. Akron, Ohio. Made sponge rubber dolls including *Patsy, Polly, Pa, Ma* and *Junior.*★

Millicent. 1927. Trade name of a doll.

Millière, Maurice. 1925–30 and later. Paris. Created dolls.★

Milligan (Millikin) & Lawley. 1881–82. London. Distributed dressed dolls, talking dolls and dolls' accessories. See THE COLLECTOR'S BOOK OF DOLLS' CLOTHES, Ill. 309.★

Million, Isabel. 1911–19. Knoxville, Tenn. Made dolls with dried apple heads that represented such people as a fussy old seamstress, a tyrannical school marm and many others.★

Mills, O. 1851–56. New York City. U.S. A toy store of this name had printed paper labels attached to the bodies of dolls with papier-mâché heads.

From **O MILLS**
Toy Store,
194 SIXTH AVENUE,
Bet. 13th & 14th sts.

Price

1915. Mark on a paper label of O. Mills Toy Store. It was found on a body having a papier-mâché shoulder head.

Milobendzka, Mme. Emilia. 1927 and earlier. Paris, then New York City. Created *Boudoir* dolls that were distributed by *Blum-Lustig Toy Co.* These long limbed dolls generally wore full trousers drawn in at the ankles and a wide cumberbund.

Milton Bradley Co. 1927 and probably other years. Springfield, Mass. Made dolls of wood flour, starch and rosin which were hot pressed into shape and finished with celluloid paint which Milton Bradley claimed could be cleaned with a damp cloth. The Kindergarten dolls were made to teach sewing, care of the hair, dressing and so on. A *Mama* doll was 16½ in. (42 cm.) tall. Style No. 9000 had painted hair, was undressed and cost $2.70. Style No. 9001 had painted hair, wore rompers and cost $3.25. Style No. 9002 had a human hair wig, wore clothes and cost $5.50.

Mimi. 1916. Trade name of an all-wood doll made by *Mme. Alexandrowicz.*

Mimi. 1918. Name of a dressed doll advertised by *Harrod.* Ht. 13 in.

Mimi. 1922–28. U.S. trademark for dolls was applied for by *Borgfeldt.* This trademark registration was granted in 1923 which probably explains why *Effanbee* changed their Mimi to Patsy.★

Mimi. 1925–26. Felt doll designed by *Dudovich* and made by *Lenci* as no. 250. It wore a pseudo 1700s costume and carried a hat box slung over its arm. Ht. 29½ in. (75 cm.). (See Ill. 840.).

Mimi. 1927. U.S. trademark for dolls was applied for by *Effanbee* but *Borgfeldt* had registered Mimi as a trademark in 1923. The Effanbee Mimi was advertised as having "It"; and the same advertisement picture was used for *Patsy* in 1928.

1916. Embossed Mimi mark on composition head dolls made by Effanbee.

Mimocculo. 1930. Trademark registered by *Steiff* in Germany for dolls.

Mimosa. 1923. Dolls made by *Mann and Mann.* The dolls had wigs, pierced nostrils and were dressed in English clothes or in Continental clothes.

Min. 1929. All-bisque doll jointed at the neck. It had molded clothes and represented the cartoon character of this name in "The Gumps," drawn by *Sidney Smith.* It was distributed by *Marshall Field.* Ht. 3½ in. (9 cm.).

Mina. Before 1911–13. Jointed felt character doll made by *Steiff* and distributed by *Borgfeldt* in the U.S. and by *Gamage* in London. It wore a print dress with a ruffled bertha and two hairbows. Six hts. 28, 35, 43, 50, 60, and 75 cm. (11, 14, 17, 19½, 23½, and 29½ in.). The 43 and 50 cm. size came with or without long hair. In 1913 the 28 cm. size came in two versions, one with long inserted hair that could be combed and carrying a bear in its arms; the other was without these attractions; the 35 cm. size came only with attractions and the 43 cm. size had a mama voice. Prices were:

Height	Style	1911 Germany	1913 New York	London
28 cm.	plain	$1.25	$2.20	$1.23
28 cm.	fancy		$2.90	
43 cm.	plain	$2.25		$2.37
43 cm.	fancy	$3.62	$4.55	

Mine. 1924. Line of dolls made by *Edmund Edelmann.*

Minerva. 1894–1930 and later. Trademark for dolls' heads made of metal and/or celluloid by *Buschow and Beck.*

Size No.	Height in.	cm.	Description
	1900–1926 SIZE–HEIGHT RELATIONSHIP OF MINERVA HEADS		
0	2¾	7	Painted hair and eyes.
0	3¾	9.5	Wigs, sleeping glass eyes, with or without teeth.
1	3	7.5	Painted hair, glass eyes.
1	4	10	Wigs, sleeping glass eyes, with or without teeth.
2	3⅜	8.5	Painted hair and eyes.
2	4⅝	11.5	Wigs, sleeping glass eyes, with or without teeth.
3	3¾	9.5	Painted hair, glass eyes.
3	4¾	12	Wigs, sleeping glass eyes, with or without teeth.
4	4⅛	10.5	Painted hair, glass eyes.
4	5½	14	Wigs, sleeping glass eyes, with or without teeth.

1898: It was advertised that when the Minerva heads were dented they could be pushed back in place.

1902: *Butler Bros.* advertised Minerva shoulder heads with painted eyes and molded hair. Six hts. of the head only, 3 to 5 in. (7.5 to 12.5 cm.); priced $1.60 to $4.00 doz. wholesale. The wigged heads came in five hts. 3¾ to 5½ in. (9.5 to 14 cm.); priced $2.20 to $5.80 doz. wholesale.

1903: *Montgomery Ward* sold five hts. of shoulder heads with molded hair and painted eyes; priced 25¢ to 75¢. There were two hts. with short hair wigs and stationary glass eyes costing 50¢ and 75¢ and five hts. of shoulder heads with long hair wigs and sleeping eyes, priced 50¢ to $1.75.

Montgomery Ward also had a doll with a Minerva head; it was dressed in removable crocheted clothes including a dress, hood and cape. Ht. 11 in. (28 cm.); priced 75¢.

1907: *Sears* advertised metal Minerva heads with painted hair and eyes or wig and sleeping eyes. The former came in seven hts. 3⅜ to 6¾ in. (8.5 to 17 cm.); priced 16¢ to 69¢. The latter came in four hts. 4 to 6⅝ in. (10 to 17 cm.); priced 38¢ to $1.00.

1909: The *Boston Store* sold eight hts. of Minerva heads with molded hair and painted eyes ranging from 3 to 5⅝ in. (7.5 to 14.5 cm.) and seven hts. with wigs and sleeping eyes ranging from 3¾ to 7¼ in. (9.5 to 18.5 cm.).

1910: The metal heads were coated with a celluloid washable enamel.

1912: *Otto Graefe* imported Minerva heads to the U.S.

1914: *John M. Smyth* advertised Minerva metal heads with molded hair and painted eyes in four sizes; with molded hair, glass eyes, and open mouth in three sizes; with wigs, glass eyes, open mouth and teeth in seven sizes. The prices ranged from 14¢ to $1.75.

Minerva heads were used on *Knockabout*, Knock-Out, Neverbreak, and *Wearwell* dolls with cloth bodies as well as Kid bodies with Universal[†] hip joints. *Marshall Field* sold these kid-bodied dolls for $17.00 and $24.00 doz. wholesale. Hts. 16 and 19½ in. (40.5 and 49.5 cm.). Sears called their Minerva head dolls on kid bodies the *Violet* line.

1924: Montgomery Ward advertised Minerva heads with molded hair. Hts. 3⅜, 4½ and 5 in. (8.5, 11.5 and 12.5 cm.); priced 32¢ to 59¢.

1926: Buschow & Beck advertised metal heads, celluloid heads and all-celluloid dolls.

Charles William advertised Minerva heads with wigs and sleeping eyes. Hts. 4¾ and 5½ in. (12 and 14 cm.); priced 98¢ and $1.15. Similar heads with open mouths and teeth came in hts. 3¼ and 3¾ in. (8 and 9.5 cm.); priced 98¢ and $1.15. See THE COLLECTOR'S BOOK OF DOLLS' CLOTHES, Ills. 757A and 761.

1927: Montgomery Ward advertised Minerva metal heads with molded hair. Six hts. 3⅜, 3¾, 4½, 5¼, 6⅜ and 6½ in. (8.5, 9.5, 11.5, 13.5, 16, and 16.5 cm.); priced 21¢ to 95¢.

In the late 1920s both composition Minerva and bisque Minerva heads were advertised by American distributors, but the relationship to the metal and celluloid Minerva heads is not known. (See **Minerva Toy Co.**)★

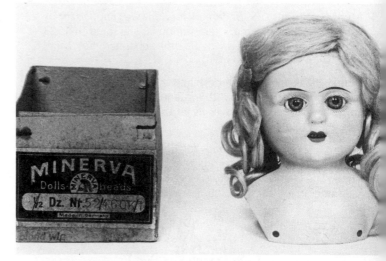

1918. Minerva metal shoulder head and its original box. The head has a blond wig, stationary blue glass eyes and an open mouth with six upper teeth. Mark on front shoulder plate: Ill. 1922. Mark on back shoulder "GERMANY//1." H. shoulder head 4 in. (10 cm.). The paper label on the box end reads: "MINERVA//Dolls' [Ill. 1922] heads//¹/₁₂ Dz. Nr. 52/460K/1 //Made in Germany." *Courtesy of the Margaret Woodbury Strong Museum. Photo by Harry Bickelhaupt.*

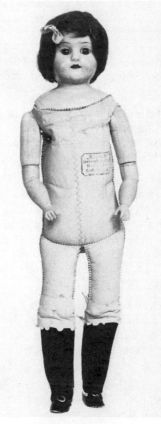

1917. Minerva metal shoulder head with a wig, stationary blue glass eyes, open mouth with four upper teeth, and a pink cotton body. The body has the typical German type reinforcement at the knees. The wooden arms that extend above the elbows resemble those on all-wood Bébé Tout en Bois dolls. Original footwear. Mark on the front of the shoulder: Ill. 1922. Mark on the back of the shoulders "GERMANY//3." Purple stamp on the left front side of the torso: "Wearwell//Unbreakable Doll//Hair Stuffed//Guaranteed Minerva Head//Made in Germany." H. of doll 17½ in. (44.5 cm.). H. of shoulder head 4¾ in. (12 cm.). *Courtesy of the Margaret Woodbury Strong Museum. Photo by Harry Bickelhaupt.*

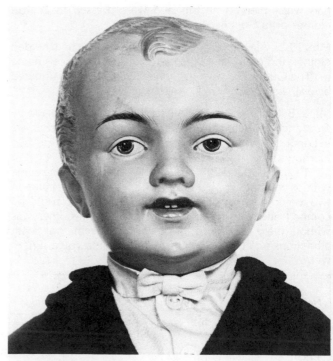

1919. Minerva celluloid socket head doll with molded and painted hair, intaglio brown eyes, open-closed mouth with two teeth, and dimple in the chin. Body not all original. Head size 6. H. of doll 19½ in. (49.5 cm.). *Courtesy of the Margaret Woodbury Strong Museum. Photo by Harry Bickelhaupt.*

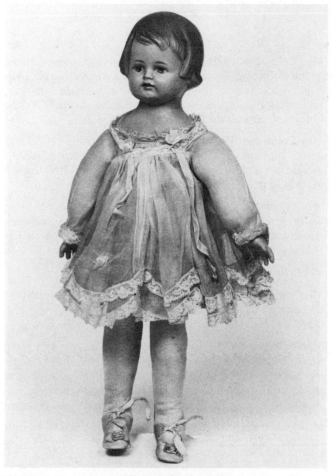

1920A & B. Minerva celluloid shoulder head and hands on a cloth body. The head has molded and painted hair and blue eyes, closed mouth, and dimple in the chin. The fingernails are molded. Original clothes. Mark on back of shoulders "GERMANY//5" embossed. The Minerva helmet is on the front of the shoulders and "2". H. 14 in. (35.5 cm.). *Courtesy of the Margaret Woodbury Strong Museum. Photos by Harry Bickelhaupt.*

1921. All-celluloid Minerva doll with molded and painted hair, sleeping glass eyes, hair eyelashes and closed mouth. Body is jointed at the neck, shoulders and hips. Mark on head: "Minerva [helmet] //Germany//No. 4 //30." Mark on body "[Ill. 1922]//Germany//32." H. 32 cm. (12½ in.). *Courtesy of Richard Withington. Photo by Barbara Jendrick.*

1922. Mark on Minerva metal or celluloid dolls' shoulder heads.

Minerva Toy Co. Brooklyn, N.Y. A composition baby in a box marked "Minerva Toy Co. Brooklyn, N.Y. No. 590 Made in U.S.A." has been reported.

Minerva Works. See **Crown Staffordshire Porcelain Co.**

Mirette. Several dolls have been found with bisque heads marked "10.731 Mirette" and the square *Gebrüder Heubach* mark. More than one of these dolls has been on a marked *Jumeau* body. Others have been found on bent limb baby bodies.

MIRETTE DOLLS SIZE–HEIGHT RELATIONSHIP (based on a small sample)				
		Height		
		Bébé	*Bent-limb baby bodies*	
Size No.	in.	cm.	in.	cm.
7	18	45.5		
11	27	68.5		
12	29	73.5	23½	60

The heights of these bébés are a little greater than the *Bébés Jumeau,* for corresponding size numbers.★

12

MIRETTE **1923.** Mirette mark on a bisque head doll.

Miriam Manuel. ca. 1902. Name of a Parisian actress who had a porcelain head portrait doll made and named for her by the *Société Française de Fabrication de Bébés & Jouets.*

Miss Babette. 1919. TOYS AND NOVELTIES reported, "The queen of all the *Rauser* dolls at present is Miss Babette, . . . This lovely doll has luxuriant curly hair, eyes which open and close, is fully jointed and may be obtained in heights of 18 or 24 in. [45.5 or 61 cm.]. It is dressed in an adorable frock of real point d'esprit net. There are miniature rosebuds with knots of baby ribbon caught about the deep tuck of the skirt. The sash is a broad satin ribbon, hand smocked at the waist. The hat is a creation of shirred net and ribbons made as expertly as any lady's chapeau; the lingerie is trimmed in fine lace; there are openwork hose and kid shoes with *real* heels, . . ."

Miss Broadway. 1912–13. Composition head doll with molded hair and painted eyes, made by *Amberg.* It wore a coat with a high collar, and a large hat.★

Miss Campbell. 1914. One of the *Campbell Kids* made by *Horsman.* It came in four versions: Style No. 130 was the same as the Campbell Kid Girl except it wore a white lawn party frock over a pink under-dress. Lace trimmed the yoke and the bottom of the skirt. Style no. 167 was the same as 130 except it had a wig with a silk hairbow and the eyes were painted to look straight ahead. Style No. 210 was the same as 130 except taller. Style No. 267, same as 210 except it had a wig and silk hairbow.★

Miss Chicago. 1921. A brunette doll designed by *Katherine Rauser* and dressed in Chicago's maroon and white colors. It was exhibited in the Pageant of Progress Exposition in Chicago.

Miss Colonial. 1918–19. Made by *Colonial Toy Manufacturing Co.* and dressed in a 1900s version of a 1700s costume. It had a white wig, gloves, a fan and two strands of pearls around its neck.

Miss Columbia. 1920. Composition doll made of wood fibre by the *Columbia Doll & Toy Co.* It had a wig with a veil, eyes painted looking to the side, watermelon-shaped mouth, jointed shoulders, and wore only an abbreviated skirt. The high boots were molded.

Miss Columbia. 1927–28. Doll with composition head and limbs, mohair wig, sleeping eyes, hair eyelashes, teeth, tongue and a cloth body. It was a dressed *Mama* doll. Ht. 25 in. (63.5 cm.); priced $5.00.

Miss Coquette. 1912–15. Composition-head doll made by *Effanbee* with either composition or cloth limbs. Sometimes marked 462 and sometimes unmarked according to Pat Schoonmaker.

1915: Renamed Naughty Marietta.

Miss Dollikin. ca. 1890. Name of a bisque-head premium doll offered by the Alpha Publishing Co. It had a wig and a kid body. Ht. 15 in. (38 cm.); priced $1.25.

Miss Fashion. 1926. Slim body doll with a dress that hung from the neckline and extended only above the knees, showing the drawers. A ribbon band was in the hair and socks and single strap slippers were the footwear. It was made by the *American Character Doll Co.* and came in various heights.

Miss Flaked Rice. 1899–1900. Cutout cloth advertising doll for *Cook's Flaked Rice Co.* was marked "My name is// Miss Flaked Rice."

My name is
Miss Flaked Rice

1924. Mark on Miss Flaked Rice cutout cloth doll.

Miss Helgett. 1892. Name of a dressed, jointed doll sold by the *Louvre* store. Ht. 45 cm. (17½ in.); priced $3.70 with a chair.

Miss Hiawatha. 1917. Composition head and hands with painted hair and features on a cloth body doll, jointed shoulders and hips, distributed by *Butler Bros.* The doll was made in the U.S.A. and wore a felt Indian costume. Ht. 14½ in. (37 cm.).

Miss Ima Walker. 1919–23. Walking doll distributed and/or made by *Transogram Co.;* priced 10¢ and 25¢.

Miss Janet. 1912–14. The composition head was copyrighted by *Horsman* in 1912 and resembled *Sunshine.* The eyes looked straight ahead and the composition hands were the same as those used for the *Campbell Kids.* It wore a white lawn dress trimmed with lace around the yoke and sleeves, and a white hair ribbon. There were two versions, style no. 163 sold for $8.50 doz. wholesale and the larger style No. 273 sold for $13.50 doz. wholesale. The heads and costumes were similar on both dolls.

Miss Jeanette. 1919. Name of a doll that came with its trousseau in a steel riveted trunk, made by the *Jeanette Doll Co.*

No. 163

"MISS JANET"

Trade Mark

(Head copyrighted, 1912, by
E. I. Horsman Co.)

Most attractive little maiden, all spic and span, in a fresh white lawn frock tastefully trimmed with lace, half length socks and buckled shoes. She wears a white ribbon fastened to her hair.

Per Dozen........$8.50

No. 163 "Miss Janet"

1925A & B. Miss Janet advertised in the Horsman catalog of ca. 1914. The composition head had been copyrighted in 1912. It had molded and painted hair and painted eyes, closed mouth, cloth body with composition Campbell Kid type hands. Came in two sizes. *Catalog courtesy of Bernard Barenholtz.*

No. 273

LARGE SIZE

"MISS JANET"

Trade Mark

(Head copyrighted, 1912, by
E. I. Horsman Co.)

A duplicate of "Miss Janet" No. 163—one of our most beautiful and popular dolls in a larger and finer edition. Dress is of fresh white lawn, lace trimmed with a pretty yoke, and in the hair a broad white silk bow of ribbon, white half-hose and white felt booties. A real little American lass, about three years of age.

Per Dozen..............$13.50

No. 273 Large "Miss Janet"

Miss Kellerman. Portrait doll of the famous swimmer of this name, Annette Kellerman.

Miss Korn Krisp. Cloth doll with painted hair and features. Ht. 26½ in. (67.5 cm.).

Miss Liberty. 1918. Name of a doll made by *Horsman.* It wore a white dress with a blue sash and a red hat.

Miss Liberty. See **Patriotic Dolls.**

My name is
Miss Korn-Crisp

1926. Mark on Miss Korn Krisp cutout cloth doll.

Miss Lily White. 1912. Name of a cloth premium doll offered by the Faultless Starch Co.

Miss Malto-Rice. Ca. 1900. Cutout cloth doll advertising *The American Rice Foods Manufacturing Co.*★

My name is
Miss Malto-Rice

1927. Mark on Miss Malto-Rice cutout cloth doll.

Miss Mary Mix-up. See **Little Mary Mix-up.**

Miss Merryheart. 1884–87. Wax-over-composition head doll handled by *Lauer,* had various hair styles with bangs, composition arms and legs with painted stockings and boots.

		MISS MERRYHEART		
	1884:	SIZE–HEIGHT RELATIONSHIP		
Size No.	Height		Price doz. wholesale	
	In.	cm.	Stationary eyes	Sleeping eyes
0	15½	39.5	$1.90	$2.50
1	17½	44.5	$2.40	$3.00
2	19½	49.5	$2.75	$4.00
3	21½	54.5	$3.75	$4.80
4	23	58.5	$4.50	$6.00
5	25½	65	$6.00	$8.00
6	28½	72.5	$7.50	$9.00

1887: Came only in size numbers 2, 4, 5, and 6, had only stationary eyes, and cost $2.25 to $6.25.

Miss Millionaire. 1910–13. Bisque head doll on a kid body. See Ill. 1928 for mark.

1912: Name of a bisque shoulder head, kid body doll with open mouth and teeth distributed by *Butler Bros.* Six hts. 14, 19 (with hair eyebrows and eyelashes), 21, 25, 27½, and 28½ in. (35.5, 48, 53.5, 63.5, 70, and 72 cm.); priced 33¢ to $2.50 each wholesale.★

1928. Miss Millionaire trademark found on some German kid bodies.

Miss Mischief. 1911–12. Composition head with blond wig, painted eyes looking to the side, on a *Horsman* doll that wore a dress similar to that of the *Campbell Kid* girl. Style No. 188; priced $10.80 doz. wholesale.★

Miss Moppie Topp. See **Moppietopp.**

Miss Muffet. 1909–13. Cutout cloth doll with a printed ankle length dress and a necklace, advertised by *Selchow & Righter.* Ht. 9 in. (23 cm.); priced 5¢ or 38¢ doz. wholesale.★

Miss Muffet. 1912–13. Flat face cloth doll stuffed with cork and sawdust was advertised by *Selchow & Righter.* The printed dress had a high neckline and an ankle length skirt. Ht. 9 in. (23 cm.); priced 5¢ or 40¢ a doz. wholesale.

Miss Muffet. 1920–21. Stockinet doll made by *Chad Valley* as No. 27. Ht. 9 in. (23 cm.).

Miss Muffet. 1924. *Mama* doll with composition head, arms and legs, mohair wig and cloth body distributed by *Montgomery Ward.* It wore a dimity dress and bonnet. Ht. 20½ in. (52 cm.); priced $3.19.

Miss Muffet. 1926. Name of a doll made by the *Jeanette Doll Co.*, came in two heights.

Miss Muffet. 1926–27. Cloth doll with a flat face, painted features except for round rolling eyes, distributed by *Charles William* stores and *American Wholesale Corp.*

It had a squeak voice, mitten type hands, jointed limbs and wore a lawn dress and hood with a bow under the chin. Ht. 14 in. (35.5 cm.); price 89¢.

Miss Muffet. See **Little Miss Muffet.**

Miss 1927, Miss 1928, Miss 1929. 1927–29. All composition *Boudoir* doll distributed by *Butler Bros.* It had a bobbed mohair wig, painted features with a facsimile cigarette in its mouth. The body was jointed at the shoulders, elbows, hips, and knees. It wore a felt lounging suit and high heeled pumps. Ht. 25 in. (63.5 cm.); priced $2.85. See Ill. 1153 and THE COLLECTOR'S BOOK OF DOLLS' CLOTHES, Ill. 770K.

Miss 1928. Dressed doll advertised by *Hitz, Jacobs & Kassler* in 1928. Ht. 13 in. (33 cm.). See Ill. 1207.

Miss Peggy. 1919. Stockinet doll designed by *E. E. Houghton,* made by *Shanklin.* It wore a muslin dress and a hairbow.

Miss Phoebe Primm. 1912. Name of a cloth premium doll offered by the Faultless Starch Co.

Miss Polly Wise. 1921. Black cloth doll made by *Horsman* and representing the daughter of *Mammie Wise.* It was advertised as having "saucy eyes and flashy clothes."

Miss Priscilla. See **Lifelike Babyland Dolls.**

Miss Sam. 1917. Name of a doll with composition head and hands, painted hair and eyes made by the *Standard Doll Co.* Its dress had red and white stripes with the yoke and band around the bottom of the skirt made of plain blue fabric. The sleeves were white. Ht. 16 in. (40.5 cm.).

Miss Snowy Eskimo. 1927. Cloth doll to be made at home according to instructions in THE LADIES' HOME JOURNAL. It was all of eiderdown except for the stockinet face and silk floss hair. The body was one piece, seamed around the edges, and the head, arms and legs were attached separately. The belt tied in front and the pointed cap had ties under the chin. Ht. 8½ in. (21.5 cm.), width hand to hand 7½ in. (19 cm.), head 2½ in. (6.5 cm.) long, legs 2 in. (5 cm.) long, waist 3½ in. (9 cm.) across.

Miss Sunshine. 1916–18. In 1918 *Butler Bros.* advertised this *Jessie M. Raleigh* doll as being all-composition with straight legs, five piece body, steel spring jointed. There was a molded barette in the hair and the doll wore a lawn dress. Ht. 13½ in. (34 cm.).★

Miss Sunshine. 1920. Dressed doll with composition head and arms advertised by *Sears.* It had a wig, sleeping eyes and a silk dress. Ht. 24 in. (61 cm.); priced $11.50.

Miss Sunshine. 1929. Doll with composition head, arms and legs, mohair wig, sleeping eyes, hair eyelashes, open mouth, tongue, and celluloid teeth distributed by *Butler Bros.* It had a crying voice, a cotton stuffed cloth body and wore an organdy dress and matching bonnet. Hts. 20, 24, and 27 in. (51, 61, and 68.5 cm.): priced $2.25 to $3.75. Both *Sol Bergfeld* and *Reisman, Barron* produced a Sunshine line of dolls. See THE COLLECTOR'S BOOK OF DOLLS' CLOTHES, Ill. 775G.

Miss Sweet-Flower. 1925–26. *Lenci* felt doll, style No. 165/6, dressed in a romantic period costume with a large brimmed hat and carried a handkerchief. Ht. 29½ in. (75 cm.).

Miss Traveler. 1916–18. Composition-head doll made by *Jessie M. Raleigh.*★

Miss Vamp. 1920. Name of an all-composition doll, jointed at the shoulders but having practically no neck. The straight legs were apart and the only clothes were a dotted net veil covering the molded hair and face. This doll was advertised by the *Southern Bargain House.* Ht. 14½ in. (37 cm.): priced $2.25.

Misska Dolls. 1919–21. Trade name of plush covered, kapok filled cloth dolls with velvet faces, made by the *Art Toy Manufacturing Co.* The plush was white, pink and/or blue with stamped trimming. They came in several styles; Style No. A. had long plaits and style No. B had a muff. They also represented Dutch Boys and *Pierrots.* A toy trade magazine suggested that the Misska dolls might rival the Teddy Bear. U.S. design patent for this doll obtained by Serge de Kazarin[†] & Mary de Porohovchikova.

One of these dolls reportedly had a paper label reading "The Prettiest Doll in England = Vide DAILY SKETCH 15/9/19 Registered No. 672300."

These dolls came in hts. from 9 to 30 in. (23 to 76 cm.).

Mistinguette. 1928. French art dolls made mostly of composition and representing a theatrical figure.

Mitchell & Co. 1917–19. Bradford, England. Manufactured and exported dolls' eyes, wigs, stuffing, and so on. They claimed their real hair wigs could be washed, brushed, and combed. Their wigs were made of wool, mohair, crepe hair, curly mohair or human hair. They dyed the hair as well as making the wigs.

Mitlacher, G. N. 1883 and probably other years. Thür. A manufacturer who served on the committee to found the *Sonneberg Industrial School.*

Mitred Box Co. 1911–17. New York City. Claimed the eyes could not come out of their *Yankee Dolls*. The Factory Representative was *McClurg & Keen*.★

Mittelland Gummiwerke. 1924–27. Hannover, Germany. Made rubber dolls which they claimed were without seams or joints and yet were movable and washable.

1926: Obtained a German patent for dolls and dolls' parts. Registered *Der neue Mensch* as a trademark in Germany.

1927: *Eisenman & Co.* was their London agent.

Mitzi. 1928. A doll made by *Maxine Doll Co.* imitating *Patsy*. It was discontinued because of the court order against the infringement.

Miyako Boeki Goshi Kaisha. 1921–28. Kyoto, Japan. Manufactured dolls.

Mizpah Toy and Novelty Co. 1930 and later. New York City. Made *Boudoir* dolls of rayon silk in various shades of rose, green and orchid. The hair, shoes and stockings matched the colors. Ht. 36 in. (91.5 cm.).

Mlle. Chrysanthème. 1910. Name of a doll with a bisque head, sleeping eyes, dressed in a Japanese costume and sold by *Printemps*. The head and costume resembled the *Simon & Halbig* Oriental dolls. Hts. 30, 38 and 44 cm. (12, 15 and 17.5 in.); priced 78¢ to $1.38.

Mobilia Cie. 1930. Strasbourg, France. Manufactured dolls.

Mochidzuki, Manjiro. 1926–30 and later. Kyoto, Japan. Manufactured dolls.

Möckel, Carl. 1928–30. Buchholz, Saxony, Nürnberg, Bavaria and Berlin. Advertised chenille dolls and automobile dolls.

Model Doll. The term "Model" was applied to various types of dolls and seems to have had several meanings. It probably referred to a doll that was a portrait, not necessarily of any well-known person but someone who posed as a model for the doll; or it may have been originally modeled after one of the children of Queen Victoria. It also may refer to a doll that wore fashionable clothes. Wax dolls were frequently called "Model" wax dolls and "Half Model" wax dolls were also listed in the 19th century. The Half Model wax dolls were less expensive than the Model wax dolls. There were wax-over composition dolls and possibly either the wax did not cover as much of the doll or was less thick, or both, on the Half Model dolls.

1852: THE DOLL AND HER FRIENDS state, "I am . . . not one of those splendid specimens of wax, modeled from the Princess Royal, with distinct fingers and toes, eyes that shut, and tongues that wag."

Ca. 1860: *Pierotti* claimed that he was the inventor of Royal Model Dolls.

1876–89: *Silber & Fleming* advertised large numbers of Model dolls. These included sitting dolls, baby dolls, infant dolls with modeled limbs, boy dolls, crying dolls, large dolls, small dolls, dolls with and without inserted hair, dressed dolls, and undressed dolls.

1882: One of the "Model Cry dolls" sold by Silber & Fleming had *Prince Charlie's Model Best Made Body*.

1885: *Horsman* listed "Model Rag Doll" and "Model Wax Dolls" in their catalog.

1920s: *Dean* patented their *Evripoze* dolls, one of which was described on its box as "One Model." (See also **Model Patent Washable Dolls** and **Montanaris**.)

Model Doll Co. 1920–21. Brooklyn, N.Y. Made popular priced dolls and dolls' heads. The dolls came with or without mohair wigs and with outside joints on the excelsior stuffed bodies. Hts. 9½ to 24 in. (24 to 61 cm.). The heads came in a variety of styles. Ht. of head only, 1 to 7 in. (2.5 to 18 cm.).★

Model Doll Manufacturing Co. 1928–30 and later. New York City. Manufactured a line of cloth-bodied dolls.

1928: Dolls representing young ladies cost 25¢ to $10.00.

Model Patent Washable Dolls. 1899–1907. Dolls with composition head and arms, cloth body including legs with tasseled boots, distributed by *Butler Bros.*

1899: Four hts. 27, 31, 33, and 35 in. (68.5, 78.5, 84, and 89 cm.).★

Model Sam. Ca. 1900. Name found incised on the back shoulder of a turned bisque shoulder head. The mark was either "Model Sam" or "Model Sam//Our best American boy//His new line." The doll had a wig, glass eyes, an open mouth with four teeth. Usually these German heads were found on kid bodies.

Most of the research on the Model Sam dolls has been the work of Patricia Hartwell.

SIZE–HEIGHT RELATIONSHIP OF MODEL SAM DOLLS				
	Heights			
Size	Head only		Entire doll	
No.	in.	cm.	in.	cm.
3/0	4	10	15½	39.5
3	5½	14	22	56
7	5⅞	15	24	61
8	6½	16.5		

*model Sam
Our best american boy
His new line*

1929. Model Sam mark incised on a bisque shoulder head.

Modern, Samuel. 1917–18. New York City. Obtained a U.S. patent for dolls' sleeping eyes; each eye was to have a lateral stem and a pendulum was made to revolve with these stems.

Modern Doll. 1930. Cloth doll made by *Dean,* wore velvet clothes trimmed with silk. Came in nine sizes.

Modern Doll Co. 1926–27. Brooklyn, N.Y. Irving Kaufman formerly with *Modern Toy Co.* formed his owned company and manufactured a general line of dolls including *Mama* dolls and sleeping dolls.

1927: Used the initials M. D. C. as a trademark. Modern Doll Co. was licensed by *Voices, Inc.* to use their patented mama voices and criers.

MODERN DOLLS
WALKING TALKING
SLEEPING

Wide Assortment of Styles, Embracing New Numbers of High Quality. Experienced Doll Buyers Know What Modern Quality Means—And That We Always Have Some Exclusive Features for the Jobbing Trade.

Modern Doll Co., Inc.
260 Stone Avenue, Brooklyn, N. Y.

1930. Advertisement for the Modern Doll Co. in PLAYTHINGS, May 1927. Their dolls appear to have been primarily Mama dolls with sleeping eyes.

Modern Toy Co. 1914–26. Brooklyn, N.Y. Company was formed by Max Roth and Julius Jacobson. They made composition dolls, later including *Mama* dolls.

1915: Dolls had composition heads and feet so that they could stand alone.

1917: Made a line of dressed character dolls, priced 50¢ to $3.00. Some of their dolls had wigs.

1920: Advertisement showed two bent-limb baby dolls. Style No. 901 had a wig, sleeping eyes, cork stuffed body with inside joints. Ht. 23 in. (58.5 cm.). Style No. 950, a composition baby, had a wig, sleeping eyes and was 20 in. (51 cm.) tall. A strike closed the factory for six weeks.

1923: A new line of dressed Mama dolls wore lace trimmed dresses with sash and bonnet to match, socks and ankle strap slippers. The doll pictured in the advertisement had painted hair.

1924: Used the mark "M.T.C.//DOLLS" and a picture of a Mama doll. Mama dolls came in 12 styles. Ht. 15 in. (38 cm.).

1926: Advertised Mama dolls, baby dolls and a new line of soft dolls called *Hug Me Dollies.* Ht. 11½ in. (29 cm.). Before the year ended the company was dissolved.★

Modernes. 1902–30 according to the catalogs found. Paris. A store that distributed dolls. During the period 1902–14 they sold *Bébé Tout en Bois.* From 1927–30 Modernes was listed in Paris directories.

1910: Advertised *Bébé Bru.*

1911: Advertised *Bébé l'Avenir* and *Eden Bébé.*

Moehling, M. J. 1870–1930 and later. Aich near Carlsbad (Karlovy Vary), Bohemia. Anger & Moehling was a successor. By 1910 it was Ludwig Engel & Sohn with 300 employees. In 1918 the Porzellanfabrik Aich was operated by Menzel & Co. consisting of Josef Theodor Menzel, Leo Höhnel and Eduard Wolf, Jr. This factory used A e M and/or Eduardo Juan as their marks. It is uncertain whether the A e M stood for Anger & Moehling or as suggested by the Ciesliks Aich and Menzel. The name Eduardo Juan was perhaps the name of one of the children of the owners. The doll may have been a portrait of the child but it seems to have a dolly face. Many of the dolls also had the mold number 1904 and the size-height relationship of all these dolls appears to be similar. A sample mark was "1904–6// A e M// Made in Austria," the 6 being the size number.

These bisque heads marked "A e M, Austria" should not be confused with bisque heads made by *Armand Marseille* or *Amandus Michaelis* marked "A. M." The A e M heads usually had a wig, sleeping glass eyes, open mouth with teeth, and a ball-jointed composition body. (See Ills. 156, 1931 and 1932).★

The size-height relationship was roughly:

Size No.	Height cm.	in.
7/0	26.5	10½
6	56	22
10	61	24

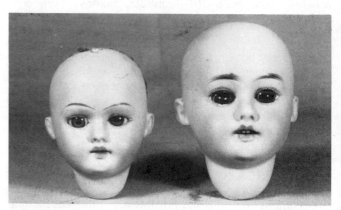

1931. Two bisque socket heads made by M. J. Moehling in Austria. These dolly face heads have sleeping eyes, open mouth with teeth. The larger head has decal or stencil eyebrows while the smaller head has a single line eyebrow. The smaller head has a small hole at the top of the forehead in front of the large pate hole. The larger head does not have a similar small hole. Mark III. 1932. Hs. of heads only, 3½ and 4½ in. (9 and 11.5 cm.). *Coleman Collection.*

1904 - 4/0

A.eM.
Made in Austria

1932. Mark on bisque heads made by M. J. Moehling. Size 4/0 head is 3½ in. (9 cm.) tall.

Moglette. 1926–30 and later. Trademark registered in France for dolls by *Lucien Kahn* in 1926. The name of these stuffed dolls also appeared as La Moglette.

Mogridge, W. H., & Co. 1918. Bristol, England. Made cloth shoulder heads and entire dolls including *Little Red Riding Hood.* According to an advertisement their dolls had heads of "linen faced cardboard." The heads had stationary or sleeping glass eyes and sometimes the eyes were "printed on paper and stuck in the socket."

Mohair Wigs. See **Manufacture of Wigs** and **Wigs.**

Mohawk Novelty Co. 1923. New York City. Advertised dressed and jointed dolls at various prices.★

Mohr, M. 1878. Sonneberg, Thür. Made dolls.

Mokiewsky, S. 1927–30 and later. Paris. Made art dolls.

Moko.† See **Kohnstam, M., & Co.**

Molds for Dolls. Among the makers of molds or dies for dolls were *American Doll Mold Co., Desfosses,* (1824), *Carl Geffers, Anton Kunst, Marquer & Garnot* (aluminum molds), *Metal Cast Products Co., Ch. Ruchot,* and *Simart Fils.* Sulphur molds were still being used for composition heads in the 1900s.★

Moll, Johann. 1901. Lübeck, Germany. Commissioned *Hertwig & Co.* to make *Snow Babies.*

Möller, August, & Sohn. 1911–28. Georgenthal, Thür. Made dolls and dolls' heads.

1911: Applied for three German patents (D.R.G.M.), two of them for dolls' eyes and the third for doll's tongue.

1919: Advertised child and baby dolls with socket heads or shoulder heads of porcelain or of celluloid. They had real hair or mohair wigs. There were also accessories for dolls.

1925: Registered the name *Amuso* for dolls.

1926–28: Advertised in a French directory that they made dolls and bébés with ball jointed composition bodies.★

Möller, F. H., & Co. 1910–26. Möhrenbach, Thür. Made and/or distributed woolen dolls.★

Möller, Georg. 1911–30 and later. Sönneberg, Thür. Manufactured dolls. *M. Sieve & Co.* was his agent in Manchester, England.★

Moller, Miss Muriel. 1917–19. London. Distributed and exported various lines of dolls including *Rock China Dolls, New Century* Composition Dolls, *Vogue* Rag Dolls and the *F. E. Houghton* Soft Dolls. She was the agent for *Nottingham* and *Shanklin.* (See also **British Dolls Ltd.**)

Möller, Prof. Reinhard. 1893–1910. Sonneberg, Thür. Director of the *Sonneberg Industrial School.*★

Möller, Rudolf. 1914. Herrenhof/Gotha, Thür. Applied for a German patent (D.R.G.M.) for the eyes of a doll.

Möller & Dippe. 1846–94. Unterködiţz, Thür. A porcelain factory that made dolls' heads, arms and legs.

1894: The owners were Fritz Möller, Hermann Dippe, Hugo Baehr and widow Anna Möller. There were 60 employees.

Moll-Es. 1926 and before. Philadelphia, Pa. Made clothes for *Mama,* infant and character dolls. The successor in 1926 was C. M. Roberts.

Molly-'es (Molly 'ES). 1929–30 and later. Trademark used by Molly Goldman of Philadelphia, Pa., for dolls' clothes which she designed and made.

1929: Advertised dolls' outfits and costumes including knitted goods and brushed wool sets. She made some of the clothes for *Hoest.*

1930: Dolls' clothes included hand-smocked and hand-embroidered dresses, hats, coats, and pajamas. Molly-'es clothes were on permanent display at the *Horsman* office. They were also made to fit other domestic dolls as well as imported dolls. Over 100 people were engaged in the production of these clothes.

1931: *Meyer Goldman* registered the trademark Molly-'es in the U.S. for dolls' apparel.

1935: Molly-'es Doll Outfitters registered in U.S. two trademarks for dolls and dolls' clothes. One was "Self Help Educational Toy" and the other was "Raggedy Ann" with a picture of a dress hanger. (See also **International Doll Co.**)

Momijiya Ning Yo-Ten. 1923–30. Fukuoka, Japan. Exported dolls.

Momson, Mlle. Valentene. 1915. France. Organized *La Vie Femmes* to make bodies and clothes for dolls. (See **French Dolls.**)

Mon Amour de Poupée. Words found with a bisque head doll having a ball jointed composition toddler body, made by the *Société Française de Fabrication de Bébés & Jouets.* The head was marked "S.F.B.J.//247//Paris."

Mon Baby. 1926. Trademark registered in France by *Bonin & Lefort* for dolls and dolls' heads.

Mon Chéri (My Cherished). 1922 and probably other years. Name of a doll made by *L. Prieur* with a poured bisque head, wig, glass eyes, open mouth, on a jointed composition body or other types of bodies. The head marked "Mon//Chéri// L P //Paris" was probably made by *Couty.* Size number 9 was 55 cm. (21½ in.) and size number 12 was 70 cm. (27½ in.).

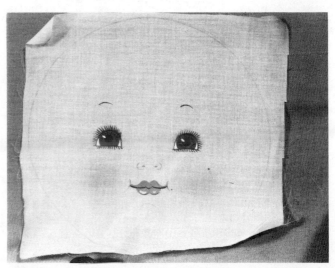

1933. Cutout hand-painted cloth face used by Molly-'es to make her dolls. Note the highlights on the lower lip. H. of face 7 in. (18 cm.). *Coleman Collection. Gift of Molly Goldman.*

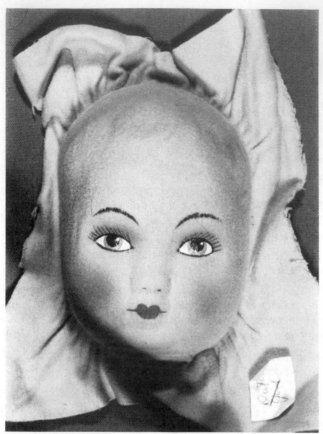

1934. Cotton velvet over buckram mask face used by Molly-'es for her Dutch Doll, painted features. Mask was made in Britain. H. of mask face 5 in. (12.5 cm.). *Coleman Collection. Gift of Molly Goldman.*

1936. Mon Chéri bisque socket head doll made by L. Prieur. It has stationary black glass eyes, ears pierced into the head, open mouth and a body made with wire armatures. Original clothes. Mark: Ill. 1937. H. 11 in. (28 cm.). H. of head 2 in. (5 cm.). *Courtesy of Helen Read. Photo by Steven Read.*

1935. Mark for Molly-'es cloth dolls or clothes for dolls.

MON
CHÉRI
ℒℙ
PARIS
0ỡ

1937. Mon Chéri mark on a bisque head.

Mon Chéri. See **Mein Liebling.**

Mon Fétiche. 1928. Trademark registered in France by *Robert Darcy* for dolls made of turtle leather.

Mon Petit Coeur (My Little Heart). Line of dolls made by *Bruno Schmidt.* One of these dolls had a bisque head with Oriental features, an Oriental style wig, and was on a ball jointed composition body.

Mon Petit Rimailho. 1915. Registered in France by *L. Prieur* for dolls.

Mon Petit Trésor. 1915. Registered in France by *L. Prieur* for dolls.

Mon Tempoivre. A factory that claimed to have produced 5,500,000 composition dolls' bodies a year.

Mon Trésor. 1914–16. Trademark of dolls made by *Henri Rostal* whose address was the rue de Trésor. Size number 7 was 48 cm. (19 in.) high.★

Mona. 1924. Line of dolls made by *Edmund Edelmann.*

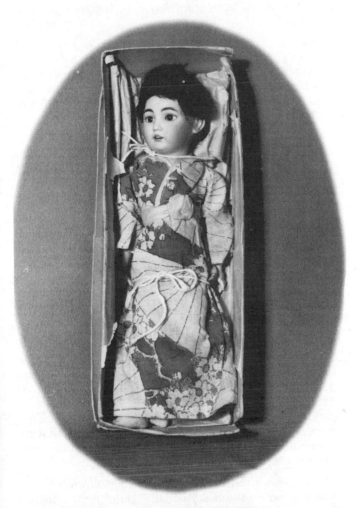

1938A & B. Mon Petit Coeur, name of a bisque socket head doll with a Simon and Halbig head made for Bruno Schmidt. It has a black wig, dark glass eyes, an open mouth with teeth, and a ball-jointed composition body. Original clothes consisting of a Japanese style cotton kimono and pearl pins in the hair. Mark on head "1329//Germany//SIMON & HALBIG//S & H // 4." The label on the end of the original box has "Japanerin" stamped on it in faint letters. The printed words are in French and translated mean "My Little Heart. No. _____ Trademark. Height 36. Wig ___ Eyes ___" H. 36 cm. (14 in.). *Courtesy of the late Magda Byfield.*

28.
MON
TRESOR.

1939. Mon Trésor mark used by Henri Rostal for dolls.

Monette. 1928–30. Bisque head, *Kiss-Throwing*, walking and talking doll distributed by *Bon Marché.* It had a wig, sleeping eyes, hair eyelashes and a silk dress. Ht. 58 or 59 cm. (23 in.).

Monique. 1926–30 and possibly other years. Name of a cloth dressed doll.

1926: Distributed by *Printemps* and came in four sizes.

1930: Had removable clothes including a hat and was distributed by *Bon Marché.* Hts. 38, 48, and 58 cm. (15, 19, and 23 in.).

Monkey Man. 1930. One of the *Plaything Toy* line of the *Atlanta Playthings Co.* This doll had a felt face with large ears and nose; the rest of the doll was made of wool plush, mohair plush and felt. The fingers were separate and a plush monkey was in its arms. It wore checked trousers and had a music box instead of a voice. Ht. 12 in. (30.5 cm.).

Montagne, E. 1929–30 and later. Argenteuil, Seine et Oise and Paris. Made footwear for dolls.

1929: Advertised slippers, boots and sandals for character bébés.

1930: Advertised Louis XV slippers for decorative dolls, stockings, and girdles for dolls.

Montagnola, Guido. 1929–30 and later. Milan, Italy. Manufactured dolls.

Montanari, Mme. Augusta. 1851–84. London. She claimed that she originated the Royal *Model Doll.* But other makers of wax dolls also claimed that they had originated the portrait dolls representing the children of Queen Victoria.

A wax child doll with inserted hair and a glazed cotton body has been found stamped with the royal coat of arms and "By appointment Montanari Manufacturers, 231 Regent St. and 280 Soho Bazar."

A wax baby doll had "Montanari" written in ink on the lower part of the cloth torso. This doll had a wax shoulder head including the top of the arms. The wax arms and legs were slightly curved. There were no grommets to attach the wax parts to the cloth torso. The head had hair inserted in the scalp, the eyebrows and eyelashes; blue glass eyes, and a closed mouth. The doll wore a long white baby dress and a lace bonnet with blue silk ribbon bows. Ht. 14½ in. (37 cm.). Ht. of shoulder head 3¾ in. (9.5 cm.).

A wooden box containing the above mentioned Montanari wax doll was marked, as nearly decipherable as possible, as follows:

Model ——r the
Patron —— majesty and Royal Family
(Royal Cipher)

"THE PRIZE MEDAL OF THE GREAT EXHIBITION OF 1851//
Unanimously awarded to Madame Montanari by the//
Jurors of Class 29 for the unique and unrivalled pro-//
duction of the MODEL DOLLS for beauty of[??]
[???] imitation Natu[??]ined with durability."

1869: Mme. Montanari had died and her son, Richard, was carrying on the business. A British edition of THE GIRLS' OWN BOOK stated:

"In fact rag dolls are not to be despised. The Mexicans make exquisite little figures of rag coated over with wax, some indeed so perfect as to approach the sculptor's art. Specimens of these may be seen at Montanari's in Charles Street, Soho Square; and it would afford our little friends a great treat if they could induce their mamas to take them to see this miniature world of . . . dolls of all sizes and representing all ages." (See also **Mexican Dolls.**)★

1940. Montanari mark found on dolls.

Montastiers & Perier. 1882 and later. Limoges, France. This porcelain factory used the initials M. R. and these initials were found on a bisque head doll of about 1910 but it is not certain that the doll was made in this factory. It seems more likely that the M. R. stood for Max Rudolph. See Ill. 2260.

Montgomery Ward & Co. 1872–1930 and later. Chicago, Ill. Imported dolls and distributed dolls by mail order. In the 1920s Montgomery Ward used a wreath surrounding the initials "M/W" as a trademark.

1889: Sold all-china dolls; china heads on cloth bodies; composition heads on cloth bodies; bisque heads on kid bodies; bisque heads on cloth bodies; wax-over-composition dolls; knitted *worsted* dolls; Japanese dolls; papier-mâché cowboy dolls, ht. 8 in. (20.5 cm.); *Cymbalier;* separate bisque heads and separate cloth bodies including the *Philip Goldsmith* bodies.

1894: Their bisque heads on kid bodies had sleeping eyes, teeth, and Ne Plus Ultra joints.[†] Some of their dressed dolls were described as having "American Bisque Heads." These had painted hair and were on cloth bodies. The picture illustrating these dolls was the same as the one illustrating composition head dolls in 1889. By 1894 *Solomon Hoffmann* was making a type of composition that might have

been known as "American bisque." *Marottes* were also advertised.

1896: Advertised four sizes of bisque head dolls on jointed composition bodies, hts. 14 to 25 in. (35.5 to 63.5 cm.); four sizes of bisque head dolls on ne plus ultra kid bodies, hts. 14 to 23 in. (35.5 to 58.5 cm.); and five sizes of bisque head dolls on gusset jointed kid bodies, hts. 12 to 25 in. (30.5 to 63.5 cm.).

1903: They sold *Kestner* kid-body dolls including the "Fat Baby." Among the cloth dolls were American Lady,[†] *Daisy,* Dusky Dude,[†] *Mammy* and *Sailor Boy.* There was also a *Multi-head* cloth doll. *Schoenhut* clowns were in their circus sets. *Minerva* metal head dolls and separate heads were advertised as well as cloth bodies, wigs, dolls' clothes and accessories.

1904: The dolls were similar to those offered in 1903 but there was more emphasis on bisque head dolls. They came with stationary or sleeping eyes, dressed or undressed. The dressed dolls ranged in price from 50¢ to $150.00. A doll was dressed in a Dutch costume. Ht. 16½ in. (42 cm.); priced $1.25. There was also a *Topsy Turvy* doll.

1919: Among the dolls advertised were *Eskimo Baby; Our Nurse Doll; Our Sailor Lad; Our Soldier Boy.* Composition infant dolls wore long dresses, hts. 11 and 14 in. (28 and 35.5 cm.); priced 29¢ and 50¢; with sleeping eyes priced $1.27. A 6 in. (15 cm.) composition doll with jointed shoulders was dressed in a bathing suit. Other composition dolls were 11½ to 25 in. (29 to 63.5 cm.) tall. With mohair wigs, cork stuffed bodies and composition hands they came dressed and undressed.

1922: Sold *Armand Marseille* bisque head dolls on composition and on imitation kid bodies; one of these imitation kid-body dolls, 18 in. (45.5 cm.) tall, cost $2.48. Separate Armand Marseille heads were also listed. The genuine kid body dolls had composition heads, arms (with jointed wrists) and legs, as well as wigs and sleeping eyes. Hts. 16 and 18 in. (40.5 and 45.5 cm.); priced $3.48 and $4.48. A bisque-head, composition-body doll with a wardrobe, ht. 7⅞ in. (19.5 cm.), cost 98¢ and $1.19.

Other dolls advertised by Montgomery Ward were Clowns, *La Petite Dolls, Mama* dolls, *Princess Dolls, Tootsie Baby Dolls,* and *Whistling Tom.* There were imported dressed baby dolls having bisque heads with or without dimples. Hts. 12 and 15 in. (30.5 and 38 cm.) as well as other sizes. The all-celluloid dolls had wigs and were jointed at the shoulders and hips. Hts. 9¾ and 12 in. (25 and 30.5 cm.); priced 98¢ and $1.38.

1924: The new dolls advertised were Mama dolls named *Baby Mine, Blue Bonnet, Goldilocks, Kiddie Dolls,* and *Miss Muffet* as well as cloth clowns, *Baby Peggy, Flanders Boy* representing Jackie Coogan, and *Sweetheart* Dolly. Nearly all of the other dolls had bisque heads on jointed composition bodies. These were probably nearly all from Germany. The heads had wigs, sleeping eyes, and many of them had hair eyelashes, open mouths with teeth, and wore chemises. Heights for the child type jointed composition body dolls ranged from 9 to 28 in. (23 to 71 cm.). Heights for the bent limb baby dolls ranged from 12½ to 21 in. (31.5 to 53.5 cm.).

1927: Advertised *Bubbles, Annabelle, Betty Ann, Bottletot, Boudoir* dolls, *Bye Lo Baby* with a composition head, *Christobel, Dorothy, Dolly, Gloria, Gwendolyn, Honey, Little Mary Sunshine*, Mama dolls, *Marilyn, Martha Ann, Mary Louise, Naughty Eyes*, and *Rosalie*. They handled dolls made by *Averill Mfg. Co., American Character Doll Co., Cameo, Effanbee, Gem*, and *Royal Toy Mfg. Co.*

1928: Among their dolls were *Bottletot, Boudoir* dolls, *Dolls' House Dolls, Glad Eyes, Laughing Eyes, Mary Sue*, and *Rose-Marie*.

1930: New dolls appear to have been *Baby Fleur, Boots, Marilee, Patsy*, and *Lady* dolls with bisque heads on thin composition bodies, wore high-heeled shoes. Ht. 13 in. (33 cm.); priced $3.33 and $5.89 when wearing a coat.★

Monty. 1929. Trademark registered in Germany by *Jos. Susskind* for dolls.

Moody. 1929. The *Doll Corporation of America* advertised this two-faced doll, one face laughing and one crying. The bonnet hid one of the faces and a new shoulder plate-socket head arrangement permitted the head to move in any direction; it came in three sizes. This Moody doll was also called "Good bad little girl."

Moody, E. Late 1800s. London. Distributed dolls made by Charles *Marsh*. "E. Moody" appears in the Marsh mark that was similar to the mark used with *C. Gooch*.†

Moon Mullins. Cutout cloth doll representing the cartoon character of this name and licensed by Famous Artists Syndicate. Ht. ca. 8 in. (20.5 cm.).

Moon Mullins. 1926–30. Style No. 25 of the *Live Long Toys* made of oilcloth. It was dressed in four colors, wore a derby, had a cigar in its mouth and a trick spring in its legs. The doll bore the names "Moon Mullins" and "Frank Willard," the designer of the cartoon character on which the doll was based. Ht. 18½ in. (47 cm.); price $12.00 doz. wholesale.

Moon Mullins. 1929. All-bisque dolls with molded clothes and jointed neck, made in Germany and distributed wholesale exclusively by *Marshall Field* and *Shackman*. The doll represented the cartoon character created by Frank Willard in 1923. Ht. 3¾ in. (9.5 cm.); priced 25¢.

Moore, H. A., & Co. 1925–27. London. Distributed *American Character Doll Co.* dolls and Effanbee dolls.

Moore & Gibson Corp. 1917–30 and later. New York City. Made cloth dolls including dolls made of terry cloth and of oilcloth, stuffed with kapok. Claimed the paint would not crack or come off.

1930: Advertised that all the dolls could stand alone and had a noise device. Among their dolls were Scotch Laddies and Scotch Lassies in Scottish attire and *Red Riding Hood* which came in two sizes.★

Moo-V-Doll Manufacturing Co. 1919–20. Bridgeport, Conn. Made patented dolls with composition head, lower arms and legs, wigs, pink cloth body and a head that turned by pushing on the nose. The five painted eyes appeared as follows: both eyes open and the face smiling, both eyes open and the face frowning, left eye closed, both eyes closed, right eye closed. There was a raised "M. V. D. Co." on the back of the shoulders. Ht. 16 in. (40.5 cm.).★

Moppietopp (Miss Moppie Topp, Moppie Topp). 1914. Cloth doll made by *Dean* with a woolly mop of curly hair, jointed neck, shoulders and hips. It had 12 styles of removable clothes and came with a booklet entitled, "All about Miss Moppie Topp." Came in three sizes namely size number 1, priced 88¢; size number 3, priced $1.13, and size number 5, priced $1.50.★

1941. Moppietopp mark used by Dean for cloth dolls.

Mora, A. L. 1887. London. Obtained a German patent (D.R.P.) for a jumping doll. The Berlin agent was J. Brandt & G. W. Von Nawrocki.

Moravian Dolls. See **Czechoslovakian Dolls** and **Holland, John.**

Moreau. See **Chéret & Moreau.**

Morel, Mme. 1918–29. Paris. Made dolls' faces of kid, satinette or georgette and dolls' clothes including hats of straw, felt or silk.

Morf, Erika. 1912. Zurich. Applied for a German patent (D.R.G.M.) for a metal doll's head.

Morgenthaler, Sasha. 1924–30 and later. Zurich. Born in 1893, she began in 1924 to make cloth dolls for her children; later she organized a team of people who produced handmade dolls.

Morhardt. 1861 and probably other years. Nürnberg, Bavaria. Supplied *Louise Amadine Prieur* with dolls' heads according to Mme. Florence Poisson, curator of the Roybet Fould Museum.

Mori, Susan Tucker. 1916. Atascadero, Calif. Applied for a German patent (D.R.G.M.) for a doll's head with sleeping eyes. This was possibly for the *Dooly Dolls*.

Morimura Bros. 1915–26. New York City. The company actually existed from the 1870s until 1941 but dolls were handled only 1915–26. Morimura Bros. appear to have used a size number on their bisque head dolls. For example a size 8 on a toddler body was 19 in. (48 cm.) tall. One of their dolls was named *Cho-Cho San*, another doll was named *Sonny*. (See Ills. 1942, 1943, and 1944.)★

Morin, L. 1921–28. Paris. Made composition character bébés and *Poupards*.★

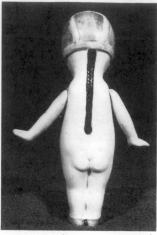

1942A & B. All-bisque Queue San Baby doll produced by Morimura Bros. ca. 1916. It has molded and painted cap, queue and slippers. The body is jointed at the shoulders. Mark: red and white sticker on chest "QUEUE//SAN//BABY." H. 4½ in. (11.5 cm.). *Coleman Collection.*

1943. Bisque socket head made for Morimura Bros. has a wig, sleeping blue glass eyes, an open mouth with two teeth, and a bent limb composition baby body. Mark: Ill. 1944. H. 7½ in. (19 cm.). Circumference of head 5¾ in. (14.5 cm.). *Courtesy of Helen Read. Photo by Steven Read.*

1944. Mark on bisque heads made for Morimura Bros.

Moritz. See **Max and Moritz.**

Moroder. Early 1800s–1896 and probably later. St. Ulrich, Grödner Tal, Austria. Several generations of this family were *Verlegers* of wooden dolls. They collected, stored and distributed the carved and turned dolls made as a local home industry. Johann Dominick Moroder was the first Verleger, he was succeeded by *Josef Purger* who in turn was succeeded by the sons of Johann Moroder who formed the firm called Josef Moroder & Co. The firm members were Josef Moroder, Dominik Moroder and Johann Peter Moroder. It is probable that this firm was also known as Gebrüder (Bros.) Moroder.

1891: Franz Moroder wrote a history of the making of wooden dolls in the Grödner Tal. (See also **Mauroner.**)★

Morrell. 1870–1930 and later. London. Horace W. Morrell, Charles Morrell and their successors handled dolls, especially wax dolls.

See color plate 21 in the COLLECTOR'S BOOK OF DOLLS' CLOTHES showing dressed bisque head dolls offered by Charles Morrel in 1910.★

Morrill Manufacturing Co. 1929. America. Founded by Mrs. Charles Morrill. The company made felt and velvet capes and caps for dolls.

1945. Mark used by Charles Morrell for wax head dolls.

1946A & B. Mark used by H. W. Morrell for dressed dolls.

Morris, Becker K., and Boullester, Jeremiah. See **Claire P. McAuley.**

Morris, Miss Claire. 1926–27. Los Angeles, Calif. Made and dressed long limbed *Boudoir* type dolls with features that resembled friends and acquaintances of Miss Morris. The dolls had highly polished fingernails, hair in the latest style and were dressed in silk and satin with shoes of silver and gold cloth. It is possible that Miss Claire Morris was Mrs. Claire McAuley who assigned her patent to Becker Morris.

Morse, Amelia. 1916–17. New York City. Obtained a U.S. and a Canadian patent for a doll with a hollow head and hollow body that were connected by a "stem." A loose pebble was placed in the head.

Morse, Leo. 1920–23. New York City. Made turned wood dolls in six styles representing boys, girls and men. Represented the *Rite Specialty Co.* in 1920. Advertised as "the shield of RITE Sanitary Playthings for Baby"; priced 25¢ to $2.00.

Mortara, Ed. 1929–30. Paris. Made dolls.

Moruzzi. 1927–28. Paris. Made dolls.

Moss, Charles Hutton. See **Sandow, Eugene.**

Moss, Leo. Late 1800s–and/or 1900s. Macon, Georgia. According to his granddaughter he made black dolls of papier-mâché. Each head was individually molded and represented a portrait of a member of the Moss family or of a neighbor. Some of these dolls had sad expressions and "tears" on their cheeks.

Mosse, Rudolf. 1878. Hamburg, Germany. Distributed and exported dolls on commission.

Mossman Toy Co. 1926. New York City. Commission house for *Bimblick* wooden bead dolls.

Most, Gebrüder. 1836 and probably other years. Vienna. The brothers Carl Most and Johann Most produced dolls.

Mother Blighty. 1917. Name in advertisement of *Tah Toys* that claimed this name was registered by *Heath Robinson*. The doll had a melon slice shaped mouth, wore a plaid dress, a cape with a hood, and spectacles.

Mother Goose. 1916–18. Line of 56 dolls made by *Samuel Gabriel Sons & Co.* who acquired new dies and molds to make these dolls in various sizes. The dolls had faces representing American children and an artist was hired to design the dresses.★

Mother Goose. 1920. Flat faced cloth dolls made by *Dean* as style No. D240. The dolls included Bo Peep, Blue Bell, Mary Mary, Mother Goose, and Red Riding Hood. Ht. 9 in. (23 cm.); priced 20¢.

Mother Goose. 1920–22. Hand painted dolls made of felt and other fabrics, cork, and rubber sponge by *Rees Davis*. The dolls had real hair and represented *Curly Locks, Little Bo-Peep, Little Boy Blue. Little Miss Muffet, Red Riding Hood* and *Tommy Tucker.*

Mother Goose. 1923. Doll made by *Pollyanna Co.* It wore a plaid shawl and white bonnet.

Mother Goose. 1923–30. Line of cloth dolls made by *Squier.*

Mother Goose. 1924. *Mama* doll made by *The Toy Shop.* It had a composition shoulder head, forearms, and legs; a mohair wig and a cloth body. It wore a percale dress with a Mother Goose nursery rhyme band all around the bottom of the skirt. The bloomers and cap matched the dress.

Mother Goose. 1926. Line of handpainted stockinet dolls designed by Mary Phillips and made by the *Rushton Co.* The 50 style nos. represented Mother Goose characters and each had its Mother Goose rhyme attached. Hts. 12 and 16 in. (30.5 and 40.5 cm.); priced 50¢ to $2.95. See Ill. 1850.

Mother Goose. 1928–29. Oilcloth dolls decorated with washable colors and stuffed with cotton, made by the *Twinzy Toy Co.* Each doll had a voice in its body and the appropriate nursery rhyme on its back.

Mother Goose. 1929. One of the *Kiddie Karakters* made by *Averill Manufacturing Co.* A *Mama* Doll type, it wore an ankle length dress, a cape and a peaked hat.

Mother Hubbard. 1882. Cloth doll sold by *Silber & Fleming,* price $2.13 doz. wholesale.

Mother Hubbard. See **Hubbard.**

Mothereau. See **Bébé Mothereau.**

Mother's Darling. 1917. Doll with composition head, hands and feet on a pink and white flannel covered coil spring body. When pressed down it cries as it rises. This doll was imported and distributed by *Butler Bros.* Ht. 5 in. (12.5 cm.).

Mother's Darling. 1925. Dressed baby doll with bisque head and bent limbs made by *Alt, Beck & Gottschalck.*

Mother's Darling. 1925. A newborn infant type doll with a wobbly head as designed by a well known artist. The head, resembling the *Armand Marseille* mold #341, had sleeping eyes and chubby cheeks. The doll, claimed to have been made by W. & R. *Eckart,* had a self activating voice.

Motion Picture Celebrity Dolls. Among these portrait dolls were: *Alkali Ike, Baby Peggy, Betty Bronson, Charlie Chaplin, Jackie Coogan, John Bunny, Marguerite Clark, Mary Pickford, Our Gang* (Hal Roach), *Rudolph Valentino,* and others.

Motschmann, Ch. 1855–60s. Sonneberg, Thür. Because his name has been found on several special type baby dolls with a cloth torso having a pelvic section of a hard material, these dolls have become known as Motschmann-type dolls. (An excellent example was illustrated in the frontispiece of GODEY'S LADY'S BOOK, January, 1860.) Further research has revealed that Motschmann was not the only manufacturer, nor was he the first one who made this type of doll. According to the research of the Ciesliks, *Edmund Lindner* appears to have made these so-called Motschmann-type dolls as early as 1851. A doll of this type bore the paper label of the successor of *Munnier* in France. See Ill. 1959. According to the Ciesliks this type of doll was called a *Täufling* in Germany. The 1880 Louis Lindner catalog showed these dolls were still available. Over the years they were made of bisque, china, composition, wax-over composition, wood, or a combination of some of the above mentioned materials. The heads and faces of wooden ones were similar to those found on *Bébé Tout en Bois*. (See also **Chinese Crying Babies** and **Motschmann & Hüffner**.)★

Motschmann & Hüffner (Hüfener). 1874–98. Sonneberg, Thür. Made and exported dolls especially *Täuflinge* (probably *Motschmann*-type dolls).

1878: Registered for Täuflinge numbers: 8337 1/0, 8337 5/0, 8338 2/0, 8340 2/0, 8341 4/0, 8343 5/0, 8353 4/0, 8355 4/0, 8359, 10286/1, 10287/1, 10288, 10738, 10742, 10793, 10796.

1879: Registered for Täuflinge with moving heads numbers: 8382 0/0, 8383 5/0, 8384 2/0, 12208, 12209; other Täuflinge numbers: 12639, 12640, 12641, 12642, 12643, 12644, 12645; also a rubber papier Täufling with curly hair wig and boots was number 8451.

1895: Applied for a German patent (D.R.G.M.) for interchangeable clothes for dolls.

1898: Advertised jointed and non-jointed dolls, specialized in ball jointed dolls. The "Changeable doll with its trousseau" was based on the 1895 patent. The above information is based on the research of the Ciesliks.★

Mourning Dolls. 1893–1910 and probably other years. Dolls dressed in black to represent a person in mourning.

1893: Jointed dolls dressed in black with a hat and veil, produced by *Horsman*. Four prices $2.00 to $18.00 doz. wholesale.

1910: *Amandus Michaelis* advertised dolls dressed to mourn the death of Edward VII. (See Color Ill. 11 in THE COLLECTOR'S BOOK OF DOLLS' CLOTHES, with the description on page 276.)

Mousmé. 1926. Trademark registered in France by *Jean Carles* for dolls.

Move. 1919–21. These were the Hungarian initials for the "Union of the Hungarian Militia." a patriotic society of ladies designed to aid middle class Christian women by providing them with work which they could do at home. This included making dolls and *Anna Dely* was one of the teachers.

Moving Lips. 1870–1930 and later. White or black dolls had mouths that opened and closed when the bellows in the chest was pressed. There were other mechanisms for making dolls' mouths move.

1899: *Butler Bros.* advertised dolls with moving lips, composition heads, arms and legs, glass eyes and cloth bodies. These dolls were dressed as *Nursing* babies, a cook, a china-

1947. Composition flange head with molded brown hair, stationary black glass eyes, closed mouth and a Motschmann-type body with a squeaker, composition hip section and limbs with floating joints. Original clothes. H. 12 in. (30.5 cm.). H. of head 3 in. (7.5 cm.). *Courtesy of Jessie Parsons.*

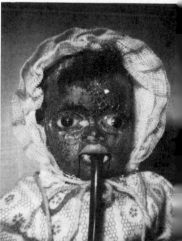

1948. Black nursing baby doll with moving lips and a baby bottle as advertised by Butler Bros. in 1899. It has a composition head, arms and legs on a cloth body, glass eyes and ethnic features. H. 10 in. (25.5 cm.). *Courtesy of the late Henrietta Van Sise.*

man, and black cake walker with a high hat. Hts. 10 and 13 in. (25.5 and 33 cm.).

1913: *Robert Maaser* applied for two German patents (D.R.G.M.) for dolls with moving lips.

1930: *Alfred Munzer* made dolls with moving lips.★

Moving Teeth. 1913. *Albert Messing* applied for a German patent (D.R.G.M.) for dolls with moving teeth.

Moxie, C. 1926–27. Boston, Mass. Registered Moxie as a U.S. trademark for dolls.

Mozart. 1925–30 and later. *Lenci* felt doll, style no. 253, dressed in a 1920s version of a 1700s boy. Hts. 14½ and 20 in. (37 and 51 cm.).

Mr. Bailey, The Boss. 1929. All-bisque doll with jointed neck and molded clothes based on the character in the *Smitty* cartoon created by *Walter Berndt.* These dolls, made in Germany, were distributed by *Marshall Field* and *Shackman.*★

Mr. Tumble-It. See **Tumble It.**

Mr. Twee Deedle. See **Twee Deedle.**

1950. Mrs. Blossom mark on an oilcloth doll.

1951. Gray advertising envelope of Mueller & Westfall which has black and gold printing on it. The back of the envelope reads: "MUELLER & WESTFALL,// IMPORTER OF //TOYS AND DOLLS// CHINA, BISQUE AND LAVA WARE, GLASS, AND //FANCY GOODS, MASKS,// GOLD AND SILVER LACES AND TRIMMINGS, // No. 373 BROADWAY//Bet White and Franklin Str. //NEW YORK." *Coleman Collection.*

1949. A nearly flat oilcloth doll made by Live Long Toys and printed to represent Mrs. Blossom. Marked on back. The printed clothes represent a fur trimmed coat and hat. Mark: Ill. 1950. H. 16½ in. (42 cm.). *Coleman Collection.*

Mrs. (Auntie) Blossom. 1924–28. Oilcloth doll made by *Live Long Toys* and representing one of the cartoon characters in Gasoline Alley. (See also **Auntie Blossom.**)★

Mrs. Captain, Mrs. Fatty. See **Mi.**

Mrs. Spaulding's Children. 1927. U.S. trademark registered by *Eleanor Spaulding* for dolls.

Mrs. Tom Thumb. 1920. Name of a doll with composition head and hands, painted hair and eyes, cloth body made by *E. Goldberger*. Its dresses came in a variety of colors. Ht. 12 in. (31.5 cm.).

Mueller & Westfall. 1880s. New York City. Imported and distributed dolls. (See Ill. 1951.)

Muhl, Georg. 1925–27. Nürnberg, Bavaria. In 1926–27 it was listed as the widow of Georg Muhl. She manufactured dolls' clothes and handled baby bottle sets for dolls.★

Muk. 1924–26. Name of dressed cloth dolls made by *Elise Israel*. Some dolls had felt heads and satin bodies.

Müller. See **Rühm & Müller.**

Müller, Albert. 1918–30 and later. Nossen, Saxony. Manufactured dolls.

Müller, B. Ch., & Mälzer. 1888–1907. Ilmenau, Thür. Made dressed dolls.

Müller, C. G. 1797 and other years. Sonneberg, Thür. Listed a variety of dolls.

Müller, Carl (Karl). 1895–1930. Sonneberg, Thür. This may be the Carl Müller of Köpplesdorf who applied for two German patents (D.R.G.M.), one in 1897 for a doll's voice and the other in 1904 for a doll with a moving head. It also may be the Carl (Karl) Müller of Neustadt, who advertised baby dolls, 1926–30. In 1923 Rehberger & Saul were factory agents in New York and Chicago for a Karl Müller doll factory in Germany.

It is also possible that this Carl Müller made porcelain dolls' heads at the Sonneberger Porzellanfabrik. See Ill. 1254 in THE COLLECTOR'S ENCYCLOPEDIA OF DOLLS.

Made in Germany
S.P. 6/0

Made in Germany.
SP 4.

1952A & B. Marks on bisque dolls' heads, possibly made by Carl Müller in the Sonneberger Porzellanfabrik.

Müller, Emil. 1878. Sonneberg, Thür. Produced dolls.

Müller, Franz. 1905–30 and later. Sonneberg, Thür. Manufactured dolls.

Müller, Friedrich. Early 1800s–1893. Sonneberg, Thür. A leading manufacturer of papier-mâché dolls according to his son's obituary. The son, Louis Müller, co-partner in the firm of Müller & Strassburger, died in 1889 at the age of 48.

According to the Ciesliks, Friedrich Müller, a sculptor, had been taught how to make papier-mâché by a French soldier in 1805. Friedrich was joined by his brother and first they made decorative ornaments, but soon they began to make papier-mâché dolls' heads. An article in DEUTSCHE SPIELWAREN ZEITUNG in 1930 gave 1807 as the date of the introduction by Müller of papier-mâché as a raw material for making dolls, replacing the bread dough used by the *Embossers*. In 1815 the Müllers devised the method of producing heads by pressure molding in sulphur molds which enabled them to mass produce dolls' heads. At first the wet papier-mâché had to be pressed into a mold by hand. Soon Müller had a positive mold made which was pushed down on top of the material in the negative mold. The molds were made by pouring liquid sulphur over a clay model and each head had a mold for the front and a mold for the back. From 1820 on, papier-mâché in Germany was made of white argillaceous washed sand, strips of paper, and animal glue. The sulphur molds were brushed inside with oil and the papier-mâché mixture put into the mold. After pressure molding, the papier-mâché was removed from the mold and dried in a coke oven or in the air. The edges were removed with a knife and the head was sanded smooth. Then the heads were painted or covered with a secret formula mix or with wax. A harder composition was sometimes made by adding plaster of paris to the papier-mâché mixture. Sulphur molds were still used to make composition dolls in the 1900s. It seems more likely that Louis Müller born in 1841 according to his obituary could have been the son of a second generation Friedrich Müller rather than the man who was making papier-mâché objects in 1805 but the latter is possible. Some records show J. F. Müller & Strassburger instead of Louis Müller and Strassburger. It is possible that both Louis and J. F. Müller belonged to this firm. J. F. Müller appeared alone as a German exhibitor at the 1873 Vienna Exhibition.

One of the composition dolls' heads marked "M & S//Superior" has been reported as having the name "Müller & Strassburger" written in ink on the inside back of the head, together with "To A. & P. Co." Allegedly the doll had always been in the owner's family.

1880: Müller & Strassburger displayed dolls at the Melbourne Exhibition.

1888: Dolls that would nod their heads to say "No" were patented by *Josef Bergmann* and distributed by Müller & Strassburger.★

Müller, H. B. See **Puppenfabrik Herzlieb.**

Müller, Heinrich, 1921–29. Nürnberg, Bavaria. From 1921 to 1925 he obtained five German patents (D.R.P.) for dolls with movable heads, one German patent (D.R.P.) for cloth covering of a doll.

1925: Obtained a British patent for the eyes of a stuffed doll which were held in place by a piece of sheet metal or celluloid.

1926: Obtained a U.S. patent for a doll with pressed metal parts covered with cloth. The metal had pointed teeth along its edge that were bent inward and securely held the cloth covering.

Obtained a German patent (D.R.P.) for eyes for a plush doll.

1927–29: Obtained six German patents (D.R.P.) for dolls having movement such as the movement of the hand turning the head.

1953A & B. Papier-mâché shoulder head probably made by Müller & Strassburger since it is marked M & S Superior. It has molded and painted hair and blue eyes, closed mouth and is on a cloth Goldsmith body with leather arms and boots. Contemporary dress. H. 16 in. (40.5 cm.). H. of shoulder head 4½ in. (11.5 cm.). *Courtesy of Cherry Bou.*

1954. M & S Superior, mark that possibly was used by Müller & Strassburger.

Müller, Helene (née Buttner). 1905. Schalkau, Thür. Obtained an Austrian patent for eyelashes for dolls.★

Müller, Herm. 1907. Sonneberg, Thür. Applied for a German patent (D.R.G.M.) for a celluloid head with sleeping eyes.

Müller, Karl, & Co. 1924–29. Sonneberg and Effelder, Thür. Made bisque-head baby dolls, dressed and undressed dolls and *Elie* dolls.★

Müller, Wilhelm G. Before 1900–30 and later. Sonneberg, Thür. Made and exported dolls and baby dolls with bisque heads, both shoulder and socket heads with wigs or molded and painted hair. Müller also advertised separate wigs and clothes for dolls. He used *Wee Gem* as a mark.

1910: One of the Sonneberg group of Grand Prize winners at the Brussels Exposition.

1926: Created character babies, fully jointed dolls, novelty dolls and dressed dolls, "of all kinds."

1930: Used *Armand Marseille* bisque head molds #s 390, 520 and 1330. He also used mold #s 221, 441, 5067, 5074, 5079 and 5080. *W. Seelig* was his London agent and Müller had an advertisement in a Paris directory.★

Müller & Fröbel. 1900–30 and later. Sonneberg, Thür. Manufactured dolls.

1910: One of the Sonneberg group of Grand Prize winners at the Brussels Exposition.★

Müller & Kaltwasser. 1930. Rauenstein, Thür. Made cloth or cloth-body dolls which were distributed by *G.F. Hertzog & Co.*

Müller & Strassburger. See **Müller, Friedrich.**

Multi-face Dolls. At least by 1866–1930 and later. Dolls with two or more faces. *Bru* used a multi face head with one face awake and one face sleeping on some of his lady dolls. Some of the three face dolls were marked D.R.P. signifying that they were patented in Germany.

A cloth doll with two faces, one happy and one sad, on one end of a *Topsy Turvy* doll had a black head on the other end.

Dolls sometimes had detachable masks which provided the doll with multi-faces. This type was most often found on cloth dolls but *Gebrüder Heubach* also used this technique for bisque heads.

An all-bisque infant doll has been found with a swivel head having one face with eyes molded asleep and the other side with open eyes. On the back of the lower torso was stamped "PATENT//30702." This doll had diagonal hip joints and bent legs.

1888: Baby dolls advertised by *Ridley* had bisque heads with two faces, one laughing and one crying. The head revolved leaving the one face exposed and the other hidden in the cap. The change was made by turning a ring on the top. Three hts.; priced 69¢ to $1.19. A similar wax-head doll had two strings at its side which when pulled caused the head to turn, crying "Mama" and "Papa" as it turned. Ht. 15 in. (38 cm.); priced $1.25. This was probably the *Fritz Bartenstein* two-faced doll.

1893: *Horsman* advertised laughing and crying composition head dolls. They came in five sizes, priced $9.00 to $18.00 doz. wholesale.

1897: *Samaritaine* advertised *Le Sonneur*, a two-faced clown with a bell in each hand.

1898: *Butler Bros.* advertised a three-face doll, one face laughing, one crying and one sleeping. It had a bisque head, composition arms and legs with ball joints at the elbows and knees, cloth torso with two pull-cords, one for "Mama" and one for "Papa." Ht. 16 in. (40.5 cm.).

1899: A French advertisement listed an "English two-faced doll" in a long dress. Priced $3.30 and $4.39.

1903: *Tapis Rouge* advertised a three-faced doll, one face laughing, one crying, and one sleeping. The head turned by means of a knob on top. The doll wore a chemise and bonnet but no footwear. Two cords when pulled said "Mama" and "Papa." Ht. 34 cm. (13½ in.); priced 70¢.

1908: The Sonneberg Museum had a four-faced doll which they attributed to *Carl Bergner* in this year.

1912: *Effanbee* made *Johnny Tu Face. Kley & Hahn* made a two-faced baby doll.
    Wilhelm Struwe used detachable masks on some of his dolls.

Ca. 1913: A celluloid multi-face head has been reported with a *Billiken* type on one side and a *Kewpie* type on the other side.
    Elizabeth Lesser created dolls with multi-face masks.

1913–14: Multi-face cloth doll with four faces. One face was that of a white baby, one face was black, and there were two white child faces, one with eyes looking upwards and the other with eyes looking straight ahead. These dolls were made by Horsman.

1916: *Amberg* made a multi-face doll.

1923: *Faultless Rubber Co.* made two-faced rubber dolls.

1926: *William Duncan* applied for a patent for a multi-face doll.

1928: *Reisman, Barron* made a two-face clown in their *Adora-Belle* line.

1929: *The Doll Corporation of America* made multi-face dolls named *Moody.* ★

1955. Bisque head multiface dolls with wigs and stationary glass eyes. Doll on left has three faces, one smiling, one crying and one sleeping. The body is imitation leather with composition and wood arms and legs. Mark on head "C.B." probably for Carl Bergner. H. 12½ in. (31.5 cm.).
    Doll on right has two faces, one smiling and one crying. The head is turned by a brass ring at the top. The body is composition and wood. H. 13 in. (33 cm.). *Courtesy of Sotheby Parke Bernet Inc., N.Y.*

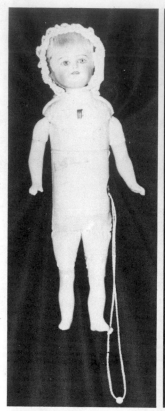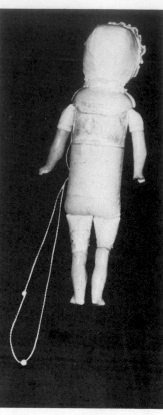

1956A & B. Multiface doll with an awake and a sleeping face operated by pulling the strings shown in the pictures. The doll says "Mama" when the button on the chest is pressed at the same time that the wake-up cord is pulled. Hair is at the edge of the cap. The head, lower arms and legs are composition while the torso and upper limbs are cloth. The eyes are stationary blue glass. It is reported that this doll was purchased at an auction in the 1890s for 10¢. H. 15 in. (38 cm.). *Courtesy of Marjorie Tatnall.*

Multi-head Dolls. Before 1849–1930 and later. There were two types: in one the various heads were affixed at the neck of the body and in the other was a two-headed *Topsy Turvy* doll with only a partial body. One of these Topsy Turvy cloth dolls had a black head at one end and a two-faced white doll at the other end.

1865: In an interview with Cremer Jr. in THE ENGLISH WOMAN'S DOMESTIC MAGAZINE, he described an unusual feature of wax dolls. "One of the most ingenious things . . . is the shifting of heads. Thus dolly, to-day a girl in the middle of her teens, is tomorrow a coquette looking out of them and the next day a bride, and the next a matron, and the next a very mature and stately lady, and the next wrinkled and white-headed, to be the next by merely twisting her head off and substituting another, a blooming girl again."

1893: *Horsman* advertised dolls with a black head and a baby's head, priced $2.00 doz. wholesale.

1894: *Bon Marché* advertised a doll sold in a box which included two separate heads. Ht. 30 cm. (12 in.); priced $1.05. (See THE COLLECTOR'S BOOK OF DOLLS' CLOTHES, Ill. 428.)

1957A & B. Composition head doll with three attachable heads. In the neck a thick ring fits over a wooden pole and is attached with a wire hook in back. This in turn is hooked by wire attached to elastic which is inserted in a hole in the middle of the back. Two of the wigs are blond and one is red. Stationary glass eyes on two are brown and one set of eyes is blue. All three heads have open mouths. The body is composition fully jointed, except at the wrists. Contemporary clothes. Mark: "D.R.G.M. Sch 16647 3/0." This doll was patented by Hermann Wegner in 1893. 3/0 is probably the size number. H. 13 in. (33 cm.). *Courtesy of the Margaret Woodbury Strong Museum. Photo by Harry Bickelhaupt.*

1895: *Butler Bros.* advertised a dressed Topsy Turvy doll with a white bisque head and a black composition head, glass eyes. Ht. 14 in. (35.5 cm.); priced $2.05 doz. wholesale.

1900: The Sonneberg Museum had a Topsy Turvy doll with papier-mâché heads, one white and one black. The swaddling clothes hid the torso joining. Ht. 19 cm. (7½ in.).

1902: Butler Bros. advertised a Topsy Turvy doll with bisque heads, one a white baby and the other black with woolly hair. Heads had glass eyes and open mouth. Ht. 12 in. (30.5 cm.); price $2.00 doz. wholesale.

1903: *Montgomery Ward* advertised a Topsy Turvy doll with a laughing and a crying lithographed face with hair bangs. It came dressed. Ht. 12½ in. (31.5 cm.); price 50¢.

1907: *Siegel Cooper* advertised two multi-head dolls. On one doll there was a laughing head and a crying baby head. This doll had a cloth body and sold dressed for $1.25. The

1958. Munich Art Doll created by Marion Kaulitz as shown in the INTERNATIONAL STUDIO, May 1909.

other multi-head doll had one end white and one end black. It had a cloth body and sold for $1.00.

1909: *Julius Dorst* produced a multi-head doll.

1911: YOUTH'S COMPANION offered as a premium an all-celluloid doll with five heads. Each head fitted into the neck socket and the heads were as follows:
1. Boy's head with "sand papered" hair.
2. Girl's head with real hair.
3. Cat's head.
4. Girl's head with molded hair.
5. Boy's head with molded hair.
Ht. 9½ in. (24 cm.); price $1.25.

1912: Bon Marché advertised dolls with three interchangeable heads, one plain, one smiling and one crying. They had short hair and there were three sets of clothes. Hts. 34 and 36 cm. (13½ and 14 in.); priced $3.15 and $3.95.

1914: A cloth Topsy Turvy doll had two celluloid faces, one white and one black. Ht. 12 in. (30.5 cm.).

Early 1900s: *Kestner* used various heads to make multi-head dolls called *Das Wunderkind;* most of the heads were mold numbers in the 170s or 180s, some had sleeping eyes and some had painted eyes. The sets usually had three of four heads.

1921: Reportedly the heads made by *Bucherer* were designed to be interchangeable.

1923: *Baby Surprise* was a multi-head doll.

1924: *Charles William* advertised Topsy Turvy dolls with celluloid faces, one black and one white, cloth body and arms. This doll is very similar to the one listed in 1914. Ht. 12 in. (30.5 cm.); priced $1.10.

1925–29: *Twinjoy Doll Co.* made Topsy Turvy type multi-head dolls representing Little Red Riding Hood and Grand-

ma; Betsy Ross and Uncle Sam; Jack and Jill; Topsy and Eva; Cinderella in rags and in silk.

1926: *Betty Bronson* as Cinderella in rags and in a ball gown.

1930: *European Doll Manufacturing Co.* produced multi-head dolls.★

Muncie Doll. 1921. Composition doll with wigs of various colors. It represented a young lady with silk gowns in a variety of colors, distributed by *Doremus & Benzer.* Hts. 8, 12, and 14 in. (20.5, 30.5, and 35.5 cm.).

Munhard, Alan Ross. 1924–26. London. Obtained a German patent (D.R.P.) for a doll.

Munich Art Dolls. 1908–20s. *Marion Kaulitz* was the originator of these dolls. The heads were designed by *Marie Marc-Schnür, Paul Vogelsanger* and *Josef Wackerle.* The faces were handpainted by Marion Kaulitz and the dolls were dressed by *Lilian Frobenius* and Alice Hagemann. These dolls usually had composition heads with wigs, painted eyes, and ball jointed composition bodies some of which were supplied by *Cuno & Otto Dressel.* They wore clothes that resembled those of German children. Sometimes the costumes were German or French regional ones. *Hermann Tietz* displayed some of these dolls.

Ca. 1908: Dolls with Wackerle heads were distributed by Cuno & Otto Dressel. Some of these are now in the Sonneberg Museum. Hts. 42, 45, and 55 cm. (16½, 17½, and 21½ in.).

1912: Distributed by *Arnoldt Doll Co.* in the U.S.A. These dolls wore German regional costumes.★

Munich Street Car Girl. 1908. Body and dress made by *Eugenie Derdzakian.* The head was created by *Marie Marc-Schnür.*

Munition Doll. 1918. Line made by *Bell & Francis.*

Munnier (Munier or Monnier), Maison. 1834–70s and later. Paris. Also known as Vve. (Widow) Munnier, was succeeded in 1863 by Benon & Cie., who occupied the same address which was called *Aux Enfant Sages* in the 1870s. Later Guiton took over Aux Enfant Sages and was in operation at least until the 1890s. The Maison Munnier handled dolls including wax-over-composition dolls, like the so-called *Motschmann* type and bisque dolls marked "E. B." for *E. Barrois*. A few of the marks found on these doll included the following:

"Maison Munnier//Passage Jouffroy// No. 15 & 17// Paris."

"AUX ENFANTS SAGES//—[?]—Mson. Monnier// BENON & Cie Succre// Passage Jouffroy, Nos 13 & 17// PARIS// Spécialité de Jouets d'Enfants & Jeux de Société // COMMISSION, EXPORTATION."

"AUX ENFANTS SAGES//GUITON//Passage JOUFFROY// Paris."★

Munro, Harold. 1924. Providence, R.I. Made celluloid dolls.

Munroe, J. C. 1844 and probably other years. Concord, N.H. Advertised "Wax and kid dolls."

Munson, Craig D. 1925–26. Wallingford, Conn. Obtained a U.S. patent for dolls.★

Munyard, Alan Ross. 1923–26. London. Obtained a German patent (D.R.P.) for moving eyes in a doll's head.★

Münzberg, A. 1926–30 and later. Prague, Czechoslovakia. Manufactured dolls.

Munzer, Alfred. 1917–30 and later. New York City. Manufactured dolls including a line of composition *Gaby* dolls designed by Mr. Gaby that had a pull string to move the lips so the doll could say "Mama."

1917: Made *Kewpie*-type dolls.

1929: Made Gaby Buttons in a short jacket, Gaby Kid Clown and Gaby Joe in overalls.★

1960. Bisque head on a kid body with a mark of Guiton, a later successor of Munnier. Mark: Ill. 1962. It has a wig, stationary blue glass eyes, applied and pierced ears and a closed mouth. The neck swivels on a bisque shoulder plate. Dolls with heads from this same mold have been found on Goldsmith, on Kintzback and on Lacmann bodies. H. 28 in. (71 cm.). H. of shoulder head 7 in. (18 cm.). *Courtesy of Richard Withington. Photo by Barbara Jendrick.*

1959A — C. Wax over papier-mâché infant doll having a paper sticker on the stomach. Mark: Ill. 1961 for Benon & Cie. who were the successors of Maison Munnier. The doll has painted wisps of hair, sleeping blue glass eyes and four glass teeth. It is on a cloth, wood, and composition body having a solid lower torso section and floating joints for the wrists and ankles. Pull strings operate the voice box in the upper torso. Dressed in period white clothes from England representing an older baby. H. 17 in. (43 cm.). *Coleman Collection.*

AUX ENFANTS SAGES
ANcne Mson MONNIER
BENON & Cie Succrs
Passage Jouffroy, Nos 13 & 17
——— PARIS ———
Specialité de Jouets d'Enfants & Jeux de Société
COMMISSION - EXPORTATION

AUX ENFANTS SAGES
GUITON
Passage JOUFFROY
PARIS

1961–1962. Marks on the front of the torsos of dolls handled by the successors of Munnier. No. 1962 is a blue stamp. No. 1961 is a paper sticker.

Münzer, Paul. 1898. Pössneck, Thür. Made dolls.

Münzer & Schneider. 1899–1918. Pössneck, Thür. Applied for two German patents (D.R.G.M.) for dolls. One of these patents pertained to a voice in the body.

Murphy (American Soldier). Before 1911–13. Jointed felt doll made by *Steiff* and distributed in the U.S. by *Borgfeldt*. It was dressed as an American soldier with three chevrons on its arm but without equipment. Ht. 35 cm. (14 in.); priced 90¢ in Germany in 1911 and $1.55 in New York in 1913. (See also **Sharkey.**)

Murphy, Albert E. 1926. Chicago, Ill. Obtained a U.S. patent for an aquatic doll.

Murray, Mrs. Getchen. 1923. Designed clothes for dolls made by *Martha Chase;* also sold other clothes for dolls.

Muschi. 1928. Trademark registered in Germany by *Martha Lehmann* (née Kohl) for dolls.

Musette. 1925–26. *Lenci* felt doll style No. 256. It wore a romantic period costume with a fringed shawl around its shoulders. Ht. 29½ in. (75 cm.).

Musette. 1929. Trademark registered in France for a doll that was produced by *Henri Ribiere.*

Mush. 1929. One of the oilcloth dolls made by *Live Long Toys* and based on the cartoon of Ad. Carter. This was style No. 30 and represented a boy wearing a red and black suit with coat and long trousers. Ht. 10 in. (25.5 cm.); price $4.00 doz. wholesale.

Mushmouth. 1929. All-bisque doll with jointed neck based on the *Moon Mullins* cartoon drawn by *Frank Willard.* The

doll wore molded clothes, was made in Germany and distributed exclusively by *Marshall Field* and *Shackman.*

Muth, Erna. Ca. 1919–20. Dresden, Saxony. Made art dolls of colored silk, crêpe paper, and wire, dressed in crêpe paper.

Mutt & Jeff. 1914. Dolls that could stand, walk or tumble; represented the cartoon pair.

Mutt & Jeff. 1923–26. All-metal ball jointed dolls made by *Bucherer* representing the cartoon pair. Dolls were distributed by *F. A. O. Schwarz;* price $3.00 for the pair.

Mutt & Jeff. 1925. All-celluloid dolls with jointed arms and molded clothes, representing the cartoon pair and distributed by *Shackman.*

Mutual Doll Co. 1919–26. New York City. Made *Bundie, Charms,* and *Lassie* as well as other composition dolls. Some of their dolls had bisque heads. The dolls came with or without wigs, with painted or glass eyes and dressed in chiffon, silk or satin gowns as well as tailored outfits. A doll representing a cabaret singer wore a large hat.★

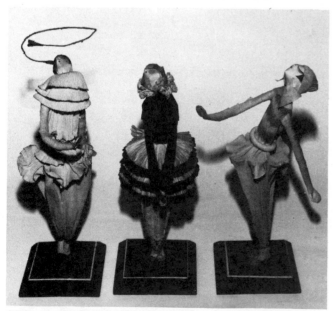

1963. Three art dolls of crepe paper and wire made by Erna Muth. The hair is made of painted paper and the eyes are painted. The Art Deco style original clothes are made of crepe paper. H. including stand 9 in. (23 cm.). *Courtesy of the late Magda Byfield.*

1964. All-composition Boudoir doll probably made by the Mutual Novelty Corp. It has a wig, painted eyes, mouth holds a cigarette. The body is jointed at the neck, shoulders, elbows, hips, and knees. Original clothes. H. 24 in. (61 cm.). *Courtesy of and photo by Stephanie and Fred Farago.*

Mutual Novelty Corp. 1925–29. New York City. Made *Mama* dolls, *Boudoir* dolls, Art dolls, infant dolls and novelty decorative dolls.

1925: Advertised that they owned the design patent granted to *Haskell* for a Boudoir doll with a cigarette known as a *Parisienne* or French Flapper or *Cigarette Doll.*

1926: Advertised an "Egyptian" doll dressed in silk ruffled pajamas.

1927: The Boudoir Dolls came dressed or undressed. Some of them had cigarettes in their mouths and wore pants suits. Mutual Novelty Corp., a member of the *American Doll Manufacturers' Association,* won an infringement suit against the *Fair Trading Co.* The infringement suit pertained to a doll for which a design patent had been granted to S. Haskell.

1929: The Boudoir dolls had fully jointed composition bodies. The art dolls, a little smaller than the Boudoir dolls, had "felt finished faces" which were not actually felt. These came dressed; priced $1.00 and $2.00.

My Baby. 1922. Line of dolls made by *Wonderland Toymaking Co.*

My Best Dolly. 1919. Cutout cloth doll made by *Saalfield.*

My Big Dolly. 1915–19. Cutout cloth doll style No. 167 made by *Saalfield.* The large doll had a photographic face and wore a combination underskirt and drawers. The shoes had a separate sole. It was recommended that a cardboard lining be placed in the sole and that the doll be stuffed with cotton batting. Ht. 24 in. (61 cm.). There were also two similar small dolls 7 in. (18 cm.).

My Cherub. 1912–30 and later. Trade name used by *Schoenau & Hoffmeister* for a bisque-head doll with hair eyelashes and open mouth. A box holding such a doll was marked "MY NEW CHERUB//Every Child's Favorite//Made in Germany." A My Cherub box was marked 1909; this appears to have been a mold number and not a date.★

My Clothes Take Off. 1917. Name of a line of dolls distributed by *Hopkins & Co.* (See also **Rosette.**)

My Daisy. 1928. Doll with bisque head, blond bobbed hair, sleeping eyes, hair eyelashes and jointed composition body. It wore a chemise and was distributed by *Gamage.* Seven hts. 12, 14, 17, 20, 22, 25 and 27 in. (30.5, 35.5, 43, 51, 56, 63.5 and 68.5 cm.).

My Daisy Baby. 1928. Doll with bisque head, dark hair wig and hair eyelashes, bent limb composition body, distributed by *Gamage.* With sleeping eyes and a voice the five hts. were 14, 16, 18, 20 and 21 in. (35.5, 40.5, 45.5, 51 and 53.5 cm.). Without sleeping eyes and voice the four hts. were 16, 17, 18, and 22 in. (40.5, 43, 45.5, and 56 cm.).

My Darling. 1887. Wax doll with Rembrandt-style hairdo, jointed arms and legs.

These dolls, distributed by *C. F. Lauer,* wore a chemise lettered "My Darling" and footwear. Six hts. 14, 14½, 16, 20, 22 and 24 in. (35.5, 37, 40.5, 51, 56, and 61 cm.). The 14, 14½, and 20 in. (35.5, 37, and 51 cm.) hts. had sleeping eyes. The 14 in. (35.5 cm.) ht. came with painted footwear or real footwear. The former was $1.25 doz. wholesale; and the largest doll was the most expensive at $4.50. doz. wholesale.

My Darling. 1919–21. Doll imported from Japan by *Morimura Bros.*★

My Darling. 1930 and later. Baby doll line with composition head, arms and legs, sleeping eyes, cloth body stuffed with kapok, made by the *Goodyear Toy Co.*

My Darling. See **Favorite.**

My Darling. See **Mein Liebling.**

My Dearie. 1908–24. A doll with a bisque head on a jointed composition body had the head marked "My Dearie." Ht. 22 in. (56 cm.). Another doll with a dolly-face bisque head, wig, open mouth and four teeth, pierced ears, had its head marked "SIMON & HALBIG//W.S.K. 4½" for a 24 in. (61 cm.) doll. This same doll had a tag reading "Germany//My Dearie//CELEBRATE." The *Celebrate* was in a circle under a crown.

1922: *Otto Gans* used this trade name.

1924: *Wiesenthal, Schindel & Kallenberg* used this trade name.★

1965. Printed cutout cloth doll named "My Big Dolly" made by Saalfield as number 167 around 1915. The sheet contains a large doll with a photographic face and two small dolls. Mark: Ill. 1966. H. of large doll 26 in. (66 cm.). H. of small doll 6¼ in. (16 cm.). *Coleman Collection.*

1966. Mark on a cloth cutout doll made by Saalfield named My Big Dolly.

My Doll. Name stamped in purple on the front of a cloth *Philip Goldsmith* body under the shoulder plate. The letters are in a Gothic style.

My Dolly. See **My Big Dolly.**

My Dream Baby. 1924–30 and later. Bisque heads made by *Armand Marseille* represented a newborn infant. They came in white, brown and black versions. Mold # 341 had a closed mouth and mold # 351 had an open mouth. The marks that ended in a K were on socket heads, the others were on heads with flange necks. The bodies were either cloth or composition. *Arranbee*, a distributor, claimed that their My Dream Babies had rubber hands as an exclusive feature. A box containing one of these dolls was marked "Celebrate 342." *Foulds & Freure* had their heads marked 342.

Dolls with heads marked 341, 342, or 351 were not necessarily named "My Dream Baby". Various companies used these heads and gave the doll, names such as *Lullaby Baby, My Playmate, My Prince, Rock-A-Bye Baby,* and *Tee Wee.*

The Size-Height Relationship for some of My Dream Baby Dolls is roughly as follows:

| Size | Height | |
No.	in.	cm.
4/0	8½	21.5
2/0	9½	24
1/0	10	25.5
2	12	30.5
3	14	35.5
4	16	40.5
5	18	45.5
6	20	51
7	22	56
8	24	61

1926: Doll held a celluloid nursing bottle containing milky white liquid and was called *Nursing Bottle Baby.*

1928: Advertised as being clothed in white, blue, or pink organdy dress and matching bonnet, shoes and stockings. It had a "baby voice." Ht. 15 in. (38 cm.); priced $3.45.

1929: Costume consisted of an organdy dress and brushed wool outer garments.

1931: Composition head doll with sleeping eyes, a voice, and a body representing a six-months-old baby bore a round tag marked "Arranbee Doll//My//Dream//Baby." Ht. 14 in. (35.5 cm.); priced $4.00.★

My Favorite. 1916–18. Composition doll made by *Jessie M. Raleigh.*★

My Girlie. 1912–22 and probably later. Trademark used by *Borgfeldt* for bisque head dolly-faced dolls on composition bodies which sometimes had wire spring joints. See Ill. 1970.★

My Girlie Girl. 1917–18. Jointed doll that could be placed in a running pose, made by *Dolls' Supplies.*

My Gold Pearl (Meine Goldperle). 1914–30. Trade name for a dressed, ball jointed character doll made by *Adolf Heller.*

My Gold Star. 1926. Trade name for dolls used by *C. M. Bergmann.*

1967A & B. Bisque flange neck version of My Dream Baby made by Armand Marseille around 1925. It has painted hair, sleeping glass eyes, closed mouth, cloth body with composition hands. This is mold # 341, size number 2. H. 10 in. (25.5 cm.); circumference of head 9 in. (23 cm.). *Coleman Collection.*

1968. Bisque socket head infant doll known as My Dream Baby. It has painted hair, sleeping blue glass eyes, open mouth, and a bent limb composition baby body. Marked "351 2K"; 351 is the mold #, 2 is the size number and K stands for socket head. H. 12 in. (30.5 cm.). *Courtesy of Sotheby Parke Bernet Inc., N.Y.*

1969. Dream Baby mark used by Arranbee on clothes that were probably designed for My Dream Baby dolls.

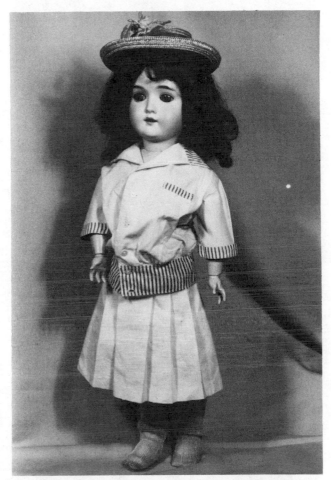

1970. My Girlie bisque socket head with wig, sleeping eyes, hair eyelashes, open mouth, and teeth, and a wire spring strung composition body. Contemporary clothes. Mark: My Girlie//III //Germany." H. 25 in. (63.5 cm.). *Courtesy of the Washington Dolls' House and Toy Museum.*

My Honey. 1921–24. Bisque head doll with wig, googly eyes, dressed as a little girl or a little boy.

1924: Distributed by *Foulds & Freure.* Wore a large hair bow and carried a round tag reading, "My// Honey."★

My Kiddie. 1917–18. Stockinet doll with wig. Made by *Fretwell.*

My Little Beauty. 1908. Imported doll advertised by *Samstag & Hilder Bros.* had a *Duchess* bisque head, wig, sleeping eyes, and removable clothes.

My Name is Miss Flake Rice. See **Miss Flaked Rice.**

My Only One. See **Meine Einzige.**

My Pet. 1905. Name on a celluloid doll's head made by *Buschow & Beck.*

My Pet. Name of a doll made by *Adolf Hülss.* (See Ill. 1971.)

1971. My Pet mark for dolls made by Adolf Hülss.

My Playmate. 1903–29. *Borgfeldt* used this name for various types of imported dolls; among them *Armand Marseille's Florodora* and mold # 390 as well as *König & Wernicke* dolls.

1909: Advertised by *Siegel Cooper* as a doll with flirting and sleeping eyes. It had a wig, a jointed composition body, wore a chemise, hair ribbon and footwear. Hts. 18 and 26 In. (45.5 and 66 cm.); priced $2.50 and $5.00.

1928–29: Trade name for dressed felt dolls.★

My Precious. 1929. All-composition bent limb baby with painted hair and features, wore a short baby dress and halo bonnet. It was distributed by *Butler Bros.* Ht. 10½ in. (26.5 cm.); priced $4.90 doz. wholesale. See THE COLLECTOR'S BOOK OF DOLLS' CLOTHES, Ill. 775 G.

My Pride. See **Mein Stolz.**

My Prince and **My Queen.** 1929–30 and later. Trade names used by *W. Cohen* for baby dolls with *Armand Marseille* heads mold #351 and mold #990 respectively. Composition bodies were toddler type for My Prince (black version named Black Prince) and bent limb type for My Queen which had a wig, and came in nine hts.

My Queen Doll. 1919. Advertised by *Gebrüder Ohlhaver.*

My Rosy Darling (Mein Rosiger Liebling). 1927–30 and later. All-celluloid or celluloid head on a composition or cloth body doll produced by *Kämmer & Reinhardt* and distributed by *B. Illfelder* and *Louis Wolf.* These dressed dolls were also called "Roli." The bodies represented babies; toddlers, including fat little dolls; and children, including the slender-bodied ones. Some of the dolls in this line were of the new-born baby type. (See Ill. 1972.)

My Sweet Baby. After 1910. Name of a doll with bisque head, wig, glass sleeping eyes, open mouth and teeth, on a bent limb composition baby style body. Ht. 14 in. (35.5 cm.).

My Sweetheart. ca. 1910. Doll with bisque head and jointed composition body. Ht. 23½ in. (59.5 cm.). (See also **Sweetheart.**)★

My Sweetheart. 1920–21. Doll imported from Japan by *Morimura Bros.*★

Mysette. 1920s. Name of a French doll exhibited in New York City.

N

N. T. I. See **Nottingham Toy Industry.**

N. V. Sales Co. 1924–26. New York City. Made dolls.

Nabob. 1930. Name of a series of black cloth dolls made by *Chad Valley.* They wore wide collars, full trousers of printed fabric and large headwear. Chad Valley labels found on the bottom of the feet. No. 685/1, 11 in. (28 cm.) tall, and No. 685/2, 14 in. (35.5 cm.) tall.

Nadaud, Mlle. A. 1878–90s. Paris. Handled dolls, especially Bébé Nadaud. The dolls usually had bisque heads, glass eyes, wigs and were on ball-jointed composition bodies. Mlle. Nadaud sold so-called "long face" (Bébé Triste) *Jumeaus.* Nadaud labels have been found on the feet of dolls and on boxes. (See Ill. 1246 in the first COLLECTOR'S ENCYCLOPEDIA OF DOLLS.) One of the labeled Nadaud dolls wore a nursemaid's costume and carried a veiled infant doll.★

Nadel & Shimmel. 1926. New York City. Imported dolls.

Nagai & Co. 1917–18. New York City. Advertised dolls with bisque heads imported from Japan. Their bent-limb composition body baby dolls wore short baby dresses. Some of their dolls had silk wigs but most of them had mohair wigs.★

Nagel (Negel), C. (née Andrews). 1897–1918. Neustadt near Coburg, Thür., and Hamburg, Germany. She was the widow of Johannes Nagel. Made cloth bodies for dolls.★

Naiad. 1884–87. Composition-head dolls handled by *Lauer,* had skin wigs, a lace-trimmed chemise, cloth stockings and leather boots.

1884: SIZE–HEIGHT RELATIONSHIP OF NAIAD DOLLS			
Size No.	Height in.	cm.	Price doz. wholesale
3/0	13	33	$2.25
2/0	14½	37	$2.80
0	16	40.5	$3.40
1	17	43	$4.25
2	19	48	$5.50
3	20½	52	$6.75
4	22	56	$8.50

1887: Size 3/0 cost $1.65 and 2/0 cost $2.00 a doz. wholesale.

1972. Advertisement for "My Rosy Darling Baby" by Louis Wolf and B. Illfelder for Kämmer & Reinhardt dolls in PLAYTHINGS, September, 1928. The tag reads "Mein Lieblings Baby" (My Darling Baby). This is a celluloid head on a toddler style body.

1973. Bisque socket head doll named My Sweet Baby. It has a wig, sleeping brown glass eyes, open mouth with teeth, and a bent limb composition baby body. Head is marked "My Sweet Baby." H. 14 in. (35.5 cm.). *Courtesy of Sotheby Parke Bernet Inc., N.Y.*

1974. Poured wax head doll handled by Mlle. Nadaud. It has inserted hair, stationary blue glass eyes, closed mouth, and a cloth body with wax arms and legs. Original clothes. Mark on shoe "Bébé Nadaud//34 Rue du Septembre// Paris Deposé." H. 27½ in. (70 cm.). *Courtesy of Betty Davis.*

1975. Bisque socket head doll that appears to be a long-face Jumeau. The ball jointed composition body is marked Nadaud. The head marked size 9 has a blond wig, stationary glass eyes, applied and pierced ears, and a closed mouth. H. 20 in. (51 cm.). *Courtesy of Sotheby Parke Bernet Inc., N.Y.*

Nain Morys and Her Son John. 1917. Name of soft character dolls made by the *Vale of Clwyd Toymakers.* The faces were handpainted.

Najo.† See **National-Joint Limb Doll Co.**

Nakayama, Shozaburo. 1928–30 and later. Kyoto, Japan. Manufactured dolls.

Nakazawa, Totaro. 1929–30 and later. Kyoto, Japan. Manufactured dolls.

Nalty, Herbert. See **Gourdel Vales & Co.**

Names. McCALL'S MAGAZINE, December 1905, published the names that children had given to the dolls they brought to the doll hospital of Mrs. Charles (Mary Ann) *Marsh* in London.

The favorite names for girl or lady dolls were: Beatrice, Daisy, Gladys, Gwendoline, Lily, and Rosalind. Other names were: Lady Helen, Marion, Matilda, May, Pauline, and Violet.

The favorite names for boy or men dolls were: Drake, Jimmy, Johnny, Kitchener, Napoleon, Nelson, Roberts, Sammy, and Wellington. No doubt some of these dolls belonged to little boys since many of the dolls were named for military heroes.

Dolls were sometimes given the name of the street on which they were made and/or distributed. *Bébé Madeleine* was named for the Blvd. Madeleine.

The Caversham doll was probably named for Caversham Street.

Mon Trésor was made on the rue de Trésor. (See also **Pet Name.**)★

Nancy. 1912–14. Name of a doll with celluloid face and cloth body produced by *Horsman.* It was similar to *Stella* except for the celluloid face. No. H/C; priced 25¢.

Nancy. 1927. Trademark registered in U.S. by *Dennison* for dolls.

Nancy. 1930 and later. Line of dolls made by *Arranbee.* The trademark for these dolls, registered in U.S. in 1930 and renewed in 1951, read, "Nancy//Arranbee//Dolls."

1931: Advertised as an all-composition doll jointed at the neck, shoulders and hips. Ht. 11½ in. (29 cm.). This doll was similar to *Patsy.*

Nancy Ann. 1923. *Mama* doll made by *Effanbee* as a big sister to *Mary Ann.* The doll had composition head and limbs. The arms were curved and there were dimples in the knees. It wore a knee-length organdy dress with elbow-length sleeves trimmed with crocheted lace, and a matching bonnet; lace trimmed lawn undergarments; fancy baby socks and ankle-strap slippers with buckles on the toes. ★

Nancy B. 1909. Dressed doll with bisque head, wig, sleeping eyes, and hair eyelashes, distributed by the *Boston Store* in Chicago. Ht. 19 in. (48 cm.).

Nancy Jane. 1922–23. *Mama* doll made by *Ideal.* It could wink or go to sleep and had a Dutch bob wig. It wore a lace-trimmed flowered lawn dress and a knitted silk cap. The round tag read "LEAD ME HOME//FOR I AM A//WALKING //DOLL//PAT. PEND."

1923: FARM LIFE, a periodical, claimed that they had sent out 2,000 of these dolls as premiums.★

Nancy Lee. 1887. Dressed bisque head doll distributed by *Ehrich Bros.* It was jointed at the neck, shoulders, and hips. Ht. 8 in. (20.5 cm.); priced 25¢.

Nancy Lee. 1911–12. Doll produced and copyrighted by *Horsman.* It was designed by *Helen Trowbridge.* The composition head appears to have been the same as that used for *Annette, Fairy,* and *Polly Prue,* with molded and bobbed hair, a curl on the forehead and painted eyes. It wore a two-piece middy dress of white duck trimmed with red. This doll No. 138, a mate to *Jack Tar,* was one of the American Kid Series.★

Nanette. 1926. Trademark registered in Germany by *M. Kohnstam & Co.*

Nani. 1930. Celluloid dolls made by *Convert.*

Nanikawa, Chujiro. 1930 and later. Kyoto, Japan. Made dolls.

Nankeen (Nanking) Dolls. ca. 1860–1930 and later. Dolls with porcelain heads, porcelain lower arms and legs, and muslin bodies. The earlier dolls usually had china heads and the later ones often had bisque heads.

1860–61: *John D. Robbins* recorded that he imported Nankeen dolls with china heads in sizes 8/0 to 4. These were priced from 75¢ to $4.50 doz. wholesale. Dressed china-head dolls were priced as high as $9.00 a doz. wholesale. China head dolls with wigs came in size 3/0, priced $3.00 a doz. wholesale.

1879–80: Dressed Nankeen dolls sold by *Silber & Fleming* came in various styles and 15 sizes.

1882: Dressed Nankeen dolls sold by Silber & Fleming came in 16 sizes. The ones with fancy hairdos, glass eyes, and painted boots came in 12 sizes. China head Nankeen dolls undressed, having molded black hair, came in 21 sizes. Silber & Fleming also sold bisque head Nankeen dolls.

1889: Silber & Fleming sold undressed Nankeen dolls in 16 sizes and dressed ones in 10 sizes. The Nankeen dolls with bisque heads came in five sizes.

1914: Nankeen dolls with china heads having molded low-brow hairdos sold by *Marshall Field* came in hts. 9 and 11½ in. (23 and 29 cm.). Bisque-head Nankeen dolls sold by Marshall Field had hairdos representing girls. Hts. 8½ and 11½ in. (21.5 and 29 cm.). The bisque head Nankeen dolls with boys' hairdos came only in the 11½ in. (29 cm.) hts.

1920–21: Nankeen dolls made in Japan were imported and distributed by *Morimura.*

1926: Nankeen dolls imported from Japan or China were distributed by *Berrick Bros.*

1928: Nanking dolls were advertised by *C. F. Kling.*

Nano. 1930. Celluloid doll made by *Convert.*

Nap-Time. 1928. Line of dressed dolls made of a crepe fabric stuffed with cotton, handpainted features, distributed by *Butler Bros.* The trade names were Tiny Tod and Little Girl. Ht. 12 in. (30.5 cm.); price $4.00 doz. wholesale.

Nathan, Fernand, & Cie. 1925–29. Paris. Made cutout cloth dolls that were to be stuffed with kapok, wool, sawdust or bran. Each doll came with its miniature version on the sheet. The trade names of these dolls were: *Aïcha* (a black doll), *Arlequin, Denise,* Jean-Jacques, *Lisette,* Madelon, *Poum* (a larger version of Jean-Jacques), *Suzy* and *Zette* (a larger version of Madelon). Hts. 27 to 80 cm. (10½ to 31½ in.).

Nathan, R. & W. 1912. Frankfurt, Germany. Applied for a German patent (D.R.G.M.) for decorating dolls' shoes.

National (Nation's). See **Le National.**

National Doll Co. 1923–30 and later. New York City. Made *Mama* dolls and were licensed by *Voices, Inc.* to use their patented mama voices and criers.

1924: Made *Betsy Ross* dolls. Their sole agent was *Borgfeldt.* (See Ills. 1976, 1977 and 1978.)★

National Doll & Glass Eye Manufacturing Co. Ltd. 1919–20. Manchester, Eng. Made fully jointed kid body dolls with moving eyes and glass eyes for dolls.

National Doll League. 1915–17. London. League formed to make money for the Red Cross, advertised the patented *Doll Exerciser,* "British born and bred."

National Doll Outfit Co. 1921–30. New York City. Made complete outfits for dolls, including stockings.

National French Fancy Novelty Co. See **Bergfeld, Sol, & Son.**

National Joint-Limb Doll Co. 1917–22. New York City. Made Najo[†] and Miss Najo[†] dolls.

1918: Bisque head dolls on ball-jointed composition bodies with patented joint so that the doll could sit or stand. Some of the thighs and upper arms were made of wood. The dolls had sleeping eyes, human hair wigs in different colors. Besides the dolls representing babies and girls there were large display dolls and little all-bisque dolls called "Najo bisque dolls." These dolls allegedly resembled *Charles M. Bergmann* or *Kestner* dolls.★

National Merchandise Supply Co. 1890–92. Chicago, Ill. Handled rubber dolls.

1892: The dolls with molded hair wore chemises. Jointed dolls, ht. 9 in. (23 cm.), cost $1.25 for the white version and $1.30 for the black version. Dolls without joints, 10½ in. (26.5 cm.) high, cost 75¢, and 12 in. (30.5 cm.) high, cost $1.25.

National Patent Products Co. 1923. Newark, N.J. Manufactured three kinds of voices for dolls which they claimed were patented. These voices were mama voices, crying voices and "cat's meow voices."

National Toy Manufacturing Co. See **Q. B. Toy and Novelty Co.**

Natura. 1927. Trademark registered in Germany by *Dr. Paul Hunaeus* for dolls and heads of dolls.

Natural Doll Co. 1914–30 and later. New York City. Manufactured composition dolls' heads, arms and legs. Used "It's Natural" as a trademark.

1914: Company was established.

1926: Advertised that moving eyes were their specialty.

1927: Member of the *American Doll Manufacturers' Association.*

1929: Made smiling baby dolls' heads.

1931: Advertised that they had made dolls' parts for leading American doll manufacturers since 1917. They made *Mama Dolls,* baby dolls, the *Just-Lyk* line of dolls and *Ritzi.*

1965: Still in business.

Nature Babies. 1912–15. Line of composition head baby dolls made by *Horsman.* The line included 20 styles. Priced 50¢ to $10.00.★

Nature Children. 1921–23. Trade name for a line of dolls made by *Amberg.*★

N D Co

N. D. Co.
© 1923

1977–1978. Marks on composition heads probably made by the Natural Doll Co. but possibly made by the National Doll Co.

Naughty (Der Unart). 1915–27 and probably later. *Kämmer & Reinhardt* obtained a German patent (D.R.P.) for a mechanism whereby the eyes of the dolls stayed open when it was laid down horizontally but a handle released the eyes so that they would close and become sleeping eyes. This feature was found on some of the character dolls. The n incised after the mold number does not refer to the Naughty mechanism but to the new (neuer) mold style of the head.★

Naughty Eyes. 1927. Name of an *Effanbee* dressed *Mama* doll with composition head, arms and legs, distributed by

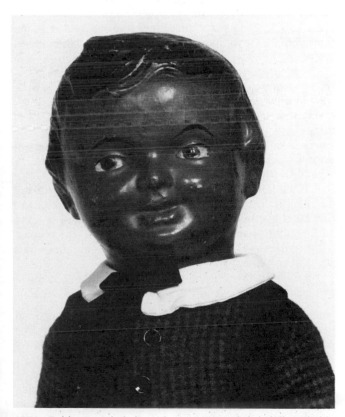

1976. Cold press dark brown composition head doll probably made by the Natural Doll Co. It has molded black hair, brown painted eyes, and a closed mouth. The flange neck fits into a cloth body with gauntlet type composition hands. Disk-type joints are at the hips and shoulders. Original footwear with striped stockings forming the leg. Embossed mark on head: "N D Co." H. 14 in. (35.5 cm.). *Courtesy of the Margaret Woodbury Strong Museum. Photo by Harry Bickelhaupt.*

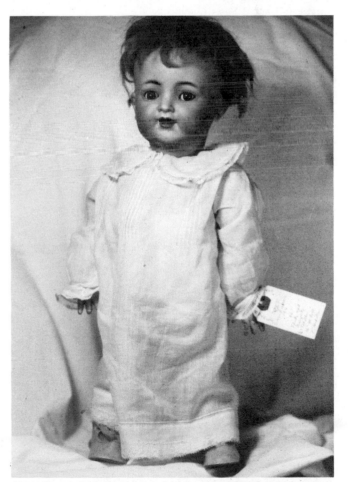

1979. Simon & Halbig bisque head with patented Naughty (Der Unart) eyes. That is the eyes can be fixed by moving a lever so that they stay open when the doll is laid down. It has a wig. Mark on head: "K & R //SIMON & HALBIG//126//36." The 126 is the mold number and the 36 (14 in.) is the height in cm. *Courtesy of Helen Read. Photo by Steven Read.*

Montgomery Ward. It had a mohair wig, sleeping eyes that rolled from side to side, hair eyelashes, open mouth, and teeth. Four hts. 14½, 16, 18, and 21 in. (37, 40.5, 45.5, and 53.5 cm.); priced $2.19 to $5.39.

Naughty Marietta. See **Miss Coquette.**

Naughty Sisters. See **Three Little Sisters.**

Nautical Nancy. 1914. Name of a cloth doll made by *Dean.*

Navy Boy. 1917. Stuffed leather doll with colored features made by the *Western Art Leather Co.* It wore a sailor suit and cap with "U.S.N." and an anchor on it.

Naylor, John. 1826–27. London. Made dolls.

Ne Plus Ultra.[†] See **Butler Bros.**

Neale, T. 1920. London. Made celluloid faces for dolls.

Neapolitan Flower Girl. 1878. Name of a lady-type doll with jointed neck, dressed in a silk costume. Ht. 13½ in. (34 cm.).

Near East Industries. 1920–30s and later. Athens. The Near East Foundation sponsored the making of cloth dolls by Greek refugees. See Ill. 1980.

Nebel & Seelhoff. 1887 and possibly other years. Paris. Advertised supplies for making dolls' heads in a German

1980. A cloth doll with molded, painted face made by Greek refugees in the 1930s for the Near East Industries. This doll with a mustache is costumed as an Albanian. H. 8 in. (20.5 cm.). *Coleman Collection.*

ceramic trade journal (SPRECHSAAL) published in Coburg, Thür. Their advertisement read, "For Dolls' head-making we recommend our admittedly superior Flesh and Cheek colors 'à la Jumeau' . . . also the finest French porcelain paste."

This important advertisement was found by the Ciesliks and indicates that some of the porcelain paste used for bisque dolls' heads came from France. It should be noted that *Kestner* later obtained some of his porcelain supplies from Bohemia. These two facts emphasize the international aspect of manufacturing dolls.

Neck Joints. Some of the heads in the second half of the 1800s ended in a flat rim that fitted over a wooden dowel. This method was used especially for untinted bisque heads to enable the head to turn.

Most of the neck joints from around the third quarter of the 1800s up until about 1928 were composed of a neck ending in a dome shape that fitted into a socket in the shoulders, which enabled the head to move in many directions. However, this neck construction formed an unsightly line which was often hidden with a choker bead necklace. In France *Schmitt & Fils* made some early attempts to make the neck joint with the reverse arrangement of the ball and socket. See Ill. 1675 in the first COLLECTOR'S ENCY-CLOPEDIA OF DOLLS.

Around 1927 with the introduction of *Patsy* the necks began to be made in the reverse position with the neck ending in a dome shape that fitted into the socket at the bottom of the head, thus eliminating the line at the base of the neck.

Flange necks were also popular for heads but they could only turn horizontally. Flange-type necks with grooves were sometimes used in the late 1800s. More often a flange neck had a rim with a slight projection. An example of these flange necks on dolls are the neck joints on *Bye-Lo Babies, My Dream* Baby and so forth. Here the projection of the rim fitted under the cloth at the top of the body which was drawn together with a string.

In the late 1920s *Amberg* produced a New Born Baby type doll named *Baby Nod* for which a patent (D.R.G.M.) had been granted. It had a ball neck which fitted into the socket in the head and into the shoulder piece which had a flange edge over which the neckline of the cloth body was sewn. (See Ill. 201.)

Similar ball neck joints were incorporated into many of the segmented wooden dolls.

Necklaces. In the early 1800s dolls often wore colored beaded necklaces. The small beads formed a V with the point attached to the neckline of the doll's dress. (See Ills. 69 A & B in THE COLLECTOR'S BOOK OF DOLLS' CLOTHES.)

In the 1860s and 70s *Ed Rocharde* produced bisque dolls' heads with necklaces having parts through which scenes could be viewed. (See Ill. 2230.)

Bisque socket-head dolls of the better grades, usually originally had a choker-type necklace often of pearls to hide the neck joints. The *E. J. Jumeau* dolls sometimes wore necklaces having the initial "J."

China-head dolls with molded hair sometimes had molded necklaces; these included: 1901 *Vanity Fair*, 1902 *Jeweled* and 1904 *Daisy.*

1981A & B. Highly decorated untinted bisque shoulder head that has a flanged flat swivel neck. The blonde hair is caught up in a green snood trimmed with pink luster band, feathers and a tassel. The eyes are painted blue and the mouth is closed. The shoulder plate is decorated with molded gold bead necklace with a crucifix. V shaped luster ruching with a blue fan shaped ruching in the lower part of the V. H. of head 4¾ in. (12 cm.). *Courtesy of Sara Kocher.*

1982. Untinted bisque head with a swivel flange type neck joint under the neck band. The head has molded blonde hair, molded blue eyes, pierced ears, closed mouth, cloth body, bisque lower arms and legs. The boots are molded. H. 14½ in. (37 cm.). *Courtesy of Estelle Johnston.*

1983A & B. A bisque head with a flat type neck joint. There are three small holes in the crown under the brown wig. The head has stationary blue glass eyes, a closed mouth. The body is composition probably with a dowel at the top. Mark on head "5." H. 13 in. (33 cm.). Circumference of head 7 in. (18 cm.). *Courtesy of Betty Lou Weicksel.*

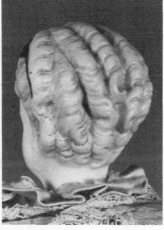

1985A & B. Socket bisque shoulder head with molded and painted features including the blond hair and eyes. Molded in the hair is a bow. There are both the upper and lower eyelashes. The body is cloth with bisque limbs. **B.** shows the mass of curls in back. H. without legs 8¾ in. (22 cm.). *Courtesy of Robert and Katrin Burlin.*

1984. China socket head on a china shoulder plate can turn in many directions. It has a blond wig, painted blue eyes and a closed mouth. The cloth body has china limbs. H. 12½ in. (31.5 cm.). H. of shoulder head 3¼ in. (8 cm.). *Courtesy of Sara Kocher.*

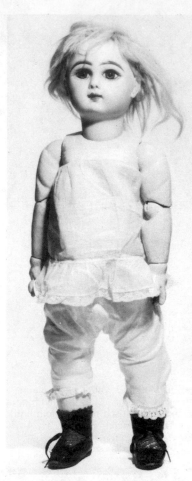

1986. Bisque Jumeau doll with a socket neck joint. It has a wig, stationary blue eyes, pierced ears, closed mouth, and a ball jointed composition body. Mark on head: "Tête Jumeau." Mark on body: "Jumeau, Medaille d'Or." H. 19 in. (48 cm.). *Courtesy of Sotheby Parke Bernet Inc., N.Y.*

Nedco. See **Utley Co.**

Neg. (Neger [Black]). 1903–16 and probably other years. Jointed felt character doll made by *Steiff* and distributed by *Borgfeldt*. Ht. 35 cm. (14 in.); priced $1.85 in 1913 in New York.

Negel, C. (née Andrews).[†] See **Nagel, C.**

Negro Dolls.[†] See **Black Dolls.**

Negro Dude. Ca. 1904–24. Name of *Schoenhut* wooden dolls that wore a high hat, long coat, checked trousers and carried a cane.

1924: Came in two sizes.★

Nehren, Ambros. See **Niko, Ferdinand.**

Neiff, Edmund. 1904. Nürnberg, Bavaria. Applied for a German patent (D.R.G.M.) for making articles of clothing for dolls.

Neiff, G. 1902. Nürnberg, Bavaria. Applied for a German patent (D.R.G.M.) for producing articles of clothing for dolls without the use of hand labor.

Neissner (Neisser), A. C. 1907–30. Vienna. Made dolls.

Nekola, Rudolf. 1800's. Viechtau near Gmunden in the Balkans. A *Verleger* who collected and distributed wooden dolls made in the homes of this area.

Nelke Corp. 1917–30. Philadelphia, Pa. As early as 1901 the company made lisle underwear for women and children. In 1917 the idea arose of making dolls for charity out of their stockinet fabric. The success of these dolls led to the making of dolls in commercial quantities which were sold all over the U.S. by 1919. By 1920 *Weeks & Co.* handled Nelke dolls in England. *E. A. Runnells* was the Nelke distributor at first.

1918: Faces were handpainted and no two were alike. Clothes in assorted styles were sewed on the dolls. Caps or toques were on the dolls' heads. The earliest dolls were made in black and orange.

1920: By this year Nelke was using red and green or blue and green, as well as white also for the dolls. The dolls were patented. Hts. 11 and 14 in. (28 and 35.5 cm.); priced 98¢. Nelke Boy, style No. 112, was produced.

1921: Nelke Girl came in white trimmed with blue, blue trimmed with white, or rose trimmed with white. Nelke Boy came in blue, green, orange, red, rose, and white.

Nelke Romper came in light blue, pink, or white.

Nelke Clown came in black and orange, black and green, blue and orange, red and green, red and white, or white and blue. Each had a matching cap.

1922: Same types of dolls as in 1921 but more sizes. Faces varied; most of the larger dolls had open-closed mouths but all had smiling mouths.

Dolls came dressed or ready to be sewed together. Price 50¢ and up. *Sears* advertised that the dolls had no pins.

1923: Produced 400,000 dolls a year and used the trade mark "The World's Happiest Family." According to their advertisements Nelke no longer used brazen orange, red or deep blue, instead they used the new Parisian shades called "Citrine, Mayflower, Confetti, Bluebird and Rosewood." The Nelke Boy, Nelke Clown, Nelke Girl and Nelke Cop were white, pink, light orange, or blue and came in four hts. 10, 12, 14, and 16 in. (25.5, 30.5, 35.5, and 40.5 cm.).

The Nelke Boy and Nelke Clown in pink and orange also came in an 8 in. (20.5 cm.) ht. Other styles of dolls included Indians, *Kewpies,* Sailors, and Imps. The Imps had voices, ht. 10 in. (25.5 cm.). *Hitz, Jacobs & Kassler* distributed these dolls.

1924: Features and hair handpainted, claimed to be water proof. The patented bodies were one-piece stockinet. Indian Maid doll had a feather in its headwear and came in three sizes. The Kewpies in two sizes cost 50¢ and $1.00. The Nelke Sailor dolls wore a white or dark blue sailor's uniform. *Butler Bros.* advertised the Nelke Boy, Girl, Clown, and Policeman as being 8½, 12, and 14 in. (21.5, 30.5, and 35.5 cm.).

1925: Dolls priced 50¢, 75¢ and $1.00. They registered in the U.S. their trademark of the name NELKE in a diamond-shaped frame. This trademark had been in use since 1919.

1926: The seven style dolls in the Nelke series came in five heights; four of these were also made in a 30 in. (76 cm.) ht. An even larger Nelke clown was exhibited in Philadelphia at the Sesquicentennial.

1927: Butler Bros. advertised the Girl and Clown, ht. 8½ in. (21.5 cm.); and the Girl and Boy, ht. 12 in. (30.5 cm.). Some of these dolls wore a worsted bow tie.

1928: Advertised that the dolls were made of "Powder Puff, knitted fabric, and silk in the brightest colors." There were 60 new numbers ranging in price from 25¢ to $3.00 each. Among these were Bo-Peep, Dutch Boy, Dutch Girl, and Cuddles, 10 in. (25.5 cm.) tall. Cuddles was only $2.00 doz. wholesale while the others with two tone bodies were $3.90 doz. wholesale. The Nelke dolls were distributed by *A. S. Ferguson.*

1929: The factory was enlarged and a finer stockinet cloth with a silky look began to be used. The faces and hair were still being painted by hand. The dolls were stuffed with kapok. One of the Nelke dolls represented a soldier. Butler Bros advertised Bo-Peep, Dutch Boy, Dutch Girl, and Cuddles. (See Ills. 905, 1987–1990.)★

Nellfoy & Co. (Nell Foy). 1916–21. Chelsea, London. Made dolls of original design in large quantities, especially wax-over-composition dolls. Artists were employed in the factory to make designs and models. Models could be supplied to order. Also the molds for casting the various parts of the dolls were made in the factory. The baby dolls had chubby faces with "iris" eyes, and bodies with "natural" hands and fingers and stocky legs. The dolls representing "early grown-up" children had jointed bodies, cloth bodies, or kid bodies. Nellfoy dolls came dressed or undressed. The dressed dolls represented Bo-Peep; Jack and Jill; Mary, Mary; Red Riding Hood; or were in Irish, Welsh, Scottish, or Russian peasant costumes.★

Nelson-Young Manufacturing Co. See **Pollyanna Co.**

Nemo. See **Little Nemo.**

Nenco.[+] See **New Era Novelty Co.**

Néné. 1927–28. Name of a felt doll made by *Lenci* as No. 700/5. It represented a school-age girl wearing a dress with a high waistline and a full skirt covering the knees.

Nénette. 1913–18. Doll designed by *Poulbot* and distributed by the large stores in Paris such as Galeries *Lafayette*. It wore a checked pinafore or apron and was a mate to *Rintintin*. Ht. 36 cm. (14 in.); price $1.78. See THE COLLECTOR'S BOOK OF DOLLS' CLOTHES, Ill. 639.

Nénette. 1916. All-bisque doll with molded hair and features, jointed with wire at the shoulders and hips. It wore crocheted clothes and was sold in Paris. *Rintintin* was its mate. Ht. 3 cm. (1¼ in.).

Nénette (Ninette) and Rintintin. 1917–19. *Mascot* dolls first created in Paris out of wool yarn, silk, knitting cotton or even dried vegetables. These dolls, most popular as mascots during German air raids and bombardments, were dressed in French or American military uniforms, as Red Cross Nurses, Alsatian peasants, black people and so forth. These good luck charms were worn by Parisians and poilus for protection. The soldiers in the field carried them in their pockets. Women wore them on cords around their necks. A pair made of blue and white woolly yarn with features of crimson embroidery silk belongs to the Newark Museum in New Jersey. Ht. 2 in. (5 cm.).

1918: DELINEATOR gave directions for making Nénette and Rintintin from knitting cotton or yarn left over from sweaters. A rose colored dress with a blue sash was suggested for Nénette but any colors could be used.

Claretie in LES ARTS FRANÇAIS, "Les Jouets," showed an extensive variety of Nénette and Rintintin dolls made of wool, silk, and even dried vegetables that were made in *Mme. Lazarski*'s workshop during the bombardments of Paris in March to July 1918.

1919: Mlle. de Bittencourt was in charge of the Nénette and Rintintin dolls shown at a London doll exhibit for charity sponsored by Mrs. Lloyd George and the ladies of the British court.

1927: Edward F. Schlee, co-pilot of the airplane "Pride of Detroit" on its successful trans-Atlantic flight to London, took the Nénette and Rintintin dolls that had been carried by a French officer during World War I. The French officer had survived the war unscathed. (See Ills. 1991 and 1992.)

Nerville. Early 1800s. Paris. A doll shop that made dolls.

Nesthäkchen (The smallest baby a little spoiled). 1927. Trademark registered in Germany by *Adolf Hülss* for dolls.

Nestler, Arthur Rudolf, and Walter, Richard. 1922–25. Wiesau near Annaberg, Germany. Obtained a German patent (D.R.P.) for making dolls of a plastic composition material. The dolls had hollow jointed bodies.

Nestler & Co. Ca. 1930. Hamburg, Germany. Distributed *Kestner* dolls.

Netherlands. Dutch regional costumes have been favorites throughout the 1800s and early 1900s. Dolls with papier-mâché heads, wigs or molded hair, glass eyes, wooden arms and cloth bodies were often dressed in various Dutch costumes during the last quarter of the 1800s. See Ill. 2196.

Gebr. Douwes, R. Eekhoff[+], *Gerzon, P. J. Trynes* and *Van Tussenbroek* made and/or dressed dolls in the Netherlands. Eekhoff used *Simon & Halbig* heads while other manufacturers often used *Armand Marseille* heads.

Many American companies dressed some of their dolls in Dutch costumes for example *Averill Manufacturing Co.* and *Horsman*.

Queen Wilhelmina was an important collector of dolls in the late 1800s.

Neugebauer (Neubauer), Albert. 1930 and later. Mönchroden, Bavaria. Made accessories for dolls.

Neugebauer (Neubauer), Ed. 1930 and later. Mönchroden, Bavaria. Manufactured dolls.

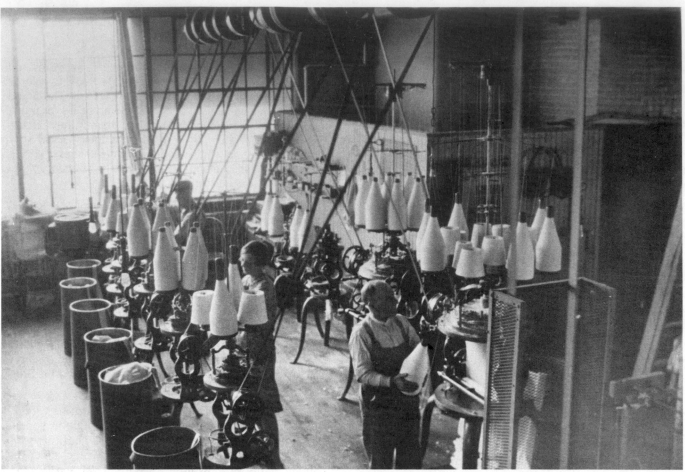

1987. Manufacturing the stockinet fabric for the Nelke Dolls. On the left the threads are being wound on the spindles. On the right the stockinet fabric is being created from the thread by machines. *Photo courtesy of Jean Nelke West and Mrs. Moreland G. Smith.*

1988. Scene in the Nelke factory. The women in the foreground appear to be painting the dolls by hand. Some of the finished dolls are also shown. The two women standing are probably assembling parts of the dolls. *Photo courtesy of Jean Nelke West and Mrs. Moreland G. Smith.*

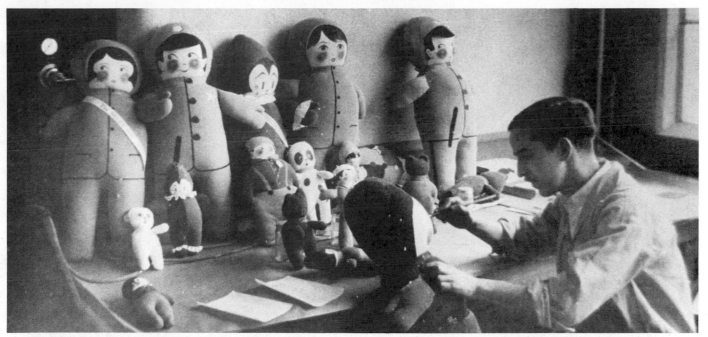

1989. Various sizes and types of Nelke stockinet dolls produced in the 1920s. The artist is shown painting the face of one of the larger dolls. This old photograph was reproduced by Mrs. Moreland G. Smith and made available by Jean Nelke West; both ladies are grandchildren of the original owner.

1990. Mark used for Nelke stockinet cloth dolls.

*Acceptez ce charmant fétiche
Il est le seul assurément
Avec lequel l'on peut se fiche
Des bombes et du bombardement*

Nénette, Rintintin et Radadou
Porte-Bonheur

1992. Postcard showing the French mascot dolls during World War I. These dolls were known as Nénette and Rintintin.

1991. Nénette & Rintintin dolls created from silk, wool and even dried vegetables by Mme. Lazarski's workshop and used as mascots during the bombardment of Paris in March and July 1918. This is an illustration from an article by Léo Claretie in LES ARTS FRANÇAIS, 1918. Note that there were black dolls as well as white dolls and at least four of the couples carry a baby.

Neugebauer (Neubauer), Heinrich. 1898. Neustadt near Coburg, Thür. Made cloth bodies for dolls.

Neumayer-Somossy, Elizabeth. See **Paar, Katarina.**

Neumeister, H. 1883. Thür. Manufacturer, on the committee to found the Sonneberg Industrial School.

Neumeyer, Joseph. 1859 and probably other years. Vienna. Handled wooden dolls of the type made in Berchtesgaden. He was Merchant of the Court for the Imperial Castles.

Neumont, Maurice Louis Henri. 1918–30. Paris. Painter and lithographer, born 1868, died 1930. He was a Chevalier of the Legion of Honor and won a gold medal in 1920. During World War I he created dolls and made war posters.

Neustadter & Son. 1926. New York City. Handled and/or made dolls.

Neutrality Kid. 1917. Dolls with composition head and hands on a cloth body distributed by *Butler Bros.* It had painted hair and features, body with jointed shoulders and hips; dressed in a felt Dutch boy costume. Ht. 30 in. (76 cm.). This may also have been called Neutrality Jim⁺.

Neverbreak. 1914. Name of a doll with a metal head, mohair wig, glass eyes, pink "silesia" (cloth) body. The jointed arms appear to be composition below the elbows. Hts. 15, 17, and 20½ in. (38, 43, and 52 cm.).

New Baby Darling. See **Baby Darling.**⁺

New Born Babe. 1914–26 and later. Made by *Amberg.* One of these dolls with a bisque head, composition body was marked "© L. Amberg & Son//Germany//886//5/0 K." Ht. 8 in. (20.5 cm.).

1926: Price 50¢ and up. (See also **New Born Basket Babe** and **New Born Bottle Babe.**)★

New Born Baby (New Born Bébé, Nouveau-né). Ca. 1910–30 and later. Generic name for dolls representing an infant. The name first seems to appear in the Paris store catalogs for bent limb character babies with bisque heads.

Ca. 1910: *Printemps* advertised New Born Baby, ht. 35 cm. (14 in.); price $1.30.

1912: *Louvre* store advertised a New Born Baby wearing a chemise and sitting on a cushion. Ht. 30 cm. (12 in.); price $1.90.

1913: Louvre store advertised undressed New Born Babies in seven hts. 20, 25, 31, 37, 42, 48, and 65 cm. (8, 10, 12, 14½, 16½, 19, and 25½ in.); priced 58¢ to $3.75. The dressed New Born Babies wore a short baby dress, jacket, knitted wool cap and bootees. These came in five hts. 31, 37, 42, 48, and 65 cm. (12, 14½, 16½, 19, and 25½ in.); priced $2.30 to $7.80.

TOYS AND NOVELTIES reported 18 New Born Babies had been added to the line, each one dressed in white.

1915: Louvre store advertised New Born Babies with fully jointed, straight legged bodies in six hts. 34, 38, 46, 52, 61, and 70 cm. (13½, 15, 18, 20½, 24, and 27½ in.); priced $1.70 to $5.00 in a chemise and $4.00 to $11.00 dressed.

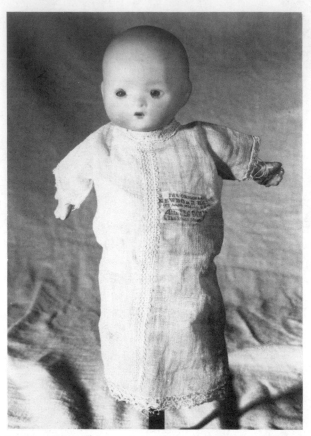

1993. New Born Babe made by Louis Amberg with a Recknagel bisque head has painted blond hair, sleeping blue glass eyes, open mouth and a flange neck on a cloth body with composition lower arms. The original chemise has a cloth label reading: "THE ORIGINAL//NEW BORN BABE//© Jan. 9th. 1914. No. GA45520 //AMBERG DOLLS//The World Standard." Mark on head "L.A. & S.// R A 241 5½//GERMANY." H. 8½ in. (21.5 cm.). *Coleman Collection.*

New Born Babies with sleeping eyes, dressed in a chemise, six hts. 32, 37, 42, 49, 58, and 66 cm. (12½, 14½, 16½, 19½, 23, and 26 in.); priced $1.30 to $4.40.

1916: Printemps advertised New Born Babies with mohair wigs, sleeping eyes, dressed in a baby dress, jacket, knitted cap and booties came in six hts. 32, 37, 42, 49, 57, and 65 cm. (12½, 14½, 16½, 19½, 22½, and 25½). The same model in chemise came in the same hts. plus 22 and 25 cm. (8½ and 10 in.); the smallest doll in a chemise cost 65¢ and the largest one dressed cost $11.00.

1921: *L'Hotel de Ville* advertised New Born Babies with short hair wig, sleeping eyes, bent limbs wearing a lace-trimmed chemise. They came in eight hts. 21, 24, 31, 37, 44, 49, 57, and 64 cm. (8½, 9½, 12, 14½, 17½, 19½, 22½, and 25 cm.).

The same dolls but with hair eyelashes and fully jointed bodies came in six hts. 33, 38, 46, 52, 60, and 68 cm. (13, 15, 18, 20½, 23½, and 27 in.).

Lesser quality undressed babies with sleeping eyes. Hts. 20 and 24 cm. (8 and 9½ in.).

1925: TOYS AND NOVELTIES reported that one fourth of the dolls sold were New Born infant types.

PLAYTHINGS in 1925 reported on New Born Baby dolls in London at Christmas time. One wholesaler said, "We've secured a reserve stock of one-half a million in various sizes. The New Born Baby doll is the biggest success we have had for years."

In the packing department of only one London warehouse many thousands of these dolls were dispatched to retailers on a single day. Some of the dolls had the wailing voice of a two or three weeks old baby. They were dressed in long white dresses.

1928: *Kestner* made some of the heads for New Born Babies.

The New Born Baby dolls with sleeping eyes wearing a short baby dress were distributed by *Hartley Sports Stores* in Australia. Hts. 12 and 16 in. (30.5 and 40.5 cm.).

1928–30: *Bon Marché* advertised New Born Baby with composition head, sleeping eyes, cloth body, a mama voice, long baby dress, and a pacifier. Hts. 30–31 cm. (12 in.). (Also see **Baby Dolls, Infant dolls,** and **Newly Born.**)

New Born Basket Babe. 1925–26. *Amberg's New Born Babe* was put into a basket with a doll blanket and sold for 65¢ to $1.25. When a pillow and mattress were also added the price rose to $5.00.

New Born Bottle Babe. 1926. *Amberg's New Born Baby* was made so that it appeared to drink a milk-colored fluid from a bottle when its arm raised the bottle to its lips. The bottle filled itself when the arm and bottle were lowered. The arm and bottle were claimed to be unbreakable. These dolls came with either bisque or composition heads.

New Century Dolls. 1917–18. Dressed composition-head dolls made by *Nottingham.*

New Doll Co. 1913–15. New York City. Company was founded by Santi Franco, John Jannonone and Emil Declyne to manufacture dolls.

New Eccles Rubber Works.† See **Eccles.**

New England Doll Co. (Nedco).† See **Utley Co.**

New England Toy Co. 1918. Boston, Mass. Manufactured dolls with composition heads and stuffed cloth or imitation leather bodies. It was claimed that the latter were washable. The dolls came dressed or undressed. There was an affiliation with the *Marks Bros.*

New Era Novelty Co. (Nenco). 1914–16. Newark, N.J. Made dolls with composition heads, bent limbs, cork-stuffed cloth bodies, and all-composition dolls. They used the acronym Nenco. *William E. Peck* was their London agent in 1915 and 1916.

1915: Advertised in England that their dolls came in four sizes. The company was amalgamated with the Politzer Toy Manufacturing Company† and they purchased a new plant in Newark, New Jersey. They advertised in TOYS AND NOVELTIES that they made high-grade dolls which they described as follows:

"In the 'New Era' doll, the house has a product that is

certainly an innovation in the toy trade. It is made of a secret composition by a new process, using a hydraulic pressure of over 3,000 pounds, and it is guaranteed unbreakable, unburnable and waterproof as well.

"The weight of this material is about one-third that of the ordinary unbreakable doll, and it takes a very high and excellent finish. The arms, legs and head of the doll are jointed in a new and unusual manner, each part being controlled by a separate spring, and the loss of an arm or leg will not affect the other members in any way.

"In addition to this feature number there is also a variety of original character dolls such as soldiers, sailors, jockeys, baby dolls, etc."

The doll pictured was a bent-limb baby, all-composition, jointed at the neck, shoulders, and hips. The hair was molded and both the head and body appear to have had good modelling.

TOYS AND NOVELTIES advertised eight styles of 26 in. (66 cm.) dolls for $2.00 each.

1916: All-composition bent-limb Nenco baby dolls came with or without wigs, dressed or undressed in four sizes. The larger dolls were jointed at the neck. Some of the dressed dolls wore a one-piece garment tied on the shoulders and pinned together between the legs like a diaper.★

New Toy Manufacturing Co. 1912–21. New York City; factory in Newark, N.J., from 1916 on; successor in 1918 was the New Toy Co. Max *Bing, Meyer Yondorf* and Alvin Cahn were the proprietors. Made composition character dolls.

THE NEW TOY CO.

1994. Mark used by the New Toy Manufacturing Co. for their composition dolls.

1913: Sales representative was *Riemann, Seabrey Co.*

1916: Employed 500 people who worked three shifts in the factory. Made all-composition dolls with sleeping eyes.

1917: Made composition-head character dolls with or without wigs. The heads were on cloth bodies. They claimed the composition was unpeelable and washable; price 50¢ to $1.00.

1918: All American material used in their dolls; priced 25¢ to $10.00. Style No. 151 all-composition doll had jointed wrists and ankles. Another doll represented *Red Riding Hood.* Style No. 300 was a baby doll in short dress with rattle on ribbon around its neck.

1919: All "New bisc" composition dolls came in 11 heights; some had moving eyes, bobbed hair and bangs style wigs. They had steel spring joints at the shoulders and diagonal hip joints. Style No. 170 W, a bent-limb baby with bobbed hair and bangs wig, wore a chemise. Style No. 200 was an all-composition, molded hair *Kewpie* type, jointed at the shoulders. It had bent arms and the legs were apart.

There were hundreds of styles of dolls with cloth bodies and "New bisc" heads.

1920: Advertised *British Ceramic* heads and an all-composition walking doll with human hair wig, wearing a tucked dress, white socks and kid shoes. Ht. 24 in. (61 cm.).★

New York Doll Co. 1921–30 and later. New York City. Manufactured dolls including novelty dolls.★

New York Rubber Co. 1851–1923. New York City. Made dressed and undressed rubber dolls. The clothes on the dressed dolls were often molded. In the early years they made rubber shoulder heads with molded hair.

1869: *H. G. Norton* was a wholesale distributor.

1922–23: Advertised baby dolls and dolls representing Santa Claus and a French Soldier with molded clothes. (See also **Goodyear Rubber.**)★

New York Stuffed Toy Co. 1924–29. New York City. Made stuffed dolls.

1923: *Riemann, Seabrey* was their agent.

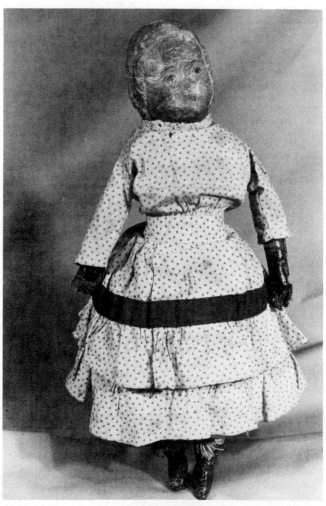

1995. Rubber shoulder head made by the New York Rubber Co. probably in the 1870s. It has molded and painted hair and features. The body appears to have been made by Philip Goldsmith before he put the corsets on his bodies. Original clothes. Marked on inside of shoulders in back: Ill. 1996. H. 14 in. (35.5 cm.) H. of shoulder head 4 in. (10 cm.). *Coleman Collection.*

1996–1997. Mark on shoulders of dolls made by the New York Rubber Co.

1926: New sitting doll that cried when it was lifted up; came in several styles; priced $1.00 and up.

Newly Born. 1927–29. Baby doll with bisque head, painted hair, sleeping glass eyes, shaped cloth or composition body with a voice and composition hands. Distributed by *Butler Bros.* who claimed that the head was modeled from a live baby. Came with long or short dresses.

1927: Bisque head on baby shaped cloth body came in hts. 5½ and 8 in. (14 and 20.5 cm.). Bisque head on toddler body with straight legs jointed at the shoulders and hips. Hts. 11, 12½ and 16 in. (28, 31.5 and 40.5 cm.).

Bisque head on composition body, wearing a long dress and/or a flannel blanket; placed in a white willow basket. Four hts. 8½, 10¼, 13, and 15 in. (21.5, 26, 33, and 38 cm.).

The bisque heads with flange necks to be used on cloth bodies were sold separately and fitted dolls 8 to 18 in. (20.5 to 45.5 cm.).

1928: Bisque head on a bent limb body came with or without the willow basket.

1929: Dolls made with composition heads having painted hair and features on cloth bodies as well as the bisque heads with sleeping eyes. The bisque-head doll was reported only in the 8 in. (20.5 cm.) ht.

Newly Wed's Kid (Baby). Ca. 1910. Composition doll based on the cartoon character of this name drawn by *McManus*. It had a curl on the top of its head and one tooth. Distributed by *Shackman*, it cost 5¢. (See the first COLLECTOR'S ENCYCLOPEDIA OF DOLLS for a cloth version of the Newly Wed Kid.) There were probably other versions.

Newmark, M., Co. 1924. Produced dolls.

Next to Nature. 1918. Line of all-composition dolls made by *Colonial Toy Manufacturing Co.* and distributed by *Butler Bros.* Came in hts. 14, 16½, and 18 in. (35.5, 42, and 45.5 cm.). Hts. 24 and 26 in. (61 and 66 cm.) also had hair eyelashes and movable tongue.★

Nez d' Hareng (Herring's Nose). 1928. Trademark registered in France by *Roger Cartier* for a mascot or a manniquin.

Nibur Novelty Co. 1914–29. New York City. Made composition heads for dolls as well as other dolls' parts. Used a

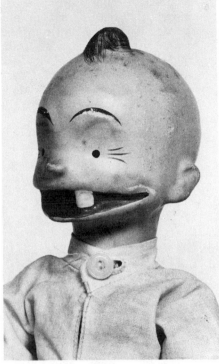

1998A & B. Composition Newly Wed's Kid has molded topknot hair, painted black eyes, open-closed mouth with one upper tooth, and a ball-jointed body. Original clothes. Mark: Ill. 1999. H. 10¼ in. (26 cm.). *Courtesy of the Margaret Woodbury Strong Museum. Photo by Harry Bickelhaupt.*

1999. Mark on the back of the body of the composition Newly Wed's Kid.

2000. Trademark of Nibur Novelty Co.

diamond shaped mark reading: "TRADE MARK//NIBUR//NOVELTY COMPANY.

Nicaput. 1930 and later. Name of a hard rubber or composition doll made by *König & Wernicke.* The name Nicaput means "unbreakable."

1932: Trademark registered in Germany by König & Wernicke for dolls and heads of dolls.

Niceray Établissements. 1928. Paris, and factory at Nice. Name of doll factory operated by *E. L. Raibault.*

Nicette. See **La Poupée Nicette.**

Nicholas, Michel. 1927. Sulphur Springs, Tex. Obtained a U.S. patent for the neck movement of a doll activated by a rod.

Nicholas & Keller. 1920s. France. Made clothes for dolls and was a member of the *Chambre Syndicale.*

Nichols, Florence. 1928. Los Angeles, Calif. She was in charge of the *California Toy Shop,* according to TOY WORLD.

Nickson, Mrs. 1919 and earlier. Tunstall, England. Manufactured dolls.

1919: Fire destroyed her materials and sewing machines.

Nicolet, H. (A.). 1927–30. Paris. Made dolls.

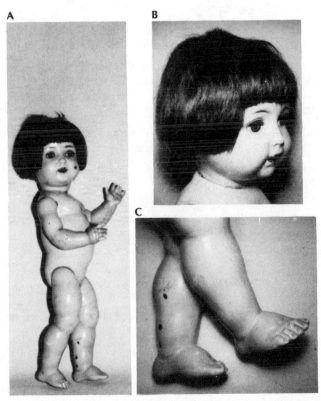

2001A, B & C. Nicaput painted hard rubber doll made by König & Wernicke. It has a wig, sleeping blue glass eyes, open mouth with two upper teeth, and a body jointed at the neck, shoulders, and hips. Mark Ill. 2002. H. 16 in. (40.5 cm.). *Courtesy of Dorothy Annunziato.*

K&W
NICAPUT
38
GERMANY

2002. Mark on hard rubber Nicaput dolls.

Niessner, Anton C. 1852–1910. Vienna. Distributed dolls and dolls' parts made in Austria and elsewhere of wood, porcelain, composition including papier-mâché and metal. The dolls had painted hair, mohair wigs or human hair wigs. The bodies were kid, cloth or jointed composition.

Nifty. 1923–28. Trademark registered in U.S. in 1928 by *Borgfeldt* for dolls.★

Nigger. 1906. Trade name of a black felt doll made by *Steiff* and distributed by *Gamage;* priced 62¢. (See also **Neg.**)

Niggers. 1930. Trade name given to a group of black cloth dolls made by *Chad Valley.* These dolls had their eyes glancing to the side, large mouths and ethnic features.

No. 616/1 wore suspenders and full trousers.

No. 618/1 wore a breast cover, fringe for a skirt and anklets.

No. 623/1 wore a shirt, Dutch-type long trousers, anklets and a hat.

All of the above dolls were 12 in. (30.5 cm.) tall. Other dolls in this group were *Nabob* and *Rajah.*

Nightingale Baby. 1927. Trade name of a doll made by *Ideal.* The name was derived from the doll's costume.

Niko, Ferdinand, and Nehren, Ambros. 1913. Herford, Westphalia, and Achern, Baden. Obtained two German patents (D.R.P.) for dolls' eyes, affixing the wig and a movable tongue.

Nini. 1910–11. Cutout cloth doll named Mademoiselle Nini was made by *Dean* and distributed by *Aux Trois Quartiers.*

Nini. 1925. Name of a cloth doll in a felt costume sold by *Bon Marché.* Four hts. 30, 37, 42, and 50 cm. (12, 14½, 16½, and 19½ in.).

Nini. 1927–28. Name of felt doll made by *Lenci* as No. 500/0. It wore sleeping coveralls with a tiny teddy bear in its pocket. Ht. 21½ in. (54.5 cm.).

Ninette. See **Nénette.**

Ninon. See **Bébé Ninon** and **Poupées Ninon.**

Niquette. 1928. Name of an all-composition dressed doll sold by *Paturel.*

Nisette. 1923–24. Name of a dressed cloth doll sold by the *Louvre* store. Ht. 50 cm. (19½ in.).

Nize Baby. 1927. Doll made by *Averill Manufacturing Co.* in their *Madame Hendren* line and representing the cartoon character created by Milt Gross. It wore a bloomer style baby costume with big felt shoes and had its name on its bib. Nize Baby was distributed by *Sears.*

2003. Mark for Nize Baby doll made by Averill Manufacturing Co.

Nizza. 1928. Line of dolls made by *Farnell.*

Nobbikid (Nobbi Kid). 1914 or earlier–1927. Name of bisque head dolls on five piece composition bodies with molded and painted footwear. They were produced by *Borgfeldt.* The heads were made by Armand Marseille often using mold # 253; other mold numbers such as 323 have been reported. They had round glass eyes looking to the side and a smiling closed mouth. These dolls had a circular tag and were usually about 7 in. (18 cm.) tall.★

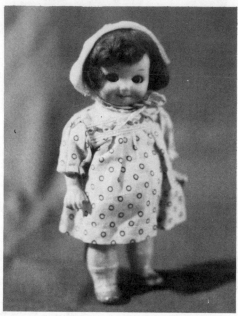

2004A. Bisque head made by Armand Marseille that is probably a Nobbi Kid. It has a wig, stationary glass roguish eyes looking to the side, a closed smiling mouth on a five piece composition body with molded footwear. Original clothes. H. 7 in. (18 cm.). *Courtesy of Gloria Modderno.*

2004B. Mark for Nobbi Kid dolls.

Noble Ned. 1923–27. One of the *Mawaphil* cloth dolls made by *Rushton Co.* It wore a Shriner's hat with sword and crescent on the hat. Came in five hts. up to 24 in. (61 cm.).

Noble & Co. 1880s. Adams, Mass. Advertised dolls on their trade card.

Nobody's Darling. 1924. Cloth doll of plush except for the flat face, made by the *Worthing Toy Factory.* It had round eyes looking to the side and was jointed at the shoulders.

Noce Village. See **Wedding Party.**

Nöckler & Tittel. 1849–1926 and later. Schneeberg, Saxony. Armin Grüning was the successor in 1893 and by 1906 Gustav Gotzke had become a partner.

The January 1925 TOY TRADER gave the following account of the history of the firm of Nöckler & Tittel:

"The firm Noekler & Tittel, manufacturers of dolls and toys, Schneeberg i. Sa. were able to celebrate their 75th anniversary towards the end of November 1924. Founded by A. Peltz in 1849, the enterprise to-day ranges amongst the largest firms in the line, and they employ 180 persons at the works and about 100 home-workers. The firm is one of the not very numerous works that are manufacturing dolls according to the vertical system from the raw material to the finished article in the most varied styles. Generally it is customary in the line to produce one part of the dolls only, or one special type. Noekler & Tittel, though, manufacture all current sorts after own models, and they are in a position to do so with their modern mechanical equipment that is arranged in every way for wholesale production. The production by the firm reaches about 3,000 freight-boxes per year, apart from the large mail-order business. The sole owner of the firm is Armin Grüning, sen., who entered the service of the firm in 1888. The firm maintains extensive exports to all foreign countries on the Continent besides the large inland business. The firm was able, luckily, to maintain manufacture during the war and was spared the many difficulties in procuring work prevailing during the last years, and could keep their plant going all the time. . . . Another remarkable fact can be stated, that the lady manager of the firm, Miss Emma Günther, has celebrated her 50th working anniversary with the firm on the 27th November, 1924."

Their London representative in 1925 was R. E. Thornton.

1889: Advertised cloth dolls, jointed dolls, baby dolls, dolls' house dolls, dolls in swaddling clothes, dolls in regional costumes, dolls' bodies, dolls' clothes including shoes and stockings.

1896: Applied for a German patent (D.R.G.M.) for a composition socket head for ball jointed dolls.

1899: Advertised jointed dolls, dolls in regional costumes; dolls in swaddling clothes; composition dolls' heads; rubber dolls' heads with molded hair or with wigs; dolls' bodies; dolls' shoes and stockings and other accessories. They also repaired dolls.

1904: Applied for a German patent (D.R.G.M.) for a wool doll with head of unbreakable material.

1910: Advertised that they made Parisian type dolls. Their dolls had bisque, celluloid, composition, wood, metal, rubber or "Lithoid" heads, bodies of kid, composition or cloth. The type of dolls included character, reform, art, sport, fashion and dolls dressed in swaddling clothes. There were 100 different models of dressed dolls, 6 to 70 cm. (2½ to 27½ in.) tall.

1911: Applied for a German patent (D.R.G.M.) for dressing baby dolls in diapers.

1913: Applied for a German patent (D.R.G.M.) for a celluloid baby doll with a voice.

Advertised character babies, googly-eyed dolls, wool dolls, dressed dolls, and dolls' bodies.

1914: Advertised character babies; *Täuflinge* (dolls in chemises); woolen dolls; ball jointed dolls marked *Schnee-*

glöckchen (Little Snow Drop); and dressed dolls including those in regional costumes.

1921: The factory employed 300 workers. They advertised baby dolls and ball-jointed dolls.

1926: Advertised in a British trade journal that they employed 300 workers and made baby dolls, jointed dolls including the Snow Drop line of dressed and undressed dolls. They also made accessories and repair parts of dolls. ★

2005. Mark on bisque dolls' heads made by Nöckler & Tittel.

Nölle, Wilh. 1908. Werdohl, Germany. Applied for a German patent (D.R.G.M.) for a jointed doll.

Nollipolli. 1930. Trade name of a doll made by *Kämmer & Reinhardt*. This name was registered as a trademark in Germany.

Nonn & Söhn G. 1907–26. Liegnitz, Silesia. Manufactured dolls.

Nono. 1921–22. Name of a seated doll with its head looking up, advertised by *Bon Marché* store. It came with a cylindrical box on which were the words: "NONO//FETICHE// PORTE BONHEUR" (Nono//Mascot// Brings Happiness). Ht. 17 cm. (6½ in.).

Noona. 1926. Name of *Boudoir*-type doll made by *Katherine Fleischmann*. It represented a French cabaret dancing girl.

Nora. 1920–21. Trade name for a stockinet doll made by *Chad Valley*. It was style No. 24, dressed and with a wig. Ht. 9 in. (23 cm.).

Nordschild, Leo. 1878–1926. Berlin. Produced Bella[+] dressed dolls. Some of these were from the *Mein Liebling* series. By 1926 dolls had roguish eyes and rubber hands.

Noris Puppen. 1905. Name of a patented doll advertised by *Debes*. The doll had a special kind of joints. See Ill. 363. ★

Normandy (Normande). See **French Regional Costume Dolls.**

Normandy Girls. 1914. Dolls advertised by *Butler Bros.* with bisque heads, wigs, sleeping eyes, dressed in costumes with Normandy style caps. Ht. 13¾ in. (35 cm.); priced $4.35 doz. wholesale.

North, Kennedy. Before 1924. Made a doll dressed to represent one of the King's Pipers with its bagpipe in a playing position. Ht. 6 in. (15 cm.). It is possible that he made some of the dolls for Queen Mary's Dolls' House since he was mentioned in a book about this dolls' house.

Norton, H. G., & Co. Ca. 1860–69. New York City. Distributed rubber shoulder heads, representing ladies and children including a black child. One lady head had a snood and flowers in its hair. There were also dressed rubber babies. George B. Thomson was their agent in St. Louis and R. Chamberlin was their agent in Rochester, N.Y. Their dolls were made by the *New York Rubber Co.*

Nos Fillettes (Our Young Girls). 1924. Name of cloth dolls sold by *Printemps.* They wore woolen dress and hat. Hts. 20, 29, and 33 cm. (8, 11½, and 13 in.).

Noso (Circus Performer). 1911. Felt art doll made by *Steiff* dressed as a Circus Performer in a felt coat with tails. Clothes came in assorted colors. Ht. 43 cm. (17 in.).

Nostrils. Pierced nostrils were often found on baby dolls in the second and third decades of the 1900s.★

2006. Pair of bisque head baby dolls with pierced nostrils. Each doll has a wig, open mouth with teeth, and a bent limb composition body. Doll on the left made by Franz Schmidt has sleeping and flirting blue glass eyes. Mark: "F.S. & Co.//1295//65." Note that the 65 in the mark is the height in centimeters. Doll on right made by Ernst Heubach of Köppelsdorf has stationary blue glass eyes. Mark "320.12." H. both dolls 25½ in. (65 cm.). *Courtesy of Sotheby Parke Bernet Inc., N.Y.*

Nosy Rosy. 1918. Trademark registered in U.S. by *Jean Friedman* for dolls. The trademark was written, "Nosy//Rosy."

Notaseme Hosiery Co. 1920–21. Philadelphia, Pa. Assignee of a U.S. patent obtained by *Horace T. Fleischer* for making dolls of knitted fabric.★

Nottingham Toy Industry. 1914–20. Nottingham, England. The company was started by Miss Wallis who first made cloth dolls with composition mask faces. Then they obtained *British Ceramic* heads designed by *Helen Fraser Rock* which were put on *Compolite* bodies and called *Rock China Dolls.* They used the initials N.T.I. which were also found on some of the *Hancock* heads. A shoulder head with a wig, stationary glass eyes, closed mouth, bore the mark "NTI//GIRL//ENGLISH MAKE." Ht. 17 in. (43 cm.).

They also made all-composition dolls and cloth dolls designed by *E. E. Houghton.*

1917: Made *June Babies, New Century* dolls, dressed dolls, and dolls' clothes.

Miss Muriel Moller was the factory agent in London.

1918: Advertised the *Vogue* Rag dolls line.

1919: Made jointed bodies, Compolite, and stuffed bodies. Handled *Daisy Dolls* which included the "Rock china" twins, Joyce & Josylin and Peter and Pauline. Another one of their dolls was called *Victory Baby.*★

NTI
GIRL
ENGLISH MAKE

2007. Mark of the Nottingham Toy Industry.

Noufflard, Mlle. Berthe (Bertha Noufflar). 1916–18. Paris. Born 1886. She was a sculptress and portrait painter who exhibited in the Paris Salons. She created baby and little girl dolls as well as dolls' clothes. Her dolls were dressed in simple clothes.★

Nourrice (Nurse). 1885–1906 and probably other years. Dolls, sold by Paris stores, representing nursemaids for baby dolls.

1885–86: Name of a painted rubber doll with molded clothes advertised by *Petit St. Thomas* as made in Paris. The nurse held a small doll representing a girl by its upstretched arms; priced 13¢.

1903: Name of a doll advertised by *Au Tapis Rouge,* dressed as a nurse in a long cape and bonnet. It held a smaller doll wearing a long baby cloak and hood. Ht. 35 cm. (14 in.); priced 99¢.

1906: Name of a doll advertised by *Aux Trois Quartiers.* It had a composition head and wore a long woolen cape and bonnet. The baby doll in the nurse's arms had long clothes including a long veil that covered its face. Hts. 40, 45, and 50 cm. (15½, 17½, and 19½ in.); priced 98¢ to $1.98. (See also **Bébé Nurse** and **Nurse.**)

Nourrice Parisienne. 1885–86. Name of a doll advertised by *Petit St. Thomas.* The doll had glass eyes, was jointed at the neck, wore a wool and silk long cape and bonnet. It held a baby doll dressed in long clothes. Four hts. 37, 39, 43, and 46 cm. (14½, 15½, 17, and 18 in.); priced $1.75 to $3.70.

Nourse, Mlle. 1918. Paris. Created bébés.

Nouveau-né. See **New Born Baby.**

Nouveaute Bébé. 1911. Name of a doll advertised by *Samaritaine.* The head represented a young infant. It had a wig and wore a chemise. Hts. 36, 43, and 51 cm. (14, 17, and 20 in.); priced 75¢ to $1.15.

Novak. 1927–29. Paris. Made dolls.

Novelty Doll Manufacturing Co. 1923–30. New York City. Made dolls and dolls' parts. Member of the *Doll Parts Manufacturing Association.*

1930: Advertised a new line of dolls called *Favorite.* They made *Mama* dolls and baby dolls. Their dolls had composition heads, arms and legs, and were distributed by jobbers, chain stores, and premium users.

Novelty Manufacturing Co. 1916–22. London. Made dolls' shoes in a variety of sizes, materials and styles.

Novelty Manufacturing Co. 1922. Milwaukee, Wis. Advertised *Eskimo* dolls dressed in sheepskin.

Nowytsky, W. 1925–27. London. Made *Lenci*-type dressed, jointed felt dolls including Ninon dolls. Claimed the dolls were cheaper than bisque-head dolls.

Noxid. See **Dixon, T. A.**

Nucraft Toys. 1930 and later. Wakefield, Mass. Paul K. Guillow, proprietor, made outfits for dolls.

Nude (Nu or Nue). A doll without any clothes. This should not be confused with a doll described as undressed which usually meant wearing a chemise and footwear. In France dolls wearing a chemise were sometimes described as "Nu" or "Nue."

Nudekin. World War I period. British version of a *Kewpie* but lacking wings. Hands were different. A lock of hair came onto the forehead.

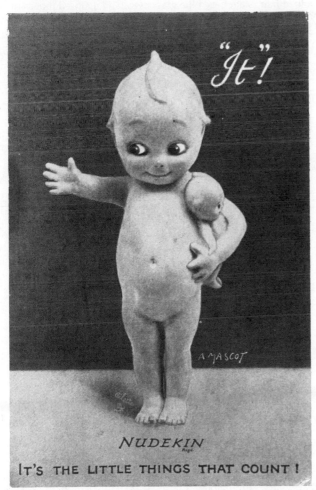

2008. Nudekin, a mascot doll as pictured on a Tuck postcard.

Nugent, B., & Bro. 1900–10 and probably other years. St. Louis, Mo. Advertised a bisque head, ball-jointed body doll imported from Sonneberg. It had a wig, sleeping eyes, openwork stockings, patent leather slippers and a chemise. It was named "*St. Louis Girl.*"

1909: Hts. 19, 22, and 24 in. (48, 56, and 61 cm.); priced $1.00 to $1.50.

1910: Ten hts. 12, 18, 20, 22, 24, 26, 29, 31, 34, and 38 in. (30.5, 45.5, 51, 56, 61, 66, 73.5, 78.5, 86.5, and 96.5 cm.); priced 75¢ to $12.50.★

Nunkey. 1917. Name registered by *Heath Robinson* for a mascot doll. It was one of the *Tah-Toys* with a large melon shaped mouth and wore a tall conical hat.

Nunn & Smeed. 1915–27. Liverpool, England. Benledi Works. Mr. George Laurence Nunn had distributed dolls for many years before forming this company. He and John James Smeed claimed that they were the first company in Britain to make an entire fully jointed composition doll even including the mold for the dolls; 27 operations were required to make the dolls. The brand name of these dolls was *Nunsuch*. Nunn & Smeed made a line of dolls named *Dolly Dimple* which they described as being pink bisque coated with wax, but this may have been a *British Ceramic* rather than a real bisque. (See **Bailey, Doris.**) Their dolls came dressed and undressed.

1915: Nunn applied for a patent for the construction of a doll.

1917: Advertised mama dolls and fully jointed dolls.

1918: Advertised character baby dolls.

Ca. 1920: Advertised Regina dolls with "porcelain heads," wigs and sleeping eyes.★

NUNSUCH

N.& S.

LIVERPOOL

No 7.

2009. Nunn & Smeed mark for their Nunsuch British Ceramic dolls.

Nunsuch. 1915–27. Brand name of dolls made by *Nunn & Smeed*. These dolls had wigs, glass eyes and were fully jointed. The heads were variously described as "imitation porcelain," having an "eggshell finish" pink bisque coated with wax. *Dolly Dimple* was one of their lines of the Nunsuch dolls that had a *British Ceramic* head, open mouth, teeth, a composition body with upper limbs of wood and plaster-like hands. A British Ceramic head character baby doll has been found marked "THE//'NUNSUCH'// N & S // LIVERPOOL //8."

1916: Hts. 21 and 24 in. (53.5 and 61 cm.); priced $2.50 and $3.00.

Nürnberger Celluloidwarenfabrik. See **Wolff, Gebrüder.**

Nürnberger Kunstlerpuppen und Stoffspielwarenfabrik. See **Zwanger, Heinrich.**

Nürnberger Stoffspielwarenfabrik. See **Köhler & Rosenwald.**

Nurse. Numerous dolls were commercially dressed as nurses from at least 1850 to 1930 and many patterns were given for dressing dolls at home as nurses. The 1872 *Bru* catalog showed a baby's nurse. In Europe Nurse dolls from the mid 1800s through the early 1900s were often dressed in regional costumes and the baby they carried was sometimes in swaddling clothes.

Popular in the 1870s–90s were French-type kid bodied lady dolls dressed as nurses. They carried a baby doll and a gift box for the christening.

Among the dolls dressed as nurses for babies were ones produced and or distributed by:

1885: *Petit St. Thomas.*

1895: *Louvre* store.

1902: *Butler Bros.* advertised a black nurse for a baby doll.

1923: *Hitz, Jacobs & Kassler* produced nurse dolls.

With changes in the social structure following World War I fewer dolls were made to represent nurses for babies.

The importance of the Red Cross during World War I caused the dressing of dolls as Red Cross nurses or other nurses for the wounded of the war instead of nurses for babies. Among the manufacturers and/or distributors of the dolls dressed as Red Cross or hospital nurses were:

1915: *Borough British Doll,* Louvre store, *Misses Lowe, W. Payne & Son,* and *Louis Wolf.* (See Ill. 1913.)

1916: *Manchester Doll Makers* (*Edith Cavell* doll), *Printemps, Robotham Bros.*

1917: *Bell & Francis, Central Doll Manufacturing Co., Doll Exerciser, Edinburgh Toy Factory, Effanbee, Gallais (Bleuette), Roberts Bros., South Wales Toy Manufacturing Co.*

1918: *Eaton, Schoenhut, Trion.*

1919: *Ideal, Maiden Toy Co., Montgomery Ward.*

1920: *Harwin.*

Dolls dressed as nurses for the sick have been popular for centuries. Often the dolls wore religious garb, since the duties of religious orders often included caring for the sick.

A fine example of a doll dressed as a nurse was advertised by F.A.O. Schwarz in 1926 as follows: It had a bisque head; mohair wig; sleeping eyes; fully jointed composition body; and wore a blue or white cotton dress, white apron, collar, cuffs and cap, stockings, kid slippers; and carried scissors and a hot water bottle. Hts. 16 and 18 in. (40.5 and 45.5 cm.); priced $6.75 and $8.50. See THE COLLECTOR'S BOOK OF DOLLS' CLOTHES, Ills. 734 and 740.

Nurse Jane Fuzzy Wuzzy. 1924. Trademark registered in U.S. for dolls by *Howard R. Garis.*

Nursery Patent Doll. 1887. Name of a doll with a wig and glass eyes, advertised by *Lauer.* The doll wore a chemise. Hts. 13½ and 15½ in. (34 and 39.5 cm.); priced $2.25 and $3.00 doz. wholesale.

2010. Nurse and baby dolls with bisque heads. The nurse has molded hair, stationary blue glass eyes, and a closed mouth. It is on a cloth body with bisque arms. Original regional costume. H. 13½ in. (34 cm.). *Courtesy of Sotheby Parke Bernet Inc., N.Y.*

2011. Nurse in regional costume as portrayed in HARPER'S BAZAR, December 1879. The directions were given for making this costume for a doll that was 17¼ in. (44 cm.) tall not including the head. The only directions for the baby doll are that it wears a long white dress trimmed with red ribbons.

2012. Brown bisque head on a doll dressed as a nurse with a tiny white bisque head baby. The nurse has a black wig, sleeping brown glass eyes, open mouth, and a fully jointed brown composition body. Mark on the nurse's head: 390 A, 6/0 M. H. 11 in. (28 cm.). *Courtesy of Sotheby Parke Bernet Inc. N.Y.*

2013. Bisque head doll with wig, sleeping blue eyes, open mouth and teeth, wearing a nurse's uniform of the Boer War period. The head is marked "1894//A M. D.E.P.//Made in Germany//2½." H. 43 cm. (17 in.). *Courtesy of the Collection Nederlands Kostuummuseum, The Hague. Photo by B. Frequin.*

2014. Pair of all-bisque dolls representing Red Cross nurses. They have wigs, painted blue eyes, and are jointed at the neck, shoulder, and hips. Original clothes bearing a Red Cross insignia. Blue boots painted on the bisque. H. 2½ in. (6.5 cm.). *Courtesy of the Washington Dolls' House and Toy Museum.*

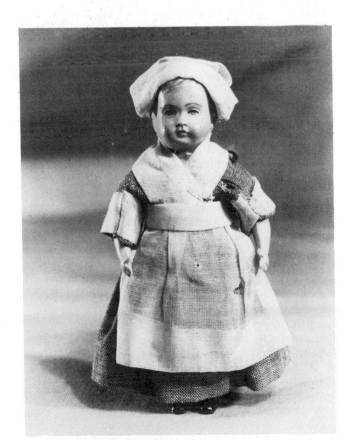

2015. All-celluloid doll with molded, painted features, jointed shoulders, molded child's style footwear. It is dressed as a medical nurse. H. 4 in. (10 cm.). *Coleman Collection.*

Nursery Rhyme and Fairy Tale Dolls. Commercial dolls representing Nursery Rhyme and Fairy Tale characters were favorites with children and consequently with people in the business of producing and/or distributing dolls. Many of these dolls were in a series that included both Nursery Rhyme and Fairy Tale characters as well as characters from other favorite children's stories. For example *Averill's Mother Goose* series included Captain Kidd which was the same doll as Little Bo Peep except for its clothes. The most popular Fairy Tale character was *Red Riding Hood,* possibly because the red cape and hood were easy clothes to make and the red was an eye-catching color. Sometimes "Little" preceded the name and sometimes the "Little" was omitted. Spellings also varied; for example, Goldielocks was also spelled Goldilocks and Goldenlocks.

The following companies were among those who made dolls representing Nursery Rhyme and/or Fairy Tale characters:

Amberg: Educational Dolls came with Nursery Rhyme booklet.
American Wholesale: Little Miss Muffet.
Arnold Print Works: Little Red Riding Hood.
Asiatic Import Co.: Fairy Tale Dolls.
Averill Manufacturing Co.: Bo Peep, Captain Kidd, Little Boy Blue, Little Lord Fauntleroy, Oliver Twist, Mary Had a Little Lamb, and Mother Goose.
Baker & Bennett: Jack & Jill.
Bell & Francis: Red Riding Hood.
Bings: Nursery Rhyme Dolls.
Borgfeldt: Jack & Jill.
British Products: Red Riding Hood.
Butler Bros.: Goldilocks, Red Riding Hood.
Buzza Co.: Jolly Jack and many others.
Callot sisters[+]: Cinderella.
Chad Valley: Jack & Jill, Little Miss Muffet, Peter Pan, Red Riding Hood.
Chase: Characters from Alice in Wonderland.
Chessler: Nursery Rhyme Dolls, Red Riding Hood.
Colonial Toy Manufacturing Co.: Bo Peep, Dillar-A-Dollar, Ding Dong Bell, Goosey Gander, Hug-Me-Tight, I love Little Pussy, Little Boy Blue, Little Mousie Bride, Ride a Cock Horse, This Little Girl, and Wee Willie Winkie.
Geo. Davis: Old Woman in a Shoe, Red Riding Hood.
Rees Davis: Bo Peep, Humpty Dumpty, Little Boy Blue, Little Miss Muffet, Red Riding Hood, Tommy Tucker.
Dean: Little Lord Fauntleroy, Mad Hatter.
Anna Dely: Fairy Tale Dolls.
Deptford Toy Co.: Cinderella, Red Riding Hood.
Eaton: GoldiLocks.
Edinburgh Toy Factory: Jack Tar.
Effanbee: Little Miss Muffet.
Franklin Studio: Nursery Rhyme Dolls.
Goodyear Toy: Peter Pan.
Grinnell Lithographic Co.: Mary Had a Little Lamb.
A. W. Hanington: Bo Peep.
Harwin & Co.: Boy Blue.
Hawksley & Co.: Bo Peep, Cinderella, Dick Turpin, Dick Whittington, Mary Had a Little Lamb, and Red Riding Hood.

Dorothy Heizer: Nursery Rhyme Dolls.
Horsman: Bo Peep, Jack Horner, Jack Robinson, Little Boy Blue, Red Riding Hood, and Tommy Tucker.
Ideal: Peter Pan, Wendy.
Indestructo Specialties Co.: Fairy Tales including Red Riding Hood.
Jeanette Doll Co.: Cinderella, Goldilocks, Little Boy Blue, Little Miss Muffet, Peter Piper, Prince Charming, Red Riding Hood, Simple Simon.
K & K Toy Co.: Red Riding Hood.
Kellogg: Bo Peep, Goldilocks, Mary and Her Little Lamb, Red Riding Hood, and Tom, Tom, the Piper's Son.
Kleinert: Goldilocks.
Knight & Cooper: Red Riding Hood.
Käthe Kruse: Red Riding Hood.
Lafayette & Co.: Little Red Riding Hood.
Lenci: Little Miss Muffet.
Marshall Field: Bo Peep.
Mawaphil: Mother Goose series. (See Ill. 1850.)
Meakin & Ridgeway: Jack & Jill.
Carl Meyer: Red Riding Hood.
W. H. Mogridge: Little Red Riding Hood.
Montgomery Ward: Little Miss Muffet.
Moore & Gibson: Red Riding Hood.
Nelke: Bo Peep, Jack & Jill, Mary Quite Contrary, Red Riding Hood.
New Toy Co.: Red Riding Hood.
Oweenee Novelty Co.: Jack & Jill.
Marie Perrault: Fairy Tale Dolls.
Printemps: Red Riding Hood.
Jessie M. Raleigh: Goldilocks, Mary Had a Little Lamb, Mary Quite Contrary, Peeps, Red Riding Hood.
Royal Crown Pottery: Red Riding Hood.
Saalfield: Goldielocks, Little Red Riding Hood.
Schoenhut: Mary Had a Little Lamb.
F.A.O. Schwarz: Red Riding Hood.
Sears: Goldilocks.
Selchow & Righter: Bo Peep, Little Boy Blue, Little Miss Muffet (two versions), Little Red Riding Hood.
Shanklin: Kate Greenaway.
Siegel Cooper: Little Red Riding Hood.
Silber & Fleming: Red Riding Hood.
Steiff: Humpty Dumpty, Mother Hubbard, Rip Van Winkle.
Strobel & Wilken: Jack & Jill.
Sun Enamel Works: Little Boy Blue, Little Polly Flinders, and Little Red Riding Hood.
Toy Shop: Mother Goose.
Twinzy Toy Co.: Little Boy Blue, Tom, Tom, the Piper's Son.
Twinjoy: Cinderella, Jack & Jill, Red Riding Hood & Grandma.
Charles William: Little Miss Muffet, Little Red Riding Hood.
Louis Wolf: Boy Blue, Cinderella.

Nearly all *Phonograph Dolls* (or dolls that could sing songs) had records that recited Nursery Rhymes.

2016. Bisque head dolls dressed in costumes representing Nursery Rhyme characters. The Old Woman Who Lived in a Shoe and Old King Cole are character face dolls. The Queen of Hearts at the bottom left is a Kestner Gibson Girl doll. The rest of the dolls have dolly type faces. The text in the middle of this page shown in THE LADIES' HOME JOURNAL, November, 15, 1910, describes the clothes on each of these dolls.

Nursery-Rhyme Dolls

By Louise Brigham

DEAR to every little girl's heart are these well-known nursery rhymes, of which the child characters are really playmates of the nursery. The dolls are described below as fully as possible, but further information will be given by letter if postage is sent.

"This old woman who lived in a shoe
Had so many children
She didn't know what to do"

"Old King Cole
Was a merry old soul,
And a merry old soul was he"

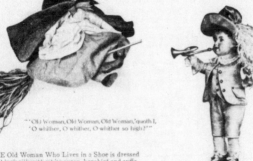

"Little Bo-Peep has lost her sheep
And can't tell where to find them"

"'Old Woman, Old Woman, Old Woman,' quoth I,
'O whither, O whither, O whither so high?'"

"Little Boy Blue, come, blow your horn;
The sheep's in the meadow, the cow's in the corn"

THE Old Woman Who Lives in a Shoe is dressed in black silk with white apron, kerchief and cuffs, mob cap of white lawn with a silk bow. Her shoe house is made of black crêpe paper on a wire frame. The buckle is gold paper. The little dolls may be purchased dressed at toy shops.

Old King Cole, dressed in royal purple velvet and white lace, sits on a throne made of five cigar boxes painted gold. The ermine on the cloak is made of white cotton wadding with black ink spots. Sandals are of pasteboard covered with purple satin trimmed with gold embroidery ribbons. The crown is of colored beads strung on wire.

Little Bo-Peep has a pink silk skirt, striped silk bodice with blue ribbons, white blouse, and a straw hat trimmed with pink ribbons. The shepherd's crook is made of a bent twig.

The Old Woman has a blue cambric skirt, white overdress, red flannel cape, hat of black satin, white stockings and black kid shoes. The broom handle is a covered stick with brush of raffia.

LITTLE BOY BLUE is in a suit of blue satin with white lace frill in sleeves, and collar of white lawn and lace. Hat of satin with white plume. Blue stockings, gold-painted shoes with blue bows.

The Pretty Milkmaid has a dress of blue muslin with white dots, white Swiss apron, kerchief and cap. She carries a toy milking-stool.

Curly-Locks is in lavender-flowered organdy trimmed with white ribbon and lace. Bonnet of black velvet with gold braid and a black plume.

The Queen of Hearts wears a dress of white satin trimmed with red velvet hearts and bands. Her crown is of gilt paper with red hearts pasted on it. She has a toy table, rolling-pin and dishes, gilded.

Mary, Mary, Quite Contrary, has a dress of blue sateen, white cambric blouse, skirt trimmed with flowered cretonne cut in scallops, a blue sateen sash with bow in back. Straw hat trimmed with cretonne and blue sateen. Black kid shoes with blue ribbon and buckles, white stockings. Toy watering-pot. Mary's garden is made of the cover of a tin box filled with clay. This makes a foundation for the flowers, trees and fence. Artificial moss covers the clay.

"'Where are you going, my pretty maid?'
'I'm going a-milking, sir,' she said"

"'Curly-Locks, Curly-Locks, wilt thou be mine?
Thou shalt not wash the dishes, nor yet feed the swine!'"

"The Queen of Hearts she made some tarts
All on a summer's day"

"'Mary, Mary, quite contrary,
How does your garden grow?'"

Nursery Rhyme Dolls. Before 1892–1930 and later. America, England, and elsewhere.

A Dillar-A-Dollar
  1915: *Hug-Me-Tight*

Bo Peep, Bo-Peep, or Little Bo-Peep
  1892: *Marshall Field*
  1912: *Horsman; Selchow & Righter*
  1915: *Hanington;* Hug-Me-Tight
  1917: H. J. Brown; *Hawksley*
  1920: *Chessler*
  1922: *Rees Davis*
  1926: *Kellogg*
  1928: *Nelke*
  1929: *Averill*

Ding Dong Bell
  1915: Hug-Me-Tight

Georgy Porgy in Mother Goose Line (See Ill. 1850.)
  1926: *Mawaphil*

Goosey Gander
  1915: Hug-Me-Tight

I Like Little Pussy
  1915: Hug-Me-Tight

Jack Horner
  1915: *Bings Ltd.*

Jack and Jill
  1921: *Baker & Bennett; Borgfeldt; Meakin & Ridgeway; Oweenee; Strobel & Wilken*
  1924: *Chad Valley*
  1927: *Twinjoy*
  1929: *Nelke*

Little Boy Blue or Boy Blue
  1912: Horsman; Selchow & Righter
  1915: Hug-Me-Tight
  1920: Chad Valley; Rees Davis; *Harwin*
  1923: *Squier*
  1924: *Jeanette; Mayfair Playthings; Louis Wolf*
  1929: *Averill; Sun Enamel Works*

Little Miss Muffet or Miss Muffet
  1909: Selchow & Righter (cutout doll)
  1912: Selchow & Righter (cloth doll)
  1915: Bings, Ltd.
  1920: Chad Valley; *Effanbee;* Rees Davis
  1924: Jeanette; *Montgomery Ward*
  1926: *American Wholesale; Charles William*
  1927: *Lenci*

Little Polly Flinders
  1929: Sun Enamel Works

Mary Had a Little Lamb or Mary and Her little Lamb
  1908: *Schoenhut*
  1915: Bings, Ltd.
  1917: *Grinnell;* Hawksley
  1919: *J. M. Raleigh*
  1926: Kellogg
  1929: Averill

Mary Quite Contrary
  1919: J. M. Raleigh
  1929: Nelke

Mother Hubbard
  1911: *Steiff*
  1915: Bings, Ltd.
  1917: Hawksley

Peter Piper
  1925: Jeanette

Queen of Hearts
  1910: *Kestner*

Ride A Cock Horse
  1915: Hug-Me-Tight

Simple Simon
  1925: Jeanette

Tom, Tom, The Piper's Son
  1923: Squier
  1926: Kellogg

Tommy Tucker
  1912: Horsman
  1920: Rees Davis

Wee Willie Winkie
  1915: Hug-Me-Tight

Some if not all of the phonograph dolls had records with nursery rhyme recitations. In 1916 *Amberg* made an Educational Doll that came with a booklet of Nursery Tales.

Nursing Bottle Baby. 1926–28. These dolls were a variant of *My Dream Baby* made by *Arranbee* and bore a rectangular tag having a picture of a baby and the words "My//Dream//Baby//Reg. U.S. Pat. Off. // Arranbee// Doll Co." This bisque head doll held a celluloid bottle containing a white liquid that disappeared when the bottle was raised to the doll's mouth. The bottle refilled when the arm was lowered. The doll wore a short baby dress, rubber panties, a halo style bonnet, knitted booties and cost $1.00 and up.

Nursing Dolls. 1866–1930 and later. In addition to the Feeding Dolls[+] listed in the first COLLECTOR'S ENCYCLOPEDIA OF DOLLS there were other nursing dolls, especially the infant dolls made after 1925 in order to prolong the infant dolls' popularity.

1892: The Rudolph Steiner[+] nursing bottle doll on a chair was distributed by *Marshall Field.* Ht. 11 in. (28 cm.); priced $16.50 doz. wholesale.

1899: *Butler Bros.* advertised white and black Nursing Baby dolls with *Moving Lips.* These dolls had bellows and the larger ones had sleeping eyes. Ht. 10 and 13 in. (25.5 and 33 cm.); priced 92¢ and $1.80 doz. wholesale.

1902: *Max Carl* obtained a patent for a nursing baby doll.

1928: One of the Paris baby dolls was able to consume the contents of a nursing bottle and then the hinged back had to be opened, a sponge removed and pressed dry before being put back in place.

1928–29: *E. Chapsal* produced nursing dolls. (See also **Bébé Teteur.**)

Nusspickel, Ernst. 1912. Neustadt near Coburg. Thür. Applied for a German patent (D.R.G.M.) for a doll's head with stationary eyes and eyelashes.

Nyce, Helen (Helene). 1914–21. New Jersey. Illustrator and doll collector. It is alleged by Virginia Schwarz that the mold 245 *Hilda* made by *Kestner* was inspired by Helen Nyce's drawings.

Nye, Miss E. L. 1919–20. London. An instructress in design and embroidery for the London County Council, she designed and made clothes for dolls. These removable clothes included indoor and outdoor costumes as well as baby clothes.

Nymphenburg. 1761–1930 and later. Nymphenburg near Munich, Bavaria. A famous porcelain factory. In the early 1900s their sculptor *Josef Wackerle* designed dolls' heads for the *Munich Art Dolls.*

1908: Made porcelain dolls' heads possibly designed by Wackerle for dolls that were dressed in 18th century period costumes by *Frau Kommerzienrat.* ★

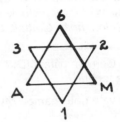

JRGM   GERMANY
20/0/3

2017. Mark found on a doll made between ca. 1890 when the D.R.G.M. patents began and ca. 1930. This six pointed star with the same arrangement of numerals and letters was used as a blue mark on porcelain figures by Nymphenburg in the 1760s according to Danckert.

O

O.K. Toy Manufacturing Co. 1920–21. New York City. Manufactured dolls with composition heads having wigs or molded hair and painted eyes, on cloth bodies, some of which had composition hands. Hts. 11, 14, and 17 in. (28, 35.5 and 43 cm.).

O. U. Kid. 1919. Line of dolls made by *Gem* included Bathing Kid, Dough Boy and Grass Widow. Ht. 11 in. (28 cm.).

O You Kid (O-U-Kid). 1914 and later. All-bisque doll had short wispy molded hair, painted eyes looking to the side, single curved line mouth, rotund body in blue molded night clothes with molded buttons in back. Arms were molded against the body, bare feet together. The round sticker on the chest read "O//You//Kid//Germany." ★

Oakhurst Studios. 1925 and later. New York City and Lynbrook, L. I. Manufactured cloth or cloth body dolls including the *Cuddlekins* line.

Oakland Stationery & Toy Co. 1928. Oakland, Calif. Importers and jobbers who distributed *Horsman, American Character* and *Steiff* dolls.

Oates Wax Studio. 1927–28. Los Angeles, Calif. Made wax figures and composition dolls.

Oberender, Hilmar. 1927 and probably other years. Sonneberg, Thür. Made voices for dolls.

Oberender, Nikolaus. 1908–27 and possibly later. Oeslau, Thür., later Bavaria. Founded a porcelain factory with *Johann Walther.* By 1910 the partnership had split and Oberender had his own porcelain factory with 110 employees, where bisque dolls' heads were made. In 1927 the company was known as Wilhelmine Oberender.

Oberender, Richard. Lived from 1858 to 1919. Probably the German sculptor who modeled dolls' heads made in porcelain by *Knoch* and *Süssenguth.*

Obletter. 1825–1859 and possibly longer. Coldeflan, Grödner Tal. Wooden doll *Verleger,* Johann Baptist Obletter, appears to have founded the business which was continued by his son Anton Obletter about 1840. During the 1850s at

A

MadeinGermany
125
7

B

Germany
2000   y·y   8/0

C

A·r DEP
y·y 2010
Germany 8/0

2018A–C. Marks on bisque dolls' heads made by Nikolaus Oberender.

the same address, Anton Obletter, Josef Obletter and Magdalena Obletter were listed as doll and toy distributors in a Vienna directory.

Obry, Jules. 1910 and probably other years. Paris. Won a silver medal at the Brussels Exposition for his dolls.★

Occupational Costumes. Many dolls were dressed in clothes representing those worn by people in various occupations. Sometimes it is difficult to distinguish between occupational and regional attire. Moreover often different regions had different costumes for the same occupation. Nursemaids for children often wore the regional costume of the place from which most of the nurses came. For example in Denmark, nursemaids usually wore the costume of a particular island that supplied many of the nursemaids regardless of the area from which the nurse actually came. A large number of dolls dressed as nursemaids wore Alsatian costumes. Many of the dolls' house dolls represented servants—butlers, chauffeurs, cooks, maids, and so forth. Also many dolls have been dressed to represent pedlars.

Among the dolls dressed in occupational costumes were:

1856: Fireman.

1888: Milkmaid.

1903–16: *Steiff* made many dolls wearing occupational attire including a barkeeper, butcher, circus performer, cowboy farmer, fisherman, jockey, messenger boy, postillion, postman, sailor, shoe maker, and soldier.

1903–24: *Schoenhut*'s circus performers, farmer and milkmaid.

1911: Milkmaid, Teachers.

World War I: Offered many female occupations for which dolls were dressed. Besides nurses there were bus drivers, chauffeurs, coachmen, conductors, mail carriers, mechanics, parcel carriers, subway employees, and workers on shells for guns.

Post World War I: There were bakers, bell hops, bullfighters, butchers, chimney sweep, doctor, Italian gondolier, magician, Newsboys, poultry keeper, railway fireman. (See also **Clowns, Costume Dolls, Cowboys, Dolls' House Dolls, Military Nurses, Policeman, Regional Costume Dolls,** and **Sports Dolls.**)

Och & Brückner. 1930. Stockheim, Bavaria. Manufactured dolls.

O'Conner, Florence Madelen. 1921–23. Ottawa, Canada. Obtained a U.S. patent for a floating doll with a cloth body.

Odette. 1928–29. Name of a cloth doll dressed in felt.

1928: Advertised by *J. Paturel & Cie.*

1929–30: Advertised by *Bon Marché*. Hts. 37, 41, and 43 cm. (14½, 16, and 17 in.).

Oeller, Albertine. 1907. Vienna. Listed in a directory under Dolls and Dolls' Heads.

Oester, Julie de. 1910. Vienna. Listed in a directory under Dolls and Dolls' Heads.

Oeuvre des Enfants des Flandres (Work of the children of Flanders). 1918. Paris. Name given to the dolls made by Flemish children.

Oeuvre du Travail. See **Mme. Sautter.**

Oeuvre du Travail à Domicile. See **Mlle. Desaubliaux.**

Off. (French Officer). 1911. Felt doll with a long nose and long feet made by *Steiff*, dressed as a French military officer with fringed epaulettes and a kepi. Ht. 35 cm. (14 in.).

Offenbacher, S., & Co. 1923–29. London. Handled dolls.

Oga. 1925. Name of a walking, talking doll and a talking baby doll advertised by *Otto Gans.*

Ohlbaum, Karl, & Son. 1929–30 and later. New York City. Manufactured and imported dolls and dolls' parts including heads, celluloid arms and legs for *Boudoir* dolls, dolls' voices and dolls' shoes.

Ohlhaver, Gebrüder. 1913–30 and later. Sonneberg, Thür. Their line of dolls was called *Revalo* which is Ohlhaver spelled backwards, omitting the two hs. They made dolls with bisque socket and shoulder heads as well as composition heads. The dolls came dressed or wearing only a chemise. According to the research of the Ciesliks, *Ernst Heubach* supplied many of the Revalo heads and the Revalo dolls were used by *Johannes Gotthilf Dietrich* and *Carl Harmus, Jr.*

1913: Applied for a German patent (D.R.G.M.) for a doll's head with a moving tongue.

1921: Advertised Revalo dolls named *My Queen Doll* and *Bébé Princesse.*

1925: Applied for a German patent (D.R.P.) for a screaming doll.

1928: Applied for a German patent (D.R.G.M.) relating to eyes in composition heads.★

Oil Cloth Dolls. 1927. Name of a line of composition head, cloth body dolls dressed in oilcloth and advertised by *Butler Bros.* The costumes represented nursery rhyme or fairy tale characters such as Jack and Jill, Hans and Gretel, Mistress Mary, Rose Red and Snow White. The girls generally wore capes and the boys wore coats. Hts. 14 and 18 in. (35.5 and 45.5 cm.). Other dolls have been found dressed in oilcloth such as soldier dolls.

Oilcloth Dolls. During the 1920s many manufacturers made and/or handled dolls of oilcloth, including *Asiatic Import Co., Fleming, Kat-A-Korner, Live Long Toys, Jack Brydone* and *Oz Doll & Toy Co.* The oilcloth dolls should not be confused with cloth dolls painted with oil paint. Oilcloth dolls were sometimes called imitation leather or Art Leather dolls.

1927: LADIES' HOME JOURNAL gave instructions for making dolls for boys out of oilcloth. These dolls were made of "pebbly white oilcloth with the face, hair and clothing painted on with oil or fabric paints. . . . the two pieces of oilcloth that compose each figure are stitched together around the sides with edges left raw, and stuffed with cotton." Colored pictures showed how the painting was done. The dolls were Tom, Tom, the Piper's Son; Chuck, the cowboy; Copper, the policeman; Sam, the Sailor and Leatherneck Marine. Hts. ca. 11½ in. (29 cm.); width ca. 5½ in. (14 cm.).

Olaf (Dutch, Volendam). 1909–16. Felt character doll made by *Steiff* and distributed by *Borgfeldt* in the U.S. It was dressed as a boy in a Volendam, Holland, costume. Five hts. 28, 35, 43, 50 and 60 cm. (11, 14, 17, 19½ and 23½ in.).

Old Country Doll, The. 1928. Trademark registered in U.S. for dolls by *Krestine Knudsen*.

Old Dutch Cleanser Dolls. 1916. Composition-head doll representing the Old Dutch Cleanser trademark, was distributed by *Butler Bros.* It had a mohair wig, painted eyes, cork stuffed body jointed at the shoulders and hips, and wore a blue percale dress, white waist-high apron, a white Dutch-style bonnet, felt shoes, open work stockings, and lace trimmed underwear. The doll carried a stick in its hand. Ht. 15 in. (38 cm.); priced $1.25.

Old Mammy. 1908–09. Cloth doll made by *Bach Bros.* as one of the *Bye Bye Kids.* This brown colored doll had a flat painted face and painted hair, an open-closed mouth showing teeth and was jointed at the shoulders and hips. It had painted orange stockings and black single strap slippers. In the lower front of the torso was a printed label, "BYE BYE KIDS//STRICTLY SANITARY// OLD MAMMY." Ht. 14 in. (35.5 cm.). (See Ills. 454 and 455.)

Ole Bill. Ca. 1915. Cloth doll with embroidered black mustache and painted features, dressed as a soldier and having a knitted scarf. Made by *Farnell,* it represented the cartoon character named "Ole Bill" drawn by Bruce Bairnsfather. Round paper tag reads, "Regd. No.//662457// OLE BILL// MASCOT//Made in//England."

Olga. 1913–16. Felt character doll made by *Steiff* and distributed in the U.S. by *Borgfeldt* in 1913. It wore a dress with a pleated skirt. Ht. 14 in. (35.5 cm.); priced $2.65.

Olga. 1924. Name of a *Chad Valley* cloth doll in their La Petite *Caresse* line. It had real hair, a hand colored face, an *Aerolite* or kapok stuffed body and carried a six-sided tag reading "Chad Valley//Hygienic//Fabric Toys." It wore a Russian style velveteen outfit trimmed with white woolly fur around the hat, neck, cuffs, bottom of the skirt, and top of the high boots. The boots were laced in front. Four hts. 11 (number 266), 13 (number 267), 16 (number 268), and 18 in. (number 269) (28, 33, 40.5 and 45.5 cm.); priced $1.25 to $2.50. Number 269 also came with a mama voice and cost $2.88.

Olhmé, Henry. 1854. Waldkirchen, Saxony. One of the creditors of the doll maker *Simon August Brouillet* when he failed.

Olida Doll & Toy Manufacturing Co. 1920. Liverpool, England. Specialized in baby dolls.

Oliver, Charles A. 1850 and probably other years. Philadelphia, Pa. Imported and distributed wax dolls and dolls with kid bodies.

Oliver Twist. 1914. Name of a composition Can't Break 'Em[†] head doll made by *Aetna Doll and Toy Co.* for *Horsman.* Designated number 187 it had a mohair wig, glass eyes, cloth body with the early Campbell Kid type hands. The head resembled *Baby Beauty.* It wore an Oliver Twist style suit with a double breasted white shirt having four buttons, blue short trousers and a brimmed white hat. Price $12.00 doz. wholesale.

No. 187 "Oliver Twist"

2019. Oliver Twist, produced by Horsman and advertised in their catalog of ca. 1914. It has a composition head and hands, mohair wig, and painted eyes. The hands resemble those of the early Campbell Kids. It is dressed in an Oliver Twist style suit.

Olsen, Herbert Villiam Bodenhoff. 1922–25. Copenhagen. Obtained a Danish and a German patents for dolls.★

Olympia Puppenconfection. 1923–29. Vienna. Manufactured dolls.

Ombry, (Felix). 1865. Paris. Wholesale distributor of rubber dolls.

Omega Brand. 1917–29. A line of jointed and stiff limbed, dressed and undressed dolls, made by the *British United Toy Manufacturing Co.* Omega was registered in Britain as a trademark.

Omega Workshop. See **Fry, Roger.**

On My Lap. 1926. Trademark in U.S. for dolls by *M. J. Frank & Co.*

O'Neill, M., & Co. 1880. New York City. Advertised a variety of dolls.

O'Neill, Rose (Mrs. Rose O'Neill Wilson). 1909–30 and later. Wilkes-Barre, Pa.; New York City; Bonniebrook, Day, Mo. The artist who created the *Kewpies* and *Scootles*.

1930: Created cloth *Cuddle Kewpies* which were manufactured and distributed by *King Innovations.*★

Onondaga Indian Wigwam Co.† See **Wigwam Co.**

Ontario Textile Co. 1921–23. Chicago, Ill. Made cloth *Kunnin-Kids.*★

OO-Gug-Luk. 1915. Composition-head, cloth body doll made by *Amberg,* using the same mold for the head as was used for their *Charlie Chaplin* dolls except that the head was painted as a black African and the doll was dressed in regional attire.★

Opera Star Character Dolls. 1920. Name of dolls with composition heads and arms, hair wigs covered with dotted veils, sleeping eyes, cloth body jointed at shoulders and hips. These dolls were dressed, some with marabou neck pieces. They were distributed by the *Southern Bargain House.* Hts. 15, 17 and 18 in. (38, 43 and 45.5 cm.); priced $24.00 a doz. to $7.00 each wholesale. (See also **Carmen, Madame Butterfly, Manon,** and **Melba.**)

2020A. Composition head doll made by Amberg to represent a black Zulu named Oo-Gug-Luk. Amberg used his Charlie Chaplin head mold for this doll but painted it black. It has molded black hair, eyes painted black with a surrounding white area, open-closed mouth also with a surrounding white area, and black cloth body jointed at the shoulders and hips. The gauntlet type hands are made of black composition. Original clothes include earrings and nose ring. Mark: Ill. 2020B. H. 13 in. (33 cm.). *Courtesy of the late Henrietta Van Sise.*

OO·GUG·LUK
ZULU LUCKY DOLL
TRADE MARK
Originated – Design Patented – by J. W. LONG
Copyrighted 1915 and Mfg'd by Louis Amberg & Son. N.Y.

2020B. Mark on the front of the cloth torso of Oo-Gug-Luk.

Oppenheimer, A. & Co. 1920 and other years. London, Montreal, New York City, Paris, and Sydney. Handled dolls.

Oppenheimer, M. F. 1923–26. New York City. Advertised popular-priced dolls including *Mama* dolls. Agent for *New York Stuffed Toy Co., Self Sell Doll Co.* and *T. & T. Toy Co.*

Orben, Knabe & Co. 1909 and later. Geschwenda, Thür. Porcelain factory that used the initials "O.K." A china head with a lowbrow style of hairdo has the initials O.K. on the back of its shoulders.

2021. China shoulder head with low-brow style molded, black painted hair, made by Orben, Knabe & Co in Geschwenda, Thür., after 1909. It has molded brown boots and blue garters. The body is pink cloth. Mark: Ill. 2022. H. 13½ in. (34 cm.). H. of shoulder head 2¾ in. (7 cm.). *Coleman Collection.*

OK

2022. Mark on a china head probably made by Orben, Knabe & Co.

Organdie. 1926. Name of an *Aerolite* cloth doll made by *Chad Valley.* It had a hand-colored face, real hair, a kapok stuffed body and wore an organdy dress and cap trimmed with felt flowers in contrasting colors. The skirt was very short. There were four numbers: 420, 421, 422, and 423 for the four hts. 11, 13, 16 and 18 in. (28, 33, 40.5 and 45.5 cm.). The largest size came with or without a mama voice.

Organization des Vents et Concours des Poupées des Allies au Bazar de la Charité. See **Brunnel.**

Oriental. Many companies or people made or handled dolls representing Orientals. Among them were:

Arnold Print Works 1893
Averill Manufacturing Co. 1923
Borgfeldt
Butler Bros.
Cissna 1897–98
Door of Hope 1901–41
Eaton 1918
Effanbee 1918
Gamage
Gerzon 1930
Hamley 1922
Hitz, Jacobs & Kassler 1923
Horsman 1910–16
Irwin-Smith 1920
Kestner 1899–1930 and later
Liberty & Co. 1913
Live Long Toys 1929
Armand Marseille, one version in 1925
Marshall Field 1889 and later
Montgomery Ward 1889 and later
Morimura Bros. 1915
Oakhurst Studios 1930
Poppy Doll Co. 1929
Scantlebury 1907–13
Schoenhut 1918
Schwerdtmann
Shackman
Simon & Halbig
Steiff 1913
YOUTH'S COMPANION 1895

Some of the popular names for Oriental dolls were *Kintarō, Mah-Jongg, Pitti Sing* and *Sum Fun.* (See also **Chinese Dolls, Friendship Dolls, Japanese Dolls** and **Regional Costume Dolls.**) (See Ills. 2023–2028.)★

Original Condition. Collectors of dolls seek those that are in as original condition as possible. The prices of dolls in original condition tend to be far higher than for the dolls that have obviously extraneous parts and are redressed. But the problem is that it is often very difficult to determine whether a doll's body and head always were together and whether the clothes were original, contemporary or even made recently.

Dolls were the playthings of children and as such they were frequently handled roughly. It is no surprise that doll hospitals have flourished through the years and great numbers of existing dolls today have replaced heads, wigs, eyes, arms, clothes and other parts. One hospital supplier even advertised teeth for Shirley Temple dolls. A documented parian type doll was given to a little girl about 1870 and within a couple of weeks the head was broken and replaced with a similar style of head, though obviously larger in size. Most famous doll makers advertised replacement parts, for example *Gesland, Kämmer & Reinhardt, Kestner, Marsh,* and many others.

All jointed composition bodies with elastic stringing must be restrung periodically. Since stringing a doll is a relatively easy task, many dolls have been shipped from Europe to American dealers and collectors unstrung for easier packing and less duty. When several similar dolls were thus shipped it was not always possible to sort them out with their correct original parts.

The problem of original parts is especially acute with dolls that have to be strung. But broken heads or mutilated limbs can be replaced on almost all types of dolls. Regretfully sometimes collectors even change original bodies because they do not like the body and wish their doll to have a different shape. One bisque turned head lady doll (See Ill. 1060 in the first COLLECTOR'S ENCYCLOPEDIA OF DOLLS) originally came on a cloth body that has a childish shape with composition limbs, the legs having molded Mary Jane style shoes. This head is frequently removed and put on a more adult shaped body. The original body on the *Schoenau & Hoffmeister Princess Elizabeth* doll (See Ill. 2145) appears to be too short for the size of the head. But that is the way it was originally. Dolls have been redressed for many reasons: the clothes may have been worn and ragged, or they may have been in good condition and not of a type that appealed to the collector. Sometimes a doll is redressed to be appropriate in a special exhibit.

Certain types of dolls are more likely to have their original heads and bodies than others. These include the early molded hair papier-mâché head doll on kid bodies with wooden limbs, and the peg jointed wooden dolls, as well as many of the cloth dolls especially those with felt faces.

China and bisque heads, both the socket and the shoulder head type, were made in the porcelain factories and then generally sold to other manufacturers who put them on bodies. Thus the same type of head did not necessarily always belong originally to the same type of body. Often heads and bodies were sold separately and many cloth bodies were made at home by the family of the child recipient of the doll. A large proportion of dolls in the 1800s were sold in chemises and the purchaser selected the commercially made clothes for it or made the clothes themselves. In these cases it is almost impossible to differentiate between original clothes and contemporary ones unless there is documentation to prove the originality.

The gauze-like dresses trimmed with narrow silk ribbon especially on early molded hair papier-mâché head dolls and other dolls of the mid 1800s, are usually original commercially made costumes. Dolls dressed in regional costumes are generally all original. For the most part these dolls were purchased by tourists and they did not undergo the difficult vicissitudes of a play doll even when given to children. The art dolls such as *Lenci, Kaulitz, Heizer, Steiff,* and so forth have nearly always retained their original condition, if kept in a suitable climate. They were expensive when new and thus they were treasured more than the usual play doll. Often the originality of a doll can be verified by comparison with a manufacturer's or distributor's catalog or other early advertisement if the doll is clearly shown in a photograph. Due to artistic license a drawing of a doll usually does not suffice. Sometimes a doll was photographed with its original owner and the picture has been preserved with the doll as documentation of its originality.

When a doll is purchased from the family of its original owner, there is no proof that the doll is all original. It could have made many trips to a doll hospital for replaced parts but the chances of originality are nevertheless greater than for a doll that has passed through the hands of many dealers. While some replacements are obvious such as poorly fitted parts, rayon dresses or saran wigs on dolls made before World War I, other replacements can be very difficult to detect. Some of the challenge and charm in collecting dolls lies in the need for knowledge so that the originality or lack of it can be determined. (See also **Repairing Dolls.**)★

Original Doll Co. 1925–29. New York City. Made *Mama*, baby, and infant dolls with sleeping eyes.

1926: A 15 in. (33 cm.) doll cost $1.00 while other dolls cost up to $25.00 retail.

1927: Licensed by *Voices, Inc.* to use their patented mama voices and criers in dolls.

Original Toy Co. 1915–24. New York City. Firm members were A. A. *Gerling* and Hersh. Made composition character dolls.

1917: Advertised Jockeys, Oliver Twist, Red Riding Hood, Sailors, Soldier Boys, and others; priced 25¢ to $1.50.★

2024. All-bisque Oriental type doll with a black wig, stationary black glass eyes and closed mouth. The body is jointed at the neck, shoulders and hips. Original clothes that include paper decoration. H. 5½ in. (14 cm.). *Coleman Collection.*

2023. Bisque head Oriental type doll with a bald head, stationary brown glass eyes, pierced ears, slightly smiling closed mouth, and a carton body with bisque hands and wooden feet. H. 17½ in. (44.5 cm.). *Courtesy of Sotheby Parke Bernet Inc., N.Y.*

2025. Composition head doll representing an Oriental probably ca. 1880s–90s. It has a black hair queue, stationary black glass eyes, and a closed mouth. The cloth body with composition arms is jointed at the shoulders and hips. Original clothes. H. 11½ in. (29 cm.). *Courtesy of Sotheby Parke Bernet Inc., N.Y.*

2026. Oriental type doll with olive tinted bisque socket head, black mohair wig, stationary brown glass eyes, open mouth with four upper teeth, and a five-piece composition body with molded and painted footwear. Original clothes. Mark on head 7/0. H. 9 in. (23 cm.). *Courtesy of Ian Foulke. Photo by Howard Foulke.*

2027A & B. Oriental type doll with bisque head, glazed hair and scarf, painted black eyes, closed mouth, and a ball-jointed wire strung wooden body. The head turns slightly. Hands are carved and there is no wrist joint. The slippers are carved and painted. Original clothes. H. 12 in. (30.5 cm.). *Courtesy of Richard Withington. Photo by Barbara Jendrick.*

2028. Mark on an Oriental bisque head doll.

Ormond. 1923–30. Dressed dolls made by *D. H. Wagner* had molded hair and painted eyes. Piasta, Pipa, Pitty, and Pirola were all-bisque. Pimonta and Pirouette were all-celluloid, black and white dolls.

Ormos, Gustétav. See **Elsó Magyar Játékbabagyá.**

Oro (Circus Performer). 1911. Felt art doll made by *Steiff* and dressed as a circus-type clown wearing a tailcoat. The costume came in assorted colors. Ht. 43 cm. (17 in.).

Orphan Annie. See **Little Orphan Annie.**

Ornstein, Dr. Martha (née Brunner). 1922. Vienna. Obtained an Austrian patent for a cloth doll with a reversible cloth coat that enabled it to change from representing a woman to representing a man.

Orsini, Jeanne I. 1916–30 and later. New York City. Her all-bisque dolls came in 5 and 7 in (12.5 and 18 cm.) hts. Later she also designed Infant and baby dolls that were made in Europe of Biscoloid. These dolls had painted heads or wigs, sleeping eyes and hair eyelashes, flange necks. The heads were 13½ to 15 in. (34 to 38 cm.) in circumference and cost about $12.00 to $21.00 wholesale.

A bisque head baby doll designed by Jeanne Orsini for the *Kiddie Joy* line and made by *Armand Marseille* has been reported.

1919: A doll copyrighted in 1919 had a wig, glass eyes, an open-closed mouth. The head was marked "J. I. O. © 1919 47." The sticker on the chest read "Vivi// Reg. U.S. Patent Office//Copr. 1920. J. I. Orsini// Patent Applied For// Germany." Ht. 5 in. (12.5 cm.).

1920: A doll copyrighted in 1920 with a wig, sleeping eyes, and open mouth was marked "J. I. O. © 1920//44." Ht. 5 in. (12.5 cm.)★

Országos Magyar Háziipari Szövetség (National Hungarian House Industry League). 1926. Budapest. Made dolls in Hungarian costumes and had shops also in Vienna and Berlin.★

Ortyz (Ortiz), M. Joseph. 1916–21. Paris. With H. Delcourt he became a successor to *Gesland.* Made bodies for dolls.

1916: Registered Excelsior Bébé[+] as a trademark in France for bébés.

1918: Made bodies for the porcelain Lanternier dolls' heads.

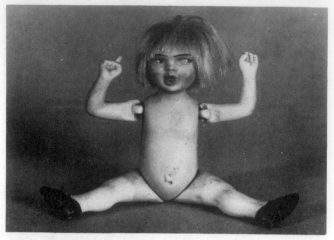

2029. All-bisque doll known as Mimi, copyrighted by Jeanne I. Orsini in 1920. It has a wig, eyes painted looking to the side, an open-closed mouth with lower teeth, and is jointed at the shoulders and hips. The footwear is molded and painted. Mark: J. I. O. © 1920//44. H. 13 cm. (5 in.). *Courtesy of Claire Hennig. Photo by Margie Landolt of Basel, Switzerland.*

2030. Bisque shoulder head copyrighted by Jeanne I. Orsini. It has a wig, sleeping brown glass eyes, and a smiling open mouth with two upper teeth. The bisque shoulders are narrow and are on a kid body that appears to be a replacement. Mark: Ill. 2031. H. of shoulder head 6 in. (15 cm.). H. of doll 21 in. (53.5 cm.). *Courtesy of the Margaret Woodbury Strong Museum. Photo by Harry Bickelhaupt.*

1423
Copr by
Jeanne F Orsini
Germany

2031. Mark on a Jeanne I. Orsini bisque shoulder head. Note that the J and I are the same and that they resemble an American script F.

This was in conjunction with the *Association d'Aide aux Veuves de la Guerre* (Association to Aid War Widows).

Osburn, Walter. See **Slicer, William.**

Oscar (Oskar). 1916. Felt doll made by *Steiff*. Five hts. 28, 35, 43, 50, and 60 cm. (11, 14, 17, 19½, 23½ in.).

Oschmann, Ernst. 1925–27. Finisterbergen, Thür. Made dolls.★

Oster, Mme. 1918. Auvergne, France. Created wooden dolls.

Österreich. See **Austrian.**

Osterreichischer Werkband (Austrian Workshop). 1920. Vienna. Listed under Character Dolls in an Austrian directory.

Oteecee. 1915–24. Name of a doll made by the *Original Toy Co.* in America. These dolls were distributed by *Bredow & Dubreuil* in London.★

Ott, Gebhardt. 1883. Steinbuhl, Germany. Made dolls.

(+G.O+)

2032. Mark of Gebhardt Ott according to Gwen White.

Ottakar, Philipp. See **Heubach, Gebrüder.**

Ottilie. 1916. Felt doll made by *Steiff*. Five hts. 28, 35, 43, 50 and 60 cm. (11, 14, 17, 19½, 23½ in.).

Otto, Franz. 1907. Vienna. Listed in a directory under Dolls and Dolls' Heads.

Otto, Robert. 1926–30. Berlin. Manufactured and exported dolls, dolls' clothes and accessories.

Otto, Rudolf. 1903–09. Sonneberg, Thür. Distributed dolls.

1903: Applied for a German patent (D.R.G.M.) for a doll with a mama-papa voice.★

Otto Doll Supply Co. 1917–18. New York City. Manufactured composition dolls and dolls' heads.

Our. Sometimes only a pronoun used by the maker or distributor, and the real name followed the pronoun.

Our Ann Ella. 1921. Name of a doll made by the *Jeanette Doll Co.* The arms were folded across the chest and the legs were apart. Four hts. 10, 12, 15, and 19 in. (25.5, 30.5, 38 and 48 cm.).

Our Anne. Name in capital letters on an elliptical green paper label affixed to kid body. Between "OUR" and the ANNE" was a circular monogram with the initials P. D. G. Co. At the bottom of the elipse was the word GERMANY.★

2033. Paper label attached to the kid body of a doll marked Our Anne.

No. G1½ "Our Baby"

2034A. Our Baby dolls produced by Horsman and advertised in their catalog of ca. 1914. The composition head came with molded and painted hair and eyes. *Courtesy of Bernard Barenholtz.*

No. 144½
"OUR BABY"
With Wig.

2034B. Our Baby dolls produced by Horsman and advertised in their catalog of ca. 1914. The composition head came with brown or blond short mohair wig and painted eyes. *Courtesy of Bernard Barenholtz.*

118

2035. Mark on the composition head of Our Baby doll.

Our Baby. 1912–16. Name of a bent limb baby doll with composition head and hands, cloth body made by *Horsman.* It came with painted molded hair or wig, painted eyes, or glass eyes, dressed in baby dresses, wore caps if it did not have a wig. Sometimes it had a bell rattle on a ribbon around its neck. Style no. 183 wore a white cape and hood lined with pink. It came in junior (No. G/O and 87) and standard (No. G/1½ and 144) sizes. Hts. 10½ and 13 in. (26.5 and 33 cm.); priced $4.25–$13.50 doz. wholesale.★

Our Baby. 1913. Composition-head doll advertised by *Gamage.* It had molded hair and wore a long or short baby dress; priced 73¢ and $1.37.

Our Baby. 1915–18. Line of dressed dolls made by *Effanbee.* It had composition head and lower arms, molded hair resembled that of *Baby Grumpy,* painted eyes, open-closed mouth with two teeth, cork stuffed cloth body, straight or bent legs. Hts. 14 and 21 in. (35.5 and 53.5 cm.). Pat Schoonmaker suggests that some of these dolls were marked 108.

1918: Distributed by *Butler Bros.* Also came with a mohair wig and an open mouth with pacifier; wore a white lawn dress and cap. Ht. 20 in. (51 cm.); priced $28.00 doz. wholesale.

Our Belle. 1909. Distributed by the *Boston Store.* Ht. 20 in. (51 cm.); priced $1.25.

Our Betty. 1929. Name of a doll produced by *C. & O. Dressel.*

Our Bobby. 1926. Name of a doll made by *Carl Harmus, Jr.,* and distributed by *Heller & Co.* In Sonneberg, Thur., and in England.

Our Darling. Early 1900s. All-bisque doll with wig, sleeping eyes, open mouth, teeth, marked on head and limbs "83/100." It came in a box labeled "Our Darling 83/100 Baby, Made in Germany." Ht. 5½ in. (14 cm.). This may have been *Baby Darling.*

Our Darling. 1917. Name of a *Horsman* doll with a Can't Break 'Em[†] composition head and limbs on a cloth body, distributed by *Charles William.* This doll had molded hair with a ribbon. Ht. 16 in. (40.5 cm.); priced 98¢.

Our Dolly-Kar Pet. 1928. Trademark registered in U.S. for dolls by *Strauss-Eckhardt Co.*

Our Fairy. 1914. All-bisque doll with wig, blue or brown glass eyes, and open-closed mouth. It was jointed at the shoulders. The height was marked in centimeters on the back of the head under the mold number 222. Four hts. 4½, 7, 9, and 11½ in. (11, 18, 22 and 29 cm.). It was made by *Hertel, Schwab.*★

Our Foreign Cousins. 1919–21. Cutout cloth dolls made by *Saalfield.* There were six styles, each 9 by 11 in. (23 by 28 cm.).

Our Gang. 1925–30. Five dolls representing the Hal Roach juvenile movie stars of this name. These clockwork winding dolls bore a scroll shaped tag and came five in a box. They were made by *Schoen & Yondorf* and distributed by *Borg-*

feldt and *Charles William.* The five dolls were *Farina, Fatty, Freckles, Mary* and *Jackie.*

Our Lindy. 1928–29. Portrait doll representing a smiling Charles *Lindbergh,* designed by *Ernesto Peruggi,* made by *Regal.* It had a composition head with molded hair and a long limbed body. The khaki aviator's costume had a fur collar, leather belt, and puttees. A round tag pinned to the chest of the suit with a safety pin had "OUR LINDY" on it. The copyright registration No. 83, 336 was claimed. Ht. 33 in. (84 cm.).

© REGAL DOLL CO.

SCULP E. PERRUGI

1928

OUR LINDY

mfg by REGAL DOLL Mfg. Co

N.Y.C.

© 83336

2036–2037. Marks for the Our Lindy composition head doll made by Regal Doll Manufacturing Co.

Our Mary. All-bisque doll with wig and glass eyes. On its stomach was a red sticker with "Our Mary//Trademark" on it; on the doll's back was Germany and 607.

Our Nancy. 1909. Distributed by the *Boston Store.* Ht. 19 in. (48 cm.); priced 98¢.

Our Nurse Doll. 1919. Name of a doll with composition head and hands distributed by *Montgomery Ward.* It had a mohair wig, cork stuffed body and wore a Red Cross nurse's outfit with a red cross insignia on its cap and apron. Hts. 12, 14½ and 18½ in. (30.5, 37 and 47 cm.); price $1.52 to $2.99.

Our Own. 1895. Trade name of a line of low-brow china head dolls with china-limbs and printed cloth bodies, distributed by *Butler Bros.* These dolls had molded collars or molded ruching at the neckline. Eight hts. 7½, 10¼, 11, 13, 16, 16½, 17½ and 19¾ in. (19, 26, 28, 33, 40.5, 42, 44.5 and 50 cm.); priced 42¢ to $3.20 doz. wholesale.

Our Pet. 1926–30 and later. Line of infant dolls resembling *My Dream Baby,* made with Biscaloid type composition socket heads for *Gebrüder Eckardt* and *Adolph Strauss* by *Armand Marseille.* They had a wig, glass eyes and a closed mouth. Frequently they came in a basket or blanket and one style in a square wicker playpen was called "Our Playyard Pet." They usually had a round tag with "Our Pet" on it. The 3¾ in. (9.5 cm.) head was marked 5/0 and the 4½ in (11.5 cm.) heads was marked 2/0.

1926: Some of the dolls were dressed in swaddling clothes and there were sets of twins; 10 heights were advertised.

1927: Two German patents (D.R.G.M.) and an American patent were applied for and claimed to relate to this line of dolls. The name Our Playyard Pet was registered as a trademark in the U.S. The ten hts. cost $1.00 and up.★

Our Pet
Germany
5/0

2038. Mark on Our Pet dolls.

Our Playmates. 1929. Name of dolls made by *Reisman, Barron.*

Our Playyard Pet. See **Our Pet.**

Our Rosebud. See **Rosebud.**

Our Sailor Lad. 1919. Name of a doll with composition head and hands, distributed by *Montgomery Ward.* It wore a navy blue uniform with bell bottom trousers, buttons indicating the fall and a white sailor's cap. Ht. 15 in. (38 cm.); priced $1.89. Fall is the name for the opening found on sailor's pants.

Our Shop. 1922–26. Budapest. Sold art dolls that were probably made by the owners of the shop, who were Jolán Jaszay, Anna Rucsimszky, Melanie Duha, and Sarolta Lukács.

Our Soldier Boy. 1919. Name of a doll with composition head and hands distributed by *Montgomery Ward.* It wore a khaki uniform with spiral puttees and a brimmed hat. Ht. 15 in. (38 cm.); priced $1.89.

Our Tommy. 1914. Name of a cloth doll with a velvet face distributed by *Whyte, Ridsdale.* It represented *Tommy Atkins.* The round tag read: "OUR//TOMMY//ARE WE // DOWNHEARTED//NO//MADE IN ENGLAND."

Our Trixie. 1921. Name of a doll with its arms folded across its chest, made by the *Jeanette Doll Co.* Four hts. 10, 12, 15 and 19 in. (25.5, 30.5, 38 and 48 cm.).

Ourine, G. 1925–30 and later. Paris. Made a line of dolls named *Poupée Royale.* These dolls were made of various kinds of materials. Ourine also made mohair or wool wigs, bodies and other parts for dolls. Advertised art dolls, dolls for decorative purposes and pincushion type dolls. Trademark see Ill. 2137.

Ouvré, Mme. Vera. 1915–18. Paris, Created cloth dolls including dolls representing Charlie Chaplin, a drummer boy wearing sabots and dolls in regional costumes with wooden shoes. One of the dolls was called Gavroche. Some of the dolls were black. (See also **Charlot.**)

Over the Bridge to Fairyland. 1926 and later. Trademark registered in 1926 in U.S. by *Hale Bros.* for dolls of bisque, celluloid, metal, rubber, or wood. Later Nancy Ann Story Book Dolls, Inc. renewed this trademark.

Overholt, Miles. 1921–23. Los Angeles, Calif. Obtained a German patent (D.R.P.) for a cloth doll.★

Overland Metal Novelty Co. 1925–27. New York City. Manufactured metal sleeping eyes and "Overland" crying voices under license by *Voices, Inc.*

1926: Placed on the center metal part of the sleeping eyes was "O. M. N. Co. Inc. // Pats. Pend."

2039. Cloth dolls made by Mme. V. Ouvré according to Léo Claretie in LES ARTS FRANÇAIS, written in 1918. The designs were registered in France. One can easily recognize Charlie Chaplin and the little African. Note that the other two dolls wear sabots (wooden shoes).

2040. Cloth doll made by Mme. V. Ouvré as seen in an illustration of an article by Léo Claretie, "Le Jouet des Pays de France" (The Native Toy of France), published in LES ARTS FRANÇAIS, 1918.

Overland Products Co. See **Zaiden, David.**

Overseas Industrial Agency. 1917. Richmond, Surrey. Handled *Pep* dolls.

Oweenee Novelty Co. 1921–23. Brooklyn, New York. Made dolls of terry cloth or of flannel. Some of the dolls had composition heads and hands on a cloth body. *Baker & Bennett, Borgfeldt, Bush Terminal,* and *Strobel & Wilken* were the distributors. The dolls were dressed to represent Black Eye Susie, *Jack and Jill Tots,* Clowns, and so forth.

1923: Advertised terry cloth dolls that could float and *Mama* dolls named "Oweenee" and *Love Me* with *Ronson* voices. Hts. 15 to 26 in. (38 to 66 cm.); priced $1.00 and up.★

Owen, C. F. 1920. Manchester, England. Produced dressed dolls at their British Doll Works.

Owens-Kreiser Co. 1912–26. New York City. Agent for various American manufacturers of dolls.

1915: Advertised *Wiggle-Waggle* dolls.

1919: Agent for *Giebeler-Falk.*

1926: Distributed *Kiddie Specialty Corp.* dolls.

Oz Doll & Toy Manufacturing Co. 1924–26. Los Angeles, Calif. Made oilcloth dolls stuffed with cotton. These dolls represented the characters in the WIZARD OF OZ.

Oz Toys and Dolls. 1924. Trademark registered in U.S. by *Frank Baum* for dolls.

Ozzeran Manufacturing Co. 1920. New York City. Made dolls including Coquette and Nettie.

P

P. & M. Doll Co. 1918–30 and later. New York City. Manufactured dolls, dolls' heads and parts of dolls. Member of the *American Doll Manufacturers' Assoc.* One of their dolls was named *Mary Ann* and another was named *Paula Mae.* The factory representative was the *Associated Toy and Doll Factories.*

1930: Advertised a baby doll with composition head and hands wearing a short baby dress, jacket and baby bonnet.★

P. R. or P. & R. See **Roma.**

P. & W. Doll Co. 1929–30 and later. Brooklyn, N.Y. Made dolls.

Pa. 1922. Name of a sponge rubber doll made by the *Miller Rubber Co.*

Paar, Katarina. World War I period–1927. Vienna. Worked with Elizabeth Neumayer making art dolls.

During World War I, Miss Paar created a new kind of cloth art doll which was sold at war benefits. Later the Paar dolls were exhibited in museums including the Brooklyn Museum in New York. Katarina Paar particularly liked to create dolls representing the 1830s period and ethnic dolls, especially black African ones.

1922: Dolls included several clowns, dolls dressed as Croatian, Spanish, or Slovak peasants; dolls in Siamese, Burmese, African and East Indian costumes; as well as dolls in costumes of the 1500s and 1700s. Among the names of the dolls were Amaravanta, Eugenie Fougère, Kalo-Mahesa, Minnesaugst, Minusiaugst, Parvati, Peter, Pua-Pua and Siva (a Hindu God).

1923: The BROOKLYN EAGLE reported an exhibit of Russian, Roumanian and Congo costumed Paar dolls at the Brooklyn Museum. "A copy of a Paar doll is no more like the original than a Montmartre sensationalist is like Cézanne or a plaster cast is like a Greek Marble. [Most of the copies are] made by girls in the workrooms of the Famous French dress makers. . . . The Vienese Werkstatte tried to commercialize them, but the artists' output is limited; she would not produce in quantities. Every doll that is created by her . . . is a personal expression." *Lanvin* dolls were shown at the same exhibit and a reporter from THE ARTS gave rave notices of the Paar dolls, stating the "Lanvin dolls pale beside them." THE BROOKLYN EVENING TRANSCRIPT described the Paar dolls as, "These objects in the opinion of the writer are the most beautiful of their kind ever made."

Pache & Son. 1852–1915. Birmingham, England. Made "True to Nature" dolls' eyes.

Pacific Doll Manufacturing Co. See **Pacific Novelty Co.**

Pacific Mills. 1927. Sales office in New York City. Made cotton fabrics used for a *Bradford* cambric cloth doll and a doll's dress of Picture Book prints.

Pacific Novelty Co. (Pacific Doll Manufacturing Co.). 1916–28. New York City. A division of *Du Pont* made *Viscoloid* dolls including bent limb baby dolls and child dolls jointed at the shoulders and hips. Dolls had wigs or molded hair; priced 10¢ and up.★

Paddlers. 1917–18. Name of cloth dolls made of stockinet or other fabric by *Shanklin*. These dolls designed by *E. E. Houghton* could either stand or sit. They wore black and white striped bathing suits and bathing hats or caps.

2042. Pair of dolls made by Katarina Paar, representing Slovak peasants. These were exhibited in 1922 at the Brooklyn Museum.

2041. Romantic costumed dolls made by Katarina Paar as shown in a 1920s exhibit arranged by Stewart Culin at the Brooklyn Museum. The men dolls both have musical instruments.

2043. A group of Katarina Paar dolls exhibited at the Brooklyn Museum in 1922. Pua-Pua and Kalo-Mahesa are 1920s Western interpretations of Eastern costumes. Peter is a Pierrot and has a musical instrument.

2044. Pair of dolls exhibited at the Brooklyn Museum ca. 1922. These dolls made by Katarina Paar represent Siva and Parvati.

Paddy. 1926–28. Name of a cloth doll designed by *Mabel Lucie Attwell,* made by *Chad Valley.* The chubby broad face of hand painted felt had veined glass eyes that looked to the side and a smiling linear mouth. The wig of real hair was allegedly combable and the body was made of velvette. It wore a coat with tails, a vest, bowtie, long plaid trousers and a high hat, carried a hexagonal tag.

1927: Three hts. 14½, 16, and 18½ in. (37, 40.5, and 47 cm.).

1928: Came 14½ in. (37 cm.) high only.

Paddy. 1930. Name of a bent-limb baby doll made in various sizes, black or white, with a wig or molded hair. Came dressed in a chemise and distributed by *Bedington, Liddiatt.*

Paderewski, Mme. Helena. 1915–18. Supervised the creation of dolls that were inspired by the dolls made by *Marie Vassilief* in Paris. The dolls were designed by *Jedrek* (Jedrick), a sculptor, and *Michèle,* a painter, both from Cracow. The dolls were made in *Mme. Lazarski*'s workshop in Paris and dressed by Sophie and Marcella.

1915: TOYS AND NOVELTIES discussed dolls made in Paris by Polish refugees as follows: "Not many months ago a group of Polish artists, sculptors and women skilled in fine needle work found themselves stranded in Paris. They had no money and no means of making money, as the market for their art had been completely destroyed, until the idea of turning their training to making dolls was suggested. The plan was immediately put into execution and the production of dolls started. The bodies were modeled by sculptors, the faces painted by portrait painters and illustrators and the costumes designed by girls and women whose early training had familiarized them with every detail of peasant costume.

"Madame Paderewski, the wife of the famous pianist, was passing through Paris at that time on the way to America. . . . She made many suggestions and encouraged the workers to put forth their best efforts, and in a short time she sent a consignment of thirty-one dolls to the Polish Victims

Relief Fund in New York. These dolls . . . represented perfectly the many types of native characters and costumes in far off Poland and they were absolutely unique in the field of stuffed dolls.

"Mr. Lyman, the capable manager of the Fund, at once saw the commercial possibilities in such dolls having a high intrinsic as well as historical value, and he immediately cabled the colony in Paris to turn out as many dolls as possible for the American market. . . . The original shipment by Madame Paderewski . . . was exhibited in the windows of the Aeolian Company . . . New York.

"The dolls shown in this display were scarcely exhibited before orders commenced to come in from collectors and museums all over the entire country. So copyright and design patents were taken out for the protection of each number, and arrangements were made with the Polish Artists' Mutual Help Society for assisting other deserving artists to obtain permission to leave Poland and join the colony in Paris.

"In order to realize as much money as possible from the initial sales of these dolls, Mr. Lyman has arranged to exhibit them at Bar Harbor, Newport, and in the Berkshires and other fashionable resorts where the first few shipments will be auctioned off at fancy prices. An especial appeal has been made to the wealthy social class and almost unbelievable prices have been obtained from the sale of every doll, but a further possibility in the commercial development of this unusual line has been discovered. At first but a few of the dolls were sold at fancy prices to people who bought them with an idea of helping the Fund, but it was soon found that the dolls in themselves were unusually attractive to the children who received them, and a real demand, far in excess of the visible supply was created.

"Two characters in particular, 'Halka' and 'Jan' . . . seemed to make a special appeal to all the children who saw them, and it was soon decided that a large enough quantity of these two numbers could be sold in this country to warrant making an attempt to have them duplicated by domestic manufacturers.

"That the dolls are attractive is an unquestionable fact, for their quaintness of costume and their originality of designs combine to make a doll which is wholly lovable and at the same time totally different from any thing which has yet been seen on the American market. The heads of the dolls are made of a heavy cloth, stuffed with cork and hand painted, while the bodies and limbs are stuffed with cork or straw. The costumes combine a multitude of high colors in a harmonious scheme, and every stitch and seam has been done by hand.

"The two characters mentioned above are about fifteen inches high, and since neither bisque nor composition enters into their makeup, they are exceedingly light in weight and unusually durable. They are in fact practically a rejuvenation of the rag dolls which were so popular some years ago, and if their initial success is any indication of what the future holds in store, it is quite possible that an era of rag dolls will again be experienced in this country.

"The plans which have so far been laid out include the manufacture of the two numbers mentioned by some domestic firm in large quantities, and a distribution covering

—HALKA

Copyright, 1915, E. B. Lyman

2045. This is a page from a booklet published in 1915 pertaining to the Paderewski dolls. Shown here are Halka and Jan, two of the cloth dolls made in the workshop of Mme. Lazarski under the supervision of Mme. Paderewski.

the entire United States is confidently expected. Several prominent department stores in New York have already arranged to handle the dolls and a number of the others are only waiting for samples before placing them in stock. The proceeds of all sales will, of course, be turned over to the Relief Fund, but if past experiences in the toy field are useful criterions, it will not be long before several manufacturers are making dolls of a similar character for themselves."

1915–16: The following dolls were produced: *Andrew, Anielka, Basia, Christine, Dominik, Franek, Halka, Henio, Jan, Jasio, Jedrek, Kasia, Little Carrot, Marcella, Michaela, Pola, Romano, Stas, Wanda, War-Man* of 1915, *Warmen* of 1794, *Water Nymph* and *Zofia*.

The dolls carried a round medal marked "Polish Victims//Relief Fund" with an armorial shield, and the dolls showed the costumes and industries of Poland. Jan and Halka were the most popular dolls. The above dolls were priced $3.00 to $15.00 with the rare ones costing even more.

1916: Mme. Paderewski and Mrs. Jerome Landfield, former-

ly a Russian princess, sold $1,400 worth of dolls in one day in San Francisco for destitute women and children in Poland.

1918: Paderewski dolls exhibited in the Art Alliance in New York were: Polish Aldermen, Polish King as a child, Polish lady of the 1300s, Polish Mountain Boys, Polish Peasants, Polish Red Indian (Polish conception of what a Red Indian looked like), Polish Street Urchins, Polish Uhlans, and Polish Zaza.

Paffert, A. 1930. Paris. Made dolls.

Page, Lewis. 1829–33. New York City. Distributed peg wooden and "varnished head" dolls that were shipped from Hamburg, Germany. Some of these dolls were produced by *Lindner.*

Page, Pat. 1929. New York City. Registered *Komie Klown* as a U.S. trademark. The name was on the pictured figure of a clown doll.

Pagliacci. See **Archie Pagliacci.**

Pahne, Harold Taylor. 1925–26. Sacramento, Calif. Obtained U.S. and German patents for a doll with changing facial expressions.

Pajama Baby. 1917. Name of a doll with moving or stationary eyes made by *Ideal.* The doll wore a coverall and hood.

Paladin Baby. 1903–14. Line of baby dolls produced by *Carl Hartmann.* These dolls with celluloid or porcelain heads and ball jointed bodies had some connection with *Kämmer & Reinhardt.*

1908: *Viktoria Luise* was the name of one of the Paladin Baby dolls.★

Palais de la Nouveauté. See **Dufayel.**

Palais Royal. 1880s. New York City. Imported dolls which they described as "French of all descriptions." They also advertised dolls' outfits. One of their advertisements showed a doll dressed as a bride, a doll in a chemise, doll's hats, shoes, fan and parasol. They sold by mail as well as from a store.★

Palais Royal. See **Marot, Maison.**

Palestine Dolls. 1927 and other years. The best dolls were imported from France but village artists also created dolls of olive wood, clay, or terra cotta.

Paloumé, Mme. 1930 and later. Toulouse, Haute-Garonne, France. Manufactured dolls.

Pamela. 1929. English dolls described in TOYS AND NOVELTIES as having "smooth, soft waxen cloth faces," auburn hair, blue eyes and green felt dresses. They came in various sizes.

Pan. 1887 and possibly later. Name of dolls made by *Henri Delcroix.*★

Pancake Baby. 1927–28. Line of cloth dolls made by *Albert Brückner's* sons in both black and white versions.

Pancho HEbee. See **HEbee-SHEbee.**

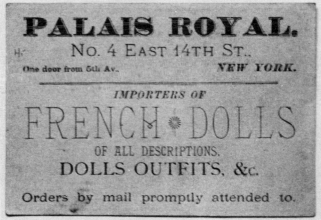

2046A & B. Palais Royal trade card advertising their French dolls and dolls' outfits; the picture on the reverse side of this card shows a little girl wearing clothes of the 1880s.

Pandora. 1915–18. Paris. Name of a workshop under the direction of *Mme. Leverrier* where dolls named Pandore†, created by *Mlle. Valentine Thomson,* were made. These dolls were distributed from this workshop. Dolls labeled "Pandora" had bisque heads, wigs, painted eyes and were on wooden stands. Their clothes showed considerable detail; one was dressed in a military khaki suit, another wore a Red Cross costume and yet another wore a couturière dress labeled "Claudinette." It is not known whether Claudinette was the name of the couturière or the gown or both.

1918: One of the dolls from France shown at the Art Alliance

2047. Bisque socket head marked Pan (see Ill. 2048). It has a blonde skin wig, glass eyes, slightly open-closed mouth and a ball jointed composition body. H. 28 in. (71 cm). *Courtesy of Vera Kramer, Dolls in Wonderland Museum.*

2048. Pan mark on a bisque socket head.

exhibit wore a Red Cross uniform and closely resembled the similar doll labeled "Pandora."★

Pandy. Name with "Germany" reported on the bisque head of a kid-body doll which was found in Austria. Ht. ca. 25 in. (63.5 cm).

Pansy (Pansy Kid). 1912–14. Name of a line of dolls with bisque head having sleeping eyes, mohair wig, kid or imitation kid body with bisque forearms; distributed by *Sears.* Four hts. 12, 16, 18½, and 20½ in. (30.5, 40.5, 47, and 52 cm.); priced 23¢ to 88¢.★

Pansy. 1927. Name of two-in-one *Twinjoy* line of *Flower Dolls* with petals for dresses created by *Berry Kollin.*

Pansy. See **Plano Toy Co.**

Pansy Doll. 1910–22. Some of the heads were made by *Schoenau & Hoffmeister*. Probably some of these dolls were the dolls marked "Pansy///III//Germany" or with some other Roman numeral. One example had a wig, sleeping blue eyes, hair eyelashes, open mouth and four upper teeth and a ball jointed composition body. Ht. 24 in. (61 cm.)★

Panta. 1930. Name used by *Kämmer & Reinhardt* for dolls' heads that they claimed were unbreakable and incombustible.

Pantalette Girl. 1919. Name of a doll made by *Ideal* and distributed by *McDonald Bros.* It had a composition head

2049. Bisque socket head doll named Pansy with a blond wig, sleeping blue glass eyes, open mouth, and a ball jointed composition body. H. 25 in. (63.5 cm.). *Courtesy of Sotheby Parke Bernet Inc., N.Y.*

2050. Mark for a Pansy doll.

and arms, a wig and sleeping eyes. Hts. 14, 15, and 16 in. (35.5, 38, and 40.5 cm.); priced $2.25 to $2.75 dressed.

Pantless Jimmie. 1919. Advertised by *Jeanette Doll Co.* It wore a stocking cap, sweater and booties.

Papayanni, J. 1928. Paris. Made dolls.

Papier-mâché Dolls. A type of doll with head made of a special kind of composition.

1860–61: Size number 12 was imported by *John D. Robbins*; priced $6.96 doz. wholesale.

1867: Jules Verne, the famous author, a passenger on the Great Eastern ship sailing from Liverpool to New York, wrote, "Among the passengers was a Frenchman who was carrying to America 30,000 papier-mâché dolls which said 'Papa' with a very successful Yankee accent."

1880: *Gottlieb Zinner & Söhne* advertised papier-mâché head dolls with black varnished molded hairdos and wooden limbs.

1929: Papier-mâché dolls cast in wooden molds were made in Florence, Italy. (See also **Friedrich Müller** and **Pappe.**)★

2051. 1830s style papier-mâché shoulder head with a modified Apollo Knot hairdo, painted eyes, closed mouth and a kid and cloth body. Original clothes. *Courtesy of the late Irene Blair Hickman.*

2052. Very high molded Apollo Knot hairdo on a papier-mâché shoulder head, painted features, kid body and wooden lower arms and legs. Original clothes. *Courtesy of the late Estelle Winthrop.*

2053A & B. Papier-mâché head has a black wig with the hair arranged in braids around the ears, stationary black glass pupilless eyes, closed mouth, kid body with wooden lower arms and legs. Original clothes. H. 15½ in. (39.5 cm.). *Courtesy of Sotheby Parke Bernet Inc., N.Y.*

This style obtained its name "Gothic" from the British coin first minted in 1847 having Gothic style letters and showing Queen Victoria with her hair in braids around the ears.

2054. Papier-mâché shoulder head with a slit into which the hair is placed, black painted pate; stationary black glass eyes, closed mouth and a cloth body with long papier-mâché arms. The lower legs are painted to resemble white stockings with red garters and yellow heelless 1840s style shoes with brown soles. Original clothes. H. 14 in. (35.5 cm.). *Courtesy of Estelle Johnston.*

2055. Papier-mâché shoulder head with a black pate, formerly covered with a wig. It has molded and painted features, closed mouth and a pink kid body of the type generally assumed to be French. Original regional costume. H. 13 in. (33 cm.). *Courtesy of Richard Withington. Photo by Barbara Jendrick.*

2056. Papier-mâché head on a kid body with wooden lower arms and legs. It has a white lamb's wool wig, molded and painted gray brown eyes, long pointed nose, open-closed mouth with teeth, appears to be smiling. Original clothes including a linen suit and a striped cotton vest. Buttons painted on legs all the way to the knees. Buckles painted on shoes. H. 8¼ in. (21 cm.). *Courtesy of Mike White.*

Papita. 1927. Trade name of a doll.

Papoose. 1907–09. Cloth cutout doll representing an Indian baby in the *Tiny Travelers* series made by *Saalfield*. Ht. 5 in. (12.5 cm.).

Papoose. 1920. Name of a handmade doll representing an Indian baby in swaddling clothes on a cradle board that could be hung anywhere. *Mary Frances Woods* made each doll with its own individual face and blanket pattern. Ht. 8 in. (20.5 cm.).

Papooski. 1916–18. Line of cloth cutout dolls representing Indian babies designed by *John Hassall* for the *Three Arts Women's Employment Fund.* Price $9.00 doz. wholesale.

Pappe. German word for cardboard or inexpensive papier-mâché used for bodies and for heads of dolls.

Pappe, Moritz. 1903–28. Liegnitz, Germany. Manufactured dolls.

1903: Applied for a German patent (D.R.G.M.) for a doll's body.

1906: Advertised dolls with felt heads, celluloid heads on cloth bodies, and small dolls, ht. 21 cm. (8½ in.), dressed and undressed. Dolls called *Hansel and Gretel.*

1907: Applied for two German patents (D.R.G.M.) for dolls with moving joints. One of these dolls wore an automobile coat.

1908–10: Applied for two German patents (D.R.G.M.) for dolls in skiing costumes and in swimming costumes. Advertised character babies, *Eskimo* dolls, dolls representing soldiers, dolls' house dolls, and dolls with celluloid heads.

1916: Applied for a German patent (D.R.G.M.) for paper dresses for dolls.

1920: Advertised *Rheinische Gummi und Celluloid Fabrik Co.* dolls.

1921: Applied for a German patent (D.R.G.M.) for jointed cloth body dolls.★

Paques-Noel, Etablissements. 1928–29. Paris. Made composition and cardboard dolls and bébés' as well as parts including wool and mohair wigs. The miniature dolls had painted, stationary glass or sleeping eyes.

Par Excellence. 1902–12 and probably other years. Name of dolls with bisque heads and kid bodies made by *Kestner* and distributed by *Butler Bros.*

1902: Five hts. 14½, 17½, 19, 21¾, and 23¾ in. (37, 44.5, 48, 55.5, and 60.5 cm.); priced 74¢ to $2.15.

1912: Dolls with painted eyebrows and eyelashes came in six hts. 14¾ to 24½ in. (37.5 to 62 cm.); priced 75¢ to $3.40 each wholesale.

Dolls with hair eyebrows and hair eyelashes came in five hts. 17½ to 26 in. (44.5 to 66 cm.); priced $1.75 to $5.00 each wholesale.★

Paradis des Enfants. See **Au Paradis des Enfants.**

Paradis des Enfants, Le. ca. 1886–1902. London. Name of a toy shop that sold dolls. This shop belonged to *Parkins & Gotto.*

Paramount Doll Co. 1926–30. New York City. Made *Mama* dolls and baby dolls. Licensed by *Voices, Inc.* to use patented voices and criers in their dolls. In 1930 Paramount was also known as *Kaufman, Levenson & Co.*

1926: Advertised a *Princess Pat* Mama doll. Another Mama doll with composition head, arms and legs, cotton stuffed body, wore an organdy dress and bonnet; priced $2.50 and up. A single baby doll with moving eyes and a crier cost $1.25. Twin babies in a pillow came in two sizes 9 by 12 in. (23 by 30.5 cm.) and 14 by 17 in. (35.5 by 43 cm.). The smaller ones had a single crier and cost $1.50; the larger ones had two criers and cost $2.50. Other baby dolls cost 50¢ and up. A satine [sic] faced Flapper doll (*Boudoir* type) with a wig cost $2.00; other Flapper dolls were $1.00 and up.

1929: Dressed dolls cost $2.00 to $15.00.

1930: Advertised *Baby Wobbles;* Mama dolls in various sizes and styles, some of them wigged and dressed; dressed baby dolls with dimpled faces, movable heads, lightweight kapok stuffed bodies. One of the baby dolls wore a short baby dress trimmed with ribbon beading and lace, a jacket and matching cap.

Parboy. 1928. Name of a molded wood-composition doll with handpainted features made by *Twistum.* It was jointed with flexible piano wire spring, anchored in a swivel. The doll represented a golfer that was described as, "He putts and drives when you twirl the wooden handle at his back." Ht. 7 in. (18 cm.); priced $1.50.

Parian. Term used by *Francis Hughes* in 1882, by *Gesland* in 1893 (Ill. 1052); the *Doll Pottery Co.* in 1916 and others.★

Parian Marble Bisque Heads. 1884–87 and possibly other years. Advertised in the *Lauer* catalogs. These bisque heads with either regular wigs or skin wigs were on "French"-type ball-jointed composition bodies but the size numbers and heights did not agree with *Bébé Jumeau* numbers and heights. (See also **Bisque Heads.**)

Paris, Richard. 1898. Oberköditz near Königsee, Thür. Applied for a German patent (D.R.G.M.) for a doll that could turn a somersault.

Paris Bébé. 1889–1941 and later. These dolls were first made by *Danel & Cie.* The *Société Française de Fabrication de Bébés & Jouets* (S.F.B.J.) renewed this trademark periodically but they used it on dolls that were also marked *Bru, Jumeau* or other names.

1906: *Aux Trois Quartiers* advertised a doll made by Jumeau with Paris Bébé on its sash. This doll, also named *Bébé Madeleine,* had sleeping eyes, hair eyelashes, and was fully jointed. Five hts. 28, 40, 45, 57, and 65 cm. (11, 15½, 17½, 22½, and 25½ in.); priced 78¢ to $4.20. The 45 and 57 cm. (17½ and 22½ in.) dolls also came "parlant"; priced $2.35 and $3.15.

1907–08: *Paris Cette* store had Paris Bébé on the sashes of their *Bébés Bru.*

1910: *Modernes* store advertised Paris Bébés.

1912: *Paris Montpelier* store advertised Paris Bébé.

1913: *Ménagère* advertised sleeping eyed, fully jointed dolls with "Paris Bébé" on the belt of the chemise. Hts. 28, 38, and 48 cm. (11, 15 and 19 in.); priced $1.00 to $1.80.

Nouvelles Galleries advertised Paris Bébé with sleeping eyes and in a chemise. Hts. 28, 38, and 41 cm. (11, 15, and 16 in.); priced 99¢ to $1.79.

1915–16: *Louvre* store advertised Paris Bébé with sleeping eyes and dressed. Eleven hts. 35, 40, 43, 45, 52, 57, 60, 63, 69, 74, and 78 cm. (14, 15½, 17, 17½, 20½, 22½, 23½, 25, 27, 29, and 30½ in.); priced $4.80 to $24.00.

1919: *Amberg* stated that Paris Bébé was the same quality as *Bébé Jumeau*.

1925: *Bon Marché* advertised Paris Bébé in seven hts. 31 to 65 cm. (12 to 25½ in.).★

Paris Cette. 1906–07 and probably other years. Paris. Store that advertised *Bébé Bru, Bébé Réclame* and *Paris Bébé* as well as other dolls.

Paris Doll. Lady doll with a bisque head and kid body was dressed to represent Saint Genevieve the patron saint of Paris. It wore the coat of arms of the city of Paris on its chest. (See Ill. 966.) TOYS AND NOVELTIES in 1927–28 reported on Paris dolls as follows: The novelty was talking dolls. Dolls walked, talked, rolled their eyes and one actually drank. The contents of a nursing bottle could be poured down the doll's throat and later a hinged back had to be opened and a sponge taken out and pressed dry. The stores had many *Eskimo* dolls due to the many trips to the North Pole. Mention was also made of "Beautiful blushing dolls." This may account for the darker coloring of some of the French dolls in this era. (See also the entries for the various Paris stores and the French manufacturers.)

Paris Montpelier. 1912 and probably other years. Paris. Store that advertised *Bébé Bru, Bébé Dormeur, Bébé Jumeau, Cymbalier, Eden Bébé, Eskimo* dolls, *Mignonnette* and *Paris Bébé.*

Paris Novelty Manufacturing Co. ca. 1919. Chicago, Ill. Made Dearie Doll.†

Pariser Dukke. Copenhagen. A purple stamp on the back of a cloth body doll with a bisque shoulder head read: "PARISER DUKKE—MAGASINET//Klinik for Dukker// 9 Østergade 9//Kjøbenhaven."

Parisettes. See Ateliers Paris-Fantaisies.

Parisian Ivory. 1913–14. Name of a celluloid made in Germany, especially in the Frankfurt-am-Main area. By 1915 celluloid was not available in Germany due to the war, according to TOYS AND NOVELTIES.

Parisienne. Generic name for dolls from Paris. Name used by Emile Jumeau for his lady dolls and also sometimes for his bébés, especially those with wardrobes of clothes. Parisienne was also a name used for *Cigarette Girl* dolls whether they were made in France, Italy, America or elsewhere.★

2057. Bisque head doll named Paris Bébé has a wig, stationary blue glass eyes, pierced ears, closed mouth and a ball jointed composition body with no joints at the wrist. Mark on head Ill. 2058. Mark on body: "JUMEAU// MEDAILLE D'OR// PARIS. H. 23½ in. (59.5 cm.). *Courtesy of Hazel Ulseth.*

PARIS BEBE
TETE DEP.

10

PARIS BEBE

2058–2059. Marks on bisque head of Paris Bébé.

Parisienne Belle. 1926. Cloth dolls with pressed faces, wigs, and cotton stuffed bodies, made by the *American Stuffed Novelty Co.* The clothes were designed by *Morris Politzer.*

Parker, Mary L. 1924. American. Designed a cloth baby doll; the design for which was stamped on a pale pink sateen and sold by the Embroidery Department of the WOMAN'S HOME COMPANION as No. 2258 A. The hair was to be made of floss and the face was to be painted. Ht. 24 in. (61 cm.); priced $1.00. For 25¢ stamped clothes patterns for this doll were obtainable.

*Doll designed
by Mary L. Parker*

A New Rag Baby

2060. Cloth doll designed by Mary L. Parker was sold by WOMAN'S HOME COMPANION. It was made of pale pink sateen with floss hair and painted features. Stamped patterns were also available for the clothes. H. 24 in. (61 cm.).

Parkhall Works. See **Dolls' Accessory Co.**

Parkins & Gotto. ca. 1886–1902 and possibly other years. London. Sold dolls.

ca. 1886: Their store was named Le *Paradis des Enfants*.

Parlez-Vous. 1928. According to TOYS AND NOVELTIES this was a new long-legged doll with "amusing and grotesque features." It was photographed by Fox News at the Chicago Toy Fair.

Parmentier. 1915–16. Cloth doll made by *Mlle. Rozmann,* described as realistic in appearance. There was also a doll representing Parmentier's sister.

Parsons, George Harry. 1924–26. New York City. Obtained several U.S. patents for dolls which he assigned to the *Averill Manufacturing Co.* One of these patents was for a doll with compressible legs having a whistle in each leg which when activated emitted a different sound in each leg. Another patent was for a doll whose eyes closed when a part of the body was pressed. After a short time the eyes opened automatically and at the same time a sound was emitted, thus simulating going to sleep for a time and then awakening with a cry.

Parsons-Jackson Co. 1910–19. Cleveland, Ohio. In 1918 or earlier the factory burned and the manufacture of the dolls was suspended for a short period but it reopened in New York City.

1912: Made both black and white dolls; smiling and crying dolls; dolls in white slips, in various colored rompers, and in blue and white sailor suits with caps.

1913: Claimed that the dolls were modeled from real live babies and were handpainted. ★

Partridge, Horace, & Co. 1873–94 and probably other years. Boston, Mass. Importers who advertised dolls on their trade card.

Party Baby. 1914. Name of a doll with composition head and arms, a mohair wig, cloth body jointed at shoulders, hips, and knees. Ht. 16½ in. (42 cm.).

Pascarel. 1930. Paris. Made or distributed dolls.

Pat. 1929. Name of an oilcloth doll made by *Live Long Toys.* It represented an Oriental child and was based on a cartoon character drawn by Ad. Carter. The stuffed doll wore a red, yellow and black costume. Ht. 10 in. (25.5 cm.); priced $4.00 doz. wholesale.

Pat M'Gee Doll. 1920. Cloth doll made by *Chad Valley.* It came in two sizes (No. R. 155 and R. 156).

Pat-A-Cake. 1918–25. Trademark registered in U.S. for dolls produced by *Horsman.* The baby doll had a place in back to insert a person's hand so that the doll could be manipulated to appear to be clapping its hands. (See also **Baby Patty Cake** and **Patty Cake.**)

Pat-A-Cake. 1925. Name used by *Amberg* for their *New Born Babe* that was claimed to be able to clap its hands, walk, and cry. It came with sleeping eyes or stationary eyes. The instructions read "To see my hands clap//Pull Jingle Bell." It cost $2.00 or $2.50.

Pataky, H. & W. 1894. Berlin. Applied for a German patent (D.R.G.M.) for dolls.

Pat-a-Pat. See **Pat-O-Pat.**

Patent Novelty Co. 1929. Fulton, Ill. Made turned, segmented wooden dolls. These articulated dolls were painted with bright colors.

Patented Absolutely Unbreakable. 1899. Words on a ribbon worn by dolls made by Mrs. *Solomon Hoffmann* and distributed by *Butler Bros.*

Patents. The information on patents published in the first COLLECTOR'S ENCYCLOPEDIA OF DOLLS was obtained from the U.S. Patent Office prior to the publication of the ENCYCLOPEDIA in 1968. A letter from the Director of the Office of Information at the U.S. Patent Office, dated April 13, 1971 gave the following information which differs in some respects from the earlier information:

The 1790 patent law provided a 14 year period of protection for a patent. The 14 years remained in effect until 1861 when the period was increased to 17 years of protection. The 17 year period still remained in 1971.

In 1842 a patent act required the owner of a patent to mark his article as patented as well as the date on which the patent was issued. Failure to mark the patent correctly or to falsely mark an article as patented resulted in a fine of $100.00. The 1861 patent act withdrew the penalty for failing to mark an article as patented, but provided that unless a manufacturer marked his article with the word "patented" he could not obtain damages from copiers.

The 1839 (sic) act permitted an American inventor to use publicly or sell his invention for two years before applying for a patent. In 1940 a patent act reduced this period from two years to one year.

An article in THE TOY TRADER, March 1926, entitled "German Patent, Model, Design and Trade-mark Protection" by Patent-attorney Dr. Oscar Arendt gave the following information:

"Patents are granted by the 'Reichspatentamt' to the applicant as main or additional patents for a period of 18 years, after the novelty of the invention has been proved. Inventors or co-inventors can be named, if desired. For inventions, which can be demonstrated by models, it is advisable to file simultaneously an application for an utility model (Eventual-Gebrauchsmuster) which is delivered when a patent is refused.

"Utility models (Gebrauchsmuster) are registered in the name of the applicant by the "Reichspatentamt" for 3 years without investigating the novelty. They can be renewed for a second period of three years. . . . Requirements for application: See Patents, but instead of drawings, one model may be submitted.

"Designs (Geschmacksmuster, surface designs or models) are registered for a period of utmost 15 years for 1 to 50 designs in one application.

"Registration at the ordinary court of law is granted to applicant without examination regarding novelty."★

Pat-O-Pat (Pat-a-Pat). 1925–28. Name of a baby doll that could clap its hands.

1926: Distributed by the *Chicago Mail Order House.* Ht. 20 in. (51 cm.); priced $1.98.★

Patriotic Dolls. 1925–26. Name used by *Shackman* for a line of all-celluloid dolls. These dolls included Miss Liberty dressed in a red, white and blue skirt and hat; Uncle Sam with beard and hair, wearing a red, white and blue sash, a hat, and carrying a cane; a doll decorated with red, white, and blue ribbon and holding a flag. Ht. 2¾ in. (7 cm.); priced $1.50 doz. wholesale. (Many other dolls were dressed in patriotic attire, especially during periods of war.)

Patsy. 1922. Name of a sponge rubber doll made by *Miller Rubber Co.*

Patsy. 1924 and probably later. Name of a composition-head doll made by *Effanbee.* They later used the name *Patsy* for an all-composition doll. The first Patsy had a stationary head marked "EFFANBEE //PATSY//COPR.//DOLL." or "EFFANBEE//PATSY." and was on a cloth body. Hts. 14 and 16 in. (35.5 and 40.5 cm.).

Patsy. 1927–30 and later. Name of a doll designed by *Bernard Lipfert,* made by *Effanbee* and distributed by *Butler Bros., Montgomery Ward,* and others. It was an all-composition doll with a ball neck going into a socket head, one arm bent and straight legs; jointed only at the neck, shoulders and hips. The design revolutionized the doll industry of the period. It was completely different from the fat *Mama* dolls that had known great popularity for nearly a decade. Effanbee in 1928 registered Patsy as a trademark in the U.S.

claiming that it had been in use since 1927. However identical (except for a name) advertisements by Effanbee appeared in PLAYTHINGS in 1927 and 1928, both showing the doll known as Patsy, but the 1927 advertisement had this same doll labeled *Mimi,* while in 1928 it was labeled Patsy. The success of Patsy caused many imitations to be produced. As early as 1928 Effanbee sued *Maxine Doll Co.* for imitating Patsy with their doll called *Mitzi.*

The progress of this litigation was described by PLAYTHINGS in 1928 as follows:

"Unfair competition" was tested in the courts in the litigation between Fleischaker & Baum, plaintiffs, and the Maxine Doll Co., defendants, over the manufacturing and selling of a doll claimed to be an imitation of "Patsy." A temporary injunction to restrain "another doll manufacturer from manufacturing, selling or handling a doll alleged to be an imitation of a doll known as 'Patsy' " was granted by Judge Goldrick. But the injunction was later denied by Judge Valente. The plaintiffs then appealed to Justice Victor J. Dowling, Presiding Judge of the Appellate Division, who ordered the defendants to "be restrained from manufacturing, handling or selling the doll stated to be the same as or simulating the appearance, size characteristics, ensemble features or general make-up of the doll, sold and distributed by the Plaintiffs under the name of 'Patsy.' "

This was a temporary stay for several months when a final decision would be made. The plaintiff contended that "where a manufacturer offers for sale a product that can be called new, novel, unique or distinctive it is not necessary to procure patent or copyright, provided that the product has been broadly advertised and distributed—and provided that this product becomes directly identified as the product of its originator and distributor."

The outcome of the case would "prove whether or not the creator of a new product (not necessarily protected by patent or copyright) successful enough to achieve a distinct commercial success, shall be able to protect his property rights represented by its origination, his investment and his new market."

Effanbee claimed that Patsy's neck arrangement was protected by their patent 1,283,558. A check on this patent showed that it had been obtained about five years earlier and did not pertain to the Patsy type neck joint.

The Patsy head, arms and legs could be turned to almost any position and it was claimed that the doll could stand alone and even stand on one leg. It came with different colored molded bobbed hair and usually its head band had a bow or rosettes. The dresses were very short, often above the crotch, and showed the drawers. A few Patsy shoulder head dolls on cloth bodies and wigged Patsy dolls have been found according to Pat Schoonmaker. Patsy dolls are usually marked with the name but the marks were not all identical.

1928: Patsy came in both black and white versions, 30 different dress styles plus a bathing suit, and by April the demand required the running of two factory shifts. Mark on back of doll "EFFANBEE//PATSY//PAT. PEND//DOLL." PLAYTHINGS published a picture of Patricia Fitzmaurice, the daughter of a trans-Atlantic aviator, holding the first Patsy doll, and suggesting that this was the origin of the name

Patsy. Ht. 13½ in. (34 cm.); priced $24.00 a doz. wholesale, $2.95 each retail.

1929: The emphasis was on Patsy's clothes. The doll came with a wardrobe. *Braitling* made special slippers for Patsy. *Katherine Rauser* designed dresses, hats and coats for Patsy. *M. L. Kahn* made outfits for Patsy.

Patsy carried the Effanbee heart-shaped tag. and was joined by her mate *Skippy* and a larger doll named *Patsy Ann.*

1930: Roller skates were an innovation for Patsy. These were attached to an extra pair of the doll's shoes. Patsy's clothes were also made by *Tailored Craft Novelty Co., Gladys Meyers,* and *Elsie R. Baunton* who made a felt cloak, a sunsuit and broad-brimmed beach hat, romper dresses, bunny slippers, and so forth. One of Patsy's new outfits was a Chinese Mandarin costume. M. L. Kahn made a snowsuit and Braitling made artificial and genuine leather shoes for Patsy as well as stockings. *Patsy Babyette* and *Patsy Kin,* both smaller dolls, were added to the Patsy family.

After 1930: Patsy Baby, Patsy Jr., Patsyette and Wee Patsy, all smaller dolls, were added to the Patsy family as well as Patsy Fluff, Patsy Joan, and Patsy Babykin.

Butterick pattern No. 442 included the following articles of apparel for Patsy: a dress, skirt with suspenders and blouse with attached bloomers, bathing suit, coat, pajamas, combination slip, cloche, and a beret. (See THE COLLECTOR'S BOOK OF DOLLS' CLOTHES, Ill. 770 I.)

2062–2065. Marks found on Patsy composition dolls.

2061. All-composition Patsy made by Effanbee with molded and painted hair and features. The eyes glance to the side; the tiny mouth is pursed. The body is jointed at the neck with the socket in the head. Shoulders and hips are jointed. Original clothes. H. 14 in. (35.5 cm.). *Courtesy of Jan Foulke and Howard Foulke. Photo by Howard Foulke.*

Patsy Ann. 1929–30 and later. All-composition doll similar to *Patsy* except larger, 19 in. (48 cm.), and described as Patsy's big sister. The clothes were more elaborate than those for Patsy. They were also made by *Tailored Craft Novelty Co., Elsie R. Baunton,* and others. Like Patsy, Patsy Ann carried a heart-shaped tag on its wrist. A red on white tape tag at the back hemline of a dress on a Patsy Ann doll of unknown date read "EFFanBEE//DOLL//FINEST & BEST// MADE IN U.S.A." All except the Made in U.S.A. was within an ellipse. This all-composition doll had tin or celluloid over tin sleeping eyes, hair eyelashes, a pursed mouth, shingled bobbed hair, rotating shoulder joints, and raised letters on the back of the doll, reading "EFFANBEE//'PATSY-ANN'// © // Pat. 1283558." The clothes on this doll consisted of a white dress with woven flowers, a square neckline edged with lace, skirt extending to just below the crotch; a red wool felt coat with red velvet collar, cuffs and belt with a silver colored buckle; the teddy matched the dress; white socks with brown tops; black single strap slippers.

1930: *Bamberger's* showed an extensive wardrobe for Patsy Ann.

1931: Dressed in a dotted swiss dress, Patsy Ann cost $4.89.

Patsy Baby. Ca. 1932. Name of doll made by *Effanbee.*

Patsy Babyette. 1930 and later. All-composition doll made by *Effanbee.* Head marked "EFFANBEE," back of the doll marked "EFFANBEE//PATSY BABYETTE." Ht. 9 in. (23 cm.).

Patsy Dobla. See **Little Shavers.**

Patsy Kin (Patsykins or Patsy Jr.). 1930 and later. All-composition doll made by *Effanbee,* distributed by *Montgomery Ward.* Mark on back "EFFANBEE//PATSY JR.//DOLL." It wore silk or dimity clothes. Ht. 11½ in. (29 cm.); priced $1.89.

1930: It came with roller skates on extra shoes. GOOD HOUSEKEEPING advertised Patsykins wearing a red, blue or green on white dotted swiss dress with matching hair ribbon and socks, and black Mary Jane slippers. Priced $1.95.

Patsy Lou. Ca. 1930 and later. One of the Patsy family of dolls made by *Effanbee.* Mark on back of body, "EFFANBEE//PATSY LOU."

Pattie Pattie Doll. 1926. Doll with a composition head, painted hair, and sleeping eyes made by *Averill Manufacturing Co.* in their *Madame Hendren* line. It wore a long baby dress and cap and carried a rectangular tag reading, "Press my body and I will clap my hands." This doll came in a variety of sizes and styles.

EFFANBEE
PATSY-ANN
⓭ C
PAT # 1283558

2067. Embossed mark on the back of Patsy Ann made by Effanbee.

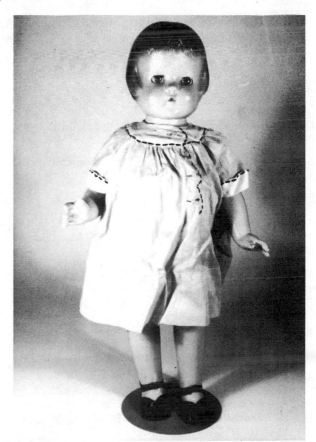

2068. All-composition doll of ca. 1932 named Patsy Baby. It has molded and painted hair, sleeping green glassine eyes, and a closed mouth. The neck socket is in the head. Five-piece bent limb baby body. Marks on head and body: "EFFanBEE//PATSY BABY." H. 10 in. (25.5 cm.). *Courtesy of John Axe. Photo by John Axe.*

2066A & B. All-composition Patsy Ann made by Effanbee starting in 1929 as a larger version of Patsy. It has molded bobbed hair, metal sleeping eyes, hair eyelashes, and a puckered mouth. Mark: Ill. 2067. H. 19 in. (48 cm.). *Coleman Collection.*

2069. All-composition doll named Patsy Lou, made by Effanbee. It is a large size Patsy with molded and painted hair, sleeping blue eyes, closed pursed mouth, and the reverse type neck joint with the socket in the head. There are joints at the shoulders and hips. H. 21 in. (53.5 cm.). *Courtesy of Richard Withington. Photo by Barbara Jendrick.*

Patty. 1917–18. Stockinet cloth doll designed by *E. E. Houghton* and made by *Shanklin*. Patty was one of the *Three Little Sisters* dolls and wore a blue and pink check or dotted dress with a white sunbonnet.

Patty. 1921. Stockinet doll imported into U.S. by *Meakin & Ridgeway*.

Patty-Cake. 1918–26. Name of a cloth baby doll produced by *Horsman* and distributed by *F. A. O. Schwarz*. It had a voice and wore a long baby dress. Hts. 12 and 15 in. (30.5 and 38 cm.); priced $1.25 and $2.00. (See also **Baby Patty Cake** and **Pat-A-Cake.**)★

Paturel, J., & Cie. 1925–28 and probably other years. Paris. Their 1928 catalog showed bisque head dolls on composition bodies; all-composition dolls; cloth dolls; rubber dolls dressed in tricot or undressed; and black or white celluloid dolls having bent limb baby bodies or straight limb child bodies. The dolls included *Boudoir* dolls, *Mignonnettes, Poupards, Esquimaux* dolls; mascots and dolls named specifically *Bobby, Colette, Lili, Niquette, Odette* and *Yvette.*

1927: Obtained a French patent for a doll's voice.

Paufler, Emil, & Co. 1876–1907. Schneeberg, Saxony. Made dolls and dolls' heads, Claimed that they were the oldest makers of dolls' heads in Saxony.

1888: Advertised papier-mâché, wax and porcelain dolls' heads as well as *Täuflinge.*

1902: Applied for a German patent (D.R.G.M.) for dolls. Advertised large, jointed dolls and a variety of dolls' house dolls.★

Paul. 1913–24. Felt character doll made by *Steiff* and distributed by *Borgfeldt*. This boy doll wore an apron or pinafore.

1913: In the U.S. the hts. were 14 and 17 in. (35 and 43 cm.); priced $2.55 and $3.50. The larger doll had a mama voice.

1916: There were five hts. 28, 35, 43, 50, and 60 cm. (11, 14, 17, 19½ and 23½ in.).

1924: Hts. were 28, 35, and 43 cm. (11, 14, and 17 in.).

Paula Mae. New York City. Name on a box containing a composition headed doll made by the *P. & M. Doll Co.* Ht. 16½ in. (42 cm.).

Paulette. 1929. Jointed cloth doll with felt clothes advertised by *Bon Marché*. Ht. 44 cm. (17½ in.).

Pauline.† See **Pet Name.**

Pauline Gilbert Dolls. 1913. Cloth dolls made by *Dean*.

Paulus, Johann Georg. See **Schlaggenwald.**

Pauvre Jacques. 1901 and other years. Paris. Name of a store that sold dolls. Among the dolls in their 1901 catalog were *Bébé Pauvre Jacques, Bébé Merveilleux, Bébé Phénix* and *Bébé Ravissant.* (See THE COLLECTOR'S BOOK OF DOLLS' CLOTHES, Ill. 525.)

Paxrainer, Anna. 1907–08. Vienna. Listed in a directory under Dolls and Dolls' Heads.

Pay. 1913: Felt comic character doll made by *Steiff* and distributed in the U.S. by *Borgfeldt*. It was dressed in a fanciful peasant costume and wore wooden (?) shoes. Ht. 17 in. (43 cm.); priced $2.95 in America.

Payne, Alec J. 1930. London. Agent for *Norah Wellings*.

Payne, W., & Son. 1772–1927. London and Paris. According to GAMES AND TOYS, April 1926:

"Dolls and dolls' accessories have always been an important feature of this House. Their dolls include lines of every description." During World War I they produced jointed, dressed and undressed dolls and imported dolls from France. After the war they manufactured some of their own dolls and imported others. In the 1920s George Ley Bevan Rees was the proprietor.

1915: Imported fully jointed dressed and undressed dolls from France. Advertised bisque head and celluloid dolls including dolls representing nurses, soldiers, Scots and Irish. One Scottish doll was described as having a "china" head, wig, sleeping eyes. "Made to Paynes' own specifications" and "dressed on the premises" in assorted tartan dresses including "sporran and glengarry."

1917: Advertised baby dolls, character dolls, dressed and undressed.

1919–21. Advertised dressed and undressed English and French dolls.

1926: The GAMES AND TOYS article continues: "A feature . . . is the miniature dressed dolls, jointed, 4¾ in. [12 cm.] high, which they can offer in great variety. They comprise Irish, Scotch, Welsh, motorists, airmen, Dutch, etc., and are packed half-a-dozen in a box. A novelty amongst dolls is a dressed baby in a rocking chair, while still further notable lines include the twins, in wedding cake boxes, and a dressed baby in a wedding cake box. Amongst the doll accessories we must mention a line known as 'Dolly's Ideal Mack.' This is beautifully made, correct in shape, and supplied in six art colours. Other lines include dolls' shoes in a variety of styles." "Dolly's Ideal Mack" must be a raincoat.

Peace Dolls. After World War I. Generic name for dolls made immediately after World War I.

Peace Family. 1918–20. Composition head portrait dolls with jointed cloth bodies. Were designed by *Ann Dailey* of Evergreen Col.

Peach. Name of an all-bisque doll made in Germany. This doll was mold # 257 and the head was marked with what appeared to be S.W.C. (Strobel & Wilken Co.?).

Peachy Pets. 1919. Line of all-composition dolls made by the *Colonial Toy Manufacturing Co.* They had mohair wigs and were jointed at the shoulders and hips. They came in both black and white versions. The line included at least 100 numbers; many of them wore bathing suits and silk bathing caps with large bows. Other numbers wore knitted or jersey outfits, or were dressed in satin ribbons with a large hair ribbon and carried a bag. The bathing suits came in assorted colors and the dolls wearing them cost $24.00 doz. wholesale. The dolls dressed in pink or blue ribbons cost

2070A. Paper sticker on an all-bisque doll named Peach.

SWC
257
19

2070B. Mark on Peach doll.

$27.00 doz. wholesale. Ht. of the dolls was 11 in. (28 cm.).★

Peacock, J. 1862–89 and probably later. London. An *Autoperipatetikos* with a china head has been found marked "July 15, 1862. J. Peacock, Doll Maker, The Rocking Horse, New Oxford St., London."★

Pearl Toy Co. 1926–27. New York City. Made dolls.

Pearlie. All-bisque doll with a wig and glass eyes, jointed at the shoulders and hips. A red sticker on the doll's stomach had the word "Pearlie." Germany and 607 were on the doll's back.

Pearlie Washable. Name on a kid body with a bisque head marked: 10 S. H. 10. for mold # 1010. Ht. 24 in. (61 cm.).

Pearly. 1908. Name of a printed cloth doll made by *Dean.* It was covered with pearl buttons to represent one of the London Pearlys.

Pearly King. Dolls have been found dressed to represent the Pearly King whose clothing was completely covered with pearl buttons. The Pearly King was a London Cockney.

Pearly King. 1916. Doll advertised by *Sunlight, Sieve & Co.*

Pearse, Ouida. ca. 1930. Plymouth, England. Head of Needlework Department, Plymouth School of Arts and Crafts. She wrote a book SOFT TOY MAKING, published in 1932. Her dolls were stuffed with kapok and usually had sheeps' wool hair.

   "Baby Doll" was a straight limbed child doll, with a commercially made cloth mask face costing 6 cents; cotton fabric body. The doll wore a bonnet, a high-collared snowsuit and mittens.

   "Arabella" was a long-limbed doll with a home-made mask face having the nose sewed on separately. It wore a tunic with a frill at the neckline and as cuffs. There was fullness at the bottom of the tunic; tight fitting trousers were ankle length. The tunic and trousers were made of artificial silk.

   "Tom," a black doll, had both the nose and ears sewed on separately. Boot buttons were used for eyes and the rest of the features were embroidered. This barefoot doll wore a short-sleeved shirt and short trousers.

   "Josephine" was made similar to Tom but was a little

2071. China shoulder head with black molded hair in corkscrew curls behind the ears, painted eyes, is on an Autoperipatetikos body bearing a J. Peacock stamp (Ill. 2073). On the bottom it states: "THIS DOLL IS ONLY INTENDED TO WALK ON SMOOTH SURFACE." and "Patented July 15, 1862, also in Europe 20 Dec. 1862." The arms are leather. H. 10½ in. (26.5 cm.). *Courtesy of Richard Withington. Photo by Barbara Jendrick.*

2072A & B. Wax head doll handled by Peacock has inserted hair, stationary blue glass eyes, closed mouth and a cloth body with wax lower arms and legs. Original clothes. Mark, black stamp on the chest: "From// PEACOCK'S // The Rocking Horse// 525 New Oxford St.// Corner of Bloomsbury St. // LONDON. W.C." H. 17½ in. (44.5 cm.). *Courtesy of Iverna and Irving Foote. Photo by Irving Foote.*

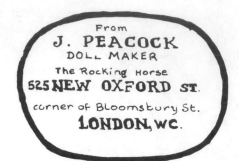

2073. Mark found on dolls handled by Peacock.

white girl with two plaits. She wore a short-sleeved printed dress and shoes.

"Golliwog" was made of black sateen and had black fur for hair. It was stuffed with kapok in the small parts and wood wool in the body, which made it harder and firmer. It wore a black velveteen coat with tails and a white silk lining, a fancy colored waistcoat and long trousers of patterned black satin.

"Miss Japanese," in an Oriental-type costume, had black hair and bent arms.

"Susanne," a 23 in. (58.5 cm.) *Boudoir* doll in a Pierrette-type costume, had long slim limbs with pointed feet and bent arms. It had a long bob wig and painted face with blue eyes.

"Belinda," 28 in. (71 cm.), was also a Boudoir doll and had long straight limbs and a painted face. It wore a long ruffled evening dress of pale blue net and a tight fitting short evening coat of blue velveteen edged with white fur. Its necklace had 2 rows of pearls in graduated sizes. The black felt high-heeled shoes had a pearl on each toe.

Peasant. 1922. Line of dolls made by *Wonderland Toymaking Co.*

Peasant. See **Regional Costume Dolls.**

Pecher, M. Ca. 1899–1925. Vienna. Listed in a directory under Dolls and Dolls' Heads.

Pechmandl, Heinrich. 1908–10. Vienna. Listed in a directory under Dolls and Dolls' Heads.

Pechthold, Oscar, Albin, and Carl. 1908. Murschnitz near Sonneberg, Thür. Applied for a German patent (D.R.G.M.) pertaining to dolls.

Peck, Mrs. Lucy (née Brightman). 1891–1930. London. She was born in 1846, married Henry Peck in 1876 and died in 1930. Some of her dolls are dark beeswax and others are a pink wax. Since she repaired wax dolls as well as making them herself, it is not always certain that a doll with a Peck label was made originally by Lucy Peck. A poured wax portrait doll of Queen Victoria has its cloth body marked "FROM Mrs. PECK, THE DOLL'S HOME 131 REGENT STREET, W." (It is known that she was at this address in 1902 and probably other years.) Height of this doll was 28 in. (71 cm.).

1922: Mrs. Peck changed from making wax dolls to modeling in clay and making plaster of Paris molds of dolls.★

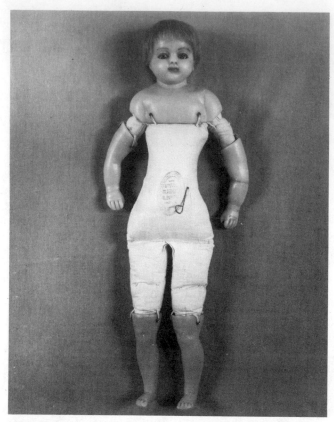

2074. Poured wax shoulder head doll made by Lucy Peck, 1902–8, has wax arms and legs, inserted hair, glass eyes, with wire mechanism for sleeping. Cloth body has an elliptical stamp reading: "MRS PECK//THE DOLL'S HOME//131 REGENT STREET //LONDON, W//DOLLS AND TOYS OF ALL DESCRIPTIONS REPAIRED.", the last group of words are in a surrounding frame. H. 54 cm. (21½ in.). *Courtesy of the Collection Nederlands Kostuummuseum, The Hague. Photo by B. Frequin.*

2075. Mark used by Lucy Peck for her wax dolls.

Peck, William E., & Co. 1911–29. London. Agent for *New Era Novelty Co., Gre-Poir* and sole agent in Britain for *Schoenhut.*★

Pedlars. 1800s–1900s. Dolls representing pedlars with their various kinds of wares in baskets or trays. The heads were primarily made of kid, papier-mâché, wax or wood and even chicken skin. The bodies were made of cloth, wood, or some other material. Pedlars were dressed as men or women; the latter usually wore a red or black cape and hood. Sometimes they wore cotton dresses with aprons and bonnets. Shells were occasionally used to indicate clothes. *C. & H. White* produced pedlar dolls.

Peek-A-Boo. 1911–20 and possibly later. In 1911 *Chloe Preston* wrote and illustrated a book called THE PEEK-A-BOOS. The children in this book had the round faces and types of eyes that were associated with *Grace Drayton*. One wonders if the name taken by the *Horsman*–Grace Drayton dolls in 1913 could have been influenced by the name of the Preston book. The name was applied to various kinds of dolls but always to those having similar faces. (See Ill. 2140.)

1913: The Horsman Peek-A-Boo dolls had bobbed molded hair, painted eyes looking to the side, single line smiling mouth, and starfish type hands.

Some of the composition Peek-A-Boos had cloth upper torsos and were 7½ in. (19 cm.) high. Cloth labels have been found on some of the clothes.

1914: The *Marshall Field* catalog used the name Peek-A-Boo for an all-bisque doll as well as composition dolls. The dolls had painted or glass googly eyes.

1916: Some of the Horsman Peek-A-Boos had wigs.

1920: A novelty Horsman doll made of Adtocolite[+] was called Peek-A-Boo. It wore costumes similar to the Horsman *Pinafore* doll and *Blue Bird* doll.★

Peeps. 1918–20. Name of an all-composition doll made by *Jessie M. Raleigh*. It had a wig of golden curly hair, a five-piece body with straight legs and was strung with steel springs. It was dressed in a white lawn dress and a sky-blue hooded cape with a yellow lining. The story of Peeps, "the Really, truly Sunshine Fairy," was written by Nancy Cox McCormack, illustrated by *Katherine Dodge* and published by P. V. Volland Co. of Chicago. The yellow lining of the cape suggested "the sunbeams on which the original Peeps of the story rides from the sky to the earth." (See Ill. 2175.)★

Peerless Doll Co. 1917–18. New York City. Made dolls with composition heads and hands on cloth bodies. They had molded painted hair including bobbed hair, and painted eyes. ★

Peg Wooden Dolls. These turned and carved dolls were made at least from the early 1700s well into the 1900s. They were made in a wide range of sizes and came chiefly from the Grödner Tal, Thüringian Wald (woods) and the Berchtesgaden, Oberammergau Tyrolian areas. The peasants living in these mountains spent their winters making dolls and other toys from the local wood usually pine. The dolls that were made in all of these areas were somewhat similar. It is believed that the earliest dolls carved in the Grödner Tal were sent north to the other areas to be painted. Around the middle of the 1800s some heads of china or composition began to be used on the wooden bodies for greater detail and realism.

Peg joints were also used on wooden dolls in other countries such as the American Joel Ellis dolls (See Ill. 438 in The first COLLECTOR'S ENCYCLOPEDIA OF DOLLS). Wooden dolls with peg joints were also made in Greenland. Some of the Oriental wooden dolls, the Swiss carved wooden dolls, and so forth also had peg joints.

1878: THE QUEEN reported, "There are many improvements even in [peg wooden dolls]; some are to be had with Chinese and other character heads."

1906: *Gamage* sold five sizes of the peg wooden dolls which they called "Dutch Dolls[+];" priced 9¢ to 68¢.

1913: Peg wooden or "Dutch Dolls" as they were commonly called were still being produced in 1913. They were described in TOYS AND NOVELTIES in January 1913: "At St. Ulrich, a picturesque Tyrolian town, the residents make carved wooden dolls. They are crude looking affairs, but the facial expressions are unusually good as some are carved to show a doll laughing and others portray a cry-baby."★

Pegard, F. 1833–50s. Paris. Manufactured dolls; according to the research of Mme. Florence Poisson, curator of the Roybet Fould Museum.★

Peggie (Peggy). 1912 and later. Cutout cloth doll made by *Dean*. It had a *Drayton* type face, a floral print dress, hairbows, socks and single strap slippers. A printed doll was in its arms. It was a mate to *Teddie*.

1920: One of the *Goo Goo* series of flat cloth dolls with eyes looking to the side. It was style no. D. 248. Ht. 8½ in. (21.5 cm.).

1979–80: It was reprinted.

Peggy. 1920–1929. Dolls made by *Chad Valley*. The first Peggy was a stockinet doll with a hand woven wig that was combable and removable clothes made of silk or other materials. This doll was style no. 6, about 12 or 13 in. (30.5 or 33 cm.) tall. It came with a wrist watch patented by Chad Valley.

The Peggy doll from 1923 to 1929 was entirely different; it was a flat-type cloth doll with its clothes printed on it. These printed clothes portrayed a cloche and rompers. The down-stuffed cloth body had its arms away from the body and its legs apart. It was style no. 40, 11 in. (28 cm.) tall.

Peggy. 1923. Name of a doll with a knitted body made by *Estelle Wheeler*. It was dressed in gingham and cost $2.00.

Peggy. 1927. *Boudoir* doll with a painted mask face, mohair wig, and cotton stuffed body. It wore a faille *Yama Yama* clown suit, silk stockings, and high heeled shoes. *Butler Bros.* distributed this doll. Ht. 34 in. (86.5 cm.).

Peggy. 1929–30. Name of an all-composition doll with painted hair and features, jointed at the shoulders and hips, made by *Horsman* and distributed by *Butler Bros.* This doll, with the same type of neck joint as Patsy, also had a bent arm and the ability to stand alone. Some of these dolls had a little pup on a leather leash.

1929: The Butler Bros. catalog (See Ill. 775G in THE COLLECTOR'S BOOK OF DOLLS' CLOTHES) described the doll as wearing a printed percale dress. Ht. 13½ in. (34 cm.); priced $8.00 doz. wholesale.

1930: PLAYTHINGS reported a variety of costumes. The print dress had a round collar and short sleeves. There were colored organdy dresses. The smallest size doll had a hair ribbon while the larger sizes had flannel or velvet coats in green, yellow, or blue with matching beret or sunbonnet. The largest size had a mama voice. Hts. 12, 14, and 20 in. (30.5, 35.5 and 51 cm.).

Peller-Hollmann, Mrs. Johanna. 1907. Vienna. Daughter of a cabinet maker, she made turned wooden dolls with some carving on them. The dolls had elaborate carved and painted clothes; for example, one doll had a ruffled skirt. Many of the dolls had wide-brimmed hats. The feet stood on round bases.

Penate. 1924. Name of dolls made by *Steiff.* Hts. 28, 35, and 43 cm. (11, 14, and 17 in.).

Péneau, Marcel. 1930 and later. Paris. Manufactured and exported dolls. Specialized in dolls with artistic heads.

Penelope. 1923. Cloth doll designed and made by *Dorothy Heizer.* Its painted face had blue eyes and a dimple in the chin. The curled hair of dark brown wool was made by coiling it around a pencil. The clothes for the doll consisted of a calico dress, a ruffled organdy dress, a duvetyn cape, a calico poke bonnet, a white nainsook night gown, a night cap, knee-length chemise, frilly full petticoat, ankle-length pantalettes, shoes and stockings. The doll cost $25.00 if made up and $2.50 if cut out ready to be made.

Penn Stuffed Toy Co. 1924–30. New York City. Manufactured *Mama* and baby dolls, and was a member of the *American Doll Manufacturers' Association.* Used a trademark of a circle with a Mama doll in the center under "Penn//Doll Trademark."

1926: Advertised walking, talking, and sleeping dolls created by *Mssrs. Tzezes and Slatin,* who had had "long experience in creating dolls."

1928: Advertised 50 style numbers; some dolls had mohair wigs or painted hair and eyes. Other dolls had human hair wigs and sleeping eyes. The dolls came dressed in a variety of frocks. Some of the dolls cost $1.00.

1929: They had a new factory.

1930: Advertised a full line of Mama and infant dolls as well as *Lialla, Quaker Dolls* and *Valencia* dolls. The Lialla and Valencia dolls were designed by *Mr. J. Green.* The Quaker doll was designed by *Julius Mangiapani.*

2076. Penn Doll, the trademark of the Penn Stuffed Toy Co., as shown in PLAYTHINGS, January 1926.

Penney, J. C., & Co. 1928–30 and later. Distributed dolls. 1928: They obtained a U.S. trademark, *Mary Lu,* for dolls. 1929: Advertised *Baby Dimples, Dolly Rosebud, Kiss Me, Peterkin, Tickletoes, Val-Encia, Mama* dolls, dolls in felt Dutch costumes, and baby dolls. (See Ill. 2077.)

Penny Dolls. 1860–61. Dolls listed as imported by J. D. Robbins in his day book owned by Elizabeth Pierce. These were probably *Peg-wooden* dolls. Size 3 cost 8¢ per doz. wholesale.

Pennsylvania Potteries. Made American redware dolls, according to Clara Fawcett.

Pensky, Alfred. 1925–30 and later. Coburg, Bavaria. Manufactured bisque and china small dolls, dolls' house dolls, baby dolls and pincushion dolls.

1926: The bent-limb baby dolls had molded hair while the straight leg child dolls had wigs.

1927–28: Advertised dressed miniature dolls, newborn baby dolls tied in a blanket, bathing girls and pincushion dolls. Mey & Edlich was the distributor in Leipzig.

1930: Advertised dressed dolls.

Pensky, Hermann. 1911–30 and later. Coburg, Thür. and later Bavaria and Eisfeld, Thür. In 1911 Hermann Pensky and Albin Michaelis owned *Amandus Michaelis & Co.* In 1922 Hermann Pensky started his own company. Manufactured dolls.

1927: Advertised *Mama* dolls.

1929–30: Advertised dressed and undressed dolls and baby dolls as well as little dolls and "artistic dolls."

Pep. 1917. Overseas Industrial Agency handled cloth dolls named Pep. The mark was a monogram ▨ .

Pépin, Silver. 1930. Paris. Listed in a directory under Dolls.

Pepita Dolls. 1920–21. Line of dolls made by *Hilda Loose.* One of these, The Ice Queen, was made of wood pulp, plaster of Paris and dextrine. Other dolls included Beach Queen, "Biedermeyer Colonial Gentleman," La Belle Helene, Marie Antoinette, Snow Fairy, and "Sportys."

Peppy Pals. 1929–30. Name of pairs of dolls made by the *S. & H. Novelty Co.* The dolls had either composition or cloth heads and were dressed as boys and girls in a variety of child costumes. A boy and girl pair could be snapped together and by moving strings they simulated dancing. When the strings were removed and the pair unsnapped, each doll became a regular play doll. They were also called "Radio Dancing Couple."

1929: Name was registered in U.S. as a trademark for dolls by the S. & H. Novelty Co. PLAYTHINGS reported the change of name to Tickle Toes.

1930: A patent was obtained for these dolls. (See also **Dean,** 1929.)

Perathoner, Johann Dominik. 1826 and other years. Tirol, Austria. Listed in a Vienna directory under Plaster Figures and Toys.

Before 1838 Peratoner *(sic)* Bros. of the Grödner Tal were *Verlegers* who sold dolls in Florence, Palermo and Naples.

The PRETTIEST DOLLS in TOYLAND!

2077. Dolls advertised in a J. C. Penney 1929 catalog.
  1. Tickletoes, composition head, rubber arms and legs, sleeping and flirting eyes, voice box. H. 16½ in. (42 cm.); priced $2.98.
  2. Dolly Rosebud Mama doll, wig, eyelashes, composition arms. H. 18 in. (45.5 cm.); priced $3.98.
  3. Kiss Me, all-composition doll. H. 12½ in. (31.5 cm.); priced 49¢.
  4. Baby Dimples, sleeping eyes, composition arms. H. 14 in. (35.5 cm.); priced $1.98.
  5. Val Encia, composition head with a felt finish, wig, composition legs and a cry voice. H. 16 in. (40.5 cm.); priced $2.98.
  6. Dutch Doll, felt costume. H. 12 in. (30.5 cm.); priced $1.90.
  7. Baby Dimples, sleeping eyes, composition arms and legs, Mamma voice. H. 22 in. (56 cm.); priced $5.90.
  8. Dutch Boy Doll, sleeping eyes, composition arms and legs, felt costume. H. 18 in. (45.5 cm.); priced $3.98.
  9. Peterkins, painted eyes, composition arms and legs. H. 14 in. (35.5 cm.); priced $1.98.
  10. Dutch Girl, sleeping eyes, composition arms and legs, felt dress. H. 18 in. (45.5 cm.); priced $3.98.
  11. Dolly Rosebud Mama doll, sleeping eyes, composition arms. H. 16 in. (40.5 cm.); priced $2.98.
  12. Baby Doll, sleeping eyes, composition arms and legs, cry voice. H. 18 in. (45.5 cm.); priced $4.98.

2078. Advertisement by Alfred Pensky for small dolls and figurines in DEUTSCHE SPIELWAREN ZEITUNG, February, 1927.

2079. Mark of Hermann Pensky.

Pehaco
Hannelore
85

2080. Mark of Hermann Pensky.

Pereyra, Manuela. ca. 1900–1930 and later. Caracas, Venezuela. Made cloth dolls representing the people of Venezuela. One of these dolls was dressed as an old lady going to mass with a shawl over her head, a long full skirt with a deep ruffle and leather shoes with heels.

Perfect Doll Shoe Co. 1925–26. New York City. Made shoes for dolls.

Perfect Toy Manufacturing Co. 1919–30 and later. New York City. Made dolls including *Mama* dolls. They were licensed by *Voices, Inc.* to use their patented mama voices and criers. Perfect Toy Manufacturing Co. was a member of the *American Doll Manufacturers' Association.*★

Perfection Doll Co. 1916–23. Long Island City, N.Y. Manufactured all-composition dolls and composition heads on cloth-body dolls.

1918–19: *Louis Wolf* was the sole agent. Came with or without wigs; stationary or sleeping eyes. Hts. 10 to 24 in. (25.5 to 61 cm.); priced $1.00 to $10.00.★

Performo Toy Co. 1926. Middletown, Pa. Made dolls representing acrobats. These dolls were finished with lacquer enamels which suggests wood or composition. They registered *Mickey* in the U.S. as a trademark for dolls.

Perger, Paul. 1834 and probably other years. Vienna. Produced dolls and toys that may have come from the Grödner Tal through the *Verleger, Josef Purger.*

Periwinkle. 1928. Name of a small bisque doll with brightly colored clothes produced by *Borgfeldt.* The doll was inspired by a character in the "Winnie Winkle" cartoons drawn by *Martin A. Branner* in the DAILY NEWS and CHICAGO TRIBUNE. The doll's sailor hat was attached by an elastic so that it could be placed in a variety of positions. (See also **Perry Winkle.**)

Perle. See **Tanagra.**

Perlico-Perlaco. 1910–13. Name registered in Germany as a trademark for dolls made by *Fleischmann & Bloedel.* These dolls had patented movable heads and legs.

Perls, Charles, Manufacturing Co. 1916–22. London. Made composition heads and dolls with celluloid heads on composition bodies during World War I. They used the initials C. P. M. Co. as a trademark. After the war they were importers and factory agents.

1917–18: Made Kiddykin, a composition doll's head.

2081. Mark of Madame Lavallée-Peronne who dressed dolls and published LA POUPÉE MODÈLE.

Permolin Products. 1918. Brooklyn, New York. Made composition dolls jointed at the neck, shoulders, and hips. Hts. 14 and 15 in. (35.5 and 38 cm.).★

Peronne, Mlle. (Mme. Lavallée-Peronne). 1864–84. Paris. Advertised lady, child, and baby dolls in *LA POUPÉE MODÈLE.*

1870: Fashion-type lady dolls with bisque heads, blond curly wigs, and kid bodies came in the following sizes:

	LAVALLÉE-PERONNE DOLLS	
Size	Height	
No.	cm.	in.
0	30	12
1	ca. 33	13
2	36–40	14–15½
3	ca. 42	16½
4	45	17½
5	50	19½
6	54	21½

Size 4 cost $2.20 undressed and $8.30 dressed.

1879: Advertised bébés of all sizes and *Le Poupon* (infant doll) as well as the fashion-type lady dolls.★

Perplex. 1913. Line of character dolls, made by *E. & H. Landgrof* who claimed these dolls could be put into a variety of positions.

Perrault, Mme. Marie. 1916. France. Made cloth dolls and dressed them in fairy tale or pseudo-medieval costumes. Some of the dolls had yarn hair.

Perrimond, Gaston. 1924–30 and later. Nice, France. Made cloth art dolls which he called Nicette (*La Poupée Nicette*). His Paris representative was *Maurice Cahen.*★

Perrin, Mme. 1916–18. Paris. Created cloth dolls and used the initials "L.P.A." for "La Poupée des Allies" (Dolls of the Allies).★

Perry Winkle. 1929. All-bisque doll with a turning head made in Germany and distributed exclusively by *Marshall Field.* It represented a character in the Winnie Winkle cartoon drawn by *Martin A. Branner.*

Perry Winkle. 1929–30. Oilcloth stuffed doll made by *Live Long Toys,* representing a character in the Winnie Winkle cartoon drawn by *Martin A. Branner.* It came in two versions. Style No. 26 wore a red and blue suit with an Eton jacket and no hat. Ht. 13 in. (33 cm.); priced $8.00 doz. wholesale. Style No. 27 wore a blue suit with an Eton jacket and a wide brimmed red hat. Ht. 11 in. (28 cm.); priced $4.00 doz. wholesale. (See also **Periwinkle.**)

Peruggi, Ernesto. 1915–28 and possibly later. New York City. Designed dolls for *Joseph Kallus* and *Regal.* The Regal dolls included *Our Lindy* and a version of a new-born baby.★

Pesendorfer. 1801 and probably other years. He made wooden dolls and allegedly made the first *Federdocken,* a carved and turned wooden doll with a real feather on its wooden hat.

Peskin, J. 1918. Dublin. Itco (Irish Toy Co.) Works. The leading line was of jointed dolls with glass eyes. These dolls came dressed and undressed.

Pet Names. 1899–1930 and later. Dolls with china heads and limbs on cloth bodies having a girl's name on the doll's chest. These dolls were controlled entirely by *Butler Bros.*

1899: The names were Edith, Esther, Florence, Mabel, Pauline and Ruth.

1902: The names were Agnes, Bertha, Dorothy, Edith, Esther, Ethel, Helen, Mabel, Marion and Ruth.

1903: The names were the same as 1902 except Florence replaced Esther.

1905: The names Edith, Florence, Helen and Ruth had been eliminated, leaving only Agnes, Bertha, Dorothy, Ethel and Marion.

1912: Same names as in 1905. Came on "A.B.C." cloth bodies. Nine hts. 7⅛ to 21 in. (18 to 53.5 cm.); priced 37¢ to $4.25 doz. wholesale.

1916: Heads came with either ribbed or plain blouse tops.

1927: Butler Bros. advertised only hts. 7½ and 12½ in. (19 and 31.5 cm.).★

Peter. 1909–11 and probably later. Name given to mold # 101 made by *Kämmer & Reinhardt*. The height in centimeters was marked on the head of the doll.★

Peter. 1920–21. Stockinet doll with combable wig and removable clothes made by *Chad Valley*. This doll No. 12 SD came with a patented wrist watch. Hts. 12 and 13 in. (30.5 and 33 cm.).

Peter. 1930. Name of a doll with flirting eyes and a toddler five-piece body made by *Franz Schmidt*. It was a mate to *Lore*.

Peter Pan. 1908. Name of a *Contortionist Doll* with a body that could be twisted into a variety of positions.

Peter Pan. 1923–1929. There were two distinctly different Peter Pan dolls made by *Chad Valley*. The first was a down-stuffed flat type cloth doll with printed clothes on it that portrayed the traditional Peter Pan costume. The arms were away from the body and the legs were apart. This 11 in. (28 cm.) doll was style number 43 and was made from 1923 to 1929.

The other Peter Pan appears to have been made only in 1926. It followed a registered design and was style number 249, 22 in. (56 cm.) tall. It had a molded face and wore removable green and brown felt clothes also of traditional type.

Peter Pan. 1925. Name of a doll with sleeping eyes and a human hair wig made by the *Goodyear Toy Co.* Ht. 17 in. (43 cm.); priced $1.50.★

Peter Pan. 1928–29. Name of a composition head doll, dressed in felt, made by *Ideal,* who obtained a U.S. trademark for this name. It was a mate to *Wendy* and sold for $2.00.

Peter Pan Drest Dolls. 1928–29. Name of an all-composition doll dressed as Peter Pan and made by *Amberg*. It had molded wind-swept hair, a waist joint, arms bent like *Patsy* and diagonal hip joints so that it could sit or stand. Marked on back "AMBERG//PAT. PEND.//L. A. & S. © 1928." Ht. 14 in. (35.5 cm.).

Peter and Joan. 1921. Pair of stockinet dolls dressed in silk jersey clothes, made in Britain and distributed in the U.S. by *Meakin & Ridgeway*.

Peter and Pauline. World War I period. Line of twin dolls made of *British Ceramic* by *Nottingham* in their *Daisy Dolls* line.

Peterhänsel, Albert. 1921–30 and later. Köppelsdorf, Thür. Made dolls.★

Peterkin. 1914–30 and possibly later. Name of a doll produced by *Horsman* and made by *Aetna Doll and Toy Co.* as well as others. *J. C. Penney* was one of the later distributors.

1914: Doll had a composition head and limbs on a cloth body. Came dressed as a boy or girl with a ribbon and bow. Ht. 11 in. (28 cm.).

1916: All composition doll.

1917: *Charles William* advertised an all-composition Peterkin doll. Ht. 11 in. (28 cm.); priced 98¢. (See THE COLLECTOR'S BOOK OF DOLLS' CLOTHES, Ill. 715.)

1918: Adtocolite[+] doll had painted hair and eyes, and bare feet. It came dressed as a boy in rompers with a brimmed straw hat or as a girl in a dress and bonnet. There were eight styles.

1919: Ht. 12½ in. (31.5 cm.); priced $1.29.

1920: Wore a ribbon and bow.

1929: The Peterkin family of dolls was introduced; besides the boy in rompers and the girl in a dress there was an Indian boy and a golf caddy. These dolls with either painted or sleeping eyes had a long rectangular tag with the name "Peterkin" on it.★

Peterl. 1923. Name of a celluloid doll representing a peasant boy made by *Rheinische Gummi und Celluloid Fabrik Co.* Its eyes glanced to the side and it had a molded tiny topknot of hair. The bent arms were movable and the shirt and trousers were painted on the doll.

Peters, Heinrich (Hermann). 1878–1928. Hannover, Prussia. The successor was Karl Peters. Made dolls' wigs.★

Peterson, Frank W., Co. 1907–30. New York City. Made segmented wooden dolls that were distributed by *Borgfeldt, B. Illfelder, Carl Silverman, Strobel & Wilken* and *Louis Wolf.*

1929: Dolls had clothes painted in three colors of waterproof lacquer. Ht. 6 in. (15 cm.); priced 25¢.

Mr. Peterson registered in the U.S. the name Petson as a trademark for dolls.

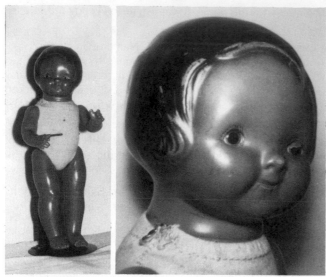

2082A & B. One of the Peterkin line of dolls produced by Horsman, has molded and painted hair and eyes. The brown eyes look straight ahead. Cloth torso contains a squeak box and there are composition arms and legs. The brown head and limbs suggest that this may have been the Indian representation in the Peterkin line. Mark on head: "E.I.H. Co. INC." H. 13½ in. (34 cm.). *Coleman Collection.*

Petit, Jacob. ca. 1790–1865. Fontainebleau, Seine-et-Marne and Belleville near Paris. In 1795 Benjamin Jacob and Aaron Smoll founded a porcelain factory at Fontainebleau. Baruch Weil was their successor and Jacob and Mardochée Petit were successors in 1830 or 1834.

The Jacob Petit porcelain factory in Paris was founded about 1790 and the Fontainebleau factory became a branch. Both factories used initials J P as a mark.

1865: The Didot "Paris Directory" listed Jacob & Petit [*sic*] as a porcelain maker, and Petit Jr. as selling Porcelain as well as Fred Petit who had obtained patents in 1850, 1853 and 1855 for "talking Marottes." Fred Petit also made an "Indian Juggler." (See also **Petit & Dumontier.**)★

Petit Saint Thomas. 1886–1914 and possibly other years. Paris department store that sold dolls.

1886: Advertised *Bébé Parisien.* (See Ill. 320 and also 324 in THE COLLECTOR'S BOOK OF DOLLS' CLOTHES.)

1894: Their dolls included *Bébé Bru, Bébé Caprice, Bébé de Paris, Bébé Directoire, Bébé Jumeau* and *Bébé Success.* (See Ill. 429 in THE COLLECTOR'S BOOK OF DOLLS' CLOTHES.)

1902–14: Advertised *Bébé Tout en Bois.*

1905: Their dolls included *Bébé Roulant, Clowns, Cymbalier, Eden Bébé, L'Elégante, Le Rêve, Marotte, Mignonnette* with a wardrobe of clothes, Nurses with baby, *Polichinelle,* and rubber doll dressed in wool. The rubber doll came in three hts. 24, 27, and 33 cm. (9½, 10½, and 13 in.).

Petit Touriste. 1911. Name of a boy and girl pair of dolls with sleeping eyes, sold at *Aux Trois Quartiers.* Ht. 37 cm. (14½ in.); priced $2.10.

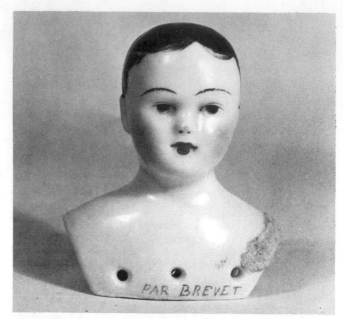

2083. China head made by Jacob Petit. It is a pressed head that has been glazed both inside and outside. The painted blue eyes have some eye shadow and there is a black line over each eye. Closed mouth with a thick lower lip. The original pink kid body is not shown. Marks: Ills. 2084A and B. (Par Brevet means "By Patent.") H. 12½ in. (31.5 cm.). *Courtesy of Margaret Woodbury Strong Museum. Photo by Barbara Jendrick.*

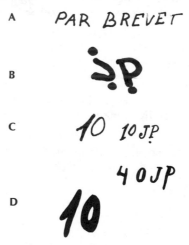

2084A–D. Marks on Jacob Petit china shoulder heads. These marks are usually painted on the shoulders.

Petit & Dumontier. 1878–90. Paris. Frederic Petit and André Dumontier exhibited dolls at the 1879 and 1889 Paris Expositions.

1881: Made dolls with bisque heads from the *François Gaultier* factory. (See also **Petit, Jacob.**)★

Petitcollin. 1860–1930 and later. Etain, Meuse; Lilas, Seine; Oyonnax; Cusset; and Paris, all in France. Started to make celluloid dolls and dolls' heads about 1909 or earlier. Their celluloid made from acetate was called celöid. Supplied Le Minor with celluloid dolls. Made celluloid heads for *L'Intrépide Bébé*.

1904: Registered in France their trademark of a side view of an eagle's head *(Tête d'Aigle).*

1907: Advertised bébés and dolls.

1925: Obtained a French patent relating to the use of celluloid for dolls according to Mme. Poisson, curator of the Roybet Fould Museum.

1930: Name of company became La Companie du Celluloid Petitcollin Oyonithe.

1930s: Made a celluloid bébé named Petit Colin.★

Petite (Baby) Dolls.† See **American Character Doll Co.**

Petite Caresse.† See **Caresse.**

Petite Écoliers. 1912. Character head bébés advertised by *Bon Marché*. They were dressed as a boy or girl in various school clothes and carried a school bag. Ht. 35 cm. (14 in.); priced $1.35.

Petite Française. 1920s. Name used by *H. Delcourt* for dolls with bisque heads or all-bisque dolls made by *J. Verlingue*. Head marked J on one side of an anchor and V on the other side of the anchor. Bisque head Petite Française dolls have been reported to be 13 to 23 in. (33 to 58.5 cm.) high. An all-bisque 6 in. (15 cm.) doll has been found.★

Petite Poucet (Little Thumb). 1910. Name of a cloth doll with removable boys' clothes sold by *Printemps*. Hts. 35 and 43 cm. (14 and 17 in.); priced $1.78.

2086. Bisque socket head doll made by Petit & Dumontier. The head was probably made by François Gaultier. It has a wig, blue glass eyes, pierced ears, closed mouth, and a ball jointed composition body with metal hands. Clothes contemporary with the doll. Mark: "P. 1 D." H. 15 in. (38 cm.). *Courtesy of Sotheby Parke Bernet Inc., N.Y.*

P 3 D

2087. Mark found on a Petit & Dumontier doll's head.

Petites Mains Parisiennes (Little Hands of Paris). 1916. Paris. Name of a workshop founded by *M. Bricon* where dolls were made.

Petites Marraines de Guerre (Little Godmothers of War). 1918. Name of dolls created by *Jean Ray* and sold at *L'Hotel de Ville* store. The godmothers were named *Lily* and *Claudette*.

Petri, John A. 1917. New York City. Advertised a line of character dolls dressed in Dutch and Spanish felt dresses of various colors as well as dolls dressed in 1917 styles, or as Continental Neapolitans or Turks. All had footwear. Priced $1.00 to $2.00.

 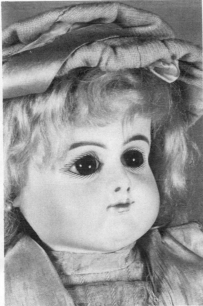

2085A & B. Bisque socket head impressed with the mark in Ill. 2087 for Petit & Dumontier. Probably made by François Gaultier, it has a blond wig, brown stationary eyes. The ball jointed composition body has metal hands. The beige clothes are contemporary. H. 20½ in. (51 cm.). *Courtesy of Z. Frances Walker.*

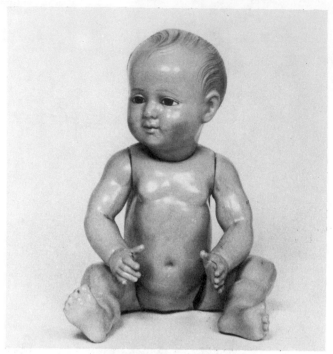

2088. All-celluloid doll made by Petitcollin. It has a socket head with molded blond hair, stationary blue glass eyes, closed mouth with only the line separating the lips painted and a bent limb baby body. Contemporary clothes. Mark on head "35". Embossed mark on body "35// [picture of an eagle's head]// FRANCE." H. 13 in. (33 cm.). *Courtesy of the Margaret Woodbury Strong Museum. Photo by Harry Bickelhaupt.*

2089–2090. Marks used by Petitcollin for their celluloid dolls.

Petri, Julius. 1924–25. Hamburg, Germany. Obtained a German patent (D.R.P.) for a parachute doll.

Petri & Blum. 1915–16. New York City. Made composition dolls with painted hair and eyes or sleeping eyes.★

Petri-Lewis Manufacturing Co. 1923–29. U.S.A. Made *Billy Bounce, Bobby Bounce* and *Jimmy Jounce* dolls. *Corcoran & Laycock* distributed these dolls, some of which were segmented wooden dolls.

Petrow, Alex. 1921–23. San Francisco. Obtained a U.S. patent for dolls' flirting eyes that moved from side to side when the doll was tilted sideways. These were also sleeping eyes.

Petsch, C. L. Berlin. Successor was M. Hilgendorf. Made and repaired dolls. This information was found on a purple stamp on the stomach of a kid body doll with a seam down the middle of the front and back of the torso. The bisque arms extended nearly to the shoulders.

Petson. See **Peterson, Frank W. Co.**

Petternell, August. 1922. Vienna. Obtained an Austrian patent for a device for fastening the iron hooks at the joints so that they were attached securely.

Petz Spielwarenfabrik. 1859–1930 and later. Neustadt near Coburg, Thür. (later Bavaria). Made and/or dressed dolls of various kinds. Factory belonged to the *Kiesewetter* family.

Petzold, Dora (née Krappe). 1919–30 and later. Berlin. Made Art dolls. Worked in *Else Hecht's* workshop in the 1920s.

1919: Dolls had heads of silk material.

1925: Dolls' heads were of "unbreakable material."

1927: *Carl Stahl* was her Berlin agent.

1927–28: Advertised cloth dolls, toy dolls, *Boudoir* dolls, grotesque dolls, dressed dolls with hats and coats, Pierrots and Pierrettes, Cavaliers, "Dollar Prinzessin" and dolls with girls' names. In August 1928 she brought out a doll called "Funny." This appears to have been the "new humorous dolls" with cloth bodies. Some of these wore eyeglasses. They were dressed as boys or girls.

1930: Advertised Baby dolls.★

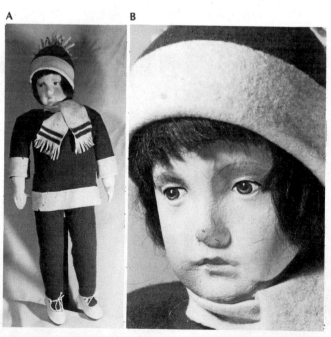

2091A & B. Dora Petzold doll has a molded composition head with painted features including brown eyes. The brown hair is shoulder length and it has bangs. The pink stockinet body has mitten shaped fingers delineated by sewing. Original blue wool suit trimmed with white felt. The pants form leggings. There is a felt scarf at the neck and a cloche-shaped hat with a felt pompon. White slippers. Mark: Ill. 2092. H. 22 in. (56 cm.). *Coleman Collection.*

C

52   DEUTSCHE SPIELWAREN-ZEITUNG   Februar II 1927

2091C. Dora Petzold Puppen cloth dolls made by Dora Petzold, as advertised in DEUTSCHE SPIELWAREN ZEITUNG, February 1927.

DORA PETZOLD
Registered
TRADE MARK
DOLL
Germany

2092. Mark stamped on the cloth body of a Dora Petzold doll.

2093. Mark used on dolls by Fritz Pfeffer.

Pfeffer, Fritz. 1892–1930 and later. Gotha, Thür. Gotha Porzellanfabrik. Made porcelain dolls' heads, *Frozen Charlottes, Nankeen* dolls, and jointed porcelain dolls. By 1930 the firm was known as Fritz Weber and Max Pfeffer; they employed 120 workers.

Pfeiffer, Emil (Gebrüder Pfeiffer). 1894–1930 and later. Vienna, Austria, and Köppelsdorf-Sonneberg, Thür. Hubert, Hans and Frank Pfeiffer were successors and by 1925 Otto Hausser had succeeded them. Gebrüder Pfeiffer of Köppelsdorf was a branch of Emil Pfeiffer. By 1927 *Hans Höning* was the Köppelsdorf successor. Produced dolls. Used *Armand Marseille* bisque heads including mold #s 560a and 1894. The 1894 may represent the date of the founding of the Emil Pfeiffer firm. One of the 560a bisque head dolls is on a composition body that has 22 impressed on the back of the torso and on one leg. This doll is 22 cm. (8.5 in.) tall and came in a box labeled "½ doz. 7350 S 22" and "Qualité supérieure// Bébé // articulé." Beneath the Pfeiffer trademark of E. P. intertwined which was registered in 1916 were shown two medals (or the two sides of a medal) with the words "Marque Déposée" under them. It is interesting to note that this doll with a head made in Germany, a body

probably made in Austria, sold in Hungary had a label entirely in French. (See Ill. 2094.)

1906: Listed in a directory under Dolls of Porcelain.

1910: Listed in an Austrian directory under Dolls and Dolls' Heads.

1917: Produced dolls named Huberta[†] and Fritz.[†] Their paper tags were similar to the *Hubsy* tag shown in Ill. 1235.

1923: Obtained an Austrian patent for toys.

1924: Hubsy had a composition or felt head, sleeping or painted eyes, ball jointed or cloth body.

1926: Specialized in *Mama* dolls and stuffed unbreakable dolls. Used the name *Hanka.*

1927: The Köppelsdorf-Sonneberg establishment was listed in a directory as making Lenci-type felt dolls.
    The Berlin agent for the Emil Pfeiffer firm was *Carl Stahl.*

1930: Listed in a directory as "Pfeiffer's Puppenparadies." (See Ills. 2094 and 2095.)★

Pfeuffer, L. 1926–30 and later. Nürnberg, Bavaria. Manufactured dolls.★

Pfiffikus. See **König & Wernicke.**

Pfohl, Maggie and Bessie. Ca. 1900. Old Salem, North Carolina. Made flat cloth dolls with painted faces.

Phénix. 1860s–70s. A doll with a wooden body that pivots at the hips on a metal sheet through the torso, and has metal hands and an eliptical metal plate with raised letters affixed to the stomach which read, "B[te] SGDG//LA POUPÉE//PHÉNIX//MARQUE DÉPOSÉ." Ht. 18 in. (45.5 cm.).

Phénix Baby. See **Bébé Phénix.**

Phenox Products. 1930 and later. Trademark registered in U.S. by *Gaess & Hollander* for composition figures.

Philadelphia Dressed Doll Co. See **Reinhardt, Ernst.**

Phillips, J. & N., Co. 1916. Manchester, England. Advertised American dolls in a British toy trade journal.

Phillips Knitting Works. 1927–29. Brooklyn, N.Y. Made outfits for dolls including stockings and boots.

Phillips, Mary Waterman.[†] See **Mawaphil.**

Phillips, Sam, Co. 1923. Chicago, Ill. Exhibited imported and domestic dolls at the Chicago Toy Fair.

Phipps, Mary. 1926. Mitchellville, Md. Obtained two U.S. design patents for dolls.

Phoebe Snow. 1917. Name of a doll with Can't Break 'Em[†] composition head and limbs, molded hair, cloth body, dressed in a white coat and hat and distributed by *Charles William.* This doll was probably the Phoebe[†] copyrighted by *Horsman* in 1914. Ht. 16 in. (40.5 cm.); priced 98¢.

Phoenix. 1856–1925. and probably later. Harburg, Germany. Made all-rubber dolls with molded and painted features and clothes. There were black dolls as well as white dolls, clowns, Dutch costume dolls, *Max and Moritz* and so on.

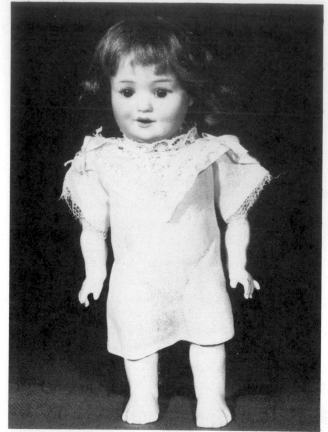

2094A & B. Doll produced by Emil Pfeiffer with an Armand Marseille bisque head, wig, glass eyes, on a toddler type composition body, probably made in the 1920s. Original chemise and box. Mark on head: Ill. 1830. Back of body marked "22," its height in cm. (8½ in.). *Coleman Collection.*

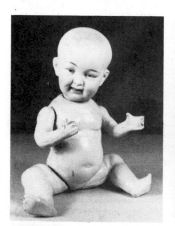

2095. Bisque head baby doll produced by Emil Pfeiffer. It has molded and painted hair and features, a bent limb composition body with the thumb on the left hand extending so that it could go into the toothless open-closed mouth. The back of the body is marked "18," the height in cm. (7 in.). (See also Ill. 1859.) *Coleman Collection.*

Phoenix Doll Co. 1921–24. New York City. Manufactured *Kewpie* type and *Mama* dolls.

1921: Made *Cutie* dolls.

1923–24. Made "Phoenix Character Dolls." These Mama dolls had composition heads with painted hair, mohair or real hair wigs with stationary or sleeping eyes. The arms and legs were composition and the cloth bodies were stuffed with cotton. They advertised 125 style numbers of these Mama dolls. Hts. 15 to 27 in. (38 to 69.5 cm.); priced $1.00 and up.★

Phonograph Dolls. 1878–1930 and later. Besides the *Edison*[†] doll and *Jumeau*'s Bébé Phonographe[†] based on *Henri Lioret*'s 1893 patent, phonograph dolls were made by *Kämmer & Reinhardt* based on an 1893 patent of *Emile Berliner*, and *Max Oscar Arnold* based on patents dating from 1903. *Benjamin Klenberg* obtained a German patent for a phonograph doll in 1904. Other manufacturers also made this type of doll.

1926: *Metal Devices Corp.* made a phonograph doll.

1928 and/or later: Several companies were producing phonograph dolls and appear to have used the same type of talking (or singing) device. *Averill Manufacturing Co.* advertised their *Dolly Record* as being an innovation, although their Dolly-Reckord[†] dated back to 1922 and the patent on

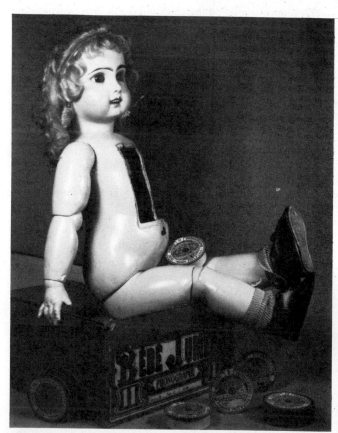

2096. Phonograph doll made by Jumeau. It has a bisque head, wig, stationary blue glass eyes, pierced ears, open mouth with six upper teeth and a fully jointed composition body with a phonograph inside the torso. Original footwear. H. 24 in. (61 cm.). *Courtesy of Cherry Bou.*

the phonograph device dated from 1920. Around 1928 or a little later there appeared in addition to Dolly Record, the *Mae Starr* doll, and *Effanbee* put a phonographic device in some of their large *Lovums* dolls. *Domec* made a doll that used a 7 in. (18 cm.) phonograph record. *Reisman, Barron Co.* made a phonograph doll named *Adora-Belle*. (See also **Talking Dolls**).★

Phyllis. 1913. Name of a bisque-head doll with wig, sleeping eyes, ball-jointed composition body distributed by *Gamage*. It wore a chemise with diagonal sash across the skirt on which was the name "PHYLLIS."

SIZE–HEIGHT RELATIONSHIP FOR PHYLLIS DOLLS			
Size No.	Height in.	cm.	Price
1	14½	37	25¢ without hair eyelashes
2	17½	44.5	48¢ with hair eyelashes
3	21	53.5	
4	25	63.5	98¢ with hair eyelashes

Phyllis. 1927–29. Name of a musical doll by the *Baby Phyllis Doll Co.* and handled by *J. Bouton & Co.* (Bouton-Woolf Co. in 1929).

It was a *Mama* doll with composition head, hands and legs, cloth body, dressed in a variety of coats and matching headwear. A heart-shaped tag on the coat read, "Phyllis." Instructions were given: "Press me and I will play sweet lullabies." This was style no. 503. Ht. 15 in. (38 cm.); priced $1.00. (See Ill. 404.)

Picaninny. 1917. Name of a doll designed by *E. E. Houghton* and made by *Shanklin* of stockinet or other fabric. It could assume standing or sitting poses.

Piccadilly Knut. 1914 and probably later. Cloth character doll made by *Dean*.

Piccolo. 1928. Doll made by *Schreyer & Co.*, appears to have been made of felt. Hts. 9 and 11 cm. (3½ and 4½ in.).

Pichot, Établissement G. 1925–26. Suresnes, Seine. Made dolls.

Pick, Filip. 1928–30 and later. Prague, Czechoslovakia. Manufactured dolls.

Pickaninnies. 1921–23. Black cloth dolls made by *Martha Chase*. Ht. 12 in. (30.5 cm.); priced $3.50 undressed, $5.50 dressed.★

Pickaninny. 1893 and later. Small size, black cutout cloth doll dressed in pink or blue made by the *Arnold Print Works*. One of a type patented in 1892. The large size was called *Topsy*.★

Pickering, J. W., & Co. 1930. Leominster, Mass. Made *Segmented Dolls* of turned birch-wood. The dolls were named *Dapper Dan*, *Sailor Sam* and *Soldier Boy*.

Pierette. See **Pierrette**.

Pierotti. 1770–1930s. London. According to Irene E. Pierotti, a niece of Charles Pierotti, the last of the Pierotti family to make wax dolls, the family history was as follows: Ca. 1770: Dominic (Domenico) Pierotti came from Tuscany, Italy, to England as a young boy. He lived with his mother's sister, a Mrs. Castelli, who made plaster wall and ceiling decorations as well as wax-covered papier-mâché dolls and from her he learned his trade. Wax-over papier-mâché dolls as collectors know them were probably not made as early as the 18th century. The following Pierotti family data is based on information supplied by Irene Pierotti:

In 1790 Dominic Pierotti married an English girl, Susanna Sleight, and they raised a large family supported by his trade.

In 1809 the son, Anericho Cephas, known as Henry, was born and he followed his father's business and also had a large family. After his marriage in 1828 to Jane Gumrell, Henry (or Harry) specialized in wax models of prominent people and high-quality wax dolls made by pouring the wax.

The model for the head was sculptured and from this model, two- or three-part plaster molds were made. Into these molds warm molten wax colored with white lead, carmine and other tints was poured and allowed to harden around the edge. The surplus was poured off and when the wax shell cooled it was taken out of the mold. The mold marks were removed and the features were enhanced by modelling tools. Holes were cut in the wax head for the blown glass eyes which were set from the inside of the head. Finally tufts of hair were inserted into slits in the wax scalp by using a sharp knife. Some of the best quality dolls had single strands of hair inserted and these also had inserted hair for eyebrows and eyelashes.

From 1849 on Henry Pierotti, the elder, showed his dolls at many exhibitions and was awarded medals. Some of his baby dolls were modeled from his own children and no doubt wore some of his family's own hair. In his advertise-

Patented July 5 & Oct. 4, '92. Reg'd, Eng., Aug. 23, '93.
PICKANINNY, 10c.

2097. Cutout cloth doll named Pickaninny as advertised in YOUTH'S COMPANION, 1894. It was a type patented in the U.S. in 1892 and registered in England in 1893.

ments he claimed that he had invented the Royal Model Doll, that is, the wax portrait dolls of Victoria's children, but other British wax doll makers made the same claim. Probably the small Princes and Princesses were a universally popular subject for dolls. The son, Henry Pierotti, made and repaired dolls for Queen Victoria. Small wax figures were also made and put on a cake for one of the royal weddings.

In 1851 Henry Pierotti showed dolls at the Crystal Palace exhibition and later opened a shop on Oxford Street which he called the Gallery, Crystal Palace Bazaar, where he sold foreign toys as well as his own dolls. He advertised that his dolls could be made to order. In addition to the London store he had shops in Bradford, Brighton, Windsor, and in Boulogne and Paris, France.

According to Faith Eaton around 1860 an advertising leaflet read: "Such beautiful dolls that will open their eyes. You may wash, comb and dress them and not hear their cries. [Signed] H. Pierotti, Inventor of the Royal Model Dolls." Pierotti made black Topsy and Uncle Tom dolls.

In 1871 several members of the Pierotti family died including Henry Pierotti. They were succeeded by Charles William Pierotti, son of Henry senior. Charles continued to use many of the original Pierotti models.

Charles William Pierotti died in 1892 of lead poisoning, a trade hazard, and he was succeeded by his wife, Anne Roache Pierotti, two sons, Charles and Harry, and three daughters, who made wax dolls as a home industry. After Harry married he moved away but continued to make wax dolls. The widow and daughters cut calico for the bodies of the dolls which they sewed together by machine. The wax head and limbs were sewed onto a stuffed fabric body.

As early as 1902 or before, the Pierottis made wax portrait dolls for *Hamleys*. Among these dolls were portraits of *King Edward VII* and *Queen Alexandra* in coronation robes.

During the 1930s, Mrs. Charles William Pierotti (Anne Roache) died and the demand for fine wax dolls diminished. After the death of her son Charles Pierotti in 1942 some of the Pierotti tools as well as finished and unfinished dolls were donated to the Toy Museum at Rottingdean, England. Other pieces of dolls and molds were donated through Irene Pierotti, granddaughter of Charles William Pierotti, to the Bethnal Green Museum. (See also **Manufacture of Wax Dolls** and **Model Doll**.)★

Pierre. 1922. Name of a doll made by *Rees Davis*. It was the mate to *Pierrot*.

Pierre Pons. See Soe (English Soldier).

Pierrette (Pierette.) Dolls have been dressed to represent this character who was the female version of Pierrot and often his mate. Some of the makers and/or distributors of these dolls were as follows:

1914–28: *Dean* made a cloth doll version which they called Pierette.

1915: Made by *St. Issell's Toy Industry*.

1916–17: Cloth doll with a silk mask face and a little hair in front produced by *Messrs. Heap & Co.* It came in various colored sateen; priced 25¢.

1917: Dolls dressed as Pierrette were popular this year as shown by the following companies: *Bell & Francis; P. J. Gallais & Co.* who made the Pierrettes designed by *A. Willette; Hamley's* advertised that *Fumsup* came in a Pierrette costume; *Laurie Hansen; Hawksley* advertised a "Fur" (plush) Pierrette with a celluloid face; and *Royal Crown Pottery Co.*

1917–20: *Knight Bros. & Cooper* made Pierrette dolls.

1918: Advertised by *Speights Ltd.*

1920: The *Art Toy Manufacturing Co.* made a Pierrette in their *Misska* line of plush dolls.

1920–21: *Chad Valley* made a stockinet version and called it Pierette, style no. S D 18.

1921–30 and later: Name of some luxury and cotillion dolls made in Paris.

1922: Produced by *Wonderland Toymaking Co.*

1927: Galeries *Lafayette* advertised a Pierrette doll.

1928: Pierrette was made by *Love Doll Co.* of Los Angeles. The costume was made of Baronette satin in black, white, turquoise blue, maise, old rose, red or nile green colors and trimmed with marabou or maline.

1930: Directions for making a *Boudoir* style Pierrette, under the name Susanne was given in SOFT TOY MAKING, written by *Ouida Pearse*. Ht. 23 in. (58.5 cm.). (See also **Clowns** and **Pierrot**.)

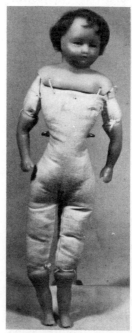 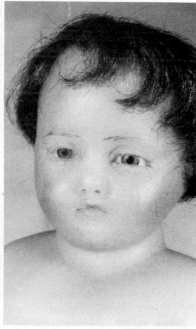

2098A & B. Poured wax head doll with a Charles Pierotti mark has reddish brown hair inserted in clumps, and blue glass stationary eyes. The turned shoulder head is sewn onto a stiff white cotton body with heavy cord. The limbs are also poured wax with the toes and fingernails delineated as are the dimples and creases. Mark: Ill. 2100. H. 12 in. (30.5 cm.). *Coleman Collection.*

2099. Poured wax shoulder head doll made by Pierotti. It has hair inserted in small groups, stationary blue glass eyes. Closed mouth, cloth body with wax arms and legs attached by grommets. Clothes contemporary with the doll. Mark on head: Pierotti. H. 18½ in. (47 cm.). *Courtesy of Sotheby Parke Bernet Inc., N.Y.*

C P

2100. Mark on a Pierotti wax head. The C. P. stands for Charles Pierotti.

Pierrot. 1600s–1930 and later. Originally represented the lover in the Italian COMMEDIA DELL'ARTE. Many dolls have represented various versions of Pierrot. The female version was called *Pierrette*. See Ills. 2101, 2102, 2103, 2104, and 2105 for some of the costumes worn by dolls dressed as Pierrots.

1901: Character face dolls in Pierrot costumes were exhibited in London. These dolls appear to have been the bisque head dolls made by the *Société Française de Fabrication de Bébés & Jouets* (S.F.B.J.) that were marked on the heads with three digit mold numbers.

1903: *Bon Marché* and *Pygmalion* stores advertised Pierrot composition head dolls. The Bon Marché's doll had its face

decorated with designs and wore a silk costume. Six hts. 37 to 59 cm. (14½ to 23 in.); priced 70¢ to $2.50. The Pygmalion all-composition doll was 45 cm. (17½ in.) tall; priced $1.10.

1904: The *Louvre*'s store's Pierrot with a composition head was a walking doll that was jointed at the neck and wore a silk costume. Hts. 35 and 41 cm. (14 and 16 in.); priced 90¢ and $1.30.

1912: *Horsman*'s Carnival Baby doll wore a costume that was similar to a Pierrot.

1913: *Gamage* sold Baby Pierrot. The Pierrot doll at *Aux Trois Quartiers* came in hts. 30 and 40 cm. (12 and 15½ in.); priced 78¢ and $1.18.

1917: *Bell & Francis* dressed character dolls as Pierrot, *British Products, Deptford, Gallais, Laurie Hansen, Hawksley, Knight Bros., Roberts Bros., Royal Crown Pottery* and *W. H. Smith* all dressed dolls in Pierrot costumes or made dolls that were so dressed or they handled such dolls. Some of the *Fumsup* dolls wore Pierrot costumes.

1918: *All British Toys* dressed dolls as Pierrot.

1919: *Spencer & Co.* advertised Pierrot dolls.

1920–21: *Chad Valley*'s stockinet Pierrot was style No. S.D.17. *Harwin & Co.* made a Pierrot doll.

1920s: S.F.B.J. continued to dress dolls as Pierrots.

1922: This was another year in which Pierrots were popular. They were produced by *Effanbee* and *Rees Davis* and sold by *Aux Trois Quartiers.*

1923: The *Louvre* store advertised a floppy long limbed Art Doll dressed in a figured satin Pierrot attire. Ht. 100 cm. (39½ in.).

1924: *Messina-Vat* and *Steiff* both dressed felt dolls as Pierrots.

1926: W. & R. *Eckart* dressed Pierrot dolls in black and orange.

1927: *Dora Petzold* dressed some of her dolls as Pierrots. The *Lafayette* store sold cloth body dolls dressed in silk, trimmed with spangles and pompons. Ht. 58 cm. (23 in.).

1929: A Pierrot cloth doll was made in Florence, Italy. (See also **Clown, Columbine, Pierrette, Polichinelles.**)

Pieter. 1907–13. Name of a doll created by *Elizabeth Scantlebury* to show school children how a Dutch boy dressed. The doll represented a brother to *Wilhelmina.*

Pietsch, Karl. 1897–1926 and possibly later. Neustadt near Coburg, Thür., and Bavaria. The successor was Adolf Pietsch. Manufactured dolls.★

Pillow Doll. 1930. Name of a *Boudoir* type doll with composition head and a pink cloth body. The costume for this doll was sold in a kit which included the fabrics marked with blue cutting lines to indicate the patterns. Also in the kit were ribbons, lace trimming, a hat, high heeled shoes and stockings. (See also **Clothes,** 1928 and **Pillowcraft.**)

N° **19157. PIERROT** habillage
soie, tête lavable incassable.

0ᵐ37	**3·50**	0ᵐ48	**7·50**
0ᵐ40	**4·50**	0ᵐ53	**8·75**
0ᵐ44	**5·90**	0ᵐ59	**10·75**

2101. Jumeau Bébé dressed in a Pierrot costume, shown in BLACK AND WHITE, 1901. It was exhibited at the Crystal Palace and was produced by the Société Française de Fabrication de Bébés & Jouets.

2102. Pierrot, advertised in Bon Marché catalog, 1903, had a "washable unbreakable" head and a silk costume. Six hs. 37, 40, 44, 48, 53, and 59 cm. (14½, 15½, 17½, 19, 21, and 23 in.). *Courtesy of Margaret Whitton.*

2103. Doll representing Pierrot shown in a 1923 Louvre store catalog. The long limbed doll had an Art type head and a satin costume that came in various colors. H. 100 cm. (39½ in.).

2104. All-bisque doll with a molded and painted Pierrot suit, brown hair, blue eyes, a mole on the cheek, and it is pegged strung at the shoulders and hips. The clown suit is white with blue buttons and shoes, pale blue cap. H. 5 in. (12.5 cm.). *Courtesy of the late Magda Byfield.*

2105. Pair of Pierrot dolls with molded felt heads. Doll on left has painted brown eyes, closed mouth, and cloth body. Original Pierrot suit of white felt with black dots. H. 20 in. (51 cm.). Doll on right has painted hair with spit curls in front of ears, brown eyes, beauty mark, closed mouth, and cloth body. Original red and black suit. H. 17½ in. (44.5 cm.). *Courtesy of Vivian Rasberry.*

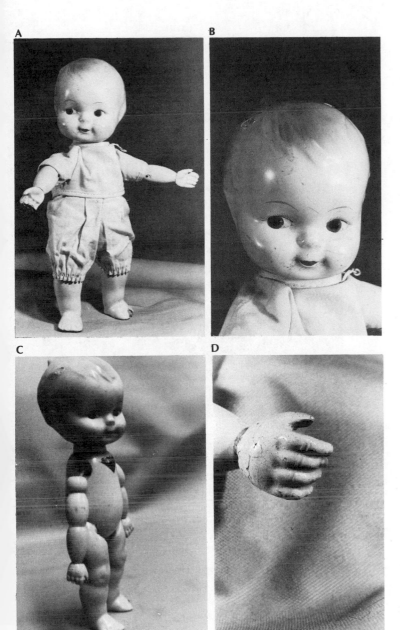

2106A–D. Pinkie, designed and made by Joseph Kallus, has composition head, legs and hands, segmented wooden torso and arms, molded hair and painted features. The neck joint has the socket in the head. The toddler type legs enable the doll to stand alone. Mark: Ill. 2107. H. 10½ in. *Coleman Collection.*

2107. Red decal mark on the chest of Pinkie designed by Joseph Kallus.

Pillowcraft. 1930 and later. Chicago, Ill. Manufactured cloth dolls. (See also **Pillow Doll.**)

Pilorgé, Alexandre Silvain. 1865. Charenton, Seine. Made porcelain heads. He was a brother-in-law of *François Gaultier.*

Pinafore Dolls. 1920. One of the flat-faced Knockabout cloth dolls made by *Dean* as style no. D255. There were six models each wearing a pinafore. Ht. 9¼ in. (23.5 cm.).

Pinafore Dolls. 1920–21. Line of dolls dressed in "Playtime Pinafores" produced by *Horsman* and representing boys and girls. These dolls came with or without wigs, with or without sleeping eyes. They appear to have included *Peek-A-Boos, Peterkins* and so forth. The clothes varied in color, material, and design but all of these dolls wore pinafores and all had bunnies somewhere as a decoration on their clothes. The sizes of the dolls varied from tiny to large.★

Pinafore Girl. 1919. Name of a doll with composition head and hands, molded hair, sleeping eyes, cloth body, made by *Ideal.* Ht. 16 in. (40.5 cm.).

Pinchon, Emile. 1904–30 and later. Designed *Bécassine* dolls representing the character in Caumery's stories.

Ping Pong. 1922. All-bisque Oriental-type doll with a queue, bead earrings and moving arms; distributed by *Hamley Bros.* It had a rectangular mark on its chest reading "PING//PONG." Came in two sizes.

Pinkie. 1930 and later. Jointed doll made of segmented wood with composition head, hands and legs by *Joseph L. Kallus* and distributed by *Borgfeldt.* The mouth was painted closed, the hair was molded and a heart-shaped paper label was on the chest. Pinkie was also made in a cloth version with its pressed face backed with buckram. In the 1960s and/or 1970s a vinyl version of Pinkie was made.

Pinner, Erna. World War I–1923. Berlin. Born in 1893, she was a painter, engraver, illustrator and writer, studied art in Berlin and Paris. During World War I a new kind of cloth art doll was created by Erna Pinner. It belonged to the "Kultur-Dolls" of Germany and reflected the unrest of the postwar period. These long-limbed dolls were described by THE BROOKLYN EAGLE as "Stiff in their baroque brocades and laces, gaze out on the world with scorn and disdain; their faces flat painted material, smile ironically and aloofly."

Also reported in 1923 in THE BROOKLYN EAGLE that the Pinner dolls were first sold at war benefits in Paris. Later copies of these dolls were made by girls in the workrooms of famous French couturiers. But the copies lacked the artistic merit of the original Pinner dolls. (See Ill. 2108.)

Pinocchio. 1929. Name of wooden dolls with movable arms and legs, made in Florence, Italy.

Pinocchio. 1930. Trademark registered in U.S. by *Bert B. Barry* for dolls.

Pintel, Henri, and Godchaux, Ernest. 1887–99. Montreuil-sous-Bois and Enghien, France. Made bébés of porcelain and of rubber including *Bébé Charmant.* Used P.G. as their incised mark. (See Ills. 2110, 2111 and 2112A.)

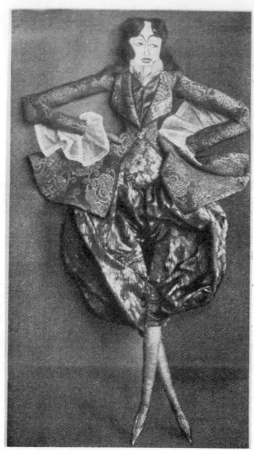

2108. Doll named "Harmonie" made by Erna Pinner and shown in DAS PUPPENBUCH, 1921.

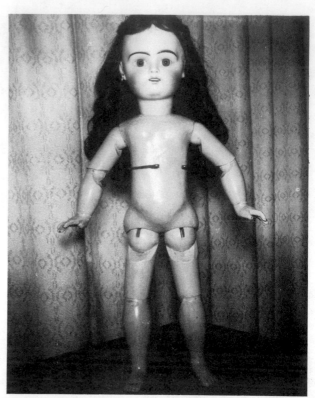

2109. Bisque head doll made by Pintel & Godchaux and handled by Guyot at the shop A la Tentation. It has a wig, cork pate, stationary glass eyes, pierced ears, open mouth with seven upper teeth, and a composition body with wood arms and legs, excluding the hands and feet. Mark incised on head: Ill. 2112A. Paper label on back of body: Ill. 3. H. 24½ in. (62. cm.). *Courtesy of Jane Thompson.*

1899: Joined the *Société Française de Fabrication de Bébés & Jouets* (S.F.B.J.) according to Mme. Poisson, curator of the Roybet Fould Museum.★

Pintel, M. 1913–28. Paris. 1920s M. Pintel Fils. Member of the *Chambre Syndicale,* made cloth dolls, including felt ones; girl and boy dolls and clown dolls. One of their dolls had a mask face with a plush body and hood.

Pionier. 1910. Name of a dressed doll exported by *Carl Hartmann* according to the research of the Ciesliks.

Pioupiou. 1896–1903 and probably other years. Name given to dolls dressed as French foot soldiers.

1896: Advertised by *Printemps.* Ht. 40 cm. (15½ in.); priced $1.10.

1903: All-composition doll sold by *Au Tapis Rouge.* Ht. 40 cm. (15½ in.); priced 29¢. (See Also **Military Dolls** and **Sof.**)

Piramovicz (Piramonie). 1915–18. Paris. Created cloth dolls.★

Pirat Baby. Name of a black doll with a Biscoloid type head, kinky wig, sleeping brown glass eyes, pierced ears, open mouth, teeth, and a black bent limb composition body. The doll was dressed to represent a pirate. The mark on the head

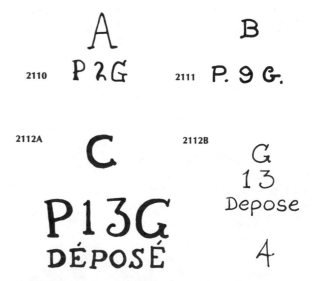

2110–2112A & B. Marks on dolls made by Pintel & Godchaux or Godchaux.

was "Heubach Köppelsdorf//418—16/0// Germany." A tag on the doll identified it as Pirat Baby made in Germany. (See Ill. 2113.) Ht. 8 in. (20.5 cm.).

Pirchan, Emil. 1907. Austria. Designed and made turned wooden dolls with painted clothes. Some of the dolls were tall and thin, others short and fat; many wore peasant costumes. They came in various sizes.

Pitschieler, Bernhard. Before 1838. Grödner Tal. A *Verleger* who sold dolls in Rome.

Pitti Sing. 1893 and later. Cutout cloth doll made by the *Arnold Print Works* (See Ill. 2114.).★

Pixie. 1920. One of the cloth flat-faced dolls made by *Dean* in their *Knockabout Series.* It was style no. D243 and wore a hood and coverall with a butterfly on its chest. Ht. 12 in. (30.5 cm.).

Pixie. 1923–29. A cloth down filled doll made by *Chad Valley* as style no. 45 in their *Aerolite* line. The arms were not against the body and the legs were apart. It wore a printed one-piece outfit with ankle-length leg covering and a pointed cap.

1927: Ht. 11 in. (28 cm.).

Pixie Dolls. 1917. Name of dolls designed by *E. O. Clark* to represent the nine countries of the Allies of World War I.

2113. Pirat Baby mark on a paper tag.

Patented July 5 & Oct. 4, '92.

PITTI-SING, (4) 10c.

2114. Pitti Sing, a cloth cutout doll, as advertised in YOUTH'S COMPANION, 1894.

Pla (American Policeman). 1905–13. Felt character doll representing an American policeman, made by *Steiff* and distributed by *Borgfeldt* in the U.S. Hts. 35, 50, and 120 cm. (14, 19½ and 47 in.); priced 82¢ to $9.75 in Germany in 1911.

Planker, B. See **Runggaldier (Rungaldier), Johann.**

Plano Toy Co. 1920–24. Plano, Ill. Made Plano Pansy, a "walking" doll made of heavy washable material printed in colors. This doll appeared to have rollers on its feet. In 1924 this company was taken over by the *Pollyanna Co.*

Plass & Roesner. 1907–30 and later. Buchau, Bohemia. Listed in an Austrian directory under Dolls' Heads, which were made in their Buchnauer Porzellanfabrik. Josef Plass and Paul Roesner probably made the bisque heads marked either "ROMA// P. 13 R.//AUSTRIA//1913" or "Made in Austria//P & R//1907//13." See Ills. 158 and 2244. (See also **Pollack & Hoffmann.**)

Plaster (Plaster of Paris). 1600s–1930 and later. Dolls and dolls' heads were made of plaster; often plaster was combined with other ingredients.

Ca. 1933: Plaster heads with flange necks were on dolls representing clowns, boys and girls. Four hts.; priced 75¢ to $1.25 doz. wholesale.★

Plastolite. 1917. Name of a type of composition made in France and Britain by *J. Roger Gault.* It was claimed to be "unbreakable, non-flammable, light in weight, can be washed without damage." Allegedly it was difficult to distinguish from porcelain.★

Plat, Emil. 1911. Coburg, Thür. Applied for a German patent (D.R.G.M.) for embroidery to decorate dolls' clothes.

Platt & Munk Co. 1923. New York City. Advertised cutout dolls. It is not certain that these were cloth but the same advertisement listed linen books.

Plaut, S. 1926. Düsseldorf, Germany. Made stuffed art dolls named *Bubl Kopf.*

Play Yard Pet. 1927–28. Trade name of dolls made by *Strauss-Eckhardt Co.*

Playmate. 1918–28. Line of cloth dolls produced by *Borgfeldt.*

1928: Many styles of felt dolls; those representing girls had curly wigs and dresses of various colors, some had bonnets and some did not.★

Playmate. 1927. Imported all-composition dolls with painted features, mohair wigs, eyes looking to the side, jointed arms, wore gingham dresses; distributed by *Butler Bros.* Ht. 5 in. (12.5 cm.).

Playmate. 1929. Name of a doll advertised by *Reisman, Barron.*

Playmate. See **My Playmate.**

Playmates. 1929. All-celluloid dolls with molded clothes representing school boys and girls, tennis, basketball players, and other sports boys and girls; distributed by *Butler*

Bros. Hts. 5¼ in. and 7¼ in. (13.5 and 18.5 cm.); priced 45¢ and 87¢ doz. wholesale.

Playpet Dolls. 1929. Segmented wooden dolls with hand-painted faces, made by the *Sun Enamel Works.* The dolls came in six color combinations and wore novelty hats. Most of the dolls represented Mother Goose Nursery Rhyme and Fairy Tale characters such as *Humpty Dumpty, Little Boy Blue, Little Polly Flinders* and *Little Red Riding Hood.*

Plaything Toys. 1930. Line of cloth dolls made by the *Atlanta Playthings Co.,* includes *Monkey Man.* Priced 50¢ to $3.00.

Playtime Baby. 1927. Imported all-composition doll distributed by *Butler Bros.* It had a wig, painted features, eyes looking to the side, jointed arms and wore a blue dress and gingham apron. Ht. 6 in. (15 cm.).

Playtime Dolls. 1926. Cloth doll made by *Dean.*

Plbe. (Belgian Policeman). 1911 and before. Felt doll made by *Steiff* representing a Belgian policeman. It had a mustache, long feet and a sword at its side. Ht. 35 cm. (14 in.); priced $1.00.

Pld. (German Policeman). 1911–16. Felt art doll made by *Steiff,* representing a German policeman. It had large feet and wore a helmet.

1911: Ht. 50 cm. (19½ in.); priced $3.25.

1916: Ht. 35 cm. (14 in.).

Ple. (English Policeman). 1903–13 and probably other years. Felt doll made by *Steiff* representing an English policeman with a long nose and a strap under its chin. It came in two versions, one short and fat and the other tall and thin. The tall, thin doll with long feet dressed in an English Police uniform resembles the one drawn by Beatrix Potter in her book A TALE OF TWO BAD MICE, 1904.

1903–05: Hts. 35 and 50 cm. (14 and 19½ in.).

1911: Same as in 1903 plus ht. 120 cm. (47 in.); priced 81¢ to $11.25 from the factory,

1913: Only the short, fat doll was advertised.

Pleiweiss, Valentine. 1853 and possibly other years. Vienna. Listed in a directory as handling Nürnberg toys.

Plf. (French Policeman). 1903–13 and probably other years. Felt doll made by *Steiff,* representing a short, fat or a tall thin French policeman.

1903: Ht. 35 cm. (14 in.).

1911: Hts. 35, 50, and 120 cm. (14, 19½, and 47 in.); priced $1.00 to $12.19.

1913: Only the short, fat doll was advertised.

Plotnick, Frank, Co. 1926–30 and later. Philadelphia, Pa. Manufactured cloth dolls.

1930: Took over the business of *American Toy & Novelty Corp.* Plotnick specialized in stockinet, plush and powder puff dolls, including *Kutie;* priced 25¢ to $2.00.

Pluci. 1927–28. Felt doll made by *Lenci.* It was one of the

950 series and represented a little girl. Ht. 28 in. (71 cm.).

Plumb, Charlie. 1925. Created together with *Bill Conselman* a cartoon character known as *Ella Cinders.*

An Ella Cinders doll was made by *Horsman* in 1928.

Pneumatic Toy Co. 1923. Racine, Wisc. Made *Goo-Goo* rubber dolls.

Pocahontas. 1910–14. Dark-skinned *Campbell Kid* composition head doll made by *Horsman.* It represented an Indian maiden mate to *Kickapoo* and wore a red head band and a tan dress trimmed with red and having tabs around the neckline and hemline. (See Ill. 1491.)★

Podhajska, Fraulein Minka. 1903–10. Vienna and Moravia. She was an artist, a craftswoman, and a pupil of Prof. Böhm at Kunstschule für Frauen Madchen (Art school for females). She made turned wooden dolls with the limbs added afterwards. These dolls were dressed in regional costumes.

Pogácar, Anton. 1910. Vienna. Listed in a directory under Dolls and Dolls' Heads.

Pogliani, O. 1916. Italy. Made papier-mâché dolls and wooden dolls which were shown at the first Italian Toy Fair in Milan.

Pogue, H. & S., Co. 1927 and probably other years. U.S. Advertised dolls, among them *Yolanda.*

Pohl. 1878–1915. Schatzlar, Bohemia. This Porzellanfabrik Schatzlar made porcelain dolls. Reinhold Pohl was listed in 1897 and Theodor Pohl was listed in 1906–15.

Pohl, Wilhelm. 1902. Vienna. Showed many kinds of dolls in various sizes at the "Art in Child Life" exhibition. Some of these dolls were dressed in regional costumes and some were in period costumes.

Pohlson Galleries. 1918. Pawtucket, R.I. Advertised the Nimble Wimbly Wops and the Flippity Flippity Flops. These were boy and girl dolls.

Poilu. See **Pioupiou.**

Poincaré. 1927. Portrait doll of the famous Frenchman created by *Mlle. Adrienne.*

Point, A. 1927–28. Saint-Chamond, Loire, and Paris. Made dolls and used the mark "A. P."

Poir. See **Gre-Poir.**

Poiret, Paul. 1910–26. Paris. Born 1878 in Paris, died 1944; he was a doll maker as well as a couturier, painter and writer.

1921: *Stewart Culin* reported that he visited Poiret's shop which had only a Pierette for sale at $11.00 in 1921. But Poiret was scheduled to exhibit dolls costing up to $50.00 later that year.

1926: Poiret created laughing dolls with humorous faces and supple legs. PLAYTHINGS reported that the Poiret "Dolls probably matching the gowns of the great couturier."★

Poiret, R. 1929. Paris. Made jewelry and parures for dolls.

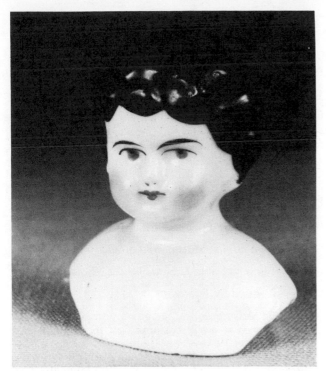

2115. China shoulder head with molded hair possibly made by Theodor Pohl in Bohemia. Mark on back: Ill. 2116A. H. of shoulder head only, 2¼ in. (5.5 cm.). *Coleman Collection.*

A **P I**

2116A. Mark on a china shoulder head that possibly was made by Theodor Pohl.

B **X⚒**
2210

C **TP**
1907
10/0

2116B & C. Other marks possibly used by Theodor Pohl.

2117. Dolls of Wilhelm Pohl exhibited in Vienna at the Art in Child Life exhibition as shown in the STUDIO, September 1902.

Poittier, F. See **Belton, Louis-Desirée.**

Pola. 1915. One of the *Paderewski* dolls made by Polish refugees in *Mme. Lazarski's* workshop. It represented a tinsmith's wife from the Tatra mountains in Galicia.

Pola. After World War I. Trademark of a factory in Waltershausen that made dolls with soft rubber heads and composition bodies.★

Pola
Germany
100
43

2118. Pola mark found on the rubber head of a doll.

Policeman. Many dolls were dressed in the police uniform of various countries.

1899: *Butler Bros.* imported and distributed dolls with painted face, a mustache, cloth body, dressed as a policeman and carrying a billy or night stick. Hts. 9½ and 12 in. (24 and 30.5 cm.).

1903: *Pygmalion* advertised an "Agent of Vehicles." This composition doll carried a billy or night stick. Ht. 45 cm. (17½ in.); price $1.65.

1904: All-composition doll with molded police uniform, jointed at the shoulders and hips, carried a billy or nightstick. Another doll, fully jointed, wore a blue policeman's uniform. Ht. 18 in. (45.5 cm.).

1906: *Gamage* advertised two types of *Steiff* felt policemen, one was fat and the other was lanky; priced 22¢ and 34¢.

1911: Steiff dressed felt dolls as American, Belgian, English, French, and German Policemen. Their code names were *Pla., Plbc., Ple., Plf.,* and *Pld.* respectively.

1913: Gamage sold two Steiff felt dolls that resembled British Bobbies. The fat doll was 17 in. (43 cm.) tall, priced 73¢, and the thin doll which Beatrix Potter had used as a model for the policeman in A TALE OF TWO BAD MICE was 20 in. (51 cm.) tall; priced 62¢.

1916: *Harwin & Co.* made a cloth doll dressed as a British Bobby.

1926: *Casey the Cop* was made by the *Wolf Doll Co.; Jeanette Doll Co.* made a doll representing a Policeman; there was also *Robert,* the Policeman; one of the *Teenie Weenies* was dressed as a Policeman.

1926: *Jedco* included a Policeman in their line of Nursery Rhyme dolls distributed by *Louis Wolf.*

1927: *The American Wholesale Corp.* made a *Traffic Cop* doll.

1930: *Whyte, Ridsdale* made a policeman doll. (See also **Fritz Brownie** and **Cymbalier.**) (See Ills. 2119 and 2120.)★

2119. Policeman or other official with a bisque socket head, blond wig, stationary blue glass eyes, open mouth with four upper teeth, and a ball-jointed composition body having straight wrists. Original clothes. Mark on head: 340. H. 10½ in. (26.5 cm.). *Private collection.*

2120. Felt Policeman with a seam down the center of its face. The eyes are black buttons. A little mustache is painted black over the closed mouth. The felt covered body contains a key wind mechanism so that the wheels on the bottom of the shoes move. The whistle is not original. H. 10 in. (25.5 cm.). *Courtesy of Clair Hennig. Photo by Margie Landolt, Basel, Switzerland.*

Polichinelle (Punchinello, Punch or Kasper). 1600s–1930 and later. These dolls had various names in different languages and were frequently in puppet form. French Polichinelles usually had strings which could manipulate their limbs and sometimes their heads, but were frequently played with just as dolls. Punch was often a hand puppet. These dolls originated as Pulcinella, the braggart, in the COMMEDIA DELL'ARTE. The following chronological list indicates the popularity, especially in France, of Polichinelles.

1848: *Barrois* made Polichinelles.

1850s: *Anton Edel* produced Polichinelle dolls.

1860–61: Imported into U.S. by *John D. Robbins.*

1878: Advertised by *Printemps.*

1882, 1892: Advertised by the *Louvre* store. Came in many sizes. The ones in a silk costume cost the most. Rubber Polichinelles wore knitted costumes.

1890: *Insam & Prinoth* produced wooden Polichinelles.

1891: Printemps advertised in their Swedish catalog that Polichinelle wore silk clothes and had strings and a bell attached to the top of its conical hat. Strings were also attached to its hands and feet. Three prices were listed.

1893: *Samaritaine* sold Polichinelles in five sizes.

1900–01: Printemps sold Polichinelles in three sizes. *Art Fabric Mills* made a cutout cloth Punch. See Ill. 140.

1902: *Gamage* advertised Polichinelles.

1903: *Bon Marché*'s Polichinelle was dressed in silk, came in six sizes. (See Ill. 2121.)

1904–15: At least six Paris stores advertised Polichinelles. These were dressed in silk or satin with lace and braid. Some had bisque heads and some had composition heads. Some had strings and some did not. Heights ranged from 35 cm. to 100 cm. (14 to 39½ in.); priced 25¢ to $5.90.

1909–10: *L'Hotel de Ville* advertised Polichinelles.

1914: *James Wisbey* handled Polichinelle dolls.

1917–18: The *Deptford Fund Toy-Making Industry* made Punch dolls.

1919–20: *Henri Bellet* produced Polichinelle dolls.

1921: The composition-head Polichinelles at L'Hotel de Ville store were nearly 30 percent less expensive than their bisque-head Polichinelles. The Louvre's Polichinelles had strings attached only to the hands, none to the legs or head.

1923–24: The Louvre sold Polichinelles dressed in satin and lace, in six sizes. (See also **Punch & Judy.**)★

Polish Dolls. Poland showed bisque head bébés at the Paris International Exhibition in 1900. *Jacob Fingerhut* produced dolls in the first decade of the 1900s. *Zast* made and/or handled celluloid dolls in the 1920s. (See also **Paderewski.**)★

N° 19012

POLICHINELLE
habillage soie, galon or.

0ᵐ39	1·25	0ᵐ52	3·90
0ᵐ42	1·75	0ᵐ59	5·50
0ᵐ46	2·45	0ᵐ66	7·75

2121. Polichinelle dressed in silk with gold braid as advertised in the 1903 Bon Marché catalog. Hs. 39, 42, 46, 52, 59, and 66 cm. (15½, 16½, 18, 20½, 23, and 26 in.); priced 25¢ to $1.55. *Courtesy of Margaret Whitton.*

17589.

Polichinelle, habillage riche.
15.90, 12.90,
9.90, 6.50, 4.90 et **3.50**

0 — 41151. POLICHINELLE
tête incassable, habillage satin
Prix
11.25 12.75 15.25
Le même, tête porcelaine.
14.50 17.25 24.50

2123. Polichinelle in the Printemps 1918 catalog. Note that the costume on this wartime Polichinelle is much simpler than in other periods. Six hs. priced 70¢ to $3.18. *Courtesy of Margaret Whitton.*

2124. Advertisement for a Polichinelle dressed in satin in the 1921 L'Hotel de Ville catalog. It came in three sizes with either a composition head or a bisque head which cost considerably more.

37263.

POLICHINELLE
très riche, costume
satin et dentelle.
10.25,   13.75,
17.90,
24.50,
29.90 et **45.**»

2125. Polichinelle shown in the 1923 Louvre store catalog. It was dressed in satin and lace, and was available in a range of six prices.

375083.

POLICHINELLE très riche,
costume satin et dentelle, galons or.

0ᵐ38	0ᵐ42	0ᵐ46	0ᵐ54
1.60	**2.45**	**3.50**	**4.90**
0ᵐ63	0ᵐ67	0ᵐ76	
6.75	**10.75**	**12.75**	

2122. Polichinelle shown in the 1916 Louvre store catalog. It has the typical humps of Polichinelle (Punch) and wears a satin and lace costume trimmed with gold braid. Seven hs. 38, 42, 46, 54, 58, 67, and 76 cm. (15, 16½, 18, 21½, 23, 26½, and 30 in.); priced 32¢ to $2.55.

2126. Bisque head doll marked F. G. for François Gaultier is dressed as a Polichinelle without its humps. The satin costume is trimmed with paper and includes green knee length pants, pink tailed jacket with black velvet cuffs and yellow vest. The bisque hands and legs have gold braid tied to them and bells are attached near the knees. The hat has a pink ornament. Mark: III. 1025. H. with hat 8 in. (20.5 cm.). H. without hat 6 in. (15 cm.). *Coleman Collection.*

Politzer, Morris. 1930 and before. Veteran designer and manufacturer of dolls.

1930: Created dolls for the *American Stuffed Novelty Co.* He may have been connected with the Politzer Toy Manufacturing Co.†

Pollak, H. 1884–88. Vienna. Obtained a German patent (D.R.P.) for fastening the hair on dolls.

Pollack & Hoffmann. 1902–07. Buchau, Bohemia. Made porcelain dolls and dolls' heads. (See Ill. 157.) (See also **Plass & Roesner.**)

Pöll-Math, Adam. 1926–27. Berlin. Made and/or exported dolls.

Poll-Parrot Shoes. Label sewed onto the front of a doll with a composition shoulder head having painted features and a cloth body. The head of this advertising doll was marked "A. M. Doll Co." During the 1920s all-bisque dolls made in Japan were used to advertise Poll-Parrot Shoes.

Polly. 1918. All-composition doll made by *Jessie M. Raleigh.* It had a five-piece steel strung body with straight legs and wore a dress of silk marquisette and a ribbon headband.★

Polly. 1920. *Mama* doll with composition head, arms and legs, made by *Paul Averill.* Ht. 26 in. (66 cm.).★

Polly. 1922. Sponge rubber doll made by the *Miller Rubber Co.*

Polly Anna. 1919. Doll with wood-fiber composition head and hands on a cloth body stuffed with cork or excelsior, made by the *American Bisque Doll Co.* It wore long or short baby dresses in various styles; some dolls had a jacket and cap. Hts. 18, 20 and 27 in. (45.5, 51, and 68.5 cm.).

Polly Heckewelder. 1872–1930 and later. Name of a dressed, flat cloth doll with a hand-painted face, made and sold by the Ladies Sewing Society of the Moravian Church Guild in Bethlehem, Pa. Some of these dolls wore a blue dress. Ht. 18 in. (45.5 cm.).

Polly of the Circus. 1908. One of the Contortionist line of dolls with a body that could be twisted into a number of positions. The doll was dressed as a circus performer with a short green and red fluffy skirt over pink leggings, white slippers and white gloves.

Polly Prue. 1911–12. Doll with composition head and hands on a cloth body designed by *Helen Trowbridge* and produced by *Horsman.* The copyrighted head design with molded bobbed hair, a curl on the forehead and painted eyes appears to be the same as was used for *Annette, Fairy* and *Nancy Lee.* Polly Prue wore a striped double breasted long "Galatea" coat, white duck skirt, and a brimmed hat. This was style No. 164.

Polly Prue. 1916. New *Horsman* doll with composition head and arms, style no. 152 dressed in figured lawn.

Polly Wobble. 1921. Aurora, Ill. Walking doll made by *C. W. Allen & Co.* The lower part of the body was rounded so that it wobbled.

Pollyanna Co. Ca. 1920–30 and later. Chicago, Ill. Appears to have developed into a conglomerate. About 1920 they took over the business of *Jessie M. Raleigh* who made dolls with composition heads having portrait sculptured faces of real children. In 1922 they took over the *Rees Davis* business and began to produce sewing sets for making dolls' clothes. By 1924 they had taken over Nelson-Young Manufacturing Co. and *Plano Toy Co.*

1922: Made character dolls and *Mama* dolls. Each doll's clothes set included a cutout dress ready to sew, needles, thread and snaps. The dresses were of organdy, batiste, voile, silk mull, or gingham. More elaborate sets included chemise and other underwear or a coat and hat or a cape. The newest set was a bloomer outfit with black sateen trimming and was called "Chin Chin." One package named "Teenie Weenies" contained a small doll, two dresses, a pair of pajamas, a cape, kimono and chemise.

1923: The Pollyanna sewing sets were adopted as standard in schools and were known as "You sew it." There were also ready-made dolls' clothes. Besides the Mama dolls and character dolls there were crying dolls, novelty dolls and cloth dolls. One of their dolls was called *Flapper Kid.*

1924: Made *Timber Tots* and other wooden dolls, formerly made by Nelson-Young. *Billy Boy* was another doll made by Pollyanna Co.

1926: Made baby dolls including Baby Bunting, Bunting Twins, and Eskimo Babies, of white eiderdown stuffed with cotton. The "Teenie Pollyanna Sewing Sets" consisted of a 7 in. (18 cm.) double jointed celluloid doll and six "You sew it" doll garments cut out and assembled on cardboard plus trimming, needle, thimble, thread and "snappers." This boxed set cost $7.50 doz. wholesale.

1927: Used the trade name Pollyanna.★

Pomarantz, A. F., & Sons. 1925–29. London. Made and/or distributed dolls.★

Pompadour. See **La Pompadour, Madame Pompadour** and **Poupée Pompadour.**

Pompeian Art Works. See **Continental Toy & Novelty Co.**

Ponchi Shokai Ayanmokoji. See **Bonchi Shokai Ayanmokoji.**

Pont Neuf. 1900–01 and probably other years. Paris. A store that sold *Bébé Jumeau, Eden Bébés, Mignonnettes, Polichinelles, Marottes,* French Soldiers, Boer War Soldiers, dolls and their trousseaux in boxes.

Pont, Nicholas Théodore. 1818–73. Méuse area, France. Born at Récicourt and made dolls when he grew up but the business failed according to Mme. Florence Poisson, curator of the Roybet Fould Museum.

Pooksie. 1914–18. All-bisque doll registered by *Hamley,* January 1914, and later made in *British Ceramic* by *Wiltshaw & Robinson* and distributed by Hamley Bros. The doll was designed by *Mabel Lucie Attwell* and registered as numbers 650718 and 650719. It had jointed shoulders and legs apart. The molded clothes consisted of a kepi, a belt, shoulder straps, and a sword. There were three sizes.★

Poore, John C. 1919–20. Boston, Mass. Obtained a U.S. patent for a doll's head with eyes that were connected with the ears and the eyes could thus be moved manually.

Popineau.† See **Guerchoux, Rémy.**

Popp, Carl. 1908–10. Murschitz near Sbg. Applied for two German patents (D.R.G.M.) for dolls.

Poppe, Mathilde. 1896. Neustadt near Coburg, Thür. Applied for a German patent (D.R.G.M.) for a jointed doll with an opening in the body.

Poppert, Isidor. 1926–28. Berlin. Manufactured dolls.

Poppets. From the mid 1800s to 1930 and later, wooden dolls were made in the Kentucky mountain area and called Poppets. These primitive hand-carved dolls were made of a fine grained light-colored and lightweight wood from buckeye trees. The features were drawn with ink or pencil and/or were carved. The hair was made of dyed wool or the skin and hair of an animal. The cheeks were stained with cohosh or poke-berries. The head and upper torso were made of one piece of wood. The arms and legs were also wood. The hands had grooves to indicate fingers and often heeled slippers were inked onto the feet. The rest of the body was cloth. The dolls were dressed in simple clothes, usually an ankle-length cotton dress. Most of the dolls were made in homes or in mission schools. These dolls show some crude relationship to the 18th century wooden dolls. Some dictionaries, especially early ones, define "Poppet" as meaning a doll.

Poppy. 1919–20. Name of a doll representing a laughing girl, made by *Jessie M. Raleigh.* (See Ill. 2175.)

Poppy. 1919–21. Stockinet doll with non-removable clothes made by *Chad Valley* as style No. 19. Ht. 11½ in. (29 cm.).

Poppy. 1924. One of the *Posy* line of cloth dolls made by *Dean.* This doll wore a knee-length dress with a flower on the chest, a jacket and cloche and carried a flower in its right hand.

Poppy Doll Co. 1925–30 and later. Atascadero, Calif. Made a line of novelty and character dolls of California redwood. The dolls were hand decorated and had a lever in back which controlled their movable parts. Factory agents were *Corcoran & Laycock.* In 1929 Troxell merged with the Poppy Doll Co. Their most famous dolls were the *Scarey Ann* line.

1928: Dolls included a clown, Santa Claus, a sailor, a tramp and a witch.

1929: *Happy Hooligan* and a *Chinaman* were added to the doll line.

Popular Dolls. 1924. Name of flat faced cloth dolls made by *Dean* in their *A 1* brand. These cloth dolls came in two models with printed clothes in assorted colors. Ht. about 17 in. (43 cm.).

Porcelite Co. (Portland Works). 1917–19. Burslem, Stoke-

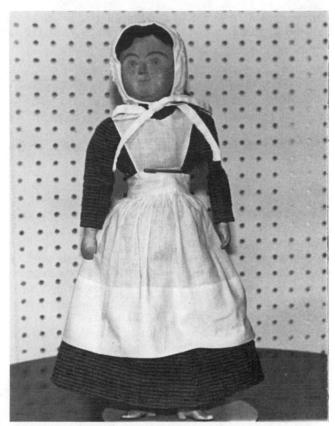

2127. Wooden doll called a Poppet made in the Kentucky mountain area. It has a wig, carved and painted features and cloth body from the waist to the knees. The arms and legs are carved wood. Original clothes with carved and painted footwear. H. 18 in. (45.5 cm.). *Courtesy of Joan Kindler.*

2128A & B. Carved and turned wooden doll made in the Kentucky mountain area and called a Poppet. Wool yarn hair; features and shoes painted with ink. H. 11 in. (28 cm.). *Coleman Collection.*

on-Trent, Staffs. Made dolls and dolls' limbs of a glossy or dull *British Ceramic*. Also made four or five sizes of dolls' limbs.

Porcheddu, Giuseppe. 1920s. He was a versatile artist who designed clothes for *Lenci* dolls. In 1918 he had been decorated by the King of Italy.

Porcellonhaus. See **Wahliss, Ernst.**

Portheim & Sohn. Mid 1800s. Carlsbad, Bohemia. Probably made porcelain dolls' heads marked "P. & S.," including heads decorated with morning glories.

Portland Works. See **Porcelite Co.**

Portrait Dolls. Many of the public personages including war heroes and politically popular people have had portrait dolls made to represent them. Famous children such as little princes and princesses, winners of baby contests and children whose parents achieved fame were all subjects represented by portrait dolls. Probably the greatest number of portrait dolls especially in the 20th century, were dolls portraying the children of the doll manufacturers who made or produced the dolls. Most dolls were inspired by drawings, paintings, sculptures or actual people especially in the entertainment field. Thus directly or indirectly nearly all of our dolls were portrait dolls. (Also see **Model Doll.**)★

Porzellanfabrik.[†] See the name of the town or owner of the porcelain factory.

Porzellanit. 1930 and other years. Name of a composition material used for some of the dolls made by *Kämmer & Reinhardt* and *Max Rudolph*.

Posner, L. M. 1922. England. Made and/or handled dolls.

Poster Girl, The. 1927. Name of a doll created by *Jane Gray* and manufactured by *Gerling*.

Postil (Postillion). 1913. Felt doll made by *Steiff* and distributed by *Borgfeldt* in the U.S. It represented a Postillion with a cornet. Ht. 19½ in. (50 cm.); priced $5.70.

Postman. See **Pse.**

Posy Dolls. 1924–28. Line of felt dolls with pressed three-dimensional faces made by *Dean*. The dolls had wigs, painted faces and eyes, and were jointed at the neck, shoulders and hips. Their clothes were decorated with flowers and resembled *Lenci* costumes. Usually they had hats. These dolls were named *Daisy, Marigold, Poppy,* and *Rose*.

Pot. An abbreviation of "pottery," Pot was a name sometimes applied to *British Ceramic* dolls. British advertisements often referred to these dolls as being "china" dolls.

Potteries Toy Co. (British Toy Co.; Potteries Doll Co.). 1914–18. Stoke-on-Trent, Staffs. Wardol Works. The making of dolls was organized by Mrs. Rittner, wife of a local member of Parliament. The ceramic heads and some of the arms of the dolls were made by W. H. Goss. The dolls themselves were made at the Wardol Works. The dolls came with glass eyes or with painted eyes, jointed or without joints, dressed or undressed.

1916: Advertised baby dolls and character dolls with movable heads. One of their largest dolls with a "flaxen curl" wig was given to the Queen. Another doll was named "Seaside Sandy." Hts. 10 to 30 in. (25.5 to 76 cm.).

1917: Dolls were dressed in the costumes of the Allies including the British Colonies and Highlanders. Some of the dolls wore clothes that would fit an 18-months child.

1918: Dolls were dressed as sailors and soldier boys.★

Poulbot, M., and Mme. Francisque. 1908–29 and possibly later. Paris. Artists who created cloth dolls and designed bisque head dolls for the *Société Française de Fabrication de Bebes & Jouets* (S.F.B.J.). Mold # 239 was sculptured by M.

2129. "L'Ecole," a group of dolls created by Poulbot and exhibited in the Salon des Humoristes. This is an illustration from THE STUDIO, November, 1908.

Poulbot. One of the cloth dolls has been found with a tag reading *Titi.* Most of the dolls represented gamins or urchins and school children of Paris. M. Poulbot, born 1879, died 1946, was a renowned artist who portrayed the children of the streets of Paris, especially Montmartre. He was not only an illustrator but he also wrote some texts. From 1918 on he won many prizes for his work which was that of a humorist, never tragic. He became a Chevalier of the Legion of Honor.

1908: Exhibited a group of cloth dolls with flexible parts at the Salon de Humoristes. This group of dolls with wigs, character faces, thin legs and rag-a-muffin type clothes was called "L'Ecole."

1913: Galeries Lafayette advertised *Nénette et Rintintin* which were designed by Poulbot. Ht. 36 cm. (14 in.) (See the COLLECTOR'S BOOK OF DOLLS' CLOTHES, Ill. 639.)

1914: The *Louvre* store advertised the "Gosses" (Mascots) of Poulbot named Nénette and Rintintin. Ht. of dolls 35 cm. (14 in.); priced dressed $1.78.

1918: M. Poulbot designed the cover for the *Bon Marché* Toy catalog.

1928: Bon Marché advertised Poulbot dolls named *Lulu* and *Riri.* ★

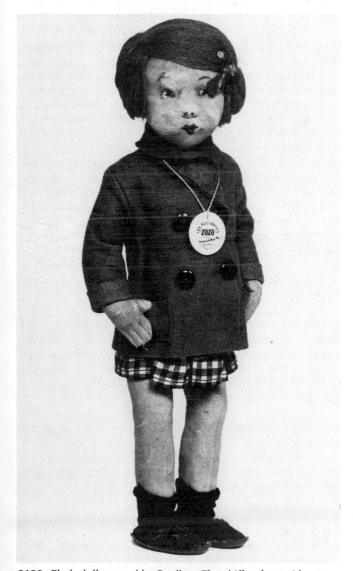

2130. Cloth doll created by Poulbot. The chiffon face with cotton backing is molded and needle sculptured. It has a mustard colored yarn wig, painted blue eyes, closed lips with a darker lip line and under the lower lip. The torso is cloth and the arms and legs are flocked buckram. The sandals are also of flocked buckram and have felt soles. Original clothes. Mark on tag: Ill. 2132. H. 15 in. (38 cm.). *Courtesy of the Margaret Woodbury Strong Museum. Photo by Harry Bickelhaupt.*

2131. Bisque-head doll designed by Poulbot has a red wig, stationary brown glass eyes, closed mouth and five-piece composition body. Original clothes. Mark: Ill. 2133. H. 36 cm. (14 in.). *Courtesy of the Margaret Woodbury Strong Museum. Photos by Harry Bickelhaupt.*

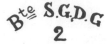

2132–2133. Marks on dolls designed by Poulbot. No. 2133 is on a bisque head. No. 2132 is on a tag on a cloth-head doll.

2135–2136. Poupée Breveté marks found on dolls indicating that the dolls have been patented.

Poum. 1925. Cutout doll with bobbed hair, bangs, eyes looking to the side, rompers and footwear all printed on the doll. These dolls were published by *Fernand Nathan* and came in two sizes, the smaller of which was called Jean-Jacques. Hts. 27 and 30 cm. (10½ and 12 in.).

Poupard. Generally the French term for *Swaddling-clothed Dolls.* In the 20th century the meaning of poupard appears to have expanded to include dolls with legs and leading strings and to have been synonymous with *Bébé Culotte.*★

Poupée. The French term for doll.

Poupée Breveté. The mark "Poupee Breveté//S.G.D.G." has been found on laminated kid bodies of the type made by Clément.[†]

Poupée Chiffon (Cloth Dolls). 1919. TOYS AND NOVELTIES reported on dolls with suede faces which were called "rag dolls" in the following United Press account:

"Rag dolls for 'Grown-Ups'. The craze of the moment in fad-loving Paris. . . . Poupée Chiffon is their regular nomenclature in their native habitat, which is Paris.

"Though reminiscent of the Polish dolls that were so much exploited both in Europe and America during the war, and also of the mascot rag dolls that had such vogue in Paris during the air raids and bombardments, these newest poupée chiffon are distinctly original. They are the work of different individual women artists, and artist is the right word. Each doll is a little master piece conceived and executed with as much art and originality as the canvas of a painter or the marble of a sculptor. There are no two alike, and each one is signed on the sole of one tiny slipper with the name of the artist.

"The face of all is of suede with embroidered features, the cheeks only touched up a la human females with a bit of paint. The hair, which is the most novel note, invariably is of yarn in exaggerated bright shades of orange, yellow and henna.

"Though there are character and period dolls among the assortment, the most typical and Parisian are the little girl dolls, long and lank of leg with their abbreviated excuses for skirts and mops of bobbed wool topped with a provocative bow or a chic chapeau. Their toilettes are worked out to the veriest detail of Frenchy perfection just like their real little human Parisian prototypes.

". . . their prices are as high as everything else now in Paris, and that certainly is beaucoup. The fact that all the returning officers are bearing gifts of these delectable dolls to their sweethearts, wives or mothers is . . . interesting. . . . Indeed, it is the big, grown-up girls who are craziest about these attractive toys."

Poupée de Modes. See **Fashion Dolls.**

Poupée Modèle, La. 1863–1924. Children's magazine published for many years by Mme. Lavallée-*Peronne*. This magazine contained paper patterns for dolls' apparel, actual clothes made of tissue paper and pieces of stamped fabric each containing all the parts needed to make a specific garment. Detailed instructions were given with the patterns. (See also **Benjamine.**)

2134. Poupard made of molded cardboard with the hair, features and clothes molded and painted, jointed at the shoulders. H. 17½ in. (44.5 cm.). *Courtesy of Ruth and R. C. Mathes.*

Poupée Musette. 1929. Trademark registered in France by *Leger Henri Ribiere* to designate dolls named *"Musette."*

Poupée Nana. 1879. Name of a doll handled by *Gregori-Olivier.*

Poupée Pompadour. 1878. Name of a fashion-type doll wearing a blue and white cashmere costume with a train and a hat, sold by *Printemps.* Ht. 38 cm. (15 in.); priced $2.95.

Poupée Royale. 1925–30 and later. Trade name for felt dolls and decorative dolls made of silk, felt, wax, or leather by *G. Ourine.* For the mark see Ill. 2137.

2137. Poupée Royale mark for felt dolls made by G. Ourine.

Poupées Arlay. 1929. Trademark registered in France by *Roger Georges Trichet* for dolls.

Poupées Artistiques. 1927. Name applied to felt dolls called *Magit.*

Poupées Chiffons. 1927. Name of art dolls made in Paris, some of them were for export. (See also **Poupée Chiffon.**)

Poupées Consuélo Fould. 1920s. Art dolls created by Consuélo Fould.[†] These lady dolls wore the extreme styles of the period with luxurious fabrics, long fringe trimming and above the knee skirts.

Poupées Georgia. 1929–30 and later. Name of dolls made by *M. Dehut.*

Poupées Gerb's. See **Gerb's.**

Poupées Grillet. See **Grillet, Albert.**

Poupées Nadine. 1930 and later. Name of some dolls made at Sèvres, France.

Poupées Ninon. 1925–30 and later. Art dolls made of "composition felt." Some of these dolls had glass eyes and hair eyelashes. The hands had the fingers separated only by sewing except for the thumb. The sole agent in the U.S. and Canada was the *French Fashion Importing Co.* The dolls were dressed as girls or boys. Hts. 11 to 23 in. (28 to 58.5 cm.).★

Poupées Parisiennes. 1910. Copenhagen, Denmark. Name of a shop that displayed dolls at the Brussels' Exposition and won a silver medal for their exhibit.

Poupées Raynal.[†] See **Raynal.**

Poupées Rosalinde, Les. 1927–30 and later. Paris. Listed under dolls in DIDOT.

Poupées Salon. 1930 and later. Felt dolls made by *Lenci* including those wearing costumes representing Spring, Summer, Autunn, and Winter, namely *Primavera, Estate, Autunno* and *Inverno.* Ht. 48 in. (122 cm.).

Poupon. French term for an infant doll.

1879: Mme. Lavallée-*Peronne* advertised Le Poupon.

1913: *Aux Trois Quartiers* advertised a black Poupon with a composition head, cloth body with bent limbs. Ht. 30 cm. (12 in.); priced 95¢.★

Pouting Bess. 1915. Flange type composition-head doll made by *Effanbee.* It had molded bobbed hair, painted eyes, closed pouting mouth and a cloth body with composition lower arms. When marked 162 it was 10 in. (25.5 cm.) tall and when marked 166 it was 15 in. (38 cm.) tall.

The head resembles the bisque Kämmer & Reinhardt head mold # 114 which was made at about the same time.

Pouty Pets (Pouting Tots). 1914–15. Names given to dolls with composition heads and hands, modeled from "real live children" and produced by *Amberg.*

1915: Dolls came dressed as boys, girls and in a nightie. Hts. 12 and 16 in. (30.5 and 40.5 cm.).★

Powell, Snelling & Co. 1835–46. Boston, Mass. London Importing Warehouse, handled a large assortment of dolls.

Powell & Zuber. 1923. Newark, N.J. Made and/or distributed dolls.

Pralong, Mme. 1918. Paris. Created cloth bébés.

Pranner, Matthaus. 1841–42. Vienna. In 1842 he was succeeded by his widow. Distributed "Nürnberg" dolls.

Premet. 1926. Made dolls representing 18th century people; a Marquise was described as "slender-waisted and coy." A Boy doll was dressed as Pierrot.

Presbyterian Doll. 1880s. Cloth doll with flat handpainted face made by the ladies of the First Presbyterian Church in Bucyrus, Ohio, in order to raise money for the church. The doll was made so that it could sit and the black material for the legs simulated black stockings. Dolls were dressed as girls or boys and cost $1.00. In the 1950s dolls were once again made from the same pattern.

President William McKinley. 1898 and probably later. Portrait doll with bisque head, molded hair, painted or glass eyes, closed mouth, five-piece composition body dressed in a naval officer's uniform.

The President McKinley doll belonging to the Wenham Museum originally came from the International Doll Collection and probably would have been new at the time that it came into that collection. The doll has a rectangular maroon leather label with gold letters and trimming. The letters read: "CUNO & OTTO DRESSEL//SONNEBERG, (Germany.)." *Admiral George Dewey* and *Admiral William Thomas Sampson* were also represented at the museum by similar dolls. These three dolls had hands bent back at the wrist and wore similar uniforms including the bicorne hats. Ht. 15½ in. (39.5 cm.).

Other similar dolls also represented such Spanish-American War heroes as *Admiral Winfield Scott Schley* and *Richmond Pearson Hobson*. President McKinley was the only one of this group found so far without a mustache or beard. These portrait dolls may have been produced by several companies with resulting variations in portraiture, uniforms, and hts. Besides the 15½ in. (39.5 cm.) doll there were smaller ones, hts. 8 and 12 in. (20.5 and 30.5 cm.).

Presles Frères. 1928. Paris. Made a *Bébé Charmant*.

Pressed versus Poured. There are two methods of filling molds in the making of china and bisque dolls, dolls' heads and limbs. The pressed method whereby the material is rolled out like dough and pressed into the mold, often with a sponge, was used for most early porcelain heads. In France this method was used until about 1890 when the pouring method which had been used in Germany much earlier began to be used. For pouring, the material was liquified to become what is called "slip" and was poured into the mold. This hardened around the edges and the remaining slip was poured off. Pressed heads can be identified by their uneven surface, often with fine striations and unequal thickness. Sometimes they have fingerprints or slight ridges where the sponge was dragged across. The poured heads are basically smooth inside except for an occasional bubble which had burst in the firing or when the liquid bisque partially hardened and retained the form of the flow with slight undulations. The porcelain is generally uniform in thickness. The bisque heads without rims or lips are usually pressed, while those having a rim or lip are usually poured. Sometimes the rim had been cut away especially on the shoulders so that they would fit over the body more snugly. The cutting away of this rim usually is detected easily.

It takes considerable study of many examples before one can feel confident to differentiate between those products made with the pressed method and those made with the poured method.

A determination of whether a head is pressed or poured helps to date dolls and it is often an indication of a French or German origin. The heads made in the mid-1800s were all pressed but at least as early as 1870 some of the German heads were poured. After about 1890 nearly all French and German heads were poured. Most of the fashion type lady heads were pressed as well as the E.J. *Bébés Jumeau*, the *Jules Steiner* bébés and so forth. Nearly all of the Tête Jumeaus and German child dolls were poured. The rarer china heads were often pressed but some of them were poured and it appears as if both methods could have been used at the same time in Germany. Some of the china heads were glazed inside making it more difficult to determine whether they had been poured or pressed. Composition-head dolls were also made by pressing or pouring. (See **Manufacture of Dolls.**)

Pressman, J., & Co. 1929–30. New York City. Made dolls with composition heads and wooden limbs called *Jerry* dolls.

Pressner, M., & Co. 1919–30 and later. New York City. Imported, exported, served as manufacturer's agent, and manufactured dressed dolls.

1920: Advertised domestic and Japanese bisque dolls and celluloid dolls.

1924: Advertised *Mama* dolls; priced $1.00.

1926: Specialized in bisque-head baby dolls. Made dressed jointed bisque or celluloid dolls some of which were called "Baby in Bed" and "Baby in Cradle."

2138. Pressed china shoulder head with a broken section showing the roughness of the interior and the uneven thickness of the china, characteristics of pressed porcelain heads. H. of shoulder head 7 in. (18 cm.). *Coleman Collection.*

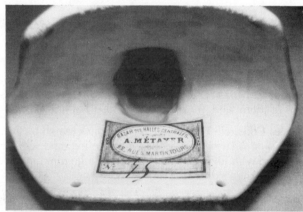

2139A & B. Inside of a pressed china shoulder head with a paper label for Métayer. Note the varying thickness around the edges, the unevenness of the surface and the irregular shape of the neck hole. The head is shown in B. and Ill. 1199 in the first COLLECTOR'S ENCYCLOPEDIA OF DOLLS. H. of shoulder head 4½ in. (11.5 cm.). *Coleman Collection.*

Preston, Chloe. 1911–30 and later. England. Illustrator who designed dolls for *Dean* and *Farnell*. The children in her drawings were round-faced, round-eyed and plump. Her book titled THE PEEK-A-BOOS was probably the inspiration for the *Horsman* composition dolls named *Peek-A-Boo*. Other dolls closely resembling her drawings had bisque heads with molded hair and features. (See Ill. 2140.) Some of these have been found on stuffed velvet bodies which comprised the dress or suit for the dolls. These were jointed at the shoulders.

Pretty. See **Fétiche Porte Bonheur//Pretty.**

Pretty Face. 1887. Name used by *Lauer* for a wax doll with a wig, glass eyes, a chemise, and painted footwear. Ht. 20 in. (51 cm.); priced $2.40 doz. wholesale.

Pretty Jane. 1924. Cloth doll made by *Chad Valley* in their La Petite *Caresse* line. It had real hair, handpainted face, a kapok-stuffed *Aerolite* body and wore a checked blouse and cap, plain skirt with a low waistline. It carried a six-sided tag that read "CHAD VALLEY//HYGIENIC//Fabric Toys." There were three heights: style no. 253 was 11 in. (28 cm.), style no. 254 was 12½ in. (31.5 cm.) and style no. 255 was 14 in. (35.5 cm.).

Pretty Peggy. 1925–26. Composition head *Mama* doll

2140. A bisque shoulder head designed by Chloe Preston. It has molded blond hair, a blue cap and round eyes looking to the side. The open-closed mouth is elliptical in shape. There is almost no neck. The cloth body may be a replacement. Mark on back of shoulder: "328 3 b." H. of head 3 in. (9.5 cm.). *Courtesy of Richard Withington. Photo by Barbara Jendrick.*

dressed in organdy and wore a hairbow, was advertised by *Louis Wolf.*★

Pretty Peggy. 1926–28. *Mama* doll designed by *Grace Corry*, and produced by *Borgfeldt*. It had a bisque head with either molded hair or a wig, sleeping eyes, cloth body with composition arms and legs.

1926: Copyright by Grace Corry Rockwell with the name Betty Jean which was changed to Pretty Peggy. This doll pictured in PLAYTHINGS wore a large hairbow and a full dress that hung from the neckline. Borgfeldt had used the name Pretty Peggy for an earlier line of dolls.★

Pretty Peggy. 1927–28. Name of a dressed doll with composition head, arms and legs, cloth body and crying voice, distributed by *Charles William*. Ht. 16 in. (40.5 cm.); priced 89¢.

Pretty Prue (Pure). 1920–21. Stockinet doll with wig, removable clothes of silk and other materials, made by *Chad Valley*. The doll had a Chad Valley patented wristwatch. Style No. 10; ht. 12 to 13 in. (30.5 to 33 cm.).

Pretz, Florence. 1909. Chicago, Ill. Created *Billiken*, "The God of things as they ought to be." Billiken in doll form was produced by *Horsman*, based on the Pretz design. See Ills. 310 and 311.

Preusser & Co. 1925–29. Oelsnitz, Germany. Made dressed and undressed dolls as well as dolls' clothes.

Prévost-Huret. See **Huret, Maison.**

Prialytine. World War I period. Name of a composition-celluloid like material that was used to make *Yerri* and *Gretel* dolls.

Price, Lenora. 1917–18. Davenport, Okla. Patented a cloth doll whose head was made of a front and back piece with a gore cut on the bias and a chin piece that was connected to the back and front below the gore to give shape to the head.★

Preusser & Co.,
G. m. b. H.
Oelsnitz i. V.
★
Fabrikation gekleideter
Puppen und Puppen-
bekleidung aller Art.
Besonders leistungsfähig in
**Puppenwäsche u. Puppen-
kleidern** in mittlerer Preislage.
★
Zur Messe in Leipzig:
Wagnerhaus Grimmaiſche Straße 6,1

2141. Preusser & Co.'s advertisement in DEUTSCHE SPIEL-WAREN ZEITUNG, February, 1927. It states that they made dressed dolls and dolls' clothes of all kinds, but were particularly excellent in washable dolls and dolls' clothes in the medium price range.

Price, Margaret Evans. 1915. U.S. Designed character-face cutout cloth dolls named *Betty and Bobby*.

Price, William. 1725–54. Boston, Mass. Distributed "London Babies" (dolls) as well as other German and English toys.

Prices of Dolls. The prices given throughout this book are THOSE QUOTED IN THE ORIGINAL SOURCES of the period listed. They are THE ORIGINAL PRICE of a doll and usually have no relationship to the current prices or value of the doll on today's market. When the source was in a foreign currency it was converted into U.S. Dollars, if the information was prior to 1920 when the relationships remained remarkably stable. Four German Marks, Four British Shillings or Five French Francs equaled $1.00. The price was for a single doll retail unless specified that it was for the wholesale trade. In a few cases the data did not make it clear whether it was the wholesale or retail price.

An analysis of original price variations in the mid-1920s is as follows: Size made a great difference in prices; roughly double the size and you have to quadruple the price. The following price comparisons were based on dolls of similar size. In general, dolls with painted hair and eyes cost about half as much as dolls with wigs and glass eyes.

Bébé Jumeau cost about twice as much as an S.F.B.J. mold # 60 or 301.

German bisque-head dolls with mohair wigs and sleeping eyes were most expensive when on real kid bodies and least expensive when on imitation kid bodies or fully jointed composition bodies. Bisque-head dolls on bent limb composition bodies were more expensive than those on the fully jointed composition bodies probably because they required a proportionately larger head. The all-bisque dolls with painted hair and eyes were the least expensive but were about the same as the china-head dolls on cloth bodies. *Käthe Kruse* cloth dolls cost about double the most expensive German bisque-head dolls.

The *Schoenhut* wooden dolls were more expensive than the *Chase* cloth dolls or the composition *Mama* dolls made in America.

Dressed dolls were usually about double the price of undressed dolls. If the clothes were elaborate and/or handmade the price was often considerably more than double.★

Prieur. 1840–1928. Paris. Several generations of Prieurs made dolls and clothes, furnishings and accessories for dolls. In the 1880s they appear to have used bisque heads made by *François Gaultier*. Later they made bébés and dolls using the mark L.P. During World War I and at least through 1920 they obtained bisque heads for dolls from Couty *(Coiffe);* probably other porcelain factories also supplied bisque heads. Shoes marked "P" may have been made by the Prieurs.

In the 1920s Louis Léon Prieur's widow was a member of the *Chambre Syndicale.* In 1928 or before, the business was purchased by L. Salomon.

1840: Mme. Louise Amadine Prieur at the age of 22 began to make clothes for dolls.

1861: Mme. Prieur declared bankruptcy but she was able to pay off 80 per cent of her creditors.

The inventory showed about 11,500 bisque or china dolls' heads of various heights. Among the creditors were *Morhardt* of Nürnberg, *Carl Heinze* of Hildburghausen, Thür., and *Blampoix* Sr. who had supplied heads with painted eyes or with glass eyes. There were also separate arms, hands, shoulders, clothes and so forth.

1865: Mme. Prieur had paid off all of her creditors and remained in business.

1880: C. Prieur was one of the creditors of Mme. Vve. (Widow) Blampoix.

1881: Claude Bastide Prieur, distributor of articles for dolls, was one of the experts who worked on the inventory of Mme. Gaultier, wife of François Gaultier. Prieur was also a customer of Gaultier.

1882 and 1890: C. Prieur was listed under Furnishings for Dolls.

1900 and 1905: L. (Léon) Prieur was listed at the same address as Claude Prieur had previously been and in the same business.

1912: L. Prieur advertised dressed and undressed dolls, *mignonnettes, Mon Trésor* heads, wigs and other furnishings for dolls.

1914: L. Prieur advertised that he made bébés and furnishings for dolls including heads of all kinds, wigs of human hair and mohair, parts of dolls, footwear, umbrellas, hats, lingerie, clothes, parures, and special models. He purchased many of his bisque heads from Couty, successor of Coiffe in Limoges.

1915: Léon Prieur registered in France the marks *Mon Petit Rimailho* and *Mon Petit Trésor.*

1916: Louis Léon Prieur died when a ship on which he was traveling was torpedoed by the Germans. He was returning to France from a fair in London.

1922: Widow Prieur advertised jointed bébés, *Bébés Maillot, Bébés Culotte* and furnishings for bébés as well as *Mon Chéri* dolls (See Ills. 1936 and 1937), mignonnettes and dolls' parts.

1927: Prieur advertised bébés, dolls' heads, limbs and clothing, including wigs, hats and footwear.

1928: The former houses of Israel[†] and Prieur were united under L. Salomon.

Part of the above information was based on the research of Mme. Florence Poisson, curator of the Roybet Fould Museum and Mme. Anne-Marie Porot.★

Prima Donna. 1895. Name of a bisque-head doll advertised by *Butler Bros.* It had glass eyes, a ball-jointed body and wore a dress advertised as having been copied from a "Worth Creation." Ht. 29 in. (73.5 cm.); priced $8.25.

Primevera (Le Printemps). 1930. Felt *Lenci* doll representing Spring in the *Poupées Salon* series of the Four Seasons, with its pink and green dress, green scarf, and bonnet. Style no. 1053. Ht. 48 in. (122 cm.).

Primrose. 1902. A black cloth doll representing a female minstrel, with woolly hair and bead eyes, distributed by *Butler Bros.* Priced $2.15 doz. wholesale.

Primrose Doll Co. 1927–30. New York City. Made dolls and patented moving eyes for their dolls.

1927: Made *Mama* dolls. Licensed by *Voices, Inc.* to use their patented mama voices and criers.

1928: Primrose line included boy and girl twin pairs of dolls called *Chums. Joseph Wolson* was the factory representative. Some of the dolls were packed in vanities.

1929: Dolls were priced $1.00 and up.

Primrose League (Junior Branch) Toy (Making) Industry. 1917–20. London. Handled washable cloth dolls made by children.

Prince Charlie. 1911–12. Copyrighted composition-head doll designed by *Helen Trowbridge* and produced by *Horsman.* It had molded bobbed hair with bangs, painted eyes, smiling open-closed mouth with teeth. The head appears to be the same as that used for *Daisy Dimple, Gretchen, Hans, Happy Hiram, Jack Tar* and *Robbie Reefer.* Prince Charlie, style no. 196, wore a "Stuart" Page costume of black velvet with a long coat and knickers, silk sash and lace collar and cuffs.

Prince Charlie's Model Best Made Bodies. Ca. 1882–89. These bodies came in six sizes and were distributed by *Silber & Fleming.* The body was advertised with a wax head, arms and legs.

Prince Charming. 1926. Line of Nursery Rhyme dolls made by *Jeanette Doll Co.* and distributed by *Louis Wolf & Co.*

Prince Edward as a doll.

2142. Portrait wax head doll of Prince Edward, who later became Edward VIII, as shown in THE LONDON MAGAZINE, 1902. This doll was handled by Hamley Bros.

Prince Edward of York (later Edward VIII). Ca. 1902. Wax-head portrait doll dressed as a boy in a white sailor suit with long trousers and a broad brimmed straw hat, probably made by *Pierotti* for *Hamley.*

Prince of Wales (later George V). Ca. 1902. Wax-head portrait doll dressed in a representation of the robes worn by the Prince at the coronation of his father, *King Edward VII,* probably made by *Pierotti* for *Hamley.*

Princess. 1914. Bisque doll representing the character of this name in the *Little Nemo* comic series drawn by Winsor McCay. This doll was imported and distributed by *Strobel & Wilken.* It wore a sleeveless, low-necked floor-length dress. Part of the skirt had large polka dots and a girdle had ends hanging in front. A small high crown ornamented the head of the doll. The two sizes were priced 25¢ to $1.00.

Princess. 1925–27. Line of composition dolls made by the *American Unbreakable Doll Corp.* ★

2143. Princess Doll mark used by the American Unbreakable Doll Corp.

Princess. 1927. Dressed felt doll advertised by *Borgfeldt.*

Princess. 1927–28. Name of a dressed doll with composition head, arms and legs, mohair wig, sleeping eyes, open mouth, teeth, tongue, cloth body and a mama voice, handled by *Charles William.* Ht. 19 in. (48 cm.); priced $1.85.

Princess Astrid Doll. 1927. A portrait doll of Princess Astrid when she married Prince Leopold. This inspired other French portrait dolls of famous people especially those in Parisian Society.

Princess Charming. After 1910. Name of a bisque head doll produced by *Kohnstam.* Reportedly the head was made by *Heubach* of Köppelsdorf in mold #320 and had a wig, flirting eyes and pierced nostrils.

Princess Doll. 1905–25 and later. Name used by *Strawbridge & Clothier.* ★

2144. Princess Doll mark used by Strawbridge and Clothier.

Princess Dolls. 1922. Name of a doll with a bisque head made by *Armand Marseille* and a fully jointed composition body made in Waltershausen, Thür. This dressed doll had sleeping eyes. Except for the smallest size it had teeth and the two larger sizes had hair eyelashes. It was distributed by *Montgomery Ward.* Nine hts. 12 to 19¾ in. (30.5 to 50 cm.); price 89¢ to $7.98.

Princess Dolls. Before 1926–30. Cloth doll made by *Dean* with a variety of faces. It wore a velveteen outfit that came in various colors and was trimmed with "white bear plush." This doll, distributed by *Gamage,* closely resembled some of the *Chad Valley* dolls.

1926: Came in eight sizes.

1928: Came in six hts. 12, 15, 18, 21, 24, and 27 in. (30.5, 38, 45.5, 53.5, 61, and 68.5 cm.).

Princess Elizabeth Doll. 1927–28. This doll was designed to resemble the baby Princess Elizabeth, born in 1926, daughter of the Duke and Duchess of York. The Princess grew up to become Queen Elizabeth II. The doll had rosy cheeks and a smiling face. Her head was covered with Titian-red curls; her frock was of white organdy with a green band at the hem decorated with clusters of flowers cut from pieces of different colored cloth. Tiny green shoes and a coat of jade-green matched her smart little hat.

Queen Mary attended a ball named in honor of her little granddaughter and she carried this doll to the ball. Other guests also brought large dolls specially made to resemble living children—preferably their own. During the ball there was a grand pageant of dolls. After this ball many copies of the Princess Elizabeth doll were made. At New Year's 1928 there were many doll balls given in England. *Harrods* specialized in dolls for these events. The dolls were made by artists. One of the chief designers was the brother of a world-famous sculptor. The dancers at the various balls either carried dolls or dressed to look like dolls. They brought their dressmakers to Harrods in order to copy the dresses on the dolls as precisely as possible.

Princess Elizabeth Doll. 1929–30. Manufactured by *Chad Valley.* According to GAMES AND TOYS, May, 1930, in 1929 Chad Valley had approached the Duke and Duchess of York for permission to make a cloth Princess Elizabeth portrait doll, "But was told that the idea was distasteful to their Royal Highnesses. Other dolls of foreign manufacture bearing the name of our Princess were marketed. Their Royal Highnesses were therefore again approached, and not only graciously withdrew their objection to the earlier proposal of the Chad Valley Co., Ltd., but instructed the Company to design a special Princess Elizabeth model, which they finally approved for sale, an example of which has been made for the Princess Elizabeth herself.

"It is . . . dressed in organdie and silk with white kid shoes and necklace, and it reproduces as nearly as possible the inimitable charm of England's most popular Princess. The doll itself is supplied in three colours of dresses, pink, blue and yellow, the last-named being the Duchess's favourite colour and the one selected for the Princess Elizabeth herself. It is interesting to record that it was the ex-

2145A. Portrait doll of Princess Elizabeth of England, born 1926. The bisque head doll was created during 1929 and has a toddler type composition body. It has a wig, sleeping blue glass eyes, and an open smiling mouth with teeth. Clothes contemporary with the doll. Mark indicates the head was made by the Burggrub Porcelain Factory and is size 5. H. 19 in. (48 cm.). *Courtesy of Sotheby Parke Bernet Inc., N.Y.*

2145B. Mark on the bisque heads of Princess Elizabeth dolls made by Schoenau & Hoffmeister.

pressed wish of their Royal Highnesses that the doll should not be made too expensive to be bought by people of average means and therefore, the retail price has been fixed at one guinea. With each doll a frame and beautiful coloured picture showcard is given, and this showcard calls attention to its special character."

This Princess Elizabeth doll was 17 in. high and was a registered design Number 752517. It had a short blond wig, a wide smiling mouth and the eyes look straight ahead.

Princess Elizabeth Doll. 1929–30. A doll with a bisque head on a ball jointed composition toddler type body was made by *Schoenau & Hoffmeister.* Alec Cohn originated the idea of making this smiling portrait doll with curly hair and closed mouth, which was designed by *Caesar Schneider.* Only about 20,000 to 30,000 of these dolls were made before the depression extinguished production. Size number 3½ was 16 in. (40.5 cm.); size 5 was 19 in. (48 cm.) tall. Taller dolls have been reported but it is not certain that the heads were on the original toddler type body which appeared visually to be too short.

Princess Elizabeth. See **Lilibeth.**

Princess Flip. See **Strobel & Wilken.**

Princess of Olie Ke Wob. See **Little Shavers.**

Princess of Wales (later Queen Mary). Ca. 1902. Wax head portrait doll dressed in a representation of the robes worn by her at the coronation of her father-in-law, *King Edward VII,* probably made by Pierotti for Hamley.

Princess Pat. 1926. Name of a *Mama* doll made by *Paramount.* It had sleeping eyes, hair eyelashes, a tongue and teeth, and wore various colored organdy dresses, trimmed with lace or rickrack. The hats and shoes matched the dress. Ht. 30 in. (76 cm.).

Princess Royal. 1906. Trademark registered by *Strawbridge & Clothier* in the U.S. for dolls.

2147. Princess Royal mark used by Strawbridge & Clothier.

2148. Cutout cloth doll representing an Indian girl made by Tambon in 1913. The doll is lithographed in six colors. It has a flat face and cardboard in the soles of its feet. Hair, features, and clothes are all printed on the doll. H. 16½ in. (42 cm.). Once part of the Laura Starr Collection. *Courtesy of the International Doll Library Foundation. Photo by Sotheby Parke Bernet Inc., N.Y.*

Princess Tambon Indian Doll. 1913. Cutout cloth doll or sold as a doll already sewed together, made by the *Tambon Co.* It was lithographed in six colors and came in three styles all wearing Indian costumes. The uncut cloth was 6 by 16 in. (15 by 40.5 cm.). (See Ill. 2148.)

Princess Wee-Wee. 1930. A *Mabel Whitman* creation made by *Regal.* (See Ill. 2149.)

Princeton Knitting Mills. 1925–26. Philadelphia, Pa. Made cloth body dolls.

Princette. 1923. Cloth baby doll made by *Mabel Bland-Hawkes.*

Prinsard, Mme. E. 1919–30 and later. Paris. Repaired and distributed dolls.

1928–30: Advertised composition heads, character heads and real hair wigs.★

H.R.H. The Princess of Wales in wax.

2146. Wax portrait doll of the Princess of Wales, later Queen Mary, wife of George V, was shown in THE LONDON MAGAZINE, 1902, in her robes for the coronation of King Edward VII. According to this magazine, "Mr. Hamley, an expert in doll portraiture, gives us some interesting details of the dolls he has made." The wax parts were possibly made by Pierotti.

2149. Princess Wee-Wee mark for one of the Kiddie Pal line of the Regal Doll Manufacturing Co.

Printemps. 1878 and earlier–1930 and later. Paris. A store that distributed dolls.

1878: Advertised *Poupée Pompadour,* a kid-body lady doll, a *Polichinelle,* and a rubber doll.

1879: Published a catalog in German advertising dressed "unbreakable" dolls. These may have been ball-jointed composition body dolls. Four hts. 41, 46, 50, and 58 cm. (16, 18, 19½, and 23 in.); priced 62¢ to $1.18.

1887–1924 and probably longer: Sold *Bébé Jumeau* and *Bébé Printemps.*

1891: Published a Scandinavian catalog for Denmark, Finland, Norway, and Sweden. This catalog listed Clowns, *Cymbaliers, Marottes, Mignonnettes, Polichinelles* with strings as well as bisque head dolls of the usual type. The latter came dressed or in a chemise. Their size-height relationship was as follows:

Size No.	Height cm.	in.
6/0	28	11
5/0	31	12
4/0	34	13½
3/0	36	14
2/0	40	15½
0	44	17½
1	48	19
2	57	22½
3	63	25
4	74	29
5	80	31½
6	90	35½

1896–1901: Advertised *Bébé Culotte, Bébé Parlant, Bébé Teteur,* Marotte, a couple dressed in Breton regional costumes, and dolls with trousseaux. In 1896 there was also *Pioupiou* and in 1901 there were also a Cymbalier and Polichinelle.

1910: Dolls included *Bébé Baptême,* Bébé Culotte, *Bébé Promenette, Bébé Pole Sud, Bébé Réclame, Chaperon Rouge, Kiss-throwing* doll, *Mlle. Chrysanthème, New Born Baby,* Petit Poucet, swaddling clothed dolls, and dolls in military costumes.

1911: Advertised *Bébé Criant* and Mignonnettes.

1916: There were dolls dressed as Red Cross Nurses and as Soldiers.

1918: A workshop for making toys, probably including dolls, was located in this store under the direction of *Guilleré.* Some of the new dolls advertised were *Charmant Bébé, Gentille Poupée, La Petite Americaine,* Japanese dolls, *Yerri & Suzel* and wooden dolls made by *M. Carlègle* and *André Hellé.* (See Ills. 2151 and 2152.)

1924: Advertised *Martine, Nos Fillettes* and dolls dressed in regional costumes of Alsace and Lorraine. (See THE COLLECTOR'S BOOK OF DOLLS' CLOTHES, Ills. 327, 614, and 756.)★

Printemps, Le. See **Primavera.**

Prinzess. 1909. Mark used for dolls by *Kley & Hahn.*

Prinzessin Wunderhold (Princess Wonder Kind). 1912. Name of a doll with a bisque head, ball jointed composition body produced by *Arthur Schoenau.*

Priscilla. 1908. Name of a dressed flat faced cloth doll offered as a premium by MODERN PRISCILLA. This doll resembled the *Babyland Rag* dolls.

Priscilla. 1919–20. Composition-head doll modeled from a real child, made by *Jessie M. Raleigh* and distributed by *Butler Bros.* It had a center-part wig, composition forearms, a cloth body, and wore Quaker style clothes with a white cap. Ht. 14 in. (35.5 cm.).

Priscilla. 1919–30 and later. Cutout cloth doll made by *Saalfield.* The dimensions were 18 × 35 in. (45.5 × 89 cm.).

Priscilla. 1924. Miniature wax or plaster art doll created by *Mr. J. S. Sant* and representing the Spirit of Dance.

Priscilla. 1929. A cloth doll made by the *American Toy & Novelty Corp.* It had a flat face, round eyes looking to the side, a mouth larger vertically than horizontally, long legs, a dress and hairbow; priced $1.00.

Prison at La Santé. See **Santé.**

Pritzel, Lotte. Before World War I–1920s. Munich, Bavaria. She originated a techique in wax modeling which gave emotional expression to her art dolls. Her dolls were made on wire frames usually dressed in silk trimmed with lace and filmy material. They were first sold at war benefits and later became some of the "Kulture-Dolls" that portrayed postwar unrest. During the 1920s Lotte Pritzel made her dolls in *Else Hecht's* workshop. Esther Singleton in her book DOLLS reported that a couple dancing the Tango was among Lotte Pritzel's most famous dolls. Singleton described some of the dolls in pseudo 1700s costumes: "How smart with glimmering brocade embroidery and glass beads. White wadding is used by hairdressers for wigs. Little arms, hands and feet

BÉBÉ tête incassable, articulé, chemise fine.

Hautrs	0m,36	0m,42	0m,51
Prix . .	3.75	4.75	5.90

BÉBÉ Plage, laine et soie, tête biscuit, articulé.

Hautrs	0m,33	0m,36	0m,42
Prix . .	4.90	5.90	6.75

BÉBÉ articulé, tête biscuit, habillage soie, costumes variés.

0m,30	0m.33	0m,36	0m,42	0m,47
2.90	3.90	5.50	6.50	8.50

BÉBÉ marin, habillage riche, tête biscuit, articulé.

Hautrs	0m,36	0m,42	0m,47
Prix . .	4.75	5.50	6.50

BÉBÉ parlant, articulé, tête biscuit, yeux mobiles, chemise soie,

hautr 0m,45 . . **5.90**

COUPLE MARIÉS BRETONS, habillage laine et soie, tête biscuit.

Hauteur 0m,30.

Prix **3.90**

BÉBÉ marchant, parlant et saluant, tête biscuit, yeux mobiles, chemise soie.

Hautrs	0m,46	0m,59	0m.70
Prix . .	10.50	15.50	21. »

BÉBÉ TÉTEUR, habillage soie, tête biscuit, articulé.

Hauteur 0m,32.

Prix **4.75**

MAROTTE A MUSIQUE, habillage soie, costumes variés. 2.75, 3.50, 3.90

Sans musique.
Prix . . **1.45 et 1.75**

POLICHINELLE habillage soie.

Prix :
1.25, 2.25 et
2.75

FILEUSE articulée, tête biscuit, avec rouet.

Hauteur 0m,22.

Prix **3.50**

LIT en vannerie fine, garni de dentelles, avec bébé dormeur articulé, hauteur 0m,29 . . **10.50**

CLOWN CYMBALIER, habillage soie, tête biscuit.

Prix :
2.25 et 3.90

TROUSSEAU avec bébé articulé et ses toilettes.

Prix . **4.50, 5.50, 6.90** et **9.50**

BERCELONNETTE en vannerie fine, avec mignonnette yeux mobiles, hauteur 0m,28 . . . . . **4.90**

BOULE ROULANTE habillage soie.

Prix **3.90**

CHEVAL SAUTEUR en peau, avec cavalier, habillage riche **6.90**

CLOWN mouvementé sur âne, pièce mécanique.

Prix **3.90**

VOITURETTE mécanique, avec lapins peau naturelle **6.50**

TOILETTE DE POUPÉE en panier vannerie fine.

Prix **3.50**

CANON en bronze ciselé, attelé de 2 chevaux peau, longueur totale 0m,42 . . . . **5.90**

PISTON TREMBLEUR en cuivre poli.

3 notes.	2 45	4 notes.	2.90	5 notes.	3.50	6 notes.	4.50

CLAIRON SCOLAIRE en cuivre, avec cordelière **4.90**

SABRE DE CAVALERIE avec ceinturon.

Prix **3.90**

2150. Printemps catalog pages in 1900/01. Left to right, top to bottom: Composition head bébé in chemise; bisque head bébé dressed for the beach; bisque head bébé dressed in silk; bisque head bébé with sleeping eyes, wearing a chemise; bisque head Bride and Groom dressed in Breton costumes; talking and walking bisque head doll with sleeping eyes, dressed in a chemise; bisque head nursing doll; Bébé Teteur dressed in silk; Marotte with music; Polichinelle; bisque head spinner with spinning wheel; baby in bed; bisque head clown Cymbalier; doll and its trousseau; small sleeping-eyed doll in a cradle. Divide the cm. by 2.55 to convert to in. and divide the francs by 5 to convert to dollars. *Coleman Collection.*

Jouets Etrennes
LUNDI 2 DÉCEMBRE et jours suivants

Les Poupées du Printemps

17560. Bébé, tête porcelaine, yeux dormeurs, perruque cheveux, costume zéphir ciel ou rose, se déshabillant.

Hauteurs :

0m,26	0m,28	0m,31
4.50	6.75	8.50
0m,34	0m,38	0m,42
11.50	14.90	19.25

17561. Bébé entièrement articulé, yeux dormeurs, perruque cheveux, costume mousseline blanche, garni ruban soie. Hrs :

0m,28	0m,33	0m,36
14.95	18.50	21.50
0m,41	0m,42	0m,46
26.50	31.50	37.25

17557. Joli Bébé Marcheur, envoyant des baisers, entièrement articulé, tête porcelaine, yeux dormeurs à ciis, perruque cheveux, costume soie nattier ou rose. Haut. 0m,70. **80 fr.**

17558. Bébé entièrement articulé, tête porcelaine, yeux dormeurs à cils, perruque cheveux, costume merveilleux orné broderie, ciel ou rose, se déshabillant. Hauteurs :

0m,28	0m,34	0m,36
22 fr.	24.75	28.90
0m,40	0m,42	0m,46
33.75	38.50	44.50

17559. Bébé entièrement articulé, tête incassable et lavable, perruque cheveux, habillage crépon soie orné de rubans. Hrs :

0m,33	0m,36	0m,40
18.50	21.50	24.75
0m,42	0m,46	0m,50
30.75	36.90	44.75

17562. "La Petite Américaine". **Poupée** entièrement articulée, yeux dormeurs, perruque fine, joli costume satin. Hauteur 0m,41. **25.90**

17563. Bébé Marcheur articulé, tête porcelaine, yeux dormeurs à cils, envoyant un baiser, costume crépon fantaisie. Hauteur 0m,49. **36.50**

17564. Charmant Bébé nouveau-né, assis, tête caractère, yeux mobiles à cils, cheveux naturels, chemise ornée dentelle. Hauteurs :

0m,20	0m,25	0m,31	0m,37	0m,42	0m,48
8.25	11.25	14.75	22.50	28 fr.	37 fr.

Le même, debout, entièrement articulé :

0m,33	0m,38	0m,45	0m,52	0m,60	0m,69
22 fr.	29 fr.	37 fr.	46 fr.	58 fr.	69 fr.

17565. Bébé Marcheur articulé, tête porcelaine, yeux dormeurs, envoyant un baiser, costume lingerie orné rubans. Hauteur 0m,55. . . **55** fr.

17566. Bébé Marcheur, fillette ou garçonnet, tête porcelaine, yeux dormeurs à cils, perruque fine, costume marin. Hauteurs.

0m,36	0m,41
Prix . . . 15.75	23.95

Pendant le mois de Décembre, les Jouets sont en vente au Rez-de-Chaussée des Nouveaux Magasins.

1 Pr. Pa.

2151. Dressed dolls except Charmant Bébé offered by Printemps in their 1918 catalog. Six of the dolls have bisque heads. One of the heads is "washable" composition. The other three heads, on La Petite Americaine (The Little American), Charmant Bébé and No. 17561, all have sleeping eyes but the material of the head is not given; No. 17560 and 17558 have removable clothes; No. 17557, 17563 and 17565 are kiss-throwing dolls; Charmant Bébé, a newborn character baby, comes with bent legs or straight legs. Divide the cm. by 2.55 to convert to in. and divide the francs by 5 to convert to dollars. *Courtesy of Margaret Whitton.*

Bébés nus et habillés — Malles de Poupées

17567. Bébé entièrement articulé, tête incassable et lavable, perruque cheveux.

0m,48	0m,52	0m,54	0m,60
19 fr.	21.50	25.50	28.50

17568. Bébé entièrement articulé, tête incassable et lavable, cheveux naturels. Hr 0m,48.

15.75

17569. Poupées Alsacienne ou Infirmière, habillage soigné, tête porcelaine. Hauteurs :

0m,21	0m,25	0m,28	0m,30	0m,32	0m,35
1.95	2.45	2.95	4.25	6.25	7.50

17570. Bébé marcheur, envoyant un baiser, tête porcelaine, yeux dormeurs, perruque cheveux. Hauteur 0m,55 :

33 fr.

17571. Bébé entièrement articulé, tête incassable et lavable, perruque cheveux.

0m,29	0m,31	0m,34	0m,36
6.25	7.50	8.75	9.50
0m,39	0m,43	0m,45	
10.75	13.75	15.50	

17572. Soldats alliés articulés, tête incassable, habillage soigné. Haut. 0m,40. **6.50**

17573. Gentille poupée articulée, habillage zéphir, tête porcelaine, yeux fixes. Hauteurs....

	0m,21	0m,22 ½
Prix........	2.25	3.25

17574. Bébé " Printemps ", articulé, tête porcelaine, yeux dormeurs à cils, cheveux naturels. Hauteurs :

0m,25	0m,28	0m,32
13.75	15.50	16.90
0m,35	0m,40	0m,44
19.90	24.50	28.50
0m,47	0m,53	0m,57
32.50	39 fr.	49 fr.
0m,60	0m,63	
59 fr.	75 fr.	

17574 bis. Bébé jumeau. Hauteurs :

0m,36	0m,41	0m,44
27.50	31 fr.	37.50
0m,49	0m,53	0m,57
44 fr.	54 fr.	63 fr.
0m,62	0m,67	0m,73
76 fr.	93 fr.	108 fr.
0m,79	0m,84	
125 fr.	158 fr.	

17575. Bébé articulé, tête incassable et lavable, perruque cheveux, habillage tablier ou couche-culotte. Hauteurs.....

	0m,33	0m,43
Prix........	10.25	16.25

17576. Bébé entièrement articulé, tête porcelaine, yeux dormeurs, perruque cheveux. Hauteur 0m,45. **14.50**

17577. Trousseau de poupée très complet, bébé articulé, en boite carton. Prix.. 9.50, 7.75, 6.25 et 4.25
17577 bis. Trousseau complet, avec poupée. 15.50, 10.25, 8.90, 6.90

17578. Bracelet-montre pour poupée. 1.95, 1.45 et 0.95

17579. Malle de poupée, fermant à clef, avec très jolie poupée et trousseau complet.
1re série. 21 fr., 15.50, 11.90, 9.90, 8.50
17579 bis. 2e Série. 31 fr., 26 fr., 20 fr., 15 fr., 11.50

NOUVEAUTÉS DE PARIS

17580. Parure de poupée, garnie bijouterie, éventail et accessoires. 7.90, 5.75, 3.90
17580 bis. Garniture de toilette pour poupée, nombreux accessoires. 9.50, 6.50 et 4.50

Costumes de Poupées

33943.
Marinière anglaise, en tissu damier noir et blanc, parure bleu ciel, pour poupée jumeau.

Numéros.	5-6	7-8	9-10	11-12
Prix..	6 fr.	6.75	7.75	8.75
Le béret.	1.75	2.10	2.40	2.65

33944. Pour poupées garçons, avec culotte. Mêmes prix.

Parure lingerie, 3 pièces, pour poupée jumeau.

Numéros.	5-6	7-8	9-10	11-12
Prix...	3.50	4.25	5 fr.	6 fr.

33946.
Pour bébé **caractérisé. Costume** tricot laine : culotte, chandail et béret, en vert, rouge, n attier.

Numéros.	4	6	8
Prix......	7.50	9 fr.	10.50
Numéros.	10	11	12
Prix......	12.50	14.50	18 fr.

33945. Pyjama en tissu blanc, rayures roses ou bleues, pour poupée jumeau.

Numéros.	5-6	7-8	9-10	11-12
Prix..	5.50	6.25	7 fr.	8 fr.

33941. Costume garçon, ottoman marine, parure bleu ciel, pour poupée jumeau.

Numéros.	5-6	7-8	9-10	11-12
Prix...	6.90	7.90	8.90	9.90
Le béret.	1.95	2.25	2.50	2.75

33942. Pour poupées filles, avec jupe plissée. Mêmes prix.

Bas et Chaussettes, blancs ou jaunes, pour poupées jumeau.

Numéros.	5-6	7-8	9-10	11-12
La paire..	0.50	0.65	0.80	1 fr.

Souliers blancs ou jaunes.

Numéros.	5-6	7-8	9-10	11-12
La paire..	0.75	1 fr.	1.25	1.50

Bottes.

	1.25	1.55	1.85	2.15

33941.

Pendant le mois de Décembre, les jouets sont en vente au Rez-de-Chaussée des Nouveaux Magasins.

2152. Printemps 1918 catalog page of bébés, undressed and dressed, as well as trunks with dolls. Among the dolls are Bébé Jumeau, Bébé Printemps and two other bisque head dolls in chemise. Three bisque head dolls are dressed; one wears an Alsatian costume, one is dressed as a Red Cross nurse, and one is "Gentille Poupée" (Pretty Doll). Five dolls have composition heads; three of these are in chemises, one wears an apron. There is a group of dolls dressed in the uniforms of the Allied soldiers. There are also dolls with trousseaux, a doll's wristwatch, clothes for dolls, and a set of doll's toilet articles. *Courtesy of Margaret Whitton.*

exhibit Lotte Pritzel's individual taste. There is a strong and original art. When you hold a doll by Lotte Pritzel in your hands, you can make it do anything you please."

1923: THE BROOKLYN EAGLE described these dolls: "The Pritzel dolls, extraordinarily graceful fantasies, in colored wax and dressed in the most exquisite laces and silks are exotic, often erotic, expressions of a spirit most prevalent in present day Germany. Lottie *[sic]* Pritzel's models were *Lilith, Faustine, Messalina* and *Madame de Pompadour.* The spirit of all of the famous courtesans is here, but attenuated and criticized."

The INTERNATIONAL STUDIO reported: "Her delightful little creations, trimmed with silk, lace and all sorts of materials. . . . uniting the unpretentiousness of a toy with the charm of an exquisite work of art."

1925: One of the art dolls was named *Simonetta,* another one was Helena. There were also a man with a crown, three ballet dancers dressed in gauze and some religious figures.

Prize Baby. 1913–30 and possibly later. Name used by *Borgfeldt* for various dolls that they produced. An all-bisque Prize Baby, mold # 208, had sleeping eyes, a wig with a side part, joints at the shoulders and hips, molded and painted footwear. A round blue sticker with white letters read, "PRIZE//BABY//REG. U.S. PAT.//OFF.//MADE IN GERMANY." Incised on the back or stamped were the words, "Made in Germany." Size number 5 was 7 in. (18 cm.); size number 7 was 8 in. (20.5 cm.). A 4 in. (10 cm.) all-bisque Prize Baby had stationary glass eyes and a closed mouth. A pair of all-bisque Prize Baby dolls had wigs, glass eyes and wore original crocheted outfits. Their heads were marked "208//0 ½" and the blue paper sticker on their chests read, "PRIZE BABY//REG. U.S.A. MADE IN GERMANY." Ht. 4½ in. (11.5 cm.).

Another all-bisque, Borgfeldt, Prize Baby appeared to have been produced in the late 1920s. These dolls had molded and painted hair, sleeping blue glass eyes, closed mouth, flange-type neck joint, shoulder joints and diagonal hip joints. The molded and painted footwear consisted of white socks and pink or blue single strap slippers. There was a round paper sticker on the chest reading "Mildred © Germany." Incised on the back of the dolls was "Copr. by//Mildred//The Prize Baby// Germany//880-17." The 880 was the mold # and the 17 was the height in centimeters (6¾ in.). A slightly smaller example had the same mark except 15 instead of 17 for a 6 in. doll.

1914: *Marshall Field* advertised a Prize Baby with a composition character head, painted hair, composition hands and a bent limb cloth body. This doll was dressed in rompers or a long baby dress and came in four hts. from 13 in. (33 cm.) up. It is NOT certain that this was the Borgfeldt Prize Baby.

1924: Name given to a *Mama* doll created by *Georgene Averill* for Borgfeldt. This doll with a composition head and hands was manufactured by *K & K.* It had a wig, a cloth body and wore a dress, baby sacque, bonnet, stockings and bootees.★

2153A. Doll named "Chichette" made by Lotte Pritzel as shown in DAS PUPPENBUCH, 1921.

"THE VIENNESE"
A Modern Doll Modeled in Wax by
Lotte B. Pritzel

2153B. Wax art doll made by Lotte Pritzel shown in the INTERNATIONAL STUDIO, April 1923.

2154. Mark on a paper label for a doll named Prize Baby.

Prize Baby. 1914. Character doll made in Germany had bobbed hair that fell in straight lines on the forehead, ears and neck of the doll. The hands were well modeled but the feet lacked details. There was a pacifier which was held in the mouth.

Production of Dolls. The following figures provide some idea of the immense number of dolls produced each year even allowing for some advertising exaggeration.

1843 and 1844: 4,000 china heads made by *Royal Copenhagen*.

1845: 2,600 china heads made by Royal Copenhagen.

1849: French workers made over a quarter of a million dollars' worth of dolls.

1850: 2,100 china heads made by Royal Copenhagen.

1868: 1,200 to 1,5000 dolls made by *Huret*.

1873: 1,500,000 peg-wooden dolls just of the 1½ in. (4 cm.) ht. were produced by *Insam & Prinoth*.

1874: 24,000,000 papier-mâché dolls were made in Sonneberg, Thür.

1878: French workers made nearly half a million dollars' worth of dolls.

1879: 10,000 bébés made by *Jumeau*.

1889: 300,000 bébés made by Jumeau.

1900: 4,500,000 bébés and dolls made by the *Société Française de Fabrication de Bébés & Jouets* (S.F.B.J.).
500,000 dolls made by *Furga*.

1902–49: Less than 50,000 *Door of Hope* dolls were made during this entire 48 year period or about 1,000 dolls per year.

1904: THE PRIZE stated, "In London alone there are at least forty manufacturers of such toy dolls giving employment to very many people, and millions of dolls are produced in France, Germany and Switzerland."

1904–06: *Fanny Zakucka-Harflinger* made about 400 wooden dolls a year.

1905: 20,000 *Bleuettes* were produced.

1907: $90,000 worth of cloth and dressed dolls made in Britain.

1909–12: 3,000 dolls a day (nearly a million a year) made by *Horsman*.

1910: Over 5,000,000 *Bébés Jumeau*. Over 1,000,000 composition dolls sent by a Sonneberg factory to America.

1913: 1,000,000 *Billikens*. Over 1,000,000 *Baby Bumps*. Several million *Campbell Kids*. About 50,000 dolls made by *Ernst Reinhardt*.

1916: 600,000 *Pullman Doll Co.*

1917: 300,000 *Wigwam Co.* 624,000 *Pullman Doll Co.* Over 500,000 *Dean*.

Ca. 1918: 1,200 *Flora's Famous Dolls*.

1919: 5,500,000 composition dolls' heads made by *Trion*. 1,000,000 *Dominion Toy Co.*

1920: 2,600,000 *Reisman, Barron Co.* 225,000 miniature dolls sold by *Bland-Hawkes*.

1922: 350,000 *Skeezix* made by *Live Long Toys*. 625,000 *Cupids* made by *Lawton*.

1923: Over 1,500,000 dolls Reisman, Barron Co. 3,000,000 dolls, *E. Goldberger*, including *Mama* dolls. 1,000,000 *Cupid Love* dolls made in Britain. 500,000 *Live Long Toys*. 400,000 *Nelke*.

1924: 4,000,000 dolls S.F.B.J. 12,000,000 dolls in Sonneberg including 1,500,000 jointed dolls. 12,000,000 dolls in Waltershausen of all types.

1925: 50,000 *Baby Bo Kaye* dolls produced by *Borgfeldt*. U.S. produced nearly twice as many dolls as Germany. 20,000,000 dolls added each year in U.S. This was 12 times the human rate.

1926: Over 1,000,000 voices for dolls, *Grubman*.

1927: 625,000 *Our Pet* baby dolls made by *Strauss-Eckhardt Co.*

1928–30: Several hundred thousand *Margies* produced.

1929: 200,000,000 dolls sold in U.S. according to the NEW YORK TIMES. This seems high but it may include some resales and exports; 2,000,000 dolls made by *Regal*.

1930 and later: 200,000 *R.C.A. Radiotrons* dolls were made by *Cameo*.

1952: 6,000,000 dolls sold by *Ideal*.★

Products Corporation of America. 1925–26. New York City. Exclusive agent for *Twinjoy*. Advertised *Mama* dolls and *Twistum Toy*.

Professor, The. See **Gr. (Grosspapa)**.

Progressive Agency of New Jersey. 1922–23. Newark, N.J. Imported dressed and undressed dolls.★

Progressive Mercantile Co. 1920. America. Imported French and English dolls, especially the *Tru-to-Life* cloth dolls made by *Dean*.

Progressive Novelty Co. 1925–30 and later. New York City. Made shoes for dolls.

Progressive Toy Co. 1917–24. New York City. Manufactured dolls which were distributed by *Riemann, Seabrey Co.*

1919: Made 40 style nos. of wood-fibre composition dolls. They had sleeping eyes, came with or without wigs. *Kewpie*-type dolls had eyes looking to the side, wigs with veils, jointed arms, and legs apart.

1920: Advertised *Sweetness,* a wood fibre doll and American bisque-head dolls with sleeping eyes, wigs, and were fully jointed. Their clothes were "Tailor made." Four hts. 14, 16, 20 and 24 in. (35.5, 40.5, 51 and 61 cm.).

1921: 30 style nos. of their bisque-head dolls.

1922: Advertised a mechanical Hula-Hula Dancer.

1923: *Admiration* line included all-composition dolls and dolls with composition heads on cloth bodies. Some of the dolls rolled their eyes.

    Chatterbox called "Mama" 60 times in 15 minutes.★

Promenette. See **Bébé Culotte.**

Pröschold, A. H. 1897–98 and probably later. Gräfenthal, Thür. Porcelain factory made all-bisque and all-china dolls.

Prouza, Wenzel. 1905–30. Satalitz and Klein-Schwadowitz, Bohemia. *Frozen Charlottes* and jointed porcelain dolls were made at his porcelain factories.

1913: Wenzel Prouza was in charge of the Klein-Schwadowitz Porzellanfabrik founded in 1908 and its 60 employees.

1920: Adolf Prouza was the successor at the Klein-Schwadowitz Porzellanfabrik. According to the Ciesliks a bisque head, probably of his, was marked "A.P. //1903//8."

Prudence. 1917–18. Name of a stockinet doll designed by *E. E. Houghton* and made by *Shanklin.* It wore a white dress trimmed with blue ribbon, and a sunbonnet.

$$1899.$$
$$WEP.$$
$$6.$$

2155A. Mark used by Wenzel Prouza on porcelain dolls.

$$A.P$$
$$1903$$
$$8$$

2155B. Mark used by the successor of Wenzel Prouza, Adolf Prouza.

Prudence. 1921. British stockinet doll distributed by *Meakin & Ridgeway* in the U.S. It had blond hair, a cap, and wore its dress above the knees.

Pse. (English Postman). 1903–13. Felt doll made by *Steiff.* It was a short fat doll or a tall thin doll with long feet and wore the uniform of a British Postman. Hts. 35 and 50 cm. (14 and 19½ in.).

1913: *Gamage* sold the larger size for 72¢.

Public Doll & Toy Co. 1929. New York City. Exhibited dolls at the New York Toy Fair.

Puck. 1913–30. Made by *Dean.*

1930: Line of dolls made with a mask face of silkeen plush and down stuffed body in a variety of color shades. The line included *Baby Puck* and Master Puck. They had large ears and a bow under the chin and at the wrists.

Puck. 1916–24. Felt doll made by *Steiff.* 1916: Hts. were 20, 30 and 40 cm. (8, 12, and 15½ in.). 1924: Hts. 20 and 30 cm. (8 and 12 in.).

Puck. 1917. Made for the *East London Toy Factory.*

Pucka Poppets Ltd. 1918. Eastbourne, England. Manufactured and handled dolls.

Pudgie. 1919–21. All-composition *Kewpie*-type doll advertised in a *Tip Top Toy Co.* catalog. The hair was usually painted but sometimes there was real hair in a net. The painted eyes glanced to the side. The boy had jointed arms and the legs were molded together. There were 16 costume variations plus an undressed version. The costumes were made of silk and included headwear. Hts. 8 and 13 in. (20.5 and 33 cm.). A *Baird-North* distributor catalog listed the 8 in. size as priced $1.25 in 1921.

Pudgy Peggy. 1928. Name of a doll made by *Century.* It was dressed like a child and had a hairbow; priced $2.95.

Pudlin, David. 1916–17. Obtained a U.S. patent for dolls' eyes connected with a bar.

Puffy. 1930. Cutout cloth doll advertising the *Quaker Oats Co.* The doll dressed as a soldier was 16 in. (40.5 cm.) high.

Puggy. 1928–30 and later. All-composition doll with molded and painted hair made by the *American Character Doll Co.* in their Petite line. It had a scowling expression and painted eyes, looking to the side. Some of these dolls (probably later ones) had a *Patsy* type neck joint with the socket in the head part. They were also jointed at the shoulders and hips. It was described in advertisements as a "mischievous little rascal," the man of the *Campbell Kids* family. It was dressed in a variety of costumes including a Boy Scout, a newsboy, a baseball player outfit, and so forth. On the back shoulder it was marked "A//PETITE//DOLL." Pat. Schoonmaker reported a round paper tag on one of these dolls reading, "A Petite Doll, Campbell Kid, Permission of Campbell Soup Company. U.S.A." Ht. 12½ in. (31.5 cm.).

Pulliche, Mme. 1922–23. New York City. Dressed dolls as Spanish ladies of the 18th century. The dolls were modeled by *Salemme* and the clothes were based on sketches by

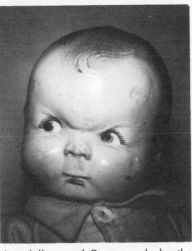

2156A & B. All-composition doll named Puggy made by the American Character Doll Co. It has molded and painted hair and eyes; the eyes look to the side; closed mouth, and a neck joint with the socket in the head. Shoulders and hips are jointed. Original clothes. Mark on body: Ill. 2157. Mark on clothes: Ill. 2158. H. 13 in. (33 cm.) *Courtesy of Dorothy Annunziato.*

A
PETITE
DOLL

PUGGY

A PETITE DOLL

2157–2158. Marks on all-composition Puggy dolls. No. 2157 is on the back of the body and No. 2158 is on the clothes.

George Barbier, used in designing clothes for the play "Don Juan." The silk fabric for the gowns was donated by *Cheney Bros.,* a silk manufacturer, and the six dressed dolls were given to the Metropolitan Museum of Art.

Pullman (Pullmann) Doll Co. 1916–17. Chicago, Ill. Made composition-head dressed dolls with flesh-colored faces and cloth bodies. Arms and legs were riveted onto the bodies.

1916: Claimed the factory had a capacity of several thousand dolls a day.

1917: Advertised new faces, new styles and new dresses.★

Pulvermacher, Albert. 1890–92. Sonneberg, Thür. Made jointed dolls. In 1892, he sold his factory to *Carl Hoffmeister,* later *Schoenau & Hoffmeister.*★

Pulvermacher & Westram, Albin (Alvin). 1895–1925 and later. Sonneberg, Thür. Manufactured dolls.

1910: One of the Sonneberg group of Grand Prize Winners at the Brussels Exposition.★

Punch. See **Polichinelle (Punchinello, Punch or Kasper).**

Punch & Judy. 1901–10 and later. Cutout cloth dolls made by *Art Fabric Mills.* These resembled the traditional puppets in design but were not actually puppets. They were used as premiums by various companies. Later *Elms & Sellon* advertised them. Ht. 27 in. (68.5 cm.)

Punch and Judy. 1915. Cloth dolls made by *Dean.*

Punfield, Frederick William. 1922–30 and later. London. Successor in 1929 was Punfield & Barstow. Sole agent in Britain for *Rheinische Gummi und Celluloid Fabrik Co.;* distributed celluloid dolls to the wholesale trade.

Puppe der Zukunft (Doll of the Future). 1904–09. Trademark used by *Süssenguth.* These dolls were produced by *Guttmann & Schiffnie.* The dolls were light in weight and allegedly unbreakable. (See also **Bébé l'Avenir.**)★

Puppel's Mary. See **Puppet's Mary.**

Puppen. German word for "dolls."

Puppen Reform. 1908–09. Instigated by *Marion Kaulitz,* both Sonneberg and Munich were involved; artists and manufacturers contributed to the movement. For example *Josef Wackerle* designed heads that were found on bodies produced by *Cuno & Otto Dressel.* Marion Kaulitz painted heads and designed clothes. Others also participated in this movement.

Puppenfabrik Georgenthal. See **Schmidt, Franz & Co.**

Puppenfabrik Gothania. 1926–30 and later. Finsterbergen and Waltershausen, Thür. Manufactured dolls.

1926: Registered "Gothania" in Germany as a trademark for dolls.

Puppenfabrik Herzlieb. 1928–30 and later. Sonneberg, Thür. Manufactured dolls; factory was operated by *H. B. Müller.*

Puppenindustrie Gotha. 1924–25. Gotha, Thür. Obtained a German patent (D.R.P.) for dolls' bodies.★

Puppet's (Puppel's) Mary. 1928–29. Trademark registered in France by *Mme. Germaine Douche* for dolls.

Pupsi. 1924–26. Celluloid dolls with molded hair and painted eyes made by *Kohl & Wengenroth.* Came dressed or undressed.

Purger, Johann Baptist. 1851–96. St. Ulrich, Grödner Tal. Son of *Josef Purger,* was a *Verleger* who collected and distributed wooden dolls made as a house industry in the area. He had one of the largest warehouses in St. Ulrich and sent his dolls all over the world.★

Purger, Josef. Early 1800s. St. Ulrich, Grödner Tal. He was the father of Johann Baptist Purger but his successor was Johann Dominik *Moroder,* who in turn was succeeded by Joseph Moroder & Co. Josef Purger was one of the early *Verlegers* who collected and distributed wooden dolls.

Putnam, Grace Storey. 1922–30 and later. California, New York City, and Sag Harbor, Long Island.

TOYS AND NOVELTIES, in January 1928, told how Grace Storey Putnam originated the *Bye-Lo Baby.*

"When Grace Storey Putnam entered Borgfeldt's to introduce a new kind of doll, she hadn't enough spare money to buy a pair of heels for her run-over shoes. Within two or three months after the first Bye-Lo Baby was sold she was on a luxurious liner with her two children starting a long trip to Europe.

"How did this charming lady think of this new doll and how does she now secure the ideas for sculpture work at her lovely Sag Harbor home and studio? . . .

"When her little girl (now also a mother) was three years old, Mrs. Putnam made for her a fine big stuffed doll, with painted face and shaped features. Then as years passed, her friends asked her for more dolls and she began to think hazily of doing something with her talent. This action was hastened by financial needs.

"Her sculptor husband became ill and finally permanently unable to provide for the family. Expenses of the two little children and of her own illnesses had taken their income, so she decided to attend normal school and begin to earn money as an art teacher.

"During the war she taught art in a school in Oakland but was thinking more and more about a doll which she could model and which would captivate the hearts of little girls. During her second year of teaching she made frequent visits to a hospital where she met the mothers who had been brought there to have their babies. . . .

"She saw young women, often dreading the ordeal and then saw them later full of pride in their eyes. Her idea at first had been to model a three months old baby but as she saw the love and joy that these tiny ones brought, she began to think of designing a new born babe. She can't point to any exact minute when she made this decision, but as she walked home from the hospital she would turn the new idea over in her mind.

"At first she feared that people would not want such a doll, but seeing the new born babes bring joy to mothers made her sure that a new born babe doll would bring happiness to little children. The idea grew and finally she began to model such a composite doll at her home. . . .

"But one day the hospital people phoned her to come over and see a three day old baby—so fine and lovable. As soon as she saw it she knew it was IT and rushed home for her clay and materials. The nurses lay the little one on a pillow and for two hours Mrs. Putnam worked feverishly to make permanent the features of the babe. She finished much of the task that day, which was fortunate, for when she returned the next day to complete the final touches, the features had already started to change. . . .

" 'Why didn't you come here first?' said a Borgfeldt man once when she was telling of her hardships in finding a home for Bye-Lo.

"Mrs. Putnam knew nothing of the commercial world but she bravely invaded New York with her wax figure ready to sell Bye-Los to the nation. At first she went to non-doll people and wasted a lot of time—several years in fact—doing the wrong things and seeing the wrong people. For instance at first she thought of making the doll of rubber. Money ran low; courage and hope almost failed. After about four years of struggle she was told to see Geo. Borgfeldt & Co. . . .

" 'Here is a little three day old baby,' said she.

" 'Well,' said one of the Borgfeldt executives, 'that is interesting, because I have a three day old baby at my home.'

"As soon as he saw the model he hurried into the office of another executive and helped fire the whole organization with enthusiasm for the new doll.

"All was not easy sailing even then for men buyers would come in and scorn the new model and say it would never sell. The men salesmen began to doubt—'crusty old bachelors,' as one man called them.

"General ideas are valueless without definite manufacturing and merchandising knowledge, and when Mrs. Putnam found the group of men who had this knowledge she was wise enough to leave these details to them. Perhaps her years of trying alone unsuccessfully gave her this wisdom.

"Her idea and later designing help, plus the Borgfeldt manufacturing and selling departments, made Bye-Lo the great success it is. . . .

"The rest of the story is known—how the first finished dolls were displayed—how some buyers approved and how some disapproved—how the flame of approval spread till all available Bye-Los were sold way before that Christmas of 1924.

"Success came so soon and so generously that Mrs. Putnam could scarcely realize it. After having had nothing but debts, she had more money than she could remember how to use; after training herself to sacrifice pleasure because of poverty she had to train herself to get pleasure from money. . . .

"Mrs. Putnam now spends much of her time at her beautiful home and studio on Long Island where she engages in sculpture. She is in constant need of ideas but finds them coming to her at odd times, more than when she sits down to a definite task. In order to have these ideas ready when needed—but let her tell us:

" 'Most of my inspirations come while I am out in the country away from commercial life and man made noise!

" 'While outdoors—walking, tending the flowers—or while doing little things around the house, ideas come to me.'

" 'These ideas I write in a little note book which is always with me. These are then transferred to a regular file in a steel cabinet. One file is for ideas on color, one for ideas on design, etc., etc.' "

Mr. *Joseph Kallus* was also designing dolls for *Borgfeldt* at this same time, namely *Baby Bo Kaye,* and he knew Mrs. Putnam well. According to Mr. Kallus the three day old baby that was the inspiration for the Bye-Lo Baby was actually a little baby who had died. The statement in the above account that the baby changed its appearance between the third and fourth day seems to lend some credence to this possibility.

1928: Designed *Fly-Lo,* "The Little Aero Baby."

1930–31: Designed *Babykins.*★

Putz. 1926. Name of a celluloid doll jointed at the shoulder, made by *Rheinische Gummi und Celluloid Fabrik,* mold # 12.

Pygmalion. 1900–07 and probably other years. Paris. A store that sold dolls.

1900–01: Advertised *Bébé Pygmalion*, *Bébé Tout Bois*, *Joli Bébé*, *Cymbalier*, *Marotte*, dolls' clothes and accessories.

1907: Advertised *Bébé Réclame*.

Q

Q. B. Toy & Novelty (Toy Manufacturing) Co. 1915 and probably before. New York City. In 1915 the company was taken over by the National Toy Manufacturing Co. The agents were *Baker & Bennett* and *Strobel & Wilken*.

Q. B. Toy & Novelty made Q. B. Bild-Me-Up Family of painted wooden dolls with interchangeable parts. The dolls included a clown, lady with parasol, maid, man with cane, nurse, policeman and two other females; priced 50¢ to $2.00.

Quaddy Playthings Manufacturing Co. 1916–17. New York City and Kansas City, Mo. This New York company bought a doll factory in Kansas City and moved their entire factory including some 20 complicated machines, half a dozen skilled artists and a score or more other employees.

They made composition dolls as well as figures based on the Thornton W. Burgess animal characters which had composition heads and cloth bodies.

1917: Made *Billy Boy*.

Quaglimo, Massimo. 1920s. Italy. Born 1899, he was an artist who designed dolls and/or ceramics for *Lenci*.

Quaker Crackels Dolls. 1930. Cutout cloth advertising doll for *Quaker Oats Co.* The doll was dressed as a Quaker boy.

Quaker Doll Co. 1915–30 and later. Philadelphia, Pa. Importer and wholesale distributor. Specialized in supplies for doll hospitals.

Ca. 1930: Advertised the following dolls: *Babie Bouquet (Baby Bo Kaye)*, *Baby Gloria*, *Babykins*, *Bonnie Babe*, *Bonser* dolls, *Borgfeldt* dolls, *Bubbles*, *Bye-Lo Baby*, *Daisy*, *Effanbee* dolls, *Flossie Flirt*, *Fly-Lo*, *Gladdie*, *Ginger*, *Horsman* dolls, *Ideal* dolls, *K & K* dolls, *Kestner* dolls, *Lovums*, *Mama* dolls, *Armand Marseille* dolls, *Orsini* dolls, *Patsy*, *Patsy Ann*, *Patsykins*, *Rock-a-Bye Baby*, *Smiles*, *Suck-a-Thumb*, *Tickle Toes* and *Tiny Tots*.★

Quaker Dolls. 1930. Designed by *Julius Mangiapani* and made by the *Penn Stuffed Toy Co.*; popular priced dolls. (See also **Religious Costumes.**)

Quaker Oats Co. 1930. Produced cutout cloth advertising dolls including *Puffy* and *Quaker Crackels Dolls*.

Qualitoy Co. 1919–20. Newark, N.J. Made dolls with composition heads, arms and legs on cloth bodies. They had either painted or sleeping eyes, and came with molded hair or wigs.

1920: 75 style nos. Hts. 11 to 22 in. (28 to 56 cm.).★

Quality Bilt. 1918–19. Name of composition dolls produced by *Century*. These dolls had a patent spring that controlled the eye movement and they wore long or short dresses. Hts. 10 to 24 in. (25.5 to 61 cm.).★

Queen Alexandra. 1902–30 and later. Portrait wax dolls made by the *Pierotti* family, distributed by *Hamley*. These dolls had the hair set into the wax and some if not all were dressed in a representation of the Queen's coronation robes. Ht. 26 in. (66 cm.) and possibly other sizes.

Queen City Novelty Co. 1920. Buffalo, N.Y. Manufactured silk sweater sets and other silk knit garments for dolls. There were three styles made to fit dolls 20, 22, and 24 in. (51, 56, and 61 cm.) tall.

Queen Elisabeth of Roumania (Carmen Sylva). Before 1874–1902 and probably later. Collected dolls. Her interest in dolls began when her mother, the Princess of Wied, asked for a few dolls dressed in Roumanian regional costume to be exhibited for a Charity Fair. Dolls representing famous people in history and dolls dressed in regional and/or occupational costumes were given to Queen Elisabeth especially by European royalty. There were wedding groups and a fancy dress ball group costumed by the leading dressmakers in Bucharest.

1899–1901: The collection totaled 1,300 dolls and toured Europe and America to raise money for charities. Most of the dolls' heads were porcelain or wax.

Queen Louise. 1910 and probably other years. The most frequently found Queen Louise is size number 7, ht. 23 in. (58.5 cm.) and the sizes go up to at least number 13.★

2159. Incised mark on bisque head Queen Louise dolls.

Queen of Beauty. 1927–28. Name of a dressed *Mama* doll with composition head and limbs, mohair wig, sleeping eyes, hair eyelashes, open mouth, teeth and tongue, distributed by *Charles William*. Ht. 26 in. (66 cm.); priced $5.48.

Queen of May. 1914. Name of a bisque-head dressed doll advertised by *Marshall Field*; had glass eyes and wore a broad brimmed hat. Ht. 11 in. (28 cm.); priced $4.00 doz. wholesale.

Queen Quality. 1910–12. Trademark registered in Germany by *Adolf Wislizenus*.

1912: A life size bent limb baby doll had a wig, sleeping eyes, and hair eyelashes.★

Queen Victoria's Dolls. Her collection has been written about by Frances Lowe and others. In 1901 Mary Lowe Dickinson wrote, "She had playthings . . . and among them was a long board with places into which the feet of her dolls fitted. As she had one hundred thirty-two dolls, you can imagine what delightful court receptions and other scenes she could arrange. Some of the dolls she dressed like Kings and Queens and other famous people whom she met." Queen Victoria's dolls are currently in the London Museum. (Also see THE COLLECTOR'S BOOK OF DOLLS' CLOTHES, Chapter 4.)

Queue San Baby. 1915–22. Most of these all-bisque dolls were jointed at the shoulders only but a few were jointed at the shoulders and hips. The molded headwear varied in shape and color. Most of these dolls had pointed Oriental style slippers but molded black Mary Jane style slippers have also been reported. These dolls produced by *Morimura Bros.* were later copied by *Gebrüder Heubach* and given the name *Chin Chin Baby*. Queue San Baby hts. 3½, 4½, 5, and 6 in. (9, 11.5, 12.5 and 15 cm.).★

Quim (Quinn). 1927–30. Paris. Made dolls.

Quint, A. 1907–08. Vienna. Listed in a directory under Dolls and Dolls' Heads.

R

R. A. C. Mascot. See **Road Scout Mascots.**

R. B. & L. Manufacturing Co. See **Roth, Joseph, Manufacturing Co.**

R. C. A. Radiotrons. 1930 and later. Segmented wooden doll designed by *Joseph Kallus* and made by *Cameo*. Its molded boots and high hat simulated a radio tube. It was marked "R. C. A. Radiotrons" on its hat and on a band across its chest. The black version represented the radio team of Amos & Andy. About 200,000 of these dolls were produced according to Mr. Kallus.

R. F. Novelty Co. 1919–20. St. Louis, Mo. Made the *Happy Doll Family* consisting of seven small dolls representing Father, Mother, Little Sister, Little Brother, Baby Love, French Maid and black Mammy. These dolls mounted on white cardboard cost $3.75 for the entire family.★

R. R. Initials found on bisque heads.

Raabe, Mme. 1920. Prague, Czechoslovakia. President of the *Klub der Kunstler* (Artists' Women's Club) in Prague, she acted as selling agent for the German artists in Bohemia. *Stewart Culin* bought several dolls from her.

Rabaut, Louis A. 1898–1901 and probably other years. Detroit, Mich. Wholesale distributor of dolls.

Rabery & Delphieu. 1856–1930 and later. Paris. In 1899 they became part of the *Société Française de Fabrication de Bébés & Jouets* (S.F.B.J.). Their bébés were sometimes

2160. Bisque head with a blond wig, stationary blue glass eyes, pierced ears, closed mouth, dimples, and a fully jointed composition body. Mark: "R 8 R" incised and "IXI" in red ink. H. 18½ in. (47 cm.). *Courtesy of the Margaret Woodbury Strong Museum. Photo by Harry Bickelhaupt.*

2161. Bisque-head doll with blond wig, glass eyes, closed mouth, and a fully jointed composition body. Original chemise and hair ribbon. Mark: R R. *Courtesy of the late Magda Byfield.*

2162. Incised R R mark on bisque-head dolls.

pressed and sometimes poured (See *Pressed versus Poured*). They carried size numbers 6/0 to 4 and probably beyond. Size number 6/0 was 28 cm. (11 in.) and size number 4 was 71 cm. (28 in.). Size 2, ht. 61 cm. (24 in.), has been seen most frequently. Shoes stamped "Rabery" have been found.

During the 1880s they purchased bisque heads for dolls and bébés as well as bisque arms from *François Gaultier*.

The Rabery & Delphieu *Chambre Syndicale* mark has been found.★

Rachel. 1923–28. Name of a black oilcloth doll made by *Live Long Toys*. The printed clothes included a circular striped skirt, an apron and cap.★

Rachel. 1929. All-bisque doll with molded and painted clothes representing the cartoon character of this name drawn by Frank King in his cartoon series "Gasoline Alley." It was jointed at the neck and distributed wholesale by *Marshall Field* and *B. Shackman*. Ht. 3½ in. (9 cm.); priced 25¢ retail, $1.80 doz. wholesale. (See Ill. 1350 in the first COLLECTOR'S ENCYCLOPEDIA OF DOLLS.)

Rachtigall, Christoph. 1925–27. Nürnberg, Bavaria. Obtained a German patent (D.R.P.) for cloth or felt dolls.

Racone Manufacturing Co. 1925. New York City. Made a device that enabled dolls to clap their hands.

Radadou. World War I period. Name of a mascot worsted doll representing a *Swaddling-clothed Baby*. This doll was shown on a postcard with *Nénette and Rintintin*.

Radiana. 1927. Paris. Made dolls including decorative dolls for autos.

Radiguet & Cordonnier. 1880 and later. Paris. Registered "R & C" as a trademark in France. Georges Cordonnier obtained two French patents for a shoulder-head doll with a swivel neck and a wood, composition, or kid body. The latter usually had bisque lower arms and legs. The patents appeared to have pertained to the stands for this doll which were metal posts that went up through the holes in the soles of the doll's feet. These posts were attached to a round wooden base.

One of these Poupée Statuettes (doll statues) had the following label on its round wooden base. "Poupée Statuette//Systeme//Breveté S.G.D.G.//Marque Déposée R & C // Buste Déposé//No. 1207// Nouveau Système//de Tied [?] Bté S.G.D.G." Some of the characteristics of these statue dolls were molded bosoms, left arm bent at the elbow and the two first fingers of the right hand extended almost like a benediction sign. See Ill. 907 in the first COLLECTOR'S ENCYCLOPEDIA OF DOLLS. The doll in this illustration had a marked *Jumeau* body. Georges Cordonnier probably had a business connection with Jumeau who had been involved in the production of these dolls. The widow Radiguet appears to have been a distributor. Bisque shoulder heads have been found marked "Déposé R. C." (See Ill. 1617 in the first COLLECTOR'S ENCYCLOPEDIA OF DOLLS.) All of the Radiguet & Cordonnier dolls found so far have been 17 in. (43 cm.) tall.

The trademark and patent information was researched by Barbara Spadaccini.

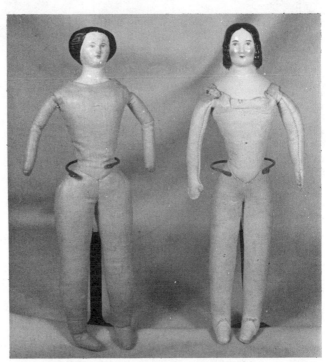

2163A. Similarly constructed dolls' bodies. The one on the left is made of pink cloth and the one on the right is made of pink kid. This suggests that these bodies could have been made by Rabery & Delphieu because in 1856 Delphieu obtained a patent to make dolls' bodies of pink cloth instead of pink kid. The head of the cloth body doll appears to be after 1856 and the head of the pink kid body could have been made before that date. H. 10½ in. (26.5 cm.). *Coleman Collection.*

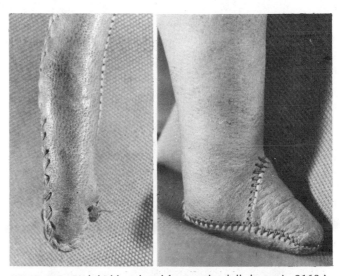

2163B & C. Pink kid hand and foot on the doll shown in 2163A. These appear to be hand sewn but commercially made. They were probably made in the 1850s before the extensive use of sewing machines. The French used pink kid to a greater extent than the Germans. H. of doll 10½ in. (26.5 cm.). *Coleman Collection.*

2164A & B. Bisque socket head on a ball jointed composition body made by Rabery & Delphieu. It has a brown wig, bangs, dark olive-green paperweight stationary glass eyes and a closed mouth. See Ill. 2167. H. 19 in. (48 cm.). *Courtesy of Z. Frances Walker.*

2165. Bisque socket head doll made by Rabery & Delphieu has a wig, stationary blue glass eyes, pierced ears, closed mouth, and is on a ball jointed composition body with straight wrists. Mark: "R 2/0 D." H. 15½ in. (39.5 cm.). *Courtesy of Sotheby Parke Bernet Inc., N.Y.*

2166. Bisque socket head doll made by Rabery & Delphieu. It has a blond wig, stationary brown eyes, pierced ears, a closed mouth, and is on a ball-jointed composition body. Mark: "R 2/0 D." H. 15 in. (38 cm.). *Courtesy of Sotheby Parke Bernet Inc., N.Y.*

R.1.D

R.3.D

2167–2168. Marks on bisque socket heads of Rabery & Delphieu dolls. The heads may have been made by François Gaultier.

Radio Dancing Couple. See **Peppy Pals.**

Rag (Rags) Bud. 1921. Cloth doll style no. 123 A made by *Sophia E. Delavan.* It had worsted hair, a triangular shaped mouth, slim neck and legs, and wore a print dress and an apron with a printed story in its pocket. There was no footwear.★

Rag Dolls.† See **Cloth Dolls.**

Rag Family. 1911. Cutout cloth dolls produced by *Saalfield.* They included *Gretchen,* a Dutch girl; *Hans,* a German boy; Juanita, a Spanish girl; Laddie, a Scottish boy; *Marie,* a French girl; and black Topsy. Ht. 8 in. (20.5 cm.).

Rag Shoppe Dolls. 1921. Cloth dolls produced by *Beck Manufacturing Co.,* made by *Van Walkenburgh* and distributed by *Severn & Long Co.* The black dolls were named *Mamie Lou* and *Aunt Caroline.*

Rag and Tag. 1926. Trademark registered in U.S. by *Borgfeldt* for dolls.

Raggedy Andy. After 1915–30 and later. First made a few years after Raggedy Ann. The doll shown in Ill. 2169 was taken to college by a girl born in 1910 and is a later doll than the Raggedy Ann in Ill. 2170. Raggedy Andy was a cloth flat face doll similar to Raggedy Ann.

2169A & B. Raggedy Andy, a cloth doll with dark maroon colored yarn hair, and a flat face with button eyes. Triangular nose and smiling mouth appear to be stenciled. The nose and center part of the mouth are red. Original clothes. H. 37 in. (94 cm.). *Courtesy of Helen Read.*

2170A & B. Raggedy Ann, a cloth doll with yarn hair, flat face having wooden spherical eyes and outlined red with black nose, black curved line for a mouth, mitten hands; black and red striped legs end in black cloth for shoes. Original clothes. H. 37 in. (94 cm.). *Courtesy of Helen Read.*

Raggedy Ann. 1915–30 and later. Cloth dolls designed by John B. Gruelle.[†] Among those making these dolls were *Georgene Novelty Co.* and *Molly-'es.* The dolls had yarn hair, button eyes, painted features on a flat face; the bodies were jointed at the shoulders and hips.

1927: Raggedy Ann wore a print dress with a high waisted apron having straps over the shoulders. The costume was unlike the one on the original patent as well as the one worn by recent dolls.★

Raggedy Man. ca. 1916. Cold press composition head doll produced by *Horsman.* It represented the character of this name in the poem by James Whitcomb Riley written in 1907. (See Ill. 2171.)

Ragtime Bill. 1914. Composition-head doll with round moving glass eyes, a cloth body jointed at the shoulders and hips, advertised by *John M. Smyth.* It wore a fur cap and removable footwear. Ht. 16 in. (40.5 cm.); priced 95¢.

Ragtime Kids. 1913–14. Cloth dolls made by *Dean* which included Ragtime Sambo.★

Ragtime Maud. 1914. Composition-head doll with round moving glass eyes, a cloth body jointed at the shoulders and hips, advertised by *John M. Smyth.* It wore a straw hat and removable footwear. Ht. 13 in. (33 cm.); priced 95¢.

Raibault, E. L. See **Niceray Établissements.**

Rainbow. 1915–16. Series of six cloth dolls made of printed fabric by *W. S. Turton.* The dolls had divided legs and cost 2¢.

Rainwater, William. 1928. Seattle, Wash. Manufactured dolls.

Rajah. 1930. Name of black cloth dolls made by *Chad Valley* of a printed fabric and wearing an East Indian style costume with full trousers, a turban, and ring earrings. The label was on the bottom of the foot. Hts. 11 and 14 in. (28 and 35.5 cm.).

Rakovsky, A. 1907–10. Vienna. Listed in a directory under Dolls and Dolls' Heads.

Rakovsky & Co. See **Blau Bela (Puppenfabrik).**

Rakuel (Rakusei), Gangu Kabushika Kaisha. 1921–27. Kyoto, Japan. Manufactured dolls.

Raleigh, Jessie McCutcheon. 1916–20. Chicago, Ill. The company was taken over by the *Pollyanna Co.* in 1920. A. D. Fleetwood was the New York representative. The dolls came in all-composition with molded hair, painted eyes, and spring joints. Hts. 13½ in. (34 cm.) and other heights. This firm also produced separate dolls' outfits.

The story of Jessie McCutcheon Raleigh and her dolls was told in several articles published in TOYS AND NOVELTIES in 1917–19.

"There is a new arrival in Dolldom. This is the Raleigh Doll. . . .

"The sponsor for the new doll is none other than Jessie McCutcheon Raleigh, a Chicago woman, who has won international fame as the orginator of the 'Good Fairy,' statuette, a work of art . . .

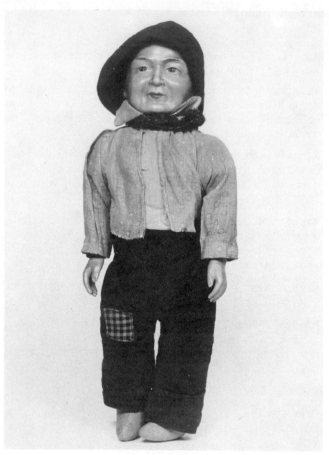

2171A & B. Composition head doll named Raggedy Man after the character in a James Whitcomb Riley poem. Doll produced by Horsman has molded hair, painted brown eyes, closed mouth, cloth body, and composition hands. It has Teddy Bear type joints. Original clothes. Mark: Ill. 2172. H. 15½ in. (39.5 cm.). *Courtesy of the Margaret Woodbury Strong Museum. Photo by Harry Bickelhaupt.*

THE RAGGEDY MAN
TRADE MARK
UNDER LICENSE FROM L. P. TUCKS
MFGD by E. I. HORSMAN

2172. Mark on the Raggedy Man, a composition head doll produced by Horsman.

"Mrs. Raleigh has now become a manufacturer of dolls and is devoting her unusual talents to the creation of dolls which express the artistic spirit that animates all her work. The dolls have been exhibited in New York and Chicago and several other cities. . . .

"The Raleigh dolls are now being made at the same studios with the 'Good Fairy,' and the corps of artists and work people engaged in the production are of the highest class.

"Mrs. Raleigh has entered the doll industry with a high artistic purpose. She believes there is a wonderful opportunity to add to the delights of American childhood by the creation of dolls which are expressive of the child spirit of this country, and are the embodiment of the childish graces peculiarly American. She believes that American children are the most lovely things in the world, distinquished by a beauty and spirituelle of face and form which superior breeding has bequeathed. Of course, these are high ideals, but she deserves respect for them. As for the realization of these ideals, she has the satisfaction of knowing that for the present the entire output of her factory is contracted for by discriminating buyers who have seen the line.

"Mrs. Raleigh has gathered about her an imposing array of talent in the field of sculpture, designing and painting. Dr. W. P. Dun Lany, after extensive research work, developed the composition of the doll itself to a point of high excellence."

The 1919 article reported:

"Jessie McCutcheon Raleigh was born in Lafayette, Indiana, and is one of the famous McCutcheon 'Big Four'—the other three being her brothers, who have international reputations as artists, authors, aviators, etc.

"Mrs. Raleigh modestly disclaims any artistic ability, laughingly declaring that she is the only one of the McCutcheon family in business, and that while she designed the Good Fairy, as well as the dolls, she did not model the former, and that the latter are put into form by skilled workers who carry out her ideas. Could you see, however, the many members of her Doll Family, you would instantly realize that Mrs. Raleigh is not only a clever industrial artist but a business woman of unusual ability as well.

"The Good Fairy was at first intended to be a model for a doll, but the 'Lugubrious Blues' took all the joy out of life by saying dolls could not be manufactured in America, there was no market, etc. but the reception accorded Mrs. Raleigh's statuette, and its increasing popularity, has proven that there is always a place in the world for Good Fairies. . . .

"Mrs. Raleigh has been manufacturing dolls since 1917 and despite the many obstacles encountered, she has helped in establishing a new industry in this country, one which promises to develop into a commercial enterprise of magnitude.

" 'American merchants have been quick to appreciate the superior qualities of the American-made doll. They have been helped by our home industries during the period of the war, and it is to be hoped this co-operation on their part will continue, and that they will give preference to home markets whenever and wherever possible,' said Mrs. Raleigh, . . .

" '. . . One source of inspiration is the letters I receive from different parts of the world, for we export to Australia, New Zealand and other Pacific points, and four of the big English merchants are among the buyers of Raleigh dolls.' . . .

"And these dolls are truly beautiful as well as companionable! A visit to the factory will readily convince one that the making of dolls is no child's play. Each process is under the supervision of skilled workmen. All [not all] the dolls have jointed limbs, light flexible bodies, moving eyes, human hair wigs and pleasing personalities. The dress question has been carefully worked out, and each doll is garbed according to name, character, and the part it takes in the doll world. A large force of women are kept busy making dolls' clothes."

Mrs. Raleigh supervised the entire production of her dolls which took place under one roof. The sculptor's model was based on a concept by Mrs. Raleigh. The various parts were molded in casts, dipped in enamel, flesh tints sprayed on, faces handpainted, hair arranged and finally the dolls were dressed. Some of the largest companies in America ordered tens of thousands of dollars' worth of these dolls according to Mrs. Raleigh.

The dolls had composition heads with molded hair or wigs, painted or sleeping eyes on cloth or on composition bodies; many of the faces were painted by students at the Chicago Art Institute. Often one arm was bent and the fingers curved so that the doll could hold an object. Since these were wartime dolls they had metal spring joints.

1918: Among the dolls were *Baby Petite, Baby Sister, Baby Stuart, Betty Bonnet, Curly Locks, Dearie, Debutante, Evelyn, Honey Bunch, Jane, Kindergarten Girlie,* Little Brother, *Marjorie, Miss Sunshine, Miss Traveler, Mother's Darling, My Favorite, Schoolgirl* and *Vacation Girl.* (See the first COLLECTOR'S ENCYCLOPEDIA OF DOLLS for additional names.) The bent-limb babies with wigs came in 12½ and 18 in. (31.5 and 45.5 cm.) hts. Those with molded hair and bent-limb bodies, five hts. 10½, 11½, 12½, 13½, and 18 in. (26.5, 29, 31.5, 34, and 45.5 cm.).

1919: TOYS AND NOVELTIES reported: "The new dolls brought out by Jessie McCutcheon Raleigh, Chicago, for the 1919 Christmas season, . . . represent beauty in design, perfection of finish, and daintiness in dress.

"There is Rose Mary, a dainty little miss whose extended arms are an invitation to gather her up; Goldilocks, of Mother Goose fame; Sweetheart, a pretty little thing in long baby dresses; Tiny-Tot, a plump little beauty with soft, short hair; Peeps, dressed in a little cape and with a peaked hood that just will not confine her curly golden locks; Mary Quite Contrary, who is quite all that her name indicates; Elise, a sedate, demure little girl with long dark curls; Helen, a lively little miss with an abundance of shining hair; Daisy Anna in a party dress; Mama's Angel Child, who is from all appear-

ances the counter part of Penny Ross's famous creation; Little Pink Lady; Little Lucille; Mary-Had-a-Lamb, with a snow-white lamb clasped in her arms; Priscilla, a dainty Quaker miss with bow tie and white cap; Doll-O'-My-Heart, a little dainty thing with long dark curls and a neat little dress; Dorothy, dressed in a party dress, with a pretty ribbon tied about her head; and Poppy, a bright, laughing, happy-go-lucky sort of a doll. . . ." (See Ills. 2173–2175.)★

Ralph, H. S. 1924. London. Made and/or distributed dolls, dolls' heads, and wigs.

Rampel, Georg. 1906. Sonneberg, Thür. Applied for a German patent (D.R.G.M.) for jointed dolls.

Randall, E. Before 1904–58. London. Distributed the *Grödner tal,* peg wooden dolls. In 1904 he paid the warehouse from 19¢ to $2.13 per gross for the 4 to 10 in. (10 to 30.5 cm.) dolls. Larger sizes up to 24 in. (61 cm.) had ball and socket joints and more detailed carving on the head.

Raphael, Martin & Co. 1921–22. London. Advertised Baby Dolls, dressed and undressed; *Melitta;* dolls' heads of bisque, celluloid, and "steel."

Rapin, Henri. Before and during World War I. Paris. Born 1873, he was an artist who received medals in 1904 and 1910 and became an Officer of the Legion of Honneur. His models were used to create expensive dolls according to a contemporary source. He designed some of the models for *Jouets de France.*

Raquel Meller. 1925–26. Felt doll made by *Lenci* as style no. 263, represented the Spanish entertainer of this name. It wore a romantic style costume and carried a carriage parasol. Ht. 28 in. (71 cm.).

Raquel Meller. 1920s. Cloth doll made in France with an imitation suede face, molded and painted features, black silk wig, dressed to represent the Spanish entertainer. It bore a cloth tag on its leg reading "Fabrication France." Ht. 10½ in. (26.5 cm.). (See Ill. 2176.)

Rassant, Mme. Elisa (née Blum). 1926. Brou, Eure et Loire, France. Registered the following trademarks in France for dressed dolls holding trays *Arlette, Bathilde, Claire, Joseph, Marie-Jeanne,* Mousmé, *Suzel, Trudy* and *Yvette.*

Rattle Doll. 1914. *Celtid* (celluloid)-head doll with a rattle, distributed by *Marshall Field,* had a cloth body and wore a knitted wool dress and felt hat. Ht. 10 in. (25.5 cm.); priced $2.50 doz. wholesale. (See also **Schepperdocken.**)

Rattle Head. 1902–05. China head doll with round china balls in its head; when shaken the balls rattled.

1902: New dolls hts. 8, 11¼, and 12½ in. (20.5, 28.5, and 31.5 cm.); priced 35¢ to 70¢ doz. wholesale.★

Rattle Head. 1930. Name of a cloth doll made by *Kat-A-Korner.*

Rattling Dolls. 1860–61. Imported by *John D. Robbins* according to a Day Book owned by Elizabeth Pierce. These were probably wooden or composition dolls with stones inside to rattle; priced $2.00 doz. wholesale.

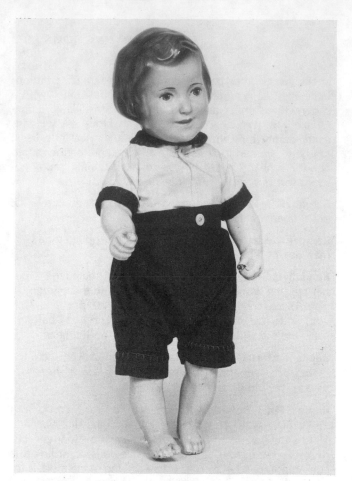

2173A & B. All-composition doll produced by Jessie M. Raleigh. It is made of a heavy dark composition painted with an ivory colored enamel on the flesh part. The hair is molded and painted as are the brown eyes. Four teeth show in the open closed mouth. Spring type joints are at the neck, shoulders and hips. The slightly bent arms have clenched fist hands. Original clothes. The modified Dutch type trousers have pockets. H. 12¾ in. (32.5 cm.). *Courtesy of the Margaret Woodbury Strong Museum. Photos by Harry Bicklehaupt.*

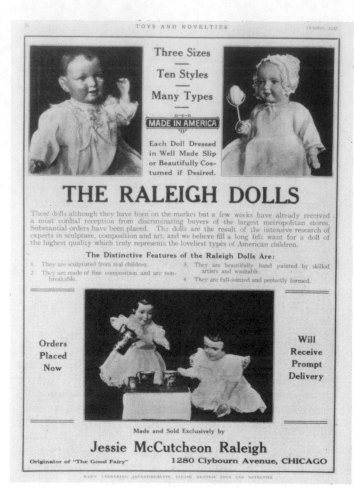

2174. Advertisement for the Raleigh dolls published in TOYS AND NOVELTIES, October, 1917. They are portraits of real children, sculptured and painted by artists.

Rauser, Mrs. Katherine A. Before 1904–30 and later. Chicago, Ill., 1930 and later; also New York. Began working for *Marshall Field* and left there in 1903. In 1904 she started to make dolls' clothes on her own which she described: "without a penny and with my workshop the borrowed dining room of a friend, who had to loan me her machine to sew." She started with the knowledge that little girls want up-to-date style removable clothes on their dolls.

In 1914 she was in charge of displays at the New York Toy Fair. By 1916 Mrs. Rauser was head of a large factory and shop. In 1919 PLAYTHINGS referred to Katherine Rauser as the "Lucile of Dolldom." "Lucile" was Lucile, *Lady Duff Gordon,* a famous couturière. *A. S. Ferguson* was Mrs. Rauser's factory representative for many years. In the late 1920s she represented other companies.

1912: Advertised dolls' clothing, dolls' hats and dolls' accessories.

1913: Advertised boy doll and lady doll outfits and rompers for dolls. TOYS AND NOVELTIES in February 1913 extolled the work of Katherine Rauser stating that she "vies with Worth or Paquin in the creation of dolls' gowns and outfits.

"Mrs. Rauser is probably the leading manufacturer of

Goldilocks   Peeps   Mama's Angel Child   Red Riding Hood   Mary-Had-a-Lamb

Christmas Dolls for the Kiddies

By Anne Wilson

I WISH I might take you with me to visit the home of Mrs. Jessie McCutcheon Raleigh, the mother of these dear little dolls, just so you can see for yourself the joy that goes into the fashioning of these little people so that they will carry happiness to all the little kiddies this Christmas. Mrs. Raleigh is a real Santa Claus and she has taken as her model for these dolls little American children. And the dresses she has made for them will delight big mothers, and little mothers as well. There are two kinds of dolls, those which open and close their eyes and those which do not.

The doll that walks is from Madam Georgine and the rag doll from Mrs. Denckla.

Mary-Quite-Contrary

Big Mary

Poppy

Doll-o'-My-Heart

This is Little Sherry

Dorothy and Fashionable Lucile are Good Friends

Little Lucile

Little Rabbit Lady

This is Miss Happy

A Darling Little Baby Who Toddles Along if You Hold its Hands

Here is a Rag Doll With Real Hair That Will Stand All Kinds of Rough Treatment

2175. Article showing Jessie McCutcheon Raleigh's composition dolls in THE LADIES' HOME JOURNAL, December, 1919. Some of these dressed dolls have stationary eyes and some have sleeping eyes. The names of the dolls clockwise starting at the upper left, are: Goldilocks, Peeps, Mama's Angel Child, Red Riding Hood, Mary Had a Lamb, Poppy, Little Lucille, and Dorothy, a rag doll made by Mrs. Denckla, and a walking toddler of Georgene Averill. Returning to the Raleigh dolls there is Miss Happy, Little Rabbit Lady, the baby Little Sherry, Doll-O-'My-Heart, Big Mary, and Mary-Quite-Contrary.

2176A & B. Molded face cloth doll reportedly made to represent Raquel Meller, a Spanish dancer of the 1920s. The face and hands are made of imitation felt. It wears a red knee length dress with black lace net skirt. Over the shoulder is a printed scarf. The stockings are loose net and the black high heel shoes have ribbon laces up the legs. Cloth tag on the leg reads, "MADE IN FRANCE." H. 10 in. (25.5 cm.). *Coleman Collection.*

fine doll outfits, dresses, underwear, aprons, hats and novelties in America. She has blazed the way in her highly specialized branch of the toy industry so surely that she is the recognized originator and authority on doll outfits in this country. She is the American Worth and Paquin of the doll world.

"Mrs. Rauser's line is always new. Each year and each month novelties are added so that the toy buyer always finds meat for the meal in her display. . . . There are scores of new items and interesting features, not the least important of which is a complete line of outfits for lady dolls. There is another for character baby dolls, one for the 62 centimeter [24½ in.] special doll, as well as outfits for boy dolls, and quaint character dolls. The new samples in top coats and hats is also of exceptional interest."

1915: Every known style was duplicated for dolls. The garments were made to measure and fitted in the making. For window displays, dolls were dressed in period costumes and as wedding parties. Mrs. Rauser made costumes for dolls representing all of the Allied Nations plus four neutral nations, including Sweden and Holland. In addition there were nurse outfits, Red Cross costumes, Peace Doll clothes and *Kewpie* outfits. Regular outfits were available for dolls from 8 to 36 in. (20.5 to 91.5 cm.) and for baby dolls 10 to 26 in. (25.5 to 66 cm.).

1916: Advertised *Dolly Modiste* sewing sets which came in three sizes with instructions on the box cover. Box No. 1 contained thimble, needle and thread, patterns, material and trimming for making two dresses for two dolls, hts. 7 and 9 in. (18 and 23 cm.); priced 50¢. Box No. 2 also had patterns and material for a coat, hat, bonnet, rompers, and an apron; priced $1.00. Box No. 3 contained instructions and material for making baby doll clothes including a dress, petticoat, stork pants, jacket, cap, and bootees. (See also **Chronology.**)

1917: Dressed dolls as babies, girls, boys, men, ladies, nurses, in costumes of various nationalities and periods. Clothes included eiderdown capes and hoods for infant dolls, toques, mittens, afghans, and leggings.

1919: TOYS AND NOVELTIES described a visit to the Rauser factory as follows: "Fashion Art in Rauser Doll Clothes Secret of Success in Chicago Woman's Doll Dress Factory Due to Painstaking Attention to Every Detail in the Costume. Fashion Writer Waxes Enthusiastic.

"A visit to the home of the Rauser doll reveals the secret of their success. Midst all the activity of busy fingers and power machines turning out garments by the hundreds and thousands, there is one mind guiding, planning, originating the ideas which have made these doll outfits famous throughout the country. This presiding genius is Katherine A. Rauser, who has a genuine love for her work, taking the same pride in creating apparel for dolls as the mother who fashions dainty garments for her children.

"Mrs. Rauser puts all those little human touches on dolls' garments which so delight children. For instance, there are *real* buttons and buttonholes. Each article is carefully finished so as to launder perfectly. All the prevailing modes are reproduced and the dresses and hats abound in beautiful hand embroidery, fine tuckings and shirrings. The materials employed are of the best.

"The scope of ideas expressed in these doll outfits is limitless. It embodies dress for all occasions. There is the romper clad doll, a veritable replica of a child's seashore outfit. There are baby dolls and beauteous fluffy gowned dolls in rose and blue and buttercup yellow, through all ages and styles, to formal evening and trousseau outfits. Mrs. Rauser scores a wonderful success in her bridal party of dolls, which is complete in costume even to the flower girls, bridesmaid and best man climaxing in a bride and groom perfectly attired.

"Perhaps one of the most irresistible attractions is the flower Kewpies. Rose has a pink velvet petalled skirt, Pansy purple and yellow and so on, with flowers for a head dress to match. Just now Mrs. Rauser and her coterie of designers are creating a special valentine, also Easter Lily Kewpie, the demand for which no doubt will be great.

"The queen of all the Rauser dolls at present is Miss Babette, . . .

"A real need of the trade is met, in that Mrs. Rauser carries on a vast business of dressing other manufacturers' dolls, supplying outfits to dealers all over the country.

"As manufacturer of artistic doll clothes; of doll outfits to be sold separately; of dolls dressed in character outfits for window dressing purposes; of special valentines and Easter Kewpies—Mrs. Rauser is known throughout the country as official outfitter to her majesty, the American doll."

The better dressed dolls had sleeping eyes, sewed wigs and fully jointed bodies. Hts. 18 to 24 in. (45.5 to 61 cm.).

1921: Designed *Miss Chicago* doll which was exhibited in the Pageant of Progress Exposition, Chicago.

1922: Pantalettes for *Mama* dolls were the fashion. A lavender garden outfit had long trousers and miniature flowers growing out of each pocket. A hat came with it. A romper outfit of one color had an appliqué representing a Japanese in another color on the front and Japanese designs on the tiny pockets. Organdy dresses were made in various pastel colors.

1923: Clothes for Mama dolls included dresses, rompers, playsuits, underwear, and accessories. Other clothes included a sports dress of crepe-knit silk and a silk street costume with matching hat, both bordered with paisley patterned silk.

1925–28: She was the factory representative of *M. & S. Shillman.*

1926: Made dolls' costumes for manufacturers, distributors and doll hospitals. New items were overnight bags and a miniature hat box with accessories for dolls.

1928: New items included racks for dolls' clothes and stands for dolls' hats, raincoats and a *Boudoir* type doll named Vanity Van, dressed in black or colored satin and having pockets, holding face powder, mirror, lipstick, purse, and handkerchief, each in a separate pocket. Katherine Rauser represented the *Berkeley Crocheters* line of dolls' clothes.

1929: Designed clothes for *Little Brother, Little Sister* and *Patsy.* Organdy dresses were the fashion. Katherine Rauser advertised doll outfits, baby doll layettes, novelty dolls, accessories for dolls, sewing sets, dolls' house furniture, and National Tinsel line.★

2177. Mark used by Katherine Rauser.

Ravca, Bernard. 1924–30 and later. Paris and later in America. According to Elsie Krug he started his career painting on silk and from his Montmartre studio came "Spanish Shawls." He made cloth dolls and in 1931 exhibited them at the Paris Colonial Exhibition. These were 24 in. (61 cm.) tall dolls. Some of his dolls were portraits of famous people. There was a similarity between his dolls and those made by *Mme. Yvonne Spaggiari.*★

Ravisé, E. 1925–29. Paris. Made dolls.★

Rawack (Rawacj), S. 1920–26. Coburg, Bavaria. Manufactured dolls.

Ray, Jean. 1917–27. Paris. Artist who created dolls for the *Société Française de Fabrication de Bébés & Jouets* and others.

1917: Designed the molded faces for the *Émile Lang* stuffed dolls.

1918: *Created Petites Marraines de Guerre* (Little God-mothers of War) named *Lily* and *Claudette*.

1921–22: *Bon Marché* advertised her *La Parisienne.*★

Rayburn Townsend & Co. 1924–25. London. Made and exported dolls; registered *Rompa* as the name of a cloth doll stuffed with kapok. The frame of the Rompa dolls could be removed and then they could be washed with soap and water.

Raynal (Poupées Raynal). 1922–30 and later. Paris. Edouard Raynal founded the firm in 1922. They made dolls of felt, cloth or with a celluloid head, especially for showrooms and festive occasions. The dolls were dressed and some of them resembled *Lenci* dolls, except that the fingers were often together when made of cloth or the hands were made of celluloid. The celluloid that they used was called rhodoid and was made by the Rhone-Poulenc factory. The dolls were marked Raynal on the soles of their shoes and/or on a pendant.

1926: *Yves de Villers & Co.* registered "Poupées Raynal" as a U.S. trademark for dolls.★

2178A & B. Raynal cloth doll with an original box. Doll has a felt head, wig, brown painted eyes glancing to the side, painted upper lashes only, two highlights on the lower lip, pink cotton body, legs seamed up the back only, blue taffeta dress, white cotton teddy trimmed with same lace as on the dress. Blue felt slippers with same buttons as on back of dress. H. 14½ in. (37 cm.) box shows "40 cm." (15½ in.). *Courtesy of Margaret F. Mandel, owner since 1938.*

2179. Mark on a Raynal cloth doll.

Rayon Princess. 1929. Doll with composition shoulder head and forearms on a cotton stuffed body distributed by *Butler Bros.* It had painted features and hair, a voice and came dressed; ht. 15½ in. (39.5 cm.); priced $8.00 doz. whole-sale; with composition legs and a mama voice, hts. 20 and 27 in. (51 and 68.5 cm.); priced $2.25 and $3.50.

R-B Dolls. See **Reisman, Barron (&) Co.**

Read, Elmer J. 1918–19. Rutherford, N.J. Obtained a U.S. patent for jointed figures, especially those made of wood.★

Reader, H., & Sons. 1926–27. New York City. Imported dolls.

Reccius Bros. 1912–13 and other years. Louisville, Ky. John and Michael Reccius owned a toy store that included a dolls' hospital. (See also **Repairing Dolls,** 1913.)

Recknagel, Phil., & Co. 1888–91. Eisfeld, Thür. Made inexpensive jointed and dressed dolls.★

Recknagel, Theodor. 1886–1930 and probably later. Alexandrinenthal near Oeslau, Thür. Made bisque heads for dolls of varying quality. Sometimes the mark was incised and sometimes it was raised. The heads had wigs or molded hair, glass eyes or painted eyes, and some of the eyes looked to the side; open mouth or closed mouth, flange neck or socket head. Heads represented children or babies. A few of the pates were cut steeply like those found on some French dolls.

1897: Registered a mark consisting of a black and a mulatto dolls' heads.

1898: Factory had 200 employees.

1900: Applied for a German patent (D.R.G.M.) for a doll's head with moving eyes.

1901: Applied for a German patent (D.R.G.M.) for dolls' eyes with eyelashes of spun yarn.

1910: Registered six mold numbers for heads namely 226, 227, 1907, R 1, RIV (in black), R XII.

1911: Applied for a German patent (D.R.G.M.) for glass dolls' eyes with elevated irises.

1912: Applied for a German patent (D.R.G.M.) for character dolls' heads of porcelain. Registered eleven mold numbers, namely 22, 23, 24, 25, 26, 27, 28, 29, 30, 31, and 32. The last two numbers were for dolls representing *Max and Moritz.* The others were for dolls' heads.

1914: Registered nineteen mold numbers for character dolls, namely 33, 34, 35, 37, 39, 41, 43, 44, 45, 46, 47, 48, 49, 50, 53, 54, 55, 56, and 57.

1925: Registered a mold number for a baby head with one tooth 128 and with two teeth 129.

1926: Registered five mold numbers for baby heads, namely 131, 132, 134, 135, and 136.

Other Recknagel numbers that have been reported are 21, 86, 121, 126, 137, 138, 1909 and 1914. The numbers seem to run in numerical order chronologically except for 226, 227, 1907, 1909 and 1914. Since the 1907 was registered in 1910 it seems doubtful that these four digit numbers represent years.

The research of the Ciesliks provided information about the dating of the registration of the mold numbers. ★

Réclame. See **Bébé Réclame.**

Red Cloud. 1923–29. Down-stuffed cloth doll made by *Chad Valley* in their *Aerolite* line as No. 44. The arms were away from the body and the legs were apart. It wore an American *Indian* type printed costume. Ht. 11 in. (28 cm.).

Red Cross Nurse. 1915. Dolls advertised by *Louis Wolf.*

Red Cross Nurse. 1915--18. Dolls with bisque heads were dressed as Red Cross Nurses and sold in the large Paris stores, especially at the *Louvre* store and *Printemps.*

1916–18: Printemps advertised Red Cross Nurse dolls; six hts. 22, 24, 28, 30, 33, and 35 cm. (8½, 9½, 11, 12, 13, and 14 in.); priced 19¢ to 75¢ in 1916 and 39¢ to $1.50 in 1918.

Red Cross Nurse. 1917. Dolls made by *Amberg* who contributed 10¢ to the American Red Cross for every one of these dolls sold.

Red Cross Nurse. 1917. Doll with composition head and hands distributed by the *Baltimore Bargain House.* It had a cloth body. Ht. 36 in. (91.5 cm.); priced $1.35.

Red Cross Nurse. 1917. Composition "Art Doll" made by *Horsman* wore blue and white lawn uniform with white cap and red insignia. Ht. 14 in. (35.5 cm.); priced $9.00 doz. wholesale.

Red Cross Nurse. 1917. Series of dolls made by the *South Wales Manufacturing Co.*

Red Cross Nurse. 1918. Composition head with molded hair on a cloth body distributed by *Eaton.* Ht. 13 in. (33 cm.); priced 50¢.

Red Cross Nurse. 1919. Composition head doll made by *Ideal* had molded hair, sleeping eyes, cloth body and composition hands. Ht. 16 in. (40.5 cm.).

Red Cross Nurse. See **Nurse.**

Red Grange. 1925–26. Trademark registered in U.S. by *Live Long Toys* for dolls. This portrait doll, made in oilcloth and wearing a football uniform with the number "77" on it, carried a miniature football.

Red Hood (Rotkäppchen). 1911–16. Jointed felt character doll made by *Steiff* and distributed by *Borgfeldt* in the U.S. and *Gamage* in England. It wore a red cape and hood over an ankle-length print dress. The two largest sizes came with or without long inserted hair and in 1913 with a mama voice. Four hts. 28, 35, 43, and 50 cm. (11, 14, 17, and 19½ in.); priced $1.38 to $3.50 with short hair or $4.69 with long hair in Germany in 1911.

1913: Gamage charged $1.22 to $3.75 for these dolls.

1916: There was also a 60 cm. (23½ in.) doll. (See also **Kruse, Käthe; Little Red Riding Hood;** and **Red Riding Hood.**)

Red Riding Hood. 1876–80. Name of a crying doll dressed

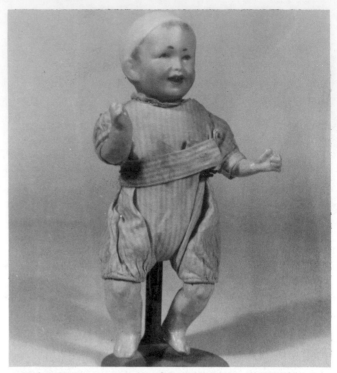

2180. Bisque head probably made by Th. Recknagel. It has molded hair and molded white bonnet with a blue pompon, intaglio blue eyes, open-closed mouth with two teeth, and a bent limb baby body. Mark: "R.A. //28–12/0." H. 8 in. (20.5 cm.). *Courtesy of Richard Withington. Photo by Barbara Jendrick.*

2181

2182

2183

2184A

2184B

2181–2184A & B. Marks on bisque heads probably made by Th. Recknagel. No. 2181 is definitely made by him.

as Red Riding Hood, advertised by *Silber & Fleming,* came in three hts.

Red Riding Hood. 1892 and later. Cutout cloth doll made by *Arnold Print Works.*

Red Riding Hood. 1893. *Horsman* advertised a *London Rag* doll type which they called Red Riding Hood; priced $4.00 doz. wholesale.

Red Riding Hood. 1910. Name of a doll made by *Carl Meyer.*

Red Riding Hood. 1912–16. Cloth doll produced by *Horsman* in their *Babyland* line, wore a dress, apron, cape and hood. It appeared to be the same doll as *American Maid* Baby and *Little Boy Blue* except the clothes. The smallest size came with either a handpainted or *Lifelike* lithographed face (2RH or 202RH); all of the larger sizes had handpainted faces. No. 9RH. was 16½ in. (42 cm.); 11RH was 20 in. (51 cm.) and 13RH was 30 in. (76 cm.).

Red Riding Hood. 1913. *Gamage* advertised two types of dolls dressed as Red Riding Hood. One came in four hts. priced $1.98 to $5.63. The other was the felt doll made by *Steiff* and was called *Red Hood* by Steiff.

Red Riding Hood. 1914. Cutout cloth doll advertised by *Butler Bros.,* made a 15 in. (38 cm.) doll; priced 79¢ doz. wholesale.

Red Riding Hood. 1916. Cloth doll made by *Harwin.*

Red Riding Hood. 1917. Character doll advertised by *Bell & Francis.*

Red Riding Hood. 1917–19. Character doll produced by the *Deptford Toy Making Industry.*

Red Riding Hood. 1918–19. Composition-head doll with molded hair, cork stuffed cloth body, was made by *K & K* and distributed by *Butler Bros.*★

Red Riding Hood. 1918. Dressed composition doll made by the *New Toy Manufacturing Co.,* came in a box with storybook and a composition wolf. Ht. of doll 12 in. (30.5 cm.).

Red Riding Hood. 1919–20. Name of a wigged doll made by *Jessie M. Raleigh* and dressed in a red cape and hood.

Red Riding Hood. 1920. Made by *Rees Davis* in her *Mother Goose* line.

Red Riding Hood. 1920–21. Stockinet cloth doll with removable clothes made by *Chad Valley.* It had a woven wig that could be brushed and combed, was dressed in silk and other materials and wore a Chad Valley patented wrist watch. Ht. 12 to 13 in. (30.5 to 33 cm.).

Red Riding Hood. 1921. Cloth doll dressed in felt, made by the *Chessler Co.*

Red Riding Hood. 1922. Line of dolls made by *Horsman* with painted hair or wigs and sleeping eyes. There were over 100 nos. in this line which included *Mama* dolls with *Lloyd* voices. They wore dresses of gingham or lace, rompers, or smocks, and were many heights.

Red Riding Hood. 1923–24. Bisque-head doll on a jointed composition body advertised by *F. A. O. Schwarz* as a *Favorite.* It had a wig, sleeping eyes, open mouth with teeth, wore a blue dress, white apron, red cape and hood and carried a basket. Hts. 13 and 16 in. (33 and 40.5 cm.); priced $7.50 and $8.50 in cotton clothes and $10.00 and $12.00 in silk clothes.

Red Riding Hood. 1926. One of a line of Nursery Rhyme dolls made by the *Jeanette Doll Co.* and distributed by *Louis Wolf.*

Red Riding Hood. 1927. See **Grandma** and **Red Riding Hood.**

Red Riding Hood. 1929. Composition shoulder head with painted features on a dressed red oilcloth body distributed by *Butler Bros.* Ht. 16 in. (40.5 cm.); priced $4.00 doz. wholesale.

Red Riding Hood. 1930. A plump doll made by *Moore & Gibson,* wore a Red Riding Hood outfit.

Red Riding Hood. See **Little Red Riding Hood, Chaperon Rouge, Rotkäppchen (Red Hood).**

Redon, Maison. Second half of the 1800s. A shop that specialized in children's toys. An oval blue "Maison Redon" stamp was found on the kid body of a bisque head lady doll with cobalt blue glass eyes and a swivel neck.

Ree-Bee Dolls. 1927. Name of some dolls distributed by *Schaeffer Bros.*

Reed, C. A. 1924 and probably other years. Williamsport, Pa. All-celluloid bride and groom dolls with crêpe paper clothes had a blue and white rectangular sticker on their bases reading "A Reed Product//C.A. Reed Co.//WILLIAMS PORT, Pa." The bride had a wig, a bridal gown, and a white net veil; the groom had molded hair and wore a black full-dress outfit. Both dolls had painted features. Ht. 3½ in. (9 cm.). (See Ills. 2185 and 2186.)

Rees Davis. See **Davis, Rees.**

Rees, L. (Leon), & Co. 1908–30 and later. London. Produced and distributed dolls. Leon Rees, born in Bavaria in 1879, died in London in 1963. He went to London and worked for *Eisenmann & Co.* In 1908 he married Maud Eisenmann and soon became a partner in Eisenmann & Co. About 1915 he left Eisenmann and helped to form Ellison, Rees & Co. By 1920 this firm became L. Rees & Co.

1920: Distributed dolls of *Bing, Kämmer & Reinhardt, Albert Schlopsnies* and *Welsch & Co.*

1921: Advertised Primrose and Fairy Queen series of dolls.

1922: Dolls included Winter Sports Girl in a white outfit trimmed with fur, and miniature dolls dressed as Irish, Scottish and Welsh girls.

1926: Cloth-body dolls were named *Cecille, Lucille* and *Lullabye Baby.* Rees was the sole distributor of Lucille Art dolls. These *Lenci*-type dolls were made chiefly by *Martin Eichhorn.* Distributed dolls of Bing and Kämmer & Reinhardt.

1930: Dolls with composition heads on cloth bodies were named Rosette and came in six different costume styles.★

2185. All-celluloid doll handled and probably dressed by the C. A. Reed Co. It has molded hair, painted black eyes looking to the side, closed mouth, and a body jointed only at the shoulders. The original clothes are made of crêpe paper. Mark: Ill. 2186. H. 3½ in. (9 cm.). *Coleman Collection.*

2186. Mark on a celluloid doll handled by C. A. Reed Co.

Reese, Charles N. 1920–26. Wilmette, Ill. Obtained a U.S. patent for a doll.

Reeves, Ruth. 1921–23. A famous couturière who designed dolls.

1923: Designed the dolls for the "Story of Silk, 3500 B. C.–1923 A. D. Told in Dolls," an Exhibit at the Second International Silk Exposition. She also designed dolls for exhibits sent to teach the history of costume in various Colleges and Universities. Ht. of silk exhibit dolls was 24 in. (61 cm.)★

Reform Movement. See **Puppen Reform.**

Regal Doll Manufacturing Co. 1918–30 and later. New York City and Jersey City, N.J.; factory built in 1929. Prede-

cessor was German American Doll Co.[†] Manufactured Regal, *Kiddie Pal* and *Kiddiejoy* lines of dolls.

1920: Made character and novelty all-composition dolls with or without sleeping eyes.

1923: Made *Mama* dolls. Dolls were designed and created by *Madame Corine Clair.*

1926: Made new born baby dolls designed by *Ernesto Peruggi,* child dolls and Mama dolls in a variety of costumes and sizes. Some of their dolls had sleeping eyes and hair eyelashes.

1927: Member of the *American Doll Manufacturers' Association.* They were licensed to use the patented mama voices and criers made by *Voices, Inc.* Advertised Kiddie Pal Baby and Kiddie Pal Dolly, both new in 1927.
    Distributed *Dolly Raindear* outfits.

1928: Made *Our Lindy,* a portrait doll of Charles Lindbergh. Registered "Kiddie Pal Dolly" as a trademark in U.S. for dolls. A doll has been seen marked "*Kiddie Pale* Baby" [sic].

1929: Continued making Kiddie Pal and Our Lindy dolls. The new doll in the Kiddy Pal line was *Kiss Me,* a character doll that raised its hand to its face as if to throw kisses.

1930: Kiddie Pal dolls included: *Billy, Dorothy Jane, Judy Kinky,* Kiss Me, *Princess Wee-Wee* created by *Mabel Whitman,* and *Sonny Boy.* Infant and Mama dolls were priced 50¢ to $5.00. The $5.00 dolls had human hair wigs, sleeping eyes, open mouth with teeth and tongue, were dressed including a hair ribbon. Ht. 27 in. (68.5 cm.).

1939: Advertised composition dolls and rubber dolls.★

Regal Sleepers. 1918–20. Name of a composition doll made by *Amberg* using the then new *Denivelle* baking process. It had a patented sleeping device. Five hts.

Reggie Rations. 1918. Name of a "soft" (cloth) character doll made by *Harwin.* Ht. 24 in. (61 cm.).

Regina. 1884. Name of a wax (wax-over-composition) doll distributed by *Lauer.* It had "French" (glass) eyes, loose hair with bangs, an embroidered chemise, cloth stockings and leather boots. Five hts. 15, 18, 22, 26, and 29½ in. (38, 45.5, 56, 66, and 75 cm.); priced $4.50 to $15.00 doz. wholesale.

Régini. 1927. Dressed cloth doll with wig sold by *Lafayette* store. Ht. 40 cm. (15½ in.).

Regional Costume Dolls. There were two kinds of Regional Dolls, those made in various countries to represent the natives and those made in Germany and elsewhere that were dressed in the costumes of the types worn in various regions. Many of the former are discussed under the name of the native country. Also included in this group were the *Door of Hope* Dolls; the wooden dolls carved in Switzerland and dressed in the costumes of the 22 different cantons; the Venezuelan cloth dolls made by *Manuela Pereyra.* Many local museums contained dolls dressed in provincial clothes. For example the museum in Arles, France, showed dolls in the variety of costumes worn in Provence over the years and for various occasions and occupations.

Many areas had special costumes for people in specific occupations. and these differed from region to region. For example French nursemaids sometimes wore an Alsatian style costume whether they came from Alsace or some other area. Danish nursemaids often wore the costume of a certain Danish island regardless of the origin of the nursemaid because many nursemaids came from that particular island. Thus the regional type costume on a doll could represent an occupation rather than a region. Regional and/or occupational costumes are seldom worn by people today except for special occasions. Collectors of dolls should realize the great importance of dolls dressed in true regional costumes. This does not include the many pseudo-regional clothes.

Tourists and travelers have nearly always been interested in dolls dressed like the natives in the places they have visited. School children studying various countries have been helped by seeing dolls dressed in regional costumes. Most of these dolls were made elsewhere, especially in Germany or France and later in the U.S. and Italy. Sometimes the clothes were made in the country represented by the costume, but more often the clothes were made in the same country as the doll or elsewhere.

Toward the end of the 1800s and the beginning of the 1900s and probably earlier, some German manufacturers of dolls used reference books on regional costumes, such as that illustrated by *Albert Kretschmer,* to dress the doll in appropriate regional attire. In fact when the *Ernst Reinhardt* family emigrated to the U.S. they brought with them such a book so that the wife, Laura, could continue to dress dolls correctly in German regional costumes.

Lenci used books on regional costumes to design some of the clothes for their dolls.

Many of the books written for young girls in the 1800s gave suggestions for dressing dolls in regional costumes. These pastime instructions were meant for educational purposes.

1831: THE GIRL'S OWN BOOK suggested, "by looking in a book called Manners and Customs, she dressed them all with great taste and propriety." The costumes represented a Laplander, African, Indian, French and Turk.

1873: Directions for dressing dolls in regional costumes including a German peasant, an Italian woman, a Norwegian peasant boy and girl, a Russian man and woman, were published in HOME GAMES FOR OLD AND YOUNG. This book stated "to [dress dolls] correctly, good pictures should be consulted, that the national dress may be faultlessly represented."

1878: THE QUEEN, a London periodical, described how to make "a doll dressed as a Russian man. High boots made of black leather or rather an old black kid glove, full trousers of blue cloth tucked into them, a long loose coat made of rough cloth, flat fur cap and long beard, the latter is best produced of dark frisette gummed on to the face."

1897: The *Samaritaine* store in Paris advertised a Russian bébé dressed in satin, velvet and gold. Hts. 37 and 43 cm. (14½ and 17 in.); priced 58¢ and 90¢. *Mignonnettes*

dressed as a Russian boy and girl had bisque heads and clothes of velvet and satin; priced 29¢ for the couple.

1899: *Nöckler & Tittel* advertised dolls in regional costumes.

Ca. 1900: Mrs. *Ernst Reinhardt* of Sonneberg dressed dolls in German regional costumes as shown in a book illustrated by A. Kretschmer, an authority on this subject. These dolls had been made by her husband.

1901: Laura Starr wrote an article for THE DELINEATOR about regional dolls. These included *Indian* dolls, *Eskimo* dolls, *Oriental* dolls, French dolls, Persian dolls, Turkish dolls, Syrian dolls, Spanish dolls and dolls from Madeira. All of these were probably made in the country of origin. Also there were an Egyptian Lady and a Russian Peasant both of which appear to have been German bisque head dolls dressed in regional costumes.

1902: Mrs. Washington Hesing had bisque and composition, including papier-mâché, dolls dressed in African, Dutch, Indian, Lapland (See Ill. 2502 for a later doll dressed as a Laplander) and other regional costumes. The dolls were of various sizes and the clothes were claimed to be removable thus permitting an examination of the details of the costume.

1906: *Carl Horn* advertised small dolls dressed in regional costumes.

1907: *Mrs. Elizabeth Scantlebury* launched her program of providing dolls clothed in regional costumes for the schools in Springfield, Mass.

1908: Laura Starr with the help of *Stewart Culin* wrote THE DOLL BOOK and described her collection of dolls. Except for the Oriental dolls nearly all of the dolls had bisque heads, probably made in Germany, and were dressed in regional costumes. These dolls represented: American Indian; Arab; Austrian Tyrol with green hat and cock's feather; Canary Islands; Danish; Dutch, Maarken and North Holland; French, Le Puy lace maker, Cannes, Arles; German Black Forest; Italian Nurse and Baby; Lebanese dressed in a Lebanon Mission; Norwegian, Hardanger Bride; Persian; Scottish; Spanish, Basque Country, Salonica, Toreador; Swedish; Swiss; and Welsh.

Saalfield published a cloth book entitled BABIES OF ALL NATIONS, containing six cutout dolls representing six nations.

Shackman advertised dolls dressed in Dutch, Indian, Italian, Japanese and Swiss costumes.

1911–13: *Steiff* dressed dolls to represent various countries and occupations in those countries.

1912: LESLIE'S ILLUSTRATED WEEKLY NEWSPAPER contained the following article, "Where Santa Claus Buys His Dolls": "A special branch of the industry is devoted to making dresses and hats. . . . The woman in charge is ever on the alert for novelties, and this year the 'character doll' has given her no little study. These dolls are made to represent different nations. They are clothed in the picturesque costumes worn in Germany and other European countries before the French fashions spread over the world, and the doll dressmakers have been compelled to study various museums of costumes in order to fashion the proper dresses. Dolls of this type have an educational value and will likely prove popular."

The dolls pictured were dressed as a Bavarian boy and girl; two Swiss women, one in a Berne costume; a Helgoland woman; a nursemaid with an infant, dressed as a North Frisian (German) girl; and an almost naked black doll which was described as, "Home-made doll which a firm is now manufacturing."

1913: TOYS AND NOVELTIES reported, "In England and on the continent many schools are equipped with complete sets of national dolls each clothed according to the prevailing fashion of that country."

Another article in TOYS AND NOVELTIES stated: "A great many doll museums have sprung into existence, the first one ever organized being in Paris. Here the children are taught the customs and costumes of the different countries with far greater success than if they learned their lesson from pictures and books. [This probably refers to Mlle. Koenig's museum.]

"In Constantinople there is a large collection of wooden dolls which present a very weird appearance, but they were made to represent all the trades and professions of the city, as well as the officials at court in various attire. But the absence of any woman in this array is very apparent. . . .

"The North American Indians have quite a number of toys, the dolls made of the bark of trees, clay, rags and wood. . . .

"The well known roly-poly doll . . . is the oldest known doll in China, and it is also seen in Korea, Japan and India, as well as all of the Western countries. . . .

"The little Korean girls make their own dolls from a bamboo stem and wisps of grass which are especially prepared for the purpose, and this is stuck into the top of the bamboo to represent hair, and a sort of white paste or powder does duty for the face, and this crude skeleton is then dressed and the effect is truly astonishing.

". . . The dolls of India which are intended as toys for the children, are made of linen with painted or embroidered features and have cotton hair, and often their clothes are very elaborate, the women wearing nose-rings and ornate head-gear, the men, ear-rings and fancy slippers."

Liberty & Co. advertised dolls dressed as East Indians, Eskimos, Laplanders, and Russians.

1914: *Carson, Pirie, Scott & Co.* advertised dolls dressed in "Old World Costumes."

1918: *Printemps* advertised bisque-head dolls in Alsatian attire. Six hts. 21, 25, 28, 30, 32, and 35 cm. (8½, 10, 11, 12, 12½, and 14 in.); priced 39¢ to $1.50. Also there were Alsatian *Yerri & Suzel* and Japanese dolls. (See also **Schoenhut.**)

1920 and later: *Lenci* dressed many of their dolls in regional costumes of people from all over the World.

1921: Both *Lotte Pritzel* and *Erna Pinner* created art dolls that represented figures from the Far East.

1922: *Averill Manufacturing Co.* dressed dolls in Irish costumes.

Mawaphil dressed dolls in Dutch costumes.

Sardeau dressed dolls in Dutch, Romany and Russian costumes.

La Salle & Koch in Toledo, Ohio, showed dolls dressed as a Hopi Indian maiden, a Javanese in a batik creation, a Chinese, a Japanese, and a peasant bride. It is not certain where these dolls were dressed.

1923: Carson, Pirie, Scott had a "well-known Chicago artist" dress dolls in regional costumes which cost as much as $25.00. The dolls, made of beaverboard, were jointed at the shoulders and hips.

A catalog of *Hitz, Jacobs and Kassler* listed turned, carved and handpainted wooden dolls dressed in various regional costumes. Hts. 6 and 9 in. (15 and 23 cm.).

1925: PLAYTHINGS reported that in London dolls dressed as various nationalities, American, French, English, Dutch, German, Swiss, and so forth, had soft bodies with wobbling necks. Some of the larger sizes weighed nearly three pounds.

Shackman advertised an all-celluloid Chinese girl doll, ht. 2¾ in. (7 cm.). All-bisque dolls included Japanese Girl, Swedish girl, Dutch boy, Spanish Toreador, and Turk with fez and sword, in crocheted costumes, ht. 1½ in. (4 cm.).

1926: PLAYTHINGS reported that an American collector on a round the world cruise found that, "in a few years, unless some philanthropist sets to work the native doll will be extinct as the dodo. . . .

"Native dolls were available to both China and Japan, and a choice of costume is possible.

"The first member of Mrs. Evan's League of Nations came from Madeira where a gaily dressed doll was picked up in a shop. Her bandanna head dress and abbreviated skirt of vivid red recall to her the native women seen on the streets of that picturesque town. At Algiers the second doll joined. Yellow pantaloons harmonized with the golden head dress from which a white veil floats. She is probably bedecked in her bridal finery.

"France added a chic lady in magenta sports attire, her face being cleverly painted on nude georgette and her hands and feet cunningly contrived of a material in flesh tone.

"Naples contributed this little girl in a bright blue skirt and handsomely embroidered apron. . . .

"The lady of Cairo wears a black dress and a scarf over her head, her eyes are visable but not her profile, for a brass nose ornament fastened to the yashmak conceals her profile most effectively.

"No native doll awarded my efforts in Bombay. . . .

"A Parsee woman . . . wears a green dress of embroidered georgette richly trimmed with gold braid. The dress is cut so that the train extends over the head and serves as a head dress.

"Number 7 is a Ceylon woman made and sold by school children on the streets of Colombo. Dressed as a Singhalese bride in voluminous skirt of yellow trimmed with gold paper she presents a unique picture. A short veil falls upon her white bouffant sleeves. The Javanesque doll is of gilded wood. The face is painted in accordance with the Javaness idea of beauty, and the arrangement of the hair has been carved and painted. Batik material is used for the dress which resembles an evening gown in that there is little above the waist. Two strips of cloth crossing behind the head serve as the bodice.

"Manila supplied another wooden doll an exact reproduction . . . of the women seen on the streets. Even the color of the skin and the straight black hair have been successfully imitated. A short-sleeved waist of the blue pineapple cloth and a skirt of printed cotton constitute the costume. A long printed train which the lady holds daintily on the tip of her fingers. . . .

"Hong Kong is represented by a doll in blue trousers and coat. Shanghai by a woman of high estate wearing an elegantly embroidered trouser and jacket suit with head dress trimmed in spray pearls. The Japanese doll came from Kiobe and is the typical doll we know, straight black hair cut across the forehead, slanting eyes and painted face."

1928: *Gerzon* advertised dolls dressed in the Dutch costumes of Goes, Marken or Volendam. Ht. 24 cm. (9½ in.).

1930: Gerzon advertised dolls similar to those offered in 1928 except the height was 35 cm. (14 in.). Lenci dressed a large number of their series 300 dolls in regional costumes. These dolls with hollow felt torsos were dressed as boy and girl pairs of Argentina, France, Eastern Europe, Holland, Lapland, the Orient, Russia, Scandinavia, Scotland, Spain, Turkey, Tyrol, and elsewhere. There were also ethnic dolls of Africa and the Orient. (See also names of individual Nations, **Douwes, Eskimo, French Regional Costume Dolls, Bécassine, Indian,** and **Oriental** as well as **Collections of Dolls** and **International Dolls.**)

Regniez, 1863 and earlier. France. Sold dolls and failed in this year according to Mme. Florence Poisson, curator of the Roybet Fould Museum.

Reich, Charles and Samuel. See Republic Doll & Toy Corp.

Reich, Ernst, Co. 1922. Chicago, Ill. Imported various kinds of German dolls including "Bobbed Hair Blondes with the mischievous eyes."

Reich, Goldmann & Co. 1890–1927. Offenbach, Germany. Made celluloid child and bent limb baby dolls. *Carl Stahl* was their Berlin agent.

Reichenauer, Anton. 1853 and probably other years. Vienna. Made dolls.

Reideler, A. 1880–1927. Königsee, Thür. Manufactured porcelain (china and bisque) dolls including all-bisque and all-china dolls. The dolls came dressed or undressed, most of them on cloth bodies.

Rein, Alex, & Co. 1926. New York City. Manufactured dies and molds for making dolls by the hot press method.

Reinecke, Otto.[†] See **Crämer & Héron.**

Reiner Manufacturing Co. 1927–29. Boonton, N.J. Created a line of dolls. J. L. Jacobi was their Denver, Colo., representative.

1929: Advertised a plush doll with a composition face and mitten hands.

Reinhardt, Christian. 1898. Neustadt near Coburg, Thür. Made dolls.

2187. Papier-mâché head with molded braided bun and comb in the bun, painted blue eyes, closed mouth. Original regional costume, similar to that in Ill. 2188 but an earlier hair style. The body construction also is similar suggesting that the heads were imported and the bodies and costumes were made locally. H. 6¼ in. (16 cm.). *Coleman Collection.*

2188A & B. Slightly pinkish china shoulder head, molded hair with a bun; brushmarks, molded and painted features, cloth body with white kid paddle shaped hands. Original regional clothes. H. 8½ in. (21.5 cm.). H. of shoulder head 2½ in. (6.5 cm.). *Coleman Collection.*

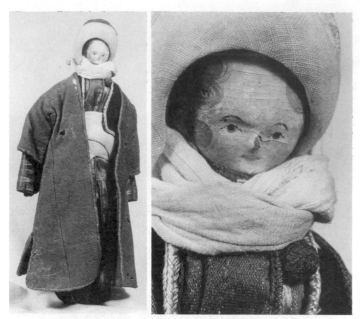

2189A & B. Peg Wooden doll in regional costume of an Arab, has a tuck comb-like headwear, brushmarks, blue painted eyes, and a closed mouth. Original costume. H. 13 in. (33 cm.). *Coleman Collection.*

2190A & B. Doll dressed in a regional costume representing a Greek of the mid 1800s. It has a composition head with molded and painted hair and features. The black hair has a bun in back. The body is wooden jointed with pegs. Original clothes. H. 16 in. (40.5 cm.). *Coleman Collection.*

2191. Papier-mâché head doll in regional costume probably of one of the French colonies. There is a very thin coating of wax over this papier-mâché. The dark brown hair is inserted in a slit in the top of the head. It has painted blue eyes, a closed mouth, and a kid body. Original clothes. H. 11 in. (28 cm.). *Courtesy of Cherry Bou*

2192. China shoulder head doll dressed in a regional costume has molded black hair in rolls in front and curls, ribbons and bow in back. The eyes are painted blue and the mouth is closed. The kid body is not jointed. Original clothes may represent a peasant costume of Germany in the 1870s when this doll was probably new. H. 12¼ in. (31 cm.). *Coleman Collection.*

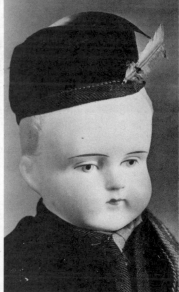

2193A & B. Bisque head doll wears a Royal Stewart tartan costume with black velvet coat and cap. Brown leather square toed slippers with buckles; knee socks are made of the same material as the kilt. Green silk ribbon trims the socks, side of the kilt and forms a bow tie at the neck. The doll's body of white kid with shapely rear made with three vertical seams and one seam around the waist. The body is without gussets. The separate fingers are stiffened with wire. H. 12½ in. (31.5 cm.). *Coleman Collection.*

2195. Regional costume on a bisque head doll with a blond wig, having a braid down the back, stationary brown glass eyes, pierced ears, closed mouth, and bisque forearms. The head and arms probably were made by Simon & Halbig. Original clothes. H. 8 in. (20.5 cm.). *Courtesy of June Jeffcott.*

2194. Fashion-type bisque head doll in regional costume. It has a brown human hair wig, stationary blue glass eyes, pierced ears, a closed mouth, socket head on a shoulder plate, and kid body. Original clothes with red predominating. The blouse is cotton, the bodice is felt, the skirt wool, cotton apron, cotton stockings, and black felt shoes. H. 13 in. (33 cm.). *Courtesy of Mike White.*

2196. Papier-mâché shoulder headed doll with black pupilless eyes. Body is cloth and the arms are wood. It is labeled as representing a fisherwoman of Marken. The hair is attached to the cap. This doll is similar to the one shown in Ill. 382 in the first COLLECTOR'S ENCYCLOPEDIA OF DOLLS, even to the bow on the apron in front. Dolls similar to this were part of the collection of Mrs. Washington Hesing. H. 10 in. (25.5 cm.). *Coleman Collection.*

2197. Doll in regional costume with a bisque head made by Armand Marseille. It has a wig, with multiple braids to which disk coins are attached, brown glass eyes, open mouth with teeth, a composition shoulder plate, and composition arms and legs. The body is pink cloth. Original clothes, representing a Near Eastern girl (possibly a bride with her dowry of coins.) Mark on head: "1894 A.M. DEP//Made in Germany 3½." H. 17 in. (43 cm.). *Courtesy of Richard Withington. Photo by Barbara Jendrick.*

2198. Regional costume on a bisque head doll with a blond wig, glass eyes, pierced ears, open mouth with teeth, and a ball jointed composition body. Original clothes. Mark: "1009 //Simon & Halbig//Germany//S & H." H. 14 in. (35.5 cm.). *Courtesy of Kay Orth. Photo by Bob Rozek.*

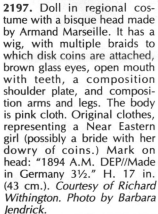

2199. All-bisque dolls in original regional costumes with molded footwear. The Alsatian girl on the left has a wig, painted eyes and a swivel neck. H. 3¾ in. (9.5 cm.). *Courtesy of Sotheby Parke Bernet Inc., N.Y.*

2202. Regional costume doll shown in THE STRAND MAGA-ZINE, September, 1902, and identified as in the collection of Mrs. Hesing of Chicago. This doll is dressed in furs and represents a gentleman in Hammerfest, Lapland, "the most northerly town in the world."

2200. Felt face doll with felt hair, glass eyes, painted features including a mustache. The body is cloth with felt hands; dressed as a South American Gaucho with its accoutrements such as spurs, a bolo and so forth. H. 13 in. (33 cm.). *Coleman Collection.*

2201. Lenci felt doll dressed as a Gaucho. This Series 300 doll has hair attached in strips, painted eyes looking to the side, closed mouth, and a hollow body, original clothes. H. 17½ in. (44.5 cm.). *Courtesy of Sotheby Parke Bernet Inc., N.Y.*

Reinhardt, Ernst. Late 1890s–1930 and possibly later. Sonneberg, Thür.; Philadelphia, Pa.; East Liverpool, Ohio; Irvington, Metuchen and Perth Amboy, N.J. Made composition dolls and bisque heads for dolls. The bisque heads usually were marked either E. R. or Reinhardt. Many of the dolls were dressed in German regional costumes based on the illustrations of *Albert Kretschmer* published after 1888 in DEUTSCHE VOLKSTRACTEN. This book with 90 large chromo-lithographic illustrations was brought to America when the Reinhardt family emigrated around 1909. It was considered a family treasure and was inherited by Ernst Reinhardt's eldest son, Herman. While still in Germany, Ernst Reinhardt applied for several German patents pertaining to dolls' eyes. There were two D.R.G.M. patents in 1904, one (D.R.P.) patent in 1906 and one (D.R.G.M.) patent in 1908.

1913: TOYS AND NOVELTIES announced the opening of the Philadelphia Dressed Doll Co., located near Wayne Junction, an important railroad junction; its proprietor was Ernst Reinhardt. He produced about 50,000 dolls a year and sold only wholesale. He made his own dolls, even his own molds for the dolls.

1917: TOYS AND NOVELTIES stated that: "One of Germany's greatest industries—in which she had a virtual monopoly for years—will soon be lost to the German people unless the war is speedily settled, according to Ernest Reinhart *[sic]*, formerly of Thüringer, Germany. Reinhart has just established a big plant at East Liverpool, Ohio, for the manufacture of bisc baby doll heads, a new industry in this country."

This was indeed the beginning of the manufacture of

2203. Mark on bisque heads made by Ernst Reinhardt.

bisque dolls' heads commercially in America. Reinhardt's production began in 1916 and was two years prior to Fulper's production.★

Reinhardt, Moritz. 1898. Neustadt near Coburg, Thür. Made dolls.

Reinhardt. See **Segitz & Reinhardt.**

Reinicke, W. 1926. Hamburg, Germany. Advertised *Hansa* dolls with either celluloid or bisque heads. These were probably made by *Buschow & Beck.*

Reisenbaby (Traveling Baby). 1912. Name used by *Kley & Hahn* for a doll.

Reisenweber. 1898. Steinach, Thür. Made dolls.

Reisenweber, Christoph. 1918–28. Steinach, Thür. Made dolls.

1926: Advertised Art dolls. London agent was *Cowan, de Groot.*★

Reisman, Barron (&) Co. 1914–30 and later. New York City. Manufactured composition dolls and dolls' heads which they claimed would not peel. Most of their dolls were on cloth bodies and were dressed.

1914: E. Matty Reisman founded his own firm as an agent.

1920: Advertised 125 style nos. The dolls had molded hair or wigs, painted eyes or sleeping eyes, straight limbs or curved limbs. They were dressed as boys, girls or babies. Hts. 10 to 30 in. (25.5 to 76 cm.); priced 25¢ to $3.00. Reisman, Barron Co. obtained toddler dolls from the *American Bisque Doll Co.*

1922: Advertised 200 style nos. including musical dolls. The company had a new factory.

1923: Advertised 250 style nos.; One of the novelty dolls wore horn-rimmed glasses on its nose. *Mama* dolls selling for 25¢ to $1.00 were the most popular dolls.

1926: Member of the *American Doll Manufacturers' Association.* Many new dolls were introduced. Total styles amounted to 300 nos. A new factory was opened. E. Reisman and Matt Reisman were in charge.

1927: There were two separate factories under one roof. Each factory had its own management and work force. One factory made R-B popular-priced dolls consisting of over 100 styles, retailing for $1.00. Some of these dolls were described as having bisque heads, wigs, sleeping eyes and composition legs. The other factory made a new Quality line of dolls called *Sunshine Dolls.* Both factories appear to have made dolls in the *Adora-Belle* line which had featherweight bodies filled with kapok. Riesman, Barron Co. was licensed by *Voices, Inc.* to use their patented mama voices and criers in the dolls. Baby dolls including infant and Mama dolls were the most popular types and there were new wardrobes for dolls. Hts. 15 to 26 in. (38 to 66 cm.).

1928: Advertised 300 regular nos. A new range of dolls wore hats and coats or sweater suits. Another innovation was the introduction of two-faced character dolls including a two-faced clown. Dolly Boudoir, a boxed set, was also new. There were about 150 nos. of Mama dolls, most of them with composition arms and legs. Hts. 16 to 28 in. (40.5 to 71 cm.). One of the Adora-Belle baby dolls had a smiling face. Others have animals embroidered around their dress hem. One baby doll was packed in a "Charleston over-night bag."

1929: Advertised *Our Playmate* dolls, *Playmates, Co-Ed Kids* and *Folly Dollies.* The baby dolls were standing, sitting, laughing, crying, or sleeping. The child dolls wore windbreaker coats and matching hats or slickers or rubber aprons; others were dressed as school girls with tiny crayons and drawing pads. Many of the dolls wore angora knitted outfits or organdy dresses.

1930: Advertised over 300 popular priced nos. including personality dolls, ensemble dolls, featherweight dolls stuffed with kapok, Folly Dollies, school girl, and infant dolls. A new featured doll had a mohair ringlet wig, sleeping eyes, teeth, tongue, a mama voice and was dressed in organdy. Ht. 23 in. (58.5 cm.); priced $5.00.★

Reismann, Franz. Ca. 1916. Sculptured the *Inge* and *Harald* portrait doll heads for *Wagner & Zetzsche.* These represented Zetzsche's children.

Reissmann, Albert. 1881–1930 and later. Neustadt near Coburg. Thür. and later Bavaria. Made dolls.

Rejall (Reiall), Johannes. 1922–23. Weisser Hirsch near Dresden, Saxony. Obtained a German patent (D.R.P.) for a doll with a metal skeleton.★

Reliable Doll & Toy Manufacturing Co. 1923–24. New York City. Manufactured composition dolls, including *Mama* dolls and parts of dolls.

1924: Mama dolls came with or without wigs and with composition legs. Dolls were 13 to 28 in. (33 to 71 cm.) tall; priced $1.00 to $5.00. They claimed they were the largest supply house of dolls' heads and parts to doll factories.

Reliable Toy Co. 1920–25 and later. Toronto, Canada. A

bent limb baby doll had molded hair with yarn tufts and was labeled "A Reliable Doll Made in Canada."★

Reliance Novelty Co. 1913–18. New York City. Made dolls.

1918: Dolls had mohair wigs, cork stuffing and inside joints.★

Reliance Rubber Co. 1925. London. Advertised dolls.

Reliance Works. See **Knight Bros. & Cooper.**

Religious Costumes. Dolls have been dressed in the costumes of various religious orders or sects and used as playthings. This was especially true for dolls representing nuns, many of which were dressed in convents and sold to raise money. Dolls have also been dressed as ministers, priests, bishops and so forth. This is especially true for dolls in wedding or coronation groups. These must not be confused with the dolls portraying Saints or Gods and used for religious purposes.

Several religious sects that wore special costumes such as the Amish, Moravians, Quakers and Shakers had dolls dressed in these costumes. Some of these dolls were played with by the children of the particular sect and others were made for tourists or for examples to show to school children. Large manufacturers of dolls often dressed some of their dolls in religious costumes, especially Quaker attire. Dolls in the Philadelphia area were frequently dressed as Quakers.

1700s or before. Many dolls were dressed as nuns in this period as shown by the number of famous paintings or prints of children holding such dolls for example the 1760s painting by Jean Baptiste Siméon Chardin (1699–1779).

1800s and early 1900s. Papier-mâché head dolls were dressed as nuns and novitiates who worked as sisters in the religious hospitals in Lyon, France.

1897: *Au Paradis des Enfants* advertised *Mignonnettes* dressed in religious costumes. (See THE COLLECTOR'S BOOK OF DOLLS' CLOTHES, Ill. 441.)

1908: Dolls dressed in Shaker outfits were advertised in LADIES' HOME JOURNAL and in catalogs. THE LADIES' HOME JOURNAL described the German bisque-head dolls dressed by the Shakers of Mount Lebanon, N.Y., as wearing a dress of mohair with long sleeves, a full pleated ankle

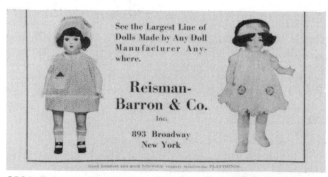

2204. Reisman, Barron Co. advertisement for dolls as shown in PLAYTHINGS, July, 1927. The Mama dolls appear to have composition heads, arms and legs. Mark: Ill. 15.

2205. All-composition doll made by Reliable. It is brown in color and has a wig, painted eyes and an original pseudo American Indian costume with a blue flannel jacket and red cotton trousers. Mark embossed on back of neck "RELIABLE//MADE IN CANADA." H. 12½ in. (31.5 cm.). *Courtesy of Richard Withington. Photo by Barbara Jendrick.*

length skirt and a silk kerchief. The coal-scuttle shaped summer bonnet was made of straw and lawn. Similar summer bonnets for dolls were made as late as the 1950s at least. For winter there was a heavy cloak (cape with a deep collar) that covered the shoulders and the cloak extended to the mid-calf of the legs. A hood was tied with a ribbon bow at the neckline. The hood was somewhat similar in shape to the summer bonnet.

Dolls made by Shakers in Alfred, Maine, included a double headed doll, one head white and one head black. The dolls made in Alfred were packed in boxes that bore the label "Shaker Goods, Alfred, Me."

1909: F. Kaempff⁺ dressed dolls as Quakers.

1912–14: *Horsman* dressed dolls as Quakers.

1913: *Liberty & Co.* sold dolls dressed as Quakers (See Ill. 1672).

1914: *Effanbee* advertised a doll called the Catholic Sister.

1915: *American Art Dolls* were dressed as Quakers.

1917–19: *Knight Bros. & Cooper* in England dressed dolls as Quakers.

1919–20: *Jessie M. Raleigh* dressed dolls as Quakers.

1930: *Penn Stuffed Toy Co.* dressed dolls as Quakers.

2206. Papier-mâché shoulder head doll dressed as a Quaker has a wig, painted eyes, closed mouth, and a kid body. Original costume of the mid-1800s. *Courtesy of the late Estelle Winthrop.*

Our doll again, dressed in a typical Shaker dress of mohair with silk kerchief. The bonnet is for summer, in straw and lawn.

An exact reproduction of the Shaker costume is shown in this little doll. Her winter cloak protects her as completely as does that of her grown-up sister.

2207. Dolls dressed in Shaker clothes for summer and winter as shown in the LADIES' HOME JOURNAL, 1908. The summer dress is made of mohair with a silk kerchief and the summer bonnet is made of straw and lawn. The winter cloak has a hood and wide collar.

Remdeo. 1914–16 and probably later. Louvain, Belgium. Name of a factory for making dolls, founded by the Countess de Mérode. It employed people wounded or harmed in the war. It was awarded a Grand Prize at an exhibit to raise money for the children of Belgian soldiers.

Remignard, Frédéric. 1884–99. Paris. Made dolls. Sometimes he used the monogram F. F. R. intertwined.

1899: Joined the *Société Française de Fabrication de Bébés & Jouets* (S.F.B.J.), granting them his rights to *Le Petit Chérubin.*★

Remond. See **Guillard, François.**

Rempel, Georg. 1904–27. Sonneberg, Thür. Applied for seven German patents (D.R.G.M.) for dolls.

Rempel & Breitung. 1920–30 and later. Sonneberg, Thür. Handled celluloid dolls and dolls' heads made by *Rheinische Gummi und Celluloid Fabrik Co.* as well as bisque heads, wigs, bodies and other items used by doll hospitals.

28
117
K.B
1¼

2208. Mark found on the bisque head of a doll which was probably produced by Rempel & Breitung.

Renault & Bon-Dufour. 1906–30 and later. Paris. Specialized in composition dolls, especially large ones similar to the one in Ill. 944. Member of the *Chambre Syndicale.* Made *Bébés Culotte,* bébé in *swaddling clothes, clowns, Mignonnettes* and soldiers.★

Renou, L. See **Dehais.**

Rentsch, E. H. 1906. Altona, Germany. Made dolls' wigs including one named "Miss Alice Roosevelt."

Renwick, Anna C. 1914–15. Flushing, N.Y. Obtained a U.S. patent for dolls.

Repairing Dolls. Make as few repairs as possible; many dolls have lost their value and their charm by repainting, rewaxing or re-dressing. Extensive repairs transform the antique doll into a modern imitation of an old doll, no matter how expertly the repairs are done. Of course there are certain repairs that may be necessary such as replacing a finger, putting a broken head together, replacing a lost eye, and so forth. Dolls have had to undergo similar repairs in the past and many of our dolls have heads that were replaced when the original owner broke the head. A badly smashed head, if it should be replaced, should have a duplicate head of the same vintage. It is not always easy to find such a head but patience and continued search will usually provide an exact antique duplicate. Replacing a broken antique head or other part of the doll with a modern reproduction is not a valid solution.

Most of the dolls on the market today have been re-dressed or are nude. A re-dressed doll even when old materials were used is still a re-dressed doll. The next best thing to original clothes is to find clothes that fit the doll and were contemporary as to period with the doll. Most dolls originally had several outfits but clothes were often separated from the doll and frequently one finds dolls' clothes offered for sale. If one has a fair sized collection there will nearly always be a doll that will fit those antique garments if the doll and the garments are of the same period and the same relative height. It is also necessary for the clothes to have belonged to a similar type doll; for example, wax dolls were plumper than wooden dolls in the same era and require a wider garment. It is necessary to have a knowledge of the correct period clothes for the various dolls and this information is available in THE COLLECTOR'S BOOK OF DOLLS' CLOTHES. Most old clothes for dolls except shoes, are still relatively reasonable and take little storage space so that if one has a supply of the old clothes on hand often a new antique acquisition can be supplied with contemporary clothes without further searching. Clothes for dolls prior to 1850 are extremely difficult to find and generally expensive. The elaborate dresses for the so-called lady fashion dolls and French Bébés can be found but their high price makes it necessary to know what size you seek. It has been found that the 22 in. (56 cm.) bisque head doll on a ball jointed composition body is one that old clothes seem to fit frequently.

Old leather shoes are relatively expensive and it is well to know the size of the foot on the doll that needs shoes. All too often one shoe has been lost but finding an exact mate is almost an impossible task; it seems to be easier to find a similar pair of old shoes.

Repairing dolls has been done throughout the ages and the following comments were made by those who did this work for the original owners many years ago.

1901: A dolls' hospital in New York City was run by a "German woman, wife of a man who made dolls in Saxony. 'Putting a finger on' and 'waxing a face over' are the two most difficult operations in doll surgery. The doctor treats fractures and wounds of every description and importers who send dolls, damaged in transportation, are very particular that dolly's new head, hand or hair shall match the rest of her; but children are her most numerous, and also her most exacting patrons—especially in the matter of heads. . . . They are not compared with the old head, but with the old head as it was when the doll was found in the Christmas stocking. That is the doll they want again."

1904: LADIES' HOME JOURNAL reported, "I went to a large toy shop and asked the proprietor if he had any dolls that needed mending or dressing up for the next holiday season. He . . . said that he had quite a number that were a loss which he would be glad if I could make salable. . . . he agreed to furnish materials for clothes, etc. A room in my home was soon turned into a workshop for mending forlorn dolls, and there I transformed them into pretty ladies and gentlemen, funny darkies, a Santa Claus and a Fairy Queen. . . . I earned $25.00 with no capital save ingenuity, patience, and determination."

1913: TOYS AND NOVELTIES reported on two toy shops that repaired dolls. One was run by E. C. Zimmer who stated: "On March 1, 1912, I opened the Tekna Shop in Omaha Neb., . . . Knowing that it was impossible to buy dolls and similar articles except during the holiday season, I decided to install a complete doll department to be maintained the year around. . . . When I was planning the doll department it occurred to me that a fully equipped doll hospital was an institution long needed in Omaha. . . . There were periods during the past fall and early winter when I found it necessary to work a force of five repairers day and night. In fact, I have already made arrangements to increase my facilities so that I will be in a position to handle repairs on 75 or more dolls a day during the present year. . . .

"When little Miss Dollie arrives she may be in a dozen pieces, or merely just have her joints all out of kilter, or an eye or a finger gone. . . . Dollie may need some new curls, which is a very simple operation, or an eye or two fastened back into her head. This latter is the most stylish ailment a doll can have, for more dolls lose their eyes than there are people who have appendicitis.

"If the doll has to have but one eye replaced, it is really quite a serious matter. She may be compelled to lose her whole head for a while, or if her head is not taken off in the operation she may temporarily lose her arms before her eyes can be replaced. But if she is just an ordinary kind of a doll, with a cavity in the back of her head, covered with a pretty wig, the operation of replacing her optics will be a simple matter.

"Dollie may only need her joints tightened up, in which case she will need to be 'restrung.' . . .

"Another common ailment is loss of sawdust, especially if she has a kid body, for she must use her various joints to please her little mother; and this vigorous exercise in time wears the kid away where the wire springs come through, and Dollie consequently loses some of her plumpness. At present the doll who is made of 'composition' with wooden joints is considered the most stylish, and strange to relate, the most practical.

"Just now there is a doll in the hospital because she has lost her voice. She does not say 'papa' and 'mamma' in the right key any more, and this distresses herself and family very much. She is French by birth, and perhaps the fresh western air of America, combined with her mamma's strenuous affection does not altogether agree with her delicate vocal organs. . . .

"Recently a well known Omaha woman brought a doll to be rejuvenated that had belonged to her grandmother. Its once fair complexion and pretty hands had turned yellow with age, its joints were stiff and refused to do their duty—in fact some of its fingers were gone, but when this ancient doll was discharged from the hospital as well and sound, she looked brand-new. . . .

"A recent distinguished patient was called the 'flirting doll' by the other doll patients. She is tall, majestic looking and a blonde, but she simply could not make her eyes behave. When they were obedient to her whims they could open and close in the style of the ordinary 'open-and-shut-eye doll,' and also roll them from right to left and left to right in a very flirty manner.

"But one day she lost some of her pretty eyelashes and her eyes refused to flirt artistically, so off to the hospital she was bundled. Now she is able to resume her flirting. . . .

"Broken heads and necks are also 'fixed up' daily. The fact that Dollie's head may be in seven or a dozen pieces only adds romance to Miss Dollie's career. 'She would not be the same child, if she had a new head put on,' explained one little mother. 'Don't you think you were rather careless to let your dollie's head get broken?' 'No,' she replied, 'company did it.'

"Dolls and their maternal ancestors are not in the least conventional in regard to the clothes they wear while patients at the doll hospital. If they are not too badly smashed, they may arrive in satin and velvet coronation gowns, bearing the impress of Paris, a chiffon evening gown, organdy and ribbon creations of a 'Peter Tompkins' dress. Sometimes a little mamma thinks her invalid child will be more comfortable in a 'nighty,' and sometimes—it is sad but true—their children are sent to the hospital garbed only in a newspaper.

"Dolls of all nationalities, colors, sizes and ages are received at the doll hospital. Recently a beautiful brown baby doll came to the hospital for repairs.

"Did you know that dolls have different seasons of popularity? It is so just the same. In the summer time the rag doll reigns almost supreme. No scientific reason has been found for this, but during the vacation period a stiff, stylishly dressed doll, that may have furnished hours of pleasure in the winter, is laid away, and the rag baby takes her place.

"Maybe it is so because the rag baby does not need so much care in the summer time—she may be left outdoors in the dew or rainstorm and recover from the exposure just as smiling and trim as ever. Rag dollie may be left . . . to bleach on the seashore, but when her little mother wants her, she is sure to find her intact and as loving as ever."

According to TOYS AND NOVELTIES in 1913 there was a trend towards toy stores including the repairing of dolls among their services.

Another toy store, owned by the *Reccius Brothers* in Louisville, Ky., repaired dolls and described their operations:

". . . there is so much sentiment stored up in the dolly, . . . that discarding a broken doll is almost comparable to abandoning a sure-enough baby. Consequently every household has its complement of time-worn dolls which are dearer to their little owners than the finest of new dolls could be.

"Realizing this feature a good many enterprising dealers have established 'doll hospitals'—to call them repair shops would be to refuse to recognize the sentiment which creates the necessity for the service. . . . The Reccius Brothers, John and Michael, have been identified with the trade in toys and novelties all their lives, a matter of 40 years, and are among the best-known men in Louisville. 'Mr. Mike' Reccius has been identified as a local Santa Claus for years and years. . . .

"The doll hospital occupies half of the store owned by Reccius Brothers. . . . Four girls are paid to confine their attention to doll surgery.

". . . Body repairs are made very infrequently, for doll

bodies as a rule are indestructible nowadays, and it is the limbs and skulls of the manikins which suffer the hard knocks.

". . . There are replacements of arms, legs and heads, readjustments for the eyes and mechanical speaking apparatus, attention to hair dressing and other features which are best taken care of by girls and which savor of the grown-up beauty parlor. Many orders arrive for doll apparel, all the way from bridal gowns to house dresses.

" '. . . Christmas is harvest time for us [Reccius Bros.], as it is with every other toy dealer, and in connection with the repair department you must remember that it is becoming the practice of many families to have all the old dolls owned by the youngsters put in tip-top condition along with whatever new ones there may be purchased at Yuletide.' "

1927: PLAYTHINGS reported "Every Christmas the Camp Fire Girls collected old dolls, repaired and redressed them and distributed them to thousands of needy children all over the U.S.A."

(See also **Gesland; Marsh; Meier, Harry; Original Condition; Toy Junkery;** and others.)

Repka, Anton. 1907–10. Vienna and Czechoslovakia. Listed in directories under Dolls and Dolls' Heads.

Reproductions. Since about 1970 a tremendous number of reproduction dolls have appeared on the market. With the introduction of commercial molds the number of people making bisque reproduction dolls has become large. Some are excellent copies and others are less artistic but most of these are well marked with the modern maker's name, and often even the date, which is good. However, there are reproductions that have only the original mark on them, thus indicating a fraudulent intent. Unfortunately it is not always easy to distinguish a well-made reproduction from its original counterpart unless it is marked by the modern maker. (Modern makers should mark their dolls with an incised mark rather than merely painting the mark on the doll's head, for the mark can be removed.)

Some collectors claim that they cannot afford to buy antique dolls and therefore must buy reproductions. This may be true for dolls currently in vogue such as bisque head French type bébés. However, many of the dolls made during the same period as the bébés or even much earlier would actually cost less than a reproduction bisque head French Bébé or Character doll. As in all works of art the genuine antique has a much greater artistic and intrinsic value than the reproduction.

Recently it has been discovered that many of the cloth dolls with pressed faces were made by using a bisque doll's head as the model from which the mold was made. Technically this would be a reproduction but because of the difference in the material of the doll, the cloth doll seems to bear little resemblance to the original bisque head. Dolls made in this manner include the *Martha Chase* dolls, the *Flora* dolls and probably others. These dolls were properly marked by their maker.

In addition the rubber head made by *Goodyear* with the patent extension of 1865, shown in Ill. 659 in the first COLLECTOR'S ENCYCLOPEDIA OF DOLLS, has been found to have its exact counterpart in a bisque shoulder head.

During the late 1930s and through the 1940s *Emma Clear* reproduced many of the china and parian-type heads that were most popular in that era. She marked nearly all of her heads.

In 1955 an article in the ANTIQUES JOURNAL stated, "I have been told on good authority that a number of French Exporters are assembling French dolls and presenting them for what they are not, originals or genuine." It should be remembered that the *Société Française de Fabrication de Bébés & Jouets* was still making *Bébés Jumeau* and *Bébés Bru* in the 1950s.

Among the many reproductions on the market in the 1980s are nearly all types of French bébés, kid-body fashion type lady dolls, German character dolls, French and German all-bisque dolls, in fact nearly every type of porcelain doll that was made in the past. Some cloth dolls have been reproduced as well as some wooden and wax dolls. So far reproductions of *British Ceramic* and most composition dolls have not appeared. Many of the wooden dolls have not been reproduced as yet, such as the Door of Hope and the Schoenhut dolls.

Many of the all-bisque and bisque head dolls of the early twentieth century had their approximate height marked on them in centimeters. When they are reproduced the firing shrinkage makes them at least one-tenth smaller than the mark indicates. Among the companies that marked some or all of their dolls with the centimeter height were *Kämmer & Reinhardt, Kestner, Franz Schmidt*.

Practically all of the bisque heads made today have slip that is relatively free of dirt while kiln dirt often is found in antique heads. Prior to about 1890 most of the French bisque heads were pressed. This was also true in Germany at an earlier date, especially for china heads. See *Pressed vers. Poured* for another way of possibly identifying a modern reproduction of an early bisque or china head.

Hopefully nearly all makers of reproductions will be proud of their work and will incise their names or initials. Collectors should shun dolls whose makers do not thus mark their dolls.★

Republic Doll & Toy Corp. 1919–21. New York City. Charles and Samuel Reich made "bisque finish" wood fibre composition dolls.

1919: Made "Salute" in soldier or sailor costume.

1920: Dolls came with or without wigs, bent limb baby bodies or straight legs; some of the dolls wore sweaters and some were dressed in chiffon. One doll type had sleeping eyes, teeth, tongue, and either a mohair or human hair wig.★

Resek (Rezek), Moritz. 1889–1927. Prague, Austria and later Czechoslovakia. Made dolls.

1889: Obtained an Austrian-Hungarian patent for dolls with movable eyes and "unbreakable bodies."

1910–25: Listed in directories under Dolls and Dolls' Heads.

Réservé Bébé. See **Bébé Réservé.**

Ressels. 1900. London. Applied for a German patent (D.R.P.) for dolls.

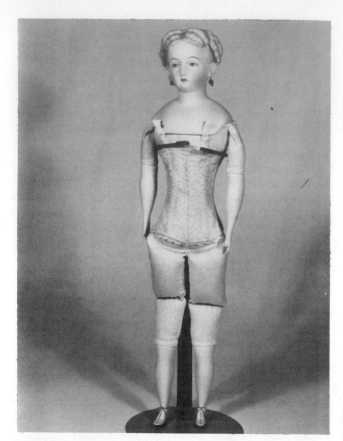

2209A. Reproduction untinted bisque shoulder head with blond hair molded in a classical style, painted eyes, pierced ears, closed mouth and a cloth body with bisque lower arms and legs. Original corset made by Emma Clear. Mark on shoulder " 42 lear." Cloth mark on body. "Humpty Dumpty// Doll Hospital." H. 15½ in. (39.5 cm.). *Courtesy of Richard Withington. Photo by Barbara Jendrick.*

2209B. China spill curl type shoulder head reproduction by Emma Clear in 1947 according to its mark. This is a poured head with stationary glass eyes, pierced ears and a closed mouth. H. 21 in. (53.5 cm.). *Courtesy of Richard Withington. Photo by Barbara Jendrick.*

2210. Reproduction of François Gaultier's bisque head lady dolls. This doll has a cork pate, threaded stationary blue glass eyes, pierced ears, closed mouth and a swivel neck on a bisque shoulder plate. The kid body is gusseted. Mark: "F + G." H. 17½ in. (44.5 cm.). *Courtesy of Sotheby Parke Bernet Inc., N.Y.*

2211. Reproduction brown Bru has a bisque socket head on a bisque shoulder plate of the Bru type and a brown kid gusseted body with brown bisque lower arms. The brown head has a dark wig, stationary brown glass eyes and a Bru type closed mouth. Mark on head, "©larmaid//1962//Bru Jne//8." Mark on shoulder plate: "Bru Jne 8." H. 18 in. (45.5 cm.). *Courtesy of Richard Withington. Photo by Barbara Jendrick.*

$$\mathcal{MR}$$
$$1895$$
$$17^5$$
$$16 \; 3/4$$

2212. Mark used by Moritz Resek on dolls.

Restall Manufacturing Co. 1918 and probably other years. Long Beach, Calif. Made *Bye-Bye Babies* and a new line of dressed dolls made of knitted woolen fabric.

Reumann, Irmgard. 1930 or before. Germany. Created dolls.

Réunis. 1907–24. Paris. Distributed dolls.

Reuss, Georg. 1915. Waltershausen, Thür. Applied for a German patent for a doll's body with a movable chest plate.

Reuther, Franz. 1927. Coburg, Bavaria. Advertised felt dolls and walking dolls of "art leather."

Revalo. 1913–26 and probably later. Line of dolls made by *Gebrüder Ohlhaver.* Revalo is Ohlhaver spelled backwards and omitting the two h's. According to the research of the Ciesliks *Ernst Heubach* made the bisque heads and some of the Revalo dolls were used by *Carl Harmus* and *Johannes Dietrich.* One of these heads has been found on an *Amkid* body made by *Amberg.*

1926: Line advertised as including child dolls, babies, toddlers and dolls' outfits.★

$$10727$$
$$Revalo$$
$$Germany$$
$$7 \; \frac{1}{4}$$

$$Revalo$$
$$3 \; Dep.$$

2213A & B. Marks found on Revalo bisque heads.

Revanc. 1885. Name on the headband of a sailor cap worn by a doll with sleeping eyes and dressed in a sailor suit with long trousers. This doll, advertised by *Bon Marché,* came in three hts. costing 70¢ to $1.28.

Revenus. Early 1800s. Paris. Name of a doll shop that made dolls according to LES JOUJOUX.

Revill, W. E. 1917. Applied for a British patent for making dolls' heads.

Revue Girl. 1927. Name of dolls made by *Eckstein & Co.*

Revue Girls. Name used by *Carl Völker* for dolls, according to the research of the Ciesliks.

Rex Kid. 1914. Composition head doll resembling a *Campbell Kid,* distributed by *Eaton.* It had a cloth body, and wore rompers. Ht. 10½ in. (26.5 cm.); priced 29¢.

Rezek, M. See **Resek, Moritz.**

Rheinboldt et Cie. 1811 and other years. Paris. A doll shop that sold French and German dolls and also made dolls.

Rheinische Gummi und Celluloid Fabrik Co. (Rhénane de Caoutchouc et Celluloid Cie.). 1873–1930 and later. Mannheim-Neckarau, Bavaria. Offices in London, Paris, Berlin and Vienna. Founded by Friedrich Bensinger. At first they made rubber products and in 1880 began to make celluloid products also. Claimed that they were the first factory to make celluloid dolls. Supplied celluloid dolls' parts including heads to *Kämmer & Reinhardt, Buschow & Beck, Kest-*

ner, *König & Wernicke, Bruno Schmidt, Carl Hoffmeister, Wagner & Zetzsche,* and others. The celluloid parts carried either the tortoise (turtle) or tortoise in a diamond mark. The molds were supplied by the other companies who also put the finishing touches on the celluloid head. The Ciesliks reported that *Karl Krausser* designed the celluloid heads for Kämmer & Reinhardt around 1902. Besides supplying other companies, Rheinische Gummi und Celluloid Fabrik Co. made all-celluloid dolls and obtained many patents for their products. They generally marked their dolls and dolls' heads with the height in centimeters.

TOYS AND NOVELTIES in 1920 reported that before 1910 this factory perfected the method of making dolls of pyroxylin plastic (celluloid) by the blowing method. About the same time this was also done by Dr. Harmonica who made animal toys. The patent rights were in dispute for years and finally the issue was decided so that both litigants continued to make toys and to export their celluloid products to America.

1897: Applied for two German patents (D.R.G.M.) for celluloid eyes for dolls. Advertised a swimming doll that moved its legs.

1898: Applied for a German patent (D.R.G.M.) for fastening glass eyes in celluloid dolls' heads.

1899: Advertised dolls with wigs, and hands for jointed dolls. Applied for several German patents both (D.R.P.) and (D.R.G.M.).

1902: Supplied celluloid heads to Kämmer & Reinhardt.

1903: Advertised celluloid socket heads and shoulder heads, heads with sleeping eyes and *Täuflinge.* Applied for a German patent (D.R.G.M.) pertaining to sleeping eyes.

1904: Applied for two German patents (D.R.G.M.) for celluloid dolls; one wore a cloth bathing suit.

1906: Granted a German patent (D.R.P.) for setting glass eyes in a celluloid head.

1910–16: Applied for three German patents (D.R.G.M.) for celluloid dolls or dolls' heads.

1913: Catalog advertised a variety of celluloid dolls and dolls' heads. Hts. for the dolls ranged from 1¼ to 39½ in. (3 to 100 cm.). The various types of celluloid bodies on dolls included ones resembling composition ball-jointed bodies, bent-limb baby bodies, five-piece sitting bodies that could sit on a chair with the feet hanging down, and five-piece standing bodies.

The dolls had either molded hair or wigs. Some dolls came with five heads, some dolls had faces on both back and front. A few dolls were in swaddling clothes. The *Happy Hooligan* series included two tramps and a policeman. Various nations and races were represented by the dolls especially the new dolls.

1920: Moritz Pappe advertised "Tortoise" dolls.

1923: Applied for a German patent (D.R.G.M.) for the joints on a rubber doll. The catalog listed *Max & Moritz, Peterle, Struwwelpeter,* and *Zappel-Philipp.*

1925: Registered the following mark number: 1925 for a character head bent-limb baby with moving arms and legs, ht. 30 cm. (12 in.), or a straight leg character doll jointed at the hips and shoulders, ht. 32 cm. (12½ in.). They also made a character girl's head, ht. 9 cm. (3½ in.) and painted dolls named *Heinz* and *Hilde.*

1926: Applied for a German patent (D.R.G.M.) for a doll's head with sleeping eyes. Made dolls named *Anneliese* and *Putz.*

König & Wernicke advertised cellowachs head dolls. The cellowachs was made by Rheinische Gummi und Celluloid Fabrik Co.

Their agent in Britain, *Punfield* & Barstow, advertised three series of dolls, *Baby, Sweetie* and *Liselotte.*

Sold celluloid and rubber dolls to *Hermann Meyer.*

1927: A new type of celluloid called *Miblu* by Kämmer & Reinhardt was an abbreviation of milk and blood which the substance was supposed to resemble. This was a wax-like celluloid and appears to have been the same or similar to cellowachs.

They claimed that this new kind of celluloid took 40 years of research to perfect and was made by a fully protected patented process. They also advertised that the sleeping eyes in their dolls' heads did not have plaster to hold the eyes.

Made celluloid versions of *Baby Bo Kaye* and *Bonnie Babe.*

Before 1929: Made celluloid head of *Father Knickerbocker* doll made by the *Averill Manufacturing Co.* in their *Madame Hendren* line. Besides the tortoise mark on this doll's head, there is the number 200/14.

1929: Made both rubber and celluloid dolls and dolls' heads as well as parts for dolls. These dolls came dressed or undressed. They were the assignee of a U.S. patent for sleeping eyes, *Albert Beyler* was the inventor. The sole London and Paris agent was *G. Sergent.*

1930: Advertised celluloid bent limb baby dolls, standing dolls and a series of New Born infant dolls.

Rhénane de Caoutchouc et Celluloid Cie. See **Rheinische Gummi und Celluloid Fabrik Co.**

Ribiere, Leger Henri. 1929. Paris. Registered Poupée-Musette as a French trademark for dolls named *Musette.*

Ricaillon. See **Rivaillon.**

Rich, William A. 1926. New York City. Distributed *Blanket Babies* dolls made by the *Wolson Novelty Co.*

Richard. 1916. Name of a felt doll made by *Steiff.*

Richards, Oscar O., & Sons. 1924. England. Made and/or distributed dolls.

Richlin, Mr. See **Acme Toy Manufacturing Co.**

Richmond Hobson Pearson. 1898–99. One of the naval heroes of the Spanish-American War who was represented by a bisque head doll with molded black hair and mustache, painted or glass eyes, closed mouth, on a five-piece composition body, wore a simulation of a U.S. naval officer's uniform. This portrait doll of Pearson was one of a series of dolls representing *Admiral Dewey, Admiral Sampson, Admiral Schley* and *President McKinley.* Hts. 8, 12, and 15½ in. (20.5, 30.5, and 39.5 cm.).

Richter, Franz. 1930 and later. Zschopau, Germany. Made clothes for dolls.

Richter, Friedrich Adolf & Co. (Richter, F. Ad., & Cie.). 1900–30. Rudolstadt, Thür. Factory named Baukastenfabrik made dolls.★

Richter, Rudolf. 1925. Prague, Czechoslovakia. Listed in an Austrian directory under Dolls and Composition Bodies.

Rickertsen, Georg. 1927. Hamburg, Germany. Applied for a German patent (D.R.P.) for a doll with changeable features.

Ride A Cock Horse. Cutout cloth doll in the *Hug-Me-Tight* line, style no. D103/200.

Ridgway. Ca. 1800–1930 and later. Cauldon, Stoke-on-Trent, Staffordshire. Dolls were produced by this factory at various times and *British Ceramic* dolls were made by *S. Hancock & Sons* during World War I.★

2215A & B. All-celluloid doll made by Rheinische Gummi und Celluloid Fabrik Co. has molded hair, painted blue eyes, closed mouth, and joints only at the shoulders. Original clothes. Mark on body: Ill. 2220. H. 32 cm. (corresponding with the 32 in the mark) (12½ in.). *Coleman Collection.*

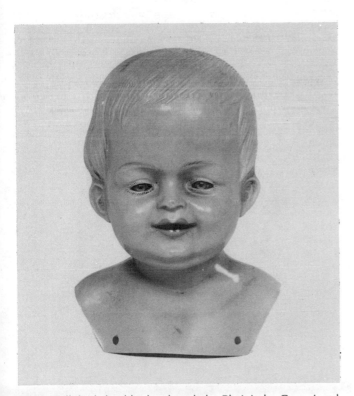

2214. Celluloid shoulder head made by Rheinische Gummi und Celluloid Fabrik Co. It has molded hair, a very high forehead, stationary blue glass eyes and an open-closed mouth with two lower teeth. There is a slight dent on the tip of the nose. The turtle mark does not have the usual diamond around the turtle which may suggest an earlier product. Under the turtle is "SCHUTZE MARKE//11½." H. of head 11½ cm. (4½ in.). *Courtesy of the Margaret Woodbury Strong Museum. Photo by Harry Bickelhaupt.*

2216. All-celluloid doll with the turtle mark of Rheinische Gummi und Celluloid Fabrik Co. It has a brown wig, blue painted eyes, open-closed mouth and the body is jointed at the shoulders and hips. Original regional costume including molded footwear. H. 4 in. (10 cm.). *Coleman Collection.*

2217. All-celluloid doll with painted hair and features and a bent limb baby body made by the Rheinische Gummi und Celluloid Fabrik Co. Mark: Turtle figure. This tiny doll, h. 3 in. (7.5 cm.), is holding an even tinier doll. *Courtesy of Dr. Eva Moskovszky.*

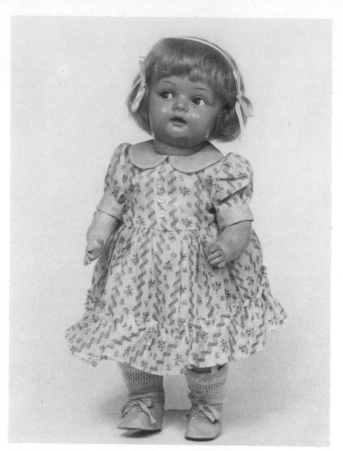

2219A & B. All-celluloid doll made by Rheinische Gummi und Celluloid Fabrik Co. for Kämmer & Reinhardt. It has a socket head with blond hair attached in strips, sleeping and flirting blue glass eyes that move from side to side, and an open mouth with tongue. The body is jointed at the neck, shoulders and hips. One of the arms is a composition replacement. Original clothes. Mark on body: K ☆ R//5. Mark on head: K ☆ R//728/5// GERMANY //38//(turtle mark). H. 38 cm. (15 in.). *Courtesy of the Margaret Woodbury Strong Museum. Photo by Harry Bickelhaupt.*

2218. Advertisement in PLAYTHINGS, December, 1927, for celluloid dolls made by "Rhenish Rubber & Celluloid Co." (Rheinische Gummi und Celluloid Fabrik Co.). The advertisement was placed by Adam Bernhard, the sole New York agent for these dolls.

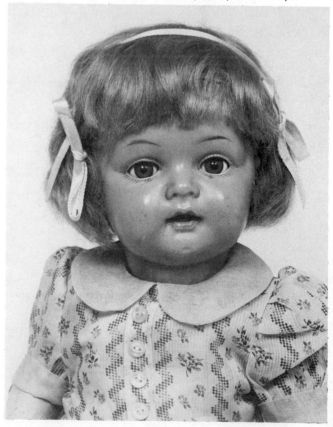

2220

2221

2222

2220–2222. Rheinische Gummi und Celluloid Fabrik Co. marks on celluloid dolls. For a head with the mark in Ill. 2221, made for Kestner, see Ill. 1448.

Ridley E., & Sons. 1884–98. New York City. Distributed dressed and undressed dolls, dolls' heads, dolls' bodies, dolls' clothes including footwear, dolls' jewelry and accessories. The dolls were bisque, china, composition, rubber or wax.

1884: All-bisque and all-china dolls in black or white versions; priced 3¢ and up. All-bisque dolls with wigs, sleeping eyes, jointed at the neck, shoulders and hips; priced $1.00 and up.

Bisque head "French Dolls" on kid or composition bodies with wigs, jointed neck, came dressed or wearing a chemise, earrings, and footwear. The chemise dolls came in size numbers 3, 4, and 5; costing $1.10 and up. The dressed dolls wore satin or plush and lace, a feather trimmed hat, silk stockings and fancy slippers. They came in six sizes; priced $3.75 to $50.00.

Dolls with china heads and limbs on cloth bodies came in ten sizes, numbers 1 to 10; priced 5¢ to 50¢. There were both hard and soft rubber dolls, black versions as well as white, priced 10¢ to $1.75.

There were 12 kinds of wax dolls with hair and these were dressed in chemises. They were of varying quality and attributes ranging from a doll with stationary eyes to those that had pull strings for speaking or the *Webber* singing doll. Prices ranged from 12¢ to $25.00. The most expensive dolls were probably poured wax with inserted hair.

Separate shoulder heads included ones of composition, wax and "French" bisque. The separate kid bodies with bisque or kid hands had size numbers 3, 4, 5, 6, 7, and 8 to correspond with the "French" bisque heads. The cloth bodies stuffed with hair were numbered 0, 1, 2, 3, 4, 5, 6, 7,

8, 9, 10, 11, and 12 to correspond with the composition and wax heads. Some of these bodies came with shaped fingers and bare feet, others had printed stockings and high-heeled kid shoes.

1886: Ridleys no longer advertised all-china dolls, black dolls or the speaking and singing wax dolls. The jointed "French" bisque head dolls in chemise came in nine hts. 10¾, 11¼, 12, 13, 14½, 16½, 20¼, 22½, and 23½ in. (27.5, 28.5, 30.5, 33, 37, 42, 51.5, 57, and 59.5 cm.); priced 25¢ to $3.25.

The jointed "French" bisque head dolls dressed in satin trimmed with plush or lace with matching hat came in four hts. 14, 16, 21 and 23½ in. (35.5, 40.5, 53.5 and 59.5 cm.); priced $2.75 to $30.00. A new offer was a jointed "French" bisque-head doll dressed as a baby in a long dress and cap; priced $1.98 to $2.17.

1888: All-china dolls were again in the catalog, priced 2¢ to 10¢.

Many new types of dolls appeared including a jointed black doll with turning head, wooly hair, earrings, and painted shoes, ht. 8 in. (20.5 cm.), priced 17¢; a composition head boy doll with loose hair, composition limbs and bare feet, 4 hts. 12½, 15½, 18, and 21½ in. (31.5, 39.5, 45.5, and 54.5 cm.), priced 25¢ to 79¢; multiface dolls with bisque heads and with wax heads; and a doll with a bisque head on a kid body came with teeth, hts. 16, 16½, and 17½ in. (40.5, 42, and 44.5 cm.); priced 98¢ to $1.25.

The jointed "French" doll with turning bisque head, wig, sleeping eyes, composition body in a chemise came in eight hts. 11, 13½, 15, 16, 18, 20½, 23½, and 26 in. (28, 34, 38, 40.5, 45.5, 52, 59.5, and 66 cm.); priced $1.12 to $15.00.

This year there were offered many more dressed dolls and separate clothes for dolls than previously. One of the dolls was a *"Jumeau"* with flowing hair, bisque head and costume of silk, satin and velvet trimmed with laces and ribbons, shoes, socks and hat to match, lace trimmed underwear; priced $3.74 and up. It is not certain that this is a true *Bébé Jumeau*.

1891–92: Rubber dolls returned to the catalog and cost 21¢ to $4.89; the more expensive ones were dressed. The black doll was 10 in. (25.5 cm.) and cost 25¢.

A "French" bisque-head doll with wig, sleeping eyes, on a ball jointed composition body, wore a satin or lace trimmed chemise; six hts. 14, 16½, 17½, 19, 21, and 24 in. (35.5, 42, 44.5, 48, 53.5 and 60.5 cm.); priced $1.49 to $4.79. A 22 in. (56 cm.) ht. was available with stationary eyes and teeth for $1.25. A bisque head with wig, on a gusset jointed kid body with bisque hands came in four hts. 12, 16, 17, and 19 in. (30.5, 40.5, 43, and 48 cm.); priced 25¢ to 98¢. A Bébé Jumeau with real hair, dressed and with hat and parasol to match came in six prices from $3.74 to $12.00.

A doll with a composition head, arms and legs, a wig and a cloth body came in six hts. 13, 15, 18½, 21, 25, and 27½ in. (33, 38, 47, 53.5, 63.5, and 70 cm.); priced 25¢ to $1.25.

1897: Catalog showed bisque head dolls with wigs, sleeping eyes, on composition bodies; cost 25¢ to $1.00; on kid bodies they were 25¢ to $1.50. Separate dolls' heads cost 19¢ to $1.50. Dressed dolls were priced 25¢ to $5.00. There were also rubber dolls, cloth dolls, separate clothes for dolls including headwear, footwear and underwear.

Riedler (Riedeler), August. 1872–1930 and later. Königsee, Thür. Made all-bisque dolls and china or bisque heads and limbs on cloth bodies. Some of the dolls had hairdos with bangs. Dolls came dressed or undressed.

1872: Made *Täuflinge*.

1895: Advertised dolls' heads, dressed all-bisque dolls, miniature dolls, nankeen bodies, and jointed dolls.

1908: The son, Carl Riedeler, and grandson became partners and ran the business with a staff of 100 plus 300 other workers.

1938: Advertised all-bisque dolls and miniature dolls.★

Riemann, Seabrey Co. 1912–30 and later. New York City. George F. Riemann (born 1865, died 1918) in 1888 became a manufacturer's agent for several American toy firms. Riemann, Seabrey Co. was established in 1912 by George F. Riemann Jr., Edgar W. Seabrey who had been in the business since 1892 (died in 1921), and *E. W. Brueninghausen.*

1913: Agent for the *New Toy Manufacturing Co.*

1918: Agent for *Famous Doll Studio.*

1919: Also agent for Artcraft Toy Products† and *Trion Toy Co.*

1921: Agent for *Limber Lou* dolls.

1923: Agent for *Atascadero, Atlas Doll & Toy Co.,* and *New York Stuffed Toy Co.*

1928: They were factory agents for American dolls. Henry W. Shaw, President, retired and Clarence W. Ely who had joined the Company in 1922, became President.★

Riera, Mlle. E. V. 1906–1912 and later. Paris. Born in the U.S., she became an art student in Paris where she designed, created, and costumed dolls.

1906: Dressed dolls for Christmas in exact imitation of portraits shown in famous paintings or sculpture. These were small, about 8 in. (20.5 cm.), manufactured wax dolls with shoulder heads. Mlle. Riera cut off the heads just below the chin and fastened them to other necks of her own molding in order to provide slender necks that would give the correct tilt to the heads. She made her own wigs and dyed fabrics so that they matched exactly the colors in the paintings. Old fabrics were often used and tiny jewels were derived from beaded lace or fringe.

1907: Mlle. Riera modeled and molded her own wax heads based on favorite portraits. She exhibited some of her dolls at the New Salon in Paris. This exhibit included the "Muff Girl," copied from the portrait of Mlle. Mollé-Rémond by Mme. Vigée Lebrun. The muff itself was made from old plush furniture covering that was dyed the precise color. Mlle. Riera made every stitch of the costume.

1908: The wax heads and bodies from the waist upwards were sent to Germany where they were reproduced in the "finest bisque." The arms and hands in various positions were also made in bisque. The fact that Mlle. Riera of Paris sent to Germany for what she termed the "finest bisque" reflected on the French bisque of that era.

By 1908 Mlle. Riera had dolls in the collections of the Musée des Arts Décoratifs (part of the Louvre), the Exposition du Theatre, Lord Northcliffe's costume collection in London, and elsewhere. Mlle. Riera won First Prize at a Paris exhibition of lady dolls in historical and regional costumes and the reviews stated, "Thus it was that the fame of a new *métier* was established, and doll-dressing numbered among the fine arts." Her work was praised extravagantly by Miss Florence Estes, an artist of note, who also exhibited at the "New Salon" of the Grand Palais.

Mlle. Riera was very particular that the costumes were precisely the same color and with the same details as those shown in the original painting or sculpture. Many of the fabrics were dyed in her own studio to obtain the exact colors. The finest detail was copied, such as the embroidery on Queen Anne's train being that of her husband's coat of arms. The tiny crest of Queen Elizabeth's gloves reproduced that shown in the painting. The clothes and accessories were made entirely by hand by Mlle. Riera.

Mlle. Riera was appreciated in America as well as abroad. *Strawbridge & Clothier* celebrated their fortieth anniversary by showing in 1908 "The Court of Historical Dolls. Miniature Fashion Models made in Paris by Mlle. Riera." These 24 costumed dolls were as follows:

1. Greece—Tanagra, wears chiffon draperies; reproduces the Tanagra statue in the Louvre.
2. Roman—Messaline [sic], jewel laden.
3. Byzantine.
4. Beginning of the Middle Ages.
5. Queen Anne of Bohemia, wife of Richard II of England (14th century).
6. Queen Isabella of Spain, wife of Ferdinand, wears many jewels and embroidered shoes.
7. Queen Elizabeth I of England in her riding costume at Tilbury.
8. Catherine de Medici, wife of Henry II of France, mother-in-law of Mary Stuart.
9. Anne of Austria, wife of Louis XIII.
10. Marie Thérèse of Austria, Infanta of Spain, from a picture by Velásquez. Marie Thérèse was nine years old when the portrait was painted.
11. Mlle. de la Valliere, favorite of Louis XIV.
12. Marie Leczinska, wife of Louis XV, from a painting by Van Loo.
13. A Flower Girl, under Louis XV.
14. Marie Antoinette at the beginning of her reign.
15. Princess de Lamballe, friend of Marie Antoinette, from a painting at Versailles.
16. Mlle. Mollé-Rémond, actress during the reign of Louis XVI, from the painting the "Muff Girl" by Mme. Vigée-Lebrun.
17. Court Lady—the reign of Louis XVI at the Petit Trianon.
18. Mlle. Lange, Directoire period, favorite of revolutionist Barras, portrait by Vernet.

19. Empress Josephine, First Empire, from the painting of "The Coronation" by David.
20. Lady of the Restoration period, about 1820.
21. Queen Amélie, wife of Louis Philippe, period of simplicity, 1830.
22. Empress Eugénie, wife of Napoleon III, 1860, from the painting by Winterhalter. She was a patron of the Senior Worth.
23. Mrs. X, 1908 period, seen at the Drags at Auteuil, June 5th.
24. Modern Directoire Style, at the Drags, 1908.

Many years later a few of these dolls or ones very similar came into the collection of Mrs. Margaret Woodbury Strong. The doll representing Mlle. Mollé-Rémond has a bisque head on a wax neck and upper torso. The other dolls are bisque from the waist upward. Some of the bisque arms are straight while others are bent.

1912: Mlle. Riera's dolls were in Museums in Moscow and Berlin. Other famous Museums had sent her so many orders for dolls that it would take two years to fill these orders. An illustrated article on her dolls entitled "Dolls that Illustrate History" was published in the December, 1912, issue of THE DELINEATOR. This article described the project on which Mlle. Riera was currently working, namely a history of costumes using 200 dolls. The first doll was all-bisque and represented an aboriginal lady, dressed only in a few strands of beads. The Egyptian and Roman dolls had bare bisque arms. The bald bisque heads were covered with wigs. Some of the curls were made by twisting flax around tiny heated knitting needles. Three of the dolls pictured, namely the Infanta of Spain from a portrait by Velásquez, one of the Flower girls of the time of Louis XV, and the "Muff Girl," (Mlle. Mollé-Rémond's portrait by Mme. Vigée-Lebrun) were similar, but not quite the same as those shown in 1908 at Strawbridge and Clothier.

Other dolls shown in the DELINEATOR article included a lady of the time of Louis XIV, in negligée, another flower girl of the time of Louis XV, a lady in street dress in the time of Louis XVI, Mlle. Lange from a different portrait, a lady with furs, a "Restoration Beauty" (ca. 1820), an 1830 Milliner or Modiste, and two fashionably dressed lady dolls of 1912.

Rigot, Mlle. Marie Georgette. 1927–30 and later. Paris. Made cloth dolls.

1928: Registered *L'Idéale* as a trademark in France for dolls made of cloth.

1929: Made stuffed art dolls.

Rilinton Toy Novelty Co. 1927–30 and later. Burlington, N.J. Made outfits for dolls; some of these were in fitted trunks or fitted hat boxes, and included accessories for dolls.

1928: Made clothes especially for small dolls. One wardrobe trunk style number had drawers, hat boxes, dress hangers, shoe boxes, and so forth all filled with dolls' clothes. The hat boxes were fitted with combs, mirrors, fans, and other items. Separate accessories included parasols, miniature vanities, and so forth.

1929: The fitted trunks and hat boxes contained small dolls and their wardrobes of clothes.

1930: Advertised Philadelphia, Pa., doll outfits.

Rina, Mme. ca. 1900. Brooklyn, N.Y. She sold dolls which she had purchased from the *Heinrich Handwerck* factory.

2223. Mlle. Riera doll that is all-bisque to the waist and a cloth covered cone below the waist. The hair, piled high on the head, has beads on top. The eyes are painted blue and the mouth is closed. The head is turned slightly. The shoulders are jointed with wooden pegs. The original embroidered and beaded gold taffeta dress and orchid colored scarf are supposed to represent Roman Messalina but they seem to have a 1907 or 1908 fashion influence (No. 2). The identifying mark is on the base. H. 8¼ in. (21 cm.). *Courtesy of the Margaret Woodbury Strong Museum. Photo by Harry Bickelhaupt.*

2225. Doll created by Mlle. Riera has bisque to the waist and a cloth covered cone below the waist. The bosom is molded and the bisque arms are jointed at the shoulders with wooden pegs. The brown hair is piled high and the crown is made of beads and braids. It has painted blue eyes and a closed mouth. Original costume represents that worn by the Empress Josephine in the painting "The Coronation" by David (No. 19). A printed paper strip label identifies this doll. The plum colored velvet robe has metallic bees (symbolic of Napoleon). H. 8 in. (20.5 cm.). *Courtesy of the Margaret Woodbury Strong Museum. Photo by Harry Bickelhaupt.*

2224. Bisque socket head doll created by Mlle. Riera has brown hair, painted blue eyes and a closed mouth. It is jointed at the neck and shoulders with the torso to the waist made of wax, and the arms bisque. The joints are contrived with wooden pegs. The body from the waist down is a cloth covered cone. Original clothes were inspired by Mme. Vigée Lebrun's portrait of Mlle. Mollé-Rémond, called the "Muff Girl" (No. 16). Identifying mark on the base. H. 7½ in. (19 cm.). *Courtesy of the Margaret Woodbury Strong Museum. Photo by Harry Bickelhaupt.*

Ring, H., & Co. 1874–1930 and later. Brieg, Silesia. Successor in 1905 was Sigismund Schwerin and successor in 1925 was Eberhard von Beden. Manufactured dolls.

1899: Advertised dolls' bodies made of a washable, leather-like material.

1905: Obtained a German patent (D.R.G.M.) for ball joints.

1925: Advertised imitation leather bodies for export.★

Ring, Karl (Carl). 1892–97. Brieg, Silesia. Applied for several German patents pertaining to dolls.

1892: Obtained a patent with Louis Meyer[+].

1894: Applied for a patent (D.R.G.M.) for ball joints.

1897: Applied for a patent (D.R.G.M.) for the movement of a doll's eyelids. This patent was assigned to *Richard Lüders.*

Ring Master. 1905–24. Wooden doll made by *Schoenhut,* had a high hat, coat with tails and carried a whip.★

Ringel, Pierre. Before 1859. Lower Rhine. Born at Wissembourg in 1805. He sold dolls but the business failed in 1859. One of his creditors was *Lindner* & Söhne. This information was supplied by Mme. Florence Poisson, Curator of the Roybet Fould Museum.

2227. Pair of cloth dolls with metal tags on which "Ringl" is marked. These tags are attached to the suspenders. The hair is tow, stitched onto the scalp. The features are needle sculptured and the eyes are painted. One of the open-closed mouths has a felt tongue that protrudes. The heads and bodies are made of stuffed linen over wire armatures. Original clothes of wool felt and linen, leather boots. Probably German. Hs. 9 and 9½ in. (23 and 24 cm.). *Courtesy of the late Magda Byfield.*

2226. Doll created by Mlle. Riera is bisque to the waist and a cloth covered cone below the waist. It has a blond wig, painted blue eyes, a closed mouth, and is jointed only at the shoulders. The straight bisque arms have hands with fingers bent so that they appear to grasp the parasol handle. Original clothes of the 1908 period represent a costume that might be seen at the Drags at Auteuil (No. 23). Identifying mark on the base. H. 8 in. (20.5 cm.). *Courtesy of the Margaret Woodbury Strong Museum. Photo by Harry Bickelhaupt.*

Ringl. Name found on metal tags attached to needle sculptured cloth dolls. (See Ill. 2227.)

Rinkes, M. 1930 and later. Frankenthal, Germany. Advertised dolls, baby dolls, miniature dolls and dolls' clothes.

Rintintin. 1912–18. Trademark registered in France by Mme. *Poulbot* for dolls. These dolls were mates to *Nénette* and were sold in the large Paris stores.

1913: *Lafayette* store advertised Rintintin designed by Poulbot and wearing knee length trousers, a small tie and suspenders over a striped shirt. Ht. 36 cm. (14 in.); priced

$1.78. See THE COLLECTOR'S BOOK OF DOLLS' CLOTHES, Ill. 639.

1914: *Samaritaine, La Place Clichy* and the *Louvre* store advertised Rintintin, designed and modeled by Poulbot. The doll was dressed as a boy. Ht. 35 or 36 cm. (14 in.); priced $1.78. (See also **Nénette and Rintintin.**)

Rip Van Winkle Gnomes. 1913. Cloth dolls made by *Steiff*.

Riri. 1928. Name of an "unbreakable" *Poulbot* doll advertised by *Bon Marché*. It wore a cape, short pants, a large cap and slippers with ribbons around the ankles. Ht. 40 cm. (15½ in.).

Rischel, A., & Co. 1893–1900. Berlin. Made, distributed, and exported dressed dolls and dolls' outfits.

1893: Advertised embroidery boxes containing dolls and their clothes.

Rita. 1927–28. Name of a felt *Lenci* doll representing a school-aged girl with braids over her ears and wearing a dress with a high waistline and full skirt that covered the knees. Style no. 700/1. Ht. 37½ in. (95 cm.).

Rite Specialty Co. 1916–20. New York City and Newark, N.J. Factories were in both places. They made dolls of handpainted "Ivorite." The dolls representing males had spherical heads and bodies, those representing females had spherical heads and bell-shaped bodies. The arms were rudimentary.

1917: Dolls included Daddy Rite, Mother Rite, Brother Rite and Sister Rite.

1920: *Leo Morse* was the factory representative. (See also **Morse, Amelia.**)★

Rittner, Mrs. See **Potteries Toy Co. (British Toy Co.; Potteries Doll Co.).**

Rittstlag, Hermann. 1910–20s. Hamburg, Germany. Wholesale distributor and exporter of dolls.

Ritz Import & Export Co. 1922–23. New York City. Handled dolls.

Ritzi. 1930 and later. Name of a Patsy-type doll made by the *Natural Doll Co.* Hts. 12 to 20 in. (30.5 to 51 cm.).

Riva, Giovanni. 1920s. Turin, Italy. Born in 1890. A sculptor who designed some of the *Lenci* ceramics and perhaps contributed to Lenci doll designs.

Rivaillon (Ricaillon), Fr., and Caroline. 1900–10. Paris. Factory at Montreuil-sous-Bois. Caroline Rivaillon's address was given as Argenteuil, France. Made bébés.

1900: Caroline Rivaillon registered the initials F.C.R. and two cherubs with the name Bébé Modèle as a trademark in France. The following year Jules Mettais, *Jules Steiner*'s successor, registered just the words Bébé Modèle as a trademark in France.

1910: F. Ch. Rivaillon made a bébé which he called *Bébé le Vrai* Modèle. It should be noted that later *Jumeau* bébés were sometimes marked on the torso *Bébé Vrai Modèle.*★

Rivière, Suzanne. 1924–29 and probably other years. Wrote instructions for making dolls and designed the patterns for making clothes for Bleuette. These were published periodically in LA SEMAINE DE SUZETTE. Her predecessor was *Tante (Aunt) Jacqueline.*

Road Scout Mascots. 1930. Dolls representing the A.A. (Automobile Association) and the R.C.A. (Royal Auto Club) Scouts in Britain. These dolls made by *Chad Valley* as styles no. 596 (A.A.) and no. 597 (R.C.A.) were officially approved and wore the uniforms of their respective clubs. They were dressed in the appropriate colored felt with puttees and

BÉBÉ
MODÈLE

F.C.R.
MARQUE
DÉPOSÉE

2228. Mark used by F. C. Rivaillon for some of their bébés.

kepis. One of the dolls had its eyes looking to the side and the other looking downwards. The right arms were made so that they could take the correct saluting position. Ht. 7½ in. (19 cm.).

Roanoke Doll. See **Smith, Ella.**

Robarts & Quantock. 1921–24. London. Handled Continental dolls. In 1921 they claimed to have over 1,000 lines of dolls.

Robbie Reefer. 1911–16. Designed by *Helen Trowbridge* and produced by *Horsman* as one of the American Kids in Toyland dolls. The head appears to have been from the same mold as *Daisy Dimple, Gretchen, Hans, Happy Hiram, Jack Tar* and *Prince Charlie*. It had molded bobbed hair and bangs, painted eyes, smiling open-closed mouth with teeth. The cloth body had *Campbell Kid* type hands and the doll was designated style no. 139.

1912: The clothes consisted of a long red double-breasted coat (reefer) over striped knickers and a sailor cap.

1914: The reefer suit was made of white duck fabric and on its head the doll wore a white beach hat. Priced $8.50 doz. wholesale.

1916: The clothes were changed and it was larger.★

Robbins, John D. 1860–61 and probably other years. U.S.A., possibly N.J. Imported and sold dolls and dolls' parts including, all-china dolls, Nankeen dolls with china heads and limbs, composition and papier-mâché heads, kid

No. 139
"ROBBIE REEFER"
Trade Mark

(Head copyrighted, 1912, by E. I. Horsman Co.)

A spruce little fellow in a suit of snowy well cut white ducks. The coat, cut reefer fashion, with an open sailor collar. Robbie wears a white beach hat, white socks and shoes. Just the sort of a boy tot every little girl will want in her doll family.

Per Dozen........**$8.50**

No. 139 Robbie Reefer"

2229. Robbie Reefer, advertised in the Horsman catalog of ca. 1914. The composition head had been copyrighted in 1912. It had molded and painted hair and eyes, closed mouth, cloth body with composition Campbell Kid type hands. *Catalog courtesy of Bernard Barenholtz.*

body dolls, varnished head dolls, peg-wooden dolls, rubber dolls made by *I. R. Comb Co.*, wax dolls, crying and speaking dolls, rattling dolls with wigs or molded hair, dolls with moving eyes or painted eyes, dressed or undressed dolls. This information was supplied by Elizabeth Pierce from a Day Book dating from 1860–61.

Robbins Leather Goods Co. 1923–27. New York City. Made shoes for dolls.

Robert. 1926. Name of a celluloid doll with molded clothes representing a Policeman; jointed at the shoulders. Ht. 6½ in. (16.5 cm.). Advertised in Britain.

Robert, Carl. Before 1926–27. Köppelsdorf, Thür. The successors manufactured dolls by 1926.

Robert, Widow. Last half of the 1800s. Versailles, France. A fashion-type doll with a bisque swivel head on a gusset jointed kid body was labeled "Vve Robert, 23 Rue Hoche, Versailles, Aux Rêves des Enfants." The boots on this doll were marked *Beaudelot* of Paris. Ht. 18 in. (45.5 cm.).

Roberts Bros. Ca. 1888–1930 and later. Gloucester and London. Made dolls. After World War I they took over *Shanklin.* According to Mary Hillier they were eventually taken over by *Chad Valley.* The Gloucester factory was known as Glevum Works, and they used the trade name "Glevum Toys." In 1921 they took over *British Toys.*

1903: Obtained a British patent for a doll on wheels.

1917: Made dressed character dolls including the Aviator, Hood dolls, Pierrot, Red Cross dolls, Sailor Boy, Smiling Face and Yachtwoman. The baby dolls had jointed arms and legs and wore short dresses, underclothes and woolen shoes.

1921: Produced *E. E. Houghton* stockinet dolls.

1926: Advertised Tiny Tots.

1929: H. O. Roberts died, aged 69. His younger brother, J. O. Roberts, survived him.

Roberts, C. M. See **Moll-Es.**

Roberts, Penelope. 1920s. Designed dolls including "Fantasy" dolls and one representing a Russian prince. These dolls were exhibited in New York City.

Robin Hood. 1923. Portrait doll of Douglas Fairbanks as he appeared in the moving picture ROBIN HOOD.

Robins, Joseph. 1826–1901. London. He and his relatives made dolls.★

Robinson, Harriet M. 1929. Tacoma, Washington. Organized the *Tillicum* Manufacturing Co. and promoted the use of dolls in school classrooms.

Robinson, Heath. 1917. Britain. Registered *Nunkey* and *Mother Blighty* as names for dolls which she designed in the *Tah Toys* line. She was a cartoonist.

Robotham Bros. & Co. 1916. Britain. Advertised in a British Toy Journal British Officer, Charlie Chaplin, Jack Tar, Red Cross Nurse and Tommy Atkins. It is not certain what kind of dolls these were.

Roch, Johann. 1910. Vienna. Listed in a directory under Dolls and Dolls' Heads.

Rochard, Ed. 1860s–70s. Patented a see-through necklace with French scenes as part of a bisque shoulder head doll. Various styles of necklaces on various sizes of dolls with wigs and glass eyes have been observed.★

Rochdale Doll Co. 1918–19. Rochdale, Lancs. Made Eclipse hair-stuffed dolls. Hts. 12 to 22 in. (30.5 to 56 cm.).

Rock, Berthold. 1895–1930. Eisfeld near Hildburghausen, Thür. Made dressed dolls.★

Rock, Helen Fraser. World War I period. England. A sculptress hired by *Nottingham* to design *British Ceramic* dolls' heads. She used real children as her models. These dolls were called *Helen's Babies* and were advertised as *Rock China Dolls.*

Rock China Dolls. 1915–19. Modeled by Helen Rock, made with *British Ceramic* heads on cloth bodies or composition bodies by *Nottingham.*

1917: The dolls were described as having "Chubby Cheeks, pleasant features and dainty coloring." There were "Sit-up baby dolls" with jointed arms and legs, wearing long dresses, cloaks and bonnets. The dolls had removable clothes and were dressed as babies, boys and girls, sailor boys and girls,

2230. Bisque head doll created by Ed Rochard has a necklace made over a hole in the bisque and a French scene of La Havre visible when one looks through the necklace toward the light. This pressed bisque head on a bisque shoulder plate has a wig, stationary blue glass eyes, pierced ears and a closed mouth. The kid body is jointed at the shoulders and has gusset hip joints. Has bisque lower arms. Mark inside the head in ink, "Ed Rochard Déposé." H. 17 in. (43 cm.). *Courtesy of Elsie and Al Potter.*

and boys and girls in nightclothes. Most of the dressed dolls were 18 in. (45.5 cm.) tall.

1918: There were 12 lines including the new composition dolls. The Rock china heads were used on *Vogue* dolls. Some of the 18 in. (45.5 cm.) dolls were dressed as school girls.

Rock & Graner. 1813–World War I. Biberach, Württemberg. There were several successors, one of these was Oskar Egelhaaf; at another time the company was known as Graner but eventually it was taken over by Märklin. Their trademark R & G N signified Rock & Graner successors (the N was for Nachfolger meaning successors).

1836: The "Biberach" catalog at Bethnal Green Museum in London probably was a Rock & Graner catalog. This catalog showed *Swaddling-clothed Babies,* dolls with Apollo knot hairdos (possibly varnished papier-mâché heads) and men dolls wearing frock coats.

1837: Factory had 100 employees according to Mary Hillier.

Ca. 1860: Dolls' house jointed porcelain dolls were included with the dolls' houses but probably were made elsewhere. The factory specialized in tin toys at this time.★

Rock-a-Bye Baby. 1920–28. Dressed composition-head dolls made by *Averill Manufacturing Co.,* had Lloyd voices. The doll came with a cradle and when rocked the eyes slowly closed and the soft crying ceased when the eyes were completely closed. When it awakened and opened its eyes, it called "Mama." The doll was distributed by *Sears.*

1921: Came in five sizes, the largest size fitted into a real baby's cradle.

1922: Came in four sizes.

1924: Came with a wire cradle. (See also other **Rock-A-Bye Baby Dolls.**)★

Rock-A-Bye Baby. 1925–30 and later. Produced by *Cuno & Otto Dressel.* In Britain this name was applied to newborn infant dolls, three weeks or three months old baby dolls. *Armand Marseille* mold #341 with a closed mouth and Armand Marseille mold #351 with an open mouth were both known as a Rock-A-Bye Baby in Britain. The black sitting version was named *Sammy* and the white sitting version was called *Sonny.*

1933: Name of a newborn baby type doll's head sold by *Quaker Doll Company.* These appear to be the same type of doll's head as the ones named *My Dream Baby* earlier. The bisque heads were made in several kinds by *Armand Marseille.* Mold # 341 had a flange neck to go on a cloth body, sleeping eyes and a closed mouth. Number 351 was similar except it had an open mouth and two teeth. Number 341 K (K for Kurbel) was the socket head version of 341 and was used on a bent-limb composition baby body. Number 351 K had an open mouth with two teeth and was otherwise similar to 341 K. These heads were made in 14 sizes as follows:

Size No.*	341 & 351 Head Circumference		341K & 351K Head Circumference	
	in.	cm.	in.	cm.
6/0	5½	14	5¾	14.5
4/0	6½	16.5	6½	16.5
3/0	7¼	18.5	7⅛	18
2/0	7½	19	7¼	18.5
0	8¼	21	8¼	21
1	8¾	22	8½	21.5
2	9	23	9	23
2½	9¾	25	9¾	25
3	10½	26.5	10¼	26
3½	11¼	28.5	11¼	28.5
4	12½	31.5	12½	31.5
5	13½	34	13	33
6	14	35.5	14	35.5
8	15	38	14½	37

*Sizes 0 thru 6 of 341K and 351K had eyelashes.

The wholesale prices for the flange neck heads ranged from $2.60 a dozen to $18.50 a dozen depending on size, while the socket heads cost $3.50 a dozen to $24 a dozen. The prices appear to have been the same for the open and closed mouth versions, but the socket heads cost about a third more than the flange neck varieties.

The Rock-A-Bye Baby heads were also made in Europe of Biscaloid composition. These heads correspond to the number 351 bisque heads. They were made in both the flange type for cloth bodies designated number 11, and the socket type for bent limb composition bodies designated number 19. They had sleeping eyes and open mouths with two teeth. All of the eyes in the socket heads were blue. These composition heads came in the following sizes:

Size No.	Flange Head Circumference		Size No.	Socket Head Circumference	
	in.	cm.		in.	cm.
			19/2/0	8	20.5
			19/0	9	23
			19/1	9¾	25
11/2	10	25.5	19/2	10	25.5
11/3	11½	29	19/3	11¾	30
11/4	14	35.5	19/4	14	35.5
11/6	15½	39.5	19/5	15	38

The prices for the flange heads ranged from $7.00 to $19.00 doz. wholesale and for the socket heads from $6.00 to $21.00 doz. wholesale. The composition heads were more expensive than the bisque heads of comparable size and again the flange heads were cheaper than the socket heads of similar size.

An *Armand Marseille* bisque head, closed mouth, infant doll on a pink cloth body with celluloid hands made by Rheinische Gummi und Celluloid Fabrik bore a round tag showing a baby in a cradle suspended from the branch of a tree. Under the cradle was the name "Rock-A-Bye Baby." On the tag in small print were "GERMANY" and "NAME// REGISTERED."

Rockendorfer, Adam. 1809 and later. He died before 1816. Vienna. Made and/or handled wooden dolls.

Rockwell, Grace Corry. See **Corry, Grace.**

Ro-Clo. 1916. Name used by *Speight* for hair wool used to stuff dolls.

Rodaer Puppenfabrik. See **Bauer & Richter.**

Rodel, Martin. 1903. Nürnberg, Bavaria. Applied for a German patent (D.R.G.M.) for dolls of various materials.

Rodler Babies. See **Kley & Hahn.**

Roffa, Heinrich. 1898. Neustadt near Coburg, Thür. Made cloth bodies for dolls.

Rogner, Hermann. 1924–26. Sonneberg, Thür., and Nürnberg, Bavaria. Made dolls.

1926: Sole British agent was *Brierly.*★

Roguish Eyes. Eyes that glance to the side; sometimes the eyes were round; they were painted or glass or tin or celluloid. When they moved from side to side they were often called flirting eyes.[†] Roguish eyes were popular in the first quarter of the 20th century and nearly all of the doll manufacturers made some of their dolls with roguish eyes.

Among the dolls with roguish eyes were mold numbers 200, 210, 252, 253, 254, 255, 258, 310, 322, 323, 324 and 325, all made by *Armand Marseille.* Dolls with roguish eyes were also made by *Bähr & Pröschild, Chad Valley, Gebrüder Heubach, Ideal, Kämmer & Reinhardt, Kestner, Lenci,* Monroe Schwarzschild[†]. *Simon & Halbig, Société Française de Fabrication de Bébés & Jouets* (S.F.B.J.), *Herm Steiner,* and many others. When the eyes were painted it is possible that they could have been painted either looking to the side or looking straight ahead. For dolls with inserted eyes the same head can be found with or without a flirting eye mechanism.★

Rohlinge (Ruffians). 1902. Name used by *Kämmer & Reinhardt.*

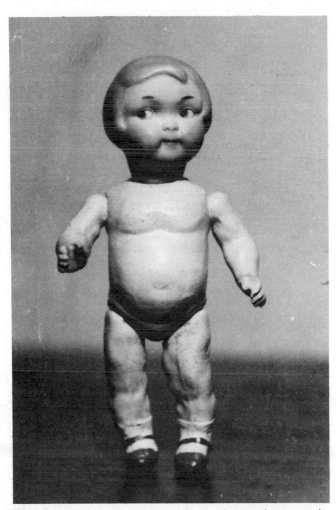

2231. Bisque-head doll with intaglio roguish eyes glancing to the side. It has molded and painted hair, closed mouth and a five-piece composition body with molded and painted footwear. H. 6¼ in. (16 cm.). *Courtesy of Dr. Eva Moskovszky.*

2232. Pair of bisque head dolls with roguish blue glass eyes, molded and painted hair, closed smiling mouths and fully jointed composition bodies. The doll on the left has eyes that sleep. Mark: 163/4. The bisque head appears to have been made by Hertel, Schwab & Co. for Strobel & Wilken. H. 13½ in. (34 cm.). The doll on the right: Mark 240.0. H. 11 in. (28 cm.). *Courtesy of Sotheby Parke Bernet Inc., N.Y.*

2233. Bisque socket head doll with roguish eyes has a blond wig, sleeping blue glass eyes that look to the side, a smiling closed mouth and fully jointed composition body. Mark: 165/4. The bisque head appears to have been made by Hertel, Schwab & Co. for Strobel & Wilken. H. 14 in. (35.5 cm.). *Courtesy of Sotheby Parke Bernet Inc., N.Y.*

2234. Bisque socket head with roguish eyes made by Simon & Halbig for Kämmer & Reinhardt, mold #131. The doll has a wig, round sleeping blue glass eyes glancing to the side, closed smiling mouth and a ball jointed composition body. The clothes are contemporary with the doll. Mark: K ✡ R//Simon & Halbig//131. H. 15½ in. (39.5 cm.). *Courtesy of Sotheby Parke Bernet Inc., N.Y.*

2235. Bisque socket head with stationary round roguish blue glass eyes; blond wig, smiling closed mouth shaped like a melon slice; five-piece composition toddler type body. Mark: J.D.K. //221. H. 13¼ in. (33.5 cm.). *Courtesy of Sotheby Parke Bernet Inc., N.Y.*

*Schieler
7/0
Germany*

2236. Mark on a bisque doll's head reading "Schieler." The translation of this German word is "squinting"; however, it was found on a doll that had roguish eyes.

Rohmer, Mme. 1857–80. Paris. Made dolls of various materials. (See THE COLLECTOR'S BOOK OF DOLLS' CLOTHES, Ill. 143 A.)★

Roig, Mme. 1915–16. Paris. Made *Gallia*, a cloth bébé.

Rolf (Winter Sports). 1911. Felt boy doll made by *Steiff* in their winter sports series; wore a red and white sweater, leather shoes, knee and elbow guards. Four hts. 28, 35, 43, and 50 cm. (11, 14, 17, and 19½ in.); priced $1.25 to $2.75.

Rolfo, Luigi. 1928–30. Turin, Italy. Made dolls.

Roli. 1928 and later. Celluloid-head doll with flirting eyes[+] and hair eyelashes, made by *Kämmer & Reinhardt;* had a cloth body and a mama voice. It was described as "*My Rosy Darling.*"

Roller, Marianne. 1906–08. Brunn and Vienna, Austria.

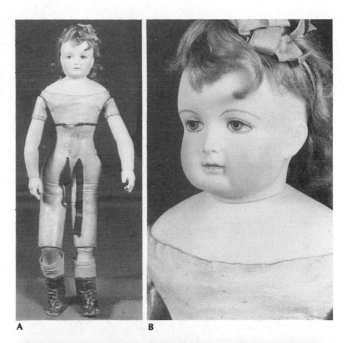

A   B

2237A & B. China shoulder head and arms on a doll made by Mme. Rohmer. It has a wig, painted blue eyes and a narrow closed mouth. The neck joint is a flat flange type. The kid body has the typical eyelet holes and oval Rohmer stamp. H. 13¾ in. (35 cm.). *Courtesy of Sara Kocher.*

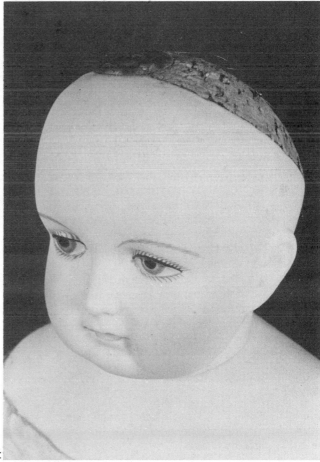

2239A & B. Bisque shoulder head and arms on a doll made by Mme. Rohmer. It has a wig, stationary blue glass eyes, pierced ears, and a closed mouth. The neck joint is the flat flange type. The body is kid and has the Rohmer stamp on the stomach. H. 17½ in. (44.5 cm.). H. of shoulder head only, 4¼ in. (11 cm.). *Courtesy of Sara Kocher.*

Made turned wood art dolls, jointed at the shoulders and with painted floor-length clothes representing everyday people.

1906: Exhibited dolls at an Edinburgh Exhibition.

Roller Skates. 1930: *Braitling* and *Canastota Sherwood* produced roller skates for dolls. The various *Patsy* dolls and *Skippy* dolls were made with feet that could wear roller skates. Roller skates were available for other dolls at various periods.

C

2238A, B & C. Bisque shoulder head and arms on a doll made by Mme. Rohmer. It has a wig, a cork pate, painted blue eyes, and a closed mouth. The short neck fits into the shoulder plate with a flat flange type joint. The kid body has the typical eyelet holes and leg construction with the upper legs being almost like pants, and it has the oval Rohmer stamped mark. H. 18 in. (45.5 cm.). *Courtesy of Sara Kocher.*

Rollinson, Gertrude F. 1916–29. Holyoke, Mass. Designed and created cloth dolls. During World War I these dolls were made by the *Utley Co.* and distributed by *Borgfeldt, Louis Wolf* and *Strobel & Wilken.* The molded faces were made of treated cloth.

1916: Designed stockinet dolls with wigs or painted hair, painted eyes, closed mouth or open-closed mouth with teeth; some of the dolls had pierced nostrils. The cloth torsos were stamped with "Rollinson Doll//Holyoke, Mass."

1917: There were 35 style nos. The painted hair was blond, tosca or dark. Each stockinet face had 20 coats of paint. After each coat, it was dried in the sun, then rubbed down with sandpaper until the final washable finish was obtained. Priced $3.00 to $35.00.

1921: Made *Kiddiekins.*

1929: TOY WORLD published the following account of Gertrude Rollinson's dolls: "Many years ago Gertrude Rollinson made her first doll. These were dolls she made at Christmas time for crippled children. Mrs. Rollinson still feels that it is a part of her Christmas to make dolls and toys and then visit the children in the hospitals and just play the part of Mrs. Santa Claus.

"It was not until 1916 that Mrs. Rollinson commercialized her doll and toy making talent. At that time the Rollinson dolls were put on the market. These dolls were sold as far as Capetown, South Africa.

"The business grew until the Utley Company bought the rights on a royalty basis. This company had the equipment to handle the business on a large scale.

"In 1921 Mrs. Rollinson made and successfully marketed the Kiddie Kins. Since that time such firms as Geo. Borgfeldt Co., Strobel-Wilkins Co. *[sic],* Inc., Louis Wolf & Co. and Bailey & Bailey have handled her line of toys.

"Mrs. Rollinson's latest creation is 'Bobby Lou,' the first of a large family of Rollinson's Bed Time Buddies.

"The dolls are made of especially prepared and treated fabric, with real fingers and toes. They are washable and stuffed with the best Kapok available. Consequently they are soft and cuddlesome.

"The 'Bed Time Buddies' are a departure from the old-fashioned rag doll in that they are waterproof and have all the features and fine points of other types of dolls now popular on the market—they even walk.

"All dolls will leave the factory fully dressed and packed in separate boxes. They come in several different sizes."★

Rolly-I-Tot. 1926. Trademark registered in U.S. for dolls by *Borgfeldt.*

Roma. 1905–09 and possibly later. Name found on bisque dolls' heads made in Bohemia, Austria. One of these heads, probably made by *Plass & Roesner,* was marked as shown in Ill. 2244. It had a wig, glass eyes, open mouth with teeth, ears not pierced, ball jointed composition body with wrists not jointed. Ht. 23½ in. (59.5 cm.).

Roma Doll Co. 1929–30. New York City. Made parts for dolls; member of the *Doll Parts Manufacturing Assoc.*

Roman Dolls. 1929. Name given to dolls made in Rome,

2240. Advertisement for Rollinson Dolls made by the Utley Co. in PLAYTHINGS, December, 1916. These stockinet dolls had painted hair or wigs and were dressed or undressed. Hs. 14 to 28 in. (35.5 to 71 cm.). Strobel & Wilken was their selling agent.

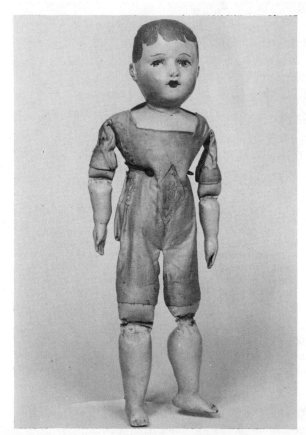

2241. Rollinson cloth doll with head, arms and legs painted with an oil paint on stockinet similar to the Martha Chase dolls. The joints and shape of the limbs are also similar to the Chase dolls. The features are molded and painted and the ears are applied. The torso and top part of the arms and legs are sateen. Mark: Ill. 2243. H. 20 in. (51 cm.). *Courtesy of the Margaret Woodbury Strong Museum. Photo by Harry Bickelhaupt.*

2242. Rollinson cloth doll with wig, molded shoulder head, painted blue eyes, molded ears, open-closed mouth with four teeth. The head, hands, limbs are painted stockinet and the torso is sateen. There are joints at the hips, shoulders and elbows. Original clothes. Mark: Ill. 2243. H. 18 in. (45.5 cm.). *Courtesy of the Margaret Woodbury Strong Museum. Photo by Harry Bickelhaupt.*

2243. Stamped mark on the front of the cloth torso of Rollinson dolls. Around the border of the diamond it reads: "ROLLINSON DOLL//HOLYOKE MASS." Inside the diamond is the drawing of a doll and the words "TRADE MARK."

2244. Roma marks found on bisque-head dolls.

Italy, of wood-pulp composition. They were advertised as being "anatomically perfect, jointed throughout and dressed in a variety of handsome costumes of different periods." Allegedly they were washable and the clothes were removable. (For Roman Dolls of the Classical Period see **Chronology**.)

Romania. See **Roumanian Dolls**.

Romano. 1914. One of the *Paderewski* dolls made by Polish refugees in Mme. Lazarski's studio, it wore a red, white, and blue (Polish national colors) costume. Romano had a red cap and its clothes were similar to those of *Henio,* except they were of different materials.

Romanowski, Karl. 1902. Elberfeld, Germany. Applied for a German patent (D.R.G.M.) for a doll with changeable rubber features.

Rommer, Isaac A. 1912–29 and later. New York City and Brooklyn, New York. Rommer was born in 1870 in Russia, came to America in 1888, joined *Ideal* in 1912, worked on improving dolls and obtained many U.S. patents for moving eyes for dolls. He was Secretary and Treasurer of Ideal when he died in 1928 and was succeeded by Dora Rommer.

1915: Obtained a U.S. patent pertaining to dolls' eyes and ears.

1929: Obtained after his death a U.S. patent for a doll with an inner and an outer eyeball. The eyelashes on the inner eyeball projected through a slot on the outer eyeball. Both eyeballs moved vertically in unison but the outer eyeball also had a lateral movement. ★

Rompa. 1924. Name of a series of cloth dolls stuffed with non-absorbent kapok, made by *Rayburn Townsend & Co.* They had handpainted faces; the frames could be removed so that the stockinet dolls could be washed in soap and water. The clothes represented those for boys and girls as well as a baby and a policeman.

Romper Baby. 1912–14. Composition character head doll distributed by *Sears,* had molded hair, pink cloth body jointed at the shoulders and hips, curved limbs and wore checked rompers. Hts. 9, 11, and 13 in. (23, 28, and 33 cm.); priced 19¢ to 85¢. The mama voice for the two smaller sizes was activated by squeezing and for the largest size by tilting the doll.

Romper Boy. Ca. 1917. Bisque head doll with jointed arms and legs, distributed by *Shackman.* Ht. 6 in. (15 cm.); priced 15¢.

Romper Boy. 1920. One of the *Madame Georgene* dolls made for *Averill,* had composition shoulder head and arms, wig, and the rompers came in four colors. Ht. 19 in. (48 cm.).

Romper Boy. 1921. Cloth doll stuffed with white cotton, designed by *Grace Corry* and made by *Century.* It was claimed that the doll could jump up and down and it was dressed in costumes of various colors. ★

Romper Doll. 1917. Made by *E. Goldberger* and dressed as a boy in short trousers or as a girl in a dress, the top part of their costume was made of a darker fabric than the bottom part.

Romper Doll. 1919. Name of the first dolls made by *Nelke* and dressed as a little girl in pink, blue, or white cotton crepe rompers, with a matching knitted cap.

Roncorone. Early 1800s. England. Made dolls of beeswax and used a rectangular label that was decorated with a border of leaves.

Ronson. 1923–27 and probably later. Name of the dolls' voices made by the *Art Metal Works*.

Rookie. 1917–19. Composition head doll produced by *Horsman,* wore a soldier's khaki uniform with puttees and hat, had a pistol in a holster.

1917–18: The hat had a brim.

1919: Wore an overseas cap. Ht. 14 in. (35.5 cm.); priced $9.00 doz. wholesale.

Roppold, Josef. 1907–10. Vienna. Listed in directories under Dolls and Dolls' Heads.

Rörstrand Porcelain Factory. 1726–1925 and later. Sweden. Porcelain factory that made china heads for dolls. Possibly they also made bisque heads. Their marks included a number, or a letter and a single digit number, located on the side of the outside of the front of the shoulder head. (See Ill. 2245)★

Rosa. 1911–24. Felt character doll made by *Steiff* and distributed by *Borgfeldt.* in the U.S. It was dressed as a peasant with a laced bodice, apron and hat.

1911: Advertised as 43 and 50 cm. (17 and 19½ in.); price $3.50 to $4.43.

1913: Advertised as 11 and 14 in. (28 and 35 cm.). The 14 in. (35 cm.) size also came with long inserted hair that could be combed and cost $3.65 in the U.S.

1924: Four hts. 28, 35, 43 and 50 cm. (11, 14, 17 and 19½ in.).

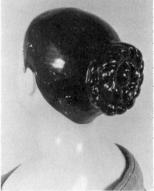

2245A & B. China shoulder head that resembles a head identified by the Swedish National Museum as having been made by the Rörstrand Factory. Note in the close-up of the front the brush marks around the widow's peak and the tiny spit curl just in front of the ear. The close-up of the back shows the molding of the braided bun hair in contrast to the smooth hair in front. It has blue painted eyes. H. 21 in. (53.5 cm.). H. of the shoulder head 5¼ in. (13 cm.). *Courtesy of Z. Frances Walker.*

Rosalie. 1927. Dressed composition head doll with mohair wig, painted eyes and crying voice, distributed by *Montgomery Ward.* This doll had composition arms and legs, and a slender body that was beginning to be fashionable. Ht. 27 in. (68.5 cm.); priced $3.00.

Rosalinde. See **Poupées Rosalinde, Les.**

Roscamp, Katarina. 1925–29. Germany. Obtained a German patent (D.R.P.) for a cloth doll made of terry cloth or felt.★

Rose. 1913. Name of a doll handled by *Whyte, Ridsdale.* Ht. 16 in. (40.5 cm.); priced $5.00 doz. wholesale.

Rose. 1924. One of the *Posy* line of cloth dolls made by *Dean;* wore a dress with a knee-length skirt made of layered semicircles, a brimmed hat and carried a flower in its right hand.

Rose. 1927. One of the *Twinjoy* line of *Flower Dolls* with a petal dress. This was two dolls in one created by *Berry Kollin.*

Rose, W. A., & Co. 1921. London. Handled dolls and used the initials W. A. R. in a diamond as a trademark.

Rose Marie. 1923–30. Line of dolls made by *K & K* and distributed by *Borgfeldt.* These dolls had slim legs and wore ensemble costumes including summer outfits and fur trimmed coats of velvet, plush or flannel.

Rose Marie.† See **Rose-Marie.**

Rose Mary. 1918–19. All-composition doll with molded hair, extended arms, straight legs, spring joints, made by *Jessie M. Raleigh* and distributed by *Butler Bros.*

1918: Wore a flowered lawn dress and sunbonnet. Hts. 11½ and 13½ in. (29 and 34 cm.).

Rose Mary. See **Dolly Rose Mary, Rosemary, and Rose-Marie.**

Rosebud. 1914. Bisque head doll with wig, sleeping eyes, and dressed, advertised by *Butler Bros.* Ht. 13 in. (33 cm.); priced $4.60 doz. wholesale. It is not known whether this Rosebud was the doll marked "Rosebud" that had an *Armand Marseille* head, or the *Schoenau & Hoffmeister* head doll marked "Rosebud" mold # 2500.

Rosebud. 1926–28 and possibly other years. Line of *Bico* dolls produced by *B. Illfelder Co.,* also known as "Our Rosebud, Our Own line."

Rosebud. See **Little Rosebud.**

2246. Mark used for Rosebud dolls by B. Illfelder.

Rosebud Babies (Baby Rosebud[†]). 1914–29. Composition head, dressed dolls produced by *Horsman.*

1916: Bent-limb baby doll with head copyrighted in 1914. Five hts. 14½ to 26 in. (37 to 66 cm.).

1929: *Mama* doll with wig; sleeping eyes, hair eyelashes; cotton-stuffed cloth body containing a *Lloyd* mama voice; doll dressed in organdy. Four hts. 17¾, 19¼, 20, and 22 in. (45, 49, 51, and 56 cm.). (See also Dolly Rosebud and Ills. 1222 and 2077.)

Rösel, Hermann. 1921–30 and later. Nürnberg, Bavaria. Made outfits for dolls, specialized in clothes for baby dolls.★

Roseland. Bisque shoulder head marked "Roseland." Ht. 25 in. (63.5 cm.).

Rose-Marie (Rose Mary). 1925–30. Composition head *Mama* doll made by *Effanbee,* had a human hair long curled wig, sleeping eyes, hair eyelashes, teeth, and tongue; on a cloth body with composition arms and long slim legs. It wore various costumes with a large hairbow or bandeau and bow, and a golden heart necklace. It was similar to *Mary Sue*

except it had long curls instead of short curls. Hts. 18 to 30 in. (45.5 to 76 cm.). *Montgomery Ward* advertised an Effanbee Rose Mary with the same description. Four hts. 18, 21, 23, and 26 in. (45.5, 53.5, 58.5, and 66 cm.); priced $6.29 to $10.93.

1929–30: Sometimes had flirting eyes when it was named Coquette or Laughing Eyes according to Pat Schoonmaker. (See also **Rosemary.**)

Rosemary. 1925–28. Generally the description was the same as for *Rose-Marie.*

1925: Came with a cloth *Mama* doll type body or a body with slanting hip joints.★

Rosemary.[†] See **Rose Mary.**

Rosenberg, Ignác. Ca. 1925–30. Budapest. Made dolls.★

Rosenthal, Gallie. 1926–29. Hamburg, Germany. Obtained three German patents (D.R.P.), for dolls' eyes.

Rosenthal Porcelain. See **Arnold, Max Oscar.**

Rosenstein, Henry, Co. 1907–30. New York City. Imported dolls and distributed domestic dolls.★

Rosetta. 1927. Trade name for a doll.

2247. Rosebud composition flange head on a shoulder plate doll. It has a brown human hair wig, sleeping blue metal eyes, hair eyelashes, open mouth with three teeth, and a felt tongue. The Mama type body is cloth with composition lower arms and legs and a mama voice inside the torso. Original dress and shoes. Mark stamped on cloth upper leg "©// E.I.H. Co. INC." Mark on body: "PATENT APPLIED FOR." H. 24 in. (61 cm.). *Courtesy of John Axe. Photo by John Axe.*

2248. Composition shoulder head Mama doll named Rosemary, made by Effanbee. It has a blond human hair wig, sleeping blue metal eyes, hair eyelashes, open mouth with teeth, and a felt tongue. The cloth body has composition arms and lower legs. Original clothes. Mark on shoulder plate in an ellipse "EFFAN-BEE//ROSEMARY//WALK TALK SLEEP." H. 21 in. (53.5 cm.). *Courtesy of John Axe. Photo by John Axe.*

Rosette. Composition-head doll whose box was marked "Rosette Indestructible, My Clothes take off. Made in Germany." Ht. 13 in. (33 cm.).

Rosette. ca. 1925. *Lafayette* store described their dressed Rosette doll as having a wig with a bow in its hair, a cloth body, and a silk costume. Hts. 42 and 65 cm. (16½ and 25½ in.).★

Rosewax. 1927 and possibly other years. A "Scientific and Artistic" composition used by *Kämmer & Reinhardt* for their *My Darling* line of dolls. This may have been a celluloid variant type of composition.

Rosie. 1893. Name of waterproof apparel for dolls, produced by *Horsman;* priced $2.25 doz. wholesale. (See also **Dollie.**)

Rosina. 1927–28. *Lenci* felt doll style no. 165/17 dressed in a romanticized costume which included an apron. Ht. 27½ in. (70 cm.).

Rosnoblet, Mme. 1918 ca. 1920. Paris. Created dolls, some of which wore Alsatian regional costumes.

Ross Dolls. 1916–22. Line of dressed composition dolls manufactured by the *Wholesale Toy Co.* The company was known as the Ross Wholesale Toy Co. by 1922.

1916: Dolls with wigs and composition legs included baby dolls and character dolls.

Ross, H. 1800s. London. A label on the chest of a wax doll in its original wooden box had the Royal cipher, below which was "H. Ross//570 Gallery// Soho Bazaar// English and Foreign// Dolls." Groups of hair were inset into the amber wax and the doll was dressed as a baby according to Margaret Glover.

A similarly marked doll had inserted short blond hair, blue glass eyes, and a cloth body. The wax head and wax arms were attached with grommets. Ht. 17½ in. (44.5 cm.). Ht. of shoulder head 4 in. (10 cm.).

Ross, Penny. 1925–26. Designed the *Flower Dolls* and *Esther Starring* as a doll; these were made of oilcloth by *Live Long Toys* in their *Mama's Angel Child* line.★

Ross & Co. 1921. London. Produced miniature dolls.

Ross & Ross. 1918–30 and later. Oakland, Calif. C. I. Ross and his two sons manufactured cloth dolls. Hilbert Ross designed the dolls which were shipped all over the Pacific areas.

1922: Dolls included *Mary Ann, Mary Jane* and *Topsy*.

1926: Dolls were distributed by *A. S. Ferguson*.

1928: Advertised *Humpty Dumpty* and plush dolls dressed as boys and girls. (See Ill. 2618.)

Rossignol, Charles. Before 1878–1900. Paris. Won a silver medal at the 1878 Paris Exposition for his dolls.★

Rostal, Henri. 1914. Paris, Rue du Trésor. A bisque-head doll marked "*Mon//Trésor*" had an open mouth and teeth. Ht. 50 cm. (19½ in.). Another one of his dolls was reported to have been a lady type on a kid body with separate toes. Ht. 76 cm. (30 in.).★

Rosy (Rosy Cheeks or Miss Rosy Cheeks). 1921–26. Composition-head *Mama* doll made by *Ideal,* had a bobbed hair wig, sleeping and winking eyes, wore a lace trimmed organdy dress or a play dress or rompers, a knitted cap, patent leather slippers. It had a patented feature that caused one foot to draw back when the other foot was pushed forward. A round tag on the doll read "Walking// Doll" plus some other words. It was offered as a premium by NEEDLECRAFT magazine. Ht. 13 in. (33 cm.).

Rosy-Posy (Rosy Posy). 1917–20. Manufactured by *Elektra.*★

Rosy-Posy (Rosy Posy). 1927–28. Trademark registered in U.S. by *Borgfeldt* for dolls.

1928: Advertised as a doll dressed in a felt Dutch girl costume; had a boy doll as a mate; priced $6.95 each.

Roszmann, Mme. 1918. Paris. Created dolls.

Roth, Joseph, Manufacturing Co. 1915–22. New York City. 1922–27. Roth, Baitz & Lipsitz† (R. B. & L. Manufacturing Co.). New York City. It was claimed that Joseph Roth had begun manufacturing dolls prior to 1908 which suggests that he may have migrated to America. Manufactured composition-head dolls made by a pressing process which they claimed could be done in all kinds of temperature both winter and summer. In the 1920s they imported German bisque-head dolls. Some of these were made by *Armand Marseille.* One of the bisque heads has been reported by Mary McCarthy as being mold # 154 having a plaster pate with R. B. L. Co. incised on it and a label reading "Real Kid, R. B. L. Co." on its kid body. The celluloid arms and legs had a *tortoise* mark.

1915: Advertised character dolls named *Grump* boy and girl, baby dolls in long dresses, sailor boys, clowns, and *Yama* dolls; priced 25¢ to $1.00.

1923: Manufactured *Mama* dolls with composition heads and arms, with or without wigs with painted eyes, cotton stuffed cloth bodies with "pink toes," *Ronson* voices, two-piece dresses with matching bonnets, mercerized socks and leatherette slippers. Some of these dolls bore a tag reading "R. B. L.//Pretty dresses, things that's fine,// Walking, Talking all the time,//Mama, Papa, crying cute,// Lusty voices, never mute."

H.R.

3
H.R.

2249–2250. Marks on bisque-head dolls believed to have been made by Henri Rostal.

1925: Advertised composition baby dolls and Mama dolls as well as *My Dream Baby* type bisque head dolls with Ronson criers in their cloth bodies, dressed in long, lace-trimmed baby dresses.

1926: Advertised *Baby Gloria,* rubber-head dolls, and a full-size "Marcel" (Marseille) bisque-head baby, with moving eyes, cloth body and Ronson voice. Bisque-head babies came in four sizes, priced $1.00 and up.

1927: Member of the *American Doll Manufacturers' Association.* They were licensed by *Voices, Inc.,* to use their patented Mama voices and criers.

Advertised Baby Gloria and other dolls with bisque or rubber heads.

1929: *Maxine Doll Co.* appears to have taken over the Baby Gloria line of dolls.★

Roth, Louis. 1895–1927. Sonneberg, Thür. Made and exported dolls.★

2251. Roth, Baitz & Lipsitz advertisement in PLAYTHINGS, January 1927. Their dolls have bisque, composition or rubber heads and include Baby Gloria, infant and Mama dolls. The infant doll closely resembles My Dream Baby.

Roth, V. See **Bauersachs, Emil.**

Roth & Rau. 1875. Nürnberg, Bavaria. Creditor of doll maker *Edouard Cerbelaud* when he failed, according to Mme. Florence Poisson, Curator of the Roybet-Fould Museum.

Rothenstein, Eugene. 1925–28. New York City. Made outfits for dolls.

Rothschild & Co. 1930. Britain. Advertised dolls including celluloid dolls in a British toy trade journal.

Rotkäppchen. See **Red Hood (Rotkäppchen)** as well as **Little Red Riding Hood** and **Red Riding Hood.**

Rotraut. 1916–24. Felt doll made by *Steiff.* Five hts. 28, 35, 43, 50 and 60 cm. (11, 14, 17, 19½ and 23½ in.). By 1924 the largest size had been discontinued.

Rouaud, Charles. 1913–20s. Paris. Member of the *Chambre Syndicale;* dressed dolls and bébés; made trunks and boxes filled with a doll and its wardrobe of clothes as well as separate dolls' clothes. Some of these items were exported.★

Rough Rider. 1899–1901. Name of a doll distributed by *Butler Bros.* Ht. 8½ in. (21 cm.).

Rough Rider. 1917. Composition head doll distributed by the *Baltimore Bargain House.* The cloth body had composition hands. Ht. 36 in. (91.5 cm.); priced $1.35.

Roullet & Decamps. 1865–1930 and later. Paris. Henriette Roullet Decamps, widow of Ernst Decamps, and her son Gaston Decamps were successors. They were members of the *Chambre Syndicale.* They made various mechanical walking dolls which usually had the initials "R D" on their keys.

1893: Made dolls named *Bébé Système.*★

Roumanian (Rumanian, Romanian) Dolls. Had heads of bisque, china or composition, and the dolls were made of cloth including felt, composition, leather or rubber.

1926–27: Roumanian refugees in Paris dressed dolls as Roumanian peasants. They wore long tunics, little bright colored wool aprons and shoes that were spangled and embroidered. (See also **Queen Elisabeth of Roumania.**)

Roussel & Dufrien. 1900–10. Paris. Made dolls.

1900: One of the Grand Prize Winners at the Paris Exposition.

1910: Received Honorable Mention at the Brussels Exposition.

Rouxel. 1927–30 and later. Paris. Created and exported art dolls including *Poupées Lumière.*

Rowan, Mr. 1922. Holland, Michigan. Made wooden shoes for dolls.

Rowe, M. & Co. 1923. London, Nürnberg, Berlin. Advertised dolls.

Roxy Doll & Toy Co. 1929. U.S.A. Member of the *Doll Parts Manufacturing Assoc.,* which required that members make heads, hands, arms, or other composition parts of dolls.

2252. Roullet & Decamps' bisque head walking doll with a blond wig, sleeping blue glass eyes, an open mouth, and a composition body containing a key wind mechanism. Contemporary clothes. H. 23 in. (58.5 cm.). *Courtesy of Dr. Eva Moskovszky.*

Roxy Factory. 1915–20. Longton, Stoke-on-Trent, Staffs. Made dolls. Probably these had *British Ceramic* heads. Thomas Dodd was the owner of this factory.

Roy, Jules. 1837–57. Paris. Made dolls.

1857: Used iron hinges for the articulation of dolls. Patented the use of zinc for dolls' heads, according to Florence Poisson, curator of the Roybet Fould Museum. A doll with its head painted on a silver colored metal and having a hair style with a molded knot has been found by Maurine Popp on a kid body with wooden limbs. This unusual doll may or may not have been made by Jules Roy.★

Royal. 1902–14. Trademark used by *Kämmer & Reinhardt.* This line of dolls included *Peter* and Marie† (See Ill. 1381) and Hans† and Gretchen† (See Ill. 1387).

1908: See THE COLLECTOR'S BOOK OF DOLLS' CLOTHES, Ill. 556.★

Royal Bébé. 1910–11: Advertised by *Aux Trois Quartiers.* It had a bisque head, wig, sleeping eyes, hair eyelashes and a fully jointed body that could walk and throw kisses. It was parlant (talking?). The elaborate clothes were removable. Hts. 62 and 66 cm. (24½ and 26 in.); priced $6.00 and $8.00.

Royal Copenhagen Manufactory. 1772–1930 and later. Denmark. The production of china dolls' heads was limited to 1843–ca. 1880 with a total production figure of only about 23,000 heads, nearly all of which were produced prior to 1860. These were marked with three lines inside the breast plate.

1977 and later: Three of the original molds were used to make china heads with colors and painting similar to that of the original dolls' heads. There were a 5½ in. (14 cm.) and a 3¾ in. (9.5 cm.) high lady's shoulder head with molded dark brown hair in a knot in back. The 3¾ in. (9.5 cm.) high boys' shoulder head had molded tan colored short hair and a side part. All three heads had three sewholes in front and in back. These dolls' heads had modern markings inside the heads along the back edge of the shoulder. One of the large heads was marked 5248 and "Denmark," in green. Probably 5248 was the mold number.★

Royal Crown Pottery Co. 1917–18. Burslem, Stoke-on-Trent, Staffs. Made dressed dolls and dolls' heads.

1917: Dressed character dolls included Pierrot, Pierrette, Scottish dolls, Jersey boys and girls and Red Riding Hood.

1918: Leading line was *Kandy Kids.*

Royal Model Dolls. Middle of the 1800s. Wax portrait dolls of the children of Queen Victoria. (See also **Model Dolls.**)

Royal Toy Manufacturing Co. 1913–30 and later. New York City. Made composition and cloth body dolls.

1920: Advertised composition baby dolls and lady dolls with painted or sleeping eyes, dressed or undressed.

1921: Advertised all-composition dolls with human hair wigs and voices that cried, "Mama, Papa." A black baby came in three sizes.

1923: Made *Mama* dolls.

1926: Member of the *American Doll Manufacturers' Association.*

1927: Advertised *Bottle Babe;* slender dolls in 20 styles and four sizes. Mama dolls came in 24 styles and five sizes. A new doll was called *Baby Joy.* This company's mark was a crowned doll's head with "Royal" on the crown and the words "ROYAL//TRADE MARK//A DOLL OF THE BETTER KIND." They were licensed by *Voices, Inc.* to use the patented Mama voices and criers in their dolls.

Produced dolls named *Annabelle* and *Gwendolyn* which were distributed by *Montgomery Ward.*

1928: Mama dolls had new faces and new clothes. Bottle Baby cost $1.00, while Baby Joy cost $4.00 and up.

1929: Bottle Baby was advertised as Bottle Babe.

1930: Advertised Bottle Babe and Baby Joy.★

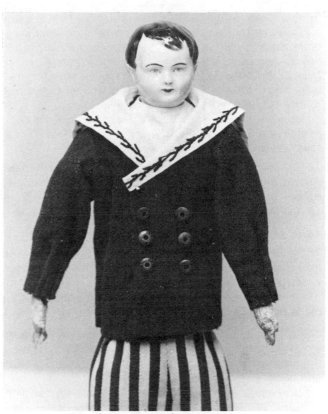

2254. Pressed china shoulder head made by Royal Copenhagen has molded short black hair, painted blue eyes, closed mouth and a body with kid arms. Mark: See Ill. 1409 in the first COLLECTOR'S ENCYCLOPEDIA OF DOLLS. Possibly contemporary clothes. *Courtesy of Paige Thornton.*

2253A, B, C & D. China shoulder head bearing the mark (See Ill. 2255) of Royal Copenhagen. **A & B** show the front and back of the shoulder head; the brown-black hair is intertwined into a bun placed at the center back of the head. In back of the exposed ears is a lock of hair ending in brushmarks. The eyes are painted blue and the eyebrows are brown. The doll can also be seen in Ill. 1408 in the first COLLECTOR'S ENCYCLOPEDIA OF DOLLS. **C** is a close-up of the hand and **D** is a close-up of the feet. The body is cloth. H. 13½ in. (34 cm.). H. of the shoulder head 4 in. (10 cm.). *Courtesy of Z. Frances Walker.*

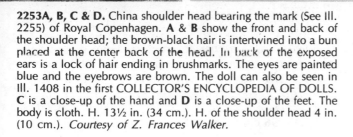

2255–2256. Mark on china shoulder heads made by Royal Copenhagen porcelain factory.

Roze Dolls. 1919–22. Composition head and arms on a cork stuffed body, made by *Federal*. It had molded hair or wigs, painted eyes, and the shoulder plate extended below the armpits so that the arms were strung with elastic. The legs had inside joints. The dolls were undressed or dressed in various costumes. Some of the dolls had sweaters over their dresses and stocking caps.

1920: 42 style Nos. Ht. 14½ in. (37 cm.)★

Rozmann, Mlle. 1915–16. Paris. Made cloth dolls, including *Parmentier*.

2257. Mark on composition Roze dolls.

Rubber Dolls. Mid 1800s–1930 and later. Made in many countries and enjoyed great popularity because they did not break easily. Unfortunately rubber deteriorated with age and few all-rubber dolls or rubber dolls' heads have survived. Most of the rubber dolls had molded clothes but when they were dressed it was usually in knitted woolen outfits. The rubber itself was red, gray, black or beige in color and often contained a whistle. The dolls tended to be small and competitive in price with dolls of other materials. Molds of the same design were used for a long time.

1850s–60s: Rubber dolls were new and a very popular type. Among the producers were: *H. G. Norton* who advertised rubber heads for dolls and dressed rubber baby dolls; *George N. Davis* advertised rubber dolls.

1872: Distributed by *S. Bloch.*

1876: *Silber & Fleming* advertised India rubber babies in long dresses, two hts., and India rubber dolls in wool dresses, three hts.

The *Louvre* store advertised rubber bébés and dolls made especially for this store.

1878: THE QUEEN reported squeaking rubber dolls dressed in crocheted colored woolen outfits representing a zouave, a drummer, a black boy or a baby in long clothes with a cloak and hood.

Printemps advertised a rubber doll in a knitted wool costume. Ht. 10 in. (25.5 cm.); priced 49¢.

1879: Dressed German rubber dolls were advertised. Hts. 24 and 29 cm. (9½ and 11½ in.).

1880: The Strasburger, Pfeiffer⁺ catalog listed baby, girl, boy and lady rubber dolls. Some of the dolls had whistles, especially the baby dolls, and some were partly painted. Hts. ranged from 3½ to 9 in. (9 to 23 cm.).

1882: Silber & Fleming's rubber dolls came undressed or wearing a chemise, in nine sizes; and dressed in wool in 15 sizes.

1884: The *Lauer* catalog listed baby, boy or girl rubber dolls in molded clothes or in worsted knitted clothes. Eight hts. 3¼ to 10¼ in. (8 to 26.5 cm.); priced $1.25 to $8.00 doz. wholesale. A rubber doll with moving head and arms was 6½ in. (16.5 cm.) tall and cost $3.50 doz. wholesale.

Bon Marché advertised rubber bébés dressed in knitted wool costumes. Three heights, priced 29¢ to 90¢.

1887: Lauer advertised imported French rubber dolls with worsted knit dresses. Six hts. 4, 4¾, 6, 8¼, 10¼, and 12 in. (10, 12, 15, 21, 26, and 30.5 cm.); priced 85¢ to $9.00 doz. wholesale. The domestic rubber boy doll with jointed neck and arms was 7 in. (18 cm.); priced $3.50 doz. wholesale. The "Little Maid from School" with a fan was 6 in. (15 cm.); priced $2.40 doz. wholesale.

1889: Silber & Fleming's rubber doll came undressed or wearing a chemise, in 13 sizes, and dressed in wool in ten sizes.

1890: A Paris store advertised rubber dolls with painted heads and knitted costumes. Hts. 22 and 26 cm. (8½ and 10½ in.); priced 29¢ and 58¢.

1891: Ridley's catalog listed dressed rubber dolls with matching hats; priced $1.49 to $4.89.

1893: *Horsman* advertised India Rubber dolls with worsted dresses and hats. The white dolls cost 75¢ to $24.00 doz. wholesale and the black ones cost $2.00 to $8.50 doz. wholesale.

1896: Printemps advertised rubber dolls dressed in wool and silk. Five hts. 21, 23, 26, 29, and 32 cm. (8½, 9, 10½, 11½, and 12½ in.). The Louvre store advertised a rubber bébé as a *Swaddling-clothed Baby.*

1902: *Butler Bros.* advertised rubber dolls with free arms and legs, dressed in worsted outfits. All except the smallest size had a "Voice." Five hts. 4½, 7½, 8¼, 8¾, and 9½ in. (11.5, 19, 21, 22.5, and 24.5 cm.); priced 75¢ to $3.85 doz. wholesale.

1903: *Tapis Rouge* advertised dressed, painted rubber dolls; hts. 24, 27, and 30 cm. (9½, 10½, and 12 in.); priced 35¢ to 55¢.

1904: Bon Marché advertised rubber dolls dressed in tricot. Six hts. 21 to 27 cm. (8½ to 10½ in.); priced 23¢ to 70¢.

1905: *Siegel Cooper* advertised dressed rubber baby dolls that looked as if they were similar to the ones in the Norton Catalog of about 1860. They had molded low neck, sleeveless dresses with high waistlines.

1908: The Louvre's rubber dolls wore knitted wool costumes and came in six hts. 21 to 30 cm. (8½ to 12 in.); priced 25¢ to $1.35.

1914: A Horsman catalog advertised six styles of dressed rubber dolls plus Buster Brown and a country girl.

Marshall Field advertised different styles of gray rubber whistling dolls, hts. 3 to 8¼ in. (7.5 to 21 cm.) and gray rubber dolls in knitted dresses, hts. 3¾ to 10½ in. (9.5 to 26.5 cm.).

1916–23: *Faultless Rubber Co.* made rubber dolls.

1926: Dolls with rubber heads, wigs, painted eyes, fully jointed composition bodies were sold by *F. A. O. Schwarz* in their *Favorite* line. The smaller sizes came dressed. Hts. 13 and 15 in. (33 and 38 cm.); priced $10.00 and $11.50. The larger sizes wore a chemise. Hts. 16, 18, and 22 in. (40.5, 45.5, and 56 cm.); priced $6.50 to $8.50.

1926–27: Rubber heads were used on composition bodies.

1927: *Montgomery Ward* advertised dolls with rubber heads, painted hair and eyes, cotton filled cloth bodies with composition hands, dressed in long baby dresses. They had cry voices. Ht. 12 in. (30.5 cm.); priced $1.19.

Ca. 1933: *Quaker Doll Co.* advertised rubber baby heads with sleeping eyes and *Patsy*-type inverted socket necks to be used on composition bodies. Also they advertised imported rubber hands for jointed composition bodies and rubber arms and crying legs for *Tickletoes.* (See also **Nicaput** and **Kämmer & Reinhardt.**)★

Rubber Hands (Separate). 1926 and later. Rubber hands were made so that dolls could grasp objects. Among those

2258. Grayish white rubber infant doll with molded clothes. Similar infant dolls were advertised by H. G. Norton in the third quarter of the 1800s; by Goodyear Rubber Co. in 1881; by Marshall Field in 1914 and the Baltimore Bargain House in 1922. H. 3¼ in. (8 cm.). *Coleman Collection.*

0 — 41160.
BÉBÉ caoutchouc, habillage
tricot laine.
4.50,
5.25, 5.95 et **6.95**

2259. Advertisement of a rubber doll in the 1921 catalog of L'Hotel de Ville. This bébé was dressed in a knitted wool outfit.

2260. Mark on Max Rudolph dolls.

who made dolls with rubber hands were *Arranbee, Ideal,* and *Kämmer & Reinhardt.* Dolls with *Armand Marseille* heads have been found on bodies with rubber hands. (See also **My Dream Baby.**)

Rube. 1929. Dressed cloth doll with long thin limbs made by the *Adler Favor and Novelty Co.* It squealed at the slightest touch.

Ruben (Rubin), J. C. 1920–21 and later. Superintendent of *Effanbee. Mr. Kallus* claimed that later Mr. Ruben made many of the dolls dressed by the *Alexander Doll Co.*

Ruchot, Ch., & Fils. 1928–29. Paris. Made molds for dolls' heads and masks for cloth dolls' heads.

Rucsimszky, Anna. See **Our Shop.**

Rudi (Swiss, Berne). 1911–13. Felt character doll made by *Steiff,* dressed in a Swiss regional costume of a Bernese girl. Ht. 35 cm. (14 in.).

Rudolph, August. 1928. Waltershausen, Thür. Manufactured baby dolls.

Rudolph, J. Doll, Co. 1924–29. Brooklyn, N.Y. Manufactured dolls. Licensed by *Voices, Inc.* to use their patented mama voices and criers in the Rudolph dolls.

Rudolph, Max. 1908–30 and later. Waltershausen, Thür. Made dolls and wigs. Used mark of M R in a W.

1907: Applied for a German patent (D.R.G.M.) for dolls' wigs.

1908: Company was founded.

1927: Advertised wigs and baby dolls.

1928: Made sitting and standing baby dolls.

1929: Applied for a German (D.R.P.) patent for a mama voice. Applied for two German (D.R.G.M.) patents, one for a doll's eyes and the other relating to a doll's voice.

1930: Distributors in Germany were: *Hermann Bischoff Jr.,* Hamburg; Karl Kraul, Leipzig; *M. Michaelis & Co.,* Berlin; Paul Teusch, Rheinland-Westfalen; Gustav Wald, Breslau; and Otto Wurster, South Germany.

The Max Rudolph catalog listed the following items: Bent limb baby dolls with mohair or human hair wig, sleeping eyes, hair eyelashes, moving tongue, a chemise and a string of beads to hide the neck joint; 10 hts. 28, 33, 36, 40, 45, 50, 55, 60, 66, and 72 cm. (11, 13, 14, 15½, 17½, 19½, 21½, 23½, 26, and 28½ in.). Toddler dolls also had five-piece bodies and were similar in other respects to the bent limb babies. Their chemises were made of silk tricot. Bisque heads only also came for two smaller size dolls, hts. 20 and 24 cm. (8 and 9½ in.). Bisque heads came in mold #98, size numbers 2/0, 1, 3, 4, 5, 7, 9, 10, 12, 13, 14½, and 16; and mold # 342 size numbers were 15/0, 10/0, 6/0, 5/0, 4/0, 0, 1, 3½, 5, 6½, 7, 8, 10, and 12.

The separate celluloid heads were of two types: the celluloid *Miblu* heads were mold # 350 and came in nine sizes, while the celluloid shoulder heads came in 14 sizes.

The *Porzellanit* (Composition) heads were mold # 399 and also came in a variety of sizes. The prices of dolls with any one of the three types of heads, bisque, celluloid, or composition, were very close for corresponding sizes. Voices and flirting eyes were each extra, but voices were not available for the 28 and 33 cm. (11 and 13 in.) dolls.

Available parts and clothes for dolls included wigs, sleeping eyes, stockings, and shoes. The two-tone oxfords were one style of shoe offered.★

Rudolph Valentino. 1928–29. *Lenci* felt portrait doll of Valentino as he appeared in THE SHEIK dressed in a striped caftan and cordovan leather boots with tassels. It carried a dagger and pistol. *Kirsch & Reale* distributed this doll in the U.S. The painted eyes looked to the side. Ht. 30 in. (76 cm.) according to the Lenci Catalog, style No. 560.

Rudolstadt. See **Bohne, Ernst.**

Rudy. 1927. Trade name used by *Borgfeldt.*

Ruf, Joseph. 1927. Made *Mama* dolls. He was licensed by *Voices, Inc.* to use their patented mama voices and criers in his dolls.

Ruffles Co. 1930 and later. Kansas City, Mo., and Los Angeles, Calif. Registered in U.S. the trademark Ruffles for dolls. The trademark was taken out by Camille C. Blair. A flat faced cloth doll with yarn hair, button eyes, embroidered nose and mouth bore the mark "Ruffles Trade Mark Reg. Design Patent 82656. The Ruffles Company, Kansas City, Missouri." Ht. 15 in. (38 cm.).

Rufus. 1929. Black doll made by *Averill Manufacturing Co.,* had composition head and arms, painted hair and eyes, cotton stuffed cloth body with a two tone whistle. The doll wore overalls and a hat. Ht. 14 in. (35.5 cm.).

Ruhling, Vergho & Co. Ca. 1855 to 1880s. Chicago, Ill. Their trade card listed dolls.

Rühm & Müller. 1910. Königsee, Thür. Applied for a German patent (D.R.G.M.) for a doll's hat.

Rumania. See **Roumanian (Rumanian, Romanian) Dolls.**

Rumplestillykin. 1917. Name of a doll made by *Shropshire Toy Industry.*

Runggaldier, Franz. Late 1700s–1844. Grödner Tal, Austria. One of the first persons to paint dolls in the Grödner Tal. He was called "Bera Franzl Moler." Moler or Maler means painter according to Dr. Eva Moskovszky.

Runggaldier (Rungaldier), Johann Anton (Antoine). Early 1800s to 1890. Janong and St. Ulrich, in the Grödner Tal, Austria. The successors were in Paris also. This was one of the *Verleger* families that collected wooden dolls made as a home industry in the Grödner Tal, and distributed them all over the world. After Johann Runggaldier died, his widow succeeded him and by 1865 she in turn was succeeded by her son Antoine Runggaldier and her son-in-law B. Planker. Both of these men were listed in a Paris directory as wholesale distributors of dolls and toys from Germany and France.

1881: Purchased bisque dolls' heads from *François Gaultier* and produced dolls according to Mme. Poisson, curator of the Roybet Fould Museum. ★

2261. Lenci felt doll dressed as Rudolph Valentino in THE SHEIK. It has hair attached to the scalp, painted brown eyes looking to the side, closed mouth, and the felt body is jointed at the neck, shoulders and hips. Original clothes. H. 29 in. (73.5 cm.). *Courtesy of Sotheby Parke Bernet Inc., N.Y.*

Runggaldier & Sennoner. Before 1838. Grödner Tal, Austria. Sold dolls in Nürnberg. (See also **Sanoner.**)

Runnells, E. A., & Co. 1887–1930. Boston, Mass., and New York City. Importers and factory agents for dolls.

1918: Factory agent for *Belgian Doll Co.* and sole agent for *Nelke.*★

Rural Dolls. 1920–21. Name given to the dolls that were sent by the Baroness de Laumont to the little French villages where they were dressed by the local peasants and shepherdesses, thus enabling them to earn a little extra money.

Rusfe (Russian Field Soldier). 1916. Felt doll made by *Steiff.* Hts. 28 and 35 cm. (11 and 14 in.).

Rushig, O. 1927. Potschappel, Germany. Assignee of a British patent obtained by Hartwig and Vogel.

Rushton Co. 1924–30 and later. Atlanta, Ga. and New York

City. Made cloth dolls, primarily the *Mawaphil* line of dolls. Most of the dolls were stockinet, handmade and hand-painted.

1927: Made plush dolls as well as stockinet.

1930: Made dolls of stockinet, plush, velveteen and terry cloth. One line of dolls had plush heads, arms and legs, handpainted faces, print costumes, felt shoes, and mercerized stockings. Ht. 10 in. (25.5 cm.); priced 50¢ to $4.00.

Russe, A.A.H. Possibly late 1800s. Paris. A doll with a bisque head made by *Simon & Halbig,* marked "S 8 H, 1009," was on a wood and composition body marked "A.A.H. Russe// Bastion 55 Bᵈ Lannes."

Russian Boy. 1912. Composition-head dolls with molded hair and molded boots, made by *Ideal,* wore a Russian style tunic. Striped cloth stockings covered the legs above the boots.

Russian Boy. 1928. *Boudoir* doll dressed as a Russian Boy and distributed by *Eisen.*

Russian Dolls. According to Russian publications, from around 1600 colored clay dolls were made in the Dimkov-skaya district. A few years later wooden dolls were made in a Sergiyevo monastery and both the clay and the wooden dolls continued to be made for generations. As early as 1787 wooden dolls began to be made by peasants and towns-people in Serhijewski near Moscow. The alleged "Father" of the doll-making industry was *Tatyha,* who carved dolls from linden (bass) wood. He trained others to make dolls including *Chirkoff.* Two of the most popular types of wooden Russian dolls were the *Trihedrals* and the *Matryoshkas* which originated in Semyonov. Many of the Trihedrals of the 1800s and 1900s were made in the Zagorsk region, the doll-making center of Russia. Both wooden and papier-mâché dolls were also made in Horodowsky, Wladymyr and Wiatsky Provinces. About 1840 *E. F. Safonoff* began making papier-mâché dolls. At first he hired a sculptor to make the models for the heads but later he was able to do this himself.

Doll making prospered in Russia during the earlier years of the 1800s and the dolls were sent all over the world. Towards the end of the century cloth dolls were made in the Orel region and some bisque head dolls were made possibly in Zagorsk. Competition grew as the 1800s ended and the craftsmen found it necessary to form a union. Russians copied many of the dolls made in other countries but one unique type of doll making in Russia was a method of carving wood using a hot iron. Not only were there the trihedrals without joints but there were also wooden dolls with many joints. Prior to the Revolution the peasant children had dolls of straw and rags.

Before 1897: Hall and Ellis of Clark University, Mass., wrote A STUDY OF DOLLS, where they reported that the Russian Toy Congress protested against the large, elegant French dolls that taught love of dress and suggested luxury.

1900: At the Paris International Exposition, Russian wooden dolls and dolls dressed in provincial costumes were displayed. The *Zemstvo* Russian dolls had strong competition from the bisque head bébés made in Poland.

1913: TOYS AND NOVELTIES showed trihedral type wooden dolls that were being made by Russian peasants. LADIES' HOME JOURNAL showed the following 7 in. (18 cm.) dolls dressed by children in a Russian orphans' asylum: a pilgrim, Russian gentleman, Russian lady, musician, nursemaid carrying a baby boy or a baby girl, water-carrier, farmer boy and girl, coachman, ice-cream peddler and broom seller.

1914: Rubber dolls were made in Russia.

1916: *Steiff* dressed a felt doll as a Russian Soldier.

1919: A collection of early clay dolls belonging to the author Denshin was given to a Toy Museum in Zagorsk. The making of these clay dolls was described as follows: the material was red clay mixed with sand. The doll dried for three or four days then it was fired. It was painted with skim milk and crushed chalk, then dried again and painted with paints mixed with egg yolks separated from the egg white. After that a mixture of water and vinegar was added and finally the gold coloring was done with crushed gold leaf.

1924: A Frenchman referred to doll babies in *swaddling clothes* made by Russian peasants and costing less than a cent.

1926: Russian refugees in Paris dressed dolls as Russian peasants in embroidered smocks and great boots; boy dolls wore full red trousers and girl dolls had flower wreaths in their yellow hair. *Marie Vassilieff,* one of the Russian doll makers, was still showing her character dolls.

1928: Dolls made by Russian peasants were distributed in America by *Am Torg.*

TOYS AND NOVELTIES reported, "Moscow Teacher's Union has decided that little girls should not be allowed to play with dolls. The doll represents the bourgeois idea of family life."

PLAYTHINGS reported that 50 more dolls that belonged to the Russian Princesses were sent to the museum at Thar-koies Selo. (See Ills. 2262–2266.)★

Ruth. Ca. 1900. Name on a bisque shoulder head. ★

Ruth (Winter Sports; Norweg). Before 1911–16. Felt character doll made by *Steiff* and distributed in the U.S. by *Borgfeldt.* It represented a girl dressed for winter sports and was a mate to *Rolf.* Ruth wore a red sweater and leather shoes. Four hts. 28, 35, 43 and 50 cm. (11, 14, 17, and 19½ in.).

1911: The two largest sizes also came with the new long hair feature. With short hair the prices were $2.00 and $3.00 but with long hair they were $3.37 and $4.20.

Ruth. 1928–29. Composition shoulder head doll with composition arms and legs that enabled it to stand; distributed by *Butler Bros.* It had painted hair and eyes, a cotton stuffed cloth body with a crying voice and wore an organdy or percale dress and bonnet. Attached to it was a round tag with "Ruth" on it. Ht. 14 in. (35.5 cm.).

Ruth. See **Pet Name.**

2262. Manufacture of dolls in Russia, 1912. Illustration from the Russian Book UTPYWKA at the Widener Library, Harvard University.

2264. Russian ceramic head of a tan color that had changed with exposure. It has sleeping glass eyes, open mouth with teeth, composition and wood cylindrical jointed body. Original Russian peasant costume. H. 16½ in. (42 cm.). *Coleman Collection.*

2266. Mark found on a Russian ceramic doll probably copied from a German prototype.

2263. A polychromed carved wood trihedral doll made in Russia in the 1800s. H. 8 in. (20.5 cm.) including base and headwear. *Coleman Collection.*

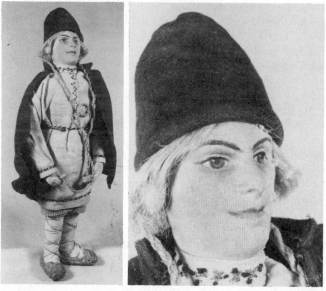

2265. Russian cloth doll, face made of painted silk stockinet, hair wig, cloth body. Dressed as a Russian Village Boy with a coarsely woven tunic, wool hat and coat, and straw shoes. H. 16 in. (40.5 cm.). *Coleman Collection.*

2267. Ruth, a name incised on a bisque head.

S

S.G.D.G. Sans Garantie du Gouvernement (Without Guarantee of the Government).

S.I.C. (S.I.M.P.). See **Société Industrielle de Celluloid.**

S.I.M.A.R.S.A. 1928. Turin, Italy. Made dolls.

S.I.R.E. 1929. Turin, Italy. Manufactured dolls.

S. J. Co-operative Society. 1920. Karachi, India. Handled dolls.

S. K. Novelty Co. (S. Kirsch & Co.†). 1917–27. Brooklyn, N.Y. and New York City. 1926–27. Known as the S. K. Doll Manufacturing Co. Made dolls of various kinds and sold them to jobbers and retailers.

1919: Advertised "America's Genuine Bisque Dolls." With or without wigs, some had colored bathing caps.

1920: Advertised all-bisque dolls, dolls named *Lovie,* also composition dolls with or without wigs, painted eyes, jointed or not jointed, dressed or undressed. The character dolls came 9 to 18 in. (23 to 45.5 cm.) tall.

1926: Advertised *Mama* dolls, infant dolls and novelty dolls; priced $1.00 and up.

1927: Licensed by *Voices, Inc.* to use their patented mama voices and criers.★

S. & C. See **Schmidt, Franz.**

S. & Co. 1910s. Sonneberg, Thür. A circular green stamp reading "Geschützt//S. & Co.//Germany." has been frequently found on bisque-head character babies. Other marks found on heads having the green stamp S. & Co. included B.P.; C.; D. I.; D. II.; D. I.P.; D.V.; F. P.; and LORI. Another head has been found incised "A//GERMANY //S & C." and having the green stamp on it. Most of these dolls have a closed or open-closed mouth. However a Lori with an open mouth had the mold number of 232.

Probably the S. & Co. stands for the porcelain manufacturer *Swaine & Co.*★

S. & H. Novelty Co. 1925–30 and later. Atlantic City, N.J. Manufactured cloth-body dolls. Factory agents were *Baker & Bennett, Borgfeldt, B. Illfelder,* and *Corcoran & Laycock.*

1927: Made *Black Bottom Vamp, Lucky Lindy,* and *Tee Wee* which was patented.

1929: Made *Peppy Pals,* the name of which they registered in the U.S. as a trademark. These dolls were also referred to as Dancing Marionettes, Radio Dancing Couple, and Tickle Toes.

1930: They unsuccessfully tried to obtain the trademark *Amos 'N Andy* for dolls.

S. & L. Manufacturing Co. 1926 and later. London. Made velveteen and stockinet dolls, including Gaby; Jim, Joyce, Pamela, Patty, and Peggy.

S. & R. 1928. Trade name used by *Selchow & Righter Co.*

S. & S. Doll Co. 1927–30 and later. New York City. Made composition-head dolls including *Mama* dolls for the jobbing trade.

2268A & B. Bisque head doll with a wig, sleeping brown glass eyes, closed mouth on a bent limb composition baby body. Contemporary clothes. Mark: Ill. 2270. H. 8½ in. (21.5 cm.). *Coleman Collection.*

2269. Pair of bisque-head dolls with closed mouths on bent limb composition baby bodies with contemporary clothes. The doll on the left has painted and molded hair, stationary blue glass eyes and is marked "D. V. //3" over the S. & Co. green stamp shown in Ill. 2270. The doll on the right has a blond wig, sleeping blue glass eyes, and is marked "D.I.P." over the S. & Co. green stamp and 3 is under it. *Courtesy of June Jeffcott.*

2270. Mark on an S. & Co. (possibly Swaine & Co.) bisque head; the upper part is incised and the lower part in the circle is a green stamp.

1927: Was licensed by *Voices, Inc.* to use their patented mama voices and criers in the dolls made by S. & S. Doll Co.

1928: Advertised 40 style nos.; the better ones had composition arms and legs.

S. & S. Sales Co. 1926–27. New York City. Made clothes and accessories for dolls.

Saalfield Publishing Co. 1907–30 and later. Akron, Ohio. Made printed cutout cloth dolls.

1907: Dolls included Baby Boy Doll (Boy Doll), Baby Girl Doll (Girl Doll), *Dotty Dimple, Japanese Kimono Doll,* Little Red Riding Hood and *Tiny Travelers* series.

1908: Made a book of cutout dolls entitled BABIES OF ALL NATIONS. It included dolls named *Ah Sid, American Girl, Gretchen, Hans, Hiawatha, Juanita, Little Peary, Marie,* and *Tokio.* A considerable amount of red was used for the costumes on these dolls. Another book was entitled DOLLIES SEWING BEE.

1909: Made *Baby Blue Eyes.*

1910: Made *Mammy Doll.*

1911: Made *Little Mary* and the *Rag Family.*

1913: Made *Golden Locks* (Goldenlocks).

1914: Made *Fritz.*

1915: Made My Big Dolly with a photographic face on the large, 26 in. (66 cm.) doll and two small versions, 6½ in. (16.5 cm.), all on a sheet 36 by 23 in. (89 by 58.5 cm.).

1916: Made *Dolly Dear* designed by *Frances Brundage.*

1919: Made Tiny Travelers, and *Our Foreign Cousins* with six dolls, size 9 × 11 in. (23 × 28 cm.); priced 5¢.

Other new cutout dolls included *Betty, Comic Kid,* Donald, *Dorothy, Girlie,* Indian Maid, *Jane, Jimmy,* Little Mary, *My Best Dolly, Priscilla* and Tootsie.

1920: *Little Princess* was a new doll.

1922: Dolly Dear came in two sizes, 17 × 23 in. (43 × 58.5 cm.) and 24 × 36 in. (61 × 91.5 cm.).

1928: The Saalfield catalog listed Baby Blue Eyes, Dolly Dear, Little Mary, Little Princess and Priscilla.

1930: The catalog listed Comic Kid, Dolly Dear, Jimmy, Little Mary and Priscilla.★

Saba. 1924–30. Turin, Italy. Advertised felt art bébés and the metal dolls made by *Bucherer.* In 1926 there were 144 types of metal dolls.

Sacajawea. 1915 and probably later. Name of an ethnic doll made by *Mary Frances Woods.* The statue honoring the Indian woman who guided Lewis and Clark on their westward expedition was the inspiration for this portrait doll. ★

Sachsenweger, Viktor. See **Harmus, Carl.**

Saemann, Martin. 1921–22. Fürth, Bavaria. Obtained a German patent for dancing dolls with movable joints.

Saenger, Carl Robert. See **Bandorf & Co.**

Safonoff, E. F. ca. 1840. Russia. Made papier-mâché dolls. At first he hired a sculptor to create the heads but later he prepared the mixture and made the dolls entirely himself.

Sailor. See **Ma (Matrose) and Military Costume Dolls.** (Dolls dressed in sailor suits were often called sailors. If it had a skirt it was a girl and pants were for the boy.)

Sailor Boy. 1903. Cloth doll with lithographed face and removable clothes distributed by *Montgomery Ward.* Ht. 13 in. (33 cm.).

Sailor Boy. 1913. Name of doll dressed in a boy's sailor suit. It had a celluloid head and a cloth body.

Sailor Boy. Ca. 1930. Cutout cloth doll representing a sailor boy. It had round eyes looking to the side and was embroidered with floss.

Sailor Dolls. 1912–16. Cloth dolls produced by *Horsman;* dressed as a girl in a middie dress or as a boy in a matching sailor suit, with long trousers and a sailor-type tam. Priced 25¢.

2272. Indian doll representing Sacajawea and her baby, made by Mary Frances Woods. The faces are crepe paper over a form that provides the portraiture. It has black hair and black glass head pins for eyes, a bead necklace and is wrapped in a red and green blanket. H. 10 in. (25.5 cm.). *Coleman Collection.*

2271. Saalfield mark on cutout cloth to be made into cloth dolls.

No. 588—"Sailor Boy"

No. 588—"Sailor Boy" Imported Doll, 14 inches tall. We are offering this doll for those who desire a doll "for the baby," as it is absolutely unbreakable, having celluloid head and cloth stuffed body. The face, hair, eyes, etc., are tinted in natural color, in the celluloid. The color cannot come off if it becomes wet, and is therefore perfectly harmless and makes the best kind of a plaything for a baby boy or girl. Sent prepaid for three yearly subscriptions at 35c each, or one subscription at 35c and 40c extra.

2273. Sailor Boy doll on a magazine subscription premium list in 1913. It has a celluloid head with molded hair and features, and a cloth body dressed in a boy's sailor suit. H. 14 in. (35.5 cm.).

Please, I Want a Mother

Won't you please give me to some little girl for Christmas? I want a home and some one to love me. I now live in a big, beautiful store but I want to belong to your little girl. They say I am beautiful. My hair is beautiful ringlet curls, tied with a pretty ribbon. My head is made of the finest bisque. My legs and arms are full ball jointed. I shut my eyes when I lie down to sleep. I have pretty shoes and lace stockings. I came from a far-off country where they make the finest dolls. You can't get as nice a doll anywhere for the money they ask for me. I have lots of sisters, all sizes, blonde and brunette. Here they are.

12 ins. high, 75c		26 ins.,	$4.00
18 " "	$1.00	29 "	5.00
20 " "	1.50	31 "	7.50
22 " "	2.25	34 "	10.00
24 " "	3.00	38 "	12.50

Send money order to-day and I'll be shipped by express, carefully packed. Say if I'm to be blonde or brunette.

B. Nugent & Bro. Dry Goods Co.
550 Broadway, St. Louis, Mo.

L.H.J.
11/15
1910

2274. B. Nugent & Bro. advertisement in the LADIES' HOME JOURNAL, November 15, 1910, for dolls named St. Louis Girl. This doll has a bisque head with a blond or brunette wig, sleeping glass eyes, open mouth and teeth, and a ball jointed composition body. Original chemise has a label reading "Our St. Louis Girl." Ten hs. 12 to 38 in. (30.5 to 96.5 cm.).

Sailor Sam. 1930. Segmented wooden doll made of birch wood by *Pickering* had a ball-shaped head with a sailor cap on it. Three balls served as arms. The clothes, represented by heavily coated lacquer colors, included bell bottom trousers. Ht. 7¾ in. (20 cm.).

Sailor, U.S. Navy. 1899. Doll with painted face having a mustache; cloth body; dressed in a flannel sailor suit and hat; was imported and distributed by *Butler Bros.* Ht. 12 in. (30.5 cm.).

Saint François. 1917. Inscription on a china socket head with wig and painted eyes, made by *Sèvres.* Ht. of head only 12 cm. (4½ in.).

St. Germain, J. N. 1919. Brooklyn, N.Y. Made dolls' shoes.

St. Issell's Toy Industry. 1915. Pembrokeshire, England. Lady Greaves of Netherwood formed classes to instruct the village girls in toy-making. They made indestructible dolls of various kinds and sizes including dolls in Welsh costumes, Punch, clowns and Pierrettes. These dolls had handpainted faces.

St. Joachim Bazar. 1870s–1880s. Boston, Mass. Sold dolls. Bartlett & Butman had a fancy goods store at this same address.

St. Louis Girl. 1910. Bisque head doll with wig having a ribbon on its blonde or brunette curls, sleeping eyes, ball jointed composition body with jointed wrist and lace stockings, distributed by *Nugent.* On the doll's chest a ribbon read, "The St. Louis Girl." 10 hts. 12, 18, 20, 22, 24, 26, 29, 31, 34, and 38 in. (30.5, 45.5, 51, 56, 61, 66, 73.5, 78.5, 86.5, and 96.5 cm.); priced 75¢ to $12.50.

Sal. 1929. Name of a cloth doll with eyes looking to the side, long thin limbs and the ability to emit a squeal at the slightest touch. It was advertised by *Adler Favor and Novelty Co.*, came dressed, wore shoes, and a pointed cap.

Sala, A. 1898. Berlin. Applied for a German patent (D.R.G.M.) for dressed dolls.

Salch, George C. See **Smith, Mrs. Putnam David.**

Salemme. 1922–23. New York City. Sculptor who modeled dolls based on the sketches of George Barbier of Paris. These dolls were dressed by *Mme. Pulliche* in costumes of the play DON JUAN.

Sally. 1926. Name of a doll with a hand-painted face made by *Kitty Fleischmann.* Hts. 14 to 16 in. (35.5 to 40.5 cm.).

Sally. 1927–30 and later. Bisque head with mohair wig, sleeping eyes, open mouth and teeth, on a bent limb composition body. It was distributed by *Montgomery Ward.*

1927: It had a tongue and wore a chemise. Five hts. 12½, 14½, 15¾, 17, and 21 in. (31.5, 37, 40, 43, and 53.5 cm.); priced $1.00 to $4.29.

1931: It had hair eyelashes, wore a chemise and necklace. Five hts. 12½, 14, 15½, 17, and 22 in. (31.5, 35.5, 39.5, 43, and 56 cm.); priced $1.10 to $3.39.

Sally. 1930 and later. All-composition doll, similar to *Patsy*, long limbs, able to stand on its own feet, made by the

American Character Doll Co. The head was embossed "A C D Inc." The doll had a wig, sleeping eyes, and turning head. It wore various dresses without waistlines, a hat and footwear. Ht. 14 in. (35.5 cm.). Three style nos.; priced $2.00 to $5.00.

Sally Jane. 1922. Cloth doll made by *Rees Davis.*

Sally Sunshine. 1929. *Mama* doll dressed as a little girl in a silk taffeta dress with matching bloomers, distributed by *Sears.*

Salome. 1913. Name of a bisque-head doll with wig and ball-jointed composition body, dressed in chemise, sold by *Gamage.* There were eight size numbers from one to eight. Hts. 15½, 18, 22, 24, 26, 28, 30, and 32 in. (39.5, 45.5, 56, 61, 66, 71, 76, and 81 cm.); priced $1.73 to $6.93.

Salome. 1920. Doll designed by *Toddi* made in a Turin factory. The dancer wore a corset, dancing skirt, headdress, bracelets and anklets and appears to have been the portrait doll representing this famous dancer made by *Lenci.* (See Ill. 4, style number 104, in LENCI DOLLS by Dorothy Coleman.)

Salome. 1920. Carved wood articulated dressed doll made by the artist *Prof. Folkmann.*

Salome. 1924. Miniature wax or plaster doll made by *J. S. Sant.*

Salomon, L. See **Israël & Prieur.**

Salt Lake Hardware Co. See **Acme Toy Manufacturing Co.**

Salter, Thomas, Ltd. 1915–30. London and Paris. Produced India rubber dolls.

1920–22. Distributed French dolls.

Salvation Army Doll. 1910. Felt doll made by *Steiff.*

Salvation Army Lass. 1921. Composition-head doll with wig, painted blue eyes, open-closed mouth, pink cloth body with composition arms, made by *Effanbee.* It wore a navy blue coat and skirt, blue blouse with a tan panel down the front, a Salvation Army type straw bonnet. On the blouse was a gold colored button with the words, "Effanbee//Dolls" under a bluebird. The shoes were usually marked "Effanbee." Ht. 15 in. (38 cm.). Each doll came with a write-up of the work of the Salvation Army. ★

Salvation Nell. 1924. Doll made by *Jeanette Doll Co.*

Salzedo Bros. & Co. 1897–1924. London. Handled and exported toys from France and Italy. Around 1915 started to produce Italian dolls in a shop called Maison d'Italie and claimed they had introduced Italian dolls into England.

1922: Distributed dolls from Germany, including those of *Carl Daum.*

Sam. 1925–26. Black felt *Lenci* doll dressed in harem trousers, bare from the waist up, carried a dagger in its sash. Style no. 260. Ht. 31 in. (78.5 cm.).

Samanthy. 1883. Comical cloth doll dressed in a calico wrapper and sun-bonnet.

2275. Composition shoulder head doll named (Petite) Sally made by the American Character Doll Co. It has molded and painted hair, brown glassine eyes, open-closed mouth and a neck joint with the socket in the head like Patsy. The cloth body with composition arms and legs is jointed at the shoulders and hips. Original clothes (except hair ribbon). Mark on head: "PETITE SALLY." H. 21½ in. (54.5 cm.). *Courtesy of John Axe. Photo by John Axe.*

2276. Salvation Army Lass made by Effanbee. This composition shoulder head doll has a wig, molded and painted blue eyes, an open-closed mouth and a pink cloth body with composition arms. Original Salvation Army uniform. The gold colored button on its outer garment has a bluebird over the words "Effanbee Doll." H. 16½ in. (42 cm.). *Courtesy of Richard Withington. Photo by Barbara Jendrick.*

2277. Doll page in the 1897 catalog of Samaritaine. The Bébé Samaritaine is in the center of the page. From left to right top to bottom is a talking bébé with open mouth and teeth, dressed in a chemise; a bébé in a Russian costume; a carton two faced clown; a bébé in a sailor outfit, a dressed bébé; a bébé made in Paris and wearing a chemise; a bébé maillot in swaddling clothes; two dressed bébés; a rubber bébé dressed in woolen clothes; a rubber bébé wearing a knitted wool outfit; a pair of mignonnettes in Russian costume; a marotte on a bone stick; and a nurse and baby.

The Bébé Samaritaine was made in Paris and had won a gold medal. It was fully jointed and wore a chemise and footwear. It also came with a voice saying Mama and Papa as well as sleeping eyes and an open mouth with teeth. The heights in centimeters can be converted to inches by dividing by 2.54 and the francs can be converted to dollars by dividing by 5. *Courtesy of Margaret Whitton.*

Samaritaine. 1897–1924 and probably other years. Paris. Store that sold dolls.

1897: Advertised *Bébé Samaritaine*, Bébé in *Swaddling clothes,* clowns with two faces, *Marotte, Mignonnettes,* Nurse with Baby, *Regional Costume Dolls, Rubber Dolls,* Soldiers and Sailors, suitcase containing a doll and its wardrobe.

1902: Advertised *Bébé Dormeur, Bébé Marcheur, Bébé Parlant, Bébé Tout en Bois.*

1909: Advertised *Bébé Culotte.*

1911: Advertised *Bébé Baptême.*

1913: Advertised *Bébé Jumeau, Bébé Maillot,* composition

character bébés, *Cymbalier, Écolière (Écolier), Esquimaux, Kiss Throwing Bébé, Polichinelle* and *Poupard.*

1914: Advertised Bébé Culotte, Bébé Jumeau, Bébé Maillot, *Bébé Premier Age,* Bébé Samaritaine, Bebe Tout en Bois, Cymbalier, Esquimaux, Googly-Eyed dolls, Kiss-Throwing dolls, Marotte, Mignonnette, *Nénette* and *Rintintin, Polichinelle,* Poupard and *Rubber* dolls.

(See THE COLLECTOR'S BOOK OF DOLLS' CLOTHES, Ills. 526, 527, 531, and 532.)

Sambo. 1910–14 and possibly other years. Cloth doll made by *Dean.*

1910–11: Dean's cutout cloth doll was named Le Petit Sambo in the *Aux Trois Quartiers* catalog.

Sambo. 1913. Black dolls advertised by *Gamage.* The Sambo family of dolls included Sambo's Little Sister with a black silky wig, sleeping eyes, a colored dress, and a "gold" beaded necklace. Hts. 14½ and 17 in. (37 and 43 cm.); priced $1.12 and $1.48. Sambo's Baby Brother had bent limbs, two teeth, and wore a chemise. Ht. 12 in. (30.5 cm.); priced 98¢. Laughing Black Sambo had short flocked hair, a jointed composition body and wore a colored suit and a gold bead necklace. Ht. 12 in. (30.5 cm.); priced 98¢. This doll resembled the mold #227 made by the *Société Française de Fabrication de Bébés & Jouets* (S.F.B.J.). See Ill. 1555 in the first COLLECTOR'S ENCYCLOPEDIA OF DOLLS.

Sambo. 1927–28. Black cloth doll made by *Chad Valley* based on a design by *Mabel Lucie Attwell;* had a hand painted chubby velvet face, wig of real kinky hair, veined glass eyes glancing to the side, velvet body, wore a long-sleeved light shirt and overalls with a knee patch. Hts. 14½, 16, and 18½ in. (37, 40.5, and 47 cm.).

1928: Came in 16 in. ht. only.

Sambo Family. 1922. Brown composition-head dolls made by *Effanbee,* included baby dolls.

Sambo Special Co. 1928. Philadelphia, Pa. Made articulated wooden dolls named Sambo. The four style nos. "walked" as they were pulled along and dragged a wagon; one of these dolls represented a Chinaman pulling a cart. Priced $1.00 to $2.00.

Samhammer, Philipp (Philip), & Co. 1872–1928. Sonneberg, Thür. Philipp Samhammer became a partner of Mathias Lambert in 1872, thus forming the doll-making firm of *Lambert & Samhammer.* By 1881 the partnership was dissolved and Samhammer went into business for himself. TOYS AND NOVELTIES in 1913 published an obituary for Philip Lamhammer of Sonneberg. It seems likely that the Lamhammer was a misspelling of Samhammer especially with the Lambert connection. This obituary stated that he had been born in 1850 and that around 1865 Philip Lamhammer served as an apprentice in the Ernst and Carl *Dressel* factory and that in 1872 he erected his own firm. This 1872 date and the given name Philip all gives credence to the possibility of a misspelling of the surname. Also an L and S in handwriting can often be mistaken for one another. Walter Samhammer was the successor in 1913 but the factory closed in 1915. After World War I a Philipp Samhammer continued at least until 1928 to be listed in DIDOT French Directories as an exporter of dolls.

1883: Served on the committee to found the Sonneberg Industrial School, according to the Ciesliks.

1888: Advertised jointed dolls, washable dolls, model dolls, bisque heads, washable heads and model wax heads.

1893: Applied for a German patent for a dressed doll with a music box.

1898: Applied for a German patent (D.R.G.M.) for a jointed doll with leather covering the torso.

1910: One of the Sonneberg group of Grand Prize Winners for their dolls at the Brussels International Exposition.★

Sammy. 1926. Trade name of a doll produced by *Cuno & Otto Dressel.* The head is painted black and it resembles the head used on the *Rock-a-Bye* babies.

Sammy (Samy) Sock. 1915–16. Cloth doll made by *Strat Manufacturing Co.* It had round eyes, a broad grin, no neck, and arms extended horizontally.★

Samojede (Eskimo). Before 1911–13. Felt doll made by *Steiff* represented an Eskimo dressed in a parka-type garment of mohair plush and high boots. Hts. 35 and 75 cm. (14 and 29½ in.). (See also **Esq.**)

Samstag & Hilder Bros. 1894–1920. Factory in Sonneberg, Thür. Distributing establishment in numerous cities in Europe, U.S.A. and Japan. They made and/or produced dolls' bodies and dressed dolls. They painted dolls' heads which were probably made elsewhere.

There appeared to have been a close business relationship between *Eisenmann* and Samstag & Hilder. The latter registered as a trademark *Hug Me Kiddies* which were patented by *Leo Rees,* a partner in Eisenmann & Co. Dolls with Hug Me Kiddies type face have been found marked "Einco" and *Gebrüder Heubach* mold #8764.

1904: Advertised *Duchess* Dolls including *My Little Beauty,* (Little Beauty, Beauty) with bodies of kid or composition. Also advertised *Majestic* dolls (their most expensive), plus all-bisque dolls, cloth dolls with linen faces and *Worsted Dolls.*

1908: PLAYTHINGS reported, "We are introducing some entirely new Doll Models for 1908—Dolls with the real child-like face. The accomplishment is announced after years of careful experiment. . . . These dolls have been modeled from living subjects under the direction of the most famous artist of Munich. . . . The line is limitless in variety, style and price range."

1919: Agent for Giebeler-Falk Doll Corp.★

Samuel & Söhne. 1907–30. Joachimstal, Bohemia, later Czechoslovakia. Manufactured dolls.★

Samulon, J. 1893–1930. Dresden, Saxony. Manufactured dolls.★

Samy Sock. See **Sammy (Samy) Sock.**

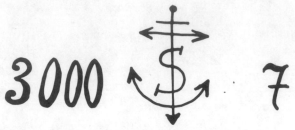

2278. Mark used on bisque dolls' heads possibly made by Armand Marseille for Samhammer.

Hug-Me-Kiddy Doll
Given for only 3 McCall subscriptions

Premium 998 — This unique doll is making a bigger hit than the Teddy Bear. Grown-ups, as well as children, fall in love with it as soon as they see it. This Doll is 11½ inches tall. One firm alone, in New York City, has sold two hundred thousand. Get 3 yearly subscriptions at once and we will send you one of these popular dolls prepaid. If you desire, you may have a girl doll.

Premium 998

2279. Boy Hug Me Kiddy produced by Samstag & Hilder and sold as a premium by McCALL'S in 1912 and 1913. H. 11½ in. (29 cm.).

San Fairy Ann. 1927. Trademark registered in France by *William Webb Sanders* for dolls. The trademark name was in a circle under the figure of a girl. A second circle also had a figure of a girl but it was over the words *"Ça Ne Fait Rien."* The girls wore capes and cloches.

San Wash Toy Co. 1930 and later. Indianapolis, Ind. Manufactured cloth dolls.

Sand, Lauth. See **Lauth-Sand, Mme. Aurore.**

Sander, G. 1926–28. Sonneberg, Thür. Exported dolls.

Sanders, Maurice. 1928–30 and later. Obtained a U.S. patent for a doll with hollow and elastic rubber arms and legs on a cloth body. A two-part mold was used, preferably with unvulcanized rubber, for each arm and each leg. The hands and feet were hollow but the fingers and toes were solid. This patent was assigned to *Ideal.*

Sanders, William Webb. 1927. Châteaudun, Eure-et-Loire, France. Registered *Ça Ne Fait Rien* and *San Fairy Ann* as trademarks in France.

Sandow, Eugene. 1915–17. Britain. Patented in England the *Doll Exerciser* with springs for arms. The *National Doll League* was formed to provide the dolls, which were made by the *All-British Doll Manufacturing Co.* The profits went to the Red Cross.

1916: There was litigation over this patent; Sandow was the successful plaintiff and Capt. Charles Hutton Moss was the defendant.

1917: The Doll Exerciser came in several styles, as a Boy Scout, *Dolly Dimple* and others. It came boxed with a chart of exercises.

Sandy. 1924. Composition-head doll with a body of heavy canvas and composition hands made by the *Lund Art Co.* Doll's hat was a removable cork and the doll could be filled with sand through this opening.

Sandy MacGregor. 1908. A *Contortionist Doll* with a body that could be twisted into an endless number of positions, was dressed as a Scotsman.

Sani-Doll. 1916–19. Composition-head doll made by *Famous Doll Studio,* wore a variety of dresses.★

San-I-Toy. 1926. Trademark registered in U.S. by *Zadek Feldstein Co.* for dolls.

Sanitrion. 1916–18. Name of a line of dolls made by *Trion* which were claimed to be capable of being taken in bathing.★

Sanoner (Senoner, Sononer). Early 1800s–1930s and later. Costa and St. Ulrich, Grödner Tal. Several generations of Sanoners were *Verlegers* who collected and distributed dolls.

Ca. 1820: The son, Ferdinand Sanoner, visited the U.S.A. and went as far west as the Mississippi with a party of men mapping the area.

1980s: Georg Senoner has a factory that makes wooden dolls. (See also **Runggaldier & Sennoner.**)★

Sans Rival. 1925–30 and later. Name of dolls made in the workshop of *Mme. de Kasparek.*

1925: These dolls were awarded the Diplôme d'Honneur at the Paris Arts Decoratifs Exhibition.★

Sant, Mr. J. S. 1924. London. Created miniature art dolls of wax or plaster. These dolls included *Priscilla, Salome,* and *Daphne.*

Santa. 1900–10. Bisque head made by *Simon & Halbig* mold #1249 usually found on a ball-jointed composition body produced by *Hamburger.* It had a wig, sleeping eyes and open mouth. Hts. included 17 and 24 in. (43 and 61 cm.).

1904–06: Priced $1.00 to $10.00, dressed in a chemise.★

Santa. Bisque head made by *Gebrüder Heubach;* marked with the square or round Heubach mark. It had a wig, sleeping eyes, molded eyebrows, open mouth with four upper teeth, jointed composition body with wooden upper arms and legs. Hts. included 10 and 20 in. (25.5 and 51

2280A. Black Santa bisque head made by Simon & Halbig. It has a wig, sleeping brown glass eyes, open mouth with four upper teeth and is on a fully jointed black composition body. Mark: S & H 1249//DEP//Germany//Santa//11. H. 24 in. (61 cm.). *Private collection.*

S & H. 1249
DEP.
Germany
SANTA
8

2280B. Mark on Santa bisque head made by Simon & Halbig.

2281. Santa bisque head made by Gebrüder Heubach has a wig, sleeping glass eyes, open mouth with four upper teeth, and a ball jointed composition body with wooden upper arms and legs. Mark: Ill. 2282. H. 10 in. (25.5 cm.). *Courtesy of Germaine Bachand.*

SANTA
2

Germany

2282. Mark on Santa bisque head made by Gebrüder Heubach.

cm.). It is possible that both Gebrüder Heubach and *Simon & Halbig* made Santa heads for *Hamburger*.

Santa Claus. 1850s–1930 and later. Many dolls were dressed to represent Santa Claus; these were generally in the Thomas Nast tradition; but sometimes they were dressed as Father Christmas, St. Nicholas or even as Ruprecht⁺. The clothes could be molded and/or painted on the doll as well as be actual fabric attire. Often the Santa Claus dolls were made of colored cotton batting with a mask face. Santa Claus figures were frequently made to hang on Christmas trees.

1856: *George N. Davis* made and/or sold India rubber Santa Claus dolls.

1860–61: Name of a doll imported by *John D. Robbins.* Priced $5.00 doz. wholesale.

1882: *Ehrichs'* advertised a walking Santa Claus with gifts in his pack. Ht. 9½ in. (24 cm.); priced $2.75.

1893: *Worsted* doll was advertised by *Horsman;* priced $4.00 doz. wholesale.

1893 and later: *Butterick* published patterns for making a Santa Claus doll and its clothes.

1897: Cloth doll with white whiskers and a flannel suit, advertised by *Zernitz.* Ht. 11 in. (28 cm.); priced $8.00 doz. wholesale.

1907: Cutout lithographed cloth doll made by *Art Fabric Mills,* made with only one side to be sewed. Ht. 6 in. (15 cm.).

1907–16: Cutout cloth doll in the *Tiny Travelers* series made by *Saalfield.* Ht. 5 in. (12.5 cm.).

1913: *Liberty & Co.* advertised Santa Claus dolls. (See Ill. 1672.)

1917: *Baltimore Bargain House* and *Hammond* advertised Santa Claus dolls.

1920: *Foulds & Freure* produced Santa Claus dolls.

1922–23: *New York Rubber Co.* made rubber Santa Claus dolls.

1927: *Carl Horn* made dolls representing Santa Claus.

1928: The *Poppy Doll Co.* made *Scarey Ann* wooden dolls painted to represent Santa Claus.

1929: Name of a doll with composition head and arms on a cloth body, had a beard and a cotton flannel Santa Claus suit. Ht. 27 in. (68.5 cm.).★

Santé. Before World War I–1923. France. Inexpensive dolls were made by the prisoners in this prison. Prior to the war they were paid so much a hundred for painting each part; for example 1¢ for painting 100 teeth, but only ⅕¢ per hundred for painting the body, arms and legs. For the larger dolls they were paid more than for the smaller ones.

1923: A large French firm supplied body parts already molded for the prisoners to file and join together. The pay was 1¢ per 100 kilos (220 pounds). The work was discontinued because of dust and competition with other workers.

Sarah Bernhardt. Ca. 1902. Porcelain head doll made at Montreuil-sous-Bois was a portrait of Sarah Bernhardt as she appeared in her role in L'AIGLON.

The *Société Française de Fabrication de Bébés & Jouets* after World War II made a doll representing Sarah Bernhardt which bore a *Jumeau* label and was mold #221.

Sarah Starer. 1914. Name of a cloth doll made by *Dean*.

Sarason, Frieda. 1909. Berlin. Applied for a German patent (D.R.G.M.) for dolls' clothes.

Sardeau, Miss Hélène. 1920–24. New York City and Palm Beach, Fla. In 1920 Hélène and her sister, Mathilde Kane, came from Antwerp, Belgium, to New York. In the winters they resided in Palm Beach. Made Portrait dolls.

1922: TOYS AND NOVELTIES described the faces of the Sardeau dolls as having been modeled of plasterine with canvas (or stockinet) stretched over it and painted in flesh colors. The dolls represented either regional types such as Romany, Russian, Dutch, or portraits of current celebrities. There were 12 portraits made of Lenore Ulric as she appeared in KIKI with short straight black hair. THEATRE MAGAZINE described the Sardeau dolls as having faces of clay painted with oils, hair of colored wool, cord or string and long thin bodies. Mathilde designed and made the colorful silk and satin costumes. One of the first dolls was a portrait of Eva Le Gallienne as Julie in LILIOM. A doll with titian hair, a Mona Lisa smile and a green silk dress was called the Green Lady and was made for Helen Dryden. The portrait doll of Pauline Lord as "Anna Christie" had ropey flaxen hair. Other dolls represented Elsie de Wolfe, Carlotta Monterey as a Spanish Beauty, Doris Keane, Margalo Gillmore and Richard Bennet in HE WHO GETS SLAPPED. Art dolls were named *Vodka, Stupid* and *Hindu Dancer.*★

Sardinian Dolls. PLAYTHINGS reported in 1929 that dolls with movable joints were dressed in various Sardinian regional costumes including shepherds, peasants, youths and old women.

Sarre (Saar). 1919–30 and later. "Made in Sarre" was a mark found on bisque dolls' heads. The Saar, an area partly in Bavaria, was under the temporary control of the League of Nations after World War I. The mark usually also included the initials "S P//S."

Sassy Sue. 1911–13. Composition head doll made by *Amberg*. Ht. 8 in. (20.5 cm.).★

Sastré. 1927–30 and later. Paris. Made dolls.

Saucy Baby. 1922. Cloth doll made by *Rees Davis*.

Sauer, August. 1907–25 and later. Sonneberg, Thür. Produced and exported dolls, especially to France before World War I.

Sauerteig, Johannes. 1888–1928. Sonneberg, Thür. Made and exported dolls especially to France.

1913–15: Applied for four German patents (D.R.G.M.) for dolls with voices.

1918: Applied for a German patent (D.R.G.M.) for jointed dolls.★

Sauerteig, Otto. 1930 and later. Neustadt near Coburg, Bavaria. Advertised jointed dolls, *Mama* dolls, and baby dolls.

Sauerzapf, Georg Andreas. 1834–51. Vienna. Hurwart Konrad was the successor in 1851. Produced papier-mâché dolls and mechanical dolls.

Saugnier, Mme. & Avard. 1848–62. Paris. In 1854 Mme. Saugnier bought a shop in the Passage Choiseul comprising five address numbers. Produced dolls and/or sold dolls.

1862: Mme. Saugnier failed and her inventory was 16 percent dolls according to Florence Poisson, curator of the Roybet Fould Museum.

Sautter, Mme. 1914–18. Paris. Founded the *Fédération du Jouet Français*. Made dolls.

1918: Supervised the operation of Oeuvre du Travail, a workshop where dolls were made using porcelain heads from *Limoges*.

Saxon Novelty Co. 1927–29. U.S.A. Made heads and other parts for dolls. Member of the *American Doll Manufacturing Assoc.* and member of the *Doll Parts Manufacturing Assoc.*

Sayco. See **Schoen & Yondorf Co.**

Scandinavian Dolls. Many dolls were dressed in Scandinavian regional costumes. Several porcelain factories such as the *Rörstrand Porcelain Factory* in Sweden and *Royal Copenhagen* in Denmark made china heads for dolls in the 1800s. Later many of the dolls dressed in Scandinavian costumes had celluloid heads.

1910: A Danish store named *Poupées Parisiennes* exhibited dolls at the Brussels Exposition.

1913: *Holmgreen* of Denmark produced dolls.

1918: *Karen Hansen* of Denmark advertised dolls.

1923: Scandinavian children were encouraged to do their

2283. Sarre mark found on bisque heads probably refers to Saar.

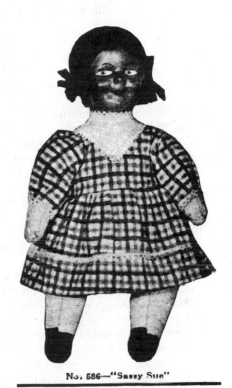

No. 586—"Sassy Sue"

No. 586—"Sassy Sue" Character Doll. This is one of the most popular of the many famous character dolls. The head is made of the unbreakable "composition" material, and the body carefully stuffed and sewed. The doll measures 8 inches tall and is neatly dressed in gingham. Sent prepaid, carefully packed, for four yearly subscriptions at 35c each, or one subscription and 75c extra.

2284. Composition-head doll named Sassy Sue, made by Amberg and shown in a subscription premium list of 1913. H. 8 in. (20.5 cm.).

2285. Mark of Johannes Sauerteig.

own repairs on dolls to make them appreciate the amount of work required, according to an article in TOYS AND NOVELTIES.

1925: Bertha Christensen and *Peder Christensen*, both of Denmark, produced dolls.

1928–29: E. Christensen advertised dolls.★

Scantlebury, Mrs. Elizabeth. 1907–20 Springfield, Mass.; Spokane, Wash.; Brooklyn, N.Y. TOYS AND NOVELTIES in 1913 discussed the educational work with dolls done by Elizabeth C. Scantlebury.

"During recent years toys and dolls have . . . become recognized as important developing agencies through which the child grows into adult mental and physical stature. . . .

"That it is of the utmost importance to the man who makes and sells toys is vouched for by the metamorphosis of the toy department from a creature destined to live two months each year to a permanent source of profit month after month. . . .

"One modern expression of the so-called 'educational toy' is found in the doll. . . . [This] serves to impress vividly anthropological essentials and racial characteristics.

". . . In England and on the Continent many schools are equipped with complete sets of national dolls, each clothed according to the prevailing fashion of that country, and each bearing the national flag to which it is supposed to swear allegiance. These are permanently on exhibition so that the children can inspect them at leisure, and they are also used as special object lessons to illustrate the more prosaic information given by illustrated text books.

"In England recently a movement was started which is intended to teach English girls some of the practical essentials of motherhood. The perfection of the modern doll, the complete clothing equipment with which it is supplied, and the increasing number of miniature home supplies which go to make life worth living to the doll, have made it possible for this movement to spread in a healthy fashion.

"But now it becomes apparent that America, and not Europe, is really the leader in this movement to give definite instruction through means of dolls. In 1907 Mrs. Elizabeth Scantlebury . . . launched the idea of a doll as a first aid to child training.

"A novel doll group which is being used by teachers in the public schools of Springfield, as well as schools in other states and foreign countries comprises representatives from the children of Holland, Japan, China, Russia, Germany, Switzerland, Arabia and Scotland. In the collection there are also two Pilgrims, a North American Indian, papoose and a woolly-woolly Eskimo.

"Of the 15 dolls used in the Springfield schools five are so 'young' that they are still in their swaddling clothes. The others are much like miniature grown-ups.

"The little Japanese girl, 'Lotus Blossom,' looks like a tiny woman. She wears just what a Japanese girl would wear, of just the fabrics that a Japanese girl would have her clothes made. She has pockets in the loose sleeves of her kimono-like upper garment and little sandals with short stilts that fit into holes in the bottom. These she puts on in rainy

weather to keep the soles off the wet ground, but when it is fair she takes the short stilts out.

"Her little brother Toyo is tied on her back. There is also a little Chinese boy exceedingly true to life. This little boy wears a loosely fitting silk coat, and red satin trousers with a band of black around the bottom of each leg.

"Another doll which interests the school children represents a Turkish girl. She wears anklets, orange colored trousers, earrings, and a scarf about her head. She is 'Gemilla,' the child of the desert.

"Then there are Pieter and Wilhelmina, two little Dutch people. . . . Pieter wears a tall hat and on his coat are two very large buttons. He wears very baggy Dutch trousers.

"The Eskimo woman doll one would certainly know by the fur and leggins, and her sex is apparent by the train on the fur coat, or coat tail, it might be called. An Eskimo man does not have any on his coat.

" 'The woman and the baby,' says Mrs. Scantlebury, 'are dressed just alike, except that the baby has moccasins sewed on the bottom of the fur trousers, and the mother has on leggins that are supposed to be made with the fur inside.

" 'Then there is the little papoose girl. She is wrapped in a blanket and tied with soft thongs to a board to which the papoose case is attached. A design from a Chippewa case is embroidered on this one, and there is a hoop to go around the front on which the baby's playthings may be hung, and in case she should happen to fall from the branch or wigwam pole from which it is suspended . . . then the hoop about the top of the case will prevent the baby's face from striking the ground.'

"It is Mrs. Scantlebury's theory that the interest added to the study of geography by the dolls will be like, but many times greater than, that produced when the child is looking through a picture book.

"[In 1907] the first set of dolls went to the Springfield schools as a 'visiting set.' The last set, November 1912, went to the children's department in the public library of Portland, Ore. In between the two dates, dolls were dressed and sent to Buenos Aires, Argentine Republic, S.A., to Kyoto, Japan, and to the various public and normal schools in the United States."

The Scantlebury dolls in the pictures illustrating this article all appeared to be dolly-faced German bisque child dolls. Besides dolls dressed in regional costumes Mrs. Scantlebury created an exhibit of dolls in Mother Goose costumes.★

Scaramouche. Name of one of the characters in the COMMEDIA DELL'ARTE, also the name of a hero in literature, which were the inspiration for dolls.★

Scarey Ann. 1924–30. A small (about 5 in. [12.5 cm.]) doll made of California redwood, which was turned, decorated by hand with lacquer enamel paint and made by the *Poppy Doll Co.* The hair stood upright on the top of the head when a small lever in the back was pressed. There were also clowns with hats that popped up, grandfathers with beards that wiggled and a sailor whose hat and nose moved up and down. All of these dolls came under *Dr. Chinn's* patent and were called Scarey Ann dolls. These dolls were distributed in Britain by H. A. Moore & Co.

1925: Doll made its debut in London.

1928: New style nos. were *Santa Claus,* Thanksgiving Pie and Witch.

1929: 11 style nos.; priced 50¢.

1930s: Advertised in HOBBIES MAGAZINE.

Scavini, Enrico, and Signora Elena König di.† See **Lenci.**

Schadelbauer, Leopold. Before and after 1853. Vienna. Handled Nürnberg wares and dolls. In 1853 his widow succeeded him according to Dr. Eva Moskovszky.

Schaedel, Th. 1924–26. London. Factory agent for the *Société Industrielle de Celluloid.*

Schaeffer Bros. 1926–27. New York City. Sole distributor of *Ree-Bee* Dolls.

1926: Advertised spring limb dolls.

Schäfer & Vater. 1890–1930 and later. Volkstedt-Rudolstadt, Thür. This porcelain factory made all-bisque dolls and bisque parts for dolls.

Schäffer, Phil. 1901. Elberfeld, Germany. Applied for a German patent (D.R.G.M.) for dolls' heads with a slit in them for holding the wig in place.

Schaitberger, Carl. 1896–1925 and later. Sonneberg, Thür.

1910: Member of the Sonneberg group who won a Grand Prize at the Brussels Exposition. ★

Schalleck, Miss Frances. Designed clothes for the *Cleo Corporation.*

Schams, Franz. 1821 and probably other years. Budapest. Distributed dolls.

Schanzer, Henry, Co. 1927. New York City. Produced small all-celluloid and all-composition dolls in either hand-knitted or machine knitted costumes. The dolls were baby dolls or *Kewpie* types.

Scharf, H. 1884–1930. Berlin. Made accessories for dolls. Agent was *G. F. Hertzog.* Used the name "Reichsverband Deutscher Spielwaren" (Imperial German Dressed Toys) and the initials "R.D.S." intertwined. ★

Scharfenberg, Carl. See **Steiner, Albin.†**

Schatzlar. See **Pohl.**

Schaulade. Bamberg, Bavaria. Used a *Kämmer & Reinhardt* head mold #800 on a doll with the patent "D.R.G.M." and Geschmacksmuster (fancy design) mark.

Schavoir Rubber Co. 1926–30 and later. New York City. Made dolls in white and red rubber. Dolls were handled by the *Wolf Doll Co.*

1926: Dolls included a boy with a musical instrument, a girl with a doll, a man with a pipe in his hand, and a chinaman.

Schear & Scher. 1929. New York City. Imported and distributed dolls from Japan for the wholesale market.

Scheffler, Karl (Carl). 1926–30 and later. Marienberg, Sax-

ony. Produced celluloid-head dolls and baby dolls with cloth bodies as well as all-celluloid dolls. Made clothing for dolls.

Schein, Hermann. 1907–10. Vienna. Listed in directories under Dolls and Dolls' Heads.

Scheler, Gustav. 1913. Mengersgereuth, Germany. Applied for a German patent (D.R.G.M.) for a doll with a voice. *Crämer & Héron* had a porcelain factory in Mengersgereuth.

Schelhorn (Schellhorn), August. 1897–30 and later. Sonneberg and Neustadt near Coburg, Thür. and later Bavaria. Manufactured dolls. Successors included *Paul Koch* in 1926–28.

1926: Advertised bent limb baby dolls; new born baby dolls; straight leg child dolls; *Mama* dolls; *Cupid* dolls; *marottes;* novelty felt dolls with unbreakable faces; and art dolls priced 12¢ and up. These dolls came dressed or undressed.

1928: *Cave & Easterling* was the sole London agent.

1930: Advertised dressed and undressed dolls, baby dolls, plaster dolls, and art dolls. ★

Schelhorn (Schellhorn), Heinrich. 1901–30. Sonneberg, Thür. Made and exported dolls and leather bodies. Fled to England in 1935 and continued with dolls.

1901: Applied for a German patent (D.R.G.M.) for a doll's body.

1912: Applied for a German patent (D.R.G.M.) for a doll's body with a musical voice.

1921: Advertised dressed baby dolls, jointed dolls wearing chemises, celluloid and porcelain heads and wigs, and bodies of cloth or imitation leather.

1925: Advertised *Mama* dolls.

1926: *Charles W. Baker* of London was the British agent; Uhlig & Co. was the agent in Hamburg. Advertised talking dolls, dressed dolls, jointed dolls, baby dolls, imitation leather and genuine leather hair stuffed bodied dolls. ★

Stoffbälle, Wiegengehänge, Stehaufs, Stoffpuppen
Karl Scheffler, Spielwarenfbk., **Marienberg** i. Sachsen

2286. Advertisement for Karl Scheffler in DEUTSCHE SPIEL-WAREN ZEITUNG, February, 1927. The dressed dolls have cloth bodies.

Schelhorn, M. A. 1853 and probably other years. Vienna. Manufactured toys and dolls according to Dr. Eva Moskovszky.

Schelhorn, Max Friedrich. 1907–20. Sonneberg, Thür. Made and exported dolls.

1903: Applied for a German patent (D.R.G.M.) relating to a doll's leg.

1909: Applied for a German patent (D.R.G.M.) for fastening a doll's head.

1913: Applied for a German patent (D.R.G.M.) for a doll's voice in a cloth body.★

2287. Max Schelhorn's mark on dolls.

Schelm. See **Flirt, The.**

Schenk, Fridolin. 1911. Schmerbach, Germany. Applied for a German patent (D.R.G.M.) for a voice in rubber dolls.

Schepperdocken. 1800s–1900s. German name for hollow wooden dolls (docken) with stones inside to form a rattle. These dolls were made as a home industry for generations in *Viechtau near Gmunden* area of the Balkans. They had movable arms. Ht. 4¼ in. (11 cm.); priced 4¼¢ doz. wholesale in the 19th century. Similar dolls were made in the Berchtesgaden and other Tirolean areas and continued to be made in the 1980s.

Scherf, Peter. 1854–1929. Sonneberg, Thür. Made and exported dolls.

1926–29: Advertised dolls and baby dolls in chemise or fully dressed.★

Scherzer & Fischer. 1887–1930 and later. Sonneberg, Thür. Also known as Richard Scherzer.[†] Made dressed and undressed dolls.

1925: Applied for a German patent (D.R.G.M.) for the limbs of a doll's body. Advertised *Mama* dolls, the *Herzlieb (Sweetheart)* line of dolls, fully jointed and bent limb baby dolls in chemise.

1926: Advertised dolls' heads and unbreakable dolls.

1927: Advertised flirting-eye dolls, and *Heio-Beio* new born dolls.

Scheu, Carl. See **Hunaeus, Dr. Paul.**

Scheuer, Max, Bert, & Harold. 1909–30 and later. New York City. Produced dolls and in 1914 founded *Century.* Max Scheuer retired in 1926 and died in 1933.

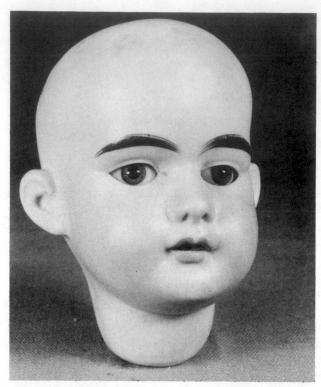

2288. Bisque socket head for a Peter Scherf doll. It had glass eyes, wide eyebrows, conspicuous ears, open mouth and teeth. Mark III. 2289A. H. head only, 3½ in. (9 cm.). *Coleman Collection.*

A

B

C

2289A, B & C. Peter Scherf marks on bisque heads made by Armand Marseille.

Germany
P Sch 1901-2

2290. Peter Scherf mark on a bisque head.

2291. Schilling mark on a metal washer on a doll.

Scheyer, O., & Co. 1925–29. Nürnberg, Bavaria; factory in Sonneberg, Thür. Made dolls and baby dolls.

1925: Used the trademark *Floresta*.

1926–29: H. & F. Keeble was the London agent.★

Schidik (Skier). 1916–24. Felt doll made by *Steiff*. Ht. 35 cm. (14 in.).

Schidun (Skier). 1916. Felt doll made by *Steiff*. Ht. 40 cm. (15½ in.).

Schleler. See **Rogulsh Eyes.**

Schiewek, Berta. 1912. Breslau, Germany. Applied for a German patent (D.R.G.M.) for dolls.

Schiffnie. See **Guttmann & Schiffnie.**

Schifra, Frau (Wintersports). 1916. Felt lady doll made by *Steiff*. Ht. 40 cm. (15½ in.).

Schilling. 1878–1928. Sonneberg, Thür. Barbara Schilling, probably the wife of Stephan Max Ferdinand Schilling, made dolls as early as 1878; Ferdinand Max Schilling was in charge of the firm 1883–1920; 1925–28 it was Max Schilling and Zitzmann. In the 1800s they specialized in *Täuflinge* and dolls' heads. The Täuflinge were made of papier-mâché, rubber, wax and other materials. In 1918 the Schillings were connected with *Borgfeldt*. For many years they exported dolls as well as making them.

Several composition head dolls with composition arms and legs on cloth bodies at the Margaret Woodbury Strong Museum had a metal disc on the shoulder plate so the head turned. The metal disc was marked "Deutsche Industre F.M.S." The number 152/2 has been found on marked Schilling heads. A pair of white leather shoes worn by a *Bébé Bon Marché* were stamped with the Schilling angel head and wings trademark. A *Bébé Tout en Bois* was marked with an angel head and wings sticker on its body. See Ills. 289 and 293. An *American Pet* doll had the mark shown in Ill. 123 stamped on its stomach, along with the name Schilling.

The angel head and wings, the Schilling trademark, was stamped on the back of a composition shoulder head near the left edge. On the right at the edge of the back were stamped what appears to be the words "Gesstzlion// Geschützt." A German variant of "patented."

One of the wax-over-composition shoulder head dolls of Queen Wilhelmina of the Netherlands had a Schilling angel impressed on it. This 1890s doll was 59 cm. (23 in.) tall.

1878: Registered numbers 360/2 and 366/0 according to the research of the Ciesliks.

1879: Registered their winged angel head trademark according to the Ciesliks.

1895: Stephan Schilling registered a winged angel head trademark in Germany. This trademark closely resembled the bottom part of the trademark registered by Fleischmann & Cramer in 1881. (See Ill. 953A.)

1896: Applied for a German patent (D.R.G.M.) for a mama-papa doll's voice activated by the movement of the legs.

1910: One of the Sonneberg group of Grand Prize Winners at the Brussels Exposition. Applied for a German patent (D.R.G.M.) for a jointed baby doll made of wood.★

**Gesstzlion
geschutzt.**

2292. Stamp on composition shoulder heads of dolls produced by Schilling.

Schima, Herr (Winter Sports). 1916. Felt gentleman doll made by Steiff. Ht. 40 cm. (15½ in.).

Schindel. See **Wiesenthal, Schindel & Kallenberg.**

Schindhelm, A. Sonneberg, Thür. Manufactured various kinds of dolls.

Schindhelm & Knauer. 1921–30 and later. Sonneberg, Thür. Manufactured dressed character dolls, trousseaux boxes, infant dolls with layettes in baskets and bodies for baby dolls. (See Ill. 2293.)★

Schitvall. 1930. Paris. Made and/or distributed dolls.

Schlaggenwald. 1793–1930 and later. Schlaggenwald, Bohemia. Lipfert & Haas were owners until in 1876 when it became Haas & Čžijžek. Various styles of china dolls' heads of the 1840s–70s have been found with the S mark for Schlaggenwald impressed on the inside of the shoulder. Often the S was made horizontally and near it was a number. More of the heads thus far observed had wigs than molded hair.

2293. Schindhelm & Knauer advertisement for dressed dolls and dolls with trousseaus in trunks and babies with layettes in baskets as shown in DEUTSCHE SPIELWAREN ZEITUNG, February, 1927.

2294. China shoulder head made by Schlaggenwald has a wig, molded and painted eyes with painted upper eyelashes and a closed mouth. Mark: Ill. 2300. H. 13 cm. (15 in.). *Courtesy of Dr. Eva Moskovszky.*

2295. China shoulder head probably made by Schlaggenwald. The hair painted black has no molding. The head has a long neck and molded bosom. Mark: see Ill. 2301. H. of shoulder head 7½ in. (19 cm.). *Courtesy of the Hungarian National Museum.*

Some of the wigged china heads had a black spot for a pate. The shoulders generally had three sew holes in both front and back and the sides were narrow compared with the long front and back. The faces usually had a long patrician look. Some of the heads had morning glories as decorations. The decorations were not always painted in multicolors but sometimes the entire hair and decorations were painted black. A few of the heads had molded blonde hair.

1793: Factory was founded by Johann Georg Paulus.

1831: Over 300 employees.★

Schlesinger, Leo. 1874–1927. New York City. In 1874, Leo Schlesinger entered the toy field and soon thereafter established his own business. By 1924 it became Schlesinger Bros. They manufactured dolls.

1922: Leo Schlesinger became the fourth President of the Toy Manufacturers of the U.S.A.★

Schlesische Spielwaren Fabrik. 1926–30. Leignitz, Silesia. Manufactured dolls under the direction of *Carl Sorneck.*

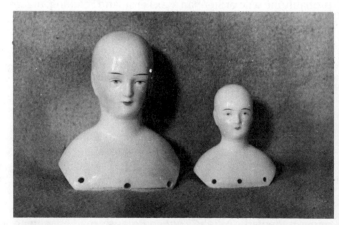

2296. Pair of china shoulder heads made by Schlaggenwald. These bald heads were made to have wigs. The molded and painted eyes are blue, closed mouth, hs. 15 and 10 cm. (6 and 4 in.). *Courtesy of Dr. Eva Moskosvszky.*

2297. Pair of china shoulder heads made by Schlaggenwald. Both heads are pressed and have molded and painted eyes and closed mouths. The head on the left has a white bald head under the wig. Its mark is Ill. 2307. H. 10 cm. (4 in.). The head on the right has molded black hair. Mark Ill. 2303. H. 4 cm. (1½ in.). *Courtesy of Gundi Groh-Pracher.*

2298A & B. China shoulder head bears the mark of Sᵒᵒ which has been attributed to Schlaggenwald. The molded hair has a coiled bun near the nape of the neck with flowers on either side, all painted black. Mark Ill. 2302. H. of head only, 3¼ in. (8.5 cm.). *Coleman Collection.*

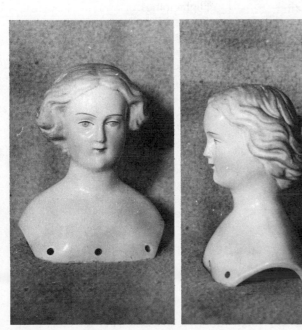

2299A & B. China shoulder head made by Schlaggenwald has molded blond hair with bun in back, molded and painted blue eyes and a closed mouth. H. 13 cm. (5 in.). *Courtesy of Dr. Eva Moskovszky.*

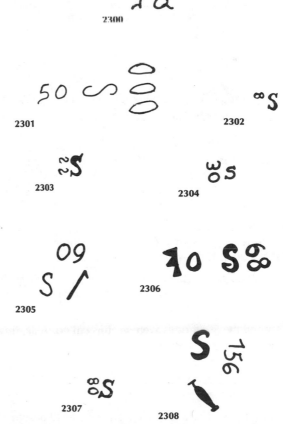

2300–2308. Schlaggenwald marks on porcelain shoulder heads.

2309A & B. All felt clown doll named Coloro, designed by Albert Schlopsnies for Steiff, shown in DEKORATIVE KUNST in 1913. Clown marking is on the face, Steiff metal button in the ear. Original costume of velveteen printed with a bear in front and an elephant in back. H. 43 cm. (17 in.). *Courtesy of Dorothy Mishler.*

Schlieff & Co. (Paul S. Schlieff & Co.) 1922–24. Made dolls and advertised in a British toy trade journal.

1922: *Simpson's Toys* was their London agent.

Schlopsnies, Albert. 1909–30 and probably other years. Munich and Nürnberg, Bavaria. An artist who designed many of the *Steiff* dolls as well as some wooden figures with spherical heads and other dolls.

Before 1912: Designed a miniature version of the Sarrasani's Circus with felt figures made by Steiff, including Clowns, Bare Back Riders, Ring Masters and so forth.

1912: Exhibited at the Bavarian Industrial Show. His dolls included fashionable ladies, children, hunters, firemen, lieutenants and tennis players.

1913: Among the Steiff dolls were groups called "A Skating Party," and "Fair in a Small Town," as shown in DEKORATIVE KUNST.

1920: His work was controlled by *Bing. L. Rees & Co.* were the London distributors.

1922–24 and possibly later: Schlopsnies in 1922 designed for Steiff a special kind of celluloid-head doll that had its features painted on the inside of the head so that the paint could not be rubbed off or washed off. These washable heads could stand rough treatment, even sandpaper, without destroying the painted features. The dolls were all 40 cm. (15½ in.) tall, and all came from identical molds. The clowns had either white or vari-colored faces. Sam and Samy were black dolls. The other 32 dolls were dressed as boys or girls and given the following names★:

Name of Doll	Costume
Adele	Red and black checked dress.
Agnes	Dressed for winter.
Anna	Dirndl style dress with yellow checks.
Axel	Dressed for winter.
Bubi (Boy)	Nightdress.
Carlos	Dressed in white.
Elsa	White trimmed with embroidery.
Ernst	White trimmed with embroidery.
Hemdmatz	Nightshirt.
Henriette	Dressed for winter in red felt.
Herbert	Dressed for winter in red felt.
Hosenmatz	Pajamas.
Klara	Dressed in white.
Kolja	Dressed in white with wool embroidery.
Lene	Dressed for winter in a knitted costume.
Madeleine	Blue felt skirt and red and white blouse.
Marga	Dressed in white with wool embroidery.
Marius	Blue felt trousers with a red and white skirt.
Meedi	Nightclothes.
Otto	Dressed for winter in knitted clothes.
Peter	Yellow checked playsuit.
Resi	Checked blouse and a green skirt.
Richard	Red and black checked costume.
Rita	Red and black checked dress.
Rolf	White shirt and red velvet trousers.
Ruth	White blouse and a red velvet skirt.
Sepp	Checked shirt and green trousers.
Theo	Red and black checked outfit.
Vera	Checked dress.
Viktor	Checked playsuit.
Yvo	Dressed for winter.
Yvonne	Dressed for winter.

Schlosser, Anton. 1853 and probably other years. Vienna. Made dolls according to Dr. Eva Moskovszky.

Schlüter, A.A. 1901. Hannover, Germany. Applied for a German patent (D.R.G.M.) for a doll.

Schmeiser, Adolf. 1907. Vienna. Listed in a directory under Dolls and Dolls' Heads.

Schmetzer, Louis. 1875–76. Chicago, Ill. But residing in Rothenburg, Bavaria. Produced dolls and used the mark shown in Ill. 2310.★

2310. Mark used by Louis Schmetzer according to Gwen White.

2311. G. Schmey's advertisement in DEUTSCHE SPIELWAREN ZEITUNG, February, 1927. He specialized in Mama walking dolls and exported dressed dolls. A newborn baby doll was one of the newest dolls.

Schmey, Gustavus. 1853–1928. Sonneberg, Thür. Made and exported dolls including *Täuflinge* and dolls' parts. By 1926 the firm was represented by *Hachmeister* & Co.

1882: Registered several marks with dolls, one was in a chemise another had a helmet and sword, according to the Ciesliks.

1894: Applied for a German patent (D.R.G.M.) for a porcelain doll's head with a moving chin.

1902: Advertised bisque heads, cloth heads, celluloid heads, metal heads, and wooden heads. Some of the bisque heads had human hair. Advertised cloth bodies, leather bodies, wooden bodies, jointed bodies and other types. The Täuflinge were described as being "ball jointed" or "stiff

jointed" and wearing a chemise. Obviously these Täuflinge were baby dolls in chemise and not the earlier so-called *Motschmann* or *Lindner* type Täuflinge.

1910: One of the Sonneberg group of Grand Prize Winners at the Brussels Exposition for their dolls. Advertised character dolls.

1913: Advertised dolls' clothing.

1916: Advertised felt soldiers.

1923: Sole London agent was *Simpson's Toys*.

1925–27: Specialized and exported *Mama* dolls and jointed dolls including *New Born Baby* dolls.★

Schmid, Julius. 1928–30. New York City. Imported *Harva* line of red rubber and colored rubber dolls. There were various designs representing boys and girls, usually with the legs apart and molded clothes.

Schmidt, Adolf. 1929–30. Schalkau, Thür. Manufactured dolls.

Schmidt, August. 1894–1927. Wilsdruff, Dresden, Saxony. Produced celluloid dolls, dolls' heads, arms and legs as well as all-celluloid dolls, including those made by *Rheinische Gummi und Celluloid Fabrik*.

1927: Made *Lona Art Dolls*.★

PLAYTHINGS   *February, 1927*

A. SCHMIDT   DRESDEN-A
10 Annen Str.   GERMANY
Founded 1894
Manufacturers of guaranteed unbreakable and washable
LONA ART DOLLS
In first-class models only, best quality of hand-work, unusually low prices. A trial of my goods will certainly pay you. Ask for my catalog.
Sample collection sent by registered mail upon receipt of $19.50, containing eleven different "LONA" Art Dolls, each 14 inches tall, except one, which is 15½ inches tall.

"LONA"-DOLLS

2312. Advertisement of Lona Art dolls made by August Schmidt in PLAYTHINGS, February, 1927. These dolls had celluloid heads and cloth bodies.

Schmidt, Bruno. 1900–30 and later. Waltershausen, Thür. Made or produced dolls of various materials including bisque and wood. Started to make celluloid dolls in 1913. It is possible that the celluloid itself was supplied by the *Rheinische Gummi und Celluloid Fabrik* the supplier of their earlier celluloid heads. In 1918 Bruno Schmidt acquired *Bähr & Pröschild*, a porcelain factory located in Ohrdruf. Many of the Bruno Schmidt dolls bore a heart-shape tag. The centimeter height of the Bruno Schmidt celluloid dolls was usually marked on the heads. Among the Bruno Schmidt mold numbers were 500, an Oriental; 535; 585; 678; 692; 2048 with painted hair; 2094; 2096; and 2097, a baby head registered in 1911.

1903: Advertised bisque, composition and wooden heads,

ball jointed dolls and stiff jointed dolls as well as wigs for dolls.

1911: Advertised bent limb baby dolls, character dolls and ball-jointed dolls.

1913: Applied for a German patent (D.R.G.M.) for a doll's tongue. Made celluloid character babies. Advertised stationary and sleeping eyes for repair shops.

1916: Used trademark *Mein Goldherz (My Golden Heart)* or just Herz for ball-jointed dolls, character babies, dolls' heads including celluloid heads and dolls. They also made wardrobes of clothes for dolls.

1919: Added series S to the earlier series G of the celluloid dolls.

1921: Applied for a German patent (D.R.G.M.) for dolls' eyes that moved. The former Bähr & Pröschild porcelain factory made china heads and limbs as well as bisque dolls and heads.

1923: Applied for a German patent (D.R.G.M.) for a speaking doll.

1924: Advertised celluloid toddlers with wigs and sleeping eyes or with painted hair.

1925: Still advertising china heads and limbs as well as bisque and celluloid dolls.

1926: Applied for a German patent (D.R.G.M.) for sleeping eyes in celluloid heads.

1927: Applied for another German patent (D.R.G.M.) for sleeping eyes in transparent celluloid heads.
    The Berlin agent was *Carl Stahl.*

1930: Advertised celluloid and papier-mâché dolls under the trade names of "Heart" "My Golden Heart" and "My Dear Heart" (in German); also dolls, babies, painted heads, and wigs. The new feature for 1930 was dolls with bisque or with celluloid heads on toddler type bodies that could sit and also could stand. A large portion of the above information was researched by the Ciesliks.★

Schmidt, Carl. 1901–26. Waltershausen, Thür. Manufactured and exported dolls and papier-mâché objects.

1901–06: Applied for three German patents (D.R.G.M.) for dolls' bodies.

Schmidt, Charles. 1880s. St. Louis, Mo. President of the Toy & Notion Co. His trade card indicated that he made and/or distributed dolls.

Schmidt, Eduard. See **Löffler & Dill.**

Schmidt, Franz, & Co. 1890–1930 and later. Georgenthal, near Waltershausen, Thür. The factory was operated by steam. Made, produced, and exported dolls with heads of various materials including bisque, wood, composition and cellulobrim (a form of celluloid). Many of the bisque heads were made by *Simon & Halbig* and pierced nostrils were found frequently on the bisque heads. Eyes moving sideways with an independent lid as well as sleeping eyes have been found on Simon & Halbig—Franz Schmidt bisque heads.

2313. Bisque head doll made by Bruno Schmidt has a wig, sleeping and flirting blue glass eyes, open mouth with teeth and a ball jointed composition body. Mark: B. S.// W. and a heart. H. 23 in. (58.5 cm.). *Courtesy of Sotheby Parke Bernet Inc., N.Y.*

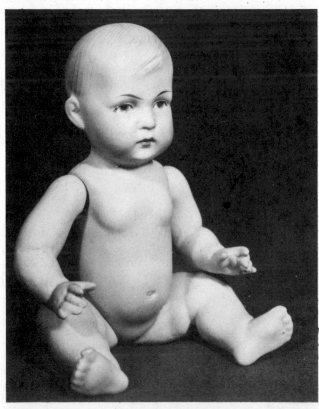

2314. All-bisque bent limb baby made by Bruno Schmidt. It has molded and painted hair and features. The head is attached to the torso; on the back is the mark: Ill. 2315. H. 6 in. (15 cm.). *Coleman Collection.*

2315–2316. Marks found on Bruno Schmidt bisque or celluloid dolls and dolls' heads.

Often the approximate height of the doll in centimeters has been found on the head.

Two dolly-faced heads with wigs, sleeping and/or flirting eyes and open mouths were marked "S & C//SIMON & HALBIG//Germany," and "S & C//SIMON & HALBIG//28." The 28 was the height of the doll in centimeters (11 in.).

Franz Schmidt appeared to have used the initials S & C on his earlier heads and F S & C on the later heads. However a head marked S & C has been found on a body marked F. S. & C. The walking dolls patented by Lander for *Imhof* sometimes had bisque heads marked F. S. & C. or S & C.

Some of the reported mold numbers on bisque heads marked S & C were 269, 293, 927, 1180, and 1310. Mold numbers reported by the Ciesliks on bisque heads marked F. S. & C. included 1250, 1253, 1259, 1262, 1263, 1266, 1267, 1270; (1910) 1271, 1272, 1274; (1911) 1293, 1295, 1296, 1297, 1298, and 1310. There was also mold #1071 (ca. 1902) that was used on Imhof walking dolls as well as mold #1250.

1891: Advertised "Pulverized composition" dolls, bisque heads, wooden heads, and ball-jointed dolls.

1898: Advertised socket and shoulder heads. Applied for a German patent (D.R.P.) for machinery to produce dolls.

1899: Applied for four German patents (two D.R.G.M. and two D.R.P.) for dolls' joints. One of the (D.R.G.M.) patents related to oval ball joints.

1901: Used a patent held by Ferdinand Imhof.

1902: A German patent (D.R.P.) was obtained for dolls. Advertised socket and shoulder type wooden heads and bisque heads for dolls. Specialized in ball jointed dolls and stiff jointed small dolls as well as composition bodies, arms and legs, wigs, and footwear.

1906: Advertised leather and cloth bodies, shoes and stockings.

1908: Franz Schmidt and distributor *Hugo Braun* formed the "Cellulobrinwerke Georgenthal G.m.b.H." to make parts for dolls.

Applied for a German patent (D.R.G.M.) for sleeping eyes operated by elastic.

1911: Applied for a German patent (D.R.G.M.) for a doll's mouth with movable teeth.

1912: Applied for two German patents (D.R.G.M.) for dolls; one of these patents pertained to pierced nostrils.

1913: Applied for two German patents (D.R.G.M.), one for a doll's wig and one for a moving tongue in a doll's head. Advertised about 120 styles of dolls in their baby series.

1914: Mentioned baby dolls with moving tongues.

1926: Manufactured dolls and bébés with ball-jointed composition bodies. Applied for a German patent (D.R.G.M.) for rubber heads to be used on dolls.

1927: There were two departments. One department made ball jointed dolls, bent limbed babies, toddlers, stiff jointed small dolls, dolls' heads, bodies, arms, legs, and wigs. The other department was a "papier-mâché factory" and "produced doll heads in all desired models."

1928: Applied for two German patents (D.R.G.M.) for dolls' eyes and for dolls' voices.

Advertised composition heads for dolls.

1930: Advertised *Lore* and *Peter* with flirting eyes and toddlers with five-piece bodies. The heads came painted or wigged.

Part of the above information was researched by the Ciesliks.★

2317. Bisque-head doll made by Franz Schmidt has molded and painted hair and eyes, open-closed mouth with two upper teeth and a bent limb composition baby body. H. 11 in. (28 cm.). *Courtesy of Richard Withington. Photo by Barbara Jendrick.*

2318A & B. Bisque head character baby with a bent limb composition baby body made by Franz Schmidt. The head with molded and painted baby hair, stationary glass eyes, dimples, open-closed mouth with two teeth and tongue was obtained from a porcelain factory. Mold #1271. H. 10 in. (25 cm.). H. marked on head. *Coleman Collection.*

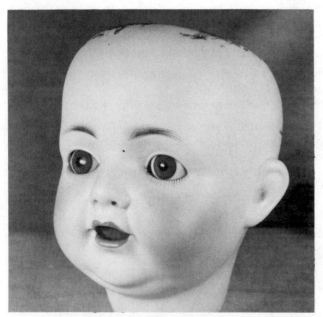

2319. Bisque socket head made by Simon & Halbig for Franz Schmidt. It has a wig, sleeping brown glass eyes, hair eyelashes, pierced nostrils and an open mouth with teeth and tongue. Mark: III. 2324. H. of head 5 in. (12.5 cm.). *Coleman Collection.*

2320. Franz Schmidt's advertisement in PLAYTHINGS, September, 1927, in which their doll products in Department I and Department II are listed. They made chiefly the various composition and papier-mâché parts of dolls.

F S & C
12 53
28

2321

F S. & C⁰
1272/40 Z
Deponiert

2322

F.S. & Co.
SIMON & HALBIG
1295
Made in
Germany
56

2323A

1310
F.S.& C
SIMON & HALBIG
Made in
Germany
48.

2323B

S & C
SIMON & HALBIG

2324A

S & C
Made in Germany

4 °/x   68

2324B

2321–2324A, B, C & D. Marks found on bisque head dolls produced by Franz Schmidt.

14

S & C

S & C

Germany

Germany **2324C**

2324D

Size No.	Height	
	cm.	in.
0	37	14
1	40	15½
2	43	17
8	78	30½

Wax was sometimes used to cover bisque or composition heads for dolls. A wax-over-composition head Bébé Schmitt[†] also had the stamp of *Au Paradis des Enfants.*

Some dolls with marked Schmitt bodies have the neck joint with the socket in the head like the ones on *Patsy* dolls.★

Schmuckler, Heinrich (Erst Schlesische Puppenfabrik). 1891–1928. Liegnitz, Silesia. Produced cloth dolls and celluloid dolls including babies.

1924: Advertised dressed porcelain dolls. The London agent was *Gross & Schild.*

1927: Advertised Hesli.[†]★

Schnabel, Gebrüder. 1923–26. Neustadt near Coburg, Bavaria. Made dressed dolls.

Schneegass, Louis, & Co. 1923–30 and later. Waltershausen, Thür. This company appears to have been called D. Schneegass & Söhne in 1926 and Gebrüder Schneegass after 1927. Made dolls and papier-mâché objects.★

Schmidt, Gebrüder. 1930. Gräfenroda, Thür. Made dolls representing cowboys, Indians, and circus trainers. Dolls were distributed by *G. F. Hertzog & Co.*

Schmidt, Georg. 1910–14. Gotha, Germany. Showed elegantly dressed dolls at the Leipzig Fair in 1914.

Schmidt, Gustav. 1913–14. Sonneberg, Thür. Made leather-body dolls. Applied for a German patent (D.R.G.M.) for dolls' voices. The application was with *Richard Steiner.*

1913: Applied for two German patents (D.R.G.M.) for leather dolls' bodies with crying voices.

Schmidt, H. 1930. Monchröden, Bavaria. Listed in a directory as manufacturing dolls' accessories.

Schmidt, Minna Moschersch. Before 1875–1930 and later. Germany and America. In Sindelfinger, Germany, at the age of six she created Snow White and the Seven Dwarfs. The heads were lacquered chestnuts, bodies were potatoes, sticks formed arms and legs and wool was used for wigs and dwarfs' beards.

In 1923 she began to make wax "portrait dolls" that represented Chicago women who had lived since 1804 and had benefited humanity. Some of the materials used for the clothes came from garments actually worn by the person represented by the doll. There were 71 dolls, each 16 in. (40.5 cm.) high and it took Minna Schmidt four years to complete this group in time for the 75th *Marshall Field* anniversary celebration in 1927. After this she continued to make dolls. There were 120 dolls in her historical series which included literary characters as well. The clothes on many of the dolls (as was typical of her era) reflected the styles when they were made more than the period they were supposed to represent. Minna Schmidt later wrote a book about her collection.

Schmidt, Paul. 1921–30 and later. Sonneberg, Thür. Successor in 1927 was M. L. Schmidt. Used an oval trademark containing the initials P. S. S. Th. Made dolls with voices and mechanical moving heads.

Schmiedeknecht, Reinhold. 1930. Neustadt near Coburg, Bavaria. Produced wardrobes of clothes for dolls.

Schmitt (Schmitt & Fils). 1854–91. Nogent-sur-Marne and Paris, France. Made dolls and bébés with porcelain heads. All of the heads examined so far have been pressed. The

2325. Schmitt & Fils' bisque head doll with a wig, stationary blue glass eyes, pierced ears, closed mouth, and a ball jointed Schmitt type composition and wood body. Contemporary clothes. Schmitt mark on the head. H. 16 in. (40.5 cm.). *Courtesy of Elsie and Al Potter.*

2326. Doll made by Schmitt & Fils with a pressed bisque socket head, wig, stationary blue glass eyes, pierced ears, closed mouth and a ball jointed composition and wood body without joints at the wrists. Original clothes. Mark: "6" embossed, shield incised. H. 15 in. (37.5 cm.). *Courtesy of and photo by Cherry Bou.*

2327. Bisque head doll made by Schmitt & Fils had a wig, blue glass eyes, pierced ears; open-closed mouth, ball jointed composition body, and contemporary clothes. Schmitt mark on head and body. Under the shield on the head is 4.5. H. 23 in. (58.5 cm.). *Courtesy of Sotheby Parke Bernet Inc., N.Y.*

2328. Schmitt & Fils bébé with bisque head wig, stationary blue glass eyes, and fully jointed composition body. Mark on head: Schmitt shield. H. 11 in. (28 cm.). *Courtesy of Richard Withington. Photo by Barbara Jendrick.*

2329–2330. Mark on Schmitt & Fils' dolls.

Schneeglöckchen (Little Snowdrop). 1914–26. A line of ball jointed dolls made by *Nöckler & Tittel* of Schneeberg. These dolls came dressed or undressed. Also called Snow-Bell. One of these bisque head dolls was marked "Schneeglöcken //562//2/0."

1926: Snowdrop babies and Snowdrop jointed dolls were advertised by *W. Cohen & Sons* in London.

Schneewittchen (Snow White). 1909–27. Name of bisque-head ball-jointed dolls made by *Kley & Hahn*. This trade-mark was in a circle.★

Schneid (Schneider, Tailor). 1913–16. Felt doll representing a tailor, made by *Steiff* and distributed by *Borgfeldt*. Ht. 14 in. (35 cm.); priced $2.10 in New York in 1913.

Schneider. 1858–96. Paris. Produced dolls.

1881: Bought bisque dolls' heads from *François Gaultier*, according to Mme. Poisson.★

Schneider, Caesar. 1926–29. Waltershausen, Thür. Designed and made dolls.

1926: Listed in directory as making dolls and baby dolls.

1929: According to Arthur Schoenau, Caesar Schneider was a free-lance designer who designed *Princess Elizabeth* doll for *Schoenau & Hoffmeister* of Burggrub, Bavaria.

Schneider Carl. See **Gräfenthal Porzellanfabrik.**

Schneider, Frank G. 1922–23. Brooklyn, N.Y. Obtained a U.S. patent for dolls' voices.

Schneider, Johannes Georg. 1895 and later. Lauscha, Thür. Possibly made the bisque doll heads marked "J S."★

Schneider, Karl. See **Heine & Schneider.**

Schneider, Otto. 1913–18 and possibly other years. Sonneberg, Thür. Made and exported dressed dolls.

1913: Advertised miniature ball-jointed and stiff-jointed dolls.

Schneider, Robert. 1867–1925 and later. Sonneberg and Coburg, Thür. Made and exported dolls.

1925: Advertised *Mama* dolls and jointed dolls.★

Schneider, Rudolf. Before 1914–25 and later. Sonneberg, Thür. Some of his wooden dolls carried the label "*Bébé Tout en Bois.*"★

Schnepff, Albert. 1903–18. Coburg, Thür. Made dolls and dolls' clothes and accessories.

1903: Applied for a German patent (D.R.G.M.) for a cloth doll's hat with straw or other trimming material.

1906: Obtained a German patent (D.R.P.) for a doll's head with moving features made of a combination of composition and rubber.

1908: Applied for a German patent (D.R.G.M.) for dolls with movable legs.★

Schnickel-Fritz. 1911. Trade name of an all-wood doll made by *Schoenhut*. See Ill. 2333.★

Schnötzinger, Joh. Ev. 1930 and later. Vienna. Distributor for *Kestner.*

2331. Bisque-head portrait doll designed by Caesar Schneider to look like Princess Elizabeth as a two or three year old child was made in 1929–30. This doll made by Schoenau & Hoffmeister has a wig, sleeping blue glass eyes, a closed smiling mouth and a five-piece composition body. The clothes are partly original. Mark on head: Porzellanfabrik Burggrub// Princess Elizabeth// 3½// Made in Germany D.R.G.M. H. 16 in. (40.5 cm.). *Courtesy of Sotheby Parke Bernet Inc., N.Y.*

5

J S

5

2332. Mark on bisque heads possibly made by Johannes Schneider.

2333. All-wood doll named Schnickel-Fritz made by Schoenhut has molded and carved hair and features, open-closed mouth with two upper and two lower teeth. It is fully jointed with metal springs. Original union suit and footwear. A Schoenhut button is on the collar. H. 15½ in. (39.5 cm.). *Courtesy of and photo by Becky Moncrief.*

2334. All-celluloid doll made by Schöberl & Becker (Cellba). After 1930 has molded and painted hair plus a roll of real hair across the top of the forehead, stationary blue glass eyes, open-closed mouth, and is jointed at the shoulder and hips. Original regional Dutch costume. Mark on back of neck is similar to Ill. 2335. Cloth label on bottom of apron reads "Dovina//Rotterdam Holland." H. 25 cm. as marked on the back (10 in.). *Coleman Collection.*

2335. Mermaid mark used by Schöberl & Becker on celluloid dolls.

Schnür, Marie. See **Marc-Schnür, Marie.**

Schöberl & Becker (Celluloidwarenfabrik Babenhausen). 1923–30 and later. Babenhausen, Hesse. Manufactured celluloid dolls and babies, dressed and undressed, with shiny or mat finish. Some of these were black or mulatto. The mark was a shield with a mermaid in it. Schöberl & Becker used *Cellba* as the trade name for their products. Some of the dolls had molded hair, glass eyes and cloth bodies with celluloid hands, others were all-celluloid.

1926: Obtained a German patent (D.R.P.) for the joints of a celluloid doll.

1927: Obtained a German patent (D.R.P.) for connecting the parts of a celluloid doll's body. Applied for a German patent (D.R.P.) for glass eyes in a doll's head.

Schoen, Joseph. 1886. Reichenbach, Silesia. Applied for a German patent for making a doll's head of two or more pieces of sheet metal.

Schoen & Yondorf Co. (Sayco). 1907–30 and later. New York City. Made composition dolls and dolls with cloth bodies. Myer (Meyer) Yondorf, before 1922 when he joined Schoen Co., had been with *E. Goldberger* and the *New Toy Manufacturing Co.*

1923: Company was described as an old company with a new name. Advertised 50 numbers of *Mama* dolls with painted hair or wigs. *Ronson* voices, cloth bodies stuffed with cotton. Hts. 15 to 25 in. (38 to 63.5 cm.); priced $1.00 and up.

1924: Advertised Jiggles the Clown, dressed dolls, and character dolls.

1925: Advertised 80 numbers of Mama dolls most of them with composition heads, hands and legs, wigs, sleeping eyes, dressed in silk often with matching hat. A few of the Mama dolls had painted hair and eyes. There were also 10 numbers of baby dolls one of which was a *"New-born baby"* type.

1926: The Mama dolls wore lace-trimmed dresses and hair ribbons. Besides the *Our Gang* dancing dolls there was a creeping baby doll and a baby with composition head and hands on a cloth body wrapped in a blanket and attached to a baby scale with a ribbon. Ht. of doll 12 in. (30.5 cm.); priced $1.75. The Schoen & Yondorf Co. was a member of the *American Doll Manufacturers' Assoc.*

1927: Licensed by *Voices, Inc.* to use their patented Mama voices and criers. New numbers were introduced, among them *Merriwinkle* created by *Grace Corry*. Myer Yondorf, Vice President of the American Doll Manufacturer's Association, predicted 80 per cent of their business would be in the new long slim Mama dolls which had superseded the earlier chubby Mama dolls. The remaining 20 percent would be baby dolls. *A. S. Ferguson* was their factory representative.

1929: *Maurice Long* appears to have taken the place of Schoen.★

2336. Advertisement for dolls made by Schoen & Yondorf (Sayco) in PLAYTHINGS, August, 1924. The Mama dolls came with or without wigs, painted or sleeping eyes, composition arms and legs or cloth arms and legs.

2337. Sayco mark on Schoen & Yondorf dolls.

2338

2339

2340

2338–2340. Marks of the Gebrüder Schoenau porcelain factory.

Schoenau, Arthur. See **Bauersachs & Henninger** and **Schoenau & Hoffmeister.**

Schoenau, Gebrüder (Gebrüder Schoenau, Swaine & Co.). 1865 and later. Hüttensteinach and North Köppelsdorf, Thür porcelain factories.★

Schoenau & Hoffmeister. 1901–53. Sonneberg, Thür. and Burggrub, Bavaria. Porzellanfabrik Burggrub was founded by Arthur Schoenau (Schönau[+]) and Carl Hoffmeister to produce the bisque heads needed for their dolls and for other doll manufacturers. Schoenau had made dolls since 1884 and he used socket heads primarily while Hoffmeister required shoulder heads for the kid-body or cloth-body dolls that he had been making. In 1907 Leube succeeded Hoffmeister. The firm Schoenhau & Hoffmeister supplied bisque heads to *Kurt Brückner, Canzler & Hoffmann, Cuno & Otto Dressel, E. Edelmann, Gebr. Eckhardt, E. Knoch, R. Leschhorn, E. Liebermann, Eg. M. Luthardt, Werner Luthardt, E. Maar & Sohn, H. Süssenguth, Friedrich Voight* and *H. Von Berg.* according to the research of the Ciesliks. The Schoenaus married into the *Dressel* family.

The mold #s included 70, 169, 900, 914, 1800, 1904, 1906, 1909, 1916, 1923, 1930, 2500, 4000, 4500, 4600, 4700, 4900, 5000, 5300, 5500, 5700, and 5800.

Dolls made by Arthur Schoenau were also marked *Hanna, My Cherub* and *Das Laschende Baby.*

1904: Applied for a German patent (D.R.G.M.) for attaching a wig to a bisque head.

1911: Applied for a German patent (D.R.G.M.) relating to dolls' eyes.

1912: Arthur Schoenau advertised ball jointed dolls marked *Prinzessin Wunderhold*, My Cherub, *Carmencita* and *Autoliebchen* as well as baby dolls.

1920: Arthur Schoenau advertised Hanna, My Cherub and Bébé Carmencita.

1923: Arthur Schoenau applied for a German patent (D.R.G.M.) for a walking doll.

1929: Advertised "all kinds of porcelain dolls' heads" and spare parts for dolls. PLAYTHINGS showed two character baby heads, one was a socket head and the other had a flange neck. Arthur Schoenau advertised dressed and undressed dolls.

The *Princess Elizabeth* portrait doll was the original idea of Alec Cohen. It represented the three year old British Princess and was designed by *Caesar Schneider*. The bisque head was made in the Porzellanfabrik Burggrub.

1930: Arthur Schoenau advertised in a British trade journal My Cherub, *Fairy Belle*, the "Elizabeth series," smiling babies (possibly Das Laschende Baby), the Happy Prize-Winner and jointed dolls. *Alec Cohen & Randall* was the sole London agent. They had to send their regrets that they could not fill all the orders for the Princess Elizabeth doll.

1938: Arthur Schoenau was still making dolls.

The research of the Ciesliks provided some of the above information.★

2342. Bisque-head doll made by Schoenau & Hoffmeister has a wig, sleeping glass eyes, open mouth with four upper teeth and a ball jointed composition and wood body. Original clothes. Mark Ill. 2348. H. 12 in. (30.5 cm.). *Coleman Collection.*

2341. Schoenau and Hoffmeister bisque head doll having a wig, sleeping blue glass eyes, open mouth with teeth and a composition body with part of the limbs made of wood. Original clothes. Mark: Ill. 2345. H. 15 in. (38 cm.). *Courtesy of the late Henrietta Van Sise.*

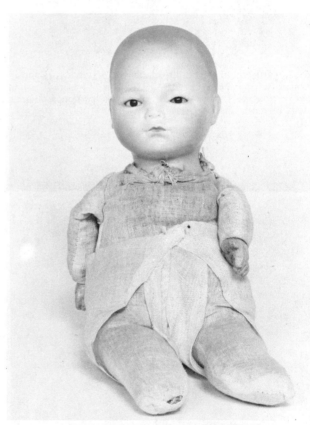

2343. Doll with a bisque head made by Schoenau & Hoffmeister has sleeping eyes, open mouth on a ball jointed composition body. Head marked: "KÜNSTLERKOPF//S ☆ H. //2/0 Germany." H. 15 in. (38 cm.). *Courtesy of the Hungarian National Museum.*

2344. Infant doll made by Schoenau and Hoffmeister has painted hair, sleeping brown glass eyes, closed mouth and a cloth body stuffed with straw. The hands are composition. Mark: Ill. 2347. H. 10½ in. (26.5 cm.). *Courtesy of the Margaret Woodbury Strong Museum. Photo by Harry Bickelhaupt.*

5500

10/0

2345

2346

2347A

2347B

2348

2349

241-5
Germany
Burggrub

2345-2349. Schoenau & Hoffmeister marks on bisque-head dolls.

Schoenhut, A., & Co. 1872–1930 and later. Philadelphia, Pa. Made their first wooden dolls in 1903 and Otto Schoenhut was still making wooden dolls in 1939. Around 1950 Otto Schoenhut gave permission to the Humpty Dumpty Toy Co. to make Humpty Dumpty Circus dolls. Several unusual dolls have been attributed to Schoenhut; among them was a doll representing an Oriental with molded and painted black hair. Ht. 17½ in. (44.5 cm.). *Borgfeldt* was the sole licensee of an all-wood doll representing *Happy Hooligan*. Ht. 9½ in. (24 cm.). According to TOYS AND NOVELTIES in 1915 the Schoenhut dolls were made of basswood, the softest of hard woods which could be easily worked, would not warp or check badly, was tough and took paint well. Unfortunately the paint has chipped off many of the Schoenhut dolls.

Julius Dorst made wooden circus dolls that closely resembled those of Schoenhut.

1906: Schoenhut circus figures sold by *Gamage* as follows:

Clowns in cotton costumes 29¢; *Hobo* for 32¢; *Chinaman, Gent, Lady Acrobats,* and *Lady Circus Rider* for 50¢ each; *Negro* (Black) *Dude, Lion Tamer* and *Ring Master* for 56¢.

1908: PLAYTHINGS reported that the Schoenhut factory employed 450 to 500 people. "A tour through the factory showed case after case of bodies, legs, arms, and heads for figures. . . . The painting of the various toys is a most interesting process. The first coat is applied in nearly all cases by dipping, but after that brush coats are used. The operatives become exceedingly expert in their work and the uniformity of the faces on the clowns, acrobats, grotesque figures and doll heads is splendid proof of their dexterity."

1909: McCALL'S MAGAZINE commented, "Ex-President Roosevelt's African hunting expedition was another source of inspiration to the toy makers . . . the ex-President himself in shooting costume . . . is accompanied by his son Kermit and two African Spearmen." These jointed wooden figures were also sold separately.

Siegel Cooper advertised a new *Mary Had a Little Lamb.*

1911–14: *Marshall Field, Montgomery Ward, Sears,* and *Wanamaker* all showed Schoenhut All-wood Art Dolls in their catalogs. The least expensive dolls were the 15 in. (35.5 cm.) ones with carved hair wearing a union suit and the most expensive ones were the 21 in. (53.5 cm.) dressed dolls with angora wigs that sold for $90.00 doz. wholesale.

1913: Circus dolls representing *Max and Moritz* were advertised. The Baby's Head[+] copyrighted by Harry Schoenhut bore a close resemblance to the Duquesnois' head which was the inspiration for many other dolls' heads, including those of *Käthe Kruse.*

1916: *Wanamaker* advertised various dressed Schoenhut dolls including girl, boy and baby dolls. These came with painted hair or the more expensive ones had wigs. Four hts. 14, 16, 19, and 21 in. (35.5, 40.5, 48, and 53.5 cm.); priced $3.50 to $11.25.

1917: *Columbus Merchandise Co.* advertised several Schoenhut dolls. One girl doll had molded and painted braided hair, a stockinet union suit, shoes and stockings. Ht. 14½ in. (37 cm.); priced $3.00. Other girl dolls had curly mohair wigs, with ribbon bows and side parts. Hts. 16 and 19 in. (40.5 and 48 cm.); priced $4.50 and $6.00.

A boy doll with a Buster Brown style mohair wig was 15 in. (38 cm.) tall; priced $3.80. A baby doll in a lace trimmed slip was 13½ in. (34 cm.) tall; priced $3.50.

1918: LADIES' HOME JOURNAL showed a full colored page of Schoenhut dolls captioned, "Dolls dressed in the costumes of our Allies for gifts or Bazars." The dolls with the baby style face wore the following costumes: Alsatian, American Sailor, Belgian, Blue Devil (French), Brittany, Chinese, Italian, Japanese, Red Cross Nurse, Russian, Scottish, Serbian, Welsh, and Yankee Soldiers.

Schoenhut made a *Barney Google.*

Eaton distributed wigged Schoenhut dolls wearing union suits. Ht. 15 in. (38 cm.); priced $5.25.

1923: Advertised that their dolls had moving or stationary eyes and mohair wigs. The baby came in two sizes and wore either a long dress or a short little girl-style dress. All the girl dolls wore large hair bows and had either bobbed hair or short ringlets and teeth. Other dolls were Clubby Clowns, Walkable Dolls and Golf Dolls. The outdoor golf dolls were named Bill-Caddie and Mary-Hit; the indoor golf dolls were named Tommy Green and Sissie Lofter. *Strobel & Wilken* as well as Borgfeldt and *A. S. Ferguson* were distributors.

The *F. A. O. Schwarz* catalog listed Schoenhut walking dolls with curly wigs, dressed in a chemise as follows:

Style	Height		Price
No.	in.	cm.	
39	16	40.5	$ 4.00
46	18	45.5	$ 5.00
53	19½	49.5	$ 6.50
62	25	63.5	$ 8.00
76	29	73.5	$15.00

Schwarz also advertised Barney Google and Spark Plug for $2.75.

1924: The elastic strung dolls were cheaper than the dolls with steel springs. The wooden head on the cloth body dolls was hollow in order to make the dolls light in weight.

A box containing one of these wooden-head *Mama* dolls had on the box end "Schoenhut's Unbreakable Wooden Head//Soft Body Mamma Doll// Dressed Mohair Wig// 41/107W S Made in U.S.A."

Schoenhut catalog advertised clowns named *Cracker Jack, Humpty,* and *Dumpty,* Hobo, Negro Dude, Lady Circus Rider and Ring Master, all made in two sizes. Schoenhut was also making in one size the Lion Tamer; Lady, Gent and Chinaman Acrobats; Max and Moritz; the *Farmer; Milk Maid* and Mary (Mary Had a Little Lamb). See Ills. 2356 and 2357.

1926: Advertised dolly-type dolls, bent limb baby dolls and the Humpty Dumpty Circus† which cost $1.00 to $35.00 per set. The Circus came in two sizes with four to 34 pieces. The pieces including the tent could be purchased separately. London agent was *William Peck.*

1928: Advertised a *Ski Jumper* and a new Circus tent made of lithographed muslin; including the side shows on either side of the tent, it was about nine feet wide. Among the dolls was one with a carved and painted bonnet having a chin strap and painted flowers as trimming. Carved hair was shown around the face.

1929: The *Big Game Hunter (Teddy Roosevelt)* set was still being advertised.

1930: Advertised the all-wood dolls, the circus dolls and a new composition doll. The all-composition doll had molded hair, painted eyes, jointed at the neck, shoulders and hips. There were eight style nos. 13/21 to 13/28. These dolls were 12 or 13 in. (30.5 or 33 cm.); priced $30.00 doz. wholesale. (See THE COLLECTOR'S BOOK OF DOLLS' CLOTHES, Ills. 650, 651, and 784.) (See Ills. 2354–2360.)★

Schoepfer, G. 1926–30 and later. New York City. Made eyes for dolls.

2350. Schoenhut wooden doll with molded, carved and painted hair and features, blue eyes, closed mouth, original clothes, Schoenhut button and outside of a Schoenhut box lid. The doll is marked: Schoenhut Doll//Pat. Jan. 17, '11 U.S.A.//Foreign Countries. H. 15¾ in. (40 cm.). *Courtesy of and photo by Becky Moncrief.*

2351. Pair of all-wood Schoenhut dolls with molded, carved and painted hair and features. They have brown eyes, closed mouths, and metal spring joints throughout. Original clothes except the dress may be contemporary and not original, original stands. Doll on left has an oval sticker on its back: "Schoenhut Doll//Pat. Jan. 17th 1911// U.S.A." H. 16½ in. (42 cm.). Doll on the right is incised on the back shoulder: "Schoenhut Doll//Pat. Jan. 17, '11, U.S.A.// 6 Foreign Countries." H. 19½ in. (49.5 cm.). *Courtesy of and photo by Becky Moncrief.*

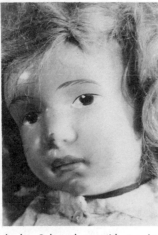

2352A & B. All-wood doll made by Schoenhut, with a wig, painted features, intaglio eyes and spring joints. It has the so-called pouty face. Homemade clothes of the period of the doll, original stockings with holes in the sole for the stand. H. 16 in. (40.5 cm.). *Coleman Collection.*

2353. All-wood bent limb baby doll made by Schoenhut with wig, sleeping brown eyes, open mouth, and teeth. H. 12 in. (30.5 cm.). *Courtesy of Richard Withington. Photo by Barbara Jendrick.*

Scholz, Franz. 1866–73. Vienna. Exhibited dolls at the Vienna Exposition in 1873.

Schön, Joseph. 1886–88. Reichenbach, Silesia. Obtained patents for making metal dolls' heads.★

Schönfeld's Toys. 1920s. New York City. Distributed dolls.

School (College) Boy or Girl. Dolls were often dressed to represent school children or college boys and girls. Some of them were identified by the college colors that they wore. Sometimes they carried school bags, slates or other accessories identified with school children.

The following dolls were among those representing school boys and girls.

1903: Eton Boy advertised by *F.A.O. Schwarz.*

1904: *Harvard Boy.*

1911–15: *Horsman* made a school boy and girl. The boy was style No. 151. In 1914 he had a new head that resembled *Billy Boy;* priced $8.50 doz. wholesale. The girl was style No. 192 in 1912 and cost $12.00 doz. wholesale. It also had a new head in 1914, which was style No. 150 and resembled *Daisy Dimple.* It wore a lawn dress with red trimming and a red hair bow. (See Ills. 2361 and 2362.)

1913: *Écolière* (School Girl) advertised by *Samaritaine.*

1914: College Kid Mascots made by Horsman, These were *Campbell Kids* dressed in college colors.
James Wisbey's dolls.

World War I. *Yerri* and *Gretel* created by *Hansi.*

1916–24. *Schülerpuppen* (School boy or girl dolls) made by *Steiff.*

1918: Name of an all-composition doll made by *Jessie M. Raleigh.* It had molded hair; five piece steel spring-jointed body.

1921: Name of a cloth-body doll dressed in felt garments and made by *Chessler Co.*

1922–24: *Flapper Novelty Doll Co.* made *Boudoir* dolls in the colors of various colleges.

1925–26. *Collegiate Dolls* were advertised by *Shackman.* Red Grange was made by *Live Long Toys.*

1926: *Eton Boy* was advertised by *J. Bloch.*

1926–29: Cloth doll made by *Chad Valley* wore spectacles, an academic robe and mortar board.

1927: *Star* was made by *Twistum Toy Factory.*

1929: *Reisman, Barron* advertised a school girl.

1929–30: *Hollywood Imps* advertised by *Woodward* included a college girl (See also **Bube** and **Mädchen**).★

School for Scandal Dolls. 1918–30 and later. Wooden dolls wearing 1700s style clothes similar to the ones worn in the play of this name. These dolls have long necks, round glass eyes and generally wigs, but sometimes painted black hair. Some of them were created and dressed in old fabrics by *Hugh Hugo.* The *Lepapes* created some dolls that resembled the School for Scandal dolls.

The Easily Made Christmas Doll That Fits the Times

Dolls Dressed in the Costumes of Our Allies

For Gifts or Bazaars: By Jane Porter

A good seller for a bazaar. Children both old and young will love our little Scotch laddie in his Highland costume.

The Serbian lady on the left is brilliant in her green satin skirt, blue bodice with bronze braid and bright red kerchief over the stiff green hat.

The little Russian lady on the right is also gay in color. Her skirt is red silk, her apron made of bits of lace, and the sleeves of her waist decorated in cross-stitch in bright colors.

The Chinese boy is sure to bring a smile to everyone's face—he is so very serious. Odd bits of silk or ribbon can be used to make his costume.

Our little Welsh doll, with her bright red hood and her stiff black hat and basket, makes you think of Little Red Riding Hood, does she not?

And who could resist this pair? The little Yankee soldier is telling his new French brother, the Blue Devil, that he is with him to the end.

Both the American soldier doll in khaki and the Blue Devil in horizon blue are sure to attract attention and will sell well separately or as a pair.

The kiddies will love the Red Cross doll in her gray dress, with white apron. Her blue cape, lined with bright red, is much admired by all France.

Here is a little Alsatian maid, with her friend from Brittany. The headdress of each is quaint; the most characteristic feature of the costumes is that the bow of the Alsatian child is black, as is the cap of the Brittany child. These are never in color.

You all know the little Japanese lady in her bright-flowered kimono made of bits of ribbon, with a broad sash which is made of cherry-colored silk.

The little Italian flower girl has a purple cotton skirt, with a bit of Roman striped ribbon as an apron. Her headdress is white and reaches to the waist at the back.

Our brave little sailor boy is telling his new little Belgian friend, Suzanna, that things will soon be better now that he is there. Her skirt is red, her apron black and the cap and surplice part of her waist yellow with a black edge.

2354. Schoenhut all-wood dolls shown in THE LADIES' HOME JOURNAL. December, 1918. These dolls are dressed in the regional costumes of the Allies of World War I, namely Alsatian, Belgian, Brittany girl, Italian, Japanese, Russian, Scottish, Serbian and Welsh, as well as dressed in military outfits of an American soldier, sailor and Red Cross Nurse and a French Blue Devil. Also included is a Chinese boy. These pictures represent suggestions for dressing dolls at home so that they can be sold at Bazars or given for Christmas gifts. These dolls all appear to have the head copyrighted in 1913 which was usually referred to as a Baby head; the Oriental dolls were painted differently from the others. (This baby head appears to have been based on a sculpture done by François Duquesnois in the 1600s.)

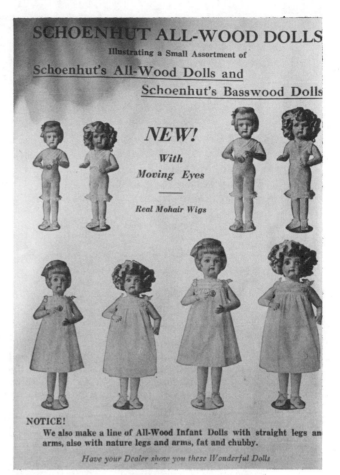

2355. Advertisement for Schoenhut All-Wood Dolls in the LADIES' HOME JOURNAL, November, 1922.

2356. Schoenhut's all-wood dolls and Schoenhut's Basswood Dolls shown in a 1924 Schoenhut catalog. These dolls have mohair wigs, sleeping eyes and wear a union suit or chemise, a hair ribbon and footwear. Some of the dolls are shown wearing Schoenhut buttons.

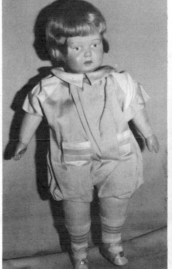

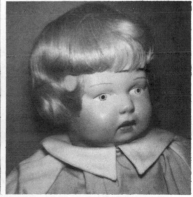

2357. Catalog page of a 1924 Schoenhut catalog showing various Humpty Dumpty Circus dolls and novelty dolls including Max, Moritz, Farmer, Milk Maid and Mary. The clowns are shown dressed in cotton on the left and dressed in silk on the right.

2358A & B. Mama doll with wooden shoulder head and wooden hands on a cloth body made by Schoenhut and first advertised in 1924. It has a wig, painted eyes, closed mouth, and original clothes. H. 17 in. (43 cm.). *Courtesy of Sylvia Brockmon.*

2359. All-composition Schoenhut doll has molded and painted blond hair and blue eyes, closed mouth and is jointed at the neck, shoulders and hips with rubber elastic. Mark: Ill. 2360. H. 13 in. (33 cm.). The papier-mâché rolly-dolly was also made by Schoenhut. *Courtesy of and photo by Becky Moncrief.*

2360. Mark on Schoenhut dolls.

Schoolmaster. See **Le.**

Schools. There were several schools for designing and making dolls in Germany. The most famous one was in Sonneberg. In 1914 TOYS AND NOVELTIES reported that the *Sonneberg Industrial School* had a model room containing many excellent pieces of sculpture and rare old prints. Modeling dolls was a difficult task, "it is truly wonderful what perfect figures the students are able to produce." These students had finished regular school and in the Academy of Design expert workmen were the teachers.

The school at Grünhainichen was established by the German government.★

Schott, Hermann. 1918–30. Schalkau, Thür. Manufactured dolls.

Schramm, Franz. 1921–30 and later. Neustadt near Coburg, Bavaria. Made cloth bodied dolls and baby dolls.

Schranz & Bieber Co. (Esanbe). 1895–1930. Jersey City, N.J. and New York City. Wholesale distributor and jobber.

1921: Advertised new stuffed stockinet clowns.★

No. 151
"SCHOOL BOY"
Trade Mark

(Head copyrighted, 1912, by E. I. Horsman Co.)

This has been, and remains, one of our most successful character kids. He is a healthy, husky youngster, just school-going age, and he has been well dressed evidently by a careful mother.

Per Dozen........**$8.50**

No. 151 "Schoolboy"

2361. School Boy advertised in the Horsman catalog of ca. 1914. The composition head had been copyrighted in 1912. It had molded and painted hair and eyes, closed mouth, cloth body with composition Campbell Kid type hands. *Catalog courtesy of Bernard Barenholtz.*

No. 150
"SCHOOL GIRL"
Trade Mark

(Head copyrighted, 1913, by E. I. Horsman Co.)

A new and very pretty Girl Doll dressed in a dainty lawn costume, with contrasting trimming, with bright red ribbons at the yoke of the dress, and a hair ribbon to match. Half length socks and buckled slippers.

Per Dozen........**$8.50**

No. 150 "School Girl"

2362. School girl as advertised in the Horsman catalog of ca. 1914. The composition head had been copyrighted in 1913. It had molded and painted hair and eyes, closed mouth, cloth body with composition Campbell Kid type hands. *Catalog courtesy of Bernard Barenholtz.*

Schreyer & Co. (Schuco). 1912–30 and later. Nürnberg, Bavaria. Successor in 1950 was Heinrich Müller

1924: Produced bisque, china, celluloid, composition, or metal head dolls on kid or cloth (including felt) bodies. Some of the composition heads resembled *Käthe Kruse* dolls, series I.

1928: Advertised *Piccolo.*

1929: Made a doll representing *Lindbergh.*★

Schroeder, Alfred. 1921–30 and later. Waltershausen, Thür. Made dolls and papier-mâché objects.

1924: Advertised that he had recently designed a doll with a movable head that bowed when its hand was shaken.★

Schubart, Gottlieb, and Berghold, Albin. 1909. Sonneberg, Thür. Applied for a German patent (D.R.G.M.) for a doll's arm.

Schubert, Franz. 1925 and before. Reichenberg, Bohemia. Listed in an Austrian directory under Dolls.

Schubert, H. 1891–1928. Berlin Made dolls.★

Schuco. See **Schreyer.**

Schudze, Max. 1864–78. Paris. Made and exported dressed dolls and mechanical dolls including pantins, which he exhibited at the 1867 and 1878 Paris Expositions.

Schuetzmeister & Quendt. 1889–1930 and later. Boilstadt, Gotha, Thür. A porcelain factory that made and exported bisque dolls' heads, all-bisque dolls and *Nankeen* dolls. They used the initials S. & Q. Their mold # 301 was sometimes incised Jeannette. (See also Ills. 105 and 106 in the first COLLECTOR'S ENCYCLOPEDIA OF DOLLS.)

1889: Made bisque dolls' heads.

1893–98: Advertised dressed dolls.

1894: Made all-bisque dolls and dolls with cloth bodies.

1918: Affiliated with *Bing* and produced bisque heads for *Kämmer & Reinhardt* and *Welsch & Co.*

1920: Applied for two German patents (D.R.G.M.) for porcelain dolls with moving joints.★

Schufinsky, Prof. Victor. 1909–10. Austria. Made turned wooden dolls and taught classes how to make them. Some of the dolls had skirts to the floor in order to support them, others had disks on which they stood. Many of the dolls had high hats and often accessories such as a muff or a cane or umbrella.

Schuh, Joh. 1927. Sonneberg, Thür. Made dolls.

Schuhmann, F. & H. 1915. Coburg, Thür. Applied for a German patent (D.R.G.M.) for artistic hairdos on dolls' heads.

Schülerpuppen (School boy or girl). 1916–24. Felt dolls made by *Steiff.* Hts. 28, 35, 43, 50, and 60 cm. (11, 14, 17, 19½, and 23½ in.). In 1924 there was only a 28 cm. (11 in.) doll.

Schultz, Adolphe. 1893. Paris. Made dolls.

2363. Schuetzmeister & Quendt doll with a bisque head on a composition bent limb baby body. It has a wig, glass eyes, and an open mouth. Mark: Ill. 2364. H. 21 in. (53.5 cm.). *Courtesy of Victoria Harper.*

2O1
Ⓢ₍Q₎
Germany

2O1
Ⓢ₍Q₎
Germany

2364–2365. Marks on bisque head dolls made by Schuetzmeister & Quendt.

Schultz, Clarence. 1893. Berlin. Applied for a German patent (D.R.G.M.) for a doll with a spiral spring foot.

Schultz, Frederick B. 1892–1917. New York City. Obtained German and U.S. patents for dolls.

1897: Applied for a German patent (D.R.G.M.) for stringing dolls. This patent was assigned to E. F. *Dressel.*★

Schulze, Alfred. See **Alt, Beck & Gottschalck.**

Schulze, Johannes V. 1927–29. Chemnitz-Hilb, Germany. Made crocheted and knitted outfits for dolls including dresses, sacks, sweaters, caps, petticoats, panties, combinations, and shoes.

Schus (Schuster, Shoemaker). 1913–16. Felt doll made by *Steiff* and distributed by *Borgfeldt* in the U.S.; represented a shoemaker. Ht. 14 in. (35 cm.); priced $2.20 in New York in 1913.

Schusterbistl. 1920s and '30s. Berchtesgaden, Bavaria. Name of a family that made wooden dolls as *Swaddling-clothed* Babies *(poupards).*

Schütteläuglein (Eyes that open and close). 1927. Trademark registered in Germany by *C. M. Bergmann* for dolls.

Schutzmarke. German for Trademark.

Schützmeister, Margarethe (née Zabel). 1916. Gotha, Thür. Applied for a German patent (D.R.G.M.) for a jointed doll.

Schützmeister & Quendt. See **Schuetzmeister & Quendt.**

Schwab & Co. 1926–30. Ohrdruf, Thür. Made porcelain objects probably including bisque dolls' heads. (See also **Hertel, Schwab & Co.**)

Schwäbische Celluloidwarenfabrik. 1913–30 and later. Mengen, Germany. Made celluloid dolls.

Schwabl, Frères. 1928–30 and later. Paris. Advertised dolls' shoulder heads of porcelain and of wax.

Schwarte, Jennie. 1926. Lawton, Ohio. Obtained a U.S. patent for joints on a cloth doll.

Schwartz, René. 1910. Berlin. Applied for a German patent (D.R.G.M.) for ornamenting dolls' clothes.

Schwartz, Sig., Co. 1917–26. New York City. Manufactured dolls.

1925: Advertised cloth body dolls.★

Schwartz, V. 1930 and later. Listed in a British toy trade journal under Dolls.

Schwarz. 1848–1930 and later. Baltimore, Md.; Boston, Mass.; Philadelphia, Pa.; and New York City. The Baltimore store was known as Schwertman and Schwarz in its beginning. F.A.O. Schwarz in New York City was founded in 1862. The G. A. Schwarz store in Philadelphia went out of business about 1917. The four Schwarz brothers imported dolls from Germany, France and England and had agents in Berlin, Nürnberg, Paris and Vienna. F.A.O. Schwarz's special doll was called *Favorite* and most of these had bisque heads made by *Simon & Halbig* and composition bodies made by *Kämmer & Reinhardt.*

A *Kestner* doll with a bisque head marked "made in // A Germany 5// 143" has been found with a paper label on the body reading: "Manufactured for F.A.O. Schwarz Toys, Fifth Avenue and Thirty-First Street, New York," along with the customary red stamp for Germany used by Kestner.

1873: The METROPOLITAN, December, 1873, gave the following report on Schwarz dolls for Christmas, "Dolls representing every station from nurse to belle, come in all the customary materials and sizes, and cost from a penny up to $150. Flora McFlimsy dolls, with Saratoga trunks full of wearing apparel, sit in grand state in elegantly furnished parlors, . . ."

1875: F.A.O. Schwarz advertised model wax dolls with natural hair, crying baby dolls, walking and talking dolls, dolls with jointed composition bodies and dressed dolls. Some of the dolls had "trousseaux designed by our special Modiste in Paris."

1884–1934: One doll outfitter made the dresses for Schwarz. Some of these garments required a considerable amount of handwork.

1903: Advertised Favorite dolls; bisque-head, so-called French dolls with wigs, sleeping eyes, teeth, ball-jointed composition bodies with jointed wrists, dressed in chemise and footwear. Five hts. 16, 18, 21, 25, and 28 in. (40.5, 45.5, 53.5, 63.5, and 71 cm.); priced $1.00 to $5.00. When these dolls had mama-papa voices they came in hts. 13, 18, and 19½ in. (33, 45.5, and 49.5 cm.); priced $1.50 to $2.50. Small dolls with bisque heads, sleeping eyes, molded and painted footwear, and fully jointed bodies. Five hts. 6, 7, 8, 9, and 10 in. (15, 18, 20.5, 23, and 25.5 cm.); priced 65¢ to $1.00. When the dolls were jointed only at the shoulders and hips, there were six hts. 4½, 5, 6, 6½, 7, and 8 in. (11.5, 12.5, 15, 16.5, 18, and 20.5 cm.); priced 25¢ to 50¢. Baby face dolls with short hair wigs, sleeping eyes, jointed composition bodies, wearing "long baby shirt." Nine hts. 6, 9, 10, 12, 13, 16, 18, 21, and 23 in. (15, 23, 25.5, 30.5, 33, 40.5, 45.5, 53.5, and 58.5 cm.); priced 50¢ to $3.50. These same dolls with mama-papa voices, hts. 16, 18, and 23 in. (40.5, 45.5, and 58.5 cm.); priced $2.25 to $3.75.

Dolls with composition heads, sheepskin wigs, stationary glass eyes, cloth bodies, hts. 11, 13, and 14 in. (28, 33, and 35.5 cm.); priced 50¢ to 70¢. Similar dolls with sleeping eyes, curly wigs and painted footwear, hts. 10 and 12 in. (25.5 and 30.5 cm.); priced 65¢ and $1.00, the latter had a mama-papa voice.

Dolls with china heads and limbs came in seven hts. 3½ to 10 in. (9 to 25.5 cm.); priced 4¢ to 20¢. *Frozen Charlottes* were also listed.

Cloth dolls included *Chase* dolls, *Foxy Grandpa* and the boys, *Buster Brown, Topsy Turvy,* and a black doll, ht. 14 in. (35.5 cm.); priced $1.00; and a boy, ht. 20 in. (51 cm.); priced $1.25.

Dressed walking dolls, hts. 7, 9, and 11½ in. (18, 23, and 29 cm.); priced $1.00 to $2.00. A jointed doll dressed in a high silk hat and representing an Eton Boy, hts. 15 and 17 in. (38 and 43 cm.); priced $7.00 and $8.00.

1917: The last shipment of German dolls prior to the war was sold in Holland by F.A.O. Schwarz.

1919: Began to see the German dolls that had been in stock since before the war.

1923–24: F.A.O. Schwarz advertised bisque-head dolls with mohair wigs, sleeping eyes, jointed composition bodies, six hts. 10½, 12, 13½, 15, 16½, and 19 in. (26.5, 30.5, 34, 38, 42, and 48 cm.); priced $1.25 to $3.50. The bent limb baby dolls had bisque heads mold #235 and were dressed. More than six hts. 11, 13, 15, 16½, 19, and 20 in. (28, 33, 38, 42, 48, and 51 cm.); priced $5.50 to $12.00; and larger sizes which cost up to $30.00 dressed. Infant dolls in long dresses came in the same five shorter hts. and cost the same as the baby dolls.

Bisque-head dolls with mohair wigs, sleeping eyes, hair eyelashes, kid bodies with composition arms and lower legs, undressed, hts. 13, 16, and 19 in. (33, 40.5, and 48 cm.); priced $2.50 to $5.50.

Composition-head dolls with wig, cloth body dressed, hts. 14, 17, and 19 in. (35.5, 43, and 48 cm.), priced $6.00 to $10.00 with crocheted dresses and $7.50 to $12.00 with silk dresses.

Schwarz listed dolls made by *Brückner*, Chase, *Käthe Kruse, Lenci,* and *Schoenhut* as well as Favorite dolls, *Mama* dolls, *Patty-Cake* dolls, and Walking dolls.

1926: Advertised Favorite dolls made by Kämmer & Reinhardt who probably supplied the rubber head baby dolls on composition bodies. There were also *Bye-Lo Babies, Tynie Baby,* Mama dolls, dolls in chemise and dolls dressed as little girls, nurses, and Scottish boys. Dressed dolls, hts. 22 to 31 in. (56 to 78.5 cm.); priced $12.00 to $22.50. In addition there were dolls with trousseaux, dolls' dresses, coats, jackets, nightgowns, and underwear. Slippers came in sizes 0 to 14, stockings in sizes 00 to 12. Dolls' raincoats with matching hat and umbrella cost $3.50 to $5.50. Jewelry sets containing necklaces, watches, bracelets, mirrors, fans and so forth cost from 35¢ to $2.00. (See THE COLLECTOR'S BOOK OF DOLLS' CLOTHES, Ill. 274).★

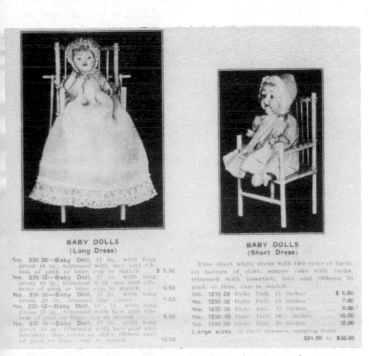

BABY DOLLS
(Long Dress)

BABY DOLLS
(Short Dress)

2366. Baby dolls in long or in short dresses and a non-mechanical walking doll sold by F.A.O. Schwarz in 1923–24. The baby dolls came in five or more hs. 11 to 20 in. (28 to 51 cm.) and larger; priced $5.50 to $30.00.

Schwarz, Josef. 1899–1910. Vienna. Made dolls and dolls' heads.

Schwarz, Julius. 1931. Hamburg, Germany. Registered "Skara" in Germany as a trademark for dolls.

Schwarz, Pauline. 1894. Breslau, Germany. Applied for a German patent (D.R.G.M.) for an embroidered cloth doll.

Schwarzkopf & Fröber. 1891–1927. Sonneberg, Thür. Made dolls.

1891: Advertised jointed dolls named *Anna* and dressed dolls.★

Schweigländer, Alban Leimgrube. 1816 and probably other years. Vienna. Produced wooden dolls.

Schwenker. See **Marottes.**

Schwerdt Bros. 1925–26. Eltingeville, L.I., N.Y. Made cloth body dolls.

Schwerdt Manufacturing Co. 1910–30 and later. Jersey City, N.J.; 1930 on, Union City, N.J. Made stuffed dolls of powder-puff velvet, crushed plush, terry cloth or crêpe.

1929: There were three models of velvet dolls. Hts. of dolls 9½ to 11½ (24 to 29 cm.).

1930: The chubby faces of the dolls were flat and had eyes glancing to the side. The mouth was indicated by a single line and the dolls represented boys or girls.

Schwerdtfeger & Co. 1904–30. Rosswein, Saxony. Manufactured felt dolls.

1904: Applied for a German patent (D.R.G.M.) for a wool felt doll.

1905: Applied for a German patent (D.R.G.M.) for a felt doll's head covered with a celluloid coating.

Schwerdtmann Toy Co. 1914 and earlier. St. Louis, Mo. Exhibited Japanese dolls.

Schwerin, Sigismund. See **Ring, H., & Co.**

Schwimmer & Rakovsky. 1925–30. Vienna. Made dolls.

Scoll, Jacob. 1923–26. Evanston, Ill. Obtained U.S. design patents for dolls.

Scootles. 1925–30 and later. Designed by *Rose O'Neill,* it came in all-bisque, all-composition and cloth. The hair was molded; the painted brown or blue eyes looked to the side or straight ahead. A few of the dolls had sleeping glass eyes. There were black as well as white Scootles. Most of the Scootles were jointed only at the shoulders but many of the composition Scootles were jointed at the neck, shoulders and hips. The bisque Scootles often had the name "Scootles" incised on the sole of the foot. Among the hts. for the bisque Scootles were 5¾ and 8 in. (14.5 and 20.5 cm.), while the hts. of the composition Scootles included 7½, 10, 12, 13, 15, and 16 in. (19, 25.5, 30.5, 33, 38, and 40.5 cm.) for the white version; the black version came 12 in. (30.5 cm.) tall.

1930: Rose O'Neill Wilson and Calista O'Neill Schuber registered a U.S. trademark for cloth Scootles with printed faces.★

Scotch Bud Golf Beauty. 1921. Cloth doll with worsted hair, triangular mouth, slim neck and limbs and having a printed story in its pocket. Made by *S. E. Delavan.*★

Scotch Highlander. 1917. Composition head and hands, painted hair and eyes, made by the *Standard Doll Co.* It wore a jacket, cap, plaid skirt and socks.★

Scotch Highlander. See **Highlander.**

Scotch Laddie and Scotch Lassie. 1930. Names of plump dolls dressed in Scottish plaid attire. They could stand and could squeak.

Scott, Herbert, Co. 1929. Harding, West Va. Obtained a U.S. patent for a doll with legs that moved by means of a spring.

Scott, J. Fred, & Co. 1915–17. Manchester and Liverpool, England. Made cloth dolls, wax dolls, *Eskimo* dolls and especially masks for dolls. The face masks were pressed out of cardboard and had handpainted sateen covers. These dolls' masks were unstuffed and were made chiefly for large inexpensive dolls.

1917: Advertised dressed and undressed dolls, knitted coats, hats, and shoes for dolls.

Scott, Walter B. 1925–26. Marblehead, Mass. Registered "*Daddy Scott*" in the U.S. as a trademark for wooden dolls.

Scottish Dolls. 1915. Dundee, Scotland. Manufactured composition dolls' heads that were cast or molded from a stiff paste.

Scottish Kilts. 1915. Name of dolls created by an English professional man and dressed as Scottish soldiers.

Scottish Lass. 1918. All-composition dolls with wig, five-piece body, steel spring joints made by *Jessie M. Raleigh* and distributed by *Butler Bros.* It wore a dress with plaid trimming, a shoulder sash and a plaid tam. Hts. 11½ and 13½ in. (29 and 34 cm.).

Scotty. 1928–29. Cloth doll, one of the *Alpha* line, made by *Farnell* and distributed by *Louis Wolf.*

Scouby, Basil. World War I-1921. Harlow, Essex. Manufactured dolls.

Scout Boy. See **Bob.**

Scouts. 1900–30 and later. Dolls were often dressed as Boy Scouts, Girl Scouts, Girl Guides or Campfire Girls. Among these were:

Ca. 1900: *Young John Bull.* (See Ill. 2776.)

1902: *General Baden-Powell,* the founder of the Boy Scouts.

1915: Girl Guide doll made by *East London Toy Factory.*

World War I period: Boy Scout doll made by *Henry Jeffrey Hughes.*

1916: Doll made by *Sunlight, Sieve.*

1917: Doll made by *Edinburgh Toy Factory.*

1925–26: *Camp Fire Girl* made by *Jeanette Doll Co.*

1928: *Puggy.*

1930: *Skippy.* (See also **Boy Scout.**)

Scovell Novelty Manufacturing Co. 1930 and later. Los Angeles, Calif. Manufactured cloth dolls.

Sea Island Sugar Co. 1900s. Their sugar sacks had cutout dolls printed on them. These advertising dolls included *Grocer, Toy Soldier* and *Gretchen.*

Seagull, Henry, & Wechsler, Oscar H. 1918. New York City. Obtained a U.S. patent for a doll with movable eyes operating on a pivot bar.

Seams down center of face. 1893 and later. *Ida Gutsell* patented a doll in 1893 with a seam down the center of the face. In 1894 *Butterick* published patterns for dolls with a seam down the center of the face. In 1902 the Gussie Decker[+] all-leather doll made by *M. S. Davis* had a seam down the center of its face. By 1903 *Steiff* made felt dolls with seams down the center of the face.

Other manufacturers also used this technique of sewing a seam down the center of a doll's face. (See also **French Dolls,** 1914–16.)

Sear, John, Ltd. 1927–29. London. Made dolls.

Sears, Roebuck & Co. 1888–1930 and later. Chicago, Ill. Distributed and copyrighted dolls.

1902: Advertised bisque shoulder heads with wigs, stationary or sleeping eyes, open mouths with teeth. Eight hts. of heads only, 3¾ to 7½ in. (9.5 to 19 cm.); there were also *Minerva* metal heads with molded hair or wigs as well as dressed and undressed rubber dolls.

1907: Advertised *Kestner* bisque shoulder heads; *Buster Brown; Farmer Boy; Indian* dolls; *Japanese* dolls; leather dolls; *Worsted* Clowns; dressed dolls; *Esquimo* dolls. The bisque shoulder heads came with wigs, stationary or sleeping eyes, seven hts. 3⅞ to 9 in. (10 to 23 cm.). The celluloid shoulder heads came with wigs or molded hair, glass eyes in five hts. 3½ to 6¼ in. (9 to 16 cm.).

1908: Dolls advertised by Sears that were not listed above included *Knock About* dolls and "Mama Papa" dolls.

1910: Copyrighted *Sunshine* and *Violet.*

1912: Advertised *Baby Ruth, Cymbaliers, Dorothy Dainty, Daisy Dimple,* Eskimo dolls, *Funny Fritzie, Little Athlete, Little Cherub, Maybelle, Pansy, Romper Baby, Schoenhut* dolls and Sunshine.

1918: Sears offered to give to the Red Cross the profits from a cargo of German dolls bought by Sears in 1914, but the offer was refused. These dolls had been stored in Holland and were shipped to the U.S. in 1918.

1919: Advertised all-composition dolls, *Dolly Dear, Kewpies, Little Orphan Annie, Peterkin,* rubber dolls, *Tom Tinker,* dolls' shoes, stockings and wigs.

1920: Advertised *American Beauty Babies,* Bath Towel Dolls, Birthday Dolls, Clowns, dolls dressed as children or babies including cloth dolls, *Fulper* bisque dolls, *Goldi-*

locks, *Humpty Dumpty,* dressed and undressed *Kewpies,*
Mary Jane, Miss Sunshine, Nelke boy and girl dolls, *Shoe-button Sue* and *Topsy.*

1921: *Rock-a-Bye Baby* was the new doll advertised.

1922: The doll department was expanded and a few German
products were again included such as the Minerva metal
heads and the Violet dolls made especially for Sears with
Minerva metal heads. The dolls this year also included
Chime Dolls, Chubby Kid, Dainty Dorothy, dolls' clothes,
Dolly Dear, dressed bisque or composition head dolls,
Horsman dolls, *Jackie Coogan Kid,* Kewpies, *Mama* dolls,
Mibs, Nelke dolls, *Playmate,* Rock-a-Bye Baby, rubber
dolls, Sunshine and Tom Tinker.

1927: Advertised dolls with bisque, composition or metal
heads; shoulder heads, socket heads or flange neck heads,
as well as *Bottle Baby, Flossie Flirt, Happy Flossie,* Mama
dolls, *Nize Baby,* rubber dolls, *Sunny Girl,* Sunshine kid
body dolls, and *Vanta Baby.*

1930–31: Registered as a U.S. trademark Dainty Dorothy for
dolls.★

Seaside Sandy. See Potteries Toy Co.

Seaside Sue. 1920–21. Stockinet doll made by *Chad Valley.*
It wore a beach costume or a bathing suit and cap with a big
bow on the front of the cap. Ht. 9½ in. (24 cm.).

Seasons. Dolls were dressed in garments indicative of the
seasons. Among them were:

1917: *Knight Bros. & Cooper* dressed dolls as Summer and
Winter

1922: *Steiff* dressed their *Schlopsnies* dolls in costumes
appropriate to the four seasons.

1930: *Lenci* dressed four large felt dolls in costumes representing the four seasons and named them accordingly.

Seco. See Strauss, Adolph.

Seelemann, Paul. 1926–27. Sonneberg, Thür. Manufactured dolls.

Seelig, William. 1922–30 and later. London. Handled dolls
and acted as an agent for *Käthe Kruse* and other makers of
dolls.

1925: Agent for *Emma Günther* and *Wagner & Zetzsche* for
dolls.

1926: Advertised celluloid dolls and that Seelig would give
to charity 6¢ for every *Sico* doll and 12¢ for every Käthe
Kruse doll that they sold. Seelig was the agent for *Beck &
Glaser.*

1930: Advertised Wee Gem celluloid dolls. Agent for the
Marvell doll of *E. Chantrain,* for *Gebr. Fleischmann* and
W. G. Müller.★

Segitz & Reinhardt. 1904. Applied for a German patent
(D.R.G.M.) for dolls.

Segmented Wooden Dolls. 1919–30 and later. Many dolls
were described as segmented wooden dolls. This could or

could not mean that the head of the doll was made of wood
but that the rest of the body was made of pieces or segments
of wood which were strung together and gave it great flex-
ibility.

Some of the makers of these dolls were: *W. Bimblick,
Cameo, Durrel, Essenel Co., Louis Hoffman, Hustler Toy
Corp., Petrie-Lewis, Pickering, Ted Toy-lers, Tinker Toys,*
and *Twistum Toy Factory.*

LA SEMAINE DE SUZETTE gave directions for making
these dolls in various designs in 1928 and named them
"Auto Dolls."

Ségo, Marcel. 1928–30 and later. Paris. Made dolls.

Sehm, Frau Mathilde. 1869–1930 and later. Guben, Brandenburg, Germany. Walter Sehm was in charge of the factory in 1928 when his son Werner Sehm became his partner.
Made dolls and dolls' clothes. They were one of the earliest
factories to make dolls dressed as *Max and Moritz.*

1927: Advertised porcelain dolls, jointed dolls, bent limb
baby dolls, dolls' house dolls, miniature dolls, jointed celluloid dolls, cloth dolls, dolls' clothes including shoes and
wardrobes of clothes for dolls. *Gustav Burmester* of Hamburg was the factory representative.

1929: Advertised things similar to that in 1927 except
dressed and undressed dolls were also listed. (See Ill.
2367.)★

Seidel, Paul. 1926. U.S. Tried to obtain a U.S. patent for a
drinking arm doll which would be assigned exclusively to
Century. A court case was in process because *Leon Wallach*
was seeking a similar patent.

Seifert, Erich. 1921–30. Eisfeld, Thür. Manufactured
dressed dolls.

Seifert, Ernst. 1904. Eisfeld, Thür. Applied for a German
patent (D.R.G.M.) for a doll's face of paper covered with
cloth.

Seifert, Max. 1902–30 and later. Eisfeld, Thür. Made
dressed bébés and *mignonnettes* (small dolls). *Jullien Messin*
was his Paris agent and *Carl Stahl* was his Berlin agent.

Selchow & Righter. 1864–1929. New York City. Elisha G.
Selchow was in the toy business as early as 1864 but later he
became John H. Righter's partner. They were jobbers, distributors and importers of dolls. By 1926 they had a factory
in Brooklyn, N.Y.

1874: Advertised the *Crandall* acrobats.

1876: Handled the *Slade* patterns for dolls' clothes.

1885: Advertised *Marottes.*

1892 and later: Distributed the cutout cloth dolls made by
the *Art Fabric Mills.* In 1911 Selchow & Righter took over the
business of the Art Fabric Mills. These colored lithographed
cloth dolls came in various sizes and were shown dressed or
in their underclothes.

1911: Advertised that they imported from 13 leading doll
factories in Europe. They handled dolls' heads, wigs and
shoes.

M. SEHM, GUBEN

Fabrik gekleideter Puppen
und Puppengarderobe

Gegründet 1869.

⊹

Schönste Kollektion in

gekleideten Puppenstubenpuppen jeder Art, ff. gekleidete Gelenksteh- und Sitzbabies, gekleidete Zelluloidpuppen, Werfpuppen in billiger und mittlerer Preislage, 1.— Mk. und 2.— Mk. Artikel. Puppengarderobe, Wäsche, handgehäkelte Wollbekleidung.

Zur Messe in Leipzig Neumarkt 10, III. Stock, Fahrstuhl.

2367. M. Sehm advertisement in DEUTSCHE SPIELWAREN ZEITUNG, February 1927. Their products included dressed dolls' house dolls, dressed bent limb baby dolls, dressed child dolls, dressed celluloid dolls, dressed cloth dolls, and dolls' wardrobes.

1912–13: Advertised all-bisque dolls; bisque socket head dolls with wigs and sleeping eyes on fully jointed composition bodies, came in 15 hts. 12 to 33 in. (30.5 to 84 cm.); priced $2.00 to $45.00 doz. wholesale. Similar bisque shoulder heads on kidlyne bodies came in 8 hts. 12½ to 18 in. (31.5 to 45.5 cm.); priced $2.25 to $8.50 doz. wholesale, and on kid bodies they came in 17 hts. 14 to 28 in. (35.5 to 71 cm.); priced $4.00 to $27.00 doz. wholesale. The bisque heads also came on kidlyne bodies with wigs and stationary eyes, hts. 11 and 12 in. (28 and 30.5 cm.); priced $2.00 and $2.25 doz. wholesale. In addition there were cloth dolls; domestic and imported character dolls; *Schoenhut* circuses; grey or red rubber dolls including ones in knit dresses; other dressed dolls came in hts. 7¾ to 25 in. (19.5 to 63.5 cm.); priced 90¢ to $30.00 doz. wholesale. All-celluloid dolls appear to have been a specialty. They came with molded hair, jointed at the shoulders with or without painted shoes and stockings. Nine hts. 5¼ to 13½ in. (13.5 to 34 cm.); priced 75¢ to $12.00 doz. wholesale. When they were jointed at the shoulders and hips there were six hts. 4 to 12 in. (10 to 30.5 cm.); priced 75¢ to $9.00 doz. wholesale. Special all-celluloid dolls such as *Mignon*.

1913: Advertised celluloid and cloth dolls, character dolls, imported and domestic jointed and kid body dolls, dressed and undressed dolls. The cutout cloth dolls were made of lithographed heavy drill in six or eight colors. Hts. 20, 27, and 30 in. (51, 68.5, and 76 cm.).

1915: Duplicated their 1914 orders for German dolls except for *Rheinische Gummi und Celluloid Fabrik Co.* who raised their prices.

1916: Advertised that they had a full line of imported dolls. A picture showed a German bisque-head child doll.

1919: Imported bisque-head child dolls with wigs, sleeping eyes, hair eyelashes, composition bodies, jointed at the wrist and wearing a chemise and footwear. Eight hts. 12, 14, 16, 18, 21, 23, 25, and 27 in. (30.5, 35.5, 40.5, 45.5, 53.5, 58.5, 63.5, and 68.5 cm.); priced $1.50 to $6.50.

1923: Advertised imported and domestic dolls.

1926: Still advertising *Merrie Marie.*★

Self Sell Doll Co. 1924–28. Brooklyn, N.Y. Made dolls, especially *Mama* dolls.

1924: Dressed Mama dolls came with or without sleeping eyes.

1927: Advertised Mama, infant, and character dolls dressed in fashionable costumes, some of these dolls had voices.

Seligmann & Mayer. 1925–30 and probably other years. Sonneberg, Thür. Made dolls. *Alfred Goldsmith* was their sole London agent. Used initials S. & M. as a mark.

1930: Registered *Mi Encanto* as a trademark in Germany for dolls.

Sem. Before World War I. France. Artist whose models were used to create expensive dolls.

Senegalaise (Senegalese). Dolls dressed in Senegalaise costumes were made and sold in Europe (not to be confused with *Singhalese* natives of Ceylon.)

1903: *Tapis Rouge*, a Paris store, advertised a doll in a

Senegalaise costume. Ht. 34 cm. (13½ in.); priced 29¢.

1915: *Kley & Hahn* made portrait dolls of Senegalese prisoners. (See also **Black Dolls** and **African Dolls.**)

Senni. 1925. Name of a doll made by *Cuno & Otto Dressel.*

Sennoner (Senoner). See **Runggaldier & Sennoner,** and **Sanoner.**

Seppl (Tirolese). 1911–16. Felt character boy doll made by *Steiff* and dressed in a Tyrolean costume. Ht. 35 cm. (14 in.); priced $1.58 in 1911.

September Morn. 1914. All-bisque doll produced by *Borgfeldt.* It had molded blond hair, painted round eyes and a round open-closed mouth. Size 2 was 5 in. (12.5 cm.). Mark, Ill. 2368.

2368. Mark on a doll named September Morn, but the mark reads "September Morning."

Sergent, G. 1929–30 and later. London and Paris. Agent for *Rheinische Gummi und celluloid Fabrik*'s celluloid dolls and dolls' heads.

Sesselmann, Ernst. 1928–30 and later. Steinach, Thür. Made dolls' eyes.

Seutter. 1854 and other years. Nürnberg, Bavaria. Handled dolls, creditor of *Brouillet* when he failed according to Mme. Florence Poisson, Curator of the Roybet Fould Museum.

77. 1926. A numeral trademark registered in U.S. for dolls by *Live Long Toys. Red Grange* wore the number 77.

Severn & Long Co. 1921–24. New York City. Advertised dolls; distributed *Beck Manufacturing Co.* dolls and *Rag Shoppe Dolls* including *Aunt Caroline.*

Sèvres. 1738–1930 and later. Sèvres, France. China dolls' heads were created at Sèvres during World War I; these were socket heads and the models were taken from 18th and 19th century busts and figures in the collections of the Sèvres Museum.

1916–17. A doll's head was modeled by *Mlle. Berthe Noufflard.* Sèvres made the following china heads with painted eyes; *Junon, La Bergère de Trianon, Louise Brongn,* (Art?): *Madame Royal, Marquisette,* and *Saint François.* Wigs were to be worn with these heads. (See Ills. 1745 and 2369.)★

Seyfarth & Reinhardt. 1922–30 and later. Waltershausen, Thür. In 1922 Seyfarth left the firm of *Gans & Seyfarth.* Otto Gans continued in the doll business and Seyfarth joined Reinhardt to form Seyfarth & Reinhardt. Used Ernst Heubach bisque heads especially mold #312. Exported dolls.

1924: Used flirting eyes invented by *Otto Gans* according to a U.S. Department of Commerce report.

1925: Advertised jointed dolls, dolls that could sit and also stand; *Mama* dolls with bisque or composition heads; infant dolls.

1926: Dolls distributed by *Louis Wolf.*

1927: Obtained a German patent (D.R.P.) and a British patent for dolls' eyes. These "living eyes" were used by *König & Wernicke* and *Alt, Beck & Gottschalck.*

Advertised jointed dolls, straight leg dolls, bent limb babies, dolls with bisque or composition heads on cloth bodies containing voices as well as walking *Mama* dolls. (See Ill. 1864, *Mein Stolz.*) (See Ills. 2370 and 2371.)★

Seyfert, Oskar. 1904. Dresden, Saxony. Designed art dolls, dressed in regional or historical costumes. See Ill. 2495.

Seyfert, Paul. 1899. Dresden, Saxony. Applied for a German patent (D.R.G.M.) for dolls' joints.

Seyfried, Albert, and his wife Jacobina. 1880–90 and perhaps later. Philadelphia, Pa. Mrs. Seyfried had been born in 1823 in Worms, Germany. They made bodies for dolls and colored leather shoes which were sold by Gustav *Schwarz, Wanamaker,* and other toy stores.

Seymour, Russell & Co. 1924. London. Advertised *Mama* dolls dressed in printed rompers and matching bonnet.

Sgt. Kelly.[†] See **Kelly.**

Shackman, B., & Co. 1898–1930 and later. New York City. Founded by Bertha Shackman. Imported and distributed dolls, especially small dolls of various materials.

1908: Advertised china dolls; bisque dolls; a dolls' house chambermaid, dolls in regional costumes included Dutch, Italian, Japanese Geisha, and Swiss; other dressed dolls were Beau Brummell with cane, Bride and groom, Hussar soldier with sword, Jockey with whip, Policeman with club, Witch with broom. Ht. 2¾ in. (7 cm.); priced 20¢ and 25¢; clothes were made of cotton or silk. Specialty dolls included an *Automobile Doll;* a black *Frozen Charlotte* in a peanut shell, ht. 3 in. (7.5 cm.); priced 5¢; Bride with bouquet, hts. 4½, 6½, and 11 in. (11.5, 16.5 and 28 cm.); priced 75¢ to $5.00; Indian dolls; Sailor dressed in velvet, ht. 10 in. (25.5 cm.); priced 35¢.

Ca. 1910: Advertised *Newly Wed's Baby,* made of papier-mâché; *Snow Babies; Cymbaliers* dressed in silk.

Ca. 1916: Advertised bisque dolls, composition dolls, *Kewpies,*® *Kidlets* and dolls' clothes.

1925: Advertised all-bisque and all-celluloid Kewpies in crêpe paper clothes; all-bisque dolls jointed at the shoulders and hips wearing hand crocheted costumes, ht. 1½ in. (4 cm.): all-bisque dolls in regional costumes, including Indian and black dolls; all-bisque dolls representing various occupations—blacksmith, college student, cowboy, goose girl, jockey, nursemaid, patriot, sailor, soldier, sports doll, toreador and wedding party; all-bisque *Bye-Lo* and *Baby Peggy.* All-celluloid Kewpie was 3¼ in. (8.5 cm.). Other all-celluloid dolls dressed as a chef, *clown,* doctor, minister, sailor, shepherdess or soldier. Ht. 2¾ in. (7 cm.); priced $1.50 doz. wholesale. There were also dolls with silk faces.

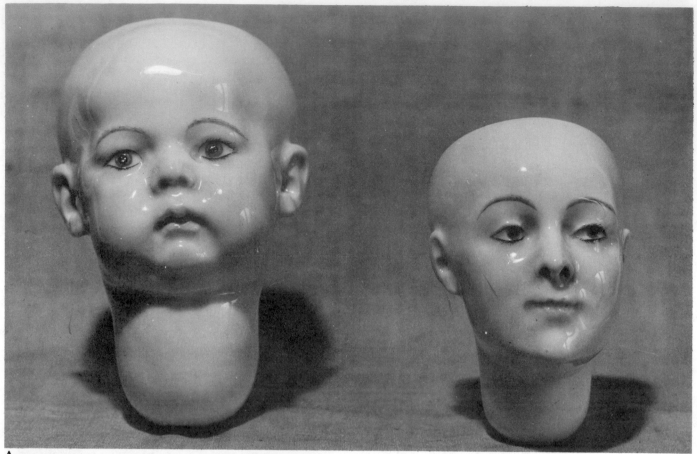

A

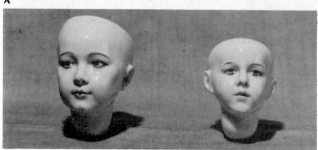

B

C

2369A, B & C. China socket heads made by Sèvres. These heads had painted eyes and were made to have wigs. Reading from left to right. Heads represented:

A. Saint François, h. 12 cm. (5 in.), and Marquisette, h. 7.5 cm. (3 in.).

B. Louise Brongn (Art?), h. 7.5 cm. (3 in.), and La Bèrgère de Trianon, h. 7.5 cm. (3 in.).

C. An unknown, h. 7.5 cm. (3 in.); Madame Royal, h. 5 cm. (2 in.); and Junon (?), h. 5 cm. (2 in.). *Courtesy of The Musée des Arts Decoratifs, Paris.*

2370—2371. Marks on bisque heads produced by Seyfarth & Reinhardt and made by Armand Marseille.

2372. Black Frozen Charlotte with molded white tunic encased in a cardboard peanut shell and sold by Shackman in the first decade of the 1900s. H. of doll 2 in. (5 cm.). *Coleman Collection.*

1929: Licensed by *Marshall Field* to distribute wholesale the all-bisque comic character dolls jointed at the neck and having molded features and clothes. These dolls represented *Andy Gump, Chester Gump, Ching Chow, Herby, Kayo, Moon Mullins, Little Orphan Annie, Rachel, Smitty, Skeezix,* and *Uncle Walt.* Hts. 2½ to 3½ in. (6.5 to 9 cm.); priced $1.10 to $1.80 doz. wholesale.

1930: Advertised George Washington on horseback as a special for George Washington's birthday. This was advertised for several years thereafter and the horse appears to have been a candy box container. Also advertised reclining china (bisque) bathing figures and dolls.

Shaker Dolls. See Religious Costumes.

Shaland, William. 1919. New York City. Importer and manufacturers' agent for dolls.

Shamin. Early 1920s. Constantinople. Sculptor who was a Russian refugee, made dolls with heads and limbs of wax or clay, bodies of wire and sticks covered with cotton clothes. The dressed dolls in Russian costumes were dipped in a gum arabic solution.

Shanklin Toy Industry, Ltd. 1915–20. Shanklin, Isle of Wight, and London. Founded by *E. E. Houghton.* Later became *Nottingham* and Shanklin Toy Industry, also known as the British Toys, based in London. At first it was funded by the *Three Arts Women's Employment Fund.* After World War I *Roberts Bros.* of Gloucester took over the business. Shanklin made cloth dolls and dolls with composition heads or mask faces and cloth bodies especially of stockinet. They made baby dolls, both black and white.

1917: Among the dolls they advertised were *Baby Bunting, Bambino, Betty* and *Kate Greenaway* children.

1918: Advertised British Babes, *Bye-Bye Babies, Christopher, Jane, Jim, Patty, Prudence, Shirley* and *Suzanne. Miss Muriel Moller* was the London agent.

1919: New dolls included *Baby Ann, Miss Peggy,* a Toddler, and a Bather wearing beach sandals. ★

Sharkey (Private Sharkey). 1909–13. Felt doll made by *Steiff* and distributed by *Borgfeldt* in the U.S.; represented an American enlisted soldier. The doll had long feet and carried a gun. Ht. 35 cm. (14 in.).

1913: Priced in New York $2.65. ★

Shaver, Elsie. Before 1919–20. New York City. Made *Little Shavers* dolls. ★

Shaw Doll Co. 1927–30 and later. New York City. Benjamin Shaw, the President, had formerly been President of the *Well Made Doll Co.* He had been in the doll manufacturing business for many years. The Shaw Doll Co. name appeared on all of their dolls' heads. They were members of the *American Doll Manufacturers' Association* and sold chiefly to jobbers.

1927: Advertised *Mama* dolls and new slim body dolls dressed in various costumes. Priced 25¢ to $10.00.

1928: Advertised about 100 style nos. with real hair or mohair wigs, the real hair dolls had sleeping eyes, others had painted eyes. Some dolls had composition arms and legs, others had cloth limbs.

1929: Introduced a smiling baby doll line with composition heads manufactured exclusively for this company. The arms were composition and the dolls wore short lace-trimmed baby dresses and halo style bonnets. They came in three sizes, priced $1.00 to $3.00. Other dolls were priced 25¢ to $10.00.

1930: Advertised 75 style nos. including infant and Mama dolls. A new doll had sleeping eyes, hair eyelashes, tongue and teeth, composition head and limbs, dressed. Ht. 25 in. (63.5 cm.); priced $3.00.

2373. Advertisement for Shaw Doll Co. in PLAYTHINGS, May, 1927. The doll shown has a composition head and limbs, wig and a slimmer body than the Mama dolls.

Shaw, Mrs. G. See **Wolstan Doll Co.**

Shearer, Lillian J. 1917–19. Denver, Colo. Made dolls.★

Sheldon, Anna M. 1921–23. Pawtucket, R.I. Obtained a U.S. patent for attaching an ornament to the socket opening of a doll's head.

Shepard, Norwell. 1873–94 and other years. Boston, Mass. Dry goods store that distributed *Jumeau* dolls.

Sheppard, J. B., & Co. Philadelphia, Pa. Handled cloth dolls. (See Ills. 2374 and 2375.)★

Sherwin Products Corp. 1922. New York City. Advertised *Checker Bobby* and *Checker Betty*.

Shikishima Shokai. 1929–30 and later. Kyoto, Japan. Manufactured dolls.

Shillman, M. & S. 1925–30. Brooklyn, N.Y. Made outfits and accessories for dolls. Used the trademark *Sun-Joy-Toy*; *Katherine Rauser* was a factory representative as well as *Joseph Wolson*. Sold chiefly to jobbers.

1926: Advertised dolls with their outfits in boxes, trunks, hat boxes, and suitcases. A new item was twin dolls on a silk sleeping pad with two silk petticoats, two jackets, two pillows, two blankets and two bottles, in a box priced $1.00 and up. When the twins were in a trunk they had two silk capes, two silk caps and two diapers instead of the petticoat, jackets, and bottles. Two sizes $3.00 to $5.00. Also sold blankets for dolls separately. These came in a variety of styles and sizes. Priced 15¢ and up.

1927: Advertised dolls' trousseaux, accessories and buntings as well as brushed wool sets for dolls of all sizes.

1928: A "*Teddy-Bear*" suit for dolls was new as well as knitted angora outfits. Advertised that the dolls' clothes went directly from the loom to the store.

1929: Advertised brushed wool sets to fit any doll. Priced $6.00 doz. wholesale and up.

1930: Advertised a suitcase with a baby doll in a long dress and various clothes and accessories also in the suitcase.

Shimizu, Katsuzo (Kita Shimizu & Co.). 1900–30. Kyoto, Japan. Manufactured dolls.★

Shinn, Lita, & Shinn, Bessie. 1916–26. Muskogee, Okla., and White Sulphur Springs, W. Va. Made cloth dolls. Their U.S. patent gave a pattern for the doll.★

Shirley. 1918. Line of dolls made by *Shanklin*. They were cloth dolls with wool hair and jointed legs. Shirley was *Christopher*'s mate.

Shoe Marks. These are generally found on the soles of the shoes. A bee was a trademark registered in France by *Jumeau* in 1891 and the *Societe Française de Fabrication de Bébés & Jouets* (S.F.B.J.) in 1906. *Eugene Alart* registered in France his trademark of a standing girl in 1913. Bordentown used two shoes with the heels together as the trademark for their shoes. Names such as *Bru* or initials such as C. M. in an oval or the *Fischer, Naumann* monogram are sometimes found on shoes. Sometimes a sticker with the name of the distribu-

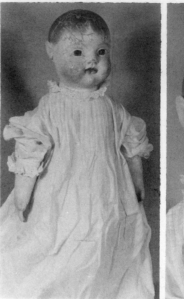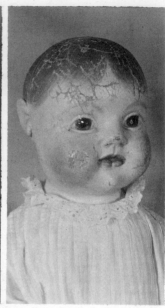

2374A & B. Molded stockinet doll with features painted with oils, including the brush marks for the hair. The eyes are brown, the ears are applied. These dolls were reportedly made for the Sheppard store in Philadelphia. H. 21 in. (53.5 cm.). *Courtesy of Z. Frances Walker.*

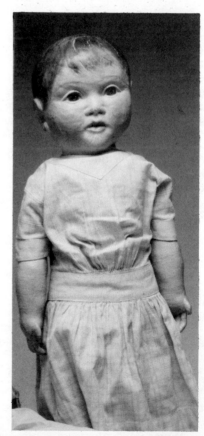

2375. Cloth doll with oil painted head made for J.B. Sheppard & Co. of Philadelphia. It has molded and painted blond hair, brown eyes and a closed mouth. Contemporary clothes. H. 20½ in. (52 cm.). *Courtesy of Sotheby Parke Bernet Inc., N.Y.*

MARQUE
DÉPOSÉE

2376–2377. Unidentified marks found on the soles of doll shoes.

tor is found on the sole of a shoe. (See **A la Récompense, Wagner & Zetzsche** and others.)

Unknown marks have been found on shoes such as NONPAREIL; TRADE MARK with a star in the center, all in a circle; the C. M. with France was stamped on the inside of the sole. A size number within a keystone mark is often found on dolls' shoes.

Shoe, Molded Composition on Cloth Body. 1914–19. Made by *Ideal* and were usually in the form of boots with cloth legs representing stockings. Examples were *Knickerbocker Boy, Sunbonnet Girl, Uneeda Kid* and *Zu-Zu Kid.* Other companies may have also made this type of shoe. Dolls bearing the mark of *de Fuisseaux* have been found with bodies having molded composition oxford-tie style shoes. See Ill. 741. These are not to be confused with the molded shoes having leather over them made by *Lacmann* in the 1870s or the composition legs with molded shoes and stockings.

1917: *Columbus Merchandise Co.* advertised dolls with composition heads, arms and boots; dressed as a boy they were 12½ in. (31.5 cm.) high; priced $9.00 doz. wholesale; dressed as a girl they were 16 in. (40.5 cm.) high; priced $18.00 doz. wholesale. See Ills. 1251, 1252, 1253, and 1583. (See THE COLLECTOR'S BOOK OF DOLLS' CLOTHES, Ill. 717.)

Shoe-Button Sam and Shoe-Button Sue. 1920–21. Cloth dolls with broad smiles made by *Jessie M. Raleigh.* Sam wore an Oliver Twist style suit and pointed hat. It had an attached verse:

Shoe-Button Sam is so plumb full of fun.
That he wins the affection of most everyone.
You can't make him cry.
You can't make him blue.
He is just like his sister, Shoe-Button Sue.

Sue's verse was:

Shoe-Button Sue is so jolly and gay,
That she smiles in the night
And she smiles in the day.
And whenever you're naughty or peevish or blue
Dear Shoe-Button Sue snuggles closer to you.

1920: Shoe Button Sue was advertised by *Sears* as having black shoe-button eyes, a big wide smiling mouth and removable clothes. Ht. 15½ in. (39.5 cm.); priced $1.19.★

Show Dolls. Large dolls that were used for display, especially in shop windows or for demonstration purposes such as the *Chase* hospital doll. Among the producers were:

1876: *Silber & Fleming* advertised undressed Show dolls costing up to $25.00.

1882: Silber & Fleming advertised Show dolls. Hts. 30 to 54 in. (76 to 137 cm.).

1895–96: *Butler Bros.* advertised an *Exhibition Baby.*

1898: Our Halma was advertised by *Cissna* as being a "Show piece in your window." Ht. 23 in. (58.5 cm.).

1902: *Emil Paufler & Co.* advertised large dressed show dolls with composition heads.

1914: *Société Industrielle de Celluloid* made dolls the size of an actual baby for demonstration purposes.

1916–18: *Mrs. P. D. Smith* made life-size dolls.

1920: *Victory Doll* made by *Amberg* wore clothes of a two year old child. Ht. 30 in. (76 cm.).

1927: TOYS AND NOVELTIES reported that a court decision was made concerning the required duty on large dolls of 70 percent ad valorem instead of a lesser duty for papier-mâché manufactures. The subject of the litigation was a 32 inch (81 cm.) doll weighing five and half pounds. It had a wig, sleeping eyes, and movable joints. The reported testimony proved that these dolls were used as children's playthings and generally not as display figures.

1927–30: The baby size *Vanta Baby* dolls made by Amberg were used to show Vanta undergarments.

1928: *Hermann Brandner* advertised mannikins for shop windows.

1930 and later: *Lenci* life-size baby dolls were called "mannequins."

Shrieking Susan. 1914. Cloth character doll made by *Dean.*

Shriner Dolls. 1920s. A few dolls were dressed as Shriners, among them:

1923: *Noble Ned,* a *Mawaphil* doll, made by *Rushton Co.*

1924: Doll made by the *Jeanette Doll Co.*

Shropshire Toy Industry. 1917. Oswestry, England. Made dolls with *British Ceramic* heads and cloth bodies. The dolls were dressed as: Alice in Wonderland characters; Ally Clowns; Humpty Dumpty; Mother-Hubbard; Officers in Scottish uniforms, English uniforms and Naval uniforms;

Puss-in-Boots; *Rumplestillykin [sic]*; Tom Tiddler; Tommy Tucker; Tweedledum and Tweedledee.

Shuco. See **Schreyer & Co. (Schuco).**

Shynall Rag Doll Co.† See **Kirkham, George William Chambers.**

Siamy. 1930. Trademark registered in Germany by *Steiff* for dolls.

Sibyl Fortune Telling Doll Co. 1925–30 and later. Los Angeles, Calif. Made dolls with composition heads and hands on cloth torsos. The faces resembled an old Gypsy. Multicolored leaves of paper printed with questions and answers formed the skirt. The torso was attached with a spindle to a cardboard base on which were the days of the week, the months of the year and the signs of the zodiac. Ht. 10 in. (25.5 cm.).

2378. Mark on base of Sibyl Fortune Telling Doll.

Sibley, Lindsay & Curr Co. 1913–14. Rochester, N.Y. Imported and distributed dolls.

1913: Advertised dolls with bisque heads, wigs, sleeping eyes (except for the 12 in. [30.5 cm.] doll), hair eyelashes (except for the 12 and 13½ in. [30.5 and 34 cm.] dolls). These dolls had kid bodies with rivet joints. 11 hts. 12 to 23½ in. (30.5 to 59.5 cm.).★

Sichert, C. See **Mandel, H.**

Sico & Sicora. See **Löffler & Dill.**

Sicoid. See **Société Industrielle de Celluloid.**

Sicoine. 1916–20. Name of a celluloid-like material made by *Société Industrielle de Celluloid* and used for dolls.★

Sieber, Oswald. 1930 and later. Chemnitz, Saxony. Advertised dolls' clothes.

Siedar, Johann. 1907–08. Vienna. Listed in directories under Dolls and Dolls' Heads. Manufactured walking dolls.

Siedenhoff, Alma (née Buscher). 1926–27. Deffan, Germany. Obtained a German patent (D.R.P.) for a doll.

Siegel, Albin. 1913–14. Neustadt, near Coburg, Thür. Applied for two German patents (D.R.G.M.) relating to dolls' bodies.

Siegel Cooper Co. Ca. 1890–1930 and later. New York City. Distributed dolls which were made or produced by *Art Fabric Mills, Borgfeldt, Brückner, M. S. Davis Co., Horsman, Kestner,* Knickerbocker Specialty,† *Armand Marseille, Schoenhut* and *Süssenguth*. Some of the imported dolls were made expressly for Siegel Cooper. Many of the dressed dolls wore clothes that were made and designed by Americans in the Siegel Cooper workrooms.

1905–06: Advertised bisque heads with wigs and sleeping eyes on ball-jointed composition bodies wearing a chemise. Hts. 24½, 26¼, and 32 in. (62, 66.5, and 81 cm.); priced $3.50 to $6.50. Similar dolls with kid bodies. Hts. 13½, 16, and 20½ in. (34, 40.5, and 52 cm.); priced 25¢ to $1.00. Other dolls were all-bisque; all-celluloid; all-rubber; *American Maid;* dressed "American Unbreakable Dolls made in the United States" (probably by the *First American Doll Factory*); dolls with composition heads and hands, wigs, and glass eyes; *Topsy* and *Topsy Turvy.* Siegel Cooper also sold separate bisque shoulder heads with wigs and sleeping eyes; metal shoulder heads with molded hair or wigs, and glass eyes; celluloid shoulder heads with painted hair and glass eyes as well as crocheted clothes for dolls.

1907: The bisque-head dolls were a little smaller than in 1906 and their having open mouths with teeth was mentioned. Dolls with flirting eyes were featured. Hts. 21 and 26 in. (53.5 and 66 cm.); priced $1.95 to $3.50. Celluloid dolls with molded hair, painted features were jointed at the shoulders. Five hts. 3½, 6½, 7¾, 10¾, and 12½, in. (9, 16.5, 18.5, 27.5, and 31.5 cm.); priced 10¢ to $1.00. Dressed dolls included an "American" dressed baby doll with bisque face, wig, sleeping eyes, long dress and cap; priced 79¢. Other dressed bisque head dolls cost 25¢ to $8.00. Novelties were a multihead doll and dolls with composition faces, body covered with plush and a felt hood; priced $1.25. These were called Teddy Bear dolls.

1909: The dolls were all-bisque; bisque heads on composition bodies or bisque heads on kid bodies; all-celluloid; celluloid head or face on cloth bodies; cloth dolls included cutout cloth dolls, plush dolls and worsted dolls; all-composition and composition head on cloth body dolls; leather dolls; rubber dolls. Some of the names of these dolls were *Billiken, Buster Brown,* Doll of the Future (*Bébé L'Avenir*), *Florodora, Knockabout, Life Size Doll, Little Red Riding Hood, Mary Had a Little Lamb,* Playmate (*My Playmate?*), and Topsy Turvy.

Most of the wigs were curly hair with a side part, a feature usually noted in the advertised description, the few with a center part were on bisque-head kid body dolls of the less expensive type. The most expensive bisque head doll (relative to its sizes) wearing a chemise had flirting eyes and was called "Playmate." Several of the bisque-head dolls were advertised as having eyelashes. Most of the dolls had open mouths, even a 5¾ in. (14.5 cm.) all-bisque doll. A bent limb baby with painted hair and eyes came with either a stationary head or a movable head.

Most of the "undressed" dolls had footwear. Over a third of the dolls were dressed. When the same doll came dressed or undressed but with footwear the dressed doll cost about four times as much as the same undressed doll. The undressed all-bisque dolls with wigs, sleeping eyes, and stationary necks cost 25¢. The undressed bisque-head dolls ranged in price from 35¢ to $5.50 while the dressed bisque-head dolls ranged in price from 25¢ to $16.50. For all dolls the height was an important factor in determining the price. Large dolls were far more expensive than their smaller counterparts. Bisque-head dolls ranged in ht. from 9 in. or less to 28½ in. (23 to 72.5 cm.).

Siegel Cooper sold dolls' clothes and accessories as well

as dolls. The clothes included eight styles of dresses, sold with accompanying underwear and advertised as fitting dolls with as much as an 8 in. (20.5 cm.) height differential; underwear; four styles of hats; a muff and scarf set; corsets, a *trousseau trunk* filled with clothes. The accessories included five styles of parasols; pocketbooks and purses; a perfume atomizer; "Alpha" nursing bottle; and fans.

Dolls' parts were not advertised in this catalog.

1910: Advertised Kestner bisque heads on ball-jointed composition or kid bodies. Cloth dolls included Buster Brown and a girl doll. Some of Siegel Cooper's dolls wore chemises while others were dressed. (See Ill. 2379.)

Siegert, Christ. 1898. Neustadt near Coburg, Thür. Made cloth bodies for dolls.

Siegfried (Winter Sports). Before 1911–13. Felt boy doll made by *Steiff* and dressed as a skier in a red or white sweater and leather shoes. Mate to *Silva*. Four hts. 28, 35, 43, and 50 cm. (11, 14, 17, and 19½ in.). (See Ill. 2380.)

Siegfried. After 1910. Name found on bisque baby type heads that are usually on a bent limb baby body. (See Ill. 2381.)

Siemens & Schuckert. See **Leven, H. Josef.**

Siering, Hermann. 1927. Berlin. Handled dolls.

Sieve, M., & Co. 1922–26. Manchester, England. Advertised dolls.

1926: They were agents for *Georg Möller.*

Siewert, Helene. Ca. 1908. Berlin. One of the *Puppen Reform* artists. Her dolls were generally distributed by *Hermann Tietz.*

Siewert, Klara. Ca. 1910–20. One of the artists who worked with *Marion Kaulitz.*★

Silber & Fleming. 1872–98 and probably other years. England. Distributed a variety of dolls including china, bisque, wax, *Frozen Charlottes, Model Dolls, Show Dolls,* and so forth.

The dolls came dressed or undressed. See Ill. 331 in THE COLLECTOR'S BOOK OF DOLLS' CLOTHES, which shows the variety of dolls offered for sale in 1889.

1876: Advertised the new *Alexandra* doll.

1882: Advertised *Prince Charlie's Model Best Made Bodies.*

Silbersteine, S. 1911. Berlin. Applied for a German patent (D.R.G.M.) for dolls' heads.

Silk Face. 1925. Name of a painted silk-face doll with hair and a wire body, dressed as a member of a wedding party, sold by *Shackman.* Ht. 6 in. (15 cm.). Many other dolls had silk faces.

Silk Flapper. 1926. *Boudoir* doll with hand-painted pressed cloth face, wig, cotton stuffed cloth body made by the *American Stuffed Novelty Co.* Its clothes were designed by *Morris Politzer.*

Silly Guss. See **Caro.**

Silly Sally. 1921–23. Dressed cloth doll made by *Martha Chase.* Ht. 12 in. (30.5 cm.).

Sil-Kov Art Pillow Co. See **Continental Toy and Novelty Co.**

Silva (Winter Sports). Before 1911–13. Felt girl doll made by *Steiff* and dressed as a skier in a red or white sweater, large hat and leather shoes. Mate to *Siegfried.* Four hts. 28, 35, 43, and 50 cm. (11, 14, 17, and 19½ in.); priced up to $3.50.

1911: Silva also came with the new long hair in the two largest sizes and cost about $1.00 more than the short-hair doll.

1913: Silva was advertised by *Borgfeldt* in the U.S. as wearing a large hat with a veil tied under its chin. Ht. 14 in. (35 cm.); priced $2.25.

Silver Doll (and Toy Manufacturing) Co. 1923–24. New York City. Owned by Mr. *Freundlich,* made dolls with composition heads, arms and legs, painted or sleeping eyes, cloth bodies stuffed with excelsior or cotton, dressed in organdy or dotted swiss. Hts. 9 to 27 in. (23 to 68.5 cm.).★

Silver Series. 1918. Line of sleeping-eyed, dressed dolls with *British Ceramic* heads, arms and legs made by the *Elite Doll Co.* Seven hts. 10, 12, 14, 16, 18, 22 and 26 in. (25.5, 30.5, 35.5, 40.5, 45.5, 56 and 66 cm.).

Silverman, B. 1922 and probably earlier–1929. New York City. Had long experience in designing and manufacturing dolls.

1929: Was in charge of *Maxine Doll Co.*

Silvermann, Carl. 1913–30 and later. New York City. Imported and distributed dolls as a factory agent or on commission.

1915: Added domestic lines of dressed composition headed character dolls.

1918: Accepted a shipment of German dolls that had been stored in Holland since their purchase in 1914.

1928: Advertised lines of dolls at factory prices. Handled American, European, and Japanese dolls.

1929: Distributed *F. W. Peterson Co.* dolls.★

Simart Fils. 1825. France. Made molds for dolls according to Mme. Florence Poisson, curator of the Roybet Fould Museum.

Simmonds, Mr. 1917 and before. London. Made dolls.

1917: Became manager of *Hammond.*

Simon, L. H., Gebrüder (Bros.). 1895–1928. Coburg, Thür., and later. Bavaria. Made dolls.

1896: Applied for two German patents (D.R.G.M.) for stuffed dolls, one patent pertained to the voice and the other to adjustable eyes.

1910: Applied for a German patent for a baby doll with jointed arms and legs.

1926–28: Made dressed dolls.★

Bisque Dolls, Novelty Dolls, Teddy Bears, Etc.

No. 27X120. Fashionably Dressed Dolls; have jointed bodies with bisque heads; sleeping eyes with eyelashes; side-parted curly hair; these dolls are imported expressly for us, and are then dressed in our own workroom by tasty and experienced American designers; we have a large variety at $2.50, $3.00, $3.50, $4.50, $5.00, $6.50, $8.00, $10.00, $14.50 and $16.50 The illustration shows one of the $14.50 models.

No. 27X121. Doll's Parasols; a large variety of neat styles; prices, 25c, 50c, $1.00, $1.50, $2.00 Illustration shows a $2.00 parasol.

No. 27X122. "La Petite" Hot Water Bag; no doll's outfit is complete without one; price..10c

No. 27X123. Baby's First Doll; made of rubber, with whistle; there are no sharp edges to hurt baby's tender gums; 6-inch doll............19c

No. 27X124. Latest Member of the Doll Family; a paper doll set, consisting of 4 dolls: 2 boys and 2 girls, with changeable crepe paper costumes; the arms and legs of these dolls are adjustable; price of set, complete..........50c

No. 27X125. Small Jointed Dressed Doll; stands 9 inches high; has a full jointed body; fine quality bisque head with sewed curly wig; sleeping eyes; open mouth, showing pearly teeth; is fitted with shoes and stockings; the

dress and hat on this doll are made in our own workrooms and are designed by skilled American designers; doll complete, as shown in illustration; price..............$1.35

No. 27X125A. The same doll as No. 27X125, not dressed, but fitted with shoes and stockings; price..............35c

No. 27X126. Topsy-Turvy; swing it one way and you see a white baby; swing it the other way and you have a little colored baby; in fact, two dolls in one; belongs to the popular family of rag dolls; price............$1.00

No. 27X127. Bisque Position Babe in China Tub; a very cute novelty for either ornament or a plaything for baby; complete..........15c

No. 27X128. Little Red Riding Hood, with soft body, tinted features, curly locks showing at edge of bonnet; white dress and underwear; red cape and bonnet; shoes and stockings; 12-inch doll, 50c; 15-inch doll............$1.00

No. 27X129. Baby's Knock-a-Bout Rag Doll; a fine doll for the little ones; no china head to break; always perfect and ready for play; three sizes: 25c, 50c and............$1.00 Illustration shows one of our $1.00 styles.

No. 27X130. Fat Baby Rag Doll; stands 9½ inches high; felt shoes; crocheted head with

celluloid face; hand-crocheted hat and dress; has loud voice; price..............50c

No. 27X131. Dressed Dolls, in stylish costumes; bisque head with curly hair and moving eyes; in a great variety of up-to-date American styles; prices: 25c, 50c, $1.00, $1.50 and $2.00 Illustration shows one of our $1.00 styles.

No. 27X132. Miniature Fine Jointed Dressed Doll; stands 9 inches high; has a ball-jointed body; prettily shaped bisque head, with sleeping eyes and sewed curly wig; has shoes and stockings; dressed in our own workrooms; price..............$1.75

No. 27X132A. The same doll as No. 27X132, not dressed, but fitted with shoes and stockings; price..............35c

No. 27X133. Teddy Bear Dolls; a doll with a Teddy plush body; full jointed and fitted with loud voice; unbreakable celluloid head; prices, 25c, 50c and............$1.00

No. 27X134. The "Old Reliable" Teddy Bear; full jointed and with loud voice; either cinnamon or white; we have Teddies at 25c, 50c, $1.00, $1.50, $2.00 and up to............$6.50 You can rest assured you will get the biggest and best bear for your money in Toy Town.

2379A & B. Two pages from the 1909–10 catalog of Siegel Cooper. All of the dolls have the numbers 27x and then their individual number. Nos. 42 and 56 were made by Kestner. 43 and 51 had heads made by Armand Marseille. No. 55, a flirting eyed doll named "Playmate," was probably produced by Borgfeldt. No. 45 was designed by Gussie Decker. No. 47 was a Billiken; 44, 50 and 130 had celluloid heads. No. 123 was a rubber doll; 126 was a Topsy Turvy two-head doll.

These Beautiful
DOLLS

have been priced exceedingly low so that they will be quick to find little mothers.

No. 27X40. The American Dressed Baby Doll; full jointed body; open mouth, showing pearly teeth; sleeping eyes; long, curly wig; baby dress made of white lawn; cap trimmed with tucks; price......75c

No. 27X41. Fine Quality Kid Doll; extra quality kid body; full jointed arms and legs; beautiful bisque features; sleeping eyes, with eyelashes; sewed curly wig, side parted; shoes and stockings; prices are: 17 inch doll, $1.85 each; 19 inch doll, $2.45 each; 21 inch doll, $3.15 each, and 22 inch doll..................$3.85 each

No. 27X42. A Kestner Kid Body Doll at $1.00. Kestner dolls are considered the acme of perfection in the doll market; this one has full jointed arms and riveted hip joints; the finely modeled bisque head is fitted with sleeping eyes and sewed curly wig; this doll is 16½ inches tall; price..................$1.00

No. 27X43. The Florodora Kid Doll; has hip joint; kid forearms; curly wig with center part; sleeping eyes with eyelashes; shoes and stockings; stands 14½ inches tall; price, each......50c

No. 27X44. A Novelty Knockabout Doll, with muslin body and full celluloid head; kid forearms; shoes and stockings; this doll is 19 inches tall; price, each......50c

No. 27X45. Baby's First Doll; a leather doll that will not break when thrown around by the baby; not breakable, not hurtable; a doll that is sanitary; price......50c

No. 27X46. Infant's Doll, with lifelike features; this doll is the nearest approach to a real infant in looks and model that the doll-maker has as yet devised; every feature bespeaks the live baby; fat, chubby legs and arms, double chin and painted hair and eyes; this doll stands 14 inches high; price, with stationary head, $1.50; price, with movable head..................$2.00

No. 27X47. The "Billiken" Teddy Doll; fitted with a "can't-break-'em" head; has a "bear plush" body; movable arms and legs; nothing funnier made; brings joy to all; price..................$1.00

No. 27X48. A Novelty Bisque Baby; jointed at shoulders and hips; open mouth, showing two baby teeth; short, curly baby wig, and sleeping eyes; stands 5¾ inches high; price......25c

No. 27X49. A Special Bisque Doll; stands 5½ inches tall; jointed arms and legs; sleeping eyes; side-parted curly wig; price, each......25c

No. 27X50. Celluloid Dolls that float when in the water; painted eyes and features; jointed arms; prices are: 4 inch, 10c; 5½ inch, 19c; 6½ inch, 25c; 7½ inch, 50c; 9½ inch, 75c; 12½ inch, $1.00; 14½ inch...$1.65

No. 27X51. A Popular Priced Jointed Doll; fitted with papier-macha body; full jointed arms and legs; Marcel bisque head; sleeping eyes; sewed curly wig, side parted; this doll stands 14½ inches tall and is equipped with shoes and stockings; price..................50c

No. 27X52. The Doll of the Future; a doll made with patent body; full jointed arms and legs; the head is made of a material that is extremely hard to break; has lifelike eyes and side-parted wig; also shoes and stockings; this doll stands 13 inches tall; price..................50c

No. 27X53. High-Grade Jointed Doll, with superior papier-maché body; finely featured bisque head; fitted with sleeping eyes; parted lips, showing teeth; fine quality sewed wig, side parted; also has shoes and stockings; prices are: 19 inch size, $1.75; 20½ inches, $2.25; 22½ inches, $2.65; 24½ inches, $3.25; 26½ inches, $4.50; 28½ inches..................$5.50

No. 27X54. Our Leader Jointed Doll; this doll is 24½ inches tall; has a strong papier-mache body; full jointed arms and legs; finely featured bisque head; sleeping eyes and eyelashes; sewed curly wig with side part; the greatest doll value in America; price..................$1.00

No. 27X55. The "Playmate" Flirting Eye Doll; a very fetching member of the doll family; the body is full jointed; the head is made of fine bisque, and is fitted with sleeping eyes that have the "goo-goo" attachment; the wig is hand sewed, and has the side part; shoes and stockings are fitted to these dolls; two sizes; prices are: 18 inch, $2.50; 26 inch..................$5.00

No. 27X56. The Celebrated "Kestner" Full Jointed Doll; the body is made of papier-maché, highly enameled; the arms and legs are fitted with ball joints; the head is made of fine Bohemian bisque; has sleeping eyes and side-parted wig; also shoes and stockings; this doll is 22½ inches tall; price..................$1.50

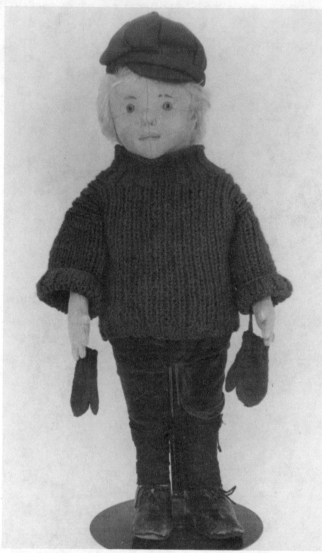

2380. Siegfried, one of the winter sports felt dolls made by Steiff. It has blond mohair sewn to its scalp, and stationary bead-like blue glass eyes; seams extend down the center of the face and from the eyes to the hairline on each side. Wide lips make the mouth appear open-closed. A hole in back of the ear indicates where the button was attached. The cap and mittens may not be original. The 1911 Steiff catalog description of Siegfried lists a red sweater, leggings and leather shoes, all of which this doll has. He should also have a scarf. H. 16 in. (40.5 cm.). *Courtesy of Richard Wright. Photo by A. Jackson.*

Siegfried
made in Germany
272

2381. Siegfried incised mark on a newborn type bisque head doll.

Simon, Mme. Eugene. 1914–18. Paris. Created dolls.

Simon (Wilhelm) & Co. 1907–30 and later. Hildburghausen, Thür.; moved to Nürnberg, Bavaria, around 1910. Manufactured dressed dolls. Did business as the Spielwarenfabrik (Toy Factory) Wilhelm Simon. It is not known what the connection, if any, was with the earlier Wilhelm Simon.†

1910: Advertised miniature dolls, character dolls and clothes for dolls.

1911: Advertised dolls' house dolls.

Simon & Halbig. 1869–1930 and later. Hildburghausen and Gräfenhain near Ohrdruf, Thür. In the 1700s Hildburghausen was one of the most important porcelain manufacturing areas in Thüringia. The *Kloster Veilsdorf* Greiner factory was located there. The Wilhelm Simon & Co.† factory founded in 1846 in Hildburghausen made dolls. The Ciesliks question whether this was a porcelain factory. It is not known whether it was this early Wilhelm Simon or his son or namesake who joined with Carl Halbig to found Simon & Halbig in 1869 and died in 1894. In the 1860s Ohrdruf had become an important area for making porcelain dolls' heads. Both *Kling* and *Kestner* had factories located there; *Alt, Beck & Gottschalck* was nearby. Simon and Halbig chose Gräfenhain, a suburb of Ohrdruf, to locate their porcelain factory. As yet no china Simon & Halbig heads have been reported but many doll makers used the bisque Simon and Halbig heads.

Among these were *Bawo & Dotter, C. M. Bergmann, Carl Bergner, Bing, Borgfeldt, Cuno & Otto Dressel, Edison, Eekhoff,† Fleischmann & Bloedel, Gimbel Bros., Hamburger & Co.* for their *Imperial*, Old Glory and *Santa* lines, *Heinrich Handwerck, Hülss, Kämmer & Reinhardt, Kley & Hahn;* Louis Lindner & Sons, *Franz Schmidt, Schwarz (Favorite), Société Française de Fabrication de Bébés & Jouets* (S.F.B.J.), *Strobel & Wilken, Wagner & Zetzsche, Wanamaker (Baby Blanche), Welsch & Co., Wiesenthal, Schindel & Kallenberg,* and *Wislizenus.*

Members of the S.F.B.J. such as *Roullet & Decamps* used Simon & Halbig heads during the period 1900–14. Often Simon & Halbig heads are found on Jumeau marked bodies. These generally have composition pates made of a composition similar to that found in the S.F.B.J. hands and feet of 1900–14. Usually the French pates (except for Jules *Steiner*) were cork and the other German pates were either cardboard or plaster. Many French authors complained that the Germans were supplying the bisque dolls' heads used in France prior to World War I and it seems likely that Simon & Halbig supplied most of these heads.

Generally a given Simon & Halbig mold number was used by only one other company. Where more than one company was involved it was probably due to the fact that the companies performed different functions in the production of the doll. Some of the mold #s found on Simon and Halbig bisque heads, shoulder plates, and all-bisque dolls were as follows:

SIMON & HALBIG MOLD NUMBERS

Mold #s	Dates Registered and/or First Used	Maker of Doll	Type of Head
22	1926	Kämmer & Reinhardt	Me-Lie-Ba Baby
100–113	1909 and later	Kämmer & Reinhardt	Character face*
114		Kämmer & Reinhardt	Character face*
115–117	1910 and later	Kämmer & Reinhardt	Character face*
118		Kämmer & Reinhardt	Baby face*
120	1912 and later	Kämmer & Reinhardt	Baby face*
121–124	1913 and later	Kämmer & Reinhardt	Character face*
126	1914 and later	Kämmer & Reinhardt	Baby face*
127	1922–27 and other years	Kämmer & Reinhardt	*
128	1927 and other years	Kämmer & Reinhardt	Baby face*
129	1922	Kämmer & Reinhardt	*
131	1922–1927 and other years	Kämmer & Reinhardt	Character face*
135		Kämmer & Reinhardt	Character face*
138		Kämmer & Reinhardt	*
144		Kämmer & Reinhardt	*
150		Kämmer & Reinhardt	*
151			Character face
152			Adult, Character face
153			Character face
155		Kämmer & Reinhardt	*
156	Probably after 1914	Hülss, Adols	Baby face
160		Handwerck, Heinrich	Character face
165		Kämmer & Reinhardt	*
170		Kämmer & Reinhardt	Baby face*
171		Kämmer & Reinhardt	Baby face*
172		Kämmer & Reinhardt	Character baby face*
173		Kämmer & Reinhardt	*
176	Probably after 1914	Hülss, Adols	
196		Kämmer & Reinhardt	*
200–214		Kämmer & Reinhardt	Shoulder heads*
351–354	1879		
400–403		Kämmer & Reinhardt	Dolly face*
530		Handwerck, Heinrich	Dolly face
540		Handwerck, Heinrich	Dolly face
541		Wiesenthal, Schindel & Kallenberg	
550		Handwerck (Gimbel's)	Dolly face
570			Dolly face, ears not pierced
600			Character face
601			
607			Oriental or Caucasian
612		Bergmann, Charles M.	Character face
615		Bergmann, Charles M.	
719	1889 and other years	Some used for Edison's Phonograph doll	Dolly face; sometimes the so-called Belton type
720			Shoulder head
729	Before 1900		Character face
739			Black or white
740			Shoulder head, sometimes a Belton type
750			Shoulder head
759			Character face
769			Closed mouth
837			All-bisque
886			All-bisque

SIMON & HALBIG MOLD NUMBERS

Mold #s	Dates Registered and/or First Used	Maker of Doll	Type of Head
905			Swivel head on a shoulder plate. Both head and shoulders marked 905
908			Swivel head usually on a shoulder plate
909			
919			Character face
927		Handwerck, Heinrich	Character face
929			Character face
939	Late 1880s?		Long face
941			Shoulder plate
947			
949	1888 or before	Wagner & Zetzsche and probably others	Belton type or cut-out crown Long face
950			Shoulder head
969			Character face
970			Shoulder head
979			Character face
989			
1000			
1008			
1009		Has been found on marked Jumeau bodies. Head also marked DEP	Black or white
1010	1880s		Shoulder head
1018			
1019		Has been found on marked Jumeau bodies	
1029			Socket head on shoulder plate
1038–1047	1895		
(1039)		Sometimes found on Jumeau or S.F.B.J. bodies, also on Roullet & Decamps walking dolls.	Black or white. Sometimes this head has the red Wimpern (Eyelashes) stamp
(1040)			Shoulder head, one of these has been found with a pull string for flirting eyes. Sometimes has "Wimpern" stamp
(1041)			Shoulder plate
1049	1899 or earlier	Cuno & Otto Dressel	
1059			Character face
1061			Shoulder plate
1069			
1078			Brown or white. Dolly face
1079		Has been found on marked Jumeau bodies, S.F.B.J. bodies and Roullet & Decamps walking dolls. Ondine Swimming dolls, Au Nain Bleu and Nadaud marked dolls.	
1080			Dolly face, shoulder head
1098–1117	1894		Child head. Some of these were heads representing Chinese or other Orientals
(1099)			Oriental child
(1109)			Dolly face
1129			Oriental child
1148–1167	1894		
(1159)		Found on marked bodies of Jumeau and of Handwerck	Adult, socket head

SIMON & HALBIG MOLD NUMBERS

Mold #s	Dates Registered and/or First Used	Maker of Doll	Type of Head
(1160)	As late as W.W.I.		Adult doll shoulder head with wigs of the rococo or baroque style
1170		Also marked "D"	Shoulder head
1199			Oriental (Burmese, Japanese, etc.)
1248	ca. 1900		Dolly face
1249	1900	Hamburger, Santa line	Dolly face, brown or white
1250	ca. 1900	Hamburger, Imperial line	Shoulder head
1260	ca. 1900		Shoulder head
1261			Baby face
1269			Dolly face
1279		Bergmann	Character face
1280		Bergmann, Columbia line	Shoulder head
1289			Dolly face
1290			
1293–1296		Franz Schmidt	
(1294)			Brown or white
(1296)			Baby face
1299			Dolly face
1300			Dolly face
1301			Black ethnic features
1302			Black ethnic features, closed thick lips, found on black lady composition body marked with a star and a B
1303			Lady or child character face, painted or glass eyes
1304			Character face, narrow eyes
1305			Long nose, protruding chin
1307			Lady, long face
1308			Character face; one of these dolls represents a coke burner; one is a man with a mustache; and another is a girl in regional costume
1310		Franz Schmidt	Character face
1329			Oriental
1339		Louis Lindner & Sons	Dolly face
1348		Cuno & Otto Dressel, Jutta Line	Dolly face
1349		Cuno & Otto Dressel, Jutta Line	Dolly face
1358			Black ethnic features
1368			Black
1385			Lady, closed mouth
1388			Character face, smiling
1397			Character face, smiling
1398			Character face, smiling
1428			Character face, open-closed mouth
1440			Lady
1468		Cuno & Otto Dressel	Lady
1469		Cuno & Otto Dressel	Lady
1478			Character face, closed mouth
1488			Baby or child character face
1489			Erika, character face
1498			Baby with molded hair
1616			
1914		Cuno & Otto Dressel, Jutta line	Baby or child character face

*For further descriptions, see the table in the Kämmer & Reinhardt entry, except for mold #s 113, 400, and 401.

Some of the mold numbers were owned by the maker of the doll (i.e. the factory who made the composition body and/or the firm who produced the doll) and were produced by other porcelain factories as well as Simon & Halbig. Often a given mold number came with either an open mouth or a closed mouth; pates were cut differently for dolls from the same mold, and the piercing of the ears was not always done on heads made from the same mold.

Some Simon & Halbig heads had a Roman numeral mark such as II or IV.

It should be noted that many of the mold #s were registered in 1894, the year in which Wilhelm Simon died according to the Ciesliks, and relatively few mold #s were registered after his death.

The earlier Simon & Halbig bisque heads had a size code as well as the initials S H and no mold numbers. Later heads were marked with Simon & Halbig and still later Halbig alone but the Halbig appears to have been used at the same time as some of the Simon & Halbig marks. The size code ran at least from 9/0 to 17½; dolls have been reported from 6 to 36 in. (15 to 91.5 cm.) tall. Matching the size code with exact heights is impossible because Simon and Halbig heads were used on many different kinds of bodies. In the twentieth century the height of the doll in centimeters was often found on the heads. This was especially true for the Kämmer & Reinhardt character dolls, the Hülss dolls and the Franz Schmidt dolls.

Practically all types of bisque heads have been found with Simon & Halbig marks—bald heads of so-called "*Belton-type*," molded hair, wigs or flocked hair; eyes painted, stationary or sleeping glass eyes, flirting eyes, open, open-closed or closed mouth; pierced or not pierced ears; most of nineteenth and early twentieth century Simon and Halbig dolls had pierced ears.

A "W" sometimes is found on the upper forehead of dolls marked Simon & Halbig, K ✡ R, or Simon & Halbig-Handwerck. which probably stands for the *Waltershauser Puppenfabrik*. Sometimes Simon and Halbig dolls have one or two holes on the upper forehead under the wig.

1896: Applied for a German patent (D.R.G.M.) for eyelashes made of threads.

1910: Applied for a German patent (D.R.G.M.) for eyelid movement in a doll's head.

1913: Applied for a German patent (D.R.G.M.) for flirting eyes which were used in Simon & Halbig head mold #122 on a Kämmer & Reinhardt body. This head bore a green stamp reading D.R.G.M.// 552425.

1920: Merged with Kämmer & Reinhardt and thus became part of the Bing conglomerate.

1930 and later: Made bisque heads and composition heads. Sometime in the 1930s the factory became known as Keramisches Werk Gräfenhain. Part of the above data, especially the information on the registration dates of the mold numbers, was researched by the Ciesliks.★

2382. Bisque head made by Simon & Halbig with molded blond hair having a braid on top, stationary glass eyes, pierced ears and a cloth body with lower arms of kid. Original clothes. Mark: III. 2415. H. 17½ in. (44.5 cm.). *Courtesy of Gundi Groh-Pracher.*

2383A, B & C. Molded hair bisque shoulder head marked S O H in front for Simon & Halbig. It has a black bow, curls falling to the shoulders, brush marks around the face, feathered eyebrows, blue threaded stationary glass eyes and pierced ears. The cloth body has bisque limbs. The feet have molded black, heeled boots. The regional style clothes are hand sewn. H. 12 in. (30.5 cm.). *Coleman Collection.*

2384. Simon and Halbig bisque shoulder head, bisque lower arms and bisque legs on a cloth body. It has a brown wig, stationary blue glass eyes, pierced ears and a closed mouth. Mark on front of shoulders: S. H. H. 9½ in. (24 cm.). *Courtesy of Sotheby Parke Bernet Inc., N.Y.*

2385. Bisque shoulder heads with wigs, blue glass eyes, pierced ears, bisque arms; dressed in costumes of ca. 1880. Left, marked "S 6 H." H. 40 cm. (15½ in.). Right, marked "S 5 H." H. 35 cm. (14 in.). *Courtesy of the Collection Nederlands Kostuummuseum, The Hague. Photo by B. Frequin.*

2386. Bisque shoulder head, bisque lower arms and lower legs with molded high boots made by Simon & Halbig. The doll has molded blond curls, painted eyes, pierced ears, closed mouth, and cloth body. Original commercial clothes representing a bride of ca. 1880. Mark: "S. H." H. 9¼ in. (23.5 cm.). *Courtesy of Gundi Groh-Pracher.*

2387A & B. Dolls' house doll with bisque shoulder head, lower arms and lower legs made by Simon & Halbig. It has molded and painted hair, blue eyes, closed mouth, and a cloth body. Original clothes. Mark: S. H. on the front shoulder. H. 5¼ in. (13.5 cm.). *Courtesy of Claire Hennig. Photos by Margie Landolt of Basel, Switzerland.*

2388A & B. Untinted bisque shoulder head made by Simon & Halbig has molded black hair, molded and painted eyes, and a cloth body with bisque arms and legs. Mark: "S. H." H. 10 in. (25.5 cm.). *Courtesy of Richard Withington. Photo by Barbara Jendrick.*

2389. Bisque shoulder head made by Simon and Halbig. The S & H initials are on the shoulder in front. It has molded and painted hair and features. The hair is in the so-called Alice-in-Wonderland style. The mouth is closed and there are no sew holes in the shoulders. H. 8½ in. (21.5 cm.). H. of shoulder head 2¼ in. (5.5 cm.). *Coleman Collection.*

2390. Bisque shoulder head, bisque lower arms and legs made by Simon and Halbig. The doll has molded hair similar to that shown in Ill. 2391, except this doll is 5½ in. (14 cm.) tall, an intermediate size. Original regional costume. Mark S. H. on the front shoulder. *Courtesy of Yvonne Baird.*

2391A, B & C. Bisque shoulder head made by Simon and Halbig with molded and painted hair and features. The hairdo is identical to that found on the dolls' house doll in Ill. 2390. There is a lip line and pierced ears. The cloth body has typical Simon and Halbig bisque arms; the feet are replacements. Original clothes of the late 1890s. Mark on the front of the shoulders is "S 3 H." H. 11½ in. (29 cm.). H. of shoulder head 3¼ in. (8 cm.). *Coleman Collection.*

A   B   C

2392. Bisque shoulder head probably made by Simon and Halbig for a dolls' house doll. It has molded and painted hair, features, and boots, on a pink cloth body. This head is identical, except for size, to a larger head marked S & H. See Ill. 2391. H. 3¾ in. (9.5 cm.). This doll was purchased new ca. 1920. *Coleman Collection.*

2393. Bisque shoulder head marked S H on the front shoulder is on a cloth body with bisque lower arms. It has a blond mohair wig with two plaits, brown glass eyes, closed mouth and pierced ears. The crown is solid. It is dressed in a regional costume of red wool. H. 10 in. (25.5 cm.). *Coleman Collection.*

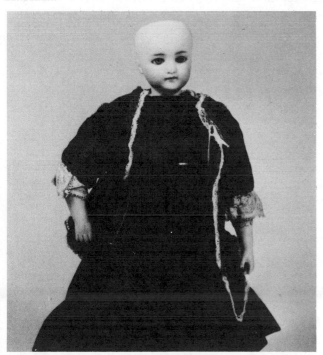

2394. Simon and Halbig bisque head has a missing wig, sleeping glass eyes, pierced ears, and a closed mouth. Bisque lower arms made by Simon and Halbig are on a small kid body. Marks: S. H. 3 //905. This small doll has an open pate but a larger mold, #905 size 9, has a bald head with a line indicating possibly where the pate could be cut. *Courtesy of Richard Withington. Photo by Barbara Jendrick.*

2395. Simon and Halbig bisque head with a solid crown, a pink wig, stationary blue glass eyes, pierced ears, a closed mouth and a composition and wood ball-jointed body. The wrists are not jointed. Original pink costume. Mark: Ill. 2422. H. 12½ in. (31.5 cm.). *Coleman Collection.*

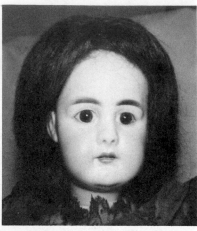

2396A & B. Bisque shoulder head and possibly lower arms were made by Simon and Halbig. The doll has a wig, stationary brown glass eyes, pierced ears, dimple in the chin, open mouth with two upper teeth and one lower tooth. The head has a swivel neck and the kid body is gusseted at the elbows, hips and knees. Mark on head: S 11 H//949. Mark on shoulder: S 10 H//941. H. 22 in. (56 cm.). *Coleman Collection.*

2397. Dark brown bisque head made by Simon and Halbig on a dark brown ball-jointed wood and composition body. It has a black kinky skin wig, brown glass eyes, pierced ears, an open mouth and four upper teeth. Clothes are contemporary with the doll. Mark: "S. & H. 1039 8½ DEP." H. 21 in. (53.5 cm.). *Courtesy of Richard Withington. Photo by Barbara Jendrick.*

2398. Bisque head made by Simon and Halbig with wig, sleeping eyes, open mouth and teeth, pierced ears, mold #1078, size 2/0. Five piece composition body with molded and painted footwear. Original costume. H. 8 in. (20.5 cm.). *Coleman Collection.*

2399. Bisque head made by Simon and Halbig with wig, sleeping eyes, open mouth and teeth, mold #1078, size 3/0. Five-piece composition body with molded and painted footwear. Original regional costume. H. 8 in. (20.5 cm.). *Coleman Collection.*

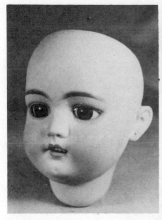

2400. Bisque socket head made by Simon and Halbig has a wig, sleeping blue glass eyes, pierced ears and an open mouth with four teeth. Mark: Ill. 2426. H. 4 in. (10 cm.). *Coleman Collection.*

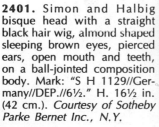

2401. Simon and Halbig bisque head with a straight black hair wig, almond shaped sleeping brown eyes, pierced ears, open mouth and teeth, on a ball-jointed composition body. Mark: "S H 1129//Germany//DEP.//6½." H. 16½ in. (42 cm.). *Courtesy of Sotheby Parke Bernet Inc., N.Y.*

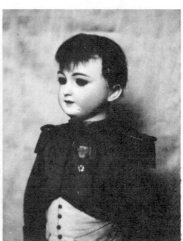

2402A & B. Bisque head made by Simon and Halbig on a ball jointed composition body that appears to have been made by the Société Française de Fabrication de Bébés & Jouets (S.F.B.J.). The doll was made to represent Napoleon I. The hair style of the wig, the stationary blue glass eyes, the open mouth with teeth, the padding of the body in appropriate places and the costume all contribute to the portraiture. The pierced ears seem to be a little out of character but are typical of Simon and Halbig heads. Mark: "1159//Germany//SIMON & HALBIG//S. & H.//10." H. 25 in. (63.5 cm.). Circumference of head 11¼ in. (28.5 cm.). *Private collection.*

2403A & B. Bisque head made by Simon and Halbig has a wig, sleeping brown glass eyes, hair eyelashes, open mouth with teeth and a lady type ball-jointed composition and wood body. The head has a red stamp "Wimpern" which means "eyelashes" in German. Mark incised on head: "S & H DEP 1159, 9½." H. 23 in. (58.5 cm.). *Courtesy of Sotheby Parke Bernet Inc., N.Y.*

2404A & B. Bisque shoulder head made by Simon and Halbig has a period hair style wig, stationary brown glass eyes, pierced ears, closed mouth, and a cloth body with bisque lower arms and legs having black molded boots. Mark: "S & H // 1160—2/0." H. 11 in. (28 cm.). *Courtesy of Jessica Norman.*

2405A & B. Simon and Halbig bisque head with a wig, sleeping brown glass eyes, pierced ears, open-closed mouth, three upper teeth, and a ball-jointed body of composition and wood. Purchased in Budapest, Hungary. Mark: "S & H. 1269//Germany//DEP//6½." H. 18 in. (45.5 cm.). *Courtesy of Helen Read. Photos by Steven Read.*

2406. Bisque socket head made by Simon and Halbig has a wig, stationary glass eyes, closed wide mouth and a ball jointed composition body. The face has lines around the eyes and smudge marks characteristic of a coke maker as portrayed by this doll which is in an appropriate costume for this trade. The suit is black broadcloth with a red vest. The black leatherette shoes are marked 1. Mark: "S & H//1308//D.// 4." H. 14 in. (35.5 cm.). *Courtesy of the Museum of the City of Neustadt near Coburg.*

2407. Simon & Halbig bisque head on a black jointed composition body. It has a black wig, brown sleeping eyes and 6 teeth in an open mouth. Mark on this head is "1358// Germany//SIMON & HALBIG//S & H //6." H. 18 in. (45.5 cm.). *Courtesy of Becky and Jaye Lowe. Photo by Bill Holland.*

2408. Simon & Halbig bisque head on a jointed composition body. It has brown glass eyes, and a slight opening to the mouth which has 6 teeth. This marked Simon & Halbig doll's head is mold #1388. H. 27 in. (68.5 cm.). *Courtesy of Becky and Jaye Lowe. Photo by Bill Holland.*

2409. Simon & Halbig bisque head mold #1428, size 6, on a composition bent limb baby body. It has a blond wig, sleeping blue glass eyes, pierced ears, and an open-closed mouth. H. 12½ in. (31.5 cm.). *Courtesy of Sotheby Parke Bernet Inc., N.Y.*

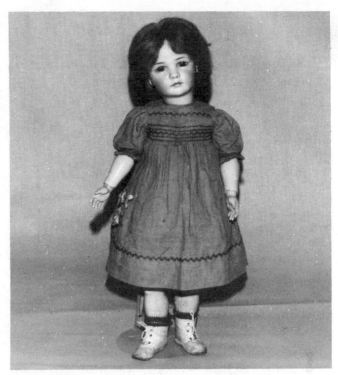

2410. Simon & Halbig bisque head mold #1448 with wig, sleeping glass eyes, pierced ears, closed mouth on a fully jointed composition body. The face closely resembles the Simon & Halbig mold # IV doll shown in Ill. 1514.† Clothes are contemporary with the doll. Mark "SIMON & HALBIG//1448//S & H." *Courtesy of the late Magda Byfield.*

2411. Bisque head made by Simon & Halbig has a wig, blue glass eyes, closed mouth and is on a jointed composition body. Original clothes for a lady doll. Mark: Simon & Halbig// 1?69 2. This mold may be a 1469. H. 14½ in. (37 cm.). *Courtesy of Sotheby Parke Bernet Inc., N.Y.*

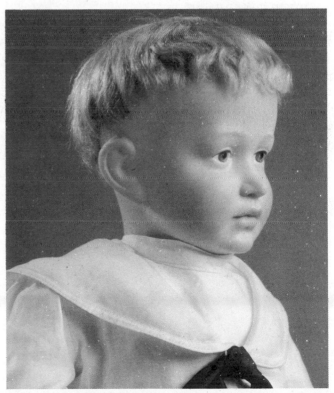

2412. Bisque character head made by Simon & Halbig. It has a wig, painted blue eyes, closed mouth and a jointed composition body. Mark: "150//S & H//3." H. 24 in. (61 cm.). Circumference of head 12½ in. (31.5 cm.). *Courtesy of Becky and Jaye Lowe. Photo by Bill Holland.*

2413A & B. Bisque character head made by Simon & Halbig has a blond wig, stationary blue glass eyes, open-closed mouth, teeth, dimples, and a ball-jointed composition body, clothes contemporary with the doll. Mark: (S & H, 12). H. 28 in. (71 cm.). *Courtesy of Sotheby Parke Bernet Inc., N.Y.*

2414. Bisque character head made by Simon and Halbig has a brown wig, blue intaglio eyes, dimples, and an open-closed mouth with four teeth. It is on a ball jointed composition body. Mark: 151//S & H //3. H. 23 in. (58.5 cm.). *Courtesy of Richard Withington. Photo by Barbara Jendrick.*

S. & H.
2415

S & H 9
DEP.
St.
2416

DEP
S H
Germany
2417

SIMON&HALBIG
Germany
2418

S&H
GS1
DEP.
2419

10 S H 9 Germany
2420

S 15 H
939
2421

S H 4
949
2422

S 8½ H 1009
DEP
St
2423

S & H. 1019
DEP.
Germany
6
2424

S 1041   8½ H
2425

2415–2433. Marks on Simon and Halbig bisque heads.

S&H. 1079
DEP.
Germany.
8

2426

S&H 1079-6
DEP.
Germany

2427

S H 1079
4½
DEP

2428

S H 1109
DEP.
6

2429

S & H
1160 - 2/0

2430A

S & H
1160.
8/0

2430B

K.W.
G.
136
12

A

K W
G
134
12/0

B

K.W.G.
1382
3

C

2434A, B & C. Later marks of the successor of Simon & Halbig, Keramisches Werk Gräfenhain.

S&H·1269
Germany.
DEP.
6½

2431

1308
S D & H
2

2432

151
S & H
3

2433

2435. All-bisque Simon and Halbig doll with a wig on a dome head, stationary brown glass eyes, closed mouth and joints at the neck, shoulders and hips. Original clothes. Mark: "S H 3/0." H. 4½ in. (11.5 cm.). *Courtesy of Joan Kindler.*

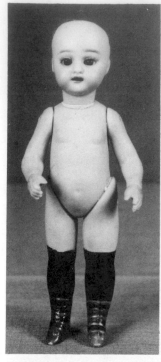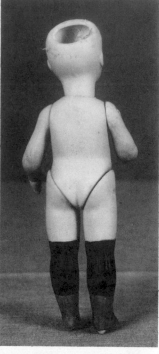

2436A & B. All-bisque doll made by Simon and Halbig has a wig, glass eyes and an open mouth with teeth. It is jointed at the neck, shoulders and hips and has kid lining at the neck joint. Molded stockings and multi-strap boots. Notice how similar the hands are to the other Simon and Halbig bisque hands and the resemblance to Ill. 2437. Mark: S & H. *Courtesy of Jan Foulke. Photos by Howard Foulke.*

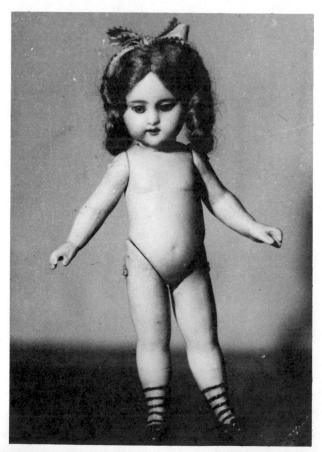

2437. All-bisque doll made by Simon and Halbig has a wig, stationary blue glass eyes and joints at the neck, shoulders and hips. The joints are lined with kid. The body and footwear molding is the same as in Ill. 2436, only the colors are different. H. 7 in. (18 cm.). *Courtesy of Dr. Eva Moskovszky.*

Simonetta. Late 1920s. Name of an art doll made by *Lotte Pritzel.*

Simonne, F. 1842–81 and possibly later. Paris. Produced bisque head lady dolls and bébés, including those made by *Jules Steiner.*

1881: Bought bisque heads from *François Gaultier* according to Mme. Florence Poisson, curator of the Roybet Fould Museum.★

Simons, E. 1924–26. London. Advertised New-born baby dolls and walking dolls with "Mama-Papa" voices. The dolls came dressed or undressed.

Simpson, Fawcett & Co. 1915–19. Leeds, England. Manufactured cloth body dolls.

Simpson-Crawford Co. 1904–06 and possibly other years. New York City. Early in the Spring they bought undressed dolls directly from the factories and had the German peasants make the clothes very inexpensively.

1904: Advertised dressed and undressed dolls; the doll in chemise cost 25¢ to $25 and included *Santa* dolls. In the same price range one could buy dolls dressed as girls, boys or babies. One of their dolls was a *Cymbalier.* Separate dolls' heads and dolls' bodies were sold as well as accessories such as parasols, jewelry sets, shoes, and watches.★

Simpson's Toys. 1922–23. London. Agent for the dolls of *G. Schmey.*

Sindacato Italiano D'Importazione E. D'Esportazione. 1919–20. Turin, Italy. Made baby dolls.

Sindall, Frederick. 1895–23. London and Derby. Made cloth dolls.★

Sing (Singhalese). 1911–13. Felt doll made by *Steiff* and distributed in U.S. by *Borgfeldt.* It represented an East Indian of Ceylon (not to be confused with *Senegalaise*) and had long feet. Ht. 17 in. (43 cm.); priced $2.95.

Singing Dolls. 1928. Trade name of dolls made by *Domec.*

Singing and Talking Dolls. 1927. Trade name of dolls made by *L. Cohen & Sons.* (See also **Phonograph Dolls.**)

Sir John French. See **General French.**

Siren Tinker. 1921–29. Doll made by *Tinker Toys,* resembled a mermaid. Ht. 8½ in. (21.5 cm.).

Sis. 1924. Trade name of a cloth doll. See Ill. 801.★

Sis. 1929. Name of a doll advertised by *Reisman, Barron.*

Sis Hopkins. 1911–12 and probably later. Composition head doll made by *Louis Amberg.* Rose Melville carried the doll on stage when she played the part of Sis Hopkins. Sis Hopkins was also a joke-book character. Several postcards advertised this doll.★

Sissy (Sissie). 1928–29. All-composition doll with painted features and hair, jointed at the shoulders and hips so that it could stand alone. Made by *Cameo* and distributed by *Butler Bros.* It wore a printed percale dress. Ht. 12 in. (30.5 cm.); priced $4.90 doz. wholesale.

1928: Copyrighted by *Joseph Kallus.*

2438. Doll with bisque head and arms on a body labeled Simonne. It has a blond wig, stationary blue glass eyes, and a closed mouth. Original clothes. H. 18½ in. (47 cm.). *Courtesy of Elsie and Al Potter.*

2439–2440. Marks on the bodies of dolls produced by Simonne. Ill. 2440 is on a paper label of Simonne's found on the composition body of a Jules Steiner doll.

Sister Lou. 1930. Character doll dressed as a child and made by *Schoen & Yondorf.*

Sister Suzy. 1929. Composition-head doll, cotton stuffed body, dressed as a girl in an organdy dress, coat and beret; distributed by *Butler Bros.* and carried a square tag. Hts. 14 and 18 in. (35.5 and 45.5 cm.); priced $8.00 and $16.50 doz. wholesale.

Sitzendorf Porzellanfabrik. See **Voight, Gebrüder.**

Skalek, Therese. 1907. Vienna. Listed in directories under Dolls and Dolls' Heads according to Dr. Eva Moskovszky.

Skara. 1931. Trademark registered in Germany by *Julius Schwarz* for dolls.

Skating Girl. 1917–18. Name of a character doll designed by *Hilda Cowham* and made by *Laurie Hansen.*

Skeezix. 1922–30. Name of a doll made of stuffed art leather (oilcloth) with the clothes and features printed on the leather. It represented a character in the comics drawn by *Frank King;* was created by *William and Eileen Benoliel* and made by *Live Long Toys.* The name "Skeezix" was in black on the lower back of the doll.

1922: Skeezix was first made as a toddler with yellow hair having an upright lock in front, and baggy red rompers. 50,000 dolls were made the first 40 days. Ht. 13 in. (33 cm.).

1924: Skeezix was also made as a little boy in a blue one-piece suit with short trousers. Ht. 14 in. (35.5 cm.).

Among the distributors was *Supplee-Biddle Hardware Co.*

1926: Skeezix was also made as an older boy in long trousers, but with the same upright lock of hair as on the toddler Skeezix. Three versions of Skeezix had him dressed in overalls, in a bathing suit and in pajamas.

1927: The toddler Skeezix was available in two new hts. 10 and 11½ in. (25.5 and 29 cm.) and the larger size was stamped "Skeezix//Reg. U.S. Pat. Off.// Pat.// Feb. 27. 1923." Skeezix as a little boy also came in two sizes.

1929: There were three versions of Skeezix as a baby in red rompers. Hts. 9 and 13 in. (23 and 33 cm.); priced $4.00 and $8.00 doz. wholesale. Over one million Skeezixes as a baby had been sold so far. There was also a standing version of Skeezix. This doll wore a necktie and pants and came in assorted colors. Ht. 14½ in. (37 cm.); priced $8.00 doz. wholesale. These dolls bore the name "Skeezix" and "Frank King." (See Ills. 2441 and 2442.)★

Skeezix. 1929 and probably later. All-bisque dolls with jointed necks and molded clothes representing a character in comics drawn by *Frank King.* Made in Germany and distributed wholesale by *Marshall Field* and *Shackman.* Priced 15¢.

Skeezix. 1930. Part of the *Trixy Toys* line of dolls made by *Durrel Co.*

Skerry, F. H. 1880s. Salem, Mass. Distributed dolls.

Ski Jumper. 1928. Name of a wooden doll made by *A. Schoenhut.*

Skinney. See **Gene Carr Kids.**

Skippy. 1928–30 and later. All-composition doll with molded hair and painted features, eyes looked to the side, the neck joint was an inverted socket like *Patsy's* neck. It was also made with a composition head, arms, and legs on a cloth body. The legs had brown molded ribbed stockings, and oxfords. The doll represented a newspaper character drawn by *Percy Crosby* and was made by *Effanbee* as a mate

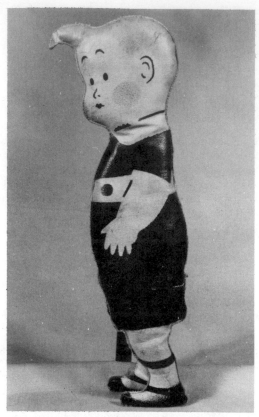

2441. Nearly flat oilcloth doll with printed features made by Live Long Toys to represent Skeezix in rompers. The legs are apart. Mark: Ill. 2442. H. 13½ in. (34 cm.). *Coleman Collection.*

2442. Stamped mark on Skeezix oilcloth doll.

to Patsy. The raised mark on the back of the neck read, "EFFANBEE//SKIPPY//©//P.L. Crosby." The body was marked "EFFANBEE//PATSY//PAT. PEND.//DOLL." Ht. 14 in. (35.5 cm.), for the all-composition doll; the cloth body Skippy was slightly taller.

1929: At first Skippy wore a white shirt with a standing collar, dark short trousers and a four-in-hand red necktie with a heart shaped label attached to the tie. The doll carried a book with a picture of Skippy on the cover.

Later Skippy also came dressed in a baseball outfit, a cowboy suit, long trousers, overalls, an Oliver Twist suit, and a soldier's uniform.

1930 and later: Skippy's clothes were designed by *Elsie R. Baunton. Gladys Meyers* made some of the clothes for Skippy including a black tailored suit representing a bridegroom's attire. Skippy's blue sailor suit consisted of a high-neck jacket with gold braid on the shoulders to simulate epaulettes and three gold buttons with anchors on them down the front. The trousers were long. Skippy also came dressed as a Boy Scout and when he wore his cowboy outfit the price was $3.50. His feet were made so that they could wear roller skates. TOYS AND NOVELTIES reported that Skippy was used in the movies.

1931: *Montgomery Ward* described their Skippy as wearing a white piqué shirt, green trousers, a leather belt, and a felt cap; priced $2.89.

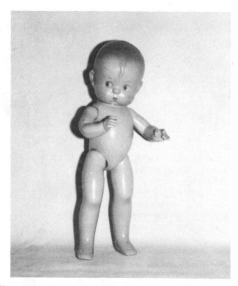

2443. All-composition Skippy has molded and painted hair and eyes. The eyes look to the side and the mouth is pursed. The neck joint and body are the same as for Patsy. In fact the mark on the body is: EFFANBEE//PATSY//DOLL. Mark on head: Ill. 2445. H. 13½ in. (34 cm.). *Courtesy of Dorothy Annunziato.*

2444. Advertisement for Skippy as shown in PLAYTHINGS, May, 1929. Skippy is shown in his various costumes and possible poses.

EFFANBEE
SKIPPY
©
P.L. CROSBY

2445. Mark on composition head of Effanbee's Skippy.

Skookum Indian Dolls. 1913–30 and later. Heads made of dried apples and later of composition by various companies. *Mary McAboy* originated and designed these dolls.

1914: A squaw with a dried apple head, hair of darning cotton and black glass pin eyes, carried a papoose with pins for eyes. The squaw carried an orange sticker with a serrated edge, black letters, and a black frame. The sticker read, "SKOOKUM//INDIAN//Patented// February// 17, 1914."

1918: TOYS AND NOVELTIES reported, "The Scholt Company, Denver Colo. . . . featured the Skookum dolls, whose heads were made of dried apples and painted to represent the countenances of various Indians, the dolls themselves ranging in height from 3 to 9 inches [7.5 to 23 cm.]. [There] were braves and squaws of three different tribes—the Navajos, Utes, and Apaches—each in appropriate tribal garb."

1920: Mrs. F. E. McAboy, the designer of the Skookum doll, wrote an article titled "The Origin of Skookum Indian Doll" for PLAYTHINGS, March, 1920.

"It is now almost seven years since the most prolific tribe of Indians—known as Skookums were discovered. . . .

"As to their origin . . . the casual remark of a friend in the grocery business, 'What became of those little apple-faced dolls your mother used to make? . . . We talked about the little Indian dummies whose novelties was a wrinkled life-like face made out of a dried apple. Each one had a different look that was peculiarly human. Wrapped in their little blankets they looked like the old squaws and bucks we knew so well in our Montana home. Mother used to give them to friends. . . . They were even sold sometimes at Church Socials and Sewing Circles. . . . The result was that I worked up a little Indian village for a window display in the grocery store. . . . The Naughty Marietta Opera Co. was playing in town at the time and bought the whole village—paid actual money. Of course, I made another village and put more Indians in it, and they kept selling. . . . I applied for Government Patents. . . . and spread my new business all over my father's home. I enlisted the house maids and hired more help as soon as I could pay them. . . . I took all the publicity that I could get which was mostly in the Sunday Society Column of western papers. I even got into a New York paper on account of a display in the Women's Suffrage Head quarters. . . .

". . . I milled around some time before I found [a name]. 'Skookum' is the Siwash for 'Bully Good.' They are 'Bully Good Indians.' . . . I am associated with a western factory where I attend exclusively to the making of the Skookums and my partners do the rest. . . . We look with pride upon the weazed old ancestors who still keep guard over the present day Skookums that emerge from an up-to-date factory in numbers 'great as the stars.'

"Nearly every Indian tribe is represented. They are copied in detail, having real leather moccasins, characteristic headdress and blankets and individual make-up. The Pueblo Squaw in wrapped legging meets the Sioux Chief in Warbonnet. The Apache Papoose in his little sheltered carrier rests cosily beside the little Chippewa strapped to a board.

"We also make Skookums with an indestructible composition face that is painted and lined to life-like imitation.

"The apple-face of course is not indestructible. We find that our customers have decided opinions—some will have nothing but the apple, others only composition. . . . I doubt if I could do as well without the satisfaction and pleasure derived from the commendation of my customers and such authorities on Indian Life as Edgar S. Paxson, who was given foremost honors in august circles of London and Paris as well as this country and our own Charley Russell who is a recognized and admired authority on western art." (Charles Manson Russell, born 1865, died 1926, was a famous painter of Indians.)

1920–21: The *Arrow Novelty Co.* made the dolls with composition faces, colored blankets, moccasins and beads. These came in ten styles and three heights.

1929: *H. H. Tammen Co.* made composition-head dolls in various styles and sizes.★

Slade, Charlotte L. 1872–77. New York City. Made patterns for dolls' clothes and handled wax dolls and baby dolls. The wax dolls had blond hair and came in three hts. 12, 16, and 20 in. (30.5, 40.5, and 51 cm.); priced with patterns for their clothes $1.50 to $2.25. The baby dolls had light hair, lace caps and also came with clothes patterns. Ht. 16 in. (40.5 cm.); priced $1.75.

Charlotte Slade copyrighted her patterns in 1872 and patented them in 1874. The patterns were for a dress, a sacque, polonaise, postilion waist, talma, Russian cloak, waterproof, hood, wrapper, apron, and underclothes. (See Ill. 2446.) The group of patterns were sold in an envelope with directions and the suggestion that the fabric should be "cut half inch larger, for wax dolls." The tissue paper pieces of the pattern for each garment were of a single color but the color varied from garment to garment. (See THE COLLECTOR'S BOOK OF DOLLS' CLOTHES, pp. 159–160, and the 1874 CS patterns at the back of the book.)

Envelopes of patterns with only the 1872 copyright date on them show sizes 4 and 6 as 15 and 21 in. (38 and 53.5 cm.). An advertising leaflet with the 1874 patent date on it has the verse:

Of cloth that's old, colored or white,
They cut and baste to view:
And when they have them all to suit,
They make of cloth that's new.

In other words use old cloth to experiment with the patterns before cutting up new cloth.

The patterns were sold in envelopes each containing 10 or 12 patterns, to fit a doll of one of 10 hts. 10, 12, 15, 18,

Patterns of Dolls' Clothes,

OR THE

DOLLS' TROUSSEAU.

No. *4* LENGTH OF DOLL *15* Inches.

Dress and Sacque, Polonaise, Talma, Russian Cloak, Waterproof, Wrapper, Apron, Hood and Underclothes.

Entered according to act of Congress in the year 1872, by C. L. Slade, in the office of the Librarian of Congress, at Washington.

TRADE MARK.

2446. Doll pattern envelope cover. The patterns for the garments shown on the left were copyrighted in 1872 by Charlotte Slade. The patterns for the various pieces of each garment came in a distinctive color so that all the blue patterns belonged to one garment, all the yellow patterns to another garment and so forth. The patterns in this envelope were for a 15 in. (38 cm.) doll.

21, 24, 27, 30, 33, and 36 in. (25.5, 30.5, 38, 45.5, 53.5, 61, 68.5, 76, 84, and 91.5 cm.); priced 25¢ to 35¢ for the patterns.

1874 and later: E. G. Selchow & Co. *(Selchow & Righter)* sold patterns for dolls' clothes patented by Charlotte Slade; priced $1.75 doz. wholesale. (See THE COLLECTOR'S BOOK OF DOLLS' CLOTHES, Ill. 224.)

Slater, Mabel (née Hunt). 1921–27. New York City. Obtained several patents for dolls.★

Slater, Thomas. 1922 and probably other years. London, Paris. Distributed French dolls in England.

Sleeping Beauty. 1884–87. Wax doll with long hair and bangs, sleeping eyes, composition arms and legs, distributed by *C. F. Lauer.* The doll wore a chemise, earrings, and had painted footwear.

1884: Eight hts. 15, 16½, 18, 20, 22, 24, 26, and 28 in. (38, 42, 45.5, 51, 56, 61, 66, and 71 cm.); priced $2.75 to $9.25 doz. wholesale.

1887: Four hts. 16, 18, 22, and 28 in. (40.5, 45.5, 56, and 71 cm.); priced $2.20 to $6.50 doz. wholesale.

Slender Leg Dolls. 1926 and later. In the early 1920s the plump proportioned *Mama* dolls were popular, but in 1926 dolls with more slender legs were introduced. Among the first of these were *Century* dolls with *Kestner* bisque heads and *Effanbee's Lovey Mary* and *Rose-Marie* with composition heads.

Slicer, William, and Osburn, Walter. 1769–71 and possibly other years. Annapolis and London-town, Maryland. Adver-

tised that they used a trade sign of a doll and "carries on all sorts of turning." They probably made wooden dolls.

Slicker Dolls. 1929. Advertised by *Reisman, Barron.*

Sloan & Co. 1915–18. Liverpool, England. Made composition-head dolls and dolls with *British Ceramic* heads. The dolls came undressed or dressed in regional costumes or in historical English costumes.

1915: Gertrude Sloan applied for a patent for composition heads for dolls.

1917: Advertised baby dolls.★

Slovak. 1925. Name of cloth dolls dressed to represent a Slovakian man and young woman, made by the *Hungarian Dolldom.* Other dolls have also been dressed in Slovak costumes.

Slovav Shepherd. Early 1900s. Wooden dolls with carved features, hair, hands and feet, and painted clothes. They stood on wooden bases.

Slovenly Peter. See **Struwwelpeter (Shock Head Peter).**

Smart Set. 1927. Dolls dressed in the latest fashion by *Dean.* The dolls represented children at first and later ladies.

Smiles. 1919–20. Name of doll made by *Republic Doll & Toy;* some of these dolls were bent limb baby dolls dressed in sweaters, others wore chiffon of assorted colors.★

Smiles. 1927–30 and later. Composition head doll with sleeping eyes, sucked its thumbs, clapped its hands, had a bent limb baby body with rubber legs that emitted a cry when squeezed, wore a white lawn dress, matching halo bonnet, and rubber panties. These dolls were made by *Ideal* and distributed by *Butler Bros.*

1928: Hts. 15 and 17 in. (38 and 43 cm.); priced $2.35 and $3.00. (See THE COLLECTOR'S BOOK OF DOLLS' CLOTHES, Ill. 770 D.)

Ca. 1933: Had celluloid-metal sleeping eyes, distributed by *Quaker Doll Co.*

Smiles. 1930. Doll in the *Kiddie Pal* line made by *Regal.*

Smiling Face. 1928. Name of a doll made by *Arranbee Doll Co.*

Smiling Sammy. 1918. Doll made by *Trion* had a military trench helmet attached to its head.

Smiling Sue. 1910–14. Name of a doll with composition head and arms, painted hair, cork stuffed cloth body, and dressed. Ht. 15½ in. (39.5 cm.).★

Smith, Celia and Charity. 1889–1911 and later. Ithaca, N.Y. Created cutout cloth dolls.

1893: THE GIRLS' OWN PAPER described some of the Smith dolls as follows: "We have now to mention a very different kind of rag-doll, for which we are indebted to the ingenuity of our American cousins. This is a doll whose shape is printed upon a sheet of calico, and that requires sewing together and stuffing. . . . The back and the front of this doll are provided, and a line is traced round the outer edges of the printed creature to indicate the exact parts that are to be cut out and where they join when sewn together. The face of the doll, its hands, feet, boots and under-garments are all indicated and printed in colours, and the worker has nothing to do but cut out the two pieces that make up the doll, face them so that the right side of the colouring is inside, and sew the two together leaving an opening at the waist. The linen shape is then turned so that its right side is outwards, and the stuffing commenced. The head is the first part stuffed, either with cotton wool or with finely-shredded crewel and Berlin wools, in fact with any-thing that is at hand and that is soft and pliable. When stuffing the head some regard to the shape of a head is necessary, as also are a few stitches through the head to keep the nose, eyes and mouth together and shapeable. The junction of neck and head is a little wide in the printed design and cannot be altered, as the head is stuffed through it; it therefore requires to be slightly drawn together with a thread; this thread narrows the neck and gives support to the head.

"Having stuffed the neck and head, fill the arms and legs with wadding and keep them as little cumbersome as possi-ble, and yet stuff them full, as unless well-stuffed they be-come limp and out of shape. When the body is well filled up and no wrinkles are visible at the joints of any of the limbs, the space through which the stuffing is introduced is sewn up, and the doll is ready for dressing.

"The under-garments, boots and stockings being already indicated on the printed linen, a dress is all that is necessary, and a pretty pink or blue silk frock trimmed with white lace makes a good garment to complete one of the cheapest rag-dolls in existence, as the sheet of coloured

linen that forms the foundation is sold for sixpence. [12½ cents.]

"One very good sheet represents a black baby. This baby is made of three pieces, the front of the child, the back, and an oval-shaped piece, sewn in after the stuffing is finished, and forming a stand which makes the baby seem standing on its feet. The black doll is dressed in a long pink garment, and holds a blue hat in one black hand. The queer one with its white eyeballs showing out of the dusky face, its solemn look and the novelty of the article renders this black baby highly appreciated by the youngsters. Being already clothed, it needs no more trouble expended on it than being cut out and sewn together, well-stuffed and the third piece lined with cardboard and sewn round the bottom of the skirt to form a stand."

1894: Applied for a German patent (D.R.G.M.) for Charity Smith's cloth dolls.★

Smith, Ella (née Gauntt). 1900–25. Roanoke, Ala. Made cloth dolls in a factory built by her husband, S. S. Smith. She had as many as 12 workers but each doll was handmade. The painted feet varied; some represented bare feet with stitched toes but most of them were one button slippers or low boots. The shoes were painted brown, black, pink or bright blue. At one time the dolls were made in as many as seven hts. from 12 to 27 in. (30.5 to 68.5 cm.). The factory closed in 1925 and Mrs. Smith died in 1932.

1921: Obtained a German patent for dolls' heads and parts. Dolls were dressed as boys or girls. (See Ill. 2451.)★

Smith, J. H. 1919. Applied for a British patent for dolls.

Smith, Mrs. Putnam David (Mabel). 1913–22. Santa Cruz, Calif. Mrs. P. D. Smith, a portrait painter, and her daughter, Margaret, modeled the heads for dolls. Their composition

2447. Cutout cloth doll designed by Celia and Charity Smith in 1889 manufactured by Cocheco. The hair and features are printed. Uncut sheet h. of dolls 15½ in. (39.5 cm.). *Coleman Collection.*

The dolls shown in Ills. 2448 and 2449 are versions of this same doll that have been sewn together to make a doll and then dressed.

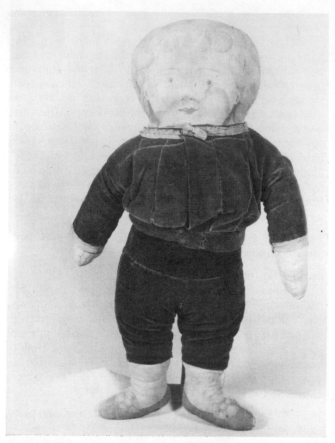

2448. Cut-out cloth doll designed by Celia and Charity Smith in 1889 made up into a doll and dressed. The hair and features are printed. H. 15 in. (38 cm.). *Coleman Collection.*

FIG. 2.

2449. Cutout cloth doll made up and described in THE GIRL'S OWN ANNUAL, December, 1893, a British periodical. The doll appears to be one of the dolls designed by Celia and Charity Smith in America. The directions suggest stuffing the head with "Cotton wool or with finely-shredded crewel and Berlin wools [and making] a few stitches through the head to keep the nose, eyes and mouth together and shapable." In other words do a little needle sculpturing.

Patented September 26, 1893.
JOINTED CLOTH DOLL, 10c.

2450. Jointed cloth doll patented by Celia and Charity Smith in 1893. This advertisement was in YOUTH'S COMPANION, 1894. The doll had a flat chromolithographed face and came on cotton yard goods ready for the purchaser to cut out, sew up and stuff.

MRS. S.S. SMITH
Manufacturer of and Dealer in
The Alabama Indestructible Doll
ROANOKE, ALA.

PATENTED
Sept. 26, 1905.

2451. Mark on Ella Smith's cloth doll.

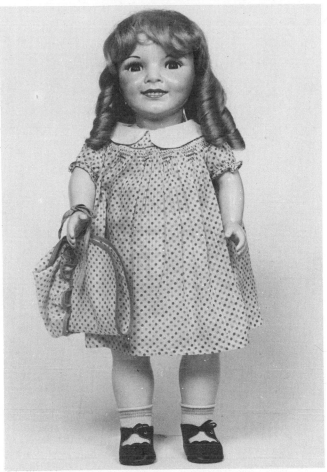

2452A & B. All-composition doll made by P.D. Smith has a wig, sleeping and flirting blue glass eyes, dimples and an open-closed mouth with six teeth. The socket head is on a composition shoulder plate that extends below the arms. The torso is flannel and there are composition arms and composition legs. The shoulders and hips have diagonal joints while the upper legs end in balls that fit into the sockets at the top of the lower legs. The knees and hands are dimpled and the fingernails are molded. Original clothes. Mark on head III. 2453. Stamp on body is a © within another circle and some words between the circles. H. 21½ in. (54.5 cm.). *Courtesy of the Margaret Woodbury Strong Museum. Photo by Harry Bickelhaupt.*

Mrs P. D. Smith

2453. Mark in ink on composition head of doll made by Mrs. P. D. Smith.

heads and arms were put on cloth bodies or old German composition bodies with the help of Mr. P. D. Smith. Most of the heads had glass eyes and many of them had dimples. The P. D. Smith dolls came in black as well as white versions and in various sizes from small dolls to life-size display dolls. Prices ranged from $5.00 to $8.00. The dolls were distributed by George C. Salch Co. of San Francisco.

1918: George Salch built a $100,000 factory to increase the business and produce more cheaply the P. D. Smith "Santa Cruz Dolls." But when the factory took over the business the dolls became inferior and demand declined.★

Smith, Sidney. 1926–29 and probably later. Drew "The Gumps" cartoon with characters that inspired the making of dolls.

1926: *Live Long Toys* started to make *Chester Gump* of "Art Leather" (oilcloth).

1929: *Andy Gump,* Chester Gump, *Ching Chow,* and *Uncle Bim* were made in all-bisque as dolls with jointed necks.

Smith, W. H., & Son. 1916–18. Shelton, Stoke-on-Trent, Staffs. Famous bookseller, produced dolls during World War I. They bought the *British Ceramic* heads and some of the limbs from local factories. In their own factory, named Toyland, they made dolls of various kinds; with or without wigs, dressed or undressed in a variety of sizes.

1916: Started with 14 designs and soon had 35 designs of dressed dolls, priced 25¢ to $1.48.

1917: Advertised 150 designs, some of the dolls had imitation leather bodies but most of them had cloth bodies. The limbs were composition or British Ceramic. A few of the dolls were celluloid such as a Pierrot or had celluloid faces; the latter were especially the Eskimo dolls in brown hair cloth or white fur. Other dolls included sports dolls, character dolls, *Wounded Tommies,* Wounded Tars, Nurses, Sailors and *Territorials* all with British Ceramic heads. Undressed dolls with British Ceramic heads, wigs, and cloth bodies were priced as low as 12¢.

1918: Advertised over 150 designs and a new better quality line. Hts. 17, 20, 24 and 30 in. (43, 51, 61 and 76 cm.). Advertised "French Dolls, dressed and undressed."

Smith & Hoyle (Clarendon Works). 1916–17. Longton, Stoke-on-Trent, Staffs. Made dolls with *British Ceramic* heads and limbs, wigs, dressed or undressed. Hts. 12 to 20 in. (30.5 to 51 cm.). The largest size cost $6.25 doz. wholesale undressed and $8.00 doz. wholesale dressed in a delaine frock and straw hat.

Smitty. Cutout cloth doll portraying the cartoon character drawn by *Walter Berndt* and licensed by Famous Artists Syndicate. Ht. ca. 8 in. (20.5 cm.).

Smitty. 1926–30. Made by *Live Long Toys* of printed Art Leather (oilcloth) stuffed with cotton. It represented the cartoon character drawn by *Walter Berndt* and bore the names "Smitty" and "Walter Berndt" on it.

1929: The doll wore a printed bright blue coat, a removable cap and necktie. Ht. 10 in. (25.5 cm.); priced $6.00 doz. wholesale.

Smitty. 1929. All-bisque doll with jointed neck and molded clothes made in Germany and distributed by *Marshall Field* and *Shackman*. It represented the cartoon character of this name drawn by *Walter Berndt*. Priced $1.80 doz. wholesale.

Smyth, John M., & Co. 1867–1914 and probably later. Chicago. Distributed dolls.

1914: Advertised *Kestner* bisque head dolls. Seven hts. 23 to 34 in. (58.5 to 86.5 cm.). There were also seven hts. of *Florodora* bisque head dolls with kid bodies, plus Mama-Papa talking bisque head dolls. A series of four composition head dolls with big round eyes and cloth bodies were named *Happy Gallagher, Big Eyed Gretchen, Ragtime Bill* and *Ragtime Maud*. Metal head dolls had either kidlyne or kid bodies. They also sold separate metal heads of various kinds including *Minerva* heads. Shoulder head celluloid dolls with cloth bodies and composition arms were described as "Knockabout unbreakable dolls." Celluloid shoulder heads came with wigs and glass eyes or with molded hair, in eight hts.

Snak. 1911–13. Felt doll representing a Gnome with a high hat, long nose, beard, and mules on its feet made by *Steiff* and distributed by *Borgfeldt* in the U.S. Hts. 22, 30, 43, and 50 cm. (8½, 12, 17, and 19½ in.); priced $1.44 to $3.30 in Germany in 1911 and $2.75 and up in New York in 1913. (See also **Snik.**)

Snappy Dolls. 1930. Cloth dolls made by *Live Long Toys* represented boys and girls. They had snaps concealed in their hands so that the two dolls could be joined together and with their feet apart, they could stand. Four styles; priced 25¢ to $1.00. Other manufacturers also made dolls that snapped together for example *S. & H. Novelty Co.*

Snéquireff, Leon. 1906. Paris. Imported *Koustari* dolls from Russia.

Snik. 1911–13. Felt doll representing a Gnome with a pointed hat, beard and mules on its feet, made by *Steiff* and distributed in the U.S. by *Borgfeldt*. Four hts. 22, 30, 43, and 50 cm. (8½, 12, 17, and 19½ in.); priced $2.75 and up, in New York in 1913.

Similar dolls were made at least until 1924 and probably only in the 22 cm. (8½ in.) size. They were named Gnome in 1916 and Dwarf in a catalog published for the English trade in 1924. (See also **Snak.**)

Snookums. 1927–28. Composition-head doll made by *Averill Manufacturing Co.* with a laughing mouth and two rows of teeth.

1927: Described in PLAYTHINGS, 1927, as "a faithful reproduction of the famous movie star in Universal-Stern Bros.

2454. Snik, one of the felt Gnomes made by Steiff. It has the Steiff button in its ear. The hair including the beard and eyebrows is sewed into place and is a grayish brown color. The stationary green glass eyes are inserted. It has a closed mouth, swivel neck and hips but the shoulder joint does not swivel. The hands and feet are extremely large. Original clothes with purple felt vest, white muslin shirt, blue plaid cotton pants, brown felt hat. The shoes have leather uppers and wooden soles. H. 30 cm. (12 in.). *Courtesy of Richard Wright. Photo by A. Jackson.*

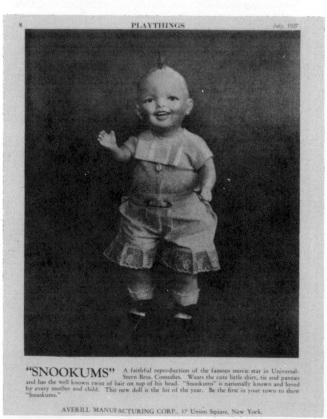

2455. Advertisement for Snookums dolls made by Averill Manufacturing Co. as shown in PLAYTHINGS, July, 1927.

2456. Bisque bonnet head covered with bisque granules to simulate snow thus making it a Snow Baby. The doll has painted features, a cloth body and bisque lower limbs. H. 8 in. (20.5 cm.). H. of shoulder head 1¾ in. (14.5 cm.). *Coleman Collection.*

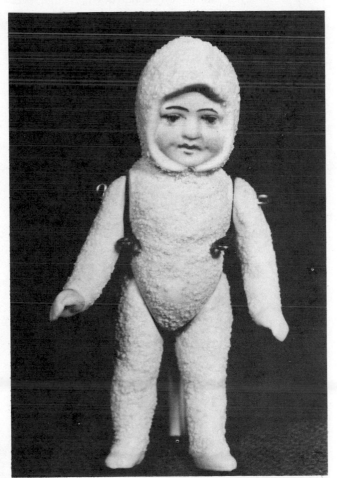

2457. All-bisque Snow Baby with porcelain granules sprinkled over it, painted features and wire joints at the shoulders and hips. Original molded snowsuit. H. 3½ in. (9 cm.). *Coleman Collection.*

comedies. Wears a cute little shirt [bow] tie and panties and has the well-known twist of hair on top of his head." The pants were attached to the shirt with a safety pin in front.

1928: New costume consisted of white rompers with flowered cuffs.

Snookums. 1930. Cloth doll designed by *Mabel Lucie Attwell* and made by *Chad Valley*. It had its mouth in a broad grin, wispy hair gathered into a topknot and wore a short sleeved shirt and long trousers. Ht. 16 in. (40.5 cm.).

Snow Babies. 1901–30 and later. All-bisque dolls made by *Bähr & Pröschild, Hertwig, C. F. Kling, Kley & Hahn* (all of these factories except Hertwig were in the Ohrdruf area) and probably other manufacturers of dolls. These dolls were covered from head to toe with bits of ground porcelain to resemble snow. Most of them had no joints but a few were jointed at the shoulders and hips. Sometimes only a shoulder head wore the snow baby cap and the body was made of cloth. The name "Snow Baby" was given to Peary's daughter, Marie Ahnighito Peary, born 1893, by the Eskimos. Mrs. Peary wrote a book, published in 1901, in which she called her daughter "Snow Baby" and showed a picture of the little girl in a white snow suit. Hts. usually 1 to 6 in. (2.5 to 15 cm.).

1910: Advertised by *Shackman,* had no joints. Ht. 3 in. (7.5 cm.); priced 20¢ with a sled.

1914: Advertised by *Marshall Field* and also called "Alaska Tots." Four styles, two with skis. Hts. 1½ to 3 in. (4 to 7.5 cm.); priced 70¢ to $1.50 doz. wholesale.

1928: About the time Byrd went to the South Pole, Snow Babies were distributed by *Butler Bros.* Dolls without joints came in three positions. Ht. 2½ in. (6.5 cm.); priced 80¢ doz. wholesale.

Snow Baby. 1918. Doll made by *Effanbee,* had a composition-head with sleeping eyes and wore an angora suit and cap.

Snow Bird. 1913. Doll advertised in TOYS AND NOVELTIES by *Claflin & Co.* was dressed for winter sports allegedly in the latest costumes from St. Moritz; priced 50¢ and up.

Snow Boys and Girls. 1927. Cloth dolls of powder puff plush with embroidered facial features; made by *Woolnough* and distributed by *Davis & Voetsch.*

Snow Doll. 1915. Name of a doll with beady black eyes, rosy cheeks, body stuffed with a buoyant material so that it floated, dressed in white terry cloth and handled by *Whyte, Ridsdale.* Four hts.; priced 13¢ to 62¢.

Snow Fairy. See **Schneewittchen.**

Snow Flake. 1929. All-bisque doll with rolling eyes and molded clothes, represented a black cartoon character; distributed by *Butler Bros.* Ht. 2¼ in. (6 cm.); priced 84¢ doz. wholesale.

Snow Girls. See **Snow Boys and Girls.**

Snow White. 1917–19. Portrait doll of Marguerite Clark as she appeared in the title role of the movie SNOW WHITE:

made by the *American Toy & Manufacturing Co.* The doll wore a pink dress, a silver crown studded with rosebuds and topped with a filmy veil that fell to the hem of the dress in back. On its feet were Princess style slippers. ★

Snowbell. 1917–18. Line of wigged, stockinet dolls made by *Fretwell.*

Snow-Bell. See **Schneeglöcken (Little Snowdrop).**

Snowdrop. See **Schneeglöcken (Little Snowdrop).**

Sobe. (Belgian Soldier). Before 1911–16. Felt doll made by *Steiff* represented a Belgian soldier wearing a shoulder sash. Hts. 28 and 35 cm. (11 and 14 in.).

Société Anct. Sustrac. See **Fantaisies Parisiennes.**

Société Art ésienne. 1926. Fruges, Pas-de-Calais. France. Made clothes for dolls.

Société au Bébé Rose. 1910. Paris. Registered a trademark in France for dolls. The trademark was usually printed in violet. See Ill. 2458. ★

2458. Mark used by the Société au Bébé Rose.

Société de Celluloid Industrielle. See **Société Industrielle de Celluloid.**

Société des "Yeux Expression" et "Poupée Mystère." 1926. Paris. Manufactured dolls.

Société du Caoutchouc Manufacturé. 1920s. France. Member of the *Chambre Syndicale,* advertised rubber bébés and undressed dolls.

Société Etna. 1926. Paris. Asmiérs, Limoges, and Marseille, France. Manufactured jointed dolls. Had a London representative.

Société Française de Fabrication de Bébés & Jouets (S.F.B.J.). 1899–1930 and later. Paris and Montreuil-sous-Bois. Towards the end of the nineteenth century competition grew with the increasing number of Germans producing dolls and the fact that dolls could be made more cheaply in Germany than in France. According to Mme. Florence Poisson, curator of the Roybet Fould Museum, the following companies joined together in 1899 to form the Société Française de Fabrication de Bébés & Jouets (S.F.B.J.): *Adolph-Henri Bouchet,* Salomon *Fleischmann, Gaultier* Frères, Emile-Louis Genty *(Rabery & Delphieu),* Paul Girard *(Bru), Adolphe-Benoit Gobert,* Emile-Louis *Jumeau* and Mme. Jumeau, *Henri Pintel & Ernest Godchaux, Frédéric Remignard* and *Arthur Wertheimer.* These companies brought to the S.F.B.J. the rights for the following dolls: *Bébé Bru, Bébé Charmant, Bébé Colosse, Bébé de Paris, Bébé Géant, Bébé*

Jumeau, Eden Bébé, Le Baby, and *Le Petit Chérubin.*

The Jumeaus rented their factories to the S.F.B.J.

Gaultier Frères, another company with a factory having ovens for making porcelain heads, may have also leased their factory to the S.F.B.J., since it was not listed as being transferred. Only Fleischmann, the head of the S.F.B.J., appeared to have transferred his factories. But there is no evidence that the Fleischmann factories had ovens for making porcelain heads. It is known that Fleischmann used some *Simon & Halbig* heads.

Fleischmann was the largest stockholder when the S.F.B.J. was formed and was in charge until 1914 when he was sequestered. The editors of DOLL WORLD in 1952 had been corresponding with M. Moynot then head of the S.F.B.J. According to him, Fleischmann's son-in-law was M. Arnaud and M. Moynot was Arnaud's son-in-law. On the other hand it has been reported that the Girard family were heads of the S.F.B.J. after Fleischmann left, namely Paul Eugene Girard, then Eugene Girard and finally André Girard. M. Moynot reported that Girard's grandson, presumably André Girard, was the commercial manager of the S.F.B.J.

M. M. Moynot and Girard were the ones who originated the error in the name of François Gaultier, calling him Fernand Gautier by mistake. This is an excellent example of the importance of primary, contemporary sources and the lack of accuracy of information handed down through several generations. In 1952 two elderly female members of the Jumeau family were still stockholders in the S.F.B.J. according to M. Moynot. Mme. Porot is searching primary sources for information on the S.F.B.J.

The S.F.B.J. used a size number code extending from at least 13/0 to 16 but the variations make it impossible to match a height with a size number; only the upward trend is apparent. Since the S.F.B.J. heads were made in several different porcelain factories and with a variety of molds belonging to a number of companies, the differences seem logical. In the first COLLECTOR'S ENCYCLOPEDIA OF DOLLS, it was stated "Character faces . . . seem to have been numbered from at least 203 to 252." The mold numbers 201 through 225 were usually marked "Tête Jumeau." Mme. Porot has discovered that some and possibly all of these mold numbers under 226 were in existence in 1896. Mold numbers 226 and above were marked S.F.B.J. These character head dolls were definitely made by the S.F.B.J. and included mold numbers 226, 227 (black), 229 (a walker), 230, 233, 234, 235, 236, 237, 238, 239 *(Poulbot),* 242, (nursing doll based on a 1910 patent), 245 (roguish eyes), 247 (pouty), 248 (pouty), 250, 251 and 252 (pouty). Mold numbers 263 (black), 271 (character baby), 284, 301, 306, and 337 probably were made later.

The mark on the doll in illustration 390 in the first COLLECTOR'S ENCYCLOPEDIA OF DOLLS should read "S.F.B.J. //248" instead of "S.F.B.J.//2LS."

1900: 2000 people were employed in making 15,000 bébés per day; 200 different pieces of heads, arms, and legs were molded each day. Dolls were of all types from a poupard costing a sou (fraction of a cent) to a dressed bébé costing $30.00 or more.

1905: Started to make *Bleuette*.

1913: *Gamage* advertised several dolls, black and white, that resembled the S.F.B.J. character head dolls. These were named Laughing Black *Sambo*, Sambo's Little Sister and Sailor Boy. The latter had a bisque head resembling mold #237, ball jointed composition body, long sailor trousers, sailor hat with an inscription. Hts. 15 and 18 in. (38 and 45.5 cm.); priced $1.94 and $2.69.

1914–23: London agent was *Henry S. Benjamin*. S.F.B.J. undressed and dressed character dolls were advertised in England.

1916: TOYS AND NOVELTIES advertised S.F.B.J. character dolls dressed as soldiers.

The 35 S.F.B.J. dolls purchased by the Carnegie Museum had bisque heads, stationary glass eyes, open mouths with teeth, ball-jointed composition bodies with wooden upper legs and arms. The two mold #237 dolls had flocked hair while the remaining mold #238 dolls all had wigs; 26 of these dolls wore French historical or regional costumes, six dolls wore Russian style costumes. The remaining three were in British, Italian, and Swiss costumes. The marks on the dolls were "S.F.B.J.//237// Paris//4" and "S.F.B.J.//238//Paris//4." Ht. for both was 18½ in. (47 cm.).

1917: *Marshall Field* advertised S.F.B.J. dolls dressed as soldiers of various nations including a Turk.

1918: French Bébé sold in England included Bébé Caractére, *Bébé Français*, *Bébé Merveille*, *Bébé Soleil*, Eden Bébé, and *Paris Bébé*.

1919: TOYS AND NOVELTIES called the S.F.B.J. "Société Française des Bébés Jumeaux."

1920: Dolls handled by Benjamin included Bébé Français, Bébé Jumeau, Eden Bébé, Merveille, Paris Bébé, and *Victory Doll*, which seems to have been made by S.F.B.J.

1920s: The S.F.B.J. Chambre Syndicale number 149 was generally included in the *Unis France* mark. The ANNUAIRE CHAMBRE SYNDICALE listed S.F.B.J. factories or shops at 8 rue Pastourelle; 160 rue de Picpus; 6 rue Montempoivre, all in Paris; plus Montreuil-sous-Bois; Champigneulles, Meurthe and Moselle. The ANNUAIRE advertised for S.F.B.J., Bébé Bru, Bébé Jumeau (in familiar flowered print chemise with "Bébé Jumeau" on the belt) and Eden Bébé; bébés with stationary eyes and bébés with sleeping eyes; walking bébés; talking bébés; bébés maillot; bébés culottes; bébés with composition heads; undressed bébés and dolls; dressed bébés and dolls in various costumes including regional French costumes and costumes of other countries; *mignonnettes*; dressed and undressed *carton poupards*; cloth dolls; *Esquimaux*; clowns; *cymbaliers*; *Gugusses*; *Marottes*; Pierrots; *Polichinelles*; clothes for dolls included footwear and trunks containing trousseaux.

Made Roullet & Decamps' *Clauderies*, according to the Porots.

1924: LES JOUJOUX reported that the S.F.B.J. was now entirely a French firm. There were 250 office employees and 1000 men and women workers who produced 71,000

pieces, that is arms, legs, hands, and bodies representing 11,000 to 12,000 dozen dolls. Articulated dolls had 11 pieces and non-articulated dolls had five pieces. A single doll passed through the hands of 20 different people, nine for the body and 11 for the head. Four million dolls a year were produced with a wide range in price.

Registered a short, fat, felt-head doll with wig, painted teeth, fingers together, thumb separate, arms bent, and toe delineated.

1925: Won a Grand Prize for bébés and dolls at the Paris Exposition of Arts Décoratifs.

1926: Renewed the trademark registered for Bébé Français, Bébé Jumeau, *Bébé Prodige* and Paris Bébé.

1927: Listed in Paris directory as "Sté de Bébés Jumeau" with a shop at 8 rue Pastourel and eight factories.

1928: Advertised Bébé Bru, Bébé Jumeau, Eden Bébé, silent or talking Poupards, Esquimaux, and stuffed dolls of plush or muslin. Made *Bambino*, infant brother of Bleuette.

Ca. 1930: Bisque head bébés on composition bodies marked *Bébé Vrai Modèle*.

1938: Made the Princess dolls for the two little British Princesses. The bisque heads were marked "JUMEAU//PARIS//PRINCESS."

1950s: Janet Johl reported that S.F.B.J. was using the Bébé Jumeau and Eden Bébé molds as late as the 1950s and the Bébé Bru molds until 1930. But they registered their Bébé Bru and Eden Bébé trademarks in 1953. In 1952 M. Moynot stated, "The company has all of the old Jumeau molds and can reproduce them in finest bisque with closed mouths or open. They are making a limited number of each model, numbering them and dressing them in high fashion." These dolls were a continuing production. At the time of Queen Elizabeth's coronation in 1953 the S.F.B.J. made a large bisque head doll which was not a real portrait, but was named for the Queen. It had a human hair wig, glass eyes, open mouth, composition body and a deluxe costume. The name Jumeau was "enameled" on the back of the head or neck. See also **Bébé Jumeau,** after 1898 and **Manufacture of Dolls, Commercial: Made in France and Germany Compared.** (See Ills. 2459–2478.)★

Société Fouquet & Douville. See **Fouquet & Douville.†**

Société Guttmann & Schiffnie. See **Guttmann & Schiffnie.**

Société Industrielle de Celluloid. 1902–30 and later. Paris and elsewhere in France. In 1900 it was known as the Société Industrielle de Cellulose and in 1906 the Cellulose in the name became "Celluloid." They appeared to have begun making celluloid dolls about 1902. They used the trade names Sicoid and *Sicoine* for their celluloid and the initials S.I.C. and S.I.M.P. Sicoid was a combination of acetate and cellulose. This company was involved in several mergers and during World War I they made explosives. *Henry S. Benjamin* and Th. Shaedel (Schaedeli) were their London agents.

1910: The Bonet Celluloid factory at Geilles near Oyonnax

was taken over by the Société Industrielle de Celluloid.

1911: Patented a celluloid swimming doll in France.

1912: Patented a drinking baby in France.

1913: Patented in France a doll that combined talking and eye movement.

1924: Merged with the Société Général pour la Fabrication des Matières Plastiques with factories at Chauffry, at Oyonnax and at Villetaneuse. The parent company had been Compagnie Française du Celluloid, founded in 1875.

1927: The successor of these companies was Société Nobel Française which used the initials S N F and inherited the trade name Sicoid. Their trademark was a Wyvern. (See Ills. 2479–2486.)★

Société Industrielle de Ferblanterie. 1918. Paris. Produced rubber dolls that were dressed and undressed. Dolls distributed by *Henry Benjamin*.

Société Industrielle de Jouets Français. See **Gesland.**

Société Nobel Française. See **Société Industrielle de Celluloid.**

Société Nouvelle des Bébés Réclames. 1929–30 and later. Montreuil-sous-Bois, France. Made dressed and undressed bébés with composition heads.

Société Nouvelle des Établissements. See **A. D. T.**

Société Radiguet & Cordonnier. See **Radiguet & Cordonnier.**

Society Belle. 1895. Name of a doll with a bisque head, wig, dressed; distributed by *Butler Bros.* Ht. 20 in. (51 cm.); priced $4.25 doz. wholesale.

Society Buds. 1914. Name of a doll with bisque head, wig, sleeping eyes, composition body jointed at the shoulders, elbows, hips and knees, removable clothes; distributed by *Butler Bros.* Ht. 17 in. (43 cm.); priced $11.00 doz. wholesale.

Society Miss. 1921. Name of a cloth-body doll with removable felt garments including a cape; made by *Chessler Co.*

Soe (English Soldier). 1905–13. Felt doll with long feet made by *Steiff*, representing a short, fat English soldier with a long nose, or a tall thin English soldier. Each wore a pill box style hat with a strap under the chin. A representation of this doll was the hero of a book entitled PIERRE PONS. The 1929 English translation of the book was illustrated by Paul Guignebault.

1905–11: Hts. 35 and 50 cm. (15 and 19½ in.); priced 82¢ in Germany in 1911.

1913: Sold by *Gamage* in two versions, one as a fat doll which was portrayed in PIERRE PONS wearing a red jacket and blue trousers. Ht. 17 in. (43 cm.). The tall thin soldier was advertised as being 20 in. (51 cm.) tall; both dolls cost 88¢.

Sof. (French Soldier). Before 1911–16. Felt doll with long feet made by *Steiff* and representing a French soldier. It wore

a kepi. Hts. 28 and 35 cm. (11 and 14 in.). This doll was portrayed as a character in the 1929 English translation of the French book, PIERRE PONS, illustrated by Paul Guignebault.

2459A & B. Bisque head doll made by the Société Française de Fabrication de Bébés & Jouets (S.F.B.J.). It has a wig, painted blue eyes, an open-closed mouth with four teeth, and a five-piece jointed composition body. Original regional costume. A note that came with the doll states, "Albania? costume called 'Chalwar' balloon pants." Mark: S.F.B.J.//60//PARIS//11/0. H. 11 in. (28 cm.). *Coleman Collection.*

2460A & B. Bisque head doll made by the S.F.B.J. has flocked hair and blond lamb's wool mustache and beard, stationary blue glass eyes (the two eyebrows differ in depth), open mouth with six upper teeth, and a fully jointed composition body. Original uniform has "11" embroidered on the collar. Mark: S.F.B.J.//227 //PARIS. H. 24½ in. (62 cm.). *Private collection.*

2461. Bisque head doll made by S.F.B.J. from mold #230 with black wig, stationary blue glass eyes, pierced ears, open mouth with teeth, dimple in chin and a ball-jointed composition body with the usual brown composition. Mark: Ill. 2472. H. 25 in. (63.5 cm.). *Courtesy of Iverna and Irving Foote. Photo by Irving Foote.*

2462. S.F.B.J. bisque head mold #230 doll has a wig, sleeping blue glass eyes, pierced ears, open mouth with four upper teeth, and a fully jointed composition body of the typical brown composition. Mark: Ill. 2473. H. 17½ in. (44.5 cm.). *Courtesy of Iverna and Irving Foote. Photo by Irving Foote.*

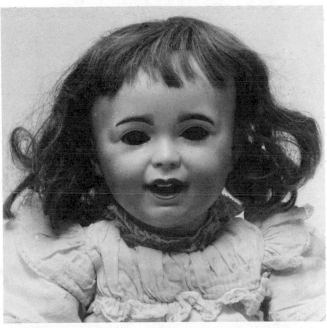

2463. S.F.B.J. bisque head doll with wig, sleeping brown glass eyes, open-closed mouth with two upper teeth, and a jointed composition body. Original clothes. Mark: S.F.B.J.//236//PARIS //10. H. 20 in. (51 cm.). *Courtesy of Sotheby Parke Bernet Inc., N.Y.*

2464. Pair of bisque-head dolls made by S.F.B.J. dressed in clothes contemporary with the dolls. Doll on the left has a blond wig, sleeping blue glass eyes with hair eyelashes and a fully jointed toddler body. Mark: S.F.B.J.//247//PARIS//8. H. 18½ in. (47 cm.). Doll on right has flocked hair, narrow stationary blue glass eyes, open mouth with teeth, and a ball-jointed composition body. Mark: S.F.B.J.//237//PARIS//6. H. 17½ in. (44.5 cm.). *Courtesy of Sotheby Parke Bernet Inc., N.Y.*

2465. Bisque head doll made by the S.F.B.J. with a wig, stationary blue glass eyes, open mouth with four upper teeth, and a fully jointed composition body. Clothes contemporary with the doll. Mark: S.F.B.J. //238//PARIS//4. H. 16 in. (40.5 cm.). *Private collection.*

2466. S.F.B.J. bisque-head doll with wig, stationary blue glass roguish eyes, closed mouth almost a single line, and five piece composition body. Original Alsatian costume with molded and painted footwear. Mark: S.F.B.J.//245//PARIS. H. 7 in. (18 cm.). *Courtesy of Sotheby Parke Bernet Inc., N.Y.*

2467. Bisque head lady doll made by the S.F.B.J. with a wig, sleeping glass eyes, pierced ears, open-closed mouth with four upper teeth and a ball-jointed wood and composition lady-type body. Clothes are contemporary with the doll. Mark: S.F.B.J.// 250// PARIS. H. 19 in. (48 cm.). *Courtesy of June Jeffcott.*

2468. Bisque head mold #251, doll made by S.F.B.J. has a wig, sleeping blue glass eyes, open mouth with teeth and a fully jointed toddler composition body. H. 15 in. (38 cm.). *Courtesy of Sotheby Parke Bernet Inc., N.Y.*

2469. S.F.B.J. bisque-head doll with a wig, sleeping blue glass eyes, closed mouth and a jointed composition body. Mark: S.F.B.J.//252//PARIS//6. H. 15 in. (38 cm.). *Courtesy of Sotheby Parke Bernet Inc., N.Y.*

2470. Black S.F.B.J. bisque-head doll with a black wig, sleeping brown glass eyes, and five-piece composition body with painted slippers. Mark: S.F.B.J.//301//PARIS. H. 12 in. (30.5 cm.). *Courtesy of the Margaret Woodbury Strong Museum. Photo by Harry Bickelhaupt.*

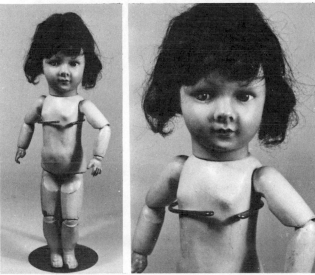

2471A & B. All-composition doll with mohair wig, painted features, flange neck, wooden arms and upper legs. Composition of the feet resembles the brown composition found in S.F.B.J. dolls. The face closely resembles the bisque head S.F.B.J. mold # 306. Soles of the feet are marked "4." H. 14½ in. (37 cm.). *Coleman Collection.*

2472. S.F.B.J. 230 PARIS 10

2473. S.F.B.J. 230 PARIS

2474. 23 S.F.B.J. 236 PARIS 4

2475. 22 S.F.B.J. 251 PARIS 4

2476. R. S.F.B.J. 301 PARIS 8.

2477. + S.F.B.J. 301 PARIS 11

2478.

2472–2478. Marks on S.F.B.J. bisque-head dolls.

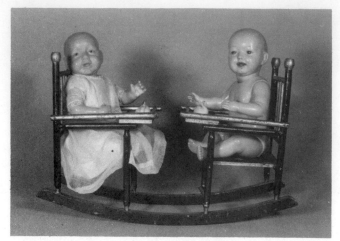

2479. All-celluloid doll made by the Société Industrielle de Celluloid has blond painted hair, blue intaglio eyes, and a closed mouth. It is jointed at the neck, shoulders and hips on a bent limb baby body. Body marked: (Picture of a Wyvern) //France// 30. H. 30 cm. (12 in.). *Courtesy of Shirley Buchholz.*

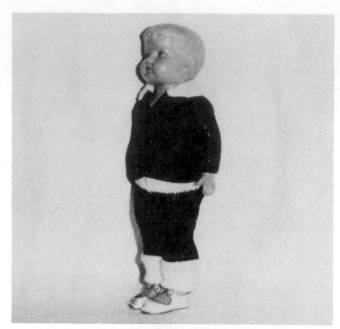

2480. All celluloid doll made by the Société Industrielle de Celluloid has molded and painted hair and eyes, closed mouth, is jointed at the shoulders, legs apart. Mark: Ill. 2482. H. 13½ in. (34 cm.). *Courtesy of Ruth Whittier.*

2481. Celluloid head made by the Société Industrielle de Celluloid has molded and painted bobbed hair, plastic brown eyes, hair eyelashes, a pursed closed mouth and a ball jointed composition body. Mark: Ill. 2483. H. 16 in. (40.5 cm.). *Courtesy of Richard Withington. Photo by Barbara Jendrick.*

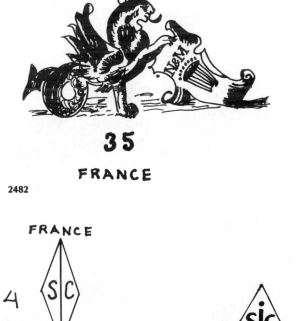

2482–2484. Marks used by the Société Industrielle de Celluloid and its successors.

2485. All-celluloid black doll made by the Société Nobel Française has molded black kinky hair, molded brown painted eyes, ethnic type nose and mouth. The bent limb baby body is jointed at the neck, shoulders and hips. Mark embossed on head: FRANCE//SNF [in a diamond] //FRANCE//45. H. 45 cm. (18 in.). *Courtesy of the Margaret Woodbury Strong Museum. Photos by Harry Bickelhaupt.*

2486. Société Nobel Française mark on a celluloid doll.

Soff, Konrad, & Co. Ca. 1930 and later. Nürnberg, Bavaria. Distributed *Kestner* dolls.

Softanlite. 1921. *Mama* type doll in the *Madame Hendren* line made by *Averill Manufacturing Co.*

Softanlite. 1930. Name of a doll made by the *Teddy Toy Co.*

Soho (Dutch Soldier). 1911 and earlier. Felt doll with long feet made by *Steiff* and representing a soldier of Holland. It wore a kepi and belt. Hts. 28 and 35 cm. (11 and 14 in.).

Soho Bazar. London. Area where many early dolls were sold including those of *Mme. Montanari* and Charles *Marsh.*

Soldier Boy. 1914–15. Composition head, full jointed doll was dressed in representations of the regulation uniforms of various nations. These dolls made by *Amberg* carried their national flag and a gun that it was claimed would actually shoot. Ht. 15 in. (38 cm.); priced $1.00 and up.

Soldier Boy. 1917. Stuffed leather doll with colors on the leather representing the uniform of an army private with a belt having U.S.A. on it, puttees and a brimmed hat. The doll made by *Western Art Leather Co.* carried a rifle and an American flag.

Soldier Boy. 1926. One of a line of Nursery Rhyme dolls made by *Jedco* and distributed by *Louis Wolf & Co.*

Soldier Boy. 1930. Segmented doll made of turned birch wood by *J. W. Pickering & Co.* It had a ball-shaped head with a pillbox hat, three balls for the arms and long bell-bottom trousers. Heavily coated lacquer provided the color for the doll. Ht. 7¾ in. (19.5 cm.).

Soldier Dolls. See Military Costume Dolls.

Soldier Joy. 1929. Doll made of wooden beads and advertised by *Blimlick.*

Solomon, Mannie, & Co. 1923. New York City. Exhibited miniature wooden dolls dressed in "authentic" costumes of Mandalay, Burma which had been designed and made by this company.

Sommer, Karl. 1907–10. Vienna. Listed in directories under Dolls and Dolls' Heads according to Dr. Eva Moskovszky.

Sommer, W. L. 1880s. New York City. Distributed dolls.

Sommereisen, Karl. 1897–98. Iserlohn, Germany. Obtained a German patent for an aluminum doll's head.★

Sommers, E. L., & Co. 1921–30. New York City. Produced rubber dolls and dolls that were activated by squeezing a ball connected to a bellows inside the doll.

1926: Advertised *Kewpie*-type dolls.

1927: Produced colorful rubber dolls which took off their hats and crawling *Buttercup* which was activated by a rubber squeeze ball.
Distributed baby dolls in baskets and cradles.

Sommers, G., & Co. 1924. St. Paul, Minn. Distributed wholesale all-bisque dolls with or without wigs, celluloid dolls, composition head dolls with cloth bodies including *Mama* dolls, especially those made by *K & K.*

Son Brothers & Co. 1917–19. San Francisco, Calif. Their lines of dolls were created in Japan under their own supervision and the dolls and dolls' heads were imported into the U.S.

1919: Advertised 100 style nos. of bisque heads with movable eyes.

Sonia. 1927. Trade name for a doll.

Sonneberg, Thür. (in the Duchy of Saxe-Meiningen). 1600s–1930 and later. Sonneberg and its satellite towns such as Bettelhecken, Hüttensteinach, Judenbach, Köppelsdorf, Oberlind and Wildenheid were known all over the world for the dolls produced in this area. According to *Adolf Fleischmann* carved wooden dolls were made in this area in the 1600s before the 30 Years War (1618–48) and in the 1700s. They were sent to Nürnberg for distribution. At the Neustadt Museum only a couple of miles from Sonneberg there are two wooden dolls of the 1700s that belonged to the Fleischmann family according to the Neustadt Museum records. These dolls resemble very closely the wooden dolls which are thought to have an English origin of the 1700s. (See Ill. 2748.)

DEUTSCHE SPIELWAREN ZEITUNG in 1930 gave a history of Sonneberg as follows:

By 1700 Painters used "bright shining colours which were dissolved in size and in order to get a polish they were given a thin coating of size solution after drying." All the Painters were called *Bismuth Painters* although Bismuth, a gray paint, was not used; instead, colored paints were used.

Around 1735 documents state that painters were in Sonneberg in large numbers. The people of Sonneberg traded toys all over the world. INTERNATIONAL STUDIO of 1923 claimed that the Sonneberg dolls of this period were made of turned wood.

By 1770 the dolls were carved of white wood in the area surrounding Sonneberg and then painted by the 19 Bismuth Painters in Sonneberg.

Beginning in 1780 the Embossers worked on dolls. Previously Embossers had covered and impressed the features and details of carved or turned wooden figures with a dough made of lime-water and black flour. By 1780 they were using this so-called dough to mold into dolls. Unfortunately the dough became moldy and mice and insects ate it.

In 1807 papier-mâché was introduced by *Friedrich Müller* as a raw material for making dolls. The papier-mâché was used for the heads and at first the body and limbs were made of wood. Later the heads and limbs were made of papier-mâché or china and the bodies of kid or canvas stuffed with sawdust according to an article in INTERNATIONAL STUDIO.

The removal of the continental blockade in 1813 and the expanding use of papier-mâché caused the doll making industry to thrive.

At first molding had been done freehand but by about 1820 plaster, sulphur (brimstone), and wooden molds began to be used in making dolls.

After 1820 dolls with papier-mâché heads on kid bodies having wooden limbs, both dressed and undressed, were most in demand.

1851 was the beginning of the Golden Era of Sonneberg dolls. Dolls began to have wax heads and limbs as well as porcelain. Up to this time the dolls had represented adults or older children. But when *Edmund Lindner* returned from visiting the Great London Exhibition he brought back information on the construction of baby dolls which were then called *Täuflinge*. Later the word Täufling seems to have been used for any doll dressed in a chemise. Soon many of the doll makers in Sonneberg were producing Täufling dolls.

By 1928 more than 40,000 people or over half the population of Sonneberg were engaged in the toy industry which was largely the making of dolls. Formerly home workers prevailed but by 1928 factory work had been instituted.

From other sources it is learned that most of the buildings in Sonneberg were factories for making dolls or their parts. Business prospered especially from around 1885 when *Armand Marseille* and *Ernst Heubach* started their porcelain factories where bisque heads were made in Köppelsdorf, a suburb of Sonneberg. Many of the dolls were made by home workers and their families of all ages. These people were poorly paid and if they could sell their dolls to American dealers they made more money than if they sold to local dealers. However they seldom had enough money to invest in required materials and to wait until the Americans came. Thus they had to sell their dolls to local *Verlegers* who controlled large businesses.

1860s: One of the dolls in the Sonneberg Museum, made in the 1860s had a mama-papa voice. This was probably one of the early Täuflinge (so-called *Motschmann* type).

1899–1902: The STRAND magazine in 1902 published the following: "In 1899 the German doll makers made a special effort to please the American customers. . . . The inhabitants of the Philippine Islands according to the Sonneberg designers are a race of huge savages . . . their Cuban brothers if not so formidable in size, are fully as terrifying to look upon, whilst the representatives of the United States Army and Navy seemed strangely teutonic in appearance, both as regard their uniforms and features. Another [doll was] Colonel Roosevelt, very fierce of aspect, in the uniform of the Rough Riders. This . . . was intended to appeal to the patriotism of the youthful American, who was not expected to object to his hero being made in Germany. (See Ill. 2588.)

"Most of the dolls treasured by the American children of to-day come from Germany. Sonneberg, the center of the doll-making industry, is a town of 12,000 inhabitants, most of whom are engaged throughout the year in the manufacture of [dolls]."

1910: McCALL'S MAGAZINE reported that one of the largest Sonneberg factories sent to America over a million dolls each year. This factory possessed a secret formula for making the powder from which the enamel paint used on papier-mâché heads and bodies was manufactured.

1911: TOYS AND NOVELTIES reported that wood and papier-mâché dolls were made in the Sonneberg homes while large factories produced the bisque-head dolls. Most of these dolls were exported to the U.S. and England.

1914: An American toy buyer reported his impressions of Sonneberg in TOYS AND NOVELTIES, April 1914.

"Sonneberg, beyond all doubt is the largest doll-making city in the world. The factories give employment to thousands of workmen, but as a rule only a few [actually] work at the factory. Toward the end of the week you will see the good old Saxon women walking through the streets of the city with their week's product in large baskets on their heads or shoulders or strapped to their backs, wending their way to the office of the company by whom they are engaged to exchange their toys for their money. Here is where the cheap labor is encountered. In some instances whole families of toy-makers work for what one man should receive. There are hundreds of families there who have been making toys for centuries. It used to be said in Germany 'once a toy-maker always a toy-maker,' and this is true in a degree yet. In some of the little cottages toys have been made for years and years—the work having been done possibly by three or four generations. Aged men and women devote all of their time to making toys, and as their children grow up they, too, are put to work, and from that day on they are toy-makers.

"The toy-makers of Sonneberg have no labor organizations, such as exist in Nuremberg. . . . The business is carried on there today very much, one would imagine[,] as it was a century ago."

1917: TOYS AND NOVELTIES reported that 30,000 people in Sonneberg, who were formerly producing dolls, were currently employed in war contracts.

1919–23: An article in INTERNATIONAL STUDIO entitled, "Dolls—Art of all Rages," emphasized the fact that dolls with natural expressions and not just "sweet faces" were popular. This article stated, "Almost all the single parts and accessories are made by home workers in the villages, while the dolls are finished [assembled] in special shops and then delivered to firms in Sonneberg for export. Several American firms have branches in Sonneberg and ship dolls direct to the United States and to other parts of the world. In this industrial art, the latest developments are the ultra modernistic dolls of the post-war time."

1920: TOYS AND NOVELTIES stated "The pretty dolls of Sonneberg are out of favour. . . . They are found fault with now, their eyes seem too light for real eyes, their hair too curly, their bodies too dumpy for artistic merit."

1923: TOYS AND NOVELTIES reported that few new lines were presented by the Sonneberg manufacturers, that they showed mostly pre-war lines. *Borgfeldt* and *Strobel & Wilken* moved permanently to Sonneberg and the German doll trade with America began to prosper once again. This can also be seen by the following account from the British journal TOYS AND FANCY GOODS TRADER, March, 1923.

"A number of American firms have established permanent buying and storage premises at Sonneberg, but some, amongst them Woolworths, have obtained control of certain factories and collecting agencies. . . . The later novelties are characteristic of special American demands. . . . Sonneberg is now turning out all kinds of American celebration novelties, from George Washington with miniature cherry tree and hatchet complete. . . . The aspect of the streets, factories and storage structures is now American. Important firms from Detroit & Pittsburg [sic] have recently established permanent premises at Sonneberg, and others from various American cities are now negotiating for sites on which to build structures for buying and storage. Naturally the bulk of the output in the future will be for American export."

1924: A U.S. Department of Commerce Report stated that the majority of Sonneberg inhabitants were protestants, possibly descendants of persecuted French Huguenots. Before the days of railways, toy shipments from Nürnberg going north passed through Sonneberg which encouraged

the toy industry there. In 1924 about 20,000 people were employed in the making of dolls of the medium and better grades. These were made exclusively by home workers; bisque and china heads were made in factories in and around Sonneberg.

This report stated that, "95 percent of the dolls produced in Sonneberg were exported."

1926: PLAYTHINGS reported that crowds of women in Sonneberg carried large baskets of dolls strapped upon their backs. These burdens sometimes six feet above their heads were carried from the homes to the assembling plants.

1928: PLAYTHINGS stated "The demand for dolls which used to constitute the principal item of manufacture in the Sonneberg district, is now relatively small, and several factories are said to have taken up the manufacture of textiles instead." (See also **Dressel, Fleischmann** and **Lindner** for the genealogy of three of the important old Sonneberg doll-making families, and also **Schools.**)★

Sonneberg Industrial School. Various dates have been given for the founding of this school. One source puts it as early as 1851. In 1910 McCALL'S MAGAZINE stated that it was founded in 1857. While according to the Ciesliks' research it was not founded until 1883 and the founders were: Josef Bergmann; *C. Bergner; C. Crämer; Julius Dorst, Otto Dressel,* Sen.; *A. Fleischmann;* Oscar *Heubach;* G. N. Mitlacher; H. Neumeister; C. P. Pfarr; Ph. *Samhammer; G. Spindler.* One of the most famous Directors of this school was *Prof. R. Möller.* He designed and was in charge of the Sonneberg exhibit at the World Expositions 1893–1910, all of which received the Grand Prize. These exhibits contained dolls from various Sonneberg producers and were as follows:

1893: Chicago	A horse-drawn coach with Santa enthroned among dolls and toys.
1900: Paris	A winter landscape in the Thüringian mountains with a sleigh drawn by two stags and filled with dolls and toys.
1904: St. Louis	A caravan with the leader on horseback followed by a fairy Princess on a camel loaded with dolls and toys.
1910: Brussels	A Thüringian village fair with a merry-go-round on which large dolls were seated, booths showing dolls' parts and other toys. A circus procession with a camel and horses, which may have been used in earlier exhibits, and a multitude of merrymakers. (This remarkable exhibit is now shown in the basement of the Sonneberg Museum.)

In 1913 *Karl Stadinger* was the School Director. The designs for the dolls were drawings and paintings produced from living models. The modeling of the dolls' heads was done largely by students in a plastic form.★

Sonny. 1920–21. All-bisque doll produced by *Morimura Bros.* It had molded and painted hair and features, eyes looking to the side, open-mouth with teeth, jointed at the shoulders, blue socks and black slippers. Ht. 4½ in. (11.5 cm.) This doll was sold with various colored wigs under the name Miss Fuzzy-Wuzz by *Whyte, Ridsdale.*

Sonny (Sunnie). 1926. Baby doll produced by *Cuno & Otto Dressel* and distributed in England by *G. Greiner.* This was the white version of their *Rock-a-Bye* baby.

Sonny Boy. 1929–30. Trademark registered for dolls in England by *Cowan, de Groot & Co.* and in Germany it was registered by *Hugo Wiegand.*

Sonny Boy. 1930. Composition head doll made by *Regal* in their *Kiddie Pal* line. A doll has been reported wearing knitted baby's clothes with a shield on its shirt containing the words, "Sonny Boy."

Sonophone Co. 1918. Advertised a line of cloth dolls; four style nos. handpainted and hand embroidered; hands had separate fingers; clothing corresponded with the faces and the dresses had snap fasteners. Ht. 18 in. (45.5 cm.); priced $4.00.

Soo. (Austrian Soldier). Before 1911–16. Felt doll made by *Steiff* had a mustache, thin limbs, long feet, and wore a kepi. Hts. 28, 35, and 50 cm. (11, 14, and 19½ in.); priced 75¢ to 90¢ in 1911. The largest size was discontinued by 1916.

Soozie Smiles. 1923–28. Two-faced composition head *Mama* doll made by *Ideal* and distributed in England by *H. S. Benjamin.* It had molded hair, painted eyes, composition arms, flange neck on a cloth body. Ht. 16 in. (40.5 cm.).★

Sophie. 1916. Name of a cloth doll created by *Mme. Manson.*

Sörgel, Johanna (née Dotze). 1915. Waltershausen, Thür. Applied for a German patent (D.R.G.M.) for a doll's wig.

Sörgel, Otto. 1896–97. Waltershausen, Thür. Obtained a German patent (D.R.G.M.) for the waist joints of a *Täufling* which was assigned to *Wislizenus.*

Sörgel, Wademar. See **Kämmer & Reinhardt.**

Sorna. 1923–27. Down stuffed cloth doll made by *Chad Valley* in their *Aerolite* line. The arms were away from the body and the legs were apart. The doll had a printed ethnic costume consisting of striped trousers and apron and a turban. Ht. 11 in. (28 cm.).

Sorneck, Karl (Carl). 1926–30. Liegnitz, Silesia. Manufactured small dolls in the *Schlesische Spielwaren Fabrik* (Silesian Toy Factory).

Sou Bros. & Co. 1919. San Francisco, Calif. Imported bisque dolls from Japan.

Soubrette, Louis XV. 1879. Name of a lady doll made in

2487. Dolls in the Sonneberg City museum collection as shown on a postcard dated 1921. Left to right: Aunt from Ritzebüttel, Parisian, Married Lady of the City of Goethe. *Coleman Collection.*

2488A & B. Gesso-over-wood head on a peg-jointed wood body of the type made in Sonneberg. The molded and painted black hair is in a pompadour in front and a braided bun in back. The eyes are painted blue. The mouth is a long line. Original clothes of the 1860s. H. 6¼ in. (16 cm.). *Coleman Collection.*

2489. Mark for an all-bisque doll named Sonny produced by Morimura Bros.

2490. Sonny Boy mark for dolls in the Kiddie Pal line.

Germany, with a jointed neck, dressed in a satin pseudo-period costume. Ht. 34 cm. (13½ in.).

Soulié, Mme. 1908. Won a second prize at the 1908 Paris Exhibition for dolls dressed as ladies and little girls at a contemporary garden party.

South American Dolls. *Stewart Culin* in 1920 described some of the early South American bone and shell dolls as well as the more recent sexed clay dolls with simulated tattooing on their faces. Other dolls had their ear plugs indicated by white shell disks.

A doll with a felt swivel head and felt hands, black felt hair, glass eyes and a painted mustache was dressed as a South American Gaucho. It wore a black bolero jacket, full wrap around trousers trimmed with red silk, a wide belt from which a bolo hung, a black felt hat with chin strap, and spurs attached to its shoes. The doll carried a lasso and whip. Ht. 12½ in. (31.5 cm.). (See also the individual names of the various countries.) *Kämmer & Reinhardt* had several agents in South America. (See Ills. 2000 and 2001.)

South Sea Baby (Südsee Baby). 1927–30. A brown bent limb composition baby doll produced by *A. Luge & Co.* It wore a grass skirt, straw hat, beaded necklace and a star-shaped paper tag reading "South Sea//Baby." (See also **Südsee [South Sea Baby].**)

South Wales (Toy) Manufacturing Co. 1916–22. Cardiff, Wales. Made *Madingland* line of dolls including Baby dolls, *Eskimo* dolls, and *Red Cross Nurse* dolls. M. H. Gigot and his French wife were in charge of this business.

Southern Bargain House. 1920–21 and other years. Richmond, Va. Wholesale distributor of American and imported dolls of various kinds.

1920–21: Bisque head dolls included those with wig, open mouth and teeth, jointed composition body and chemise in 10 hts. 7 to 23 in. (18 to 58.5 cm.); priced $4.50 doz. to $8.00 each wholesale. The dolls that were 12 in. (30.5 cm.) or larger had sleeping eyes. Similar dolls with molded and painted hair were only made in hts. 7 to 14 in. (18 to 35.5 cm.). A character head doll with sleeping eyes was 10¼ in. (26 cm.) tall; priced $18.00 doz. wholesale.

Bisque-head dolls with wigs, open mouths showing teeth, imitation kid bodies with bisque lower arms, and footwear came in five hts. 12, 15, 16, 18 and 21 in. (30.5, 38, 40.5, 45.5 and 53.5 cm.); priced $24.00 doz. to $5.50 each, wholesale.

All-bisque dolls with molded and painted hair, features, and footwear were 3 or 3¾ in. (7.5 or 9.5 cm.) high and cost 45¢ to 75¢ doz. wholesale. All-bisque dolls with molded and painted costumes were 4 in. (10 cm.) high; priced 90¢ doz. wholesale.

Dolls with china head and limbs on cloth bodies had molded and painted hair and features. Hts. 5⅜ and 8½ in. (13.5 and 21.5 cm.); priced 75¢ and $1.25 doz. wholesale.

A *Japanese* bisque head doll with wig, sleeping eyes, open mouth and teeth on a jointed composition body dressed in a Japanese kimono. Hts. 13 and 16 in. (33 and 40.5 cm.); priced $5.00 and $6.00 each wholesale.

Dressed bisque head dolls with hats, had wigs, sleeping eyes, open mouths with teeth, jointed composition bodies. Hts. 10, 12½, and 13½ in. (25.5, 31.5, and 34 cm.); priced $9.00 to $24.00 doz. wholesale.

Dressed boy and girl dolls had character bisque heads with painted features and open mouths. The girl had a wig of short hair and wore a dress; the boy had molded hair and wore rompers. Hts. 14, 15, and 18 in. (35.5, 38, and 45.5 cm.); priced $18.00 to $36.00 doz. wholesale.

There were also numerous composition dolls including ones with composition heads on cloth bodies and all-composition dolls, among them *Miss Vamp.* One of the composition-head dolls, named Romper Boy, had molded hair, painted features, cloth body with composition hands, and wore rompers. Ht. 14 in. (35.5 cm.); priced $12.00 doz. wholesale. A black all-composition doll named "Fiji Island Negro" had woolly hair, painted features, movable arms, metal earrings and collar, and a fur girdle. Priced 45¢ doz. wholesale. Dressed composition dolls cost up to $45.00 doz. wholesale.

Dolls of celluloid or with celluloid heads, all-metal dolls, all-rubber dolls, and cloth dolls were offered in a variety of forms. The bent limb all-celluloid naked dolls cost up to $4.50 each wholesale for one with molded hair and painted features. Ht. 18½ in. (47 cm.). The all-metal dolls with wig, sleeping eyes and wearing a chemise. Ht. 12 in. (30.5 cm.); priced $24.00 doz. wholesale.

All-rubber dolls with whistles. Hts. 5 and 5½ in. (12.5 and 14 cm.) cost $2.25 doz. wholesale. The cloth dolls cost the same as the all-rubber dolls but were about twice as tall. A small all-rubber doll with molded and painted hair and features was 3¾ in. (9.5 cm.) tall and cost $1.25 doz. wholesale.

A few composition shoulder heads were also shown in the Southern Bargain House catalog.

Southern California Statuary Co. 1927–28. Los Angeles, Calif. Manufactured plaster dolls including *Kewpie* type dolls.

Southern Doll & Candy Manufacturing Co. 1930 and later. Manufactured dolls.

Spaggiari, Mme. Yvonne. 1927–30. Paris. Made cloth dolls dressed in regional costumes. These dolls usually wore wooden sabots and closely resembled the dolls made by Ravca.[†]

1927: Registered five models portraying elderly men and women.

Registered *Les Originaux* and *De Vovonne* in France as trademarks for peasant style dolls.

Spalteholtz, Mrs. Gertrude. World War I period and later. San Francisco, Calif. Made dolls.

Spanish Dolls. The *Hosta* porcelain factory in Barcelona made porcelain dolls in the 1800s. *Stewart Culin* purchased Seville pottery dolls in 1892 for ¼¢ each. Large crude composition dolls with painted features and clothes were made in Spain in the late 1800s and early 1900s. Ca. 1925 E. *Llacer*[†] produced dolls. Lenci and many other makers dressed dolls in Spanish costumes.★

Sparkle Twins. 1929. Composition dolls made by *Amberg;* some of the girls wore short dresses and the boys wore overalls; priced 75¢ and up.

Spatz, Ulmer. 1927. Ulm, Germany. Advertised cloth art dolls and dolls' clothes.

Spaulding, Eleanor. 1927. Swampscott, Mass. Registered *Mrs. Spaulding's Children* as a U.S. trademark for dolls.

Speaking Babies. 1860–61. Name of some imported dolls listed in the Day Book of *John D. Robbins* as style no. 1529. Size 2 cost $36.00 doz. wholesale and size 4 cost $48.00 doz. wholesale. These may have been *Täufling* type dolls.

Spear, J. W., & Sons (Spear Works). 1928–30 and probably later. New York City; Bavaria; Canada; and Great Britain. Made sewing sets for children. "Wool Mascot Making" contained a little doll and patterns for wool costumes. "Our Little Dressmaker" was another set. "Knitting Nancy" was a wooden doll.

1929: "Dolly and Her Dresses" was designed in England and made at the Spear Works in Bavaria. The box contained a bisque-head doll with a wig, sleeping eyes, open mouth on a five-piece composition body. Ht. 7½ in. (19 cm.). There were several dresses, a bonnet, some underclothes and accessories. The doll and clothes pictured on the cover of the box differed from those contained in the box but appear to be original.

Spearmint Kid. 1915–17. Name of a cloth doll with a celluloid face, squeak voice, and a dress trimmed with arrows on its chest and belt. It had a three-cornered hat and spearmint leaves in its hair. *Baker and Bennett* held the license for this doll and distributed it. Ht. 13 in. (33 cm.).

1917: Doll was shown in the *Wyman, Partridge* catalog.★

Special. Both *Armand Marseille* and *Schoenau & Hoffmeis-ter* made bisque dolls' heads marked Special. (Also see **Spezial.**)★

Specialty Toy (Doll) Co. 1919–20. Leamington Spa., Warwickshire. Manufactured various kinds of dressed dolls. Some of the dolls had *British Ceramic* heads and limbs. These dolls had wigs, glass eyes and hair-stuffed bodies.

2491. Large all-papier-mâché doll probably made in Spain has molded and painted reddish brown hair, painted brown eyes and a closed mouth. There are joints at the shoulders and hips, molded and painted boots, and clothes that are contemporary with the doll. H. 31 in. (78.5 cm.). *Courtesy of Sotheby Parke Bernet Inc., N.Y.*

2492. All-bisque doll probably of a Spanish origin since it has "Aragon" painted on the back shoulder and a tag with the name "Aragon" on it. The original costume looks as if it might represent a Spanish Province. The doll has a blond wig, large eyes painted black, and a closed mouth. The body is jointed at the neck, shoulders and hips. The footwear is molded and painted. This doll does not look like the usual German or French all-bisque doll. H. 4 in. (10 cm.). *Coleman Collection.*

2493. Spearmint Kid doll with a celluloid mask face, cloth arms and wooden legs. It had a squeaker inside its body. The clothes represented the Wrigley chewing gum trademark. *Courtesy of Richard Withington. Photo by Barbara Jendrick.*

Special

Germany

2494. "Special" mark on doll but the maker is not known.

Other dolls were cloth. Arthur Kitson was their sole agent for wholesale and export distribution. Hts. of dolls 15 to 22 in. (38 to 56 cm.). Handled American, Japanese and Italian dolls.

Speer, Helen. 1916. New York City. TOYS AND NOVELTIES reported: "It is a long, long reach from the stiff, kid-bodied, bisque-headed dolls of a few years ago to the life-like infant that the modern little girl mothers. That is one of the results accomplished by Mrs. Helen Speer, of New York.

"The new dolls are things to marvel at with their short plump little bodies and dimpled knees and cheeks. Their hair does not grow in long, inconsistent curls, but is short

and sparse as babies' hair should be. But the dolls are only a part of the work of Mrs. Speer. . . .

"She never creates a toy that does not wear a cheerful expression."

Speier, Emil. 1888–1902 and possibly other years. Berlin. Manufactured dressed dolls.

1896: Advertised dolls' heads, wigs, hats, shoes and stockings as well as "jointed Taufling." It is not known whether *Täufling* meant a baby doll or a doll dressed in a chemise.

Speights Ltd. (Classic Works). 1900–24 and later. Dewsbury, Yorkshire, and Mirfield, England. Prior to World War I they made dolls' wigs and sent some of them to Germany and Austria. After making wigs for dolls they started around 1915 to make bodies and then the entire doll. The *British Ceramic* heads were made by *Mayer & Sherratt* and probably others. See Ills. 1855, 1856 and 1857. Speights' first dolls were described as having a shoulder plate, wig with side part, cloth body jointed at the hips and elbows, mitten hands and stump feet. Later their dolls often had composition lower arms and legs. Their two lines of dolls were named *Classic* and *Kidette.*

1916: Employed about 400 workers. Dolls had British Ceramic heads and limbs, human hair or mohair wigs, glass or painted eyes and washable Kidette bodies stuffed with hair or wool filling. Made a portrait doll of the actress Miss Gertie Miller in a Pierrette costume. Used the trade name "Ro-Clo" for their dolls' hair. Dolls came dressed and undressed; priced 13¢ to $5.25.

1917: Had 500 employees and 1,000 style numbers (many of these differed only in their clothes); there were over 150 lines of undressed dolls. The factory had machines for making composition parts, wood turning, painting, drying, stuffing, assembling, dress making, shoe making, and box making. The eyes had to be fixed in place and the wigs glued. Wigs made of hair rolls, frizettes, crêpe hair, or curly mohair. The heads were glued to the cloth or imitation kid bodies. Hands and feet were sometimes molded. Dolls wore fanciful costumes, period costumes or were dressed as children. Undressed dolls cost 12¢ to $5.25, while dressed dolls cost 48¢ to $5.25.

1919: Advertised dolls named *Cecily* and *Dazzle Dazzle.* In one of their advertisements they claimed that, "Some say they have French heads," referring to their dolls.

1920: They had upward of 300 workers and about 1,000 designs of dolls. Style number 4019/w/D16 (girl model), hts. 12, 16 and 19 in. (30.5, 40.5 and 48.5 cm.).

The Speights' catalog listed the following dolls but they differed chiefly in their clothes; Classic Baby Doll; Countess; Country Girl; Dazzle; Dinkie Dolls; Dutch Boy; Dutch Girl; Fairy; Flossy; Georgette; Marchioness; Marie; Miss Muffet; Nighty Girl; Princess; Pyjama Girl; Red Riding Hood; River Girl; and Seaside Viscountess. *Meakin & Ridgeway* were their representatives in the U.S. and Canada.

1924: Made all-British Wembley Doll that was given as a prize at the Wembley Exhibition. ★

2495. Group of dolls dressed in regional and historical costumes exhibited in Dresden in 1904. These dolls were among those designed by Hugo Spieler, Karl Gross, Otto Gussmann, Wilhelm Kreis, William Lossow, Oskar Seyfert and Wilhelm Thiele, according to DEKORATIVE KUNST, 1904. (See also Ill. 1594.)

Spencer & Co. 1916–20 and later. Cardiff, Wales. Successor in 1919 was *Leda Dolls*. Made composition-head dolls with glass eyes, cloth bodies, came undressed or dressed in short clothes or long clothes; some of the clothes were woolen. Spencer used the trade name Leda for these dolls. They also made a line of dressed dolls with *British Ceramic* heads.

1917: The jointed baby doll with pacifier in its mouth could be posed to sit up. Other dolls represented infants, boys or girls. The latter were dressed character dolls.

The Leda trademark was registered by Thomas Charles Salisbury in England.

1919: Made 15 style Nos. of dolls, which included a jointed composition baby doll with pacifier, a Pierrot doll and a "soft-bodied" doll dressed in silk or muslin, with a British Ceramic head. Some of their dolls had molded hair.

Spenkuch, Georg. 1897. Nürnberg, Bavaria. Applied for a German patent (D.R.G.M.) for a standing doll.

Sperrhake, Arno. 1891–1930 and later. Eisenberg, Thür. Manufactured dolls.

1929: Made dressed and undressed dolls.

1930: Dolls' house children made of porcelain or celluloid

came with or without wigs. Also made dolls' house men and women.★

Spezial. 1913. Line of dolls made by *Franz Kühles,* according to the research of the Ciesliks.★

Spicer, Gilbert H. 1916–17. Leamington, England. Made dolls and dolls' parts including baby dolls, dolls' house dolls, mascots, molds, and dolls' clothes. Advertised dolls with composition, *British Ceramic* or wax heads.

1916: Some of the dolls had wigs and glass eyes. Advertised that their dolls were made to withstand tropical climates. Hts. 8 and 13 in. (20.5 and 33 cm.); priced up to $6.75 doz. wholesale.

Spiegel, May, Stern Co. 1920s. America. Advertised *Hush-a-Bye* baby dolls, *Mama* dolls and dressed dolls.

Spielberger, Armin. 1920–30 and later. Budapest. Wholesale distributor of dolls.

Spieler, Hugo. 1904. Dresden, Germany. Designed art dolls dressed in regional or historical costumes.

Spielwarenfabrik Wilhelm Simon. See **Simon (Wilhelm) & Co.**

Spiffy. 1926. *Boudoir* doll with "saucy hat," made by *Kitty Fleischmann.*

Spindler, Georg. 1862–1930. Sonneberg, Thür. Made dolls. One of the founders of the *Sonneberg Industrial School.*

Spitz, Ph. J. 1895. Cologne, Germany. Applied for a German patent (D.R.G.M.) for dolls' joints.

Splendide Bébé. 1892–1906. Name of a doll made by Cosman Frères.[†]

December 1, 1894, JOURNAL DES DAMES ET DES DEMOISELLES published the same advertisement as had been published in January 1893. Both of these were in Goubaud publications but the 1894 price was $2.50 in contrast to the $1.60 for which this 50 cm. (19½ in.) doll had been offered earlier. Both offers included "patterns to make a complete trousseau: chemise, drawers, skirt, dress, coat, etc." The doll came packed in a wooden box.

1906: *Aux Trois Quartiers* described Splendide Bébé as having sleeping eyes, hair eyelashes, jointed, talking; costume with English embroidery and ribbon trimming. Ht. 50 cm. (19½ in.); priced $1.58.★

Spo. (Sportsman). 1911–13. Felt art doll made by *Steiff,* represents a "globe trotter" in an elegant sports outfit with a visored cap. Ht. 50 cm. (19½ in.).

Sporlin, Michael, & Rahn, Heinrich. 1835–41. Gumpendorf, Haupstra, Austria. By 1840 it was Sporlin & Heinrich Zimmerman. Made various kinds of dolls with papiermâché heads according to Dr. Eva Moskovszky.

Sports Dolls. Dolls have been dressed in costumes representing nearly all the sports including the following: Automobile drivers, Aviators usually with a parachute, bathers, baseball players, diabolo players, cricket players, croquet players, fishermen, football players (see **Fu**), golfers, hunters, jockeys, mountain climbers, oarsmen, polo players, prize fighters, sailors, skaters, skiers, tennis players.

These dolls were made in a variety of materials and sizes from the mid 19th century until the present day by a great variety of companies, including *Amberg, Horsman, Lenci* and *Steiff.* (See Ills. 389 and 694 in THE COLLECTOR'S BOOK OF DOLLS' CLOTHES.)

2496. Composition head doll wearing a black and red wool bathing suit of the 1860s. Its molded black hair has a bun in back. The eyes are painted blue, the mouth is closed. H. 11½ in. (29 cm.). H. of shoulder head 2½ in. (6.5 cm.). *Coleman Collection.*

2497. Sports clothes for dolls shown in THE SEASON, January, 1897. The dolls are shown dressed as a boy pushing a cart, a boy and girl playing tennis, boys and girl playing croquet and a girl on gymnastic bars. This picture first appeared in DIE MODEN WELT, the parent magazine.

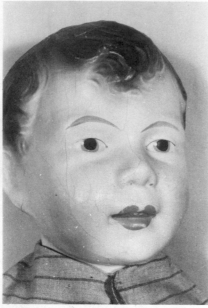

2498A & B. Composition shoulder-head doll with a cloth body dressed as a Baseball Player. It has molded and painted blond hair, molded and painted blue eyes, and a closed mouth. The body is jointed at the shoulders and hips. Original uniform. H. 31 in. (78.5 cm.). *Courtesy of the Washington Dolls' House and Toy Museum.*

2499. Harvard football player, probably a favor in the form of a celluloid Kewpie with crepe paper helmet and pants, carrying a crepe paper football. The crimson shirt and H are painted on the upper part of the body. The doll is a regular Kewpie type with blue wings. H. 2¼ in. (5.5 cm.). *Coleman Collection.*

2500. Three Lenci felt dolls dressed in sports outfits. They have blond hair sewed on in strips, painted eyes, closed mouths.

Doll on the left is the golfer shown in the 1925/26 Lenci catalog; the other two dolls are in the 300 series and are dressed to represent a polo player and a tennis player. Original clothes and accessories. H. of all three dolls 17 in. (43 cm.). *Courtesy of Sotheby Parke Bernet Inc., N.Y.*

Sports Girl. 1916. Line of dolls made by the *Atlas Manufacturing Co.*

Sportsman. See **Spo.**

Spree-wald. 1913. Name of dressed art dolls imported by *Claflin & Co.;* priced $1.00 to $2.00.

Spring-jointed Bodies. Many dolls were made with springs for joints during and shortly after World War I when there was difficulty in obtaining rubber. Among the companies that used metal springs for dolls' joints were: *Borgfeldt, Jessie M. Raleigh* and *New Era Novelty Co.*★

Spurin, E. C., Toy Warehouse. 1851–67 and probably other years. London. Followed *Edlin's* and represented *Adolf Fleischmann* in the 1851 Exhibition of Gulliver in Lilliput.

Squaw. 1920. Handmade Indian doll; each doll with an individual face and blanket pattern, made by *Mary Frances Woods* as style no. 5. Ht. 12 in. (30.5 cm.).

Squaw. 1927. Cloth doll representing an Indian woman mate to Buck; made by the *Henderson Glove Co.*

2501. Mark used by E. C. Spurin.

Squier Twins Toy Co. 1920–30 and later. Battle Creek, Mich. In 1923 the name was changed to Twinzy Toy Co. They used both Squier Twins and Twinzy Toys as trade names. Company was operated by Bernice and Blanche Squier. Made dolls of leatherette, cloth or yarn.

1923: *Mother Goose* line included Boy Blue and Tom, Tom, the Piper's Son. Priced $4.80 doz. wholesale and $5.75 doz. wholesale with a voice. Other dolls in colored leatherette included Big Buddy, Bings, and Jumbo Jim.

1927–28: Registered in U.S. Twinzy as a trademark for dolls.

1928: Made an aviator doll in leatherette stuffed with cotton and having its parachute equipment. Mother Goose line, also made of leatherette stuffed with cotton, had the appropriate Mother Goose verse on its back. *Cradle-Time Twinzies* were cloth dolls. A new doll was the *Alphabet Man.* All dolls had voices.

1929: Advertised a cloth pull toy representing a little girl or a little boy; Sailor and Soldier dolls; Twinzy twins, priced $1.00 and Mother Goose dolls, priced 50¢.★

Stadinger, Karl. 1911–13 and later. Sonneberg, Thür. Designed dolls and by 1913 he was the Director of the *Sonneberg Industrial School.*

1911: At an International Doll Exposition in Frankfurt he exhibited dolls representing an Alps climber, automobilist, aviator, hunter, taxidermist and rag picker.

Stadler, Johann. 1809–16. Vienna. Made wooden dolls; his shop was called "Zum Schwarzen Adler" (At the Black Eagle), according to Dr. Eva Moskovszky.

Städt Porzellan-Manufactur. See **Nymphenburg.**

Stahl, Carl. 1899–1930 and later. Berlin. Produced, distributed and exported dolls.

1899: Factory agent for *Cuno and Otto Dressel.*

1927: Agent for *Alt, Beck & Gottschalck, Fleischmann & Crämer, Reich, Goldman & Co., Heinrich Horn, Dora Petzold, Emil Pfeiffer, Bruno Schmidt,* and *Max Seifert.*

Stähr, Gustav. 1899 and possibly other years. Hamburg, Germany. Factory agent for *Cuno & Otto Dressel.*

Stammberger, Louis. 1903. Sonneberg, Thür. Applied for a German patent (D.R.G.M.) for a walking doll.

Standard Doll Co. 1917. New York City. Made *Miss Sam.* Handled dolls and dolls' accessories including wigs.★

Standard Jewelry Co. 1902. Boston, Mass. Advertised a premium doll imported from Europe with the purchase of 30 collar buttons. The turning bisque head doll had a wig, sleeping eyes, teeth, jointed body and wore removable clothes including footwear. Ht. 18 in. (45.5 cm.).

Standard Solophone Manufacturing Co. 1926–30. New York City. Manufactured dolls' clothing and art needlework outfits such as the *Little Dressmaker.* which contained a sleeping eye doll, a sewing machine, dresses stamped for embroidery, floss to do the embroidery, buttons, ribbons, thimble, and so forth. The "Art Needlework Outfits" cost 10¢ to $3.00.

1930: A doll's outfit consisting of a dress, rompers, nightgown, and floss for embroidery cost $1.00.

Standard Toy Co. 1920. Brooklyn, N.Y. Manufactured dressed dolls with and without sleeping eyes, cork and excelsior stuffed inside and outside joints.

Standard Toy & Novelty Co. 1929. New York City. Made dolls.

Standfuss, Karl (Carl). 1898–1930. Deuben near Dresden, Saxony. Made metal and celluloid dolls. The Ciesliks report that like *Buschow & Beck* their metal heads often had a celluloid surface.

1898: Applied for two German patents (D.R.G.M.), one for metal dolls' heads and the other for moving eyes.

1899: Advertised that they used zinc in their metal heads and the dolls had glass eyes.

1902: Applied for a German patent (D.R.G.M.) for doll's head with sleeping eyes.

1903: Applied for a German patent (D.R.G.M.) for a celluloid covering for their metal heads to protect the coloring.

    Advertised metal dolls' heads with a celluloid surface; dolls marked "Juno"[+] and cloth dolls.

1911: Applied for a German patent (D.R.G.M.) for a celluloid soldier doll.

1912: Both celluloid and metal heads came with wigs or with painted hair.

1913: Advertised *Cupido.*

1921: Advertised celluloid *Kewpies.*

1926: Advertised *Newborn Baby.*

1927: Advertised dressed celluloid dolls.

1927: Advertised dressed and undressed dolls, dolls' parts including painted heads, dolls' house dolls and other small dolls as well as "artistic dolls."

1930: Kewpies came dressed or undressed and with a shield-shape label. *G. F. Hertzog* distributed the Standfuss products. (See Ills. 2502–2504.)★

Standish No Brake Life Size Doll. 1918. Cutout cloth doll made by *Elms & Sellon Co.* had shaped foot. Dimensions 24 by 7½ in. (61 by 19 cm.).

Stangl, Martin. See **Fulper Pottery Co.**

Star. 1927–28. Name of a wood-composition doll assembled with wire springs and handpainted, made by *Twistum Toy Factory.* The doll represented a football player; a football and goal posts were packed with each doll. Letters of various colleges were on the chest of the dolls which were painted in colors appropriate to the letter. These dolls were intended to be college mascots. Ht. 7½ in. (18 cm.); priced $1.50.

2502A & B. Juno celluloid shoulder head doll with blond molded hair, blue painted eyes, open-closed mouth and a cloth body jointed at the shoulders, made by Standfuss. Original costume of a Laplander. Mark: Ill. 2503. H. of shoulder head 7½ cm. (3 in.) as indicated in the mark. H. 11 in. (28 cm.). *Coleman Collection.*

JUNO

GERMANY

7 ½

JUNO

2503–2504. Marks embossed on celluloid shoulder heads made by Carl Standfuss.

Star Doll Shoe Co. 1925–27. New York City. Made shoes for dolls.

Star Doll & Toy Co. 1915–30 and later. New York City. Made dolls for jobbers, especially including *Mama* and baby dolls. They were members of the *American Doll Manufacturers' Association.*

1927: Licensed by *Voices, Inc.* to use the patented Mama voices and criers in their dolls.★

Star Manufacturing Co. 1887–1925 and later. London; factory at Cubitt town, England. Produced dressed dolls, dolls' clothes, *Golliwoggs,* and repaired dolls.

1917: Made *Swan* brand dolls with *British Ceramic* heads and cloth bodies as well as composition-head dolls. Some of the baby dolls were dressed in furs; these may have been their *Eskimo* dolls. They also dressed dolls as Scottish lads and lassies, Red Riding Hood; and Sailor boys and girls. *Golliwoggs* were made in three style nos. Ht. 15 in. (38 cm.). The dolls' clothes that they made included sports coats and trimmed hats.

1920: Incorporated with John G. Murdoch & Co.

Star Toy & Novelty Co. 1914–21. New York City. Made composition dolls and wooden dolls.

1921: Dolls priced 25¢ to $1.00.★

Stark, Christian. 1926. Berlin. Manufactured and/or exported dolls.

Stas. 1915. One of the cloth *Paderewski* dolls made in *Mme. Lazarski's* workshop. It represented a tinsmith from the Tatra Mountains in Galicia, Poland. (A tinsmith sold tinware and mended pieces of tin such as pots and pans.)

Staudt, Ferdinand. 1926. Nürnberg, Bavaria. Handled and distributed dolls made by *Hans Süssenguth.*

Staudt, Fritz. 1885. Nürnberg, Bavaria. Applied for a German patent (D.R.P.) for the mechanism for a moving doll.

Stearn Co. 1927 and probably other years. Cleveland, Ohio. The toy department was run by Mr. Altman. Dolls were assembled and distributed. One room was for infant dolls and another room was for *Mama* dolls.

Stearns, R. H., & Co. 1873–1930 and later. Boston, Mass. Imported and distributed dolls.

1880s: Had a "Paris Doll Department."

Stecher Lithographic Co. 1916. Rochester, N.Y. Advertised cutout cloth dolls designed by *Margaret Evans. Bobby* and *Betty* were the names of two of the dolls. Sometimes these dolls were used as premiums.

Steevan's Manufacturing Co. 1917. England. Made walking dolls without springs or clockwork mechanism. The dolls were dressed as a clown in a dark jacket, checked pants, and big shoes or as a little girl with long hair and wearing a coat.

Stefan. (Winter Sports). 1911 and before. Felt character doll made by *Steiff.* It was dressed as a boy in a winter sports outfit with a sweater, velvet pants, and leather shoes. Four hts. 28, 35, 43, and 50 cm. (11, 14, 17, and 19½ in.).

Stefania. 1927–28. Felt doll made by *Lenci* as style no. 800/D. was dressed as a girl in period costume. Ht. 45 in. (114.5 cm.).

Stegner, Max. 1913. Neustadt near Coburg, Thür. Applied for a German patent (D.R.G.M.) for hair for dolls' heads of paper or papier-mâché.

Steiff, Kaete, Co. 1924. Germany. Showed art dolls at the Leipzig fair. Dolls wore fancy costumes and were sought by American buyers; priced $4.00 to $5.00 for the smallest size up to $12.00 for the largest size. There was demand especially for dolls wearing real lambskin coats and costing up to $14.00.

Steiff, Fräulein Margarete. 1877–1930 and later. Giengen, Württemburg. Made clothes for dolls and then made felt toys in 1880, dolls with mask heads in 1889 according to the research of the Ciesliks, and clown dolls by 1898. Steiff claimed this was the first factory in Germany to make felt toys. Nearby felt factories supplied scraps of felt, and Margarete Steiff designed the dolls until she died in 1909, when she was over 70. The drawings of *Schlopsnies* were the basis for many of the dolls. By 1899 there were factory agents in Berlin, Hamburg, Paris and London. At one time in the early twentieth century *Borgfeldt* was the sole distributor in the U.S. and *G. Greiner & Co.* was the sole distributor in Britain and the British Colonies. In 1908 Margarete's nephews were in charge of the factory and looking after the many home workers in the area. By 1930 Paul, Richard, Hugo and Otto Steiff ran the factory. The dolls were sold all over the world. Most of the early Steiff dolls were made with a seam down the center of the face but not all of them, even among the early ones, had this feature. Steiff claimed that they had originated the term "Character dolls," and dolls which were later so named had appeared at least as early as 1903.

STUDIO "Talk," 1911, reported historically, "Even before Margarete Steiff's animal figures took the juvenile world by storm, she had already experimented in the production of dolls for little girls, which should be free from the sugary smartness and insipid 'dollishness' of the average factory product. Jovial lads and buxom maidens that could stand something more than a puff and looked quite becoming in the gay national costume were followed in due course by the village schoolmaster . . . the group of village musicians [and] . . . a company of infantry at drill [with a] raucous Captain."

Beatrix Potter used a Steiff Policeman as a model for one of the pictures in her book A TALE OF TWO BAD MICE.

At least four of the Steiff dolls, Grandpa *(Gr.)*, Ma, Soe, and *Sof.* were portrayed in the book PIERRE PONS, illustrated by Paul Guignebault.

The Swedish painter *Carl Larsson* used Steiff's *Mi* and *Al* in one of his paintings and he held a Mi in his own self portrait.

Many of the Steiff character dolls closely resembled the comic characters of the period prior to World War I. Foxy Grandpa (Grandpa, Gr.), Happy Hooligan *(Ho)*, and the Katzenjammer Kids' family, namely, Fat Captain *(Ka)* and Mrs. Fatty *(Mi)*. There were also popular characters in German children's literature, such as *Max and Moritz, Struwwelpeter,* and so forth. Many of the Steiff names, used as entries in this book, were abbreviations but these appeared sometimes with or sometimes without a period after the abbreviations.

1894: Advertised nine styles of dolls with unbreakable heads, felt bodies and felt clothes, plus dressed dolls with porcelain heads. The unbreakable-head dolls represented farmers of various areas, shepherds, a sailor, boys and girls, and Red Riding Hood. Ht. 26 cm. (10½ in.).

1897: Used a tag with an elephant whose trunk formed an S for "Steiff."

1898: Dolls still had heads other than felt except possibly some clowns. Among the dolls were a harlequin and a jockey. Elephant tags were used on the dolls.

1900: Began to export dolls to France; a French writer in 1916 criticised the Steiff dolls as being "Squinting eyed." (See **French Dolls,** 1914–16.)

1902: Advertised clowns in several sizes; some of the dolls had celluloid faces. There were timely dolls such as those representing Boer and English soldiers, with bisque dolly-face heads having wigs and glass eyes, as well as Nansen, a doll representing an Eskimo.

1903: Advertised felt-faced dolls representing an English policeman, an English Postman, white and black football players, a French Policeman, a Negro and others. *Borgfeldt* was handling Steiff products in America.

1904: First button in the ear was used; in the beginning they were blank buttons. Won a Grand Prize at the St. Louis Exhibition.

1905: Used a small metal button in the ear with the name in raised block letters.

The Steiff catalog listed the following dolls: Al (Alphons); *Bu* (Bube, Boy); *Fu* (Football Player); *Ga* (Gaston); Gr (Foxy Grandpa); Ho (Happy Hooligan); Ka (Kaptain); Mi (Missis); *Pla* (American Policeman); *Ple* (English Policeman); *Plf* (French Policeman); *Pse* (English Postman); Soe (English Soldier).

1906: Became a corporation with Margarete Steiff as the manager and her nephews Paul, Richard and Franz-Josef Steiff assisting her.

Gamage advertised the following Steiff dolls: Fat Captain (Ka), Frenchman, Grandpa (Gr.), Hooligan (Ho), Jack Tar, Mrs. Fatty (Mi, Missis), Nigger, Fat or Lanky Policeman, Fat or Lanky Postman (Pse), Sailor, Soldier and *Sunny Jim*.

1909: Wholesale agents in London were Arthur A. *Abrahams;* Faudel's; Foster; Porter & Co.; J. Howell & Co.; J. Rotherham & Co.; *C. E. Turnbull & Co.;* and *Whyte, Ridsdale & Co.*

1910: Applied for a German patent (D.R.G.M.) relating to dolls' feet. The *Puppen Reform* movement influenced the Steiff dolls. New dolls supposedly representing American characters were: Chinamen, Cowboys, Gibson Girls, Indians, Policemen, Negroes, Sailors, Salvation Army Workers and Yankees.

Aux Trois Quarticrs advertised what appeared to be dolls made by Steiff. These included dolls resembling *Alida, Anthony,* a *clown,* Eskimos, *Lisl* and *Olaf.*

A Steiff advertisement in PLAYTHINGS showed *Alfred, Daisy, Dora,* Krackjack *(Krack,* a *Billiken*-type), *Mabel, Martha,* Max, Moritz, *Samojede* (Eskimo) and *Walter.* Won a Grand Prize at the Brussels Exhibition.

1911: Applied for a German patent (D.R.G.M.) for dolls' ears. The Steiff German catalog advertised the following dolls: *Akro* (Acrobat), Al (Alphons), *Alb* (Farmer), Alfred (Norwegian), Alida (Dutch, Marken), *Anthony* (Anton, Tirolese), *Artil* (German Soldier), *Bob* (Scout Boy), *Bre* (French, Brittany), *Brz.* (Brenz Farmer), *Brown* (Musician), Bu (Bube, Boy), *Bube* (School boy, French and German), *Caro* (Silly Gus), *Chev* (German Soldier), *Chi* (Chinaman), *Cl.* (Clown), *Coloro* (Clown), *Dach.* (German, Dachau),

Daisy (Bather), *Di* (porter), *Dick* (English Soldier), *Do* (Baby), Dora (Bather), *Drag* (German Dragoon), *Else* (Winter Sports), *Esq* (Esk, Eskimo), *Felix* (Knitted clothes), *Franz* (Fisherman), *Fritz* (Knitted clothes), Fu (Football Player), *Ga.* (Gaston), *Gef.* (French Gendarme), *Gow.* (Golliwog), Gr. (Foxy Grandpa), *Green* (Footman), *Gusto* (Circus Usher), *Hans* (Farmer Boy), *Harry* (Dutch Fisherman), *Hellen* (Dutch Fisherwoman), *Helma* (Dutch woman), *Herbert, Hiasl* (Tirolese Boy), *Hilde* (Toddler), Ho. (Happy Hooligan), *Hubbard* (Mother Hubbard), *Hubertus* (Hunter Boy), *Ida* (Bather), *Ind.* (Indian), *Inf* (German Infantryman), *Inge* (Dutch, Volendam), *Jäg* (Hunter with gun), *Jansen* (Dutch boy), Ka. (Kaptain, Captain), *Kalo* (Austrian Hunter), *Karl* (Bather), *Kathi* (Regional), *Kelly* (Sgt. Kelly[+], American Soldier), Knut (Dutchman), Krack (Krackjack, Billiken-type), *Kuni* (Swiss, Berne), *Kurt* (Winter Sports), *Laura* (German, Spreewald), *Le.* (Lehrer, Schoolmaster), *Lisl* (Lizzie, Loni, Bavarian Tirolese), Ma. (Matrose, Sailor), Mabel (Bather), *Mädchen* (German and French Schoolgirls). *Markus,* Martha (Bather), Max and Moritz (Bad Boys), Mi (Missis), *Mich* (Michel), *Mina, Murphy* (American Soldier), *Noso* (Circus Performer), *Off* (French Officer), *Olaf* (Dutch, Volendam), *Oro* (Circus Performer), *Pla* (American Policeman), *Plbe.* (Belgian Policeman), *Pld.* (German Policeman), *Ple.* (English Policeman), *Plf.* (French Policeman), *Pse.* (English Postman), *Red Hood* (Red Riding Hood), *Rolf* (Winter Sports), *Rosa* (Peasant), *Rudi* (Swiss girl, Berne), *Ruth* (Winter Sports) Samojede (Eskimo), *Seppl* (Tirolese), *Sharkey* (American Soldier with gun), *Siegfried* (Winter Sports), *Silva* (Winter Sports), *Sing* (Singhalese), *Snak* (Gnome), *Snik* (Gnome), *Sobe.* (Belgian Soldier), Soe (English Soldier), Sof. (French Soldier), *Soho* (Dutch Soldier), Soica (carabinier), Soibe (Italian Soldier), Soo. (Austrian Soldier), Spo. (Sportsman), *Stefan* (Winter Sports), Stru. (Struwwelpeter, Mophead), *Therese* (German, Dachau), *Tommy* (English Soldier), *Train.* (Trainee, Military), *Uffi* (Italian Officer), *Ulan* (German Soldier), Walter (Bather), Zep. (Uncle Zeppelin).

These included caricature dolls, art dolls and character dolls. Many of these dolls were dressed in military outfits and large feet were typical of the caricature dolls.

In 1911 Steiff reported that they had 2,000 employees.

1912: Applied for a German patent (D.R.G.M.) for a stuffed doll with limited joint movement. Borgfeldt, the sole U.S. agent, advertised Steiff dolls: Chinaman, Clowns, Huntsman, Piper's Son with Pig, Red Riding Hood and Sailors.

1913: The Borgfeldt catalog which listed Steiff dolls included the following: *Akro.* (Acrobat), Al (Alphons), Alb (Farmer Bauer), *Albert* (Boy with hoop), Alfred, Alida (Dutch, Marken), Anthony (Anton, Tirolese), Artil, Baby, *Baseb* (Baseball-Player), *Berta,* Bob (Scout boy), *Boy* (Messenger Boy), Brz., Bu. (Bube, Boy), Caro (Silly Gus), Cl (Clown), Coloro (Clown), *Cowboy* (Mexican), Dach (German, Dachau), *Daum* (Pigmy), Do (Baby), Else, *Erich,* Esq (Esk, Eskimo), Felix, Franz, Ga (Gaston), Gef (French Gendarme), Gow. (Golliwog), Hans (Farmer Boy), Harry (Dutch Fisherman), Hellen (Dutch Fisherwoman), Helma, Hiasl, Hilde (Toddler), Hubertus (Hunter), Ind (Indian), Inf. (Infantryman), Jäg (Hunter with gun), *Jansen, Jok.* (Jockey), *Juge,* Ka (Kaptain, Captain), Kalo (Austrian hunter), Karl, Kathi,

Kelly (Sgt. Kelly, American Soldier), Knut, Krack (Krackjack, Billiken-type), Kuni, Laura, Le, Lilly, Lisl (*Lizzie,* Loni, Bavarian Tirolese), Ma (Matrose, Sailor), Mädchen, Markus, Max and Moritz, *Mezg.* (Butcher), Mi. (Missis), Mich. (Michel), Mina, Murphy (American Soldier), *Neg* (Black), Olaf (Dutch, Volendam), *Olga, Paul, Pay,* Pla (American Policeman), *Postil* (Postillion), Red Hood (Red Riding Hood), Rosa (Peasant), Rudi, Ruth (Winter sports), Samojede, *Schneid* (Tailor), *Schus* (Shoemaker), *Seppl,* Sharkey (American soldier with gun), Siegfried, Silva (Winter Sports), Sing (Singhalese), Snak (Gnome), Snik (Gnome), Soo. (Austrian Soldier, Spo. (Sportsman), Stru. (Struwwelpeter, Mophead), Tommy (English Soldier), *Tweedeedle,* Ulan, and Walter (Bather).

Lafayette store in Paris advertised a cloth Boy Scout doll that looked like the Steiff Bob and had a Steiff height 35 cm. (14 in.).

A British Toy Journal listed Steiff football players, golfers, various baseball players, tennis players, cricketeers, Texas cowboys and cowgirls, Indian chiefs, squaws as well as Mr. Twee Deedle.

Gamage advertised the following Steiff dolls: Alfons; Boy in delaine suit (Markus): Captain; Girl in delaine dress (Mina); Golliwog; Harry, a Dutch boy; Helen (Hellen), a Dutch girl; *Highlander;* Hunter (Hubertus); Mrs. Captain; Policeman; Thin Postman; Red Riding Hood; Fat Soldier. Ht. 17 in. (43 cm.). Thin Soldier. Ht. 20 in. (51 cm.).

Steiff applied for a German patent (D.R.G.M.) for a mama voice in dolls.

TOYS AND NOVELTIES described the Steiff dolls: "Borgfeldt & Company are now the sole Steiff . . . agents. . . .

"The quaint Steiff character figures, dressed in the costumes of all nationalities, are shown in wonderful array. There is an assortment of sailors, soldiers, messenger boys, sportsman, a tutor with that 'teacher look,' clowns that squeak, firemen with their buckets, policemen, regular Rip Van Winkle gnomes and countless other novel creations.

"A great many American toy dealers are following the successful example of European dealers in having a display set of Steiff toys and figures made after their own ideas, or from original drawings.

"One cannot help but be impressed by the minute painstaking attention to detail that each animal and figure has received in the manufacture, and which is found both in structure and dress. . . . There is a realism about them that children of the present age demand."

Another report in TOYS AND NOVELTIES stated: "The Steiff character dolls have been on [display in] the Borgfeldt building. . . .

"One of the features of the display represents a football game which, to all appearances, is at its height. The players, all Steiff character dolls, are realistically attired in football clothes, and equipped with all the paraphernalia necessary to safety in the game, tousley heads and all.

". . . The Steiff character dolls and figures, because of their distinct individuality, their great durability and lasting qualities, are winning their way into the hearts of the doll-loving world."

1915: Advertised soldiers in field gray uniforms.

1916: The Steiff German catalog advertised the following dolls: Albert, Alb Bauer, Alphons (Al.) Alida, Anton, Artil, *August,* Baby Puppen, Bauer Michel, Bersi (Italian), Berta, Betty (Tennis player), Blanca (Winter Sports). Böck, Brenz Bauer, Brenz Bauerin, Bretagne Bauer, Bu, Buben, (Bob), Clown, Coloro, Cowboy (Mexican), Dauchauer Bauer, Dienstmann, Erich, Erika, Felix, Footballer, Franz, Fritz, Ful, Gaston (Ga.) Gaucho (Argentinian), Gnome, Golliwogg (Gow.) Grete, Hans, Harry, Helma, Hellen, Hiasl, Hilde, Hooligan, Hubertus (Hunter), Ind (Indian), Inf, Inf Leute, Inf Maj., Inf Ski, Johann, Jorg, Juge, Kaptain (Ka.), Karl, Kicker, Knabe, Knut, Kofem (Field uniform with mantle), Kospa (Cossack), Krackjack, Landsturm, Laura, Lehrer, Lisa, Lisl, Loni, Lothar, Lotte, Mädchen, Markus, Matrose (Ma), Max and Moritz, Metzger, Missis (Mi), Neg. (Negroknabe), Olaf, Onkel Fritz, Oskar, Ottilie, Paul, Pld, Plo., Puck, Rotkäppchen (Red Riding Hood), Rotraut, Rusfe (Russian Field Soldier) Schidik, Schidun, Schifra, Schima, Schneider, Schülerpuppen, Schuster, Seppl, Sobe, Sof, Soo (Austrian Soldier), Stu (Student), Stru (Struwwelpeter), Tommy, Türfe (Field uniform), Turko, Türpa, Ulan (Cavalry Lancer), Wilma, Wirt, Widow Bolte, Zuave (dark skin).

1922: The Albert Schlopsnies dolls had a trademark *Armring.* These dolls had patented celluloid heads that were painted on the inside so that they could be washed without harm or even rubbed with sandpaper. They had regular Steiff bodies and removable clothes. Ht. 40 cm. (15½ in.). They were dressed to represent one of the four seasons or in nightclothes. The names of these dolls included: Adele, Agnes, Anna, Axel, Bubi, Carlos, Elsa, Ernst, Hemdmatz, Henriette, Herbert, Hosenmatz, Klara, Kolja, Lene, Madeleine, Marga, Marius, Meedi, Otto, Peter, Resi, Richard, Rita, Rolf, Ruth, Sepp, Theo, Vera, Viktor, Yvo, Yvonne. (See table under Schlopsnies.)

The black dolls were named Sam and Samy. The clowns came with white faces or with vari-colored faces.

1923: H. E. Hughes was the sole British agent.

1924: The following dolls with felt faces and removable clothes were advertised by Steiff, in a catalog printed in English.

Al. (Alphons), Anthony, August, Berta, Bu, Clown, Dach, Dwarf, Erich, Erika, Fu (Football player), Ga. (Gaston), Grete, Gretel, Hans, Hänsel, Harry, Heinz, Hellen, Helmut, Hilmar, Ho (Hooligan), Hubertus (Hunter), Lisa, Lizzie, Mat (Ma, Matrose) but in different clothes than earlier, Max & Moritz, Paul, Penate, Pierrot, Puck, Rosa, Rotraut, Schidik, School Boy, School Girl, Stru (Struwwelpeter), *Toni,* Tramp, Trene, Wintersports, and Xaver. *John Hess* advertised some of these dolls plus one named "Strolch."

Steiff continued to advertise the Albert Schlopsnies dolls.

Sole agent in Britain was G. Greiner.

1925–30 and later: Made dolls with pressed felt faces, having the seam at the back of the neck. The wigs could be washed and combed. The eyes were glass.

In 1925 the football player, Hubertus (the Hunter), and others were still being made in the earlier manner.

1926: Still advertising the celluloid dolls designed by Schlopsnies.

1927: DEUTSCHE SPIELWAREN ZEITUNG listed Steiff cloth dolls and molds for dolls.

Steiff used tags with a bear's head on them.

1930: Borgfeldt had a permanent display of Steiff dolls. Registered Mimocculo and Siamy as trademarks in Germany.

1931: Used the trademark BÄRKOPF (Bearhead).

1938: They were making dolls with felt pressed heads, mohair, wigs and glass eyes. Among their dolls were Autopuppen, Clowns, Glucks-Fager (Chimney Sweep) Glucks-Hexe, Gudrun, Heidi, Matrose, Melia, Puck, Rosemarie, A. Schlopsnies doll, and Snik. (See also **Seams down center of face.**)★

2505. Three felt Steiff dolls representing a schoolmaster and his two pupils. The schoolmaster is named Le (Lehrer). According to THE STUDIO, Le was the first character doll made by Steiff. All three dolls have mohair attached to the scalp, button-type eyes, closed mouth and a seam down the middle of each face. Original clothes. Hs. of the Schoolmaster, 50 cm. (19.5 in.), children 30 cm. (12 in.). *Courtesy of Claire Hennig. Photo by Margie Landolt of Basel.*

2506. Steiff felt dolls representing the musicians in "The Village Band," as shown in THE STUDIO, December 15, 1911, p. 234. The dolls are, left to right: Al (Alphonse), two Dachs (Dachau peasants), two Les or Lehrers (Schoolmasters).

2507. All-felt Steiff school boy and girl. They have hair sewn on their heads, beads for eyes. Dolls have Steiff buttons in the ears. Original clothes. Hs. 13 and 13½ in. (33 and 34 cm.). *Courtesy of and photo by Phyllis Salak.*

2508. All-felt doll made by Steiff. It has a seam down the middle of the face, a Steiff metal button in the ear. Hair sewn onto the head. Original ring-master's costume, a full dress black felt suit with tails, a hat with a high crown and black leather knee boots. It holds a wooden handled whip. H. 45 cm. (17½ in.). *Courtesy of Dorothy Mishler.*

2509A & B. One of the Steiff gnomes, has brown wiry hair attached to the scalp, to the cheeks, chin and as eyebrows. The imbedded round green glass eyes have black pupils. The painted smiling mouth is closed. The neck swivels. Hands and feet are large, typical of Steiff gnomes. The big toe is separate from the other toes. Original clothes but the hat is missing. Steiff button is in the ear. H. 9 in. (23 cm.). *Courtesy of and photo by Mike White.*

2510. Steiff gnome with the characteristic hair on the head including the beard and the eyebrows. Some of this hair has been worn away. The green glass eyes with black pupils are imbedded in the felt. The open-closed mouth has large lips. The hands and feet are large and the big toe is separate from the other toes. The Steiff button is in the ear. H. 16 in. (40.5 cm.). *Courtesy of Richard Wright. Photo by A. Jackson.*

2511. Steiff doll dressed to represent a player engaged in sports. The blond mohair is sewed to the scalp and the round white glass eyes have a black pupil looking to the side. There is a seam down the center of the face to the mouth. The doll resembles *Baseb* and the clothes resemble those worn by *Fu*. The neck, hips and shoulders are jointed. A hole in back of the ears suggests that there might have been a button. H. 17 in. (43 cm.). *Courtesy of Richard Wright. Photo by A. Jackson.*

2512. Steiff felt doll representing a Nazi soldier. It has a swastika insignia on the armband and tie pin. The arms and legs are jointed so that they can simulate goose step marching. The hair is painted and the eyes are bead-like blue glass. A seam is down the center of the face. Original brown felt uniform. Hat is sewed onto the head. It has a button in its ear and a red tag reading: "Steiff//Original //Geschutzt//22 Made in Germany." H. 9½ in. (24 cm.) including hat. *Courtesy of Richard Wright. Photo by A. Jackson.*

2513A & B. Marks sometimes used by Steiff.

Stein, Charles, and Heller, William M. 1927. Atlantic City, N.J. Obtained a U.S. design patent for a *Black Bottom Vamp* doll and a U.S. patent for an infant doll on a pillow, known as *Tee Wee*. The infant doll could be made to move like a hand puppet. These dolls were produced by the *S. & H. Novelty Co.*

Stein, H. 1918–30 and later. Prague (Praha), Czechoslovakia. Appears to have been associated with Ignác Stein. Made dolls.

Steinberg. 1927. Cologne, Germany. Produced rubber dolls.

Steinbrinks', B. B. Late 1800s. New York City. Their tradecard advertised a doll and toy bazaar.

Steiner, Albin. 1904–14. Sonneberg, Thür. Applied for two German patents (D.R.G.M.) in 1904 and 1912 for dolls' voices. ★

Steiner, Edmund Ulrich. 1864–1916. Sonneberg, Thür. and New York City. Produced, patented, imported and distributed dolls.

According to PLAYTHINGS, 1908: "June 1907 was the month set for the launching of this Human Face Doll campaign and Mr. Steiner left for his Fatherland, where he could personally direct operations and supervise very little details which went into the making of the new doll. Life face dolls have appeared before, but Mr. Steiner wanted to give his customers an article which would be the direct result of his own genius and long experience. He stayed in and around Sonneberg for the rest of the year, gathering his skilled workmen about him, and instilling into their minds and hearts the hopes which had so long been the very companion of his dreams.

"To more fully carry out his true-to-life doll, human hair was procured for the new line of dolls, long blonde, brunette and Titian tresses, which hung below the waist and which might be dressed simply or in any of the elaborate coiffures which the mood of Dame Fashion might dictate. The doll is made in many different styles, every one of which portrays perfectly, a beautiful child or an age corresponding to that represented by the doll, a brilliant feature in itself. This doll was given a kid body. . . .

"With the idea in mind that the very young child prefers a toy or doll which requires some effort of the owner to put in motion, rather than one which is wholly automatic, Mr.

Steiner has also evolved a new Walking and Sitting Doll. He claims that the effort is good for the child, and also is a great educator. Once more the great artist from Munich was called in, again the hair dressers had to respond to a second call, and he had to go after new workmen and machinery, for it took special mechanism to construct this walking and sitting doll. In the end the doll was finished. She will walk along, rolling her eyes at each step, guided by the slightest touch on the head or shoulder, and the new girlie will also sit on the floor.

"The dashing, heartrending 'Merry Widow'[†] doll came out of those buzzing German factories, and the splendid line of Peter Pan [Play Dolls][†] and his bold, bad pirates, all under the personal direction of the same hand. The work finished, Mr. Steiner and his little coterie of fellow workers took the results of their labors to the art galleries in Berlin. There they were shown for three days and elicited the most enthusiastic notes of approval that the staid old German museum has heard for many a day. The women and children went wild over the new dolls and the artist was awarded many medals."

1908: PLAYTHINGS advertised his walking and sitting dolls made with a variety of hair styles, came dressed or undressed; priced $1.00 to $5.00.★

Steiner, Erich. 1924–25. Sonneberg, Thür. Obtained two German patents (D.R.P.) for dolls' voices including a mama-papa voice.

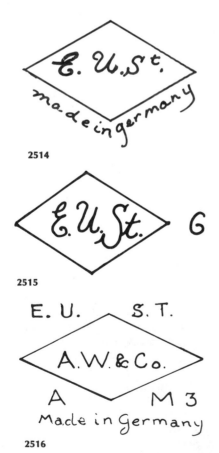

2514–2516. Marks on dolls produced by Edmund Ulrich Steiner. No. 2516 appears to be on a head made by Armand Marseille and probably the body was made by Adolf Wislizenus for E. U. Steiner.

Steiner, Fa. Georg. 1922–28. Sonneberg, Thür. Obtained two German patents (D.R.P.) for dolls' voices including a mama-papa voice.

Steiner, Gustav, Jr. 1914. Neufang, Germany. Applied for a German patent (D.R.G.M.) for a doll's voice.

Steiner, Heinrich. 1898. Schalkau, Thür. Made and exported wax and jointed dolls.

Steiner, Hermann. 1911–30 and later. Sonneberg, and Neustadt near Coburg, Thür., and Bavaria. Company founded in 1911 and made plush animals at first. Bisque head dolls were made in the 1920s and later. Composition and celluloid-head dolls were produced. A composition head *Boudoir* doll had a Hermann Steiner mark.

1920: Founded a porcelain factory and made bisque dolls' heads; employed 300 workers. Advertised jointed dolls. See *Steiner Porzellanfabrik.*

1925: Applied for a German patent (D.R.G.M.) for dolls.

1926: Applied for a German patent (D.R.G.M.) for eyes with movable pupils.

1927: Obtained a German patent (D.R.P.) for sleeping eyes. A British patent was for a glass lens-shaped eyeball containing a pupil that moved freely. The eyeballs were fixed in the head with plaster of Paris which formed the whites of the eyes. Applied for a German patent (D.R.G.M.) for eyes in composition or celluloid heads. Advertised all kinds of porcelain dolls' heads; new-born babies a specialty; the living Steiner Eye was patented in many countries. The new "Life like Steiner-Eye" appeared to be a flirting eye. PLAYTHINGS stated that these eyes moved sideways at the least touch as well as slept. Registered *Das Lebende Steiner-Auge* (The Living Steiner Eye) as a trademark in Germany.

1928: Obtained a German patent (D.R.P.) for sleeping eyes. Advertised "Natural eyelashes for dolls."

1929: Obtained a German patent (D.R.P.) for dolls' sleeping eyes.

Ca. 1930: Composition-head dolls were marked STEHA, a name formed from STEiner and HAuser.★

2517A & B. Bisque head with wig, sleeping eyes, open mouth, teeth, on a five-piece composition body made by Hermann Steiner. Original regional costume, molded footwear. Mark: III. 2521. H. 7 in. (18 cm.). *Coleman Collection.*

2518. Bisque-head infant doll made by Hermann Steiner. It has a painted dome head, sleeping blue glass eyes, closed mouth and a cloth infant type body with celluloid hands. Clothes contemporary with the doll. Mark: H and S intertwined under 14. H. 9 in. (23 cm.). Cir. of head 7½ in. (19 cm.). *Private collection.*

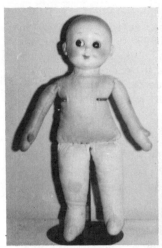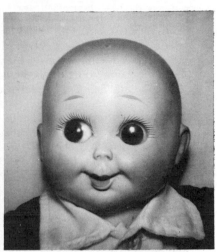

2519A & B. Plaster-type composition-head doll with eyes patented by Hermann Steiner, Also see Ills. 1583 and 1585 in the first COLLECTOR'S ENCYCLOPEDIA OF DOLLS. H. 12½ in. (31.5 cm.). *Courtesy of Ollie Leavister.*

2520. Bisque head doll made by Hermann Steiner has blond molded hair and molded pink hair ribbon. The round blue eyes have unattached discs which float around behind clear glassine covers. The open-closed mouth is wide open. The flange neck fits into a cloth body (a possible replacement). Mark: D.R.G.M.// Germany//22372. H. of head only, 3½ in. (9 cm.). *Courtesy of the Margaret Woodbury Strong Museum. Photo by Harry Bickelhaupt.*

Made in
Germany
HermSteiner
18/0

2521

H. 401 0½ S
made in Germany

2522

402
H. 5/0 S

2523

Made in
Germany

H
St.
10.

2524

2521–2524. Marks found on dolls made by Hermann Steiner.

Steiner, Jules Nicholas (Société Steiner). 1855–91. Paris. The successors were: 1892 Amedée Lafosse; 1893–98 Widow Lafosse, née Lambert; 1899–1901 Jules Mettais; 1904–08, Edmond Daspres. Many of the Steiner dolls also have the name *Bourgoin* on them. The connection between Bourgoin and Steiner has been ascertained from the following doll. A wire-eyed bisque head was incised, "S^te·C 4." and stamped in red "J. STEINER B^te. S.G.D.G. J. BOURGOIN SUCCe." The glass eyes were impressed on the back "STEINER B^te. S.G.D.G. 4." The composition body was stamped in purple "LE PETIT PARISIEN J. ST. B^te. S.G.D.G. SUCCe. PARIS." Ht. 57 cm. (22½ in.). SUCCe stands for Successeur (Successor). By 1882 a Paris directory included the successor information.

In 1943 Fred Kolb, then president of *Borgfeldt,* stated in a letter that he had made his first trip to Paris in 1892 and that the Steiner Co. of Paris had German affiliations and also a doll factory in Germany. Kolb was "under the impression that at that time [1892] the heads of the dolls turned out by the Paris factory were produced in Germany." It should be noted that this statement was made 51 years after the trip.

All of the Jules Steiner dolls examined by the authors so far have been pressed which was a French characteristic. There is some evidence that Steiner pressed their heads even after *Jumeau* changed to the pouring technique. The Steiner dolls marked *Le Parisien* generally had longer fingers than most of the other Steiner hands which were often very short. The sleeping eyes operated manually by a wire behind the ear were usually marked "J. Steiner." A marked Le Parisien body had a pressed head with eyes operated with a wire. The kicking Steiner dolls had a bald head under their wigs. One of these kicking Steiners at the Wenham Museum has written on it in an ink stamp, "Le PETIT STEINER//MEDAILLE D'OR //PARIS 1889//PREMIER CHOIX//DU MAGASIN JOUETS// PASSAGE DE L'OPERA//PARIS." The caduseus mark used by Steiner was sometimes impressed on the hips of the doll's composition body.

The Steiner head often had a F., FI^RE or FIGURE (Translated into English means face or countenance.) followed generally by one of four letters, namely, A, B, C or D. "A" being the most common one. There were two distinct size-height relationships. One went with the four letters mentioned above and was approximately as follows:

Size No.	Height	
	cm.	in.
4/0	18	8
3/0	23	10
2/0	28	11
0	33	13
1	41	16
2	46	18
3	51	20
4	56	22
5	61	24
6	71	28
7	86	34

The other size-height relationship went almost entirely with the A (one C has been reported) and is roughly as follows:

Size No.	Height	
	cm.	in.
4	23	9
7	31	12
9	38	15
11	46	18
13	51	20
14	56	22
15	61	24
19	71	28

1865: Advertised dolls and Bébés; talking and other mechanical dolls. Applied for a patent for a doll that could make a sound.

1870s: A walking Steiner on wheels with a bisque head and arms, an open mouth and teeth carried a tag with red and brown letters reading "I'm the Pretty Dolly that walks, calls Papa and Mamma and if you lay me down I cry."

1889: Obtained a patent for reinforcing porcelain or bisque dolls' heads with a piece of heavy fabric, leather, felt or rubber material in order to hold the pieces together when the head is broken. This also reinforces the plaster that holds the eyes in place. (Some Steiner dolls have been found with wax pates.)

1890 or later: The directions for a walking Steiner which was patented in 1890 are as follows: The directions for operating the mechanical walking Steiner came with the doll in four languages, French, English, German and Spanish. The directions in English are as follows: "To make the mechanism work it is sufficient to wind up with the brass key attached to the baby, turning to the right, just as one winds up a watch or clock.

"When the movement is wound up, one must, to obtain the work, push behind the iron-wire which is near the key; one can stop the movement, as one whises [sic] in pulling to one's self the iron-wire.

"When the baby is wound up, not to forget to lift up the arms like those of a child who calls, holding out his arms. Even children can wind up this mechanism themselves, without danger."

At the bottom of the page is "J. St., breveté s.g.d.g., Paris."

It is not known whether these directions were for *Bébé Premier Pas* or *Bébé Marcheur* both of which were patented in 1890.

Au Nain Bleu sold Le Petit Parisien, a Steiner doll, with the "Medaille d'Or, Paris 1889" mark.

A dressed boy Jules Steiner doll has been found wearing a miniature copy of the Steiner's Paris Exhibition Medal.★

Steiner, Louis. 1909–24. Sonneberg, Thür. From 1909 through 1915 he applied for six German patents (4 D.R.G.M.) and (2 D.R.P.) for dolls' wigs and hair eyebrows.★

2525. Jules Steiner bisque head doll has a wig, stationary glass eyes, open mouth with eight upper and seven lower teeth. The body is marked "J. Steiner, fabricante, rue de Saintonge, No. 25 a [???] Paris, Prisette, Imp. Pass. du Carre 17." Original clothes including the "puddin" helmet to protect a baby's head. H. 11½ in. (29 cm.). *Private collection.*

2526. Bisque-head Jules Steiner doll with wig, stationary blue glass eyes, pierced ears, closed mouth and a ball jointed composition body. Size 4. H. 21½ in. (54.5 cm.). *Courtesy of Sotheby Parke Bernet Inc., N.Y.*

2527. Jules Steiner bisque-head doll has a wig, stationary blue glass eyes, pierced ears, closed mouth and a ball-jointed composition body. Mark: Ste C. H. 14½ in. (37 cm.). *Courtesy of Sotheby Parke Bernet Inc., N.Y.*

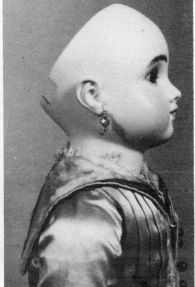

2528A & B. Pressed bisque-head doll made by Jules Steiner has a wig, stationary blue glass eyes, pierced ears, and a closed mouth. The ball jointed composition body has no joints at the wrists. Mark: "FIGURE C N° 2 //J. STEINER B^te S.G.D.G.// PARIS." H. 18½ in. (47 cm.). *Courtesy of Cherry Bou.*

2529. Pressed bisque-head doll made by Jules Steiner with a wig, wire-eyed sleeping blue eyes operated with a lever, pierced ears, open mouth and a ball jointed composition body containing a voice box. Probably original clothes. Marked: Figure B. No. 5. H. 24 in. (61 cm.). *Courtesy of Sotheby Parke Bernet Inc., N.Y.*

2530. Jules Steiner bisque-head doll with a blond wig, stationary brown glass eyes, applied ears, closed mouth, and a ball jointed composition body. Original clothes. H. 13 in. (33 cm.). *Courtesy of Sylvia Brockmon.*

2531. Jules Steiner bisque-head doll with black wig, stationary blue glass eyes, pierced ears, closed mouth, and a ball-jointed composition body. Mark on head: STEINER//PARIS//F^{RE} A 10. Mark on body: Le Petite Parisien//Bébé Steiner//Medaille d'Or Paris 1889. H. 17 in. (43 cm.). *Courtesy of Sotheby Parke Bernet Inc., N.Y.*

2532A & B. Pressed bisque-head doll made by Jules Steiner. It has a wig, stationary blue glass eyes, pierced ears, closed mouth and is on a fully jointed composition body. Original clothes. Mark: J. STEINER//B^{te} S G D G//PARIS// FI^{re} A 19. H. 30 in. (76 cm.). *Courtesy of Cherry Bou.*

2533. Jules Steiner doll with a bisque head having its face painted like a clown. A black silk cap covers its head. There are stationary brown glass eyes, pierced ears, a closed mouth, and a five-piece composition body. Original costume. Mark on head: STEINER//PARIS//F^{RE} A 4. A paper label on the back has "Le Petit Parisien" on a flag held by a doll. H. 12 in. (30.5 cm.). *Private collection.*

J. Steiner.   B^{te} S. G. D. G.   S^{ie} C · 7   J. Bourgoin. Sr.

2534

S^{TE} A O

J. Steiner B^{te} S.g.D.g. J. Bourgoin S^r

2535

FIGURE C N° 2
J. STEINER B^{TE} S.G.D.G.
PARIS

2536

FIGURE   A 18
J. STEINER B^{TE} S.G.D.G.
PARIS

2537

FIGURE A N·12
J · STEINER B_{TE} S.G.D.G
P A R I S

2538

J. STEINER
B^{TE} S.G.D.G.
PARIS
F^{IRE} A 19

2539

11
PARIS

2540

2541

STEINER
4
S.G.D.G.

2542

2534–2542. Marks on Bisque-head Jules Steiner dolls.

Steiner, Nicol. 1911–20. Neustadt near Coburg, Thür. Made dolls.

1911: Applied for a German patent (D.R.G.M.) for a jointed doll.★

Steiner Porzellanfabrik. 1920–26 and later. Neustadt near Coburg, Bavaria. Advertised for workers to make dolls' heads and "child dolls." Child dolls probably were all-bisque dolls if they were made in a porcelain factory. This factory made dolls' heads and all-bisque dolls for *Hermann Steiner.*

Steiner, Richard. 1912–13. Neufang, Sbg. Applied for two German patents (D.R.G.M.); both were for dolls' voices and one was obtained with *Gustav Schmidt.*

Steiner, Victor (Viktor). 1903–30. Sonneberg, Thür. Made dolls especially dolls with voices.

1922: Advertised that all his dolls had voices and were patented in many countries. One of these dolls was named *Lotte Talking Baby.*

1926: Obtained a German patent (D.R.P.) for sleeping eyes.

1927: Obtained a German patent (D.R.P.) for a mama voice.

1928: Obtained a German patent (D.R.P.) for a mama voice. Advertised wooden dolls and voices for dolls including mama voices.

1930: Advertised talking and singing voices for dolls. *M. Michaelis & Co.* was his Berlin agent.★

Steiner, Willi. 1925–29. Freiburg, Bavaria. Made cloth dolls and embroidery patterns including material to dress dolls.★

Steiner & Co., Messrs. 1915. London. Made dolls and claimed that all members of the firm were British born or American. Advertised 20 unbreakable models of "Mama" dolls. These were American dolls with voices but did not walk like the later real *Mama* dolls. The dolls were dressed as a Dutch Girl, an Indian, Mama's Baby in Long Clothes, a Piccaninny, a Red Cross Nurse, a Sailor, a Scotsman and *Tommy Atkins.*

Steinfeld Bros. 1898–1919. New York City. Made and imported dolls.

1919: Advertised 45 style nos. made of a composition containing cork fibre, painted or sleeping eyes, fully jointed. Hts. 13 to 25 in. (33 to 63.5 cm.).★

Steinhardt, A., & Bro. 1910–19. New York City. Made and imported dolls.

Ca. 1912: Advertised *Flossie.*

1919: They were agents for *Giebeler-Falk.*★

Steinhauser, A., & Co. † See **Henze & Steinhauser.**

DEP
A.S.
1900-9

2543. Mark possibly used by A. Steinhardt.

Steinmann, Violet D. 1930. Los Angeles, Calif. Registered in U.S. the trademark *The Hart Doll* for dolls.

Steinmeier, J. E., Bronze Works. 1903–29. New York City. Made dies and *Molds for Dolls*.

1920: Claimed they were the originators of the *Hot Press* baking dies.

1929: Advertised dies and molds for dolls and parts of dolls.

Stella. 1884. Name of a wax doll (probably wax-over-composition) advertised by *Lauer*. It had a wig, earrings, a lace trimmed chemise, stockings, and boots. Five hts. 13, 16, 20, 23½, and 27½ in. (33, 40.5, 51, 59.5, and 70 cm.); priced $2.00 to $8.00 doz. wholesale.

Stella. 1909. Name of a Knock-about cloth doll with a chromolithographed face, distributed by the *Boston Store* in Chicago. Ht. 14 in. (35.5 cm.); priced 25¢.

Stella. 1903–14. Trade name of a cloth doll produced by *Horsman* and probably made by *Albert Brückner*.

1912: Style no. H/O had a compressed fabric face and wore a low-waisted print dress having bretelles and a bonnet; priced 25¢.

Style no H/C had a celluloid mask face and wore a dress with a yoke and bertha.

1914: H/O was the same but H/C was named *Nancy* instead of Stella.★

Stellmacher, J. 1909–20. Steinheid, Germany. Made a doll named Stella.

1909: Applied for a German patent (D.R.G.M.) for a doll's head with spun glass hair.

Stephan, Carl (Karl). 1907–10. Hernals near Vienna. Listed in directories under Dolls and Dolls' Heads. Several dolls have been reported with their bodies marked "Aus der Puppen Klinik und Reparatur Austalt von Carl Stephan, Hernals. (From the doll clinic and repairing workshop of Carl Stephan, Hernals.).

Steppin' Baby. 1926–27. Name of a key-wind walking and dancing doll made by *E. Goldberger*. The dolls had composition heads, painted eyes, metal bodies and were dressed as a Dutch boy, a Dutch girl or a baby in a sacque and in an ankle length dress; priced $1.00 and up.

Stergard (Stergard-Manuel), Georges. 1930 and later. Paris. Made dolls' clothes including dresses, hats, bonnets, coats, lingerie, and footwear.

1930: Registered in France the trademark *Géo* to designate dolls.

Sterling Doll Co. 1930 and later. Made dolls including cloth dolls.

1930: Advertised baby dolls, *Boudoir* dolls and other kinds of dolls.

Sterling Toys. After 1900. New York City. Turned wooden dolls, painted and water-proofed with valspar, representing girls and boys. These dolls were originated by W. S. Sterling, exhibited and sold at The Children's Gift Shop formerly (around 1900) the Stryvelyne Shop. Hts. 4 to 6 in. (10 to 15 cm.); priced 25¢.

Stern, Ernst, Johann & Alexander. 1926–27. Vienna. Obtained Austrian and German patents (D.R.P.) for a walking doll.

Stern, Helene. 1908. Berlin. One of the Puppen Reform artists. She dressed dolls in crinoline (1860s) period costumes. These dolls were written about in the art periodical KIND & KUNST (Children & Art) and were distributed by *Hermann Tietz*.

Stern Bros. 1883–84 and probably other years. American. Advertised all their dolls as being "French"; they included all-bisque dolls and bisque-head bébés. Hts. 4 to 36 in. (10 to 91.5 cm.); priced undressed 25¢ to $30.00, dressed 50¢ to $100.00.

1883–84: Stern Bros. catalog gave the following information on "French Dolls" with bisque heads:

| | Jointed Composition Body | | | | Kid Body | |
| | Sleeping Eyes | | Stationary Eyes | | Sleeping Eyes | |
Size No.	in.	cm.	in.	cm.	in.	cm.
0	14	35.5	10½	26.5		
1	15½	39.5	11½	29		
2	17½	44.5	13	33	14	35.5
3	19½	49.5	14½	37	15	38
4	21½	54.5	15½	39.5	16½	42
5	24½	62	17	43	17½	44.5
6	26	66	19½	49.5		

SIZE HEIGHT RELATION FOR "FRENCH DOLLS" SOLD BY STERN BROS.*

(*See table in All-Bisque Dolls for additional Stern Bros. data.)

The kid-body dolls were a little less expensive than the composition-body dolls. The undressed dolls wearing only a chemise cost about one third as much as the dressed dolls.

This size-height relationship does not fit *Jumeau* or *Jules Steiner* or *Gaultier* or any of the other known French manufacturers that have been studied.

Stern Specialty Co. 1912. New York City. Made dolls' auto goggles and dolls' rubberized auto coats.

Steuber, Mary. 1878 and probably later. Philadelphia, Pa. Legs on dolls' bodies have been found bearing the stamped date of her patent.★

Stich, Hedwig. 1908. Germany. One of the Puppen Reform artists; she dressed dolls as boys and girls in the style of the 1800s. These dolls were written about in an art periodical, KIND & KUNST (Children & Art), and were distributed by *Hermann Tietz.*

Stiebel, David. 1928. London. Agent for *Hunaeus* and *H. Josef Leven.*

Stier, Heinrich. 1830 through the 1880s. Sonneberg, Thür. Heinrich, visited America and England in the 1830s and 1840s before he established a doll factory in Sonneberg where he made chiefly wax-over-composition dolls. The Sonneberg Museum has one of his wax-over-composition heads with molded-hair and glass eyes. Ht. 13 cm. (5 in.) head only.

Heinrich Stier, born 1814, died 1888, was related to Gustav Stier who founded a doll factory in 1871. Gustav's sister was *Barbara Schilling.*

Doll bodies bearing the mark of Heinrich Stier, which had the so-called *Belton-type* heads, have been reported though not seen by the authors.★

Stoddart's. 1921. London. Advertised metal dolls.

Stoke-on-Trent Doll Supplies Co. 1920. Stoke-on-Trent, Staffs. Factory named Victory Works made dolls' heads with sleeping eyes.

Stolfa, Hermann. 1924. Vienna. Obtained an Austrian patent for a baby doll that kicked when in a lying position according to Dr. Eva Moskovszky.

Stoll & Edwards Co. 1925–30 and later. New York City. Made cloth-body dolls.

Storch, Inc. 1925–26. Breslau, Silesia. Manufactured dolls.

Stos. Early 1800s. Paris. Made and/or distributed dolls.

Stöter, Otto. 1906–07. Cologne, Germany. Applied for several German patents (D.R.G.M.) and (D.R.P.) relating to dolls' eyes.★

Strasser. 1920s. Germany. Made art dolls in *Else Hecht's* workshop.

Strasserpuppen Werkstatten (Strasser† Doll Workshop). 1924–30. Berlin. The workshop of Hedwig Maria Huldschinsky† where portrait art dolls were made. Some of these dolls were made for export and it was advertised that dolls with movable and washable heads were suitable for the

2544. Cloth body with legs patented by Mary Steuber. The doll has a dome shaped bisque shoulder head, blond wig, stationary blue glass eyes and a closed mouth. The body has leather arms and the shoes and socks are part of the legs. Mark: Ill. 2545, stamped on the upper part of a lower leg. H. 13½ in. (34 cm.). *Private collection.*

STEUBER'S PATENT June 25 78

2545. Stamped mark on a cloth leg made according to Mary Steuber's patent.

tropics. *John Hess* distributed these rubber head dolls in 1924, named Babs, Gerda, Hansl, and Maria. Hts. 30 to 60 cm. (12 to 23½ in.). In 1926 Hess described the dolls as of "soft elastic material," and included Buby and Plumsi.

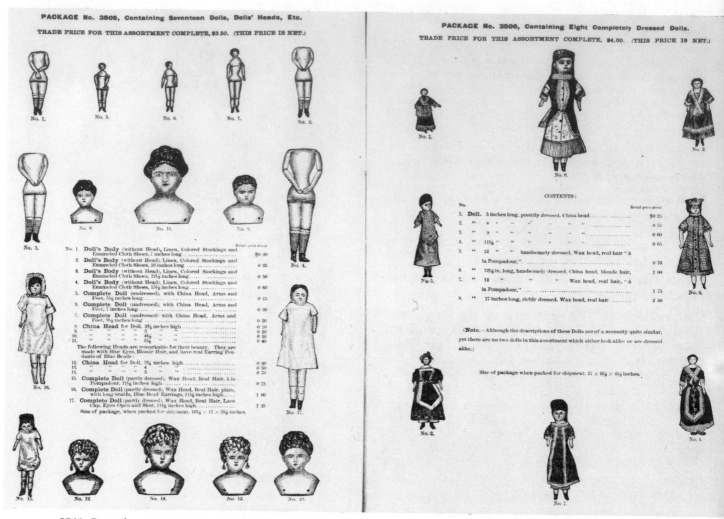

2546. Pages from a J.F. Stratton Co. Catalog of the 1880s showing doll bodies with striped stockings and "Enameled cloth shoes"; small dolls with china heads and cloth bodies; wax-head dolls in chemise; china shoulder heads, some with pierced ears; dressed dolls with china or wax heads. Hs. of dolls 5 to 17 in. (12.5 to 43 cm.). *Courtesy of the Henry Francis Du Pont Winterthur Museum.*

Strassner, Ernst. 1910. Sonneberg, Thür. Applied for a German patent (D.R.G.M.) for dolls' eyebrows of imitation silk.

Strat Manufacturing (Game) Co. 1915–16. New York City. Made *Sammy Sock* and other cloth dolls. Before 1916 made a 75¢ line. In 1916 started a new line of smaller dolls, two styles in various colors; priced 50¢.

Stratton, John F., Co. 1880s. America. His catalog listed:
Dolls with china head and limbs on cloth bodies. Hts. 5½, 7, and 9½ in. (14, 18, and 24 cm.); priced 15¢ to 30¢.
China heads with blue eyes, blond hair and blue bead earrings; priced 30¢ to 70¢.
All-china dolls, jointed at the shoulders and hips dressed in a chemise. Ht. 5½ in. (14 cm.); priced 50¢ and 65¢.
All-china dolls in molded sailor suits. Ht. 4 in. (10 cm.); priced 40¢. (China may refer to unglazed porcelain or bisque.)

Wax-head dolls with real hair. Ht. 11½ in. (29 cm.); priced 75¢; with earrings $1.00; with sleeping eyes $1.25.
Linen dolls' bodies with "colored stocking and enamel cloth shoes." Hts. without head 7 to 15½ in. (18 to 39.5 cm.); priced 20¢ to 60¢. Dressed dolls with china heads, hts. 5, 8, 9, 11½, and 12½ in. (12.5, 20.5, 23, 29, and 31.5 cm.); priced 25¢ to $1.00. Dressed dolls with wax heads and real hair. Hts. 12, 14, and 17 in. (30.5, 35.5, and 37 cm.); priced 70¢ to $2.50.

Straube, William. See **Kling, C. F., & Co.**

Strauss, Adolph & Co. 1857–1930 and later. New York City. In 1923 the successor was Strauss-Eckhardt Co. or "Seco." Imported and distributed dolls. One of the Seco dolls has been found with a bisque head made by *Heubach* of Köppelsdorf on a five-piece stapled composition body that could sit or stand upright. This firm made a doll named *Fan Kid* dressed as a baseball catcher.

1926: Advertised an infant doll in a basket called *Our Pet*, also baby dolls with layettes.

1927: New factory in Sonneberg, opened to produce Our Pet dolls; the bisque heads look like *My Dream Baby.* Our Pet was wrapped in a blanket and lying in a wicker basket, came in five style nos. 100, 150, 200, 250 (twins) and 300. There were 10 sizes. A round tag had "Our Pet" on it. Seco produced 2000 dolls called "Our Play Yard Pet" each week. These babies in a play pen came in ten sizes; priced $1.00 and up. These dolls came with a nursing bottle, rattle and /or pacifier. The total number of Our Pet dolls produced each year was 624,000. Applied for two German (D.R.G.M.) and one U.S. patent for Our Pet dolls. *Hermann V. Eckhardt* was the assignee of the U.S. patent for an opaque white glass nursing bottle with a red rubber nipple that fitted into the doll's mouth. Registered in U.S. Our Play Yard Pet as a trademark for dolls.

1928: Registered in U.S. *Our Dolly-Kar Pet* as a trademark for dolls. Their advertisement stated, "Dolls like motor cars must be changed yearly in design and construction to meet the constant demand for something different, something new, something novel."

1929: Imported nude papier-mâché dolls representing American Indians, squaws, and papooses in a standing position. After importation they were dressed or wrapped in colored cloth or pockets inscribed, "Asheville, N.C.," "Devil's Lake" and so forth. These were dutiable at 70 percent as dolls because they were suitable for the amusement of children. Hts. 2½ to 6 in. (6.5 to 15 cm.). Probably these dolls resembled the Mary McAboy dolls, and some of them were marked "Made in Germany."

1931: Advertised Our Pet line of dolls, *Boudoir* dolls, Play yard dolls, Basket dolls, cradle dolls and hundreds of other imported dolls.★

Strauss, Haas & Co. 1908. U.S.A. Imported dolls.

Strauss-Eckhardt. See *Eckardt; Eckart & Co.; Eckhardt, Gebr.* and *Strauss, Adolph.*

Strawbridge & Clothier. 1868–1930 and later. Philadelphia, Pa. Distributed dolls.

1906: Registered *Princess Royal* in U.S. as a trademark for dolls.

1908: Celebrated their 40th anniversary by showing, "The Court of Historical Dolls. Miniature fashion Models made in Paris by *Mlle. Riera.*"

1913: Dolls included *Baby Edith, Baby Helen, Baby Marguerite* and *Dolly Penn.* Hts. 18 to 24 in. (45.5 to 61 cm.).★

Strawman. 1921–22. Name of a doll that could float, made by the *Rees Davis* Toy Co. It had a painted face.

Strehl, Max. 1912–13. Zuckelhausen near Leipzig, Germany. Obtained a German patent (D.R.P.) for walking dolls.

2547. Strauss & Eckhardt's Seco mark for dolls.

Striking Dolls. 1928. Name used by *Arranbee* for some of their dolls.

Strobel & Wilken Co. 1864–1930 and later. Cincinnati, Ohio, New York City, and Sonneburg, Thür. Importers and manufacturers' agent for domestic dolls. According to the Ciesliks the marks attributed to Strobel and Wilken may have belonged to *Walther & Sohn.*

1881: Strobel of Cincinnati stayed at a hotel while visiting Sonneberg.

1913: Advertised *Käthe Kruse* dolls, other dolls with celluloid faces and dolls with light or black hair. Hts. a few to 48 in. (122 cm.).

1914: Made special arrangements with Winsor McCay to make bisque dolls in two sizes representing *Little Nemo,* *Princess Flip, Impie* and *Dr. Pill.*

1915: Had exclusive control of the *American Art Dolls,* such as the *Susie's Sister* line, *Tootsie* line and others. Agent for *National Toy Manufacturing Co.*

1916: The President, Emil Strobel, died.

1917: Advertised Japanese dolls as well as the American Art Dolls.

1918: Advertised Rag Bag dolls, price 25¢. A shipment of German dolls that had been bought and paid for in 1914 before the War started, arrived from Holland and was accepted by Strobel & Wilken, despite protests.

1921: Distributed dolls made by *Oweenee Novelty Co.*

1923: The Ohio business was liquidated and Andrew K. Ackerman who had been with Strobel & Wilken since 1870 became President of the Company. Strobel & Wilken established themselves permanently in Sonneberg and tried to restore the old market conditions. The few German lines they offered were mostly prewar ones.

1924: Became agent for the red rubber dolls made by the *Ungarische Gummiwaren-Fabrik* (Hungarian Rubber Goods Factory) in Budapest. Their own line of *Mama* walking dolls was added to the American lines of dolls.

1926: George Wilken died. He had been active in the business until 1917, when he retired but stayed on the Board of Directors. Jeter A. Penny became President of the Company in 1926. Strobel & Wilken were direct manufacturers' or factory representative for dolls. They were the sole selling agents for the *Arabesque* line of baby and Mama dolls, the cloth *Cuddlekins* line and the commission house for *W. Bimblick & Co.*'s wooden head dolls. They distributed *Kid-*

die Specialty Corp. dolls and represented 600 lines of toys, part of them doll manufacturers.

1927: Advertised *Jubilee Art Dolls* and *Baby Dahne.*

1929: Factory representative for *Schoenhut.* Distributed the cloth dolls created by *Gertrude Rollinson* and the *F. W. Peterson Co.* dolls.

1930: *American Beauty* dolls were their own line.★

Strome & Co. 1892–1930 and later. London. Made and/or distributed celluloid dolls.

Stroup, Thomas H. 1926. Seattle, Wash. Obtained a U.S. patent for a dancing character doll.

Stru. (Struwwelpeter, Strubelpeter†, Mop-head). Before 1911–24. Felt doll made by *Steiff,* representing the character *Struwwelpeter* in the children's storybook of this name. The doll had unruly hair and very long fingernails. Hts. 30, 35 and 43 cm. (12, 14, and 17 in.); priced 87¢ in Germany in 1911 and $1.50 in New York in 1913 for the smallest size dolls. Only the smallest size was advertised in 1924.★

Strunz, Wilhelm. 1909–11. Nürnberg, Bavaria. Made cloth dolls.★

Struwe, Wilhelm. 1912. Nürnberg, Bavaria. Applied for a German patent (D.R.G.M.) for a doll with changeable heads.

2548. Doll named Darling handled by Strobel & Wilken has a bisque head, dark wig, sleeping brown glass eyes, open mouth, and a kid body with bisque hands and cloth feet. Mark: Darling //3/0. H. 19½ in. (49.5 cm.). *Courtesy of Sotheby Parke Bernet Inc., N.Y.* (See Ills. 734–736.)

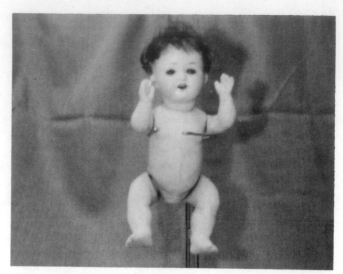

2549. Bisque-head doll produced perhaps by Strobel & Wilken but more likely by Walther & Sohn. It has a wig, sleeping blue glass eyes, an open mouth with two upper teeth, dimples in the cheeks, and a bent limb composition baby body. Mark: Ill. 2550. *Courtesy of Helen Ralph.*

2550–2551. Marks used by Strobel & Wilken or Walther & Sohn, for various types of dolls.

Struwwelpeter (Shock Head Peter). Several dolls were made to represent the character of this name in the Struwwelpeter storybook, especially ones made of various kinds of cloth, sometimes with leather heads and limbs. (See also **Stru.**)

Struwwelpeter. 1912–23. Celluloid doll with jointed arms and molded clothes made by *Rheinische Gummi und Celluloid Fabrik Co.* The doll represented the boy in the verse "Struwwelpeter." Ht. 14 cm. (5½ in.). This series also in-

Der Struwwelpeter.

2552. Directions for making this doll representing Struwwelpeter are given in DIE WELT DER FRAU (THE LADY'S WORLD), 1908. It has leather head, arms and legs, wool yarn hair, needle sculptured face with embroidered features and black glass bead eyes. H. 23 to 25 cm. (9 to 10 in.).

cluded Daumenlutscher (Thumb sucker) and *Suppen Kasper* in 1913; *Zappel-Philipp* was in the 1923 series. (See also **Stru.**)

Stryker, Mrs. Edward. 1900–29. Seattle, Wash. Born in Norway and came to America in 1900. According to TOY WORLD the "best stores in America bought her dolls' clothes and sewing sets." She made the clothes as diminutive as possible.

1928: She was proprietor of the *Toinette Fashion Shop.*

1929: Elected Secretary of the Toy Makers Guild of the State of Washington.

Stu (Student). 1916. Felt doll made by *Steiff.* Ht. 43 cm. (17 in.).

Stupid. 1922. Name of a doll with a face of tricot cloth over a plaster cast made by the *Sardeau* sisters. It had long blond braids made of rope and tied with green satin bows. Its orange satin costume with a tight bodice and puff sleeves was trimmed with Armenian embroidery. It was the mate to *Vodka.*

Sturani, Mario. 1920s. Italy. Born 1906 in Ancona. He was a ceramist and a painter who assisted in the production of the *Lenci* ceramics. He may have contributed to the designing of the Lenci dolls. According to Beppe Garella, head of the Lenci firm in 1980s, Sturani joined the Lenci firm about 1925 and in 1930 devised a washable felt with a lacquer (cellulose) finish.

Stutgarter Holz & Spielwarenfabrik (Stuttgart Wood and Toy Factory). 1923–24. Stuttgart, Germany. Obtained a German patent for the movement of a doll.

Stutzhauser Porzellanfabrik. See Hertel, Schwab & Co.

Styl. 1921. Pistyan, Central Europe. Shop that distributed dolls, among them dolls dressed in costumes of Slovak peasants at a Fair. The garments of these dolls were embroidered by hand. *Stewart Culin* purchased some of these dolls.

Suck-a-Thumb. 1911–16. Trade name of a doll designed by *Helen Trowbridge,* allegedly from a life model; produced by *Horsman* as one of their Nature Baby dolls; copyrighted in 1911; distributed by *Wanamaker,* price $1.00 retail, and *Marshall Field.* This composition-head cloth body doll was shown in both the 1912 and 1914 Horsman catalogs as Number 146 but the two dolls did not have identical heads. Both dolls had short molded hair with a slight topknot, painted eyes glancing to the side, open mouth and a patented right arm and hand made so that the doll could simulate sucking its thumb. The doll was 10 in. (25.5 cm.) high and with its long dress it was 19 in. (48 cm.).

1914: In the Horsman catalog besides No. 146 there was a No. 726, also called "Baby Suck-a-Thumb." This doll was one of the *Gold Medal Babies,* and was totally different from Number 146 since its mouth and arm did not appear to permit the sucking of its thumb. With its long dress it measured 30 in. (76 cm.) and cost $27.00 doz. wholesale. (See Sucker Thumb[†].)

Suck-a-Thumb (Sucker Thumb Baby). 1924–30 and later. Designed by *Bernard Lipfert* and made by *Ideal.* It had a composition head, sleeping celluloid covered eyes, "Composition rubber" arms and its open mouth could suck a thumb or pacifier. Similar heads were used on *Smiles* and *Tickletoes.*

1926: Wore a short organdy dress trimmed with lace, and single strap slippers. Ht. 15 in. (38 cm.).

1927–28: Distributed by *Charles William,* it had a movable neck, runner arms and hands, cloth body and legs, crying voice. Ht. 16 in. (40.5 cm.); priced $2.75.

1928: Had molded hair, a flange neck joint, cotton stuffed cloth body with voice, rubber arms and legs. Wore a white short organdy baby dress and halo cap. Hts. 12½, 15, and 17 in. (31.5, 38, and 43 cm.); priced $1.98 to $3.98.

Ca. 1930 or later: Larger sizes were added and the dolls were distributed by *Quaker Doll Co.*★

Suck-Thumb-Baby. 1929. Name of a doll manufactured by *Carl Heumann.*

Südsee (South Sea Baby). 1930 and later. Brown bisque-head baby doll with sleeping or painted eyes, brown composition baby body, wore a grass skirt, large metal earrings and anklet and a bead necklace. Some of these dolls were made by *Heubach* of Köppelsdorf, and distributed by *Montgomery Ward.* Ht. 8½ in. (21.5 cm.); priced 68¢. (See also **South Sea Baby.**)

Sue. 1929. All-composition doll with a waist joint made by *Amberg,* based on the patent for the *It* doll. Sue had molded side-part hair, painted eyes, bent arms and diagonal hip joints. Ht. 14 in. (35.5 cm.).

Suedine. See **Eisen, Louis.**

Suez. 1927. Trade name of a doll.

Suffragette. 1918. Name of a composition doll made by *K & K*, distributed by *Borgfeldt.* It was dressed in the same material as children wore.

Sugar Baby. 1930 and probably other years. Made by *Effanbee,* had a kapok-filled cloth body, came in three sizes.★

Sugar Plum. 1921–28. Cloth doll had real hair and big blue eyes.

1921: Wore a pink or blue dress and hat; priced $2.75.

1928: Trademark registered in U.S. by *Borgfeldt* for dolls.

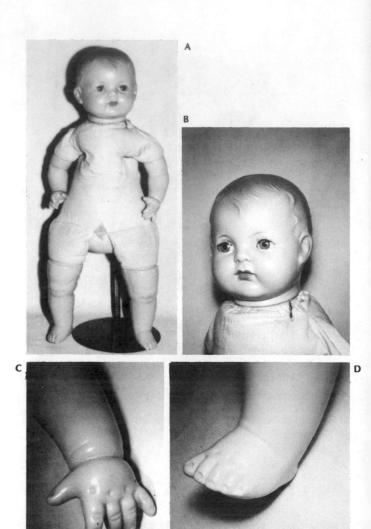

2554A–D. Composition-head doll named Sugar Baby, made by Effanbee. It has molded blond hair, sleeping blue celluloid covered eyes, hair eyelashes, closed mouth, a flange neck and a cloth Mama doll body with composition arms and legs. Mark: Ill. 2555. H. 22 in. (56 cm.). *Courtesy of Dorothy Annunziato.*

EFFANBEE
SUGAR BABY

2555. Sugar Baby embossed mark on a composition head made by Effanbee.

Suitcase Dolly. 1915–17. *Amberg* produced a dressed baby doll with an extra dress, underwear and a rattle all placed in a 12 in. (30.5 cm.) suitcase.

Sully, George, & Co. 1921. New York City. Made and/or distributed cutout cloth dolls.

Sum Fun. See **Kitts, J. DeLancy.**

Summer Girl. 1914. Bisque-head doll with wig, sleeping eyes, composition body jointed at the shoulders, elbows,

No. 146 "Suck-a-Thumb"

2553. Baby Suck-a-Thumb produced by Horsman and advertised in their catalog of ca. 1914. The design of the composition head was copyrighted in 1911 and it appears to be the same as Baby Blossom's head. The right arm on this doll is made so that its thumb can go into its open mouth.

hips and knees, wore removable clothes; and distributed by *Butler Bros.* Ht. 16 in. (40.5 cm.); priced $10.00 doz. wholesale.

Summer Girl. 1916. Cloth doll made by *Atlas Manufacturing Co.* It had stub hands and wore a short flowered print dress with matching bonnet. Three hts.

Summer Girl. 1919. Doll with composition head and hands, wig, sleeping eyes, made by *Ideal.* It wore a knee-length white organdy dress and a ribbon bandeau on its hair. Ht. 15 in. (38 cm.); priced $2.25.

Sun Enamel Works. 1929. Leominster, Mass. Made *Playpet Dolls,* a line of turned wood segmented dolls including Mother Goose, Nursery Rhyme characters such as *Little Boy Blue, Little Polly Flinders,* and *Humpty Dumpty.*

Sun Rubber Co. Ca. 1930. Barberton, Ohio. Made and patented rubber dolls in the U.S. An all-rubber doll with molded hair and features, painted eyes was marked "MF'D BY//THE SUN RUBBER CO.//BARBERTON, O.//U.S.A." It wore a crocheted woolen outfit.

Sunbonnet Girl. 1919. Composition head doll with molded hair, sleeping eyes, composition arms and molded composition boots, made by *Ideal.* Wore a checked cotton dress and sunbonnet. Ht. 14 in. (35.5 cm.); priced $10.80 doz. wholesale.

Sunbonnet Girl. 1927. Cloth doll made of powder puff plush with embroidered facial features, made by *Woolnough.*

Sunbonnet Lassie. 1914. Composition head doll with composition hands distributed by *Marshall Field.* It wore a plaid dress trimmed with lace, a pinafore and a sunbonnet with a very large bow. Ht. 14 in. (35.5 cm.); priced $17.00 doz. wholesale.

Sunbonnet Sal (Sunbonnet Sallie). 1912–16. Composition head doll with molded hair, painted eyes, produced by *Horsman* as style no. 143. It appears to be a smaller version of the doll called *Milkmaid Mary.*

1912: Wore a checked gingham dress and sunbonnet, and a pinafore.

1914: Wore a dress and sunbonnet of plain pink fabric and a pinafore trimmed with lace. Ht. 14 in. (35.5 cm.); priced $8.50 doz. wholesale.★

Sunbonnet Sal SHEbee. See **HEbee-SHEbee.**

Sunbonnet Sue. 1909–14. One of the Life Like *Babyland* dolls. Produced by *Horsman.*★

Sunbonnet Sue. Ca. 1918. Doll wearing a blue dress and sunbonnet distributed by *Shackman.* Ht. 16 in. (40.5 cm.): priced $1.00.

Sun-Joy-Toy. 1926–30. Trademark used by *M. & S. Shillman* for their dolls' clothes and infant dolls' accessories. The trademark was a circle within which were the words "Dolls up the Doll//The Sun-Joy-Toy//Line//and its household."

Sunlight, Sieve & Co. (Crescent Works). 1915–20. Manchester, England. Made cloth dolls printed back and front.

No. 143
"SUNBONNET SAL"
Trade Mark

(Head copyrighted, 1912, by E. I. Horsman Co.)

Another winsome lassie with roguish eyes, all dressed for daisy picking in the fields. Over her pink frock, which matches her sunbonnet, she wears a pretty lace trimmed overdress, and short white socks and white shoes. Her head, too, is unbreakable, and body cork stuffed and fully jointed.

Per Dozen........**$8.50**

No. 143 "Sunbonnet Sal"

2556. Sunbonnet Sal advertised in the Horsman catalog of ca. 1914. The composition head had been copyrighted in 1912. It had molded and painted hair and eyes, closed mouth, cloth body with composition Campbell Kid early type hands. *Catalog courtesy of Bernard Barenholtz.*

Later they made dolls with *British Ceramic* or composition heads or celluloid faces.

1915: Advertised cloth soldiers and sailors; special export lines; priced 2¢ to 12¢.

1916: Advertised dolls representing soldiers, sailors, nurses, Scouts, Colonials, *Pearly King,* "Gollywog" (*Golliwogg*) and dressed dolls. London agent was *Charles W. Baker.*

1917: Made over 50 numbers of dressed and undressed dolls with composition heads; priced 12¢ and up.

1918: One of their leading lines was Eskimo dolls.

Sunny. 1915. Doll representing a girl was dressed in a ribbon sash and hair ribbon; made by *Trion* as style no. 234.

Sunny Babe, Sunny Boy, and Sunny Girl. 1927–29. Names given to dolls made by *Averill Manufacturing Co.*

1927: *Mama* Doll type had a celluloid head with molded hair, glass eyes, composition arms and legs, slender cloth body. Various costumes included a lace trimmed Little Lord Fauntleroy style suit and Tam. Tag on Sunny girl read "Sunny//Girl//the doll with the//beautiful bright eyes." Five hts. 14, 17, 19, 20, and 22 in. (35.5, 43, 48, 51, and 56 cm.). The 20 in. (51 cm.) size was priced $4.00 to $10.00. One Sunny Girl wore a coat, hat and leggings, the rest wore organdy, voile or a linen dress.

1928: Sunny Babe had composition head and arms, cloth body and legs, open mouth with two teeth, dimples, a crying

November, 1927   PLAYTHINGS   9

"SUNNY GIRL"—"SUNNY BOY"

Outstanding Successes of 1927

ARE

Madame Hendren
DOLLS
"*Everybody Loves Them*"

POPULARIZED BY OUR
1927 ADVERTISING
CAMPAIGN IN "LADIES
HOME JOURNAL" AND
OTHER MEDIUMS. THEY
ARE DIFFERENT FROM OR-
DINARY DOLLS AND
THEIR QUALITY IS EASILY
RECOGNIZED.

"SUNNY GIRL" *and* "SUNNY BOY"

WILL BE THE LEADERS IN ALL SHOPS AT CHRISTMAS TIME.

PERMIT US TO SEND YOU A SAMPLE DOZEN ASSORTED
STYLES TO RETAIL FROM $4.00 TO $10.00 EACH.
ORDER BY EXPRESS TODAY.

AVERILL MANUFACTURING CORP.
37 UNION SQUARE, W.   NEW YORK CITY

2557. Sunny Boy and Sunny Girl dressed dolls shown in PLAY-THINGS, November, 1927. These dolls had celluloid heads and were made by the Averill Manufacturing Co. See Averill Ill. 166 for the picture of the matching Sunny Girl, and her mark, Ill. 2558.

2558. Sunny Girl mark.

voice, and wore a short organdy baby dress and halo bonnet. Ht. 21 in. (53.5 cm.); priced 98¢.

Sunny Boy and Sunny Girl were the new names for the composition head dolls once known as *Little Brother* and *Little Sister*. They had a wig or molded hair, glass eyes with separate closing lids and hair eyelashes, cotton filled cloth body, composition arms and legs, mama voice. Sunny Girl had a rectangular card reading "Sunny//Girl" under the Averill trademark. The 19 in. (48 cm.) size wore a flowered voile dress and cost $4.25. The 20 in. (51 cm.) size wore a "chinchilla" coat, hat and leggings over its voile dress, cost $7.25.

1929: Still came with celluloid heads as well as composi-

tion, with wigs or with molded hair, glass eyes, cotton stuffed cloth bodies, composition limbs and *Lloyd Manufacturing Co.* Mama voices. Sunny Boy wore either the Little Lord Fauntleroy or Oliver Twist suit. Ht. 19 in. (48 cm.). Sunny Girl wore dresses and bonnets of voile, organdy, dimity or taffeta. Hts. 14, 17, 19, 20, and 21 in. (35.5, 43, 48, 51, and 53.5 cm.).

Sunny Boy. 1914. One of the *Dolly Varden* series of cutout cloth dolls, distributed by *Marshall Field.* The doll had a Buster Brown hairdo; double breasted tan Buster Brown suit; red tie with white dots; white socks with red around the top; tan sandals. Ht. 14 in. (35.5 cm.); priced 90¢ doz. wholesale.

Sunny Jane. 1914. Name of a doll with composition head and hands; cork stuffed cloth body, jointed at the shoulders, hips and knees. Ht. 14 in. (35.5 cm.).

Sunny Jim. 1904 and later. Doll jointed at the neck, limbs and wrists; wore a red swallow-tail coat, yellow vest, white pants, black footwear, hat and spectacles. ★

Sunny Jim. 1906. Felt doll (possibly *Steiff*) distributed by *Gamage;* priced 49¢.

Sunny Jim. 1910–14. Name of a doll with composition head and cloth body.

1914: Distributed by *Butler Bros.* Ht. 11½ in. (29 cm.); priced $2.20 doz. wholesale. ★

Sunny Orange Blossom. 1924–25. Name of a doll made by *Amberg* with a composition head and a *Mama* type body. ★

Sunny-Twin Dolly Co. 1919–20. Los Angeles, Calif. Dressed Sunny Twin celluloid dolls in hand-embroidered clothes, silk socks and white kid Mary Jane type slippers. Dolls had bent limbs and were dressed as a girl in a sunbonnet or as a boy.

1919: Price was $12.00 doz. wholesale.

1920: Regular size cost $13.50 doz. wholesale and the large size cost $45.00 doz. wholesale, $7.00 each retail. ★

Sunshine. 1884. Name of a wax doll with Rembrandt style wig, sleeping eyes, embroidered chemise, distributed by *Lauer.* Hts. 16 and 24 in. (40.5 and 61 cm.); priced $4.00 and $7.50.

Sunshine. 1910–29. Line of dolls distributed by *Sears* who copyrighted them in 1910. Prior to World War I, they had *Armand Marseille* bisque heads, mold #370, mohair wigs, sleeping eyes and kid bodies. In the 1920s they were also *Mama* doll types representing babies and girls and were named *Baby Sunshine, Mary Sunshine, Sally Sunshine,* and *Sunshine Ann.* Also in this line was *Miss Sunshine.*

1912: Bodies had rivet joints at the hips and knees. Five hts. 15, 17, 20, 22½, and 25 in. (38, 43, 51, 57 and 63.5 cm.); priced 59¢ to $2.45.

Ca. 1914: Dolls had hair eyelashes, bisque forearms, rivet joints at the shoulders, hips and knees, and wore stockings and sandals. Five hts. 16, 19, 21½, 24 and 25½ in. (40.5, 48, 54.5, 61 and 65 cm.). Priced 59¢ to $1.98.

2559. Sunny Orange Blossom, a composition head doll made by Amberg. The molded bonnet resembles an orange and has holes on each side where probably originally the ribbon ties were affixed. The face has painted blue eyes and a closed mouth. The cloth Mama body has composition gauntlet hands and composition legs to above the knees. Original clothes, Mark: Ill. 2560. H. 14½ in. *Courtesy of the Margaret Woodbury Strong Museum. Photo by Harry Bickelhaupt.*

©
L. A. & S.
1924

2560. Mark on a Sunny Orange Blossom composition head.

2561. Mark for Sunny Twin celluloid dolls shown in PLAY-THINGS, 1920.

1927: Same as 1914 but also had a hair ribbon. Hts. 15¾, 21½, and 23¼ in. (40, 54.5, and 59 cm.); priced $1.98 to $3.75.★

Sunshine. 1912–14. Dolls produced by *Horsman* as style no. 174 had a composition-head copyrighted in 1912 that resembled *Miss Janet;* and *Campbell Kid* type composition hands. It wore a white dress, coat of tinted ribbed fabric and a matching lace frilled close-fitting bonnet; priced $8.50 doz. wholesale.

1914: New doll in a smaller size was named Sunshine Jr. and listed as style no. 83. It wore a lawn dress with a ribbon sash; priced $4.25 doz. wholesale.★

Sunshine. 1915. Composition-head doll made by *Trion* as style no. 231.★

Sunshine. 1917. Character doll advertised by *Bell & Francis* in a British toy trade journal.

Sunshine. See **Charlotte Dolls.**

Sunshine Ann. 1927–29. One of the Sunshine line of dolls distributed by *Sears.* It was a *Mama* doll dressed as a little girl in a cotton dress.

2562. Mark found on dolls named Sunshine handled by Sears

2563. Sunshine mark for dolls produced by Reisman, Barron.

Sunshine Dolls. 1927. Line made by *Reisman, Barron.* There were various models including *Mama* dolls and they were marked "Brighten the HEART of every child//SUNSHINE//DOLLS//REISMAN, BARRON CO."

Sunshine Dolls. 1928–30. Cloth baby dolls made by *Dean.*

Sunshine Girl. 1914. Bisque-head dressed dolls with heads of the same mold as *Baby Betty,* wig, glass eyes, teeth, shoulder and hip joints. Ht. 11 in. (28 cm.); priced $2.20 doz. wholesale.

Sunshine Girl. 1917. Name of a doll handled by the *Columbus Merchandise Co.* It had a composition head and arms, a cloth body jointed at the shoulders and hips and it wore a lawn dress. Ht. 12 in. (30.5 cm.); priced $8.50 doz. wholesale.

Sunshine Girl. 1928. *Boudoir* type dolls in assorted colors, made by *Kat-A-Korner Kompany.*

Sunshine Kids. 1915–16. All-composition dolls with wigs, flirting and sleeping eyes, made by the *Indestructo Specialties Co.* Ht. 15 in. (38 cm.).★

Superb. 1902–24. Trade name of a bisque-head doll with bisque forearms on a kid body.

1902: Bisque heads usually made by *Armand Marseille.* The kid body had gusset joints at the hips and knees. The mark on the chest was, "W. (F. [?]) //SUPERB//MADE IN GERMANY." Seven hts. from 12¾ to 18¾ in. (32.5 to 47.5 cm.). The 14, 16½ and 18¾ in. (35.5, 42, and 47.5 cm.) dolls had sleeping eyes.

These dolls were distributed wholesale by *Webb-Freyschlag.*

1924: The lower legs as well as the arms were bisque and the kid body had Universal Joints at the shoulders, elbows, hips and knees. The only clothes were footwear. Six hts. 12, 14, 16½, 18½, 21, and 23 in. (30.5, 35.5, 42, 47, 53.5, and 58.5 cm.).

Superior Doll Co. 1930 and later. Manufactured dolls.

Suppenkaspar. 1908. Name of a doll representing a character in a German children's verse, "Die Geschichte vom Suppen-Kaspar." The story is about a bad boy who refused to eat his soup and got thinner and thinner until he died. The plump doll shown in Ill. 2564 must represent Suppenkaspar before he refused to eat his soup.

Suppenkasper. 1912 and later. Celluloid doll with jointed arms and molded clothes made by *Rheinische Gummi und Celluloid Fabrik* in the *Struwwelpeter* series.

Der Suppenkaspar.

2564. This fat boy doll representing Suppenkaspar has a leather head, yarn hair and a stuffed cloth body. It was made in accordance with the directions in DIE WELT DER FRAU (THE LADY'S WORLD), 1908.

Supplee-Biddle Hardware Co. 1924. Philadelphia, Pa. Distributed wholesale *Cliquot Club Kid, Live Long Toys, Mama* dolls and *Nelke* dolls.

Supreme Doll & Toy Co. 1919. New York City. Produced all-composition dolls; one of them had a *Baby Grumpy* type face, bent arms, jointed only at the shoulders, legs apart.

Surprise Doll. 1927. Made by *Roth,* Baitz, & Lipsitz.

Surprise Shop. 1925–30 and later. Salem, Mass. Made cloth dolls.

Susan and Bobby. 1921. Pair of British stockinet dolls dressed in nightgowns and also known as the Bye-Bye Twins; distributed in the U.S. by *Meakin & Ridgeway.*

Susanne. 1920–21. Stockinet doll with hand-woven wig, removable clothes made by *Chad Valley* as style no. 1. S. D.

1921: Dressed in silk or other fabric and had a Chad Valley patent wrist watch. Hts. 12 to 13 in. (30.5 to 33 cm.).

Susie. 1916. Cloth doll manufactured by the *Atlas Manufacturing Co.* It wore a lace trimmed floral print dress and bonnet. Came in three sizes.

Susie. 1925–26. Name of a cloth doll with a molded felt face produced by *Cuno and Otto Dressel* and distributed in England by *G. Greiner.*

1926: Doll also came with a new composition face, with or without a voice.

Susie. 1925–26. Felt doll made by *Lenci* as style no. 165/3. It represented a girl dressed in a tight sleeveless bodice, full striped calf-length skirt with a big bow in back and a wide brimmed hat. Ht. 29½ in. (75 cm.).

Susie. 1926. Doll created by *Kitty Fleischmann,* had a hand-painted face. Hts. 14 to 16 in. (35.5 to 40.5 cm.).

Susie's Sister. 1915–16. Line of *American Art* character cloth dolls similar to the *Käthe Kruse* dolls and distributed by *Strobel & Wilken.* The dolls had handpainted faces, painted hair, stuffed bodies with jointed arms and legs. They wore colored dresses, caps or sunbonnets, shoes and stockings and sometimes aprons.★

Süssenguth, Gebrüder. 1894–1930. Neustadt near Coburg, Thür., and later, Bavaria. Christian Süssenguth† appears to have been one of the brothers. They made dolls' bodies and used *Revalo* heads but their specialty was *Bébé L'Avenir* (French), Puppe der Zukunft (German); both of these names mean Doll of the Future. Bébé L'Avenir was a trademark registered in France by *Guttmann & Schiffnie Société* in 1907, while Gebrüder Süssenguth had registered Puppe der Zukunft as a German trademark in 1904. The trademark also included the initials "G. S." which could stand for Gebrüder Sussenguth or Guttmann & Schiffnie. It has been reported that *Richard Oberender* modeled some of the porcelain heads used by Süssenguth in the 20th century.

1898: Applied for two German patents (D.R.G.M.) for dolls' bodies.

1904: Applied for a German patent (D.R.G.M.) for dolls' bodies. *Max Oscar Arnold* used this patent.

1909: *Siegel Cooper* advertised the "Doll of the Future" which was made by Süssenguth.

1911: Bébé l'Avenir was exported to Belgium, France, Italy and North America.

1930: A Süssenguth Catalog in the Ciesliks' collection showed dressed *Mama* dolls with composition heads, arms and legs. They had wigs or molded hair. Ht. 47 cm. (18½ in.). *Kewpies* were all-composition and babies had composition heads. Dolls with composition heads on cloth bodies came in nine hts. 30 to 55 cm. (12 to 21½ in.). Jointed dolls probably with patent leather paste-board bodies, came dressed or in a chemise. Eight hts. 26 to 50 cm. (10½ to 19½ in.).★

Süssenguth, Hans. 1918–30 and later. Sonneberg, Thür. Manufactured and exported dressed dolls. Used *Schoenau & Hoffmeister* heads.

1926: Advertised *New Born Baby* dolls and unbreakable dolls.

1927: Advertised Art dolls, molded cloth dolls and life-like baby dolls.

Sussfeld & Cie. (Co.). 1863–1930. Paris and London. Distributed and exported dolls. Known as Sussfeld Frères in the 1920s. Claimed they were the oldest exporting firm of French dolls.

1915: Advertised in England, porcelain-head dolls with stationary or sleeping eyes, fully jointed dressed or undressed dolls. Mr. G. H. Metzler was their London manager.

1919: G. H. Glenn was their London representative.

1923: Advertised "Teddy" Toys which were all-British cloth toys.

1924–26: Advertised that they dealt only in French products and specialized in celluloid dolls.

1930: Advertised under the name *Teddy Toy Co.* their line of Softanlite dolls which included *Christopher Robin.* ★

Susskind, Jos. 1929–30 and later. Hamburg, Germany. Handled character dolls.

1929: Registered *Monty* in Germany as a trademark for dolls.

1931: Registered *Bosco* in Germany as a trademark for dolls.

Sustrac, Ph. & P. See **Thomas, Maurice.**

Sutherland Doll Co. (Sutherland Works). 1918. Fenton, Stoke-on-Trent, Staffs. Made dolls with *British Ceramic* heads. Most of the dolls were dressed and the leading line was named *Arcadian Babs.*

Sutter, Prof. Conrad. 1914. Hesse, Germany. Designed wooden dolls that were made in his workshop called Hessische Spielwaren-Manufaktur. These dolls represented typical city and country folks especially laborers and peasants. The dolls were exhibited in Cologne and were described in a German art journal.

Suzanne. 1917–18. Stockinet doll designed by *E. E. Houghton* and made by *Shanklin;* dressed in a knitted wool coat and bonnet. It was one of three similar dolls called *Three Little Sisters.*

Suzanne. 1928. *Boudoir* doll distributed by *Eisen,* came dressed in red, orange or purple.

Suzel. 1918–26. Doll represented an Alsatian peasant.

1918: Doll shown in a catalog of *Printemps* without a tray. (It is not certain that this was the Mme. Rassant doll.)

1926: Suzel was registered as a French trademark for a regional costume doll holding a tray by *Mme. Elisa Rassant (née Blum).* ★

Suzette. 1923–30. Dressed doll with felt character head, distributed by Paris stores.

1923–24: Sold by the *Louvre* store. Ht. 28 cm. (11 in.).

1930: Sold by *Bon Marché.* It had a wig and wore a felt dress. Ht. 65 cm. (25½ in.).

Suzon. 1927. Doll sold by the *Lafayette* store. It had a wig, hair eyelashes and wore a taffeta dress. Hts. 50 and 56 cm. (19½ and 25½ in.).

Suzy. 1925. Cutout printed cloth doll published by *Fernand Nathan.* A miniature Suzy was also on the sheet. Suzy had a smile and the teeth showed. It wore a printed teddy, a bow in the curly printed hair and footwear. Ht. 80 cm. (31½ in.). Smaller versions of Suzy were called *Lisette* and *Denise.*

Swaddling-clothed Dolls. 1700s and probably earlier–1930 and later. These dolls were usually called *Poupards* in France but they were also known as *Bébé Maillot* and even *Bébé Teteur.* Many of the prints of the 1700s and early 1800s such as those by Boilly show children playing with this kind of doll. At the beginning of the 1800s bébés in swaddling clothes (poupards) were made of wood at Notre-Dame de Liesse in Laonnais, France, as a cottage industry to compete with the German toys. These brilliantly colored, inexpensive bébés were exported to America, England and Belgium.

Most of the poupards with a French origin were made of cardboard or papier-mâché. Léo Claretie reported from an early source "Lady what do you wish? One is no longer able to give you Venus de Milo for a sou. It is as a poupard in swaddling clothes without arms or legs with the head painted, the hair stained with shoe blackening, the eyebrows shaped like parenthesis, heart-shaped mouth, ruddy cheeks, blue eyes and three pebbles inside the torso." Gray poupards of cardboard were made in Villers-Cotterêts and sent to Paris where they were finished with a coat of varnish. The sizes of the poupards varied from a couple of inches to 25 or 30 inches (63.5 or 76 cm.).

Several early German catalogs show dolls in swaddling clothes which were called "Wickelpuppen" in German. Among these catalogs were the two *Lindner* catalogs of about 1830 and 1841 and the Biberach catalog dated 1836 by the Bethnal Green Museum. The early Lindner catalog shows Wickelpuppen with arms and with ruffs around their necks. In the 1841 catalog they were colorful painted wooden dolls without arms. The catalog showed seven styles or sizes.

1840s–60s: *Dehais* specialized in poupards.

1848: The inventory of *E. Barrois* listed poupards.

1884: *Bon Marché* advertised a bébé in swaddling clothes with a wig, sleeping eyes, arms free. The doll came with a baby bottle and was shown with the nipple in its mouth. Three hts.; priced 70¢ to $1.28.

1890: A French advertisement listed composition bébés in molded swaddling clothes, ht. 24 cm. (9½ in.) for 15¢. Composition bébés with sleeping eyes, dressed in swaddling clothes came in hts. 29, 33, and 50 cm. (11½, 13, and 19½ in.); priced $1.10 to $2.70. Small bisque sleeping eyed bébés in swaddling clothes, hts. 17 and 20 cm. (6½ to 8 in.); priced 70¢ and 90¢. The sleeping-eyed dolls came with bottles.
  Petit St. Thomas advertised a doll dressed in swaddling clothes with a baby bottle. Ht. 60 cm. (23½ in.): priced $1.10 dressed in flannel and $1.38 dressed in white piqué and ribbons.

1891: *Printemps'* Swedish catalog showed dolls in swaddling clothes. Ht. 55 cm. (21½ in.).

1892: *Louvre* store advertised composition head bébés in swaddling clothes with arms away from the body. Ht. 60 cm. (23½ in.): priced 98¢.

1896: Louvre store advertised a composition head bébé in swaddling clothes, 60 cm. (23½ in.) tall; priced 98¢. Also a rubber bébé in swaddling clothes, 20 cm. (8 in.) tall for 29¢.

1897: *La Samaritaine* advertised a bébé in white piqué swaddling clothes trimmed with ribbons and wearing a baby cap. Ht. 45 cm. (17½ in.); priced 59¢.

1901: Louvre store advertised composition head bébés in swaddling clothes. Hts. 45 and 60 cm. (17½ and 23½ in.); priced 58¢ and 98¢. Also rubber dolls with arms attached to the body, dressed in swaddling clothes. Hts. 20, 23, and 26 cm. (8, 9 and 10½ in.); priced 19¢ to 35¢.
  Samaritaine advertised rubber bébés, decorated in colors. Ht. 25 cm. (10 in.); priced 38¢.

1902: Louvre store advertised an "unbreakable" (probably composition) swaddling clothed bébé with sleeping eyes, hair eyelashes and a bib. Four hts. 24, 29, 36, and 43 cm. (9½, 11½, 14 and 17 in.); priced 70¢ to $2.10. The carton (cardboard) swaddling clothed bébé had jointed arms. Hts. 55 and 60 cm. (21½ and 23½ in.); priced 68¢, and 90¢. Colored rubber swaddling clothed bébés came in hts. 20, 23 and 26 cm. (8, 9 and 10½ in.); priced 18¢ to 35¢.

1903: Bon Marché advertisd a carton bébé in swaddling clothes. This doll came in four hts. 36, 42, 53, and 58 cm. (14, 16½, 21, and 23 in.); priced 33¢ to 90¢. The smallest and cheapest bébés in swaddling clothes were sold at *Tapis Rouge*. Their *mignonnettes* in swaddling clothes were 15 cm. (6 in.) tall; priced 15¢, while a crying wooden poupard in swaddling clothes, ht. 23 cm. (9 in.) cost 29¢.
  Ville de St. Denis advertised a poupard with moving head and arms, dressed in piqué. Ht. 46 cm. (18 in.); priced 59¢.

1904: Louvre store advertised a rubber swaddling clothed bébé called "Joli Poupard" (Pretty Poupard). Hts. 19, 23,

and 26 cm. (7½, 9, and 10½ in.): priced 19¢ to 39¢.

1906: Louvre store advertised composition swaddling clothed bébés with head and arms jointed and "enamel eyes." Four hts. 36, 40, 45, and 52 cm. (14, 15½, 17½, and 20½ in.); priced 39¢ to 95¢. The rubber poupards had attached arms. Four hts. 16, 19, 23, and 26 cm. (6½, 7½, 9, and 10½ in.); priced 13¢ to 28¢.

1908–20s: *Les Fils de N. Clerc* made poupards with joints at the neck and shoulders.

1908: Louvre store sold poupards similar to the Clerc ones in composition. Four hts. 35, 40, 45, and 50 cm. (14, 15½, 17½, and 19½ in.); priced 38¢ to 90¢.
  Samaritaine advertised decorated rubber bébés in swaddling clothes. Ht. 26 cm. (10½ in.); priced 38¢.

1910: Louvre store advertised a composition head bébé in swaddling clothes with removable clothes such as the bib. Hts. 37 cm. and 46 cm. (14½ and 18 in.); priced 78¢ and $1.18.
  Printemps offered the same bébés as the Louvre except they gave the hts. as 2 cm. (1 in.) shorter but the prices were the same.

1912–14: *La Place Clichy* offered the same dolls at the same prices as Printemps in 1910.

1913–14: Samaritaine advertised painted rubber swaddling clothed dolls; priced 29¢ to 58¢.

1919–21: *Henri Bellet* made papier-mâché poupards.

Ca. 1921: *Alexandre Lefebvre & Cie.* advertised poupards.

1921–30 and later: *Société Française de Fabrication de Bébés & Jouets* (S.F.B.J.) made swaddling clothed bébés (poupards) of carton paté (cardboard). Other companies probably also made cardboard dolls and poupards.

1927: *Société Industrielle de Jouet Français* made poupards. (See THE COLLECTOR'S BOOK OF DOLLS' CLOTHES, Ills. 101, 428B, 429A, 526, 529, 562, and 614.)

Swaine & Co. 1854–1927. Hüttensteinach (North Köppelsdorf), Thür. Made porcelain dolls' heads. It is probable that the "S. & Co." found in the green stamp on bisque head dolls stands for this company. (See Ill. 2569.)★

Swan Dolls. 1917–20. Name of dressed dolls sold by the *Star Manufacturing Co.* The dolls had *British Ceramic* heads and cloth bodies including the limbs.

1917: Advertised Sailor Boys and Sailor Girls.

Sweater Babies. 1918. Dolls dressed in sweaters, made by *Effanbee*. Hts. 12 to 25 in. (30.5 to 63.5 cm.).

Sweater Girl. 1917. Name of a doll made by *Ideal* with painted hair, stationary or sleeping eyes. It wore a turban and high boots and was a mate to Sweater Boy.[†]

Swedlin, J. See **Gund Manufacturing Co.**

Sweeney Lithographing Co. 1930 and later. Belleville, N.J. Made cloth dolls.

2565. Gesso-over-wood doll representing a baby in swaddling clothes has painted brown hair. The painted swaddling clothes are decorated with ribbons, bows and roses. H. 3¾ in. (9 cm.). *Coleman Collection.*

2566. Turned, carved, and painted wooden doll representing a baby in swaddling clothes. The back of the doll is flat except for the head. The hair is painted black, blue painted eyes. The swaddling clothes are painted red and black, blue and white trimming. H. 6¼ in. (16 cm.). *Courtesy of the Margaret Woodbury Strong Museum. Photo by Harry Bickelhaupt.*

2568A. Wax-over-composition head with wig, sleeping blue glass eyes, teeth, on a cloth body with composition hands and feet. The upper thigh is impressed with three letters of the old German script. It is dressed as a swaddling clothed baby on a pillow. This type of doll was called a *Täufling* in Germany. H. 34 cm. (13½ in.). *Courtesy of the Collection of Nederlands Kostuummuseum, The Hague. Photo by B. Frequin.*

BOHEMIAN PAINTED WOODEN DOLL   LITHUANIAN DOLL CARVED IN WOOD

2567. Wooden dolls carved and painted to represent babies in swaddling clothes as shown in INTERNATIONAL STUDIO, April 1923. The doll on the left was made in Bohemia (Czechoslovakia). The doll on the right was made in Lithuania.

N° 19018. BÉBÉ MAILLOT
cartonnage incassable.
0ᵐ36. **1.65** | 0ᵐ53. **3.40**
0ᵐ42. **2.40** | 0ᵐ58. **4.50**

2568B. Swaddling clothed bébé made of "unbreakable" carton as advertised in the Bon Marché 1903 catalog. Four hs. 36, 42, 53, and 58 cm. (14, 16½, 21, and 23 in.).

2569. An incised mark and a stamped mark both used by Swaine & Co. on their dolls' heads. The green stamp was used consistently.

Sweet Alice. 1895. Bisque-head dressed doll with wig, distributed by *Butler Bros.* Hts. 27 in. (68.5 cm.); priced $5.50 doz. wholesale.

Sweet Nell. 1925–28. Line of dolls made by *Hugo Wiegand.*

1926: Described in DEUTSCHE SPIELWAREN ZEITUNG as *Mama* dolls.

1928: Advertised as dolls that could stand or sit, having composition toddler bodies. They had wigs and glass eyes.★

Sweet Pea. 1927. Name of two dolls in one; part of the *Twinjoy* line of *Flower Dolls* with petal dresses, created by *Berry Kollin.*

Sweetheart. 1910–28. Trade name of a line of child and baby dolls belonging to *B. Illfelder & Co.*★

Sweetheart. 1915. Name of dressed baby doll made by *Amberg;* had molded hair. Style Nos. 212 and 214 wore short dresses; style Nos. 222 and 214R wore long baby dresses.★

Sweetheart. 1918. Line of cloth dolls with celluloid faces made by *Marks Bros.;* priced 25¢ to $1.00.

Sweetheart. 1919. Name of a baby doll in a long dress, made by *Jessie M. Raleigh.*

Sweetheart. 1924. *Mama* doll with composition head, hands and legs; wig and sleeping eyes; distributed by *Montgomery Ward.* It wore an organdy dress and bonnet. Ht. 22 in. (56 cm.): priced $3.59.

Sweetheart. 1930. Doll representing Princess Elizabeth was exhibited by *H. Josef Leven.*

Sweetheart. See **Little Sweetheart** and **Herzlieb.**

Sweetie. 1917–21. All-rubber doll made by *Faultless Rubber Co.*

1920–21: Priced 65¢ doz. wholesale.★

Sweetie. 1918. All-composition *Kewpie*-type doll, jointed at the shoulders, legs apart, distributed by *Butler Bros.* Ht. 12 in. (30.5 cm.).

Sweetie. 1921–28. Name of a doll made by *Anna Keenan.*

Sweetie. 1926. Line of all-celluloid dolls with molded short hair, body jointed at the neck, shoulders and hips, arms bent, made by the *Rheinische Gummi und Celluloid Fabrik.*

Sweetie. 1930. One of the *Kiddie Pal* line of dolls made by *Regal.*

Sweetness. 1920. Wood fibre composition doll advertised by *Progressive Toy Co.*

Sweets. Ca. 1930s. A *Georgene* cloth doll designed by *Maude Tousey Fangel.* It had a flat, painted face and wore pink cotton clothes including a bonnet.

Sweetums. 1925 and probably other years. Bisque head made by *Kestner* for *Century.* (See Ills. 2570 and 2571.)★

Sweetums. 1930. Line of dolls made by the *Uneeda Doll Co.*

Swiecka (Swieka, Swieczka), Mlle. 1915–18. Russia and Paris. Created dolls of cloth or of leather.

1916: The French author, Doin, mentioned her Zobéida and Haroun-al-Raschid dolls.★

2570. Century infant doll made by Kestner probably called "Sweetums." It has a bisque flange neck, head with molded blond hair, sleeping blue glass eyes, cloth body with celluloid hands. Mark: Century Doll Co. // Kestner. H. 11 in. (28 cm.). Circumference of head 11 in. (28 cm.). *Courtesy of Sotheby Parke Bernet Inc., N.Y.*

2571. Sweetums tag mark on a doll made for Century.

2572A & B. All-wood doll carved including the fingernails, in Switzerland. It has painted brown hair and eyes. The hair is upswept in a loop in back. The mouth is closed. There are joints at the neck, shoulders, elbows, hips and knees. Original Sunday peasant costume of the Engadine area. The dress is red wool. H. 14½ in. (37 cm.). *Courtesy of the Margaret Woodbury Strong Museum. Photos by Harry Bickelhaupt.*

Swiss Dolls. The native dolls in Swiss Museums usually had cloth bodies with wooden lower arms or kid bodies or were all-wood. Many of the Swiss dolls wore regional costumes, especially popular were those representing Bern. Often this costume was found on German dolls that perhaps had been dressed in Switzerland. A major Swiss carving center for dolls was Brienz where Peter Huggler-Huggler employed several carvers. Some of these dolls were sold by Dr. Lauer to the Heimatwerk in Zurich.

Early 1900s; Th. *Anderegg* carved wooden dolls; *Mme. Louise Bureau* created dolls.

1912: *Erika Morf* produced dolls.

1915: TOYS AND NOVELTIES reported that the U.S. Government encouraged the making of Swiss dolls.

1923: TOYS AND NOVELTIES commented that Swiss dolls were works of arts, "From the manicuring of the nails to the dressing of the hair, each detail is complete."

1924: *Sasha Morgenthaler* began to make dolls.

1925: *Pauline Laar* obtained a patent for dolls.★

Sylver, Jane. 1927–30 and later. Paris. Made dolls.

Sylvie Dolls. 1930. Cloth dolls made by *Dean.* They had wigs, jointed shoulders and hips and were dressed in velvet and silkeen with plush trimming. Clothes included a knee-length coat, hat and boots. Nine hts.

Syndicate de la Couture Parisienne. 1921. Paris. Made clothes for the dolls supplied by *Stewart Culin,* curator of the Brooklyn Museum, where these dolls were exhibited. The Syndicate de la Couture Parisienne paid for the materials and work required for making the clothes. Edouard Ziegler was the Syndicate's administrator of this project. Ziegler and Mr. Marot dressed the dolls.

Synthetic. 1929. Name of a doll with interchangeable parts such as the head, wig, arms and legs.

Szégo, R. 1927–30. and later. Paris. Made dolls.

Szerelemhegyi, Mrs. Marga. 1920s–30 and later. Hungary. Made and exported *Marga* dolls with felt or composition heads and cotton bodies. The clothes were copies of various peasant costumes, those worn in the villages, as well as the countryside throughout Hungary. She never mixed styles. Mrs. Szerelemhegyi had a shop in Budapest. Dr. Eva Moskovszky supplied the information on these Hungarian dolls.

Some of these dolls were exhibited at the 1939 World's Fair.

2573A & B. Carved and turned jointed wooden doll made in Switzerland. The head and hair are carved and painted. The limbs are turned. Original regional costume made of handwoven fabric. H. 16½ in. (42 cm.). *Coleman Collection.*

T

T.S. Dolls. 1923–28. Trademark used by *The Toy Shop.*

T. W. Toy & Novelty Co. 1922–23. Rochester, N.Y. Made and/or distributed dolls.

T. & T. Toy Co. 1924. New York City. Advertised *Mama* dolls in various sizes including 25¢ doll lines for jobbers.★

Ta Ta. 1917–30. Line of flat-faced cloth dolls made by *Dean;* by 1930 the name was spelled Ta-Ta.

1917: Inexpensive character dolls with patented skirts that were separate from the body; made in five styles; one wore a Scottish outfit and another wore a coat, tam and leggings.

1920: Style number D239. Ht. 11 in. (28 cm.).

1930: Made of a new soft fabric for dolls; came in various shades and in six sizes. It wore a low waisted coat, leggings and bonnet.

Taeuber, Sophie. 1915–30 and later. Paris and Zurich, Switzerland. She was an artist who designed dolls and textiles.

Taft, James Scholly. Bisque heads have been found marked "D//Taft//1910" over a size number. The D was written in script. The heads had sleeping eyes and open mouths and were on jointed composition bodies. Size number six has been found on a 25 in. (63.5 cm.) doll.

According to Paul Evans, James Scholly Taft during World War I in Keene, N.H., made bisque dolls' heads marked "Taft" at his Hampshire Pottery.

Tah Toys (Tah-Toys) Ltd. 1917–18. London. Made stockinet dolls designed by *Heath Robinson* and *Rene Bull.* These

2575. Mark on Taft bisque heads.

were in a line named *Kiddlums* which included *Nunkey* and *Mother Blighty.*

1917: Made *Dilly Dick,* a character doll.

1918: Made "Robinson Crusoe" which resembled an Eskimo doll, "Babs" and the "Pyjama Kid."

Taillandier, E. H. 1925–27. Paris. Made dolls for decoration.★

Tailored Craft Novelty Co. 1927–30 and later. Made outfits and dresses for dolls.

1928: Advertised dress outfits, blankets, bathrobes, bathing suits, hats, pajamas, parasols and so forth.

1930: Made the Kute Klothes line which included dresses for *Patsy,* and *Patsy Ann,* silk underwear and pajamas, raincoats, coats and hats sets, parasols, blankets, comforters, mattresses, sheets, and pillow cases.

Takada Kinosukee. 1930 and later. Kyoto, Japan. Made dolls.

Talking Doll & Novelty Co. 1913 and later. New York City. Company incorporated by M. S. Birkhahn, P. D. Birkhahn and J. Birkhahn to manufacture talking dolls.

Talking Dolls. Dolls that could make some sort of sound from a feeble squeak to actually saying understandable words have been popular at least since the 1850s. Among the earliest commercial dolls were the so-called *Motschmann*-type *(Edmund Lindner)* or the *Goodyear* rubber dolls. The dolls with two pull-strings usually allegedly said "Mama" when one string was pulled and "Papa" when the other string was pulled. Following World War I the *Mama* doll became popular with its two-tone voice, which was interpreted by manufacturers of dolls as saying the two syllable "Ma-ma."

French advertisements for dolls especially in the early 1900s often described the dolls as "Parlant" which meant speaking or talking. Occasionally the French dolls were described as "Disant" which also meant speaking or talking. It is not known whether there was a different meaning to these two French descriptions or whether like the English "Talking" and "Speaking," they meant practically the same

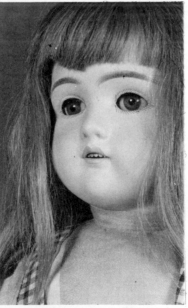

2574A & B. Bisque head doll with a Taft mark. It has a blond wig, sleeping blue glass eyes, hair eyelashes, open mouth, five upper teeth, and a fully jointed composition and wood body. The clothes are contemporary with the doll. Mark: Ill. 2575. H. 24½ in. (62 cm.). *Courtesy of Robert and Katrin Burlin.*

thing. One obvious fact is that a greater percentage of French dolls were described as "Parlant" than the percentage found today having the ability to make a sound. Whether voice boxes have been removed to a greater extent through the years or whether "Parlant" simply meant that the doll had an open mouth as if it were talking or if there were another explanation it has not been discovered as yet. Very few contemporary advertisements of dolls ever mentioned whether the mouth was open or closed.

1862: *Jules Steiner* patented a talking doll.

1872: *Silber & Fleming* advertised "Mama and Papa speaking dolls," undressed in seven sizes.

1876: Silber & Fleming advertised "Mamma and Papa speaking dolls made to talk by pulling the string," undressed in six sizes and two more sizes having inserted hair and sleeping eyes.

1879: The Silber & Fleming Mamma and Papa dolls were made to cry "Mama" and "Papa" by moving the arms upwards or sideways. Came in five sizes. Another five sizes of mama and papa dolls activated by arm movements were boy dolls "with the new fur hair." There were also baby dolls with wax arms and legs and the voice similarly activated, in three sizes. Speaking dolls came dressed or undressed.

1882: Silber & Fleming had increased their talking baby dolls to seven sizes.

1884: *Bon Marché* advertised bisque-head "Bébés Parlants" with wig, unjointed wrists, two pull strings, and chemise. Size no. 8 was 48 cm. (19 in.); priced $3.30; and size no. 9 was 51 cm. (20 in.); priced $3.90.

1885: *Horsman* advertised five sizes or style numbers of talking dolls; priced $12.00 to $48.00 doz. wholesale.

1887: *Lauer* advertised wax dolls with mama papa voices, wigs and a chemise. Ht. 24 in. (61 cm.); priced $6.50 doz. wholesale.

1887–88: The *Bon Marché's Jumeau* Bébés Parlant with two pull strings, and elaborate chemises cost 40¢ to 80¢ more than the ordinary non-parlant Jumeau bébés.

1889: Silber & Fleming advertised wax-head mama, papa dolls in chemise, 14 sizes, and dressed in "latest fashion" in eight sizes.

1890: *Emile Berliner* patented a talking doll.

1892: The British DEWSBURY REPORTER stated: "Germany was the first country to invent talking dolls. So great is the cost of their manufacture that comparatively few are made; in art as in nature, it is easier to make a baby doll say 'Mamma' than 'Papa.' " There have been many claims to the origin of the talking doll. The French catalogs of this period and later show very little increase in the prices for parlant dolls beyond the prices for non-parlant dolls.

1903: PLAYTHINGS reported that dolls saying "Mama" and "Papa" were popular.

1903 and later: *Max Oscar Arnold* obtained many German patents for talking dolls including ones for *Arnoldia*.

1904: In America Mama, Papa dolls with two strings came with bisque heads or were all-composition. The latter came in hts. 13 and 15 in. (33 and 38 cm.). The larger dolls had sleeping eyes.

1905: *Petit Saint Thomas* advertised Bébé Parlant with sleeping eyes, fully jointed body, including wrists, two pull-strings for saying "Mama and Papa," chemise and footwear. Ht. 52 cm. (20½ in.): priced $1.75.

1910: Dolls with composition heads and limbs, wig, and glass eyes, had two cords attached to bellows. Hts. 16 and 17 in. (40.5 and 43 cm.), the larger doll had sleeping eyes.

1912: TOYS AND NOVELTIES commented—"Now hardly any doll can be found which does not . . . say 'Papa and Mamma.' "

"Dolls that kick, throw up their hands, move their heads and call for their parents."

"Small music boxes are used to make a doll sing and phonographs take the place of talking starlings used in ancient Italy."

Lyra-Fahrrad-Werke sold composition head "Mama Papa" dolls with pull strings. Ht. 28 cm. (11 in.); priced 12¢.

1913: TOYS AND NOVELTIES stated that new from Paris was a doll that said several different words. A key inserted at the waist-line wound up the clockwork mechanism. The doll also rolled its eyes and walked; priced $15.00 and up.

1914: *Marshall Field* advertised composition and *Celtid* (celluloid) head dressed dolls with "double automatic crying voice" and "voice by pressure." The two strings on the doll's side had rings on them. Hts. 15 and 16 in. (38 and 40.5 cm.); priced $17.00 doz. wholesale. Other similar composition head dressed dolls without voices. Hts. 15½ and 17½ in. (39.5 and 43 cm.) were also priced $17.00 doz. wholesale.

Art Metal Works advertised "Mama Doll—I talk," and claimed the doll cried "Mama" loudly and clearly. The dressed baby doll, style number 7008 B was 17 in. (43 cm.) tall.

1915: TOYS AND NOVELTIES advertised a variety of styles and sizes of composition-head talking dolls; among them was *Amberg's* "Mama Voice Doll," priced 50¢.

A French publication, REVUE DE DEUX MONDES reported that prior to World War I the voices of dolls were imported from Germany and in 1915 bébés no longer cried.

1919: Amberg claimed the baby doll that cried, opened its eyes and wore a long dress was the company's best seller.

1920: The *Southern Bargain House* advertised dressed baby dolls with celluloid faces, painted hair and features, felt hands, wooden legs, bodies covered with rubber sheeting. The bodies contained coiled wire springs that when pressed down and allowed to rise were claimed to say "Mama" and "Papa." Hts. 6, 7½, and 11 in. (15, 19, and 28 cm.); priced $4.25 to $6.50 doz. wholesale.

1922: *Victor Steiner* advertised that all his dolls had voices.

1926: *Metal Devices Corp.* made a phonograph doll.

1930: Victor Steiner advertised talking and singing voices for

BÉBÉS PARLANTS, tête
biscuit, perruque flottante.
Nos 8. Haut. 0m48 c. **16.50**
9. — 0m51 **19.50**

2576. Talking bisque-head doll shown in the 1884/85 Bon Marché catalog. It is wearing a chemise and the Mama-Papa strings are visible. It has a wig, and a ball jointed composition body. Sizes 8 and 9, hs. 48 and 51 cm. (19 and 20 in.). Priced $3.30 and $3.90 as converted.

dolls. Dolls with Mama voices were manufactured by *Morris Politzer* for *American Stuffed Novelty Co.*

(See also **Bébé Jumeau, Kiss Throwing Doll, Mama Dolls, Phonograph Dolls, Voices** and **Wax Dolls.**)★

Tam O'Shanter Doll. 1893–1902. All-porcelain doll with molded tam, painted features distributed by *Butler Bros.*

1895: Hts. 4¾ and 7 in. (12 and 18 cm.).

1902: Hts. 5¾ and 7 in. (14.5 and 18 cm.); priced 33¢ and 84¢ doz. wholesale.★

Tambon Co. 1913. Denver, Colo. Made *Princess Tambon* cutout cloth dolls and two other Indian dolls, lithographed in six colors. These were sold in stores in the American west uncut 25¢ and made up into a doll $1.00. Hts. reported were 6 to 16 in. (15 to 40.5 cm.). See Ill. 2148. Similar dolls were later made by the *Henderson Glove Co.*

Tamlin & Rowley. 1924–26. England. Became Tamlin, Rowley & Jordan in 1926. Produced dolls.

Tamma Shanta. 1917. Name of a character doll advertised by *Bell & Francis.*

Tammen, H. H., Co. 1886–1930 and later. Denver, Colo., New York City and Los Angeles, Calif. Produced and distributed burnt leather, composition, cloth, and ceramic dolls, most of them representing American Indians.

1886: Advertised dolls (or idols) of the Apache, Moki, Santa Clara and Zuni Indians.

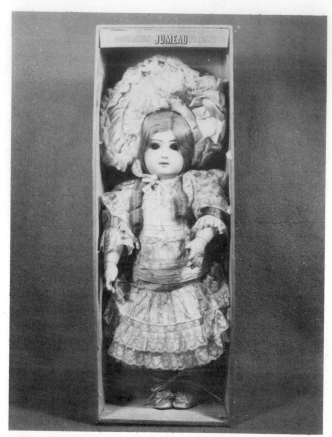

2577. Talking Bébé Jumeau with two strings to say "Mama" and "Papa." It has a wig, stationary glass eyes, pierced ears, a closed mouth, and a fully jointed composition body. Original clothes with a ribbon armband having "Bébé//JUMEAU" in gold letters. The original box has "Parlant" and "FABRICATION JUMEAU PARIS." On its shoes are marked "9//PARIS// [Bee picture]// JUMEAU." (See Ill. 1362.) H. 20 in. (51 cm.). *Courtesy of and photo by Cherry Bou.*

1925: Advertised cloth-body dolls.

1929: Dolls were dressed by workers in their homes after being instructed by *Mary McAboy*. (See Ill. 2578.)★

Tana. Ca. 1920s. Name on a doll's head. (See Ill. 2580.)★

Tanagra. 1917–30 and later. Paris and Montreuil-sous-Bois. Name used by the *Société Industrielle de Jouets Française* (successor to *H. Delcourt*). They made bébés and were members of the *Chambre Syndicale*. Tanagra made many kinds of bébés, ones with bisque or with composition heads, stationary or sleeping eyes, jointed bodies of various types, dressed or undressed bébés as well as poupards *(Swaddling-clothed babies)*. A bisque head Tanagra doll was marked "TANAGRA//PERLE DEPOSE." Perle (Pearl) appears to have been the name.

1960: The trademark "Tanagra" was again registered in France by Mme. Marguerite Clemm, née Lemounier, and Mme. Marguerite Schambre, née Cadel. (See Ills. 2582–2584.)★

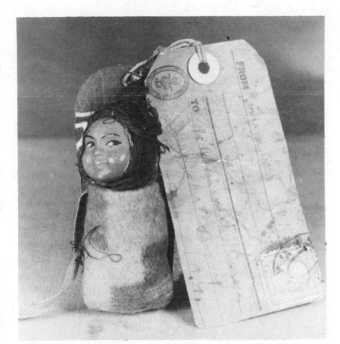

2578. Composition mask faced head representing an Indian papoose, created by Mary McAboy and produced by H.H. Tammen Co. It has black string hair, painted features, and is wrapped in a blanket attached to a painted board. Mark Ill. 2579. H. of doll 3 in. (7.5 cm.). *Coleman Collection.*

2579. Paper label mark on Mary McAboy's Skookum Indian dolls produced by Tammen.

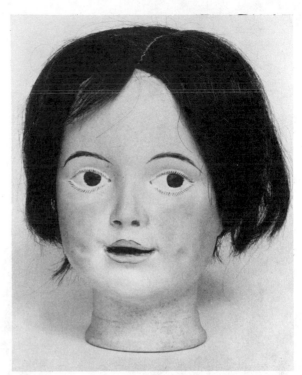

2580. Biscoid flange neck head incised "TANA." It has a bald head covered with a brown wig, the painted eyes look to the side; the mouth is open-closed and there are dimples in the cheeks. Mark: Ill. 2581. H. of head only, 6¼ in. (16 cm.). *Courtesy of the Margaret Woodbury Strong Museum. Photo by Harry Bickelhaupt.*

TANA

2581. Incised mark found on a head marked Tana.

Tango Kiddies. See Betty Bounce.

Tango Tar Baby. 1926–27. Black cloth doll made by *Chad Valley* as style number 368. They claimed it could walk and dance on its long legs. It wore a short double-breasted jacket, striped long trousers and striped high hat. Ht. 21 in. (53.5 cm.).

Tango Tots. 1914. Pair of dolls made by *Amberg* who claimed they could dance. The female was a coquette⁺ type doll, had molded hair and wore a dress with a full skirt almost to the ankles and a hat with a ruffle. Its partner had short molded hair and wore a tuxedo-type suit.

Tapis Rouge. 1903 and possibly other years. Paris. Store that advertised *Bébé L'Avenir; Bébé Merveilleux;* celluloid dolls in bathing suits. Ht. 20 cm. (8 in.); *Mignonnettes,* black or white jointed or as a baby in swaddling clothes with a bottle; three-faced bébé, laughing, crying or sleeping; walking dolls with head that turned when it walked or with a voice; rubber dolls, painted or gray, some were in swaddling

clothes; wooden dolls in swaddling clothes or a wooden head on a kid body; a Pioupiou (French soldier doll); dolls in regional costumes. Tapis Rouge claimed their best doll had a bisque head, sewn wig, open mouth with teeth, fully jointed body, chemise and footwear. Seven hts. 28, 36, 45, 53, 62, 74, and 84 cm. (11, 14, 17½, 21, 24½, 29, and 33 in.): priced 59¢ to $5.80.

Tarian et Marie. 1927–30 and later. Paris. Listed in Paris directory under Poupées de Salon (Dolls for decoration).

Tariff. The Tariff Act of 1922 doubled the previous duty on toys in order to help domestic manufacturing which had grown and prospered during and immediately after World War I. Bisque dolls and celluloid dolls could still be imported advantageously.

In 1930 PLAYTHINGS compared the previous tariff bill with the new act. Under the previous bill dressed dolls in which the clothes were over 50 percent of the value were assessed at 90 percent of ad valorem, provided lace embroidery, etc., were on the clothes. But where the value

2582. Tanagra bisque head doll with a blond wig, stationary blue glass eyes, open mouth, four upper teeth and a ball jointed composition body. Mark: TANAGRA//PERLE-DEPOSE//5//PARIS. H. 16 in. (40.5 cm.). *Courtesy of the Margaret Woodbury Strong Museum. Photo by Harry Bickelhaupt.*

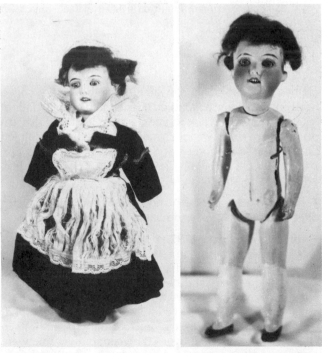

2583A & B. Bisque head Tanagra doll with a dark brown mohair wig, sleeping blue glass eyes, open mouth with four upper teeth and a five-piece composition body. Original clothes including molded and painted footwear. Mark: Ill. 2584. H. 13 in. (33 cm.). *Courtesy of Helen Read. Photo by Steven Read.*

2584. Incised Tanagra mark on bisque head dolls.

of the doll was greater than the clothes it was assessed at 70 percent ad valorem, regardless of whether there was lace, embroidery, etc.

According to the New Tariff Bill, dolls and dolls' clothing composed in any part of laces or nets or fringes or braids or any type of embroidery or beads were charged 90 percent ad valorem. Celluloid dolls with joints were charged 1¢ each and 60 percent ad valorem; celluloid dolls without joints were charged 1¢ each and 50 percent ad valorem. All other dolls, parts of dolls including dolls' heads and clothing were charged at 70 percent ad valorem. (See also **Duty on Dolls** and **Strauss, Adolph, & Co.,** 1929.)

Taroli Leoing. Name found on a doll with a composition face and a cloth body having a *Marga* tag. The clothes had a black stamp "Made in Hungary" and consisted of a red print jacket, a black fringed apron with red and white cross-stitch embroidery.

Tata. World War I–1930. A key wind waddling doll dressed as a girl. The keys were marked "R.D." for *Roullet & Decamps.* The composition head modeled by Gaston Descamps had a wig, painted eyes and a smiling expression in the *Poulbot* style. The cardboard body had iron wire arms and legs with composition hands and feet. The head turned as the doll waddled along. The doll was dressed and sometimes carried a small doll in its arm. The use of Tata as a pet name for girls in France and part of the information about this doll were based on the research of Anne-Marie & Jacques Porot.

Ta-Ta. See **Ta Ta.**

Tatem & Co. 1915. Cardiff, Wales. Distributed jointed dolls, kid-body dolls and dressed dolls.

Tatterstall, J. 1919–25. London and Southport. Manufacturer of dolls' parts including limbs for jointed dolls and celluloid mask faces.

Tatyha. Late 1700s Russia. Allegedly the founder of the Russian doll-making industry. He carved his dolls from the wood of linden trees. His dolls grew in popularity and he trained other people to make similar dolls. (See also **Chirkoff.**)

Täuflinge. This is apparently a generic term used in Germany which refers to almost any kind of doll that was dressed only in a chemise and sometimes footwear. Despite the fact that the German word Täuflinge literally meant babies of christening age (and it appears that it was first used for the *Motschmann* or *Lindner* type dolls that actually represented babies), it soon began to be used for dolls representing various ages. A 1928 article in DEUTSCHE SPIELWAREN ZEITUNG attributes the origin of the Täuflinge to baby dolls with wax heads, arms and legs shown at the 1851 London Exhibition. This article described a Täufling of 1880 as having a bisque head and limbs, sleeping eyes, and a mama-papa voice. It is difficult to determine the age represented by dolls dressed in a commercial chemise, but the proportions of some of the later dolls that were called "Täuflinge" were those of children or even young adults. These dolls were on the standard type jointed composition bodies that were usually dressed as girls or children, rather than babies. Note that the e on the end of Täuflinge makes it plural. The singular is without the final e. (See also **Sonneberg, Thür.**)

ca. 1860: A German catalog at Winterthur showed several Täuflinge. These dolls were probably composition or wax-over-composition with wooden limbs. All except some of the smallest sizes had peg jointed knees. The torso on the white dolls appeared to be cloth while those on the black dolls that can be seen appeared to be wood. The torsos of the black dolls were white but the heads and limbs were black.

All of the dolls except one had molded hair, several had snoods. The one doll with a wig (no. 4599 D/1) had wavy hair nearly to the shoulders and with a center part. This doll was shown with its head turned to the side and tilted down. Several of the dolls had a string but it is not known whether the string operated the closing of the eyes or a voice box. The largest white doll and the two largest black dolls were shown with their eyes closed. All of the dolls wore chemises of mid-calf length. Boots, probably carved and painted, were on all of the white dolls except two with bare feet and wearing baby bonnets. These two dolls may have had composition limbs and were sizes 1 and 3. All of the black dolls were shown wearing slippers.

SIZE–HEIGHT RELATIONSHIPS OF TÄUFLINGE, Ca. 1860				
			Height	
Size	White		Black (with letter N)	
No.	in.	cm.	in.	cm.
4/0	9	23	4	10
3/0	10	25.5	4¾	12
2/0	11½	29	6½	16.5
0	13	33	8½	21.5
1	14½	37	10½	26.5
2	16	40.5	12¾	32.5
3	17½	44.5		
4	19½	49.5		

See in THE COLLECTOR'S BOOK OF DOLLS' CLOTHES, Ill. 140 B, a Nürnberg catalog page of ca. 1860s that shows "Tauflinge" dressed as girls.

1907: *Kaufhaus* advertised several "Tauflinge." They had bisque heads wigs, sleeping eyes, composition bodies, and wore chemises. The ones of five-piece composition bodies were hts. 43, 48, and 60 cm. (17, 19, and 23½ in.); priced 24¢ to 73¢. The ones on ball-jointed composition bodies came in four hts. 30, 42, 55, and 62 cm. (12, 16½, 21½, and 24½ in.); priced 24¢ to 98¢. The pictorial representation of these dolls showed a standard dolly-faced doll with shoulder length curls and jointed wrists. They bore no rela-

2585. Täufling, an infant china Motschmann-type doll, with china hips and legs. The head is bald, the eyes are painted blue, and the mouth is closed. H. 11 in. (28 cm.). *Courtesy of Sotheby Parke Bernet Inc., N.Y.*

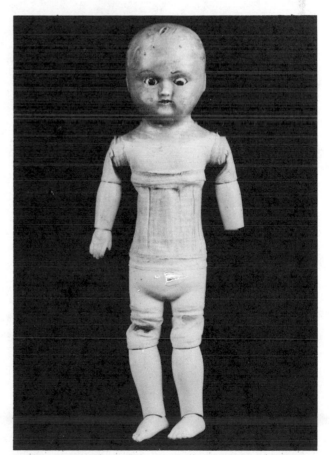

2586. Täufling or baby doll of the type referred to as a Motschmann-type. The head is wax-over-composition, molded and painted hair, sleeping eyes, open mouth with teeth. The cloth torso contains a voice box. The composition and wooden arms and legs have floating joints at the wrists and ankles. *Courtesy of the Collection Nederlands Kostuummuseum, The Hague. Photo by B. Frequin.*

2587. Wax-over-composition Täufling type early baby doll. It has a bald head, painted blue eyes, closed mouth, body jointed at the neck, shoulders and hips, wooden arms and legs. Orange boots are painted on the legs. Original infant style clothes. H. 7 in. (18 cm.). *Coleman Collection.*

tionship in appearance to the earlier Täuflinge of the mid 1800s and they were definitely not babies of a christening age.

Tawka Toys. 1930. Line of cloth-body dolls, some with celluloid heads made by *Irwin & Co.*

Tears. *George John Hoefler* in 1916–18 obtained a U.S. patent for a doll that would cry watery tears.★

Tebbets, Marian Curry, & Tebbets, Miss. 1921–30 and later. Pittsburgh, Pa. Made flat face cloth dolls and dolls with needle modeling.★

Ted Toy-lers. 1924–28. New Bedford, Mass. Company founded by E. V. (Ted) Babbitt, an engineer who made segmented wooden toys for his own children and then opened a production line type of factory with an output of 5000 wooden toys a day (Not all the toys were dolls). By 1928 the factory was a branch of the *International Toy Corp.*

1926: Advertised *Teddy Acrobat, Teddy Blue Walking Sailor, Teddy Jockey* and *Teddy Soldier.*

1927: Advertised Teddy Giant Sailor, Teddy Blue Sailor, Teddy White Sailor, Teddy Giant Soldier, Teddy Red Soldier, Teddy Giant Klown, Teddy Yellow Klown. The Teddy dolls came in six hts. from 7½ to 17 in. (19 to 43 cm.). There were also Giant Teddies. Hts. 13½ to 19 in. (34 to 48 cm.).

1928: Advertised Teddy Blue Sailor, Teddy Yellow Klown and Teddy Soldier.

Teddie (Teddy). 1912 and later. Cutout cloth doll made by *Dean.* It had a *Drayton* style face and was a mate to *Peggie.*

1920: One of the *Goo Goo* line of flat faced cloth dolls with eyes looking to the side. It was style no. D 248. Ht. 8½ in. (21.5 cm.).

1980: Reprinted.

Teddy. 1918. Doll with composition head and hands, molded hair, produced by the *Made in America Manufacturing Co.* It wore a red, white, and blue suit including vertical striped trousers, a cap and footwear. *Baby Glory* was its mate and it was given as a subscription premium by NEEDLECRAFT. Ht. 14 in. (35.5 cm.).

Teddy Acrobat. 1926. Segmented wooden doll with painted clothes made by *Ted Toy-lers* as style no. 103.

Teddy Bear Doll. 1909. Name used by *Siegel Cooper* for a doll with a celluloid face and a plush covered Teddy Bear type body with a crier; priced 25¢ to $1.00.

Teddy Blue (Walking) Sailor. 1926–28. Segmented turned wooden doll made by the *Ted Toy-lers* as style nos. 102B and 50. It had a painted blue sailor's outfit including a sailor's cap.

1927: Also came as Teddy White Sailor in a white outfit.

1927–28. Came in two sizes, the larger one was called Teddy Giant Sailor. Hts. 7½ and 15⅜ in. (19 and 39 cm.).

Teddy Clown. 1928. Cloth doll made by *Steiff* and distributed by *Borgfeldt.*

Teddy Doll. ca. 1913–17. Name of a doll with composition head, painted hair and eyes, felt hands and feet and a "Baby lamb cloth" covered body which simulated a boy's suit. It had a patent leather belt, a white "baby lamb cloth" collar and toque. This doll was distributed by *Butler Bros.*★

Teddy Giant. 1927–28. Large size segmented wooden dolls with painted clothes including *Teddy* Giant *Sailor, Teddy* Giant *Soldier,* and *Teddy Giant* Klown made by *Ted Toy-lers.* Hts. 13½ to 19 in. (34 to 48 cm.). The 19 in. (48 cm.) Giants were new in 1927.

Teddy Jockey. 1926. Segmented wooden doll with painted clothes made by the *Ted Toy-lers* as style no. 101.

Teddy Red Soldier. See **Teddy Soldier.**

Teddy Roosevelt. Ca. 1900. Stockinet portrait doll. (See also **Sonneberg, Thür.** 1899–1902.)

2588. Cloth portrait doll of Teddy Roosevelt has a stockinet needle sculptured head, black wool yarn hair, blue eyes behind embroidered glasses, embroidered mustache, and an open-closed mouth with teeth. The body is formed by the brown felt pseudo Rough Riders' uniform. H. 10¼ in. (26 cm.). This doll was once in the Laura Starr Collection. *Courtesy of The International Doll Library. Photo by Sotheby Parke Bernet Inc., N.Y.*

Teddy Roosevelt. 1909–29. Wooden portrait doll made by *Schoenhut* and belonging to the "Teddy in Africa" set. The doll had a hunter's costume with a sun helmet on its head and a gun in its hand.

1929: This doll was advertised as a "Big Game Hunter."★

Teddy Soldier. 1926–28. Segmented turned wooden doll made by *Ted Toy-lers* as style no. 100. It had a painted uniform of a soldier with a tall busby and a shoulder sash.

1927: Advertised as Teddy Red Soldier.

1928: Came in two sizes, the larger one was called *Teddy Giant* Soldier. Hts. 8½ and 16¼ in. (21.5 and 41 cm.).

Teddy Toy Co. 1914–30 and later. London. Advertised a portrait doll of A. A. Milne's character *Christopher Robin* in 1930. One of a *Softanlite* line of *Sussfeld & Co.* The doll wore an oil-skin coat and sou'wester hat.

Teddy White Sailor. See **Teddy Blue (Walking) Sailor.**

Teddy Yellow Klown. 1927–28. Segmented, turned wooden doll made by *Ted Toy-lers* as style no. 502. It had a painted yellow costume including a conical hat and came in two sizes, the larger one was called *Teddy Giant* Klown. Hts. 8¾ and 17 in. (22.5 and 43 cm.).

Teddy-Bear Suit. 1928. Name of a new doll's outfit made by *M. & S. Shillman* of brushed angora wool. It covered the doll completely so that no dress or footwear was needed and the doll resembled an *Eskimo* baby; priced $2.95.

Tee Wee. 1927–30. Hand puppet infant on a pillow made by *S. & H. Novelty Co.*, distributed by *Baker & Bennett Co.* The bisque heads were *My Dream Baby* heads made by *Armand Marseille.* The hands were usually celluloid. The pillow was made of sheer white fabric, lace and ribbons on pink or blue satin. In the back of the pillow was an aperture through which a hand could be inserted. The thumb and middle finger fit into the arms while the first or index finger fit into the head of the doll. When a voice was added the voice box was held in the palm of one's hand.

1927: A U.S. patent for this doll was obtained by Charles Stein; a Canadian patent and a U.S. design patent were pending. Doll was priced $3.00. Tee Wee was shown in Fox Weekly News reels in motion picture theaters.

1928: New Tee Wee number had a body and voice. Tee Wee also came as a regular baby doll in a long dress or as a boudoir pillow baby. Queen Mary of England chose one of the Tee Wee hand puppets for a Christmas gift. Came in four sizes, 10 × 7, 10 × 7½, 11½ × 8½, and 12 × 13 in. (25.5 × 18, 25.5 × 19, 29 × 21.5 and 30.5 × 33 cm.). Sold at *Gamage* and was priced in England $4.37 to $7.50.

1929: The pillows were made in a square or heart shape, size 12 × 12 in. (30.5 × 30.5 cm.); priced $2.00. *Harrods* sold these dolls. A heart-shaped tag was pinned to the baby dolls. Hts. 17 and 21 in. (43 and 53.5 cm.); priced $2.00 and $3.00.

1930: Tee Wee was made as twin doll sets.

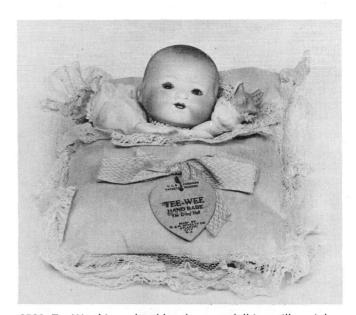

2589. Tee Wee bisque head hand puppet doll in a pillow. It has painted hair, stationary glass eyes, open mouth with two lower teeth, a flange neck and a cloth body with celluloid hands, a voice box but no legs. Original clothes and pillow. Blue tag with black letters, Ill. 2590. The opposite side of the tag reads: "Directions//Place your thumb//in my left hand and // your first finger//in my head and // your second fin-//ger in my right// hand and you//can use your//fourth finger// to make me//cry." The head is marked "A.M.//Germany." H. of head 3½ in. (9 cm.). *Courtesy of the Margaret Woodbury Strong Museum. Photo by Harry Bickelhaupt.*

2590. Cardboard tag attached to a Tee Wee hand puppet doll.

2591. Teenie Weenie mark on composition-head dolls made by the American Character Doll Co.

Teenie Weenie. 1925 and probably later. *Bye-Lo* type doll made by the *American Character Doll Co.* (See Ill. 2591.)★

Teenie Weenies. 1924–26. Dolls representing the Sunday comic characters of this name were designed by *William Donahey* and made by *Live Long Toys.* They were made of stuffed oilcloth (imitation leather) and represented a Chinese, an Indian, a black person, a lady of fashion, a policeman, and a boy. Either the black person or the boy was named "Gogo." Ht. 6 in. (15 cm.).

Teenie Weenies. 1929. All-composition dolls made by *Amberg* with his new patented body motion; priced 75¢. (See also **It** and **Tiny Tots.**)

Teeth. Some of the unusual teeth found in dolls' heads included: A china head having an open mouth and teeth.

A character doll with teeth; the lower set and tongue fell back and disappeared when the doll was placed horizontally. This head was marked "Germany//410//3/0." Ht. 12 in. (30.5 cm.). Patents for moving teeth were applied for by *Franz Schmidt* in 1911, and by *Albert Messing* in 1913.

A *Bye-Lo Baby* with bisque head marked "Grace S. Putnam// Germany 4½ 15/48," had glass eyes, four teeth in a smiling mouth, and a cloth body. Ht. 18 in. (45.5 cm.).

1928: A dolls' hospital reported that it made dolls' teeth by carving them out of bits of shell found on beaches. (See also **Manufacture of Dolls, Commercial; Made in France and Germany Compared.**)★

Telma Manufacturing Co. 1917–18. London. Manufactured dressed dolls with removable clothes, undressed dolls, woolen dolls and dolls' heads. The dolls had either *British Ceramic* or composition heads and limbs. *Joseph Hopkins* was their agent.

Tempier. 1843–ca. 1850. Paris. Two dolls have been found with Tempier marks. One had a printed sticker having the name "Tempier" placed on the shoes of a *Jacob Petit* bald china head doll on a kid body in the collection of the Swiss National Museum in Zurich. Ht. 29 cm. (11½ in.). The other mark was a square paper label with the words "TEMPIER//27 BOULEVARD des ITALIENS" found on a papier-mâché head with painted eyes, papier-mâché body except for wooden lower arms.★

Tennis Dolls. Name of dolls dressed as boys, girls or ladies in tennis outfits.

1880: Wax doll in tennis attire was dressed by the Powell family in England. (See illustration 389 in THE COLLECTOR'S BOOK OF DOLLS' CLOTHES.)

Before 1914: German bisque-head dolls sometimes were dressed commercially as boys and girls in tennis costumes, usually carrying a tennis racquet. MODENWELT (FASHION WORLD) pictured dolls dressed for tennis. (See Ill. 2497.)

1916: *Steiff* advertised Betty and Eduard as being dressed in tennis clothes.

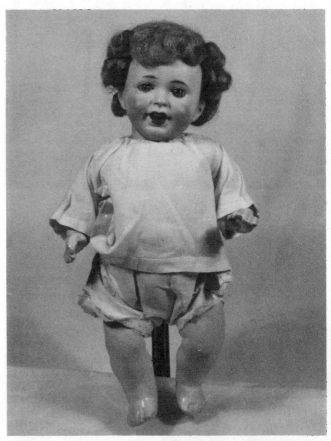

2592. Bisque head doll with an open-closed mouth and teeth made by the Société Française de Fabrication de Bébés & Jouets. It has a wig, blue glass eyes and a bent limb composition baby body. Mark: 23 S.F.B.J.//236//PARIS. H. 12 in. (30.5 cm.). Cir. of head 9 in. (23 cm.). *Courtesy of Richard Withington. Photo by Barbara Jendrick.*

1927–29: Felt dolls made by *Lenci;* girl had fluffy flax hair, tennis shoes and racquet. The boy, style no. 1004, had a racquet. He was 17½ in. (44 cm.) tall.

1928: *Hartleys Sports Stores* advertised tennis dolls. (See also **Sports Dolls.**)★

Terra Cotta or Earthen Dolls. An early and often crude type of doll.

Early 1800s: Earthen dolls' heads were made by Moravians in North Carolina.★

Terrène. 1863–90. Paris. Made bodies for dolls.★

Territorial. 1915. Cloth body doll distributed by *Hyman Abrahams.* Allegedly this doll's features could change to express various emotions. It appeared also with the name "Fall In."

Territorial. 1915 and later. Cloth body dolls dressed as soldiers. Line of dolls obtainable from many wholesale distributors. (See also **Military Costume Dolls.**)

Terry, John, Co. 1923–26. Obtained a U.S. patent for a cloth, composition or celluloid doll that was wrapped like an Egyptian mummy; that is, the bodies including the limbs were wrapped diagonally with ribbon on which was printed writing and pictures of nursery rhymes in imitation of hieroglyphics.

2593A & B. Jacob Petit china shoulder head doll with shoes marked Tempier. The doll has a bald head covered with a wig, painted eyes, a closed mouth and a kid body, gusset jointed at the shoulders, hips, and knees. Original clothes. Mark on shoes: Ill. 2594. H. 29 cm. (11½ in.). *Courtesy of the Musée National Suisse.*

TEMPIER
Blvd. des Italiens, 23

2594. Tempier mark on the sole of the shoe of a china-head doll.

2595. Bisque swivel neck shoulder head on a kid and aluminum body which resembles dolls bearing the Terrène mark. It has a blond wig, blue stationary glass eyes. The green dress makes the doll represent a young girl of either the late 1870s or early 1880s. H. 17½ in. (44.5 cm.). H. of head only, 4 in. (10 cm.). *Courtesy of Z. Frances Walker.*

Terry, William J. (Welbury Works). 1890–1915 and possibly later. London. Made and distributed cloth dolls including *Eskimo* dolls, including Billy Esquimaux and Susie Esquimau.

Tersch, M., Firm, Kunstwerkstätten. 1920–30. Berlin. Manufactured dolls. ★

Tesmine. 1927. Paris. Made dolls.

Tessie. 1919–20. Name of an all-composition doll with molded bobbed hair, eyes painted looking to the side, teeth, jointed at the shoulders, legs apart, It was made by the *American Toy & Novelty Co.*

Tessie. 1930. Trade name of dressed dolls made by *M. Kohnstam & Co.*

Tête Bois. Name on the wooden shoulder head of a doll with a kid body and jointed wooden arms. See Ill. 2596. There is some similarity between this doll and the *Bébé Tout en Bois* dolls.

Tête d'Aigle (Eagle's head). 1904–30 and later. Trademark used by *Petitcollin* for celluloid dolls.

Tête Jumeau. See **Bébé Jumeau.**

Textile Novelty Co. See **Kirkham, George William Chambers.**

Thames Valley Toy Co. 1930. Created a series of dolls known as *Winnie The Pooh.* This included Christopher Robin.

Thanhauser, S. 1913. Philadelphia, Pa. Imported dolls.

Thanksgiving Pie. See **Scarey Ann.**

2596. Wooden shoulder head marked Tête Bois on the lower front edge. The head with a wig, sleeping brown glass eyes, hair eyebrows and an open-closed mouth is on a kid body with wooden jointed arms. H. 14 in. (35.5 cm.). *Courtesy of the Margaret Woodbury Strong Museum. Photo by Barbara Jendrick.*

Therese (German, Dachau). 1911 and before. Felt doll made by *Steiff,* wore the regional costume of Dachau, Germany. Ht. 35 cm. (14 in.).

Théroude, Alexandre Nicholas. 1837–95. Paris. Manufactured dolls. The beginning date was based on research by Mme. Florence Poisson, curator of the Roybet Fould Museum.★

Theyer, Martin. Before 1836–53. Vienna. In 1836 Franz Theyer was managing director of his father's firm. They produced and distributed dolls according to the research of Dr. Eva Moskovszky.

Thiele, Anna. 1885–1930 and later. Waltershausen, Thür. From 1920 to at least 1931 Gustav Theile was head of this firm that made dolls' wigs, dolls and papier-mâché objects.

1930: Used the mark "Trade Mark//Getefrisur// Schutzmarke."★

Thiele, Arthur. 1926. Dresden, Germany. Manufactured dolls.

Thiele, Max. 1930 and before. Germany. Created dolls representing historical and fictional characters.

Thiele, Wilhelm. 1904. Dresden, Germany. Designed art dolls dressed in regional or historical costumes according to an Art Journal. See Ill. 2495.

Thiem, Adolf. 1900. Waltershausen, Thür. Applied for a German patent (D.R.G.M.) for dolls' joints.

Thierer, Charles. 1930. New York City. Made dolls including one named *Faerie Princess.*

Thirsty. 1928. Name of a cloth doll made by *Dean.*

This Little Girl. 1915–17. Cutout cloth doll in the *Hug-Me-Tight* line, style no. 110/200.

Thomas. Early 1800s. London. His tradecard read "Doll Maker//Wholesale, Retail & for Exportation."

Thomas, Mme. Ambroise. 1915–16. Paris. Created cloth dolls with French characteristics according to Doin.

Thomas, Maurice. 1925–29. Paris. By 1928 Ph. & P. Sustrac were the successors of Maurice Thomas. Made dolls.★

Thomas, Queen G. 1921. American. Designed dresses for *Buds and Buddies* dolls made by *S. E. Delavan.*

Thomas Edison. Jr. 1916. Composition head doll, produced by Horsman, based on the comic character drawn by Fontaine Fox. (See also **Edison, Thomas.**)

Thomas Squeelix. See **Little Shavers.**

Thomas & Heinrichs. 1915. New York City. Formerly connected with Turner and Thomas. Represented *Amberg.*

Thomee, Edmund. 1913. Sonneberg, Thür. Applied for a German patent (D.R.G.M.) for celluloid joints for dolls.

Thomle, P. 1880. Queensland, Australia. Exhibited mechanical dolls at the Melbourne Exposition.

Thompson, Thos. R. 1919. Registered in U.S. *Tots Toie* as a trademark for wooden dolls.

Thompson, Victor C. 1926. Los Angeles, Calif. Obtained a U.S. design patent for a doll.

Thompson's Mail Order Premium House. Bridgewater, Conn. Name found on a *Dolly Dimple* uncut cloth doll.

Thomson, Mlle. Valentine. 1914–18. Paris. Designed and created dolls.

1916: The models for one of her dolls was made by the sculptor, *M. Lejeune.*

1918: Her dolls were distributed by a shop named *Pandora.* (See also **Momson, V.**)★

Thormolhlen, Emma. 1905. Hamburg, Germany. Applied for a German patent (D.R.G.M.) for a *Topsy Turvy* doll with one head white and the other head black.

Thorne Bros. 1915–18. London. Their leading line was *Tumble It* with a carved wooden head.

Other dolls were *Long Jack and Little Jack, Brownie* and squeaker dolls.

Three Arts Toy Industry. 1920–27. London. This may have been the successor of the *Three Arts Women's Employment*

Fund. In 1927 became the Artistic Novelty Co. Ltd. Made cuddly dolls of plush, velvet or felt.

1920: Advertised dolls named Fairies, *Joibelles* and Midgets.

1921: Advertised "Cuddley Doll" "Joli Chap" and *Pierrot.*

Three Arts Women's Employment Fund. 1915–20. London. At the beginning it funded *Shanklin.* Then in 1916 they began to make cloth dolls such as *Papooski* and *Cuddley Ones.* The dolls were designed or created by artists such as *John Hassall* or by actresses.

1917: Cloth dolls were their leading line and the dolls came dressed or undressed. (See also **Three Arts Toy Industry.**)

Three Little Sisters. 1917. Cloth dolls designed by *E. E. Houghton* and made by *Shanklin.* They came in standing and sitting types and included the Good Sisters, Patty, Prudence, and another doll and the Naughty Sisters, with untidy hair, one of whom was named *Betty.*

Thuillier, A. 1875–93. Paris. Made dolls with various kinds of bodies. He purchased at least some of his bisque heads from *François Gaultier.* His dolls ranged at least from size number 2 to 15.

1881: Listed in a Gaultier inventory as owing money for bisque dolls' heads that he had bought, according to the research by Mme. Florence Poisson, curator of the Roybet Fould Museum. (See also **De La Thuilerie, A.**)★

2598. Bisque head possibly made by Gaultier who is known to have made bisque heads for A. Thuillier, who probably made the doll. It has blue glass eyes, slight white area between the lips and a ball jointed composition body. Head marked "A 9 T." H. 17½ in. (44.5 cm.). *Courtesy of Becky and Jaye Lowe. Photo by Bill Holland.*

2597. Bisque head doll probably made by Thuillier. It has a blond mohair wig, cork pate, blue paperweight glass eyes, deep pink shadow above the eyes, closed mouth with slight white between the lips, pierced ears, ball jointed composition body, wrists not jointed. Head marked "A 6 T." H. 16½ in. (42 cm.). *Courtesy of Becky and Jaye Lowe. Photo by Bill Holland.*

2599. Bisque head marked "A 9 T," probably for A. Thuillier, has a black wig, stationary blue eyes, pierced ears, closed mouth and a ball jointed composition body. H. 18 in. (45.5 cm.). *Courtesy of Sotheby Parke Bernet Inc., N.Y.*

2600. Mark on bisque head doll probably made by or for Thuillier.

Thumbs up! //Haut les Mains! 1921. Trademark registered in France for dolls by Herbert Nalty doing business as *Gourdel Vales & Co.* (See also **Fumsup.**)★

Thüringer Puppen-Industrie. 1922–23 and probably other years. Waltershausen, Thür. Bisque head character face doll with a wig and an open mouth on a toddler body. Ht. 12 in. (30.5 cm.); had the mark of the Thüringer Puppen-Industrie according to the Richard Merrills.

2601–2602. Marks for dolls of the Thüringer Puppen-Industrie.

Thüringer Puppen & Spielwarenexport Co. 1923–28. Berlin. Distributed and exported dolls.★

Thüringer Spielwarenfabrik See **Freytag, F. W., & Co.**

Thüringia. 1902. Name used as a mark for jointed dolls by *Carl Hartmann.*

Thüringian Dolls. See **Sonneberg** and **Waltershausen Dolls.**

Tibbals, Lewis P. 1880s and probably earlier. New York City. The successor was George F. Langenbacker whose trade card listed dolls.

Tickletoes. 1928–30 and later. Composition head, bent-limb baby doll with rubber limbs made by *Ideal* and distributed by *Butler Bros., J. C. Penney, Quaker Doll Co.* and probably others. The doll had molded hair, sleeping, flirting and winking eyes, an open mouth into which a thumb or pacifier could be placed. The rubber hands could hold objects and the doll cried when the rubber legs were squeezed. It had a cloth torso.

1929: Wore a short lawn dress, matching bonnet, rubber panties, socks, baby moccasins and had a pacifier. Doll cried not only when its leg was squeezed but also when it was tilted forward. Ideal claimed the doll could clap its hands, hold a teacup or pray. "Tickletoes" was registered in U.S. as a trademark for dolls by Ideal. Four hts. including 15, 17, and 19 in. (38, 43, and 48 cm.); priced $3.50 to $7.50.

1930: Doll cried when it was turned on its side as well as when the leg was squeezed. It was described as having a smiling face and blue eyes, dressed in silk coat or handknitted coat and bonnet and in trimmed organdy.

Ca. 1933: Head was described as similar to that on *Smiles*

and on *Suck-a-Thumb.* Tickletoes came with a skin wig as well as molded hair. The sleeping, flirting eyes were celluloid; sometimes doll was dressed in rompers. Six hts.

Tickle Toes. See **Radio Dancing Couple** and **S. & H. Novelty Co.**

Tietz, Hermann. Probably before 1908–26. Munich, Bavaria, and Berlin. He collected, exhibited and distributed in his stores the Puppen Reform dolls created by *Lilli Frobenius,* Alice Hagemann, *Marion Kaulitz, Marie Marc-Schnür, Paul Vogelsanger,* and *Joseph Wackerle.* The dolls were dressed by *Eugenie Derdzakian,* M. Heinz, *Helene Siewert, Helene Stern, Hedwig Stich,* and others. He also exhibited the early *Kämmer & Reinhardt* character dolls and early *Käthe Kruse* dolls.

„G'sundheit!"

2603. Puppen Reform doll exhibited by Hermann Tietz, shown in DIE WELT DER FRAU, November, 1908. "G'sundheit!" (A sneeze).

2604. Group of Marion Kaulitz dolls of the type exhibited by Hermann Tietz in Munich as shown in DEKORATIVE KUNST, February, 1912.

2605. Munich Art Dolls of the type exhibited by Hermann Tietz. The girl has a mohair wig and painted brown eyes. H. 18½ in. (47 cm.). The taller boy has painted brown hair and eyes. H. 18½ in. (47 cm.). The shorter boy has a mohair wig and painted blue eyes. H. 13½ in. (34 cm.). All three dolls have original clothes. *Courtesy of Becky and Jaye Lowe. Photo by Bill Holland.*

1926: Had 14 stores in Germany. Amalgamated with M Conitzer & Sohne and combined they had 38 establishments.

Tietz, Léonhard. ca. 1910. Antwerp, Belgium. Name of a store owner that had a doll exhibit and competition for charity.

Tilda. 1929. All-bisque doll with turning head, molded and painted clothes, represented one of the characters in "The Gumps" cartoon drawn by *Sidney Smith.* Tilda was made in Germany and distributed wholesale by *Marshall Field.*

Tilde. 1927–28. Felt doll made by *Lenci* as style no. 700. It represented a school-age girl with braids over its ears, wearing a dress with a high waistline and a full skirt that covered the knees. Ht. 37½ in. (95 cm.).

Tiller, William. 1850. Philadelphia, Pa. Imported and distributed dolls according to an advertisement in the PUBLIC LEDGER.

Tillicum Toys. 1926–30. Tacoma, Washington. *Harriet M. Robinson* organized the Tillicum Manufacturing Co. to create toys which she had designed for classroom use. Kennard Weddell was President of the Company. In 1928, they merged with Craigcraft but continued to use the Tillicum name. Manufactured wooden dolls from kindling wood.

Concours de la « POUPÉE CHARITABLE, » aux Magasins Léonhard Tietz, au profit des œuvres « *Le Lait pour les Petits* » et Soc. prot. des « *Enfants Martyrs* »
Phot. G. Hauck. Anvers.

Concours de la « POUPÉE CHARITABLE, » aux Magasins Léonhard Tietz, au profit des œuvres « *Le Lait pour les Petits* » et Soc. prot. des « *Enfants Martyrs* »
Phot. G. Hauck. Anvers.

2606A & B. Léonhard Tietz exhibited dolls in his store in Antwerp, Belgium ca. 1910. The exhibit was to raise money in order to buy milk for children under the auspices of the Soc. prot. des "Enfants Martyrs." A series of postcards commemorated this event (Also see Ills. 914 A-C.). The first card shows two women with their babies at the window where the nurse is located. The second picture shows dolls in various costumes. The dolls in these pictures appear to have German bisque heads.

Concours de la « POUPÉE CHARITABLE, » aux Magasins Léonhard Tietz, au profit des œuvres « *Le Lait pour les Petits* » et Soc. prot. des « *Enfants Martyrs* »
Phot. G. Hauck. Anvers.

2607. Bisque head dolls in period costume exhibited in Léonhard Tietz store in Antwerp, Belgium. The three dolls on the left possibly represent the children of Charles the First of England.

1927: Made turned all-wood dolls named *Tiny Tot Dolls.*

1928: The Tiny Tot Dolls were used in classrooms. Tillicum Toys claimed that they paid $4.50 for a load of wood and sold it as toys for $72.50.

Tilp, Adolf. 1904. Nürnberg, Bavaria. Applied for a German patent (D.R.G.M.) for dolls with spherical forms.

Timber Tots. 1924. Colored and dressed little wooden art dolls made by Nelson-Young Manufacturing Co., a subsidiary of the *Pollyanna Co.*

Tina. 1916. Felt doll representing an Argentinian woman, made by *Steiff.* Ht. 43 cm. (17 in.).

Tinker, E. London. A doll with a wax-over-composition head and glass eyes had written on its body "To be had of E. Tinker, 54 Bishopsgate and nowhere else."

Tinker Toys. 1919–30 and later. Evanston, Ill. Trade name of dolls made by the Toy Tinkers of enameled painted wooden beads of various shapes.

1919: Distributed by *Sears.*

1921: Advertised *Siren Tinker* and *Tom Tinker.*

1923: Advertised *Belle Tinker,* Follo-Me Tinker, Giant Tinker, Jump Rope Tinker, Tilly Tinker and Whirling Tinker.

1926: New doll with leather arms and legs was called *Lanky Tinker.* Distributed in Britain by H. A. Moore & Co.

1927: Doll with bell shaped segments was called *Belle Tinker.*

1928: A new doll representing a baby was introduced.

1929: Advertised *Baby Doll Tinker, Gym Tinker,* and *Tip Toe Tinker.*

Tinkle Belle. 1924. *Aerolite* rattle art doll of plush stuffed with kapok. It had bells on its fingers and toes and wore a pointed hat. Came in assorted colors, made by *Chad Valley* as style no. 193. Ht. 6½ in. (16.5 cm.).

Tiny Tads. 1915. Line of dolls representing infants, boys and girls made by *Effanbee* as style nos. 221 A, 221 B, 221 C and 222 which were the infants in long dresses. These dolls had composition heads with molded hair, cloth bodies and limbs; priced 35¢. (See Ill. 647 in THE COLLECTOR'S BOOK OF DOLLS' CLOTHES.).★

Tiny Tim. 1909–16: Cutout cloth doll with a Lord Fauntleroy style suit printed on it. The jacket had rounded corners. This doll was produced by *Selchow & Righter* and was a mate to *Dolly Dimple;* priced 75¢ doz. wholesale in 1912.

1915–16: It was advertised by the National Cloak & Suit Co. Ht. 13½ in. (34 cm.); priced 10¢.★

Tiny Toddler. Ca. 1917. A doll that could walk when operated by one's fingers, advertised by *Shackman.* Ht. 8 in. (20.5 cm.); priced 50¢.

Tiny Tot. 1920s. Bisque-head made by *Armand Marseille* had a wig; sleeping eyes; open mouth with four teeth; composition body, jointed at the neck, shoulders and hips; long legs, painted white; molded and painted high heel tan single strap slippers. One of these dolls wore a very short lace net dress with a silk ribbon at the waistline and a silk ribbon hairbow. Mark on head "Germany// A 12/0 M." Round blue tag with white letters "TINY TOT// REG. U.S. PAT. OFF.//GERMANY." Ht. 7½ in. (19 cm.).

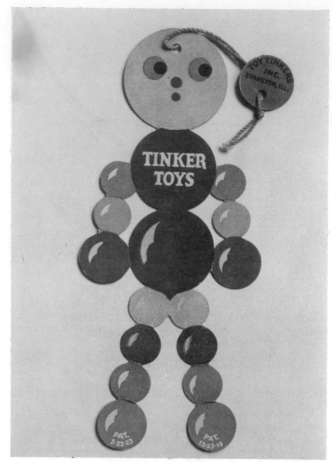

2608. Tinker Toy advertisement representing the painted face and the segmented wooden body made of wooden spheres of various colors and various sizes. The 1919 and 1923 patent dates are shown on the feet. *Coleman Collection.*

Tiny Tot. 1927. Cloth doll, not embossed, made of cotton crepe with handpainted features and clothes; distributed by *Butler Bros.* Ht. 11½ in. (29 cm.).

Tiny Tot Dolls. 1927–28. All-wood turned dolls with painted hair and features, jointed at the shoulders and standing on a round bottom; made by *Tillicum Toys.* These dolls represented a Father, Mother, Girl and Boy in various walks of life and were used in classrooms. They were approximately dolls' house size.

Tiny Tots. 1913–14. Composition head dolls representing boys and girls made by *Amberg.*

1913: Doll had composition head and hands which had all the fingers apart. The hair was molded, the eyes were painted looking to the side and the body was cloth. Came in five styles as boys and girls wearing rompers or dresses. Ht. of at least one of the dolls was 13 in. (33 cm.).

1914: The bodies were stuffed with cork and the legs were straight to enable the doll to stand. Ht. of at least one of the dolls was 11 in. (28 cm.); priced $8.00 doz. wholesale.★

Tiny Tots. 1928–30 and later. All-composition dolls with a

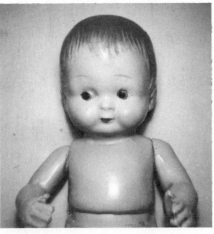

2609A & B. All-composition doll named Tiny Tot made by Amberg. It had molded brown short hair, molded brown eyes looking to the side, closed mouth, almost no neck, jointed at the shoulders, and a ball and socket joint at the waist. The footwear was molded. Mark: Ill. 2610. H. 9 in. (23 cm.). *Courtesy of Dorothy Annunziato.*

PAT.APPL'D.FOR
L.A.& S.©1928

2610. Embossed mark on the back shoulders of an all-composition Tiny Tot.

waist joint like the *It* dolls which were also produced by *Amberg,* until the company was taken over by *Horsman* in 1930 after which Horsman produced these dolls. (See also **Teenie Weenies.**)

1929: They had molded and painted hair, features and footwear. The girl had bobbed hair while the boy had short hair. The back of the upper torso was marked "PAT. APPL'D FOR// L.A. & S. © 1928." The boy wore long overalls and the girl wore a short-sleeved print dress. Both a dressed boy and girl came in a box with extra clothes. The label on the clothes read, "AN AMBERG DOLL with //BODY TWIST//All its own //PAT. PEND. SER. NO. 32018." Ht. 8 in. (20.5 cm.); priced $2.00.

1930: Named Tynie Tots by Horsman.

Tiny Travelers. 1907–21. Cutout cloth dolls made by *Saalfield.* There were six versions, each one 6 by 8 in. (15 × 20.5 cm.); priced 3¢ each including *Santa Claus.*

Tiny-Tot (Tiny Tot). 1919–20. Composition doll made by *Jessie M. Raleigh.* It had short hair and was a "plump little doll."★

Tip Toe Tinker. 1929. Wooden doll made by *Tinker Toys,* represented a toe dancer and came with a detachable jump rope. Ht. 7⅛ in. (18 cm.); priced 65¢.

Tip Top Toy Co. 1912–21. New York City. By 1921, facto-

ries were located in Brooklyn, Jersey City and Hoboken. Made and distributed dolls.

1919: *Joseph Kaempfer* doing business as the Tip Top Toy Co. obtained a U.S. design patent for dolls.

1920: Trademark was a spinning top under which was an ellipse with the words "TIP TOP//TOY//COMPANY" in it.

Composition dolls were made of a treated wood pulp (method of treating was secret) which was run into flame-heated brass molds and allowed to remain until it set. After it was removed it was given a rough finish and placed on racks to dry. This composition was called "bisque finish."

Baby dolls with "bisque finish" composition heads had wigs, sleeping eyes, bent limb composition bodies and a chemise. Hts. 18 and 24 in. (45.5 and 61 cm.).

Child dolls with "bisque finish" composition heads had human hair wigs with a pair of hair ribbons and sleeping eyes. Their kid bodies had wooden ball joints at the shoulders, elbows, and knees. The hips had a pin joint and the upper legs as well as the torso were kid. Undressed the dolls came in five hts. 16, 18, 20, 22, and 24 in. (40.5, 45.5, 51, 56, and 61 cm.).

The all-composition *Kewpie*-type doll had painted hair or hair under a net, painted eyes glancing to the side. Undressed they were called *Pudgie.* Hts. 8 and 13 in. (20.5 and 33 cm.). The 8 in. (20.5 cm.) size also came dressed in differing costumes of silk and satin when it was given other names such as: La Belle, La France, La Mode, La Petite, Pansy, Patricia, Peggy, Pierrot, Polly, Valeska, Viola and Vivien depending on the costume.

1921: Advertised a walking doll which could sit down. (See also **Manufacture of Dolls, Commercial: Made in United States.**) (See Ills. 2611 and 2612.)★

Tipperary Tom. 1916. Line of dolls made by the *Atlas Manufacturing Co.*

Tipry. 1915. Cloth doll wearing a British territorial uniform was handled by *Whyte, Ridsdale.* Three hts.; priced $4.50 to $5.00 doz. wholesale.

Tiroler Docken. At least from the late 1700s to the 1900s. Name of wooden dolls representing the people from the Tyrol. (See also **Grödner Tal Wooden Dolls** and **Viechtau near Gmunden.**)

Tiss Me (Tiss-Me). 1921–27. All-composition doll with molded hair or wig, jointed at the shoulders; created by Hy Mayer. Distributed by *Borgfeldt* and *Butler Bros.*

1921: Painted eyes, dressed and with ribbon wristbands. Hts. 5, 7 and 9 in. (12.5, 18 and 23 cm.); largest size cost $1.00 without wig and $1.15 with wig. See THE COLLECTOR'S BOOK OF DOLLS' CLOTHES, Ill. 727.

1927: Borgfeldt advertised that their Tiss-Me had sleeping eyes and was part of their import line.★

Tissier & Cie. 1920s and probably earlier. Paris. Factories at Oyonnax, Ain, and at Muzy, Eure. Member of the *Chambre Syndicale.* Listed in DIDOT as Giselle Paul Tissier until 1929. Successor was Anel & Fils *(Anel & Fraisse).* Made dolls and bébés of celluloid and "Galatith," made deluxe dolls and fetishes; some of the dolls were undressed and some were dressed.

Titche-Goettinger's. 1927 and possibly other years. Dallas, Texas. Store called "The Doll's House" advertised baby dolls, walking dolls, talking dolls, dolls that cry and go to sleep, dolls dressed in the costumes of "all lands," dolls of various sizes, even including dolls that were the size of six year old children.

Titi. Cloth doll designed by *Poulbot;* molded and painted features; mouth was a straight line, felt ears; cotton stuffing in body, dressed as boys or girls; most of the clothes were made of felt. Mark was "LES POULBOTTES//'TiTi'// de Poulbot//'DOUMKA'//EDITEUR EXCLUSIF" and "MODÈLE DÉPOSÉ." Ht. 40 cm. (15½ in.).

Tóbiás, Mrs. Károly. 1920s. Budapest. Created dolls that were lent by the Brooklyn Museum for an exhibit in New York City.

Toddi. 1920. Italy. Artist who designed dolls. His *Salome* was made in a large Turin factory, probably *Lenci.* (See also **Italian Dolls.**)

Toddle Tot. 1928–30 and later. Composition head *Mama* doll with sleeping eyes made by the *American Character Doll Co.* in their Petite line. It came dressed in various outfits.

1929: Costumes included tailored, formal or street wear outfits.

1930: This doll was advertised as being able to turn its head,

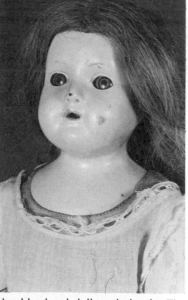

2611A & B. Composition shoulder head doll made by the Tip Top Toy Co. The brown wig is a replacement. The sleeping eyes are metal painted with cellulose and the mouth is open. The body has a kid torso and upper legs. The lower legs are composition, as are the hands. The upper arms are wood with ball joints. It wears a commercial chemise. Mark: Ill. 2612. H. 18½ in. (47 cm.); head only, 5½ in. (14 cm.). *Courtesy of Robert and Katrin Burlin.*

2612. Mark on the composition head of a doll made by the Tip Top Toy Co.

2613. Mark on a Poulbot Titi doll.

hands and feet in any direction and walk when one held its hand. It had upper teeth and wore knitted suits or frilled dresses; priced $8.00 to $25.00.

Toddler. 1919. Name of a doll with head and hands made of wood-fibre composition by the *American Bisque Doll Co.* It had a cloth baby body and removable clothes including a short baby dress. Hts. 18, 20, and 25 in. (45.5, 51, and 63.5 cm.).

Toddler. 1921. Name of a stockinet cloth doll made in England and imported into America by *Meakin & Ridgeway.*

Toddlers. See **Clauderies, Tata** and **Toto.**

Toddling Toodles. 1925–27. Trade name of a line of walking dolls produced by *Louis Wolf* with a mechanism patented by *Butsum.*

1926: Dolls dressed in various costumes as boys and girls.

1927: Walked 25 feet by itself.★

Todhunter, M. E. 1926–28. Windermere, Westmorland. Dolls made with a copper skeleton, a molded clay head and leather glued over the clay and colored with oil paints. The body was covered with cotton batting and bound with strips of calico. The hands covered with leather allegedly could hold small objects. The suede clothes created the dolls as representations of elves, pipers, pierrots, and so forth.

1928: Obtained a patent for these dolls.

Tódor Kertész. 1861–1926 and later. Budapest. One of the largest shops in Hungary, distributed dolls.

Toinette Fashion Shop of Toyland. 1928–29. Produced sewing sets for making dolls' clothes. The proprietor was *Mrs. Edward Stryker.*

Tokio. 1908. Cutout cloth doll with a printed Japanese costume, made by *Saalfield.* Ht. 7¾ in. (20 cm.).

Tom Thumb. 1909–13. Cutout cloth doll portraying a boy in a middy suit, produced by *Selchow & Righter*. In 1912 ht. 9 in. (23 cm.); priced 5¢ to 38¢ doz. wholesale.★

Tom Tinker. 1919–30. Wooden enameled bead doll made by *Tinker Toys*. It had painted features.

1919–22: Distributed by *Sears*, Ht. 7 in. (18 cm.); priced 45¢.

1923: Priced 50¢; Tom Tinker II with a new type of pastel colored enamel; priced 75¢.

1927: Ht. 8 in. (20.5 cm.).

Tom, Tom, the Piper's Son. 1928. Cutout cloth doll used for advertising *Kellogg Co.* products.

Tomboy. 1921. Stockinet doll made in England and imported into America by *Meakin & Ridgeway*. It wore a short dress and bloomers of the same fabric. Bloomers showed below the dress.

Tommy (English Soldier). Before 1911–16. Felt doll representing a British soldier, made by *Steiff* and distributed by *Borgfeldt*. It wore a kepi and came with or without equipment. Ht. 35 cm. (14 in.); priced $1.55 in New York City in 1913.

Tommy Atkins. World War I period. Name given to dolls representing British privates. Some of these dolls wore a shirt, short trousers and a broad brimmed hat; others wore a soldier's jacket, puttees and a kepi. One such doll was called *Our Tommy*. (See also **Steiner & Co.**)★

Tommy Snooks. 1921–23. Dressed cloth doll made by *Martha Chase*. Ht. 12 in. (30.5 cm.).★

Tommy Toodles. 1922. Cloth walking doll made by *Rees Davis*.

Tommy Trim. Early 1900s. Cutout lithographed cloth doll produced by *Horsman*. The boy doll wore a blue Lord Fauntleroy style knee length suit with a large white collar. Ht. 13 in. (33 cm.). (See Ill. 2614.)★

Tommy Tucker. 1920–21. Cloth doll, handpainted and real hair, made by *Rees Davis* in her *Mother Goose* line.

Tommy Tucker. See **Babyland**.

Tompkin, James, Ltd. 1877–1925 and possibly later. London. Known as the Rubber House which produced an "Eton" Boy with detachable Topper or straw hat designed by *Chloe Preston*.

Toni (Girl). 1924. Felt doll made by *Steiff*. Ht. 35 cm. (14 in.).

Toodles. 1910–16. Composition-head doll copyrighted 1910, designed by *Helen Trowbridge* for *Horsman* as style no. 148. In 1914 a new model head that had been copyrighted in 1912 was used. This head resembled *Farmer Boy*. Toodles with *Campbell Kid* type hands represented a boy of toddling age and its smock and knickers of a striped cotton fabric were of the same clothes pattern as the outfit worn by *Carnival Baby*.

1914: Two sizes were distributed by *Marshall Field*. The Jr.

2614. Cutout chromolithographed cloth doll named Tommy Trim, produced by Horsman. It is dressed in a blue Little Lord Fauntleroy style suit and a wide white collar and red socks. *Courtesy of Margaret Whitton.*

No. 148 "Toodles"

No. 148.   "TOODLES"
Trade Mark
(Head Copyrighted, 1912, by
E. I. Horsman Co.)
This is a stocky little fellow just able to toddle. Dressed in a pretty patterned suit of rompers with a smock blouse. The head is an especially beautiful model. One of our most popular character dolls—always in demand.
Per Dozen........**$8.50**

2615. Toodles as advertised in a Horsman catalog of ca. 1914. It has a composition head with molded and painted hair and eyes, closed mouth, Campbell Kid type composition hands on a cloth body. The head was copyrighted in 1912. *Catalog courtesy of Bernard Barenholtz.*

size, style no. 82, also wore a "Carter's" smock and knickers. The regular size was reported as being 12 in. (30.5 cm.); priced $17.00 doz. wholesale, while the Jr. size cost only $4.24 doz. wholesale. Another distributor's catalog listed the regular size as being 13½ in. (34 cm.).★

Toodles. 1919. Wood fibre composition dolls made by the *American Bisque Doll Co.* as style Nos. 9 BBC and 9C. These dolls dressed in various costumes had molded hair or wigs. Ht. 11 in. (28 cm.).★

Tootle Campbell Dry Goods Co. 1916. St. Louis, Mo. The catalog of this company showed composition dolls that resembled *Coquette* and *Whistling Jim,* which were probably made by *Effanbee.* The girl doll wore circular striped stockings.

Tootse. 1928. All-composition doll distributed wholesale by *Butler Bros.* It wore various dresses, sometimes with bonnets and sometimes with bandeaus.

Tootsie. 1911–12. Composition head doll, copyrighted and designed by *Helen Trowbridge,* and produced by *Horsman.* It had molded bobbed hair with bangs and wore a white lawn-over-blue party dress with satin ribbons. Because of the elaborate dress this doll cost $10.80 doz. wholesale, over $2.00 more than similar regular dressed dolls.★

Tootsie. 1915–16. Line of character baby dolls known as *American Art Dolls.*★

Tootsie. 1919. Stuffed muslin cloth doll produced by *Saalfield.* Ht. 10½ in. (26.5 cm.).

Tootsie Baby Dolls. 1922. Name of a doll with mohair wig, sleeping eyes and composition bent limb baby body. It wore a chemise and was distributed by *Montgomery Ward.* Five hts. 12½, 14¼, 15¾, 18, and 21 in. (31.5, 36, 40, 45.5, and 53.5 cm.); priced 98¢ to $4.48.

Tootsie Baby Dolls. 1930. Advertised in PLAYTHINGS as made by *Borgfeldt* in their own factory. Came dressed in various costumes.

Tootsie Wootsie. 1916–20. Made by *Elektra.*★

Tootsie-Toothums. 1927. Name of a doll with molded hair, two upper teeth, dimpled cheeks, made completely by *The Toy Shop.*

Topics. 1920. Prague, Czechoslovakia. Name of an art store. Miss *Giblet* and the store's bookkeeper had a workshop over the store, where they painted and dressed dolls. The unpainted dolls were purchased from a manufacturer.

Topsey. 1904–05: Black cutout cloth doll made as a premium for the Malted Cereal Co.

Topsy. 1893 and later. Black cutout cloth doll made by *Arnold Print Works.* It had a printed pink or blue dress in a large size. A similar smaller version was called *Pickaninny.* (See also **Smith, Celia and Charity.**)★

Topsy. 1900–02. Black cutout cloth doll made by *Art Fabric Mills.* Printed on the doll was one-piece underwear. Ht. 20 in. (51 cm.); priced 25¢.★

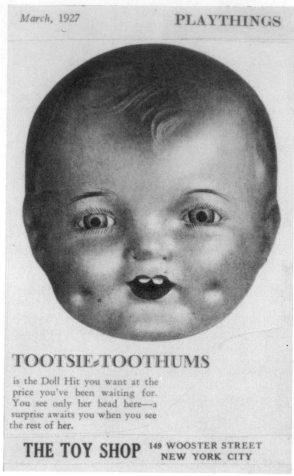

March, 1927 **PLAYTHINGS**

TOOTSIE-TOOTHUMS

is the Doll Hit you want at the price you've been waiting for. You see only her head here—a surprise awaits you when you see the rest of her.

THE TOY SHOP 149 WOOSTER STREET
NEW YORK CITY

2616. Head of a Tootsie-Toothums doll made by *The* Toy Shop and advertised in PLAYTHINGS, March, 1927.

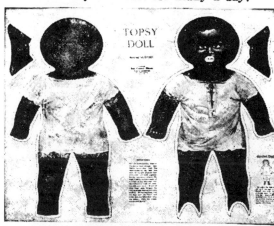

*Here's something to entertain 'em.
To help 'em in their play.
Mama can make 'em,
Baby can't break 'em,
And they will last for many a day.*

TOPSY DOLL

(THIS CUT SHOWS THE DOLLS AS SOLD.)

2617. Cutout cloth black Topsy doll made by the Art Fabric Mills as shown in the DELINEATOR in 1900. This lithographed doll wears a union suit, is 20 in. (51 cm.) high and retailed for 25¢.

Topsy. First decade of the 1900s–1910s. Black doll with a pressed cloth face jointed at the shoulders and hips, made by *Albert Brückner*. It could have been one of the Topsy dolls produced by *Horsman*. Hts. 10 and 12 in. (25.5 and 30.5 cm.).

1905: Distributed by *Siegel Cooper;* priced $1.00.

1912–14: Listed in Horsman catalog as style no. H/T. It wore a plaid gingham dress and bandana on its head; priced 25¢.

Topsy. 1912–13. Black cutout cloth doll produced by *Selchow & Righter*. This doll had a printed African costume. Ht. 8 in. (20.5 cm.); priced 40¢ doz. wholesale.

Topsy. 1920. Black cloth doll with a flat face, a patch for the eyes and mouth, distributed by *Sears*. Hts. 15½ in. (39.5 cm.); priced 98¢.

Topsy. 1922. Cloth doll stuffed with silk floss or kapok produced by *Ross & Ross*.

2618. Mark on a Ross and Ross' Topsy cloth doll.

Topsy. 1926–27. A two-in-one character doll created by *Berry Kollin* and made by *Twinjoy Doll Co*. It was paired with Eva and wore an apron on which was printed an appropriate poem.

Topsy. 1927. Black all-composition doll with pigtails, rompers and hair ribbons distributed by the *American Wholesale Corp*. Ht. 8½ in. (21.5 cm.); priced $5.50 doz. wholesale.

Topsy. 1927–28. Black doll with composition shoulder head and arms, three pigtails, painted features, cloth body, distributed by *American Wholesale Corp*. and by *Butler Bros*. It wore figured percale rompers and hair ribbons. Ht. 14½ in. (37 cm.); priced $8.50 doz. wholesale.

Topsy. 1930. Black faced doll with kinky hair made by *W. R. Woodard* as a *Hollywood Imp*.

Topsy Baby. See Babyland and **Life Like (Lifelike) Babyland Dolls.**

Topsy Lou. 1921. Black stockinet doll with yarn hair, button eyes, and printed calico dress; a commercial substitute for early home-made dolls.

Topsy Turvy Dolls. Dolls had two heads, two arms, one body and no legs. The skirt was reversible so that it could cover the head at the opposite end.

1899: *Dewitt C. Bouton* patented a Topsy Turvy doll.

1903: *F. A. O. Schwarz* advertised Topsy Turvy dolls. Hts. 14 and 20 in. (35.5 and 51 cm.); priced $1.25 and $3.50.

1904: Dressed cloth Topsy Turvy doll with chromolithographed faces, one head white with hair having bangs and one black, distributed by *Montgomery Ward*. Ht. 12½ in. (31.5 cm.); priced 50¢.

1905: Dressed Topsy Turvy doll with one head white and one black produced by *Horsman* and distributed by *Siegel Cooper*. The black head had short pigtails; priced $1.25.

1908: One end of the Topsy Turvy doll represented the Goddess of Liberty, clad in long red, white and blue robes. The other end also dressed in patriotic colors represented "Uncle Sam Cat." When the doll was rolled from side to side it gave a simulated "Me-ow" sound.

1911: Numerous stores advertised a Topsy Turvy doll, one head white and the other black. The one at *Wanamakers* resembled the *Albert Brückner* Topsy Turvy doll. *Woodward & Lothrop* advertised a cloth one that was 10 in. (25.5 cm.) tall, costing $1.00.

1912–14: *Babyland* cloth dolls with two heads produced by Horsman. Style no. 7 had embossed faces, one white and the other black (probably made by Brückner). Style no. 207 had the black and white Lifelike faces. Style no. 207½ represented a baby with one face laughing and one face crying. These dolls cost $8.50 in 1912 and $8.00 in 1914 per doz. wholesale.

1915: A Topsy Turvy doll was distributed by *Best & Co*. Ht. 12 in. (30.5 cm.); priced $1.00.

1919: Cutout cloth Topsy Turvy doll made by *Saalfield* was 22 × 32 in. (56 × 81 cm.).

1926: The Brückner Topsy Turvy doll with a white girl's head at one end and a black mammy's head at the other end had its name changed to *Tu-N-One*. (See also **Betty Bronson Cinderella Doll** and **Multi-head dolls**.)★

Tortoise Brand. See Rheinische Gummi und Celluloid Fabrik.

Tosalli, Felice. 1929–30. Turin, Italy. Born 1883, died 1958, he was a ceramist and sculptor. In 1929 and 1930 he was involved with *Lenci* ceramics and may have contributed to the design of Lenci dolls.

Tot Bumps. 1914. Composition head, arms and legs on a cloth torso; doll distributed by *Marshall Field*. It resembled *Horsman's Gold Medal Baby* and had painted hair and eyes; wore a white lawn dress. Ht. 12 in. (30.5 cm.); priced $17.00 doz. wholesale.

Toto. Ca. World War I. period. Name of a doll with a bisque head made by *Lanternier* in Limoges. The doll had a wig, glass eyes, open-closed mouth with teeth and a composition body. It was marked "DÉPOSÉ TOTO//LIMOGES." One of these was dressed as a clown and at the Margaret Woodbury Strong Museum are ones 11 and 18½ in. (28 and 47 cm.) tall.

Toto. World War I–1929. A mechanical waddling doll with a key marked "R.D." for *Roullet & Decamps* was the mate to *Tata*. The composition head designed by Gaston Decamps had an impish smiling expression resembling the *Poulbot* style and it turned from side to side as the doll advanced. It had painted or glass eyes. The arms and legs were iron wire, the hands and feet were composition and the body was molded cardboard. It represented a school boy dressed in a checked school pinafore over trousers and there was a school bag on the doll's back. Toto was a pet name for boys in France. This information was researched by Anne-Marie and Jacques Porot.

Toto. 1920. Name of a doll designed by *Georgene Averill.* It had a composition shoulder head and arms, a wig and was dressed as a clown.

Toto. 1928–29. Composition-head dressed doll with glass eyes and a cloth body was advertised by *Bon Marché.* It said "Mama." Ht. 40 cm. (15½ in.).

Tots Toie. 1919. Trademark registered in U.S. by *Thos. Thompson* for wooden dolls.

Touche du Bois//Touch Wood! 1921. Trademark for dolls registered in France by Herbert Nalty doing business as *Gourdel Vales & Co.*

Tousel (Tousle) Head. 1930 and later. Name of a baby boy doll made by *Effanbee* and distributed by *Montgomery Ward.* It had "silky infant hair" a lamb's skin wig that could be brushed and combed. The composition head had sleeping eyes and hair eyelashes. The body was all composition or it had a kapok stuffed torso with a cry voice. It was dressed in rompers and wore an Effanbee locket. Ht. 18 in. (45.5 cm.); priced $4.89.

Tout Bois. See **Bébé Tout en Bois.**

Tout Va Bien. 1919. Trademark registered in France by *M. Fernand Gratieux* for toys of all kinds which should include dolls.

Toy Junkery. 1927. Iowa. Advertised in TOYS AND NOVELTIES that if "hopeless dolls" were brought and sold to that shop any usable part would be salvaged for use by a dolls' hospital.

Toy Pack Corp. 1929. New Haven, Conn. Registered in U.S. the trademark "Toy Pak" for rubber dolls.

Toy Products Manufacturing Co. 1925–30. New York City. Made all-composition dolls, composition heads and other parts of dolls. Member of the *Doll Parts Manufacturing Association.* Dolls made for jobbers and quantity buyers. Dolls marked "TOY PRODUCTS//MFG. CO."

1926–28: Advertised all-composition dolls with molded hair and painted eyes. Style no. 25 had a googly type face, jointed shoulders, legs together, no clothes. Ht. 7 in. (18 cm.); priced 10¢.

Style no. 200 was a jointed baby in a long dress and wrapped in a blanket. Ht. 7 in. (18 cm.); priced 39¢.

Style no. 250 and 257, twins, two white or one white and one black, wrapped in a blanket. Ht. 7 in. (18 cm.); priced 39¢.

Style no. 300, bent limb baby, jointed at the shoulders and hips, wore a chemise, came white or black. Ht. 9 in. (23 cm.); priced 25¢.

Style no. 340, same as no. 300 except it wore a long lace-trimmed dress. Ht. 9 in. (23 cm.); priced 39¢.

Style no. 350, same as no. 25 except it was wrapped in a blanket. Ht. 9 in. (23 cm.); priced 25¢.

Style no. 375, same as 340, except it was white twins wrapped in a blanket. Ht. 9 in. (23 cm.); priced 75¢.

Style no. 425, same as no. 340. Ht. 10½ in. (26.5 cm.); priced 50¢.

Style no. 450, same as no. 350. Ht. 10½ in. (26.5 cm.); priced 50¢.

Style no. 475, same as no. 425 except there were twins, both white or one white and one black. Ht. 10½ in. (26.5 cm.); priced $1.00.

1930: Made *We Dolls.*

2619. Mark on composition dolls made by Toy Products Manufacturing Co.

Toy Shop, The. 1922–29. New York City. Made entire dolls in their own factory; sold to jobbers and quantity buyers; used the trademark "T.S."; specialized in *Mama* dolls.

Mr. Joseph Kallus said that *Mme. Alexander's* future husband, Mr. Behrman, was connected with the Toy Shop at one time.

1924: Advertised black Mama dolls with or without sleeping eyes, in many styles and costumes as well as white *Mother Goose* dolls.

1926: Member of the *American Doll Manufacturers' Association.* The trademark was a seal with an intertwined **S** in an inner circle and around the circle were the words "THE MARK **S** OF QUALITY **S** THE STANDARD **S** OF PERFECTION **S**."

1927: Advertised *Aunt Jemima, Tootsie-Toothums,* "T. S." slim body dolls and chubby body Mama dolls. The Toy Shop was licensed by *Voices, Inc.* to use their patented voices and criers in the Toy Shop dolls.

1928: New line of baby dolls including black babies and Wee Ones. A mulatto lady doll had fluffy hair. The dolls were dressed in costumes of original designs.

1929: Mama dolls were still their specialty. ★

Toy Soldier. Cutout cloth advertising doll used on sugar sacks by *Sea Island Sugar Co.* according to Frances Walker and Margaret Whitton. Ht. 8 in. (20.5 cm.).

2620. Mark used by The Toy Shop for dolls that they made.

Toy Tinkers, The. 1923–30 and later. Evanston, Ill. Made segmented wooden dolls under the trade name *Tinker Toys.* Advertised that they had obtained several patents for their dolls.

Toy & Notion Co. See **Schmidt, Charles.**

Toyland. 1912. Buffalo, N.Y. Distributed and repaired dolls. Advertised "Dolls that really say things."

Toyland. See **Smith, W. H., & Son.**

Toyland Works. See **Imperial Toy Co.**

Toyo. 1907–13. Name of a doll dressed as a Japanese boy, designed by *Elizabeth Scantlebury* as a teaching aid. This doll represented the brother of *Lotus Blossom.*

Trademarks. An article in THE TOY TRADER, March 1926, entitled, "German Patent, Model, Design and Trade-Mark Protection" by Patent-attorney, Dr. Oscar Arendt gave the following information:
"Trademarks are registered in the name of the applicant by the 'Reichspatentamt' for the unlimited time, first however, for a period of 10 years, after due examination."★

Traffic Cop. 1927. All-celluloid doll with jointed arms and molded clothes including a large white glove on its right hand, distributed by the *American Wholesale Corp.*

Train (Trainee, Military). 1911 and before. Felt doll made by *Steiff.* It wore a pill-box type cap and carried a sword. Hts. 28 and 35 cm. (11 and 14 in.).

Tramp. 1916. Felt doll made by *Steiff.* Ht. 35 cm. (14 in.).

Tramp. 1928. Small wooden doll made by the *Poppy Doll Co.*

Transogram Co. 1915–30 and later. Brooklyn, N.Y. and New York City. Made walking dolls and dolls' outfits.

1920: Named their doll *Miss Ima Walker.*

1930: Advertised outfits for dolls.★

Trautmann, Carl. See **Catterfelder Puppenfabrik.**

Travel Tots. 1928. Cloth dolls made by *Dean.*

Travelers, The. 1914. Bisque-head dolls with wigs, sleeping eyes, composition bodies jointed at the shoulders, elbows, hips, and knees, removable clothes, distributed by *Butler Bros.* Ht. 15½ in. (39.5 cm.); priced $10.00 doz. wholesale.

Travers, Geo. W., Co. 1912. East Templeton, Mass., and New York City. The factory was located in Massachusetts. They also imported dolls.

Travertine Art Co. 1927–28. Calif. Manufactured art dolls.

Treat-'Em-Rough Kiddie. 1919–20. All-metal, talking and sleeping jointed dolls made by the *Art Metal Works.* The parts were stamped into place allegedly eliminating springs. These dolls came in 24 different styles. The larger dolls had eyelids that closed while the eyes remained stationary.★

Trebor. Name found on bisque-head dolls with wigs, sleeping eyes, sometimes hair eyelashes, open mouth with teeth, and ball-jointed composition bodies. The bisque heads were possibly made by *Cråmer and Héron* at their Porzellanfabrik Mengersgereuth. The heads were marked "Trebor// Germany//22//P 2/0 M." The 2/0 represented the size number and varied with the height of the doll. Examples seen have been as follows:

Size No.	Height cm.	in.
7/0	26	10½
5/0	30	12
2/0	40	15½

All of these dolls had the number 22 which was probably the mold #. According to the Ciesliks *Carl Harmus* produced dolls with the Trebor heads.

Trebor.
Germany
22.
P. 2. M

2621. Trebor mark on bisque head dolls.

Trego Doll Manufacturing Co. 1918–21. New York City. Valentine Treat was President of the Company. Made dolls with imported bisque heads or with composition heads on composition bodies. Used "TREGO//MADE IN U.S.A." as their mark. Distributed in Britain.

1919: All-composition fully jointed dolls had a mat or glazed finish; human hair wigs. The composition head dolls had sleeping eyes, wore a chemise and hair bows.

1920: Represented by *Bush Terminal.*

1921: Made black dolls and dolls representing American Indians.★

2622. Mark used by Trego Doll Manufacturing Co. for their dolls.

Treidler, Friedrich, and Treidler, Josef. 1853 and possibly other years. Vienna. Manufactured dolls, according to the research of Dr. Eva Moskovszky.

Tremaco. See **Treng Manufacturing Co.**

Trene (Girl). 1924. Felt doll made by *Steiff*. Hts. 28, 35, 43 cm. (11, 14 and 17 in.).

Treng Manufacturing Co. 1926–27. Astoria, Long Island, N.Y. Made dolls' clothes and "art embroidery clothing sets." Used the trademark of a diamond enclosing the word TRE-MACO and the words TRADE MARK under the diamond.

1926: Art embroidery clothing sets included Doll's Dress, Doll's Feeding Bib, Doll's Play Apron, Doll's Peter Pan Collar and Cuffs, and Doll's Rompers; priced 25¢ to $3.00.

1927: Each set came in three styles: (1) Junior with simple embroidery stitches; (2) Regular and (3) DeLuxe with better grade materials. New sets included a Doll's Sunbonnet and a Doll's Combing Jacket. The garments were for dolls of seven hts. 5, 7, 10, 14, 16, 20 and 24 in. (12.5, 18, 25.5, 35.5, 40.5, 51, and 61 cm.) but the individual sets were not for all of these hts. nor for all of the garments.

Trenthan, Therese. 1908. Austria. The art magazine KIND & KUNST (Children & Art) wrote about the carved wooden dolls made by Therese Trenthan. These dolls shown in a Vienna Art Exhibition had wigs, painted features and separate fingers. The dolls were dressed as men and women and some of the men wore glasses.

Treskow, Pudor & Co. 1925–28. Showed stuffed dolls at the Leipzig Fair.

Trichet, M. Roger Georges. 1929. Paris. Registered in France the trademark *Poupées Arlay* for dolls.

Trihedral Dolls. 1700s–1930 and later. Made chiefly in the Sergius Community (now Zagorsk) and Bogorodskoye on the outskirts of Moscow, Russia. These were all-wooden dolls carved from three-sided pieces of wood; they had carved and painted features and clothes. The dolls represented ladies, children, peasants, craftsmen, soldiers and officers. These dolls had no joints and were usually on a carved base so that they could stand. The colorful clothes generally included a hat or headdress. The making of these dolls flourished in the first half of the 1800s and declined during the second half of the 1800s. At the end of the 1800s Russian artists came to help the artisans revive this art form. After the Russian Revolution these were stamped "Soviet Union." (See also **Russian Dolls**.)

Trilby. 1895. Bisque-head dressed doll with wig, distributed by *Butler Bros*. Ht. 23½ in. (59.5 cm.); priced $4.50 doz. wholesale.

Trion Toy Co. 1911–21. Brooklyn, N.Y. Manufactured composition-head character dolls and exported dolls.

Adolph Cohen became factory manager in 1914. He had manufactured dolls in America for 12 years and prior to that he had spent 20 years in French and German doll factories. He had been educated in Moscow. The Trion dolls were allegedly made by a special process that allowed their manufacture despite unfavorable conditions of temperature and weather which prevented the manufacture of many early American composition dolls. Trion stressed the quality of their dolls' clothes and claimed that some of their dresses were designed from imported models by an assistant to *Lady*

2623. Four Russian dolls carved from triangular pieces of wood and hence called Trihedrals. The clothes are carved and painted. Stamped "Soviet Union." H. 8 in. (20.5 cm.) includes base. *Coleman Collection.*

TRION.TOY.CO.

2624. Mark on composition head dolls made by Trion Toy Co.

Duff Gordon. The name "Trion" was an inscription on the dresses or suits.

1915: Some of the new dolls included: *Sunshine, Little Rascal, Sunny,* and *Happy.* Several of these dolls had kid bodies. Dolls cost 50¢ and $1.00 according to size.

1916: The new dolls included *Cheery Boy,* another version of Happy, *Goldie Girl* and *Wiggsie.* The *Sanitrion* dolls had loofah bodies, so that they could be taken in bathing.

1917: Dolls had composition heads and hands, molded hair or wig, cloth bodies and legs with circular stripes and cloth boots. Dressed as girls, boys or babies in long or short clothes. The name "Trion" was in script on the dresses or suits. Hts. 13 in. (33 cm.), the girl dolls were also 17½ in. (44.5 cm.). Wholesale distributor was *Wyman, Partridge.*

1918: Advertised 100 style nos. of lads, lassies and baby dolls. The wigged dolls had composition scalps and sleeping eyes. *Babs Baby* was a new doll as well as *Smiling Sammy,* Red Cross nurses, doctors, and sailors. A 10 in. (25.5 cm.) doll had a wig with bangs and bobbed hair and wore a silk bathing suit; priced 75¢. Two large dolls of the same style were 11 and 14 in. (28 and 35.5 cm.).

1919: Factory production was 5,500,000 dolls' heads. Advertised that the tinting on the face was life-like and that the color of the composition arms and cloth legs matched. ★

Triumph Bébé. 1902. Ball-jointed doll that could sit, stand or walk. Its head turned when it walked; made by *Max Handwerck.*

Trixie. 1924. Cloth doll with a *Tru-To-Life* three-dimensional face, one of the *A 1 Brand* made by *Dean*. It was stuffed with down and wore a pleated crepe muslin print dress with a ribbon sash and glossy black shoes. Ht. 12 in. (30.5 cm.).

Trixie. 1929. All-composition doll, painted hair and features, jointed neck, shoulders and hips; could stand alone; wore a floral print organdy dress and silk hair ribbon. It was distributed by *Butler Bros.* Ht. 18 in. (45.5 cm.); priced $18.00 doz. wholesale. See THE COLLECTOR'S BOOK OF DOLLS' CLOTHES, Ill. 775G.

Trixy Toys. 1930. Line of turned wood dolls made by *Durrel Co.* The clothes painted on the dolls included representations of peasant costumes; *Skeezix,* and *Little Orphan Annie;* priced 10¢ to $1.00.

Trois Quartiers. See **Aux Trois Quartiers.**

Trost, William. 1916–17. Seattle, Wash. Obtained a U.S. patent for the moving eyes of a doll.

Trotman, Walter Knowles, and Grout, William Edward. 1904. London. Applied for a German patent (D.R.G.M.) for a doll with moving legs.

Trousseau Trunk. See **Trunk Trousseaux.**

Trowbridge, Helen. 1910–22. Montclair, N.J. Evidence suggests that *Grace Wiederseim Drayton*'s drawings of the *Campbell Kids* were sculptured into a three-dimensional model by Helen Trowbridge who made the models for most of the Can't Break 'Em[+] *Horsman* dolls. Often the same model was used for several dolls with different names and the name on the original copyright papers was not always the same as the name finally given to the doll by Horsman.

1910 11: Helen Trowbridge appears to have made the models for the following dolls:

Campbell Kid, Pocahontas.
Baby *Suck-a-Thumb.*
Carnival Baby, Candy Kid.
Daisy Dimple, Hans, Gretchen, Happy Hiram, Jack Tar, Prince Charlie. Robbie Reefer.
Fairy, Annette, Nancy Lee, Polly Prue.
Gold Medal Prize Baby, Kickapoo.
Jap Rose Kids.
School Boy.
Toodles.

Other dolls, some of them from the same models as above, were listed in the first COLLECTOR'S ENCYCLOPEDIA OF DOLLS.

1922: Created *Bye Bye Baby* for Horsman. ★

Troxell. See **Poppy Doll Co.**

Tru-Craft Doll Co. 1930 and later. U.S.A. Made clothes for dolls.

Trudy. 1926. Trademark registered in France by *Mme. Elisa Rassant* for a doll dressed in a French peasant costume and holding a tray.

Trunk Trousseaux. Name of trunks of various types and sizes containing a doll and its wardrobe of clothes. The dolls were usually one of the type popular in the period of the trunk. The early trunks usually had one or more trays while in the 1920s wardrobe trunks were introduced. The number of garments varied but there was usually at least one other dress besides the one worn on the doll and frequently there were several other dresses, plus hats, nightwear, underwear, accessories and so forth. Most of the large Paris stores and toy shops sold these trunk trousseaux. The dolls tended to be small; for example *F.A.O. Schwarz* in 1926 advertised dolls in their trunks as coming in five hts. 6, 7, 12, 15, and 18 in. (15, 18, 30.5, 38 and 45.5 cm.). Layettes occasionally came in trunks but more often they were in a basket.

Tru-Shu. 1917–20 and probably later. Three dimensional printed shoes used by *Dean* on their *Tru-To-Life* cloth dolls. These included babies, boys and girls.

Tru-To-Life (True to Life). 1913–28. Three dimensional cloth dolls with embossed faces made by *Dean*. The later ones had Tru-Shu feet. They had painted features and removable clothes.

1913: Advertised baby dolls, ht. over 24 in. (61 cm.); *Betty Blue*. Ht. 20 in. (51 cm.), and one other size; priced 37¢ to 87¢.

1915: Advertised 30 models including style no. 1007, a girl in dress and cap; style no. 1014, girl in dress, cape and bonnet; style no. 1015, girl in dress, coat and bonnet; style no. 1017, girl in dress with pleated skirt and bonnet; style nos. 1117 and 1120, babies in long dresses; priced 62¢ to $6.25.

1917: Dolls had Tru-Shu feet, jointed arms and legs. A series of these dolls was designed by *Hilda Cowham*. There were also *Airman, Colonial Doll* and *Dolly Dips*. Some of the dolls came with a dress and striped pajamas for the doll to wear at night.

1920: Dean's catalog listed *Baby Puck*, Betty Blue, *Big Baby*

37258.
MALLE fermant à clef, avec bébé dormeur articulé et son trousseau.
0ᵐ28 0ᵐ32 0ᵐ35 0ᵐ39 0ᵐ42 0ᵐ45
55.» 67.» 73.» 85.» 104.» 115.»
MALLE avec mignonnette.
0ᵐ26. **19.75** | 0ᵐ30. **25.50** | 0ᵐ34. **33.** »

2625. Trunks containing a sleeping-eyed jointed bébé with its clothes as shown in the 1923 Louvre store catalog. The trunk came with a key and lock as well as a tray. Hs. 28, 32, 35, 39, 42, and 45 cm. (11, 12½, 14, 15½, 16½, and 17½ in.). A trunk with a mignonnette (small doll). Hs. 26, 30 and 34 cm. (10½, 12, and 13½ in.).

Doll, Bow Belles, Curly Locks, Dolly Dips, *Florrie the Flapper* and the Hilda Cowham dolls. The dolls came with or without wigs. The wigged dolls came in two hts. 14 and 16 in. (35.5 and 40.5 cm.). The smaller dolls were dressed as girls or babies in short dresses and coats. The larger dolls were dressed as boys or babies in long clothes.

1922: Advertised *A 1 Dolls.* There were six models without wigs; three models with or without wigs that were dressed in 14 styles. A doll with "the Disc" came semi-dressed in three sizes and dressed in 13 styles.

1924: Advertised A 1 Dolls named *Trixie* and *Wendy.*

1928: *Gamage* advertised Tru-To-Life dolls with and without wigs. Ht. 24 in. (61 cm.).

Trynes, P. J., P. Jzn. 1850–1930. Arnhem, Netherlands. Made and exported Dutch costumes including wooden shoes for dolls.

Trznice Zadruhv. Ca. 1900. Prague Name on some wooden dolls.

Tsau Guo Gui. 1925–26. Felt doll made by *Lenci* as style no. 255. It wore an Oriental costume with a hat resembling a stocking cap having a square end on top. Ht. 23 in. (58 cm.).

Tubbins. 1921–24. Made of a single piece of Kraft Kloth. The head was stuffed with cotton; the face and trimming were embroidered in colors. Representations of animals such as lambs, ducks, kittens and so forth ornamented the doll's dress.★

Tubby-Tot. 1926–30. Cloth dolls made by *Albert Brückner*'s Sons. The body was made of flesh-colored rubberized cloth stuffed with kapok. It wore a removable red or green rubberized bathing suit and cap. The doll could float and allegedly dried rapidly.

1926: Priced $1.50 to $2.00.

1930: Priced $1.00 to $1.25.

Tuco Doll. 1917–18. "Papier-mâché" dolls made by *Utley Co.* and claimed to be washable. They had wigs, socket heads, jointed shoulders and diagonal hip joints, ball joints at the elbows and knees. The dolly dolls came in hts. 14 to 26 in. (35.5 to 66 cm.) and the character dolls came in hts. 14 to 20 in. (35.5 to 51 cm.).★

Tuftex. 1917–18. Name of a composition used for dolls' heads, bodies, arms, and legs made by the *Art Statue Co.*

Tum Tum Toys. 1922–24. Colorful floating rubber dolls stuffed with silk floss, representing boys and girls and made by *Fleming.* The seven style nos. included a girl with plaid skirt. One retailer claimed that he sold over 1,500 of the Tum Tum dolls during 24 days in August, 1923; priced 25¢.★

Tumble It. 1917. Dolls that tumbled over and over down a board were made by *Thorne Bros.* The line included Mr. Tumble It and there was a Billiken Tumble It.

Tunkler Von Treuinfeld. 1786–1847. Prague, Bohemia. Large toy store that distributed dolls, according to research by Dr. Eva Moskovszky.

TU-N-ONE (Tu in One). 1926–30. Cloth doll formerly known as *Topsy Turvy.* It was made by *Albert Brückner*'s Sons. One end was a white girl and the other end was a black mammy. The name was changed in April, 1926.

1926–28: Advertised with this poem:
Turn Me Up
Turn Me Back
First I'm white
Then I'm Black

Priced in 1926; $1.50 to $1.75.

Tupper, Arthur W. 1926. Riverdale, Md. Obtained a U.S. patent for a doll.

Türfe. 1916. Felt doll dressed in a military field uniform, made by *Steiff.* Ht. 35 cm (14 in.).

Turko. 1916. Felt doll made by *Steiff.* Ht. 35 cm. (14 in.).

Turnbull, Charles Edward, & Co. 1895–1925 and later. London. Imported, dressed, and distributed dolls from France and Germany. They had two large warehouses where dolls were dressed and stored. Claimed they had many thousands of dolls consisting of wax, china, bisque, cloth and other materials as well as dolls' clothing and accessories such as hats, bonnets, shoes, socks, parasols, and so forth.

1909: Agent for *Steiff.* Turnbull was one of the creditors when *J. W. Merrill* went bankrupt.

1917–18: Advertised *Charterhouse* babies.

Turner, Ernst. 1929–30. London. Registered in Britain the trademark *Kalutu* in 1929. He dressed and distributed the Kalutu series and other dolls of *Karl Kalbitz* as well as the *My Gold Pearl* dolls of *Adolf Heller.*

Turner, H. Francis, & Co. 1894–1924 and later. England. Imported celluloid dolls from Japan.

Turner's Toy and Fancy Store. 1890s. Hereford, England. Sold dolls, among them ones made by *Jumeau* and marked "Tête Jumeau."

Türpa. 1916. Felt doll dressed in a military parade uniform, made by *Steiff.* Ht. 35 cm. (14 in.).

Turton, W. S. 1915–18. Manchester, England. Made cloth dolls called the *Rainbow* series.

Tuttle, George W. Before 1853 and later. New York City. Received an Honorable Mention for his exhibit of dolls at the 1853 Exhibition, with the comment, "The specimens of dressed dolls here exhibited certainly surpass anything we have ever seen, both in tasteful design and beauty of decoration." See THE COLLECTOR'S BOOK OF DOLLS' CLOTHES, Ill. 139.

Twee Deedle (Mr. Twee Deedle). 1911–12. Can't Break 'Em[+] composition head doll with a broad toothy grin, produced by *Horsman* and distributed by *Gimbel Bros.* It wore a red and yellow tunic, a pointed cap and green stockings. Ht. to top of cap 18 in. (45.5 cm.); priced $1.00. The all-felt Twee Deedle[+] had bells on its vandyked collar.

Tweedeedle. 1913. Felt doll made by *Steiff,* dressed as a clown with a conical pointed hat. Ht. 14 in. (35 cm.); priced $1.70.

Tweedle-dee and Tweedle-dum. 1921–23. Pair of dressed stockinet dolls representing the characters of this name in ALICE IN WONDERLAND as drawn by John Tenniel and made by *Martha Chase.* Ht. 12 in. (30.5 cm.); priced $6.00.

Tweedledum and Tweedledee. 1917. Dolls made by the *Shropshire Toy Industries.*

Twelvetrees, Charles. 1925–26. Drew the *Twelvetrees Kids* for PICTORIAL REVIEW and other leading newspapers. ★

Twelvetrees Kids. 1925–26. Dolls produced by *Horsman* based on the *HEbee-SHEbee* drawings by *Charles Twelvetrees.*

Twinjoy Doll Co. 1925–29. New York City. Made Twinjoy Dolls, two dolls in one, created by *Berry Kollin.* These dolls often represented characters from fairy tales or Nursery Rhymes such as Little Red Riding Hood and *Grandma* with horn-rimmed spectacles; *Betsy Ross and Uncle Sam; Jack and Jill* with a little tin bucket; *Topsy* and Eva; *Cinderella* in rags and Cinderella in silk. Dolls had either an apron or a tag with an appropriate poem on it. Agent was the *Products Corporation of America.*

1927: New dolls were the *Flower Dolls* that wore petal dresses to represent various flowers. Other new dolls were the *Messenger Boy* and a pajama doll, the latter priced 49¢.

1928: Advertised that their dolls were suitable for girls of around six years old. There was a new series of flower dolls with composition heads and cotton stuffed bodies dressed with colorful flower effect. New washable baby dolls wore colored rompers. There were many styles of felt dolls that were claimed to have rivaled the French and Italian imported dolls. The heads, bodies and frocks were made of felt; the features were handpainted; some of the felt dolls had real hair. Each model was given a child's name.

1929: Dolls represented boys as well as girls.

Twinkie. 1927. All-bisque advertising doll used by the Hamilton Brown Shoe Co. See Ill. 2626.

Twinkie Dolls. 1928–30 and later. Produced by *Borgfeldt.*

Ca. 1933: Cloth-body dolls with rolling, sleeping eyes representing a boy, distributed by *Quaker Doll Co.* Ht. 13½ in. (34 cm.); priced $24.00 doz. wholesale.

Twinkle Toes. 1927. Trademark registered in U.S. by *Ideal* for a doll with a laughing, dimpled face, rubber arms and legs, toes separated, dressed in a creeper. It cried when a leg was pinched and "Gurgled" when danced up and down.

Twinkle Twins. 1929. Composition dolls representing baby girls, made by *Amberg;* priced $2.50.

Twinzy Toy Co. See **Squier Twins Toy Co.**

Twist body. See **Waist Joints.**

Twistum Toy Factory. 1921–29. Atascadero and Oakland, Calif. Made segmented molded wood-composition and

2626. All-bisque doll with molded hair and clothes, painted eyes looking to the side. An advertising doll named Twinkie, of the Hamilton Brown Shoe Co. in 1927. H. 2¾ in. (7 cm.). *Coleman Collection.*

TWINKIE
COPR 1927 BY
Hamilton Brown
Shoe Co.

2627. Mark on an all-bisque advertising doll of the Hamilton Brown Shoe Co. The doll was named Twinkie.

wood dolls called Twistums. New models were added each year.

1921: Factory opened in Atascadero.

1922: Second factory opened in Oakland. Made several thousand dolls and toys a day. Then fire destroyed the Oakland factory and the factories were consolidated into one factory in Oakland.

1927: The processes for making the dolls were: molding under high heat and pressure or baking, trimming and filling, blowing dust from parts before dipping, glue dipping, lacquer spraying, hand painting, assembling the parts. The factory made 25 styles of dolls and animals. The clothes were turned and painted on the dolls.

1928: Style no. 64 was named *Parboy* and represented a golfer. Style no. 65 was named *Star* and represented a football player.

1929: Developed a large export business. Introduced the

Funny Fuzzee line made of twisted flexible wire covered with colored knotted yarn. This line included *Brownee, Clownee, Fairee* and *Jerree* and other acrobats. Another new doll was the clown *Archie Pagliacci* who came with barbells, dumbbells, ball and stick.

1930: Archie Pagliacci was advertised as a segmented wooden balancing clown doll.

Tyneside Toys. 1918–19. Newcastle-on-Tyne, England. Produced dolls with *British Ceramic* or composition heads on plush bodies. The leading line was black dolls, including *Black Topsie.* J.A. Brothers was their agent.

Tynie Baby. 1924–late 1920s. Made with bisque or composition head. The early composition heads were marked "E.I.H. Co. 1924" on the flange-type necks. Some of these dolls had the celluloid-over-metal type sleeping eyes. Bisque heads sometimes came with bent composition arms on cloth bodies. Ht. 12 in. (30.5 cm.). All-bisque versions of this doll have been found.

1926: *F.A.O. Schwarz* advertised composition-head Tynie Baby dolls with sleeping eyes, cloth body having a crying voice. It came in a long dress either wrapped in a blanket or

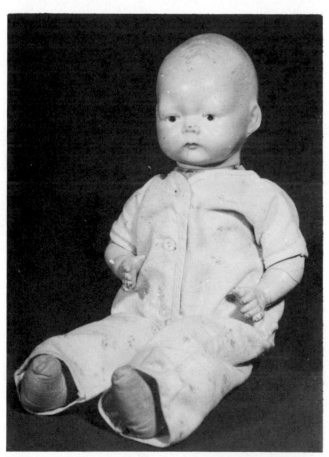

2628. Tynie Baby composition head version produced by Horsman. It has molded hair, painted features, bent limb cloth body with composition arms. Mark III. 2629. H. 16 in. (40.5 cm.). *Coleman Collection.*

© 1924
E.I. HORSMAN
CO. INC.

© 1924 by
E.I. Horsman Co. INC.
Germany
37

2629–2630. Tynie Baby embossed mark on composition heads and incised mark on bisque heads.

with lace trimming the dress. Hts. 12 and 15 in. (30.5 and 38 cm.); twins also came in the smaller size.

Late 1920s: *Horsman* sued *Acme* for copying Tynie Baby but Horsman lost because they had only "E.I.H." on the dolls and not the full name. Thereafter the dolls were marked "E.I.H. 1924 Horsman."★

Tynie Tots. See **Tiny Tots.**

Tyrolers. 1914. Boy and girl composition head dolls produced by *Horsman,* same dolls as the Bauerkind (Peasant [farmer] Child) boy and girl except for their costumes. This girl, style No. 135½, wore a green blouse, a red skirt with suspenders and a green Tyrolean hat and feather. The boy, style No. 136½, wore a green and red costume with blouse and overralls and a Tyrolean style hat.

Many other dolls have been dressed in the costumes representing those worn in the Tyrol such as dolls made by *Lenci, Steiff, Wagner & Zetzsche,* and many others. (See also **Regional Costume Dolls** and **Tiroler Docken.**)★

Tzar (Nicholas). 1915. Composition head portrait doll of the Russian Tzar distributed by *Hamley Bros.,* made by the *Women's Emergency Corps Workshop.*

Tzezes & Slatin, Mssrs. 1926 and earlier. U.S.A. Created dolls, among them the dolls made by the *Penn Stuffed Toy Co.*

U

U.S. Doll Co. 1923–26. New York City. Made dolls.★

U.S. Toy & Novelty Co. 1919–20. New York City. Advertised *Wauketoi* walking dolls, Nurses, and Farmer Boy.★

Übler & Beck. 1922–24. Nürnberg, Bavaria. Made dolls. London agent was *W. Franklin & Son.*

Uffi (Italian Officer). 1911 and before. Felt doll representing an Italian officer having a mustache and long feet, made by *Steiff*. Ht. 35 cm. (14 in.).

Ulan (German Soldier). Before 1911–16. Felt doll representing a German soldier (cavalry lancer) wearing a Bell-hop type cap, carrying a sword and having long feet, made by *Steiff*. Hts. 28 and 35 cm. (11 and 14 in.); priced in 1911 75¢ and $1.00. (Ulan was German generic term for a lancer and was used for other dolls. See Ill. 1907.)

Ulhenhuth, Henry, & Cie. 1876–1919. Paris, and later, Lagny, Seine-et-Oise. Made dolls and bébés including *Bébé Merveilleux*. Probably joined the *Société Française de Fabrication de Bébés & Jouets* (S.F.B.J.).★

Ulla Puppe. 1921–30. Made by *Gotthelf*.

1926: *John Hess* handled Ulla dolls with wigs, glass eyes, five-piece bodies, dressed in silks. Under 12 cm. (4½ in.) dolls were all-bisque, larger dolls up to 26 cm. (10 in.) had bisque heads.

1929: Advertised as being small dolls with bisque heads, five-piece bodies, dressed and wearing hats or bows. Their round paper tags with a scalloped edge read, "GES. GESCH //ULLA//PUPPE."★

Ullmann, Alois. 1914–23. Teplitz, Bohemia, later Czechoslovakia. Was listed in an Austrian directory under Wool and Stuffed Dolls with celluloid heads.

Ullmann & Engelmann. 1901. Fürth, Bavaria. Applied for a German patent (D.R.G.M.) for a walking doll with a voice.

Ulmcke, Carl, Co. 1912–27. New York City. Imported and distributed dolls.

Unbreakable Heads. Descriptive name on a paper label found on the back shoulder of a papier-mâché shoulder head doll.★

2631. Mark on papier-mâché shoulder heads indicating that they were supposedly unbreakable.

Uncle Bim. 1929. All-bisque doll with moving head based on "The Gumps" cartoon series drawn by *Sidney Smith*. It was made in Germany and distributed wholesale exclusively by *Marshall Field* and *Shackman*.

Uncle Mose. 1908–30 and later. Cutout cloth doll produced by the *Davis Milling Co.* (Aunt Jemima Mills Co.).

1910: It was bare headed and the arms were crossed. Ht. 15 in. (37.5 cm.).

1924: Wore a hat and had hands in pockets.★

Uncle Sam. Many dolls have been dressed to represent Uncle Sam as he appeared in the line drawings. This costume included a top hat, a tail coat and long striped trousers.

1898: A character bisque head doll which resembled the one shown in Ill. 2632 was pictured in LADIES' HOME JOURNAL.

1899: Doll with painted face had a vandyked beard, cloth body and was dressed as Uncle Sam. It was imported and distributed wholesale by *Butler Bros.* Hts. 9 and 11½ in. (23 and 29 cm.).

1917: *Standard Doll Co.* made dolls with composition head and hands representing Uncle Sam. It had painted eyes.

Baltimore Bargain House distributed an Uncle Sam doll with composition head and hands on a cloth body. Ht. 36 in. (91.5 cm.); priced $1.45.

Western Art Leather Co. made a stuffed leather doll representing Uncle Sam.

1918: *Horsman* distributed felt dolls dressed to represent Uncle Sam. (See also **Patriotic Dolls; Fritz Brownie**.)★

Uncle Sam and Betsy Ross. 1926. Character doll created by *Mrs. Berry Kollin* and made by *Twinjoy*. It was a two-in-one character doll. Uncle Sam was paired with Betsy Ross and had a round tag.

2632. Bisque head Uncle Sam doll with a white wig and beard, stationary brown glass eyes, closed smiling mouth and a fully jointed composition body. Original clothes. Mark: Ill. 2633. H. 13½ in. (34 cm.). *Courtesy of Sotheby Parke Bernet Inc., N.Y.*

2633. Mark on a bisque head of a doll representing Uncle Sam.

Uncle Tom. Ca. 1860. Black wax headed doll made by *Pierotti*.

Uncle Walt. 1923–28. Oilcloth doll with printed clothes made by *Live Long Toys*. The name "Uncle Walt" was in black on the lower back.★

Uncle Walt. 1929. Cartoon character in Gasoline Alley drawn by Frank King, made in Germany as an all-bisque doll with movable head and molded clothes. Distributed wholesale exclusively by *Marshall Field* and *Shackman*. Priced $1.80 wholesale and 25¢ retail.★

Under the China-berry Tree. 1930 and later. *Bamberger* began to sell these dolls in 1930 and registered the name as a U.S. trademark for cloth dolls in 1931.

Undressed. Usually meant wearing a chemise. Sometimes. the doll wore only footwear or jewelry and hair ornaments. (See also **Nude** and **Clothes.**)

Uneeda Biscuit Boy.† See **Uneeda Kid.**

Uneeda Doll Co. 1917–30 and later. New York City. Made composition-head dolls including *Mama* dolls.

1920: Made dolls from 13 to 21 in. (33 to 53.5 cm.); priced 50¢ to $4.00. Represented by *Bush Terminal.*

1921: Advertised 100 numbers which were either cork or excelsior stuffed, joints inside or outside of the body, with painted or sleeping eyes, and with or without wigs. Priced 10¢ to $5.00.

1926: Advertised "high grade Mama dolls." Dolls priced from 25¢ to $15.00.

1927: Moved to larger quarters, made dolls for jobbers, mail-order houses and stores. Julius Jacobson and Ben Slarsky represented them at a Toy Fair.

1929: Advertised 250 styles of dolls.

1930: Advertised *Sweetums* line of dolls and Mama dolls.★

Uneeda Kid (Uneeda Biscuit Boy†). 1914–19. Made by *Ideal* and distributed by *Butler Bros., McDonald Bros.* and *Shackman*. It was one of the Character Art dolls with composition head, hands, and boots, painted features and hair, cloth body. Label on sleeve of yellow sou'wester coat read: "Uneeda Kid//Patented Dec. 8, 1914//Ideal Novelty & Toy Co. Brooklyn, N.Y." There were striped rompers under the coat.

Uneke. 1928. Trademark registered in U.S. for dolls by Helen N. Gove, doing business as *Gove Manufacturing Co.*

Ungarische Gummiwaren-Fabrik (Magyar Ruggyantaárugyár Rt. [Hungarian Rubber Factory Articles]). 1894–1930 and later. Budapest. Made rubber dolls' heads, rubber dolls and celluloid dolls.

1894: Applied for a German patent (D.R.P.) for a doll's head.

1899: Applied for a German patent (D.R.G.M.) for fastening a doll's head.

1924: *Strobel & Wilken* became their American agent.

1929: Was granted a German patent (D.R.P.) for a doll with movement.

1930: *Jacob, Son & Co.* was their London distributor.

Unger, Robert. 1909–29. Waltershausen, Thür. Manufactured dolls.★

Unger, Schneider & Hutschenreuther. See **Gräfenthal Porzellanfabrik.**

Unger & Co. 1920s–30 and later. Buchholz, Saxony. Made chenille dressed dolls. Some of which resembled *Kewpies*®. Four of the 58 dolls shown in a catalog were brown.

Unger Doll & Toy Co. 1929–30. Milwaukee, Wis. Manufactured "Cellupon" dolls with cellulose lacquer enamel finish and representing comic characters. Hts. 8 to 15 in. (20.5 to 38 cm.).

Union Jack Baby. 1916. Trade name of a doll made by *Ellison, Rees.* It had sleeping eyes, allegedly the first doll with sleeping eyes in Britain. The body had ball joints.

Union Nationale Inter-Syndicale. See **Unis France.**

Unique Novelty Doll Co. 1925–30 and later. New York City. Made dolls including three styles of *Boudoir* dolls. Ht. 32 in. (81 cm.) and dolls with silk wigs.

Unis France. 1916–30 and later. Mark used by *Société Française de Fabrication de Bébés & Jouets* (S.F.B.J.). The initials UNIS stood for Union Nationale Inter-Syndicale. The letters UNIS FRANCE are often found in a circle or football-shaped mark and were accompanied by numbers. The number on the left was the Syndicale number, for example, 71 for the *Chambre Syndicale,* the number on the right was the company number, for example, 149 stood for S.F.B.J., and the number underneath the UNIS appears to have represented the mold number.★

United Hoisery Mills Corp. (Buster Brown Hosiery Mills). 1921. Chattanooga, Tenn. Registered *Dixie Doll* as a U.S. trademark for dolls.

2634. Mark used by the Uneeda Doll Co.

Uneeda Kid
Patented Dec. 8, 1914
IDEAL TOY and NOVELTY Co.
BROOKLYN, N.Y.

2635. Mark on the Uneeda Kid doll made by Ideal.

2636–2637. Marks on bisque heads made by the S.F.B.J. The initials UNIS stand for Union Nationale Inter-Syndicale.

2638. Corn husk doll dressed in the style fashionable in the late 1890s or early 1900s. To her side is the typical parasol. The hair is braided corn silk which is cut in front. The face is a piece of paper printed in colors to denote the features. The costume details are created by the use of the differing shades of the corn husks including a purple color. Also pins and beads are used as decoration. H. 10½ in. (26.5 cm.). *Coleman Collection.*

United States (U.S.) Emblem. 1902–05. Name used by *Butler Bros.* for dolls with china heads and limbs; cloth bodies with a printed emblem of the U.S. on the front of the body and the names of the states on the rest of the body; 12 hts. 7⅛, 8, 10¼, 11, 12, 13, 14, 16, 17, 17½, 19⅓, and 20⅓ in. (18, 20.5, 26, 28, 30.5, 33, 35, 40.5, 43, 44.5, 49, and 51.5 cm.); priced 33¢ to $3.75 doz. wholesale.

United States Rubber Co. Before 1918–1920. Cleveland, Ohio. By 1918 the Mechanical Rubber Co.† merged with the United States Rubber Co.

1920: Advertised rubber dolls with whistles.

Universal Dolls' Outfitters. 1918–21. New York City. Made knitted clothes including sacques, caps, mittens, bootees, and a variety of two- three- and four-piece outfits for dolls ranging in hts. from 10 to 24 in. (25.5 to 61 cm.). They supplied garments for large *Madame Hendren* dolls and *Colonial* dolls, as well as a line for *Kewpie®* dolls.

Universal Fashion Co. 1884–87 and probably other years. New York City, London, Paris, Amsterdam, Antwerp, Havana, Sydney, Melbourne, Yokohama, and other principal cities in U.S., U.K., and Canada. Sold dolls' clothes patterns.

Unsere Kleine Mammy (Our Little Mammy). Ca. 1930. Name of baby dolls representing a newborn up to a year old baby, with bisque or celluloid painted hair heads on cloth bodies, was advertised by *Kämmer & Reinhardt.*

Untley and Palmer. 1926. Paris. Made dolls.

Unusual Materials for Making Dolls. Dolls have been made of some of the following materials: bread crumbs; corn husks; corncobs; dried apples; bamboo sawdust; egg shells; flowers; hollyhocks; lead swords; lobster claws; long neck squash; nuts; pinecones; poppy blossoms; potatoes; sea shells; fossilized shellfish; seeds; sponges; straw paper.

In 1881 ST. NICHOLAS described a doll as follows: "Flower lady doll underskirt is a petunia, canterbury-bell forms the overskirt and waist, small twigs or broom straws, stuck through buds of the phlox are the arms; the head is made of a green pea, with a phlox blossom for a bonnet. A reversed daisy makes a very nice parasol."

Various species of eggs were used by *James French* to make dolls' heads commercially.

1916: TOYS AND NOVELTIES published a list of unusual materials of which dolls were made. This included corn husks, carved oak balls, bark of trees, knots of wood and egg shells.

1928: Dolls made of turtle leather were mentioned in a trademark registered by *Robert Darcy.*

Unwin & Wigglesworth. 1759–60 and possibly other years. London. Handled dolls and supplied dolls to George Washington.

Up-to-Date Manfacturing Co. 1926–29. Jersey City, N.J. Made dolls' voices; *Albert Brückner* was the treasurer.

Urbanek, B. 1925. Hartmanitz, Böhmerwald, Czechoslovakia. Listed under Walking Dolls in an Austrian directory.

2639. Advertisement in PLAYTHINGS, February, 1917, for the Rollinson cloth dolls made by Utley. The dolls distributed by Strobel & Wilken and Louis Wolf in this picture are all dressed and have wigs but they also came undressed and came with painted hair. There are boy, girl and baby dolls. Hs. 14 to 28 in. (35.5 to 71 cm.).

U-Shab-Ti. 1923. Made with a dark composition face by the *Averill Mfg. Co.* shortly after the discovery of King Tutankhamen's Tomb.★

Utley Co. 1914–22. Holyoke, Mass. In 1919 it became a subsidiary of the American Tissue Mills and affiliated with the Japanese Tissue Mills. The name was changed to New England Doll Co. Their dolls were then called NEDCO dolls; NEDCO being an acronym for "*N*ew, *E*xquisite, *D*elightful, *C*omely, *O*riginal" as well as the initials of the Company.

The cloth dolls were created by *Gertrude Rollinson* and bore a diamond-shaped stamp with the Rollinson name on it. Many of the dolls were described as "cloth papier-mâché."

1917: The Rollinson dolls had painted hair or wigs, came dressed or undressed. Hts. 14 to 28 in. (35.5 to 71 cm.).

1918: Advertised dolls with head and body of "cloth papier-mâché." These dolls had sleeping eyes, straight limbs and came in seven hts. 14 to 26 in. (35.5 to 66 cm.). Also advertised Tuco[+] and *Fabco* dolls.

1919: Advertised human hair or mohair wigs on their dolls which had socket heads, sleeping eyes, and were fully jointed including the wrists. They claimed the dolls were washable in hot or cold water. Due to their diagonal hip joints the dolls could stand alone.

1921: Described their dolls as made of papier-mâché with aluminum arms, wooden wrists, human hair wigs, glass eyes, hair eyelashes, teeth and tongue. These dolls were available with a "high glaze or dull finish" and the claim was still made that they were washable.★

V

Vacation Girl. 1918. Made by *Jessie M. Raleigh,* had a five-piece all-composition body with steel spring joints. Came dressed in a white dress and a ribbon headband.★

Vacchetti, Sandro. 1920–30 and later. Turin, Italy. Born 1889, died 1975. A painter and ceramist, he joined the *Lenci* firm in 1920 and later became Art Director. He designed some of the dolls' faces.

1926: Mentioned in TOY WORLD as working with Madame Lenci as a painter.

1933: He left the Lenci firm to found his own ceramic studio.

Val Gardena. See **Grödner Tal.**

Valdivielso, M. Pablo. 1929. Paris. Registered as a French trademark *FÉTICHE PORTE BONHEUR//PRETTY* (Mascot Brings Happiness) for Mascot dolls.

Vale of Clwyd Toymakers. 1917 and later. Trefnant, Wales. Made a line of cloth dolls with handpainted faces. Among them was "Nain Morys and her son John," a swing made Nain Morys rock John to sleep.

Val-encia. 1928–29. Trade name of a *Mme. Hendren* wigged *Mama* doll in the *Lyf-Lyk* line of the *Averill Manufacturing Co.*

Valencia. 1930. Trade name of a line of dolls made by *Penn Stuffed Toy Co.* They were designed by *Mr. J. Green* who supervised the manufacture.

Vamp. 1928. Trade name of a *Viscoloid* doll made by the *Pacific Novelty Co.* division of *Du Pont*'s *Viscoloid Co.* Dolls had molded hair, painted eyes glancing to the side, shoulders jointed, legs together and were dressed in crepe paper. Ht. 7 in. (18 cm.).

Vampir. 1927–28. Made by *Lenci* mold # 800 C. It had bobbed hair and a Flapper-style costume with gloves and high-heeled shoes. Ht. 45 in. (115 cm.).

Vamps. 1920. Made by *Duckme Doll Co.* of all-wood fibre composition. The dolls came with or without wigs, jointed at the shoulders, and feet apart with molded footwear. Dressed in ribbons gathered at the top or undressed. Style no. 106. Ht. 9½ in. (24 cm.); Style no. 121. Ht. 13½ in. (34 cm.).★

Van Briggle, Artus. 1886. Cincinnati, Ohio. Painted the faces on white bisque and china heads imported by *Arnoldt Doll Co.* Later Artus Van Briggle made famous art pottery.

Van Hollebeke—De Potter. Around 1850. Bruges, Belgium. According to a blue and gold label they made and distributed dolls, dolls' heads and automatons.

Van Laar, Pauline Henriette (née Petitmaitre). 1925–26. Gerzensee, Switzerland. Obtained a German patent (D.R.P.) for dolls.

Van Look. 1930. Paris. Made and/or distributed dolls.

Van Rozen, J. World War I period. Paris. Belgian refugee who designed dolls' heads which were made of a bisque-like ceramic material. These were marked "VAN ROZEN// FRANCE//DÉPOSÉ" in a circle. His dolls were distributed by La Maison Bossier and La Maison Rouzaud. He also made ceramic figurines that wore fabric representations of French military uniforms. These were displayed at the Musée de L'Armée. Hts. of figurines were 9 to 16 in. (23 to 40.5 cm.). One of the Van Rozen dolls is shown in Ill. 2640 and a similar one has been found wearing a pair of shoes bearing the *Fischer, Naumann* mark.

Slightly similar dolls were made by the *De Fuisseaux* factory in Belgium prior to World War I.

Van Tussenbroek, Harry. 1929. Rotterdam, Netherlands. Created art dolls.

Van Walkenburgh, R. 1920–21. Made a line of terry cloth crepe dolls known as *Rag Shoppe Dolls* for *Beck Manufacturing Co.* Some of these were dressed in rompers.

Vanity Fair Dolls. 1901. China shoulder head dolls with molded and painted hair and features. They had a diamond-shaped mirror in their molded and gilded pendants.★

Vanity Fair. See **Vanity Flossie.**

Vanity Flossie (Vanity Fair). 1926–29. Trade name of a doll made by *Ideal.* When it first appeared in 1926 it was called

2640A & B. Character head designed by Van Rozen of France. It has a wig, stationary blue glass eyes; open-closed smiling mouth and a fully jointed composition body. The clothes are contemporary with the doll. Mark: Ill. 2641. H. 16 in. (40.5 cm.). *Courtesy of the Margaret Woodbury Strong Museum. Photos by Harry Bickelhaupt.*

2641. Mark on a bisque-like ceramic doll's head designed by Van Rozen. (See Ill. 2640.)

2642. China shoulder head doll with molded and painted hair, eyes and necklace, named Vanity Fair. The pendant has a diamond shaped mirror. There is no gilding on the necklace in the back. The body is cloth with china limbs and the legs have molded and painted footwear. H. 10 in. (25.5 cm.). *Courtesy of Richard Withington. Photo by Barbara Jendrick.*

Vanity Fair. This composition-head *Mama* doll had flirting eyes, rubber arms and legs, and a hand that could hold a mirror.

1927: Advertised as being the "half-sister" of *Flossie Flirt* and that the doll had a vampish look.

Vanner, Emile. 1929–30 and later. Paris. French representative for *Lenci* dolls.

Vannier, Mme. Hippolyte. 1864–65. Paris. Made dressed dolls and bébés.★

Vanta Baby. 1927–30. Trade name of a bisque or composition-head doll produced by *Amberg* and dressed in Vanta baby undergarments. The doll had sleeping eyes, generally

metal, or painted eyes, a crier, and a bent limb cloth body. It was distributed by *Sears.*

1927: Doll was guaranteed washable, unbreakable and had no pins or buttons. It wore an organdy dress, Vanta shirt, and Vanta panties, all tied with Vanta tape, socks, and handmade moccasins. The doll cost 50¢ extra if it came with Vanta shirt, Vanta panties, and a four-piece dress outfit. The three largest sizes had hair eyelashes. Each doll came with a celluloid baby rattle, gift card, "Dolly Record Book," and a gold tag. Five hts. 14½, 17, 19, 21 and 25 in. (37, 43, 48, 53.5 and 63.5 cm.); priced $4.50 to $14.00.

1928: A 10 in. (25.5 cm.) size wearing Vanta pants and shirt costing $1.00 and an 11 in. (28 cm.) size wearing a frock and cap costing $2.00 were added, while the 19 and 25 in. (48 and 63.5 cm.) sizes were deleted. The dolls were advertised as being able to stand on their own.

1929: Vanta Baby wore a short infant's dress having short sleeves, a halo-style bonnet and moccasins.

1930: Was one of the dolls acquired by *Horsman* when Amberg sold his business. Vanta Baby was dressed in a new Horsman creation.

Varale, A., & Co. 1927–30 and later. Turin, Italy. Made Art dolls. Their dolls were distributed in Britain.

Vargas, Antonio. 1915–30 and later. New Orleans, La. The Vargas family made wax doll figures representing old street hucksters and other workers. Many of these were black. They also repaired wax dolls.

Varnished Head Dolls. 1820s–80s. Trade name used by importing concerns in the U.S. to describe molded hair

2643

2644

2645

2643–2645. Marks on Vanta Baby dolls produced by Amberg.

papier-mâché head dolls with kid or cloth bodies having wooden limbs.

1829–31: Lewis Page used this term in his account book.

1860–61: John D. Robbins used this term in his Day Book (belonging to Elizabeth Pierce). Priced 25¢ to $2.50 doz. wholesale.

Vassilief (Vasilyeff), Marie. Before World War I–1926. Moscow and Paris. Was a painter and sculptor who made dolls. According to ARTS AND DECORATION, her dolls were exhibited at the Morozov Museum of Decorative Arts in Moscow. Early in World War I she opened a school of modern art in Paris which Leon Trotsky and other revolutionists frequented. She was arrested and was jailed for a year. The BROOKLYN EAGLE gave the following account: "During World War I a new type of art cloth doll was created by Mme. Vassilief which inspired the *Madame Paderewski* dolls. Copies of the Vassilief dolls were made by the girls in the workrooms of the famous French dressmakers. But the copies had no real artistic merit when compared with the original Vassilief dolls."

1923: Made character dolls of the modernistic style.

1925: Designed portrait dolls of famous people including a caricature of Marie Vassilief herself, and Mr. Brenswige, a California business man. These cloth dolls had holes for inserting the eyes, thus making the eyes look large.

1926: Made dolls representing Matisse, Picasso, and *Paul Poiret* as well as those representing Spanish dancers and

2646. Three dolls with varnished shoulder heads of papier-mâché. They have fancy molded hair, painted eyes, closed mouths on kid bodies with wooden arms and legs. Doll on the left has green eyes and a so-called Apollo's knot hairdo. H. 9¼ in. (23.5 cm.). Doll in the center has brown eyes, corkscrew curls and an original dress. H. 9¼ in. (23.5 cm.). Doll on the right has a high braided knot hairdo, blue-green eyes and a contemporary dress. H. 7 in. (18 cm.). *Courtesy of Sotheby Parke Bernet Inc., N.Y.*

velvet-eyed Italians and dolls with chamois skin faces and limbs.★

Vat. See **Messina-Vat.**

Veldeman, Mme. 1916. Belgium. Dressed dolls that were shown in the Exposition of Dolls for Children of Belgian Soldiers.

Veelo Manufacturing Co. 1928–30. New York City, and Adrian, Mich. Made terry cloth dolls. Factory agent was *Corcoran & Laycock.*

1929: Advertised dolls with round eyes glancing to the side and a doll with an apron and pigtails.

Veilsdorf. See **Kloster Veilsdorf Porzellan Fabrik Co.**

Veller, Diana. Signature on the foot of a felt doll made or distributed by *Krauhs* of Vienna.

Velponer Bros. Before 1838. Grödner Tal, Austria. *Verlegers* who sold dolls in Lisbon and elsewhere.

Velter. See **Borreau.**

Venezuela. See **Pereyra, Manuela.**

Venus. 1902 and possibly other years. The word "Venus" over a heart has been found on a metal doll's head by the Cieśliks. This mark was used on dolls made by *Gebrüder Lokesch.* (See Ill. 1715.)

Venus (La Vénus†). 1923–30. Trade name of cloth dolls made by *Adrien Carvaillo* and distributed by *Bon Marché.*

1925: Came dressed in felt. Hts. 40, 50, and 60 cm. (15½, 19½, and 23½ in.

1928–29: Bon Marché advertised dressed cloth Venus dolls. Hts. 37 and 45 cm. (14½ and 17½ in.).

1930: Bon Marché advertised dressed cloth Venus dolls with wigs. Hts. 39, 47, and 55 cm. (15½, 18½, and 21½ in.). (See Ills. 2647 and 2648.)

Vera. 1913–19. Dolls with ball-jointed composition bodies first produced by J. *Kohnstam (Keen & Co.†).* Bodies contained 20 parts.

In 1916 the patented equipment for making the Vera dolls was taken over by *Lord Roberts' Memorial Workshops.*

1913: Vera dolls had bisque heads imported from Germany and carried a shield-shaped tag. The dolls were dressed in a lingerie factory.

1916: The dolls came in seven hts. Including a long limbed lady doll which slightly resembled the *Hilda Cowham* dolls. This lady doll wore a red, white and blue outfit. Vera dolls were distributed by *Laurie Hansen.*

1917: The dolls came in three styles including those with composition heads, *British Ceramic* heads with painted eyes, and those with glass eyes.

1918: The seven hts. ranged from 15½ to 27 in. (39.5 to 68.5 cm.): priced $2.50 and up.

Verchaly, A L'Industrie. After 1880. Anger, France. Handled *Bébé Jumeau* dolls. Mark: Ill. 2649.

2647A & B. Venus, a cloth doll with molded head made by A. Carvaillo, mohair wig, painted features, Original felt clothes. Mark: Ill. 2648. Mark on original box: "Les Poupées en Etoff// FABRICATION FRANÇAISE// A. C. PARIS//VENUS // Série—No. 100." H. 14 in. (35.5 cm.). *Coleman Collection.*

VÉNUS

2648. Mark for a Venus cloth doll.

2649. Mark of Verchaly used on boxes containing Bébés Jumeau.

2650. Cloth dolls made by Mlle. Verita. The doll on the right is called Bébé "Vérité." The dolls have molded features with a seam down the middle of the face. *The illustration is from REN-AISSANCE DE LA POUPÉE, by Doin, 1916.*

Verdavainne, Alphonso. 1847–72. Paris. Exhibited dolls at the Paris Exposition.★

Vereinigte (United) Berliner und Erdmannsdorfer Fabriken. 1903. Berlin. The factory was owned by Ed. Boehm and Th. Haroske. They applied for a German patent (D.R.G.M.) for stringing dolls.

Vereinigte Gummiwaren-Fabriken (United Rubberware Factory). See **Menier-Reihoffer, J.N.**

Verger. See **Dehais.**

Verita, Mlle. Gabrielle. 1915–18. Paris. Created cloth character dolls representing children, toddlers, and babies in her Vérité line.★

Verleger was a special term used in the German doll industry but there is no precise English word that conveys a true translation relating to the doll industry. The Verleger was the major company in charge of the production of dolls. He or one of his employees designed and modeled the dolls; he financed, organized, collected, and distributed the dolls. He was in charge of the central office to which the dolls and/or doll parts were brought. In the case of large companies there were the Grand Verleger and subsidiary Verlegers. Usually the patents and trademarks were in the name of the Verleger. However the Verleger did not actually manufacture dolls. He generally had no factory nor did he directly make dolls, he hired others to do so. Collectors have been in the habit of calling Verlegers such as Cuno and Otto Dressel manufacturers which is not precisely correct. The interrelationship of companies involved in the production of dolls is often very complex and changed from time to time.

The difficult job of discovering these relationships has received greater attention and emphasis in this ENCYCLOPEDIA, Vol. Two than it did in the first COLLECTOR'S ENCYCLOPEDIA OF DOLLS. (See also **Assemblers.**)

Verlingue, J. 1915–20s. Boulogne-sur-Mer, Montreuil-sous-Bois, and Paris. In a 1920s ANNUAIRE CHAMBRE SYNDICALE the listing for H. Delcourt included J. V. and "Petite Française." H. Delcourt, the successor to *Gesland,* had the same address as J. Verlingue in Paris in 1921. Verlingue dolls' heads have been found on dolls with bodies labeled "Jumeau Diplôme d' Honneur."★

Verone, Maria. 1914–15. France. Created dolls.

Verry Fils. 1865–73. Paris. Name found on dolls' bodies.★

2651. Verry Fils mark found stamped on bodies of dolls. This mark may be more accurate than the one shown in Ill. 1643 in the first COLLECTOR'S ENCYCLOPEDIA OF DOLLS.

Vetter, Herm. Göppingen, Germany. 1927–29. Listed under Dolls' Clothes in DEUTSCHE SPIELWAREN ZEITUNG.

Vialard, Pierre. 1900–30 and later. Paris. Distributed and repaired dolls. Used a blue and white sticker that has been found on the back of composition bodies.

He used the initials P. V. During World War I he handled Japanese dolls.

2652. Vialard mark found on composition bodies of dolls.

Vichy, G. 1862–1900 and later. Paris. G. Vichy, Vichy Jr., G. P. Vichy Fils (Sons), G. & H. Vichy, and Henry Vichy were listed in this chronological order. They were best known for their mechanical dolls, some of which were with music, but they also advertised bébés and "Artistic shoulder heads."

1862: Obtained a French patent for a mechanical doll.

1878: Won a silver medal at the Paris Exposition.

1879: Won a silver medal at the Cherbourg Exposition.

1880: Won a bronze medal at the Melbourne Exhibition.

1881: Owed money to *François Gaultier* for porcelain dolls' heads and/or parts.

1884: Won a gold medal at the New Orleans Exhibition.

1888: Won a gold medal at the Melbourne Exhibition.

1889: Won a gold medal at the Paris Exposition.

1893: Showed dolls at the Chicago Exhibition.

1900: Won a Grand Prize at the Paris Exposition.

Vickers, Ltd. 1920. London; and factory at Dartford. Made dolls including cloth dolls. During World War I, they made guns and munitions.

Victoria (Viktoria). Name found on several bisque-head dolls. Among the porcelain factories that used Victoria as a mark were *Julius Hering* and the Altrohlau factory in Bohemia near Carlsbad. The Cartwright and Edwards factory in Longton, England, also used Victoria as a mark. It is known that Julius Hering and his successor Hering & Weithase made bisque heads for dolls marked Victoria (or Viktoria). (See Ills. 2653 and 2654.) These heads were usually highly colored. One of the Victoria bisque-head dolls had a wig, sleeping eyes, composition body jointed at the shoulder and hips, arms slightly bent, straight legs. Ht. 36 cm. (14 in.): size 2/0.★

MADE IN GERMANY

Viktoria

J. 🏳 H.

²⁄₀

VictoriA
H&W
²⁄₀
Germany

2653–2654. Victoria marks on bisque dolls' heads made by Julius Hering and Viktoria mark used by his successor Hering & Weithase.

Victoria Doll Co. 1919–30 and later. U.S.A. Made dolls including cloth dolls.

1919: Advertised 50 style nos.

Victoria Toy Works. See **Wellings, Norah.**

Victory Baby. 1919. Trade name of a doll advertised by *Nottingham.*

Victory Doll. 1917–20. Line of all-composition ball-jointed dolls made by *Amberg.* Unpainted molded hair was often found under the wig. The head and bodies were marked and the marks usually included the doll's height in centimeters.

1917: Advertised as having a wig, sleeping eyes, and a hair bow. Four hts. 40, 50, 60, and 70 cm. (16, 20, 24 and 28 in.).

1919: Advertised as being a character baby or fully jointed child doll with patented eyelashes. Both styles came in four sizes.

1920: Advertised baby and girl dolls, dressed and undressed; seven sizes. A 30 in. (76 cm.) Victory doll could display clothes for a two-year-old child in a shop window.★

L.A & S
50
AMBERG'S
VICTORY
DOLL
50

2655. Mark impressed on Victory all-composition dolls made by Amberg.

Victory Doll. World War I Period–1923. A box has been reported labeled, "Victory Doll. No. F. J. 100." It contained a doll with a bisque head marked "S.F.B.J." (*Société Française de Fabrication de Bébés & Jouets).* This doll had sleeping eyes and a jointed composition body. Ht. 19 in. (48 cm.). Dolls by this name were advertised by H. Benjamin in Britain. They had sleeping eyes with eyelashes.

Vida Nisbet Sales Co. 1922. Cleveland, Ohio. Made cloth patterns for Van Doll Clothes which came with full instructions and were sold through the mails. (See THE COLLECTOR'S BOOK OF DOLLS' CLOTHES, Ills. 751 and 752.)

Viechtau near Gmunden. 1800s. Balkan area. Region where wooden dolls were made as a home industry. The quality was poor and the same types were made for generations. Dolls were named *Federdocken* (Feather doll), *Gmunderdocken, Linzerdocken, Schepperdocken* and *Tiroler Docken.* (Docken means wooden doll.)

Dolls were exported to Albania, Bosnia, Bulgaria, southern Hungary and Serbia. *Rudolf Nekola* was the *Ver-*

leger who collected and distributed these dolls. In the 1880s there were 137 families with 329 people carving wooden dolls. The prices did not vary from 1850 to 1880. Some of these dolls had movable arms and in 1881 cost less than a cent each.

Vier Bros. 1928–30. Los Angeles, Calif. Jobbers and distributors of dolls made by *Acme.* In 1928 and 1930 they distributed *Cuddly Kewpies.*

Viktoria. See **Victoria.**

Viktoria Luise. 1908. Trade name of a dressed doll produced by *Carl Hartmann* in the *Paladin* line. The doll had a porcelain head with hair eyelashes.

Villard & Weill. 1834–1928. Paris and Lunéville, France. Made dolls.

1905: Won a Grand Prize at Liège.

1927: Had a capital of 1,875,000 francs.★

Ville de St. Denis. 1901–14 and possibly other years. Paris. A department store that handled dolls including *Bébé Ville de St. Denis* made by *Jumeau* while it was part of the *Société Française de Fabrication de Bébés & Jouets, Cymbaliers* and *Marottes.*

1903: Handled *Bébés Maillot* and *Polichinelles.*

1910: Handled *Bébé Jumeau,* Bébé Maillot, *Bébé Promenette, Bébé Tout (en) Bois, Clowns, Eden Bébé, Esquimau, Mignonnette,* Polichinelle, Rubber Bébés, and composition soldiers representing cavalrymen, Turks, and Zouaves.

1914: Handled Eden Bébé, Esquimau, *Kiss Throwing* dolls, Mignonnette and Tout en Bois dolls. (See COLLECTOR'S BOOK OF DOLLS' CLOTHES, Ill. 528.)

Viola. 1902–07. Produced by *Hamburger & Co.* who in 1907 sent a postcard to Goldzcher & Co., a store in Bayonne, New Jersey, advertising Viola. These dolls have been found in hts. 20½, 24, and 25 in. (52, 61, and 63.5 cm.).★

Viola Doll Co. 1917–26. New York City. Manufactured dolls.

1918: Composition-head dolls ranged in hts. 12 to 24 in. (30.5 to 61 cm.); priced 50¢ to $5.00.★

Violet. 1901–02. THE FAMILY HOME JOURNAL offered as a subscription premium this dressed "French" doll with sleeping eyes; jointed body; wearing a silk finished dress, hat and removable footwear.

Violet. 1910–22. Line of dolls distributed by *Sears.*

Ca. 1914: Advertised as having *Minerva* metal heads with sleeping eyes, hair eyelashes, a cork stuffed white kid body with celluloid forearms and footwear. Hts. 16, 18, and 20 in. (40.5, 45.5 and 51 cm.); priced 98¢ to $1.65.★

Violet Dolls. 1924. Trade name used by *M. Kohnstam & Co.*

Violett (Violet). Before 1927–30. Trademark for dolls used by *Ernst Liebermann.*

Violetta. 1927–28. Trade name of a *Lenci* doll, No. 165/18.

2656. Postcard picture of a German bisque-head doll named Viola sent to Goldzcher's Department Store in Bayonne, N.J. The message is "I leave with all the Kids for//New York this month, will you make//a date with me? Yours sincerely//Miss Viola// c/o Hamburger & Co.//28–30 West 4th St// New York."

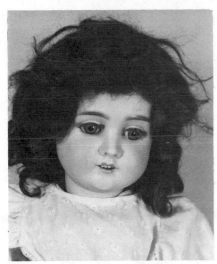

2657. Bisque head Viola doll with a dark wig, sleeping blue glass eyes, hair eyelashes, open mouth, four upper teeth, and a fully jointed composition body. Mark: Ill. 2658. H. 25 in. (63.5 cm.). *Courtesy of Richard Withington. Photo by Barbara Jendrick.*

Made in Germany Viola H & Co. 8

2658. Mark on Viola bisque heads.

It wore a pseudo mid-19th century style costume with an organdy dress. Ht. 27½ in. (70 cm.).

Violette. 1925–27. New York City. Made dolls' outfits including those for *Mama,* infant and jointed dolls. These were original designs, reproductions of imported models, character and period costumes.

Vipi. 1915. Cloth doll wearing a Scottish uniform was handled by *Whyte, Ridsdale.* Three hts.; $4.50 to $5.50 doz. wholesale.

Virginia, Ginny for Short. 1927. Trademark registered in Germany by *Borgfeldt* for dolls.

Virginia Pop-eye (Virginia). 1927–28. Trade name of a doll with fuzzy hair produced by *Borgfeldt.*

Virnich. 1874–1930 and later. Cologne and Nürnberg, Germany. In 1902 B. H. Virnich was succeeded by P. H. Virnich. Handled dolls. ★

Viscoloid. 1923–28. Trade name for the celluloid-like material used by the *Pacific Novelty Co.* division of the *Du Pont Viscoloid Co.,* for making dolls.

Vitale Doll Co. 1927. New York City. Member of the *American Doll Manufacturers' Association.*

Vivandière†. See **Military Costume Dolls.**

Vivet, Mme. Vve. (Widow). Marseille, France. A bisque-head has been found marked "Paris Bébé 260 Tété Dep. 11," on a composition body bearing Mme. Vivet's label. It also stated that she repaired dolls.

Vodka. 1922. Name of a doll with a tricot cloth over a plaster cast face made by the *Sardeau* sisters and it represented a drunken Russian peasant with flaxen hair cropped in a zig-zag fashion, red nose and a tipsy-type smile. It wore a blue satin peasant jacket, red satin trousers, blue cap with a visor tilted sideways and bronze shoes. He was the mate to *Stupid.*

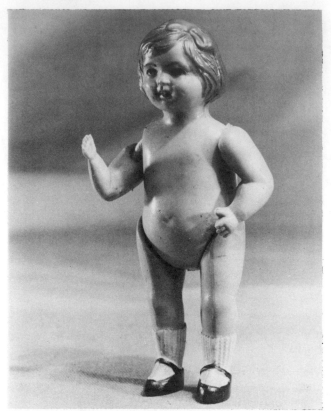

2659. Viscoloid doll made by the Pacific Novelty Division of the Du Pont Viscoloid Co. The doll resembles an all-celluloid doll with molded hair and bow, painted features, molded footwear. H. 3¾ in. (9 cm.). *Coleman Collection.*

2660. Mark probably used by the Du Pont Viscoloid Co. on Viscoloid (celluloid type) dolls.

Voetsch, Fred W. See **Davis & Voetsch.**

Vogel, Max. 1930. Sonneberg-Oberlind, Thür. Produced celluloid headed dolls which had either a mat or glossy finish. *M. Michaelis & Co.* was the Berlin agent.

Vogelsanger, Paul. 1908–18. Munich, Bavaria. Sculptured art dolls' heads which were made of a composition material, and were handled by *Hermann Tietz.*★

Vogler. ca. 1810. Grödner Tal, Austria. A *Verleger* who produced dolls.

Vogt, Anna. 1914. Gussmeyer in Ravenburg, Germany. Applied for a German patent (D.R.G.M.) for jointed felt dolls without visible seams.

Vogt, Prof. 1925. Nürnberg, Bavaria. Designed art dolls for *Bing.*

Vogue. 1917–19. Line of dolls produced by *Nottingham.* Some of these had *Rock China* heads *(British Ceramic);* others had composition masks on cloth dolls or they may have been cloth dolls designed by *E. E. Houghton.*

1917: In the line there were 17 style nos. including *Wounded Tommies,* Sailors and Red Riding Hood. These had composition mask faces.

1918: The Rock China heads had glass eyes and leatherette bodies. A line of cloth dolls was called *June Babies.*

Vogue Doll Shoppe. 1922–30 and later. Sommerville, Mass. Made dolls' clothes designed by Jennie H. Graves as a cottage industry. Probably made clothes for *Patsy* and for *Just Me.* (See Ill. 1364.)

1930: Made clothes for fitted trunks, suitcases and bassinettes.

Voices. Dolls voices can be only a squeak, a two syllable sound or an actual phonographic-type reproduction of the human voice.

1924: According to a U.S. DEPARTMENT OF COMMERCE REPORT: German manufacturers made arrangements with

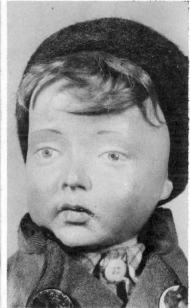

2661. Composition head modeled by Paul Vogelsanger for Marion Kaulitz who probably painted the face. It has a wig, detailed features and is on a German ball jointed body. Original clothes. Mark: Ill. 2662. H. 15 in. (38 cm.). *Coleman Collection.*

V 2

2662. Vogelsanger mark incised on the rear top of a doll's bald head.

the patentees of the *Lloyd Manufacturing Co.* and *Grubman* patents to duplicate their Mama voices in German dolls.

1926: The three types of voice mechanism found in American dolls were the crying voice, the Mama voice and the talking voice.

1927: *Victor Steiner* obtained a German patent (D.R.G.M.) for a Mama voice.

1929: *Voices, Inc.* stated that three million dolls sold in the U.S. as saying "Mama" could only give out a squawk. (See also **Mama Dolls, Phonograph Dolls** and **Talking Dolls**.)★

Voices, Inc. 1923–30. Newark, New Jersey. A conglomerate of the three principal manufacturers of voices[†] for dolls. Licensed 57 doll manufacturers to use their patented Mama voices and criers; included were *Acme, Ad Rena Co., Amberg, American Character, Averill, Cameo, Effanbee, Gerling Toy Co., Horsman, Ideal, Kampes, Marks Bros.* and *Overland Metal Novelty Co.* Aronson was president and *Grubman* was the secretary of Voices, Inc., which was the assignee of the U.S. patent obtained by Leo J. Grubman in 1926. The patent was for a sound device placed behind an opening in the lower middle front of the doll's torso. This sound device was mounted so that it could not be easily damaged if the doll were dropped or abusively handled.

Voight, Armin. 1918–29. Herschdorf, Thür. Manufactured dolls.

Voight, Friedrich. 1879–1930 and later. Sonneberg, Thür. He and his successors made jointed and unjointed dolls; they used *Schoenau & Hoffmeister* bisque heads.

1912: Advertised dolls and babies with celluloid, wood or porcelain (bisque) heads, and with wigs.★

Voigt (Voight), A. 1892–99 and possibly later. Grossbreitenbach, Thür. Owned the *Marienfeld Porcelain Factory*, where china and bisque dolls' heads and limbs were made.

Voigt, Gebrüder. 1850–1911. Sitzendorf, Thür. Possibly made porcelain dolls' heads in their Sitzendorf Porzellanfabrik. One of their marks was ⚹ but it is not known whether this factory made any of the many dolls' heads with ⚹ between the mold number and the size number. (See also **Alt, Beck & Gottschalck**.)

Voivides. 1898. Portrait dolls representing Romanian aristocrats given to Elizabeth, Queen of Romania for her collection of dolls.

Völker, Carl (Karl). 1888–1930 and later. Sonneberg, Oberlind, Thür. Produced, probably as a *Verleger,* all-bisque dolls, all-celluloid dolls and bisque-head dolls or celluloid-head dolls on composition bodies with ball joints or bent limbs. He had a special factory for making baby dolls. Also produced *Boudoir* dolls.

1908: Applied for a German patent (D.R.G.M.) for a jointed doll having forearms, and legs with molded shoes, made of celluloid.

1910: Advertised shoulder and socket heads with wigs; character babies with bisque or celluloid heads; mama dolls with a switch for disconnecting the voice and mechanism for the eye movement.

1914: Advertised bisque and celluloid heads and *Kewpies*®, dressed baby dolls, wigs, and bodies.

1926: Advertised ball jointed and character dolls, standing and sitting babies in chemise; bisque and celluloid heads; ornamental dolls including *Revue Girls* and Auto puppen (*Auto Dolls*).

1928: Advertised jointed dolls in chemise, character dolls, baby dolls, Mascot dolls for motor cars. The picture showed one black doll and two white dolls, one in a dress and the other in a chemise, plus a long-limbed Boudoir doll dressed in a *Pierrot* costume.

1930: Advertised mulatto dolls and black babies with the hair in three spots on the head.★

Volland, P. F., Co. Joliet, Ill. 1930 and later. Manufactured cloth dolls.

Vollée, Mme. 1921–30. Paris. Made dolls' clothes.★

Von Berg. See **Berg, Hermann**.

Von de Henden, Max. 1922–24. Berlin. Was granted a German patent (D.R.P.) for rubber dolls.

Von der Lipp, Baron Adolf. 1926–27. Ludwigsburg, Germany. Was granted a German patent (D.R.P.) for a doll's head with two faces.

Von der Wehd, Adolf. 1925–26. Sonneberg and Köppelsdorf, Thür. Manufactured dolls.★

Von Hindenburg. 1917. Wood portrait doll carved by Austrians from the Tyrol, while in the World War I trenches. Dolls were sold by the Red Cross.

Von Uchatius, Fräulein. 1900–06. Vienna. Made dolls of several layers of small pieces of wood which were cemented together and then painted; the process, called Brettle or Brettlein (Little Boards), was claimed to have been invented by Fräulein Von Uchatius. She studied art in Nürnberg and at the Imperial Kunstgewerbeschule (Applied Art School), in Vienna.

1906: She won a prize for her Noah's Ark and her work was written up in STUDIO.

Vuaquelin, M. 1925–27. Paris. Made dolls.

Vrai Modèle. See **Bébé Vrai Modèle**.

W

W.D. Mark found on bisque heads of dolls (see Ills. 2663 and 2664) possibly made by W. Dehler.

W. & F. Manufacturing Co. 1930 and later. Buffalo, N.Y. Made dolls.

Wabbly Wally. 1928. Cloth doll made and patented by *Dean.*

2663. A poured bisque head with blue glass eyes possibly made by Wilhelm Dehler, pierced ears, closed mouth, on a ball jointed composition body. Mark: Ill. 2664. *Courtesy of Richard Withington. Photo by Barbara Jendrick.*

W.D.
8

2664. W. D. incised mark found on bisque head dolls. See Ill. 2663.

Wachuda, Franz. 1910. Vienna and Czechoslovakia. Listed in directories under Dolls and Dolls' Heads.

Wacker, Albert. Before 1904–30 and later. Nürnberg, Bavaria. By 1904 became Bayerische Celluloidwarenfabrik. Made celluloid dolls, dolls' bodies and dolls' accessories.

1904: Applied for a German patent (D.R.G.M.) for dolls' bodies.

1910: Applied for a German patent (D.R.G.M.) for a toy figure.

1924: Applied for two German patents (D.R.G.M.) for celluloid dolls.

1926: Applied for a German patent (D.R.G.M.) for celluloid

dolls with interchangeable wigs. Was granted a German patent (D.R.P.) for a toy figure. Registered in Germany *Kleiner Spatz* (Little Sparrow) and *Cleo* as trademarks.

1927: Advertised doll outfits, celluloid dolls and bent limb babies.

1928: All-celluloid bent limb babies had molded hair.

1929: Advertised dressed and undressed dolls. Distributed in London by G. Greiner & Co.

1930: Obtained a German patent (D.R.P.) for a figure with machinery inside. Advertised babies, dolls, little dolls and dolls' trousseaux.★

Wacker, Andreas. 1899–1912. Waltershausen, Thür. Applied for several German patents (D.R.G.M.).

1899: Applied for a German patent for dolls' heads of pressed wood.

1912: Applied for a German patent for the movement of a doll's jaw by an external stick.

2665. All-celluloid doll produced by Albert Wacker, has molded hair with black silk floss over it which is caught up into a comb. The eyes are molded and painted black; closed mouth; jointed only at the shoulders. Original clothes including molded and painted footwear. Mark on body: Ill. 2666. H. 11 cm. (4½ in.). *Coleman Collection.*

GERMANY
11

2666. Mark on an Albert Wacker celluloid doll.

Wacker, Hugo. 1901. Sonneberg, Thür. Applied for a German patent (D.R.G.M.) for a doll's chemise.

Wacker. See **Henze, L., & Steinhäuser.**

Wackerle, Prof. Josef (Joseph). 1907–18. Munich, Bavaria. Born in 1880 in Partenkirchen, Bavaria. He was a noted sculptor and artist who participated in the *Puppen Reform* movement. STUDIO in 1907 described him as a "Sculptor employed at *Nymphenburg* who creates porcelain figurines, either leaves them white or colors them with strong harmonious tones under the glaze. This method is adopted for the first time in porcelain figures. He has precise and sharp line modelling. Wackerle may be destined to immortalise modern female types in porcelain portraits." The original models were done in colored pastes by the Nymphenburg porcelain factory. When the Puppen Reform took place in 1908 according to DEKORATIVE KUNST, Wackerle was "One of the principal artists who designed heads for the *Marion Kaulitz* dolls. At first they were known as Wackerle dolls." Marion Kaulitz instigated the Puppen Reform and dressed the dolls. They used ordinary German jointed composition bodies and the heads were made of a hard grayish white composition painted by hand. According to data from the Sonneberg Museum *Cuno and Otto Dressel* handled many of these dolls. Hts. reported were 42, 45, and 55 cm. (16½, 17½, and 21½ in.

1908: Wackerle's dolls were exhibited by *Hermann Tietz.*

1911: Designed dolls that were dressed by *Marta J. Langer-Schlaffke.* These dolls were exhibited at the Museum of Applied Arts in Silesia.★

Waddington, Florence. 1912. Baltimore, Md. Applied for a German patent (D.R.G.M.) for dressed dolls.

Waddlers. See **Clauderies, Tata** and **Toto.**

2667A & B. A Kaulitz all-composition doll with the socket head probably designed by Josef Wackerle. It has a blond mohair wig with two braids. There is detailed modeling around the eyes which look to the side. The pointed nose is a Josef Wackerle characteristic. The mouth is open-closed and the fully jointed body has some wood in the limbs. Original regional costume. H. 17 in. (43 cm.). *Coleman Collection.*

Wade Davis. 1908–25 and later. Black cutout cloth doll.

1910: Shown with hands in his pockets, made by the *Davis Milling Co.* Ht. 11½ in. (29 cm.).

1924: Same except held his hat.★

Wagner, D. H., & Sohn. 1742–1930 and later. Grünhainichen, Saxony; Sonneberg, Thür.; and Nürnberg, Bavaria. Handled and exported dolls.

1926: Advertised carnival dolls including *Ormond* dolls and *Marottes.*

1927: Advertised celluloid and porcelain dolls as well as "little dolls."★

Wagner, Ed. L. 1902. Lauscha, Thür. Applied for a German patent (D.R.G.M.) for fastening a head to a doll's body.

Wagner, Emil. 1925. Sonneberg, Thür. Designed art dolls for *Bing* of Nürnberg.

Wagner, Fritz. 1895. Berlin. Applied for a German patent (D.R.G.M.) for a doll attached to a pillow.

Wagner, Hermann. 1922. England. Distributed dolls.

Wagner & Zetzsche. 1875–1930 and later. Ilmenau, Thür. Manufactured dolls, parts of dolls and dolls' clothes especially shoes. Richard Wagner and Richard Zetzsche worked for *Fischer, Naumann* before starting their own company on Jan. 1, 1875. Wagner was the business administrator and Zetzsche was the designer and sculptor. Max Zetzsche, son of Richard, had four children all of whom were models for dolls. The most famous were the boy *Harald* and the two girls *Hansi* and *Inge.* The fourth child may have been *Barbele.* Later the grandsons of Richard Wagner, namely, Richard Wagner and Otto Rehm, were partners of Inge Zetzsche.

Many of the marked kid bodies made by Wagner & Zetzsche during their early period had very fine quality bisque or china heads marked on the back with three- or four-digit mold #s ranging from 639 to 1288; following the number was either #, // or No. and then the size number of the head. These shoulder heads were in a variety of types. (See **Alt, Beck & Gottschalck** for further details.) After about 1910 Wagner and Zetzsche sometimes used bisque heads made by *Gebrüder Heubach* (some of these had the square Heubach mark) and in the 1930s they used *Armand Marseille* bisque heads. Sometimes heads made by *Buschow & Beck* were used, especially for Liese. In the 1930s they advertised products from the *Rheinische Gummi und Celluloid Fabrik Co.* In 1917 Haralit, a hard celluloid type composition, was patented and used for many of the Wagner & Zetzsche dolls. These dolls were often marked with "W. & Z." and with the name of the doll if it were a portrait doll.

Wagner & Zetzsche made cloth bodies especially for the dolls with china heads and limbs. One of these china heads was marked "2 K." Later they made "Linnen" and imitation leather bodies. Marks included "W u Z" and a dark blue and gold trefoil tag with "W//1875" on it.

1880s and later: Used bisque and china heads that were probably made by *Alt, Beck and Gottschalck.* The heads usually represented children and sometimes had molded headwear.

By the 1880s Wagner & Zetzsche made shoes for dolls. The shoes were made in styles that had been popular since the 1840s suggesting that some of their dolls may have been dressed in period costumes. Most of their shoes were in the styles of the early 1900s. Many of them were marked "W & Z" and "Gesetzlich//Geschutz" in an oval. The shoe sizes were one to six and larger.

1881: Mr. Zetzsche of Ilmenau visited Sonneberg, Thür. according to the Ciesliks.

1888: They used *Simon & Halbig* bisque heads, mold # 949, on some of their kid bodies that had the blue Wagner & Zetzsche stickers. Some of these dolls wore leather shoes marked "W & Z."

1892: Louis Wolf handled Wagner & Zetzsche dolls.

1894: Applied for a German patent (D.R.G.M.) for arm movement.

1895: Applied for a German patent (D.R.G.M.) for making dolls' bodies of satin.

1897: The factory employed 25 men and 205 women to make dolls, dolls' bodies of leather and of cloth, dolls' shoes and stockings and other dolls' articles. The dolls were ex-ported to Australia, Belgium, Denmark, England, Holland, Italy, North America, Norway and Sweden according to a contemporary HISTORY OF ILMENAU.

1898: Applied for a German patent (D.R.G.M.) for a doll's body to go with a shoulder plate and a turning head.

1900: At the 25th anniversary congratulations were sent by Fischer, Naumann, *Ilmenauer* Porzellanfabrik, *Metzler & Ortloff* and *Louis Wolf.*

1907: Applied for a German patent (D.R.G.M.) for making dolls' bodies of pink fabric art leather (oilcloth).

1910: Applied for three German patents for the hip joints on character dolls.

1911: Advertised character dolls with leather or cloth bodies having hip and knee joints so that the dolls could sit like a bent limb baby. Also advertised dolls' heads, bodies, wigs, shoes and stockings, and accessories for dolls.

1912: Applied for a German patent (D.R.G.M.) for dolls' shoes.

1913: Applied for a German patent (D.R.G.M.) for dolls' bodies to go with turning heads.

1916: Applied for three German patents (D.R.G.M.) for jointed dolls of cellulose and of cloth impregnated with celluloid.

Advertised Harald and Inge portrait dolls with Haralit heads.

A

B

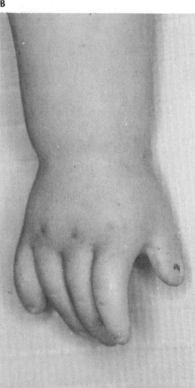

C

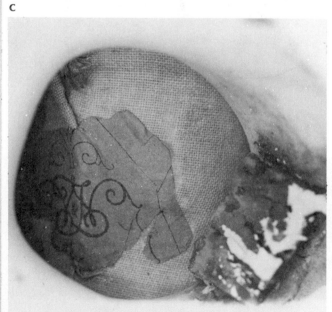

2668A–C. Bisque shoulder head that closely resembles mold # 639 (See Alt, Beck & Gottschalck.) but has only the size number 8, closed mouth, kid gusseted body with bisque lower arms. Body has the Wagner & Zetzsche blue paper bearing the mark of the company placed between the shoulders under the head. H. 20 in. (51 cm.). H. of shoulder head 5 in. (12.5 cm.). *Courtesy of Kathryn Reilly.*

1924: Applied for a German patent (D.R.G.M.) for a doll with a ball jointed arm and movable head.

1925: 50th anniversary, advertised Art dolls known as Harald, Hansi and Inge. Dolls were made dressed or undressed. Limbs of bodies were gusset or button jointed; they had composition or bisque lower arms. Hats came four to six in a box, stockings came in sizes 6, 7, 8, 9, 10, 12, 14, 16, and 45; style A shoes came in size numbers 4/0, 3/0, 2/0, 0, 1 through 15; Style B shoes came in size numbers 3/0, 2/0, 0, 1 through 16. The company had distributors in Berlin, Hamburg, Leipzig, Nürnberg, Amsterdam (*A. A. Van der Kolk*), London (*W. Seelig*) and Vienna (*Max Felix*).

1927: Advertised *Mama* dolls, Art dolls, heads, bodies, wigs, shoes, and clothes.

1929: Applied for a German patent (D.R.G.M.) for dolls. Registered *Wildfang* as a trademark in Germany for dolls.

1936: Advertised Hansi, Hans'chen, Liese, Peter, Mein Wildfang (My Madcap), Waldtraut (Beloved Wood Nymph), and other dolls. They used Armand Marseille mold #390 bisque heads and Rheinische Gummi und Celluloid Fabrik celluloid dolls and heads as well as their own composition heads. The heads came with or without wigs, with painted or glass eyes including flirting eyes and were either socket, shoulder, or flange heads. The bodies were usually covered with imitation leather or tricot.

1938: Still making leather bodies for dolls.★

2670. Bisque head made by Heubach of Köppelsdorf with flirty glass eyes and an open mouth. Doll has a five-piece composition body with straight legs, made by Wagner & Zetzsche. Mark on head: Ill. 2675. Mark on back of body: Ill. 2674. H. 21 in. (53.5 cm.). *Courtesy of Kathryn Reilly.*

 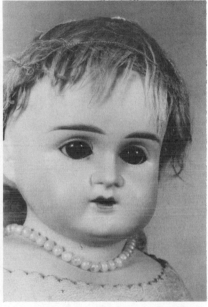

2669A & B. Bisque shoulder head on a Wagner & Zetzsche kid body. It has a wig, sleeping eyes, open mouth, teeth, two sew holes on each side and two arm creases on each side in front. The gusseted kid body has a scalloped edge and bisque lower arms. Original clothes of the 1890s. H. 22 in. (56 cm.). H. of shoulder head 6 in. (15 cm.). *Coleman Collection.*

2671. Wagner & Zetzsche advertisement in DEUTSCHE SPIELWAREN ZEITUNG, February, 1927. They listed dressed Mama and Art dolls, dolls' bodies, arms, shoes, stockings, heads, wigs, dolls' clothes and repair items for dolls' hospitals.

2672A & B. Pair of dolls with bisque heads having fired paint as well as being painted over after the firing. They have mohair wigs, sleeping eyes, hair eyelashes, open mouth, teeth, five-piece cloth bodies made by Wagner & Zetzsche in their Helga line in the 1930s. Original removable regional costumes. Marks: Ills. 2676 and 2677. H. 12½ in. (31.5 cm.). *Coleman Collection.*

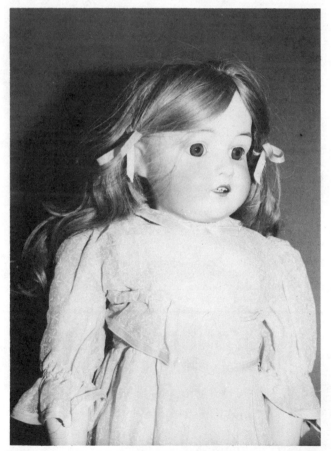

2673. Bisque head doll with wig, glass eyes, open mouth and teeth on a body made by Wagner & Zetzsche. The head was made by Gebrüder Heubach and is marked for both Heubach and Wagner & Zetzsche. Mark see Ill. 1195. *Courtesy of Richard Wright. Photo by Howard Foulke.*

2674   W Z

2675   Heubach·Koppelsdorf
342·5
Germany

2676   W.Z.
J.

2677   Helga
ges. gesch.

2678A   1875
2678B   18 17 75
2678C   Wag Wag

2679   10585
6
W. Z
J.

2680   W. u. Z
J.
Germany
200/4
HEU BACH

2674–2680. Marks on Wagner & Zetzsche dolls. The J stands for Ilmenau in Ills. 2676, 2679 and 2680. Helga is a paper tag mark used after 1930. Wagner & Zetzsche used Gebrüder Heubach bisque heads as shown by Ill. 2680. A doll with the body marked "W.Z." (see Ill. 2674) had its bisque head marked as shown in Ill. 2675, a Heubach of Köppelsdorf mark.

Wahliss, Ernst. Vienna. An all-bisque doll with molded hair, intaglio painted eyes, jointed only at the shoulders, bore his mark. The hands had the two middle fingers together and other fingers were apart. Marked "Ernst Wahliss// Porcellanhaus// Wien//Kartnerstrasse 17." Arms marked "80." Ht. 8 in. (20.5 cm.).

Wahn, Professor. 1902–07. Troppau, Silesia. Made flat wooden dolls that were first drawn then transferred to a piece of hardwood which was cut along the grain, sanded and then painted. The dolls represented people of Silesia and Vienna and were exhibited in Vienna in 1902.

Waist Joints. Dolls that had a joint at the waistline included:
Martin, Benoit[†] (1863).
Bru (1869).
Huret.
Wislizenus (1897).
Schoenhut (1915).
Amberg (1928–29): Including *It, Peter Pan Drest Doll, Sue* and *Tiny Tots.*
Horsman (1930). Took over the American branch of the Amberg business.
Averill (1930 or later).
Mme. Alexander and Mary Hoyer (after 1930).

An all-bisque doll with wig, glass eyes, socket head, molded bosom, white stockings to the knees and high black boots had joints at the shoulders, waist and diagonal hip joints. There was a 3 marked on the back of the head and a 3 on the hip section at the joint. Kid was around all the joining sections.

Another doll with a waistline joint was reported as having a *Simon & Halbig* bisque head. This doll had a dark wood-pulp composition body.

Waite, John. 1928–30 and later. Philadelphia, Pa. Owner of the *Quaker Doll Co.*

Walch, Gustav. 1909–18. Unterweid, Thür. Applied for two German patents (D.R.G.M.) for dolls: 1913 for hip joints and 1915 for wire arm and leg joints.★

Walch, Karl. 1925–27. Munich and Nürnberg, Bavaria. He was granted a German patent (D.R.P.) for dolls.

Walch, Rudolf. 1910–13. Unterweid, Thür. Applied for three German patents (D.R.G.M.) for dolls' legs and ball and socket joints in 1910, 1911 and 1913.

Waldorf Toy Corp. (Waldorf Spielzeug & Verlag). 1927–30. Stuttgart, Würtemberg and New York City. Produced dolls of cloth and of wood designed by children for children.

1929: The cloth dolls had yarn hair.

2681. Ball jointed waist on a wooden body with a composition head. The head has a wig, painted blue eyes and a closed mouth. Except for the waist joint the body is similar to those found on Bébé Tout en Bois (all-wood dolls). This doll was made in the Sonneberg-Neustadt area. *Courtesy of the Museum of the City of Neustadt near Coburg.*

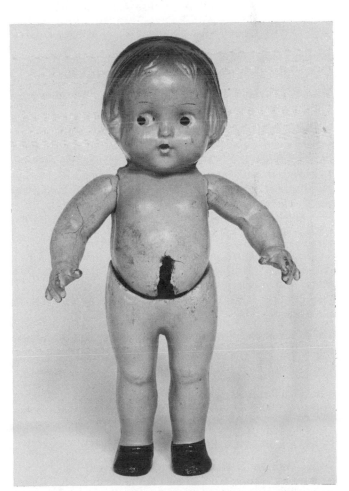

2682. All-composition doll with a waist joint has molded blond, bobbed hair, blue eyes painted glancing to the side, closed pursed mouth, joints at the shoulders and waist. Molded shoes. Mark embossed on back PAT. APPL'D. H. 10¼ in. (26 cm.). *Courtesy of the Margaret Woodbury Strong Museum. Photo by Harry Bickelhaupt.*

2683 AMBERG
PAT. PEND.
L.A.&S. ©1928

2684 PAT. APPL'D. FOR
L.A.&S.© 1928

2685 AN AMBERG DOLL WITH
BODY TWIST
all, all its own
PAT. PEND. SER.NO. 32018

2683–2685. Marks found on dolls with waist joints.

Waldtraut (Beloved Wood Nymph). See **Wagner & Zetzsche.**

Walker, Izannah F. Ca. 3rd quarter of the 1800s. Central Falls, R.I. Made cloth dolls with pressed features painted with oils to look like children. These seem to resemble many of the American folk art paintings. The connection between *Martha Chase* and Walker dolls has not been proven yet.★

Walker, Lida Kingsley. 1925–26. St. Catharines, Ontario. Obtained a U.S. design patent for dolls in 1926.★

Walker's Toyland. 1928. Los Angeles, Calif. Advertised that "Mrs. Santa Claus is making doll clothes."

Walking Dolls. Many dolls had mechanisms to make them walk or were balanced so that they appeared to walk when led by the hand. In 1912 TOYS AND NOVELTIES gave the following report, "In 1813 an inventor named Benton applied a small steam engine to the legs, which moved alternately like human feet."

Among the many offerings of walking dolls were the following:

1870s: *Jules Steiner* made a clockwork walking doll with a paper label, "J. Steiner, fabricant//Rue de Saintong No. 25 à Paris." The mechanism was marked "Steiner Bte S G D G." (See the first COLLECTOR'S ENCYCLOPEDIA OF DOLLS, Ill. 1588.)

1872: *Silber* and *Fleming* advertised three sizes of walking dolls.

1896: *Printemps* advertised that *Bébé Printemps* walked.

1903: *Au Tapis Rouge* advertised several kinds of walking dolls. *Bon Marché* advertised a doll that walked step by step.

1904: Walking Doll advertised by *Amberg* & Brill. (See THE COLLECTOR'S BOOK OF DOLLS' CLOTHES, Ill. 536.)

1905: *Petit St. Thomas* advertised a dressed walking doll which had a cone with wheels at the bottom. Ht. 27 cm. (10½ in.); priced 98¢.

1914: *Marshall Field* advertised a celtid (celluloid) head doll

2686. Izannah Walker cloth doll with oil painted molded head. The short hair is painted brown and has brushmarks. The eyes are painted blue and the mouth is closed. Joints are sewn at the shoulders and hips. Original red flannel suit and cap with gold colored buttons. H. 19 in. (48 cm.). *Private collection.*

2687. Cloth doll made by Izannah Walker with molded oil painted head, dark brown hair, blue eyes, and closed mouth. Original clothes including molded and painted footwear. H. 18 in. (47 cm.). *Courtesy of Sotheby Parke Bernet Inc., N.Y.*

I.F. WALKER'S
PATENT
NOV. 4TH 1873.

2688. Mark found on an Izannah Walker cloth doll.

which walked with spring motion. Ht. 7½ in. (19 cm.); priced $7.50 doz. wholesale.

1919: *Wauketoi* made by the *U.S. Toy and Novelty Co.*

1922: By 1922 some of the companies making walking dolls in the U.S. were: *C.W. Allen Co.; Aronson; Averill* (Madame Georgene's Wonder[+] Walking Doll was the original *Mama* doll); *Favor Toy & Novelty Importing Corp., Federal; E. M. Leavens Co.; Plano Toy Co.; Reisman, Barron; Tip Top Toy Co.;* and *Transogram Co.*

1923: *F.A.O. Schwarz* advertised walking dolls with bisque heads and composition bodies that could be lead by the hand. These did not have clock-work mechanisms. They wore an organdy dress and large hair ribbon. Hts. 20 and 25 in. (51 and 63.5 cm.); priced $14.00 to $20.00.

1924: By 1924 German manufacturers were making Mama dolls. (See also **Kiss-throwing** dolls, **Bébé Marcheur** and **Waddlers.**)★

Walküre (Valkurie). 1902–27 and possibly later. Ball jointed composition body dolls produced by *Kley & Hahn.* The bisque heads were possibly made by *Kestner.* A size 12 has been reported as 24 in. (61 cm.) tall.★

WALKÜRE		
Size No.	Height in.	cm.
2/0	15	38
2	21	53.5
2¼	23	57.5

2690A. Bisque head walking doll made by the S.F.B.J. has a blond wig, stationary brown glass eyes, pierced ears, open mouth with teeth and a brown composition body of the S.F.B.J. type. Original clothes. Red marks on head. Ribbon label on clothes: "BÉBÉ QUI MARCHE//WALKING BABY." H. 13½ in. (34 cm.). *Courtesy of Sotheby Parke Bernet Inc., N.Y.*

2689A & B. Pressed bisque head walking doll with a wig, stationary glass eyes, pierced ears and a closed mouth. The socket head has a bisque shoulder plate with H inside the plate and O on the outside of the plate. There is some resemblance to the so-called smiling Bru lady doll heads. The cloth body is glued onto cardboard which encases the three wheel walking mechanism. Leather lower arms have hands stuffed with twigs. On the body are printed directions about how to operate the mechanism: "Wind up the doll, holding it in the left hand; Turn the key towards you. To start the doll, turn the lever on the bottom forward; to stop, reverse the lever." H. ca. 11 in. (28 cm.). *Courtesy of and photo by Cherry Bou.*

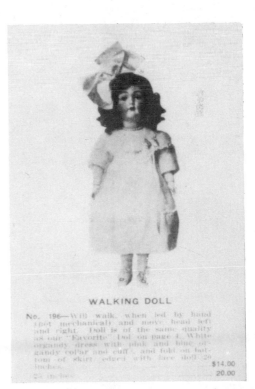

WALKING DOLL

No. 196—Will walk when led by hand
(not mechanical) and move head left
and right. Doll is of the same quality
as our "Favorite" Doll on page 4. White
organdy dress with pink and blue organdy collar and cuff, and told on bottom of skirt, edged with lace doll 20
inches $14.00
25 inches 20.00

2690B. Walking doll advertised by F. A. O. Schwarz in their 1923/24 catalog. It is not a mechanical doll but when led by the hand the head moves from side to side. Hs. 20 and 25 in. (51 and 63.5 cm.); priced $14.00 and $20.00.

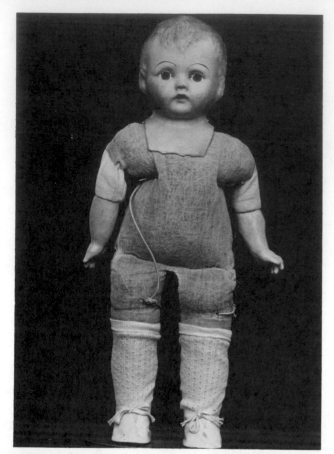

2691. Composition shoulder head walking doll has molded blond hair, painted blue eyes, closed mouth and a cloth body with composition lower arms. The head is stapled together at the seams. The cord is attached under the shoulder plate in the back and to the front of each upper leg. When the cord in the back is pulled it raises the legs to simulate walking. This doll was a Christmas present in South Africa in 1927. H. 16 in. (40.5 cm.). *Courtesy of Victoria Harper.*

K.H.
Walküre
6
2692 Germany

2694
2693 **Wälkure**
Germany
Walküre **7½**
Germany

2692–2694. Marks on Walküre bisque head dolls.

Wallach. ca. 1914. Munich, Bavaria. Produced composition-head dolls on pink cloth bodies with celluloid arms; dressed in costumes, especially regional costumes, copied from those worn by performers of the Theatre Company of Munich. Ht. 15 in.

Wallach, Leon. 1926. U.S.A. Tried to obtain a U.S. patent for a drinking-arm doll. A court case was in process because *Paul Seidel* was seeking a similar patent.

Wallendorf. 1764–1930 and later. Wallendorf, Thür. Porcelain factory that used a W mark, similar to the W often attributed to Berlin. (See also **Kämpfe & Heubach.**)

2695–2696. Marks used by the Wallendorf Porcelain Factory.

Wallis, Miss. See **Nottingham Toy Industry.**

Wally. Name found on the back of a bisque socket head with wig, sleeping eyes and open mouth. It was marked "Wally //Limbach" and was apparently made by the *Limbach Porzellanfabrik.*★

Walter (Bather). Before 1910–1913. Felt character doll dressed in a removable blue jersey bathing suit and beach hat. Made by *Steiff* and distributed in the U.S. by *Borgfeldt.* Came in four hts. 28, 35, 43, and 50 cm. (11, 14, 17 and 19½ in.).

In New York in 1913 the largest size came with a mama voice and cost $3.75.

Walter, Gebrüder. 1923–26. Berlin. Manufactured and exported dolls.

Waltershausen. A town in northern Thüringia where some of the finest German dolls were produced. In fact sometimes the name Waltershausen was given to describe the quality of a doll rather than its place of origin. Occasionally the name "Waltershausen" was put on bisque heads just as French dolls were marked "Paris" or "Parisienne."

1924 The U.S. DEPARTMENT OF COMMERCE REPORT discussed the Waltershausen dolls at length. This report said that the earliest dolls made in Waltershausen had cloth bodies and papier-mâché limbs, a type still being sold in 1924. In that year there were 20 firms making dolls and employing 50 to 200 factory hands and an even greater number of home workers. This town produced over 1,500,000 jointed dolls a year as well as wooden dolls, papier-mâché dolls and others. *Kestner* was founded here in 1805 but their bisque heads were made in nearby Ohrdruf. *A. Wislizenus* came to Waltershausen in 1851 and a few years later in 1858 *Wiesenthal, Schindel & Kallenberg* founded their factory. This report stated that Kestner and *Kämmer & Reinhardt* made the finest jointed dolls but it also mentioned *C. M. Bergmann, Otto Gans, Max Handwerck, Adolf Heller, Alfred Schroeder, Seyfarth & Reinhardt,* Gebrüder *Wernicke* and *Hugo Wiegand.* Some of the Walters-

2697. Three bent limb babies made in Waltershausen. The doll on the left was made by Kämmer & Reinhardt with a Simon & Halbig head number 126 and the other two dolls on the right were made by Kestner and have heads with mold numbers 211 and 260. *Courtesy of Sotheby Parke Bernet Inc., N.Y.*

hausen dolls could walk, talk and one of them bowed its head when its hand was shaken. The 1924 Report continued: *Waltershäuser Puppenfabrik,* the name given to *Heinrich Handwerck*'s factory after his death in 1902, was affiliated with Kämmer & Reinhardt but it was owned by Bing. The Waltershauser Puppenfabrik made its own wooden parts for dolls' joints and also supplied Kämmer & Reinhardt. The dolls were made by large scale machines with die-forming and stamping production processes. They made bent limb baby dolls and ball-jointed child dolls.

1926: PLAYTHINGS described the sights of Waltershausen, "Huge crowds of women with large baskets strapped upon their backs, carrying toys made at home to assembling plants. The burdens often six feet above their heads."★

Waltershäuser Puppenfabrik. 1902–30 and possibly later. Waltershausen, Thür. The name given to *Heinrich Handwerck*'s factory after he died. This factory was a subsidiary of *Kämmer & Reinhardt* and by 1924 became part of the *Bing* conglomerate. The factory had large scale die-forming and stamping process machinery. They made their own wooden parts for dolls' joints.

Often a W was incised in the middle of the forehead just below the cutout crown of the bisque head dolls. These Ws have been found on both Heinrich Handwerck marked dolls and Kämmer & Reinhardt-Simon & Halbig marked dolls. It seems likely that these Ws stood for Waltershauser since the name of the factory where the dolls were made was the Waltershauser Puppenfabrik.

1924: Made ball-jointed and bent-limb baby bodies for dolls.

1926: *John Hess* distributed Waltershäuser bisque-head dolly-face dolls in 21 hts. 32 to 100 cm. (12 to 39½ in.).★

Walther, Georg. 1914. Oeslau, near Coburg, Thür. Applied for a German patent (D.R.G.M.) for attaching eyes to a moving tongue.

Walther, Johann. 1900–30 and later. Oeslau, Thür., later Bavaria. Made dressed dolls at first, then in 1908 acquired a porcelain factory with *Nikolaus Oberender* where they made bisque heads for dolls. By 1910 Walther and Oberender had separated and each had his own porcelain factory. By 1921 the firm had become J. Walther & Sohn.

According to the Ciesliks the monogram marks attributed to *Strobel & Wilken* may have belonged to Walther & Sohn (See Ills. 2549, 2550, and 2551e). It should be noted that Nikolaus Oberender used his initials as a monogram in his marks. (See also Ill. 2018.)

1930: Produced all-bisque dolls and bisque dolls' heads including those for baby dolls.

Wampl, Josef. 1853 and possibly other years. Vienna. Distributed dolls.

Wanamaker, John. 1880–1930 and later. Philadelphia, Pa., New York City, and Paris. Imported, dressed, and distributed dolls. *Baby Blanche* and the more expensive *Baby Dorothy* appear to have been their own special dolls in the early 1900s. *John Doll, Jr.,* of he Philadelphia Doll family started the Wanamaker Toy Department in Philadelphia and was still manager of this department when he traveled on the LUSITANIA in 1915.

1887: Advertised *Bébés Jumeau;* dolls with bisque heads on jointed composition bodies or on muslin bodies; china heads and limbs on muslin bodies; composition heads on muslin bodies; knitted dolls and rubber dolls as well as all-bisque dolls with wigs, sleeping eyes and jointed bodies. Six hts. 5½, 6¼, 7¼, 8½, 9½ and 11 in. (14, 16, 18.5, 21.5, 24 and 28 cm.).

In addition they sold separate muslin bodies with footwear; kid bodies; bisque heads with glass eyes and wig or painted hair and eyes; composition heads with wigs and glass eyes or painted eyes and hair, as well as separate wigs. Also they sold accessories for dolls including hair brushes, combs, glasses, nursing bottles, soap, watches, kid gloves, jewelry sets and puff boxes.

1896: Advertised Bébés Jumeau.

1902: Advertised two qualities of undressed dolls having bisque heads, wigs, ball jointed composition bodies, wearing footwear and chemise. The lesser quality came in five hts. 21½, 22½, 25, 27½, and 30 in. (54.5, 57, 63.5, 70, and 76 cm.); priced $1.00 to $4.00, while the better quality came in six hts. 15½, 18, 21, 23, 24½, and 29 in. (39.5, 45.5, 53.5, 58.5, 62, and 73.5 cm.); priced $1.50 to $5.50. They also offered poorer quality dolls, which were dressed; priced 25¢ to $1.00. Among these was style no. 4370, which is shown in THE COLLECTOR'S BOOK OF DOLLS' CLOTHES, color plate 19. The head on this doll was made by *Armand Marseille* and the mark on the tag indicates that the doll was produced by *Cuno and Otto Dressel.*

1903: Baby Blanche came in five hts. 21½, 22½, 24½, 28½ and 30 in. (54.5, 57, 62, 72.5 and 76 cm.); priced

2698. Bisque head made by Armand Marseille on a Cuno & Otto Dressel doll handled and probably dressed by John Wanamaker. The doll has a blond wig, sleeping glass eyes, an open mouth and a composition body jointed at the neck, shoulders, elbows, hips and knees. Original clothes. Mark on head: "1894//A M 5 DEP// MADE IN GERMANY." Mark on clothes: Ill. 2699. There is also a Cuno & Otto Dressel Holz Masse tag. H. 19 in. (48 cm.). *Courtesy of the late Henrietta Van Sise.*

2699. Mark on a ribbon label attached to a doll handled by John Wanamaker.

$1.00 to $4.00. The best grade was sold under the name Baby Dorothy and came in 10 hts. 13, 15½, 17, 18½, 21, 23, 25½, 27½, 29½, and 35 in. (33, 39.5, 43, 47, 53.5, 58.5, 65, 70, 75, and 89 cm.); priced $1.50 to $9.50. (See THE COLLECTOR'S BOOK OF DOLLS' CLOTHES, Ill. 538.)

1916: Advertised dressed German bisque head dolls with wigs and ball jointed bodies; American composition-head dolls including those made by the *Averill Manufacturing Co;* *Schoenhut* all-wood dolls and another all-wood baby doll; celluloid dolls; *Martha Chase* dolls; and stockinet cloth dolls. Dolls' hats were a specialty and came made of straw, silk or velvet. Hats could be made to order and cost up to $18.00. Wanamaker stated that "The dolls have also their Dressmaking Department in the Toy Store, and can be further fitted there for dresses for every occasion." They also had a dolls' hospital.

1918: Sold 900 life size baby dolls made by Averill; priced at $10.00 each.

1921: Advertised dolls with composition heads covered with chamois made by disabled French soldiers.

1923–24: According to *Joseph Kallus,* Wanamaker's was the first store that stocked *Bye-Lo Babies.*★

Wanda. 1915. Made in *Mme. Lazarski*'s workshop as a *Paderewski* doll. It represented a girl going to market from her village home dressed in her best clothes.

Wangenheim, N. 1925–26. Freiberg, Saxony. Manufactured dolls.

Wanner, Mme., Paul. 1918. Paris. Created dolls.

Wannez et Rayer. 1891. Handled *Bébé Loulou* dolls.

War Bonnet. 1920. Name of doll made by *Mary Frances Woods* as style no. 1. It was an Indian doll wearing a feather war bonnet and had a blanket wrapped around its shoulders. Ht. 16 in. (40.5 cm.).

War Doll. 1898–99. Name for dolls used by *Butler Bros.;* included so-called lowbrow hair style china heads with china limbs on cloth bodies having "Flags of all Nations in their true colors" and the name of the country underneath each flag. A third of these dolls were blonds; the rest had black hair. Five hts. 10¼, 10¾, 11½, 13, and 16 in. (26, 27.5, 29, 33, and 40.5 cm.). *Filipino* and *Filipino Belle* were also shown as War Dolls.

Wardol Works. See **Potteries Toy Co. (British Toy Co.; Potteries Doll Co.)**

War-Man, The. 1915. Made by *Mme. Lazarski*'s workshop as a *Paderewski* doll. It represented the enemy in World War I.

Warmen. 1916. Carved wooden dolls made for *Mme. Paderewski.* They represented the peasants who fought for Poland's independence under General Thaddeus Kosciusko in 1794.

Warren, A. E., & Co. 1922. London. Advertised dolls in an English toy journal.

Warren Pattern Co. 1914–16. Roxbury, Mass. Advertised cutout chromolithographed cloth dolls that probably were made by *Saalfield.*

Wassy. 1930 and later. Name registered as a U.S. trademark for dolls by *Augusta Wasson Whitestone* in 1931.

Water Nymph. 1915. Made in the Mme. *Lazarski* workshop as a *Paderewski* doll. It was considered to be a doll of ill omen because of the association with water lilies.

Watford Toy Manufacturers. 1915. England. Produced dressed and undressed cloth body dolls.

Wauketoi. 1919–20. Made under a U.S. patent by the *U.S. Toy and Novelty Co.*★

Wax Dolls. Ancient times–1930 and later. A popular but perishable type of doll, made in many lands and often artistic and expensive. The wax-over-composition dolls were usually less attractive, less expensive and more durable than the wax dolls.

The Sonneberg Museum gave the provenance of one of their wax shoulder heads with painted hair and glass eyes as having been made in Hildburghausen about 1800. Ht. 15 cm. (6 in.).

Ca. 1850, Henry Mayhew commented, "They can't make wax dolls in America, Sir, so we [English doll makers] ship off a great many there. The reason why they can't produce dolls in America is owing to the climate."

The wax dolls from Paris melted in the summer heat at the 1876 Philadelphia Centennial Exhibition.

Early 1800s: Wax-head doll with wig, wire pull glass eyes, wax lower arms and red heelless ankle boots of wax was on a homespun cloth body. Ht. 9 in. (23 cm.).

1851 or later: Paper label on a *Montanari* wooden box that contained a marked Montanari wax-head doll stated that it was a *Model* doll under the patronage of the Royal family which suggests that "model dolls" were portrait dolls. Many of the wax dolls were described as "model wax dolls" or "half model wax dolls." These were usually more expensive than other wax dolls, A fine wax-over-composition doll was in what appeared to be its original box that was labeled "Model wax doll."

1856: Directions were given in GODEY'S LADY'S MAGAZINE for making Wax Dolls at home. (See **Manufacture of Wax Dolls.**)

1860: John D. Robbins in his Day Book in the collection of Elizabeth Pierce listed the following imported wax dolls. Six number 2/0; priced $3.00 to $4.75 doz. wholesale.
Dressed wax dolls size number 1; priced $2.00 doz. wholesale.
Dressed wax dolls size number 9; priced $48.00 doz. wholesale.
Dressed wax dolls size number 18; priced $60.00 doz. wholesale.
Wax sleeping babies, size numbers 2/0 to 4; priced $5.00 to $16.60 doz. wholesale.
Wax speaking babies priced $36.00 doz. wholesale.
Crying wax dolls with sleeping eyes, size number 3; priced $30.00 doz. wholesale.

Ca. 1860s. *Munnier* of Paris and his successors made and/or distributed wax-over-composition headed dolls, especially the *Motschmann type* and mechanical baby dolls,

1865: THE ENGLISHWOMAN'S DOMESTIC MAGAZINE had an article titled "Lilliput in Regent Street" which described the store of *Cremer*, Jr.

"As to dolly herself, her face and head and neck are made of wax, so are her limbs; her body is made of kid, stuffed with fine wool. Some of her poorer sisters are compelled to be content with a linen epidermis. . . . Most of the miniature ladies can be made to move their heads and to exercise their joints; some of them open and shut their eyes, and we were introduced to a baby that shrieked and kicked its arms and legs."

Ca. 1870s: *Au Paradis des Enfants* appears to have distributed wax-over-composition baby dolls.

1872: *Silber & Fleming* advertised "Best model wax dolls with wax arms, legs, and inserted hair," undressed in two sizes.

1876: Silber & Fleming advertised "Wax face ladies, the bodies stuffed with wool"; undressed, three sizes; English model wax dolls with wax arms and legs, inserted hair, 17 sizes, dressed.

1878: THE QUEEN reported, "There are the ordinary English dolls with wax heads and curling tresses, calico bodies stuffed with sawdust, and wax or, in inferior kinds—leather arms and wax legs. They vary with regard to size, 29 in. [73.5 cm.] being the largest usually sold, though we occasionally come across monsters as big as children of two or three years old, but they are generally intended as advertisements, and are too large to be played with. The baby [generic meaning] dolls in this class particularly excel, and they can be had with the hair arranged in a variety of ways, suitable either for dressing as men, women of fashion, or children, and with the eyes open and shut."

1879: Silber & Fleming advertised dolls with wax faces, stiff bodies, painted wooden legs and feet, five sizes; same doll with sleeping eyes, four sizes; dolls with wax faces, painted band or comb, earrings, fancy painted boots, long chemise, nine sizes; same dolls with sleeping eyes, five sizes; dressed model crying dolls, 15 sizes; dressed lady dolls with wax faces, stiff bodies and wooden legs, five sizes. The large show dolls had wax faces and arms, wig, and painted boots.

Ca. 1882: Silber & Fleming advertised "Wax English Model Dolls" with golden color inserted hair, wax arms and legs. Cotton cloth body stuffed with wool, 20 sizes or varieties, 13½ to over 32½ in. (34 to over 82.5 cm.); wax babies in removable clothes, 12 sizes; wax dolls in wool costumes, eight sizes; in Llama costumes 12 sizes; crying wax face dolls, stiff bodies, painted legs and feet, sleeping eyes, two sizes; with painted band or comb, earrings, painted boots, long chemise, five sizes; model crying wax head dolls with glass eyes, wax limbs, long hair, *Prince Charlie's Model Best Made Bodies,* six sizes; "Mama" and "Papa" wax head baby dolls, fur wigs, glass eyes, lace trimmed chemises, seven sizes. These dolls cried when their hands were raised.

1884: *Lauer* advertised more wax dolls than any other kind, probably many of these were wax-over-composition. They had molded hair or real hair; painted eyes, glass eyes or sleeping eyes; undressed, wearing a chemise or dressed. Many of the dolls had earrings. The two "speaking" dolls had "hoods." One also wore a chemise. Ht. 16½ in. (42 cm.); priced $9.00 doz. wholesale. Only the hood was mentioned for the second speaking doll but it had an open mouth and teeth, was 2 in. (5 cm.) taller and cost the same as the other speaking doll. "Talking" wax dolls with earrings were hts. 14 and 15 in. (35.5 and 38 cm.); priced $7.50 and $9.50 doz. wholesale.

Lauer's wax dolls were named *Baby Mine, Beauty's Daughter, Daisey, Department, Fairy Lilyan, Fairy Moonbeam, Miss Merryheart, Regina, Sleeping Beauty, Stella* and *Sunshine.*

1885: *Horsman* advertised model wax dolls with shoes and stockings, 11 sizes or styles; priced $4.00 to $36.00 doz. wholesale. Extra large wax dolls in 12 sizes or styles were priced $2.00 to $18.00 doz. wholesale; with sleeping eyes these heads came in ten sizes or styles $8.00 to $48.00 doz. wholesale.

1887: Lauer advertised wax dolls with wig, glass eyes, composition arms and legs, wearing a crocheted chemise. Hts. 8½ and 12 in. (21.5 and 30.5 cm.); priced 40¢ and 75¢ wholesale. Other wax dolls included speaking "Mama, Papa" dolls; dressed dolls with glass eyes 5½ in. (14 cm.) tall costing 33¢ doz. wholesale and large wax dolls up to 33 in. tall costing $9.75 doz. wholesale.

New named wax dolls since 1884 were *Celestia, My Darling* and *Pretty Face.*

1889: Silber & Fleming advertised wax-faced dolls with stiff bodies, four sizes; crying dolls with wax faces, painted feet, eight sizes; crying dolls with wax faces, painted band or comb, earrings, painted boots and long chemise, nine sizes; model crying dolls with wax heads and model limbs, inserted hair, glass eyes, chemise, six sizes; same with fur wigs, seven sizes or with long flowing hair, ten sizes. Sometimes the dolls had composition arms instead of wax arms; these came in nine sizes. Model wax head "Mama" and "Papa" dolls with or without glass eyes, composition limbs, chemises, 14 sizes.

1899: An advertisement in the Louvre Library listed wax dolls without chemise. Six sizes; priced $1.39 to $6.40. Half wax dolls that said, "Mama, Papa," dressed in Liberty satin were $5.10.

1900: THE GIRL'S OWN ANNUAL quoted a maker of dolls' bodies and *London Rag Dolls* in Shoreditch, England, as saying, about wax dolls, "British doll-makers have never pretended to make those exquisite creatures that are bought for the nurseries of the wealthy. These have always come from France." The owners of fine Montanari or *Pierotti* wax dolls might have differed from this opinion.

1902: The Pierottis made a group of wax portrait dolls, which were sold by *Hamleys.* These included *King Edward VII, Queen Alexandra, Lord Kitchener* and other important personages of that period.

1908: At a Paris Exposition were shown wax dolls created by *Mme. Jungbluth, Mmes. Lafitte and Désirat,* and *Mlle. Riera.*

1912: TOYS AND NOVELTIES reported "The days of the old wax dolls are over."

1914: TOYS AND NOVELTIES reported "The old style wax doll, either put out in a little shift [chemise] or dressed is still of course a tremendous seller." This seems to refute the statement made two years earlier.

1915: THE ILLUSTRATED WEEKLY JOURNAL OF HANDICRAFTS described three methods of making wax dolls at home in England.

(1) A warm liquid wax was poured into a water saturated plaster mold, allowed to cool and the excess drained off. "A doll's head made like this is rather fragile. It can be made stronger by pouring a second coat of wax; but as this makes the head heavier, the wax is sometimes reinforced in places by a layer of fine muslin, cheese cloth, or very fine papier-

mâché." This was the process most used by English doll makers.

(2) Dip wood or composition heads in wax.

(3) Carve a lump of wax to make a small doll.

East London (Federation of Suffragettes) Toy Factory made wax dolls.

1916: Doris Sylvia Bailey and Sarah Jane Baxter[+] obtained a British patent for coating dolls' heads, arms, legs, and even bodies with wax. This patent was applied to *British Ceramic* dolls.

1917: Wax dolls or wax heads were made in England by the local villagers of Braxted. *Gilbert H. Spicer* and *Laurie Hansen* also made dressed wax dolls.

1920s: *Lotte Pritzel* made wax dolls.

1926: *John Hess* distributed Art dolls of "Wax Composition." These were dressed as ladies, clowns, and men in period costumes. (See also **Manufacture of Dolls, Commercial: Made in Britian** and **Manufacture of Wax Dolls.**)★

2700. Wax shoulder head with a blond wig, stationary black pupilless eyes, closed mouth. The handsewn linen body has wax lower arms and brown wax shoes. Original clothes include a high hat of stiffened paper trimmed with ribbons and feathers. H. 11 in. (28 cm.). *Courtesy of a Estelle Johnston.*

2701. Wax head, arms and lower legs on a cloth body. It has a blond human hair wig nailed to the scalp, stationary blue glass eyes, and a closed mouth. Original clothes. H. 7½ in. (19 cm.). *Private collection.*

2702. Poured wax head doll of the 1850s period. Painted black hair, black bead-like eyes, cloth body with wax limbs. Original clothes including rosettes over the ears, white cotton gauze dress with short lace sleeves. H. 3½ in. (9 cm.). *Coleman Collection.*

2703. Poured wax head with inserted hair, stationary blue glass eyes, closed mouth, cloth body and wax arms and legs. Original clothes. *Courtesy of the late Blair Hickman.*

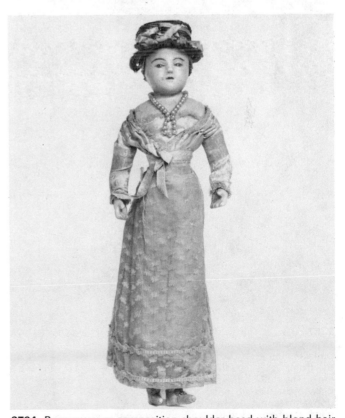

2704. Beeswax over composition shoulder head with blond hair in strips, sleeping blue glass eyes, closed mouth, a linen body, and wax-over-composition lower arms. Original clothes including pink kid boots. H. 20 in. (51 cm.). H. of shoulder head 5 in. (12.5 cm.). *Courtesy of the Margaret Woodbury Strong Museum. Photo by Harry Bickelhaupt.*

2705A & B. Papier-mâché shoulder head with a thin wax coating, on a gusseted pink kid body has a wig and painted features. Original French type regional costume of about 1850s. H. 16 in. (40.5 cm.). *Coleman Collection.*

2706. Wax-over-composition shoulder head with black wig, stationary glass eyes, closed mouth, and a cloth body with wooden arms. Original clothes of the 1850s. H. 50 cm. (19½ in.). *Courtesy of the Collection Nederlands Kostuummuseum, The Hague. Photo by B. Frequin.*

2707. Pair of wax-over-composition shoulder head dolls with cloth bodies. The doll on the left has hair inserted in a slit, wire pull sleeping glass eyes, closed mouth and kid arms. The note on the front was allegedly dated Dec. 24, 1859. H. 15½ in. (39.5 cm.). The doll on the right has molded blond hair, sleeping blue glass eyes, pierced ears, closed mouth and wax-over-composition arms and legs. Molded footwear includes high boots. The glass earrings and glass bead necklace only across the front are original. H. 15 in. (38 cm.). *Courtesy of Sotheby Parke Bernet Inc., N.Y.*

2708. Pair of wax-over-composition shoulder head dolls with molded blonde hair having a molded comb in back and glass eyes. It is on a cloth body with wooden arms and legs. Original clothes. H. 16 in. (40.5 cm.). *Private collection.*

2709A & B. Wax-over-composition shoulder head, arms and legs. It has a wig, sleeping eyes, closed mouth, cloth body with molded high heeled boots trimmed with tassels. The original clothes date this doll as ca. 1870s. H. 16 in. (40.5 cm.). *Coleman Collection.*

2710. Wax-over-composition shoulder head with a blond pompadour style wig, sleeping glass eyes, pierced ears, closed mouth and a cloth body having wax-over-composition arms and legs. Molded footwear includes tasseled boots. Clothes contemporary with the doll. H. 17½ in. (44.5 cm.). *Courtesy of Richard Withington. Photo by Barbara Jendrick.*

2711A & B. Wax-over-composition head with a blond wig, sleeping blue glass eyes, closed mouth and a cloth body with composition arms and boots. Original clothes with pink cloth stockings, blue sateen garters and paper decorations on the high button tasseled boots. H. 22 in. (56 cm.). *Courtesy of Cherry Bou.*

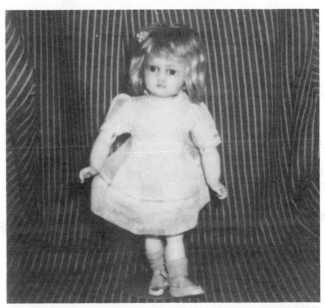

2712. Wax-over-composition socket head with blond mohair wig, sleeping brown glass eyes, closed mouth and a ball jointed composition body. Clothes are contemporary with the doll. H. 10 in. (25.5 cm.). *Private collection.*

We Dolls. 1930. Line made by the *Toy Products Manufacturing Co.* included baby and girl dolls. The all-composition babies wore short dresses with short sleeves and halo bonnets; priced 25¢ to $10.00.

Wearwell Brand. Ca. 1914–22. *Minerva* head dolls advertised by *Sears.*

Ca. 1914: Hts. 14¾, 17 and 20 in. (37.5, 43 and 51 cm.).★

Webber, William Augustus (Webber Co.). 1882–85. Medford and later Cambridge, Mass. Patented a singing doll. It appears to have been made in hts. 18 to 26 in. (45.5 to 66 cm.).

1884: Was advertised by *Ridley* in three sizes costing from $2.95 to $4.45.★

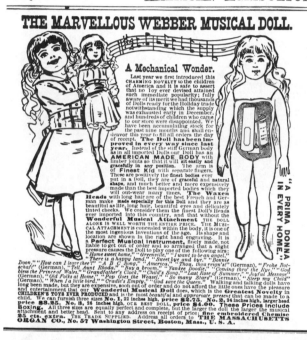

2713. Advertisement for the Webber Musical Doll in THE AMERICAN AGRICULTURIST, 1883. This doll had a French or German wax (wax-over-composition) shoulder head on an American cloth body with kid arms, Rembrandt-style wig and a musical device inside the torso. Hs. 22, 24, and 26 in. (56, 61, and 66 cm.). *Photo by Richard Merrill.*

Webb-Freyschlag. 1902. Kansas City, Mo. Distributed wholesale *Superb* kid body dolls with *Armand Marseille* bisque shoulder heads as well as separate Armand Marseille heads.

Weber. Sonneberg, Thür. Made arms and legs for dolls in his factory on Jutta Street, Sonneberg.

Weber, Franz Carl. Before 1897–1930 and later. Zurich. Distributed dolls.

1897: Catalog listed dressed dolls, dolls' articles such as hats, shoes, collars, muffs, jewelry sets and Agnes Lucas

DOLL MOTHER SEWING SCHOOL containing a 29 cm. (11½ in.) doll plus patterns and material for dressing dolls.

Late 1940s–early 1950s: Handled dolls carrying the *Jumeau* label, including those similar to the Jumeaus shown in Ill. 1340.★

Weber, Gustav. 1906. Hamburg, Germany. Applied for a German patent (D.R.G.M.) for the moving arms on a doll.

Weber, R. See **Kubelka, Josef.**

Weber Co. 1860s or 1870s. Philadelphia, Pa. Carved and turned articulated wooden doll marked "Weber Co. Phila." No paint visible, wore homespun drawers. Ht. 19 in. (48 cm.).

Webster, Stella N. Before World War I–1930 and later. Los Angeles, Calif. Stella Webster, born 1860, died 1941, was a painter who designed dolls and/or dolls' clothes. According to Agnes Daisey, a relative of Stella Webster, the dolls began as watercolor sketches.

Before World War I the all-bisque undressed dolls came from Germany, later they came from Japan.

These dolls called *Birthday Dolls* were dressed by Stella Webster. She also created a doll of a plaster composition with human hair wig and painted features. Ht. 7½ in. (19 cm.).★

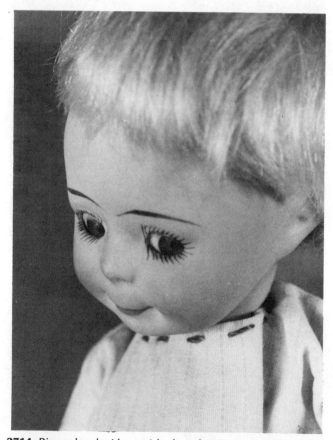

2714. Bisque head with roguish glass sleeping eyes, wig, smiling closed mouth, distributed by Franz Carl Weber. The Mark "131–16" incised on the head is identical to that on the small size Kämmer & Reinhardt mold #131 dolls. H. with replaced body is 7½ in. (19 cm.). Probably on its original body it would have been 16 cm. (6½ in.) tall. (See Mein Dicker Kleiner Liebling.) *Coleman Collection.*

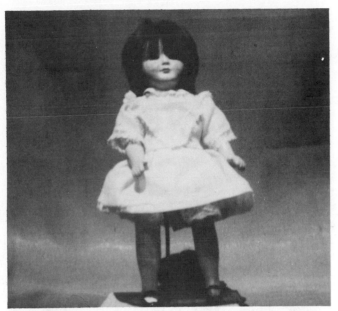

2715. Plaster composition doll made by Stella Webster. It has a wig, molded footwear and original clothes. *Courtesy of Agnes A. Daisey.*

Wedding Party. Small dolls were sometimes dressed as a wedding party and sold as a group. Large dolls were often dressed as a Bride and Groom and occasionally as a complete wedding party. Sometimes these wore miniature versions of the actual dresses of a real bride and her attendants. (See THE COLLECTOR'S BOOK OF DOLLS' CLOTHES, Ill. 417.)

1900: *La Place Clichy* advertised a village wedding party called "Noce Villageoise" which included eight small dolls representing the bride and groom, the clergyman, a female attendant, a male attendant, two parents and an official. Three of the men wore top hats and one wore a bicorne and knee breeches. These were boxed under glass and cost $1.95 for the set.

1922: *Mrs. Adj. Lowry* dressed dolls in wedding clothes.

1925: *Shackman* advertised numerous dressed all-bisque and all-celluloid dolls that could have been used as souvenirs at a wedding or on the wedding cake. Hts. 1½ to 5½ in. (4 to 14 cm.); priced $1.50 to $13.80 doz. wholesale.

1926: *HEbee-SHEbee* dolls were dressed in wedding clothes.

1927: *Efird's* advertised bride and groom dolls.

1930: *Gladys Meyers* dressed *Skippy* as a bridegroom and eight other dolls as bridesmaids.

1931: In the *Lenci* catalog the last four photographs show scenes from a marriage, including the wedding.

Ca. 1933: Quaker Doll Co. distributed dolls' house dolls dressed as brides and grooms. Hts. 3½ to 6¼ in. (9 to 16 cm.); priced $7.00 to $36.00 doz. wholesale. (See also Ill. 2185.)

Wedgewood Toy Factory. See **Keats & Co.**

Wee Gem Dolls. 1930. Produced by *W. G. Müller.*

Wee Willie Winkie. 1917. One of the *Hug-Me-Tight* cutout cloth dolls, style no. D. 105/200.

Wee-Baby. 1925–26. Line of new-born infant dolls with bisque or composition heads made by *Gustav Förster.* They had half-closed eyes, full cheeks, dimples, sunken chin and a crying voice.

Weeks & Co. 1920–22. Distributed *Nelke* dolls in England.

Weeping Dolls. 1918. TOYS AND NOVELTIES reported a patent for a weeping doll sought by *George John Hoefler.* Later dolls such as Tiny Tears had this feature.★

Weezer. 1920s. All-bisque doll with jointed neck, wore molded and painted clothes representing one of the *Our Gang* boys.

Wegner, Heinrich. 1910. Sonneberg, Thür. Applied for a German patent (D.R.G.M.) for a doll with jointed arms and legs.

Wegner, Hermann. 1886–1930 and later. Sonneberg, Thür. Applied for numerous German patents (D.R.G.M.) for dolls; 1893 patent No. 16,647 for a multi-head doll (See Ill. 1957); 1904 patent for dolls joints; 1908 patent No. 357,529 for dolls' voices (See Ill. 1697) which shows a head with *Simon & Halbig* and *Louis Lindner* marks; and 1910–12 a patent each year. By 1926 Wegner represented *Hachmeister* and advertised in Britain, dressed baby dolls.★

Wehd, Adolf. 1924–25. Hüttensteinach, Thür. Obtained a German patent (D.R.P.) for a doll's voice box.

Weibezahl, Rudolf. 1912. Halle, Germany. Applied for a German patent (D.R.G.M.) for a doll's head. (See also **Harania, Joachim.**)

Weide, Gisella. See **Weyde, Gisella.**

Weidemann Co. 1922–23. New York City. Importers, advertised kid and kidoline dolls. (See Ill. 2718.)★

Weidmann, Carl. 1900–02. Leipzig, Saxony. Applied for three German patents (two D.R.G.M.) and (one D.R.P.) for dolls' heads and/or bodies.★

Weiersmüller, Willy. 1925–30. Nürnberg, Bavaria. Made cloth dolls including baby dolls. He had distributors in Amsterdam *(A. A. Van der Kolk)*, Berlin, Hamburg, Stockholm and Vienna.

Weigirt, Leo. 1928. Nürnberg, Bavaria. Made art dolls including *Boudoir* and *Auto* dolls; some had Parisian type masks. (See also **Heho Art Dolls.**)

Weignerova, H. 1929–30 and later. Rakovnik, Czechoslovakia. Manufactured dolls.

Weill, Armand. 1927–29. Paris. Made cloth dolls including plush dolls. The dolls represented *Polichinelle, Esquimaux* and so forth. He was a member of the *Chambre Syndicale.*

Weinland, V. 1930 and later. Sonneberg, Thür. Made dolls.

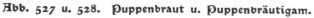

Abb. 527 u. 528. Puppenbraut u. Puppenbräutigam.

Abb. 529. Wäsche
für die Brautpuppe.

2716. Wedding dolls dressed as a bride and groom as shown in DIE WELT DER FRAU (Woman's World), 1908. The directions for making these clothes for dolls 38 to 40 cm. (15 to 15½ in.) tall were given.

2717. Wedding group of all-bisque dolls; each doll has a blond wig, painted eyes, closed mouth and is jointed at the shoulders and hips. Original clothes. Hs. 4¾ to 6 in. (12 to 15 cm.). *Courtesy of Sotheby Parke Bernet Inc., N.Y.*

2718. Marks used by Weidmann Co. for their kid and kidoline dolls.

4702
WEISS KÜHNERT & CO.
GRÄFENTHAL THÜR.
MADE IN GERMANY
6

4703
Weiss Kühnert
&
Co
Gräfenthal.
5
Made in
Germany

2719A & B. Weiss, Kühnert marks used on porcelain dolls' heads.

Weinschenk (Wemschenk), Marc, Fils, & Benda, G. 1865–67. Listed in a French directory as selling German dolls wholesale. (See Benda, Gabriel.[†])

Weinschenker, J., & Co. 1923–24. New York City. Made a line of *Mama* dolls including custom made dolls.

Weise, Bruno. 1897. Breslau, Silesia. Applied for a German patent (D.R.G.M.) for a cloth or leather doll's body.

Weiss, J. 1907–25. Vienna. Listed in directories under Dolls and Dolls' Heads.

Weiss, Kopfovi. 1920–21. Prague, Czechoslovakia. Handled *Käthe Kruse* dolls and an imitation of the Kruse dolls made in Czechoslovakia that was of a poorer quality, especially the features. Also handled *Steiff* dolls and leather dolls made by *Miss Friedmann*. Weiss was the President of the Toy Sellers Society of Bohemia.

Weiss, Kühnert & Co. 1891–1930 and later. Gräfenthal, Thür. Porcelain factory made dolls' heads. The Ciesliks have found a head marked "4703// Weiss, Kühnert//&//Co.// Gräfenthal//5//Made in//Germany." This company also used the initials "W.K.C."

Weiss, Mr. See **Knickerbocker Toy Co.**

Weiss, S., & Bruder (Brother). 1930 and later. Vienna. Made dolls.

Weissengruben, Johann. 1853 and possibly other years. Vienna. Distributed dolls according to Dr. Moskovszky.

Well Made Doll Co. 1911–30 and later. New York City. B. *Shaw* was in charge at first and later it was *S. Kalner* and S. Gershowitz. Made *Mama* dolls and stuffed character dolls, composition dolls' heads and hands.

1926–27: Member of the *American Doll Manufacturers' Association*. Made a line of infant dolls.

1928: Factory moved into a five story building. Made popular priced and high grade lines of dolls. Made dolls' heads used by *Anita Novelty Co*. Composition-head *Boudoir* dolls with silk wigs was a new line. Other lines had new dresses.

1929: Advertised baby dolls, Mama dolls and child dolls.★

Wellings, Norah (Victoria Toy Works). 1926–30 and later. Wellington, Shropshire. Chief designer for *Chad Valley* until the mid 1920s when she and her brother, Leonard Wellings, started their own factory for making cloth dolls. They specialized in making sailor dolls to be sold as souvenirs on the large steamships, especially the Cunard line. The dolls, made of velvet, velveteen, plush and felt, represented children and adults including blacks and other ethnic groups as well as fantasy characters.

The Norah Wellings cloth labels were usually on the sole of the foot of the doll. One type of label read, "Made in England//by//Norah Wellings." A round tag with a picture of a standing doll in the center had "NORAH WELLINGS'// PRODUCTIONS" around the edge.

1926–28: Applied for and was granted a British patent for a felt doll's head backed with buckram and having the inner forehead coated with a waterproof material such as plastic wood to which was attached the plaster of Paris used to hold the stationary or sleeping glass eyes in place. The head was strengthened by a wooden strut on its inside.

1927: One of the dolls was named *Cora*.

1928: Advertised that she designed models to the customer's requirements. Her dolls included Bambimine, "Daily Mail" Newsboy and So Soft.

1930: Dolls included *Dudu, Zuzu* and black dolls. The London agent was *Alec J. Payne*.

World War II. Norah Wellings was made Dollmaker to the British Commonwealth of Nations. She made dolls representing the Army, Navy, Air Force and Auxiliary Services. Harry the Hawk, a doll with a parachute, had a special label saying that a percentage of his sales was given to the R.A.F. Comforts Fund in England.

2720A & B. Felt doll with a cloth torso made by Norah Wellings. It has brown hair in strips and arranged in two pigtails, painted blue eyes looking to the side, a closed mouth and a flange joint at the neck, joints at the shoulders and hips. Original clothes including extra outfits in its original box. Marks: Ills. 2723 and 2724. H. of doll 14½ in. (37 cm.). *Courtesy of the Margaret Woodbury Strong Museum. Photo by Harry Bickelhaupt.*

Wellington, Martha L. 1883 and probably later. Brookline, Mass. Made a stockinet baby doll with pressed features including eyes and eyelids. The face, arms and lower legs were painted with oil paints, the rest of the body made of flesh colored stockinet was unpainted. The thumbs were separate and the fingers were curved. Ht. 23 in. (58.5 cm.).★

Wells, Florence. 1918–19. New York City. Obtained a U.S. patent for a cloth doll made from a sock.

2721. Norah Wellings cloth doll with a felt head and velveteen arms and legs. It has blond hair, painted blue eyes looking to the side and a closed mouth. Original clothes and a bunch of felt flowers. Mark: cloth label on wrist. Ill. 2723. H. 15 in. (38 cm.). *Courtesy of the Margaret Woodbury Strong Museum. Photo by Harry Bickelhaupt.*

Welmaid Toys. 1920. Manchester, England. Produced dolls.

Welsch, Friederike. 1925–30 and later. Breslau, Silesia. Made dolls.

Welsh Toy Industries. 1919. Cardiff, Wales, and London. Manufactured dolls with *British Ceramic* or composition heads. Their trademark was "WE-TO."

Welsch & Co. 1911–28. Sonneberg, Thür. The owners in 1911 were Ferdinand Welsch and Otto Mühlhausen. In 1917 the company was taken over by *Bing* but Welsch & Co. retained its name. Before the merger their bisque heads were made by *Max Oscar Arnold* and after the merger their bisque heads were made by *Simon & Halbig* and *Schuetzmeister & Quendt.* The mold #s used by Welsch & Co. included 200 and 201.

1920: *L. Rees & Co.* was their London distributor.

1921: Applied for two German patents (D.R.G.M.) for dolls' voices. One of these pertained to activating the voice by raising the doll's arm.

1927: Advertised in PLAYTHINGS "Welsch Specialty Dolls," dressed and undressed as well as baby dolls in baskets.★

 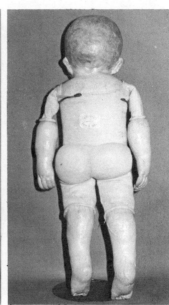

2725A & B. Oil painted stockinet head, arms and legs on a stockinet torso. The facial features are needle sculptured and molded over a wire frame, in accordance with 1883 patent of Martha Wellington. The blond painted hair has brushmarks and the large eyes are painted blue. The ears are applied and the mouth is closed. Mark: Ill. 2725C. H. 22½ in. (57 cm.). *Courtesy of Nancy Slattery.*

2722. Cloth doll made by Norah Wellings has a molded felt face, hair sewed to the scalp, painted features with side glancing eyes. Original felt clothes and a velvet cap, Wellings' tag. H. 14½ in. (37 cm.). *Courtesy of Sotheby Parke Bernet Inc., N.Y.*

2725C. Mark on a cloth label attached to the back of a Wellington doll.

F. W.
B.
GERMANY

2726. Possible mark for Friederike Welsch of Breslau.

2723–2724. Norah Wellings marks: No. 2724 is a box end or a paper tag. No. 2723 is a cloth label often found on the sole of the foot or attached to the clothes or to the wrist.

Wendenburg, Katharine. 1910. Vienna. Listed in directories under Dolls and Dolls' Heads.

Wendt, Theodor. 1924. Hamburg, Germany. Handled dolls. (See Ill. 2727.)★

Wendy. 1924. A *Tru-to-Life A 1* brand cloth doll made by *Dean.* It had a pressed face and came in two versions, one had printed clothes and the other costing nearly twice as much was fully dressed and wore a bonnet. Ht. 12 in. (30.5 cm.).

121.
Made in Germany

2727. Mark used by Theodor Wendt for dolls.

Wendy. 1925. Composition head doll with human hair and sleeping eyes made by *Goodyear Toy Co.* Ht. 17 in. (43 cm.); priced $1.50.★

Wendy. 1929. Doll dressed in felt, made by *Ideal* as a mate to *Peter Pan.* The name Wendy was registered by Ideal as a U.S. trademark for dolls; priced $2.00.

Wengel, Rt. 1929. Oberlind, Thür. Made dolls.

Wenz, Rat L. 1912–13. Exhibited costume dolls at a Bavarian Industrial Show. The dolls included ones in regional costumes such as Hungarians, Indians, Russians, Schwabians, Spaniards of the sixteenth century, and blacks. There were also dolls named "Buam" and "Dirudin."

Wenzel, Georg, & Stroh, Alfred. 1921–22. Breslau, Silesia. Obtained a German patent (D.R.P.) for dolls.

Werfpuppen. A German name for cloth body dolls.

Werkstätte der Käthe Kruse-Puppen (Workshop for Käthe Kruse Dolls). See **Kruse, Käthe.**

Werkstätte Fur Künstlerische Dekorationspuppen und Kunstgewerbe. See **Ens-Puppen.**

Wernicke Family. Ca. 1850–1930 and later. Ilmenau and Waltershausen, Thür. The father of Rudolf Wernicke worked in the doll industry in Ilmenau around 1850. Rudolf worked with *Fischer, Naumann* in Ilmenau until around 1912. He and Mr. König founded *König & Wernicke.* Two of Rudolf's brothers were also with König & Wernicke. Some of their first dolls were *Pfiffikus* with googly eyes, mulatto and Japanese dolls. During World War I crepe paper was used instead of textiles and wire coils instead of rubber elastic for stringing the dolls. At that time the demand was so great that there was no need to create new models according to Mr. Wernicke.

1924: U.S. DEPARTMENT OF COMMERCE REPORT said that the Wernicke Brothers had recently made flirting-eye dolls.

1924–28: Paul Wernicke[+] made dolls.

1925: Used disk joints as well as toddler type bodies.

1929: *Cellowachs* was their name for the celluloid heads that resembled wax.

Wernovsky, Samuel. 1930 and later. New York City. Made outfits for dolls.

Wertheimer, Arthur. 1898–99. Paris. Made dolls.

1899: Contributed materials, goodwill and rights to *Le Baby* to the *Société Française de Fabrication de Bebes & Jouets* (S.F.B.J.) valued at $5,000.★

Western Art Leather Co. 1917. Denver, Colo. Advertised stuffed leather dolls with colors on them; called "Fisher's Famous Kiddies." The nine styles were Big Chief, *Cow Boy, Cow Girl, Dutch Boy* (Hans), *Dutch Girl,* Indian Girl, *Navy Boy, Soldier Boy* and *Uncle Sam;* priced $3.00 doz. wholesale.

Western News Co. 1904 and probably other years. U.S.A. Advertised the following dolls:

All-bisque dolls with painted hair and eyes. Hts. 3⅜ to 4½ in. (8.5 to 11.5 cm.): 80¢ to $1.30 doz. wholesale.
All-bisque dolls with wigs and glass eyes. Hts. 4⅞ to 6¼ in. (12.5 to 16 cm.); priced $2.60 to $4.20 doz. wholesale.
Dolls named Fifth Avenue Dolls had bisque heads with wigs, kid bodies and footwear. Hts. 11 to 22 in. (28 to 56 cm.) came with stationary eyes. Hts. 19 to 23 in. (48 to 58.5 cm.) came with sleeping eyes.
Dressed bisque head dolls generally with stationary eyes and ball jointed bodies. Hts. 5 to 26 in. (12.5 to 66 cm.); priced $1.68 to $84.00 doz. wholesale.
Baby dolls with sleeping eyes, dressed in long muslin dresses. Ht. 20 in. (51 cm.); priced $17.00 doz. wholesale.
All-china dolls. Hts. 2 to 5¼ in. (5 to 13.5 cm.).
Dolls with china heads and limbs on cloth bodies. Hts. 4½ to 17 in. (11.5 to 43 cm.); priced 42¢ to $3.80 doz. wholesale.
Dressed cloth dolls with painted faces. Hts. 14 to 20 in. (35.5 to 51 cm.); priced $1.60 to $4.50 doz. wholesale.
Leather dolls made by *M. S. Davis Co.*
Rubber dolls. Hts. 3½ to 9½ in. (9 to 24 cm.); priced 80¢ to $8.70 doz. wholesale.
They also sold separate bisque or china shoulder heads as well as *Diana* metal heads.

Weston, Samuel, & Weston, William James. 1921–23. Applied in England and Germany for patents pertaining to dolls' eyes.★

Weston & Wells Manufacturing Co. 1913. Philadelphia, Pa. Made outfits for dolls.

Westwood, Mrs. Ethel P. 1923–27. New York City. Dressed and sold *Boudoir* dolls. The dolls wore silk and satin clothes in Mrs. Westwood's idea of the 1850s styles.

Weszely, G. 1906. Hungary. Designed wooden dolls. These dolls had turned wooden heads, and flat bodies jointed at the shoulders.

Weyde (Weide), Gisella. 1920–22 and possibly other years. Bratislava, Czecholsovakia. An artist who made dolls that were sold in Bratislava at the store *Am Munchen* and Budapest. She won prizes for her dolls at an exhibit of Artistic Dolls in Vienna. These cloth dolls were made of silk, muslin or linen. *Stewart Culin* described them as being more vital and interesting than the pictures he saw in curio shops. He especially liked a doll representing a Toreador and a lady doll with powdered hair and face patches.

Weyh, Kurt. 1930. Sonneberg, Thür. Made art dolls.

Weyh, Max. 1911–18. Wildenheid near Sonneberg, Thür. Made dolls.

1911–12: Applied for three German patents (D.R.G.M.) for character dolls' heads with glass eyes.

Weyh, Willy. 1925. Sonneberg, Thür. Bisque head *Bye-Lo* type baby dolls were marked "Germany//W. Weyh." One of these had molded and painted hair, sleeping glass eyes, closed mouth, flange neck and a cloth body with bent composition arms and legs. Size 4 was 16 in. (40.5 cm.) tall; circumference of head was 12 in. (30.5 cm.). (See also **Wohlleben, H.**)★

2728. Mark incised on the bisque head of a doll made by W. Weyh.

Wezel & Naumann. 1896. Leipzig-Rendnitz. Germany. Applied for a German patent (D.R.G.M.) for dressed dolls.

Whaley, Mrs. Charles H. Ca. 1880s–90s. Norwich, Conn. Several trade cards advertised that Mrs. Whaley was a "Manufacturer and Dealer in Dolls' Wardrobes. Dolls dressed to order in the latest styles at short notice."

Wheeler, Estelle. 1923. Los Angeles, Calif. Made a doll named *Peggy*.

Wheeler, Mrs. Grace, and Wheeler, Florence. 1915–28, Graaf-Reinet and Somerset East, Cape Province, South Africa. Mother and daughter made *Flora's Famous Dolls,* cloth dolls with pressed faces. They used an *Armand Marseille* mold #390 as their model and produced about 100 dolls a month. Archie Jameson distributed the dolls. Florence became Mrs. Bowker and in the 1980s made some reissues of the Flora's Famous Dolls using the same techniques as were used originally.

Wheeler, John. 1879. London. Handled dolls and dolls' clothes.

Wheeler, T. M. 1917–20. London. Agent for *Knight Bros. & Cooper.*

Wheelhouse, James. 1908–23. London. Made dolls.★

2729. Mark used by John Wheeler.

Whistling Boy. 1914. Doll with composition head and hands, wore a striped cotton suit and a stocking cap; distributed by *Marshall Field.* Hts. 11 and 15 in. (28 and 38 cm.); priced $4.50 and $8.00 doz. wholesale.

Whistling Boy. 1927. Composition-head doll with molded hair, puckered lips, jointed limbs, wore a colored felt suit. The doll whistled when the body was pressed; distributed by the *American Wholesale Corporation.* Ht. 9½ in. (24 cm.); priced $1.75 doz. wholesale.

Whistling Clown. 1914. Name of a doll with a composition head, cloth body, that turned its head and whistled when its chest was pressed.

Whistling Dolls. 1913–20s. Various companies made whistling dolls. Dolls with round holes in their mouth sometimes were dolls that smoked including the *Cigarette* dolls of the 1920s. Rubber dolls often contained whistles. *Marotte* sticks were made sometimes with whistles.

1894: *M. La Fossa* produced whistling dolls.

1912: *Le Petit Siffleur* was a whistling doll.

1914: *Bellas Hess* advertised Whistling Willie.[†]

1922: *Louis Wolf* handled whistling dolls.

1924–26: *George Harry Parsons* produced whistling dolls.

1926: *Averill Manufacturing Co.* made several whistling dolls and named them Whistling Cowboy, Whistling Dutch Boy, Whistling Indian, and Whistling Sailor.

1929: *Dan* and *Dolly Dingle* were produced as Whistling Dolls.

Whistling Jim. 1913–24. Bisque head made by *Gebrüder Heubach.* The head had the square Heubach mark and mold # 8774. Size number 2 was 11 in. (28 cm.); number 3 was 12 in. (30.5 cm.).

1924: *Montgomery Ward* called a doll *Whistling Tom* that looked like Whistling Jim. ★

Whistling Jim. 1916. Composition head doll made by *Effanbee.* It had molded hair in the same style as *Baby Grumpy,* painted eyes, a round mouth with a hole, a flange type neck, a cloth body stuffed with cork, that contained the whistling mechanism. The lower arms were composition. It wore a red and white striped shirt and blue overalls trimmed with red tape. The black cloth shoes were part of the feet. On the clothes was a cloth ribbon label reading "EFFANBEE//Whistling Jim// TRADE MARK." Ht. 16½ in. (42 cm.).

It is not known whether this was the doll advertised by the *Tootle Campbell Dry Goods Co.* or whether that doll had a bisque head made by *Gebrüder Heubach.*

2730. Bisque head made by Gebrüder Heubach called Whistling Jim. It has molded blond hair, intaglio blue eyes and a round hole in the mouth. The flange neck is on a cloth body with composition hands. The numbers on the head are 49587 74. H. 13 in. (33 cm.). *Courtesy of Sotheby Parke Bernet Inc., N.Y.*

EFFANBEE
Whistling Jim
TRADE MARK

2731. Mark on Whistling Jim composition-head dolls made by Effanbee.

Whistling Pete. Ca. 1918. Celluloid-head doll dressed as a boy and distributed by *Shackman.* When the doll's head was pressed it whistled and cried with a double voice. Ht. 6 in. (15 cm.); priced 35¢.

Whistling Tom. 1922–24. Name given to two different dolls distributed by *Montgomery Ward.*

1922: Imported doll with composition head, metal wire body, wooden legs, and dressed in a blouse and pants extending to just below the knees. It whistled and turned its head when the chest was pressed. Ht. 13¼ in. (33.5 cm.); priced 49¢.

1924: Montgomery Ward described Whistling Tom as having a bisque head, molded hair, composition hands on a cloth body. The doll whistled when the chest was pressed. By 1924 the patent on the earlier *Whistling Jim* would have probably expired.

White, C. & H. First half of the 1800s. Milton, Portsmouth, England. Made doll with leather heads. These dolls were often dressed as *Pedlars.*

White Daisy. 1917. Name of a doll with composition head and hands, molded hair, cloth body, distributed by *Charles William.* Ht. 11 in. (28 cm.); priced 49¢.

White, James C. 1928. Sewickley, Pa. Obtained a U.S. patent for, "Movable eyes which can be moved at will by the child by moving a lever at the back of the head or by pulling a cord. . . . The purpose is to enable the child to move the eyes of the doll to simulate winking."

White House Toys. 1918. England. Listed under Dolls in a British trade journal directory.

Whitehouse, John N. 1913–28. New York City. In 1928 he assigned to *Markon* a U.S. patent for operating the eyes of a doll so that it appears to sleep.★

Whitestone, Augusta Wasson. 1931. Long Island City, N.Y. Registered *Wassy* as a trademark in the U.S. for dolls.

Whitlock, Edwin L., and Madison, James. 1923–26. New York City. In 1926 they obtained a U.S. design patent for dolls.★

Whitman, Mabel. 1930. Creator of *Princess Wee-Wee* which was made by *Regal.*

Whitney & Co. 1927 and probably other years. San Diego, Calif. Distributed dolls made by *American Character Doll Co.* and *Averill Manufacturing Co.* In 1927 Whitney won a special award for their window display of dolls.

Wholesale Toy Co. 1915–21. London. Made baby and character dolls with composition heads and limbs, cloth bodies. These included a line which they called *Ross Dolls.* The entire doll was made in their factory, even the wig and the removable clothes for their dressed dolls.

1915: Made *Esquimaux* dolls.

1917: Agent was *Joseph Hopkins.*

Wholesalers. Used manufacturers' catalogs from which they took retailers' orders. When manufacturers did not have catalogs the wholesalers often had their own catalogs or even used clippings from PLAYTHINGS or other magazines.

Whoopee. 1929. Name of a *Boudoir* doll made by *Gerling.*

Whyte, Ridsdale & Co. 1867–1927. London. Handled *British Ceramic,* bisque, wax, composition, celluloid, and cloth dolls.

1913: Advertised *Iris, Lily* and *Rose.* Other dolls priced 52¢ doz. wholesale and up.

2732. C. & H. White paper label found on dolls with leather heads.

1914: Advertised all-bisque *Kewpies,* a dressed Dolly Dimple which they described as having a "china head," a squeeze doll that said "Mama" and a "floating" doll.

1915: Advertised first British Ceramic head dolls on the market. These had British Ceramic shoulder heads, hands and forearms on pink cloth bodies. Among the dressed British Ceramic dolls was one in a sailor suit and a baby doll in a long dress. The French dolls included jointed ones with bisque heads, dressed or undressed. Many more sizes were available for the French dolls than for the British dolls but the prices appeared to be roughly the same except for some of the very elaborately dressed French dolls. The French dolls also included celluloid child and bent limb baby dolls as well as India rubber dolls. Also there were floating *Snow Dolls* and cloth dolls named *Arctic Baby, Meg, Tipry* and *Vipi.*

1916: Advertised *Doris* and a range of dressed dolls with composition faces; priced $1.25 doz. wholesale and up.

1917: Advertised many new baby doll numbers, some of them crying and some of them dressed in long silk robes. The British Ceramic jointed dolls had glass eyes or painted eyes and the bodies were usually stuffed with hair. Some of these appear to have a wax finish. The French dolls had bisque or composition heads. Some of the dolls were talking dolls. Dolls' heads and wigs were sold separately.

1926: Advertised felt dolls a new series, dressed in colored felt, style Nos. L. 3/1318 and L3/1483. Hts. 7 and 10 in. (18 and 25.5 cm.); priced $1.13 and $2.13 doz. wholesale. Other dolls included *Cherub; Harold, the College Boy; Robert; New Born* Babies.

1927: Advertised a doll named *Black Bird.*

Wide-Awake Doll. 1913–14. All-bisque doll whose height in centimeters was marked on the sole of its feet.★

Widget. 1926. U.S. trademark for dolls registered by *Ray W. Dumont.*

WIDGET

2733. Widget mark used by Ray Dumont for dolls.

Widmann, O., & Co. 1924–30 and later. Great Britain. Advertised dolls.

1930: Sole British agent for *Löffler & Dill.*

Wiederseim, Grace. See **Drayton, Grace.**

Widows Industrial Home. India. Made dolls.

Wiefel & Co. 1912–30 and later. Steinbach near Sonneberg, Thür. Their Erste Steinbacher Porzellanfabrik (First Steinbach Porcelain Factory) made dolls' heads and used the initials "E. st. P." This factory had been founded in 1900 by Max Kiesewetter and was taken over by Hugo Wiefel in

1912 when they appear to have begun the making of dolls' heads. Wiefel retired in 1926 and the successors were a Robert Carl and Gustav Heubach.

Wiegand, Carl. 1876–83. New York City. Made papier-mâché heads for dolls. These were stamped with black ink between the shoulder blades. The stamp read "WIEGAND'S PATENT//May 23, 1876." Hts. of head only, 4, 4½, and 7 in. (10, 11.5, and 18 cm.). (See Ill. 2735.)★

Wiegand, Hugo. 1911–30 and later. Waltershausen, Thür. Manufactured dolls and baby dolls.

1923: Applied for a German patent (D.R.G.M.) for dolls.

1926: Applied for two German patents (D.R.G.M.), one for the limb movements of a doll and the other for dolls' eyes.

Advertised *Mama* dolls, baby dolls that could sit or stand wearing a chemise, or fully dressed. *Gustav Burmester* of Hamburg was a factory representative. British agent was *Cowan, de Groot & Co.*

1927: Advertised clockwork dolls and parts for dolls as well as dolls including Sweet Nell[+] (Nel) and *Edelkind.*

1928: Applied for a German patent (D.R.G.M.) for jointed dolls. Obtained a German patent (D.R.P.) relating to the pendulum movement of dolls' eyes. Dolls had bead necklaces to hide the neck joint. The toddler type bodies could sit with their legs out straight.

1929: Obtained a German patent (D.R.P.) for a doll's jointed body. One of their dolls was named Sonny Boy.

1930: Berlin agent was *M. Michaelis & Co.* Wiegand advertised "Waltershausen" jointed dolls and babies. He registered Sonny Boy as a trademark in Germany for dolls. ★

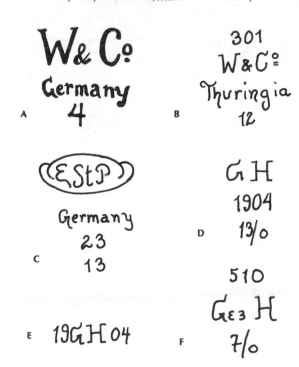

2734A, B, C, D, E & F. Marks of Wiefel & Co. found on bisque dolls' heads.

2735A. Wax-over-composition head which was made in accordance with the patent obtained by Carl Wiegand. It has molded hair, painted eyes, closed mouth, and a cloth body. Original clothes. Mark: III. 2735B. H. 20½ in. (52 cm.). H. of shoulder head 6 in. (15 cm.). *Courtesy of Z. Frances Walker.*

Wiegand's Patent
MAY 23, 1876

2735B. Mark on a doll's head made by Carl Wiegand.

2736A. Hugo Wiegand advertisement for dolls in DEUTSCHE SPIELWAREN ZEITUNG, February, 1927. The dolls include Edelkind and Sweet Nell dolls, and baby dolls.

Germany
H.W.

2736B. Mark found on Hugo Wiegand dolls.

Wiele, A. Munich, Bavaria. 1898. Assignee of a German patent (D.R.G.M.) by *Peter Cadie* for turning a doll's head.

Wiener, August. 1903–30. Köppelsdorf, Thür. Made porcelain dolls' heads of various kinds with and without wigs.

1903: Applied for a German patent (D.R.G.M.) pertaining to dolls' eyes.

1930: *M. Michaelis & Co.* handled the products.

Wiener (Weiner), David. 1918–26. New York City. Obtained at least three U.S. patents for dolls.★

Wiener, Ferdinand. 1909–20. Köppelsdorf, Thür. Manufactured dolls.

1909: Applied for a German patent (D.R.G.M.) for sleeping eyes in a celluloid doll's head.

Wiesendanger, Mme. 1930. Paris. Made and/or distributed dolls.

Wiesenthal, Schindel & Kallenberg. 1858–1926 and possibly later. Waltershausen, Thür. In the late 1800s this company specialized in wax dolls. Bisque head dolls have been found marked "Simon & Halbig//W S K." The W S K were the initials used by this company.

1898: Made and exported dolls.

1904: Applied for a German patent (D.R.G.M.) for dolls.

1911: Applied for a German patent (D.R.G.M.) for sleeping eyes in bisque dolls' heads.

1913: Specialized in jointed child and baby dolls.

1924: U.S. DEPARTMENT OF COMMERCE REPORT stated that Wiesenthal, Schindel & Kallenberg made *My Dearie* type dolls.★

Wiesner, H., & Co. 1925–26. Germany. Obtained a British patent for dolls' eyes comprised of a transparent disc in which there was a pupil that moved freely.

Wiggle-Waggle Dolls. 1915. Trade name used by *Owens-Kreiser* for dolls made of various materials including metal, cloth and so forth; priced 50¢ and $1.00.

Wiggsie. 1916. Name of style no. 575 made by *Trion* and representing a girl with a short hair wig with bangs and a straw hat.

Wigs. Most dolls had either a wig or hair attached to the doll's head. Various grades of wigs were made; the human hair sewed wigs were the most expensive. Especially in the early 1900s some dolls with molded hair also had wigs. Unfortunately wigs seem to have suffered the ravages of time more than any other part of a doll. Also the right wig can vastly improve the appearance of a doll. Most wigs before the days of saran were made of mohair which came from Tibetan goats and was sometimes called Thibet.

According to various reports in 1912 and 1918 in TOYS AND NOVELTIES, mohair was not spun in Germany at all. It was an English industry; mohair yarn needed moisture which was available in Britain but insufficient in Germany. Prior to World War I mohair was manufactured in Bradford,

2737. Bisque head doll made by Wiesenthal, Schindel & Kallenberg. It has a wig, sleeping blue glass eyes, pierced ears, open mouth with teeth, and a ball jointed composition body. Mark: II W S K Germany. H. 19 in. (48 cm.). *Courtesy of Richard Withington. Photo by Barbara Jendrick.*

WSK
541
21

2738. Mark on bisque-head dolls made by Wiesenthal, Schindel & Kallenberg.

England, and England had a monopoly of this commodity made of the long hair of the Angora goat which was found in Asia Minor.

Some Angora goats were raised in Southern France for mohair.

Before the war, Sonneberg alone worked up several million marks' worth of wigs annually. (A mark was then worth about 25¢.) Mohair wigs were not made during World War I.

In the late 1800s Rembrandt wigs (See Ill. 1328) were most popular. After 1900 the hair was often parted on the side instead of the middle and in the 1920s bobbed hair was popular.

1806 or earlier: 250 Tibetan goats were brought from Asia to France for breeding purposes.

1860–61: "China" dolls with natural hair were imported by *John D. Robbins.* Natural hair could be human or animal hair. Doll size 3/0; priced $3.00 doz. wholesale.

1865: THE ENGLISH WOMAN'S DOMESTIC MAGAZINE describes wigs for dolls: "Dolly simply shifts her head of hair. Cunning she is, and may sometimes be seen in curlpapers, knowing well that her ringlets are all ready for her in a drawer up-stairs. Whatever be the prevailing fashion of the hair, dolly's wigs are made accordingly; for morning calls, for the park, for dinner, for the opera, she takes one off and puts another on." It sounds as though the well-dressed doll had many wigs, but collectors today are fortunate to find even one original wig.

1885: *Horsman* advertised bisque-head dolls and composition-head dolls with white fur hair. Their "French" bisque heads had natural hair.

Late 1800s and early 1900s: In Germany hair dressing shops specialized also in repairing dolls because they had access to hair that could be used for making wigs. Contemporary photographs showed such shops with wigs both for humans and dolls plus parts for the composition bodies of dolls.

1903: The pompadour was a popular coiffure style. Human hair was used for American dolls' wigs, mohair and Angora wool were used for imported dolls' wigs.

1904: THE PRIZE reported that girls from Switzerland sold their blond hair for very little money; however, most flaxen hair dolls' wigs were made of mohair.

1908: The new color for dolls' wigs was a dull gold called "Tosca." This and the bright yellow wigs were the most popular in color.

1917: *Max Handwerck* made wigs of glass fibers.

1920s: Wool yarn, silk yarn, tow, flax, and even string were used for wigs as well as mohair and human hair. The fluffy flax used by *Lenci* was sewed to the scalp of the doll in strips. TOYS AND NOVELTIES in 1923 reported that it was common to find black thread used to sew up light-haired wigs while for dark haired wigs white stitching was common.

PLAYTHINGS in 1927 reported that most of the dolls' wigs were made by hand using the same method as had been used for at least 20 years. China was the principal source for human hair. The hair was cleansed, softened and changed to any desirable shade. "Then it is woven, several hairs at a time into long strings and these strings are sewed on forms of cloth. Each style of wig requires a different method of sewing. Then the hair is either curled into the desired long curls, ringlets, roll curls, marcelles, and any number of other styles."

1939: Emma Clear advertised mohair wigs priced 35¢; factory made "real hair" wigs of split Oriental hair, bleached and dyed to desired shade, 75¢ and up; Caucasian hair $2.00 to $3.75. (See also **Manufacture of Dolls,** including **Manufacture of Wigs.**)★

2739. Mark used by the Wigwam Co. for their dolls.

Wigwam Co. 1917–18. Syracuse, N.Y. Formerly Onondaga Indian Wigwam Co.† Made dolls with composition heads and hands and cloth bodies, came with or without wigs, painted stationary or sleeping eyes, dressed as babies, boys, girls, clowns, soldiers, or nurses. The removable clothes buttoned on.

1917: Priced 50¢ to $5.00.

1918: Made hundreds of dolls a day, hoped to make thousands of dolls each day with the specially designed machinery.★

Wild, Lewis. 1884–1926 and later. London and Sonneberg, Thür. Sole agent of "Made in Canada Doll" *(Dominion Toy Co.)* for Great Britain, Australia, India and New Zealand.

1915: Canadian dolls priced 25¢ to $10.50.

1925: Distributed dolls of *Arthur Schoenau* including the Cherub doll.

1926: Sole agent for *Buschow & Beck*'s *Minerva* metal heads.★

Wild West Dolls. 1895. Name of bisque-head dolls with glass eyes, open mouth, teeth, fully jointed composition body, dressed as an Indian Brave, Indian Squaw or a Mexican Cowboy, distributed by *Butler Bros.* Ht. 13¾ in. (35 cm.); priced $8.35 doz. wholesale. Many other dolls wore Wild West costumes. (See also **Cowboys, Indians,** and Ill. 914.)

Wildfang. 1929. Trademark registered in Germany by *Wagner & Zetzsche* for dolls.

Wilhelm, Grete (née Hujber [Huiber]). 1919–20. Vienna. According to Dr. Eva Moskovszky, Grete Wilhelm obtained an Austrian patent for a process for producing dolls' heads by pressing newspapers into a ball, covering the ball with linen, pulling out a small part of the fabric to form the nose and rolling the end of the fabric around a wooden stick to form the neck. The head was dipped into a glue solution and while still wet the features were formed and then it was painted. It was claimed that this was a process to produce dolls very inexpensively.★

Wilhelmina. 1912–14. Composition head doll with mohair wig, painted eyes, open-closed mouth made by *Horsman* as style No. 194. It wore a Dutch type costume with felt simulated wooden shoes; mate to *Willem*. It was advertised by *Bellas Hess* in 1914.

Willard, Frank. 1926–29 and probably other years. United States. An artist who drew cartoons. The oilcloth and all-bisque dolls which represented *Moon Mullins* and *Kayo* were based on his designs.

Willem. 1912. Composition head dolls with mohair wig, painted eyes, open-closed mouth, cloth body with composition hands, produced by *Horsman*. It wore a Dutch costume consisting of a striped shirt, knickers, plain dark stockings, felt simulated wooden shoes, and a turban. It was a mate to *Wilhelmina*.

Willerton & Roberts. 1768 and possibly other years. Turners who made and repaired dolls. They also sold "Dutch dolls," the wooden dolls probably made in the Grödner Tal, according to Mary Hillier. The shop was in London.

Willette, Adolphe Léon. 1910–26. Paris. Born 1857 in Châlons-sur-Marne, died 1926 in Paris. He was a painter, lithographer, illustrator, and designer, as well as an officer of the Legion of Honor. He designed jointed dolls, especially *Columbine, Pierrot and Pierrette* for *Gallais*. These dolls in the Watteau style were marked on the arm -W-. He designed the covers for French store catalogs such as the "Toy Gifts" ones for La *Samaritaine* in 1906 and 1909.

Willhelmina. 1907–13. One of the dolls created by *Elizabeth Scantlebury*. It was dressed as a Dutch girl and a sister to Pieter to show American school children how people in Holland dressed.

William, Charles. 1915–30 and probably other years. New York City. Mail-order distributor who advertised a variety of dolls.

1915: Advertised *Campbell Kids, Parsons-Jackson* dolls and *Uneeda Biscuit Boy*.

1917: Advertised Can't Break 'Em† dolls, Everybody's Pet, *Lady Fuller, Peterkin,* Picnic Girl, *Phoebe Snow, Romper Boy, Summer Girl* and *White Daisy*. (See THE COLLECTOR'S BOOK OF DOLLS' CLOTHES, Ill. 715.)

1924: Advertised *K & K* dolls, *Little Sister; Mama* dolls, *Minerva* metal dolls, *Topsy Turvy* with a celluloid face, all-metal bent limb baby doll with wig, sleeping eyes and chemise, ht. 12 in. (30.5 cm.), priced $1.89; low-brow dolls with china heads and limbs, and cloth bodies, ht 11⅜ in. (29 cm.); priced 25¢. Bisque head dolls were the same price for the same height whether they had fully jointed composition bodies or kidlyne bodies with universal joints. The bisque-head dolls on composition bodies came dressed or wearing only a chemise. The latter came in four hts. 13, 17¼, 20, and 26¾ in. (33, 44, 51 and 68 cm.); priced 98¢ to $4.48. They also advertised separate bisque shoulder heads and dolls' accessories. (See THE COLLECTOR'S BOOK OF DOLLS' CLOTHES, Ill. 757.)

1926: Advertised *Boudoir* dolls, *Bye-Lo* Baby, china head dolls, cutout cloth dolls, *Dolly Mine, Flossie Flirt, Golf Boy,* Hush-a-Bye Baby, K & K dolls, *Life-Like Baby, Little Red Riding Hood,* Mama dolls, Minerva metal heads, *Miss Muffet* and *Our Gang*. They still advertised bisque-head dolls on composition bodies either fully jointed or bent limb, and kidlyne bodies, but there were only two of each type, the majority of the dolls were composition heads on plush cloth bodies. A wooden-head doll had metal balls for its hands and feet. Ht. 6¾ in. (17 cm.); priced 25¢. (See THE COLLECTOR'S BOOK OF DOLLS' CLOTHES, Ill. 761.)

Williams, J. A., & Co. 1923–30. Pittsburgh, Pa., and New York City. Factory distributor of *Averill Manufacturing Co., Nelke* dolls and *Tinker Toys.*★

Williamson, Mr. 1924. Great Britain. Artist who designed newspaper cartoons especially for the Children's Corner. *Chad Valley* made dolls based on his designs called *Dan* and *Dolly.*

Willie Frog. 1923. Doll advertised as having a human form, wiggly arms and legs. It squeaked when the stomach was pressed. This *Mawaphil* cloth doll was made by *Rushton Co.*

Willie Walk. 1921. Name of a doll dressed as a clown and made by *C. W. Allen Co.* The doll was attached to a wheel so that the legs moved as the wheel turned.

Willie Winkle. Early 1900s. Cutout chromolithographed cloth doll produced by *Horsman.* The boy doll wore a blue knee-length sailor suit with red trimming. Ht. 9½ in. (24 cm.).

Willmann, Carl. 1878. Germany. Produced *Täuflinge* type dolls.

Willow Pottery. See **Hewitt & Leadbeater.**

Wilma. 1916. Felt doll made by *Steiff.* Five hts. 28, 35, 43, 50 and 60 cm. (11, 14, 17, 19½ and 23½ in.).

Wilson Bros. Ltd. 1923–30 and later. London. Made dolls.

1926: Advertised bent limb baby dolls in chemises.

Wilson Doll Co. 1920–21. Birmingham, England. Assembled dolls, distributed dolls and dolls' parts, repaired dolls.

1920: Advertised dolls' heads and dolls' limbs.

1921: Advertised latest models in heads, bodies, limbs, wigs, moving and fixed eyes, celluloid dolls made to order; all kinds of repairs for trade or private persons.

1910
W

made in Germany

6

2740. Mark used by Ernst Winkler for dolls.

Wiltshaw & Robinson (Carlton Works). 1915–23. Stoke-on-Trent, Staff. Made *British Ceramic* dolls' heads and all-British Ceramic dolls including Pooksie, which was designed by *Mabel Lucie Attwell,* as well as those made from the comic designs of *John Hassall.*

Winkler, Ernst, Firm. 1908–25 and later. Sonneberg, Thür. Made and exported dolls and dolls' parts.

1910: One of the Sonneberg group of Grand Prize Winners at the Brussels Exposition. ★

Winnie The Pooh. 1930. Series of cloth dolls made by the *Thames Valley Toy Co.* This series probably represented characters, including Christopher Robin, in the Milne book of this name.

Winnie Winkle. 1929. All-bisque doll with jointed neck, molded and painted clothes, based on the "Winnie Winkle" cartoon drawn by *Martin A. Branner. Marshall Field* had the exclusive wholesale distribution rights.

Winsome Baby. 1926–29. Infant dolls with bisque or composition heads made by *Gerling.* These dolls wore various infant attires. The trademark showed a girl seated in a chair, holding a doll upright and the words, "Winsome//Trademark//Baby Doll//THE GERLING TOY CO., N.Y."

Winsome Winnie. 1929. Trademark for dolls registered in the U.S. by *Ideal.*

Winters, Anton. 1861–1913. Philadelphia, Pa. Louis L. Reinecke was born in 1861 the year Anton Winters started his business. In 1880 Louis Reinecke began working for Winters. In 1893 Winters died and Reinecke handled the firm for Winters' estate. In 1904 the name became Winters & Reinecke.† They were importers and wholesale distributors of dolls.

1912: Advertised *Kestner* and *Heinrich Handwerck* jointed dolls, kid body dolls, cloth dolls, celluloid dolls, dressed dolls, and parts for doll hospitals.

Wirt. 1913–16. Felt doll made by *Steiff,* distributed by *Borgfeldt* in the U.S. It represented a barkeeper. Ht. 35 cm. (14 in.); priced $2.35 in New York in 1913.

Wisbey, James, & Co. 1838–1929. London. Imported and distributed dolls.

1914: Advertised "Dame of Fashion," Polichinelle, Red Riding Hood, "School Girl and Boy," and dolls dressed as

2741. Mark used by Gerling for their Winsome Baby dolls.

Albanians, Brigands, Bulgarians, Generals, Golfers, Magicians, Montenegrins, Mountaineers, Princes, Serbians, Soldiers and Tennis Players.

1917: Advertised "Hard and soft dolls of all types," including leading lines of British and Allied dolls.

Wisconsin Deluxe Doll and Dress Co. 1927–30 and later. Milwaukee, Wisc. Manufactured dolls.

Wise Dolls. 1921. Black cloth dolls produced by *Horsman*. They included *Baby Wise, Lizzie Wise, Mammie Wise* and *Miss Polly Wise.*

Wislizenus, Adolf. 1851–1930 and later. Waltershausen, Thür. In 1894 W. Heinecke was the successor and by 1911 *Hans Heinecke* was the owner of the firm. Before World War I *Mr. Eckardt* was the chief modeller. They used *Ernst Heubach* bisque heads for the dolls that they made. A bisque head has been found marked "28 A.W. Special II Germany."

1867: Wislizenus was a creditor of *Chatel et Louapt* according to Mme. Florence Poisson, Curator of the Roybet Fould Museum.

1894: Applied for a German patent (D.R.G.M.) for a jointed doll.

1897: Assignee of a patent for a *waist jointed Täufling* by *Otto Sörgel*. Made a doll with the hips forming a ball joint at the waist so that the upper torso could move.

1910: Applied for a German patent (D.R.G.M.) for ball-jointed character baby dolls. Registered *Queen Quality*.

1911: Advertised a line of heads with painted eyes or with sleeping eyes and eyelashes as well as a doll named *Gretchen*.

1912: Advertised ball jointed dolls of *Mattlack*. Applied for a German patent (D.R.G.M.) for baby dolls. One of the Queen Quality dolls was a life sized baby doll.

1916: Advertised Art Waltershäuser dolls.

1920: Advertised *Mein Glückskind* (My Lucky Child).

1921: Used a four leaf clover and the initials "A.W.//W." as a trademark.

1925: Applied for a German patent (D.R.G.M.) for a mechanical walking doll.

1927: Applied for a German patent (D.R.G.M.) for dolls.★

Witch. See **Scarey Ann.**

Witch. Dolls in Welsh costumes and/or pedlar costumes sometimes resembled dolls dressed as Witches.†

Wittenberg, Louis C. Before 1897–1927. Brooklyn, N.Y. and elsewhere. According to PLAYTHINGS he was one of the best known doll salesmen. Born in 1859 in Indianapolis; worked for Edward A. Prior & Co. of Baltimore, Md.

1897: Became commission salesman for *Horsman*.

1907: Joined Horsman as a firm member.

1927: Died in Brooklyn, N.Y.

Witthauer, Carl Otto. 1909–26. Neustadt near Coburg, Thür. and Bavaria. Made dressed dolls.

1910–11: Applied for two German patents (D.R.G.M.) for dolls.★

Witthauer, Christopher. 1862–1909. Neustadt near Coburg, Thür. Manufactured dolls.

1899: Applied for a German patent (D.R.G.M.) for a doll made by covering molded papier-mâché with felt or another textile.

1903: Applied for a German patent (D.R.G.M.) improving the 1899 patent.★

Wittzack, Emil. 1862–1921. Gotha, Thür. Firm was founded in 1862 but Emil Wittzack did not assume control until 1878. Made wool dolls which were given the trade name *Worsted Dolls*. Factory agent was *H. E. Eckart* at least from 1891–1914 when they published catalogs of the Wittzack dolls.

1891–1914: The dolls included knitted dressed dolls representing clowns, boys, girls, soldiers and dolls in regional costumes; plus dolls' clothes.

1913: Advertised woolen dolls with celluloid heads and character babies.

1921: Advertised character babies, cloth dolls and clowns.★

Woerlein, Eugenia. 1912. Germany. Used *Meissen* porcelain heads on Biedermeier figures to be used as Tea Cozies. Exhibited at a Bavarian Industrial Show dolls representing fairy tale dwarfs and old peasant women with pointed shawls.

Wohlleben, A. H. 1921–30 and later. Baltimore, Md. Made and imported dolls.★

Wohlleben, H. 1909–30 and later. Sonneberg, Thür. Successor was Wohlleben & *Willy Weyh*. Manufactured dolls.

Wolf, Gustav. 1930. Neuköln, Germany. Made dolls' shoes, which were distributed by *G.F. Hertzog & Co.*

Wolf, Louis, & Co. 1870–1930 and possibly later. Sonneberg, Thür., Nürnberg, Bavaria, Boston, Mass., and New York City. Their Sonneberg office and factories were taken over by *Leutheuser* during World War I. In 1928 they merged with *Bing* forming the Bing-Wolf Corp. Louis Wolf & Co. were *Verlegers* who produced and distributed dolls. Some of the bisque head baby dolls with mold # 152 were also marked "L. W. & Co." These heads were made by *Hertel, Schwab.*

The size-height relationship for these 152 baby dolls was:

Size	Height		Circumference	
No.	in.	cm.	in.	cm.
2	12	30.5	8¼	21
5	14	35.5	10	25.5
10	17	43		
12	21	53.5		

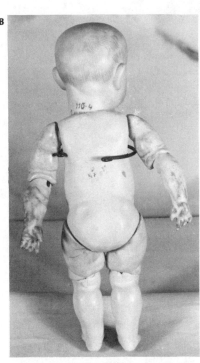
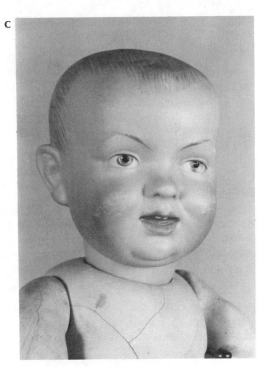

2742A, B & C. Composition body with rubber half-ball joints patented by Adolf Wislizenus in Germany in 1911 (No. 421481). The bisque head has molded and painted brown hair, blue eyes and an open-closed mouth with two upper teeth. Marks shown in the first COLLECTOR'S ENCYCLOPEDIA OF DOLLS, Ills. 1692 and 1694. H. 12 in. (30.5 cm.). *Private collection.*

2743

2744A

2744B

2743–2744A & B. Marks found on Wislizenus bisque head dolls.

2745–2746. Marks used by Louis Wolf for dolls, with heads made by Hertel, Schwab.

1907: Applied for a German patent (D.R.G.M.) for dolls.

1913: Emil Eschwege became a member of the firm after 20 years of service with the Company.

1915: Advertised that they controlled four large toy factories in Sonneberg as well as many "House-workers." They had about 1,000 models including bisque and composition character dolls in various sizes. They specialized in baby dolls and Red Cross Nurses.

1918: Advertised that the American branch refused to accept dolls made in Germany when a shipment from Holland arrived in Oct. 1918. These dolls ordered before the war had been bought and paid for in 1914. Louis Wolf was the sole agent for the all-composition *Perfection* dolls. Also they advertised over 300 styles other than all-composition dolls at various prices.

1919: Agent for *Giebeler-Falk Doll Corp.*

1922: Advertised 1500 to 1800 style numbers of dolls with fully jointed composition bodies, kid bodies, kidaline bodies and hair stuffed bodies. Dolls had bisque heads or were all-composition. Some dolls had sleeping eyes, others winked, as well as slept and some dolls whistled. The newest fashions in dolls' clothes were French and Dutch costumes. Some of the felt dolls were dressed as Dutch peasants. Marottes on sticks were made with musical chimes so that the faster they were turned the more they played.

1923: Advertised an *Aunt Jemima* doll with a red polka dot umbrella and basket.

1925: Producer and sole distributor of *Happiness Dolls.*

1926: Represented over 400 manufacturers in America, Austria, Canada, Czechoslovakia, England, France and Germany including *W. Bimblick & Co., Chad Valley,* Jedco *(Jeanette Doll Co.),* Kiddie Specialty Corp., *W. G. Müller,* and *Seyfarth & Reinhardt.*

Their dolls included *Pretty Peggy, Nursery Rhyme* line; *Baby Tunes, Mama* dolls, character dolls, fully jointed dolls and novelty dolls.

1927: Registered "Baby Tunes" in U.S. as a trademark. Obtained a U.S. patent for improving musical dolls such as Baby Tunes but complained that other companies were imitating their doll. Happiness Dolls were still being advertised. Distributed *Baby Dahne* made by *Hoest & Henderson.*

A Louis Wolf representative stated in TOYS AND NOVELTIES that infants in long dresses were here to stay but the real sellers were the chubby Mama dolls. (This was the year that the thinner, long-legged dolls were introduced.)

1928: Distributed *Kämmer & Reinhardt's* line of *My Rosy Darling* dolls. The firm representatives were Max Bing, M. Du Koff and W. W. Vail.

1929: Handled cloth dolls made by *J. K. Farnell,* and the cloth dolls created by *Gertrude Rollinson* as well as a line of dolls called *Kiddie Karakters.*

Exhibited on the American Pacific coast Bing, Kämmer & Reinhardt and Louis Wolf dolls.★

Wolf, Otto. 1912. Rottweil, Würtemberg. Applied for a German patent (D.R.G.M.) for character dolls.

Wolf, Wilhelm. 1898. Neustadt near Coburg, Thür. Made cloth bodies for dolls.

Wolf Doll Co. 1905–27. New York City. Manufactured dolls.

1919: Advertised a line of American made character dolls.

1926: Harry Wolf doing business as the Wolf Doll Co. registered a U.S. trademark of a circular frame surrounded by the words "Wolf Doll Company, N.Y." In the circle was a picture of a wolf and a doll. Under the circle were the words "Trade Mark."

Advertised a doll named *Casey the Cop* and *Schavoir Rubber Dolls.*

1927: Made *Mama* dolls and *I-C-U Baby* dolls for which the patent was pending. When the head of the I-C-U Baby doll was depressed it sprang back while uttering a cry. The Wolf Doll Co. was licensed by *Voices, Inc.* to use patented mama voices and criers in their dolls. They were members of the *American Doll Manufacturers' Association.*★

Wolff, Gebrüder (Nürnberger Celluloidwaren Fabrik). 1912–30 and later. Nürnberg, Bavaria. Made celluloid dolls, baby dolls and parts of dolls.

1930: Made patented mechanical swimming dolls of celluloid named Lya die Schwimmerin.★

Wolff, L. A. See **M'Ginn, Peter.**

Wolson, Joseph. 1928–30. New York City. Factory representative for *Primrose Doll Co., M. & S. Shillman* and other doll-making companies.

Wolson Novelty Co. 1925–26. Bronx, N.Y. Made a line of dolls named *Blanket Babies;* priced 25¢, 50¢ and $1.00.

Wolstan Doll Co. 1918–28. Wolstan, Stoke-on-Trent, Staffs. Made *British Ceramic* dolls' heads, both shoulder and socket heads, and dolls' limbs. Also made wigs for dolls and clothing including hats for dolls. Used the trade names *Dorothea* and *Dorothy.* Under the direction of Mrs. Shaw, the Director, the firm continued to make British Ceramic heads during the 1920s, which inspired other British potteries to resume production of dolls.

1923: Made a line of mascot dolls.

Women's Emergency Corps Workshop. 1914–17. London. According to Caroline Goodfellow, Curator of Dolls at the Bethnal Green Museum, this workshop made the bisque-like composition-head portrait dolls of *Admiral Jellicoe, King Albert of the Belgians, King George V* and *Lord Kitchener.* (See Ill. 744, THE COLLECTOR'S BOOK OF DOLLS' CLOTHES.) There were probably other dolls in this series including the Russian *Tzar (Nicholas), General French* and *General Joffre.* All of these dolls were distributed by *Hamley.*

They also made dolls representing babies, Alsatian peasants, Boulogne Fishwives, and Soldier Dolls.

Wonder Baby, The. 1913. Life size baby doll made by *Amberg* from a sculptor's model of the head. It wore long or short dresses in a variety of styles and a cap.★

Wonder Baby. See **Bottletot.**

Wonder Dolls. See **Wunderpuppen.**

Wonderland Toymaking Co. 1921–23. London. Produced dolls.

1922: Advertised *Bathing Dolls, Billy Sitter,* Candy Boxes with dolls, *Cossack, Darkie, Jazz Nigger, Laddie, Lady Charmana, Lady Di, Lady Sheila, Lassie, My Baby, Peasant,* and *Pierrette.*

Wood Toy Co. 1919–20. New York City. Made *Dolly Walker.*★

Woodard (Woodward), W.R., & Co. 1929–30 and later. Los Angeles, Calif. Made *Hollywood Imps* which appear to have been cloth dolls. Claimed the dolls were manufactured almost entirely by machine.

1929: Hollywood Imp price $1.00.

1930: Line had about 30 styles with handpainted faces and either yarn or felt hair; priced 50¢ to $1.00.

Woode, R., Toy Co. 1917. England. Manufactured composition dolls' heads.

Wooden Dolls. Wood has been used for commercial dolls, for folk art type dolls and for homemade one of a kind dolls. Basswood (also known as linden wood) was a favorite type of wood because of its ease of carving. The *Bébé Tout en Bois* dolls and *Schoenhut* dolls were made of basswood. A considerable number of the wooden dolls were made of the local pine trees in the wooded areas of Thüringia and the Tyrol. The following represent some of the important places where wooden dolls have been made: The American West Coast; Berchtesgaden; Bohemia; England; Erzgebirge; Grödner Tal; Greenland; Kentucky Mountain area *(Poppets);* New England; Oberammergau; Pennsylvania; Russia; Shanghai; Sonneberg; Switzerland; Viechtau; and Wales.

According to an article in the INTERNATIONAL STUDIO, the oldest wooden doll in the Sonneberg Museum was dated ca. 1735. Later these skittle[†] shaped types of dolls were painted with oil paints and still later in the 1700s the dolls were made so that their arms moved. One type had a string which protruded and when it was pulled it activated the arm movement. (See Ill. 2750.)

Two mid-1700s wooden dolls in the Neustadt-near-Coburg Museum belonged to the *Fleischmann* family and according to the Museum's records were made in the Sonneberg area. These dolls resembled the wooden dolls that have heretofore been considered to have an English origin. This type of doll usually had hair, painted or glass eyes and clothes of a handmade fabric. Once again we probably have an example of the fact that dolls that were of the same era look similar rather than that dolls of the same country or manufacturer looked alike over a long period of time.

During the 1800s most of the German toy catalogs showed wooden dolls that had been made in the Tyrol, the Erzgebirge or in Viechtau. See Ills. 482, 2750, 2751 and 2777 for a special type of wooden doll. The Erzgebirge dolls often came in groups and sometimes represented whole villages. From the 1840s on the peg wooden dolls had china, a plaster type composition or wax heads.

By about the 1890s Bébé Tout en Bois dolls began to be made. These were sold chiefly in France but there is ample evidence that most, if not all, of them were made in Germany. A doll resembling a Bébé Tout en Bois has been found with the *Schilling* mark. See the year listing for 1896 through 1913 below.

A doll with its wooden shoulder head and arms like the Bébés Tout en Bois has been found with a wig, sleeping glass eyes, closed mouth, a red stamp reading "*Tête bois,*" on the front of the shoulders and a kid body with Universal joints. Ht. 14½ in. (37 cm.); ht. of shoulder head 4½ in. (11.5 cm.). See Ill. 2596.

1860–61: Jointed wooden dolls were imported by *John D. Robbins* according to his Day Book in Elizabeth Pierce's collection. Hts. 3 to 4 in. (7.5 to 10 cm.); priced 6½¢ a doz. wholesale.

1872: *Silber & Fleming* advertised nine sizes of undressed "Woolyhead wood dolls" and five sizes of undressed jointed wooden dolls.

1876: Silber & Fleming advertised four sizes of jointed wooden dolls as well as dressed carved wooden dolls.

1878: THE QUEEN described wooden *Dutch* dolls, with stiff joints, recently made with Chinese and other character heads. One of these dolls had a fez painted on its head, it wore a blue lama jacket, full red lama trousers and green shoes. It was claimed to have been dressed in France. This magazine continued by saying "Quite a novelty is the un-

breakable wooden doll with joints that move any way even to the ankles and wrists; the usual size from 10 in. to 16 in. (25.5 to 40.5 cm.)." These could have been the dolls with wooden bodies based on the earlier *Bru* patent.

1879: Silber & Fleming advertised wooden Dutch dolls with movable joints made in five sizes.

1880: Date attributed to a carved wooden doll's head made in Catterfeld, Thür., according to the Sonneberg Museum. Ht. of head only, 8 cm. (3 in.).

1882: Silber & Fleming advertised Dutch dolls of wood with movable joints in six sizes.

1884: *Lauer* advertised carved wooden heads with enameled surfaces, sizes 1, 2, and 3; priced $3.00 to $3.75 a doz. wholesale. Their jointed wooden doll ht. 7 in. (18 cm.) cost 5¢.

1885–1912: *Richard Metzler* of Sonneberg made wooden dolls and dolls' heads.

1887: Hundreds of peg-wooden dolls were described and/or illustrated in a book entitled SYBIL'S DUTCH DOLLS (See THE COLLECTOR'S BOOK OF DOLLS' CLOTHES, pp. 243–244.).

Lauer advertised jointed wooden dolls for 6½¢ doz. wholesale. All-wooden "patent" dolls with movable head and jointed limbs came in the following sizes:

Size No.	Height in.	cm.	Price per doz. wholesale
6/0	7½	19	60¢
2/0	10½	26.5	75¢
0	12	30.5	$1.25

1891: *A. Kröhl* advertised wooden dolls.

1896: *Kämmer & Reinhardt* advertised wooden dolls.

1902: *G. Schmey* successors advertised wooden dolls.
Franz Schmidt & Co. advertised wooden heads for dolls.

1903: *Bruno Schmidt* advertised wooden dolls.

1910: ARTS ET DECORATION reported carved wooden dolls that sold for $10.00 in France. Ht. 6 in. (15 cm.).

1911: *E. Dehler* advertised dressed and undressed wooden dolls.

1912: TOYS AND NOVELTIES reported two-dimensional wooden dolls jointed at the neck, shoulders, elbows, hips and knees having their feet at right angles to their legs.

1913: *Gamage* advertised *Bass-Wood* dolls.
R. Grundig & Co. advertised wooden dolls' heads.

1916: *Wanamaker* advertised a bent limb wooden baby doll with painted hair and wearing a chemise. These were probably the Schoenhut baby dolls with painted hair. Ht. 13 in. (33 cm.); priced $2.50, with a mohair wig. Ht. 15 in. (38 cm.); priced $3.50.

1917: According to TOYS AND NOVELTIES the wood carvers of the Austrian Tyrol carved wooden dolls while they were in the trenches. *Von Hindenburg* was the most popular subject. Other subjects were an English suffragette; a German soldier; an Italian Brigand and the Italian poet *D'Annunzio.* The Red Cross hoped to collect these dolls and sell them to make money.

1920: Carved wooden dolls were imported from Switzerland and sold by *Marshall Field.* These dolls were dressed in Swiss Provincial costumes of 15 to 20 different designs; priced $10.00 to $37.50. Similar dolls were still being sold as new in the 1950s.

1919–30 and later: Many companies made *Segmented Wooden Dolls.*

1923: *Hitz, Jacobs & Kassler* advertised a wide variety of dressed wooden dolls with turned and carved features that were handpainted. (See Ill. 2762 for a pair of dolls that they probably imported.) Peg-wooden dolls were still being made in the Grödner Tal (called Val Gardena), after World War I. (See also **German Dolls,** 1913.)★

Woodflour (Wood Flower). 1920s. The principal ingredient of many composition dolls made following World War I. Sometimes dolls made of wood flour were inaccurately described as wooden dolls.

1926: PLAYTHINGS reported that Schmalz Dairy Farm and State Chemical Co. imported wood flour because it was of a uniform quality. (See also **Manufacture of Dolls, Commercial: Made in United States.**)

Woodflour Novelty Co. 1927. New York City. Made woodflour dolls and belonged to the *American Doll Manufacturers' Association.*

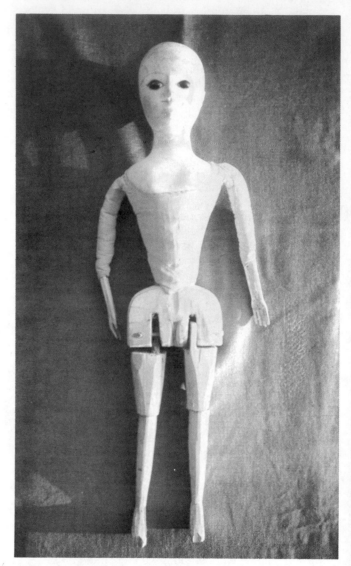

2748. Carved and turned wooden doll made in Germany in the mid-1700s. This doll belonged to the Fleischmann family and is now in the Neustadt Museum. *Courtesy of the Museum of the City of Neustadt near Coburg.*

2747. All-wood doll of the 1700s. It has a wig, glass pupilless eyes. There is some carving of the features as well as a gesso covering of the face. Original clothes. H. 17 in. (43 cm.). *Courtesy of Sylvia Brockmon.*

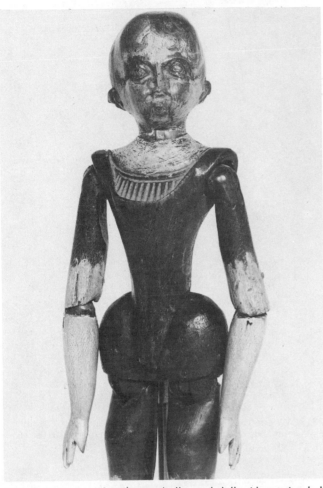

2749A & B. Carved and turned all-wood doll with rotating ball joints including a neck joint. The painted brown hair has brush marks; the eyes are carved; the mouth is closed, and the chin is pointed. The chemise and base for the stomacher are carved. H. 14 in. (35.5 cm.). *Courtesy of the Margaret Woodbury Strong Museum. Photos by Harry Bickelhaupt.*

2750A & B. Carved wooden lady doll holding a baby. When the string in back is pulled the arms rise, thus rocking the baby to and fro. The shape of the doll suggests a trihedral but the wooden doll rocking a baby is a German type feature. H. 7¼ in. (18.5 cm.). *Courtesy of Winifred Moor.* (See also Ills. 482, 2751 and 2777.)

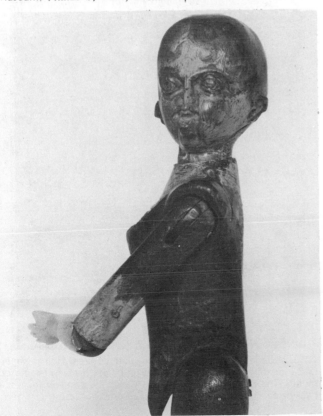

2752. Wooden doll with wig, gessoed face, painted features, cloth arms, peg jointed legs. Original clothes of the 1810s. H. 7 in. (18 cm.). *Coleman Collection.*

2751. All-wood doll made in the late 1800s in the Berchtesgaden or other Tyrolean areas. Came from a collection in Beszterc-zebánya. When a string at the back of the doll is pulled the arms and the baby in swaddling clothes are raised. *Courtesy of the Hungarian National Museum.*

2753. Wooden doll with a gessoed, painted face. Hair is nailed to the head. It has stationary black pupilless eyes and a closed mouth. The clothes are contemporary with the doll and suggest a date of ca. 1805–10. H. 11½ in. (29 cm.). *Courtesy of Cherry Bou.*

2754. Carved and painted wooden doll with ball joints at the shoulders, elbows, hips, and knees. It has black carved and painted hair, painted blue eyes, dots for eyelashes, pierced ears, closed mouth, and a carved and painted bosom. H. 21 in. (53.5 cm.). *Courtesy of and photo by Estelle Johnston.*

2755A & B. Ball jointed wooden doll ca. 1810s. It has a painted windswept hair style, molded and painted eyes, pierced ears and a closed mouth. Original clothes. H. 11 in. (28 cm.). *Coleman Collection.*

2756. Carved wooden doll of about 1810–15, painted hair and eyes. Original dress of blue silk with gold colored trimming, high net collar and red shoes. *Courtesy of the Hungarian National Museum.*

2757. Carved and painted wooden doll with ball joints. Doll was dated 1819, dress dated 1822 and hat dated 1823. H. 73.5 cm. (29 in.). *Courtesy of the Nordiska Museet in Stockholm.*

2758. Swivel jointed wooden doll with black painted hair and a brunette wig. The eyes are painted brown and wire loops are attached to the ears. The mouth is closed. There are joints at the shoulders, elbows, hips, and knees. Original clothes of the 1820s including long white mitts. H. 22 in. (56 cm.). *Courtesy of Estelle Johnston.*

2759. Peg-wooden doll with painted black hair having brush marks, painted blue eyes, closed mouth. Original clothes appear to be a German interpretation of a Scottish outfit. The button and trimming are paper. The slippers are painted red. H. 7½ in. (19 cm.). *Courtesy of the Margaret Woodbury Strong Museum. Photo by Harry Bickelhaupt.*

2760. Tuck comb wooden doll with peg joints has painted black hair, painted eyes, pierced ears and a closed mouth. The clothes appear to be contemporary with the doll. H. 14 in. (35.5 cm.). *Courtesy of Richard Withington. Photo by Barbara Jendrick.*

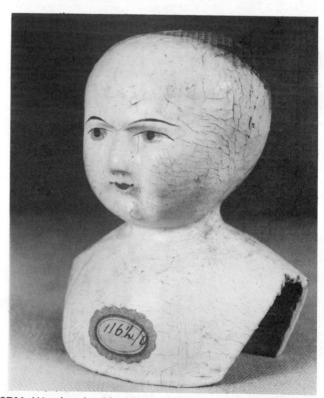

2761. Wooden shoulder head with a bald crown for a wig to be placed on it has painted and carved features. The short neck suggests that it represents a baby. The sticker on the front has only a number on it. H. 3¼ in. (8 cm.). *Coleman Collection.*

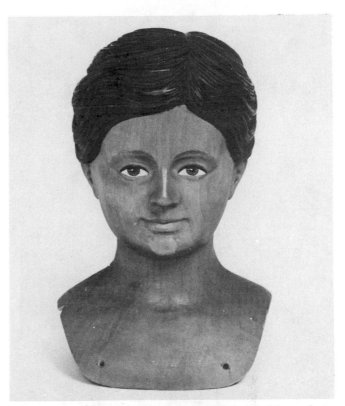

2763A & B. Carved wooden shoulder head probably made in Switzerland. The hair has a side part and a bun in back. The painted brown eyes are threaded. The mouth is closed. H. of shoulder head 7 in. (18 cm.). *Courtesy of the Margaret Woodbury Strong Museum. Photos by Harry Bickelhaupt.*

2762. Pair of all-wood dolls with painted hair and features. The boy has a spherical head with a conical hat and the girl has an egg-shaped head. They have scoop hands with separate thumbs. Original clothes. Dolls similar to these were advertised by Hitz, Jacobs and Kassler in 1923 as being imported. Hs. 8¼ (including the hat) and 7¾ in. (21 and 19.5 cm.). *Courtesy of Richard Withington. Photo by Barbara Jendrick.*

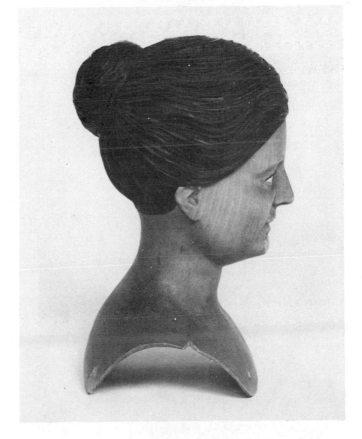

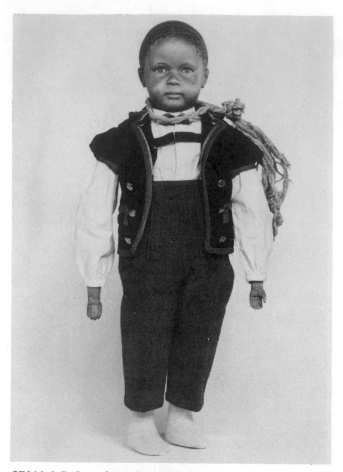

2764A & B. Carved wooden shoulder head and hands of the type made in Switzerland. The hair, cap and features are carved. The painted blue eyes are threaded. The mouth is closed. The arms have ball joints and the cloth body has sewn joints at the shoulders and hips. Original clothes. H. 23 in. (58.5 cm.). H. of shoulder head 7 in. (18 cm.). *Courtesy of the Margaret Woodbury Strong Museum. Photos by Harry Bickelhaupt.*

Woodford, Orin F. 1840–55. Boston, Mass. In 1851 listed under Fancy Goods Stores as Woodford & Merrill. Probably made bodies and clothes for china and papier-mâché head dolls, and distributed dolls. One doll had a pink china head with a dark brown boyish hairdo, wooden arms and a cloth body on which was glued a paper label reading "From Woodford's//FANCY STORE//309 Washington Street//Boston." Another doll had a china head with a dark brown boyish hairdo longer than the other doll. This head was marked with the red orb and blue eagle of the *Königliche Porzellan Manufaktur* (K.P.M.). The paper label on its chest read: "From Woodford & Merrill's// Fancy Store//309 Washington St.// Boston." The Merrill part of the label had been crossed out by pen. A third doll had the same words as the first china doll stamped on its cloth torso in black. This was a French type papier-mâché head doll with a thin wax coating. The black pate had a slit for the hair. The black glass eyes were pupilless and the nostrils were pierced. Both of the china Woodford dolls had well-made clothes.

Woods, Mrs. Mary Frances. 1904–20. Portland, Ore. 1920–30 and later, her successor was her son G. B. Woods. Made dolls representing American Indians. *Konstructo Co.* was the sole distributor in the early 1920s.

1920: TOYS AND NOVELTIES published an advertisement and an article on the Mary Frances Woods' dolls. The following dolls were advertised: Style No. 1 War Bonnet; No. 2 Chief; No. 3 Madonna; No. 4 Cigarette Buck; No. 5 Squaw; No. 6 Little Buck; No. 7 Little Squaw; No. 9 Papoose. Each doll had an individual handpainted face and an individually patterned blanket. Hts. 8 to 16 in. (20.5 to 40.5 cm.).

2765A & B. China shoulder head with short molded dark brown hair on a cloth body with wooden arms. The German head is on a body that was possibly made by Woodford in Boston, Mass., in the early 1850s. The original clothes represent a boy of that period. Mark on body: Ill. 2766. H. 13 in. (33 cm.). H. of shoulder head 3½ in. (9 cm.). *Coleman Collection.*

From
WOODFORD'S
FANCY STORE,
309 Washington Street,
BOSTON

FROM
WOODFORD & MERRILL'S
FANCY STORE
309 WASHINGTON STREET
BOSTON

2766–2767. Woodford paper labels on the cloth bodies of china-head dolls. Other Woodford marks have been found stamped on bodies.

The article titled "Indian Dolls" by Western Artist, Mrs. Woods of Portland was as follows: ". . . Each figure was an artistic triumph—a representative of an individual type of the American Indian. . . . Here, a squaw bent beneath the burden of heavy boughs on her shoulders; there a young princess in her savage glory; here, a warrior stoical but conscious of his achievements; there, a majestic chief in war bonnet and plume.

"Easterners for the first time are having a chance to see the dolls of this western artist. . . .

"Twice have these dolls found their way to the White House. At the time of President Taft's trip to the Pacific Coast, Mrs. Taft, accompanied by her sister and Helen Taft, chanced to go into a Portland shop where one of these Indian figures leaned against the cash register. Immediately it caught her eye and she exclaimed that she must have one to carry home. Of course, she and her party were soon supplied with the dolls of their choice. When the presidential party came to Portland last fall, Mrs. Woodrow Wilson, also was presented with a realistic Pocahontas, likewise, with a Multnomah who would have done credit to that grand old chief of Oregon. . . .

"Splendid as are the costumes from the standpoint of Indian dress, more wonderful are the heads in point of shape, color, and lineaments. The faces are made from a non-breakable composition which after modeling hardens and preserves the features. The final tinting and touching up requires the hand of an artist. One of the interesting points, in this connection, is that the faces like in old paintings—seem to grow more human with age. Mrs. Woods explains that in time the paint is absorbed by the composition as well as more perfectly blended by exposure to dust and other elements of the atmosphere.

"So real are these dolls, so true to primitive character, that Indians looking upon them are deeply moved. When Chief White Elk, the Cherokee baritone . . ., visited Mrs. Woods' studio a few years ago, he gazed at the figures in silence and then finally said, 'They look just like my grandparents.' He was touched by her work and by her understanding of his people. . . .

"Mrs. Woods, like any true artist, has not been satisfied with the acquiring of an academic technique merely but has grounded her art in the realities of human life and of existence. In her case this has meant the devotion of the greater portion of a life time to the study of the history, tradition, and habits of the American Indian.

" 'Each Indian is a personality unto himself,' she said as she told how she had always tried to get into communication with the individuals of the race when the opportunity presented itself. 'Merely show that you have a personal interest in an Indian's tribe and you have reached his heart.'

"Her purpose is to show, whether by means of portraits or of dolls, a character that is true to some type in one of the three tribes intimately studied—the Nez Perce, the Umatilla or the Cheyenne.

"To understand something of the labor and the love that has gone into the making of these native dolls, one must know, at least, the outstanding facts in the life of the artist, herself. She was born in Michigan and received her early training at a convent in Monroe, Michigan. Her artistic education began in Chicago at the Julian school, a branch of a well known institution in Paris. Possessing a love for history as well as a highly imaginative type of mind, she conceived a glowing interest in the West. She was thrilled with the story of the trend of civilization toward the Pacific; and she was gripped by the pathos in the fortunes of the native American tribes. To see the buffalo, to study the Indian at first hand was her dearest desire. And so it was that she left Chicago and came West. By living on reservations, she came to know the tribes intimately. For instance, she became acquainted with the Nez Perces while on the Lapwai Reservation near Lewiston, Idaho.

"About 1903 she went to New York City to continue her artistic studies. After some time spent in modelling at the Chase School, she returned to the West, the source from which she has drawn all her original inspiration.

"For awhile she devoted her efforts to portraiture of the Indian. These splendid heads painted on leather, used to be displayed in a cigar and curio store of Portland and thus several were sold to tourists from various parts of the United States.

"The story of the evolution of the Indian dolls is interesting, as Mrs. Woods gives it. In the beginning, she used leather for faces on which features were painted. The bodies, originally, had pedestals. Then came the struggle of making feet which would not only have a life-like appearance but which would enable the figure to stand. With the naive honesty of the true artist, Mrs. Woods describes her difficulties.

" 'For commercial reasons, the feet had to have three qualities. They must be cheap, they must be light, and they must stand. Once when I was working on the feet of an old chief, I nearly gave up. "I'm whipped," I said to him. Just then his expression seemed to change. A surprised look came over his face as if he said, What? Is it possible? Why, I guess not! At that moment an idea came to me and I began again.'

"As the dolls are today [1920], there are wooden feet with all the appearance of beaded moccasins. The hair—once a serious problem—seems to be real Indian hair, too.

"After years spent in perfecting the methods of manufacturing the dolls, the studio is beginning to take on a commercial aspect. The old quarters have been outgrown, and a new and larger place has been leased. G. B. Woods is now associated with his mother in the business.

"These Indian dolls in time will doubtless have great popularity both here and abroad. That Europe will like them, seems to be indicated by the fact that the French officers, who were in Portland at the time of the Rose Festival last summer, bought several to take back to France. Realizing their possibilities in European markets as well as the growing demand for American toys in the United States, several firms have recently tried to secure from Mrs. Woods various kinds of rights. A contract, however, has just been drawn which makes the Konstructo Company sole distributors. The two distributing points will be Portland, Oregon, and New York City, respectively. So at last with provisions made for publicity, the future of these western dolls seems assured."

1921: Another article in TOYS AND NOVELTIES entitled "Indian Dolls Find World Market" discussed the Woods dolls.

"The recent development of the M.F. Woods Company, manufacturer of American Indian dolls, is quite remarkable. A year ago this business was scarcely known outside of Portland [Oregon] as it was dependent on an indifferent local trade and a small occasional tourist demand. Today, however, these unique dolls are sold abroad as well as in the most representative shops and stores of the United States.

"The new home of the Woods' toy presents a great contrast to the crowded space of the old studio, where Mrs. Woods and a few assistants used to make dolls for the seasonal trade. In the shipping room are rows of great paper boxes containing dozens of dolls, which are destined to go to American firms, or to toy dealers of England, Australia, Spain, Mexico, Chile and Argentina. . . .

"Inquiries from dealers regarding these realistic Indian figures today come from almost all parts of the world, from Cuba, Australia, the Philippines and the East Indies. . . . A group of the Indian figures in all their tribal glory proved to be a great attraction at the benefit given a short time ago by the Emergency Aid for the Philadelphia General Hospital. . . . Illustrative of how widespread has become the trade of this Western company is the amusing incident of a well known Portlander who on a recent trip to Juarez, Mexico, purchased an Indian doll. . . . On his return to Portland, he called on Mr. Woods at the factory one day to exhibit the trophy picked up on the southern tour, and great was the surprise and chagrin when his friend quietly pointed to the Woods trademark on the bottom of the doll's foot.

"Mr. Woods, who had been associated with his mother in business since the close of the war, assumed entire control, after her death last year. With distributors in New York as well as in Portland and with an aggressive advertising campaign well under way, sales began to increase at an extraordinary rate. With great energy and enthusiasm Mr. Woods threw himself into the work, enlarging its scope and adding new equipment as rapidly as permitted."★

2769. Portrait doll of an Indian Brave made by Mary Frances Woods. It has a molded crepe paper face, long black hair, black pin head for eyes, blue cloth over cardboard body wrapped in a blanket. Mark on the sole of one wooden foot: Ill. 2770. H. 15 in. (38 cm.). *Coleman Collection.*

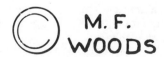

2770. Mark on the feet of dolls made by Mary Frances Woods.

2768. Advertisement for dolls created by Mary Frances Woods in the style of American Indians as shown in PLAYTHINGS, October 1920. The dolls shown are Little Buck and Little Squaw, h. 10 in. (25.5 cm.); Little Papoose and Little Princess, h. 8 in. (20.5 cm.). Each one of these handmade dolls has an individual face and blanket.

Woodward & Lothrop. 1880–1930 and later. Washington, D.C. Known at first as the Boston House. Distributed dolls and dressed some of their dolls. Handled the *Kämmer & Reinhardt* dolls with *Simon & Halbig* bisque heads.

1911: A German doll was made expressly for Woodward & Lothrop so they had to take several thousands of these dolls which had bisque heads, wigs, sleeping eyes, hair eyelashes, fully jointed composition bodies in a chemise. Ht. 22 in. (56 cm.); priced $1.00. Other similar bisque head dolls of this size cost $3.75.

They also advertised *Babyland Rag* dolls produced by *Horsman;* flirting eyed German bisque head dolls. Eight hts. 18 to 32 in. (45.5 to 81 cm.); priced $2.50 to $8.50; and celluloid heads with wigs on kid bodies. Six hts. 14 to 27 in. (35.5 to 68.5 cm.); priced $3.50 to $10.00. These celluloid-head dolls were the most expensive ones offered. Small all-celluloid bent limb babies. Hts. 5 to 13 in. (12.5 to 33 cm.); priced 25¢ to $2.00. Bisque head character babies on bent limb bodies (probably made by Kämmer & Reinhardt) came with painted hair and eyes or with wig and sleeping eyes. Various heights; priced $1.00 to $5.00. They also advertised *Campbell Kids, Topsy Turvy* cloth dolls, stockinet dolls, *Eskimo* dolls and rubber dolls as well as dolls' clothes and accessories.

Wool Yarn Dolls. 1915–20 and later. Dolls knitted or crocheted of wool yarn (See *Worsted Dolls*) had been made for many years prior to World War I when the technique of making dolls of wrapped wool yarn around pieces of wire became popular. One author of the period commented that these wool yarn dolls "appeared on the market in such numbers and variety that they practically may be considered a new branch of art." The faces were made of linen or other fabric or of the wool yarn with embroidered facial features. The wool used to make these dolls was usually in various shades and colors and the wire armatures permitted them to be bent into a variety of positions. Generally these dolls were small in size and often they were an adult diversion or mascot as well as a child's plaything. Some of the *Nénette* and *Rintintin* dolls were made in this manner. (See also **Yerri & Suzel.**)

Woolly-Wags. 1929. Trade name used by *Chad Valley.*

Woolly Wally. 1921. Trade name of a *Golliwogg* made by *Dean.*

Woolnough. 1927. U.S.A. Made cloth dolls of powder puff plush. These dolls had embroidered facial features and were named *Ballet Skirt Girls,* French Gamins, Snow Boys, Snow Girls, Sunbonnet Girls. *Davis & Voetsch* was their factory representative.

Woolworth, F. W., Co. Before 1913–30 and later. Sonneberg, Thür. and stores in many places in U.S. and Europe. They were known as 5 and 10¢ stores; allegedly their top price was 10¢ but as inflation progressed so did their prices.

1913: Bought the business of *Wilhelm Dressel* in Sonneberg.

World War I: Viktor Roth of *Emil Bauersachs* took over their Sonneberg offices.

1925: Started to build a big warehouse and offices in Sonneberg. Over 800 suppliers and home workers in the Sonneberg area worked for Woolworth.

World War II: The large warehouse was blown up by the Germans.

Woop. 1921–22. Advertised in VOGUE as a *Boudoir* doll which was sold in a New York shop that claimed to handle French goods. Ht. 34 in. (86.5 cm.); priced $2.50.

Worms, Dr. R. 1895. Applied for a German patent (D.R.G.M.) for a rubber doll's head.

Worrell, Lola Carrier. 1922–23. New York City. Advertised a doll named *Floppy Flo.*★

Worsted Dolls (Woolen Dolls). 1880s to about 1917. These commercial dolls usually had stockinet faces, worsted hair and knitted or crocheted worsted clothes. Sometimes parts of the dolls such as mouths, hands, shoes, and so forth were made of fabric. The eyes were beads, buttons or other articles. *Emil Wittzack* and probably other manufacturers made these dolls. Various distributors handled these dolls. A typical worsted doll had a flesh colored stockinet face with pink painted cheeks, worsted hair, black bead eyes, red woolen mouth; the nose had a backing which made it stick out. The body was made of white knitted (stockinet) material with white cotton hands and black cloth feet. The dress and hat were crocheted. Often the bodies were made of a woven fabric. Besides boys and girls these dolls represented Clowns, Sailors, *Santa Claus,* soldiers, and so forth. They were sometimes called *Knockabout* Worsted dolls.

1886: *Ridley* advertised cloth body dolls dressed in worsted; priced 20¢ to $1.00.

1888: Ridley's worsted dolls had worsted faces, hair and hands as well as clothes; priced 18¢ and up.

1889: *Montgomery Ward* advertised worsted dolls dressed as boys and girls, a sailor, and a clown. Hts. 9½ to 15 in. (24 to 38 cm.); priced 20¢ to 85¢.

1893: *Butler Bros.* advertised dolls in worsted clothes dressed as girls, boys or clowns. Hts. 7, 10, and 13 in. (18, 25.5, and 33 cm.).

Horsman's catalog listed *Harlequins* and clowns under Worsted dolls, these had knitted worsted clothes in 13 styles or sizes; priced 90¢ to $8.50 doz. wholesale. One of these dolls had a voice, many had bells attached to their costume and hands. (See Ill. 2771.)

Selchow & Righter advertised three styles of worsted dolls. Hts. 9, 9¼, and 10 in. (23, 23.5, and 25.5 cm.).

1894: Montgomery Ward advertised worsted dolls dressed to represent girls and a clown. Hts. 10, 12½, and 15 in. (25.5, 31.5, and 38 cm.).

Selchow & Righter advertised six style nos. dressed as boys and girls. Hts. 10 to 18 in. (25.5 to 33 cm.).

1897: *Zernitz* advertised worsted dolls with cloth bodies and knitted clothes, representing boys, girls and clowns. Hts. 7 to 14 in. (18 to 35.5 cm.).

1898: *Cissna* advertised worsted dolls dressed as girls, boys, and clowns. Some of these had clothes with tufted trimming and bells at the end of each arm. Hts. 9 to 13 in. (23 to 33 cm.); priced 80¢ to $1.88 doz. wholesale.

ca. 1905: *H. E. Eckart & Co.* showed a photograph containing some Worsted dolls which they captioned "View of Mr. Emil Wittzach's sample collection."

1907: *Sears'* catalog contained knitted clowns. Hts. 15 and 17 in. (38 and 43 cm.); priced 25¢ and 40¢.

1909: *Siegel Cooper* advertised worsted dolls with celluloid faces on crocheted heads and with crocheted clothes except for the felt shoes. With a voice the price was 50¢.

1912: Butler Bros. advertised ten styles of dressed worsted dolls. There were clowns, Pierrots, boys and girls represented. Hts. 7½ to 14 in. (19 to 35.5 cm.); priced 42¢ to $2.25 doz. wholesale.

1914: *Marshall Field* offered dolls with celtid (celluloid) faces or heads, wearing "knitted" (crocheted) dresses or coats.

1917: The *Columbus Merchandise Co.* advertised worsted dolls with celluloid faces and ribbon bows. Ht. 9½ in. (24 cm.): priced $4.00 doz. wholesale.

Worthing Toy Factory. 1924. Worthing, Sussex. Advertised a cloth doll named *Nobody's Darling,* and introduced Cry Baby and Baby Bunting.

Worthitt & Co. 1916–17. Hull, Yorkshire. Made cloth (or cloth body) dolls, dressed dolls. Sole agent was *Mr. A. Bell.*

Worthy Doll Co. See **Eclipse Doll Manufacturing Co.**

Wörz, Bartholomäus. 1853 and possibly other years. Vienna. Distributed dolls.

Wounded Tommies. World War I period. Generic term for a variety of dolls. (See also **Tommy Atkins.**)

Wray, Eugene. 1928. New York City. Made knitted clothes for dolls, especially dolls dressed as men.

Wright. 1924. London. Made dolls.

Wu Wu. 1915–17. *British Ceramic* mascot dolls with jointed shoulders distributed by *Hamley Bros.* ★

Wunderlich, Ernst. 1913–18. Ibenhain near Waltershausen, Thür. Made dolls.

1913: Applied for a German patent (D.R.G.M.) for a doll's body that could sit.

Wunderpuppen (Wonder Dolls). 1928. Trade name of dolls made by *Eduard Schmidt.*

Wunderschön (Wonderfully Beautiful). 1914. Name of a composition-head baby doll made by *Kämmer & Reinhardt.* It was jointed at the neck, shoulders and hips. One arm was made so that it could be raised to lift a bottle to its mouth.

Würtembergische Puppenwerkstätte (Würtemberg doll workshop). 1926–27. Ulm, Würtemberg. Made character dolls with celluloid heads and cloth bodies. These came naked or with handmade clothes. There were also jointed celluloid baby dolls.

2771. Worsted doll like the one shown in the Horsman 1893 catalog. It has black bead eyes, a mustache, open-closed mouth. Original clothes on a stuffed body; the garment is knotted worsted and trimmed with bells. H. 14 in. (35.5 cm.). *Part of the Laura Starr Collection which became part of the International Doll Library. Photo by Sotheby Parke Bernet Inc., N.Y.*

Wurzburg, F. A., & Son. 1916. Grand Rapids, Mich. Made cloth dolls with *Grace Drayton* type faces. These dolls had tinted faces. The clothes were either printed on the doll or were separate. They were to be completed at home with embroidery. The styles included white dolls, black dolls; boy, girl and baby dolls. The smaller dolls were named Bed-Time Dolls and the larger ones were named Character Cuddle Dolls. (See Ill. 300.)

Wutschka, Georg. 1925–27. Fürth, Bavaria. Applied for a German patent (D.R.G.M.) for a doll with a moving head.

Wyman, Partridge & Co. 1917. Minneapolis, Minn. Wholesale distributors of dolls including the *Hug-Me-Tight* line of Mother Goose cloth dolls designed by *Grace*

Württembergische Puppenwerkstätte G. m. b. H.

Fernruf Nr. 1037   **Ulm a. D.**   Drahtanschrift: Spielwa

Charakter-Puppen

weich gestopft (Werfpuppen mit Celluloidkopf)
nackte und gekleidete Celluloidbabies
handgehäkelte Kleidchen
Holzspielwaren.

Verlangen Sie unseren Katalog.

2772. Advertisement in DEUTSCHE SPIELWAREN ZEITUNG, February, 1927, for celluloid-head dolls with cloth bodies and celluloid babies made by the Württembergische Puppenwerkstätte. These came dressed and undressed; hand crocheted clothes.

Drayton. The trademark of this company was a pennant with "W. P. Co." on it. Their catalog listed *Bloomin' Kids,* flat face cloth clowns, composition head character dolls, *Eskimo* dolls, *Kewpies®, Maiden America, Marjorie* and *Spearmint Kid.*

Wyse-Bailey Inc. 1926. New York City. Helen Haldane Wyse was a member of this firm. They were agents for *Bonser.*

Wywelecka, Appollonie. 1907. Vienna and Bohemia. Listed in directories under Dolls and Dolls' Heads according to Dr. Eva Moskovszky.

X

Xaver (Boy). 1924. Felt doll made by *Steiff.* Ht. 35 cm. (14 in.).

Y

Yaaka Hula. Ca. 1918. Doll with celluloid head, cloth body, dressed as a Hawaiian native was distributed by *Shackman.* Ht. 10 in. (25.5 cm.); priced 25¢.

Yabsley, A. W. See **Bringlee.**

Yagoda Bros. & Africk. 1925–30. New York City. Made composition head dolls; specialized in infant and *Mama* dolls costing $1.00 and up. Also made separate composition heads.

1925: Advertised dolls' heads.

1926: Infant dolls had composition heads, sleeping eyes, mama voices and wore long dresses, priced $1.00.

1927: Was licensed by *Voices, Inc.* to use their patented Mama voices and criers in their dolls.

1929–30: Advertised new faces and new costumes on their dolls each year.

Yama Doll. 1926. Made by *American Stuffed Novelty Co.* It had a handpainted pressed cloth face, mohair or silk wig and a long-limbed cotton stuffed body. Its removable silk clown costume, designed by *Morris Politzer,* had a dark top and light trousers. Ht. 26 in. (66 cm.).

Yama Yama. 1915–18. Doll with composition head and hands, painted features, molded hair, cloth body, jointed at the shoulders and hips, dressed in a clown costume with matching pointed cap. Made by *New Era Novelty Co.*

1917–18: The 13½ in. (34 cm.) size wore a suit with black polka dots on a white ground. The 30 in. (76 cm.) size wore black and white striped suit.★

Yama Yama. 1925. *Shackman* advertised all-celluloid and all-bisque *Kewpie* type dolls dressed in Yama crepe paper costumes.

Yama Yama. 1927. *Butler Bros.* advertised *Peggy,* a *Boudoir* doll, dressed in a Yama Yama suit.

Yama Yama Kid. 1917. Doll with composition head and hands, cloth body, advertised by the *Baltimore Bargain House.* Ht. 36 in. (91.5 cm.); priced $1.35.

Yama-Yama. 1920. *Elektra Toy & Novelty Co.* manufactured dolls in Yama Yama costumes.

Yankee. 1897. Handmade cloth doll distributed by *Jordan, Marsh & Co.;* priced 50¢ and $1.00.

Yankee Doll. Ca. World War I. U.S.A. Name of a composition head doll.

YANKEE DOLL
MADE IN USA

2773. Yankee mark on composition heads for dolls.

Yankee Doodle Kids. 1917. Line of dolls dressed in red, white and blue, made by *Averill Manufacturing Co.* They included Miss U.S.A.[†] and Uncle Sam Jr.[†]

Yerri. 1917–18. Name of a doll based on the drawings of *L'Oncle Hansi* and made of *Prialytine,* a composition-celluloid type substance. It had molded hair, molded footwear, joints at the neck, shoulders, hips, and wore the costume of a peasant school boy. In its left hand was a school slate with the signature of Hansi written on one side. In its right hand was a bouquet or a tricolor flag.★

Yerri & Suzel. 1918. Pair of good luck *Wool Yarn* Dolls made of wound wool. *Printemps* advertised them for 58¢.★

Yolanda. 1927. Advertised by *H. & S. Pogue Co.* as "A lifelike French Doll—can be dry cleaned"; priced $6.00.

Yondorf, Meyer. See **Schoen & Yondorf.**

Young John Bull. Ca. 1900. Stockinet doll with worsted hair, bead eyes, features embroidered with yarn, wearing a scarf, short pants, felt hat, and boots. This doll was in the Laura Starr collection and looks like a Boy Scout.

Yves. 1916. Cloth bébé made by *Mme. d'Eichthal.*

Yves and Yvette. 1920s. Pair of cloth dolls advertised in the Annuaire de la *Chambre Syndicale* by *Les Poupées Artistiques Française.*

Yvette. 1926–28. Trademark registered in France by Mme. *Elisa Rassant.* It showed a doll holding a tray.

1928: *Paturel* advertised a cloth doll with this name.

Yvonne. See **Maison Yvonne.**

591486. *"Yerri et Suzel".* Couple alsacien, fétiche porte-bonheur, en laine . . **2.90**

2775. War-time French mascot dolls named Yerri & Suzel, made of wool yarn and representing an Alsatian girl and boy. They were shown in the Printemps 1918 catalog; priced 58¢. *Courtesy of Margaret Whitton.*

2774. Yerri, a doll made of Prialytine, has painted hair and eyes looking to the side. The mouth is a curved line. Original clothes and original box identify the doll as a registered model created by J. P. Gallais to represent an articulated version of the Yerri drawings by L'Oncle Hansi. This doll received first prize at the 1917 Paris Exhibition. *Courtesy of the Margaret Woodbury Strong Museum. Photo by Harry Bickelhaupt.*

2776. Stockinet cloth doll representing "Young John Bull" resembles a Boy Scout. It has yarn hair, black bead eyes, and closed mouth. Original clothes include a felt hat. H. 10 in. (25.5 cm.). Part of the Laura Starr Collection. *Courtesy of the International Doll Library. Photo by Sotheby Parke Bernet Inc., N.Y.*

Z

Zadek Feldstein Co. See **Feldstein, Zadek, Co.**

Zaiden, David. 1906–30 and later. New York City, Newark, N.J. and Brooklyn, N.Y. By 1929 Zaiden mechanical dolls were being advertised by Overland Products Co.

1921: Products of Zaiden Toy Works included a wood fibre composition used to make dolls; moving eyes and moving and flirting eyes for dolls' heads, walking dolls.★

Zakucka-Harlfinger, Frau Fanny. 1903–07. Vienna and Salzburg, Austria. Studied the making of dolls under Professor Böhm at the Kunstschule für Frauen und Mädchen (An Art School for females) in Vienna. An artist and craftswoman, she specialized in making turned wooden dolls which she painted, thus no two were alike. The articulation was worked by strings. Dolls were dressed in bonnets, muffs, and period costumes as well as representing people of Salzburg and Bohemia. They came in various sizes.

1904–06: Sold about 400 dolls a year and taught others to make these dolls.

1907: Exported them to remote parts. (See Ills. 482, 2750, 2751 and 2777.)

2777. Wooden dolls created by Fanny Zakucka-Harlfinger. The clothes are painted on the dolls. The doll in the center raises and lowers its arms which hold a baby doll in swaddling clothes. For an earlier example, see Ill. 2750. These Zakucka-Harlfinger dolls are shown in STUDIO, August, 1906. *Courtesy of the Brooklyn Museum.*

Zapon. 1919. Name of a type of lacquer and enamel made by the Celluloid Zapon Co. and used to spray paint dolls.

Zappel-Philipp. 1923. Celluloid doll shown in a *Rheinische Gummi und Celluloid Fabrik* catalog as style no. 14. It had jointed arms, fixed legs and molded clothes. *Struwwelpeter* was also style no. 14. Zappel-Philipp represented a bad boy who rocked his chair at the table.

Zast, P.R. 1920s. Poland. Made celluloid dolls.★

Zayda. 1927. Trade name for a doll.

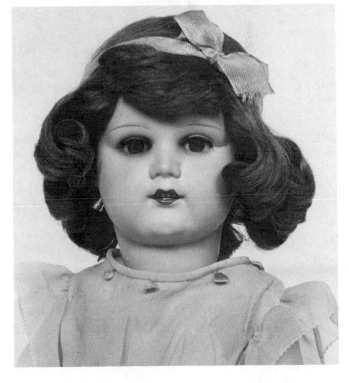

2778A & B. All-celluloid doll made in Poland and possibly handled by Zast. It has a socket head, wig, sleeping blue glass eyes, open mouth with four upper teeth. Original clothes. Mark: Ill. 2779. H. 16½ in. (42 cm.). *Courtesy of the Margaret Woodbury Strong Museum. Photos by Harry Bickelhaupt.*

2779. Mark on an all-celluloid doll that was possibly handled by Zast.

Zboray, Jánosne. 1920 and probably other years. Budapest. A professor who designed dolls and supervised the making of them in his workshop. The dolls represented people and types that he knew. *Stewart Culin* purchased two of the Budapest type dolls.

Zeh, Eduard. 1913. Sonneberg, Thür. Applied for a German patent (D.R.G.M.) for a jointed doll.★

Zehner, Bernhard. 1895–1930 and later. Schalkau, Thür. Manufactured and exported dolls.

1902: Applied for a German patent (D.R.G.M.) for walking dolls.

1908: Advertised walking and dancing dolls.

1910: Advertised jointed dolls including a doll 28 cm. (11 in.) tall; priced 10¢.

1911–12: Advertised a doll with a shoe having rollers on it as well as dancing dolls and the 28 cm. (11 in.) doll.

1921: Made dressed dolls that were handled by *Gross & Schild.*

1925: Advertised baby bodies with patented (D.R.G.M.) works and mama voices. Hts. 20 to 80 cm. (8 to 31½ in.).

1926: Advertised five piece and fully jointed dolls including the *Waltershausen* type, mechanical dolls, *Mama* dolls, dolls' heads and bodies for the English and American markets.

1927: Advertised a baby doll with a mama voice and turning head based on a German patent (D.R.G.M.) as well as other dolls.★

Zehner, Edmund Carl. 1925–26. Schalkau, Thür. Advertised cloth dolls; some of their dolls had wigs and were dressed.★

Zehner, Ferdinand. 1926–30. Oberlind, Thür. Produced dolls.

Zeiner, Gustav. 1898. Jena, Thür. Applied for a German patent (D.R.G.M.) for jointed dolls. The patent was used by *Carl Feiler.*

Zeller-Stevens, Inc. 1918–23. New York City. Importer and exporter of dolls including handmade lines. Represented over 40 German factories that made dolls and toys.

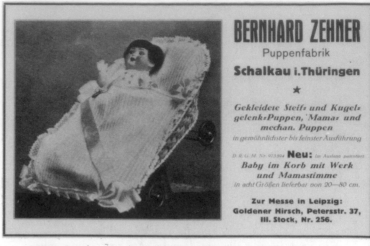

2780. Bernhard Zehner's advertisement in DEUTSCHE SPIEL-WAREN ZEITUNG, February, 1927. This lists dressed, "stiff" and ball jointed dolls, dolls with Mama voices and Mama dolls as well as mechanical dolls.

2781. Zep, name of a Steiff felt doll representing Count Zeppelin. It has hair attached to its head, hair mustache and beard, button black glass eyes, and joints at the shoulders and hips. Original clothes are attached to the body. The hat band reads "L'Onkel Zeppelin." H. 30 cm. (12 in.). *Courtesy of Claire Hennig. Photo by Margie Landolt of Basel.*

Zello Wax. See **König & Wernicke.**

Zemstvo. Ca. 1900. Name of a type of Russian doll, possibly a bisque bébé.

Zep (L'Onkel Zeppelin, Zeppl or Zeppelin). 1911 or before. Felt doll made by *Steiff.* It had a mustache and wore an outfit with a tuxedo type collar and kepi. Ht. 35 cm. (14 in.). Price 82¢.

Zerbi. See **De Zerbi, A.**

Zernitz, John D., Co. 1887–97. Chicago, Ill. Imported and distributed dolls. (See THE COLLECTOR'S BOOK OF DOLLS' CLOTHES, Ill. 442.)★

Zette. 1925. Cutout cloth doll produced by *Fernand Nathan*. It had bobbed hair, wore a dress, footwear and a ribbon bow in its hair. Ht. 55 cm. (21½ in.). Madelon was a smaller version, ht. 27 cm. (10½ in.).

Zeuch & Lausmann. 1893–1925 and later. Sonneberg, Thür. By 1910 the owner was Werner Zeuch. Distributed dolls.

1894: Advertised jointed dolls, *Täuflinge*, musical dolls and washable dolls; dolls' heads of bisque, wood, and model (wax).

1910: Advertised jointed dolls and Täuflinge as well as musical dolls.★

Zezette. 1923–24. Cloth doll advertised by the *Louvre* store. It had a wig, articulation and wore a colored taffeta dress and hair ribbon. Ht. 76 cm. (30 in.).

Zierow, Paul R. 1897–1930 and later. Berlin. Manufactured and exported dolls.

1905: Applied for a German patent (D.R.G.M.) for dolls' bodies with celluloid ball joints.★

Zig Zag Chap. 1915. Doll that wiggled as it walked, made by *Ferguson Novelty Co.* One of these was black and one was a Charlie Chaplin doll.

Zimmer, S. D. Ca. 1840–1929. Fürth, Bavaria. Handled Nürnberg, Olbernhau, and Sonneberg dolls. London agent was *Cowan de Groot.*

Zimmermann. See **Böhnke, Clara, and Zimmermann, Helene.**

Zina. 1924–30. Name of dolls made and distributed by *André Lambert.*★

Zinner, Adolf. 1899–1929. Schalkau, Thür. Manufactured dolls.

1904: Applied for a German patent (D.R.G.M.) for a doll with a voice.

1905: Applied for a German patent (D.R.G.M.) for a doll with a walking wheel.

1911: Applied for a German patent (D.R.G.M.) for a crawling baby.

1927: Advertised *Mama* dolls.

Zinner, Gottlieb, & Söhne. 1845–1926. Schalkau, Thür. Produced dolls with bisque, papier-mâché or wax-over-composition heads.

1880: Advertised bisque-head dolls with glass eyes, jointed bodies and vari-colored chemises or with painted eyes and white chemises; china heads on cloth bodies; papier-mâché head dolls with black varnished molded hairdos and wooden limbs; wax-over-composition dolls with cloth bodies and wooden limbs; wax *Täuflinge* with wigs, glass eyes and vari-colored chemises.

1897: Advertised musical dolls, wooden and papier-mâché dolls.

1925: Advertised five piece and fully jointed dolls, and *clowns* with music.★

Zitzmann, Emil. 1911–30 and later. Steinach, Thür. Emil Zitzmann died in 1913. Manufactured dolls' heads and leather or imitation leather (Art leather) bodies for dolls, especially those with the Universal joints.† Advertised bisque or composition heads and lower limbs.

1930: Was granted a German patent (D.R.P.) for the simultaneous movement of a doll's leg and head.

1931: Advertised large dolls wearing Seiden (silk) clothes and having a Bubicut hair style (Bobbed hair). Hts. 58 and 68 cm. (23 and 27 in.).★

Zitzmann, Mlle. 1915. Lichte, Thür. According to the Sonneberg Museum she created the model for a porcelain head with painted hair made by *Gebrüder Heubach*. Ht. of head only, 9 cm. (3½ in.).

Zoe. 1921. Stockinet doll with handwoven wig, removable clothes made by *Chad Valley.*

1921: Had a Chad Valley patented wrist watch and was dressed in silk and other materials. Hts. 12 to 13 in. (30.5 to 33 cm.).

Zofia. 1915. Name of a doll made in *Mme. Lazarski's* workshop as a *Mme. Paderewski* doll. It represented a woman of Lodz, Poland.

Zöllner, Georg. 1927–30 and later. Rosswein, Saxony. Produced and/or distributed dressed and undressed dolls, cloth dolls including felt dolls, baby dolls, dolls' parts, molds for dolls and *Matryoshkas.*

1930: *G. H. Hertzog & Co.* was an agent for them.

Zoo Soft Toy Co. 1928. London. Made soft plush toys including Fondle Dolley.

Zoo Toy Co. See **Burman, J. and A. J.**

Zorn, Friedrich. 1927. Greifswald near Bonn, Germany. Applied for a German patent (D.R.P.) for a "Mama Papa" voice for dolls.

Zouaves.† See **Military Costume Dolls.**

Zsigmond Liebner (Uncle Liebner). Before 1930 and later. Budapest. Large toy shop that sold dolls.

Zuave (Dark skin). 1916. Name of a felt doll made by *Steiff*. Ht. 35 cm. (14 in.).

Zulema. 1927–28. Felt doll made by *Lenci* as style no. 165/19. It wore a contemporary fashionable outfit with high heels and held a cigarette. Ht. 27½ in. (70 cm.).

Zulu. 1893. Name of dolls possibly with bisque heads, advertised by *Horsman* in their catalog. These came in three sizes or styles; priced 37¢ to $2.00 doz. wholesale.

Zur Puppendoktorim (At the Dolls' Lady Doctor). 1907–10. Vienna. Name of the doll repair shop of *Josef Kubelka.*

Zuzu. 1930. Trade name of a cloth doll made by *Norah Wellings.*

Zu-Zu Kid. 1916–19. Advertising doll with composition head, painted or sleeping eyes, and cork stuffed cloth body with molded composition shoes; made by *Ideal* and distributed by *Butler Bros.* Hts. 13 and 15½ in. (33 and 39.5 cm.).

1917: *Columbus Merchandise Co.* advertised Zu-Zu Kid with molded hair, teeth, composition arms and flesh tinted cloth body jointed at the shoulders and hips. The clown suit had red pompons on it and a bell on the cap. Ht. 15 in. (38 cm.); priced $18.00 doz. wholesale.

1919: The name of the doll was changed to *Farmerette* and it wore a new style outfit.★

Zwanger, Heinrich. 1928–30 and later. Nürnberg, Bavaria. His firm, known as the Nürnberger Kunstlerpuppen und Stoffspielwarenfabrik (Nürnberg Art Doll and Cloth Toy Factory), made art dolls. Some of the dolls had composition heads, cloth bodies and wore regional costumes.

The authors have endeavored to provide a tremendous amount of information in a readily accessible, clear but condensed form which includes some abbreviations and symbols that are used throughout this book.

ABBREVIATIONS AND SYMBOLS

Ca.	= about	no.	=	number (used with "style" as style no.)
Cie.	= Company	nos.	=	numbers (used with "style" as style nos.)
cir.	= circumference	Vve.	=	Widow
cm.	= centimeter (centimeters)	#	=	number (used with "mold" as mold #)
Co.	= Company	★		Placed at the end of an entry signifies that additional information on that entry can be found in the first COLLECTOR'S ENCYCLOPEDIA OF DOLLS.
Gebr.	= Gebrüder (Brothers)			
in.	= inch (inches)			
h.	= height (used only in captions)			
ht.	= height (used only in text)	†		Placed at the end of a name indicates that additional information about this name can be found in the first COLLECTOR'S ENCYCLOPEDIA OF DOLLS, but not in Volume Two.
hts.	= heights (used only in text)			
Ill.	= Illustration			
Inc.	= Incorporated			
Mfg.	= Manufacturing	*		Used for a footnote reference.
née	= maiden name			

SELECTED BIBLIOGRAPHY

The most important sources of information are the marks and labels on the dolls themselves, on their clothes, on their jewelry, or on their containers.

Other sources of information about the dolls include early contemporary photographs; advertising and exhibit postcards; and small promotional leaflets that were distributed when the doll was new.

Also see the bibliographies in the first *Collector's Encyclopedia of Dolls* and *The Collector's Book of Dolls' Clothes* for additional sources, many of which were used in this book. Some of the books and articles listed in the two earlier bibliographies have been repeated because they were used to a considerable extent in this volume.

I. OFFICIAL SOURCES

Austrian *Patents*, 1920ff.
French *Patents*, 1824ff.
German *Patents (D.R.P.)*, 1878ff.
Grey, Arthur J. *Postwar Conditions in the German Toy Industry.* U.S. Department of Commerce Report No. 267. Washington, D.C.: GPO, 1924.
Italian *Patents*, 1919ff.
Livre D'Or de l'Exposition de Poupées, Jouets, Vêtements et Literies. Belgium: Union Amicale des Oeuvres Patriotiques, 1916.
Schutrumpf. *World Trade in Toys.* U.S. Department of Commerce Trade Promotion Series No. 192. Washington, D.C.: GPO, 1939.
United States *Design Patents*, 1886ff.
United States *Patents*, 1858ff.
United States *Trademarks*, 1871ff.

II. DIRECTORIES

Adressbuch der Sächsisch-Thüringischen Industrie, 1907ff.
Annuaire de la Chambre Syndicale des Fabricants de Jouets, Jeux et Engins Sportifs. Paris, ca. 1920s.
Boston City Directories
    Charles Stimpson, Jr., 1829ff.
    Boston Annual Advertiser, 1840.
    S. N. Dickinson, 1846ff.
    Boston, Almanac, 1851.
    Business Directory, 1852ff.
    Bufford's, 1867ff.
    Sampson, Davenport, & Co., 1873ff.
    Sampson, Murdock, & Co., 1887ff.
Deutsches Reichs Adressbuch, 1909ff.
Didot-Bottin, France, 1842ff.
Export Hand-Adressbuch von Deutschland, Berlin, 1891.
Leuchs Adressbuch, Germany, 1828ff.
Osterreichischen Industrie, Austrian Industry, Rudolf Hanel, 1906ff.
Pigot, J., & Co., England, 1823–24.
Rochester, New York, Directories
    Boyd, 1863–69.
    Drew, 1869ff.
    Anthony, 1895ff.
Vienna Directory, 1839ff.

III. CATALOGS
A. MANUFACTURER'S AND/OR DISTRIBUTOR'S CATALOGS

American Cereal Co. (Cereta), Chicago, Ill., 1904.
Amusement, Novelty Supply Co., Elmira, N.Y., 1926ff.
Averill Manufacturing Co., New York, ca. 1925.
Baird-North Co., Providence, R.I., 1920–21.
Baltimore Bargain House, 1902ff. (successor, American Wholesale Corp., ca. 1920ff.).
Bellas, Hess & Co., New York, 1914ff.
Berwick Doll Co., New York, ca. 1923.
Bestelmeier, Nürnberg, 1793ff.

Biberach, Germany, ca. 1836.
Boggs & Buhl, Allegheny, Pa., 1894–95.
Bon Marché, Paris, 1884ff.
Boston Store, Chicago, Ill., 1886ff.
Bru Jne. & Cie., Paris, 1872.
Butler Bros., Chicago, Ill., Dallas, Tex., Minneapolis, Minn., New York, and St. Louis, Mo., 1886ff.
Butterick Publishing Co., New York, 1882ff.
Chad Valley, Harborne, England, 1920ff.
Chicago Mail Order House, Chicago, Ill., 1926.
Colgate & Co., New York, 1908.
Columbian Dolls, Oswego Center, N.Y., ca. 1893.
Columbus Merchandise Co., Columbus, Ohio, 1917.
Dean's Rag Book Co., London, Rye, Sussex, 1920ff.
Dorst, Julius, Sonneberg, Thür., n.d.
Dufayel, Paris, 1923.
Dunham Manufacturing Co., New York, 1893.
Eaton, T., Toronto, Canada, 1901ff.
Eckart, H. E., & Co., London, 1905.
Effanbee, New York, 1915ff.
Elms & Sellon, New York, n.d.
Escher, J. G., Sonneberg, Thür., 1920–21.
Faultless Rubber Co., Ashland, Ohio, 1923.
Forbes & Wallace, Springfield, Mass., 1887.
Gamage, London, 1902ff.
Gerzon, Netherlands, 1925ff.
Gimbel Bros., Philadelphia, Pa., 1904ff.
Goodyear Rubber Co., New York, 1881.
Gordon, M., Boston, 1904ff.
Hamley's, London, 1900ff.
Harleys Sports Stores, Melbourne, Australia, 1928.
Harrods, London, 1898ff.
Hitz, Jacobs & Kassler, Fürth, Bavaria, and New York, 1923ff.
Horsman, E. I., New York, 1880ff.
Hotel de Ville, Paris, 1907ff.
Hughes, Francis L., Rochester, N.Y., 1882ff.
Hutzler Bros., Baltimore, Md., 1906.
Insam & Prinoth, Grödner Tal, Austria, 1890.
Jordan, Marsh & Co., Boston, Mass., 1889ff.
Kämmer & Reinhardt, Waltershausen, Thür., 1922ff.
Käthe Kruse, Bad Kösen, Germany, 1915ff.
Kaufhaus, Des Westens, Berlin, 1908.
Kellogg, Robert W., Springfield, Mass., 1925.
Kimport Dolls, Independence, Mo., 1937ff.
La Place Clichy, Paris, 1900ff.
Lafayette, Galleries, Paris, 1909ff.
Larkin Co., Buffalo, N.Y., 1913ff.
Lauer, C. F., New York, 1884ff.
Lenci, Turin, Italy, 1925ff.
Leuchars, William, London, 1867.
Liberty & Co. (Metz & Co.), Amsterdam branch of the London company, 1913ff.
Lichenstein, B. T., 1889.
Lindholms, Hanna, Scandinavia, 1915.
Lindner, Fa., Sonneberg, Thür., 1831ff.

Linington's, C. M., Chicago, Ill., 1883ff.
Louvre (store), Paris, 1876ff.
Lyra-Fahrrad-Werke, Prenzlau, Germany, 1912.
Macy, R. H., & Co., New York, 1884ff.
Magenta, Grand Bazar, Paris, 1896ff.
Mandel Bros., Chicago, Ill., 1915.
Marshall Field, Chicago, Ill., 1888ff.
McCall's, New York, 1913.
McKim Studios, Independence, Mo., 1931ff.
Ménagère, Paris, 1903ff.
Metropole, Galleries, Paris, 1900.
Millikin & Lawley, London, 1881ff.
Montgomery Ward & Co., Chicago, Ill., 1887ff.
Morrell, Charles, London, 1900.
Müller, W. G., Sonneberg, Thür., 1930+ff.
Nathan, Fernand, Paris, 1925.
Paris Cette, Paris, 1907ff.
Paturel, J., & Cie., Paris, 1928.
Pauvre Jacques, Paris, 1901.
Penney, J. C., Frederick, Md., 1929.
People's Home Journal, New York, 1921.
Petit Saint Thomas, Paris, 1886ff.
Pohlson, Galleries, Pawtucket, R.I., ca. 1915.
Pont Neuf, Paris, 1900.
Printemps, Paris, 1882ff.
    Printemps, printed in Scandinavia, 1891.
Pygmalion, Paris, 1900ff.
Rheinische Gummi und Celluloid-Fabrik (Schildkröt-Puppen), Mannheim-Neckarau, Germany, 1913ff.
Ridley, E., & Sons, New York, 1884ff.
Rudolph, Max, Waltershausen, Thür., 1929.
Rumford Chemical Works, Providence, R.I., 1917.
Samaritaine, Paris, 1898ff.
Samstag & Hilder, New York and Sonneberg, Thür., 1904.
Schoenhut, A., Co., Philadelphia, Pa., 1915ff.
Schwarz, F. A. O., New York, 1878ff.
Shackman, B., New York, 1908ff.
Siegel Cooper Co., New York, 1905ff.
Silber & Fleming, London, 1872ff.
Simpson-Crawford Co., New York, 1904.
Smyth, John, & Co., Chicago, Ill., 1914.
Spiegel, May, Stern Co., Chicago, Ill., 1920s.
Steiff, Margarete, Giengen an der Brenz, Germany, 1898ff.
Stern Bros., U.S.A., 1883.
Supplee-Biddle Hardware Co., Philadelphia, Pa., 1924.
Strawbridge & Clothier, Philadelphia, Pa., 1912.
Tip Top Toy Co., New York, 1920–21.
Tapis Rouge, Paris, 1903.
Trois Quartiers, Paris, 1905ff.
Unger & Co., Bruchlos, 1920s.
Ville de Paris, Versailles, France, 1903.
Ville de St. Denis, Paris, 1901ff.
Wagner & Zetzsche, Ilmenau, Thür., 1936.
Weber, Franz Carl, Zurich, 1893ff.
Wellings, Norah, Wellington, Shropshire, 1936.
Western News Co., U.S.A., 1904.

William Charles, New York, 1915ff.

Wyman, Partridge & Co., Minneapolis, Minn., 1917.

B. MANUFACTURER AND/OR DISTRIBUTOR, MULTICATALOG REPRINTS

Bachmann, Manfred. *Das Waldkirchner Spielzeug Musterbuch um 1850.* Leipzig: Heimeran, 1977.

Cook, Dorothy. *Doll Pages from Old Catalogs.* Malibu, Calif., 1967.

Long, Ernest and Ida. *A Catalog of Dolls 1877–1961.* Mokelumne Hill, Calif., 1978.

Parry-Crooke, Charlotte. *Toys—Dolls—Games, Paris 1903–1914.* Reprints of Paris store catalogs. London: Denys Ingram; New York: Hastings House, 1981.

Pieska, Christa. *Schones Spielzeug aus alten Nürnberger Musterbuchern.* Munich: Idion, 1979.

Schroeder, Joseph J., Jr. *The Wonderful World of Toys, Games & Dolls, 1860–1930.* Chicago, Ill.: Follett Publishing Co., 1970.

Westbrook, Dorothy Figg, and Sherry Ehrhardt. *Encyclopedia of American Collector Dolls.* Kansas City, Mo.: Heart of America Press, 1975.

C. AUCTION CATALOGS

Bourne, Richard, Hyannis, Mass., 1972ff.

Bruce & Crandall, Bloomingburg, N.Y., 1973.

Christie's, New York, 1979ff.; and London, 1968ff.

Cohen, Marvin, New Lebanon, N.Y., 1982ff.

Early Auction Co., Milford, Ohio, 1973ff.

Freeman, Samuel, Philadelphia, Pa., 1953ff.

Galerie de Chartres (Lelievre), Chartres, France, 1977ff.

Garth, Stratford Auction, Delaware, Ohio, 1979ff.

Hays, Kenneth S., Pewee Valley, Ky., 1982ff.

Ineichen, Zurich, 1973ff.

Merrill, Duane, South Burlington, Vt., 1980.

Moore, Walter E., Ludlow, Mass., 1969ff.

Neret-Minet, Paris, 1982ff.

Patton, Gerald M., Duncansville, Pa., 1973.

Phillips, London, Geneva, and New York, 1981ff.

Poulain, Hervé, Paris, 1982ff.

Skinner, Robert W., Bolton, Mass., 1983ff.

Smith, William A., Plainfield, N.H., 1972ff.

Sotheby Parke Bernet, New York and London, 1970ff.

Weschler, Adam, & Son, Washington, D.C., 1962ff.

Withington, Richard, Concord, N.H., 1975ff.

IV. GENERAL REFERENCE BOOKS

Ackerman, Evelyn, and Fredrick Keller. *Schoenhut's Humpty Dumpty Circus from A to Z.* Los Angeles: Era Industries Inc., 1975.

Anderton, Johana Gast. *Twentieth Century Dolls From Bisque to Vinyl.* North Kansas City, Mo.: Trojan Press, 1971.

————. *More Twentieth Century Dolls From Bisque to Vinyl.* North Kansas City, Mo.: Athena Publishing Co., 1974.

————. *The Collector's Encyclopedia of Cloth Dolls.* Lombard, Ill.: Wallace-Homestead Book Co., 1984.

Angione, Genevieve, and Judith Whorton. *All Dolls are Collectible.* Hanover, Pa.: Everybody's Press Inc., 1977.

Anka, Georgine, and Ursula Gauder. *An Example of Dolls made in Waltershausen by Koenig & Wernicke.* Stuttgart: Ritter, 1976.

————. *Die Deutsche Puppenindustrie, 1815–1940.* Stuttgart: Puppen und Spielzeug, 1978.

Axe, John. *The Encyclopedia of Celebrity Dolls.* Cumberland, Md.: Hobby House Press, 1983.

Bachmann, Manfred, and Claus Hansmann. *Dolls the Wide World Over.* Translated by Ruth Michaelis, Jena and Patrick Murray. New York: Crown Publishers, 1973.

Bachmann, Manfred, and Reinhold Langner. *Bergtesgadener Volkkunst.* Leipzig: Friedrich Hofmeister, 1957.

Baker, Roger. *Dolls and Dolls' Houses.* New York: Crescent Books, division of Crown Publishers, 1973.

Bartram, N. D. *UTPYWKA.* Moscow: Russian publisher, 1912.

Bateman, Thelma, and Jan Foulke. *Blue Book of Dolls and Values.* Riverdale, Md.: Hobby House Press, 1974.

Bénézit, E. *Dictionnaire, Critique et Documentaire des Peintres, Sculpteurs, Dessinateurs, et Graveurs.* Librairie Grund, 1976.

Benson, A. C., and Sir Laurence Weaver. *Everybody's Book of The Queen's Dolls' House.* London: The Daily Telegraph, 1924.

Bittner, Herbert. *Verlag und Fabrik in der Spielwarenindustrie Sonneberg.* Halle-Wittenberg, Germany: Universität Friedrichs, 1927.

Bivins, John, Jr. *The Moravian Potters in North Carolina.* Chapel Hill, N.C.: University of North Carolina Press, 1972.

Böhmer, Bettina. *Püppchen.* Cologne, West Germany: Verlag M. DuMont Schauberg, 1963.

Borger, Mona. *Chinas, Dolls for Study and Admiration.* San Francisco: Borger Publications, 1983.

Borràs, Maria Lluisa. *Mundo de Los Juguetes* (World of toys). Barcelona, Spain: Ediciónes Poligrafa, S.A., 1969.

Brecht, Ursula. *Kostbare Puppen* (English version titled *Precious Dolls*). Weingarten, West Germany: Kunstverlag Weingarten GmbH, 1981.

Brisou, Catherine. *Poupées du Temps Passé Histoire d'une Collection.* Editeur, Pierre Gauthier. France: Printer Goubault, 1980.

Brovarone, Adelina Rauccib. *Pupeide Discorso Intorno Alla Bambola.* Torino, Italy: Priuli & Verlucca, editori, 1973.

Buchholz, Shirley. *A Century of Celluloid Dolls.* Cumberland, Md.: Hobby House Press, 1983.

Bullard, Helen. *Dorothy Heizer, the Artist and Her Dolls.* New York: National Institute of American Doll Artists, 1972.

Burdick, Loraine. *A Doll for Christmas or Any Time.* Puyallup, Wash.: Quest Books, 1971.

Burger, Doralee Whitten. *History and Price Guide of English Cloth Dolls.* Privately published, 1979.

Buser, M. Elaine, and Dan Buser. *Guide to Schoenhut's Dolls, Toys and Circus, 1872–1976.* Paducah, Ky.: Schroeder Publishing Co., 1976.

Byfield, Magdalena. *Dolls' House Dolls, 1850–1900.* Enfield, Middlesex: Living Dolls Publications, 1977.

————. *In a Miniature Garden.* Cumberland, Md.: Hobby House Press, 1981.

Byford, Peggy (Pegby). *Unique and Interesting Antique Wood Dolls & History in Their Time.* Haywards Heath, Sussex: Key Books, 1983.

Cadbury, Betty. *Playthings Past.* Newton Abbot, England: David & Charles, 1976.

Calmettes, Pierre. *Les Joujoux, Leur Histoire, Leur Technique Les Artisans et Les Ouvriers, Les Ateliers et Les Usines.* Paris: Bibliothéque Sociale Des Metiers, 1924.

Canning-Wright, H. W. *Peeps at the World's Dolls.* London: A & C Black, 1922.

Capia, Robert. *Le Manuel de L' Amateur, Les Poupées Françaises.* France: Hachette, 1979.

————. *Les Poupées Anciennes.* France: Ouest Rennes, 1980.

Centro Internazionale Brera. *Le Ceramiche Lenci Gli Artisti—Secessionisté.* Sugar Co. Edizioni, n.d.

Chérau, Gaston. *Les Albums D'Art Druet XXV Albert Marque.* Paris: F. Sant' Andrea, after 1930.

Cieslik, Jürgen and Marianne. *Puppen Handbuch.* Bad Honnef-Rhondorf, West Germany: Verlag Marianne Cieslik, 1976.

————. *Silbernes Jubilaum Einer Puppenfabrik, 1886–1911.* Reprint. Bad Honnef-Rhondorf, West Germany: Verlag Marianne Cieslik, 1978.

————. *Dolls, European Dolls, 1800–1930.* London: Studio Vista, Christie's, Cassell Ltd., 1979.

————. *Puppen Sammeln.* Munich: Emil Vollmer, 1980.

————. *German Doll Encyclopedia, 1800–1939.* Cumberland, Md.: Hobby House Press, 1985.

————. *Puppen Bestimmungsbuch.* Jülich, West Germany: Marianne Cieslik, 1985.

Claretie, Léo. "Les Jouets des Pays de France." In *Les Arts Français.* Paris: Librairie Larousse, 1918.

————. *Les Jouets de France.* Paris: Librairie Delagrave, 1920.

Coleman, Dorothy S. *Lenci Dolls, Fabulous Figures of Felt.* Riverdale, Md.: Hobby House Press, 1977.

Coleman, Dorothy S., Elizabeth Ann, and Evelyn Jane. *The Collector's Encyclopedia of Dolls.* New York: Crown Publishers, Inc., 1968.

————. *The Collector's Book of Dolls' Clothes, Costumes in Miniature: 1700–1929.* New York: Crown Publishers, Inc., 1975.

Cooper, Marlow, and Madalaine Selfridge. *Dimples and Sawdust.* Privately published, n.d.

Cooper, Marlow. *Dimples and Sawdust. Vol. 2.* Privately published, 1968.

————. Doll Home Library Series. Boulder, Colo.: Marlow Cooper.

Vol. 1. *S.F.B.J. French Characters.* 1969.

Vol. 3. *Grace Drayton Collectibles.* 1970.

Vol. 5. *Doll Costumes and Dresses.* N.d.

Vol. 6. *Doll Costumes and Dresses.* 1970.

Vol. 7. *Les Parisiennes.* 1971.

Vol. 8. *Les Petites.* 1971.

Vol. 9. *The Schoenhuts, Their Book.* 1972.

Vol. 10. *Collectible Baby Dolls.* 1972.

Vol. 13. The Second *A Potpourri of Collectible Dolls.* 1973.

Vol. 14. *Mini Maids.* 1974.

Cooper, Marlow, and Dee Van Kampen. *A*

Taste of Honey. Escondido, Calif.: Omni Publishers, 1976.

Cramer, Martha. *China Heads.* Forest, Ohio: Heart of Ohio Doll Club, 1971.

Cramer, Mary E. *Little Treasures of Long Ago.* Hastings, Mich.: Um. & Mary E. Cramer, 1964.

Cremer, W. H., Jr. *The Toy Kingdom.* London, 1873.

Culff, Robert. *The World of Toys.* Feltham, Middlesex: Hamlyn Publishing Group, 1969.

Daiken, Leslie. *Children's Toys Throughout the Ages.* London: Spring Books, 1963.

———. *World of Toys.* London: Lambarde Press, 1963.

Danckert, Ludwig. *Handbuch des Europaischen Porzellans.* Munich, West Germany: Prestel, 1967.

Darrah, Marjorie Merritt. *Dolls in Color.* Des Moines, Iowa: Wallace-Homestead Book Co., 1971.

Das Puppenbuch. Published by Franz Peffer, Berlin, 1921.

Davies, Nina S. *Classics of the Doll World.* New Orleans, La.: Pelican Publishing Co., 1969.

De Chabreul, Mme. *Jeux et Exercices des Jeunes Filles.* 2d ed. Paris: Librairie de L. Hachette et Cie., 1860.

Demoulin, Mme. Gustave. *Les Jouets D'Enfants.* Paris: Librairie Hachette et Cie., 1884.

Desmond, Kay. *Dolls & Dolls' Houses.* London: Charles Letts & Co., 1972.

———. *All Color Book of Dolls.* London: Octopus Books, 1974.

Dicicco, Laurel M. *Doll Collector's Treasures.* New York: Hearthstone, 1970.

Doll Collectors of America, The Doll Collectors Manuals. *First Doll Exhibit.* Winchester, Mass.: Winchester Public Library, May, 1938.

———. *American Made Dolls & Figurines.* Winchester, 1940.

———. *Supplement to American Made Dolls & Figurines.* Boston, 1942.

———. *Dolls.* Boston, 1946.

———. *Doll Collectors Manual.* 1949.

———. *Doll Collectors Manual.* 1956–57.

———. *Doll Collectors Manual.* 1964.

———. *Doll Collectors Manual.* 1967.

———. *Doll Collectors Manual.* 1973.

———. *Doll Collectors Manual.* Cumberland, Md.: Hobby House Press, 1983.

———. *Index* to the nine manuals of the Doll Collectors of America Inc., 1940–1983.

Dröscher, Elke. *Puppenwelt.* Dortmund, Harenberg, West Germany, 1978.

———. *Puppenleben.* Dortmund, Harenberg, West Germany, 1979.

———. *Puppengrusse.* Dortmund, Harenberg, West Germany, 1981.

———. *Puppen im Wandel der Zeit.* Munich, Bavaria: Keysersche Verlagsbuchhandlung, 1982.

Eaton, Faith. *Dolls in Color.* New York: Macmillan Publishing Co., 1975.

Ehret, Gloria, and Marlon Gischer. *Battenberg, Antiquetaten—Kataloge Puppen.* Munich, Bavaria: Battenberg, 1980.

Ellenburg, M. Kelly. *Effanbee, the Dolls with the Golden Hearts.* North Kansas City, Mo.: Trojan Press, 1973.

Ernst, Hannelore. *Puppen.* Munich, Bavaria: Wilhelm Heyne, 1981.

Flick, Pauline. *Discovering Toys & Toy Museums.* Aylesbury, Bucks: Shire Publications, 1977.

———. *Old Toys.* Aylesbury, Bucks: Shire Publications, 1985.

Follett Studios. *The Old Doll Maker.* Books 1 and 2. Moorhead, Minn., n.d.

Foulke, Jan. *Focusing on Effanbee Composition Dolls.* Riverdale, Md.: Hobby House Press, 1978.

———. *Focusing on Gebrüder Heubach Dolls.* Cumberland, Md.: Hobby House Press, 1980.

———. *Kestner, King of Dollmakers.* Cumberland, Md.: Hobby House Press, 1982.

———. *Simon & Halbig Dolls, The Artful Aspect.* Cumberland, Md.: Hobby House Press, 1984.

———. *2nd Blue Book of Dolls & Values.* Riverdale, Md.: Hobby House Press, 1976.

———. *3rd Blue Book of Dolls & Values.* Riverdale, Md.: Hobby House Press, 1978.

———. *4th Blue Book of Dolls & Values.* Cumberland, Md.: Hobby House Press, 1980.

———. *5th Blue Book of Dolls & Values.* Cumberland, Md.: Hobby House Press, 1982.

———. *6th Blue Book of Dolls & Values.* Cumberland, Md.: Hobby House Press, 1984.

Fournier, Louis Édouard. *Histoire Des Jouets Et Des Jeux D'Enfants.* Paris: Libraire de la Société des Gens de Lettres, 1888.

Fox, Carl. *The Doll.* New York: Harry N. Abrams, 1973.

Francis, Jean. *A Collector's Guide to Canadian Dolls.* Whitby, Ontario: Canada Yearbook Services Ltd., 1979.

Fritzsch, Karl Ewald, and Manfred Bachmann. *An Illustrated History of Toys.* Translated by Ruth Michaelis, Jena and Patrick Murray. London: Abbey Library, 1966.

Fyleman, Rose. *The Katy Kruse Play Book.* Philadelphia, Pa.: David Mckay Co., 1930.

Gantner, Theo, and Waltraut Hartmann. *Das Spielzeug Buch.* Frankfurt/Main, Germany: Umschau; Innsbruck, Austria: Pinguin, 1973.

Gauss, Hans, and Gudrun Volk. *Puppen Aus Dem Spielzeugmuseum Sonneberg.* Sonneburg, Thür.: Volksdruckerei, 1983.

———. *Spielzeug Gestern und Heute Spielzeug Spielzeugmuseum.* Sonneberg, Thür., n.d.

Gerken, Jo Elizabeth. *Wonderful Dolls of Papier-Mâché.* Lincoln, Neb.: Doll Research Associates, Union College Press, 1970.

Glubok, Shirley. *Dolls Dolls Dolls.* Chicago, Ill.: Follett Publishing Co., 1975.

Goodfellow, Caroline G. *Dolls.* London: Victoria & Albert Museum and Bethnal Green Museum, Her Majesty's Stationery Office, 1975.

———. *Understanding Dolls.* Woodbridge, Suffolk: Antique Collector's Club, Baron Publishing, 1983.

Grein, Gerd J. *Spielzeug aus Hessen.* Langen, West Germany: Weisenborn & Potthoff, 1978.

Griffith, Ralph W. *Once Upon a Time . . . & Now!* Books 1 and 2. Parkville, Mo.: Ralph's Antique Dolls, n.d.

Grünspan, Siegfried. *Die Deutsche Spiel-*

warenindustrie unter Besonderer Berucksichtigung des Exporter und der Auslandischen Konkurrenz. Sonneberg, Thür., 1931.

Gulick, Sidney L., Committee on World Friendship Among Children. *Dolls of Friendship.* New York: Friendship Press, 1929.

Guthrie, Dorothy L., and Margaret T. Haley. *A Portfolio of Armand Marseille Dolls.* Allen Park, Mich.: The Fine Print, 1981.

Hall, Stanley, and A. Caswell Ellis. *A Study of Dolls.* New York and Chicago, Ill.: E. L. Kellogg & Co., 1897.

Hamil, Kathryn. *Antique Dolls.* Schenectady, N.Y., n.d.

Hansi, L'Oncle. *Le Paradis Tricolore.* Paris: H. Floury, 1918.

Hart, Luella. *The Japanese Dolls.* Middletown, Conn.: Elizabeth Andrews Fisher, 1952.

———. *Dolls Tell the Story of Hawaii.* Privately published, 1954.

Heede, Frau Christine. *Alte Puppensammlung von Frau Christine Heede.* Cologne, West Germany: Heiligenhaus, 1973.

Hennig, Clair. *So lebten die alten Puppen.* Frankfurt am Main, Germany: Wolfgang Krüger, 1979.

Hillier, Mary. *Automata & Mechanical Toys.* London: Jupiter Books, 1976.

———. *History of Wax Dolls.* Cumberland, Md.: Hobby House Press, 1985.

Hooper, Elizabeth. *Dolls The World Over.* Privately published. Baltimore, Md., 1936.

Hopkinson, Isabella and William. *Dolls and Miniatures with Their Prices at Auction.* Concord, N.H.: Rumford Press, 1976.

Horine, Maude M. *Memories of Rose O'Neill, Creator of the Kewpie Doll.* Bronson, Mo.: A. C. Offset Printing Co., 1950.

Jacobs, Flora Gill. *Dolls' Houses in America, Historic Preservation in Miniature.* New York: Charles Scribner's Sons, 1974.

Jacobsen, Carol L. *Portrait of Dolls.* Vol. 1. Seattle, Wash.: University Printing Co., 1973.

———. *Portrait of Dolls.* Vol. 2. Hong Kong: Mandarin Publishers, n.d.

———. *Portrait of Dolls.* Vol. 3. Chas. M. Henry Printing Co., 1977.

Johnston, LaVaughn C. *Open Mouth Dolls.* Downey, Calif.: Elena Quinn, 1974.

Jones, Iris Sanderson. *Early North American Dollmaking.* New York: Charles Scribner's Sons; Toronto, Canada: Van Nostrand, 1976.

Jordan, Nina R. *Homemade Dolls in Foreign Dress.* New York: Harcourt, Brace and Co., 1939.

Kerler, Christine, and Gertrud Rosemann. *Trachtepuppen aus Aller Welt.* Frankfurt, Germany: Rosenheimer, 1980.

King, Constance Eileen. *Toys and Dolls for Collectors.* London: Hamlyn, 1973.

———. *Dolls and Dolls' Houses.* London: Hamlyn, 1977.

———. *The Collector's History of Dolls.* London: Robert Hale, 1977; New York: St. Martin's Press, 1978.

———. *The Encyclopedia of Toys.* New York: Crown Publishers, 1978.

———. *Jumeau, Prince of Dollmakers.* Cumberland, Md.: Hobby House Press, 1983.

Kobayashi, Kei. *American Antique Dolls.* Japan, 1980.

Koenig, Marie. *Poupées et Legendes de France.* Paris: Librairie Centrale des Beaux-Arts, 1900.

———. *Musée de Poupées.* Paris: Hachette, 1909.

Kruse, Käthe. *Käthe Kruse, Das Grosse Puppenspiel.* Heidelberg, West Germany: Kurt Vonwinkel, 1951.

Kutschera, Volker. *Spielzeug, Spiegelbild der Kulturgeschichte.* Munich, West Germany: Deutscher Taschenbuch, 1979.

Lammèr, Jutta. *Handbuch für Puppensammler.* Ravensburg, West Germany: Otto Maier, 1981.

Lavitt, Wendy. *Children's Children.* New York: Museum of American Folk Art, n.d.

———. *American Folk Dolls.* New York: Alfred A. Knopf, 1982.

———. *Dolls: The Knopf Collectors' Guides to American Antiques.* New York: Alfred A. Knopf, 1983.

Lehmann, Emmy. *Die Puppe im Wandel der Zeiten.* Sonneberg Spielzeugmuseum, Urania–Verlag, 1957.

Leuzzie, Marlene, and Robert J. Kershner. *Kewpies in Action.* Englewood, Colo., 1971.

MacDowell, Robert and Karin. *The Collector's Digest of German Character Dolls.* Cumberland, Md.: Hobby House Press, 1981.

Machen, Patti. *Do You Know?* Saratoga, Calif., n.d.

Manos, Susan. *Schoenhut Dolls & Toys.* Paducah, Ky.: Schroeder Publishing Co., 1976.

Marwitz, Christa von der. *Spielzeug aus Frankfurter Familienbesitz.* Frankfurt am Main, West Germany: Waldemar Kramer, 1965.

———. *Der Kleiner Kinder Zeitvertreib.* Darmstadt: Reba, 1967.

Merrill, Madeline O. *Handbook of Collectible Dolls.* Vol. 1 (1969), with Nellie Perkins. Vols. 2 (1976) and 3 (1977), with Richard Merrill. Saugus, Mass.: Richard Merrill.

———. *The Art of Dolls, 1700–1940.* Cumberland, Md.: Hobby House Press, 1985.

Moore, Lorene. *Dolls of the North American Indians.* Lore, A Milwaukee Public Museum Publication, 1964.

Morgenthaler, Sasha. *Autobiography.* Zurich, Switzerland: Sasha Morgenthaler Doll Museum, n.d.

Morrison, Lucile Phillips. *Doll Dreams.* Hollywood, Calif., 1932.

Moskovsky, Eva. *A Day At The Dolls.* Budapest: Móra Publishers, 1984.

Noble, John. *A Treasury of Beautiful Dolls.* New York: Hawthorn Books, 1971.

Nolan, Helen. *Antique Doll Photo Postcards.* New York: Dover Publications, 1985.

Oehley, Arthur L. *Saga of the Famous Flora Dolls.* South Africa: Somerset East Museum, 1981.

Ogilvie, Jean. *The Wax Doll's Story.* Brighton, Sussex: Dolphin Press, 1974.

Pearse, Ouida. *Soft Toy Making.* London: Sir Isaac Pitman & Sons, 1932.

Petersen, Grete. *Dolls in Danish Dresses.* Denmark: Høst & Søn, 1960.

Poe, Marion Ball. *Schoenhut Treasures.* Kansas, 1974.

Pollock. *Pollock's History of English Dolls & Toys.* London: Ernest Benn, 1979.

———. *The Story of Benjamin Pollock and Pollock's Toy Museum.* London: Richard Metcalfe, 1981.

———. *Pollock's Dictionary of English Dolls.* New York: Crown Publishers, 1982.

Porot, Anne-Marie. *Les Poupées de Caractère de la S.F.B.J.* Paris, 1980.

———, **and Jacques Porot.** *La Poupée Ce Qu'il Y A Dedans.* Paris, 1982.

———. *Les Poupées Mecaniques de Roullet et Decamps.* Paris, 1982.

Practical Toymaker, The. London: Home Industries, 1921.

Proverbio, L. *Lenci, Le Ceramishe, 1919–1937.* Torino, Italy: Tipostampa, n.d.

Rabecq-Maillard, M. M. *Jeux & Jouets.* Paris: Institut Pedagogue National, 1961.

Reible, Karl. "Die Deutsche Spielwarenindustrie, Ihre Entwicklung und Ihr Gegenwärtiger Stand." Dissertation. Giessen, Germany, 1925.

Remise, Jac. *L'Argus Des Jouets Anciens, 1850–1918.* Dijon-Quetigny: Balland, Imprimerie Darantiere, 1978.

Richter, Lydia. *The Beloved Käthe-Kruse-Dolls, Yesterday and Today.* Cumberland, Md.: Hobby House Press, 1983.

———. *Treasury of Käthe Kruse Dolls, Album 3.* Tucson, Ariz.: H. P. Books, 1984.

Robinson, Julia A. *Dolls, An Anthology.* Chicago, Ill.: Albert Whitman, 1938.

Saxby, Lewis. *The Life of A Wooden Doll.* New York: Fox Duffield, 1903.

Scherf, Helmut. *Thüringer Porzellan.* Wiesbaden, West Germany: Ebeling, 1980.

Scholbel, A. *Thüringen.* Leipzig, Germany: Fischer & Wittig, 1902.

Schoonmaker, Patricia N. *The Effanbee Patsy Family & Related Types.* North Hollywood, Calif.: Doll Research Projects, 1971.

———. *Effanbee Dolls.* Cumberland, Md.: Hobby House Press, 1984.

Schroeder, Bill. *The Standard Antique Doll Identification & Value Guide, 1700–1935.* Paducah, Ky.: Collector Books, 1976.

Schwarz, Erica, and Nikolai Molodovsky. *Berchtesgadener Handwerkskunst.* Freilassing, West Germany: Pannonia, 1977.

Schweitzer, John C. *The A B C's of Doll Collecting.* New York: Sterling Publishing Co., 1981.

Schwindrazheim, Hildamarie. *Altes Spielzeug aus Schleswig-Holstein.* Heide in Holstein, West Germany: Boyens & Co., 1957.

Seeley, Mildred. *The Doll House Doll.* Oneonta, N.Y.: Seeley's Ceramic Service, 1976.

Selfridge, Madalaine. *Wendy and Friends.* Escondido, Calif.: Swadell Lithographers, 1969.

———. *Dolls, Images of Love.* Jim and Madalaine Selfridge, 1973.

Seyffert, Oskar, and W. Trier. *Spielzeug.* Berlin: Ernst Wasmuth, 1922.

Shea, Ralph A. *Doll Mark Clues.* Ridgefield, N.J.: Ralph A. Shea.

———. *Dictionary of Antique Doll Marks.* Vol. 1. 1972.

———. *Numbers in Antique Doll Marks.* Vol. 2. 1973.

———. Part B, vol. 3. 1974.

———. Part C, vol. 4. 1975.

———. Part D, vol. 5. 1976.

———. Part E, vol. 6. 1977.

———. Vol. 8. *Antique German Mystery Dolls Identified—A Key.* 1981.

Shoemaker, Rhoda. *Compo Dolls, Cute and Collectible.* Menlo Park, Calif.: 1971.

———. *Compo Dolls, Cute and Collectible.* Vol. 2. Menlo Park, Calif.: 1973.

Shpikalov, A. *Russian Toys.* Moscow: Progress Publishers, 1974.

Smith, Patricia. (All of the titles below were published by Bill Schroeder of Collector Books, Paducah, Ky.)

———. *Armand Marseille Dolls, 1865–1928.* 1975.

———. *First Series, Antique Collector's Dolls.* 1975.

———. *Kestner and Simon & Halbig Dolls, 1804–1930.* 1976.

———. *Second Series, Antique Collector's Dolls.* 1976.

———. *French Dolls in Color.* 1979.

———. *Oriental Dolls in Color.* 1979.

———. *German Dolls, Featuring Character Children & Babies.* 1979.

———. *China and Parian Dolls.* 1980.

South, Brenda B. *Heirloom Dolls.* Colorado Springs, Colo.: Graphic Services, 1969.

Spinning Wheel's Complete Book of Dolls. Edited by Albert Christian Revi. Hanover, Pa.: Everybody's Press, 1975.

Stäblein, Rita. *Altes Holzspielzeug aus Gröden.* Bozen, Italy: Athensia, 1980.

Staniland, Kay. *Fashion in Miniature, The Gallery of English Costume.* Picture Book No. 9. Manchester, England: William Morris Press, 1970.

Stanton, Carol Ann. *Heubach's Little Characters, Dolls and Figurines, 1850–1930.* Enfield, Middlesex: Living Dolls Publications, 1978.

Stewart, Ethel, and Katherine Dennis. *A Collector's Guide to the Patsy Dolls.* Seattle, Washington, 1974.

Symons, Harry. *Playthings of Yesterday.* Toronto: The Ryerson Press, 1963.

Tavares, Olinda. *The Armchair Museum of Dolls.* New York: Vantage Press, 1973.

Theimer, François. *Si Huret m'etait Conté.* Paris: Polichinelle, 1980.

———. *Madame la Poupée Bleuette.* Paris: Polytechnique d'Impression, 1982.

———. *Le Bébé Jumeau.* Paris: Polichinelle, 1985.

United Federation of Doll Clubs, Inc. *Glossary, Standardized Terminology for Doll Collectors.* United Federation of Doll Clubs, 1978.

Vollmer, Hans. *Allgemeines Lexikon der Bildenden Kunstler.* Leipzig, Germany: E. A. Seemann, 1930.

Walker, Frances, and Margaret Whitton. *Playthings By the Yard.* South Hadley, Mass.: Hadley Printing Co., 1973.

White, Gwen. *A Picture Book of Ancient & Modern Dolls.* London: A. & C. Black, 1928.

———. *Toys and Dolls, Marks and Labels.* Newton, Mass.: Charles T. Branford, 1975.

Whitton, Margaret. *The Jumeau Doll.* New York: Dover Publications, 1980.

Wilson, Jean, and Shirley Conway. *Steiff, Teddy Bears, Dolls and Toys.* West Des Moines, Iowa: Wallace-Homestead, 1984.

Yamada, Tokubei. *Japanese Dolls.* Tokyo: Japan Travel Bureau, 1955.

Young, Helen. *The Complete Book of Doll Collecting.* New York: G. P. Putnam's Sons, 1967.

V. GENERAL REFERENCE PERIODICALS

Antique Dealer & Collectors Guide, Juvenilia and Children's Antiques. London: City Magazines, 1973ff.

Antiques. New York: Straight Enterprises, 1936ff.

Art Center Bulletin. New York, 1920ff.

Art et Décoration. Paris, 1896ff.

Avocations. New York: Lindquist, 1938ff.

Cabinet Des Modes. Paris: Buisson, 1785, p. 2.

Centre d'Etude et de Recherche Sur la Poupée (C.E.R.P.). Bulletins No. 7, 8, and 9. Courbevoie, France, n.d.

Child Life. Chicago, Ill., 1926ff.

Collector's Showcase. San Diego, Calif.: D. Keith Kaonis, 1980ff.

Country Life. England, 1974ff.

Craftsman. 1914ff.

Creative Arts. New York edition of *The Studio*, 1927ff.

Dekorative Kunst. Germany, 1897ff.

Delineator. New York: Butterick Publishers, 1875ff.

Design, The. 1898ff.

Deutsche Kunst und Dekoration. Darmstadt, Germany, 1896ff.

Deutsche Spielwaren Zeitung. Nürnberg, Bavaria: Meisenbach, 1909. (Later *Das Spielzeug*, Bamberg.)

Die Hausfrau. Milwaukee, Wis., 1903ff.

Die Modenwelt. Berlin, 1865ff. Foreign editions include *The Season*, New York, 1882ff.

Die Welt der Frau. Leipzig, Germany: Ernst Keil, 1908.

Doll News. United Federation of Doll Clubs, 1953ff.

Doll Reader. Riverdale and Cumberland, Md.: Hobby House Press, 1972ff.

Dolls' Dressmaker, A Magazine For Girls. Ed. Jennie Wren [pseud.]. New York: Vols. 1–3 (1891–93).

Dolls, The Collector's Magazine. New York: Collector Communications Corp., 1981ff.

Femina. Paris, 1908ff.

Fillette. Paris, 1912ff.

Friendly Neighbors. Danvers, Mass.: Tower Press, 1970ff.

Games & Toys. London: International Trades Press, 1914ff.

Gazette des Beaux-Arts. Paris, 1858ff.

Girl's Own. London, ca. 1915.

Girl's Own Annual, The (The Girl's Own Paper). London, ca. 1878ff.

Girls' Own Book. England, 1869ff.

Good Housekeeping. New York, 1910ff.

Harper's Magazine. New York, 1900.

Illustrated London News. London, 1842ff.

International Studio. New York: John Lane Co., 1897ff.

La Poupée Modèle. Paris: Bureau du Journal des Demoiselles, 1863ff.

La Semaine de Suzette. Paris: Gautier-Languereau, 1905ff.

Ladies' Home Journal. Philadelphia, Pa., 1890ff.

Ladies' Standard Magazine. Standard Publishers, 1895ff.

Life. Chicago, 1938ff.

Little Folks Magazine. England, 1884ff.

London Magazine, The. London, 1902.

Modern Priscilla. Boston, 1909ff.

Myra's Journal of Dress and Fashion. England, 1883.

Needlecraft. Augusta, Maine, 1914ff.

People's Home Journal, 1923.

Pictorial Review, 1907.

Playthings. New York: McCready Publishing Co., 1903ff.

———. "Story of the Growth of an Industry from Infancy to World Leadership." Thirty-fifth Anniversary Issue of *Playthings*, Sept. 1938.

Queen, The. London, 1861ff.

Souvenir Journals. United Federation of Doll Clubs, 1961ff.

Standard Delineator, The. Standard Publishing Co., 1895–96.

Standard Designer, The. Standard Publishing Co., 1897.

Strand Magazine, The. London and New York: The International News Company, 1889ff.

Studio, An Illustrated Magazine of Fine and Applied Arts. London, 1893ff.

Toy and Fancy Goods Trader, The. England, 1915–23. Became *The Toy Trader* in 1923ff.

Toy World. California, 1927ff.

Toys and Novelties. Chicago, 1913ff.

Toyshop and Fancy Goods Journal. London, 1916–21.

Woman's World. Chicago, 1928ff.

VI. ARTICLES OF SPECIAL INTEREST

(Listed by author)

Capia, Robert. "La Poupée Bleuette." *Art Antiquites Artisanat l'Estampille*, Oct. 1975, 22–32.

Claretie, Léo. "Un Musée De Jouets." *Le Monde Moderne*, 15 March 1902, 469–80.

Cleveland, S. D. "Dolls and Dolls' Houses at Heaton Hall, Manchester." *The Connoisseur, incorporated with International Studio*, Feb. 1935, 83–86.

Darrach, Doris. "Collecting Antique Dolls Today." *Canadian Collector*, Nov.–Dec. 1978, 21–25.

D'Avenel, Georges, le Vicomte. "Jouets Français Contre Jouets Allemands." *Revue Des Deux Mondes*, Paris, 15 May 1915, 340–68.

Dickinson, Velvalee. "Dolls, The Story of A Doll." *The Compleat Collector*, Jan.–Feb. 1941, 17.

Doin, Jeanne. "La Renaissance De La Poupée Française." *Gazette Des Beaux-Arts* (Paris), 1916, 1–17.

Feder, Norman. "The Side Fold Dress." *American Indian Art*, Winter 1984, 49–55, 75–77.

H.W.F. "Dolls and Dolls." *Our Little Men and Women*, 1893, 10–11.

Heard, James. (Curator of Toys at Pollock's.) "Dolls." *Pollock's World of Toys.* n.d.

Hillier, Mary. "Victorian Dolls." *Discovering Antiques*, 1972, 1839–1843.

Kendall, Evelyn. "Doll Collecting." *Ellis Memorial Antiques Show*, 1960, 41–44.

Larmon, Leila. "Dolls, People for a Make-believe World." *The Encyclopedia of Collectibles.* Vol.: *Dogs—Fishing Tackle.* Alexandria, Va.: Time-Life Books, 1978.

Mount, Harry A. "The Ancestors of a Jazz Baby." *Leslie's (Illustrated Magazine)*, Oct. 1921, 454–66.

Raines, Leonora S. "Where Christmas Toys Come From." *Woman's Home Companion*, Dec. 1904, 14–15.

Reinhardt, Herman. "Ernst Reinhardt: Inventor, Manufacturer, Craftsman, Artisan." *Co-operator*, Dec. 1972, 4–5.

Robinson, Marie M. "French Dolls Were Always Beauties." *Carnegie Magazine* (Pittsburgh, Pa.), Dec. 1971, 423–25.

Seabury, Katharine. "With A Doll Land All Her Own." *The Spur*, Feb. 1934, 30–31, 60.

Seidenberg, Judy. "Playthings of the Past." *Museum News*, Dec. 1967, 24–27.

Stanton, Carol Ann. "Popularity of Bisque-Head Dolls Increases." *Art & Antiques Weekly*, 18 Sept. 1971, 27–29.

Wilson, Marion B. "Ludwig Greiner, Doll Head Maker." *The American Review*, Dec.–Jan. 1959–60, 29–33.

(Listed by title)

"Lilliput in Regent Street." *Englishwoman's Domestic Magazine*, Dec. 1865, 359–61.

"Art of Making Wax Fruit and Flowers, The." *Godey's Lady's Book.* 1856. Jan.: 20–22; Feb.: 134–35; Mar.: 231–32; April: 325–26; May: 404–405; June: 500–502.

"Peddlers in Miniature." *Public Employees News* (Pen), Dec. 1971, 4–8.

"Rather Too Much of A Good Thing." *Harper's New Monthly Magazine*, Feb. 1852, 429.

VII. EXHIBITS, MUSEUMS

Musée Des Arts Décoratifs. "Jouets, Une Sélection Du Musée De Sonneberg, R.D.A." Palais du Louvre, Paris, 1973–74.

———. "Jouets Americains de la petite enfances, 1925–1975," Paris, 1977–78.

———. "Jouets Français, 1800–1980," Paris, 1982–83.

Barcelona Museum. "Guia Abreviada del Museo Romantico Provincial," Barcelona, 1968.

Dolls in Wonderland. "Dolls in Wonderland," by Vera Kramer. Brighton, England: Planet House Press, n.d.

Essex Institute. "Dolls & Toys at the Essex Institute," by Madeline O. & Richard Merrill. Salem, Mass.: Essex Institute, 1976.

Finland National Museum. "Dockor Och Tennsoldater" (Dolls and toy soldiers). Helsinki: Riitta Pylkkänen, 1961.

Hessischer Museumsverband. "Trachtenpuppen aus Hessen," 1983.

Hessisches Puppenmuseum. Hanau-Wilhelmsbad, Germany, n.d.

Historische Museum Basle (Basel). "Old Toys from Basle," Basel, Switzerland, 1973.

Institut Pédagogique National. "Jeux & Jouets d'Autrefois," Paris, 12 December 1961–10 March 1962.

Købbtadtmuseet. "En Dukke Fra, 1830–40," 1967.

Musée de La Mode Et Du Costume, Ville De Paris. "La Mode Et Les Poupées Du XVIIIe Siècle A Nos Jours," Paris, 1981–82.

Legoland Museum. "The Book About Little People in Legoland's Doll Collection," Legoland, Denmark, 1977.

Musée de L'Homme at Muséum National d' Histoire Naturelle. "Poupée-Jouet, Poupée-Reflet," Paris, 1983.

Louisiana State Museum. "Playthings of the Past," 1972.

Mary Merritt Museum. "Mary Merritt's Doll Museum," by Dan Weidner, Pennsylvania, 1963.

Monaco Musée National. "Dolls and Automatons of the Past," De Galléa Collection, Monaco: Studio Bazzoli, 1972.

Morris Museum of Arts and Science. "Dolls of American Childhood," Morristown, N.J., 1976.

Munich City Museum. "Aus Münchner Kinderstuben, 1750–1930," Munich: Kall M. Lipp, 1976.

Nebraska State Historical Society. "The Doll Show, 1850–1949," April 30–Nov. 15, 1982.

Nederlands Kostuummuseum. "Poppen + Mode 18e eeuw-heden," Den Haag, Netherlands, n.d.

Neustadt bei Coburg Museum. "Chronik des Trachten-Puppen-Museum," by Erwin Drobik, Neustadt bei Coburg, 1980.

Newark Museum. "Make Believe and Whimsey, European and American Dolls in the Collection of the Newark Museum," by Margaret E. White, *The Museum,* Newark, N.J., 1955.

———. "19th & 20th Century Dolls and Their Manufacturers in the Collection of the Newark Museum," by Elizabeth Ann Coleman, *The Museum* 20, no. 3 (1968), Newark, N.J.

Nürnberg Museum. "City of Nuremberg Toy Museum," by Lydia Bayer, Nürnberg, Germany, 1978.

Pollock's Toy Museum. "The Evolution of the Baby Doll and the Human Nursery," London, n.d.

Rijksmuseum. "Poppenhuizen Dolls' Houses," Amsterdam, 1967.

Colección Rocamora, Museo de Indumentaria. "Ayuntamiento de Barcelona Museos de Arte," Barcelona: Gráficas Europeas, S.A., 1970.

Romantico Museo Provincial. "Colección de Muñecas Antiguas 'Lola Anglada,' " Escuela, Spain, 1968.

Rottingdean Grange, The. "Guide to the Display from the Toy Museum Collections," County Borough of Brighton, Sussex, n.d.

Musée Roybet Fould. "La Poupée Française," by Florence Poisson and Michel Manson, Courbevoie, France, 1980.

Salzburg Museum, Museum Carolina Augusteum. "Spielzeugmuseum Sammlung Folk Salzburg," by Volker Kutschera. Braunschweig: Westermann, 1983.

Schweizerischen Landesmuseum. "Spielzeug des 18 and 19 Jahrhunderts," by Dr. Jenny Schneider. Bern, Switzerland: Paul Haupt, 1969.

South Dakota Museum. "Old Style Plains Indians from Collections in South Dakota," by Joanita Kant. Vol. 2, no. 1, University of South Dakota, 1975.

Spielzeug Museum Sonneberg. "Spielzeug," by Otto Kiel. Leipzig, East Germany: Zenner und Gurchott, 1963.

———. "Spielzeuggestern und Heute Spielzeug," by Hans Gauss et al., Sonneberg, Thür., n.d.

Victoria & Albert Museum. "Dolls," Her Majesty's Stationery Office, London, 1960.

Warwick Doll Museum. "The Story of Dolls and the Joy Robinson Collection," Joy Robinson, Warwick, England, 1955.

Wenham Museum. "Notes on the Collection of Dolls and Figurines at the Wenham Museum, Claflin-Richards House, Wenham, Massachusetts," by Adeline P. Cole, Wenham Historical Association, 1951.

Historisches Museum Der Stadt, Wein (city of Vienna). "Das Kind und Seine Welt," Vienna, 1959–60.

Worthing Museum. "Dolls in the Worthing Museum. Compiled by K. J. Evans," Museum Publication no. 9, 1969. 2d ed. 1977.

VIII. EXHIBITS OF COLLECTIONS

Anderson, Imogene. *Early American Dolls, The Imogene Anderson Collection,* by Edward P. Alexander, Ticonderoga, N.Y., 1937. (Also as an article in the *Journal of the New York Historical Association,* 1937.)

———. *Early American Dolls and Dolls' Furniture.* Collection of Imogene Anderson and Charles B. Jopp, New York, 1934.

Crawford, M. D. *The Philosophy of Dress.* Exhibit at Bonwit Teller & Co. Manikins designed by Stewart Culin, 1925.

De Galea, E. *Poupées et Automates Depuis La Renaissance. Collection de Madame E. De Galea,* Paris, 1952.

Doll Collectors Guild, The. *Dolls from the Collections of the Members,* 1964.

———. *Dolls from the Collections of the Members and Dolls Made by Members,* 1974.

Doll 76. Conference Report and Magazine. Kelvedon, Essex: Printwize, 1976.

Exhibition Catalogs, Dolls Through The Ages. London, 1954ff.

Figures in boldface type are illustration numbers, that is, pictures or marks, not page numbers. The letter "C" preceding a number refers to a color illustration.

The names in the index are supplementary to the text entries. There is no listing of the names in reference to their text entry or to their accompanying illustrations. This index includes references to the names that appeared as entries in Volume One but were omitted in this volume. Due to the increased size of Volume Two, some of the longer index entries in Volume One have been omitted. The names of associates are listed only when they appear in the text entry itself. References to companies, people, and dolls in general entries such as Chronology, Clothes, etc., are listed herein.

People are indexed by their surname, dolls are indexed by full names, except for portrait dolls. Names are given without prepositions and sometimes without descriptive adjectives, such as "La," "Little," etc., as given in the text entries

The names in this index include many of the numerous wording and spelling variations, which are due to the fact that information on dolls is derived from many countries and numerous languages (see Introduction). Names of European stores are indexed because of the importance of the detailed information about the dolls that they sold. Sculptors and other artists who created dolls are indexed as well as new features such as the Tables and Charts. See also Indexes of Marks found on dolls.

TABLES AND CHARTS INDEXES

INDEXES OF MARKS FOUND ON DOLLS

Index reference numerals in boldface type are illustration numbers. The letter "C" preceding a number refers to a color illustration.

The important parts of the marks shown in this book are listed by category as follows:

I. NUMERALS, except for obvious size numbers less than 10, are chiefly arabic numbers and represent mold or model numbers, occasionally a date. Style numbers based on clothes are not included. See Index of Tables and Charts.

II. ADDRESSES: streets, towns and/or countries as given in marks except for Paris and Germany which are too numerous to include. It should be noted that "Paris" did not always refer to the French city.

III. LETTERS AND INITIALS: marks were often handwritten by people of varying backgrounds using different ways of writing letters. This index tries to identify letters not only as they were intended but also as they might appear to a reader. Letters are often super-

imposed in which case the letters are listed in both ways in which they could be read. Initials are sometimes separated by a size number; if this happens to be a zero it can be mistaken for an "O." Many of the initials found in this index as capital letters could have appeared as small letters.

IV. NAMES, WORDS, PHRASES, AND ABBREVIATIONS other than initials: sometimes, these can also be found in the General Index; this is particularly true of acronyms such as Effanbee. The information in this index is valuable in deciphering hard to read marks and relating them to specific dolls and/or makers.

V. SYMBOLS AND SHAPES: includes the outline and configuration of marks. Marks that might have more than one name for their shape are also listed under some of the additional names.

See the entry entitled "Marks" in order to fully understand the problems encountered in reading and interpreting marks.

I. NUMERALS

I, 669–672, 977; **1566**
II, 207, 1072, 1208; **2744**
III, 207, 914; **1970, 2255, 2256**
IV, 207, 977, 1072; **2050, C34**
V, 309; **698**
VII, 669, 670; **1566**
VIII, 309, 669, 670
IX, 309; **2181**
XI, **331, 336**
XII, 977; **1347**
XV, **826**
XXXVIII, **827**
A1, 331, 332; **5**
Z1, 480
1X1, **2160**
01, 181
9/18, 332
13/15, 332
0, 13, 14
1, 1, 13, 14; **4, 5, 2017**
2, **638, 2017**
3, 13, 1183; **2017**
4, 1, 13
5, 14
6, **2017**
8, 14
9, 44
10, 208, 650, 917; **1341, 1342, 1352, 1405, 1466, 2084, 2420, 2472, 2524, 2531, 2645, 2746, C33**
11, 628, 1004, 1175; **921, 1195, 1338, 1349, 2214, 2376, 2540, 2666**
12, 208, 372, 628, 723, 966; **844, 1189, 1337, 1432, 1457, 1458, 1472, 1870, 2006, 2538**
13, 1, 560, 941; **1167, 1248, 1467, 1473, 1698, 2112, 2734**
14, **1335, 1843, 2600**
15, 854, 871, 962, 1146; **1406, 1539, 1553, 1748, 1822, 2315**
16, **1190, 2212, 2714**
17, 5, 44, 871, 962; **2525, 2678**
18, 612; **1859, 2095, 2521, 2537, 2539**
19, 854, 1004, 1453, 2070, 2532
20, 208; **2017**

21, 977; **1355, 1398, 1408, 1409, 2184, C40**
22, 933, 977, 1069, 1159; **770, 1057, 1190, 1246, 1295, 1944, 2094, 2475, 2512, 2621**
23, 314, 977, 2734; **1692, 2474, 2592**
24, 44, 75, 977
25, 731, 977; **1338, 2525, 2545**
26, 977
27, 977
28, 977, 1039, 1208; **845, 1138, 1939, 2180, 2208, 2321**
29, 731, 977; **1404**
30, 977; **1242, 1755, 1921, 2304**
31, 977; **1404, 1468, 1469**
32, 560, 977, **1240, 1397, 1921, 2215, 2220**
33, 977
34, 588, 589, 977; **1, 1247**
35, 309, 977; **2088, 2266, 2482**
36, 309; **51, 1136, 1406, 1532, 1533, 1979**
37, 309, 977; **698**
38, 486, 499, 1368, 1388, 2002, 2219**
39, 977; **1403, 1412, 1413**
40, 7, 605, 2084, 2483; **1735, 2322**
41, 977, 1048
42, **995, 2209**
43, 977; **2118**
44, 905, 977; **2029**
45, 977; **163, 485, 1268, 1751, 2485**
46, 7, 480, 800, 977; **775**
47, 905, 977
48, 977, 1146; **1734, 2323**
49, 977; **776, 1189**
50, 76, 977; **206, 1534, 2301, 2335, 2486, 2655**
52, **1918**
53, 977
54, 480, 977
55, 977, 1019
56, 977; **1367, 2323**
57, 977
60, 115, 154, 519, 612, 954; **984, 1909, 2459**
62, 344; **779**
64, **1069**

65, **2006**
66, **1379**
67, **777**
68, 83; **2306, 2324**
69, 363; **819**
70, 1045; **886, 1189, 1393**
71, 154, 1166; **353, 984, 2637**
72, 630
74, **2730**
76, **483**
77, 978; **2347**
78, **2545**
79, **1134**
80, 1183; **2307**
81, **1192**
83, 907; **1192**
84, **514**
85, **2080**
86, 977; **1189**
88, 663
89, **2306**
90, 663; **1197**
91, **487**
92, **200**
93, 803, 807; **835**
94, 27
95, 803; **1197, 1818**
98, 526, 663, 1017
99, 526
100, 66, 95, 130, 222, 224, 545, 609–611, 702, 726, 907, 1069, 1174; **125, 1039, 1210, 1380, 2118, 2647**
101, 2, 610–612, 929, 994, 1069; **307, 1266, 1381, 1382**
102, 610, 611, 1069; **200**
103, 610, 611, 1069; **1883**
104, 610, 611, 1069
105, 610, 611, 1069; **33, 1384**
106, 481, 610, 611, 663, 1069; **1385**
107, 80, 481, 610, 611, 1069; **211, 1048, 1382**
108, 610, 611, 907, 1069
109, 609–611, 702, 703, 1069; **1382**
110, 481, 610, 611, 702, 703, 803, 1069; **1644**
111, 481, 610, 611, 663, 1069; **592, 1646, 1647, C38**
112, 610, 611, 663, 1069; **1386**
113, 1069

114, 481, 610–612, 654, 951, 1069; **1387, C14**
115, 139, 610, 612, 827, 1069; **1388**
116, 130, 139, 610, 654, 1069; **378, 1389–1391, C36**
117, 130, 610, 612, 827, 829, 1069; **1038 (117A), 1392, 1393, 2208**
118, 610, 1069
119, 654; **1135, 1259**
120, 130, 610, 628, 1069
121, 610, 612, 628, 803, 977, 1069; **2727**
122, 1, 481, 610, 612, 628, 654, 827, 830, 1069, 1072; **1394**
123, 481, 610, 612, 628, 654, 821, 1069; **1395, 1854**
124, 481, 610, 612, 628, 821, 1069; **185, 1396, 1854**
125, 481, 610, 628; **2018**
126, 418, 481, 482, 610–612, 628, 826–829, 977, 1069; **659, 1008, 1397, 1398, 1406, 1979, 2697**
127, 130, 610, 628, 827–829, 1069; **1399**
128, 610, 628, 654, 977, 1069; **1394, 1452**
129, 136, 610, 628, 654, 977, 1069; **1456**
130, 526; **1446**
131, 610, 628, 654, 826–828, 977, 1069; **1400, 2234, 2714**
132, 526, 628, 977; **1209**
133, 526, 628, 652, 654; **498**
134, 526, 628, 977; **2434**
135, 526, 610, 628, 652, 654, 977, 1069; **1515, 1525**
136, 628, 977; **2434**
137, 130, 628, 654, 977
138, 526, 610, 628, 652, 977, 1069
140, 628, 654; **178**
141, 526, 628, 654; **521, 1767**
142, 526, 628, 654
143, 80, 526, 628, 1054; **1040, 1432, 1457**
144, 181, 610, 628, 1069
145, 628; **177**
146, 630

1255

II. ADDRESSES

III. LETTERS AND INITIALS

IV. NAMES, WORDS, PHRASES, AND ABBREVIATIONS

V. SYMBOLS AND SHAPES